W9-AQS-460

CollegeBoard

2010 Getting Financial Aid HANDBOOK

$21.95

Library
Ivy Tech Community College
200 Daniels Way
Bloomington, IN 47404-9772

2010 Getting Financial Aid

HANDBOOK

CollegeBoard

Fourth Edition

The College Board, New York

CollegeBoard

The College Board

The College Board is a not-for-profit membership association whose mission is to connect students to college success and opportunity. Founded in 1900, the College Board is composed of more than 5,600 schools, colleges universities and other educational organizations. Each year, the College Board serves seven million students and their parents, 23,000 high schools and 3,800 colleges through major programs and services in college readiness, college admissions, guidance, assessment, financial aid, enrollment, and teaching and learning. Among its best-known programs are the SAT®, the PSAT/NMSQT® and the Advanced Placement Program® (AP®). The College Board is committed to the principles of excellence and equity, and that commitment is embodied in all of its programs, services, activities and concerns.

For further information, visit the College Board on the Web: www.collegeboard.com.

Editorial inquiries concerning this book should be directed to College Planning Services, College Board, 45 Columbus Avenue, New York, NY 10023-6992, or telephone 212-713-8000.

Copies of this book are available from your local bookseller or may be ordered from College Board Publications, P.O. Box 869010, Plano, TX 75074-0998. The book may also be ordered online through the College Board Store at www.collegeboard.com. The price is $21.95.

© 2009 The College Board. All rights reserved. College Board, Advanced Placement Program, AP, CLEP, CollegeCredit, College-Level Examination Program, College Scholarship Service, CSS, CSS/Financial Aid PROFILE, SAT and the acorn logo are registered trademarks of the College Board. inspiring minds, SAT Reasoning Test, SAT Subject Tests, The Official SAT Online Course, The Official SAT Study Guide and The Official Study Guide for all SAT Subject Tests are trademarks owned by the College Board. PSAT/NMSQT is a registered trademark of the College Board and National Merit Scholarship Corporation. All other products and services may be trademarks of their respective owners.

ISBN: 978-0-87447-848-8

Printed in the United States of America

Distributed by Macmillan

Contents

List of Figures

List of Tables

List of Worksheets

Preface

Financial aid is a great equalizer. In 2008, over $143 billion in aid was awarded from government and private sources. Coupled with the wide range of lower-cost college options available, financial aid should make a college education affordable for just about everyone.

Yet a recent study by the American Council on Education shows that each year almost *two million* students who are eligible for this boon don't even apply for it. We assume these students are either unaware of the possibility of aid, or mistakenly believe financial aid is not for them.

And many parents and students who apply for financial aid find the process to be confusing, even intimidating. Like the tax code, the forms and guidelines appear to be full of exceptions, convolutions and incomprehensible terms.

But it doesn't have to be that way. A central aim of this book is to take the confusion and intimidation out of the process by giving clear and direct explanations of what financial aid is all about and simple, step-by-step directions for how to get it. By combining these explanations and directions with costs and financial aid facts for every accredited college that reports this data, we hope this book will achieve our ultimate goal of connecting students to colleges that match both their needs and their means.

Acknowledgments

We gratefully acknowledge the contributions of the many individuals who helped bring the first edition of this book into being. George Ochoa, our writer for Part I of this book, "Financial Aid, Step by Step," transformed a complicated and intricate subject into clear and simple prose. Without his talent, the purpose of this guide could not have been achieved.

Renée Gernand provided leadership and editorial guidance throughout the project. Kathie Little and Jack Joyce, our resident experts on financial aid, reviewed the content and kept our course true, as did Sandy Baum, Cindy Bailey, Myra Baas Smith and Linda Peckham. Kate Crane copyedited the manuscript, and Betty Keim proofread the finished book.

While we had the advantage of many "in house" resources, we also relied upon the knowledge and advice of seven financial aid officers who took time from their busy schedules to give us interviews: Vincent Amoroso of the University of North Carolina at Chapel Hill (now at Johns Hopkins University), Bonnie Lee Behm of Villanova University, Elizabeth Bickford of the University of Oregon, Joe Paul Case of Amherst College, Mary San Agustin of Palomar College, Mike Scott of Texas Christian University and Forrest Stuart of Rhodes College (now at Furman University). We hope you will find their insight and advice, quoted throughout Part I, as illuminating as we did.

For the current edition, the descriptions of colleges presented in Part III, "Financial Aid, College by College," were compiled from the College Board's Annual Survey of Colleges. A team of editors, led by Stan Bernstein, edited, verified and double-checked the data with the colleges. Finally, we would like to thank the team of programmers and composers at Content Data Solutions, Inc., who converted the database into readable pages.

Tom Vanderberg, Senior Editor
College Planning Services
Michael Polizzi, Assistant Editor

How to Use This Book

Part I: Financial Aid, Step by Step

The first chapter, "Yes, You Can Afford College," establishes our central point: a college can be found to fit any budget. If you are skeptical about that, please start here — we think we make a strong case.

Steps 1 through 11 provide easy-to-follow directions on how to get financial aid, including what you need to know, what you need to do, and when you need to do it.

These "steps" are presented in a logical sequence. But depending upon your own circumstances — where you are in the college application process, your family's finances, what kinds of colleges you're applying to, and the policies of those individual colleges — you may need to take the steps in a slightly different order, skip some steps, or do some steps simultaneously. To keep track of what should be done when, consult the planning calendar on the inside front cover.

Financial aid officers and the forms you need to fill out often use jargon that can at times seem vague or confusing. Terms like "need" and "cost of attendance" have specific meanings that might not be the same as what you would assume. Throughout Part I, you'll find key terms defined in "Know the Lingo" sidebars (you'll also find a detailed, comprehensive glossary at the end of this book). Other sidebars emphasize or illustrate the main points of each step.

Throughout Part I, you'll find graphs and charts that also illustrate key points, and tables that summarize information and let you compare different financial aid options. You'll also find checklists and prefilled sample worksheets that will help you plan and keep track of your applications. Blank copies of those worksheets for you to fill in are in Part II.

Part II: Tables and Worksheets

One of the worksheets that you'll find in Part II will help you compare the financial aid award letters that you'll receive from colleges. To drive home the point that no two award letters are alike, we've included two samples in Part II, immediately after the comparison worksheet. These are actual award letters that were sent to the same aid applicant by two different universities, the names of which we've changed.

Part II also includes a series of worksheets that you can use to estimate how much the federal government will say you should pay for college out of pocket — that's your "expected family contribution" (EFC) used by colleges to award financial aid. (You'll learn more about the EFC and how it's calculated in Part I.) These worksheets are designed for dependent students and their parents. If you are an independent student, you can do the same thing with the online tools at the collegeboard.com Web site. In addition to worksheets, Part II includes a sample of the preapplication worksheet for the Free Application for Federal Student Aid (FAFSA). This worksheet shows all of the questions included on *last year's* FAFSA; it may be that some questions will change somewhat in the year you fill this out. Finally, in Part II you'll find lists of state aid programs, state-sponsored 529 college savings plans and other useful places to find more information.

Part III: Financial Aid College by College

This is where we help you get the "financial aid picture" at specific colleges, including scholarships the colleges offer to entering students, and required forms and deadlines. To place this picture in context, we give you brief facts about the kind of college it is, and its basic costs. This information can help you compare the colleges you are considering and find colleges that look affordable. But keep in mind that the financial aid figures are mostly based on averages, meaning many students will be above or below these benchmarks.

The college descriptions in Part III are arranged alphabetically by state or territory. Running headers at the top of each page will help you orient yourself and find schools quickly. An alphabetical index of all the colleges in the book appears in Part IV.

Every college described in this book is accredited by an agency recognized by the U.S. Department of Education. Accreditation is a process in which an outside agency ensures that a college meets certain basic standards — it's a stamp of approval on the college's teaching, facilities and administration. For financial aid purposes, accreditation by a federally recognized agency means that federal student aid dollars can be used to attend the institution.

The College Board College Handbook also includes full descriptions of the colleges in this book, going beyond the cost and financial aid details presented here to include information about admissions requirements, academics, housing, student life, athletics and more.

Where the College Information Comes From

The information in the college descriptions comes from the College Board's most recent Annual Survey of Colleges, which was conducted in the spring of 2009. Every college reported its own cost and financial aid information to us. Where possible, our staff of editors verified the information by consulting third-party sources, including public university system or district offices, state education departments and the federal government's Integrated Postsecondary Educational Database System. The information presented was current at the time this book went to press in May 2009 — but be warned that it may have changed by the time you're reading this. Once you have narrowed down a list of colleges that you're interested in, you should confirm critical information, such as financial aid application deadlines and requirements, by visiting the colleges' Web sites or contacting their financial aid offices.

What's in the College Descriptions

Each college description begins with a shaded box that contains the name of the college, the city or town where it's located, and its Web site address. For every college, its six-digit "federal code" — the code you will need in order to have your FAFSA information sent to the college — appears in this box. If a college requires the College Board's CSS/Financial Aid PROFILE®, its four-digit CSS® code also appears in this box. (The CSS code is the same code you use to send SAT® and SAT Subject Test scores and AP® Exam scores to a college; the federal code is only used for the FAFSA.)

Below the college name box you'll find a brief summary of what type of college it is — whether it's a four-year private university, a two-year community college or a four-year culinary school run on a for-profit basis. (Definitions of all the different types of schools you might find here are in the glossary.) You'll also find information about the number of students who were enrolled in the 2008-09 school year, and the relative difficulty of obtaining admission to the college.

BASIC COSTS

"Basic Costs" lists the tuition, fees, room and board charged by the college. The date indicates the school year for which these numbers apply — if the college was unable to report final or projected figures for the upcoming school year, last year's figures are given. If the college combines tuition, fees, and room and board expenses, that single figure is given as a comprehensive fee.

It's important to note that these figures do not include other out-of-pocket costs, such as books, supplies, transportation and personal expenses. These costs can be substantial, depending upon where and how you live, and what you study. But since these costs vary widely from student to student, we felt it would be misleading to display average amounts.

FINANCIAL AID PICTURE

The core of each college's description is the information about the financial aid it offers. Again, the date indicates the school year for which the college reported numbers — either the current year or the prior year. Depending on the aid programs offered by the college and the figures they reported, you may see one or several of these elements of the financial aid picture:

- **Students with Need.** This shows how financial aid was given to students who could not afford the full cost of attending the college on their own (a full explanation of how "need" is determined is found in Part I, Step 1). The focus is on the entering freshman class but, if a college was unable to provide that breakdown, the numbers are for all undergraduates. Most colleges disclosed the average percentage of need met by financial aid packages, and the relative proportion of aid given as scholarships and grants as opposed to loans or work-study jobs. Use this data to get a sense of how likely a college is to meet your full need, and how much aid will probably come in the form of loans.
- **Students Without Need.** Even though a student does not need financial aid, it's still possible that a college will provide aid based on merit or other criteria, such as alumni affiliation or minority status. That's what is shown here. If a college has a policy of only awarding aid to students who have need, this is also stated here.
- **Scholarships Offered.** This gives details on merit scholarships offered by the college and their criteria for being awarded. Here you can get a sense of whether your GPA or SAT scores put you in the right ballpark for a merit-based grant. You'll also find information about the number of student-athletes who were given a scholarship by the college, and the average award.
- **Cumulative Student Debt.** This tells you how many students borrowed money to pay for college and how much they owed, on average, when they graduated. This is another way for you to measure how much of a college's aid will be loan based. The numbers here only include student loans taken out through the college — not PLUS loans, private education loans or other borrowing done through a third-party lender.

FINANCIAL AID PROCEDURES

The financial aid application forms required by the college, and the priority date and/or deadlines that the financial aid office has set, appear here. This section also includes information about notification — that is, when you can expect to hear back from the financial aid office after applying, and by when they will need your final answer about whether you'll be attending. Unless otherwise noted, all dates given in this section are for applicants who intend to enroll in the fall of 2010. If you plan to apply for admission to the spring 2011 term, contact the college's financial aid office to find out about their policies and deadlines.

CONTACT

The final section of each college description lists the mailing address of the school's financial aid office.

Part IV: Scholarship Lists

If you want to zero in on colleges that offer scholarships for your particular talents and interests, the lists in Part IV will help you do that. Arranged alphabetically by state, these lists will point you to colleges that offer scholarships for a variety of achievements. Please note that, in many cases, merit is not the only criterion used by the college when awarding aid: It may require recipients to also demonstrate financial need by submitting the FAFSA or another financial aid form.

At some colleges, every applicant is automatically considered for merit scholarships. At others, you have to specifically apply for a given scholarship. And in some cases, a scholarship is only open to you if you've been recommended by your principal, school counselor or teacher.

What's in the Scholarship Lists

Each list points to colleges that offer aid for a specific talent or area of interest.

Academics. This list names colleges that offer merit aid for academic achievement. Typical criteria include the classes you've taken, your GPA and your standardized test scores.

Art. This list includes colleges that offer merit aid for artistic ability, as reflected by grades in art classes, teacher recommendations and/or a portfolio you submit to the college.

Athletics. If a college offers scholarships for a certain sport, it will be listed here. The letters "M" and "W" indicate whether the scholarship is available to men, women or both. Please note that, at most colleges, only a very few athletes receive significant scholarships. No one should rely on athletic achievements alone to get into college or to pay for it. Instead, make sure your academic record is solid, and be sure to apply for need-based financial aid by submitting the FAFSA and any other required forms.

Music/Drama. This list includes colleges and conservatories that offer merit aid for talent in the performing arts, as reflected by grades in music, dance or drama classes; teacher recommendations; and/or an audition or a submitted tape.

ROTC. Three lists are included here, one each for the Air Force, Army and Naval Reserve Officers' Training Corps. (Marine Corps ROTC is included in Naval ROTC; the Coast Guard and Merchant Marine do not have ROTC programs.) The schools listed may not necessarily have all their ROTC programs on campus; they may have a sponsorship agreement with a neighboring college or university instead. If you enroll in ROTC, you will need to apply separately for the actual ROTC scholarship from the service branch you've chosen — the money doesn't come automatically. (For information on how much money is awarded and how to apply, consult *The College Board Scholarship Handbook*, or visit your local recruiting station.) Some colleges offer additional institutional scholarships for ROTC candidates from their own funds, beyond what's awarded by the Department of Defense.

Part I

Financial Aid Step by Step

Yes, You Can Afford College

Yes, you can afford college. How do we know? Because most colleges are not as expensive as you think. Because if a college wants you as a student, it will try to help you with financial aid. Because most students get financial aid. And because there are ways to reduce the amount you have to pay now, including working part-time and taking out loans.

This is not what everyone will tell you. You may hear discouraging words like, "Most colleges are expensive" and "You won't qualify for financial aid." People may hint that college is not worth all the trouble. The financial aid forms may look complicated and confusing.

We will show you how to get past these doubts. You *can* afford college, and we will show you how. College is worth the expense; you should apply for financial aid. With our step-by-step guide through the process, you'll sidestep confusion and be able to focus on the important decisions in front of you.

This book will help you if you have already saved some money for college — and also if you have not. It will help if you are a student, or a parent of a student. It will help if you have already decided what colleges to apply to, and also if you are not sure where you'd like to go. You may be the first in your family to consider college, or the latest in a family tradition. You might think your family doesn't make enough money to afford college, or that it makes too much to be awarded financial aid. You may have an expensive "dream college" you hope to attend, or you may be looking only for the best buy. You may plan to work or not to work, commute or live on campus, rely on your parents' money or pay your own way. No matter what your situation, you can afford college and we will help you do it.

Why You Can Afford College

Despite media hype about pricey colleges and the soaring cost of higher education, most colleges are not as expensive as you might think. In addition, the published prices of many colleges, though high, are not the whole story. If a college wants you as a student, and if you and your parents don't have enough money, the college will usually offer help so you can attend. That help is financial aid — and because of it, **a college's published tuition and fees are not what most people pay.**

Financial aid is a great equalizer, and most students benefit from it. Two-thirds of all full-time college students receive grants or scholarships to help them foot the bill. Those grants come either from the government, the college or both, and do not have to be paid back. Many students also receive other forms of help, including federal tax credits and deductions that allow their families to keep more of their money at tax time. Thanks to all this assistance, full-time college students pay, on average, much less than the advertised price of their education. In 2008-09, for example, students at four-year private colleges paid an average net price of $14,900 in tuition and fees instead of the published price of $25,143. Students at four-year public universities received a proportionally similar discount.

Even expensive colleges are less costly than you might think because they offer more financial aid. Since a high-priced college often awards more assistance than a low-priced one, a particular student might end up paying the same out-of-pocket cost at both, or even less at the college with a higher sticker price. **That's why you shouldn't rule out your "dream college" as too expensive until you find out if it wants you and what kind of financial aid package it will give you.**

MYTH/FACT

Myth: Most colleges are expensive.

Fact: The most expensive colleges get the most media attention, which creates the illusion that all colleges are expensive. The truth is that colleges vary greatly in price, and most are much more affordable than people think, especially once financial aid is factored in.

That said, there are great deals to be found. At a public college — one supported by a state or local government — the average tuition and fees in 2008-09 were $6,585 a year. That's a 74 percent saving over the $25,143 a year charged by private colleges. Another way to save money is to spend your first two years at a community college, which is a public college that specializes in two-year education programs. Published tuition and fees at community colleges averaged just over $2,400 a year — a 64 percent saving over the average at a public four-year college.

Here's one last reason you can afford college: you don't have to pay every penny up front. You can borrow money at a low interest rate and pay it back after your studies are over. There are also ways to reduce the amount you have to pay right now. *(See Step 11 for more on these "out-of-pocket" options.)*

Figure 1:
Average Total Costs by Type of College

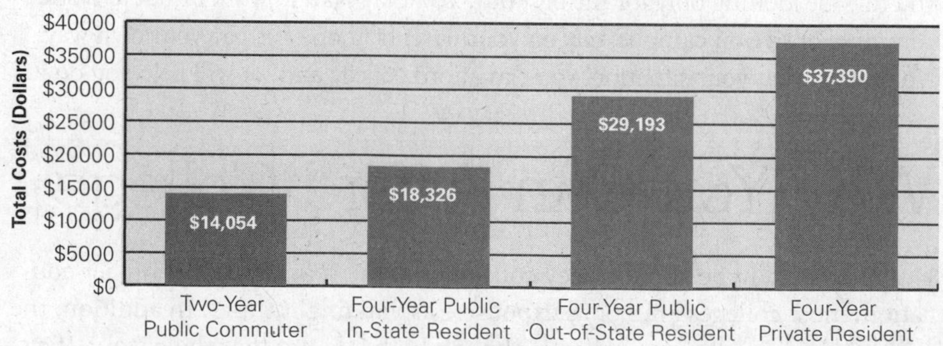

Prices given here are for the total cost of attendance: tuition, fees, room, board, books and supplies, transportation and personal expenses. See Step 3 for more about the components of college costs.

Is College Worth It?

Even if you can afford college, is it a good idea? No matter how much financial aid you get, college will still require a sacrifice of money, time, and effort. Kids who go straight to work after high school have more spending money sooner. Does college give enough bang for the buck?

The answer is yes for many reasons including money, job insurance and personal growth.

In terms of money, college clearly pays. The difference in earnings between college graduates and high school graduates has increased sharply over the past three decades. The typical male college graduate now earns 65 percent more than the typical male high school graduate; for women, the difference is 60 percent. **College graduates earn an average of $1 million more over their careers than high school graduates.** Even if you borrow to pay for part of your education, it's still worth it. Provided you borrow intelligently, your increased earnings will help you pay back the loan. (*See Step 11 for more about loans.*)

You might think that the increased earnings from your college education won't make up for the total costs and the years that you won't be in the work force. But Figure 3 on the next page shows otherwise. The grey line shows the cumulative earnings at each age for the average high school graduate

Figure 2:
Median Annual Earnings by Education Level

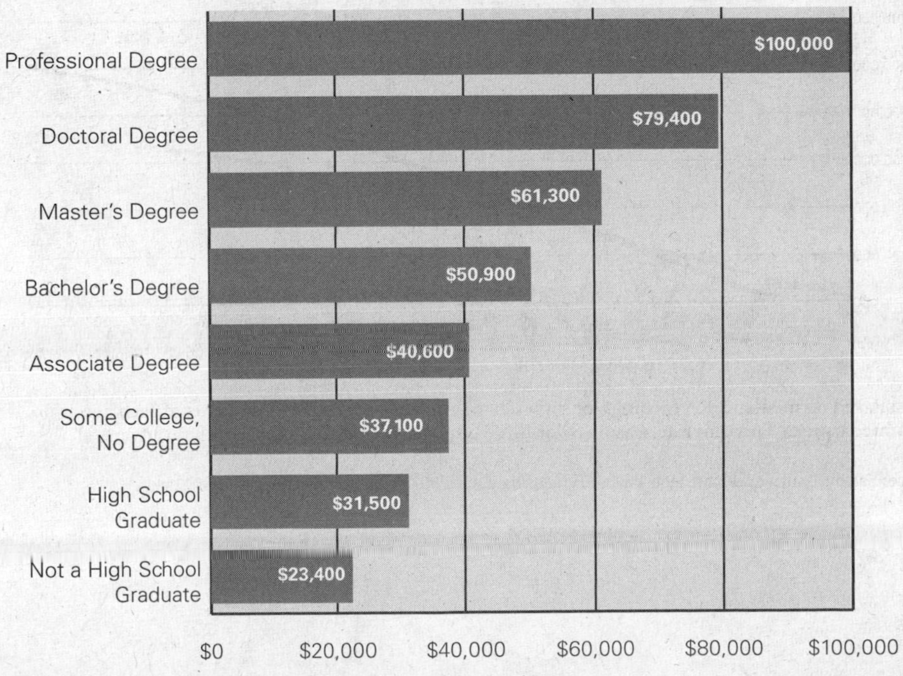

Note: Includes full-time, year-round workers age 25 and older.
Sources: U.S. Census Bureau, 2006, PINC-03; Internal Revenue Service, 2006; McIntyre, et al., 2003; calculations by the authors.

who enters the workforce full time at the age of 18. The black line shows the cumulative earnings at each age for the average college graduate who enters the workforce at age 22, after subtracting average tuition and fees paid over four years at a public college or university. As you can see, by age 32 the lines intersect. From that point on, the investment in college pays off.

College also provides job insurance in a world whose economy is constantly changing. As new industries develop and many jobs are outsourced to foreign countries, you can compete better with a college degree. A college degree teaches you how to acquire knowledge and put it to use no matter what the circumstances. In fact, some higher-education credential — at least an associate degree — is a minimum to stay employed in the "knowledge economy" of the 21st century. **A mere high school diploma is obsolete; college helps to ensure employment.**

But the value of college can't be reduced to dollars alone. It involves intangibles, things you can't touch directly: how you value yourself, your dreams and your ambitions. If you are an artist, a musician, a writer, a builder, a scientist or a thinker, college will help you cultivate those talents. If you are hoping to find yourself, meet people who are more like you, and meet people who are different and interesting, college can contribute to that search too. College provides rich ground for personal growth.

On every front, as a matter of value for dollars, college is a good buy. You can afford college — and it is worth the price.

Figure 3:

Estimated Cumulative Earnings Minus College Costs

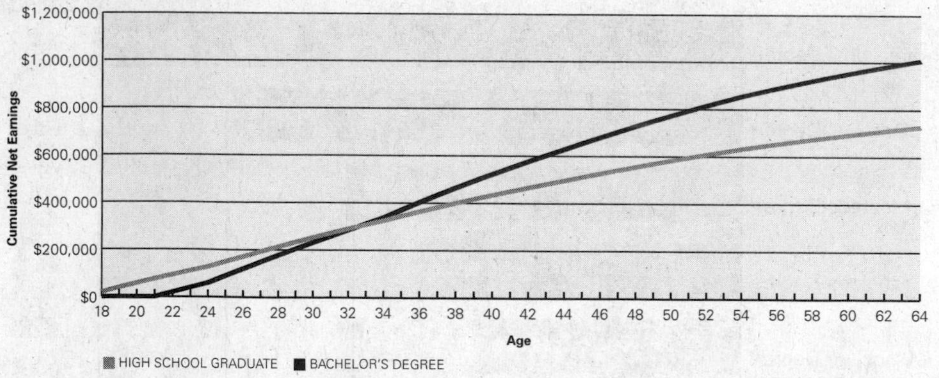

Notes: Based on median 2005 earnings for high school graduates and college graduates at each age and discounted using a 3 percent rate. Earnings for B.A. recipients include only those with no advanced degree.

Source: Sandy Baum and Kathleen Payea, *Education Pays 2007*, The College Board, New York.

How This Book Will Help You

KEEP IN MIND

Don't approach the chronology of this book too rigidly — **not all steps have to come in this order.** For example, Step 9, "Look for Other Sources of Money," can be done at any time. Since outside scholarships aren't tied to a particular college, you can start researching and applying for them before you've even made a short list of schools. In fact, this is a good idea because the application deadline for these scholarships may be as early as Nov. 1, before most college admissions applications are due.

Through this book, you will learn how to make college affordable for you. You'll find out exactly what you need to know so you can apply for financial aid, choose an affordable college and control costs while at college. In Part I, we will walk you step-by-step through the process. There are 11 steps in all:

- **Step 1:** You'll find out the key facts about financial aid.
- **Step 2:** You'll get an idea of how much financial aid you can get.
- **Step 3:** You'll see how and why college costs vary.
- **Step 4:** You'll figure out which forms you need to fill out, and when.
- **Step 5:** You'll learn how to fill out the Free Application for Federal Student Aid (FAFSA).
- **Step 6:** You'll find out how to complete the CSS/Financial Aid PROFILE® form (called the PROFILE for short), if your colleges require it.
- **Step 7:** You'll learn how to fill out any other forms a particular college might require.
- **Step 8:** If your family has special circumstances, you'll find out the best way to explain them to colleges.
- **Step 9:** You'll learn about scholarships and other aid you can get from sources outside of a college.
- **Step 10:** You'll learn how to compare award letters from colleges and decide which offer is best for you.
- **Step 11:** You'll learn how to pay your share of the cost of college through work, loans and other means.

In Part II of the book, tables and worksheets will help you make informed decisions and stay in control of the financial aid process. Part III will paint a clear picture of the financial facts about each college you might want to investigate. That includes its costs and its approach to financial aid.

No one will tell you that paying for college is fun. But what you're getting — a college education — is worth it and is within reach. College is a big-ticket purchase that requires careful thought and preparation, like a house or a car. And it shouldn't be done in the dark. This book will guide you into one of the most important purchases you'll ever make — with your eyes wide open.

Step 1: Let's Go Over the Basics

QUICK OVERVIEW

The first step to getting financial aid is to understand the basic facts about it. In this step we will explain what financial aid is (money to help you pay for college), what types there are (the kind that comes free and the kind that doesn't), who gets it and where it comes from.

The most important point: almost everyone qualifies for at least one form of financial aid. As long as you apply, the chances are excellent that you will get some.

Just What Is Financial Aid?

Financial aid is money given or loaned to you to help you pay for college. Different forms have different rules. The vast majority of aid comes from the federal government, and most of it consists of loans that you must pay back. However, some aid does not require repayment — which makes it the best kind of aid to get.

If you qualify for financial aid, your college will put together an aid "package," usually with different types of aid bundled together. You and your parents will almost certainly still have to pay something, but the aid package will help. Most students qualify for some form of financial aid, so it makes sense to apply for it.

You'll apply for financial aid either at the same time or soon after you apply for admission. You may have to fill out more than one application. At the very least you will fill out the FAFSA, or federal government form. You may also fill out another form, the PROFILE, which many colleges require. And some colleges and state aid agencies require their own financial aid forms, too. The colleges to which you apply will use the forms to figure out what your family can afford to pay and what your "need" is — that is, the difference between what you can pay and what the college actually costs. If the school wants you as a student but sees that you can't handle the whole bill, it will make you a financial aid offer to help you meet your need. If you accept, that financial aid package is your award.

KNOW THE LINGO

Grant — money that is given away for free, usually on the basis of who needs it

Merit scholarship — money that is given away for free on the basis of academic qualifications or special talents

Subsidized loan — money that you have to pay back with interest; however, the federal government pays the interest for you while you are in college

Work-study — a program in which you take a part-time job to earn money for your education; the federal government pays part of your salary

Financial aid package — what a college offers to an accepted student who has applied for aid. Usually a mix of grants, loans and/or work-study.

You will need to apply for financial aid every year that you are in college, mainly because your family's financial situation changes yearly. As a result, your financial aid package will probably be somewhat different from year to year.

Financial aid is a helping hand, not a free pass. In the United States, everyone has a right to a free public school education, but not to a free college education. The federal government and most colleges agree that students and their parents are the ones most responsible for paying for college. "The primary responsibility of paying for the student's education lies with the student and his or her parents," says Forrest M. Stuart, the director of financial aid at Rhodes College in Memphis, Tenn. "Financial aid comes in to fill that gap, if you will, between what they can afford and what the college costs." Even so, financial aid can be the deciding factor in whether or not a student attends college.

Types of Aid

Financial aid may come in many forms. However, all forms can be grouped into two major categories: gift aid and self-help aid.

GIFT AID

Gift aid is free money, money that you don't have to pay back or work for. Naturally, this is the kind of aid most people want. It can take the form of grants or scholarships.

The terms "grant" and "scholarship" are often used interchangeably to mean free money. But here's the difference. A grant is usually given only on the basis of need, or your family's inability to pay the full cost of college. Scholarships are usually awarded only to those who have "merit," such as proven ability in academics, the arts or athletics. Once you're in college, you may have to maintain a minimum GPA or take certain courses to continue receiving a scholarship.

SELF-HELP AID

Self-help aid is money that requires a contribution from you. That can mean paying back the money (if the aid is a loan) or working for the money (if the aid is a work-study job).

The most common form of self-help aid is also the most common of any form of financial aid: the loan. A loan is money that you have to pay back with interest. In light of that, you might not consider this aid at all. But it is — a loan means you don't have to pay the full price of college all at once: You can stretch the payments over time, as you would when buying a house or a car. Furthermore, some student loans are subsidized by the federal government. With these loans, you don't have to pay the interest that comes due while you're in college. The federal government subsidizes, or helps to pay, the loan by paying that interest while you're enrolled and for the first few months after you graduate.

EXPERT ADVICE

"One of the **most important things for students** to understand is what loans are about, and what indebtedness means, so that they don't stumble through four years of college having signed promissory notes blindly, and then come to the end of their senior year and say, I really owe that much money? They should know that they have to pay loans back, and they should **think about their total indebtedness** in relation to what their prospective income is and how it might affect some life choices."

— Joe Paul Case, dean and director of financial aid, Amherst College, Amherst, Mass.

Subsidized loans, which are awarded based on need and administered by the college, are the best kind. But you can also take out unsubsidized student loans and parent loans, which are not packaged by most colleges. However, be careful not to take on more debt than necessary. No matter what kind of loan you take out, you will have to pay it back.

Another form of self-help is work-study. This is financial aid in the form of a job. Since you earn the money through your work, this too may not seem like aid. But it is, because the federal work-study program pays most of your wages. And work-study jobs are usually available right on campus, with limits on your hours so that you won't be unduly distracted from studying.

Aid can also come in the form of tax cuts — income tax deductions and credits for education. But colleges don't award this variety, and you don't apply for it in the same way as you would loans or grants, so we will discuss it separately, in Step 11.

Who Gets Aid?

Grants and loans are not just for the poorest of the poor, nor are scholarships only for the smartest of the smart. The truth about who gets financial aid is somewhat different from what many people think.

Those Who Need It

Most financial aid is based on need, not merit. There is money for merit, but since the 1950s most colleges in the United States have focused their financial aid packages on meeting financial need.

However, there is a lot of confusion about what need means. Many people think it means a state of dire poverty, so that no working-class or middle-class student need apply. "A lot of people think that they either have to be on welfare or Social Security — really poor — to get financial aid, and that's not correct," says Mary San Agustin, director of financial aid and scholarships at Palomar College in San Marcos, Calif. On the other hand, some rich families mistakenly think they are needy because their high living expenses leave them little money for college. "It's this expectation of, I pay my taxes, so my kid should be entitled to some federal financial aid regardless of how much money I make," says Ms. San Agustin.

Need simply means that your family can't afford to pay the full cost of a particular college. The *amount* of your need will vary from college to college, because it depends on the cost of attending an individual college. Whether your family has need is determined not by whether you think you are rich or poor, but by the financial aid forms you fill out.

Just fill out the forms. If you do have need, you will be considered for financial aid.

Those Who Don't

Despite the overall emphasis on need, many colleges do give away money on the basis of merit. They do this to attract the students they want most, and they may award this money even if it is more than the student needs. However, in many cases, the student both needs the money and has earned it on the basis of merit.

Don't think that only geniuses get merit aid. At many colleges a "B"-average GPA can put you in the running for merit money. Sometimes a separate application for merit aid is required to put you into consideration; sometimes your application for admission is enough. In either case, don't count yourself out by not applying; apply and let the college decide.

Grants are sometimes awarded based on neither need nor merit. For example, you may get a grant if you are in a certain field of study, are a resident of the state or are a student from the same town as the college. *(See Step 9 for more about grants and scholarships.)*

KNOW THE LINGO

Merit aid — aid awarded on the basis of academics, character or talent

Need-based aid — aid awarded on the basis of a family's inability to pay the cost of attending a particular college

Non-need-based aid — aid awarded on some basis other than need or merit, such as grants with eligibility requirements related to field of study or state residence

Part-Time Students

Some kinds of aid are only available to students enrolled in college full time — usually 12 or more credit hours of courses per semester. But part-time students are eligible for some financial aid. For example, federal programs such as the Stafford loan require only that students be enrolled at least half-time, whereas others, like the Pell Grant, are available to students enrolled less than half-time. Also, some employers offer tuition reimbursement benefits to students who work full time and go to college parttime.

Where the Money Comes From

Financial aid comes from three basic sources: governments (both federal and state), colleges and outside benefactors.

From the Government

The lion's share of total financial aid awarded in this country comes from the federal government. Fully 65 percent of all student aid is sent from Washington. The largest chunk of that consists of federal loans, which total $43.8 billion a year and represent 41 percent of all student aid. The loans take multiple shapes. Perkins and Stafford loans are for students, while parents may take out a PLUS loan to help pay for their children's educations.

The federal government also funds several grants, including the Pell Grant, the Supplemental Educational Opportunity Grant (SEOG), the Academic Competitiveness Grant and the SMART Grant. The Pell and SEOG are strictly needbased, while the last two are based on both need and academic criteria. The government also funds the federal work-study program.

A much smaller piece of the financial aid pie (7 percent) comes from individual state governments. Most of this aid is for use only at colleges within the state, though a few states offer "portable" aid, which state residents can take with them to a college in another state.

From the College

A great deal of financial aid comes from individual colleges, using their own "institutional" funds. In fact, colleges award nearly half of all grants. Many, though not all, award merit scholarships as well as need-based grants. They may also offer on-campus job opportunities and loans.

Private colleges give more financial aid than public ones, but their tuition is usually higher as well. Public colleges award less aid, but taxpayer support keeps their tuition lower.

Outside Grants and Scholarships

Outside grants and scholarships come from sources other than the government or the college. These sources may include corporations like Coca-Cola or community groups like the Elks Club. Some are well known, such as the National Merit Scholarship, but altogether they are the smallest piece of the financial aid pie: **only 7 percent of all student aid comes from this source**. Pursue them, but don't expect them to outweigh the other aid you will get.

Bear in mind also that your outside scholarship is unlikely to expand the total aid you receive. Most colleges will use an outside scholarship to substitute for some other piece of aid rather than increase the total aid package. Think of your financial aid package as a barrel: when the barrel is full, no more can be added unless something is taken away. The last thing colleges will take away is whatever sum of money your family is expected to contribute. However, at many colleges, the first thing taken away is self-help aid such as loans. Since that could reduce the total amount you will have to pay back

Figure 4:
Undergraduate Student Aid (in billions) by Source, 2007-08

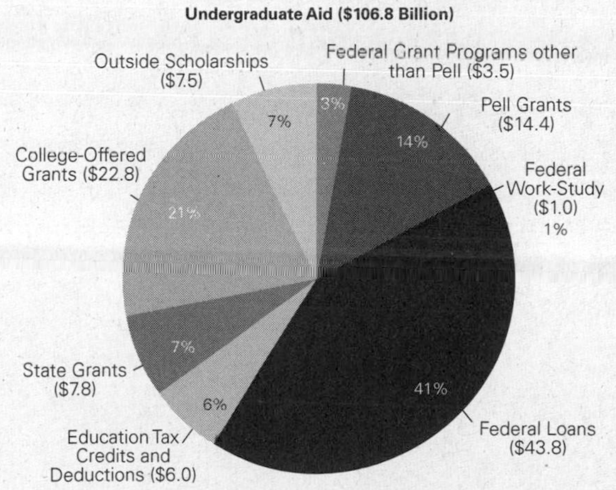

later, it is worth applying for outside scholarships. (*See Step 9 for more on these sources of aid.*)

QUICK RECAP

There is a lot of financial aid out there, in many forms. Apply for it — there is a good chance you will get some. These are the main things to know about financial aid:

- It is money to help you pay for college.
- It may come in the form of a gift (grants and scholarships) or in the form of self-help (loans and work-study).
- Most people get it because they need it, though some get it solely because of merit.
- The federal government funds most of it, but states, colleges and outside sources also help.

Step 2: Estimate How Financial Aid Will Work for *You*

QUICK OVERVIEW

Only rarely does a student get a "free ride" scholarship. You and your parents will have to contribute some money to your education — the precise amount will be determined by the college's analysis of financial aid forms you'll fill out. But even before you fill out the forms, you can estimate your share of the cost and begin planning for how to pay it.

Don't Count Yourself Out

Most college students get some financial aid, but few receive exactly the same financial aid package. Financial aid packages are as individual as the financial circumstances of the students who apply. One family makes $50,000 a year and has two children, a house and a savings account; another makes $50,000 a year but has only one child, a rented apartment and no savings. What financial aid package will each family receive? The answer: It depends on several factors. Families must first submit their applications for consideration by the colleges.

"Probably the question I'm most often asked is, 'Is there a cutoff?'" says Joe Paul Case, the dean and director of financial aid at Amherst College in Amherst, Mass. Financial aid officers agree that there is no single salary cutoff for financial aid — no one income figure that will definitely exclude a student from receiving financial aid. Income is only one criterion for giving out aid: Colleges also consider such factors as family size, number of children in college, and savings. Many students who would be eligible for financial aid fail to apply because they don't realize this.

EXPERT ADVICE

"We always encourage students to **go ahead and apply** for financial aid even though you may not qualify for anything but a student loan. **At least get the paperwork in**, because if something happens in the middle of the year, we already have the financial aid data we need to make adjustments."

— Forrest M. Stuart, director of financial aid, Rhodes College, Memphis, Tenn.

"I always tell families, don't cut yourself off from the application process," says Bonnie Lee Behm, the director of financial assistance at Villanova University in Villanova, Pa. "Apply and let it work through the system."

Even if you feel absolutely sure that your family doesn't qualify for financial aid, fill out the forms. Your family circumstances might change suddenly — a lost job, health problems, a new child. Then you may need financial aid, and it will help to be in the system already. A college can assist you faster if your financial aid application is on file.

What "Expected Family Contribution" Means

Even though you probably will qualify for some financial aid, it's very unlikely that you will get the fabled "full ride." Colleges do sometimes award full tuition — or even full room and board — to a student they greatly want to attract, but that is rare. Almost always, the family is expected to contribute some money. The exact dollar amount will be based on the family's ability to pay. That dollar amount is the expected family contribution, or EFC.

The EFC is carefully calculated to be your "fair share." It is what you can afford to pay based on your financial circumstances — no more and no less. The formulas that the federal government and colleges use to calculate EFC are ultimately intended to make sure that the EFC is fair.

In some ways, the concept of EFC works in your favor. No matter what a college costs, so long as it awards you the full financial aid you need you won't have to pay more than your EFC — the amount your family is able to pay. Say your EFC is $8,000. At a college with a total cost of attendance of $11,000, you could get up to $3,000 in financial aid. At a college where the total cost is $25,000, you could get up to $17,000 in aid. **Because of financial aid, any college is at least worth considering; no college should be ruled out in advance as too expensive.**

On the other hand, even though the expected family contribution is based on ability to pay, that does not simply mean how much the family would like to pay. For any purchase, most people would *like* to pay zero dollars. But what they are *able* to pay is how much money they have minus how much they need to keep for other things, such as food, rent, heat and retirement. When colleges award financial aid, they calculate your ability to pay by looking at your income and financial assets as you lay them out in your financial aid application. Using what are called need-analysis formulas, they analyze your data to see how much of the college costs you are able to pay (your EFC) and how much you are unable to pay (your need). How much you would like to pay is not part of the calculation.

Costs – EFC = Need

Your expected family contribution is your family's share of college costs. Any cost greater than that is your need. Need varies from college to college because it depends on the cost of the individual college. **It's simple arithmetic: College costs minus your EFC equals the amount of aid you need.** At colleges that award enough financial aid to meet your need, the aid package will equal the amount of your need. Costs minus aid equals what you pay.

Unmet Need (a.k.a. "Gap")

KEEP IN MIND

If a college offers you a financial aid award that doesn't meet your full need, you may be able to fill the "gap" in your package with an **outside scholarship**. For more on outside scholarships, see Step 9.

Unfortunately, not all colleges will award enough aid to meet your full need. Some colleges may "gap" your package — that is, not meet your full need. Economics plays a part here. While some colleges may have enough aid dollars available to meet every student's full need, some colleges lack such funds. If your college cannot meet your full need, costs minus aid will still equal what you pay. But what you pay will be more than your EFC. (*See Step 11 for more information on loans* and other ways to help fill such a gap.)

If you do encounter a "gap" in your award, compare the package with the ones you've gotten from other schools, and consider your priorities. Do you want to go to that college, no matter the cost? Or does cost matter more? (*For more on this topic, see Step 10.*)

It Depends on the College

The amount of aid you get — along with the kind of aid you get, whether gift or self-help — ultimately depends on the college. Formulas and forms are important, but so is the professional judgment of the financial aid officer. And so is the desire of the college to attract you to its campus.

How Colleges Calculate Your Need

As you saw in Step 1, financial aid comes from two main sources: government money (usually in the form of loans and work-study), and the college's own "institutional" money — usually in the form of grants and scholarships. Your financial aid package will probably contain money from both sources.

Just as there are two main sources of aid, there are two main formulas that colleges use to figure out how much aid you should get. One is called the "Federal Methodology," used for aid coming from government money. Most colleges use it to award their own institutional funds as well. The Federal Methodology is based on the FAFSA, the federal financial aid form.

For aid coming out of their own money, some colleges and scholarship programs use a different formula called the "Institutional Methodology." This is based on the PROFILE (more formally known as the College Board's CSS/Financial Aid PROFILE application) and/or the college's own financial aid application form. (*For more about these forms, see Steps 6 and 7.*) Colleges that require the Institutional Methodology do so because they think it presents a fuller picture of your family's financial situation. "I just think it does a much better job of measuring ability to pay," says Forrest M. Stuart, whose institution, Rhodes College, requires the PROFILE.

So what does all this mean to you? The differences between the two formulas make it possible that your expected family contribution will be lower under one or the other; it all depends on your individual family circumstances, and the individual college(s) you are applying to. You don't have to know how these formulas work or remember what they are called. The thing to remember is that if you apply to several colleges, because of these different formulas you might end up with a different EFC for one college than you do for another.

KNOW THE LINGO

EFC (Expected Family Contribution) — How much money a family is expected to pay for college.

Need — The difference between your EFC and the cost of attending a particular college you've chosen. Financial aid is designed to meet your need, not your EFC.

Unmet need — The difference (if any) between the your need and the financial aid offered by a particular college. Informally, unmet need is also called a **gap**.

Asset protection allowance — The amount of money considered reasonable to set aside for educational savings and emergencies, and is therefore not part of your EFC.

Will College Savings Count Against You?

While some families save diligently for their children's college educations, others think this is a mistake. They worry that having a lot of savings will keep colleges from awarding financial aid. **But savings help you more than they hurt you**, and here is why.

When calculating your EFC, colleges subtract what they call an "asset protection allowance" from the amount you have saved. This "allowance" is the amount of money considered reasonable to set aside for educational savings and family emergencies. These "free" savings are not assessed at all. In Federal Methodology, the allowance varies based on the age of the oldest parent, and it can be several tens of thousands of dollars for a married couple in their 40s or 50s. These savings are clearly worth having, since they aren't included when calculating your EFC. (See Table 12 on page 136 to get an estimate of what your parents' asset protection allowance may be.)

Even if your family saves more than the asset protection allowance, those savings will be assessed at a maximum rate of only 5.6 percent. So even if 5.6 percent of your excess savings count "against" you when it comes to federal need determination, 94.4 percent count "for" you. You can use them to meet your expected contribution, whatever it turns out to be. That's good news, because your family will be expected to pay much more out of income than out of savings. Most colleges will expect your parents to contribute between 22 and 47 percent of their income toward your EFC.

Essentially, your family will be expected to pay some part of your college costs out of pocket, and if you have savings, you have a pot to draw from. The alternatives are to pay it out of your monthly income or to borrow it — both of which are less appealing choices than using savings. "If I were preparing to send a son or daughter off to school, I would want to have as much savings available to me as I realistically could," says Vincent Amoroso, deputy director of the Office of Scholarships and Student Aid at the University of North Carolina at Chapel Hill. "The reason is because, just like in other situations, having money on hand makes it easier for me to make choices that are good for myself and my child."

To be sure, there are other factors your family should consider before saving for college, such as whether they have enough money to save for retirement. But if they can put away any money for college, they should do so without hesitating. (*See Step 11 for information on tax-free college savings plans.*)

Responsibilities Within the Family

Who should pay for college? Is it entirely the parents' duty, or should the student be responsible? If both, which combination of both? There is no single right answer to questions like these. But families need to discuss the topic, and the sooner the better. Your college will expect someone in the family to make a contribution, and you and your parents should figure out who that is before the bill comes due.

"Families should discuss college costs, family budget, financial aid and financing options at the beginning of the college application process, not at the end," says Carlene Riccelli, a college adviser at Amherst Regional High School in Amherst, Mass. Try to reach decisions that are as specific as possible, so that you each know what's expected of you. Try to make the decisions fair, so that no one feels used. What portion of your summer job income should go toward college? If your family takes out loans, should they be in your name your parents' name or both? Don't forget to discuss ways of keeping costs down, such as living at home and taking community college courses.

If your family is nontraditional, the discussion should include all adults involved in your care. When considering the financial need of students with divorced parents, for example, some colleges that use the Institutional Methodology will assess the income and assets of both natural parents. It will be up to the family to decide how to pay the expected family contribution, but part of that contribution will be based on the income and assets of the parent without custody. (*See Step 8 for more about parental custody and financial aid.*)

While it's important to talk about money, your family also needs to talk about other aspects of choosing a college, such as its academic and social environment. Some of the discussion will have nothing to do with money, but others will have financial aspects: for example, going away to an expensive college versus staying home and commuting to a cheaper one. Step 3 will further explore how to think about these issues. But the important thing is to start having the discussions — financial and otherwise — as early as possible.

Crunch Some Numbers

If you want a sneak peek at what your expected family contribution will be, crunch some numbers. Part II contains worksheets and tables that you can use to calculate the EFC of a "typical" family under the Federal Methodology. Use the worksheets to add up your income, then subtract deductions and allowances. Total up your assets, too. Apply the formulas in the worksheets to calculate the contribution that is expected from you as a student. Then use the next set of worksheets and tables to calculate your parents' expected contribution. When you're finished, you will have your estimated EFC.

The figure you come up with will only be an estimate. Your actual EFC may be higher or lower, depending on the exact data you ultimately submit and the particular college's financial aid policies. But at least this exercise will give you a ballpark figure for what you can expect to pay.

Online Calculators

If you'd prefer to estimate your EFC online, there are several Web sites with special calculators. They include:

- **collegeboard.com** — Our Financial Aid EasyPlanner lets you "Do the Math" not only on EFC but on college costs, savings and loans.
- **College and university Web sites** — These sites sometimes include calculators geared to their individual financial aid policies.

Figure 5:
Sample EFC Illustration

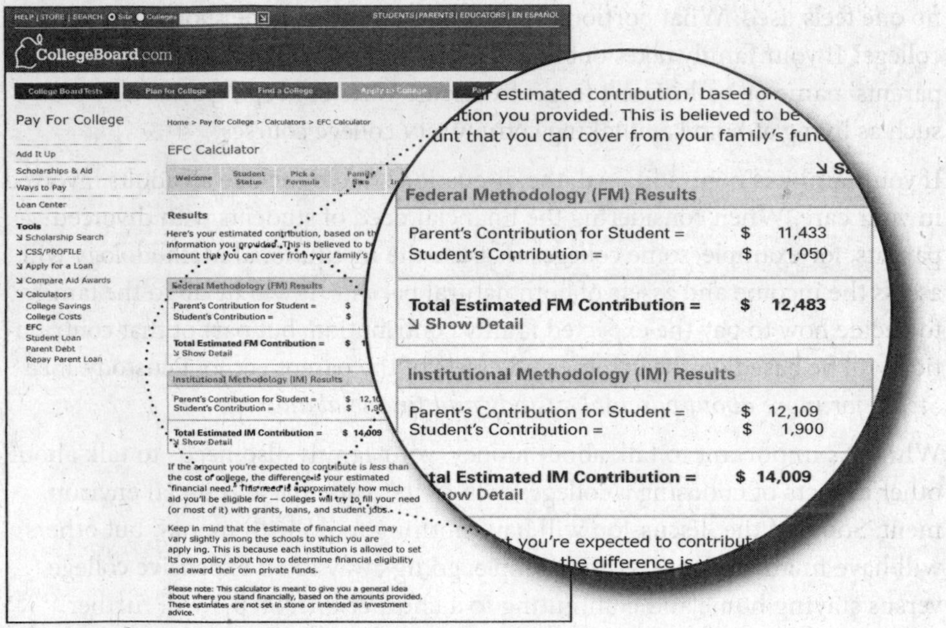

Online calculators like the one at www.collgeboard.com can help you estimate your expected family contribution.

Your Unique Situation Counts Too

Colleges expect families to contribute some money toward students' education, and the amount they expect is your EFC. But colleges are not just faceless buildings of stone, and your EFC is not fixed in cement. The financial aid officer in charge of distributing a college's financial aid is a human being, and he or she does have some room to adjust how the EFC calculations are made based on your individual circumstances.

Step 8 will go into greater detail on how to notify your college about changes in your family's financial situation, such as a lost job. And Step 10 will discuss how to appeal if you think the college hasn't taken all your circumstances into account. Generally, financial aid officers are sympathetic if you are struggling with problems such as caring for an elderly parent or a lost job. They will be less sympathetic if it seems that you've chosen your financial problems — such as buying a new motorcycle with money that could have gone to pay your college bill. Still, financial aid officers are not heartless, and they will try to help when there is genuine distress.

QUICK RECAP

The American education system expects families to bear as much responsibility for the costs of higher education as they can, but not more. Your family will have to contribute to your college costs, but will also receive help.

- Your family will be required to pay an expected family contribution, or EFC.
- The costs of the college you attend minus the financial aid you receive equals what you pay.
- College savings will not be held against you.

Step 3: Choosing Colleges, Thinking Costs

QUICK OVERVIEW

This step shows you how to think about cost when choosing a college. You'll see why you shouldn't exclude any college from consideration just because of its price. You'll learn what your different college expenses will be, from tuition to pizza money; how costs can vary from college to college; and how to factor in the financial aid package the college is likely to give.

KNOW THE LINGO

Total cost of attendance — Not just tuition, but also all fees, room and board, transportation, books and supplies, and personal expenses.

Public college — A college or university that is subsidized by taxes and other public revenues and governed by a county, state or federal government agency.

Community college — A two-year public college subsidized by a local government, such as a county or city.

Out-of-state tuition — What public colleges charge students from other states; often more than double the rate for in-state residents.

Reciprocity agreement — A deal between neighboring states that allows residents to attend a public college in either state at the in-state tuition rate.

How to Think About College Costs

When you're thinking about where to apply for college, its "list price" should not be the main consideration. Because financial aid will probably be available to help meet your need, even a college that appears exorbitant may in fact be within reach. A college's published costs are only one part of the equation when it comes to what you'll actually pay. **Until you've applied for and received an offer of financial aid, you won't know the real cost to your family.**

Remember that financial aid works like this: Total cost of attendance *minus* your family's expected family contribution (EFC) *equals* your financial need. As long as the college meets your need, the amount you pay stays the same whatever the price of the college. "I don't think college cost really should be a factor in where students apply for admission," says Vincent Amoroso of the University of North Carolina. "I say that because your family contribution, in theory, is the same whether you apply to a school that costs $4,000 or to a school that costs $40,000."

In practice, your expected family contribution may actually vary somewhat from college to college. As noted in Step 2, a college using the Federal Methodology to assess your ability to pay might calculate a higher or lower EFC than a college that uses the Institutional Methodology. Even two institutions using the same methodology might calculate slightly different EFCs, depending on how they have treated any special circumstances that may apply to your family. (*See Step 8 for more on special circumstances.*) But in general, the principle holds that your EFC will be constant from college to college, while your need will vary depending on the price of each college.

The main thing to consider when applying for college is whether you and that school will be a good fit. Look for the academic and social aspects that are likely to make you happy and successful there. Are you artistic? Are you mathematical? Do you love to learn for learning's sake? Do you have strong career ambitions in a particular field? Do you long to get away and see the world? Or does it matter more to stay near your family and the place where you grew up? "Students should not just look at a school because it's affordable," says Bonnie Lee Behm of Villanova University. "They should look at a school because it's the right fit for them academically, socially, spiritually and physically. Is cost an important part? Yes. It's a consideration, but only one among many." **And remember — you can find a good fit at more than one college.**

To discover what specific colleges have to offer, research them. You can find a lot of information about majors offered, the composition of the student body, academic policies, and extracurricular and athletic offerings in *The College Board College Handbook*. You can also learn more on the College Search engine on collegeboard.com, and from college guidebooks and Web sites. If you know people who have gone to the colleges you're considering, talk to them and get their opinions.

So, when deciding which colleges to apply to, don't focus too much on cost. But do be aware of what the costs are; cost may become a factor depending on what financial aid packages you are ultimately offered. Even though your EFC should in principle be the same at all colleges, not all schools always meet full need. And even those that do may meet it with different packages — some with more loans, others with more grants. It makes sense to know what kinds of packages a particular school is likely to give.

By using Part III of this book as a guide, and also by contacting the admissions and financial aid offices of the colleges you're considering, gather as much information as you can about the costs of the school and the type of aid they offer. The rest of Step 3 suggests the kinds of information you should be seeking from each school.

Choosing Colleges

Both you and your parents should be involved in the discussion about where to apply for college. You will share the responsibility for paying for college, so you should all have a voice. Furthermore, your parents can give you good advice about what colleges to consider based on their life experiences, their knowledge of you, and their understanding of the family finances — even if they themselves have never been to college. The deciding vote, however, should be yours. You are the one who will have to start and finish college, and you are more likely to do so successfully if you have chosen the college yourself. "Only the student knows the fit that he or she will have at a particular institution academically, socially and financially as well," says Forrest Stuart of Rhodes College.

When you begin choosing where to apply, don't exclude any college. Let every college be on the table, even if it seems too difficult academically or financially. Aim high. Shop around. The best colleges for you may not be the ones that occur to you first.

If a college is a good fit for you, there is probably a way to make it work financially. "Apply to those colleges that you think, okay, maybe we could afford these, but also apply above that level, because some schools may be much more manageable than you expect," says Bonnie Lee Behm of Villanova University.

Do Consider a "Financial Safety"

KNOW THE LINGO

Need-blind admissions — If a college has a "need-blind admissions" policy, this means that it will admit a student solely on the basis of his or her academic merit or other characteristics, regardless of their ability to pay. However, it does not mean the college guarantees to meet full need. You may be admitted, but the college may be unable to offer a financial aid package equal to your need.

Even though all colleges should be on the drawing board, you should also consider applying to a financial "safety" school — one that is a good academic fit and that you feel fairly confident you can afford. Your financial safety school is one you would be happy attending and that has either low published costs or will almost certainly offer enough grant money to make attendance affordable. A public university in your state, a local community college or a private university where you are highly likely to win a merit scholarship might all be financial safeties.

A financial safety is a good idea because your top choices may not give you as much financial aid as you want. "We know students who are really strong academically, but they're not at the top of their class, and they apply to the college of their dreams," says Elizabeth Bickford, director of the Office of Student Financial Aid and Scholarships at the University of Oregon in Eugene. Despite their hopes for a full merit scholarship, such students may find that they can enroll only if they are willing to take out a large amount in unsubsidized loans — something their family may not be willing to do.

In these and other situations, a financial safety is a good backup. For example, if you accept admission to a far-off university, but find that you can't get used to it and want to come back to the financial safety school near home, it will be easier to transfer if you've already applied and been admitted. Still, Elizabeth Bickford says she encourages students to "dream large, because it's your one opportunity. When you go from high school to that first year in college, that's where most of the scholarships are — for entering freshmen. It's your opportunity to make that big step away from home."

Figure 6:
Distribution of Full-Time Undergraduates at Four-Year Institutions by Tuition and Fee Charges

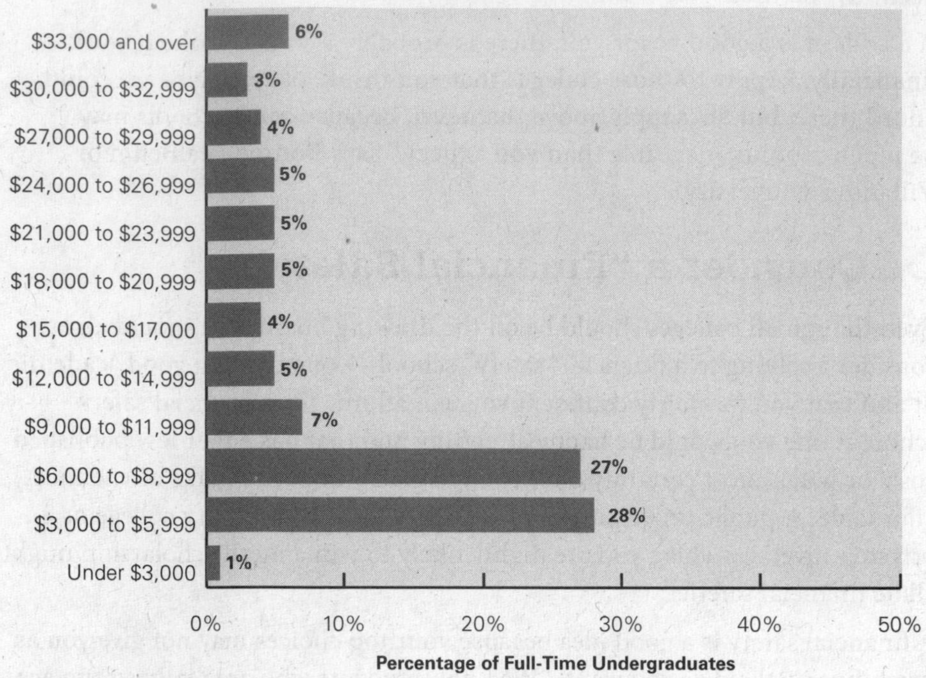

Fifty-five percent of full-time undergraduates attend colleges with published tuition and fee charges of under $9,000. After financial aid, many of those students pay an even lower "net price" for tuition.

Source: *Annual Survey of Colleges*, The College Board, New York, N.Y.

Components of College Costs

The price of a college education has several parts. The most obvious is tuition, the cost of taking courses. Tuition varies depending on how many courses you take, but full time students pay a flat rate for a full schedule of courses. If you attend part time, you will likely pay by credit hours, a measure of how long each class is. Most courses are three credit hours apiece, which usually translates to three one-hour classes each week. Most full-time students take an average of four or five courses per semester, for a total of 12 to 15 credit hours per semester for a full load.

Fees are another component of college costs. Fees are usually billed to all students as funding for the college's general expenses, such as the library or student activities. But there may be additional special fees for students enrolled in certain classes or activities. A chemistry student may pay lab fees, for example.

Tuition and fees are just one part of what you'll pay for college, and often not even half. Another large component is room and board. "Room" is the cost of housing you, and "board" is the cost of food. You may live in a dorm on campus, or off campus — in an apartment or a house with other students or at home with your parents. You may be on a meal plan where all your meals are prepared for you for one price, or you may fend for yourself, buying groceries and cooking meals. Either way, these basic living expenses are your room and board.

Taken together, tuition, fees, room and board are the largest chunk of college costs. On average, at four-year public colleges across the nation, these elements together make up 78 percent of what students pay for college — tuition and fees 36 percent, room and board 42 percent. Yet there is still another 22 percent of costs to be accounted for. These include:

- Books and supplies — class expenses that are not covered by tuition and will vary depending on the courses you take.
- Transportation expenses — for on-campus students, this is the cost of trips home during holidays; for commuters, this is the cost of either mass transit or a car. Car costs include parking, gas, insurance and maintenance.
- Computer equipment costs — if required by the college. Some colleges may insist that you buy a certain model of computer, or bring your own computer but have special hardware and software installed to make it work on the campus network.
- Personal expenses — everything from snacks outside the meal plan to newspaper subscriptions to haircuts and toothpaste to membership fees for student groups.

How Costs Can Vary

Each college has different price tags for each of the cost components. For example, on average, books and supplies cost $800 for the first year at the University of Nebraska, but $1,500 at the Kansas City Art Institute. Table 1 on page 28 shows national averages for cost components.

To get specifics for a particular college that you're considering, check its Web site and look for the school's published estimate of what the average student spends on the different expense categories. The college will use these averages as part of the calculation of your "total cost of attendance," which will partly determine how much aid you're awarded. You can also consult Part III of this book for a school-by-school summary of costs.

However, remember that these average costs are only averages. You are an individual, and you may pay more or less than average, depending on your individual circumstances. For example, if you attend college in California but your family lives in New York, you will pay more for traveling to and from home than if your family is also in California.

Textbook and supply costs can also vary widely depending on your major. If you are an architecture or drafting student, you might have to buy an expensive computer-aided design program that your English major friends won't need. Science students might need to buy a statistical-modeling software package; studio artists a graphic-design suite. At least software like this only has to be bought once and is then used to do work for several classes; furthermore, educational discounts may be available for such purchases. In some programs, students might have to buy supplies that frequently get used up and must be replenished, such as brushes and paints for art students.

Rooming costs will vary a little between different dorm complexes on campus — for example, newer dorms may cost more, and a single room is always more expensive than one shared with a roommate. There will also be differences between various off-campus rooming locations.

Finally, your personal expenses may be higher or lower than average depending on lifestyle factors — but they will almost always be higher than you think. As James Schembari wrote in the *New York Times*, there is always a need for "pizza money" — money to buy pizza, go on a road trip, or hang out at the student union. Books, supplies, travel and everyday expenses "can add $3,000 or more a year, depending on parents' generosity and where their child goes to college," wrote Mr. Schembari.

Table 1:

Average Estimated Undergraduate Budgets, 2008-09

SECTOR	TUITION AND FEES	BOOKS AND SUPPLIES	ROOM AND BOARD	TRANSPORTATION	OTHER EXPENSES	TOTAL EXPENSES*
Public Two-Year						
Resident	$2,402	$1,036	—	—	—	—
Commuter	$2,402	$1,036	$7,341	$1,380	$1,895	$14,054
Public Four-Year						
Resident	$6,585	$1,077	$7,748	$1,010	$1,906	$18,326
Commuter	$6,585	$1,077	$7,748	$1,380	$2,138	$18,928
Out-of-State	$17,452	$1,077	$7,748	$1,010	$1,906	$29,193
Private Four-Year						
Resident	$25,143	$1,054	$8,989	$807	$1,397	$37,390
Commuter	$25,143	$1,054	$7,748	$1,380	$1,895	$37,220

— Sample too small to provide meaningful information.
* Average total expenses include room and board costs for commuter students, which are average estimated living expenses for students living off campus but not with parents.
Note: Estimates of individual budget items are based on reporting by institutional financial aid offices.
Source: *Annual Survey of Colleges*, The College Board, New York, N.Y.

Ways to Reduce Costs

There are a few time-tested ways of saving money on some of the major cost components of college. To save money on tuition and fees, many students have attended public colleges and community colleges. To save money on room and board, many have commuted rather than roomed on campus. Here are the pros and cons for these money-saving techniques.

Public vs. Private, In-State vs. Out-of-State

GOOD TO KNOW

This section discusses ways to **find inexpensive colleges** during your college search. For tips on how to cut costs once you've enrolled, see Step 11.

Attending a public college in your own state is an excellent way to save money on tuition and fees. Public colleges are subsidized by state taxes, so their tuition and fees for state residents are usually much less than at private colleges — 74 percent less, on average. Depending on the school, the quality of education may be as good or even better than what you would get at a private college.

On the other hand, the true cost picture is more complicated than it looks. Even though private colleges charge more for tuition and fees, most of them also give more scholarships and grants than public colleges do, which helps to even out the costs. "There's an adage that the more expensive the school, the more money they give away," says Mike Scott of Texas Christian University, a private institution.

Cost isn't everything. If a particular private school has some valuable characteristic that you want — smaller classes, professors with whom you want to study — it may be worth the extra tuition money. But cost is a factor to consider. If a certain state school can give you all that you want from college, why not go there and save some money?

If you would like to study at a public college or university in another state, be aware that most public schools charge higher tuition to students from out of state than they do to in-state students. Public colleges currently charge an average of $6,585 in tuition and fees to a state resident, but $17,452 to an out-of-state student. The in- and out-of-state rates for specific public colleges and universities are listed in Part III.

PAYING IN-STATE RATES IN ANOTHER STATE

It is sometimes possible to get the in-state tuition rate, or at least a lowered tuition rate, even if you are an out-of-state student. For example, some state universities have "reciprocity agreements" with neighboring states. South Dakota residents pay tuition rates comparable to state residents at the University of Minnesota and vice versa. There are also discipline-based "consortiums" of public colleges that let you get the in-state tuition rate at another state's public college if your desired major is not available at any public college in your own state.

Your school counselor and state board of education Web site can give you more information about programs for paying in-state rates in another state.

Community Colleges

Community colleges are another great way of saving money on tuition and fees. A community college is a two-year school subsidized by a state, county or city. Its cost for tuition and fees is usually much lower than that of a four-year institution — 64 percent lower, on average, than a public four-year college. Community colleges often charge tuition in three tiers — in district, in state and out of state — with the lowest price for those who live in the local district. Though most community colleges do not offer a four-year bachelor's degree (though the number that do are on the rise), they do provide courses whose credits can be transferred toward a bachelor's degree at another college. Because those courses cost much less, this can be a way to save money in your first two years of college — money you can use to help pay for the last two years. Four out of 10 college-bound high school graduates start their college education this way.

There are other reasons to attend a community college besides saving money. If you aren't sure whether you want to go to a four-year college, a community college will give you a sense of what the college experience is like. If you don't know what kind of program you want to pursue — science, art, business or something else — you can explore different subject areas at a community college before committing to a program. And if you need to be able to work, perhaps to support a family, you can work out a more flexible schedule at a community college, where many students work full time and attend classes at night and on weekends.

A community college is also a golden opportunity for students who didn't do well enough in high school to win admission to the college of their choice. Community colleges are open to everyone, and some have agreements with four-year colleges that guarantee admission in the third year for students who have maintained good grades. This is the case in California, according to Mary San Agustin of Palomar College, a community college. If students, she says, "have their heart set in going, let's say, to Stanford or U.C. Berkeley, we have an excellent articulation program that allows them to take the two-year required courses and get guaranteed admissions in their junior year at those schools that they prefer to go to." In this way, **a community college can open the door to a four-year college for you.**

Of course, there are advantages to entering a four-year college as a freshman rather than two years later as a transfer from a community college. Socially and academically, you may enjoy a fuller college experience. "It's all the things that you can't quite name," says Elizabeth Bickford of the University of Oregon. "There is something that you do lose in that transition as an 18- or 19-year-old." But those factors have to be balanced against financial realities, as Ms. Bickford found when she was making her own college decisions. "I'm a community college transfer to a four-year myself. So is my husband. We wouldn't have financially been able to make it if we hadn't done it that way. I think it's a good way to make it if all the support isn't there."

Living at Home

A good way to save money on room and board is to commute. Instead of paying for campus housing and meals — an average cost of $8,989 a year for private colleges — you continue to live at home. There your housing and meal costs remain whatever they have been, and you commute to campus daily by train, bus, car or other means. This will probably be more inconvenient than living on campus, where you would only have to walk a few steps from your dorm to the classroom. But you will almost certainly save a lot of money.

However, commuting has hidden costs. You will have transportation expenses that you wouldn't have if you lived on campus. If you can use mass transit, these costs will probably be low enough to make economic sense. But if you have to buy a car and pay for gas and insurance, your transportation costs might end up being close to the costs of on-campus room and board. And if you're thinking of relying on family and friends for rides to and from campus, remember that their schedules may not overlap with yours. Your own schedule may change day to day and semester to semester, depending on your classes and activities. You probably will need your own car if mass transit isn't available.

Also, don't forget that you cost money at home, too. You're still eating and using utilities at home, and you'll inevitably add pick-up meals on campus to those costs. Financial aid packages usually offer help in paying for room and board as well as tuition and fees, so your actual cost for living on campus would probably not be as high as the published price.

We're not saying that commuting isn't a bargain — it usually is. (There are other good reasons to live at home, too.) But if you are thinking of commuting just to save money, don't commit to it until you weigh all the costs and assess the financial aid offers from any "live away" colleges to which you may apply.

Living Off-Campus

If you don't want to commute but still want to save money on room and board, you might want to consider living off-campus. By residing near campus in an apartment that you share with classmates, you may be able to live more cheaply than you could in the dorms. **But be sure to check the college's policies** — many do not allow freshmen to live off campus if they're under 21 and not living with their parents.

How to Factor in Financial Aid

Every college publishes an average price for the various cost components, but that published price is probably not the price you will end up paying. Your financial aid package will reduce your actual costs. Yet financial aid packages vary from college to college as much as costs do. In thinking about where you will apply, you need to find out some financial aid basics about each college on your short list. How great a percentage of need does it usually meet? How much aid does it award in grants and how much in loans? Does the college offer any merit scholarships or other forms of aid not based on need?

Part III of this book, "Financial Aid College by College," gives you these financial aid basics, along with a number of other essential facts. These include:

- the school's Web address
- what type of school it is, such as public or private
- how many students are enrolled
- how selective the school is
- basic costs, including tuition, fees, room and board
- financial aid application procedures, including deadlines and required forms
- contact information for the financial aid office

In addition, the "Financial Aid Picture" section of each college's profile tells you how much aid is being distributed to how many students and in what form. This information is useful, but note that it only shows averages. Since few families are "average," the numbers in the financial aid profile shouldn't be considered a guarantee of what you'll get or how much you'll have to pay. For example, in-state students at public colleges usually borrow much less than the average debt per student listed in the profiles, while out-of-state students usually borrow more. You can, however, use the profiles to compare colleges: This college meets a greater percentage of need than most; this college awards a relatively large portion of aid in grants.

KEEP IN MIND

The **college profiles in Part III** of this book give the "financial aid picture" for each college, based on averages. Use these profiles to **compare colleges only**; the aid you would get at any college is based on your own individual circumstances, so the amount might be higher or lower than the average for that college.

Check with the Financial Aid Office Before You Apply

Before you apply for financial aid, check with the financial aid offices of the colleges to which you're planning to apply for admission — by simply visiting their Web site, or by talking to them on the phone or in person. Confirm which forms you need to complete and the deadlines. Better to get these details right before you get started than to find out after the fact that you filed too late or didn't file the proper form.

Bear in mind also that each college has its own financial aid policies, such as how outside scholarships are treated and whether or not aid awards can be appealed. When you contact the office, whether long distance or in a campus visit, find out as much as you can about these policies, along with facts about costs and the financial aid process. If possible, schedule an interview with a member of the financial aid staff. They'll give you a lot of information, but don't expect them to offer you aid until they've seen your forms.

Questions to Ask Colleges

Here are some questions worth asking the aid office:

✔ What are your average costs for the first year for:
- tuition and fees
- room and board
- books and supplies
- transportation
- other personal expenses

✔ What is the range of costs for:
- rooms (single, double)
- board (different meal plans)
- tuition rates (flat rate, per credit, etc.)

✔ By how much will total costs increase each year?

✔ How much have tuition and fees and room and board increased over the past three to five years?

✔ Does financial need have an impact on admissions decisions?

✔ Does the school offer both need-based and merit-based financial aid?

✔ Do I need to file a separate application for merit-based scholarships?

✔ If the financial aid package isn't enough, under what conditions, if any, will the aid office reconsider the offer?

✔ How will the aid package change from year to year?

✔ What will happen if my family's financial situation changes?

✔ What are the terms and conditions of your aid programs? For example, what are the academic requirements or other conditions for renewing financial aid from year to year?

✔ When can we expect to receive bills from the college? Is there an option to spread the yearly payment over equal monthly installments?

QUICK RECAP

When deciding where to apply to college, cost is a factor, but not the most important factor. Don't exclude any college from consideration because of its "sticker price" — what you will actually pay might be much less. Remember:

- Each school has different costs and financial aid policies.
- When choosing colleges to apply to, consider a "financial safety."
- Your costs might vary from the published averages.
- You might be able to save money at a public college or community college or by commuting — but there are pros and cons to all those strategies.
- Research the colleges you're considering and contact their financial aid offices early.

Step 4: Get Ready for the Forms

QUICK OVERVIEW

Depending on where you'll apply, you may need to file up to three kinds of forms to get financial aid: the FAFSA, the CSS/Financial Aid PROFILE and forms for individual colleges or states. Step 4 gets you ready for those forms. There are two main things to remember. First, file before the deadlines. The early bird — or at least the timely bird — gets the worm. Second, don't be intimidated. The forms are easier to fill out than they look.

Forms You'll Fill Out

Applying for financial aid is basically a matter of filling out a few financial aid forms on time. The forms may look complicated and be hard to face, but they are simpler than they look, and millions of people fill them out every year. We will guide you through them so they make sense.

The three steps that follow this one walk you through the forms you may need to complete: the FAFSA (Step 5), the PROFILE (Step 6) and whatever forms your individual colleges may require (Step 7). This step will help you create a timeline of which colleges require which forms when.

You may not need to fill out all the forms we describe. Most colleges require only one form, the FAFSA. If you do need to fill out more than one form, take heart. Most of the other forms ask for information similar to what the FAFSA requests. Repeating that information may be annoying, but it isn't hard.

KEEP IN MIND

Even though this book presents the financial aid forms in order of FAFSA, PROFILE and institutional forms, **you may need to submit these forms in a different order** depending on the financial aid deadlines of your colleges. In some cases, you may have to file PROFILE a few weeks before FAFSA, or the institutional form on the same day as FAFSA.

FAFSA: The Federal Form

This is the big one. The FAFSA, or Free Application for Federal Student Aid, must be completed by everyone who wants federal government aid. Just about every college financial aid program requires it, even if they also require other forms. Most schools and states use nothing but the FAFSA to determine eligibility for aid.

There is no charge for completing the FAFSA, which you should fill out online if possible at www.fafsa.ed.gov.

FILING THE FAFSA

You cannot file the FAFSA before Jan. 1 of the year for which you're seeking aid. For example, if you will start college in September 2010, you cannot file the FAFSA before Jan. 1, 2010. If you want a head start, visit the FAFSA Web site earlier so you can familiarize yourself with the form and start working on your application as soon after Jan. 1 as possible. If you don't have all your tax documents together before you need to file, you can estimate your tax information using your end-of-year pay stubs and last year's income tax return (see "Get Your Stuff Together" on page 41).

Once it's Jan. 1, however, you should aim to file your FAFSA as soon as possible. Don't be fooled by the federal filing deadline (June 30). **Most college deadlines for financial aid are in February or March**, and they need your FAFSA information by then. The window of time between Jan. 1 and the financial aid deadlines, some of which fall as early as Feb. 1, isn't big. So, come January, the earlier that you start working on the FAFSA, the better. **Don't worry about filing your tax return first**: If you don't have all your tax documents together before you need to file your FAFSA, you can estimate your tax information using your end-of-year pay stubs and last year's income tax returns (see "Get Your Stuff Together" on page 41). You can correct your FAFSA with actual tax figures later.

The most important thing is to leave time for your FAFSA to be processed after it's filed. If you're filing on paper, leave at least four weeks before your earliest college or state deadline. If you're filing online, you can wait until only a week before the earliest deadline.

The FAFSA may seem complicated, but it's a lot easier than it looks. We'll walk you through it in Step 5.

On the FAFSA, you'll provide financial information about yourself and also about your parents, if you're a dependent student. The information will be based on your income tax returns plus your own reporting of your financial assets, such as bank accounts and savings bonds. The federal government will use that data to calculate your Expected Family Contribution, or EFC.

Soon after you've submitted the FAFSA, you'll receive the Student Aid Report (SAR). This lists the information you reported on your FAFSA and tells you what your EFC is. This report is important. Check it over as soon as possible and, if necessary, update it with your family's latest tax return information. **Don't sit on the SAR: keep the process moving quickly.**

GOOD TO KNOW

If you're filing both the PROFILE and the FAFSA, it might help to **do the PROFILE first**. One feature of the PROFILE Web site is that once you've completed your application, it will create a worksheet you can use to fill out the FAFSA.

WHERE TO GET A PAPER FAFSA

If you don't have Internet access or just prefer to work on paper, you can request the paper FAFSA by calling 800-433-3243. After you submit the paper FAFSA you'll have to allow at least four weeks for mailing and processing before your earliest deadline.

If you use the paper FAFSA, you can only list four colleges to receive your information. You can add up to six more later, but you'll have to wait until your FAFSA is processed and you've received your Student Aid Report (SAR).

KNOW THE LINGO

FAFSA (Free Application for Federal Student Aid) — The form that must be completed by everyone applying for federal government aid.

PROFILE (CSS/Financial Aid PROFILE) — A Web-based form offered by the College Board and used by some colleges and scholarship programs to award their own financial aid.

PIN (Personal Identification Number) — A number that serves as your electronic signature for filing the FAFSA on the Web.

SAR (Student Aid Report) — A report based on the information you provided in your FAFSA that reports your federally calculated EFC. The SAR is sent to every student who files a FAFSA.

Priority date — The date by which applications for financial aid must be received in order to be offered the best possible package. After the priority date, applicants are considered on a first-come, first-served basis, and are offered grants, scholarships and work-study only if the college still has money remaining.

PROFILE

In addition to the FAFSA, some colleges and scholarship programs also require that you fill out the CSS/Financial Aid PROFILE to award their own nonfederal funds. They believe this form gives a more complete picture of students' financial circumstances, allowing them to allocate money as fairly as possible. The PROFILE service is administered by the College Board, though the College Board itself does not give out any need-based scholarships.

A few colleges require PROFILE only if you're applying for early decision or early action. Others require it for all applicants. If your college requires it and you're applying early, it is often the first form to fill out — ahead of even FAFSA. To find out if your colleges require PROFILE, look them up in Part III of this book or refer to the college's Web sites.

PROFILE is online only; there are no paper forms. You can register for PROFILE at www.collegeboard.com beginning Oct. 1 of the year before you intend to start college. Once you register, you can either complete your application then and there or return to it at a later time. It's best if you submit it at least one week before your earliest college financial aid deadline. You can use the same application for multiple colleges, and you'll receive an online acknowledgment confirming the schools to which you're sending the information.

There is a $25 fee to send your PROFILE to one college, plus a fee of $16 for each additional institution. However, depending on the information you submit, you may qualify for a fee waiver. Automatically awarded to low-income, first-time applicants, the fee waiver covers the costs of the PROFILE registration and up to six school reports.

College Forms

Some colleges — most of them private — require you to complete their own financial aid form as well as the FAFSA. Usually the forms are not complicated, and filling them out is not a big deal. Mike Scott of Texas Christian University says, "We have a very simple online form, where we just ask a couple of extra questions." Some of the questions are about projected enrollment: "Are they going to be full time or part time? When do they think they're going to graduate?" Others are aimed at matching students to outside sources of aid.

Find out if your colleges require you to file their own form, and if they do, file them on time.

State Forms

Most states offer need-based financial aid to their residents, and most colleges will require you to apply for it. Ask your school counselor for information on what form you need to complete to apply for state scholarship or grant programs. In many states, the FAFSA alone is enough to establish eligibility for state aid — but some states require their own form. If your state does, find out the deadline and add it to your master timeline for applying for aid. (*A table showing the deadlines for state aid, and which forms each state requires, appears on page 70 of this book.*)

Know the Deadlines!

Deadlines count. If you're on time, the colleges to which you've applied will have more money to give you; if you're late, they will have less money — or even none. **Late means less money, so be on time!** That means knowing and keeping track of all the financial aid deadlines you have to meet.

This can be tricky, because the deadlines are not all the same. Many schools and states may require you to fill out their own financial aid forms, and those forms may have deadlines that differ from those of the FAFSA or PROFILE. And **keep in mind that a college's due date for financial aid applications is typically different from its due date for admissions applications.**

Many colleges have no firm deadline or closing date for applying for financial aid; rather, they have a "priority" date. Often falling in February or March, the priority date is the date by which the school needs to receive your application to make its most attractive aid offer. After that date, funds may be limited or used up, and you may not get as much aid as you need. "I urge my students to apply for aid by the priority date," says Lauri Benton, a counselor at Columbia High School in Decatur, Ga. "They are more likely to get the aid they need early in the process, when the colleges have ample money to award."

Some colleges accept financial aid applications on a "rolling" basis. This means that applications are reviewed as they come in on a first-come, first-reviewed basis. Applicants are notified — that is, sent a financial aid award letter — a few weeks after they submit their forms. Most colleges that have a priority date will review late applications on a rolling basis. If you're applying to a rolling-applications college that doesn't have any set deadlines or priority dates, you're best off applying by mid-February or early March, when they will probably still have enough money available to meet your need.

Part III of this book, "Financial Aid College by College," lists deadlines and priority dates for colleges, along with their required forms. But it is worth confirming this information with the schools to which you're applying — at least by visiting their Web sites in November or December. Remember: Time is money. To get the most aid available, apply by the priority date. (*See also "Do You Get More Money If You Apply Early?" on page 40.*)

EXPERT ADVICE

"If you **meet our priority date**, we're going to guarantee you a full package here. You'll get 100 percent of need if you meet that priority deadline. If you don't, then it's what's left over, if we have money left over. And we typically do — but we don't have enough to meet 100 percent of the need of every late applicant."

— Vincent Amoroso, deputy director, Office of Scholarships and Student Aid, University of North Carolina at Chapel Hill

Creating a Timeline for Aid Applications

There are a lot of dates to remember as you apply for financial aid, but they don't have to be overwhelming. You can stay on top of them by making a timeline.

When you've found out the priority dates of the colleges and scholarship programs to which you're applying, as well as those of your state financial aid agency, list them in chronological order. Make that list part of a month-by-month timeline. Don't worry about the past; start the timeline with whatever month you're in now. The chart on the opposite page is an example of the sort of timeline you might construct. (*A blank copy of this chart for you to fill in appears in Part II on page 119.*)

SAMPLE WORKSHEET 1:

Meet Your Application Deadlines

		COLLEGE 1:	COLLEGE 2:	COLLEGE 3:
	College Name	*1st Choice Univ.*	*Private Univ.*	*Financial Safety*
FORMS REQUIRED	FAFSA	*Yes*	*Yes*	*Yes*
	PROFILE	*For ED (by 11/1)*	*Yes*	*No*
	State form	*Yes*	*No*	*Yes*
	Institutional form	*No*	*Laptop loaner*	*Yes*
	Tax returns	*Verification only*	*Verification only*	*Yes*
	Other			
SCHOOL CODES	Federal code	*999999*	*888888*	*777777*
	CSS code	*999Z*	*999X*	
PRIORITY DATE		*3/1 (FAFSA, State Form)*	*2/1*	*3/15*
CLOSING DATE		*None*	*2/15*	*None*
AFTER APPLYING	Need to send letter?			
	Documentation required?			
COMPARE AWARDS	Notification date	*12/15*	*4/1*	*2 weeks after applying*
	Reply-by date	*Immediately (if accepted ED)*	*5/1*	*4 weeks after notification*

For a blank version of this worksheet that you can photocopy for your own use, see page 119.

Throughout the period that you're applying for aid, keep your timeline where you can see it, check off what you've done, and remind yourself of what to do next. This will put the deadlines in your control. (*See the inside front cover of this book for a calendar of important dates and reminders.*)

Do You Get More Money If You Apply Early?

No. If you apply for financial aid Tuesday and another student applies Wednesday, you don't get more money than that student — so long as both of you apply by the deadline (or the priority date). However, when it comes to the college's own funds, and certain "campus-based" federal student aid programs (such as federal work-study), aid is distributed first-come, first-served once that date has passed. If you apply for aid after the college's deadline or priority date, the pool of funds may be used up. So always apply on time.

WHAT ABOUT EARLY DECISION?

Many schools allow students to apply for admission under early-decision or early-action programs. Whether early acceptance to a school affects the student's financial aid package varies from school to school. Depending on the college, the student accepted early may get more financial aid, less, or the same.

If you are considering early-decision programs, ask each school's financial aid officer: How is financial aid affected if I apply early decision? You may not know exactly what aid you'll get until after you accept. Don't panic: The rules of early decision allow you to turn down the college's acceptance offer if it doesn't offer you enough aid. Just don't put all your eggs into one basket — be sure to apply to a "financial safety school" as well.

The Benefits of Web-Based Applications

The FAFSA can be filled out and submitted online at www.fafsa.ed.gov. A limited number of paper FAFSAs are available for students who do not have access to a computer (see page 36 for information) but it is better to file online. Doing so cuts processing time by several weeks — essential if you're running late. It can also reduce delays due to errors because the site edits your information before you submit it, allowing you to correct it before submitting. Also, once you have submitted the form online, you will instantly get your EFC back from the Web site, which reduces some of the anxiety in the process. The FAFSA Web site gives lots of help in completing the form.

If you do file online, save and print out a hard copy of the confirmation you'll receive after submitting your application. If you file a paper form, make a photocopy for your records.

KEEP IN MIND

When you fill out the FAFSA, both you and one of your parents need a **Personal Identification Number**. This is important: the PIN will allow you to sign your FAFSA electronically, which will cut down your processing time. **You and one of your parents must each request a PIN** at **www.pin.ed.gov**. You should register for your PINs **before you fill out the FAFSA**. A good time to ask for your PINs is November of your senior year. **Remember your PIN and write it down in a safe place:** If you forget it, the government can't "remind" you of it later on.

PROFILE is only available online. If you don't have a computer at home, find out if one of your parents can use a computer at work, or use a computer at your school's guidance office or the library. After you register for the PROFILE, you can print a customized preapplication worksheet to help you gather the information you'll need, then complete the application online.

Figure 7:

FAFSA PIN Site

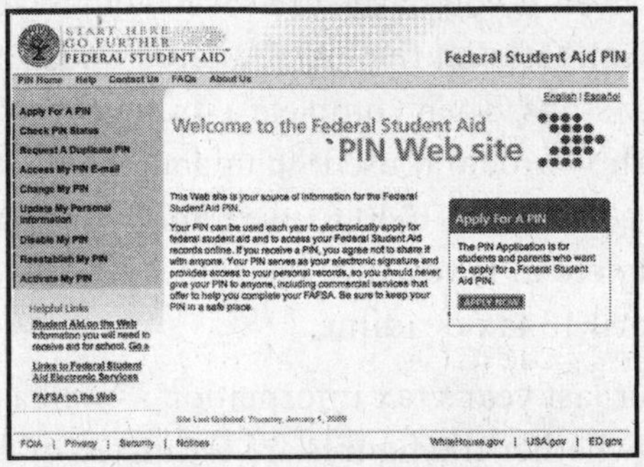

Get Your Stuff Together

EXPERT ADVICE

If, like many students, you've never filed a tax return, you'll probably find it helpful to **get a blank copy of IRS Form 1040EZ** and the instructions that come with it. This is the simplest tax return form there is, and most high school and college students use it to report their summer and after-school job earnings. If your parents have filed for you in past years, **ask them to walk you through your return** for the last year.

For maximum efficiency, gather all the records you need to complete the forms before you sit down to work on them. That will save you a lot of time getting up, hunting around and forgetting where you left off. For both you and your parents, you'll probably need tax returns and related documents (such as W-2 forms) for the year that just ended, as well as end-of-year pay stubs, bank statements and other financial records. If you're filling out the PROFILE, you will also need tax documents from the previous year. If your parents own their home, you will need current value and mortgage information to fill out the PROFILE.

The FAFSA and PROFILE preapplication worksheets are basically a way to help you gather your information before filling out the actual application. Use them that way. Add a list of all the records you need to assemble. It should be comprehensive and indicate which records are for all forms and which are for PROFILE only.

Establish Eligibility

To be eligible for federal financial aid, among other requirements, you'll have to:

- be a U.S. citizen or eligible noncitizen
- have a valid Social Security number
- not have been convicted of sale or possession of drugs
- if male and at least 18 years old, be registered with the Selective Service (in most cases)

Most of these requirements will not require extra work for most students. But two of them may. If you don't have a Social Security number, get one as soon as possible (go to www.ssa.gov to learn how), and certainly before you file your

FAFSA. And if you are male, you can register for the Selective Service through the FAFSA application if you haven't already. If you do have a drug conviction, you may still be able to establish eligibility by completing a treatment program.

Tax Forms and Other Records

Income tax returns are due on April 15, but most colleges want your financial aid forms much sooner. **Don't wait until your taxes are done to file your financial aid forms**. Even if you haven't received your W-2s yet, you can still file the FAFSA. Use estimates on the FAFSA based on last year's return and your current-year pay stubs. Then complete a draft of your 1040 tax return as soon as possible afterward, and use it to update the SAR if necessary. You don't necessarily have to file the 1040 to use it for your financial aid forms; you just need to complete it. If you owe tax, you can wait to file the tax return until closer to the April 15 tax deadline.

PROFILE asks you for last year's tax information as well as for this year's. For this year, it asks you whether the figures are estimated or final. It also asks for estimated income for next year, which you can base on this year's information.

QUICK RECAP

You'll have to file some forms to get financial aid, but they aren't as difficult as they might look. The main forms are FAFSA and PROFILE, plus whatever other forms your colleges or state may require.

- File on time — filing late can cost you money.
- File your FAFSA online. Get a PIN for yourself and for one of your parents early — and don't lose them.
- Make a timeline to keep track of your deadlines, including college priority dates.
- As early as possible, check with your colleges to be sure you know what forms they each require.
- Gather together the records you need to fill out the forms.
- If you don't have one already, get a Social Security number.

Step 5: Fill Out the FAFSA

QUICK OVERVIEW

The FAFSA may look intimidating, but it's actually pretty easy to fill out. The questions mainly concern your income and assets and those of your parents, but they also touch on other matters, such as your citizenship status and the schools to which you want the FAFSA to be sent. We'll walk you through it, and give you tips about how to avoid delays. Above all: File on time!

General Advice

Nobody likes to fill out forms, with their cramped boxes and unfamiliar terms. And no one enjoys having to share information about family finances. But the potential result — money to help you pay for college — is well worth it. And you will see in this step that the FAFSA is really pretty simple. While the form for 2009-10 has eight sections, only two require financial information, and one is, essentially, "sign here."

Again, remember that you don't have to do the steps in this book in exactly the order presented. If the colleges require you to submit the PROFILE before the FAFSA, then do the PROFILE first, even though we present the FAFSA first. In fact, one nice thing about the PROFILE is that, after you've submitted it, you'll receive a worksheet that you can use to fill out the FAFSA, making this step much easier.

EXPERT ADVICE

"Our job is to get students through this maze. You'd call a mechanic if your car is broken. Well, why not call us if you have a question about financial aid applications? That's our job — to get you through the process."

— Bonnie Lee Behm, director of financial assistance, Villanova University

Help is available by phone and online if you have questions about FAFSA (see the "Good to Know" sidebar on page 45). And don't be afraid to call the financial aid offices of the colleges to which you're applying. If you're confused about this or any other aspect of the financial aid process, these offices can help. "People look at the FAFSA and they find it a bit overwhelming initially," says Vincent Amoroso, of the University of North Carolina at Chapel Hill. "They come to us seeking guidance and reassurance on how to get through the application process. We show them that it's not as complicated as it looks."

Apply on Time

You can't file your FAFSA before Jan. 1 of the year you're applying for aid. Most college deadlines for financial aid are in March, and some fall as early as February, so the window for filing is narrow. You have to leave time for your FAFSA to be processed. Be sure to file your online form at least one week before the earliest deadline.

Don't wait until the April 15 tax deadline to file your FAFSA. Most priority dates will be long over by then. If your earliest deadline doesn't fall until March, you can wait for W-2s, 1099s and other official tax documents to arrive from employers and banks and then complete draft income tax returns. You don't have to file those draft returns with the IRS, but you can use the information from them on your FAFSA. The advantage of using draft tax returns this way is that you probably won't have to correct your FAFSA after you've submitted it, and it will be easier to answer the questions on the form that refer directly to lines on the 1040.

If your earliest deadline falls in February, however, you should have a backup plan in case W-2s don't arrive in time. The best thing to do in this case is to use end-of-year pay stubs, quarterly bank statements and similar records to estimate your and your parents' income. You can also use 1040 forms for the previous year as a frame of reference, but don't just plug in the information from last year's returns into the FAFSA — you really do need to estimate the current information, not duplicate old information. (Also, be warned that the numbers assigned to each line of the 1040 tend to change whenever the IRS adds new credits or deductions, so the references on the FAFSA you're filling out may not match old 1040s.)

No matter how you derive the numbers, remember this above all: Get the FAFSA in on time.

Read Instructions Carefully; Fill Out the Form Accurately

With the FAFSA as with all financial aid forms, accuracy is vital. Read the directions. Understand the terms that are being used. Many terms, such as "date of birth," are straightforward, but others, such as "investments," require you to read the instructions carefully so you know what they mean in this context. Even the term "parent," as discussed below, has a special meaning on the FAFSA.

Be as complete and accurate as you can about your financial circumstances. If you submit incorrect data, you might create delays that could endanger your aid. By avoiding errors, you will increase your chances of getting all the aid for which you are eligible.

Keep Track of Your Pin and Password

You can submit a paper FAFSA, but it's easier and faster to submit your FAFSA online at www.fafsa.ed.gov. Filing the FAFSA on the Web can reduce processing time by a couple of weeks. It also reduces delays due to errors: The site edits your information before you submit it, so if you made errors or left out information, you can correct it before submitting it.

KNOW THE LINGO

If you've never filed an income tax return before — or if your parents file for you — you may not be familiar with these IRS forms:

1040 — the main form of your tax return, this is a summary of all the taxable income you or your parents made last year, possible deductions from that income, the tax owed on that income, and credits that give some of that tax back.

W-2 — a tax form prepared by the employer stating how much taxable income they paid you last year, as well as untaxed benefits you or your parents received from them. Information on this form is used on both the 1040 and the FAFSA.

1099 — a form similar to the W-2 that shows income you received from anyone other than an employer. For example, if one of your parents is an independent contractor, he or she may receive a 1099-MISC showing the nonemployee compensation a client paid them.

1098 — a tax form showing payments for which you can take a deduction or credit. For example, if you take out a student loan, once you begin repaying it you will receive a 1098-E from your lender every year showing how much interest you paid on the loan.

You don't have to complete the FAFSA on the Web in one sitting. At the start, you'll supply a password that will allow you to leave the application before completing it and to return later, so long as you come back within 45 days. But **make sure you write down the password and keep it in a safe place** where you can find it again. Unlike most Web sites, the FAFSA site provides no hint or reminder to aid your memory. If you forget the password, there will be no way to retrieve your data, and you'll have to start over.

GOOD TO KNOW

Detailed information on how to complete the paper FAFSA is available on the Web at **www.studentaid.ed.gov/completefafsa.** If you're filing the FAFSA online at **www.fafsa.ed.gov**, that same site offers help screens for each question and live, one-on-one online help with a customer service representative. Click the "help" icon to access that feature. For help over the phone with either the paper or online FAFSA, call **1-800-4-FED-AID** (**1-800-433-3243**).

Avoid any Web site that offers to help you file the FAFSA for a fee. The federal government offers its help for free and does not endorse any site that charges money for assistance.

Get PINs ahead of time for both yourself and for one of your parents so you can sign the form electronically. The PINs can be ordered at www.pin.ed.gov. You should do this in advance because it will take a week to get the PINs — a delay you may not be able to afford later in the process. Write down the PIN in a safe place; if you forget it, that could make you miss your deadline.

Figure 8:

FAFSA on the Web

Let's Walk Through It

The FAFSA consists of seven sections, or "steps," each of which contains a number of questions with a common theme. The exact order or wording of these questions may change from year to year (last year's preapplication worksheet is in Part II), but the substance remains more or less the same. And the purpose never changes: to provide information about yourself and your family that colleges will use to figure out how much federal student aid you qualify for.

There are a few general tips to keep in mind while filling out the FAFSA:

- The word "you" always means you, the student.
- The word "college" means a college, university, community college or any other school beyond high school.
- The phrase "net worth" means the current value of an asset (such as a business) minus the amount of debt owed on it.

- Questions about income are for the previous year; questions about assets ask for their value as of the day you fill out the form.
- When entering dollar figures, round to the nearest dollar and don't use commas or decimal points.
- If you have special financial circumstances that you need to explain, you can't do it on the FAFSA. Instead, write to your colleges directly. (*See Step 8 of this book, "Make Your Special Circumstances Known."*)

Here is a step-by-step walk-through of the key questions on the FAFSA. Since the online form is interactive, it will automatically skip over some questions or sections depending on how you answer. For example, if you say that you're not married, you won't be asked questions about your spouse. Worksheets are available for download as PDFs from the Web site.

FAFSA Step One: About Yourself

These questions gather basic information used to identify you and determine which federal and state programs you may qualify for. For example, the question about your citizenship is there because only U.S. citizens (or eligible noncitizens) can get federal student aid.

Here's the main information this section will ask for:

Your name. Enter your name exactly as it appears on your Social Security card. If the two don't match, you will be asked for more documentation through the mail, slowing down the whole process.

Where you live. Use a permanent home mailing address here, not a school or office address.

Your Social Security number (SSN). As noted in Step 4 of this book, you need to have an SSN to apply for federal aid (you can't even open the online FAFSA without one).

Your date of birth.

Your permanent telephone number. Use a permanent home or cell phone number, not a school or office number.

Your driver's license number (if any).

Whether you are a citizen or an eligible noncitizen. You are a citizen if you were born in this country or became a citizen through the naturalization process. An eligible noncitizen is someone such as a U.S. permanent resident holding a green card (Permanent Resident Card), or someone who has refugee status who is allowed to live permanently in the United States. It is not someone visiting on a student visa. If you're an eligible noncitizen, you'll have to fill in your Alien Registration Number. If you're neither a citizen nor an eligible noncitizen, you can't get federal aid, but you may be eligible for state or college aid — so you should still fill out the FAFSA, unless you don't have a Social Security number. In that case, call your colleges.

Your e-mail address. This is optional, but if you provide it, the government can send you your Student Aid Report (SAR) by e-mail instead of snail mail, so it will reach you faster.

Whether you're single, married, divorced, widowed or separated.

The state in which you legally reside. Your answer will determine whether you're eligible for scholarships and grants from your state. It's also used to estimate how much state income tax you pay. In some cases, your state of legal residence — where you officially live — might be different from the state where you're actually living at the time you fill out the FAFSA. This might be the case if you've recently moved or one of your parents is in the military.

Whether you're male or female. If you are male and you haven't registered with the Selective Service yet, you'll have the option of registering now via the FAFSA. To get federal aid, male students 18 years or older must be registered with the Selective Service, the agency responsible for providing drafted men to the armed forces in an emergency.

Whether you've ever been convicted of possessing or selling illegal drugs. Say "yes" only if the offense occurred while you were receiving federal student aid (unlikely if this is your first FAFSA, in which case you won't even see this question online), it's still on your record, and you were tried as an adult.

The highest level of education completed by your father and mother. This won't affect your federal aid, but some states use this information to award scholarships to students who are the first in their family to attend college.

What year of college you'll be in next year. Your answer determines which aid programs you qualify for. For example, the SMART grant is only available to students in their junior or senior year of college.

What degree will you be working on in the next school year. Some aid programs are not available for graduate study, a second bachelor's degree or nondegree study. If you are undecided about what type of degree you will be pursuing (for example, if you're applying to both two-year and four-year colleges), check "undecided," but be sure to follow up with each college you're applying to after you've submitted the FAFSA.

Your enrollment status next school year. Most aid programs are not available to students who will be attending less than half-time (that is, taking fewer than six credits per semester). Some are only available for full-time students. If you're not sure how many credits you will take, check "undecided," but be sure to follow up with each college you're applying to after you've submitted the FAFSA.

Whether you're interested in loans and work-study. The best answer is "both." Preserve your options. It doesn't matter if you aren't sure. Answering no won't make colleges more likely to give you grants, but it might keep you from getting loan or work-study aid if you change your mind later. By the time you change your mind, all the funds might be gone.

FAFSA Step Two: Are You Independent?

The questions in this step determine whether or not you're an independent student. To be considered independent for the purpose of federal student aid eligibility, it doesn't matter if you feel independent, have a job, or even live on your own. It also has nothing to do with whether your parents claim you as a dependent on their tax return. But if you can truthfully answer "yes" to at least one of the questions in this step, you will be considered independent.

The things that would classify you as independent are:

- You turn age 24 or older in the year you start college.
- You'll be enrolled in a graduate degree program in the year for which you're seeking aid.
- You're married.
- You have children who get more than half of their support from you.
- You have dependents other than your children or spouse who live with you and get more than half their support from you.
- You're an orphan, or you've been a ward/dependent of the court.
- You're currently serving in, or are a veteran of, the active-duty U.S. armed forces. (If you served only as a reservist and were never activated for reasons other than training, answer "no.")

If you are independent, then you can skip FAFSA Step Three, which asks about your parents' income and assets. But there are certain cases where a college financial aid office will want to know about your parents' finances even if you are an independent. If you do meet one of the criteria on the list above, it's a good idea to ask the colleges to which you're applying whether they'll consider you fully independent for the purpose of awarding their own institutional funds. If one or more of them won't, you should fill out FAFSA Step Three. The online application will ask you whether you want to fill it out or skip it.

FAFSA Step Three: Your Parents' Income and Assets

These questions are about your parents' income and assets. If you're a dependent student, you have to answer these questions even if you don't live with your parents. When you're ready to submit the application, you will also need one of your parents to sign it, either on the paper form or by using a PIN on the electronic version.

Modern family life can make the definition of "parent" complicated. But the FAFSA definitions are fairly clear:

- If both your parents are living and married to each other, answer the questions about both of them.
- If only one of your parents is living, answer the questions about him or her.
- If your widowed parent remarried, answer the questions about your stepparent too.
- If you were raised by a single parent, answer the questions about him or her.
- If your parents are divorced or separated, answer the questions about the parent you lived with the most during the past 12 months.
- If that parent remarried, answer the questions about your stepparent, too.
- Don't provide information about grandparents, legal guardians or foster parents. FAFSA doesn't consider them your parents unless they have legally adopted you.

This step is the most work, but it's not hard. Here's a run-down of the important questions:

Their Social Security numbers: Unlike you, your parents are not required to have Social Security numbers in order for you to file the FAFSA (but in that case you have to enter zeroes). But if they do have Social Security numbers, they must provide them.

Their names: Again, if they have social security cards, their names must exactly match.

The number of people in your parents' household: These include you and your parents. The number who will be in college during the next year is also asked for: that also includes you (but not your parents). These questions affect how much money your parents will be expected to contribute to your education.

Whether they've completed a tax return for the past year. This means the return that is due the coming April 15.

Whether they're eligible to file the 1040A or 1040EZ tax form. It's to your advantage if they can answer yes, they're eligible to file this form. If they would normally file the 1040A but filed the full 1040 only to take advantage of an education tax benefit relating to a child already in college, they can still check this box.

GOOD TO KNOW

Most students are eligible to file IRS Form 1040EZ or 1040A as their tax return. Some parents can, too. (The rules determining whether you can are explained in the FAFSA instructions.) **If both you and your parents are eligible to file the 1040A or 1040EZ**, you may qualify for a "simplified needs analysis," wherein only your income (not your assets) will be assessed when calculating your expected family contribution.

If either of your parents is a "dislocated worker." Answer "yes" if one (or both) of your parents has been laid off or has lost their business due to the economic downturn, and is still unemployed. "Dislocated worker" also includes a stay-at-home mom or dad who no longer receives support from a spouse and can't find a job. If you answer "yes" to this question, you should also contact the financial aid office at each college you are applying to. *(See Step 8, "Make Your Special Circumstances Known.")*

Their income tax information: These questions are easy to answer if they've already completed a draft of their tax return. But if they haven't, ask them to give estimates, using W-2s or pay stubs, bank statements and last year's return. **Don't miss any college deadlines or priority dates because**

your parents haven't done their taxes yet. After you submit your FAFSA, you'll be able to correct the estimated figures on your SAR.

What their untaxed income and benefits are. These include items like earned income credits, welfare benefits, Social Security benefits, child support and other money that didn't get taxed. It also includes any contributions your parents made for the last tax year to deductible Individual Retirement Accounts (IRAs) or employer-sponsored retirement plans such as 401(k)s or 403(b)s. Add this up on worksheets and fill in the totals on the FAFSA. If you're filling out the worksheets online, the information will appear on the confirmation page you'll see after submitting, which you should print out and keep on file in case a financial aid administrator asks about them later.

Veterans' education benefits. Here your parents would report any education benefits they get as a result of military service, such as GI Bill funds. (They should report the monthly benefit amount, not the annual amount.) These are not used in calculating your EFC, but colleges take them into account when putting together an aid package, as described in Step 9 of this book.

What their assets are. These include cash, savings and the value of investments, such as stocks and bonds. The amounts to put down are "as of" the day you fill out the FAFSA. Often that is just a best guess, using the most recent bank statements. (Keep in mind that the amount of aid you are entitled to is based much more on family income than on assets.) They do *not* include the home where your parents primarily live (a summer cottage would be included), a family-owned business of less than 100 employees, or a family farm that they live on and operate. However, if your parents own more than one home — a summer cottage, for example, or an investment property — they also should report their equity in that home on the "investments" line. If they own a farm that they don't live on, they also should report the value of that farm as a business. Another thing your parents do not need to include here is any money they have in tax-advantaged retirement accounts, such as IRAs, 401(k)s, 403(b)s and the like.

FAFSA Step Four: Your Own Income and Assets

These questions ask about *your* income and assets — the student's. Income is how much money you made last year; assets are what you own and the savings you have. If you are married, they also want to know about your spouse's income and assets.

These are the main things that this section asks for:

Whether you've completed a tax return for the past year. This means the return that is due the coming April 15, not the one you filed a year ago. If you have filed a return or plan to file one, they will ask what form you're using, for example, the 1040 or 1040A. If you're not going to file any tax return, they will still ask how much you (and, if you have one, your spouse) earned from working.

EXPERT ADVICE

"**Some people overthink the FAFSA** questions. They'll get to what we would see as straightforward questions: 'How many are in your household?' And then 'How many in your household go to college?' Well, some families will list every person who's ever lived in the household and then every member who has ever attended college. And actually **what we want to know** is, how many are living in your household now, and how many of them are in college now."

— Elizabeth Bickford, director, Office of Student Financial Aid and Scholarships, University of Oregon, Eugene

GOOD TO KNOW

The FAFSA asks both you and your parents to report the amount of income tax you will have to pay on last year's income. The **amount they want here is only the federal income tax amount** — don't include Social Security, Medicare, or any of the taxes that are reported in the "other taxes" section of Form 1040. If you or one of your parents is self-employed or has to self-report tip income from a restaurant job, you should keep this in mind.

Whether you're eligible to file the 1040A or 1040EZ tax form. The instructions on the FAFSA explain who can file these forms. Most students can. If you can, say yes.

What income and tax information you and your spouse will report on your tax returns. Again, these questions are easy to answer if you've already completed a draft of your tax return. But if you haven't completed your tax return yet, you should estimate what the information on the completed return will be and update the information later. Use pay stubs and, if you have one, your prior-year tax return to make the income estimates. Just don't put off filing the FAFSA because you haven't done your taxes yet. **You're not required to file your tax return before completing the FAFSA.**

The number of people in your household: This question refers to the number of people in *your* household, if you have one — not your parents'.

What your untaxed income and benefits are. Once again, these include items like earned income credits, welfare benefits, Social Security benefits, child support and other money that came to you without being taxed. You will be asked about these in a series of questions on screen. (If you are filling out the paper FAFSA, you should use the worksheets that come with the form to add them all up, then fill in the totals on your FAFSA. Don't submit the worksheets, but keep copies of them on file. A financial aid office may want those details later.)

Veterans' noneducation benefits. If you are a veteran, the untaxed-income worksheets will ask you to list your noneducation benefits. But if you're receiving veteran's education benefits (for example, GI Bill funds) that are paid directly to a college, do not report those as income in this section (you'll report them a little later in a separate question). Do report any military pensions, health benefits or the like.

What your assets are. This question is meant to provide a snapshot of your assets, the money or property you currently own. Using current banking statements and investment records, say how much cash and savings you have, as well the total value of any stocks, other investments or investment properties that you might own. If you're still in high school, chances are that you only have a small savings or checking account, which you should report on the line asking for "cash, savings accounts and checking accounts." You may also have some government savings bonds, certificates of deposit (CDs) or a few shares of stock; those should be reported on the line asking about "investments."

Don't include any college savings accounts in this step unless you are independent (you answered "yes" to any question in FAFSA Step 2) and they are owned by you in your own name.

FAFSA Step Five: College Codes

Now you're in the home stretch. There are no more questions about your family's finances or personal life. All this section of the FAFSA asks is which colleges should receive your FAFSA information. You list the colleges, and the government will send the processed information to them for free.

You can list up to 10 colleges online; but if you are using the paper FAFSA, you can only list four. In either case you can add additional schools later, when you get your Student Aid Report (SAR). In choosing which colleges to list first, *pick the ones whose financial aid deadlines come first.*

Identify each college by its federal school code. You can find the federal school code in Part III of this book (see Figure 9 below). You can also get it from www.fafsa.ed.gov or the colleges' financial aid Web sites.

For each college, you have to say whether you plan to live on campus, off campus or with your parents. Your answer will affect the housing costs that the school will estimate for you, and therefore your financial need. If you haven't made a decision yet, assume you'll live on campus.

You don't need to request that your information be sent to a state agency; the government will automatically send your processed information to the agency of your state government that administers financial aid programs for state residents, whether scholarships, grants or loans. Do be aware, however, that some states require an additional financial aid form, as discussed in Step 7 of this book.

Figure 9:

Finding a College's Federal Code

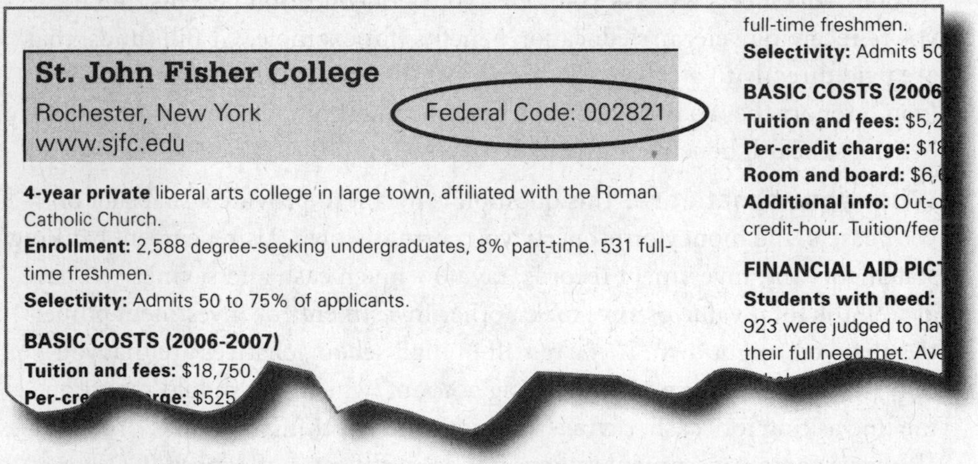

The Federal Code for each college in Part III of this book can be found in its college description.

FAFSA Step Six: Preparer's Information

If you or your family paid a fee to someone to fill out your FAFSA, or to advise you on how to fill it out, that person must provide his or her Social Security number or Employment Identification number (EIN), and must also sign and date the form. This requirement does not apply to school counselors, financial aid administrators, friends or mentors who helped but did not charge a fee.

Pay heed to this warning from the FAFSA Web site: "Be wary of organizations that charge a fee to submit your application, or to find you money for school. Some are legitimate and some are scams. Generally, **any help that you pay for can be received free** from your school or Federal Student Aid."

KEEP IN MIND

You have to leave time for your FAFSA to be processed. If you're filing on paper, allow at least four weeks before your earliest college or state deadline. If you're filing online, leave at least one week before the earliest deadline.

FAFSA Step Seven: Review Your Answers, Then Sign

This is easy, but it's still an important step. Take the time to carefully review all your answers for accuracy and spelling — even your name. When you're satisfied, it's time to sign.

You'll see a list of terms you must agree to by signing. There is nothing onerous here, but there is a scary-sounding penalty for giving "false or misleading information." This does *not* mean honest mistakes or estimates that turn out to be way off; they're talking about intentional fraud.

If your parents provided financial information in FAFSA Step Two, one of them also needs to sign. Use your PINs to sign electronically — don't use the "print signature page and mail" option. It just wastes time.

Be sure to keep clicking on "next" until you get to the confirmation page! Your FAFSA is not truly submitted until then.

FAFSA Step Eight: Submit

You're done! Be sure to print the confirmation page, and save it to your hard drive as well. If you don't have a printer, write down the confirmation number, date and time. This is your proof that your FAFSA was received.

If you file using the paper form, make a photocopy of it before mailing it, and keep that photocopy together with the worksheets you filled out and all the records you used.

Check Your Student Aid Report!

After you submit your FAFSA, you'll receive your Student Aid Report, or SAR. How long it will take for you to receive it, and in what form, will depend on how you filed the FAFSA. If you filed FAFSA on the Web and signed it with your PIN, you should recieve it immediately, or at most within one to three days. If you filed a paper FAFSA and did not provide an e-mail address, you'll receive a paper SAR within about four weeks.

In whatever form the SAR reaches you, check it over carefully. It will include a summary detailing the information you supplied on the FAFSA. Make sure this information is correct. If not, then you must make corrections. It's easy to do — just go back to www.fafsa.ed.gov and follow the link under "FAFSA Follow Up."

Make corrections only if the data on the SAR doesn't accurately represent your family's financial situation at the time the FAFSA was originally filed. For example, if you estimated the previous year's income but have since filed a tax return with exact figures, substitute those figures now. Or if you mistyped a number, or if the federal data-entry clerk misread your handwriting, correct that. But **don't make changes that reflect changes to your income or assets since you filed the FAFSA**. If important changes of that sort have happened — such as a lost job — inform your colleges individually rather than through the FAFSA. (*See Step 8, "Make Your Special Circumstances Known."*)

KEEP IN MIND

Eligibility for **federal student aid does not automatically continue** from one year to the next. You have to reapply every year that you're in college. Do that by filling out a **Renewal FAFSA**. This is a partially preformatted version of the FAFSA that you can use so long as you applied for federal aid the previous year.

At the top of the SAR's front page, you should also see an estimate of your EFC: the amount of money your family is expected to contribute toward college costs. The only reason you won't see it is if your SAR has been rejected because you didn't provide required signatures, valid Social Security numbers or enough data to calculate the EFC. If that happens to you, submit the necessary corrections and you'll get your EFC estimate. **The actual EFC calculated by a given college may be different than what you'll see here**, especially if that college uses a different formula, or if its financial aid office has adjusted your EFC based on special circumstances that you brought to the college's attention.

The colleges you requested to receive your FAFSA information will automatically get your SAR. At the corrections stage, you'll have an opportunity to add more colleges to receive your FAFSA information. You can also give a school permission to add itself to the list. Just provide the college with the Data Release Number (DRN) at the bottom-left corner of the first page of the SAR. The school will use your DRN to access your application record.

The SAR gives you an estimate of how much money your family is expected to pay for college, but not how much financial aid you'll receive. You'll find that out when your individual colleges send you their award letters. Even so, by filing your FAFSA, you've taken a big step toward getting those letters.

If the expected family contribution (EFC) indicated on the SAR looks too high for your family to afford, you should talk to your parents and discuss other financing options with them. (*See Step 11, "Consider Your Out-of-Pocket Options."*) It could also mean that you need to explain some special financial circumstances to the colleges to which you've applied (see Step 8).

QUICK RECAP

The FAFSA is easier than it looks. Most of it is about your income and assets, and that of your parents. It's organized in seven steps. Remember:

- File on time. Submit your FAFSA as soon as possible, beginning Jan. 1 of the year you'll start college.
- It helps to have your tax return finished first, but don't let that delay you. You can estimate your figures and correct them later.
- Read instructions.
- Be accurate.
- Reapply every year.

Step 6: Fill Out the PROFILE (If Required)

QUICK OVERVIEW

Whether you have to fill out the CSS/Financial Aid PROFILE depends on the colleges to which you're applying. If you do, you'll find it mainly asks for "more of the same" — information about your family's income, expenses and assets — rather than something completely new. The online form is customized to your situation, so you won't be presented with too many questions that don't apply to you. However, the application does take time to fill out, so leave yourself plenty of time to submit it before your colleges' deadlines.

General Advice

Step 6 is to fill out the CSS/Financial Aid PROFILE — but only if you need to. If the schools to which you're applying don't require this financial aid form, you don't have to complete it. Find out if they require it by checking Part III of this book or the colleges' Web sites.

The PROFILE is administered by the College Board, a not-for-profit association of schools and colleges (and the publisher of this book). It is available online only: You can't file on paper. The upside of this is that PROFILE is available 24 hours a day, seven days a week. Furthermore, its system of online edits alerts you to missing or incorrect information before you submit the application, eliminating a potential source of delays. Firewall protection and data encryption protect the information you submit about your family and its finances. The downside is that if you don't have a computer with Internet access at home, you will have to use one at your school, a library or a parent's workplace.

The PROFILE doesn't replace the FAFSA: You still need to complete that, too, because that's the form required for federal student aid, which any college will expect you to seek before they give away their own institutional funds. The schools that require the PROFILE do so because they believe it gives a more complete account of your financial situation to guide them in awarding their own funds. The College Board provides the colleges with your PROFILE information, and the colleges use it to calculate your expected family contribution and your need.

Since it's designed to give a more complete picture of your finances, it is not surprising that the PROFILE is longer than the FAFSA. It's the same general concept, but you'll need to gather more records to answer all the questions, and it will take more time to fill out.

EXPERT ADVICE

"Chapel Hill is no different than most schools that require the PROFILE and use it when they're investing a lot of their own institutional dollars into need-based programs. We use it because **the PROFILE gives us an added, more in-depth look** at a family's financial strength. Our ultimate goal is to give the right dollars to the right students at the right time, and this PROFILE application helps us do that."

— Vincent Amoroso, deputy director, Office of Scholarships and Student Aid, University of North Carolina, Chapel Hill

Figure 10:
CSS/Financial Aid PROFILE Online

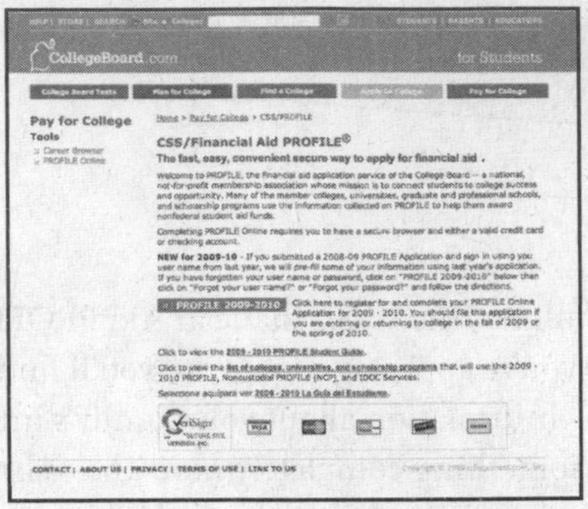

Register and File Early

Because the PROFILE form is more involved, and because colleges may ask for additional information even after the form is filed (such as data on a family-owned farm or store), register well before your colleges' deadlines and leave yourself lots of time to fill out the application. The College Board usually processes your PROFILE information overnight, but delays can happen — especially in late January and early February. Also, don't assume it can all be completed in one session; you may need to gather additional information to complete the form (especially if a college asks for additional information in section SQ). Fortunately, you can go back and forth to your application online, rather than having to finish it in one sitting.

It's best to submit the PROFILE at least one week before your earliest financial aid priority date. Remember, colleges use PROFILE information to determine who gets their limited grant dollars. If you file late, you will have to make do with whatever funds, if any, are left over.

You may need to submit the PROFILE ahead of the FAFSA, depending on the deadlines your colleges set. In fact, some of the colleges that require the PROFILE will ask you to submit it before you submit your FAFSA. This is especially likely if you're applying early decision or early action for admission to the college. If a college requires the PROFILE before Jan. 1, you can submit a PROFILE with estimated income figures for this year based on your year-to-date pay stubs and your previous year's tax return, then send corrections to the college later if necessary.

Even if college deadlines don't require the PROFILE first, it may save you time to complete it before the FAFSA. The PROFILE collects all the information asked for by the FAFSA, and when you complete the application, PROFILE

GOOD TO KNOW

Help is available to get you through the PROFILE application. If you're not sure about how to answer any question, **check the online Help Desk** that's built into the online application. If you can't find an answer to your question there, contact the PROFILE help line, either by e-mail (**help@cssprofile.org**) or by phone (**305-829-9793**; TTD 800-915-9990). From January to April, PROFILE customer service hours are Monday through Friday, 8 a.m. to 10 p.m. Eastern Time.

You can also contact the financial aid office at the college to which you're applying. In addition, your high school counselor may be able to answer your questions.

will generate a worksheet that you can print out and use to complete the FAFSA.

Preparing for the PROFILE

You can get ready to complete the PROFILE with the Pre-Application Worksheet, available from the PROFILE site at collegeboard.com. (The worksheet is customized for you after you have registered.) You can also download and print out the PROFILE Registration Guide and Application Instructions from the same site. All of these materials are available in both English and Spanish.

The Pre-Application Worksheet can save you a lot of time by helping you gather all your necessary family financial information before starting the application. Filling it out on paper can also speed your way if you have to file the application on a computer where your log-in time is limited, such as at school or a library.

Whether you're filling out the Pre-Application Worksheet or the PROFILE itself, you'll need to gather more records to fill out the PROFILE than you will for the FAFSA. For example, in addition to asking about your parents' income for the year before you plan to enter college, the PROFILE asks about their income the year before that, as well as their projected income in the year to come. There are also questions about your projected summer and school-year earnings during your first year in college. The purpose of this is to give financial aid officers a better idea of whether last year's income was typical or unusually low or high. But it also means that you must collect more documents, such as tax returns for the prior year, and you'll need to estimate future income.

Documents You'll Need Before You Fill Out Your PROFILE

It's a good idea to gather the necessary records before you start and have them handy as you work on the PROFILE. You'll need records for both yourself and your parents.

- ✔ U.S. income tax return for the year before you start college, if completed, or pay stubs and other income-related records for estimates
- ✔ U.S. income tax return for the year before that
- ✔ W-2 forms and other records of money earned the year before you start college
- ✔ Records of untaxed income for those two years
- ✔ Current bank statements and mortgage information
- ✔ Records of stocks, bonds, trusts and other investments

As with the FAFSA, it's easiest if you've already completed your tax return for the most recent tax year before you start filling out the PROFILE. But don't let that hold you up. Estimate your tax return information if you haven't completed your return by the time you need to file the PROFILE. (There are tools on the PROFILE site to help you and your parents estimate this information.) You can correct PROFILE information, if necessary, directly with the colleges after filing your return.

How to Register/File on the Web

Just like registering ahead of time for a FAFSA PIN, **it's best to register for the PROFILE well before the first college's deadline.** Since the PROFILE is entirely Web based, you do this online at www.collegeboard.com. You'll need to create a collegeboard.com account (with a username and password) before you can file; setting up the account is free. (If you previously registered online for the SAT, you already have this account: It's the same one you used then.) If you don't have Internet access at home, ask your school counselor or librarian if you can use one of the school's computers.

It's smart to register for PROFILE as soon as you're sure about where you'll be applying for aid, but in any case at least one week before the earliest financial aid filing date you need to meet. Registrations are accepted beginning Oct. 1 of the year before you intend to start college. Once you register, you can either complete your application then and there or return to it at a later time. Your PROFILE application will be customized to your circumstances based on the information you give when you register.

Most families will have to pay a fee of $25 to have their PROFILE sent to one college, plus $16 for each additional college. The fee can be paid with most major credit cards, with some bank debit cards or by an electronic withdrawal from your checking account. Low-income families applying for the first time may qualify for a fee waiver (see sidebar).

Registration will involve providing some preliminary information such as your date of birth; mailing address; the year in school for which you're seeking aid; whether you are a U.S. citizen, a veteran or an orphan; whether you have dependents or have separated or divorced parents; and whether your parents own a home, or all or part of a business or farm. The questions usually won't involve looking up documents; just answer them straightforwardly. Some of them (such as the questions about date of birth and being a veteran) are intended to clarify whether you're a dependent or independent student.

GOOD TO KNOW

If your family's income and assets are very low, and you are applying for financial aid for the first time, **you may be eligible for a fee waiver** covering registration costs and up to six school reports. Whether you qualify will be determined based on the information that you provide in the PROFILE form itself. **You will automatically get the fee waiver if you qualify** — you don't have to apply for it separately.

Figure 11:
Finding a College's CSS code

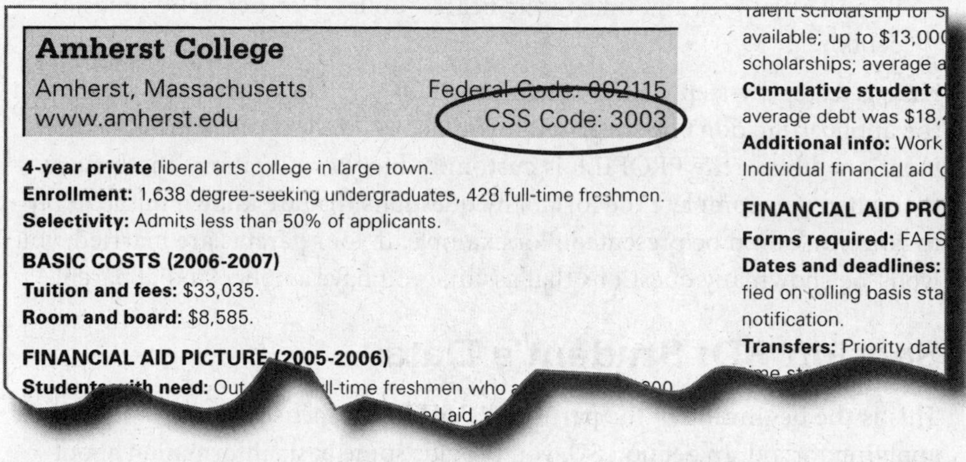

Amherst College
Amherst, Massachusetts
www.amherst.edu
Federal Code: 002115
CSS Code: 3003

4-year private liberal arts college in large town.
Enrollment: 1,638 degree-seeking undergraduates, 428 full-time freshmen.
Selectivity: Admits less than 50% of applicants.

BASIC COSTS (2006-2007)
Tuition and fees: $33,035.
Room and board: $8,585.

FINANCIAL AID PICTURE (2005-2006)
Student with need: Out ll-time freshmen who a

available; up to $13,00
scholarships; average a
Cumulative student d
average debt was $18,
Additional info: Work
Individual financial aid c

FINANCIAL AID PRO
Forms required: FAFS
Dates and deadlines:
fied on rolling basis sta
notification.
Transfers: Priority date

The College Scholarship Service® (CSS) Code for each college in Part III of this book can be found in its college description.

During registration you will also be asked a few very basic questions about your family's finances; these determine whether you will be asked certain questions that usually don't apply to low-income families. For example, if your parents rent their house, they won't be asked about home equity in the Parents' Assets section.

You will also have to select the colleges or scholarship programs to which you would like to have your PROFILE report sent. Colleges and programs can be selected on collegeboard.com by name, code or state. You can add more colleges or programs to this list after you register, or even after filing your application. (See "After Submitting Your PROFILE" on page 65.)

Let's Walk Through It

Your PROFILE application may contain up to 15 sections, depending on your family's situation. The application includes questions about you and your finances and questions about your parents and their finances. There is a place for you to explain in writing any special financial circumstances (section ES) and a place for any additional questions that may be required by one or more of the schools to which you're applying (section SQ). In addition, if your parents are divorced or separated, your noncustodial parent might need to complete an online Noncustodial PROFILE.

To help you fill out the PROFILE, there are instructions online that you can follow, along with other avenues for help (see sidebar on page 57). A few general points to keep in mind:

- If a financial question (such as one about income or assets) doesn't apply to you, enter a zero (0).

- If a nonfinancial question (such as a year or a name) doesn't apply to you, leave it blank.
- Round all money amounts to the nearest dollar. Don't enter commas or cents.

Here is a step-by-step walk through the PROFILE. However, when you fill out the application, don't be surprised if you don't see all the questions that are mentioned here. The PROFILE is customized to your situation. That means that when you complete the form, any questions that are known not to apply to you won't even be presented. For example, if your parents are married, you won't be shown any questions that assume you have a noncustodial parent.

Section SD: Student's Data

This is the beginning of the part of PROFILE that focuses on you, the student applying for aid. In Section SD, you provide some basic information about yourself. Much like on the FAFSA, you'll be asked to name your current legal state of residence, which may not be the same as the state you're actually living in now (see page 47).

Section SI: Student's Income and Benefits for the Previous Year

This section asks about your income and benefits in the year before you intend to start college.

If you have a completed tax return for that year, this section is mostly a matter of copying the amounts from the correct lines, such as the adjusted gross income and income tax paid. If you haven't filed a return but plan to do so later, you'll have to fill in estimates. If you don't plan to file a return but you did make some money last year, you'll have to report it. Untaxed income also goes in this section. A worksheet is available for you to tally it up.

Section SR: Student's Expected Summer/ School-Year Resources for the Coming School Year

Here you're asked to state your expected resources for this coming summer and this coming school year. You're also asked about scholarships you expect to get from sources other than the colleges to which you're applying and how much money your parents think they'll be able to pay for your college expenses.

This may seem like a strange series of questions, especially if you don't know yet where you'll be going to college next year, or where (even if) you'll be working. But colleges that use the PROFILE want to have as clear a picture as possible of your future resources, not just your past ones. For example, if you currently have an after-school job but will leave that job when you graduate, the financial aid offices need to know that the income from that job won't be available to you anymore once you've started college.

Do the best you can to estimate these figures. If you're not sure how to answer in your particular case, check the PROFILE help online or contact the financial aid office at the college to which you're applying.

Section SA: Student's Assets

This section asks about your assets — the money or property you, the student, currently own. These too affect your ability to pay for college. You need to list any cash you have and any checking or savings accounts in your name. Give their value as of the day you're filling out the application. You should also include any investments, such as certificates of deposit, savings bonds, stocks or real estate that you own. If you have any Individual Retirement Accounts (IRAs) or other tax-advantaged retirement accounts, you should also list them here.

If you're an independent student, then any money you have in 529 prepaid tuition or college savings plans or Coverdell savings accounts should be included here. If you're a dependent, those will be considered your parents' assets, and the information about them should go in Section PA.

This section will also ask you to answer questions about any trust accounts your parents or other relatives may have established for you. A trust account is money that is held for you by somebody else until you reach a certain age, at which point it becomes yours. Colleges want to know about this because if you have a trust, that money will eventually reach your hands, lowering your ultimate financial need. If you have any trust accounts, list their value here and answer the questions about them. But don't include money in Section 529 plans; those aren't the same as trusts.

Section SE: Student's Expenses for the Previous Year

You'll only see these questions if you're an independent student. If you are, you'll be asked about any child support you or your spouse paid to a former spouse and any medical and dental expenses you had last year that weren't covered by insurance. Most colleges will consider these expenses in determining your financial need.

Section PD: Parents' Data

Now the PROFILE application switches its focus from you, the student, to your parents. The term "parents" as PROFILE understands it might need some defining. It basically means your custodial parents, the people with whom you live. If both your parents are living, married to each other, and have custody of you, answer the questions about both of them. But if that isn't the case, follow these rules:

- If your birth or adoptive parents are divorced, separated or were never married, then you only need to provide information about the parent with whom you live. If you lived with both equally in the past 12 months, answer the questions about the parent who provided most of your financial support.

- If you have a widowed or single parent or a legal guardian, answer the questions only about that person.
- If your parent (as defined above) has married or remarried, include information about your stepparent too.

Your parents should use this section to provide information about themselves, including name, date of birth, employment status and whether they themselves are in college or graduate school. Some of these questions have to do with clarifying financial strength — for example, the question about what kind of retirement plans your parents have. Some are just matters of housekeeping, such as their preferred daytime telephone number in case they need to be contacted.

Section PH: Parents' Household Information

Here your parents give basic information about their household, such as how many members are in their household and how many of them will be in college. The more dependents your parents have, and the more college educations they have to pay for, the less they will be expected to contribute to your own college education.

Section FM: Dependent Family Member Listing

This section asks questions about other dependent members of your household. If you're an independent student, the household in question here is the one you described in Section SD; if you're a dependent, it's your parents' household as described in Section PD.

The questions in Section FM ask for more information about these household members: their names, how they're related to you, their ages, and to what extent you or your parents are required to pay for their school or college education last year and next year. The reason for these questions is that if household members other than you are enrolled in college, and your family is paying heavily to fund those educations, the colleges may take this into account when they determine the expected family contribution (EFC) to your own education. If there are younger children in the family, the colleges will assume that a certain portion of the household's income and assets need to be saved for their college educations, which will also affect your EFC.

Section PI: Parents' Income and Benefits for the Previous Year

In this section, your parents report their income and benefits for the year before you intend to start college. Just as with the section about your income, this is important in establishing the resources they have available to pay for college.

If your parents have a completed tax return, filling in this section is mostly a matter of copying from the right lines. If they haven't filed a return but will do so later, they'll need to estimate the amounts. If they don't plan to file a return, they still have to report income. Again they have to list untaxed income and benefits, such as Social Security benefits or child support.

Section PP: Parents' Income and Benefits for the Year Before Last

Here your parents are asked to give information about income and benefits not for the year before you intend to start college, but the year before that year. Together with sections PI and PF, this is meant to give the PROFILE colleges a long-term view of your family's finances in order to clarify whether or not last year was typical. This section is fairly easy to fill out: for most of the questions — e.g., adjusted gross income, income taxes and itemized deductions — your family has only to look up their tax return for that year. You also have to calculate any untaxed income and benefits, using a worksheet that's provided.

Section PF: Parents' Expected Income and Benefits for This Year

Here your parents have to estimate how much they expect to receive in income and benefits during the year in which you start college. Again, the idea is to establish as clear a picture as possible about your family's finances in the long term, and to show whether the year before you started college was typical or not. Your parents will have to estimate work income, other taxable income, and untaxed income and benefits. In Section ES, explain any unusual increases or decreases in income and benefits (10 percent or more) from last year.

Section PA: Parents' Assets

This section asks about your parents' assets because these are resources that can help them finance college. There are questions about cash and savings and checking accounts (with their value as of the day you fill out the form). If they own their home, there are questions to determine home equity, the difference between the current market value of their home and the outstanding mortgage debt.

There are also questions about the current market value of any other assets they own, including investments and other real estate. They also need to include educational savings accounts, such as 529 prepaid tuition or college savings plans or Coverdell savings accounts that they've opened for you or your siblings.

Sections BA and FA: Business Assets and Farm Assets

These sections will only appear if your parents indicated ownership in a business or farm. There will be questions about value, debt, number of employees, tax form filed and if you live on the farm.

Section PE: Parents' Expenses

This section asks about certain special expenses your parents might have. These are not just any expenses, such as grocery bills or vacation airfare, but specific costs that might legitimately affect their ability to pay for college. Included here are child support payments, certain educational costs, and medical and dental expenses not covered by insurance.

Section NP: Information About a Noncustodial Parent

If your parents are divorced or separated, this section asks for information about the parent who doesn't have custody of you. But it should be filled out by your custodial parent. If for any reason you can't get sufficient information about the noncustodial parent, explain why in Section ES. Many colleges want this information because they believe it is the responsibility of both your biological or adoptive parents to pay for your college costs, even if they no longer live together, and even if the parent who does have custody of you has remarried. That's why, after you've filled out this section and submitted your PROFILE, they may request that your noncustodial parent fill out a supplemental form, the Noncustodial PROFILE. (See "After Submitting Your PROFILE" on page 65.) The section you're filling out here is not that supplemental form; your noncustodial parent will fill out that form if it's required.

Section ES: Explanations/ Special Circumstances

This is the one free-form part of the PROFILE, where you write rather than fill in boxes. This section gives you a chance to explain anything unusual in your application or any special circumstances that affect your family's ability to pay for college. You can mention, for example, reasons for unusually high medical or dental expenses, steep rises or falls in income from year to year, or loss of employment. You should also give information about any outside scholarships you've been awarded. This allows the PROFILE colleges to better understand your financial picture.

In addition to telling the colleges about anything you think it's important that they know about, you should also use this section to expand on your answers to certain questions in previous sections, per the instructions that you'll find on the PROFILE Web site. For example, if there are more than six dependent members of your household, you won't be able to list them all in section FM. The instructions will tell you to list the additional members here.

You're limited to 27 lines of information in this section. If you need more space, send the information on paper directly to your colleges, including your name and Social Security number on all correspondence. (**See Step 8 for tips on how to let your college know about your special circumstances.**)

Section SQ: Supplemental Information

Section SQ may not be included in your application. You will only see it if one or more of the colleges to which you're applying requires more information. In that case, you'll see additional questions here. Your answers to these questions will be used only by the colleges that ask for them. Some of the questions colleges ask here are used to determine your eligibility for purely need-based financial aid; others are used to determine if you're eligible for scholarships that have non-need-based criteria.

Here are some examples of the types of questions you might see:

- What is the year, make and model of the family's primary car?
- Do you or either of your parents receive free food or housing as a job benefit?
- What is your family's religious denomination? (This information will be used to determine scholarship eligibility.)
- In what field of study do you plan to major?

After Submitting Your PROFILE

After you complete your PROFILE, you'll receive an online PROFILE acknowledgment that confirms the colleges to which you're sending the information and gives you the opportunity to correct any data you submitted. You should print the acknowledgment, which includes the list of colleges and the data you entered on the form. Once you submit your PROFILE, you can't revise your information online for the colleges you selected. Use the printed acknowledgment to make changes, if necessary, to the PROFILE information, and send those corrections directly to your colleges.

GOOD TO KNOW

If only one of your birth parents has custody of you, your college may still require information from both parents. If that happens, the main PROFILE application collects information from one parent, and the **Noncustodial PROFILE** collects information from the other. After the information is processed, the college will complete the EFC calculation. How to divide up payment of the EFC among you and your parents is a family decision.

The College Board analyzes your data and reports it to the colleges to which you're applying. The schools then apply their own institutional policies to figure out your expected family contribution (EFC). From this analysis, they determine how great your need is and how much institutional financial aid to give you.

SENDING YOUR PROFILE TO ADDITIONAL COLLEGES

You can delete colleges from your list of schools only before you submit the application. After that, all the listed colleges will get your information.

But you can add colleges whenever you want, even after you submit the application. Just go to the PROFILE Web site and click on "Add Colleges to Submitted Application." The fee is $16 for each additional college or program to which you want your information sent.

When you add additional colleges, you will also be given the opportunity to update or correct any of the information on your original application. Please note, however, that this new information will only be sent to the colleges you're adding. You should directly contact the colleges to which you submitted your original application to update your information with them.

SUPPLEMENTAL PROFILE FORMS

Some colleges require supplemental information that's not on the PROFILE application. For example, a college may require a Noncustodial PROFILE if you don't live with both of your birth parents. When you register for the PROFILE and indicate that your biological or adoptive parents are not married, you will receive an e-mail with instructions, a temporary password and a link to forward an application to your noncustodial parent to complete. This form can be completed only by the noncustodial parent.

Be aware that these follow-ups take additional time. All the more reason to leave yourself plenty of time to file the PROFILE before your college financial aid deadlines.

QUICK RECAP

Since the PROFILE form is customized, the application may not necessarily be the same length as the FAFSA. In some cases the PROFILE will contain more questions than the FAFSA and in some cases it will contain fewer. The main difference is that it tries to get a more complete picture of your family's finances. A few points to keep in mind:

- File early.
- The PROFILE is online only, so you have to submit it on a computer.
- Prepare by using the Pre-Application Worksheet.
- There are fees, but students from low-income families may qualify for a fee waiver.
- After you submit your PROFILE, you'll get an online acknowledgment confirming that you submitted it. To make corrections to your information, you should write your colleges directly.
- Depending on your circumstances, you or one of your parents may have to submit supplemental information to one or more of your colleges.

Step 7: Fill Out Any Other Required Forms

QUICK OVERVIEW

The FAFSA and PROFILE are the big ones, but don't forget to file any other forms that may be required by your state or by the colleges to which you're applying. You don't want to have your application for financial aid marked "incomplete" because you didn't file a one-page form. These forms can vary widely from college to college, and from state to state.

Some Colleges Have Their Own Financial Aid Application

Some colleges have their own forms that you have to submit in addition to the FAFSA and the PROFILE. A purpose of the form may be to get more information about your finances, or to find out if you're a member of a particular group that is eligible for a special scholarship or grant. If a college requires such a form from all first-time applicants, its description in Part III of the book will say "institutional form required" under the "application procedures" section. Contact the financial aid office at your colleges to find out more.

The good news is that these forms are generally not long or complicated — they are usually just a page or two in length. They manage to stay short because they are intended not to duplicate the FAFSA or PROFILE forms but to supplement them and help the financial aid office keep track of applications. Such a "one pager" might, for example, ask for basic identifying information, some demographic facts and whether you are interested in loans and work-study. This kind of form is typical at community colleges and most four-year public colleges. "It's almost like an update form," Mary San Agustin says of the institutional form currently in use at her institution, Palomar College. "It's basically just a supplemental form in case any changes occurred since the time the student applied for admission or completed the FAFSA."

Sometimes a college might require a longer form that asks questions about your finances that are about as broad and deep as the FAFSA or PROFILE. Usually this only happens with colleges that use their own formulas to calculate need, but choose not to use the PROFILE to help them with it.

Another reason a college might require its own financial aid form is if it requires every student to have a computer on campus. Such schools sometimes have a supplemental form that qualifies needy applicants for a stipend to buy a computer, or places them in a "loaner" program so they can borrow one. The University of Virginia has two forms that deal with computers. One form is for its "laptop loaner" program, and a different form is for a "one-time computer expense" that allows students who want to buy a laptop to add the purchase price to their cost of attendance; that way their aid package may cover the cost.

Still another kind of institutional form is one for early-decision applicants. Such a form works as a sort of "pre-read" meant to help students get an early estimate of their expected family contribution and the financial aid package they will receive if they accept an early-decision offer. (The rules of early decision require them to accept the offer if the college offers enough financial aid for them to attend.) Some schools offer a similar pre-read form for student athletes who are being recruited by a coach.

Scholarship and Grant Forms

Some colleges require a separate form for students applying for merit scholarships. This isn't always the case: At many schools, every student who applies for admission is automatically considered for merit scholarships. But at some schools, you must file a separate application for merit scholarships. The rules may even differ from department to department, depending on your major. "Theater majors may have to audition," says Bonnie Lee Behm of Villanova University. "Or a film major may need to send in a tape." Contact the financial aid office at your colleges for more details, and check with the department in which you're interested in majoring.

Some institutional forms ask questions to find out if you qualify for financial aid funds set aside for students with particular characteristics. For example, the college might offer grants that are only available to children of alumni or descendants of the town's founding families. At most colleges, these grants are part of the need-based aid program, so you have to demonstrate need through the FAFSA along with proving you have the right characteristics for the grant.

Verification of Your Tax Return

Some colleges require you to send copies of your family's federal or state tax returns. They may tell you to mail them with your initial application, or they may require them for only a few applicants who have been selected for verification.

"Verification" doesn't mean that you did something wrong. It's not like an IRS audit, where only suspicious tax returns are selected for special scrutiny. Since colleges disburse federal money — in the form of grants, work-study and loans — they are required by law to check the information that a certain percentage of financial aid applicants have submitted. Some colleges exceed this minimum requirement and, for the sake of safety and fairness, verify all applications.

If you are selected for verification by one or more colleges, you'll have to submit tax documents: for example, the 1040 and any attached schedules, along with the W-2s or 1099s you received from employers and banks. Usually you'll also have to fill out a form that allows colleges to confirm details, like how many of your siblings are enrolled in college. The college may ask you to send your documents directly to the financial aid office, or it might ask you to send them to the College Board's Institutional Documentation (IDOC) service.

Some colleges will request verification if the data you submitted on the FAFSA looks unusual. As an extreme example, people who reported that they had no income last year may be asked how they supported themselves.

State Forms

Most states rely on the FAFSA to award their need-based grants and loans to students. But a few states have their own financial aid forms. For example, New York State has an application for its Tuition Assistance Program (TAP) that is sent to eligible students who submit a FAFSA. See Table 2 on the next page for a list of states that require their own forms; the list gives the name of each form and the program's Web site and mailing address.

Even though the thought of filling out yet another form may seem burdensome, and you feel sure that you won't qualify for the state aid program, fill it out. If you don't, your application might be marked "incomplete" at your colleges. These state forms are usually short and don't take long to fill out, especially once you do the prep work of filling out the FAFSA. **When you file the FAFSA online, you'll be automatically directed to your state's form.** (If you file the FAFSA paper form, you'll usually have to send away for a paper copy of your state form.)

Table 2:
State Aid Deadlines

STATE	FORM(S) REQUIRED	DEADLINE	NOTES
Alaska	FAFSA	4/15	
Arizona	FAFSA	3/1	
Arkansas	FAFSA	6/1	Higher Education Opportunity Grant Academic Challenge awards
California	FAFSA, state form	3/2	Initial awards
		9/2	Additional community college awards
Connecticut	FAFSA	2/15	
Delaware	FAFSA	4/15	
District of Columbia	FAFSA, DC form	6/30	
Florida	FAFSA	5/15	
Illinois	FAFSA	9/30	First-time applicants
		8/15	Continuing applicants
Indiana	FAFSA	3/10	
Iowa	FAFSA	7/1	
Kansas	FAFSA, state form	4/1	
Kentucky	FAFSA	3/15	
Louisiana	FAFSA	7/1	Closing date
Maine	FAFSA	5/1	
Maryland	FAFSA	3/1	
Massachusetts	FAFSA	5/1	
Michigan	FAFSA	3/1	
Minnesota	FAFSA	30 days after start of term	
Missouri	FAFSA	4/1	
Montana	FAFSA	3/1	
New Hampshire	FAFSA	5/1	
New Jersey	FAFSA	6/1	Tuition Aid Grant applicants
		10/1	All other applicants
		3/1	Spring-term applicants only
New York	FAFSA, state form	5/1	
North Carolina	FAFSA	3/15	
North Dakota	FAFSA	3/15	
Ohio	FAFSA	10/1	
Oklahoma	FAFSA	4/15	Priority date
Pennsylvania	FAFSA, state form	5/1	Degree program candidates
		8/1	Other applicants
Rhode Island	FAFSA	3/1	
South Carolina	FAFSA	6/30	
Tennessee	FAFSA	3/1	
West Virginia	FAFSA, state form	3/1	

Residents of states not listed in this table should contact their state aid office directly. See page 137 for a list of addresses, phone numbers and Web sites for each state's aid office.

QUICK RECAP

In addition to the FAFSA and PROFILE, some states and colleges have financial aid forms of their own. Here's what to know about them:

- They're usually short.
- Their questions vary from school to school and from state to state.
- They may determine if you're eligible for special grants.
- They may help verify your financial information, perhaps through questions about your tax returns.
- If state aid is available, apply for it, or your colleges might consider your financial aid application incomplete.
- If one of your colleges requires an institutional application, fill it out, or you'll disqualify yourself from financial aid.

Step 8: Make Your Special Circumstances Known

QUICK OVERVIEW

If something in your family's financial life can't be explained on the financial aid forms, make sure your colleges know about it. These "special circumstances" may include a lost job, high medical expenses or supporting an extended family. Colleges are willing to listen and, if you make your case, may be able to improve your financial aid package by taking those circumstances into account. This step is about how to prepare your case.

Be a Person, Not Just a Form

Sometimes the financial aid forms you fill out don't tell the whole story. They may not show that your family sends money every month to support relatives in another country. Since the forms are based on last year's tax forms, they may not reveal this year's events: how one of your parents just lost a job, or will be shifting from full-time to half-time work. When the forms don't adequately report a special circumstance that affects your family's ability to pay for college, let your college know — it may change how much financial aid you get!

Even if you're not sure your circumstance qualifies as special, speak up. The financial aid office will let you know whether it qualifies. Don't think you're limited to communicating with your college only through the financial aid forms. If there's any doubt in your mind about whether those forms give a true picture of your family's situation, feel free to go beyond the form and contact the financial aid office. **Be a person, not just a form**. There are two reasons to do this: It guarantees that the college knows how much you are able to pay, and it shows that you're interested in the college — which may affect the lengths to which they'll go to help you.

Using the Financial Aid Forms

In some cases, you can inform your colleges of special circumstances through the financial aid forms themselves — the FAFSA, PROFILE and institutional forms (Steps 5, 6 and 7, respectively, of this book). If you're supporting children, if you've been in the military, or if your parents are divorced, your FAFSA will make that clear. For colleges requiring PROFILE, you can use Section ES of that form to describe special financial circumstances. Elsewhere on the PROFILE form, you can list special family expenses, such as your family's medical and dental expenses, or any private school tuition that your parents might pay for your younger siblings. While forms may serve well enough, it may still be a good idea to write a letter or schedule a visit. If there's any doubt in your mind about whether forms convey your situation, definitely contact the college.

Going Beyond the Forms

You may have special circumstances that aren't covered by the forms. Or financially significant events may happen after you submit the forms — events that may be too complicated to explain in a simple correction. If that happens, communicate with the aid office as soon as possible after you realize you have special circumstances or after any financial hardships arise. The sooner you act, the sooner the college can adjust your award — and the more likely they are to still have the funds available to do so.

Even after you start college, if a financial emergency occurs, let the school know. The financial aid director can often help needy students with unusual expenses, such as medical costs, emergency trips home or funding to allow them to take an unpaid internship in the summer instead of working for money.

How to Contact the College

A letter to the financial aid office explaining your circumstances is often the best way to state your case. Some schools have a form specifically for explaining special circumstances; it's worth asking your colleges what they prefer. The more closely you follow their procedures, the more likely you are to be heard.

No matter how you communicate with your college, be polite, clear and specific. There's no need for a despairing or bullying tone. **Remember, you're trying to put a face to the form, so make it a friendly one.** You'll get further by calmly presenting your situation and giving as many relevant specifics as possible. A school will want to know not only that a parent got laid off, but what the prospects for reemployment might be, whether the parent has filed for unemployment benefits and, if so, the amount of the benefit payments awarded to the parent. Don't be surprised or offended if the college responds to you with a request for documentation, such as a copy of your tax return or a recent pay stub.

The Special Circumstances Form

Some colleges have a form through which you can let them know about special circumstances. At Rhodes College, it's called the Special Financial Circumstances Form, and it is available on the school's Web site. "The purpose of the form is not to make everybody jump through a hoop," says Forrest

Stuart, the director of financial aid at Rhodes. "It's to help the parents and the student put on paper all the information we need to help them out."

The form asks the student for the specific data — such as about changes in income and expenses — that the financial aid office will need to reach a decision about their case. It helps the school treat students equally, and it prevents the vagueness that might be found in a letter. "A lot of time we'll just get letters — I've lost my job, I need more aid," says Stuart. "Well, that doesn't tell me a whole lot. But if I can see some concrete information, then that gives me an idea of how I can help this student."

Communicating by Letter

With many schools, the best way to contact the aid office is in a letter. Often, it can strengthen your case to enclose photocopies of supporting documentation with the letter — for example, a paper showing your parent was laid off. The aid officer may also ask you for specific documentation.

After sending your letter, follow up with the financial aid office a week or two later to make sure they received it and to see if they have any questions. You can do this by e-mail or telephone. If you live close by, or have scheduled a campus visit, you should also visit the aid office, but call first to make an appointment.

EXPERT ADVICE

"**We must have documentation**, and what we really like too is a nice **letter explaining the situation**. But on top of that, we also like to have a phone call or, if the student's already on campus, to have them come in and talk to us. That way, we can have a **dialogue about the situation** and give them some direction on what to provide to us and how to provide it."

— Vincent Amoroso, deputy director, Office of Scholarships and Student Aid, University of North Carolina, Chapel Hill

E-Mail

Some colleges prefer to have you contact them by e-mail. At the University of Oregon, applicants can communicate their special financial circumstances through the school's Web site, where they can find an e-mail address for the financial aid office. "That way, they can do it whenever they think about it," says Elizabeth Bickford, the financial aid director.

Examples of Special Situations

Many circumstances can affect your family's ability to pay for college. They may include a change in your financial situation from what was reported in the financial aid forms, such as a lost job, emergency expenses, health problems or even a windfall that misrepresents your usual level of income.

Family ties can also have financial implications, such as supporting an extended family or going through a divorce. And if you've served in the military, there are some special instructions you need to follow on the financial aid forms.

Change in Financial Situation

Financial aid officers want to know not only that your financial aid situation changed, but why it changed. Certain types of changes are more likely than others to persuade them to give you more financial aid. Generally, aid officers will look more kindly on circumstances that are beyond your control, rather than the result of poor planning. For example, if your father gets laid off because his company has fallen on hard times, that is more likely to get attention than if he retires early to spend more time golfing. And the college is more likely to turn a sympathetic eye to necessary roof repairs than a loan to install a backyard Jacuzzi.

GOOD TO KNOW

If you're explaining your special financial circumstances by letter, it's best to send it to the financial aid office via mail or fax, so that it can be **easily incorporated into your file**. Write and format it as a standard business letter. **Put your name and Social Security Number** in the first paragraph, so the financial aid office won't have trouble matching the letter to your file.

LOST JOB OR LOST INCOME

If you or your parents had a job when you filled out the FAFSA, and now don't, that will clearly affect your ability to pay. Even if you receive a severance package or collect unemployment benefits, your long-term ability to pay will still be reduced. This is information your financial aid office needs to know. For Palomar College, you would fill out a form that allows the financial aid office to override the FAFSA data with the new data. "You have to still report the prior year's income," according to Palomar's Mary San Agustin, "but we override it with the current-year income."

The FAFSA form for 2009-10 asks if you or a parent is a "dislocated worker." But don't think answering "yes" to that question is sufficient to alert colleges to the problem. They will want to know more, and the more information you give them, the more likely they can help you. And given the large number of job losses caused by the current recession, you should try to give them this information as soon as possible. Remember, there is a limit to the amount of financial aid funds available.

Equally important are unusual changes in other sources of income besides wages and salaries. For example, suppose a student's mother becomes disabled in August and has to stop working, and her employer's disability insurance plan gives her a large percentage of her salary for the first six months (through February), but a much lower percentage afterward. The FAFSA will show a larger income than she will be receiving once the student arrives in college. This change in disability benefits, like a lost job, needs to be explained to the college.

EMERGENCY SAVINGS DRAWDOWN

An emergency may force your family to spend some of the savings that you reported on the financial aid forms. For example, suppose your house is damaged by a fire the day after you submit the FAFSA. Your family needs to spend a large amount of money to pay for the repairs. Depending on where the money comes from — regular savings, a retirement account, borrowing through a home-equity loan — this will have different effects on your need calculation. But no matter what the emergency or the source of the money you wind up spending is, you should tell the aid office.

Sometimes one crisis will have several different effects. Hurricane Katrina in 2005 might not only have destroyed an applicant's home in Louisiana, but put the family breadwinners temporarily out of work. In such a case, make sure the aid office knows about all the different effects on your financial situation.

HEALTH PROBLEMS

A serious health problem in your family can have financial as well as medical effects. It may involve both an emergency savings drawdown to pay for medical expenses, and loss of income if the patient is too sick to work. If someone in your family has recently become disabled, developed a chronic illness or had major surgery, this has a clear impact on your family's ability to pay for college. Your college's financial aid office should be able to help.

A letter, or the school's own "special circumstances" form (if they have one), is a good way to let a college know about your family's medical problem. But the financial aid forms provide some paths as well. The PROFILE form allows you to list medical expenses that weren't covered by insurance last year, and estimate the same for this year. You can also explain high medical expenses in the "Explanations/Special Circumstances" box (Section ES). The FAFSA, on the other hand, doesn't ask specifically about medical expenses. If your college only uses the FAFSA, and you have unusually high medical expenses, a letter to the college makes sense.

WINDFALL

In financial terms, a windfall is a sum of money you didn't expect to get, which is normally a good thing — but even a windfall can have its downside. On your financial aid forms, if you received a windfall last year, that makes your annual income look higher than it normally is, which will tend to raise your expected family contribution (EFC).

Some windfalls are better than others. A windfall is usually understood as a genuine, one-time boost to your finances. It might be an inheritance from an aunt you never knew or an unusually high year-end bonus from your job. If you get such a windfall, inform the aid office that your income was higher than usual last year, and that they shouldn't expect a repeat performance next year.

But some windfalls not only make your annual income look bigger than it is, but represent an overall loss to your financial position. Examples include a severance package on losing your job, or an early withdrawal from a retirement plan, such as an IRA, to cover an emergency. In both situations, your records for that year show a boost in income, but that apparent good news conceals bad financial news — that you lost your job, in one case, and suffered a massive hit to your retirement savings in the other. If you experience this kind of windfall, explain the reality to your aid office.

Family Ties

Not every family has two parents married to each other. And some families have stronger ties to grandparents, uncles, aunts and cousins than others. Different families live in different ways. The way your family lives may have financial implications that your financial aid office should recognize.

SUPPORTING EXTENDED FAMILY

The financial aid forms tell the colleges about how many people live in your household, including you, your parents and your siblings. But many families give financial support to an extended family of relatives who live outside the household. Immigrant families, for example, often send money regularly to grandparents, aunts or uncles in another country. Since that decreases the amount you have available to pay for college, make sure the financial aid office knows about it.

DIVORCED OR SEPARATED PARENTS

If your parents have divorced or separated, make sure the colleges know how that has affected your ability to pay. To do this, follow the rules on the financial aid forms. For the FAFSA, provide only the information on the parent you lived with more during the past 12 months (your custodial parent) — and, if that parent has remarried, your stepparent. For the PROFILE, provide not only that data but also information on your other parent, the one who does not have custody of you — your noncustodial parent. That information goes in Section NP of the PROFILE.

Some colleges that use PROFILE will also want your noncustodial parent to submit information separately on the Noncustodial PROFILE. That information will be confidential; you and your custodial parent won't be able to see the data the other parent provides, nor will that parent see yours. However, the information submitted by your noncustodial parent will affect the college's calculation of your total expected family contribution (EFC). If you don't think it will be possible to get your noncustodial parent to fill out the form, let the college know. However, the school isn't likely to waive its requirement for the form for anything less than a significant reason.

In the parent-income section of either the FAFSA or PROFILE, a custodial parent who is receiving alimony or child support payments should report only what he or she received, not what he or she was supposed to receive. In certain circumstances, documented evidence that your noncustodial parent is behind in payments could help support your case if you appeal your award.

Military Service

If you're currently serving in the active-duty military or the reserves, or if you are a veteran, don't assume that your military benefits alone will meet your full financial need. At most institutions, they no longer will. Benefits or not, you should apply for financial aid by submitting the FAFSA and any other required forms.

When filling out these forms, there are a few points to remember. Read the instructions carefully to make sure you qualify as a veteran for purposes of federal student aid. You should report housing allowances, subsistence allowances and untaxed combat pay as income. But don't include veterans' education benefits or ROTC scholarships when answering the questions about your untaxed income. The colleges consider them outside resources to be reported separately. (*See Step 9 for more information on outside resources.*)

Veterans are as liable as anyone to the special situations discussed earlier, from lost jobs to medical crises. That includes windfalls. For example, if you received a lot of combat pay last year but have now been discharged and won't receive it again, you should explain that to the colleges.

For more information on the intricacies of how veterans' benefits affect the FAFSA, see www.gibill.va.gov.

QUICK RECAP

If there are special circumstances that affect your ability to pay for college, let your college know.

- Tell the college financial aid office as soon as you know about your special circumstances — either before you get your award or afterward.
- If you have to go beyond the forms, write a letter, e-mail, call or visit.
- Explain your situation clearly, documenting it where appropriate.
- The situations that may affect your ability to pay range from a lost job or high medical bills to status as a veteran or an undocumented immigrant.

Step 9: Look for Scholarships

QUICK OVERVIEW

It's worth it to look for financial aid beyond what you'll get from colleges and federal student aid programs. This "outside money" probably won't amount to a "full ride," but it can help. Begin your search for outside scholarships around the time you start looking for a college because many scholarships have early deadlines.

KNOW THE LINGO

Outside money — Grants and scholarships that come from sources other than colleges or the federal government, such as states and private organizations.

Portable money — Grants and scholarships that you can take with you to whichever college you attend.

College-offered money Grants and scholarships that colleges award from their own funds.

Scholarships Colleges Give You vs. Scholarships You Get on Your Own

Financial aid doesn't come only from the government and colleges. It also comes in the form of scholarships from outside sources, including states and private donors. This money doesn't come looking for you: You have to find the programs that fit you and apply. You will have to qualify for the scholarship in some way, whether through academic merit, artistic talent or fitting some set of criteria, such as being a person of Japanese descent living in either Connecticut, New York or New Jersey. **Very few outside scholarships offer anything close to full tuition, fees, room and board.** But they're worth the search because every little bit helps.

The scholarships you can get from outside sources are not exactly like the scholarships you might get from your college. These are the basic facts to know about each type.

Collogo-Offered Scholarships

In most cases, you don't have to apply separately for the scholarships that colleges award. You're automatically considered for them when you apply to the school. If you qualify, the college will include the scholarship in your financial aid package as they see fit. However, some colleges have merit-based scholarships for which you must apply separately.

To find out what the rules are for scholarship aid at your colleges, contact the schools or look at their Web sites, which usually describe the process for applying for scholarships under "admissions" and then under "financial aid." Be sure to do this research *before* you submit your application for admission. At some colleges, you have to indicate on your admissions application that you are applying for a special scholarship; for example, this is true of Boston University's Trustee Scholar Program. At others, you don't have to apply for special scholarships until after you've submitted your application for admission.

Many college merit scholarships have to be renewed from year to year. To make sure yours is renewed, know the school's criteria for keeping it — for example, maintaining a certain GPA. Different scholarships will have different criteria at each college.

Outside Scholarships: State Sources

Almost every state offers scholarships to their residents. These scholarships are usually available only for state residents attending colleges within the state, though a few states offer "portable" aid that a state resident can take to a college in another state.

Take the time to research scholarships and grants in your state. Almost every state has a department of education Web site that describes state scholarships and how to apply for them. These are usually separate from the state-sponsored, need-based financial aid programs that you apply for through the FAFSA or the state's own financial aid form, such as the Tuition Assistance Program (TAP) in New York State. An example of a state-sponsored, merit-based scholarship program with a separate application process is Florida's Merit Scholars Award, for which applicants must show high academic achievement.

Outside Scholarships: Private Sources

Private scholarships are offered by many sources, including foundations, corporations, civic groups, religious organizations, veterans' associations and the military. The Society of Women Engineers offers the Bechtel Corporation Scholarship to high-achieving female students of engineering. United Methodist Scholarships are available to students who belong to that Christian denomination. The Senator George J. Mitchell Scholarship Research Institute offers awards to Maine residents studying in state.

Don't assume you have to be a genius to get a private scholarship. Although many scholarship programs consider academic merit, a range of conditions may qualify you for a scholarship, including interests, ethnic background and community work. The Los Padres Foundation grants scholarships to low-income Latino students. California students pursuing a career in agriculture are eligible for a California Farm Bureau Scholarship.

Most scholarships come with limits. Though a few programs will pay full tuition, the amount of most awards is much smaller, as little as $500 or $1,000.

MYTH/FACT

Myth: "Untold millions" of scholarship dollars are available for use every year.

Fact: Private scholarships are only a small segment of the overall money available for college — **just 7 percent**. True, that share amounts to $7.5 billion a year, but that's dwarfed by the $99.2 billion paid out by other sources. Money from federal, college-granted, and state funds, in that order, are likely to be much more important in your overall financial aid package. It's worth looking for private scholarships, but don't count on them as your sole source of funding.

Many awards are limited to the freshman year of study. Fortunately, other scholarships are only for later years. The Bechtel Corporation Scholarship, for example, is just for women in their sophomore, junior or senior year of study. And once you've declared a major you may find yourself eligible for a scholarship that is aimed only at students in your academic discipline.

Searching for Scholarships

Searching for private scholarships takes effort. But there are a number of Web-based scholarship search engines, like the ones on collegeboard.com and fastweb.com, that can help you zero in on scholarships for which you may qualify. If you like using this book, you might prefer to search for scholarships using the *College Board Scholarship Handbook*. It describes more than 2,100 outside scholarships, internships and loan programs, and is indexed by eligibility requirements — such as minority status, religious affiliation and state of residence — to help you match yourself to the programs.

Beware of commercial scholarship search companies that offer to help you find scholarships for a fee. Some do a responsible job, but many charge exorbitant fees and make fraudulent claims. For example, if they "guarantee" you a scholarship or promise to "do all the work for you," they are probably lying. Getting a scholarship is never guaranteed and, no matter what, you are going to have to do some work to apply.

Your school counselor may be of more help. Many private scholarships send application forms directly to school counselors. Tell your counselor in your junior year or early in your senior year that you are interested in applying for private scholarships.

Figure 12:
collegboard.com's Scholarship Search

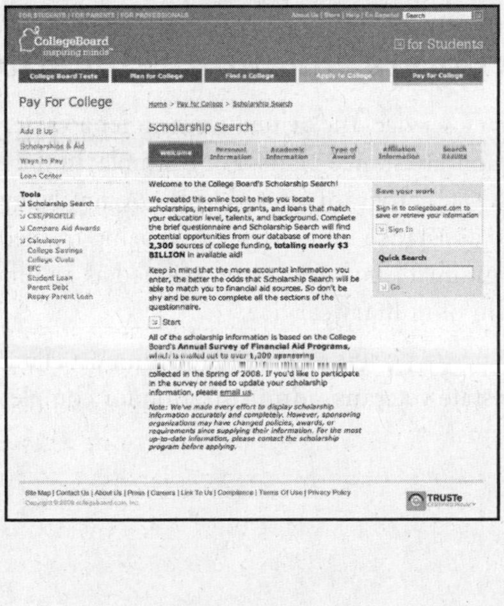

Start researching options as soon as possible. You'll need time to learn about scholarships, request information and application materials, and complete your application. Some programs, such as the Discover Card Tribute Award Scholarship Program (see sidebar on page 87), are looking only for students in their junior year of high school. Even if you're past that point, look as soon as you can — in the summer before your senior year, or by October or November of that year.

Look Locally

The national and state programs that you'll find on Web-based scholarship search engines and in print directories are good sources of scholarship aid. But don't forget to look even closer to home: your own county, city, town, employer or church. When looking for scholarships, it pays to look locally.

The fact is, you are more likely to obtain a scholarship from a local organization than from a state or national one. On the local level, you will be competing with a smaller pool of applicants and are more likely to have characteristics that interest the donors. Again, your school counselor can help. The counseling office will have a file of local scholarships — from banks, the Kiwanis, the local garden club and other groups. Let your counselor know you are looking for scholarships; stop by the counseling office regularly to read the scholarship files or check the scholarship bulletin board. The office may also use Internet announcements, e-mail postings or newsletters to spread the word about scholarship programs to interested students.

Employers can also be a source of scholarship money. If you have a part-time job after school or a summer job, check to see if the company that employs you has a scholarship program or offers tuition assistance. For example, Chick-fil-A has a well-known scholarship program for its restaurant employees. Some companies provide their employees with a dependent tuition-assistance benefit. That means one of your parents might be able to get his or her employer to pay some of your tuition.

Military Scholarships and Education Benefits

In return for military service, the armed forces offer a variety of college scholarships and education-assistance plans. For example, in the Reserve Officer Training Corps (ROTC) program offered by the Army, Navy and Air Force, you get scholarship assistance for college while being trained as a military officer. When you graduate, you are commissioned as an officer in the reserves and begin your term of military service.

Educational assistance for veterans is available in most states. If you're a veteran, contact your state veterans' administration for complete information and application forms.

Applying for Scholarships

Once you find the programs for which you qualify, you have to apply. This may mean not only another form to fill out, but compiling supporting documents, such as transcripts, recommendations and an essay. Depending on the program, you may have to provide evidence of leadership, patriotism, depth of character, desire to serve or financial need. Get to know the requirements of each scholarship as early as possible, so you can do any necessary extra work on time.

A few pointers to remember:

Apply early! Apply as early as possible to scholarship programs. If you can, do it in the fall of your senior year, even if the deadlines aren't until February or March. Very often, scholarship programs will have awarded all their funds for the year on a first-come, first-served basis before their stated deadline.

Follow directions. Read instructions carefully and do what they say. Scholarship programs receive hundreds and even thousands of applications. Don't lose out because of failure to submit a typewritten essay versus a handwritten one if required, or to provide appropriate recommendations. If you have a question about your eligibility for a particular scholarship or how to complete the application, contact the scholarship sponsors.

Be organized. It's a good idea to create a separate file for each scholarship and sort them by their due dates. Track application deadlines and requirements using Worksheet 2 (**a blank copy of this worksheet appears on page 120**). In one place, store the different supporting documents you may need, such as transcripts, standardized test scores and letters of recommendation.

Check your work. Proofread your applications for spelling or grammatical errors, fill in all blanks, and make sure your handwriting is legible.

Keep copies of everything. If application materials get lost, having copies on file will make it easier to resend the application quickly.

Reapply. Some programs only offer money for the first year of college, but others can be renewed each subsequent year. If your program is one of them, it pays to reapply once you're in college.

SAMPLE WORKSHEET 2:
Scholarship Application Planner

	PROGRAM 1	PROGRAM 2	PROGRAM 3
PROGRAM/SPONSOR	*National Merit Scholarship*	*Young Epidemiology Scholars*	*First Bank*
ELIGIBILITY REQUIREMENTS	*Academic merit*	*Academic merit*	*Need, local residency*
TYPE OF AWARD	*Scholarship*	*Scholarship*	*Internship*
AMOUNT OF AWARD	*$2,500*	*$1,000 or more*	*$2,500*
CAN BE USED FOR	*Tuition/fees*	*Any expense*	*Any expense*
CAN BE USED AT	*First-choice college*	*Any college*	*In-state colleges*
DEADLINE	*Oct. 1 (give essay to English teacher for review)*	*Feb. 1*	*April 1*
FORMS REQUIRED	*NMSC application*	*Web form*	*Application (includes need analysis)*
TEST SCORES REQUIRED	*PSAT/NMSQT (already took), SAT (by December)*	*None*	*SAT*
ESSAY OR ACADEMIC SAMPLE	*Personal statement, academic transcript*	*Essay, research project*	*None required*
RECOMMENDATIONS	*Principal*	*None*	*One teacher (Mr. Filmer), Local branch manager*
NOTIFICATION BEGINS	*February*	*Not sure*	*May 15*
REQUIREMENTS TO KEEP AFTER FRESHMAN YEAR	*One-time payment only*	*One-time payment only*	*Based on performance during internship*

For a blank version of this worksheet that you can photocopy for your own use, see page 120.

How a Scholarship Can Affect Your Financial Aid Package

SCHOLARSHIP PROFILE

The **Discover Card Tribute Award Scholarship** is one example of the many sources of private scholarship aid. Run by Discover Financial Services, Inc., and the American Association of School Administrators, this national program issues up to 10 scholarships of $30,000 each. To be eligible, you must be a high school junior who demonstrates achievement in three of four areas: special talents, leadership, community service and obstacles overcome. You also need a minimum cumulative GPA of 2.75 for the 9th and 10th grades.

If a college to which you're applying hasn't met your full need — that is, if there's a "gap" in your financial aid award — outside scholarships can be used to fill that gap. That will make the college much more affordable and give you more choices when it comes time to decide which college you want to attend.

If, on the other hand, a college is already meeting your full need, it works a little differently. It would be nice if your outside scholarship were added on top of all your other financial aid to make your total aid package even bigger. But it probably won't be. Following federal policy, your college will most likely count any outside scholarship or tuition assistance you receive as an "outside resource" that decreases your aid package dollar for dollar. So the total amount of your financial aid package will be exactly the same.

You might think this is unfair: This is money you found and, in the case of employer tuition assistance and veteran's benefits, money you earned. On the other hand, it is money that's available to pay for your education without your having to dip into your income and assets. The philosophy behind financial aid is that everyone should pay what they can out of income and assets (your expected family contribution, or EFC), and then financial aid, including any outside resources, makes up the difference. The only way you can pay less than your EFC is if you get so many outside scholarships that they exceed your financial need. This is highly unlikely.

However, **it is still worth getting outside scholarships**. For one thing, it increases your freedom to choose a college regardless of cost. "If I'm a student, the more money that I can bring to the table for myself, the better position I'm going to be in to exercise choices that I might want to make," says Vincent Amoroso of the University of North Carolina at Chapel Hill. For another thing, many colleges will use your outside scholarship money to reduce the self-help part of your aid package first — loans and work-study. This can significantly reduce the amount of money you'll owe after college or the time you'll need to spend working during college.

At some colleges, your outside scholarships will not be used to reduce your gift aid (grants and scholarships) unless the amount exceeds your self-help aid. Others use a formula in which at least a portion of your outside money will be used to decrease loans. For example, the first $500 in outside scholarships might be used to reduce your loans, then any funds remaining would be split 50/50 between reducing loans and cutting grants. Colleges that don't meet your full financial need may first apply outside scholarships toward filling the gap. Most colleges decide these issues on a case-by-case basis, but a few have stated policies that they publish on their financial aid Web page or will share with you if asked.

No matter what their policies, colleges welcome outside scholarships because they may reduce the amounts of college funds that have to be spent. Indeed, some schools encourage students to look for outside scholarships. According to Vincent Amoroso, the institutional financial aid form at his college asks students for data related to outside sources of financial aid, including global foundations, to "help us know [if] the student might match up to one of these other foundations that's awarding money."

In making admissions decisions, admissions offices are likely to look on outside scholarships favorably. Students who have searched for and found outside scholarships on their own will probably be seen as students with initiative and a sense of responsibility. That makes the student a stronger candidate for admission.

If you win a scholarship after you've already submitted your FAFSA and/or PROFILE, tell the colleges to which you've applied. Many schools have a special form specifically designed for you to submit this information. If you don't tell the colleges about a scholarship, it could jeopardize your eligibility for federal aid.

Tax Effects

Your outside scholarship may be taxed as income — this depends on the use for which it's designated by the program that awards the scholarship. Generally, scholarship dollars used for costs that are purely educational, such as tuition and fees, will be tax free. But money used for living expenses, transportation or books will be taxed as unearned income. The scholarship program will let you know how much (if any) of your award is taxable, and will send you a copy of the IRS's Form 1098 at the end of each tax year.

If your employer gives you tuition assistance, it's tax free up to $5,250 a year. After that amount, it's taxable. If you get tuition assistance from your parent's employer, the entire amount will be added to your parents' taxable income, but they might be able to deduct some of that amount (see Table 7 on page 110 for more info.)

QUICK RECAP

It takes work to hunt down and apply for outside scholarships, but it's worth it. Just remember:

- Outside scholarships will probably provide only a small part of the money you need for college, but every little bit helps.
- There are national and statewide scholarships programs, but look locally too.
- Web sites, books and your school counselor can help you match outside scholarships to your qualifications.
- Search and apply early, and follow instructions.
- Your outside scholarship may affect the financial aid package awarded by your college, and it may be taxable as income.

Step 10: Weigh the Offers

QUICK OVERVIEW

After you've submitted all the financial aid forms, you'll receive offers of financial aid from the colleges that have accepted you. This step will help you weigh these award letters and make an informed decision based on an "apples to apples" comparison of the packages. If an award leaves you with a larger out-of-pocket share than you think your family can handle, you can appeal.

Comparing Award Letters from Colleges

Sometime after a college accepts you for admission, it will send you a financial aid award letter. The letter will detail your award — the financial aid package the college is offering you. It will contain an outline of the expected costs you will incur during a year at the college, your expected family contribution (EFC) toward those costs, and the types and amounts of financial aid the college is offering to make up the difference between the costs and the EFC.

The letter will also contain instructions on how to accept the aid package and how to contact the aid office if you have any questions or want to appeal the award. Often, the award letter will come with a thick packet of supplementary documents, including promissory notes for any loans offered and information about work-study jobs, if you've been offered those.

It's best to wait until you have the award letters from all the different colleges that have accepted you before deciding which one to accept. If you have questions, wait until you've gotten answers from all the financial aid offices involved before you decide.

The offers in your award letters will differ. The amount and type of aid given will vary, and the letters may also differ in format, especially in how they itemize costs. In weighing the offers, the important thing is to compare apples to apples and not apples to oranges. For example, just because School A offers $10,000 in financial aid while School B only offers $8,000 doesn't necessarily

KNOW THE LINGO

Aid package — The total amount of all financial aid being offered to a student by a college.

Award letter — A document that a college sends to a student detailing the financial aid package. It indicates the type and amount of each scholarship, grant, loan or work-study opportunity being offered.

Appeal — A request that a college reconsider its financial aid package.

SAMPLE WORKSHEET 3:

Compare Your Awards

	COLLEGE 1	COLLEGE 2	COLLEGE 3
Step 1. List the name of each college you want to consider attending, the award deadline, and the total cost of attendance. This figure should be in your award letter. If not, refer to the college catalog or contact the college financial aid office.			
Name of college	*Private Univ.*	*Small College*	*Regional State*
Award deadline date	*5/1*	*5/1*	*4 weeks*
Total cost of attendance	*$31,825*	*$33,410*	*$15,566*
Step 2. List the financial aid awards each school is offering. Don't forget that grants, scholarships and work-study do not have to be repaid, while all loans must be repaid.			
Grants and scholarships			
• Pell Grant (federal)			
• SEOG (federal)			
• State	*can't use*	*$2,000*	*$2,000*
• College	*$12,700*	*$13,785*	*$941*
• Other			
Total grants/scholarships	*$12,700*	*$15,785*	*$2,941*
Percentage of package that is grant/scholarship	*60%*	*74%*	*53%*
Work-study opportunities	*$2,000*	*$1,000*	
Loans			
• Stafford-Direct (federal)	*$2,625*	*$2,625*	*$2,625*
• Perkins (federal)	*$4,000*	*$2,000*	
• Other			
Total loans	*$6,625*	*$4,625*	*$2,625*
Percentage of package that is work or loans	*40%*	*26%*	*47%*
Total financial aid award	*$21,325*	*$21,410*	*$5,566*
Grants and scholarships + work-study + loans			
Step 3. Calculate what it will cost you to attend each college you are considering. For each college, enter the total cost of attendance. Then, subtract the total financial aid award from the total cost of attendance. That number is the net cost, or what it will cost you to attend that college.			
a) Total cost of attendance	*$31,825*	*$33,410*	*$15,566*
b) Total financial aid award	*$21,325*	*$21,410*	*$5,566*
c) Net cost to attend (a minus b)	*$10,500*	*$12,000*	*$10,000*

For a blank version of this worksheet that you can photocopy for your own use, see page 121.

EXPERT ADVICE

"It's **not simply the dollar amount of the grant or scholarship** that families should focus on. They need to **lay out, side by side, the full picture**. What's the cost of attendance, including out-of-pocket expenses? What's the family contribution? What are the elements of aid? What's going to happen with loans, with work?"

— Joe Paul Case, dean and director of financial aid, Amherst College, Amherst, Mass.

mean School A has the better deal. If School A's aid package has $3,000 in grants and $7,000 in loans, but School B has $6,000 in grants and $2,000 in loans, School B is offering you more free money (grants) than School A.

There is another reason why a financial aid package may not be as big as it seems: higher costs. If one school's costs are higher than another's, you may be left with a higher out-of-pocket expense even after subtracting a "bigger" aid package. **Don't be dazzled by a large award. Instead, look for the bottom line: your net cost to attend the school.**

Here's a true story to illustrate this further. **Two sample award letters appear in Part II** (see pages 122, 123). These were taken from actual letters received by a student. Only the names of the colleges involved have been changed, to "Blue University" and "Green University." The student's first-choice college was Blue U, which cost about $2,000 more than Green U. When she first compared the letters, she was very upset because it looked like Green U was giving her a much bigger scholarship, and much more total aid.

But her school counselor showed her that Blue U was actually offering the better deal. First of all, the grants and scholarship from Green U only looked bigger because they were presented as a total. Secondly, the student loans offered by Blue U (Stafford and Perkins) were subsidized, while the Stafford loan offered by Green U was not. That meant at Green U she would have to pay interest on the loan while she was in college. And third, the $14,810 Green U was "offering" as a parent PLUS loan wasn't really aid at all, but just an option for how her family could pay for their contribution. Bottom line, the true cost to her would be about the same at both colleges, even though Blue U is more expensive.

Collegeboard.com has an online "Compare Your Aid Awards" tool that lets you do this kind of side-by-side comparison of your awards. You can also use Worksheet 3 to break out the different components of costs and aid packages and compare them side by side (a blank copy of this worksheet appears on page 121). When doing this analysis, keep an eye out for both quantity and quality. On the quantity side, for example, the "Family Share of Costs" figure tells you the amount of money your family will be expected to contribute. Your family will need to decide whether this amount is affordable. Look especially for evidence of "gapping," the practice of leaving a gap between the cost of attendance and the money accounted for by aid and EFC. You will be expected to fill that gap — in effect increasing your EFC.

On the quality side, consider the figures for "% of Award That Is Gift Aid" and "% of Award That Is Loan." The higher the proportion of gift aid (grant or scholarships) to loans, the better the award.

Loans vs. Grants

All other things being equal, it's better to receive a grant or scholarship than a loan. For that reason, a financial aid package with a high percentage of gift aid is more attractive, on the face of it, than one with a high percentage of loans. But there are circumstances where you might take the award that offers more loans and less gift aid: For example, if that college is a better fit for you overall.

In any event, don't be surprised if your award includes loans. Most aid packages contain them. Loans are optional; you don't have to take them out. But if offered as part of a need-based aid package, they can be an excellent way to help finance your education. The alternative — taking only grant aid and trying to pay the costs that the loans would cover out-of-pocket — could put your family under much more financial stress than the loan would.

It's usually in your best interest to accept subsidized Stafford and Perkins loans that are part of the aid package: The repayment terms are good and the government pays the interest while you're in school. Unsubsidized loans — such as unsubsidized Stafford, PLUS loan and private loans from a bank — should be studied more carefully to make sure the terms are acceptable. You should understand the specific terms of each loan, including its interest rate, the origination fee, the term of the loan and the grace period before repayment begins. You should also realize that unsubsidized loans are not need based and are typically used to help your families pay their EFC. If a college offers them as part of your aid package, consider them as an option, but don't weigh them equally with subsidized loans in the package.

Work-study jobs are also optional, but if you're offered one and you can manage the time, take it. Having a job on campus brings in income, expands your social networks, allows you to make contacts with professors and administrators, and gives you experience that can improve your résumé.

KEEP IN MIND

Just because you're awarded a loan to pay part of your college costs **doesn't mean you have to accept it**. If your family has funds available in savings or current income, you can use these funds if you prefer. The downside is that you'll have less money available now, which could put your family under financial stress. The upside is that you won't have to pay the money back later with interest.

Appealing Your Award

Even though your award letters are printed in black and white, they aren't necessarily the last word. It is possible to appeal the awards: to ask the colleges to reconsider their aid packages. There is no guarantee that they will grant your request, but there are circumstances where it's worth trying.

One reason you might appeal a package is if it has a lot of unsubsidized loans. However, bear in the mind that the college probably offered those loans because there wasn't enough gift aid to go around. Another reason to appeal is if you don't think you can afford the expected family contribution. You will need to have evidence to make that case. The college based its calculation of your EFC on the financial information you submitted. If you think this calculation was wrong, ask the financial aid office how it was made and see if you can find out if a mistake occurred. It will help if you have special circumstances that weren't communicated in your financial aid forms, such as a recent layoff; situations like this will clearly demonstrate why your family would have difficulty paying its EFC. (*See Step 8, "Make Your Special Circumstances Known."*)

"I've changed financial aid packages on appeal if somebody can demonstrate why they can't afford it," says Forrest Stuart of Rhodes College. "It may be the need analysis just didn't take some things into account. If they can show me where there's a real problem, even to the point where they show me their monthly

KNOW THE LINGO

There are three types of federal loans for educational expenses:

Stafford — Loan to students. May be subsidized (if student demonstrates need) or unsubsidized. If subsidized, the government pays the interest on the loan while the student is in college.

PLUS — A federal loan for parents to cover college costs not met by financial aid. Not subsidized.

Perkins — Subsidized loan to students with exceptional need. Perkins-loan debt may be forgiven if the borrower enters a career in the public service.

Questions to Ask About Your Award

These are some questions to ask your college financial aid office if you're awarded gift aid:

- ✔ What do I have to do to keep my scholarship — do I have to do anything more than maintain satisfactory academic progress?
- ✔ Is there a minimum GPA or other condition?
- ✔ Is the scholarship renewable in subsequent years?
- ✔ If I win an outside scholarship, what happens to my aid?

Questions to ask if you're awarded a loan:

- ✔ What are the terms of my loan?
- ✔ What is the interest rate, and when do I start repayment?
- ✔ How much will I owe by the time I graduate?
- ✔ What will my monthly repayment be?
- ✔ By how much will my loan increase after my first year?

Questions to ask if you're awarded work-study:

- ✔ Do I have a "guaranteed" job, or will I have to find one?
- ✔ How are jobs assigned?
- ✔ How many hours per week will I be expected to work?
- ✔ What is the hourly wage?
- ✔ How often will I be paid?
- ✔ Will I be paid directly, or will my student account get credited?

budget, I might say, 'Man, you are right. You've got these medical expenses or you've got this and that. Let me see if I can help you.' I am not perfect, and the need analysis is not perfect, and we'll sometimes overlook something."

Still another reason for appealing an award is if you have better offers from other colleges, and would like to see if this college can match them. Some aid offices will consider matching a better offer from another college. But most will only hear an appeal that's based on your family's financial circumstances. "We don't bargain," says Mike Scott of Texas Christian University. "We just don't want to play that game of, 'Well, we'll give you more money simply because another school gave you more money.'"

You might see the entire appeal process as essentially negotiation or bargaining — trying to get as much as possible from the school you'd like to attend. However, most financial aid officers loathe the term "negotiate." Your appeal will have a better chance of success if it appears not a matter of haggling but of providing information not previously available to the financial aid office.

It will also help your cause if you are obviously doing your part to fund your education. A student who accepts the self-help components of a school's financial aid package will be more likely to get extra help than one who declined them. "If the student is not willing to somehow contribute, either by working or taking out a student loan, then we are very unlikely to give them any extra money," says Mike Scott.

A phone call is a good way to start the appeal process, even though most colleges will want you to put your reasons for an appeal in writing. Some have a specific form for appeals; others would like for you to state your case in a letter. Find out the college's preferred procedure by calling or checking their Web site. No matter how you file your appeal, your case will be stronger if you can provide data to back it up. A few days after filing your appeal, follow up with a phone call or, if possible, by visiting the aid office. Within a short time, the college will let you know its decision.

If you receive a revised award, take the new award letter and compare it to your other aid packages. **It's best not to decide where to enroll until you've received the final offer from each college.** But keep in mind the deadline set by each college for acceptance of its award. If you miss the deadline, you could lose the package. If you do need more time, try asking the college for an extension.

EXPERT ADVICE

"I tell families **not to use the word 'negotiate.'** If an aid package is much lower than what's being offered by similar institutions, families should call and ask if there is additional information that may make a difference."

— Carlene Riccelli, college adviser, Amherst Regional High School, Amherst, Mass.

Follow Up: Accepting an Award

Once you've compared all the awards and any appeals have been ruled upon, you and your family will have to decide on a college. Many factors, including costs and financial aid, will be in play. If your first-choice college has accepted you but not given as much aid as you'd hoped, the choice may be difficult. Do you go to your first-choice college even though it's a financial risk for your family, or to a second-choice college your family can safely afford? In the end, your own preferences should have the greatest weight. Most of the loan debt, payable after graduation, will be on your shoulders. And your personal happiness at the school will have a major influence on whether you graduate successfully. If your family can put together a sensible financial plan to pay the costs, the best choice is the one that fits you best academically and personally.

Once you've decided which offer to accept, it's polite to send a note declining the offers of the colleges you're rejecting. That way any funds they offered you can be made available to other students. As for the offer you're accepting, follow whatever instructions came in the award packet. If you're being asked for more information, send it. Complete any forms that came with the award letter. Sign the letter and return it by the due date.

QUICK RECAP

When you receive your award letters from colleges, you'll have to decide which offer to accept.

- Compare apples to apples, analyzing the awards to see what the real costs and financial aid elements are.
- Just because loans are offered, you don't have to accept them. But they're worth considering, especially if they're subsidized loans.
- If you appeal an award, you'll be on stronger ground if you can demonstrate circumstances that weren't previously made clear to the school.
- Your decision about which offer to accept should be based not just on cost but on how well the college fits you academically, socially and personally.

Step 11: Consider Your Out-of-Pocket Options

QUICK OVERVIEW

Financial aid is intended to cover the difference between your expected family contribution (EFC) and the total cost of college. However, you still have to pay your EFC and whatever gap there might be between the aid you received and your financial need. This step is about ways to meet those out-of-pocket costs.

Making Up the Difference

For almost every family, college is going to cost money. Even a generous financial aid package will usually leave you with some bills to pay. Some packages will meet less than your full need and leave you spending more than your EFC. You can afford to make up this difference between the total cost of attendance and the aid you're receiving if you take advantage of the various resources available to you. Most families use a combination of savings, current income and loans to pay their out-of-pocket costs. You'll have to decide how to do that in a way that fits your own particular situation. But you'll have help, because there are a number of programs and strategies that can help you save, pay or borrow for college.

KNOW THE LINGO

EFC (Expected Family Contribution) — How much money a family is expected to pay for college out of pocket, based on the family's ability to pay.

Need — The difference between your EFC and the cost of attending a particular college you've chosen. Financial aid is designed to meet your need, not your EFC.

Unmet need — The difference (if any) between your need and the financial aid offered by a particular college. Informally, unmet need is also called a **gap**.

Save for It

You shouldn't spend your entire family savings on college: You need to leave some for other uses, such as retirement and emergency medical costs. But it makes sense to use some of your savings for college.

Don't worry if your family doesn't already have a huge sum of money saved for college. **Every little bit helps, and it's never too late to start saving.** Even while you're applying to college, your family can start saving. Try to save as much as you can from summer and after-school jobs, and encourage your parents to set aside some money from every paycheck. Talk with your parents about how much money you and they already have saved for your college costs, and discuss how your family can afford the rest of the bill.

Don't believe anyone who says you shouldn't save for college because it will reduce your chances of getting financial aid. As noted in Step 2, savings are worth having so you can pay out-of-pocket costs without having to borrow. Very little, if any, of your parents' savings are counted against you when your financial need is determined. "Parents should not avoid saving because, frankly, a family that has saved has a resource to draw on, whereas a family that hasn't is totally dependent on current income and loans," says Joe Paul Case, dean and director of financial aid at Amherst College in Amherst, Mass.

There are a number of places families can put their savings. The most traditional is a regular bank savings account, which pays a little interest and offers freedom to withdraw and deposit money at any time. A certificate of deposit (CD) has stricter rules about when you can withdraw money, but it usually pays higher interest than a savings account. Both of these options are good for short-term, flexible savings. But neither has any tax incentives — tax breaks that make them especially attractive for college savings.

The following savings vehicles do come with tax breaks. For more details, see Table 3 on page 100:

529 college savings plan. Also known as the QTP (Qualified Tuition Program), these are tax-advantaged accounts sponsored by the various states. Interest earned in these plans is not taxed as income, and some states also offer a state income-tax deduction for contributions their residents make to the state's plan. There are no income restrictions, and contribution limits are high. Grandparents, uncles and aunts are also allowed to contribute to the plan, even if they don't live in the same state as you and your parents — in fact, you don't have to be a resident of a state to contribute to its plan, and you can withdraw funds from a state's plan to pay for expenses at a college in another state. Most plans offer a few different investment types, such as a fund that invests in stocks or one that invests in bonds.

Coverdell Education Savings Account. These tax-free trust or custodial accounts are similar to 529s, but they're sponsored by banks and brokerage houses instead of states, and therefore offer a greater range of investment choices. They can be used to pay private elementary and high school costs as well as college costs, unlike 529s, which can only be used for college costs. Total contributions for the student can't be more than $2,000 in a given year, and your family income has to be less than $110,000 (for single filers) or $220,000 (for joint filers). You can contribute to both a 529 and a Coverdell in the same year for the same student.

529 prepaid tuition plan. Like the 529 college savings plans, these are sponsored by the states, but they work differently. A 529 prepaid tuition plan lets a family make advance tuition payments years before their children will enter college. That allows them to "lock in" today's tuition rates instead of paying the higher rates likely to prevail years from now. Provided the student is admitted, the plans are guaranteed to be honored by public universities and some private colleges in the state that sponsors the plan. However, these plans have drawbacks. They can only be used for tuition and fees, not for room, board or other supplemental costs. When that's combined with the fact that the tuition rates are only locked in for in-state colleges, most parents prefer the more flexible 529 savings plans.

Independent 529 prepaid tuition plan. This is a special 529 prepaid tuition plan sponsored by a group of private colleges and universities and administered by TIAA-CREF. For more information, visit www.independent529plan.org.

U.S. savings bonds. If your parents pay for some of your college costs by cashing in U.S. government savings bonds, the interest that has accumulated on the bond may be tax exempt. That means the interest won't be taxed as income and your tax bill will be smaller. There's a penalty if you cash in the bonds less than five years after the date of issue, and there are some restrictions on the tax exemption. The bond must be issued after 1989 and your parent must have been age 24 or older when the bond was issued. This deduction can't overlap with any other education tax break. You can't use two different tax breaks to pay for the same expense. The family income must be less than $82,100 (for single filers) or $130,650 (for joint filers).

Uniform Gifts to Minors Act (UGMA) or Uniform Transfers to Minors Act (UTMA) account. These accounts allow parents to put money in the child's name so it will receive preferential tax treatment. Much of the earnings are taxed at the child's rate rather than the parent's rate. Such accounts were popular in the 1980s, but the advent of tax-free 529s and Coverdells has made them nearly obsolete as a college-savings vehicle.

Individual Retirement Account (IRA). Generally, it's not a good idea to raid the family retirement funds, such as IRAs, to pay for college. "We tell parents all the time, you can borrow money to pay for your kid's education. You cannot borrow money to retire with," says Mike Scott of Texas Christian University. It's usually better to take out a PLUS loan than to diminish retirement assets. Still, if your family does need to go into an IRA to pay college expenses, the government doesn't charge the 10 percent additional tax you would ordinarily have to pay for breaking open an IRA before age 59½.

Table 3:
Comparison of Education Savings Options

	COVERDELL EDUCATION SAVINGS ACCOUNT	529 COLLEGE SAVINGS PLAN (QUALIFIED TUITION PROGRAM)	529 PREPAID TUITION PLAN	U.S. GOVERNMENT SAVINGS BONDS	UNIFORM GIFTS TO MINORS ACT ACCOUNT	INDIVIDUAL RETIREMENT ACCOUNT
Tax advantages	Earnings in account not taxed as income	Earnings in account not taxed as income Some states allow residents to deduct contributions for state income tax purposes	Earnings in account not taxed as income Some states allow residents to deduct contributions for state income tax purposes	Interest earned is not taxed if used for qualified expenses	Interest earned is taxed at child's rate	Exception to the 10% early withdrawal penalty rule
Expenses that qualify	• Tuition & fees • Books & supplies • Room & board (if at least half-time) • Expenses for special needs services • K-12 education expenses	• Tuition & fees • Books & supplies • Room & board (if at least half-time)	Tuition & fees	• Tuition & fees • Contributions to a Coverdell or 529	Any expense (not limited to education)	• Tuition & fees • Books & supplies • Room & board (if at least half-time)
Contribution limits	$2,000 per year	None	None	None	None	$4,000 per year ($5,000 if over 50)
Income phaseout for benefits	$95,000-$110,000 (single filers) $190,000-$220,000 (joint filers)	None	None	$67,100-$82,100 (single filers) $100,650-$130,650 (joint filers)	None	Varies by type of account
Other limitations	Assets must be distributed by age 30 Must pay 10% penalty if distributions not used for qualified expenses	Must pay 10% penalty if distributions not used for qualified expenses	Benefits may only be used at colleges that participate in the plan Must pay 10% penalty if distributions not used for qualified expenses	Applies only to Series EE or Series I bonds issued after 1989 and purchased after owner turned 24	Counted as student asset for financial aid purposes	Interest earned will still be taxed at your regular rate

Work for It

Besides a summer job, you might also want to consider working during the school year to help meet expenses. There are two basic approaches. You can go to college full time while working part-time, or you can hold a full-time job while attending college part time.

Full-Time Student, Part-Time Job

If you're offered a work-study job as part of your financial aid package, the earnings from that job will go toward your college costs. Even if you're not offered work-study, you may still be able to find a part-time job on or near campus. You can also work during the summer to make money to put toward college.

Work has benefits beyond the extra income it generates. It can help you structure your time, which can make you a more disciplined student. Studies have shown that students who work part-time get better grades and are more likely to finish college than those who don't work at all. If the job is on campus, it enhances the college experience by connecting students more closely with the school and giving them a chance to meet people they wouldn't meet in classes.

On the other hand, don't work so many hours that you jeopardize your ability to get through college. **If you're going to college full time, the recommended workload is about 10 to 15 hours a week**. If you work more than 20 hours a week, you're likely to get overloaded and put yourself at risk of dropping out. If you take fewer courses to make time for work, you may drop below full-time status, which could make you ineligible for many grants and scholarships. If your financial situation makes you feel that you have to work more hours, it might be better to borrow more money so you don't have to work so much.

EXPERT ADVICE

"**Work gives students structure.** First, they have to be somewhere. They have to be doing something at certain times of the week, which helps them manage their time. Second, if the job is on campus, they get involved with an office or a department or a faculty member, and that helps to **strengthen that student's connection with that school**, which always enhances the academic experience."

— Vincent Amoroso, deputy director, Office of Scholarships and Student Aid, University of North Carolina, Chapel Hill

Part-Time Student, Full-Time Job

A different (and much more difficult) way of approaching work is to be a full-time worker who goes to college part time. This is possible as long as you don't take too many credits in one semester. If you try for more than six to eight credits (two courses) while working full time, you'll probably have trouble getting everything done. On the other hand, if you take fewer than six credits a semester, you won't be eligible for need-based subsidized Stafford or Perkins loans or a Pell Grant.

Working full time while going to school part time is an especially attractive way to pay for an associate degree or a vocational certificate. Most community colleges cater to working students and offer classes at night to meet their needs. If you take six credits per semester, you can probably earn an associate degree in four or five years.

If you're planning on earning a bachelor's degree, however, you should strongly consider attending college full time and borrowing money to replace the income that you won't be earning through a job. Why? If you take only six credits a semester, it will take 10 years to earn a bachelor's! You will probably earn more money in the long run if you get that bachelor's in the usual four or five years, and concentrate on your career after you've earned that degree.

Some employers offer tuition assistance or scholarship money to employees who are attending college. Check to see if your employer is one of them. For a typical educational assistance program, up to $5,250 of those benefits will be tax free each year.

KEEP IN MIND

As noted in Step 2, you will be **expected to contribute** a larger percentage of your **work income to college costs** than your parents will. This is because it is expected that you have fewer financial responsibilities and will benefit more from college than your parents will. In general, you will be expected to pay about 50 percent of your earnings toward the EFC.

Co-op and Internship Programs

Many colleges sponsor internships or "co-op" (cooperative) programs with local employers. Some interns and almost all co-op participants receive payment from their employers along with academic credit. In co-op programs, you may be able to alternate periods of full-time work and full-time study. Often the business at which you intern hires you after graduation, or at least recommends you to others. Internship and co-op programs can help you make money, get academic credit, gain job experience and make contacts with potential employers.

Promising to Work Later

Holding a job during college is not the only way of using work to pay your college costs. There are several programs that allow you to commit to work in public service after graduation in exchange for either a non-need-based scholarship while in college or a stipend that can be used to repay student loans after college. The ROTC program is an example of the former, and AmeriCorps is an example of the latter.

ROTC

In return for military service, the armed forces offer career training and a number of educational benefits to help pay for college, including full college scholarships and education assistance plans. If you're interested in training to be a military officer during college in return for educational benefits, check with the Reserve Officers' Training Corps (ROTC) office at your high school or on your college campus. Each branch of the military offers ROTC training. Part IV of this book contains lists of colleges that offer ROTC programs for each service branch.

OTHER SERVICE PROGRAMS

AmeriCorps is a network of national service programs for which you can work as a volunteer, full or part time, for up to a year. After completing a term of service with AmeriCorps, you're eligible for an education award, which can be used either to repay student loans or to pay for college tuition. The amount of the award depends on how long you worked for the program, and for how many hours each week. (Currently, completion of one year's full-time service earns an award of $4,725.) For more information, go to www.americorps.org.

Another type of program is one that hinges on your financial aid package and the profession you choose after college. If you received a Perkins loan as part of your package, the loan may be forgiven if you enter certain professions serving the public, such as teaching, nursing or law enforcement.

Borrow It

To borrow money is to spend today what you'll earn in the future. You will have to pay the loan back, with interest, when you start earning money after college. A loan can be intimidating because it assumes you'll have the money for repayment, and you may not feel sure of that. But rest assured that college will increase your earning power, which will make it possible to repay your loans.

There are many forms of "bad debt" in our society, such as credit card debt, where you borrow money on unfavorable terms to buy consumer goods that will have little or no value in a year. By comparison, an education loan is a "good debt." You are borrowing money on favorable terms to achieve an outcome — higher lifetime earnings — that will more than pay back the loan.

GOOD TO KNOW

To apply for EFC-meeting loans, shop around on the Internet. The FinAid Web site (www.finaid.com) maintains lists of lenders. Your college financial aid office may also be able to recommend their "preferred" lenders.

Subsidized Stafford loans, Perkins loans and need-based state loans all have excellent terms that make them worth considering. Some institutions also offer their own need-based loans to qualified students. However, these loans are intended as financial aid to cover your need. In general, you won't be able to use them towards your expected family contribution.

However, loans are available that are not based on need and that your family can use to borrow money to meet their EFC. The terms are not as favorable as the need-based loans, but the loans may be helpful just the same. The most common types are the unsubsidized Stafford and the PLUS loan, both of which are guaranteed by the federal government, but there are also state and private sources.

How Much Should You Borrow?

If your family decides to borrow money to pay for college, they should consider the total debt that you will carry after graduation. That total debt includes any subsidized, need-meeting loans that you accept as part of the college's aid package as well as any non-need-based loans your family takes out to meet the EFC. When you pay back that debt, you'll do so in the form of monthly payments, and those payments should be reasonable ones that you can afford to pay from the income you're likely to have. The total monthly payment will usually be similar to a car payment — $200 to $300 a month. But the amount will vary with the amount borrowed and interest rate offered. See Table 4 on the next page for help in determining what your monthly payment will be. It shows monthly repayment over 10 years for a loan of $10,000 at various interest rates. To calculate a monthly payment for a loan amount not listed on the table, multiply the amount borrowed by the repayment factor for your interest rate. For example, if you borrowed $12,500 at 7.5 percent, your monthly payment would be $148.46 ($12,500 × .0118770).

KNOW THE LINGO

Principal — the portion of debt that is left over from the amount you originally borrowed.

Interest — the portion of debt that has been charged to you by the lender as a fee for loaning you the principal.

There are some ways to make your repayment burden lighter after college. Many lenders will offer to cut your interest rate a bit if you make your first 12 monthly payments on time. If you borrow from multiple federal loan programs, such as the Perkins, subsidized Stafford and unsubsidized Stafford, you can consolidate these loans after graduation, which will simplify things by allowing you to make only one payment a month. Consolidation also gives you the option of "re-amortizing" your loans — that means stretching your payments over a longer period of time than you would normally have left to repay the debt. If you re-amortize when you consolidate, you will usually have a lower monthly payment, but will pay more interest over the total life of all the loans.

Table 4:
Calculating Your Monthly Loan Payment

AMOUNT OF LOAN	INTEREST RATE	REPAYMENT FACTOR	MONTHLY PAYMENT
$10,000	4.00%	.010125	$101.25
	4.50%	.010364	$103.64
	5.00%	.010607	$106.07
	5.50%	.010853	$108.53
	6.00%	.011102	$111.02
	6.50%	.011355	$113.55
	7.00%	.011611	$116.11
	7.50%	.011870	$118.70
	8.00%	.012133	$121.33
	8.50%	.012399	$123.99
	9.00%	.012668	$126.68

GOOD TO KNOW

When you start paying back your educational loan, remember that the **interest may be tax deductible**. To a maximum of $2,500 per year, you can deduct the interest you pay from your income, which will lower your tax bite. In effect, the government will be subsidizing your loan. This is true for every kind of education loan, including PLUS loans.

Types of Non-Need-Based Loans

There are three basic types of loans you can use to pay your out-of-pocket costs: federal, state and private.

FEDERAL LOANS

Federal loans have relatively low interest rates and are guaranteed by the federal government. This means that if you don't pay your loan back to the lender (though, of course, you should), the federal government will. That encourages lenders to lend you money even if you're a student with no credit history and little employment record.

Two basic kinds of federal loans are used for paying an EFC, one for students, one for parents:

- **Student Loans (Unsubsidized Stafford).** With an unsubsidized Stafford loan, you borrow money through participating colleges or directly from a bank or other lender. You'll be charged only interest while you're in school, and can either pay it while you're in school or let it accrue (accumulate) for payment after school. If you let the interest accrue, the bank will "capitalize" it into the principal of the loan when you start sending them payments after graduation. Table 5 shows the effects of interest accrual. The calculations on the table are for example only — they assume that you borrow $3,500 at the beginning of your freshman year and don't borrow any more to fund subsequent years of education. With this amount and the interest rate shown, letting the interest accrue saves you a $20 monthly payment while you're in college, but it ends up costing you about $407 more over the life of the loan. Whether or not you let interest accrue, six months after leaving school (your grace period), you have to begin paying back both the principal and the interest. To apply for an unsubsidized Stafford loan, ask your college financial aid office; they will refer you to lenders.

Table 5:
Effects of Letting Interest Accrue While You're in College

	INTEREST RATE IN COLLEGE	MONTHLY PAYMENT IN COLLEGE	DEBT REMAINING AFTER COLLEGE	INTEREST RATE AFTER COLLEGE*	MONTHLY PAYMENT AFTER COLLEGE	TOTAL INTEREST PAID OVER LIFE OF THE LOAN
Subsidized Stafford	0%	$0	$3,500.00	4.5%	$36.27	$852.40
Unsubsidized Stafford (no interest accrual)	6.8%	$19.83	$3,500.00	6.8%	$40.28	$2,404.60
Unsubsidized Stafford (interest accrual option)	6.8%	$0	$4,571.00	6.8%	$52.60	$2,812.00

*After July 1, 2010

- **Parent Loans (PLUS).** With a PLUS loan, your parents borrow money to pay for your education either through the school or a third-party lender. They can borrow any amount up to the student's total cost of attendance minus the financial aid you receive. To get a PLUS loan, your parents have to fill out an application and pass a credit review. They will have to start making payments on the entire debt — both the principal and the interest — as soon as the loan money is disbursed to the school.

If you take out a federal loan, you'll receive a loan repayment schedule that spells out when your first payment is due and the number, frequency and amounts of the payments. You'll have to pay back the loan on schedule or go into default, an official state of failure to repay a loan. That would hurt your credit rating — your ability to borrow more money later.

Under certain circumstances, such as economic hardship, you can postpone repayment of a federal student loan by applying for a deferment (during which no interest accumulates) or forbearance (during which it does). Under exceptional circumstances, such as total disability or teaching in a designated low-income school, some borrowers get a loan discharge, or cancellation of the debt. These rules apply to all federal student loans, but not to PLUS loans.

STATE LOANS

Some states sponsor loan programs for students and parents in their state. These loans are usually neither subsidized nor based on need. Check with your state financial aid agency to find out more.

PRIVATE LOANS

Many banks, credit unions and other organizations offer their own education loans. These usually have slightly higher interest rates than federal loans, but they have lower interest rates than other consumer borrowing options, and may have attractive features, such as deferred repayment while in school. The borrowers — usually parents — have to prove their creditworthiness to get these loans.

HOME-EQUITY LOANS

Many parents consider taking out a loan against their home equity to pay for their children's higher education. While this may be an attractive option for your family, you should keep in mind that, unlike PLUS loans and other education loans, home-equity loans do come with the condition that if you can't pay back the loan, the bank can foreclose on your house.

Table 6:
Comparison of Education Loan Options

	SUBSIDIZED STAFFORD	PERKINS	UNSUBSIDIZED STAFFORD	PLUS	PRIVATE/ ALTERNATIVE EDUCATION LOAN	HOME EQUITY LOAN OR LINE OF CREDIT
BORROWING LIMIT	$3,500 first year $4,500 second year $5,500 third and fourth years Higher limits for independent students and for graduate study	$5,500/year $27,500 undergraduate maximum	$5,500 first year $6,500 second year $7,500 third and fourth years Higher limits if parents were denied a PLUS loan	Maximum is difference between total cost of attendance and financial aid awarded	Depends on credit check Maximum is difference between total cost of attendance and financial aid awarded	Depends on credit check and home equity
INTEREST RATES FOR 2010-11	In school: 0% In repayment: 4.5% (fixed)	In school: 0% In repayment: 5% (fixed)	In school: 6.8% (fixed) In repayment: 6.8% (fixed)	8.5% (fixed)	Depends on lender and credit check; range from 7% to 12%; may be fixed or variable	Depends on lender and credit check; may be fixed or variable
PROS	Interest that accumulates while you're in college paid by federal government	No origination fee Interest that accumulates while you're in college paid by federal government Debt may be forgiven if you enter a career in the public service	Option of not making payments during college and "capitalizing" accrued interest into the loan upon graduation Same deferment, and forbearance rules as subsidized loans	No collateral required	Available for nondegree programs and adult continuing education Repayment term may be longer than for federal loans	Can use money for noneducational purposes Repayment term may be longer than for federal loans
CONS	Only available to students with financial need 2% origination fee (may be discounted by lender)	Only available to students with financial need Amount of loan you're offered subject to college financial aid office's discretion	4% origination fee (may be discounted by lender)	Parents must pass credit check to take out loan Parents must begin paying interest immediately 4% origination fee	Student must pass credit check Parents may have to cosign promissory note May have high origination fees	Home used as collateral for loan Can take several months to secure loan; may need to have house appraised

KNOW THE LINGO

Advanced placement — Admission into an advanced-level course in a certain subject on the basis of an exam or other evidence that the student has already completed the equivalent of the introductory course in that subject.

Credit by examination — College credit earned for prior knowledge, usually demonstrated on either an AP Exam or CLEP exam.

Accelerated program — A program of study completed in fewer semesters than normal, usually by taking extra courses and attending classes over the summer.

Cut It

In addition to spending past, present and future resources to pay your college bill, you can also take steps to make that bill smaller. This is an especially smart move if it looks like college won't be affordable otherwise, even when you contribute all you can from savings, current income and loans. But some strategies to cut college costs are worth using even if your family is financially comfortable.

Tuition "On the Cheap"

Tuition, the cost of taking classes, is usually high at four-year colleges. But you can get a reduced rate on those classes by taking them ahead of time at your own high school or a community college. By doing this, you may also be able to reduce the number of semesters you have to spend in college, which will cut not only your tuition costs but all other costs, such as room and board. Some colleges offer accelerated programs that will help you do that.

AP®/CLEP®

Several programs let you earn college credit or advanced placement. They include the Advanced Placement Program® (AP) and the College-Level Examination Program® (CLEP®), which are sponsored by the College Board. The programs differ in various ways. For example, students take AP courses as part of their high school curriculum, but they can prepare to take the CLEP examinations by any number of means — in school, on the job or by just reading books in their spare time. These programs are similar, however, in that you earn credit by taking an examination and receiving a score that your college accepts.

Colleges differ as to which programs, courses and scores they accept and how much credit they grant. But every credit you receive means a credit you don't have to pay for in college. Depending on your exam scores and your college's policies, you may be able to graduate a semester or even a year early if you've taken enough AP exams.

CLEP exams can be taken on your campus or at a nearby campus, and can be used to bypass introductory-level courses. For more information see collegeboard.com/clep. To find out about your college's policy on AP credit, go to collegeboard.com and use the AP Credit Policy Info tool.

TAKE COMMUNITY COLLEGE CLASSES OVER THE SUMMER

Courses at a community college usually cost much less than at a four-year college. Find out if there are courses you can take at a local community college in the summers and transfer to your four-year college. For example, if you don't have the knowledge of a certain subject that you need to pass a CLEP exam, you may still be able to take that course at a community college over the summer and transfer the credit to your four-year college.

OTHER ACCELERATED PROGRAMS

Some colleges offer an "accelerated program" designed for students who want to graduate in three years. These programs require a lot of work and dedication, but they will cut your college costs substantially by eliminating an entire year of expenses. It's possible to get through these programs if you're determined.

Cutting Other Expenses

Tuition is not the only college cost you can cut. Room, board, books, supplies, transportation — all of these add substantially to your total college bill. (Most people are shocked at what college textbooks cost these days.) Here are some suggestions to reduce these expenses:

BOOKS

- ✔ Buy used textbooks instead of new ones.
- ✔ Comparison shop for textbooks online.
- ✔ Sell your textbooks at the end of the semester.

ROOM AND BOARD

- ✔ Live off campus in a house or apartment that you share with classmates. That can be cheaper than a college dorm. (But check the policy at the college you want to attend — many require freshmen to live on campus.)
- ✔ If you plan to live in a dorm in your sophomore year and beyond, try to get a position as a resident adviser and the free room and board that comes with it.

TRANSPORTATION

- ✔ If you're commuting to school, carpool with a classmate from your area.

Education Tax Breaks

Federal student aid isn't the only way that Uncle Sam can help you pay for college. There are also tax breaks available for higher-education costs. By reducing the amount your family has to pay the government at tax time, these programs amount to federal subsidies for out-of-pocket costs. Some of them take the form of tax credits, which cut your taxes dollar for dollar: That is, a $1 tax credit would make your tax bill $1 smaller. Others take the form of tax deductions,

GOOD TO KNOW

The information about higher-education tax breaks printed here is current as of early 2009. **To make sure you qualify for a deduction or credit** before you file, download IRS Publication 970, "Tax Benefits for Education," from www.irs.gov.

which lower the amount of your income that is subject to tax, indirectly lowering your tax bill.

There are two federal income tax credits for higher-education expenses: **the Hope tax credit and the Lifetime Learning tax credit.** Both of these benefits let your family reduce the tax they pay by a fraction of their out-of-pocket costs, but the criteria for eligibility are different. The Hope tax credit, which is worth up to $1,800 per student per year, is available to families that have a first- or second-year student enrolled at least half-time in an undergraduate degree program. To be eligible for the Lifetime Learning tax credit, you don't have to be enrolled half time or even be in a degree program. It's available for almost any kind of postsecondary education and training. The Lifetime Learning tax credit is equal to 20 percent of your family's tuition expenses, up to a $2,000 credit for $10,000 in tuition. Unlike the Hope Scholarship Credit, the Lifetime Learning Credit is calculated on a per-family, not a per-student, basis, so the maximum credit has to be shared among all students in the family.

Your family can't use both of these credits for the same student in the same year, though they can use both credits if they're applied to separate students. For either tax credit, the amount depends in part on your family's income, as calculated according to a formula called modified adjusted gross income. The more your family makes, the less money they'll be eligible for. Past a certain level of income ($58,000 for single filers; $116,000 for joint filers), your family won't be eligible at all. Still, for many people, the tax credits are a big help in paying the tuition bills.

If your family's income is too high to qualify for either the Hope or Lifetime Learning credits, there's also a tax deduction that may help. With the tuition and fees deduction, you can deduct up to $4,000 of college tuition and fees as long as your family income isn't more than $80,000 (for single filers) or $160,000 (for joint filers). If you claim this deduction, you can't claim the Hope or Lifetime Learning credits for the same student that year.

Interest paid on student loans is tax deductible to a maximum of $2,500 per year. This benefit applies to all loans used to pay for college, including PLUS loans. To be eligible for this deduction, your income has to be lower than $70,000 (for single filers) or $145,000 (for joint filers). The tax break is only for interest — the amount you pay the lender as the price for borrowing a sum of money, rather than the starting sum itself (the principal). If you take out a student loan, the lender will send a 1098 form to you at the end of each tax year telling you how much of your payments went to interest that year.

Some states also allow you to take tax credits or deductions off your state income taxes. Find out about yours from your state government.

Table 7:
Federal Income Tax Benefits for Higher Education

	HOPE EDUCATION CREDIT	LIFETIME LEARNING CREDIT	TUITION AND FEES DEDUCTION	STUDENT LOAN INTEREST DEDUCTION
AVAILABLE FOR	Tuition and fees only 1st two years of undergraduate study only Associate and bachelor's degree programs only	Tuition and fees only All years of study Any degree program, also nondegree courses to acquire job skills	Tuition and fees only All years of study Attendance at any postsecondary institution participating in a federal student aid program	Any higher education cost All years of study Any degree program
MAXIMUM VALUE	$1,800 credit per student	$2,000 credit per family	$4,000 deduction taken as an adjustment to gross income	$2,500 deduction from taxable income
MAXIMUM INCOME FOR ELIGIBILITY	$48,000-$58,000 (single filers) $96,000-$116,000 (joint filers)		$80,000 (single filers) $160,000 (joint filers)	$55,000-$70,000 (single filers) $115,000-$145,000 (joint filers)
CONDITIONS	Student must be enrolled at least half-time Student may not have felony drug conviction(s) Can be claimed for only two tax years for each student	Cannot claim both Lifetime Learning and Hope credits for same student in same year	May not claim if married and filing singly Cannot claim a Lifetime Learning or Hope credit for same student in the same year	Student must have been enrolled at least half-time May not claim if married and filing singly

QUICK RECAP

To deal with out-of-pocket college costs, you have several options. You can draw on savings or current income to pay, or you can borrow some portion of the total bill. And you can cut the costs.

- Several savings options, including U.S. savings bonds, 529s and Coverdell accounts, have tax benefits that can also help.
- You can work during college or promise to work later through programs like ROTC or AmeriCorps.
- You can borrow through student or parent loans.
- You can reduce your costs by such means as taking college-level courses for credit before you enter college.
- Tax breaks can help you meet college costs.

Once You're in College

QUICK OVERVIEW

Once you're in college, you shouldn't be preoccupied with paying for it. Academics, extracurricular activities and making friends are more important. But there are some things you need to do to stay on target financially. This chapter will tell you what they are.

Reapply for Aid Each Year!

Don't forget to reapply to renew your aid package every year! Check at your financial aid office to make sure you have the right forms and know what the deadlines are. Most colleges have a renewal deadline for financial aid that's a week or two later than the deadline for new applicants.

When you renew, don't expect your aid package to stay exactly the same. It may become more loan heavy each year, with more money in subsidized loans. The borrowing limits on the subsidized Stafford loan are higher for sophomores than for freshmen, and even higher for juniors and seniors. Also, keep in mind that some scholarships and grants are for freshmen only.

While you're reapplying for the financial aid you already have, keep an eye out for new opportunities. As you move on to higher grades and declare a major, you may become eligible for outside scholarships that weren't open to you in the past. Follow the guidelines in Step 9 to look for outside sources of money.

EXPERT ADVICE

"There are students who tell me that the reason they didn't pass their class was they're **too busy working**, because they need the money to support themselves. And I tell them, you need to determine your priorities. There's a limit of how much financial aid I can give you to help offset that."

— Mary San Agustin, director of financial aid and scholarships, Palomar College, San Marcos, Calif.

Stay on Track

The next thing to keep in mind is that you have to maintain eligibility for financial aid. For federal student aid, stay in school at least half time, and avoid illegal drugs. A drug-related conviction can lead to suspension or revocation of your federal-aid eligibility.

You don't have to maintain a particular GPA to maintain federal eligibility (though you do have to meet your individual school's standards for "satisfactory academic progress"). But the financial aid your college gives you, such as scholarships, may have specific academic requirements. Do your best in all your classes and stay on track academically, not only because it will help you get the most out of college but because it will help you keep your financial aid. To maintain or establish eligibility for academic scholarships, an on-campus job as a teaching or research assistant, or a "co-op" program between your department and a local employer, you'll need to be in good academic standing.

Maintain Grades

To keep up your grades, you'll have to make decisions about how to spend your time. It's important to build social relationships, pursue extracurricular activities, and earn money through work, but balance those against the need to maintain a good academic record. If you have a job, don't work so hard at it that you jeopardize your aid eligibility. (See "Expert Advice" sidebar on page 11.)

Don't Stay Too Long (Pick a Major, Any Major)

Did you know that only about one-third of all students who enter a four-year college graduate in four years? Most take six or more years to earn a bachelor's degree. Obviously, the longer you stay in college, the more it's going to cost you — not only in tuition, fees, room, board and other expenses, but also in lost earnings from a delayed career.

Make it a goal to graduate on time. Make sure you are on track to complete your college's core requirements, as well as the core requirements for your major.

Speaking of majors, don't feel that you need to rush into choosing one. Except for some very specialized career and technical institutes, most colleges and universities allow you to take time during your first two years to take classes in different fields and make sure you know enough to choose a major that fits your interests and abilities. On the other hand, don't wait so long that you neglect to take the courses that are requirements for a major. You don't want to have to pay for an extra semester to get your biology degree because you didn't take that required organic chemistry course your sophomore year.

Transferring from a Community College

If you're going to a community college, and plan to transfer to a four-year college, **make sure you know all the transfer requirements** — including whatever courses are needed for the major you intend to declare. It helps if your community college has an articulation agreement with the four-year college specifying exactly what courses are required for transfer. Almost all community colleges have a transfer adviser on staff who can help you make sure you're on track. Get to know your adviser and check in with him or her regularly.

MYTH/FACT

Myth: Only certain majors will lead to high earnings after graduation.

Fact: Don't be fooled. If you're not drawn to the major, you probably won't like the work and will leave that field before you ever reach the high earnings. Instead, **choose a major based on your interests and talents**, not on someone else's predictions of industrial trends. And remember that many of today's highest paying fields — such as marketing and software engineering — require critical thinking skills that you will acquire in courses like anthropology and philosophy. To learn more about specific academic fields and what it's like to major in them, read the College Board's *Book of Majors*.

Watch Your Personal Expenses

The purpose of financial aid is to give you the money you need to pay for college costs. But that aid can quickly become too little if you spend too much. To avoid overspending, live within your means and don't run up frivolous debt. That means sticking to a budget and avoiding credit cards.

Student Budgeting

To live within your means, all you have to do is not spend more than you receive in income. The best way to do that is to create a budget at the beginning of each semester and stick to it. Your budget should list the funds you will receive (such as money from parents, savings, work, grants and loans), subtract how much money you plan to spend on given items (such as tuition, fees, room, board, books, clothes and recreation), and calculate the difference — the bottom line. If the bottom line is a negative number — that is, if your expenses exceed your income — you're overspending. Once you have a budget where your income is equal to or greater than your expenses, follow it, and you'll be living within your means.

To create a budget, first examine what you have actually been spending, then **set priorities if you're spending too much**. That alone can help you to spend less, as you realize you can make do with one latte a day instead of two. "You start making conscious decisions about what it is that you want to do," says Elizabeth Bickford of the University of Oregon at Eugene. "You're actually just taking control over your financial spending."

By all means have fun, but don't spend too much money on nonessential items like DVDs, high-end clothes or trips to the beach. Some of your friends at college may have more money than you, but don't let social pressure push you into trying to spend like they do. Learn to suggest ordering pizza from the local hangout instead of driving to an expensive restaurant.

Save money wherever you can — for example, limit your cell phone use to free times. Comparison shop for groceries and supplies. And don't visit the ATM too often: It's too easy to withdraw money and overspend. See collegeboard.com for more advice on budgeting and financial planning.

Credit Card Debt

Be especially careful with your credit cards. They can be convenient for paying for big-ticket items like textbooks and airplane tickets, if you use them sparingly and pay off the entire amount when you get the bill. But if you abuse them, they can land you in a world of trouble.

A credit card is essentially a high-interest loan. Pulling it out at a cash register to make an impulse purchase may give you a feeling of freedom, but you won't feel free once you get the bill — especially when you're still paying interest on that impulse purchase months or years later. If you let the debt accumulate, it may swell so much that you won't be able to pay down the debt. This can affect your future academic career. If you miss payments on your credit cards, or if your credit card debt is high, you can hurt your credit rating. A bad credit rating can harm your chances of getting student loans to pay for graduate school, or a car loan when you start working. It can even prevent you from getting a job with certain security-conscious employers, such as banks or government agencies.

Use credit cards only when you know you can repay the debt promptly. Save them for emergencies. (A spring-break vacation is not an emergency.) Think through each credit card purchase before you spend. If you do get in over your head with credit card use, cut your expenses and talk to your family and financial aid administrator for more guidance.

Saving for Future Needs

While you're trying to live within your means, it's also wise to save for the future. Savings will give you greater freedom to cope with college and personal costs to come. If at all possible, make sure your budget includes money set aside for future needs. Your parents, of course, should do the same.

Try to save what you can from the jobs you have during the school year and in the summer. Think about the following as goals for your savings:

Students Should Think About…

- ✔ Next year's college expenses
- ✔ Application fees and tuition for graduate school
- ✔ A vacation with friends after you graduate
- ✔ Moving to another city after you graduate
- ✔ The unexpected (such as traveling to a friend's wedding or a family funeral)

Parents Should Think About…

- ✔ Next year's college expenses
- ✔ College expenses for younger children (if any)
- ✔ Retirement
- ✔ The unexpected (such as making it through a layoff or paying for a child's wedding)

Final Thoughts

Once you're in college, you may sometimes wonder if it's worth it. Can your family afford the expense? Will you be able to repay your student loans? If you've made reasonable choices along the way, the answer is yes. If you ever have doubts, visit your school's career center and do some research into the fields of work you might enter. Find out how much money you're likely to be earning when you first graduate, and how much five years later. A light might go on for you, as Elizabeth Bickford has often observed with other students. "When they see that relationship, many students say, 'Oh, wait a second, I can do that.'"

You will be able to pay back your student loans. College is a sound investment. You can afford college!

QUICK RECAP

Once you're in college, make sure you stay on track financially.

- Reapply for aid every year.
- Maintain your federal eligibility by staying in school the right number of hours and avoiding illegal drugs.
- Keep up your grades. Don't let them get derailed by too much time spent on work or other nonacademic activities.
- Declare a major at a suitable time.
- Make a budget and stick to it.
- Be wary of credit cards.
- Save for future expenses.
- Keep an eye out for new sources of outside scholarships.
- Remember that college is worth it!

Part II

Tables and Worksheets

WORKSHEET 1:
Meet Your Application Deadlines

		COLLEGE 1:	COLLEGE 2:	COLLEGE 3:
	College Name	*1st Choice Univ.*	*Private Univ.*	*Financial Safety*
FORMS REQUIRED	FAFSA			
	PROFILE			
	State form			
	Institutional form			
	Tax returns			
	Other			
SCHOOL CODES	Federal code			
	CSS code			
PRIORITY DATE				
CLOSING DATE				
AFTER APPLYING	Need to send letter?			
	Documentation required?			
COMPARE AWARDS	Notification date			
	Reply-by date			

WORKSHEET 2:
Scholarship Application Planner

	PROGRAM 1	PROGRAM 2	PROGRAM 3
PROGRAM/SPONSOR			
ELIGIBILITY REQUIREMENTS			
TYPE OF AWARD			
AMOUNT OF AWARD			
CAN BE USED FOR			
CAN BE USED AT			
DEADLINE			
FORMS REQUIRED			
TEST SCORES REQUIRED			
ESSAY OR ACADEMIC SAMPLE			
RECOMMENDATIONS			
NOTIFICATION BEGINS			
REQUIREMENTS TO KEEP AFTER FRESHMAN YEAR			

WORKSHEET 3:
Compare Your Awards

	COLLEGE 1	COLLEGE 2	COLLEGE 3
Step 1. List the name of each college you want to consider attending, the award deadline and the total cost of attendance. This figure should be in your award letter. If not, refer to the college catalog or contact the college financial aid office.			
Name of college			
Award deadline date			
Total cost of attendance			
Step 2. List the financial aid awards each school is offering. Don't forget that grants, scholarships and work-study do not have to be repaid, while all loans must be repaid.			
Grants and scholarships			
• Pell Grant (federal)			
• SEOG (federal)			
• State			
• College			
• Other			
Total grants/scholarships			
Percentage of package that is grant/scholarship			
Work-study opportunities			
Loans			
• Stafford-Direct (federal)			
• Perkins (federal)			
• Other			
Total loans			
Percentage of package that is work or loans			
Total financial aid award			
Grants and scholarships + work-study + loans			
Step 3. Calculate what it will cost you to attend each college you are considering. For each college, enter the total cost of attendance. Then, subtract the total financial aid award from the total cost of attendance. That number is the net cost, or what it will cost you to attend that college.			
a) Total cost of attendance			
b) Total financial aid award			
c) Net cost to attend (a minus b)			

Figure 13:
Sample Financial Aid Award Letter 1

Blue University Cost of Attendance: $ 28,706.00

CLASS: 01

March 22, 2009

TENTATIVE
FINANCIAL AWARD NOTIFICATION FOR 2009-2010

Based on the information that you submitted on your FAFSA and to our office, **Blue University** can offer you the following TENTATIVE awards.

This package is based on an award period from 09/10/09 to 06/06/10.

AID AWARD	ACCEPT AWARD Yes	NO	OFFERED AMOUNT
FEDERAL PERKINS LOAN	______	______	$1,143
STATE WORK-STUDY	______	______	$2,400
BLUE EDUCATIONAL GRANT	______	______	$3,538
UNIVERSITY SCHOLARSHIP	______	______	$2,000
RESIDENCE HALL GRANT	______	______	$2,000
FEDERAL STAFFORD LOAN – SUB.	______	______	$2,625

Finalize your financial aid award as soon as possible by forwarding to our office the forms listed on the Missing Documents Form included with this letter.

Please read the important information pamphlet! Indicate your intent by checking whether or not you accept each aid award, then sign and return this letter in order to reserve your award(s).

Please refer to the Cost Worksheet to help determine your expenses for the academic year.

If direct loan amounts desired are less than above, please indicate below:

Requested Federal Stafford Loan (Sub.) $ ____________
Requested Federal Perkins Loan $ ____________

I acknowledge that I have read and will comply with all the supporting information in the Important Information Pamphlet. Furthermore, if I receive any financial assistance not included in this award letter, including tuition waivers or employer reimbursement, I will notify your office immediately.

Signature ______________________ Date ______________

Figure 14:
Sample Financial Aid Award Letter 2

Green University | Office of Student Financial Planning

Cost of Attendance: $ 26,005.00

March 1, 2009

Step 1. Circle A for Accept or D for Decline for each individual award where indicated below:

	Fall 2009	Spring 2010	Total	A / D
Presidential Freshman Scholarship	$3,250	$3,250	$6,500	A / D
Green University Grant	$705	$705	$1,410	A / D
Total Grants and Scholarships			**$7,910**	
Federal Unsubsidized Stafford Loan	$1,313	$1,312	$2,625	A / D
Total Student Loans			**$2,625**	
Federal College Work-Study	$330	$330	$660	A / D
Federal PLUS Loan and/or Green Partnership Loan	$7,405	$7,405	$14,810	

Step 2. Please note the following:

Your awards are based on full-time enrollment for the fall and spring terms and residence hall occupancy for the fall and spring terms (for financial aid purposes, full-time is defined as 12 credits or more per term).

You have been offered loan(s) that require separate loan materials.

The amount of your Green University Grant was based upon residence hall occupancy for the fall and spring terms. A change in housing status may result in a reduction of this award.

Step 3. Please list other financial assistance, scholarships or loans you will receive not indicated above. List the scholarship/donor name and the expected amount (example: Elks Club $100).

Name	Amount

Step 4. Attention: Your awards are not final until you complete the items on the ACTION REQUESTED page.

FAFSA U.S. DEPARTMENT OF EDUCATION FEDERAL STUDENT AID

2009–2010
FAFSA ON THE WEB WORKSHEET
www.fafsa.ed.gov

START HERE GO FURTHER FEDERAL STUDENT AID

DO NOT MAIL THIS WORKSHEET.

You must complete and submit a *Free Application for Federal Student Aid* (FAFSA) to apply for federal student aid and to apply for most state and college aid. Applying online with *FAFSA on the Web* at **www.fafsa.ed.gov** is faster and easier than using a paper FAFSA.

For state or college aid, the deadline may be as early as January 2009. See the table to the right for state deadlines. Check with your high school counselor or your college's financial aid administrator about other deadlines.

- **This Worksheet is optional and should only be completed if you plan to use *FAFSA on the Web*.**
- Sections in gray are for parent information.
- In parentheses after each question is the number that is used on *FAFSA on the Web* and the paper FAFSA. However, not all of the questions appear on this worksheet.
- **Submit your FAFSA early, but not before January 1, 2009.**

Apply Faster—Sign your FAFSA with a Federal Student Aid PIN.
If you do not have a PIN, you can apply for one at **www.pin.ed.gov.** Your PIN allows you to electronically sign when you submit your FAFSA. If you are providing parent information, one parent must also sign your FAFSA. To sign electronically, your parent should also apply for a PIN.

You will need the following information to complete this Worksheet:

- ❑ Your Social Security Number and your parents' Social Security Numbers if you are providing parental information.
- ❑ Your driver's license number if you have one.
- ❑ Your Alien Registration Number if you are not a U.S. citizen.
- ❑ 2008 federal tax information or tax returns (including IRS W-2 information) for yourself (and spouse if you are married) and for your parents if you are providing parental information. If you have not yet filed a 2008 income tax return, you can still submit your FAFSA but you must provide income and tax information.
- ❑ Information on savings, investments, and business and farm assets for yourself and your parents if you are providing parental information.

WARNING!
Be wary of organizations that charge a fee to submit your application or to find you money for college. In general, the help you pay for can be obtained for free from your college or from Federal Student Aid.

NOTE:
If you or your family have unusual circumstances (such as loss of employment), complete *FAFSA on the Web* to the extent you can, then submit the application and consult the financial aid office at the college you plan to attend.

STATE AID DEADLINES

Check with your financial aid administrator for these states and territories:
AL, *AS, CO, *FM, GA, *GU, *HI, *MH, *MP, NC, NE, *NM, *NV, OR, PR, *PW, *SD, *TX, UT, *VA, *VI, *VT, WA, WI and *WY.

AK	April 15, 2009 *(date received)*
AR	Academic Challenge - June 1, 2009 Workforce Grant - Contact your financial aid administrator Higher Education Opportunity Grant - June 1, 2009 (fall term) - November 1, 2009 (spring term) *(date received)*
AZ	March 1, 2009 *(date received)*
*CA	Initial awards - March 2, 2009 Additional community college awards - September 2, 2009 *(date postmarked)*
#*CT	February 15, 2009 *(date received)*
*DC	June 30, 2009 *(date received by state)*
DE	April 15, 2009 *(date received)*
FL	May 15, 2009 *(date processed)*
IA	July 1, 2009 *(date received)*
#*ID	Opportunity Grant - March 1, 2009 *(date received)*
#IL	First-time applicants - September 30, 2009 Continuing applicants - August 15, 2009 *(date received)*
IN	March 10, 2009 *(date received)*
#*KS	April 1, 2009 *(date received)*
#KY	March 15, 2009 *(date received)*
LA	July 1, 2009 *(date received)*
#MA	May 1, 2009 *(date received)*
MD	March 1, 2009 *(date received)*
ME	May 1, 2009 *(date received)*
MI	March 1, 2009 *(date received)*
MN	30 days after term starts *(date received)*
MO	April 1, 2009 *(date received)*
#MS	MTAG and MESG Grants - September 15, 2009 HELP Scholarship - March 31, 2009 *(date processed)*
#MT	March 1, 2009 *(date received)*
ND	March 15, 2009 *(date received)*
NH	May 1, 2009 *(date received)*
NJ	June 1, 2009, if you received a Tuition Aid Grant in 2008 -2009 All other applicants - October 1, 2009, fall & spring terms - March 1, 2010, spring term only *(date received)*
*NY	May 1, 2010 *(date received)*
OH	October 1, 2009 *(date received)*
#OK	April 15, 2009 *(date received)* for best consideration
*PA	All 2008 - 2009 State Grant recipients & all non-2008 - 2009 State Grant recipients in degree programs - May 1, 2009 All other applicants - August 1, 2009 *(date received)*
#RI	March 1, 2009 *(date received)*
SC	Tuition Grants - June 30, 2009 *(date received)*
#TN	State Grant - March 1, 2009 State Lottery - September 1, 2009 *(date received)*
# *WV	March 1, 2009 *(date received)*

For priority consideration, submit application by date specified.

* Additional form may be required.

SECTION 1 – STUDENT INFORMATION

Questions are ordered as they appear on *FAFSA on the Web*, but after you are online you may be able to skip some questions based on your answers to earlier questions.

Your last name (Q1) [ ]

Your Social Security Number (Q8) [ ][ ][ ] - [ ][ ] - [ ][ ][ ][ ]

Your driver's license number (optional) (Q11) [ ]

Are you a U.S. citizen? (Q14)

If you are neither a citizen nor an eligible noncitizen, you are not eligible for federal student aid. However, you should still complete the application, because you may be eligible for state or college aid.

If you are in the U.S. on an F1 or F2 student visa, or a J1 or J2 exchange visitor visa, or a G series visa (pertaining to international organizations), you must answer "Neither citizen nor eligible noncitizen."

❑ U.S. citizen (U.S. national)
❑ Eligible noncitizen Generally, you are an eligible noncitizen if you are:
- A permanent U.S. resident with a Permanent Resident Card (I-551);
- A conditional permanent resident (I-551C); or
- The holder of an Arrival-Departure Record (I-94) from the Department of Homeland Security showing any of the following designations: "Refugee," "Asylum Granted," "Parolee" (I-94 confirms paroled for a minimum of one year and status has not expired), "Victim of human trafficking," T-Visa holder (T-1, T-2, T-3, etc.) or "Cuban-Haitian Entrant."

❑ Neither citizen nor eligible noncitizen

Your Alien Registration Number (Q15)
If you are an eligible noncitizen, enter your eight- or nine-digit Alien Registration Number. [A][ ][ ][ ][ ][ ][ ][ ][ ][ ]

What is your marital status as of today? (Q16)
"As of today" refers to the day that you sign your FAFSA.

❑ Single, divorced or widowed
❑ Married or remarried ❑ Separated

Month and year you were married, separated, divorced or widowed (Q17)
(Example: Month and year: 05/1998) [M][M][Y][Y][Y][Y]

What is your state of legal residence? (Q18) [ ]

Enter the date you became a legal resident of your state if it was not before January 1, 2004. (Q20) (Example: Month and year: 05/2005) [M][M][Y][Y][Y][Y]

Most male students must register with Selective Service to get federal aid. If you are male, age 18-25 and **NOT** registered, select "Register me." (Q22)

❑ Register me

Have you ever received federal student aid?
Answer "No" if you have never received federal student grants, federal student loans or federal work-study. You should also answer "No" if you have never attended college. If you answer "No" to this question, skip question 23.

❑ Yes
❑ No

Have you been convicted for the possession or sale of illegal drugs for an offense that occurred while you were receiving federal student aid (grants, loans or work-study)? (Q23)
Do not count convictions that have been removed from your record or that occurred before you turned age 18, unless you were tried as an adult. If you answer "Yes," you can use an interactive worksheet when completing the FAFSA online. Based on your answers to the worksheet questions, you can determine if the conviction affects your eligibility for federal student aid. If the conviction does affect your eligibility for federal aid, you should still submit your application because you may qualify for state or college aid.

❑ Yes
❑ No

Highest school your father completed (Q24)
Some states and colleges offer aid based on the level of schooling your parents completed.

❑ Middle school/Jr. high ❑ College or beyond
❑ High school ❑ Other/unknown

Highest school your mother completed (Q25)
Some states and colleges offer aid based on the level of schooling your parents completed.

❑ Middle school/Jr. high ❑ College or beyond
❑ High school ❑ Other/unknown

When you begin the 2009-2010 school year, what degree or certificate will you be working on? (Q29)

❑ 1st bachelor's degree
❑ 2nd bachelor's degree
❑ Associate degree (occupational or technical program)
❑ Associate degree (general education or transfer program)
❑ Certificate or diploma (occupational, technical or educational program of less than two years)
❑ Certificate or diploma (occupational, technical or educational program of two or more years)
❑ Teaching credential (nondegree program)
❑ Graduate or professional degree
❑ Other/undecided

SECTION 1 (CONTINUED) – STUDENT INFORMATION

When you begin the 2009-2010 school year, what do you expect your enrollment status to be? (Q30) (Enrollment definitions refer to undergraduate study.)	❑ Full-time (at least 12 credit hours in a term or 24 clock hours per week) ❑ 3/4-time (at least 9 credit hours in a term or 18 clock hours per week) ❑ Half-time (at least 6 credit hours in a term or 12 clock hours per week) ❑ Less than half-time (fewer than 6 credit hours in a term or less than 12 clock hours per week) ❑ Don't know
In addition to grants, are you interested in being considered for work-study or student loans? (Q31)	❑ Work-study (aid earned through work) ❑ Student loans (which you must pay back) ❑ Both work-study and student loans ❑ Neither ❑ Don't know

SECTION 2 – STUDENT DEPENDENCY STATUS

Were you born before January 1, 1986? (Q48)	❑ Yes ❑ No
As of today, are you married? (Q49) (Answer "Yes" if you are separated but not divorced.) "As of today" refers to the day that you sign your FAFSA.	❑ Yes ❑ No
At the beginning of the 2009-2010 school year, will you be working on a master's or doctorate program (such as an MA, MBA, MD, JD, PhD, EdD, graduate certificate, etc.)? (Q50)	❑ Yes ❑ No
Are you currently serving on active duty in the U.S. Armed Forces for purposes other than training? (Q51)	❑ Yes ❑ No
Are you a veteran of the U.S. Armed Forces? (Q52) Answer "Yes" (you are a veteran) if you (1) have engaged in active duty in the U.S. Armed Forces (Army, Navy, Air Force, Marines or Coast Guard) or are a National Guard or Reserve enlistee who was called to active duty for other than state or training purposes, or were a cadet or midshipman at one of the service academies, **and** (2) were released under a condition other than dishonorable. Also answer "Yes" if you are not a veteran now but will be by June 30, 2010. Answer "No" (you are not a veteran) if you (1) have never engaged in active duty in the U.S. Armed Forces, (2) are currently an ROTC student or a cadet or midshipman at a service academy, (3) are a National Guard or Reserve enlistee activated only for state or training purposes, or (4) were engaged in active duty in the U.S. Armed Forces but released under dishonorable conditions.	❑ Yes ❑ No
Do you have children who will receive more than half of their support from you between July 1, 2009 and June 30, 2010? (Q53)	❑ Yes ❑ No
Do you have dependents (other than your children or spouse) who live with you and who receive more than half of their support from you, now and through June 30, 2010? (Q54)	❑ Yes ❑ No
At any time since you turned age 13, were both your parents deceased, were you in foster care or were you a dependent or ward of the court? (Q55) Answer "Yes" if you had no living parent (biological or adoptive) at any time since you turned age 13, even if you are now adopted. Answer "Yes" if you were in foster care at any time since you turned age 13, even if you are no longer in foster care as of today. Answer "Yes" if you were a dependent or ward of the court at any time since you turned age 13, even if you are no longer a dependent or ward of the court as of today. Note that the financial aid administrator at your school may require you to provide proof that you were in foster care or a dependent or ward of the court.	❑ Yes ❑ No
Use these instructions to answer questions 56-57 Answer "Yes" if you can provide a copy of a court's decision that as of today you are an emancipated minor or are in legal guardianship. Also answer "Yes" if you can provide a copy of a court's decision that you were an emancipated minor or were in legal guardianship immediately before you reached the age of being an adult in your state. The court must be located in your state of legal residence at the time the court's decision was issued.	
Are you or were you an emancipated minor as determined by a court in your state of legal residence? (Q56)	❑ Yes ❑ No
Are you or were you in legal guardianship as determined by a court in your state of legal residence? (Q57)	❑ Yes ❑ No
Use these instructions to answer questions 58-60 Answer "Yes" if you received a determination at any time on or after July 1, 2008, that you were an unaccompanied youth who was homeless or, for question 60, at risk of being homeless. • "Homeless" means lacking fixed, regular and adequate housing, which includes living in shelters, motels or cars, or temporarily living with other people because you had nowhere else to go. • "Unaccompanied" means you are not living in the physical custody of your parent or guardian. • "Youth" means you are 21 years of age or younger or you are still enrolled in high school as of the day you sign this application.	
At any time on or after July 1, 2008, did your high school or school district homeless liaison determine that you were an unaccompanied youth who was homeless? (Q58)	❑ Yes ❑ No
At any time on or after July 1, 2008, did the director of an emergency shelter or transitional housing program funded by the U.S. Department of Housing and Urban Development determine that you were an unaccompanied youth who was homeless? (Q59)	❑ Yes ❑ No
At any time on or after July 1, 2008, did the director of a runaway or homeless youth basic center or transitional living program determine that you were an unaccompanied youth who was homeless or were self-supporting and at risk of being homeless? (Q60)	❑ Yes ❑ No

If you answered "YES" to ANY of the previous questions, you do not have to provide parental information. Skip to Section 4 on page 6.
If you answered "NO" to ALL of the previous questions, then you must provide parental information. Complete Section 3 on the next page.

SECTION 3 – PARENTAL INFORMATION

If you answered "No" to all of the questions in Section 2, you must provide parental information. Refer to your parents' IRS tax return when necessary. Answer the questions as of the date you will complete and sign your FAFSA.

- Grandparents, foster parents and legal guardians are not considered parents on this form unless they have legally adopted you.
- If your parent is widowed or single, answer the questions about that parent. If your widowed parent is remarried, answer the questions about that parent and your stepparent.
- If your parents are divorced or separated, answer the questions about the parent you lived with more during the past 12 months. If you did not live with one parent more than the other, give answers about the parent who provided more financial support during the past 12 months. If this parent is remarried, answer the questions about that parent and your stepparent.

Federal law provides that, under very limited special circumstances, you may submit your FAFSA without parental information. If you have a special circumstance and are unable to provide parental information, *FAFSA on the Web* will instruct you on how to proceed. The following **are examples** of special circumstances.

- Your parents are incarcerated; or
- You have left home due to an abusive family environment; or
- You do not know where your parents are and are unable to contact them (and you have not been adopted).

What is your parents' marital status as of today? (Q61) "As of today" refers to the day that you sign your FAFSA.	❑ Married or remarried ❑ Divorced or separated ❑ Single ❑ Widowed
Month and year your parents were married, separated, divorced or widowed. (Q62) (Example: Month and year: 05/1998)	M M / Y Y Y Y
What is your parents' e-mail address? (Q71) If you provide your parents' e-mail address, we will let them know your FAFSA has been processed.	
What is your father's (or stepfather's) Social Security Number? (Q63)	_ _ _ - _ _ - _ _ _ _
What is your father's (or stepfather's) last name? (Q64)	
What is your father's (or stepfather's) date of birth? (Q66) (Example: Month, day and year: 05/07/1962)	M M D D Y Y Y Y
What is your mother's (or stepmother's) Social Security Number? (Q67)	_ _ _ - _ _ - _ _ _ _
What is your mother's (or stepmother's) last name? (Q68)	
What is your mother's (or stepmother's) date of birth? (Q70) (Example: Month, day and year: 05/07/1962)	M M D D Y Y Y Y
What is your parents' state of legal residence? (Q72)	
Enter the date of legal residency for the parent who has lived in the state the longest, if it was not before January 1, 2004. (Q74) (Example: Month and year: 05/2005)	M M Y Y Y Y
What income tax return did your parents file or will they file for 2008? (Q83)	❑ IRS 1040 ❑ IRS 1040A, 1040EZ ❑ A foreign tax return ❑ A tax return with Puerto Rico, another U.S. territory or a Freely Associated State
If your parents have filed or will file a 1040, were they eligible to file a 1040A or 1040EZ? (Q84) A person is not eligible to file a 1040A or 1040EZ if he or she makes $100,000 or more, itemizes deductions, receives income from his or her own business or farm, is self-employed, receives alimony or is required to file Schedule D for capital gains. If your parents were not required to file a tax return or they filed a 1040 only to claim Hope or Lifetime Learning tax credits, and would have otherwise been eligible for a 1040A or 1040EZ, answer "Yes."	❑ Yes ❑ No ❑ Don't know
In 2007 or 2008, did you, your parents or anyone in your parents' household receive benefits from any of the federal benefits programs listed? (Q77-81) ***Mark all the programs that apply.*** Select benefits received for all of your parents' household members. Include in your parents' household: (1) your parents and yourself, even if you don't live with your parents; (2) your parents' other children if (a) your parents will provide more than half of their support between July 1, 2009, and June 30, 2010, or (b) the children could answer "No" to every question in Section 2 of this worksheet; and (3) other people only if they live with your parents, your parents provide more than half of their support and your parents will continue to provide more than half of their support between July 1, 2009, and June 30, 2010. TANF may have a different name in your parents' state. Call 1-800-4-FED-AID to find out the name of the state's program.	❑ Supplemental Security Income ❑ Food Stamps ❑ Free or Reduced Price School Lunch ❑ Temporary Assistance for Needy Families (TANF) ❑ Special Supplemental Nutrition Program for Women, Infants and Children (WIC)

SECTION 3 (CONTINUED) – PARENTAL INFORMATION

As of today, is either of your parents a dislocated worker? (Q85) In general, a person may be considered a dislocated worker if he or she is receiving unemployment benefits due to being laid off or losing a job and is unlikely to return to a previous occupation; has been laid off or received a lay-off notice from a job; was self-employed but is now unemployed due to economic conditions or natural disaster; or is a displaced homemaker. A displaced homemaker is generally a person who previously provided unpaid services to the family (e.g., a stay-at-home mom or dad), is no longer supported by the husband or wife, is unemployed or underemployed and is having trouble finding or upgrading employment.	❑ Yes ❑ No ❑ Don't know
What was your parents' adjusted gross income for 2008? (Q86) Adjusted gross income is on IRS form 1040—line 37; 1040A—line 21; or 1040EZ—line 4.	$
Questions 89 and 90 ask about earnings (wages, salaries, tips, etc.) in 2008. Answer the questions whether or not a tax return was filed. This information may be on the W-2 forms, or on IRS Form 1040—lines 7 + 12 + 18 + Box 14 of IRS Schedule K-1 (Form 1065); 1040A—line 7; or 1040EZ—line 1.	
How much did your father/stepfather earn from working in 2008? (Q89)	$
How much did your mother/stepmother earn from working in 2008? (Q90)	$
Enter the amount of your parents' income tax for 2008. (Q87) Income tax amount is on IRS Form 1040—line 56; 1040A—line 35; or 1040EZ—line 11.	$
Enter your parents' exemptions for 2008. (Q88) Exemptions are on IRS Form 1040—line 6d or 1040A—line 6d. On the 1040EZ, if a person checked either the "you" or "spouse" box on line 5, use 1040EZ worksheet line F to determine the number of exemptions ($3,500 equals one exemption). If a person didn't check either box on line 5, enter 01 if he or she is single, or 02 if he or she is married.	
Your parents' number of family members in 2009-2010. (Q75) Include in your parents' household: (1) your parents and yourself, even if you don't live with your parents, (2) your parents' other children if (a) your parents will provide more than half of their support between July 1, 2009, and June 30, 2010, or (b) the children could answer "No" to every question in Section 2 of this worksheet, and (3) other people only if they live with your parents, your parents provide more than half of their support and your parents will continue to provide more than half of their support between July 1, 2009, and June 30, 2010.	
How many people in your parents' household will be college students between July 1, 2009 and June 30, 2010? (Q76) Always count yourself. **Do not include your parents.** Include others only if they will attend, at least half-time in 2009-2010, a program that leads to a college degree or certificate.	

Your parents' 2008 Additional Financial Information (Q94) **Complete the left column of the table on page 8.**

Your parents' 2008 Untaxed Income (Q95) **Complete the left column of the table on page 8.**

Parent Asset Information

As of today, what is your parents' total current balance of cash, savings and checking accounts? (Q91)	$

- Investments include real estate (do not include the family home), trust funds, UGMA and UTMA accounts, money market funds, mutual funds, certificates of deposit, stocks, stock options, bonds, other securities, Coverdell savings accounts, 529 college savings plans, the refund value of 529 prepaid tuition plans, installment and land sale contracts (including mortgages held), commodities, etc. For more information about reporting educational savings plans call 1-800-4-FED-AID. Investment value means the current balance or market value of these investments as of today. Investment debt means only those debts that are related to the investments.
- Do not include the value of life insurance, retirement plans (401[k] plans, pension funds, annuities, noneducation IRAs, Keogh plans, etc.) or cash, savings and checking accounts already reported in questions 41 and 91.
- Business and/or investment farm value includes the market value of land, buildings, machinery, equipment, inventory, etc. Business and/or investment farm debt means only those debts for which the business or investment farm was used as collateral.

As of today, what is the net worth of your parents' investments, including real estate (not your parents' home)? (Q92) Net worth means current value minus debt.	$
As of today, what is the net worth of your parents' current businesses and/or investment farms? (Q93) **Do not include** the value of a family farm that your parents live on and operate. **Do not include** the value of a small business if your family owns and controls more than 50 percent of the business and the business has 100 or fewer full-time or full-time equivalent employees. For small business value, your family includes (1) persons directly related to you, such as a parent, sister or cousin, or (2) persons who are or were related to you by marriage, such as a spouse, stepparent or sister-in-law.	$

SECTION 4 – STUDENT FINANCES

- Answer the questions as of the date you will complete and sign your FAFSA. Refer to the IRS tax return as needed.
- If you filed a foreign tax return, use the exchange rate at **www.federalreserve.gov/releases/h10/update** to convert monetary units to U.S. dollars.
- If you are married as of today, report your and your spouse's income, even if you were not married in 2008. Ignore references to spouse if you are single, divorced, separated or widowed.

What income tax return did you file or will you file for 2008? (Q34)

❑ IRS 1040
❑ IRS 1040A, 1040EZ
❑ A foreign tax return
❑ A tax return with Puerto Rico, another U.S. territory or a Freely Associated State

If you have filed or will file a 1040, were you eligible to file a 1040A or 1040EZ? (Q35)

A person is not eligible to file a 1040A or 1040EZ if he or she makes $100,000 or more, itemizes deductions, receives income from his or her own business or farm, is self-employed, receives alimony or is required to file Schedule D for capital gains. If you were not required to file a tax return or you filed a 1040 only to claim Hope or Lifetime Learning tax credits, and you would otherwise have been eligible for a 1040A or 1040EZ, answer "Yes."

❑ Yes
❑ No
❑ Don't know

What was your (and your spouse's) adjusted gross income for 2008? (Q36)

Adjusted gross income is on IRS Form 1040—line 37; 1040A—line 21; or 1040EZ—line 4.

$

Questions 39 and 40 ask about earnings (wages, salaries, tips, etc.) in 2008. Answer the questions whether or not a tax return was filed. This information may be on the W-2 forms, or on IRS Form 1040—lines 7 + 12 + 18 + Box 14 of IRS Schedule K-1 (Form 1065); 1040A—line 7; or 1040EZ—line 1.

How much did you earn from working in 2008? (Q39) $

How much did your spouse earn from working in 2008? (Q40) $

What type of veterans' education benefits will you receive? (Q45)

Answer this question only if you will receive these benefits between July 1, 2009 and June 30, 2010.

❑ Montgomery GI Bill - Active Duty (Chapter 30)
❑ Post-9/11 GI Bill (Chapter 33)
❑ Montgomery GI Bill - Selected Reserve (Chapter 1606)
❑ Reserve Educational Assistance Program (Chapter 1607)
❑ Vocational Rehabilitation and Employment (Chapter 31)
❑ Dependents' Educational Assistance (Chapter 35)
❑ Any other type of veterans education benefits

If you answered "YES" to ANY question in Section 2, answer the following questions.
If you answered "NO" to all the questions in Section 2, skip to page 7.

Your number of family members in 2009-2010. (Q96)

Include in your household: (1) yourself (and your spouse), (2) your children, if you will provide more than half of their support between July 1, 2009, and June 30, 2010, and (3) other people if they now live with you, you provide more than half of their support and you will continue to provide more than half of their support between July 1, 2009, and June 30, 2010.

How many people in your (and your spouse's) household will be college students between July 1, 2009 and June 30, 2010? (Q97)

Always count yourself. Include others only if they will attend, at least half time in 2009-2010, a program that leads to a college degree or certificate.

In 2007 or 2008, did you (or your spouse) or anyone in your household (from question 96) receive benefits from any of the federal benefits programs listed? (Q98-102) ***Mark all the programs that apply.***

Select benefits received for all of your household members. Use the instructions in question 96 to identify who is included in your household. Answering these questions will not reduce your eligibility for student aid or these other federal benefits. TANF may have a different name in your state. Call 1-800-4-FED-AID to find out the name of your state's program.

❑ Supplemental Security Income
❑ Food Stamps
❑ Free or Reduced Price School Lunch
❑ Temporary Assistance for Needy Families (TANF)
❑ Special Supplemental Nutrition Program for Women, Infants and Children (WIC)

As of today, are you (or your spouse) a dislocated worker? (Q103)

In general, a person may be considered a dislocated worker if he or she is receiving unemployment benefits due to being laid off or losing a job and is unlikely to return to a previous occupation; has been laid off or received a lay-off notice from a job; was self-employed but is now unemployed due to economic conditions or natural disaster; or is a displaced homemaker. A displaced homemaker is generally a person who previously provided unpaid services to the family (e.g., a stay-at-home mom or dad), is no longer supported by the husband or wife, is unemployed or underemployed, and is having trouble finding or upgrading employment.

❑ Yes
❑ No
❑ Don't know

SECTION 4 (CONTINUED) – STUDENT FINANCES

Enter the amount of your (and your spouse's) income tax for 2008. (Q37) Income tax amount is on IRS Form 1040—line 56; 1040A—line 35; or 1040EZ—line 11.	$
Enter your (and your spouse's) exemptions for 2008. (Q38) Exemptions are on IRS Form 1040—line 6d or 1040A—line 6d. On the 1040EZ, if a person checked either the "you" or "spouse" box on line 5, use 1040EZ worksheet line F to determine the number of exemptions ($3,500 equals one exemption). If a person didn't check either box on line 5, enter 01 if he or she is single, or 02 if he or she is married.	

Your 2008 Additional Financial Information amount (Q46) Complete the right column of the table on page 8.

Your 2008 Untaxed Income amount (Q47) Complete the right column of the table on page 8.

Student Asset Information (See "Parent Asset Information" on page 5 for instructions on reporting assets.)

As of today, what is your (and your spouse's) total current balance of cash, savings and checking accounts? (Q41) **Do not include** student financial aid.	$
As of today, what is the net worth of your (and your spouse's) investments, including real estate (not your home)? (Q42) Net worth means current value minus debt.	$
As of today, what is the net worth of your (and your spouse's) current businesses and/or investment farms? (Q43) **Do not include** the value of a family farm that you (and your spouse) live on and operate. **Do not include** the value of a small business if your family owns and controls more than 50 percent of the business and the business has 100 or fewer full-time or full-time equivalent employees. For small business value, your family includes (1) persons directly related to you, such as a parent, sister or cousin, or (2) persons who are or were related to you by marriage, such as a spouse, stepparent or sister-in-law.	$

SECTION 5 – COLLEGES TO RECEIVE INFORMATION

- **If you do not know the school code, write the college's name. You will have a chance online to search for the school code.**
- **For each college, indicate the corresponding housing plan.**

	1st college	2nd college	3rd college	4th college	5th college
Federal School Code	______ (Q104.a)	______ (Q104.c)	______ (Q104.e)	______ (Q104.g)	______ (Q104.i)
Housing Plan	❑ on campus ❑ with parent ❑ off campus (Q104.b)	❑ on campus ❑ with parent ❑ off campus (Q104.d)	❑ on campus ❑ with parent ❑ off campus (Q104.f)	❑ on campus ❑ with parent ❑ off campus (Q104.h)	❑ on campus ❑ with parent ❑ off campus (Q104.j)

	6th college	7th college	8th college	9th college	10th college
Federal School Code	______ (Q104.k)	______ (Q104.m)	______ (Q104.o)	______ (Q104.q)	______ (Q104.s)
Housing Plan	❑ on campus ❑ with parent ❑ off campus (Q104.l)	❑ on campus ❑ with parent ❑ off campus (Q104.n)	❑ on campus ❑ with parent ❑ off campus (Q104.p)	❑ on campus ❑ with parent ❑ off campus (Q104.r)	❑ on campus ❑ with parent ❑ off campus (Q104.t)

Go to www.fafsa.ed.gov and enter the information from this worksheet.

Additional help is available online, or you can call 1-800-4-FED-AID. TTY users (hearing impaired) may call 1-800-730-8913. For more information on federal student aid, visit **www.FederalStudentAid.ed.gov**.

You can also talk with your college's financial aid office about other types of student aid that may be available.

DO NOT MAIL THIS WORKSHEET.

Use the tables below to report annual amounts.

For the Parents' column, enter the amount for the student's parent(s). For the Student's column, enter the amount for the student (and his or her spouse).

Parents' (Q94)	2008 Additional Financial Information	Student's (Q46)
$	a. Education credits (Hope and Lifetime Learning tax credits) from IRS Form 1040—line 50 or 1040A—line 31.	$
$	b. Child support paid because of divorce or separation or as a result of a legal requirement. Don't include support for children in your (or your parents') household, as reported in question 96 (or question 75 for your parents).	$
$	c. Taxable earnings from need-based employment programs, such as Federal Work-Study and need-based employment portions of fellowships and assistantships.	$
$	d. Grant and scholarship aid reported to the IRS in the adjusted gross income. Includes AmeriCorps benefits (awards, living allowances and interest accrual payments), as well as grant and scholarship portions of fellowships and assistantships.	$
$	e. Combat pay or special combat pay. Only enter the amount that was taxable and included in the adjusted gross income. Do not enter untaxed combat pay reported on the W-2 (Box 12, Code Q).	$

Parents' (Q95)	2008 Untaxed Income	Student's (Q47)
$	a. Payments to tax-deferred pension and savings plans (paid directly or withheld from earnings), including, but not limited to, amounts reported on the W-2 forms in Boxes 12a through 12d, codes D, E, F, G, H and S.	$
$	b. IRA deductions and payments to self-employed SEP, SIMPLE, Keogh and other qualified plans from IRS Form 1040—line 28 + line 32 or 1040A—line 17.	$
$	c. Child support received for all children. Don't include foster care or adoption payments.	$
$	d. Tax exempt interest income from IRS Form 1040—line 8b or 1040A—line 8b.	$
$	e. Untaxed portions of IRA distributions from IRS Form 1040—lines (15a minus 15b) or 1040A—lines (11a minus 11b). Exclude rollovers. If negative, enter a zero here.	$
$	f. Untaxed portions of pensions from IRS Form 1040—lines (16a minus 16b) or 1040A—lines (12a minus 12b). Exclude rollovers. If negative, enter a zero here.	$
$	g. Housing, food and other living allowances paid to members of the military, clergy and others (including cash payments and cash value of benefits).	$
$	h. Veterans noneducation benefits such as Disability, Death Pension, or Dependency & Indemnity Compensation (DIC) and/or VA Educational Work-Study allowances.	$
$	i. Other untaxed income not reported, such as workers' compensation, disability, etc. **Don't include** student aid, earned income credit, additional child tax credit, welfare payments, untaxed Social Security benefits, Supplemental Security Income, Workforce Investment Act educational benefits, combat pay, benefits from flexible spending arrangements (e.g., cafeteria plans), foreign income exclusion or credit for federal tax on special fuels.	$
XXXXXXXXXX	j. Money received, or paid on your behalf (e.g., bills), not reported elsewhere on this form.	$

Estimate Your EFC Under Federal Methodology

WORKSHEET 4A: Estimate a Dependent Student's Expected Contribution

STUDENT'S INCOME	
1. Taxable income ("adjusted gross income" from IRS Form 1040)	$
2. Untaxed income/benefits	+
3. Taxable student aid	-
4. Total student's income (sum of lines 1 and 2, minus line 3)	=
Allowances	
5. U.S. income tax paid (from IRS Form 1040)	
6. State taxes paid (% from Table 8 x line 4)	+
7. F.I.C.A. (Table 2)	+
8. Income protection allowance	$3,000
9. Parents' negative available income offset (line 11 of parents' worksheet, if negative)	+
10. Total allowances (sum of lines 5-9)	=
11. Available income (line 4 minus line 10)	=
12. Available income assessment rate	x 0.50
13. Contribution from income (line 11 x line 12; if negative, enter $0)	=
Student's Assets*	
14. Cash, savings and checking accounts	
15. Other real estate/investment equity	+
16. Business/nonfamily farm equity	+
17. Net assets (sum of lines 14-16)	=
18. Asset assessment rate	x 0.20
19. Contribution from assets (line 17 x line 18; if simple needs test or negative, enter $0)	=
Contribution**	
20. Total Student Contribution (sum of lines 13 and 19)	=

* If you are eligible to file an IRS 1040A or 1040EZ form, or you are not required to file a tax return, and your parents' taxable income is less than $50,000, no assets are included in the methodology.

** If your parents' adjusted gross income is $15,000 or less, and they file or are eligible to file an IRS 1040A or 1040EZ form, no contribution is expected.

WORKSHEET 4B:
Estimate the Parents' Expected Contribution

Parents' Income	
1. Taxable income ("adjusted gross income" from IRS Form 1040)	$
2. Untaxed income/benefits	+
3. Income exclusions (child support paid + education tax credits)	-
4. Total parents' income (sum of lines 1 and 2, minus line 3)	=
Allowances	
5. U.S. income tax paid (from IRS Form 1040)	
6. State taxes paid (% from Table 8 x line 4)	+
7. F.I.C.A. paid (Table 9)	+
8. Employment allowance (Table 9)	+
9. Income protection allowance (Table 10)	+
10. Total allowances (sum of lines 5-9)	=
11. Available income (line 4 minus line 10)	=
Parents' Assets*	
12. Cash, savings and checking accounts	
13. Other real estate/investment equity	+
14. Adjusted business/nonfamily farm equity (Table 11)	+
15. Net worth (sum of lines 12-14)	=
16. Education Savings and Asset protection allowance (Table 12)	-
17. Discretionary net worth (line 15 minus line 16)	=
18. Conversion percentage	x 12%
19. Contribution from assets (line 17 x line 18; if simple needs test or negative, enter $0)	=
20. Adjusted available income (sum of line 11 and line 19)	=
Contribution**	
21. Total contribution (calculate using line 20 and Table 13)	=
22. Number of dependent children in college at least half time	÷
23. Parents' contribution for student (line 21 divided by line 22; if negative, enter $0)	=

* If your parents are eligible to file an IRS 1040A or 1040EZ form, or are not required to file a tax return and their taxable income is less than $50,000, no assets are included in the methodology.

** If your parents' adjusted gross income is $15,000 or less, and they are eligible to file an IRS 1040A or 1040EZ form, or are not required to file a tax return, no contribution is expected.

TABLE 8: 2009-2010 Federal EFC Allowances for State Taxes

	Parents TOTAL INCOME $ 0-14,999	Parents TOTAL INCOME $15,000 or more	Student TOTAL INCOME Any amount
Alabama (AL)	3%	2%	2%
Alaska (AK)	2	1	0
American Samoa (AS)	3	2	2
Arizona (AZ)	4	3	3
Arkansas (AR)	4	3	3
California (CA)	8	7	5
Canada (CN)	3	2	2
Colorado (CO)	5	4	3
Connecticut (CT)	8	7	4
Delaware (DE)	4	3	3
District of Columbia (DC)	7	6	6
Federated States of Micronesia (FM)	3	2	2
Florida (FL)	3	2	1
Georgia (GA)	5	4	4
Guam (GU)	3	2	2
Hawaii (HI)	5	4	4
Idaho (ID)	5	4	3
Illinois (IL)	5	4	2
Indiana (IN)	4	3	3
Iowa (IA)	5	4	3
Kansas (KS)	5	4	3
Kentucky (KY)	5	4	4
Louisiana (LA)	3	2	2
Maine (ME)	6	5	4
Marshall Islands (MH)	3	2	2
Maryland (MD)	8	7	5
Massachusetts (MA)	7	6	4
Mexico (MX)	3	2	2
Michigan (MI)	5	4	3
Minnesota (MN)	6	5	4
Mississippi	3	2	2
Missouri (MO)	5	4	3
Montana (MT)	5	4	3
Nebraska (NE)	5	4	3
Nevada (NV)	3	2	1
New Hampshire (NH)	5	4	1
New Jersey (NJ)	9	8	4
New Mexico (NM)	3	2	3
New York (NY)	9	8	6
North Carolina (NC)	6	5	4
North Dakota (ND)	3%	2%	1%
Northern Mariana Islands (MP)	3	2	2
Ohio (OH)	6	5	4
Oklahoma (OK)	4	3	3
Oregon (OR)	7	6	5
Palau (PW)	3	2	2
Pennsylvania (PA)	6	5	3
Puerto Rico (PR)	3	2	2
Rhode Island (RI)	7	6	4
South Carolina (SC)	5	4	3
South Dakota (SD)	2	1	1
Tennessee (TN)	2	1	1
Texas (TX)	3	2	1
Utah (UT)	5	4	4
Vermont (VT)	5	4	3
Virgin Islands (VI)	3	2	2
Virginia (VA)	6	5	4
Washington (WA)	4	3	1
West Virginia (WV)	3	2	2
Wisconsin (WI)	7	6	4
Wyoming (WY)	2	1	1
Not Reported (NR)	3	2	2

TABLE 9. Federal EFC Allowances for FICA and Employment

FICA: WAGES	
$1 to $102,00	7.65% of income earned by each wage earner (maximum $7,312.50 per person)
$97,501 or more	$7,803 + 1.45% of income earned above $102,000 by each wage earner
EMPLOYMENT ALLOWANCE	35% of lesser earned income to a maximum $3,500 (single parent: 35% of earned income to a maximum of $3,500)

TABLE 10. Federal EFC Income Protection Allowance for Parents

Family Size (including student)	Number in College				
	1	2	3	4	5
2	$ 15,840	$ 13,130			
3	19,730	17,030	$ 14,320		
4	24,370	21,660	18,960	$ 16,250	
5	28,750	26,040	23,340	20,630	$ 17,940
6	33,630	30,920	28,220	25,510	22,820

For each additional family member, add $3,800.
For each additional college student, subtract $2,700.

TABLE 11. Federal EFC Adjusted Net Worth of a Business or Farm

NET WORTH	ADJUSTED NET WORTH		
Less than $1	$ 0		
$1 to 115,000	$ 0	+	40% of net worth
$115,001 to 340,000	$ 46,000	+	50% of net worth over $115,000
$340,001 to 565,000	$ 158,500	+	60% of net worth over $340,000
$565,001 or more	$ 293,500	+	100% of net worth over $565,000

TABLE 12. Federal EFC Education Savings and Asset Protection Allowance for Parents

AGE OF OLDER PARENT OR STUDENT	COUPLE/ MARRIED	UNMARRIED/ SINGLE
25 or under	$ 0	$ 0
26	2,900	1,200
27	5,800	2,400
28	8,700	3,600
29	11,600	4,800
30	14,500	6,000
31	17,400	7,200
32	20,300	8,400
33	23,100	9,500
34	26,000	10,700
35	28,900	11,900
36	31,800	13,100
37	34,700	14,300
38	37,600	15,500
39	40,500	16,700
40	43,400	17,900
41	44,200	18,200
42	45,300	18,600
43	46,400	19,100
44	47,600	19,500
45	48,700	19,900
46	49,900	20,400
47	51,200	20,900
48	52,400	21,400
49	53,700	21,900
50	55,300	22,400
51	56,700	22,900
52	58,000	23,500
53	59,800	24,000
54	61,200	24,600
55	63,000	25,300
56	64,900	25,900
57	66,400	26,500
58	68,300	27,200
59	70,300	27,900
60	72,300	28,700
61	74,400	29,500
62	76,600	30,300
63	79,100	31,100
64	81,300	32,000
65 or over	84,000	32,800

TABLE 13. Federal EFC Parents' Contribution from Adjusted Available Income (AAI)

ADJUSTED AVAILABLE INCOME (AAI)	TOTAL CONTRIBUTIONS FROM INCOME
Less than $ -3,409 (3,409)	$ -750
$(3,409) to 14,200	22% of AI
$ 14,201 to 17,800	$ 3,124 + 25% of AAI over $ 14,200
$ 17,801 to 21,400	$ 4,024 + 29% of AAI over $ 17,800
$ 21,401 to 25,000	$ 5,068 + 34% of AAI over $ 21,400
$ 25,001 to 28,600	$ 6,292 + 40% of AAI over $ 25,000
$ 28,601 or more	$ 7,732 + 47% of AAI over $ 28,600

Contact Information for State Aid Programs

ALABAMA
Alabama Commission on Higher Education
P.O. Box 302000
Montgomery, AL 36130-2000
334-242-1998
www.ache.state.al.us

ALASKA
Alaska Commission on Postsecondary Education
P.O. Box 110505
Juneau, AK 99811-0505
800-441-2962
www.state.ak.us/acpe

ARIZONA
Arizona Department of Education
1535 W. Jefferson Street
Phoenix, AZ 85007
800-352-4558
www.ade.state.az.us

ARKANSAS
Arkansas Department of Higher Education
114 East Capitol Avenue
Little Rock, AR 72201
501-371-2000
www.adhe.edu

CALIFORNIA
California Student Aid Commission
P.O. Box 419026
Rancho Cordova, CA 95741-9026
888-224-7268
www.csac.ca.gov

COLORADO
Colorado Department of Education
201 East Colfax Avenue
Denver, CO 80203-1799
303-866-6600
www.cde.state.co.us

CONNECTICUT
Connecticut Department of Higher Education
61 Woodland Street
Hartford, CT 06105-2326
860-947-1800
www.ctdhe.org

DELAWARE
Delaware Higher Education Commission
820 North French Street
Wilmington, DE 19801-3509
800-292-7935
www.doe.state.de.us/high-ed

DISTRICT OF COLUMBIA
State Education Office
441 4th St., N.W., Suite 350 North
Washington, DC 20001
202-727-6436
www.seo.dc.gov

FLORIDA
Florida Department of Education
Office of Student Financial Assistance
1940 N. Monroe Street, Suite 70
Tallahassee, FL 32303-4759
888-827-2004
www.floridastudentfinancialaid.org

GEORGIA
Georgia Student Finance Commission
2082 East Exchange Place
Tucker, GA 30084
800-505-4732
www.gsfc.org

HAWAII
Hawaii State Department of Education
P.O. Box 2360
Honolulu, HI 96804
808-586-3230
www.doe.k12.hi.us

IDAHO
Idaho State Department of Education
P.O. Box 83720
650 West State Street
Boise, ID 83720-0027
800-432-4601
www.sde.state.id.us

ILLINOIS
Illinois Student Assistance Commission
1755 Lake Cook Road
Deerfield, IL 60015-5209
800-899-4722
www.collegezone.com

INDIANA
State Student Assistance Commission of Indiana
150 W. Market Street, Suite 500
Indianapolis, IN 46204
888-528-4719
www.in.gov/ssaci

IOWA
Iowa College Student Aid Commission
200 10th Street, Fourth Floor
Des Moines, IA 50309-3609
877-272-4456
www.iowacollegeaid.org

KANSAS
Kansas Board of Regents
1000 SW Jackson Street, Suite 520
Topeka, KS 66612-1368
785-296-3421
www.kansasregents.org

KENTUCKY
KHEAA Student Aid Branch
P.O. Box 798
Frankfort, KY 40602
800-928-8926
www.kheaa.com

LOUISIANA
Louisiana Office of Student Financial Assistance
P.O. Box 91202
Baton Rouge, LA 70821-9202
800-259-5626
www.osfa.state.la.us

MAINE
Finance Authority of Maine
Education Assistance Division
P.O. Box 949
5 Community Drive
Augusta, ME 04332
800-228-3734
www.famemaine.com

MARYLAND
Maryland Higher Education Commission
Office of Student Financial Assistance
839 Bestgate Road, Suite 400
Annapolis, MD 21401
800-974-0203
www.mhec.state.md.us

MASSACHUSETTS
Massachusetts Board of Higher Education
Office of Student Financial Assistance
454 Broadway, Suite 200
Revere, MA 02151-3034
617-727-9420
www.osfa.mass.edu

MICHIGAN
Michigan Higher Education Assistance Authority
Office of Scholarships and Grants
P.O. Box 30462
Lansing, MI 48909-7962
888-447-2687
www.michigan.gov/mistudentaid

MINNESOTA
Minnesota Office of Higher Education
1450 Energy Park Drive, Suite 350
St. Paul, MN 55108-5227
800-657-3866
www.ohe.state.mn.us

MISSISSIPPI
Mississippi Office of Student Financial Aid
3825 Ridgewood Road
Jackson, MS 39211-6453
800-327-2980
www.ihl.state.ms.us/financialaid

MISSOURI
Missouri Department of Higher Education
3515 Amazonas Drive
Jefferson City, MO 65109-5717
800-473-6757
www.dhe.mo.gov

MONTANA
Montana Board of Regents
P.O. Box 203201
2500 Broadway Street
Helena, MT 59620-3201
406-444-6570
www.mus.edu

NEBRASKA
Nebraska Coordination Commission for Postsecondary Education
P.O. Box 95005
Lincoln, NE 68509-5005
402-471-2847
www.ccpe.state.ne.us

NEVADA
Nevada Department of Education
700 East 5th Street
Carson City, NV 89701
775-687-9228
www.doe.nv.gov

NEW HAMPSHIRE
New Hampshire Postsecondary Education Commission
3 Barrell Court, Suite 300
Concord, NH 03301-8543
603-271-2555
www.nh.gov/postsecondary

NEW JERSEY
New Jersey Higher Education Student Assistance Authority
P.O. Box 540
Trenton, NJ 08625
800-792-8670
www.hesaa.org

NEW MEXICO
New Mexico Higher Education Department
2048 Galisteo Street
Santa Fe, NM 87505
505-476-8400
www.hed.state.nm.us

NEW YORK
New York State Higher Education Services Corporation
99 Washington Avenue
Albany, NY 12255
888-697-4372
www.hesc.state.ny.us

NORTH CAROLINA
North Carolina State Education Assistance Authority
P.O. Box 14103
Research Triangle Park, NC 27709
919-549-8614
www.ncseaa.edu

NORTH DAKOTA
North Dakota University System
600 East Boulevard, Dept. 215
Bismarck, ND 58505-0230
701-328-2960
www.ndus.nodak.edu

OHIO
Ohio Board of Regents
30 East Broad Street, 36th floor
Columbus, OH 43215-3414
614-466-6000
www.regents.ohio.gov

OKLAHOMA
Oklahoma State Regents for Higher Education
Tuition Aid Grant Program
655 Research Parkway, Suite 200
Oklahoma City, OK 73104
405-225-9100
www.okhighered.org

OREGON
Oregon Student Assistance Commission
1500 Valley River Drive, Suite 100
Eugene, OR 97401
800-452-8807
www.osac.state.or.us

PENNSYLVANIA
Pennsylvania Higher Education Assistance Agency
1200 N. Seventh Street
Harrisburg, PA 17102-1444
800-233-0557
www.pheaa.org

PUERTO RICO
Departmento de Educacion
P.O. Box 190759
San Juan, PR 00919-0759
787-759-2000
www.de.gobierno.pr

RHODE ISLAND
Rhode Island Higher Education Assistance Authority
560 Jefferson Boulevard, Suite 100
Warwick, RI 02886
401-736-1100
www.riheaa.org

SOUTH CAROLINA
South Carolina Commission on Higher Education
1333 Main Street, Suite 200
Columbia, SC 29201
803-737-2260
www.che.sc.gov

SOUTH DAKOTA
South Dakota Department of Education
Office of Finance and Management
700 Governors Drive
Pierre, SD 57501
605-773-3134
www.doe.sd.gov/stateaid

TENNESSEE
Tennessee Student Assistance Corporation
404 James Robertson Parkway
Suite 1510, Parkway Towers
Nashville, TN 37243-0820
800-342-1663
www.state.tn.us/tsac

TEXAS
Texas Higher Education Coordinating Board
Division of Student Services
P.O. Box 12788, Capital Station
Austin, TX 78711
800-242-3062
www.hhloans.com

UTAH
Utah Higher Education Assistance Authority
Board of Regents Building, The Gateway
60 South 400 West
Salt Lake City, UT 84101-1284
877-336-7378
www.uheaa.org

VERMONT
Vermont Student Assistance Corporation
P.O. Box 999
Winooski, VT 05404
800-798-8722
www.vsac.org

VIRGINIA
State Council of Higher Education for Virginia
101 North 14th Street
Richmond, VA 23219
804-225-2600
www.schev.edu

WASHINGTON
Washington Higher Education Coordination Board
917 Lakeridge Way
P.O. Box 43430
Olympia, WA 98504-3430
360-753-7800
www.hecb.wa.gov

WEST VIRGINIA
West Virginia Higher Education Policy Commission
Central Office, Higher Education Grant Program
1018 Kanawha Boulevard East, Suite 700
Charleston, WV 25301-2800
304-558-4614
www.hepc.wvnet.edu

WISCONSIN
Wisconsin Higher Educational Aids Board
P. O. Box 7885
Madison, WI 53707
608-267-2206
www.heab.state.wi.us

WYOMING
Wyoming Department of Education
2300 Capitol Avenue
Hathaway Building, Second Floor
Cheyenne, WY 82002-0050
307-777-7690
www.k12.wy.us

GUAM
University of Guam
Student Financial Aid Office
UOG Station
Mangilao, GU 96923
671-735-2287
www.uog.edu

VIRGIN ISLANDS
Financial Aid Office, Virgin Islands Board of Education
P.O. Box 11900
St. Thomas, VI 00801
340-774-4546

Part III

Financial Aid College by College

Alabama

Alabama Agricultural and Mechanical University

Huntsville, Alabama
www.aamu.edu Federal Code: 001002

4-year public university and agricultural college in small city.
Enrollment: 4,290 undergrads, 6% part-time. 1,044 full-time freshmen.
Selectivity: Admits less than 50% of applicants.

BASIC COSTS (2008-2009)

Tuition and fees: $4,930; out-of-state residents $9,220.
Per-credit charge: $143; out-of-state residents $286.
Room and board: $3,592.
Additional info: Part-time student required fees are $440. Tuition/fee waivers available for minority students.

FINANCIAL AID PICTURE

Students with need: Need-based aid available for full-time and part-time students. Work study available weekends and for part-time students.
Students without need: No-need awards available for athletics, minority status.
Scholarships offered: Presidential Scholarship; full tuition, course fees, room and board, $1,000 for books and supplies per semester; for students with 3.5 GPA or higher. Provost Scholarship; full tuition, course fees, room and board, $800 for books and supplies per semester; for students with 3.4 GPA or higher. Dean's Scholarship; full tuition, course fees, room and board, $500 for books and supplies per semester; for students with 3.3 GPA or higher.

FINANCIAL AID PROCEDURES

Forms required: FAFSA, institutional form.
Dates and Deadlines: Applicants notified on a rolling basis; must reply within 2 week(s) of notification.

CONTACT

Sybrenna Harris, Director of Financial Aid
Box 908, Normal, AL 35762
(256) 372-4862

Alabama State University

Montgomery, Alabama
www.alasu.edu Federal Code: 001005

4-year public university in small city.
Enrollment: 4,695 undergrads, 11% part-time. 1,334 full-time freshmen.
Selectivity: Admits less than 50% of applicants.

BASIC COSTS (2008-2009)

Tuition and fees: $5,460; out-of-state residents $10,068.
Per-credit charge: $192; out-of-state residents $384.
Room and board: $4,600.

FINANCIAL AID PICTURE (2008-2009)

Students with need: Average financial aid package met 66% of need; average scholarship/grant was $4,673; average loan was $3,508. For part-time students, average financial aid package was $12,190.
Students without need: No-need awards available for academics, alumni affiliation, art, athletics, job skills, leadership, minority status, music/drama, ROTC, state/district residency.
Cumulative student debt: 91% of graduating class had student loans; average debt was $30,005.

FINANCIAL AID PROCEDURES

Forms required: FAFSA.
Dates and Deadlines: Priority date 4/1; no closing date. Applicants notified on a rolling basis starting 5/15.
Transfers: Applicants notified on a rolling basis starting 5/1.

CONTACT

Dorenda Adams, Director of Financial Aid
PO Box 271, Montgomery, AL 36101-0271
(334) 229-4323

Amridge University

Montgomery, Alabama
www.amridgeuniversity.edu Federal Code: 016885

4-year private university and seminary college in small city, affiliated with Church of Christ.
Enrollment: 356 undergrads, 35% part-time.
Selectivity: Open admission; but selective for some programs.

BASIC COSTS (2009-2010)

Additional info: $300 per-semester-hour charge; full-time students receive a $150 credit per semester.

FINANCIAL AID PICTURE (2007-2008)

Students with need: Need-based aid available for full-time and part-time students.
Students without need: No-need awards available for academics, leadership.

FINANCIAL AID PROCEDURES

Forms required: FAFSA, institutional form.
Dates and Deadlines: Priority date 5/1; closing date 6/30. Applicants notified by 6/30; must reply by 8/15 or within 2 week(s) of notification.
Transfers: No deadline.

CONTACT

Louise Hicks, Financial Aid Director
PO Box 240240, Montgomery, AL 36124-0240
(800) 351-4040 ext. 7525

Athens State University

Athens, Alabama
www.athens.edu Federal Code: 001008

Upper-division public business and liberal arts and teachers college in large town.
Enrollment: 3,114 undergrads, 53% part-time.

BASIC COSTS (2009-2010)

Tuition and fees: $4,350; out-of-state residents $7,950.
Per-credit charge: $120; out-of-state residents $240.

FINANCIAL AID PICTURE (2007-2008)

Students with need: 98% of average financial aid package awarded as scholarships/grants, 2% awarded as loans/jobs. Need-based aid available for part-time students. Work study available nights, weekends, and for part-time students.
Students without need: No-need awards available for academics, alumni affiliation, art, athletics, leadership, minority status.

FINANCIAL AID PROCEDURES

Forms required: FAFSA.
Dates and Deadlines: No deadline. Applicants notified on a rolling basis starting 6/1; must reply within 3 week(s) of notification.

CONTACT
Sarah McAbee, Director, Student Financial Services
300 North Beaty Street, Athens, AL 35611
(256) 233-8122

Auburn University
Auburn, Alabama
www.auburn.edu Federal Code: 001009

4-year public university in large town.
Enrollment: 20,031 undergrads, 8% part-time. 4,191 full-time freshmen.
Selectivity: Admits 50 to 75% of applicants.

BASIC COSTS (2008-2009)
Tuition and fees: $6,500; out-of-state residents $18,260.
Per-credit charge: $243; out-of-state residents $729.
Room and board: $8,260.

FINANCIAL AID PICTURE (2007-2008)
Students with need: Out of 2,133 full-time freshmen who applied for aid, 1,179 were judged to have need. Of these, 1,179 received aid, and 252 had their full need met. Average financial aid package met 58% of need; average scholarship/grant was $5,555; average loan was $3,872. For part-time students, average financial aid package was $5,623.
Students without need: 718 full-time freshmen who did not demonstrate need for aid received scholarships/grants; average award was $4,427.
Scholarships offered: ***Merit:*** Freshmen and General Scholarships; up to full-tuition; require 28 ACT/1240 SAT and 3.25 GPA. National Merit and National Achievement Finalists; full-tuition plus additional benefits. ***Athletic:*** 95 full-time freshmen received athletic scholarships; average amount $17,730.
Cumulative student debt: 39% of graduating class had student loans; average debt was $34,398.
Additional info: State of Alabama has pre-paid college tuition plan for residents.

FINANCIAL AID PROCEDURES
Forms required: FAFSA, institutional form.
Dates and Deadlines: No deadline. Applicants notified on a rolling basis.
Transfers: No deadline. Applicants notified on a rolling basis; must reply within 2 week(s) of notification.

CONTACT
Mike Reynolds, Director of Student Financial Services
Quad Center, Auburn, AL 36849-5111
(334) 844-4080

Auburn University at Montgomery
Montgomery, Alabama
www.aum.edu Federal Code: 008310

4-year public university in small city.
Enrollment: 4,323 undergrads, 33% part-time. 709 full-time freshmen.
Selectivity: Admits over 75% of applicants.

BASIC COSTS (2008-2009)
Tuition and fees: $5,580; out-of-state residents $16,200.
Per-credit charge: $177; out-of-state residents $531.
Room only: $3,420.

FINANCIAL AID PICTURE (2008-2009)
Students with need: 23% of average financial aid package awarded as scholarships/grants, 77% awarded as loans/jobs. Need-based aid available for part-time students. Work study available nights, weekends, and for part-time students.
Students without need: No-need awards available for academics, alumni affiliation, art, athletics, job skills, leadership, minority status, music/drama, religious affiliation, ROTC.

FINANCIAL AID PROCEDURES
Forms required: FAFSA.
Dates and Deadlines: Priority date 3/15; no closing date. Applicants notified on a rolling basis starting 5/1; must reply within 2 week(s) of notification.
Transfers: Priority date 3/1. Aid awarded based on need and the availability of funds.

CONTACT
Anthony Richey, Director of Financial Aid
7400 East Drive, Room 139 Taylor Center, Montgomery, AL 36124-4023
(334) 244-3571

Bevill State Community College
Sumiton, Alabama
www.bscc.edu Federal Code: 005733

2-year public community college in small town.
Enrollment: 3,899 undergrads. 747 full-time freshmen.
Selectivity: Open admission; but selective for some programs.

BASIC COSTS (2008-2009)
Tuition and fees: $2,730; out-of-state residents $4,860.
Per-credit charge: $71; out-of-state residents $142.
Room only: $1,350.

FINANCIAL AID PICTURE (2007-2008)
Students with need: Need-based aid available for full-time and part-time students.
Students without need: No-need awards available for academics, athletics, leadership, music/drama.

FINANCIAL AID PROCEDURES
Forms required: FAFSA.
Dates and Deadlines: Priority date 5/1; no closing date. Applicants notified on a rolling basis starting 7/1.

CONTACT
Susanne Bush, Assistant to the Dean of Student Services
Box 800, Sumiton, AL 35148
(205) 387-0511 ext. 5814

Birmingham-Southern College
Birmingham, Alabama
www.bsc.edu Federal Code: 001012

4-year private liberal arts college in very large city, affiliated with United Methodist Church.
Enrollment: 1,412 undergrads, 2% part-time. 445 full-time freshmen.
Selectivity: Admits 50 to 75% of applicants.

BASIC COSTS (2008-2009)
Tuition and fees: $25,586.
Per-credit charge: $1,033.
Room and board: $8,595.

FINANCIAL AID PICTURE (2008-2009)
Students with need: Out of 299 full-time freshmen who applied for aid, 236 were judged to have need. Of these, 236 received aid, and 143 had their full need met. Average financial aid package met 99% of need; average scholarship/grant was $4,857; average loan was $3,395. For part-time students, average financial aid package was $19,080.
Students without need: 190 full-time freshmen who did not demonstrate need for aid received scholarships/grants; average award was $10,302. No-

need awards available for academics, alumni affiliation, art, job skills, leadership, minority status, music/drama, religious affiliation, state/district residency.

Scholarships offered: Neal and Anne Berte Scholarship; full tuition; based on academic achievement; 1 awarded. Blount-Monaghan/Vulcan Materials Company Scholarship; full tuition; based on academic achievement; 1 awarded. William Jones and Elizabeth Perry Rushton Scholarship; full tuition, room and board, fees, books, $2,000 travel stipend; based on academic achievement; 1 awarded. Phi Beta Kappa; full tuition; based on academic achievement. United Methodist Scholarship; $1,000-$2,500; awarded to United Methodist with recommendation from senior United Methodist Minister.

Cumulative student debt: 79% of graduating class had student loans; average debt was $27,798.

Additional info: Auditions required for music, theatre, dance applicants seeking scholarships. Portfolios required for art applicants seeking scholarships, and essays recommended for all applicants seeking scholarships.

FINANCIAL AID PROCEDURES

Forms required: FAFSA.

Dates and Deadlines: Closing date 3/1. Applicants notified on a rolling basis starting 3/1; must reply by 8/21.

Transfers: No deadline. Applicants notified on a rolling basis starting 3/1; must reply within 2 week(s) of notification.

CONTACT

Fred Carter, Director of Financial Aid Services
900 Arkadelphia Road, Birmingham, AL 35254
(205) 226-4688

Chattahoochee Valley Community College

Phenix City, Alabama
www.cv.edu Federal Code: 012182

2-year public community college in small city.

Enrollment: 1,925 undergrads.

Selectivity: Open admission; but selective for some programs.

BASIC COSTS (2008-2009)

Tuition and fees: $2,700; out-of-state residents $4,830.

Per-credit charge: $71; out-of-state residents $142.

FINANCIAL AID PICTURE (2007-2008)

Students with need: 59% of average financial aid package awarded as scholarships/grants, 41% awarded as loans/jobs. Need-based aid available for part-time students. Work study available nights, weekends, and for part-time students.

Students without need: No-need awards available for academics, art, athletics, leadership, music/drama.

FINANCIAL AID PROCEDURES

Forms required: FAFSA.

Dates and Deadlines: Priority date 7/1; no closing date. Applicants notified on a rolling basis; must reply within 1 week(s) of notification.

CONTACT

Joan Waters, Director of Financial Aid
2602 College Drive, Phenix City, AL 36869
(334) 291-4915

Faulkner University

Montgomery, Alabama
www.faulkner.edu Federal Code: 001003

4-year private university and liberal arts college in large city, affiliated with Church of Christ.

Enrollment: 2,483 undergrads, 19% part-time. 262 full-time freshmen.

Selectivity: Admits 50 to 75% of applicants.

BASIC COSTS (2008-2009)

Tuition and fees: $12,770.

Per-credit charge: $445.

Room and board: $6,350.

Additional info: Tuition/fee waivers available for adults, minority students, unemployed or children of unemployed.

FINANCIAL AID PICTURE (2008-2009)

Students with need: Average financial aid package met 60% of need; average scholarship/grant was $2,650; average loan was $3,500. For part-time students, average financial aid package was $3,900.

Students without need: No-need awards available for academics, alumni affiliation, art, athletics, leadership, music/drama, religious affiliation, ROTC, state/district residency.

Cumulative student debt: 89% of graduating class had student loans; average debt was $21,000.

FINANCIAL AID PROCEDURES

Forms required: FAFSA, state aid form, institutional form.

Dates and Deadlines: Priority date 5/1; no closing date. Applicants notified on a rolling basis starting 6/1; must reply within 3 week(s) of notification.

Transfers: No deadline. Applicants notified on a rolling basis.

CONTACT

William Jackson, Director of Financial Aid
5345 Atlanta Highway, Montgomery, AL 36109-3398
(334) 386-7195

Gadsden State Community College

Gadsden, Alabama
www.gadsdenstate.edu Federal Code: 001017

2-year public community and technical college in large town.

Enrollment: 4,467 undergrads, 43% part-time. 906 full-time freshmen.

Selectivity: Open admission; but selective for some programs.

BASIC COSTS (2008-2009)

Tuition and fees: $2,700; out-of-state residents $4,830.

Per-credit charge: $71; out-of-state residents $142.

Room and board: $3,200.

Additional info: Tuition/fee waivers available for minority students, unemployed or children of unemployed.

FINANCIAL AID PICTURE (2007-2008)

Students with need: For part-time students, average financial aid package was $902.

Students without need: No-need awards available for academics, alumni affiliation, art, athletics, job skills, leadership, minority status, music/drama, state/district residency.

Cumulative student debt: 95% of graduating class had student loans; average debt was $1,796.

FINANCIAL AID PROCEDURES

Forms required: FAFSA, institutional form.

Dates and Deadlines: Priority date 4/15; no closing date. Applicants notified on a rolling basis starting 6/10.

CONTACT

Kelly D'Eath, Director of Financial Aid
1001 George Wallace Drive, Gadsden, AL 35902-0227
(256) 549-8267

Heritage Christian University

Florence, Alabama
www.hcu.edu Federal Code: 015370

4-year private Bible college in large town, affiliated with Church of Christ.
Enrollment: 73 undergrads.
Selectivity: Admits over 75% of applicants.

BASIC COSTS (2008-2009)

Tuition and fees: $10,140.
Per-credit charge: $322.
Room only: $3,000.

FINANCIAL AID PICTURE (2008-2009)

Students with need: Need-based aid available for full-time and part-time students.

FINANCIAL AID PROCEDURES

Forms required: FAFSA.
Dates and Deadlines: Priority date 6/1; no closing date. Applicants notified on a rolling basis starting 6/1; must reply by 7/28 or within 2 week(s) of notification.
Transfers: No deadline. Applicants notified on a rolling basis; must reply by 7/28 or within 3 week(s) of notification.

CONTACT

Mechelle Thompson, Financial Aid Counselor
3625 Helton Drive, Florence, AL 35630
(256) 766-6610 ext. 224

Huntingdon College

Montgomery, Alabama
www.huntingdon.edu Federal Code: 001019

4-year private liberal arts college in small city, affiliated with United Methodist Church.
Enrollment: 1,076 undergrads, 21% part-time. 253 full-time freshmen.
Selectivity: Admits 50 to 75% of applicants.

BASIC COSTS (2009-2010)

Tuition and fees: $20,990.
Per-credit charge: $830.
Room and board: $7,500.
Additional info: Tuition at time of enrollment locked for 4 years.

FINANCIAL AID PICTURE (2008-2009)

Students with need: Out of 218 full-time freshmen who applied for aid, 187 were judged to have need. Of these, 187 received aid, and 124 had their full need met. Average financial aid package met 92% of need; average scholarship/grant was $6,264; average loan was $3,650. For part-time students, average financial aid package was $8,051.
Students without need: 66 full-time freshmen who did not demonstrate need for aid received scholarships/grants; average award was $9,383. No-need awards available for academics, alumni affiliation, music/drama, religious affiliation, ROTC, state/district residency.
Cumulative student debt: 73% of graduating class had student loans; average debt was $14,758.

FINANCIAL AID PROCEDURES

Forms required: institutional form.
Dates and Deadlines: Priority date 4/14; no closing date. Applicants notified on a rolling basis starting 3/14; must reply by 5/14 or within 2 week(s) of notification.
Transfers: Priority date 4/15; no deadline. Applicants notified on a rolling basis starting 3/1; must reply by 5/1 or within 2 week(s) of notification.

CONTACT

Belinda Duett, Director of Student Financial Services
1500 East Fairview Avenue, Montgomery, AL 36106-2148
(334) 833-4519

Jacksonville State University

Jacksonville, Alabama
www.jsu.edu Federal Code: 001020

4-year public university in small town.
Enrollment: 7,522 undergrads, 21% part-time. 1,243 full-time freshmen.
Selectivity: Admits over 75% of applicants.

BASIC COSTS (2008-2009)

Tuition and fees: $5,700; out-of-state residents $11,400.
Per-credit charge: $190; out-of-state residents $380.
Room and board: $4,215.

FINANCIAL AID PICTURE (2007-2008)

Students with need: Need-based aid available for full-time and part-time students. Work study available nights, weekends, and for part-time students.
Students without need: No-need awards available for academics, alumni affiliation, art, athletics, music/drama, ROTC.
Scholarships offered: 4-year tuition scholarship; for entering freshmen from Alabama with 28 ACT or 1230 SAT are eligible.

FINANCIAL AID PROCEDURES

Forms required: FAFSA, institutional form.
Dates and Deadlines: Priority date 3/15; no closing date. Applicants notified on a rolling basis starting 5/15; must reply within 2 week(s) of notification.

CONTACT

Vickie Adams, Director of Financial Aid
700 Pelham Road North, Jacksonville, AL 36265-1602
(256) 782-5006

Jefferson Davis Community College

Brewton, Alabama
www.jdcc.edu Federal Code: 001021

2-year public nursing and community college in small town.
Enrollment: 1,099 undergrads.
Selectivity: Open admission; but selective for some programs.

BASIC COSTS (2008-2009)

Tuition and fees: $2,700; out-of-state residents $4,830.
Per-credit charge: $71; out-of-state residents $142.
Room only: $1,866.

FINANCIAL AID PICTURE (2007-2008)

Students with need: 89% of average financial aid package awarded as scholarships/grants, 11% awarded as loans/jobs. Need-based aid available for part-time students. Work study available nights.
Students without need: No-need awards available for academics, athletics, leadership.

FINANCIAL AID PROCEDURES

Forms required: FAFSA.
Dates and Deadlines: Priority date 5/8; no closing date. Applicants notified on a rolling basis; must reply within 2 week(s) of notification.
Transfers: Must reply within 2 week(s) of notification.

CONTACT

Vanessa Kyles, Director of Financial Aid
PO Box 958, Brewton, AL 36427
(251) 809-1516

Jefferson State Community College

Birmingham, Alabama
www.jeffstateonline.com Federal Code: 001022

2-year public community college in very large city.
Enrollment: 6,404 undergrads, 55% part-time. 919 full-time freshmen.
Selectivity: Open admission; but selective for some programs.

BASIC COSTS (2008-2009)

Tuition and fees: $3,060; out-of-state residents $5,190.
Per-credit charge: $71; out-of-state residents $142.

FINANCIAL AID PICTURE (2007-2008)

Students with need: Need-based aid available for full-time and part-time students. Work study available nights.
Students without need: No-need awards available for academics, art, athletics, leadership, music/drama.
Additional info: Any Alabama resident over age 60 may attend classes tuition free, on a space available basis.

FINANCIAL AID PROCEDURES

Forms required: FAFSA, institutional form.
Dates and Deadlines: Priority date 5/1; no closing date. Applicants notified on a rolling basis starting 6/1.
Transfers: Transfer students not eligible for academic scholarships until 12 hours have been completed on campus.

CONTACT

Tracy Adams, Director, Financial Aid
2601 Carson Road, Birmingham, AL 35215-3098
(205) 856-8509

Judson College

Marion, Alabama
www.judson.edu Federal Code: 001023

4-year private liberal arts college for women in small town, affiliated with Baptist faith.
Enrollment: 313 undergrads, 16% part-time. 95 full-time freshmen.
Selectivity: Admits over 75% of applicants.

BASIC COSTS (2009-2010)

Tuition and fees: $12,547.
Per-credit charge: $410.
Room and board: $7,969.

FINANCIAL AID PICTURE (2008-2009)

Students with need: Out of 87 full-time freshmen who applied for aid, 73 were judged to have need. Of these, 73 received aid, and 16 had their full need met. Average financial aid package met 79% of need; average scholarship/grant was $10,923; average loan was $3,440. For part-time students, average financial aid package was $2,775.
Students without need: 15 full-time freshmen who did not demonstrate need for aid received scholarships/grants; average award was $6,910. No-need awards available for academics, alumni affiliation, art, athletics, music/drama, religious affiliation, state/district residency.
Scholarships offered: ***Merit:*** Garner-Webb Honors Scholarship; full tuition; given to applicants who are National Merit Finalists or have 30 ACT; up to 5 awarded. Lockhart Competitive Scholarships; 1 for full tuition, 2 for $2,500, 3 for $2,000; awarded based on exam scores. Music scholarships; $1,500; awarded based on audition. ***Athletic:*** 11 full-time freshmen received athletic scholarships; average amount $3,591.
Cumulative student debt: 74% of graduating class had student loans; average debt was $17,185.

FINANCIAL AID PROCEDURES

Forms required: FAFSA, state aid form, institutional form.
Dates and Deadlines: Priority date 3/1; no closing date. Applicants notified on a rolling basis starting 3/1; must reply within 2 week(s) of notification.
Transfers: No deadline. Applicants notified on a rolling basis starting 3/1; must reply within 2 week(s) of notification.

CONTACT

Doris Wilson, Director of Financial Aid
302 Bibb Street, Marion, AL 36756
(334) 683-5157

Lawson State Community College

Birmingham, Alabama
www.lawsonstate.edu Federal Code: 001059

2-year public community college in small city.
Enrollment: 3,609 undergrads, 47% part-time. 776 full-time freshmen.
Selectivity: Open admission; but selective for some programs.

BASIC COSTS (2008-2009)

Tuition and fees: $3,000; out-of-state residents $5,130.
Per-credit charge: $71; out-of-state residents $142.

FINANCIAL AID PICTURE (2008-2009)

Students with need: 96% of average financial aid package awarded as scholarships/grants, 4% awarded as loans/jobs. Need-based aid available for part-time students. Work study available nights.
Students without need: This college awards aid only to students with need.

FINANCIAL AID PROCEDURES

Forms required: FAFSA.
Dates and Deadlines: Priority date 6/1; no closing date. Applicants notified on a rolling basis starting 8/1; must reply within 2 week(s) of notification.

CONTACT

Cassandra Byrd, Director of Student Financial Services
3060 Wilson Road SW, Birmingham, AL 35221-1717
(205) 929-6380

Marion Military Institute

Marion, Alabama
www.marionmilitary.edu Federal Code: 001026

2-year public junior and military college in small town.
Enrollment: 398 undergrads. 273 full-time freshmen.
Selectivity: Admits less than 50% of applicants.

BASIC COSTS (2008-2009)

Tuition and fees: $8,570; out-of-state residents $14,570.
Per-credit charge: $200; out-of-state residents $400.
Room and board: $3,450.
Additional info: Required fees include one-time uniform fee of $1,850 and accident insurance of $150 per academic year.

FINANCIAL AID PICTURE (2007-2008)

Students with need: Need-based aid available for full-time and part-time students.

FINANCIAL AID PROCEDURES

Forms required: FAFSA.

Dates and Deadlines: No deadline. Applicants notified on a rolling basis starting 6/15; must reply within 6 week(s) of notification.

CONTACT

Jacquita Smith, Director of Financial Aid
1101 Washington Street, Marion, AL 36756-0420
(334) 683-2309

Miles College

Birmingham, Alabama
www.miles.edu Federal Code: 001028

4-year private liberal arts college in very large city, affiliated with Christian Methodist Episcopal Church.
Enrollment: 1,800 undergrads.
Selectivity: Open admission; but selective for some programs.

BASIC COSTS (2008-2009)
Tuition and fees: $7,968.
Per-credit charge: $311.
Room and board: $5,516.

FINANCIAL AID PICTURE (2007-2008)
Students with need: Need-based aid available for full-time and part-time students.
Students without need: This college awards aid only to students with need.

FINANCIAL AID PROCEDURES
Forms required: FAFSA, state aid form.
Dates and Deadlines: Priority date 4/15; no closing date. Applicants notified on a rolling basis starting 7/15; must reply within 2 week(s) of notification.

CONTACT

Percy Lanier, Director of Financial Aid
5500 Myron-Massey Boulevard, Fairfield, AL 35064
(205) 929-1665

Northeast Alabama Community College

Rainsville, Alabama
www.nacc.edu Federal Code: 001031

2-year public community college in rural community.
Enrollment: 2,050 undergrads.
Selectivity: Open admission; but selective for some programs.

BASIC COSTS (2008-2009)
Tuition and fees: $2,850; out-of-state residents $4,980.
Per-credit charge: $71; out-of-state residents $142.
Additional info: In-state costs apply to on-campus or distance-learning courses. Out-of-state distance-learning students pay $5,400 for academic year (or $180 per-credit-hour).

FINANCIAL AID PICTURE
Students with need: Need-based aid available for full-time and part-time students.
Students without need: No-need awards available for academics, art, leadership, minority status, music/drama.

FINANCIAL AID PROCEDURES
Forms required: FAFSA.
Dates and Deadlines: No deadline. Applicants notified on a rolling basis.

CONTACT

Nixon Willmon, Director of Financial Aid
Admissions Office, NACC, Rainsville, AL 35986-0159
(256) 228-6001 ext. 327

Northwest-Shoals Community College

Muscle Shoals, Alabama
www.nwscc.edu Federal Code: 005697

2-year public community and technical college in large town.
Enrollment: 4,055 undergrads.
Selectivity: Open admission; but selective for some programs.

BASIC COSTS (2008-2009)
Tuition and fees: $2,880; out-of-state residents $5,010.
Per-credit charge: $71; out-of-state residents $142.
Room only: $1,600.
Additional info: Tuition at time of enrollment locked for 2 years; tuition/fee waivers available for minority students, unemployed or children of unemployed.

FINANCIAL AID PICTURE (2007-2008)
Students with need: 51% of average financial aid package awarded as scholarships/grants, 49% awarded as loans/jobs. Need-based aid available for part-time students. Work study available nights, weekends, and for part-time students.
Students without need: No-need awards available for academics, art, athletics, leadership, minority status, music/drama.

FINANCIAL AID PROCEDURES
Forms required: FAFSA, institutional form.
Dates and Deadlines: Priority date 4/1; closing date 8/1. Applicants notified on a rolling basis; must reply within 2 week(s) of notification.
Transfers: No deadline. Applicants notified on a rolling basis; must reply within 2 week(s) of notification. Students without 1-year Alabama residency before fall term ineligible for state grant.

CONTACT

Joel Parris, Director of Student Financial Aid Services
PO Box 2545, Muscle Shoals, AL 35662
(256) 331-5368

Oakwood University

Huntsville, Alabama
www.oakwood.edu Federal Code: 001033

4-year private liberal arts college in small city, affiliated with Seventh-day Adventists.
Enrollment: 1,789 undergrads, 6% part-time. 485 full-time freshmen.
Selectivity: Admits 50 to 75% of applicants.

BASIC COSTS (2009-2010)
Tuition and fees: $13,834.
Room and board: $8,464.

FINANCIAL AID PICTURE
Students with need: Need-based aid available for full-time students.
Students without need: No-need awards available for academics, leadership, religious affiliation, state/district residency.

FINANCIAL AID PROCEDURES
Forms required: FAFSA, state aid form.
Dates and Deadlines: Priority date 3/31; no closing date. Applicants notified on a rolling basis starting 4/1.

CONTACT

Compton Brathwaite, Director of Financial Aid
7000 Adventist Boulevard, NW, Huntsville, AL 35896
(256) 726-7208

Prince Institute of Professional Studies

Montgomery, Alabama
www.princeinstitute.edu Federal Code: 022960

2-year for-profit technical college in large city.
Enrollment: 59 undergrads.
Selectivity: Open admission.

BASIC COSTS (2008-2009)

Tuition and fees: $6,895.
Per-credit charge: $183.

FINANCIAL AID PICTURE (2008-2009)

Students with need: Need-based aid available for full-time and part-time students.
Students without need: This college awards aid only to students with need.

FINANCIAL AID PROCEDURES

Forms required: FAFSA.
Dates and Deadlines: No deadline.

CONTACT

Reginald James, Financial Aid Administrator
7735 Atlanta Highway, Montgomery, AL 36117-4231
(334) 271-1670

Remington College: Mobile

Mobile, Alabama
www.remingtoncollege.edu Federal Code: 026055

2-year private technical college in large city.
Enrollment: 145 undergrads.
Selectivity: Open admission.

BASIC COSTS (2008-2009)

Additional info: Associate degree programs annual tuition $19,500 plus $50 fees. 8-month diploma program full tuition $13,900 plus $50 fees. Tuition includes textbooks and supplies.

FINANCIAL AID PICTURE (2007-2008)

Students with need: Need-based aid available for full-time students. Work study available nights.
Students without need: This college awards aid only to students with need.

FINANCIAL AID PROCEDURES

Forms required: FAFSA.

CONTACT

Linda Calvanese, Financial Aid Director
828 Downtowner Loop West, Mobile, AL 36609-5404
(251) 343-8200

Samford University

Birmingham, Alabama
www.samford.edu Federal Code: 001036

4-year private university in small city, affiliated with Southern Baptist Convention.
Enrollment: 2,824 undergrads, 7% part-time. 713 full-time freshmen.
Selectivity: Admits over 75% of applicants.

BASIC COSTS (2009-2010)

Tuition and fees: $20,420.
Room and board: $6,624.

FINANCIAL AID PICTURE (2007-2008)

Students with need: Out of 427 full-time freshmen who applied for aid, 277 were judged to have need. Of these, 277 received aid, and 81 had their full need met. Average financial aid package met 82% of need; average scholarship/grant was $10,669; average loan was $4,068. For part-time students, average financial aid package was $7,280.
Students without need: 213 full-time freshmen who did not demonstrate need for aid received scholarships/grants; average award was $5,697. No-need awards available for academics, athletics, leadership, music/drama, religious affiliation, ROTC, state/district residency.
Scholarships offered: 53 full-time freshmen received athletic scholarships; average amount $16,441.
Cumulative student debt: 46% of graduating class had student loans; average debt was $18,700.
Additional info: Consideration for merit scholarships automatically given to students with admission files completed by December 15.

FINANCIAL AID PROCEDURES

Forms required: FAFSA, state aid form.
Dates and Deadlines: Priority date 3/1; no closing date. Applicants notified by 4/1; must reply by 5/1.

CONTACT

Lane Smith, Director of Financial Aid
800 Lakeshore Drive, Birmingham, AL 35229
(205) 726-2905

Selma University

Selma, Alabama
www.selmauniversity.org Federal Code: 001037

4-year private university in large town, affiliated with Baptist faith.
Enrollment: 125 undergrads.
Selectivity: Open admission.

BASIC COSTS (2008-2009)

Tuition and fees: $4,600.
Per-credit charge: $175.

FINANCIAL AID PICTURE (2008-2009)

Students with need: 50% of average financial aid package awarded as scholarships/grants, 50% awarded as loans/jobs.

FINANCIAL AID PROCEDURES

Forms required: FAFSA.
Dates and Deadlines: Priority date 9/15; no closing date. Applicants notified on a rolling basis starting 8/23; must reply within 2 week(s) of notification.

CONTACT

Erika Roberson, Student Financial Aid Administrator
1501 Lapsley Street, Selma, AL 36701

Shelton State Community College

Tuscaloosa, Alabama
www.sheltonstate.edu Federal Code: 005691

2-year public community and technical college in small city.
Enrollment: 5,350 undergrads.
Selectivity: Open admission.

BASIC COSTS (2008-2009)

Tuition and fees: $2,700; out-of-state residents $4,830.
Per-credit charge: $71; out-of-state residents $142.

FINANCIAL AID PICTURE

Students with need: Need-based aid available for full-time and part-time students. Work study available nights.

Students without need: This college awards aid only to students with need.

FINANCIAL AID PROCEDURES

Forms required: FAFSA.

Dates and Deadlines: Priority date 6/30; no closing date. Applicants notified on a rolling basis starting 7/30.

CONTACT

JoeAnn Cousette, Financial Aid Coordinator
9500 Old Greensboro Road, Tuscaloosa, AL 35405-8522
(205) 391-2376

Snead State Community College

Boaz, Alabama
www.snead.edu Federal Code: 001038

2-year public community college in small town.
Enrollment: 2,249 undergrads.
Selectivity: Open admission; but selective for some programs.

BASIC COSTS (2008-2009)

Tuition and fees: $2,820; out-of-state residents $4,950.
Per-credit charge: $71; out-of-state residents $142.
Room and board: $3,290.

FINANCIAL AID PICTURE

Students with need: Need-based aid available for full-time and part-time students. Work study available nights.

Students without need: No-need awards available for academics, alumni affiliation, art, athletics, leadership, music/drama.

FINANCIAL AID PROCEDURES

Forms required: FAFSA.

Dates and Deadlines: Priority date 4/15; no closing date. Applicants notified on a rolling basis starting 4/15.

CONTACT

Amanda Harbison, Financial Aid Officer
PO Box 734, Boaz, AL 35957-0734
(256) 840-4127

South University: Montgomery

Montgomery, Alabama
www.southuniversity.edu Federal Code: 004463

4-year for-profit business and health science college in small city.
Enrollment: 513 undergrads, 45% part-time. 60 full-time freshmen.

BASIC COSTS (2008-2009)

Tuition and fees: $14,085.

FINANCIAL AID PICTURE (2007-2008)

Students with need: Need-based aid available for full-time and part-time students.

Students without need: This college awards aid only to students with need.

FINANCIAL AID PROCEDURES

Forms required: FAFSA.

Dates and Deadlines: No deadline. Applicants notified on a rolling basis starting 6/1.

Transfers: No deadline. Applicants notified on a rolling basis.

CONTACT

Yvonne Miller, Director of Financial Aid
5355 Vaughn Road, Montgomery, AL 36116-1120
(334) 395-8800

Southeastern Bible College

Birmingham, Alabama
www.sebc.edu Federal Code: 013857

4-year private Bible college in very large city, affiliated with nondenominational tradition.
Enrollment: 197 undergrads, 18% part-time. 18 full-time freshmen.
Selectivity: Admits over 75% of applicants.

BASIC COSTS (2008-2009)

Tuition and fees: $10,610.
Per-credit charge: $345.
Room only: $2,450.

FINANCIAL AID PICTURE (2008-2009)

Students with need: 24% of average financial aid package awarded as scholarships/grants, 76% awarded as loans/jobs. Need-based aid available for part-time students.

Students without need: No-need awards available for academics, leadership, music/drama, state/district residency.

FINANCIAL AID PROCEDURES

Forms required: FAFSA, institutional form.

Dates and Deadlines: No deadline.

Transfers: No deadline. Applicants notified on a rolling basis.

CONTACT

Ann Campbell, Director of Financial Aid
2545 Valleydale Road, Birmingham, AL 35244-2083
(205) 970-9215

Southern Union State Community College

Wadley, Alabama
www.suscc.edu Federal Code: 001040

2-year public community and technical college in small city.
Enrollment: 4,810 undergrads.
Selectivity: Open admission; but selective for some programs.

BASIC COSTS (2008-2009)

Tuition and fees: $2,700; out-of-state residents $4,830.
Per-credit charge: $71; out-of-state residents $142.
Room and board: $3,200.

FINANCIAL AID PICTURE

Students with need: Need-based aid available for full-time and part-time students.

FINANCIAL AID PROCEDURES

Forms required: FAFSA.

Dates and Deadlines: Priority date 7/1; no closing date. Applicants notified on a rolling basis.

CONTACT

Ellen Canada, Director of Financial Aid
750 Roberts Street, Wadley, AL 36276
(256) 395-2215

Spring Hill College

Mobile, Alabama
www.shc.edu Federal Code: 001041

4-year private liberal arts college in large city, affiliated with Roman Catholic Church.
Enrollment: 1,308 undergrads, 11% part-time. 343 full-time freshmen.
Selectivity: Admits 50 to 75% of applicants.

BASIC COSTS (2009-2010)
Tuition and fees: $25,450.
Per-credit charge: $890.
Room and board: $9,730.

FINANCIAL AID PICTURE (2008-2009)
Students with need: Out of 303 full-time freshmen who applied for aid, 265 were judged to have need. Of these, 265 received aid, and 68 had their full need met. Average financial aid package met 85% of need; average scholarship/grant was $17,302; average loan was $4,325. For part-time students, average financial aid package was $6,560.
Students without need: 80 full-time freshmen who did not demonstrate need for aid received scholarships/grants; average award was $13,104. No-need awards available for academics, alumni affiliation, athletics, job skills, leadership, minority status, state/district residency.
Scholarships offered: ***Merit:*** Spring Hill Scholars scholarships; full tuition and fees annually for 4 years; based on academic excellence, leadership, service, 3.5 GPA and 28 ACT/1230 SAT; 10 awarded. Trustee Honors Scholarship; $16,000-$18,000 annually; based on 3.5 GPA and 28 ACT/1230 SAT. Presidential Honors Scholarship; $13,000-$15,000 annually; based on grades, test scores, and leadership potential. Portier Scholarship; $12,000-$14,000 annually; based on grades, test scores, and leadership potential. Ignatian Leadership Award; $11,000-$13,000 annually; based on grades, test scores, and leadership potential. Gautrelet Award; $5,000-$7,500 annually; based on leadership, service, and potential contributions to the college community. ***Athletic:*** 20 full-time freshmen received athletic scholarships; average amount $5,429.
Cumulative student debt: 72% of graduating class had student loans; average debt was $13,761.

FINANCIAL AID PROCEDURES
Forms required: FAFSA, state aid form.
Dates and Deadlines: Priority date 3/1; no closing date. Applicants notified on a rolling basis starting 2/15; must reply by 5/1 or within 2 week(s) of notification.
Transfers: No deadline. Applicants notified on a rolling basis starting 2/1; must reply within 2 week(s) of notification. Transfer scholarships awarded to students transferring from an accredited college or university with 3.0 GPA. Scholarships range from $4,000-$10,000 annually and are renewable with 2.5 GPA. Transfer students who are members of Phi Theta Kappa and/or transfer students who plan to pursue a degree in nursing may receive additional scholarship funding.

CONTACT
Ellen Foster, Director of Financial Aid
4000 Dauphin Street, Mobile, AL 36608-1791
(251) 380-3460

Talladega College

Talladega, Alabama — Federal Code: 001046
www.talladega.edu — CSS Code: 1800

4-year private liberal arts college in large town, affiliated with United Church of Christ.
Enrollment: 631 undergrads, 15% part-time. 254 full-time freshmen.
Selectivity: Open admission; but selective for some programs.

BASIC COSTS (2008-2009)
Tuition and fees: $7,348.
Per-credit charge: $280.
Room and board: $4,420.

FINANCIAL AID PICTURE (2008-2009)
Students with need: Need-based aid available for full-time and part-time students.
Students without need: This college awards aid only to students with need.

FINANCIAL AID PROCEDURES
Forms required: FAFSA, CSS PROFILE, state aid form, institutional form.
Dates and Deadlines: Priority date 4/15; no closing date. Applicants notified on a rolling basis; must reply within 2 week(s) of notification.
Transfers: No deadline. Applicants notified on a rolling basis.

CONTACT
Michelle Burwell, Director of Financial Aid
627 West Battle Street, Talladega, AL 35160
(256) 761-6256

Troy University

Troy, Alabama
www.troy.edu — Federal Code: 001047

4-year public university in large town.
Enrollment: 20,899 undergrads, 51% part-time. 1,827 full-time freshmen.
Selectivity: Admits 50 to 75% of applicants.

BASIC COSTS (2008-2009)
Tuition and fees: $5,410; out-of-state residents $10,900.
Per-credit charge: $200; out-of-state residents $400.
Room and board: $5,286.

FINANCIAL AID PICTURE (2008-2009)
Students with need: For part-time students, average financial aid package was $4,353.
Students without need: No-need awards available for academics, alumni affiliation, art, athletics, leadership, minority status, music/drama, ROTC.

FINANCIAL AID PROCEDURES
Forms required: FAFSA, institutional form.
Dates and Deadlines: Closing date 5/1. Applicants notified on a rolling basis starting 5/1; must reply within 2 week(s) of notification.

CONTACT
Carol Supri, Director, Financial Aid
University Avenue, Adams Administration 111, Troy, AL 36082
(334) 670-3186

Tuskegee University

Tuskegee, Alabama — Federal Code: 001050
www.tuskegee.edu — CSS Code: 1813

4-year private university and liberal arts college in small town.
Enrollment: 2,541 undergrads, 3% part-time. 723 full-time freshmen.
Selectivity: Admits 50 to 75% of applicants.

BASIC COSTS (2009-2010)
Tuition and fees: $16,160.
Per-credit charge: $500.
Room and board: $7,350.

FINANCIAL AID PICTURE (2008-2009)
Students with need: 37% of average financial aid package awarded as scholarships/grants, 63% awarded as loans/jobs. Need-based aid available for part-time students.
Students without need: No-need awards available for academics, athletics, ROTC, state/district residency.

FINANCIAL AID PROCEDURES
Forms required: FAFSA, CSS PROFILE, institutional form.
Dates and Deadlines: Closing date 3/31. Applicants notified on a rolling basis starting 5/15; must reply within 2 week(s) of notification.

CONTACT

A. James, Director, Financial Aid Services
102 Old Administration Building, Tuskegee, AL 36088
(334) 724-4733

University of Alabama

Tuscaloosa, Alabama
www.ua.edu Federal Code: 001051

4-year public university in small city.
Enrollment: 22,046 undergrads, 7% part-time. 4,493 full-time freshmen.
Selectivity: Admits 50 to 75% of applicants.

BASIC COSTS (2008-2009)

Tuition and fees: $6,400; out-of-state residents $18,000.
Room and board: $6,430.

FINANCIAL AID PICTURE (2007-2008)

Students with need: Out of 2,170 full-time freshmen who applied for aid, 1,429 were judged to have need. Of these, 1,378 received aid, and 278 had their full need met. Average financial aid package met 73% of need; average scholarship/grant was $4,119; average loan was $3,596. For part-time students, average financial aid package was $8,860.
Students without need: 1,718 full-time freshmen who did not demonstrate need for aid received scholarships/grants; average award was $5,072. No-need awards available for academics, alumni affiliation, art, athletics, leadership, minority status, music/drama, ROTC, state/district residency.
Scholarships offered: 96 full-time freshmen received athletic scholarships; average amount $18,897.
Cumulative student debt: 49% of graduating class had student loans; average debt was $18,896.

FINANCIAL AID PROCEDURES

Forms required: FAFSA.
Dates and Deadlines: Priority date 3/1; no closing date. Applicants notified on a rolling basis starting 4/1; must reply within 3 week(s) of notification.
Transfers: No deadline. Applicants notified on a rolling basis. Scholarship opportunities for transfer students.

CONTACT

Jeanetta Allen, Director, Student Financial Aid
Box 870132, Tuscaloosa, AL 35487-0132
(205) 348-6756

University of Alabama at Birmingham

Birmingham, Alabama
www.uab.edu Federal Code: 001052

4-year public university in very large city.
Enrollment: 9,989 undergrads, 25% part-time. 1,392 full-time freshmen.
Selectivity: Admits over 75% of applicants.

BASIC COSTS (2008-2009)

Tuition and fees: $5,696; out-of-state residents $12,806.
Per-credit charge: $158; out-of-state residents $395.
Room and board: $7,500.

FINANCIAL AID PICTURE (2007-2008)

Students with need: Out of 885 full-time freshmen who applied for aid, 632 were judged to have need. Of these, 619 received aid, and 110 had their full need met. Average financial aid package met 43% of need; average scholarship/grant was $4,087; average loan was $3,776. For part-time students, average financial aid package was $6,198.
Students without need: 348 full-time freshmen who did not demonstrate need for aid received scholarships/grants; average award was $6,803. No-need awards available for academics, alumni affiliation, art, athletics, leadership, minority status, music/drama, ROTC.
Scholarships offered: 81 full-time freshmen received athletic scholarships; average amount $13,354.

FINANCIAL AID PROCEDURES

Forms required: FAFSA, institutional form.
Dates and Deadlines: Priority date 4/1; no closing date. Applicants notified on a rolling basis starting 4/1; must reply within 4 week(s) of notification.
Transfers: Must reply within 4 week(s) of notification.

CONTACT

Jan May, Director of Financial Aid
HUC 260, 1530 Third Avenue South, Birmingham, AL 35294-1150
(205) 934-8223

University of Alabama in Huntsville

Huntsville, Alabama
www.uah.edu Federal Code: 001055

4-year public university in small city.
Enrollment: 5,689 undergrads, 24% part-time. 765 full-time freshmen.
Selectivity: Admits over 75% of applicants.

BASIC COSTS (2008-2009)

Tuition and fees: $5,952; out-of-state residents $13,092.
Per-credit charge: $193; out-of-state residents $425.
Room and board: $6,100.
Additional info: Per-credit-hour rate decreases as number of hours registered increases.

FINANCIAL AID PICTURE (2008-2009)

Students with need: Out of 680 full-time freshmen who applied for aid, 317 were judged to have need. Of these, 316 received aid, and 64 had their full need met. Average financial aid package met 68% of need; average scholarship/grant was $5,054; average loan was $4,521. For part-time students, average financial aid package was $6,093.
Students without need: 266 full-time freshmen who did not demonstrate need for aid received scholarships/grants; average award was $3,788. No-need awards available for academics, art, athletics, leadership, minority status, music/drama, ROTC.
Scholarships offered: ***Merit:*** Application deadline for institutional scholarships is December 1st. ***Athletic:*** 43 full-time freshmen received athletic scholarships; average amount $5,668.
Cumulative student debt: 32% of graduating class had student loans; average debt was $21,882.

FINANCIAL AID PROCEDURES

Forms required: FAFSA.
Dates and Deadlines: Priority date 4/1; closing date 7/31. Applicants notified on a rolling basis starting 4/1; must reply within 2 week(s) of notification.
Transfers: First-time regularly admitted transfer students who have earned transfer credits from an accredited 2-year institution of higher learning considered for one-time transfer scholarship award. Preference given to students who have demonstrated academic potential and leadership and are members of Phi Theta Kappa. Super Scholar Transfer Scholarship requires 3.75 college GPA and is currently valued at $2,000 plus a $500 textbook scholarship, renewable for an additional year. UAH Transfer Merit Scholarship requires 3.25 college GPA and is currently valued at $1,000 plus a $500 textbook scholarship, renewable for an additional year. Eligible students should submit the UAH Scholarship Application to apply.

CONTACT

Andy Weaver, Director of Student Financial Services
UAH Office of Undergraduate Admissions, Huntsville, AL 35899
(256) 824-6241

University of Mobile
Mobile, Alabama
www.umobile.edu Federal Code: 001029

4-year private university and liberal arts college in small city, affiliated with Baptist faith.
Enrollment: 1,422 undergrads, 11% part-time. 248 full-time freshmen.
Selectivity: Admits 50 to 75% of applicants.

BASIC COSTS (2008-2009)
Tuition and fees: $13,970.
Per-credit charge: $480.
Room and board: $7,170.

FINANCIAL AID PICTURE (2008-2009)
Students with need: Out of 194 full-time freshmen who applied for aid, 194 were judged to have need. Of these, 193 received aid. Average financial aid package met 70% of need; average scholarship/grant was $8,469; average loan was $3,302. For part-time students, average financial aid package was $3,004.
Students without need: 9 full-time freshmen who did not demonstrate need for aid received scholarships/grants; average award was $5,210. No-need awards available for academics, alumni affiliation, athletics, music/drama, religious affiliation, ROTC, state/district residency.
Scholarships offered: 17 full-time freshmen received athletic scholarships; average amount $13,572.

FINANCIAL AID PROCEDURES
Forms required: FAFSA, state aid form, institutional form.
Dates and Deadlines: Priority date 2/28; no closing date. Applicants notified on a rolling basis starting 2/1; must reply within 2 week(s) of notification.

CONTACT
Marie Batson, Associate Vice President for Enrollment Management
5735 College Parkway, Mobile, AL 36613-2842
(251) 442-2252

University of Montevallo
Montevallo, Alabama
www.montevallo.edu Federal Code: 001004

4-year public university and liberal arts college in small town.
Enrollment: 2,558 undergrads. 402 full-time freshmen.
Selectivity: Admits 50 to 75% of applicants.

BASIC COSTS (2008-2009)
Tuition and fees: $6,620; out-of-state residents $12,770.
Per-credit charge: $205; out-of-state residents $410.
Room and board: $4,356.

FINANCIAL AID PICTURE (2007-2008)
Students with need: Out of 269 full-time freshmen who applied for aid, 205 were judged to have need. Of these, 198 received aid, and 46 had their full need met. Average financial aid package met 70% of need; average scholarship/grant was $3,995; average loan was $3,275. For part-time students, average financial aid package was $4,509.
Students without need: 129 full-time freshmen who did not demonstrate need for aid received scholarships/grants; average award was $4,960. No-need awards available for academics, art, athletics, job skills, leadership, minority status, music/drama, religious affiliation, ROTC.
Scholarships offered: 30 full-time freshmen received athletic scholarships; average amount $6,542.

FINANCIAL AID PROCEDURES
Forms required: FAFSA.
Dates and Deadlines: Priority date 4/1; no closing date. Applicants notified by 5/10; must reply within 2 week(s) of notification.

CONTACT
Maria Parker, Director of Financial Aid
Station 6030, Montevallo, AL 35115-6030
(205) 665-6050

University of North Alabama
Florence, Alabama
www.una.edu Federal Code: 001016

4-year public university in large town.
Enrollment: 5,486 undergrads.
Selectivity: Admits over 75% of applicants.

BASIC COSTS (2008-2009)
Tuition and fees: $5,598; out-of-state residents $10,188.
Per-credit charge: $153; out-of-state residents $306.
Room and board: $4,658.

FINANCIAL AID PICTURE (2007-2008)
Students with need: Need-based aid available for full-time and part-time students. Work study available nights, weekends, and for part-time students.
Students without need: No-need awards available for academics, art, athletics, leadership, minority status, music/drama, ROTC, state/district residency.

FINANCIAL AID PROCEDURES
Forms required: FAFSA.
Dates and Deadlines: Priority date 4/1; no closing date. Applicants notified on a rolling basis starting 5/31; must reply within 2 week(s) of notification.

CONTACT
Ben Baker, Director of Student Financial Services
One Harrison Plaza, UNA Box 5011, Florence, AL 35632-0001
(256) 765-4590

University of South Alabama
Mobile, Alabama
www.southalabama.edu Federal Code: 001057

4-year public university in small city.
Enrollment: 10,701 undergrads, 25% part-time. 1,543 full-time freshmen.
Selectivity: Admits over 75% of applicants.

BASIC COSTS (2008-2009)
Tuition and fees: $5,512; out-of-state residents $9,922.
Per-credit charge: $147; out-of-state residents $294.
Room and board: $5,308.
Additional info: Tuition/fee waivers available for minority students.

FINANCIAL AID PICTURE (2007-2008)
Students with need: Need-based aid available for full-time and part-time students.
Students without need: No-need awards available for academics, alumni affiliation, art, athletics, minority status, music/drama, ROTC, state/district residency.

FINANCIAL AID PROCEDURES
Forms required: FAFSA, institutional form.
Dates and Deadlines: Priority date 5/1; no closing date. Applicants notified on a rolling basis starting 5/15.

CONTACT
Emily Johnston, Director of Financial Aid
Meisler Hall, Suite 2500, Mobile, AL 36688-0002
(251) 460-6231

University of West Alabama

Livingston, Alabama
www.uwa.edu Federal Code: 001024

4-year public university in small town.
Enrollment: 1,867 undergrads, 10% part-time. 298 full-time freshmen.
Selectivity: Admits 50 to 75% of applicants.

BASIC COSTS (2008-2009)

Tuition and fees: $5,200; out-of-state residents $9,800.
Per-credit charge: $195; out-of-state residents $390.
Room and board: $4,104.

FINANCIAL AID PICTURE (2008-2009)

Students with need: Average financial aid package met 68% of need; average scholarship/grant was $3,102; average loan was $3,116. Need-based aid available for part-time students.
Students without need: No-need awards available for academics, alumni affiliation, athletics, leadership, music/drama, state/district residency.
Cumulative student debt: 76% of graduating class had student loans; average debt was $18,540.

FINANCIAL AID PROCEDURES

Forms required: FAFSA.
Dates and Deadlines: Priority date 4/1; no closing date. Applicants notified on a rolling basis starting 6/1; must reply within 2 week(s) of notification.

CONTACT

Don Rainer, Director of Financial Aid
Station 4, Livingston, AL 35470
(205) 652-3576

Wallace State Community College at Hanceville

Hanceville, Alabama
www.wallacestate.edu Federal Code: 007871

2-year public health science and community college in rural community.
Enrollment: 3,078 full-time undergrads.
Selectivity: Open admission; but selective for some programs.

BASIC COSTS (2008-2009)

Tuition and fees: $2,700; out-of-state residents $4,830.
Per-credit charge: $71; out-of-state residents $142.
Room only: $1,450.
Additional info: Room only-Dorms $1,550; House $1,100.

FINANCIAL AID PICTURE

Students with need: Need-based aid available for full-time and part-time students. Work study available nights.
Students without need: This college awards aid only to students with need.

FINANCIAL AID PROCEDURES

Forms required: FAFSA.
Dates and Deadlines: Priority date 5/1; no closing date. Applicants notified on a rolling basis starting 7/15; must reply within 2 week(s) of notification.
Transfers: No deadline.

CONTACT

Becky Graves, Director of Student Financial Aid
PO Box 2000, Hanceville, AL 35077-2000
(256) 352-8182

Alaska

Alaska Bible College

Glennallen, Alaska
www.akbible.edu Federal Code: 014325

4-year private Bible college in rural community, affiliated with nondenominational tradition.
Enrollment: 26 undergrads.
Selectivity: Open admission; but selective for some programs.

BASIC COSTS (2009-2010)

Tuition and fees: $7,524.
Per-credit charge: $315.
Room and board: $5,540.

FINANCIAL AID PICTURE (2008-2009)

Students with need: Need-based aid available for full-time students.
Students without need: This college awards aid only to students with need.

FINANCIAL AID PROCEDURES

Forms required: institutional form.
Dates and Deadlines: Priority date 4/30; closing date 8/1. Applicants notified on a rolling basis; must reply within 2 week(s) of notification.

CONTACT

Bill Lambert, Financial Aid Officer
Box 289, Glennallen, AK 99588-0289
(907) 822-3201

Alaska Pacific University

Anchorage, Alaska
www.alaskapacific.edu Federal Code: 001061

4-year private university and liberal arts college in large city.
Enrollment: 493 undergrads, 34% part-time. 66 full-time freshmen.
Selectivity: Admits less than 50% of applicants.

BASIC COSTS (2008-2009)

Tuition and fees: $22,610.
Per-credit charge: $940.
Room and board: $8,884.
Additional info: Tuition at time of enrollment locked for 4 years.

FINANCIAL AID PICTURE (2008-2009)

Students with need: Average financial aid package met 89% of need; average scholarship/grant was $7,500; average loan was $3,375. For part-time students, average financial aid package was $4,251.
Students without need: No-need awards available for academics, alumni affiliation, leadership, religious affiliation, state/district residency.

FINANCIAL AID PROCEDURES

Forms required: FAFSA.
Dates and Deadlines: Priority date 4/15; no closing date. Applicants notified on a rolling basis starting 2/1; must reply within 4 week(s) of notification.
Transfers: Priority date 6/1; no deadline. Applicants notified on a rolling basis; must reply within 2 week(s) of notification.

CONTACT

Jo Holland, Director, Student Financial Services
4101 University Drive, Anchorage, AK 99508
(907) 564-8341

Prince William Sound Community College

Valdez, Alaska
www.pwscc.edu Federal Code: 011462

2-year public community college in small town.
Enrollment: 155 undergrads.
Selectivity: Open admission.

BASIC COSTS (2008-2009)

Tuition and fees: $3,840.
Per-credit charge: $116.
Room and board: $4,730.

FINANCIAL AID PICTURE

Students with need: Need-based aid available for full-time and part-time students.
Students without need: No-need awards available for state/district residency.

FINANCIAL AID PROCEDURES

Forms required: FAFSA.
Dates and Deadlines: Priority date 6/30; no closing date. Applicants notified on a rolling basis.
Transfers: Priority date 4/1; closing date 5/1.

CONTACT

Gianna Thornton, Assistant to the Director of Student Services
Box 97, Valdez, AK 99686
(907) 834-1666

University of Alaska Anchorage

Anchorage, Alaska
www.uaa.alaska.edu Federal Code: 011462

4-year public university in large city.
Enrollment: 10,854 undergrads, 41% part-time. 1,287 full-time freshmen.
Selectivity: Open admission; but selective for some programs.

BASIC COSTS (2008-2009)

Tuition and fees: $4,580; out-of-state residents $14,000.
Per-credit charge: $134; out-of-state residents $448.
Room and board: $7,982.

FINANCIAL AID PICTURE

Students with need: Need-based aid available for full-time and part-time students. Work study available nights, weekends, and for part-time students.
Students without need: No-need awards available for academics, athletics.

FINANCIAL AID PROCEDURES

Forms required: FAFSA, institutional form.
Dates and Deadlines: Priority date 4/1; closing date 8/1. Applicants notified on a rolling basis starting 3/15; must reply within 4 week(s) of notification.
Transfers: Closing date 4/15.

CONTACT

Ted Malone, Director of Financial Aid
PO Box 141020, Anchorage, AK 99514 1629
(907) 786-1586

University of Alaska Fairbanks

Fairbanks, Alaska
www.uaf.edu Federal Code: 001063

4-year public university in small city.
Enrollment: 4,883 undergrads, 33% part-time. 763 full-time freshmen.
Selectivity: Admits 50 to 75% of applicants. GED not accepted.

BASIC COSTS (2008-2009)

Tuition and fees: $4,828; out-of-state residents $14,248.
Per-credit charge: $134; out-of-state residents $448.
Room and board: $7,190.
Additional info: Estimated course and lab fees: $500 per year.

FINANCIAL AID PICTURE (2007-2008)

Students with need: Out of 617 full-time freshmen who applied for aid, 346 were judged to have need. Of these, 326 received aid, and 135 had their full need met. Average financial aid package met 55% of need; average scholarship/grant was $4,999; average loan was $8,604. For part-time students, average financial aid package was $8,821.
Students without need: 210 full-time freshmen who did not demonstrate need for aid received scholarships/grants; average award was $7,552. No-need awards available for academics, art, athletics, leadership, music/drama, ROTC, state/district residency.
Scholarships offered: 17 full-time freshmen received athletic scholarships; average amount $14,009.
Cumulative student debt: 54% of graduating class had student loans; average debt was $28,597.

FINANCIAL AID PROCEDURES

Forms required: FAFSA.
Dates and Deadlines: Priority date 2/15; closing date 7/1. Applicants notified on a rolling basis starting 3/1; must reply within 2 week(s) of notification.

CONTACT

Deanna Dieringer, Director of Financial Aid
PO Box 757480, Fairbanks, AK 99775-7480
(888) 474-7256

University of Alaska Southeast

Juneau, Alaska
www.uas.alaska.edu Federal Code: 001065

4-year public university and liberal arts college in large town.
Enrollment: 1,145 undergrads, 50% part-time. 160 full-time freshmen.
Selectivity: Admits over 75% of applicants.

BASIC COSTS (2008-2009)

Tuition and fees: $4,303; out-of-state residents $11,839.
Per-credit charge: $143; out-of-state residents $457.
Room and board: $7,583.
Additional info: Tuition reported is for lower division offerings.

FINANCIAL AID PICTURE (2008-2009)

Students with need: Average financial aid package met 45% of need; average scholarship/grant was $3,517; average loan was $3,264. For part-time students, average financial aid package was $3,564.
Students without need: No-need awards available for academics, leadership.
Cumulative student debt: 41% of graduating class had student loans; average debt was $20,815.
Additional info: Transfer, continuing, and freshman scholarship deadline March 1.

FINANCIAL AID PROCEDURES

Forms required: FAFSA.
Dates and Deadlines: Priority date 6/1; no closing date. Applicants notified on a rolling basis starting 2/15; must reply within 3 week(s) of notification.

CONTACT

Barbara Burnett, Manager of Financial Aid
11120 Glacier Highway, Juneau, AK 99801-8681
(907) 796-6255

Arizona

Anthem College
Phoenix, Arizona
www.hightechinstitute.edu Federal Code: 022631

2-year for-profit technical college in very large city.
Enrollment: 5,745 undergrads.
Selectivity: Open admission.

BASIC COSTS (2008-2009)
Additional info: Costs for diploma programs range from $12,150 to $25,850. Fees, books, uniforms and tools included.

FINANCIAL AID PICTURE
Students with need: Need-based aid available for full-time students.
Students without need: This college awards aid only to students with need.

FINANCIAL AID PROCEDURES
Dates and Deadlines: No deadline.

CONTACT
Joshua Esquivel, Financial Aid Director
1515 East Indian School Road, Phoenix, AZ 85014-4901
(602) 279-9700

Arizona State University
Tempe, Arizona
www.asu.edu Federal Code: 001081

4-year public university in very large city.
Enrollment: 52,883 undergrads, 19% part-time. 8,664 full-time freshmen.
Selectivity: Admits over 75% of applicants.

BASIC COSTS (2008-2009)
Tuition and fees: $5,661; out-of-state residents $17,949.
Per-credit charge: $386; out-of-state residents $737.
Room and board: $8,790.

FINANCIAL AID PICTURE (2007-2008)
Students with need: Out of 5,188 full-time freshmen who applied for aid, 3,472 were judged to have need. Of these, 3,472 received aid, and 900 had their full need met. Average financial aid package met 63% of need; average scholarship/grant was $7,181; average loan was $3,098. For part-time students, average financial aid package was $6,595.
Students without need: 2,058 full-time freshmen who did not demonstrate need for aid received scholarships/grants; average award was $7,054. No-need awards available for academics, art, athletics, leadership, music/drama, ROTC.
Scholarships offered: 57 full-time freshmen received athletic scholarships; average amount $14,116.
Cumulative student debt: 43% of graduating class had student loans; average debt was $17,732.

FINANCIAL AID PROCEDURES
Forms required: FAFSA.
Dates and Deadlines: Priority date 3/1; no closing date. Applicants notified on a rolling basis.

CONTACT
Craig Fennell, Director of Student Financial Assistance
Box 870112, Tempe, AZ 85287-0112
(480) 965-3355

Arizona Western College
Yuma, Arizona
www.azwestern.edu Federal Code: 001071

2-year public community college in small city.
Enrollment: 6,690 undergrads, 66% part-time. 442 full-time freshmen.
Selectivity: Open admission; but selective for some programs.

BASIC COSTS (2008-2009)
Tuition and fees: $1,680; out-of-state residents $6,240.
Per-credit charge: $56; out-of-state residents $208.
Room and board: $4,898.

FINANCIAL AID PICTURE (2008-2009)
Students with need: Need-based aid available for part-time students. Work study available nights, weekends, and for part-time students.
Students without need: No-need awards available for academics, athletics.

FINANCIAL AID PROCEDURES
Forms required: FAFSA, institutional form.
Dates and Deadlines: Priority date 4/1; no closing date. Applicants notified on a rolling basis starting 5/1.

CONTACT
Lisa Seale, Director of Financial Aid
PO Box 929, Yuma, AZ 85366-0929
(928) 344-7634

Art Center Design College
Tucson, Arizona
www.theartcenter.edu Federal Code: 024915

4-year for-profit visual arts college in very large city.
Enrollment: 346 undergrads. 29 full-time freshmen.
Selectivity: Admits over 75% of applicants.

BASIC COSTS (2008-2009)
Tuition and fees: $16,320.
Per-credit charge: $680.

FINANCIAL AID PICTURE
Students with need: Need-based aid available for full-time and part-time students. Work study available nights, weekends, and for part-time students.
Students without need: This college awards aid only to students with need.
Scholarships offered: Board of Trustees Scholarship, Transfer Student Scholarship, Scholarship for Continuing Students.

FINANCIAL AID PROCEDURES
Forms required: FAFSA.
Dates and Deadlines: No deadline.
Transfers: No deadline. Applicants notified on a rolling basis.

CONTACT
Amy Woods, Director of Student Services
2525 North Country Club Road, Tucson, AZ 85716
(520) 325-0123

Art Institute of Phoenix
Phoenix, Arizona
www.artinstitutes.edu/phoenix Federal Code: 040513

3-year for-profit culinary school and visual arts college in very large city.
Enrollment: 1,125 undergrads.

BASIC COSTS (2008-2009)
Tuition and fees: $20,405.
Per-credit charge: $449.

FINANCIAL AID PICTURE
Students with need: Need-based aid available for full-time and part-time students.

FINANCIAL AID PROCEDURES
Forms required: FAFSA.
Dates and Deadlines: No deadline.

CONTACT
Lori Ryan, Director of Administrative and Financial Services
2233 West Dunlap Avenue, Phoenix, AZ 85021-2859

Central Arizona College
Coolidge, Arizona
www.centralaz.edu Federal Code: 007283

2-year public community college in rural community.
Enrollment: 1,300 full-time undergrads.
Selectivity: Open admission; but selective for some programs.

BASIC COSTS (2008-2009)
Tuition and fees: $1,705; out-of-state residents $7,501.
Per-credit charge: $60; out-of-state residents $120.
Room and board: $4,645.

FINANCIAL AID PICTURE
Students with need: Need-based aid available for full-time and part-time students. Work study available nights, weekends, and for part-time students.

FINANCIAL AID PROCEDURES
Forms required: FAFSA.
Dates and Deadlines: Priority date 5/1; closing date 7/15. Must reply within 3 week(s) of notification.

CONTACT
Russ Banta, Finance Office
8470 North Overfield Road, Coolidge, AZ 85228-9778
(520) 494-5425

Chandler-Gilbert Community College: Pecos
Chandler, Arizona
www.cgc.maricopa.edu Federal Code: 030722

2-year public community college in small city.
Enrollment: 1,776 undergrads, 58% part-time. 311 full-time freshmen.
Selectivity: Open admission.

BASIC COSTS (2008-2009)
Tuition and fees: $2,145; out-of-state residents $8,595.
Per-credit charge: $71; out-of-state residents $286.

FINANCIAL AID PICTURE (2008-2009)
Students with need: Work study available nights, weekends, and for part-time students.

CONTACT
Doug Bullock, Director of Financial Aid
2626 East Pecos Road, Chandler, AZ 85225

Cochise College
Douglas, Arizona
www.cochise.edu Federal Code: 001072

2-year public community college in large town.
Enrollment: 2,879 undergrads, 68% part-time. 2,464 full-time freshmen.
Selectivity: Open admission; but selective for some programs.

BASIC COSTS (2009-2010)
Tuition and fees: $1,630; out-of-state residents $8,770.
Per-credit charge: $52; out-of-state residents $290.
Room and board: $5,300.

FINANCIAL AID PICTURE (2007-2008)
Students with need: Out of 329 full-time freshmen who applied for aid, 274 were judged to have need. Of these, 266 received aid. For part-time students, average financial aid package was $6,118.
Students without need: 17 full-time freshmen who did not demonstrate need for aid received scholarships/grants; average award was $830. No-need awards available for academics, athletics.
Cumulative student debt: 25% of graduating class had student loans; average debt was $7,434.

FINANCIAL AID PROCEDURES
Forms required: FAFSA, institutional form.
Dates and Deadlines: Closing date 4/15. Applicants notified on a rolling basis starting 6/15; must reply within 2 week(s) of notification.
Transfers: Priority date 4/15; no deadline. Applicants notified on a rolling basis.

CONTACT
Dartle Atherton, Director of Financial Aid
901 North Colombo Avenue, Sierra Vista, AZ 85635
(520) 515-5417

DeVry University: Phoenix
Phoenix, Arizona
www.devry.edu Federal Code: 008322

4-year for-profit university in large city.
Enrollment: 1,081 undergrads, 37% part-time. 160 full-time freshmen.
Selectivity: Admits over 75% of applicants.

BASIC COSTS (2008-2009)
Tuition and fees: $14,130.
Per-credit charge: $515.

FINANCIAL AID PICTURE (2007-2008)
Students with need: Need-based aid available for full-time and part-time students.
Students without need: This college awards aid only to students with need.

FINANCIAL AID PROCEDURES
Forms required: FAFSA.
Dates and Deadlines: No deadline. Applicants notified on a rolling basis.

CONTACT
Kathy Wyse, Dean of Student Finances
2149 West Dunlap Avenue, Phoenix, AZ 85021-2995
(602) 870-9229

Dine College
Tsaile, Arizona
www.dinecollege.edu Federal Code: 008246

2-year public community college in rural community.
Enrollment: 550 full-time undergrads.
Selectivity: Open admission.

BASIC COSTS (2008-2009)
Tuition and fees: $850.
Per-credit charge: $30.
Room and board: $3,764.

FINANCIAL AID PICTURE (2007-2008)
Students with need: Need-based aid available for full-time and part-time students.
Students without need: This college awards aid only to students with need.

FINANCIAL AID PROCEDURES
Forms required: FAFSA, institutional form.
Dates and Deadlines: Priority date 4/15; no closing date. Applicants notified on a rolling basis starting 5/1; must reply within 4 week(s) of notification.
Transfers: Priority date 3/1; no deadline. Applicants notified on a rolling basis starting 1/1; must reply within 6 week(s) of notification.

CONTACT
Gary Segay, Director of Financial Aid
Box 67, Tsaile, AZ 86556
(928) 724-6738

Eastern Arizona College
Thatcher, Arizona
www.eac.edu Federal Code: 001073

2-year public community college in large town.
Enrollment: 4,224 undergrads, 58% part-time. 707 full-time freshmen.
Selectivity: Open admission; but selective for some programs.

BASIC COSTS (2008-2009)
Tuition and fees: $1,380; out-of-state residents $7,440.
Per-credit charge: $60; out-of-state residents $120.
Room and board: $4,703.

FINANCIAL AID PICTURE (2008-2009)
Students with need: Average financial aid package met 43% of need; average scholarship/grant was $4,137. For part-time students, average financial aid package was $2,571.
Students without need: No-need awards available for academics, art, athletics, leadership, music/drama, state/district residency.
Scholarships offered: Departmental Scholarships; in-state tuition; based on 2.5 GPA. Academic Scholarships; in-state tuition; based on 3.0 GPA. Performing Arts Scholarships; amounts vary; based on 2.5 GPA and audition.
Additional info: Limited number of tuition waivers for New Mexico residents. Unlimited number of waivers for those meeting WUE requirements.

FINANCIAL AID PROCEDURES
Forms required: FAFSA, institutional form.
Dates and Deadlines: Priority date 3/1; no closing date. Applicants notified on a rolling basis starting 3/15.
Transfers: No deadline. Applicants notified on a rolling basis starting 3/15.

CONTACT
Sharon Montoya, Associate Director of Financial Aid
615 North Stadium Avenue, Thatcher, AZ 85552-0769
(928) 428-8287

Embry-Riddle Aeronautical University: Prescott Campus
Prescott, Arizona
www.embryriddle.edu Federal Code: 014797

4-year private university in large town.
Enrollment: 1,672 undergrads, 8% part-time. 416 full-time freshmen.
Selectivity: Admits over 75% of applicants.

BASIC COSTS (2009-2010)
Tuition and fees: $27,740.
Per-credit charge: $1,120.
Room and board: $8,008.

FINANCIAL AID PICTURE (2008-2009)
Students with need: Out of 347 full-time freshmen who applied for aid, 295 were judged to have need. Of these, 294 received aid. For part-time students, average financial aid package was $14,060.
Students without need: No-need awards available for academics, alumni affiliation, athletics, leadership, ROTC.
Scholarships offered: 15 full-time freshmen received athletic scholarships; average amount $8,982.

FINANCIAL AID PROCEDURES
Forms required: FAFSA.
Dates and Deadlines: No deadline. Applicants notified on a rolling basis starting 3/1; must reply within 4 week(s) of notification.

CONTACT
Barbara Dryden, Director of Financial Aid
3700 Willow Creek Road, Prescott, AZ 86301-3720
(928) 777-3765

Estrella Mountain Community College
Avondale, Arizona
www.estrellamountain.edu Federal Code: 031563

2-year public community college in small city.
Enrollment: 2,156 undergrads, 63% part-time. 273 full-time freshmen.
Selectivity: Open admission.

BASIC COSTS (2008-2009)
Tuition and fees: $2,145; out-of-state residents $8,595.
Per-credit charge: $71; out-of-state residents $286.

FINANCIAL AID PICTURE (2007-2008)
Students with need: Need-based aid available for full-time and part-time students. Work study available nights.
Students without need: No-need awards available for leadership.

FINANCIAL AID PROCEDURES
Dates and Deadlines: Priority date 4/1; no closing date. Applicants notified on a rolling basis starting 4/15.

CONTACT
Rosanna Short, Director, Financial Aid
3000 North Dysart Road, Avondale, AZ 85392-1010
(623) 935-8930

Gateway Community College
Phoenix, Arizona
www.gatewaycc.edu Federal Code: 008303

2-year public community and technical college in very large city.
Enrollment: 5,810 undergrads.

Selectivity: Open admission; but selective for some programs.

BASIC COSTS (2008-2009)

Tuition and fees: $2,145; out-of-state residents $8,085.

Per-credit charge: $71; out-of-state residents $269.

FINANCIAL AID PICTURE (2007-2008)

Students with need: Need-based aid available for full-time and part-time students. Work study available nights, weekends, and for part-time students.

Students without need: No-need awards available for athletics.

FINANCIAL AID PROCEDURES

Forms required: FAFSA, institutional form.

Dates and Deadlines: Priority date 4/15; no closing date. Applicants notified on a rolling basis starting 7/1; must reply within 4 week(s) of notification.

CONTACT

Suzanne Ringle, Director of Financial Aid
108 North 40th Street, Phoenix, AZ 85034
(602) 286-8115

Glendale Community College

Glendale, Arizona
www.gccaz.edu Federal Code: 001076

2-year public community college in small city.

Enrollment: 5,792 undergrads, 60% part-time.

Selectivity: Open admission; but selective for some programs.

BASIC COSTS (2008-2009)

Tuition and fees: $2,115; out-of-state residents $8,595.

Per-credit charge: $71; out-of-state residents $286.

FINANCIAL AID PICTURE (2007-2008)

Students with need: Need-based aid available for full-time and part-time students. Work study available nights, weekends, and for part-time students.

FINANCIAL AID PROCEDURES

Forms required: FAFSA.

Dates and Deadlines: Priority date 4/30; closing date 8/1. Applicants notified on a rolling basis starting 6/1.

CONTACT

Ellen Neel, Director of Financial Aid
6000 West Olive Avenue, Glendale, AZ 85302
(623) 845-3366

Grand Canyon University

Phoenix, Arizona
www.gcu.edu/clgbrd Federal Code: 001074

4-year for-profit university in very large city.

Enrollment: 4,800 undergrads. 366 full-time freshmen.

Selectivity: Admits over 75% of applicants.

BASIC COSTS (2009-2010)

Tuition and fees: $17,050.

Per-credit charge: $687.

Room and board: $8,064.

FINANCIAL AID PICTURE (2008-2009)

Students with need: 15% of average financial aid package awarded as scholarships/grants, 85% awarded as loans/jobs. Need-based aid available for part-time students. Work study available nights, weekends, and for part-time students.

Students without need: No-need awards available for academics, alumni affiliation, athletics, leadership, religious affiliation, ROTC.

FINANCIAL AID PROCEDURES

Forms required: FAFSA.

Dates and Deadlines: No deadline. Applicants notified on a rolling basis.

Transfers: No deadline. Applicants notified on a rolling basis.

CONTACT

David Weems, Director of Financial Aid
3300 West Camelback Road, Phoenix, AZ 85017
(602) 639-6522

IIA College: Mesa

Mesa, Arizona
www.iia.edu Federal Code: 022188

2-year for-profit branch campus and career college in very large city.

Enrollment: 191 undergrads.

Selectivity: Open admission; but selective for some programs.

BASIC COSTS (2009-2010)

Tuition and fees: $11,750.

Additional info: Tuition and fees may vary by program.

FINANCIAL AID PICTURE

Students with need: Need-based aid available for full-time students.

Students without need: This college awards aid only to students with need.

FINANCIAL AID PROCEDURES

Forms required: FAFSA, institutional form.

CONTACT

Rich Dombrowski, Corporate Director of Financial Aid
925 South Gilbert Road, Suite 201, Mesa, AZ 85204-4448
(480) 545-8755

IIA College: Phoenix

Phoenix, Arizona
www.iia.edu Federal Code: 022188

2-year for-profit career college in very large city.

Enrollment: 609 undergrads.

Selectivity: Open admission; but selective for some programs.

BASIC COSTS (2009-2010)

Tuition and fees: $11,750.

Additional info: Tuition and fees may vary by program.

FINANCIAL AID PICTURE

Students with need: Need-based aid available for full-time students.

Students without need: This college awards aid only to students with need.

FINANCIAL AID PROCEDURES

Forms required: FAFSA, institutional form.

Dates and Deadlines: No deadline.

CONTACT

Rich Dombrowski, Corporate Director of Financial Aid
4240 West Bethany Home Road, Phoenix, AZ 85019-1808
(602) 644-7090

IIA College: Tucson

Tucson, Arizona
www.iia.edu Federal Code: 022188

2-year for-profit branch campus and career college in very large city.
Enrollment: 317 undergrads.
Selectivity: Open admission; but selective for some programs.

BASIC COSTS (2009-2010)

Tuition and fees: $11,750.
Additional info: Tuition and fees may vary by program.

FINANCIAL AID PICTURE

Students with need: Need-based aid available for full-time and part-time students.
Students without need: This college awards aid only to students with need.

FINANCIAL AID PROCEDURES

Forms required: FAFSA, institutional form.
Dates and Deadlines: No deadline.

CONTACT

Rich Dombrowski, Corporate Director of Financial Aid
5441 East 22nd Street, Suite 125, Tucson, AZ 85711-5444
(602) 644-7090

Lamson College

Tempe, Arizona
www.lamsoncollege.com Federal Code: 005186

2-year for-profit junior and technical college in very large city.
Enrollment: 460 full-time undergrads.
Selectivity: Open admission.

BASIC COSTS (2008-2009)

Additional info: Per-credit-hour charges vary according to program: $250 to $271; cost of books and supplies ranges from $995 to $3,000, depending on program of study.

FINANCIAL AID PICTURE

Students with need: Need-based aid available for full-time and part-time students.

FINANCIAL AID PROCEDURES

Forms required: FAFSA.
Dates and Deadlines: No deadline. Applicants notified on a rolling basis.

CONTACT

Massus Lindsley, Director of Financial Aid
1126 North Scottsdale Road, Suite 17, Tempe, AZ 85281-1700
(480) 898-7000

Mohave Community College

Kingman, Arizona
www.mohave.edu Federal Code: 011864

2-year public community college in small city.
Enrollment: 5,539 undergrads.
Selectivity: Open admission; but selective for some programs.

BASIC COSTS (2008-2009)

Tuition and fees: $1,850; out-of-state residents $5,390.
Per-credit charge: $59; out-of-state residents $177.

FINANCIAL AID PICTURE

Students with need: Need-based aid available for full-time and part-time students. Work study available nights.

FINANCIAL AID PROCEDURES

Forms required: FAFSA, institutional form.
Dates and Deadlines: Priority date 4/15; no closing date. Applicants notified on a rolling basis starting 5/1; must reply within 2 week(s) of notification.

CONTACT

Bill Osborn, Director of Financial Aid
1971 Jagerson Avenue, Kingman, AZ 86409
(866) 664-2832

Northern Arizona University

Flagstaff, Arizona
www.nau.edu Federal Code: 001082

4-year public university in small city.
Enrollment: 16,887 undergrads, 16% part-time. 2,931 full-time freshmen.
Selectivity: Admits 50 to 75% of applicants.

BASIC COSTS (2008-2009)

Tuition and fees: $5,446; out-of-state residents $16,544.
Per-credit charge: $257; out-of-state residents $635.
Room and board: $7,086.
Additional info: Tuition at time of enrollment locked for 4 years.

FINANCIAL AID PICTURE (2007-2008)

Students with need: Out of 2,217 full-time freshmen who applied for aid, 1,339 were judged to have need. Of these, 1,296 received aid, and 330 had their full need met. Average financial aid package met 72% of need; average scholarship/grant was $5,537; average loan was $3,144. For part-time students, average financial aid package was $7,073.
Students without need: 653 full-time freshmen who did not demonstrate need for aid received scholarships/grants; average award was $3,393. No-need awards available for academics, alumni affiliation, art, athletics, leadership, minority status, music/drama, ROTC, state/district residency.
Scholarships offered: 84 full-time freshmen received athletic scholarships; average amount $10,054.
Cumulative student debt: 53% of graduating class had student loans; average debt was $14,714.

FINANCIAL AID PROCEDURES

Forms required: FAFSA.
Dates and Deadlines: Priority date 2/14; no closing date. Applicants notified on a rolling basis starting 3/15.

CONTACT

Jack Edwards, Director of Financial Aid
PO Box 4084, Flagstaff, AZ 86011-4084
(928) 523-4951

Northland Pioneer College

Holbrook, Arizona
www.npc.edu Federal Code: 011862

2-year public community and technical college in small town.
Enrollment: 3,649 undergrads.
Selectivity: Open admission; but selective for some programs.

BASIC COSTS (2008-2009)

Tuition and fees: $1,440; out-of-state residents $7,050.
Per-credit charge: $48; out-of-state residents $80.

FINANCIAL AID PICTURE (2007-2008)

Students with need: Average financial aid package for all full-time undergraduates was $2,356; for part-time $2,356. 95% awarded as scholarships/grants, 5% awarded as loans/jobs. Work study available nights, weekends, and for part-time students.

Students without need: No-need awards available for academics, art, job skills, leadership, minority status, music/drama, state/district residency.

FINANCIAL AID PROCEDURES

Forms required: FAFSA, institutional form.

Dates and Deadlines: Priority date 6/1; no closing date. Applicants notified on a rolling basis starting 5/15; must reply within 2 week(s) of notification.

Transfers: No deadline. Applicants notified on a rolling basis.

CONTACT

Beaulah Bob-Pennypacker, Financial Aid Coordinator
PO Box 610, Holbrook, AZ 86025-0610
(928) 524-7626

Paradise Valley Community College

Phoenix, Arizona
www.pvc.maricopa.edu Federal Code: 026236

2-year public community college in very large city.

Enrollment: 3,290 undergrads.

Selectivity: Open admission.

BASIC COSTS (2008-2009)

Tuition and fees: $2,160; out-of-state residents $8,610.

Per-credit charge: $71; out-of-state residents $286.

FINANCIAL AID PICTURE

Students with need: Need-based aid available for full-time and part-time students.

FINANCIAL AID PROCEDURES

Forms required: FAFSA.

Dates and Deadlines: No deadline. Applicants notified on a rolling basis starting 6/1.

CONTACT

Ken Clarke, Director of Financial Aid
18401 North 32nd Street, Phoenix, AZ 85032
(602) 787-7100

Phoenix College

Phoenix, Arizona
www.pc.maricopa.edu Federal Code: 001078

2-year public community college in very large city.

Enrollment: 2,633 full-time undergrads.

Selectivity: Open admission; but selective for some programs.

BASIC COSTS (2008-2009)

Tuition and fees: $2,160; out-of-state residents $8,610.

Per-credit charge: $71; out-of-state residents $286.

FINANCIAL AID PICTURE

Students with need: Work study available weekends and for part-time students.

FINANCIAL AID PROCEDURES

Forms required: FAFSA.

Dates and Deadlines: Priority date 6/30; no closing date. Applicants notified on a rolling basis starting 5/1.

CONTACT

Genevieve Watson, Director of Financial Aid
1202 West Thomas Road, Phoenix, AZ 85013
(602) 285-7404

Pima Community College

Tucson, Arizona
www.pima.edu Federal Code: 007266

2-year public community and technical college in very large city.

Enrollment: 27,190 undergrads.

Selectivity: Open admission; but selective for some programs.

BASIC COSTS (2008-2009)

Tuition and fees: $1,625; out-of-state residents $7,610.

Per-credit charge: $50; out-of-state residents $84.

FINANCIAL AID PICTURE

Students with need: Need-based aid available for full-time and part-time students.

Students without need: No-need awards available for academics, alumni affiliation, art, athletics, minority status, music/drama.

FINANCIAL AID PROCEDURES

Forms required: FAFSA.

Dates and Deadlines: Priority date 3/15; no closing date. Applicants notified on a rolling basis starting 7/1; must reply within 2 week(s) of notification.

CONTACT

Anna Reese, Executive Director of Financial Aid
4905B East Broadway, Tucson, AZ 85709-1120
(520) 206-4950

Prescott College

Prescott, Arizona
www.prescott.edu Federal Code: 013659

4-year private liberal arts college in large town.

Enrollment: 717 undergrads, 11% part-time. 89 full-time freshmen.

Selectivity: Admits over 75% of applicants.

BASIC COSTS (2009-2010)

Tuition and fees: $23,643.

Room only: $3,630.

Additional info: Health insurance is required; cost of school's health insurance is $482 for fall term and $675 for spring term.

FINANCIAL AID PICTURE (2008-2009)

Students with need: Average financial aid package met 53% of need; average scholarship/grant was $10,256; average loan was $3,422. For part-time students, average financial aid package was $7,216.

Students without need: No-need awards available for academics, alumni affiliation, minority status, state/district residency.

Cumulative student debt: 72% of graduating class had student loans; average debt was $11,495.

FINANCIAL AID PROCEDURES

Forms required: FAFSA.

Dates and Deadlines: Priority date 4/1; no closing date. Applicants notified on a rolling basis starting 3/15; must reply within 12 week(s) of notification.

Transfers: No deadline. Applicants notified on a rolling basis; must reply within 12 week(s) of notification.

CONTACT

Terri Eckel, Director of Financial Aid
220 Grove Avenue, Prescott, AZ 86301
(928) 776-5225

Rio Salado College

Tempe, Arizona
www.riosalado.edu Federal Code: 014483

2-year public virtual community college in very large city.
Enrollment: 4,849 undergrads.
Selectivity: Open admission; but selective for some programs.

BASIC COSTS (2008-2009)

Tuition and fees: $2,160; out-of-state residents $8,610.
Per-credit charge: $71; out-of-state residents $286.

FINANCIAL AID PICTURE (2007-2008)

Students with need: Need-based aid available for full-time and part-time students.
Students without need: This college awards aid only to students with need.

FINANCIAL AID PROCEDURES

Forms required: FAFSA, institutional form.
Dates and Deadlines: Priority date 6/30; no closing date. Applicants notified on a rolling basis starting 6/30.

CONTACT

Linda Ross, Director of Financial Aid
2323 West 14th Street, Tempe, AZ 85281
(480) 517-8310

South Mountain Community College

Phoenix, Arizona
www.smc.maricopa.edu Federal Code: 015001

2-year public community college in very large city.
Enrollment: 870 undergrads.
Selectivity: Open admission.

BASIC COSTS (2008-2009)

Tuition and fees: $2,160; out-of-state residents $8,610.
Per-credit charge: $71; out-of-state residents $286.

FINANCIAL AID PICTURE

Students with need: Need-based aid available for full-time and part-time students. Work study available nights, weekends, and for part-time students.
Students without need: No-need awards available for academics, athletics, minority status, music/drama.

FINANCIAL AID PROCEDURES

Forms required: FAFSA.
Dates and Deadlines: Priority date 5/1; no closing date. Applicants notified on a rolling basis starting 5/15; must reply within 3 week(s) of notification.

CONTACT

Inez Moreno-Weinert, Director of Financial Aid and Placement
7050 South 24th Street, Phoenix, AZ 85042
(602) 243-8300

Southwestern College

Phoenix, Arizona
www.swcaz.edu Federal Code: 007113

4-year private Bible and liberal arts college in very large city, affiliated with Baptist faith.
Enrollment: 365 undergrads.

BASIC COSTS (2008-2009)

Tuition and fees: $14,364.
Per-credit charge: $570.
Room and board: $5,046.

FINANCIAL AID PICTURE

Students with need: Need-based aid available for full-time and part-time students.
Students without need: No-need awards available for academics, alumni affiliation, athletics, leadership, minority status, music/drama, religious affiliation.

FINANCIAL AID PROCEDURES

Forms required: FAFSA, state aid form, institutional form.
Dates and Deadlines: Priority date 3/15; closing date 8/31. Applicants notified on a rolling basis.

CONTACT

Cheryl Hansen, Director of Financial Aid
2625 East Cactus Road, Phoenix, AZ 85032-7042
(602) 489-5500 ext. 115

Tohono O'odham Community College

Sells, Arizona
www.tocc.cc.az.us Federal Code: 037844

2-year public Tribal College in rural community.
Enrollment: 100 undergrads.
Selectivity: Open admission.

BASIC COSTS (2008-2009)

Tuition and fees: $1,270; out-of-state residents $6,340.
Per-credit charge: $42; out-of-state residents $72.

FINANCIAL AID PICTURE (2007-2008)

Students with need: Need-based aid available for full-time and part-time students.
Students without need: This college awards aid only to students with need.

FINANCIAL AID PROCEDURES

Forms required: FAFSA, institutional form.
Dates and Deadlines: No deadline. Applicants notified on a rolling basis.

CONTACT

Alvaro Rivera, Financial Aid Director
PO Box 3129, Sells, AZ 85634-3129
(520) 383-8401 ext. 41

University of Advancing Technology

Tempe, Arizona
www.uat.edu Federal Code: 017188

4-year for-profit university in very large city.
Enrollment: 1,152 undergrads. 185 full-time freshmen.

BASIC COSTS (2009-2010)

Tuition and fees: $17,900.
Room and board: $10,548.

FINANCIAL AID PICTURE (2007-2008)

Students with need: 31% of average financial aid package awarded as scholarships/grants, 69% awarded as loans/jobs. Need-based aid available for part-time students.

FINANCIAL AID PROCEDURES

Forms required: FAFSA.

Dates and Deadlines: Priority date 4/15; no closing date. Applicants notified on a rolling basis; must reply within 2 week(s) of notification.
Transfers: No deadline. Must reply within 2 week(s) of notification. Loan periods may not overlap.

CONTACT
Lisa Frankowski, Senior Financial Aid Administrator
2625 West Baseline Road, Tempe, AZ 85283-1056
(602) 383-8217

University of Arizona
Tucson, Arizona
www.arizona.edu Federal Code: 001083

4-year public university in very large city.
Enrollment: 29,340 undergrads, 12% part-time. 6,231 full-time freshmen.
Selectivity: Admits over 75% of applicants.

BASIC COSTS (2008-2009)
Tuition and fees: $5,531; out-of-state residents $18,665.
Per-credit charge: $276; out-of-state residents $767.
Room and board: $8,058.
Additional info: Tuition/fee waivers available for minority students.

FINANCIAL AID PICTURE (2007-2008)
Students with need: Out of 3,798 full-time freshmen who applied for aid, 2,374 were judged to have need. Of these, 2,255 received aid, and 448 had their full need met. Average financial aid package met 66% of need; average scholarship/grant was $6,706; average loan was $3,515. For part-time students, average financial aid package was $6,134.
Students without need: 2,167 full-time freshmen who did not demonstrate need for aid received scholarships/grants; average award was $4,662. No-need awards available for academics, art.
Scholarships offered: ***Merit:*** Various merit scholarships available. National Merit scholarship; $6,000-$10,000 a year. ***Athletic:*** 42 full-time freshmen received athletic scholarships.
Cumulative student debt: 44% of graduating class had student loans; average debt was $18,025.
Additional info: Arizona Assurance Program: provides housing, books, and tuition for all new, incoming resident freshmen; must be Pell-eligible with combined family income less than $42,500; funding provided as grants, scholarships, and federal work-study.

FINANCIAL AID PROCEDURES
Forms required: FAFSA.
Dates and Deadlines: Priority date 3/1; no closing date. Applicants notified on a rolling basis starting 4/1; must reply within 3 week(s) of notification.
Transfers: Some waivers available for Arizona Community College transfer students with 3.2 GPA who are Arizona residents.

CONTACT
John Nametz, Director of Student Financial Aid
Robert L. Nugent Building, Tucson, AZ 85721-0040
(520) 621-1858

University of Phoenix
Phoenix, Arizona
www.phoenix.edu Federal Code: 014593

4-year for-profit virtual university in very large city.
Enrollment: 174,818 undergrads. 35,898 full-time freshmen.
Selectivity: Open admission; but selective for some programs.

BASIC COSTS (2008-2009)
Tuition and fees: $10,849.
Per-credit charge: $362.

FINANCIAL AID PICTURE
Students with need: Need-based aid available for full-time students.

FINANCIAL AID PROCEDURES
Forms required: FAFSA, institutional form.
Dates and Deadlines: No deadline. Applicants notified on a rolling basis.

CONTACT
Robert Collins, Vice President, Student Financial Aid
4035 South Riverpoint Parkway, Phoenix, AZ 85040-0723
(480) 804-7600

Western International University
Phoenix, Arizona
www.wintu.edu Federal Code: 014970

4-year for-profit university and business college in very large city.
Enrollment: 1,980 undergrads. 31 full-time freshmen.
Selectivity: Open admission.

BASIC COSTS (2008-2009)
Tuition and fees: $10,950.
Per-credit charge: $365.

FINANCIAL AID PICTURE (2007-2008)
Students with need: Average financial aid package for all full-time undergraduates was $10,500.
Students without need: This college awards aid only to students with need.
Cumulative student debt: 40% of graduating class had student loans; average debt was $22,364.

FINANCIAL AID PROCEDURES
Forms required: FAFSA, institutional form.
Dates and Deadlines: No deadline. Applicants notified on a rolling basis.
Transfers: No deadline. Applicants notified on a rolling basis.

CONTACT
Ella Owen, Associate Director of Financial Services
9215 North Black Canyon Highway, Phoenix, AZ 85021
(602) 943-2311

Yavapai College
Prescott, Arizona
www.yc.edu Federal Code: 001079

2-year public community college in large town.
Enrollment: 4,720 undergrads.
Selectivity: Open admission; but selective for some programs.

BASIC COSTS (2008-2009)
Tuition and fees: $1,560; out-of-state residents $8,230.
Per-credit charge: $52; out-of-state residents $330.
Room and board: $4,530.

FINANCIAL AID PICTURE (2008-2009)
Students with need: Need-based aid available for full-time and part-time students.
Students without need: No-need awards available for academics, athletics.

FINANCIAL AID PROCEDURES
Forms required: FAFSA.
Dates and Deadlines: Priority date 4/1; no closing date. Applicants notified on a rolling basis.

CONTACT
Vikki Gill, Director of Financial Aid
1100 East Sheldon Street, Prescott, AZ 86301
(928) 776-2152

Arkansas

Arkansas Baptist College
Little Rock, Arkansas
www.arkansasbaptist.edu Federal Code: 001087

4-year private liberal arts college in large city, affiliated with American Baptist Churches in the USA.
Enrollment: 625 undergrads.
Selectivity: Open admission.

BASIC COSTS (2008-2009)
Tuition and fees: $5,700.
Per-credit charge: $216.
Room and board: $6,710.

FINANCIAL AID PICTURE
Students with need: Need-based aid available for full-time and part-time students.
Students without need: This college awards aid only to students with need.

FINANCIAL AID PROCEDURES
Forms required: FAFSA.
Dates and Deadlines: Closing date 5/1. Applicants notified on a rolling basis starting 6/15.

CONTACT
Rosie Toney, Director of Admissions and Financial Aid
1621 Dr. Martin Luther King Drive, Little Rock, AR 72202
(501) 374-6135

Arkansas Northeastern College
Blytheville, Arkansas
www.anc.edu Federal Code: 012860

2-year public community college in large town.
Enrollment: 1,425 undergrads.
Selectivity: Open admission; but selective for some programs.

BASIC COSTS (2008-2009)
Tuition and fees: $1,720; out-of-district residents $2,020; out-of-state residents $3,520.
Per-credit charge: $50; out-of-district residents $60; out-of-state residents $110.

FINANCIAL AID PICTURE (2007-2008)
Students with need: 82% of average financial aid package awarded as scholarships/grants, 18% awarded as loans/jobs. Need-based aid available for part-time students. Work study available nights.
Students without need: No-need awards available for academics, minority status, music/drama, state/district residency.

FINANCIAL AID PROCEDURES
Forms required: FAFSA, institutional form.
Dates and Deadlines: Priority date 4/15; no closing date. Applicants notified on a rolling basis starting 5/1; must reply within 2 week(s) of notification.

CONTACT
Laura Yarbrough, Director of Financial Aid
Box 1109, Blytheville, AR 72316-1109
(870) 762-1020 ext. 1160

Arkansas State University
State University, Arkansas
www.astate.edu Federal Code: 001090

4-year public university in small city.
Enrollment: 9,200 undergrads, 18% part-time. 1,752 full-time freshmen.
Selectivity: Admits over 75% of applicants.

BASIC COSTS (2008-2009)
Tuition and fees: $6,370; out-of-state residents $14,290.
Per-credit charge: $163; out-of-state residents $427.
Room and board: $5,406.

FINANCIAL AID PICTURE (2008-2009)
Students with need: Out of 1,576 full-time freshmen who applied for aid, 1,558 were judged to have need. Of these, 1,558 received aid, and 423 had their full need met. Average financial aid package met 63% of need; average scholarship/grant was $6,800; average loan was $3,400. Need-based aid available for part-time students.
Students without need: 111 full-time freshmen who did not demonstrate need for aid received scholarships/grants; average award was $5,100. No-need awards available for academics, alumni affiliation, art, athletics, leadership, minority status, music/drama, ROTC, state/district residency.
Scholarships offered: 61 full-time freshmen received athletic scholarships; average amount $8,800.
Cumulative student debt: 68% of graduating class had student loans; average debt was $18,750.

FINANCIAL AID PROCEDURES
Forms required: FAFSA, institutional form.
Dates and Deadlines: Priority date 2/15; closing date 7/1. Applicants notified on a rolling basis starting 6/1; must reply within 2 week(s) of notification.
Transfers: Applicants notified on a rolling basis starting 6/1; must reply within 2 week(s) of notification.

CONTACT
Robin Kaloghirou, Director of Financial Aid
PO Box 1630, State University, AR 72467-1630
(870) 972-2310

Arkansas State University: Beebe
Beebe, Arkansas
www.asub.edu Federal Code: 001090

2-year public community college in small town.
Enrollment: 3,489 undergrads.
Selectivity: Open admission.

BASIC COSTS (2008-2009)
Tuition and fees: $2,670; out-of-state residents $4,350.
Per-credit charge: $78; out-of-state residents $134.
Room and board: $2,930.

FINANCIAL AID PICTURE (2007-2008)
Students with need: 17% of average financial aid package awarded as scholarships/grants, 83% awarded as loans/jobs. Need-based aid available for part-time students. Work study available nights, weekends, and for part-time students.
Students without need: No-need awards available for academics, leadership, music/drama.

FINANCIAL AID PROCEDURES

Forms required: FAFSA, institutional form.

Dates and Deadlines: Priority date 6/1; no closing date. Applicants notified on a rolling basis starting 6/1; must reply within 2 week(s) of notification.

Transfers: No deadline. Applicants notified on a rolling basis.

CONTACT

Linda Yelder, Director of Student Aid
PO Box 1000, Beebe, AR 72012-1000
(501) 882-8245

Arkansas State University: Mountain Home

Mountain Home, Arkansas
www.asumh.edu Federal Code: 001090

2-year public community and technical college in large town.

Enrollment: 1,173 undergrads, 37% part-time. 267 full-time freshmen.

Selectivity: Open admission; but selective for some programs.

BASIC COSTS (2008-2009)

Tuition and fees: $2,760; out-of-state residents $4,410.

Per-credit charge: $77; out-of-state residents $132.

FINANCIAL AID PICTURE (2008-2009)

Students with need: Need-based aid available for full-time and part-time students.

Students without need: No-need awards available for academics, state/district residency.

FINANCIAL AID PROCEDURES

Forms required: FAFSA, institutional form.

Dates and Deadlines: Priority date 7/1; no closing date. Applicants notified on a rolling basis starting 5/1; must reply within 2 week(s) of notification.

CONTACT

Lyndle McCurley, Vice Chancellor Administrative Affairs
1600 South College Street, Mountain Home, AR 72653
(870) 508-6195

Arkansas Tech University

Russellville, Arkansas
www.atu.edu Federal Code: 001089

4-year public university and liberal arts college in large town.

Enrollment: 6,581 undergrads, 13% part-time. 1,552 full-time freshmen.

Selectivity: Admits over 75% of applicants.

BASIC COSTS (2008-2009)

Tuition and fees: $5,430; out-of-state residents $10,260.

Per-credit charge: $161; out-of-state residents $322.

Room and board: $4,888.

FINANCIAL AID PICTURE (2007-2008)

Students with need: Out of 1,208 full-time freshmen who applied for aid, 846 were judged to have need. Of those, 811 received aid, and 119 had their full need met. Average financial aid package met 68% of need; average scholarship/grant was $4,000; average loan was $2,750. For part-time students, average financial aid package was $5,140.

Students without need: 445 full-time freshmen who did not demonstrate need for aid received scholarships/grants; average award was $6,150. No-need awards available for academics, athletics, leadership, music/drama, ROTC, state/district residency.

Scholarships offered: 62 full-time freshmen received athletic scholarships; average amount $3,420.

Cumulative student debt: 51% of graduating class had student loans; average debt was $6,142.

FINANCIAL AID PROCEDURES

Forms required: FAFSA.

Dates and Deadlines: Priority date 4/15; no closing date. Applicants notified on a rolling basis starting 5/1; must reply within 2 week(s) of notification.

CONTACT

Shirley Goines, Director of Student Financial Aid
1605 Coliseum Diver Suite 141, Russellville, AR 72801-2222
(479) 968-0399

Central Baptist College

Conway, Arkansas
www.cbc.edu Federal Code: 001093

4-year private Bible and junior college in large town, affiliated with Baptist faith.

Enrollment: 547 undergrads, 19% part-time. 104 full-time freshmen.

Selectivity: Admits over 75% of applicants.

BASIC COSTS (2008-2009)

Tuition and fees: $9,650.

Room and board: $5,000.

FINANCIAL AID PICTURE

Students with need: Need-based aid available for full-time and part-time students.

Students without need: No-need awards available for academics, athletics, music/drama, religious affiliation.

FINANCIAL AID PROCEDURES

Forms required: FAFSA.

Dates and Deadlines: Priority date 7/1; closing date 8/1. Applicants notified on a rolling basis starting 4/1.

Transfers: No deadline.

CONTACT

Christi Bell, Director of Financial Aid
1501 College Avenue, Conway, AR 72034
(501) 329-6872 ext. 185

Cossatot Community College of the University of Arkansas

De Queen, Arkansas
www.cccua.edu Federal Code: 012432

2-year public community college in small town.

Enrollment: 1,396 undergrads.

Selectivity: Open admission; but selective for some programs.

BASIC COSTS (2008-2009)

Tuition and fees: $1,710; out-of-district residents $2,010; out-of-state residents $5,310.

Per-credit charge: $45; out-of-district residents $55; out-of-state residents $165.

Additional info: Residents of bordering out-of-state counties may qualify for in-state tuition.

FINANCIAL AID PICTURE (2007-2008)

Students with need: Need-based aid available for full-time and part-time students. Work study available nights.

Additional info: Active or honorably discharged military and their dependents receive tuition discounts.

FINANCIAL AID PROCEDURES

Forms required: FAFSA, institutional form.

Dates and Deadlines: Priority date 5/1; no closing date. Applicants notified on a rolling basis starting 3/1.
Transfers: Applicants notified on a rolling basis starting 3/1.

CONTACT

Denise Hammond, Director of Financial Aid
183 Highway 399, De Queen, AR 71832
(870) 584-4471

Crowley's Ridge College

Paragould, Arkansas
www.crowleysridgecollege.edu Federal Code: 001095

2-year private junior college in large town, affiliated with Church of Christ.
Enrollment: 136 undergrads.
Selectivity: Open admission.

BASIC COSTS (2008-2009)

Tuition and fees: $8,650.
Per-credit charge: $245.
Room and board: $5,300.
Additional info: Tuition/fee waivers available for adults.

FINANCIAL AID PICTURE (2008-2009)

Students with need: Work study available nights, weekends, and for part-time students.
Students without need: No-need awards available for academics, leadership, music/drama.

FINANCIAL AID PROCEDURES

Forms required: FAFSA.
Dates and Deadlines: No deadline.

CONTACT

David Goff, Director of Financial Aid
100 College Drive, Paragould, AR 72450
(870) 236-6901

East Arkansas Community College

Forrest City, Arkansas
www.eacc.edu Federal Code: 012260

2-year public community college in large town.
Enrollment: 1,139 undergrads.
Selectivity: Open admission.

BASIC COSTS (2008-2009)

Tuition and fees: $1,890; out-of-district residents $2,130; out-of-state residents $2,550.
Per-credit charge: $55; out-of-district residents $63; out-of-state residents $77.

FINANCIAL AID PICTURE

Students with need: Need-based aid available for full-time and part-time students.
Students without need: This college awards aid only to students with need.

FINANCIAL AID PROCEDURES

Forms required: FAFSA.
Dates and Deadlines: Priority date 3/1; closing date 7/1. Applicants notified on a rolling basis starting 5/15; must reply within 2 week(s) of notification.

CONTACT

Alvin Coleman, Director of Financial Aid
1700 Newcastle Road, Forrest City, AR 72335-9598
(870) 633-4480 ext. 225

Ecclesia College

Springdale, Arkansas
www.ecollege.edu Federal Code: 038553

4-year private liberal arts college in large town, affiliated with interdenominational tradition.
Enrollment: 126 undergrads.
Selectivity: Open admission; but selective for some programs.

BASIC COSTS (2009-2010)

Tuition and fees: $15,050.
Per-credit charge: $475.
Room and board: $5,010.
Additional info: Full-time students not living on campus may be subject to additional $750 nonresidents fee/semester. Tuition/fee waivers available for adults.

FINANCIAL AID PICTURE (2007-2008)

Students with need: Need-based aid available for full-time and part-time students. Work study available nights, weekends, and for part-time students.
Students without need: No-need awards available for academics, athletics, leadership, music/drama.

FINANCIAL AID PROCEDURES

Forms required: FAFSA.
Dates and Deadlines: No deadline. Applicants notified on a rolling basis starting 7/1.

CONTACT

Jesse Wadkins, Financial Aid Officer
9653 Nations Drive, Springdale, AR 72762
(479) 248-7236 ext. 212

Harding University

Searcy, Arkansas
www.harding.edu Federal Code: 001097

4-year private university in large town, affiliated with Church of Christ.
Enrollment: 4,132 undergrads, 6% part-time. 981 full-time freshmen.
Selectivity: Admits 50 to 75% of applicants.

BASIC COSTS (2009-2010)

Tuition and fees: $13,580.
Per-credit charge: $438.
Room and board: $5,814.

FINANCIAL AID PICTURE (2007-2008)

Students with need: Need-based aid available for full-time and part-time students. Work study available nights, weekends, and for part-time students.
Students without need: No-need awards available for academics, art, athletics, music/drama, religious affiliation, ROTC, state/district residency.
Additional info: Music scholarships available, audition required.

FINANCIAL AID PROCEDURES

Forms required: FAFSA, institutional form.
Dates and Deadlines: Priority date 4/1; no closing date. Applicants notified on a rolling basis starting 2/15; must reply within 2 week(s) of notification.
Transfers: No deadline.

CONTACT

Jon Roberts, Director of Student Financial Services
915 East Market Avenue, Searcy, AR 72149-2255
(501) 279-4257

Henderson State University
Arkadelphia, Arkansas
www.getreddie.com Federal Code: 001098

4-year public university and liberal arts college in large town.
Enrollment: 2,833 undergrads.
Selectivity: Admits 50 to 75% of applicants.

BASIC COSTS (2008-2009)
Tuition and fees: $6,024; out-of-state residents $10,944.
Room and board: $4,790.

FINANCIAL AID PICTURE (2007-2008)
Students with need: Need-based aid available for full-time and part-time students.
Students without need: No-need awards available for academics, alumni affiliation, art, athletics, leadership, minority status, music/drama, state/district residency.

FINANCIAL AID PROCEDURES
Forms required: FAFSA.
Dates and Deadlines: Priority date 6/1; no closing date. Applicants notified on a rolling basis starting 4/1; must reply within 2 week(s) of notification.

CONTACT
Vicky Taylor, Director of Financial Aid
1100 Henderson Street, Arkadelphia, AR 71999-0001
(870) 230-5094

Hendrix College
Conway, Arkansas
www.hendrix.edu Federal Code: 001099

4-year private liberal arts college in small city, affiliated with United Methodist Church.
Enrollment: 1,341 undergrads, 1% part-time. 437 full-time freshmen.
Selectivity: Admits over 75% of applicants.

BASIC COSTS (2008-2009)
Tuition and fees: $26,080.
Room and board: $7,950.

FINANCIAL AID PICTURE (2008-2009)
Students with need: Out of 365 full-time freshmen who applied for aid, 250 were judged to have need. Of these, 250 received aid, and 102 had their full need met. Average financial aid package met 87% of need; average scholarship/grant was $17,774; average loan was $4,301. For part-time students, average financial aid package was $3,500.
Students without need: 190 full-time freshmen who did not demonstrate need for aid received scholarships/grants; average award was $19,277. No-need awards available for academics, art, leadership, music/drama, religious affiliation.
Scholarships offered: Hays Memorial Scholarship: full tuition, room, board, mandatory fees; based on academic excellence. Visual and Performing Arts Scholarships (music, theatre, art): $2,000 to $5,000 per year; auditions/portfolios required. Leadership and United Methodist (UMYF) scholarships: $2,000 to $3,500.
Cumulative student debt: 81% of graduating class had student loans; average debt was $17,484.

FINANCIAL AID PROCEDURES
Forms required: FAFSA.
Dates and Deadlines: Priority date 2/15; no closing date. Applicants notified on a rolling basis starting 2/15; must reply by 5/1 or within 4 week(s) of notification.
Transfers: Applicants notified by 2/15.

CONTACT
Mark Bandre, Director of Financial Aid
1600 Washington Avenue, Conway, AR 72032-3080
(501) 450-1368

John Brown University
Siloam Springs, Arkansas
www.jbu.edu Federal Code: 001100

4-year private liberal arts college in large town, affiliated with interdenominational tradition.
Enrollment: 1,674 undergrads, 5% part-time. 310 full-time freshmen.
Selectivity: Admits 50 to 75% of applicants.

BASIC COSTS (2009-2010)
Tuition and fees: $18,880.
Per-credit charge: $720.
Room and board: $6,876.
Additional info: Tuition/fee waivers available for adults.

FINANCIAL AID PICTURE (2008-2009)
Students with need: Average financial aid package for all full-time undergraduates was $13,260; for part-time $6,106. 51% awarded as scholarships/grants, 49% awarded as loans/jobs.
Students without need: No-need awards available for academics, alumni affiliation, art, athletics, leadership, music/drama, ROTC.
Cumulative student debt: 60% of graduating class had student loans; average debt was $18,066.

FINANCIAL AID PROCEDURES
Forms required: FAFSA, institutional form.
Dates and Deadlines: Priority date 3/1; no closing date. Applicants notified on a rolling basis starting 3/1; must reply within 4 week(s) of notification.
Transfers: No deadline. Applicants notified on a rolling basis; must reply within 4 week(s) of notification.

CONTACT
Kim Eldridge, Director of Financial Aid
2000 West University Street, Siloam Springs, AR 72761-2121
(877) 528-4636

Lyon College
Batesville, Arkansas
www.lyon.edu Federal Code: 001088

4-year private liberal arts college in small town, affiliated with Presbyterian Church (USA).
Enrollment: 453 undergrads, 4% part-time. 109 full-time freshmen.
Selectivity: Admits 50 to 75% of applicants.

BASIC COSTS (2009-2010)
Tuition and fees: $19,968.
Per-credit charge: $730.
Room and board: $7,340.

FINANCIAL AID PICTURE (2008-2009)
Students with need: Out of 93 full-time freshmen who applied for aid, 79 were judged to have need. Of these, 79 received aid, and 20 had their full need met. Average financial aid package met 82% of need; average scholarship/grant was $13,609; average loan was $3,863. For part-time students, average financial aid package was $7,222.
Students without need: 30 full-time freshmen who did not demonstrate need for aid received scholarships/grants; average award was $7,350. No-need awards available for academics, art, athletics, leadership, minority status, music/drama, religious affiliation, state/district residency.

Scholarships offered: ***Merit:*** Brown Scholarship; tuition, room, board, mandatory fees and books; based on high school record, standardized test scores; 4 awarded. Anderson Scholarship; tuition, mandatory fees and books; based on high school record, test scores; 4 awarded. Lyon Fellowship; $10,000; based on high school record, test scores, with a preference for students with a career interest in business or public service or a strong academic interest in computer science or the fine arts; up to 8 awarded. ***Athletic:*** 22 full-time freshmen received athletic scholarships; average amount $7,618.
Cumulative student debt: 64% of graduating class had student loans; average debt was $18,428.

FINANCIAL AID PROCEDURES
Forms required: FAFSA.
Dates and Deadlines: Priority date 3/15; no closing date. Applicants notified on a rolling basis starting 3/1; must reply by 8/15.
Transfers: No deadline. Applicants notified on a rolling basis starting 3/1; must reply within 2 week(s) of notification.

CONTACT
Tommy Tucker, Director of Financial Aid
PO Box 2317, Batesville, AR 72503-2317
(870) 307-7257

Mid-South Community College
West Memphis, Arkansas
www.midsouthcc.edu Federal Code: 015862

2-year public community and junior college in large town.
Enrollment: 1,133 undergrads, 61% part-time. 171 full-time freshmen.
Selectivity: Open admission.

BASIC COSTS (2008-2009)
Tuition and fees: $1,950; out-of-district residents $2,280; out-of-state residents $3,930.
Per-credit charge: $55; out-of-district residents $66; out-of-state residents $121.

FINANCIAL AID PICTURE (2007-2008)
Students with need: Need-based aid available for full-time and part-time students. Work study available nights.
Students without need: No-need awards available for academics, state/district residency.

FINANCIAL AID PROCEDURES
Forms required: FAFSA, institutional form.
Dates and Deadlines: No deadline. Applicants notified on a rolling basis starting 6/1; must reply within 2 week(s) of notification.

CONTACT
Jackie Brubaker, Director of FInancial Aid
2000 West Broadway, West Memphis, AR 72301
(870) 733-6741

National Park Community College
Hot Springs, Arkansas
www.npcc.edu Federal Code: 012105

2-year public liberal arts and technical college in large town.
Enrollment: 1,529 full-time undergrads.
Selectivity: Open admission; but selective for some programs.

BASIC COSTS (2008-2009)
Tuition and fees: $1,925; out-of-district residents $2,225; out-of-state residents $4,145.
Per-credit charge: $60; out-of-district residents $70; out-of-state residents $134.

FINANCIAL AID PICTURE
Students with need: Need-based aid available for full-time and part-time students. Work study available nights, weekends, and for part-time students.
Students without need: No-need awards available for academics, minority status, music/drama, state/district residency.

FINANCIAL AID PROCEDURES
Forms required: FAFSA, institutional form.
Dates and Deadlines: Priority date 7/1; no closing date. Applicants notified on a rolling basis starting 3/1.
Transfers: Transfer applicants must furnish evidence of good standing at previous institution to qualify for financial aid.

CONTACT
Lisa Hopper, Counselor and Financial Aid Adviser
101 College Drive, Hot Springs, AR 71913
(501) 760-4235

North Arkansas College
Harrison, Arkansas
www.northark.edu Federal Code: 012261

2-year public community and technical college in large town.
Enrollment: 1,789 undergrads, 28% part-time. 426 full-time freshmen.
Selectivity: Open admission; but selective for some programs.

BASIC COSTS (2008-2009)
Tuition and fees: $1,800; out-of-district residents $2,460; out-of-state residents $4,590.
Per-credit charge: $60; out-of-district residents $82; out-of-state residents $153.

FINANCIAL AID PICTURE (2007-2008)
Students with need: Need-based aid available for full-time and part-time students. Work study available nights.
Students without need: No-need awards available for academics, athletics, state/district residency.

FINANCIAL AID PROCEDURES
Forms required: FAFSA, institutional form.
Dates and Deadlines: Priority date 5/1; no closing date. Applicants notified on a rolling basis starting 5/1.
Transfers: No deadline. Applicants notified on a rolling basis starting 5/1.

CONTACT
Jennifer Haddock, Director of Financial Aid
1515 Pioneer Drive, Harrison, AR 72601
(870) 391-3266

Northwest Arkansas Community College
Bentonville, Arkansas
www.nwacc.edu Federal Code: 030633

2-year public community college in small city.
Enrollment: 5,385 undergrads, 59% part-time. 668 full-time freshmen.
Selectivity: Open admission; but selective for some programs.

BASIC COSTS (2008-2009)
Tuition and fees: $2,410; out-of-district residents $3,460; out-of-state residents $4,652.
Per-credit charge: $63; out-of-district residents $98; out-of-state residents $138.

FINANCIAL AID PICTURE

Students with need: Need-based aid available for full-time and part-time students. Work study available nights, weekends, and for part-time students.
Students without need: No-need awards available for academics, leadership, music/drama, state/district residency.

FINANCIAL AID PROCEDURES

Forms required: FAFSA, institutional form.
Dates and Deadlines: Priority date 4/1; no closing date. Applicants notified on a rolling basis starting 4/1; must reply within 2 week(s) of notification.

CONTACT

Michelle Cordell, Director of Financial Aid
One College Drive, Bentonville, AR 72712
(479) 619-4129

Ouachita Baptist University

Arkadelphia, Arkansas
www.obu.edu Federal Code: 001102

4-year private liberal arts college in large town, affiliated with Southern Baptist Convention.
Enrollment: 1,437 undergrads, 1% part-time. 404 full-time freshmen.
Selectivity: Admits 50 to 75% of applicants.

BASIC COSTS (2009-2010)

Tuition and fees: $18,940.
Per-credit charge: $525.
Room and board: $5,660.

FINANCIAL AID PICTURE (2008-2009)

Students with need: Need-based aid available for full-time students. Work study available nights, weekends, and for part-time students.
Students without need: No-need awards available for academics, alumni affiliation, athletics, job skills, leadership, minority status, music/drama, religious affiliation, ROTC, state/district residency.

FINANCIAL AID PROCEDURES

Forms required: FAFSA.
Dates and Deadlines: Priority date 1/15; closing date 6/1. Applicants notified on a rolling basis starting 11/1; must reply by 5/1.

CONTACT

Chris Kear, Director of Student Financial Services
OBU Box 3776, Arkadelphia, AR 71998-0001
(870) 245-5570

Ouachita Technical College

Malvern, Arkansas
www.otcweb.edu Federal Code: 009976

2-year public community and technical college in small town.
Enrollment: 821 undergrads, 36% part-time. 163 full-time freshmen.
Selectivity: Open admission; but selective for some programs.

BASIC COSTS (2008-2009)

Tuition and fees: $2,150; out-of-state residents $3,830.
Per-credit charge: $56; out-of-state residents $112.

FINANCIAL AID PICTURE

Students with need: Need-based aid available for full-time and part-time students. Work study available nights.

FINANCIAL AID PROCEDURES

Forms required: FAFSA.
Dates and Deadlines: Closing date 6/30. Applicants notified on a rolling basis starting 7/1; must reply within 6 week(s) of notification.

CONTACT

Teresa Avery, Director of Financial Aid
One College Circle, Malvern, AR 72104
(501) 337-5000 ext. 1122

Ozarka College

Melbourne, Arkansas
www.ozarka.edu Federal Code: 013217

2-year public community and technical college in rural community.
Enrollment: 944 undergrads.
Selectivity: Open admission; but selective for some programs.

BASIC COSTS (2008-2009)

Tuition and fees: $2,310; out-of-state residents $5,400.
Per-credit charge: $70; out-of-state residents $173.

FINANCIAL AID PICTURE (2008-2009)

Students with need: Need-based aid available for full-time and part-time students.

FINANCIAL AID PROCEDURES

Forms required: FAFSA.
Dates and Deadlines: No deadline. Applicants notified on a rolling basis; must reply within 2 week(s) of notification.

CONTACT

Joyce Goff, Financial Aid Officer
218 College Drive, Melbourne, AR 72556-0010
(870) 368-7371 ext. 2010

Philander Smith College

Little Rock, Arkansas
www.philander.edu Federal Code: 001103

4-year private liberal arts college in small city, affiliated with United Methodist Church.
Enrollment: 587 undergrads.
Selectivity: Admits over 75% of applicants.

BASIC COSTS (2008-2009)

Tuition and fees: $8,740.
Room and board: $6,650.

FINANCIAL AID PICTURE (2008-2009)

Students with need: Need-based aid available for full-time and part-time students.
Students without need: This college awards aid only to students with need.

FINANCIAL AID PROCEDURES

Forms required: FAFSA, institutional form.
Dates and Deadlines: Priority date 3/1; no closing date. Applicants notified on a rolling basis starting 5/1; must reply within 2 week(s) of notification.
Transfers: Closing date 6/30.

CONTACT

David Page, Director of Financial Aid
One Trudie Kibbe Reed Drive, Little Rock, AR 72202-3718
(501) 370-5350

Phillips Community College of the University of Arkansas

Helena, Arkansas
www.pccua.edu
Federal Code: 001104

2-year public community college in large town.
Enrollment: 1,154 undergrads, 42% part-time. 142 full-time freshmen.
Selectivity: Open admission; but selective for some programs.

BASIC COSTS (2008-2009)
Tuition and fees: $2,020; out-of-district residents $2,290; out-of-state residents $3,430.
Per-credit charge: $55; out-of-district residents $64; out-of-state residents $102.

FINANCIAL AID PICTURE (2007-2008)
Students with need: 85% of average financial aid package awarded as scholarships/grants, 15% awarded as loans/jobs. Need-based aid available for part-time students. Work study available nights.
Students without need: This college awards aid only to students with need.
Additional info: Tuition waivers are given to firefighters and law enforcement officers.

FINANCIAL AID PROCEDURES
Forms required: FAFSA.
Dates and Deadlines: Priority date 4/1; closing date 6/30. Applicants notified on a rolling basis starting 4/1; must reply within 2 week(s) of notification.

CONTACT
Barbra Stevenson, Director of Financial Aid
1000 Campus Drive, Helena, AR 72342
(870) 338-6474 ext. 1160

Pulaski Technical College

North Little Rock, Arkansas
www.pulaskitech.edu
Federal Code: 014167

2-year public community and technical college in small city.
Enrollment: 7,984 undergrads, 51% part-time. 812 full-time freshmen.
Selectivity: Open admission; but selective for some programs.

BASIC COSTS (2008-2009)
Tuition and fees: $2,630; out-of-state residents $4,160.
Per-credit charge: $77; out-of-state residents $128.

FINANCIAL AID PICTURE (2008-2009)
Students with need: Need-based aid available for full-time and part-time students.

FINANCIAL AID PROCEDURES
Forms required: FAFSA, institutional form.
Dates and Deadlines: Priority date 5/15; no closing date. Applicants notified on a rolling basis starting 5/1; must reply within 2 week(s) of notification.

CONTACT
Kris Burford, Director Financial Aid
3000 West Scenic Drive, North Little Rock, AR 72118-3347
(501) 812-2289

Rich Mountain Community College

Mena, Arkansas
www.rmcc.edu
Federal Code: 012435

2-year public community college in small town.
Enrollment: 367 full-time undergrads.
Selectivity: Open admission; but selective for some programs.

BASIC COSTS (2008-2009)
Tuition and fees: $1,620; out-of-district residents $2,010; out-of-state residents $5,190.
Per-credit charge: $51; out-of-district residents $64; out-of-state residents $170.

FINANCIAL AID PICTURE (2007-2008)
Students with need: Need-based aid available for full-time and part-time students.
Students without need: No-need awards available for academics.

FINANCIAL AID PROCEDURES
Forms required: FAFSA, institutional form.
Dates and Deadlines: Priority date 7/1; no closing date. Applicants notified on a rolling basis starting 6/1; must reply within 2 week(s) of notification.

CONTACT
Mary Stenderfer, Director of Financial Aid
1100 College Drive, Mena, AR 71953
(479) 394-7622 ext. 1420

South Arkansas Community College

El Dorado, Arkansas
www.southark.edu
Federal Code: 013858

2-year public community and junior college in large town.
Enrollment: 1,525 undergrads.
Selectivity: Open admission.

BASIC COSTS (2008-2009)
Tuition and fees: $2,180; out-of-district residents $2,420; out-of-state residents $4,250.
Per-credit charge: $66; out-of-district residents $74; out-of-state residents $135.
Additional info: $25 lab fee for most courses.

FINANCIAL AID PICTURE (2007-2008)
Students with need: Need-based aid available for full-time and part-time students.

FINANCIAL AID PROCEDURES
Forms required: FAFSA, institutional form.
Dates and Deadlines: Closing date 8/1. Applicants notified on a rolling basis starting 7/1; must reply within 2 week(s) of notification.

CONTACT
Veronda Tatum, Director of Financial Aid
Box 7010, El Dorado, AR 71731-7010
(870) 864-7133

Southeast Arkansas College

Pine Bluff, Arkansas
www.seark.edu
Federal Code: 005707

2-year public community and technical college in small city.
Enrollment: 1,605 undergrads, 43% part-time. 192 full-time freshmen.
Selectivity: Open admission; but selective for some programs.

BASIC COSTS (2008-2009)
Tuition and fees: $2,290; out-of-state residents $4,330.
Per-credit charge: $68; out-of-state residents $136.

FINANCIAL AID PICTURE
Students with need: Need-based aid available for full-time and part-time students. Work study available nights, weekends, and for part-time students.

Students without need: No-need awards available for academics, leadership, state/district residency.

FINANCIAL AID PROCEDURES

Forms required: FAFSA.
Dates and Deadlines: Priority date 6/1; no closing date. Applicants notified on a rolling basis starting 5/1; must reply within 2 week(s) of notification.

CONTACT

Donna Cox, Director of Financial Aid
1900 Hazel Street, Pine Bluff, AR 71603
(870) 543-5909

Southern Arkansas University

Magnolia, Arkansas
www.saumag.edu Federal Code: 001107

4-year public university in large town.
Enrollment: 2,546 undergrads, 12% part-time. 621 full-time freshmen.
Selectivity: Admits 50 to 75% of applicants.

BASIC COSTS (2008-2009)

Tuition and fees: $5,760; out-of-state residents $8,220.
Per-credit charge: $160; out-of-state residents $242.
Room and board: $4,200.

FINANCIAL AID PICTURE (2007-2008)

Students with need: 40% of average financial aid package awarded as scholarships/grants, 60% awarded as loans/jobs. Need-based aid available for part-time students. Work study available nights, weekends, and for part-time students.
Students without need: No-need awards available for academics, alumni affiliation, art, athletics, leadership, minority status, music/drama, state/district residency.

FINANCIAL AID PROCEDURES

Forms required: FAFSA.
Dates and Deadlines: Priority date 7/1; no closing date. Applicants notified on a rolling basis starting 4/15; must reply within 2 week(s) of notification.

CONTACT

Bronwyn Sneed, Director of Financial Aid
Box 9382, Magnolia, AR 71754-9382
(870) 235-4023

Southern Arkansas University Tech

Camden, Arkansas
www.sautech.edu Federal Code: 007738

2-year public community and technical college in large town.
Enrollment: 871 undergrads, 34% part-time. 211 full-time freshmen.
Selectivity: Open admission; but selective for some programs.

BASIC COSTS (2008-2009)

Tuition and fees: $3,008; out-of-state residents $4,238.
Per-credit charge: $80; out-of-state residents $121.

FINANCIAL AID PICTURE (2007-2008)

Students with need: 71% of average financial aid package awarded as scholarships/grants, 29% awarded as loans/jobs. Need-based aid available for part-time students. Work study available nights, weekends, and for part-time students.
Students without need: No-need awards available for academics, state/district residency.

FINANCIAL AID PROCEDURES

Forms required: FAFSA.
Dates and Deadlines: Priority date 6/1; no closing date. Applicants notified on a rolling basis starting 5/1.
Transfers: Priority date 4/15; closing date 6/1. Applicants notified on a rolling basis starting 5/1.

CONTACT

John Jefferson, Director of Financial Aid
PO Box 3499, Camden, AR 71711-1599
(870) 574-4511

University of Arkansas

Fayetteville, Arkansas
www.uark.edu Federal Code: 001108

4-year public university in small city.
Enrollment: 14,861 undergrads, 13% part-time. 2,879 full-time freshmen.
Selectivity: Admits 50 to 75% of applicants.

BASIC COSTS (2008-2009)

Tuition and fees: $6,400; out-of-state residents $15,278.
Per-credit charge: $167; out-of-state residents $463.
Room and board: $7,422.

FINANCIAL AID PICTURE (2007-2008)

Students with need: Out of 1,642 full-time freshmen who applied for aid, 1,089 were judged to have need. Of these, 1,063 received aid, and 332 had their full need met. Average financial aid package met 78% of need; average scholarship/grant was $6,656; average loan was $3,590. For part-time students, average financial aid package was $5,719.
Students without need: 549 full-time freshmen who did not demonstrate need for aid received scholarships/grants; average award was $5,764. No-need awards available for academics, alumni affiliation, art, athletics, leadership, minority status, music/drama, ROTC, state/district residency.
Scholarships offered: ***Merit:*** Sturgis Fellowship: $11,500, based on exceptional academic performance, 10 awards available to arts and sciences majors. Bodenhamer Fellowship: $11,000, based on strong academic performance and leadership. Chancellor's Scholarships: tuition, fees, room and board. University Scholarships: $4,000, based on rank in top 5-10% of high school class. Non-resident Tuition Award: non-resident tuition, for entering freshmen from neighboring states, based on minimum ACT score of 25 or SAT of 1130 (exclusive of writing) and 3.5 high school GPA. ***Athletic:*** 84 full-time freshmen received athletic scholarships; average amount $7,933.
Cumulative student debt: 44% of graduating class had student loans; average debt was $19,248.

FINANCIAL AID PROCEDURES

Forms required: FAFSA.
Dates and Deadlines: Priority date 3/15; no closing date. Applicants notified on a rolling basis starting 4/1; must reply within 4 week(s) of notification

CONTACT

Kattie Wing, Director of Student Financial Services
232 Silas Hunt Hall, Fayetteville, AR 72701
(479) 575-3806

University of Arkansas at Fort Smith

Fort Smith, Arkansas
www.uafortsmith.edu Federal Code: 001110

4-year public university in small city.
Enrollment: 6,110 undergrads, 27% part-time. 1,074 full-time freshmen.
Selectivity: Open admission; but selective for some programs.

BASIC COSTS (2008-2009)

Tuition and fees: $4,410; out-of-state residents $9,600.
Per-credit charge: $110; out-of-state residents $283.

Room only: $4,282.

FINANCIAL AID PICTURE (2007-2008)

Students with need: Out of 812 full-time freshmen who applied for aid, 460 were judged to have need. Of these, 443 received aid, and 56 had their full need met. Average financial aid package met 60% of need; average scholarship/grant was $3,849; average loan was $2,732. For part-time students, average financial aid package was $4,786.

Students without need: 300 full-time freshmen who did not demonstrate need for aid received scholarships/grants; average award was $3,376. No-need awards available for academics, athletics, job skills, leadership, music/drama.

Scholarships offered: 27 full-time freshmen received athletic scholarships; average amount $4,778.

Cumulative student debt: 47% of graduating class had student loans; average debt was $14,234.

FINANCIAL AID PROCEDURES

Forms required: FAFSA.

Dates and Deadlines: Priority date 6/15; no closing date. Applicants notified on a rolling basis starting 3/1; must reply within 4 week(s) of notification.

Transfers: No deadline. Applicants notified on a rolling basis starting 3/1; must reply within 4 week(s) of notification.

CONTACT

Alan Pixley, Director of Financial Aid
PO Box 3649, Fort Smith, AR 72913-3649
(479) 788-7090

University of Arkansas at Little Rock

Little Rock, Arkansas
www.ualr.edu Federal Code: 001161

4-year public university in small city.
Enrollment: 9,195 undergrads.
Selectivity: Admits over 75% of applicants.

BASIC COSTS (2008-2009)

Tuition and fees: $6,121; out-of-state residents $14,304.
Per-credit charge: $163; out-of-state residents $436.
Room only: $3,100.

FINANCIAL AID PICTURE

Students with need: Need-based aid available for full-time and part-time students.

FINANCIAL AID PROCEDURES

Forms required: FAFSA.

Dates and Deadlines: Closing date 8/1. Applicants notified on a rolling basis starting 5/1.

CONTACT

Tammy Harrison, Director of Admissions and Financial Aid
2801 South University Avenue, Little Rock, AR 72204
(501) 569-3035

University of Arkansas at Monticello

Monticello, Arkansas
www.uamont.edu Federal Code: 001085

4-year public university and technical college in large town.
Enrollment: 2,616 undergrads, 18% part-time. 612 full-time freshmen.
Selectivity: Admits 50 to 75% of applicants.

BASIC COSTS (2008-2009)

Tuition and fees: $4,600; out-of-state residents $8,770.
Per-credit charge: $114; out-of-state residents $253.
Room and board: $3,870.

FINANCIAL AID PICTURE (2007-2008)

Students with need: 59% of average financial aid package awarded as scholarships/grants, 41% awarded as loans/jobs. Need-based aid available for part-time students. Work study available nights, weekends, and for part-time students.

Students without need: No-need awards available for academics, athletics, job skills, leadership, music/drama, ROTC, state/district residency.

FINANCIAL AID PROCEDURES

Forms required: FAFSA, institutional form.

Dates and Deadlines: Priority date 5/1; no closing date. Applicants notified on a rolling basis starting 4/1; must reply within 2 week(s) of notification.

CONTACT

Susan Brewer, Director of Financial Aid
Box 3600, Monticello, AR 71656
(870) 460-1050

University of Arkansas at Pine Bluff

Pine Bluff, Arkansas
www.uapb.edu Federal Code: 001086

4-year public university in small city.
Enrollment: 3,352 undergrads, 10% part-time. 954 full-time freshmen.
Selectivity: Admits 50 to 75% of applicants.

BASIC COSTS (2008-2009)

Tuition and fees: $4,676; out-of-state residents $9,236.
Per-credit charge: $115; out-of-state residents $267.
Room and board: $6,100.
Additional info: Tuition/fee waivers available for minority students.

FINANCIAL AID PICTURE (2007-2008)

Students with need: Need-based aid available for full-time and part-time students. Work study available weekends and for part-time students.

Students without need: No-need awards available for academics, alumni affiliation, art, athletics, leadership, minority status, music/drama, religious affiliation, ROTC, state/district residency.

FINANCIAL AID PROCEDURES

Forms required: FAFSA.

Dates and Deadlines: Priority date 4/15; no closing date. Applicants notified on a rolling basis starting 3/1.

Transfers: Must supply financial aid transcript from prior college or university.

CONTACT

Janice Kearney, Director of Financial Aid
1200 North University Drive, Mail Slot 4981, Pine Bluff, AR 71601-2799
(870) 575-8302

University of Arkansas Community College at Morrilton

Morrilton, Arkansas Federal Code: 005245
www.uaccm.edu CSS Code: 3881

2-year public community college in small town.
Enrollment: 1,855 undergrads, 30% part-time. 473 full-time freshmen.
Selectivity: Admits 50 to 75% of applicants.

BASIC COSTS (2008-2009)

Tuition and fees: $2,520; out-of-district residents $2,730; out-of-state residents $3,720.
Per-credit charge: $67; out-of-district residents $74; out-of-state residents $107.

FINANCIAL AID PICTURE (2008-2009)

Students with need: Out of 351 full-time freshmen who applied for aid, 309 were judged to have need. Of these, 278 received aid, and 19 had their full need met. Average financial aid package met 53% of need; average scholarship/grant was $1,531; average loan was $1,204. For part-time students, average financial aid package was $1,418.

Students without need: 14 full-time freshmen who did not demonstrate need for aid received scholarships/grants; average award was $1,068. No-need awards available for academics, leadership, state/district residency.

FINANCIAL AID PROCEDURES

Forms required: FAFSA, CSS PROFILE, institutional form.

Dates and Deadlines: Priority date 7/1; no closing date. Applicants notified by 5/1.

CONTACT

Teresa Cash, Director of Financial Aid
1537 University Boulevard, Morrilton, AR 72110
(501) 977-2055

University of Arkansas for Medical Sciences

Little Rock, Arkansas
www.uams.edu Federal Code: 001109

4-year public university and health science college in large city.

Enrollment: 900 undergrads.

BASIC COSTS (2008-2009)

Additional info: In-state students pay $190 per credit hour for the following programs: dental hygiene, diagnostic medical sonography, nuclear medicine imaging sciences and radiologic technology. In-state students pay $180 per credit hour for the following programs: cytotechnology, health information management, medical dosimetry, medical technology, ophthalmic medical technology, radiation therapy, respiratory care and surgical technology. All out-of-state students pay tuition of $436 per credit hour for programs. Emergency medical sciences/paramedic students pay according to program: 4-semester program, $905 tuition; 5-semester program, $724 tuition. Additional required fees vary by program.

FINANCIAL AID PICTURE

Students with need: Need-based aid available for full-time and part-time students.

FINANCIAL AID PROCEDURES

Forms required: FAFSA.

Dates and Deadlines: No deadline. Applicants notified on a rolling basis starting 5/1; must reply within 2 week(s) of notification.

CONTACT

Phyllis Lloyd, Registrar
4301 West Markham Street, Little Rock, AR 72205
(501) 686-5454

University of Arkansas: Community College at Batesville

Batesville, Arkansas
www.uaccb.edu Federal Code: 020735

2-year public community college in small town.

Enrollment: 1,333 undergrads.

Selectivity: Open admission; but selective for some programs.

BASIC COSTS (2008-2009)

Tuition and fees: $2,077; out-of-district residents $2,377; out-of-state residents $4,117.

Per-credit charge: $52; out-of-district residents $62; out-of-state residents $120.

FINANCIAL AID PICTURE

Students with need: Need-based aid available for full-time students. Work study available nights, weekends, and for part-time students.

Students without need: This college awards aid only to students with need.

FINANCIAL AID PROCEDURES

Forms required: FAFSA.

Dates and Deadlines: No deadline. Applicants notified on a rolling basis starting 3/1; must reply within 2 week(s) of notification.

CONTACT

Gayle Cooper, Vice Chancellor for Finance and Administration
Box 3350, Batesville, AR 72503
(870) 612-2036

University of Arkansas: Community College at Hope

Hope, Arkansas
www.uacch.edu Federal Code: 005732

2-year public community and technical college in small town.

Enrollment: 964 undergrads.

Selectivity: Open admission; but selective for some programs.

BASIC COSTS (2008-2009)

Tuition and fees: $1,790; out-of-district residents $1,940; out-of-state residents $3,620.

Per-credit charge: $54; out-of-district residents $59; out-of-state residents $115.

FINANCIAL AID PICTURE (2007-2008)

Students with need: Need-based aid available for full-time and part-time students. Work study available nights.

Students without need: No-need awards available for academics.

FINANCIAL AID PROCEDURES

Forms required: FAFSA, institutional form.

Dates and Deadlines: Priority date 7/6; no closing date. Applicants notified on a rolling basis starting 1/1; must reply within 4 week(s) of notification.

CONTACT

Brian Lee, Director of Financial Aid
2500 South Main, Hope, AR 71802-0140
(870) 722-8264

University of Central Arkansas

Conway, Arkansas
www.uca.edu Federal Code: 001092

4-year public university in small city.

Enrollment: 9,669 undergrads, 9% part-time. 2,075 full-time freshmen.

Selectivity: Admits 50 to 75% of applicants.

BASIC COSTS (2008-2009)

Tuition and fees: $6,505; out-of-state residents $11,605.

Per-credit charge: $170; out-of-state residents $340.

Room and board: $4,740.

FINANCIAL AID PICTURE (2007-2008)

Students with need: 39% of average financial aid package awarded as scholarships/grants, 61% awarded as loans/jobs. Work study available nights, weekends, and for part-time students.

Students without need: No-need awards available for academics, art, athletics, leadership, minority status, music/drama, ROTC, state/district residency.
Additional info: Room and board may be paid monthly.

FINANCIAL AID PROCEDURES
Forms required: FAFSA.
Dates and Deadlines: Priority date 4/15; closing date 7/1. Applicants notified on a rolling basis starting 5/4.

CONTACT
Cheryl Lyons, Director of Financial Aid
201 Donaghey Avenue, Conway, AR 72035
(501) 450-3140

University of the Ozarks
Clarksville, Arkansas
www.ozarks.edu Federal Code: 001094

4-year private university and liberal arts college in small town, affiliated with Presbyterian Church (USA).
Enrollment: 636 undergrads, 2% part-time. 195 full-time freshmen.
Selectivity: Admits over 75% of applicants.

BASIC COSTS (2008-2009)
Tuition and fees: $17,330.
Per-credit charge: $700.
Room and board: $5,725.
Additional info: Tuition/fee waivers available for minority students.

FINANCIAL AID PICTURE (2008-2009)
Students with need: Out of 155 full-time freshmen who applied for aid, 143 were judged to have need. Of these, 143 received aid, and 35 had their full need met. Average financial aid package met 87% of need; average scholarship/grant was $15,183; average loan was $6,476. For part-time students, average financial aid package was $11,161.
Students without need: 44 full-time freshmen who did not demonstrate need for aid received scholarships/grants; average award was $15,077. No-need awards available for academics, alumni affiliation, art, leadership, minority status, music/drama, religious affiliation, state/district residency.
Cumulative student debt: 44% of graduating class had student loans; average debt was $16,852.
Additional info: Walton International Scholarship Program provides full scholarships to selected Central American and Mexican residents.

FINANCIAL AID PROCEDURES
Forms required: FAFSA.
Dates and Deadlines: Priority date 2/15; no closing date. Applicants notified on a rolling basis starting 3/1; must reply within 2 week(s) of notification.

CONTACT
Jana Hart, Dean of Admissions and Financial Aid
415 North College Avenue, Clarksville, AR 72830-2880
(479) 979-1221

Williams Baptist College
Walnut Ridge, Arkansas
www.wbcoll.edu Federal Code: 001106

4-year private liberal arts college in small town, affiliated with Southern Baptist Convention.
Enrollment: 486 undergrads, 3% part-time. 134 full-time freshmen.
Selectivity: Admits 50 to 75% of applicants.

BASIC COSTS (2009-2010)
Tuition and fees: $11,400.
Per-credit charge: $442.
Room and board: $5,200.

FINANCIAL AID PICTURE (2007-2008)
Students with need: Out of 122 full-time freshmen who applied for aid, 94 were judged to have need. Of these, 94 received aid. For part-time students, average financial aid package was $5,712.
Students without need: No-need awards available for academics, art, athletics, leadership, minority status, music/drama, religious affiliation, state/district residency.
Scholarships offered: ***Merit:*** Trustee's Scholarship: up to full tuition and room and board; based on minimum ACT composite score of 30 and minimum 3.5 high school GPA; 1 awarded; deadline March 1, renewable for 4 years with 3.25 cumulative GPA on at least 15 credit hours per semester. ***Athletic:*** 53 full-time freshmen received athletic scholarships; average amount $3,164.
Cumulative student debt: 65% of graduating class had student loans; average debt was $15,878.
Additional info: Art scholarship applicants must submit portfolio.

FINANCIAL AID PROCEDURES
Forms required: FAFSA.
Dates and Deadlines: Priority date 5/1; no closing date. Applicants notified on a rolling basis starting 4/1; must reply within 2 week(s) of notification.
Transfers: Priority date 4/1; no deadline. Applicants notified on a rolling basis starting 4/1; must reply within 2 week(s) of notification.

CONTACT
Barbara Turner, Director of Financial Aid
PO Box 3665, Walnut Ridge, AR 72476
(870) 759-4112

California

Academy of Art University
San Francisco, California
www.academyart.edu Federal Code: 007531

4-year for-profit university and visual arts college in very large city.
Enrollment: 9,400 undergrads, 36% part-time. 717 full-time freshmen.
Selectivity: Open admission.

BASIC COSTS (2009-2010)
Tuition and fees: $22,490.
Per-credit charge: $740.
Room and board: $13,400.

FINANCIAL AID PICTURE (2007-2008)
Students with need: Out of 512 full-time freshmen who applied for aid, 446 were judged to have need. Of these, 443 received aid, and 2 had their full need met. Average financial aid package met 25% of need; average scholarship/grant was $4,275; average loan was $2,839. For part-time students, average financial aid package was $4,962.
Students without need: No-need awards available for academics, art.
Additional info: Numerous summer grant programs available.

FINANCIAL AID PROCEDURES
Forms required: FAFSA, institutional form.
Dates and Deadlines: Priority date 7/10; no closing date. Applicants notified on a rolling basis.
Transfers: Priority date 3/1; no deadline. Applicants notified on a rolling basis.

CONTACT

Joe Vollaro, Executive Vice President for Financial Aid/Compliance
79 New Montgomery Street, San Francisco, CA 94105-3410
(415) 618-6273

Allan Hancock College

Santa Maria, California
www.hancockcollege.edu Federal Code: 001111

2-year public community college in small city.
Enrollment: 6,481 undergrads.
Selectivity: Open admission; but selective for some programs.

BASIC COSTS (2008-2009)
Tuition and fees: $647; out-of-state residents $6,077.
Per-credit charge: $20; out-of-state residents $201.

FINANCIAL AID PICTURE
Students with need: Need-based aid available for full-time and part-time students.
Students without need: This college awards aid only to students with need.

FINANCIAL AID PROCEDURES
Forms required: FAFSA.
Dates and Deadlines: Priority date 5/1; no closing date. Applicants notified on a rolling basis starting 6/1.

CONTACT
Robert Parisi, Financial Aid Director
800 South College Drive, Santa Maria, CA 93454-6399
(805) 922-6966 ext. 3200

Alliant International University

San Diego, California
www.alliant.edu Federal Code: 011117

Upper-division private university in very large city.
Enrollment: 192 undergrads, 36% part-time.

BASIC COSTS (2008-2009)
Tuition and fees: $15,210.
Per-credit charge: $550.
Room and board: $8,540.
Additional info: Tuition/fee waivers available for minority students.

FINANCIAL AID PICTURE (2008-2009)
Students with need: 29% of average financial aid package awarded as scholarships/grants, 71% awarded as loans/jobs. Need-based aid available for part-time students. Work study available nights, weekends, and for part-time students.
Students without need: No-need awards available for academics, alumni affiliation, athletics, leadership.
Scholarships offered: Grants and scholarships available based on GPA and SAT/ACT scores.

FINANCIAL AID PROCEDURES
Forms required: FAFSA.
Dates and Deadlines: Priority date 3/2; no closing date. Applicants notified on a rolling basis starting 2/1; must reply within 3 week(s) of notification.

CONTACT
Deborah Spindler, Director of Financial Aid
10455 Pomerado Road, San Diego, CA 92131-1799
(858) 635-4559

American Jewish University

Los Angeles, California
www.ajula.edu Federal Code: 002741

4-year private university and liberal arts college in very large city, affiliated with Jewish faith.
Enrollment: 100 undergrads. 29 full-time freshmen.
Selectivity: Admits 50 to 75% of applicants.

BASIC COSTS (2008-2009)
Tuition and fees: $22,352.
Room and board: $11,416.

FINANCIAL AID PICTURE (2008-2009)
Students with need: Need-based aid available for full-time and part-time students. Work study available nights, weekends, and for part-time students.
Students without need: No-need awards available for academics, leadership.
Scholarships offered: President's Scholarship: offered to incoming students with a GPA of 3.5 or higher. Ambassador's Scholarship: offered to incoming students with a GPA of 3.0 or higher; renewable for 4 years based on good academic standing. Transfer Excellence Award: offered to transfer students with GPA of 3.3 or higher; renewable based on good academic standing. Additional merit-based scholarships: Dean's Scholarship, Leadership & Service, Israel Experience, IDF/Bagrut Scholarship.

FINANCIAL AID PROCEDURES
Forms required: FAFSA, state aid form, institutional form.
Dates and Deadlines: Priority date 3/2; no closing date. Applicants notified on a rolling basis starting 3/15; must reply within 3 week(s) of notification.
Transfers: Priority date 2/16; no deadline. Applicants notified on a rolling basis starting 5/18; must reply within 3 week(s) of notification. Excellence awards: $7,500 towards tuition for a transfer student with a GPA of 3.3 or higher, and $5,000 towards tuition for transfer students with a GPA of 3.0 or higher. Both of these awards are renewable based on good academic standing (at least a 3.0 GPA).

CONTACT
Larisa Zadoyen, Director of Financial Aid
15600 Mulholland Drive, Los Angeles, CA 90077
(310) 476-9777 ext. 252

American River College

Sacramento, California
www.arc.losrios.edu Federal Code: 001232

2-year public community college in large city.
Enrollment: 21,549 undergrads.
Selectivity: Open admission; but selective for some programs.

BASIC COSTS (2008-2009)
Tuition and fees: $632; out-of-state residents $6,062.
Per-credit charge: $20; out-of-state residents $201.
Additional info: Tuition/fee waivers available for minority students.

FINANCIAL AID PICTURE
Students with need: Need-based aid available for full-time and part-time students.
Students without need: This college awards aid only to students with need.

FINANCIAL AID PROCEDURES
Forms required: FAFSA.
Dates and Deadlines: Priority date 3/2; no closing date. Applicants notified on a rolling basis starting 7/1; must reply within 2 week(s) of notification.

CONTACT
Roy Beckhorn, Financial Aid Supervisor
4700 College Oak Drive, Sacramento, CA 95841
(916) 484-8437

Antelope Valley College

Lancaster, California
www.avc.edu Federal Code: 001113

2-year public community college in large city.
Enrollment: 10,505 undergrads.
Selectivity: Open admission; but selective for some programs.

BASIC COSTS (2008-2009)
Tuition and fees: $602; out-of-state residents $6,032.
Per-credit charge: $20; out-of-state residents $201.

FINANCIAL AID PICTURE
Students with need: Need-based aid available for full-time and part-time students.

FINANCIAL AID PROCEDURES
Forms required: FAFSA, state aid form, institutional form.
Dates and Deadlines: Priority date 3/2; no closing date. Applicants notified on a rolling basis starting 7/15; must reply within 2 week(s) of notification.

CONTACT
Sherrie Padilla, Director of Financial Aid
3041 West Avenue K, Lancaster, CA 93536-5426
(661) 722-6336

Antioch University Santa Barbara

Santa Barbara, California
www.antiochsb.edu Federal Code: 003010

Upper-division private university and liberal arts college in small city.
Enrollment: 105 undergrads, 65% part-time.

BASIC COSTS (2008-2009)
Tuition and fees: $15,401.
Per-credit charge: $515.

FINANCIAL AID PICTURE (2007-2008)
Students with need: Average financial aid package for all full-time undergraduates was $10,500. 22% awarded as scholarships/grants, 78% awarded as loans/jobs. Need-based aid available for part-time students. Work study available nights, weekends, and for part-time students.
Cumulative student debt: 75% of graduating class had student loans; average debt was $25,000.

FINANCIAL AID PROCEDURES
Forms required: FAFSA, institutional form.
Dates and Deadlines: Priority date 4/15; no closing date. Applicants notified on a rolling basis; must reply within 4 week(s) of notification.
Transfers: Priority date 4/1; no deadline.

CONTACT
Cecilia Schneider, Financial Aid Director
801 Garden Street, Suite 101, Santa Barbara, CA 93101-1581
(805) 962-8179 ext. 108

Art Center College of Design

Pasadena, California
www.artcenter.edu Federal Code: 001116

4-year private visual arts college in small city.
Enrollment: 1,504 undergrads.
Selectivity: Admits 50 to 75% of applicants.

BASIC COSTS (2008-2009)
Tuition and fees: $30,284.

FINANCIAL AID PICTURE (2007-2008)
Students with need: Need-based aid available for full-time students.
Students without need: This college awards aid only to students with need.
Additional info: Students may apply for scholarships after they enroll while progressing through the program.

FINANCIAL AID PROCEDURES
Forms required: FAFSA.
Dates and Deadlines: Priority date 3/1; no closing date. Applicants notified on a rolling basis starting 5/15; must reply within 4 week(s) of notification.
Transfers: Applicants notified on a rolling basis starting 1/1.

CONTACT
Clema McKenzie, Director of Financial Aid
1700 Lida Street, Pasadena, CA 91103
(626) 396-2215

Art Institute of California: Hollywood

Los Angeles, California
www.artinstitutes.edu/hollywood Federal Code: 031254

4-year for-profit visual arts and technical and career college in very large city.
Enrollment: 918 undergrads, 46% part-time. 227 full-time freshmen.
Selectivity: Open admission.

BASIC COSTS (2008-2009)
Tuition and fees: $21,835.
Per-credit charge: $483.
Room only: $9,285.
Additional info: Cost for 7-quarter continuous enrollment associate degree program $52,118; cost for 12-quarter continuous enrollment bachelor's degree program $88,938. Fees vary by program.

FINANCIAL AID PICTURE (2007-2008)
Students with need: Out of 119 full-time freshmen who applied for aid, 119 were judged to have need. Of these, 119 received aid. For part-time students, average financial aid package was $7,098.

CONTACT
Adis Ceballos, Director of Student Financial Services
3440 Wilshire Boulevard, 10th Floor, Los Angeles, CA 90010

Art Institute of California: Los Angeles

Santa Monica, California
www.artinstitutes.edu/losangeles Federal Code: 007470

2-year for-profit visual arts college in small city.
Enrollment: 2,179 undergrads.

BASIC COSTS (2008-2009)
Tuition and fees: $23,234.
Per-credit charge: $483.
Additional info: Apartment-style housing: $2,663/quarter for 2-bedroom, $3,227/quarter for 1-bedroom unit.

FINANCIAL AID PICTURE (2008-2009)

Students with need: Need-based aid available for full-time and part-time students. Work study available nights, weekends, and for part-time students.

Students without need: No-need awards available for academics.

FINANCIAL AID PROCEDURES

Forms required: FAFSA.

Dates and Deadlines: No deadline. Applicants notified on a rolling basis.

CONTACT

Kathleen Harris, Director of Student Financial Services
2900 31st Street, Santa Monica, CA 90405-3035
(310) 752-4700

Art Institute of California: Orange County

Santa Ana, California
www.artinstitutes.edu/orangecounty Federal Code: 007236

3-year for-profit culinary school and visual arts college in very large city.

Enrollment: 1,694 undergrads, 23% part-time. 430 full-time freshmen.

Selectivity: Open admission; but selective for some programs.

BASIC COSTS (2008-2009)

Tuition and fees: $23,384.

Per-credit charge: $483.

Room only: $3,025.

Additional info: Typical full-time load 16 credit hours per quarter. Culinary lab fee $315 per quarter, online fee $100 per class per quarter.

FINANCIAL AID PICTURE

Students with need: Need-based aid available for full-time and part time students. Work study available nights, weekends, and for part-time students.

Students without need: No-need awards available for academics, art, minority status.

FINANCIAL AID PROCEDURES

Forms required: FAFSA, state aid form.

Dates and Deadlines: No deadline. Applicants notified on a rolling basis; must reply within 2 week(s) of notification.

CONTACT

Silvia Guzman, Director of Student Financial Services
3601 West Sunflower Avenue, Santa Ana, CA 92704-7931
(714) 830-0202

Art Institute of California: San Diego

San Diego, California
www.artinstitutes.edu/sandiego Federal Code: 016471

3-year for-profit visual arts college in very large city.

Enrollment: 1,974 undergrads.

BASIC COSTS (2008-2009)

Tuition and fees: $22,272.

Per-credit charge: $4[illegible].

FINANCIAL AID PICTURE

Students with need: Need-based aid available for full-time students.

FINANCIAL AID PROCEDURES

Forms required: FAFSA.

Dates and Deadlines: No deadline.

CONTACT

Director of Student Financial Services
7650 Mission Valley Road, San Diego, CA 92108-4423

Art Institute of California: San Francisco

San Francisco, California
www.artinstitutes.edu/sanfrancisco

4-year for-profit visual arts college in very large city.

Enrollment: 1,539 undergrads.

BASIC COSTS (2008-2009)

Tuition and fees: $21,375.

Per-credit charge: $475.

Additional info: Starter kits additional $750-$1,300 estimate for all programs.

FINANCIAL AID PICTURE (2007-2008)

Students with need: 42% of average financial aid package awarded as scholarships/grants, 58% awarded as loans/jobs.

Scholarships offered: The Art Institutes and Americans for the Arts Poster Design Competition; $2,000-$3,000 locally, up to $25,000 nationally; 2 awarded per Art Institute location, 10 awarded nationally. Evelyn Keedy Memorial Scholarship; $30,000; 1 awarded nationally.

FINANCIAL AID PROCEDURES

Forms required: FAFSA.

Dates and Deadlines: No deadline. Applicants notified on a rolling basis.

CONTACT

Maria Juravic, Director of Student Financial Services
1170 Market Street, San Francisco, CA 94102
(415) 865-0198

Azusa Pacific University

Azusa, California
www.apu.edu Federal Code: 001117

4-year private university in small city, affiliated with interdenominational tradition.

Enrollment: 4,858 undergrads, 16% part-time. 848 full-time freshmen.

Selectivity: Admits 50 to 75% of applicants.

BASIC COSTS (2009-2010)

Tuition and fees: $26,640.

Per-credit charge: $1,075.

Room and board: $7,742.

Additional info: Tuition/fee waivers available for minority students.

FINANCIAL AID PICTURE (2007-2008)

Students with need: Out of 845 full-time freshmen who applied for aid, 541 were judged to have need. Of these, 539 received aid, and 92 had their full need met. Average financial aid package met 56% of need; average scholarship/grant was $12,004; average loan was $8,271. For part-time students, average financial aid package was $3,842.

Students without need: 242 full-time freshmen who did not demonstrate need for aid received scholarships/grants; average award was $5,980. No-need awards available for academics, athletics, leadership, minority status, music/drama, religious affiliation, ROTC.

Scholarships offered: 9 full-time freshmen received athletic scholarships; average amount $15,615.

FINANCIAL AID PROCEDURES

Forms required: FAFSA, institutional form.

Dates and Deadlines: Priority date 3/2; closing date 7/1. Applicants notified on a rolling basis starting 3/1; must reply within 3 week(s) of notification.

Transfers: Cal Grants not available to first time applicants who are seniors.

CONTACT

Todd Ross, Director of Student Financial Services
901 East Alosta Avenue, Azusa, CA 91702-7000
(626) 812-3009

Barstow Community College

Barstow, California
www.barstow.edu Federal Code: 001119

2-year public community college in large town.
Enrollment: 1,581 undergrads.
Selectivity: Open admission.

BASIC COSTS (2008-2009)
Tuition and fees: $600; out-of-state residents $5,520.
Per-credit charge: $20; out-of-state residents $184.

FINANCIAL AID PICTURE (2007-2008)
Students with need: 98% of average financial aid package awarded as scholarships/grants, 2% awarded as loans/jobs. Need-based aid available for part-time students.
Students without need: This college awards aid only to students with need.

FINANCIAL AID PROCEDURES
Forms required: FAFSA.
Dates and Deadlines: Closing date 5/22. Applicants notified on a rolling basis starting 7/1.

CONTACT
Danielle Cordova, Financial Aid Officer
2700 Barstow Road, Barstow, CA 92311-9984
(760) 252-2411 ext. 7205

Berkeley City College

Berkeley, California
www.berkeleycitycollege.edu Federal Code: 014311

2-year public community college in small city.
Enrollment: 2,634 undergrads.
Selectivity: Open admission.

BASIC COSTS (2008-2009)
Tuition and fees: $604; out-of-state residents $6,034.
Per-credit charge: $20; out-of-state residents $201.

FINANCIAL AID PICTURE
Students with need: Need-based aid available for full-time and part-time students.
Students without need: This college awards aid only to students with need.

FINANCIAL AID PROCEDURES
Dates and Deadlines: No deadline. Applicants notified on a rolling basis.

CONTACT
Nohemy Ornelas, Financial Aid Program Supervisor
2050 Center Street, Berkeley, CA 94704
(510) 981-2878

Bethany University

Scotts Valley, California
www.bethany.edu Federal Code: 001121

4-year private Bible and liberal arts college in small town, affiliated with Assemblies of God.
Enrollment: 441 undergrads, 13% part-time. 108 full-time freshmen.
Selectivity: Admits 50 to 75% of applicants.

BASIC COSTS (2009-2010)
Tuition and fees: $18,150.
Per-credit charge: $735.
Room and board: $7,450.

FINANCIAL AID PICTURE (2008-2009)
Students with need: Need-based aid available for full-time and part-time students. Work study available nights, weekends, and for part-time students.
Students without need: No-need awards available for academics, alumni affiliation, athletics, leadership, minority status, music/drama, religious affiliation.

FINANCIAL AID PROCEDURES
Forms required: FAFSA, institutional form.
Dates and Deadlines: Priority date 3/2; no closing date. Applicants notified on a rolling basis starting 4/15; must reply within 2 week(s) of notification.

CONTACT
Sharon Anderson, VP of Enrollment and Student Development
800 Bethany Drive, Scotts Valley, CA 95066-2898
(831) 438-3800 ext. 3901

Bethesda Christian University

Anaheim, California
www.bcu.edu Federal Code: 032663

4-year private university in large city, affiliated with Christian Church.
Enrollment: 245 undergrads.
Selectivity: Open admission. GED not accepted.

BASIC COSTS (2009-2010)
Tuition and fees: $7,160.
Per-credit charge: $231.
Room and board: $3,200.

FINANCIAL AID PICTURE (2008-2009)
Students with need: Need-based aid available for full-time and part-time students.
Students without need: This college awards aid only to students with need.

FINANCIAL AID PROCEDURES
Forms required: FAFSA, institutional form.
Dates and Deadlines: Closing date 3/14. Applicants notified on a rolling basis starting 6/30.
Transfers: No deadline.

CONTACT
Tony Chiang, Director of Financial Aid
730 North Euclid Street, Anaheim, CA 92801
(714) 517-1945

Biola University

La Mirada, California
www.biola.edu Federal Code: 001122

4-year private university and Bible college in large town, affiliated with interdenominational tradition.
Enrollment: 3,610 undergrads, 2% part-time. 840 full-time freshmen.
Selectivity: Admits over 75% of applicants.

BASIC COSTS (2009-2010)
Tuition and fees: $27,744.
Per-credit charge: $1,156.
Room and board: $8,080.
Additional info: Tuition/fee waivers available for minority students.

FINANCIAL AID PICTURE (2007-2008)

Students with need: Average financial aid package met 68% of need; average scholarship/grant was $11,339; average loan was $1,796. Need-based aid available for part-time students.

Students without need: No-need awards available for academics, alumni affiliation, art, athletics, leadership, minority status, music/drama, state/district residency.

Scholarships offered: Scholarships for Underrepresented Groups of Ethnicity; up to $6,500; based on GPA and ethnicity. Community Service Scholarship; $2,700; based on demonstration of outstanding spiritual leadership. Alumni Dependent Scholarship; $500; given to students whose parents completed 30 units of coursework at Biola University.

FINANCIAL AID PROCEDURES

Forms required: FAFSA, state aid form.

Dates and Deadlines: Priority date 1/1; no closing date. Applicants notified on a rolling basis starting 3/1.

Transfers: No deadline. Applicants notified on a rolling basis starting 3/1.

CONTACT

Jonathan Choy, Director of Financial Aid
13800 Biola Avenue, La Mirada, CA 90639-0001
(562) 903-4742

Brooks Institute

Santa Barbara, California
www.brooks.edu Federal Code: 001123

3-year for-profit visual arts college in small city.

Enrollment: 1,185 undergrads. 136 full-time freshmen.

BASIC COSTS (2008-2009)

Tuition and fees: $17,840.

FINANCIAL AID PICTURE (2007-2008)

Students with need: 28% of average financial aid package awarded as scholarships/grants, 72% awarded as loans/jobs.

FINANCIAL AID PROCEDURES

Forms required: FAFSA, institutional form.

Dates and Deadlines: Priority date 3/2; no closing date. Applicants notified on a rolling basis starting 5/1.

CONTACT

Andy Rahimi, Director of Student Finance
27 East Cota Street, Santa Barbara, CA 93101
(805) 966-3888

Cabrillo College

Aptos, California
www.cabrillo.edu Federal Code: 001124

2-year public community college in large town.

Enrollment: 7,631 undergrads

Selectivity: Open admission, but selective for some programs.

BASIC COSTS (2008-2009)

Tuition and fees: $636; out-of-state residents $6,066.

Per-credit charge: $20; out-of-state residents $201.

FINANCIAL AID PICTURE (2007-2008)

Students with need: Need-based aid available for full-time and part-time students.

FINANCIAL AID PROCEDURES

Forms required: FAFSA, institutional form.

Dates and Deadlines: No deadline. Applicants notified on a rolling basis starting 7/31; must reply within 3 week(s) of notification.

Transfers: Academic transcript required.

CONTACT

Debbie Soria, Director of Financial Aid and Scholarships
6500 Soquel Drive, Aptos, CA 95003
(831) 479-6100

California Baptist University

Riverside, California
www.calbaptist.edu Federal Code: 001125

4-year private university and liberal arts college in large city, affiliated with Southern Baptist Convention.

Enrollment: 3,072 undergrads, 12% part-time. 438 full-time freshmen.

Selectivity: Admits 50 to 75% of applicants.

BASIC COSTS (2009-2010)

Tuition and fees: $23,266.

Per-credit charge: $841.

Room and board: $8,170.

FINANCIAL AID PICTURE (2007-2008)

Students with need: Need-based aid available for full-time and part-time students. Work study available nights, weekends, and for part-time students.

Students without need: No-need awards available for academics, art, athletics, leadership, music/drama, religious affiliation, ROTC.

Scholarships offered: Matching room and board scholarship for recipients of the ROTC scholarships.

FINANCIAL AID PROCEDURES

Forms required: FAFSA, state aid form.

Dates and Deadlines: Priority date 3/2; no closing date. Applicants notified on a rolling basis starting 3/2; must reply by 5/1 or within 3 week(s) of notification.

Transfers: No deadline. Applicants notified on a rolling basis starting 12/15.

CONTACT

Rebecca Sanchez, Director of Financial Aid
8432 Magnolia Avenue, Riverside, CA 92504-3297
(951) 343-4236

California College of the Arts

San Francisco, California
www.cca.edu Federal Code: 001127

4-year private visual arts college in very large city.

Enrollment: 1,336 undergrads, 7% part-time. 247 full-time freshmen.

Selectivity: Admits over 75% of applicants.

BASIC COSTS (2009-2010)

Tuition and fees: $33,254.

Per-credit charge: $1,371

Room only: $6,870.

Additional info: No meal plan offered. Residence halls equipped with kitchens on each floor. Estimated food cost: $2,850.

FINANCIAL AID PICTURE (2008-2009)

Students with need: Out of 141 full-time freshmen who applied for aid, 123 were judged to have need. Of these, 123 received aid, and 4 had their full need met. Average financial aid package met 64% of need; average scholarship/grant was $16,391; average loan was $3,656. For part-time students, average financial aid package was $9,955.

Students without need: 38 full-time freshmen who did not demonstrate need for aid received scholarships/grants; average award was $4,947. No-need awards available for academics, art.
Scholarships offered: Creative Achievement Scholarship; up to $18,000 annually; renewable; based on academic achievement and strength of admissions portfolios.
Cumulative student debt: 61% of graduating class had student loans; average debt was $35,924.
Additional info: Application deadline for merit scholarships February 1.

FINANCIAL AID PROCEDURES

Forms required: FAFSA.
Dates and Deadlines: Priority date 3/1; no closing date. Applicants notified on a rolling basis starting 3/15; must reply by 5/1 or within 3 week(s) of notification.
Transfers: No deadline. Applicants notified on a rolling basis starting 3/15; must reply by 5/1 or within 3 week(s) of notification. Scholarships available for community college transfer students.

CONTACT

Shawn Brick, Director of Financial Aid
1111 Eighth Street, San Francisco, CA 94107-2247
(415) 703-9528

California Institute of Integral Studies

San Francisco, California
www.ciis.edu Federal Code: 012154

Upper-division private liberal arts college in very large city.
Enrollment: 83 undergrads, 13% part-time.

BASIC COSTS (2009-2010)

Tuition and fees: $14,460.
Per-credit charge: $585.
Additional info: Cost quoted for 2 semesters; 3-semester attendance mandatory.

FINANCIAL AID PICTURE (2007-2008)

Students with need: Average financial aid package for all full-time undergraduates was $7,607; for part-time $6,110. 20% awarded as scholarships/grants, 80% awarded as loans/jobs. Work study available nights, weekends, and for part-time students.
Students without need: No-need awards available for academics, alumni affiliation, art, job skills, leadership, minority status, ROTC, state/district residency.

FINANCIAL AID PROCEDURES

Dates and Deadlines: Closing date 4/15.

CONTACT

Marisol Mendoza, Financial Aid Director
1453 Mission Street, San Francisco, CA 94103
(415) 575-6156

California Institute of Technology

Pasadena, California Federal Code: 001131
www.caltech.edu CSS Code: 4034

4-year private university in small city.
Enrollment: 921 undergrads. 236 full-time freshmen.
Selectivity: Admits less than 50% of applicants.

BASIC COSTS (2008-2009)

Tuition and fees: $34,437.
Per-credit charge: $873.
Room and board: $10,146.

FINANCIAL AID PICTURE (2008-2009)

Students with need: Out of 166 full-time freshmen who applied for aid, 116 were judged to have need. Of these, 116 received aid, and 116 had their full need met. Average financial aid package met 100% of need; average scholarship/grant was $28,846; average loan was $2,261.
Students without need: 5 full-time freshmen who did not demonstrate need for aid received scholarships/grants; average award was $30,190. No-need awards available for academics.
Scholarships offered: Merit scholarships available up to full tuition and room and board. Special application not required.
Cumulative student debt: 39% of graduating class had student loans; average debt was $9,871.

FINANCIAL AID PROCEDURES

Forms required: FAFSA, CSS PROFILE, state aid form, institutional form.
Dates and Deadlines: Closing date 1/15. Applicants notified by 4/1; must reply by 5/1.
Transfers: Priority date 3/2; no deadline.

CONTACT

Don Crewell, Director of Financial Aid
1200 East California Boulevard, MC 1-94, Pasadena, CA 91125
(626) 395-6280

California Institute of the Arts

Valencia, California
www.calarts.edu Federal Code: 001132

4-year private visual arts and performing arts college in small city.
Enrollment: 863 undergrads, 1% part-time. 172 full-time freshmen.
Selectivity: Admits less than 50% of applicants.

BASIC COSTS (2009-2010)

Tuition and fees: $35,406.
Room and board: $9,070.

FINANCIAL AID PICTURE (2008-2009)

Students with need: Out of 133 full-time freshmen who applied for aid, 103 were judged to have need. Of these, 102 received aid, and 5 had their full need met. Average financial aid package met 72% of need; average scholarship/grant was $13,917; average loan was $4,907. Need-based aid available for part-time students.
Students without need: 19 full-time freshmen who did not demonstrate need for aid received scholarships/grants; average award was $3,826. No-need awards available for academics, art, minority status, music/drama.
Cumulative student debt: 71% of graduating class had student loans; average debt was $40,668.

FINANCIAL AID PROCEDURES

Forms required: FAFSA.
Dates and Deadlines: Priority date 3/2; no closing date. Applicants notified on a rolling basis starting 4/1; must reply by 5/1 or within 3 week(s) of notification.

CONTACT

Bobbi Heuer, Financial Aid Director
24700 McBean Parkway, Valencia, CA 91355
(661) 253-7869

California Lutheran University

Thousand Oaks, California
www.callutheran.edu Federal Code: 001133

4-year private university and liberal arts college in small city, affiliated with Evangelical Lutheran Church in America.
Enrollment: 2,199 undergrads, 9% part-time. 482 full-time freshmen.

Selectivity: Admits 50 to 75% of applicants.

BASIC COSTS (2008-2009)

Tuition and fees: $27,850.
Room and board: $9,650.

FINANCIAL AID PICTURE (2008-2009)

Students with need: Out of 471 full-time freshmen who applied for aid, 317 were judged to have need. Of these, 317 received aid, and 74 had their full need met. Average financial aid package met 79% of need; average scholarship/grant was $18,030; average loan was $3,440. For part-time students, average financial aid package was $6,115.
Students without need: 165 full-time freshmen who did not demonstrate need for aid received scholarships/grants; average award was $11,360. No-need awards available for academics, alumni affiliation, art, leadership, minority status, music/drama, religious affiliation, state/district residency.
Scholarships offered: Academic Scholarships; range from $3,000 up to $15,000 per year; based on GPA, test scores, and class rank at time of Admission. Presidential Scholarship Program; $17,000 up to full tuition; additional application required. UC Guarantee; 2008-2009 amount was $15,994; student must be admitted to CLU and UCLA or UCSB. Visual and Performing Arts Scholarships; $1,000-$6,000; application deadline of February 1 and audition with department deadline of February 22.
Cumulative student debt: 74% of graduating class had student loans; average debt was $21,288.

FINANCIAL AID PROCEDURES

Forms required: FAFSA.
Dates and Deadlines: Priority date 3/1; no closing date. Applicants notified on a rolling basis starting 3/15; must reply within 2 week(s) of notification.
Transfers: No deadline. Applicants notified on a rolling basis starting 3/15; must reply within 2 week(s) of notification.

CONTACT

60 West Olsen Road #1350, Thousand Oaks, CA 91360-2787
(805) 493-3115

California Maritime Academy

Vallejo, California
www.csum.edu Federal Code: 001134

4-year public university and maritime college in small city.
Enrollment: 810 undergrads.
Selectivity: Admits 50 to 75% of applicants.

BASIC COSTS (2008-2009)

Tuition and fees: $4,112; out-of-state residents $14,282.
Room and board: $8,830.
Additional info: Each student participates in at least one cruise and one internship prior to graduation. Some majors have additional cruise requirements. The cost for a cruise is $3,800. The cost for an internship/co-op is $225. Additionally, each incoming student must purchase a uniform. Prices range from $1,550-$1,785 depending on the major. Reduced out-of-state tuition for residents of AK, AZ, CO, HI, ID, MT, NV, NM, ND, OR, SD, UT, WA, WY available under the Western Undergraduate Exchange (WUE) program. WUE students pay one-and-a half the State University Fee ($3,048 this year), which is $4,572.

FINANCIAL AID PICTURE

Students with need: Need-based aid available for full-time and part-time students.
Students without need: This college awards aid only to students with need.
Additional info: US Maritime Administration provides annual incentive payment of $3,000 per student, with certain conditions. Tuition waiver for children of deceased or disabled California veterans.

FINANCIAL AID PROCEDURES

Forms required: FAFSA.
Dates and Deadlines: Priority date 4/2; no closing date. Applicants notified on a rolling basis starting 4/1.

CONTACT

Ken Walsh, Director of Financial Aid
200 Maritime Academy Drive, Vallejo, CA 94590
(707) 654-1275

California Polytechnic State University: San Luis Obispo

San Luis Obispo, California
www.calpoly.edu Federal Code: 001143

4-year public university in large town.
Enrollment: 18,400 undergrads, 4% part-time. 4,286 full-time freshmen.
Selectivity: Admits less than 50% of applicants.

BASIC COSTS (2008-2009)

Tuition and fees: $5,043; out-of-state residents $15,213.
Room and board: $9,369.
Additional info: Required fees vary by program.

FINANCIAL AID PICTURE (2007-2008)

Students with need: Out of 2,816 full-time freshmen who applied for aid, 1,417 were judged to have need. Of these, 1,244 received aid, and 207 had their full need met. Average financial aid package met 65% of need; average scholarship/grant was $1,882; average loan was $3,024. For part-time students, average financial aid package was $5,935.
Students without need: 175 full-time freshmen who did not demonstrate need for aid received scholarships/grants; average award was $2,135. No-need awards available for academics, alumni affiliation, art, athletics, job skills, leadership, music/drama, ROTC, state/district residency.
Scholarships offered: 83 full-time freshmen received athletic scholarships; average amount $2,327.
Additional info: College-administered financial aid is not available for undergraduate international students.

FINANCIAL AID PROCEDURES

Forms required: FAFSA.
Dates and Deadlines: Priority date 3/2; no closing date. Applicants notified on a rolling basis starting 4/15; must reply within 8 week(s) of notification.

CONTACT

Lois Kelly, Director, Financial Aid
Admissions Office, Cal Poly, San Luis Obispo, CA 93407-0031
(805) 756-2927

California School of Culinary Arts

Pasadena, California
www.csca.edu Federal Code: 032103

2-year for-profit culinary school in very large city.
Enrollment: 1,536 undergrads.
Selectivity: Open admission.

BASIC COSTS (2008-2009)

Additional info: Diploma programs vary in cost. Associate of occupational studies in culinary arts program tuition: $43,950, fees $3,000. Associate of occupational students in hospitality/restaurant management tuition: $31,000, fees $4,015.

FINANCIAL AID PICTURE (2007-2008)

Students with need: Need-based aid available for full-time and part-time students. Work study available nights, weekends, and for part-time students.

FINANCIAL AID PROCEDURES
Forms required: FAFSA.
Dates and Deadlines: No deadline. Applicants notified on a rolling basis.
Transfers: No deadline.

CONTACT
Kristin Hanle, Director of Student Finance
530 East Colorado Boulevard, Pasadena, CA 91101
(626) 229-1300

California State Polytechnic University: Pomona
Pomona, California
www.csupomona.edu Federal Code: 001144

4-year public university in small city.
Enrollment: 19,220 undergrads, 17% part-time. 2,538 full-time freshmen.
Selectivity: Admits 50 to 75% of applicants.

BASIC COSTS (2008-2009)
Tuition and fees: $3,564; out-of-state residents $13,734.
Room and board: $9,120.

FINANCIAL AID PICTURE (2008-2009)
Students with need: Out of 1,853 full-time freshmen who applied for aid, 1,260 were judged to have need. Of these, 1,195 received aid, and 237 had their full need met. Average financial aid package met 76% of need; average scholarship/grant was $7,622; average loan was $2,926. For part-time students, average financial aid package was $7,759.
Students without need: 7 full-time freshmen who did not demonstrate need for aid received scholarships/grants; average award was $1,957. No-need awards available for academics, alumni affiliation, athletics, leadership, state/district residency.
Scholarships offered: 26 full-time freshmen received athletic scholarships; average amount $3,901.
Cumulative student debt: 37% of graduating class had student loans; average debt was $12,527.

FINANCIAL AID PROCEDURES
Forms required: FAFSA.
Dates and Deadlines: Priority date 3/3; no closing date. Applicants notified on a rolling basis starting 4/1; must reply within 2 week(s) of notification.

CONTACT
Diana Minor, Director of Financial Aid
3801 West Temple Avenue, Pomona, CA 91768-4019
(909) 869-3700

California State University: Bakersfield
Bakersfield, California
www.csub.edu Federal Code: 007993

4-year public university and liberal arts college in small city.
Enrollment: 6,078 undergrads.
Selectivity: Admits 50 to 75% of applicants.

BASIC COSTS (2008-2009)
Tuition and fees: $4,077; out-of-state residents $14,241.
Room and board: $6,852.
Additional info: Reduced out-of-state tuition for residents of AK, AZ, CO, HI, ID, MT, NV, NM, ND, OR, SD, UT, WA, WY available under the Western Undergraduate Exchange (WUE) program. WUE students pay one-and-a half the State University Fees plus campus-based fees, which is $5,601 for the 2008/2009 academic year.

FINANCIAL AID PICTURE (2007-2008)
Students with need: 69% of average financial aid package awarded as scholarships/grants, 31% awarded as loans/jobs. Need-based aid available for part-time students.
Students without need: This college awards aid only to students with need.

FINANCIAL AID PROCEDURES
Forms required: FAFSA.
Dates and Deadlines: Priority date 3/2; closing date 4/1. Applicants notified on a rolling basis; must reply within 2 week(s) of notification.

CONTACT
Ron Radney, Dean of Financial Aid
9001 Stockdale Highway, Bakersfield, CA 93311-1099
(661) 664-2011

California State University: Chico
Chico, California
www.csuchico.edu Federal Code: 001146

4-year public university and liberal arts college in small city.
Enrollment: 15,804 undergrads, 9% part-time. 2,710 full-time freshmen.
Selectivity: Admits over 75% of applicants.

BASIC COSTS (2008-2009)
Tuition and fees: $4,008; out-of-state residents $14,178.
Room and board: $9,300.
Additional info: Reduced out-of-state tuition for residents of AK, AZ, CO. HI, ID, MT, NV, NM, ND, OR, SD, UT, WA, WY may be available under the Western Undergraduate Exchange (WUE) program.

FINANCIAL AID PICTURE (2008-2009)
Students with need: Out of 1,836 full-time freshmen who applied for aid, 1,158 were judged to have need. Of these, 1,138 received aid, and 314 had their full need met. Average financial aid package met 88% of need; average scholarship/grant was $7,913; average loan was $3,538. For part-time students, average financial aid package was $9,075.
Students without need: 126 full-time freshmen who did not demonstrate need for aid received scholarships/grants; average award was $1,467. No-need awards available for academics, art, athletics, leadership, minority status, music/drama, religious affiliation.
Scholarships offered: ***Merit:*** President's Scholar Award: 10 awards at $12,000 each; 12 awards at $1,000 each. ***Athletic:*** 23 full-time freshmen received athletic scholarships; average amount $1,743.

FINANCIAL AID PROCEDURES
Forms required: FAFSA.
Dates and Deadlines: Priority date 3/2; no closing date. Applicants notified on a rolling basis starting 3/2.

CONTACT
Dan Reed, Director of Financial Aid
400 West First Street, Chico, CA 95929-0722
(530) 898-6451

California State University: Dominguez Hills
Carson, California
www.csudh.edu Federal Code: 001141

4-year public university in small city.
Enrollment: 8,639 undergrads, 37% part-time. 913 full-time freshmen.
Selectivity: Admits over 75% of applicants.

BASIC COSTS (2008-2009)

Tuition and fees: $3,663; out-of-state residents $13,833.

Room and board: $8,955.

Additional info: Reduced out-of-state tuition for residents of AK, AZ, CO, HI, ID, MT, NV, NM, ND, OR, SD, UT, WA, WY available under the Western Undergraduate Exchange (WUE) program. Tuition/fee waivers available for adults.

FINANCIAL AID PICTURE (2007-2008)

Students with need: Out of 659 full-time freshmen who applied for aid, 652 were judged to have need. Of these, 647 received aid, and 45 had their full need met. Average financial aid package met 65% of need; average scholarship/grant was $5,980; average loan was $2,907. For part-time students, average financial aid package was $5,618.

Students without need: 3 full-time freshmen who did not demonstrate need for aid received scholarships/grants; average award was $1,822. No-need awards available for academics, alumni affiliation, art, athletics, leadership, music/drama.

Scholarships offered: 5 full-time freshmen received athletic scholarships; average amount $2,690.

Cumulative student debt: 35% of graduating class had student loans; average debt was $16,319.

FINANCIAL AID PROCEDURES

Forms required: FAFSA.

Dates and Deadlines: Priority date 3/2; closing date 4/15. Applicants notified on a rolling basis starting 2/28; must reply within 4 week(s) of notification.

CONTACT

Delores Lee, Director of Financial Aid
1000 East Victoria Street, Carson, CA 90747
(310) 243-3696

California State University: East Bay

Hayward, California
www.csueastbay.edu Federal Code: 001138

4-year public university in small city.

Enrollment: 10,336 undergrads, 18% part-time. 1,343 full-time freshmen.

Selectivity: Admits 50 to 75% of applicants.

BASIC COSTS (2008-2009)

Tuition and fees: $3,392; out-of-state residents $13,562.

Room and board: $9,228.

Additional info: Quoted freshman room-only charge is for suite shared by 6 to 8 students. Additional $3,200 advance purchase of flexible retail meal credits required. (Standard meal plans not available).

FINANCIAL AID PICTURE (2007-2008)

Students with need: Need-based aid available for full-time and part-time students.

Students without need: No-need awards available for music/drama.

FINANCIAL AID PROCEDURES

Forms required: FAFSA.

Dates and Deadlines: Priority date 3/2; no closing date. Applicants notified on a rolling basis; must reply within 3 week(s) of notification.

CONTACT

Rhonda Johnson, Financial Aid Department
25800 Carlos Bee Boulevard, Hayward, CA 94542-3095
(510) 885-4746

California State University: Fresno

Fresno, California
www.csufresno.edu Federal Code: 001147

4-year public university in very large city.

Enrollment: 19,245 undergrads, 18% part-time. 2,732 full-time freshmen.

Selectivity: Admits 50 to 75% of applicants.

BASIC COSTS (2008-2009)

Tuition and fees: $3,687; out-of-state residents $13,857.

Room and board: $8,590.

Additional info: Tuition/fee waivers available for adults, minority students, unemployed or children of unemployed.

FINANCIAL AID PICTURE (2008-2009)

Students with need: Out of 2,220 full-time freshmen who applied for aid, 1,825 were judged to have need. Of these, 1,775 received aid, and 296 had their full need met. Average financial aid package met 74% of need; average scholarship/grant was $8,599; average loan was $3,030. For part-time students, average financial aid package was $8,042.

Students without need: 119 full-time freshmen who did not demonstrate need for aid received scholarships/grants; average award was $2,998. No-need awards available for academics, art, athletics, leadership, music/drama, ROTC, state/district residency.

Scholarships offered: 67 full-time freshmen received athletic scholarships; average amount $10,237.

Cumulative student debt: 36% of graduating class had student loans; average debt was $10,754.

FINANCIAL AID PROCEDURES

Forms required: FAFSA.

Dates and Deadlines: Priority date 3/3; no closing date. Applicants notified on a rolling basis starting 4/1; must reply within 3 week(s) of notification.

CONTACT

Maria Hernandez, Director of Financial Aid
5150 North Maple Avenue, M/S JA 57, Fresno, CA 93740-8026
(559) 278-2182

California State University: Fullerton

Fullerton, California
www.fullerton.edu Federal Code: 001137

4-year public university in small city.

Enrollment: 29,868 undergrads, 23% part-time. 4,042 full-time freshmen.

Selectivity: Admits 50 to 75% of applicants.

BASIC COSTS (2008-2009)

Tuition and fees: $3,658; out-of-state residents $13,828.

Room only: $5,608.

FINANCIAL AID PICTURE (2007-2008)

Students with need: Out of 2,907 full-time freshmen who applied for aid, 1,953 were judged to have need. Of these, 1,535 received aid, and 35 had their full need met. Average financial aid package met 59% of need; average scholarship/grant was $6,644; average loan was $3,237. For part-time students, average financial aid package was $6,076.

Students without need: 355 full-time freshmen who did not demonstrate need for aid received scholarships/grants; average award was $4,551. No-need awards available for academics.

Scholarships offered: 52 full-time freshmen received athletic scholarships; average amount $6,112.

Cumulative student debt: 39% of graduating class had student loans; average debt was $14,556.

Additional info: Fee waiver for children of veterans killed in action or with service-connected disability whose annual income is $5,000 or less.

FINANCIAL AID PROCEDURES

Forms required: FAFSA.
Dates and Deadlines: Priority date 3/2; no closing date. Applicants notified on a rolling basis starting 3/31; must reply within 4 week(s) of notification.
Transfers: No deadline. Applicants notified on a rolling basis starting 3/31; must reply within 4 week(s) of notification.

CONTACT

Deborah McCracken, Director of Financial Aid
800 North State College Boulevard, Langsdorf Hall-114, Fullerton, CA 92831-6900
(657) 278-3125

California State University: Long Beach

Long Beach, California
www.csulb.edu Federal Code: 001139

4-year public university in large city.
Enrollment: 31,564 undergrads, 19% part-time. 4,537 full-time freshmen.
Selectivity: Admits less than 50% of applicants.

BASIC COSTS (2008-2009)

Tuition and fees: $3,392; out-of-state residents $13,562.
Room and board: $7,940.

FINANCIAL AID PICTURE (2008-2009)

Students with need: Out of 3,239 full-time freshmen who applied for aid, 2,364 were judged to have need. Of these, 2,158 received aid, and 1,596 had their full need met. Average financial aid package met 80% of need; average scholarship/grant was $5,450; average loan was $2,952. For part-time students, average financial aid package was $9,570.
Students without need: 170 full-time freshmen who did not demonstrate need for aid received scholarships/grants; average award was $2,044. No-need awards available for academics, art, athletics, music/drama.
Scholarships offered: President's Scholar Award: full tuition and fees, campus housing, books.
Cumulative student debt: 41% of graduating class had student loans; average debt was $10,671.

FINANCIAL AID PROCEDURES

Forms required: FAFSA.
Dates and Deadlines: Priority date 3/2; no closing date. Applicants notified on a rolling basis starting 3/30; must reply within 3 week(s) of notification.
Transfers: Community college EOPS students may apply as EOP students and thus be eligible for an EOP Grant.

CONTACT

Nicholas Valdivia, Director of Financial Aid
1250 Bellflower Boulevard, Long Beach, CA 90840-0106
(562) 985-4641

California State University: Los Angeles

Los Angeles, California
www.calstatela.edu/index2.htm Federal Code: 001140

4-year public university in very large city.
Enrollment: 15,588 undergrads, 25% part-time. 1,670 full-time freshmen.
Selectivity: Admits over 75% of applicants.

BASIC COSTS (2008-2009)

Tuition and fees: $3,661; out-of-state residents $13,831.
Room only: $4,050.

FINANCIAL AID PICTURE (2008-2009)

Students with need: Need-based aid available for full-time and part-time students.

FINANCIAL AID PROCEDURES

Forms required: FAFSA.
Dates and Deadlines: Priority date 3/1; no closing date. Applicants notified on a rolling basis starting 4/1; must reply within 3 week(s) of notification.

CONTACT

Arlie Stops, Associate Director of Center for Student Financial Aid
5151 State University Drive SA101, Los Angeles, CA 90032
(323) 343-6260

California State University: Monterey Bay

Seaside, California
www.csumb.edu Federal Code: 032603

4-year public liberal arts and teachers college in large town.
Enrollment: 3,889 undergrads, 10% part-time. 899 full-time freshmen.
Selectivity: Admits 50 to 75% of applicants.

BASIC COSTS (2008-2009)

Tuition and fees: $3,301; out-of-state residents $13,471.
Room and board: $9,152.
Additional info: Tuition/fee waivers available for unemployed or children of unemployed.

FINANCIAL AID PICTURE (2008-2009)

Students with need: Out of 691 full-time freshmen who applied for aid, 463 were judged to have need. Of these, 411 received aid, and 86 had their full need met. Average financial aid package met 73% of need; average scholarship/grant was $7,942; average loan was $3,347. For part-time students, average financial aid package was $6,163.
Students without need: No-need awards available for academics, alumni affiliation, athletics, leadership, state/district residency.
Scholarships offered: 29 full-time freshmen received athletic scholarships; average amount $1,995.
Cumulative student debt: 64% of graduating class had student loans; average debt was $15,305.

FINANCIAL AID PROCEDURES

Forms required: FAFSA, state aid form, institutional form.
Dates and Deadlines: Priority date 3/2; no closing date. Applicants notified by 3/1; must reply within 2 week(s) of notification.

CONTACT

Angeles Fuentes, Director of Financial Aid
100 Campus Center, Building 47, Seaside, CA 93955-8001
(831) 582-5100

California State University: Northridge

Northridge, California
www.csun.edu Federal Code: 001153

4-year public university in very large city.
Enrollment: 30,235 undergrads, 23% part-time. 3,982 full-time freshmen.
Selectivity: Admits 50 to 75% of applicants.

BASIC COSTS (2008-2009)

Tuition and fees: $3,702; out-of-state residents $13,872.
Room and board: $10,152.

FINANCIAL AID PICTURE (2007-2008)

Students with need: Out of 2,897 full-time freshmen who applied for aid, 2,448 were judged to have need. Of these, 2,448 received aid. For part-time students, average financial aid package was $5,787.
Students without need: 81 full-time freshmen who did not demonstrate need for aid received scholarships/grants; average award was $1,705. No-need awards available for academics, athletics, state/district residency.

Scholarships offered: 56 full-time freshmen received athletic scholarships; average amount $5,525.
Cumulative student debt: 40% of graduating class had student loans; average debt was $14,009.

FINANCIAL AID PROCEDURES
Forms required: FAFSA.
Dates and Deadlines: Priority date 3/1; no closing date. Applicants notified on a rolling basis starting 4/1.

CONTACT
Lili Vidal, Director of Financial Aid
18111 Nordhoff Street, Northridge, CA 91328-8207
(818) 677-4085

California State University: Sacramento
Sacramento, California
www.csus.edu Federal Code: 001233

4-year public university in very large city.
Enrollment: 21,505 undergrads, 19% part-time. 2,708 full-time freshmen.
Selectivity: Admits 50 to 75% of applicants.

BASIC COSTS (2008-2009)
Tuition and fees: $3,854; out-of-state residents $14,024.
Room and board: $11,210.

FINANCIAL AID PICTURE (2007-2008)
Students with need: Out of 2,499 full-time freshmen who applied for aid, 2,163 were judged to have need. Of these, 1,411 received aid, and 158 had their full need met. Average financial aid package met 47% of need; average scholarship/grant was $3,828; average loan was $1,584. For part-time students, average financial aid package was $3,192.
Cumulative student debt: 35% of graduating class had student loans; average debt was $11,152.

FINANCIAL AID PROCEDURES
Forms required: FAFSA.
Dates and Deadlines: Applicants notified on a rolling basis starting 4/1; must reply within 4 week(s) of notification.

CONTACT
Craig Yamamoto, Financial Aid Director
6000 J Street, Sacramento, CA 95819-6048
(916) 278-6554

California State University: San Bernardino
San Bernardino, California
www.csusb.edu Federal Code: 001142

4-year public university and liberal arts college in small city.
Enrollment: 13,947 undergrads, 15% part-time. 1,917 full-time freshmen.

BASIC COSTS (2008-2009)
Tuition and fees: $3,779; out-of-state residents $13,949.
Room and board: $9,624.

FINANCIAL AID PICTURE (2008-2009)
Students with need: Need-based aid available for full-time students. Work study available weekends and for part-time students.

FINANCIAL AID PROCEDURES
Forms required: FAFSA.
Dates and Deadlines: Priority date 3/2; no closing date. Applicants notified on a rolling basis starting 4/1.

CONTACT
Roseanna Ruiz, Director of Financial Aid
5500 University Parkway, San Bernardino, CA 92407-2397
(909) 537-7800

California State University: Stanislaus
Turlock, California
www.csustan.edu Federal Code: 001157

4-year public business and liberal arts college in small city.
Enrollment: 6,559 undergrads. 899 full-time freshmen.
Selectivity: Admits 50 to 75% of applicants.

BASIC COSTS (2008-2009)
Tuition and fees: $3,819; out-of-state residents $13,989.
Room and board: $8,820.
Additional info: Tuition/fee waivers available for adults.

FINANCIAL AID PICTURE (2008-2009)
Students with need: Out of 573 full-time freshmen who applied for aid, 447 were judged to have need. Of these, 429 received aid, and 55 had their full need met. Average financial aid package met 68% of need; average scholarship/grant was $5,190; average loan was $4,309. For part-time students, average financial aid package was $5,041.
Students without need: 10 full-time freshmen who did not demonstrate need for aid received scholarships/grants; average award was $4,750. No-need awards available for academics, alumni affiliation, art, athletics, leadership, minority status, music/drama, state/district residency.
Scholarships offered: ***Merit:*** President's Scholarships: $12,500, renewable for up to 4 years, awards based on GPA minimum of 3.8 and SAT of at least 1350 or ACT of at least 30, 20 available; Provost's Scholarships: $3,500, renewable for up to 4 years, awards based on GPA minimum of 3.5 and SAT of at least 1250 or ACT of at least 28, 20 available; Provost's Achievement Award for community college transfers: $2,000, renewable for up to 2 years, awards based on GPA minimum of 3.5 and completion of at least 45 transferable credits at time of application, 10 available. ***Athletic:*** 21 full-time freshmen received athletic scholarships; average amount $2,307.
Cumulative student debt: 23% of graduating class had student loans; average debt was $17,000.

FINANCIAL AID PROCEDURES
Forms required: FAFSA.
Dates and Deadlines: Priority date 3/2; no closing date. Applicants notified on a rolling basis starting 3/15; must reply within 3 week(s) of notification.
Transfers: No deadline. Applicants notified on a rolling basis; must reply within 3 week(s) of notification.

CONTACT
Noelia Gonzales, Director of Financial Aid
One University Cirlce, Turlock, CA 95382-0256
(209) 667-3336

Cerro Coso Community College
Ridgecrest, California
www.cerrocoso.edu Federal Code: 010111

2-year public community college in large town.
Enrollment: 2,159 undergrads.
Selectivity: Open admission.

BASIC COSTS (2008-2009)
Tuition and fees: $600; out-of-state residents $6,510.
Per-credit charge: $20; out-of-state residents $217.

FINANCIAL AID PICTURE

Students with need: Need-based aid available for full-time and part-time students. Work study available nights.

FINANCIAL AID PROCEDURES

Forms required: FAFSA.

Dates and Deadlines: Priority date 5/15; no closing date. Applicants notified on a rolling basis starting 6/1; must reply within 2 week(s) of notification.

CONTACT

Joanne Spiller, Director of Financial Aid and Scholarships
3000 College Heights Boulevard, Ridgecrest, CA 93555-7777
(760) 384-6221

Chabot College

Hayward, California
www.chabotcollege.edu Federal Code: 001162

2-year public community college in large city.
Enrollment: 8,752 undergrads.
Selectivity: Open admission; but selective for some programs.

BASIC COSTS (2008-2009)

Tuition and fees: $626; out-of-state residents $6,026.
Per-credit charge: $20; out-of-state residents $200.

FINANCIAL AID PICTURE

Students with need: Work study available nights, weekends, and for part-time students.
Additional info: Tuition and/or fee waivers for low-income students.

FINANCIAL AID PROCEDURES

Forms required: FAFSA, institutional form.
Dates and Deadlines: Priority date 8/1; no closing date. Applicants notified on a rolling basis.

CONTACT

Kathryn Linzmeyer, Director of Financial Aid
25555 Hesperian Boulevard, Hayward, CA 94545
(510) 723-6746

Chaffey College

Rancho Cucamonga, California
www.chaffey.edu Federal Code: 001163

2-year public community college in small city.
Enrollment: 13,295 undergrads.
Selectivity: Open admission.

BASIC COSTS (2008-2009)

Tuition and fees: $630; out-of-state residents $6,060.
Per-credit charge: $20; out-of-state residents $201.
Additional info: Tuition/fee waivers available for adults.

FINANCIAL AID PICTURE

Students with need: Need-based aid available for full-time and part-time students.
Students without need: No-need awards available for academics.
Additional info: State of California Board of Governors fee waivers to qualified state residents. Criteria for eligibility: households which receive public assistance, meet state's low income guidelines, and demonstrate need as defined by Title IV programs.

FINANCIAL AID PROCEDURES

Forms required: FAFSA.
Dates and Deadlines: No deadline. Applicants notified on a rolling basis starting 7/15; must reply within 2 week(s) of notification.

CONTACT

Karen Sanders, Financial Aid Supervisor
5885 Haven Avenue, Rancho Cucamonga, CA 91701-3002
(909) 652-6006

Chapman University

Orange, California
www.chapman.edu Federal Code: 001164

4-year private university and liberal arts college in very large city, affiliated with Christian Church (Disciples of Christ).
Enrollment: 4,264 undergrads, 5% part-time. 961 full-time freshmen.
Selectivity: Admits 50 to 75% of applicants.

BASIC COSTS (2009-2010)

Tuition and fees: $36,764.
Per-credit charge: $1,115.
Room and board: $12,832.

FINANCIAL AID PICTURE (2007-2008)

Students with need: Need-based aid available for full-time and part-time students. Work study available nights, weekends, and for part-time students.
Students without need: No-need awards available for academics, alumni affiliation, art, music/drama, religious affiliation, ROTC.

FINANCIAL AID PROCEDURES

Forms required: FAFSA, state aid form.
Dates and Deadlines: Priority date 3/2; no closing date. Applicants notified on a rolling basis starting 3/15; must reply within 3 week(s) of notification.
Transfers: No deadline. Applicants notified on a rolling basis starting 3/15; must reply within 3 week(s) of notification.

CONTACT

Gregory Ball, Director of Financial Aid
One University Drive, Orange, CA 92866
(714) 997-6815

Charles R. Drew University of Medicine and Science

Los Angeles, California
www.cdrewu.edu

4-year private university and health science college in very large city.
Enrollment: 213 undergrads.
Selectivity: Admits over 75% of applicants.

BASIC COSTS (2008-2009)

Additional info: Tuition $250/unit for associate degree programs, $312/unit for bachelor's degree programs. Required fees vary by program and enrollment.

FINANCIAL AID PICTURE (2008-2009)

Students with need: 38% of average financial aid package awarded as scholarships/grants, 62% awarded as loans/jobs. Work study available nights, weekends, and for part-time students.

CONTACT

Pierre Flood, Director of Financial Aid
1731 East 120th Street, Los Angeles, CA 90059
(323) 563-4824

Citrus College

Glendora, California
www.citruscollege.edu Federal Code: 001166

2-year public community college in large town.
Enrollment: 6,812 undergrads.
Selectivity: Open admission.

BASIC COSTS (2008-2009)

Tuition and fees: $617; out-of-state residents $6,047.
Per-credit charge: $20; out-of-state residents $201.

FINANCIAL AID PICTURE (2008-2009)

Students with need: Need-based aid available for full-time and part-time students. Work study available nights, weekends, and for part-time students.

FINANCIAL AID PROCEDURES

Forms required: FAFSA.
Dates and Deadlines: Priority date 3/1; no closing date. Applicants notified on a rolling basis; must reply within 2 week(s) of notification.

CONTACT

Lilia Medina, Director of Financial Aid
1000 West Foothill Boulevard, Glendora, CA 91741-1899
(626) 914-8592

City College of San Francisco

San Francisco, California
www.ccsf.edu Federal Code: 012874

2-year public community college in very large city.
Enrollment: 18,393 undergrads.
Selectivity: Open admission; but selective for some programs.

BASIC COSTS (2008-2009)

Tuition and fees: $632; out-of-state residents $6,002.
Per-credit charge: $20; out-of-state residents $199.
Additional info: Tuition/fee waivers available for unemployed or children of unemployed.

FINANCIAL AID PICTURE

Students with need: Work study available nights, weekends, and for part-time students.
Additional info: Board of Governor fee waiver for low income students.

FINANCIAL AID PROCEDURES

Forms required: FAFSA.
Dates and Deadlines: Priority date 3/1; no closing date. Applicants notified on a rolling basis starting 7/1.

CONTACT

Jorge Bell, Dean, Financial Aid
Office of Admissions and Records E-107, San Francisco, CA 94112
(415) 239-3576

Claremont McKenna College

Claremont, California Federal Code: 001170
www.claremontmckenna.edu CSS Code: 4054

4-year private liberal arts college in large town.
Enrollment: 1,211 undergrads. 320 full-time freshmen.
Selectivity: Admits less than 50% of applicants.

BASIC COSTS (2009-2010)

Tuition and fees: $38,510.
Room and board: $12,525.

FINANCIAL AID PICTURE (2008-2009)

Students with need: Out of 178 full-time freshmen who applied for aid, 145 were judged to have need. Of these, 145 received aid, and 145 had their full need met. Average financial aid package met 100% of need; average scholarship/grant was $32,151. Need-based aid available for part-time students.
Students without need: 22 full-time freshmen who did not demonstrate need for aid received scholarships/grants; average award was $5,539. No-need awards available for academics.
Scholarships offered: McKenna Achievement Award: $10,000; based on strong academic record and outstanding leadership and involvement; 9 are awarded, renewable for total of 4 years. The Frank Seaver Leadership Scholarship: full tuition; awarded to students who demonstrate exceptional promise to become leaders intent on making a positive impact in the world; renewable for 4 years. Interdisciplinary Science Scholarship: full tuition for all four years; awarded to students who want to major in science and a non-science.
Cumulative student debt: 35% of graduating class had student loans; average debt was $11,164.

FINANCIAL AID PROCEDURES

Forms required: FAFSA, CSS PROFILE.
Dates and Deadlines: Closing date 2/1. Applicants notified by 4/1; must reply by 5/1.
Transfers: Closing date 3/2. Applicants notified by 5/15.

CONTACT

Georgette DeVeres, Associate Vice President of Admission & Financial Aid
890 Columbia Avenue, Claremont, CA 91711-6425
(909) 621-8088

Coastline Community College

Fountain Valley, California
www.coastline.edu Federal Code: 013536

2-year public community college in small city.
Enrollment: 5,520 undergrads.
Selectivity: Open admission.

BASIC COSTS (2008-2009)

Tuition and fees: $658; out-of-state residents $6,088.
Per-credit charge: $20; out-of-state residents $201.
Additional info: Tuition/fee waivers available for unemployed or children of unemployed.

FINANCIAL AID PICTURE (2007-2008)

Students with need: Need-based aid available for full-time and part-timo students.
Students without need: This college awards aid only to students with need.
Additional info: Board of Governor's Grant: statewide fee waiver program for students or dependents receiving HFOL/TANF, SSI, General Relief, or whose income meets set standards or who are considered eligible through Federal needs analysis.

FINANCIAL AID PROCEDURES

Forms required: FAFSA, institutional form.
Dates and Deadlines: Priority date 3/2; no closing date. Applicants notified on a rolling basis starting 8/1; must reply within 2 week(s) of notification.

CONTACT

Cynthia Pienkowski, Director of Financial Aid
11460 Warner Avenue, Fountain Valley, CA 92708
(714) 241-6239

Cogswell Polytechnical College

Sunnyvale, California
www.cogswell.edu Federal Code: 001177

4-year private visual arts and engineering college in small city.
Enrollment: 224 undergrads, 52% part-time. 16 full-time freshmen.
Selectivity: Admits 50 to 75% of applicants.

BASIC COSTS (2009-2010)

Tuition and fees: $18,036.
Per-credit charge: $744.

FINANCIAL AID PICTURE (2007-2008)

Students with need: Out of 11 full-time freshmen who applied for aid, 11 were judged to have need. Of these, 11 received aid. Need-based aid available for part-time students.
Students without need: No-need awards available for academics.

FINANCIAL AID PROCEDURES

Forms required: FAFSA.
Dates and Deadlines: Priority date 3/2; no closing date. Applicants notified on a rolling basis starting 4/30; must reply within 4 week(s) of notification.
Transfers: No deadline. Applicants notified by 4/1; must reply within 4 week(s) of notification.

CONTACT

Andrew Hagedorn, Director of Financial Aid
1175 Bordeaux Drive, Sunnyvale, CA 94089-1299
(408) 541-0100

College of Alameda

Alameda, California
alameda.peralta.edu Federal Code: 006720

2-year public community college in small city.
Enrollment: 2,703 undergrads.
Selectivity: Open admission.

BASIC COSTS (2008-2009)

Tuition and fees: $604; out-of-state residents $6,034.
Per-credit charge: $20; out-of-state residents $201.

FINANCIAL AID PICTURE (2007-2008)

Students with need: 94% of average financial aid package awarded as scholarships/grants, 6% awarded as loans/jobs.

FINANCIAL AID PROCEDURES

Forms required: FAFSA.
Dates and Deadlines: Priority date 3/2; no closing date. Applicants notified on a rolling basis starting 7/1; must reply within 2 week(s) of notification.

CONTACT

Angelita Martinez-Finlayson, Financial Aid Supervisor
555 Ralph Appezzato Memorial Parkway, Alameda, CA 94501
(510) 522-7221

College of Marin: Kentfield

Kentfield, California
www.marin.edu Federal Code: 001178

2-year public community college in small town.
Enrollment: 2,768 undergrads.
Selectivity: Open admission.

BASIC COSTS (2008-2009)

Tuition and fees: $636; out-of-state residents $6,126.
Per-credit charge: $20; out-of-state residents $203.

FINANCIAL AID PICTURE

Students with need: Need-based aid available for full-time and part-time students.

FINANCIAL AID PROCEDURES

Forms required: FAFSA.
Dates and Deadlines: Priority date 3/1; no closing date. Applicants notified on a rolling basis starting 5/15.

CONTACT

David Cook, Director of Financial Aid
835 College Avenue, Kentfield, CA 94904
(415) 457-8811 ext. 7405

College of San Mateo

San Mateo, California
www.collegeofsanmateo.edu Federal Code: 001181

2-year public community college in small city.
Enrollment: 5,598 undergrads.
Selectivity: Open admission; but selective for some programs.

BASIC COSTS (2008-2009)

Tuition and fees: $628; out-of-state residents $6,358.
Per-credit charge: $20; out-of-state residents $211.

FINANCIAL AID PICTURE (2007-2008)

Students with need: 87% of average financial aid package awarded as scholarships/grants, 13% awarded as loans/jobs.

FINANCIAL AID PROCEDURES

Forms required: FAFSA, institutional form.
Dates and Deadlines: Priority date 3/2; no closing date. Applicants notified on a rolling basis starting 6/15.

CONTACT

Claudia Menjivar, Director of Financial Aid
1700 West Hillsdale Boulevard, San Mateo, CA 94402-3784
(650) 574-6147

College of the Canyons

Santa Clarita, California
www.canyons.edu Federal Code: 008903

2-year public community college in large city.
Enrollment: 8,572 undergrads. 2,828 full-time freshmen.
Selectivity: Open admission; but selective for some programs.

BASIC COSTS (2008-2009)

Tuition and fees: $612; out-of-state residents $5,262.
Per-credit charge: $20; out-of-state residents $175.

FINANCIAL AID PICTURE (2007-2008)

Students with need: 69% of average financial aid package awarded as scholarships/grants, 31% awarded as loans/jobs. Need-based aid available for part-time students. Work study available nights, weekends, and for part-time students.
Students without need: No-need awards available for academics, alumni affiliation, art, leadership, minority status, music/drama, state/district residency.

FINANCIAL AID PROCEDURES

Forms required: FAFSA, state aid form.

Dates and Deadlines: Closing date 3/2. Applicants notified on a rolling basis starting 6/1; must reply within 4 week(s) of notification.
Transfers: No deadline.

CONTACT

Thomas Bilbruck, Director, Financial Aid and Scholarships
26455 Rockwell Canyon Road, Santa Clarita, CA 91355
(661) 362-3242

College of the Desert

Palm Desert, California
www.collegeofthedesert.edu Federal Code: 001182

2-year public community college in small city.
Enrollment: 5,426 undergrads. 273 full-time freshmen.
Selectivity: Open admission; but selective for some programs.

BASIC COSTS (2008-2009)

Tuition and fees: $630; out-of-state residents $5,730.
Per-credit charge: $20; out-of-state residents $190.
Additional info: Tuition/fee waivers available for adults, minority students, unemployed or children of unemployed.

FINANCIAL AID PICTURE (2007-2008)

Students with need: 92% of average financial aid package awarded as scholarships/grants, 8% awarded as loans/jobs. Need-based aid available for part-time students. Work study available weekends and for part-time students.
Students without need: This college awards aid only to students with need.

FINANCIAL AID PROCEDURES

Forms required: FAFSA.
Dates and Deadlines: Priority date 3/2; no closing date. Applicants notified on a rolling basis starting 7/1.

CONTACT

Heidi Granger, Director of Financial Aid
43-500 Monterey Avenue, Palm Desert, CA 92260
(760) 773-2532

College of the Redwoods

Eureka, California
www.redwoods.edu Federal Code: 001185

2-year public community college in large town.
Enrollment: 4,410 undergrads.
Selectivity: Open admission; but selective for some programs.

BASIC COSTS (2008-2009)

Tuition and fees: $624; out-of-state residents $7,794.
Per-credit charge: $20; out-of-state residents $259.
Room and board: $6,284.

FINANCIAL AID PICTURE (2008-2009)

Students with need: Need-based aid available for full-time and part-time students.

FINANCIAL AID PROCEDURES

Forms required: FAFSA, institutional form.
Dates and Deadlines: Priority date 4/15; no closing date. Applicants notified on a rolling basis starting 5/1; must reply within 6 week(s) of notification.

CONTACT

Lynn Thiesen, Director of Financial Aid
7351 Tompkins Hill Road, Eureka, CA 95501-9300
(707) 476-4182

College of the Siskiyous

Weed, California
www.siskiyous.edu Federal Code: 001187

2-year public community and junior college in small town.
Enrollment: 1,424 undergrads.
Selectivity: Open admission; but selective for some programs.

BASIC COSTS (2008-2009)

Tuition and fees: $630; out-of-state residents $6,330.
Per-credit charge: $20; out-of-state residents $210.
Room and board: $7,550.
Additional info: Oregon residents with interstate exchange program: $42 per unit (no enrollment fee).

FINANCIAL AID PICTURE (2007-2008)

Students with need: Need-based aid available for full-time and part-time students. Work study available nights, weekends, and for part-time students.
Students without need: This college awards aid only to students with need.

FINANCIAL AID PROCEDURES

Forms required: FAFSA.
Dates and Deadlines: Priority date 4/30; no closing date. Applicants notified on a rolling basis starting 6/1; must reply within 2 week(s) of notification.
Transfers: No deadline. Applicants notified on a rolling basis. Academic transcripts required.

CONTACT

Vicki Wrobel, Director of Financial Aid
800 College Avenue, Weed, CA 96094-2899
(530) 938-5209

Columbia College

Sonora, California
www.gocolumbia.edu Federal Code: 007707

2-year public community college in small town.
Enrollment: 1,806 undergrads.
Selectivity: Open admission.

BASIC COSTS (2008-2009)

Tuition and fees: $646; out-of-state residents $6,076.
Per-credit charge: $20; out-of-state residents $201.

FINANCIAL AID PICTURE (2008-2009)

Students with need: Need-based aid available for full-time and part-time students.
Students without need: No-need awards available for academics.

FINANCIAL AID PROCEDURES

Forms required: FAFSA, state aid form, institutional form.
Dates and Deadlines: Priority date 3/2; no closing date. Applicants notified on a rolling basis starting 6/15; must reply within 2 week(s) of notification.

CONTACT

Marnie Shively, Financial Aid Specialist
11600 Columbia College Drive, Sonora, CA 95370
(209) 588-5105

Concordia University

Irvine, California
www.cui.edu Federal Code: 013885

4-year private university and liberal arts college in small city, affiliated with Lutheran Church - Missouri Synod.
Enrollment: 1,331 undergrads.
Selectivity: Admits 50 to 75% of applicants.

BASIC COSTS (2009-2010)
Tuition and fees: $24,950.
Per-credit charge: $725.
Room and board: $7,990.
Additional info: Tuition/fee waivers available for minority students.

FINANCIAL AID PICTURE (2008-2009)
Students with need: 76% of average financial aid package awarded as scholarships/grants, 24% awarded as loans/jobs. Work study available weekends and for part-time students.
Students without need: No-need awards available for academics, alumni affiliation, art, athletics, leadership, music/drama, religious affiliation.
Scholarships offered: President: full tuition. National Merit finalist is a requirement. Honors: up to $10,000; based on 3.9-4.0 GPA. Honors applicant must also score 1300 SAT or 29 ACT. Regent: up to $8,000; based on 3.8-4.0 GPA. Provost: up to $5,000; based on 3.5-3.79 GPA. Dean's: up to $3,000; based on 3.2-3.49 GPA. Various other academic, music, theater, athletic scholarships; amounts vary. Freshman students must score 1000 SAT or 21 ACT. Academic scholarships are based on cumulative GPA.

FINANCIAL AID PROCEDURES
Forms required: FAFSA, state aid form, institutional form.
Dates and Deadlines: Priority date 3/2; no closing date. Applicants notified on a rolling basis starting 2/1; must reply within 4 week(s) of notification.
Transfers: Must reply within 4 week(s) of notification.

CONTACT
Lori McDonald, Executive Director, Student Financial Services
1530 Concordia West, Irvine, CA 92612-3299
(949) 854-8002 ext. 1136

Copper Mountain College

Joshua Tree, California
www.cmccd.edu Federal Code: 035424

2-year public community college in small town.
Enrollment: 1,101 undergrads. 1,120 full-time freshmen.
Selectivity: Open admission.

BASIC COSTS (2008-2009)
Tuition and fees: $602; out-of-state residents $6,032.
Per-credit charge: $20; out-of-state residents $201.

FINANCIAL AID PICTURE (2007-2008)
Students with need: Out of 1,016 full-time freshmen who applied for aid, 600 were judged to have need. Of these, 340 received aid, and 65 had their full need met. Need-based aid available for part-time students.

FINANCIAL AID PROCEDURES
Forms required: FAFSA.
Dates and Deadlines: Priority date 3/2; no closing date.

CONTACT
Brian Heinemann, Director of Financial Aid
6162 Rotary Way, Joshua Tree, CA 92252
(866) 366-3791 ext. 4235

Crafton Hills College

Yucaipa, California
www.craftonhills.edu Federal Code: 009272

2-year public community college in large town.
Enrollment: 4,211 undergrads. 34 full-time freshmen.
Selectivity: Open admission.

BASIC COSTS (2008-2009)
Tuition and fees: $642; out-of-state residents $6,222.
Per-credit charge: $20; out-of-state residents $206.
Additional info: Tuition/fee waivers available for adults, minority students, unemployed or children of unemployed.

FINANCIAL AID PICTURE
Students with need: Need-based aid available for full-time and part-time students. Work study available nights.
Students without need: This college awards aid only to students with need.

FINANCIAL AID PROCEDURES
Forms required: FAFSA, institutional form.
Dates and Deadlines: Priority date 4/15; closing date 6/2. Applicants notified on a rolling basis starting 7/31; must reply within 2 week(s) of notification.
Transfers: Priority date 1/2; closing date 3/2.

CONTACT
John Muskavitch, Director of Financial Aid
11711 Sand Canyon Road, Yucaipa, CA 92399-1799
(909) 794-2161 ext. 3242

Cuyamaca College

El Cajon, California
www.cuyamaca.net Federal Code: 014435

2-year public community college in small city.
Enrollment: 4,947 undergrads.
Selectivity: Open admission; but selective for some programs.

BASIC COSTS (2008-2009)
Tuition and fees: $638; out-of-state residents $6,068.
Per-credit charge: $20; out-of-state residents $201.

FINANCIAL AID PICTURE (2007-2008)
Students with need: Work study available nights, weekends, and for part-time students.

FINANCIAL AID PROCEDURES
Forms required: FAFSA.
Dates and Deadlines: Priority date 3/2; no closing date. Applicants notified on a rolling basis; must reply within 2 week(s) of notification.

CONTACT
900 Rancho San Diego Parkway, El Cajon, CA 92019-4304
(619) 660-4201

De Anza College

Cupertino, California
www.deanza.edu Federal Code: 004480

2-year public community college in large town.
Enrollment: 18,138 undergrads.
Selectivity: Open admission; but selective for some programs.

BASIC COSTS (2008-2009)
Tuition and fees: $675; out-of-state residents $5,850.
Per-credit charge: $13; out-of-state residents $128.

FINANCIAL AID PICTURE
Students with need: Need-based aid available for full-time and part-time students.
Students without need: This college awards aid only to students with need.

FINANCIAL AID PROCEDURES
Forms required: FAFSA.
Dates and Deadlines: No deadline. Applicants notified on a rolling basis starting 5/15; must reply within 2 week(s) of notification.

CONTACT
Cindy Castillo, Director of Financial Aid
21250 Stevens Creek Boulevard, Cupertino, CA 95014
(408) 864-8718

Deep Springs College
Dyer, Nevada
www.deepsprings.edu Federal Code: 015483

2-year private liberal arts college for men in rural community.
Enrollment: 26 undergrads.
Selectivity: Admits less than 50% of applicants.

BASIC COSTS (2009-2010)
Additional info: All students receive full scholarship covering tuition, room, and board valued at $50,000. Tuition at time of enrollment locked for 2 years.

FINANCIAL AID PICTURE
Students with need: Work study available nights, weekends, and for part-time students.
Students without need: No-need awards available for academics.

FINANCIAL AID PROCEDURES
Dates and Deadlines: No deadline.

CONTACT
David Neidorf, President
Applications Committee, Dyer, NV 89010-9803
(760) 872-2000 ext. 45

DeVry University: Fremont
Fremont, California
www.devry.edu Federal Code: 008322

4-year for-profit university in small city.
Enrollment: 1,255 undergrads, 39% part-time. 154 full-time freshmen.

BASIC COSTS (2008-2009)
Tuition and fees: $14,800.
Per-credit charge: [illegible].

FINANCIAL AID PICTURE (2007-2008)
Students with need: Need-based aid available for full-time and part-time students.
Students without need: This college awards aid only to students with need.

FINANCIAL AID PROCEDURES
Forms required: FAFSA.
Dates and Deadlines: No deadline. Applicants notified on a rolling basis.

CONTACT
Kim Kane, Director of Financial Aid
6600 Dumbarton Circle, Fremont, CA 94555-3615
(510) 574-1120

DeVry University: Long Beach
Long Beach, California
www.devry.edu Federal Code: 023329

4-year for-profit university in large town.
Enrollment: 878 undergrads, 57% part-time. 71 full-time freshmen.

BASIC COSTS (2008-2009)
Tuition and fees: $14,130.
Per-credit charge: $515.

FINANCIAL AID PICTURE (2007-2008)
Students with need: Need-based aid available for full-time and part-time students.
Students without need: This college awards aid only to students with need.

FINANCIAL AID PROCEDURES
Forms required: FAFSA.
Dates and Deadlines: No deadline. Applicants notified on a rolling basis.

CONTACT
Brenda Woods, Associate Director of Student Finance
3880 Kilroy Airport Way, Long Beach, CA 90806
(562) 427-0861

DeVry University: Pomona
Pomona, California
www.devry.edu Federal Code: 023329

4-year for-profit university in small city.
Enrollment: 1,707 undergrads, 54% part-time. 136 full-time freshmen.

BASIC COSTS (2008-2009)
Tuition and fees: $14,130.
Per-credit charge: $515.

FINANCIAL AID PICTURE (2007-2008)
Students with need: Need-based aid available for full-time and part-time students.
Students without need: This college awards aid only to students with need.

FINANCIAL AID PROCEDURES
Forms required: FAFSA.
Dates and Deadlines: No deadline. Applicants notified on a rolling basis.

CONTACT
Kathy Odom, Director of Financial Aid
901 Corporate Center Drive, Pomona, CA 91768-2642

DeVry University: Sherman Oaks
Sherman Oaks, California
www.devry.edu Federal Code: 016219

4-year for-profit university in large city.
Enrollment: 573 undergrads, 41% part-time. 72 full-time freshmen.

BASIC COSTS (2008-2009)
Tuition and fees: $14,130.
Per-credit charge: $515.

FINANCIAL AID PICTURE (2007-2008)
Students with need: Need-based aid available for full-time and part-time students.
Students without need: This college awards aid only to students with need.

FINANCIAL AID PROCEDURES
Forms required: FAFSA.
Dates and Deadlines: No deadline. Applicants notified on a rolling basis.

CONTACT
Lou LaSota, Director of Financial Aid
15301 Ventura Boulevard, D-100, Sherman Oaks, CA 91403
(818) 932-3111

Diablo Valley College
Pleasant Hill, California
www.dvc.edu Federal Code: 001191

2-year public community college in large town.
Enrollment: 12,058 undergrads.
Selectivity: Open admission.

BASIC COSTS (2008-2009)
Tuition and fees: $600; out-of-state residents $5,700.
Per-credit charge: $20; out-of-state residents $190.

FINANCIAL AID PICTURE (2007-2008)
Students with need: 89% of average financial aid package awarded as scholarships/grants, 11% awarded as loans/jobs. Need-based aid available for part-time students.

FINANCIAL AID PROCEDURES
Forms required: FAFSA, state aid form, institutional form.
Dates and Deadlines: Priority date 3/2; closing date 5/1. Applicants notified on a rolling basis starting 6/1; must reply within 2 week(s) of notification.

CONTACT
Brenda Jerez, Financial Aid Director
321 Golf Club Road, Pleasant Hill, CA 94523
(925) 685-1230 ext. 2290

Dominican University of California
San Rafael, California
www.dominican.edu Federal Code: 001196

4-year private university and liberal arts college in small city, affiliated with Roman Catholic Church.
Enrollment: 1,426 undergrads, 19% part-time. 296 full-time freshmen.
Selectivity: Admits 50 to 75% of applicants.

BASIC COSTS (2009-2010)
Tuition and fees: $33,840.
Per-credit charge: $1,400.
Room and board: $13,150.

FINANCIAL AID PICTURE (2007-2008)
Students with need: Out of 255 full-time freshmen who applied for aid, 225 were judged to have need. Of these, 225 received aid, and 17 had their full need met. Average financial aid package met 63% of need; average scholarship/grant was $17,310; average loan was $3,593. For part-time students, average financial aid package was $7,019.
Students without need: 57 full-time freshmen who did not demonstrate need for aid received scholarships/grants; average award was $11,203. No-need awards available for academics, alumni affiliation, athletics, leadership, minority status, music/drama.
Scholarships offered: 9 full-time freshmen received athletic scholarships; average amount $2,790.
Cumulative student debt: 93% of graduating class had student loans; average debt was $19,806.
Additional info: 4-year guarantee program.

FINANCIAL AID PROCEDURES
Forms required: FAFSA, institutional form.
Dates and Deadlines: Priority date 3/2; no closing date. Applicants notified on a rolling basis starting 3/15; must reply within 2 week(s) of notification.
Transfers: Priority date 5/9. Applicants notified on a rolling basis starting 3/9; must reply within 2 week(s) of notification.

CONTACT
Mary-Frances Causey, Director of Financial Aid
50 Acacia Avenue, San Rafael, CA 94901-2298
(415) 257-1350

East Los Angeles College
Monterey Park, California
www.elac.edu Federal Code: 001222

2-year public community college in very large city.
Enrollment: 11,105 undergrads. 1,323 full-time freshmen.
Selectivity: Open admission; but selective for some programs.

BASIC COSTS (2008-2009)
Tuition and fees: $622; out-of-state residents $6,052.
Per-credit charge: $20; out-of-state residents $201.
Additional info: Tuition/fee waivers available for adults, minority students.

FINANCIAL AID PICTURE (2007-2008)
Students with need: 97% of average financial aid package awarded as scholarships/grants, 3% awarded as loans/jobs. Need-based aid available for part-time students. Work study available nights, weekends, and for part-time students.
Students without need: This college awards aid only to students with need.
Additional info: Need-based enrollment fee waivers available through a state aid program.

FINANCIAL AID PROCEDURES
Forms required: FAFSA.
Dates and Deadlines: Closing date 3/2.
Transfers: No deadline.

CONTACT
Lindy Fong, Director of Financial Aid
1301 Avenida Cesar Chavez, Monterey Park, CA 91754
(323) 265-8738

El Camino College
Torrance, California
www.elcamino.edu Federal Code: 001197

2-year public community college in very large city.
Enrollment: 14,100 undergrads. 1,538 full-time freshmen.
Selectivity: Open admission.

BASIC COSTS (2008-2009)
Tuition and fees: $629; out-of-state residents $6,059.
Per-credit charge: $20; out-of-state residents $201.
Additional info: Tuition/fee waivers available for adults.

FINANCIAL AID PICTURE (2007-2008)

Students with need: 86% of average financial aid package awarded as scholarships/grants, 14% awarded as loans/jobs. Need-based aid available for part-time students.

Students without need: No-need awards available for academics, art, athletics, leadership, music/drama.

Additional info: Students may apply for Pell grants until June 30.

FINANCIAL AID PROCEDURES

Forms required: FAFSA, institutional form.

Dates and Deadlines: Priority date 3/2; closing date 6/30. Applicants notified on a rolling basis starting 7/15.

Transfers: Outside scholarships must be reported to financial aid office.

CONTACT

Hortense Cooper, Director of Financial Aid
16007 Crenshaw Boulevard, Torrance, CA 90506
(310) 660-3593 ext. 3493

Empire College

Santa Rosa, California
www.empcol.edu Federal Code: 009032

2-year for-profit business college in small city.

Enrollment: 202 undergrads. 202 full-time freshmen.

Selectivity: Open admission.

BASIC COSTS (2008-2009)

Tuition and fees: $8,625.

FINANCIAL AID PICTURE (2008-2009)

Students with need: Need-based aid available for full-time students.

Students without need: This college awards aid only to students with need.

Scholarships offered: Dean's Scholarship for high school seniors; 10 awarded; range from $250-$1,500. Dean's Scholarships for Empire College students; 7 awarded; range from $250-$1,000. Based on academic achievement, letter of intent, extracurricular activities and letter of recommendation.

FINANCIAL AID PROCEDURES

Forms required: FAFSA.

Dates and Deadlines: No deadline. Applicants notified on a rolling basis.

CONTACT

Mary O'Brien, Financial Aid Officer
3035 Cleveland Avenue, Santa Rosa, CA 95403-2100
(707) 546-4000

Feather River College

Quincy, California
www.frc.edu Federal Code: 008597

2-year public community and liberal arts college in small town.

Enrollment: 757 undergrads.

Selectivity: Open admission.

BASIC COSTS (2008-2009)

Tuition and fees: $664; out-of-state residents $6,124.

Per-credit charge: $20; out-of-state residents $202.

Room only: $4,208.

Additional info: Good neighbor per unit fee is $42/unit for Nevada residents. Tuition/fee waivers available for adults, unemployed or children of unemployed.

FINANCIAL AID PICTURE

Students with need: Need-based aid available for full-time and part-time students. Work study available nights, weekends, and for part-time students.

FINANCIAL AID PROCEDURES

Forms required: FAFSA.

Dates and Deadlines: No deadline. Applicants notified on a rolling basis starting 7/30; must reply within 3 week(s) of notification.

CONTACT

Barbara Cormack, Financial Aid Director
570 Golden Eagle Avenue, Quincy, CA 95971
(530) 283-0202 ext. 296

Foothill College

Los Altos Hills, California
www.foothill.edu Federal Code: 001199

2-year public community college in large town.

Enrollment: 8,223 undergrads.

Selectivity: Open admission; but selective for some programs.

BASIC COSTS (2008-2009)

Tuition and fees: $628; out-of-state residents $5,803.

Per-credit charge: $13; out-of-state residents $128.

FINANCIAL AID PICTURE

Students with need: Need-based aid available for full-time and part-time students.

Students without need: This college awards aid only to students with need.

Scholarships offered: Chancellor's Scholarship for first-time freshmen who graduate in the top 20 percent of high school class as Chancellor's Scholar; $1,200 for two years.

FINANCIAL AID PROCEDURES

Forms required: FAFSA, institutional form.

Dates and Deadlines: Priority date 3/30; no closing date. Applicants notified on a rolling basis; must reply within 2 week(s) of notification.

Transfers: Application required for CDL grants, March 2 due date for CAL grant application.

CONTACT

Kevin Harral, Director, Financial Aid
12345 El Monte Road, Los Altos Hills, CA 94022
(650) 949-7245

Fremont College

Cerritos, California
www.fremont.edu Federal Code: 030399

2-year for-profit health science and career college in very large city.

Enrollment: 131 undergrads.

Selectivity: Open admission; but selective for some programs.

BASIC COSTS (2008-2009)

Additional info: Paralegal: $22,000. Sports therapy: $21,600. Massage Therapy: $13,600. Tuition at time of enrollment locked for 2 years; tuition/fee waivers available for unemployed or children of unemployed.

FINANCIAL AID PICTURE (2007-2008)

Students with need: Need-based aid available for full-time students.

Students without need: This college awards aid only to students with need.

FINANCIAL AID PROCEDURES

Forms required: FAFSA, institutional form.

CONTACT
Neeyah Francois, Director of Financial Aid
18000 Studebaker Road, 900A, Cerritos, CA 90703-5342
(562) 809-5100

Fresno City College
Fresno, California
www.fresnocitycollege.edu Federal Code: 001307

2-year public community and liberal arts college in large city.
Enrollment: 12,583 undergrads.
Selectivity: Open admission; but selective for some programs.

BASIC COSTS (2008-2009)
Tuition and fees: $630; out-of-state residents $6,060.
Per-credit charge: $20; out-of-state residents $201.
Additional info: Tuition/fee waivers available for adults, minority students, unemployed or children of unemployed.

FINANCIAL AID PICTURE
Students with need: Need-based aid available for full-time and part-time students.
Students without need: This college awards aid only to students with need.
Additional info: Board of Governors Grant Program to offset enrollment fees based on untaxed income, low income, or calculated need. Students qualifying for program also automatically exempt from health fees. March 2 application deadline for California grants.

FINANCIAL AID PROCEDURES
Forms required: FAFSA, state aid form.
Dates and Deadlines: Priority date 4/15; no closing date. Applicants notified on a rolling basis starting 4/1.

CONTACT
Frank Ramon, Financial Aid Director
1101 East University Avenue, Fresno, CA 93741
(559) 442-8279

Fresno Pacific University
Fresno, California
www.fresno.edu Federal Code: 001253

4-year private university and liberal arts college in large city, affiliated with Mennonite Brethren Church.
Enrollment: 1,583 undergrads.
Selectivity: Admits 50 to 75% of applicants.

BASIC COSTS (2009-2010)
Tuition and fees: $23,898.
Per-credit charge: $845.
Room and board: $6,180.

FINANCIAL AID PICTURE (2008-2009)
Students with need: 57% of average financial aid package awarded as scholarships/grants, 43% awarded as loans/jobs. Need-based aid available for part-time students. Work study available nights, weekends, and for part-time students.
Students without need: No-need awards available for academics, athletics, music/drama.
Scholarships offered: Paragon Scholarship; 2 awarded; full tuition; requires 3.65 GPA, demonstrated Christian leadership, SAT 1150 or higher. President's Scholarship; 40 awarded; $6,500-$9,500; requires 3.65 GPA, demonstrated Christian leadership, SAT 1150 or higher. Provost Scholarship; 20 awarded; $4,000-$8,000; for transfer students with 3.5 GPA and demonstrated Christian leadership. SAT scores exclusive of Writing.

FINANCIAL AID PROCEDURES
Forms required: FAFSA, institutional form.
Dates and Deadlines: Priority date 3/2; no closing date. Applicants notified on a rolling basis starting 3/2; must reply by 7/30 or within 3 week(s) of notification.
Transfers: No deadline.

CONTACT
Ken Isaak, Director of Student Financial Services
1717 South Chestnut Avenue, Fresno, CA 93702-4709
(559) 453-2041

Glendale Community College
Glendale, California
www.glendale.edu Federal Code: 001203

2-year public community college in small city.
Enrollment: 12,517 undergrads. 978 full-time freshmen.
Selectivity: Open admission; but selective for some programs.

BASIC COSTS (2008-2009)
Tuition and fees: $633; out-of-state residents $6,063.
Per-credit charge: $20; out-of-state residents $201.

FINANCIAL AID PICTURE (2007-2008)
Students with need: Need-based aid available for full-time and part-time students. Work study available nights, weekends, and for part-time students.
Students without need: This college awards aid only to students with need.

FINANCIAL AID PROCEDURES
Forms required: FAFSA, institutional form.
Dates and Deadlines: Priority date 4/15; no closing date. Applicants notified on a rolling basis starting 6/15; must reply within 2 week(s) of notification.
Transfers: No deadline.

CONTACT
Patricia Hurley, Director of Financial Aid
1500 North Verdugo Road, Glendale, CA 91208-2809
(818) 240-1000 ext. 5916

Golden Gate University
San Francisco, California
www.ggu.edu Federal Code: 001205

4-year private university in very large city.
Enrollment: 413 undergrads, 84% part-time. 2 full-time freshmen.
Selectivity: Admits over 75% of applicants.

BASIC COSTS (2009-2010)
Tuition and fees: $16,950.
Per-credit charge: $565.

FINANCIAL AID PICTURE (2008-2009)
Students with need: Need-based aid available for full-time and part-time students. Work study available nights.
Students without need: This college awards aid only to students with need.

FINANCIAL AID PROCEDURES
Forms required: FAFSA, institutional form.
Dates and Deadlines: Priority date 1/2; no closing date. Applicants notified on a rolling basis starting 4/1; must reply within 3 week(s) of notification.
Transfers: Priority date 6/14; no deadline. Applicants notified on a rolling basis starting 1/2; must reply within 3 week(s) of notification.

CONTACT

Louis Riccardi
536 Mission Street, San Francisco, CA 94105-2968
(415) 442-7270

Grossmont College

El Cajon, California
www.grossmont.edu Federal Code: 001208

2-year public community college in small city.
Enrollment: 12,595 undergrads.
Selectivity: Open admission; but selective for some programs.

BASIC COSTS (2008-2009)

Tuition and fees: $630; out-of-state residents $6,060.
Per-credit charge: $20; out-of-state residents $201.

FINANCIAL AID PICTURE (2007-2008)

Students with need: 86% of average financial aid package awarded as scholarships/grants, 14% awarded as loans/jobs. Need-based aid available for part-time students. Work study available nights, weekends, and for part-time students.
Students without need: This college awards aid only to students with need.

FINANCIAL AID PROCEDURES

Forms required: FAFSA.
Dates and Deadlines: Priority date 2/1; no closing date. Applicants notified on a rolling basis starting 7/15; must reply within 2 week(s) of notification.

CONTACT

Michael Copenhaver, Director of Financial Aid
8800 Grossmont College Drive, El Cajon, CA 92020
(619) 644-7129

Hartnell College

Salinas, California
www.hartnell.edu Federal Code: 001209

2-year public community college in small city.
Enrollment: 4,092 undergrads.
Selectivity: Open admission; but selective for some programs.

BASIC COSTS (2008-2009)

Tuition and fees: $608; out-of-state residents $6,038.
Per-credit charge: $20; out-of-state residents $201.

FINANCIAL AID PICTURE (2007-2008)

Students with need: 96% of average financial aid package awarded as scholarships/grants, 4% awarded as loans/jobs.

FINANCIAL AID PROCEDURES

Forms required: FAFSA.
Dates and Deadlines: Priority date 8/1; no closing date. Applicants notified on a rolling basis.

CONTACT

Mary Helen Dorado, Director, Financial Aid
156 Homestead Avenue, Salinas, CA 93901

Harvey Mudd College

Claremont, California Federal Code: 001171
www.hmc.edu CSS Code: 4341

4-year private engineering and liberal arts college in small city.
Enrollment: 738 undergrads. 196 full-time freshmen.
Selectivity: Admits less than 50% of applicants.

BASIC COSTS (2009-2010)

Tuition and fees: $38,567.
Room and board: $12,570.
Additional info: Room and board expense covers 16-meal plan.

FINANCIAL AID PICTURE (2007-2008)

Students with need: Out of 139 full-time freshmen who applied for aid, 115 were judged to have need. Of these, 115 received aid, and 115 had their full need met. Average financial aid package met 100% of need; average scholarship/grant was $26,872; average loan was $3,436. For part-time students, average financial aid package was $844.
Students without need: 50 full-time freshmen who did not demonstrate need for aid received scholarships/grants; average award was $9,512. No-need awards available for academics.
Scholarships offered: Harvey S. Mudd Scholarship: for first-time freshmen in science and technology programs; $10,000 annually for 4 years; must maintain minimum 2.75 GPA. Harvey Mudd College-sponsored National Merit Scholarships: from $750 to $2,000 based on need.
Cumulative student debt: 53% of graduating class had student loans; average debt was $21,018.

FINANCIAL AID PROCEDURES

Forms required: FAFSA, CSS PROFILE, state aid form.
Dates and Deadlines: Closing date 2/1. Applicants notified by 4/1; must reply by 5/1 or within 2 week(s) of notification.
Transfers: Closing date 3/2. Applicants notified by 5/15; must reply by 6/10 or within 2 week(s) of notification.

CONTACT

Gilma Lopez, Director of Financial Aid
301 Platt Boulevard, Claremont, CA 91711-5901
(909) 621-8055

Heald College: Concord

Concord, California
www.heald.edu Federal Code: 030693

2-year for-profit business college in small city.
Enrollment: 983 undergrads.

BASIC COSTS (2008-2009)

Tuition and fees: $11,550.

FINANCIAL AID PICTURE

Students with need: Need-based aid available for full-time and part-time students. Work study available nights, weekends, and for part-time students.
Students without need: This college awards aid only to students with need.

FINANCIAL AID PROCEDURES

Forms required: FAFSA.
Dates and Deadlines: No deadline. Applicants notified on a rolling basis.

CONTACT

Maria Duenas, Director of Financial Aid
5130 Commercial Circle, Concord, CA 94520
[illegible]

Heald College: Hayward

Hayward, California
www.heald.edu Federal Code: 008532

2-year for-profit technical college in small city.
Enrollment: 829 undergrads.

BASIC COSTS (2008-2009)
Tuition and fees: $11,550.

FINANCIAL AID PICTURE
Students with need: Need-based aid available for full-time and part-time students. Work study available nights, weekends, and for part-time students.
Students without need: This college awards aid only to students with need.

FINANCIAL AID PROCEDURES
Forms required: FAFSA.
Dates and Deadlines: No deadline.

CONTACT
Wylodin Banez, Director of Financial Aid
25500 Industrial Boulevard, Hayward, CA 94545
(510) 783-2100

Heald College: Rancho Cordova
Rancho Cordova, California
www.heald.edu Federal Code: 025931

2-year for-profit technical college in large city.
Enrollment: 566 undergrads.

BASIC COSTS (2008-2009)
Tuition and fees: $11,550.

FINANCIAL AID PICTURE
Students with need: Need-based aid available for full-time and part-time students. Work study available nights, weekends, and for part-time students.
Students without need: This college awards aid only to students with need.

FINANCIAL AID PROCEDURES
Forms required: FAFSA.
Dates and Deadlines: No deadline.

CONTACT
Karen Haro, Director of Financial Aid
2910 Prospect Park Drive, Rancho Cordova, CA 95670
(916) 638-1616

Heald College: Roseville
Roseville, California
www.heald.edu

2-year for-profit business and junior college in small city.
Enrollment: 685 undergrads.

BASIC COSTS (2008-2009)
Tuition and fees: $11,550.

FINANCIAL AID PICTURE
Students with need: Need-based aid available for full-time and part-time students. Work study available nights, weekends, and for part-time students.
Students without need: This college awards aid only to students with need.

FINANCIAL AID PROCEDURES
Forms required: FAFSA.
Dates and Deadlines: No deadline.

CONTACT
Rhonda Shaw, Director of Financial Aid
7 Sierra Gate Plaza, Roseville, CA 95678
(916) 789-8600

Heald College: Salinas
Salinas, California
www.heald.edu Federal Code: 030340

2-year for-profit business college in small city.
Enrollment: 573 undergrads.

BASIC COSTS (2008-2009)
Tuition and fees: $11,550.

FINANCIAL AID PICTURE
Students with need: Need-based aid available for full-time and part-time students. Work study available nights, weekends, and for part-time students.
Students without need: This college awards aid only to students with need.

FINANCIAL AID PROCEDURES
Forms required: FAFSA.
Dates and Deadlines: No deadline.

CONTACT
Heloise Mata, Director of Financial Aid
1450 North Main Street, Salinas, CA 93906
(831) 443-1700

Heald College: San Francisco
San Francisco, California
www.heald.edu Federal Code: 007234

2-year for-profit business college in very large city.
Enrollment: 650 undergrads.

BASIC COSTS (2008-2009)
Tuition and fees: $11,550.

FINANCIAL AID PICTURE
Students with need: Need-based aid available for full-time and part-time students. Work study available nights, weekends, and for part-time students.
Students without need: This college awards aid only to students with need.

FINANCIAL AID PROCEDURES
Forms required: FAFSA.
Dates and Deadlines: No deadline.

CONTACT
Judy Bacchus, Director of Financial Aid
350 Mission Street, San Francisco, CA 94103
(415) 808-3000

Heald College: San Jose
Milpitas, California
www.heald.edu Federal Code: 025932

2-year for-profit business college in very large city.
Enrollment: 761 undergrads.

BASIC COSTS (2008-2009)
Tuition and fees: $11,550.

FINANCIAL AID PICTURE
Students with need: Need-based aid available for full-time and part-time students. Work study available nights, weekends, and for part-time students.
Students without need: This college awards aid only to students with need.

FINANCIAL AID PROCEDURES

Forms required: FAFSA.

Dates and Deadlines: No deadline. Applicants notified on a rolling basis starting 6/15; must reply within 2 week(s) of notification.

CONTACT

Lidia Hurtado, Director of Financial Aid
341 Great Mall Parkway, Milpitas, CA 95035
(408) 934-4900

Heald College: Stockton

Stockton, California
www.heald.edu Federal Code: 025933

2-year for-profit business college in large city.

Enrollment: 1,095 undergrads.

Selectivity: Open admission.

BASIC COSTS (2008-2009)

Tuition and fees: $11,550.

FINANCIAL AID PICTURE

Students with need: Need-based aid available for full-time students.

FINANCIAL AID PROCEDURES

Forms required: FAFSA.

Dates and Deadlines: No deadline.

CONTACT

Valerie Edwards-Bendy, Director of Financial Aid
1605 East March Lane, Stockton, CA 95210
(209) 473-5200

Holy Names University

Oakland, California
www.hnu.edu Federal Code: 001183

4-year private university in large city, affiliated with Roman Catholic Church.

Enrollment: 669 undergrads, 22% part-time. 66 full-time freshmen.

Selectivity: Admits 50 to 75% of applicants.

BASIC COSTS (2009-2010)

Tuition and fees: $27,340.

Per-credit charge: $905.

Room and board: $9,320.

FINANCIAL AID PICTURE (2007-2008)

Students with need: Out of 63 full-time freshmen who applied for aid, 63 were judged to have need. Of these, 63 received aid, and 21 had their full need met. Average financial aid package met 37% of need; average scholarship/grant was $17,631; average loan was $3,357. For part-time students, average financial aid package was $7,211.

Students without need: 20 full-time freshmen who did not demonstrate need for aid received scholarships/grants; average award was $8,825. No-need awards available for academics, athletics, leadership, music/drama, religious affiliation.

Scholarships offered: ***Merit:*** Aspiring Leadership Grant, $5,500 annually, based on 2.70-2.99 GPA. Honors Scholarship; $8,500 annually, based on 3.00-3.29 GPA. Dean's Scholarship; $9,500 annually, based on 3.30-3.49 GPA. President's Scholarship; $11,000 annually, based on 3.50-3.74 GPA. Regent's Scholarship; $12,000 annually, based on 3.75+ GPA. Durocher Scholarship; full tuition, campus residency required; based on evidence of leadership, contributions to school and/or community and academic achievement, minimum GPA 3.75, minimum SAT 1100 (exclusive of writing); 1 awarded per year. ***Athletic:*** 13 full-time freshmen received athletic scholarships; average amount $7,715.

Cumulative student debt: 75% of graduating class had student loans; average debt was $11,167.

FINANCIAL AID PROCEDURES

Forms required: FAFSA, state aid form.

Dates and Deadlines: Priority date 3/2; closing date 6/30. Applicants notified on a rolling basis starting 9/1; must reply by 5/1 or within 2 week(s) of notification.

Transfers: Applicants notified on a rolling basis starting 9/1; must reply by 5/1 or within 2 week(s) of notification.

CONTACT

Murad Dibbini, Dean of Enrollment Services
3500 Mountain Boulevard, Oakland, CA 94619-1699
(510) 436-1327

Hope International University

Fullerton, California
www.hiu.edu Federal Code: 001252

4-year private university and liberal arts college in small city, affiliated with Independent Christian Churches and Churches of Christ.

Enrollment: 652 undergrads. 90 full-time freshmen.

Selectivity: Admits over 75% of applicants.

BASIC COSTS (2009-2010)

Tuition and fees: $22,520.

Per-credit charge: $825.

Room and board: $8,800.

FINANCIAL AID PICTURE (2008-2009)

Students with need: Out of 81 full-time freshmen who applied for aid, 75 were judged to have need. Of these, 74 received aid, and 11 had their full need met. Average financial aid package met 70% of need; average scholarship/grant was $13,837; average loan was $3,929. For part-time students, average financial aid package was $11,168.

Students without need: 15 full-time freshmen who did not demonstrate need for aid received scholarships/grants; average award was $19,880. No-need awards available for academics, job skills, leadership, music/drama, state/district residency.

Cumulative student debt: 100% of graduating class had student loans; average debt was $14,602.

FINANCIAL AID PROCEDURES

Forms required: FAFSA, institutional form.

Dates and Deadlines: Closing date 3/2. Applicants notified on a rolling basis starting 3/15; must reply within 2 week(s) of notification.

Transfers: Priority date 3/2; no deadline. Applicants notified on a rolling basis starting 4/1; must reply within 2 week(s) of notification.

CONTACT

Shannon O'Shields, Director of Student Financial Aid
2500 East Nutwood Avenue, Fullerton, CA 92831-3199
(714) 879-3901 ext. 2232

Humboldt State University

Arcata, California
www.humboldt.edu Federal Code: 001149

4-year public university and liberal arts college in large town.

Enrollment: 6,685 undergrads, 9% part-time. 1,038 full-time freshmen.

Selectivity: Admits over 75% of applicants.

BASIC COSTS (2008-2009)

Tuition and fees: $4,139; out-of-state residents $14,309.

Room and board: $8,972.

FINANCIAL AID PICTURE (2007-2008)

Students with need: Out of 808 full-time freshmen who applied for aid, 569 were judged to have need. Of these, 535 received aid, and 26 had their full need met. Average financial aid package met 71% of need; average scholarship/grant was $4,403; average loan was $222. For part-time students, average financial aid package was $7,191.

Students without need: 6 full-time freshmen who did not demonstrate need for aid received scholarships/grants; average award was $917. No-need awards available for academics.

Scholarships offered: 15 full-time freshmen received athletic scholarships; average amount $1,700.

Cumulative student debt: 47% of graduating class had student loans; average debt was $14,178.

FINANCIAL AID PROCEDURES

Forms required: FAFSA.

Dates and Deadlines: Priority date 3/2; no closing date. Applicants notified on a rolling basis starting 4/15; must reply within 6 week(s) of notification.

Transfers: Need is most salient factor for some programs.

CONTACT

Kim Coughlin-Lamphear, Director of Financial Aid
One Harpst Street, Arcata, CA 95521-8299
(707) 826-4321

Humphreys College

Stockton, California
www.humphreys.edu Federal Code: 001212

4-year private business and liberal arts college in large city.

Enrollment: 649 undergrads.

Selectivity: Open admission.

BASIC COSTS (2008-2009)

Tuition and fees: $12,240.

Per-credit charge: $255.

Room only: $3,150.

Additional info: School-controlled apartment housing cost quoted, not including utilities.

FINANCIAL AID PICTURE (2008-2009)

Students with need: Need-based aid available for full-time and part-time students. Work study available nights, weekends, and for part-time students.

Students without need: No-need awards available for academics, state/district residency.

FINANCIAL AID PROCEDURES

Forms required: FAFSA.

Dates and Deadlines: Closing date 6/30. Applicants notified on a rolling basis; must reply within 2 week(s) of notification.

CONTACT

Judi Lafeber, Director of Financial Aid
6650 Inglewood Avenue, Stockton, CA 95207-3896
(209) 478-0800 ext. 3

Imperial Valley College

Imperial, California
www.imperial.edu Federal Code: 001214

2-year public community college in rural community.

Enrollment: 5,701 undergrads. 1,156 full-time freshmen.

Selectivity: Open admission; but selective for some programs.

BASIC COSTS (2008-2009)

Tuition and fees: $630; out-of-state residents $5,820.

Per-credit charge: $20; out-of-state residents $193.

FINANCIAL AID PICTURE (2007-2008)

Students with need: Need-based aid available for full-time and part-time students.

FINANCIAL AID PROCEDURES

Forms required: FAFSA.

Dates and Deadlines: Priority date 3/2; no closing date. Applicants notified on a rolling basis.

Transfers: Closing date 3/2. Academic transcripts from previous institutions required.

CONTACT

Janis Magno, Dean of Financial Aid
Box 158, Imperial, CA 92251-0158
(760) 355-6266

Irvine Valley College

Irvine, California
www.ivc.edu Federal Code: 025395

2-year public community college in small city.

Enrollment: 4,818 undergrads.

Selectivity: Open admission.

BASIC COSTS (2008-2009)

Tuition and fees: $647; out-of-state residents $6,077.

Per-credit charge: $20; out-of-state residents $201.

Additional info: Tuition/fee waivers available for minority students.

FINANCIAL AID PICTURE (2007-2008)

Students with need: 81% of average financial aid package awarded as scholarships/grants, 19% awarded as loans/jobs. Need-based aid available for part-time students. Work study available nights.

Students without need: This college awards aid only to students with need.

FINANCIAL AID PROCEDURES

Forms required: FAFSA, state aid form, institutional form.

Dates and Deadlines: No deadline. Applicants notified on a rolling basis starting 4/30.

CONTACT

Darryl Cox, Director of Financial Aid
5500 Irvine Center Drive, Irvine, CA 92618-4399
(949) 451-5287

John F. Kennedy University

Pleasant Hill, California
www.jfku.edu Federal Code: 004484

Upper-division private university in large town.

Enrollment: 225 undergrads, 79% part-time.

Selectivity: Open admission; but selective for some programs.

BASIC COSTS (2008-2009)

Tuition and fees: $15,468.

Per-credit charge: $340.

FINANCIAL AID PICTURE (2007-2008)

Students with need: Need-based aid available for full-time and part-time students.

Students without need: This college awards aid only to students with need.

FINANCIAL AID PROCEDURES
Forms required: FAFSA, institutional form.
Dates and Deadlines: Priority date 3/2; no closing date. Applicants notified on a rolling basis; must reply within 4 week(s) of notification.
Transfers: Priority date 4/1.

CONTACT
Mindy Bergeron, Director of Financial Aid
100 Ellinwood Way, Pleasant Hill, CA 94523-4817
(925) 969-3385

Kaplan College: Panorama City
Panorama City, California
www.mariccollege.edu Federal Code: 030445

2-year for-profit junior and technical college in very large city.
Enrollment: 40 undergrads.
Selectivity: Open admission.

BASIC COSTS (2008-2009)
Additional info: Tuition varies by program from $12,720 (fees $45) to $26,175 (fees $45).

FINANCIAL AID PICTURE
Students with need: Need-based aid available for full-time students. Work study available nights.
Students without need: This college awards aid only to students with need.

FINANCIAL AID PROCEDURES
Forms required: FAFSA, institutional form.
Dates and Deadlines: No deadline.
Transfers: No deadline.

CONTACT
Cynthia Arevalo
14355 Roscoe Boulevard, Panorama City, CA 91402
(818) 672-8907

The King's College and Seminary
Van Nuys, California
www.kingscollege.edu

4-year private Bible and seminary college in very large city, affiliated with non-denominational tradition.
Enrollment: 525 undergrads.

BASIC COSTS (2009-2010)
Tuition and fees: $8,385.
Per-credit charge: $180.
Additional info: Seminary students pay $195 per credit hour.

FINANCIAL AID PICTURE
Students with need: Need-based aid available for full-time and part-time students. Work study available nights, weekends, and for part-time students.
Students without need: No-need awards available for academics, leadership.
Additional info: Specific scholarships may require specific essays.

FINANCIAL AID PROCEDURES
Forms required: FAFSA.
Dates and Deadlines: No deadline. Applicants notified on a rolling basis.

CONTACT
Norman Stoppenbrink, Financial Aid Director
14800 Sherman Way, Van Nuys, CA 91405-2233
(818) 779-8040

La Sierra University
Riverside, California
www.lasierra.edu Federal Code: 001215

4-year private university in large city, affiliated with Seventh-day Adventists.
Enrollment: 1,442 undergrads, 9% part-time. 327 full-time freshmen.
Selectivity: Admits 50 to 75% of applicants.

BASIC COSTS (2009-2010)
Tuition and fees: $24,917.
Per-credit charge: $660.
Room and board: $6,990.

FINANCIAL AID PICTURE (2007-2008)
Students with need: Out of 252 full-time freshmen who applied for aid, 213 were judged to have need. Of these, 213 received aid, and 37 had their full need met. Average financial aid package met 68% of need; average scholarship/grant was $14,683; average loan was $3,321. For part-time students, average financial aid package was $8,779.
Students without need: 111 full-time freshmen who did not demonstrate need for aid received scholarships/grants; average award was $8,476. No-need awards available for academics, leadership, music/drama, religious affiliation.
Cumulative student debt: 74% of graduating class had student loans; average debt was $34,247.

FINANCIAL AID PROCEDURES
Forms required: FAFSA, state aid form.
Dates and Deadlines: Priority date 3/2; no closing date. Applicants notified on a rolling basis starting 4/15; must reply by 9/1.
Transfers: No deadline. Applicants notified on a rolling basis.

CONTACT
Esther Kinzer, Director of Student Financial Services
4500 Riverwalk Parkway, Riverside, CA 92515-8247
(951) 785-2175

Las Positas College
Livermore, California
www.laspositascollege.edu Federal Code: 030357

2-year public community college in small city.
Enrollment: 5,593 undergrads.
Selectivity: Open admission.

BASIC COSTS (2008-2009)
Tuition and fees: $622; out-of-state residents $6,022.
Per-credit charge: $20; out-of-state residents $200.
Additional info: Tuition/fee waivers available for unemployed or children of unemployed.

FINANCIAL AID PICTURE (2007-2008)
Students with need: 88% of average financial aid package awarded as scholarships/grants, 12% awarded as loans/jobs.

FINANCIAL AID PROCEDURES
Forms required: institutional form.
Dates and Deadlines: Priority date 5/1; no closing date. Applicants notified on a rolling basis starting 7/1; must reply within 2 week(s) of notification.

CONTACT
Andi Schreibman, Financial Aid Officer
3033 Collier Canyon Road, Livermore, CA 94551
(925) 424-1580

Lassen Community College
Susanville, California
www.lassencollege.edu Federal Code: 001217

2-year public community college in small town.
Enrollment: 923 undergrads.
Selectivity: Open admission; but selective for some programs.

BASIC COSTS (2008-2009)
Tuition and fees: $616; out-of-state residents $6,106.
Per-credit charge: $20; out-of-state residents $203.
Room and board: $6,960.
Additional info: Nevada residents pay $42 per-credit-hour with good neighbor policy.

FINANCIAL AID PICTURE (2007-2008)
Students with need: 95% of average financial aid package awarded as scholarships/grants, 5% awarded as loans/jobs.
Additional info: Board of Governors Grant: low-income California residents can have registration fees waived.

FINANCIAL AID PROCEDURES
Forms required: FAFSA.
Dates and Deadlines: Priority date 7/1; no closing date. Applicants notified on a rolling basis starting 7/1; must reply within 2 week(s) of notification.

CONTACT
Matt Levine, Financial Aid Director
Box 3000, Susanville, CA 96130
(530) 257-6181 ext. 8649

Life Pacific College
San Dimas, California
www.lifepacific.edu Federal Code: 016029

4-year private Bible college in large town, affiliated with The Foursquare Church.
Enrollment: 414 undergrads, 25% part-time. 52 full-time freshmen.
Selectivity: Open admission; but selective for some programs..

BASIC COSTS (2009-2010)
Tuition and fees: $12,250.
Per-credit charge: $400.
Room and board: $6,000.

FINANCIAL AID PICTURE (2008-2009)
Students with need: Need-based aid available for full-time and part-time students.
Students without need: No-need awards available for academics, alumni affiliation.

FINANCIAL AID PROCEDURES
Forms required: FAFSA.
Dates and Deadlines: Closing date 7/1. Applicants notified on a rolling basis starting 6/1.

CONTACT
Becky Huyck, Director of Financial Aid
Attn: Admissions, San Dimas, CA 91773-3203
(909) 599-5433 ext. 325

Lincoln University
Oakland, California
www.lincolnuca.edu Federal Code: 006975

4-year private university and business college in very large city.
Enrollment: 89 undergrads, 25% part-time. 9 full-time freshmen.
Selectivity: Admits over 75% of applicants.

BASIC COSTS (2009-2010)
Tuition and fees: $8,920.
Per-credit charge: $335.
Additional info: Tuition for Intensive English program $2,860 per 16 weeks.

FINANCIAL AID PICTURE (2007-2008)
Students with need: Out of 9 full-time freshmen who applied for aid, 9 were judged to have need. Of these, 9 received aid, and 9 had their full need met. Average financial aid package met 100% of need; average scholarship/grant was $4,730; average loan was $3,720. For part-time students, average financial aid package was $12,250.
Students without need: This college awards aid only to students with need.
Cumulative student debt: 35% of graduating class had student loans; average debt was $16,400.

FINANCIAL AID PROCEDURES
Forms required: FAFSA.
Dates and Deadlines: Priority date 3/22; closing date 8/22. Applicants notified by 12/1; must reply by 1/2.
Transfers: Applicants notified by 12/1; must reply by 1/1.

CONTACT
James Peterson, Chief Financial Aid Director
401 15th Street, Oakland, CA 94612
(510) 628-8023

Loma Linda University
Loma Linda, California
www.llu.edu Federal Code: 001218

3-year private university and health science college in large town, affiliated with Seventh-day Adventists.
Enrollment: 1,092 undergrads, 20% part-time.

BASIC COSTS (2009-2010)
Tuition and fees: $25,164.
Per-credit charge: $525.
Room only: $2,520.
Additional info: Tuition quoted for nursing program. Full-time tuition for dental hygiene program: $23,833 plus $1,590 fees. For allied health program $450/credit hour; for certificate programs, $338/credit. Application fee may vary by program; tuition may vary by grade level in program.

FINANCIAL AID PICTURE (2007-2008)
Students with need: Need-based aid available for full-time and part-time students.

FINANCIAL AID PROCEDURES
Forms required: FAFSA.
Transfers: Priority date 3/2; no deadline. Applicants notified on a rolling basis starting 4/1; must reply within 4 week(s) of notification.

CONTACT
Verdell Schaefer, Director of Financial Aid
Admissions Processing, Loma Linda, CA 92350
(909) 558-4509

Long Beach City College
Long Beach, California
www.lbcc.edu Federal Code: 001219

2-year public community college in large city.
Enrollment: 15,613 undergrads.
Selectivity: Open admission.

BASIC COSTS (2008-2009)
Tuition and fees: $628; out-of-state residents $5,848.
Per-credit charge: $20; out-of-state residents $194.

FINANCIAL AID PICTURE
Students with need: Need-based aid available for full-time and part-time students.
Students without need: This college awards aid only to students with need.

FINANCIAL AID PROCEDURES
Forms required: FAFSA, institutional form.
Dates and Deadlines: Priority date 5/6; no closing date. Applicants notified on a rolling basis starting 7/6; must reply within 2 week(s) of notification.

CONTACT
Mike MacCallum, Director of Financial Aid and Veterans Affairs
4901 East Carson Street, Long Beach, CA 90808
(562) 938-4257

Los Angeles City College
Los Angeles, California
www.lacitycollege.edu Federal Code: 001223

2-year public community college in very large city.
Enrollment: 6,912 undergrads.
Selectivity: Open admission.

BASIC COSTS (2008-2009)
Tuition and fees: $622; out-of-state residents $6,052.
Per-credit charge: $20; out-of-state residents $201.

FINANCIAL AID PICTURE (2007-2008)
Students with need: Need-based aid available for full-time and part-time students.
Students without need: This college awards aid only to students with need.
Additional info: Fee waivers available for public assistance and Social Security insurance recipients; fee credits available for low income families.

FINANCIAL AID PROCEDURES
Forms required: FAFSA.
Dates and Deadlines: Priority date 3/2; no closing date. Applicants notified on a rolling basis starting 7/6; must reply within 2 week(s) of notification.
Transfers: No deadline. Applicants notified by 7/1.

CONTACT
Jeremy Villar, Dean of Student Services
855 North Vermont Avenue, Los Angeles, CA 90029-3589
(323) 953-4000 ext. 2025

Los Angeles Harbor College
Wilmington, California
www.lahc.edu Federal Code: 001224

2-year public community college in small city.
Enrollment: 4,054 undergrads. 726 full-time freshmen.
Selectivity: Open admission.

BASIC COSTS (2008-2009)
Tuition and fees: $622; out-of-state residents $6,052.
Per-credit charge: $20; out-of-state residents $201.

FINANCIAL AID PICTURE
Students with need: Need-based aid available for full-time and part-time students. Work study available nights, weekends, and for part-time students.
Students without need: This college awards aid only to students with need.

FINANCIAL AID PROCEDURES
Forms required: FAFSA, institutional form.
Dates and Deadlines: Priority date 3/2; no closing date. Applicants notified on a rolling basis; must reply within 2 week(s) of notification.
Transfers: Closing date 5/15.

CONTACT
Sheila Millman, Financial Aid Manager
1111 Figueroa Place, Wilmington, CA 90744-2397
(310) 233-4320

Los Angeles Mission College
Sylmar, California
www.lamission.edu Federal Code: 012550

2-year public community college in large town.
Enrollment: 3,895 undergrads.
Selectivity: Open admission.

BASIC COSTS (2008-2009)
Tuition and fees: $612; out-of-state residents $5,802.
Per-credit charge: $20; out-of-state residents $193.

FINANCIAL AID PICTURE (2007-2008)
Students with need: 92% of average financial aid package awarded as scholarships/grants, 8% awarded as loans/jobs.
Additional info: Board of Governors Grant available to those in receipt of AFDC, Social Security Insurance, or General Relief. If not in receipt of program, may qualify based on income.

FINANCIAL AID PROCEDURES
Forms required: FAFSA.
Dates and Deadlines: Priority date 8/1; no closing date. Applicants notified on a rolling basis starting 8/15.
Transfers: Financial aid transcripts required from previous institutions.

CONTACT
Dennis Schroeder, Financial Aid Manager
13356 Eldridge Avenue, Sylmar, CA 91342-3245
(818) 364-7648

Los Angeles Pierce College
Woodland Hills, California
www.piercecollege.edu Federal Code: 001226

2-year public community college in very large city.
Enrollment: 10,995 undergrads.
Selectivity: Open admission; but selective for some programs.

BASIC COSTS (2008-2009)
Tuition and fees: $622; out-of-state residents $6,052.
Per-credit charge: $20; out-of-state residents $201.

FINANCIAL AID PICTURE
Students with need: Need-based aid available for full-time and part-time students. Work study available nights, weekends, and for part-time students.
Students without need: This college awards aid only to students with need.

FINANCIAL AID PROCEDURES
Forms required: FAFSA, institutional form.
Dates and Deadlines: Priority date 5/1; no closing date. Applicants notified on a rolling basis starting 8/1.

CONTACT
Anafe Robinson, Director of Financial Aid
6201 Winnetka Avenue, Woodland Hills, CA 91371
(818) 719-6428

Los Angeles Southwest College
Los Angeles, California
www.lasc.edu Federal Code: 007047

2-year public community college in very large city.
Enrollment: 2,965 undergrads.
Selectivity: Open admission; but selective for some programs.

BASIC COSTS (2008-2009)
Tuition and fees: $622; out-of-state residents $6,052.
Per-credit charge: $20; out-of-state residents $201.

FINANCIAL AID PICTURE
Students with need: Need-based aid available for full-time and part-time students.
Additional info: Board of Governors Enrollment Fee Waiver available to students receiving AFDC, SSI/SSP, or General Assistance. May also qualify on basis of income.

FINANCIAL AID PROCEDURES
Forms required: FAFSA.
Dates and Deadlines: No deadline. Applicants notified on a rolling basis; must reply within 2 week(s) of notification.

CONTACT
Oscar Cobian, Dean, TRIO Programs
1600 West Imperial Highway, Los Angeles, CA 90047-4899
(323) 241-5328

Los Angeles Trade and Technical College
Los Angeles, California
www.lattc.edu Federal Code: 001227

2-year public community and technical college in very large city.
Enrollment: 4,473 undergrads.
Selectivity: Open admission.

BASIC COSTS (2008-2009)
Tuition and fees: $622; out-of-state residents $6,052.
Per-credit charge: $20; out-of-state residents $201.

FINANCIAL AID PICTURE
Students with need: Need-based aid available for full-time and part-time students. Work study available nights, weekends, and for part-time students.
Students without need: This college awards aid only to students with need.

FINANCIAL AID PROCEDURES
Forms required: FAFSA.
Dates and Deadlines: Priority date 5/1; no closing date. Applicants notified on a rolling basis.
Transfers: No deadline.

CONTACT
Leann Roque, Financial Aid Manager
400 West Washington Boulevard, Los Angeles, CA 90015-4181
(213) 744-9016

Los Angeles Valley College
Valley Glen, California
www.lavc.edu Federal Code: 001228

2-year public community college in very large city.
Enrollment: 8,810 undergrads.
Selectivity: Open admission; but selective for some programs.

BASIC COSTS (2008-2009)
Tuition and fees: $624; out-of-state residents $6,054.
Per-credit charge: $20; out-of-state residents $201.

FINANCIAL AID PICTURE
Students with need: Need-based aid available for full-time and part-time students.
Students without need: This college awards aid only to students with need.

FINANCIAL AID PROCEDURES
Forms required: FAFSA.
Dates and Deadlines: Priority date 6/12; no closing date. Applicants notified on a rolling basis.

CONTACT
Barbara Ralston, Associate Dean of Financial Aid
5800 Fulton Avenue, Valley Glen, CA 91401-4096
(818) 947-2412

Los Medanos College
Pittsburg, California
www.losmedanos.edu Federal Code: 010340

2-year public community college in small city.
Enrollment: 4,818 undergrads.
Selectivity: Open admission.

BASIC COSTS (2008-2009)
Tuition and fees: $610; out-of-state residents $6,040.
Per-credit charge: $20; out-of-state residents $201.

FINANCIAL AID PICTURE (2007-2008)
Students with need: 94% of average financial aid package awarded as scholarships/grants, 6% awarded as loans/jobs.

FINANCIAL AID PROCEDURES
Forms required: FAFSA.
Dates and Deadlines: Priority date 3/2; no closing date. Applicants notified on a rolling basis starting 7/1; must reply within 2 week(s) of notification.

CONTACT
Loretta Canto-Williams, Director of Financial Aid
2700 East Leland Road, Pittsburg, CA 94565
(925) 439-2181

Loyola Marymount University
Los Angeles, California Federal Code: 001234
www.lmu.edu CSS Code: 4403

4-year private university in very large city, affiliated with Roman Catholic Church.
Enrollment: 5,509 undergrads, 2% part-time. 1,267 full-time freshmen.
Selectivity: Admits 50 to 75% of applicants.

BASIC COSTS (2009-2010)
Tuition and fees: $35,419.
Per-credit charge: $1,447.
Room and board: $13,260.

FINANCIAL AID PICTURE (2007-2008)

Students with need: Out of 953 full-time freshmen who applied for aid, 669 were judged to have need. Of these, 659 received aid, and 121 had their full need met. Average financial aid package met 70% of need; average scholarship/grant was $15,704; average loan was $4,658. For part-time students, average financial aid package was $8,037.

Students without need: 157 full-time freshmen who did not demonstrate need for aid received scholarships/grants; average award was $11,510. No-need awards available for academics, alumni affiliation, art, athletics, music/drama, religious affiliation, ROTC.

Scholarships offered: 29 full-time freshmen received athletic scholarships; average amount $16,165.

Cumulative student debt: 58% of graduating class had student loans; average debt was $26,550.

FINANCIAL AID PROCEDURES

Forms required: FAFSA, CSS PROFILE.

Dates and Deadlines: Priority date 2/1; closing date 5/15. Applicants notified on a rolling basis starting 3/15; must reply by 5/1 or within 4 week(s) of notification.

CONTACT

Catherine Graham, Director of Financial Aid
Admissions, 1 LMU Drive, Los Angeles, CA 90045-8350
(310) 338-2700

Marymount College

Rancho Palos Verdes, California
www.marymountpv.edu Federal Code: 010474

2-year private junior and liberal arts college in large town, affiliated with Roman Catholic Church.

Enrollment: 617 undergrads. 315 full-time freshmen.

Selectivity: Admits over 75% of applicants.

BASIC COSTS (2009-2010)

Tuition and fees: $24,422.

Per-credit charge: $825.

Room and board: $10,600.

FINANCIAL AID PICTURE (2007-2008)

Students with need: Need-based aid available for full-time students.

Students without need: No-need awards available for academics.

Scholarships offered: President's Scholarship: $8,000; Academic GPA: 3.30 and above; SAT 1530 or ACT 22. Dean's Scholarship: $6,000; Academic GPA 3.00-3.29; SAT 1410 or ACT 20. Achievement Scholarship: $4,500; Academic GPA 2.80-2.99; SAT 1210 or ACT 17. Deadline May 1. All admitted students considered. Renewable for one additional, consecutive year.

FINANCIAL AID PROCEDURES

Forms required: FAFSA.

Dates and Deadlines: Priority date 3/1; no closing date. Applicants notified on a rolling basis starting 2/1; must reply by 5/1 or within 4 week(s) of notification.

CONTACT

Ray Parris, Director of Financial Aid
30800 Palos Verdes Drive East, Rancho Palos Verdes, CA 90275-6299
(310) 303-7217

The Master's College

Santa Clarita, California
www.masters.edu Federal Code: 001220

4-year private liberal arts and seminary college in small city, affiliated with Christian Church.

Enrollment: 1,039 undergrads, 14% part-time. 158 full-time freshmen.

Selectivity: Admits 50 to 75% of applicants.

BASIC COSTS (2009-2010)

Tuition and fees: $24,280.

Per-credit charge: $1,015.

Room and board: $8,000.

FINANCIAL AID PICTURE (2007-2008)

Students with need: Out of 158 full-time freshmen who applied for aid, 128 were judged to have need. Of these, 128 received aid, and 25 had their full need met. Average financial aid package met 71% of need; average scholarship/grant was $13,042; average loan was $3,766. For part-time students, average financial aid package was $7,319.

Students without need: 21 full-time freshmen who did not demonstrate need for aid received scholarships/grants; average award was $5,309. No-need awards available for academics, alumni affiliation, art, athletics, leadership, music/drama.

Scholarships offered: 9 full-time freshmen received athletic scholarships; average amount $7,166.

Cumulative student debt: 46% of graduating class had student loans; average debt was $18,994.

FINANCIAL AID PROCEDURES

Forms required: FAFSA, state aid form, institutional form.

Dates and Deadlines: Priority date 3/2; no closing date. Applicants notified on a rolling basis starting 2/18; must reply by 5/1 or within 2 week(s) of notification.

Transfers: Closing date 3/2.

CONTACT

Gary Edwards, Director of Financial Aid
21726 Placerita Canyon Road, Santa Clarita, CA 91321-1200
(661) 259-3540 ext. 3391

Mendocino College

Ukiah, California
www.mendocino.edu Federal Code: 011672

2-year public community college in large town.

Enrollment: 2,186 undergrads. 304 full-time freshmen.

Selectivity: Open admission.

BASIC COSTS (2008-2009)

Tuition and fees: $634; out-of-state residents $6,184.

Per-credit charge: $20; out-of-state residents $205.

Additional info: Tuition/fee waivers available for unemployed or children of unemployed.

FINANCIAL AID PICTURE (2007-2008)

Students with need: Out of 207 full-time freshmen who applied for aid, 196 were judged to have need. Of these, 195 received aid. For part-time students, average financial aid package was $1,805.

Students without need: 59 full-time freshmen who did not demonstrate need for aid received scholarships/grants; average award was $3,637. No-need awards available for academics, leadership, state/district residency.

FINANCIAL AID PROCEDURES

Forms required: FAFSA.

Dates and Deadlines: Priority date 5/31; no closing date. Applicants notified on a rolling basis starting 7/1; must reply within 2 week(s) of notification.

CONTACT

Jacqueline Bradley, Director of Financial Aid
1000 Hensley Creek/Box 3000, Ukiah, CA 95482
(707) 468-3110

Menlo College

Atherton, California
www.menlo.edu Federal Code: 001236

4-year private business and liberal arts college in small city.
Enrollment: 593 undergrads, 4% part-time. 158 full-time freshmen.
Selectivity: Admits 50 to 75% of applicants.

BASIC COSTS (2009-2010)

Tuition and fees: $32,120.
Per-credit charge: $1,322.
Room and board: $11,330.

FINANCIAL AID PICTURE (2008-2009)

Students with need: Out of 91 full-time freshmen who applied for aid, 79 were judged to have need. Of these, 79 received aid, and 3 had their full need met. Average financial aid package met 69% of need; average scholarship/grant was $22,458; average loan was $2,785. For part-time students, average financial aid package was $7,340.
Students without need: 54 full-time freshmen who did not demonstrate need for aid received scholarships/grants; average award was $11,860. No-need awards available for academics.
Cumulative student debt: 92% of graduating class had student loans; average debt was $12,653.

FINANCIAL AID PROCEDURES

Forms required: FAFSA, state aid form.
Dates and Deadlines: Priority date 3/2; closing date 8/1. Applicants notified on a rolling basis starting 12/15; must reply by 5/1 or within 2 week(s) of notification.
Transfers: No deadline. Must reply by 5/1 or within 2 week(s) of notification.

CONTACT

Anne Heaton-Dunlap, Director, Office of Financial Aid
1000 El Camino Real, Atherton, CA 94027
(650) 543-3880

Merritt College

Oakland, California
www.merritt.edu Federal Code: 001267

2-year public community college in large city.
Enrollment: 2,544 undergrads.
Selectivity: Open admission.

BASIC COSTS (2008-2009)

Tuition and fees: $604; out-of-state residents $6,034.
Per-credit charge: $20; out-of-state residents $201.
Additional info: Tuition/fee waivers available for unemployed or children of unemployed.

FINANCIAL AID PICTURE

Students with need: Need-based aid available for full-time and part-time students.

FINANCIAL AID PROCEDURES

Forms required: FAFSA, institutional form.
Dates and Deadlines: Priority date 4/1; closing date 6/30. Applicants notified on a rolling basis starting 6/1.

CONTACT

Alice Freeman, Financial Aid Coordinator
12500 Campus Drive, Oakland, CA 94619
(510) 436-2465

Mills College

Oakland, California
www.mills.edu Federal Code: 001238

4-year private liberal arts college for women in large city.
Enrollment: 956 undergrads, 6% part-time. 200 full-time freshmen.
Selectivity: Admits 50 to 75% of applicants.

BASIC COSTS (2008-2009)

Tuition and fees: $35,190.
Room and board: $10,550.

FINANCIAL AID PICTURE (2008-2009)

Students with need: Out of 184 full-time freshmen who applied for aid, 171 were judged to have need. Of these, 171 received aid, and 71 had their full need met. Average financial aid package met 87% of need; average scholarship/grant was $27,283; average loan was $3,450. For part-time students, average financial aid package was $10,254.
Students without need: 21 full-time freshmen who did not demonstrate need for aid received scholarships/grants; average award was $17,285. No-need awards available for academics, leadership, minority status, music/drama.
Cumulative student debt: 97% of graduating class had student loans; average debt was $24,255.

FINANCIAL AID PROCEDURES

Forms required: FAFSA, institutional form.
Dates and Deadlines: Priority date 2/15; no closing date. Applicants notified on a rolling basis starting 3/1; must reply by 5/1 or within 2 week(s) of notification.
Transfers: Priority date 3/2. Applicants notified on a rolling basis starting 4/15; must reply by 5/1 or within 2 week(s) of notification. Applications by March 2 for California residents, April 1 for out-of-state students.

CONTACT

David Gin, Associate Vice President for Student Finance and Administration Services
5000 MacArthur Boulevard, Oakland, CA 94613
(510) 430-2000

MiraCosta College

Oceanside, California
www.miracosta.edu Federal Code: 001239

2-year public community college in large city.
Enrollment: 8,834 undergrads. 892 full-time freshmen.
Selectivity: Open admission; but selective for some programs.

BASIC COSTS (2008-2009)

Tuition and fees: $644; out-of-state residents $6,074.
Per-credit charge: $20; out-of-state residents $201.

FINANCIAL AID PICTURE (2007-2008)

Students with need: 14% of average financial aid package awarded as scholarships/grants, 86% awarded as loans/jobs. Need-based aid available for part-time students. Work study available nights.
Additional info: Waiver of in-state fees for eligible low-income students.

FINANCIAL AID PROCEDURES

Forms required: FAFSA, state aid form, institutional form.

Dates and Deadlines: Priority date 4/9; no closing date. Applicants notified on a rolling basis; must reply within 4 week(s) of notification.

CONTACT

JoAnn Bernard, Financial Aid Director
One Barnard Drive, Oceanside, CA 92056-3899
(760) 795-6711

Modesto Junior College

Modesto, California
www.mjc.edu Federal Code: 001240

2-year public community college in small city.
Enrollment: 14,518 undergrads.
Selectivity: Open admission; but selective for some programs.

BASIC COSTS (2008-2009)

Tuition and fees: $642; out-of-state residents $6,072.
Per-credit charge: $20; out-of-state residents $201.

FINANCIAL AID PICTURE (2008-2009)

Students with need: Need-based aid available for full-time and part-time students. Work study available nights, weekends, and for part-time students.
Students without need: This college awards aid only to students with need.
Additional info: Modesto Junior College scholarship priority deadline 12/15.

FINANCIAL AID PROCEDURES

Forms required: FAFSA, state aid form, institutional form.
Dates and Deadlines: Priority date 3/2; no closing date. Applicants notified on a rolling basis starting 5/1; must reply within 2 week(s) of notification.

CONTACT

Myra Rush, Director of Financial Aid and Scholarships
435 College Avenue, Modesto, CA 95350-5800
(209) 575-6023

Monterey Peninsula College

Monterey, California
www.mpc.edu Federal Code: 001242

2-year public community college in large town.
Enrollment: 4,011 undergrads.
Selectivity: Open admission; but selective for some programs.

BASIC COSTS (2008-2009)

Tuition and fees: $662; out-of-state residents $6,092.
Per-credit charge: $20; out-of-state residents $201.
Additional info: Tuition/fee waivers available for adults, minority students, unemployed or children of unemployed.

FINANCIAL AID PICTURE

Students with need: Need-based aid available for full-time and part-time students.

FINANCIAL AID PROCEDURES

Forms required: FAFSA, institutional form.
Dates and Deadlines: Priority date 3/2; no closing date. Applicants notified on a rolling basis starting 6/1.

CONTACT

Claudia Martin, Director of Financial Aid
980 Fremont Street, Monterey, CA 93940-4799
(831) 646-4000

Mount St. Mary's College

Los Angeles, California
www.msmc.la.edu Federal Code: 001243

4-year private liberal arts college in very large city, affiliated with Roman Catholic Church.
Enrollment: 1,880 undergrads, 25% part-time. 323 full-time freshmen.
Selectivity: Admits over 75% of applicants.

BASIC COSTS (2008-2009)

Tuition and fees: $27,100.
Per-credit charge: $1,012.
Room and board: $9,830.

FINANCIAL AID PICTURE (2008-2009)

Students with need: Average financial aid package for all full-time undergraduates was $26,842. Need-based aid available for part-time students.
Students without need: No-need awards available for academics, alumni affiliation, art, leadership, music/drama.

FINANCIAL AID PROCEDURES

Forms required: FAFSA, institutional form.
Dates and Deadlines: Priority date 3/1; closing date 4/30. Applicants notified on a rolling basis starting 2/1.
Transfers: No deadline.

CONTACT

La Royce Dodd, Director of Student Financing
12001 Chalon Road, Los Angeles, CA 90049
(310) 954-4195

Mount San Antonio College

Walnut, California
www.mtsac.edu Federal Code: 001245

2-year public community college in small city.
Enrollment: 21,447 undergrads.
Selectivity: Open admission.

BASIC COSTS (2008-2009)

Tuition and fees: $664; out-of-state residents $6,094.
Per-credit charge: $20; out-of-state residents $201.

FINANCIAL AID PICTURE

Students with need: Need-based aid available for full-time and part-time students.
Students without need: This college awards aid only to students with need.

FINANCIAL AID PROCEDURES

Forms required: FAFSA, institutional form.
Dates and Deadlines: Closing date 3/2. Applicants notified on a rolling basis starting 6/1; must reply within 4 week(s) of notification.

CONTACT

Susanna Jones, Director Financial Aid
1100 North Grand Avenue, Walnut, CA 91789
(909) 594-5611

Mount San Jacinto College

San Jacinto, California
www.msjc.edu Federal Code: 001246

2-year public community college in small city.
Enrollment: 8,794 undergrads.
Selectivity: Open admission; but selective for some programs.

BASIC COSTS (2008-2009)
Tuition and fees: $600; out-of-state residents $6,030.
Per-credit charge: $20; out-of-state residents $201.

FINANCIAL AID PICTURE
Students with need: Need-based aid available for full-time and part-time students. Work study available nights.
Students without need: This college awards aid only to students with need.
Additional info: Board of Governors Grant Program for state residents to defray cost of enrollment fee.

FINANCIAL AID PROCEDURES
Forms required: FAFSA, institutional form.
Dates and Deadlines: Priority date 3/2; no closing date. Applicants notified on a rolling basis starting 5/1; must reply within 3 week(s) of notification.
Transfers: No deadline.

CONTACT
Lisa Navarro, Financial Aid Director
1499 North State Street, San Jacinto, CA 92583
(951) 487-6752

Mt. Sierra College
Monrovia, California
www.mtsierra.edu Federal Code: 031287

3-year for-profit technical college in very large city.
Enrollment: 458 undergrads, 44% part-time. 11 full-time freshmen.
Selectivity: Admits over 75% of applicants.

BASIC COSTS (2008-2009)
Tuition and fees: $15,064.
Per-credit charge: $308.
Additional info: Additional lab fees may apply; varies by program of study.

FINANCIAL AID PICTURE (2007-2008)
Students with need: Out of 11 full-time freshmen who applied for aid, 11 were judged to have need. Of these, 11 received aid, and 11 had their full need met. Average financial aid package met 80% of need; average scholarship/grant was $8,110; average loan was $3,500. For part-time students, average financial aid package was $1,078.
Cumulative student debt: 79% of graduating class had student loans; average debt was $9,500.

FINANCIAL AID PROCEDURES
Forms required: FAFSA.

CONTACT
Mary Olmos, Senior Student Finance Administrator
101 East Huntington Drive, Monrovia, CA 91016
(626) 873-2144 ext. 210

MTI College
Sacramento, California
www.mticollege.edu Federal Code: 012912

2-year for-profit business and technical college in large city.
Enrollment: 300 undergrads.

BASIC COSTS (2008-2009)
Tuition and fees: $11,025.

FINANCIAL AID PICTURE
Students with need: Need-based aid available for full-time students. Work study available nights.

CONTACT
Paula Perez, Director of Financial Aid
5221 Madison Avenue, Sacramento, CA 95841
(916) 339-1500

National Hispanic University
San Jose, California
www.nhu.edu Federal Code: 016968

4-year private university in very large city.
Enrollment: 367 undergrads, 38% part-time. 40 full-time freshmen.
Selectivity: Admits 50 to 75% of applicants.

BASIC COSTS (2009-2010)
Tuition and fees: $8,000.
Per-credit charge: $260.

FINANCIAL AID PICTURE (2007-2008)
Students with need: 63% of average financial aid package awarded as scholarships/grants, 37% awarded as loans/jobs.
Students without need: No-need awards available for academics.

FINANCIAL AID PROCEDURES
Forms required: FAFSA.
Dates and Deadlines: No deadline.

CONTACT
Wilbert Lleses, Director, Office of Financial Aid and Scholarship
14271 Story Road, San Jose, CA 95127-3823
(408) 254-6900

National Polytechnic College of Science
San Diego, California
www.natpoly.edu Federal Code: 011696

2-year private health science and maritime college in large city.
Enrollment: 236 undergrads.
Selectivity: Open admission.

BASIC COSTS (2008-2009)
Additional info: Associate degree program charge (covering 12 months), $17,360; per-credit-hour charge, $280. Academic year is comprised of 30 weeks (36 quarter credits), with courses offered in five-week sessions. Undergraduate courses are scheduled, typically, for eight to ten hours per day (two days each week, five-week period). Some courses require basic supplies (e.g., wet suit, fins, weights, work boots) that are not covered by tuition; additional cost of these supplies could amount to $500 or more.

FINANCIAL AID PICTURE
Students with need: Need-based aid available for full-time students.
Additional info: Work-study programs available.

FINANCIAL AID PROCEDURES
Forms required: FAFSA, institutional form.
Dates and Deadlines: No deadline. Applicants notified on a rolling basis; must reply within 3 week(s) of notification.

CONTACT
Lida Castillo, Financial Aid Officer
3580 Aero Court, San Diego, CA 92123
(310) 834-2501

National University

La Jolla, California
www.nu.edu Federal Code: 011460

4-year private university in very large city.
Enrollment: 6,092 undergrads, 64% part-time.
Selectivity: Open admission; but selective for some programs.

BASIC COSTS (2008-2009)

Tuition and fees: $10,224.

FINANCIAL AID PICTURE (2007-2008)

Students with need: 4% of average financial aid package awarded as scholarships/grants, 96% awarded as loans/jobs. Need-based aid available for part-time students.

FINANCIAL AID PROCEDURES

Forms required: FAFSA, state aid form, institutional form.
Dates and Deadlines: No deadline. Applicants notified on a rolling basis.
Transfers: No deadline.

CONTACT

Valerie Ryan, Director of Financial Aid
11255 North Torrey Pines Road, La Jolla, CA 92037-1011
(858) 642-8500

NewSchool of Architecture & Design

San Diego, California
www.newschoolarch.edu Federal Code: 030439

5-year for-profit visual arts and liberal arts college in very large city.
Enrollment: 309 undergrads.
Selectivity: Admits over 75% of applicants.

BASIC COSTS (2008-2009)

Tuition and fees: $19,845.
Per-credit charge: $600.

FINANCIAL AID PICTURE (2008-2009)

Students with need: 15% of average financial aid package awarded as scholarships/grants, 85% awarded as loans/jobs. Work study available nights.
Students without need: No-need awards available for academics.
Scholarships offered: Presidential Scholarship; $5,000 annually for 2 years; for incoming freshmen based on GPA, activity, recommendations, portfolio; 15 recipients.

FINANCIAL AID PROCEDURES

Forms required: FAFSA.
Dates and Deadlines: No deadline. Applicants notified on a rolling basis.
Transfers: Priority date 4/1; no deadline.

CONTACT

Matt Wakeman, Director of Financial Aid
1249 F Street, San Diego, CA 92101
(619) 235-4100 ext. 206

Notre Dame de Namur University

Belmont, California
www.ndnu.edu Federal Code: 001179

4-year private university and liberal arts college in large town, affiliated with Roman Catholic Church.
Enrollment: 799 undergrads, 35% part-time. 147 full-time freshmen.
Selectivity: Admits over 75% of applicants.

BASIC COSTS (2009-2010)

Tuition and fees: $27,110.
Per-credit charge: $545.
Room and board: $11,210.

FINANCIAL AID PICTURE

Students with need: Need-based aid available for full-time and part-time students. Work study available nights, weekends, and for part-time students.
Students without need: No-need awards available for academics, alumni affiliation, athletics, leadership, music/drama, religious affiliation.
Scholarships offered: Presidential Scholarships: up to $12,000 per semester; based on academic merit and leadership; variable number available. Leadership Scholarship: up to $9,000 annually; based on academic merit and leadership or service; variable number available. Emerging Artist Scholarship: up to $9,500 annually; based on demonstrated talent in the performing and fine arts; variable number available. Belmont Scholarships: up to $8,000 annually; based on merit; variable number available. Bay Area Catholic High School: up to $7,500 per year to one student from each of Bay Area Catholic high schools in their freshman year at NDNU.

FINANCIAL AID PROCEDURES

Forms required: FAFSA. CSS PROFILE accepted but not required.
Dates and Deadlines: Priority date 3/2; no closing date. Applicants notified on a rolling basis starting 1/15.

CONTACT

Susan Pace, Director of Financial Aid
1500 Ralston Avenue, Belmont, CA 94002-1908
(650) 508-3600

Occidental College

Los Angeles, California Federal Code: 001249
www.oxy.edu CSS Code: 4581

4-year private liberal arts college in very large city, affiliated with nondenominational tradition.
Enrollment: 1,834 undergrads. 459 full-time freshmen.
Selectivity: Admits less than 50% of applicants.

BASIC COSTS (2008-2009)

Tuition and fees: $37,071.
Room and board: $10,270.

FINANCIAL AID PICTURE (2007-2008)

Students with need: Out of 307 full-time freshmen who applied for aid, 239 were judged to have need. Of these, 239 received aid, and 118 had their full need met. Average financial aid package met 92% of need; average scholarship/grant was $25,556; average loan was $4,565. For part-time students, average financial aid package was $30,944.
Students without need: 115 full-time freshmen who did not demonstrate need for aid received scholarships/grants; average award was $8,285. No-need awards available for academics, leadership, music/drama, state/district residency.
Scholarships offered: Margaret Bundy Scott Scholarship: $20,000. President's Scholarship: $15,000; awarded to top 10-15% of incoming class based on academic achievement, leadership, and citizenship.
Cumulative student debt: 73% of graduating class had student loans; average debt was $21,002.

FINANCIAL AID PROCEDURES

Forms required: FAFSA, CSS PROFILE, state aid form.
Dates and Deadlines: Priority date 2/1; closing date 2/1. Applicants notified by 4/1; must reply by 5/1.
Transfers: Priority date 3/15; closing date 3/15. Applicants notified on a rolling basis; must reply within 2 week(s) of notification. California residents must apply for Cal Grant by completing FAFSA and CSAC's GPA verification form by March 2.

CONTACT
Maureen McRae, Director of Financial Aid
1600 Campus Road, Los Angeles, CA 90041
(323) 259-2548

Ohlone College

Fremont, California
www.ohlone.edu Federal Code: 004481

2-year public community college in large city.
Enrollment: 4,910 undergrads.
Selectivity: Open admission; but selective for some programs.

BASIC COSTS (2008-2009)
Tuition and fees: $652; out-of-state residents $6,082.
Per-credit charge: $20; out-of-state residents $201.
Additional info: Tuition/fee waivers available for adults, minority students, unemployed or children of unemployed.

FINANCIAL AID PICTURE
Students with need: Need-based aid available for full-time and part-time students.
Students without need: No-need awards available for academics.

FINANCIAL AID PROCEDURES
Forms required: FAFSA, state aid form, institutional form.
Dates and Deadlines: Priority date 7/1; no closing date. Applicants notified on a rolling basis starting 7/30; must reply within 2 week(s) of notification.

CONTACT
Debra Griffin, Financial Aid Director
43600 Mission Boulevard, Fremont, CA 94539-0390
(510) 659-6150

Orange Coast College

Costa Mesa, California
www.orangecoastcollege.edu Federal Code: 001250

2-year public community college in large city.
Enrollment: 18,711 undergrads. 2,337 full-time freshmen.
Selectivity: Open admission.

BASIC COSTS (2008-2009)
Tuition and fees: $658; out-of-state residents $6,088.
Per-credit charge: $20; out-of-state residents $201.
Additional info: Tuition/fee waivers available for adults, minority students, unemployed or children of unemployed.

FINANCIAL AID PICTURE (2007-2008)
Students with need: Need-based aid available for full-time and part-time students.
Students without need: No-need awards available for academics.

FINANCIAL AID PROCEDURES
Forms required: FAFSA, institutional form.
Dates and Deadlines: Priority date 3/2; closing date 5/31. Applicants notified on a rolling basis; must reply within 2 week(s) of notification.

CONTACT
Melissa Moser, Financial Aid Director
2701 Fairview Road, Costa Mesa, CA 92628-5005
(714) 432-5508

Otis College of Art and Design

Los Angeles, California
www.otis.edu Federal Code: 001251

4-year private visual arts college in very large city.
Enrollment: 1,139 undergrads, 2% part-time. 225 full-time freshmen.
Selectivity: Admits 50 to 75% of applicants.

BASIC COSTS (2009-2010)
Tuition and fees: $32,060.
Per-credit charge: $1,022.

FINANCIAL AID PICTURE (2008-2009)
Students with need: Out of 182 full-time freshmen who applied for aid, 143 were judged to have need. Of these, 143 received aid. Average financial aid package met 54% of need; average scholarship/grant was $9,089; average loan was $3,323. Need-based aid available for part-time students.
Students without need: 36 full-time freshmen who did not demonstrate need for aid received scholarships/grants; average award was $5,613. No-need awards available for academics, art.
Cumulative student debt: 66% of graduating class had student loans; average debt was $37,356.

FINANCIAL AID PROCEDURES
Forms required: FAFSA, state aid form.
Dates and Deadlines: Priority date 2/15; no closing date. Applicants notified on a rolling basis starting 3/1; must reply within 2 week(s) of notification.

CONTACT
Ji Choi, Director of Financial Aid
9045 Lincoln Boulevard, Los Angeles, CA 90045-9785
(310) 665-6880

Pacific Oaks College

Pasadena, California
www.pacificoaks.edu Federal Code: 001255

Upper-division private teachers college in small city.
Enrollment: 239 undergrads, 95% part-time.

BASIC COSTS (2009-2010)
Tuition and fees: $26,100.
Per-credit charge: $868.

FINANCIAL AID PICTURE (2008-2009)
Students with need: Need-based aid available for full-time and part-time students. Work study available nights, weekends, and for part-time students.
Students without need: This college awards aid only to students with need.

FINANCIAL AID PROCEDURES
Dates and Deadlines: Priority date 4/15; no closing date. Applicants notified on a rolling basis starting 5/1; must reply by 5/15 or within 4 week(s) of notification.

CONTACT
Seph Rodriguez, Director of Financial Aid
5 Westmoreland Place, Pasadena, CA 91103
(626) 397-1350

Pacific States University

Los Angeles, California
www.psuca.edu Federal Code: 031633

4-year private university in very large city.
Enrollment: 55 undergrads.

Selectivity: Open admission; but selective for some programs.

BASIC COSTS (2009-2010)
Tuition and fees: $13,400.
Per-credit charge: $210.

FINANCIAL AID PICTURE
Students with need: Need-based aid available for full-time and part-time students.
Students without need: No-need awards available for academics.

FINANCIAL AID PROCEDURES
Forms required: FAFSA, institutional form.
Dates and Deadlines: No deadline.

CONTACT
Min Kim, Financial Aid Officer
1516 South Western Avenue, Los Angeles, CA 90006
(323) 731-2383 ext. 14

Pacific Union College
Angwin, California
www.puc.edu Federal Code: 001258

4-year private liberal arts college in small town, affiliated with Seventh-day Adventists.
Enrollment: 1,203 undergrads.
Selectivity: Admits over 75% of applicants.

BASIC COSTS (2009-2010)
Tuition and fees: $23,979.
Room and board: $6,750.

FINANCIAL AID PICTURE (2007-2008)
Students with need: Need-based aid available for full-time and part-time students.
Students without need: No-need awards available for leadership, religious affiliation.

FINANCIAL AID PROCEDURES
Forms required: FAFSA, state aid form, institutional form.
Dates and Deadlines: No deadline. Applicants notified on a rolling basis; must reply within 3 week(s) of notification.

CONTACT
Laurie Wheeler, Director of Student Financial Services
One Angwin Avenue, Angwin, CA 94508
(707) 965-7200

Palo Verde College
Blythe, California
www.paloverde.edu Federal Code: 001259

2-year public community college in large town.
Enrollment: 1,371 undergrads.
Selectivity: Open admission; but selective for some programs.

BASIC COSTS (2008-2009)
Tuition and fees: $600; out-of-state residents $6,030.
Per-credit charge: $20; out-of-state residents $201.

FINANCIAL AID PICTURE (2007-2008)
Students with need: Need-based aid available for full-time and part-time students. Work study available nights.
Students without need: This college awards aid only to students with need.

FINANCIAL AID PROCEDURES
Forms required: FAFSA, institutional form.
Dates and Deadlines: No deadline. Applicants notified on a rolling basis starting 7/1; must reply within 4 week(s) of notification.

CONTACT
Linda Pratt, Director of Financial Aid
One College Drive, Blythe, CA 92225
(760) 921-5410

Palomar College
San Marcos, California
www.palomar.edu Federal Code: 001260

2-year public community college in large town.
Enrollment: 15,698 undergrads.
Selectivity: Open admission; but selective for some programs.

BASIC COSTS (2008-2009)
Tuition and fees: $627; out-of-state residents $5,997.
Per-credit charge: $20; out-of-state residents $199.

FINANCIAL AID PICTURE
Students with need: Need-based aid available for full-time and part-time students. Work study available nights.
Students without need: This college awards aid only to students with need.

FINANCIAL AID PROCEDURES
Forms required: FAFSA, institutional form.
Dates and Deadlines: Priority date 4/1; no closing date. Applicants notified on a rolling basis starting 6/1.
Transfers: No deadline.

CONTACT
Mary San Agustin, Financial Aid Director
1140 West Mission Road, San Marcos, CA 92069-1487
(760) 744-1150

Patten University
Oakland, California
www.patten.edu Federal Code: 004490

4-year private university and liberal arts college in very large city, affiliated with interdenominational tradition.
Enrollment: 525 undergrads.

BASIC COSTS (2009-2010)
Tuition and fees: $13,440.
Per-credit charge: $560.
Room and board: $7,090.

FINANCIAL AID PICTURE
Students with need: Need-based aid available for full-time and part-time students.
Students without need: No-need awards available for academics, athletics, state/district residency.

FINANCIAL AID PROCEDURES
Forms required: FAFSA, institutional form.
Dates and Deadlines: Priority date 3/31; no closing date. Applicants notified on a rolling basis starting 5/31.
Transfers: No deadline.

CONTACT
Dennis Clark, Financial Aid Director
2433 Coolidge Avenue, Oakland, CA 94601-2699
(510) 261-8500 ext. 7747

Pepperdine University
Malibu, California
www.pepperdine.edu Federal Code: 001264

4-year private university and liberal arts college in small city, affiliated with Church of Christ.
Enrollment: 3,386 undergrads.
Selectivity: Admits less than 50% of applicants.

BASIC COSTS (2009-2010)
Tuition and fees: $37,850.
Per-credit charge: $1,170.
Room and board: $10,900.

FINANCIAL AID PICTURE (2008-2009)
Students with need: Need-based aid available for full-time and part-time students.
Students without need: No-need awards available for academics, art, athletics, minority status, music/drama, religious affiliation.

FINANCIAL AID PROCEDURES
Forms required: FAFSA, institutional form.
Dates and Deadlines: Closing date 2/15. Applicants notified by 4/15; must reply within 2 week(s) of notification.

CONTACT
Janet Lockhart, Director of Financial Assistance
24255 Pacific Coast Highway, Malibu, CA 90263-4392
(310) 506-4301

Pitzer College
Claremont, California Federal Code: 001172
www.pitzer.edu CSS Code: 4619

4-year private liberal arts college in large town.
Enrollment: 1,025 undergrads, 5% part-time. 257 full-time freshmen.
Selectivity: Admits less than 50% of applicants.

BASIC COSTS (2008-2009)
Tuition and fees: $37,870.
Room and board: $10,930.
Additional info: Part-time tuition: $4,313 per course.

FINANCIAL AID PICTURE (2008-2009)
Students with need: Out of 139 full-time freshmen who applied for aid, 107 were judged to have need. Of these, 107 received aid, and 107 had their full need met. Average financial aid package met 100% of need; average scholarship/grant was $27,064; average loan was $2,613. For part-time students, average financial aid package was $18,958.
Students without need: 28 full-time freshmen who did not demonstrate need for aid received scholarships/grants; average award was $5,000. No-need awards available for academics, leadership.
Scholarships offered: Trustee Community Scholar Award; $10,000 per year; based on extraordinary academic achievement, outstanding leadership or exceptional community service; 20 awarded.
Cumulative student debt: 37% of graduating class had student loans; average debt was $21,044.

FINANCIAL AID PROCEDURES
Forms required: FAFSA, CSS PROFILE, state aid form.
Dates and Deadlines: Closing date 2/1. Applicants notified by 4/1; must reply by 5/1.
Transfers: Closing date 3/1. Applicants notified by 5/15; must reply by 6/15.

CONTACT
Margaret Carothers, Director of Financial Aid
1050 North Mills Avenue, Claremont, CA 91711-6101
(909) 621-8208

Platt College: Los Angeles
Alhambra, California
www.plattcollege.edu Federal Code: 030627

2-year for-profit visual arts and technical college in very large city.
Enrollment: 185 undergrads.

BASIC COSTS (2008-2009)
Additional info: Varies by program: associate degree cost range $26,780 (paralegal) to $28,370 (information technology).

FINANCIAL AID PICTURE
Students with need: Need-based aid available for full-time and part-time students. Work study available nights.

FINANCIAL AID PROCEDURES
Forms required: FAFSA, institutional form.
Dates and Deadlines: Priority date 3/2; no closing date. Applicants notified on a rolling basis starting 1/1.

CONTACT
Syrena Sokolis, Financial Aid Director
1000 South Fremont Avenue A9W, Alhambra, CA 91803
(626) 300-5444 ext. 230

Platt College: San Diego
San Diego, California
www.platt.edu Federal Code: 023043

4-year for-profit visual arts and technical college in very large city.
Enrollment: 286 undergrads. 162 full-time freshmen.
Selectivity: Open admission; but selective for some programs and for out-of-state students.

BASIC COSTS (2008-2009)
Tuition and fees: $15,010.
Per-credit charge: $497.
Additional info: Total program costs range from $17,710 to $35,810, depending on the program chosen. Tuition at time of enrollment locked for 4 years.

FINANCIAL AID PICTURE (2007-2008)
Students with need: 35% of average financial aid package awarded as scholarships/grants, 65% awarded as loans/jobs. Need-based aid available for part-time students.

FINANCIAL AID PROCEDURES
Forms required: FAFSA, state aid form, institutional form.
Dates and Deadlines: Closing date 3/2. Applicants notified on a rolling basis; must reply within 1 week(s) of notification.

CONTACT
Opel Oliver, Director of Financial Aid
6250 El Cajon Boulevard, San Diego, CA 92115
(619) 265-0107

Point Loma Nazarene University
San Diego, California
www.pointloma.edu Federal Code: 001262

4-year private university and liberal arts college in very large city, affiliated with Church of the Nazarene.
Enrollment: 2,385 undergrads, 3% part-time. 538 full-time freshmen.
Selectivity: Admits over 75% of applicants.

BASIC COSTS (2009-2010)
Tuition and fees: $25,840.
Per-credit charge: $1,055.
Room and board: $8,100.

FINANCIAL AID PICTURE (2007-2008)
Students with need: Need-based aid available for full-time students.

FINANCIAL AID PROCEDURES
Forms required: FAFSA, institutional form.
Dates and Deadlines: Closing date 3/2. Applicants notified on a rolling basis starting 3/1.
Transfers: Must reply within 4 week(s) of notification.

CONTACT
Pam Macias, Director of Financial Aid
3900 Lomaland Drive, San Diego, CA 92106-2899
(619) 849-2068

Pomona College
Claremont, California Federal Code: 001173
www.pomona.edu CSS Code: 4607

4-year private liberal arts college in large town.
Enrollment: 1,516 undergrads. 375 full-time freshmen.
Selectivity: Admits less than 50% of applicants.

BASIC COSTS (2008-2009)
Tuition and fees: $35,625.
Room and board: $12,220.

FINANCIAL AID PICTURE (2007-2008)
Students with need: Out of 241 full-time freshmen who applied for aid, 195 were judged to have need. Of these, 195 received aid, and 195 had their full need met. Average financial aid package met 100% of need; average scholarship/grant was $31,000; average loan was $2,000. Need-based aid available for part-time students.
Students without need: This college awards aid only to students with need.
Cumulative student debt: 54% of graduating class had student loans; average debt was $11,300.

FINANCIAL AID PROCEDURES
Forms required: FAFSA, CSS PROFILE.
Dates and Deadlines: Closing date 2/1. Applicants notified by 4/10; must reply by 5/1.
Transfers: Closing date 3/1. Candidates required to submit finanical aid transcript from previous institution directly to the college.

CONTACT
Patricia Coye, Director of Financial Aid
333 North College Way, Claremont, CA 91711-6312
(909) 621-8205

Professional Golfers Career College
Temecula, California
www.golfcollege.edu Federal Code: 033673

2-year for-profit golf academy in small city.
Enrollment: 160 undergrads.
Selectivity: Admits over 75% of applicants.

BASIC COSTS (2009-2010)
Additional info: Tuition $5,590/semester for domestic students and $5,890/semester for international students; program lasts 4 semesters.

FINANCIAL AID PICTURE
Students with need: Need-based aid available for full-time students.

FINANCIAL AID PROCEDURES
Dates and Deadlines: No deadline.
Transfers: No deadline.

CONTACT
Maria Fons, FAO
26109 Ynez Road, Temecula, CA 92591
(800) 877-4380

Reedley College
Reedley, California
www.reedleycollege.edu Federal Code: 001308

2-year public community college in large town.
Enrollment: 7,718 undergrads.
Selectivity: Open admission.

BASIC COSTS (2008-2009)
Tuition and fees: $632; out-of-state residents $6,062.
Per-credit charge: $20; out-of-state residents $201.
Room and board: $8,942.
Additional info: Tuition/fee waivers available for adults, minority students, unemployed or children of unemployed.

FINANCIAL AID PICTURE
Students with need: Need-based aid available for full-time and part-time students.
Students without need: This college awards aid only to students with need.
Additional info: Board of Governors fee waiver available for low-income students. Book voucher available for EOPS students.

FINANCIAL AID PROCEDURES
Forms required: FAFSA, state aid form.
Dates and Deadlines: Priority date 3/2; no closing date. Applicants notified on a rolling basis starting 3/2; must reply within 3 week(s) of notification.
Transfers: Priority date 4/15. March 2 deadline for California grants.

CONTACT
Christina Cortes, Director of Financial Aid
995 North Reed Avenue, Reedley, CA 93654
(559) 638-3641

Rio Hondo College
Whittier, California
www.riohondo.edu Federal Code: 001269

2-year public community college in small city.
Enrollment: 9,040 undergrads.
Selectivity: Open admission; but selective for some programs.

BASIC COSTS (2008-2009)
Tuition and fees: $623; out-of-state residents $5,723.
Per-credit charge: $20; out-of-state residents $190.

FINANCIAL AID PICTURE (2007-2008)
Students with need: Need-based aid available for full-time and part-time students.

FINANCIAL AID PROCEDURES
Forms required: FAFSA.
Dates and Deadlines: Priority date 7/15; no closing date. Applicants notified on a rolling basis.

CONTACT
Elizabeth Coria, Director Financial Aid
3600 Workman Mill Road, Whittier, CA 90601-1699
(562) 908-3411

Riverside Community College
Riverside, California
www.rcc.edu Federal Code: 001270

2-year public community college in large city.
Enrollment: 23,722 undergrads.
Selectivity: Open admission; but selective for some programs.

BASIC COSTS (2008-2009)
Tuition and fees: $634; out-of-state residents $6,064.
Per-credit charge: $20; out-of-state residents $201.
Additional info: Tuition/fee waivers available for adults, unemployed or children of unemployed.

FINANCIAL AID PICTURE (2007-2008)
Students with need: Need-based aid available for full-time and part-time students. Work study available nights, weekends, and for part-time students.
Students without need: No-need awards available for academics, alumni affiliation, art, leadership, minority status, music/drama, state/district residency.

FINANCIAL AID PROCEDURES
Forms required: FAFSA, institutional form.
Dates and Deadlines: Priority date 3/1; no closing date. Applicants notified on a rolling basis starting 7/1.
Transfers: Students who received financial aid at another institution and earned less than 2.0 GPA ineligible for aid during first semester. Students must complete 6 units and earn 2.0 GPA to be eligible.

CONTACT
Eugenia Vincent, District Dean of Student Financial Services
4800 Magnolia Avenue, Riverside, CA 92506
(951) 222-8709

Sacramento City College
Sacramento, California
www.scc.losrios.edu Federal Code: 001233

2-year public community college in large city.
Enrollment: 15,997 undergrads.
Selectivity: Open admission.

BASIC COSTS (2008-2009)
Tuition and fees: $632; out-of-state residents $6,062.
Per-credit charge: $20; out-of-state residents $201.

FINANCIAL AID PICTURE
Students with need: Need-based aid available for full-time and part-time students. Work study available nights, weekends, and for part-time students.

FINANCIAL AID PROCEDURES
Forms required: FAFSA, state aid form.
Dates and Deadlines: Priority date 3/2; no closing date. Applicants notified on a rolling basis starting 7/1; must reply within 2 week(s) of notification.
Transfers: Priority date 5/30.

CONTACT
3835 Freeport Boulevard, Sacramento, CA 95822
(916) 558-2546

Saddleback College
Mission Viejo, California
www.saddleback.edu Federal Code: 008918

2-year public community college in small city.
Enrollment: 9,466 undergrads.
Selectivity: Open admission; but selective for some programs.

BASIC COSTS (2008-2009)
Tuition and fees: $628; out-of-state residents $6,058.
Per-credit charge: $20; out-of-state residents $201.

FINANCIAL AID PICTURE (2007-2008)
Students with need: Need-based aid available for full-time and part-time students.
Students without need: This college awards aid only to students with need.

FINANCIAL AID PROCEDURES
Forms required: FAFSA.
Dates and Deadlines: Closing date 6/30. Applicants notified on a rolling basis starting 4/1.

CONTACT
Mary Hall, Director, Financial Aid
28000 Marguerite Parkway, Mission Viejo, CA 92692
(949) 582-4860

St. Mary's College of California
Moraga, California
www.stmarys-ca.edu Federal Code: 001302

4-year private liberal arts college in large town, affiliated with Roman Catholic Church.
Enrollment: 2,514 undergrads, 3% part-time. 675 full-time freshmen.
Selectivity: Admits over 75% of applicants.

BASIC COSTS (2009-2010)
Tuition and fees: $33,910.
Per-credit charge: $1,378.
Room and board: $11,940.

FINANCIAL AID PICTURE (2008-2009)
Students with need: Out of 566 full-time freshmen who applied for aid, 489 were judged to have need. Of these, 489 received aid, and 36 had their full need met. Average financial aid package met 86% of need; average scholarship/grant was $24,277; average loan was $3,979. For part-time students, average financial aid package was $13,221.
Students without need: 30 full-time freshmen who did not demonstrate need for aid received scholarships/grants; average award was $15,564. No-need awards available for academics, alumni affiliation, athletics, leadership.
Scholarships offered: ***Merit:*** Honors at Entrance Scholarship Awards: $12,000 annually; freshman students admitted with a GPA of at least 3.7 or higher and a combined SAT score of at least 1200 (or a 27 on the ACT); transfers with 30 + transferable academic semester units and 3.5 GPA. Honors at Entrance Scholarship Awards: $10,000 annually; fall term applicants;

must be admitted by March 1. Presidential Scholars Scholarships: $10,000 annually; freshmen with 3.8 GPA or higher and combined SAT score of at least 1350 (exclusive of writing). Students who receive Presidential Scholarship will also receive Honors at Entrance Scholarship for total of $22,000 annually. ***Athletic:*** 51 full-time freshmen received athletic scholarships; average amount $26,249.
Cumulative student debt: 71% of graduating class had student loans; average debt was $23,389.

FINANCIAL AID PROCEDURES
Forms required: FAFSA, state aid form.
Dates and Deadlines: Priority date 2/15; no closing date. Applicants notified on a rolling basis starting 3/15; must reply by 5/1 or within 2 week(s) of notification.
Transfers: Must reply by 5/1 or within 2 week(s) of notification. To receive consideration for all types of financial aid, transfer students must be admitted by March 1 prior to enrolling in the following fall term.

CONTACT
Priscilla Muha, Director of Financial Aid
Box 4800, Moraga, CA 94575-4800
(925) 631-4370

Samuel Merritt University
Oakland, California
www.samuelmerritt.edu Federal Code: 007012

Upper-division private health science and nursing college in large city.
Enrollment: 441 undergrads, 1% part-time.
Selectivity: GED not accepted.

BASIC COSTS (2009-2010)
Tuition and fees: $35,398.
Per-credit charge: $1,439.
Additional info: $2,958 per semester health insurance mandatory unless student covered by existing insurance.

FINANCIAL AID PICTURE (2007-2008)
Students with need: Average financial aid package for all full-time undergraduates was $20,000. 43% awarded as scholarships/grants, 57% awarded as loans/jobs. Need-based aid available for part-time students. Work study available nights, weekends, and for part-time students.
Students without need: No-need awards available for academics, leadership, minority status.
Cumulative student debt: 97% of graduating class had student loans; average debt was $53,582.
Additional info: Ongoing private scholarships available. Students eligible to work in Medical Center (associated with college).

FINANCIAL AID PROCEDURES
Dates and Deadlines: No deadline.
Transfers: Priority date 3/2; no deadline. Applicants notified on a rolling basis; must reply within 3 week(s) of notification.

CONTACT
Mary Robinson, Director of Financial Aid
370 Hawthorne Avenue, Oakland, CA 94609-9954
(510) 869-1550

San Bernardino Valley College
San Bernardino, California
www.valleycollege.edu Federal Code: 001272

2-year public community college in small city.
Enrollment: 9,325 undergrads.
Selectivity: Open admission; but selective for some programs.

BASIC COSTS (2008-2009)
Tuition and fees: $644; out-of-state residents $6,224.
Per-credit charge: $20; out-of-state residents $206.
Additional info: Tuition/fee waivers available for unemployed or children of unemployed.

FINANCIAL AID PICTURE (2007-2008)
Students with need: 89% of average financial aid package awarded as scholarships/grants, 11% awarded as loans/jobs.

FINANCIAL AID PROCEDURES
Dates and Deadlines: Priority date 5/25; no closing date. Applicants notified on a rolling basis starting 5/1; must reply within 2 week(s) of notification.

CONTACT
Nancy Davis, Director of Financial Aid
701 South Mount Vernon Avenue, San Bernardino, CA 92410

San Diego Christian College
El Cajon, California
www.sdcc.edu Federal Code: 012031

4-year private liberal arts college in small city, affiliated with nondenominational tradition.
Enrollment: 384 undergrads, 10% part-time. 56 full-time freshmen.
Selectivity: Admits 50 to 75% of applicants.

BASIC COSTS (2009-2010)
Tuition and fees: $21,610.
Per-credit charge: $833.
Room and board: $8,000.

FINANCIAL AID PICTURE (2008-2009)
Students with need: Out of 45 full-time freshmen who applied for aid, 33 were judged to have need. Of these, 33 received aid, and 23 had their full need met. Average financial aid package met 85% of need; average scholarship/grant was $8,405; average loan was $3,500. For part-time students, average financial aid package was $8,958.
Students without need: 10 full-time freshmen who did not demonstrate need for aid received scholarships/grants; average award was $6,614. No-need awards available for academics, alumni affiliation, athletics, leadership, music/drama, state/district residency.
Scholarships offered: 11 full-time freshmen received athletic scholarships; average amount $10,365.
Cumulative student debt: 88% of graduating class had student loans; average debt was $16,000.

FINANCIAL AID PROCEDURES
Forms required: FAFSA, state aid form, institutional form.
Dates and Deadlines: Priority date 3/2; closing date 7/15. Applicants notified on a rolling basis starting 4/1; must reply by 5/1 or within 4 week(s) of notification.

CONTACT
Nancy DeMars, Financial Aid Director
2100 Greenfield Drive, El Cajon, CA 92019-1157
(619) 590-1786 ext. 3

San Diego City College
San Diego, California
www.sdccd.edu Federal Code: 001273

2-year public community and junior college in very large city.
Enrollment: 10,062 undergrads.
Selectivity: Open admission.

BASIC COSTS (2008-2009)
Tuition and fees: $632; out-of-state residents $6,002.
Per-credit charge: $20; out-of-state residents $199.
Additional info: Tuition/fee waivers available for unemployed or children of unemployed.

FINANCIAL AID PICTURE (2007-2008)
Students with need: 79% of average financial aid package awarded as scholarships/grants, 21% awarded as loans/jobs. Need-based aid available for part-time students.
Students without need: This college awards aid only to students with need.

FINANCIAL AID PROCEDURES
Forms required: FAFSA.
Dates and Deadlines: Priority date 4/15; no closing date. Applicants notified on a rolling basis starting 7/1; must reply within 4 week(s) of notification.
Transfers: No deadline. Aid is limited to remaining eligibility based on receipt of aid from previous college.

CONTACT
Greg Sanchez, Director of Financial Aid
1313 Park Boulevard, San Diego, CA 92101-4787
(619) 388-3501

San Diego Miramar College
San Diego, California
www.miramarcollege.net Federal Code: 014172

2-year public community college in very large city.
Enrollment: 5,972 undergrads.
Selectivity: Open admission.

BASIC COSTS (2008-2009)
Tuition and fees: $626; out-of-state residents $5,996.
Per-credit charge: $20; out-of-state residents $199.
Additional info: Tuition/fee waivers available for unemployed or children of unemployed.

FINANCIAL AID PICTURE (2007-2008)
Students with need: Need-based aid available for part-time students.
Additional info: Private scholarships available.

FINANCIAL AID PROCEDURES
Forms required: FAFSA.
Dates and Deadlines: Priority date 3/2; no closing date. Applicants notified on a rolling basis; must reply within 3 week(s) of notification.
Transfers: No deadline. Transfers advised to apply early.

CONTACT
Teresa Vilaboy, Financial Aid Officer
10440 Black Mountain Road, San Diego, CA 92126-2999
(619) 388-7864

San Diego State University
San Diego, California
www.sdsu.edu Federal Code: 001151

4-year public university in very large city.
Enrollment: 29,481 undergrads, 15% part-time. 3,600 full-time freshmen.
Selectivity: Admits less than 50% of applicants.

BASIC COSTS (2008-2009)
Tuition and fees: $3,754; out-of-state residents $13,924.
Room and board: $11,266.

FINANCIAL AID PICTURE (2008-2009)
Students with need: Out of 3,600 full-time freshmen who applied for aid, 2,400 were judged to have need. Of these, 2,300 received aid, and 500 had their full need met. Average financial aid package met 67% of need; average scholarship/grant was $7,100; average loan was $3,100. For part-time students, average financial aid package was $6,900.
Students without need: 150 full-time freshmen who did not demonstrate need for aid received scholarships/grants; average award was $2,400. No-need awards available for academics, alumni affiliation, art, athletics, leadership, music/drama, ROTC, state/district residency.
Scholarships offered: ***Merit:*** Various departmental scholarships are open to first time freshman with declared majors. Brian Schultz Memorial Scholarship, amount varies (1 awarded); recipient must be a cancer survivor or have been affected by cancer. ***Athletic:*** 100 full-time freshmen received athletic scholarships; average amount $11,000.
Cumulative student debt: 44% of graduating class had student loans; average debt was $14,700.

FINANCIAL AID PROCEDURES
Forms required: FAFSA, state aid form.
Dates and Deadlines: Priority date 3/2; no closing date. Applicants notified on a rolling basis starting 2/14.
Transfers: No deadline. Applicants notified on a rolling basis.

CONTACT
Chrys Dutton, Director of Financial Aid
5500 Campanile Drive, San Diego, CA 92182-7455
(619) 594-6323

San Francisco Art Institute
San Francisco, California
www.sfai.edu Federal Code: 003948

4-year private visual arts college in very large city.
Enrollment: 346 undergrads, 8% part-time. 63 full-time freshmen.
Selectivity: Admits 50 to 75% of applicants.

BASIC COSTS (2009-2010)
Tuition and fees: $31,700.
Per-credit charge: $1,450.
Room and board: $10,800.

FINANCIAL AID PICTURE (2007-2008)
Students with need: Out of 43 full-time freshmen who applied for aid, 37 were judged to have need. Of these, 36 received aid, and 1 had their full need met. Average financial aid package met 41% of need; average scholarship/grant was $12,477; average loan was $3,297. For part-time students, average financial aid package was $6,114.
Students without need: 20 full-time freshmen who did not demonstrate need for aid received scholarships/grants; average award was $4,925. No-need awards available for academics, art.
Scholarships offered: Several awards based on portfolio reviews during application for admissions process.
Cumulative student debt: 67% of graduating class had student loans; average debt was $28,828.

FINANCIAL AID PROCEDURES
Forms required: FAFSA.
Dates and Deadlines: Priority date 3/1; closing date 5/31. Applicants notified on a rolling basis starting 4/15; must reply within 3 week(s) of notification.
Transfers: Priority date 6/30; no deadline. Applicants notified on a rolling basis starting 4/1; must reply within 3 week(s) of notification.

CONTACT
Daryl Cullen, Director of Financial Aid
800 Chestnut Street, San Francisco, CA 94133-2299
(415) 749-4520

San Francisco Conservatory of Music

San Francisco, California
www.sfcm.edu Federal Code: 001278

4-year private music college in very large city.
Enrollment: 200 undergrads, 3% part-time. 37 full-time freshmen.
Selectivity: Admits less than 50% of applicants.

BASIC COSTS (2009-2010)

Tuition and fees: $33,528.
Per-credit charge: $1,500.
Room only: $6,000.

FINANCIAL AID PICTURE (2008-2009)

Students with need: Out of 30 full-time freshmen who applied for aid, 28 were judged to have need. Of these, 28 received aid, and 24 had their full need met. Average financial aid package met 89% of need; average scholarship/grant was $11,600; average loan was $3,500. For part-time students, average financial aid package was $24,200.
Students without need: 34 full-time freshmen who did not demonstrate need for aid received scholarships/grants; average award was $7,500. No-need awards available for music/drama.
Cumulative student debt: 95% of graduating class had student loans; average debt was $22,000.

FINANCIAL AID PROCEDURES

Forms required: FAFSA, institutional form.
Dates and Deadlines: Priority date 3/1; no closing date. Applicants notified on a rolling basis starting 3/15; must reply by 5/1 or within 2 week(s) of notification.
Transfers: Priority date 2/1; closing date 4/1. Applicants notified on a rolling basis starting 4/1; must reply by 5/1 or within 2 week(s) of notification.

CONTACT

Doris Howard, Financial Aid Officer
50 Oak Street, San Francisco, CA 94102
(415) 503-6235

San Francisco State University

San Francisco, California
www.sfsu.edu Federal Code: 001154

4-year public university in very large city.
Enrollment: 24,378 undergrads, 18% part-time. 3,512 full-time freshmen.
Selectivity: Admits 50 to 75% of applicants.

BASIC COSTS (2008-2009)

Tuition and fees: $3,762; out-of-state residents $13,932.
Room and board: $11,500.

FINANCIAL AID PICTURE (2008-2009)

Students with need: Need-based aid available for full-time and part-time students.
Students without need: This college awards aid only to students with need.
Scholarships offered: Presidential Scholarship; 3.8 GPA and California residency required.

FINANCIAL AID PROCEDURES

Forms required: FAFSA.
Dates and Deadlines: Priority date 3/2; no closing date. Applicants notified on a rolling basis starting 2/1; must reply within 2 week(s) of notification.

CONTACT

Barbara Hubler, Director of Financial Aid
1600 Holloway Avenue, San Francisco, CA 94132
(415) 338-7000

San Joaquin Delta College

Stockton, California
www.deltacollege.edu Federal Code: 001280

2-year public community college in large city.
Enrollment: 8,003 undergrads. 2,938 full-time freshmen.
Selectivity: Open admission; but selective for some programs.

BASIC COSTS (2008-2009)

Tuition and fees: $602; out-of-state residents $6,032.
Per-credit charge: $20; out-of-state residents $201.

FINANCIAL AID PICTURE (2007-2008)

Students with need: Out of 2,938 full-time freshmen who applied for aid, 2,297 were judged to have need. Of these, 1,997 received aid, and 14 had their full need met. Average financial aid package met 30% of need; average scholarship/grant was $3,326; average loan was $2,662. For part-time students, average financial aid package was $3,368.
Students without need: No-need awards available for academics, athletics.
Cumulative student debt: 98% of graduating class had student loans; average debt was $7,648.
Additional info: Enrollment fee waivers available for low-income California residents.

FINANCIAL AID PROCEDURES

Forms required: FAFSA, institutional form.
Dates and Deadlines: Priority date 4/15; no closing date. Applicants notified on a rolling basis starting 5/1; must reply within 3 week(s) of notification.
Transfers: No deadline.

CONTACT

Denise Donn, Director of Financial Aid
5151 Pacific Avenue, Stockton, CA 95207-6370
(209) 954-5115

San Joaquin Valley College

Visalia, California
www.sjvc.edu Federal Code: 021207

2-year for-profit junior college in small city.
Enrollment: 820 undergrads.
Selectivity: Open admission; but selective for some programs.

BASIC COSTS (2008-2009)

Tuition and fees: $12,190.
Additional info: Costs may vary by program, annual tuition includes textbooks and supplies.

FINANCIAL AID PICTURE

Students with need. Need-based aid available for full-time students.

FINANCIAL AID PROCEDURES

Forms required: FAFSA, state aid form, institutional form.
Dates and Deadlines: No deadline.

CONTACT

Kevin Robinson, Vice President of Student Financial Services
8400 West Mineral King Avenue, Visalia, CA 93291-9283
(559) 651-2500

San Jose State University

San Jose, California
www.sjsu.edu Federal Code: 001155

4-year public university and liberal arts college in very large city.
Enrollment: 25,187 undergrads, 21% part-time. 3,085 full-time freshmen.

Selectivity: Admits 50 to 75% of applicants.

BASIC COSTS (2008-2009)

Tuition and fees: $3,992; out-of-state residents $14,162.
Room and board: $10,153.

FINANCIAL AID PICTURE (2007-2008)

Students with need: Out of 2,311 full-time freshmen who applied for aid, 2,112 were judged to have need. Of these, 2,035 received aid, and 706 had their full need met. Average financial aid package met 87% of need; average scholarship/grant was $5,864; average loan was $5,632. For part-time students, average financial aid package was $8,791.
Students without need: This college awards aid only to students with need.
Scholarships offered: 5 full-time freshmen received athletic scholarships; average amount $9,234.
Cumulative student debt: 50% of graduating class had student loans; average debt was $11,815.

FINANCIAL AID PROCEDURES

Forms required: FAFSA.
Dates and Deadlines: Priority date 3/2; closing date 6/12. Applicants notified on a rolling basis starting 4/10; must reply within 2 week(s) of notification.

CONTACT

Colleen Brown, Director of Financial Aid
One Washington Square, San Jose, CA 95192-0011
(408) 283-7500

Santa Ana College

Santa Ana, California
www.sac.edu Federal Code: 001284

2-year public community college in large city.
Enrollment: 13,409 undergrads. 332 full-time freshmen.
Selectivity: Open admission.

BASIC COSTS (2008-2009)

Tuition and fees: $628; out-of-state residents $6,058.
Per-credit charge: $20; out-of-state residents $201.

FINANCIAL AID PICTURE (2007-2008)

Students with need: Out of 332 full-time freshmen who applied for aid, 327 were judged to have need. Of these, 326 received aid, and 5 had their full need met. Average financial aid package met 50% of need; average scholarship/grant was $4,408; average loan was $1,064. For part-time students, average financial aid package was $2,954.
Cumulative student debt: 100% of graduating class had student loans; average debt was $3,980.

FINANCIAL AID PROCEDURES

Forms required: FAFSA.
Dates and Deadlines: Priority date 6/30; no closing date. Applicants notified on a rolling basis starting 6/1; must reply within 2 week(s) of notification.

CONTACT

Mark Liang, Financial Aid Director
1530 West 17th Street, Santa Ana, CA 92706
(714) 564-6242

Santa Barbara City College

Santa Barbara, California
www.sbcc.edu Federal Code: 001285

2-year public community college in small city.
Enrollment: 11,298 undergrads. 1,763 full-time freshmen.
Selectivity: Open admission; but selective for some programs.

BASIC COSTS (2008-2009)

Tuition and fees: $670; out-of-state residents $6,100.
Per-credit charge: $20; out-of-state residents $201.
Additional info: Tuition/fee waivers available for unemployed or children of unemployed.

FINANCIAL AID PICTURE (2008-2009)

Students with need: Need-based aid available for full-time and part-time students.
Additional info: California residents may qualify for Board of Governor's Financial Assistance Program, which will allow institutions to waive enrollment fee.

FINANCIAL AID PROCEDURES

Forms required: FAFSA.
Dates and Deadlines: No deadline. Applicants notified on a rolling basis starting 5/1; must reply within 2 week(s) of notification.

CONTACT

Brad Hardison, Director, Financial Aid
721 Cliff Drive, Santa Barbara, CA 93109-2394
(805) 965-0581 ext. 2716

Santa Clara University

Santa Clara, California Federal Code: 001326
www.scu.edu CSS Code: 4851

4-year private university in small city, affiliated with Roman Catholic Church.
Enrollment: 5,234 undergrads, 2% part-time. 1,219 full-time freshmen.
Selectivity: Admits 50 to 75% of applicants. GED not accepted.

BASIC COSTS (2008-2009)

Tuition and fees: $34,950.
Per-credit charge: $1,165.
Room and board: $11,070.

FINANCIAL AID PICTURE (2008-2009)

Students with need: Out of 767 full-time freshmen who applied for aid, 522 were judged to have need. Of these, 513 received aid, and 209 had their full need met. Average financial aid package met 77% of need; average scholarship/grant was $20,490; average loan was $3,270. Need-based aid available for part-time students.
Students without need: 378 full-time freshmen who did not demonstrate need for aid received scholarships/grants; average award was $8,047. No-need awards available for academics, alumni affiliation, athletics, music/drama, ROTC.
Scholarships offered: ***Merit:*** Presidential Scholar at Entry: full tuition; 10 students awarded; admitted with distinction. Provost Scholar: half tuition; 40 students awarded; admitted with distinction. National Merit Scholarship: $2,000; 4 students awarded. Dean's Scholarship: $3,000 to $12,000; admitted with distinction. Honors Program Scholarship: $2,000; by invitation and based on high academic achievement. Bannan Merit Scholarship: amount varies; based on high academic achievement. Jesuit Ignation Award: amount varies, to students of Jesuit high schools. ***Athletic:*** 76 full-time freshmen received athletic scholarships; average amount $21,512.
Cumulative student debt: 44% of graduating class had student loans; average debt was $25,438.

FINANCIAL AID PROCEDURES

Forms required: FAFSA, CSS PROFILE.
Dates and Deadlines: Priority date 2/1; no closing date. Applicants notified by 4/1; must reply by 5/1 or within 2 week(s) of notification.
Transfers: No deadline. Applicants notified on a rolling basis starting 4/1; must reply by 5/1 or within 2 week(s) of notification.

CONTACT

Richard Toomey, Dean of Financial Services
500 El Camino Real, Santa Clara, CA 95053
(408) 554-4505

Santa Monica College

Santa Monica, California
www.smc.edu Federal Code: 001286

2-year public community college in small city.
Enrollment: 21,976 undergrads.
Selectivity: Open admission; but selective for some programs.

BASIC COSTS (2008-2009)

Tuition and fees: $632; out-of-state residents $5,552.
Per-credit charge: $20; out-of-state residents $184.

FINANCIAL AID PICTURE (2007-2008)

Students with need: Need-based aid available for full-time and part-time students.

FINANCIAL AID PROCEDURES

Forms required: FAFSA, institutional form.
Dates and Deadlines: No deadline. Applicants notified on a rolling basis starting 7/1; must reply within 2 week(s) of notification.
Transfers: No deadline.

CONTACT

Steve Myrow, Director of Financial Aid
1900 Pico Boulevard, Santa Monica, CA 90405-1628
(310) 434 4871

Santa Rosa Junior College

Santa Rosa, California
www.santarosa.edu Federal Code: 001287

2-year public community college in small city.
Enrollment: 12,663 undergrads.
Selectivity: Open admission; but selective for some programs.

BASIC COSTS (2008-2009)

Tuition and fees: $634; out-of-state residents $6,064.
Per-credit charge: $20; out-of-state residents $201.

FINANCIAL AID PICTURE (2007-2008)

Students with need: Need-based aid available for full-time and part-time students. Work study available nights, weekends, and for part-time students.
Students without need: No-need awards available for academics, art, leadership, music/drama.
Scholarships offered: Doyle Scholarships available (need-based and GPA based) for high school graduates or college applicants with 2.75 GPA or higher.
Additional info: California's Board of Governors Program provides fee waivers for applicants with need.

FINANCIAL AID PROCEDURES

Forms required: FAFSA.
Dates and Deadlines: Priority date 3/1; no closing date. Applicants notified on a rolling basis starting 4/5.

CONTACT

Kristin Shear, Director of Financial Services
1501 Mendocino Avenue, Santa Rosa, CA 95401
(707) 527-4471

Santiago Canyon College

Orange, California
www.sccollege.edu

2-year public community college in small city.
Enrollment: 7,202 undergrads. 845 full-time freshmen.
Selectivity: Open admission.

BASIC COSTS (2008-2009)

Tuition and fees: $628; out-of-state residents $6,358.
Per-credit charge: $20; out-of-state residents $211.
Additional info: Tuition/fee waivers available for adults, minority students, unemployed or children of unemployed.

FINANCIAL AID PICTURE (2007-2008)

Students with need: Need-based aid available for full-time and part-time students.
Students without need: This college awards aid only to students with need.

FINANCIAL AID PROCEDURES

Forms required: FAFSA, state aid form, institutional form.
Dates and Deadlines: Priority date 7/1; no closing date. Applicants notified on a rolling basis starting 6/1.
Transfers: No deadline. Applicants notified by 6/1.

CONTACT

Syed Rizvi, Financial Aid Coordinator
8045 East Chapman Avenue, Orange, CA 92869
(714) 628-4876

School of Urban Missions: Oakland

Oakland, California
www.sum.edu Federal Code: 037524

4-year private Bible college in very large city, affiliated with Assemblies of God.
Enrollment: 71 undergrads, 3% part-time. 25 full-time freshmen.
Selectivity: Admits over 75% of applicants.

BASIC COSTS (2009-2010)

Tuition and fees: $7,155.
Per-credit charge: $235.
Room only: $2,400.

FINANCIAL AID PICTURE (2007-2008)

Students with need: 69% of average financial aid package awarded as scholarships/grants, 31% awarded as loans/jobs. Need-based aid available for part-time students.
Students without need: No-need awards available for academics, leadership, religious affiliation.

FINANCIAL AID PROCEDURES

Forms required: FAFSA, state aid form, institutional form.
Dates and Deadlines: No deadline.
Transfers: No deadline. Applicants notified on a rolling basis.

CONTACT

Dave Wallace, Financial Aid Director
735 105th Avenue, Oakland, CA 94603
(510) 567-6174

Scripps College

Claremont, California
www.scrippscollege.edu
Federal Code: 001174
CSS Code: 4693

4-year private liberal arts college for women in large town.
Enrollment: 944 undergrads. 252 full-time freshmen.
Selectivity: Admits less than 50% of applicants.

BASIC COSTS (2009-2010)

Tuition and fees: $38,700.
Per-credit charge: $1,203.
Room and board: $11,850.

FINANCIAL AID PICTURE (2008-2009)

Students with need: Out of 157 full-time freshmen who applied for aid, 111 were judged to have need. Of these, 111 received aid, and 111 had their full need met. Average financial aid package met 100% of need; average scholarship/grant was $31,650; average loan was $2,935. Need-based aid available for part-time students.
Students without need: 31 full-time freshmen who did not demonstrate need for aid received scholarships/grants; average award was $18,022. No-need awards available for academics, leadership.
Scholarships offered: James E. Scripps Scholarship; variable amount up to half-tuition; renewable; for distinguished young women whose intellectual and personal promise can be developed with a Scripps education.
Cumulative student debt: 48% of graduating class had student loans; average debt was $13,207.

FINANCIAL AID PROCEDURES

Forms required: FAFSA, CSS PROFILE, state aid form.
Dates and Deadlines: Priority date 1/15; closing date 5/1. Applicants notified by 4/1; must reply by 5/1.
Transfers: Priority date 4/1; no deadline. Applicants notified by 5/1; must reply by 6/1 or within 2 week(s) of notification. Students applying for admission as a transfer student should be aware that financial aid may be limited or unavailable.

CONTACT

David Levy, Director of Financial Aid
1030 Columbia Avenue, Claremont, CA 91711-3905
(909) 621-8275

Shasta College

Redding, California
www.shastacollege.edu
Federal Code: 001289

2-year public community college in small city.
Enrollment: 5,388 undergrads.
Selectivity: Open admission; but selective for some programs.

BASIC COSTS (2008-2009)

Tuition and fees: $675; out-of-state residents $6,195.
Per-credit charge: $20; out-of-state residents $204.
Room only: $2,610.

FINANCIAL AID PICTURE

Students with need: Need-based aid available for full-time and part-time students.
Students without need: This college awards aid only to students with need.

FINANCIAL AID PROCEDURES

Forms required: FAFSA, institutional form.
Dates and Deadlines: Priority date 3/2; no closing date. Applicants notified on a rolling basis starting 7/1.

CONTACT

Benna Starrett, Director of Financial Aid
Box 496006, Redding, CA 96049-6006
(530) 225-4735

Sierra College

Rocklin, California
www.sierracollege.edu
Federal Code: 001290

2-year public community college in large town.
Enrollment: 13,403 undergrads.
Selectivity: Open admission.

BASIC COSTS (2008-2009)

Tuition and fees: $640; out-of-state residents $6,070.
Per-credit charge: $20; out-of-state residents $201.
Room and board: $7,090.
Additional info: Tuition/fee waivers available for unemployed or children of unemployed.

FINANCIAL AID PICTURE (2008-2009)

Students with need: 75% of average financial aid package awarded as scholarships/grants, 25% awarded as loans/jobs. Need-based aid available for part-time students. Work study available nights, weekends, and for part-time students.

FINANCIAL AID PROCEDURES

Forms required: FAFSA.
Dates and Deadlines: Priority date 3/2; no closing date. Applicants notified on a rolling basis starting 5/15.
Transfers: No deadline.

CONTACT

Linda Williams, Financial Aid Program Manager
5000 Rocklin Road, Rocklin, CA 95677
(916) 781-0568

Simpson University

Redding, California
www.simpsonuniversity.edu
Federal Code: 001291

4-year private liberal arts college in small city, affiliated with Christian and Missionary Alliance.
Enrollment: 935 undergrads, 3% part-time. 214 full-time freshmen.
Selectivity: Admits 50 to 75% of applicants.

BASIC COSTS (2009-2010)

Tuition and fees: $20,400.
Per-credit charge: $850.
Room and board: $6,900.
Additional info: Tuition/fee waivers available for minority students.

FINANCIAL AID PICTURE (2007-2008)

Students with need: Need-based aid available for full-time and part-time students. Work study available nights, weekends, and for part-time students.
Students without need: No-need awards available for academics, alumni affiliation, athletics, leadership, minority status, music/drama, religious affiliation, state/district residency.
Scholarships offered: Academic awards; up to full tuition for 4.0 GPA and 1200 minimum SAT (exclusive of Writing).
Additional info: Work-study programs available.

FINANCIAL AID PROCEDURES

Forms required: FAFSA, institutional form.
Dates and Deadlines: Priority date 3/2; no closing date. Applicants notified on a rolling basis starting 3/1; must reply within 4 week(s) of notification.

Transfers: No deadline. Applicants notified on a rolling basis starting 3/1; must reply within 4 week(s) of notification.

CONTACT

James Herberger, Director of Enrollment Management
2211 College View Drive, Redding, CA 96003-8606
(530) 226-4111

Skyline College

San Bruno, California
www.skylinecollege.edu Federal Code: 007713

2-year public community college in small city.
Enrollment: 5,387 undergrads.
Selectivity: Open admission; but selective for some programs.

BASIC COSTS (2008-2009)

Tuition and fees: $628; out-of-state residents $6,358.
Per-credit charge: $20; out-of-state residents $211.

FINANCIAL AID PICTURE

Students with need: Need-based aid available for full-time and part-time students.

FINANCIAL AID PROCEDURES

Forms required: FAFSA, institutional form.
Dates and Deadlines: Priority date 5/2; no closing date. Applicants notified on a rolling basis starting 5/1; must reply within 2 week(s) of notification.

CONTACT

Maria Escobar, Director of Financial Aid
3300 College Drive, San Bruno, CA 94066-1662
(650) 738-4484

Soka University of America

Aliso Viejo, California
www.soka.edu Federal Code: 038144

4-year private university and liberal arts college in large town.
Enrollment: 388 undergrads. 101 full-time freshmen.
Selectivity: Admits 50 to 75% of applicants.

BASIC COSTS (2009-2010)

Tuition and fees: $24,606.
Room and board: $9,360.

FINANCIAL AID PICTURE (2007-2008)

Students with need: Out of 101 full-time freshmen who applied for aid, 101 were judged to have need. Of these, 91 received aid, and 81 had their full need met. Average financial aid package met 85% of need; average scholarship/grant was $12,000; average loan was $3,500. Need-based aid available for part-time students.
Students without need: 9 full-time freshmen who did not demonstrate need for aid received scholarships/grants; average award was $10,000. No-need awards available for academics, athletics.
Cumulative student debt: 56% of graduating class had student loans; average debt was $18,500.

FINANCIAL AID PROCEDURES

Forms required: FAFSA.
Dates and Deadlines: Closing date 3/1. Applicants notified on a rolling basis starting 3/15; must reply within 4 week(s) of notification.

CONTACT

Christopher Brown, Director of Admission and Financial Aid
One University Drive, Aliso Viejo, CA 92656-8081
(949) 480-4150

Sonoma State University

Rohnert Park, California
www.sonoma.edu Federal Code: 001156

4-year public university and liberal arts college in large town.
Enrollment: 7,709 undergrads, 11% part-time. 1,577 full-time freshmen.
Selectivity: Admits over 75% of applicants.

BASIC COSTS (2008-2009)

Tuition and fees: $4,272; out-of-state residents $14,442.
Room and board: $10,115.

FINANCIAL AID PICTURE (2007-2008)

Students with need: Out of 683 full-time freshmen who applied for aid, 413 were judged to have need. Of these, 336 received aid, and 97 had their full need met. Average financial aid package met 65% of need; average scholarship/grant was $7,117; average loan was $3,100. For part-time students, average financial aid package was $10,038.
Students without need: 6 full-time freshmen who did not demonstrate need for aid received scholarships/grants; average award was $733. No-need awards available for academics, alumni affiliation, art, athletics, leadership, minority status, music/drama.
Scholarships offered: 4 full-time freshmen received athletic scholarships; average amount $875.
Cumulative student debt: 37% of graduating class had student loans; average debt was $14,410.

FINANCIAL AID PROCEDURES

Forms required: FAFSA.
Dates and Deadlines: Priority date 1/31; no closing date. Applicants notified on a rolling basis starting 3/15; must reply within 2 week(s) of notification.

CONTACT

Susan Gutierrez, Director, Financial Aid
1801 East Cotati Avenue, Rohnert Park, CA 94928-3609
(707) 664-2389

Southern California Institute of Architecture

Los Angeles, California
www.sciarc.edu Federal Code: 014073

5-year private visual arts college in very large city.
Enrollment: 278 undergrads. 69 full-time freshmen.
Selectivity: Admits over 75% of applicants.

BASIC COSTS (2009-2010)

Tuition and fees: $24,000.
Additional info: International student fee (one-time only) $500. International student mandatory health insurance premium $822 per year.

FINANCIAL AID PICTURE (2008-2009)

Students with need: Need-based aid available for part-time students. Work study available nights, weekends, and for part-time students.
Students without need: No-need awards available for academics, state/district residency.

FINANCIAL AID PROCEDURES

Forms required: FAFSA, institutional form.
Dates and Deadlines: No deadline. Must reply within 2 week(s) of notification.
Transfers: Priority date 3/2; closing date 5/2. Applicants notified on a rolling basis starting 4/15.

CONTACT
Helen Lara, Financial Aid Director
960 East Third Street, Los Angeles, CA 90013
(213) 613-2200 ext. 326

Southern California Institute of Technology
Anaheim, California
www.scit-scu.edu Federal Code: 031136

4-year for-profit business and engineering college in large city.
Enrollment: 501 undergrads.
Selectivity: Open admission; but selective for some programs.

BASIC COSTS (2008-2009)
Tuition and fees: $14,670.
Per-credit charge: $191.
Additional info: Tuition and fees quoted for electronic engineering program. Costs vary by program.

FINANCIAL AID PICTURE (2007-2008)
Students with need: 36% of average financial aid package awarded as scholarships/grants, 64% awarded as loans/jobs.

CONTACT
Mylinh Pham, Director of Financial Aid
222 South Harbor Boulevard, Suite 200, Anaheim, CA 92805
(714) 300-0300

Southwestern College
Chula Vista, California
www.swccd.edu Federal Code: 001294

2-year public community college in small city.
Enrollment: 12,999 undergrads.
Selectivity: Open admission; but selective for some programs.

BASIC COSTS (2008-2009)
Tuition and fees: $624; out-of-state residents $6,054.
Per-credit charge: $20; out-of-state residents $201.

FINANCIAL AID PICTURE
Students with need: Need-based aid available for full-time and part-time students. Work study available nights, weekends, and for part-time students.

FINANCIAL AID PROCEDURES
Forms required: FAFSA, state aid form.
Dates and Deadlines: Closing date 3/2. Applicants notified on a rolling basis starting 7/1.

CONTACT
Linda Thrower, Director of Financial Aid
900 Otay Lakes Road, Chula Vista, CA 91910-7297
(619) 482-6357

Stanford University
Stanford, California Federal Code: 001305
www.stanford.edu CSS Code: 4704

4-year private university in small city.
Enrollment: 6,502 undergrads. 1,723 full-time freshmen.
Selectivity: Admits less than 50% of applicants.

BASIC COSTS (2008-2009)
Tuition and fees: $36,030.
Room and board: $11,182.

FINANCIAL AID PICTURE (2007-2008)
Students with need: Out of 1,020 full-time freshmen who applied for aid, 761 were judged to have need. Of these, 756 received aid, and 574 had their full need met. Average financial aid package met 100% of need; average scholarship/grant was $31,794; average loan was $2,401. Need-based aid available for part-time students.
Students without need: This college awards aid only to students with need.
Scholarships offered: 126 full-time freshmen received athletic scholarships; average amount $24,963.
Cumulative student debt: 40% of graduating class had student loans; average debt was $15,724.

FINANCIAL AID PROCEDURES
Forms required: FAFSA, CSS PROFILE.
Dates and Deadlines: Priority date 2/15; no closing date. Applicants notified on a rolling basis starting 4/3; must reply by 5/1.
Transfers: Priority date 3/15.

CONTACT
Karen Cooper, Director, Financial Aid
Montag Hall, Stanford, CA 94305-6106
(650) 723-3058

Taft College
Taft, California
www.taftcollege.edu Federal Code: 001309

2-year public community college in small town.
Enrollment: 1,684 undergrads. 272 full-time freshmen.
Selectivity: Open admission.

BASIC COSTS (2008-2009)
Tuition and fees: $600; out-of-state residents $6,030.
Per-credit charge: $20; out-of-state residents $201.
Room and board: $3,640.

FINANCIAL AID PICTURE (2007-2008)
Students with need: 81% of average financial aid package awarded as scholarships/grants, 19% awarded as loans/jobs. Need-based aid available for part-time students. Work study available nights.
Students without need: No-need awards available for academics.
Scholarships offered: Taft College Merit Awards: $250; for students from local high schools; available for 2 years; based on GPA of 3.0 or higher. Taft College High School Merit Award: $600; for students from local high schools. Taft College Nonresident Awards: $4,230; applied to nonresident tuition; available for 1 year; based on GPA of 3.0 or higher.

FINANCIAL AID PROCEDURES
Forms required: FAFSA, institutional form.
Dates and Deadlines: No deadline. Applicants notified on a rolling basis; must reply within 4 week(s) of notification.
Transfers: No deadline.

CONTACT
Gayle Roberts, Director of Financial Aid
29 Emmons Park Drive, Taft, CA 93268
(661) 763-7762

Thomas Aquinas College

Santa Paula, California
www.thomasaquinas.edu Federal Code: 023580

4-year private liberal arts college in rural community, affiliated with Roman Catholic Church.
Enrollment: 340 undergrads. 102 full-time freshmen.
Selectivity: Admits 50 to 75% of applicants.

BASIC COSTS (2009-2010)

Tuition and fees: $22,400.
Room and board: $7,400.

FINANCIAL AID PICTURE (2008-2009)

Students with need: Out of 74 full-time freshmen who applied for aid, 68 were judged to have need. Of these, 68 received aid, and 68 had their full need met. Average financial aid package met 100% of need; average scholarship/grant was $11,916; average loan was $3,036.
Students without need: This college awards aid only to students with need.
Cumulative student debt: 71% of graduating class had student loans; average debt was $14,000.

FINANCIAL AID PROCEDURES

Forms required: FAFSA, state aid form, institutional form.
Dates and Deadlines: Closing date 3/2. Applicants notified on a rolling basis starting 1/1; must reply by 5/1 or within 2 week(s) of notification.

CONTACT

Gregory Becher, Director of Financial Aid
10000 North Ojai Road, Santa Paula, CA 93060-9621
(800) 634-9797

University of California: Berkeley

Berkeley, California
www.berkeley.edu Federal Code: 001312

4-year public university in small city.
Enrollment: 25,151 undergrads, 3% part-time. 4,239 full-time freshmen.
Selectivity: Admits less than 50% of applicants.

BASIC COSTS (2008-2009)

Tuition and fees: $7,656; out-of-state residents $28,264.
Room and board: $14,494.

FINANCIAL AID PICTURE (2008-2009)

Students with need: Need-based aid available for full-time and part-time students.
Students without need: No-need awards available for academics.
Scholarships offered: University Scholarship, President's Undergraduate Fellowships, Regents and Chancellor's Scholarships, Alumni Scholarships.

FINANCIAL AID PROCEDURES

Forms required: FAFSA, state aid form.
Dates and Deadlines: Closing date 3/2. Applicants notified by 4/15.

CONTACT

Cheryl Resh, Director, Financial Aid
110 Sproul Hall, #5800, Berkeley, CA 94720-5800
(510) 642-6000

University of California: Davis

Davis, California
www.ucdavis.edu Federal Code: 001313

4-year public university in small city.
Enrollment: 24,017 undergrads, 1% part-time. 4,972 full-time freshmen.
Selectivity: Admits 50 to 75% of applicants.

BASIC COSTS (2008-2009)

Tuition and fees: $8,635; out-of-state residents $29,243.
Room and board: $11,978.
Additional info: Students must purchase the Student Health Insurance Plan (SHIP) unless they are able to prove comparable coverage.

FINANCIAL AID PICTURE (2008-2009)

Students with need: Need-based aid available for full-time and part-time students. Work study available nights, weekends, and for part-time students.
Students without need: This college awards aid only to students with need.

FINANCIAL AID PROCEDURES

Forms required: FAFSA, state aid form.
Dates and Deadlines: Priority date 3/2; no closing date. Applicants notified on a rolling basis starting 3/15.

CONTACT

Kathryn Maloney, Interim Director, Financial Aid
One Shields Ave, Davis, CA 95616
(530) 752-2390

University of California: Irvine

Irvine, California
www.uci.edu Federal Code: 001314

4-year public university in small city.
Enrollment: 22,122 undergrads, 3% part-time. 4,918 full-time freshmen.
Selectivity: Admits less than 50% of applicants.

BASIC COSTS (2008-2009)

Tuition and fees: $8,046; out-of-state residents $28,654.
Room and board: $10,527.

FINANCIAL AID PICTURE (2007-2008)

Students with need: Out of 3,726 full-time freshmen who applied for aid, 2,546 were judged to have need. Of these, 2,456 received aid, and 1,158 had their full need met. Average financial aid package met 82% of need; average scholarship/grant was $10,685; average loan was $5,897. For part-time students, average financial aid package was $11,438.
Students without need: 164 full-time freshmen who did not demonstrate need for aid received scholarships/grants; average award was $8,526. No-need awards available for academics, alumni affiliation, art, athletics, job skills, leadership, music/drama, state/district residency.
Scholarships offered: 44 full-time freshmen received athletic scholarships; average amount $10,719.
Cumulative student debt: 49% of graduating class had student loans; average debt was $17,282.

FINANCIAL AID PROCEDURES

Forms required: FAFSA, state aid form.
Dates and Deadlines: Closing date 3/2. Applicants notified by 4/1; must reply by 5/1.

CONTACT

Christopher Shultz, Director of Financial Aid
204 Aldrich Hall, Irvine, CA 92697-1075
(949) 824-8262

University of California: Los Angeles

Los Angeles, California
www.ucla.edu Federal Code: 001315

4-year public university in very large city.
Enrollment: 26,536 undergrads, 3% part-time. 4,555 full-time freshmen.
Selectivity: Admits less than 50% of applicants.

BASIC COSTS (2008-2009)

Tuition and fees: $7,551; out-of-state residents $28,162.
Room and board: $12,891.

FINANCIAL AID PICTURE (2007-2008)

Students with need: Out of 2,579 full-time freshmen who applied for aid, 2,085 were judged to have need. Of these, 2,085 received aid, and 478 had their full need met. Average financial aid package met 80% of need; average scholarship/grant was $12,017; average loan was $5,360. For part-time students, average financial aid package was $11,242.
Students without need: 277 full-time freshmen who did not demonstrate need for aid received scholarships/grants; average award was $5,511. No-need awards available for academics, alumni affiliation, athletics, ROTC.
Scholarships offered: 80 full-time freshmen received athletic scholarships; average amount $12,593.

FINANCIAL AID PROCEDURES

Forms required: FAFSA.
Dates and Deadlines: Priority date 3/2; no closing date. Applicants notified on a rolling basis starting 3/15; must reply within 3 week(s) of notification.

CONTACT

Ronald Johnson, Director, Financial Aid Office
1147 Murphy Hall, Los Angeles, CA 90095-1436
(310) 206-0400

University of California: Merced

Merced, California
www.ucmerced.edu Federal Code: 041271

4-year public university in small city.
Enrollment: 2,533 undergrads. 925 full-time freshmen.
Selectivity: Admits over 75% of applicants.

BASIC COSTS (2008-2009)

Tuition and fees: $7,749; out-of-state residents $28,357.
Room and board: $11,692.

FINANCIAL AID PICTURE (2008-2009)

Students with need: Need-based aid available for full-time and part-time students. Work study available nights, weekends, and for part-time students.
Students without need: No-need awards available for academics.
Scholarships offered: Regents' Scholarships; based on strength and breadth of academic program, grades, personal statement, extracurricular activities, community activities, first-generation attendance, other indicators of academic excellence and promise.

FINANCIAL AID PROCEDURES

Forms required: FAFSA.
Dates and Deadlines: Priority date 3/2; no closing date. Applicants notified on a rolling basis starting 3/2.
Transfers: Priority date 3/2. Applicants notified on a rolling basis; must reply by 6/1.

CONTACT

Diana Ralls, Director of Financial Aid & Scholarships
5200 North Lake Road, Merced, CA 95343-5603
(209) 228-4243

University of California: Riverside

Riverside, California
www.ucr.edu Federal Code: 001316

4-year public university in large city.
Enrollment: 15,708 undergrads, 2% part-time. 4,404 full-time freshmen.
Selectivity: Admits over 75% of applicants.

BASIC COSTS (2008-2009)

Tuition and fees: $7,846; out-of-state residents $28,453.
Room and board: $10,850.

FINANCIAL AID PICTURE (2008-2009)

Students with need: Out of 3,729 full-time freshmen who applied for aid, 2,948 were judged to have need. Of these, 2,867 received aid, and 1,653 had their full need met. Average financial aid package met 89% of need; average scholarship/grant was $13,463; average loan was $4,463. For part-time students, average financial aid package was $11,762.
Students without need: 83 full-time freshmen who did not demonstrate need for aid received scholarships/grants; average award was $7,012. No-need awards available for academics, art, athletics, job skills, leadership, music/drama, state/district residency.
Scholarships offered: ***Merit:*** Regents and Chancellor's Scholarships: available to top-ranked incoming freshmen, including international and home-schooled admits. ***Athletic:*** 26 full-time freshmen received athletic scholarships; average amount $10,165.
Cumulative student debt: 62% of graduating class had student loans; average debt was $15,414.

FINANCIAL AID PROCEDURES

Forms required: FAFSA, state aid form.
Dates and Deadlines: Closing date 3/2. Applicants notified on a rolling basis starting 3/1; must reply by 5/1 or within 3 week(s) of notification.
Transfers: Deadlines may be extended for mid-year admissions.

CONTACT

Sheryl Hayes, Director of Financial Aid
Admissions Office, Riverside, CA 92521
(951) 827-3878

University of California: San Diego

La Jolla, California
www.ucsd.edu Federal Code: 001317

4-year public university in large town.
Enrollment: 22,518 undergrads, 1% part-time. 4,132 full-time freshmen.
Selectivity: Admits less than 50% of applicants.

BASIC COSTS (2008-2009)

Tuition and fees: $8,062; out-of-state residents $28,670.
Room and board: $10,787.

FINANCIAL AID PICTURE (2007-2008)

Students with need: Out of 3,243 full-time freshmen who applied for aid, 2,440 were judged to have need. Of these, 2,344 received aid, and 433 had their full need met. Average financial aid package met 83% of need; average scholarship/grant was $11,343; average loan was $4,254. For part-time students, average financial aid package was $11,173.
Students without need: 130 full-time freshmen who did not demonstrate need for aid received scholarships/grants; average award was $8,257. No-need awards available for academics, art, leadership, minority status, music/drama.
Scholarships offered: 82 full-time freshmen received athletic scholarships; average amount $537.

FINANCIAL AID PROCEDURES

Forms required: FAFSA, state aid form.

Dates and Deadlines: Priority date 3/2; no closing date. Applicants notified on a rolling basis starting 3/15; must reply within 3 week(s) of notification.
Transfers: Applicants notified on a rolling basis; must reply within 3 week(s) of notification.

CONTACT
Ann Klein, Director of Financial Aid
9500 Gilman Drive, 0021, La Jolla, CA 92093-0021
(858) 534-4480

University of California: Santa Barbara

Santa Barbara, California
www.ucsb.edu Federal Code: 001320

4-year public university in small city.
Enrollment: 18,888 undergrads, 2% part-time. 4,320 full-time freshmen.
Selectivity: Admits less than 50% of applicants.

BASIC COSTS (2008-2009)
Tuition and fees: $8,386; out-of-state residents $28,994.
Room and board: $12,485.

FINANCIAL AID PICTURE (2007-2008)
Students with need: Out of 3,122 full-time freshmen who applied for aid, 2,130 were judged to have need. Of these, 1,899 received aid, and 453 had their full need met. Average financial aid package met 80% of need; average scholarship/grant was $14,034; average loan was $5,398. For part-time students, average financial aid package was $11,922.
Students without need: 63 full-time freshmen who did not demonstrate need for aid received scholarships/grants; average award was $7,659. No-need awards available for academics, athletics.
Scholarships offered: 68 full-time freshmen received athletic scholarships; average amount $9,008.
Cumulative student debt: 48% of graduating class had student loans; average debt was $15,201.

FINANCIAL AID PROCEDURES
Forms required: FAFSA.
Dates and Deadlines: Priority date 3/2; closing date 5/31. Applicants notified on a rolling basis starting 3/15; must reply within 2 week(s) of notification.
Transfers: California residents must apply for a CAL grant from the California Student Aid Commission; must complete and submit FAFSA by March 2.

CONTACT
Ron Andrade, Director of Financial Aid
1210 Cheadle Hall, Santa Barbara, CA 93106-2014
(805) 893-2432

University of California: Santa Cruz

Santa Cruz, California
www.ucsc.edu Federal Code: 001321

4-year public university in small city.
Enrollment: 15,125 undergrads, 3% part-time. 3,689 full-time freshmen.
Selectivity: Admits 50 to 75% of applicants.

BASIC COSTS (2008-2009)
Tuition and fees: $8,200; out-of-state residents $28,808.
Room and board: $13,038.
Additional info: Tuition/fee waivers available for unemployed or children of unemployed.

FINANCIAL AID PICTURE (2007-2008)
Students with need: Out of 2,593 full-time freshmen who applied for aid, 1,828 were judged to have need. Of these, 1,718 received aid, and 618 had their full need met. Average financial aid package met 87% of need; average scholarship/grant was $10,836; average loan was $5,326. For part-time students, average financial aid package was $12,057.
Students without need: 54 full-time freshmen who did not demonstrate need for aid received scholarships/grants; average award was $9,707. No-need awards available for academics, alumni affiliation, art, leadership, music/drama.
Cumulative student debt: 51% of graduating class had student loans; average debt was $14,932.

FINANCIAL AID PROCEDURES
Forms required: FAFSA, state aid form.
Dates and Deadlines: Closing date 3/2. Applicants notified on a rolling basis starting 4/1; must reply within 4 week(s) of notification.

CONTACT
Ann Draper, Director of Financial Aid
Cook House, 1156 High Street, Santa Cruz, CA 95064
(831) 459-2963

University of La Verne

La Verne, California
www.laverne.edu Federal Code: 001216

4-year private university and liberal arts college in large town.
Enrollment: 1,528 undergrads, 4% part-time. 297 full-time freshmen.
Selectivity: Admits 50 to 75% of applicants.

BASIC COSTS (2009-2010)
Tuition and fees: $28,250.
Per-credit charge: $800.
Room and board: $11,110.

FINANCIAL AID PICTURE (2008-2009)
Students with need: Out of 258 full-time freshmen who applied for aid, 240 were judged to have need. Of these, 239 received aid, and 2 had their full need met. Average financial aid package met 50% of need; average scholarship/grant was $12,209; average loan was $4,798. For part-time students, average financial aid package was $14,978.
Students without need: 30 full-time freshmen who did not demonstrate need for aid received scholarships/grants; average award was $11,333. No-need awards available for academics, alumni affiliation, art, leadership, minority status, music/drama, religious affiliation.
Cumulative student debt: 81% of graduating class had student loans; average debt was $19,467.

FINANCIAL AID PROCEDURES
Forms required: FAFSA, state aid form.
Dates and Deadlines: Priority date 3/2; no closing date. Applicants notified on a rolling basis starting 3/17; must reply within 2 week(s) of notification.
Transfers: No deadline.

CONTACT
Leatha Webster, Director of Financial Aid
1950 Third Street, La Verne, CA 91750
(800) 649-0160

University of Redlands

Redlands, California
www.redlands.edu Federal Code: 001322

4-year private university and liberal arts college in small city.
Enrollment: 2,335 undergrads, 1% part-time. 572 full-time freshmen.

Selectivity: Admits 50 to 75% of applicants.

BASIC COSTS (2008-2009)

Tuition and fees: $32,294.
Per-credit charge: $1,000.
Room and board: $10,122.

FINANCIAL AID PICTURE (2008-2009)

Students with need: Out of 467 full-time freshmen who applied for aid, 353 were judged to have need. Of these, 353 received aid, and 155 had their full need met. Average financial aid package met 81% of need; average scholarship/grant was $21,661; average loan was $5,313. For part-time students, average financial aid package was $15,564.
Students without need: 61 full-time freshmen who did not demonstrate need for aid received scholarships/grants; average award was $11,672. No-need awards available for academics, art, music/drama.
Cumulative student debt: 70% of graduating class had student loans; average debt was $17,290.

FINANCIAL AID PROCEDURES

Forms required: FAFSA, state aid form.
Dates and Deadlines: Priority date 2/15; no closing date. Applicants notified on a rolling basis starting 2/28; must reply by 5/1.
Transfers: No deadline.

CONTACT

Bethann Corey, Financial Aid Director
1200 East Colton Avenue, Redlands, CA 92373-0999
(909) 748-8047

University of San Diego

San Diego, California
www.sandiego.edu Federal Code: 010395

4-year private university in very large city, affiliated with Roman Catholic Church.
Enrollment: 5,097 undergrads, 4% part-time. 1,090 full-time freshmen.
Selectivity: Admits 50 to 75% of applicants.

BASIC COSTS (2009-2010)

Tuition and fees: $36,292.
Per-credit charge: $1,240.
Room and board: $12,602.

FINANCIAL AID PICTURE (2007-2008)

Students with need: Out of 673 full-time freshmen who applied for aid, 523 were judged to have need. Of these, 520 received aid, and 71 had their full need met. Average financial aid package met 72% of need; average scholarship/grant was $17,887; average loan was $5,098. For part-time students, average financial aid package was $11,434.
Students without need: 192 full-time freshmen who did not demonstrate need for aid received scholarships/grants; average award was $11,790. No-need awards available for academics, athletics, leadership, music/drama, religious affiliation, ROTC.
Scholarships offered: 31 full-time freshmen received athletic scholarships; average amount $31,066.
Cumulative student debt: 48% of graduating class had student loans; average debt was $23,343.

FINANCIAL AID PROCEDURES

Forms required: FAFSA.
Dates and Deadlines: Priority date 3/2; no closing date. Applicants notified on a rolling basis starting 3/1; must reply by 5/1 or within 3 week(s) of notification.
Transfers: No deadline. Entering transfer students not eligible for institutional merit-based scholarships.

CONTACT

Judith Lewis Logue, Director of Financial Aid Services
5998 Alcala Park, San Diego, CA 92110
(619) 260-4514

University of San Francisco

San Francisco, California
www.usfca.edu Federal Code: 001325

4-year private university in very large city, affiliated with Roman Catholic Church.
Enrollment: 4,934 undergrads, 3% part-time. 1,040 full-time freshmen.
Selectivity: Admits 50 to 75% of applicants.

BASIC COSTS (2009-2010)

Tuition and fees: $34,770.
Per-credit charge: $1,225.
Room and board: $11,540.
Additional info: Nursing undergraduate clinical lab $100 per lab, clinical lab malpractice insurance $25 per lab.

FINANCIAL AID PICTURE (2008-2009)

Students with need: Need-based aid available for full-time and part-time students.
Students without need: No-need awards available for academics, athletics, ROTC.
Scholarships offered: University Scholars Program: $19,500 per year for 4 years; must have 3.8 weighted GPA and combined SAT of 1320 on Critical Reading and Math sections or ACT composite of 30. Applicants must apply for admission by November 15.
Additional info: Individualized installment plans available.

FINANCIAL AID PROCEDURES

Forms required: FAFSA.
Dates and Deadlines: Priority date 2/1; no closing date. Applicants notified on a rolling basis starting 4/1; must reply within 4 week(s) of notification.

CONTACT

Susan Murphy, Senior Associate Dean, Director, Enrollment and Financial Services
2130 Fulton Street, San Francisco, CA 94117-1046
(415) 422-6303

University of Southern California

Los Angeles, California Federal Code: 001328
www.usc.edu CSS Code: 4852

4-year private university in very large city.
Enrollment: 16,283 undergrads, 3% part-time. 2,963 full-time freshmen.
Selectivity: Admits less than 50% of applicants. GED not accepted.

BASIC COSTS (2008-2009)

Tuition and fees: $37,844.
Per-credit charge: $1,249.
Room and board: $11,298.

FINANCIAL AID PICTURE (2007-2008)

Students with need: Out of 1,849 full-time freshmen who applied for aid, 1,194 were judged to have need. Of these, 1,193 received aid, and 1,166 had their full need met. Average financial aid package met 100% of need; average scholarship/grant was $23,131; average loan was $4,046. For part-time students, average financial aid package was $14,672.
Students without need: 772 full-time freshmen who did not demonstrate need for aid received scholarships/grants; average award was $14,721. No-need awards available for academics, alumni affiliation, art, athletics, leadership, music/drama, ROTC.

Scholarships offered: ***Merit:*** Trustee Scholarship: full tuition; approximately 100 awards annually; finalists invited to a mandatory interview. Presidential Scholarship: one-half tuition; approximately 200 awarded annually; finalists invited to a mandatory interview. National Merit Presidential Scholarship: one-half tuition; number of awards varies; admitted Freshmen who are National Merit Finalists and who designate USC as their first-choice college will receive this award. Deans Scholarship: one-quarter tuition; approximately 50 awards annually. ***Athletic:*** 80 full-time freshmen received athletic scholarships; average amount $34,438.
Cumulative student debt: 51% of graduating class had student loans; average debt was $27,692.

FINANCIAL AID PROCEDURES
Forms required: FAFSA, CSS PROFILE.
Dates and Deadlines: Priority date 2/9; no closing date. Applicants notified on a rolling basis starting 3/15; must reply by 5/1.
Transfers: Priority date 2/2. Applicants notified by 5/1.

CONTACT
Susan Ikerd, Associate Dean and Director
Office of Admission, Los Angeles, CA 90089-0911
(213) 740-1111

University of the Pacific
Stockton, California
www.pacific.edu Federal Code: 001329

4-year private university in large city.
Enrollment: 3,443 undergrads, 3% part-time. 880 full-time freshmen.
Selectivity: Admits 50 to 75% of applicants.

BASIC COSTS (2009-2010)
Tuition and fees: $30,880.
Per-credit charge: $1,048.
Room and board: $10,118.

FINANCIAL AID PICTURE (2008-2009)
Students with need: Out of 716 full-time freshmen who applied for aid, 605 were judged to have need. Of these, 605 received aid, and 160 had their full need met. For part-time students, average financial aid package was $18,733.
Students without need: 155 full-time freshmen who did not demonstrate need for aid received scholarships/grants; average award was $9,164. No-need awards available for academics, athletics, leadership, music/drama, religious affiliation.
Scholarships offered: 21 full-time freshmen received athletic scholarships; average amount $18,653.

FINANCIAL AID PROCEDURES
Forms required: FAFSA.
Dates and Deadlines: Priority date 2/15; no closing date. Applicants notified on a rolling basis starting 3/15.

CONTACT
Lynn Fox, Director of Financial Aid
3601 Pacific Avenue, Stockton, CA 95211-0197
(209) 946-2011

Vanguard University of Southern California
Costa Mesa, California
www.vanguard.edu Federal Code: 001293

4-year private university and liberal arts college in small city, affiliated with Assemblies of God.
Enrollment: 1,796 undergrads, 19% part-time. 380 full-time freshmen.
Selectivity: Admits over 75% of applicants.

BASIC COSTS (2009-2010)
Tuition and fees: $25,452.
Per-credit charge: $1,039.
Room and board: $7,994.

FINANCIAL AID PICTURE (2007-2008)
Students with need: Out of 318 full-time freshmen who applied for aid, 235 were judged to have need. Of these, 234 received aid, and 74 had their full need met. Average financial aid package met 82% of need; average scholarship/grant was $14,614; average loan was $3,036. For part-time students, average financial aid package was $15,670.
Students without need: 83 full-time freshmen who did not demonstrate need for aid received scholarships/grants; average award was $8,414. No-need awards available for academics, athletics, music/drama, religious affiliation.
Scholarships offered: 36 full-time freshmen received athletic scholarships; average amount $9,388.
Cumulative student debt: 78% of graduating class had student loans; average debt was $18,762.

FINANCIAL AID PROCEDURES
Forms required: FAFSA, state aid form.
Dates and Deadlines: Priority date 3/2; closing date 3/2. Applicants notified on a rolling basis starting 4/1; must reply within 3 week(s) of notification.
Transfers: Applicants notified on a rolling basis.

CONTACT
Robyn Fournier, Director of Financial Aid
55 Fair Drive, Costa Mesa, CA 92626-9601
(714) 556-3610 ext. 4250

Ventura College
Ventura, California
www.venturacollege.edu Federal Code: 001334

2-year public community college in small city.
Enrollment: 7,041 undergrads. 1,034 full-time freshmen.
Selectivity: Open admission; but selective for some programs.

BASIC COSTS (2008-2009)
Tuition and fees: $642; out-of-state residents $6,072.
Per-credit charge: $20; out-of-state residents $201.

FINANCIAL AID PICTURE
Students with need: Need-based aid available for full-time and part-time students.

FINANCIAL AID PROCEDURES
Forms required: FAFSA, state aid form.
Dates and Deadlines: Priority date 3/2; no closing date. Applicants notified on a rolling basis.

CONTACT
Dora Washington, Director, Financial Aid
4667 Telegraph Road, Ventura, CA 93003
(805) 654-6369

Victor Valley College
Victorville, California Federal Code: 001335
www.vvc.edu CSS Code: 4932

2-year public community college in small city.
Enrollment: 4,933 undergrads.
Selectivity: Open admission; but selective for some programs.

BASIC COSTS (2008-2009)
Tuition and fees: $610; out-of-state residents $6,040.
Per-credit charge: $20; out-of-state residents $201.
Additional info: Nevada residents may qualify for tuition reduction program as part of Good Neighbor policy.

FINANCIAL AID PICTURE
Students with need: Need-based aid available for full-time and part-time students.
Additional info: Board of Governors grant pays enrollment fee in full for low-income students.

FINANCIAL AID PROCEDURES
Forms required: FAFSA, CSS PROFILE, state aid form, institutional form.
Dates and Deadlines: Priority date 3/2; no closing date. Applicants notified on a rolling basis starting 8/1; must reply within 4 week(s) of notification.

CONTACT
Greg Ryan, Associate Director, Office of Financial Aid
18422 Bear Valley Road, Victorville, CA 92392-5849
(760) 245-4271 ext. 2277

West Hills College: Coalinga

Coalinga, California
www.westhillscollege.com Federal Code: 001176

2-year public community college in small town.
Enrollment: 1,765 undergrads. 251 full-time freshmen.
Selectivity: Open admission.

BASIC COSTS (2008-2009)
Tuition and fees: $600; out-of-state residents $6,030.
Per-credit charge: $20; out-of-state residents $201.
Room and board: $5,321.
Additional info: Additional $250 refundable deposit for room and board plan. Tuition/fee waivers available for unemployed or children of unemployed.

FINANCIAL AID PICTURE
Students with need: Need-based aid available for full-time and part-time students.

FINANCIAL AID PROCEDURES
Forms required: FAFSA.
Dates and Deadlines: Priority date 3/2; no closing date. Applicants notified on a rolling basis starting 6/1.

CONTACT
Dolores Smith, District Director of Financial Aid
300 Cherry Lane, Coalinga, CA 93210
(559) 934-2310

West Los Angeles College

Culver City, California
www.wlac.edu Federal Code: 008596

2-year public community college in large town.
Enrollment: 4,656 undergrads.
Selectivity: Open admission.

BASIC COSTS (2008-2009)
Tuition and fees: $622; out-of-state residents $6,052.
Per-credit charge: $20; out-of-state residents $201.
Additional info: Tuition/fee waivers available for unemployed or children of unemployed.

FINANCIAL AID PICTURE (2008-2009)
Students with need: Need-based aid available for full-time and part-time students.
Students without need: This college awards aid only to students with need.
Additional info: California residents may qualify for Board of Governors Grant Program.

FINANCIAL AID PROCEDURES
Forms required: FAFSA.
Dates and Deadlines: No deadline. Applicants notified on a rolling basis; must reply within 4 week(s) of notification.
Transfers: No deadline.

CONTACT
Glenn Schenk, Financial Aid Manager
9000 Overland Avenue, Culver City, CA 90230
(310) 287-4533

West Valley College

Saratoga, California
www.westvalley.edu Federal Code: 001338

2-year public community college in large town.
Enrollment: 6,028 undergrads.
Selectivity: Open admission.

BASIC COSTS (2008-2009)
Tuition and fees: $658; out-of-state residents $6,088.
Per-credit charge: $20; out-of-state residents $201.
Additional info: Tuition/fee waivers available for unemployed or children of unemployed.

FINANCIAL AID PICTURE
Students with need: Need-based aid available for full-time and part-time students.
Students without need: This college awards aid only to students with need.

FINANCIAL AID PROCEDURES
Forms required: FAFSA.
Dates and Deadlines: Priority date 5/31; no closing date. Applicants notified on a rolling basis starting 7/1.

CONTACT
Maritza Cantarero, Director of Financial Aid
14000 Fruitvale Avenue, Saratoga, CA 95070-5698
(408) 867-2200

Westmont College

Santa Barbara, California
www.westmont.edu Federal Code: 001341

4-year private liberal arts college in small city, affiliated with nondenominational tradition.
Enrollment: 1,327 undergrads, 1% part-time. 331 full-time freshmen.
Selectivity: Admits 50 to 75% of applicants.

BASIC COSTS (2009-2010)
Tuition and fees: $33,190.
Room and board: $10,550.

FINANCIAL AID PICTURE (2008-2009)
Students with need: Out of 273 full-time freshmen who applied for aid, 223 were judged to have need. Of these, 223 received aid, and 19 had their full need met. Average financial aid package met 72% of need; average scholarship/grant was $19,597; average loan was $4,440.

Students without need: 111 full-time freshmen who did not demonstrate need for aid received scholarships/grants; average award was $12,073. No-need awards available for academics, art, athletics, leadership, minority status, music/drama.
Scholarships offered: ***Merit:*** Scholarships automatically awarded to entering students based on high school GPA and SAT or ACT scores (first-year students) or college academic GPA (transfers): renewable annually; unlimited number awarded until class is full. First-year scholarships: Presidential ($11,000), must maintain 3.25 GPA; Provost ($9,000), must maintain 3.0 GPA; Dean's ($7,000), must maintain 2.75 GPA. Transfer scholarships: Presidential ($5,000), must have 3.75 GPA and 24 or more transferable credits; Provost ($4,000), must have 3.35 GPA and 24 or more transferable credits. ***Athletic:*** 13 full-time freshmen received athletic scholarships; average amount $5,844.
Cumulative student debt: 59% of graduating class had student loans; average debt was $26,032.

FINANCIAL AID PROCEDURES
Forms required: FAFSA.
Dates and Deadlines: Priority date 3/1; no closing date. Applicants notified on a rolling basis starting 3/15; must reply by 5/1 or within 2 week(s) of notification.
Transfers: Applicants notified on a rolling basis starting 4/1; must reply by 5/1 or within 2 week(s) of notification. Transfer students may qualify for academic merit scholarships.

CONTACT
Diane Horvath, Director of Financial Aid
955 La Paz Road, Santa Barbara, CA 93108-1089
(888) 963-4624

Westwood College: Inland Empire
Upland, California
www.westwood.edu Federal Code: 007548

3-year for-profit business and technical college in small city.
Enrollment: 993 undergrads.

BASIC COSTS (2008-2009)
Tuition and fees: $14,061.

FINANCIAL AID PICTURE
Students with need: Need-based aid available for full-time and part-time students. Work study available nights, weekends, and for part-time students.
Students without need: No-need awards available for academics.

FINANCIAL AID PROCEDURES
Forms required: FAFSA, institutional form.
Dates and Deadlines: No deadline. Must reply within 1 week(s) of notification.
Transfers: No deadline.

CONTACT
Erin Vargas, Director of Financial Aid
20 West Seventh Street, Upland, CA 91786
(909) 931-7599

Whittier College
Whittier, California Federal Code: 001342
www.whittier.edu CSS Code: 4952

4-year private liberal arts college in small city.
Enrollment: 1,291 undergrads. 341 full-time freshmen.
Selectivity: Admits 50 to 75% of applicants.

BASIC COSTS (2009-2010)
Tuition and fees: $34,088.
Per-credit charge: $1,430.
Room and board: $9,548.

FINANCIAL AID PICTURE (2008-2009)
Students with need: Out of 341 full-time freshmen who applied for aid, 213 were judged to have need. Of these, 210 received aid, and 56 had their full need met. Average financial aid package met 94% of need; average scholarship/grant was $15,995; average loan was $6,331. For part-time students, average financial aid package was $23,346.
Students without need: 75 full-time freshmen who did not demonstrate need for aid received scholarships/grants; average award was $8,093. No-need awards available for academics, alumni affiliation, art, leadership, minority status.
Cumulative student debt: 73% of graduating class had student loans; average debt was $31,179.
Additional info: Auditions required for talent scholarship applicants in art, music, and theater.

FINANCIAL AID PROCEDURES
Forms required: FAFSA, CSS PROFILE, institutional form.
Dates and Deadlines: Priority date 3/1; closing date 6/30. Applicants notified on a rolling basis starting 2/15; must reply within 2 week(s) of notification.
Transfers: Priority date 2/1. Applicants notified on a rolling basis starting 3/1; must reply by 6/1 or within 2 week(s) of notification.

CONTACT
David Carnevale, Director of Student Financing
13406 East Philadelphia Street, Whittier, CA 90608-0634
(562) 907-4285

William Jessup University
Rocklin, California
www.jessup.edu Federal Code: 001281

4-year private Bible and liberal arts college in small city, affiliated with nondenominational tradition.
Enrollment: 453 undergrads, 21% part-time. 57 full-time freshmen.
Selectivity: Admits 50 to 75% of applicants.

BASIC COSTS (2009-2010)
Tuition and fees: $19,980.
Per-credit charge: $850.
Room and board: $7,840.

FINANCIAL AID PICTURE (2008-2009)
Students with need: Out of 54 full-time freshmen who applied for aid, 41 were judged to have need. Of these, 41 received aid, and 8 had their full need met. Average financial aid package met 74% of need; average scholarship/grant was $10,033; average loan was $3,257. For part-time students, average financial aid package was $6,789.
Students without need: 10 full-time freshmen who did not demonstrate need for aid received scholarships/grants; average award was $6,900. No-need awards available for academics, athletics, leadership, minority status, music/drama, religious affiliation.
Scholarships offered: 21 full-time freshmen received athletic scholarships; average amount $7,488.
Cumulative student debt: 65% of graduating class had student loans; average debt was $15,802.

FINANCIAL AID PROCEDURES
Forms required: FAFSA.
Dates and Deadlines: Priority date 3/2; no closing date. Applicants notified on a rolling basis starting 3/2; must reply within 3 week(s) of notification.

CONTACT

Korey Compaan, Director of Financial Aid
333 Sunset Boulevard, Rocklin, CA 95765
(916) 577-2233

Woodbury University

Burbank, California
www.woodbury.edu Federal Code: 001343

4-year private university in very large city.
Enrollment: 1,254 undergrads.
Selectivity: Admits 50 to 75% of applicants.

BASIC COSTS (2008-2009)

Tuition and fees: $26,978.
Per-credit charge: $869.
Room and board: $9,093.

FINANCIAL AID PICTURE (2008-2009)

Students with need: 58% of average financial aid package awarded as scholarships/grants, 42% awarded as loans/jobs. Need-based aid available for part-time students. Work study available nights, weekends, and for part-time students.
Students without need: No-need awards available for academics.

FINANCIAL AID PROCEDURES

Forms required: FAFSA, institutional form.
Dates and Deadlines: Priority date 3/2; no closing date. Applicants notified on a rolling basis starting 3/15; must reply by 5/1 or within 2 week(s) of notification.
Transfers: No deadline. Applicants notified on a rolling basis starting 3/15; must reply by 5/1 or within 2 week(s) of notification.

CONTACT

Celeastia Williams, Director of Enrollment Services
7500 Glenoaks Boulevard, Burbank, CA 91510-7846
(818) 767-0888 ext. 273

Yuba Community College District

Marysville, California
www.yccd.edu Federal Code: 001344

2-year public community college in small city.
Enrollment: 4,891 undergrads.
Selectivity: Open admission; but selective for some programs.

BASIC COSTS (2008-2009)

Tuition and fees: $612; out-of-state residents $6,042.
Per-credit charge: $20; out-of-state residents $201.
Additional info: Tuition/fee waivers available for adults.

FINANCIAL AID PICTURE

Students with need: Need-based aid available for full-time and part-time students.
Students without need: No-need awards available for academics, athletics, job skills, minority status, music/drama.
Additional info: Tuition fee waiver based on Board of Governors Grant.

FINANCIAL AID PROCEDURES

Forms required: FAFSA.
Dates and Deadlines: Closing date 3/1. Applicants notified on a rolling basis starting 4/1.

CONTACT

Marisela Arce, Dean for EOP&S and Financial Aid
2088 North Beale Road, Marysville, CA 95901
(530) 741-6781

Colorado

Adams State College

Alamosa, Colorado
www.adams.edu Federal Code: 001345

4-year public liberal arts college in small town.
Enrollment: 2,110 undergrads, 21% part-time. 463 full-time freshmen.
Selectivity: Admits 50 to 75% of applicants.

BASIC COSTS (2008-2009)

Tuition and fees: $3,790; out-of-state residents $12,919.
Room and board: $6,640.

FINANCIAL AID PICTURE (2007-2008)

Students with need: Need-based aid available for full-time and part-time students. Work study available nights, weekends, and for part-time students.
Students without need: No-need awards available for academics, alumni affiliation, art, athletics, leadership, minority status, music/drama, state/district residency.

FINANCIAL AID PROCEDURES

Forms required: FAFSA.
Dates and Deadlines: Priority date 3/1; closing date 4/15. Applicants notified on a rolling basis starting 4/30; must reply within 4 week(s) of notification.
Transfers: No deadline. Applicants notified on a rolling basis starting 4/30.

CONTACT

Philip Schroeder, Director of Financial Aid
208 Edgemont Boulevard, Alamosa, CO 81102
(719) 587-7306

Aims Community College

Greeley, Colorado
www.aims.edu Federal Code: 007582

2-year public community college in small city.
Enrollment: 3,547 undergrads.
Selectivity: Open admission; but selective for some programs.

BASIC COSTS (2008-2009)

Tuition and fees: $2,115; out-of-district residents $2,925; out-of-state residents $11,085.
Per-credit charge: $55; out-of-district residents $82; out-of-state residents $354.
Additional info: Tuition/fee waivers available for adults.

FINANCIAL AID PICTURE (2007-2008)

Students with need: 51% of average financial aid package awarded as scholarships/grants, 49% awarded as loans/jobs.

FINANCIAL AID PROCEDURES

Forms required: FAFSA.
Dates and Deadlines: Priority date 4/15; no closing date. Applicants notified on a rolling basis starting 6/1.

CONTACT

Teri Dorchuck, Financial Aid Director
5401 West 20th Street, Greeley, CO 80632
(970) 330-8008 ext. 6304

Arapahoe Community College

Littleton, Colorado
www.arapahoe.edu Federal Code: 001346

2-year public community college in large town.
Enrollment: 5,250 undergrads, 68% part-time. 372 full-time freshmen.
Selectivity: Open admission; but selective for some programs.

BASIC COSTS (2008-2009)

Tuition and fees: $2,631; out-of-state residents $11,455.
Per-credit charge: $81; out-of-state residents $375.
Additional info: In-state tuition based upon assumption of Colorado Opportunity Fund waiver of $92 per-credit-hour.

FINANCIAL AID PICTURE (2007-2008)

Students with need: Need-based aid available for full-time and part-time students. Work study available nights, weekends, and for part-time students.
Students without need: No-need awards available for academics, leadership, state/district residency.
Scholarships offered: President's Scholarship; based on minimum 3.0 GPA, references. College Bound Scholarship; based on high GED score. All awards $750 for full-time students, $375 for half-time, $563 for three-quarters time. Awards made on first-come first-served basis.

FINANCIAL AID PROCEDURES

Forms required: FAFSA, institutional form.
Dates and Deadlines: Priority date 5/1; no closing date. Applicants notified on a rolling basis starting 5/1; must reply within 3 week(s) of notification.
Transfers: No deadline. Applicants notified on a rolling basis starting 5/1.

CONTACT

Thad Spaulding, Associate Director of Financial Aid
PO Box 9002, Littleton, CO 80160-9002
(303) 797-5661

Art Institute of Colorado

Denver, Colorado
www.aic.artinstitutes.edu Federal Code: 013961

4-year for-profit culinary school and visual arts college in very large city.
Enrollment: 2,404 undergrads, 41% part-time. 406 full-time freshmen.

BASIC COSTS (2008-2009)

Tuition and fees: $21,992.
Per-credit charge: $454.
Additional info: Supply kit $585-$1,965 depending on program. Tuition at time of enrollment locked for 4 years.

FINANCIAL AID PICTURE (2008-2009)

Students with need: Need-based aid available for full-time and part-time students. Work study available nights, weekends, and for part-time students.
Additional info: Tuition at time of first enrollment guaranteed to students for 4 years providing student maintains continuous attendance and completes program within 150% of program length.

FINANCIAL AID PROCEDURES

Forms required: FAFSA, institutional form.
Dates and Deadlines: No deadline. Applicants notified on a rolling basis.
Transfers: No deadline.

CONTACT

Shannon May, Director of Student Financial Services
1200 Lincoln Street, Denver, CO 80203-2983
(303) 824-4757

Bel-Rea Institute of Animal Technology

Denver, Colorado
www.bel-rea.com Federal Code: 012670

2-year for-profit technical college in very large city.
Enrollment: 645 undergrads.

BASIC COSTS (2008-2009)

Additional info: Tuition for full associate program $22,750 including fees.

FINANCIAL AID PICTURE

Students with need: Need-based aid available for full-time students.
Students without need: This college awards aid only to students with need.

FINANCIAL AID PROCEDURES

Forms required: FAFSA.
Dates and Deadlines: Priority date 8/31; no closing date. Applicants notified on a rolling basis starting 8/15.
Transfers: No deadline.

CONTACT

Stasi Botinelli, Financial Aid Director
1681 South Dayton Street, Denver, CO 80247
(303) 751-8700

Boulder College of Massage Therapy

Boulder, Colorado
www.bcmt.org Federal Code: 030131

2-year private health science college in small city.
Enrollment: 185 undergrads.
Selectivity: Open admission; but selective for some programs.

BASIC COSTS (2008-2009)

Additional info: Program costs range from $13,700-$17,500.

FINANCIAL AID PICTURE

Students with need: Need-based aid available for full-time and part-time students.
Students without need: This college awards aid only to students with need.

FINANCIAL AID PROCEDURES

Forms required: FAFSA.
Dates and Deadlines: No deadline.

CONTACT

Debbie Clarke, Director of Financial Aid
6255 Longbow Drive, Boulder, CO 80301
(303) 530-2100 ext. 106

Cambridge College

Aurora, Colorado
www.cambridgecollege.com Federal Code: 021829

2-year for-profit technical college in small city.
Enrollment: 585 undergrads.

BASIC COSTS (2008-2009)

Additional info: Tuition for associate degree programs ranges from $22,950 to $24,500 depending on program; tuition for diploma programs ranges from $11,550 to $23,550. Items such as books, uniforms and other fees are included in the total cost.

FINANCIAL AID PICTURE

Students with need: Need-based aid available for full-time students.

Students without need: This college awards aid only to students with need.

FINANCIAL AID PROCEDURES

Forms required: FAFSA, institutional form.

Dates and Deadlines: No deadline. Applicants notified on a rolling basis.

CONTACT

Gerry Major, Director of Financial Aid
350 Blackhawk Street, Aurora, CO 80011
(720) 859-7900

CollegeAmerica: Colorado Springs

Colorado Springs, Colorado
www.collegeamerica.edu

4-year for-profit career college in large city.

Enrollment: 388 undergrads. 82 full-time freshmen.

Selectivity: Open admission.

BASIC COSTS (2008-2009)

Additional info: Tuition ranges from $342 to $392 per quarter credit depending on program. First-year tuition for associates degree is $14,505 and $14,215 for bachelor's degree.

FINANCIAL AID PICTURE

Students with need: Need-based aid available for full-time and part-time students.

FINANCIAL AID PROCEDURES

Forms required: FAFSA, institutional form.

Dates and Deadlines: No deadline.

CONTACT

3645 Citadel Drive South, Colorado Springs, CO 80909

Colorado Christian University

Lakewood, Colorado
www.ccu.edu Federal Code: 009401

4-year private university and liberal arts college in large city, affiliated with nondenominational tradition.

Enrollment: 2,024 undergrads, 38% part-time. 209 full-time freshmen.

Selectivity: Admits less than 50% of applicants.

BASIC COSTS (2009-2010)

Tuition and fees: $21,130.

Per-credit charge: $950.

Room and board: $8,455.

FINANCIAL AID PICTURE (2007-2008)

Students with need: Out of 157 full-time freshmen who applied for aid, 117 were judged to have need. Of these, 117 received aid. Average financial aid package met 35% of need; average scholarship/grant was $8,678; average loan was $3,326. For part-time students, average financial aid package was $5,500.

Students without need: 68 full-time freshmen who did not demonstrate need for aid received scholarships/grants; average award was $7,071. No-need awards available for academics, athletics, leadership, music/drama.

Scholarships offered: 49 full-time freshmen received athletic scholarships; average amount $1,735.

Cumulative student debt: 61% of graduating class had student loans; average debt was $17,539.

FINANCIAL AID PROCEDURES

Forms required: FAFSA.

Dates and Deadlines: Priority date 3/15; no closing date. Applicants notified on a rolling basis starting 4/1; must reply by 5/1 or within 4 week(s) of notification.

Transfers: Priority date 3/1; no deadline. Applicants notified by 3/10; must reply within 4 week(s) of notification.

CONTACT

Steve Woodburn, Director of Student Financial Aid
8787 West Alameda Avenue, Lakewood, CO 80226
(303) 963-3230

Colorado College

Colorado Springs, Colorado Federal Code: 001347
www.coloradocollege.edu CSS Code: 4072

4-year private liberal arts college in large city.

Enrollment: 1,972 undergrads. 550 full-time freshmen.

Selectivity: Admits less than 50% of applicants.

BASIC COSTS (2009-2010)

Tuition and fees: $37,478.

Per-credit charge: $1,165.

Room and board: $9,624.

FINANCIAL AID PICTURE (2008-2009)

Students with need: Out of 286 full-time freshmen who applied for aid, 236 were judged to have need. Of these, 236 received aid, and 45 had their full need met. Average financial aid package met 95% of need; average scholarship/grant was $29,371; average loan was $1,861. For part-time students, average financial aid package was $21,056.

Students without need: 49 full-time freshmen who did not demonstrate need for aid received scholarships/grants; average award was $10,098. No-need awards available for academics, athletics.

Scholarships offered: ***Merit:*** Barnes Scholarship; full tuition; available in all natural sciences; 4 or 5 awarded in chemistry, 4 available in remaining natural sciences. Trustee Scholarship; $7,000; based on highly rated entering students; 10 awarded. Merit Awards; up to $2,000; for National Merit finalists. Men's Ice Hockey and Women's Soccer merit awards. Colorado College Scholars; 10 merit awards for highly rated entering students from Colorado. ***Athletic:*** 6 full-time freshmen received athletic scholarships; average amount $31,899.

Cumulative student debt: 39% of graduating class had student loans; average debt was $16,041.

Additional info: Need-based financial aid available only to students enrolled half-time or more.

FINANCIAL AID PROCEDURES

Forms required: FAFSA, CSS PROFILE.

Dates and Deadlines: Closing date 2/15. Applicants notified by 3/20; must reply by 5/1.

Transfers: Closing date 4/1. Transfer students might not receive full-need package during first year.

CONTACT

James Swanson, Director of Financial Aid
14 East Cache La Poudre Street, Colorado Springs, CO 80903-9854
(719) 389-6651

Colorado Mountain College

Glenwood Springs, Colorado
www.coloradomtn.edu Federal Code: 004506

2-year public community and liberal arts college in small town.

Enrollment: 5,200 undergrads.

Selectivity: Open admission; but selective for some programs.

BASIC COSTS (2008-2009)
Tuition and fees: $1,550; out-of-district residents $2,450; out-of-state residents $7,250.
Per-credit charge: $45; out-of-district residents $75; out-of-state residents $235.
Room and board: $7,040.

FINANCIAL AID PICTURE (2007-2008)
Students with need: Need-based aid available for full-time and part-time students. Work study available nights, weekends, and for part-time students.
Students without need: This college awards aid only to students with need.

FINANCIAL AID PROCEDURES
Forms required: FAFSA.
Dates and Deadlines: Priority date 3/31; no closing date. Applicants notified on a rolling basis starting 5/15; must reply within 4 week(s) of notification.
Transfers: Transfer scholarships available for Colorado residents with 3.0 GPA and minimum 20 credit hours from previous schools.

CONTACT
Gary Lewis, Director of Student Financial Aid
831 Grand Avenue, Glenwood Springs, CO 81601
(970) 947-8277

Colorado Northwestern Community College
Rangely, Colorado
www.cncc.edu Federal Code: 001359

2-year public community college in rural community.
Enrollment: 1,000 undergrads.
Selectivity: Open admission; but selective for some programs.

BASIC COSTS (2008-2009)
Tuition and fees: $2,648; out-of-state residents $5,408.
Per-credit charge: $81; out-of-state residents $173.
Room and board: $5,650.
Additional info: In-state tuition based upon assumption of Colorado Opportunity Fund waiver of $92 per-credit-hour.

FINANCIAL AID PICTURE (2007-2008)
Students with need: Need-based aid available for full-time and part-time students. Work study available nights, weekends, and for part-time students.
Students without need: No-need awards available for academics, athletics, state/district residency.
Scholarships offered: Academic Scholarships; $200-$1,000; for Colorado residents based on grades, specific talent, area of study; requires application, essay, informal interview, 2.5 GPA.

FINANCIAL AID PROCEDURES
Forms required: FAFSA, institutional form.
Dates and Deadlines: Priority date 5/1; no closing date. Applicants notified on a rolling basis starting 5/15; must reply within 4 week(s) of notification.
Transfers: No deadline.

CONTACT
Merrie Byers, Financial Aid Technician
500 Kennedy Drive, Rangely, CO 81648
(970) 675-3204

Colorado School of Healing Arts
Lakewood, Colorado
www.csha.net Federal Code: 035844

2-year for-profit career college in small city.
Enrollment: 196 undergrads.
Selectivity: Open admission.

BASIC COSTS (2008-2009)
Tuition and fees: $11,275.
Per-credit charge: $150.
Additional info: Books, massage table package, materials fees, and insurance are included in required fees.

FINANCIAL AID PICTURE (2007-2008)
Students with need: Need-based aid available for full-time and part-time students.
Students without need: This college awards aid only to students with need.

FINANCIAL AID PROCEDURES
Forms required: FAFSA.
Dates and Deadlines: No deadline.

CONTACT
Gina Simpson, Director of Financial Aid
7655 West Mississippi, Suite 100, Lakewood, CO 80226
(303) 986-2320

Colorado School of Mines
Golden, Colorado
www.mines.edu Federal Code: 001348

4-year public university and engineering college in large town.
Enrollment: 3,400 undergrads, 5% part-time. 810 full-time freshmen.
Selectivity: Admits 50 to 75% of applicants.

BASIC COSTS (2008-2009)
Tuition and fees: $11,238; out-of-state residents $25,248.
Per-credit charge: $327; out-of-state residents $794.
Room and board: $7,626.

FINANCIAL AID PICTURE (2008-2009)
Students with need: Out of 605 full-time freshmen who applied for aid, 550 were judged to have need. Of these, 550 received aid, and 450 had their full need met. Average financial aid package met 93% of need; average scholarship/grant was $8,750; average loan was $5,450. Need-based aid available for part-time students.
Students without need: 90 full-time freshmen who did not demonstrate need for aid received scholarships/grants; average award was $5,500. No-need awards available for academics, alumni affiliation, athletics, music/drama, ROTC.
Scholarships offered: 125 full-time freshmen received athletic scholarships; average amount $3,000.
Cumulative student debt. 95% of graduating class had student loans; average debt was $22,500.

FINANCIAL AID PROCEDURES
Forms required: FAFSA.
Dates and Deadlines: Priority date 2/15; no closing date. Applicants notified on a rolling basis starting 3/15; must reply by 5/1 or within 2 week(s) of notification.
Transfers: Applicants notified on a rolling basis starting 3/15; must reply by 5/1 or within 2 week(s) of notification. Federal aid only (Pell grant and Stafford loan) available for second undergraduate degree candidates.

CONTACT

Roger Koester, Director of Financial Aid
Undergraduate Admissions, Golden, CO 80401
(303) 273-3220

Colorado School of Trades

Lakewood, Colorado
www.schooloftrades.com Federal Code: 013513

2-year for-profit technical college in small city.
Enrollment: 145 undergrads.
Selectivity: Open admission.

BASIC COSTS (2008-2009)

Additional info: For gunsmithing program: tuition, $18,000; tools $3,000, miscellaneous $154. Farrier science program is no longer offered.

FINANCIAL AID PICTURE (2008-2009)

Students with need: Need-based aid available for full-time students.

FINANCIAL AID PROCEDURES

Forms required: FAFSA, institutional form.

CONTACT

Robert Martin, President
1575 Hoyt Street, Lakewood, CO 80215
(303) 233-4697 ext. 14

Colorado State University

Fort Collins, Colorado
www.colostate.edu Federal Code: 001350

4-year public university in small city.
Enrollment: 20,829 undergrads, 7% part-time. 4,351 full-time freshmen.
Selectivity: Admits over 75% of applicants.

BASIC COSTS (2008-2009)

Tuition and fees: $5,874; out-of-state residents $21,590.
Per-credit charge: $221; out-of-state residents $1,007.
Room and board: $8,134.

FINANCIAL AID PICTURE (2007-2008)

Students with need: Out of 2,515 full-time freshmen who applied for aid, 1,442 were judged to have need. Of these, 1,442 received aid, and 461 had their full need met. Average financial aid package met 66% of need; average scholarship/grant was $5,422; average loan was $3,999. For part-time students, average financial aid package was $6,944.
Students without need: 209 full-time freshmen who did not demonstrate need for aid received scholarships/grants; average award was $2,453. No-need awards available for academics, art, athletics, leadership, music/drama, ROTC, state/district residency.
Scholarships offered: 43 full-time freshmen received athletic scholarships; average amount $17,693.
Cumulative student debt: 61% of graduating class had student loans; average debt was $18,607.
Additional info: High-need CO residents put into Economically Disadvantaged group, providing scholarships, grants and work study for the first year. CSU Land Grant Award guarantees full-time Pell-eligible CO residents are funded at minimum of tuition and fees.

FINANCIAL AID PROCEDURES

Forms required: FAFSA.
Dates and Deadlines: Priority date 3/1; no closing date. Applicants notified on a rolling basis starting 3/1.

CONTACT

Sandra Calhoun, Director of Student Financial Aid/Registrar
Office of Admissions/Colorado State University, Fort Collins, CO 80523-1062
(970) 491-6321

Colorado State University: Pueblo

Pueblo, Colorado
www.colostate-pueblo.edu Federal Code: 001365

4-year public university in small city.
Enrollment: 4,401 undergrads, 21% part-time. 983 full-time freshmen.
Selectivity: Admits over 75% of applicants.

BASIC COSTS (2008-2009)

Tuition and fees: $4,667; out-of-state residents $14,788.
Room and board: $6,300.
Additional info: WUE tuition is $2,713 less per semester than out-of-state rate. Differential tuition charged for business, nursing, computer information systems, and engineering courses at $18 more per-credit-hour.

FINANCIAL AID PICTURE (2008-2009)

Students with need: Average financial aid package met 63% of need; average scholarship/grant was $5,498; average loan was $3,249. For part-time students, average financial aid package was $7,141.
Students without need: No-need awards available for academics, alumni affiliation, art, athletics, job skills, leadership, minority status, music/drama, ROTC, state/district residency.
Cumulative student debt: 54% of graduating class had student loans; average debt was $16,981.

FINANCIAL AID PROCEDURES

Forms required: FAFSA, institutional form.
Dates and Deadlines: Priority date 3/1; no closing date. Applicants notified on a rolling basis starting 3/13; must reply within 3 week(s) of notification.

CONTACT

Sean McGivney, Director of Financial Aid
2200 Bonforte Boulevard, Pueblo, CO 81001-4901
(719) 549-2753

Colorado Technical University

Colorado Springs, Colorado
www.coloradotech.edu Federal Code: 010148

4-year for-profit university and technical college in large city.
Enrollment: 1,200 undergrads.

BASIC COSTS (2008-2009)

Tuition and fees: $13,025.
Per-credit charge: $285.
Additional info: Lab fees $30 per lab class.

FINANCIAL AID PICTURE

Students with need: Need-based aid available for full-time and part-time students. Work study available nights, weekends, and for part-time students.
Students without need: No-need awards available for academics, ROTC.

FINANCIAL AID PROCEDURES

Forms required: FAFSA.
Dates and Deadlines: No deadline. Applicants notified on a rolling basis starting 6/30.
Transfers: No deadline.

CONTACT

Cindy Rubek, Director of Student Financial Services
4435 North Chestnut Street, Colorado Springs, CO 80907
(719) 598-0200

Community College of Aurora

Aurora, Colorado
www.ccaurora.edu Federal Code: 016058

2-year public community college in large city.
Enrollment: 1,285 full-time undergrads.
Selectivity: Open admission.

BASIC COSTS (2008-2009)
Tuition and fees: $2,576; out-of-state residents $11,400.
Per-credit charge: $81; out-of-state residents $375.
Additional info: In-state tuition based upon assumption of Colorado Opportunity Fund waiver of $92 per-credit-hour.

FINANCIAL AID PICTURE
Students with need: Need-based aid available for full-time and part-time students. Work study available nights.

FINANCIAL AID PROCEDURES
Forms required: FAFSA, institutional form.
Dates and Deadlines: Priority date 6/1; no closing date. Applicants notified on a rolling basis starting 7/15.

CONTACT
John Young, Executive Director, Financial Aid
16000 East CentreTech Parkway, Aurora, CO 80011-9036
(303) 360-4709

Community College of Denver

Denver, Colorado
www.ccd.edu Federal Code: 009542

2-year public community college in very large city.
Enrollment: 5,260 undergrads, 68% part-time. 713 full-time freshmen.
Selectivity: Open admission; but selective for some programs.

BASIC COSTS (2008-2009)
Tuition and fees: $2,942; out-of-state residents $11,766.
Per-credit charge: $81; out-of-state residents $375.
Additional info: In-state tuition based upon assumption of Colorado Opportunity Fund waiver of $92 per-credit-hour.

FINANCIAL AID PICTURE (2007-2008)
Students with need: Need-based aid available for full-time and part-time students.
Students without need: No-need awards available for academics, leadership, state/district residency.

FINANCIAL AID PROCEDURES
Forms required: FAFSA, institutional form.
Dates and Deadlines: Priority date 3/1; no closing date.

CONTACT
Karla Nash, Director of Financial Aid
Campus Box 201, PO Box 173363, Denver, CO 80217-3363
(303) 556-2420

DeVry University: Westminster

Westminster, Colorado
www.devry.edu Federal Code: 014831

4-year for-profit university in very large city.
Enrollment: 718 undergrads, 59% part-time. 43 full-time freshmen.

BASIC COSTS (2008-2009)
Tuition and fees: $14,130.
Per-credit charge: $515.

FINANCIAL AID PICTURE (2007-2008)
Students with need: Out of 29 full-time freshmen who applied for aid, 25 were judged to have need. Of these, 25 received aid, and 4 had their full need met. Average financial aid package met 35% of need; average scholarship/grant was $5,510; average loan was $6,000. For part-time students, average financial aid package was $9,942.
Students without need: This college awards aid only to students with need.
Cumulative student debt: 100% of graduating class had student loans; average debt was $11,071.

FINANCIAL AID PROCEDURES
Forms required: FAFSA.
Dates and Deadlines: No deadline. Applicants notified on a rolling basis.

CONTACT
Terry Bargas, Director of Financial Aid
1870 West 122 Avenue, Westminster, CO 80234-2010
(303) 329-3340

Everest College: Aurora

Aurora, Colorado
www.cci.edu Federal Code: 004507

2-year for-profit branch campus and technical college in large city.
Enrollment: 65 undergrads.
Selectivity: Open admission.

BASIC COSTS (2008-2009)
Additional info: $352 per credit hour for all linear programs; $500 estimated cost per term for books, kits and supplies.

FINANCIAL AID PICTURE (2008-2009)
Students with need: Need-based aid available for full-time and part-time students. Work study available nights.
Students without need: This college awards aid only to students with need.

FINANCIAL AID PROCEDURES
Forms required: FAFSA, state aid form, institutional form.
Dates and Deadlines: No deadline. Applicants notified on a rolling basis; must reply within 4 week(s) of notification.
Transfers: $4,500 limitation on Colorado State Grant per award year.

CONTACT
Ray Hamel, Finance Director
14280 East Jewell Suite 100, Aurora, CO 80012
(303) 745-6244 ext. 104

Everest College: Colorado Springs

Colorado Springs, Colorado
www.cci.edu Federal Code: 004503

2-year for-profit business and junior college in large city.
Enrollment: 454 undergrads.
Selectivity: Open admission.

BASIC COSTS (2008-2009)

Additional info: Accounting, Business Administration, Administrative Assistant, Criminal Justice and Paralegal programs are $328 per credit hour. CIS ? Networking, Programming and Web Design are $330 per credit hour. Business Accounting is $331 per credit hour. Diploma programs for Medical Assisting, Medical Administrative Assistant and Medical Billing and Coding are $13,140 (includes books) for the entire 8-month program. No additional fees.

FINANCIAL AID PICTURE

Students with need: Need-based aid available for full-time and part-time students. Work study available nights.

FINANCIAL AID PROCEDURES

Forms required: FAFSA, institutional form.
Dates and Deadlines: No deadline. Applicants notified on a rolling basis starting 7/1.
Transfers: No deadline.

CONTACT

Meng Johnson, FA Director
1815 Jet Wing Drive, Colorado Springs, CO 80916
(719) 638-6580 ext. 103

Fort Lewis College

Durango, Colorado
www.fortlewis.edu Federal Code: 001353

4-year public liberal arts college in large town.
Enrollment: 3,611 undergrads, 8% part-time. 893 full-time freshmen.
Selectivity: Admits 50 to 75% of applicants.

BASIC COSTS (2008-2009)

Tuition and fees: $4,196; out-of-state residents $16,512.
Per-credit charge: $142; out-of-state residents $758.
Room and board: $7,170.
Additional info: Tuition/fee waivers available for minority students.

FINANCIAL AID PICTURE (2007-2008)

Students with need: Out of 646 full-time freshmen who applied for aid, 440 were judged to have need. Of these, 438 received aid, and 83 had their full need met. Average financial aid package met 66% of need; average scholarship/grant was $3,950; average loan was $3,333. For part-time students, average financial aid package was $6,034.
Students without need: 258 full-time freshmen who did not demonstrate need for aid received scholarships/grants; average award was $670. No-need awards available for academics, alumni affiliation, art, athletics, job skills, leadership, minority status, music/drama, state/district residency.
Scholarships offered: ***Merit:*** Presidential Scholarship; $8,000 out-of-state, $2,000 in-state; 121 admission index required. Provost Scholarship; $7,000 out-of-state, $1,500 in-state; 110-120 admission index required. Dean's Scholarship; $6,000 out-of-state, $1,000 in-state; 101-109 admission index required. Academic Promise Scholarship; $4,000 out-of-state, $750 in-state; 92-100 admission index required. New Mexico Reciprocal Scholarship; New Mexico residents are given in-state tuition rates; must have 3.5 GPA or higher; number of awards limited. ***Athletic:*** 31 full-time freshmen received athletic scholarships; average amount $3,416.
Cumulative student debt: 52% of graduating class had student loans; average debt was $17,962.
Additional info: Tuition waived for Native Americans of federally recognized tribes; census number and Certificate of Indian Blood must accompany application.

FINANCIAL AID PROCEDURES

Forms required: FAFSA.
Dates and Deadlines: Priority date 2/15; no closing date. Applicants notified on a rolling basis starting 3/15; must reply within 2 week(s) of notification.
Transfers: Closing date 2/15. Applicants notified on a rolling basis starting 3/15; must reply within 2 week(s) of notification.

CONTACT

Elaine Redwine, Director of Financial Aid
1000 Rim Drive, Durango, CO 81301-3999
(970) 247-7142

Front Range Community College

Westminster, Colorado
www.frontrange.edu Federal Code: 007933

2-year public community college in large city.
Enrollment: 12,583 undergrads, 61% part-time. 1,136 full-time freshmen.
Selectivity: Open admission.

BASIC COSTS (2008-2009)

Tuition and fees: $2,715; out-of-state residents $11,539.
Per-credit charge: $81; out-of-state residents $375.
Additional info: In-state tuition based upon assumption of Colorado Opportunity Fund waiver of $92 per-credit-hour.

FINANCIAL AID PICTURE (2007-2008)

Students with need: 40% of average financial aid package awarded as scholarships/grants, 60% awarded as loans/jobs. Need-based aid available for part-time students. Work study available nights, weekends, and for part-time students.
Students without need: No-need awards available for academics, job skills, leadership, ROTC, state/district residency.

FINANCIAL AID PROCEDURES

Forms required: FAFSA, institutional form.
Dates and Deadlines: Priority date 5/1; no closing date. Applicants notified on a rolling basis starting 7/1; must reply within 3 week(s) of notification.

CONTACT

Director of Financial Aid
3645 West 112th Avenue, Westminster, CO 80031
(303) 439-9454

IntelliTec College

Colorado Springs, Colorado
www.intelliteccollege.com Federal Code: 008635

2-year for-profit technical college in large city.
Enrollment: 500 undergrads.
Selectivity: Open admission.

BASIC COSTS (2008-2009)

Additional info: HVAC $24,177; CNSA $24,969; ATM $24,822; DAS $21,828; DMECH $22,122.

FINANCIAL AID PICTURE

Students with need: Need-based aid available for full-time and part-time students. Work study available nights.
Students without need: This college awards aid only to students with need.

FINANCIAL AID PROCEDURES

Forms required: FAFSA, state aid form, institutional form.
Dates and Deadlines: No deadline. Applicants notified on a rolling basis.
Transfers: No deadline.

CONTACT

Laurie Roth, Financial Services Representative
2315 East Pikes Peak Avenue, Colorado Springs, CO 80909
(719) 632-7626

IntelliTec College: Grand Junction

Grand Junction, Colorado
www.intelliteccollege.edu Federal Code: 030669

2-year for-profit technical college in small city.
Enrollment: 152 undergrads. 64 full-time freshmen.
Selectivity: Open admission.

BASIC COSTS (2008-2009)

Additional info: $200 per-credit-hour charge for all programs. Number of credits required for completion varies by program. Total costs for some programs include: Medical Assistant, $18,200; Massage Therapist, $14,600; Architectural/Structural Drafting, $22,200. Tuition at time of enrollment locked for 2 years.

FINANCIAL AID PICTURE

Students with need: Need-based aid available for full-time students.
Students without need: This college awards aid only to students with need.

FINANCIAL AID PROCEDURES

Forms required: FAFSA.
Dates and Deadlines: No deadline. Applicants notified on a rolling basis.
Transfers: No deadline.

CONTACT

Lisa Watson, Director of Financial Sevices
772 Horizon Drive, Grand Junction, CO 81506
(970) 245-8101

Johnson & Wales University: Denver

Denver, Colorado
www.jwu.edu Federal Code: 003404

4-year private university in large city.
Enrollment: 1,454 undergrads, 3% part-time. 395 full-time freshmen.
Selectivity: Admits 50 to 75% of applicants.

BASIC COSTS (2009-2010)

Tuition and fees: $23,490.
Room and board: $9,249.
Additional info: Optional weekend meal plan available for $1,068.

FINANCIAL AID PICTURE (2008-2009)

Students with need: Out of 377 full-time freshmen who applied for aid, 295 were judged to have need. Of these, 295 received aid, and 30 had their full need met. Average financial aid package met 66% of need; average scholarship/grant was $7,226; average loan was $3,260. For part-time students, average financial aid package was $9,715.
Students without need: 77 full-time freshmen who did not demonstrate need for aid received scholarships/grants; average award was $6,025. No-need awards available for academics, alumni affiliation, job skills, leadership, state/district residency.
Cumulative student debt: 82% of graduating class had student loans; average debt was $28,354.

FINANCIAL AID PROCEDURES

Forms required: FAFSA.
Dates and Deadlines: No deadline. Applicants notified on a rolling basis starting 3/1; must reply within 2 week(s) of notification.

CONTACT

Lynn Robinson, Chief Financial Aid Officer
7150 Montview Boulevard, Denver, CO 80220
(800) 342-5598 ext. 4648

Lamar Community College

Lamar, Colorado
www.lamarcc.edu Federal Code: 001355

2-year public community college in large town.
Enrollment: 612 undergrads.
Selectivity: Open admission; but selective for some programs.

BASIC COSTS (2008-2009)

Tuition and fees: $2,812; out-of-state residents $5,572.
Per-credit charge: $81; out-of-state residents $173.
Room and board: $4,995.
Additional info: In-state tuition based upon assumption of Colorado Opportunity Fund waiver of $92 per-credit-hour.

FINANCIAL AID PICTURE

Students with need: Need-based aid available for full-time and part-time students.

FINANCIAL AID PROCEDURES

Forms required: FAFSA, institutional form.
Dates and Deadlines: Priority date 4/1; no closing date. Applicants notified on a rolling basis starting 7/1.
Transfers: No deadline.

CONTACT

Linda Becker, Director of Financial Aid
2401 South Main Street, Lamar, CO 81052-3999

Mesa State College

Grand Junction, Colorado
www.mesastate.edu Federal Code: 001358

4-year public community and liberal arts college in small city.
Enrollment: 5,617 undergrads, 23% part-time. 1,207 full-time freshmen.
Selectivity: Admits over 75% of applicants.

BASIC COSTS (2008-2009)

Tuition and fees: $4,738; out-of-state residents $13,512.
Per-credit charge: $154; out-of-state residents $468.
Room and board: $7,355.

FINANCIAL AID PICTURE (2007-2008)

Students with need: Out of 1,082 full-time freshmen who applied for aid, 1,004 were judged to have need. Of these, 1,004 received aid, and 129 had their full need met. Average financial aid package met 45% of need; average scholarship/grant was $3,762; average loan was $3,666. For part-time students, average financial aid package was $5,254.
Students without need: No-need awards available for academics, art, athletics, leadership, minority status, music/drama.
Scholarships offered: 86 full-time freshmen received athletic scholarships; average amount $3,104.
Cumulative student debt: 56% of graduating class had student loans; average debt was $19,178.

FINANCIAL AID PROCEDURES

Forms required: FAFSA.
Dates and Deadlines: Priority date 3/1; no closing date. Applicants notified on a rolling basis starting 4/1; must reply within 5 week(s) of notification.

CONTACT

Curt Martin, Director of Financial Aid
1100 North Avenue, Grand Junction, CO 81501
(970) 248-1396

Metropolitan State College of Denver

Denver, Colorado
www.mscd.edu Federal Code: 001360

4-year public liberal arts college in very large city.
Enrollment: 20,662 undergrads, 39% part-time. 1,994 full-time freshmen.
Selectivity: Admits 50 to 75% of applicants.

BASIC COSTS (2008-2009)

Tuition and fees: $3,241; out-of-state residents $11,949.
Per-credit charge: $109; out-of-state residents $472.

FINANCIAL AID PICTURE (2007-2008)

Students with need: 34% of average financial aid package awarded as scholarships/grants, 66% awarded as loans/jobs. Need-based aid available for part-time students.
Students without need: No-need awards available for academics, art, athletics, job skills, music/drama, state/district residency.

FINANCIAL AID PROCEDURES

Forms required: FAFSA.
Dates and Deadlines: Priority date 2/15; no closing date. Applicants notified on a rolling basis starting 3/1.
Transfers: No deadline.

CONTACT

Cindy Hejl, Director of Financial Aid
Campus Box 16, Denver, CO 80217

Morgan Community College

Fort Morgan, Colorado
www.morgancc.edu Federal Code: 009981

2-year public community college in large town.
Enrollment: 365 full-time undergrads.
Selectivity: Open admission; but selective for some programs.

BASIC COSTS (2008-2009)

Tuition and fees: $2,597; out-of-state residents $11,421.
Per-credit charge: $81; out-of-state residents $375.
Additional info: In-state tuition based upon assumption of Colorado Opportunity Fund waiver of $92 per-credit-hour.

FINANCIAL AID PICTURE (2008-2009)

Students with need: Need-based aid available for full-time and part-time students. Work study available nights, weekends, and for part-time students.

FINANCIAL AID PROCEDURES

Forms required: FAFSA.
Dates and Deadlines: Priority date 6/1; no closing date. Applicants notified on a rolling basis.

CONTACT

Sally Nestor, Director of Financial Aid
920 Barlow Road, Fort Morgan, CO 80701
(970) 542-3100

Naropa University

Boulder, Colorado
www.naropa.edu Federal Code: 014652

4-year private liberal arts college in small city.
Enrollment: 444 undergrads, 7% part-time. 56 full-time freshmen.
Selectivity: Admits over 75% of applicants.

BASIC COSTS (2009-2010)

Tuition and fees: $23,520.
Per-credit charge: $760.
Room and board: $8,478.

FINANCIAL AID PICTURE (2008-2009)

Students with need: Out of 38 full-time freshmen who applied for aid, 34 were judged to have need. Of these, 34 received aid. Average financial aid package met 88% of need; average scholarship/grant was $14,474; average loan was $4,344. For part-time students, average financial aid package was $10,164.
Students without need: This college awards aid only to students with need.
Cumulative student debt: 68% of graduating class had student loans; average debt was $19,359.

FINANCIAL AID PROCEDURES

Forms required: FAFSA.
Dates and Deadlines: Priority date 1/15; closing date 7/1. Applicants notified on a rolling basis starting 1/15; must reply within 4 week(s) of notification.
Transfers: No deadline. Applicants notified on a rolling basis starting 1/15; must reply within 4 week(s) of notification.

CONTACT

Cheryl Barbour, Assistant Vice President of Student Administrative Services
2130 Arapahoe Avenue, Boulder, CO 80302-6697
(303) 546-3534

Nazarene Bible College

Colorado Springs, Colorado
www.nbc.edu Federal Code: 013007

4-year private Bible college in very large city, affiliated with Church of the Nazarene.
Enrollment: 975 undergrads, 81% part-time.
Selectivity: Open admission; but selective for some programs.

BASIC COSTS (2008-2009)

Tuition and fees: $8,580.
Per-credit charge: $275.

FINANCIAL AID PICTURE (2007-2008)

Students with need: Need-based aid available for full-time and part-time students.
Students without need: No-need awards available for religious affiliation.
Additional info: Tuition waiver available to students serving as student body officers.

FINANCIAL AID PROCEDURES

Forms required: FAFSA.
Dates and Deadlines: Priority date 6/1; no closing date. Applicants notified on a rolling basis starting 6/15; must reply within 2 week(s) of notification.

CONTACT

Mal Britton, Director of Financial Aid
1111 Academy Park Loop, Colorado Springs, CO 80910-3704
(719) 884-5050 ext. 5050

Northeastern Junior College

Sterling, Colorado
www.njc.edu Federal Code: 001361

2-year public community and junior college in large town.
Enrollment: 1,421 undergrads, 37% part-time. 440 full-time freshmen.
Selectivity: Open admission; but selective for some programs.

BASIC COSTS (2008-2009)

Tuition and fees: $3,038; out-of-state residents $9,609.

Per-credit charge: $81; out-of-state residents $300.

Room and board: $5,444.

Additional info: In-state tuition based upon assumption of Colorado Opportunity Fund waiver of $92 per-credit-hour. Reduced out-of-state tuition for residents of AK, AZ, CA, HI, ID MT, NV NM, ND, OR, SD, UT, WA, WY may be available under the Western Undergraduate Exchange (WUE) program, and for residents of NE, KS, OK under the Border State Incentive (BUI). Tuition/fee waivers available for adults, minority students.

FINANCIAL AID PICTURE (2007-2008)

Students with need: 56% of average financial aid package awarded as scholarships/grants, 44% awarded as loans/jobs. Need-based aid available for part-time students.

Students without need: No-need awards available for academics, alumni affiliation, art, athletics, job skills, leadership, music/drama, state/district residency.

Additional info: Need-based financial aid available to part-time students taking 6 credits or more per semester.

FINANCIAL AID PROCEDURES

Forms required: FAFSA, institutional form.

Dates and Deadlines: Priority date 3/1; no closing date. Applicants notified on a rolling basis starting 4/15; must reply within 3 week(s) of notification.

Transfers: No deadline. Applicants notified on a rolling basis starting 4/15; must reply within 3 week(s) of notification.

CONTACT

Alice Weingardt, Financial Aid Director
100 College Avenue, Sterling, CO 80751
(970) 521-6800

Otero Junior College

La Junta, Colorado
www.ojc.edu Federal Code: 001362

2-year public community and junior college in small town.

Enrollment: 1,350 undergrads.

Selectivity: Open admission; but selective for some programs.

BASIC COSTS (2008-2009)

Tuition and fees: $2,652; out-of-state residents $5,412.

Per-credit charge: $81; out-of-state residents $173.

Room and board: $4,926.

Additional info: In-state tuition based upon assumption of Colorado Opportunity Fund waiver of $92 per-credit-hour.

FINANCIAL AID PICTURE (2008-2009)

Students with need: Need-based aid available for full-time and part-time students. Work study available nights, weekends, and for part-time students.

Students without need: No-need awards available for academics, athletics, state/district residency.

FINANCIAL AID PROCEDURES

Forms required: FAFSA.

Dates and Deadlines: Priority date 4/15; no closing date. Applicants notified on a rolling basis starting 4/15; must reply within 2 week(s) of notification.

Transfers: No deadline. Applicants notified on a rolling basis starting 4/15; must reply within 2 week(s) of notification.

CONTACT

Janet Carrillo, Financial Aid Director
1802 Colorado Avenue, La Junta, CO 81050
(719) 384-6834

Pikes Peak Community College

Colorado Springs, Colorado
www.ppcc.edu Federal Code: 008896

2-year public community college in large city.

Enrollment: 10,800 undergrads.

Selectivity: Open admission.

BASIC COSTS (2008-2009)

Tuition and fees: $2,658; out-of-state residents $11,482.

Per-credit charge: $81; out-of-state residents $375.

Additional info: In-state tuition eligible for Colorado Opportunity Fund (COF) waiver, currently $92 per credit hour.

FINANCIAL AID PICTURE

Students with need: Need-based aid available for full-time and part-time students. Work study available nights.

FINANCIAL AID PROCEDURES

Forms required: FAFSA.

Dates and Deadlines: Priority date 7/1; no closing date. Applicants notified on a rolling basis starting 8/1; must reply within 2 week(s) of notification.

CONTACT

Sherri McCullough, Assistant Director of Financial Aid
5675 South Academy Boulevard, Colorado Springs, CO 80906-5498
(719) 502-3000

Platt College: Aurora

Aurora, Colorado
www.plattcolorado.edu Federal Code: 030149

4-year for-profit visual arts and nursing college in very large city.

Enrollment: 160 undergrads.

BASIC COSTS (2008-2009)

Additional info: Visual and Performing Arts: associate program: $34,000; Bachelor's program: $50,107. Nursing program (RN): $68,000. Costs include tuition, registration fee, lab fees, supplies. Cost of books, art kit vary with program.

FINANCIAL AID PICTURE

Students with need: Need-based aid available for full-time students.

Students without need: This college awards aid only to students with need.

FINANCIAL AID PROCEDURES

Forms required: FAFSA, institutional form.

Dates and Deadlines: No deadline. Applicants notified on a rolling basis.

CONTACT

Margie Rose, Director of Financial Aid
3100 South Parker Road, Aurora, CO 80014-3141
(303) 369-5151

Pueblo Community College

Pueblo, Colorado
www.pueblocc.edu Federal Code: 014829

2-year public community college in small city.

Enrollment: 4,343 undergrads, 57% part-time. 316 full-time freshmen.

Selectivity: Open admission; but selective for some programs.

BASIC COSTS (2008-2009)

Tuition and fees: $2,700; out-of-state residents $11,524.

Per-credit charge: $81; out-of-state residents $375.

Additional info: In-state tuition based upon assumption of Colorado Opportunity Fund waiver of $92 per-credit-hour.

FINANCIAL AID PICTURE (2007-2008)

Students with need: Average financial aid package met 40% of need; average scholarship/grant was $2,920; average loan was $2,200. For part-time students, average financial aid package was $3,010.

Students without need: 20 full-time freshmen who did not demonstrate need for aid received scholarships/grants; average award was $305. No-need awards available for academics, art, job skills, leadership, music/drama.

Cumulative student debt: 62% of graduating class had student loans; average debt was $11,565.

FINANCIAL AID PROCEDURES

Forms required: FAFSA.

Dates and Deadlines: Priority date 3/15; no closing date. Applicants notified on a rolling basis starting 4/1.

Transfers: No deadline. Applicants notified on a rolling basis starting 4/1.

CONTACT

Ron Swartwood, Director of Financial Aid
900 West Orman Avenue, Pueblo, CO 81004-1499
(719) 549-3020

Red Rocks Community College

Lakewood, Colorado
www.rrcc.edu Federal Code: 009543

2-year public community college in small city.

Enrollment: 5,536 undergrads.

Selectivity: Open admission.

BASIC COSTS (2008-2009)

Tuition and fees: $2,719; out-of-state residents $11,543.

Per-credit charge: $81; out-of-state residents $375.

Additional info: In-state tuition based upon assumption of Colorado Opportunity Fund waiver of $92 per-credit-hour.

FINANCIAL AID PICTURE (2007-2008)

Students with need: Need-based aid available for full-time and part-time students. Work study available nights, weekends, and for part-time students.

FINANCIAL AID PROCEDURES

Forms required: FAFSA, institutional form.

Dates and Deadlines: Priority date 4/1; no closing date. Applicants notified on a rolling basis starting 6/1; must reply within 2 week(s) of notification.

CONTACT

Linda Crook, Director of Financial Aid
13300 West Sixth Avenue, Lakewood, CO 80228-1255
(303) 914-6256

Redstone College

Broomfield, Colorado
www.redstonecollege.com Federal Code: 007297

2-year for-profit technical college in small city.

Enrollment: 440 undergrads.

Selectivity: Open admission.

BASIC COSTS (2008-2009)

Additional info: Tuition for entire associate degree ranges from $30,891 to $35,000 depending on program of study.

FINANCIAL AID PICTURE (2008-2009)

Students with need: Need-based aid available for full-time students.

Students without need: This college awards aid only to students with need.

FINANCIAL AID PROCEDURES

Forms required: FAFSA, state aid form.

Dates and Deadlines: No deadline. Applicants notified on a rolling basis; must reply within 2 week(s) of notification.

CONTACT

Alicia Harbin, Financial Aid Director
10851 West 120th Avenue, Broomfield, CO 80021-3401

Regis University

Denver, Colorado
www.regis.edu Federal Code: 001363

4-year private university and liberal arts college in very large city, affiliated with Roman Catholic Church.

Enrollment: 1,277 undergrads, 3% part-time. 345 full-time freshmen.

Selectivity: Admits 50 to 75% of applicants.

BASIC COSTS (2008-2009)

Tuition and fees: $28,700.

Per-credit charge: $888.

Room and board: $8,982.

Additional info: Tuition-free for any student who does not graduate in 4 years while maintaining required amount of credit hours.

FINANCIAL AID PICTURE (2007-2008)

Students with need: Need-based aid available for full-time and part-time students. Work study available nights, weekends, and for part-time students.

Students without need: No-need awards available for academics, athletics, leadership, minority status, religious affiliation, ROTC, state/district residency.

FINANCIAL AID PROCEDURES

Forms required: FAFSA.

Dates and Deadlines: Priority date 3/1; no closing date. Applicants notified on a rolling basis starting 3/15.

CONTACT

Ellie Miller, Director of Financial Aid
3333 Regis Boulevard, Mail Code B20, Denver, CO 80221-1099
(800) 388-2366 ext. 4126

Remington College: Colorado Springs

Colorado Springs, Colorado
www.remingtoncollege.com Federal Code: 030121

2-year for-profit technical college in very large city.

Enrollment: 170 undergrads.

Selectivity: Open admission; but selective for some programs.

BASIC COSTS (2008-2009)

Additional info: Associate degree programs annual tuition $19,500 plus $50 fees. 8-month diploma program full tuition $13,900 plus $50 fees. Tuition includes textbooks and supplies.

FINANCIAL AID PICTURE (2008-2009)

Students with need: Need-based aid available for full-time and part-time students.

Students without need: This college awards aid only to students with need.

FINANCIAL AID PROCEDURES

Forms required: FAFSA.

Dates and Deadlines: No deadline. Applicants notified on a rolling basis; must reply within 3 week(s) of notification.

Transfers: No deadline. Applicants notified on a rolling basis.

CONTACT

Tara Miller, Director of Student Finance
6050 Erin Park Drive, Colorado Springs, CO 80918
(719) 532-1234 ext. 202

Rocky Mountain College of Art & Design

Denver, Colorado
www.rmcad.edu Federal Code: 013991

4-year for-profit visual arts college in very large city.
Enrollment: 568 undergrads, 15% part-time. 135 full-time freshmen.
Selectivity: Admits over 75% of applicants.

BASIC COSTS (2009-2010)

Tuition and fees: $24,840.
Per-credit charge: $1,035.
Additional info: Flat fee of $12,420 per term for students taking 12 to 18 credits.

FINANCIAL AID PICTURE (2008-2009)

Students with need: Out of 110 full-time freshmen who applied for aid, 103 were judged to have need. Of these, 103 received aid, and 9 had their full need met. Average financial aid package met 60% of need; average scholarship/grant was $3,776; average loan was $3,136. For part-time students, average financial aid package was $8,510.
Students without need: 24 full-time freshmen who did not demonstrate need for aid received scholarships/grants; average award was $5,668. No-need awards available for academics, art, state/district residency.
Cumulative student debt: 74% of graduating class had student loans; average debt was $27,831.

FINANCIAL AID PROCEDURES

Forms required: FAFSA, state aid form, institutional form.
Dates and Deadlines: Priority date 3/15; no closing date. Applicants notified on a rolling basis starting 4/15; must reply within 2 week(s) of notification.

CONTACT

Tammy Dybdahl, Director of Financial Aid
1600 Pierce Street, Denver, CO 80214
(303) 753-6046

Trinidad State Junior College

Trinidad, Colorado
www.trinidadstate.edu Federal Code: 001368

2-year public community and junior college in small town.
Enrollment: 1,692 undergrads.
Selectivity: Open admission; but selective for some programs.

BASIC COSTS (2008-2009)

Tuition and fees: $2,820; out-of-state residents $5,580.
Per-credit charge: $81; out-of-state residents $173.
Room and board: $4,692.
Additional info: In-state tuition based upon assumption of Colorado Opportunity Fund waiver of $92 per-credit-hour.

FINANCIAL AID PICTURE (2007-2008)

Students with need: 70% of average financial aid package awarded as scholarships/grants, 30% awarded as loans/jobs. Need-based aid available for part-time students. Work study available nights.
Students without need: No-need awards available for academics, athletics, state/district residency.

FINANCIAL AID PROCEDURES

Forms required: FAFSA, institutional form.
Dates and Deadlines: Priority date 5/1; no closing date. Applicants notified on a rolling basis starting 6/15.

CONTACT

Wilma Atencio, Financial Aid Director
600 Prospect Street, Trinidad, CO 81082
(719) 846-5553

United States Air Force Academy

USAF Academy, Colorado
www.usafa.edu Federal Code: 001369

4-year public military college in large city.
Enrollment: 4,537 undergrads. 1,286 full-time freshmen.
Selectivity: Admits less than 50% of applicants.

BASIC COSTS (2008-2009)

Additional info: Tuition, room, board, medical and dental care paid by U.S. Government. Each cadet receives monthly salary to pay for uniforms, supplies and personal expenses. A government loan is advanced to each member of the freshman class.

CONTACT

HQ USAF/RRS, 2304 Cadet Drive, Suite 2300, USAF Academy, CO 80840

University of Colorado at Boulder

Boulder, Colorado
www.colorado.edu Federal Code: 001370

4-year public university in small city.
Enrollment: 26,111 undergrads, 7% part-time. 5,797 full-time freshmen.
Selectivity: Admits over 75% of applicants.

BASIC COSTS (2008-2009)

Tuition and fees: $7,278; out-of-state residents $26,756.
Room and board: $9,860.
Additional info: One-time matriculation fee of $112.

FINANCIAL AID PICTURE (2008-2009)

Students with need: Out of 4,170 full-time freshmen who applied for aid, 1,928 were judged to have need. Of these, 1,924 received aid, and 1,418 had their full need met. Average financial aid package met 93% of need; average scholarship/grant was $7,460; average loan was $5,000. For part-time students, average financial aid package was $13,609.
Students without need: 1,740 full-time freshmen who did not demonstrate need for aid received scholarships/grants; average award was $6,355. No-need awards available for academics, alumni affiliation, art, athletics, leadership, music/drama, ROTC, state/district residency.
Scholarships offered: ***Merit:*** Presidential Scholars Program; $10,000 annual tuition reduction for 4 years; for entering non-resident freshmen in the top 3-5% of admitted non-resident freshman class based on GPA, class rank, and test scores; must maintain 2.75 college GPA for renewal. Chancellor's Achievement Scholarship; $15,000 over 4 years; for entering non-resident freshmen in the top 25% of admitted non-resident freshman class based on GPA and test scores; must maintain 2.75 college GPA for renewal. CU Parents Association Freshmen Scholarship; $1,000; based on full-time entering freshman status with 3.5 GPA, academic excellence and extracurricular activities; 10-20 awarded annually; nonrenewable. Norlin Scholars Program; $3,000 per academic year; based on excellent academic or creative ability; 25 awards; renewable for 2 or 4 years, contingent upon academic progress. ***Athletic:*** 59 full-time freshmen received athletic scholarships; average amount $16,466.
Cumulative student debt: 42% of graduating class had student loans; average debt was $18,361.

FINANCIAL AID PROCEDURES

Forms required: FAFSA.

Dates and Deadlines: Priority date 4/1; no closing date. Applicants notified on a rolling basis starting 2/1; must reply within 3 week(s) of notification.

Transfers: Some financial aid programs available exclusively to transfer students.

CONTACT

Gwen Pomper, Director of Financial Aid
552 UCB, Boulder, CO 80309-0552
(303) 492-5091

University of Colorado at Colorado Springs

Colorado Springs, Colorado
www.uccs.edu Federal Code: 004509

4-year public university in large city.

Enrollment: 6,495 undergrads, 21% part-time. 667 full-time freshmen.

Selectivity: Admits 50 to 75% of applicants.

BASIC COSTS (2008-2009)

Tuition and fees: $5,770; out-of-state residents $16,394.

Room and board: $7,204.

Additional info: Tuition varies by program. One-time matriculation fee of $25 required.

FINANCIAL AID PICTURE (2007-2008)

Students with need: Out of 574 full-time freshmen who applied for aid, 306 were judged to have need. Of these, 287 received aid, and 59 had their full need met. Average financial aid package met 54% of need; average scholarship/grant was $5,537; average loan was $2,523. For part-time students, average financial aid package was $4,886.

Students without need: 126 full-time freshmen who did not demonstrate need for aid received scholarships/grants; average award was $1,546. No-need awards available for academics, alumni affiliation, athletics, state/district residency.

Scholarships offered: ***Merit:*** College Opportunity Fund for in-state undergraduates. ***Athletic:*** 8 full-time freshmen received athletic scholarships; average amount $2,138.

Cumulative student debt: 59% of graduating class had student loans; average debt was $20,860.

FINANCIAL AID PROCEDURES

Forms required: FAFSA.

Dates and Deadlines: Priority date 4/1; no closing date. Applicants notified on a rolling basis starting 4/15.

CONTACT

Lee Noble, Director of Financial Aid
PO Box 7150, Colorado Springs, CO 80933-7150
(719) 255-3460

University of Colorado at Denver

Denver, Colorado
www.ucdenver.edu Federal Code: 006740

4-year public university in very large city.

Enrollment: 8,721 undergrads, 26% part-time. 1,012 full-time freshmen.

Selectivity: Admits 50 to 75% of applicants.

BASIC COSTS (2008-2009)

Tuition and fees: $6,279; out-of-state residents $19,251.

Additional info: Tuition varies by program. One-time matriculation fee of $115 required.

FINANCIAL AID PICTURE (2008-2009)

Students with need: Average financial aid package met 52% of need; average scholarship/grant was $4,334; average loan was $2,628. For part-time students, average financial aid package was $5,991.

Students without need: No-need awards available for academics, alumni affiliation, art, job skills, leadership, music/drama, ROTC, state/district residency.

Cumulative student debt: 46% of graduating class had student loans; average debt was $17,441.

FINANCIAL AID PROCEDURES

Forms required: FAFSA, institutional form.

Dates and Deadlines: Priority date 4/1; no closing date. Applicants notified on a rolling basis starting 5/1.

CONTACT

Patrick McTee, Director of Financial Aid
Box 173364, Campus Box 167, Denver, CO 80217-3364
(303) 556-2886

University of Denver

Denver, Colorado Federal Code: 001371
www.du.edu CSS Code: 4842

4-year private university in very large city, affiliated with United Methodist Church.

Enrollment: 5,305 undergrads, 9% part-time. 1,131 full-time freshmen.

Selectivity: Admits 50 to 75% of applicants.

BASIC COSTS (2009-2010)

Tuition and fees: $35,481.

Per-credit charge: $961.

Room and board: $9,900.

FINANCIAL AID PICTURE (2007-2008)

Students with need: Out of 646 full-time freshmen who applied for aid, 489 were judged to have need. Of these, 488 received aid, and 137 had their full need met. Average financial aid package met 77% of need; average scholarship/grant was $18,908; average loan was $3,252. For part-time students, average financial aid package was $7,503.

Students without need: 387 full-time freshmen who did not demonstrate need for aid received scholarships/grants; average award was $10,376. No-need awards available for academics, art, athletics, leadership, music/drama, state/district residency.

Scholarships offered: 46 full-time freshmen received athletic scholarships; average amount $24,236.

Cumulative student debt: 34% of graduating class had student loans; average debt was $11,218.

FINANCIAL AID PROCEDURES

Forms required: FAFSA, CSS PROFILE.

Dates and Deadlines: Priority date 3/1; no closing date.

CONTACT

Barbara McFall, Director of Financial Aid
2197 South University Boulevard, Denver, CO 80208
(303) 871-4020

University of Northern Colorado

Greeley, Colorado
www.unco.edu Federal Code: 001349

4-year public university in small city.

Enrollment: 9,690 undergrads, 9% part-time. 2,161 full-time freshmen.

Selectivity: Admits over 75% of applicants.

BASIC COSTS (2008-2009)

Tuition and fees: $4,680; out-of-state residents $14,082.

Per-credit charge: $164; out-of-state residents $556.

Room and board: $7,784.

Additional info: Costs reflect student share of tuition after the Colorado College Opportunity Fund.

FINANCIAL AID PICTURE (2007-2008)

Students with need: Out of 1,684 full-time freshmen who applied for aid, 995 were judged to have need. Of these, 932 received aid, and 527 had their full need met. Average financial aid package met 100% of need; average scholarship/grant was $4,405; average loan was $3,788. For part-time students, average financial aid package was $10,083.

Students without need: 397 full-time freshmen who did not demonstrate need for aid received scholarships/grants; average award was $2,198. No-need awards available for academics, art, athletics, music/drama.

Scholarships offered: 8 full-time freshmen received athletic scholarships; average amount $6,993.

FINANCIAL AID PROCEDURES

Forms required: FAFSA.

Dates and Deadlines: Priority date 3/1; no closing date. Applicants notified on a rolling basis starting 4/15; must reply within 4 week(s) of notification.

CONTACT

Donni Clark, Director of Financial Aid
1862 10th Avenue, Campus Box 10, Greeley, CO 80639
(970) 351-2502

Western State College of Colorado

Gunnison, Colorado
www.western.edu Federal Code: 001372

4-year public liberal arts college in small town.

Enrollment: 1,875 full-time undergrads.

Selectivity: Admits over 75% of applicants.

BASIC COSTS (2008-2009)

Tuition and fees: $3,778; out-of-state residents $12,754.

Per-credit charge: $120; out-of-state residents $494.

Room and board: $7,516.

Additional info: Tuition/fee waivers available for unemployed or children of unemployed.

FINANCIAL AID PICTURE (2008-2009)

Students with need: Need-based aid available for full-time students. Work study available nights, weekends, and for part-time students.

Students without need: No-need awards available for academics, alumni affiliation, art, athletics, leadership, music/drama.

Scholarships offered: Academic Excellence Award; $1,000; based on 3.5 GPA and 22 ACT/1010 SAT. Non-resident Leadership Award; $2,500; based on 3.2 GPA, 990 SAT, leadership activities. SAT scores exclusive of Writing.

FINANCIAL AID PROCEDURES

Forms required: FAFSA.

Dates and Deadlines: Priority date 4/1; no closing date. Applicants notified on a rolling basis starting 4/1; must reply within 4 week(s) of notification.

CONTACT

Marty Somero, Director of Financial Aid
600 North Adams Street, Gunnison, CO 81231
(970) 943-3085

Westwood College: Denver North

Denver, Colorado
www.westwood.edu Federal Code: 007548

4-year for-profit technical college in very large city.

Enrollment: 3,755 full-time undergrads.

BASIC COSTS (2008-2009)

Additional info: Full-time costs per 10-week term for most programs: $4,463 for tuition. Tuition and fees may vary.

FINANCIAL AID PICTURE

Students with need: Need-based aid available for full-time and part-time students. Work study available nights.

Students without need: No-need awards available for academics, state/district residency.

FINANCIAL AID PROCEDURES

Forms required: FAFSA, state aid form, institutional form.

Dates and Deadlines: No deadline. Applicants notified on a rolling basis starting 1/1; must reply within 2 week(s) of notification.

Transfers: No deadline.

CONTACT

Amy Argyris, Director, Financial Aid
7350 North Broadway, Denver, CO 80221
(303) 426-7000

Westwood College: Denver South

Denver, Colorado
www.westwood.edu Federal Code: 007548

4-year for-profit technical college in very large city.

Enrollment: 377 undergrads.

Selectivity: Admits over 75% of applicants.

BASIC COSTS (2009-2010)

Tuition and fees: $25,630.

Per-credit charge: $559.

Additional info: Tuition and fees may vary by program.

FINANCIAL AID PICTURE (2008-2009)

Students with need: Need-based aid available for full-time and part-time students. Work study available nights.

FINANCIAL AID PROCEDURES

Forms required: FAFSA, state aid form, institutional form.

Dates and Deadlines: No deadline. Applicants notified on a rolling basis; must reply within 2 week(s) of notification.

CONTACT

Maureen Wallace, Director of Student Affairs
3150 South Sheridan Boulevard, Denver, CO 80227-5507
(303) 934-1122

Connecticut

Albertus Magnus College

New Haven, Connecticut
www.albertus.edu Federal Code: 001374

4-year private liberal arts college in small city, affiliated with Roman Catholic Church.

Enrollment: 1,714 undergrads, 8% part-time. 185 full-time freshmen.

Selectivity: Admits over 75% of applicants.

BASIC COSTS (2008-2009)
Tuition and fees: $22,724.
Per-credit charge: $907.
Room and board: $9,442.

FINANCIAL AID PICTURE (2008-2009)
Students with need: Average financial aid package met 52% of need; average scholarship/grant was $12,529; average loan was $3,416. For part-time students, average financial aid package was $5,670.
Students without need: No-need awards available for academics, art, job skills, leadership, music/drama, religious affiliation, state/district residency.
Cumulative student debt: 93% of graduating class had student loans; average debt was $18,733.

FINANCIAL AID PROCEDURES
Forms required: FAFSA.
Dates and Deadlines: Closing date 2/28. Applicants notified on a rolling basis starting 3/1; must reply within 2 week(s) of notification.
Transfers: No deadline. Must reply within 2 week(s) of notification.

CONTACT
Andrew Foster, Director of Financial Aid
700 Prospect Street, New Haven, CT 06511-1189
(203) 773-8508

Asnuntuck Community College
Enfield, Connecticut
www.acc.commnet.edu Federal Code: 011150

2-year public community and technical college in large town.
Enrollment: 1,122 undergrads.
Selectivity: Open admission.

BASIC COSTS (2008-2009)
Tuition and fees: $2,984; out-of-state residents $8,912.
Per-credit charge: $110; out-of-state residents $330.

FINANCIAL AID PICTURE (2007-2008)
Students with need: 85% of average financial aid package awarded as scholarships/grants, 15% awarded as loans/jobs. Need-based aid available for part-time students. Work study available nights, weekends, and for part-time students.
Students without need: This college awards aid only to students with need.

FINANCIAL AID PROCEDURES
Forms required: FAFSA, institutional form.
Dates and Deadlines: Priority date 6/1; no closing date. Applicants notified on a rolling basis starting 7/1; must reply within 2 week(s) of notification.
Transfers: Financial aid transcript required.

CONTACT
Donna Jones-Searle, Director of Financial Aid
170 Elm Street, Enfield, CT 06082
(860) 253-3030

Briarwood College
Southington, Connecticut
www.briarwood.edu Federal Code: 009407

2-year for-profit junior college in large town.
Enrollment: 702 undergrads.
Selectivity: Open admission; but selective for some programs.

BASIC COSTS (2008-2009)
Tuition and fees: $17,835.
Per-credit charge: $570.
Room only: $4,000.

FINANCIAL AID PICTURE
Students with need: Need-based aid available for full-time and part-time students. Work study available nights, weekends, and for part-time students.
Students without need: No-need awards available for academics, alumni affiliation, leadership.

FINANCIAL AID PROCEDURES
Forms required: FAFSA.
Dates and Deadlines: Priority date 4/30; no closing date. Applicants notified on a rolling basis starting 3/15; must reply within 2 week(s) of notification.
Transfers: Priority date 4/15.

CONTACT
Gina Swenton, Assistant Director of Student Financial Services
2279 Mount Vernon Road, Southington, CT 06489-1057
(860) 628-4751 ext. 213

Capital Community College
Hartford, Connecticut
www.ccc.commnet.edu Federal Code: 007635

2-year public community and technical college in small city.
Enrollment: 3,422 undergrads, 69% part-time. 372 full-time freshmen.
Selectivity: Open admission; but selective for some programs.

BASIC COSTS (2009-2010)
Tuition and fees: $3,200; out-of-state residents $9,560.
Per-credit charge: $118; out-of-state residents $354.
Additional info: Tuition/fee waivers available for minority students.

FINANCIAL AID PICTURE
Students with need: Need-based aid available for full-time and part-time students. Work study available nights, weekends, and for part-time students.
Students without need: This college awards aid only to students with need.

FINANCIAL AID PROCEDURES
Forms required: FAFSA.
Dates and Deadlines: Closing date 7/15. Applicants notified on a rolling basis starting 7/15; must reply within 2 week(s) of notification.
Transfers: Closing date 7/1.

CONTACT
Margaret Wolf, Director of Financial Aid
950 Main Street, Hartford, CT 06103-1207
(860) 906-5127

Central Connecticut State University
New Britain, Connecticut
www.ccsu.edu Federal Code: 001378

4-year public university in small city.
Enrollment: 9,479 undergrads, 18% part-time. 1,303 full-time freshmen.
Selectivity: Admits 50 to 75% of applicants.

BASIC COSTS (2008-2009)
Tuition and fees: $7,042; out-of-state residents $16,179.
Room and board: $8,838.

FINANCIAL AID PICTURE (2007-2008)

Students with need: Out of 1,107 full-time freshmen who applied for aid, 747 were judged to have need. Of these, 737 received aid, and 124 had their full need met. Average financial aid package met 64% of need; average scholarship/grant was $5,039; average loan was $2,811. For part-time students, average financial aid package was $5,716.

Students without need: 68 full-time freshmen who did not demonstrate need for aid received scholarships/grants; average award was $2,674. No-need awards available for academics, athletics, minority status.

Scholarships offered: 54 full-time freshmen received athletic scholarships; average amount $9,494.

FINANCIAL AID PROCEDURES

Forms required: FAFSA.

Dates and Deadlines: Priority date 3/1; closing date 9/15. Applicants notified on a rolling basis starting 3/30; must reply within 2 week(s) of notification.

CONTACT

Richard Bishop, Director of Financial Aid
1615 Stanley Street, New Britain, CT 06050
(860) 832-2200

Charter Oak State College

New Britain, Connecticut
www.charteroak.edu Federal Code: 032343

4-year public virtual liberal arts college in small city.

Enrollment: 1,599 undergrads, 92% part-time.

BASIC COSTS (2008-2009)

Per-credit charge: $186; out-of-state residents $256.

Additional info: Academic Services Fee: In-state Bachelor's degree $1,015; In-state Associate's Degree $700; Out-of state Bachelor's degree $1,335; Out-of-state Associate's degree $985. Books and supplies $1,000. Cost of education varies due to students having the option to take courses at other institutions.

FINANCIAL AID PICTURE (2007-2008)

Students with need: Need-based aid available for full-time and part-time students.

Students without need: This college awards aid only to students with need.

FINANCIAL AID PROCEDURES

Forms required: FAFSA, institutional form.

Dates and Deadlines: No deadline. Applicants notified on a rolling basis starting 8/23.

CONTACT

Deborah Flinn, Director of Financial Aid
55 Paul Manafort Drive, New Britain, CT 06053-2150
(860) 832-3872

Clemens College

Suffield, Connecticut
www.clemenscollege.edu

2-year for-profit culinary school and business college in small town.

Enrollment: 75 undergrads.

BASIC COSTS (2008-2009)

Tuition and fees: $19,770.

Room and board: $5,690.

Additional info: International students without health insurance are required to purchase it for $350 per 11-week term. Culinary students pay an extra $668 for cutlery and tools.

FINANCIAL AID PICTURE

Students with need: Need-based aid available for full-time and part-time students. Work study available nights, weekends, and for part-time students.

Students without need: No-need awards available for academics.

FINANCIAL AID PROCEDURES

Dates and Deadlines: No deadline. Applicants notified on a rolling basis starting 1/1.

CONTACT

Joanne Seymour, Director of Financial Aid
1760 Mapleton Avenue, Suffield, CT 06078
(860) 668-3515

Connecticut College

New London, Connecticut Federal Code: 001379
www.conncoll.edu CSS Code: 3284

4-year private liberal arts college in large town.

Enrollment: 1,741 undergrads. 493 full-time freshmen.

Selectivity: Admits less than 50% of applicants.

BASIC COSTS (2009-2010)

Tuition and fees: $42,335.

Room and board: $8,780.

FINANCIAL AID PICTURE (2008-2009)

Students with need: Out of 263 full-time freshmen who applied for aid, 203 were judged to have need. Of these, 203 received aid, and 203 had their full need met. Average financial aid package met 100% of need; average scholarship/grant was $31,003; average loan was $3,445. For part-time students, average financial aid package was $678.

Students without need: This college awards aid only to students with need.

Cumulative student debt: 41% of graduating class had student loans; average debt was $21,283.

FINANCIAL AID PROCEDURES

Forms required: FAFSA, CSS PROFILE.

Dates and Deadlines: Closing date 2/1. Applicants notified by 4/1; must reply by 5/1.

Transfers: Closing date 4/1.

CONTACT

Elaine Solinga, Director of Financial Aid
270 Mohegan Avenue, New London, CT 06320-4196
(860) 439-2058

Eastern Connecticut State University

Willimantic, Connecticut
www.easternct.edu Federal Code: 001425

4-year public university and liberal arts college in large town.

Enrollment: 4,896 undergrads, 16% part-time. 843 full-time freshmen.

Selectivity: Admits 50 to 75% of applicants.

BASIC COSTS (2008-2009)

Tuition and fees: $7,400; out-of-state residents $16,543.

Per-credit charge: $336.

Room and board: $8,855.

FINANCIAL AID PICTURE (2007-2008)

Students with need: Out of 756 full-time freshmen who applied for aid, 575 were judged to have need. Of these, 472 received aid, and 57 had their full need met. Average financial aid package met 62% of need; average scholarship/grant was $6,207; average loan was $3,254. For part-time students, average financial aid package was $2,654.

Students without need: 44 full-time freshmen who did not demonstrate need for aid received scholarships/grants; average award was $2,625. No-need awards available for academics.
Cumulative student debt: 57% of graduating class had student loans; average debt was $14,829.
Additional info: Tuition waiver for veterans and members of National Guard.

FINANCIAL AID PROCEDURES

Forms required: FAFSA.
Dates and Deadlines: Priority date 3/15; no closing date. Applicants notified on a rolling basis starting 2/15; must reply within 2 week(s) of notification.
Transfers: Must reply within 2 week(s) of notification.

CONTACT

Mona Lucas, Director of Financial Aid
83 Windham Street, Willimantic, CT 06226-2295
(860) 465-5286

Fairfield University

Fairfield, Connecticut
www.fairfield.edu
Federal Code: 001385
CSS Code: 3390

4-year private university in small city, affiliated with Roman Catholic Church.
Enrollment: 3,948 undergrads, 13% part-time. 899 full-time freshmen.
Selectivity: Admits 50 to 75% of applicants. GED not accepted.

BASIC COSTS (2009-2010)

Tuition and fees: $37,490.
Per-credit charge: $495.
Room and board: $11,270.
Additional info: Standard meal plan covers 12 meals per week; 14-meal plan available with "dining dollars" (i.e., cash value added by deposit to student ID). Proof of health insurance required in order to waive health insurance fee.

FINANCIAL AID PICTURE (2008-2009)

Students with need: Out of 618 full-time freshmen who applied for aid, 495 were judged to have need. Of these, 493 received aid, and 127 had their full need met. Average financial aid package met 86% of need; average scholarship/grant was $21,344; average loan was $3,980. Need-based aid available for part-time students.
Students without need: 37 full-time freshmen who did not demonstrate need for aid received scholarships/grants; average award was $12,649. No-need awards available for academics, alumni affiliation, art, athletics, leadership, music/drama.
Scholarships offered: ***Merit:*** Magis scholarship; $20,000 annually; renewable for 4 years with 3.0 GPA; based on academics and participation in high school, community or church activities; 70-75 awared annually. ***Athletic:*** 82 full-time freshmen received athletic scholarships; average amount $17,952.
Cumulative student debt: 59% of graduating class had student loans; average debt was $32,857.
Additional info: Free tuition to any eligible student from Bridgeport, CT with family income below $50,000. Enhanced financial aid available for veterans.

FINANCIAL AID PROCEDURES

Forms required: FAFSA, CSS PROFILE.
Dates and Deadlines: Closing date 2/15. Applicants notified by 4/1; must reply by 5/1.
Transfers: Closing date 5/1. Applicants notified on a rolling basis starting 5/1; must reply within 3 week(s) of notification.

CONTACT

Erin Chiaro, Director of Financial Aid
1073 North Benson Road, Fairfield, CT 06824-5195
(203) 254-4125

Gateway Community College

New Haven, Connecticut
www.gwcc.commnet.edu
Federal Code: 008303

2-year public community college in small city.
Enrollment: 5,140 undergrads, 56% part-time. 1,087 full-time freshmen.
Selectivity: Open admission; but selective for some programs.

BASIC COSTS (2009-2010)

Tuition and fees: $3,200; out-of-state residents $9,560.
Per-credit charge: $118; out-of-state residents $354.

FINANCIAL AID PICTURE

Students with need: Need-based aid available for full-time and part-time students. Work study available nights, weekends, and for part-time students.
Students without need: This college awards aid only to students with need.

FINANCIAL AID PROCEDURES

Forms required: FAFSA, institutional form.
Dates and Deadlines: No deadline. Applicants notified on a rolling basis; must reply within 2 week(s) of notification.

CONTACT

Raymond Zeek, Director of Financial Aid
60 Sargent Drive, New Haven, CT 06511-5970
(203) 285-2013

Goodwin College

East Hartford, Connecticut
www.goodwin.edu
Federal Code: 015833

2-year private health science and career college in small city.
Enrollment: 1,572 undergrads, 79% part-time. 117 full-time freshmen.
Selectivity: Open admission; but selective for some programs.

BASIC COSTS (2008-2009)

Tuition and fees: $16,250.
Per-credit charge: $490.

FINANCIAL AID PICTURE (2007-2008)

Students with need: Out of 114 full-time freshmen who applied for aid, 113 were judged to have need. Of these, 113 received aid. Average financial aid package met 85% of need; average scholarship/grant was $2,415; average loan was $2,831. For part-time students, average financial aid package was $7,187.
Students without need: This college awards aid only to students with need.
Cumulative student debt: 87% of graduating class had student loans; average debt was $15,175.

FINANCIAL AID PROCEDURES

Forms required: FAFSA.
Dates and Deadlines: No deadline. Applicants notified on a rolling basis starting 8/1.
Transfers: No deadline. Applicants notified on a rolling basis starting 8/1.

CONTACT

Bill Mangini, Director of Financial Aid
One RIverside Drive, East Hartford, CT 06118
(860) 727-6723

Holy Apostles College and Seminary
Cromwell, Connecticut
www.holyapostles.edu Federal Code: 001389

4-year private liberal arts and seminary college in large town, affiliated with Roman Catholic Church.
Enrollment: 39 undergrads, 33% part-time. 2 full-time freshmen.
Selectivity: Admits over 75% of applicants.

BASIC COSTS (2008-2009)
Tuition and fees: $8,640.
Per-credit charge: $360.

FINANCIAL AID PICTURE (2008-2009)
Students with need: Out of 2 full-time freshmen who applied for aid, 2 were judged to have need. Of these, 2 received aid, and 2 had their full need met. Average financial aid package met 70% of need; average loan was $4,811. Need-based aid available for part-time students.
Students without need: This college awards aid only to students with need.
Cumulative student debt: 35% of graduating class had student loans; average debt was $9,100.

FINANCIAL AID PROCEDURES
Forms required: FAFSA, institutional form.
Dates and Deadlines: Priority date 7/11; no closing date. Applicants notified on a rolling basis starting 8/25; must reply within 2 week(s) of notification.
Transfers: No deadline. Applicants notified on a rolling basis; must reply within 2 week(s) of notification.

CONTACT
Henry Miller, Financial Aid Director
33 Prospect Hill Road, Cromwell, CT 06416-2005
(860) 632-8120

Housatonic Community College
Bridgeport, Connecticut
www.hcc.commnet.edu Federal Code: 004513

2-year public community college in small city.
Enrollment: 1,650 full-time undergrads.
Selectivity: Open admission; but selective for some programs.

BASIC COSTS (2008-2009)
Tuition and fees: $2,984; out-of-state residents $8,912.
Per-credit charge: $110; out-of-state residents $330.

FINANCIAL AID PICTURE (2007-2008)
Students with need: Need-based aid available for full-time and part-time students.
Students without need: This college awards aid only to students with need.

FINANCIAL AID PROCEDURES
Forms required: FAFSA.
Dates and Deadlines: Priority date 11/1; closing date 5/1. Applicants notified on a rolling basis starting 6/1.

CONTACT
Barbara Surowiec, Director of Financial Aid
900 Lafayette Boulevard, Bridgeport, CT 06604-4704
(203) 332-5047

Lyme Academy College of Fine Arts
Old Lyme, Connecticut
www.lymeacademy.edu Federal Code: 030794

4-year private visual arts college in small town.
Enrollment: 96 undergrads, 9% part-time. 11 full-time freshmen.
Selectivity: Admits over 75% of applicants.

BASIC COSTS (2009-2010)
Tuition and fees: $23,092.
Per-credit charge: $908.

FINANCIAL AID PICTURE (2008-2009)
Students with need: Out of 11 full-time freshmen who applied for aid, 11 were judged to have need. Of these, 11 received aid. Need-based aid available for part-time students.
Students without need: No-need awards available for academics, art, leadership.

FINANCIAL AID PROCEDURES
Forms required: FAFSA.
Dates and Deadlines: Priority date 2/15; closing date 4/15. Applicants notified on a rolling basis starting 3/1; must reply by 5/1 or within 2 week(s) of notification.
Transfers: Closing date 7/31. Applicants notified on a rolling basis starting 2/15; must reply by 5/1 or within 2 week(s) of notification.

CONTACT
Jim Falconer, Director of Financial Aid
84 Lyme Street, Old Lyme, CT 06371
(860) 434-3571 ext. 114

Manchester Community College
Manchester, Connecticut
www.mcc.commnet.edu Federal Code: 001392

2-year public community college in small city.
Enrollment: 5,710 undergrads, 47% part-time. 1,225 full-time freshmen.
Selectivity: Open admission; but selective for some programs.

BASIC COSTS (2008-2009)
Tuition and fees: $2,984; out-of-state residents $8,912.
Per-credit charge: $110; out-of-state residents $330.

FINANCIAL AID PICTURE (2007-2008)
Students with need: Need-based aid available for full-time and part-time students.

FINANCIAL AID PROCEDURES
Forms required: FAFSA
Dates and Deadlines: Priority date 5/15; no closing date. Applicants notified on a rolling basis starting 5/1; must reply within 2 week(s) of notification.

CONTACT
Ivette Rivera-Dreyer, Director of Financial Aid
Great Path PO Box 1046, MS 12, Manchester, CT 06040-1046
(860) 512-3380

Middlesex Community College
Middletown, Connecticut
www.mxcc.commnet.edu Federal Code: 008038

2-year public community college in large town.
Enrollment: 1,940 undergrads, 52% part-time. 355 full-time freshmen.
Selectivity: Open admission; but selective for some programs.

BASIC COSTS (2009-2010)

Tuition and fees: $3,200; out-of-state residents $9,560.

Per-credit charge: $118; out-of-state residents $354.

Additional info: Out-of-state tuition includes fees.

FINANCIAL AID PICTURE

Students with need: Need-based aid available for full-time and part-time students.

Students without need: This college awards aid only to students with need.

Additional info: Tuition and/or fee waiver for veterans.

FINANCIAL AID PROCEDURES

Forms required: FAFSA, institutional form.

Dates and Deadlines: Priority date 6/1; no closing date. Applicants notified on a rolling basis starting 7/1; must reply within 2 week(s) of notification.

Transfers: Closing date 9/1.

CONTACT

Irene Martin, Director of Financial Aid
100 Training Hill Road, Middletown, CT 06457
(860) 343-5741

Mitchell College

New London, Connecticut
www.mitchell.edu Federal Code: 001393

4-year private liberal arts college in small city.

Enrollment: 890 undergrads, 12% part-time. 266 full-time freshmen.

Selectivity: Admits less than 50% of applicants.

BASIC COSTS (2008-2009)

Tuition and fees: $24,358.

Per-credit charge: $275.

Room and board: $10,977.

FINANCIAL AID PICTURE

Students with need: Need-based aid available for full-time and part-time students. Work study available nights, weekends, and for part-time students.

Students without need: No-need awards available for academics, alumni affiliation, leadership.

FINANCIAL AID PROCEDURES

Forms required: FAFSA.

Dates and Deadlines: Priority date 3/1; no closing date. Applicants notified on a rolling basis starting 2/15; must reply within 2 week(s) of notification.

CONTACT

Jacklyn Stoltz, Director of Financial Aid
437 Pequot Avenue, New London, CT 06320-4498
(860) 701-5040

Naugatuck Valley Community College

Waterbury, Connecticut
www.nvcc.commnet.edu Federal Code: 006982

2-year public community and technical college in small city.

Enrollment: 5,086 undergrads, 52% part-time. 930 full-time freshmen.

Selectivity: Open admission; but selective for some programs.

BASIC COSTS (2009-2010)

Tuition and fees: $3,200; out-of-state residents $9,560.

Per-credit charge: $118; out-of-state residents $354.

Additional info: Non-resident fees $1,064.

FINANCIAL AID PICTURE (2007-2008)

Students with need: Need-based aid available for full-time and part-time students.

Students without need: This college awards aid only to students with need.

FINANCIAL AID PROCEDURES

Forms required: FAFSA.

Dates and Deadlines: Priority date 4/1; no closing date. Applicants notified on a rolling basis starting 6/1.

Transfers: Financial aid transcripts required from all previous schools attended.

CONTACT

Catherine Hardy, Director of Financial Aid Services
750 Chase Parkway, Waterbury, CT 06708-3089
(203) 575-8006

Norwalk Community College

Norwalk, Connecticut
www.ncc.commnet.edu Federal Code: 001399

2-year public community and technical college in small city.

Enrollment: 4,580 undergrads, 56% part-time. 606 full-time freshmen.

Selectivity: Open admission; but selective for some programs.

BASIC COSTS (2008-2009)

Tuition and fees: $2,984; out-of-state residents $8,912.

Per-credit charge: $110; out-of-state residents $330.

Additional info: New England Regional Student Program: $241.25 per credit-hour.

FINANCIAL AID PICTURE

Students with need: Need-based aid available for full-time and part-time students.

Students without need: No-need awards available for academics, alumni affiliation.

FINANCIAL AID PROCEDURES

Forms required: FAFSA, institutional form.

Dates and Deadlines: Priority date 7/1; no closing date. Applicants notified on a rolling basis starting 7/1; must reply within 2 week(s) of notification.

CONTACT

Norma McNerney, Director of Financial Aid
188 Richards Avenue, Norwalk, CT 06854-1655
(203) 857-7023

Paier College of Art

Hamden, Connecticut
www.paiercollegeofart.edu Federal Code: 007459

4-year for-profit visual arts college in small city.

Enrollment: 207 undergrads, 21% part-time. 13 full-time freshmen.

Selectivity: Admits 50 to 75% of applicants.

BASIC COSTS (2009-2010)

Tuition and fees: $12,365.

Per-credit charge: $380.

FINANCIAL AID PICTURE (2007-2008)

Students with need: Out of 13 full-time freshmen who applied for aid, 9 were judged to have need. Of these, 9 received aid. Average financial aid package met 64% of need; average scholarship/grant was $5,497; average loan was $3,788. For part-time students, average financial aid package was $5,576.

Cumulative student debt: 76% of graduating class had student loans; average debt was $20,330.

FINANCIAL AID PROCEDURES

Forms required: FAFSA.

Dates and Deadlines: Priority date 4/15; no closing date. Applicants notified on a rolling basis starting 6/1; must reply within 3 week(s) of notification.

Transfers: No deadline. Applicants notified on a rolling basis starting 6/1; must reply within 3 week(s) of notification.

CONTACT

John DeRose, Director of Financial Aid
20 Gorham Avenue, Hamden, CT 06514-3902
(203) 287-3034

Post University

Waterbury, Connecticut
www.post.edu Federal Code: 001401

4-year for-profit university and business college in small city.

Enrollment: 1,320 undergrads. 96 full-time freshmen.

Selectivity: Admits 50 to 75% of applicants.

BASIC COSTS (2008-2009)

Tuition and fees: $23,425.

Per-credit charge: $750.

Room and board: $9,000.

FINANCIAL AID PICTURE (2007-2008)

Students with need: Out of 96 full-time freshmen who applied for aid, 90 were judged to have need. Of these, 90 received aid, and 1 had their full need met. Average financial aid package met 73% of need; average scholarship/grant was $5,000; average loan was $2,600.

Additional info: Academic merit scholarships available based on GPA and test scores. Renewable contingent upon maintaining specific GPA.

FINANCIAL AID PROCEDURES

Forms required: FAFSA.

Dates and Deadlines: Priority date 3/15; no closing date. Applicants notified on a rolling basis starting 4/15; must reply by 5/1 or within 3 week(s) of notification.

Transfers: No deadline. Applicants notified on a rolling basis starting 4/15; must reply within 1 week(s) of notification.

CONTACT

Claire Dwyer, Director of Office of Student Finance
800 Country Club Road, Waterbury, CT 06723-2540
(203) 596-4571

Quinebaug Valley Community College

Danielson, Connecticut
www.qvcc.commnet.edu Federal Code: 010530

2-year public community and technical college in large town.

Enrollment: 1,660 undergrads, 59% part-time. 272 full-time freshmen.

Selectivity: Open admission; but selective for some programs.

BASIC COSTS (2008-2009)

Tuition and fees: $2,984; out-of-state residents $8,912.

Per-credit charge: $110; out-of-state residents $330.

FINANCIAL AID PICTURE (2008-2009)

Students with need: 96% of average financial aid package awarded as scholarships/grants, 4% awarded as loans/jobs. Need-based aid available for part-time students. Work study available nights, weekends, and for part-time students.

Students without need: This college awards aid only to students with need.

FINANCIAL AID PROCEDURES

Forms required: FAFSA.

Dates and Deadlines: Closing date 10/1. Applicants notified on a rolling basis starting 5/1.

CONTACT

Alfred Williams, Director of Financial Aid
742 Upper Maple Street, Danielson, CT 06239-1440
(860) 412-7208

Quinnipiac University

Hamden, Connecticut
www.quinnipiac.edu Federal Code: 001402

4-year private university in small city.

Enrollment: 5,747 undergrads, 3% part-time. 1,481 full-time freshmen.

Selectivity: Admits less than 50% of applicants.

BASIC COSTS (2009-2010)

Tuition and fees: $32,400.

Per-credit charge: $745.

Room and board: $12,380.

FINANCIAL AID PICTURE (2008-2009)

Students with need: Out of 1,111 full-time freshmen who applied for aid, 835 were judged to have need. Of these, 834 received aid, and 131 had their full need met. Average financial aid package met 69% of need; average scholarship/grant was $13,813; average loan was $3,567. For part-time students, average financial aid package was $7,203.

Students without need: 233 full-time freshmen who did not demonstrate need for aid received scholarships/grants; average award was $10,265. No-need awards available for academics, athletics.

Scholarships offered: ***Merit:*** Available; $4,000-$16,000 per year; based on high school class rank and SAT/ACT scores; renewable with full-time status and 3.0 GPA. ***Athletic:*** 68 full-time freshmen received athletic scholarships; average amount $26,400.

Cumulative student debt: 70% of graduating class had student loans; average debt was $37,849.

FINANCIAL AID PROCEDURES

Forms required: FAFSA.

Dates and Deadlines: Priority date 3/1; no closing date. Applicants notified on a rolling basis starting 2/15; must reply by 5/1 or within 2 week(s) of notification.

Transfers: No deadline. Applicants notified on a rolling basis starting 3/1; must reply by 5/1 or within 2 week(s) of notification. Students transferring with 2 years of full-time college work and 3.5 GPA may be eligible for transfer scholarship.

CONTACT

Dominic Yoia, Director of Financial Aid
275 Mount Carmel Avenue, Hamden, CT 06518-1908
(800) 462-1944

Sacred Heart University

Fairfield, Connecticut Federal Code: 001403
www.sacredheart.edu CSS Code: 3780

4-year private university and liberal arts college in large town, affiliated with Roman Catholic Church.

Enrollment: 4,239 undergrads, 17% part-time. 980 full-time freshmen.

Selectivity: Admits 50 to 75% of applicants.

BASIC COSTS (2008-2009)

Tuition and fees: $28,990.
Per-credit charge: $445.
Room and board: $11,330.
Additional info: Tuition/fee waivers available for minority students.

FINANCIAL AID PICTURE (2008-2009)

Students with need: Out of 880 full-time freshmen who applied for aid, 671 were judged to have need. Of these, 671 received aid, and 280 had their full need met. Average financial aid package met 67% of need; average scholarship/grant was $14,220; average loan was $3,660. For part-time students, average financial aid package was $20,745.
Students without need: 198 full-time freshmen who did not demonstrate need for aid received scholarships/grants; average award was $6,115. No-need awards available for academics, alumni affiliation, art, athletics, leadership, minority status, music/drama.
Scholarships offered: 55 full-time freshmen received athletic scholarships; average amount $16,235.
Cumulative student debt: 96% of graduating class had student loans; average debt was $27,516.
Additional info: Financial aid for first-year, full-time students from Fairfield County, CT who have family income at or below $50,000 will cover 100% tuition.

FINANCIAL AID PROCEDURES

Forms required: FAFSA, CSS PROFILE.
Dates and Deadlines: Priority date 2/15; no closing date. Applicants notified on a rolling basis starting 3/1; must reply within 2 week(s) of notification.
Transfers: Priority date 5/1; no deadline. Applicants notified on a rolling basis.

CONTACT

Julie Savino, Dean of University Financial Assistance
5151 Park Avenue, Fairfield, CT 06825
(203) 371-7980

St. Joseph College

West Hartford, Connecticut
www.sjc.edu Federal Code: 001409

4-year private liberal arts college for women in small city, affiliated with Roman Catholic Church.
Enrollment: 1,037 undergrads, 21% part-time. 225 full-time freshmen.
Selectivity: Admits over 75% of applicants.

BASIC COSTS (2009-2010)

Tuition and fees: $27,202.
Per-credit charge: $595.
Room and board: $12,437.

FINANCIAL AID PICTURE (2008-2009)

Students with need: Need-based aid available for full-time and part-time students.
Students without need: No-need awards available for academics.

FINANCIAL AID PROCEDURES

Forms required: FAFSA.
Dates and Deadlines: Priority date 2/15; no closing date. Applicants notified on a rolling basis starting 3/1.

CONTACT

Elizabeth Baker, Director of Financial Aid
1678 Asylum Avenue, West Hartford, CT 06117
(866) 442-8752

Southern Connecticut State University

New Haven, Connecticut
www.southernct.edu Federal Code: 001406

4-year public university in small city.
Enrollment: 8,496 undergrads, 16% part-time. 1,288 full-time freshmen.
Selectivity: Admits 50 to 75% of applicants.

BASIC COSTS (2008-2009)

Tuition and fees: $7,179; out-of-state residents $15,038.
Per-credit charge: $357.
Room and board: $8,966.
Additional info: Out-of-state students pay an additional $1,278 in fees.

FINANCIAL AID PICTURE (2007-2008)

Students with need: Need-based aid available for full-time and part-time students. Work study available nights, weekends, and for part-time students.
Scholarships offered: General Academic Achievement Awards; 90 awarded. Presidential Scholarships, Trustees Scholarships available.

FINANCIAL AID PROCEDURES

Dates and Deadlines: Priority date 3/6; no closing date. Must reply within 2 week(s) of notification.
Transfers: Applicants notified on a rolling basis starting 6/15; must reply within 2 week(s) of notification.

CONTACT

Avon Dennis, Director, Financial Aid & Scholarships
131 Farnham Avenue, New Haven, CT 06515-1202
(203) 392-5222

Three Rivers Community College

Norwich, Connecticut
www.trcc.commnet.edu Federal Code: 009765

2-year public community and technical college in large town.
Enrollment: 3,712 undergrads, 63% part-time. 594 full-time freshmen.
Selectivity: Open admission; but selective for some programs.

BASIC COSTS (2009-2010)

Tuition and fees: $3,200; out-of-state residents $9,560.
Per-credit charge: $118; out-of-state residents $354.
Additional info: Out-of-state required fees $1,064. New England state students pay $4,248 for tuition and $542 for fees.

FINANCIAL AID PICTURE (2007-2008)

Students with need: Out of 293 full-time freshmen who applied for aid, 286 were judged to have need. Of these, 280 received aid, and 125 had their full need met. Average financial aid package met 53% of need; average scholarship/grant was $2,011; average loan was $1,971. For part-time students, average financial aid package was $1,317.
Students without need: This college awards aid only to students with need.
Scholarships offered: Available, $75 to $500.

FINANCIAL AID PROCEDURES

Forms required: FAFSA.
Dates and Deadlines: Priority date 7/15; no closing date. Applicants notified on a rolling basis; must reply within 2 week(s) of notification.

CONTACT

Hong-Yu Kovic, Financial Aid Counselor
New London Turnpike, Norwich, CT 06360-6598
(860) 823-2870

Trinity College

Hartford, Connecticut
www.trincoll.edu
Federal Code: 001414
CSS Code: 3899

4-year private liberal arts college in large city.
Enrollment: 2,263 undergrads, 2% part-time. 589 full-time freshmen.
Selectivity: Admits less than 50% of applicants.

BASIC COSTS (2009-2010)

Tuition and fees: $40,840.
Room and board: $10,560.
Additional info: One-time $25 transcript fee for new students only. Tuition/fee waivers available for adults.

FINANCIAL AID PICTURE (2008-2009)

Students with need: Average financial aid package met 100% of need; average scholarship/grant was $34,175; average loan was $3,564. Need-based aid available for part-time students.
Students without need: No-need awards available for academics, leadership.
Cumulative student debt: 45% of graduating class had student loans; average debt was $17,218.

FINANCIAL AID PROCEDURES

Forms required: FAFSA, CSS PROFILE.
Dates and Deadlines: Priority date 2/1; closing date 3/1. Applicants notified by 4/1; must reply by 5/1 or within 2 week(s) of notification.
Transfers: Closing date 4/1. Applicants notified on a rolling basis starting 5/15; must reply within 2 week(s) of notification.

CONTACT

Kelly O'Brien, Director of Financial Aid
300 Summit Street, Hartford, CT 06106
(860) 297-2046

Tunxis Community College

Farmington, Connecticut
www.tunxis.commnet.edu
Federal Code: 009764

2-year public community college in large town.
Enrollment: 3,317 undergrads, 49% part-time. 591 full-time freshmen.
Selectivity: Open admission; but selective for some programs.

BASIC COSTS (2009-2010)

Tuition and fees: $3,200; out-of-state residents $9,560.
Per-credit charge: $118; out-of-state residents $364.
Additional info: Out-of-state required fees: $1,064.

FINANCIAL AID PICTURE (2007-2008)

Students with need: Need-based aid available for full-time and part-time students. Work study available nights, weekends, and for part-time students.
Students without need: No-need awards available for academics, leadership.
Additional info: Financial aid available to all students showing need. Part-time students encouraged to apply.

FINANCIAL AID PROCEDURES

Forms required: FAFSA.
Dates and Deadlines: Priority date 6/1; no closing date. Applicants notified on a rolling basis starting 3/1.

CONTACT

David Welsh, Director of Financial Aid
271 Scott Swamp Road, Farmington, CT 06032-3187
(860) 255-3555

United States Coast Guard Academy

New London, Connecticut
www.uscga.edu
Federal Code: 001415

4-year public engineering and maritime college in small city.
Enrollment: 973 undergrads. 271 full-time freshmen.
Selectivity: Admits less than 50% of applicants.

BASIC COSTS (2009-2010)

Additional info: All tuition, room and board paid for by U.S. government. Students make one-time entrance deposit of $3,000 to help defray cost of uniforms, books, supplies and personal computer. All students paid monthly stipend of $734.

FINANCIAL AID PROCEDURES

Dates and Deadlines: No deadline.

CONTACT

31 Mohegan Avenue, New London, CT 06320
(860) 444-8309

University of Bridgeport

Bridgeport, Connecticut
www.bridgeport.edu
Federal Code: 001416

4-year private university in small city.
Enrollment: 2,028 undergrads, 31% part-time. 333 full-time freshmen.
Selectivity: Admits 50 to 75% of applicants.

BASIC COSTS (2008-2009)

Tuition and fees: $24,470.
Per-credit charge: $750.
Room and board: $10,600.

FINANCIAL AID PICTURE (2007-2008)

Students with need: Out of 268 full-time freshmen who applied for aid, 263 were judged to have need. Of these, 263 received aid, and 21 had their full need met. Average financial aid package met 69% of need; average scholarship/grant was $6,725; average loan was $4,915. For part-time students, average financial aid package was $7,155.
Students without need: 36 full-time freshmen who did not demonstrate need for aid received scholarships/grants; average award was $9,417. No-need awards available for academics, athletics, music/drama, state/district residency.
Scholarships offered: ***Merit:*** Academic Excellence and Leadership Scholarship; up to full tuition, room, and board; for students ranking in the top quarter of high school class with 1200 SAT. Academic Scholarship; up to full tuition; for students in the top quarter of class and 1100 SAT. Academic Grant; up to half-tuition; for students in top half of class and 1100 SAT. Challenge Grant; $3,000; for students in the top half of class and 1000 SAT. All SAT scores exclusive of writing. ***Athletic:*** 9 full-time freshmen received athletic scholarships; average amount $22,213.

FINANCIAL AID PROCEDURES

Forms required: FAFSA.
Dates and Deadlines: Priority date 4/1; no closing date. Applicants notified on a rolling basis starting 4/1; must reply within 4 week(s) of notification.

CONTACT

Kathleen Gailor, Director of Financial Aid
126 Park Avenue, Bridgeport, CT 06604
(203) 576-4568

University of Connecticut

Storrs, Connecticut
www.uconn.edu Federal Code: 007997

4-year public university in large town.

Enrollment: 16,459 undergrads, 3% part-time. 3,596 full-time freshmen.

Selectivity: Admits 50 to 75% of applicants.

BASIC COSTS (2008-2009)

Tuition and fees: $9,338; out-of-state residents $24,050.

Per-credit charge: $300; out-of-state residents $913.

Room and board: $9,300.

Additional info: Incoming out-of-state New England residents pay 175% of in-state tuition rate for programs of study not offered at their home state university.

FINANCIAL AID PICTURE (2008-2009)

Students with need: Out of 2,866 full-time freshmen who applied for aid, 1,812 were judged to have need. Of these, 1,754 received aid, and 362 had their full need met. Average financial aid package met 72% of need; average scholarship/grant was $7,389; average loan was $3,835. For part-time students, average financial aid package was $7,248.

Students without need: 395 full-time freshmen who did not demonstrate need for aid received scholarships/grants; average award was $6,609. No-need awards available for academics, art, athletics, leadership, minority status, music/drama.

Scholarships offered: 87 full-time freshmen received athletic scholarships; average amount $22,254.

Cumulative student debt: 61% of graduating class had student loans; average debt was $21,521.

Additional info: Institution offers variety of need-based financial aid programs. Financial assistance packages may include grants, loans and work-study awards.

FINANCIAL AID PROCEDURES

Forms required: FAFSA.

Dates and Deadlines: Priority date 3/1; no closing date. Applicants notified on a rolling basis starting 3/1; must reply within 4 week(s) of notification.

CONTACT

Jean Main, Director of Financial Aid
2131 Hillside Road, Unit 3088, Storrs, CT 06269-3088
(860) 486-2819

University of Hartford

West Hartford, Connecticut
www.hartford.edu Federal Code: 001422

4-year private university in small city.

Enrollment: 5,449 undergrads, 12% part-time. 1,458 full-time freshmen.

Selectivity: Admits 50 to 75% of applicants.

BASIC COSTS (2009-2010)

Tuition and fees: $28,980.

Per-credit charge: $410.

Room and board: $11,238.

Additional info: Tuition/fee waivers available for minority students.

FINANCIAL AID PICTURE (2007-2008)

Students with need: Out of 1,198 full-time freshmen who applied for aid, 1,043 were judged to have need. Of these, 1,042 received aid, and 204 had their full need met. Average financial aid package met 81% of need; average scholarship/grant was $15,135; average loan was $3,014. For part-time students, average financial aid package was $10,470.

Students without need: 348 full-time freshmen who did not demonstrate need for aid received scholarships/grants; average award was $7,258. No-need awards available for academics, art, athletics, music/drama.

Scholarships offered: 16 full-time freshmen received athletic scholarships; average amount $28,602.

Cumulative student debt: 70% of graduating class had student loans; average debt was $34,126.

FINANCIAL AID PROCEDURES

Forms required: FAFSA, institutional form.

Dates and Deadlines: Priority date 2/1; no closing date. Applicants notified on a rolling basis starting 3/1; must reply by 5/1.

CONTACT

Jennifer Fuhrmann, Director of Student Financial Assistance
Bates House, West Hartford, CT 06117-1599
(860) 768-4296

University of New Haven

West Haven, Connecticut
www.newhaven.edu Federal Code: 001397

4-year private university in small city.

Enrollment: 3,494 undergrads, 12% part-time. 1,129 full-time freshmen.

Selectivity: Admits 50 to 75% of applicants.

BASIC COSTS (2009-2010)

Tuition and fees: $29,470.

Per-credit charge: $940.

Room and board: $12,372.

FINANCIAL AID PICTURE (2008-2009)

Students with need: Out of 1,038 full-time freshmen who applied for aid, 936 were judged to have need. Of these, 936 received aid, and 131 had their full need met. Average financial aid package met 68% of need; average scholarship/grant was $15,807; average loan was $3,502. For part-time students, average financial aid package was $5,736.

Students without need: 167 full-time freshmen who did not demonstrate need for aid received scholarships/grants; average award was $9,007. No-need awards available for academics, alumni affiliation, athletics, leadership.

Scholarships offered: ***Merit:*** Presidential Scholarship; half-tuition; for applicants in top 15% of class with 1200 SAT (exclusive of Writing) or ACT equivalent. Academic Achievement Awards. ***Athletic:*** 8 full-time freshmen received athletic scholarships; average amount $8,500.

FINANCIAL AID PROCEDURES

Forms required: FAFSA.

Dates and Deadlines: Priority date 3/1; no closing date. Applicants notified on a rolling basis starting 3/1; must reply by 5/1 or within 2 week(s) of notification.

CONTACT

Karen Flynn, Director of Financial Aid
300 Boston Post Road, West Haven, CT 06516
(203) 932-7315

Wesleyan University

Middletown, Connecticut
www.wesleyan.edu CSS Code: 3959

4-year private university and liberal arts college in large town.

Enrollment: 2,748 undergrads. 733 full-time freshmen.

Selectivity: Admits less than 50% of applicants.

BASIC COSTS (2009-2010)

Tuition and fees: $40,392.

Room and board: $11,040.

FINANCIAL AID PICTURE (2007-2008)

Students with need: Out of 390 full-time freshmen who applied for aid, 329 were judged to have need. Of these, 329 received aid, and 329 had their full need met. Average financial aid package met 100% of need; average scholarship/grant was $26,348; average loan was $3,217.

Students without need: This college awards aid only to students with need.

Scholarships offered: Freeman Asian Scholars; for international first-year applicants from select East and Southeast Asian countries; 22 awarded.

FINANCIAL AID PROCEDURES

Forms required: FAFSA, CSS PROFILE.

Dates and Deadlines: Closing date 2/15. Applicants notified by 4/1; must reply by 5/1.

Transfers: Priority date 2/15; closing date 3/15. Applicants notified by 5/15; must reply by 6/1 or within 2 week(s) of notification. No financial aid available for international transfer candidates.

CONTACT

Jennifer Lawton, Director of Financial Aid
70 Wyllys Avenue, Middletown, CT 06459-0260
(860) 685-2800

Western Connecticut State University

Danbury, Connecticut
www.wcsu.edu Federal Code: 001380

4-year public university in small city.

Enrollment: 5,348 undergrads, 14% part-time. 913 full-time freshmen.

Selectivity: Admits 50 to 75% of applicants.

BASIC COSTS (2008-2009)

Tuition and fees: $7,088; out-of-state residents $16,225.

Per-credit charge: $319.

Room and board: $9,158.

FINANCIAL AID PICTURE (2007-2008)

Students with need: Out of 686 full-time freshmen who applied for aid, 614 were judged to have need. Of these, 593 received aid, and 186 had their full need met. Average financial aid package met 55% of need; average scholarship/grant was $4,725; average loan was $2,823. For part-time students, average financial aid package was $4,699.

Students without need: 27 full-time freshmen who did not demonstrate need for aid received scholarships/grants; average award was $2,084. No-need awards available for academics.

Cumulative student debt: 63% of graduating class had student loans; average debt was $15,045.

FINANCIAL AID PROCEDURES

Forms required: FAFSA, institutional form.

Dates and Deadlines: Priority date 3/15; closing date 4/15. Applicants notified on a rolling basis starting 4/15; must reply by 5/1 or within 2 week(s) of notification.

CONTACT

Nancy Barton, Director, Financial Aid/Veterans Affairs
181 White Street, Danbury, CT 06810-6826
(203) 837-8580

Yale University

New Haven, Connecticut Federal Code: 001426
www.yale.edu CSS Code: 3987

4-year private university in small city.

Enrollment: 5,256 undergrads. 1,319 full-time freshmen.

Selectivity: Admits less than 50% of applicants.

BASIC COSTS (2009-2010)

Tuition and fees: $36,500.

Room and board: $11,000.

FINANCIAL AID PICTURE (2007-2008)

Students with need: Out of 750 full-time freshmen who applied for aid, 611 were judged to have need. Of these, 611 received aid, and 611 had their full need met. Average financial aid package met 100% of need; average scholarship/grant was $32,138; average loan was $2,921. Need-based aid available for part-time students.

Students without need: This college awards aid only to students with need.

Cumulative student debt: 34% of graduating class had student loans; average debt was $12,237.

Additional info: All scholarships based on demonstrated need.

FINANCIAL AID PROCEDURES

Forms required: FAFSA, CSS PROFILE.

Dates and Deadlines: Closing date 3/1. Applicants notified by 4/1; must reply by 5/1 or within 1 week(s) of notification.

CONTACT

Caesar Storlazzi, Director of University Financial Aid
Box 208234, New Haven, CT 06520-8234
(203) 432-2700

Delaware

Delaware College of Art and Design

Wilmington, Delaware
www.dcad.edu

2-year private visual arts college in large city.

Enrollment: 227 undergrads, 7% part-time. 102 full-time freshmen.

Selectivity: Admits 50 to 75% of applicants.

BASIC COSTS (2008-2009)

Tuition and fees: $17,300.

Room only: $6,400.

FINANCIAL AID PICTURE (2007-2008)

Students with need: Out of 96 full-time freshmen who applied for aid, 70 were judged to have need. Of these, 70 received aid, and 18 had their full need met. Average financial aid package met 98% of need; average scholarship/grant was $4,000; average loan was $3,500.

Students without need: 16 full-time freshmen who did not demonstrate need for aid received scholarships/grants; average award was $4,167.

CONTACT

Teresa Haman, Director of Financial Aid
600 North Market Street, Wilmington, DE 19801

Delaware State University
Dover, Delaware
www.desu.edu Federal Code: 001428

4-year public university in large town.
Enrollment: 3,159 undergrads, 9% part-time. 798 full-time freshmen.
Selectivity: Admits less than 50% of applicants.

BASIC COSTS (2008-2009)
Tuition and fees: $6,481; out-of-state residents $13,742.
Per-credit charge: $238; out-of-state residents $540.
Room and board: $9,112.

FINANCIAL AID PICTURE (2007-2008)
Students with need: Out of 764 full-time freshmen who applied for aid, 687 were judged to have need. Of these, 668 received aid, and 215 had their full need met. Average financial aid package met 77% of need; average scholarship/grant was $2,392; average loan was $93. For part-time students, average financial aid package was $9,097.
Students without need: This college awards aid only to students with need.
Scholarships offered: 15 full-time freshmen received athletic scholarships; average amount $19,379.
Additional info: Students must file FAFSA by March 17 every year.

FINANCIAL AID PROCEDURES
Forms required: FAFSA.
Dates and Deadlines: Priority date 3/1; closing date 7/1. Applicants notified on a rolling basis starting 4/1; must reply by 8/20.
Transfers: Closing date 2/15.

CONTACT
Lynn Iocono, Executive Director of Student Financial Services
1200 North DuPont Highway, Dover, DE 19901
(302) 857-6250

Delaware Technical and Community College: Owens
Georgetown, Delaware
www.dtcc.edu Federal Code: 007053

2-year public community and technical college in rural community.
Enrollment: 3,768 undergrads, 49% part-time. 733 full-time freshmen.
Selectivity: Open admission; but selective for some programs.

BASIC COSTS (2008-2009)
Tuition and fees: $2,631; out-of-state residents $6,141.
Per-credit charge: $98; out-of-state residents $244.

FINANCIAL AID PICTURE
Students with need: Need-based aid available for full-time and part-time students.
Students without need: This college awards aid only to students with need.

FINANCIAL AID PROCEDURES
Forms required: FAFSA.
Dates and Deadlines: Priority date 6/15; no closing date. Applicants notified on a rolling basis; must reply within 2 week(s) of notification.

CONTACT
Veronica Oney, Financial Aid Officer
PO Box 610, Georgetown, DE 19947
(302) 855-5692

Delaware Technical and Community College: Stanton/Wilmington
Newark, Delaware
www.dtcc.edu Federal Code: 021449

2-year public community and technical college in small city.
Enrollment: 6,665 undergrads, 58% part-time. 1,152 full-time freshmen.
Selectivity: Open admission; but selective for some programs.

BASIC COSTS (2008-2009)
Tuition and fees: $2,631; out-of-state residents $6,141.
Per-credit charge: $98; out-of-state residents $244.

FINANCIAL AID PICTURE
Students with need: Need-based aid available for full-time and part-time students.
Students without need: This college awards aid only to students with need.

FINANCIAL AID PROCEDURES
Forms required: FAFSA.
Dates and Deadlines: Priority date 6/15; no closing date. Applicants notified on a rolling basis; must reply within 2 week(s) of notification.

CONTACT
Debra Troxler, Student Financial Aid Officer
400 Stanton-Christiana Road, Newark, DE 19713
(302) 571-5380

Delaware Technical and Community College: Terry
Dover, Delaware
www.dtcc.edu Federal Code: 011727

2-year public community and technical college in large town.
Enrollment: 3,062 undergrads, 55% part-time. 589 full-time freshmen.
Selectivity: Open admission; but selective for some programs.

BASIC COSTS (2008-2009)
Tuition and fees: $2,631; out-of-state residents $6,141.
Per-credit charge: $98; out-of-state residents $244.

FINANCIAL AID PICTURE
Students with need: Need-based aid available for full-time and part-time students.
Students without need: This college awards aid only to students with need.

FINANCIAL AID PROCEDURES
Forms required: FAFSA.
Dates and Deadlines: Priority date 6/15; no closing date. Applicants notified on a rolling basis starting 7/1; must reply within 2 week(s) of notification.

CONTACT
Jennifer Grunden, Financial Aid Director
100 Campus Drive, Dover, DE 19901
(302) 857-1040

Goldey-Beacom College
Wilmington, Delaware
www.gbc.edu Federal Code: 001429

4-year private business college in small city.
Enrollment: 998 undergrads, 33% part-time. 95 full-time freshmen.

BASIC COSTS (2009-2010)

Tuition and fees: $17,880.

Room only: $4,982.

FINANCIAL AID PICTURE (2008-2009)

Students with need: 60% of average financial aid package awarded as scholarships/grants, 40% awarded as loans/jobs. Need-based aid available for part-time students. Work study available nights, weekends, and for part-time students.

Students without need: No-need awards available for academics.

Additional info: Essays required for scholarship applicants.

FINANCIAL AID PROCEDURES

Forms required: FAFSA.

Dates and Deadlines: Priority date 4/1; no closing date. Applicants notified on a rolling basis starting 2/15; must reply within 2 week(s) of notification.

Transfers: No deadline. Applicants notified on a rolling basis starting 2/15; must reply within 2 week(s) of notification.

CONTACT

Jane Lysle, Dean of Enrollment Management
4701 Limestone Road, Wilmington, DE 19808
(302) 225-6265

University of Delaware

Newark, Delaware
www.udel.edu Federal Code: 001431

4-year public university in large town.

Enrollment: 15,407 undergrads, 5% part-time. 3,826 full-time freshmen.

Selectivity: Admits 50 to 75% of applicants.

BASIC COSTS (2008-2009)

Tuition and fees: $8,646; out-of-state residents $21,126.

Per-credit charge: $325; out-of-state residents $845.

Room and board: $8,478.

FINANCIAL AID PICTURE (2007-2008)

Students with need: Out of 2,901 full-time freshmen who applied for aid, 1,484 were judged to have need. Of these, 1,444 received aid, and 744 had their full need met. Average financial aid package met 73% of need; average scholarship/grant was $5,892; average loan was $5,634. For part-time students, average financial aid package was $8,152.

Students without need: This college awards aid only to students with need.

Scholarships offered: ***Merit:*** All freshman applicants evaluated for a wide range of merit scholarships ranging from $1,000 to full cost of education. ***Athletic:*** 65 full-time freshmen received athletic scholarships; average amount $12,840.

Cumulative student debt: 44% of graduating class had student loans; average debt was $17,200.

Additional info: December 15 application deadline to receive scholarship consideration. Sibling/parent tuition credit plan. Senior citizen tuition credit for state residents over 60.

FINANCIAL AID PROCEDURES

Forms required: FAFSA.

Dates and Deadlines: Priority date 2/1; closing date 3/15. Applicants notified on a rolling basis starting 3/15; must reply by 5/1 or within 3 week(s) of notification.

Transfers: No deadline. Aid usualy limited to federal and state programs.

CONTACT

Johnie Burton, Director of Financial Aid
116 Hullihen Hall, Newark, DE 19716
(302) 831-8761

Wesley College

Dover, Delaware
www.wesley.edu Federal Code: 001433

4-year private liberal arts college in large town, affiliated with United Methodist Church.

Enrollment: 1,869 undergrads.

BASIC COSTS (2009-2010)

Tuition and fees: $19,830.

Per-credit charge: $800.

Room and board: $9,000.

FINANCIAL AID PICTURE (2007-2008)

Students with need: Need-based aid available for full-time and part-time students. Work study available nights, weekends, and for part-time students.

Students without need: This college awards aid only to students with need.

FINANCIAL AID PROCEDURES

Forms required: FAFSA, institutional form.

Dates and Deadlines: Priority date 2/1; no closing date. Applicants notified on a rolling basis starting 1/1; must reply within 2 week(s) of notification.

Transfers: No deadline. Applicants notified on a rolling basis; must reply within 2 week(s) of notification.

CONTACT

James Marks, Director of Student Financial Planning
120 North State Street, Dover, DE 19901-3875
(302) 736-2334

Wilmington University

New Castle, Delaware
www.wilmu.edu Federal Code: 007948

4-year private liberal arts college in large town.

Enrollment: 5,461 undergrads, 49% part-time. 335 full-time freshmen.

Selectivity: Open admission.

BASIC COSTS (2008-2009)

Tuition and fees: $8,760.

Per-credit charge: $292.

FINANCIAL AID PICTURE

Students with need: Need-based aid available for full-time and part-time students. Work study available nights, weekends, and for part-time students.

Students without need: No-need awards available for academics, athletics.

FINANCIAL AID PROCEDURES

Forms required: FAFSA.

Dates and Deadlines: Priority date 4/30; no closing date. Applicants notified on a rolling basis starting 8/5; must reply within 2 week(s) of notification.

CONTACT

Trudy Yingling, Director of Student Financial Services
320 Dupont Highway, New Castle, DE 19720
(302) 328-9401 ext. 107

District of Columbia

American University
Washington, District of Columbia
www.american.edu Federal Code: 001434

4-year private university in very large city, affiliated with United Methodist Church.
Enrollment: 6,028 undergrads, 3% part-time. 1,573 full-time freshmen.
Selectivity: Admits 50 to 75% of applicants.

BASIC COSTS (2008-2009)
Tuition and fees: $33,283.
Per-credit charge: $1,093.
Room and board: $12,418.

FINANCIAL AID PICTURE (2008-2009)
Students with need: Out of 1,076 full-time freshmen who applied for aid, 759 were judged to have need. Of these, 756 received aid, and 248 had their full need met. Average financial aid package met 93% of need; average scholarship/grant was $11,448; average loan was $3,918. For part-time students, average financial aid package was $17,000.
Students without need: This college awards aid only to students with need.
Scholarships offered: ***Merit:*** United Methodist scholarship; supplemental application required. ***Athletic:*** 49 full-time freshmen received athletic scholarships; average amount $20,009.
Additional info: Early decision applicants must submit estimated AU institutional financial aid application by 11/15 and a FASFA as soon as possible after Jan 1.

FINANCIAL AID PROCEDURES
Forms required: FAFSA, institutional form.
Dates and Deadlines: Closing date 2/15. Applicants notified by 4/1; must reply by 5/1 or within 4 week(s) of notification.
Transfers: Priority date 3/1. Phi Theta Kappa scholarship available.

CONTACT
Brian Lee-Sang, Director of Financial Aid
4400 Massachusetts Avenue NW, Washington, DC 20016-8001
(202) 885-6100

Catholic University of America
Washington, District of Columbia
www.cua.edu Federal Code: 001437

4-year private university in very large city, affiliated with Roman Catholic Church.
Enrollment: 3,431 undergrads, 7% part-time. 901 full-time freshmen.
Selectivity: Admits over 75% of applicants.

BASIC COSTS (2008-2009)
Tuition and fees: $30,670.
Per-credit charge: $1,125.
Room and board: $11,320.
Additional info: Tuition/fee waivers available for adults.

FINANCIAL AID PICTURE (2008-2009)
Students with need: Out of 721 full-time freshmen who applied for aid, 561 were judged to have need. Of these, 561 received aid, and 273 had their full need met. Average financial aid package met 80% of need; average scholarship/grant was $15,519; average loan was $4,011. For part-time students, average financial aid package was $5,429.
Students without need: 279 full-time freshmen who did not demonstrate need for aid received scholarships/grants; average award was $10,458. No-need awards available for academics, alumni affiliation, music/drama, religious affiliation.

FINANCIAL AID PROCEDURES
Forms required: FAFSA.
Dates and Deadlines: Priority date 2/15; no closing date. Applicants notified on a rolling basis starting 4/1; must reply by 5/1 or within 2 week(s) of notification.
Transfers: No deadline. Applicants notified on a rolling basis starting 4/1; must reply by 5/1 or within 2 week(s) of notification.

CONTACT
Donald Bosse, Director of Financial Aid
102 McMahon Hall, Washington, DC 20064
(202) 319-5307

Corcoran College of Art and Design
Washington, District of Columbia
www.corcoran.edu Federal Code: 011950

4-year private visual arts college in very large city.
Enrollment: 320 undergrads, 12% part-time. 44 full-time freshmen.
Selectivity: Admits 50 to 75% of applicants.

BASIC COSTS (2008-2009)
Tuition and fees: $27,380.
Room only: $9,694.

FINANCIAL AID PICTURE (2007-2008)
Students with need: Out of 36 full-time freshmen who applied for aid, 36 were judged to have need. Of these, 36 received aid. Average financial aid package met 24% of need; average scholarship/grant was $7,281; average loan was $4,194. For part-time students, average financial aid package was $5,264.
Students without need: 9 full-time freshmen who did not demonstrate need for aid received scholarships/grants; average award was $4,600. No-need awards available for academics, art.
Cumulative student debt: 87% of graduating class had student loans; average debt was $32,236.

FINANCIAL AID PROCEDURES
Forms required: FAFSA, institutional form.
Dates and Deadlines: Priority date 3/15; no closing date. Applicants notified on a rolling basis starting 4/15; must reply by 5/1 or within 2 week(s) of notification.
Transfers: No deadline. Applicants notified on a rolling basis; must reply within 2 week(s) of notification.

CONTACT
Diane Morris, Director of Financial Aid
500 17th Street, NW, Washington, DC 20006-4804
(202) 639-1816

Gallaudet University
Washington, District of Columbia
www.gallaudet.edu Federal Code: 001443

4-year private university and liberal arts college in very large city.
Enrollment: 964 undergrads, 4% part-time. 179 full-time freshmen.
Selectivity: Admits 50 to 75% of applicants.

BASIC COSTS (2008-2009)
Tuition and fees: $11,226.
Per-credit charge: $542.

Room and board: $9,340.
Additional info: Students from developing countries may apply for reduction in percentage of tuition surcharge.

FINANCIAL AID PICTURE (2007-2008)
Students with need: Need-based aid available for full-time and part-time students.
Students without need: No-need awards available for academics.
Additional info: Institution receives substantial aid from state vocational rehabilitation agencies, supplemented by institutional grants when needed.

FINANCIAL AID PROCEDURES
Forms required: FAFSA, institutional form.
Dates and Deadlines: Priority date 7/1; no closing date. Applicants notified on a rolling basis starting 4/1; must reply within 4 week(s) of notification.

CONTACT
Nancy Goodman, Director of Financial Aid
800 Florida Avenue, NE, Washington, DC 20002
(202) 651-5290

George Washington University
Washington, District of Columbia Federal Code: 001444
www.gwu.edu CSS Code: 5246

4-year private university in very large city.
Enrollment: 10,291 undergrads, 7% part-time. 2,123 full-time freshmen.
Selectivity: Admits less than 50% of applicants. GED not accepted.

BASIC COSTS (2008-2009)
Tuition and fees: $40,437.
Per-credit charge: $1,123.
Room and board: $9,920.
Additional info: Tuition stays fixed until student graduates, for a maximum of five years.

FINANCIAL AID PICTURE (2007-2008)
Students with need: Out of 1,028 full-time freshmen who applied for aid, 774 were judged to have need. Of these, 730 received aid, and 498 had their full need met. Average financial aid package met 92% of need; average scholarship/grant was $22,804; average loan was $5,561. For part-time students, average financial aid package was $12,707.
Students without need: 330 full-time freshmen who did not demonstrate need for aid received scholarships/grants; average award was $19,014. No-need awards available for academics, art, athletics, music/drama, ROTC.
Scholarships offered: 18 full-time freshmen received athletic scholarships; average amount $23,031.
Cumulative student debt: 49% of graduating class had student loans; average debt was $30,817.
Additional info: Auditions required for performing arts scholarships.

FINANCIAL AID PROCEDURES
Forms required: FAFSA, CSS PROFILE.
Dates and Deadlines: Closing date 2/1. Applicants notified on a rolling basis starting 3/24; must reply by 5/1.
Transfers: Priority date 4/1; closing date 5/1.

CONTACT
Daniel Small, Director of Student Financial Assistance
2121 I Street NW, Suite 201, Washington, DC 20052
(202) 994-6620

Georgetown University
Washington, District of Columbia Federal Code: 001445
www.georgetown.edu CSS Code: 5244

4-year private university in very large city, affiliated with Roman Catholic Church.
Enrollment: 6,692 undergrads, 2% part-time. 1,571 full-time freshmen.
Selectivity: Admits less than 50% of applicants.

BASIC COSTS (2008-2009)
Tuition and fees: $37,947.
Per-credit charge: $1,564.
Room and board: $12,753.

FINANCIAL AID PICTURE (2008-2009)
Students with need: Need-based aid available for full-time and part-time students. Work study available nights, weekends, and for part-time students.
Students without need: No-need awards available for athletics.

FINANCIAL AID PROCEDURES
Forms required: FAFSA, CSS PROFILE.
Dates and Deadlines: Closing date 2/1. Applicants notified by 4/1; must reply by 5/1 or within 2 week(s) of notification.
Transfers: Priority date 3/1. Applicants notified by 5/15; must reply by 5/30 or within 2 week(s) of notification.

CONTACT
Patricia McWade, Dean of Student Financial Services
103 White-Gravenor, Washington, DC 20057-1002
(202) 687-4547

Howard University
Washington, District of Columbia
www.howard.edu Federal Code: 001448

4-year private university in very large city.
Enrollment: 7,086 undergrads, 6% part-time. 1,476 full-time freshmen.
Selectivity: Admits less than 50% of applicants.

BASIC COSTS (2008-2009)
Tuition and fees: $15,010.
Per-credit charge: $592.
Room and board: $7,436.

FINANCIAL AID PICTURE (2007-2008)
Students with need: Out of 1,396 full-time freshmen who applied for aid, 1,270 were judged to have need. Of these, 1,210 received aid, and 316 had their full need met. For part-time students, average financial aid package was $790.
Students without need: 122 full-time freshmen who did not demonstrate need for aid received scholarships/grants; average award was $6,479. No-need awards available for academics, art, athletics, music/drama.
Scholarships offered: 33 full-time freshmen received athletic scholarships; average amount $578.
Cumulative student debt: 80% of graduating class had student loans; average debt was $16,798.

FINANCIAL AID PROCEDURES
Forms required: FAFSA, institutional form.
Dates and Deadlines: Priority date 2/15; closing date 8/15. Applicants notified on a rolling basis starting 4/1; must reply by 8/1 or within 4 week(s) of notification.

CONTACT
Marcus DeCosta, Associate Director, Office of Financial Aid, Scholarships, and Student Employment
2400 Sixth Street NW, Washington, DC 20059
(202) 806-2820

Potomac College
Washington, District of Columbia
www.potomac.edu Federal Code: 032183

3-year for-profit business college in very large city.
Enrollment: 450 undergrads.
Selectivity: Open admission.

BASIC COSTS (2008-2009)
Tuition and fees: $13,480.
Per-credit charge: $445.

FINANCIAL AID PICTURE
Students with need: Need-based aid available for full-time and part-time students.

FINANCIAL AID PROCEDURES
Forms required: FAFSA, institutional form.
Dates and Deadlines: No deadline. Applicants notified on a rolling basis; must reply within 4 week(s) of notification.

CONTACT
Jan Stanley, Director of Compliance
4000 Chesapeake Street NW, Washington, DC 20016
(202) 686-0876

Southeastern University
Washington, District of Columbia
www.seu.edu Federal Code: 001456

4-year private university and business college in very large city.
Enrollment: 467 undergrads, 82% part-time. 4 full-time freshmen.
Selectivity: Admits 50 to 75% of applicants.

BASIC COSTS (2009-2010)
Tuition and fees: $14,010.
Per-credit charge: $270.

FINANCIAL AID PICTURE (2007-2008)
Students with need: 20% of average financial aid package awarded as scholarships/grants, 80% awarded as loans/jobs. Need-based aid available for part-time students.
Students without need: No-need awards available for academics, state/district residency.

FINANCIAL AID PROCEDURES
Forms required: FAFSA, institutional form.
Dates and Deadlines: Closing date 8/15. Applicants notified on a rolling basis; must reply within 2 week(s) of notification.

CONTACT
Peter Canine, CFO & Director of Financial Aid
501 I Street,SW, Washington, DC 20024
(202) 478-8214 ext. 276

Trinity Washington University
Washington, District of Columbia
www.trinitydc.edu Federal Code: 001460

4-year private liberal arts college for women in very large city, affiliated with Roman Catholic Church.
Enrollment: 1,127 undergrads.
Selectivity: Admits 50 to 75% of applicants.

BASIC COSTS (2008-2009)
Tuition and fees: $18,960.
Per-credit charge: $650.
Room and board: $8,450.
Additional info: Mandatory health insurance.

FINANCIAL AID PICTURE (2008-2009)
Students with need: 54% of average financial aid package awarded as scholarships/grants, 46% awarded as loans/jobs. Need-based aid available for part-time students.
Students without need: No-need awards available for academics, alumni affiliation, leadership.

FINANCIAL AID PROCEDURES
Forms required: FAFSA.
Dates and Deadlines: Priority date 3/1; no closing date. Applicants notified on a rolling basis starting 2/1; must reply within 2 week(s) of notification.

CONTACT
Dana Baumgartner, Director of Financial Aid
125 Michigan Avenue, NE, Washington, DC 20017
(202) 884-9530

University of the District of Columbia
Washington, District of Columbia
www.udc.edu Federal Code: 007015

4-year public university and liberal arts college in very large city.
Enrollment: 5,121 undergrads, 49% part-time. 694 full-time freshmen.
Selectivity: Open admission.

BASIC COSTS (2008-2009)
Tuition and fees: $3,770; out-of-state residents $7,070.
Per-credit charge: $105; out-of-state residents $215.

FINANCIAL AID PICTURE
Students with need: Need-based aid available for full-time and part-time students. Work study available nights, weekends, and for part-time students.
Students without need: This college awards aid only to students with need.

FINANCIAL AID PROCEDURES
Forms required: FAFSA.
Dates and Deadlines: Priority date 3/15; no closing date. Applicants notified on a rolling basis starting 5/1; must reply within 2 week(s) of notification.

CONTACT
Willis Parker, Director of Financial Aid
4200 Connecticut Avenue NW, Washington, DC 20008
(202) 274-5060

Florida

Art Institute of Fort Lauderdale
Fort Lauderdale, Florida
www.aifl.edu Federal Code: 010195

4-year for-profit visual arts and technical college in large city.
Enrollment: 2,827 undergrads, 42% part-time. 473 full-time freshmen.

BASIC COSTS (2009-2010)
Tuition and fees: $21,555.
Per-credit charge: $479.
Additional info: Tuition at time of enrollment locked for 4 years.

FINANCIAL AID PICTURE (2007-2008)

Students with need: 75% of average financial aid package awarded as scholarships/grants, 25% awarded as loans/jobs. Need-based aid available for part-time students. Work study available nights, weekends, and for part-time students.

Students without need: No-need awards available for academics.

Scholarships offered: Art Institute's International Excellence Award: $200-$300 per quarter; based on GPA.

Additional info: Internal scholarships available. Financial planning program allows personalized service to budget and meet college costs through individualized payment plans.

FINANCIAL AID PROCEDURES

Forms required: FAFSA.

Dates and Deadlines: No deadline.

CONTACT

Joy Cummings, Director of Student Financial Service
1799 Southeast 17th Street, Fort Lauderdale, FL 33316
(954) 308-2165

Ave Maria University

Ave Maria, Florida
www.avemaria.edu

4-year private university and liberal arts college in small town, affiliated with Roman Catholic Church.

Enrollment: 516 undergrads.

Selectivity: Admits 50 to 75% of applicants.

BASIC COSTS (2009-2010)

Tuition and fees: $17,745.

Room and board: $7,980.

FINANCIAL AID PICTURE (2008-2009)

Students with need: Average financial aid package met 51% of need; average scholarship/grant was $2,864; average loan was $3,500. For part-time students, average financial aid package was $7,544.

CONTACT

Anne Hart, Director of Financial Aid
5050 Ave Maria Boulevard, Ave Maria, FL 34142-9505

Baptist College of Florida

Graceville, Florida
www.baptistcollege.edu Federal Code: 013001

4-year private Bible and teachers college in small town, affiliated with Southern Baptist Convention.

Enrollment: 565 undergrads, 27% part-time. 70 full-time freshmen.

Selectivity: Admits less than 50% of applicants.

BASIC COSTS (2008-2009)

Tuition and fees: $8,150.

Per-credit charge: $260.

Room and board: $3,886.

FINANCIAL AID PICTURE (2007-2008)

Students with need: Out of 53 full-time freshmen who applied for aid, 45 were judged to have need. Of these, 41 received aid, and 7 had their full need met. Average financial aid package met 50% of need; average scholarship/grant was $3,715; average loan was $2,552. For part-time students, average financial aid package was $5,344.

Students without need: 3 full-time freshmen who did not demonstrate need for aid received scholarships/grants; average award was $1,333. No-need awards available for academics, minority status, music/drama, religious affiliation.

FINANCIAL AID PROCEDURES

Forms required: FAFSA, state aid form, institutional form.

Dates and Deadlines: Priority date 4/1; closing date 4/15. Applicants notified on a rolling basis starting 6/15; must reply within 4 week(s) of notification.

Transfers: No deadline.

CONTACT

Angela Rathel, Director of Financial Aid
5400 College Drive, Graceville, FL 32440-3306
(850) 263-3261 ext. 461

Barry University

Miami Shores, Florida
www.barry.edu Federal Code: 001466

4-year private university in large town, affiliated with Roman Catholic Church.

Enrollment: 4,963 undergrads, 18% part-time. 584 full-time freshmen.

Selectivity: Admits 50 to 75% of applicants.

BASIC COSTS (2009-2010)

Tuition and fees: $26,400.

Per-credit charge: $790.

Room and board: $8,504.

FINANCIAL AID PICTURE (2008-2009)

Students with need: Out of 503 full-time freshmen who applied for aid, 457 were judged to have need. Of these, 456 received aid, and 49 had their full need met. Average financial aid package met 74% of need; average scholarship/grant was $7,985; average loan was $3,507. For part-time students, average financial aid package was $6,263.

Students without need: 62 full-time freshmen who did not demonstrate need for aid received scholarships/grants; average award was $8,868. No-need awards available for academics, art, athletics, music/drama.

Scholarships offered: 19 full-time freshmen received athletic scholarships; average amount $11,885.

FINANCIAL AID PROCEDURES

Forms required: FAFSA.

Dates and Deadlines: No deadline. Applicants notified on a rolling basis starting 1/25.

CONTACT

H. Dart Humeston, Director of Financial Aid
11300 Northeast Second Avenue, Miami Shores, FL 33161-6695
(305) 899-3673

Beacon College

Leesburg, Florida
www.beaconcollege.edu Federal Code: 033733

4-year private liberal arts college in large town.

Enrollment: 122 undergrads. 22 full-time freshmen.

Selectivity: Admits 50 to 75% of applicants.

BASIC COSTS (2009-2010)

Tuition and fees: $27,400.

Per-credit charge: $510.

Room and board: $8,150.

Additional info: Tuition/fee waivers available for minority students, unemployed or children of unemployed.

FINANCIAL AID PICTURE (2007-2008)

Students with need: Out of 4 full-time freshmen who applied for aid, 4 were judged to have need. Of these, 4 received aid. Average financial aid package met 90% of need; average scholarship/grant was $15,000. Need-based aid available for part-time students.

Students without need: This college awards aid only to students with need.

Scholarships offered: Paul and Dorothy Heim Civic Award: $500; awarded annually. Ehil E. Brodbeck Book Scholarship: pays complete book costs for 1 semester; awarded annually based on merit or financial need.

Additional info: Work-study programs offered based on financial need.

FINANCIAL AID PROCEDURES

Forms required: FAFSA, state aid form, institutional form.

Dates and Deadlines: Priority date 4/1; no closing date. Applicants notified on a rolling basis starting 4/1; must reply within 2 week(s) of notification.

Transfers: No deadline. Applicants notified on a rolling basis starting 4/1; must reply within 2 week(s) of notification.

CONTACT

Kimberly Padget, Financial Aid Coordinator
105 East Main Street, Leesburg, FL 34748
(352) 787-7660

Bethune-Cookman University

Daytona Beach, Florida
www.cookman.edu Federal Code: 001467

4-year private liberal arts college in small city, affiliated with United Methodist Church.

Enrollment: 3,596 undergrads, 3% part-time. 1,193 full-time freshmen.

Selectivity: Admits 50 to 75% of applicants.

BASIC COSTS (2009-2010)

Tuition and fees: $12,936.

Per-credit charge: $537.

Room and board: $7,672.

FINANCIAL AID PICTURE (2008-2009)

Students with need: Need-based aid available for full-time and part-time students. Work study available nights, weekends, and for part-time students.

Students without need: This college awards aid only to students with need.

FINANCIAL AID PROCEDURES

Forms required: FAFSA.

Dates and Deadlines: Priority date 4/1; no closing date. Applicants notified on a rolling basis starting 4/1; must reply within 3 week(s) of notification.

CONTACT

Joseph Coleman, Director of Financial Aid
Dr. Mary McLeod Bethune Boulevard, Daytona Beach, FL 32114-3099
(800) 553-9369

Brevard Community College

Cocoa, Florida
www.brevardcc.edu Federal Code: 001470

2-year public community college in large town.

Enrollment: 14,403 undergrads, 58% part-time. 1,288 full-time freshmen.

Selectivity: Open admission; but selective for some programs.

BASIC COSTS (2008-2009)

Tuition and fees: $2,280; out-of-state residents $8,490.

FINANCIAL AID PICTURE (2007-2008)

Students with need: Need-based aid available for full-time and part-time students.

Students without need: No-need awards available for academics, athletics.

FINANCIAL AID PROCEDURES

Forms required: FAFSA.

Dates and Deadlines: Priority date 4/15; closing date 6/30. Applicants notified on a rolling basis starting 6/1; must reply within 2 week(s) of notification.

Transfers: Transfer students must complete at least 15 credit hours with 3.5 GPA to be considered for merit scholarship.

CONTACT

Indira Dzadovsky, Director of Financial Aid/ Veteran Affairs
1519 Clearlake Road, Cocoa, FL 32922-9987
(321) 433-5530

Broward College

Fort Lauderdale, Florida
www.broward.edu Federal Code: 001500

2-year public community college in small city.

Enrollment: 29,234 undergrads, 62% part-time. 3,363 full-time freshmen.

Selectivity: Open admission; but selective for some programs.

BASIC COSTS (2008-2009)

Tuition and fees: $2,245; out-of-state residents $8,018.

Additional info: Tuition/fee waivers available for adults, minority students.

FINANCIAL AID PICTURE (2007-2008)

Students with need: 72% of average financial aid package awarded as scholarships/grants, 28% awarded as loans/jobs. Need-based aid available for part-time students. Work study available nights, weekends, and for part-time students.

Students without need: No-need awards available for academics, athletics, leadership, state/district residency.

FINANCIAL AID PROCEDURES

Forms required: FAFSA, institutional form.

Dates and Deadlines: Priority date 4/15; closing date 7/1. Applicants notified on a rolling basis starting 7/15.

Transfers: No deadline.

CONTACT

Marcia Conliffe, Student Success and Enrollment Management Services
225 East Las Olas Boulevard, Fort Lauderdale, FL 33301
(954) 201-7635

Carlos Albizu University

Miami, Florida
www.albizu.edu Federal Code: 010724

4-year private university in very large city.

Enrollment: 407 undergrads.

BASIC COSTS (2008-2009)

Tuition and fees: $14,269.

Additional info: Reported tuition, fees and per credit hour charge are for bachelor's degree program in business. Other programs individually priced.

FINANCIAL AID PICTURE

Students with need: Need-based aid available for full-time and part-time students. Work study available nights.

Students without need: This college awards aid only to students with need.

FINANCIAL AID PROCEDURES

Forms required: FAFSA, institutional form.

Dates and Deadlines: Priority date 6/1; no closing date. Applicants notified on a rolling basis starting 2/1.

Transfers: No deadline. Applicants notified on a rolling basis.

CONTACT

Ramona Morales, Financial Aid Director
2173 NW 99th Avenue, Miami, FL 33172
(305) 593-1223 ext. 153

Central Florida College

Winter Park, Florida
www.centralfloridacollege.edu Federal Code: 022455

2-year for-profit technical college in very large city.

Enrollment: 450 undergrads.

Selectivity: Open admission.

FINANCIAL AID PICTURE

Students with need: Need-based aid available for full-time students.

Students without need: This college awards aid only to students with need.

FINANCIAL AID PROCEDURES

Forms required: FAFSA.

Dates and Deadlines: No deadline.

CONTACT

Cathy Lane, Corporate Finance Director
1573 West Fairbanks Avenue, Winter Park, FL 32789
(407) 843-3984

Central Florida Community College

Ocala, Florida
www.cf.edu Federal Code: 001471

2-year public community college in small city.

Enrollment: 5,057 undergrads.

Selectivity: Open admission; but selective for some programs.

BASIC COSTS (2008-2009)

Tuition and fees: $2,314; out-of-state residents $8,433.

Additional info: Tuition/fee waivers available for minority students.

FINANCIAL AID PICTURE (2007-2008)

Students with need: Need-based aid available for full-time and part-time students.

Students without need: No-need awards available for academics, athletics, minority status, music/drama, state/district residency.

FINANCIAL AID PROCEDURES

Forms required: FAFSA.

Dates and Deadlines: No deadline.

CONTACT

Walter Fleming, Director, Financial Aid
3001 SW College Road, Ocala, FL 34474-4415
(352) 873-5803 ext. 1310

Chipola College

Marianna, Florida
www.chipola.edu Federal Code: 001472

4-year public community and junior college in small town.

Enrollment: 1,563 undergrads, 37% part-time. 262 full-time freshmen.

Selectivity: Open admission; but selective for some programs.

BASIC COSTS (2008-2009)

Tuition and fees: $2,250; out-of-state residents $6,662.

FINANCIAL AID PICTURE (2007-2008)

Students with need: 91% of average financial aid package awarded as scholarships/grants, 9% awarded as loans/jobs. Need-based aid available for part-time students. Work study available nights.

Students without need: No-need awards available for academics, alumni affiliation, art, athletics, job skills, leadership, minority status, music/drama.

FINANCIAL AID PROCEDURES

Forms required: FAFSA, institutional form.

Dates and Deadlines: Priority date 5/1; no closing date. Applicants notified on a rolling basis starting 1/2; must reply within 2 week(s) of notification.

CONTACT

Sybil Cloud, Director of Financial Aid
3094 Indian Circle, Marianna, FL 32446
(850) 718-2223

City College: Miami

Miami, Florida
www.citycollege.edu Federal Code: 025154

2-year for-profit business and health science college in large city.

Enrollment: 270 undergrads.

BASIC COSTS (2008-2009)

Tuition and fees: $10,975.

FINANCIAL AID PICTURE

Students with need: Need-based aid available for full-time and part-time students.

Students without need: This college awards aid only to students with need.

FINANCIAL AID PROCEDURES

Forms required: FAFSA, institutional form.

Dates and Deadlines: No deadline. Applicants notified on a rolling basis.

CONTACT

Esther Fike, President
9300 South Dadeland Boulevard, Miami, FL 33156
(305) 666-9242

Clearwater Christian College

Clearwater, Florida
www.clearwater.edu Federal Code: 015025

4-year private liberal arts college in small city, affiliated with nondenominational tradition.

Enrollment: 586 undergrads, 3% part-time. 151 full-time freshmen.

Selectivity: Admits over 75% of applicants.

BASIC COSTS (2008-2009)

Tuition and fees: $14,040.

Per-credit charge: $515.

Room and board: $5,900.

FINANCIAL AID PICTURE (2008-2009)

Students with need: Need-based aid available for full-time and part-time students. Work study available nights, weekends, and for part-time students.

Students without need: No-need awards available for academics, alumni affiliation, leadership, music/drama, religious affiliation, ROTC.

Additional info: Special consideration given to children of Christian service workers; need-based scholarships available to first-generation students; scholarships up to $3,000 available to dual-enrolled students.

FINANCIAL AID PROCEDURES

Forms required: FAFSA, state aid form, institutional form.

Dates and Deadlines: Priority date 3/15; no closing date. Applicants notified on a rolling basis starting 4/15; must reply within 2 week(s) of notification.

Transfers: Transfer academic scholarship of $750 per semester awarded to sophomore or junior transfer with at least 3.25 cumulative GPA. After transferring, student must maintain 3.5 GPA.

CONTACT

Ruth Strum, Director of Financial Aid
3400 Gulf-to-Bay Boulevard, Clearwater, FL 33759-4595
(727) 726-1153 ext. 214

College of Business and Technology: Flagler

Miami, Florida
www.cbt.edu Federal Code: 030716

2-year private junior and technical college in very large city.

Enrollment: 153 undergrads. 77 full-time freshmen.

Selectivity: Open admission.

BASIC COSTS (2008-2009)

Tuition and fees: $12,830.

Per-credit charge: $360.

FINANCIAL AID PICTURE

Students with need: Need-based aid available for full-time and part-time students. Work study available nights.

Students without need: This college awards aid only to students with need.

FINANCIAL AID PROCEDURES

Forms required: FAFSA.

Dates and Deadlines: No deadline.

CONTACT

Yazmin Palma, Financial Aid Director
8230 West Flagler Street, Miami, FL 33144

Daytona State College

Daytona Beach, Florida
www.daytonastate.edu Federal Code: 001475

2-year public community and technical college in large city.

Enrollment: 10,327 undergrads, 56% part-time. 1,209 full-time freshmen.

Selectivity: Open admission; but selective for some programs.

BASIC COSTS (2008-2009)

Tuition and fees: $2,348; out-of-state residents $8,830.

FINANCIAL AID PICTURE (2007-2008)

Students with need: 60% of average financial aid package awarded as scholarships/grants, 40% awarded as loans/jobs. Need-based aid available for part-time students.

Students without need: No-need awards available for athletics, leadership, music/drama.

FINANCIAL AID PROCEDURES

Forms required: FAFSA.

Dates and Deadlines: No deadline. Applicants notified on a rolling basis starting 2/15.

CONTACT

Aileen Morrissey, Director of Financial Aid
Daytona State College Admissions Office, Daytona Beach, FL 32114-2811
(386) 506-3000 ext. 3015

DeVry University: Miramar

Miramar, Florida
www.devry.edu

4-year for-profit university in large town.

Enrollment: 955 undergrads, 52% part-time. 84 full-time freshmen.

BASIC COSTS (2008-2009)

Tuition and fees: $14,130.

Per-credit charge: $515.

FINANCIAL AID PICTURE (2007-2008)

Students with need: Need-based aid available for full-time and part-time students.

Students without need: This college awards aid only to students with need.

FINANCIAL AID PROCEDURES

Forms required: FAFSA.

Dates and Deadlines: No deadline. Applicants notified on a rolling basis.

CONTACT

Scott Howard, Assistant Director of Student Finance
2300 Southwest 145th Avenue, Miramar, FL 33027
(954) 499-9700

DeVry University: Orlando

Orlando, Florida
www.devry.edu Federal Code: 022966

4-year for-profit university in very large city.

Enrollment: 1,403 undergrads, 51% part-time. 145 full-time freshmen.

BASIC COSTS (2008-2009)

Tuition and fees: $14,130.

Per-credit charge: $515.

FINANCIAL AID PICTURE (2007-2008)

Students with need: Need-based aid available for full-time and part-time students.

Students without need: This college awards aid only to students with need.

FINANCIAL AID PROCEDURES

Forms required: FAFSA.

Dates and Deadlines: No deadline. Applicants notified on a rolling basis.

CONTACT

Estrella Velasquez Domenech, Director of Student Finance
4000 Millennia Boulevard, Orlando, FL 32839-2426
(407) 345-2800

Eckerd College

St. Petersburg, Florida
www.eckerd.edu Federal Code: 001487

4-year private liberal arts college in large city, affiliated with Presbyterian Church (USA).

Enrollment: 1,808 undergrads, 1% part-time. 486 full-time freshmen.

Selectivity: Admits 50 to 75% of applicants.

BASIC COSTS (2008-2009)

Tuition and fees: $30,590.
Per-credit charge: $1,043.
Room and board: $8,754.

FINANCIAL AID PICTURE (2008-2009)

Students with need: Need-based aid available for full-time and part-time students.
Students without need: No-need awards available for academics, art, athletics, music/drama.
Scholarships offered: Academic scholarships: ranging from $7,500 to $13,000 per year; available to entering freshmen regardless of financial need. Trustee, Presidential, and Dean's Scholarships: range from $13,000 to $25,000 awarded to outstanding freshmen with strong scholastic records and leadership potential. Limited number of Artistic Achievement Awards in music, theater, visual art and creative writing also available through separate application process.

FINANCIAL AID PROCEDURES

Forms required: FAFSA.
Dates and Deadlines: Priority date 3/1; no closing date. Applicants notified on a rolling basis starting 2/1.

CONTACT

Patricia Watkins, Director of Financial Aid
4200 54th Avenue South, St. Petersburg, FL 33711-4700
(727) 864-8334

Edison State College

Fort Myers, Florida
www.edison.edu Federal Code: 001477

4-year public liberal arts college in very large city.
Enrollment: 13,740 undergrads.
Selectivity: Open admission; but selective for some programs.

BASIC COSTS (2008-2009)

Tuition and fees: $2,348; out-of-state residents $8,830.

FINANCIAL AID PICTURE

Students with need: Need-based aid available for full-time and part-time students. Work study available nights, weekends, and for part-time students.
Students without need: No-need awards available for art, music/drama.

FINANCIAL AID PROCEDURES

Forms required: FAFSA.
Dates and Deadlines: Priority date 5/1; no closing date. Applicants notified on a rolling basis starting 6/1; must reply within 2 week(s) of notification.

CONTACT

Cindy Lewis, District Director of Financial Aid
Box 60210, Fort Myers, FL 33906-6210
(239) 489-9346

Edward Waters College

Jacksonville, Florida
www.ewc.edu Federal Code: 001478

4-year private liberal arts college in very large city, affiliated with African Methodist Episcopal Church.
Enrollment: 847 undergrads.
Selectivity: Open admission.

BASIC COSTS (2008-2009)

Tuition and fees: $9,196.
Per-credit charge: $382.
Room and board: $6,474.

FINANCIAL AID PICTURE (2007-2008)

Students with need: Need-based aid available for full-time and part-time students. Work study available nights, weekends, and for part-time students.

FINANCIAL AID PROCEDURES

Forms required: FAFSA.
Dates and Deadlines: Closing date 4/15. Applicants notified on a rolling basis starting 5/1; must reply within 2 week(s) of notification.

CONTACT

Roslyn Lopez, Director of Financial Aid
1658 Kings Road, Jacksonville, FL 32209
(904) 470-8190

Embry-Riddle Aeronautical University

Daytona Beach, Florida
www.embryriddle.edu Federal Code: 001479

4-year private university in small city.
Enrollment: 4,632 undergrads, 6% part-time. 1,059 full-time freshmen.
Selectivity: Admits over 75% of applicants.

BASIC COSTS (2008-2009)

Tuition and fees: $27,540.
Per-credit charge: $1,100.
Room and board: $9,580.

FINANCIAL AID PICTURE (2008-2009)

Students with need: Out of 876 full-time freshmen who applied for aid, 738 were judged to have need. Of these, 738 received aid. For part-time students, average financial aid package was $10,550.
Students without need: No-need awards available for academics, alumni affiliation, athletics, leadership, ROTC.
Scholarships offered: 27 full-time freshmen received athletic scholarships; average amount $7,737.

FINANCIAL AID PROCEDURES

Forms required: FAFSA.
Dates and Deadlines: No deadline. Applicants notified on a rolling basis starting 3/1; must reply within 4 week(s) of notification.

CONTACT

Barbara Dryden, Director of Financial Aid
600 South Clyde Morris Boulevard, Daytona Beach, FL 32114-3900
(386) 226-6300

Embry-Riddle Aeronautical University: Worldwide Campus

Daytona Beach, Florida
www.embryriddle.edu Federal Code: 001479

4-year private university in small city.
Enrollment: 11,591 undergrads, 83% part-time. 46 full-time freshmen.

BASIC COSTS (2009-2010)

Additional info: Per credit hour charges range from $221 - $309.

FINANCIAL AID PICTURE (2008-2009)

Students with need: Out of 7 full-time freshmen who applied for aid, 7 were judged to have need. Of these, 7 received aid. For part-time students, average financial aid package was $5,236.
Students without need: No-need awards available for academics.

FINANCIAL AID PROCEDURES

Forms required: FAFSA.
Dates and Deadlines: Priority date 4/15; no closing date. Applicants notified on a rolling basis starting 3/1; must reply within 4 week(s) of notification.

CONTACT
Barbara Dryden, Director of Financial Aid
600 South Clyde Morris Boulevard, Daytona Beach, FL 32114-3900
(386) 226-6300

Everest University: Brandon

Tampa, Florida
www.everest.edu Federal Code: 001534

4-year for-profit university and business college in very large city.
Enrollment: 1,165 undergrads.

BASIC COSTS (2008-2009)
Tuition and fees: $15,750.
Per-credit charge: $350.

FINANCIAL AID PICTURE
Students with need: Need-based aid available for full-time and part-time students.
Students without need: This college awards aid only to students with need.

FINANCIAL AID PROCEDURES
Forms required: FAFSA, institutional form.
Dates and Deadlines: No deadline. Applicants notified on a rolling basis; must reply within 2 week(s) of notification.

CONTACT
Jose Nieves, Director of Financial Aid
3924 Coconut Palm Drive, Tampa, FL 33619
(813) 621-0041 ext. 118

Everest University: Lakeland

Lakeland, Florida
www.everest.edu Federal Code: 025998

4-year for-profit university and branch campus college in small city.
Enrollment: 700 undergrads.

BASIC COSTS (2008-2009)
Tuition and fees: $15,750.
Per-credit charge: $350.
Additional info: Tuition and fees may vary by program.

FINANCIAL AID PICTURE
Students with need: Need-based aid available for full-time and part-time students.
Students without need: This college awards aid only to students with need.

FINANCIAL AID PROCEDURES
Dates and Deadlines: No deadline.

CONTACT
Andrew Feldberg
995 East Memorial Boulevard, Suite 110, Lakeland, FL 33801-1919
(863) 686-1449 ext. 101

Everest University: Largo

Largo, Florida
www.everest.edu Federal Code: 025998

4-year for-profit university and business college in large city.
Enrollment: 536 undergrads.

BASIC COSTS (2008-2009)
Tuition and fees: $15,750.
Per-credit charge: $350.
Additional info: Tuition and fees may vary by program.

FINANCIAL AID PICTURE
Students with need: Need-based aid available for full-time and part-time students. Work study available nights.

FINANCIAL AID PROCEDURES
Forms required: FAFSA, institutional form.
Dates and Deadlines: No deadline. Applicants notified on a rolling basis.

CONTACT
David Destrooper, Director of Financial aid
1199 East Bay Drive Largo, Largo, FL 33770
(727) 725-2688

Everest University: North Orlando

Orlando, Florida
www.everest.edu Federal Code: 001499

4-year for-profit business college in very large city.
Enrollment: 1,250 undergrads.

BASIC COSTS (2008-2009)
Tuition and fees: $15,750.
Per-credit charge: $350.
Additional info: Tuition and fees may vary by program.

FINANCIAL AID PICTURE
Students with need: Need-based aid available for full-time and part-time students.

FINANCIAL AID PROCEDURES
Forms required: FAFSA.
Dates and Deadlines: No deadline. Applicants notified on a rolling basis starting 6/1.

CONTACT
Linda Kaisrlik, Senior Financial Aid Administrator
5421 Diplomat Circle, Orlando, FL 32810
(407) 628-5870 ext. 118

Everest University: Tampa

Tampa, Florida
www.everest.edu Federal Code: 001534

4-year for-profit university and business college in large city.
Enrollment: 946 undergrads.

BASIC COSTS (2008-2009)
Tuition and fees: $15,750.
Per-credit charge: $350.
Additional info: Cost of tuition may vary with program.

FINANCIAL AID PICTURE
Students with need: Need-based aid available for full-time and part-time students.
Students without need: This college awards aid only to students with need.

FINANCIAL AID PROCEDURES
Forms required: FAFSA.
Dates and Deadlines: No deadline. Applicants notified on a rolling basis.

CONTACT
Jennifer Hayne, Director of Financial Aid
3319 West Hillsborough Avenue, Tampa, FL 33614
(813) 879-6000 ext. 145

Flagler College
St. Augustine, Florida
www.flagler.edu Federal Code: 007893

4-year private liberal arts college in large town.
Enrollment: 2,762 undergrads, 3% part-time. 646 full-time freshmen.
Selectivity: Admits less than 50% of applicants.

BASIC COSTS (2009-2010)
Tuition and fees: $13,300.
Per-credit charge: $443.
Room and board: $7,190.

FINANCIAL AID PICTURE (2008-2009)
Students with need: Average financial aid package met 90% of need; average scholarship/grant was $4,494; average loan was $3,586. For part-time students, average financial aid package was $2,142.
Students without need: No-need awards available for academics, art, athletics, job skills, leadership, minority status, music/drama, state/district residency.
Cumulative student debt: 61% of graduating class had student loans; average debt was $18,415.

FINANCIAL AID PROCEDURES
Forms required: FAFSA, state aid form, institutional form.
Dates and Deadlines: Priority date 4/1; no closing date. Applicants notified on a rolling basis starting 4/1; must reply within 2 week(s) of notification.
Transfers: No deadline. Applicants notified on a rolling basis starting 3/1, must reply within 2 week(s) of notification. Transfer students receiving Florida-sponsored aid must notify Florida Office of Student Financial Assistance of their transfer.

CONTACT
Christopher Haffner, Director of Financial Aid
74 King Street, St. Augustine, FL 32084
(800) 304-4208

Florida Agricultural and Mechanical University
Tallahassee, Florida
www.famu.edu Federal Code: 001480

4-year public university in small city.
Enrollment: 9,457 undergrads, 9% part-time. 2,092 full-time freshmen.
Selectivity: Admits 50 to 75% of applicants.

BASIC COSTS (2008-2009)
Tuition and fees: $3,572; out-of-state residents $15,513.
Room and board: $6,508.

FINANCIAL AID PICTURE (2007-2008)
Students with need: Need-based aid available for full-time and part-time students.
Students without need: No-need awards available for academics, art, leadership.

FINANCIAL AID PROCEDURES
Forms required: FAFSA.
Dates and Deadlines: Priority date 3/1; closing date 6/30. Applicants notified on a rolling basis starting 3/1; must reply within 2 week(s) of notification.
Transfers: No deadline. Applicants notified on a rolling basis.

CONTACT
Marcia Boyd, Director of Financial Aid
FHAC, G-9, Tallahassee, FL 32307-3200
(850) 599-3730

Florida Atlantic University
Boca Raton, Florida
www.fau.edu Federal Code: 001481

4-year public university in small city.
Enrollment: 20,946 undergrads, 41% part-time. 2,520 full-time freshmen.
Selectivity: Admits less than 50% of applicants.

BASIC COSTS (2008-2009)
Tuition and fees: $3,782; out-of-state residents $17,506.
Room and board: $9,170.

FINANCIAL AID PICTURE (2008-2009)
Students with need: Out of 2,113 full-time freshmen who applied for aid, 1,135 were judged to have need. Of these, 1,111 received aid, and 259 had their full need met. Average financial aid package met 97% of need; average scholarship/grant was $7,338; average loan was $3,165. For part-time students, average financial aid package was $5,604.
Students without need: 115 full-time freshmen who did not demonstrate need for aid received scholarships/grants; average award was $1,993. No-need awards available for academics, athletics, music/drama, state/district residency.
Scholarships offered: 41 full-time freshmen received athletic scholarships; average amount $7,925.

FINANCIAL AID PROCEDURES
Forms required: FAFSA.
Dates and Deadlines: Priority date 3/1; no closing date. Applicants notified on a rolling basis starting 4/1; must reply within 3 week(s) of notification.

CONTACT
Carol Pfeilsticker, Director of Financial Aid
777 Glades Road, Boca Raton, FL 33431
(561) 297-2738

Florida Christian College
Kissimmee, Florida
www.fcc.edu Federal Code: 015192

4-year private Bible and teachers college in small city, affiliated with Christian Churches and Churches of Christ.
Enrollment: 230 undergrads, 26% part-time. 51 full-time freshmen.
Selectivity: Admits less than 50% of applicants.

BASIC COSTS (2008-2009)
Tuition and fees: $10,200.
Per-credit charge: $325.
Room only: $2,400.
Additional info: Tuition at time of enrollment locked for 4 years.

FINANCIAL AID PICTURE (2007-2008)
Students with need: Need-based aid available for full-time and part-time students. Work study available nights, weekends, and for part-time students.
Students without need: No-need awards available for academics, alumni affiliation, leadership, music/drama, religious affiliation, state/district residency.

FINANCIAL AID PROCEDURES
Forms required: FAFSA, institutional form.
Dates and Deadlines: Priority date 5/1; closing date 7/15. Applicants notified on a rolling basis starting 3/1.

Transfers: Available only if funding remains.

CONTACT

Bruce Dusterhoft, Director of Student Financial Aid
1011 Bill Beck Boulevard, Kissimmee, FL 34744-4402
(407) 569-1365

Florida College

Temple Terrace, Florida
www.floridacollege.edu Federal Code: 001482

4-year private liberal arts college in large town.
Enrollment: 506 undergrads, 4% part-time. 178 full-time freshmen.
Selectivity: Admits 50 to 75% of applicants.

BASIC COSTS (2008-2009)

Tuition and fees: $12,060.
Per-credit charge: $450.
Room and board: $6,300.

FINANCIAL AID PICTURE (2008-2009)

Students with need: Average financial aid package met 47% of need; average scholarship/grant was $1,121; average loan was $1,743. For part-time students, average financial aid package was $2,750.
Students without need: No-need awards available for academics, athletics, music/drama, state/district residency.

FINANCIAL AID PROCEDURES

Forms required: FAFSA, state aid form, institutional form.
Dates and Deadlines: Applicants notified on a rolling basis starting 3/1; must reply within 2 week(s) of notification.
Transfers: No deadline.

CONTACT

Lisa McClister, Financial Aid Director
119 North Glen Arven Avenue, Temple Terrace, FL 33617
(813) 899-6720

Florida College of Natural Health: Bradenton

Bradenton, Florida
www.fcnh.com

2-year for-profit health science and career college in small city.
Enrollment: 100 undergrads.
Selectivity: Open admission; but selective for some programs.

BASIC COSTS (2008-2009)

Tuition and fees: $20,948.

FINANCIAL AID PICTURE

Students with need: Need-based aid available for full-time students.
Students without need: This college awards aid only to students with need.

FINANCIAL AID PROCEDURES

Forms required: FAFSA.
Dates and Deadlines: No deadline. Applicants notified on a rolling basis.

CONTACT

Theofani Kalogeropoulos, Director
616 67th Street Circle East, Bradenton, FL 34208

Florida Community College at Jacksonville

Jacksonville, Florida
www.fccj.edu Federal Code: 001484

2-year public community college in very large city.
Enrollment: 23,901 undergrads, 68% part-time. 1,963 full-time freshmen.
Selectivity: Open admission; but selective for some programs.

BASIC COSTS (2008-2009)

Tuition and fees: $2,226; out-of-state residents $8,418.

FINANCIAL AID PICTURE (2008-2009)

Students with need: Need-based aid available for full-time and part-time students. Work study available nights, weekends, and for part-time students.
Students without need: No-need awards available for academics, alumni affiliation, art, athletics, job skills, leadership, minority status, music/drama.

FINANCIAL AID PROCEDURES

Forms required: FAFSA, institutional form.
Dates and Deadlines: Priority date 8/1; no closing date. Applicants notified by 7/1.

CONTACT

Joel Friedman, Director of Student Aid
501 West State Street, Jacksonville, FL 32202
(904) 632-3352

Florida Gulf Coast University

Ft. Myers, Florida
www.fgcu.edu Federal Code: 032553

4-year public university in small city.
Enrollment: 8,645 undergrads, 19% part-time. 1,785 full-time freshmen.
Selectivity: Admits 50 to 75% of applicants.

BASIC COSTS (2008-2009)

Tuition and fees: $3,969; out-of-state residents $17,238.
Room and board: $7,450.

FINANCIAL AID PICTURE (2007-2008)

Students with need: Out of 1,491 full-time freshmen who applied for aid, 619 were judged to have need. Of these, 619 received aid, and 50 had their full need met. Average financial aid package met 65% of need; average scholarship/grant was $4,012; average loan was $3,308. For part-time students, average financial aid package was $4,953.
Students without need: 111 full-time freshmen who did not demonstrate need for aid received scholarships/grants; average award was $5,292. No-need awards available for academics, alumni affiliation, athletics, leadership, minority status, music/drama, religious affiliation, state/district residency.
Scholarships offered: 21 full-time freshmen received athletic scholarships; average amount $4,996.
Cumulative student debt: 36% of graduating class had student loans; average debt was $11,747.

FINANCIAL AID PROCEDURES

Forms required: FAFSA.
Dates and Deadlines: Priority date 3/1; closing date 6/30. Applicants notified on a rolling basis starting 2/15.
Transfers: Applicants notified on a rolling basis.

CONTACT

Jorge Lopez-Rosado, Director, Student Financial Aid
10501 FGCU Boulevard South, Ft. Myers, FL 33965-6565
(239) 590-7920

Florida Hospital College of Health Sciences

Orlando, Florida
www.FHCHS.edu Federal Code: 031155

4-year private health science and nursing college, in large city, affiliated with Seventh-day Adventists.
Enrollment: 2,369 undergrads.

BASIC COSTS (2008-2009)

Tuition and fees: $8,540.
Per-credit charge: $275.
Room only: $3,360.
Additional info: Fees vary according to program.

FINANCIAL AID PICTURE (2007-2008)

Students with need: 52% of average financial aid package awarded as scholarships/grants, 48% awarded as loans/jobs. Need-based aid available for part-time students.
Students without need: No-need awards available for state/district residency.

FINANCIAL AID PROCEDURES

Forms required: FAFSA, institutional form.
Dates and Deadlines: Priority date 4/12; no closing date. Applicants notified on a rolling basis starting 3/1.

CONTACT

Starr Bender, Director of Financial Aid
671 Winyah Drive, Orlando, FL 32803
(407) 303-6963

Florida Institute of Technology

Melbourne, Florida
www.fit.edu Federal Code: 001469

4-year private university in small city.
Enrollment: 3,557 undergrads, 17% part-time. 635 full-time freshmen.
Selectivity: Admits over 75% of applicants.

BASIC COSTS (2009-2010)

Tuition and fees: $31,520.
Per-credit charge: $930.
Room and board: $10,630.
Additional info: Tuition $28,260 for aeronautics, business, psychology, and humanities programs.

FINANCIAL AID PICTURE (2008-2009)

Students with need: Out of 475 full-time freshmen who applied for aid, 394 were judged to have need. Of these, 392 received aid, and 104 had their full need met. Average financial aid package met 84% of need; average scholarship/grant was $20,050; average loan was $3,432. For part-time students, average financial aid package was $9,840.
Students without need: 216 full-time freshmen who did not demonstrate need for aid received scholarships/grants; average award was $9,230. No-need awards available for academics, alumni affiliation, athletics, ROTC, state/district residency.
Scholarships offered: 23 full-time freshmen received athletic scholarships; average amount $19,324.
Cumulative student debt: 70% of graduating class had student loans; average debt was $35,106.

FINANCIAL AID PROCEDURES

Forms required: FAFSA, state aid form.
Dates and Deadlines: Priority date 3/1; no closing date. Applicants notified on a rolling basis starting 2/15; must reply by 5/1 or within 4 week(s) of notification.
Transfers: No deadline. Applicants notified on a rolling basis starting 2/15; must reply by 5/1 or within 4 week(s) of notification.

CONTACT

Jay Lally, Director of Financial Aid
150 West University Boulevard, Melbourne, FL 32901-6975
(321) 674-8070

Florida International University

Miami, Florida
www.fiu.edu Federal Code: 009635

4-year public university in very large city.
Enrollment: 30,717 undergrads, 38% part-time. 2,759 full-time freshmen.
Selectivity: Admits less than 50% of applicants.

BASIC COSTS (2008-2009)

Tuition and fees: $3,975; out-of-state residents $16,374.
Room and board: $11,120.

FINANCIAL AID PICTURE (2008-2009)

Students with need: Need-based aid available for full-time and part-time students.
Students without need: No-need awards available for academics, art, athletics, minority status, music/drama, state/district residency.

FINANCIAL AID PROCEDURES

Forms required: FAFSA.
Dates and Deadlines: Priority date 3/1; closing date 5/15. Applicants notified on a rolling basis; must reply by 5/1 or within 4 week(s) of notification.

CONTACT

Francisco Valines, Director of Financial Aid
University Park Campus, PC 140, Miami, FL 33199
(305) 348-7272

Florida Keys Community College

Key West, Florida
www.fkcc.edu Federal Code: 001485

2-year public nursing and community college in large town.
Enrollment: 1,000 undergrads, 73% part-time. 22 full-time freshmen.
Selectivity: Open admission; but selective for some programs.

BASIC COSTS (2008-2009)

Tuition and fees: $2,385; out-of-state residents $8,980.

FINANCIAL AID PICTURE

Students with need: Need-based aid available for full-time and part-time students.
Students without need: No-need awards available for academics, art, leadership, minority status.

FINANCIAL AID PROCEDURES

Forms required: FAFSA, institutional form.
Dates and Deadlines: Priority date 5/1; no closing date. Applicants notified on a rolling basis starting 6/15; must reply within 2 week(s) of notification.
Transfers: Closing date 5/1. Florida Student Assistance Grant available to students paying Florida resident tuition.

CONTACT

Lynn Burris, Financial Aid Director
5901 College Road, Key West, FL 33040
(305) 809-3523

Florida Memorial University

Miami Gardens, Florida
www.fmuniv.edu Federal Code: 001486

4-year private liberal arts college in very large city, affiliated with American Baptist Churches in the USA.

Enrollment: 1,738 undergrads, 8% part-time. 543 full-time freshmen.

BASIC COSTS (2008-2009)

Tuition and fees: $12,254.
Per-credit charge: $438.
Room and board: $5,340.

FINANCIAL AID PICTURE

Students with need: Need-based aid available for full-time and part-time students.

Additional info: Need-based financial aid available to part-time students taking 6 credits or more per semester.

FINANCIAL AID PROCEDURES

Dates and Deadlines: No deadline. Applicants notified on a rolling basis; must reply within 2 week(s) of notification.

Transfers: Priority date 3/15; closing date 4/15.

CONTACT

Brian Phillip, Director of Financial Aid
15800 Northwest 42 Avenue, Miami Gardens, FL 33054
(305) 430-1168

Florida National College

Hialeah, Florida
www.fnc.edu Federal Code: 017069

2-year for-profit liberal arts college in very large city.

Enrollment: 2,387 undergrads, 27% part-time. 522 full-time freshmen.

Selectivity: Open admission; but selective for some programs.

BASIC COSTS (2008-2009)

Tuition and fees: $12,594.
Per-credit charge: $400.

FINANCIAL AID PICTURE (2007-2008)

Students with need: Out of 522 full-time freshmen who applied for aid, 516 were judged to have need. Of these, 516 received aid. Need-based aid available for part-time students.

Students without need: This college awards aid only to students with need.

FINANCIAL AID PROCEDURES

Forms required: FAFSA, institutional form.

Dates and Deadlines: No deadline.

CONTACT

Omar Sanchez, Vice President for Planning and Research
4425 West 20th Avenue, Hialeah, FL 33012
(305) 821-3333 ext. 1003

Florida Southern College

Lakeland, Florida
www.flsouthern.edu Federal Code: 001488

4-year private liberal arts college in small city, affiliated with United Methodist Church.

Enrollment: 1,736 undergrads, 3% part-time. 497 full-time freshmen.

Selectivity: Admits 50 to 75% of applicants.

BASIC COSTS (2008-2009)

Tuition and fees: $22,145.
Per-credit charge: $650.
Room and board: $7,850.

FINANCIAL AID PICTURE (2008-2009)

Students with need: Out of 397 full-time freshmen who applied for aid, 327 were judged to have need. Of these, 327 received aid, and 87 had their full need met. Average financial aid package met 73% of need; average scholarship/grant was $6,576; average loan was $4,054. For part-time students, average financial aid package was $4,791.

Students without need: 93 full-time freshmen who did not demonstrate need for aid received scholarships/grants; average award was $8,915. No-need awards available for academics, alumni affiliation, art, athletics, job skills, leadership, minority status, music/drama, religious affiliation, ROTC, state/district residency.

Scholarships offered: 49 full-time freshmen received athletic scholarships; average amount $9,063.

Cumulative student debt: 66% of graduating class had student loans; average debt was $19,864.

FINANCIAL AID PROCEDURES

Forms required: FAFSA, institutional form.

Dates and Deadlines: Priority date 3/1; closing date 7/1. Applicants notified on a rolling basis starting 3/1; must reply within 3 week(s) of notification.

Transfers: No deadline. Applicants notified on a rolling basis; must reply within 2 week(s) of notification.

CONTACT

William Healy, Director of Financial Aid
111 Lake Hollingsworth Drive, Lakeland, FL 33801-5698
(863) 680-4140

Florida State University

Tallahassee, Florida
www.fsu.edu Federal Code: 001489

4-year public university in small city.

Enrollment: 29,405 undergrads, 11% part-time. 4,834 full-time freshmen.

Selectivity: Admits less than 50% of applicants.

BASIC COSTS (2008-2009)

Tuition and fees: $3,799; out-of-state residents $18,243.
Room and board: $8,178.

FINANCIAL AID PICTURE (2008-2009)

Students with need: Out of 3,411 full-time freshmen who applied for aid, 1,625 were judged to have need. Of these, 1,625 received aid, and 1,300 had their full need met. Average financial aid package met 76% of need; average scholarship/grant was $4,212; average loan was $2,692. Need-based aid available for part-time students.

Students without need: 485 full-time freshmen who did not demonstrate need for aid received scholarships/grants; average award was $2,272. No-need awards available for academics, athletics, state/district residency.

Cumulative student debt: 48% of graduating class had student loans; average debt was $16,927.

FINANCIAL AID PROCEDURES

Forms required: FAFSA.

Dates and Deadlines: No deadline. Applicants notified on a rolling basis starting 3/15.

CONTACT

Darryl Marshall, Director of Financial Aid
PO Box 3062400, Tallahassee, FL 32306-2400
(850) 644-0539

Florida Technical College: Deland

Deland, Florida
www.flatech.edu

2-year for-profit junior and technical college in small city.
Enrollment: 188 undergrads.
Selectivity: Open admission.

FINANCIAL AID PICTURE

Students with need: Need-based aid available for full-time and part-time students. Work study available nights.
Students without need: This college awards aid only to students with need.

FINANCIAL AID PROCEDURES

Forms required: FAFSA.
Dates and Deadlines: No deadline. Applicants notified on a rolling basis.
Transfers: No deadline. Applicants notified on a rolling basis.

CONTACT

Sandra Follmar, Financial Aid Administrator
1199 South Woodland Boulevard, Deland, FL 32720

Florida Technical College: Orlando

Orlando, Florida
www.flatech.edu Federal Code: 015670

2-year for-profit junior and technical college in large city.
Enrollment: 435 undergrads.
Selectivity: Open admission.

FINANCIAL AID PICTURE (2008-2009)

Students with need: Need-based aid available for full-time and part-time students.
Students without need: This college awards aid only to students with need.

FINANCIAL AID PROCEDURES

Forms required: FAFSA.
Dates and Deadlines: No deadline. Applicants notified on a rolling basis.

CONTACT

Jennie Gomeztagle, Financial Services
12689 Challenger Parkway, #130, Orlando, FL 32826-2707
(407) 447-7300

Full Sail University

Winter Park, Florida
www.fullsail.edu Federal Code: 016812

2-year for-profit visual arts and technical college in very large city.
Enrollment: 6,717 undergrads.
Selectivity: Open admission; but selective for some programs.

BASIC COSTS (2008-2009)

Additional info: Degree programs leading to an associate and bachelor range from $34,775 - $72,775. Includes books and supplies.

FINANCIAL AID PICTURE

Students with need: Need-based aid available for full-time students. Work study available nights, weekends, and for part-time students.

FINANCIAL AID PROCEDURES

Forms required: FAFSA.
Dates and Deadlines: No deadline. Applicants notified on a rolling basis; must reply within 2 week(s) of notification.

CONTACT

3300 University Boulevard, Winter Park, FL 32792-7429
(407) 679-0100 ext. 2300

Gulf Coast Community College

Panama City, Florida
www.gulfcoast.edu Federal Code: 001490

2-year public community college in small city.
Enrollment: 4,551 undergrads, 54% part-time. 405 full-time freshmen.
Selectivity: Open admission; but selective for some programs.

BASIC COSTS (2008-2009)

Tuition and fees: $2,221; out-of-state residents $7,949.

FINANCIAL AID PICTURE

Students with need: Need-based aid available for full-time and part-time students. Work study available nights, weekends, and for part-time students.
Students without need: No-need awards available for academics, athletics, job skills, leadership, minority status, music/drama, state/district residency.

FINANCIAL AID PROCEDURES

Forms required: FAFSA.
Dates and Deadlines: Priority date 4/1; closing date 7/1. Applicants notified on a rolling basis starting 7/1.
Transfers: Priority date 11/1; no deadline.

CONTACT

Chris Westlake, Director of Financial Aid
5230 West Highway 98, Panama City, FL 32401-1041
(850) 872-3845

Herzing College

Winter Park, Florida
www.herzing.edu Federal Code: 014030

2-year for-profit business and health science college in very large city.
Enrollment: 187 undergrads.
Selectivity: Open admission; but selective for some programs.

BASIC COSTS (2008-2009)

Tuition and fees: $12,150.
Per-credit charge: $380.
Additional info: Reported annual tuition is representative. Actual costs vary by program.

FINANCIAL AID PICTURE (2007-2008)

Students with need: 15% of average financial aid package awarded as scholarships/grants, 85% awarded as loans/jobs.

CONTACT

Karyn Fahey, Financial Aid Director
1595 South Semoran Boulevard, Suite 1501, Winter Park, FL 32792-5509

Hillsborough Community College

Tampa, Florida
www.hccfl.edu Federal Code: 007870

2-year public community college in large city.
Enrollment: 18,651 undergrads, 58% part-time. 2,584 full-time freshmen.
Selectivity: Open admission; but selective for some programs.

BASIC COSTS (2008-2009)

Tuition and fees: $2,348; out-of-state residents $8,451.

FINANCIAL AID PICTURE (2007-2008)

Students with need: 86% of average financial aid package awarded as scholarships/grants, 14% awarded as loans/jobs. Need-based aid available for part-time students. Work study available nights, weekends, and for part-time students.

Students without need: No-need awards available for academics, art, athletics, minority status, music/drama.

FINANCIAL AID PROCEDURES

Forms required: FAFSA, institutional form.

Dates and Deadlines: Priority date 5/15; closing date 6/30. Applicants notified on a rolling basis.

Transfers: No deadline. Transfer students must submit academic transcripts prior to obtaining student loans at sophomore level.

CONTACT

Charlotte Johns-Rich, Director of Financial Aid
Box 31127, Tampa, FL 33631-3127
(813) 253-7235

Hobe Sound Bible College

Hobe Sound, Florida
www.hsbc.edu Federal Code: 015463

4-year private Bible college in small town, affiliated with interdenominational tradition.

Enrollment: 160 undergrads.

BASIC COSTS (2008-2009)

Tuition and fees: $4,850.

Per-credit charge: $198.

Room and board: $4,400.

FINANCIAL AID PICTURE (2008-2009)

Students with need: Need-based aid available for full-time and part-time students.

Students without need: No-need awards available for academics, leadership.

FINANCIAL AID PROCEDURES

Forms required: FAFSA.

Dates and Deadlines: Closing date 8/1.

CONTACT

John Churchill, Director of Financial Aid
Box 1065, Hobe Sound, FL 33475
(772) 546-5534 ext. 1003

Hodges University

Naples, Florida
www.hodges.edu Federal Code: 030375

4-year private university and business college in small city.

Enrollment: 1,658 undergrads, 22% part-time. 170 full-time freshmen.

Selectivity: Admits over 75% of applicants.

BASIC COSTS (2008-2009)

Tuition and fees: $13,880.

Per-credit charge: $450.

FINANCIAL AID PICTURE (2008-2009)

Students with need: Out of 161 full-time freshmen who applied for aid, 144 were judged to have need. Of these, 144 received aid, and 30 had their full need met. Average financial aid package met 64% of need; average scholarship/grant was $2,400; average loan was $2,700. For part-time students, average financial aid package was $6,000.

Students without need: 28 full-time freshmen who did not demonstrate need for aid received scholarships/grants; average award was $350. No-need awards available for academics.

Cumulative student debt: 82% of graduating class had student loans; average debt was $18,600.

FINANCIAL AID PROCEDURES

Forms required: FAFSA.

Dates and Deadlines: Priority date 9/7; no closing date. Applicants notified on a rolling basis starting 7/7.

Transfers: No deadline. Applicants notified on a rolling basis.

CONTACT

Joe Gilchrist, Vice President of Student Financial Assistance
2655 Northbrooke Drive, Naples, FL 34119
(239) 513-1122

Indian River State College

Fort Pierce, Florida
www.ircc.edu Federal Code: 001493

2-year public community college in small city.

Enrollment: 9,464 undergrads.

Selectivity: Open admission; but selective for some programs.

BASIC COSTS (2008-2009)

Tuition and fees: $2,242; out-of-state residents $8,332.

FINANCIAL AID PICTURE (2007-2008)

Students with need: 78% of average financial aid package awarded as scholarships/grants, 22% awarded as loans/jobs. Need-based aid available for part-time students.

Students without need: No-need awards available for academics, athletics, minority status, music/drama, state/district residency.

FINANCIAL AID PROCEDURES

Forms required: FAFSA, institutional form.

Dates and Deadlines: Priority date 7/18; no closing date. Applicants notified on a rolling basis starting 5/15.

CONTACT

Mary Lewis, Director of Financial Aid
3209 Virginia Avenue, Fort Pierce, FL 34981-5596
(772) 462-7450

International Academy of Design and Technology: Orlando

Orlando, Florida
www.iadt.edu Federal Code: 030314

4-year for-profit career college in very large city.

Enrollment: 1,151 undergrads.

Selectivity: Open admission.

FINANCIAL AID PICTURE (2007-2008)

Students with need: 50% of average financial aid package awarded as scholarships/grants, 50% awarded as loans/jobs.

FINANCIAL AID PROCEDURES

Forms required: FAFSA.

Dates and Deadlines: No deadline.

CONTACT

Daisy Tabachow, Director of Finanacial Aid
5959 Lake Ellenor Drive, Orlando, FL 32809
(407) 857-2300

International Academy of Design and Technology: Tampa

Tampa, Florida
www.academy.edu Federal Code: 030314

4-year for-profit visual arts and technical college in very large city.
Enrollment: 2,560 undergrads.
Selectivity: Open admission.

BASIC COSTS (2008-2009)
Tuition and fees: $18,780.
Per-credit charge: $385.

FINANCIAL AID PICTURE (2007-2008)
Students with need: 26% of average financial aid package awarded as scholarships/grants, 74% awarded as loans/jobs. Need-based aid available for part-time students. Work study available nights, weekends, and for part-time students.
Students without need: No-need awards available for academics.

FINANCIAL AID PROCEDURES
Forms required: FAFSA.
Dates and Deadlines: No deadline.

CONTACT
Tim Coppola, Vice President of Finance
5104 Eisenhower Boulevard, Tampa, FL 33634
(813) 880-8056

Jacksonville University

Jacksonville, Florida
www.ju.edu Federal Code: 001495

4-year private university and liberal arts college in very large city.
Enrollment: 2,950 undergrads, 28% part-time. 539 full-time freshmen.
Selectivity: Admits 50 to 75% of applicants.

BASIC COSTS (2008-2009)
Tuition and fees: $23,900.
Per-credit charge: $795.
Room and board: $8,760.
Additional info: $540 mandatory health insurance fee charged unless proof of other coverage is provided.

FINANCIAL AID PICTURE (2008-2009)
Students with need: Average financial aid package met 52% of need; average scholarship/grant was $15,971; average loan was $3,906. For part-time students, average financial aid package was $10,398.
Students without need: No-need awards available for academics, art, athletics, job skills, leadership, music/drama, ROTC, state/district residency.

FINANCIAL AID PROCEDURES
Forms required: FAFSA, state aid form, institutional form.
Dates and Deadlines: Priority date 3/15; no closing date. Applicants notified on a rolling basis starting 2/15.
Transfers: No deadline. Applicants notified on a rolling basis.

CONTACT
Catherine Huntress, Financial Aid Director
2800 University Boulevard North, Jacksonville, FL 32211-3394
(904) 256-7060

Johnson & Wales University: North Miami

North Miami, Florida
www.jwu.edu Federal Code: 003404

4-year private university in large city.
Enrollment: 1,917 undergrads, 3% part-time. 578 full-time freshmen.
Selectivity: Admits over 75% of applicants.

BASIC COSTS (2009-2010)
Tuition and fees: $23,490.
Room and board: $8,274.

FINANCIAL AID PICTURE (2008-2009)
Students with need: Out of 563 full-time freshmen who applied for aid, 493 were judged to have need. Of these, 491 received aid, and 23 had their full need met. Average financial aid package met 66% of need; average scholarship/grant was $8,864; average loan was $3,393. For part-time students, average financial aid package was $11,398.
Students without need: 56 full-time freshmen who did not demonstrate need for aid received scholarships/grants; average award was $5,250. No-need awards available for academics, alumni affiliation, job skills, leadership, state/district residency.
Cumulative student debt: 79% of graduating class had student loans; average debt was $33,501.

FINANCIAL AID PROCEDURES
Forms required: FAFSA.
Dates and Deadlines: No deadline. Applicants notified on a rolling basis starting 3/1; must reply within 2 week(s) of notification.

CONTACT
Lynn Robinson, Director, Financial Aid
1701 Northeast 127th Street, North Miami, FL 33181
(800) 342-5598

Jones College

Jacksonville, Florida
www.jones.edu Federal Code: 001497

4-year private business and teachers college in very large city.
Enrollment: 619 undergrads, 64% part-time. 17 full-time freshmen.
Selectivity: Open admission.

BASIC COSTS (2009-2010)
Tuition and fees: $8,340.
Per-credit charge: $275.

FINANCIAL AID PICTURE
Students with need: Need-based aid available for full-time and part-time students. Work study available nights, weekends, and for part-time students.
Students without need: This college awards aid only to students with need.

FINANCIAL AID PROCEDURES
Forms required: FAFSA.
Dates and Deadlines: No deadline. Applicants notified on a rolling basis.

CONTACT
Becky Davis, Financial Assistant Director
5353 Arlington Expressway, Jacksonville, FL 32211
(904) 743-1122 ext. 100

Jones College: Miami
Miami, Florida
www.jones.edu/

4-year private branch campus and career college in very large city.

FINANCIAL AID PICTURE
Students with need: Work study available nights.

Key College
Dania Beach, Florida
www.keycollege.edu Federal Code: 015191

2-year for-profit business and technical college in very large city.
Enrollment: 175 undergrads.
Selectivity: Open admission; but selective for some programs.

BASIC COSTS (2008-2009)
Tuition and fees: $9,210.

FINANCIAL AID PICTURE
Students with need: Work study available nights.
Additional info: Federal Supplemental Educational Opportunities Grant (FSEOG), PELL grant, FFEL (federal loan program) available; direct loans offered.

FINANCIAL AID PROCEDURES
Dates and Deadlines: No deadline.

CONTACT
Jo McGrath, Director of Financial Services
225 Dania Beach Boulevard, Dania Beach, FL 33004
(954) 923-4440

Lake City Community College
Lake City, Florida
www.lakecitycc.edu Federal Code: 001501

2-year public community college in large town.
Enrollment: 2,753 undergrads.
Selectivity: Open admission; but selective for some programs.

BASIC COSTS (2008-2009)
Tuition and fees: $2,237; out-of-state residents $8,522.
Additional info: Tuition/fee waivers available for minority students.

FINANCIAL AID PICTURE
Students with need: Need-based aid available for full-time and part-time students.
Students without need: No-need awards available for academics, athletics.

FINANCIAL AID PROCEDURES
Forms required: FAFSA, institutional form.
Dates and Deadlines: Priority date 6/1; no closing date. Applicants notified on a rolling basis starting 6/1; must reply within 2 week(s) of notification.

CONTACT
Debberin Tunsil, Director of Financial Aid
149 SE College Place, Lake City, FL 32025-8703
(386) 754-4282

Lake-Sumter Community College
Leesburg, Florida
www.lscc.edu Federal Code: 001502

2-year public community college in small city.
Enrollment: 3,274 undergrads, 63% part-time. 420 full-time freshmen.
Selectivity: Open admission; but selective for some programs.

BASIC COSTS (2008-2009)
Tuition and fees: $2,326; out-of-state residents $8,743.

FINANCIAL AID PICTURE (2008-2009)
Students with need: Out of 91 full-time freshmen who applied for aid, 91 were judged to have need. Of these, 91 received aid. For part-time students, average financial aid package was $1,756.
Students without need: No-need awards available for academics, art, athletics, leadership, minority status, music/drama, state/district residency.

FINANCIAL AID PROCEDURES
Forms required: FAFSA, institutional form.
Dates and Deadlines: Priority date 4/15; no closing date. Applicants notified on a rolling basis starting 7/1.

CONTACT
Audrey Williams, Financial Aid Director
9501 U.S. Highway 441, Leesburg, FL 34788-8751
(352) 365-3512

Lynn University
Boca Raton, Florida
www.lynn.edu Federal Code: 001505

4-year private university in small city.
Enrollment: 1,972 undergrads, 10% part-time. 371 full-time freshmen.
Selectivity: Admits 50 to 75% of applicants.

BASIC COSTS (2009-2010)
Tuition and fees: $30,100.
Room and board: $10,900.

FINANCIAL AID PICTURE (2008-2009)
Students with need: Out of 269 full-time freshmen who applied for aid, 133 were judged to have need. Of these, 127 received aid, and 17 had their full need met. Average financial aid package met 58% of need; average scholarship/grant was $13,022; average loan was $4,514. For part-time students, average financial aid package was $5,945.
Students without need: 121 full-time freshmen who did not demonstrate need for aid received scholarships/grants; average award was $11,469. No-need awards available for academics, athletics, leadership, music/drama, religious affiliation, state/district residency.
Scholarships offered: 32 full-time freshmen received athletic scholarships; average amount $9,045.
Cumulative student debt: 37% of graduating class had student loans; average debt was $30,175.

FINANCIAL AID PROCEDURES
Forms required: FAFSA, institutional form.
Dates and Deadlines: Priority date 3/1; no closing date. Applicants notified on a rolling basis starting 2/1; must reply within 2 week(s) of notification.
Transfers: Scholarships and grants available.

CONTACT
Chan Park, Director of Student Financial Assistance
3601 North Military Trail, Boca Raton, FL 33431-5598
(561) 237-7185

Manatee Community College

Bradenton, Florida
www.mccfl.edu Federal Code: 001504

2-year public community college in small city.
Enrollment: 9,157 undergrads, 50% part-time. 1,342 full-time freshmen.
Selectivity: Open admission; but selective for some programs.

BASIC COSTS (2008-2009)
Tuition and fees: $2,348; out-of-state residents $8,830.

FINANCIAL AID PICTURE (2008-2009)
Students with need: Out of 890 full-time freshmen who applied for aid, 695 were judged to have need. Of these, 695 received aid, and 618 had their full need met. Need-based aid available for part-time students.
Students without need: 283 full-time freshmen who did not demonstrate need for aid received scholarships/grants; average award was $3,962. No-need awards available for academics, art, athletics, music/drama, state/district residency.

FINANCIAL AID PROCEDURES
Forms required: FAFSA.
Dates and Deadlines: Priority date 6/1; closing date 7/28. Applicants notified on a rolling basis starting 3/15.

CONTACT
Anders Nilsen, Director of Financial Aid
Box 1849, Bradenton, FL 34206-1849
(941) 752-5037

Miami Dade College

Miami, Florida
www.mdc.edu/main/ Federal Code: 001506

2-year public community college in very large city.
Enrollment: 49,147 undergrads, 60% part-time. 5,954 full-time freshmen.
Selectivity: Open admission; but selective for some programs.

BASIC COSTS (2008-2009)
Tuition and fees: $2,348; out-of-state residents $8,469.

FINANCIAL AID PICTURE (2008-2009)
Students with need: Average financial aid package met 67% of need; average scholarship/grant was $1,313; average loan was $483. For part-time students, average financial aid package was $573.
Students without need: No-need awards available for academics, art, athletics, music/drama, state/district residency.

FINANCIAL AID PROCEDURES
Forms required: FAFSA.
Dates and Deadlines: Priority date 3/15; closing date 6/30. Applicants notified on a rolling basis starting 5/15.
Transfers: No deadline. Applicants notified on a rolling basis.

CONTACT
Mercedes Amaya, Collegewide Director of Financial Aid
11011 SW 104th Street, Miami, FL 33176-3393
(305) 237-2122

New College of Florida

Sarasota, Florida
www.ncf.edu Federal Code: 039574

4-year public liberal arts college in small city.
Enrollment: 785 undergrads. 222 full-time freshmen.
Selectivity: Admits 50 to 75% of applicants.

BASIC COSTS (2008-2009)
Tuition and fees: $4,128; out-of-state residents $23,767.
Room and board: $7,464.

FINANCIAL AID PICTURE (2008-2009)
Students with need: Out of 155 full-time freshmen who applied for aid, 93 were judged to have need. Of these, 93 received aid, and 61 had their full need met. Average financial aid package met 93% of need; average scholarship/grant was $9,010; average loan was $2,908.
Students without need: 129 full-time freshmen who did not demonstrate need for aid received scholarships/grants; average award was $2,635. No-need awards available for academics, state/district residency.
Cumulative student debt: 24% of graduating class had student loans; average debt was $13,162.

FINANCIAL AID PROCEDURES
Forms required: FAFSA.
Dates and Deadlines: Priority date 2/15; no closing date. Applicants notified on a rolling basis starting 10/1; must reply by 5/1 or within 4 week(s) of notification.
Transfers: No deadline. Applicants notified on a rolling basis starting 10/1; must reply by 5/1 or within 4 week(s) of notification.

CONTACT
Monica Baldwin, Director of Financial Aid
5800 Bay Shore Road, Sarasota, FL 34243-2109
(941) 487-5001

North Florida Community College

Madison, Florida
www.nfcc.edu Federal Code: 001508

2-year public community college in rural community.
Enrollment: 820 undergrads.
Selectivity: Open admission; but selective for some programs.

BASIC COSTS (2008-2009)
Tuition and fees: $2,190; out-of-state residents $7,734.

FINANCIAL AID PICTURE (2007-2008)
Students with need: Need-based aid available for full-time and part-time students. Work study available nights, weekends, and for part-time students.
Students without need: This college awards aid only to students with need.

FINANCIAL AID PROCEDURES
Forms required: FAFSA.
Dates and Deadlines: Priority date 5/15; no closing date. Applicants notified on a rolling basis starting 6/20; must reply within 2 week(s) of notification.

CONTACT
Amelia Mulkey, Director of Financial Aid
325 NW Turner Davis Drive, Madison, FL 32340
(850) 973-1621

Northwest Florida State College

Niceville, Florida
www.nwfstatecollege.edu Federal Code: 001510

4-year public business and community college in large town.
Enrollment: 7,463 undergrads.
Selectivity: Open admission.

BASIC COSTS (2008-2009)
Tuition and fees: $2,003; out-of-state residents $8,014.
Additional info: Tuition/fee waivers available for minority students.

FINANCIAL AID PICTURE (2007-2008)

Students with need: 93% of average financial aid package awarded as scholarships/grants, 7% awarded as loans/jobs. Need-based aid available for part-time students. Work study available nights.

Students without need: No-need awards available for academics, art, athletics, leadership, minority status, music/drama.

FINANCIAL AID PROCEDURES

Forms required: FAFSA, institutional form.

Dates and Deadlines: Priority date 4/1; no closing date. Applicants notified on a rolling basis starting 2/1; must reply within 2 week(s) of notification.

Transfers: Academic transcript evaluated to determine student eligibility for financial aid.

CONTACT

Pat Bennett, Director of Financial Aid
100 College Boulevard, Niceville, FL 32578-1295
(850) 678-5111

Northwood University: Florida

West Palm Beach, Florida
www.northwood.edu Federal Code: 013040

4-year private university and business college in small city.
Enrollment: 620 undergrads, 2% part-time. 109 full-time freshmen.
Selectivity: Admits 50 to 75% of applicants.

BASIC COSTS (2008-2009)

Tuition and fees: $17,544.
Per-credit charge: $346.
Room and board: $8,404.

FINANCIAL AID PICTURE (2008-2009)

Students with need: Out of 65 full-time freshmen who applied for aid, 56 were judged to have need. Of these, 56 received aid, and 12 had their full need met. Average financial aid package met 60% of need; average scholarship/grant was $7,122; average loan was $3,309. For part-time students, average financial aid package was $8,250.

Students without need: 14 full-time freshmen who did not demonstrate need for aid received scholarships/grants; average award was $4,830. No-need awards available for academics, alumni affiliation, athletics, leadership, minority status, state/district residency.

Scholarships offered: 25 full-time freshmen received athletic scholarships; average amount $9,109.

Cumulative student debt: 61% of graduating class had student loans; average debt was $22,488.

FINANCIAL AID PROCEDURES

Forms required: FAFSA, state aid form.

Dates and Deadlines: No deadline. Applicants notified on a rolling basis starting 3/1.

Transfers: No deadline. Applicants notified on a rolling basis starting 3/1.

CONTACT

Teresa Palmer, Director of Financial Aid
2600 North Military Trail, West Palm Beach, FL 33409-2911
(561) 478-5590

Nova Southeastern University

Fort Lauderdale, Florida
www.nova.edu Federal Code: 001509

4-year private university in small city.
Enrollment: 5,562 undergrads, 34% part-time. 489 full-time freshmen.
Selectivity: Admits less than 50% of applicants.

BASIC COSTS (2009-2010)

Tuition and fees: $21,100.
Per-credit charge: $685.
Room and board: $8,634.

FINANCIAL AID PICTURE (2007-2008)

Students with need: Out of 425 full-time freshmen who applied for aid, 359 were judged to have need. Of these, 358 received aid, and 51 had their full need met. Average financial aid package met 64% of need; average scholarship/grant was $7,983; average loan was $2,786. For part-time students, average financial aid package was $14,879.

Students without need: 100 full-time freshmen who did not demonstrate need for aid received scholarships/grants; average award was $3,310. No-need awards available for academics, athletics, leadership, music/drama.

Scholarships offered: 39 full-time freshmen received athletic scholarships; average amount $8,629.

Cumulative student debt: 94% of graduating class had student loans; average debt was $24,221.

FINANCIAL AID PROCEDURES

Forms required: FAFSA, state aid form.

Dates and Deadlines: Priority date 4/15; no closing date. Applicants notified on a rolling basis starting 3/15.

CONTACT

Stephanie Brown, Associate Vice President, Enrollment and Student Services
3301 College Avenue, Fort Lauderdale, FL 33314
(954) 262-3380

Palm Beach Atlantic University

West Palm Beach, Florida
www.pba.edu Federal Code: 008849

4-year private university and liberal arts college in large city, affiliated with nondenominational tradition.
Enrollment: 2,393 undergrads, 8% part-time. 452 full-time freshmen.
Selectivity: Admits less than 50% of applicants.

BASIC COSTS (2009-2010)

Tuition and fees: $22,700.
Room and board: $8,220.

FINANCIAL AID PICTURE (2007-2008)

Students with need: Out of 369 full-time freshmen who applied for aid, 300 were judged to have need. Of these, 300 received aid, and 23 had their full need met. Average financial aid package met 66% of need; average scholarship/grant was $4,745; average loan was $3,339. For part-time students, average financial aid package was $6,468.

Students without need: 69 full-time freshmen who did not demonstrate need for aid received scholarships/grants; average award was $6,453. No-need awards available for academics, alumni affiliation, athletics, minority status, music/drama, state/district residency.

Scholarships offered: 24 full-time freshmen received athletic scholarships; average amount $9,273.

Cumulative student debt: 70% of graduating class had student loans; average debt was $17,281.

FINANCIAL AID PROCEDURES

Forms required: FAFSA, state aid form.

Dates and Deadlines: Priority date 2/1; no closing date. Applicants notified on a rolling basis starting 3/1; must reply within 3 week(s) of notification.

Transfers: Applicants notified on a rolling basis starting 3/1; must reply within 3 week(s) of notification. Florida residential undergraduate students eligible for grant from state if enrolled on full-time basis.

CONTACT

Becky Moore, Director, Student Financial Planning
PO Box 24708, West Palm Beach, FL 33416-4708
(561) 803-2126

Palm Beach Community College

Lake Worth, Florida
www.pbcc.edu Federal Code: 001512

2-year public community college in large town.
Enrollment: 19,428 undergrads, 58% part-time. 2,403 full-time freshmen.
Selectivity: Open admission; but selective for some programs.

BASIC COSTS (2008-2009)

Tuition and fees: $2,250; out-of-state residents $8,101.

FINANCIAL AID PICTURE (2008-2009)

Students with need: 77% of average financial aid package awarded as scholarships/grants, 23% awarded as loans/jobs. Work study available nights, weekends, and for part-time students.
Students without need: No-need awards available for academics, alumni affiliation, athletics, leadership, state/district residency.

FINANCIAL AID PROCEDURES

Forms required: FAFSA, institutional form.
Dates and Deadlines: Priority date 7/1; no closing date. Applicants notified on a rolling basis; must reply within 2 week(s) of notification.

CONTACT

David Bodwell, Director of Student Financial Aid
4200 Congress Avenue, Lake Worth, FL 33461
(561) 868-3330

Pasco-Hernando Community College

New Port Richey, Florida
www.phcc.edu Federal Code: 010652

2-year public community college in large town.
Enrollment: 7,747 undergrads.
Selectivity: Open admission; but selective for some programs.

BASIC COSTS (2008-2009)

Tuition and fees: $2,225; out-of-state residents $8,397.

FINANCIAL AID PICTURE

Students with need: Need-based aid available for full-time and part-time students. Work study available nights, weekends, and for part-time students.
Students without need: No-need awards available for academics, athletics, minority status.
Additional info: Childcare assistance grants available to eligible students.

FINANCIAL AID PROCEDURES

Forms required: FAFSA.
Dates and Deadlines: Priority date 4/1; no closing date. Applicants notified on a rolling basis starting 3/1.
Transfers: Priority date 3/1.

CONTACT

Rebecca Shanafelt, Director of Financial Aid/Veterans Services
10230 Ridge Road, New Port Richey, FL 34654-5199
(727) 816-3463

Polk Community College

Winter Haven, Florida
www.polk.edu Federal Code: 001514

2-year public community college in large town.
Enrollment: 6,718 undergrads, 63% part-time. 863 full-time freshmen.
Selectivity: Open admission; but selective for some programs.

BASIC COSTS (2008-2009)

Tuition and fees: $2,235; out-of-state residents $8,237.

FINANCIAL AID PICTURE

Students with need: Need-based aid available for full-time and part-time students. Work study available nights, weekends, and for part-time students.
Students without need: No-need awards available for academics, athletics, leadership, state/district residency.

FINANCIAL AID PROCEDURES

Forms required: FAFSA.
Dates and Deadlines: Priority date 5/15; no closing date. Applicants notified on a rolling basis.

CONTACT

Olivia Maultsby, Director of Financial Aid
999 Avenue H NE, Winter Haven, FL 33881-4299
(863) 297-1004

Rasmussen College: Ocala

Ocala, Florida
www.rasmussen.edu Federal Code: 008501

4-year for-profit career college in small city.
Enrollment: 1,212 undergrads.
Selectivity: Open admission; but selective for some programs.

BASIC COSTS (2008-2009)

Tuition and fees: $14,063.
Per-credit charge: $395.
Additional info: Tuition includes books and fees.

FINANCIAL AID PICTURE

Students with need: Need-based aid available for full-time and part-time students.

FINANCIAL AID PROCEDURES

Forms required: FAFSA, institutional form.
Dates and Deadlines: No deadline. Applicants notified on a rolling basis.

CONTACT

Kristen Corrigan, Director of Financial Aid
2221 Southwest 19th Avenue Road, Ocala, FL 34471
(352) 629-1941 ext. 130

Rasmussen College: Pasco County

Holiday, Florida
www.rasmussen.edu Federal Code: 008501

4-year for-profit career college in small city.
Enrollment: 568 undergrads.
Selectivity: Open admission; but selective for some programs.

BASIC COSTS (2008-2009)

Tuition and fees: $14,063.

FINANCIAL AID PICTURE

Students with need: Need-based aid available for full-time and part-time students.

FINANCIAL AID PROCEDURES
Forms required: FAFSA, institutional form.
Dates and Deadlines: No deadline. Applicants notified on a rolling basis.

CONTACT
Tina Fisher, Director of Student Financial Services
2127 Grand Boulevard, Holiday, FL 34690
(727) 942-0069

Remington College: Tampa
Tampa, Florida
www.remingtoncollege.edu Federal Code: 007586

4-year for-profit technical college in very large city.
Enrollment: 247 undergrads.

FINANCIAL AID PICTURE
Students with need: Need-based aid available for full-time students.
Students without need: This college awards aid only to students with need.

FINANCIAL AID PROCEDURES
Forms required: FAFSA, institutional form.
Dates and Deadlines: No deadline.

CONTACT
Shavonne Roberts, Director of Student Financial Services
2410 East Busch Boulevard, Tampa, FL 33612
(813) 935-5700 ext. 217

Ringling College of Art and Design
Sarasota, Florida
www.ringling.edu Federal Code: 012574

4-year private visual arts college in small city.
Enrollment: 1,229 undergrads, 4% part-time. 281 full-time freshmen.
Selectivity: Admits 50 to 75% of applicants.

BASIC COSTS (2008-2009)
Tuition and fees: $27,110.
Per-credit charge: $1,230.
Room and board: $10,750.
Additional info: Required fees may vary according to program.

FINANCIAL AID PICTURE (2008-2009)
Students with need: Out of 216 full-time freshmen who applied for aid, 187 were judged to have need. Of these, 187 received aid, and 11 had their full need met. Average financial aid package met 50% of need; average scholarship/grant was $9,266; average loan was $9,241. For part-time students, average financial aid package was $15,335.
Students without need: 21 full-time freshmen who did not demonstrate need for aid received scholarships/grants; average award was $8,642. No-need awards available for academics, art.
Scholarships offered: Presidential Scholarship: amount determined annually; based on portfolio; up to 4 awards.
Cumulative student debt: 98% of graduating class had student loans; average debt was $49,756.

FINANCIAL AID PROCEDURES
Forms required: FAFSA.
Dates and Deadlines: Priority date 3/1; no closing date. Applicants notified on a rolling basis starting 4/1; must reply within 2 week(s) of notification.
Transfers: Must reply within 2 week(s) of notification.

CONTACT
Kurt Wolf, Director of Financial Aid
2700 North Tamiami Trail, Sarasota, FL 34234-5895
(941) 359-7534

Rollins College
Winter Park, Florida
www.rollins.edu Federal Code: 001515

4-year private liberal arts college in large town.
Enrollment: 1,785 undergrads. 464 full-time freshmen.
Selectivity: Admits 50 to 75% of applicants.

BASIC COSTS (2009-2010)
Tuition and fees: $36,220.
Room and board: $11,320.

FINANCIAL AID PICTURE (2008-2009)
Students with need: Out of 242 full-time freshmen who applied for aid, 187 were judged to have need. Of these, 186 received aid, and 41 had their full need met. Average financial aid package met 90% of need; average scholarship/grant was $27,367; average loan was $4,127.
Students without need: 83 full-time freshmen who did not demonstrate need for aid received scholarships/grants; average award was $14,613. No-need awards available for academics, art, athletics, leadership, music/drama, state/district residency.
Scholarships offered: ***Merit:*** Presidential, Alonzo Rollins: $4,000-$15,000 per year; based on academic record; 130 available per year. Donald Cram: $3,000-$5,000 per year; based on academic record, science major; 10 available per year. ***Athletic:*** 14 full-time freshmen received athletic scholarships; average amount $29,269.
Cumulative student debt: 48% of graduating class had student loans; average debt was $21,904.
Additional info: Audition required for theater arts and music scholarship applicants. Portfolio required for art scholarships.

FINANCIAL AID PROCEDURES
Forms required: FAFSA, institutional form.
Dates and Deadlines: Closing date 3/1. Applicants notified on a rolling basis starting 3/1.
Transfers: Priority date 4/15; no deadline.

CONTACT
Phil Asbury, Director of Financial Aid
1000 Holt Avenue, Winter Park, FL 32789
(407) 646-2395

Saint Johns River Community College
Palatka, Florida
www.sjrcc.edu Federal Code: 001523

2-year public community college in large town.
Enrollment: 4,025 undergrads.
Selectivity: Open admission; but selective for some programs.

BASIC COSTS (2008-2009)
Tuition and fees: $2,340; out-of-state residents $8,794.

FINANCIAL AID PICTURE (2007-2008)
Students with need: Need-based aid available for full-time and part-time students.

FINANCIAL AID PROCEDURES
Forms required: FAFSA.
Dates and Deadlines: Priority date 5/15; no closing date. Applicants notified on a rolling basis.

CONTACT

Wayne Bodiford, Director of Financial Aid
5001 St. Johns Avenue, Palatka, FL 32177-3897
(386) 312-4040

St. Leo University

Saint Leo, Florida
www.saintleo.edu Federal Code: 001526

4-year private university in rural community, affiliated with Roman Catholic Church.
Enrollment: 1,699 undergrads, 5% part-time. 499 full-time freshmen.
Selectivity: Admits 50 to 75% of applicants.

BASIC COSTS (2009-2010)

Tuition and fees: $17,646.
Room and board: $8,724.

FINANCIAL AID PICTURE (2008-2009)

Students with need: Out of 454 full-time freshmen who applied for aid, 361 were judged to have need. Of these, 361 received aid, and 116 had their full need met. Average financial aid package met 84% of need; average scholarship/grant was $11,991; average loan was $4,143. For part-time students, average financial aid package was $15,079.
Students without need: No-need awards available for academics, alumni affiliation, athletics, leadership, minority status, music/drama, religious affiliation, state/district residency.
Scholarships offered: 14 full-time freshmen received athletic scholarships; average amount $6,935.
Cumulative student debt: 69% of graduating class had student loans; average debt was $23,178.

FINANCIAL AID PROCEDURES

Forms required: FAFSA.
Dates and Deadlines: Priority date 4/1; no closing date. Applicants notified on a rolling basis starting 1/31.

CONTACT

Brenda Wright, Assistant Vice President, Student Financial Services
Office of Admission, Saint Leo, FL 33574-6665
(800) 240-7658

St. Petersburg College

St. Petersburg, Florida
www.spcollege.edu Federal Code: 001528

2-year public community college in large city.
Enrollment: 19,535 undergrads, 65% part-time. 1,866 full-time freshmen.
Selectivity: Open admission; but selective for some programs.

BASIC COSTS (2008-2009)

Tuition and fees: $2,337; out-of-state residents $8,412.

FINANCIAL AID PICTURE

Students with need: Need-based aid available for full-time and part-time students. Work study available nights, weekends, and for part-time students.
Students without need: No-need awards available for academics, art, athletics, minority status, music/drama.

FINANCIAL AID PROCEDURES

Forms required: FAFSA, state aid form.
Dates and Deadlines: Priority date 4/15; no closing date. Applicants notified on a rolling basis starting 5/15; must reply within 2 week(s) of notification.

CONTACT

Marcia McConnell, Director of Financial Aid
Box 13489, St. Petersburg, FL 33733-3489
(727) 791-2443

Saint Thomas University

Miami Gardens, Florida
www.stu.edu Federal Code: 001468

4-year private university in very large city, affiliated with Roman Catholic Church.
Enrollment: 1,122 undergrads, 7% part-time. 212 full-time freshmen.
Selectivity: Admits over 75% of applicants.

BASIC COSTS (2008-2009)

Tuition and fees: $20,664.
Per-credit charge: $689.
Room and board: $6,206.

FINANCIAL AID PICTURE (2007-2008)

Students with need: Need-based aid available for full-time students.
Students without need: No-need awards available for academics, athletics, leadership, music/drama, religious affiliation, state/district residency.

FINANCIAL AID PROCEDURES

Forms required: FAFSA, state aid form.
Dates and Deadlines: Priority date 4/2; no closing date. Applicants notified on a rolling basis starting 3/1.
Transfers: Priority date 4/15.

CONTACT

Ahn Do, Director of Financial Aid
16401 Northwest 37th Avenue, Miami Gardens, FL 33054-6459
(305) 628-6547

Santa Fe College

Gainesville, Florida
www.sfcc.edu Federal Code: 001519

2-year public community college in small city.
Enrollment: 8,066 full-time undergrads.
Selectivity: Open admission; but selective for some programs.

BASIC COSTS (2008-2009)

Tuition and fees: $2,274; out-of-state residents $8,462.
Additional info: Required fees for out-of-state students taking 30 semester hours: $1,285. Tuition/fee waivers available for minority students.

FINANCIAL AID PICTURE

Students with need: Need-based aid available for full-time and part-time students.
Students without need: No-need awards available for academics, art, athletics, leadership, minority status, music/drama, state/district residency.

FINANCIAL AID PROCEDURES

Forms required: FAFSA.
Dates and Deadlines: Priority date 3/15; closing date 6/30. Applicants notified by 8/1.
Transfers: Must have minimum 2.0 GPA to be eligible for financial aid.

CONTACT

Steve Fisher, Director of Financial Aid
3000 NW 83rd Street, R-112, Gainesville, FL 32606
(352) 395-5400

Schiller International University

Largo, Florida
www.schiller.edu Federal Code: 023141

4-year for-profit university in small city.
Enrollment: 191 undergrads, 20% part-time. 16 full-time freshmen.
Selectivity: Open admission.

BASIC COSTS (2008-2009)
Tuition and fees: $17,890.
Room and board: $9,027.

FINANCIAL AID PICTURE (2007-2008)
Students with need: Out of 9 full-time freshmen who applied for aid, 9 were judged to have need. Of these, 9 received aid. Need-based aid available for part-time students.
Students without need: No-need awards available for academics, alumni affiliation, leadership, minority status, state/district residency.
Scholarships offered: Fifty one-fourth tuition awards available to students possessing an outstanding academic record and who exhibit excellent potential for academic achievement. This award is available for one or two semesters. Twenty one-quarter Knowledge Tuition Awards available for two semesters to students who with good academic records and financial need.
Additional info: Special scholarship program for US students studying abroad at European campuses of Schiller. Work-study available to students taking 2 or more courses.

FINANCIAL AID PROCEDURES
Forms required: FAFSA, state aid form, institutional form.
Dates and Deadlines: Closing date 4/1. Applicants notified on a rolling basis starting 5/1; must reply within 3 week(s) of notification.
Transfers: No deadline. Applicants notified on a rolling basis.

CONTACT
Jennifer Fraser, Director of Financial Aid
300 East Bay Drive, Largo, FL 33770-3716
(727) 736-5082 ext. 253

Seminole Community College
Sanford, Florida
www.scc-fl.edu Federal Code: 001520

2-year public community college in large town.
Enrollment: 11,705 undergrads, 53% part-time. 1,721 full-time freshmen.
Selectivity: Open admission; but selective for some programs.

BASIC COSTS (2008-2009)
Tuition and fees: $2,434; out-of-state residents $8,596.

FINANCIAL AID PICTURE (2007-2008)
Students with need: 43% of average financial aid package awarded as scholarships/grants, 57% awarded as loans/jobs. Need-based aid available for part-time students.
Students without need: No-need awards available for academics, art, athletics, leadership, minority status, music/drama, state/district residency.

FINANCIAL AID PROCEDURES
Forms required: FAFSA.
Dates and Deadlines: No deadline. Applicants notified on a rolling basis starting 4/1.
Transfers: No deadline. Applicants notified on a rolling basis starting 4/1.

CONTACT
Robert Lynn, Director of Financial Aid
100 Weldon Boulevard, Sanford, FL 32773-6199
(407) 708-4722 ext. 3422

South Florida Community College
Avon Park, Florida
www.southflorida.edu Federal Code: 001522

2-year public community and technical college in small town.
Enrollment: 2,328 undergrads, 63% part-time. 277 full-time freshmen.
Selectivity: Open admission; but selective for some programs.

BASIC COSTS (2008-2009)
Tuition and fees: $2,281; out-of-state residents $8,589.
Additional info: Tuition/fee waivers available for minority students.

FINANCIAL AID PICTURE (2007-2008)
Students with need: Need-based aid available for full-time and part-time students.
Students without need: No-need awards available for academics, athletics, leadership, minority status, music/drama, state/district residency.

FINANCIAL AID PROCEDURES
Forms required: FAFSA.
Dates and Deadlines: Priority date 3/15; no closing date. Applicants notified on a rolling basis starting 4/1.
Transfers: Students must maintain satisfactory academic progress.

CONTACT
Susie Johnson, Director of Financial Aid
600 West College Drive, Avon Park, FL 33825
(863) 453-6661 ext. 7254

South University: West Palm Beach
West Palm Beach, Florida
www.southuniversity.edu

4-year for-profit university and business and health science college in large city.
Enrollment: 699 undergrads, 31% part-time.

BASIC COSTS (2008-2009)
Tuition and fees: $13,035.

FINANCIAL AID PICTURE
Students with need: Need-based aid available for full-time and part-time students. Work study available nights.
Students without need: No-need awards available for academics.

FINANCIAL AID PROCEDURES
Forms required: FAFSA, institutional form.
Dates and Deadlines: No deadline. Applicants notified on a rolling basis; must reply within 2 week(s) of notification.

CONTACT
1760 North Congress Avenue, West Palm Beach, FL 33409-5178
(561) 697-9200

Southeastern University
Lakeland, Florida
www.seuniversity.edu Federal Code: 001521

4-year private liberal arts and teachers college in small city, affiliated with Assemblies of God.
Enrollment: 2,651 undergrads, 7% part-time. 519 full-time freshmen.
Selectivity: Open admission; but selective for some programs.

BASIC COSTS (2008-2009)
Tuition and fees: $14,470.
Per-credit charge: $540.
Room and board: $7,000.

FINANCIAL AID PICTURE (2008-2009)
Students with need: 49% of average financial aid package awarded as scholarships/grants, 51% awarded as loans/jobs. Need-based aid available for part-time students.
Students without need: No-need awards available for academics, leadership, music/drama, ROTC.

Cumulative student debt: 86% of graduating class had student loans; average debt was $13,995.

FINANCIAL AID PROCEDURES

Forms required: FAFSA, state aid form, institutional form.
Dates and Deadlines: Priority date 4/15; no closing date. Applicants notified on a rolling basis starting 2/1; must reply within 4 week(s) of notification.
Transfers: No deadline. Applicants notified on a rolling basis starting 2/1; must reply within 4 week(s) of notification.

CONTACT

Carol Bradley, Financial Aid Director
1000 Longfellow Boulevard, Lakeland, FL 33801-6034
(863) 667-5024

Southwest Florida College

Ft. Myers, Florida
www.swfc.edu Federal Code: 016068

2-year private career college in large city.
Enrollment: 1,737 undergrads, 16% part-time. 368 full-time freshmen.
Selectivity: Open admission; but selective for some programs.

BASIC COSTS (2009-2010)

Tuition and fees: $10,800.
Per-credit charge: $275.
Additional info: Required fees do not include lab or online fees.

FINANCIAL AID PICTURE

Students with need: Need-based aid available for full-time and part-time students. Work study available nights.

FINANCIAL AID PROCEDURES

Forms required: FAFSA.
Dates and Deadlines: No deadline. Applicants notified on a rolling basis.
Transfers: No deadline. Applicants notified on a rolling basis.

CONTACT

Laura Selvey, Director of Financial Aid
1685 Medical Lane, Ft. Myers, FL 33907-1108
(813) 630-4401

Stetson University

DeLand, Florida
www.stetson.edu Federal Code: 001531

4-year private university in large town.
Enrollment: 2,186 undergrads, 3% part-time. 588 full-time freshmen.
Selectivity: Admits 50 to 75% of applicants.

BASIC COSTS (2009-2010)

Tuition and fees: $31,770.
Per-credit charge: $914.
Room and board: $8,934.

FINANCIAL AID PICTURE (2008-2009)

Students with need: Average financial aid package met 88% of need; average scholarship/grant was $21,815; average loan was $3,946. For part-time students, average financial aid package was $12,388.
Students without need: No-need awards available for academics, alumni affiliation, art, athletics, leadership, minority status, music/drama, religious affiliation, ROTC, state/district residency.
Cumulative student debt: 75% of graduating class had student loans; average debt was $28,775.

FINANCIAL AID PROCEDURES

Forms required: FAFSA, institutional form.
Dates and Deadlines: Priority date 3/15; no closing date. Applicants notified on a rolling basis starting 2/15.

CONTACT

Martin Carney, Director of Financial Aid
Campus Box 8378, DeLand, FL 32723
(386) 822-7120

Tallahassee Community College

Tallahassee, Florida
www.tcc.fl.edu Federal Code: 001533

2-year public community college in small city.
Enrollment: 12,775 undergrads.
Selectivity: Open admission; but selective for some programs.

BASIC COSTS (2008-2009)

Tuition and fees: $2,086; out-of-state residents $7,523.

FINANCIAL AID PICTURE (2007-2008)

Students with need: 46% of average financial aid package awarded as scholarships/grants, 54% awarded as loans/jobs. Need-based aid available for part-time students.
Students without need: No-need awards available for academics, art, athletics, leadership, music/drama, state/district residency.

FINANCIAL AID PROCEDURES

Forms required: FAFSA, institutional form.
Dates and Deadlines: Priority date 5/1; no closing date. Applicants notified on a rolling basis starting 5/15.

CONTACT

William Spiers, Director of Financial Aid
444 Appleyard Drive, Tallahassee, FL 32304
(850) 201-8399

Talmudic College of Florida

Miami Beach, Florida
www.talmudicu.edu Federal Code: 013814

4-year private rabbinical college for men in very large city, affiliated with Jewish faith.
Enrollment: 25 undergrads.

BASIC COSTS (2008-2009)

Additional info: Tuition at time of enrollment locked for 4 years.

FINANCIAL AID PICTURE

Students with need: Need-based aid available for full-time and part-time students. Work study available nights, weekends, and for part-time students.
Students without need: This college awards aid only to students with need.

FINANCIAL AID PROCEDURES

Forms required: FAFSA, institutional form.
Dates and Deadlines: No deadline. Applicants notified on a rolling basis.

CONTACT

Peggy Loewy Wellisch, Chief Financial Aid Officer
1910 Alton Road, Miami Beach, FL 33139
(305) 534-050

Trinity College of Florida
Trinity, Florida
www.trinitycollege.edu Federal Code: 030282

4-year private Bible college in small city, affiliated with interdenominational tradition.
Enrollment: 178 undergrads, 12% part-time. 30 full-time freshmen.
Selectivity: Admits less than 50% of applicants.

BASIC COSTS (2009-2010)
Tuition and fees: $11,200.
Per-credit charge: $430.
Room and board: $6,534.

FINANCIAL AID PICTURE (2007-2008)
Students with need: Out of 30 full-time freshmen who applied for aid, 26 were judged to have need. Of these, 26 received aid, and 4 had their full need met. Average financial aid package met 78% of need; average scholarship/grant was $3,024; average loan was $1,750. For part-time students, average financial aid package was $2,756.
Students without need: This college awards aid only to students with need.
Cumulative student debt: 83% of graduating class had student loans; average debt was $15,284.

FINANCIAL AID PROCEDURES
Forms required: FAFSA, institutional form.
Dates and Deadlines: Priority date 3/15; closing date 8/2. Applicants notified on a rolling basis.
Transfers: No deadline. Applicants notified on a rolling basis.

CONTACT
Sue Wayne, Financial Aid Director
2430 Welbilt Boulevard, Trinity, FL 34655-4401
(727) 569-1413

University of Central Florida
Orlando, Florida
www.ucf.edu Federal Code: 003954

4-year public university in very large city.
Enrollment: 42,642 undergrads, 25% part-time. 6,365 full-time freshmen.
Selectivity: Admits less than 50% of applicants.

BASIC COSTS (2008-2009)
Tuition and fees: $3,947; out-of-state residents $18,689.
Room and board: $8,574.

FINANCIAL AID PICTURE (2007-2008)
Students with need: Out of 4,429 full-time freshmen who applied for aid, 2,568 were judged to have need. Of these, 2,547 received aid, and 495 had their full need met. Average financial aid package met 69% of need; average scholarship/grant was $4,196; average loan was $3,265. For part-time students, average financial aid package was $5,124.
Students without need: 671 full-time freshmen who did not demonstrate need for aid received scholarships/grants; average award was $2,177. No-need awards available for academics, alumni affiliation, athletics, leadership, ROTC, state/district residency.
Scholarships offered: ***Merit:*** Academic scholarships: $2,000-$24,000 over 4-year period, freshmen automatically considered. ***Athletic:*** 56 full-time freshmen received athletic scholarships; average amount $8,816.

FINANCIAL AID PROCEDURES
Forms required: FAFSA.
Dates and Deadlines: Priority date 3/1; closing date 6/30. Applicants notified on a rolling basis starting 3/15; must reply within 3 week(s) of notification.

CONTACT
Mary McKinney, Executive Director of Financial Aid
Box 160111, Orlando, FL 32816-0111
(407) 823-2827

University of Florida
Gainesville, Florida
www.ufl.edu Federal Code: 001535

4-year public university in small city.
Enrollment: 34,094 undergrads, 6% part-time. 6,445 full-time freshmen.
Selectivity: Admits less than 50% of applicants.

BASIC COSTS (2008-2009)
Tuition and fees: $3,790; out-of-state residents $20,640.
Per-credit charge: $89; out-of-state residents $624.
Room and board: $7,150.

FINANCIAL AID PICTURE (2007-2008)
Students with need: Out of 4,155 full-time freshmen who applied for aid, 2,653 were judged to have need. Of these, 2,648 received aid, and 1,136 had their full need met. Average financial aid package met 86% of need; average scholarship/grant was $6,149; average loan was $3,465. Need-based aid available for part-time students.
Students without need: 3,602 full-time freshmen who did not demonstrate need for aid received scholarships/grants; average award was $5,811. No-need awards available for academics, art, athletics, leadership, minority status, music/drama, ROTC, state/district residency.
Scholarships offered: 79 full-time freshmen received athletic scholarships; average amount $14,381.
Cumulative student debt: 41% of graduating class had student loans; average debt was $15,318.

FINANCIAL AID PROCEDURES
Forms required: FAFSA.
Dates and Deadlines: Priority date 3/15; no closing date. Applicants notified on a rolling basis starting 4/1.
Transfers: Priority date 3/15; no deadline. Applicants notified on a rolling basis starting 4/1.

CONTACT
Karen Fooks, Director of Student Financial Aid
201 Criser Hall-PO Box 114000, Gainesville, FL 32611-4000
(352) 392-1275

University of Miami
Coral Gables, Florida
www.miami.edu Federal Code: 001536

4-year private university in small city.
Enrollment: 10,008 undergrads, 5% part-time. 1,984 full-time freshmen.
Selectivity: Admits less than 50% of applicants.

BASIC COSTS (2009-2010)
Tuition and fees: $36,188.
Per-credit charge: $1,480.
Room and board: $10,800.

FINANCIAL AID PICTURE (2008-2009)
Students with need: Out of 1,234 full-time freshmen who applied for aid, 907 were judged to have need. Of these, 907 received aid, and 435 had their full need met. Average financial aid package met 88% of need; average scholarship/grant was $22,661; average loan was $4,554. For part-time students, average financial aid package was $18,296.

Students without need: 453 full-time freshmen who did not demonstrate need for aid received scholarships/grants; average award was $18,963. No-need awards available for academics, athletics, music/drama, ROTC.
Scholarships offered: ***Merit:*** Singer Scholarship: full tuition; minimum 1500 SAT or 34 ACT; A+ average; rank in top 1% of high school graduating class. University Scholarship (24,000), Dean Scholarship (16,000) and Trustee Scholarship(8,000): minimum 1350 or 31 ACT; minimum of a A- GPA in addition to academic rigor. ***Athletic:*** 45 full-time freshmen received athletic scholarships; average amount $21,585.
Cumulative student debt: 56% of graduating class had student loans; average debt was $24,500.

FINANCIAL AID PROCEDURES
Forms required: FAFSA.
Dates and Deadlines: Priority date 2/1; no closing date. Applicants notified on a rolling basis starting 3/1.
Transfers: Priority date 3/1; no deadline.

CONTACT
James Bauer, Assistant Dean of Enrollment Management and Director of Financial Assistance Services
132 Ashe Building, Coral Gables, FL 33124-4616
(305) 284-5212

University of North Florida
Jacksonville, Florida
www.unf.edu Federal Code: 009841

4-year public university in very large city.
Enrollment: 13,204 undergrads, 27% part-time. 1,690 full-time freshmen.
Selectivity: Admits 50 to 75% of applicants.

BASIC COSTS (2008-2009)
Tuition and fees: $3,775; out-of-state residents $15,417.
Room and board: $7,366.

FINANCIAL AID PICTURE (2008-2009)
Students with need: Average financial aid package met 90% of need; average scholarship/grant was $975; average loan was $1,717. For part-time students, average financial aid package was $1,745.
Students without need: No-need awards available for academics, athletics, leadership, minority status, music/drama, state/district residency.
Cumulative student debt: 41% of graduating class had student loans; average debt was $14,694.

FINANCIAL AID PROCEDURES
Forms required: FAFSA.
Dates and Deadlines: Priority date 4/1; no closing date. Applicants notified on a rolling basis starting 3/15; must reply within 2 week(s) of notification.
Transfers: Must reply within 2 week(s) of notification. Students must submit financial aid transcripts from previous institutions attended.

CONTACT
Anissa Agne, Director of Financial Aid
1 UNF Drive, Jacksonville, FL 32224-7699
(904) 620-2604

University of South Florida
Tampa, Florida
www.usf.edu Federal Code: 001537

4-year public university in very large city.
Enrollment: 35,104 undergrads, 29% part-time. 2,515 full-time freshmen.
Selectivity: Admits less than 50% of applicants.

BASIC COSTS (2008-2009)
Tuition and fees: $3,906; out-of-state residents $16,623.
Room and board: $8,080.
Additional info: Tuition/fee waivers available for unemployed or children of unemployed.

FINANCIAL AID PICTURE (2007-2008)
Students with need: Out of 2,515 full-time freshmen who applied for aid, 1,779 were judged to have need. Of these, 1,765 received aid, and 134 had their full need met. Average financial aid package met 32% of need; average scholarship/grant was $4,785; average loan was $2,617. For part-time students, average financial aid package was $7,752.
Students without need: 698 full-time freshmen who did not demonstrate need for aid received scholarships/grants; average award was $3,992. No-need awards available for academics, alumni affiliation, art, athletics, job skills, leadership, minority status, music/drama, religious affiliation, ROTC, state/district residency.
Scholarships offered: 41 full-time freshmen received athletic scholarships; average amount $1,643.
Cumulative student debt: 53% of graduating class had student loans; average debt was $18,568.
Additional info: Deferred tuition payment plan available for late financial aid recipients.

FINANCIAL AID PROCEDURES
Forms required: FAFSA.
Dates and Deadlines: Priority date 3/1; no closing date. Applicants notified on a rolling basis starting 3/15.

CONTACT
Billie Hamilton, Director of Financial Aid
4202 East Fowler Avenue, SVC 1036, Tampa, FL 33620-9951
(813) 974-4700

University of Tampa
Tampa, Florida
www.ut.edu Federal Code: 001538

4-year private university and liberal arts college in large city.
Enrollment: 5,081 undergrads, 7% part-time. 1,224 full-time freshmen.
Selectivity: Admits 50 to 75% of applicants.

BASIC COSTS (2009-2010)
Tuition and fees: $22,482.
Per-credit charge: $455.
Room and board: $8,296.

FINANCIAL AID PICTURE (2008-2009)
Students with need: Out of 845 full-time freshmen who applied for aid, 628 were judged to have need. Of these, 628 received aid, and 156 had their full need met. Average financial aid package met 77% of need; average scholarship/grant was $7,031; average loan was $4,230. For part-time students, average financial aid package was $6,518.
Students without need: 201 full-time freshmen who did not demonstrate need for aid received scholarships/grants; average award was $6,385. No-need awards available for academics, alumni affiliation, art, athletics, leadership, music/drama, ROTC, state/district residency.
Scholarships offered: ***Merit:*** Presidential Scholarships: up to $9,000; 3.5 GPA. Dean's Scholarships: up to $8,000; 3.2 GPA. Departmental scholarships also awarded. ***Athletic:*** 4 full-time freshmen received athletic scholarships; average amount $7,500.
Cumulative student debt: 59% of graduating class had student loans; average debt was $23,807.
Additional info: Early aid estimator service.

FINANCIAL AID PROCEDURES
Forms required: FAFSA, state aid form.

Dates and Deadlines: No deadline. Applicants notified on a rolling basis starting 2/1; must reply within 3 week(s) of notification.
Transfers: No deadline. Must reply within 3 week(s) of notification. Transfer scholarships available; Phi Theta Kappa Scholarships.

CONTACT

John Marsh, Director of Financial Aid
401 West Kennedy Boulevard, Tampa, FL 33606-1490
(813) 253-6239

University of West Florida

Pensacola, Florida
www.uwf.edu Federal Code: 003955

4-year public university in small city.
Enrollment: 8,412 undergrads, 28% part-time. 1,019 full-time freshmen.
Selectivity: Admits 50 to 75% of applicants.

BASIC COSTS (2008-2009)

Tuition and fees: $3,655; out-of-state residents $16,546.
Room and board: $7,256.
Additional info: There is a $10 per course, per semester fee for online courses.

FINANCIAL AID PICTURE (2007-2008)

Students with need: 43% of average financial aid package awarded as scholarships/grants, 57% awarded as loans/jobs. Need-based aid available for part-time students. Work study available nights, weekends, and for part-time students.
Students without need: No-need awards available for academics, alumni affiliation, art, athletics, minority status, music/drama, ROTC.
Scholarships offered: John C. Pace Scholars: $16,000; based on high school record and leadership; 8 awards. John C. Pace Honors and Presidential Scholarships: $4,000; based on high school record. Both available to Florida residents only. Non-Florida tuition reduction scholarships available to non-residents.

FINANCIAL AID PROCEDURES

Forms required: FAFSA, institutional form.
Dates and Deadlines: Priority date 3/1; no closing date. Applicants notified on a rolling basis starting 2/1.

CONTACT

Cathy Brown, Director of Student Financial Aid
11000 University Parkway, Pensacola, FL 32514-5750
(850) 474-2400

Valencia Community College

Orlando, Florida
www.valenciacc.edu Federal Code: 006750

2-year public community college in very large city.
Enrollment: 29,020 undergrads, 50% part-time. 4,683 full-time freshmen.
Selectivity: Open admission; but selective for some programs.

BASIC COSTS (2008-2009)

Tuition and fees: $2,335; out-of-state residents $8,782.

FINANCIAL AID PICTURE

Students with need: Need-based aid available for full-time and part-time students. Work study available nights.

FINANCIAL AID PROCEDURES

Forms required: FAFSA.
Dates and Deadlines: Closing date 5/15. Applicants notified on a rolling basis starting 4/2; must reply within 2 week(s) of notification.
Transfers: No deadline.

CONTACT

Brad Honious, Director, Financial Aid
PO Box 3028, Orlando, FL 32802-3028
(407) 299-5000

Warner University

Lake Wales, Florida
www.warner.edu Federal Code: 008848

4-year private liberal arts college in large town, affiliated with Church of God.
Enrollment: 1,003 undergrads, 11% part-time. 145 full-time freshmen.
Selectivity: Admits 50 to 75% of applicants.

BASIC COSTS (2008-2009)

Tuition and fees: $14,690.
Room and board: $6,580.
Additional info: One-time $50 security deposit for incoming freshmen living on campus.

FINANCIAL AID PICTURE (2007-2008)

Students with need: Need-based aid available for full-time and part-time students.
Students without need: No-need awards available for academics, alumni affiliation, art, athletics, leadership, music/drama, religious affiliation, state/district residency.

FINANCIAL AID PROCEDURES

Forms required: FAFSA, state aid form.
Dates and Deadlines: Priority date 5/1; no closing date. Applicants notified on a rolling basis starting 3/15; must reply within 2 week(s) of notification.
Transfers: Priority date 10/1; closing date 5/15. Applicants notified on a rolling basis; must reply within 2 week(s) of notification.

CONTACT

Lorrie Steedley, Financial Aid Director
13895 Highway 27, Lake Wales, FL 33859
(863) 638-7202

Webber International University

Babson Park, Florida
www.webber.edu Federal Code: 001540

4-year private university and business college in rural community.
Enrollment: 542 undergrads, 9% part-time. 126 full-time freshmen.
Selectivity: Admits 50 to 75% of applicants.

BASIC COSTS (2009-2010)

Tuition and fees: $17,850.
Per-credit charge: $247.
Room and board: $6,822.
Additional info: Tuition/fee waivers available for adults.

FINANCIAL AID PICTURE (2008-2009)

Students with need: Out of 126 full-time freshmen who applied for aid, 100 were judged to have need. Of these, 100 received aid, and 7 had their full need met. Average financial aid package met 51% of need; average scholarship/grant was $12,672; average loan was $3,357. For part-time students, average financial aid package was $5,134.
Students without need: 47 full-time freshmen who did not demonstrate need for aid received scholarships/grants; average award was $6,950. No-need awards available for academics, alumni affiliation, athletics, leadership, state/district residency.
Scholarships offered: 47 full-time freshmen received athletic scholarships; average amount $5,547.
Cumulative student debt: 66% of graduating class had student loans; average debt was $23,902.

FINANCIAL AID PROCEDURES

Forms required: FAFSA, state aid form.

Dates and Deadlines: Priority date 5/1; closing date 8/1. Applicants notified on a rolling basis starting 4/1; must reply within 4 week(s) of notification.

Transfers: Eligibility for academic scholarships predicated on 12 hours of transferable credit.

CONTACT

Kathleen Wilson, Registrar
1201 North Scenic Highway, Babson Park, FL 33827-0096
(863) 638-2930

Georgia

Agnes Scott College

Decatur, Georgia
www.agnesscott.edu Federal Code: 001542

4-year private liberal arts college for women in very large city, affiliated with Presbyterian Church (USA).

Enrollment: 757 undergrads, 2% part-time. 179 full-time freshmen.

Selectivity: Admits less than 50% of applicants.

BASIC COSTS (2009-2010)

Tuition and fees: $30,105.

Per-credit charge: $1,245.

Room and board: $9,850.

FINANCIAL AID PICTURE (2008-2009)

Students with need: Need-based aid available for full-time and part-time students. Work study available nights, weekends, and for part-time students.

Students without need: No-need awards available for academics, leadership, music/drama, religious affiliation, state/district residency.

Scholarships offered: Presidential and Honor Scholarships; $8,750 to full tuition, room and board. College will match HOPE Scholarship for HOPE-eligible Georgia residents who meet college admission criteria. Leadership and community service awards also available.

Cumulative student debt: 73% of graduating class had student loans; average debt was $25,577.

Additional info: Middle Income Assistance Grants available. Auditions required for music scholarship applicants.

FINANCIAL AID PROCEDURES

Forms required: FAFSA.

Dates and Deadlines: Priority date 2/15; closing date 5/1. Applicants notified on a rolling basis starting 3/1; must reply by 5/1 or within 2 week(s) of notification.

Transfers: Must reply by 5/1 or within 2 week(s) of notification. Merit scholarships available.

CONTACT

Patrick Bonones, Director of Financial Aid
141 East College Avenue, Decatur, GA 30030-3797
(404) 471-6395

Albany State University

Albany, Georgia
www.asurams.edu/ Federal Code: 001544

4-year public university and liberal arts college in small city.

Enrollment: 3,753 undergrads, 16% part-time. 618 full-time freshmen.

Selectivity: Admits less than 50% of applicants.

BASIC COSTS (2008-2009)

Tuition and fees: $3,710; out-of-state residents $13,002.

Per-credit charge: $130; out-of-state residents $517.

Room and board: $4,990.

Additional info: Tuition at time of enrollment locked for 4 years.

FINANCIAL AID PICTURE (2007-2008)

Students with need: Need-based aid available for full-time and part-time students. Work study available nights, weekends, and for part-time students.

Students without need: No-need awards available for academics, alumni affiliation, art, athletics, music/drama, ROTC.

FINANCIAL AID PROCEDURES

Forms required: FAFSA, state aid form.

Dates and Deadlines: Priority date 4/15; closing date 4/30. Applicants notified on a rolling basis; must reply within 2 week(s) of notification.

Transfers: Must reply within 2 week(s) of notification.

CONTACT

Thomas Harris, Director of Financial Aid
504 College Drive, Albany, GA 31705-2796
(229) 430-4649

Albany Technical College

Albany, Georgia
www.albanytech.edu Federal Code: 005601

2-year public technical college in small city.

Enrollment: 2,699 undergrads, 38% part-time. 349 full-time freshmen.

Selectivity: Open admission; but selective for some programs.

BASIC COSTS (2008-2009)

Tuition and fees: $1,539; out-of-state residents $2,835.

Per-credit charge: $36; out-of-state residents $72.

FINANCIAL AID PICTURE (2008-2009)

Students with need: 71% of average financial aid package awarded as scholarships/grants, 29% awarded as loans/jobs. Need-based aid available for part-time students. Work study available nights.

Students without need: No-need awards available for academics, state/district residency.

FINANCIAL AID PROCEDURES

Forms required: FAFSA, state aid form.

Dates and Deadlines: No deadline. Applicants notified on a rolling basis starting 5/1.

CONTACT

Helen Catt, Financial Aid Director
1704 South Slappy Boulevard, Albany, GA 31701-3514
(229) 430-3506

Andrew College

Cuthbert, Georgia
www.andrewcollege.edu Federal Code: 001545

2-year private junior and liberal arts college in small town, affiliated with United Methodist Church.

Enrollment: 266 undergrads, 2% part-time. 155 full-time freshmen.

BASIC COSTS (2009-2010)

Tuition and fees: $11,416.

Room and board: $7,170.

FINANCIAL AID PICTURE

Students with need: Need-based aid available for full-time and part-time students.

Students without need: No-need awards available for academics, art, athletics, leadership, music/drama, religious affiliation, state/district residency.

FINANCIAL AID PROCEDURES

Forms required: FAFSA, state aid form, institutional form.

Dates and Deadlines: Priority date 4/1; closing date 8/1. Applicants notified on a rolling basis starting 4/15.

CONTACT

Amy Thompson, Financial Aid Administrator
501 College Street, Cuthbert, GA 39840-1395
(229) 732-5938

Armstrong Atlantic State University

Savannah, Georgia
www.armstrong.edu Federal Code: 001546

4-year public university in small city.

Enrollment: 6,152 undergrads, 32% part-time. 797 full-time freshmen.

Selectivity: Admits 50 to 75% of applicants.

BASIC COSTS (2008-2009)

Tuition and fees: $3,876; out-of-state residents $13,168.

Per-credit charge: $130; out-of-state residents $517.

Room only: $5,048.

Additional info: Tuition at time of enrollment locked for 4 years.

FINANCIAL AID PICTURE (2007-2008)

Students with need: Need-based aid available for full-time and part-time students. Work study available nights, weekends, and for part-time students.

Students without need: No-need awards available for academics, alumni affiliation, art, athletics, leadership, minority status, music/drama, state/district residency.

FINANCIAL AID PROCEDURES

Forms required: FAFSA.

Dates and Deadlines: Priority date 3/15; no closing date. Applicants notified on a rolling basis starting 2/1; must reply by 4/15 or within 2 week(s) of notification.

CONTACT

Lee Ann Kirkland, Financial Aid Director
11935 Abercorn Street, Savannah, GA 31419-1997
(912) 344-3266

Art Institute of Atlanta

Atlanta, Georgia
www.aia.artinstitutes.edu Federal Code: 009270

4-year for-profit visual arts college in very large city.

Enrollment: 3,400 undergrads.

BASIC COSTS (2008-2009)

Tuition and fees: $19,575.

Per-credit charge: $435.

Room only: $9,075.

Additional info: Students purchase starting kits for programs; costs vary depending on programs. Some programs require lab fees.

FINANCIAL AID PICTURE (2007-2008)

Students with need: Need-based aid available for full-time and part-time students. Work study available nights, weekends, and for part-time students.

Students without need: No-need awards available for academics, art, state/district residency.

Scholarships offered: Art Institutes Scholarship Competition awards $2,000 - $56,064 depending on program to winning high school seniors selected on merits of written essay, original artwork, resume, letter(s) of recommendation, and high school academic achievement; up to 1 full-tuition, 2 half-tuition, and 24 partial-tuition scholarships available. Art Institutes Culinary Scholarship Competition awards $2,000 - $32,704 to winning high school seniors selected through three-part elimination-style competition to prove academic ability, culinary expertise, and commitment to succeed; up to 1 full-tuition or 2 partial-tuition scholarships available. Various other scholarships and awards available.

FINANCIAL AID PROCEDURES

Forms required: FAFSA, state aid form.

Dates and Deadlines: No deadline. Applicants notified on a rolling basis starting 3/15.

CONTACT

Rachel Oliver, Director of Student Financial Services
6600 Peachtree Dunwoody Road, Atlanta, GA 30328
(770) 394-8300

Athens Technical College

Athens, Georgia
www.athenstech.edu Federal Code: 005600

2-year public technical college in small city.

Enrollment: 3,592 undergrads, 60% part-time. 347 full-time freshmen.

Selectivity: Open admission; but selective for some programs.

BASIC COSTS (2008-2009)

Tuition and fees: $1,539; out-of-state residents $2,835.

Per-credit charge: $36; out-of-state residents $72.

FINANCIAL AID PICTURE (2007-2008)

Students with need: Need-based aid available for full-time and part-time students.

Students without need: No-need awards available for academics, leadership.

FINANCIAL AID PROCEDURES

Forms required: FAFSA.

Dates and Deadlines: No deadline. Applicants notified on a rolling basis starting 6/15; must reply within 2 week(s) of notification.

CONTACT

Patrick Harris, Director of Financial Aid
800 US Highway 29 North, Athens, GA 30601-1500
(706) 355-5009

Atlanta Christian College

East Point, Georgia
www.acc.edu Federal Code: 001547

4-year private Bible and liberal arts college in small city, affiliated with Christian Church.

Enrollment: 440 undergrads, 7% part-time. 87 full-time freshmen.

Selectivity: Admits over 75% of applicants.

BASIC COSTS (2009-2010)

Tuition and fees: $15,150.

Room and board: $5,580.

FINANCIAL AID PICTURE (2007-2008)

Students with need: 45% of average financial aid package awarded as scholarships/grants, 55% awarded as loans/jobs. Need-based aid available for part-time students.

FINANCIAL AID PROCEDURES

Forms required: FAFSA.

Dates and Deadlines: Priority date 6/1; closing date 8/1. Applicants notified on a rolling basis starting 3/1; must reply within 3 week(s) of notification.

CONTACT

Blair Walker, Director Financial Aid
2605 Ben Hill Road, East Point, GA 30344
(404) 460-2462

Atlanta Metropolitan College

Atlanta, Georgia
www.atlm.edu Federal Code: 012165

2-year public junior college in very large city.
Enrollment: 2,144 undergrads, 44% part-time. 319 full-time freshmen.

BASIC COSTS (2008-2009)

Tuition and fees: $2,148; out-of-state residents $7,650.
Per-credit charge: $77; out-of-state residents $306.

FINANCIAL AID PICTURE (2007-2008)

Students with need: Need-based aid available for full-time and part-time students. Work study available nights, weekends, and for part-time students.
Students without need: This college awards aid only to students with need.

FINANCIAL AID PROCEDURES

Forms required: FAFSA, state aid form.
Dates and Deadlines: Closing date 6/1. Applicants notified on a rolling basis; must reply by 6/30.
Transfers: Priority date 6/1; closing date 6/30. Applicants notified on a rolling basis; must reply by 6/30.

CONTACT

Alicia Scott, Director
1630 Metropolitan Parkway, SW, Atlanta, GA 30310-4498
(404) 756-4002

Atlanta Technical College

Atlanta, Georgia
www.atlantatech.org

2-year public community and technical college in very large city.
Enrollment: 3,026 undergrads, 48% part-time. 395 full-time freshmen.
Selectivity: Open admission; but selective for some programs.

BASIC COSTS (2008-2009)

Tuition and fees: $1,542; out-of-state residents $2,838.
Per-credit charge: $36; out-of-state residents $72.

FINANCIAL AID PICTURE (2008-2009)

Students with need: Need-based aid available for full-time and part-time students. Work study available nights.

FINANCIAL AID PROCEDURES

Forms required: state aid form.
Dates and Deadlines: Priority date 3/1; no closing date. Applicants notified on a rolling basis starting 4/15.

CONTACT

Deborah Clark, Director of Financial Aid
1560 Metropolitan Parkway, SW, Atlanta, GA 30310-4446

Augusta State University

Augusta, Georgia
www.aug.edu Federal Code: 001552

4-year public liberal arts and teachers college in small city.
Enrollment: 5,394 undergrads, 28% part-time. 897 full-time freshmen.
Selectivity: Admits 50 to 75% of applicants.

BASIC COSTS (2008-2009)

Tuition and fees: $3,644; out-of-state residents $12,936.
Per-credit charge: $130; out-of-state residents $517.

FINANCIAL AID PICTURE (2007-2008)

Students with need: Out of 545 full-time freshmen who applied for aid, 444 were judged to have need. Of these, 404 received aid, and 13 had their full need met. Average financial aid package met 70% of need; average scholarship/grant was $1,818; average loan was $1,427. For part-time students, average financial aid package was $2,938.
Students without need: 29 full-time freshmen who did not demonstrate need for aid received scholarships/grants; average award was $1,524. No-need awards available for academics, art, athletics, leadership, minority status, music/drama, ROTC, state/district residency.
Scholarships offered: 4 full-time freshmen received athletic scholarships; average amount $4,966.
Cumulative student debt: 36% of graduating class had student loans; average debt was $5,961.

FINANCIAL AID PROCEDURES

Forms required: FAFSA, institutional form.
Dates and Deadlines: Closing date 6/1. Applicants notified on a rolling basis starting 3/1; must reply within 4 week(s) of notification.

CONTACT

Willene Holmes, Director of Financial Aid
2500 Walton Way, Augusta, GA 30904-2200
(706) 737-1431

Bainbridge College

Bainbridge, Georgia
www.bainbridge.edu Federal Code: 011074

2-year public community and technical college in large town.
Enrollment: 3,050 undergrads, 59% part-time. 309 full-time freshmen.

BASIC COSTS (2008-2009)

Tuition and fees: $2,326; out-of-state residents $7,828.
Per-credit charge: $77; out-of-state residents $306.

FINANCIAL AID PICTURE (2007-2008)

Students with need: 99% of average financial aid package awarded as scholarships/grants, 1% awarded as loans/jobs. Need-based aid available for part-time students.
Students without need: This college awards aid only to students with need.
Scholarships offered: Small number of merit scholarships available.
Additional info: 30-day loans available for tuition and fees.

FINANCIAL AID PROCEDURES

Forms required: FAFSA, institutional form.
Dates and Deadlines: Priority date 6/1; closing date 8/1. Applicants notified on a rolling basis starting 6/1; must reply within 2 week(s) of notification.
Transfers: Priority date 6/11.

CONTACT

Debra Turner, Director of Financial Aid
2500 East Shotwell Street, Bainbridge, GA 39818-0990
(229) 248-2505

Bauder College

Atlanta, Georgia
www.bauder.edu Federal Code: 011574

4-year for-profit career college in very large city.
Enrollment: 1,078 undergrads.
Selectivity: Open admission.

BASIC COSTS (2008-2009)
Tuition and fees: $13,639.
Additional info: Additional book fee of $1280.

FINANCIAL AID PICTURE
Students with need: Need-based aid available for full-time and part-time students. Work study available nights, weekends, and for part-time students.
Students without need: This college awards aid only to students with need.

FINANCIAL AID PROCEDURES
Forms required: FAFSA, institutional form.
Dates and Deadlines: No deadline. Applicants notified on a rolling basis starting 7/15.

CONTACT
Bela Akbasheva, Director of Financial Aid
384 Northyards Boulevard NW, Ste 190, Atlanta, GA 30313
(404) 237-7573

Berry College

Mount Berry, Georgia
www.berry.edu Federal Code: 001554

4-year private liberal arts college in large town.
Enrollment: 1,681 undergrads, 2% part-time. 461 full-time freshmen.
Selectivity: Admits 50 to 75% of applicants.

BASIC COSTS (2009-2010)
Tuition and fees: $23,360.
Per-credit charge: $772.
Room and board: $8,340.

FINANCIAL AID PICTURE (2008-2009)
Students with need: Out of 371 full-time freshmen who applied for aid, 275 were judged to have need. Of these, 275 received aid, and 69 had their full need met. Average financial aid package met 84% of need; average scholarship/grant was $15,269; average loan was $3,044. For part-time students, average financial aid package was $8,410.
Students without need: 178 full-time freshmen who did not demonstrate need for aid received scholarships/grants; average award was $8,511. No-need awards available for academics, art, athletics, leadership, minority status, music/drama, state/district residency.
Scholarships offered: ***Merit:*** HOPE Scholarship: $3,500 annually; for entering freshmen based on legal residence in Georgia and graduation from eligible high school with at least a B average in college preparatory coursework. ***Athletic:*** 38 full-time freshmen received athletic scholarships; average amount $11,751.
Cumulative student debt: 76% of graduating class had student loans; average debt was $15,808.
Additional info: Students are encouraged to work on-campus up to 20 hours per week.

FINANCIAL AID PROCEDURES
Forms required: institutional form.
Dates and Deadlines: Priority date 4/1; no closing date. Applicants notified on a rolling basis starting 2/1.
Transfers: No deadline. Applicants notified on a rolling basis starting 4/1.

CONTACT
J. Elmore, Director of Student Financial Aid
PO Box 490159, Mount Berry, GA 30149-0159
(706) 236-1714

Brenau University

Gainesville, Georgia
www.brenau.edu Federal Code: 001556

4-year private liberal arts college for women in small city.
Enrollment: 805 undergrads, 4% part-time. 173 full-time freshmen.
Selectivity: Admits less than 50% of applicants.

BASIC COSTS (2008-2009)
Tuition and fees: $18,800.
Per-credit charge: $618.
Room and board: $9,487.

FINANCIAL AID PICTURE (2008-2009)
Students with need: Need-based aid available for full-time and part-time students. Work study available nights, weekends, and for part-time students.
Students without need: No-need awards available for academics, art, athletics, leadership, minority status, music/drama.

FINANCIAL AID PROCEDURES
Forms required: FAFSA, state aid form.
Dates and Deadlines: Priority date 4/1; no closing date. Applicants notified on a rolling basis starting 3/1.

CONTACT
Pam Barrett, Director of Financial Aid
500 Washington Street SE, Gainesville, GA 30501
(770) 534-6152

Brewton-Parker College

Mount Vernon, Georgia
www.bpc.edu Federal Code: 001557

4-year private liberal arts college in small town, affiliated with Southern Baptist Convention.
Enrollment: 1,007 undergrads, 27% part-time. 229 full-time freshmen.
Selectivity: Admits over 75% of applicants.

BASIC COSTS (2008-2009)
Tuition and fees: $14,730.
Per-credit charge: $420.
Room and board: $6,240.
Additional info: $130 per-credit fee for applied music surcharge.

FINANCIAL AID PICTURE (2007-2008)
Students with need: Need-based aid available for part-time students.
Students without need: No-need awards available for academics, athletics, music/drama, religious affiliation, state/district residency.
Scholarships offered: Scholarships available for academic achievement and SAT scores for incoming freshman transfer students, ranging from $1,500-$3,000 per academic year, available for four years.
Cumulative student debt: 89% of graduating class had student loans; average debt was $24,592.

FINANCIAL AID PROCEDURES
Forms required: FAFSA, state aid form.
Dates and Deadlines: Priority date 5/1; no closing date. Applicants notified on a rolling basis starting 2/27; must reply within 2 week(s) of notification.

CONTACT

Jackie White, Assistant Director of Financial Aid
Brewton-Parker College # 2011, Mount Vernon, GA 30445
(912) 583-2241 ext. 209

Central Georgia Technical College

Macon, Georgia
www.cgtcollege.edu Federal Code: 005763

2-year public community and technical college in small city.
Enrollment: 5,308 undergrads, 49% part-time. 579 full-time freshmen.
Selectivity: Open admission; but selective for some programs.

BASIC COSTS (2008-2009)

Tuition and fees: $1,539; out-of-state residents $2,835.
Per-credit charge: $36; out-of-state residents $72.

FINANCIAL AID PICTURE (2007-2008)

Students with need: Need-based aid available for full-time and part-time students.

FINANCIAL AID PROCEDURES

Forms required: FAFSA, state aid form, institutional form.
Dates and Deadlines: Closing date 7/14.

CONTACT

Pennie Strong, Director, Financial Aid
3300 Macon Tech Drive, Macon, GA 31206
(478) 757-3422

Chattahoochee Technical College

Marietta, Georgia
www.chattcollege.com Federal Code: 005620

2-year public technical college in large city.
Enrollment: 4,597 undergrads, 52% part-time. 711 full-time freshmen.
Selectivity: Open admission; but selective for some programs.

BASIC COSTS (2008-2009)

Tuition and fees: $1,560; out-of-state residents $2,856.
Per-credit charge: $36; out-of-state residents $72.

FINANCIAL AID PICTURE (2007-2008)

Students with need: 97% of average financial aid package awarded as scholarships/grants, 3% awarded as loans/jobs. Need-based aid available for part-time students. Work study available nights, weekends, and for part-time students.
Students without need: No-need awards available for state/district residency.

FINANCIAL AID PROCEDURES

Forms required: FAFSA, institutional form.
Dates and Deadlines: Priority date 7/15; no closing date. Applicants notified on a rolling basis starting 6/15.

CONTACT

Lori Burnette, Director of Financial Aid
980 South Cobb Drive, Marietta, GA 30060-3300
(770) 528-4531

Clark Atlanta University

Atlanta, Georgia
www.cau.edu Federal Code: 001559

4-year private university in very large city, affiliated with United Methodist Church.
Enrollment: 3,380 undergrads, 4% part-time. 814 full-time freshmen.
Selectivity: Admits 50 to 75% of applicants.

BASIC COSTS (2009-2010)

Tuition and fees: $17,038.
Per-credit charge: $680.
Room and board: $7,620.
Additional info: Tuition at time of enrollment locked for 4 years.

FINANCIAL AID PICTURE (2008-2009)

Students with need: Out of 789 full-time freshmen who applied for aid, 762 were judged to have need. Of these, 762 received aid, and 11 had their full need met. Average financial aid package met 12% of need; average scholarship/grant was $5,500; average loan was $3,500. For part-time students, average financial aid package was $5,400.
Students without need: 15 full-time freshmen who did not demonstrate need for aid received scholarships/grants; average award was $8,900. No-need awards available for academics, art, athletics, leadership, minority status, music/drama, religious affiliation, ROTC, state/district residency.
Scholarships offered: 65 full-time freshmen received athletic scholarships; average amount $5,400.
Cumulative student debt: 95% of graduating class had student loans; average debt was $36,000.

FINANCIAL AID PROCEDURES

Forms required: FAFSA, state aid form.
Dates and Deadlines: Priority date 3/1; no closing date. Applicants notified on a rolling basis starting 4/1.

CONTACT

Mark Adkins, Director
223 James P. Brawley Drive, SW, Atlanta, GA 30314-4391
(404) 880-6018

Clayton State University

Morrow, Georgia
www.clayton.edu Federal Code: 008976

4-year public liberal arts and technical college in small city.
Enrollment: 5,773 undergrads, 44% part-time. 373 full-time freshmen.

BASIC COSTS (2008-2009)

Tuition and fees: $3,852; out-of-state residents $13,144.
Per-credit charge: $130; out-of-state residents $517.

FINANCIAL AID PICTURE (2008-2009)

Students with need: Need-based aid available for full-time and part-time students.
Students without need: No-need awards available for academics.

FINANCIAL AID PROCEDURES

Forms required: FAFSA, state aid form.
Dates and Deadlines: Priority date 7/18; no closing date. Applicants notified on a rolling basis starting 3/12.

CONTACT

Patricia Barton, Director of Financial Aid
2000 Clayton State Boulevard, Morrow, GA 30260-0285
(678) 466-4185

College of Coastal Georgia

Brunswick, Georgia
www.ccga.edu Federal Code: 001558

2-year public junior college in large town.
Enrollment: 2,794 undergrads, 63% part-time. 449 full-time freshmen.
Selectivity: Open admission; but selective for some programs.

BASIC COSTS (2008-2009)
Tuition and fees: $2,050; out-of-state residents $7,552.
Per-credit charge: $77; out-of-state residents $306.
Additional info: Costs may vary among students.

FINANCIAL AID PICTURE (2007-2008)
Students with need: Need-based aid available for full-time and part-time students. Work study available nights, weekends, and for part-time students.
Students without need: No-need awards available for academics, athletics, leadership, state/district residency.

FINANCIAL AID PROCEDURES
Forms required: FAFSA.
Dates and Deadlines: Priority date 5/1; no closing date. Applicants notified on a rolling basis starting 7/1.
Transfers: No deadline. Applicants notified on a rolling basis.

CONTACT
Rodney Clements, Financial Aid Director
3700 Altama Avenue, Brunswick, GA 31520
(912) 279-5722

Columbus State University
Columbus, Georgia
www.colstate.edu Federal Code: 001561

4-year public university and liberal arts college in large city.
Enrollment: 6,668 undergrads, 30% part-time. 1,068 full-time freshmen.
Selectivity: Admits 50 to 75% of applicants. GED not accepted.

BASIC COSTS (2008-2009)
Tuition and fees: $3,772; out-of-state residents $13,064.
Per-credit charge: $130; out-of-state residents $517.
Room and board: $6,300.
Additional info: Tuition at time of enrollment locked for 4 years.

FINANCIAL AID PICTURE (2008-2009)
Students with need: Out of 927 full-time freshmen who applied for aid, 590 were judged to have need. Of these, 572 received aid, and 389 had their full need met. Average financial aid package met 66% of need; average scholarship/grant was $3,146; average loan was $2,899. For part-time students, average financial aid package was $3,311.
Students without need: 351 full-time freshmen who did not demonstrate need for aid received scholarships/grants; average award was $1,671. No-need awards available for academics, alumni affiliation, art, athletics, job skills, leadership, minority status, music/drama, ROTC.
Scholarships offered: 17 full-time freshmen received athletic scholarships; average amount $2,460.
Cumulative student debt: 75% of graduating class had student loans; average debt was $26,905.

FINANCIAL AID PROCEDURES
Forms required: FAFSA.
Dates and Deadlines: Priority date 5/1; no closing date. Applicants notified on a rolling basis starting 5/15; must reply within 4 week(s) of notification.

CONTACT
Janis Bowles, Director of Financial Aid
4225 University Avenue, Columbus, GA 31907-5645
(706) 507-8800

Columbus Technical College
Columbus, Georgia
www.columbustech.org Federal Code: 005624

2-year public technical college in small city.
Enrollment: 3,621 undergrads, 57% part-time. 373 full-time freshmen.
Selectivity: Open admission; but selective for some programs.

BASIC COSTS (2008-2009)
Tuition and fees: $1,539; out-of-state residents $2,835.
Per-credit charge: $36; out-of-state residents $72.

FINANCIAL AID PICTURE
Students with need: Need-based aid available for full-time and part-time students.

FINANCIAL AID PROCEDURES
Forms required: FAFSA.
Dates and Deadlines: No deadline. Applicants notified on a rolling basis.

CONTACT
Debbie Henshaw, Director, Financial Aid
928 Manchester Expressway, Columbus, GA 31904
(706) 649-1859

Covenant College
Lookout Mountain, Georgia
www.covenant.edu Federal Code: 003484

4-year private liberal arts college in small city, affiliated with Presbyterian Church in America.
Enrollment: 983 undergrads, 2% part-time. 291 full-time freshmen.
Selectivity: Admits 50 to 75% of applicants.

BASIC COSTS (2009-2010)
Tuition and fees: $25,270.
Per-credit charge: $1,025.
Room and board: $7,170.

FINANCIAL AID PICTURE (2007-2008)
Students with need: Out of 244 full-time freshmen who applied for aid, 211 were judged to have need. Of these, 211 received aid, and 36 had their full need met. Average financial aid package met 79% of need; average scholarship/grant was $13,388; average loan was $4,335. For part-time students, average financial aid package was $11,023.
Students without need: 69 full-time freshmen who did not demonstrate need for aid received scholarships/grants; average award was $6,022. No-need awards available for academics, alumni affiliation, art, athletics, job skills, leadership, minority status, music/drama, religious affiliation, state/district residency.
Scholarships offered: ***Merit:*** Maclellan Scholars Program; minimum SAT 1200 (exclusive of Writing) or ACT 27, high school GPA 3.3. Presidential Scholarship; based on GPA, leadership, Christian commitment, extracurricular activities, work experience, references. ***Athletic:*** 27 full-time freshmen received athletic scholarships; average amount $5,941.
Cumulative student debt: 61% of graduating class had student loans; average debt was $19,478.

FINANCIAL AID PROCEDURES
Forms required: FAFSA, state aid form.
Dates and Deadlines: No deadline. Applicants notified on a rolling basis starting 2/1; must reply within 3 week(s) of notification.
Transfers: Some scholarships may be depleted for mid-semester transfers, such as athletic, diversity or music.

CONTACT

Brenda Rapier, Director of Financial Aid
14049 Scenic Highway, Lookout Mountain, GA 30750
(706) 419-1126

Dalton State College

Dalton, Georgia
www.daltonstate.edu Federal Code: 003956

4-year public liberal arts and teachers college in large town.
Enrollment: 4,957 undergrads, 46% part-time. 958 full-time freshmen.
Selectivity: Admits 50 to 75% of applicants.

BASIC COSTS (2008-2009)
Tuition and fees: $2,340; out-of-state residents $8,322.
Per-credit charge: $84; out-of-state residents $333.

FINANCIAL AID PICTURE (2007-2008)
Students with need: Need-based aid available for full-time and part-time students.
Students without need: No-need awards available for academics, leadership, minority status, state/district residency.

FINANCIAL AID PROCEDURES
Forms required: FAFSA, state aid form, institutional form.
Dates and Deadlines: Priority date 7/1; no closing date. Applicants notified on a rolling basis starting 7/1.
Transfers: No deadline. Applicants notified on a rolling basis.

CONTACT

Dianne Cox, Director of Student Financial Aid
650 College Drive, Dalton, GA 30720
(706) 272-4545

Darton College

Albany, Georgia
www.darton.edu Federal Code: 001543

2-year public community college in small city.
Enrollment: 4,528 undergrads, 50% part-time. 904 full-time freshmen.
Selectivity: Admits over 75% of applicants.

BASIC COSTS (2008-2009)
Tuition and fees: $2,412; out-of-state residents $7,914.
Per-credit charge: $77; out of state residents $306.

FINANCIAL AID PICTURE (2007-2008)
Students with need: Need-based aid available for full-time and part-time students. Work study available nights, weekends, and for part-time students.
Students without need: No-need awards available for academics, alumni affiliation, art, athletics, music/drama, state/district residency.
Additional info: Auditions, portfolios, essays, extracurricular activities impact scholarship decisions.

FINANCIAL AID PROCEDURES
Forms required: FAFSA, state aid form, institutional form.
Dates and Deadlines: No deadline. Applicants notified on a rolling basis; must reply within 3 week(s) of notification.

CONTACT

Martha Whittle, Director of Financial Aid
2400 Gillionville Road, Albany, GA 31707-3098
(229) 317-6746

DeKalb Technical College

Clarkston, Georgia
www.dekalbtech.edu Federal Code: 016582

2-year public technical college in large city.
Enrollment: 3,805 undergrads, 60% part-time. 350 full-time freshmen.
Selectivity: Open admission; but selective for some programs.

BASIC COSTS (2008-2009)
Tuition and fees: $1,587; out-of-state residents $2,883.
Per-credit charge: $36; out-of-state residents $72.
Additional info: Truck driving and flight technology are higher cost programs.

FINANCIAL AID PICTURE (2008-2009)
Students with need: Need-based aid available for full-time and part-time students. Work study available nights, weekends, and for part-time students.

FINANCIAL AID PROCEDURES
Forms required: FAFSA.
Dates and Deadlines: Priority date 7/15; closing date 8/20. Applicants notified on a rolling basis starting 6/1.
Transfers: No deadline.

CONTACT

John Gottardy, Director of Financial Aid
495 North Indian Creek Drive, Clarkston, GA 30021-2397
(404) 297-9522 ext. 1166

DeVry University: Alpharetta

Alpharetta, Georgia
www.devry.edu Federal Code: 009224

4-year for-profit university in large town.
Enrollment: 708 undergrads, 52% part-time. 65 full-time freshmen.

BASIC COSTS (2008-2009)
Tuition and fees: $14,130.
Per-credit charge: $515.

FINANCIAL AID PICTURE (2007-2008)
Students with need: Need-based aid available for full-time and part-time students.
Students without need: This college awards aid only to students with need.

FINANCIAL AID PROCEDURES
Forms required: FAFSA.
Dates and Deadlines: No deadline. Applicants notified on a rolling basis.

CONTACT

David Pickett, Assistant Director of Financial Aid
2555 Northwinds Parkway, Alpharetta, GA 30004
(770) 521-4900

DeVry University: Decatur

Decatur, Georgia
www.devry.edu Federal Code: 009224

4-year for-profit university in large town.
Enrollment: 2,376 undergrads, 48% part-time. 197 full-time freshmen.

BASIC COSTS (2008-2009)
Tuition and fees: $14,130.
Per-credit charge: $515.

FINANCIAL AID PICTURE (2007-2008)
Students with need: Need-based aid available for full-time and part-time students.
Students without need: This college awards aid only to students with need.

FINANCIAL AID PROCEDURES
Forms required: FAFSA.
Dates and Deadlines: No deadline. Applicants notified on a rolling basis.

CONTACT
Robin Winston, Director of Financial Aid
250 North Arcadia Avenue, Decatur, GA 30030-2198
(404) 292-7900

East Georgia College
Swainsboro, Georgia
www.ega.edu Federal Code: 010997

2-year public community and junior college in small town.
Enrollment: 2,555 undergrads.

BASIC COSTS (2008-2009)
Tuition and fees: $2,010; out-of-state residents $7,512.
Per-credit charge: $77; out-of-state residents $306.

FINANCIAL AID PICTURE
Students with need: Need-based aid available for full-time and part-time students.
Students without need: No-need awards available for academics, leadership, state/district residency.

FINANCIAL AID PROCEDURES
Forms required: FAFSA, institutional form.
Dates and Deadlines: Priority date 6/15; no closing date. Applicants notified on a rolling basis starting 6/15; must reply within 2 week(s) of notification.

CONTACT
Barbara Green, Director of Financial Aid
131 College Circle, Swainsboro, GA 30401-2699
(478) 289-2009

Emmanuel College
Franklin Springs, Georgia
www.ec.edu Federal Code: 001563

4-year private liberal arts college in rural community, affiliated with Pentecostal Holiness Church.
Enrollment: 645 undergrads, 5% part-time. 126 full-time freshmen.
Selectivity: Admits 50 to 75% of applicants.

BASIC COSTS (2009-2010)
Tuition and fees: $12,880.
Per-credit charge: $530.
Room and board: $5,520.

FINANCIAL AID PICTURE (2008-2009)
Students with need: Out of 120 full-time freshmen who applied for aid, 103 were judged to have need. Of these, 103 received aid, and 15 had their full need met. Average financial aid package met 81% of need; average scholarship/grant was $8,481; average loan was $3,304. For part-time students, average financial aid package was $8,390.
Students without need: 16 full-time freshmen who did not demonstrate need for aid received scholarships/grants; average award was $3,334. No-need awards available for academics, art, athletics, leadership, music/drama, religious affiliation, state/district residency.
Scholarships offered: 8 full-time freshmen received athletic scholarships; average amount $3,313.
Cumulative student debt: 85% of graduating class had student loans; average debt was $23,880.

FINANCIAL AID PROCEDURES
Forms required: FAFSA, state aid form, institutional form.
Dates and Deadlines: Priority date 5/1; closing date 7/1. Applicants notified on a rolling basis starting 3/1; must reply within 2 week(s) of notification.
Transfers: Students on probation at previous institution may be accepted and funded for one semester. Continued funding dependent on satisfactory performance.

CONTACT
Gloria Hambrick, Financial Aid Director
181 Spring Street, Franklin Springs, GA 30639-0129
(706) 245-7226

Emory University
Atlanta, Georgia Federal Code: 001564
www.emory.edu CSS Code: 5187

4-year private university in very large city, affiliated with United Methodist Church.
Enrollment: 5,169 undergrads, 1% part-time. 1,277 full-time freshmen.
Selectivity: Admits less than 50% of applicants. GED not accepted.

BASIC COSTS (2008-2009)
Tuition and fees: $36,336.
Room and board: $10,572.

FINANCIAL AID PICTURE (2008-2009)
Students with need: Out of 853 full-time freshmen who applied for aid, 680 were judged to have need. Of these, 680 received aid, and 680 had their full need met. Average financial aid package met 100% of need; average scholarship/grant was $27,850; average loan was $3,399. Need-based aid available for part-time students.
Students without need: 217 full-time freshmen who did not demonstrate need for aid received scholarships/grants; average award was $13,094. No-need awards available for academics, art, leadership, music/drama, state/district residency.
Scholarships offered: Emory Scholars program: two-thirds tuition to full cost; based on academic merit of incoming first-year students, requires nomination by appropriate high school official by November 1 of senior year; renewable for four years of undergraduate study.
Cumulative student debt: 42% of graduating class had student loans; average debt was $23,181.
Additional info: Loan replacement grant and loan cap program available to students from families with total annual incomes of $100,000 or less who demonstrate need for financial aid.

FINANCIAL AID PROCEDURES
Forms required: FAFSA, CSS PROFILE.
Dates and Deadlines: Priority date 2/15; closing date 3/1. Applicants notified by 4/1; must reply by 5/1 or within 4 week(s) of notification.
Transfers: No deadline. Applicants notified on a rolling basis. Limitations on aid available to transfer students. Financial aid filing deadline for transfers is 30 days following transfer student admission date.

CONTACT
Dean Bentley, Director of Financial Aid
200 Boisfeuillet Jones Center, Atlanta, GA 30322
(800) 727-6039

Fort Valley State University
Fort Valley, Georgia
www.fvsu.edu Federal Code: 001566

4-year public liberal arts and teachers college in small town.
Enrollment: 2,969 undergrads, 7% part-time. 1,049 full-time freshmen.
Selectivity: Admits less than 50% of applicants.

BASIC COSTS (2008-2009)
Tuition and fees: $4,018; out-of-state residents $13,310.
Per-credit charge: $130; out-of-state residents $517.
Room and board: $6,410.

FINANCIAL AID PICTURE (2008-2009)
Students with need: Out of 1,045 full-time freshmen who applied for aid, 1,038 were judged to have need. Of these, 1,035 received aid. Average financial aid package met 96% of need; average scholarship/grant was $2,140; average loan was $2,300. For part-time students, average financial aid package was $400.
Students without need: 132 full-time freshmen who did not demonstrate need for aid received scholarships/grants; average award was $1,780. No-need awards available for academics, job skills.
Scholarships offered: 58 full-time freshmen received athletic scholarships; average amount $1,639.
Cumulative student debt: 98% of graduating class had student loans; average debt was $36,700.
Additional info: Loans decreased and grant aid offered to make institution more affordable.

FINANCIAL AID PROCEDURES
Forms required: FAFSA, state aid form.
Dates and Deadlines: Priority date 4/15; closing date 6/30. Applicants notified on a rolling basis starting 7/1; must reply within 1 week(s) of notification.
Transfers: Financial aid transcripts must be received from former institutions before application for aid will be considered complete and reviewed for awards.

CONTACT
Eula Solomon, Director of Financial Aid
1005 State University Drive, Fort Valley, GA 31030-4313
(478) 825-6351

Gainesville State College
Gainesville, Georgia
www.gsc.edu Federal Code: 001567

2-year public junior college in large town.
Enrollment: 8,035 undergrads.
Selectivity: Admits over 75% of applicants.

BASIC COSTS (2008-2009)
Tuition and fees: $2,324; out-of-state residents $8,306.
Per-credit charge: $84; out-of-state residents $333.

FINANCIAL AID PICTURE (2007-2008)
Students with need: 55% of average financial aid package awarded as scholarships/grants, 45% awarded as loans/jobs. Need-based aid available for part-time students. Work study available nights, weekends, and for part-time students.
Students without need: No-need awards available for academics, art, leadership, music/drama.

FINANCIAL AID PROCEDURES
Forms required: FAFSA.
Dates and Deadlines: Priority date 6/1; no closing date. Applicants notified on a rolling basis starting 5/1; must reply within 2 week(s) of notification.
Transfers: No deadline. Applicants notified on a rolling basis starting 5/1; must reply within 2 week(s) of notification. Must have minimum 2.0 GPA to be eligible for financial aid.

CONTACT
Susan Smith, Financial Aid Director
PO Box 1358, Gainesville, GA 30503
(678) 717-3642

Georgia College and State University
Milledgeville, Georgia
www.gcsu.edu Federal Code: 001602

4-year public university and liberal arts college in large town.
Enrollment: 5,464 undergrads, 9% part-time. 1,094 full-time freshmen.
Selectivity: Admits 50 to 75% of applicants.

BASIC COSTS (2008-2009)
Tuition and fees: $5,476; out-of-state residents $19,108.
Per-credit charge: $190; out-of-state residents $758.
Room and board: $7,698.

FINANCIAL AID PICTURE (2007-2008)
Students with need: For part-time students, average financial aid package was $5,228.
Students without need: 26 full-time freshmen who did not demonstrate need for aid received scholarships/grants; average award was $1,756. No-need awards available for academics, alumni affiliation, art, athletics, job skills, leadership, minority status, music/drama, religious affiliation, ROTC, state/district residency.
Scholarships offered: Presidential Scholarship: $4,000 per year, renewable; 1250 SAT/ equivalent ACT, 3.5 high school GPA. Distinguished Scholars Award: $6,000-$13,000, renewable; available to non Georgia residents who demonstrate high academic merit. Lucille Vincent Scholarshop: up to 4000 per year, renewable; 3.3 GPA.
Cumulative student debt: 55% of graduating class had student loans; average debt was $15,197.

FINANCIAL AID PROCEDURES
Forms required: FAFSA, institutional form.
Dates and Deadlines: Priority date 3/1; no closing date. Applicants notified on a rolling basis starting 3/1; must reply within 2 week(s) of notification.
Transfers: No deadline. Applicants notified on a rolling basis starting 3/1; must reply within 2 week(s) of notification.

CONTACT
Cathy Crawley, Director of Financial Aid
Campus Box 23, Milledgeville, GA 31061-0490
(478) 445-5149

Georgia Highlands College
Rome, Georgia
www.highlands.edu Federal Code: 009507

2-year public community and liberal arts college in small city.
Enrollment: 4,700 undergrads, 43% part-time. 1,078 full-time freshmen.
Selectivity: Admits over 75% of applicants.

BASIC COSTS (2008-2009)
Tuition and fees: $2,056; out-of-state residents $7,558.
Per-credit charge: $77; out-of-state residents $306.

FINANCIAL AID PICTURE (2007-2008)
Students with need: Need-based aid available for full-time and part-time students. Work study available nights.
Students without need: No-need awards available for academics, art.

FINANCIAL AID PROCEDURES

Forms required: FAFSA.

Dates and Deadlines: Closing date 4/1. Applicants notified on a rolling basis starting 4/1; must reply within 2 week(s) of notification.

CONTACT

Donna Childres, Director of Financial Aid
3175 Cedartown Highway, Rome, GA 30161
(706) 295-6311

Georgia Institute of Technology

Atlanta, Georgia
www.gatech.edu Federal Code: 001569

4-year public university in very large city.
Enrollment: 12,533 undergrads, 5% part-time. 2,637 full-time freshmen.
Selectivity: Admits 50 to 75% of applicants.

BASIC COSTS (2008-2009)

Tuition and fees: $6,040; out-of-state residents $25,182.
Per-credit charge: $203; out-of-state residents $1,000.
Room and board: $7,694.

FINANCIAL AID PICTURE (2008-2009)

Students with need: Out of 1,976 full-time freshmen who applied for aid, 808 were judged to have need. Of these, 777 received aid, and 428 had their full need met. Average financial aid package met 87% of need; average scholarship/grant was $8,947; average loan was $4,666. For part-time students, average financial aid package was $6,396.

Students without need: 1,229 full-time freshmen who did not demonstrate need for aid received scholarships/grants; average award was $6,431. No-need awards available for academics, alumni affiliation, athletics, leadership, state/district residency.

Scholarships offered: ***Merit:*** President's Scholarship Program; 4-year awards range from half to full tuition; for freshmen with outstanding academic/leadership qualities. ***Athletic:*** 55 full-time freshmen received athletic scholarships; average amount $10,206.

Cumulative student debt: 48% of graduating class had student loans; average debt was $20,881.

Additional info: Georgia Tech Promise Program offers a debt-free degree to qualified Georgia residents with family income less than $33,300.

FINANCIAL AID PROCEDURES

Forms required: FAFSA, institutional form.

Dates and Deadlines: Closing date 3/1. Applicants notified on a rolling basis starting 4/1; must reply by 5/1.

Transfers: Closing date 5/1. Applicants notified on a rolling basis starting 6/1. Student must be officially admitted, all final transcripts must be received, and transcripts must be articulated.

CONTACT

Marie Mons, Director of Student Financial Planning and Services
Georgia Institute of Technology, Atlanta, GA 30332-0320
(404) 894-4160

Georgia Military College

Milledgeville, Georgia
www.gmc.cc.ga.us Federal Code: 001571

2-year public community and military college in large town.
Enrollment: 5,047 undergrads, 26% part-time. 2,573 full-time freshmen.
Selectivity: Open admission; but selective for some programs.

BASIC COSTS (2008-2009)

Tuition and fees: $6,300.
Per-credit charge: $102.
Room and board: $5,535.
Additional info: Tuition and fees for cadet students: $12,150 with $1,150 additional for uniforms.

FINANCIAL AID PICTURE (2007-2008)

Students with need: Need-based aid available for full-time and part-time students. Work study available nights.

Students without need: No-need awards available for athletics, leadership, ROTC, state/district residency.

Additional info: Institutional aid offered to those enrolled in Cadet Corps who reside on campus.

FINANCIAL AID PROCEDURES

Forms required: FAFSA, state aid form.

Dates and Deadlines: No deadline. Applicants notified on a rolling basis starting 3/1.

CONTACT

Alisa Stephens, Director of Financial Aid
201 East Greene Street, Milledgeville, GA 31061
(478) 445-0840

Georgia Perimeter College

Clarkston, Georgia
www.gpc.edu Federal Code: 001562

2-year public junior and liberal arts college in very large city.
Enrollment: 21,036 undergrads, 54% part-time. 2,989 full-time freshmen.
Selectivity: Admits 50 to 75% of applicants.

BASIC COSTS (2008-2009)

Tuition and fees: $2,322; out-of-state residents $7,824.
Per-credit charge: $77; out-of-state residents $306.

FINANCIAL AID PICTURE (2007-2008)

Students with need: Need-based aid available for full-time and part-time students. Work study available nights, weekends, and for part-time students.

FINANCIAL AID PROCEDURES

Forms required: FAFSA.

Dates and Deadlines: Closing date 6/1. Applicants notified on a rolling basis; must reply within 3 week(s) of notification.

Transfers: Priority date 6/1; no deadline.

CONTACT

Sheletha Champion, Director, Student Financial Services
555 North Indian Creek Drive, Clarkston, GA 30021-2361
(678) 891-3400

Georgia Southern University

Statesboro, Georgia
www.georgiasouthern.edu Federal Code: 001572

4-year public university in large town.
Enrollment: 14,598 undergrads, 6% part-time. 3,029 full-time freshmen.
Selectivity: Admits 50 to 75% of applicants. GED not accepted.

BASIC COSTS (2008-2009)

Tuition and fees: $4,348; out-of-state residents $13,930.
Per-credit charge: $134; out-of-state residents $533.
Room and board: $7,300.

FINANCIAL AID PICTURE (2007-2008)

Students with need: Out of 2,750 full-time freshmen who applied for aid, 1,538 were judged to have need. Of these, 1,488 received aid, and 243 had their full need met. Average financial aid package met 60% of need; average scholarship/grant was $5,619; average loan was $3,230. For part-time students, average financial aid package was $5,355.

Students without need: 175 full-time freshmen who did not demonstrate need for aid received scholarships/grants; average award was $2,121. No-need awards available for academics, alumni affiliation, art, athletics, leadership, minority status, music/drama, ROTC, state/district residency.

Scholarships offered: 36 full-time freshmen received athletic scholarships; average amount $4,618.

Cumulative student debt: 66% of graduating class had student loans; average debt was $18,518.

Additional info: The majority of scholarships available are need-blind.

FINANCIAL AID PROCEDURES

Forms required: FAFSA.

Dates and Deadlines: Priority date 4/20; no closing date. Applicants notified on a rolling basis starting 4/20.

Transfers: No deadline. Applicants notified on a rolling basis starting 4/20.

CONTACT

Connie Murphey, Director of Financial Aid
PO Box 8024, Statesboro, GA 30460
(912) 478-5413

Georgia Southwestern State University

Americus, Georgia
www.gsw.edu Federal Code: 001573

4-year public university and liberal arts college in large town.

Enrollment: 2,368 undergrads, 26% part-time. 418 full-time freshmen.

Selectivity: Admits 50 to 75% of applicants.

BASIC COSTS (2008-2009)

Tuition and fees: $3,836; out-of-state residents $13,128.

Per-credit charge: $130; out-of-state residents $517.

Room and board: $5,694.

FINANCIAL AID PICTURE (2007-2008)

Students with need: Need-based aid available for full-time and part-time students.

Students without need: No-need awards available for academics, athletics, leadership.

Scholarships offered: Wheatley Scholarship: $2,000-2,500; 3.0 in college preparatory course and either 1100 SAT (exclusive of Writing) or 24 ACT.

FINANCIAL AID PROCEDURES

Forms required: FAFSA, institutional form.

Dates and Deadlines: Priority date 4/1; closing date 6/1. Applicants notified on a rolling basis starting 3/1.

CONTACT

Freida Jones, Director of Financial Aid
800 Georgia Southwestern State University Drive, Americus, GA 31709-9957
(229) 928-1378

Georgia State University

Atlanta, Georgia
www.gsu.edu Federal Code: 001574

4-year public university in very large city.

Enrollment: 20,179 undergrads, 24% part-time. 2,849 full-time freshmen.

Selectivity: Admits 50 to 75% of applicants. GED not accepted.

BASIC COSTS (2008-2009)

Tuition and fees: $6,056; out-of-state residents $20,624.

Per-credit charge: $203; out-of-state residents $810.

Room only: $6,550.

FINANCIAL AID PICTURE (2008-2009)

Students with need: Out of 2,342 full-time freshmen who applied for aid, 1,783 were judged to have need. Of these, 1,713 received aid, and 412 had their full need met. Average financial aid package met 27% of need; average scholarship/grant was $2,684; average loan was $2,994. For part-time students, average financial aid package was $9,841.

Students without need: This college awards aid only to students with need.

Scholarships offered: 38 full-time freshmen received athletic scholarships; average amount $12,389.

Cumulative student debt: 55% of graduating class had student loans; average debt was $15,950.

FINANCIAL AID PROCEDURES

Forms required: FAFSA.

Dates and Deadlines: Priority date 4/1; closing date 11/1. Applicants notified on a rolling basis starting 3/30; must reply within 2 week(s) of notification.

CONTACT

Louis Scott, Director of Student Financial Aid
Box 4009, Atlanta, GA 30302-4009
(404) 413-2400

Gordon College

Barnesville, Georgia
www.gdn.edu Federal Code: 001575

2-year public junior college in small town.

Enrollment: 3,794 undergrads, 30% part-time. 1,158 full-time freshmen.

Selectivity: Admits 50 to 75% of applicants.

BASIC COSTS (2008-2009)

Tuition and fees: $2,362; out-of-state residents $8,344.

Per-credit charge: $84; out-of-state residents $333.

Room and board: $4,560.

FINANCIAL AID PICTURE (2007-2008)

Students with need: Need-based aid available for full-time and part-time students. Work study available nights, weekends, and for part-time students.

Students without need: No-need awards available for academics, athletics, music/drama, state/district residency.

FINANCIAL AID PROCEDURES

Forms required: FAFSA, institutional form.

Dates and Deadlines: Priority date 5/1; no closing date. Applicants notified on a rolling basis starting 5/1.

CONTACT

Larry Mitcham, Director of Financial Aid
419 College Drive, Barnesville, GA 30204
(678) 359-5990

Gupton Jones College of Funeral Service

Decatur, Georgia
www.gupton-jones.edu Federal Code: 010771

2-year private technical college in very large city.

Enrollment: 135 undergrads. 75 full-time freshmen.

Selectivity: Open admission.

BASIC COSTS (2008-2009)
Tuition and fees: $9,000.
Per-credit charge: $200.
Additional info: Tuition costs include all textbooks and supplies needed.

FINANCIAL AID PICTURE
Students with need: Need-based aid available for full-time and part-time students.
Students without need: This college awards aid only to students with need.

FINANCIAL AID PROCEDURES
Forms required: FAFSA.
Dates and Deadlines: No deadline. Applicants notified on a rolling basis.

CONTACT
James Hinz, Dean
5141 Snapfinger Woods Drive, Decatur, GA 30035
(770) 593-2257

Gwinnett College
Lilburn, Georgia
www.gwinnettcollege.edu Federal Code: 025830

2-year for-profit junior and career college in large city.
Enrollment: 360 undergrads.
Selectivity: Open admission; but selective for some programs.

BASIC COSTS (2009-2010)
Tuition and fees: $8,725.

FINANCIAL AID PICTURE (2008-2009)
Students with need: Need-based aid available for full-time and part-time students.

FINANCIAL AID PROCEDURES
Forms required: FAFSA.

CONTACT
James Davidson, Director of Financial Aid
4230 Highway 29, Lilburn, GA 30047
(770) 381-7200

Gwinnett Technical College
Lawrenceville, Georgia
www.gwinnetttech.edu Federal Code: 016139

2-year public technical college in large town.
Enrollment: 5,120 undergrads, 53% part-time. 563 full-time freshmen.
Selectivity: Open admission; but selective for some programs.

BASIC COSTS (2008-2009)
Tuition and fees: $1,605; out-of-state residents $2,901.
Per-credit charge: $36; out-of-state residents $72.

FINANCIAL AID PICTURE (2008-2009)
Students with need: Need-based aid available for full-time and part-time students.

FINANCIAL AID PROCEDURES
Forms required: FAFSA.
Dates and Deadlines: Closing date 7/1.
Transfers: Priority date 7/1; no deadline.

CONTACT
Stephen Whitaker, Director of Financial Aid
5150 Sugarloaf Parkway, Lawrenceville, GA 30243
(770) 962-7580 ext. 6637

Herzing College
Atlanta, Georgia
www.herzing.edu Federal Code: 014030

3-year for-profit business and technical college in very large city.
Selectivity: Admits 50 to 75% of applicants.

BASIC COSTS (2008-2009)
Tuition and fees: $11,640.
Per-credit charge: $388.
Additional info: Costs may vary by program.

FINANCIAL AID PICTURE
Students with need: Need-based aid available for full-time and part-time students. Work study available nights.
Students without need: No-need awards available for academics.

FINANCIAL AID PROCEDURES
Forms required: FAFSA, institutional form.
Dates and Deadlines: No deadline. Applicants notified on a rolling basis.

CONTACT
Stephanie Gunby, Director of Financial Services
3393 Peachtree Road NE, Suite 1003, Atlanta, GA 30326
(404) 816-4533

Kennesaw State University
Kennesaw, Georgia
www.kennesaw.edu Federal Code: 001577

4-year public university in large town.
Enrollment: 19,113 undergrads, 25% part-time. 2,544 full-time freshmen.
Selectivity: Admits 50 to 75% of applicants. GED not accepted.

BASIC COSTS (2008-2009)
Tuition and fees: $4,144; out-of-state residents $13,726.
Per-credit charge: $134; out-of-state residents $533.
Room only: $5,100.

FINANCIAL AID PICTURE (2008-2009)
Students with need: 48% of average financial aid package awarded as scholarships/grants, 52% awarded as loans/jobs. Need-based aid available for part-time students. Work study available nights.
Students without need: No-need awards available for academics, alumni affiliation, art, athletics, job skills, leadership, minority status, music/drama, ROTC, state/district residency.

FINANCIAL AID PROCEDURES
Forms required: FAFSA.
Dates and Deadlines: Priority date 4/1; closing date 7/1. Applicants notified on a rolling basis starting 5/15.
Transfers: No deadline. Applicants notified on a rolling basis starting 5/15.

CONTACT
Ron Day, Director of Financial Aid
1000 Chastain Road, Kennesaw, GA 30144-5591
(770) 423-6074

LaGrange College
LaGrange, Georgia
www.lagrange.edu Federal Code: 001578

4-year private liberal arts college in large town, affiliated with United Methodist Church.
Enrollment: 834 undergrads, 8% part-time. 220 full-time freshmen.
Selectivity: Admits 50 to 75% of applicants.

BASIC COSTS (2009-2010)
Tuition and fees: $21,094.
Per-credit charge: $869.
Room and board: $8,576.

FINANCIAL AID PICTURE (2007-2008)
Students with need: Out of 207 full-time freshmen who applied for aid, 171 were judged to have need. Of these, 170 received aid, and 55 had their full need met. Average financial aid package met 87% of need; average scholarship/grant was $10,329; average loan was $3,231. For part-time students, average financial aid package was $9,443.
Students without need: 39 full-time freshmen who did not demonstrate need for aid received scholarships/grants; average award was $5,754. No-need awards available for academics, art, leadership, music/drama, religious affiliation, state/district residency.
Scholarships offered: Presidential: tuition, room and board. Fellows: $12,000 per year. Deans: $10,000 per year. Founders: $8,000 per year. Lafayette: $ 6,000 per year. Quadrangle: $ 4,500 per year. All competitive.
Cumulative student debt: 76% of graduating class had student loans; average debt was $19,224.

FINANCIAL AID PROCEDURES
Forms required: FAFSA, state aid form.
Dates and Deadlines: Priority date 3/1; no closing date. Applicants notified on a rolling basis starting 3/15; must reply by 8/15 or within 2 week(s) of notification.
Transfers: No deadline. Applicants notified on a rolling basis; must reply within 2 week(s) of notification.

CONTACT
Sylvia Smith, Director of Financial Aid
601 Broad Street, LaGrange, GA 30240-2999
(706) 880-8241

Life University
Marietta, Georgia
www.life.edu Federal Code: 014170

4-year private university in very large city.
Enrollment: 597 undergrads, 30% part-time. 107 full-time freshmen.
Selectivity: Admits less than 50% of applicants.

BASIC COSTS (2008-2009)
Tuition and fees: $7,830.
Per-credit charge: $163.

FINANCIAL AID PICTURE (2008-2009)
Students with need: Out of 76 full-time freshmen who applied for aid, 62 were judged to have need. Of these, 58 received aid. For part-time students, average financial aid package was $2,050.
Students without need: 2 full-time freshmen who did not demonstrate need for aid received scholarships/grants; average award was $2,600. No-need awards available for academics.
Scholarships offered: 5 full-time freshmen received athletic scholarships; average amount $2,500.
Cumulative student debt: 36% of graduating class had student loans; average debt was $17,500.

FINANCIAL AID PROCEDURES
Forms required: FAFSA.
Dates and Deadlines: No deadline. Applicants notified on a rolling basis starting 5/1.

CONTACT
Michelle Nixon, Director of Financial Aid
1269 Barclay Circle, Marietta, GA 30060
(770) 426-2901

Macon State College
Macon, Georgia
www.maconstate.edu Federal Code: 007728

4-year public business and health science college in small city.
Enrollment: 6,303 undergrads.
Selectivity: Admits 50 to 75% of applicants.

BASIC COSTS (2008-2009)
Tuition and fees: $2,182; out-of-state residents $8,164.
Per-credit charge: $84; out-of-state residents $333.

FINANCIAL AID PICTURE (2007-2008)
Students with need: Need-based aid available for full-time and part-time students. Work study available nights, weekends, and for part-time students.
Students without need: This college awards aid only to students with need.

FINANCIAL AID PROCEDURES
Forms required: FAFSA.
Dates and Deadlines: Priority date 4/1; no closing date. Applicants notified on a rolling basis starting 4/15; must reply within 2 week(s) of notification.

CONTACT
Pat Simmons, Director of Financial Aid
100 College Station Drive, Macon, GA 31206-5145
(478) 803-1200

Medical College of Georgia
Augusta, Georgia
www.mcg.edu Federal Code: 001579

Upper-division public health science college in large city.
Enrollment: 582 undergrads, 11% part-time.

BASIC COSTS (2008-2009)
Tuition and fees: $5,568; out-of-state residents $20,136.
Per-credit charge: $202; out-of-state residents $723.
Room only: $1,952.
Additional info: Declining balance account available for meals.

FINANCIAL AID PICTURE (2008-2009)
Students with need: Need-based aid available for full-time and part-time students. Work study available nights, weekends, and for part-time students.
Students without need: No-need awards available for academics, state/district residency.
Additional info: State Hope scholarships only available to Georgia residents.

FINANCIAL AID PROCEDURES
Forms required: FAFSA, state aid form, institutional form.
Dates and Deadlines: No deadline. Applicants notified on a rolling basis; must reply within 2 week(s) of notification.
Transfers: Priority date 3/31; closing date 5/30. Applicants notified on a rolling basis; must reply within 2 week(s) of notification.

CONTACT
Beverly Boggs, Director of Financial Aid
Office of Academic Admissions, Room 170 Kelly Building, Augusta, GA 30912-7310
(706) 721-4901

Mercer University
Macon, Georgia
www.mercer.edu Federal Code: 001580

4-year private university in small city, affiliated with Baptist faith.
Enrollment: 2,228 undergrads, 3% part-time. 592 full-time freshmen.
Selectivity: Admits 50 to 75% of applicants. GED not accepted.

BASIC COSTS (2009-2010)
Tuition and fees: $29,540.
Per-credit charge: $978.
Room and board: $8,788.

FINANCIAL AID PICTURE (2008-2009)
Students with need: Out of 508 full-time freshmen who applied for aid, 409 were judged to have need. Of these, 409 received aid, and 244 had their full need met. Average financial aid package met 94% of need; average scholarship/grant was $21,158; average loan was $6,897. For part-time students, average financial aid package was $13,160.
Students without need: 177 full-time freshmen who did not demonstrate need for aid received scholarships/grants; average award was $21,339. No-need awards available for academics, art, athletics, job skills, leadership, music/drama, religious affiliation, ROTC, state/district residency.
Scholarships offered: ***Merit:*** Various scholarships: primarily based on high school GPA, SAT/ACT scores, and personal interview (for some); early applications given highest consideration. National Merit finalists and semi-finalists guaranteed full-tuition scholarships. ***Athletic:*** 51 full-time freshmen received athletic scholarships; average amount $15,167.
Cumulative student debt: 66% of graduating class had student loans; average debt was $22,835.

FINANCIAL AID PROCEDURES
Forms required: FAFSA, state aid form, institutional form.
Dates and Deadlines: Priority date 4/1; no closing date. Applicants notified on a rolling basis starting 3/15; must reply within 2 week(s) of notification.
Transfers: Priority date 6/1; no deadline.

CONTACT
Carol Williams, Associate Vice President, Student Financial Planning
1400 Coleman Avenue, Macon, GA 31207-0001
(478) 301-2670

Middle Georgia College
Cochran, Georgia
www.mgc.edu Federal Code: 001581

2-year public junior college in small town.
Enrollment: 3,111 undergrads.

BASIC COSTS (2008-2009)
Tuition and fees: $2,368; out-of-state residents $8,350.
Per-credit charge: $84; out-of-state residents $333.
Room and board: $4,800.

FINANCIAL AID PICTURE (2007-2008)
Students with need: Need-based aid available for full-time and part-time students. Work study available nights, weekends, and for part-time students.
Students without need: No-need awards available for academics, alumni affiliation, art, athletics, job skills, leadership, minority status, music/drama, state/district residency.

FINANCIAL AID PROCEDURES
Forms required: FAFSA.
Dates and Deadlines: Priority date 4/1; no closing date. Applicants notified on a rolling basis starting 5/1.

CONTACT
Jon Finkelstein, Director of Financial Aid
1100 Second Street SE, Cochran, GA 31014
(478) 934-3133

Morehouse College
Atlanta, Georgia Federal Code: 001582
www.morehouse.edu CSS Code: 5415

4-year private liberal arts college for men in very large city.
Enrollment: 2,781 undergrads, 6% part-time. 668 full-time freshmen.
Selectivity: Admits 50 to 75% of applicants.

BASIC COSTS (2009-2010)
Tuition and fees: $21,376.
Per-credit charge: $809.
Room and board: $10,946.

FINANCIAL AID PICTURE (2008-2009)
Students with need: Out of 653 full-time freshmen who applied for aid, 653 were judged to have need. Of these, 653 received aid, and 38 had their full need met. Average financial aid package met 25% of need; average scholarship/grant was $9,250; average loan was $3,500. Need-based aid available for part-time students.
Students without need: No-need awards available for academics, alumni affiliation, art, athletics, leadership, music/drama, ROTC, state/district residency.
Cumulative student debt: 94% of graduating class had student loans; average debt was $30,000.

FINANCIAL AID PROCEDURES
Forms required: FAFSA, CSS PROFILE, state aid form, institutional form.
Dates and Deadlines: Priority date 2/15; closing date 4/1. Must reply by 5/1.
Transfers: Applicants notified by 4/1; must reply by 5/1.

CONTACT
James Stotts, Director of Financial Aid
830 Westview Drive SW, Atlanta, GA 30314
(404) 215-2638

North Georgia College & State University
Dahlonega, Georgia
www.ngcsu.edu Federal Code: 001585

4-year public university and military college in small town.
Enrollment: 4,719 undergrads, 17% part-time. 843 full-time freshmen.
Selectivity: Admits 50 to 75% of applicants.

BASIC COSTS (2008-2009)
Tuition and fees: $4,070; out-of-state residents $13,362.
Per-credit charge: $130; out-of-state residents $517.
Room and board: $5,244.

FINANCIAL AID PICTURE (2007-2008)
Students with need: Average financial aid package for all full-time undergraduates was $8,200. 40% awarded as scholarships/grants, 60% awarded as loans/jobs. Need-based aid available for part-time students.
Students without need: No-need awards available for academics, alumni affiliation, art, athletics, job skills, leadership, minority status, music/drama, religious affiliation, ROTC, state/district residency.
Scholarships offered: ROTC grant: $1,500 a year; available to Georgia residents. Out-of-state tuition waiver; $5,628 per year.
Cumulative student debt: 56% of graduating class had student loans; average debt was $9,815.

FINANCIAL AID PROCEDURES
Forms required: FAFSA, state aid form.
Dates and Deadlines: Priority date 3/17; no closing date. Applicants notified on a rolling basis starting 3/1; must reply within 3 week(s) of notification.

CONTACT
Jill Rayner, Director of Financial Aid
82 College Circle, Dahlonega, GA 30597
(706) 864-1412

North Georgia Technical College
Clarkesville, Georgia
www.northgatech.edu Federal Code: 005619

2-year public community and technical college in large town.
Enrollment: 2,036 undergrads, 40% part-time. 428 full-time freshmen.
Selectivity: Open admission; but selective for some programs.

BASIC COSTS (2008-2009)
Tuition and fees: $1,566; out-of-state residents $2,862.
Per-credit charge: $36; out-of-state residents $72.
Additional info: Higher per-credit-hour charges for some programs. Cost of complete CDL program: $2784;. Tuition/fee waivers available for unemployed or children of unemployed.

FINANCIAL AID PICTURE
Students with need: Need-based aid available for full-time and part-time students. Work study available nights, weekends, and for part-time students.

CONTACT
Kim Kelley, Director of Financial Aid
1500 Highway 197 North, Clarkesville, GA 30523

Northwestern Technical College
Rock Spring, Georgia
www.northwesterntech.edu Federal Code: 005257

2-year public technical college in small town.
Enrollment: 1,576 undergrads, 48% part-time. 224 full-time freshmen.
Selectivity: Open admission; but selective for some programs.

BASIC COSTS (2008-2009)
Tuition and fees: $1,539; out-of-state residents $2,835.
Per-credit charge: $36; out-of-state residents $72.
Additional info: Truck driving and flight technology are higher cost programs.

FINANCIAL AID PICTURE
Students with need: Need-based aid available for full-time and part-time students.

FINANCIAL AID PROCEDURES
Forms required: FAFSA, institutional form.
Dates and Deadlines: No deadline.

CONTACT
Sarah Twiggs, Director of Financial Aid
265 Bicentennial Trail, Rock Spring, GA 30739
(706) 764-3575

Oglethorpe University
Atlanta, Georgia
www.oglethorpe.edu Federal Code: 001586

4-year private liberal arts college in very large city.
Enrollment: 958 undergrads, 10% part-time. 245 full-time freshmen.
Selectivity: Admits less than 50% of applicants.

BASIC COSTS (2008-2009)
Tuition and fees: $25,580.
Room and board: $9,500.

FINANCIAL AID PICTURE (2008-2009)
Students with need: Out of 206 full-time freshmen who applied for aid, 179 were judged to have need. Of these, 179 received aid, and 23 had their full need met. Average financial aid package met 75% of need; average scholarship/grant was $20,488; average loan was $4,747. For part-time students, average financial aid package was $16,076.
Students without need: 27 full-time freshmen who did not demonstrate need for aid received scholarships/grants; average award was $10,204. No-need awards available for academics, music/drama.

FINANCIAL AID PROCEDURES
Forms required: FAFSA, institutional form.
Dates and Deadlines: Priority date 2/1; no closing date. Applicants notified on a rolling basis starting 3/1; must reply by 5/1 or within 3 week(s) of notification.
Transfers: No deadline.

CONTACT
Patrick Bonones, Director of Financial Aid
4484 Peachtree Road NE, Atlanta, GA 30319-2797
(404) 364-8356

Oxford College of Emory University
Oxford, Georgia Federal Code: 001565
www.oxford.emory.edu CSS Code: 5186

2-year private branch campus and liberal arts college in large town, affiliated with United Methodist Church.
Enrollment: 753 undergrads. 422 full-time freshmen.
Selectivity: Admits less than 50% of applicants. GED not accepted.

BASIC COSTS (2009-2010)
Tuition and fees: $31,862.
Per-credit charge: $981.
Room and board: $8,924.

FINANCIAL AID PICTURE (2007-2008)
Students with need: 82% of average financial aid package awarded as scholarships/grants, 18% awarded as loans/jobs. Need-based aid available for part-time students. Work study available nights, weekends, and for part-time students.
Students without need: No-need awards available for academics, leadership, religious affiliation, state/district residency.
Scholarships offered: Woodruff Scholarships; full tuition, room and board for 4 years. Dean's Scholarship; full tuition for 4 years. Faculty Scholarships; half tuition for 4 years. 2-year scholarships; range from $8,000-$10,000 a year.
Additional info: Deadline of November 1 to apply for Oxford College Scholars Program.

FINANCIAL AID PROCEDURES
Forms required: FAFSA, CSS PROFILE.
Dates and Deadlines: Priority date 2/1; closing date 3/1. Applicants notified by 4/1; must reply by 5/1 or within 2 week(s) of notification.

CONTACT
Jennifer Taylor, Dean of Enrollment Services
100 Hamill Street, Oxford, GA 30054-1418
(770) 784-8303

Paine College

Augusta, Georgia
www.paine.edu Federal Code: 001587

4-year private liberal arts college in large city, affiliated with Christian Methodist Episcopal Church and United Methodist Church.
Enrollment: 855 undergrads, 4% part-time. 242 full-time freshmen.
Selectivity: Admits less than 50% of applicants.

BASIC COSTS (2008-2009)

Tuition and fees: $11,224.
Per-credit charge: $432.
Room and board: $5,476.

FINANCIAL AID PICTURE (2008-2009)

Students with need: Average financial aid package met 53% of need; average scholarship/grant was $5,732; average loan was $3,303. For part-time students, average financial aid package was $5,702.
Students without need: No-need awards available for academics, alumni affiliation, athletics, music/drama, religious affiliation, ROTC.
Cumulative student debt: 97% of graduating class had student loans; average debt was $33,836.

FINANCIAL AID PROCEDURES

Forms required: FAFSA, state aid form.
Dates and Deadlines: Priority date 3/1; no closing date. Applicants notified on a rolling basis starting 5/1; must reply within 2 week(s) of notification.

CONTACT

Gerri Bogan, Director of Financial Aid
1235 15th Street, Augusta, GA 30901-3182
(706) 821-8262

Piedmont College

Demorest, Georgia
www.piedmont.edu Federal Code: 001588

4-year private liberal arts and teachers college in rural community, affiliated with United Church of Christ.
Enrollment: 1,135 undergrads, 13% part-time. 206 full-time freshmen.
Selectivity: Admits 50 to 75% of applicants.

BASIC COSTS (2009-2010)

Tuition and fees: $18,000.
Per-credit charge: $750.
Room and board: $6,000.
Additional info: Tuition/fee waivers available for adults.

FINANCIAL AID PICTURE (2008-2009)

Students with need: Out of 161 full-time freshmen who applied for aid, 120 were judged to have need. Of these, 109 received aid, and 42 had their full need met. Average financial aid package met 61% of need; average scholarship/grant was $1,155; average loan was $3,415. For part-time students, average financial aid package was $5,964.
Students without need: 64 full-time freshmen who did not demonstrate need for aid received scholarships/grants; average award was $8,165. No-need awards available for academics, art, leadership, music/drama, religious affiliation, state/district residency.
Scholarships offered: Highest academic scholarships awarded to high school seniors superior in academics, leadership, and extracurricular activities.
Cumulative student debt: 72% of graduating class had student loans; average debt was $16,940.
Additional info: College meets 100% of unmet direct financial need for early applicants through grants, scholarships, and loan programs.

FINANCIAL AID PROCEDURES

Forms required: FAFSA, state aid form, institutional form.
Dates and Deadlines: Priority date 5/1; no closing date. Applicants notified on a rolling basis; must reply within 2 week(s) of notification.
Transfers: Priority date 4/1. Must reply within 2 week(s) of notification.

CONTACT

Kimberly Lovell, Director of Financial Aid
165 Central Avenue, Demorest, GA 30535-0010
(706) 776-0114 ext. 1191

Reinhardt College

Waleska, Georgia
www.reinhardt.edu Federal Code: 001589

4-year private business and teachers college in rural community, affiliated with United Methodist Church.
Enrollment: 994 undergrads, 8% part-time. 263 full-time freshmen.
Selectivity: Admits 50 to 75% of applicants.

BASIC COSTS (2009-2010)

Tuition and fees: $16,670.
Per-credit charge: $550.
Room and board: $6,272.

FINANCIAL AID PICTURE (2008-2009)

Students with need: Need-based aid available for full-time and part-time students.
Students without need: No-need awards available for academics, art, athletics.

FINANCIAL AID PROCEDURES

Forms required: state aid form.
Dates and Deadlines: Priority date 5/1; no closing date. Applicants notified on a rolling basis starting 3/15; must reply within 2 week(s) of notification.

CONTACT

Robert Gregory, Director of Financial Aid
7300 Reinhardt College Circle, Waleska, GA 30183
(770) 720-5667

Savannah College of Art and Design

Savannah, Georgia
www.scad.edu Federal Code: 015022

4-year private visual arts and performing arts college in small city.
Enrollment: 7,745 undergrads, 10% part-time. 1,396 full-time freshmen.
Selectivity: Admits 50 to 75% of applicants.

BASIC COSTS (2009-2010)

Tuition and fees: $27,765.
Per-credit charge: $617.
Room and board: $11,710.
Additional info: A one-time matriculation fee of $500 is required of all students.

FINANCIAL AID PICTURE (2008-2009)

Students with need: Out of 1,004 full-time freshmen who applied for aid, 751 were judged to have need. Of these, 747 received aid, and 426 had their full need met. Average financial aid package met 10% of need; average scholarship/grant was $4,198; average loan was $3,379. For part-time students, average financial aid package was $9,643.
Students without need: 301 full-time freshmen who did not demonstrate need for aid received scholarships/grants; average award was $7,234. No-need awards available for academics, art, athletics, music/drama.

Scholarships offered: 56 full-time freshmen received athletic scholarships; average amount $4,877.
Additional info: Degree-seeking students may be awarded maximum of one scholarship from college, but may receive additional scholarships from other sources, as well as additional forms of financial aid. Scholarships based on academic achievement are awarded through admission office.

FINANCIAL AID PROCEDURES

Forms required: FAFSA, state aid form, institutional form.
Dates and Deadlines: Priority date 2/15; no closing date. Applicants notified on a rolling basis starting 6/1.
Transfers: Priority date 4/1; no deadline. Applicants notified on a rolling basis. Transfer students eligible to apply for academic and portfolio scholarships.

CONTACT

Director of Financial Aid
PO Box 2072, Savannah, GA 31402-2072
(912) 525-6109

Savannah River College

Augusta, Georgia
www.savannahrivercollege.edu Federal Code: 013115

2-year for-profit junior and technical college in small city.
Enrollment: 268 undergrads.
Selectivity: Admits over 75% of applicants.

BASIC COSTS (2008-2009)

Tuition and fees: $10,495.

FINANCIAL AID PICTURE (2008-2009)

Students with need: Need-based aid available for full-time and part-time students.
Students without need: This college awards aid only to students with need.

FINANCIAL AID PROCEDURES

Forms required: FAFSA, institutional form.
Dates and Deadlines: No deadline.

CONTACT

Amy Barnett, Financial Aid Officer
2528 Center West Parkway, Building A, Augusta, GA 30909

Savannah Technical College

Savannah, Georgia
www.savannahtech.edu Federal Code: 005618

2-year public technical college in small city.
Enrollment: 4,068 undergrads, 54% part-time. 538 full-time freshmen.
Selectivity: Open admission; but selective for some programs.

BASIC COSTS (2008-2009)

Tuition and fees: $1,539; out-of-state residents $2,835.
Per-credit charge: $36; out-of-state residents $72.

FINANCIAL AID PICTURE (2007-2008)

Students with need: Need-based aid available for part-time students.
Students without need: No-need awards available for academics, leadership, minority status, state/district residency.

FINANCIAL AID PROCEDURES

Forms required: FAFSA.
Dates and Deadlines: No deadline. Applicants notified on a rolling basis.

CONTACT

Timothy Cranford, Financial Aid Director
5717 White Bluff Road, Savannah, GA 31405-5521
(912) 443-5705

Shorter College

Rome, Georgia
www.shorter.edu Federal Code: 001591

4-year private liberal arts college in large town, affiliated with Southern Baptist Convention.
Enrollment: 1,116 undergrads, 2% part-time. 330 full-time freshmen.
Selectivity: Admits 50 to 75% of applicants.

BASIC COSTS (2008-2009)

Tuition and fees: $15,770.
Per-credit charge: $420.
Room and board: $7,400.

FINANCIAL AID PICTURE (2008-2009)

Students with need: Out of 283 full-time freshmen who applied for aid, 235 were judged to have need. Of these, 235 received aid, and 72 had their full need met. Average financial aid package met 75% of need; average scholarship/grant was $11,934; average loan was $3,013. For part-time students, average financial aid package was $4,838.
Students without need: 47 full-time freshmen who did not demonstrate need for aid received scholarships/grants; average award was $5,585. No-need awards available for academics, art, athletics, music/drama, religious affiliation.
Scholarships offered: 53 full-time freshmen received athletic scholarships; average amount $7,242.
Additional info: Cost is reduced for all in-state students by state tuition equalization grant program. College matches for out-of-state full-time students.

FINANCIAL AID PROCEDURES

Forms required: FAFSA, state aid form, institutional form.
Dates and Deadlines: Priority date 4/1; no closing date. Applicants notified on a rolling basis starting 4/1; must reply within 2 week(s) of notification.
Transfers: Priority date 4/15; no deadline. Applicants notified on a rolling basis starting 3/31; must reply within 2 week(s) of notification.

CONTACT

Tara Jones, Director of Financial Aid
315 Shorter Avenue, Rome, GA 30165
(706) 233-7227

South Georgia College

Douglas, Georgia
www.sgc.edu Federal Code: 001592

2-year public community and junior college in large town.
Enrollment: 1,860 undergrads.
Selectivity: Open admission

BASIC COSTS (2008-2009)

Tuition and fees: $2,272; out-of-state residents $7,774.
Per-credit charge: $77; out-of-state residents $306.
Room and board: $7,350.

FINANCIAL AID PICTURE

Students with need: Need-based aid available for full-time and part-time students.
Students without need: No-need awards available for academics.

FINANCIAL AID PROCEDURES

Forms required: FAFSA, institutional form.
Dates and Deadlines: Priority date 4/1; no closing date. Applicants notified on a rolling basis starting 7/6; must reply within 2 week(s) of notification.

CONTACT

Wes Brown, Director of Financial Aid
100 West College Park Drive, Douglas, GA 31533-5098
(912) 389-4285

Southeastern Technical College

Vidalia, Georgia
www.southeasterntech.edu

2-year public technical college in large town.
Enrollment: 1,003 undergrads.
Selectivity: Open admission.

BASIC COSTS (2008-2009)

Tuition and fees: $1,539; out-of-state residents $2,835.
Per-credit charge: $36; out-of-state residents $62.

FINANCIAL AID PICTURE (2007-2008)

Students with need: Need-based aid available for full-time and part-time students. Work study available nights.
Students without need: No-need awards available for state/district residency.

FINANCIAL AID PROCEDURES

Forms required: FAFSA, state aid form, institutional form.
Dates and Deadlines: No deadline. Applicants notified on a rolling basis starting 4/6.

CONTACT

Rebecca Ethredge, Financial Aid Director
3001 East First Street, Vidalia, GA 30474

Southern Polytechnic State University

Marietta, Georgia
www.spsu.edu Federal Code: 001570

4-year public university and engineering college in small city.
Enrollment: 4,126 undergrads, 28% part-time. 502 full-time freshmen.
Selectivity: Admits 50 to 75% of applicants. GED not accepted.

BASIC COSTS (2008-2009)

Tuition and fees: $4,232; out-of-state residents $14,728.
Per-credit charge: $146; out-of-state residents $584.
Room and board: $5,870.

FINANCIAL AID PICTURE (2007-2008)

Students with need: Out of 408 full-time freshmen who applied for aid, 408 were judged to have need. Of these, 398 received aid, and 159 had their full need met. Average financial aid package met 76% of need; average scholarship/grant was $2,656; average loan was $3,082. For part-time students, average financial aid package was $2,511.
Students without need: 3 full-time freshmen who did not demonstrate need for aid received scholarships/grants; average award was $7,117. No-need awards available for academics, athletics.
Scholarships offered: 9 full-time freshmen received athletic scholarships; average amount $4,813.
Cumulative student debt: 42% of graduating class had student loans; average debt was $13,244.

FINANCIAL AID PROCEDURES

Forms required: FAFSA.
Dates and Deadlines: Priority date 4/1; no closing date. Applicants notified on a rolling basis starting 6/1.
Transfers: No deadline. Applicants notified on a rolling basis starting 5/1.

CONTACT

Gary Bush, Director of Financial Aid
1100 South Marietta Parkway, Marietta, GA 30060-2896
(678) 915-7290

Southwest Georgia Technical College

Thomasville, Georgia
www.southwestgatech.edu Federal Code: 005615

2-year public technical college in large town.
Enrollment: 1,208 undergrads, 58% part-time. 122 full-time freshmen.
Selectivity: Open admission; but selective for some programs.

BASIC COSTS (2008-2009)

Tuition and fees: $1,539; out-of-state residents $2,835.
Per-credit charge: $36; out-of-state residents $72.
Additional info: Truck driving and flight technology are higher cost programs.

FINANCIAL AID PICTURE (2007-2008)

Students with need: Need-based aid available for full-time and part-time students. Work study available nights.
Students without need: No-need awards available for state/district residency.
Scholarships offered: Hope Scholarship; full tuition; available to GA residents with 3.0 minimum GPA.

FINANCIAL AID PROCEDURES

Forms required: FAFSA, institutional form.
Dates and Deadlines: No deadline. Applicants notified on a rolling basis starting 7/1.

CONTACT

Michael Rayburn, Director of Financial Aid
15689 US Highway 19N, Thomasville, GA 31792
(229) 225-5221

Spelman College

Atlanta, Georgia
www.spelman.edu Federal Code: 001594

4-year private liberal arts college for women in very large city.
Enrollment: 2,270 undergrads, 5% part-time. 540 full-time freshmen.
Selectivity: Admits less than 50% of applicants.

BASIC COSTS (2008-2009)

Tuition and fees: $20,281.
Room and board: $9,734.

FINANCIAL AID PICTURE (2007-2008)

Students with need: 56% of average financial aid package awarded as scholarships/grants, 44% awarded as loans/jobs. Need-based aid available for part-time students. Work study available nights, weekends, and for part-time students.
Students without need: No-need awards available for academics, alumni affiliation, leadership, music/drama, state/district residency.

FINANCIAL AID PROCEDURES

Forms required: FAFSA, institutional form.
Dates and Deadlines: Priority date 3/1; no closing date. Applicants notified on a rolling basis starting 2/15; must reply within 2 week(s) of notification.
Transfers: Closing date 10/1. No special aid for transfer students for the first year.

CONTACT

Lenora Jackson, Director of Student Financial Services
350 Spelman Lane SW, Campus Box 277, Atlanta, GA 30314
(404) 270-5212

Thomas University

Thomasville, Georgia
www.thomasu.edu Federal Code: 001555

4-year private university and liberal arts college in large town.
Enrollment: 748 undergrads, 41% part-time. 98 full-time freshmen.
Selectivity: Open admission; but selective for some programs.

BASIC COSTS (2008-2009)

Tuition and fees: $11,664.
Per-credit charge: $436.
Room only: $2,766.

FINANCIAL AID PICTURE (2007-2008)

Students with need: Need-based aid available for full-time and part-time students.
Students without need: No-need awards available for academics, athletics, leadership, state/district residency.

FINANCIAL AID PROCEDURES

Forms required: FAFSA, state aid form.
Dates and Deadlines: Priority date 5/1; no closing date. Applicants notified on a rolling basis.
Transfers: Student must submit official academic transcripts from all colleges attended. Financial aid received during current academic year from previous school will be verified through the National Student Loan Data System (NSLDS).

CONTACT

Angela Keys, Director of Financial Aid
1501 Millpond Road, Thomasville, GA 31792-7499
(229) 227-6931

Toccoa Falls College

Toccoa Falls, Georgia
www.tfc.edu Federal Code: 001596

4-year private Bible and liberal arts college in large town, affiliated with Christian and Missionary Alliance.
Enrollment: 877 undergrads, 5% part-time. 162 full-time freshmen.
Selectivity: Admits less than 50% of applicants.

BASIC COSTS (2009-2010)

Tuition and fees: $15,575.
Per-credit charge: $644.
Room and board: $5,650.

FINANCIAL AID PICTURE (2007-2008)

Students with need: Need-based aid available for full-time and part-time students.
Students without need: No-need awards available for academics, alumni affiliation, leadership, music/drama, religious affiliation, state/district residency.
Scholarships offered: Trustee: $7,500; ACT score of 28 or SAT score of 1250 and high school GPA of 3.8; renewable with GPA of 3.5. President: $6,000; ACT score of 26 or SAT score 1200 and high school GPA of 3.5; renewable with GPA of 3.25. Dean: $4,500; ACT score of 25 or SAT score of 1150 and high school GPA of 3.2; renewable with GPA of 3.0. Director: $4,000; ACT score of 21 or SAT score of 1000 and high school GPA of 3.0; renewable with GPA of 2.75. Faculty: $5,000; have earned at least 24 college credits and college GPA of 3.5; renewable with GPA of 3.5. Home School: $5,500; ACT score of 26 or SAT score of 1200 and home school GPA of 3.0; renewable with a GPA of 3.0. Leadership: $6,000; ACT score of 22 or SAT score of 1050 and high school GPA of 3.00 and two letters of recommendation, personal essay, application by April 1; 10 available, renewable by maintaining leadership standards and a GPA of 2.75. Music: $5,000; ACT score of 22 or SAT score of 1050 and high school GPA of 3.0 and audition, May 1 deadline; 8 available, renewable by maintaining music standards and a GPA of 2.75.

FINANCIAL AID PROCEDURES

Forms required: FAFSA, institutional form.
Dates and Deadlines: Priority date 5/1; closing date 8/1. Applicants notified on a rolling basis starting 3/1; must reply within 2 week(s) of notification.
Transfers: Priority date 12/15; no deadline. Applicants notified on a rolling basis starting 10/1; must reply within 2 week(s) of notification.

CONTACT

Holly Howard, Director of Financial Aid
PO Box 800899, Toccoa Falls, GA 30598-0368
(706) 886-6831 ext. 5435

Truett-McConnell College

Cleveland, Georgia
www.truett.edu Federal Code: 001597

4-year private liberal arts college in small town, affiliated with Southern Baptist Convention.
Enrollment: 389 undergrads.

BASIC COSTS (2009-2010)

Tuition and fees: $14,000.
Per-credit charge: $450.
Room and board: $5,700.

FINANCIAL AID PICTURE

Students with need: Need-based aid available for full-time and part-time students.
Students without need: No-need awards available for academics, athletics, music/drama, religious affiliation, state/district residency.
Additional info: Installment plan available.

FINANCIAL AID PROCEDURES

Forms required: FAFSA, state aid form, institutional form.
Dates and Deadlines: Priority date 6/1; no closing date. Applicants notified on a rolling basis starting 4/1; must reply within 2 week(s) of notification.

CONTACT

Becky Moore, Director of Financial Aid
100 Alumni Drive, Cleveland, GA 30528
(800) 226-8621

University of Georgia

Athens, Georgia
www.uga.edu Federal Code: 001598

4-year public university in small city.
Enrollment: 25,150 undergrads, 6% part-time. 4,775 full-time freshmen.
Selectivity: Admits 50 to 75% of applicants.

BASIC COSTS (2008-2009)

Tuition and fees: $6,031; out-of-state residents $22,343.
Per-credit charge: $203; out-of-state residents $882.
Room and board: $7,528.

FINANCIAL AID PICTURE (2008-2009)

Students with need: Out of 3,068 full-time freshmen who applied for aid, 1,439 were judged to have need. Of these, 1,433 received aid, and 638 had their full need met. Average financial aid package met 81% of need; average scholarship/grant was $8,153; average loan was $2,900. For part-time students, average financial aid package was $5,827.

Students without need: 360 full-time freshmen who did not demonstrate need for aid received scholarships/grants; average award was $1,791. No-need awards available for academics, athletics, ROTC, state/district residency.

Scholarships offered: 98 full-time freshmen received athletic scholarships; average amount $10,998.

Cumulative student debt: 39% of graduating class had student loans; average debt was $14,343.

FINANCIAL AID PROCEDURES

Forms required: FAFSA.

Dates and Deadlines: Priority date 3/1; no closing date. Applicants notified on a rolling basis starting 5/15; must reply within 2 week(s) of notification.

CONTACT

Susan Little, Director, Student Financial Aid
Office of Undergraduate Admissions, Athens, GA 30602-1633
(706) 542-6147

University of West Georgia

Carrollton, Georgia
www.westga.edu Federal Code: 001601

4-year public university in large town.

Enrollment: 9,230 undergrads, 15% part-time. 2,023 full-time freshmen.

Selectivity: Admits 50 to 75% of applicants. GED not accepted.

BASIC COSTS (2008-2009)

Tuition and fees: $4,316; out-of-state residents $13,898.

Per-credit charge: $134; out-of-state residents $533.

Room and board: $5,714.

Additional info: Tuition/fee waivers available for adults, minority students.

FINANCIAL AID PICTURE (2008-2009)

Students with need: Out of 1,689 full-time freshmen who applied for aid, 1,169 were judged to have need. Of these, 1,145 received aid, and 233 had their full need met. Average financial aid package met 66% of need; average scholarship/grant was $5,540; average loan was $3,185. For part-time students, average financial aid package was $3,652.

Students without need: 35 full-time freshmen who did not demonstrate need for aid received scholarships/grants; average award was $2,091. No-need awards available for academics, alumni affiliation, art, athletics, leadership, music/drama.

Scholarships offered: 31 full-time freshmen received athletic scholarships; average amount $5,414.

FINANCIAL AID PROCEDURES

Forms required: FAFSA.

Dates and Deadlines: Priority date 4/1; closing date 7/1. Applicants notified on a rolling basis starting 5/15; must reply within 4 week(s) of notification.

CONTACT

Kimberly Jordan, Director of Financial Aid
1601 Maple Street, Carrollton, GA 30118
(678) 839-6421

Valdosta State University

Valdosta, Georgia
www.valdosta.edu Federal Code: 001599

4-year public university in small city.

Enrollment: 9,654 undergrads, 13% part-time. 1,987 full-time freshmen.

Selectivity: Admits 50 to 75% of applicants. GED not accepted.

BASIC COSTS (2008-2009)

Tuition and fees: $4,456; out-of-state residents $14,038.

Per-credit charge: $134; out-of-state residents $533.

Room and board: $6,290.

Additional info: Tuition at time of enrollment locked for 4 years.

FINANCIAL AID PICTURE (2007-2008)

Students with need: Out of 1,622 full-time freshmen who applied for aid, 1,170 were judged to have need. Of these, 1,160 received aid, and 660 had their full need met. Average financial aid package met 89% of need; average scholarship/grant was $5,309; average loan was $4,559. For part-time students, average financial aid package was $12,575.

Students without need: 18 full-time freshmen who did not demonstrate need for aid received scholarships/grants; average award was $1,778. No-need awards available for academics, alumni affiliation, art, athletics, minority status, music/drama, ROTC, state/district residency.

Scholarships offered: 3 full-time freshmen received athletic scholarships; average amount $3,838.

Cumulative student debt: 62% of graduating class had student loans; average debt was $16,736.

FINANCIAL AID PROCEDURES

Forms required: FAFSA.

Dates and Deadlines: Priority date 5/1; no closing date. Applicants notified on a rolling basis starting 6/1.

CONTACT

Doug Tanner, Director of Financial Aid
1500 North Patterson Street, Valdosta, GA 31698-0170
(229) 333-5935

Waycross College

Waycross, Georgia
www.waycross.edu Federal Code: 013537

2-year public community and liberal arts college in large town.

Enrollment: 970 undergrads.

BASIC COSTS (2008-2009)

Tuition and fees: $1,992; out-of-state residents $7,494.

Per-credit charge: $77; out-of-state residents $306.

Additional info: Tuition/fee waivers available for adults.

FINANCIAL AID PICTURE (2007-2008)

Students with need: Need-based aid available for full-time and part-time students. Work study available nights.

Students without need: No-need awards available for academics, alumni affiliation, leadership.

FINANCIAL AID PROCEDURES

Forms required: FAFSA, institutional form.

Dates and Deadlines: Priority date 6/1; no closing date. Applicants notified on a rolling basis; must reply within 2 week(s) of notification.

CONTACT

Debbie Howard, Assistant Director of Financial Aid
2001 South Georgia Parkway, Waycross, GA 31503
(912) 285-6035

Wesleyan College
Macon, Georgia
www.wesleyancollege.edu Federal Code: 001600

4-year private liberal arts college for women in small city, affiliated with United Methodist Church.
Enrollment: 557 undergrads, 32% part-time. 83 full-time freshmen.
Selectivity: Admits 50 to 75% of applicants.

BASIC COSTS (2009-2010)
Tuition and fees: $17,500.
Per-credit charge: $415.
Room and board: $8,000.
Additional info: Tuition/fee waivers available for adults.

FINANCIAL AID PICTURE (2008-2009)
Students with need: Out of 76 full-time freshmen who applied for aid, 62 were judged to have need. Of these, 62 received aid, and 23 had their full need met. Average financial aid package met 85% of need; average scholarship/grant was $13,018; average loan was $3,807. For part-time students, average financial aid package was $5,585.
Students without need: 26 full-time freshmen who did not demonstrate need for aid received scholarships/grants; average award was $20,404. No-need awards available for academics, alumni affiliation, art, job skills, leadership, minority status, music/drama, religious affiliation, state/district residency.
Scholarships offered: Academic Scholarships; $1,000 to $16,000; based on minimum 1100 SAT (exclusive of Writing) or 25 ACT and 3.75 GPA, or 1200 SAT (exclusive of Writing) or 27 ACT and 3.5 GPA. Leadership Awards and scholarships for music, art and theater; range from $1,000-$3,000.
Cumulative student debt: 57% of graduating class had student loans; average debt was $14,186.

FINANCIAL AID PROCEDURES
Forms required: FAFSA, state aid form, institutional form.
Dates and Deadlines: Priority date 2/15; closing date 6/3. Applicants notified on a rolling basis starting 3/1; must reply by 5/1 or within 3 week(s) of notification.
Transfers: Fellowships available based on number of hours and GPA transferred in, with minimum 30 semester or 45 quarter hours and 3.0 GPA required.

CONTACT
Richard Maier, Vice President for Enrollment Services
4760 Forsyth Road, Macon, GA 31210-4462
(478) 757-3902

West Central Technical College
Waco, Georgia
www.westcentraltech.edu Federal Code: 010487

2-year public technical college in rural community.
Enrollment: 3,748 undergrads, 68% part-time. 427 full-time freshmen.
Selectivity: Open admission; but selective for some programs.

BASIC COSTS (2008-2009)
Tuition and fees: $1,539; out-of-state residents $2,835.
Per-credit charge: $36; out-of-state residents $72.
Additional info: Truck driving and flight technology are higher cost programs.Tuition reciprocity with bordering states. Commercial truck driving program is $2,784. EMT programs are $45 per-credit-hour. Additional fees may apply.

FINANCIAL AID PICTURE
Students with need: Need-based aid available for full-time and part-time students.

CONTACT
David Robinson, Director of Financial Aid
176 Murphy Campus Boulevard, Waco, GA 30182

West Georgia Technical College
LaGrange, Georgia
www.westgatech.edu Federal Code: 005614

2-year public technical college in small city.
Enrollment: 1,682 undergrads, 57% part-time. 231 full-time freshmen.
Selectivity: Open admission; but selective for some programs.

BASIC COSTS (2008-2009)
Tuition and fees: $1,539; out-of-state residents $2,835.
Per-credit charge: $36; out-of-state residents $72.
Additional info: Tuition reciprocity with bordering states. Commercial truck driving program is $2,784. Basic welding and EMT programs are $45 per-credit-hour.

FINANCIAL AID PICTURE
Students with need: Need-based aid available for full-time and part-time students. Work study available nights.
Students without need: No-need awards available for state/district residency.

FINANCIAL AID PROCEDURES
Forms required: FAFSA, state aid form, institutional form.
Dates and Deadlines: No deadline. Applicants notified on a rolling basis; must reply within 1 week(s) of notification.
Transfers: Aid must be in order or cash paid at registration for classes.

CONTACT
Dorothy Cantor, Financial Aid Coordinator
One College Circle, LaGrange, GA 30240
(706) 845-4323

Young Harris College
Young Harris, Georgia
www.yhc.edu Federal Code: 001604

2-year private liberal arts college in rural community, affiliated with United Methodist Church.
Enrollment: 649 undergrads, 4% part-time. 339 full-time freshmen.
Selectivity: Admits 50 to 75% of applicants.

BASIC COSTS (2008-2009)
Tuition and fees: $16,630.
Per-credit charge: $500.
Room and board: $5,878.

FINANCIAL AID PICTURE (2007-2008)
Students with need: Out of 252 full-time freshmen who applied for aid, 187 were judged to have need. Of these, 187 received aid, and 67 had their full need met. Average financial aid package met 78% of need; average scholarship/grant was $9,841; average loan was $2,783. For part-time students, average financial aid package was $13,302.
Students without need: 150 full-time freshmen who did not demonstrate need for aid received scholarships/grants; average award was $10,023. No-need awards available for academics, art, athletics, job skills, music/drama, state/district residency.
Scholarships offered: Academic Scholarships; $3,500-$8,500; based on index including GPA and SAT/ACT. Additional awards to a percentage of recipients range from additional $1,000 to full tuition, room and board.

FINANCIAL AID PROCEDURES
Forms required: FAFSA, state aid form, institutional form.

Dates and Deadlines: Priority date 4/1; no closing date. Applicants notified on a rolling basis starting 3/1; must reply within 2 week(s) of notification.

CONTACT

Clinton Hobbs, Vice President for Enrollment Management
PO Box 116, Young Harris, GA 30582-0116
(706) 379-3111

Hawaii

Brigham Young University-Hawaii

Laie, Hawaii
www.byuh.edu Federal Code: 001606

4-year private university and liberal arts college in small town, affiliated with Church of Jesus Christ of Latter-day Saints.
Enrollment: 2,309 undergrads, 6% part-time. 294 full-time freshmen.
Selectivity: Admits less than 50% of applicants. GED not accepted.

BASIC COSTS (2008-2009)

Tuition and fees: $3,600.
Room and board: $5,568.
Additional info: 100% higher tuition and per-credit-hour charges for students who are not members of The Church of Jesus Christ of Latter-day Saints.

FINANCIAL AID PICTURE (2007-2008)

Students with need: Need-based aid available for full-time and part-time students.
Students without need: No-need awards available for academics, art, athletics, leadership, music/drama, state/district residency.

FINANCIAL AID PROCEDURES

Forms required: FAFSA.
Dates and Deadlines: Closing date 3/15. Applicants notified by 5/1; must reply by 8/31.
Transfers: Closing date 3/15.

CONTACT

Pepper Muae, Financial Aid and Student Accounts Manager
55-220 Kulanui Street, #1973, Laie, HI 96762-1294
(808) 675-3539

Chaminade University of Honolulu

Honolulu, Hawaii
www.chaminade.edu Federal Code: 001605

4-year private university in large city, affiliated with Roman Catholic Church.
Enrollment: 1,046 undergrads.
Selectivity: Admits over 75% of applicants.

BASIC COSTS (2009-2010)

Tuition and fees: $17,040.
Per-credit charge: $563.
Room and board: $10,420.

FINANCIAL AID PICTURE (2008-2009)

Students with need: Need-based aid available for full-time and part-time students.
Students without need: No-need awards available for academics, art, athletics, leadership, religious affiliation, ROTC, state/district residency.
Additional info: For students whose eligibility for federal and institutional aid does not meet entire costs, alternative student loans may be secured for eligible applicants.

FINANCIAL AID PROCEDURES

Forms required: FAFSA.
Dates and Deadlines: Priority date 2/15; no closing date. Applicants notified on a rolling basis starting 2/15; must reply within 4 week(s) of notification.

CONTACT

Eric Nemoto, Associate Dean of Enrollment Management
3140 Waialae Avenue, Honolulu, HI 96816
(808) 735-4780

Hawaii Pacific University

Honolulu, Hawaii
www.hpu.edu Federal Code: 007279

4-year private university and liberal arts college in large city.
Enrollment: 6,505 undergrads, 46% part-time. 569 full-time freshmen.
Selectivity: Admits over 75% of applicants.

BASIC COSTS (2009-2010)

Tuition and fees: $14,960.
Per-credit charge: $619.
Room and board: $11,094.

FINANCIAL AID PICTURE (2008-2009)

Students with need: Out of 501 full-time freshmen who applied for aid, 283 were judged to have need. Of these, 275 received aid, and 1 had their full need met. Average financial aid package met 83% of need; average scholarship/grant was $4,428; average loan was $6,003. For part-time students, average financial aid package was $10,981.
Students without need: 77 full-time freshmen who did not demonstrate need for aid received scholarships/grants; average award was $2,070. No-need awards available for academics, alumni affiliation, athletics, job skills, leadership, music/drama, religious affiliation, ROTC.
Scholarships offered: Makana Scholarship: $2,600; 3.5 GPA or higher. Phi Theta Kappa Scholarship: $6,500; for member of Phi Theta Kappa.

FINANCIAL AID PROCEDURES

Forms required: FAFSA.
Dates and Deadlines: Priority date 3/1; no closing date. Applicants notified on a rolling basis starting 4/1; must reply within 3 week(s) of notification.

CONTACT

Adam Hatch, Director of Financial Aid
1164 Bishop Street, Suite 200, Honolulu, HI 96813
(808) 544-0253

Heald College: Honolulu

Honolulu, Hawaii
www.heald.edu Federal Code: E00886

2-year for-profit technical and career college in very large city.
Enrollment: 1,139 undergrads.
Selectivity: Open admission.

BASIC COSTS (2008-2009)

Tuition and fees: $11,550.
Additional info: Fees vary by program.

FINANCIAL AID PICTURE

Students with need: Need-based aid available for full-time and part-time students. Work study available nights, weekends, and for part-time students.
Students without need: This college awards aid only to students with need.

FINANCIAL AID PROCEDURES

Forms required: FAFSA.
Dates and Deadlines: No deadline.

CONTACT
Candice Wong, Director of Financial Aid
1500 Kapiolani Boulevard, Honolulu, HI 96814-3715
(808) 955-1500 ext. 504

University of Hawaii at Hilo
Hilo, Hawaii
www.uhh.hawaii.edu Federal Code: 001611

4-year public university in large town.
Enrollment: 3,208 undergrads, 16% part-time. 533 full-time freshmen.

BASIC COSTS (2008-2009)
Tuition and fees: $4,360; out-of-state residents $12,880.
Per-credit charge: $169; out-of-state residents $524.
Room and board: $7,014.

FINANCIAL AID PICTURE (2008-2009)
Students with need: Need-based aid available for full-time and part-time students. Work study available nights, weekends, and for part-time students.
Additional info: Hawaii student incentive grants and tuition waivers (merit and need-based) available to Hawaii residents at participating institutions.

FINANCIAL AID PROCEDURES
Forms required: FAFSA.
Dates and Deadlines: Priority date 3/1; no closing date. Applicants notified on a rolling basis starting 4/15; must reply within 2 week(s) of notification.

CONTACT
Jeff Schofield, Financial Aid Director
200 West Kawili Street, Hilo, HI 96720-4091
(808) 974-7324

University of Hawaii at Manoa
Honolulu, Hawaii
www.manoa.hawaii.edu Federal Code: 001610

4-year public university in very large city.
Enrollment: 13,438 undergrads, 18% part-time. 1,626 full-time freshmen.
Selectivity: Admits 50 to 75% of applicants.

BASIC COSTS (2008-2009)
Tuition and fees: $6,259; out-of-state residents $16,915.
Per-credit charge: $248; out-of-state residents $692.
Room and board: $7,564.
Additional info: Tuition/fee waivers available for minority students.

FINANCIAL AID PICTURE (2007-2008)
Students with need: Out of 1,220 full-time freshmen who applied for aid, 589 were judged to have need. Of these, 514 received aid, and 119 had their full need met. Average financial aid package met 59% of need; average scholarship/grant was $5,119; average loan was $3,088. For part-time students, average financial aid package was $5,958.
Students without need: 334 full-time freshmen who did not demonstrate need for aid received scholarships/grants; average award was $5,632. No-need awards available for academics, alumni affiliation, art, athletics, job skills, leadership, minority status, music/drama, religious affiliation, ROTC, state/district residency.
Scholarships offered: 36 full-time freshmen received athletic scholarships; average amount $7,136.
Cumulative student debt: 35% of graduating class had student loans; average debt was $14,818.
Additional info: Hawaii student incentive grants and tuition waivers (merit and need-based) available to Hawaii residents at participating institutions.

FINANCIAL AID PROCEDURES
Forms required: FAFSA.
Dates and Deadlines: Priority date 3/1; no closing date. Applicants notified on a rolling basis starting 3/15; must reply within 4 week(s) of notification.
Transfers: No deadline. Applicants notified on a rolling basis starting 3/15; must reply within 4 week(s) of notification.

CONTACT
Linda Clemons, Director of Financial Aid
2600 Campus Road, QLC Rm 001, Honolulu, HI 96822
(808) 956-7251

University of Hawaii: Hawaii Community College
Hilo, Hawaii
www.hawcc.hawaii.edu Federal Code: 005258

2-year public community college in small city.
Enrollment: 2,378 undergrads.
Selectivity: Open admission.

BASIC COSTS (2008-2009)
Tuition and fees: $2,264; out-of-state residents $8,054.
Per-credit charge: $71; out-of-state residents $264.

FINANCIAL AID PICTURE
Students with need: Need-based aid available for full-time and part-time students.
Students without need: This college awards aid only to students with need.
Additional info: Hawaii student incentive grants and tuition waivers (merit and need-based) available to Hawaii residents.

FINANCIAL AID PROCEDURES
Forms required: FAFSA.
Dates and Deadlines: Priority date 4/1; no closing date. Applicants notified on a rolling basis starting 5/1; must reply within 2 week(s) of notification.
Transfers: Residents of Guam, Federated States of Micronesia, Palau, Marianas Islands and certain other island nations considered residents for tuition purpose.

CONTACT
Sheryl Lundberg-Spregue, Financial Aid Officer
200 West Kawili Street, Hilo, HI 96720-4091
(808) 974-7663

University of Hawaii: Honolulu Community College
Honolulu, Hawaii
honolulu.hawaii.edu Federal Code: 001612

2-year public community and technical college in very large city.
Enrollment: 3,300 undergrads.
Selectivity: Open admission; but selective for out-of-state students.

BASIC COSTS (2008-2009)
Tuition and fees: $2,160; out-of-state residents $7,950.
Per-credit charge: $71; out-of-state residents $264.

FINANCIAL AID PICTURE (2007-2008)
Students with need: Need-based aid available for full-time and part-time students.
Students without need: No-need awards available for academics, state/district residency.
Additional info: Hawaii student incentive grants and tuition waivers (merit and need-based) available to Hawaii residents at participating institutions.

FINANCIAL AID PROCEDURES

Forms required: FAFSA.

Dates and Deadlines: Priority date 4/1; no closing date. Applicants notified on a rolling basis starting 7/1; must reply within 3 week(s) of notification.

CONTACT

Jannine Oyama, Financial Aid Officer
874 Dillingham Boulevard, Honolulu, HI 96817
(808) 845-9116

University of Hawaii: Kapiolani Community College

Honolulu, Hawaii
www.kcc.hawaii.edu Federal Code: 001613

2-year public community college in very large city.

Enrollment: 4,909 undergrads.

Selectivity: Open admission; but selective for some programs.

BASIC COSTS (2008-2009)

Tuition and fees: $2,190; out-of-state residents $7,980.

Per-credit charge: $71; out-of-state residents $264.

FINANCIAL AID PICTURE

Students with need: Need-based aid available for full-time and part-time students.

Students without need: This college awards aid only to students with need.

Additional info: Hawaii student incentive grants and tuition waivers (merit and need-based) available to Hawaii residents.

FINANCIAL AID PROCEDURES

Forms required: FAFSA.

Dates and Deadlines: Priority date 4/1; no closing date. Applicants notified on a rolling basis; must reply within 2 week(s) of notification.

CONTACT

Coleen Oshiro, Financial Aid Officer
4303 Diamond Head Road, Honolulu, HI 96816-4421
(808) 734-9555

University of Hawaii: Kauai Community College

Lihue, Hawaii
www.kauai.hawaii.edu Federal Code: 001614

2-year public community college in small city.

Enrollment: 840 undergrads.

Selectivity: Open admission; but selective for out-of-state students.

BASIC COSTS (2008-2009)

Tuition and fees: $2,190; out-of-state residents $7,980.

Per-credit charge: $71; out-of-state residents $264.

FINANCIAL AID PICTURE (2008-2009)

Students with need: Work study available nights.

Additional info: Hawaii student incentive grants and tuition waivers (merit and need-based) available to Hawaii residents.

FINANCIAL AID PROCEDURES

Forms required: FAFSA, institutional form.

Dates and Deadlines: Priority date 4/1; closing date 5/1. Applicants notified on a rolling basis starting 5/1.

Transfers: Academic transcript evaluation by end of first semester is required.

CONTACT

Financial Aid Officer
3-1901 Kaumualii Highway, Lihue, HI 96766-9500
(808) 245-8256

University of Hawaii: Leeward Community College

Pearl City, Hawaii
www.lcc.hawaii.edu Federal Code: 004549

2-year public community college in large town.

Enrollment: 5,887 undergrads.

Selectivity: Open admission.

BASIC COSTS (2008-2009)

Tuition and fees: $2,155; out-of-state residents $7,945.

Per-credit charge: $71; out-of-state residents $264.

FINANCIAL AID PICTURE

Students with need: Need-based aid available for full-time and part-time students.

Additional info: Leveraging Educational Assistance Partnership (LEAP) funds or tuition waivers available to students with financial need.

FINANCIAL AID PROCEDURES

Forms required: FAFSA.

Dates and Deadlines: Priority date 4/15; no closing date. Applicants notified on a rolling basis starting 6/1; must reply within 2 week(s) of notification.

CONTACT

Valerie Chun, Financial Aid Officer
96-045 Ala Ike, Pearl City, HI 96782
(808) 455-0606

University of Hawaii: Maui Community College

Kahului, Hawaii
www.maui.hawaii.edu

2-year public community college in small city.

Enrollment: 2,659 undergrads, 55% part-time. 456 full-time freshmen.

Selectivity: Open admission; but selective for some programs.

BASIC COSTS (2008-2009)

Tuition and fees: $2,252; out-of-state residents $10,922.

Per-credit charge: $71; out-of-state residents $360.

Room and board: $7,478.

Additional info: Tuition/fee waivers available for minority students.

FINANCIAL AID PICTURE (2007-2008)

Students with need: Need-based aid available for full-time and part-time students. Work study available nights.

FINANCIAL AID PROCEDURES

Forms required: FAFSA, institutional form.

Dates and Deadlines: Priority date 4/1; no closing date. Applicants notified on a rolling basis starting 6/1; must reply within 4 week(s) of notification.

CONTACT

Cathy Bio
310 West Kaahumanu Avenue, Kahului, HI 96732-1617
(808) 984-3277

University of Hawaii: West Oahu

Pearl City, Hawaii
www.uhwo.hawaii.edu Federal Code: 014315

4-year public liberal arts and teachers college in large town.
Enrollment: 1,094 undergrads, 64% part-time. 22 full-time freshmen.
Selectivity: Admits 50 to 75% of applicants.

BASIC COSTS (2008-2009)
Tuition and fees: $3,706; out-of-state residents $11,578.
Per-credit charge: $154; out-of-state residents $482.
Additional info: Foreign students pay out-of-state tuition rates. However, citizens of an eligible Pacific island district, commonwealth, territory or insular jurisdiction, state or nation which does not provide public institutions that grant baccalaureate degrees may be allowed to pay 150% of the resident tuition.

FINANCIAL AID PICTURE (2007-2008)
Students with need: Out of 9 full-time freshmen who applied for aid, 7 were judged to have need. Of these, 7 received aid, and 1 had their full need met. Average financial aid package met 70% of need; average scholarship/grant was $3,467; average loan was $3,500. For part-time students, average financial aid package was $5,048.
Students without need: 13 full-time freshmen who did not demonstrate need for aid received scholarships/grants; average award was $1,170. No-need awards available for academics, alumni affiliation, leadership, state/district residency.

FINANCIAL AID PROCEDURES
Forms required: FAFSA.
Dates and Deadlines: Priority date 4/1; no closing date. Applicants notified on a rolling basis starting 4/1.
Transfers: No deadline. Applicants notified by 7/1.

CONTACT
Jodie Kuba, Financial Aid Officer
96-129 Ala Ike, Pearl City, HI 96782
(808) 454-4700

University of Hawaii: Windward Community College

Kaneohe, Hawaii
www.wcc.hawaii.edu Federal Code: 010390

2-year public community college in small city.
Enrollment: 1,824 undergrads.
Selectivity: Open admission.

BASIC COSTS (2008-2009)
Tuition and fees: $2,170; out-of-state residents $7,960.
Per-credit charge: $71; out-of-state residents $264.
Additional info: Tuition/fee waivers available for minority students.

FINANCIAL AID PICTURE
Students with need: Need-based aid available for full-time and part-time students.
Additional info: Hawaii student incentive grants and tuition waivers (merit and need-based) available to Hawaii residents.

FINANCIAL AID PROCEDURES
Forms required: FAFSA.
Dates and Deadlines: Priority date 4/1; no closing date. Applicants notified on a rolling basis starting 3/15; must reply within 2 week(s) of notification.

CONTACT
Steven Chigawa, Financial Aid Officer
45-720 Kea'ahala Road, Kaneohe, HI 96744
(808) 235-7449

Idaho

Boise Bible College

Boise, Idaho
www.boisebible.edu Federal Code: 015783

4-year private Bible college in small city, affiliated with nondenominational tradition.
Enrollment: 170 undergrads.
Selectivity: Admits over 75% of applicants.

BASIC COSTS (2008-2009)
Tuition and fees: $8,100.
Per-credit charge: $330.
Room and board: $5,400.

FINANCIAL AID PICTURE
Students with need: Need-based aid available for full-time and part-time students.
Students without need: No-need awards available for academics, leadership, music/drama, religious affiliation.

FINANCIAL AID PROCEDURES
Forms required: FAFSA, institutional form.
Dates and Deadlines: Priority date 5/1; no closing date. Applicants notified on a rolling basis starting 5/2; must reply by 8/1 or within 2 week(s) of notification.
Transfers: Financial aid and academic transcripts must be on file before federal aid is awarded.

CONTACT
Joyce Anderson, Financial Aid Officer
8695 West Marigold Street, Boise, ID 83714-1220
(800) 893-7755

Boise State University

Boise, Idaho
www.boisestate.edu Federal Code: 001616

4-year public university in small city.
Enrollment: 16,485 undergrads, 30% part-time. 2,261 full-time freshmen.
Selectivity: Admits over 75% of applicants.

BASIC COSTS (2008-2009)
Tuition and fees: $4,632; out-of-state residents $13,208.
Per-credit charge: $238; out-of-state residents $313.
Room and board: $5,938.
Additional info: Out-of-state students (undergraduate and graduate) taking less than 8 credit hours pay in-state rate.

FINANCIAL AID PICTURE (2008-2009)
Students with need: Out of 1,626 full-time freshmen who applied for aid, 1,623 were judged to have need. Of these, 1,623 received aid, and 444 had their full need met. Average financial aid package met 21% of need; average scholarship/grant was $3,300; average loan was $4,333. For part-time students, average financial aid package was $5,433.
Students without need: 423 full-time freshmen who did not demonstrate need for aid received scholarships/grants; average award was $913. No-need

awards available for academics, athletics, music/drama, ROTC, state/district residency.
Scholarships offered: 12 full-time freshmen received athletic scholarships; average amount $10,545.
Cumulative student debt: 64% of graduating class had student loans; average debt was $21,064.

FINANCIAL AID PROCEDURES
Forms required: FAFSA.
Dates and Deadlines: Priority date 4/1; no closing date. Applicants notified on a rolling basis starting 6/1; must reply within 2 week(s) of notification.
Transfers: Financial aid transcripts required from all postsecondary schools attended whether or not financial aid was received.

CONTACT
David Tolman, Director of Financial Aid
1910 University Drive, Boise, ID 83725
(208) 426-1664

Brigham Young University-Idaho
Rexburg, Idaho
www.byui.edu Federal Code: 001625

4-year private university in large town, affiliated with Church of Jesus Christ of Latter-day Saints.
Enrollment: 13,759 undergrads.
Selectivity: Admits over 75% of applicants.

BASIC COSTS (2008-2009)
Tuition and fees: $3,470.
Room and board: $6,600.
Additional info: Tuition for students who are not members of The Church of Jesus Christ of Latter-day Saints is $6,340 for academic year.

FINANCIAL AID PICTURE
Students with need: Need-based aid available for full-time and part-time students.
Students without need: No-need awards available for academics, athletics, leadership.
Additional info: Application deadline for merit scholarships 3/1.

FINANCIAL AID PROCEDURES
Forms required: FAFSA.
Dates and Deadlines: Priority date 5/1; no closing date. Applicants notified on a rolling basis starting 2/1.

CONTACT
Aaron Sanns, Financial Aid and Scholarship Director
120 Kimball Building, Rexburg, ID 83460-1615
(208) 496-1015

College of Idaho
Caldwell, Idaho
www.collegeofidaho.edu Federal Code: 001617

4-year private liberal arts college in large town.
Enrollment: 920 undergrads, 3% part-time. 272 full-time freshmen.
Selectivity: Admits 50 to 75% of applicants.

BASIC COSTS (2009-2010)
Tuition and fees: $20,070.
Per-credit charge: $810.
Room and board: $7,478.
Additional info: Tuition/fee waivers available for adults.

FINANCIAL AID PICTURE (2008-2009)
Students with need: Out of 179 full-time freshmen who applied for aid, 179 were judged to have need. Of these, 179 received aid, and 35 had their full need met. Average financial aid package met 88% of need; average scholarship/grant was $4,888; average loan was $3,729. For part-time students, average financial aid package was $8,185.
Students without need: 93 full-time freshmen who did not demonstrate need for aid received scholarships/grants; average award was $13,521. No-need awards available for academics, alumni affiliation, art, athletics, leadership, minority status, music/drama, religious affiliation, ROTC.
Scholarships offered: ***Merit:*** Albertson Heritage Scholarship: full tuition; minimum 3.85-4.0 GPA and 31-33 ACT or 1380-1470 SAT. Presidential Scholarship: $10,000/year; requirements range from 2.9 GPA and 36 ACT or 1590 SAT to 4.0 GPA and 29 ACT or 1280 SAT. Trustee Scholarship: $7,500/year; requirements range from 2.50 GPA and 36 ACT or 1590 SAT to 4.0 GPA and 25 ACT or 1125 SAT. Dean Grant: $5,000/year; requirements range from 2.5 GPA and 32 ACT or 1400 SAT to 4.0 GPA and 24 ACT or 1090 SAT. All SAT scores exclusive of Writing. Alumni Scholarship: $2,500; 2.5 GPA and 27 ACT or 1200 SAT. ***Athletic:*** 56 full-time freshmen received athletic scholarships; average amount $4,315.
Cumulative student debt: 76% of graduating class had student loans; average debt was $24,919.

FINANCIAL AID PROCEDURES
Forms required: FAFSA, institutional form.
Dates and Deadlines: Priority date 2/15; no closing date. Applicants notified on a rolling basis starting 2/1; must reply within 3 week(s) of notification.
Transfers: No deadline. Applicants notified on a rolling basis starting 1/31; must reply within 3 week(s) of notification.

CONTACT
Juanitta Pearson, Director of Student Financial Services
2112 Cleveland Boulevard, Caldwell, ID 83605
(208) 459-5308

College of Southern Idaho
Twin Falls, Idaho
www.csi.edu Federal Code: 001619

2-year public community and junior college in large town.
Enrollment: 4,960 undergrads.
Selectivity: Open admission; but selective for some programs.

BASIC COSTS (2008-2009)
Tuition and fees: $2,280; out-of-state residents $6,360.
Per-credit charge: $95; out-of-state residents $265.
Room and board: $4,700.

FINANCIAL AID PICTURE
Students with need: Need-based aid available for full-time and part-time students.
Additional info: Out-of-state tuition waivers based on GPA and activities.

FINANCIAL AID PROCEDURES
Forms required: FAFSA.
Dates and Deadlines: Priority date 3/1; no closing date. Applicants notified on a rolling basis starting 4/30; must reply within 3 week(s) of notification.

CONTACT
Colin Randolph, Director of Student Financial Aid
Box 1238, Twin Falls, ID 83303-1238
(208) 732-6273

Eastern Idaho Technical College

Idaho Falls, Idaho
www.eitc.edu Federal Code: 011133

2-year public technical college in small city.
Enrollment: 651 undergrads.
Selectivity: Open admission; but selective for some programs.

BASIC COSTS (2008-2009)

Tuition and fees: $1,796; out-of-state residents $6,238.
Per-credit charge: $85; out-of-state residents $170.
Additional info: Fees may vary according to the program of study.

FINANCIAL AID PICTURE

Students with need: Need-based aid available for full-time and part-time students.
Students without need: No-need awards available for academics, job skills, state/district residency.

FINANCIAL AID PROCEDURES

Forms required: FAFSA, institutional form.
Dates and Deadlines: Priority date 6/1; no closing date. Applicants notified on a rolling basis starting 6/6; must reply within 4 week(s) of notification.

CONTACT

Shayna Sharp, Director of Financial Aid
1600 South 25th East, Idaho Falls, ID 83404-5788
(208) 524-3000 ext. 3389

Idaho State University

Pocatello, Idaho
www.isu.edu Federal Code: 001620

4-year public university in small city.
Enrollment: 9,249 undergrads, 24% part-time. 980 full-time freshmen.
Selectivity: Admits over 75% of applicants.

BASIC COSTS (2008-2009)

Tuition and fees: $4,664; out-of-state residents $13,868.
Per-credit charge: $236; out-of-state residents $364.
Room and board: $5,270.
Additional info: $1,046 refundable health insurance.

FINANCIAL AID PICTURE (2007-2008)

Students with need: Out of 776 full-time freshmen who applied for aid, 568 were judged to have need. Of these, 555 received aid, and 79 had their full need met. Average financial aid package met 40% of need; average scholarship/grant was $4,223; average loan was $3,034. For part-time students, average financial aid package was $4,921.
Students without need: 284 full-time freshmen who did not demonstrate need for aid received scholarships/grants; average award was $2,590. No-need awards available for academics, alumni affiliation, art, athletics, leadership, minority status, music/drama, ROTC, state/district residency.
Scholarships offered: 28 full-time freshmen received athletic scholarships; average amount $10,339.
Cumulative student debt: 73% of graduating class had student loans; average debt was $22,237.

FINANCIAL AID PROCEDURES

Forms required: FAFSA.
Dates and Deadlines: Priority date 3/1; no closing date. Applicants notified on a rolling basis starting 4/1.

CONTACT

Doug Severs, Director of Financial Aid
921 South 8th Stop 8270, Pocatello, ID 83209-8270
(208) 282-2756

Lewis-Clark State College

Lewiston, Idaho
www.lcsc.edu Federal Code: 001621

4-year public liberal arts and technical college in small city.
Enrollment: 3,027 undergrads, 23% part-time. 540 full-time freshmen.
Selectivity: Admits 50 to 75% of applicants.

BASIC COSTS (2008-2009)

Tuition and fees: $4,296; out-of-state residents $11,920.
Per-credit charge: $215.
Room and board: $5,400.

FINANCIAL AID PICTURE (2007-2008)

Students with need: Out of 416 full-time freshmen who applied for aid, 367 were judged to have need. Of these, 347 received aid, and 32 had their full need met. Average financial aid package met 9% of need; average scholarship/grant was $3,074; average loan was $2,841. For part-time students, average financial aid package was $5,511.
Students without need: 64 full-time freshmen who did not demonstrate need for aid received scholarships/grants; average award was $1,501. No-need awards available for academics, alumni affiliation, art, athletics, leadership, minority status, music/drama.
Scholarships offered: 25 full-time freshmen received athletic scholarships; average amount $6,029.

FINANCIAL AID PROCEDURES

Forms required: FAFSA.
Dates and Deadlines: Priority date 3/1; no closing date. Applicants notified on a rolling basis starting 4/15; must reply within 2 week(s) of notification.

CONTACT

Laura Hughes, Director of Financial Aid
500 Eighth Avenue, Lewiston, ID 83501-2698
(208) 792-2224

North Idaho College

Coeur d'Alene, Idaho
www.nic.edu Federal Code: 001623

2-year public community college in large town.
Enrollment: 3,958 undergrads, 36% part-time. 842 full-time freshmen.
Selectivity: Open admission; but selective for some programs.

BASIC COSTS (2008-2009)

Tuition and fees: $2,246; out-of-district residents $3,246; out-of-state residents $7,798.
Per-credit charge: $150; out-of-district residents $213; out-of-state residents $435.
Room and board: $5,680.
Additional info: Tuition/fee waivers available for minority students.

FINANCIAL AID PICTURE (2007-2008)

Students with need: Need-based aid available for full-time and part-time students. Work study available weekends and for part-time students.
Students without need: No-need awards available for academics, art, athletics, leadership, minority status, music/drama, state/district residency

FINANCIAL AID PROCEDURES

Forms required: FAFSA.
Dates and Deadlines: Priority date 3/15; no closing date. Applicants notified on a rolling basis starting 4/1; must reply within 2 week(s) of notification.

CONTACT

Victor Cazun, Director of Financial Aid
1000 West Garden Avenue, Coeur d'Alene, ID 83814-2199
(208) 769-3368

Northwest Nazarene University
Nampa, Idaho
www.nnu.edu Federal Code: 001624

4-year private university in small city, affiliated with Church of the Nazarene.
Enrollment: 1,281 undergrads, 5% part-time. 303 full-time freshmen.
Selectivity: Admits 50 to 75% of applicants.

BASIC COSTS (2009-2010)
Tuition and fees: $22,250.
Per-credit charge: $950.
Room and board: $5,790.

FINANCIAL AID PICTURE (2008-2009)
Students with need: Need-based aid available for full-time and part-time students. Work study available nights, weekends, and for part-time students.
Students without need: No-need awards available for academics, alumni affiliation, art, athletics, leadership, minority status, music/drama, religious affiliation, ROTC.
Scholarships offered: Merit scholarships for freshmen based primarily on cumulative high school GPA and ACT test scores.

FINANCIAL AID PROCEDURES
Forms required: FAFSA, institutional form.
Dates and Deadlines: Priority date 3/1; no closing date. Applicants notified on a rolling basis starting 3/1; must reply within 3 week(s) of notification.

CONTACT
Wes Maggard, Director of Financial Aid
623 Holly Street, Nampa, ID 83686-5897
(208) 467-8347

Stevens-Henager College: Boise
Boise, Idaho
www.stevenshenager.edu/shc/campus/boise.cfm
Federal Code: 003674

2-year for-profit technical and career college in small city.
Enrollment: 503 undergrads. 503 full-time freshmen.
Selectivity: Open admission; but selective for some programs.

BASIC COSTS (2009-2010)
Tuition and fees: $14,560.
Additional info: Tuition and fees can vary by program.

FINANCIAL AID PICTURE (2007-2008)
Students with need: 17% of average financial aid package awarded as scholarships/grants, 83% awarded as loans/jobs.

CONTACT
George Thomas, Business Officer
1444 S Entertainment Avenue, Boise, ID 83709
(208) 345-0700

University of Idaho
Moscow, Idaho
www.uidaho.edu Federal Code: 001626

4-year public university in large town.
Enrollment: 8,542 undergrads, 6% part-time. 1,663 full-time freshmen.
Selectivity: Admits over 75% of applicants.

BASIC COSTS (2008-2009)
Tuition and fees: $4,632; out-of-state residents $14,712.
Per-credit charge: $238; out-of-state residents $574.
Room and board: $6,762.
Additional info: Tuition/fee waivers available for minority students.

FINANCIAL AID PICTURE (2007-2008)
Students with need: Out of 1,300 full-time freshmen who applied for aid, 947 were judged to have need. Of these, 931 received aid, and 299 had their full need met. Average financial aid package met 78% of need; average scholarship/grant was $3,469; average loan was $4,066. For part-time students, average financial aid package was $7,113.
Students without need: 507 full-time freshmen who did not demonstrate need for aid received scholarships/grants; average award was $3,892. No-need awards available for academics, alumni affiliation, art, athletics, leadership, minority status, music/drama, religious affiliation, ROTC, state/district residency.
Scholarships offered: 48 full-time freshmen received athletic scholarships; average amount $16,288.
Cumulative student debt: 66% of graduating class had student loans; average debt was $21,702.

FINANCIAL AID PROCEDURES
Forms required: FAFSA.
Dates and Deadlines: Priority date 2/15; no closing date. Applicants notified on a rolling basis starting 3/30; must reply within 4 week(s) of notification.
Transfers: No deadline. Applicants notified on a rolling basis starting 3/30; must reply within 4 week(s) of notification.

CONTACT
Daniel Davenport, Director of Admissions and Student Financial Aid
PO Box 444264, Moscow, ID 83844-4264
(208) 885-6312

Illinois

American Academy of Art
Chicago, Illinois
www.aaart.edu Federal Code: 001628

4-year for-profit visual arts college in very large city.
Enrollment: 383 undergrads.
Selectivity: Open admission.

BASIC COSTS (2008-2009)
Tuition and fees: $22,780.

FINANCIAL AID PICTURE
Students with need: Work study available nights.
Students without need: No-need awards available for art.

FINANCIAL AID PROCEDURES
Forms required: FAFSA, institutional form.
Dates and Deadlines: No deadline. Applicants notified on a rolling basis.
Transfers: Financial aid transcript from previously attended college required.

CONTACT
Ione Fitzgerald, Financial Aid Director
332 South Michigan Avenue, Suite 300, Chicago, IL 60604-4302
(312) 461-0600

Augustana College
Rock Island, Illinois
www.augustana.edu Federal Code: 001633

4-year private liberal arts college in large city, affiliated with Evangelical Lutheran Church in America.
Enrollment: 2,530 undergrads, 1% part-time. 639 full-time freshmen.
Selectivity: Admits 50 to 75% of applicants.

BASIC COSTS (2009-2010)
Tuition and fees: $31,326.
Per-credit charge: $1,350.
Room and board: $7,950.

FINANCIAL AID PICTURE (2007-2008)
Students with need: Average financial aid package met 88% of need; average scholarship/grant was $14,274; average loan was $5,136.
Students without need: 203 full-time freshmen who did not demonstrate need for aid received scholarships/grants; average award was $11,497. No-need awards available for academics, alumni affiliation, art, leadership, music/drama, religious affiliation.
Scholarships offered: Presidential Scholarship; $10,000 to full tuition; 28 ACT composite score (1260 combined SAT score in critical reading and mathematics) and rank in the top ten percent of high school class. Dean's Scholarship; $7,750-$9,000; 25 ACT composite score or above (1140 combined SAT score in critical reading and mathematics) and rank in the top 20 percent of their high school class. Founders Scholarship; $5,000-$7,500; must plan to enroll full-time at Augustana College. Transfer Scholarship; $3,000-$6,000; demonstrated outstanding academic performance in previous college studies.

FINANCIAL AID PROCEDURES
Forms required: FAFSA, institutional form.
Dates and Deadlines: Priority date 4/1; no closing date. Applicants notified on a rolling basis.
Transfers: Priority date 5/1. Financial aid transcripts from previous institutions required.

CONTACT
Sue Standley, Director of Financial Assistance
639 38th Street, Rock Island, IL 61201-2296
(309) 794-7207

Aurora University
Aurora, Illinois
www.aurora.edu Federal Code: 001634

4-year private university in small city.
Enrollment: 2,181 undergrads, 15% part-time. 377 full-time freshmen.
Selectivity: Admits over 75% of applicants.

BASIC COSTS (2009-2010)
Tuition and fees: $18,100.
Per-credit charge: $540.
Room and board: $7,850.
Additional info: Course laboratory fees in sciences, photography, nursing, physical education and student teaching. Tuition will vary for several adult degree completion programs.

FINANCIAL AID PICTURE (2008-2009)
Students with need: Out of 352 full-time freshmen who applied for aid, 301 were judged to have need. Of these, 301 received aid, and 123 had their full need met. Average financial aid package met 88% of need; average scholarship/grant was $6,851; average loan was $3,238. For part-time students, average financial aid package was $7,112.
Students without need: 74 full-time freshmen who did not demonstrate need for aid received scholarships/grants; average award was $9,047. No-need awards available for academics, alumni affiliation, art, music/drama, religious affiliation, ROTC, state/district residency.
Scholarships offered: Board of Trustees scholarships: $10,000. James E. Crimi Presidential Scholarships: $9,500. Dean's Scholarships: $8,500. Aurora University Opportunity Grants: $6,500. AU Promise Grant: $2,000.
Cumulative student debt: 79% of graduating class had student loans; average debt was $20,092.

FINANCIAL AID PROCEDURES
Forms required: FAFSA.
Dates and Deadlines: Priority date 4/15; no closing date. Applicants notified on a rolling basis starting 3/1; must reply by 5/1 or within 3 week(s) of notification.

CONTACT
Heather McKane, Dean of Student Financial Services
347 South Gladstone Avenue, Aurora, IL 60506-4892
(630) 844-6190

Benedictine University
Lisle, Illinois
www.ben.edu Federal Code: 001767

4-year private university and liberal arts college in large town, affiliated with Roman Catholic Church.
Enrollment: 3,185 undergrads, 33% part-time. 394 full-time freshmen.
Selectivity: Admits over 75% of applicants.

BASIC COSTS (2009-2010)
Tuition and fees: $22,310.
Per-credit charge: $720.
Room and board: $6,945.
Additional info: Tuition freeze for all students 2009-2010 academic year. Tuition/fee waivers available for adults, minority students.

FINANCIAL AID PICTURE (2007-2008)
Students with need: Out of 326 full-time freshmen who applied for aid, 273 were judged to have need. Of these, 273 received aid. For part-time students, average financial aid package was $5,858.
Students without need: 52 full-time freshmen who did not demonstrate need for aid received scholarships/grants; average award was $7,419. No-need awards available for academics, alumni affiliation, minority status, music/drama, ROTC, state/district residency.
Cumulative student debt: 78% of graduating class had student loans; average debt was $16,802.

FINANCIAL AID PROCEDURES
Forms required: FAFSA.
Dates and Deadlines: Priority date 4/15; no closing date. Applicants notified on a rolling basis starting 2/15; must reply within 2 week(s) of notification.
Transfers: No deadline. Applicants notified on a rolling basis; must reply within 2 week(s) of notification.

CONTACT
Diane Battistella, Associate Dean
5700 College Road, Lisle, IL 60532
(630) 829-6100

Black Hawk College
Moline, Illinois
www.bhc.edu Federal Code: 001638

2-year public community college in large town.
Enrollment: 4,263 undergrads, 44% part-time. 549 full-time freshmen.
Selectivity: Open admission; but selective for some programs.

BASIC COSTS (2008-2009)
Tuition and fees: $2,535; out-of-district residents $4,755; out-of-state residents $8,325.
Per-credit charge: $77; out-of-district residents $151; out-of-state residents $270.
Additional info: Agreement with 5 contiguous Iowa counties for special tuition rate of $111 per credit plus required fees. Online courses are $91 (tuition only) per credit hour in-state; $270, out-of-state.

FINANCIAL AID PICTURE (2007-2008)

Students with need: Out of 530 full-time freshmen who applied for aid, 328 were judged to have need. Of these, 293 received aid, and 35 had their full need met. Average financial aid package met 64% of need; average scholarship/grant was $2,137; average loan was $1,445. For part-time students, average financial aid package was $1,418.

Students without need: 33 full-time freshmen who did not demonstrate need for aid received scholarships/grants; average award was $885. No-need awards available for academics, art, athletics, leadership, music/drama, state/district residency.

Scholarships offered: ***Merit:*** Scholarship program; based on need and/or merit. Tuition awards; awarded to students who graduate in the top 10% of their class. ***Athletic:*** 49 full-time freshmen received athletic scholarships; average amount $1,936.

Cumulative student debt: 32% of graduating class had student loans; average debt was $5,069.

Additional info: 5/15 deadline for scholarships.

FINANCIAL AID PROCEDURES

Forms required: FAFSA.

Dates and Deadlines: Priority date 5/15; no closing date. Applicants notified on a rolling basis starting 5/1.

CONTACT

Joanna Dye, Director, Financial Aid
6600 34th Avenue, Moline, IL 61265-5899
(309) 796-5400

Blackburn College

Carlinville, Illinois
www.blackburn.edu — Federal Code: 001639

4-year private liberal arts college in small town, affiliated with Presbyterian Church (USA).

Enrollment: 619 undergrads.

Selectivity: Admits 50 to 75% of applicants.

BASIC COSTS (2008-2009)

Tuition and fees: $13,610.

Per-credit charge: $450.

Room and board: $4,363.

Additional info: All on-campus students participate in a work program which reduces net tuition costs.

FINANCIAL AID PICTURE (2008-2009)

Students with need: Need-based aid available for full-time and part-time students.

Students without need: No-need awards available for academics, state/district residency.

Additional info: Each resident student works 160 hours per semester.

FINANCIAL AID PROCEDURES

Forms required: FAFSA.

Dates and Deadlines: Priority date 4/1; no closing date. Applicants notified on a rolling basis starting 3/1; must reply within 4 week(s) of notification.

Transfers: No deadline. Applicants notified on a rolling basis; must reply within 4 week(s) of notification.

CONTACT

Jane Kelsey, Director of Financial Aid
700 College Avenue, Carlinville, IL 62626
(217) 854-3231 ext. 4283

Blessing-Rieman College of Nursing

Quincy, Illinois
www.brcn.edu — Federal Code: 006214

4-year private nursing college in large town.

Enrollment: 201 undergrads, 9% part-time.

BASIC COSTS (2009-2010)

Tuition and fees: $22,050.

Per-credit charge: $490.

Room and board: $7,145.

Additional info: Tuition and fees are average costs charged to freshman. Partnered with Quincy University and Culver-Stockton College. Freshmen and sophomores pay partnering school's tuition rate.

FINANCIAL AID PICTURE (2008-2009)

Students with need: Need-based aid available for full-time and part-time students.

Additional info: Financial aid for freshmen and sophomores administered by Culver-Stockton College and Quincy University.

FINANCIAL AID PROCEDURES

Forms required: FAFSA.

Dates and Deadlines: No deadline.

CONTACT

Sara Brehm, Financial Aid Officer
PO Box 7005, Quincy, IL 62305-7005
(217) 228-5520 ext. 6993

Bradley University

Peoria, Illinois
www.bradley.edu — Federal Code: 001641

4-year private university in large city.

Enrollment: 5,064 undergrads, 6% part-time. 1,081 full-time freshmen.

Selectivity: Admits 50 to 75% of applicants.

BASIC COSTS (2008-2009)

Tuition and fees: $22,814.

Room and board: $7,350.

FINANCIAL AID PICTURE (2007-2008)

Students with need: Out of 918 full-time freshmen who applied for aid, 696 were judged to have need. Of these, 694 received aid, and 258 had their full need met. Average financial aid package met 74% of need; average scholarship/grant was $11,624; average loan was $3,525. Need-based aid available for part-time students.

Students without need: 207 full-time freshmen who did not demonstrate need for aid received scholarships/grants; average award was $10,844. No-need awards available for academics, alumni affiliation, art, athletics, leadership, music/drama.

Scholarships offered: 18 full-time freshmen received athletic scholarships; average amount $16,106.

FINANCIAL AID PROCEDURES

Forms required: FAFSA.

Dates and Deadlines: Priority date 3/1; no closing date. Applicants notified on a rolling basis starting 2/15.

CONTACT

Dave Pardieck, Financial Assistance Director
1501 West Bradley Avenue, Peoria, IL 61625
(309) 677-3089

Carl Sandburg College

Galesburg, Illinois
www.sandburg.edu Federal Code: 007265

2-year public community college in large town.
Enrollment: 1,976 undergrads, 42% part-time. 99 full-time freshmen.
Selectivity: Open admission; but selective for some programs.

BASIC COSTS (2008-2009)

Tuition and fees: $3,810; out-of-district residents $4,320; out-of-state residents $6,360.
Additional info: Tuition at time of enrollment locked for 2 years.

FINANCIAL AID PICTURE (2007-2008)

Students with need: Out of 80 full-time freshmen who applied for aid, 72 were judged to have need. Of these, 72 received aid, and 18 had their full need met. Average financial aid package met 25% of need; average scholarship/grant was $4,019; average loan was $2,212. For part-time students, average financial aid package was $3,545.
Students without need: 16 full-time freshmen who did not demonstrate need for aid received scholarships/grants; average award was $1,189. No-need awards available for academics, art, athletics, music/drama.
Scholarships offered: 10 full-time freshmen received athletic scholarships; average amount $2,817.

FINANCIAL AID PROCEDURES

Forms required: FAFSA, institutional form.
Dates and Deadlines: Priority date 5/1; no closing date. Applicants notified on a rolling basis starting 5/1; must reply by 8/25 or within 2 week(s) of notification.
Transfers: Must reply by 8/25. Tuition guarantee provides no increase in tuition up to three years as long as enrolled full-time.

CONTACT

Lisa Hanson, Director of Financial Aid
2400 Tom L. Wilson Boulevard, Galesburg, IL 61401
(309) 341-5283

City Colleges of Chicago: Harold Washington College

Chicago, Illinois
www.ccc.edu Federal Code: 001652

2-year public community college in very large city.
Enrollment: 7,748 undergrads.
Selectivity: Open admission; but selective for some programs.

BASIC COSTS (2008-2009)

Tuition and fees: $2,510; out-of-district residents $8,120; out-of-state residents $9,557.
Per-credit charge: $72; out-of-district residents $259; out-of-state residents $307.

FINANCIAL AID PICTURE

Students with need: Need-based aid available for full-time and part-time students. Work study available nights.
Students without need: This college awards aid only to students with need.

FINANCIAL AID PROCEDURES

Forms required: FAFSA.
Dates and Deadlines: Priority date 5/1; closing date 6/30. Applicants notified on a rolling basis starting 7/1; must reply within 2 week(s) of notification.

CONTACT

Francois Hasouk, Director of Financial Aid
30 East Lake Street, Chicago, IL 60601
(312) 553-6041

City Colleges of Chicago: Harry S. Truman College

Chicago, Illinois
www.ccc.edu Federal Code: 001648

2-year public community college in very large city.
Enrollment: 5,092 undergrads.
Selectivity: Open admission; but selective for some programs.

BASIC COSTS (2008-2009)

Tuition and fees: $2,510; out-of-district residents $8,120; out-of-state residents $9,557.
Per-credit charge: $72; out-of-district residents $259; out-of-state residents $307.

FINANCIAL AID PICTURE

Students with need: Need-based aid available for full-time and part-time students. Work study available nights, weekends, and for part-time students.
Students without need: This college awards aid only to students with need.

FINANCIAL AID PROCEDURES

Forms required: FAFSA.
Dates and Deadlines: No deadline. Applicants notified on a rolling basis starting 7/1; must reply within 3 week(s) of notification.

CONTACT

Shirley Howell, Director of Financial Aid
1145 West Wilson Avenue, Chicago, IL 60640
(773) 907-4810

City Colleges of Chicago: Kennedy-King College

Chicago, Illinois
www.ccc.edu Federal Code: 001654

2-year public community college in very large city.
Enrollment: 4,581 undergrads.
Selectivity: Open admission.

BASIC COSTS (2008-2009)

Tuition and fees: $2,510; out-of-district residents $8,120; out-of-state residents $9,557.
Per-credit charge: $72; out-of-district residents $259; out-of-state residents $307.
Additional info: Lab fee of $30 for technical and vocational courses.

FINANCIAL AID PICTURE

Students with need: Need-based aid available for full-time and part-time students.
Students without need: This college awards aid only to students with need.

FINANCIAL AID PROCEDURES

Forms required: FAFSA.
Dates and Deadlines: Priority date 8/1; no closing date. Applicants notified on a rolling basis starting 8/15; must reply within 2 week(s) of notification.

CONTACT

Alicia Williams, Financial Aid Supervisor
6800 South Wentworth Avenue, Chicago, IL 60621
(773) 602-5133

City Colleges of Chicago: Malcolm X College

Chicago, Illinois
www.malcolmx.ccc.edu Federal Code: 001650

2-year public community and junior college in very large city.
Enrollment: 3,534 undergrads.
Selectivity: Open admission; but selective for some programs.

BASIC COSTS (2008-2009)

Tuition and fees: $2,510; out-of-district residents $8,120; out-of-state residents $9,557.
Per-credit charge: $72; out-of-district residents $259; out-of-state residents $307.
Additional info: Some courses require a $30 lab fee.

FINANCIAL AID PICTURE

Students with need: Need-based aid available for full-time and part-time students. Work study available nights, weekends, and for part-time students.
Students without need: This college awards aid only to students with need.

FINANCIAL AID PROCEDURES

Forms required: FAFSA, institutional form.
Dates and Deadlines: Priority date 7/1; no closing date. Applicants notified on a rolling basis starting 7/1; must reply within 2 week(s) of notification.

CONTACT

Patricia Burke, Director, Financial Aid
1900 West Van Buren Street, Chicago, IL 60612
(312) 850-7146

City Colleges of Chicago: Olive-Harvey College

Chicago, Illinois
www.ccc.edu Federal Code: 009767

2-year public community college in very large city.
Enrollment: 2,526 undergrads.
Selectivity: Open admission; but selective for some programs.

BASIC COSTS (2008-2009)

Tuition and fees: $2,510; out-of-district residents $8,120; out-of-state residents $9,557.
Per-credit charge: $72; out-of-district residents $259; out-of-state residents $307.

FINANCIAL AID PICTURE

Students with need: Need-based aid available for full-time and part-time students.

FINANCIAL AID PROCEDURES

Forms required: FAFSA.
Dates and Deadlines: Priority date 8/15; no closing date. Applicants notified on a rolling basis; must reply within 3 week(s) of notification.

CONTACT

Michael Shields, Director of Financial Aid
10001 South Woodlawn Avenue, Chicago, IL 60628
(773) 291-6391

City Colleges of Chicago: Richard J. Daley College

Chicago, Illinois
www.daley.ccc.edu/ Federal Code: 001649

2-year public community college in very large city.
Enrollment: 4,107 undergrads.
Selectivity: Open admission; but selective for some programs.

BASIC COSTS (2008-2009)

Tuition and fees: $2,510; out-of-district residents $8,120; out-of-state residents $9,557.
Per-credit charge: $72; out-of-district residents $259; out-of-state residents $307.

FINANCIAL AID PICTURE

Students with need: Need-based aid available for full-time students.

FINANCIAL AID PROCEDURES

Forms required: FAFSA.
Dates and Deadlines: No deadline. Applicants notified on a rolling basis.
Transfers: College workstudy jobs and Federal Supplemental Educational Opportunity Grant (SEOG) may not be available to transfers.

CONTACT

Thelma Barnes, Dean of Student Services
7500 South Pulaski Road, Chicago, IL 60652
(773) 838-7579

City Colleges of Chicago: Wright College

Chicago, Illinois
www.ccc.edu Federal Code: 001655

2-year public community college in very large city.
Enrollment: 7,571 undergrads.
Selectivity: Open admission.

BASIC COSTS (2008-2009)

Tuition and fees: $2,510; out-of-district residents $8,120; out-of-state residents $9,557.
Per-credit charge: $72; out-of-district residents $259; out-of-state residents $307.

FINANCIAL AID PICTURE

Students with need: Need-based aid available for full-time and part-time students. Work study available nights, weekends, and for part-time students.

FINANCIAL AID PROCEDURES

Forms required: FAFSA, institutional form.
Dates and Deadlines: Priority date 6/1; no closing date. Applicants notified on a rolling basis starting 7/15.

CONTACT

Marco Sepulveda, Financial Aid Director
4300 North Narragansett Avenue, Chicago, IL 60634-4276
(773) 481-8100

College of DuPage

Glen Ellyn, Illinois
www.cod.edu Federal Code: 006656

2-year public community college in large town.
Enrollment: 21,978 undergrads, 57% part-time. 1,900 full-time freshmen.
Selectivity: Open admission; but selective for some programs.

BASIC COSTS (2008-2009)

Tuition and fees: $3,240; out-of-district residents $8,880; out-of-state residents $10,770.

Per-credit charge: $88; out-of-district residents $276; out-of-state residents $339.

FINANCIAL AID PICTURE (2007-2008)

Students with need: Out of 766 full-time freshmen who applied for aid, 550 were judged to have need. Of these, 439 received aid, and 42 had their full need met. Average financial aid package met 63% of need; average scholarship/grant was $4,087; average loan was $2,815. For part-time students, average financial aid package was $4,302.

Students without need: 43 full-time freshmen who did not demonstrate need for aid received scholarships/grants; average award was $1,279. No-need awards available for academics, art, leadership, minority status, music/drama, state/district residency.

FINANCIAL AID PROCEDURES

Forms required: FAFSA.

Dates and Deadlines: Priority date 4/30; no closing date. Applicants notified on a rolling basis starting 6/1; must reply within 2 week(s) of notification.

Transfers: No deadline. Applicants notified on a rolling basis; must reply within 2 week(s) of notification. Must have financial aid application on file indicating previous institutions attended.

CONTACT

Mark Holysz, Director of Student Financial Aid
425 Fawell Boulevard, Glen Ellyn, IL 60137-6599
(630) 942-2251

College of Lake County

Grayslake, Illinois
www.clcillinois.edu Federal Code: 007694

2-year public community college in large town.

Enrollment: 11,999 undergrads, 62% part-time. 1,342 full-time freshmen.

Selectivity: Open admission; but selective for some programs.

BASIC COSTS (2009-2010)

Tuition and fees: $2,850; out-of-district residents $6,600; out-of-state residents $8,730.

Per-credit charge: $81; out-of-district residents $206; out-of-state residents $277.

Additional info: Tuition/fee waivers available for minority students.

FINANCIAL AID PICTURE

Students with need: Need-based aid available for full-time and part-time students. Work study available nights.

Students without need: No-need awards available for academics, alumni affiliation, art, athletics, leadership, minority status, music/drama.

Scholarships offered: Academic Achievement Scholarship: based on GPA and student essay; tuition and fees.

FINANCIAL AID PROCEDURES

Forms required: FAFSA.

Dates and Deadlines: Priority date 6/5; no closing date. Applicants notified on a rolling basis starting 6/15; must reply within 2 week(s) of notification.

CONTACT

Karen Hlavin, Assistant Vice President, Student Development
19351 West Washington Street, Grayslake, IL 60030-1198
(847) 543-2062

College of Office Technology

Chicago, Illinois
www.cot.edu Federal Code: 017378

2-year for-profit business college in very large city.

Enrollment: 270 undergrads.

Selectivity: Open admission.

BASIC COSTS (2008-2009)

Tuition and fees: $10,368.

FINANCIAL AID PICTURE

Students with need: Need-based aid available for full-time and part-time students.

Students without need: This college awards aid only to students with need.

FINANCIAL AID PROCEDURES

Forms required: FAFSA.

Dates and Deadlines: No deadline. Applicants notified on a rolling basis.

CONTACT

Paula Terronez, Educational Operations and Financial Aid Director
1520 West Division Street, Chicago, IL 60622-3312
(773) 278-0042

Columbia College Chicago

Chicago, Illinois
www.colum.edu Federal Code: 001665

4-year private visual arts and liberal arts college in very large city.

Enrollment: 11,749 undergrads, 10% part-time. 2,333 full-time freshmen.

Selectivity: Open admission; but selective for some programs.

BASIC COSTS (2008-2009)

Tuition and fees: $18,430.

Per-credit charge: $621.

Room and board: $12,926.

FINANCIAL AID PICTURE (2007-2008)

Students with need: Average financial aid package met 48% of need; average scholarship/grant was $3,912; average loan was $3,241. For part-time students, average financial aid package was $6,299.

Students without need: No-need awards available for academics, art, leadership, music/drama, state/district residency.

FINANCIAL AID PROCEDURES

Forms required: FAFSA, institutional form.

Dates and Deadlines: Priority date 5/1; no closing date. Applicants notified on a rolling basis.

CONTACT

Jennifer Waters, Executive Director of Student Financial Services
600 South Michigan Avenue, Chicago, IL 60605-1996
(866) 705-0200

Concordia University Chicago

River Forest, Illinois
www.cuchicago.edu Federal Code: 001666

4-year private university and teachers college in large town, affiliated with Lutheran Church - Missouri Synod.

Enrollment: 1,067 undergrads, 4% part-time. 221 full-time freshmen.

Selectivity: Admits over 75% of applicants.

BASIC COSTS (2009-2010)
Tuition and fees: $23,458.
Per-credit charge: $719.
Room and board: $7,700.

FINANCIAL AID PICTURE (2007-2008)
Students with need: Out of 207 full-time freshmen who applied for aid, 173 were judged to have need. Of these, 173 received aid, and 41 had their full need met. Average financial aid package met 79% of need; average scholarship/grant was $11,675; average loan was $4,271. For part-time students, average financial aid package was $11,353.
Students without need: 48 full-time freshmen who did not demonstrate need for aid received scholarships/grants; average award was $9,420. No-need awards available for academics, alumni affiliation, music/drama, religious affiliation, state/district residency.
Scholarships offered: Presidential Honors: full tuition; selection by essay; 5 per year. Presidential Scholarships: up to $12,000; selection by ACT and GP. Community Awards: up to $7000; selection by ACT and GPA. Transfer Honors: up to $10,000; selection by GPA. Music Scholarships: amount varies; selection by audition.
Cumulative student debt: 79% of graduating class had student loans; average debt was $21,697.

FINANCIAL AID PROCEDURES
Forms required: FAFSA.
Dates and Deadlines: Priority date 4/1; no closing date. Applicants notified on a rolling basis starting 3/1; must reply within 4 week(s) of notification.
Transfers: No deadline. Applicants notified on a rolling basis; must reply within 4 week(s) of notification.

CONTACT
Patricia Williamson, Director of Student Financial Planning
7400 Augusta Street, River Forest, IL 60305-1499
(708) 209-3113

Cooking & Hospitality Institute of Chicago
Chicago, Illinois
www.chic.edu Federal Code: 016758

2-year for-profit culinary school in very large city.
Enrollment: 1,004 undergrads. 154 full-time freshmen.
Selectivity: Open admission.

BASIC COSTS (2008-2009)
Additional info: Tuition for associate of applied science in Le Cordon Bleu Culinary Arts: $39,950; associate of applied science in Le Cordon Bleu Patisserie and Baking: $38,500; certificate in Le Cordon Bleu Culinary Arts: $12,200. Tuition at time of enrollment locked for 2 years.

FINANCIAL AID PICTURE
Students with need: Need-based aid available for full-time and part-time students. Work study available nights.

FINANCIAL AID PROCEDURES
Forms required: FAFSA, institutional form.
Dates and Deadlines: No deadline. Applicants notified on a rolling basis.
Transfers: No deadline. Applicants notified on a rolling basis.

CONTACT
Loren Mokrzycki, Director of Student Finance
361 West Chestnut, Chicago, IL 60610-3050
(312) 944-0882

Danville Area Community College
Danville, Illinois
www.dacc.edu Federal Code: 001669

2-year public community college in large town.
Enrollment: 2,491 undergrads, 55% part-time. 259 full-time freshmen.
Selectivity: Open admission.

BASIC COSTS (2008-2009)
Tuition and fees: $2,520; out-of-district residents $4,800; out-of-state residents $4,800.
Per-credit charge: $74; out-of-district residents $150; out-of-state residents $150.

FINANCIAL AID PICTURE (2007-2008)
Students with need: Average financial aid package met 67% of need; average scholarship/grant was $1,620; average loan was $2,625. Need-based aid available for part-time students.
Students without need: No-need awards available for academics, athletics, minority status.

FINANCIAL AID PROCEDURES
Forms required: FAFSA, institutional form.
Dates and Deadlines: Priority date 7/1; no closing date. Applicants notified on a rolling basis starting 4/1.
Transfers: NSLDS reviewed before aid disbursed.

CONTACT
Janet Ingargiola, Director of Financial Aid
2000 East Main Street, Danville, IL 61832
(217) 443-8891

DePaul University
Chicago, Illinois
www.depaul.edu Federal Code: 001671

4-year private university in very large city, affiliated with Roman Catholic Church.
Enrollment: 15,449 undergrads, 18% part-time. 2,555 full-time freshmen.
Selectivity: Admits 50 to 75% of applicants.

BASIC COSTS (2009-2010)
Tuition and fees: $27,342.
Per-credit charge: $475.
Room and board: $10,617.

FINANCIAL AID PICTURE (2008-2009)
Students with need: Out of 2,195 full-time freshmen who applied for aid, 1,674 were judged to have need. Of these, 1,637 received aid, and 159 had their full need met. Average financial aid package met 65% of need; average scholarship/grant was $14,229; average loan was $3,739. For part-time students, average financial aid package was $8,847.
Students without need: 176 full-time freshmen who did not demonstrate need for aid received scholarships/grants; average award was $9,492. No-need awards available for academics, art, athletics, leadership, music/drama, ROTC, state/district residency.
Scholarships offered: ***Merit:*** Various scholarships; based on top 10% of class, 1100 SAT (exclusive of writing) or 26 ACT, and active in student/community organizations. ***Athletic:*** 49 full-time freshmen received athletic scholarships; average amount $19,653.
Cumulative student debt: 66% of graduating class had student loans; average debt was $19,375.

FINANCIAL AID PROCEDURES
Forms required: FAFSA.
Dates and Deadlines: Priority date 3/1; no closing date. Applicants notified on a rolling basis starting 3/15; must reply by 5/1 or within 4 week(s) of notification.

Transfers: Closing date 4/1. Applicants notified by 6/1. 5 different scholarships awarded to fall incoming transfer students who have been admitted and have submitted scholarship application by April 1. Scholarships range from $3,000-$7,000, and vary based on competitiveness of pool and student's qualifications.

CONTACT

Paula Luff, Director of Financial Aid
One East Jackson Boulevard, Chicago, IL 60604-2287
(312) 362-8091

DeVry University: Addison

Addison, Illinois
www.devry.edu Federal Code: 016219

4-year for-profit university in large town.
Enrollment: 1,397 undergrads, 35% part-time. 181 full-time freshmen.

BASIC COSTS (2008-2009)

Tuition and fees: $14,130.
Per-credit charge: $515.

FINANCIAL AID PICTURE (2007-2008)

Students with need: Need-based aid available for full-time and part-time students.
Students without need: This college awards aid only to students with need.

FINANCIAL AID PROCEDURES

Forms required: FAFSA.
Dates and Deadlines: No deadline. Applicants notified on a rolling basis.

CONTACT

Sajel Anin, Director of Student Finance
1221 North Swift Road, Addison, IL 60101-6106
(630) 953-1300

DeVry University: Chicago

Chicago, Illinois
www.devry.edu Federal Code: 010727

4-year for-profit university in very large city.
Enrollment: 1,882 undergrads, 42% part-time. 194 full-time freshmen.

BASIC COSTS (2008-2009)

Tuition and fees: $14,130.
Per-credit charge: $515.

FINANCIAL AID PICTURE (2007-2008)

Students with need: Need-based aid available for full-time and part-time students.
Students without need: This college awards aid only to students with need.

FINANCIAL AID PROCEDURES

Forms required: FAFSA.
Dates and Deadlines: No deadline. Applicants notified on a rolling basis.

CONTACT

Milena Dobrina, Director of Financial Aid
3300 North Campbell Avenue, Chicago, IL 60618-5994
(773) 929-8509

DeVry University: Tinley Park

Tinley Park, Illinois
www.devry.edu Federal Code: 022966

4-year for-profit university in large town.
Enrollment: 1,088 undergrads, 40% part-time. 145 full-time freshmen.

BASIC COSTS (2008-2009)

Tuition and fees: $14,130.
Per-credit charge: $515.

FINANCIAL AID PICTURE (2007-2008)

Students with need: Need-based aid available for full-time and part-time students.
Students without need: This college awards aid only to students with need.

FINANCIAL AID PROCEDURES

Forms required: FAFSA.
Dates and Deadlines: No deadline. Applicants notified on a rolling basis.

CONTACT

Sejal Amin, Director of Student Finance
18624 West Creek Drive, Tinley Park, IL 60477-6243
(708) 342-3219

Dominican University

River Forest, Illinois
www.dom.edu Federal Code: 001750

4-year private university and liberal arts college in large town, affiliated with Roman Catholic Church.
Enrollment: 1,608 undergrads, 8% part-time. 412 full-time freshmen.
Selectivity: Admits over 75% of applicants.

BASIC COSTS (2008-2009)

Tuition and fees: $23,950.
Per-credit charge: $790.
Room and board: $7,350.

FINANCIAL AID PICTURE (2008-2009)

Students with need: Out of 382 full-time freshmen who applied for aid, 350 were judged to have need. Of these, 350 received aid, and 68 had their full need met. Average financial aid package met 85% of need; average scholarship/grant was $15,411; average loan was $3,289. For part-time students, average financial aid package was $7,803.
Students without need: 54 full-time freshmen who did not demonstrate need for aid received scholarships/grants; average award was $10,187. No-need awards available for academics, alumni affiliation, leadership.
Scholarships offered: Presidential Scholarships: $14,000. Dean's Scholarships: $12,000. University Honor Scholarships: $10.000. Achievement Scholarships: $8,000. All based on ACT/SAT scores and class rank. Ida Brechtel Scholarships: $7,500 up to full tuition; for students majoring in chemistry of biology/chemistry.
Cumulative student debt: 90% of graduating class had student loans; average debt was $18,200.

FINANCIAL AID PROCEDURES

Forms required: FAFSA.
Dates and Deadlines: Priority date 6/1; no closing date. Applicants notified on a rolling basis starting 2/15; must reply within 2 week(s) of notification.
Transfers: No deadline. Applicants notified on a rolling basis starting 3/15; must reply within 3 week(s) of notification. Merit scholarships available to full-time students with GPA of 3.3 from previous institution. Phi Theta Kappa scholarships available to PTK members.

CONTACT
Michael Shields, Director of Financial Aid
7900 West Division Street, River Forest, IL 60305-1099
(708) 524-6809

East-West University
Chicago, Illinois
www.eastwest.edu Federal Code: 015310

4-year private university in very large city.
Enrollment: 1,150 undergrads.
Selectivity: Open admission.

BASIC COSTS (2008-2009)
Tuition and fees: $13,530.

FINANCIAL AID PICTURE
Students with need: Need-based aid available for full-time and part-time students.
Students without need: No-need awards available for academics.
Additional info: Foreign students eligible for institutional scholarship.

FINANCIAL AID PROCEDURES
Forms required: FAFSA.
Dates and Deadlines: No deadline. Applicants notified on a rolling basis starting 1/4; must reply within 4 week(s) of notification.
Transfers: Closing date 4/1.

CONTACT
Elizabeth Guzman, Director of Financial Aid
816 South Michigan Avenue, Chicago, IL 60605
(312) 939-0111

Eastern Illinois University
Charleston, Illinois
www.eiu.edu Federal Code: 001674

4-year public university and teachers college in large town.
Enrollment: 10,065 undergrads, 10% part-time. 1,762 full-time freshmen.
Selectivity: Admits 50 to 75% of applicants.

BASIC COSTS (2008-2009)
Tuition and fees: $8,782; out-of-state residents $21,862.
Per-credit charge: $218; out-of-state residents $654.
Room and board: $7,588.
Additional info: Tuition at time of enrollment locked for 4 years.

FINANCIAL AID PICTURE (2008-2009)
Students with need: Out of 1,539 full-time freshmen who applied for aid, 995 were judged to have need. Of these, 978 received aid, and 95 had their full need met. Average financial aid package met 69% of need; average scholarship/grant was $2,625; average loan was $3,188. For part-time students, average financial aid package was $7,112.
Students without need: 88 full-time freshmen who did not demonstrate need for aid received scholarships/grants; average award was $3,808. No-need awards available for academics, art, athletics, leadership, music/drama, ROTC.
Scholarships offered: 42 full-time freshmen received athletic scholarships; average amount $11,171.
Cumulative student debt: 59% of graduating class had student loans; average debt was $14,233.

FINANCIAL AID PROCEDURES
Forms required: FAFSA.
Dates and Deadlines: Priority date 3/1; no closing date. Applicants notified on a rolling basis starting 2/1; must reply within 2 week(s) of notification.

CONTACT
Jone Zieren, Director of Financial Aid
600 Lincoln Avenue, Charleston, IL 61920-3011
(217) 581-3713

Elgin Community College
Elgin, Illinois
www.elgin.edu Federal Code: 001675

2-year public community college in small city.
Enrollment: 6,746 undergrads, 55% part-time. 785 full-time freshmen.
Selectivity: Open admission; but selective for some programs.

BASIC COSTS (2008-2009)
Tuition and fees: $2,740; out-of-district residents $11,778; out-of-state residents $14,184.
Per-credit charge: $91; out-of-district residents $392; out-of-state residents $472.

FINANCIAL AID PICTURE
Students with need: Need-based aid available for full-time and part-time students. Work study available nights, weekends, and for part-time students.
Students without need: No-need awards available for academics, alumni affiliation, art, athletics, job skills, leadership, minority status, music/drama, religious affiliation, ROTC, state/district residency.

FINANCIAL AID PROCEDURES
Forms required: FAFSA, institutional form.
Dates and Deadlines: Priority date 6/1; no closing date. Applicants notified on a rolling basis starting 4/6; must reply within 3 week(s) of notification.

CONTACT
Amy Perrin, Director of Student Financial Assistance
1700 Spartan Drive, Elgin, IL 60123-7193
(847) 214-7520

Elmhurst College
Elmhurst, Illinois
www.elmhurst.edu Federal Code: 001676

4-year private liberal arts college in large town, affiliated with United Church of Christ.
Enrollment: 2,960 undergrads, 7% part-time. 508 full-time freshmen.
Selectivity: Admits 50 to 75% of applicants.

BASIC COSTS (2008-2009)
Tuition and fees: $26,060.
Per-credit charge: $740.
Room and board: $8,476.

FINANCIAL AID PICTURE (2007-2008)
Students with need: Out of 420 full-time freshmen who applied for aid, 384 were judged to have need. Of these, 384 received aid, and 75 had their full need met. Average financial aid package met 91% of need; average scholarship/grant was $14,576; average loan was $3,957. For part-time students, average financial aid package was $6,011.
Students without need: 112 full-time freshmen who did not demonstrate need for aid received scholarships/grants; average award was $9,113. No-need awards available for academics, alumni affiliation, art, minority status, music/drama, religious affiliation, state/district residency.
Scholarships offered: Presidential Scholarship: $13,000-$18,000; 412 awarded. Dean's Scholarship: 9,000-$12,000; 487 awarded. Founder's Scholarship: $4,000-$8,000; 347 awarded. Combination of class rank, test scores, and GPA considered.
Additional info: Must be admitted to the college by 1/15 to be considered for scholarships.

FINANCIAL AID PROCEDURES

Forms required: FAFSA.

Dates and Deadlines: Priority date 4/15; no closing date. Applicants notified on a rolling basis starting 2/21; must reply within 3 week(s) of notification.

CONTACT

Ruth Pusich, Director of Financial Aid
190 South Prospect Avenue, Elmhurst, IL 60126-3296
(630) 617-3075

Eureka College

Eureka, Illinois
www.eureka.edu Federal Code: 001678

4-year private liberal arts college in small town, affiliated with Christian Church (Disciples of Christ).

Enrollment: 728 undergrads.

Selectivity: Admits 50 to 75% of applicants.

BASIC COSTS (2008-2009)

Tuition and fees: $16,255.

Per-credit charge: $450.

Room and board: $7,130.

FINANCIAL AID PICTURE (2008-2009)

Students with need: Need-based aid available for full-time and part-time students. Work study available nights, weekends, and for part-time students.

Students without need: No-need awards available for academics, alumni affiliation, art, leadership, music/drama, religious affiliation.

Scholarships offered: Reagan Fellows Program: full tuition; 5 awarded. Sandifer Mentorships: fully paid mentorship anywhere in the world at end of sophomore year; all freshmen eligible. Eureka College Ministry Fellowship: full tuition scholarships; 2 available each year.

FINANCIAL AID PROCEDURES

Forms required: FAFSA.

Dates and Deadlines: Priority date 4/15; no closing date. Applicants notified on a rolling basis starting 2/15; must reply by 5/1 or within 3 week(s) of notification.

Transfers: No deadline. Applicants notified on a rolling basis; must reply within 2 week(s) of notification.

CONTACT

Ellen Rigsby, Director of Financial Aid
300 East College Avenue, Eureka, IL 61530-1500
(309) 467-6311

Governors State University

University Park, Illinois
www.govst.edu Federal Code: 009145

Upper-division public university in large town.

Enrollment: 2,583 undergrads, 63% part-time.

BASIC COSTS (2008-2009)

Tuition and fees: $7,542; out-of-state residents $19,782.

Per-credit charge: $204; out-of-state residents $612.

Additional info: Tuition/fee waivers available for minority students.

FINANCIAL AID PICTURE

Students with need: Need-based aid available for full-time and part-time students. Work study available nights, weekends, and for part-time students.

Students without need: No-need awards available for academics, ROTC, state/district residency.

FINANCIAL AID PROCEDURES

Forms required: FAFSA.

Dates and Deadlines: Priority date 5/1; closing date 10/1. Applicants notified on a rolling basis.

CONTACT

Freda Whisenton-Comer, Office of Financial Aid
One University Parkway, University Park, IL 60466
(708) 534-4480

Greenville College

Greenville, Illinois
www.greenville.edu Federal Code: 001684

4-year private liberal arts college in small town, affiliated with Free Methodist Church of North America.

Enrollment: 1,418 undergrads, 2% part-time. 307 full-time freshmen.

Selectivity: Admits over 75% of applicants.

BASIC COSTS (2009-2010)

Tuition and fees: $20,216.

Per-credit charge: $422.

Room and board: $6,878.

FINANCIAL AID PICTURE (2007-2008)

Students with need: Out of 294 full-time freshmen who applied for aid, 254 were judged to have need. Of these, 254 received aid, and 49 had their full need met. Average financial aid package met 86% of need; average scholarship/grant was $11,964; average loan was $4,214. For part-time students, average financial aid package was $8,025.

Students without need: 55 full-time freshmen who did not demonstrate need for aid received scholarships/grants; average award was $9,868. No-need awards available for academics, alumni affiliation, art, leadership, minority status, music/drama, religious affiliation, state/district residency.

Scholarships offered: President's Scholarships; $8,000; requiring cumulative GPA of 3.0, ACT of 27 or SAT of 1210, and leadership qualities. Dean's Scholarship; $6,000; for GPA of 3.0, ACT of 22 or SAT of 1020, and leadership qualities. Leadership Scholarships; $500-$4,000; for GPA of 2.5, ACT of 18 or SAT 860, and leadership qualities. (All SAT scores are exclusive of Writing.).

Cumulative student debt: 88% of graduating class had student loans; average debt was $15,073.

FINANCIAL AID PROCEDURES

Forms required: FAFSA.

Dates and Deadlines: Priority date 5/1; no closing date. Applicants notified on a rolling basis starting 3/15; must reply within 3 week(s) of notification.

Transfers: No deadline. Applicants notified on a rolling basis; must reply within 3 week(s) of notification.

CONTACT

Marilae Latham, Director of Financial Aid
315 East College Avenue, Greenville, IL 62246-0159
(618) 664-7111

Harper College

Palatine, Illinois
www.harpercollege.edu Federal Code: 003901

2-year public community college in small city.

Enrollment: 13,302 undergrads, 50% part-time. 2,088 full-time freshmen.

Selectivity: Open admission; but selective for some programs.

BASIC COSTS (2008-2009)

Tuition and fees: $3,234; out-of-district residents $10,194; out-of-state residents $12,504.

Per-credit charge: $90; out-of-district residents $322; out-of-state residents $399.

Additional info: In-district tuition rates available to employees of in-district companies who reside outside college district.

FINANCIAL AID PICTURE (2007-2008)

Students with need: Need-based aid available for full-time and part-time students. Work study available nights, weekends, and for part-time students.
Students without need: No-need awards available for academics, art, leadership, minority status, music/drama, state/district residency.
Scholarships offered: Distinguished Scholar Award; full tuition and fees; available to full-time students during regular academic year who graduate in top 10% of class from district high school; renewable for second year.

FINANCIAL AID PROCEDURES

Forms required: FAFSA, institutional form.
Dates and Deadlines: Priority date 3/1; no closing date. Applicants notified on a rolling basis starting 3/1; must reply within 2 week(s) of notification.
Transfers: No deadline. Applicants notified on a rolling basis starting 3/1; must reply within 2 week(s) of notification.

CONTACT

Earl Dowling, Director, Scholarships and Financial Assistance
1200 West Algonquin Road, Palatine, IL 60067-7398
(847) 925-6248

Harrington College of Design

Chicago, Illinois
www.harringtoncollege.com Federal Code: 013601

4-year for-profit visual arts college in very large city.
Enrollment: 1,279 undergrads.

BASIC COSTS (2008-2009)

Tuition and fees: $16,565.
Per-credit charge: $656.
Additional info: Required fees vary depending on a program.

FINANCIAL AID PICTURE

Students with need: Need-based aid available for full-time and part-time students.
Students without need: This college awards aid only to students with need.

FINANCIAL AID PROCEDURES

Forms required: FAFSA.
Dates and Deadlines: Closing date 7/15. Applicants notified on a rolling basis; must reply within 2 week(s) of notification.
Transfers: No deadline.

CONTACT

Renee Darosky, Director of Financial Aid
200 West Madison Avenue, Chicago, IL 60606
(877) 939-4975

Heartland Community College

Normal, Illinois
www.heartland.edu Federal Code: 030838

2-year public community college in small city.
Enrollment: 4,952 undergrads, 54% part-time. 653 full-time freshmen.
Selectivity: Open admission; but selective for some programs.

BASIC COSTS (2009-2010)

Tuition and fees: $2,850; out-of-district residents $5,490; out-of-state residents $8,130.
Per-credit charge: $88; out-of-district residents $176; out-of-state residents $264.

FINANCIAL AID PICTURE (2007-2008)

Students with need: 96% of average financial aid package awarded as scholarships/grants, 4% awarded as loans/jobs. Need-based aid available for part-time students. Work study available nights, weekends, and for part-time students.
Students without need: No-need awards available for academics, alumni affiliation, athletics, job skills, leadership, minority status, state/district residency.

FINANCIAL AID PROCEDURES

Forms required: FAFSA, institutional form.
Dates and Deadlines: Priority date 4/1; no closing date. Applicants notified on a rolling basis starting 5/15; must reply within 2 week(s) of notification.

CONTACT

Cheryl Schaffer, Director of Financial Aid
1500 West Raab Road, Normal, IL 61761
(309) 268-8020

Highland Community College

Freeport, Illinois
www.highland.edu Federal Code: 001681

2-year public community college in large town.
Enrollment: 1,876 undergrads, 44% part-time. 317 full-time freshmen.
Selectivity: Open admission; but selective for some programs.

BASIC COSTS (2008-2009)

Tuition and fees: $2,490; out-of-district residents $4,050; out-of-state residents $4,050.
Per-credit charge: $76; out-of-district residents $128; out-of-state residents $128.

FINANCIAL AID PICTURE (2007-2008)

Students with need: 74% of average financial aid package awarded as scholarships/grants, 26% awarded as loans/jobs. Need-based aid available for part-time students. Work study available nights.
Students without need: No-need awards available for academics, athletics.

FINANCIAL AID PROCEDURES

Forms required: FAFSA, institutional form.
Dates and Deadlines: No deadline. Applicants notified on a rolling basis starting 8/1; must reply within 2 week(s) of notification.
Transfers: No deadline. Applicants notified on a rolling basis starting 4/1.

CONTACT

Kathy Bangasser, Director of Financial Aid
2998 West Pearl City Road, Freeport, IL 61032-9341
(815) 599-3559

Illinois College

Jacksonville, Illinois
www.ic.edu Federal Code: 001688

4-year private liberal arts college in large town, affiliated with United Church of Christ and Presbyterian Church (USA).
Enrollment: 870 undergrads, 1% part-time. 166 full-time freshmen.
Selectivity: Admits 50 to 75% of applicants.

BASIC COSTS (2008-2009)

Tuition and fees: $20,300.
Room and board: $7,230.

FINANCIAL AID PICTURE (2008-2009)

Students with need: Out of 160 full-time freshmen who applied for aid, 147 were judged to have need. Of these, 147 received aid, and 68 had their full need met. Average financial aid package met 91% of need; average scholarship/grant was $9,813; average loan was $4,650. For part-time students, average financial aid package was $9,026.

Students without need: 16 full-time freshmen who did not demonstrate need for aid received scholarships/grants; average award was $7,681. No-need awards available for academics, art, minority status, music/drama.

Scholarships offered: College transfer scholarship; available with 12 transferable credit hours and minimum 3.0 GPA.

Cumulative student debt: 81% of graduating class had student loans; average debt was $20,466.

FINANCIAL AID PROCEDURES

Forms required: FAFSA.

Dates and Deadlines: Priority date 3/1; no closing date. Applicants notified on a rolling basis starting 3/1; must reply within 2 week(s) of notification.

Transfers: No deadline. Applicants notified on a rolling basis starting 6/1; must reply within 2 week(s) of notification.

CONTACT

Katherine Taylor, Director of Financial Aid
1101 West College Avenue, Jacksonville, IL 62650
(217) 245-3035

Illinois Eastern Community Colleges: Frontier Community College

Fairfield, Illinois
www.iecc.edu/fcc Federal Code: 014090

2-year public community college in small town.

Enrollment: 1,529 undergrads, 81% part-time. 31 full-time freshmen.

Selectivity: Open admission; but selective for some programs.

BASIC COSTS (2008-2009)

Tuition and fees: $1,910; out-of-district residents $5,736; out-of-state residents $7,140.

Per-credit charge: $60; out-of-district residents $188; out-of-state residents $234.

Additional info: Students in qualifying Indiana districts pay per-credit-hour rate of $114.

FINANCIAL AID PICTURE

Students with need: Need-based aid available for full-time and part-time students.

Students without need: No-need awards available for academics, state/district residency.

FINANCIAL AID PROCEDURES

Forms required: FAFSA, institutional form.

Dates and Deadlines: No deadline. Applicants notified on a rolling basis starting 8/1; must reply within 2 week(s) of notification.

CONTACT

Carroll Hilliard, Associate Dean of Student Services
2 Frontier Drive, Fairfield, IL 62837-9801
(618) 842-3711

Illinois Eastern Community Colleges: Lincoln Trail College

Robinson, Illinois
www.iecc.edu/ltc Federal Code: 009786

2-year public community college in small town.

Enrollment: 1,036 undergrads, 53% part-time. 77 full-time freshmen.

Selectivity: Open admission.

BASIC COSTS (2008-2009)

Tuition and fees: $1,910; out-of-district residents $5,736; out-of-state residents $7,140.

Per-credit charge: $60; out-of-district residents $188; out-of-state residents $234.

Additional info: Students in qualifying Indiana districts pay per-credit-hour rate of $114.

FINANCIAL AID PICTURE

Students with need: Need-based aid available for full-time and part-time students.

Students without need: No-need awards available for academics, athletics, state/district residency.

FINANCIAL AID PROCEDURES

Forms required: FAFSA, institutional form.

Dates and Deadlines: No deadline. Applicants notified on a rolling basis starting 8/1; must reply within 2 week(s) of notification.

CONTACT

Jennifer Barthelemy, Coordinator of Financial Aid
11220 State Highway 1, Robinson, IL 62454-5707
(618) 544-8657

Illinois Eastern Community Colleges: Olney Central College

Olney, Illinois
www.iecc.edu/occ Federal Code: 001742

2-year public community college in small town.

Enrollment: 963 undergrads, 25% part-time. 126 full-time freshmen.

Selectivity: Open admission; but selective for some programs.

BASIC COSTS (2008-2009)

Tuition and fees: $1,910; out-of-district residents $5,736; out-of-state residents $7,140.

Per-credit charge: $60; out-of-district residents $188; out-of-state residents $234.

Additional info: Students in qualifying Indiana districts pay per-credit-hour rate of $114.

FINANCIAL AID PICTURE

Students with need: Need-based aid available for full-time and part-time students.

Students without need: No-need awards available for academics, athletics, state/district residency.

FINANCIAL AID PROCEDURES

Forms required: FAFSA, institutional form.

Dates and Deadlines: No deadline. Applicants notified on a rolling basis starting 8/1; must reply within 2 week(s) of notification.

CONTACT

Vicki Stuckey, Financial Aid Coordinator
305 North West Street, Olney, IL 62450
(618) 395-7777

Illinois Eastern Community Colleges: Wabash Valley College

Mount Carmel, Illinois
www.iecc.edu/wvc Federal Code: 001779

2-year public community college in small town.
Enrollment: 621 full-time undergrads.
Selectivity: Open admission.

BASIC COSTS (2008-2009)

Tuition and fees: $1,910; out-of-district residents $5,736; out-of-state residents $7,140.
Per-credit charge: $60; out-of-district residents $188; out-of-state residents $234.
Additional info: Students in qualifying Indiana districts pay per-credit-hour rate of $114.

FINANCIAL AID PICTURE

Students with need: Need-based aid available for full-time and part-time students.
Students without need: No-need awards available for academics, athletics, state/district residency.

FINANCIAL AID PROCEDURES

Forms required: FAFSA, institutional form.
Dates and Deadlines: No deadline. Applicants notified on a rolling basis starting 8/1; must reply within 2 week(s) of notification.

CONTACT

Melinda Silvernale, Financial Aid Coordinator
2200 College Drive, Mount Carmel, IL 62863-2657
(618) 262-8641

Illinois Institute of Art: Chicago

Chicago, Illinois
www.ilic.artinstitutes.edu Federal Code: 012584

4-year for-profit visual arts college in very large city.
Enrollment: 3,000 undergrads.

BASIC COSTS (2008-2009)

Tuition and fees: $21,648.
Per-credit charge: $451.
Room and board: $10,155.

FINANCIAL AID PICTURE

Students with need: Need-based aid available for full-time and part-time students.

FINANCIAL AID PROCEDURES

Forms required: FAFSA.
Dates and Deadlines: Priority date 5/1; no closing date. Applicants notified on a rolling basis.

CONTACT

Charles Munro, Financial Aid Officer
350 North Orleans Street, Chicago, IL 60654

Illinois Institute of Art: Schaumburg

Schaumburg, Illinois
www.artinstitutes.edu/schaumburg Federal Code: 012584

3-year for-profit visual arts college in small city.
Enrollment: 1,240 undergrads.
Selectivity: Open admission; but selective for some programs.

BASIC COSTS (2008-2009)

Tuition and fees: $21,600.
Per-credit charge: $450.
Room and board: $7,080.

FINANCIAL AID PICTURE

Students with need: Need-based aid available for full-time and part-time students. Work study available nights, weekends, and for part-time students.
Students without need: No-need awards available for academics, art.
Scholarships offered: Scholarships based on GPA and talent-based scholarships available.

FINANCIAL AID PROCEDURES

Forms required: FAFSA.
Dates and Deadlines: Priority date 3/1; no closing date.
Transfers: No deadline. Applicants notified on a rolling basis.

CONTACT

Joe Payne, Director of Student Financial Services
1000 North Plaza Drive, Schaumburg, IL 60173
(800) 314-3450

Illinois Institute of Technology

Chicago, Illinois
www.iit.edu Federal Code: 001691

4-year private university and engineering college in very large city.
Enrollment: 2,590 undergrads, 7% part-time. 520 full-time freshmen.
Selectivity: Admits 50 to 75% of applicants.

BASIC COSTS (2008-2009)

Tuition and fees: $27,513.
Per-credit charge: $832.
Room and board: $9,226.
Additional info: Tuition and fees cover unlimited number of courses during academic year and include library and computer usage fees.

FINANCIAL AID PICTURE (2007-2008)

Students with need: Out of 380 full-time freshmen who applied for aid, 333 were judged to have need. Of these, 331 received aid, and 103 had their full need met. Average financial aid package met 89% of need; average scholarship/grant was $18,002; average loan was $4,403. For part-time students, average financial aid package was $9,188.
Students without need: 183 full-time freshmen who did not demonstrate need for aid received scholarships/grants; average award was $12,712. No-need awards available for academics, alumni affiliation, athletics, leadership, ROTC.
Scholarships offered: ***Merit:*** Henry Heald Scholarship: up to $10,000; based on student application. University Scholarship: up to $10,000; based on student application. Crown Scholarship (College of Architecture): full-tuition; based on student application, on-campus interview and portfolio. Camras Scholarship: 3/4-tuition and full-tuition; based on student application, on-campus interview and essay. Leadership Edge Scholarship (Stuart School of Business): based on student application, on-campus interview and essay. ***Athletic:*** 21 full-time freshmen received athletic scholarships; average amount $11,086.
Cumulative student debt: 60% of graduating class had student loans; average debt was $20,308.

FINANCIAL AID PROCEDURES

Forms required: FAFSA.
Dates and Deadlines: Priority date 4/15; no closing date. Applicants notified on a rolling basis starting 3/5.
Transfers: No deadline.

CONTACT

Gerald Doyle, Associate Vice President, Undergraduate Enrollment and Financial Aid
10 West 33rd Street, Chicago, IL 60616
(312) 567-7219

Illinois State University

Normal, Illinois
www.ilstu.edu Federal Code: 001692

4-year public university in small city.
Enrollment: 17,997 undergrads, 6% part-time. 3,388 full-time freshmen.
Selectivity: Admits 50 to 75% of applicants.

BASIC COSTS (2008-2009)

Tuition and fees: $9,814; out-of-state residents $16,444.
Per-credit charge: $256; out-of-state residents $477.
Room and board: $7,860.
Additional info: Tuition at time of enrollment locked for 4 years.

FINANCIAL AID PICTURE (2008-2009)

Students with need: Out of 2,596 full-time freshmen who applied for aid, 1,787 were judged to have need. Of these, 1,609 received aid, and 818 had their full need met. Average financial aid package met 81% of need; average scholarship/grant was $8,621; average loan was $5,967. For part-time students, average financial aid package was $10,550.
Students without need: 56 full-time freshmen who did not demonstrate need for aid received scholarships/grants; average award was $3,219. No-need awards available for academics, art, athletics, music/drama.
Scholarships offered: ***Merit:*** Various non-need based merit scholarships available, including Presidential Scholars' Program, Provost's Scholarship, and Dean's Scholarship. ***Athletic:*** 30 full-time freshmen received athletic scholarships; average amount $12,587.
Cumulative student debt: 57% of graduating class had student loans; average debt was $18,854.

FINANCIAL AID PROCEDURES

Forms required: FAFSA.
Dates and Deadlines: Priority date 3/1; no closing date. Applicants notified on a rolling basis starting 4/1; must reply within 2 week(s) of notification.

CONTACT

Jana Albrecht, Director of Financial Aid
Campus Box 2200, Normal, IL 61790-2200
(309) 438-2231

Illinois Valley Community College

Oglesby, Illinois
www.ivcc.edu Federal Code: 001705

2-year public community college in small town.
Enrollment: 2,940 undergrads.
Selectivity: Open admission; but selective for some programs.

BASIC COSTS (2008-2009)

Tuition and fees: $2,168; out-of-district residents $7,992; out-of-state residents $9,092.
Per-credit charge: $61; out-of-district residents $243; out-of-state residents $277.

FINANCIAL AID PICTURE (2007-2008)

Students with need: Need-based aid available for full-time and part-time students.

FINANCIAL AID PROCEDURES

Forms required: FAFSA.
Dates and Deadlines: Priority date 5/1; no closing date. Applicants notified on a rolling basis starting 5/1.

CONTACT

Steve Crick, Director, Financial Aid
815 North Orlando Smith Avenue, Oglesby, IL 61348-9693
(815) 224-0438

Illinois Wesleyan University

Bloomington, Illinois Federal Code: 001696
www.iwu.edu CSS Code: 1320

4-year private university and liberal arts college in small city.
Enrollment: 2,115 undergrads. 562 full-time freshmen.
Selectivity: Admits 50 to 75% of applicants.

BASIC COSTS (2009-2010)

Tuition and fees: $33,982.
Per-credit charge: $1,057.
Room and board: $7,776.

FINANCIAL AID PICTURE (2008-2009)

Students with need: Out of 421 full-time freshmen who applied for aid, 360 were judged to have need. Of these, 360 received aid, and 230 had their full need met. Average financial aid package met 95% of need; average scholarship/grant was $18,287; average loan was $4,627.
Students without need: 186 full-time freshmen who did not demonstrate need for aid received scholarships/grants; average award was $12,580. No-need awards available for academics, art, music/drama.
Scholarships offered: Academic scholarships based on high school academic performance, recommendations, testing. Talent awards available in music, art, theater, and musical theater. Limited number of full-tuition awards in music.
Cumulative student debt: 62% of graduating class had student loans; average debt was $26,555.

FINANCIAL AID PROCEDURES

Forms required: FAFSA, CSS PROFILE, institutional form.
Dates and Deadlines: Closing date 3/1. Applicants notified on a rolling basis starting 2/15; must reply by 5/1 or within 3 week(s) of notification.
Transfers: No deadline. Applicants notified on a rolling basis; must reply by 5/1 or within 3 week(s) of notification.

CONTACT

Scott Seibring, Director of Financial Aid
PO Box 2900, Bloomington, IL 61702-2900
(309) 556-3096

International Academy of Design and Technology: Chicago

Chicago, Illinois
www.iadtchicago.edu Federal Code: 021603

4-year for-profit visual arts and technical college in very large city.
Enrollment: 1,736 undergrads.
Selectivity: Open admission.

BASIC COSTS (2008-2009)

Tuition and fees: $17,730.

FINANCIAL AID PICTURE (2007-2008)

Students with need: 35% of average financial aid package awarded as scholarships/grants, 65% awarded as loans/jobs. Need-based aid available for part-time students.
Students without need: This college awards aid only to students with need.

Additional info: College work study programs available to day and evening students.

FINANCIAL AID PROCEDURES

Forms required: FAFSA.

Dates and Deadlines: No deadline. Applicants notified on a rolling basis.

Transfers: No deadline. Applicants notified on a rolling basis; must reply within 2 week(s) of notification.

CONTACT

Andrea Watkins, Associate Director of Financial Aid
One North State Street, Suite 500, Chicago, IL 60602
(312) 980-9200 ext. 9251

International Academy of Design and Technology: Schaumburg

Schaumburg, Illinois
www.iadtschaumburg.com

4-year for-profit visual arts and technical college in small city.

Enrollment: 214 undergrads.

Selectivity: Open admission.

BASIC COSTS (2008-2009)

Tuition and fees: $16,140.

FINANCIAL AID PICTURE (2007-2008)

Students with need: 21% of average financial aid package awarded as scholarships/grants, 79% awarded as loans/jobs.

CONTACT

Chris Miller, Assistant Financial Aid Director
915 National Parkway, Schaumburg, IL 60173

John A. Logan College

Carterville, Illinois
www.jalc.edu Federal Code: 008076

2-year public community college in small town.

Enrollment: 2,306 undergrads.

Selectivity: Open admission; but selective for some programs.

BASIC COSTS (2008-2009)

Tuition and fees: $2,130; out-of-district residents $5,030; out-of-state residents $6,984.

Per-credit charge: $71; out-of-district residents $168; out-of-state residents $233.

FINANCIAL AID PICTURE

Students with need: Need-based aid available for full-time and part-time students.

Students without need: This college awards aid only to students with need.

FINANCIAL AID PROCEDURES

Forms required: FAFSA, institutional form.

Dates and Deadlines: Priority date 5/1; no closing date. Applicants notified on a rolling basis starting 5/1.

CONTACT

Stacy Holloway, Director for Student Financial Assistance
700 Logan College Road, Carterville, IL 62918
(618) 985-3741 ext. 8308

John Wood Community College

Quincy, Illinois
www.jwcc.edu Federal Code: 012813

2-year public community college in large town.

Enrollment: 1,889 undergrads, 40% part-time. 422 full-time freshmen.

Selectivity: Open admission; but selective for some programs.

BASIC COSTS (2008-2009)

Tuition and fees: $3,120; out-of-state residents $6,120.

Per-credit charge: $96; out-of-state residents $196.

FINANCIAL AID PICTURE

Students with need: Need-based aid available for full-time and part-time students. Work study available nights, weekends, and for part-time students.

FINANCIAL AID PROCEDURES

Forms required: FAFSA.

Dates and Deadlines: No deadline. Applicants notified on a rolling basis starting 3/1.

CONTACT

Melanie Lechtenberg, Director of Financial Aid
1301 South 48th Street, Quincy, IL 62305-8736
(217) 641-4336

Joliet Junior College

Joliet, Illinois
www.jjc.edu Federal Code: 001699

2-year public community college in small city.

Enrollment: 11,788 undergrads.

Selectivity: Open admission; but selective for some programs and for out-of-state students.

BASIC COSTS (2008-2009)

Tuition and fees: $2,640; out-of-district residents $7,193; out-of-state residents $8,042.

Per-credit charge: $64; out-of-district residents $216; out-of-state residents $244.

Additional info: Additional course fees range from $3 to $90.

FINANCIAL AID PICTURE (2007-2008)

Students with need: 63% of average financial aid package awarded as scholarships/grants, 37% awarded as loans/jobs. Need-based aid available for part-time students. Work study available nights, weekends, and for part-time students.

Students without need: No-need awards available for academics.

FINANCIAL AID PROCEDURES

Forms required: FAFSA, institutional form.

Dates and Deadlines: Closing date 5/1. Applicants notified on a rolling basis starting 5/15.

CONTACT

David Seward, Director of Financial Aid
1215 Houbolt Road, Joliet, IL 60431-8938
(815) 729-9020 ext. 2701

Judson University

Elgin, Illinois
www.judsonu.edu Federal Code: 001700

4-year private university and liberal arts college in small city, affiliated with American Baptist Churches in the USA.

Enrollment: 926 full-time undergrads. 132 full-time freshmen.

Selectivity: Admits 50 to 75% of applicants.

BASIC COSTS (2009-2010)

Tuition and fees: $23,500.
Room and board: $8,200.

FINANCIAL AID PICTURE (2007-2008)

Students with need: Out of 116 full-time freshmen who applied for aid, 99 were judged to have need. Of these, 99 received aid.
Students without need: 12 full-time freshmen who did not demonstrate need for aid received scholarships/grants; average award was $5,416. No-need awards available for academics, alumni affiliation, art, athletics, music/drama.
Scholarships offered: ***Merit:*** Academic Merit Award: 1 awarded; $7,000; incoming freshmen with ACT score of 25 (1140 SAT) or higher with at least 3.33 GPA. Academic Merit Award: 2 awarded; $5,000; incoming freshmen with ACT score of 25 (1140 SAT) or higher with a 3.32 GPA or less. Academic Merit Award: 3 awarded; $5,000; incoming freshmen with ACT score from 19-24 (910-1110 SAT) with 3.3 GPA or higher. ***Athletic:*** 15 full-time freshmen received athletic scholarships; average amount $14,195.
Cumulative student debt: 58% of graduating class had student loans; average debt was $22,948.

FINANCIAL AID PROCEDURES

Forms required: FAFSA.
Dates and Deadlines: Priority date 3/15; closing date 5/1. Applicants notified on a rolling basis starting 3/1; must reply within 4 week(s) of notification.
Transfers: Must reply within 4 week(s) of notification.

CONTACT

Michael Davis, Director of Financial Aid
1151 North State Street, Elgin, IL 60123-1404
(800) 879-5376

Kankakee Community College

Kankakee, Illinois
www.kcc.edu Federal Code: 007690

2-year public community college in large town.
Enrollment: 2,906 undergrads, 54% part-time. 266 full-time freshmen.
Selectivity: Open admission; but selective for some programs.

BASIC COSTS (2009-2010)

Tuition and fees: $2,310; out-of-district residents $5,160; out-of-state residents $11,460.
Per-credit charge: $77; out-of-district residents $172; out-of-state residents $382.

FINANCIAL AID PICTURE (2007-2008)

Students with need: 90% of average financial aid package awarded as scholarships/grants, 10% awarded as loans/jobs. Need-based aid available for part-time students.
Students without need: No-need awards available for athletics.

FINANCIAL AID PROCEDURES

Forms required: FAFSA.
Dates and Deadlines: Priority date 0/1, no closing date. Applicants notified on a rolling basis; must reply within 4 week(s) of notification.

CONTACT

John Perry, Director of Financial Aid
100 College Drive, Kankakee, IL 60901-6505
(815) 802-8550

Kaskaskia College

Centralia, Illinois
www.kaskaskia.edu Federal Code: 001701

2-year public community college in large town.
Enrollment: 1,824 full-time undergrads.
Selectivity: Open admission; but selective for some programs.

BASIC COSTS (2008-2009)

Tuition and fees: $2,190; out-of-district residents $4,140; out-of-state residents $9,240.
Per-credit charge: $65; out-of-district residents $130; out-of-state residents $300.

FINANCIAL AID PICTURE (2008-2009)

Students with need: Need-based aid available for full-time and part-time students.
Students without need: No-need awards available for academics, athletics, state/district residency.

FINANCIAL AID PROCEDURES

Forms required: FAFSA.
Dates and Deadlines: Priority date 5/15; no closing date. Applicants notified on a rolling basis starting 4/1; must reply within 2 week(s) of notification.
Transfers: No deadline. Applicants notified on a rolling basis.

CONTACT

Lisa Collier, Director of Financial Aid
27210 College Road, Centralia, IL 62801
(618) 545-3080

Kendall College

Chicago, Illinois
www.kendall.edu Federal Code: 001703

4-year private culinary school and business and teachers college in very large city, affiliated with United Methodist Church.
Enrollment: 1,842 undergrads, 34% part-time. 170 full-time freshmen.

BASIC COSTS (2008-2009)

Room and board: $10,485.
Additional info: Tuition costs range from $7,200 to $21,450 per academic year. Required fees: $675.

FINANCIAL AID PICTURE (2007-2008)

Students with need: 33% of average financial aid package awarded as scholarships/grants, 67% awarded as loans/jobs. Need-based aid available for part-time students. Work study available nights, weekends, and for part-time students.
Students without need: No-need awards available for academics.

FINANCIAL AID PROCEDURES

Forms required: FAFSA.
Dates and Deadlines: Priority date 6/1; no closing date. Applicants notified on a rolling basis starting 4/1; must reply within 2 week(s) of notification.
Transfers: Priority date 4/15; no deadline.

CONTACT

Sharon Clough, Associate VP for Financial Aid
900 North Branch Street North, Chicago, IL 60642-4278
(866) 803-9988

Kishwaukee College

Malta, Illinois
www.kishwaukeecollege.edu Federal Code: 007684

2-year public community college in rural community.
Enrollment: 3,083 undergrads.
Selectivity: Open admission; but selective for some programs.

BASIC COSTS (2008-2009)

Tuition and fees: $2,430; out-of-district residents $7,410; out-of-state residents $8,340.
Per-credit charge: $71; out-of-district residents $237; out-of-state residents $268.

FINANCIAL AID PICTURE (2007-2008)

Students with need: Need-based aid available for full-time and part-time students. Work study available nights, weekends, and for part-time students.
Students without need: No-need awards available for academics, athletics, leadership, music/drama, state/district residency.

FINANCIAL AID PROCEDURES

Forms required: FAFSA, institutional form.
Dates and Deadlines: Priority date 5/1; no closing date. Applicants notified on a rolling basis starting 5/1; must reply within 2 week(s) of notification.
Transfers: Must reply within 2 week(s) of notification. Some state programs not available to sophomore status students.

CONTACT

Pamela Wagener, Director, Financial Aid/Veterans Affairs
21193 Malta Road, Malta, IL 60150-9699
(815) 825-2086 ext. 224

Knox College

Galesburg, Illinois
www.knox.edu Federal Code: 001704

4-year private liberal arts college in large town.
Enrollment: 1,360 undergrads. 367 full-time freshmen.
Selectivity: Admits 50 to 75% of applicants.

BASIC COSTS (2009-2010)

Tuition and fees: $31,911.
Room and board: $7,164.

FINANCIAL AID PICTURE (2008-2009)

Students with need: Need-based aid available for full-time and part-time students. Work study available nights, weekends, and for part-time students.
Students without need: No-need awards available for academics, art, music/drama.
Scholarships offered: Academic scholarship; up to $15,000; based on high school academic performance and class rank. Visual and performing arts scholarships (in music, art, theater, dance, writing); up to $4,000; based on auditions or submission of portfolios. Social Concerns Scholarships; up to $4,000; based on community service activity.

FINANCIAL AID PROCEDURES

Forms required: FAFSA, institutional form.
Dates and Deadlines: Priority date 2/1; no closing date. Applicants notified on a rolling basis starting 3/15; must reply by 5/1 or within 2 week(s) of notification.
Transfers: Priority date 4/1. Applicants notified on a rolling basis starting 4/15; must reply by 6/1 or within 2 week(s) of notification.

CONTACT

Ann Brill, Director of Financial Aid
Knox College - Campus Box 148, Galesburg, IL 61401-4999
(309) 341-7149

Lake Forest College

Lake Forest, Illinois
www.lakeforest.edu Federal Code: 001706

4-year private liberal arts college in large town, affiliated with Presbyterian Church (USA).
Enrollment: 1,350 undergrads, 1% part-time. 379 full-time freshmen.
Selectivity: Admits 50 to 75% of applicants.

BASIC COSTS (2008-2009)

Tuition and fees: $32,520.
Per-credit charge: $1,004.
Room and board: $7,724.

FINANCIAL AID PICTURE (2008-2009)

Students with need: Out of 311 full-time freshmen who applied for aid, 284 were judged to have need. Of these, 284 received aid, and 105 had their full need met. Average financial aid package met 92% of need; average scholarship/grant was $22,988; average loan was $4,674.
Students without need: 57 full-time freshmen who did not demonstrate need for aid received scholarships/grants; average award was $11,193. No-need awards available for academics, alumni affiliation, art, leadership, music/drama, state/district residency.
Scholarships offered: Academic Scholarships; up to $16,000; non-need based. Forester Scholarships; $1,000-$5,000; awarded in art, modern languages, leadership, music, math and computer science, science, theater, and writing; non-need based.
Cumulative student debt: 74% of graduating class had student loans; average debt was $23,962.

FINANCIAL AID PROCEDURES

Forms required: FAFSA, institutional form.
Dates and Deadlines: Priority date 3/1; no closing date. Applicants notified on a rolling basis starting 3/15; must reply by 5/1 or within 3 week(s) of notification.
Transfers: Closing date 6/1. Applicants notified on a rolling basis starting 1/3; must reply within 3 week(s) of notification.

CONTACT

Gerard Cebrzynski, Financial Aid Director
555 North Sheridan Road, Lake Forest, IL 60045-2338
(847) 735-5015

Lake Land College

Mattoon, Illinois
www.lakelandcollege.edu Federal Code: 007644

2-year public community college in large town.
Enrollment: 5,134 undergrads.
Selectivity: Open admission; but selective for some programs.

BASIC COSTS (2008-2009)

Tuition and fees: $2,394; out-of-district residents $5,087; out-of-state residents $9,264.
Per-credit charge: $64; out-of-district residents $153; out-of-state residents $293.

FINANCIAL AID PICTURE (2007-2008)

Students with need: 74% of average financial aid package awarded as scholarships/grants, 26% awarded as loans/jobs. Need-based aid available for part-time students. Work study available nights, weekends, and for part-time students.
Students without need: No-need awards available for academics, athletics.

FINANCIAL AID PROCEDURES

Forms required: FAFSA.

Dates and Deadlines: Priority date 5/1; no closing date. Applicants notified on a rolling basis starting 6/1.
Transfers: No deadline.

CONTACT

Paula Carpenter, Director of Financial Aid and Veteran Services
5001 Lake Land Boulevard, Mattoon, IL 61938-9366
(217) 234-5231

Lakeview College of Nursing

Danville, Illinois
www.lakeviewcol.edu Federal Code: 010501

Upper-division private nursing college in large town.
Enrollment: 283 undergrads, 20% part-time.

BASIC COSTS (2009-2010)

Tuition and fees: $11,850.
Per-credit charge: $395.

FINANCIAL AID PICTURE

Students with need: Need-based aid available for full-time and part-time students.
Students without need: This college awards aid only to students with need.

FINANCIAL AID PROCEDURES

Forms required: FAFSA, institutional form.
Dates and Deadlines: Closing date 4/15.
Transfers: Priority date 4/15; no deadline.

CONTACT

Janet Ingargiola, Director of Financial Aid
903 North Logan Avenue, Danville, IL 61832
(217) 554-6887

Lewis and Clark Community College

Godfrey, Illinois
www.lc.edu Federal Code: 010020

2-year public community college in large town.
Enrollment: 2,813 full-time undergrads.
Selectivity: Open admission; but selective for some programs.

BASIC COSTS (2009-2010)

Tuition and fees: $2,820; out-of-district residents $7,620; out-of-state residents $10,020.
Per-credit charge: $80; out-of-district residents $254; out-of-state residents $334.

FINANCIAL AID PICTURE (2008-2009)

Students with need: Need-based aid available for full-time and part-time students.

FINANCIAL AID PROCEDURES

Forms required: FAFSA.
Dates and Deadlines: Priority date 6/1; no closing date. Applicants notified on a rolling basis starting 8/1; must reply within 3 week(s) of notification.
Transfers: No deadline. Applicants notified on a rolling basis.

CONTACT

Angela Weaver, Director, Financial Aid
5800 Godfrey Road, Godfrey, IL 62035-2466
(618) 468-2223

Lewis University

Romeoville, Illinois
www.lewisu.edu Federal Code: 001707

4-year private university in large town, affiliated with Roman Catholic Church.
Enrollment: 3,913 undergrads, 21% part-time. 655 full-time freshmen.
Selectivity: Admits 50 to 75% of applicants.

BASIC COSTS (2008-2009)

Tuition and fees: $21,990.
Per-credit charge: $705.
Room and board: $8,000.
Additional info: Tuition/fee waivers available for adults.

FINANCIAL AID PICTURE (2008-2009)

Students with need: Average financial aid package met 79% of need; average scholarship/grant was $8,718; average loan was $3,391. For part-time students, average financial aid package was $6,304.
Students without need: No-need awards available for academics, alumni affiliation, art, athletics, leadership, music/drama, religious affiliation, ROTC.
Cumulative student debt: 24% of graduating class had student loans; average debt was $24,451.

FINANCIAL AID PROCEDURES

Forms required: FAFSA.
Dates and Deadlines: Closing date 5/1. Applicants notified on a rolling basis starting 2/1; must reply within 2 week(s) of notification.
Transfers: No deadline. Applicants notified on a rolling basis; must reply by 8/1 or within 2 week(s) of notification.

CONTACT

Janeen Decharinte, Director of Financial Aid
One University Parkway, Romeoville, IL 60446-2200
(815) 836-5262

Lexington College

Chicago, Illinois
www.lexingtoncollege.edu Federal Code: 016942

4-year private hospitality management college for women in very large city, affiliated with Roman Catholic Church.
Enrollment: 60 undergrads.
Selectivity: Admits 50 to 75% of applicants.

BASIC COSTS (2008-2009)

Tuition and fees: $22,800.
Per-credit charge: $727.
Room and board: $8,000.

FINANCIAL AID PICTURE (2008-2009)

Students with need: Need-based aid available for full-time and part-time students.
Students without need: This college awards aid only to students with need.
Additional info: Work-study is available.

FINANCIAL AID PROCEDURES

Forms required: FAFSA.
Dates and Deadlines: Priority date 5/15; no closing date. Applicants notified on a rolling basis starting 7/1; must reply within 2 week(s) of notification.
Transfers: Closing date 5/15. Students who enroll and then transfer to another college within a given term can only receive Illinois state aid at one institution per academic year.

CONTACT
Maria LeBron, Director of Financial Aid
310 South Peoria Street, Suite 512, Chicago, IL 60607-3534
(312) 226-6294 ext. 227

Lincoln Christian College and Seminary
Lincoln, Illinois
www.lccs.edu Federal Code: 001708

4-year private Bible and seminary college in large town, affiliated with Church of Christ.
Enrollment: 672 undergrads.

BASIC COSTS (2009-2010)
Tuition and fees: $13,020.
Per-credit charge: $434.
Room and board: $5,623.

FINANCIAL AID PICTURE
Students with need: Need-based aid available for full-time and part-time students. Work study available nights, weekends, and for part-time students.
Students without need: No-need awards available for academics.
Cumulative student debt: 69% of graduating class had student loans; average debt was $19,594.

FINANCIAL AID PROCEDURES
Forms required: FAFSA, institutional form.
Dates and Deadlines: Priority date 8/10; no closing date. Applicants notified on a rolling basis starting 3/1; must reply within 2 week(s) of notification.

CONTACT
Nancy Siddens, Director of Student Financial Aid
100 Campus View Drive, Lincoln, IL 62656-2167
(217) 732-3168 ext. 2304

Lincoln College
Lincoln, Illinois
www.lincolncollege.edu Federal Code: 001709

2-year private junior and liberal arts college in large town.
Enrollment: 1,090 undergrads.
Selectivity: Admits 50 to 75% of applicants.

BASIC COSTS (2008-2009)
Tuition and fees: $20,000.
Per-credit charge: $250.
Room and board: $6,200.

FINANCIAL AID PICTURE (2008-2009)
Students with need: Average financial aid package met 48% of need; average scholarship/grant was $11,202; average loan was $3,020. For part-time students, average financial aid package was $6,358.
Students without need: No-need awards available for academics, art, athletics, music/drama.
Cumulative student debt: 73% of graduating class had student loans; average debt was $8,275.
Additional info: Auditions recommended for music, speech, theater, broadcasting, and dance scholarship candidates, portfolios recommended for art and technical theater scholarship candidates.

FINANCIAL AID PROCEDURES
Forms required: FAFSA.
Dates and Deadlines: Priority date 6/1; closing date 7/1. Applicants notified on a rolling basis starting 6/1; must reply within 3 week(s) of notification.

CONTACT
Kevin Stephens, Director of Financial Aid
300 Keokuk Street, Lincoln, IL 62656
(217) 732-3155 ext. 230

Lincoln Land Community College
Springfield, Illinois
www.llcc.edu Federal Code: 007170

2-year public community and junior college in small city.
Enrollment: 4,937 undergrads, 53% part-time. 513 full-time freshmen.
Selectivity: Open admission; but selective for some programs.

BASIC COSTS (2008-2009)
Tuition and fees: $2,505; out-of-district residents $4,710; out-of-state residents $6,915.
Per-credit charge: $74; out-of-district residents $147; out-of-state residents $221.
Additional info: Tuition/fee waivers available for minority students.

FINANCIAL AID PICTURE
Students with need: Need-based aid available for full-time and part-time students. Work study available nights.
Students without need: No-need awards available for academics, athletics, minority status, state/district residency.

FINANCIAL AID PROCEDURES
Forms required: FAFSA, institutional form.
Dates and Deadlines: Priority date 5/1; no closing date. Applicants notified on a rolling basis starting 4/15; must reply within 2 week(s) of notification.

CONTACT
Lee Bursi, Associate Vice President, Financial Aid
5250 Shepherd Road, Springfield, IL 62794-9256
(217) 786-2237

Loyola University Chicago
Chicago, Illinois
www.luc.edu Federal Code: 001710

4-year private university in very large city, affiliated with Roman Catholic Church.
Enrollment: 9,586 undergrads, 5% part-time. 2,031 full-time freshmen.
Selectivity: Admits 50 to 75% of applicants.

BASIC COSTS (2008-2009)
Tuition and fees: $29,486.
Per-credit charge: $580.
Room and board: $10,490.

FINANCIAL AID PICTURE (2007-2008)
Students with need: Out of 1,748 full-time freshmen who applied for aid, 1,475 were judged to have need. Of these, 1,470 received aid, and 174 had their full need met. Average financial aid package met 83% of need; average scholarship/grant was $15,514; average loan was $3,849. For part-time students, average financial aid package was $12,801.
Students without need: 405 full-time freshmen who did not demonstrate need for aid received scholarships/grants; average award was $7,089. No-need awards available for academics, athletics, leadership, music/drama, religious affiliation.
Scholarships offered: 15 full-time freshmen received athletic scholarships; average amount $19,435.
Cumulative student debt: 69% of graduating class had student loans; average debt was $26,874.

FINANCIAL AID PROCEDURES
Forms required: FAFSA.

Dates and Deadlines: Priority date 3/1; no closing date. Applicants notified on a rolling basis starting 2/15; must reply within 3 week(s) of notification.
Transfers: FAFSA must be filed by July 1 to receive Illinois map grant.

CONTACT

Eric Weems, Director, Student Financial Assistance
820 North Michigan Avenue, Chicago, IL 60611-9810
(773) 508-3155

MacMurray College

Jacksonville, Illinois
www.mac.edu Federal Code: 001717

4-year private liberal arts college in large town, affiliated with United Methodist Church.
Enrollment: 581 undergrads.
Selectivity: Admits less than 50% of applicants.

BASIC COSTS (2008-2009)

Tuition and fees: $17,450.
Per-credit charge: $565.
Room and board: $6,995.

FINANCIAL AID PICTURE (2008-2009)

Students with need: 93% of average financial aid package awarded as scholarships/grants, 7% awarded as loans/jobs. Need-based aid available for part-time students. Work study available nights, weekends, and for part-time students.
Students without need: No-need awards available for academics, alumni affiliation, art, leadership, music/drama, religious affiliation.
Scholarships offered: Academic scholarships: $500-$1,4000; based on merit. Music performance and art competition scholarships available. Transfer scholarships: to $10,000; based on academic merit. Leadership scholarships: available based on committee selection.
Additional info: Merit scholarships for accepted, enrolled freshman based on academic record. Need-based program meets 100% of direct tuition charges after family contribution and financial aid.

FINANCIAL AID PROCEDURES

Forms required: FAFSA.
Dates and Deadlines: Priority date 5/1; no closing date. Applicants notified on a rolling basis starting 2/1; must reply within 2 week(s) of notification.
Transfers: No deadline.

CONTACT

Charles Carothers, Director of Financial Aid
447 East College Avenue, Jacksonville, IL 62650-2590
(217) 479-7041

McHenry County College

Crystal Lake, Illinois
www.mchenry.edu Federal Code: 007691

2-year public community college in large town.
Enrollment: 5,374 undergrads.
Selectivity: Open admission; but selective for some programs.

BASIC COSTS (2008-2009)

Tuition and fees: $2,594; out-of-district residents $8,483; out-of-state residents $9,619.
Per-credit charge: $77; out-of-district residents $273; out-of-state residents $311.

FINANCIAL AID PICTURE (2007-2008)

Students with need: Need-based aid available for full-time and part-time students. Work study available nights, weekends, and for part-time students.
Students without need: No-need awards available for academics, athletics, leadership, music/drama, state/district residency.
Scholarships offered: President's Scholarship: full tuition for two years; based on talent in academic areas; students must complete portfolio and have 3.0 GPA. Founding Faculty Scholarship: full tuition for 2 years; based on GPA and essay.
Additional info: Students can apply throughout the award year for federal and state aid. Students with physical handicaps or learning disabilities may apply for special needs scholarship.

FINANCIAL AID PROCEDURES

Forms required: FAFSA, institutional form.
Dates and Deadlines: Priority date 6/1; no closing date. Applicants notified on a rolling basis starting 5/1.

CONTACT

Marianne Devenny, Director, Office of Financial Aid and Records
8900 U.S. Highway 14, Crystal Lake, IL 60012-2761
(815) 455-8761

McKendree University

Lebanon, Illinois
www.mckendree.edu Federal Code: 001722

4-year private university and liberal arts college in small town, affiliated with United Methodist Church.
Enrollment: 2,222 undergrads, 27% part-time. 319 full-time freshmen.
Selectivity: Admits 50 to 75% of applicants.

BASIC COSTS (2008-2009)

Tuition and fees: $21,270.
Per-credit charge: $690.
Room and board: $8,220.

FINANCIAL AID PICTURE (2008-2009)

Students with need: Out of 295 full-time freshmen who applied for aid, 269 were judged to have need. Of these, 267 received aid, and 73 had their full need met. Average financial aid package met 87% of need; average scholarship/grant was $16,620; average loan was $3,502. For part-time students, average financial aid package was $5,823.
Students without need: 44 full-time freshmen who did not demonstrate need for aid received scholarships/grants; average award was $8,189. No-need awards available for academics, alumni affiliation, art, athletics, leadership, minority status, music/drama, religious affiliation.
Scholarships offered: ***Merit:*** Academic Scholarships; $4,000 to $17,000; 25 ACT or 3.4 GPA. ***Athletic:*** 40 full-time freshmen received athletic scholarships; average amount $7,408.
Cumulative student debt: 72% of graduating class had student loans; average debt was $18,291.

FINANCIAL AID PROCEDURES

Forms required: FAFSA.
Dates and Deadlines: Priority date 5/31; no closing date. Applicants notified on a rolling basis starting 3/1; must reply within 4 week(s) of notification.
Transfers: No deadline. Applicants notified on a rolling basis starting 3/1.

CONTACT

Chris Hall, Vice President for Admission and Financial Aid
701 College Road, Lebanon, IL 62254
(618) 537-6829

Midstate College
Peoria, Illinois
www.midstate.edu Federal Code: 004568

4-year for-profit business college in small city.
Enrollment: 584 undergrads, 54% part-time. 15 full-time freshmen.
Selectivity: Admits over 75% of applicants.

BASIC COSTS (2009-2010)
Tuition and fees: $12,506.
Per-credit charge: $347.
Additional info: Fees vary according to program.

FINANCIAL AID PICTURE (2008-2009)
Students with need: Work study available nights, weekends, and for part-time students.

FINANCIAL AID PROCEDURES
Forms required: FAFSA, institutional form.
Dates and Deadlines: No deadline. Applicants notified on a rolling basis; must reply within 4 week(s) of notification.

CONTACT
Mike Bunch, Business Manager
411 West Northmoor Road, Peoria, IL 61614-3558
(800) 251-4299

Millikin University
Decatur, Illinois
www.millikin.edu Federal Code: 001724

4-year private university in small city, affiliated with Presbyterian Church (USA).
Enrollment: 2,238 undergrads, 5% part-time. 475 full-time freshmen.
Selectivity: Admits over 75% of applicants.

BASIC COSTS (2009-2010)
Tuition and fees: $26,445.
Per-credit charge: $860.
Room and board: $7,866.

FINANCIAL AID PICTURE (2007-2008)
Students with need: Out of 447 full-time freshmen who applied for aid, 378 were judged to have need. Of these, 378 received aid, and 191 had their full need met. Average financial aid package met 92% of need; average scholarship/grant was $7,714; average loan was $3,976. For part-time students, average financial aid package was $7,114.
Students without need: 69 full-time freshmen who did not demonstrate need for aid received scholarships/grants; average award was $8,510. No-need awards available for academics, alumni affiliation, art, leadership, minority status, music/drama.
Scholarships offered: Millikin University Merit Scholarships: $5,000 to $13,000; guaranteed for four years of attendance.
Cumulative student debt: 82% of graduating class had student loans; average debt was $27,375.

FINANCIAL AID PROCEDURES
Forms required: FAFSA.
Dates and Deadlines: Priority date 3/15; no closing date. Applicants notified on a rolling basis starting 3/15; must reply by 5/1 or within 4 week(s) of notification.
Transfers: Must reply by 5/1 or within 4 week(s) of notification.

CONTACT
Cheryl Howerton, Director of Financial Aid
1184 West Main Street, Decatur, IL 62522-2084
(217) 424-6317

Monmouth College
Monmouth, Illinois
www.monm.edu Federal Code: 001725

4-year private liberal arts college in large town, affiliated with Presbyterian Church (USA).
Enrollment: 1,318 undergrads. 383 full-time freshmen.
Selectivity: Admits 50 to 75% of applicants.

BASIC COSTS (2009-2010)
Tuition and fees: $25,400.
Per-credit charge: $800.
Room and board: $7,300.

FINANCIAL AID PICTURE (2008-2009)
Students with need: Out of 372 full-time freshmen who applied for aid, 310 were judged to have need. Of these, 310 received aid, and 80 had their full need met. Average financial aid package met 91% of need; average scholarship/grant was $16,780; average loan was $3,775. For part-time students, average financial aid package was $10,328.
Students without need: 72 full-time freshmen who did not demonstrate need for aid received scholarships/grants; average award was $9,822. No-need awards available for academics, art, music/drama, ROTC.
Cumulative student debt: 80% of graduating class had student loans; average debt was $23,726.

FINANCIAL AID PROCEDURES
Forms required: FAFSA.
Dates and Deadlines: Priority date 3/1; no closing date. Applicants notified on a rolling basis starting 3/1.

CONTACT
Jayne Whiteside, Director of Financial Aid
700 East Broadway, Monmouth, IL 61462-1998
(309) 457-2129

Moody Bible Institute
Chicago, Illinois
www.moody.edu Federal Code: 001727

4-year private Bible college in very large city, affiliated with interdenominational tradition.
Enrollment: 1,821 full-time undergrads.

BASIC COSTS (2008-2009)
Additional info: Undergraduate students in the BA and BMus programs on main campus are not charged tuition. Undergraduate students taking courses through distance learning programs (ABS, BSBS) and in BSMAT (Bachelor of Science in Missionary Aviation) program pay tuition of $220 per credit hour. Students pay required fees of $1,569 and room/board of $8,040 per year.

FINANCIAL AID PICTURE
Students with need: Need-based aid available for full-time students.
Students without need: This college awards aid only to students with need.
Additional info: Aid available to upperclassmen is based on private and not federal/state sources.

FINANCIAL AID PROCEDURES
Dates and Deadlines: No deadline.
Transfers: Students should complete two semesters of study in residence before applying for aid.

CONTACT
Esther Kim, Financial Aid Coordinator
820 North La Salle Boulevard, Chicago, IL 60610
(312) 329-4178

Moraine Valley Community College

Palos Hills, Illinois
www.morainevalley.edu Federal Code: 007692

2-year public community college in large town.
Enrollment: 11,133 undergrads, 46% part-time. 1,313 full-time freshmen.
Selectivity: Open admission; but selective for some programs.

BASIC COSTS (2009-2010)

Tuition and fees: $2,466; out-of-district residents $6,816; out-of-state residents $8,016.
Per-credit charge: $82; out-of-district residents $227; out-of-state residents $267.

FINANCIAL AID PICTURE (2007-2008)

Students with need: 88% of average financial aid package awarded as scholarships/grants, 12% awarded as loans/jobs. Need-based aid available for part-time students. Work study available nights.
Students without need: No-need awards available for academics, athletics, leadership.

FINANCIAL AID PROCEDURES

Forms required: FAFSA, institutional form.
Dates and Deadlines: Priority date 5/1; no closing date. Applicants notified on a rolling basis starting 3/1; must reply within 4 week(s) of notification.

CONTACT

Laurie Anema, Director of Financial Aid
9000 West College Parkway, Palos Hills, IL 60465-0937
(708) 974-5726

Morrison Institute of Technology

Morrison, Illinois
www.morrison.tec.il.us Federal Code: 008880

2-year private junior and technical college in small town.
Enrollment: 132 undergrads.
Selectivity: Open admission.

BASIC COSTS (2008-2009)

Tuition and fees: $13,360.
Per-credit charge: $545.
Room only: $2,700.

FINANCIAL AID PICTURE (2007-2008)

Students with need: Need-based aid available for part-time students. Work study available nights, weekends, and for part-time students.
Students without need: No-need awards available for academics.

FINANCIAL AID PROCEDURES

Forms required: FAFSA, institutional form.
Dates and Deadlines: No deadline. Applicants notified on a rolling basis; must reply within 2 week(s) of notification.

CONTACT

Julie Damhoff, Financial Aid Officer
701 Portland Avenue, Morrison, IL 61270-2959
(815) 772-7218

Morton College

Cicero, Illinois
www.morton.edu Federal Code: 001728

2-year public community college in small city.
Enrollment: 2,271 undergrads, 58% part-time. 268 full-time freshmen.
Selectivity: Open admission; but selective for some programs and for out-of-state students.

BASIC COSTS (2008-2009)

Tuition and fees: $2,580; out-of-district residents $6,676; out-of-state residents $8,724.
Per-credit charge: $64; out-of-district residents $192; out-of-state residents $256.

FINANCIAL AID PICTURE (2007-2008)

Students with need: Need-based aid available for full-time and part-time students. Work study available nights, weekends, and for part-time students.

FINANCIAL AID PROCEDURES

Forms required: FAFSA, institutional form.
Dates and Deadlines: Priority date 6/1; no closing date. Applicants notified on a rolling basis starting 8/3.

CONTACT

Barbara Moore, Coordinator of Financial Aid
3801 South Central Avenue, Cicero, IL 60804-4398
(708) 656-8000 ext. 428

North Central College

Naperville, Illinois
www.northcentralcollege.edu Federal Code: 001734

4-year private liberal arts college in small city, affiliated with United Methodist Church.
Enrollment: 2,302 undergrads, 6% part-time. 528 full-time freshmen.
Selectivity: Admits 50 to 75% of applicants.

BASIC COSTS (2009-2010)

Tuition and fees: $26,916.
Per-credit charge: $645.
Room and board: $8,379.

FINANCIAL AID PICTURE (2008-2009)

Students with need: Out of 462 full-time freshmen who applied for aid, 398 were judged to have need. Of these, 395 received aid, and 116 had their full need met. Average financial aid package met 82% of need; average scholarship/grant was $15,907; average loan was $3,306. For part-time students, average financial aid package was $10,639.
Students without need: 115 full-time freshmen who did not demonstrate need for aid received scholarships/grants; average award was $10,873. No-need awards available for academics, art, leadership, minority status, music/drama, religious affiliation, ROTC, state/district residency.
Scholarships offered: Numerous merit and talent scholarship opportunities available.
Cumulative student debt: 76% of graduating class had student loans; average debt was $26,395.

FINANCIAL AID PROCEDURES

Forms required: FAFSA, institutional form.
Dates and Deadlines: No deadline. Applicants notified on a rolling basis starting 3/1; must reply within 4 week(s) of notification.

CONTACT

Marty Rossman, Director of Financial Aid
PO Box 3063, Naperville, IL 60566-7063
(630) 637-5600

North Park University
Chicago, Illinois
www.northpark.edu Federal Code: 001735

4-year private university and liberal arts college in very large city, affiliated with Evangelical Covenant Church.
Enrollment: 2,188 undergrads, 17% part-time. 410 full-time freshmen.
Selectivity: Admits 50 to 75% of applicants.

BASIC COSTS (2009-2010)
Tuition and fees: $18,800.
Per-credit charge: $750.
Room and board: $8,140.

FINANCIAL AID PICTURE (2007-2008)
Students with need: Out of 361 full-time freshmen who applied for aid, 289 were judged to have need. Of these, 289 received aid, and 37 had their full need met. Average financial aid package met 69% of need; average scholarship/grant was $4,793; average loan was $3,700.
Students without need: 64 full-time freshmen who did not demonstrate need for aid received scholarships/grants; average award was $2,700. No-need awards available for academics, art, music/drama, religious affiliation.
Cumulative student debt: 79% of graduating class had student loans; average debt was $21,140.

FINANCIAL AID PROCEDURES
Forms required: FAFSA.
Dates and Deadlines: Priority date 5/1; closing date 8/1. Applicants notified on a rolling basis starting 10/1; must reply by 5/1 or within 4 week(s) of notification.
Transfers: Applicants notified on a rolling basis starting 10/1; must reply within 3 week(s) of notification.

CONTACT
Lucy Shaker, Director of Financial Aid
3225 West Foster Avenue Box 19, Chicago, IL 60625-4895
(773) 244-5506

Northeastern Illinois University
Chicago, Illinois
www.neiu.edu Federal Code: 001693

4-year public university in very large city.
Enrollment: 8,787 undergrads, 44% part-time. 952 full-time freshmen.
Selectivity: Admits 50 to 75% of applicants.

BASIC COSTS (2008-2009)
Tuition and fees: $8,016; out-of-state residents $14,616.
Per-credit charge: $220; out-of-state residents $440.

FINANCIAL AID PICTURE (2008-2009)
Students with need: Need-based aid available for full-time and part-time students.
Students without need: No-need awards available for academics, art, leadership, music/drama.

FINANCIAL AID PROCEDURES
Forms required: FAFSA, institutional form.
Dates and Deadlines: Priority date 2/28; no closing date. Applicants notified on a rolling basis starting 4/1; must reply within 3 week(s) of notification.

CONTACT
J. Jennings, Director of Financial Aid
5500 North St. Louis Avenue, Chicago, IL 60625
(773) 442-5000

Northern Illinois University
DeKalb, Illinois
www.niu.edu Federal Code: 001737

4-year public university in large town.
Enrollment: 18,398 undergrads, 10% part-time. 2,995 full-time freshmen.
Selectivity: Admits 50 to 75% of applicants.

BASIC COSTS (2008-2009)
Tuition and fees: $8,524; out-of-state residents $15,244.
Per-credit charge: $249; out-of-state residents $498.
Room and board: $8,970.
Additional info: Tuition/fee waivers available for minority students.

FINANCIAL AID PICTURE (2007-2008)
Students with need: Out of 2,671 full-time freshmen who applied for aid, 2,128 were judged to have need. Of these, 1,928 received aid. For part-time students, average financial aid package was $7,700.
Students without need: 57 full-time freshmen who did not demonstrate need for aid received scholarships/grants; average award was $1,139. No-need awards available for academics, athletics, ROTC.
Scholarships offered: 67 full-time freshmen received athletic scholarships; average amount $15,303.

FINANCIAL AID PROCEDURES
Forms required: FAFSA, institutional form.
Dates and Deadlines: Priority date 3/1; no closing date. Applicants notified on a rolling basis starting 4/15.

CONTACT
Kathleen Brunson, Director of Student Financial Aid DeKalb, IL 60115-2854
(815) 753-1395

Northwestern Business College
Chicago, Illinois
www.northwesternbc.edu Federal Code: 012362

2-year for-profit technical college in very large city.
Enrollment: 1,372 undergrads, 55% part-time. 275 full-time freshmen.
Selectivity: Admits over 75% of applicants.

BASIC COSTS (2008-2009)
Tuition and fees: $17,890.
Per-credit charge: $390.
Additional info: Tuition may be higher for some classes.

FINANCIAL AID PICTURE (2008-2009)
Students with need: Need-based aid available for full-time and part-time students. Work study available nights.
Students without need: No-need awards available for academics.
Scholarships offered: President's Scholarship: $400 per quarter, up to $2,400. Vice-Presidential Scholarship: $300 per quarter, up to $1,800. Early bird scholarships: $750 first year, $1,500 sophomore year; must enroll by May 31 for fall quarter, must be full time.
Additional info: State grant programs for Illinois residents and alternative loans offered.

FINANCIAL AID PROCEDURES
Forms required: FAFSA, institutional form.
Dates and Deadlines: Priority date 6/30; no closing date. Applicants notified on a rolling basis starting 8/15; must reply within 4 week(s) of notification.

CONTACT
Frank McClinton, Director of Financial Assistance
4839 North Milwaukee Avenue, Chicago, IL 60630
(708) 237-5050

Northwestern University

Evanston, Illinois — Federal Code: 001739
www.northwestern.edu — CSS Code: 1565

4-year private university in small city.
Enrollment: 8,364 undergrads, 1% part-time. 2,078 full-time freshmen.
Selectivity: Admits less than 50% of applicants.

BASIC COSTS (2008-2009)
Tuition and fees: $37,125.
Room and board: $11,295.

FINANCIAL AID PICTURE (2008-2009)
Students with need: Out of 1,095 full-time freshmen who applied for aid, 841 were judged to have need. Of these, 841 received aid, and 841 had their full need met. Average financial aid package met 100% of need; average scholarship/grant was $26,100; average loan was $3,651.
Students without need: 105 full-time freshmen who did not demonstrate need for aid received scholarships/grants; average award was $2,634. No-need awards available for academics, athletics, music/drama, ROTC.
Scholarships offered: 102 full-time freshmen received athletic scholarships; average amount $30,783.
Cumulative student debt: 49% of graduating class had student loans; average debt was $19,808.

FINANCIAL AID PROCEDURES
Forms required: FAFSA, CSS PROFILE.
Dates and Deadlines: Closing date 2/15. Applicants notified by 4/15; must reply by 5/1 or within 2 week(s) of notification.
Transfers: Closing date 6/1. Transfer student aid limited for first year.

CONTACT
Carolyn Lindley, Director of University Financial Aid
1801 Hinman Avenue, Evanston, IL 60204-3060
(847) 491-7400

Oakton Community College

Des Plaines, Illinois
www.oakton.edu — Federal Code: 009896

2-year public community college in small city.
Enrollment: 5,529 undergrads.
Selectivity: Open admission; but selective for some programs.

BASIC COSTS (2008-2009)
Tuition and fees: $2,678; out-of-district residents $8,002; out-of-state residents $9,677.
Per-credit charge: $84; out-of-district residents $261; out-of-state residents $317.

FINANCIAL AID PICTURE (2007-2008)
Students with need: 93% of average financial aid package awarded as scholarships/grants, 7% awarded as loans/jobs. Need-based aid available for part-time students. Work study available nights, weekends, and for part-time students.
Students without need: No-need awards available for academics, art, athletics, leadership, minority status, music/drama, state/district residency.
Scholarships offered: Oakton Merit Scholarship Program; tuition and related fees, first-time, in-district, freshmen in top 10% of high school class, U.S. citizens or permanent residents only.

FINANCIAL AID PROCEDURES
Forms required: FAFSA, institutional form.
Dates and Deadlines: Priority date 3/1; no closing date. Applicants notified on a rolling basis starting 3/1; must reply within 2 week(s) of notification.
Transfers: Applicants notified on a rolling basis starting 5/1.

CONTACT
Cheryl Warmann, Director of Financial Aid
1600 East Golf Road, Des Plaines, IL 60016
(847) 635-1708

Olivet Nazarene University

Bourbonnais, Illinois
www.olivet.edu — Federal Code: 001741

4-year private university and liberal arts college in small city, affiliated with Church of the Nazarene.
Enrollment: 3,028 undergrads, 19% part-time. 688 full-time freshmen.
Selectivity: Admits over 75% of applicants.

BASIC COSTS (2009-2010)
Tuition and fees: $23,590.
Per-credit charge: $948.
Room and board: $6,400.

FINANCIAL AID PICTURE (2007-2008)
Students with need: Out of 688 full-time freshmen who applied for aid, 609 were judged to have need. Of these, 530 received aid, and 118 had their full need met. Average financial aid package met 94% of need; average scholarship/grant was $10,896; average loan was $3,662. Need-based aid available for part-time students.
Students without need: 158 full-time freshmen who did not demonstrate need for aid received scholarships/grants; average award was $8,188. No-need awards available for academics, art, athletics, leadership, music/drama, religious affiliation, ROTC, state/district residency.
Scholarships offered: 82 full-time freshmen received athletic scholarships; average amount $4,882.
Cumulative student debt: 72% of graduating class had student loans; average debt was $24,960.

FINANCIAL AID PROCEDURES
Forms required: FAFSA, institutional form.
Dates and Deadlines: Priority date 3/1; no closing date. Applicants notified on a rolling basis starting 1/15; must reply within 2 week(s) of notification.
Transfers: No deadline. Applicants notified on a rolling basis; must reply within 2 week(s) of notification.

CONTACT
Greg Bruner, Director of Financial Aid
One University Avenue, Bourbonnais, IL 60914
(815) 939-5249

Parkland College

Champaign, Illinois
www.parkland.edu — Federal Code: 007118

2-year public community college in small city.
Enrollment: 6,501 undergrads.
Selectivity: Open admission; but selective for some programs.

BASIC COSTS (2008-2009)
Tuition and fees: $2,610; out-of-district residents $6,900; out-of-state residents $10,740.
Per-credit charge: $87; out-of-district residents $230; out-of-state residents $358.
Additional info: For Internet classes, in-district students pay $87, all others pay $127 per credit hour.

FINANCIAL AID PICTURE (2007-2008)
Students with need: Need-based aid available for full-time students. Work study available nights.

Students without need: No-need awards available for academics, art, athletics, leadership, minority status, music/drama, state/district residency.

FINANCIAL AID PROCEDURES

Forms required: FAFSA, institutional form.
Dates and Deadlines: Priority date 3/1; no closing date. Applicants notified on a rolling basis starting 6/1; must reply within 2 week(s) of notification.

CONTACT

Tom Wendt, Director of Financial Aid
2400 West Bradley Avenue, Champaign, IL 61821-1899
(217) 351-2276

Prairie State College

Chicago Heights, Illinois
www.prairiestate.edu Federal Code: 001640

2-year public community college in large town.
Enrollment: 4,709 undergrads.
Selectivity: Open admission; but selective for some programs.

BASIC COSTS (2008-2009)

Tuition and fees: $2,620; out-of-district residents $7,340; out-of-state residents $9,980.
Per-credit charge: $87; out-of-district residents $244; out-of-state residents $332.

FINANCIAL AID PICTURE

Students with need: Need-based aid available for full-time and part-time students. Work study available nights, weekends, and for part-time students.

FINANCIAL AID PROCEDURES

Forms required: FAFSA, institutional form.
Dates and Deadlines: Priority date 7/1; no closing date. Applicants notified on a rolling basis; must reply within 2 week(s) of notification.

CONTACT

Alice Garcia, Director of Financial Aid
202 South Halsted Street, Chicago Heights, IL 60411
(708) 709-3523

Principia College

Elsah, Illinois Federal Code: 001744
www.prin.edu CSS Code: 1630

4-year private liberal arts college in rural community, affiliated with First Church of Christ, Scientist (Christian Science).
Enrollment: 514 undergrads.
Selectivity: Admits over 75% of applicants.

BASIC COSTS (2009-2010)

Tuition and fees: $22,950.
Room and board: $8,730.

FINANCIAL AID PICTURE (2008-2009)

Students with need: Average financial aid package met 100% of need. Need-based aid available for part-time students.
Students without need: No-need awards available for academics, alumni affiliation, leadership.
Scholarships offered: Trustee Scholarship: full tuition; Chairman's Scholarship: 3/4 tuition; Presidential Scholarship: 1/2 tuition; Dean's Scholarship: 1/4 tuition; Arthur Schulz, Jr. Alumni Scholarship: $4,500; 4-year scholarships based on high school GPA and test scores. Dean's and Arthur Schulz Scholarships available for transfer students who meet the above criteria with a minimum 3.5 GPA. Children and grandchildren of alumni eligible for 4-year scholarships based on high school or transfer GPA. Whole Man Character Scholarships range from 1/4 to full tuition.

Additional info: Need-based tuition reduction work plan combines job with grant.

FINANCIAL AID PROCEDURES

Forms required: CSS PROFILE, institutional form.
Dates and Deadlines: Closing date 3/1. Applicants notified by 4/1.
Transfers: Priority date 3/1.

CONTACT

Tamara Gavaletz, Director of Financial Aid
One Maybeck Place, Elsah, IL 62028-9799
(800) 277-4648 ext. 2813

Quincy University

Quincy, Illinois
www.quincy.edu Federal Code: 001745

4-year private university and liberal arts college in large town, affiliated with Roman Catholic Church.
Enrollment: 1,076 undergrads, 5% part-time. 245 full-time freshmen.
Selectivity: Admits over 75% of applicants.

BASIC COSTS (2008-2009)

Tuition and fees: $20,790.
Per-credit charge: $480.
Room and board: $7,900.

FINANCIAL AID PICTURE (2008-2009)

Students with need: Out of 238 full-time freshmen who applied for aid, 203 were judged to have need. Of these, 203 received aid, and 50 had their full need met. Average financial aid package met 81% of need; average scholarship/grant was $14,532; average loan was $5,735. For part-time students, average financial aid package was $6,843.
Students without need: 33 full-time freshmen who did not demonstrate need for aid received scholarships/grants; average award was $1,007. No-need awards available for academics, alumni affiliation, art, athletics, music/drama.
Scholarships offered: ***Merit:*** Academic scholarships; $5,000-$11,000 per year; based on ACT and high school GPA; unlimited number awarded. ***Athletic:*** 12 full-time freshmen received athletic scholarships; average amount $6,995.
Cumulative student debt: 88% of graduating class had student loans; average debt was $22,376.

FINANCIAL AID PROCEDURES

Forms required: FAFSA.
Dates and Deadlines: Priority date 3/15; no closing date. Applicants notified on a rolling basis starting 2/15; must reply by 5/1 or within 2 week(s) of notification.

CONTACT

Kevin Brown, Director of Financial Aid
1800 College Avenue, Quincy, IL 62301-2699
(217) 228-5260

Rend Lake College

Ina, Illinois
www.rlc.edu Federal Code: 007119

2-year public community college in rural community.
Enrollment: 4,821 undergrads.
Selectivity: Open admission; but selective for some programs.

BASIC COSTS (2008-2009)

Tuition and fees: $2,220; out-of-district residents $3,375; out-of-state residents $4,500.

Per-credit charge: $74; out-of-district residents $113; out-of-state residents $150.

FINANCIAL AID PICTURE (2007-2008)

Students with need: 73% of average financial aid package awarded as scholarships/grants, 27% awarded as loans/jobs. Need-based aid available for part-time students.

Students without need: No-need awards available for academics, art, athletics, leadership, music/drama, state/district residency.

FINANCIAL AID PROCEDURES

Forms required: FAFSA.

Dates and Deadlines: No deadline. Applicants notified on a rolling basis starting 3/15; must reply within 4 week(s) of notification.

CONTACT

Douglas Carlson, Director of Financial Aid
468 North Ken Gray Parkway, Ina, IL 62846
(618) 437-5321 ext. 1385

Richland Community College

Decatur, Illinois
www.richland.edu Federal Code: 010879

2-year public community college in small city.

Enrollment: 2,131 undergrads, 60% part-time. 267 full-time freshmen.

Selectivity: Open admission; but selective for some programs.

BASIC COSTS (2008-2009)

Tuition and fees: $2,230; out-of-district residents $11,304; out-of-state residents $14,768.

Per-credit charge: $70; out-of-district residents $372; out-of-state residents $487.

FINANCIAL AID PICTURE (2007-2008)

Students with need: Out of 152 full-time freshmen who applied for aid, 85 were judged to have need. Of these, 73 received aid, and 1 had their full need met. Average financial aid package met 48% of need; average scholarship/grant was $3,578; average loan was $2,687. For part-time students, average financial aid package was $3,328.

Students without need: 6 full-time freshmen who did not demonstrate need for aid received scholarships/grants; average award was $602. No-need awards available for academics.

FINANCIAL AID PROCEDURES

Forms required: FAFSA.

Dates and Deadlines: Closing date 6/30. Applicants notified on a rolling basis starting 3/20.

Transfers: No deadline. Applicants notified on a rolling basis.

CONTACT

Carmin Ross, Director of Financial Aid
One College Park, Decatur, IL 62521
(217) 875-7200 ext. 271

Robert Morris College: Chicago

Chicago, Illinois
www.robertmorris.edu Federal Code: 001746

4-year private university in very large city.

Enrollment: 4,223 undergrads, 6% part-time. 1,437 full-time freshmen.

Selectivity: Admits over 75% of applicants.

BASIC COSTS (2009-2010)

Tuition and fees: $19,200.

Per-credit charge: $533.

Room and board: $9,900.

FINANCIAL AID PICTURE (2007-2008)

Students with need: Out of 1,342 full-time freshmen who applied for aid, 1,307 were judged to have need. Of these, 1,269 received aid, and 26 had their full need met. Average financial aid package met 42% of need; average scholarship/grant was $8,583; average loan was $4,890. For part-time students, average financial aid package was $9,183.

Students without need: 21 full-time freshmen who did not demonstrate need for aid received scholarships/grants; average award was $683. No-need awards available for academics, art, athletics, state/district residency.

Scholarships offered: 18 full-time freshmen received athletic scholarships; average amount $7,420.

Cumulative student debt: 92% of graduating class had student loans; average debt was $24,601.

FINANCIAL AID PROCEDURES

Forms required: FAFSA.

Dates and Deadlines: No deadline. Applicants notified on a rolling basis.

Transfers: No deadline. Applicants notified on a rolling basis.

CONTACT

Leigh Taylor, Vice President of Financial Aid
401South State Street, Chicago, IL 60605
(312) 935-4075

Rock Valley College

Rockford, Illinois
www.rockvalleycollege.edu

2-year public community college in small city.

Enrollment: 5,871 undergrads.

Selectivity: Open admission; but selective for some programs.

BASIC COSTS (2008-2009)

Tuition and fees: $2,220; out-of-district residents $8,670; out-of-state residents $13,560.

Per-credit charge: $66; out-of-district residents $281; out-of-state residents $444.

Additional info: Costs vary by program.

FINANCIAL AID PICTURE (2007-2008)

Students with need: 70% of average financial aid package awarded as scholarships/grants, 30% awarded as loans/jobs. Need-based aid available for part-time students. Work study available nights.

Students without need: No-need awards available for academics, ROTC.

FINANCIAL AID PROCEDURES

Forms required: FAFSA.

Dates and Deadlines: Closing date 5/1. Applicants notified on a rolling basis starting 4/1; must reply within 2 week(s) of notification.

CONTACT

Cyndi Stonesifer, Director of Financial Aid
3301 North Mulford Road, Rockford, IL 61114-5699
(815) 921-4150

Rockford Business College

Rockford, Illinois
www.rockfordcareercollege.edu Federal Code: 008545

2-year for-profit career college in small city.

Enrollment: 560 undergrads.

Selectivity: Open admission.

BASIC COSTS (2009-2010)

Tuition and fees: $7,350.

Per-credit charge: $200.

FINANCIAL AID PICTURE

Students with need: Need-based aid available for full-time and part-time students. Work study available nights.

Students without need: This college awards aid only to students with need.

FINANCIAL AID PROCEDURES

Forms required: FAFSA.

Dates and Deadlines: No deadline. Applicants notified on a rolling basis.

CONTACT

Garry Kirk, Director of Financial Aid
1130 South Alpine Road, Rockford, IL 61108
(815) 967-7311

Rockford College

Rockford, Illinois
www.rockford.edu Federal Code: 001748

4-year private liberal arts college in small city.

Enrollment: 861 undergrads, 13% part-time. 111 full-time freshmen.

Selectivity: Admits 50 to 75% of applicants.

BASIC COSTS (2009-2010)

Tuition and fees: $24,250.

Per-credit charge: $650.

Room and board: $6,750.

FINANCIAL AID PICTURE (2007-2008)

Students with need: Out of 104 full-time freshmen who applied for aid, 94 were judged to have need. Of these, 94 received aid, and 12 had their full need met. Average financial aid package met 73% of need; average scholarship/grant was $14,972; average loan was $3,256. For part-time students, average financial aid package was $10,944.

Students without need: 17 full-time freshmen who did not demonstrate need for aid received scholarships/grants; average award was $10,964. No-need awards available for academics, alumni affiliation, leadership, minority status, music/drama, state/district residency.

Cumulative student debt: 92% of graduating class had student loans; average debt was $25,148.

FINANCIAL AID PROCEDURES

Forms required: FAFSA.

Dates and Deadlines: Priority date 3/1; no closing date. Applicants notified on a rolling basis starting 3/1; must reply within 4 week(s) of notification.

CONTACT

Todd Free, Assistant Vice President of Student Administrative Services
5050 East State Street, Rockford, IL 61108-2393
(815) 226-3383

Roosevelt University

Chicago, Illinois
www.roosevelt.edu Federal Code: 001749

4-year private university in very large city.

Enrollment: 4,264 undergrads, 36% part-time. 482 full-time freshmen.

Selectivity: Admits over 75% of applicants.

BASIC COSTS (2009-2010)

Tuition and fees: $21,000.

Per-credit charge: $689.

Room and board: $11,100.

Additional info: Tuition for Chicago College of the Performing Arts is $28,000 per year.

FINANCIAL AID PICTURE (2007-2008)

Students with need: Need-based aid available for full-time students.

Students without need: No-need awards available for academics, alumni affiliation, leadership, minority status, music/drama, state/district residency.

Scholarships offered: Presidential Award: full tuition; based on GPA, SAT or ACT test scores, and community involvement; 5 awarded. Honors Program: $14,000-$42,000 over 4 years; 3.5 GPA, ACT of 23, and involvement; 20-30 awarded. Recognition Award: $1,500-$6,000 annually; for transfers and freshmen; 60 awarded. Music and Theater Scholarships: tuition and housing; for transfers and freshmen based on talent; approximately 90 awarded.

FINANCIAL AID PROCEDURES

Forms required: FAFSA, institutional form.

Dates and Deadlines: Priority date 4/1; no closing date. Applicants notified on a rolling basis starting 3/15; must reply within 2 week(s) of notification.

CONTACT

Walter O'Neill, Director of Financial Aid
430 South Michigan Avenue, Chicago, IL 60605-1394
(312) 341-3565

Rosalind Franklin University of Medicine and Science

North Chicago, Illinois
www.rosalindfranklin.edu Federal Code: 001659

Upper-division private university and health science college in large town.

Enrollment: 5 undergrads.

BASIC COSTS (2008-2009)

Tuition and fees: $15,200.

Additional info: Full-time tuition rate is for bachelor's degree program in Medical Technology.

FINANCIAL AID PICTURE

Students with need: Need-based aid available for full-time and part-time students.

Students without need: This college awards aid only to students with need.

Additional info: Financial aid application deadline 60 days prior to program start.

FINANCIAL AID PROCEDURES

Forms required: FAFSA, institutional form.

Dates and Deadlines: No deadline. Applicants notified on a rolling basis.

CONTACT

Maryann DeCaire, Executive Director Admissions, Records & Financial Aid
3333 Green Bay Road, North Chicago, IL 60064-3095
(847) 578-3217

Rush University

Chicago, Illinois
www.rushu.rush.edu Federal Code: 009800

Upper-division private health science and nursing college in very large city.

Enrollment: 166 undergrads.

BASIC COSTS (2008-2009)

Tuition and fees: $20,352.

Room only: $8,658.

Additional info: Tuition costs vary by program.

FINANCIAL AID PICTURE (2007-2008)

Students with need: Average financial aid package for all full-time undergraduates was $21,000. 28% awarded as scholarships/grants, 72% awarded as loans/jobs. Need-based aid available for part-time students. Work study available nights, weekends, and for part-time students.

FINANCIAL AID PROCEDURES

Forms required: FAFSA, institutional form.
Dates and Deadlines: No deadline.
Transfers: Priority date 5/1; no deadline. Applicants notified on a rolling basis starting 4/1; must reply within 3 week(s) of notification.

CONTACT

David Nelson, Director of Student Financial Aid
College Admissions, Chicago, IL 60612
(312) 942-6256

Saint Anthony College of Nursing

Rockford, Illinois
www.sacn.edu Federal Code: 009987

Upper-division private nursing college in small city, affiliated with Roman Catholic Church.
Enrollment: 151 undergrads.

BASIC COSTS (2009-2010)

Tuition and fees: $19,086.
Per-credit charge: $590.
Additional info: Required fees may vary.

FINANCIAL AID PICTURE (2008-2009)

Students with need: Need-based aid available for full-time and part-time students.
Students without need: No-need awards available for academics, leadership, state/district residency.

FINANCIAL AID PROCEDURES

Forms required: FAFSA.
Dates and Deadlines: Priority date 4/15; no closing date.
Transfers: No deadline. Applicants notified on a rolling basis starting 8/18.

CONTACT

Serrita Woods, Financial Aid Officer
5658 East State Street, Rockford, IL 61108-2468
(815) 395-5089

St. Francis Medical Center College of Nursing

Peoria, Illinois
www.sfmccon.edu Federal Code: 006240

Upper-division private nursing college in small city, affiliated with Roman Catholic Church.
Enrollment: 333 undergrads, 19% part-time.

BASIC COSTS (2009-2010)

Tuition and fees: $14,420.
Per-credit charge: $472.
Room only: $2,400.

FINANCIAL AID PICTURE (2007-2008)

Students with need: Average financial aid package for all full-time undergraduates was $11,615; for part-time $8,994. 48% awarded as scholarships/grants, 52% awarded as loans/jobs.
Students without need: No-need awards available for academics, alumni affiliation.
Additional info: OSF Saint Francis Medical Center Education student loan available to full-time students on a limited basis. Tuition waiver program for hospital employees available.

FINANCIAL AID PROCEDURES

Forms required: FAFSA, institutional form.
Dates and Deadlines: Priority date 6/1; no closing date. Applicants notified by 10/30; must reply within 4 week(s) of notification.
Transfers: No deadline. Applicants notified on a rolling basis starting 5/15; must reply within 2 week(s) of notification.

CONTACT

Laura Simmons, Coordinator Student Account & Business Services
511 NE Greenleaf Street, Peoria, IL 61603-3783
(309) 655-4119

St. Xavier University

Chicago, Illinois
www.sxu.edu Federal Code: 001768

4-year private university in very large city, affiliated with Roman Catholic Church.
Enrollment: 3,160 undergrads, 18% part-time. 510 full-time freshmen.
Selectivity: Admits 50 to 75% of applicants.

BASIC COSTS (2008-2009)

Tuition and fees: $22,926.
Per-credit charge: $753.
Room and board: $8,007.

FINANCIAL AID PICTURE (2007-2008)

Students with need: Out of 484 full-time freshmen who applied for aid, 449 were judged to have need. Of these, 449 received aid, and 103 had their full need met. Average financial aid package met 87% of need; average scholarship/grant was $6,977; average loan was $1,703. For part-time students, average financial aid package was $4,352.
Students without need: 51 full-time freshmen who did not demonstrate need for aid received scholarships/grants; average award was $3,711. No-need awards available for academics, athletics, music/drama.
Scholarships offered: 7 full-time freshmen received athletic scholarships; average amount $3,250.
Cumulative student debt: 74% of graduating class had student loans; average debt was $22,621.

FINANCIAL AID PROCEDURES

Forms required: FAFSA.
Dates and Deadlines: Priority date 3/1; no closing date. Applicants notified on a rolling basis starting 2/1; must reply by 5/1 or within 2 week(s) of notification.

CONTACT

Susan Swisher, Director of Financial Aid
3700 West 103rd Street, Chicago, IL 60655
(773) 298-3070

Sauk Valley Community College

Dixon, Illinois
www.svcc.edu Federal Code: 001752

2-year public community college in large town.
Enrollment: 1,905 undergrads.
Selectivity: Open admission; but selective for some programs.

BASIC COSTS (2008-2009)

Tuition and fees: $2,550; out-of-district residents $7,500; out-of-state residents $8,460.

Per-credit charge: $85; out-of-district residents $250; out-of-state residents $282.
Room only: $4,131.

FINANCIAL AID PICTURE (2007-2008)
Students with need: 73% of average financial aid package awarded as scholarships/grants, 27% awarded as loans/jobs. Need-based aid available for part-time students. Work study available nights, weekends, and for part-time students.
Students without need: No-need awards available for academics, art, athletics, leadership, minority status, ROTC, state/district residency.

FINANCIAL AID PROCEDURES
Forms required: FAFSA, state aid form, institutional form.
Dates and Deadlines: Priority date 3/1; no closing date. Applicants notified on a rolling basis starting 5/1; must reply within 4 week(s) of notification.
Transfers: Priority date 3/9; no deadline. Applicants notified on a rolling basis starting 3/1; must reply within 4 week(s) of notification.

CONTACT
Debra Stiefel, Coordinator of Financial Aid
173 Illinois Route 2, Dixon, IL 61021-9110
(815) 288-5511 ext. 339

School of the Art Institute of Chicago
Chicago, Illinois
www.saic.edu Federal Code: 001753

4-year private visual arts college in very large city.
Enrollment: 2,359 undergrads, 6% part-time. 453 full-time freshmen.
Selectivity: Admits over 75% of applicants.

BASIC COSTS (2009-2010)
Tuition and fees: $34,600.
Per-credit charge: $1,140.
Room only: $9,200.
Additional info: Students will be required to purchase a laptop through SAIC. Costs range from $2,000 to $2,200.

FINANCIAL AID PICTURE (2007-2008)
Students with need: Out of 299 full-time freshmen who applied for aid, 260 were judged to have need. Of these, 259 received aid, and 24 had their full need met. Average financial aid package met 76% of need; average scholarship/grant was $12,783; average loan was $3,668. For part-time students, average financial aid package was $16,529.
Students without need: 176 full-time freshmen who did not demonstrate need for aid received scholarships/grants; average award was $5,410. No-need awards available for academics, art.
Scholarships offered: Merit scholarships; $2,000 to full tuition; renewable.
Cumulative student debt: 63% of graduating class had student loans; average debt was $33,563.

FINANCIAL AID PROCEDURES
Forms required: FAFSA.
Dates and Deadlines: Priority date 3/15; no closing date. Applicants notified on a rolling basis starting 3/1.

CONTACT
Patrick James, Director of Financial Aid
36 South Wabash Avenue, Chicago, IL 60603
(312) 629-6600

Shawnee Community College
Ullin, Illinois
www.shawneecc.edu Federal Code: 007693

2-year public community college in rural community.
Enrollment: 1,954 undergrads.
Selectivity: Open admission; but selective for some programs.

BASIC COSTS (2008-2009)
Tuition and fees: $2,160; out-of-state residents $3,240.
Per-credit charge: $66; out-of-state residents $102.

FINANCIAL AID PICTURE
Students with need: Need-based aid available for full-time and part-time students.
Students without need: This college awards aid only to students with need.

FINANCIAL AID PROCEDURES
Forms required: FAFSA.
Dates and Deadlines: Priority date 9/1; no closing date. Applicants notified on a rolling basis; must reply within 2 week(s) of notification.

CONTACT
Tammy Capps, Director of Financial Aid
8364 Shawnee College Road, Ullin, IL 62992
(618) 634-3280 ext. 3280

Shimer College
Chicago, Illinois
www.shimer.edu Federal Code: 001756

4-year private liberal arts college in very large city.
Enrollment: 91 undergrads, 14% part-time. 25 full-time freshmen.
Selectivity: Admits over 75% of applicants.

BASIC COSTS (2009-2010)
Tuition and fees: $25,960.
Per-credit charge: $850.
Room and board: $10,500.
Additional info: Required fees include cost of books. Tuition/fee waivers available for adults.

FINANCIAL AID PICTURE (2008-2009)
Students with need: Out of 23 full-time freshmen who applied for aid, 18 were judged to have need. Of these, 18 received aid, and 3 had their full need met. Average financial aid package met 62% of need; average scholarship/grant was $9,000; average loan was $5,400. For part-time students, average financial aid package was $14,000.
Students without need: 5 full-time freshmen who did not demonstrate need for aid received scholarships/grants; average award was $3,100. No-need awards available for academics, alumni affiliation.
Scholarships offered: Michel de Montaigne Scholarship: half or full tuition; awarded to new students on the basis of merit in writing and discussion; 2 full and 2 half tuition scholarships awarded each year.
Cumulative student debt: 100% of graduating class had student loans; average debt was $35,000.

FINANCIAL AID PROCEDURES
Forms required: FAFSA, institutional form.
Dates and Deadlines: Priority date 3/1; no closing date. Applicants notified on a rolling basis starting 4/1; must reply by 5/1 or within 3 week(s) of notification.
Transfers: Closing date 8/1. Applicants notified on a rolling basis; must reply by 5/1 or within 3 week(s) of notification.

CONTACT

Janet Henthorn, Financial Aid Officer
3424 South State Street, Chicago, IL 60616
(312) 235-3507

South Suburban College of Cook County

South Holland, Illinois
www.southsuburbancollege.edu Federal Code: 001769

2-year public community college in large town.
Enrollment: 4,983 undergrads.
Selectivity: Open admission; but selective for some programs.

BASIC COSTS (2009-2010)

Tuition and fees: $3,112; out-of-district residents $8,452; out-of-state residents $10,102.
Per-credit charge: $90; out-of-district residents $268; out-of-state residents $323.
Additional info: Some students may qualify for a tuition rate of $105 per credit hour for special programs in other in-state community college districts, in Lake County Illinois and in Chicago. Tuition/fee waivers available for adults.

FINANCIAL AID PICTURE (2007-2008)

Students with need: 98% of average financial aid package awarded as scholarships/grants, 2% awarded as loans/jobs. Need-based aid available for part-time students. Work study available nights.
Students without need: No-need awards available for academics, art, athletics, music/drama, state/district residency.

FINANCIAL AID PROCEDURES

Forms required: FAFSA.
Dates and Deadlines: No deadline. Applicants notified on a rolling basis.
Transfers: No deadline. Applicants notified on a rolling basis.

CONTACT

John Semple, Director of Financial Aid
15800 South State Street, South Holland, IL 60473
(708) 596-2000 ext. 2321

Southeastern Illinois College

Harrisburg, Illinois
www.sic.edu Federal Code: 001757

2-year public community college in small town.
Enrollment: 848 full-time undergrads.
Selectivity: Open admission; but selective for some programs.

BASIC COSTS (2008-2009)

Tuition and fees: $2,220; out-of-district residents $3,300; out-of-state residents $3,660.
Per-credit charge: $72; out-of-district residents $108; out-of-state residents $120.

FINANCIAL AID PICTURE (2007-2008)

Students with need: Need-based aid available for full-time and part-time students.
Students without need: No-need awards available for academics, alumni affiliation, art, athletics, music/drama.

FINANCIAL AID PROCEDURES

Forms required: FAFSA.
Dates and Deadlines: No deadline. Applicants notified on a rolling basis starting 4/15; must reply within 2 week(s) of notification.

CONTACT

Joseph Schmitt, Director of Financial Aid
3575 College Road, Harrisburg, IL 62946
(618) 252-5400 ext. 2450

Southern Illinois University Carbondale

Carbondale, Illinois
www.siuc.edu Federal Code: 001758

4-year public university in large town.
Enrollment: 15,921 undergrads, 10% part-time. 2,660 full-time freshmen.
Selectivity: Admits 50 to 75% of applicants.

BASIC COSTS (2008-2009)

Tuition and fees: $9,813; out-of-state residents $20,276.
Per-credit charge: $233; out-of-state residents $581.
Room and board: $7,137.
Additional info: Tuition at time of enrollment locked for 4 years.

FINANCIAL AID PICTURE (2008-2009)

Students with need: Out of 2,214 full-time freshmen who applied for aid, 1,767 were judged to have need. Of these, 1,726 received aid, and 1,537 had their full need met. Average financial aid package met 96% of need; average scholarship/grant was $7,954; average loan was $3,895. For part-time students, average financial aid package was $9,556.
Students without need: 148 full-time freshmen who did not demonstrate need for aid received scholarships/grants; average award was $6,480. No-need awards available for academics, alumni affiliation, art, athletics, leadership, minority status, music/drama, ROTC.
Scholarships offered: 23 full-time freshmen received athletic scholarships; average amount $13,374.
Cumulative student debt: 45% of graduating class had student loans; average debt was $18,603.
Additional info: Need-based financial aid available to part-time students enrolled in minimum of 6 semester hours.

FINANCIAL AID PROCEDURES

Forms required: FAFSA.
Dates and Deadlines: Priority date 4/1; no closing date. Applicants notified on a rolling basis starting 3/21; must reply within 3 week(s) of notification.

CONTACT

Linda Clemons, Director, Financial Aid
Mailcode 4701, Carbondale, IL 62901-4701
(618) 453-4334

Southern Illinois University Edwardsville

Edwardsville, Illinois
www.siue.edu Federal Code: 001759

4-year public university in very large city.
Enrollment: 10,892 undergrads, 14% part-time. 1,902 full-time freshmen.
Selectivity: Admits over 75% of applicants.

BASIC COSTS (2008-2009)

Tuition and fees: $7,831; out-of-state residents $16,606.
Per-credit charge: $195; out-of-state residents $488.
Room and board: $7,071.
Additional info: Required fees include book rental. Tuition at time of enrollment locked for 4 years.

FINANCIAL AID PICTURE (2007-2008)

Students with need: Out of 1,385 full-time freshmen who applied for aid, 1,086 were judged to have need. Of these, 1,016 received aid, and 417 had their full need met. Average financial aid package met 63% of need; average scholarship/grant was $8,999; average loan was $9,272. For part-time students, average financial aid package was $15,091.

Students without need: This college awards aid only to students with need.

Scholarships offered: 14 full-time freshmen received athletic scholarships; average amount $3,634.

FINANCIAL AID PROCEDURES

Forms required: FAFSA.

Dates and Deadlines: Priority date 3/1; closing date 6/1. Applicants notified on a rolling basis starting 3/15; must reply within 4 week(s) of notification.

CONTACT

Sharon Berry, Director of Student Financial Aid
Campus Box 1600, Rendleman Hall, Rm 2120, Edwardsville, IL 62026-1600
(618) 650-3880

Spoon River College

Canton, Illinois
www.src.edu Federal Code: 001643

2-year public community college in large town.
Enrollment: 1,616 undergrads.
Selectivity: Open admission; but selective for some programs.

BASIC COSTS (2008-2009)

Tuition and fees: $2,640; out-of-district residents $6,030; out-of-state residents $7,110.

Per-credit charge: $78; out-of-district residents $191; out-of-state residents $227.

FINANCIAL AID PICTURE (2007-2008)

Students with need: Need-based aid available for full-time and part-time students. Work study available nights.

Students without need: No-need awards available for academics, athletics.

FINANCIAL AID PROCEDURES

Forms required: FAFSA.

Dates and Deadlines: Closing date 7/2. Applicants notified on a rolling basis starting 3/15.

CONTACT

Jo Branson, Director of Financial Aid
23235 North County Road 22, Canton, IL 61520
(309) 649-7030

Springfield College in Illinois

Springfield, Illinois
www.sci.edu Federal Code: 001761

2-year private junior and liberal arts college in small city, affiliated with Roman Catholic Church.
Enrollment: 522 undergrads.

BASIC COSTS (2009-2010)

Tuition and fees: $8,870.
Room and board: $6,900.
Additional info: 15 meals per week provded.

FINANCIAL AID PICTURE

Students with need: Need-based aid available for full-time and part-time students. Work study available nights, weekends, and for part-time students.

Students without need: No-need awards available for academics, art, athletics, leadership, religious affiliation.

FINANCIAL AID PROCEDURES

Forms required: FAFSA, institutional form.

Dates and Deadlines: Priority date 3/1; no closing date. Applicants notified on a rolling basis starting 3/15; must reply within 2 week(s) of notification.

CONTACT

Josephine Negro, Director of Financial Aid
1500 North Fifth Street, Springfield, IL 62702-2694
(217) 525-1420 ext. 244

Taylor Business Institute

Chicago, Illinois
www.tbiil.edu Federal Code: 011810

2-year for-profit business college in very large city.
Enrollment: 185 undergrads.
Selectivity: Open admission.

FINANCIAL AID PICTURE

Students with need: Need-based aid available for full-time students. Work study available nights.

FINANCIAL AID PROCEDURES

Forms required: FAFSA, state aid form, institutional form.

CONTACT

Florence Davis, Financial Aid Director
318 West Adams Street, 5th Floor, Chicago, IL 60606
(312) 658-5100

Trinity Christian College

Palos Heights, Illinois
www.trnty.edu Federal Code: 001771

4-year private liberal arts college in very large city, affiliated with Reformed (unaffiliated).
Enrollment: 1,271 undergrads, 17% part-time. 235 full-time freshmen.
Selectivity: Admits over 75% of applicants.

BASIC COSTS (2008-2009)

Tuition and fees: $20,256.
Per-credit charge: $664.
Room and board: $7,420.

FINANCIAL AID PICTURE (2008-2009)

Students with need: Out of 205 full-time freshmen who applied for aid, 191 were judged to have need. Of these, 191 received aid, and 12 had their full need met. Average financial aid package met 47% of need; average scholarship/grant was $6,879; average loan was $4,231. Need-based aid available for part-time students.

Students without need: 31 full-time freshmen who did not demonstrate need for aid received scholarships/grants; average award was $5,718. No-need awards available for academics, alumni affiliation, art, athletics, leadership, minority status, music/drama, religious affiliation.

Scholarships offered: 44 full-time freshmen received athletic scholarships; average amount $6,777.

Cumulative student debt: 89% of graduating class had student loans; average debt was $42,375.

Additional info: High school transcripts and ACT or SAT scores required for merit scholarships.

FINANCIAL AID PROCEDURES

Forms required: FAFSA, institutional form.

Dates and Deadlines: Priority date 2/15; closing date 4/15. Applicants notified on a rolling basis starting 4/1; must reply by 5/1 or within 2 week(s) of notification.
Transfers: Applicants notified by 2/28; must reply by 5/1 or within 2 week(s) of notification.

CONTACT
Denise Coleman, Director of Financial Aid
6601 West College Drive, Palos Heights, IL 60463
(708) 239-4706

Trinity College of Nursing and Health Sciences

Rock Island, Illinois
www.trinitycollegeqc.edu Federal Code: 006225

4-year private nursing college in very large city.
Enrollment: 230 undergrads.

BASIC COSTS (2008-2009)
Tuition and fees: $11,105.
Per-credit charge: $366.
Additional info: Students are required to have a uniform and other health equipment.

FINANCIAL AID PICTURE (2007-2008)
Students with need: 25% of average financial aid package awarded as scholarships/grants, 75% awarded as loans/jobs.

CONTACT
Kris Hodgerson, Financial Aid Specialist
2122 25th Avenue, Rock Island, IL 61201
(309) 779-7740

Trinity International University

Deerfield, Illinois
www.tiu.edu Federal Code: 001772

4-year private university and liberal arts college in large town, affiliated with Evangelical Free Church of America.
Enrollment: 950 undergrads, 11% part-time. 133 full-time freshmen.
Selectivity: Admits 50 to 75% of applicants.

BASIC COSTS (2008-2009)
Tuition and fees: $21,930.
Per-credit charge: $900.
Room and board: $7,270.
Additional info: Tuition/fee waivers available for minority students.

FINANCIAL AID PICTURE (2008-2009)
Students with need: Need-based aid available for full-time and part-time students. Work study available nights, weekends, and for part-time students.
Students without need: No-need awards available for academics, alumni affiliation, athletics, minority status, music/drama, religious affiliation.

FINANCIAL AID PROCEDURES
Forms required: FAFSA.
Dates and Deadlines: Priority date 4/1; no closing date. Applicants notified on a rolling basis starting 2/15; must reply within 4 week(s) of notification.
Transfers: No deadline. Applicants notified on a rolling basis; must reply within 4 week(s) of notification.

CONTACT
Ron Campbell, Director of Financial Aid
2065 Half Day Road, Deerfield, IL 60015
(847) 317-8060

Triton College

River Grove, Illinois
www.triton.edu Federal Code: 001773

2-year public community and junior college in large town.
Enrollment: 9,610 undergrads, 60% part-time. 1,145 full-time freshmen.
Selectivity: Open admission; but selective for some programs.

BASIC COSTS (2008-2009)
Tuition and fees: $2,170; out-of-district residents $5,740; out-of-state residents $7,150.
Per-credit charge: $64; out-of-district residents $183; out-of-state residents $230.

FINANCIAL AID PICTURE (2007-2008)
Students with need: Out of 634 full-time freshmen who applied for aid, 428 were judged to have need. Of these, 428 received aid. For part-time students, average financial aid package was $2,276.
Students without need: 23 full-time freshmen who did not demonstrate need for aid received scholarships/grants; average award was $1,120. No-need awards available for academics, athletics, leadership.
Scholarships offered: ***Merit:*** Board of Trustees Honor Scholarship; covers tuition and fees; for in-district high school students in top 10% of graduating class. ***Athletic:*** 11 full-time freshmen received athletic scholarships; average amount $856.

FINANCIAL AID PROCEDURES
Forms required: FAFSA, institutional form.
Dates and Deadlines: Priority date 4/15; no closing date. Applicants notified on a rolling basis starting 4/1; must reply within 2 week(s) of notification.

CONTACT
Pat Zinga, Director of Financial Aid
2000 North Fifth Avenue, River Grove, IL 60171
(708) 456-0300 ext. 3441

University of Chicago

Chicago, Illinois Federal Code: 001774
www.uchicago.edu CSS Code: 1832

4-year private university and liberal arts college in very large city.
Enrollment: 5,027 undergrads, 1% part-time. 1,306 full-time freshmen.
Selectivity: Admits less than 50% of applicants.

BASIC COSTS (2008-2009)
Tuition and fees: $37,632.
Room and board: $11,697.

FINANCIAL AID PICTURE (2008-2009)
Students with need: Out of 890 full-time freshmen who applied for aid, 636 were judged to have need. Of these, 636 received aid, and 636 had their full need met. Average financial aid package met 100% of need; average scholarship/grant was $33,838; average loan was $4,264.
Students without need: 156 full-time freshmen who did not demonstrate need for aid received scholarships/grants; average award was $11,520. No-need awards available for academics, leadership.
Cumulative student debt: 41% of graduating class had student loans; average debt was $27,562.

FINANCIAL AID PROCEDURES
Forms required: FAFSA, CSS PROFILE, institutional form.
Dates and Deadlines: Closing date 2/1. Applicants notified by 4/15; must reply by 5/1.
Transfers: Closing date 3/1. Applicants notified on a rolling basis starting 4/15; must reply by 6/1.

CONTACT

Alicia Reyes, Director of College Aid
1101 East 58th Street, Chicago, IL 60637
(773) 702-8666

University of Illinois at Chicago

Chicago, Illinois
www.uic.edu Federal Code: 001776

4-year public university in very large city.
Enrollment: 15,576 undergrads, 7% part-time. 3,248 full-time freshmen.
Selectivity: Admits 50 to 75% of applicants.

BASIC COSTS (2008-2009)

Tuition and fees: $11,710; out-of-state residents $24,100.
Room and board: $8,774.
Additional info: Tuition at time of enrollment locked for 4 years; tuition/fee waivers available for minority students.

FINANCIAL AID PICTURE (2007-2008)

Students with need: Out of 2,577 full-time freshmen who applied for aid, 2,112 were judged to have need. Of these, 1,992 received aid, and 562 had their full need met. Average financial aid package met 75% of need; average scholarship/grant was $10,580; average loan was $3,941. For part-time students, average financial aid package was $7,362.
Students without need: 218 full-time freshmen who did not demonstrate need for aid received scholarships/grants; average award was $2,233. No-need awards available for academics, art, athletics, music/drama, ROTC.
Scholarships offered: 35 full-time freshmen received athletic scholarships; average amount $16,743.
Cumulative student debt: 57% of graduating class had student loans; average debt was $16,715.

FINANCIAL AID PROCEDURES

Forms required: FAFSA.
Dates and Deadlines: Priority date 3/1; no closing date. Applicants notified on a rolling basis starting 3/15; must reply by 5/1 or within 2 week(s) of notification.

CONTACT

Timothy Opgenorth, Director of the Office of Student Financial Aid
PO Box 5220, Chicago, IL 60680-5220
(312) 996-3126

University of Illinois at Urbana-Champaign

Champaign, Illinois
www.illinois.edu Federal Code: 001775

4-year public university in small city.
Enrollment: 30,400 undergrads.
Selectivity: Admits 50 to 75% of applicants.

BASIC COSTS (2008-2009)

Tuition and fees: $12,240; out-of-state residents $26,024.
Room and board: $8,764.
Additional info: Tuition at time of enrollment locked for 4 years.

FINANCIAL AID PICTURE (2007-2008)

Students with need: Need-based aid available for full-time and part-time students. Work study available nights, weekends, and for part-time students.
Students without need: No-need awards available for academics, alumni affiliation, art, athletics, leadership, music/drama, ROTC, state/district residency.
Scholarships offered: President's Award Program: $1,000 - $4,000 for 4 years; for members of historically underrepresented group, with ACT score of 22-23 and in the top quarter of their class, or who have an ACT score of 24 or higher and are in the top half of their class. University Achievement Scholarship: $8,000; criteria set by each college, renewable with 3.0 GPA; 50 available. Matthews Scholars: $2,000 per year, renewable for 4 years if GPA of 3.3 is maintained; criteria includes academic achievement, leadership skills, commitment to campus and community efforts, good sponsor relations, diversity of college gender and ethnicity; approximately 150 available. FMC Award of Excellence: $1,000 a year, non-renewable; criteria set by individual colleges; 20 available. Provost Scholarship: full tuition, renewable with 3.0 GPA; National Achievement, National Hispanic Scholar finalists, or National Merit finalists who have indicated the University of Illinois at Urbana-Champaign as their top choice. Campus Merit: $3,000; students in historically under-represented groups who are in the top 10 percent of their graduating class. National Merit: $500; National Merit finalists who indicated the University of Illinois as their top choice, renewable with 3.0 GPA. James Hunter Anthony and Gerald Blackshear Scholarship: 1 year of tuition and fees, renewable with 3.0 GPA; incoming freshmen who are graduates of an Illinois high school, with superior academic and leadership qualities; need may be considered.

FINANCIAL AID PROCEDURES

Forms required: FAFSA.
Dates and Deadlines: Priority date 3/15; no closing date.

CONTACT

Daniel Mann, Director of Student Financial Aid
901 West Illinois, Urbana, IL 61801-3028
(217) 333-0100

University of Illinois: Springfield

Springfield, Illinois
www.uis.edu Federal Code: 009333

4-year public university and liberal arts college in small city.
Enrollment: 2,798 undergrads, 37% part-time. 255 full-time freshmen.
Selectivity: Admits over 75% of applicants.

BASIC COSTS (2008-2009)

Tuition and fees: $8,605; out-of-state residents $17,755.
Per-credit charge: $241; out-of-state residents $546.
Room and board: $8,840.
Additional info: Tuition at time of enrollment locked for 4 years.

FINANCIAL AID PICTURE (2007-2008)

Students with need: Out of 215 full-time freshmen who applied for aid, 159 were judged to have need. Of these, 156 received aid, and 24 had their full need met. Average financial aid package met 74% of need; average scholarship/grant was $7,722; average loan was $2,943. For part-time students, average financial aid package was $5,635.
Students without need: 65 full-time freshmen who did not demonstrate need for aid received scholarships/grants; average award was $2,726. No-need awards available for academics, alumni affiliation, art, athletics, job skills, leadership, minority status, music/drama, state/district residency.
Scholarships offered: 4 full-time freshmen received athletic scholarships; average amount $9,285.
Cumulative student debt: 76% of graduating class had student loans; average debt was $14,226.

FINANCIAL AID PROCEDURES

Forms required: FAFSA.
Dates and Deadlines: Priority date 4/1; closing date 11/15. Applicants notified on a rolling basis starting 1/1; must reply within 3 week(s) of notification.
Transfers: No deadline. Applicants notified on a rolling basis.

CONTACT
Gerard Joseph, Director of Financial Aid
One University Plaza, MS UHB 1080, Springfield, IL 62703
(217) 206-6724

University of St. Francis
Joliet, Illinois
www.stfrancis.edu Federal Code: 001664

4-year private university and liberal arts college in small city, affiliated with Roman Catholic Church.
Enrollment: 1,255 undergrads, 3% part-time. 203 full-time freshmen.
Selectivity: Admits 50 to 75% of applicants.

BASIC COSTS (2008-2009)
Tuition and fees: $21,860.
Per-credit charge: $715.
Room and board: $7,744.

FINANCIAL AID PICTURE (2008-2009)
Students with need: Out of 192 full-time freshmen who applied for aid, 163 were judged to have need. Of these, 163 received aid, and 105 had their full need met. Average financial aid package met 82% of need; average scholarship/grant was $8,129; average loan was $3,866. For part-time students, average financial aid package was $4,802.
Students without need: 38 full-time freshmen who did not demonstrate need for aid received scholarships/grants; average award was $7,342. No-need awards available for academics, alumni affiliation, art, athletics, leadership, music/drama, religious affiliation, state/district residency.
Scholarships offered: 17 full-time freshmen received athletic scholarships; average amount $10,698.
Cumulative student debt: 75% of graduating class had student loans; average debt was $21,996.

FINANCIAL AID PROCEDURES
Forms required: FAFSA, institutional form.
Dates and Deadlines: Priority date 3/15; no closing date. Applicants notified on a rolling basis starting 2/15.

CONTACT
Bruce Foote, Executive Director Financial Aid Services
500 Wilcox Street, Joliet, IL 60435
(866) 890-8331

Waubonsee Community College
Sugar Grove, Illinois
www.waubonsee.edu Federal Code: 006931

2-year public community college in small town.
Enrollment: 6,813 undergrads, 52% part-time. 1,017 full-time freshmen.
Selectivity: Open admission; but selective for some programs.

BASIC COSTS (2009-2010)
Tuition and fees: $2,460; out-of-district residents $8,027; out-of-state residents $8,838.
Per-credit charge: $79; out-of-district residents $265; out-of-state residents $292.

FINANCIAL AID PICTURE (2007-2008)
Students with need: 74% of average financial aid package awarded as scholarships/grants, 26% awarded as loans/jobs. Need-based aid available for part-time students. Work study available nights.
Students without need: No-need awards available for academics, art, athletics, leadership, minority status, music/drama.
Scholarships offered: Gustafson Scholarship; provides tuition for 64 semester hours; selected graduates from each in-district school.

FINANCIAL AID PROCEDURES
Forms required: FAFSA.
Dates and Deadlines: Closing date 12/1. Applicants notified on a rolling basis.

CONTACT
Charles Boudreau, Director of Student Financial Aid Services
Route 47 at Waubonsee Drive, Sugar Grove, IL 60554-9454
(630) 466-7900 ext. 5774

West Suburban College of Nursing
Oak Park, Illinois
www.wscn.edu Federal Code: 022141

Upper-division private nursing college in very large city, affiliated with Roman Catholic Church.
Enrollment: 237 undergrads, 23% part-time.

BASIC COSTS (2008-2009)
Tuition and fees: $20,910.
Per-credit charge: $697.

FINANCIAL AID PICTURE (2007-2008)
Students with need: 45% of average financial aid package awarded as scholarships/grants, 55% awarded as loans/jobs. Need-based aid available for part-time students. Work study available nights, weekends, and for part-time students.
Students without need: No-need awards available for academics, alumni affiliation.

FINANCIAL AID PROCEDURES
Forms required: FAFSA.
Transfers: Priority date 4/15; no deadline. Applicants notified on a rolling basis; must reply within 3 week(s) of notification.

CONTACT
Shirley Howell, Financial Aid Officer
Three Erie Court, Oak Park, IL 60302
(708) 763-1426

Western Illinois University
Macomb, Illinois
www.wiu.edu Federal Code: 001780

4-year public university in large town.
Enrollment: 10,730 undergrads, 9% part-time. 1,810 full-time freshmen.
Selectivity: Admits 50 to 75% of applicants.

BASIC COSTS (2008-2009)
Tuition and fees: $8,828; out-of-state residents $12,056.
Per-credit charge: $215; out-of-state residents $323.
Room and board: $7,210.
Additional info: Residents of nearby counties in Iowa and Missouri pay in-state tuition during first year. Tuition at time of enrollment locked for 4 years.

FINANCIAL AID PICTURE (2008-2009)
Students with need: Need-based aid available for full-time and part-time students.
Students without need: No-need awards available for academics, alumni affiliation, art, athletics, leadership, minority status, music/drama, ROTC.

FINANCIAL AID PROCEDURES
Forms required: FAFSA.
Dates and Deadlines: Priority date 2/15; no closing date. Applicants notified on a rolling basis starting 1/15.
Transfers: Priority date 1/31; no deadline. Applicants notified on a rolling basis.

CONTACT
William Bushaw, Director of Financial Aid
One University Circle, Macomb, IL 61455-1390
(309) 298-2446

Westwood College: DuPage
Woodridge, Illinois
www.westwood.edu Federal Code: 030792

4-year for-profit technical college in large city.
Enrollment: 519 undergrads, 18% part-time. 108 full-time freshmen.

BASIC COSTS (2008-2009)
Additional info: Expenses vary by program; however, average cost for academic year is $14,867, which includes tuition, fees and books.

FINANCIAL AID PICTURE (2007-2008)
Students with need: 38% of average financial aid package awarded as scholarships/grants, 62% awarded as loans/jobs.

CONTACT
Patty Zavala, Financial Aid Specialist
7155 Janes Avenue, Woodridge, IL 60517
(630) 434-8250 ext. 65330

Westwood College: O'Hare Airport
Chicago, Illinois
www.westwood.edu Federal Code: 023139

4-year for-profit technical and career college in very large city.
Enrollment: 730 undergrads, 17% part-time. 462 full-time freshmen.

BASIC COSTS (2008-2009)
Tuition and fees: $14,570.
Per-credit charge: $508.

FINANCIAL AID PICTURE (2007-2008)
Students with need: Need-based aid available for full-time and part-time students. Work study available nights, weekends, and for part-time students.

FINANCIAL AID PROCEDURES
Forms required: FAFSA, institutional form.
Dates and Deadlines: Priority date 3/1; closing date 6/30.

CONTACT
Denise Brown, Director of Financial Aid
8501 West Higgins Road, Chicago, IL 60631
(773) 380-6800

Wheaton College
Wheaton, Illinois
www.wheaton.edu Federal Code: 001781

4-year private liberal arts college in small city, affiliated with nondenominational tradition.
Enrollment: 2,344 undergrads, 3% part-time. 581 full-time freshmen.
Selectivity: Admits 50 to 75% of applicants.

BASIC COSTS (2009-2010)
Tuition and fees: $26,520.
Per-credit charge: $1,105.
Room and board: $7,770.

FINANCIAL AID PICTURE (2008-2009)
Students with need: Average financial aid package met 85% of need; average scholarship/grant was $14,776; average loan was $4,423. For part-time students, average financial aid package was $19,055.
Students without need: No-need awards available for academics, alumni affiliation, art, minority status, music/drama.
Scholarships offered: President's Award; $1,000 per year for 4 years; U.S. citizens with 3.6 GPA on 4.0 scale, plus minimum 1400 SAT or 32 ACT; unlimited number.
Additional info: First $500 to $2,000 of need awarded as grant instead of loan.

FINANCIAL AID PROCEDURES
Forms required: FAFSA, institutional form.
Dates and Deadlines: Priority date 2/15; no closing date. Applicants notified on a rolling basis starting 3/1.
Transfers: Priority date 3/1; no deadline. Applicants notified on a rolling basis.

CONTACT
Donna Peltz, Director of Financial Aid
501 College Avenue, Wheaton, IL 60187-5593
(630) 752-5021

Indiana

Ancilla College
Donaldson, Indiana
www.ancilla.edu Federal Code: 001784

2-year private community and liberal arts college in rural community, affiliated with Roman Catholic Church.
Enrollment: 495 undergrads.
Selectivity: Open admission; but selective for some programs.

BASIC COSTS (2008-2009)
Tuition and fees: $12,080.
Per-credit charge: $395.

FINANCIAL AID PICTURE (2008-2009)
Students with need: Need-based aid available for full-time and part-time students.
Students without need: No-need awards available for academics, athletics, job skills, leadership.

FINANCIAL AID PROCEDURES
Forms required: FAFSA, institutional form.
Dates and Deadlines: Closing date 3/1. Applicants notified on a rolling basis starting 3/1; must reply within 2 week(s) of notification.

CONTACT
Katherine Mills, Director of Financial Aid
9001 Union Road, Donaldson, IN 46513
(574) 936-8898 ext. 307

Anderson University
Anderson, Indiana
www.anderson.edu Federal Code: 001785

4-year private liberal arts college in small city, affiliated with Church of God.
Enrollment: 2,147 undergrads, 8% part-time. 541 full-time freshmen.
Selectivity: Admits 50 to 75% of applicants. GED not accepted.

BASIC COSTS (2008-2009)
Tuition and fees: $21,920.
Per-credit charge: $914.

Room and board: $7,600.
Additional info: Tuition/fee waivers available for adults.

FINANCIAL AID PICTURE

Students with need: Need-based aid available for full-time and part-time students. Work study available nights, weekends, and for part-time students.
Students without need: No-need awards available for academics, leadership, minority status, music/drama, state/district residency.

FINANCIAL AID PROCEDURES

Forms required: FAFSA.
Dates and Deadlines: Priority date 3/1; no closing date. Applicants notified on a rolling basis starting 3/1.

CONTACT

Kenneth Nieman, Director of Financial Aid
1100 East Fifth Street, Anderson, IN 46012-3495
(765) 641-4182

Aviation Institute of Maintenance: Indianapolis

Indianapolis, Indiana
www.aviationmaintenance.edu Federal Code: 031763

2-year for-profit technical college in very large city.
Enrollment: 157 undergrads.
Selectivity: Open admission; but selective for some programs.

BASIC COSTS (2008-2009)

Additional info: Tuition: $240 per credit hour.

FINANCIAL AID PICTURE

Students with need: Need-based aid available for full-time students.

FINANCIAL AID PROCEDURES

Forms required: FAFSA.

CONTACT

Stacey Bruton, Financial Aid Coordinator
7251 West McCarty Street, Indianapolis, IN 46241-1445
(317) 243-4514

Ball State University

Muncie, Indiana
www.bsu.edu Federal Code: 001786

4-year public university in small city.
Enrollment: 16,575 undergrads, 6% part-time. 4,013 full-time freshmen.
Selectivity: Admits 50 to 75% of applicants.

BASIC COSTS (2008-2009)

Tuition and fees: $7,500; out-of-state residents $19,304.
Room and board: $7,598.

FINANCIAL AID PICTURE (2008-2009)

Students with need: Out of 3,501 full-time freshmen who applied for aid, 2,479 were judged to have need. Of these, 2,433 received aid, and 666 had their full need met. Average financial aid package met 63% of need; average scholarship/grant was $5,692; average loan was $3,501. For part-time students, average financial aid package was $7,587.
Students without need: 279 full-time freshmen who did not demonstrate need for aid received scholarships/grants; average award was $5,653. No-need awards available for academics, athletics, leadership, minority status, music/drama, ROTC, state/district residency.
Scholarships offered: 74 full-time freshmen received athletic scholarships; average amount $14,661.
Cumulative student debt: 67% of graduating class had student loans; average debt was $20,326.

FINANCIAL AID PROCEDURES

Forms required: FAFSA.
Dates and Deadlines: Priority date 3/10; no closing date. Applicants notified on a rolling basis starting 4/1.
Transfers: No deadline. Applicants notified on a rolling basis.

CONTACT

Robert Zellers, Director of Scholarships/Financial Aid
2000 University Avenue, Muncie, IN 47306-1022
(765) 285-5600

Bethel College

Mishawaka, Indiana
www.bethelcollege.edu Federal Code: 001787

4-year private liberal arts college in large town, affiliated with Missionary Church.
Enrollment: 1,802 undergrads.
Selectivity: Admits over 75% of applicants.

BASIC COSTS (2009-2010)

Tuition and fees: $20,978.
Room and board: $6,120.
Additional info: All first-time, full-time students must pay a one-time student activity and technology fee of $600. Tuition/fee waivers available for adults, minority students.

FINANCIAL AID PICTURE (2007-2008)

Students with need: 43% of average financial aid package awarded as scholarships/grants, 57% awarded as loans/jobs. Need-based aid available for part-time students.
Students without need: No-need awards available for academics, art, athletics, job skills, leadership, minority status, music/drama, religious affiliation, ROTC, state/district residency.

FINANCIAL AID PROCEDURES

Forms required: FAFSA.
Dates and Deadlines: Priority date 3/1; closing date 3/10. Applicants notified by 4/15; must reply within 3 week(s) of notification.

CONTACT

Guy Fisher, Director of Financial Aid
1001 Bethel Circle, Mishawaka, IN 46545
(574) 257-3316

Brown Mackie College: South Bend

South Bend, Indiana
www.brownmackie.edu Federal Code: 004583

2-year for-profit community and technical college in small city.
Enrollment: 905 undergrads.
Selectivity: Open admission.

BASIC COSTS (2008-2009)

Additional info: Nursing program tuition $295 per credit hour. Occupational therapy courses $350 per credit hour; general education courses for occupational therapy $235 per credit hour. Fees are $15 per credit hour for all programs except nursing which is $20.

FINANCIAL AID PICTURE (2008-2009)

Students with need: 30% of average financial aid package awarded as scholarships/grants, 70% awarded as loans/jobs. Need-based aid available for part-time students.
Students without need: This college awards aid only to students with need.

FINANCIAL AID PROCEDURES

Forms required: FAFSA.

Dates and Deadlines: No deadline. Applicants notified on a rolling basis; must reply within 1 week(s) of notification.

CONTACT

Sue Kempt, Senior Financial Aid Officer
1030 East Jefferson Boulevard, South Bend, IN 46617

Butler University

Indianapolis, Indiana
www.butler.edu Federal Code: 001788

4-year private university in very large city.

Enrollment: 3,607 undergrads, 1% part-time. 934 full-time freshmen.

Selectivity: Admits 50 to 75% of applicants.

BASIC COSTS (2008-2009)

Tuition and fees: $28,266.

Per-credit charge: $1,150.

Room and board: $9,410.

FINANCIAL AID PICTURE (2008-2009)

Students with need: 63% of average financial aid package awarded as scholarships/grants, 37% awarded as loans/jobs. Need-based aid available for part-time students. Work study available nights, weekends, and for part-time students.

Students without need: No-need awards available for academics, athletics, music/drama.

Cumulative student debt: 60% of graduating class had student loans; average debt was $23,500.

FINANCIAL AID PROCEDURES

Forms required: FAFSA.

Dates and Deadlines: Priority date 3/1; no closing date. Applicants notified on a rolling basis starting 3/15; must reply within 3 week(s) of notification.

Transfers: Priority date 3/15; no deadline.

CONTACT

Richard Bellows, Executive Director of Financial Aid
4600 Sunset Avenue, Indianapolis, IN 46208
(317) 940-8200

Calumet College of St. Joseph

Whiting, Indiana
www.ccsj.edu Federal Code: 001834

4-year private liberal arts college in small city, affiliated with Roman Catholic Church.

Enrollment: 1,051 undergrads, 53% part-time. 138 full-time freshmen.

Selectivity: Admits 50 to 75% of applicants.

BASIC COSTS (2009-2010)

Tuition and fees: $13,220.

Per-credit charge: $405.

FINANCIAL AID PICTURE (2007-2008)

Students with need: Need-based aid available for full-time and part-time students.

Students without need: No-need awards available for academics, alumni affiliation, religious affiliation.

Additional info: Immediate computerized estimate of financial aid eligibility available to students applying in person.

FINANCIAL AID PROCEDURES

Forms required: FAFSA.

Dates and Deadlines: Priority date 3/1; no closing date. Applicants notified on a rolling basis; must reply within 2 week(s) of notification.

CONTACT

Chuck Walz, Director of Financial Aid
2400 New York Avenue, Whiting, IN 46394-2195
(219) 473-4296

DePauw University

Greencastle, Indiana
www.depauw.edu Federal Code: 001792

4-year private liberal arts college in small town, affiliated with United Methodist Church.

Enrollment: 2,241 undergrads. 600 full-time freshmen.

Selectivity: Admits 50 to 75% of applicants.

BASIC COSTS (2009-2010)

Tuition and fees: $33,250.

Room and board: $8,740.

FINANCIAL AID PICTURE (2008-2009)

Students with need: Need-based aid available for full-time and part-time students. Work study available nights, weekends, and for part-time students.

Students without need: No-need awards available for academics, alumni affiliation, leadership, minority status, music/drama, ROTC.

Scholarships offered: Holton Scholarships; $1,000 to full tuition; based on exceptional leadership and/or service; 50 awarded.

FINANCIAL AID PROCEDURES

Forms required: FAFSA, institutional form.

Dates and Deadlines: Closing date 2/15. Applicants notified by 3/27; must reply by 5/1.

Transfers: Applicants notified by 3/27; must reply by 5/1.

CONTACT

Craig Slaughter, Director of Financial Aid
101 East Seminary Street, Greencastle, IN 46135-1611
(765) 658-4030

DeVry University: Indianapolis

Indianapolis, Indiana
www.devry.edu

4-year for-profit university in very large city.

Enrollment: 184 undergrads, 70% part-time. 2 full-time freshmen.

BASIC COSTS (2008-2009)

Tuition and fees: $13,930.

Per-credit charge: $515.

FINANCIAL AID PICTURE (2007-2008)

Students with need: Out of 1 full-time freshmen who applied for aid, 1 were judged to have need. Of these, 1 received aid. Average financial aid package met 21% of need; average loan was $3,500. For part-time students, average financial aid package was $11,287.

Students without need: No-need awards available for academics.

FINANCIAL AID PROCEDURES

Forms required: FAFSA.

Dates and Deadlines: No deadline. Applicants notified on a rolling basis.

CONTACT

9100 Keystone Crossing, Suite 350, Indianapolis, IN 46240

Earlham College
Richmond, Indiana
www.earlham.edu Federal Code: 001793

4-year private liberal arts and seminary college in large town, affiliated with Society of Friends (Quaker).
Enrollment: 1,146 undergrads, 1% part-time. 302 full-time freshmen.
Selectivity: Admits over 75% of applicants.

BASIC COSTS (2009-2010)
Tuition and fees: $35,164.
Per-credit charge: $1,147.
Room and board: $7,160.

FINANCIAL AID PICTURE (2007-2008)
Students with need: Out of 196 full-time freshmen who applied for aid, 177 were judged to have need. Of these, 176 received aid, and 87 had their full need met. Average financial aid package met 96% of need; average scholarship/grant was $17,016; average loan was $4,594. Need-based aid available for part-time students.
Students without need: 64 full-time freshmen who did not demonstrate need for aid received scholarships/grants; average award was $8,582. No-need awards available for academics, minority status.
Cumulative student debt: 64% of graduating class had student loans; average debt was $20,287.

FINANCIAL AID PROCEDURES
Forms required: FAFSA, institutional form.
Dates and Deadlines: Closing date 3/1. Applicants notified on a rolling basis starting 2/15; must reply by 5/1.
Transfers: Priority date 3/1; no deadline. Deadline for State of Indiana Grants, 3/1 (FAFSA date).

CONTACT
Robert Arnold, Director of Financial Aid
801 National Road West, Richmond, IN 47374-4095
(765) 983-1217

Franklin College
Franklin, Indiana
www.franklincollege.edu Federal Code: 001798

4-year private liberal arts college in large town, affiliated with American Baptist Churches in the USA.
Enrollment: 1,153 undergrads, 12% part-time. 394 full-time freshmen.
Selectivity: Admits 50 to 75% of applicants.

BASIC COSTS (2009-2010)
Tuition and fees: $23,275.
Room and board: $6,885.

FINANCIAL AID PICTURE (2007-2008)
Students with need: Out of 360 full-time freshmen who applied for aid, 318 were judged to have need. Of these, 317 received aid, and 53 had their full need met. Average financial aid package met 78% of need; average scholarship/grant was $12,438; average loan was $3,610. For part-time students, average financial aid package was $9,508.
Students without need: This college awards aid only to students with need.
Cumulative student debt: 83% of graduating class had student loans; average debt was $42,908.

FINANCIAL AID PROCEDURES
Forms required: FAFSA, institutional form.
Dates and Deadlines: Closing date 3/1. Applicants notified by 4/1; must reply by 5/1 or within 4 week(s) of notification.
Transfers: Must reply by 5/1 or within 2 week(s) of notification.

CONTACT
Elizabeth Sappenfield, Director of Financial Aid
101 Branigin Boulevard, Franklin, IN 46131-2623
(317) 738-8075

Goshen College
Goshen, Indiana
www.goshen.edu Federal Code: 001799

4-year private liberal arts college in large town, affiliated with Mennonite Church.
Enrollment: 913 undergrads, 6% part-time. 172 full-time freshmen.
Selectivity: Admits 50 to 75% of applicants.

BASIC COSTS (2009-2010)
Tuition and fees: $23,400.
Per-credit charge: $935.
Room and board: $7,900.

FINANCIAL AID PICTURE (2007-2008)
Students with need: 69% of average financial aid package awarded as scholarships/grants, 31% awarded as loans/jobs. Need-based aid available for part-time students. Work study available nights, weekends, and for part-time students.
Students without need: No-need awards available for academics, art, athletics, leadership, music/drama.
Scholarships offered: President's Leadership Award; $15,000; must meet 2 of the following criteria: 3.8 GPA, 1270 SAT (exclusive of writing) or 29 ACT, top 5% of class, National Merit semi-finalist; 15 awards offered each year, renews annually with 3.20 GPA. Menno Simons Scholarships; $8,000; 3.75 GPA and 1200 SAT (exclusive of Writing) or 26 ACT required. Wens Honors Scholarship; $7,000; 3.50 GPA and 1100 SAT (exclusive of Writing) or ACT of 25. Yoder Honors Scholarship; $6,000; 3.30 GPA and 1050 SAT or 22 ACT. Kratz Honors Scholarship; $3,000; 3.0 GPA required.

FINANCIAL AID PROCEDURES
Forms required: FAFSA, institutional form.
Dates and Deadlines: Priority date 2/1; no closing date. Applicants notified by 3/1; must reply by 5/1 or within 2 week(s) of notification.
Transfers: Priority date 3/10; no deadline. Applicants notified by 3/1; must reply by 5/1 or within 2 week(s) of notification.

CONTACT
James Histand, Vice President for Finance
1700 South Main Street, Goshen, IN 46526-4724
(574) 535-7522

Grace College
Winona Lake, Indiana
www.grace.edu Federal Code: 001800

4-year private liberal arts college in large town, affiliated with Brethren Church.
Enrollment: 1,265 undergrads, 7% part-time. 303 full-time freshmen.
Selectivity: Admits over 75% of applicants.

BASIC COSTS (2009-2010)
Tuition and fees: $21,100.
Per-credit charge: $466.
Room and board: $6,880.
Additional info: Tuition/fee waivers available for minority students.

FINANCIAL AID PICTURE (2007-2008)
Students with need: 71% of average financial aid package awarded as scholarships/grants, 29% awarded as loans/jobs. Need-based aid available for part-time students. Work study available nights, weekends, and for part-time students.

Students without need: No-need awards available for academics, art, athletics, leadership, minority status, music/drama, religious affiliation.

FINANCIAL AID PROCEDURES

Forms required: FAFSA.

Dates and Deadlines: Closing date 3/1. Applicants notified on a rolling basis starting 3/1; must reply by 5/1.

Transfers: Applicants notified by 3/15; must reply by 5/1. Applicants who miss dates for admission and financial aid are notified on rolling basis until class is full.

CONTACT

Charlette Sauders, Director of Financial Aid Services
200 Seminary Drive, Winona Lake, IN 46590
(574) 372-5100 ext. 6162

Hanover College

Hanover, Indiana
www.hanover.edu Federal Code: 001801

4-year private liberal arts college in rural community, affiliated with Presbyterian Church (USA).

Enrollment: 921 undergrads. 231 full-time freshmen.

Selectivity: Admits 50 to 75% of applicants. GED not accepted.

BASIC COSTS (2009-2010)

Tuition and fees: $26,350.

Per-credit charge: $715.

Room and board: $7,900.

FINANCIAL AID PICTURE (2007-2008)

Students with need: Out of 200 full-time freshmen who applied for aid, 167 were judged to have need. Of these, 167 received aid, and 73 had their full need met. Average financial aid package met 91% of need; average scholarship/grant was $17,874; average loan was $2,616. For part-time students, average financial aid package was $10,859.

Students without need: 60 full-time freshmen who did not demonstrate need for aid received scholarships/grants; average award was $16,903. No-need awards available for academics, alumni affiliation, leadership, music/drama, religious affiliation, state/district residency.

Cumulative student debt: 67% of graduating class had student loans; average debt was $21,296.

Additional info: Academic Honors Diploma Scholarship is a grant program committed to meeting 100% of Indiana student's demonstrated need. Available to Indiana students who graduate with an Academic Honors Diploma (AHD), have completed their application for admission by January 15, and file a complete and valid FAFSA by March 10.

FINANCIAL AID PROCEDURES

Forms required: FAFSA.

Dates and Deadlines: Priority date 3/1; no closing date. Applicants notified on a rolling basis starting 3/1; must reply by 5/1.

Transfers: No deadline. Applicants notified on a rolling basis starting 3/1; must reply by 5/1 or within 2 week(s) of notification.

CONTACT

Jon Riester, Associate Dean of Financial Assistance and Admission
PO Box 108, Hanover, IN 47243-0108
(812) 866-7030

Holy Cross College

Notre Dame, Indiana
www.hcc-nd.edu Federal Code: 007263

4-year private liberal arts college in small city, affiliated with Roman Catholic Church.

Enrollment: 510 undergrads.

Selectivity: Admits over 75% of applicants.

BASIC COSTS (2008-2009)

Tuition and fees: $17,900.

Per-credit charge: $560.

Room and board: $8,500.

FINANCIAL AID PICTURE

Students with need: Need-based aid available for full-time and part-time students. Work study available nights, weekends, and for part-time students.

Students without need: No-need awards available for academics, leadership.

FINANCIAL AID PROCEDURES

Forms required: FAFSA.

Dates and Deadlines: Closing date 3/1. Applicants notified on a rolling basis starting 5/1; must reply within 2 week(s) of notification.

CONTACT

Robert Benjamin, Director of Financial Aid
54515 State Road 933N, Notre Dame, IN 46556-0308
(574) 239-8400

Huntington University

Huntington, Indiana
www.huntington.edu Federal Code: 001803

4-year private university and liberal arts college in large town, affiliated with United Brethren in Christ.

Enrollment: 941 undergrads, 2% part-time. 271 full-time freshmen.

Selectivity: Admits over 75% of applicants.

BASIC COSTS (2009-2010)

Tuition and fees: $21,290.

Room and board: $7,180.

FINANCIAL AID PICTURE (2008-2009)

Students with need: Out of 250 full-time freshmen who applied for aid, 215 were judged to have need. Of these, 215 received aid, and 22 had their full need met. Average financial aid package met 79% of need; average scholarship/grant was $13,495; average loan was $3,950. For part-time students, average financial aid package was $6,290.

Students without need: 46 full-time freshmen who did not demonstrate need for aid received scholarships/grants; average award was $8,045. No-need awards available for academics, alumni affiliation, art, athletics, leadership, music/drama, religious affiliation.

Scholarships offered: ***Merit:*** The Horizon Leader Scholarship covers all fees associated with tuition and housing costs for up to 10 semesters. ***Athletic:*** 9 full-time freshmen received athletic scholarships; average amount $3,222.

Cumulative student debt: 73% of graduating class had student loans; average debt was $23,898.

FINANCIAL AID PROCEDURES

Forms required: FAFSA.

Dates and Deadlines: Priority date 3/1; no closing date. Applicants notified on a rolling basis starting 3/1; must reply by 5/1 or within 2 week(s) of notification.

Transfers: No deadline. Applicants notified on a rolling basis; must reply by 5/1 or within 2 week(s) of notification.

CONTACT
Sharon Woods, Director of Financial Aid
2303 College Avenue, Huntington, IN 46750-1237
(260) 359-4015

Indiana Business College: Anderson
Anderson, Indiana
www.ibcschools.edu Federal Code: 015227

2-year for-profit business and health science college in small city.
Enrollment: 174 undergrads.

BASIC COSTS (2008-2009)
Tuition and fees: $10,770.
Additional info: Tuition and fees vary by program.

FINANCIAL AID PICTURE
Students with need: Need-based aid available for full-time and part-time students.
Additional info: Work-study programs available.

FINANCIAL AID PROCEDURES
Forms required: FAFSA.
Dates and Deadlines: Applicants notified on a rolling basis.

CONTACT
140 East 53rd Street, Anderson, IN 46013
(800) 422-4723

Indiana Business College: Columbus
Columbus, Indiana
www.ibcschools.edu Federal Code: 015226

2-year for-profit business and health science college in large town.
Enrollment: 207 undergrads.

BASIC COSTS (2008-2009)
Tuition and fees: $10,770.
Additional info: Tuition and fees vary by program.

FINANCIAL AID PICTURE
Students with need: Need-based aid available for full-time and part-time students.
Additional info: Work-study programs available.

FINANCIAL AID PROCEDURES
Forms required: FAFSA.
Dates and Deadlines: Applicants notified on a rolling basis.

CONTACT
2222 Poshard Drive, Columbus, IN 47203
(800) 422-4723

Indiana Business College: Evansville
Evansville, Indiana
www.ibcschools.edu Federal Code: E00778

2-year for-profit business and health science college in small city.
Enrollment: 226 undergrads.

BASIC COSTS (2008-2009)
Tuition and fees: $10,770.
Additional info: Tuition and fees vary by program.

FINANCIAL AID PICTURE
Students with need: Need-based aid available for full-time and part-time students.
Additional info: Work-study programs available.

FINANCIAL AID PROCEDURES
Forms required: FAFSA.
Dates and Deadlines: Applicants notified on a rolling basis.

CONTACT
4601 Theater Drive, Evansville, IN 47715
(800) 422-4723

Indiana Business College: Fort Wayne
Fort Wayne, Indiana
www.ibcschools.edu

2-year for-profit business and health science college in large city.
Enrollment: 492 undergrads.

BASIC COSTS (2008-2009)
Tuition and fees: $10,770.
Additional info: Tuition and fees vary by program.

FINANCIAL AID PICTURE
Students with need: Need-based aid available for full-time and part-time students.
Additional info: Work-study programs available.

FINANCIAL AID PROCEDURES
Forms required: FAFSA.
Transfers: Applicants notified on a rolling basis.

CONTACT
6413 North Clinton Street, Fort Wayne, IN 46825
(800) 422-4723

Indiana Business College: Indianapolis
Indianapolis, Indiana
www.ibcschools.edu Federal Code: 075218

2-year for-profit business and health science college in very large city.
Enrollment: 1,889 undergrads.

BASIC COSTS (2008-2009)
Tuition and fees: $10,770.
Additional info: Tuition and fees vary by program.

FINANCIAL AID PICTURE
Students with need: Need-based aid available for full-time and part-time students.
Additional info: Work-study programs available.

FINANCIAL AID PROCEDURES
Forms required: FAFSA.
Dates and Deadlines: Applicants notified on a rolling basis.

CONTACT
550 East Washington Street, Indianapolis, IN 46204
(800) 422-4723

Indiana Business College: Indianapolis Northwest

Indianapolis, Indiana
www.ibcschools.edu Federal Code: E01209

2-year for-profit business and health science college in very large city.
Enrollment: 247 undergrads.

BASIC COSTS (2008-2009)
Tuition and fees: $10,770.
Additional info: Tuition and fees vary by program.

FINANCIAL AID PICTURE
Students with need: Need-based aid available for full-time students.

FINANCIAL AID PROCEDURES
Forms required: FAFSA.

CONTACT
6300 Technology Center Drive, Indianapolis, IN 46278

Indiana Business College: Lafayette

Lafayette, Indiana
www.ibcschools.edu Federal Code: 015224

2-year for-profit business and health science college in small city.
Enrollment: 272 undergrads.

BASIC COSTS (2008-2009)
Tuition and fees: $10,770.
Additional info: Tuition and fees vary by program.

FINANCIAL AID PICTURE
Students with need: Need-based aid available for full-time and part-time students.
Additional info: Work-study programs available.

FINANCIAL AID PROCEDURES
Forms required: FAFSA.
Dates and Deadlines: Applicants notified on a rolling basis.
Transfers: Applicants notified on a rolling basis.

CONTACT
4705 Meijer Court, Lafayette, IN 47905
(800) 422-4723

Indiana Business College: Marion

Marion, Indiana
www.ibcschools.edu Federal Code: 015223

2-year for-profit business and health science college in large town.
Enrollment: 114 undergrads.

BASIC COSTS (2008-2009)
Tuition and fees: $10,770.
Additional info: Tuition and fees vary by program.

FINANCIAL AID PICTURE
Students with need: Need-based aid available for full-time and part-time students.
Additional info: Work-study programs available.

FINANCIAL AID PROCEDURES
Forms required: FAFSA.
Dates and Deadlines: Applicants notified on a rolling basis.

CONTACT
830 North Miller Avenue, Marion, IN 46952
(800) 422-4723

Indiana Business College: Medical

Indianapolis, Indiana
www.ibcschools.edu Federal Code: E00777

2-year for-profit health science college in very large city.
Enrollment: 458 undergrads.

BASIC COSTS (2008-2009)
Tuition and fees: $10,770.
Additional info: Tuition and fees vary by program.

FINANCIAL AID PICTURE
Students with need: Need-based aid available for full-time and part-time students.
Additional info: Work-study programs available.

FINANCIAL AID PROCEDURES
Forms required: FAFSA.
Dates and Deadlines: Applicants notified on a rolling basis.
Transfers: Applicants notified on a rolling basis.

CONTACT
8150 Brookville Road, Indianapolis, IN 46239
(800) 422-4723

Indiana Business College: Muncie

Muncie, Indiana
www.ibcschools.edu Federal Code: 015222

2-year for-profit business and health science college in small city.
Enrollment: 201 undergrads.

BASIC COSTS (2008-2009)
Tuition and fees: $10,770.
Additional info: Tuition and fees vary by program.

FINANCIAL AID PICTURE
Students with need: Need-based aid available for full-time and part-time students.
Additional info: Work-study programs available.

FINANCIAL AID PROCEDURES
Forms required: FAFSA.
Dates and Deadlines: Applicants notified on a rolling basis.
Transfers: Applicants notified on a rolling basis.

CONTACT
411 West Riggin Road, Muncie, IN 47303
(800) 422-4723

Indiana Business College: Terre Haute

Terre Haute, Indiana
www.ibcschools.edu Federal Code: 015220

2-year for-profit business and health science college in small city.
Enrollment: 257 undergrads.

BASIC COSTS (2008-2009)
Tuition and fees: $10,770.
Additional info: Tuition and fees vary by program.

FINANCIAL AID PICTURE

Students with need: Need-based aid available for full-time and part-time students.

Additional info: Work-study programs available.

FINANCIAL AID PROCEDURES

Forms required: FAFSA.

Dates and Deadlines: Applicants notified on a rolling basis.

Transfers: Applicants notified on a rolling basis.

CONTACT

David Marshall, Director of Financial Aid
1378 South State Road 46, Terre Haute, IN 47803
(812) 877-2100

Indiana Institute of Technology

Fort Wayne, Indiana
www.indianatech.edu Federal Code: 001805

4-year private business and engineering college in large city.

Enrollment: 3,133 undergrads, 38% part-time. 333 full-time freshmen.

Selectivity: Admits 50 to 75% of applicants.

BASIC COSTS (2009-2010)

Tuition and fees: $21,400.

Per-credit charge: $703.

Room and board: $8,040.

Additional info: Tuition/fee waivers available for adults.

FINANCIAL AID PICTURE (2008-2009)

Students with need: Need-based aid available for full-time and part-time students. Work study available nights, weekends, and for part-time students.

Students without need: No-need awards available for academics, alumni affiliation, athletics, leadership, minority status, music/drama, state/district residency.

FINANCIAL AID PROCEDURES

Forms required: FAFSA, institutional form.

Dates and Deadlines: Closing date 3/10. Applicants notified on a rolling basis starting 2/2; must reply within 2 week(s) of notification.

Transfers: Priority date 3/10; no deadline. Applicants notified on a rolling basis starting 2/2; must reply within 2 week(s) of notification.

CONTACT

Judy Roy, Vice President of Finance and Administration
1600 East Washington Boulevard, Fort Wayne, IN 46803-1297
(260) 422-5561 ext. 2208

Indiana State University

Terre Haute, Indiana
www.indstate.edu Federal Code: 001807

4-year public university in small city.

Enrollment: 8,200 undergrads, 12% part-time. 1,824 full-time freshmen.

Selectivity: Admits 50 to 75% of applicants.

BASIC COSTS (2008-2009)

Tuition and fees: $7,148; out-of-state residents $15,402.

Per-credit charge: $245; out-of-state residents $530.

Room and board: $6,972.

FINANCIAL AID PICTURE (2007-2008)

Students with need: Out of 1,607 full-time freshmen who applied for aid, 1,296 were judged to have need. Of these, 1,291 received aid, and 152 had their full need met. For part-time students, average financial aid package was $4,568.

Students without need: This college awards aid only to students with need.

Scholarships offered: 56 full-time freshmen received athletic scholarships; average amount $10,554.

Cumulative student debt: 66% of graduating class had student loans; average debt was $21,772.

Additional info: Financial aid application deadline March 1 for Indiana residents applying for state grant.

FINANCIAL AID PROCEDURES

Forms required: FAFSA.

Dates and Deadlines: Priority date 3/1; no closing date. Applicants notified on a rolling basis starting 4/15.

CONTACT

Kim Donat, Director of Student Financial Aid
Office of Admissions, Erickson 114, Terre Haute, IN 47809-9989
(800) 841-4744

Indiana University Bloomington

Bloomington, Indiana
www.iub.edu Federal Code: 001809

4-year public university in small city.

Enrollment: 31,087 undergrads, 3% part-time. 7,182 full-time freshmen.

Selectivity: Admits 50 to 75% of applicants.

BASIC COSTS (2008-2009)

Tuition and fees: $8,231; out-of-state residents $24,769.

Per-credit charge: $230; out-of-state residents $747.

Room and board: $7,138.

FINANCIAL AID PICTURE (2007-2008)

Students with need: Out of 4,671 full-time freshmen who applied for aid, 2,940 were judged to have need. Of these, 2,848 received aid, and 845 had their full need met. Average financial aid package met 93% of need; average scholarship/grant was $8,207; average loan was $4,032. For part-time students, average financial aid package was $6,076.

Students without need: 1,868 full-time freshmen who did not demonstrate need for aid received scholarships/grants; average award was $5,556. No-need awards available for academics, art, athletics, leadership, minority status, music/drama, religious affiliation, ROTC.

Scholarships offered: ***Merit:*** Wells Scholarship; all costs for 4 years; individual schools nominate students; 25 students selected each year. Honors College Scholarship; $1,000-$6,000; 1300 SAT (30 ACT), top 10% class rank. Hudson & Holland; $4,000-$7,000; 1000 SAT (25 ACT), top 20% class rank, 3.0 GPA, based on African, Hispanic, Native American ethnicity. Mathematics and Science Scholarship; $5,000-$6,000; 1000 SAT (25 ACT), top 20% class rank, 3.0 GPA. E.W. Kelley Scholars Program; tuition, room and board, books (overseas study funding, if requested); business major, 1300 SAT (30 ACT), top 10% class rank. School of Music Dean's Award; amounts vary; exceptional talent displayed in audition. Residence Scholarship (via Honors College); $1,500; 1100 SAT (27 ACT), top 10% class rank. Faculty Scholarship: amounts vary; for out-of-state residents with superior test scores and class rank. Valedictorian Award; $1,000; for valedictorians from Indiana schools. 21st Century Scholars Award; in-state Instructional fees; Indiana residence, fulfilled terms of pledged in eighth grade, filed FAFSA before March 1 of senior year. Army and Air Force ROTC Scholarships; tuition, fees, books, $200 monthly stipend. All SAT scores listed exclusive of the writing portion. ***Athletic:*** 76 full-time freshmen received athletic scholarships; average amount $18,685.

Cumulative student debt: 56% of graduating class had student loans; average debt was $22,015.

Additional info: Majority of institutional gift aid merit-based. Some need-based grants go to merit winners with financial need.

FINANCIAL AID PROCEDURES

Forms required: FAFSA.

Dates and Deadlines: Priority date 3/1; no closing date. Applicants notified on a rolling basis starting 4/1.

Transfers: Except for school of music, no merit-based aid for transfer students.

CONTACT

Susan Pugh, Director of Student Financial Assistance
300 North Jordan Avenue, Bloomington, IN 47405
(812) 855-0321

Indiana University East

Richmond, Indiana
www.iue.edu Federal Code: 001811

4-year public university and branch campus college in large town.

Enrollment: 2,081 undergrads, 35% part-time. 268 full-time freshmen.

Selectivity: Open admission; but selective for some programs.

BASIC COSTS (2008-2009)

Tuition and fees: $5,556; out-of-state residents $13,722.

Per-credit charge: $173; out-of-state residents $445.

FINANCIAL AID PICTURE (2007-2008)

Students with need: Out of 236 full-time freshmen who applied for aid, 187 were judged to have need. Of these, 180 received aid, and 16 had their full need met. Average financial aid package met 94% of need; average scholarship/grant was $4,849; average loan was $2,953. For part-time students, average financial aid package was $4,654.

Students without need: 21 full-time freshmen who did not demonstrate need for aid received scholarships/grants; average award was $976. No-need awards available for academics, alumni affiliation, leadership.

Cumulative student debt: 78% of graduating class had student loans; average debt was $24,309.

FINANCIAL AID PROCEDURES

Forms required: FAFSA, institutional form.

Dates and Deadlines: Priority date 3/1; no closing date. Applicants notified on a rolling basis starting 5/1; must reply within 2 week(s) of notification.

CONTACT

William Gill, Director of Financial Aid
2325 Chester Boulevard, Richmond, IN 47374-1289
(765) 973-8288

Indiana University Kokomo

Kokomo, Indiana
www.iuk.edu Federal Code: 001814

4-year public university in large town.

Enrollment: 2,204 undergrads, 41% part-time. 382 full-time freshmen.

Selectivity: Admits over 75% of applicants.

BASIC COSTS (2008-2009)

Tuition and fees: $5,591; out-of-state residents $13,754.

Per-credit charge: $172; out-of-state residents $445.

FINANCIAL AID PICTURE (2007-2008)

Students with need: Out of 302 full-time freshmen who applied for aid, 215 were judged to have need. Of these, 195 received aid, and 16 had their full need met. Average financial aid package met 92% of need; average scholarship/grant was $5,140; average loan was $2,741. For part-time students, average financial aid package was $5,267.

Students without need: 23 full-time freshmen who did not demonstrate need for aid received scholarships/grants; average award was $1,562. No-need awards available for academics.

Cumulative student debt: 63% of graduating class had student loans; average debt was $20,492.

FINANCIAL AID PROCEDURES

Forms required: FAFSA, institutional form.

Dates and Deadlines: Closing date 3/1. Applicants notified on a rolling basis starting 5/1; must reply within 4 week(s) of notification.

CONTACT

David Campbell, Director of Financial Aid
Box 9003, KC 230A, Kokomo, IN 46904-9003
(765) 455-9217

Indiana University Northwest

Gary, Indiana
www.iun.edu Federal Code: 001815

4-year public university in small city.

Enrollment: 3,974 undergrads, 36% part-time. 556 full-time freshmen.

Selectivity: Admits over 75% of applicants.

BASIC COSTS (2008-2009)

Tuition and fees: $5,669.

Per-credit charge: $174; out-of-state residents $445.

FINANCIAL AID PICTURE (2007-2008)

Students with need: Out of 424 full-time freshmen who applied for aid, 326 were judged to have need. Of these, 302 received aid, and 38 had their full need met. Average financial aid package met 91% of need; average scholarship/grant was $5,160; average loan was $2,902. For part-time students, average financial aid package was $5,311.

Students without need: 34 full-time freshmen who did not demonstrate need for aid received scholarships/grants; average award was $3,051. No-need awards available for academics, athletics.

Cumulative student debt: 69% of graduating class had student loans; average debt was $22,335.

FINANCIAL AID PROCEDURES

Forms required: FAFSA, institutional form.

Dates and Deadlines: Priority date 3/1; no closing date. Applicants notified on a rolling basis starting 5/1; must reply within 2 week(s) of notification.

CONTACT

Harold Burtley, Financial Aid Director
3400 Broadway, Gary, IN 46408
(219) 980-6778

Indiana University South Bend

South Bend, Indiana
www.iusb.edu Federal Code: 001816

4-year public university in small city.

Enrollment: 5,875 undergrads, 34% part-time. 884 full-time freshmen.

Selectivity: Admits over 75% of applicants.

BASIC COSTS (2008-2009)

Tuition and fees: $5,763; out-of-state residents $14,880.

Per-credit charge: $177; out-of-state residents $481.

FINANCIAL AID PICTURE (2007-2008)

Students with need: Out of 694 full-time freshmen who applied for aid, 517 were judged to have need. Of these, 482 received aid, and 43 had their full need met. Average financial aid package met 94% of need; average scholarship/grant was $5,090; average loan was $2,788. For part-time students, average financial aid package was $4,696.

Students without need: 34 full-time freshmen who did not demonstrate need for aid received scholarships/grants; average award was $1,744. No-need awards available for academics, athletics.

Scholarships offered: ***Merit:*** Honors Scholarship; $1,200 per academic year (full-time); based on 1200 SAT (exclusive of Writing) or 27 ACT, rank in top 10%, and 3.5 GPA; renewable up to 8 semesters. Alumni Scholarship; $3,500 freshman year; must be first-time freshman from Northern Indiana, meet Honors Scholarship criteria, submit essay and 3 letters of recommendation. ***Athletic:*** 4 full-time freshmen received athletic scholarships; average amount $7,745.

Cumulative student debt: 72% of graduating class had student loans; average debt was $22,235.

FINANCIAL AID PROCEDURES

Forms required: FAFSA, institutional form.

Dates and Deadlines: Closing date 3/1. Applicants notified on a rolling basis starting 5/1.

Transfers: No deadline.

CONTACT

Cyndi Lang, Director of Financial Aid
1700 Mishawaka Avenue, South Bend, IN 46634-7111
(574) 520-4357

Indiana University Southeast

New Albany, Indiana
www.ius.edu Federal Code: 001817

4-year public university in large town.

Enrollment: 5,352 undergrads, 34% part-time. 787 full-time freshmen.

Selectivity: Admits over 75% of applicants.

BASIC COSTS (2008-2009)

Tuition and fees: $5,644; out-of-state residents $13,804.

Per-credit charge: $173; out-of-state residents $445.

Room and board: $6,240.

Additional info: Room and board includes $600 meal plan. Meal plans can be purchased for $100, $300 or $600.

FINANCIAL AID PICTURE (2007-2008)

Students with need: Out of 585 full-time freshmen who applied for aid, 455 were judged to have need. Of these, 420 received aid, and 44 had their full need met. Average financial aid package met 91% of need; average scholarship/grant was $5,226; average loan was $2,675. For part-time students, average financial aid package was $4,723.

Students without need: 56 full-time freshmen who did not demonstrate need for aid received scholarships/grants; average award was $1,735. No-need awards available for academics, art, athletics, leadership, minority status, music/drama.

Scholarships offered: 6 full-time freshmen received athletic scholarships; average amount $1,200.

Cumulative student debt: 57% of graduating class had student loans; average debt was $19,592.

FINANCIAL AID PROCEDURES

Forms required: FAFSA.

Dates and Deadlines: Priority date 3/1; no closing date. Applicants notified on a rolling basis starting 5/1; must reply within 3 week(s) of notification.

CONTACT

Brittany Hubbard, Director of Financial Aid
4201 Grant Line Road, New Albany, IN 47150-6405
(812) 941-2246 ext. 2260

Indiana University-Purdue University Fort Wayne

Fort Wayne, Indiana
www.ipfw.edu Federal Code: 001828

4-year public university and branch campus college in large city.

Enrollment: 10,787 undergrads, 30% part-time. 1,854 full-time freshmen.

Selectivity: Admits over 75% of applicants.

BASIC COSTS (2008-2009)

Tuition and fees: $6,596; out-of-state residents $15,545.

Per-credit charge: $192; out-of-state residents $490.

Room only: $5,400.

FINANCIAL AID PICTURE (2007-2008)

Students with need: Out of 1,554 full-time freshmen who applied for aid, 1,208 were judged to have need. Of these, 1,119 received aid, and 42 had their full need met. Average financial aid package met 50% of need; average scholarship/grant was $4,780; average loan was $3,157. For part-time students, average financial aid package was $5,829.

Students without need: 16 full-time freshmen who did not demonstrate need for aid received scholarships/grants; average award was $1,396. No-need awards available for academics, athletics, state/district residency.

Scholarships offered: 22 full-time freshmen received athletic scholarships; average amount $11,645.

Cumulative student debt: 62% of graduating class had student loans; average debt was $20,335.

FINANCIAL AID PROCEDURES

Forms required: FAFSA.

Dates and Deadlines: Priority date 3/10; no closing date. Applicants notified on a rolling basis starting 5/15; must reply within 3 week(s) of notification.

CONTACT

Judith Cramer, Director of Financial Aid
2101 East Coliseum Boulevard, Fort Wayne, IN 46805-1499
(260) 481-6820

Indiana University-Purdue University Indianapolis

Indianapolis, Indiana
www.iupui.edu Federal Code: 001813

4-year public university in very large city.

Enrollment: 20,390 undergrads, 28% part-time. 2,744 full-time freshmen.

Selectivity: Admits 50 to 75% of applicants.

BASIC COSTS (2008-2009)

Tuition and fees: $7,191; out-of-state residents $20,579.

Per-credit charge: $218; out-of-state residents $664.

Room only: $3,140.

FINANCIAL AID PICTURE (2007-2008)

Students with need: Out of 2,202 full-time freshmen who applied for aid, 1,672 were judged to have need. Of these, 1,618 received aid, and 167 had their full need met. Average financial aid package met 80% of need; average scholarship/grant was $6,696; average loan was $2,880. For part-time students, average financial aid package was $5,414.

Students without need: 354 full-time freshmen who did not demonstrate need for aid received scholarships/grants; average award was $2,748. No-need awards available for academics, ROTC.
Scholarships offered: 23 full-time freshmen received athletic scholarships; average amount $7,170.
Cumulative student debt: 70% of graduating class had student loans; average debt was $25,241.

FINANCIAL AID PROCEDURES
Forms required: FAFSA.
Dates and Deadlines: Priority date 3/1; no closing date. Applicants notified on a rolling basis starting 4/1.

CONTACT
Kathy Purvis, Director of Scholarships and Financial Aid
420 North University Boulevard, Cavanaugh Hall R129, Indianapolis, IN 46202-5143
(317) 274-4162

Indiana Wesleyan University

Marion, Indiana
www.indwes.edu Federal Code: 001822

4-year private university and liberal arts college in large town, affiliated with Wesleyan Church.
Enrollment: 3,109 undergrads, 3% part-time. 885 full-time freshmen.
Selectivity: Admits over 75% of applicants.

BASIC COSTS (2009-2010)
Tuition and fees: $20,496.
Per-credit charge: $732.
Room and board: $6,770.
Additional info: Required fees vary by program.

FINANCIAL AID PICTURE (2008-2009)
Students with need: Out of 773 full-time freshmen who applied for aid, 649 were judged to have need. Of these, 648 received aid, and 67 had their full need met. Average financial aid package met 50% of need; average scholarship/grant was $6,442; average loan was $4,172. For part-time students, average financial aid package was $5,223.
Students without need: 113 full-time freshmen who did not demonstrate need for aid received scholarships/grants; average award was $23,741. No-need awards available for academics, alumni affiliation, art, athletics, music/drama, ROTC.
Scholarships offered: ***Merit:*** Academic Scholarships; $750-$6,000; 3.2 GPA and 1050 SAT (exclusive of Writing) or 23 ACT required. ***Athletic:*** 42 full-time freshmen received athletic scholarships; average amount $3,245.

FINANCIAL AID PROCEDURES
Forms required: FAFSA.
Dates and Deadlines: Closing date 3/1. Applicants notified by 4/1.

CONTACT
Thomas Ratliff, Associate Vice President for Financial Aid
4201 South Washington Street, Marion, IN 46953-4999
(765) 677-2116

Ivy Tech Community College: Bloomington

Bloomington, Indiana
www.ivytech.edu Federal Code: 035213

2-year public community college in small city.
Enrollment: 5,136 undergrads, 48% part-time. 811 full-time freshmen.
Selectivity: Open admission; but selective for some programs.

BASIC COSTS (2008-2009)
Tuition and fees: $2,930; out-of-state residents $5,879.
Per-credit charge: $95; out-of-state residents $193.
Additional info: Out-of-state distance education tuition: $124 per credit hour ($3,731 for academic year).

FINANCIAL AID PICTURE (2007-2008)
Students with need: Need-based aid available for full-time and part-time students. Work study available nights.

FINANCIAL AID PROCEDURES
Forms required: FAFSA.
Dates and Deadlines: Priority date 3/1; no closing date. Applicants notified on a rolling basis starting 7/1.

CONTACT
Patt McCafferty, Director of Financial Aid
200 Daniels Way, Bloomington, IN 47404-1511
(812) 332-1559

Ivy Tech Community College: Central Indiana

Indianapolis, Indiana
www.ivytech.edu Federal Code: 009917

2-year public community college in very large city.
Enrollment: 15,795 undergrads, 67% part-time. 1,725 full-time freshmen.
Selectivity: Open admission; but selective for some programs.

BASIC COSTS (2008-2009)
Tuition and fees: $2,930; out-of-state residents $5,879.
Per-credit charge: $95; out-of-state residents $193.
Additional info: Out-of-state distance education tuition: $124 per credit hour ($3,731 for academic year).

FINANCIAL AID PICTURE (2007-2008)
Students with need: Need-based aid available for full-time and part-time students. Work study available nights.

FINANCIAL AID PROCEDURES
Forms required: FAFSA.
Dates and Deadlines: Priority date 3/1; no closing date. Applicants notified on a rolling basis starting 7/1.

CONTACT
Daniel Adams, Director of Financial Aid
50 West Fall Creek Parkway North Drive, Indianapolis, IN 46208-5752
(317) 921-4882

Ivy Tech Community College: Columbus

Columbus, Indiana
www.ivytech.edu Federal Code: 010038

2-year public community college in large town.
Enrollment: 3,174 undergrads, 60% part-time. 333 full-time freshmen.
Selectivity: Open admission; but selective for some programs.

BASIC COSTS (2008-2009)
Tuition and fees: $2,930; out-of-state residents $5,879.
Per-credit charge: $95; out-of-state residents $193.
Additional info: Out-of-state distance education tuition: $124 per credit hour ($3,731 for academic year).

FINANCIAL AID PICTURE (2007-2008)
Students with need: Need-based aid available for full-time and part-time students. Work study available nights.

FINANCIAL AID PROCEDURES
Forms required: FAFSA.
Dates and Deadlines: Priority date 3/1; no closing date. Applicants notified on a rolling basis starting 7/1.

CONTACT
Nina Loesch, Director of Financial Aid
4475 Central Avenue, Columbus, IN 47203-1868
(812) 372-9925

Ivy Tech Community College: East Central
Muncie, Indiana
www.ivytech.edu Federal Code: 009924

2-year public community college in small city.
Enrollment: 6,702 undergrads, 52% part-time. 908 full-time freshmen.
Selectivity: Open admission; but selective for some programs.

BASIC COSTS (2008-2009)
Tuition and fees: $2,930; out-of-state residents $5,879.
Per-credit charge: $95; out-of-state residents $193.
Additional info: Out-of-state distance education tuition: $124 per credit hour ($3,731 for academic year).

FINANCIAL AID PICTURE (2007-2008)
Students with need: Need-based aid available for full-time and part-time students. Work study available nights.
Additional info: Higher Education Aid (HEA), Child of Disabled/Deceased Veterans (CDV), Ivy Tech Scholarships (IVTC) and grants, vocational rehabilitation and veteran's assistance available. None require repayment.

FINANCIAL AID PROCEDURES
Forms required: FAFSA.
Dates and Deadlines: Priority date 3/1; no closing date. Applicants notified on a rolling basis starting 7/1.

CONTACT
Sylvia Bogle, Director of Financial Aid
4301 South Cowan Road, Muncie, IN 47302-9448
(765) 289-2291 ext. 1222

Ivy Tech Community College: Kokomo
Kokomo, Indiana
www.ivytech.edu Federal Code: 010041

2-year public community college in large town.
Enrollment: 3,905 undergrads, 63% part-time. 302 full-time freshmen.
Selectivity: Open admission; but selective for some programs.

BASIC COSTS (2008-2009)
Tuition and fees: $2,930; out-of-state residents $5,879.
Per-credit charge: $95; out-of-state residents $193.
Additional info: Out-of-state distance education tuition: $124 per credit hour ($3,731 for academic year).

FINANCIAL AID PICTURE (2007-2008)
Students with need: Need-based aid available for full-time and part-time students. Work study available nights.

FINANCIAL AID PROCEDURES
Forms required: FAFSA.
Dates and Deadlines: Priority date 3/1; no closing date. Applicants notified on a rolling basis starting 7/1.
Transfers: Applicants notified on a rolling basis starting 7/1.

CONTACT
David Scheblo, Director of Financial Aid
1815 East Morgan Street, Kokomo, IN 46903-1373
(765) 459-0561

Ivy Tech Community College: Lafayette
Lafayette, Indiana
www.ivytech.edu Federal Code: 010039

2-year public community college in large town.
Enrollment: 5,563 undergrads, 49% part-time. 753 full-time freshmen.
Selectivity: Open admission; but selective for some programs.

BASIC COSTS (2008-2009)
Tuition and fees: $2,930; out-of-state residents $5,879.
Per-credit charge: $95; out-of-state residents $193.
Additional info: Out-of-state distance education tuition: $124 per credit hour ($3,731 for academic year).

FINANCIAL AID PICTURE (2007-2008)
Students with need: Need-based aid available for full-time and part-time students. Work study available nights.

FINANCIAL AID PROCEDURES
Forms required: FAFSA.
Dates and Deadlines: Priority date 3/1; no closing date. Applicants notified on a rolling basis starting 7/1.

CONTACT
Christina Coon, Director of Financial Aid
3101 South Creasy Lane, Lafayette, IN 47905-6299
(765) 772-9100

Ivy Tech Community College: North Central
South Bend, Indiana
www.ivytech.edu Federal Code: 008423

2-year public community college in small city.
Enrollment: 6,090 undergrads, 69% part-time. 497 full-time freshmen.
Selectivity: Open admission; but selective for some programs.

BASIC COSTS (2008-2009)
Tuition and fees: $2,930; out-of-state residents $5,879.
Per-credit charge: $95; out-of-state residents $193.
Additional info: Out-of-state distance education tuition: $124 per credit hour ($3,731 for academic year).

FINANCIAL AID PICTURE (2007-2008)
Students with need: Need-based aid available for full-time and part-time students. Work study available nights.

FINANCIAL AID PROCEDURES
Forms required: FAFSA.
Dates and Deadlines: Priority date 3/1; no closing date. Applicants notified on a rolling basis starting 7/1.

CONTACT
Jeff Fisher, Director of Financial Aid
220 Dean Johnson Boulevard, South Bend, IN 46601-3415
(219) 289-7001

Ivy Tech Community College: Northeast

Fort Wayne, Indiana
www.ivytech.edu Federal Code: 009926

2-year public community college in small city.
Enrollment: 7,458 undergrads, 60% part-time. 806 full-time freshmen.
Selectivity: Open admission; but selective for some programs.

BASIC COSTS (2008-2009)

Tuition and fees: $2,930; out-of-state residents $5,879.
Per-credit charge: $95; out-of-state residents $193.
Additional info: Out-of-state distance education tuition: $124 per credit hour ($3,731 for academic year).

FINANCIAL AID PICTURE (2007-2008)

Students with need: Need-based aid available for full-time and part-time students. Work study available nights.

FINANCIAL AID PROCEDURES

Forms required: FAFSA.
Dates and Deadlines: Priority date 3/1; no closing date. Applicants notified on a rolling basis starting 7/1.

CONTACT

Teresa Sweazey, Director of Financial Aid
3800 North Anthony Boulevard, Fort Wayne, IN 46805-1489
(260) 482-9171

Ivy Tech Community College: Northwest

Gary, Indiana
www.ivytech.edu Federal Code: 010040

2-year public community college in small city.
Enrollment: 5,701 undergrads, 61% part-time. 633 full-time freshmen.
Selectivity: Open admission; but selective for some programs.

BASIC COSTS (2008-2009)

Tuition and fees: $2,930; out-of-state residents $5,879.
Per-credit charge: $95; out-of-state residents $193.
Additional info: Out-of-state distance education tuition: $124 per credit hour ($3,731 for academic year).

FINANCIAL AID PICTURE (2007-2008)

Students with need: Need-based aid available for full-time and part-time students. Work study available nights.

FINANCIAL AID PROCEDURES

Forms required: FAFSA.
Dates and Deadlines: Priority date 3/1; no closing date. Applicants notified on a rolling basis starting 7/1.

CONTACT

Barb Jerzyk, Director of Financial Aid
1440 East 35th Avenue, Gary, IN 46409-1499
(219) 981-1111

Ivy Tech Community College: Richmond

Richmond, Indiana
www.ivytech.edu Federal Code: 010037

2-year public community college in large town.
Enrollment: 2,457 undergrads, 64% part-time. 172 full-time freshmen.
Selectivity: Open admission; but selective for some programs.

BASIC COSTS (2008-2009)

Tuition and fees: $2,930; out-of-state residents $5,879.
Per-credit charge: $95; out-of-state residents $193.
Additional info: Out-of-state distance education tuition: $124 per credit hour ($3,731 for academic year).

FINANCIAL AID PICTURE (2007-2008)

Students with need: Need-based aid available for full-time and part-time students. Work study available nights.

FINANCIAL AID PROCEDURES

Forms required: FAFSA.
Dates and Deadlines: Priority date 3/1; no closing date. Applicants notified on a rolling basis starting 7/1.

CONTACT

Ann Franzen-Roha, Director of Financial Aid
2357 Chester Boulevard, Richmond, IN 47374-1298
(765) 966-2656

Ivy Tech Community College: South Central

Sellersburg, Indiana
www.ivytech.edu Federal Code: 010109

2-year public community college in small town.
Enrollment: 3,826 undergrads, 64% part-time. 403 full-time freshmen.
Selectivity: Open admission; but selective for some programs.

BASIC COSTS (2008-2009)

Tuition and fees: $2,930; out-of-state residents $5,879.
Per-credit charge: $95; out-of-state residents $193.
Additional info: Out-of-state distance education tuition: $124 per credit hour ($3,731 for academic year).

FINANCIAL AID PICTURE (2007-2008)

Students with need: Need-based aid available for full-time and part-time students. Work study available nights.

FINANCIAL AID PROCEDURES

Forms required: FAFSA.
Dates and Deadlines: Priority date 3/1; no closing date. Applicants notified on a rolling basis starting 7/1.

CONTACT

Gary Cottrill, Director of Financial Aid
8204 Highway 311, Sellersburg, IN 47172-1897
(812) 246-3301

Ivy Tech Community College: Southeast

Madison, Indiana
www.ivytech.edu Federal Code: 009923

2-year public community college in large town.
Enrollment: 2,056 undergrads, 55% part-time. 253 full-time freshmen.
Selectivity: Open admission; but selective for some programs.

BASIC COSTS (2008-2009)

Tuition and fees: $2,930; out-of-state residents $5,879.
Per-credit charge: $95; out-of-state residents $193.
Additional info: Out-of-state distance education tuition: $124 per credit hour ($3,731 for academic year).

FINANCIAL AID PICTURE (2007-2008)

Students with need: Need-based aid available for full-time and part-time students. Work study available nights.

FINANCIAL AID PROCEDURES
Forms required: FAFSA.
Dates and Deadlines: Priority date 3/1; no closing date. Applicants notified on a rolling basis starting 7/1.

CONTACT
Richard Hill, Director of Financial Aid
590 Ivy Tech Drive, Madison, IN 47250-1881
(812) 265-2580 ext. 4148

Ivy Tech Community College: Southwest

Evansville, Indiana
www.ivytech.edu Federal Code: 009925

2-year public community college in small city.
Enrollment: 4,783 undergrads, 59% part-time. 516 full-time freshmen.
Selectivity: Open admission; but selective for some programs.

BASIC COSTS (2008-2009)
Tuition and fees: $2,930; out-of-state residents $5,879.
Per-credit charge: $95; out-of-state residents $193.
Additional info: Out-of-state distance education tuition: $124 per credit hour ($3,731 for academic year).

FINANCIAL AID PICTURE (2007-2008)
Students with need: Need-based aid available for full-time and part-time students. Work study available nights.

FINANCIAL AID PROCEDURES
Forms required: FAFSA.
Dates and Deadlines: Priority date 3/1; no closing date. Applicants notified on a rolling basis starting 7/1.

CONTACT
Kristi Eidson-Spahn, Director of Financial Aid
3501 First Avenue, Evansville, IN 47710-3398
(812) 426-2865

Ivy Tech Community College: Wabash Valley

Terre Haute, Indiana
www.ivytech.edu Federal Code: 008547

2-year public community college in small city.
Enrollment: 5,084 undergrads, 55% part-time. 522 full-time freshmen.
Selectivity: Open admission; but selective for some programs.

BASIC COSTS (2008-2009)
Tuition and fees: $2,930; out-of-state residents $5,879.
Per-credit charge: $95; out-of-state residents $193.
Additional info: Out-of-state distance education tuition: $124 per credit hour ($3,731 for academic year).

FINANCIAL AID PICTURE (2007-2008)
Students with need: Need-based aid available for full-time and part-time students. Work study available nights.

FINANCIAL AID PROCEDURES
Forms required: FAFSA.
Dates and Deadlines: Priority date 3/1; no closing date. Applicants notified on a rolling basis starting 7/1.
Transfers: Applicants notified on a rolling basis starting 7/1.

CONTACT
Julie Wonderlin, Director of Financial Aid
8000 South Education Drive, Terre Haute, IN 47802-4898
(812) 299-1121

Kaplan College: Merrillville

Merrillville, Indiana
www.sawyercollege.edu Federal Code: 022018

2-year for-profit technical college in large town.
Enrollment: 390 undergrads.
Selectivity: Open admission.

BASIC COSTS (2008-2009)
Tuition and fees: $12,316.

FINANCIAL AID PICTURE
Students with need: Need-based aid available for full-time and part-time students.

FINANCIAL AID PROCEDURES
Forms required: FAFSA.
Dates and Deadlines: No deadline. Applicants notified on a rolling basis.

CONTACT
Lisa Coff, Director of Financial Aid
3803 East Lincoln Highway, Merrillville, IN 46410
(219) 947-8400 ext. 8409

Manchester College

North Manchester, Indiana
www.manchester.edu Federal Code: 001820

4-year private liberal arts college in small town, affiliated with Church of the Brethren.
Enrollment: 1,120 undergrads, 1% part-time. 396 full-time freshmen.
Selectivity: Admits over 75% of applicants.

BASIC COSTS (2009-2010)
Tuition and fees: $23,790.
Per-credit charge: $700.
Room and board: $8,050.
Additional info: Health insurance and other fees as required.

FINANCIAL AID PICTURE (2008-2009)
Students with need: Out of 380 full-time freshmen who applied for aid, 337 were judged to have need. Of these, 337 received aid, and 40 had their full need met. Average financial aid package met 87% of need; average scholarship/grant was $16,557; average loan was $4,580. For part-time students, average financial aid package was $22,011.
Students without need: 43 full-time freshmen who did not demonstrate need for aid received scholarships/grants; average award was $10,519. No-need awards available for academics, alumni affiliation, minority status, music/drama, religious affiliation.
Scholarships offered: Honors Fellowship; full tuition; based on academics; 2 awarded. Presidential Leadership Award; $2,500 travel grant; 3 awarded. Trustee Scholarships; $12,000; based on merit; 40 awarded to each incoming class. Presidential Scholarships; $9,000; based on merit. Arts, service, modern language scholarships; $9,000; based on merit/ability.
Additional info: Students are automatically considered for all scholarship programs.

FINANCIAL AID PROCEDURES
Forms required: FAFSA.
Dates and Deadlines: Priority date 3/1; no closing date. Applicants notified on a rolling basis starting 2/15; must reply within 2 week(s) of notification.
Transfers: Aid eligibility remaining determined by reviewing total credit hours transferred and financial aid transcripts.

CONTACT

Gina Voelz, Director of Financial Aid
604 East College Avenue, North Manchester, IN 46962-0365
(260) 982-5066

Marian College

Indianapolis, Indiana
www.marian.edu Federal Code: 001821

4-year private liberal arts college in very large city, affiliated with Roman Catholic Church.
Enrollment: 1,892 undergrads, 25% part-time. 322 full-time freshmen.
Selectivity: Admits 50 to 75% of applicants.

BASIC COSTS (2008-2009)

Tuition and fees: $22,400.
Per-credit charge: $940.
Room and board: $7,228.

FINANCIAL AID PICTURE (2008-2009)

Students with need: Out of 309 full-time freshmen who applied for aid, 264 were judged to have need. Of these, 264 received aid, and 77 had their full need met. Average financial aid package met 87% of need; average scholarship/grant was $11,257; average loan was $3,506. For part-time students, average financial aid package was $8,553.
Students without need: 57 full-time freshmen who did not demonstrate need for aid received scholarships/grants; average award was $12,759. No-need awards available for academics, alumni affiliation, art, athletics, leadership, music/drama, religious affiliation.
Scholarships offered: 25 full-time freshmen received athletic scholarships; average amount $9,620.
Cumulative student debt: 92% of graduating class had student loans; average debt was $23,467.

FINANCIAL AID PROCEDURES

Forms required: FAFSA, institutional form.
Dates and Deadlines: Priority date 3/15; no closing date. Applicants notified on a rolling basis starting 3/15; must reply within 2 week(s) of notification.
Transfers: No deadline. Applicants notified on a rolling basis starting 3/15; must reply within 2 week(s) of notification.

CONTACT

John Shelton, Dean for Financial Aid and Enrollment
3200 Cold Spring Road, Indianapolis, IN 46222-1997
(317) 955-6040

Oakland City University

Oakland City, Indiana
www.oak.edu Federal Code: 001824

4-year private university and liberal arts college in small town, affiliated with Baptist General Conference.
Enrollment: 1,529 undergrads.
Selectivity: Open admission; but selective for some programs.

BASIC COSTS (2009-2010)

Tuition and fees: $15,400.
Per-credit charge: $500.
Room and board: $6,700.
Additional info: Tuition/fee waivers available for minority students, unemployed or children of unemployed.

FINANCIAL AID PICTURE (2008-2009)

Students with need: Need-based aid available for full-time and part-time students. Work study available nights, weekends, and for part-time students.
Students without need: No-need awards available for academics, alumni affiliation, art, athletics, minority status, music/drama, religious affiliation.

FINANCIAL AID PROCEDURES

Forms required: FAFSA.
Dates and Deadlines: Closing date 3/1. Applicants notified on a rolling basis starting 5/1.

CONTACT

Caren Richeson, Director of Financial Aid
138 North Lucretia Street, Oakland City, IN 47660
(812) 749-1224

Purdue University

West Lafayette, Indiana
www.purdue.edu Federal Code: 001825

4-year public university in small city.
Enrollment: 31,491 undergrads, 4% part-time. 6,792 full-time freshmen.
Selectivity: Admits 50 to 75% of applicants.

BASIC COSTS (2008-2009)

Tuition and fees: $7,750; out-of-state residents $23,224.
Per-credit charge: $262; out-of-state residents $755.
Room and board: $7,930.
Additional info: Engineering students pay additional $656 fee per year. Management students pay additional $1,022 fee per year.

FINANCIAL AID PICTURE (2008-2009)

Students with need: Need-based aid available for full-time and part-time students.
Students without need: No-need awards available for academics, athletics, leadership, music/drama, ROTC, state/district residency.
Additional info: Cooperative work for credit available in many programs.

FINANCIAL AID PROCEDURES

Forms required: FAFSA.
Dates and Deadlines: Priority date 3/1; no closing date. Applicants notified by 4/15.

CONTACT

Joyce Hall, Director of Financial Aid
475 Stadium Mall Drive, West Lafayette, IN 47907-2050
(765) 494-5050

Purdue University Calumet

Hammond, Indiana
www.calumet.purdue.edu Federal Code: 001827

4-year public university and branch campus college in small city.
Enrollment: 8,053 undergrads, 32% part-time. 1,267 full-time freshmen.
Selectivity: Admits 50 to 75% of applicants.

BASIC COSTS (2008-2009)

Tuition and fees: $5,970; out-of-state residents $13,279.
Per-credit charge: $181; out-of-state residents $424.

FINANCIAL AID PICTURE (2007-2008)

Students with need: Out of 920 full-time freshmen who applied for aid, 712 were judged to have need. Of these, 632 received aid, and 199 had their full need met. Average financial aid package met 11% of need; average scholarship/grant was $2,812; average loan was $1,816. For part-time students, average financial aid package was $3,618.
Students without need: 77 full-time freshmen who did not demonstrate need for aid received scholarships/grants; average award was $1,340. No-need awards available for academics, alumni affiliation, athletics, minority status, state/district residency.

Scholarships offered: 8 full-time freshmen received athletic scholarships; average amount $2,000.
Cumulative student debt: 58% of graduating class had student loans; average debt was $18,735.

FINANCIAL AID PROCEDURES

Forms required: FAFSA.
Dates and Deadlines: Priority date 3/10; closing date 6/30. Applicants notified on a rolling basis starting 5/1; must reply within 2 week(s) of notification.

CONTACT

Carol Zencka, Director of Financial Aid and Student Accounts
2200 169th Street, Hammond, IN 46323-2094
(219) 989-2301

Purdue University North Central

Westville, Indiana
www.pnc.edu Federal Code: 001826

4-year public branch campus college in rural community.
Enrollment: 3,762 undergrads, 33% part-time. 753 full-time freshmen.
Selectivity: Admits over 75% of applicants.

BASIC COSTS (2008-2009)

Tuition and fees: $6,080; out-of-state residents $14,205.
Per-credit charge: $182; out-of-state residents $452.
Additional info: Tuition/fee waivers available for minority students.

FINANCIAL AID PICTURE (2008-2009)

Students with need: Out of 562 full-time freshmen who applied for aid, 443 were judged to have need. Of these, 405 received aid, and 53 had their full need met. Average financial aid package met 36% of need; average scholarship/grant was $3,960; average loan was $3,092. For part-time students, average financial aid package was $5,192.
Students without need: This college awards aid only to students with need.
Scholarships offered: 15 full-time freshmen received athletic scholarships; average amount $670.
Cumulative student debt: 61% of graduating class had student loans; average debt was $19,536.

FINANCIAL AID PROCEDURES

Forms required: FAFSA.
Dates and Deadlines: Priority date 3/10; closing date 6/30. Applicants notified on a rolling basis starting 5/31; must reply within 2 week(s) of notification.
Transfers: No deadline. Transfer students not considered for campus-based financial aid.

CONTACT

Bryant Dabney, Director of Financial Aid
1401 South US Highway 421, Westville, IN 46391-9542
(219) 785-5278

Rose-Hulman Institute of Technology

Terre Haute, Indiana
www.rose-hulman.edu Federal Code: 001830

4-year private engineering college in small city.
Enrollment: 1,818 undergrads. 482 full-time freshmen.
Selectivity: Admits 50 to 75% of applicants. GED not accepted.

BASIC COSTS (2009-2010)

Tuition and fees: $34,560.
Per-credit charge: $987.
Room and board: $9,441.
Additional info: Purchase of laptop computer (approximately $2,800) required of freshmen.

FINANCIAL AID PICTURE (2008-2009)

Students with need: Out of 419 full-time freshmen who applied for aid, 351 were judged to have need. Of these, 351 received aid, and 53 had their full need met. Average financial aid package met 85% of need; average scholarship/grant was $20,042; average loan was $12,642. For part-time students, average financial aid package was $22,981.
Students without need: 125 full-time freshmen who did not demonstrate need for aid received scholarships/grants; average award was $10,269. No-need awards available for academics, minority status, ROTC.
Cumulative student debt: 78% of graduating class had student loans; average debt was $36,818.

FINANCIAL AID PROCEDURES

Forms required: FAFSA.
Dates and Deadlines: Priority date 3/1; no closing date. Applicants notified on a rolling basis starting 3/10.
Transfers: No deadline. Applicants notified on a rolling basis; must reply by 6/1.

CONTACT

Melinda Middleton, Director of Financial Aid
Office of Admissions, Terre Haute, IN 47803-3999
(800) 248-7448

Saint Joseph's College

Rensselaer, Indiana
www.saintjoe.edu Federal Code: 001833

4-year private liberal arts college in small town, affiliated with Roman Catholic Church.
Enrollment: 1,057 undergrads, 4% part-time. 286 full-time freshmen.
Selectivity: Admits 50 to 75% of applicants.

BASIC COSTS (2009-2010)

Tuition and fees: $24,530.
Per-credit charge: $810.
Room and board: $7,420.

FINANCIAL AID PICTURE (2007-2008)

Students with need: Out of 286 full-time freshmen who applied for aid, 231 were judged to have need. Of these, 231 received aid, and 70 had their full need met. Average financial aid package met 81% of need; average scholarship/grant was $13,873; average loan was $3,609. For part-time students, average financial aid package was $8,423.
Students without need: 56 full-time freshmen who did not demonstrate need for aid received scholarships/grants; average award was $12,174. No-need awards available for academics, alumni affiliation, athletics, minority status, music/drama.
Scholarships offered: 19 full-time freshmen received athletic scholarships; average amount $6,699.
Cumulative student debt: 77% of graduating class had student loans; average debt was $28,135.

FINANCIAL AID PROCEDURES

Forms required: FAFSA.
Dates and Deadlines: Priority date 3/1; no closing date. Applicants notified on a rolling basis starting 3/1; must reply by 5/1 or within 2 week(s) of notification.
Transfers: No deadline. Applicants notified on a rolling basis; must reply by 5/1 or within 2 week(s) of notification. Limited institutional academic scholarship.

CONTACT

Debra Sizemore, Director of Student Financial Services
Box 890, Rensselaer, IN 47978
(219) 866-6163

St. Mary-of-the-Woods College

St. Mary-of-the-Woods, Indiana
www.smwc.edu Federal Code: 001835

4-year private liberal arts college for women in rural community, affiliated with Roman Catholic Church.
Enrollment: 1,176 undergrads, 58% part-time. 104 full-time freshmen.
Selectivity: Admits 50 to 75% of applicants.

BASIC COSTS (2009-2010)

Tuition and fees: $23,060.
Per-credit charge: $424.
Room and board: $8,450.
Additional info: Tuition/fee waivers available for minority students.

FINANCIAL AID PICTURE (2007-2008)

Students with need: Out of 74 full-time freshmen who applied for aid, 68 were judged to have need. Of these, 68 received aid, and 24 had their full need met. Average financial aid package met 84% of need; average scholarship/grant was $16,413; average loan was $2,888. For part-time students, average financial aid package was $4,954.
Students without need: 35 full-time freshmen who did not demonstrate need for aid received scholarships/grants; average award was $17,200. No-need awards available for academics, alumni affiliation, art, athletics, leadership, minority status, music/drama, state/district residency.
Scholarships offered: ***Merit:*** Saint Mother Theodore Guerin Scholarships; 2 per year at $20,000 a year for 4 years, 8 per year at $13,000 a year for 4 years; based on academics, service and leadership. Top Ten on 10 Scholarships; 2 per year at $20,000 a year for 4 years, 8 per year at $13,000 a year for four years; for local students based on academics, service and leadership. Trustees Scholarships; up to $11,000 a year for 4 years; based on academics. Presidential Scholasrhips; up to $9,000 a year for 4 years; based on academics. Dean's Scholarships; up to $6,000 a year for 4 years; based on academics. Woods Scholarships; up to $4,000 per year for 4 years; based on academics. ***Athletic:*** 6 full-time freshmen received athletic scholarships; average amount $6,566.
Cumulative student debt: 100% of graduating class had student loans; average debt was $11025.8.
Additional info: Portfolio or audition required of applicants who wish to be considered for Creative Arts Scholarship.

FINANCIAL AID PROCEDURES

Forms required: FAFSA.
Dates and Deadlines: Priority date 3/1; no closing date. Applicants notified on a rolling basis starting 12/1; must reply within 6 week(s) of notification.
Transfers: Priority date 7/1; no deadline. Applicants notified on a rolling basis; must reply within 8 week(s) of notification. Transfer grants available for students graduating or transferring from Ivy Tech Community College.

CONTACT

Jacki Switzer, Director of Financial Aid
Guerin Hall, SMWC, St. Mary of the Woods, IN 47876
(812) 535-5109

Saint Mary's College

Notre Dame, Indiana Federal Code: 001836
www.saintmarys.edu CSS Code: 1702

4-year private liberal arts college for women in small city, affiliated with Roman Catholic Church.
Enrollment: 1,613 undergrads. 455 full-time freshmen.
Selectivity: Admits over 75% of applicants.

BASIC COSTS (2009-2010)

Tuition and fees: $29,616.
Per-credit charge: $1,146.
Room and board: $9,206.

FINANCIAL AID PICTURE (2008-2009)

Students with need: Out of 442 full-time freshmen who applied for aid, 288 were judged to have need. Of these, 287 received aid, and 79 had their full need met. Average financial aid package met 84% of need; average scholarship/grant was $17,804; average loan was $3,702. Need-based aid available for part-time students.
Students without need: 140 full-time freshmen who did not demonstrate need for aid received scholarships/grants; average award was $10,498. No-need awards available for academics, art.
Cumulative student debt: 70% of graduating class had student loans; average debt was $26,684.

FINANCIAL AID PROCEDURES

Forms required: FAFSA, CSS PROFILE.
Dates and Deadlines: Priority date 3/1; no closing date. Applicants notified on a rolling basis starting 12/15; must reply by 5/1.
Transfers: Priority date 5/15; no deadline. Applicants notified on a rolling basis. To meet Indiana grant deadlines, Indiana residents must submit FAFSA by March 1.

CONTACT

Kathleen Brown, Director of Financial Aid Notre Dame, IN 46556-5001
(574) 284-4557

Taylor University

Upland, Indiana
www.taylor.edu Federal Code: 001838

4-year private university and liberal arts college in small town, affiliated with interdenominational tradition.
Enrollment: 1,841 undergrads, 2% part-time. 465 full-time freshmen.
Selectivity: Admits over 75% of applicants.

BASIC COSTS (2009-2010)

Tuition and fees: $25,396.
Per-credit charge: $715.
Room and board: $6,708.

FINANCIAL AID PICTURE (2008-2009)

Students with need: Out of 339 full-time freshmen who applied for aid, 266 were judged to have need. Of these, 266 received aid, and 63 had their full need met. Average financial aid package met 76% of need; average scholarship/grant was $13,352; average loan was $4,421. For part-time students, average financial aid package was $9,150.
Students without need: 141 full-time freshmen who did not demonstrate need for aid received scholarships/grants; average award was $4,346. No-need awards available for academics, alumni affiliation, art, athletics, leadership, minority status, music/drama, religious affiliation, state/district residency.
Scholarships offered: 19 full-time freshmen received athletic scholarships; average amount $7,368.

Cumulative student debt: 54% of graduating class had student loans; average debt was $22,942.

FINANCIAL AID PROCEDURES

Forms required: FAFSA.

Dates and Deadlines: Closing date 3/10. Applicants notified on a rolling basis starting 3/1; must reply by 5/1.

CONTACT

Tim Nace, Assistant Dean, Enrollment Management
236 West Reade Avenue, Upland, IN 46989-1001
(765) 998-5358

Trine University

Angola, Indiana
www.trine.edu Federal Code: 001839

4-year private university and engineering college in small town.

Enrollment: 1,384 undergrads, 6% part-time. 423 full-time freshmen.

Selectivity: Admits 50 to 75% of applicants.

BASIC COSTS (2009-2010)

Tuition and fees: $24,200.

Per-credit charge: $750.

Room and board: $8,300.

FINANCIAL AID PICTURE (2008-2009)

Students with need: Out of 420 full-time freshmen who applied for aid, 288 were judged to have need. Of these, 288 received aid, and 288 had their full need met. Average financial aid package met 93% of need; average scholarship/grant was $5,127; average loan was $3,350.

Students without need: 67 full-time freshmen who did not demonstrate need for aid received scholarships/grants; average award was $9,397. No-need awards available for academics, alumni affiliation, minority status, music/drama, ROTC.

Cumulative student debt: 79% of graduating class had student loans; average debt was $17,380.

FINANCIAL AID PROCEDURES

Forms required: FAFSA.

Dates and Deadlines: Priority date 3/10; closing date 3/10. Applicants notified on a rolling basis starting 2/15; must reply by 5/1 or within 2 week(s) of notification.

Transfers: Applicants notified on a rolling basis starting 3/1; must reply by 5/1 or within 2 week(s) of notification.

CONTACT

Kim Bennett, Executive Director of Admission and Financial Aid
One University Avenue, Angola, IN 46703
(260) 665-4158

University of Evansville

Evansville, Indiana
www.evansville.edu Federal Code: 001795

4-year private university and liberal arts college in small city, affiliated with United Methodist Church.

Enrollment: 2,443 undergrads, 4% part-time. 619 full-time freshmen.

Selectivity: Admits over 75% of applicants.

BASIC COSTS (2009-2010)

Tuition and fees: $26,756.

Per-credit charge: $725.

Room and board: $8,670.

FINANCIAL AID PICTURE (2008-2009)

Students with need: Out of 520 full-time freshmen who applied for aid, 452 were judged to have need. Of these, 452 received aid, and 142 had their full need met. Average financial aid package met 92% of need; average scholarship/grant was $20,695; average loan was $4,040. For part-time students, average financial aid package was $5,256.

Students without need: 142 full-time freshmen who did not demonstrate need for aid received scholarships/grants; average award was $13,011. No-need awards available for academics, alumni affiliation, art, athletics, leadership, minority status, music/drama, religious affiliation, state/district residency.

Scholarships offered: ***Merit:*** Scouting Scholarship; $13,750; awarded to students who have earned the Boy Scouts of America Eagle Scout, Girl Scouts of the USA Gold Award, Sea Scouting Quartermaster Award, or Venturing Silver Award, renewable for 4 years with 2.5 GPA. ***Athletic:*** 27 full-time freshmen received athletic scholarships; average amount $22,440.

Cumulative student debt: 70% of graduating class had student loans; average debt was $25,390.

Additional info: Early financial planning service allows prospective students to get free estimate of available aid.

FINANCIAL AID PROCEDURES

Forms required: FAFSA.

Dates and Deadlines: Priority date 3/10; no closing date. Applicants notified on a rolling basis starting 3/25; must reply by 5/1.

Transfers: Must reply by 6/1. Indiana state aid is available for a total of 8 semesters.

CONTACT

JoAnn Laugel, Director of Financial Aid
1800 Lincoln Avenue, Evansville, IN 47722
(812) 488-2364

University of Indianapolis

Indianapolis, Indiana
www.uindy.edu Federal Code: 001804

4-year private university and liberal arts college in very large city, affiliated with United Methodist Church.

Enrollment: 3,548 undergrads, 24% part-time. 742 full-time freshmen.

Selectivity: Admits over 75% of applicants.

BASIC COSTS (2009-2010)

Tuition and fees: $21,170.

Per-credit charge: $874.

Room and board: $8,040.

FINANCIAL AID PICTURE (2007-2008)

Students with need: Need-based aid available for full-time and part-time students. Work study available nights, weekends, and for part-time students.

Students without need: No-need awards available for academics, alumni affiliation, art, athletics, job skills, leadership, music/drama, religious affiliation, state/district residency.

Scholarships offered: Presidential Scholarship; full tuition; upper 5% of class, 1270 SAT/29 ACT, strong college prep required. Dean's Scholarship; 50% tuition; upper 7% of class, 1270 SAT/29 ACT, demonstrated leadership, strong college prep required. Alumni Scholarship; 30% tuition; upper 15% of class, 1100 SAT/24 ACT, alumnus connection to school required. Service Award; $2,500; based on demonstrated commitment to community volunteerism. United Methodist Award; $2,500; based on demonstrated commitment to church, activities. SAT scores listed are exclusive of the writing portion.

FINANCIAL AID PROCEDURES

Forms required: FAFSA, institutional form.

Dates and Deadlines: Priority date 3/10; no closing date. Applicants notified on a rolling basis starting 3/1; must reply within 3 week(s) of notification.

Transfers: No deadline. Applicants notified on a rolling basis starting 3/1.

CONTACT

Linda Handy, Director of Financial Aid
1400 East Hanna Avenue, Indianapolis, IN 46227-3697
(317) 788-3217

University of Notre Dame

Notre Dame, Indiana — Federal Code: 001840
www.nd.edu — CSS Code: 1841

4-year private university in small city, affiliated with Roman Catholic Church.
Enrollment: 8,354 undergrads. 2,000 full-time freshmen.
Selectivity: Admits less than 50% of applicants. GED not accepted.

BASIC COSTS (2009-2010)

Tuition and fees: $38,477.
Per-credit charge: $1,582.
Room and board: $10,368.

FINANCIAL AID PICTURE (2008-2009)

Students with need: Out of 1,393 full-time freshmen who applied for aid, 939 were judged to have need. Of these, 938 received aid, and 937 had their full need met. Average financial aid package met 100% of need; average scholarship/grant was $25,757; average loan was $3,547. Need-based aid available for part-time students.
Students without need: 42 full-time freshmen who did not demonstrate need for aid received scholarships/grants; average award was $5,806. No-need awards available for athletics, ROTC.
Scholarships offered: 96 full-time freshmen received athletic scholarships; average amount $27,014.
Cumulative student debt: 57% of graduating class had student loans; average debt was $29,835.

FINANCIAL AID PROCEDURES

Forms required: FAFSA, CSS PROFILE.
Dates and Deadlines: Closing date 2/15. Applicants notified by 4/1; must reply by 5/1.
Transfers: Closing date 3/31. Applicants notified on a rolling basis; must reply within 2 week(s) of notification. Require signed and completed federal tax returns, including all schedules and W-2 forms from both the applicant and the parents of the applicant.

CONTACT

Joseph Russo, Director, Student Finance Strategies
220 Main Building, Notre Dame, IN 46556
(574) 631-6436

University of St. Francis

Fort Wayne, Indiana
www.sf.edu — Federal Code: 001832

4-year private university and liberal arts college in small city, affiliated with Roman Catholic Church.
Enrollment: 1,750 undergrads, 17% part-time. 299 full-time freshmen.
Selectivity: Admits less than 50% of applicants.

BASIC COSTS (2009-2010)

Tuition and fees: $21,760.
Per-credit charge: $660.
Room and board: $6,750.
Additional info: Tuition/fee waivers available for adults.

FINANCIAL AID PICTURE (2007-2008)

Students with need: Out of 289 full-time freshmen who applied for aid, 260 were judged to have need. Of these, 259 received aid, and 86 had their full need met. Average financial aid package met 80% of need; average scholarship/grant was $11,729; average loan was $3,031. For part-time students, average financial aid package was $11,184.
Students without need: 29 full-time freshmen who did not demonstrate need for aid received scholarships/grants; average award was $11,624. No-need awards available for academics, alumni affiliation, art, athletics, music/drama.
Scholarships offered: 39 full-time freshmen received athletic scholarships; average amount $5,540.
Cumulative student debt: 96% of graduating class had student loans; average debt was $25,397.

FINANCIAL AID PROCEDURES

Forms required: FAFSA.
Dates and Deadlines: Priority date 3/10; no closing date. Applicants notified on a rolling basis starting 3/1.

CONTACT

Jamie McGrath, Director of Financial Aid
2701 Spring Street, Fort Wayne, IN 46808
(260) 399-8003

University of Southern Indiana

Evansville, Indiana
www.usi.edu — Federal Code: 001808

4-year public university and liberal arts college in small city.
Enrollment: 9,137 undergrads, 16% part-time. 2,059 full-time freshmen.
Selectivity: Admits over 75% of applicants.

BASIC COSTS (2008-2009)

Tuition and fees: $5,210; out-of-state residents $12,140.
Per-credit charge: $167; out-of-state residents $398.
Room and board: $6,570.

FINANCIAL AID PICTURE (2008-2009)

Students with need: Out of 1,715 full-time freshmen who applied for aid, 1,165 were judged to have need. Of these, 1,142 received aid, and 250 had their full need met. Average financial aid package met 83% of need; average scholarship/grant was $5,593; average loan was $2,136. For part-time students, average financial aid package was $9,579.
Students without need: 255 full-time freshmen who did not demonstrate need for aid received scholarships/grants; average award was $3,672. No-need awards available for academics, alumni affiliation, art, athletics, job skills, leadership, music/drama, state/district residency.
Scholarships offered: 17 full-time freshmen received athletic scholarships; average amount $3,961.

FINANCIAL AID PROCEDURES

Forms required: FAFSA, institutional form.
Dates and Deadlines: Closing date 3/1. Applicants notified on a rolling basis starting 4/1.

CONTACT

Mary Harper, Director of Student Financial Assistance
8600 University Boulevard, Evansville, IN 47712
(812) 464-1767

Valparaiso University

Valparaiso, Indiana
www.valpo.edu Federal Code: 001842

4-year private university in large town, affiliated with Lutheran Church.
Enrollment: 2,824 undergrads, 4% part-time. 713 full-time freshmen.
Selectivity: Admits over 75% of applicants.

BASIC COSTS (2009-2010)

Tuition and fees: $28,320.
Per-credit charge: $640.
Room and board: $7,960.

FINANCIAL AID PICTURE (2007-2008)

Students with need: Out of 657 full-time freshmen who applied for aid, 545 were judged to have need. Of these, 545 received aid, and 141 had their full need met. Average financial aid package met 86% of need; average scholarship/grant was $16,375; average loan was $5,243. For part-time students, average financial aid package was $8,797.
Students without need: 138 full-time freshmen who did not demonstrate need for aid received scholarships/grants; average award was $9,145. No-need awards available for academics, alumni affiliation, art, athletics, leadership, music/drama, religious affiliation, ROTC.
Scholarships offered: ***Merit:*** Academic Scholarships; $6,000 to full-tuition. Departmental and Lutheran Scholarships; amounts vary. ***Athletic:*** 16 full-time freshmen received athletic scholarships; average amount $18,292.
Cumulative student debt: 73% of graduating class had student loans; average debt was $28,784.
Additional info: Financial assistance based on need, academic record, talent available through university.

FINANCIAL AID PROCEDURES

Forms required: FAFSA.
Dates and Deadlines: Priority date 3/1; no closing date. Applicants notified on a rolling basis starting 3/1; must reply by 5/1.
Transfers: Transfer students eligible for scholarships based on previous college work. Scholarship amounts vary depending on the GPA at previous institutions.

CONTACT

Robert Helgeson, Director of Financial Aid
Kretzmann Hall, 1700 Chapel Drive, Valparaiso, IN 46383-6493
(219) 464-5015

Vincennes University

Vincennes, Indiana
www.vinu.edu Federal Code: 001843

2-year public junior college in large town.
Enrollment: 8,848 undergrads, 42% part-time. 1,956 full-time freshmen.
Selectivity: Open admission; but selective for some programs.

BASIC COSTS (2008-2009)

Tuition and fees: $4,398; out-of-state residents $10,126.
Per-credit charge: $134; out-of-state residents $325.
Room and board: $7,036.
Additional info: Students from Crawford, Richland, Lawrence and Wabash counties in Illinois pay tuition of $209 per credit hour (including capital improvement and technology fees, not including student activity fee).

FINANCIAL AID PICTURE

Students with need: Need-based aid available for full-time and part-time students. Work study available nights, weekends, and for part-time students.
Students without need: No-need awards available for academics, art, athletics, leadership, music/drama, state/district residency.
Scholarships offered: Presidential Scholarship; $2,000 annually; 1100 SAT and rank in upper 10% of class; 10 awarded. Blue & Gold Scholarship; $1,100 annually; 1010 SAT and rank in upper half of class; 40 awarded. Indiana Academic Honors Diploma; $900 annually. Walters Scholarship; tuition, room and board; for candidates in good standing. Education Scholarship; for education majors, based on SAT scores and rank in upper 10% of class; 1 awarded. Validictorian/Salutatorian scholarship; full costs.

FINANCIAL AID PROCEDURES

Forms required: FAFSA.
Dates and Deadlines: Priority date 3/1; closing date 5/1. Applicants notified on a rolling basis starting 5/1; must reply by 8/24.
Transfers: No deadline. Applicants notified on a rolling basis starting 4/1. Transfer students must notify state student assistance commission within 30 days of start of term.

CONTACT

Stanley Werne, Director of Financial Aid
1002 North First Street, Vincennes, IN 47591
(812) 888-4361

Wabash College

Crawfordsville, Indiana Federal Code: 001844
www.wabash.edu CSS Code: 1895

4-year private liberal arts college for men in large town.
Enrollment: 903 undergrads. 255 full-time freshmen.
Selectivity: Admits less than 50% of applicants.

BASIC COSTS (2008-2009)

Tuition and fees: $27,950.
Room and board: $7,900.

FINANCIAL AID PICTURE (2008-2009)

Students with need: Out of 239 full-time freshmen who applied for aid, 222 were judged to have need. Of these, 222 received aid, and 221 had their full need met. Average financial aid package met 100% of need; average scholarship/grant was $19,159; average loan was $4,597. Need-based aid available for part-time students.
Students without need: 29 full-time freshmen who did not demonstrate need for aid received scholarships/grants; average award was $16,356. No-need awards available for academics, art, leadership, music/drama, state/district residency.
Scholarships offered: Lilly Awards Program; full tuition, room, board, fees, and travel stipend; recognizes outstanding personal achievement and potential for leadership. Fine Arts Fellows; up to $15,000; based on creativity/ability; approximately 16 awarded each year. Honor Scholarships; up to $15,000; based on competitive exams; approximately 40 awarded each year. President's Scholarships; based on class rank, SAT scores; unlimited number awarded. Top-10 Scholarships; up to $15,000 per year; unlimited number awarded.
Cumulative student debt: 90% of graduating class had student loans; average debt was $21,423.

FINANCIAL AID PROCEDURES

Forms required: FAFSA, CSS PROFILE.
Dates and Deadlines: Priority date 2/15; closing date 3/1. Applicants notified by 4/1; must reply by 5/1 or within 2 week(s) of notification.
Transfers: Applicants notified by 4/1; must reply by 5/1 or within 2 week(s) of notification.

CONTACT

Clint Gasaway, Director of Financial Aid
PO Box 352, Crawfordsville, IN 47933
(800) 718-9746

Iowa

AIB College of Business
Des Moines, Iowa
www.aib.edu Federal Code: 003963

2-year private business college in large city.
Enrollment: 975 undergrads, 42% part-time. 130 full-time freshmen.
Selectivity: Admits 50 to 75% of applicants.

BASIC COSTS (2008-2009)
Tuition and fees: $12,120.
Per-credit charge: $220.
Room only: $3,150.
Additional info: Tuition/fee waivers available for minority students.

FINANCIAL AID PICTURE (2007-2008)
Students with need: Need-based aid available for full-time and part-time students. Work study available nights, weekends, and for part-time students.
Students without need: No-need awards available for academics, alumni affiliation, leadership.
Scholarships offered: Founder's Scholarship; full tuition; 3.75 GPA and upper 10% of high school graduating class or 3.75 GPA and 28 ACT required; up to 4 students per year.

FINANCIAL AID PROCEDURES
Forms required: FAFSA, institutional form.
Dates and Deadlines: Priority date 4/1; no closing date. Applicants notified on a rolling basis starting 3/1; must reply within 2 week(s) of notification.
Transfers: No deadline. Applicants notified on a rolling basis starting 3/1; must reply within 2 week(s) of notification. Prior aid from previous institutions considered.

CONTACT
Connie Loven, Financial Aid Director
2500 Fleur Drive, Des Moines, IA 50321-1799
(515) 244-4221

Allen College
Waterloo, Iowa
www.allencollege.edu Federal Code: 030691

4-year private health science and nursing college in small city.
Enrollment: 308 undergrads, 23% part-time. 4 full-time freshmen.
Selectivity: Admits less than 50% of applicants.

BASIC COSTS (2008-2009)
Tuition and fees: $14,895.
Per-credit charge: $458.
Room and board: $6,178.

FINANCIAL AID PICTURE (2007-2008)
Students with need: Need-based aid available for full-time and part-time students.
Students without need: No-need awards available for academics, leadership, minority status, ROTC.

FINANCIAL AID PROCEDURES
Forms required: FAFSA, institutional form.
Dates and Deadlines: Priority date 6/1; no closing date. Applicants notified on a rolling basis starting 4/1; must reply within 2 week(s) of notification.
Transfers: No deadline. Applicants notified on a rolling basis starting 4/1; must reply within 2 week(s) of notification.

CONTACT
Kathie Walters, Financial Aid Director
1825 Logan Avenue, Waterloo, IA 50703
(319) 226-2003

Ashford University
Clinton, Iowa
www.ashford.edu Federal Code: 001881

4-year for-profit university in large town.
Enrollment: 23,665 undergrads. 1,656 full-time freshmen.

BASIC COSTS (2008-2009)
Tuition and fees: $15,890.
Per-credit charge: $447.
Room and board: $5,800.
Additional info: Tuition/fee waivers available for minority students, unemployed or children of unemployed.

FINANCIAL AID PICTURE (2008-2009)
Students with need: 17% of average financial aid package awarded as scholarships/grants, 83% awarded as loans/jobs. Need-based aid available for part-time students. Work study available nights, weekends, and for part-time students.
Students without need: No-need awards available for academics, art, athletics, music/drama.
Scholarships offered: Divisional Award; up to full tuition; based on 3.2 GPA/23-26 ACT. Presidential Scholarships; $1,500-$5,000; based on rank in top 20% of class, or 26 ACT, or 3.2 GPA. Departmental Awards; maximum $1,500; based on competitive exams in various departments. Leadership Awards; maximum $1,000; based on extracurricular activities and 2.3 GPA. Counselor's Choice Awards; $500; based on recommendation from guidance counselor, 2.5-3.19 GPA, 19-25 ACT, and at least one extracurricular activity.

FINANCIAL AID PROCEDURES
Forms required: FAFSA, institutional form.
Dates and Deadlines: Priority date 3/1; no closing date. Applicants notified on a rolling basis starting 2/15; must reply within 2 week(s) of notification.
Transfers: Students with 3.0 GPA eligible for Presidential Scholarship.

CONTACT
Lisa Kramer, Director of Financial Aid
400 North Bluff Boulevard, Clinton, IA 52733-2967
(563) 242-4023 ext. 1242

Briar Cliff University
Sioux City, Iowa
www.briarcliff.edu Federal Code: 001846

4-year private liberal arts college in small city, affiliated with Roman Catholic Church.
Enrollment: 1,026 undergrads, 12% part-time. 252 full-time freshmen.
Selectivity: Admits 50 to 75% of applicants.

BASIC COSTS (2008-2009)
Tuition and fees: $21,510.
Per-credit charge: $696.
Room and board: $6,411.

FINANCIAL AID PICTURE (2008-2009)
Students with need: Out of 246 full-time freshmen who applied for aid, 184 were judged to have need. Of these, 184 received aid, and 147 had their full need met. Average financial aid package met 90% of need; average scholarship/grant was $6,500; average loan was $3,900. Need-based aid available for part-time students.

Students without need: 68 full-time freshmen who did not demonstrate need for aid received scholarships/grants; average award was $10,100. No-need awards available for academics, alumni affiliation, art, athletics, leadership, music/drama, religious affiliation, state/district residency.
Scholarships offered: ***Merit:*** Presidential Scholarships; awarded each year for achievement and demonstrated leadership, based on application and on-campus interview; 2-5 awarded. ***Athletic:*** 60 full-time freshmen received athletic scholarships; average amount $520.
Cumulative student debt: 88% of graduating class had student loans; average debt was $31,853.

FINANCIAL AID PROCEDURES

Forms required: FAFSA.
Dates and Deadlines: Priority date 3/15; no closing date. Applicants notified on a rolling basis starting 3/15; must reply by 5/1 or within 2 week(s) of notification.
Transfers: Closing date 3/15.

CONTACT

Robert Piechota, Director of Financial Aid
3303 Rebecca Street, Sioux City, IA 51104-0100
(712) 279-5200

Buena Vista University

Storm Lake, Iowa
www.bvu.edu Federal Code: 001847

4-year private liberal arts college in large town, affiliated with Presbyterian Church (USA).
Enrollment: 957 undergrads, 1% part-time. 264 full-time freshmen.
Selectivity: Admits over 75% of applicants.

BASIC COSTS (2009-2010)

Tuition and fees: $25,540.
Per-credit charge: $858.
Room and board: $7,292.

FINANCIAL AID PICTURE (2008-2009)

Students with need: Out of 250 full-time freshmen who applied for aid, 233 were judged to have need. Of these, 233 received aid, and 149 had their full need met. Average financial aid package met 62% of need; average scholarship/grant was $11,583; average loan was $4,511. For part-time students, average financial aid package was $16,872.
Students without need: 20 full-time freshmen who did not demonstrate need for aid received scholarships/grants; average award was $11,674. No-need awards available for academics, art, minority status, music/drama, religious affiliation.
Cumulative student debt: 96% of graduating class had student loans; average debt was $34,029.
Additional info: Portfolio required of art scholarship applicants, audition required of music and drama scholarship applicants.

FINANCIAL AID PROCEDURES

Forms required: FAFSA.
Dates and Deadlines: Priority date 6/1; no closing date. Applicants notified on a rolling basis starting 2/20.

CONTACT

Leanne Valentine, Director of Financial Assistance
610 West Fourth Street, Storm Lake, IA 50588
(714) 749-2164

Central College

Pella, Iowa
www.central.edu Federal Code: 001850

4-year private liberal arts college in large town, affiliated with Reformed Church in America.
Enrollment: 1,445 undergrads, 1% part-time. 405 full-time freshmen.
Selectivity: Admits over 75% of applicants.

BASIC COSTS (2008-2009)

Tuition and fees: $23,944.
Per-credit charge: $818.
Room and board: $8,006.
Additional info: Costs provided are for main campus only. International location costs may vary by program location.

FINANCIAL AID PICTURE (2008-2009)

Students with need: Need-based aid available for full-time and part-time students. Work study available nights, weekends, and for part-time students.
Students without need: No-need awards available for academics, alumni affiliation, art, leadership, minority status, music/drama, religious affiliation, state/district residency.
Additional info: Institutional parent loan program and interest-earning, tuition prepayment savings account available.

FINANCIAL AID PROCEDURES

Forms required: FAFSA.
Dates and Deadlines: Priority date 3/15; no closing date. Applicants notified on a rolling basis starting 3/15; must reply by 5/1 or within 2 week(s) of notification.
Transfers: Applicants notified on a rolling basis starting 3/15; must reply by 5/1 or within 2 week(s) of notification. Transfers only eligible for total of 4 years of state funds.

CONTACT

Jean Vander Wert, Financial Aid Director
812 University Street, Pella, IA 50219-1999
(641) 628-5336

Clarke College

Dubuque, Iowa
www.clarke.edu Federal Code: 001852

4-year private liberal arts college in small city, affiliated with Roman Catholic Church.
Enrollment: 940 undergrads, 13% part-time. 138 full-time freshmen.
Selectivity: Admits 50 to 75% of applicants.

BASIC COSTS (2009-2010)

Tuition and fees: $23,520.
Per-credit charge: $578.
Room and board: $6,840.

FINANCIAL AID PICTURE (2008-2009)

Students with need: Out of 132 full-time freshmen who applied for aid, 111 were judged to have need. Of these, 111 received aid, and 35 had their full need met. Average financial aid package met 92% of need; average scholarship/grant was $17,066; average loan was $3,406. For part-time students, average financial aid package was $7,005.
Students without need: 26 full-time freshmen who did not demonstrate need for aid received scholarships/grants; average award was $19,457. No-need awards available for academics, alumni affiliation, art, athletics, leadership, music/drama, religious affiliation, state/district residency.
Scholarships offered: ***Merit:*** Mary Frances Clarke Scholarship; full tuition; based on 3.8 GPA, 28 ACT, participation in campus competition. Trustee's Scholarship; 75% tuition; based on 3.8 GPA, 28 ACT, participation in campus

competition; 4 awarded. View/Leadership Award; $1,000-$5,000; based on 2.9 GPA, participation in weekend competition, selected components of credentials and activities during the competition considered; up to 15 awarded. ***Athletic:*** 65 full-time freshmen received athletic scholarships; average amount $6,646.
Additional info: Reduced tuition for family members of BVMs.

FINANCIAL AID PROCEDURES

Dates and Deadlines: Priority date 4/15; no closing date. Applicants notified on a rolling basis starting 3/11; must reply by 5/1 or within 2 week(s) of notification.

CONTACT

Sharon Willenborg, Director of Financial Aid
1550 Clarke Drive, Dubuque, IA 52001-3198
(563) 588-6327

Coe College

Cedar Rapids, Iowa
www.coe.edu Federal Code: 001854

4-year private nursing and liberal arts college in small city, affiliated with Presbyterian Church (USA).
Enrollment: 1,269 undergrads, 2% part-time. 342 full-time freshmen.
Selectivity: Admits 50 to 75% of applicants.

BASIC COSTS (2009-2010)

Tuition and fees: $29,270.
Room and board: $7,150.
Additional info: Cost per course for part-time students (fewer than 3 course credits) is $3,620. Tuition/fee waivers available for adults.

FINANCIAL AID PICTURE (2008-2009)

Students with need: Out of 292 full-time freshmen who applied for aid, 252 were judged to have need. Of these, 251 received aid, and 92 had their full need met. Average financial aid package met 95% of need; average scholarship/grant was $18,422; average loan was $5,255. For part-time students, average financial aid package was $13,821.
Students without need: 89 full-time freshmen who did not demonstrate need for aid received scholarships/grants; average award was $16,478. No-need awards available for academics, alumni affiliation, art, leadership, music/drama, ROTC.
Scholarships offered: Scholarships for business/economics, music, art, theater, writing, foreign language, science; based on portfolio or audition; available for non-majors except in science and business/economics. Academic Awards; $6,000-$19,000; based on high school achievement.

FINANCIAL AID PROCEDURES

Forms required: FAFSA.
Dates and Deadlines: Priority date 3/1; no closing date. Applicants notified on a rolling basis starting 3/15; must reply by 5/1 or within 2 week(s) of notification.

CONTACT

Barb Hoffman, Director of Financial Aid
1220 First Avenue NE, Cedar Rapids, IA 52402
(319) 399-8540

Cornell College

Mount Vernon, Iowa
www.cornellcollege.edu Federal Code: 001856

4-year private liberal arts college in small town, affiliated with United Methodist Church.
Enrollment: 1,102 undergrads.
Selectivity: Admits less than 50% of applicants.

BASIC COSTS (2009-2010)

Tuition and fees: $29,580.
Room and board: $7,350.
Additional info: Tuition/fee waivers available for adults, minority students.

FINANCIAL AID PICTURE (2007-2008)

Students with need: 83% of average financial aid package awarded as scholarships/grants, 17% awarded as loans/jobs. Need-based aid available for part-time students. Work study available nights, weekends, and for part-time students.
Students without need: No-need awards available for academics, art, leadership, minority status, music/drama, religious affiliation, state/district residency.
Additional info: Portfolio required for art scholarship applicants. Audition required for music scholarship applicants.

FINANCIAL AID PROCEDURES

Forms required: FAFSA, institutional form.
Dates and Deadlines: Closing date 3/1. Applicants notified on a rolling basis starting 3/1; must reply by 5/1 or within 2 week(s) of notification.
Transfers: Priority date 3/1; no deadline. Applicants notified on a rolling basis starting 3/1; must reply by 5/1 or within 2 week(s) of notification.

CONTACT

Cindi Reints, Director of Financial Assistance
600 First Street SW, Mount Vernon, IA 52314-1098
(319) 895-4216

Des Moines Area Community College

Ankeny, Iowa
www.dmacc.edu Federal Code: 004589

2-year public community college in large town.
Enrollment: 13,443 undergrads, 46% part-time. 2,147 full-time freshmen.
Selectivity: Open admission; but selective for some programs.

BASIC COSTS (2008-2009)

Tuition and fees: $3,210; out-of-state residents $6,420.
Per-credit charge: $107; out-of-state residents $214.

FINANCIAL AID PICTURE (2007-2008)

Students with need: 29% of average financial aid package awarded as scholarships/grants, 71% awarded as loans/jobs. Need-based aid available for part-time students. Work study available nights, weekends, and for part-time students.
Students without need: No-need awards available for academics, athletics, state/district residency.
Scholarships offered: Foundation Freshmen Scholar Award; full tuition, fees and books for maximum of 15 credit hours per semester based on available funds; open to all high school seniors in top 10% of graduating class.

FINANCIAL AID PROCEDURES

Forms required: FAFSA.
Dates and Deadlines: Priority date 4/1; no closing date. Applicants notified on a rolling basis starting 4/1; must reply within 2 week(s) of notification.

CONTACT

DeLores Hawkins, Director of Financial Aid
2006 South Ankeny Boulevard, Ankeny, IA 50023-3993
(515) 964-6282

Dordt College

Sioux Center, Iowa
www.dordt.edu Federal Code: 001859

4-year private liberal arts college in small town, affiliated with Christian Reformed Church.
Enrollment: 1,314 undergrads, 4% part-time. 402 full-time freshmen.
Selectivity: Admits over 75% of applicants.

BASIC COSTS (2009-2010)

Tuition and fees: $22,080.
Per-credit charge: $860.
Room and board: $6,010.
Additional info: Tuition/fee waivers available for adults.

FINANCIAL AID PICTURE (2007-2008)

Students with need: Out of 362 full-time freshmen who applied for aid, 303 were judged to have need. Of these, 303 received aid, and 59 had their full need met. Average financial aid package met 91% of need; average scholarship/grant was $11,295; average loan was $5,399. For part-time students, average financial aid package was $3,825.
Students without need: 79 full-time freshmen who did not demonstrate need for aid received scholarships/grants; average award was $12,925. No-need awards available for academics, alumni affiliation, art, athletics, job skills, leadership, minority status, music/drama, religious affiliation, state/district residency.
Scholarships offered: 31 full-time freshmen received athletic scholarships; average amount $4,737.
Cumulative student debt: 87% of graduating class had student loans; average debt was $19,208.

FINANCIAL AID PROCEDURES

Forms required: FAFSA, institutional form.
Dates and Deadlines: Priority date 4/1; no closing date. Applicants notified on a rolling basis starting 3/15; must reply within 3 week(s) of notification.
Transfers: Closing date 6/1. Applicants notified on a rolling basis starting 10/1.

CONTACT

Michael Epema, Director of Financial Aid
498 Fourth Avenue, NE, Sioux Center, IA 51250
(712) 722-6087

Drake University

Des Moines, Iowa
www.drake.edu Federal Code: 001860

4-year private university in large city.
Enrollment: 3,465 undergrads, 5% part-time. 902 full-time freshmen.
Selectivity: Admits 50 to 75% of applicants.

BASIC COSTS (2009-2010)

Tuition and fees: $25,680.
Per-credit charge: $520.
Room and board: $7,800.

FINANCIAL AID PICTURE (2008-2009)

Students with need: Out of 725 full-time freshmen who applied for aid, 534 were judged to have need. Of these, 534 received aid, and 195 had their full need met. Average financial aid package met 89% of need; average scholarship/grant was $14,176; average loan was $5,051. For part-time students, average financial aid package was $9,248.
Students without need: 321 full-time freshmen who did not demonstrate need for aid received scholarships/grants; average award was $10,898. No-need awards available for academics, alumni affiliation, art, athletics, music/drama, ROTC, state/district residency.
Scholarships offered: ***Merit:*** Drake University Presidential Scholarship; $7,000-$12,000; based on academic merit and awards; unlimited available. National Alumni Scholarship Competition; 6 full-time tuition with room and board and 10 full-time tuition; available to top students. ***Athletic:*** 19 full-time freshmen received athletic scholarships; average amount $18,046.
Cumulative student debt: 64% of graduating class had student loans; average debt was $32,318.

FINANCIAL AID PROCEDURES

Forms required: FAFSA.
Dates and Deadlines: Priority date 3/1; no closing date. Applicants notified on a rolling basis starting 3/1; must reply by 5/1 or within 3 week(s) of notification.
Transfers: No deadline. Applicants notified on a rolling basis starting 3/1; must reply by 5/1 or within 2 week(s) of notification. FAFSA must be filed by July 1 for Iowa Tuition Grant deadline.

CONTACT

Susan Ladd, Director of Student Financial Planning
2507 University Avenue, Des Moines, IA 50311-4505
(515) 271-2905

Ellsworth Community College

Iowa Falls, Iowa
www.iavalley.cc.ia.us/ecc Federal Code: 001862

2-year public community college in small town.
Enrollment: 1,106 undergrads.
Selectivity: Open admission; but selective for some programs.

BASIC COSTS (2008-2009)

Tuition and fees: $4,290; out-of-state residents $5,190.
Per-credit charge: $119; out-of-state residents $149.
Room and board: $4,852.
Additional info: Tuition/fee waivers available for adults.

FINANCIAL AID PICTURE (2007-2008)

Students with need: Need-based aid available for full-time and part-time students. Work study available nights, weekends, and for part-time students.
Students without need: No-need awards available for academics, art, athletics, leadership, minority status, music/drama.
Scholarships offered: Academic scholarships; $500-$1,800; based on ACT and GPA; unlimited number offered. Directors Scholarship; $2,300; for those who are 1st or 2nd in class; unlimited number offered.

FINANCIAL AID PROCEDURES

Forms required: FAFSA, institutional form.
Dates and Deadlines: Priority date 4/1; no closing date. Applicants notified on a rolling basis starting 2/15; must reply within 4 week(s) of notification.
Transfers: Priority date 4/15.

CONTACT

Tara Miller, Financial Aid Administrator
1100 College Avenue, Iowa Falls, IA 50126
(641) 648-4611 ext. 432

Emmaus Bible College

Dubuque, Iowa
www.emmaus.edu Federal Code: 016487

4-year private Bible college in small city, affiliated with Brethren Church.
Enrollment: 238 undergrads, 7% part-time. 61 full-time freshmen.
Selectivity: Admits over 75% of applicants.

BASIC COSTS (2008-2009)
Tuition and fees: $11,030.
Room and board: $5,212.

FINANCIAL AID PICTURE
Students with need: Need-based aid available for full-time and part-time students.
Students without need: No-need awards available for academics, music/drama.

FINANCIAL AID PROCEDURES
Forms required: FAFSA, institutional form.
Dates and Deadlines: Priority date 5/15; closing date 7/1. Applicants notified on a rolling basis starting 3/1; must reply within 2 week(s) of notification.

CONTACT
Steve Seeman, Financial Aid Director
2570 Asbury Road, Dubuque, IA 52001
(563) 588-8000 ext. 1309

Faith Baptist Bible College and Theological Seminary

Ankeny, Iowa
www.faith.edu Federal Code: 007121

4-year private Bible and seminary college in large town, affiliated with General Association of Regular Baptist Churches.
Enrollment: 310 undergrads, 8% part-time. 92 full-time freshmen.
Selectivity: Admits over 75% of applicants.

BASIC COSTS (2009-2010)
Tuition and fees: $13,260.
Per-credit charge: $470.
Room and board: $5,510.

FINANCIAL AID PICTURE (2007-2008)
Students with need: Need-based aid available for full-time and part-time students.
Students without need: No-need awards available for academics, leadership, music/drama.

FINANCIAL AID PROCEDURES
Forms required: FAFSA.
Dates and Deadlines: Priority date 4/1; no closing date. Applicants notified on a rolling basis starting 3/15.

CONTACT
Breck Appell, Financial Assistance Director
1900 NW Fourth Street, Ankeny, IA 50023
(515) 964-0601 ext. 216

Graceland University

Lamoni, Iowa
www.graceland.edu Federal Code: 001866

4-year private university and liberal arts college in rural community, affiliated with Community of Christ.
Enrollment: 1,383 undergrads, 15% part-time. 205 full-time freshmen.
Selectivity: Admits 50 to 75% of applicants.

BASIC COSTS (2009-2010)
Tuition and fees: $20,090.
Per-credit charge: $630.
Room and board: $6,780.

FINANCIAL AID PICTURE (2008-2009)
Students with need: Out of 169 full-time freshmen who applied for aid, 151 were judged to have need. Of these, 147 received aid, and 47 had their full need met. Average financial aid package met 89% of need; average scholarship/grant was $15,109; average loan was $5,202. For part-time students, average financial aid package was $6,522.
Students without need: 49 full-time freshmen who did not demonstrate need for aid received scholarships/grants; average award was $10,079. No-need awards available for academics, alumni affiliation, art, athletics, job skills, leadership, music/drama, religious affiliation.
Scholarships offered: 35 full-time freshmen received athletic scholarships; average amount $4,258.
Cumulative student debt: 87% of graduating class had student loans; average debt was $28,347.

FINANCIAL AID PROCEDURES
Forms required: FAFSA.
Dates and Deadlines: No deadline. Applicants notified on a rolling basis starting 3/1; must reply within 2 week(s) of notification.
Transfers: Must reply within 2 week(s) of notification.

CONTACT
Christine McGee, Director of Student Finance
One University Place, Lamoni, IA 50140
(641) 784-5140

Grand View University

Des Moines, Iowa
www.grandview.edu Federal Code: 001867

4-year private liberal arts college in large city, affiliated with Evangelical Lutheran Church in America.
Enrollment: 1,887 undergrads, 18% part-time. 343 full-time freshmen.
Selectivity: Admits over 75% of applicants.

BASIC COSTS (2009-2010)
Tuition and fees: $19,274.
Per-credit charge: $485.
Room and board: $6,736.

FINANCIAL AID PICTURE (2008-2009)
Students with need: Out of 331 full-time freshmen who applied for aid, 281 were judged to have need. Of these, 281 received aid, and 132 had their full need met. Average financial aid package met 92% of need; average scholarship/grant was $13,428; average loan was $3,554. For part-time students, average financial aid package was $12,029.
Students without need: 58 full-time freshmen who did not demonstrate need for aid received scholarships/grants; average award was $6,876. No-need awards available for academics, alumni affiliation, art, athletics, leadership, music/drama, religious affiliation.
Scholarships offered: ***Merit:*** Presidential Scholarship; $8,000. Honors Scholarship; $7,000. Viking Incentive Program; $6,500. All for first-time, full-time freshmen. ***Athletic:*** 36 full-time freshmen received athletic scholarships; average amount $5,633.
Cumulative student debt: 83% of graduating class had student loans; average debt was $27,337.

FINANCIAL AID PROCEDURES
Forms required: FAFSA.
Dates and Deadlines: Priority date 3/1; no closing date. Applicants notified on a rolling basis starting 3/1; must reply by 5/1 or within 4 week(s) of notification.

CONTACT
Michele Dunne, Director of Financial Aid
1200 Grandview Avenue, Des Moines, IA 50316-1599
(515) 263-2963

Grinnell College

Grinnell, Iowa
www.grinnell.edu Federal Code: 001868

4-year private liberal arts college in small town.
Enrollment: 1,639 undergrads. 464 full-time freshmen.
Selectivity: Admits less than 50% of applicants.

BASIC COSTS (2009-2010)

Tuition and fees: $36,476.
Per-credit charge: $1,092.
Room and board: $8,536.

FINANCIAL AID PICTURE (2008-2009)

Students with need: Out of 388 full-time freshmen who applied for aid, 318 were judged to have need. Of these, 318 received aid, and 318 had their full need met. Average financial aid package met 100% of need; average scholarship/grant was $28,159; average loan was $2,787. For part-time students, average financial aid package was $10,146.
Students without need: 93 full-time freshmen who did not demonstrate need for aid received scholarships/grants; average award was $10,137. No-need awards available for academics.
Cumulative student debt: 53% of graduating class had student loans; average debt was $19,526.
Additional info: Need-blind admission policy, meets 100% of demonstrated institutional need for all domestic students, with loan cap programs. Students may apply financial aid to off-campus study programs.

FINANCIAL AID PROCEDURES

Forms required: FAFSA, institutional form.
Dates and Deadlines: Closing date 2/1. Applicants notified by 4/1; must reply by 5/1.

CONTACT

Arnold Woods, Director of Student Financial Aid
1103 Park Street, Grinnell, IA 50112-1690
(641) 269-3250

Hawkeye Community College

Waterloo, Iowa
www.hawkeyecollege.edu Federal Code: 004595

2-year public community and technical college in small city.
Enrollment: 4,086 undergrads, 24% part-time. 1,111 full-time freshmen.
Selectivity: Open admission; but selective for some programs.

BASIC COSTS (2008-2009)

Tuition and fees: $4,050; out-of-state residents $5,910.
Per-credit charge: $124; out-of-state residents $186.

FINANCIAL AID PICTURE (2008-2009)

Students with need: Need-based aid available for full-time students. Work study available nights, weekends, and for part-time students.
Students without need: No-need awards available for academics, state/district residency.

FINANCIAL AID PROCEDURES

Forms required: FAFSA.
Dates and Deadlines: Priority date 7/1; no closing date. Applicants notified on a rolling basis starting 5/1; must reply within 2 week(s) of notification.

CONTACT

Lois Mulbrook, Director of Financial Aid
Box 8015, Waterloo, IA 50704-8015
(319) 296-4020

Indian Hills Community College

Ottumwa, Iowa
www.indianhills.edu Federal Code: 008298

2-year public community and technical college in large town.
Enrollment: 2,863 undergrads, 21% part-time. 925 full-time freshmen.
Selectivity: Open admission; but selective for some programs.

BASIC COSTS (2008-2009)

Tuition and fees: $3,540; out-of-state residents $5,310.
Per-credit charge: $118; out-of-state residents $177.
Room and board: $5,175.

FINANCIAL AID PICTURE (2007-2008)

Students with need: Need-based aid available for part-time students. Work study available nights, weekends, and for part-time students.
Students without need: No-need awards available for academics, athletics, state/district residency.

FINANCIAL AID PROCEDURES

Forms required: FAFSA, institutional form.
Dates and Deadlines: Priority date 4/1; no closing date. Applicants notified on a rolling basis starting 6/1; must reply within 2 week(s) of notification.

CONTACT

Jo Altheide, Financial Aid
623 Indian Hills Drive, Building 12, Ottumwa, IA 52501

Iowa Central Community College

Fort Dodge, Iowa
www.iowacentral.edu Federal Code: 004597

2-year public community college in large town.
Enrollment: 5,731 undergrads.
Selectivity: Open admission; but selective for some programs.

BASIC COSTS (2008-2009)

Tuition and fees: $3,600; out-of-state residents $5,235.
Per-credit charge: $109; out-of-state residents $164.
Room and board: $4,850.

FINANCIAL AID PICTURE

Students with need: Need-based aid available for full-time and part-time students. Work study available nights, weekends, and for part-time students.
Students without need: No-need awards available for academics, art, athletics, leadership, music/drama.

FINANCIAL AID PROCEDURES

Forms required: FAFSA.
Dates and Deadlines: Priority date 3/8; no closing date. Applicants notified on a rolling basis starting 4/15; must reply within 2 week(s) of notification.

CONTACT

Angie Martin, Director of Financial Aid
One Triton Circle, Fort Dodge, IA 50501

Iowa Lakes Community College

Estherville, Iowa
www.iowalakes.edu Federal Code: 001864

2-year public community college in small town.
Enrollment: 1,973 undergrads, 21% part-time. 657 full-time freshmen.
Selectivity: Open admission; but selective for some programs.

BASIC COSTS (2008-2009)

Tuition and fees: $4,121; out-of-state residents $4,181.
Per-credit charge: $120; out-of-state residents $122.
Room and board: $4,600.

FINANCIAL AID PICTURE (2008-2009)

Students with need: Need-based aid available for full-time and part-time students.
Students without need: This college awards aid only to students with need.

FINANCIAL AID PROCEDURES

Forms required: FAFSA, institutional form.
Dates and Deadlines: Priority date 4/22; no closing date. Applicants notified on a rolling basis starting 4/15.

CONTACT

John Beneke, Director of Financial Aid
300 South 18th Street, Estherville, IA 51334-2725
(712) 362-7917

Iowa State University

Ames, Iowa
www.iastate.edu Federal Code: 001869

4-year public university in small city.
Enrollment: 21,169 undergrads, 5% part-time. 4,338 full-time freshmen.
Selectivity: Admits over 75% of applicants.

BASIC COSTS (2008-2009)

Tuition and fees: $6,360; out-of-state residents $17,350.
Per-credit charge: $231; out-of-state residents $688.
Room and board: $6,884.
Additional info: Additional tuition of $500 for junior and senior engineering students; increased fees of $171 for engineering and computer science programs; additional $50 in fees for business program.

FINANCIAL AID PICTURE (2008-2009)

Students with need: Out of 3,522 full-time freshmen who applied for aid, 2,362 were judged to have need. Of these, 2,314 received aid, and 953 had their full need met. Average financial aid package met 80% of need; average scholarship/grant was $5,938; average loan was $3,698. For part-time students, average financial aid package was $8,385.
Students without need: 1,443 full-time freshmen who did not demonstrate need for aid received scholarships/grants; average award was $2,693. No-need awards available for academics, art, athletics, leadership, minority status, music/drama, ROTC, state/district residency.
Scholarships offered: 68 full-time freshmen received athletic scholarships; average amount $15,315.
Cumulative student debt: 71% of graduating class had student loans; average debt was $31,616.
Additional info: Short-term loan program available to meet unplanned needs. Financial counseling clinic provides budget and credit education assistance.

FINANCIAL AID PROCEDURES

Forms required: FAFSA.
Dates and Deadlines: Priority date 3/1; no closing date. Applicants notified on a rolling basis starting 4/1.
Transfers: Priority date 2/15.

CONTACT

Roberta Johnson, Director of Student Financial Aid
100 Enrollment Services Center, Ames, IA 50011-2011
(515) 294-0066

Iowa Wesleyan College

Mount Pleasant, Iowa
www.iwc.edu Federal Code: 001871

4-year private liberal arts college in small town, affiliated with United Methodist Church.
Enrollment: 842 undergrads, 25% part-time. 150 full-time freshmen.
Selectivity: Admits 50 to 75% of applicants.

BASIC COSTS (2008-2009)

Tuition and fees: $20,000.
Per-credit charge: $495.
Room and board: $6,240.

FINANCIAL AID PICTURE (2007-2008)

Students with need: 59% of average financial aid package awarded as scholarships/grants, 41% awarded as loans/jobs. Work study available nights, weekends, and for part-time students.
Students without need: No-need awards available for academics, art, athletics, music/drama.
Scholarships offered: Unlimited merit based scholarships; based on ACT/SAT and GPA.

FINANCIAL AID PROCEDURES

Forms required: FAFSA.
Dates and Deadlines: Priority date 4/1; no closing date. Applicants notified on a rolling basis starting 1/1; must reply within 2 week(s) of notification.

CONTACT

Deb Morrissey, Director of Financial Aid
601 North Main Street, Mount Pleasant, IA 52641-1398
(319) 385-6242

Iowa Western Community College

Council Bluffs, Iowa
www.iwcc.edu Federal Code: 004598

2-year public community and technical college in small city.
Enrollment: 3,897 undergrads.
Selectivity: Open admission; but selective for some programs.

BASIC COSTS (2008-2009)

Tuition and fees: $3,660; out-of-state residents $5,325.
Per-credit charge: $111; out-of-state residents $167.
Room and board: $5,910.

FINANCIAL AID PICTURE (2007-2008)

Students with need: 83% of average financial aid package awarded as scholarships/grants, 17% awarded as loans/jobs. Need-based aid available for part-time students.
Students without need: No-need awards available for athletics, music/drama.

FINANCIAL AID PROCEDURES

Forms required: FAFSA.
Dates and Deadlines: Priority date 7/1; no closing date. Applicants notified on a rolling basis starting 3/1; must reply within 3 week(s) of notification.

CONTACT

Blaine Duistermars, Director of Financial Aid
2700 College Road, Council Bluffs, IA 51502-3004
(800) 432-5852 ext. 292

Kaplan University: Cedar Falls

Cedar Falls, Iowa
www.kucampus.edu Federal Code: 004586

4-year for-profit university and branch campus college in small city.
Enrollment: 506 undergrads, 32% part-time. 106 full-time freshmen.
Selectivity: Open admission; but selective for some programs.

BASIC COSTS (2008-2009)
Tuition and fees: $14,070.
Additional info: Cost is for 3 terms of 12 hours each. Tuition includes books and supplies; may vary by program.

FINANCIAL AID PICTURE (2007-2008)
Students with need: Need-based aid available for full-time and part-time students. Work study available nights, weekends, and for part-time students.
Students without need: This college awards aid only to students with need.

FINANCIAL AID PROCEDURES
Forms required: FAFSA, institutional form.
Dates and Deadlines: No deadline. Applicants notified on a rolling basis.
Transfers: No deadline. Applicants notified on a rolling basis.

CONTACT
Amy Kramer, Director of Finance
7009 Nordic Drive, Cedar Falls, IA 50613

Kaplan University: Cedar Rapids

Cedar Rapids, Iowa
www.kucampus.edu Federal Code: 004220

2-year for-profit liberal arts college in small city.
Enrollment: 572 undergrads, 34% part-time. 140 full-time freshmen.
Selectivity: Open admission; but selective for some programs.

BASIC COSTS (2008-2009)
Tuition and fees: $14,075.
Per-credit charge: $390.
Additional info: Cost is for 3 terms of 12 hours each. Tuition includes books and supplies; may vary by program.

FINANCIAL AID PICTURE (2007-2008)
Students with need: Need-based aid available for full-time and part-time students. Work study available nights, weekends, and for part-time students.
Students without need: No-need awards available for academics.

FINANCIAL AID PROCEDURES
Forms required: FAFSA, institutional form.
Dates and Deadlines: Priority date 6/30; no closing date. Applicants notified on a rolling basis.
Transfers: Priority date of 07/08 for filing Iowa Tuition Grant application.

CONTACT
Susan Spivey, President
3165 Edgewood Parkway, SW, Cedar Rapids, IA 52404
(319) 363-0481

Kaplan University: Davenport

Davenport, Iowa
www.kucampus.edu Federal Code: 004586

4-year for-profit university in large city.
Enrollment: 35,797 undergrads.
Selectivity: Open admission; but selective for some programs.

BASIC COSTS (2008-2009)
Tuition and fees: $14,120.
Additional info: Cost is for 3 terms of 12 hours each. Tuition includes books and supplies; may vary by program.

FINANCIAL AID PICTURE
Students with need: Need-based aid available for full-time and part-time students. Work study available nights.
Students without need: No-need awards available for academics.

FINANCIAL AID PROCEDURES
Forms required: FAFSA, institutional form.
Dates and Deadlines: No deadline. Applicants notified on a rolling basis starting 3/4; must reply by 6/15 or within 2 week(s) of notification.

CONTACT
1801 East Kimberly Road, Suite 1, Davenport, IA 52807-2095

Kaplan University: Des Moines

Urbandale, Iowa
www.kucampus.edu Federal Code: 004220

4-year for-profit university in large city.
Enrollment: 767 undergrads.
Selectivity: Open admission; but selective for some programs.

BASIC COSTS (2008-2009)
Tuition and fees: $14,070.
Additional info: Cost is for 3 terms of 12 hours each. Tuition includes books and supplies; may vary by program.

FINANCIAL AID PICTURE
Students with need: Need-based aid available for full-time and part-time students. Work study available nights, weekends, and for part-time students.
Students without need: This college awards aid only to students with need.

FINANCIAL AID PROCEDURES
Forms required: FAFSA, institutional form.
Dates and Deadlines: Priority date 6/30; no closing date.

CONTACT
Summer Vaselaar, Assistant Director of Student Finance
4655 121st Street, Urbandale, IA 50323
(515) 727-2100

Kaplan University: Mason City

Mason City, Iowa
www.kucampus.edu Federal Code: 004586

4-year for-profit branch campus college in large town.
Enrollment: 327 undergrads, 35% part-time. 55 full-time freshmen.
Selectivity: Open admission.

BASIC COSTS (2008-2009)
Tuition and fees: $14,025.
Additional info: Cost is for 3 terms of 12 hours each. Tuition includes books and supplies; may vary by program.

FINANCIAL AID PICTURE (2007-2008)
Students with need: 41% of average financial aid package awarded as scholarships/grants, 59% awarded as loans/jobs.
Students without need: No-need awards available for academics.

FINANCIAL AID PROCEDURES
Forms required: FAFSA.
Dates and Deadlines: Closing date 6/1. Applicants notified on a rolling basis.

CONTACT

Cathy Gomez, Director of Financial Aid
2570 Fourth Street, SW, Mason City, IA 50401
(641) 423-2530

Kirkwood Community College

Cedar Rapids, Iowa
www.kirkwood.edu Federal Code: 004076

2-year public community college in small city.
Enrollment: 12,563 undergrads, 36% part-time. 2,753 full-time freshmen.
Selectivity: Open admission; but selective for some programs.

BASIC COSTS (2008-2009)

Tuition and fees: $3,210; out-of-state residents $3,960.
Per-credit charge: $107; out-of-state residents $132.

FINANCIAL AID PICTURE

Students with need: Need-based aid available for full-time and part-time students. Work study available nights, weekends, and for part-time students.
Students without need: No-need awards available for art, athletics, leadership, music/drama.

FINANCIAL AID PROCEDURES

Forms required: FAFSA.
Dates and Deadlines: Priority date 7/1; no closing date. Applicants notified on a rolling basis starting 4/1.

CONTACT

Peg Julius, Director of Financial Aid
6301 Kirkwood Boulevard SW, Cedar Rapids, IA 52406
(319) 398-1274

Loras College

Dubuque, Iowa
www.loras.edu Federal Code: 001873

4-year private liberal arts college in small city, affiliated with Roman Catholic Church.
Enrollment: 1,512 undergrads.
Selectivity: Admits 50 to 75% of applicants.

BASIC COSTS (2009-2010)

Tuition and fees: $25,348.
Per-credit charge: $475.
Room and board: $7,026.
Additional info: Tuition/fee waivers available for minority students.

FINANCIAL AID PICTURE (2008-2009)

Students with need: Need-based aid available for full-time and part-time students. Work study available nights, weekends, and for part-time students.
Students without need: No-need awards available for academics, alumni affiliation, leadership, minority status, music/drama.
Additional info: Audition or portfolio recommended for music and art financial aid applicants.

FINANCIAL AID PROCEDURES

Forms required: FAFSA.
Dates and Deadlines: Priority date 4/15; no closing date. Applicants notified on a rolling basis starting 3/1; must reply within 3 week(s) of notification.

CONTACT

Julie Dunn, Director of Financial Planning
1450 Alta Vista Street, Dubuque, IA 52004-0178
(563) 588-7136

Luther College

Decorah, Iowa
www.luther.edu Federal Code: 001874

4-year private liberal arts college in small town, affiliated with Evangelical Lutheran Church in America.
Enrollment: 2,355 undergrads. 630 full-time freshmen.
Selectivity: Admits over 75% of applicants.

BASIC COSTS (2009-2010)

Tuition and fees: $32,290.
Per-credit charge: $1,148.
Room and board: $5,380.

FINANCIAL AID PICTURE (2008-2009)

Students with need: Out of 541 full-time freshmen who applied for aid, 428 were judged to have need. Of these, 428 received aid, and 153 had their full need met. Average financial aid package met 92% of need; average scholarship/grant was $17,526; average loan was $5,376. For part-time students, average financial aid package was $12,249.
Students without need: 113 full-time freshmen who did not demonstrate need for aid received scholarships/grants; average award was $1,117. No-need awards available for academics, alumni affiliation, art, minority status, music/drama.
Scholarships offered: Academic scholarship; $4,000-$17,000; based on class rank and SAT/ACT. National Merit Scholarship; $1,000-$2,000; depending on qualifications. Diversity Enrichment Scholarship; $3,000-$5,000 awarded to students with broadly diverse and distinctive backgrounds. Church Matching Scholarship; up to $750; for students from member churches. Music scholarship; $1,000-$4,000, plus one scholarship that covers one credit hour of private instruction. Legacy Award; $1,000 for children of Luther College alumni. Competitive Nursing scholarship; $1,000; determined by nursing faculty and strength of admission file. Art scholarship; $150-$500; determined by evaluation of portfolio.
Cumulative student debt: 81% of graduating class had student loans; average debt was $18,581.

FINANCIAL AID PROCEDURES

Forms required: FAFSA, institutional form.
Dates and Deadlines: Priority date 3/1; no closing date. Applicants notified on a rolling basis starting 3/15; must reply by 5/1 or within 4 week(s) of notification.

CONTACT

Janice Cordell, Director of Student Financial Planning
700 College Drive, Decorah, IA 52101-1042
(563) 387-1018

Maharishi University of Management

Fairfield, Iowa
www.mum.edu Federal Code: 011113

4-year private university and liberal arts college in small town.
Enrollment: 236 undergrads, 9% part-time. 40 full-time freshmen.

BASIC COSTS (2008-2009)

Tuition and fees: $24,430.
Per-credit charge: $550.
Room and board: $6,000.

FINANCIAL AID PICTURE (2007-2008)

Students with need: Need-based aid available for full-time and part-time students. Work study available nights, weekends, and for part-time students.
Scholarships offered: Shelley Hoffman Scholarship; $500-$900; based on creative writing and/or cerebral palsy; 7 awarded. National Merit Scholarship; full tuition; for NMS finalists; 4 awarded. Ray Prat Scholarship; $500-$1,750;

for musically-talented undergraduates; 4 awarded. Girl Scout Gold Award Scholarship; $1,500 renewable; for GS Gold Award recipients; 5 awarded. DeRoy D. Thomas Scholarship; $3,000 each; open to outstanding African American; 1 awarded.
Additional info: Students may earn scholarships through volunteer staff program.

FINANCIAL AID PROCEDURES
Forms required: FAFSA.
Dates and Deadlines: Priority date 7/15; closing date 7/30. Applicants notified on a rolling basis starting 3/1; must reply within 4 week(s) of notification.
Transfers: No deadline. Applicants notified on a rolling basis starting 3/15; must reply within 4 week(s) of notification.

CONTACT
Bill Christensen, Director of Financial Aid
Office of Admissions, Fairfield, IA 52557
(641) 472-1156

Mercy College of Health Sciences
Des Moines, Iowa
www.mchs.edu Federal Code: 006273

4-year private health science college in large city, affiliated with Roman Catholic Church.
Enrollment: 669 undergrads, 43% part-time. 56 full-time freshmen.
Selectivity: Admits 50 to 75% of applicants.

BASIC COSTS (2008-2009)
Tuition and fees: $13,000.
Per-credit charge: $440.

FINANCIAL AID PICTURE (2007-2008)
Students with need: Out of 55 full-time freshmen who applied for aid, 52 were judged to have need. Of these, 52 received aid, and 1 had their full need met. Average financial aid package met 35% of need; average scholarship/grant was $5,145; average loan was $2,918. For part-time students, average financial aid package was $8,059.
Students without need: 1 full-time freshmen who did not demonstrate need for aid received scholarships/grants; average award was $3,000. No-need awards available for academics.

FINANCIAL AID PROCEDURES
Forms required: FAFSA.
Dates and Deadlines: Closing date 7/1. Applicants notified on a rolling basis; must reply by 1/1 or within 3 week(s) of notification.
Transfers: Students must submit information by 7/1 to be eligible for Iowa Tuition Grant.

CONTACT
Wayne Dillo, Financial Aid Director
921 Sixth Avenue, Des Moines, IA 50309
(515) 643-6611

Morningside College
Sioux City, Iowa
www.morningside.edu Federal Code: 001879

4-year private liberal arts college in small city, affiliated with United Methodist Church.
Enrollment: 1,180 undergrads, 3% part-time. 302 full-time freshmen.
Selectivity: Admits 50 to 75% of applicants.

BASIC COSTS (2009-2010)
Tuition and fees: $22,246.
Room and board: $6,729.
Additional info: Tuition/fee waivers available for adults.

FINANCIAL AID PICTURE (2008-2009)
Students with need: Need-based aid available for full-time and part-time students. Work study available nights, weekends, and for part-time students.
Students without need: No-need awards available for academics, alumni affiliation, art, athletics, job skills, leadership, music/drama, religious affiliation, ROTC, state/district residency.
Scholarships offered: President's Scholarship; $6,000 to $10,000; based on 27 ACT and top 10% of class. Dean's Scholarship; $3,000 to $6,000; based on 23 ACT or top 20% of class. Mustang Co-Curricular Award; up to $3,000; based on leadership and involvement. National Merit; full tuition. Talent Awards; up to $4,000; based on talents in the areas of art, cheerleading, creative writing, computer technology, mass communications, music, and/or theater.

FINANCIAL AID PROCEDURES
Forms required: FAFSA.
Dates and Deadlines: Priority date 3/1; no closing date. Applicants notified on a rolling basis starting 3/31.

CONTACT
Karen Gagnon, Director Student Financial Planning
1501 Morningside Avenue, Sioux City, IA 51106
(712) 274-5159

Mount Mercy College
Cedar Rapids, Iowa
www.mtmercy.edu Federal Code: 001880

4-year private liberal arts college in small city, affiliated with Roman Catholic Church.
Enrollment: 1,446 undergrads, 38% part-time. 170 full-time freshmen.
Selectivity: Admits over 75% of applicants.

BASIC COSTS (2008-2009)
Tuition and fees: $21,125.
Per-credit charge: $585.
Room and board: $6,650.

FINANCIAL AID PICTURE (2008-2009)
Students with need: Out of 158 full-time freshmen who applied for aid, 114 were judged to have need. Of these, 114 received aid, and 53 had their full need met. Average financial aid package met 72% of need; average scholarship/grant was $17,274; average loan was $5,491. For part-time students, average financial aid package was $9,839.
Students without need: 22 full-time freshmen who did not demonstrate need for aid received scholarships/grants; average award was $7,579. No-need awards available for academics, alumni affiliation, art, athletics, leadership, music/drama, religious affiliation.
Scholarships offered: 8 full-time freshmen received athletic scholarships; average amount $12,799.
Cumulative student debt: 89% of graduating class had student loans; average debt was $27,803.

FINANCIAL AID PROCEDURES
Forms required: FAFSA.
Dates and Deadlines: Priority date 3/1; no closing date. Applicants notified on a rolling basis starting 3/15; must reply by 5/1 or within 3 week(s) of notification.
Transfers: No deadline. Applicants notified on a rolling basis starting 3/1; must reply within 3 week(s) of notification.

CONTACT
Bethany Rinderknecht, Director of Financial Aid
1330 Elmhurst Drive NE, Cedar Rapids, IA 52402-4797
(319) 368-6467

North Iowa Area Community College

Mason City, Iowa
www.niacc.edu Federal Code: 001877

2-year public community college in large town.
Enrollment: 3,335 undergrads, 45% part-time. 766 full-time freshmen.
Selectivity: Open admission; but selective for some programs.

BASIC COSTS (2008-2009)

Tuition and fees: $3,487; out-of-state residents $5,041.
Per-credit charge: $103; out-of-state residents $155.
Room and board: $4,536.

FINANCIAL AID PICTURE (2007-2008)

Students with need: Out of 705 full-time freshmen who applied for aid, 585 were judged to have need. Of these, 562 received aid, and 73 had their full need met. Average financial aid package met 68% of need; average scholarship/grant was $3,794; average loan was $4,391. For part-time students, average financial aid package was $3,116.
Students without need: No-need awards available for academics, alumni affiliation, art, athletics, leadership, music/drama.

FINANCIAL AID PROCEDURES

Forms required: FAFSA, institutional form.
Dates and Deadlines: Priority date 3/1; no closing date. Applicants notified on a rolling basis starting 4/1; must reply within 2 week(s) of notification.

CONTACT

Mary Bloomingdale, Director of Financial Aid
500 College Drive, Mason City, IA 50401
(641) 422-4351

Northeast Iowa Community College

Calmar, Iowa
www.nicc.edu Federal Code: 004587

2-year public community college in rural community.
Enrollment: 3,200 undergrads.
Selectivity: Open admission; but selective for some programs.

BASIC COSTS (2008-2009)

Tuition and fees: $4,050.
Per-credit charge: $122.

FINANCIAL AID PICTURE

Students with need: Need-based aid available for full-time and part-time students. Work study available nights.
Students without need: No-need awards available for academics, leadership.

FINANCIAL AID PROCEDURES

Forms required: FAFSA.
Dates and Deadlines: Priority date 7/1; no closing date. Applicants notified on a rolling basis starting 5/1.

CONTACT

Jeff Murphy, Director of Financial Aid
Box 400, Calmar, IA 52132
(563) 526-3263 ext. 447

Northwest Iowa Community College

Sheldon, Iowa
www.nwicc.edu Federal Code: 004600

2-year public community college in small town.
Enrollment: 1,256 undergrads.
Selectivity: Open admission; but selective for some programs.

BASIC COSTS (2008-2009)

Tuition and fees: $4,110; out-of-state residents $5,160.
Per-credit charge: $113; out-of-state residents $148.
Room and board: $3,550.

FINANCIAL AID PICTURE

Students with need: Need-based aid available for full-time and part-time students.

FINANCIAL AID PROCEDURES

Forms required: FAFSA, institutional form.
Dates and Deadlines: Priority date 4/1; no closing date. Applicants notified on a rolling basis starting 5/1.

CONTACT

Karna Hofmeyer, Financial Aid Director
603 West Park Street, Sheldon, IA 51201
(712) 324-5061 ext. 138

Northwestern College

Orange City, Iowa
www.nwciowa.edu Federal Code: 001883

4-year private liberal arts college in small town, affiliated with Reformed Church in America.
Enrollment: 1,201 undergrads, 2% part-time. 320 full-time freshmen.
Selectivity: Admits over 75% of applicants.

BASIC COSTS (2008-2009)

Tuition and fees: $22,950.
Room and board: $6,580.
Additional info: 1-4 credits, $445 per credit hour; 5-8 credits, $660 per credit hour; 9-11 credits, $870 per credit hour. Tuition/fee waivers available for adults.

FINANCIAL AID PICTURE (2007-2008)

Students with need: Out of 256 full-time freshmen who applied for aid, 256 were judged to have need. Of these, 256 received aid, and 84 had their full need met. Average financial aid package met 83% of need; average scholarship/grant was $6,133; average loan was $3,894. For part-time students, average financial aid package was $9,260.
Students without need: 56 full-time freshmen who did not demonstrate need for aid received scholarships/grants; average award was $5,880. No-need awards available for academics, art, athletics, music/drama, religious affiliation, state/district residency.
Scholarships offered: 121 full-time freshmen received athletic scholarships; average amount $4,009.

FINANCIAL AID PROCEDURES

Forms required: FAFSA.
Dates and Deadlines: Priority date 4/1; closing date 6/30. Applicants notified on a rolling basis starting 3/15; must reply within 3 week(s) of notification.
Transfers: No deadline. Financial aid transcript required for aid.

CONTACT

Teresa Gunderson, Director of Financial Aid
101 Seventh Street, SW, Orange City, IA 51041
(712) 707-7131

St. Ambrose University

Davenport, Iowa
www.sau.edu Federal Code: 001889

4-year private university and liberal arts college in small city, affiliated with Roman Catholic Church.

Enrollment: 2,845 undergrads, 15% part-time. 572 full-time freshmen.

Selectivity: Admits over 75% of applicants.

BASIC COSTS (2008-2009)

Tuition and fees: $21,610.

Per-credit charge: $672.

Room and board: $7,825.

Additional info: Tuition/fee waivers available for adults.

FINANCIAL AID PICTURE (2008-2009)

Students with need: Need-based aid available for full-time and part-time students. Work study available nights, weekends, and for part-time students.

Students without need: No-need awards available for academics, alumni affiliation, art, athletics, job skills, music/drama.

Scholarships offered: Ambrose Scholarship; 4.0 GPA and 30 ACT or 1320 SAT score required. Presidential Scholarship; 3.8 GPA and ACT 26-29 or SAT 1170-1319 required. SAT scores listed are exclusive of Writing.

Additional info: Iowa applicants must apply for financial aid by July 1. Audition required for music, drama scholarship applicants.

FINANCIAL AID PROCEDURES

Forms required: FAFSA.

Dates and Deadlines: Priority date 3/15; no closing date. Applicants notified on a rolling basis starting 2/1; must reply within 2 week(s) of notification.

Transfers: No deadline. Must reply within 2 week(s) of notification.

CONTACT

Julie Haack, Director of Financial Aid
518 West Locust Street, Davenport, IA 52803-2898
(563) 333-6314

St. Luke's College

Sioux City, Iowa
www.stlukescollege.edu Federal Code: 007291

2-year private health science college in small city, affiliated with Lutheran and Methodist churches.

Enrollment: 149 undergrads, 31% part-time. 4 full-time freshmen.

Selectivity: Admits 50 to 75% of applicants.

BASIC COSTS (2009-2010)

Tuition and fees: $14,270.

Per-credit charge: $390.

Additional info: Summer general fee: $125.

FINANCIAL AID PICTURE (2008-2009)

Students with need: 28% of average financial aid package awarded as scholarships/grants, 72% awarded as loans/jobs. Need-based aid available for part-time students. Work study available nights, weekends, and for part-time students.

Students without need: No-need awards available for academics, job skills, leadership.

FINANCIAL AID PROCEDURES

Forms required: FAFSA.

Dates and Deadlines: Priority date 3/1; no closing date. Applicants notified on a rolling basis starting 4/1; must reply within 2 week(s) of notification.

CONTACT

Danelle Johannsen, Director, Student and Administrative Services
2720 Stone Park Boulevard, Sioux City, IA 51104
(712) 279-3377

Simpson College

Indianola, Iowa
www.simpson.edu Federal Code: 001887

4-year private liberal arts college in large town, affiliated with United Methodist Church.

Enrollment: 1,929 undergrads, 24% part-time. 384 full-time freshmen.

Selectivity: Admits over 75% of applicants.

BASIC COSTS (2008-2009)

Tuition and fees: $24,771.

Per-credit charge: $275.

Room and board: $6,988.

Additional info: Tuition/fee waivers available for adults, minority students.

FINANCIAL AID PICTURE (2008-2009)

Students with need: Out of 384 full-time freshmen who applied for aid, 322 were judged to have need. Of these, 322 received aid, and 94 had their full need met. Average financial aid package met 93% of need; average scholarship/grant was $17,812; average loan was $3,052. For part-time students, average financial aid package was $9,117.

Students without need: 62 full-time freshmen who did not demonstrate need for aid received scholarships/grants; average award was $11,987. No-need awards available for academics, alumni affiliation, art, leadership, minority status, music/drama, religious affiliation, state/district residency.

Cumulative student debt: 92% of graduating class had student loans; average debt was $31,115.

Additional info: Music and theater scholarships based on audition. Art scholarships based on portfolio.

FINANCIAL AID PROCEDURES

Forms required: FAFSA.

Dates and Deadlines: Priority date 4/1; no closing date. Applicants notified on a rolling basis starting 3/12; must reply by 5/1 or within 3 week(s) of notification.

CONTACT

Tracie Pavon, Assistant Vice President for Enrollment and Financial Assistance
701 North C Street, Indianola, IA 50125
(515) 961-1630

Southeastern Community College: North Campus

West Burlington, Iowa
www.scciowa.edu Federal Code: 004603

2-year public community and junior college in large town.

Enrollment: 2,363 undergrads, 37% part-time. 308 full-time freshmen.

Selectivity: Open admission; but selective for some programs.

BASIC COSTS (2008-2009)

Tuition and fees: $3,450; out-of-state residents $3,600.

Per-credit charge: $115; out-of-state residents $120.

FINANCIAL AID PICTURE (2007-2008)

Students with need: Out of 261 full-time freshmen who applied for aid, 210 were judged to have need. Of these, 201 received aid. For part-time students, average financial aid package was $5,561.

Students without need: 4 full-time freshmen who did not demonstrate need for aid received scholarships/grants; average award was $2,223. No-need awards available for academics, art, athletics, minority status.
Scholarships offered: 7 full-time freshmen received athletic scholarships; average amount $1,656.

FINANCIAL AID PROCEDURES
Forms required: FAFSA.
Dates and Deadlines: Priority date 7/1; no closing date. Applicants notified on a rolling basis starting 3/1; must reply within 4 week(s) of notification.

CONTACT
Gwen Scholer, Financial Aid Director
1500 West Agency Road, West Burlington, IA 52655-0605
(319) 752-2731 ext. 5014

Southwestern Community College
Creston, Iowa
www.swcciowa.edu Federal Code: 001857

2-year public community college in small town.
Enrollment: 908 undergrads, 24% part-time. 173 full-time freshmen.
Selectivity: Open admission; but selective for some programs.

BASIC COSTS (2008-2009)
Tuition and fees: $3,920; out-of-state residents $4,934.
Per-credit charge: $111; out-of-state residents $143.
Room and board: $4,700.

FINANCIAL AID PICTURE (2007-2008)
Students with need: Need-based aid available for full-time and part-time students. Work study available nights, weekends, and for part-time students.
Students without need: No-need awards available for academics, athletics, leadership, music/drama, state/district residency.

FINANCIAL AID PROCEDURES
Forms required: FAFSA.
Dates and Deadlines: Priority date 7/1; no closing date. Applicants notified on a rolling basis starting 6/1; must reply within 2 week(s) of notification.

CONTACT
Tracy Sleep, Financial Aid Officer
1501 West Townline Street, Creston, IA 50801
(641) 782-1333

University of Dubuque
Dubuque, Iowa
www.dbq.edu Federal Code: 001891

4-year private university and seminary college in small city, affiliated with Presbyterian Church (USA).
Enrollment: 1,321 undergrads, 3% part-time. 337 full-time freshmen.
Selectivity: Admits 50 to 75% of applicants.

BASIC COSTS (2008-2009)
Tuition and fees: $20,020.
Per-credit charge: $445.
Room and board: $6,750.

FINANCIAL AID PICTURE (2008-2009)
Students with need: Average financial aid package met 77% of need; average scholarship/grant was $11,263; average loan was $7,033. For part-time students, average financial aid package was $9,150.
Students without need: No-need awards available for academics, alumni affiliation, music/drama, ROTC.
Scholarships offered: Presidential Scholarship; $6,000 for 4 years; top 20% of class and top 20% of ACT. Honors Scholarship; top 20% of class, or top 20% of ACT/SAT, or 3.5 GPA or greater.
Cumulative student debt: 97% of graduating class had student loans; average debt was $37,936.

FINANCIAL AID PROCEDURES
Forms required: FAFSA.
Dates and Deadlines: Priority date 4/1; no closing date. Applicants notified on a rolling basis starting 3/1; must reply within 3 week(s) of notification.
Transfers: No deadline. Applicants notified on a rolling basis starting 3/1; must reply within 3 week(s) of notification. Iowa Tuition Grant available to Iowa residents.

CONTACT
Timothy Kremer, Dean of Student Financial Planning and Scholarships
2000 University Avenue, Dubuque, IA 52001-5099
(563) 589-3396

University of Iowa
Iowa City, Iowa
www.uiowa.edu Federal Code: 001892

4-year public university in small city.
Enrollment: 20,079 undergrads, 8% part-time. 4,182 full-time freshmen.
Selectivity: Admits over 75% of applicants.

BASIC COSTS (2008-2009)
Tuition and fees: $6,544; out-of-state residents $20,658.
Room and board: $7,079.

FINANCIAL AID PICTURE (2007-2008)
Students with need: Out of 3,420 full-time freshmen who applied for aid, 2,302 were judged to have need. Of these, 2,086 received aid, and 1,085 had their full need met. Average financial aid package met 52% of need; average scholarship/grant was $4,179; average loan was $2,904. Need-based aid available for part-time students.
Students without need: 911 full-time freshmen who did not demonstrate need for aid received scholarships/grants; average award was $2,313. No-need awards available for academics, alumni affiliation, art, athletics, leadership, minority status, music/drama, ROTC.
Scholarships offered: ***Merit:*** Presidential Scholarship; $52,000 over 4 years; based on ACT/SAT, GPA, essay; 20 awarded. Old Gold Scholarship; $12,000 over 4 years; awarded to runners-up for Presidential Scholarship; 350 awarded. National Scholars Award; $12,080; for non-residents based on admission index. Iowa Heritage Award; $6,000; for nonresident students who have a parent, step-parent, legal guardian, or grandparent who graduated from UI. Advantage Iowa Award; $2,000 to full tuition; race/ethnic background, socioeconomic factors considered; other criteria include U.S. citizenship or permanent residency, whether student is a first-generation college student, participant in federal TRIO program. ***Athletic:*** 84 full-time freshmen received athletic scholarships; average amount $14,117.
Cumulative student debt: 61% of graduating class had student loans; average debt was $22,856.

FINANCIAL AID PROCEDURES
Forms required: FAFSA, institutional form.
Dates and Deadlines: Priority date 1/1; no closing date. Applicants notified on a rolling basis starting 3/15.
Transfers: No deadline. Applicants notified on a rolling basis starting 3/15.

CONTACT
Mark Warner, Assistant Provost for Enrollment Services
107 Calvin Hall, Iowa City, IA 52242-1396
(319) 335-1450

University of Northern Iowa
Cedar Falls, Iowa
www.uni.edu Federal Code: 001890

4-year public university in small city.
Enrollment: 10,835 undergrads, 8% part-time. 1,986 full-time freshmen.
Selectivity: Admits over 75% of applicants.

BASIC COSTS (2008-2009)
Tuition and fees: $6,376; out-of-state residents $14,596.
Per-credit charge: $231; out-of-state residents $573.
Room and board: $6,810.

FINANCIAL AID PICTURE (2008-2009)
Students with need: Out of 1,693 full-time freshmen who applied for aid, 1,134 were judged to have need. Of these, 1,109 received aid, and 313 had their full need met. Average financial aid package met 72% of need; average scholarship/grant was $3,825; average loan was $3,213. For part-time students, average financial aid package was $7,220.
Students without need: 508 full-time freshmen who did not demonstrate need for aid received scholarships/grants; average award was $2,590. No-need awards available for academics, alumni affiliation, art, athletics, leadership, minority status, music/drama, ROTC, state/district residency.
Scholarships offered: ***Merit:*** Presidential Scholarship Award; $8,000/year for up to 4 years; must be in upper 10% of high school class with 29 ACT or Regent Admission Index of 335 and involved in leadership and service activities; 20 available. Distinguished Scholar Award for Iowans; $1,500/year, renewable for a 2nd year; Iowa residents in upper 20% of high school class or 26 ACT with college GPA of 3.0. ***Athletic:*** 70 full-time freshmen received athletic scholarships; average amount $11,369.
Cumulative student debt: 78% of graduating class had student loans; average debt was $24,176.

FINANCIAL AID PROCEDURES
Forms required: FAFSA.
Dates and Deadlines: No deadline. Applicants notified on a rolling basis starting 3/1.

CONTACT
Roland Carrillo, Director Financial Aid and Student Employment
1227 West 27th Street, Cedar Falls, IA 50614-0018
(319) 273-2700

Upper Iowa University
Fayette, Iowa
www.uiu.edu Federal Code: 001893

4-year private university in rural community.
Enrollment: 767 undergrads.
Selectivity: Admits 50 to 75% of applicants.

BASIC COSTS (2009-2010)
Tuition and fees: $21,418.
Room and board: $6,578.

FINANCIAL AID PICTURE (2007-2008)
Students with need: 42% of average financial aid package awarded as scholarships/grants, 58% awarded as loans/jobs. Need-based aid available for part-time students. Work study available nights, weekends, and for part-time students.
Students without need: No-need awards available for academics..

FINANCIAL AID PROCEDURES
Forms required: FAFSA.
Dates and Deadlines: Priority date 3/1; no closing date. Applicants notified on a rolling basis starting 3/1.

CONTACT
Jobyna Johnston, Director of Financial Aid
Parker Fox Hall, Fayette, IA 52142
(800) 553-4150 ext. 3

Vatterott College
Des Moines, Iowa
www.vatterott-college.edu Federal Code: 026092

2-year for-profit health science and technical college in large city.
Enrollment: 238 undergrads.
Selectivity: Open admission.

BASIC COSTS (2008-2009)
Additional info: Program cost ranges: $14,300 to $22,000 (certificate/diploma); $21,450 to $31,050 (associate degree).

FINANCIAL AID PICTURE
Students with need: Need-based aid available for full-time students.
Students without need: This college awards aid only to students with need.
Scholarships offered: Make the Grade Scholarship; up to $1,000; based on final semester grades; available for 1 year after high school graduation.

FINANCIAL AID PROCEDURES
Forms required: FAFSA.
Dates and Deadlines: No deadline. Applicants notified on a rolling basis.

CONTACT
Ryan Williams, Financial Aid Administrator
6100 Thornton, Suite 290, Des Moines, IA 50321
(515) 309-9000

Waldorf College
Forest City, Iowa
www.waldorf.edu Federal Code: 001895

4-year private liberal arts college in small town, affiliated with Evangelical Lutheran Church in America.
Enrollment: 524 undergrads, 3% part-time. 167 full-time freshmen.
Selectivity: Admits 50 to 75% of applicants.

BASIC COSTS (2008-2009)
Tuition and fees: $20,054.
Room and board: $5,810.

FINANCIAL AID PICTURE (2007-2008)
Students with need: Out of 119 full-time freshmen who applied for aid, 105 were judged to have need. Of these, 104 received aid, and 31 had their full need met. Average financial aid package met 84% of need; average scholarship/grant was $12,898; average loan was $4,582. For part-time students, average financial aid package was $12,498.
Students without need: 59 full-time freshmen who did not demonstrate need for aid received scholarships/grants; average award was $11,146. No-need awards available for academics, alumni affiliation, athletics, job skills, leadership, music/drama, religious affiliation, state/district residency.
Scholarships offered: 29 full-time freshmen received athletic scholarships; average amount $2,947.

FINANCIAL AID PROCEDURES
Forms required: FAFSA, institutional form.
Dates and Deadlines: Priority date 3/1; no closing date. Applicants notified on a rolling basis starting 3/1; must reply within 2 week(s) of notification.
Transfers: Applicants notified on a rolling basis starting 3/1; must reply within 2 week(s) of notification.

CONTACT

Duane Polsdofer, Director of Student Financial Aid
106 South Sixth Street, Forest City, IA 50436-1713
(641) 585-8120

Wartburg College

Waverly, Iowa
www.wartburg.edu Federal Code: 001896

4-year private liberal arts college in small town, affiliated with Evangelical Lutheran Church in America.
Enrollment: 1,757 undergrads, 2% part-time. 545 full-time freshmen.
Selectivity: Admits 50 to 75% of applicants.

BASIC COSTS (2009-2010)

Tuition and fees: $27,450.
Room and board: $7,615.

FINANCIAL AID PICTURE (2007-2008)

Students with need: Out of 504 full-time freshmen who applied for aid, 418 were judged to have need. Of these, 418 received aid, and 150 had their full need met. Average financial aid package met 90% of need; average scholarship/grant was $15,882; average loan was $5,324. For part-time students, average financial aid package was $7,222.
Students without need: 126 full-time freshmen who did not demonstrate need for aid received scholarships/grants; average award was $15,074. No-need awards available for academics, alumni affiliation, leadership, music/drama.
Scholarships offered: Regents scholarship; up to full tuition, fees, room and board; based on 28 ACT (1240 SAT, exclusive of writing) or rank in top 10% of class; renewable for 4 years with 3.0 GPA. Presidential Scholarship; up to $6,000 per year; based on 25 ACT (1140 SAT, exclusive of writing) or rank in top 20% of class or 3.5 GPA; renewable for 4 years with 2.7 GPA. Students who participate in Regents Scholarship competition not eligible for Presidential Scholarship.
Cumulative student debt: 89% of graduating class had student loans; average debt was $31,063.

FINANCIAL AID PROCEDURES

Forms required: FAFSA.
Dates and Deadlines: Priority date 3/1; no closing date. Applicants notified on a rolling basis starting 3/1; must reply within 2 week(s) of notification.

CONTACT

Jennifer Sassman, Director of Financial Aid
100 Wartburg Boulevard, PO Box 1003, Waverly, IA 50677-0903
(319) 352-8262

Western Iowa Tech Community College

Sioux City, Iowa
www.witcc.com Federal Code: 004590

2-year public community college in small city.
Enrollment: 2,426 undergrads, 36% part-time. 269 full-time freshmen.
Selectivity: Open admission; but selective for some programs.

BASIC COSTS (2008-2009)

Tuition and fees: $3,735; out-of-state residents $4,455.
Per-credit charge: $109; out-of-state residents $133.
Room and board: $4,887.

FINANCIAL AID PICTURE (2007-2008)

Students with need: Need-based aid available for full-time and part-time students. Work study available nights, weekends, and for part-time students.
Students without need: No-need awards available for academics, leadership, music/drama.

FINANCIAL AID PROCEDURES

Forms required: FAFSA.
Dates and Deadlines: No deadline. Applicants notified on a rolling basis starting 4/1.

CONTACT

Donald Duzik, Director of Financial Aid
Box 5199, Sioux City, IA 51102-5199
(712) 274-6402

William Penn University

Oskaloosa, Iowa
www.wmpenn.edu Federal Code: 001900

4-year private liberal arts college in small town, affiliated with Society of Friends (Quaker).
Enrollment: 1,697 undergrads, 3% part-time. 209 full-time freshmen.
Selectivity: Admits 50 to 75% of applicants.

BASIC COSTS (2008-2009)

Tuition and fees: $18,034.
Room and board: $5,132.
Additional info: Per-credit-hour charge of $215 for 1-7 credits, $425 for credits in excess of 18.

FINANCIAL AID PICTURE (2007-2008)

Students with need: 56% of average financial aid package awarded as scholarships/grants, 44% awarded as loans/jobs. Need-based aid available for part-time students. Work study available nights, weekends, and for part-time students.
Students without need: No-need awards available for academics, alumni affiliation, athletics, leadership, music/drama, religious affiliation.
Scholarships offered: Participation awards; up to $3,000; for music, drama, media, cheerleading, dance, religious leadership. Academic scholarships; based on high school GPA, ACT/SAT, class rank.

FINANCIAL AID PROCEDURES

Forms required: FAFSA.
Dates and Deadlines: Priority date 4/15; no closing date. Applicants notified on a rolling basis starting 1/1; must reply within 3 week(s) of notification.
Transfers: No deadline. Applicants notified on a rolling basis starting 1/1.

CONTACT

Cyndi Peiffer, Director of Financial Aid
201 Trueblood Avenue, Oskaloosa, IA 52577
(641) 673-1060

Kansas

Allen County Community College

Iola, Kansas
www.allencc.edu Federal Code: 001901

2-year public community college in small town.
Enrollment: 2,821 undergrads.
Selectivity: Open admission.

BASIC COSTS (2008-2009)

Tuition and fees: $1,710; out-of-district residents $1,800; out-of-state residents $1,800.
Per-credit charge: $41; out-of-district residents $44; out-of-state residents $44.
Room and board: $4,100.

FINANCIAL AID PICTURE (2007-2008)

Students with need: 53% of average financial aid package awarded as scholarships/grants, 47% awarded as loans/jobs. Need-based aid available for part-time students. Work study available nights, weekends, and for part-time students.

Students without need: No-need awards available for academics, art, athletics, music/drama, state/district residency.

Additional info: Scholarships for livestock judging, cheerleading, choir, dance, drama, art, academic challenge, and student ambassadors.

FINANCIAL AID PROCEDURES

Forms required: FAFSA.

Dates and Deadlines: Closing date 6/1. Applicants notified on a rolling basis starting 6/1; must reply within 2 week(s) of notification.

CONTACT

Vicki Curry, Director of Financial Aid/Registrar
1801 North Cottonwood, Iola, KS 66749
(620) 365-5116 ext. 221

Baker University

Baldwin City, Kansas
www.bakeru.edu Federal Code: 001903

4-year private liberal arts and teachers college in small town, affiliated with United Methodist Church.

Enrollment: 906 undergrads, 1% part-time. 239 full-time freshmen.

Selectivity: Admits 50 to 75% of applicants.

BASIC COSTS (2009-2010)

Tuition and fees: $21,130.

Per-credit charge: $640.

Room and board: $6,800.

Additional info: Tuition/fee waivers available for minority students.

FINANCIAL AID PICTURE (2008-2009)

Students with need: Average financial aid package met 85% of need; average scholarship/grant was $6,358; average loan was $4,136. For part-time students, average financial aid package was $8,006.

Students without need: No-need awards available for academics, alumni affiliation, art, athletics, leadership, music/drama, religious affiliation, ROTC.

Scholarships offered: Presidential Scholarships, $8,000; 28 ACT or 1260 SAT, 3.70 GPA, top 10% class rank. Faculty Merit Scholarships, $7,000; 25 ACT or 1140 SAT, 3.40 GPA, top 25% class rank. University Scholarships, $6,000; 22 ACT or 1030 SAT, 3.10 GPA, top 50% class rank. Academic Leadership Scholarships, $1,500; 22 ACT or 1030 SAT, 3.10 GPA, top 50% class rank. SAT scores listed are exclusive of the writing portion.

FINANCIAL AID PROCEDURES

Forms required: FAFSA, institutional form.

Dates and Deadlines: Priority date 3/1; no closing date. Applicants notified on a rolling basis starting 3/1; must reply by 5/1 or within 6 week(s) of notification.

Transfers: No deadline. Applicants notified on a rolling basis starting 3/1; must reply within 6 week(s) of notification.

CONTACT

Jeanne Mott, Director of Financial Aid
618 Eighth Street, Baldwin City, KS 66006-0065
(785) 594-4595

Barclay College

Haviland, Kansas
www.barclaycollege.edu Federal Code: 001917

4-year private Bible college in rural community, affiliated with Evangelical Friends Alliance and Friends United Meeting.

Enrollment: 138 undergrads, 5% part-time. 34 full-time freshmen.

Selectivity: Admits over 75% of applicants.

BASIC COSTS (2008-2009)

Tuition and fees: $13,000.

Per-credit charge: $350.

Room and board: $6,300.

FINANCIAL AID PICTURE (2008-2009)

Students with need: 68% of average financial aid package awarded as scholarships/grants, 32% awarded as loans/jobs. Need-based aid available for part-time students. Work study available nights, weekends, and for part-time students.

Students without need: No-need awards available for academics, alumni affiliation, leadership, music/drama, state/district residency.

Scholarships offered: President's Academic Award; $2,600 for 3.8 GPA or ACT score of 30. Dean's Academic Award; $2,000 for 3.6 GPA or ACT scores of 27-29. Trustees Academic Award; $1,600; for 3.4 GPA or ACT scores of 25-26.

FINANCIAL AID PROCEDURES

Forms required: FAFSA, institutional form.

Dates and Deadlines: Priority date 5/31; closing date 7/15. Applicants notified on a rolling basis starting 1/1; must reply within 4 week(s) of notification.

CONTACT

Ryan Haase, Director of Student Financial Services
607 North Kingman, Haviland, KS 67059
(620) 862-5252 ext. 41

Barton County Community College

Great Bend, Kansas
www.bartonccc.edu Federal Code: 004608

2-year public community college in large town.

Enrollment: 3,060 undergrads.

Selectivity: Open admission; but selective for some programs.

BASIC COSTS (2008-2009)

Tuition and fees: $2,130; out-of-state residents $2,700.

Per-credit charge: $49; out-of-state residents $68.

Room and board: $4,342.

FINANCIAL AID PICTURE (2007-2008)

Students with need: Need-based aid available for full-time and part-time students.

Students without need: No-need awards available for academics, athletics.

FINANCIAL AID PROCEDURES

Forms required: FAFSA, state aid form.

Dates and Deadlines: Priority date 3/1; no closing date. Applicants notified on a rolling basis starting 6/1; must reply within 4 week(s) of notification.

CONTACT

Myrna Perkins, Assistant Dean of Student Services/Director of Financial Aid
245 North East 30th Road, Great Bend, KS 67530-9283
(620) 792-2701

Benedictine College
Atchison, Kansas
www.benedictine.edu Federal Code: 010256

4-year private liberal arts college in large town, affiliated with Roman Catholic Church.
Enrollment: 1,364 undergrads, 1% part-time. 396 full-time freshmen.
Selectivity: Admits less than 50% of applicants.

BASIC COSTS (2009-2010)
Tuition and fees: $19,800.
Per-credit charge: $540.
Room and board: $6,575.

FINANCIAL AID PICTURE (2008-2009)
Students with need: Out of 360 full-time freshmen who applied for aid, 295 were judged to have need. Of these, 295 received aid, and 63 had their full need met. Average financial aid package met 69% of need; average scholarship/grant was $4,065; average loan was $3,780. For part-time students, average financial aid package was $6,303.
Students without need: 100 full-time freshmen who did not demonstrate need for aid received scholarships/grants; average award was $8,685. No-need awards available for academics, alumni affiliation, art, athletics, job skills, leadership, minority status, music/drama, religious affiliation, ROTC.
Scholarships offered: ***Merit:*** Presidential Scholarship; full tuition. Dean's Scholarship; partial tuition. Both renewable every year, 5 recipients each, must maintain 3.5 GPA. Students must be admitted by Jan. 31. Academic Scholarships; renewable every year; ranges from $2,500-$7,500 depending on ACT scores; unlimited number. ***Athletic:*** 138 full-time freshmen received athletic scholarships; average amount $4,415.
Cumulative student debt: 98% of graduating class had student loans; average debt was $26,000.

FINANCIAL AID PROCEDURES
Forms required: FAFSA.
Dates and Deadlines: Priority date 3/15; no closing date. Applicants notified on a rolling basis starting 2/1; must reply within 2 week(s) of notification.
Transfers: No deadline. Applicants notified on a rolling basis. Scholarship available for students transferring 2.0 cumulative GPA.

CONTACT
Tony Tanking, Director Financial Aid
1020 North Second Street, Atchison, KS 66002-1499
(913) 367-5340 ext. 2484

Bethany College
Lindsborg, Kansas
www.bethanylb.edu Federal Code: 001904

4-year private liberal arts college in small town, affiliated with Evangelical Lutheran Church in America.
Enrollment: 569 undergrads, 3% part-time. 176 full-time freshmen.
Selectivity: Admits 50 to 75% of applicants.

BASIC COSTS (2008-2009)
Tuition and fees: $18,124.
Per-credit charge: $300.
Room and board: $5,650.

FINANCIAL AID PICTURE (2008-2009)
Students with need: Out of 175 full-time freshmen who applied for aid, 145 were judged to have need. Of these, 145 received aid, and 69 had their full need met. Average financial aid package met 89% of need; average scholarship/grant was $7,254; average loan was $4,304. For part-time students, average financial aid package was $7,500.
Students without need: 10 full-time freshmen who did not demonstrate need for aid received scholarships/grants; average award was $4,580. No-need awards available for academics, alumni affiliation, art, athletics, leadership, music/drama, religious affiliation.
Cumulative student debt: 82% of graduating class had student loans; average debt was $17,161.
Additional info: State financial aid deadline March 15.

FINANCIAL AID PROCEDURES
Forms required: FAFSA.
Dates and Deadlines: Priority date 3/15; no closing date. Applicants notified on a rolling basis starting 2/1; must reply within 3 week(s) of notification.

CONTACT
Brenda Meagher, Director of Financial Aid
335 East Swensson, Lindsborg, KS 67456-1897
(785) 227-3311 ext. 8114

Bethel College
North Newton, Kansas
www.bethelks.edu Federal Code: 001905

4-year private liberal arts college in large town, affiliated with Mennonite Church.
Enrollment: 500 undergrads, 5% part-time. 107 full-time freshmen.
Selectivity: Admits 50 to 75% of applicants.

BASIC COSTS (2009-2010)
Tuition and fees: $19,990.
Per-credit charge: $720.
Room and board: $6,770.

FINANCIAL AID PICTURE (2007-2008)
Students with need: Out of 91 full-time freshmen who applied for aid, 89 were judged to have need. Of these, 89 received aid, and 37 had their full need met. Average financial aid package met 87% of need; average scholarship/grant was $4,317; average loan was $4,768. For part-time students, average financial aid package was $14,842.
Students without need: 17 full-time freshmen who did not demonstrate need for aid received scholarships/grants; average award was $7,126. No-need awards available for academics, alumni affiliation, art, athletics, minority status, music/drama, religious affiliation, state/district residency.
Scholarships offered: ***Merit:*** Scholarships for academically talented students, ranging from 16% to 50% of tuition. ***Athletic:*** 52 full-time freshmen received athletic scholarships; average amount $3,734.
Cumulative student debt: 81% of graduating class had student loans; average debt was $22,818.

FINANCIAL AID PROCEDURES
Forms required: FAFSA.
Dates and Deadlines: Priority date 4/1; no closing date. Applicants notified on a rolling basis starting 2/1; must reply within 2 week(s) of notification.
Transfers: Applicants notified on a rolling basis starting 2/1; must reply within 2 week(s) of notification.

CONTACT
Tony Graber, Director of Financial Aid
300 East 27th Street, North Newton, KS 67117-0531
(800) 522-1887 ext. 232

Central Christian College of Kansas
McPherson, Kansas
www.centralchristian.edu Federal Code: 001908

4-year private liberal arts college in large town, affiliated with Free Methodist Church of North America.
Enrollment: 309 undergrads. 94 full-time freshmen.

Selectivity: Admits 50 to 75% of applicants.

BASIC COSTS (2009-2010)

Tuition and fees: $17,000.
Per-credit charge: $475.
Room and board: $5,900.

FINANCIAL AID PICTURE (2007-2008)

Students with need: Out of 90 full-time freshmen who applied for aid, 87 were judged to have need. Of these, 87 received aid. Average financial aid package met 72% of need; average scholarship/grant was $4,847; average loan was $4,749. Need-based aid available for part-time students.
Students without need: 7 full-time freshmen who did not demonstrate need for aid received scholarships/grants; average award was $5,446. No-need awards available for academics, alumni affiliation, athletics, leadership, music/drama, religious affiliation.
Scholarships offered: ***Merit:*** National Merit Scholarship: full tuition; National Merit semifinalists. Trustees Scholarship: 60% tuition; minimum score of 30 on ACT/1340 on SAT and minimum 3.5 high school GPA. Valedictorian Scholarship: half tuition; for students who are first in their class, with minimum 27 ACT/1220 SAT and 3.5 GPA. SAT scores listed are exclusive of the writing portion. ***Athletic:*** 6 full-time freshmen received athletic scholarships; average amount $1,750.

FINANCIAL AID PROCEDURES

Forms required: FAFSA.
Dates and Deadlines: Priority date 3/1; no closing date. Applicants notified on a rolling basis starting 3/1; must reply within 4 week(s) of notification.
Transfers: No deadline. Applicants notified on a rolling basis starting 3/1; must reply within 4 week(s) of notification.

CONTACT

Mike Heimer, Director of Financial Aid
1200 South Main, McPherson, KS 67460-5740
(620) 241-0723 ext. 333

Cloud County Community College

Concordia, Kansas
www.cloud.edu Federal Code: 001909

2-year public community college in small town.
Enrollment: 800 undergrads, 32% part-time. 193 full-time freshmen.
Selectivity: Open admission.

BASIC COSTS (2008-2009)

Tuition and fees: $2,438; out-of-state residents $2,438.
Per-credit charge: $61.
Room and board: $4,540.

FINANCIAL AID PICTURE

Students with need: Need-based aid available for full-time and part-time students. Work study available nights, weekends, and for part-time students.

FINANCIAL AID PROCEDURES

Forms required: FAFSA.
Dates and Deadlines: Priority date 4/1; no closing date. Applicants notified on a rolling basis starting 5/1; must reply within 4 week(s) of notification.

CONTACT

Sherry Campbell, Director of Student Financial Aid
2221 Campus Drive, Concordia, KS 66901-1002
(785) 243-1435 ext. 280

Coffeyville Community College

Coffeyville, Kansas
www.coffeyville.edu Federal Code: 001910

2-year public community and technical college in large town.
Enrollment: 1,500 undergrads, 25% part-time. 607 full-time freshmen.
Selectivity: Open admission.

BASIC COSTS (2008-2009)

Tuition and fees: $1,840; out-of-state residents $3,240.
Per-credit charge: $27; out-of-state residents $67.
Room and board: $4,796.
Additional info: Oklahoma border county resident tuition: $35 per-credit-hour.

FINANCIAL AID PICTURE (2007-2008)

Students with need: Need-based aid available for full-time and part-time students. Work study available nights, weekends, and for part-time students.
Students without need: No-need awards available for academics, alumni affiliation, art, athletics, leadership, music/drama, state/district residency.

FINANCIAL AID PROCEDURES

Forms required: FAFSA.
Dates and Deadlines: Priority date 8/1; no closing date. Applicants notified on a rolling basis starting 6/20.

CONTACT

Rhonda Baker, Director of Financial Aid
400 West 11th Street, Coffeyville, KS 67337-5064
(620) 252-7357

Colby Community College

Colby, Kansas
www.colbycc.edu Federal Code: 001911

2-year public community college in small town.
Enrollment: 577 undergrads, 11% part-time. 259 full-time freshmen.
Selectivity: Open admission; but selective for some programs.

BASIC COSTS (2008-2009)

Tuition and fees: $2,430; out-of-state residents $3,600.
Per-credit charge: $48; out-of-state residents $87.
Room and board: $3,900.
Additional info: Nebraska and Colorado border county residents pay $58 per credit hour for tuition, and additional $33 per credit hour for required fees.

FINANCIAL AID PICTURE (2007-2008)

Students with need: Out of 163 full-time freshmen who applied for aid, 132 were judged to have need. Of these, 129 received aid, and 19 had their full need met. Average financial aid package met 77% of need; average scholarship/grant was $4,405; average loan was $1,583. For part-time students, average financial aid package was $4,980.
Students without need: 35 full-time freshmen who did not demonstrate need for aid received scholarships/grants; average award was $1,190. No-need awards available for academics, athletics, music/drama.
Scholarships offered: 38 full-time freshmen received athletic scholarships; average amount $2,709.

FINANCIAL AID PROCEDURES

Forms required: FAFSA, state aid form.
Dates and Deadlines: Priority date 6/1; no closing date. Applicants notified on a rolling basis starting 5/1.

CONTACT

Paula Halvorson, Director of Financial Aid
1255 South Range Avenue, Colby, KS 67701
(785) 460-4695

Cowley County Community College

Arkansas City, Kansas
www.cowley.edu Federal Code: 001902

2-year public community and technical college in large town.
Enrollment: 3,372 undergrads, 55% part-time. 389 full-time freshmen.
Selectivity: Open admission; but selective for some programs.

BASIC COSTS (2008-2009)

Tuition and fees: $2,040; out-of-district residents $2,190; out-of-state residents $3,750.
Per-credit charge: $45; out-of-district residents $50; out-of-state residents $102.
Room and board: $4,200.
Additional info: Oklahoma border county resident tuition: $50 per-credit-hour.

FINANCIAL AID PICTURE (2008-2009)

Students with need: For part-time students, average financial aid package was $2,948.
Students without need: No-need awards available for academics, alumni affiliation, art, athletics, leadership, music/drama, state/district residency.

FINANCIAL AID PROCEDURES

Forms required: FAFSA.
Dates and Deadlines: Priority date 4/15; no closing date. Applicants notified on a rolling basis starting 1/15; must reply within 2 week(s) of notification.

CONTACT

Sally Palmer, Director of Financial Aid
PO Box 1147, Arkansas City, KS 67005-1147
(620) 442-0430 ext. 5248

Dodge City Community College

Dodge City, Kansas
www.dc3.edu Federal Code: 001913

2-year public community and technical college in large town.
Enrollment: 1,554 undergrads.
Selectivity: Open admission; but selective for some programs.

BASIC COSTS (2008-2009)

Tuition and fees: $1,950; out-of-state residents $2,700.
Per-credit charge: $35; out-of-district residents $35; out-of-state residents $45.
Room and board: $4,370.

FINANCIAL AID PICTURE (2007-2008)

Students with need: Need-based aid available for full-time and part-time students. Work study available nights, weekends, and for part-time students.
Students without need: No-need awards available for academics, athletics, music/drama, state/district residency.

FINANCIAL AID PROCEDURES

Forms required: FAFSA, institutional form.
Dates and Deadlines: Priority date 3/15; no closing date. Applicants notified on a rolling basis; must reply within 2 week(s) of notification.

CONTACT

Anthony Lyons, Dean of Students
2501 North 14th Avenue, Dodge City, KS 67801-2399
(620) 227-9336

Donnelly College

Kansas City, Kansas
www.donnelly.edu Federal Code: 001914

2-year private junior and liberal arts college in large city, affiliated with Roman Catholic Church.
Enrollment: 631 undergrads, 53% part-time. 41 full-time freshmen.
Selectivity: Open admission.

BASIC COSTS (2008-2009)

Tuition and fees: $5,040.
Per-credit charge: $180.

FINANCIAL AID PICTURE (2008-2009)

Students with need: Out of 39 full-time freshmen who applied for aid, 39 were judged to have need. Of these, 39 received aid. Average financial aid package met 99% of need; average scholarship/grant was $2,057; average loan was $1,290. For part-time students, average financial aid package was $1,468.
Students without need: No-need awards available for academics, religious affiliation.

FINANCIAL AID PROCEDURES

Forms required: FAFSA, institutional form.
Dates and Deadlines: Priority date 4/1; no closing date. Applicants notified on a rolling basis starting 7/1.
Transfers: Applicants notified on a rolling basis.

CONTACT

Belinda Ogan, Director of Financial Aid
608 North 18th Street, Kansas City, KS 66102-4210
(913) 621-8740

Emporia State University

Emporia, Kansas
www.emporia.edu Federal Code: 001927

4-year public university in large town.
Enrollment: 4,148 undergrads, 10% part-time. 655 full-time freshmen.
Selectivity: Admits over 75% of applicants.

BASIC COSTS (2008-2009)

Tuition and fees: $4,136; out-of-state residents $12,648.
Per-credit charge: $110; out-of-state residents $394.
Room and board: $5,858.

FINANCIAL AID PICTURE (2007-2008)

Students with need: Average financial aid package met 45% of need; average scholarship/grant was $3,342; average loan was $3,093. For part-time students, average financial aid package was $6,471.
Students without need: No-need awards available for academics, alumni affiliation, art, athletics, job skills, leadership, minority status, music/drama, religious affiliation, state/district residency.
Scholarships offered: Presidential Academic Awards; $1,000 to $1,200 (unlimited number) based on ACT. Challenge Awards; $500 (unlimited number) based on ACT/GPA. Transfer President's Academic Award; $500 to $1,000; based on cumulative GPA or Phi Theta Kappa membership. Guaranteed GPA Scholarship; $500 to $1,200; based on GPA for continuing full-time undergraduates.
Additional info: Institution's own payment plan is available.

FINANCIAL AID PROCEDURES

Forms required: FAFSA, state aid form.
Dates and Deadlines: Priority date 3/15; no closing date. Applicants notified on a rolling basis starting 2/2; must reply within 2 week(s) of notification.

CONTACT

M Henrie, Director of Financial Aid
1200 Commercial, Campus Box 4034, Emporia, KS 66801-5087
(620) 341-5457

Fort Hays State University

Hays, Kansas
www.fhsu.edu Federal Code: 001915

4-year public university in large town.
Enrollment: 8,670 undergrads. 849 full-time freshmen.

BASIC COSTS (2008-2009)

Tuition and fees: $3,540; out-of-state residents $11,125.
Per-credit charge: $118; out-of-state residents $370.
Room and board: $6,252.

FINANCIAL AID PICTURE (2007-2008)

Students with need: Out of 644 full-time freshmen who applied for aid, 494 were judged to have need. Of these, 489 received aid, and 106 had their full need met. Average financial aid package met 68% of need; average scholarship/grant was $4,311; average loan was $2,944. For part-time students, average financial aid package was $5,125.
Students without need: 314 full-time freshmen who did not demonstrate need for aid received scholarships/grants; average award was $3,388. No-need awards available for academics, art, athletics, leadership, minority status, music/drama.
Scholarships offered: 44 full-time freshmen received athletic scholarships; average amount $3,186.

FINANCIAL AID PROCEDURES

Forms required: FAFSA.
Dates and Deadlines: Priority date 3/15; no closing date. Applicants notified on a rolling basis starting 3/15; must reply within 2 week(s) of notification.
Transfers: No deadline. Applicants notified on a rolling basis starting 3/15; must reply within 3 week(s) of notification.

CONTACT

Craig Karlin, Director of Student Financial Aid
600 Park Street, Hays, KS 67601
(785) 628-4408

Friends University

Wichita, Kansas
www.friends.edu Federal Code: 001918

4-year private business and liberal arts college in large city, affiliated with nondenominational tradition.
Enrollment: 1,183 full-time undergrads.
Selectivity: Admits 50 to 75% of applicants.

BASIC COSTS (2008-2009)

Tuition and fees: $18,320.
Per-credit charge: $607.
Room and board: $5,450.

FINANCIAL AID PICTURE (2008-2009)

Students with need: Need-based aid available for full-time and part-time students.
Students without need: No-need awards available for academics, alumni affiliation, art, athletics, leadership, music/drama.
Additional info: Scholarships for clergy/family of clergy available.

FINANCIAL AID PROCEDURES

Forms required: FAFSA, institutional form.
Dates and Deadlines: Priority date 3/15; no closing date. Applicants notified on a rolling basis; must reply within 3 week(s) of notification.

CONTACT

Brandon Pierce, Director of Financial Aid
2100 University, Wichita, KS 67213
(316) 295-5200

Garden City Community College

Garden City, Kansas
www.gcccks.edu Federal Code: 001919

2-year public community college in large town.
Enrollment: 1,984 undergrads.
Selectivity: Open admission; but selective for some programs.

BASIC COSTS (2008-2009)

Tuition and fees: $1,860; out-of-state residents $2,580.
Per-credit charge: $41; out-of-state residents $65.
Room and board: $4,350.

FINANCIAL AID PICTURE (2007-2008)

Students with need: 73% of average financial aid package awarded as scholarships/grants, 27% awarded as loans/jobs. Need-based aid available for part-time students. Work study available nights, weekends, and for part-time students.
Students without need: No-need awards available for academics, art, athletics, job skills, leadership, minority status, music/drama, state/district residency.

FINANCIAL AID PROCEDURES

Forms required: FAFSA, institutional form.
Dates and Deadlines: Priority date 3/1; no closing date. Applicants notified on a rolling basis starting 4/15; must reply within 2 week(s) of notification.

CONTACT

Kathleen Blau, Director of Financial Aid
801 Campus Drive, Garden City, KS 67846-6333
(620) 276-9519

Hesston College

Hesston, Kansas
www.hesston.edu Federal Code: 001920

2-year private junior college in small town, affiliated with Mennonite Church.
Enrollment: 419 undergrads, 11% part-time. 176 full-time freshmen.
Selectivity: Open admission; but selective for some programs.

BASIC COSTS (2009-2010)

Tuition and fees: $19,906.
Room and board: $6,590.

FINANCIAL AID PICTURE (2007-2008)

Students with need: Out of 165 full-time freshmen who applied for aid, 149 were judged to have need. Of these, 149 received aid, and 21 had their full need met. Average financial aid package met 80% of need; average scholarship/grant was $10,237; average loan was $3,750. Need-based aid available for part-time students.
Students without need: 24 full-time freshmen who did not demonstrate need for aid received scholarships/grants; average award was $1,750. No-need awards available for academics, alumni affiliation, art, athletics, job skills, music/drama.
Scholarships offered: 7 full-time freshmen received athletic scholarships; average amount $1,250.

FINANCIAL AID PROCEDURES

Forms required: FAFSA.

Dates and Deadlines: Priority date 4/1; no closing date. Applicants notified on a rolling basis starting 2/1; must reply within 4 week(s) of notification.

CONTACT

Marcia Mendez, Financial Aid Director
Box 3000, Hesston, KS 67062-2093
(800) 995-2757

Highland Community College

Highland, Kansas
www.highlandcc.edu Federal Code: 001921

2-year public community college in rural community.
Enrollment: 1,689 undergrads.
Selectivity: Open admission; but selective for out-of-state students.

BASIC COSTS (2008-2009)

Tuition and fees: $1,980; out-of-district residents $2,370; out-of-state residents $3,900.
Per-credit charge: $39; out-of-district residents $52; out-of-state residents $103.
Room and board: $4,690.
Additional info: Out-of-state within 150 miles: $65 per-credit-hour.

FINANCIAL AID PICTURE (2007-2008)

Students with need: 58% of average financial aid package awarded as scholarships/grants, 42% awarded as loans/jobs. Need-based aid available for part-time students. Work study available nights, weekends, and for part-time students.
Students without need: No-need awards available for academics, alumni affiliation, art, athletics, job skills, leadership, music/drama.
Additional info: Auditions and portfolios important for certain scholarship candidates.

FINANCIAL AID PROCEDURES

Forms required: FAFSA, institutional form.
Dates and Deadlines: Priority date 4/1; no closing date. Applicants notified on a rolling basis starting 4/15; must reply within 14 week(s) of notification.
Transfers: No deadline. Applicants notified on a rolling basis starting 4/1; must reply within 2 week(s) of notification.

CONTACT

Kelly Twombly, Director of Student Financial Aid
606 West Main Street, Highland, KS 66035-0068
(785) 442-6023

Hutchinson Community College

Hutchinson, Kansas
www.hutchcc.edu Federal Code: 001923

2-year public community college in large town.
Enrollment: 3,475 undergrads, 39% part-time. 902 full-time freshmen.
Selectivity: Open admission; but selective for some programs.

BASIC COSTS (2008-2009)

Tuition and fees: $2,130; out-of-state residents $3,150.
Per-credit charge: $55; out-of-state residents $89.
Room and board: $4,724.

FINANCIAL AID PICTURE

Students with need: Need-based aid available for full-time and part-time students.
Students without need: No-need awards available for academics, athletics, minority status, state/district residency.

FINANCIAL AID PROCEDURES

Forms required: FAFSA, institutional form.
Dates and Deadlines: Priority date 2/1; no closing date. Applicants notified on a rolling basis starting 4/1; must reply within 2 week(s) of notification.

CONTACT

Ron Menefee, Financial Aid Director
1300 North Plum, Hutchinson, KS 67501
(620) 665-3400

Independence Community College

Independence, Kansas
www.indycc.edu Federal Code: 001924

2-year public community and junior college in large town.
Enrollment: 622 undergrads.
Selectivity: Open admission.

BASIC COSTS (2008-2009)

Tuition and fees: $1,575; out-of-district residents $1,650; out-of-state residents $2,850.
Per-credit charge: $25; out-of-district residents $28; out-of-state residents $68.
Room and board: $4,400.

FINANCIAL AID PICTURE

Students with need: Need-based aid available for full-time and part-time students.
Students without need: No-need awards available for academics, athletics.

FINANCIAL AID PROCEDURES

Forms required: FAFSA.
Dates and Deadlines: Priority date 4/1; no closing date. Applicants notified on a rolling basis.

CONTACT

Sheila Smither, Director of Financial Aid
1057 West College Avenue, Independence, KS 67301

Johnson County Community College

Overland Park, Kansas
www.jccc.edu Federal Code: 008244

2-year public community college in very large city.
Enrollment: 19,056 undergrads.
Selectivity: Open admission; but selective for some programs.

BASIC COSTS (2008-2009)

Tuition and fees: $1,950; out-of-district residents $2,400; out-of-state residents $4,470.
Per-credit charge: $65; out-of-district residents $80; out-of-state residents $149.

FINANCIAL AID PICTURE (2008-2009)

Students with need: Need-based aid available for full-time and part-time students.
Students without need: No-need awards available for academics.

FINANCIAL AID PROCEDURES

Forms required: FAFSA, state aid form.
Dates and Deadlines: Priority date 4/1; no closing date. Applicants notified on a rolling basis starting 4/15; must reply within 2 week(s) of notification.

CONTACT

Chris Christensen, Program Director for Student Financial Aid
12345 College Boulevard, Overland Park, KS 66210-1299
(913) 469-3840

Kansas City Kansas Community College
Kansas City, Kansas
www.kckcc.edu Federal Code: 001925

2-year public community and junior college in very large city.
Enrollment: 4,364 undergrads, 58% part-time. 457 full-time freshmen.
Selectivity: Open admission; but selective for some programs.

BASIC COSTS (2008-2009)
Tuition and fees: $1,770; out-of-state residents $4,710.
Per-credit charge: $49; out-of-state residents $147.
Additional info: Fees vary by program.

FINANCIAL AID PICTURE (2007-2008)
Students with need: 43% of average financial aid package awarded as scholarships/grants, 57% awarded as loans/jobs. Need-based aid available for part-time students. Work study available nights, weekends, and for part-time students.
Students without need: No-need awards available for academics, art, athletics, music/drama.

FINANCIAL AID PROCEDURES
Forms required: FAFSA.
Dates and Deadlines: Priority date 4/15; no closing date. Applicants notified on a rolling basis starting 5/1; must reply within 4 week(s) of notification.

CONTACT
Mary Dorr, Director of Financial Aid
7250 State Avenue, Kansas City, KS 66112
(913) 288-7697

Kansas State University
Manhattan, Kansas
www.k-state.edu Federal Code: 001928

4-year public university in large town.
Enrollment: 18,114 undergrads, 11% part-time. 3,633 full-time freshmen.
Selectivity: Admits over 75% of applicants.

BASIC COSTS (2008-2009)
Tuition and fees: $6,627; out-of-state residents $16,931.
Per-credit charge: $198; out-of-state residents $542.
Room and board: $6,448.

FINANCIAL AID PICTURE (2007-2008)
Students with need: Out of 2,715 full-time freshmen who applied for aid, 1,892 were judged to have need. Of these, 1,851 received aid, and 369 had their full need met. Average financial aid package met 67% of need; average scholarship/grant was $3,889; average loan was $3,297. For part-time students, average financial aid package was $4,639.
Students without need: 561 full-time freshmen who did not demonstrate need for aid received scholarships/grants; average award was $3,556. No-need awards available for academics, alumni affiliation, art, athletics, leadership, music/drama, ROTC, state/district residency.
Scholarships offered: 98 full-time freshmen received athletic scholarships; average amount $10,016.

FINANCIAL AID PROCEDURES
Forms required: FAFSA.
Dates and Deadlines: Priority date 3/1; no closing date. Applicants notified on a rolling basis starting 4/1; must reply within 2 week(s) of notification.

CONTACT
Larry Moeder, Assistant Vice President for Student Financial Assistance and Admissions
119 Anderson Hall, Manhattan, KS 66506
(785) 532-6420

Kansas Wesleyan University
Salina, Kansas
www.kwu.edu Federal Code: 001929

4-year private liberal arts college in large town, affiliated with United Methodist Church.
Enrollment: 766 undergrads.

BASIC COSTS (2008-2009)
Tuition and fees: $18,200.
Room and board: $6,400.
Additional info: $200 per-credit-hour charge for 1-5 credit hours; $1,800 per semester for 6-8 credit hours; $3,600 per semester for 9-11 credit hours. Tuition/fee waivers available for adults.

FINANCIAL AID PICTURE
Students with need: Need-based aid available for full-time and part-time students.
Students without need: No-need awards available for academics, alumni affiliation, art, athletics, music/drama, state/district residency.
Additional info: Awards available for residence hall students: minimum $7,000 for 3.0 GPA plus ACT score of 22 or SAT of 950 (exclusive of Writing); minimum $8,000 for 3.5 GPA plus ACT score of 22 or SAT score of 1030 (exclusive of Writing); minimum $9,000 for 3.75 GPA plus ACT score of 25 or SAT score of 1140 (exclusive of Writing). Application deadline March 15.

FINANCIAL AID PROCEDURES
Forms required: FAFSA.
Dates and Deadlines: Closing date 3/15. Applicants notified on a rolling basis starting 1/1; must reply by 8/1 or within 3 week(s) of notification.
Transfers: Academic scholarships based upon cumulative GPA of transferring credit hours.

CONTACT
Glenna Alexander, Director of Enrollment & Financial Services
100 East Claflin Avenue, Salina, KS 67401-6196
(785) 827-5541 ext. 1130

Labette Community College
Parsons, Kansas
www.labette.edu Federal Code: 001930

2-year public community college in large town.
Enrollment: 934 undergrads.
Selectivity: Open admission; but selective for some programs.

BASIC COSTS (2008-2009)
Tuition and fees: $2,130; out-of-state residents $2,880.
Per-credit charge: $42; out-of-state residents $67.
Additional info: Residents of neighboring states (AR, MO, OK) pay per-credit-hour tuition rate of $63. Tuition/fee waivers available for adults, minority students, unemployed or children of unemployed.

FINANCIAL AID PICTURE
Students with need: Need-based aid available for full-time and part-time students. Work study available nights.
Students without need: No-need awards available for academics, leadership.
Scholarships offered: Foundation Scholarships.

FINANCIAL AID PROCEDURES
Forms required: FAFSA.
Dates and Deadlines: No deadline. Applicants notified on a rolling basis starting 4/4; must reply within 2 week(s) of notification.

CONTACT
Kathy Johnston, Director of Financial Aid
200 South 14th Street, Parsons, KS 67357
(620) 820-1219

Manhattan Christian College
Manhattan, Kansas
www.mccks.edu Federal Code: 001931

4-year private Bible college in large town, affiliated with Christian Church.
Enrollment: 380 undergrads.

BASIC COSTS (2008-2009)
Tuition and fees: $10,932.
Per-credit charge: $449.
Room and board: $6,720.
Additional info: Additional $6 required fee per-credit-hour, up to $72; $140 per-credit-hour charge for part-time, non-degree-seeking students. Part time non-degree and/or audit at $170 per-credit-hour.

FINANCIAL AID PICTURE (2007-2008)
Students with need: 38% of average financial aid package awarded as scholarships/grants, 62% awarded as loans/jobs. Need-based aid available for part-time students.
Students without need: No-need awards available for academics, leadership.

FINANCIAL AID PROCEDURES
Forms required: FAFSA.
Dates and Deadlines: Priority date 4/1; no closing date. Applicants notified on a rolling basis starting 5/1; must reply within 2 week(s) of notification.
Transfers: No deadline. Applicants notified on a rolling basis; must reply within 2 week(s) of notification.

CONTACT
Margaret Carlisle, Director of Financial Aid
1415 Anderson Avenue, Manhattan, KS 66502
(785) 539-3571 ext. 207

McPherson College
McPherson, Kansas
www.mcpherson.edu Federal Code: 001933

4-year private liberal arts college in large town, affiliated with Church of the Brethren.
Enrollment: 535 undergrads.
Selectivity: Admits over 75% of applicants.

BASIC COSTS (2009-2010)
Tuition and fees: $18,400.
Per-credit charge: $250.
Room and board: $6,910.

FINANCIAL AID PICTURE (2008-2009)
Students with need: Need-based aid available for full-time and part-time students. Work study available nights, weekends, and for part-time students.
Students without need: No-need awards available for academics, alumni affiliation, art, athletics, music/drama, religious affiliation, state/district residency.
Scholarships offered: Presidential Scholarship; $10,000 each year of attendance for four years; competition in fall and spring; 10 awards given per year.

FINANCIAL AID PROCEDURES
Forms required: FAFSA.
Dates and Deadlines: Priority date 3/1; no closing date. Applicants notified on a rolling basis starting 3/1; must reply within 3 week(s) of notification.
Transfers: No deadline. Applicants notified on a rolling basis; must reply within 3 week(s) of notification.

CONTACT
Steve Frick, Director of Financial Aid
1600 East Euclid Street, McPherson, KS 67460-1402
(620) 241-0731

MidAmerica Nazarene University
Olathe, Kansas
www.mnu.edu Federal Code: 007032

4-year private university and liberal arts college in small city, affiliated with Church of the Nazarene.
Enrollment: 1,296 undergrads, 13% part-time. 204 full-time freshmen.
Selectivity: Admits 50 to 75% of applicants.

BASIC COSTS (2009-2010)
Tuition and fees: $19,146.
Per-credit charge: $607.
Room and board: $6,452.

FINANCIAL AID PICTURE (2008-2009)
Students with need: Out of 176 full-time freshmen who applied for aid, 143 were judged to have need. Of these, 143 received aid, and 25 had their full need met. Average financial aid package met 71% of need; average scholarship/grant was $10,410; average loan was $4,821. For part-time students, average financial aid package was $5,974.
Students without need: 57 full-time freshmen who did not demonstrate need for aid received scholarships/grants; average award was $5,249. No-need awards available for academics, athletics, leadership, music/drama, religious affiliation, ROTC.
Scholarships offered: 50 full-time freshmen received athletic scholarships; average amount $5,912.
Cumulative student debt: 84% of graduating class had student loans; average debt was $28,859.

FINANCIAL AID PROCEDURES
Forms required: FAFSA.
Dates and Deadlines: Priority date 3/1; no closing date. Applicants notified on a rolling basis starting 1/30; must reply within 2 week(s) of notification.

CONTACT
Rhonda Cole, Director of Student Financial Services
2030 East College Way, Olathe, KS 66062-1899
(913) 917-3298

Neosho County Community College
Chanute, Kansas
www.neosho.edu Federal Code: 001936

2-year public community college in small town.
Enrollment: 2,025 undergrads.
Selectivity: Open admission; but selective for some programs.

BASIC COSTS (2008-2009)
Tuition and fees: $2,010; out-of-district residents $2,310; out-of-state residents $3,030.
Per-credit charge: $44.
Room and board: $4,400.

FINANCIAL AID PICTURE (2007-2008)
Students with need: Need-based aid available for full-time and part-time students. Work study available nights, weekends, and for part-time students.
Students without need: No-need awards available for academics, art, athletics, leadership, music/drama, state/district residency.

Scholarships offered: Visual and performing arts, Academic Challenge stipends, industrial engineering and business scholarship.

FINANCIAL AID PROCEDURES

Forms required: FAFSA.

Dates and Deadlines: Priority date 4/1; no closing date. Applicants notified on a rolling basis; must reply within 6 week(s) of notification.

Transfers: All academic transcripts and financial aid transcripts must be on file before aid will be awarded.

CONTACT

Kerrie Coomes, Director of Financial Aid
800 West 14th Street, Chanute, KS 66720
(620) 431-2820 ext. 278

Newman University

Wichita, Kansas
www.newmanu.edu Federal Code: 001939

4-year private university and liberal arts college in large city, affiliated with Roman Catholic Church.

Enrollment: 1,015 undergrads, 16% part-time. 115 full-time freshmen.

Selectivity: Admits less than 50% of applicants.

BASIC COSTS (2009-2010)

Tuition and fees: $19,650.

Per-credit charge: $640.

Room and board: $6,500.

Additional info: Tuition/fee waivers available for adults.

FINANCIAL AID PICTURE (2008-2009)

Students with need: Average financial aid package met 77% of need; average scholarship/grant was $5,306; average loan was $2,943. For part-time students, average financial aid package was $5,584.

Students without need: No-need awards available for academics, alumni affiliation, art, athletics, leadership, music/drama.

Cumulative student debt: 71% of graduating class had student loans; average debt was $26,938.

FINANCIAL AID PROCEDURES

Forms required: FAFSA.

Dates and Deadlines: Priority date 3/1; no closing date. Applicants notified on a rolling basis starting 2/1.

CONTACT

Brenda Krehbiel, Director of Financial Aid
3100 McCormick, Wichita, KS 67213-2097
(316) 942-4291

North Central Kansas Technical College

Beloit, Kansas
www.ncktc.edu Federal Code: 005265

2-year public technical college in small town.

Enrollment: 355 undergrads.

Selectivity: Open admission.

BASIC COSTS (2008-2009)

Tuition and fees: $3,497.

Room and board: $4,150.

FINANCIAL AID PICTURE (2008-2009)

Students with need: Need-based aid available for full-time and part-time students. Work study available nights.

Students without need: This college awards aid only to students with need.

FINANCIAL AID PROCEDURES

Forms required: FAFSA, state aid form.

Dates and Deadlines: No deadline.

CONTACT

Gary Odle, Financial Aid Director
P.O. Box 507, Beloit, KS 67420
(800) 658-4655

Ottawa University

Ottawa, Kansas
www.ottawa.edu Federal Code: 001937

4-year private liberal arts college in large town, affiliated with American Baptist Churches in the USA.

Enrollment: 541 undergrads.

Selectivity: Admits 50 to 75% of applicants.

BASIC COSTS (2008-2009)

Tuition and fees: $18,420.

Per-credit charge: $605.

Room and board: $5,700.

FINANCIAL AID PICTURE (2007-2008)

Students with need: Need-based aid available for full-time and part-time students. Work study available nights, weekends, and for part-time students.

Students without need: No-need awards available for academics, alumni affiliation, athletics, music/drama, religious affiliation.

FINANCIAL AID PROCEDURES

Forms required: FAFSA.

Dates and Deadlines: Priority date 3/15; no closing date. Applicants notified on a rolling basis starting 2/1; must reply within 4 week(s) of notification.

Transfers: No deadline.

CONTACT

Gary Bateman, Financial Aid Director
1001 South Cedar Street, #17, Ottawa, KS 66067-3399
(785) 242-5200 ext. 5571

Pittsburg State University

Pittsburg, Kansas
www.pittstate.edu Federal Code: 001926

4-year public university in large town.

Enrollment: 5,694 undergrads, 6% part-time. 905 full-time freshmen.

Selectivity: Admits over 75% of applicants.

BASIC COSTS (2008-2009)

Tuition and fees: $4,322; out-of-state residents $12,576.

Per-credit charge: $114; out-of-state residents $460.

Room and board: $5,394.

FINANCIAL AID PICTURE (2008-2009)

Students with need: Average financial aid package met 89% of need; average scholarship/grant was $4,742; average loan was $3,470. For part-time students, average financial aid package was $5,738.

Students without need: No-need awards available for academics, alumni affiliation, art, athletics, leadership, music/drama, ROTC.

Cumulative student debt: 60% of graduating class had student loans; average debt was $15,643.

FINANCIAL AID PROCEDURES

Forms required: FAFSA, state aid form, institutional form.

Dates and Deadlines: Priority date 3/1; no closing date. Applicants notified on a rolling basis; must reply within 2 week(s) of notification.

Transfers: Transfer student scholarships available.

CONTACT
Marilyn Haverly, Director of Student Financial Assistance
1701 South Broadway, Pittsburg, KS 66762
(620) 235-4240

Pratt Community College
Pratt, Kansas
www.prattcc.edu Federal Code: 001938

2-year public community and technical college in small town.
Enrollment: 705 undergrads, 13% part-time. 270 full-time freshmen.
Selectivity: Open admission; but selective for some programs.

BASIC COSTS (2008-2009)
Tuition and fees: $2,220; out-of-state residents $2,280.
Per-credit charge: $45; out-of-state residents $47.
Room and board: $4,576.
Additional info: Out-of-district Kansas residents have additional fee of $100; out-of-state $200, and international students $300 for the year. Technology fee applicable for auto, ag power, and electrical power areas.

FINANCIAL AID PICTURE (2008-2009)
Students with need: Average financial aid package for all full-time undergraduates was $5,608; for part-time $2,328. 69% awarded as scholarships/grants, 31% awarded as loans/jobs.
Students without need: No-need awards available for academics, art, athletics, leadership, minority status, music/drama, state/district residency.

FINANCIAL AID PROCEDURES
Forms required: FAFSA, institutional form.
Dates and Deadlines: Priority date 5/1; closing date 8/1. Applicants notified on a rolling basis starting 2/1; must reply within 2 week(s) of notification.

CONTACT
Debbie Boley, Director of Financial Aid
348 Northeast State Road 61, Pratt, KS 67124-8317
(620) 672-9800 ext. 248

Seward County Community College
Liberal, Kansas
www.sccc.edu Federal Code: 008228

2-year public community college in large town.
Enrollment: 1,687 undergrads.
Selectivity: Open admission; but selective for some programs.

BASIC COSTS (2008-2009)
Tuition and fees: $1,860; out-of-state residents $2,550.
Per-credit charge: $40; out-of-state residents $63.
Room and board: $4,100.
Additional info: Residents of neighboring counties in OK, TX and CO pay per-credit-hour rate of $50.

FINANCIAL AID PICTURE (2007-2008)
Students with need: Need-based aid available for part-time students.
Students without need: No-need awards available for academics, athletics.

FINANCIAL AID PROCEDURES
Forms required: FAFSA, institutional form.
Dates and Deadlines: Priority date 4/1; no closing date. Applicants notified on a rolling basis starting 6/15; must reply within 4 week(s) of notification.

CONTACT
Donna Fisher, Financial Aid Director
1801 North Kansas Avenue, Liberal, KS 67905-1137
(620) 417-1110

Southwestern College
Winfield, Kansas
www.sckans.edu Federal Code: 001940

4-year private liberal arts college in large town, affiliated with United Methodist Church.
Enrollment: 1,545 undergrads, 64% part-time. 159 full-time freshmen.
Selectivity: Admits over 75% of applicants.

BASIC COSTS (2009-2010)
Tuition and fees: $19,630.
Per-credit charge: $814.
Room and board: $5,750.

FINANCIAL AID PICTURE (2008-2009)
Students with need: Out of 138 full-time freshmen who applied for aid, 114 were judged to have need. Of these, 114 received aid, and 52 had their full need met. Average financial aid package met 90% of need; average scholarship/grant was $14,299; average loan was $3,306. For part-time students, average financial aid package was $12,268.
Students without need: 24 full-time freshmen who did not demonstrate need for aid received scholarships/grants; average award was $7,583. No-need awards available for academics, alumni affiliation, athletics, leadership, minority status, music/drama, religious affiliation.
Scholarships offered: ***Merit:*** Presidential Scholarship based on GPA, SAT/ACT scores, essay, resume, leadership, community service. Scholarships for major based on GPA, SAT scores, essay, interview; 3 awarded. ***Athletic:*** 88 full-time freshmen received athletic scholarships; average amount $3,200.
Additional info: Academic and activity grants available.

FINANCIAL AID PROCEDURES
Forms required: FAFSA, institutional form.
Dates and Deadlines: Priority date 4/1; closing date 8/15. Applicants notified on a rolling basis starting 2/1; must reply within 2 week(s) of notification.
Transfers: Activity grants and scholarships, except for presidential scholarship and premier scholarships, available to transfer students. Phi Theta Kappa scholarship available for transfer students who are members.

CONTACT
Brenda Hicks, Director of Financial Aid
100 College Street, Winfield, KS 67156
(620) 229-6215

Sterling College
Sterling, Kansas
www.sterling.edu Federal Code: 001945

4-year private liberal arts college in rural community, affiliated with Presbyterian Church (USA).
Enrollment: 611 undergrads, 7% part-time. 138 full-time freshmen.
Selectivity: Admits 50 to 75% of applicants.

BASIC COSTS (2009-2010)
Tuition and fees: $18,100.
Room and board: $6,430.

FINANCIAL AID PICTURE (2007-2008)
Students with need: Out of 86 full-time freshmen who applied for aid, 76 were judged to have need. Of these, 76 received aid, and 15 had their full need met. Average financial aid package met 73% of need; average scholarship/grant was $6,367; average loan was $2,233. For part-time students, average financial aid package was $11,777.
Students without need: 9 full-time freshmen who did not demonstrate need for aid received scholarships/grants; average award was $4,206. No-need awards available for academics, athletics.

Scholarships offered: 9 full-time freshmen received athletic scholarships; average amount $6,189.
Cumulative student debt: 73% of graduating class had student loans; average debt was $19,187.

FINANCIAL AID PROCEDURES

Forms required: FAFSA.
Dates and Deadlines: Priority date 3/1; no closing date. Applicants notified on a rolling basis starting 2/1; must reply within 3 week(s) of notification.
Transfers: No deadline. Applicants notified on a rolling basis; must reply within 2 week(s) of notification.

CONTACT

Tricia Brothers, Financial Aid Coordinator
125 West Cooper, Sterling, KS 67579
(620) 278-4207

Tabor College

Hillsboro, Kansas
www.tabor.edu Federal Code: 001946

4-year private liberal arts college in small town, affiliated with Mennonite Brethren Church.
Enrollment: 583 undergrads, 20% part-time. 141 full-time freshmen.
Selectivity: Admits over 75% of applicants.

BASIC COSTS (2009-2010)

Tuition and fees: $19,660.
Per-credit charge: $800.
Room and board: $6,870.
Additional info: Tuition/fee waivers available for adults.

FINANCIAL AID PICTURE (2008-2009)

Students with need: Need-based aid available for full-time and part-time students. Work study available nights, weekends, and for part-time students.
Students without need: No-need awards available for academics, alumni affiliation, athletics, music/drama, religious affiliation, state/district residency.

FINANCIAL AID PROCEDURES

Forms required: FAFSA, state aid form.
Dates and Deadlines: Priority date 3/1; closing date 8/30. Applicants notified on a rolling basis starting 3/15; must reply within 4 week(s) of notification.
Transfers: Transfer students not eligible for Presidential, National Merit or Dean's scholarships.

CONTACT

Scott Franz, Director of Student Financial Assistance
400 South Jefferson, Hillsboro, KS 67063-1799
(620) 947-3121 ext. 1726

University of Kansas

Lawrence, Kansas
www.ku.edu Federal Code: 001948

4-year public university in small city.
Enrollment: 20,555 undergrads, 9% part-time. 4,034 full-time freshmen.
Selectivity: Admits over 75% of applicants.

BASIC COSTS (2008-2009)

Tuition and fees: $7,725; out-of-state residents $18,909.
Per-credit charge: $229; out-of-state residents $602.
Room and board: $6,474.
Additional info: Tuition at time of enrollment locked for 4 years.

FINANCIAL AID PICTURE (2007-2008)

Students with need: Out of 3,173 full-time freshmen who applied for aid, 1,584 were judged to have need. Of these, 1,512 received aid, and 359 had their full need met. Average financial aid package met 58% of need; average scholarship/grant was $4,550; average loan was $2,873. For part-time students, average financial aid package was $6,497.
Students without need: 882 full-time freshmen who did not demonstrate need for aid received scholarships/grants; average award was $3,282. No-need awards available for academics, alumni affiliation, art, athletics, leadership, minority status, music/drama, ROTC, state/district residency.
Scholarships offered: 83 full-time freshmen received athletic scholarships; average amount $14,119.
Cumulative student debt: 46% of graduating class had student loans; average debt was $20,902.
Additional info: Students awarded federal work study are responsible for securing their own jobs on campus. There are positions on campus with a variety of schedules beyond 8-5.

FINANCIAL AID PROCEDURES

Forms required: FAFSA.
Dates and Deadlines: Priority date 3/1; no closing date. Applicants notified on a rolling basis starting 4/1; must reply within 2 week(s) of notification.

CONTACT

Brenda Maigaard, Director of Student Financial Aid
1502 Iowa Street, Lawrence, KS 66045-7576
(785) 864-4700

University of Kansas Medical Center

Kansas City, Kansas
www.kumc.edu Federal Code: 001948

Upper-division public university and health science college in small city.
Enrollment: 490 undergrads, 21% part-time.
Selectivity: Open admission; but selective for some programs.

BASIC COSTS (2008-2009)

Tuition and fees: $6,554; out-of-state residents $16,631.
Per-credit charge: $207; out-of-state residents $542.

FINANCIAL AID PICTURE (2007-2008)

Students with need: Average financial aid package for all full-time undergraduates was $10,100; for part-time $9,789. 24% awarded as scholarships/grants, 76% awarded as loans/jobs. Work study available nights, weekends, and for part-time students.
Students without need: No-need awards available for academics, leadership, state/district residency.

FINANCIAL AID PROCEDURES

Dates and Deadlines: No deadline.
Transfers: Priority date 2/14; no deadline. Applicants notified on a rolling basis starting 4/1.

CONTACT

Sara Honeck, Director of Student Financial Aid
3901 Rainbow Boulevard, Kansas City, KS 66160-7116
(913) 588-5170

University of St. Mary

Leavenworth, Kansas
www.stmary.edu Federal Code: 001943

4-year private university in large town, affiliated with Roman Catholic Church.
Enrollment: 575 undergrads, 18% part-time. 112 full-time freshmen.
Selectivity: Admits 50 to 75% of applicants.

BASIC COSTS (2008-2009)
Tuition and fees: $18,090.
Per-credit charge: $590.
Room and board: $6,050.

FINANCIAL AID PICTURE (2008-2009)
Students with need: Out of 103 full-time freshmen who applied for aid, 86 were judged to have need. Of these, 86 received aid, and 16 had their full need met. Average financial aid package met 76% of need; average scholarship/grant was $10,927; average loan was $3,741. For part-time students, average financial aid package was $5,452.
Students without need: 17 full-time freshmen who did not demonstrate need for aid received scholarships/grants; average award was $7,985. No-need awards available for academics, art, athletics, leadership, music/drama.
Scholarships offered: ***Merit:*** Essays may be required for scholarship applicants. Auditions recommended for music and drama scholarship applicants. Portfolio reviews for art award applicants. ***Athletic:*** 10 full-time freshmen received athletic scholarships; average amount $2,930.
Cumulative student debt: 96% of graduating class had student loans; average debt was $23,509.

FINANCIAL AID PROCEDURES
Forms required: FAFSA.
Dates and Deadlines: Priority date 4/1; no closing date. Applicants notified on a rolling basis starting 2/8; must reply within 2 week(s) of notification.
Transfers: No deadline. Applicants notified on a rolling basis; must reply within 2 week(s) of notification.

CONTACT
Judy Wiedower, Director of Financial Aid
4100 South Fourth Street Trafficway, Leavenworth, KS 66048
(913) 758-6314

Washburn University
Topeka, Kansas
www.washburn.edu Federal Code: 001949

4-year public university in small city.
Enrollment: 5,396 undergrads, 29% part-time. 726 full-time freshmen.
Selectivity: Open admission; but selective for some programs.

BASIC COSTS (2008-2009)
Tuition and fees: $5,996; out-of-state residents $13,496.
Per-credit charge: $197; out-of-state residents $447.
Room and board: $5,602.

FINANCIAL AID PICTURE (2008-2009)
Students with need: Out of 632 full-time freshmen who applied for aid, 443 were judged to have need. Of these, 441 received aid, and 83 had their full need met. Average financial aid package met 43% of need; average scholarship/grant was $4,296; average loan was $3,338. For part-time students, average financial aid package was $7,101.
Students without need: 103 full-time freshmen who did not demonstrate need for aid received scholarships/grants; average award was $2,029. No-need awards available for academics, alumni affiliation, art, athletics, job skills, leadership, minority status, music/drama, religious affiliation, ROTC, state/district residency.
Scholarships offered: 31 full-time freshmen received athletic scholarships; average amount $6,470.
Cumulative student debt: 59% of graduating class had student loans; average debt was $20,562.

FINANCIAL AID PROCEDURES
Forms required: FAFSA.
Dates and Deadlines: Priority date 2/15; no closing date. Applicants notified on a rolling basis starting 3/15; must reply within 4 week(s) of notification.
Transfers: No deadline. Applicants notified on a rolling basis starting 3/15; must reply within 4 week(s) of notification.

CONTACT
Gail Palmer, Associate Director of Financial Aid
1700 SW College Avenue, Morgan 114, Topeka, KS 66621
(785) 670-1151

Wichita State University
Wichita, Kansas
www.wichita.edu Federal Code: 001950

4-year public university in large city.
Enrollment: 10,590 undergrads, 27% part-time. 1,352 full-time freshmen.
Selectivity: Admits over 75% of applicants.

BASIC COSTS (2008-2009)
Tuition and fees: $5,084; out-of-state residents $12,761.
Per-credit charge: $138; out-of-state residents $394.
Room and board: $5,860.

FINANCIAL AID PICTURE (2008-2009)
Students with need: Out of 1,157 full-time freshmen who applied for aid, 578 were judged to have need. Of these, 565 received aid. Average financial aid package met 48% of need; average scholarship/grant was $3,661; average loan was $2,933. For part-time students, average financial aid package was $7,669.
Students without need: 398 full-time freshmen who did not demonstrate need for aid received scholarships/grants; average award was $3,756. No-need awards available for academics, alumni affiliation, art, athletics, leadership, music/drama.
Scholarships offered: 27 full-time freshmen received athletic scholarships; average amount $8,945.
Cumulative student debt: 59% of graduating class had student loans; average debt was $22,116.
Additional info: Top freshman applicants admitted by October 1 invited to university scholarship competition.

FINANCIAL AID PROCEDURES
Forms required: FAFSA, state aid form.
Dates and Deadlines: Priority date 3/1; no closing date. Applicants notified on a rolling basis starting 3/1; must reply within 2 week(s) of notification.

CONTACT
Deborah Byers, Director of Financial Aid
1845 Fairmount Box 124, Wichita, KS 67260-0124
(316) 978-3430

Kentucky

Alice Lloyd College
Pippa Passes, Kentucky
www.alc.edu Federal Code: 001951

4-year private liberal arts college in rural community.
Enrollment: 615 undergrads.
Selectivity: Admits less than 50% of applicants.

BASIC COSTS (2008-2009)
Tuition and fees: $7,300.
Room and board: $5,450.
Additional info: Guaranteed tuition for students from 108-county central Appalachian service area in Kentucky, West Virginia, Virginia, Tennessee, and Ohio. Tuition/fee waivers available for minority students.

FINANCIAL AID PICTURE (2007-2008)

Students with need: Need-based aid available for full-time and part-time students. Work study available nights, weekends, and for part-time students.

Students without need: No-need awards available for athletics, minority status, state/district residency.

Scholarships offered: Students meeting admissions criteria from one of 108 counties in West Virginia, Virginia, Tennessee, Ohio and Kentucky guaranteed free tuition of up to $3,180 per semester; based on admission application; no limit on awards given. Minority scholarships; tuition, room, and board; offered to students from 108 service areas. Alice Lloyd Scholars Program; tuition, room, board, fees, and books; awarded to up to 3 freshmen a year.

Additional info: All students receive financial aid through student work program. No student denied admission because of inability to pay. All full-time students required to work minimum of 10 hours per week.

FINANCIAL AID PROCEDURES

Forms required: FAFSA.

Dates and Deadlines: Priority date 3/15; no closing date. Applicants notified on a rolling basis starting 4/1; must reply within 6 week(s) of notification.

Transfers: Closing date 3/15. Tuition guarantee only for total of 10 semesters of course work from all schools attended.

CONTACT

Barbara Begley, Director of Financial Aid
100 Purpose Road, Pippa Passes, KY 41844
(606) 368-6058

Asbury College

Wilmore, Kentucky
www.asbury.edu Federal Code: 001952

4-year private liberal arts college in small town, affiliated with interdenominational tradition.

Enrollment: 1,216 undergrads, 2% part-time. 311 full-time freshmen.

Selectivity: Admits 50 to 75% of applicants.

BASIC COSTS (2009-2010)

Tuition and fees: $23,748.

Per-credit charge: $907.

Room and board: $5,620.

Additional info: Tuition/fee waivers available for minority students.

FINANCIAL AID PICTURE

Students with need: Need-based aid available for full-time and part-time students. Work study available nights, weekends, and for part-time students.

Students without need: No-need awards available for academics, alumni affiliation, art, athletics, leadership, minority status, music/drama, religious affiliation, ROTC.

FINANCIAL AID PROCEDURES

Forms required: institutional form.

Dates and Deadlines: Priority date 3/1; no closing date. Applicants notified on a rolling basis starting 1/31; must reply within 4 week(s) of notification.

CONTACT

Ronald Anderson, Director of Financial Aid
One Macklem Drive, Wilmore, KY 40390-1198
(859) 858-3511 ext. 2195

Beckfield College

Florence, Kentucky
www.beckfield.edu Federal Code: 016726

4-year for-profit business and health science and nursing college in large town.

Enrollment: 600 undergrads.

Selectivity: Open admission; but selective for some programs.

BASIC COSTS (2008-2009)

Tuition and fees: $12,927.

Per-credit charge: $266.

Additional info: Fees vary by program.

FINANCIAL AID PICTURE (2007-2008)

Students with need: Need-based aid available for full-time and part-time students.

Students without need: This college awards aid only to students with need.

Scholarships offered: High School scholarship; tuition for one course per quarter for maximum of 8 quarters; must achieve and maintain 3.0 GPA, be enrolled full-time, and enter college in July or October following graduation from high school. Merit scholarship; $100 per quarter; must maintain 4.0 GPA, perfect attendance, and carry at least 8 quarter credit hours.

Additional info: Deadline for filing of financial aid forms is end of first week of classes.

FINANCIAL AID PROCEDURES

Forms required: FAFSA.

Dates and Deadlines: Applicants notified on a rolling basis.

CONTACT

Pat Nettleton, Corporate Director of Financial Aid
16 Spiral Drive, Florence, KY 41042
(859) 371-9393

Bellarmine University

Louisville, Kentucky
www.bellarmine.edu Federal Code: 001954

4-year private university and liberal arts college in very large city, affiliated with Roman Catholic Church.

Enrollment: 2,068 undergrads, 7% part-time. 567 full-time freshmen.

Selectivity: Admits 50 to 75% of applicants.

BASIC COSTS (2009-2010)

Tuition and fees: $28,900.

Per-credit charge: $660.

Room and board: $8,400.

Additional info: Room and board based on 10 meal per week plan.

FINANCIAL AID PICTURE (2008-2009)

Students with need: Out of 500 full-time freshmen who applied for aid, 428 were judged to have need. Of these, 428 received aid, and 127 had their full need met. Average financial aid package met 74% of need; average scholarship/grant was $19,981; average loan was $3,586. For part-time students, average financial aid package was $8,815.

Students without need: 138 full-time freshmen who did not demonstrate need for aid received scholarships/grants; average award was $18,504. No-need awards available for academics, alumni affiliation, art, athletics, leadership, minority status, music/drama, religious affiliation, ROTC, state/district residency.

Scholarships offered: ***Merit:*** Merit awards range from $5,500 to full tuition. ***Athletic:*** 48 full-time freshmen received athletic scholarships; average amount $6,789.

Cumulative student debt: 66% of graduating class had student loans; average debt was $19,055.

FINANCIAL AID PROCEDURES

Forms required: FAFSA.

Dates and Deadlines: Priority date 3/1; no closing date. Applicants notified on a rolling basis starting 3/15; must reply by 5/1 or within 3 week(s) of notification.

Transfers: Applicants notified on a rolling basis starting 4/15; must reply within 3 week(s) of notification.

CONTACT

Heather Boutell, Director of Financial Aid
2001 Newburg Road, Louisville, KY 40205
(502) 452-8124

Berea College

Berea, Kentucky
www.berea.edu Federal Code: 001955

4-year private liberal arts college in small town.
Enrollment: 1,491 undergrads. 413 full-time freshmen.
Selectivity: Admits less than 50% of applicants.

BASIC COSTS (2009-2010)

Additional info: Only those with financial need admitted. All students awarded a 4-year tuition scholarship. The amount of the scholarship will vary depending on financial need and the presence of any additional outside scholarships. These resources cover the entire cost of tuition, which totals $25,500 for the 2009-2010 school year. The actual cost, for tuition, to students and their families is $0. Financial aid and scholarships available for meeting the additional costs of room/board ($5,768) and fees ($876), depending on financial need. About 1/3 of students pay $0 their first year of enrollment for these costs.

FINANCIAL AID PICTURE (2008-2009)

Students with need: Out of 413 full-time freshmen who applied for aid, 413 were judged to have need. Of these, 413 received aid. Average financial aid package met 94% of need; average scholarship/grant was $31,200; average loan was $927. Need-based aid available for part-time students.
Students without need: This college awards aid only to students with need.
Cumulative student debt: 78% of graduating class had student loans; average debt was $8,505.

FINANCIAL AID PROCEDURES

Forms required: FAFSA.
Dates and Deadlines: Priority date 3/15; no closing date. Applicants notified on a rolling basis starting 4/15.
Transfers: Financial aid transcript from previous school(s) must be received before awarding aid.

CONTACT

Theresa Lowder, Associate Director of Student Financial Aid Services
CPO 2220, Berea, KY 40404
(859) 985-3310

Big Sandy Community and Technical College

Prestonsburg, Kentucky
www.bigsandy.kctcs.edu Federal Code: 001996

2-year public community and technical college in small town.
Enrollment: 1,880 full-time undergrads.
Selectivity: Open admission; but selective for some programs.

BASIC COSTS (2008-2009)

Tuition and fees: $3,630; out-of-state residents $11,700.
Per-credit charge: $121; out-of-state residents $390.
Additional info: Tuition reduction program available for qualified residents of contiguous states.

FINANCIAL AID PICTURE (2008-2009)

Students with need: Need-based aid available for full-time and part-time students.
Students without need: No-need awards available for academics.

FINANCIAL AID PROCEDURES

Forms required: FAFSA.
Dates and Deadlines: Priority date 4/1; no closing date. Applicants notified on a rolling basis; must reply within 2 week(s) of notification.
Transfers: Kentucky State Grant must be transferred by August 1 for fall semester, December 1 for spring semester.

CONTACT

Denise Trusty, Director of Financial Aid
One Bert T. Combs Drive, Prestonsburg, KY 41653
(606) 886-3863 ext. 67255

Brescia University

Owensboro, Kentucky
www.brescia.edu Federal Code: 001958

4-year private university and liberal arts college in small city, affiliated with Roman Catholic Church.
Enrollment: 462 undergrads, 10% part-time. 113 full-time freshmen.
Selectivity: Admits 50 to 75% of applicants.

BASIC COSTS (2009-2010)

Tuition and fees: $16,040.
Per-credit charge: $495.
Room and board: $7,600.

FINANCIAL AID PICTURE (2008-2009)

Students with need: Need-based aid available for full-time and part-time students. Work study available nights, weekends, and for part-time students.
Students without need: No-need awards available for academics, alumni affiliation, art, athletics, minority status, music/drama, religious affiliation, state/district residency.

FINANCIAL AID PROCEDURES

Forms required: FAFSA.
Dates and Deadlines: Priority date 8/1; closing date 8/23. Applicants notified on a rolling basis starting 3/1; must reply within 3 week(s) of notification.

CONTACT

Marcie Tilleet, Director of Financial Aid
717 Frederica Street, Owensboro, KY 42301-3023
(270) 685-3131 ext. 4216

Campbellsville University

Campbellsville, Kentucky
www.campbellsville.edu Federal Code: 001959

4-year private university in large town, affiliated with Baptist faith.
Enrollment: 1,714 undergrads, 9% part-time. 443 full-time freshmen.
Selectivity: Admits 50 to 75% of applicants.

BASIC COSTS (2008-2009)

Tuition and fees: $18,100.
Per-credit charge: $738.
Room and board: $6,410.
Additional info: Tuition/fee waivers available for adults, minority students, unemployed or children of unemployed.

FINANCIAL AID PICTURE (2007-2008)

Students with need: Need-based aid available for full-time and part-time students. Work study available nights, weekends, and for part-time students.
Additional info: Matching scholarships available for students whose church contributes $200 annually. Performance grants available to members of marching band.

FINANCIAL AID PROCEDURES

Forms required: FAFSA.

Dates and Deadlines: Priority date 4/1; no closing date. Applicants notified on a rolling basis starting 5/15.

CONTACT

Chris Tolson, Director of Financial Aid
1 University Drive, Campbellsville, KY 42718-2799
(270) 789-5013

Centre College

Danville, Kentucky
www.centre.edu Federal Code: 001961

4-year private liberal arts college in large town, affiliated with Presbyterian Church (USA).

Enrollment: 1,193 undergrads. 336 full-time freshmen.
Selectivity: Admits 50 to 75% of applicants.

BASIC COSTS (2008-2009)

Per-credit charge: $1,070.
Comprehensive fee: $37,000.
Additional info: Reduced comprehensive fee may be available if student is approved to live off-campus by dean of students.

FINANCIAL AID PICTURE (2008-2009)

Students with need: Out of 266 full-time freshmen who applied for aid, 203 were judged to have need. Of these, 203 received aid, and 73 had their full need met. Average financial aid package met 88% of need; average scholarship/grant was $21,160; average loan was $3,488.
Students without need: 122 full-time freshmen who did not demonstrate need for aid received scholarships/grants; average award was $13,302. No-need awards available for academics, alumni affiliation, music/drama, ROTC.
Scholarships offered: Institutional Merit Award: $9,500 to full tuition; applications must be on file by February 1; renewable. Music and Drama Scholarships: up to $7,500. Guaranteed minimum award available to admitted Centre Fellows and Kentucky Governor's Scholars.
Cumulative student debt: 56% of graduating class had student loans; average debt was $17,600.

FINANCIAL AID PROCEDURES

Forms required: FAFSA, institutional form.
Dates and Deadlines: Closing date 3/1. Applicants notified by 3/25; must reply by 5/1 or within 2 week(s) of notification.
Transfers: No deadline. Applicants notified on a rolling basis starting 3/1; must reply within 2 week(s) of notification. Financial aid transcript required.

CONTACT

Elaine Larson, Director of Student Financial Planning
600 West Walnut Street, Danville, KY 40422-1394
(859) 238-5365

Clear Creek Baptist Bible College

Pineville, Kentucky
www.ccbbc.edu Federal Code: 017044

4-year private Bible college in small town, affiliated with Southern Baptist Convention.

Enrollment: 145 undergrads, 20% part-time. 21 full-time freshmen.
Selectivity: Open admission.

BASIC COSTS (2008-2009)

Tuition and fees: $5,322.
Per-credit charge: $226.
Room and board: $3,750.

FINANCIAL AID PICTURE (2007-2008)

Students with need: Out of 21 full-time freshmen who applied for aid, 17 were judged to have need. Of these, 17 received aid. Average financial aid package met 49% of need; average scholarship/grant was $3,411. For part-time students, average financial aid package was $1,902.
Students without need: 4 full-time freshmen who did not demonstrate need for aid received scholarships/grants; average award was $450. No-need awards available for academics.

FINANCIAL AID PROCEDURES

Forms required: FAFSA, institutional form.
Dates and Deadlines: Priority date 6/30; no closing date. Applicants notified on a rolling basis; must reply by 8/1.
Transfers: Priority date 5/5; no deadline. Applicants notified on a rolling basis starting 5/5; must reply by 8/1.

CONTACT

Sam Risner, Director of Financial Aid
300 Clear Creek Road, Pineville, KY 40977-9754
(606) 337-3196 ext. 142

Daymar College: Owensboro

Owensboro, Kentucky
www.daymarcollege.edu Federal Code: 009313

2-year for-profit business and junior college in small city.

Enrollment: 300 undergrads.
Selectivity: Open admission.

BASIC COSTS (2008-2009)

Tuition and fees: $12,000.

FINANCIAL AID PICTURE

Students with need: Need-based aid available for full-time and part-time students.
Students without need: This college awards aid only to students with need.

FINANCIAL AID PROCEDURES

Forms required: FAFSA.
Dates and Deadlines: No deadline. Applicants notified on a rolling basis.

CONTACT

Denise Jernigan, Director of Financial Services
3361 Buckland Square, Owensboro, KY 42301
(270) 926-4040

Daymar College: Paducah

Paducah, Kentucky Federal Code: 013661
www.daymarcollege.edu CSS Code: 0669

2-year for-profit technical college in small city.

Enrollment: 350 undergrads.
Selectivity: Open admission.

BASIC COSTS (2008-2009)

Tuition and fees: $12,000.

FINANCIAL AID PICTURE

Students with need: Need-based aid available for full-time students.

FINANCIAL AID PROCEDURES

Forms required: FAFSA, CSS PROFILE.
Dates and Deadlines: No deadline. Applicants notified on a rolling basis; must reply within 3 week(s) of notification.

CONTACT

JoAnn Price, Financial Aid Officer
509 South 30th Street, Paducah, KY 42001

Eastern Kentucky University

Richmond, Kentucky
www.eku.edu Federal Code: 001963

4-year public university in large town.
Enrollment: 12,710 undergrads. 2,464 full-time freshmen.
Selectivity: Admits 50 to 75% of applicants.

BASIC COSTS (2008-2009)
Tuition and fees: $6,080; out-of-state residents $16,612.
Per-credit charge: $253; out-of-state residents $692.
Room and board: $6,360.
Additional info: Targeted out-of-state tuition: $9,596.

FINANCIAL AID PICTURE (2008-2009)
Students with need: Out of 2,119 full-time freshmen who applied for aid, 1,580 were judged to have need. Of these, 1,558 received aid, and 199 had their full need met. Average financial aid package met 87% of need; average scholarship/grant was $5,704; average loan was $2,506. For part-time students, average financial aid package was $6,486.
Students without need: 340 full-time freshmen who did not demonstrate need for aid received scholarships/grants; average award was $5,426. No-need awards available for academics, alumni affiliation, art, athletics, job skills, leadership, minority status, music/drama, ROTC.
Scholarships offered: 38 full-time freshmen received athletic scholarships; average amount $11,470.
Cumulative student debt: 69% of graduating class had student loans; average debt was $14,976.

FINANCIAL AID PROCEDURES
Forms required: FAFSA.
Dates and Deadlines: Priority date 3/15; no closing date. Applicants notified on a rolling basis starting 4/1.

CONTACT

Shelley Park, Director of Financial Aid
SSB CPO 54, 521 Lancaster Avenue, Richmond, KY 40475-3102

Elizabethtown Community and Technical College

Elizabethtown, Kentucky
www.elizabethtown.kctcs.edu Federal Code: 001991

2-year public community and technical college in large town.
Enrollment: 2,481 full-time undergrads.
Selectivity: Open admission; but selective for some programs.

BASIC COSTS (2008-2009)
Tuition and fees: $3,630; out-of-state residents $11,700.
Per-credit charge: $121; out-of-state residents $390.
Additional info: Tuition reduction program available for qualified residents of contiguous states.

FINANCIAL AID PICTURE
Students with need: Need-based aid available for full-time and part-time students. Work study available nights, weekends, and for part-time students.
Students without need: This college awards aid only to students with need.

FINANCIAL AID PROCEDURES
Forms required: FAFSA.
Dates and Deadlines: Priority date 4/1; no closing date. Applicants notified on a rolling basis starting 6/1; must reply within 2 week(s) of notification.
Transfers: Must reply within 2 week(s) of notification.

CONTACT

Michael Barlow, Director of Financial Aid
600 College Street Road, Elizabethtown, KY 42701
(270) 769-2371 ext. 68614

Georgetown College

Georgetown, Kentucky
www.georgetowncollege.edu Federal Code: 001964

4-year private liberal arts college in large town, affiliated with Southern Baptist Convention.
Enrollment: 1,321 undergrads, 1% part-time. 378 full-time freshmen.
Selectivity: Admits over 75% of applicants.

BASIC COSTS (2009-2010)
Tuition and fees: $26,080.
Per-credit charge: $1,080.
Room and board: $7,030.
Additional info: Per-credit-hour charge for one course is $800; for more than one course or hours over 18 the per-credit-hour charge is $1,080.

FINANCIAL AID PICTURE (2008-2009)
Students with need: Out of 324 full-time freshmen who applied for aid, 283 were judged to have need. Of these, 283 received aid, and 144 had their full need met. Average financial aid package met 92% of need; average scholarship/grant was $21,085; average loan was $3,686.
Students without need: 77 full-time freshmen who did not demonstrate need for aid received scholarships/grants; average award was $12,027. No-need awards available for academics, alumni affiliation, art, athletics, leadership, minority status, music/drama, religious affiliation, ROTC, state/district residency.
Scholarships offered: 16 full-time freshmen received athletic scholarships; average amount $9,091.
Cumulative student debt: 66% of graduating class had student loans; average debt was $22,241.

FINANCIAL AID PROCEDURES
Forms required: FAFSA, institutional form.
Dates and Deadlines: Priority date 2/15; closing date 8/1. Applicants notified on a rolling basis starting 3/1; must reply by 5/1.

CONTACT

Rhyan Conyers, Director of Student Financial Planning
400 East College Street, Georgetown, KY 40324
(502) 863-8027

Hazard Community and Technical College

Hazard, Kentucky
www.hazard.kctcs.edu Federal Code: 006962

2-year public community and technical college in small town.
Enrollment: 2,065 undergrads.
Selectivity: Open admission; but selective for some programs.

BASIC COSTS (2008-2009)
Tuition and fees: $3,630; out-of-state residents $11,700.
Per-credit charge: $121; out-of-state residents $390.
Additional info: Tuition reduction program available for qualified residents of contiguous states.

FINANCIAL AID PICTURE (2008-2009)

Students with need: Need-based aid available for full-time and part-time students.

Students without need: This college awards aid only to students with need.

FINANCIAL AID PROCEDURES

Forms required: FAFSA.

Dates and Deadlines: Priority date 4/1; no closing date. Applicants notified on a rolling basis starting 6/15; must reply within 2 week(s) of notification.

CONTACT

Chuck Anderson, Financial Aid Director
One Community College Drive, Hazard, KY 41701
(606) 487-3061

Hopkinsville Community College

Hopkinsville, Kentucky
www.hopkinsville.kctcs.edu Federal Code: 001994

2-year public community college in small city.

Enrollment: 2,430 undergrads, 60% part-time. 254 full-time freshmen.

Selectivity: Open admission.

BASIC COSTS (2008-2009)

Tuition and fees: $3,630; out-of-state residents $11,700.

Per-credit charge: $121; out-of-state residents $390.

Additional info: Tuition reduction program available for qualified residents of contiguous states.

FINANCIAL AID PICTURE

Students with need: Need-based aid available for full-time and part-time students. Work study available nights.

Students without need: No-need awards available for academics, leadership, minority status, state/district residency.

Additional info: ACT required for academic scholarships.

FINANCIAL AID PROCEDURES

Forms required: FAFSA.

Dates and Deadlines: No deadline. Applicants notified on a rolling basis starting 7/1.

Transfers: No deadline. Applicants notified on a rolling basis.

CONTACT

Katraya Williams, Director, Financial Aid
PO Box 2100, Hopkinsville, KY 42241-2100
(270) 707-3831

Jefferson Community and Technical College

Louisville, Kentucky
www.jefferson.kctcs.edu Federal Code: 006961

2-year public community and technical college in large city.

Enrollment: 11,230 undergrads.

Selectivity: Open admission; but selective for some programs.

BASIC COSTS (2008-2009)

Tuition and fees: $3,630; out-of-state residents $11,700.

Per-credit charge: $121; out-of-state residents $390.

Additional info: Tuition reduction program available for qualified residents of contiguous states.

FINANCIAL AID PICTURE

Students with need: Need-based aid available for full-time and part-time students.

Students without need: No-need awards available for academics, art, minority status.

FINANCIAL AID PROCEDURES

Forms required: FAFSA, institutional form.

Dates and Deadlines: Priority date 3/15; no closing date. Applicants notified on a rolling basis starting 6/15; must reply within 3 week(s) of notification.

CONTACT

Lisa Schrenger, Financial Aid Officer
109 East Broadway, Louisville, KY 40202
(502) 213-2137

Kentucky Christian University

Grayson, Kentucky
www.kcu.edu Federal Code: 001965

4-year private Bible and liberal arts college in small town, affiliated with Independent Christian Church/Church of Christ.

Enrollment: 599 undergrads, 5% part-time. 191 full-time freshmen.

Selectivity: Admits 50 to 75% of applicants.

BASIC COSTS (2009-2010)

Tuition and fees: $13,220.

Per-credit charge: $434.

Room and board: $5,800.

FINANCIAL AID PICTURE (2008-2009)

Students with need: Need-based aid available for full-time and part-time students. Work study available nights, weekends, and for part-time students.

Students without need: No need awards available for academics, alumni affiliation, leadership, minority status, music/drama, religious affiliation.

FINANCIAL AID PROCEDURES

Forms required: FAFSA.

Dates and Deadlines: Priority date 3/1; no closing date. Applicants notified on a rolling basis starting 3/15; must reply within 2 week(s) of notification.

CONTACT

Jennie Bender, Director of Financial Aid
100 Academic Parkway, Grayson, KY 41143-2205
(606) 474-3226

Kentucky Mountain Bible College

Vancleve, Kentucky
www.kmbc.edu Federal Code: 030021

4-year private Bible college in rural community, affiliated with Kentucky Mountain Holiness Association.

Enrollment: 59 undergrads, 15% part-time. 11 full-time freshmen.

Selectivity: Open admission; but selective for some programs and for out-of-state students.

BASIC COSTS (2008-2009)

Tuition and fees: $5,940.

Per-credit charge: $180.

Room and board: $3,700.

FINANCIAL AID PICTURE (2007-2008)

Students with need: Out of 8 full-time freshmen who applied for aid, 8 were judged to have need. Of these, 8 received aid. Need-based aid available for part-time students.

Students without need: No-need awards available for academics, job skills, leadership, music/drama.

FINANCIAL AID PROCEDURES

Forms required: FAFSA, institutional form.

Dates and Deadlines: Priority date 4/1; closing date 6/30. Applicants notified on a rolling basis starting 3/15; must reply by 7/1.
Transfers: No deadline. Applicants notified on a rolling basis starting 8/30; must reply within 6 week(s) of notification.

CONTACT

Carla Frazier, Director of Financial Aid
Box 10, Vancleve, KY 41385-0010
(606) 693-5000 ext. 175

Kentucky State University

Frankfort, Kentucky
www.kysu.edu Federal Code: 001968

4-year public university and liberal arts college in large town.
Enrollment: 2,209 undergrads, 15% part-time. 664 full-time freshmen.
Selectivity: Admits less than 50% of applicants.

BASIC COSTS (2008-2009)

Tuition and fees: $5,692; out-of-state residents $13,490.
Per-credit charge: $190; out-of-state residents $450.
Room and board: $6,392.

FINANCIAL AID PICTURE (2008-2009)

Students with need: For part-time students, average financial aid package was $2,182.
Students without need: No-need awards available for academics, alumni affiliation, art, athletics, minority status, music/drama.
Scholarships offered: 35 full-time freshmen received athletic scholarships; average amount $3,467.
Cumulative student debt: 90% of graduating class had student loans; average debt was $27,356.

FINANCIAL AID PROCEDURES

Forms required: FAFSA.
Dates and Deadlines: Closing date 4/15.
Transfers: No deadline. Applicants notified on a rolling basis; must reply within 4 week(s) of notification.

CONTACT

Carmella Conner, Director of Financial Aid
400 East Main Street, ASB 312, Frankfort, KY 40601
(502) 597-5960

Kentucky Wesleyan College

Owensboro, Kentucky
www.kwc.edu Federal Code: 001969

4-year private liberal arts college in small city, affiliated with United Methodist Church.
Enrollment: 893 undergrads, 3% part-time. 281 full-time freshmen.
Selectivity: Admits 50 to 75% of applicants.

BASIC COSTS (2009-2010)

Tuition and fees: $16,870.
Per-credit charge: $490.
Room and board: $6,440.

FINANCIAL AID PICTURE (2007-2008)

Students with need: Out of 273 full-time freshmen who applied for aid, 247 were judged to have need. Of these, 242 received aid, and 38 had their full need met. Average financial aid package met 70% of need; average scholarship/grant was $11,157; average loan was $3,052. For part-time students, average financial aid package was $8,684.
Students without need: 31 full-time freshmen who did not demonstrate need for aid received scholarships/grants; average award was $6,900. No-need awards available for academics, alumni affiliation, art, athletics, leadership, music/drama, religious affiliation, state/district residency.
Scholarships offered: Scholarships range from $1,000 to full tuition. Students compete in on-campus scholarship competitions.
Cumulative student debt: 94% of graduating class had student loans; average debt was $18,785.

FINANCIAL AID PROCEDURES

Forms required: FAFSA.
Dates and Deadlines: Closing date 3/15. Applicants notified on a rolling basis starting 2/15; must reply within 2 week(s) of notification.

CONTACT

Samantha Hayes, Director of Financial Aid
3000 Frederica Street, Owensboro, KY 42301
(270) 852-3130

Lindsey Wilson College

Columbia, Kentucky
www.lindsey.edu Federal Code: 001972

4-year private liberal arts college in small town, affiliated with United Methodist Church.
Enrollment: 1,615 undergrads.
Selectivity: Open admission; but selective for some programs.

BASIC COSTS (2008-2009)

Tuition and fees: $16,670.
Per-credit charge: $685.
Room and board: $6,925.

FINANCIAL AID PICTURE (2007-2008)

Students with need: Need-based aid available for full-time and part-time students.
Students without need: This college awards aid only to students with need.

FINANCIAL AID PROCEDURES

Forms required: FAFSA, institutional form.
Dates and Deadlines: Priority date 4/15; no closing date. Applicants notified on a rolling basis starting 5/1; must reply within 2 week(s) of notification.
Transfers: Applicants notified on a rolling basis.

CONTACT

Roger Drake, Vice President for Administration and Finance
210 Lindsey Wilson Street, Columbia, KY 42728
(270) 384-8022

Louisville Technical Institute

Louisville, Kentucky
www.louisvilletech.edu Federal Code: 012088

2-year for-profit visual arts and technical and career college in very large city.
Enrollment: 575 undergrads, 46% part-time. 123 full-time freshmen.
Selectivity: Admits over 75% of applicants.

BASIC COSTS (2008-2009)

Additional info: For 2008-09, the cost of associate degree programs range from $29,820 to $34,790. The Computer Graphic Design and Dynamic Web tech fee is $610 per quarter; the tech fee for Computer Network Administration and information Systems Security is $525 per quarter. Tuition at time of enrollment locked for 2 years; tuition/fee waivers available for adults.

FINANCIAL AID PICTURE (2007-2008)

Students with need: 25% of average financial aid package awarded as scholarships/grants, 75% awarded as loans/jobs. Need-based aid available for part-time students. Work study available nights.

Students without need: No-need awards available for academics, art, job skills.
Scholarships offered: Academic Scholarships; up to $3,000; based on class rank, GPA, essay. Scholarship Day Competition; up to $1,500 based upon testing scores. Scholarship Fair Competition; up to $3,000; based upon open competition in electronics, drafting, interior design, computer networking and art skills. Kentucky Skills USA Scholarships; up to $1,500; based upon state championship competitions in such fields as drafting, electronics, etc.

FINANCIAL AID PROCEDURES
Forms required: FAFSA.
Dates and Deadlines: No deadline. Applicants notified on a rolling basis; must reply within 2 week(s) of notification.
Transfers: No deadline. Applicants notified on a rolling basis.

CONTACT
Kelley Hornback, Financial Planning Director
3901 Atkinson Square Drive, Louisville, KY 40218-4524
(502) 456-6509

Madisonville Community College
Madisonville, Kentucky
www.madisonville.kctcs.edu Federal Code: 009010

2-year public community college in large town.
Enrollment: 4,000 undergrads.
Selectivity: Open admission.

BASIC COSTS (2008-2009)
Tuition and fees: $3,630; out of state residents $11,700.
Per-credit charge: $121; out-of-state residents $390.
Additional info: Tuition reduction program available for qualified residents of contiguous states. Tuition/fee waivers available for minority students, unemployed or children of unemployed.

FINANCIAL AID PICTURE (2007-2008)
Students with need: Need-based aid available for full-time and part-time students. Work study available nights, weekends, and for part-time students.
Students without need: No-need awards available for minority status.

FINANCIAL AID PROCEDURES
Forms required: FAFSA, institutional form.
Dates and Deadlines: Priority date 3/15; no closing date. Applicants notified on a rolling basis; must reply within 3 week(s) of notification.

CONTACT
Caroline Clayton, Director of Financial Aid
2000 College Drive, Madisonville, KY 42431
(270) 821-6514

Maysville Community and Technical College
Maysville, Kentucky
www.maysville.kctcs.edu Federal Code: 006960

2-year public community and technical college in small town.
Enrollment: 2,086 undergrads.
Selectivity: Open admission; but selective for some programs.

BASIC COSTS (2008-2009)
Tuition and fees: $3,630; out-of-state residents $11,700.
Per-credit charge: $121; out-of-state residents $390.
Additional info: Tuition reduction program available for qualified residents of contiguous states.

FINANCIAL AID PICTURE (2007-2008)
Students with need: 57% of average financial aid package awarded as scholarships/grants, 43% awarded as loans/jobs. Need-based aid available for part-time students. Work study available nights.
Students without need: No-need awards available for academics.

FINANCIAL AID PROCEDURES
Forms required: FAFSA, institutional form.
Dates and Deadlines: Priority date 4/1; no closing date. Applicants notified on a rolling basis starting 3/1; must reply within 3 week(s) of notification.

CONTACT
Leslie McCord, Financial Aid Director
1755 US HIghway 68, Maysville, KY 41056
(606) 759-7141 ext. 66207

Mid-Continent University
Mayfield, Kentucky
www.midcontinent.edu Federal Code: 025762

4-year private Bible and liberal arts college in large town, affiliated with Southern Baptist Convention.
Enrollment: 1,634 undergrads, 14% part-time. 141 full-time freshmen.
Selectivity: Admits 50 to 75% of applicants.

BASIC COSTS (2008-2009)
Tuition and fees: $13,100.
Per-credit charge: $395.
Room and board: $6,300.

FINANCIAL AID PICTURE (2007-2008)
Students with need: Out of 122 full-time freshmen who applied for aid, 112 were judged to have need. Of these, 111 received aid, and 8 had their full need met. Average financial aid package met 43% of need; average scholarship/grant was $6,160; average loan was $2,609. For part-time students, average financial aid package was $5,564.
Students without need: 18 full-time freshmen who did not demonstrate need for aid received scholarships/grants; average award was $9,085. No-need awards available for academics.
Cumulative student debt: 65% of graduating class had student loans; average debt was $8,805.

FINANCIAL AID PROCEDURES
Forms required: FAFSA, institutional form.
Dates and Deadlines: Priority date 3/15; closing date 5/30. Applicants notified on a rolling basis starting 4/1; must reply within 2 week(s) of notification.
Transfers: No deadline. Must reply within 2 week(s) of notification.

CONTACT
Kent Youngblood, Director of Financial Aid
99 Powell Road East, Mayfield, KY 42066-0357
(270) 247 8521 ext. 260

Midway College
Midway, Kentucky
www.midway.edu Federal Code: 001975

4-year private liberal arts college for women in small town, affiliated with Christian Church (Disciples of Christ).
Enrollment: 1,284 undergrads, 29% part-time. 119 full-time freshmen.
Selectivity: Open admission; but selective for some programs.

BASIC COSTS (2009-2010)
Tuition and fees: $18,000.
Per-credit charge: $600.
Room and board: $6,800.

FINANCIAL AID PICTURE

Students with need: Need-based aid available for full-time and part-time students.

Students without need: No-need awards available for academics, alumni affiliation, art, athletics, leadership, minority status, religious affiliation.

Additional info: Audition required of applicants for music scholarships. Portfolio required for art scholarships.

FINANCIAL AID PROCEDURES

Forms required: FAFSA, institutional form.

Dates and Deadlines: Priority date 4/1; closing date 8/1. Applicants notified on a rolling basis; must reply within 4 week(s) of notification.

CONTACT

Katie Conrad, Director of Financial Aid
512 East Stephens Street, Midway, KY 40347-1120
(859) 846-5410

Morehead State University

Morehead, Kentucky
www.moreheadstate.edu Federal Code: 001976

4-year public university in small town.

Enrollment: 6,773 undergrads, 17% part-time. 1,373 full-time freshmen.

Selectivity: Admits 50 to 75% of applicants.

BASIC COSTS (2008-2009)

Tuition and fees: $5,670; out-of-state residents $14,742.

Per-credit charge: $225; out-of-state residents $585.

Room and board: $5,852.

Additional info: Tuition is based on enrollment of 15 credit hours.

FINANCIAL AID PICTURE (2007-2008)

Students with need: Out of 1,226 full-time freshmen who applied for aid, 957 were judged to have need. Of these, 947 received aid, and 295 had their full need met. Average financial aid package met 71% of need; average scholarship/grant was $4,416; average loan was $2,896. For part-time students, average financial aid package was $5,302.

Students without need: 167 full-time freshmen who did not demonstrate need for aid received scholarships/grants; average award was $5,239. No-need awards available for academics, alumni affiliation, art, athletics, leadership, minority status, music/drama, ROTC, state/district residency.

Scholarships offered: 65 full-time freshmen received athletic scholarships; average amount $3,771.

Cumulative student debt: 69% of graduating class had student loans; average debt was $18,204.

FINANCIAL AID PROCEDURES

Forms required: FAFSA, institutional form.

Dates and Deadlines: Priority date 3/15; no closing date. Applicants notified on a rolling basis.

Transfers: Transfer scholarships available.

CONTACT

Donna King, Director of Financial Aid
100 Admissions Center, Morehead, KY 40351
(606) 783-2011

Murray State University

Murray, Kentucky
www.murraystate.edu Federal Code: 001977

4-year public university in large town.

Enrollment: 7,630 undergrads, 10% part-time. 1,452 full-time freshmen.

Selectivity: Admits over 75% of applicants.

BASIC COSTS (2008-2009)

Tuition and fees: $5,748; out-of-district residents $8,242; out-of-state residents $15,612.

Per-credit charge: $240; out-of-state residents $650.

Room and board: $6,004.

Additional info: Tuition/fee waivers available for minority students.

FINANCIAL AID PICTURE (2008-2009)

Students with need: Out of 1,161 full-time freshmen who applied for aid, 697 were judged to have need. Of these, 655 received aid, and 616 had their full need met. Average financial aid package met 92% of need; average scholarship/grant was $2,610; average loan was $1,857. For part-time students, average financial aid package was $4,014.

Students without need: 523 full-time freshmen who did not demonstrate need for aid received scholarships/grants; average award was $2,530. No-need awards available for academics, alumni affiliation, art, athletics, job skills, leadership, minority status, music/drama, ROTC, state/district residency.

Scholarships offered: 62 full-time freshmen received athletic scholarships; average amount $7,380.

Additional info: Tuition discount for children and grandchildren of out-of-state alumni. Regional tuition for students from certain counties in Illinois, Tennessee, Missouri, and Indiana.

FINANCIAL AID PROCEDURES

Forms required: FAFSA, institutional form.

Dates and Deadlines: Priority date 4/1; no closing date. Applicants notified on a rolling basis starting 4/15.

Transfers: No deadline. Applicants notified on a rolling basis starting 4/15.

CONTACT

Lori Mitchum, Director of Financial Aid
113 Sparks Hall, Murray, KY 42071
(270) 809-2546

National College: Danville

Danville, Kentucky
www.ncbt.edu Federal Code: 010489

2-year for-profit business college in large town.

Enrollment: 295 undergrads.

Selectivity: Open admission.

BASIC COSTS (2008-2009)

Tuition and fees: $9,585.

Per-credit charge: $212.

FINANCIAL AID PICTURE

Students with need: Need-based aid available for full-time and part-time students.

Students without need: This college awards aid only to students with need.

FINANCIAL AID PROCEDURES

Forms required: FAFSA.

Dates and Deadlines: No deadline. Applicants notified on a rolling basis.

CONTACT

Pamela Cotton, Director of Financial Aid and Compliance Officer
PO Box 6400, Roanoke, VA 24017
(540) 986-1800

National College: Florence

Florence, Kentucky
www.ncbt.edu Federal Code: 010489

2-year for-profit business college in large town.
Enrollment: 137 undergrads.
Selectivity: Open admission.

BASIC COSTS (2008-2009)
Tuition and fees: $9,585.
Per-credit charge: $212.

FINANCIAL AID PICTURE
Students with need: Need-based aid available for full-time and part-time students.
Students without need: This college awards aid only to students with need.

FINANCIAL AID PROCEDURES
Forms required: FAFSA.
Dates and Deadlines: No deadline. Applicants notified on a rolling basis.

CONTACT
Pamela Cotton, Director of Financial Aid and Compliance Officer
PO Box 6400, Roanoke, VA 24017
(540) 986-1800

National College: Lexington

Lexington, Kentucky
www.ncbt.edu Federal Code: 010489

2-year for-profit business and junior college in small city.
Enrollment: 548 undergrads.
Selectivity: Open admission.

BASIC COSTS (2008-2009)
Tuition and fees: $9,585.
Per-credit charge: $212.

FINANCIAL AID PICTURE
Students with need: Need-based aid available for full-time and part-time students.
Students without need: This college awards aid only to students with need.

FINANCIAL AID PROCEDURES
Forms required: FAFSA.
Dates and Deadlines: No deadline. Applicants notified on a rolling basis.

CONTACT
Pamela Cotton, Director of Financial Aid and Compliance Officer
PO Box 6400, Roanoke, VA 24017
(859) 255-0621

National College: Louisville

Louisville, Kentucky
www.ncbt.edu Federal Code: 010489

2-year for-profit business college in large city.
Enrollment: 767 undergrads.
Selectivity: Open admission.

BASIC COSTS (2008-2009)
Tuition and fees: $9,585.
Per-credit charge: $212.

FINANCIAL AID PICTURE
Students with need: Need-based aid available for full-time and part-time students.
Students without need: This college awards aid only to students with need.

FINANCIAL AID PROCEDURES
Forms required: FAFSA.
Dates and Deadlines: No deadline. Applicants notified on a rolling basis.

CONTACT
Pamela Cotton, Director of Financial Aid and Compliance Officer
PO Box 6400, Roanoke, VA 24017
(540) 986-1800

National College: Pikeville

Pikeville, Kentucky
www.ncbt.edu Federal Code: 010489

2-year for-profit business college in large town.
Enrollment: 191 undergrads.
Selectivity: Open admission.

BASIC COSTS (2008-2009)
Tuition and fees: $9,585.
Per-credit charge: $212.

FINANCIAL AID PICTURE
Students with need: Need-based aid available for full-time and part-time students.
Students without need: This college awards aid only to students with need.

FINANCIAL AID PROCEDURES
Forms required: FAFSA.
Dates and Deadlines: No deadline.

CONTACT
Pamela Cotton, Director of Financial Aid and Compliance Officer
PO Box 6400, Roanoke, VA 24017
(540) 986-1800

National College: Richmond

Richmond, Kentucky
www.ncbt.edu Federal Code: 010489

2-year for-profit business college in large town.
Enrollment: 306 undergrads.
Selectivity: Open admission.

BASIC COSTS (2008-2009)
Tuition and fees: $9,585.
Per-credit charge: $212.

FINANCIAL AID PICTURE
Students with need: Need-based aid available for full-time and part-time students.
Students without need: This college awards aid only to students with need.

FINANCIAL AID PROCEDURES
Forms required: FAFSA.
Dates and Deadlines: No deadline. Applicants notified on a rolling basis.

CONTACT
Pamela Cotton, Director of Financial Aid and Compliance Officer
PO Box 6400, Roanoke, VA 24017
(540) 986-1800

Northern Kentucky University

Highland Heights, Kentucky
www.nku.edu Federal Code: 009275

4-year public university in large city.
Enrollment: 12,296 undergrads, 23% part-time. 1,884 full-time freshmen.
Selectivity: Open admission; but selective for some programs.

BASIC COSTS (2008-2009)

Tuition and fees: $6,528; out-of-state residents $11,952.
Per-credit charge: $272; out-of-state residents $498.
Room and board: $6,082.

FINANCIAL AID PICTURE (2007-2008)

Students with need: Out of 1,441 full-time freshmen who applied for aid, 1,035 were judged to have need. Of these, 1,024 received aid, and 227 had their full need met. Average financial aid package met 62% of need; average scholarship/grant was $5,134; average loan was $2,940. For part-time students, average financial aid package was $5,481.
Students without need: 189 full-time freshmen who did not demonstrate need for aid received scholarships/grants; average award was $3,858. No-need awards available for academics, alumni affiliation, art, athletics, leadership, music/drama, state/district residency.
Scholarships offered: 21 full-time freshmen received athletic scholarships; average amount $4,341.
Cumulative student debt: 68% of graduating class had student loans; average debt was $22,743.

FINANCIAL AID PROCEDURES

Forms required: FAFSA.
Dates and Deadlines: Priority date 3/1; no closing date. Applicants notified on a rolling basis starting 4/1.
Transfers: Applicants notified by 5/30.

CONTACT

Leah Stewart, Director of Financial Assistance
Administrative Center 401, Northern Kentucky University, Highland Heights, KY 41099
(859) 572-5143

Owensboro Community and Technical College

Owensboro, Kentucky
www.octc.kctcs.edu Federal Code: 030345

2-year public community and technical college in small city.
Enrollment: 2,986 undergrads, 42% part-time. 507 full-time freshmen.
Selectivity: Open admission; but selective for some programs.

BASIC COSTS (2008-2009)

Tuition and fees: $3,630; out-of-state residents $11,700.
Per-credit charge: $121; out-of-state residents $390.
Additional info: Tuition reduction program available for qualified residents of contiguous states.

FINANCIAL AID PICTURE (2007-2008)

Students with need: Need-based aid available for full-time and part-time students.
Students without need: No-need awards available for academics, state/district residency.

FINANCIAL AID PROCEDURES

Forms required: FAFSA.
Dates and Deadlines: Priority date 3/16; no closing date. Applicants notified by 6/1; must reply within 2 week(s) of notification.
Transfers: Must have financial aid transcripts from previous institutions.

CONTACT

Bernice Ayer, Financial Aid Officer
4800 New Hartford Road, Owensboro, KY 42303-1899
(270) 686-4520

Pikeville College

Pikeville, Kentucky
www.pc.edu Federal Code: 001980

4-year private liberal arts college in small town, affiliated with Presbyterian Church (USA).
Enrollment: 755 undergrads, 9% part-time. 180 full-time freshmen.
Selectivity: Open admission; but selective for some programs.

BASIC COSTS (2009-2010)

Tuition and fees: $14,535.
Per-credit charge: $606.
Room and board: $6,000.

FINANCIAL AID PICTURE (2008-2009)

Students with need: Out of 180 full-time freshmen who applied for aid, 179 were judged to have need. Of these, 179 received aid, and 110 had their full need met. Average financial aid package met 93% of need; average scholarship/grant was $12,971; average loan was $4,573. For part-time students, average financial aid package was $10,815.
Students without need: This college awards aid only to students with need.
Cumulative student debt: 71% of graduating class had student loans; average debt was $14,908.

FINANCIAL AID PROCEDURES

Forms required: FAFSA, institutional form.
Dates and Deadlines: Priority date 3/15; no closing date. Applicants notified on a rolling basis starting 1/15; must reply by 5/1 or within 2 week(s) of notification.
Transfers: No deadline. Must reply by 5/1 or within 2 week(s) of notification.

CONTACT

Judy Bradley, Financial Aid Director
147 Sycamore Street, Pikeville, KY 41501-1194
(606) 218-5251

St. Catharine College

St. Catharine, Kentucky
www.sccky.edu Federal Code: 001983

4-year private health science and liberal arts college in small town, affiliated with Roman Catholic Church.
Enrollment: 552 full-time undergrads.
Selectivity: Open admission.

BASIC COSTS (2008-2009)

Tuition and fees: $13,600.
Per-credit charge: $465.
Room and board: $6,740.
Additional info: Higher tuition applies for health science program.

FINANCIAL AID PICTURE

Students with need: Need-based aid available for full-time and part-time students.
Students without need: This college awards aid only to students with need.

FINANCIAL AID PROCEDURES

Forms required: FAFSA, institutional form.

Dates and Deadlines: Priority date 3/15; no closing date. Applicants notified on a rolling basis; must reply by 8/15.

CONTACT

Laura Dean, Financial Aid Director
2735 Bardstown Road, St. Catharine, KY 40061
(502) 336-5082

Somerset Community College

Somerset, Kentucky
www.somerset.kctcs.edu Federal Code: 001997

2-year public community and technical college in large town.
Enrollment: 4,860 undergrads.
Selectivity: Open admission; but selective for some programs.

BASIC COSTS (2008-2009)

Tuition and fees: $3,630; out-of-state residents $11,700.
Per-credit charge: $121; out-of-state residents $390.
Additional info: Tuition reduction program available for qualified residents of contiguous states.

FINANCIAL AID PICTURE (2007-2008)

Students with need: 79% of average financial aid package awarded as scholarships/grants, 21% awarded as loans/jobs. Need-based aid available for part-time students.
Students without need: This college awards aid only to students with need.

FINANCIAL AID PROCEDURES

Forms required: FAFSA.
Dates and Deadlines: Priority date 3/1; no closing date. Applicants notified on a rolling basis starting 5/1; must reply within 2 week(s) of notification.
Transfers: Priority date 3/15; closing date 8/15. Applicants notified on a rolling basis starting 5/1; must reply within 2 week(s) of notification.

CONTACT

Shawn Anderson, Chief Financial Aid Officer
808 Monticello Street, Somerset, KY 42501
(606) 679-8501 ext. 16640

Southeast Kentucky Community and Technical College

Cumberland, Kentucky
www.secc.kctcs.edu Federal Code: 001998

2-year public community and technical college in small town.
Enrollment: 2,104 undergrads, 39% part-time. 610 full-time freshmen.
Selectivity: Open admission; but selective for some programs.

BASIC COSTS (2008-2009)

Tuition and fees: $3,630; out-of-state residents $11,844.
Per-credit charge: $121; out-of-state residents $390.
Additional info: Tuition reduction program available for qualified residents of contiguous states.

FINANCIAL AID PICTURE (2008-2009)

Students with need: Need-based aid available for full-time and part-time students.
Students without need: This college awards aid only to students with need.
Additional info: March 15 deadline for state financial aid.

FINANCIAL AID PROCEDURES

Forms required: FAFSA.
Dates and Deadlines: Priority date 3/15; no closing date. Applicants notified by 6/15; must reply within 2 week(s) of notification.

CONTACT

Rebecca Robbins, Associate Dean of Student Affairs/Director Financial Aid
700 College Road, Cumberland, KY 40823
(606) 589-2145

Southwestern College: Florence

Florence, Kentucky
www.swcollege.net Federal Code: 012128

2-year for-profit health science and career college in small city.
Enrollment: 315 undergrads. 300 full-time freshmen.
Selectivity: Open admission.

BASIC COSTS (2008-2009)

Tuition and fees: $10,825.

FINANCIAL AID PICTURE (2007-2008)

Students with need: Out of 300 full-time freshmen who applied for aid, 280 were judged to have need. Of these, 280 received aid, and 270 had their full need met. Average financial aid package met 100% of need; average scholarship/grant was $400. For part-time students, average financial aid package was $384.
Students without need: This college awards aid only to students with need.
Cumulative student debt: 100% of graduating class had student loans; average debt was $3,500.

FINANCIAL AID PROCEDURES

Forms required: FAFSA.
Dates and Deadlines: No deadline. Applicants notified on a rolling basis.
Transfers: No deadline. Applicants notified on a rolling basis.

CONTACT

Kay Boone, Director of Financial Aid
8095 Connector Drive, Florence, KY 41042
(859) 282-9999

Spalding University

Louisville, Kentucky
www.spalding.edu Federal Code: 001960

4-year private university in large city, affiliated with Roman Catholic Church.
Enrollment: 1,057 undergrads, 32% part-time. 102 full-time freshmen.
Selectivity: Admits less than 50% of applicants.

BASIC COSTS (2008-2009)

Tuition and fees: $17,700.
Per-credit charge: $560.
Room and board: $4,560.

FINANCIAL AID PICTURE (2007-2008)

Students with need: 18% of average financial aid package awarded as scholarships/grants, 82% awarded as loans/jobs. Need-based aid available for part-time students. Work study available nights, weekends, and for part-time students.
Students without need: No-need awards available for academics, religious affiliation.
Scholarships offered: Angela Garcia Residence Hall Scholarship: covers cost of a double room on campus; up to 12 awards per year; awarded to students who demonstrate leadership in campus activities, especially in residence halls.

FINANCIAL AID PROCEDURES

Forms required: FAFSA.
Dates and Deadlines: Priority date 3/1; no closing date. Applicants notified on a rolling basis starting 3/31; must reply within 2 week(s) of notification.

CONTACT

Gina Kuzuoka, Director of Financial Aid
845 S. Third Street, Louisville, KY 40203
(502) 588-7185

Spencerian College: Lexington

Lexington, Kentucky
www.spencerian.edu Federal Code: 004618

2-year for-profit branch campus and technical college in small city.

Enrollment: 601 undergrads, 41% part-time. 100 full-time freshmen.

Selectivity: Open admission; but selective for some programs.

BASIC COSTS (2008-2009)

Tuition and fees: $2,775.

Additional info: Cost of programs ranges from $9,000 to $41,000; program-specific fees are additional. Cost of housing is $520 per month. Per-credit-hour charge ranges from $235 to $380 depending on program. Tuition at time of enrollment locked for 2 years.

FINANCIAL AID PICTURE (2008-2009)

Students with need: 41% of average financial aid package awarded as scholarships/grants, 59% awarded as loans/jobs. Need-based aid available for part-time students.

Students without need: This college awards aid only to students with need.

FINANCIAL AID PROCEDURES

Forms required: FAFSA, state aid form, institutional form.

Dates and Deadlines: No deadline. Applicants notified on a rolling basis starting 1/1.

Transfers: No deadline. Applicants notified on a rolling basis.

CONTACT

Brian Highley, Director of Financial Planning
1575 Winchester Road, Lexington, KY 40505
(859) 223-9608 ext. 5421

Sullivan University

Louisville, Kentucky
www.sullivan.edu Federal Code: 004619

4-year for-profit university in large city.

Enrollment: 4,338 undergrads.

BASIC COSTS (2008-2009)

Room only: $4,680.

Additional info: Tuition at time of enrollment locked for 4 years.

FINANCIAL AID PICTURE

Students with need: Need-based aid available for full-time and part-time students. Work study available nights.

Students without need: This college awards aid only to students with need.

FINANCIAL AID PROCEDURES

Forms required: FAFSA.

Dates and Deadlines: No deadline. Applicants notified on a rolling basis starting 1/2.

CONTACT

Lisa Wright, Financial Planning Director
3101 Bardstown Road, Louisville, KY 40205
(502) 456-6505

Thomas More College

Crestview Hills, Kentucky
www.thomasmore.edu Federal Code: 002001

4-year private liberal arts college in small town, affiliated with Roman Catholic Church.

Enrollment: 1,397 undergrads. 274 full-time freshmen.

Selectivity: Admits over 75% of applicants.

BASIC COSTS (2009-2010)

Tuition and fees: $23,220.

Per-credit charge: $530.

Room and board: $6,560.

Additional info: Tiered tuition with a guaranteed 3% increase pre year which allows planning the cost of a degree. Each level has different tuition and figures given are for incoming Freshmen only, with other classes lower. Tuition/fee waivers available for minority students.

FINANCIAL AID PICTURE (2007-2008)

Students with need: Need-based aid available for full-time and part-time students. Work study available nights, weekends, and for part-time students.

Students without need: No-need awards available for academics, alumni affiliation, art, job skills, leadership, minority status, music/drama, religious affiliation, ROTC, state/district residency.

FINANCIAL AID PROCEDURES

Forms required: FAFSA, institutional form.

Dates and Deadlines: Priority date 3/15; no closing date. Applicants notified on a rolling basis; must reply by 5/1.

Transfers: No deadline. Applicants notified on a rolling basis; must reply by 5/1.

CONTACT

Mary Givhan, Director of Financial Aid
333 Thomas More Parkway, Crestview Hills, KY 41017-3495
(859) 344-4043

Transylvania University

Lexington, Kentucky
www.transy.edu Federal Code: 001987

4-year private liberal arts college in large city, affiliated with Christian Church (Disciples of Christ).

Enrollment: 1,154 undergrads, 1% part-time. 315 full-time freshmen.

Selectivity: Admits over 75% of applicants.

BASIC COSTS (2008-2009)

Tuition and fees: $23,810.

Room and board: $7,450.

Additional info: Tuition/fee waivers available for minority students.

FINANCIAL AID PICTURE (2008-2009)

Students with need: Out of 272 full-time freshmen who applied for aid, 217 were judged to have need. Of these, 217 received aid, and 66 had their full need met. Average financial aid package met 86% of need; average scholarship/grant was $15,690; average loan was $4,250. For part-time students, average financial aid package was $5,148.

Students without need: 96 full-time freshmen who did not demonstrate need for aid received scholarships/grants; average award was $14,662. No-need awards available for academics, art, leadership, minority status, music/drama, religious affiliation, ROTC, state/district residency.

Scholarships offered: William T. Young Merit Scholarships: 25 awarded; tuition and fees.

Cumulative student debt: 63% of graduating class had student loans; average debt was $17,885.

Additional info: Auditions and portfolios required for music and art scholarships respectively. Essays required for other scholarship programs. Applications for William T. Young scholarships must be received by December 1.

FINANCIAL AID PROCEDURES

Forms required: FAFSA.

Dates and Deadlines: Priority date 3/1; no closing date. Applicants notified on a rolling basis starting 3/15; must reply by 5/1 or within 2 week(s) of notification.

Transfers: No deadline. Applicants notified on a rolling basis starting 3/15; must reply by 8/6.

CONTACT

David Cecil, Director of Financial Aid
300 North Broadway, Lexington, KY 40508-1797
(859) 233-8239

Union College

Barbourville, Kentucky
www.unionky.edu Federal Code: 001988

4-year private liberal arts and teachers college in small town, affiliated with United Methodist Church.

Enrollment: 804 undergrads, 5% part-time. 231 full-time freshmen.

Selectivity: Open admission; but selective for some programs.

BASIC COSTS (2009-2010)

Tuition and fees: $17,894.

Per-credit charge: $280.

Room and board: $3,300.

FINANCIAL AID PICTURE (2007-2008)

Students with need: Out of 231 full-time freshmen who applied for aid, 215 were judged to have need. Of these, 215 received aid, and 67 had their full need met. Average financial aid package met 82% of need; average scholarship/grant was $11,460; average loan was $6,118. For part-time students, average financial aid package was $7,542.

Students without need: 16 full-time freshmen who did not demonstrate need for aid received scholarships/grants; average award was $18,791. No-need awards available for academics, athletics, leadership, minority status, music/drama, religious affiliation, state/district residency.

FINANCIAL AID PROCEDURES

Forms required: FAFSA.

Dates and Deadlines: Priority date 3/15; no closing date. Applicants notified on a rolling basis starting 3/1; must reply within 2 week(s) of notification.

CONTACT

Sue Buttery, Associate Dean for Financial Aid
310 College Street, Box 005, Barbourville, KY 40906
(606) 546-1618

University of Kentucky

Lexington, Kentucky
www.uky.edu Federal Code: 001989

4-year public university in large city.

Enrollment: 18,591 undergrads, 7% part-time. 4,079 full-time freshmen.

Selectivity: Admits over 75% of applicants.

BASIC COSTS (2008-2009)

Tuition and fees: $7,736; out-of-state residents $15,884.

Per-credit charge: $307; out-of-state residents $647.

Room and board: $5,887.

Additional info: Tuition charges include fees. Upper division tuition $7,302, in-state; $15,094, out-of-state. Tuition/fee waivers available for adults, minority students.

FINANCIAL AID PICTURE (2008-2009)

Students with need: Need-based aid available for full-time and part-time students. Work study available weekends and for part-time students.

Students without need: No-need awards available for academics, alumni affiliation, art, athletics, job skills, leadership, minority status, music/drama, ROTC, state/district residency.

FINANCIAL AID PROCEDURES

Forms required: FAFSA.

Dates and Deadlines: Priority date 2/15; no closing date. Applicants notified on a rolling basis starting 4/1; must reply within 3 week(s) of notification.

Transfers: Priority date 4/1.

CONTACT

Lynda George, Director of Student Financial Aid
100 W.D. Funkhouser Building, Lexington, KY 40506-0054
(859) 257-3172

University of Louisville

Louisville, Kentucky
www.louisville.edu Federal Code: 001999

4-year public university in very large city.

Enrollment: 14,524 undergrads, 20% part-time. 2,549 full-time freshmen.

Selectivity: Admits 50 to 75% of applicants.

BASIC COSTS (2008-2009)

Tuition and fees: $7,564; out-of-state residents $18,354.

Per-credit charge: $316; out-of-state residents $765.

Room and board: $6,288.

FINANCIAL AID PICTURE (2008-2009)

Students with need: Need-based aid available for full-time and part-time students.

Students without need: No-need awards available for academics, art, athletics, leadership, minority status, music/drama, ROTC.

FINANCIAL AID PROCEDURES

Forms required: FAFSA.

Dates and Deadlines: Priority date 3/15; no closing date. Applicants notified on a rolling basis starting 4/1; must reply by 5/1.

Transfers: Priority date 3/1.

CONTACT

Patricia Arauz, Director of Student Financial Aid
2211 South Brook Street, Louisville, KY 40292
(502) 852-5511

University of the Cumberlands

Williamsburg, Kentucky
www.ucumberlands.edu Federal Code: 001962

4-year private university and liberal arts college in small town, affiliated with Baptist faith.

Enrollment: 1,429 undergrads, 3% part-time. 432 full-time freshmen.

Selectivity: Admits over 75% of applicants.

BASIC COSTS (2009-2010)

Tuition and fees: $15,658.

Per-credit charge: $490.

Room and board: $6,826.

FINANCIAL AID PICTURE (2008-2009)

Students with need: Out of 420 full-time freshmen who applied for aid, 386 were judged to have need. Of these, 386 received aid, and 119 had their full need met. Average financial aid package met 86% of need; average scholarship/grant was $11,734; average loan was $3,478. For part-time students, average financial aid package was $7,827.

Students without need: 38 full-time freshmen who did not demonstrate need for aid received scholarships/grants; average award was $5,656. No-need awards available for academics, alumni affiliation, art, athletics, leadership, music/drama, religious affiliation, ROTC, state/district residency.

Scholarships offered: 29 full-time freshmen received athletic scholarships; average amount $5,271.

Cumulative student debt: 78% of graduating class had student loans; average debt was $19,339.

FINANCIAL AID PROCEDURES

Forms required: FAFSA.

Dates and Deadlines: Priority date 3/1; no closing date. Applicants notified on a rolling basis starting 4/1; must reply within 2 week(s) of notification.

CONTACT

Steve Allen, Director of Financial Planning
6178 College Station Drive, Williamsburg, KY 40769
(800) 343-1609

West Kentucky Community and Technical College

Paducah, Kentucky
www.westkentucky.kctcs.edu Federal Code: 001979

2-year public community and technical college in large town.

Enrollment: 3,514 undergrads.

Selectivity: Open admission; but selective for some programs.

BASIC COSTS (2008-2009)

Tuition and fees: $3,630; out-of-state residents $11,700.

Per-credit charge: $121; out-of-state residents $390.

Additional info: Tuition reduction program available for qualified residents of contiguous states.

FINANCIAL AID PICTURE

Students with need: Need-based aid available for full-time and part-time students.

FINANCIAL AID PROCEDURES

Forms required: FAFSA.

Dates and Deadlines: Priority date 4/1; no closing date. Applicants notified on a rolling basis starting 7/15; must reply within 4 week(s) of notification.

CONTACT

Sandy Barlow, Financial Aid Officer
4810 Alben Barkley Drive/ Box 7380, Paducah, KY 42002-7380
(270) 534-3248

Western Kentucky University

Bowling Green, Kentucky
www.wku.edu Federal Code: 002002

4-year public university in small city.

Enrollment: 15,731 undergrads, 15% part-time. 3,024 full-time freshmen.

Selectivity: Open admission; but selective for some programs.

BASIC COSTS (2008-2009)

Tuition and fees: $6,930; out-of-state residents $17,088.

Per-credit charge: $289; out-of-state residents $712.

Room and board: $6,248.

FINANCIAL AID PICTURE (2007-2008)

Students with need: Out of 2,433 full-time freshmen who applied for aid, 1,833 were judged to have need. Of these, 1,815 received aid, and 643 had their full need met. Average financial aid package met 35% of need; average scholarship/grant was $4,730; average loan was $2,962. For part-time students, average financial aid package was $7,391.

Students without need: 319 full-time freshmen who did not demonstrate need for aid received scholarships/grants; average award was $4,550. No-need awards available for academics, alumni affiliation, art, athletics, job skills, leadership, minority status, music/drama, religious affiliation, ROTC, state/district residency.

Scholarships offered: ***Merit:*** Academic scholarships; $200 to full tuition; number awarded varies. ***Athletic:*** 91 full-time freshmen received athletic scholarships; average amount $9,329.

Cumulative student debt: 57% of graduating class had student loans; average debt was $15,042.

FINANCIAL AID PROCEDURES

Forms required: FAFSA.

Dates and Deadlines: Priority date 4/1; no closing date. Applicants notified on a rolling basis starting 3/1.

Transfers: Transfer students receiving CAP Grant must notify the state agency by December 1 of each year.

CONTACT

Cynthia Burnette, Director of Financial Assistance
1906 College Heights Boulevard, Bowling Green, KY 42101
(270) 745-2755

Louisiana

Baton Rouge Community College

Baton Rouge, Louisiana
www.mybrcc.edu Federal Code: 037303

2-year public community college in large city.

Enrollment: 6,929 undergrads, 43% part-time. 1,133 full-time freshmen.

Selectivity: Open admission; but selective for some programs.

BASIC COSTS (2008-2009)

Tuition and fees: $1,846; out-of-state residents $4,794.

FINANCIAL AID PICTURE (2007-2008)

Students with need: 99% of average financial aid package awarded as scholarships/grants, 1% awarded as loans/jobs. Need-based aid available for part-time students. Work study available weekends and for part-time students.

Students without need: No-need awards available for academics, athletics.

FINANCIAL AID PROCEDURES

Forms required: FAFSA, institutional form.

Dates and Deadlines: Priority date 4/15; no closing date. Applicants notified on a rolling basis.

Transfers: No deadline. Applicants notified on a rolling basis.

CONTACT

Calaundra Brown, Director of Financial Aid
201 Community College Drive, Baton Rouge, LA 70806
(225) 216-8005

Bossier Parish Community College
Bossier City, Louisiana
www.bpcc.edu Federal Code: 012033

2-year public community college in small city.
Enrollment: 3,828 undergrads, 35% part-time. 776 full-time freshmen.
Selectivity: Open admission; but selective for out-of-state students.

BASIC COSTS (2008-2009)
Tuition and fees: $1,760; out-of-state residents $3,900.

FINANCIAL AID PICTURE (2007-2008)
Students with need: Out of 655 full-time freshmen who applied for aid, 530 were judged to have need. Of these, 491 received aid. Average financial aid package met 74% of need; average scholarship/grant was $5,730; average loan was $4,377. For part-time students, average financial aid package was $5,799.
Students without need: 99 full-time freshmen who did not demonstrate need for aid received scholarships/grants; average award was $1,947. No-need awards available for academics, alumni affiliation, athletics, minority status, music/drama.
Scholarships offered: 38 full-time freshmen received athletic scholarships; average amount $2,466.

FINANCIAL AID PROCEDURES
Forms required: FAFSA.
Dates and Deadlines: Closing date 7/1. Applicants notified on a rolling basis.
Transfers: Priority date 6/1; no deadline.

CONTACT
Vickie Temple, Financial Aid Director
6220 East Texas Street, Bossier City, LA 71111-6922
(318) 678-6026

Centenary College of Louisiana
Shreveport, Louisiana
www.centenary.edu Federal Code: 002003

4-year private liberal arts college in small city, affiliated with United Methodist Church.
Enrollment: 816 full-time undergrads.
Selectivity: Admits 50 to 75% of applicants.

BASIC COSTS (2008-2009)
Tuition and fees: $21,630.
Per-credit charge: $700.
Room and board: $7,360.

FINANCIAL AID PICTURE (2007-2008)
Students with need: Need-based aid available for full-time and part-time students. Work study available nights, weekends, and for part-time students.
Students without need: No-need awards available for academics, art, athletics, leadership, music/drama, religious affiliation, state/district residency.

FINANCIAL AID PROCEDURES
Forms required: FAFSA, institutional form.
Dates and Deadlines: Priority date 2/15; no closing date. Applicants notified on a rolling basis starting 2/15.

CONTACT
Mary Sue Rix, Director of Financial Aid
Box 41188, Shreveport, LA 71134-1188
(318) 869-5137

Delgado Community College
New Orleans, Louisiana
www.dcc.edu Federal Code: 004626

2-year public community college in very large city.
Enrollment: 13,015 undergrads, 54% part-time. 1,606 full-time freshmen.
Selectivity: Open admission; but selective for some programs.

BASIC COSTS (2008-2009)
Tuition and fees: $1,928; out-of-state residents $4,908.

FINANCIAL AID PICTURE
Students with need: Need-based aid available for full-time and part-time students. Work study available nights, weekends, and for part-time students.
Students without need: No-need awards available for academics, athletics, leadership, music/drama, state/district residency.

FINANCIAL AID PROCEDURES
Forms required: FAFSA, institutional form.
Dates and Deadlines: Priority date 5/1; closing date 7/15. Applicants notified on a rolling basis starting 4/1; must reply within 2 week(s) of notification.

CONTACT
Germaine Edwards, Director of Student Financial Assistance
615 City Park Avenue, New Orleans, LA 70119

Dillard University
New Orleans, Louisiana
www.dillard.edu Federal Code: 002004

4-year private university and liberal arts college in very large city, affiliated with United Church of Christ and United Methodist Church.
Enrollment: 781 full-time undergrads.
Selectivity: Admits less than 50% of applicants.

BASIC COSTS (2008-2009)
Tuition and fees: $13,540.
Per-credit charge: $542.
Room and board: $8,210.

FINANCIAL AID PICTURE
Students with need: Need-based aid available for full-time and part-time students. Work study available nights, weekends, and for part-time students.
Students without need: This college awards aid only to students with need.

FINANCIAL AID PROCEDURES
Forms required: FAFSA, institutional form.
Dates and Deadlines: Priority date 12/1; closing date 5/1. Applicants notified on a rolling basis starting 3/1; must reply by 5/1 or within 2 week(s) of notification.

CONTACT
Michael White, Director of Financial Aid
2601 Gentilly Boulevard, New Orleans, LA 70122-3097
(800) 216-8094

Grambling State University
Grambling, Louisiana
www.gram.edu Federal Code: 002006

4-year public university in small town.
Enrollment: 4,799 undergrads, 6% part-time. 1,205 full-time freshmen.
Selectivity: Admits over 75% of applicants. GED not accepted.

BASIC COSTS (2008-2009)

Tuition and fees: $3,804; out-of-state residents $9,154.

Per-credit charge: $101.

Room and board: $5,202.

FINANCIAL AID PICTURE (2008-2009)

Students with need: For part-time students, average financial aid package was $1,249.

Students without need: No-need awards available for academics, alumni affiliation, art, athletics, job skills, leadership, minority status, music/drama, religious affiliation, ROTC, state/district residency.

Scholarships offered: 97 full-time freshmen received athletic scholarships; average amount $2,159.

FINANCIAL AID PROCEDURES

Forms required: FAFSA.

Dates and Deadlines: Priority date 4/1; closing date 6/1. Applicants notified on a rolling basis starting 3/1; must reply within 2 week(s) of notification.

Transfers: Applicants notified on a rolling basis starting 3/1; must reply within 2 week(s) of notification.

CONTACT

Jackie Greer, Director of Student Financial Aid
403 Main Street, GSU Box 4200, Grambling, LA 71245
(318) 274-6190

Herzing College

Kenner, Louisiana
www.herzing.edu Federal Code: 020897

4-year for-profit branch campus and technical college in very large city.

Enrollment: 90 full-time undergrads.

BASIC COSTS (2008-2009)

Additional info: Tuition costs vary by program, $315-$375 per credit hour.

FINANCIAL AID PICTURE

Students with need: Work study available nights, weekends, and for part-time students.

CONTACT

Ava Gomez, Financial Aid Director
2400 Veterans Boulevard, Suite 410, Kenner, LA 70062

ITI Technical College

Baton Rouge, Louisiana
www.iticollege.edu Federal Code: 015270

2-year for-profit technical college in large city.

Enrollment: 370 undergrads. 163 full-time freshmen.

Selectivity: Open admission.

BASIC COSTS (2008-2009)

Additional info: Full-time tuition varies by program from $12,000 to $24,100.

FINANCIAL AID PICTURE

Students with need: Need-based aid available for full-time and part-time students.

Students without need: This college awards aid only to students with need.

FINANCIAL AID PROCEDURES

Forms required: FAFSA.

Dates and Deadlines: No deadline.

CONTACT

Connie Roubique, Financial Aid Director
13944 Airline Highway, Baton Rouge, LA 70817
(225) 752-4233

Louisiana College

Pineville, Louisiana
www.lacollege.edu Federal Code: 002007

4-year private liberal arts college in small city, affiliated with Southern Baptist Convention.

Enrollment: 858 undergrads, 5% part-time. 276 full-time freshmen.

Selectivity: Admits 50 to 75% of applicants.

BASIC COSTS (2008-2009)

Tuition and fees: $12,030.

Per-credit charge: $355.

Room and board: $4,316.

Additional info: Tuition at time of enrollment locked for 4 years.

FINANCIAL AID PICTURE

Students with need: Need-based aid available for full-time and part-time students. Work study available nights, weekends, and for part-time students.

Students without need: No-need awards available for academics, art, leadership, music/drama, ROTC.

FINANCIAL AID PROCEDURES

Forms required: FAFSA, institutional form.

Dates and Deadlines: Priority date 3/31; no closing date. Applicants notified on a rolling basis starting 3/1; must reply by 5/1 or within 2 week(s) of notification.

Transfers: Scholarships available.

CONTACT

Ronnie LaLande, Director of Financial Aid
LC Box 566, Pineville, LA 71359
(318) 487-7386

Louisiana State University and Agricultural and Mechanical College

Baton Rouge, Louisiana
www.lsu.edu Federal Code: 002010

4-year public university and agricultural college in large city.

Enrollment: 23,057 undergrads, 6% part-time. 4,588 full-time freshmen.

Selectivity: Admits 50 to 75% of applicants.

BASIC COSTS (2008-2009)

Tuition and fees: $5,086; out-of-state residents $13,800.

Room and board: $7,238.

FINANCIAL AID PICTURE (2007-2008)

Students with need: Out of 2,752 full-time freshmen who applied for aid, 1,573 were judged to have need. Of these, 1,573 received aid, and 337 had their full need met. Average financial aid package met 75% of need; average scholarship/grant was $8,083; average loan was $3,324. For part-time students, average financial aid package was $5,721.

Students without need: 1,288 full-time freshmen who did not demonstrate need for aid received scholarships/grants; average award was $3,276. No-need awards available for academics, alumni affiliation, art, athletics, leadership, music/drama, ROTC, state/district residency.

Scholarships offered: 105 full-time freshmen received athletic scholarships; average amount $14,345.

Cumulative student debt: 40% of graduating class had student loans; average debt was $17,060.

FINANCIAL AID PROCEDURES

Forms required: FAFSA, institutional form.

Dates and Deadlines: No deadline. Applicants notified on a rolling basis starting 3/1; must reply within 3 week(s) of notification.

Transfers: No deadline. Applicants notified on a rolling basis.

CONTACT

Mary Parker, Executive Director of Undergraduate Admissions & Student Aid
1146 Pleasant Halll, Baton Rouge, LA 70803-2750
(225) 578-3103

Louisiana State University at Alexandria

Alexandria, Louisiana
www.lsua.edu Federal Code: 002011

4-year public university in small city.
Enrollment: 2,950 undergrads.
Selectivity: Admits over 75% of applicants.

BASIC COSTS (2008-2009)

Tuition and fees: $3,381; out-of-state residents $5,963.
Per-credit charge: $132; out-of-state residents $239.
Additional info: On-campus housing (double-occupancy) $510 per month; meal plan $608 per 160 meals.

FINANCIAL AID PICTURE

Students with need: Need-based aid available for full-time and part-time students. Work study available nights.
Students without need: No-need awards available for academics, state/district residency.

FINANCIAL AID PROCEDURES

Forms required: FAFSA, institutional form.
Dates and Deadlines: Priority date 4/1; no closing date. Applicants notified on a rolling basis starting 4/20; must reply within 3 week(s) of notification.

CONTACT

Paul Monteleone, Director of Student Aid and Scholarships
8100 Highway 71 South, Alexandria, LA 71302-9121
(318) 473-6423

Louisiana State University at Eunice

Eunice, Louisiana
www.lsue.edu Federal Code: 002012

2-year public branch campus and community college in large town.
Enrollment: 3,031 undergrads.
Selectivity: Open admission; but selective for some programs.

BASIC COSTS (2008-2009)

Tuition and fees: $2,355; out-of-state residents $5,445.
Per-credit charge: $110.

FINANCIAL AID PICTURE (2008-2009)

Students with need: Need-based aid available for full-time and part-time students.

FINANCIAL AID PROCEDURES

Forms required: FAFSA, institutional form.
Dates and Deadlines: Priority date 6/1; no closing date. Applicants notified on a rolling basis starting 4/1; must reply within 2 week(s) of notification.

CONTACT

Jacqueline LaChapelle, Director of Financial Aid
Box 1129, Eunice, LA 70535
(337) 550-1282

Louisiana State University Health Sciences Center

New Orleans, Louisiana
www.lsuhsc.edu Federal Code: 002014

Upper-division public health science and nursing college in large city.
Enrollment: 747 undergrads.

BASIC COSTS (2008-2009)

Tuition and fees: $3,978; out-of-state residents $7,110.
Room only: $2,210.

FINANCIAL AID PICTURE (2008-2009)

Students with need: Need-based aid available for full-time and part-time students. Work study available nights, weekends, and for part-time students.
Students without need: No-need awards available for academics.

FINANCIAL AID PROCEDURES

Forms required: FAFSA, institutional form.
Dates and Deadlines: Priority date 4/15; no closing date. Applicants notified on a rolling basis starting 7/1.

CONTACT

Patrick Gorman, Director of Financial Aid
433 Bolivar Street, New Orleans, LA 70112-2223
(504) 568-4820

Louisiana State University in Shreveport

Shreveport, Louisiana
www.lsus.edu Federal Code: 002013

4-year public university in large city.
Enrollment: 3,108 undergrads.
Selectivity: Admits over 75% of applicants.

BASIC COSTS (2008-2009)

Tuition and fees: $3,687; out-of-state residents $8,230.

FINANCIAL AID PICTURE

Students with need: Need-based aid available for full-time and part-time students. Work study available nights, weekends, and for part-time students.

FINANCIAL AID PROCEDURES

Dates and Deadlines: No deadline. Applicants notified on a rolling basis.

CONTACT

Betty McCrary, Director of Student Financial Aid
One University Place, Shreveport, LA 71115-2399
(318) 797-5363

Louisiana Tech University

Ruston, Louisiana
www.latech.edu Federal Code: 002008

4-year public university in large town.
Enrollment: 6,560 full-time undergrads.
Selectivity: Admits 50 to 75% of applicants.

BASIC COSTS (2008-2009)

Tuition and fees: $4,628; out-of-state residents $11,006.
Room and board: $4,770.

FINANCIAL AID PICTURE (2007-2008)

Students with need: Need-based aid available for full-time and part-time students.

Students without need: No-need awards available for academics, art, athletics, leadership, music/drama, ROTC.

FINANCIAL AID PROCEDURES

Forms required: FAFSA, institutional form.
Dates and Deadlines: Priority date 4/15; no closing date. Applicants notified on a rolling basis starting 3/18; must reply within 4 week(s) of notification.
Transfers: Priority date 8/1; no deadline. Applicants notified on a rolling basis starting 8/20; must reply within 2 week(s) of notification.

CONTACT

Roger Vick, Director of Student Financial Aid
Box 3178, Ruston, LA 71272
(318) 257-2641

Loyola University New Orleans

New Orleans, Louisiana
www.loyno.edu Federal Code: 002016

4-year private university and liberal arts college in large city, affiliated with Roman Catholic Church.
Enrollment: 2,600 undergrads, 11% part-time. 700 full-time freshmen.
Selectivity: Admits 50 to 75% of applicants.

BASIC COSTS (2009-2010)

Tuition and fees: $29,706.
Per-credit charge: $821.
Room and board: $9,826.

FINANCIAL AID PICTURE (2008-2009)

Students with need: Out of 533 full-time freshmen who applied for aid, 409 were judged to have need. Of these, 409 received aid, and 129 had their full need met. Average financial aid package met 92% of need; average scholarship/grant was $16,505; average loan was $3,565. For part-time students, average financial aid package was $8,807.
Students without need: 226 full-time freshmen who did not demonstrate need for aid received scholarships/grants; average award was $18,391. No-need awards available for academics, alumni affiliation, art, leadership, ROTC.
Scholarships offered: 1 full-time freshmen received athletic scholarships; average amount $34,670.
Cumulative student debt: 59% of graduating class had student loans; average debt was $21,401.

FINANCIAL AID PROCEDURES

Forms required: FAFSA.
Dates and Deadlines: Priority date 2/15; closing date 6/1. Applicants notified on a rolling basis starting 3/1; must reply by 5/1 or within 2 week(s) of notification.
Transfers: Priority date 3/1; closing date 5/1. Transfer scholarship deadline June 1.

CONTACT

Catherine Simoneaux, Director of Scholarships and Financial Aid
6363 St. Charles Avenue, New Orleans, LA 70118-6195
(504) 865-3231

McNeese State University

Lake Charles, Louisiana
www.mcneese.edu Federal Code: 002017

4-year public university in small city.
Enrollment: 7,256 undergrads, 19% part-time. 1,289 full-time freshmen.
Selectivity: Admits over 75% of applicants.

BASIC COSTS (2008-2009)

Tuition and fees: $3,246; out-of-state residents $9,312.
Room and board: $5,436.

FINANCIAL AID PICTURE

Students with need: Need-based aid available for full-time and part-time students. Work study available nights, weekends, and for part-time students.
Students without need: No-need awards available for academics, alumni affiliation, art, athletics, leadership, minority status, music/drama, state/district residency.
Additional info: Books may be charged and paid in 2 installments during semester.

FINANCIAL AID PROCEDURES

Forms required: FAFSA, institutional form.
Dates and Deadlines: Priority date 5/1; no closing date. Applicants notified on a rolling basis starting 4/15; must reply within 2 week(s) of notification.
Transfers: Transfer students must exhibit satisfactory academic progress at school most recently attended to be eligible for financial aid.

CONTACT

Taina Savoit, Director of Financial Aid
Box 91740 MSU, Lake Charles, LA 70609-1740
(337) 475-5065

Nicholls State University

Thibodaux, Louisiana
www.nicholls.edu Federal Code: 002005

4-year public university in large town.
Enrollment: 6,246 undergrads, 18% part-time. 1,165 full-time freshmen.
Selectivity: Admits over 75% of applicants.

BASIC COSTS (2008-2009)

Tuition and fees: $3,651; out-of-state residents $9,099.
Room and board: $6,798.

FINANCIAL AID PICTURE (2007-2008)

Students with need: Out of 1,068 full-time freshmen who applied for aid, 548 were judged to have need. Of these, 535 received aid, and 438 had their full need met. Average financial aid package met 94% of need; average scholarship/grant was $4,060; average loan was $2,598. For part-time students, average financial aid package was $5,081.
Students without need: 74 full-time freshmen who did not demonstrate need for aid received scholarships/grants; average award was $1,906. No-need awards available for academics, athletics, state/district residency.
Scholarships offered: 35 full-time freshmen received athletic scholarships; average amount $4,402.

FINANCIAL AID PROCEDURES

Forms required: FAFSA, state aid form, institutional form.
Dates and Deadlines: Priority date 4/17; no closing date. Applicants notified on a rolling basis; must reply within 2 week(s) of notification.
Transfers: Priority date 5/1; no deadline. Applicants notified on a rolling basis.

CONTACT

Director of Financial Aid
PO Box 2004-NSU, Thibodaux, LA 70310
(985) 448-4048

Northwestern State University

Natchitoches, Louisiana
www.nsula.edu Federal Code: 002021

4-year public university in large town.
Enrollment: 7,440 undergrads, 27% part-time. 1,278 full-time freshmen.

Selectivity: Admits over 75% of applicants.

BASIC COSTS (2008-2009)

Tuition and fees: $3,598; out-of-state residents $9,676.
Room and board: $6,272.

FINANCIAL AID PICTURE (2007-2008)

Students with need: Out of 994 full-time freshmen who applied for aid, 849 were judged to have need. Of these, 817 received aid, and 260 had their full need met. Average financial aid package met 51% of need; average scholarship/grant was $3,821; average loan was $4,390. For part-time students, average financial aid package was $4,906.
Students without need: 262 full-time freshmen who did not demonstrate need for aid received scholarships/grants; average award was $4,403. No-need awards available for academics, alumni affiliation, art, athletics, job skills, leadership, minority status, music/drama, religious affiliation, ROTC, state/district residency.
Scholarships offered: 54 full-time freshmen received athletic scholarships; average amount $7,371.
Cumulative student debt: 72% of graduating class had student loans; average debt was $22,045.

FINANCIAL AID PROCEDURES

Forms required: FAFSA, institutional form.
Dates and Deadlines: Priority date 5/1; no closing date. Applicants notified on a rolling basis starting 5/1; must reply within 4 week(s) of notification.
Transfers: No deadline. Applicants notified on a rolling basis starting 5/1; must reply within 4 week(s) of notification.

CONTACT

Misti Adams, Director of Financial Aid
Roy Hall, Room 209, Natchitoches, LA 71497
(800) 823-3008

Nunez Community College

Chalmette, Louisiana
www.nunez.edu Federal Code: 015130

2-year public community and technical college in large town.
Enrollment: 1,046 undergrads, 40% part-time. 74 full-time freshmen.
Selectivity: Open admission; but selective for some programs.

BASIC COSTS (2008-2009)

Tuition and fees: $1,858; out-of-state residents $4,378.
Additional info: Tuition/fee waivers available for minority students.

FINANCIAL AID PICTURE (2007-2008)

Students with need: 89% of average financial aid package awarded as scholarships/grants, 11% awarded as loans/jobs. Need-based aid available for part-time students. Work study available nights.
Scholarships offered: Louisiana TOPS Tech Award.
Additional info: Pell Grants, Stafford Loans, campus workstudy, and tuition waiver scholarships available. Louisiana National Guard tuition exemption, teacher tuition exemption, dependents of injured fire-police tuition waivers.

FINANCIAL AID PROCEDURES

Forms required: FAFSA.
Dates and Deadlines: Priority date 6/1; closing date 8/1. Applicants notified by 9/1; must reply by 10/15.
Transfers: Applicant must supply academic transcripts from every postsecondary school attended before aid is awarded.

CONTACT

Glenda Despenza, Financial Aid Officer
3710 Paris Road, Chalmette, LA 70043
(504) 278-7487

Our Lady of Holy Cross College

New Orleans, Louisiana
www.olhcc.edu Federal Code: 002023

4-year private liberal arts college in very large city, affiliated with Roman Catholic Church.
Enrollment: 610 full-time undergrads.

BASIC COSTS (2009-2010)

Tuition and fees: $10,320.
Per-credit charge: $310.

FINANCIAL AID PICTURE (2008-2009)

Students with need: Need-based aid available for full-time and part-time students. Work study available nights, weekends, and for part-time students.
Students without need: No-need awards available for academics, state/district residency.

FINANCIAL AID PROCEDURES

Forms required: FAFSA.
Dates and Deadlines: Priority date 7/1; no closing date. Applicants notified on a rolling basis starting 5/15; must reply within 4 week(s) of notification.
Transfers: Must reply within 2 week(s) of notification.

CONTACT

Donna Kennedy, Director of Financial Aid
4123 Woodland Drive, New Orleans, LA 70131-7399
(504) 394-7744

Our Lady of the Lake College

Baton Rouge, Louisiana
www.ololcollege.edu Federal Code: 031062

4-year private health science and nursing college in large city, affiliated with Roman Catholic Church.
Enrollment: 1,570 undergrads, 65% part-time. 69 full-time freshmen.
Selectivity: Open admission; but selective for some programs.

BASIC COSTS (2009-2010)

Tuition and fees: $9,217.
Per-credit charge: $280.

FINANCIAL AID PICTURE (2007-2008)

Students with need: 96% of average financial aid package awarded as scholarships/grants, 4% awarded as loans/jobs.

FINANCIAL AID PROCEDURES

Forms required: FAFSA, institutional form.
Dates and Deadlines: Closing date 3/1.

CONTACT

Tiffany MaGee, Director of Financial Aid
7434 Perkins Road, Baton Rouge, LA 70808
(225) 768-1714

Remington College: Baton Rouge

Baton Rouge, Louisiana
www.remingtoncollege.edu/batonrouge Federal Code: E00907

2-year for-profit technical college in large city.
Enrollment: 525 undergrads.
Selectivity: Open admission; but selective for some programs.

BASIC COSTS (2008-2009)

Additional info: Costs of entire programs leading to certificate, associate degree, bachelor's degree range from $13,000 to $38,880; includes books and supplies.

FINANCIAL AID PICTURE

Students with need: Need-based aid available for full-time students. Work study available nights.

Students without need: This college awards aid only to students with need.

FINANCIAL AID PROCEDURES

Forms required: FAFSA.

Dates and Deadlines: No deadline. Applicants notified on a rolling basis; must reply within 1 week(s) of notification.

CONTACT

Bill Moody, National Director of Financial Aid
10551 Coursey Boulevard, Baton Rouge, LA 70816
(225) 236-3200

Remington College: Lafayette

Lafayette, Louisiana
www.remingtoncollege.edu Federal Code: 005203

2-year for-profit junior college in small city.

Enrollment: 207 undergrads. 30 full-time freshmen.

Selectivity: Open admission; but selective for some programs.

BASIC COSTS (2008-2009)

Additional info: Costs of entire programs leading to certificate, associate degree, bachelor's degree range from $14,000 to $39,900; includes books and supplies.

FINANCIAL AID PICTURE (2007-2008)

Students with need: Need-based aid available for full-time students. Work study available nights.

Students without need: This college awards aid only to students with need.

FINANCIAL AID PROCEDURES

Forms required: FAFSA, institutional form.

Dates and Deadlines: No deadline.

CONTACT

Anabel Juarez, Director of Student Finance
303 Rue Louis XIV, Lafayette, LA 70508
(337) 981-4010

St. Joseph Seminary College

St. Benedict, Louisiana
www.sjasc.edu Federal Code: 002027

4-year private liberal arts and seminary college for men in rural community, affiliated with Roman Catholic Church.

Enrollment: 76 undergrads. 6 full-time freshmen.

Selectivity: Open admission; but selective for some programs.

BASIC COSTS (2009-2010)

Tuition and fees: $13,082.

Per-credit charge: $175.

Room and board: $11,168.

FINANCIAL AID PICTURE

Students with need: Need-based aid available for full-time and part-time students.

Students without need: No-need awards available for academics, leadership.

FINANCIAL AID PROCEDURES

Forms required: FAFSA.

Dates and Deadlines: Priority date 3/15; no closing date. Applicants notified on a rolling basis starting 7/1; must reply within 4 week(s) of notification.

Transfers: Closing date 5/1.

CONTACT

George Binder, Director of Student Financial Aid
75376 River Road, St. Benedict, LA 70457-9990
(985) 867-2248

School of Urban Missions: New Orleans

New Orleans, Louisiana
www.sum.edu Federal Code: 037524

4-year private Bible college in very large city, affiliated with Assemblies of God, Church of God in Christ.

Enrollment: 37 undergrads, 46% part-time. 7 full-time freshmen.

Selectivity: Admits over 75% of applicants.

BASIC COSTS (2009-2010)

Tuition and fees: $7,155.

Per-credit charge: $235.

Room only: $2,400.

FINANCIAL AID PICTURE (2007-2008)

Students with need: 72% of average financial aid package awarded as scholarships/grants, 28% awarded as loans/jobs. Need-based aid available for part-time students.

Students without need: No-need awards available for academics, leadership, religious affiliation.

FINANCIAL AID PROCEDURES

Forms required: FAFSA, institutional form.

Dates and Deadlines: No deadline.

Transfers: No deadline. Applicants notified on a rolling basis.

CONTACT

Dave Wallace, Financial Aid Director
511 Westbank Expressway, Gretna, LA 70053-3677
(510) 567-6174

South Louisiana Community College

Lafayette, Louisiana
www.southlouisiana.edu

2-year public community college in small city.

Enrollment: 1,711 undergrads, 45% part-time. 279 full-time freshmen.

Selectivity: Open admission; but selective for some programs.

BASIC COSTS (2008-2009)

Tuition and fees: $1,862; out-of-state residents $4,022.

FINANCIAL AID PICTURE

Students with need: Need-based aid available for full-time and part-time students.

FINANCIAL AID PROCEDURES

Forms required: FAFSA, institutional form.

Dates and Deadlines: Priority date 7/1; no closing date.

CONTACT

Shonda Rosinski, Director of Financial Aid
320 Devalcourt, Lafayette, LA 70506-4124

Southeastern Louisiana University

Hammond, Louisiana
www.selu.edu Federal Code: 002024

4-year public university in large town.
Enrollment: 12,921 undergrads, 14% part-time. 2,536 full-time freshmen.
Selectivity: Admits over 75% of applicants.

BASIC COSTS (2008-2009)

Tuition and fees: $3,721; out-of-state residents $9,721.
Per-credit charge: $99; out-of-state residents $349.
Room and board: $6,220.

FINANCIAL AID PICTURE (2007-2008)

Students with need: Out of 2,110 full-time freshmen who applied for aid, 1,297 were judged to have need. Of these, 1,151 received aid, and 308 had their full need met. For part-time students, average financial aid package was $4,450.
Students without need: 183 full-time freshmen who did not demonstrate need for aid received scholarships/grants; average award was $1,592. No-need awards available for academics, athletics, job skills, leadership, music/drama, state/district residency.
Scholarships offered: ***Merit:*** Various scholarships; $1,000-$3,500; any student admitted with 24 ACT and 3.0 GPA on a seven-semester transcript qualifies for scholarship. On-campus housing scholarships; range from half room award to full room award; based on ACT score and GPA. Presidential Honors Scholarship; $2,500-$3,500 plus on-campus housing and meals (full shared housing award and pack meal plan); 30 ACT, 3.0 GPA. ***Athletic:*** 34 full-time freshmen received athletic scholarships; average amount $4,609.
Cumulative student debt: 57% of graduating class had student loans; average debt was $18,741.

FINANCIAL AID PROCEDURES

Forms required: FAFSA, institutional form.
Dates and Deadlines: Priority date 5/1; no closing date. Applicants notified on a rolling basis starting 3/1; must reply within 2 week(s) of notification.
Transfers: Applicants notified on a rolling basis starting 3/1; must reply within 2 week(s) of notification. Financial aid is available for transfer students, including those admitted on probation.

CONTACT

Jeff Rhodes, Dean of Enrollment Management
SLU 10752, Hammond, LA 70402
(985) 549-2244

Southern University and Agricultural and Mechanical College

Baton Rouge, Louisiana
www.subr.edu Federal Code: 002025

4-year public university in large city.
Enrollment: 6,382 undergrads, 10% part-time. 1,035 full-time freshmen.
Selectivity: Admits 50 to 75% of applicants.

BASIC COSTS (2008-2009)

Tuition and fees: $3,906; out-of-state residents $9,600.
Room and board: $5,558.

FINANCIAL AID PICTURE (2007-2008)

Students with need: Need-based aid available for full-time students.
Students without need: No-need awards available for academics, athletics, ROTC, state/district résidency.

FINANCIAL AID PROCEDURES

Forms required: FAFSA.
Dates and Deadlines: Priority date 1/31; closing date 3/30. Applicants notified on a rolling basis starting 5/1; must reply within 3 week(s) of notification.
Transfers: Closing date 5/31. Applicants notified on a rolling basis starting 5/31; must reply within 3 week(s) of notification.

CONTACT

Ursula Shorty, Director of Financial Aid
T.H. Harris Hall, Baton Rouge, LA 70813
(225) 771-2790

Southern University at New Orleans

New Orleans, Louisiana
www.suno.edu Federal Code: 002026

4-year public university in large city.
Enrollment: 2,603 undergrads.
Selectivity: Open admission.

BASIC COSTS (2008-2009)

Tuition and fees: $3,002; out-of-state residents $6,742.

FINANCIAL AID PICTURE

Students with need: Need-based aid available for full-time and part-time students.
Students without need: This college awards aid only to students with need.

FINANCIAL AID PROCEDURES

Forms required: FAFSA.
Dates and Deadlines: Closing date 4/1. Applicants notified by 5/15; must reply within 1 week(s) of notification.

CONTACT

Kathy Woods, Director of Financial Aid
6801 Press Drive, New Orleans, LA 70126
(504) 286-5263

Tulane University

New Orleans, Louisiana Federal Code: 002029
www.tulane.edu CSS Code: 6832

4-year private university in very large city.
Enrollment: 6,692 undergrads, 22% part-time. 1,639 full-time freshmen.
Selectivity: Admits less than 50% of applicants.

BASIC COSTS (2009-2010)

Tuition and fees: $38,664.
Per-credit charge: $1,571.
Room and board: $9,296.

FINANCIAL AID PICTURE (2007-2008)

Students with need: Out of 801 full-time freshmen who applied for aid, 584 were judged to have need. Of these, 582 received aid, and 440 had their full need met. Average financial aid package met 95% of need; average scholarship/grant was $22,465; average loan was $5,630. For part-time students, average financial aid package was $8,851.
Students without need: 423 full-time freshmen who did not demonstrate need for aid received scholarships/grants; average award was $20,323. No-need awards available for academics, athletics, leadership, music/drama, state/district residency.
Scholarships offered: ***Merit:*** Dean's Honor Scholarship; full-tuition. Distinguished Scholars Award; up to $18,000. Founders Scholarship; up to $16,000. Urban Scholars Award; full-tuition. ***Athletic:*** 20 full-time freshmen received athletic scholarships; average amount $38,075.
Cumulative student debt: 48% of graduating class had student loans; average debt was $23,819.

Additional info: Application deadline for merit scholarships December 1.

FINANCIAL AID PROCEDURES

Forms required: FAFSA, CSS PROFILE.

Dates and Deadlines: Priority date 2/1; no closing date. Applicants notified on a rolling basis starting 2/1; must reply by 5/1 or within 2 week(s) of notification.

Transfers: Applicants notified on a rolling basis starting 2/1; must reply by 5/1 or within 2 week(s) of notification.

CONTACT

Michael Goodman, Associate Vice President for Financial Aid
6823 St. Charles Avenue, New Orleans, LA 70118-5680
(504) 865-5723

University of Louisiana at Lafayette

Lafayette, Louisiana
www.louisiana.edu Federal Code: 002031

4-year public university in small city.

Enrollment: 14,240 undergrads, 14% part-time. 2,710 full-time freshmen.

Selectivity: Admits 50 to 75% of applicants.

BASIC COSTS (2008-2009)

Tuition and fees: $3,604; out-of-state residents $9,784.

Per-credit charge: $100; out-of-state residents $358.

Room and board: $4,200.

FINANCIAL AID PICTURE (2007-2008)

Students with need: Out of 2,393 full-time freshmen who applied for aid, 1,380 were judged to have need. Of these, 1,344 received aid, and 315 had their full need met. Average financial aid package met 68% of need; average scholarship/grant was $5,285; average loan was $3,081. For part-time students, average financial aid package was $4,425.

Students without need: This college awards aid only to students with need.

Scholarships offered: 64 full-time freshmen received athletic scholarships; average amount $5,173.

FINANCIAL AID PROCEDURES

Forms required: FAFSA, institutional form.

Dates and Deadlines: Priority date 5/1; no closing date. Applicants notified on a rolling basis starting 4/1; must reply within 2 week(s) of notification.

CONTACT

Cindy Perez, Director, Student Financial Aid
Box 41210, Lafayette, LA 70504-1210
(337) 482-6506

University of Louisiana at Monroe

Monroe, Louisiana
www.ulm.edu Federal Code: 002020

4-year public university in small city.

Enrollment: 7,424 undergrads, 23% part-time. 1,200 full-time freshmen.

Selectivity: Admits over 75% of applicants.

BASIC COSTS (2008-2009)

Tuition and fees: $3,791; out-of-state residents $8,734.

Room and board: $4,350.

FINANCIAL AID PICTURE

Students with need: Need-based aid available for full-time and part-time students.

Students without need: No-need awards available for academics, alumni affiliation, art, athletics, job skills, leadership, minority status, music/drama, religious affiliation, ROTC, state/district residency.

FINANCIAL AID PROCEDURES

Forms required: FAFSA.

Dates and Deadlines: Priority date 4/1; no closing date. Applicants notified on a rolling basis starting 6/1; must reply within 2 week(s) of notification.

CONTACT

Teri Smith, Director of Financial Aid
700 University Avenue, Monroe, LA 71209-1160
(318) 342-5320

University of New Orleans

New Orleans, Louisiana
www.uno.edu Federal Code: 002015

4-year public university in very large city.

Enrollment: 8,628 undergrads, 24% part-time. 1,210 full-time freshmen.

Selectivity: Admits 50 to 75% of applicants.

BASIC COSTS (2008-2009)

Tuition and fees: $4,306; out-of-state residents $11,702.

Per-credit charge: $145; out-of-state residents $454.

Room and board: $6,130.

FINANCIAL AID PICTURE (2008-2009)

Students with need: Out of 838 full-time freshmen who applied for aid, 744 were judged to have need. Of these, 670 received aid, and 163 had their full need met. Average financial aid package met 74% of need; average scholarship/grant was $6,690; average loan was $3,212. For part-time students, average financial aid package was $7,965.

Students without need: 335 full-time freshmen who did not demonstrate need for aid received scholarships/grants; average award was $1,510. No-need awards available for academics, athletics.

Scholarships offered: 28 full-time freshmen received athletic scholarships; average amount $8,612.

Cumulative student debt: 9% of graduating class had student loans; average debt was $14,911.

Additional info: Students in good academic and financial standing eligible to participate in Extended Payment Plan option.

FINANCIAL AID PROCEDURES

Forms required: FAFSA.

Dates and Deadlines: Priority date 5/15; no closing date. Applicants notified on a rolling basis starting 4/20; must reply within 4 week(s) of notification.

Transfers: Mid-year transfers must submit financial aid transcript from all post-secondary schools attended. Others submit NSLDS.

CONTACT

Emily London-Jones, Director of Student Financial Aid
Administration Building Room 103, New Orleans, LA 70148
(504) 280-6603

Xavier University of Louisiana

New Orleans, Louisiana
www.xula.edu Federal Code: 002032

4-year private university in very large city, affiliated with Roman Catholic Church.

Enrollment: 2,435 undergrads, 4% part-time. 663 full-time freshmen.

Selectivity: Admits 50 to 75% of applicants.

BASIC COSTS (2008-2009)

Tuition and fees: $15,000.

Room and board: $6,800.

FINANCIAL AID PICTURE (2007-2008)

Students with need: Out of 639 full-time freshmen who applied for aid, 584 were judged to have need. Of these, 578 received aid, and 162 had their full need met. Average financial aid package met 86% of need; average scholarship/grant was $5,578; average loan was $3,645. For part-time students, average financial aid package was $11,323.

Students without need: 27 full-time freshmen who did not demonstrate need for aid received scholarships/grants; average award was $7,546. No-need awards available for music/drama.

Scholarships offered: 15 full-time freshmen received athletic scholarships; average amount $13,750.

Cumulative student debt: 70% of graduating class had student loans; average debt was $25,227.

FINANCIAL AID PROCEDURES

Forms required: FAFSA.

Dates and Deadlines: Priority date 1/1; no closing date. Applicants notified on a rolling basis starting 4/1; must reply within 2 week(s) of notification.

CONTACT

Mildred Higgins, Director of Financial Aid
1 Drexel Drive, New Orleans, LA 70125-1098
(504) 520-7517

Maine

Bates College

Lewiston, Maine — Federal Code: 002036
www.bates.edu — CSS Code: 3076

4-year private liberal arts college in large town.

Enrollment: 1,776 undergrads. 521 full-time freshmen.

Selectivity: Admits less than 50% of applicants. GED not accepted.

BASIC COSTS (2008-2009)

Comprehensive fee: $49,350.

FINANCIAL AID PICTURE (2008-2009)

Students with need: Out of 287 full-time freshmen who applied for aid, 238 were judged to have need. Of these, 227 received aid, and 211 had their full need met. Average financial aid package met 100% of need; average scholarship/grant was $31,175; average loan was $3,786.

Students without need: This college awards aid only to students with need.

Cumulative student debt: 40% of graduating class had student loans; average debt was $18,785.

Additional info: Priority date for filing required financial aid forms for early decision students is 11/15.

FINANCIAL AID PROCEDURES

Forms required: FAFSA, CSS PROFILE.

Dates and Deadlines: Closing date 2/1. Applicants notified by 4/1; must reply by 5/1.

Transfers: Closing date 1/1. Applicants notified by 4/15; must reply by 5/15.

CONTACT

Wendy Glass, Acting Director of Student Financial Services
23 Campus Avenue, Lindholm House, Lewiston, ME 04240-9917
(207) 786-6096

Bowdoin College

Brunswick, Maine — Federal Code: 002038
www.bowdoin.edu — CSS Code: 3089

4-year private liberal arts college in large town.

Enrollment: 1,716 undergrads. 476 full-time freshmen.

Selectivity: Admits less than 50% of applicants. GED not accepted.

BASIC COSTS (2008-2009)

Tuition and fees: $38,190.

Room and board: $10,380.

FINANCIAL AID PICTURE (2007-2008)

Students with need: Out of 268 full-time freshmen who applied for aid, 198 were judged to have need. Of these, 198 received aid, and 198 had their full need met. Average financial aid package met 100% of need; average scholarship/grant was $28,359; average loan was $3,622.

Students without need: 19 full-time freshmen who did not demonstrate need for aid received scholarships/grants; average award was $1,000. No-need awards available for academics, leadership.

Scholarships offered: National Merit Scholarships average $1,000 per year.

Additional info: Regardless of financial circumstances, students admitted will receive money they need to attend. International students for regular admission must submit their financial aid applications by January 1st.

FINANCIAL AID PROCEDURES

Forms required: FAFSA, CSS PROFILE.

Dates and Deadlines: Closing date 2/15. Applicants notified by 4/5; must reply by 5/1 or within 1 week(s) of notification.

Transfers: Closing date 3/1. Applicants notified by 5/1; must reply by 6/1 or within 1 week(s) of notification. Financial aid usually not available for transfer students. Early Decision applicants must submit financial aid applications by November 15 (ED I) and January 1 (ED II).

CONTACT

Stephen Joyce, Director of Student Aid
5000 College Station, Brunswick, ME 04011-8441
(207) 725-3273

Central Maine Community College

Auburn, Maine
www.cmcc.edu — Federal Code: 005276

2-year public community and technical college in small city.

Enrollment: 2,018 undergrads, 43% part-time. 501 full-time freshmen.

Selectivity: Open admission; but selective for some programs.

BASIC COSTS (2008-2009)

Tuition and fees: $3,192; out-of-state residents $5,652.

Per-credit charge: $82; out-of-state residents $164.

Room and board: $6,820.

Additional info: Additional lab and technology fees may apply to specific programs and courses. Tuition/fee waivers available for minority students.

FINANCIAL AID PICTURE (2008-2009)

Students with need: Need-based aid available for full-time and part-time students. Work study available nights, weekends, and for part-time students.

Students without need: This college awards aid only to students with need.

Additional info: Tuition and/or fee waivers may be available to orphans, Native Americans, fire fighters, police, disabled veterans, dependents or survivors of veterans killed in line of duty.

FINANCIAL AID PROCEDURES

Forms required: FAFSA, institutional form.

Dates and Deadlines: Priority date 5/8; no closing date. Applicants notified on a rolling basis starting 3/15; must reply within 2 week(s) of notification.

Transfers: Priority date 8/1; no deadline. Applicants notified on a rolling basis starting 1/15; must reply within 2 week(s) of notification.

CONTACT

Monique Schreiber, Financial Aid Director
1250 Turner Street, Auburn, ME 04210
(207) 755-5269

Central Maine Medical Center College of Nursing and Health Professions

Lewiston, Maine
www.cmmcson.edu Federal Code: 006305

2-year private nursing college in large town.
Enrollment: 122 undergrads, 79% part-time. 22 full-time freshmen.

BASIC COSTS (2009-2010)
Tuition and fees: $7,638.
Per-credit charge: $182.
Room only: $1,500.

FINANCIAL AID PICTURE (2007-2008)
Students with need: Out of 22 full-time freshmen who applied for aid, 21 were judged to have need. Of these, 21 received aid, and 16 had their full need met. Average financial aid package met 28% of need; average scholarship/grant was $6,800; average loan was $4,000. For part-time students, average financial aid package was $8,300.
Students without need: This college awards aid only to students with need.

FINANCIAL AID PROCEDURES
Forms required: FAFSA, institutional form.
Dates and Deadlines: Priority date 5/1; closing date 7/1. Applicants notified on a rolling basis starting 4/1; must reply within 2 week(s) of notification.

CONTACT

Keith Bourgault, Controller
70 Middle Street, Lewiston, ME 04240
(207) 795-2270

Colby College

Waterville, Maine Federal Code: 002039
www.colby.edu CSS Code: 3280

4-year private liberal arts college in large town.
Enrollment: 1,846 undergrads. 482 full-time freshmen.
Selectivity: Admits less than 50% of applicants.

BASIC COSTS (2008-2009)
Comprehensive fee: $48,520.

FINANCIAL AID PICTURE (2008-2009)
Students with need: Out of 263 full-time freshmen who applied for aid, 191 were judged to have need. Of these, 191 received aid, and 191 had their full need met. Average financial aid package met 100% of need; average scholarship/grant was $30,303; average loan was $512.
Students without need: This college awards aid only to students with need.
Cumulative student debt: 42% of graduating class had student loans; average debt was $19,200.
Additional info: Institutional loans have been replaced with institutional grants.

FINANCIAL AID PROCEDURES
Forms required: FAFSA, CSS PROFILE.
Dates and Deadlines: Closing date 2/1. Applicants notified by 4/1; must reply by 5/1.
Transfers: Priority date 2/1; closing date 3/1. Must reply within 2 week(s) of notification.

CONTACT

Lucia Whittelsey, Director of Financial Aid
4800 Mayflower Hill, Waterville, ME 04901-8848
(800) 723-3032

College of the Atlantic

Bar Harbor, Maine
www.coa.edu Federal Code: 011385

4-year private liberal arts college in small town.
Enrollment: 312 undergrads, 4% part-time. 69 full-time freshmen.
Selectivity: Admits 50 to 75% of applicants.

BASIC COSTS (2009-2010)
Tuition and fees: $33,060.
Per-credit charge: $1,086.
Room and board: $8,490.

FINANCIAL AID PICTURE (2008-2009)
Students with need: Out of 58 full-time freshmen who applied for aid, 55 were judged to have need. Of these, 55 received aid, and 29 had their full need met. Average financial aid package met 96% of need; average scholarship/grant was $28,949; average loan was $4,031. For part-time students, average financial aid package was $15,561.
Students without need: This college awards aid only to students with need.
Cumulative student debt: 56% of graduating class had student loans; average debt was $23,762.

FINANCIAL AID PROCEDURES
Forms required: FAFSA, institutional form.
Dates and Deadlines: Closing date 2/15. Applicants notified by 4/1; must reply by 5/1.
Transfers: Priority date 2/15. Applicants notified by 4/1; must reply by 5/1. FAFSA must be filed by 5/1 for Maine residents to be eligible for Maine state grant.

CONTACT

Bruce Hazam, Director of Financial Aid
105 Eden Street, Bar Harbor, ME 04609
(207) 288-5015

Eastern Maine Community College

Bangor, Maine
www.emcc.edu Federal Code: 005277

2-year public community and technical college in large town.
Enrollment: 1,607 undergrads.
Selectivity: Open admission; but selective for some programs.

BASIC COSTS (2008-2009)
Tuition and fees: $3,255; out-of-state residents $5,715.
Per-credit charge: $82; out-of-state residents $164.
Room and board: $6,360.
Additional info: Additional lab and technology fees may apply to specific programs and courses. Tuition/fee waivers available for minority students.

FINANCIAL AID PICTURE (2007-2008)
Students with need: Need-based aid available for full-time and part-time students. Work study available nights, weekends, and for part-time students.
Students without need: This college awards aid only to students with need.

FINANCIAL AID PROCEDURES

Forms required: FAFSA, institutional form.

Dates and Deadlines: Priority date 5/1; no closing date. Applicants notified on a rolling basis starting 5/1; must reply within 3 week(s) of notification.

CONTACT

Candace Ward, Registrar/Financial Aid Director
354 Hogan Road, Bangor, ME 04401
(207) 974-4625

Husson University

Bangor, Maine
www.husson.edu Federal Code: 002043

4-year private business and health science college in large town.

Enrollment: 2,196 undergrads, 17% part-time. 479 full-time freshmen.

Selectivity: Admits over 75% of applicants.

BASIC COSTS (2009-2010)

Tuition and fees: $12,990.

Per-credit charge: $423.

Room and board: $6,994.

FINANCIAL AID PICTURE (2008-2009)

Students with need: Average financial aid package met 77% of need; average scholarship/grant was $8,801; average loan was $3,265. For part-time students, average financial aid package was $5,446.

Students without need: No-need awards available for academics, leadership.

Scholarships offered: Scholarships awarded based on academics and leadership, ranging from $1,000 to $4,000 renewable up to four years.

FINANCIAL AID PROCEDURES

Forms required: FAFSA.

Dates and Deadlines: Priority date 4/15; no closing date. Applicants notified on a rolling basis starting 4/1; must reply by 5/1 or within 2 week(s) of notification.

Transfers: No deadline. Applicants notified on a rolling basis starting 2/20.

CONTACT

Linda Conant, Director of Financial Aid
One College Circle, Bangor, ME 04401-2999
(207) 941-7156

Kennebec Valley Community College

Fairfield, Maine
www.kvcc.me.edu Federal Code: 009826

2-year public community and technical college in small town.

Enrollment: 1,495 undergrads, 60% part-time. 166 full-time freshmen.

Selectivity: Open admission; but selective for some programs.

BASIC COSTS (2008-2009)

Tuition and fees: $3,012; out-of-state residents $5,472.

Per-credit charge: $82; out-of-state residents $164.

Additional info: Additional lab and technology fees apply to specific programs and courses.

FINANCIAL AID PICTURE (2007-2008)

Students with need: Out of 154 full-time freshmen who applied for aid, 128 were judged to have need. Of these, 104 received aid, and 7 had their full need met. Average financial aid package met 41% of need; average scholarship/grant was $3,880; average loan was $2,458. For part-time students, average financial aid package was $4,015.

Students without need: 18 full-time freshmen who did not demonstrate need for aid received scholarships/grants; average award was $2,590.

FINANCIAL AID PROCEDURES

Forms required: FAFSA, institutional form.

Dates and Deadlines: Priority date 4/1; no closing date. Applicants notified on a rolling basis starting 5/1.

CONTACT

Anne Connors, Director of Financial Aid
92 Western Avenue, Fairfield, ME 04937-1367
(207) 453-5121

Maine College of Art

Portland, Maine
www.meca.edu Federal Code: 011673

4-year private visual arts college in small city.

Enrollment: 341 undergrads, 5% part-time. 103 full-time freshmen.

Selectivity: Admits over 75% of applicants.

BASIC COSTS (2009-2010)

Tuition and fees: $28,090.

Per-credit charge: $1,148.

Room and board: $9,875.

Additional info: Studio fees vary per class.

FINANCIAL AID PICTURE (2008-2009)

Students with need: Need-based aid available for full-time and part-time students. Work study available nights, weekends, and for part-time students.

Students without need: No-need awards available for academics, art.

FINANCIAL AID PROCEDURES

Forms required: FAFSA.

Dates and Deadlines: Priority date 3/1, no closing date. Applicants notified on a rolling basis starting 2/15; must reply within 2 week(s) of notification.

Transfers: Closing date 4/15. Applicants notified on a rolling basis starting 2/15; must reply within 2 week(s) of notification.

CONTACT

Adrienne Amari, Director of Financial Aid
522 Congress Street, Portland, ME 04101
(207) 699-5073

Maine Maritime Academy

Castine, Maine
www.mainemaritime.edu Federal Code: 002044

4-year public maritime college in rural community.

Enrollment: 868 undergrads.

Selectivity: Admits 50 to 75% of applicants.

BASIC COSTS (2008-2009)

Tuition and fees: $9,600; out-of-district residents $13,350; out-of-state residents $16,900.

Room and board: $8,000.

Additional info: Fee of $3,000 for U.S. Coast Guard licensing programs.

FINANCIAL AID PICTURE

Students with need: Need-based aid available for full-time and part-time students. Work study available nights, weekends, and for part-time students.

Students without need: No-need awards available for academics, leadership, ROTC, state/district residency.

FINANCIAL AID PROCEDURES

Forms required: FAFSA, institutional form.

Dates and Deadlines: Priority date 4/15; no closing date. Applicants notified on a rolling basis starting 3/1; must reply within 4 week(s) of notification.

Transfers: Priority date 6/1.

CONTACT
Kathy Heath, Financial Aid Officer
66 Pleasant Street, Castine, ME 04420
(207) 326-2339

New England School of Communications
Bangor, Maine
www.nescom.edu Federal Code: 023471

4-year private college of communications in small city.
Enrollment: 440 undergrads.
Selectivity: Admits 50 to 75% of applicants.

BASIC COSTS (2009-2010)
Tuition and fees: $11,200.
Per-credit charge: $360.
Room and board: $6,994.
Additional info: Additional cost of $160 for FireWire hard drive.

FINANCIAL AID PICTURE (2007-2008)
Students with need: 29% of average financial aid package awarded as scholarships/grants, 71% awarded as loans/jobs. Need-based aid available for part-time students.
Students without need: No-need awards available for academics, leadership.
Scholarships offered: Scholarships are merit based for second semester.

FINANCIAL AID PROCEDURES
Forms required: FAFSA, institutional form.
Dates and Deadlines: Priority date 4/15; no closing date. Applicants notified on a rolling basis starting 2/1; must reply by 8/15.
Transfers: No deadline. Applicants notified on a rolling basis starting 2/15; must reply within 4 week(s) of notification.

CONTACT
Nicole Rediker, Director of Financial Aid
One College Circle, Bangor, ME 04401
(207) 941-7176

Northern Maine Community College
Presque Isle, Maine
www.nmcc.edu Federal Code: 005760

2-year public technical college in small town.
Enrollment: 840 undergrads.

BASIC COSTS (2008-2009)
Tuition and fees: $3,121; out-of-state residents $5,581.
Per-credit charge: $82; out-of-state residents $164.
Room and board: $5,500.
Additional info: Additional lab and technology fees may apply to specific programs and courses. Tuition/fee waivers available for minority students.

FINANCIAL AID PICTURE
Students with need: Need-based aid available for full-time and part-time students.

FINANCIAL AID PROCEDURES
Forms required: FAFSA, institutional form.
Dates and Deadlines: Priority date 5/1; no closing date. Applicants notified on a rolling basis starting 4/15; must reply within 2 week(s) of notification.

CONTACT
Gail Gagnon, Financial Aid Coordinator
33 Edgemont Drive, Presque Isle, ME 04769
(207) 768-2790

St. Joseph's College
Standish, Maine
www.sjcme.edu Federal Code: 002051

4-year private liberal arts college in small town, affiliated with Roman Catholic Church.
Enrollment: 1,066 undergrads.
Selectivity: Admits over 75% of applicants.

BASIC COSTS (2008-2009)
Tuition and fees: $25,049.
Per-credit charge: $800.
Room and board: $9,950.

FINANCIAL AID PICTURE (2008-2009)
Students with need: Need-based aid available for full-time and part-time students. Work study available nights, weekends, and for part-time students.
Students without need: No-need awards available for academics, leadership.

FINANCIAL AID PROCEDURES
Forms required: FAFSA, institutional form.
Dates and Deadlines: Priority date 3/1; no closing date. Applicants notified on a rolling basis starting 3/1; must reply within 3 week(s) of notification.

CONTACT
Andrea Cross, Associate Dean for Financial Aid
278 Whites Bridge Road, Standish, ME 04084-5263
(800) 752-1266

Southern Maine Community College
South Portland, Maine
www.smccme.edu Federal Code: 005525

2-year public community and technical college in large town.
Enrollment: 5,235 undergrads, 48% part-time.
Selectivity: Open admission; but selective for some programs.

BASIC COSTS (2008-2009)
Tuition and fees: $3,167; out-of-state residents $5,627.
Per-credit charge: $82; out-of-state residents $164.
Room and board: $7,746.
Additional info: Additional lab and technology fees may apply to specific programs and courses.

FINANCIAL AID PICTURE
Students with need: Need-based aid available for full-time and part-time students. Work study available nights, weekends, and for part-time students.
Students without need: This college awards aid only to students with need.

FINANCIAL AID PROCEDURES
Forms required: FAFSA.
Dates and Deadlines: Priority date 3/30; no closing date. Applicants notified on a rolling basis; must reply by 5/1 or within 2 week(s) of notification.

CONTACT
Michel Lussier, Director of Financial Aid, Transfer and Employment Services
2 Fort Road, South Portland, ME 04106
(207) 741-5518

Thomas College
Waterville, Maine
www.thomas.edu Federal Code: 002052

4-year private business and liberal arts college in large town.
Enrollment: 737 undergrads, 14% part-time. 209 full-time freshmen.
Selectivity: Admits over 75% of applicants.

BASIC COSTS (2008-2009)
Tuition and fees: $19,750.
Per-credit charge: $801.
Room and board: $8,170.

FINANCIAL AID PICTURE (2008-2009)
Students with need: Out of 204 full-time freshmen who applied for aid, 198 were judged to have need. Of these, 198 received aid, and 39 had their full need met. Average financial aid package met 85% of need; average scholarship/grant was $13,240; average loan was $4,189. For part-time students, average financial aid package was $8,902.
Students without need: 22 full-time freshmen who did not demonstrate need for aid received scholarships/grants; average award was $5,364. No-need awards available for academics, leadership, state/district residency.
Cumulative student debt: 93% of graduating class had student loans; average debt was $31,334.

FINANCIAL AID PROCEDURES
Forms required: FAFSA.
Dates and Deadlines: Priority date 2/15; no closing date. Applicants notified on a rolling basis starting 3/15; must reply within 2 week(s) of notification.

CONTACT
Jeannine Bosse, Director of Student Financial Services
180 West River Road, Waterville, ME 04901
(207) 859-1105

Unity College
Unity, Maine
www.unity.edu Federal Code: 006858

4-year private liberal arts college in rural community.
Enrollment: 544 undergrads, 2% part-time. 165 full-time freshmen.
Selectivity: Admits 50 to 75% of applicants.

BASIC COSTS (2008-2009)
Tuition and fees: $20,750.
Room and board: $7,680.

FINANCIAL AID PICTURE (2008-2009)
Students with need: Out of 154 full-time freshmen who applied for aid, 128 were judged to have need. Of these, 128 received aid, and 19 had their full need met. Average financial aid package met 77% of need; average scholarship/grant was $11,047; average loan was $4,878. For part-time students, average financial aid package was $11,648.
Students without need: 34 full-time freshmen who did not demonstrate need for aid received scholarships/grants; average award was $9,461. No-need awards available for academics, leadership, minority status.

FINANCIAL AID PROCEDURES
Forms required: FAFSA.
Dates and Deadlines: Priority date 3/1; no closing date. Applicants notified on a rolling basis starting 3/10; must reply within 2 week(s) of notification.

CONTACT
Rand Newell, Director of Financial Aid
P.O. 532, Unity, ME 04988-0532
(207) 948-3131 ext. 235

University of Maine
Orono, Maine
www.umaine.edu Federal Code: 002053

4-year public university in large town.
Enrollment: 8,868 undergrads, 9% part-time. 1,996 full-time freshmen.
Selectivity: Admits over 75% of applicants.

BASIC COSTS (2008-2009)
Tuition and fees: $9,100; out-of-state residents $22,510.
Per-credit charge: $239; out-of-state residents $686.
Room and board: $8,008.

FINANCIAL AID PICTURE (2008-2009)
Students with need: Need-based aid available for full-time and part-time students. Work study available nights, weekends, and for part-time students.
Students without need: No-need awards available for academics, alumni affiliation, art, athletics, job skills, leadership, minority status, music/drama, religious affiliation, ROTC, state/district residency.
Scholarships offered: Academic merit scholarships range in value from $1,000 to full tuition. All awards are renewable for up to eight (8) consecutive semesters, based upon academic performance. Top Scholar Awards and Tuition Scholarships pay full resident tuition or full nonresident differential per semester each academic year.
Additional info: Financial aid is available for students entering in the spring.

FINANCIAL AID PROCEDURES
Forms required: FAFSA.
Dates and Deadlines: Priority date 3/1; no closing date. Applicants notified on a rolling basis starting 3/15; must reply by 5/1 or within 2 week(s) of notification.

CONTACT
Peggy Crawford, Director of Student Financial Aid
5713 Chadbourne Hall, Orono, ME 04469-5713
(207) 581-1324

University of Maine at Augusta
Augusta, Maine
www.uma.edu Federal Code: 006760

4-year public university in large town.
Enrollment: 4,369 undergrads, 62% part-time. 345 full-time freshmen.
Selectivity: Open admission; but selective for some programs.

BASIC COSTS (2008-2009)
Tuition and fees: $6,495; out-of-state residents $14,595.
Per-credit charge: $190; out-of-state residents $460.
Additional info: New England Regional Student Program tuition is $8,580.

FINANCIAL AID PICTURE (2008-2009)
Students with need: Out of 288 full-time freshmen who applied for aid, 253 were judged to have need. Of these, 245 received aid, and 33 had their full need met. Average financial aid package met 63% of need; average scholarship/grant was $4,491; average loan was $2,941. For part-time students, average financial aid package was $4,577.
Students without need: 22 full-time freshmen who did not demonstrate need for aid received scholarships/grants; average award was $3,978. No-need awards available for academics, athletics, leadership, music/drama, state/district residency.
Scholarships offered: 4 full-time freshmen received athletic scholarships; average amount $2,500.
Cumulative student debt: 68% of graduating class had student loans; average debt was $15,842.

FINANCIAL AID PROCEDURES
Forms required: FAFSA.

Dates and Deadlines: Priority date 3/1; no closing date. Applicants notified on a rolling basis starting 3/15; must reply within 2 week(s) of notification.

CONTACT

Sherry McCollett, Director of Financial Aid
46 University Drive, Augusta, ME 04330
(207) 621-3455

University of Maine at Farmington

Farmington, Maine
www.farmington.edu Federal Code: 002040

4-year public liberal arts and teachers college in small town.
Enrollment: 2,145 undergrads, 5% part-time. 479 full-time freshmen.
Selectivity: Admits 50 to 75% of applicants.

BASIC COSTS (2008-2009)

Tuition and fees: $7,976; out-of-state residents $15,752.
Per-credit charge: $228; out-of-state residents $471.
Room and board: $7,158.
Additional info: New England Regional Student Program tuition and fees: $10,677. Tuition/fee waivers available for minority students.

FINANCIAL AID PICTURE (2007-2008)

Students with need: Out of 425 full-time freshmen who applied for aid, 379 were judged to have need. Of these, 360 received aid, and 36 had their full need met. Average financial aid package met 72% of need; average scholarship/grant was $4,935; average loan was $3,536. For part-time students, average financial aid package was $6,421.
Students without need: 13 full-time freshmen who did not demonstrate need for aid received scholarships/grants; average award was $1,738. No-need awards available for academics, leadership, minority status, state/district residency.
Scholarships offered: Presidential Scholarships; $2,000 renewable annually; for non-residents graduating in top half of high school class.
Cumulative student debt: 81% of graduating class had student loans; average debt was $19,490.
Additional info: FAFSA must arrive at Federal processor by 3/1.

FINANCIAL AID PROCEDURES

Forms required: FAFSA.
Dates and Deadlines: Priority date 3/1; no closing date. Applicants notified on a rolling basis starting 3/15; must reply within 2 week(s) of notification.

CONTACT

Ronald Milliken, Director of Financial Aid
246 Main Street, Farmington, ME 04938
(207) 778-7100

University of Maine at Fort Kent

Fort Kent, Maine
www.umfk.maine.edu Federal Code: 002041

4-year public university in small town.
Enrollment: 784 undergrads, 22% part-time. 148 full-time freshmen.
Selectivity: Admits over 75% of applicants.

BASIC COSTS (2008-2009)

Tuition and fees: $6,413; out-of-state residents $15,023.
Per-credit charge: $190; out-of-state residents $477.
Room and board: $6,940.
Additional info: New England Regional tuition is 150% of public in-district tuition.

FINANCIAL AID PICTURE (2007-2008)

Students with need: Out of 143 full-time freshmen who applied for aid, 122 were judged to have need. Of these, 122 received aid, and 46 had their full need met. Average financial aid package met 84% of need; average scholarship/grant was $5,291; average loan was $3,155. For part-time students, average financial aid package was $5,846.
Students without need: 12 full-time freshmen who did not demonstrate need for aid received scholarships/grants; average award was $4,666. No-need awards available for academics, leadership, state/district residency.

FINANCIAL AID PROCEDURES

Forms required: FAFSA, state aid form, institutional form.
Dates and Deadlines: Priority date 3/1; closing date 2/1. Applicants notified on a rolling basis starting 3/15; must reply within 2 week(s) of notification.

CONTACT

Ellen Cost, Director of Financial Aid
23 University Drive, Fort Kent, ME 04743
(207) 834-7607

University of Maine at Machias

Machias, Maine
www.umm.maine.edu Federal Code: 002055

4-year public university and liberal arts college in rural community.
Enrollment: 565 undergrads.
Selectivity: Admits over 75% of applicants.

BASIC COSTS (2008-2009)

Tuition and fees: $6,410; out-of-state residents $16,550.
Per-credit charge: $190; out-of-state residents $528.
Room and board: $6,574.
Additional info: New England Regional Student Program tuition is 150% of public in-district tuition. Tuition/fee waivers available for minority students.

FINANCIAL AID PICTURE

Students with need: Need-based aid available for full-time and part-time students.
Students without need: No-need awards available for academics, alumni affiliation, art, job skills, leadership, minority status, music/drama, state/district residency.

FINANCIAL AID PROCEDURES

Forms required: FAFSA.
Dates and Deadlines: Priority date 3/1; no closing date. Applicants notified on a rolling basis starting 2/15; must reply within 2 week(s) of notification.

CONTACT

Stephanie Larrabee, Director of Financial Aid
9 O'Brien Avenue, Machias, ME 04654
(207) 255-1203

University of Maine at Presque Isle

Presque Isle, Maine
www.umpi.edu Federal Code: 002033

4-year public university in small town.
Enrollment: 1,567 undergrads, 39% part-time. 188 full-time freshmen.

BASIC COSTS (2008-2009)

Tuition and fees: $6,340; out-of-state residents $14,950.
Per-credit charge: $190; out-of-state residents $477.
Room and board: $6,192.
Additional info: Tuition/fee waivers available for minority students.

FINANCIAL AID PICTURE (2008-2009)

Students with need: Need-based aid available for full-time and part-time students. Work study available nights, weekends, and for part-time students.

Students without need: No-need awards available for academics, alumni affiliation, art, job skills, leadership, minority status, music/drama, state/district residency.

FINANCIAL AID PROCEDURES

Forms required: FAFSA.

Dates and Deadlines: Priority date 4/1; no closing date. Applicants notified on a rolling basis starting 3/1; must reply within 2 week(s) of notification.

CONTACT

Christopher Bell, Director of Financial Aid
181 Main Street, Presque Isle, ME 04769
(207) 768-9510

University of New England

Biddeford, Maine
www.une.edu Federal Code: 002050

4-year private university in small city.

Enrollment: 2,113 undergrads, 5% part-time. 560 full-time freshmen.

Selectivity: Admits over 75% of applicants.

BASIC COSTS (2009-2010)

Tuition and fees: $27,920.

Per-credit charge: $970.

Room and board: $10,870.

FINANCIAL AID PICTURE (2007-2008)

Students with need: Need-based aid available for full time and part-time students. Work study available nights, weekends, and for part-time students.

Students without need: No-need awards available for academics, alumni affiliation, leadership.

Scholarships offered: UNE Scholarships and UNE Departmental Award; award amounts range from $1,000 to $12,000; non-need, based on academic qualifications as determined from GPA and SAT/ACT scores, must be a full-time undergraduate student and maintain a 2.5 GPA.

FINANCIAL AID PROCEDURES

Forms required: FAFSA.

Dates and Deadlines: Priority date 5/1; no closing date. Applicants notified on a rolling basis starting 2/1.

CONTACT

John Bowie, Director of Financial Aid
Hills Beach Road, Biddeford, ME 04005
(207) 602-2342

University of Southern Maine

Gorham, Maine
www.usm.maine.edu Federal Code: 009762

4-year public university and liberal arts college in small city.

Enrollment: 6,483 undergrads, 30% part-time. 980 full-time freshmen.

Selectivity: Admits over 75% of applicants.

BASIC COSTS (2008-2009)

Tuition and fees: $7,364; out-of-state residents $18,884.

Per-credit charge: $218; out-of-state residents $602.

Room and board: $8,334.

Additional info: New England Regional Student Program tuition is 150% of public in-district tuition.

FINANCIAL AID PICTURE (2008-2009)

Students with need: Average financial aid package met 62% of need; average scholarship/grant was $4,894; average loan was $3,592. For part-time students, average financial aid package was $7,697.

Students without need: No-need awards available for academics, music/drama.

Scholarships offered: Range from $1,000 to $5,500 based on academic record, school/community leadership, and potential for intellectual/social contribution.

FINANCIAL AID PROCEDURES

Forms required: FAFSA.

Dates and Deadlines: Priority date 2/15; no closing date. Applicants notified on a rolling basis starting 3/15; must reply by 5/1 or within 2 week(s) of notification.

Transfers: Applicants notified on a rolling basis; must reply by 5/1 or within 2 week(s) of notification.

CONTACT

Keith Dubois, Director of Financial Aid Office
37 College Avenue, Gorham, ME 04038
(207) 780-5250

Washington County Community College

Calais, Maine
www.wccc.me.edu Federal Code: 009231

2-year public community and technical college in small town.

Enrollment: 380 undergrads.

Selectivity: Open admission; but selective for some programs.

BASIC COSTS (2008-2009)

Tuition and fees: $3,062; out-of-state residents $5,522.

Per-credit charge: $82; out-of-state residents $164.

Room only: $2,730.

Additional info: Additional lab and technology fees may apply to specific programs and courses.

FINANCIAL AID PICTURE

Students with need: Need-based aid available for full-time and part-time students.

Students without need: No-need awards available for academics.

FINANCIAL AID PROCEDURES

Forms required: FAFSA, institutional form.

Dates and Deadlines: Priority date 5/1; no closing date. Applicants notified on a rolling basis starting 6/1; must reply within 2 week(s) of notification.

CONTACT

Joyce Maker, Financial Aid Coordinator
One College Drive, Calais, ME 04619
(207) 454-1033

York County Community College

Wells, Maine
www.yccc.edu Federal Code: 031220

2-year public community and technical college in small town.

Enrollment: 850 undergrads, 55% part-time. 153 full-time freshmen.

Selectivity: Open admission.

BASIC COSTS (2008-2009)

Tuition and fees: $3,042; out-of-state residents $5,502.

Per-credit charge: $82; out-of-state residents $164.

Additional info: Additional lab and technology fees may apply to specific programs and courses. Tuition/fee waivers available for minority students.

FINANCIAL AID PICTURE (2007-2008)

Students with need: Need-based aid available for full-time and part-time students. Work study available nights, weekends, and for part-time students.

Students without need: No-need awards available for academics, art, leadership.

FINANCIAL AID PROCEDURES

Forms required: FAFSA.

Dates and Deadlines: Priority date 5/1; no closing date. Applicants notified by 3/1; must reply within 2 week(s) of notification.

CONTACT

David Daigle, Director of Financial Aid
112 College Drive, Wells, ME 04090
(207) 646-9282 ext. 312

Maryland

Allegany College of Maryland

Cumberland, Maryland
www.allegany.edu Federal Code: 002057

2-year public community college in large town.

Enrollment: 2,994 undergrads, 31% part-time. 748 full-time freshmen.

Selectivity: Open admission; but selective for some programs.

BASIC COSTS (2009-2010)

Tuition and fees: $3,336; out-of-district residents $5,632; out-of-state residents $6,472.

Per-credit charge: $99; out-of-district residents $182; out-of-state residents $213.

FINANCIAL AID PICTURE (2007-2008)

Students with need: 66% of average financial aid package awarded as scholarships/grants, 34% awarded as loans/jobs. Need-based aid available for part-time students. Work study available nights.

Students without need: No-need awards available for academics, athletics, leadership, state/district residency.

FINANCIAL AID PROCEDURES

Forms required: FAFSA, institutional form.

Dates and Deadlines: Priority date 3/1; no closing date. Applicants notified on a rolling basis starting 4/15; must reply within 2 week(s) of notification.

CONTACT

Vicki Smith, Director of Financial Aid
12401 Willowbrook Road, SE, Cumberland, MD 21502
(301) 784-5213

Anne Arundel Community College

Arnold, Maryland
www.aacc.edu Federal Code: 002058

2-year public community college in large town.

Enrollment: 12,492 undergrads.

Selectivity: Open admission; but selective for some programs.

BASIC COSTS (2008-2009)

Tuition and fees: $2,860; out-of-district residents $5,230; out-of-state residents $9,040.

Per-credit charge: $86; out-of-district residents $165; out-of-state residents $292.

FINANCIAL AID PICTURE (2007-2008)

Students with need: 42% of average financial aid package awarded as scholarships/grants, 58% awarded as loans/jobs. Need-based aid available for part-time students. Work study available nights, weekends, and for part-time students.

FINANCIAL AID PROCEDURES

Forms required: FAFSA, institutional form.

Dates and Deadlines: Priority date 5/15; no closing date. Applicants notified on a rolling basis starting 7/1; must reply within 2 week(s) of notification.

CONTACT

Rich Heath, Director of Student Financial Services
101 College Parkway, Arnold, MD 21012-1895
(410) 777-2240

Baltimore City Community College

Baltimore, Maryland
www.bccc.edu Federal Code: 002061

2-year public community college in very large city.

Enrollment: 6,818 undergrads.

Selectivity: Open admission; but selective for some programs.

BASIC COSTS (2008-2009)

Tuition and fees: $3,062; out-of-state residents $6,722.

FINANCIAL AID PICTURE

Students with need: Need-based aid available for full-time and part-time students. Work study available nights, weekends, and for part-time students.

Students without need: This college awards aid only to students with need.

FINANCIAL AID PROCEDURES

Forms required: FAFSA, state aid form, institutional form.

Dates and Deadlines: Priority date 6/1; no closing date. Applicants notified on a rolling basis starting 7/1; must reply within 2 week(s) of notification.

CONTACT

Donald Smith, Director of Financial Aid
2901 Liberty Heights Avenue, Baltimore, MD 21215-7893
(410) 462-8348

Baltimore Hebrew University

Baltimore, Maryland
www.bhu.edu Federal Code: 002060

4-year private university and teachers college in very large city.

Enrollment: 4 undergrads.

BASIC COSTS (2008-2009)

Tuition and fees: $11,350.

Per-credit charge: $467.

FINANCIAL AID PICTURE (2007-2008)

Students with need: 34% of average financial aid package awarded as scholarships/grants, 66% awarded as loans/jobs. Need-based aid available for part-time students.

Students without need: No-need awards available for academics.

Scholarships offered: Tuition subsidy for teachers employed at any Jewish congregational day school, nursery or kindergarten; Tuition subsidy for teachers employed at a school affiliated with Center for Jewish Education; Tuition discount for full-time employees of the Associated Jewish Community Federation of Baltimore.

FINANCIAL AID PROCEDURES

Forms required: FAFSA.

Dates and Deadlines: Priority date 4/15; closing date 6/1. Applicants notified on a rolling basis starting 7/15; must reply by 9/9.
Transfers: No deadline.

CONTACT

Kerri Moseley-Hobbs, Financial Aid Counselor
5800 Park Heights Avenue, Baltimore, MD 21215
(410) 578-6913

Baltimore International College

Baltimore, Maryland
www.bic.edu Federal Code: 016376

4-year private culinary school and business college in very large city.
Enrollment: 478 undergrads.
Selectivity: Admits 50 to 75% of applicants.

BASIC COSTS (2008-2009)

Tuition and fees: $17,436.
Per-credit charge: $542.
Room and board: $9,828.
Additional info: Fees shown are for culinary school and include use of computer, culinary supplies, upgrading and maintenance of kitchen equipment and facilities. Day students provided one full meal daily. Business program students pay lower fees. ($8764).

FINANCIAL AID PICTURE (2007-2008)

Students with need: Need-based aid available for full-time students. Work study available nights, weekends, and for part-time students.
Students without need: No-need awards available for academics, alumni affiliation, job skills, leadership, state/district residency.

FINANCIAL AID PROCEDURES

Forms required: FAFSA, institutional form.
Dates and Deadlines: Priority date 3/1; no closing date. Applicants notified on a rolling basis; must reply within 2 week(s) of notification.
Transfers: No deadline. Applicants notified on a rolling basis; must reply within 2 week(s) of notification.

CONTACT

Kim Wittler, Director of Student Financial Planning
17 Commerce Street, Baltimore, MD 21202-3230
(410) 752-4710

Bowie State University

Bowie, Maryland
www.bowiestate.edu Federal Code: 002062

4-year public university in small city.
Enrollment: 4,340 undergrads.
Selectivity: Admits less than 50% of applicants.

BASIC COSTS (2008-2009)

Tuition and fees: $5,939; out-of-state residents $15,629.
Per-credit charge: $189; out-of-state residents $589.
Room and board: $9,879.

FINANCIAL AID PICTURE (2008-2009)

Students with need: Need-based aid available for full-time and part-time students. Work study available weekends and for part-time students.
Students without need: No-need awards available for academics, alumni affiliation, art, athletics, leadership, music/drama, ROTC, state/district residency.

FINANCIAL AID PROCEDURES

Forms required: FAFSA.
Dates and Deadlines: Closing date 3/1. Applicants notified on a rolling basis starting 4/1; must reply within 2 week(s) of notification.
Transfers: Applicants notified on a rolling basis starting 4/1; must reply within 2 week(s) of notification.

CONTACT

Deborah Stanley, Director of Financial Aid
14000 Jericho Park Road, Bowie, MD 20715
(301) 860-3540

Carroll Community College

Westminster, Maryland
www.carrollcc.edu Federal Code: 031007

2-year public community college in large town.
Enrollment: 3,460 undergrads, 53% part-time. 633 full-time freshmen.
Selectivity: Open admission; but selective for some programs.

BASIC COSTS (2008-2009)

Tuition and fees: $3,407; out-of-district residents $4,925; out-of-state residents $6,926.
Per-credit charge: $114; out-of-district residents $164; out-of-state residents $231.

FINANCIAL AID PICTURE (2007-2008)

Students with need: 98% of average financial aid package awarded as scholarships/grants, 2% awarded as loans/jobs. Need-based aid available for part-time students. Work study available nights, weekends, and for part-time students.
Students without need: No-need awards available for academics, art, job skills, leadership, state/district residency.

FINANCIAL AID PROCEDURES

Forms required: FAFSA.
Dates and Deadlines: Priority date 3/1; no closing date. Applicants notified by 6/1; must reply within 2 week(s) of notification.

CONTACT

Lori Henry, Director of Financial Aid
1601 Washington Road, Westminster, MD 21157
(410) 386-8435

Cecil College

North East, Maryland
www.cecil.edu Federal Code: 008308

2-year public community college in large town.
Enrollment: 2,086 undergrads, 62% part-time. 294 full-time freshmen.
Selectivity: Open admission; but selective for some programs.

BASIC COSTS (2008-2009)

Tuition and fees: $2,912; out-of-district residents $5,612; out-of-state residents $6,962.
Per-credit charge: $85; out-of-district residents $175; out-of-state residents $220.
Additional info: Tuition at time of enrollment locked for 2 years

FINANCIAL AID PICTURE (2007-2008)

Students with need: 45% of average financial aid package awarded as scholarships/grants, 55% awarded as loans/jobs. Work study available nights, weekends, and for part-time students.
Students without need: No-need awards available for academics, alumni affiliation, athletics, job skills, state/district residency.

FINANCIAL AID PROCEDURES

Forms required: FAFSA.

Dates and Deadlines: Priority date 8/1; no closing date. Applicants notified on a rolling basis; must reply within 2 week(s) of notification.

CONTACT

Kate Lockhart, Director of Financial Aid
One Seahawk Drive, North East, MD 21901
(410) 287-1003

Chesapeake College

Wye Mills, Maryland
www.chesapeake.edu Federal Code: 004650

2-year public community college in rural community.
Enrollment: 2,038 undergrads.
Selectivity: Open admission; but selective for some programs.

BASIC COSTS (2008-2009)

Tuition and fees: $3,304; out-of-district residents $5,374; out-of-state residents $7,684.
Per-credit charge: $91; out-of-district residents $159; out-of-state residents $236.

FINANCIAL AID PICTURE

Students with need: Need-based aid available for full-time and part-time students.
Students without need: No-need awards available for academics, art, athletics, state/district residency.

FINANCIAL AID PROCEDURES

Forms required: FAFSA, institutional form.
Dates and Deadlines: Priority date 5/1; no closing date. Applicants notified on a rolling basis starting 5/1; must reply within 2 week(s) of notification.

CONTACT

Mindy Schaffer, Director of Financial Aid
Box 8, Wye Mills, MD 21679-0008
(410) 822-5400 ext. 252

College of Notre Dame of Maryland

Baltimore, Maryland
www.ndm.edu Federal Code: 002065

4-year private liberal arts college for women in very large city, affiliated with Roman Catholic Church.
Enrollment: 1,338 undergrads.
Selectivity: Admits 50 to 75% of applicants.

BASIC COSTS (2009-2010)

Tuition and fees: $27,250.
Per-credit charge: $410.
Room and board: $9,100.

FINANCIAL AID PICTURE (2008-2009)

Students with need: Need-based aid available for full-time and part-time students.
Students without need: No-need awards available for academics, alumni affiliation, art, leadership, music/drama, ROTC.
Scholarships offered: Academic/achievement awards; $6,000 to full tuition. Endowed scholarships; $1,000 to $8,000; variable criteria; usually 20-35 awards.
Additional info: Maximum consideration for financial aid if application received by February 15. Auditions and portfolios in areas of art, music and writing considered for scholarships.

FINANCIAL AID PROCEDURES

Forms required: FAFSA.
Dates and Deadlines: Priority date 2/15; no closing date. Applicants notified on a rolling basis starting 3/15; must reply by 5/1 or within 2 week(s) of notification.
Transfers: Applicants notified by 3/15; must reply by 5/1 or within 2 week(s) of notification. Specific non-need based merit scholarships available for transfer students. Transfer scholarships; range from $7000 to full tuition.

CONTACT

Zhana Goltser, Director of Financial Aid
4701 North Charles Street, Baltimore, MD 21210
(410) 532-5369

College of Southern Maryland

La Plata, Maryland
www.csmd.edu Federal Code: 002064

2-year public community college in large town.
Enrollment: 6,687 undergrads, 60% part-time. 951 full-time freshmen.
Selectivity: Open admission; but selective for some programs.

BASIC COSTS (2008-2009)

Tuition and fees: $3,528; out-of-state residents $7,956.
Per-credit charge: $98; out-of-district residents $171; out-of-state residents $221.
Additional info: Out-of-district fees are an additional $420; out-of-state fees are an additional $690.

FINANCIAL AID PICTURE (2007-2008)

Students with need: 83% of average financial aid package awarded as scholarships/grants, 17% awarded as loans/jobs. Need-based aid available for part-time students. Work study available nights, weekends, and for part-time students.
Students without need: No-need awards available for academics, athletics, state/district residency.

FINANCIAL AID PROCEDURES

Forms required: FAFSA.
Dates and Deadlines: Priority date 3/1; no closing date. Applicants notified on a rolling basis starting 5/15; must reply within 2 week(s) of notification.

CONTACT

George Bachman, Director of Financial Assistance
College of Southern Maryland-AOD, La Plata, MD 20646-0910
(301) 934-7531

Columbia Union College

Takoma Park, Maryland
www.cuc.edu Federal Code: 002067

4-year private liberal arts college in large town, affiliated with Seventh-day Adventists.
Enrollment: 859 undergrads.

BASIC COSTS (2009-2010)

Tuition and fees: $19,430.
Room and board: $6,887.

FINANCIAL AID PICTURE (2007-2008)

Students with need: Need-based aid available for full-time and part-time students.
Students without need: No-need awards available for academics, athletics, leadership, music/drama, state/district residency.

FINANCIAL AID PROCEDURES

Forms required: FAFSA.
Dates and Deadlines: Closing date 3/31. Applicants notified on a rolling basis starting 5/31; must reply within 4 week(s) of notification.

CONTACT
Sharon Conway, Director of Financial Aid
7600 Flower Avenue, Takoma Park, MD 20912
(301) 891-4005

Community College of Baltimore County
Baltimore, Maryland
www.ccbcmd.edu Federal Code: 002063

2-year public community college in very large city.
Enrollment: 17,105 undergrads, 62% part-time. 2,048 full-time freshmen.
Selectivity: Open admission; but selective for some programs.

BASIC COSTS (2008-2009)
Tuition and fees: $3,080; out-of-district residents $5,600; out-of-state residents $8,210.
Per-credit charge: $90; out-of-district residents $174; out-of-state residents $261.

FINANCIAL AID PICTURE (2007-2008)
Students with need: Need-based aid available for full-time and part-time students. Work study available nights, weekends, and for part-time students.
Students without need: No-need awards available for academics, athletics, state/district residency.
Additional info: On-campus employment typically available.

FINANCIAL AID PROCEDURES
Forms required: FAFSA.
Dates and Deadlines: Closing date 3/1. Applicants notified on a rolling basis starting 5/1; must reply within 2 week(s) of notification.

CONTACT
Jerome Lovick, Director of Financial Aid
800 South Rolling Road, Baltimore, MD 21228
(443) 840-4170

Coppin State University
Baltimore, Maryland
www.coppin.edu Federal Code: 002068

4-year public liberal arts college in very large city.
Enrollment: 3,201 undergrads, 21% part-time. 570 full-time freshmen.
Selectivity: Admits less than 50% of applicants.

BASIC COSTS (2008-2009)
Tuition and fees: $5,140; out-of-state residents $13,365.
Per-credit charge: $151; out-of-state residents $404.
Room and board: $7,139.

FINANCIAL AID PICTURE (2008-2009)
Students with need: Need-based aid available for full-time and part-time students.
Students without need: No-need awards available for academics, alumni affiliation, athletics, ROTC, state/district residency.
Scholarships offered: Gold Freshman Merit Award; $1,200 per year; awarded to freshmen with 950 combined SAT and 2.5 high school GPA. Gold Transfer Merit Award; $1,200 per year, awarded to Maryland Community College transfer students with 2.8 GPA and successful completion of 56 credits. Blue Freshman Merit Award; $800 per year; awarded to freshman with 900 combined SAT and 2.5 GPA. Blue Transfer Merit Award; $600 per year; awarded to Maryland Community College transfer students with 2.5 GPA and successful completion of 25 credits. SAT scores exclusive of Writing.
Additional info: Funds allocated by State of Maryland for minority students enrolled for at least 6 credits who are Maryland residents and U.S. citizens (Other Race Grant).

FINANCIAL AID PROCEDURES
Forms required: FAFSA.
Dates and Deadlines: Priority date 3/1; no closing date. Applicants notified on a rolling basis starting 4/15; must reply within 2 week(s) of notification.

CONTACT
Lady Jenkins, Director of Financial Aid
2500 West North Avenue, Baltimore, MD 21216
(410) 951-3636

Frederick Community College
Frederick, Maryland
www.frederick.edu Federal Code: 002071

2-year public community college in small city.
Enrollment: 5,172 undergrads, 59% part-time. 837 full-time freshmen.
Selectivity: Open admission; but selective for some programs.

BASIC COSTS (2008-2009)
Tuition and fees: $3,128; out-of-district residents $6,368; out-of-state residents $8,528.
Per-credit charge: $92; out-of-district residents $200; out-of-state residents $272.

FINANCIAL AID PICTURE (2007-2008)
Students with need: 82% of average financial aid package awarded as scholarships/grants, 18% awarded as loans/jobs. Need-based aid available for part-time students.
Students without need: No-need awards available for academics, athletics, state/district residency.
Scholarships offered: Scholarships available for Frederick County Public Schools students with high gpas to participate in student ambassador program; other general scholarships available for prospective students.

FINANCIAL AID PROCEDURES
Forms required: FAFSA, institutional form.
Dates and Deadlines: Priority date 6/1; no closing date. Applicants notified on a rolling basis starting 5/15; must reply within 2 week(s) of notification.
Transfers: Applicants notified on a rolling basis starting 6/1. Financial aid transcripts from prior institutions must be submitted before awards are made.

CONTACT
Brenda Dayhoff, Director, Financial Aid
7932 Opossumtown Pike, Frederick, MD 21702
(301) 846-2480

Frostburg State University
Frostburg, Maryland
www.frostburg.edu Federal Code: 002072

4-year public university and teachers college in small town.
Enrollment: 4,470 undergrads, 5% part-time. 1,028 full-time freshmen.
Selectivity: Admits 50 to 75% of applicants.

BASIC COSTS (2008-2009)
Tuition and fees: $6,614; out-of-state residents $16,810.
Per-credit charge: $207; out-of-state residents $427.
Room and board: $7,016.

FINANCIAL AID PICTURE (2008-2009)
Students with need: Average financial aid package met 71% of need; average scholarship/grant was $5,585; average loan was $3,055. For part-time students, average financial aid package was $5,244.
Students without need: No-need awards available for academics, leadership, minority status.

Cumulative student debt: 67% of graduating class had student loans; average debt was $18,035.

FINANCIAL AID PROCEDURES

Forms required: FAFSA.

Dates and Deadlines: Priority date 3/1; no closing date. Applicants notified on a rolling basis starting 3/15; must reply within 3 week(s) of notification.

CONTACT

Angela Hovatter, Director of Financial Aid
101 Braddock Road, Frostburg, MD 21532-1099
(301) 687-4201

Garrett College

McHenry, Maryland
www.garrettcollege.edu Federal Code: 010014

2-year public community college in rural community.

Enrollment: 656 undergrads.

Selectivity: Open admission.

BASIC COSTS (2008-2009)

Tuition and fees: $2,970; out-of-district residents $6,510; out-of-state residents $7,590.

Per-credit charge: $78; out-of-district residents $196; out-of-state residents $232.

Room and board: $4,300.

FINANCIAL AID PICTURE

Students with need: Need-based aid available for full-time and part-time students.

Students without need: No-need awards available for academics, athletics, leadership.

Additional info: Many local scholarships both merit and need based.

FINANCIAL AID PROCEDURES

Forms required: FAFSA.

Dates and Deadlines: Closing date 3/1. Applicants notified on a rolling basis starting 5/15; must reply within 2 week(s) of notification.

CONTACT

Mary Peoples, Director of Financial Aid
687 Mosser Road, McHenry, MD 21541
(301) 387-3057

Goucher College

Baltimore, Maryland Federal Code: 002073
www.goucher.edu CSS Code: 5257

4-year private liberal arts college in small city.

Enrollment: 1,434 undergrads, 1% part-time. 363 full-time freshmen.

Selectivity: Admits 50 to 75% of applicants.

BASIC COSTS (2009-2010)

Tuition and fees: $33,786.

Room and board: $10,008.

FINANCIAL AID PICTURE (2008-2009)

Students with need: Out of 242 full-time freshmen who applied for aid, 192 were judged to have need. Of these, 190 received aid, and 47 had their full need met. Average financial aid package met 81% of need; average scholarship/grant was $22,609; average loan was $3,394. For part-time students, average financial aid package was $9,703.

Students without need: 66 full-time freshmen who did not demonstrate need for aid received scholarships/grants; average award was $12,670. No-need awards available for academics, art, leadership, music/drama.

Cumulative student debt: 39% of graduating class had student loans; average debt was $16,729.

FINANCIAL AID PROCEDURES

Forms required: FAFSA, CSS PROFILE.

Dates and Deadlines: Closing date 2/1. Applicants notified on a rolling basis starting 4/1; must reply by 5/1 or within 2 week(s) of notification.

Transfers: Must reply within 2 week(s) of notification.

CONTACT

Sharon Hassan, Director of Financial Aid
1021 Dulaney Valley Road, Baltimore, MD 21204-2753
(410) 337-6141

Hagerstown Community College

Hagerstown, Maryland
www.hagerstowncc.edu Federal Code: 002074

2-year public community college in small city.

Enrollment: 1,260 full-time undergrads.

Selectivity: Open admission; but selective for some programs.

BASIC COSTS (2008-2009)

Tuition and fees: $3,210; out-of-district residents $4,860; out-of-state residents $6,270.

Per-credit charge: $96; out-of-district residents $151; out-of-state residents $198.

FINANCIAL AID PICTURE (2007-2008)

Students with need: Need-based aid available for full-time and part-time students. Work study available nights, weekends, and for part-time students.

Students without need: This college awards aid only to students with need.

FINANCIAL AID PROCEDURES

Forms required: FAFSA.

Dates and Deadlines: Priority date 3/1; no closing date. Applicants notified on a rolling basis starting 5/1.

Transfers: No deadline.

CONTACT

Carolyn Cox, Director of Financial Aid
11400 Robinwood Drive, Hagerstown, MD 21742
(301) 790-2800 ext. 473

Hood College

Frederick, Maryland
www.hood.edu Federal Code: 002076

4-year private liberal arts college in small city.

Enrollment: 1,385 undergrads, 9% part-time. 308 full-time freshmen.

Selectivity: Admits over 75% of applicants.

BASIC COSTS (2009-2010)

Tuition and fees: $28,170.

Per-credit charge: $800.

Room and board: $9,440.

Additional info: Tuition/fee waivers available for adults.

FINANCIAL AID PICTURE (2008-2009)

Students with need: Out of 278 full-time freshmen who applied for aid, 230 were judged to have need. Of these, 228 received aid, and 62 had their full need met. Average financial aid package met 83% of need; average scholarship/grant was $18,092; average loan was $3,703. For part-time students, average financial aid package was $7,605.

Students without need: 69 full-time freshmen who did not demonstrate need for aid received scholarships/grants; average award was $20,939. No-need awards available for academics, alumni affiliation, music/drama, ROTC.
Scholarships offered: Hood Trust Academic Scholarship: amount varies. Hodson Scholarship: amount varies. Project Excellence Scholarship: up to full tuition. Presidential Scholarship: $10,000-$14,000. Trustee Scholarship: $8,000-$10,000.
Cumulative student debt: 71% of graduating class had student loans; average debt was $19,038.

FINANCIAL AID PROCEDURES

Forms required: FAFSA.
Dates and Deadlines: Priority date 2/15; no closing date. Applicants notified on a rolling basis starting 3/1; must reply by 5/1 or within 3 week(s) of notification.

CONTACT

Margherite Powell, Director of Financial Aid
401 Rosemont Avenue, Frederick, MD 21701-8575
(301) 696-3411

Howard Community College

Columbia, Maryland
www.howardcc.edu Federal Code: 008175

2-year public community college in small city.
Enrollment: 7,143 undergrads, 59% part-time. 1,086 full-time freshmen.
Selectivity: Open admission; but selective for some programs.

BASIC COSTS (2008-2009)

Tuition and fees: $3,993; out-of-district residents $6,483; out-of-state residents $8,193.

FINANCIAL AID PICTURE (2007-2008)

Students with need: 73% of average financial aid package awarded as scholarships/grants, 27% awarded as loans/jobs. Need-based aid available for part-time students. Work study available nights, weekends, and for part-time students.

FINANCIAL AID PROCEDURES

Forms required: FAFSA.
Dates and Deadlines: Priority date 3/1; no closing date. Applicants notified on a rolling basis starting 5/1.

CONTACT

Katherine Allen, Director of Financial Aid
10901 Little Patuxent Parkway, Columbia, MD 21044-3197
(410) 772-4898

Johns Hopkins University

Baltimore, Maryland Federal Code: 002077
www.jhu.edu CSS Code: 5332

4-year private university in very large city.
Enrollment: 4,725 undergrads. 1,236 full-time freshmen.
Selectivity: Admits less than 50% of applicants.

BASIC COSTS (2009-2010)

Tuition and fees: $39,650.
Per-credit charge: $1,305.
Room and board: $12,040.

FINANCIAL AID PICTURE (2008-2009)

Students with need: Out of 819 full-time freshmen who applied for aid, 590 were judged to have need. Of these, 575 received aid, and 555 had their full need met. Average financial aid package met 98% of need; average scholarship/grant was $28,182; average loan was $3,377.
Students without need: 16 full-time freshmen who did not demonstrate need for aid received scholarships/grants; average award was $25,406. No-need awards available for academics, athletics, leadership, ROTC, state/district residency.
Scholarships offered: ***Merit:*** Hodson Trust Scholarship; $25,500 annually for 4 years; 20 awards. Westgate Scholarship for engineering freshmen; tuition plus $1,000 for 4 years: academic excellence, leadership, demonstrated research experience required, 2 offered per year per class. Wilson Research grants; $10,000. Baltimore Scholars Program; full tuition scholarship for US citizens or permanent residents who have attended a Baltimore City public school for at least 10th, 11th, and 12th grades and meet a residency requirement. ***Athletic:*** 9 full-time freshmen received athletic scholarships; average amount $23,039.
Cumulative student debt: 50% of graduating class had student loans; average debt was $21,984.
Additional info: Selected students receive aid packages without loan expectation, grants to full need. Private merit aid does not reduce Hopkins grant.

FINANCIAL AID PROCEDURES

Forms required: FAFSA, CSS PROFILE.
Dates and Deadlines: Closing date 3/1. Applicants notified by 4/1; must reply by 5/1 or within 2 week(s) of notification.
Transfers: Closing date 3/15. Aid on funds-available basis.

CONTACT

Vincent Amoroso, Director of Student Financial Services
3400 North Charles Street, Mason Hall, Baltimore, MD 21218
(410) 516-8028

Johns Hopkins University: Peabody Conservatory of Music

Baltimore, Maryland
www.peabody.jhu.edu Federal Code: E00233

4-year private music college in very large city.
Enrollment: 329 undergrads, 3% part-time. 83 full-time freshmen.
Selectivity: Admits less than 50% of applicants.

BASIC COSTS (2009-2010)

Tuition and fees: $35,375.
Per-credit charge: $975.
Room and board: $11,100.

FINANCIAL AID PICTURE

Students with need: Need-based aid available for full-time and part-time students.
Students without need: No-need awards available for academics, music/drama.

FINANCIAL AID PROCEDURES

Forms required: FAFSA, institutional form.
Dates and Deadlines: Closing date 2/1. Applicants notified by 4/1; must reply by 5/1 or within 2 week(s) of notification.

CONTACT

Thomas McDermott, Director of Financial Aid
One East Mount Vernon Place, Baltimore, MD 21202
(410) 659-8100 ext. 3023

Kaplan College: Hagerstown

Hagerstown, Maryland
www.KC-Hagerstown.com Federal Code: 007946

2-year for-profit business and junior college in large town.
Enrollment: 611 undergrads.
Selectivity: Open admission; but selective for some programs.

FINANCIAL AID PICTURE (2007-2008)
Students with need: Need-based aid available for full-time and part-time students.

FINANCIAL AID PROCEDURES
Forms required: FAFSA, institutional form.
Dates and Deadlines: No deadline. Applicants notified on a rolling basis starting 6/1; must reply within 2 week(s) of notification.

CONTACT
Kristen Brezler, Director of Financial Aid
18618 Crestwood Drive, Hagerstown, MD 21742
(301) 739-2670

Loyola College in Maryland
Baltimore, Maryland — Federal Code: 002078
www.loyola.edu — CSS Code: 5370

4-year private business and liberal arts college in very large city, affiliated with Roman Catholic Church.
Enrollment: 3,716 undergrads, 1% part-time. 1,068 full-time freshmen.
Selectivity: Admits 50 to 75% of applicants.

BASIC COSTS (2009-2010)
Tuition and fees: $37,610.
Room and board: $10,200.

FINANCIAL AID PICTURE (2008-2009)
Students with need: Out of 768 full-time freshmen who applied for aid, 576 were judged to have need. Of these, 576 received aid, and 576 had their full need met. Average financial aid package met 100% of need; average scholarship/grant was $19,530; average loan was $5,235. For part-time students, average financial aid package was $2,960.
Students without need: 107 full-time freshmen who did not demonstrate need for aid received scholarships/grants; average award was $14,285. No-need awards available for academics, athletics, ROTC.
Scholarships offered: 32 full-time freshmen received athletic scholarships; average amount $26,960.
Cumulative student debt: 71% of graduating class had student loans; average debt was $26,340.

FINANCIAL AID PROCEDURES
Forms required: FAFSA, CSS PROFILE.
Dates and Deadlines: Closing date 2/1. Applicants notified by 4/1; must reply by 5/1.
Transfers: No deadline. Academic (merit-based) scholarships not available to transfer students.

CONTACT
Mark Lindenmeyer, Director of Financial Aid
4501 North Charles Street, Baltimore, MD 21210-2699
(410) 617-2576

Maryland Institute College of Art
Baltimore, Maryland
www.mica.edu — Federal Code: 002080

4-year private visual arts college in very large city.
Enrollment: 1,631 undergrads, 1% part-time. 429 full-time freshmen.
Selectivity: Admits 50 to 75% of applicants.

BASIC COSTS (2009-2010)
Tuition and fees: $34,090.
Per-credit charge: $1,375.
Room and board: $9,450.

FINANCIAL AID PICTURE
Students with need: Need-based aid available for full-time and part-time students. Work study available nights, weekends, and for part-time students.
Students without need: No-need awards available for academics, art.

FINANCIAL AID PROCEDURES
Forms required: FAFSA, institutional form.
Dates and Deadlines: Closing date 3/1. Applicants notified by 4/10; must reply by 5/1.
Transfers: Priority date 3/1. Applicants notified by 4/20; must reply by 5/21.

CONTACT
Diane Prengaman, Associate Vice President for Financial Aid
1300 Mount Royal Avenue, Baltimore, MD 21217-4134
(410) 225-2285

McDaniel College
Westminster, Maryland
www.mcdaniel.edu — Federal Code: 002109

4-year private liberal arts college in large town.
Enrollment: 1,739 undergrads, 3% part-time. 420 full-time freshmen.
Selectivity: Admits over 75% of applicants.

BASIC COSTS (2009-2010)
Tuition and fees: $32,000.
Per-credit charge: $1,000.
Room and board: $6,820.

FINANCIAL AID PICTURE (2008-2009)
Students with need: Out of 340 full-time freshmen who applied for aid, 285 were judged to have need. Of these, 285 received aid, and 85 had their full need met. Average financial aid package met 93% of need; average scholarship/grant was $12,559; average loan was $4,680. For part-time students, average financial aid package was $5,026.
Students without need: 135 full-time freshmen who did not demonstrate need for aid received scholarships/grants; average award was $13,368. No-need awards available for academics, ROTC, state/district residency.
Cumulative student debt: 65% of graduating class had student loans; average debt was $25,345.

FINANCIAL AID PROCEDURES
Forms required: FAFSA, institutional form.
Dates and Deadlines: Priority date 3/1; no closing date. Applicants notified on a rolling basis starting 2/15; must reply by 5/1 or within 2 week(s) of notification.
Transfers: No deadline. Applicants notified on a rolling basis starting 2/15; must reply by 8/1 or within 2 week(s) of notification.

CONTACT
Patricia Williams, Director of Financial Aid
Two College Hill, Westminster, MD 21157-4390
(410) 857-2233

Montgomery College
Rockville, Maryland
www.montgomerycollege.edu — Federal Code: 006911

2-year public community college in very large city.
Enrollment: 18,004 undergrads, 59% part-time. 2,622 full-time freshmen.
Selectivity: Open admission; but selective for some programs.

BASIC COSTS (2008-2009)
Tuition and fees: $3,984; out-of-district residents $7,728; out-of-state residents $10,320.

FINANCIAL AID PICTURE (2007-2008)

Students with need: 78% of average financial aid package awarded as scholarships/grants, 22% awarded as loans/jobs. Need-based aid available for part-time students. Work study available nights, weekends, and for part-time students.

Students without need: No-need awards available for academics, alumni affiliation, art, music/drama, state/district residency.

Scholarships offered: Board of Trustees Academic Potential Scholarship; first year of tuition; based on GPA and high school nominations; 125 awards available.

FINANCIAL AID PROCEDURES

Forms required: FAFSA, institutional form.

Dates and Deadlines: Priority date 5/15; no closing date. Applicants notified on a rolling basis starting 5/30.

Transfers: Priority date 5/15; no deadline. Applicants notified on a rolling basis starting 1/1; must reply within 4 week(s) of notification.

CONTACT

Melissa Gregory, Director of Financial Aid
51 Mannakee Street, Rockville, MD 20850
(240) 567-5100

Morgan State University

Baltimore, Maryland
www.morgan.edu Federal Code: 002083

4-year public university and liberal arts college in large city.

Enrollment: 6,114 undergrads.

Selectivity: Admits less than 50% of applicants.

BASIC COSTS (2008-2009)

Tuition and fees: $6,438; out-of-state residents $14,928.

Per-credit charge: $194; out-of-state residents $505.

Room and board: $8,030.

Additional info: Tuition/fee waivers available for minority students.

FINANCIAL AID PICTURE

Students with need: Need-based aid available for full-time and part-time students.

FINANCIAL AID PROCEDURES

Forms required: FAFSA.

Dates and Deadlines: Priority date 4/1; no closing date. Applicants notified on a rolling basis starting 6/1; must reply within 2 week(s) of notification.

CONTACT

Abraham Moore, Vice President
1700 East Cold Spring Lane, Baltimore, MD 21251
(443) 885-3000

Mount St. Mary's University

Emmitsburg, Maryland
www.msmary.edu Federal Code: 002086

4-year private university and liberal arts college in rural community, affiliated with Roman Catholic Church.

Enrollment: 1,632 undergrads, 6% part-time. 409 full-time freshmen.

Selectivity: Admits over 75% of applicants.

BASIC COSTS (2009-2010)

Tuition and fees: $29,020.

Per-credit charge: $950.

Room and board: $9,878.

Additional info: Tuition/fee waivers available for minority students.

FINANCIAL AID PICTURE (2008-2009)

Students with need: Out of 342 full-time freshmen who applied for aid, 268 were judged to have need. Of these, 266 received aid, and 63 had their full need met. Average financial aid package met 72% of need; average scholarship/grant was $14,983; average loan was $3,968. For part-time students, average financial aid package was $2,031.

Students without need: 136 full-time freshmen who did not demonstrate need for aid received scholarships/grants; average award was $14,008. No-need awards available for academics, art, athletics, leadership, minority status, ROTC.

Scholarships offered: ***Merit:*** Founder's Scholarship; full-tuition scholarship for 4 years; based on competitive examinations, strong academic records and SAT scores of 1200 or higher (exclusive of writing); 3 awards. ***Athletic:*** 38 full-time freshmen received athletic scholarships; average amount $6,636.

Cumulative student debt: 77% of graduating class had student loans; average debt was $27,230.

FINANCIAL AID PROCEDURES

Forms required: FAFSA, institutional form.

Dates and Deadlines: Closing date 3/1. Applicants notified on a rolling basis starting 2/1; must reply by 5/1.

Transfers: Scholarships available based on GPA at previous institution.

CONTACT

David Reeder, Director of Financial Aid
16300 Old Emmitsburg Road, Emmitsburg, MD 21727
(800) 448-4347

Prince George's Community College

Largo, Maryland
www.pgcc.edu Federal Code: 002089

2-year public community college in very large city.

Enrollment: 10,752 undergrads.

Selectivity: Open admission; but selective for some programs.

BASIC COSTS (2008-2009)

Tuition and fees: $3,920; out-of-district residents $6,050; out-of-state residents $8,690.

Per-credit charge: $96; out-of-district residents $167; out-of-state residents $255.

Additional info: Instructional services fees range from $27 to $37 per credit depending on course.

FINANCIAL AID PICTURE (2007-2008)

Students with need: 77% of average financial aid package awarded as scholarships/grants, 23% awarded as loans/jobs. Need-based aid available for part-time students.

Students without need: This college awards aid only to students with need.

FINANCIAL AID PROCEDURES

Forms required: FAFSA, institutional form.

Dates and Deadlines: Priority date 6/1; no closing date. Applicants notified on a rolling basis starting 6/1; must reply within 2 week(s) of notification.

CONTACT

Jane Hickey, Director of Financial Aid
301 Largo Road, Largo, MD 20774
(301) 322-0866

St. John's College

Annapolis, Maryland
www.stjohnscollege.edu

Federal Code: 002092
CSS Code: 5598

4-year private liberal arts college in large town.
Enrollment: 488 undergrads. 154 full-time freshmen.
Selectivity: Admits over 75% of applicants.

BASIC COSTS (2009-2010)

Tuition and fees: $40,392.
Room and board: $9,960.

FINANCIAL AID PICTURE (2008-2009)

Students with need: Out of 122 full-time freshmen who applied for aid, 95 were judged to have need. Of these, 95 received aid, and 65 had their full need met. Average financial aid package met 82% of need; average scholarship/grant was $26,542; average loan was $4,325. Need-based aid available for part-time students.
Students without need: This college awards aid only to students with need.

FINANCIAL AID PROCEDURES

Forms required: FAFSA, CSS PROFILE.
Dates and Deadlines: Priority date 2/15; no closing date. Applicants notified on a rolling basis starting 1/15; must reply by 5/1.

CONTACT

Paula Abernethy, Director of Financial Aid
PO Box 2800, Annapolis, MD 21404
(410) 626-2502

St. Mary's College of Maryland

St. Mary's City, Maryland
www.smcm.edu

Federal Code: 002095

4-year public liberal arts college in large town.
Enrollment: 1,988 undergrads, 2% part-time. 490 full-time freshmen.
Selectivity: Admits 50 to 75% of applicants.

BASIC COSTS (2008-2009)

Tuition and fees: $12,604; out-of-state residents $23,454.
Per-credit charge: $160.
Room and board: $9,225.

FINANCIAL AID PICTURE (2007-2008)

Students with need: Out of 345 full-time freshmen who applied for aid, 221 were judged to have need. Of these, 221 received aid. Average financial aid package met 59% of need; average scholarship/grant was $3,500; average loan was $2,625. For part-time students, average financial aid package was $3,500.
Students without need: 167 full-time freshmen who did not demonstrate need for aid received scholarships/grants; average award was $3,000. No-need awards available for academics, alumni affiliation.
Cumulative student debt: 70% of graduating class had student loans; average debt was $17,125.

FINANCIAL AID PROCEDURES

Forms required: FAFSA.
Dates and Deadlines: Priority date 2/15; closing date 3/1. Applicants notified by 4/1; must reply by 5/1.
Transfers: Priority date 3/1; closing date 6/1. Must reply by 8/1 or within 2 week(s) of notification. All financial aid recipients must have GED or high school diploma. Financial aid transcript required from previous colleges attended.

CONTACT

Timothy Wolfe, Director of Financial Aid
18952 East Fisher Road, St. Mary's City, MD 20686-3001
(240) 895-3000

Salisbury University

Salisbury, Maryland
www.salisbury.edu

Federal Code: 002091

4-year public university and liberal arts college in large town.
Enrollment: 7,025 undergrads, 5% part-time. 1,143 full-time freshmen.
Selectivity: Admits 50 to 75% of applicants.

BASIC COSTS (2008-2009)

Tuition and fees: $6,492; out-of-state residents $14,794.
Per-credit charge: $200; out-of-state residents $545.
Room and board: $7,798.

FINANCIAL AID PICTURE (2007-2008)

Students with need: Out of 874 full-time freshmen who applied for aid, 498 were judged to have need. Of these, 473 received aid, and 118 had their full need met. Average financial aid package met 61% of need; average scholarship/grant was $6,467; average loan was $3,034. For part-time students, average financial aid package was $3,960.
Students without need: 224 full-time freshmen who did not demonstrate need for aid received scholarships/grants; average award was $3,712. No-need awards available for academics, alumni affiliation, art, leadership, music/drama, state/district residency.
Cumulative student debt: 53% of graduating class had student loans; average debt was $15,939.
Additional info: Job opportunities provided for almost 17% of full-time undergraduate students. Students can expect to earn between $1,200 and $2,000 per academic year by working 10 to 15 hours per week.

FINANCIAL AID PROCEDURES

Forms required: FAFSA.
Dates and Deadlines: Closing date 3/1. Applicants notified on a rolling basis starting 3/15; must reply by 5/1 or within 2 week(s) of notification.
Transfers: No deadline. Financial aid transcripts from previous schools required.

CONTACT

Elizabeth Zimmerman, Director of Financial Aid
1200 Camden Avenue, Salisbury, MD 21801-6862
(410) 543-6165

Sojourner-Douglass College

Baltimore, Maryland
www.sdc.edu

Federal Code: 021279

4-year private liberal arts college in very large city.
Enrollment: 1,246 undergrads.
Selectivity: Open admission.

BASIC COSTS (2008-2009)

Tuition and fees: $7,478.

FINANCIAL AID PICTURE (2007-2008)

Students with need: Need-based aid available for full-time and part-time students.

FINANCIAL AID PROCEDURES

Forms required: FAFSA, institutional form.
Dates and Deadlines: Priority date 3/1; no closing date. Applicants notified on a rolling basis; must reply within 2 week(s) of notification.

CONTACT

Rebecca Chalk, Financial Aid Administrator
500 North Caroline Street, Baltimore, MD 21205
(410) 276-0306 ext. 260

Stevenson University

Stevenson, Maryland
www.stevenson.edu Federal Code: 002107

4-year private university and career college in very large city.
Enrollment: 3,118 undergrads, 17% part-time. 604 full-time freshmen.
Selectivity: Admits 50 to 75% of applicants.

BASIC COSTS (2009-2010)

Tuition and fees: $20,644.
Per-credit charge: $487.
Room and board: $10,296.
Additional info: Room and board fees includes laundry.

FINANCIAL AID PICTURE (2007-2008)

Students with need: Out of 504 full-time freshmen who applied for aid, 402 were judged to have need. Of these, 402 received aid, and 73 had their full need met. Average financial aid package met 69% of need; average scholarship/grant was $10,005; average loan was $3,287. For part-time students, average financial aid package was $4,764.
Students without need: 131 full-time freshmen who did not demonstrate need for aid received scholarships/grants; average award was $4,861. No-need awards available for academics, art, leadership, music/drama, ROTC.
Additional info: Cooperative Education Program allows students to work in their field of study with area corporations.

FINANCIAL AID PROCEDURES

Forms required: FAFSA.
Dates and Deadlines: Priority date 2/15; no closing date. Applicants notified on a rolling basis starting 3/15; must reply by 5/1 or within 2 week(s) of notification.

CONTACT

Chris Hanlon, Assistant Vice President for Enrollment Management, Director of Financial Aid
1525 Greenspring Valley Road, Stevenson, MD 21153-0641
(443) 334-2559

Towson University

Towson, Maryland
www.towson.edu Federal Code: 002099

4-year public university in large city.
Enrollment: 16,628 undergrads, 10% part-time. 2,826 full-time freshmen.
Selectivity: Admits 50 to 75% of applicants.

BASIC COSTS (2008-2009)

Tuition and fees: $7,314; out-of-state residents $17,860.
Per-credit charge: $225; out-of-state residents $588.
Room and board: $8,306.

FINANCIAL AID PICTURE (2008-2009)

Students with need: Out of 2,149 full-time freshmen who applied for aid, 1,342 were judged to have need. Of these, 1,267 received aid, and 262 had their full need met. Average financial aid package met 69% of need; average scholarship/grant was $8,416; average loan was $3,177. For part-time students, average financial aid package was $5,780.
Students without need: 288 full-time freshmen who did not demonstrate need for aid received scholarships/grants; average award was $4,768. No-need awards available for academics, alumni affiliation, art, athletics, leadership, minority status, music/drama.
Scholarships offered: ***Merit:*** Towson Scholar Award: full tuition, fees, room and board. Presidential Scholarship: full tuition and fees. University Scholarship: full tuition. Provost Scholarship: $1,000-$6,000. Selection based on GPA and combined SAT score. ***Athletic:*** 58 full-time freshmen received athletic scholarships; average amount $9,928.
Cumulative student debt: 36% of graduating class had student loans; average debt was $9,498.

FINANCIAL AID PROCEDURES

Forms required: FAFSA.
Dates and Deadlines: Closing date 2/10. Applicants notified on a rolling basis starting 3/21; must reply within 2 week(s) of notification.
Transfers: Priority date 3/1.

CONTACT

Vincent Pecora, Director of Financial Aid
8000 York Road, Towson, MD 21252-0001
(410) 704-4236

United States Naval Academy

Annapolis, Maryland
www.usna.edu Federal Code: 002101

4-year public military college in large town.
Enrollment: 4,489 undergrads. 1,232 full-time freshmen.
Selectivity: Admits less than 50% of applicants.

BASIC COSTS (2009-2010)

Additional info: First-year students pay one-time fee of $2,500 upon entering the Naval Academy for initial outfitting of uniforms and other supplies. Tuition, room and board, and medical and dental care provided by United States government. Each midshipman receives monthly salary of about $895 to cover costs of books, supplies, uniforms, laundry, and equipment, including microcomputer.

CONTACT

117 Decatur Road, Annapolis, MD 21402-5018

University of Baltimore

Baltimore, Maryland
www.ubalt.edu Federal Code: 002102

4-year public business and liberal arts college in very large city.
Enrollment: 2,710 undergrads, 45% part-time. 163 full-time freshmen.
Selectivity: Admits 50 to 75% of applicants.

BASIC COSTS (2008-2009)

Tuition and fees: $7,051; out-of-state residents $20,557.
Per-credit charge: $243; out-of-state residents $784.

FINANCIAL AID PICTURE

Students with need: Need-based aid available for full-time and part-time students.

FINANCIAL AID PROCEDURES

Forms required: FAFSA, institutional form.
Dates and Deadlines: No deadline. Applicants notified on a rolling basis.
Transfers: Closing date 5/1. Applicants notified on a rolling basis; must reply within 2 week(s) of notification. Scholarship application deadline, March 1.

CONTACT

Anne Hamill, Director, Financial Aid
1420 North Charles Street, Baltimore, MD 21201-5779
(410) 837-4763

University of Maryland: Baltimore
Baltimore, Maryland
www.umaryland.edu Federal Code: 002104

Upper-division public university and health science college in very large city.
Enrollment: 851 undergrads, 37% part-time.

BASIC COSTS (2008-2009)
Tuition and fees: $7,803; out-of-state residents $21,542.
Per-credit charge: $301; out-of-state residents $533.

FINANCIAL AID PICTURE (2007-2008)
Students with need: 36% of average financial aid package awarded as scholarships/grants, 64% awarded as loans/jobs. Need-based aid available for part-time students. Work study available nights, weekends, and for part-time students.
Additional info: Maryland state deadline 3/1.

FINANCIAL AID PROCEDURES
Forms required: FAFSA, state aid form.
Dates and Deadlines: Priority date 3/15; no closing date. Applicants notified on a rolling basis starting 4/15; must reply within 2 week(s) of notification.

CONTACT
Patricia Scott, Associate Director of Financial Aid
620 West Lexington Street, Baltimore, MD 21201
(410) 706-7347

University of Maryland: Baltimore County
Baltimore, Maryland
www.umbc.edu Federal Code: 002105

4-year public university in large city.
Enrollment: 9,468 undergrads, 13% part-time. 1,424 full-time freshmen.
Selectivity: Admits 50 to 75% of applicants.

BASIC COSTS (2008-2009)
Tuition and fees: $8,780; out-of-state residents $17,512.
Per-credit charge: $270; out-of-state residents $633.
Room and board: $8,960.

FINANCIAL AID PICTURE (2007-2008)
Students with need: Out of 981 full-time freshmen who applied for aid, 657 were judged to have need. Of these, 657 received aid, and 264 had their full need met. Average financial aid package met 86% of need; average scholarship/grant was $10,287; average loan was $3,622. For part-time students, average financial aid package was $8,262.
Students without need: 404 full-time freshmen who did not demonstrate need for aid received scholarships/grants; average award was $3,619. No-need awards available for academics, alumni affiliation, art, athletics, music/drama.
Scholarships offered: ***Merit:*** UMBC General Merit Awards, range from $500-$22,000 per year. Scholars Programs, awards range from $5,000-$22,000 per year. These programs include Center for Women and Information Technology (CWIT) Scholars Program, Humanities Scholars Program, Linehan Artist Scholars Program, Meyerhoff Scholars Program (Sciences and Engineering), and Sondheim Public Affairs Scholars Program Scholars Programs; tuition, fees, room and board. ***Athletic:*** 78 full-time freshmen received athletic scholarships; average amount $4,235.
Cumulative student debt: 50% of graduating class had student loans; average debt was $20,228.

FINANCIAL AID PROCEDURES
Forms required: FAFSA.
Dates and Deadlines: Priority date 2/14; no closing date. Applicants notified on a rolling basis starting 4/1; must reply within 2 week(s) of notification.

Transfers: Two-year merit scholarships available for transfer students from community colleges.

CONTACT
Stephanie Johnson, Director, Financial Aid
1000 Hilltop Circle, Baltimore, MD 21250
(410) 455-2387

University of Maryland: College Park
College Park, Maryland
www.maryland.edu Federal Code: 002103

4-year public university in large town.
Enrollment: 25,852 undergrads, 6% part-time. 3,900 full-time freshmen.
Selectivity: Admits less than 50% of applicants.

BASIC COSTS (2008-2009)
Tuition and fees: $8,005; out-of-state residents $23,076.
Per-credit charge: $273; out-of-state residents $902.
Room and board: $9,109.

FINANCIAL AID PICTURE (2007-2008)
Students with need: Need-based aid available for full-time and part-time students. Work study available nights, weekends, and for part-time students.
Students without need: No-need awards available for academics, art, athletics, music/drama.
Additional info: Prepaid tuition plans available through state.

FINANCIAL AID PROCEDURES
Forms required: FAFSA.
Dates and Deadlines: Priority date 2/15; no closing date. Applicants notified on a rolling basis starting 4/1.

CONTACT
Sarah Bauder, Director of Student Financial Aid
Mitchell Building, College Park, MD 20742-5235
(301) 314-9000

University of Maryland: Eastern Shore
Princess Anne, Maryland
www.umes.edu Federal Code: 002106

4-year public university in rural community.
Enrollment: 3,716 undergrads, 5% part-time. 1,038 full-time freshmen.
Selectivity: Admits 50 to 75% of applicants.

BASIC COSTS (2008-2009)
Tuition and fees: $6,042; out-of-state residents $12,830.
Per-credit charge: $171; out-of-state residents $401.
Room and board: $6,880.

FINANCIAL AID PICTURE (2007-2008)
Students with need: 74% of average financial aid package awarded as scholarships/grants, 26% awarded as loans/jobs. Need-based aid available for part-time students.
Students without need: No-need awards available for academics, alumni affiliation, art, athletics, leadership, music/drama, ROTC, state/district residency.

FINANCIAL AID PROCEDURES
Forms required: FAFSA.
Dates and Deadlines: Priority date 3/1; closing date 4/1. Applicants notified on a rolling basis starting 4/15.

CONTACT
James Kellam, Director of Financial Aid
Bird Hall, Princess Anne, MD 21853
(410) 651-6172

University of Maryland: University College

Adelphi, Maryland
www.umuc.edu Federal Code: 011644

4-year public university in large town.
Enrollment: 21,061 undergrads, 86% part-time. 108 full-time freshmen.
Selectivity: Open admission.

BASIC COSTS (2008-2009)
Tuition and fees: $5,820; out-of-state residents $12,060.
Per-credit charge: $230; out-of-state residents $490.

FINANCIAL AID PICTURE (2007-2008)
Students with need: Out of 72 full-time freshmen who applied for aid, 70 were judged to have need. Of these, 54 received aid. Average financial aid package met 18% of need; average scholarship/grant was $3,624; average loan was $2,799. For part-time students, average financial aid package was $4,767.
Students without need: No-need awards available for academics, leadership.

FINANCIAL AID PROCEDURES
Forms required: FAFSA, institutional form.
Dates and Deadlines: Priority date 6/1; no closing date. Applicants notified on a rolling basis starting 5/1; must reply within 2 week(s) of notification.

CONTACT
Cheryl Storie, Associate Vice President, Financial Aid
3501 University Boulevard East, Adelphi, MD 20783-8010
(301) 985-7000

Washington Bible College

Lanham, Maryland
www.bible.edu Federal Code: 001462

4-year private Bible and seminary college in large town, affiliated with nondenominational tradition.
Enrollment: 253 undergrads.

BASIC COSTS (2009-2010)
Tuition and fees: $13,230.
Per-credit charge: $420.
Room and board: $6,770.

FINANCIAL AID PICTURE (2007-2008)
Students with need: Need-based aid available for full-time and part-time students. Work study available nights, weekends, and for part-time students.
Students without need: No-need awards available for academics, leadership, music/drama, state/district residency.

FINANCIAL AID PROCEDURES
Forms required: FAFSA, institutional form.
Dates and Deadlines: Closing date 3/1. Applicants notified on a rolling basis starting 7/1; must reply within 2 week(s) of notification.
Transfers: Priority date 7/1; no deadline. Applicants notified on a rolling basis; must reply within 2 week(s) of notification.

CONTACT
Nichole Sefiane, Director of Financial Aid
6511 Princess Garden Parkway, Lanham, MD 20706-3599
(877) 793-7227

Washington College

Chestertown, Maryland
www.washcoll.edu Federal Code: 002108

4-year private liberal arts college in small town.
Enrollment: 1,275 undergrads. 415 full-time freshmen.
Selectivity: Admits 50 to 75% of applicants.

BASIC COSTS (2008-2009)
Tuition and fees: $34,005.
Per-credit charge: $1,391.
Room and board: $7,180.

FINANCIAL AID PICTURE (2008-2009)
Students with need: Out of 297 full-time freshmen who applied for aid, 209 were judged to have need. Of these, 209 received aid, and 105 had their full need met. Average financial aid package met 82% of need; average scholarship/grant was $19,757; average loan was $2,380. For part-time students, average financial aid package was $3,395.
Students without need: 115 full-time freshmen who did not demonstrate need for aid received scholarships/grants; average award was $11,541. No-need awards available for academics.
Scholarships offered: National Honor Society Scholarship; $40,000 over 4 years; applicant must be member of National Honor Society.
Cumulative student debt: 61% of graduating class had student loans; average debt was $20,611.

FINANCIAL AID PROCEDURES
Forms required: FAFSA, institutional form.
Dates and Deadlines: Priority date 2/15; no closing date. Applicants notified on a rolling basis starting 2/15; must reply by 5/1.

CONTACT
Jean Narcum, Director of Financial Aid
300 Washington Avenue, Chestertown, MD 21620-1197
(410) 778-7214

Wor-Wic Community College

Salisbury, Maryland
www.worwic.edu Federal Code: 013842

2-year public community college in large town.
Enrollment: 3,278 undergrads, 64% part-time. 447 full-time freshmen.
Selectivity: Open admission; but selective for some programs.

BASIC COSTS (2009-2010)
Tuition and fees: $2,594; out of district residents $6,104; out-of-state residents $7,094.
Per-credit charge: $80; out-of-district residents $197; out-of-state residents $230.

FINANCIAL AID PICTURE (2008-2009)
Students with need: Need-based aid available for full-time and part-time students. Work study available nights, weekends, and for part-time students.
Students without need: No-need awards available for academics, state/district residency.

FINANCIAL AID PROCEDURES
Forms required: FAFSA, institutional form.
Dates and Deadlines: Priority date 6/1; no closing date. Applicants notified on a rolling basis starting 4/1.

CONTACT
Deborah Jenkins, Director of Financial Aid
32000 Campus Drive, Salisbury, MD 21804
(410) 334-2905

Massachusetts

American International College
Springfield, Massachusetts
www.aic.edu Federal Code: 002114

4-year private liberal arts college in small city.
Enrollment: 1,717 undergrads, 11% part-time. 381 full-time freshmen.
Selectivity: Admits over 75% of applicants.

BASIC COSTS (2008-2009)
Tuition and fees: $24,100.
Per-credit charge: $497.
Room and board: $10,150.

FINANCIAL AID PICTURE (2008-2009)
Students with need: Out of 333 full-time freshmen who applied for aid, 316 were judged to have need. Of these, 316 received aid, and 42 had their full need met. Average financial aid package met 75% of need; average scholarship/grant was $17,778; average loan was $3,305. For part-time students, average financial aid package was $8,000.
Students without need: 59 full-time freshmen who did not demonstrate need for aid received scholarships/grants; average award was $14,399. No-need awards available for academics, alumni affiliation, athletics, leadership.
Scholarships offered: ***Merit:*** Presidential, Provost, Opportunity Scholarships; $5,000 to $11,000; based on class rank, SAT, GPA. ***Athletic:*** 44 full-time freshmen received athletic scholarships; average amount $13,565.
Cumulative student debt: 93% of graduating class had student loans; average debt was $31,893.

FINANCIAL AID PROCEDURES
Forms required: FAFSA, state aid form.
Dates and Deadlines: Priority date 5/1; no closing date. Applicants notified on a rolling basis starting 3/15; must reply by 5/1 or within 2 week(s) of notification.

CONTACT
Douglas Fish, Director of Financial Aid
1000 State Street, Springfield, MA 01109
(413) 205-3259

Amherst College
Amherst, Massachusetts Federal Code: 002115
www.amherst.edu CSS Code: 3003

4-year private liberal arts college in large town.
Enrollment: 1,697 undergrads. 438 full-time freshmen.
Selectivity: Admits less than 50% of applicants.

BASIC COSTS (2009-2010)
Tuition and fees: $38,928.
Room and board: $10,150.
Additional info: Health Insurance (waivable): $950.

FINANCIAL AID PICTURE (2008-2009)
Students with need: Out of 249 full-time freshmen who applied for aid, 224 were judged to have need. Of these, 224 received aid, and 100 had their full need met. Average financial aid package met 100% of need; average scholarship/grant was $36,075; average loan was $2,375.
Students without need: This college awards aid only to students with need.
Cumulative student debt: 46% of graduating class had student loans; average debt was $12,603.

FINANCIAL AID PROCEDURES
Forms required: FAFSA, CSS PROFILE.
Dates and Deadlines: Priority date 2/15; no closing date. Applicants notified by 4/1; must reply by 5/1.

CONTACT
Joe Case, Dean of Financial Aid
PO Box 5000, Amherst, MA 01002-5000
(413) 542-2296

Anna Maria College
Paxton, Massachusetts
www.annamaria.edu Federal Code: 002117

4-year private liberal arts college in small town, affiliated with Roman Catholic Church.
Enrollment: 978 undergrads, 20% part-time. 245 full-time freshmen.
Selectivity: Admits over 75% of applicants.

BASIC COSTS (2008-2009)
Tuition and fees: $25,850.
Per-credit charge: $783.
Room and board: $9,350.
Additional info: Annual tuition for music program: $26,500.

FINANCIAL AID PICTURE (2008-2009)
Students with need: Out of 225 full-time freshmen who applied for aid, 199 were judged to have need. Of these, 199 received aid, and 16 had their full need met. Average financial aid package met 66% of need; average scholarship/grant was $13,617; average loan was $4,443. For part-time students, average financial aid package was $13,210.
Students without need: 43 full-time freshmen who did not demonstrate need for aid received scholarships/grants; average award was $7,500. No-need awards available for academics, alumni affiliation, music/drama, religious affiliation, state/district residency.
Cumulative student debt: 92% of graduating class had student loans; average debt was $35,575.

FINANCIAL AID PROCEDURES
Forms required: FAFSA, state aid form.
Dates and Deadlines: Priority date 3/1; no closing date. Applicants notified on a rolling basis starting 4/1; must reply within 4 week(s) of notification.
Transfers: No deadline. Applicants notified on a rolling basis starting 4/1; must reply within 4 week(s) of notification. Deadline May 1 for state aid.

CONTACT
Colleen King, Director of Financial Aid
50 Sunset Lane, Box O, Paxton, MA 01612-1198
(508) 849-3363

Assumption College
Worcester, Massachusetts
www.assumption.edu Federal Code: 002118

4-year private liberal arts college in small city, affiliated with Roman Catholic Church.
Enrollment: 2,163 undergrads. 607 full-time freshmen.
Selectivity: Admits 50 to 75% of applicants.

BASIC COSTS (2009-2010)
Tuition and fees: $30,171.
Per-credit charge: $994.
Room and board: $10,070.

FINANCIAL AID PICTURE (2008-2009)

Students with need: Out of 542 full-time freshmen who applied for aid, 450 were judged to have need. Of these, 450 received aid, and 102 had their full need met. Average financial aid package met 74% of need; average scholarship/grant was $14,950; average loan was $3,756. For part-time students, average financial aid package was $8,550.

Students without need: 141 full-time freshmen who did not demonstrate need for aid received scholarships/grants; average award was $13,577. No-need awards available for academics, athletics.

Scholarships offered: ***Merit:*** Academic scholarships; $2,500-$20,000 per year; based on academic achievement and leadership talents. ***Athletic:*** 9 full-time freshmen received athletic scholarships; average amount $28,763.

Cumulative student debt: 93% of graduating class had student loans; average debt was $26,691.

FINANCIAL AID PROCEDURES

Forms required: FAFSA.

Dates and Deadlines: Closing date 2/1. Applicants notified on a rolling basis starting 2/16; must reply by 5/1.

Transfers: Closing date 3/1. Applicants notified on a rolling basis starting 5/1.

CONTACT

Linda Mularczyk, Director of Financial Aid
500 Salisbury Street, Worcester, MA 01609-1296
(508) 767-7158

Atlantic Union College

South Lancaster, Massachusetts
www.auc.edu Federal Code: 002119

4-year private liberal arts college in small town, affiliated with Seventh-day Adventists.

Enrollment: 362 undergrads, 15% part-time. 55 full-time freshmen.

Selectivity: Admits less than 50% of applicants.

BASIC COSTS (2008-2009)

Tuition and fees: $16,570.

Room and board: $5,000.

Additional info: Additional fees for nursing program. Tuition/fee waivers available for adults.

FINANCIAL AID PICTURE (2008-2009)

Students with need: Average financial aid package met 35% of need; average scholarship/grant was $4,617; average loan was $3,318. For part-time students, average financial aid package was $7,888.

Students without need: No-need awards available for academics, alumni affiliation, art, leadership.

Cumulative student debt: 33% of graduating class had student loans; average debt was $34,800.

FINANCIAL AID PROCEDURES

Forms required: FAFSA, institutional form.

Dates and Deadlines: Priority date 3/1; closing date 9/16. Applicants notified on a rolling basis starting 3/1; must reply by 9/12 or within 2 week(s) of notification.

Transfers: Applicants notified on a rolling basis starting 3/1; must reply within 2 week(s) of notification.

CONTACT

Sandra Pereira, Financial Aid Director
Main Street, South Lancaster, MA 01561
(978) 368-2275

Babson College

Babson Park, Massachusetts Federal Code: 002121
www.babson.edu CSS Code: 3075

4-year private business college in large town.

Enrollment: 1,851 undergrads. 469 full-time freshmen.

Selectivity: Admits less than 50% of applicants.

BASIC COSTS (2008-2009)

Tuition and fees: $36,096.

Room and board: $12,020.

FINANCIAL AID PICTURE (2008-2009)

Students with need: Average financial aid package met 97% of need; average scholarship/grant was $26,223; average loan was $2,684.

Students without need: This college awards aid only to students with need.

Scholarships offered: Presidential Scholarship; half tuition; based on high school record, cocurricular achievements, demonstrated leadership, writing skills, standardized test scores; approximately 40 awarded each year. Woman's Leadership Award; one quarter tuition; based on demonstrated leadership experience, future leadership potential, and academic achievement. Diversity Leadership Award; either full or half tuition; awarded to students with the greatest potential for leadership in creating a diverse Babson community.

Cumulative student debt: 47% of graduating class had student loans; average debt was $27,598.

FINANCIAL AID PROCEDURES

Forms required: FAFSA, CSS PROFILE.

Dates and Deadlines: Closing date 2/15. Applicants notified by 4/1; must reply by 5/1.

Transfers: Priority date 2/15; closing date 4/15.

CONTACT

Melissa Shaak, Director, Student Financial Services
231 Forest Street, Babson Park, MA 02457-0310
(781) 239-4219

Bard College at Simon's Rock

Great Barrington, Massachusetts Federal Code: 009645
www.simons-rock.edu CSS Code: 3795

4-year private liberal arts college in small town.

Enrollment: 427 undergrads. 185 full-time freshmen.

Selectivity: Admits over 75% of applicants.

BASIC COSTS (2008-2009)

Tuition and fees: $37,860.

Per-credit charge: $1,430.

Room and board: $10,600.

Additional info: Annual health services fee of $640. Student activity fee $150.

FINANCIAL AID PICTURE (2007-2008)

Students with need: Out of 168 full-time freshmen who applied for aid, 110 were judged to have need. Of these, 110 received aid, and 18 had their full need met. Average financial aid package met 68% of need; average scholarship/grant was $15,500; average loan was $4,425.

Students without need: 35 full-time freshmen who did not demonstrate need for aid received scholarships/grants; average award was $14,000. No-need awards available for academics, alumni affiliation, leadership, state/district residency.

Scholarships offered: Acceleration to Excellence Program; 2 years full tuition; based on excellent grades, community service, maturity; special application process required.

Cumulative student debt: 40% of graduating class had student loans; average debt was $21,000.

FINANCIAL AID PROCEDURES

Forms required: FAFSA, CSS PROFILE.
Dates and Deadlines: Priority date 4/15; no closing date. Applicants notified on a rolling basis starting 4/15; must reply within 2 week(s) of notification.

CONTACT

Ann Gitto, Director of Financial Aid
Office of Admission, Great Barrington, MA 01230-1990
(413) 528-7297

Bay Path College

Longmeadow, Massachusetts
www.baypath.edu Federal Code: 002122

4-year private business college for women in large town.
Enrollment: 1,409 undergrads, 22% part-time. 182 full-time freshmen.
Selectivity: Admits over 75% of applicants.

BASIC COSTS (2009-2010)

Tuition and fees: $24,530.
Per-credit charge: $455.
Room and board: $10,035.

FINANCIAL AID PICTURE (2008-2009)

Students with need: Out of 169 full-time freshmen who applied for aid, 155 were judged to have need. Of these, 154 received aid, and 21 had their full need met. Average financial aid package met 77% of need; average scholarship/grant was $13,941; average loan was $4,483. For part-time students, average financial aid package was $3,401.
Students without need: 24 full-time freshmen who did not demonstrate need for aid received scholarships/grants; average award was $11,318. No-need awards available for academics, state/district residency.
Cumulative student debt: 90% of graduating class had student loans; average debt was $20,662.
Additional info: Opportunity Grant program for students whose family may be facing financial difficulties paying tuition resulting from economic conditions. Additional funding available in an endowment program to assist students who qualify.

FINANCIAL AID PROCEDURES

Forms required: FAFSA.
Dates and Deadlines: Priority date 3/15; no closing date. Applicants notified on a rolling basis starting 3/1; must reply within 2 week(s) of notification.

CONTACT

Stephanie King, Director of Student Financial Services
588 Longmeadow Street, Longmeadow, MA 01106
(413) 565-1000 ext. 1345

Bay State College

Boston, Massachusetts
www.baystate.edu Federal Code: 003965

2-year private junior college in very large city.
Enrollment: 810 undergrads.

BASIC COSTS (2008-2009)

Tuition and fees: $19,350.
Per-credit charge: $788.
Room and board: $11,130.
Additional info: Program specific fees for allied health, $475 and fashion design, $300.

FINANCIAL AID PICTURE (2007-2008)

Students with need: 28% of average financial aid package awarded as scholarships/grants, 72% awarded as loans/jobs. Need-based aid available for part-time students. Work study available nights, weekends, and for part-time students.
Scholarships offered: Scholarship awards; amounts vary; need-based and merit-based.

FINANCIAL AID PROCEDURES

Forms required: FAFSA, institutional form.
Dates and Deadlines: Priority date 3/15; no closing date. Applicants notified on a rolling basis starting 3/15; must reply within 3 week(s) of notification.

CONTACT

Jeanne Stella-Devani, Director of Financial Aid
122 Commonwealth Avenue, Boston, MA 02116
(617) 217-9000

Becker College

Worcester, Massachusetts
www.becker.edu Federal Code: 002123

4-year private liberal arts college in small city.
Enrollment: 1,728 undergrads, 22% part-time. 346 full-time freshmen.
Selectivity: Admits 50 to 75% of applicants.

BASIC COSTS (2009-2010)

Tuition and fees: $24,780.
Per-credit charge: $1,040.
Room and board: $9,760.
Additional info: Additional one-time charge of $285 for nursing program.

FINANCIAL AID PICTURE (2007-2008)

Students with need: Need-based aid available for full-time and part-time students. Work study available nights, weekends, and for part-time students.
Students without need: No-need awards available for academics.

FINANCIAL AID PROCEDURES

Forms required: FAFSA.
Dates and Deadlines: Priority date 3/1; no closing date. Applicants notified on a rolling basis starting 2/1; must reply within 2 week(s) of notification.

CONTACT

61 Sever Street, Worcester, MA 01609
(508) 791-9241 ext. 242

Benjamin Franklin Institute of Technology

Boston, Massachusetts
www.bfit.edu Federal Code: 002151

2-year private technical college in very large city.
Enrollment: 529 undergrads.

BASIC COSTS (2009-2010)

Tuition and fees: $13,950.
Per-credit charge: $581.
Additional info: Cost shown is for certificate program.

FINANCIAL AID PICTURE (2007-2008)

Students with need: Need-based aid available for full-time and part-time students.
Students without need: No-need awards available for academics.

FINANCIAL AID PROCEDURES

Forms required: FAFSA.

Dates and Deadlines: Priority date 4/1; no closing date. Applicants notified on a rolling basis starting 3/1; must reply within 4 week(s) of notification.

CONTACT

Chris Verleger, Director of Financial Aid
41 Berkeley Street, Boston, MA 02116
(617) 423-4630

Bentley University

Waltham, Massachusetts — Federal Code: 002124
www.bentley.edu — CSS Code: 3096

4-year private business college in small city.
Enrollment: 4,187 undergrads, 5% part-time. 939 full-time freshmen.
Selectivity: Admits less than 50% of applicants.

BASIC COSTS (2008-2009)

Tuition and fees: $34,488.
Room and board: $11,320.

FINANCIAL AID PICTURE (2007-2008)

Students with need: Out of 687 full-time freshmen who applied for aid, 448 were judged to have need. Of these, 444 received aid, and 199 had their full need met. Average financial aid package met 95% of need; average scholarship/grant was $19,436; average loan was $4,402. For part-time students, average financial aid package was $4,210.
Students without need: 157 full-time freshmen who did not demonstrate need for aid received scholarships/grants; average award was $13,825. No-need awards available for academics, athletics, leadership, minority status.
Scholarships offered: ***Merit:*** Trustee Scholarships; full tuition; based on superior record of academic accomplishment. President's Scholarships; half or one-third tuition; based on excellent academic record. Service Learning Scholarships; $7,500; for students with excellent academic records who have demonstrated commitment to community service. ***Athletic:*** 7 full-time freshmen received athletic scholarships; average amount $35,044.
Cumulative student debt: 65% of graduating class had student loans; average debt was $30,577.
Additional info: Deadlines for receipt of CSS PROFILE: early decision 12/1, early action and regular decision 2/1.

FINANCIAL AID PROCEDURES

Forms required: FAFSA. CSS PROFILE required if student is applying for institutional grants.
Dates and Deadlines: Closing date 2/1. Applicants notified on a rolling basis starting 3/25.
Transfers: Closing date 3/1. Applicants notified on a rolling basis.

CONTACT

Donna Kendall, Director of Financial Assistance
175 Forest Street, Waltham, MA 02452-4705
(781) 891-3441

Berklee College of Music

Boston, Massachusetts
www.berklee.edu — Federal Code: 002126

4-year private music college in very large city.
Enrollment: 4,054 undergrads, 8% part-time. 605 full-time freshmen.
Selectivity: Admits less than 50% of applicants.

BASIC COSTS (2009-2010)

Tuition and fees: $33,653.
Per-credit charge: $1,053.
Room and board: $15,080.
Additional info: $2,950 one-time charge for purchase of laptop, which all freshmen must purchase.

FINANCIAL AID PICTURE (2008-2009)

Students with need: Out of 402 full-time freshmen who applied for aid, 343 were judged to have need. Of these, 341 received aid, and 28 had their full need met. Average financial aid package met 26% of need; average scholarship/grant was $6,826; average loan was $4,068. For part-time students, average financial aid package was $10,274.
Students without need: 85 full-time freshmen who did not demonstrate need for aid received scholarships/grants; average award was $11,638.

FINANCIAL AID PROCEDURES

Forms required: FAFSA.
Dates and Deadlines: Closing date 5/1. Applicants notified on a rolling basis starting 3/7; must reply within 2 week(s) of notification.

CONTACT

Julie Poorman, Director of Financial Aid
1140 Boylston Street, Boston, MA 02215
(800) 538-3844

Berkshire Community College

Pittsfield, Massachusetts
www.berkshirecc.edu — Federal Code: 002167

2-year public community college in large town.
Enrollment: 1,841 undergrads, 47% part-time. 378 full-time freshmen.
Selectivity: Open admission; but selective for some programs.

BASIC COSTS (2008-2009)

Tuition and fees: $3,930; out-of-state residents $11,550.
Per-credit charge: $26; out-of-state residents $280.

FINANCIAL AID PICTURE (2007-2008)

Students with need: Average financial aid package for all full-time undergraduates was $4,014. 68% awarded as scholarships/grants, 32% awarded as loans/jobs. Need-based aid available for part-time students. Work study available nights, weekends, and for part-time students.
Students without need: No-need awards available for academics, job skills, leadership, state/district residency.
Additional info: Tuition waivers available to Massachusetts residents who fall into one of the following categories: Department of Social Services adopted or foster children, Massachusetts Rehabilitation Commission clients, high-scoring MCAS students, National Guard members, Native Americans, state employees and their dependents, veterans.

FINANCIAL AID PROCEDURES

Forms required: FAFSA.
Dates and Deadlines: Priority date 5/1; no closing date. Applicants notified on a rolling basis starting 5/10; must reply within 2 week(s) of notification.
Transfers: No deadline. Applicants notified on a rolling basis.

CONTACT

Anne Moore, Director of Financial Aid
1350 West Street, Pittsfield, MA 01201-5786
(413) 236-1644

Boston Architectural College

Boston, Massachusetts
www.the-bac.edu — Federal Code: 003966

6-year private architecture and design college in very large city.
Enrollment: 624 undergrads, 2% part-time. 64 full-time freshmen.
Selectivity: Open admission.

BASIC COSTS (2008-2009)

Tuition and fees: $10,620.
Per-credit charge: $826.

Additional info: Academic Only program tuition is $14,200 plus $20 required fees.

FINANCIAL AID PICTURE (2007-2008)

Students with need: Out of 64 full-time freshmen who applied for aid, 44 were judged to have need. Of these, 28 received aid, and 3 had their full need met. Average financial aid package met 33% of need; average scholarship/grant was $5,960; average loan was $3,918. For part-time students, average financial aid package was $909.

Students without need: 5 full-time freshmen who did not demonstrate need for aid received scholarships/grants; average award was $10,036. No-need awards available for academics, art, leadership.

Scholarships offered: Creative Exercise Scholarship; 20% of semester's tuition; based on completion of creative exercise on admission application; 6 issued annually.

Cumulative student debt: 59% of graduating class had student loans; average debt was $31,178.

FINANCIAL AID PROCEDURES

Forms required: FAFSA.

Dates and Deadlines: Priority date 4/15; no closing date. Applicants notified on a rolling basis starting 3/1; must reply within 2 week(s) of notification.

Transfers: No deadline. Applicants notified on a rolling basis starting 3/1; must reply within 2 week(s) of notification.

CONTACT

Anne Downey, Director of Financial Aid
320 Newbury Street, Boston, MA 02115-2795
(617) 585-0125

Boston College

Chestnut Hill, Massachusetts — Federal Code: 002128
www.bc.edu — CSS Code: 3083

4-year private university in small city, affiliated with Roman Catholic Church.

Enrollment: 9,060 undergrads. 2,291 full-time freshmen.

Selectivity: Admits less than 50% of applicants.

BASIC COSTS (2008-2009)

Tuition and fees: $37,950.

Room and board: $11,610.

FINANCIAL AID PICTURE (2007-2008)

Students with need: Out of 1,214 full-time freshmen who applied for aid, 939 were judged to have need. Of these, 939 received aid, and 939 had their full need met. Average financial aid package met 100% of need; average scholarship/grant was $24,075; average loan was $3,513. Need-based aid available for part-time students.

Students without need: 23 full-time freshmen who did not demonstrate need for aid received scholarships/grants; average award was $15,193. No-need awards available for academics, athletics, leadership, ROTC.

Scholarships offered: 69 full-time freshmen received athletic scholarships; average amount $34,968.

Cumulative student debt: 53% of graduating class had student loans; average debt was $18,799.

FINANCIAL AID PROCEDURES

Forms required: FAFSA, CSS PROFILE.

Dates and Deadlines: Priority date 2/1; no closing date. Applicants notified by 4/1; must reply by 5/1.

Transfers: Priority date 3/15. Must reply within 2 week(s) of notification.

CONTACT

Mary McGranahan, Director of Financial Aid
140 Commonwealth Avenue, Devlin Hall 208, Chestnut Hill, MA 02467-3809
(617) 552-3300

Boston Conservatory

Boston, Massachusetts
www.bostonconservatory.edu — Federal Code: 002129

4-year private music and performing arts college in very large city.

Enrollment: 482 undergrads.

Selectivity: Admits less than 50% of applicants.

BASIC COSTS (2008-2009)

Tuition and fees: $32,350.

Per-credit charge: $1,260.

Room and board: $15,670.

FINANCIAL AID PICTURE (2008-2009)

Students with need: 48% of average financial aid package awarded as scholarships/grants, 52% awarded as loans/jobs. Need-based aid available for part-time students.

Students without need: No-need awards available for music/drama.

FINANCIAL AID PROCEDURES

Forms required: FAFSA, institutional form.

Dates and Deadlines: Priority date 3/1; no closing date.

CONTACT

Nicole Brennan, Director of Financial Aid
8 The Fenway, Boston, MA 02215

Boston University

Boston, Massachusetts — Federal Code: 002130
www.bu.edu — CSS Code: 3087

4-year private university in very large city.

Enrollment: 16,474 undergrads, 3% part-time. 4,131 full-time freshmen.

Selectivity: Admits 50 to 75% of applicants.

BASIC COSTS (2009-2010)

Tuition and fees: $38,440.

Per-credit charge: $1,184.

Room and board: $11,848.

FINANCIAL AID PICTURE (2008-2009)

Students with need: Out of 2,427 full-time freshmen who applied for aid, 1,954 were judged to have need. Of these, 1,952 received aid, and 930 had their full need met. Average financial aid package met 90% of need; average scholarship/grant was $21,485; average loan was $4,960. For part-time students, average financial aid package was $15,091.

Students without need: 293 full-time freshmen who did not demonstrate need for aid received scholarships/grants; average award was $18,405. No-need awards available for academics, alumni affiliation, art, athletics, leadership, music/drama, religious affiliation, ROTC, state/district residency.

Scholarships offered: ***Merit:*** Trustee Scholar Program; full tuition and fees (renewable); candidates nominated by high school principals, headmasters, or students. University Scholarships; half tuition (renewable); based on exceptionally strong high school academic record. Dean's Scholarships; $10,000 (renewable); based on strong academic credentials; for students who have applied for need-based financial aid but have financial resources which exceed, cost of attendance. Dr. Martin Luther King, Jr. Scholarship; full tuition; for academically gifted students with proven leadership abilities and strong commitment to social justice and community involvement. ***Athletic:*** 59 full-time freshmen received athletic scholarships; average amount $37,899.

Cumulative student debt: 59% of graduating class had student loans; average debt was $26,586.

Additional info: Financial aid deadline for early decision applicants: 11/01; notification date: 2/15. Graduates of Boston's public high schools who complete financial aid application and demonstrate need will be awarded financial aid packages which contain no loans and meet their full demonstrated need.

FINANCIAL AID PROCEDURES

Forms required: FAFSA, CSS PROFILE, state aid form.

Dates and Deadlines: Closing date 2/15. Applicants notified on a rolling basis starting 3/15; must reply by 5/1 or within 2 week(s) of notification.

Transfers: Priority date 4/1. Transfer students cannot receive duplicate disbursements simultaneously from different institutions.

CONTACT

Christine McGuire, Director of Financial Assistance
121 Bay State Road, Boston, MA 02215
(617) 353-2965

Brandeis University

Waltham, Massachusetts — Federal Code: 002133
www.brandeis.edu — CSS Code: 3092

4-year private university in small city.
Enrollment: 3,169 undergrads. 754 full-time freshmen.
Selectivity: Admits less than 50% of applicants.

BASIC COSTS (2008-2009)

Tuition and fees: $37,294.
Room and board: $10,354.

FINANCIAL AID PICTURE (2008-2009)

Students with need: Out of 546 full-time freshmen who applied for aid, 405 were judged to have need. Of these, 403 received aid, and 92 had their full need met. Average financial aid package met 86% of need; average scholarship/grant was $26,874; average loan was $3,990. Need-based aid available for part-time students.

Students without need: 145 full-time freshmen who did not demonstrate need for aid received scholarships/grants; average award was $21,688. No-need awards available for academics.

Scholarships offered: Justice Brandeis Scholarships; full tuition. Martin Luther King scholarships; tuition and room and board. SERP Scholarships; $20,000; based on musical ability. Presidential scholarships; $20,000. Dean's Awards; $15,000. Waltham High School scholarships; full tuition.

Cumulative student debt: 77% of graduating class had student loans; average debt was $20,095.

FINANCIAL AID PROCEDURES

Forms required: FAFSA, CSS PROFILE.

Dates and Deadlines: Priority date 2/1; no closing date. Applicants notified on a rolling basis starting 4/1.

Transfers: Priority date 4/1. International transfer students seeking scholarship or need-based financial assistance must apply by 2/1.

CONTACT

Peter Giumette, Director of Student Financial Services
Box 549110, Waltham, MA 02454-9110
(781) 736-3700

Bridgewater State College

Bridgewater, Massachusetts
www.bridgew.edu — Federal Code: 002183

4-year public liberal arts and teachers college in large town.
Enrollment: 8,310 undergrads, 15% part-time. 1,464 full-time freshmen.
Selectivity: Admits 50 to 75% of applicants.

BASIC COSTS (2008-2009)

Tuition and fees: $6,107; out-of-state residents $12,247.
Per-credit charge: $38; out-of-state residents $294.
Room and board: $8,405.
Additional info: Tuition/fee waivers available for unemployed or children of unemployed.

FINANCIAL AID PICTURE (2007-2008)

Students with need: Out of 1,369 full-time freshmen who applied for aid, 975 were judged to have need. Of these, 967 received aid. Average financial aid package met 75% of need; average scholarship/grant was $3,632; average loan was $3,400. For part-time students, average financial aid package was $4,289.

Students without need: 24 full-time freshmen who did not demonstrate need for aid received scholarships/grants; average award was $6,094. No-need awards available for academics, leadership, minority status, state/district residency.

Cumulative student debt: 72% of graduating class had student loans; average debt was $16,971.

FINANCIAL AID PROCEDURES

Forms required: FAFSA.

Dates and Deadlines: Priority date 3/1; no closing date. Applicants notified on a rolling basis starting 4/1.

CONTACT

Janet Gumbris, Director of Financial Aid
Gates House, Bridgewater, MA 02325
(508) 531-1341

Bristol Community College

Fall River, Massachusetts
www.bristolcc.edu — Federal Code: 002176

2-year public community college in small city.
Enrollment: 6,598 undergrads, 47% part-time. 1,337 full-time freshmen.
Selectivity: Open admission; but selective for some programs.

BASIC COSTS (2008-2009)

Tuition and fees: $3,840; out-of-state residents $10,020.
Per-credit charge: $24; out-of-state residents $230.
Additional info: Tuition/fee waivers available for unemployed or children of unemployed.

FINANCIAL AID PICTURE (2007-2008)

Students with need: Need-based aid available for full-time and part-time students. Work study available nights, weekends, and for part-time students.

Students without need: No-need awards available for academics, art, leadership, minority status, music/drama.

FINANCIAL AID PROCEDURES

Forms required: FAFSA, institutional form.

Dates and Deadlines: Priority date 5/1; no closing date. Applicants notified on a rolling basis starting 5/1; must reply within 2 week(s) of notification.

Transfers: No deadline. Applicants notified on a rolling basis starting 3/1.

CONTACT

David Allen, Director of Financial Aid
777 Elsbree Street, Fall River, MA 02720-7395
(508) 678-2811 ext. 2513

Bunker Hill Community College

Boston, Massachusetts
www.bhcc.mass.edu — Federal Code: 011210

2-year public community college in very large city.
Enrollment: 7,313 undergrads, 60% part-time. 862 full-time freshmen.
Selectivity: Open admission; but selective for some programs.

BASIC COSTS (2008-2009)

Tuition and fees: $3,480; out-of-state residents $9,660.
Per-credit charge: $24; out-of-state residents $230.

Additional info: New England Regional Tuition: $112 per-credit-hour. Tuition/fee waivers available for minority students.

FINANCIAL AID PICTURE (2007-2008)

Students with need: 89% of average financial aid package awarded as scholarships/grants, 11% awarded as loans/jobs. Need-based aid available for part-time students.
Students without need: No-need awards available for academics.

FINANCIAL AID PROCEDURES

Forms required: FAFSA.
Dates and Deadlines: Priority date 4/15; no closing date. Applicants notified on a rolling basis starting 6/1; must reply within 2 week(s) of notification.
Transfers: No deadline. Applicants notified on a rolling basis; must reply within 2 week(s) of notification.

CONTACT

Melissa Holster, Director of Financial Aid
250 New Rutherford Avenue, Boston, MA 02129-2925
(617) 228-2275

Cambridge College

Cambridge, Massachusetts
www.cambridgecollege.edu Federal Code: 021829

4-year private liberal arts and teachers college in very large city.
Enrollment: 1,130 undergrads, 69% part-time. 91 full-time freshmen.
Selectivity: Open admission.

BASIC COSTS (2008-2009)

Tuition and fees: $10,350.
Per-credit charge: $345.

FINANCIAL AID PICTURE (2007-2008)

Students with need: Need-based aid available for full-time and part-time students.
Students without need: This college awards aid only to students with need.

FINANCIAL AID PROCEDURES

Forms required: FAFSA, institutional form.
Dates and Deadlines: No deadline. Applicants notified on a rolling basis starting 5/1.
Transfers: No deadline. Applicants notified on a rolling basis.

CONTACT

Francis Lauder, Director of Financial Aid
1000 Massachusetts Avenue, Cambridge, MA 02138-5304
(617) 868-1000

Cape Cod Community College

West Barnstable, Massachusetts
www.capecod.edu Federal Code: 002168

2-year public community college in small town.
Enrollment: 3,432 undergrads.
Selectivity: Open admission; but selective for some programs.

BASIC COSTS (2008-2009)

Tuition and fees: $4,080; out-of-state residents $10,260.
Per-credit charge: $24; out-of-state residents $230.
Additional info: Tuition/fee waivers available for minority students.

FINANCIAL AID PICTURE (2008-2009)

Students with need: Average financial aid package for all full-time undergraduates was $4,067. Need-based aid available for part-time students.
Students without need: No-need awards available for academics, art, job skills, leadership, music/drama, state/district residency.

FINANCIAL AID PROCEDURES

Forms required: FAFSA.
Dates and Deadlines: Priority date 5/1; no closing date. Applicants notified on a rolling basis starting 5/1.

CONTACT

Sherry Andersen, Director of Financial Aid
2240 Iyannough Road, West Barnstable, MA 02668-1599
(508) 362-2131 ext. 4393

Caritas Laboure College

Boston, Massachusetts
www.laboure.edu Federal Code: 006324

2-year private health science and junior college in very large city, affiliated with Roman Catholic Church.
Enrollment: 535 undergrads.

BASIC COSTS (2008-2009)

Per-credit charge: $585.
Additional info: Cost of 4-term year is $21,878, inclusive of fees. Professional study courses are $645 per credit.

FINANCIAL AID PICTURE (2008-2009)

Students with need: Need-based aid available for full-time and part-time students. Work study available nights.
Students without need: No-need awards available for academics, alumni affiliation, leadership, religious affiliation.
Scholarships offered: Allied Health Scholarship; covers cost of general education courses for students enrolled in electroneurodiagnostic technology, health information technology, and nutrition and food management programs. Caritas Christi Scholarship; covers 25% of tuition for nursing and radiation therapy courses; also covers 50% of cost of nursing courses for students with LPN credential; for students who work 16 hours per week at a Caritas Christi healthcare agency. Evening LPN Scholarship; discounts tuition 75% for evening nursing majors with LPN credential.

FINANCIAL AID PROCEDURES

Forms required: FAFSA, institutional form.
Dates and Deadlines: Priority date 4/1; no closing date. Applicants notified on a rolling basis starting 5/15; must reply within 2 week(s) of notification.
Transfers: Priority date 12/1.

CONTACT

Erin Hanlon, Director of Financial Aid
2120 Dorchester Avenue, Boston, MA 02124-5698
(617) 296-8300 ext. 4054

Clark University

Worcester, Massachusetts Federal Code: 002139
www.clarku.edu CSS Code: 3279

4-year private university and liberal arts college in small city.
Enrollment: 2,293 undergrads, 2% part-time. 588 full-time freshmen.
Selectivity: Admits 50 to 75% of applicants.

BASIC COSTS (2009-2010)

Tuition and fees: $35,220.
Per-credit charge: $1,091.
Room and board: $6,750.
Additional info: New student contingency fee: $50. Fifth-year tuition waived for eligible undergraduates admitted to accelerated bachelor's/master's programs.

FINANCIAL AID PICTURE (2008-2009)

Students with need: Out of 418 full-time freshmen who applied for aid, 312 were judged to have need. Of these, 302 received aid, and 224 had their full need met. Average financial aid package met 95% of need; average scholarship/grant was $21,932; average loan was $4,731. Need-based aid available for part-time students.

Students without need: 173 full-time freshmen who did not demonstrate need for aid received scholarships/grants; average award was $14,472. No-need awards available for academics, leadership.

Scholarships offered: Scholarships; $10,000-$16,000; based on superior academic achievement or community service involvement.

Cumulative student debt: 90% of graduating class had student loans; average debt was $22,250.

FINANCIAL AID PROCEDURES

Forms required: FAFSA, CSS PROFILE.

Dates and Deadlines: Closing date 1/15. Applicants notified by 3/31; must reply by 5/1 or within 2 week(s) of notification.

Transfers: Priority date 4/1; no deadline. Financial aid transcript from previous institution(s) attended required.

CONTACT

Mary Ellen Severance, Director of Financial Aid and Student Employment
950 Main Street, Worcester, MA 01610-1477
(508) 793-7478

College of the Holy Cross

Worcester, Massachusetts — Federal Code: 002141
www.holycross.edu — CSS Code: 3282

4-year private liberal arts college in small city, affiliated with Roman Catholic Church.

Enrollment: 2,866 undergrads. 737 full-time freshmen.

Selectivity: Admits less than 50% of applicants.

BASIC COSTS (2009-2010)

Tuition and fees: $38,722.

Room and board: $10,620.

FINANCIAL AID PICTURE (2008-2009)

Students with need: Out of 517 full-time freshmen who applied for aid, 401 were judged to have need. Of these, 397 received aid, and 397 had their full need met. Average financial aid package met 100% of need; average scholarship/grant was $26,693; average loan was $4,673.

Students without need: 17 full-time freshmen who did not demonstrate need for aid received scholarships/grants; average award was $29,677. No-need awards available for academics, athletics, ROTC.

Scholarships offered: 4 full-time freshmen received athletic scholarships; average amount $47,849.

Additional info: Cost of tuition waived above the amount of the Pell Grant award for Worcester residents whose families earn less than $50,000.

FINANCIAL AID PROCEDURES

Forms required: FAFSA. CSS PROFILE required of all students applying for institutional aid.

Dates and Deadlines: Closing date 2/1. Applicants notified by 3/30; must reply by 5/1.

Transfers: Financial aid generally not available to transfer students.

CONTACT

Lynne Myers, Director of Financial Aid
One College Street, Worcester, MA 01610-2395
(508) 793-2265

Curry College

Milton, Massachusetts
www.curry.edu — Federal Code: 002143

4-year private nursing and liberal arts college in large town.

Enrollment: 2,598 undergrads, 22% part-time. 630 full-time freshmen.

Selectivity: Admits 50 to 75% of applicants.

BASIC COSTS (2008-2009)

Tuition and fees: $27,540.

Room and board: $11,080.

Additional info: PAL (Program for Advancement of Learning) students pay additional program participation fee of up to $5,700.

FINANCIAL AID PICTURE (2007-2008)

Students with need: Out of 445 full-time freshmen who applied for aid, 445 were judged to have need. Of these, 445 received aid, and 19 had their full need met. Average financial aid package met 63% of need; average scholarship/grant was $11,372; average loan was $3,447. For part-time students, average financial aid package was $4,694.

Students without need: 30 full-time freshmen who did not demonstrate need for aid received scholarships/grants; average award was $4,115. No-need awards available for academics, leadership.

Scholarships offered: Presidential Scholarship; $12,000 per year. Dean's Scholarship; $6,500 per year. Leadership Scholarship; $3,000 per year.

Cumulative student debt: 79% of graduating class had student loans; average debt was $47,955.

FINANCIAL AID PROCEDURES

Forms required: FAFSA.

Dates and Deadlines: Priority date 3/1; no closing date. Applicants notified on a rolling basis starting 3/1; must reply by 5/1 or within 2 week(s) of notification.

CONTACT

Stephanny Elias, Director, Student Financial Services
1071 Blue Hill Avenue, Milton, MA 02186-9984
(617) 333-2354

Dean College

Franklin, Massachusetts
www.dean.edu — Federal Code: 002144

2-year private junior and liberal arts college in large town.

Enrollment: 1,147 undergrads, 10% part-time. 572 full-time freshmen.

Selectivity: Admits 50 to 75% of applicants.

BASIC COSTS (2009-2010)

Tuition and fees: $28,020.

Room and board: $11,964.

FINANCIAL AID PICTURE (2007-2008)

Students with need: Out of 396 full-time freshmen who applied for aid, 353 were judged to have need. Of these, 353 received aid, and 42 had their full need met. Average financial aid package met 93% of need; average scholarship/grant was $12,769; average loan was $3,535. For part-time students, average financial aid package was $6,683.

Students without need: 217 full-time freshmen who did not demonstrate need for aid received scholarships/grants; average award was $10,102. No-need awards available for academics, athletics, leadership, music/drama, state/district residency.

Scholarships offered: ***Merit:*** Trustee's Scholarship; $10,000 - $12,000 per year; based on outstanding academic accomplishments or potential. President's Leadership Scholarship; $8,000 - $12,000 per year; given to students with leadership positions during their high school careers. Performing Arts Scholarship; $5,000 - $11,000 per year; based on achievement in dance or

theater. ***Athletic:*** 63 full-time freshmen received athletic scholarships; average amount $3,651.
Cumulative student debt: 52% of graduating class had student loans; average debt was $9,984.

FINANCIAL AID PROCEDURES

Forms required: FAFSA.
Dates and Deadlines: Priority date 3/15; no closing date. Applicants notified on a rolling basis starting 3/6; must reply by 5/1 or within 2 week(s) of notification.
Transfers: No deadline. Applicants notified on a rolling basis starting 3/1.

CONTACT

Jenny Aguiar, Director of Financial Aid
99 Main Street, Franklin, MA 02038-1994
(508) 541-1518

Elms College

Chicopee, Massachusetts
www.elms.edu Federal Code: 002140

4-year private liberal arts college in small city, affiliated with Roman Catholic Church.
Enrollment: 991 undergrads, 20% part-time. 208 full-time freshmen.
Selectivity: Admits over 75% of applicants.

BASIC COSTS (2008-2009)

Tuition and fees: $24,942.
Per-credit charge: $482.
Room and board: $9,260.

FINANCIAL AID PICTURE (2007-2008)

Students with need: Need-based aid available for full-time and part-time students. Work study available nights, weekends, and for part-time students.
Students without need: No-need awards available for academics, alumni affiliation, leadership, religious affiliation, state/district residency.

FINANCIAL AID PROCEDURES

Forms required: FAFSA, institutional form.
Dates and Deadlines: Priority date 3/1; no closing date. Applicants notified on a rolling basis starting 3/10; must reply by 5/1 or within 2 week(s) of notification.
Transfers: Priority date 7/1; no deadline. Applicants notified on a rolling basis starting 5/1; must reply by 9/6.

CONTACT

Troy Davis, Director of Student Financial Aid Services
291 Springfield Street, Chicopee, MA 01013
(413) 265-2249

Emerson College

Boston, Massachusetts Federal Code: 002146
www.emerson.edu CSS Code: 3367

4-year private college of communication and the arts in very large city.
Enrollment: 3,418 undergrads, 2% part-time. 773 full-time freshmen.
Selectivity: Admits less than 50% of applicants.

BASIC COSTS (2008-2009)

Tuition and fees: $28,884.
Per-credit charge: $886.
Room and board: $11,868.

FINANCIAL AID PICTURE (2007-2008)

Students with need: Out of 625 full-time freshmen who applied for aid, 468 were judged to have need. Of these, 468 received aid, and 262 had their full need met. Average financial aid package met 86% of need; average scholarship/grant was $12,792; average loan was $3,698. For part-time students, average financial aid package was $8,507.
Students without need: 192 full-time freshmen who did not demonstrate need for aid received scholarships/grants; average award was $13,092. No-need awards available for academics, music/drama, state/district residency.
Scholarships offered: Trustee's Scholarships (Honors Program); half tuition. Dean's Scholarships; approximately $8,000. Emerson Stage Scholarships; amounts vary; based on performing arts audition and academic merit.
Cumulative student debt: 65% of graduating class had student loans; average debt was $15,701.
Additional info: Massachusetts Loan Plan available for parents of dependent undergraduates.

FINANCIAL AID PROCEDURES

Forms required: FAFSA, CSS PROFILE.
Dates and Deadlines: Priority date 3/1; no closing date. Applicants notified by 4/1; must reply by 5/1 or within 3 week(s) of notification.
Transfers: Priority date 4/1.

CONTACT

Michelle Smith, Director of Student Financial Services
120 Boylston Street, Boston, MA 02116-4624
(617) 824-8655

Emmanuel College

Boston, Massachusetts
www.emmanuel.edu Federal Code: 002147

4-year private liberal arts college in very large city, affiliated with Roman Catholic Church.
Enrollment: 1,682 undergrads, 1% part-time. 480 full-time freshmen.
Selectivity: Admits 50 to 75% of applicants.

BASIC COSTS (2009-2010)

Tuition and fees: $29,490.
Per-credit charge: $921.
Room and board: $11,950.

FINANCIAL AID PICTURE (2008-2009)

Students with need: Out of 426 full-time freshmen who applied for aid, 387 were judged to have need. Of these, 387 received aid, and 135 had their full need met. Average financial aid package met 71% of need; average scholarship/grant was $16,954; average loan was $3,552. For part-time students, average financial aid package was $5,222.
Students without need: 49 full-time freshmen who did not demonstrate need for aid received scholarships/grants; average award was $8,696. No-need awards available for academics, alumni affiliation, leadership.

FINANCIAL AID PROCEDURES

Forms required: FAFSA, institutional form.
Dates and Deadlines: Priority date 4/1; no closing date. Applicants notified on a rolling basis starting 3/15.

CONTACT

Jennifer Porter, Assistant Vice President for Student Financial Services
400 The Fenway, Boston, MA 02115
(617) 735-9938

Endicott College

Beverly, Massachusetts
www.endicott.edu Federal Code: 002148

4-year private liberal arts college in large town.
Enrollment: 2,296 undergrads, 8% part-time. 587 full-time freshmen.
Selectivity: Admits less than 50% of applicants.

BASIC COSTS (2009-2010)

Tuition and fees: $25,376.
Per-credit charge: $766.
Room and board: $11,836.

FINANCIAL AID PICTURE (2008-2009)

Students with need: Out of 405 full-time freshmen who applied for aid, 283 were judged to have need. Of these, 279 received aid, and 33 had their full need met. Average financial aid package met 58% of need; average scholarship/grant was $7,651; average loan was $3,762. For part-time students, average financial aid package was $5,676.
Students without need: 94 full-time freshmen who did not demonstrate need for aid received scholarships/grants; average award was $5,746. No-need awards available for academics, alumni affiliation, art, leadership, religious affiliation, ROTC, state/district residency.
Cumulative student debt: 72% of graduating class had student loans; average debt was $28,022.

FINANCIAL AID PROCEDURES

Forms required: FAFSA, institutional form.
Dates and Deadlines: Priority date 3/15; no closing date. Applicants notified on a rolling basis starting 3/15; must reply within 2 week(s) of notification.

CONTACT

Marcia Toomey, Director of Financial Aid
376 Hale Street, Beverly, MA 01915-9985
(978) 232-2060

Fisher College

Boston, Massachusetts
www.fisher.edu Federal Code: 002150

2-year private liberal arts college in very large city.
Enrollment: 1,230 undergrads, 30% part-time. 282 full-time freshmen.

BASIC COSTS (2008-2009)

Tuition and fees: $23,225.
Room and board: $12,250.

FINANCIAL AID PICTURE (2008-2009)

Students with need: Need-based aid available for full-time and part-time students. Work study available nights, weekends, and for part-time students.
Students without need: No-need awards available for academics, alumni affiliation, state/district residency.
Scholarships offered: Fisher Honor Scholarship; $2,500; based on outstanding academic and personal achievement, contribution to school and community; renewable with 3.0 GPA. Business Administration and Computer Technology Scholarship; $1,500 for 2.5-2.99 GPA, $3,000 for 3.0 GPA; for students enrolling in associate programs in business administration or computer technology; renewable.

FINANCIAL AID PROCEDURES

Forms required: FAFSA.
Dates and Deadlines: Priority date 3/1; no closing date. Applicants notified on a rolling basis starting 3/1; must reply within 2 week(s) of notification.

CONTACT

Frank Lauder, Director of Financial Aid
118 Beacon Street, Boston, MA 02116
(617) 236-4418

Fitchburg State College

Fitchburg, Massachusetts
www.fsc.edu Federal Code: 002184

4-year public liberal arts and teachers college in small city.
Enrollment: 3,762 undergrads, 13% part-time. 763 full-time freshmen.
Selectivity: Admits 50 to 75% of applicants.

BASIC COSTS (2008-2009)

Tuition and fees: $6,400; out-of-state residents $12,480.
Per-credit charge: $40; out-of-state residents $294.
Room and board: $7,148.

FINANCIAL AID PICTURE

Students with need: Need-based aid available for full-time and part-time students. Work study available nights, weekends, and for part-time students.
Students without need: No-need awards available for academics, alumni affiliation, leadership, state/district residency.
Scholarships offered: Renewable scholarships awarded on basis of high school record and test scores.

FINANCIAL AID PROCEDURES

Forms required: FAFSA.
Dates and Deadlines: Priority date 2/1; no closing date. Applicants notified on a rolling basis starting 3/15; must reply within 2 week(s) of notification.

CONTACT

Pamela McCafferty, Dean of Enrollment Management
160 Pearl Street, Fitchburg, MA 01420-2697
(978) 665-3156

Framingham State College

Framingham, Massachusetts
www.framingham.edu Federal Code: 002185

4-year public liberal arts and teachers college in small city.
Enrollment: 3,448 undergrads, 12% part-time. 644 full-time freshmen.
Selectivity: Admits 50 to 75% of applicants.

BASIC COSTS (2008-2009)

Tuition and fees: $6,141; out-of-state residents $12,221.
Per-credit charge: $40; out-of-state residents $294.
Room and board: $7,625.
Additional info: Fees include mandatory laptop purchase by new students. New England Regional tuition rate $1,455.

FINANCIAL AID PICTURE (2007-2008)

Students with need: Need-based aid available for full-time and part-time students. Work study available nights, weekends, and for part-time students.
Students without need: No-need awards available for academics.
Scholarships offered: Senator Paul E. Tsongas Scholarship; full-tuition and fees; available to Massachusetts residents based on 3.75 GPA and test scores; 5 awarded. Merit scholarships; available to students majoring in education, natural or physical sciences based on GPA and test scores.

FINANCIAL AID PROCEDURES

Forms required: FAFSA.
Dates and Deadlines: Priority date 3/1; no closing date. Applicants notified on a rolling basis starting 4/15; must reply by 5/1 or within 2 week(s) of notification.

Transfers: Priority date 11/1; no deadline. Applicants notified on a rolling basis; must reply within 2 week(s) of notification.

CONTACT

Susan Lanzillo, Director of Financial Aid
PO Box 9101, Framingham, MA 01701-9101
(508) 626-4534

Franklin W. Olin College of Engineering

Needham, Massachusetts
www.olin.edu Federal Code: 039463

4-year private engineering college in large town.
Enrollment: 301 undergrads. 75 full-time freshmen.
Selectivity: Admits less than 50% of applicants.

BASIC COSTS (2008-2009)

Tuition and fees: $35,375.
Per-credit charge: $1,167.
Room and board: $12,400.
Additional info: Each admitted student receives 4-year full-tuition-plus-fees scholarship. Room and Board not included in scholarship. Additional $1,000 enrollment confirmation deposit required; $2,500 charge for laptop and software.

FINANCIAL AID PICTURE (2008-2009)

Students with need: 90% of average financial aid package awarded as scholarships/grants, 10% awarded as loans/jobs.
Students without need: No-need awards available for academics, leadership.
Additional info: All students receive full tuition scholarships. No financial aid forms necessary.

FINANCIAL AID PROCEDURES

Forms required: FAFSA.
Dates and Deadlines: Priority date 2/15; no closing date. Applicants notified on a rolling basis starting 3/31; must reply by 5/1.

CONTACT

Jean Ricker, Manager, Financial Aid
Olin Way, Needham, MA 02492-1245
(781) 292-2343

Gordon College

Wenham, Massachusetts
www.gordon.edu Federal Code: 002153

4-year private liberal arts college in small town, affiliated with nondenominational tradition.
Enrollment: 1,585 undergrads, 3% part-time. 430 full-time freshmen.
Selectivity: Admits 50 to 75% of applicants.

BASIC COSTS (2008-2009)

Tuition and fees: $27,294.
Room and board: $7,424.

FINANCIAL AID PICTURE (2008-2009)

Students with need: Out of 337 full-time freshmen who applied for aid, 275 were judged to have need. Of these, 275 received aid, and 54 had their full need met. Average financial aid package met 69% of need; average scholarship/grant was $12,993; average loan was $3,648. Need-based aid available for part-time students.
Students without need: 133 full-time freshmen who did not demonstrate need for aid received scholarships/grants; average award was $9,829. No-need awards available for academics, alumni affiliation, art, leadership, minority status, music/drama, religious affiliation.
Scholarships offered: A.J. Gordon Scholarship; $12,000; based on academic achievement and leadership. Dean's Scholarships; $9,000; based on academic record. Challenge Scholarships; $7,000; based on academic record. Discipleship Scholarships; $6,000; based on academic record. Choral Scholars Program; $5,000; for students with excellent ability/academic performance seeking career in vocal music field. All scholarships renewable annually.
Cumulative student debt: 80% of graduating class had student loans; average debt was $34,834.

FINANCIAL AID PROCEDURES

Forms required: FAFSA, institutional form.
Dates and Deadlines: Closing date 3/1. Applicants notified on a rolling basis starting 4/15; must reply by 5/1 or within 2 week(s) of notification.
Transfers: Priority date 3/15. Applicants notified on a rolling basis starting 4/1.

CONTACT

Silvio Vazquez, Vice President of Enrollment
255 Grapevine Road, Wenham, MA 01984
(800) 343-1379

Greenfield Community College

Greenfield, Massachusetts
www.gcc.mass.edu Federal Code: 002169

2-year public community college in large town.
Enrollment: 1,969 undergrads, 58% part-time. 195 full-time freshmen.
Selectivity: Open admission; but selective for some programs.

BASIC COSTS (2008-2009)

Tuition and fees: $4,637; out-of-state residents $12,287.
Per-credit charge: $26; out-of-state residents $281.
Additional info: Tuition/fee waivers available for adults.

FINANCIAL AID PICTURE

Students with need: Need-based aid available for full-time and part-time students. Work study available nights, weekends, and for part-time students.
Students without need: This college awards aid only to students with need.

FINANCIAL AID PROCEDURES

Forms required: FAFSA, institutional form.
Dates and Deadlines: Priority date 4/15; no closing date. Applicants notified on a rolling basis starting 5/1; must reply within 2 week(s) of notification.

CONTACT

Linda Dejardins, Director of Financial Aid
One College Drive, Greenfield, MA 01301
(413) 775-1109

Hampshire College

Amherst, Massachusetts Federal Code: 004661
www.hampshire.edu CSS Code: 3447

4-year private liberal arts college in large town.
Enrollment: 1,402 undergrads. 396 full-time freshmen.
Selectivity: Admits less than 50% of applicants.

BASIC COSTS (2009-2010)

Tuition and fees: $40,017.
Room and board: $10,433.

FINANCIAL AID PICTURE (2008-2009)

Students with need: Out of 249 full-time freshmen who applied for aid, 218 were judged to have need. Of these, 218 received aid, and 170 had their full need met. Average financial aid package met 98% of need; average scholarship/grant was $26,785; average loan was $3,500.

Students without need: 59 full-time freshmen who did not demonstrate need for aid received scholarships/grants; average award was $5,760. No-need awards available for academics, leadership.

Cumulative student debt: 63% of graduating class had student loans; average debt was $21,300.

FINANCIAL AID PROCEDURES

Forms required: FAFSA, CSS PROFILE.

Dates and Deadlines: Priority date 2/1; no closing date. Applicants notified by 4/1; must reply by 5/1.

Transfers: Closing date 2/1. Applicants notified by 4/1; must reply by 5/1.

CONTACT

Kathleen Methot, Director of Financial Aid
893 West Street, Amherst, MA 01002-9988
(413) 559-5484

Harvard College

Cambridge, Massachusetts — Federal Code: 002155
www.college.harvard.edu — CSS Code: 3434

4-year private university and liberal arts college in large city.

Enrollment: 6,678 undergrads. 1,652 full-time freshmen.

Selectivity: Admits less than 50% of applicants.

BASIC COSTS (2009-2010)

Tuition and fees: $36,828.

Room and board: $11,856.

FINANCIAL AID PICTURE (2008-2009)

Students with need: Out of 1,146 full-time freshmen who applied for aid, 999 were judged to have need. Of these, 999 received aid, and 999 had their full need met. Average financial aid package met 100% of need; average scholarship/grant was $39,164; average loan was $2,510. Need-based aid available for part-time students.

Students without need: This college awards aid only to students with need.

Cumulative student debt: 39% of graduating class had student loans; average debt was $10,813.

Additional info: Institution meets full need of all admitted students. Aid includes no loans; home equity and retirement excluded from need analysis; families with incomes below $60,000 have zero parent contribution; $60,000 to $180,000 and standard assets have parent contributions from 0-10% of income.

FINANCIAL AID PROCEDURES

Forms required: FAFSA. CSS PROFILE required of all US citizens and US permanent residents plus all Canadians.

Dates and Deadlines: Closing date 2/1. Applicants notified by 4/1; must reply by 5/1 or within 2 week(s) of notification.

Transfers: Closing date 2/15. Applicants notified by 5/30; must reply within 2 week(s) of notification.

CONTACT

Janet Irons, Senior Associate Director of Financial Aid
86 Brattle Street, Cambridge, MA 02138
(617) 495-1581

Hellenic College/Holy Cross

Brookline, Massachusetts
www.hchc.edu — Federal Code: 002154

4-year private liberal arts and seminary college in large town, affiliated with Eastern Orthodox Church.

Enrollment: 69 undergrads. 18 full-time freshmen.

BASIC COSTS (2009-2010)

Tuition and fees: $18,850.

Per-credit charge: $767.

Room and board: $11,780.

FINANCIAL AID PICTURE (2007-2008)

Students with need: Need-based aid available for full-time students. Work study available nights, weekends, and for part-time students.

Students without need: This college awards aid only to students with need.

FINANCIAL AID PROCEDURES

Forms required: FAFSA, institutional form.

Dates and Deadlines: Closing date 4/1. Applicants notified on a rolling basis starting 10/1; must reply within 2 week(s) of notification.

Transfers: No deadline. Applicants notified on a rolling basis; must reply within 2 week(s) of notification.

CONTACT

Director of Financial Aid
50 Goddard Avenue, Brookline, MA 02445
(617) 850-1297

Holyoke Community College

Holyoke, Massachusetts
www.hcc.edu — Federal Code: 002170

2-year public community college in large town.

Enrollment: 6,131 undergrads, 44% part-time. 1,310 full-time freshmen.

Selectivity: Open admission; but selective for some programs.

BASIC COSTS (2008-2009)

Tuition and fees: $3,558; out-of-state residents $9,738.

Per-credit charge: $24; out-of-state residents $230.

FINANCIAL AID PICTURE (2007-2008)

Students with need: 76% of average financial aid package awarded as scholarships/grants, 24% awarded as loans/jobs. Need-based aid available for part-time students. Work study available nights.

Students without need: No-need awards available for academics, art, leadership, music/drama.

FINANCIAL AID PROCEDURES

Forms required: FAFSA.

Dates and Deadlines: Priority date 5/1; no closing date. Applicants notified on a rolling basis starting 5/1; must reply within 2 week(s) of notification.

CONTACT

Karen Derouin, Director of Financial Aid
303 Homestead Avenue, Holyoke, MA 01040
(413) 552-2150

Lasell College

Newton, Massachusetts
www.lasell.edu — Federal Code: 002158

4-year private liberal arts college in small city.

Enrollment: 1,374 undergrads, 1% part-time. 483 full-time freshmen.

Selectivity: Admits 50 to 75% of applicants.

BASIC COSTS (2009-2010)
Tuition and fees: $25,300.
Per-credit charge: $775.
Room and board: $10,500.

FINANCIAL AID PICTURE (2008-2009)
Students with need: Need-based aid available for full-time and part-time students. Work study available nights, weekends, and for part-time students.
Students without need: No-need awards available for academics, alumni affiliation.

FINANCIAL AID PROCEDURES
Forms required: FAFSA, institutional form.
Dates and Deadlines: Priority date 3/1; no closing date. Applicants notified on a rolling basis starting 2/15; must reply by 5/1 or within 2 week(s) of notification.

CONTACT
Michele Kosboth, Director of Student Financial Planning
1844 Commonwealth Avenue, Newton, MA 02466-2709
(617) 243-2227

Lesley University
Cambridge, Massachusetts
www.lesley.edu/lc Federal Code: 002160

4-year private liberal arts and teachers college in very large city.
Enrollment: 1,261 undergrads, 5% part-time. 327 full-time freshmen.
Selectivity: Admits 50 to 75% of applicants.

BASIC COSTS (2009-2010)
Tuition and fees: $28,460.
Room and board: $12,400.

FINANCIAL AID PICTURE (2008-2009)
Students with need: Average financial aid package met 70% of need; average scholarship/grant was $15,024; average loan was $4,057. For part-time students, average financial aid package was $7,913.
Students without need: 59 full-time freshmen who did not demonstrate need for aid received scholarships/grants; average award was $10,502. No-need awards available for academics, art, leadership, minority status, state/district residency.
Scholarships offered: Freshmen scholarships; $5,000-full tuition; for students with strong academic backgrounds who have shown a commitment to community service and making a difference in the lives of others.
Cumulative student debt: 93% of graduating class had student loans; average debt was $17,000.

FINANCIAL AID PROCEDURES
Forms required: FAFSA.
Dates and Deadlines: Priority date 2/15; no closing date. Applicants notified on a rolling basis starting 2/15.
Transfers: Priority date 3/15.

CONTACT
Scott Jewell, Director of Financial Aid
29 Everett Street, Cambridge, MA 02138-2790
(617) 349-8667

Marian Court College
Swampscott, Massachusetts
www.mariancourt.edu Federal Code: 006873

2-year private junior college in large town, affiliated with Roman Catholic Church.
Enrollment: 216 full-time undergrads.
Selectivity: Admits 50 to 75% of applicants.

BASIC COSTS (2008-2009)
Tuition and fees: $13,956.
Additional info: Evening program: $675 for 3 credit course. Tuition/fee waivers available for adults.

FINANCIAL AID PICTURE (2007-2008)
Students with need: Need-based aid available for full-time and part-time students.
Students without need: No-need awards available for academics.

FINANCIAL AID PROCEDURES
Forms required: FAFSA, institutional form.
Dates and Deadlines: Priority date 4/1; no closing date. Applicants notified on a rolling basis starting 4/15.

CONTACT
Kathy Angle, Director of Financial Aid
35 Little's Point Road, Swampscott, MA 01907-2896
(781) 595-6768

Massachusetts Bay Community College
Wellesley Hills, Massachusetts
www.massbay.edu Federal Code: 002171

2-year public community college in large town.
Enrollment: 4,577 undergrads, 57% part-time. 784 full-time freshmen.
Selectivity: Open admission; but selective for some programs.

BASIC COSTS (2008-2009)
Tuition and fees: $4,530; out-of-state residents $10,710.
Per-credit charge: $24; out-of-state residents $230.
Additional info: NEBHE tuition rate is 150% of in-state cost and fees are approximately the same. Tuition/fee waivers available for unemployed or children of unemployed.

FINANCIAL AID PICTURE (2007-2008)
Students with need: Need-based aid available for full-time and part-time students.

FINANCIAL AID PROCEDURES
Forms required: FAFSA, institutional form.
Dates and Deadlines: Priority date 8/30; no closing date. Applicants notified on a rolling basis starting 4/1.

CONTACT
Paula Ogden, Director of Financial Aid/Assistant Dean of Students
50 Oakland Street, Wellesley Hills, MA 02481
(781) 239-2600

Massachusetts College of Art and Design
Boston, Massachusetts
www.massart.edu Federal Code: 002180

4-year public visual arts college in very large city.
Enrollment: 1,692 undergrads, 11% part-time. 275 full-time freshmen.
Selectivity: Admits 50 to 75% of applicants.

BASIC COSTS (2008-2009)
Tuition and fees: $7,900; out-of-state residents $23,000.
Room and board: $10,170.
Additional info: Tuition for New England resident students $14,000. Tuition/fee waivers available for unemployed or children of unemployed.

FINANCIAL AID PICTURE (2008-2009)
Students with need: Need-based aid available for full-time and part-time students.

Students without need: No-need awards available for academics, art, leadership, state/district residency.
Additional info: Tuition waiver available to Vietnam veterans.

FINANCIAL AID PROCEDURES

Forms required: FAFSA.
Dates and Deadlines: Priority date 3/1; no closing date. Applicants notified on a rolling basis starting 3/15; must reply within 3 week(s) of notification.
Transfers: Priority date 5/1. Financial aid transcripts required.

CONTACT

Aurelio Ramirez, Director of Financial Aid
621 Huntington Avenue, Boston, MA 02115-5882
(617) 879-7850

Massachusetts College of Liberal Arts

North Adams, Massachusetts
www.mcla.edu Federal Code: 002187

4-year public liberal arts college in large town.
Enrollment: 1,531 undergrads, 12% part-time. 325 full-time freshmen.
Selectivity: Admits over 75% of applicants.

BASIC COSTS (2008-2009)

Tuition and fees: $6,565; out-of-state residents $15,510.
Per-credit charge: $43; out-of-state residents $416.
Room and board: $7,754.
Additional info: Tuition/fee waivers available for unemployed or children of unemployed.

FINANCIAL AID PICTURE (2008-2009)

Students with need: Out of 301 full-time freshmen who applied for aid, 217 were judged to have need. Of these, 216 received aid. Need-based aid available for part-time students.
Students without need: 93 full-time freshmen who did not demonstrate need for aid received scholarships/grants; average award was $1,864. No-need awards available for academics, alumni affiliation, art, leadership, minority status, music/drama.
Cumulative student debt: 37% of graduating class had student loans; average debt was $19,090.

FINANCIAL AID PROCEDURES

Forms required: FAFSA, institutional form.
Dates and Deadlines: Priority date 3/1; no closing date. Applicants notified on a rolling basis starting 3/1; must reply by 5/1 or within 2 week(s) of notification.

CONTACT

Elizabeth Petri, Director of Financial Aid
375 Church Street, North Adams, MA 01247
(413) 662-5219

Massachusetts College of Pharmacy and Health Sciences

Boston, Massachusetts
www.mcphs.edu Federal Code: 002165

4-year private health science and pharmacy college in very large city.
Enrollment: 2,708 undergrads, 3% part-time. 604 full-time freshmen.
Selectivity: Admits 50 to 75% of applicants.

BASIC COSTS (2009-2010)

Tuition and fees: $24,550.
Per-credit charge: $875.
Room and board: $11,900.

FINANCIAL AID PICTURE (2008-2009)

Students with need: Need-based aid available for full-time and part-time students. Work study available weekends and for part-time students.
Students without need: No-need awards available for academics.

FINANCIAL AID PROCEDURES

Forms required: FAFSA.
Dates and Deadlines: Priority date 3/15; no closing date. Applicants notified on a rolling basis.
Transfers: Massachusetts State Grant deadline May 1.

CONTACT

Carrie Glass, Executive Director of Enrollment Services
179 Longwood Avenue, Boston, MA 02115-5896
(617) 732-2864

Massachusetts Institute of Technology

Cambridge, Massachusetts Federal Code: 002178
web.mit.edu CSS Code: 3514

4-year private university in small city.
Enrollment: 4,138 undergrads, 1% part-time. 1,073 full-time freshmen.
Selectivity: Admits less than 50% of applicants.

BASIC COSTS (2009-2010)

Tuition and fees: $37,782.
Per-credit charge: $585.
Room and board: $11,360.

FINANCIAL AID PICTURE (2007-2008)

Students with need: Out of 853 full-time freshmen who applied for aid, 667 were judged to have need. Of these, 667 received aid, and 667 had their full need met. Average financial aid package met 100% of need; average scholarship/grant was $30,232; average loan was $1,978. For part-time students, average financial aid package was $22,124.
Students without need: This college awards aid only to students with need.
Cumulative student debt: 49% of graduating class had student loans; average debt was $14,148.
Additional info: Filing deadline 2/15 for CSS PROFILE.

FINANCIAL AID PROCEDURES

Forms required: FAFSA, CSS PROFILE.
Dates and Deadlines: Closing date 2/15. Applicants notified by 4/1; must reply by 5/1.
Transfers: Closing date 3/1. Applicants notified by 4/15; must reply by 5/1. Access to MIT funds may be limited to fewer than 8 terms.

CONTACT

Charlene Chisom-Freeman, Executive Director of Student Financial Services
77 Massachusetts Avenue, Rm 3-108, Cambridge, MA 02139-4307
(617) 253-4971

Massachusetts Maritime Academy

Buzzards Bay, Massachusetts
www.maritime.edu Federal Code: 002181

4-year public military and maritime college in large town.
Enrollment: 1,050 undergrads.
Selectivity: Admits 50 to 75% of applicants.

BASIC COSTS (2008-2009)

Tuition and fees: $5,827; out-of-state residents $17,864.
Room and board: $8,607.
Additional info: Semester at Sea cost: $3,218.

FINANCIAL AID PICTURE (2007-2008)

Students with need: Need-based aid available for full-time and part-time students. Work study available nights, weekends, and for part-time students.

Students without need: No-need awards available for academics, leadership, music/drama.

FINANCIAL AID PROCEDURES

Forms required: FAFSA, institutional form.

Dates and Deadlines: Priority date 4/30; no closing date. Applicants notified on a rolling basis starting 3/1.

CONTACT

Elizabeth Benway, Financial Aid Director
101 Academy Drive, Buzzards Bay, MA 02532-1803
(508) 830-5086

Massasoit Community College

Brockton, Massachusetts
www.massasoit.mass.edu Federal Code: 002177

2-year public community college in small city.

Enrollment: 5,377 undergrads, 44% part-time. 1,285 full-time freshmen.

Selectivity: Open admission; but selective for some programs.

BASIC COSTS (2008-2009)

Tuition and fees: $3,510; out-of-state residents $9,690.

Per-credit charge: $24; out-of-state residents $230.

Additional info: Tuition/fee waivers available for unemployed or children of unemployed.

FINANCIAL AID PICTURE

Students with need: Need-based aid available for full-time students.

Students without need: This college awards aid only to students with need.

FINANCIAL AID PROCEDURES

Forms required: FAFSA.

Dates and Deadlines: Priority date 4/15; no closing date. Applicants notified on a rolling basis starting 6/1.

CONTACT

Mary Courtright, Director of Financial Aid
One Massasoit Boulevard, Brockton, MA 02302-3996
(508) 588-9100

Merrimack College

North Andover, Massachusetts
www.merrimack.edu Federal Code: 002120

4-year private business and liberal arts college in large town, affiliated with Roman Catholic Church.

Enrollment: 2,057 undergrads, 8% part-time. 588 full-time freshmen.

Selectivity: Admits over 75% of applicants.

BASIC COSTS (2008-2009)

Tuition and fees: $29,810.

Per-credit charge: $1,085.

Room and board: $10,190.

FINANCIAL AID PICTURE (2007-2008)

Students with need: Out of 485 full-time freshmen who applied for aid, 481 were judged to have need. Of these, 481 received aid, and 410 had their full need met. Average financial aid package met 70% of need; average scholarship/grant was $13,107; average loan was $3,337.

Students without need: 104 full-time freshmen who did not demonstrate need for aid received scholarships/grants; average award was $9,060. No-need awards available for academics, athletics, leadership, minority status, religious affiliation.

Scholarships offered: 79 full-time freshmen received athletic scholarships; average amount $14,432.

Cumulative student debt: 75% of graduating class had student loans; average debt was $42,000.

Additional info: Accept the Challenge program provides tuition for students from Lawrence who meet program criteria.

FINANCIAL AID PROCEDURES

Forms required: FAFSA.

Dates and Deadlines: Closing date 2/1. Applicants notified by 3/15; must reply by 5/1 or within 2 week(s) of notification.

Transfers: Priority date 3/1; closing date 4/30. Must reply within 2 week(s) of notification.

CONTACT

Christine Mordach, Director of Financial Aid
315 Turnpike Street, North Andover, MA 01845
(978) 837-5186

Middlesex Community College

Bedford, Massachusetts
www.middlesex.mass.edu Federal Code: 009936

2-year public community college in small city.

Enrollment: 7,569 undergrads.

Selectivity: Open admission; but selective for some programs.

BASIC COSTS (2008-2009)

Tuition and fees: $4,010; out-of-state residents $10,190.

Per-credit charge: $132; out-of-state residents $338.

Additional info: New England resident tuition $144 per credit hour. Tuition/fee waivers available for adults.

FINANCIAL AID PICTURE (2007-2008)

Students with need: Need-based aid available for full-time and part-time students. Work study available nights, weekends, and for part-time students.

Students without need: This college awards aid only to students with need.

Additional info: Application priority date 5/1 for Massachusetts state funds.

FINANCIAL AID PROCEDURES

Forms required: FAFSA, institutional form.

Dates and Deadlines: Priority date 5/1; no closing date. Applicants notified on a rolling basis starting 6/1; must reply within 2 week(s) of notification.

CONTACT

Robert Baumel, Financial Aid Director
33 Kearney Square, Lowell, MA 01852-1987
(978) 656-3242

Montserrat College of Art

Beverly, Massachusetts
www.montserrat.edu Federal Code: 013774

4-year private visual arts college in large town.

Enrollment: 281 undergrads, 4% part-time. 80 full-time freshmen.

Selectivity: Admits 50 to 75% of applicants.

BASIC COSTS (2008-2009)

Tuition and fees: $23,320.

Per-credit charge: $936.

Room and board: $6,000.

FINANCIAL AID PICTURE (2008-2009)

Students with need: Out of 73 full-time freshmen who applied for aid, 66 were judged to have need. Of these, 66 received aid, and 1 had their full need met. Average financial aid package met 48% of need; average scholarship/grant was $9,172; average loan was $3,862. For part-time students, average financial aid package was $10,330.

Students without need: 11 full-time freshmen who did not demonstrate need for aid received scholarships/grants; average award was $2,647. No-need awards available for academics, art.

Scholarships offered: Talent Awards; $1,000-$7,000; based on artistic and academic ability.

Cumulative student debt: 100% of graduating class had student loans; average debt was $37,980.

FINANCIAL AID PROCEDURES

Forms required: FAFSA, institutional form.

Dates and Deadlines: Closing date 3/1. Applicants notified on a rolling basis starting 12/20; must reply within 2 week(s) of notification.

Transfers: Priority date 3/1; no deadline. Applicants notified on a rolling basis starting 12/20; must reply within 2 week(s) of notification.

CONTACT

Creda Camacho, Director of Financial Aid
23 Essex Street, Beverly, MA 01915
(978) 922-8222

Mount Holyoke College

South Hadley, Massachusetts — Federal Code: 002192
www.mtholyoke.edu — CSS Code: 3529

4-year private liberal arts college for women in large town.

Enrollment: 2,182 undergrads, 1% part-time. 518 full-time freshmen.

Selectivity: Admits 50 to 75% of applicants.

BASIC COSTS (2009-2010)

Tuition and fees: $39,126.

Per-credit charge: $1,220.

Room and board: $11,450.

FINANCIAL AID PICTURE (2008-2009)

Students with need: Out of 387 full-time freshmen who applied for aid, 315 were judged to have need. Of these, 315 received aid, and 315 had their full need met. Average financial aid package met 100% of need; average scholarship/grant was $29,044; average loan was $3,008. For part-time students, average financial aid package was $25,796.

Students without need: 41 full-time freshmen who did not demonstrate need for aid received scholarships/grants; average award was $15,610. No-need awards available for academics, leadership.

Scholarships offered: Mount Holyoke College Leadership Awards; based on high school scholarship and extracurricular achievement; limited number; conditional annual renewal.

Cumulative student debt: 66% of graduating class had student loans; average debt was $23,841.

Additional info: Parent loan plans include MASSPLAN, Achievers and PLUS. 10-month payment plan offered.

FINANCIAL AID PROCEDURES

Forms required: FAFSA, CSS PROFILE.

Dates and Deadlines: Priority date 2/15; closing date 3/1. Applicants notified by 4/1; must reply by 5/1.

Transfers: Priority date 2/1; closing date 5/31. Applicants notified on a rolling basis; must reply within 4 week(s) of notification. Financial aid transcripts from all schools previously attended required.

CONTACT

Kathy Blaisdell, Director of Student Financial Services
Newhall Center, South Hadley, MA 01075-1488
(413) 538-2291

Mount Ida College

Newton, Massachusetts
www.mountida.edu — Federal Code: 002193

4-year private business and liberal arts college in small city.

Enrollment: 1,445 undergrads, 4% part-time. 410 full-time freshmen.

Selectivity: Admits 50 to 75% of applicants.

BASIC COSTS (2009-2010)

Tuition and fees: $23,100.

Per-credit charge: $625.

Room and board: $11,450.

FINANCIAL AID PICTURE (2008-2009)

Students with need: Average financial aid package met 55% of need; average scholarship/grant was $11,015; average loan was $3,462. For part-time students, average financial aid package was $11,210.

FINANCIAL AID PROCEDURES

Forms required: FAFSA, institutional form.

Dates and Deadlines: Priority date 5/1; no closing date. Applicants notified on a rolling basis starting 3/1; must reply within 3 week(s) of notification.

CONTACT

David Goldman, Director of Financial Aid
777 Dedham Street, Newton, MA 02459
(617) 928-4785

Mount Wachusett Community College

Gardner, Massachusetts
www.mwcc.edu — Federal Code: 002172

2-year public community college in large town.

Enrollment: 3,907 undergrads, 53% part-time. 650 full-time freshmen.

Selectivity: Open admission; but selective for some programs.

BASIC COSTS (2008-2009)

Tuition and fees: $4,530; out-of-state residents $10,680.

Per-credit charge: $25; out-of-state residents $230.

Additional info: New England resident tuition is $1,125.

FINANCIAL AID PICTURE (2007-2008)

Students with need: Out of 500 full-time freshmen who applied for aid, 345 were judged to have need. Of these, 320 received aid, and 52 had their full need met. Average financial aid package met 91% of need; average scholarship/grant was $3,764; average loan was $886. For part-time students, average financial aid package was $3,308.

Students without need: This college awards aid only to students with need.

FINANCIAL AID PROCEDURES

Forms required: FAFSA, institutional form.

Dates and Deadlines: Priority date 4/15; no closing date. Applicants notified on a rolling basis starting 5/1.

CONTACT

JoEllen Soucier, Director of Financial Aid
444 Green Street, Gardner, MA 01440-1000
(978) 632-6600 ext. 524

New England Conservatory of Music

Boston, Massachusetts
www.newenglandconservatory.edu Federal Code: 002194

4-year private music college in very large city.
Enrollment: 351 undergrads, 7% part-time. 81 full-time freshmen.
Selectivity: Admits less than 50% of applicants.

BASIC COSTS (2008-2009)

Tuition and fees: $33,325.
Per-credit charge: $1,050.
Room and board: $11,600.
Additional info: On-campus residents and all incoming students pay $440 health center fee.

FINANCIAL AID PICTURE (2008-2009)

Students with need: Average financial aid package met 68% of need; average scholarship/grant was $14,079; average loan was $5,323. For part-time students, average financial aid package was $3,069.
Students without need: No-need awards available for academics, music/drama.
Cumulative student debt: 71% of graduating class had student loans; average debt was $31,975.

FINANCIAL AID PROCEDURES

Forms required: FAFSA, institutional form.
Dates and Deadlines: Closing date 12/1. Applicants notified by 4/1; must reply by 5/1 or within 2 week(s) of notification.

CONTACT

Lauren Urbanek, Director of Financial Aid
290 Huntington Avenue, Boston, MA 02115
(617) 585-1110

New England Institute of Art

Brookline, Massachusetts
www.artinstitutes.edu/boston Federal Code: 007486

4-year for-profit visual arts and technical college in very large city.
Enrollment: 1,687 undergrads.
Selectivity: Admits less than 50% of applicants.

BASIC COSTS (2008-2009)

Tuition and fees: $23,288.
Per-credit charge: $715.

FINANCIAL AID PICTURE

Students with need: Need-based aid available for full-time and part-time students. Work study available nights, weekends, and for part-time students.
Students without need: No-need awards available for academics.

FINANCIAL AID PROCEDURES

Forms required: FAFSA, institutional form.
Dates and Deadlines: Priority date 5/1; no closing date. Applicants notified on a rolling basis starting 3/1.

CONTACT

Anna Kelly, Director of Student Financial Services
10 Brookline Place West, Brookline, MA 02445-7295
(617) 739-1700

Newbury College

Brookline, Massachusetts
www.newbury.edu Federal Code: 007484

4-year private business and liberal arts college in large city.
Enrollment: 1,200 undergrads.
Selectivity: Admits 50 to 75% of applicants.

BASIC COSTS (2008-2009)

Tuition and fees: $22,000.
Room and board: $10,750.

FINANCIAL AID PICTURE

Students with need: Need-based aid available for full-time and part-time students. Work study available nights.
Students without need: This college awards aid only to students with need.

FINANCIAL AID PROCEDURES

Forms required: FAFSA.
Dates and Deadlines: Closing date 5/1. Applicants notified on a rolling basis starting 3/1; must reply within 2 week(s) of notification.
Transfers: No deadline.

CONTACT

Jeannie Gonzales, Director of Financial Assistance
129 Fisher Avenue, Brookline, MA 02445
(617) 730-7196

Nichols College

Dudley, Massachusetts
www.nichols.edu Federal Code: 002197

4-year private business and liberal arts college in small town.
Enrollment: 1,285 undergrads, 14% part-time. 391 full-time freshmen.
Selectivity: Admits 50 to 75% of applicants.

BASIC COSTS (2009-2010)

Tuition and fees: $28,040.
Per-credit charge: $925.
Room and board: $9,200.

FINANCIAL AID PICTURE (2008-2009)

Students with need: Out of 379 full-time freshmen who applied for aid, 366 were judged to have need. Of these, 366 received aid, and 35 had their full need met. Average financial aid package met 76% of need; average scholarship/grant was $14,123; average loan was $3,668. For part-time students, average financial aid package was $4,789.
Students without need: 35 full-time freshmen who did not demonstrate need for aid received scholarships/grants; average award was $9,571. No-need awards available for academics, alumni affiliation, ROTC.
Cumulative student debt: 89% of graduating class had student loans; average debt was $28,091.

FINANCIAL AID PROCEDURES

Forms required: FAFSA.
Dates and Deadlines: Priority date 3/1; closing date 6/1. Applicants notified on a rolling basis starting 2/26; must reply within 4 week(s) of notification.
Transfers: Applicants notified by 3/1; must reply within 4 week(s) of notification.

CONTACT

Denise Brindle, Director of Financial Aid
PO Box 5000, Dudley, MA 01571-5000
(508) 213-2372

North Shore Community College
Danvers, Massachusetts
www.northshore.edu Federal Code: 002173

2-year public community college in small city.
Enrollment: 6,331 undergrads, 52% part-time. 1,068 full-time freshmen.
Selectivity: Open admission; but selective for some programs.

BASIC COSTS (2008-2009)
Tuition and fees: $3,750; out-of-state residents $10,710.
Per-credit charge: $25; out-of-state residents $257.
Additional info: New England regional tuition: $133.50 per credit hour.

FINANCIAL AID PICTURE (2007-2008)
Students with need: Average financial aid package for all full-time undergraduates was $4,569; for part-time $7,007. 84% awarded as scholarships/grants, 16% awarded as loans/jobs.
Students without need: This college awards aid only to students with need.

FINANCIAL AID PROCEDURES
Forms required: FAFSA.
Dates and Deadlines: Priority date 5/1; no closing date. Applicants notified on a rolling basis starting 6/1; must reply within 2 week(s) of notification.

CONTACT
Susan Sullivan, Director of Student Financial Services
One Ferncroft Road, Danvers, MA 01923-0840
(978) 762-4000

Northeastern University
Boston, Massachusetts Federal Code: 002199
www.northeastern.edu CSS Code: 3667

4-year private university in very large city.
Enrollment: 15,521 undergrads. 2,923 full-time freshmen.
Selectivity: Admits less than 50% of applicants.

BASIC COSTS (2008-2009)
Tuition and fees: $33,721.
Room and board: $11,940.

FINANCIAL AID PICTURE (2008-2009)
Students with need: 54% of average financial aid package awarded as scholarships/grants, 46% awarded as loans/jobs. Work study available nights, weekends, and for part-time students.
Students without need: No-need awards available for academics, athletics, minority status.

FINANCIAL AID PROCEDURES
Forms required: FAFSA, CSS PROFILE.
Dates and Deadlines: Closing date 2/15. Applicants notified on a rolling basis starting 2/15; must reply by 5/1.
Transfers: Institutional application and financial aid transcript from all previously attended colleges required.

CONTACT
M. Seamus Harreys, Dean and Director of Student Financial Services
360 Huntington Avenue, 150 Richards Hall, Boston, MA 02115-9959
(617) 373-3190

Northern Essex Community College
Haverhill, Massachusetts
www.necc.mass.edu Federal Code: 002174

2-year public community and junior college in small city.
Enrollment: 6,146 undergrads, 59% part-time. 920 full-time freshmen.
Selectivity: Open admission; but selective for some programs.

BASIC COSTS (2008-2009)
Tuition and fees: $3,510; out-of-state residents $10,740.
Per-credit charge: $25; out-of-state residents $266.
Additional info: New England residents pay $134 per credit hour.

FINANCIAL AID PICTURE
Students with need: Need-based aid available for full-time and part-time students.
Students without need: No-need awards available for academics.

FINANCIAL AID PROCEDURES
Forms required: FAFSA.
Dates and Deadlines: Priority date 5/1; no closing date. Applicants notified on a rolling basis starting 3/1; must reply within 2 week(s) of notification.

CONTACT
Tina Favara, Assistant Dean for Financial Aid
100 Elliott Street, Haverhill, MA 01830-2399
(978) 556-3600

Pine Manor College
Chestnut Hill, Massachusetts
www.pmc.edu Federal Code: 002201

4-year private liberal arts college for women in very large city.
Enrollment: 163 undergrads, 1% part-time. 162 full-time freshmen.
Selectivity: Admits 50 to 75% of applicants.

BASIC COSTS (2008-2009)
Tuition and fees: $18,957.
Room and board: $11,115.

FINANCIAL AID PICTURE (2007-2008)
Students with need: Need-based aid available for full-time and part-time students. Work study available nights.
Students without need: No-need awards available for academics, alumni affiliation, leadership.

FINANCIAL AID PROCEDURES
Forms required: FAFSA.
Dates and Deadlines: Priority date 5/1; no closing date. Applicants notified on a rolling basis starting 3/1; must reply by 5/1 or within 2 week(s) of notification.
Transfers: No deadline. Applicants notified on a rolling basis starting 3/1; must reply by 5/1 or within 2 week(s) of notification.

CONTACT
Barry Ward, Dean of Admissions and Financial Aid
400 Heath Street, Chestnut Hill, MA 02467
(617) 731-7104

Quinsigamond Community College
Worcester, Massachusetts
www.qcc.edu Federal Code: 002175

2-year public community college in small city.
Enrollment: 5,923 undergrads, 47% part-time. 1,243 full-time freshmen.
Selectivity: Open admission; but selective for some programs.

BASIC COSTS (2008-2009)
Tuition and fees: $3,960; out-of-state residents $10,140.
Per-credit charge: $24; out-of-state residents $230.

FINANCIAL AID PICTURE (2007-2008)
Students with need: Need-based aid available for full-time and part-time students. Work study available nights, weekends, and for part-time students.
Students without need: No-need awards available for academics, leadership, minority status.

FINANCIAL AID PROCEDURES
Forms required: FAFSA.
Dates and Deadlines: Priority date 4/1; no closing date. Applicants notified on a rolling basis starting 4/1.

CONTACT
Beverly Guerin, Director of Financial Aid
670 West Boylston Street, Worcester, MA 01606
(508) 854-4261

Regis College
Weston, Massachusetts
www.regiscollege.edu Federal Code: 002206

4-year private nursing and liberal arts college in large town, affiliated with Roman Catholic Church.
Enrollment: 991 undergrads, 22% part-time. 237 full-time freshmen.
Selectivity: Admits 50 to 75% of applicants.

BASIC COSTS (2009-2010)
Tuition and fees: $28,900.
Room and board: $12,190.
Additional info: Tuition/fee waivers available for adults.

FINANCIAL AID PICTURE (2008-2009)
Students with need: Out of 228 full-time freshmen who applied for aid, 212 were judged to have need. Of these, 210 received aid, and 28 had their full need met. Average financial aid package met 62% of need; average scholarship/grant was $14,351; average loan was $4,267. For part-time students, average financial aid package was $7,214.
Students without need: 17 full-time freshmen who did not demonstrate need for aid received scholarships/grants; average award was $8,424. No-need awards available for academics, alumni affiliation, leadership, ROTC.
Cumulative student debt: 95% of graduating class had student loans; average debt was $24,178.
Additional info: Family tuition discount scholarship; offered during any semester in which 2 or more unmarried, dependent siblings attend full-time.

FINANCIAL AID PROCEDURES
Forms required: FAFSA, institutional form.
Dates and Deadlines: Priority date 2/15; no closing date. Applicants notified on a rolling basis starting 3/15; must reply by 5/1 or within 2 week(s) of notification.
Transfers: No deadline. Applicants notified on a rolling basis.

CONTACT
Dolores Ludwick, Director of Financial Aid
235 Wellesley Street, Weston, MA 02493-1571
(781) 768-7180

Roxbury Community College
Roxbury Crossing, Massachusetts
www.rcc.mass.edu Federal Code: 011930

2-year public community college in very large city.
Enrollment: 2,154 undergrads, 61% part-time. 302 full-time freshmen.
Selectivity: Open admission; but selective for some programs.

BASIC COSTS (2008-2009)
Tuition and fees: $3,660; out-of-state residents $11,310.
Per-credit charge: $26; out-of-state residents $281.
Additional info: New England Regional per-credit-hour charge $105.

FINANCIAL AID PICTURE
Students with need: Need-based aid available for full-time and part-time students.
Students without need: This college awards aid only to students with need.

FINANCIAL AID PROCEDURES
Forms required: FAFSA, institutional form.
Dates and Deadlines: Priority date 5/1; no closing date. Applicants notified on a rolling basis starting 6/15; must reply within 2 week(s) of notification.

CONTACT
Ray O'Rourke, Director of Financial Aid
1234 Columbus Avenue, Roxbury Crossing, MA 02120-3400
(617) 541-5322

School of the Museum of Fine Arts
Boston, Massachusetts
www.smfa.edu Federal Code: 004667

4-year private visual arts college in very large city.
Enrollment: 576 undergrads, 5% part-time. 129 full-time freshmen.
Selectivity: Admits over 75% of applicants.

BASIC COSTS (2008-2009)
Tuition and fees: $29,612.
Per-credit charge: $1,680.
Room only: $12,500.

FINANCIAL AID PICTURE (2008-2009)
Students with need: Out of 92 full-time freshmen who applied for aid, 86 were judged to have need. Of these, 85 received aid, and 5 had their full need met. Average financial aid package met 42% of need; average scholarship/grant was $10,941; average loan was $3,392. For part-time students, average financial aid package was $6,183.
Students without need: 8 full-time freshmen who did not demonstrate need for aid received scholarships/grants; average award was $11,137. No-need awards available for art.
Scholarships offered: Awarded on strength of portfolio and potential for growth as an artist; no separate application needed.
Cumulative student debt: 76% of graduating class had student loans; average debt was $30,027.

FINANCIAL AID PROCEDURES
Forms required: FAFSA, institutional form.
Dates and Deadlines: Closing date 3/15. Applicants notified by 4/1; must reply by 5/1 or within 2 week(s) of notification.
Transfers: Applicants notified on a rolling basis starting 4/1; must reply by 5/1 or within 2 week(s) of notification.

CONTACT
Elizabeth Goreham, Director of Financial Aid
230 The Fenway, Boston, MA 02115
(800) 776-0135

Simmons College

Boston, Massachusetts
www.simmons.edu Federal Code: 002208

4-year private liberal arts college for women in very large city.
Enrollment: 2,023 undergrads, 9% part-time. 391 full-time freshmen.
Selectivity: Admits 50 to 75% of applicants.

BASIC COSTS (2009-2010)

Tuition and fees: $31,220.
Per-credit charge: $910.
Room and board: $12,050.

FINANCIAL AID PICTURE (2008-2009)

Students with need: Out of 321 full-time freshmen who applied for aid, 277 were judged to have need. Of these, 277 received aid, and 34 had their full need met. Average financial aid package met 63% of need; average scholarship/grant was $13,369; average loan was $3,863. For part-time students, average financial aid package was $14,133.
Students without need: 86 full-time freshmen who did not demonstrate need for aid received scholarships/grants; average award was $8,398. No-need awards available for academics, alumni affiliation, leadership, minority status.
Cumulative student debt: 78% of graduating class had student loans; average debt was $42,174.

FINANCIAL AID PROCEDURES

Forms required: FAFSA.
Dates and Deadlines: Priority date 2/15; closing date 3/1. Applicants notified on a rolling basis starting 3/15; must reply by 5/1 or within 4 week(s) of notification.
Transfers: Priority date 3/1; closing date 4/1. Applicants notified on a rolling basis starting 3/15; must reply by 5/1 or within 4 week(s) of notification. Combination of grants, loans, employment opportunities available.

CONTACT

Diane Hallisey, Director of Student Financial Services
300 The Fenway, Boston, MA 02115-5898
(617) 521-2004

Smith College

Northampton, Massachusetts Federal Code: 002209
www.smith.edu CSS Code: 3762

4-year private liberal arts college for women in large town.
Enrollment: 2,610 undergrads, 1% part-time. 656 full-time freshmen.
Selectivity: Admits less than 50% of applicants.

BASIC COSTS (2009-2010)

Tuition and fees: $37,848.
Room and board: $12,652.

FINANCIAL AID PICTURE (2007-2008)

Students with need: Out of 496 full-time freshmen who applied for aid, 396 were judged to have need. Of these, 396 received aid, and 396 had their full need met. Average financial aid package met 100% of need; average scholarship/grant was $26,630; average loan was $3,500. For part-time students, average financial aid package was $26,874.
Students without need: 30 full-time freshmen who did not demonstrate need for aid received scholarships/grants; average award was $7,651. No-need awards available for academics, state/district residency.
Scholarships offered: Zollman Scholarships; $20,000; for academic excellence; about 15 awarded. STRIDE scholarship; $15,000; about 50 awarded. Springfield Partnership; full-tuition; for academic excellence in Springfield public high schools; up to 3 awarded. Picker Engineering Scholarship; $10,000 per year.
Cumulative student debt: 71% of graduating class had student loans; average debt was $20,960.
Additional info: Financial aid policy guarantees to meet full financial need, as calculated by college, of all admitted students.

FINANCIAL AID PROCEDURES

Forms required: FAFSA, CSS PROFILE.
Dates and Deadlines: Closing date 2/15. Applicants notified by 4/1; must reply by 5/1.
Transfers: Priority date 2/15; closing date 4/1. Must reply by 5/1. Applicants who apply after admission decision is made cannot receive college aid until they complete at least 32 credits at Smith.

CONTACT

David Belanger, Director of Student Financial Services
7 College Lane, Northampton, MA 01063
(413) 585-2530

Springfield College

Springfield, Massachusetts Federal Code: 002211
www.springfieldcollege.edu CSS Code: 3763

4-year private health science and liberal arts college in small city.
Enrollment: 2,216 undergrads, 1% part-time. 618 full-time freshmen.
Selectivity: Admits 50 to 75% of applicants.

BASIC COSTS (2009-2010)

Tuition and fees: $26,480.
Per-credit charge: $790.
Room and board: $9,510.

FINANCIAL AID PICTURE (2007-2008)

Students with need: Need-based aid available for full-time students.
Additional info: Co-operative education program available to students after freshman year.

FINANCIAL AID PROCEDURES

Forms required: FAFSA, CSS PROFILE, institutional form.
Dates and Deadlines: Priority date 3/15; no closing date. Applicants notified on a rolling basis starting 3/15; must reply by 5/1 or within 2 week(s) of notification.
Transfers: Priority date 4/15.

CONTACT

Edward Ciosek, Director of Financial Aid
263 Alden Street, Springfield, MA 01109
(413) 748-3000

Springfield Technical Community College

Springfield, Massachusetts
www.stcc.edu Federal Code: 005549

2-year public community and technical college in small city.
Enrollment: 5,330 undergrads, 51% part-time. 991 full-time freshmen.
Selectivity: Open admission; but selective for some programs.

BASIC COSTS (2008-2009)

Tuition and fees: $3,696; out-of-state residents $10,206.
Per-credit charge: $25; out-of-state residents $242.
Additional info: New England reciprocal rate $237 per credit hour, including fees.

FINANCIAL AID PICTURE (2007-2008)

Students with need: 77% of average financial aid package awarded as scholarships/grants, 23% awarded as loans/jobs. Need-based aid available for part-time students.

Students without need: This college awards aid only to students with need.

FINANCIAL AID PROCEDURES

Forms required: FAFSA, institutional form.

Dates and Deadlines: Priority date 5/1; no closing date. Applicants notified on a rolling basis starting 7/1.

CONTACT

Mary Forni, Coordinator of Financial Aid Services
One Armory Square, Springfield, MA 01102-9000
(413) 755-4214

Stonehill College

Easton, Massachusetts — Federal Code: 002217
www.stonehill.edu — CSS Code: 3770

4-year private liberal arts college in large town, affiliated with Roman Catholic Church.

Enrollment: 2,408 undergrads, 2% part-time. 634 full-time freshmen.

Selectivity: Admits less than 50% of applicants.

BASIC COSTS (2009-2010)

Tuition and fees: $31,210.

Per-credit charge: $1,040.

Room and board: $12,240.

Additional info: Tuition/fee waivers available for minority students.

FINANCIAL AID PICTURE (2008-2009)

Students with need: Out of 541 full-time freshmen who applied for aid, 427 were judged to have need. Of these, 427 received aid, and 110 had their full need met. Average financial aid package met 80% of need; average scholarship/grant was $18,275; average loan was $3,755. For part-time students, average financial aid package was $9,283.

Students without need: 133 full-time freshmen who did not demonstrate need for aid received scholarships/grants; average award was $8,603. No-need awards available for academics, athletics, ROTC.

Scholarships offered: 17 full-time freshmen received athletic scholarships; average amount $7,312.

Cumulative student debt: 75% of graduating class had student loans; average debt was $25,603.

FINANCIAL AID PROCEDURES

Forms required: FAFSA, CSS PROFILE.

Dates and Deadlines: Priority date 2/1; no closing date. Applicants notified by 4/1; must reply by 5/1.

Transfers: Closing date 4/1. Applicants notified by 6/1; must reply by 6/30.

CONTACT

Eileen O'Leary, Assistant Vice President for Finance/Director of Student Aid and Finance
320 Washington Street, Easton, MA 02357-0100
(508) 565-1088

Suffolk University

Boston, Massachusetts
www.suffolk.edu — Federal Code: 002218

4-year private university in very large city.

Enrollment: 5,639 undergrads, 8% part-time. 1,559 full-time freshmen.

Selectivity: Admits over 75% of applicants.

BASIC COSTS (2009-2010)

Tuition and fees: $27,208.

Per-credit charge: $665.

Room and board: $14,544.

FINANCIAL AID PICTURE (2008-2009)

Students with need: Out of 1,121 full-time freshmen who applied for aid, 911 were judged to have need. Of these, 905 received aid, and 117 had their full need met. Average financial aid package met 62% of need; average scholarship/grant was $9,755; average loan was $3,996. For part-time students, average financial aid package was $8,447.

Students without need: 100 full-time freshmen who did not demonstrate need for aid received scholarships/grants; average award was $9,306. No-need awards available for academics, alumni affiliation.

Scholarships offered: Various scholarships; amounts vary; based on academic achievement, talent, and contribution to applicant's school and community.

Additional info: Foreign students may apply for institutional employment awards.

FINANCIAL AID PROCEDURES

Forms required: FAFSA, institutional form.

Dates and Deadlines: Closing date 3/1. Applicants notified on a rolling basis starting 2/5.

CONTACT

Christine Perry, Director of Financial Aid
8 Ashburton Place, Boston, MA 02108
(617) 573-8470

Tufts University

Medford, Massachusetts — Federal Code: 002219
www.tufts.edu — CSS Code: 3901

4-year private university in small city.

Enrollment: 5,029 undergrads. 1,297 full-time freshmen.

Selectivity: Admits less than 50% of applicants.

BASIC COSTS (2008-2009)

Tuition and fees: $38,840.

Room and board: $10,518.

FINANCIAL AID PICTURE (2008-2009)

Students with need: Need-based aid available for full-time and part-time students.

Students without need: This college awards aid only to students with need.

Scholarships offered: National Merit Scholarships; $500 for non-need; $2,000 for need.

FINANCIAL AID PROCEDURES

Forms required: FAFSA, CSS PROFILE.

Dates and Deadlines: Closing date 2/15. Applicants notified by 4/1; must reply by 5/1.

Transfers: Closing date 3/1. Applicants notified by 5/1; must reply within 2 week(s) of notification.

CONTACT

Patricia Reilly, Director of Financial Aid
Bendetson Hall, Medford, MA 02155
(617) 627-2000

University of Massachusetts Amherst

Amherst, Massachusetts
www.umass.edu — Federal Code: 002221

4-year public university in large town.

Enrollment: 19,964 undergrads, 6% part-time. 4,272 full-time freshmen.

Selectivity: Admits 50 to 75% of applicants.

BASIC COSTS (2008-2009)

Tuition and fees: $10,232; out-of-state residents $21,729.
Room and board: $8,114.

FINANCIAL AID PICTURE (2007-2008)

Students with need: Out of 3,701 full-time freshmen who applied for aid, 2,266 were judged to have need. Of these, 2,206 received aid, and 470 had their full need met. Average financial aid package met 83% of need; average scholarship/grant was $7,865; average loan was $3,577. For part-time students, average financial aid package was $10,475.
Students without need: 418 full-time freshmen who did not demonstrate need for aid received scholarships/grants; average award was $2,265. No-need awards available for academics, art, athletics, music/drama, ROTC, state/district residency.
Scholarships offered: ***Merit:*** Merit scholarships; all applicants automatically considered. ***Athletic:*** 66 full-time freshmen received athletic scholarships; average amount $10,961.
Cumulative student debt: 66% of graduating class had student loans; average debt was $21,614.

FINANCIAL AID PROCEDURES

Forms required: FAFSA.
Dates and Deadlines: Priority date 2/14; no closing date. Applicants notified on a rolling basis starting 3/1.
Transfers: Financial aid transcripts required.

CONTACT

Suzanne Peters, Director of Financial Aid
University Admissions Center, Amherst, MA 01003-9291
(413) 545-0801

University of Massachusetts Boston

Boston, Massachusetts
www.umb.edu Federal Code: 002222

4-year public university in very large city.
Enrollment: 9,564 undergrads, 27% part-time. 949 full-time freshmen.
Selectivity: Admits 50 to 75% of applicants.

BASIC COSTS (2008-2009)

Tuition and fees: $9,111; out-of-state residents $21,297.
Per-credit charge: $72; out-of-state residents $406.

FINANCIAL AID PICTURE (2007-2008)

Students with need: Out of 737 full-time freshmen who applied for aid, 616 were judged to have need. Of these, 616 received aid, and 287 had their full need met. Average financial aid package met 90% of need; average scholarship/grant was $6,757; average loan was $3,730. For part-time students, average financial aid package was $8,701.
Students without need: 72 full-time freshmen who did not demonstrate need for aid received scholarships/grants; average award was $3,618. No-need awards available for academics, leadership, state/district residency.
Cumulative student debt: 60% of graduating class had student loans; average debt was $18,902.
Additional info: Some Massachusetts state employees and Massachusetts Vietnam veterans eligible for tuition waiver. Some waivers available based on talent and academic excellence.

FINANCIAL AID PROCEDURES

Forms required: FAFSA.
Dates and Deadlines: Priority date 3/1; no closing date. Applicants notified on a rolling basis starting 3/21.

CONTACT

Judy Keyes, Director of Financial Aid Services
100 Morrissey Boulevard, Boston, MA 02125-3393
(617) 287-6300

University of Massachusetts Dartmouth

North Dartmouth, Massachusetts
www.umassd.edu Federal Code: 002210

4-year public university in large town.
Enrollment: 7,738 undergrads, 10% part-time. 1,925 full-time freshmen.
Selectivity: Admits 50 to 75% of applicants.

BASIC COSTS (2008-2009)

Tuition and fees: $8,861; out-of-state residents $18,561.
Room and board: $9,457.

FINANCIAL AID PICTURE (2007-2008)

Students with need: Out of 1,580 full-time freshmen who applied for aid, 1,155 were judged to have need. Of these, 1,155 received aid, and 703 had their full need met. Average financial aid package met 91% of need; average scholarship/grant was $6,433; average loan was $4,841. For part-time students, average financial aid package was $8,873.
Students without need: 191 full-time freshmen who did not demonstrate need for aid received scholarships/grants; average award was $2,310. No-need awards available for academics, minority status, ROTC, state/district residency.
Scholarships offered: Chancellor's Merit Scholarship; approximately $2,000; for Massachusetts high school seniors with 1250 SAT (exclusive of Writing) and in top 25% of class; 50 awarded. Solveig E.J. Balestracci Scholarship; $1,000; for academic achievement in marine-related area for residents of New Bedford, Dartmouth, Acushnet, Westport, Mattapoisett, Marion, Rochester or Lakeville; 1 awarded. Boivon Scholarship; $1,000; based on academic involvement in French language and culture. A.J. Carvalho Memorial Scholarship; approximately $5,000; for New Bedford graduates of Portuguese descent with 3.0 GPA. Cranston Foundation Scholarship; $500; for students in the Textile Science Department.
Cumulative student debt: 68% of graduating class had student loans; average debt was $21,714.

FINANCIAL AID PROCEDURES

Forms required: FAFSA.
Dates and Deadlines: Priority date 3/1; no closing date. Applicants notified on a rolling basis starting 3/25; must reply within 3 week(s) of notification.

CONTACT

Bruce Palmer, Director of Financial Aid
285 Old Westport Road, North Dartmouth, MA 02747-2300
(508) 999-8632

University of Massachusetts Lowell

Lowell, Massachusetts
www.uml.edu Federal Code: 002161

4-year public university in small city.
Enrollment: 7,151 undergrads, 9% part-time. 1,527 full-time freshmen.
Selectivity: Admits over 75% of applicants.

BASIC COSTS (2008-2009)

Tuition and fees: $9,147; out-of-state residents $21,167.
Per-credit charge: $61; out-of-state residents $367.
Room and board: $7,519.

FINANCIAL AID PICTURE (2008-2009)

Students with need: Out of 1,281 full-time freshmen who applied for aid, 853 were judged to have need. Of these, 853 received aid, and 609 had their full need met. Average financial aid package met 95% of need; average scholarship/grant was $6,287; average loan was $4,461. For part-time students, average financial aid package was $8,128.
Students without need: 232 full-time freshmen who did not demonstrate need for aid received scholarships/grants; average award was $2,940. No-

need awards available for academics, alumni affiliation, art, athletics, job skills, leadership, minority status, music/drama, ROTC, state/district residency.
Scholarships offered: 52 full-time freshmen received athletic scholarships; average amount $7,006.
Cumulative student debt: 65% of graduating class had student loans; average debt was $20,267.

FINANCIAL AID PROCEDURES
Forms required: FAFSA.
Dates and Deadlines: Priority date 3/1; no closing date. Applicants notified on a rolling basis starting 3/20.

CONTACT
Carole King, Director of Financial Aid
883 Broadway Street, Room 110, Lowell, MA 01854-5104
(978) 934-4220

Urban College of Boston
Boston, Massachusetts
www.urbancollege.edu Federal Code: 031305

2-year private community college in very large city.
Enrollment: 3 full-time undergrads.
Selectivity: Open admission.

BASIC COSTS (2008-2009)
Tuition and fees: $4,700.
Per-credit charge: $155.

FINANCIAL AID PICTURE (2007-2008)
Students with need: Need-based aid available for full-time and part-time students.
Students without need: This college awards aid only to students with need.

FINANCIAL AID PROCEDURES
Forms required: FAFSA.
Dates and Deadlines: No deadline. Applicants notified on a rolling basis starting 4/15.

CONTACT
Sandra Coswatte, Director of Financial Aid
178 Tremont Street, Seventh Floor, Boston, MA 02111
(617) 348-6220

Wellesley College
Wellesley, Massachusetts Federal Code: 002224
www.wellesley.edu CSS Code: 3957

4-year private liberal arts college for women in large town.
Enrollment: 2,212 undergrads, 1% part-time. 596 full-time freshmen.
Selectivity: Admits less than 50% of applicants.

BASIC COSTS (2008-2009)
Tuition and fees: $36,640.
Room and board: $11,336.

FINANCIAL AID PICTURE (2008-2009)
Students with need: Out of 423 full-time freshmen who applied for aid, 344 were judged to have need. Of these, 344 received aid, and 344 had their full need met. Average financial aid package met 100% of need; average scholarship/grant was $34,528; average loan was $2,417. For part-time students, average financial aid package was $9,578.
Students without need: This college awards aid only to students with need.
Cumulative student debt: 53% of graduating class had student loans; average debt was $12,639.
Additional info: Wellesley has increased scholarships and eliminated or reduced student loans for nearly all students.

FINANCIAL AID PROCEDURES
Forms required: FAFSA, CSS PROFILE, institutional form.
Dates and Deadlines: Closing date 1/15. Applicants notified by 4/1; must reply by 5/1.
Transfers: Closing date 3/1.

CONTACT
Kathryn Osmond, Director of Student Financial Services
106 Central Street, Wellesley, MA 02481-8203
(781) 283-2360

Wentworth Institute of Technology
Boston, Massachusetts
www.wit.edu Federal Code: 002225

4-year private engineering and technical college in very large city.
Enrollment: 3,764 undergrads, 10% part-time. 813 full-time freshmen.
Selectivity: Admits 50 to 75% of applicants.

BASIC COSTS (2009-2010)
Tuition and fees: $21,800.
Room and board: $10,500.
Additional info: Tuition includes cost of laptop computer; students in architecture and design programs pay $2,000 in required fees for academic year.

FINANCIAL AID PICTURE (2008-2009)
Students with need: Out of 813 full-time freshmen who applied for aid, 571 were judged to have need. Of these, 571 received aid. Average financial aid package met 38% of need; average scholarship/grant was $2,800; average loan was $3,300. For part-time students, average financial aid package was $6,650.
Students without need: 250 full-time freshmen who did not demonstrate need for aid received scholarships/grants; average award was $6,000. No-need awards available for academics, leadership, ROTC, state/district residency.
Scholarships offered: Applicants for admission automatically considered for merit scholarships.

FINANCIAL AID PROCEDURES
Forms required: FAFSA.
Dates and Deadlines: Priority date 3/1; no closing date. Applicants notified on a rolling basis starting 3/15; must reply within 2 week(s) of notification.
Transfers: Review of NSLDS history within 30 days of beginning of enrollment required.

CONTACT
Anne-Marie Caruso, Director of Financial Aid
550 Huntington Avenue, Boston, MA 02115
(617) 989-4020

Western New England College
Springfield, Massachusetts
www.wnec.edu Federal Code: 002226

4-year private university in small city.
Enrollment: 2,768 undergrads, 10% part-time. 735 full-time freshmen.
Selectivity: Admits 50 to 75% of applicants.

BASIC COSTS (2008-2009)
Tuition and fees: $27,470.
Per-credit charge: $481.

Room and board: $10,554.

FINANCIAL AID PICTURE (2008-2009)

Students with need: Out of 687 full-time freshmen who applied for aid, 558 were judged to have need. Of these, 558 received aid, and 77 had their full need met. Average financial aid package met 74% of need; average scholarship/grant was $15,099; average loan was $4,027. For part-time students, average financial aid package was $6,092.

Students without need: 92 full-time freshmen who did not demonstrate need for aid received scholarships/grants; average award was $10,245. No-need awards available for academics, music/drama, ROTC.

FINANCIAL AID PROCEDURES

Forms required: FAFSA.

Dates and Deadlines: Priority date 4/15; closing date 5/1. Applicants notified on a rolling basis starting 3/15; must reply by 5/1 or within 2 week(s) of notification.

CONTACT

Kathy Chambers, Associate Director of Financial Aid
1215 Wilbraham Road, Springfield, MA 01119-2684
(800) 325-1122 ext. 2080

Westfield State College

Westfield, Massachusetts
www.wsc.ma.edu Federal Code: 002189

4-year public liberal arts and teachers college in large town.

Enrollment: 4,739 undergrads, 7% part-time. 933 full-time freshmen.

Selectivity: Admits 50 to 75% of applicants.

BASIC COSTS (2008-2009)

Tuition and fees: $6,515; out-of-state residents $12,595.

Per-credit charge: $85; out-of-state residents $95.

Room and board: $7,204.

Additional info: New England Regional tuition and fees per year: $7,000.

FINANCIAL AID PICTURE (2007-2008)

Students with need: Out of 821 full-time freshmen who applied for aid, 471 were judged to have need. Of these, 460 received aid, and 72 had their full need met. Average financial aid package met 78% of need; average scholarship/grant was $5,121; average loan was $3,318. Need-based aid available for part-time students.

Students without need: 15 full-time freshmen who did not demonstrate need for aid received scholarships/grants; average award was $3,533.

Cumulative student debt: 72% of graduating class had student loans; average debt was $17,059.

FINANCIAL AID PROCEDURES

Forms required: FAFSA

Dates and Deadlines: Priority date 3/1; no closing date. Applicants notified on a rolling basis starting 4/1.

CONTACT

Catherine Ryan, Director of Financial Aid
577 Western Avenue, Westfield, MA 01086-1630
(413) 572-5218

Wheaton College

Norton, Massachusetts Federal Code: 002227
www.wheatoncollege.edu CSS Code: 3963

4-year private liberal arts college in large town.

Enrollment: 1,655 undergrads. 420 full-time freshmen.

Selectivity: Admits less than 50% of applicants.

BASIC COSTS (2009-2010)

Tuition and fees: $39,850.

Room and board: $9,590.

Additional info: Freshmen pay one-time $50 general fee (non-refundable).

FINANCIAL AID PICTURE (2008-2009)

Students with need: Out of 279 full-time freshmen who applied for aid, 237 were judged to have need. Of these, 237 received aid, and 136 had their full need met. Average financial aid package met 97% of need; average scholarship/grant was $26,139; average loan was $4,237. For part-time students, average financial aid package was $5,550.

Students without need: 55 full-time freshmen who did not demonstrate need for aid received scholarships/grants; average award was $11,915. No-need awards available for academics.

Scholarships offered: Balfour Scholarship; $15,000 annually plus $4,000 total in research/internship/community service stipends. Trustee Scholarship; $10,000 annually plus $4,000 total in research/internship/community service stipends. Community Scholarship; $7,500 annually plus $3,000 total in research/internship/community service stipends. All selected from top 15% of applicant pool.

Cumulative student debt: 48% of graduating class had student loans; average debt was $24,428.

FINANCIAL AID PROCEDURES

Forms required: FAFSA, CSS PROFILE.

Dates and Deadlines: Closing date 2/1. Applicants notified by 4/1; must reply by 5/1.

Transfers: Closing date 3/15. Applicants notified by 5/15; must reply by 6/1. Very limited institutional grant funds available for late transfer applicants.

CONTACT

Robin Randall, Assistant Vice President for Enrollment and Student Financial Services
26 East Main Street, Norton, MA 02766
(508) 286-8232

Wheelock College

Boston, Massachusetts
www.wheelock.edu Federal Code: 002228

4-year private liberal arts and teachers college in very large city.

Enrollment: 818 undergrads, 3% part-time. 231 full-time freshmen.

Selectivity: Admits 50 to 75% of applicants.

BASIC COSTS (2008-2009)

Tuition and fees: $27,205.

Per-credit charge: $825.

Room and board: $10,825.

FINANCIAL AID PICTURE (2008-2009)

Students with need: Out of 209 full-time freshmen who applied for aid, 178 were judged to have need. Of these, 178 received aid, and 36 had their full need met. Average financial aid package met 74% of need; average scholarship/grant was $15,734; average loan was $3,916. For part-time students, average financial aid package was $14,492.

Students without need: 49 full-time freshmen who did not demonstrate need for aid received scholarships/grants; average award was $10,685. No-need awards available for academics, job skills, leadership.

Scholarships offered: Wheelock College Grants; based on 1050 SAT (exclusive of writing) plus 3.0 GPA; renewable if 3.0 GPA maintained.

Cumulative student debt: 96% of graduating class had student loans; average debt was $43,115.

FINANCIAL AID PROCEDURES

Forms required: FAFSA.

Dates and Deadlines: Priority date 2/15; no closing date. Applicants notified on a rolling basis starting 3/1; must reply by 5/1.

Transfers: Priority date 4/15. Applicants notified by 5/1; must reply by 6/1.

CONTACT

Roxanne Dumas, Director of Financial Aid
200 The Riverway, Boston, MA 02215-4176
(617) 879-2443

Williams College

Williamstown, Massachusetts
www.williams.edu
Federal Code: 002229
CSS Code: 3965

4-year private liberal arts college in small town, affiliated with United Church of Christ.
Enrollment: 1,970 undergrads. 539 full-time freshmen.
Selectivity: Admits less than 50% of applicants.

BASIC COSTS (2009-2010)

Tuition and fees: $39,490.
Room and board: $10,390.

FINANCIAL AID PICTURE (2008-2009)

Students with need: Out of 334 full-time freshmen who applied for aid, 269 were judged to have need. Of these, 269 received aid, and 269 had their full need met. Average financial aid package met 100% of need; average scholarship/grant was $38,410. Need-based aid available for part-time students.
Students without need: This college awards aid only to students with need.
Cumulative student debt: 46% of graduating class had student loans; average debt was $9,214.

FINANCIAL AID PROCEDURES

Forms required: FAFSA, CSS PROFILE.
Dates and Deadlines: Closing date 2/1. Applicants notified by 4/1; must reply by 5/1.
Transfers: Closing date 4/1. Applicants notified by 5/15; must reply within 2 week(s) of notification.

CONTACT

Paul Boyer, Director of Financial Aid
33 Stetson Court, Williamstown, MA 01267
(413) 597-3131

Worcester Polytechnic Institute

Worcester, Massachusetts
www.wpi.edu
Federal Code: 002233
CSS Code: 3969

4-year private university in small city.
Enrollment: 3,160 undergrads, 3% part-time. 805 full-time freshmen.
Selectivity: Admits 50 to 75% of applicants.

BASIC COSTS (2009-2010)

Tuition and fees: $37,845.
Per-credit charge: $996.
Room and board: $11,315.

FINANCIAL AID PICTURE (2007-2008)

Students with need: Out of 696 full-time freshmen who applied for aid, 599 were judged to have need. Of these, 596 received aid, and 247 had their full need met. Average financial aid package met 65% of need; average scholarship/grant was $16,584; average loan was $5,806. For part-time students, average financial aid package was $14,363.
Students without need: 159 full-time freshmen who did not demonstrate need for aid received scholarships/grants; average award was $12,764. No-need awards available for academics, leadership, minority status, ROTC.
Scholarships offered: Merit scholarships; typically $12,500-$25,000; renewable for 4 years.
Cumulative student debt: 66% of graduating class had student loans; average debt was $37,032.

FINANCIAL AID PROCEDURES

Forms required: FAFSA, CSS PROFILE.
Dates and Deadlines: Closing date 2/1. Applicants notified by 4/1; must reply by 5/1.
Transfers: Priority date 2/1; closing date 3/1. Applicants notified by 4/15; must reply by 5/1.

CONTACT

Monica Blondin, Director, Financial Aid
100 Institute Road, Worcester, MA 01609-2280
(508) 831-5469

Worcester State College

Worcester, Massachusetts
www.worcester.edu
Federal Code: 002190

4-year public liberal arts and teachers college in small city.
Enrollment: 4,077 undergrads, 18% part-time. 678 full-time freshmen.
Selectivity: Admits 50 to 75% of applicants.

BASIC COSTS (2008-2009)

Tuition and fees: $6,170; out-of-state residents $12,250.
Per-credit charge: $40; out-of-state residents $294.
Room and board: $8,527.

FINANCIAL AID PICTURE (2007-2008)

Students with need: Out of 601 full-time freshmen who applied for aid, 382 were judged to have need. Of these, 372 received aid, and 148 had their full need met. Average financial aid package met 81% of need; average scholarship/grant was $4,252; average loan was $2,059. For part-time students, average financial aid package was $5,925.
Students without need: No-need awards available for academics, ROTC.
Scholarships offered: Presidential Scholarships; full in-state tuition and fees; 3.5 GPA and 1150 SAT required; 15 awarded. Tsongas Scholarships; full in-state tuition and fees to Massachusetts residents; 3.7 GPA and 1200 SAT required; 5 awarded. Access Scholarships; $1,000 per year; for underserved groups with 2.5 GPA and 920 SAT; 15 awarded. Teacher Education Scholarship; full in-state tuition and fees; for future teachers with 3.5 GPA and 1150 SAT; 15 awarded. Honors Scholarship; $1,500 per year; 3.2 GPA and 1100 SAT required; 25 awarded. All SAT scores exclusive of writing.
Cumulative student debt: 43% of graduating class had student loans; average debt was $16,063.
Additional info: Veterans, Native Americans and those certified by Massachusetts Rehabilitation Commission and Massachusetts Commission for the Blind considered for tuition waivers while funds available. Tuition also waived for needy Massachusetts residents and in-state National Guard members.

FINANCIAL AID PROCEDURES

Forms required: FAFSA.
Dates and Deadlines: Priority date 3/1; closing date 5/1. Applicants notified on a rolling basis starting 3/1; must reply within 2 week(s) of notification.
Transfers: Transfer Scholarship; $1,000; requires associate degree and 3.2 GPA; 25 awarded to Massachusetts residents.

CONTACT

Jayne McGinn, Director of Financial Aid
486 Chandler Street, Worcester, MA 01602-2597
(508) 929-8056

Zion Bible College
Haverhill, Massachusetts
www.zbc.edu Federal Code: 035705

4-year private Bible college in small city, affiliated with Assemblies of God.
Enrollment: 250 undergrads, 18% part-time. 41 full-time freshmen.
Selectivity: Open admission.

BASIC COSTS (2008-2009)
Tuition and fees: $7,640.
Per-credit charge: $235.
Room and board: $5,700.

FINANCIAL AID PICTURE (2008-2009)
Students with need: Out of 36 full-time freshmen who applied for aid, 32 were judged to have need. Of these, 31 received aid. Average financial aid package met 28% of need; average scholarship/grant was $3,530; average loan was $1,715. For part-time students, average financial aid package was $4,588.
Students without need: 2 full-time freshmen who did not demonstrate need for aid received scholarships/grants; average award was $562. No-need awards available for academics, leadership, minority status, state/district residency.

FINANCIAL AID PROCEDURES
Forms required: FAFSA.
Dates and Deadlines: Priority date 6/1; no closing date. Applicants notified on a rolling basis; must reply within 4 week(s) of notification.

CONTACT
Patricia Stauffer, Financial Aid Director
320 South Main Street, Haverhill, MA 01835

Michigan

Adrian College
Adrian, Michigan
www.adrian.edu Federal Code: 002234

4-year private liberal arts college in large town, affiliated with United Methodist Church.
Enrollment: 1,469 undergrads, 3% part-time. 492 full-time freshmen.
Selectivity: Admits 50 to 75% of applicants.

BASIC COSTS (2008-2009)
Tuition and fees: $23,390.
Per-credit charge: $670.
Room and board: $7,600.

FINANCIAL AID PICTURE (2007-2008)
Students with need: Out of 420 full-time freshmen who applied for aid, 420 were judged to have need. Of these, 420 received aid, and 420 had their full need met. Average financial aid package met 100% of need; average scholarship/grant was $9,159; average loan was $4,483. For part-time students, average financial aid package was $7,338.
Students without need: 62 full-time freshmen who did not demonstrate need for aid received scholarships/grants; average award was $11,381. No-need awards available for academics, alumni affiliation, art, leadership, music/drama, religious affiliation, state/district residency.
Scholarships offered: Academic scholarships; based on ACT score of 20 and GPA of 3.0.
Cumulative student debt: 81% of graduating class had student loans; average debt was $17,160.

FINANCIAL AID PROCEDURES
Forms required: FAFSA.
Dates and Deadlines: Priority date 3/1; no closing date. Applicants notified on a rolling basis starting 3/15; must reply by 5/1 or within 2 week(s) of notification.

CONTACT
Andrew Spohn, Director of Financial Services
110 South Madison Street, Adrian, MI 49221-2575
(517) 265-5161 ext. 4306

Albion College
Albion, Michigan
www.albion.edu Federal Code: 002235

4-year private liberal arts college in small town, affiliated with United Methodist Church.
Enrollment: 1,845 undergrads. 486 full-time freshmen.
Selectivity: Admits over 75% of applicants.

BASIC COSTS (2009-2010)
Tuition and fees: $30,272.
Per-credit charge: $1,253.
Room and board: $8,510.

FINANCIAL AID PICTURE (2008-2009)
Students with need: Out of 384 full-time freshmen who applied for aid, 318 were judged to have need. Of these, 318 received aid, and 125 had their full need met. Average financial aid package met 91% of need; average scholarship/grant was $20,133; average loan was $3,908.
Students without need: 162 full-time freshmen who did not demonstrate need for aid received scholarships/grants; average award was $13,448. No-need awards available for academics, alumni affiliation, art, music/drama, state/district residency.
Scholarships offered: Distinguished Albion Scholarships: full tuition for 4 years; awarded to students who present original research during on-campus competition; up to 10 awarded. Trustee Scholarships: $15,500; based on GPA and SAT or ACT. Presidential Scholarships: $14,000; based on GPA and SAT or ACT. Performing and Fine Arts Scholarships: up to $3,000. Speech Communication Scholarships: up to $8,000. Diversity Awards: $4,000 renewable annually; awarded to students involved with promoting and enhancing multicultural on-campus relations.

FINANCIAL AID PROCEDURES
Forms required: FAFSA.
Dates and Deadlines: Priority date 3/1; no closing date. Applicants notified on a rolling basis starting 3/15; must reply by 5/1 or within 2 week(s) of notification.
Transfers: Applicants notified on a rolling basis.

CONTACT
Doug Kellar, Associate Vice President for Enrollment and Financial Aid
611 East Porter Street, Albion, MI 49224-1831
(517) 629-0440

Alma College
Alma, Michigan
www.alma.edu Federal Code: 002236

4-year private liberal arts college in small town, affiliated with Presbyterian Church (USA).
Enrollment: 1,350 undergrads, 1% part-time. 429 full-time freshmen.
Selectivity: Admits 50 to 75% of applicants.

BASIC COSTS (2009-2010)
Tuition and fees: $26,068.
Per-credit charge: $1,000.
Room and board: $8,518.

FINANCIAL AID PICTURE (2008-2009)
Students with need: Out of 420 full-time freshmen who applied for aid, 348 were judged to have need. Of these, 348 received aid, and 102 had their full need met. Average financial aid package met 95% of need; average scholarship/grant was $18,287; average loan was $3,767. For part-time students, average financial aid package was $7,206.
Students without need: 82 full-time freshmen who did not demonstrate need for aid received scholarships/grants; average award was $12,602. No-need awards available for academics, alumni affiliation, art, minority status, music/drama.
Scholarships offered: Distinguished Scholar Award; up to full tuition; awarded to designated National Merit Scholarship Finalist. Trustee Honors Scholarship; $14,000; awarded on basis of superior academic achievement, national test scores. Presidential Scholarships; $13,000; awarded on basis of outstanding scholarship and high national test scores. Dean's Scholarship; $12,000; awarded on basis on academic achievement and high national test scores. Tartan Scholars Award ($10,000) and Achievement Awards ($8,000); both awards based on academic achievement or high national test scores. Performance Scholarships; up to $1,000; awarded to students with a demonstrated high level of accomplishment in the fine or performing arts.
Cumulative student debt: 85% of graduating class had student loans; average debt was $30,187.
Additional info: Auditions required for music, drama, dance scholarship candidates. Portfolios required for art scholarship candidates.

FINANCIAL AID PROCEDURES
Forms required: FAFSA.
Dates and Deadlines: Priority date 3/1; no closing date. Applicants notified on a rolling basis starting 3/1; must reply within 3 week(s) of notification.
Transfers: No deadline. Applicants notified on a rolling basis starting 3/1; must reply within 3 week(s) of notification.

CONTACT
Christopher Brown, Director of Financial Assistance
614 West Superior Street, Alma, MI 48801-1599
(989) 463-7347

Alpena Community College
Alpena, Michigan
www.alpenacc.edu Federal Code: 002237

2-year public community college in large town.
Enrollment: 2,047 undergrads.
Selectivity: Open admission; but selective for some programs.

BASIC COSTS (2008-2009)
Tuition and fees: $3,040; out-of-district residents $4,300; out-of-state residents $5,560.
Per-credit charge: $84; out-of-district residents $126; out-of-state residents $168.

FINANCIAL AID PICTURE (2008-2009)
Students with need: 97% of average financial aid package awarded as scholarships/grants, 3% awarded as loans/jobs. Need-based aid available for part-time students.
Students without need: No-need awards available for academics, art, athletics, job skills, leadership, music/drama.

FINANCIAL AID PROCEDURES
Forms required: FAFSA.
Dates and Deadlines: Priority date 8/1; no closing date. Applicants notified on a rolling basis starting 5/15; must reply within 3 week(s) of notification.

CONTACT
Max Lindsay, Dean of Students
665 Johnson Street, Alpena, MI 49707
(989) 358-7205

Andrews University
Berrien Springs, Michigan
www.andrews.edu Federal Code: 002238

4-year private university in small town, affiliated with Seventh-day Adventists.
Enrollment: 1,760 undergrads, 7% part-time. 386 full-time freshmen.
Selectivity: Admits 50 to 75% of applicants.

BASIC COSTS (2009-2010)
Tuition and fees: $21,170.
Per-credit charge: $855.
Room and board: $6,360.

FINANCIAL AID PICTURE (2007-2008)
Students with need: Need-based aid available for full-time and part-time students. Work study available nights, weekends, and for part-time students.
Students without need: No-need awards available for academics, alumni affiliation, leadership, music/drama, religious affiliation.

FINANCIAL AID PROCEDURES
Forms required: FAFSA, institutional form.
Dates and Deadlines: Priority date 3/31; no closing date. Applicants notified on a rolling basis starting 3/15.

CONTACT
Elynda Bedney, Director of Student Financial Services
100 US Highway 31, Berrien Springs, MI 49104

Aquinas College
Grand Rapids, Michigan
www.aquinas.edu Federal Code: 002239

4-year private liberal arts college in small city, affiliated with Roman Catholic Church.
Enrollment: 1,872 undergrads, 14% part-time. 450 full-time freshmen.
Selectivity: Admits over 75% of applicants. GED not accepted.

BASIC COSTS (2009-2010)
Tuition and fees: $22,314.
Per-credit charge: $698.
Room and board: $7,014.
Additional info: Tuition/fee waivers available for adults.

FINANCIAL AID PICTURE (2008-2009)
Students with need: Out of 436 full-time freshmen who applied for aid, 379 were judged to have need. Of these, 379 received aid, and 177 had their full need met. Average financial aid package met 90% of need; average scholarship/grant was $17,500; average loan was $3,500. For part-time students, average financial aid package was $3,489.
Students without need: 81 full-time freshmen who did not demonstrate need for aid received scholarships/grants; average award was $8,600. No-need awards available for academics, alumni affiliation, art, athletics, leadership, music/drama.
Scholarships offered: ***Merit:*** Spectrum Scholarship; $3,000 to full tuition; awarded to students who have excelled in academics, leadership or community service; renewable. ***Athletic:*** 12 full-time freshmen received athletic scholarships; average amount $3,450.

FINANCIAL AID PROCEDURES
Forms required: FAFSA.

Dates and Deadlines: Priority date 3/1; no closing date. Applicants notified on a rolling basis starting 2/15; must reply within 2 week(s) of notification.
Transfers: Priority date 4/15; closing date 7/1. Must reply within 2 week(s) of notification.

CONTACT
David Steffee, Director of Financial Aid
1607 Robinson Road Southeast, Grand Rapids, MI 49506-1799
(616) 632-2893

Baker College of Auburn Hills
Auburn Hills, Michigan
www.baker.edu Federal Code: E00466

4-year private business and technical college in small city.
Enrollment: 3,824 undergrads.
Selectivity: Open admission.

BASIC COSTS (2009-2010)
Tuition and fees: $8,775.
Per-credit charge: $195.

FINANCIAL AID PICTURE
Students with need: Work study available nights, weekends, and for part-time students.
Students without need: No-need awards available for academics, alumni affiliation.

FINANCIAL AID PROCEDURES
Forms required: FAFSA, institutional form.
Dates and Deadlines: Priority date 2/21; closing date 9/1. Applicants notified on a rolling basis starting 4/1.
Transfers: Must have been deemed financial aid-eligible at previous school.

CONTACT
Greg Little, Financial Aid Director
1500 University Drive, Auburn Hills, MI 48326
(248) 340-0600

Baker College of Cadillac
Cadillac, Michigan
www.baker.edu Federal Code: E00461

4-year private business and health science college in large town.
Enrollment: 1,952 undergrads.
Selectivity: Open admission.

BASIC COSTS (2009-2010)
Tuition and fees: $8,775.
Per-credit charge: $195.

FINANCIAL AID PICTURE
Students with need: Need-based aid available for full-time and part-time students. Work study available nights, weekends, and for part-time students.
Students without need: No-need awards available for academics.
Scholarships offered: Baker College Career Scholarships; $400 per term for 4 years; based on 2.5 GPA after junior year of high school. Board of Regents Scholarships; half tuition for 4 years; based on 3.5 GPA through grade 11.

FINANCIAL AID PROCEDURES
Forms required: FAFSA, institutional form.
Dates and Deadlines: Priority date 2/21; no closing date. Applicants notified on a rolling basis starting 5/1.
Transfers: Priority date 3/20; closing date 9/1.

CONTACT
Kristin Bonney, Financial Aid Officer
9600 East 13th Street, Cadillac, MI 49601
(231) 876-3118

Baker College of Clinton Township
Clinton Township, Michigan
www.baker.edu Federal Code: E00462

4-year private business and technical college in very large city.
Enrollment: 5,637 undergrads.
Selectivity: Open admission; but selective for some programs.

BASIC COSTS (2009-2010)
Tuition and fees: $8,775.
Per-credit charge: $195.

FINANCIAL AID PICTURE
Students with need: Need-based aid available for full-time and part-time students. Work study available nights, weekends, and for part-time students.
Students without need: No-need awards available for academics, minority status.

FINANCIAL AID PROCEDURES
Forms required: FAFSA, institutional form.
Dates and Deadlines: Priority date 2/21; closing date 9/1. Applicants notified on a rolling basis starting 4/1.

CONTACT
Lisa Harvener, Vice President of Student Services
34950 Little Mack Avenue, Clinton Township, MI 48035
(586) 790-9589

Baker College of Muskegon
Muskegon, Michigan
www.baker.edu Federal Code: E00463

4-year private business and technical college in small city.
Enrollment: 5,232 undergrads.
Selectivity: Open admission; but selective for some programs.

BASIC COSTS (2009-2010)
Tuition and fees: $8,775.
Per-credit charge: $195.
Room only: $2,965.

FINANCIAL AID PICTURE
Students with need: Need-based aid available for full-time and part-time students. Work study available nights, weekends, and for part-time students.
Students without need: No-need awards available for academics, minority status.
Scholarships offered: Career Scholarship; $4,800 over 4 years; based on GPA over 3.0. Board Regents Scholarship; one-half tuition for 4 years; based on GPA over 3.5. Alternative Scholarship; one-half tuition for 2 years; based on academic success in alternative high school education program.

FINANCIAL AID PROCEDURES
Forms required: FAFSA, institutional form.
Dates and Deadlines: Priority date 2/21; no closing date. Applicants notified on a rolling basis starting 4/1.
Transfers: Priority date 3/21.

CONTACT
Jody Zerlant, Director of Financial Aid
1903 Marquette Avenue, Muskegon, MI 49442
(231) 777-5231

Baker College of Owosso

Owosso, Michigan
www.baker.edu Federal Code: E00464

4-year private business and technical college in large town.
Enrollment: 2,996 undergrads.
Selectivity: Open admission.

BASIC COSTS (2009-2010)
Tuition and fees: $8,775.
Per-credit charge: $195.
Room only: $2,700.

FINANCIAL AID PICTURE
Students with need: Need-based aid available for full-time and part-time students. Work study available nights, weekends, and for part-time students.
Students without need: No-need awards available for academics, minority status.

FINANCIAL AID PROCEDURES
Forms required: FAFSA, institutional form.
Dates and Deadlines: Priority date 2/21; closing date 9/1. Applicants notified on a rolling basis starting 4/1.
Transfers: Priority date 3/21.

CONTACT
Nicole Patterson, Financial Aid Director
1020 South Washington Street, Owosso, MI 48867
(989) 720-3430

Baker College of Port Huron

Port Huron, Michigan
www.baker.edu Federal Code: E00465

4-year private business and technical college in large town.
Enrollment: 1,716 undergrads.
Selectivity: Open admission; but selective for some programs.

BASIC COSTS (2009-2010)
Tuition and fees: $8,775.
Per-credit charge: $195.

FINANCIAL AID PICTURE
Students with need: Need-based aid available for full-time and part-time students. Work study available nights.
Students without need: This college awards aid only to students with need.

FINANCIAL AID PROCEDURES
Forms required: FAFSA, institutional form.
Dates and Deadlines: Priority date 2/21; no closing date. Applicants notified on a rolling basis starting 4/1.
Transfers: Priority date 3/21; closing date 9/1.

CONTACT
Barbara Fosgard, Financial Aid Director
3403 Lapeer Road, Port Huron, MI 48060-2597
(810) 985-7000

Bay de Noc Community College

Escanaba, Michigan
www.baycollege.edu Federal Code: 002240

2-year public community college in large town.
Enrollment: 2,170 undergrads, 36% part-time. 471 full-time freshmen.
Selectivity: Open admission; but selective for some programs.

BASIC COSTS (2008-2009)
Tuition and fees: $2,565; out-of-district residents $4,035; out-of-state residents $5,055.
Per-credit charge: $77; out-of-district residents $126; out-of-state residents $160.
Room and board: $2,600.
Additional info: Tuition and instructional fees based on contact hours.

FINANCIAL AID PICTURE (2008-2009)
Students with need: Need-based aid available for full-time and part-time students. Work study available nights, weekends, and for part-time students.
Students without need: No-need awards available for academics.

FINANCIAL AID PROCEDURES
Forms required: FAFSA.
Dates and Deadlines: Priority date 4/1; no closing date. Applicants notified on a rolling basis starting 2/1; must reply within 2 week(s) of notification.

CONTACT
Sue Hebert, Financial Aid Director
2001 North Lincoln Road, Escanaba, MI 49829-2511
(906) 786-5802 ext. 1215

Bay Mills Community College

Brimley, Michigan
www.bmcc.edu Federal Code: 030666

2-year public community college in rural community.
Enrollment: 210 full-time undergrads.
Selectivity: Open admission.

BASIC COSTS (2008-2009)
Tuition and fees: $2,910.
Per-credit charge: $85.

FINANCIAL AID PICTURE
Students with need: Work study available nights.

FINANCIAL AID PROCEDURES
Forms required: FAFSA.
Dates and Deadlines: Priority date 6/30; no closing date.

CONTACT
Tina Miller, Financial Aid Director
12214 West Lakeshore Drive, Brimley, MI 49715
(906) 248-3354 ext. 8437

Calvin College

Grand Rapids, Michigan
www.calvin.edu Federal Code: 002241

4-year private liberal arts college in large city, affiliated with Christian Reformed Church.
Enrollment: 4,021 undergrads, 2% part-time. 936 full-time freshmen.
Selectivity: Admits over 75% of applicants.

BASIC COSTS (2009-2010)
Tuition and fees: $24,035.
Per-credit charge: $570.
Room and board: $8,275.

FINANCIAL AID PICTURE (2008-2009)
Students with need: Out of 773 full-time freshmen who applied for aid, 596 were judged to have need. Of these, 596 received aid, and 166 had their full need met. Average financial aid package met 87% of need; average scholarship/grant was $11,443; average loan was $4,670. For part-time students, average financial aid package was $12,158.

Students without need: 295 full-time freshmen who did not demonstrate need for aid received scholarships/grants; average award was $4,061. No-need awards available for academics, alumni affiliation, art, leadership, minority status, music/drama, religious affiliation, state/district residency.

Cumulative student debt: 64% of graduating class had student loans; average debt was $27,400.

FINANCIAL AID PROCEDURES

Forms required: FAFSA.

Dates and Deadlines: Priority date 2/15; no closing date. Applicants notified on a rolling basis starting 3/15.

Transfers: Priority date 3/15; closing date 8/15. Applicants notified on a rolling basis starting 3/15.

CONTACT

Dale Kuiper, Director of Admissions and Financial Aid
3201 Burton Street Southeast, Grand Rapids, MI 49546
(616) 526-6134

Central Michigan University

Mount Pleasant, Michigan
www.cmich.edu Federal Code: 002243

4-year public university in large town.

Enrollment: 20,022 undergrads, 11% part-time. 3,787 full-time freshmen.

Selectivity: Admits 50 to 75% of applicants.

BASIC COSTS (2008-2009)

Tuition and fees: $9,720; out-of-state residents $22,590.

Per-credit charge: $324; out-of-state residents $753.

Room and board: $7,067.

Additional info: Tuition at time of enrollment locked for 4 years.

FINANCIAL AID PICTURE (2007-2008)

Students with need: Out of 3,003 full-time freshmen who applied for aid, 2,128 were judged to have need. Of these, 2,087 received aid, and 1,111 had their full need met. Average financial aid package met 78% of need; average scholarship/grant was $5,113; average loan was $4,747. For part-time students, average financial aid package was $7,806.

Students without need: 487 full-time freshmen who did not demonstrate need for aid received scholarships/grants; average award was $3,337. No-need awards available for academics, alumni affiliation, art, athletics, leadership, minority status, music/drama, ROTC, state/district residency.

Scholarships offered: ***Merit:*** President's Award; differential between in and out-of-state tuition; awarded to out-of-state students; based on high school GPA of 3.0 or higher. ***Athletic:*** 47 full-time freshmen received athletic scholarships; average amount $12,912.

Cumulative student debt: 70% of graduating class had student loans; average debt was $24,236.

Additional info: Tuition waiver for Native American students qualifying under state program criteria.

FINANCIAL AID PROCEDURES

Forms required: FAFSA.

Dates and Deadlines: Priority date 3/1; no closing date. Applicants notified on a rolling basis starting 4/1.

CONTACT

Michael Owens, Director, Scholarships and Financial Aid
Admissions Office, Mount Pleasant, MI 48859
(989) 774-3674

Cleary University

Howell, Michigan
www.cleary.edu Federal Code: 002246

4-year private university and business college in small city.

Enrollment: 694 undergrads, 40% part-time. 96 full-time freshmen.

Selectivity: Open admission; but selective for some programs.

BASIC COSTS (2009-2010)

Tuition and fees: $15,600.

Per-credit charge: $325.

Additional info: Tuition prices guaranteed if student enrolled continuously. Tuition includes all books and fees. Tuition at time of enrollment locked for 4 years.

FINANCIAL AID PICTURE (2007-2008)

Students with need: Out of 66 full-time freshmen who applied for aid, 66 were judged to have need. Of these, 66 received aid, and 5 had their full need met. Average financial aid package met 43% of need; average scholarship/grant was $1,028; average loan was $1,295. For part-time students, average financial aid package was $8,814.

Students without need: 12 full-time freshmen who did not demonstrate need for aid received scholarships/grants; average award was $2,049. No-need awards available for academics.

Scholarships offered: Oren Beutler Endowed Scholarship: $750; new or continuing full-time student maintaining 3.0 GPA, demonstrated leadership and service to community; one awarded annually, renewable for 4 years.

Additional info: Filing electronically preferred; paper applications available. Tuition guarantee based on continuous enrollment. Essay and recommendations required for scholarship consideration.

FINANCIAL AID PROCEDURES

Forms required: FAFSA.

Dates and Deadlines: Priority date 3/15; closing date 8/15. Applicants notified on a rolling basis; must reply within 2 week(s) of notification.

CONTACT

Vesta Smith-Campbell, Director of Financial Aid
3750 Cleary Drive, Howell, MI 48843
(517) 548-3670

College for Creative Studies

Detroit, Michigan
www.collegeforcreativestudies.edu Federal Code: 006771

4-year private visual arts college in very large city.

Enrollment: 1,354 undergrads, 14% part-time. 226 full-time freshmen.

Selectivity: Admits less than 50% of applicants.

BASIC COSTS (2009-2010)

Tuition and fees: $29,985.

Per-credit charge: $995.

Room and board: $8,500.

FINANCIAL AID PICTURE (2007-2008)

Students with need: 52% of average financial aid package awarded as scholarships/grants, 48% awarded as loans/jobs. Need-based aid available for part-time students. Work study available nights, weekends, and for part-time students.

Students without need: No-need awards available for academics, art.

Cumulative student debt: 87% of graduating class had student loans; average debt was $45,913.

FINANCIAL AID PROCEDURES

Forms required: FAFSA.

Dates and Deadlines: Priority date 7/1; no closing date. Applicants notified on a rolling basis starting 3/15; must reply within 3 week(s) of notification.

Transfers: Priority date 3/21.

CONTACT

Kristin Moskovitz, Director of Financial Aid
201 East Kirby, Detroit, MI 48202-4034
(313) 664-7495

Concordia University

Ann Arbor, Michigan
www.cuaa.edu Federal Code: 002247

4-year private liberal arts and teachers college in small city, affiliated with Lutheran Church - Missouri Synod.
Enrollment: 459 undergrads.
Selectivity: Admits 50 to 75% of applicants.

BASIC COSTS (2009-2010)

Tuition and fees: $20,460.
Per-credit charge: $673.
Room and board: $7,606.
Additional info: Additional one-time fees for all undergraduates include: $125 pre-enrollment deposit, $100 matriculation fee.

FINANCIAL AID PICTURE (2007-2008)

Students with need: 68% of average financial aid package awarded as scholarships/grants, 32% awarded as loans/jobs. Need-based aid available for part-time students. Work study available nights, weekends, and for part-time students.
Students without need: No-need awards available for academics, alumni affiliation, art, athletics, leadership, music/drama, religious affiliation.

FINANCIAL AID PROCEDURES

Forms required: FAFSA, institutional form.
Dates and Deadlines: Closing date 3/1. Applicants notified on a rolling basis starting 3/1; must reply within 3 week(s) of notification.
Transfers: Priority date 5/1. Applicants notified on a rolling basis; must reply within 3 week(s) of notification.

CONTACT

Angela Acosta, Director of Financial Aid
4090 Geddes Road, Ann Arbor, MI 48105
(734) 995-7408

Cornerstone University

Grand Rapids, Michigan
www.cornerstone.edu Federal Code: 002266

4-year private university and liberal arts college in small city, affiliated with interdenominational tradition.
Enrollment: 1,741 undergrads, 24% part-time. 200 full-time freshmen.
Selectivity: Admits 50 to 75% of applicants.

BASIC COSTS (2009-2010)

Tuition and fees: $20,520.
Per-credit charge: $765.
Room and board: $6,510.
Additional info: Tuition includes laptop computer.

FINANCIAL AID PICTURE (2008-2009)

Students with need: Out of 185 full-time freshmen who applied for aid, 166 were judged to have need. Of these, 166 received aid, and 26 had their full need met. Average financial aid package met 88% of need; average scholarship/grant was $13,016; average loan was $3,725. For part-time students, average financial aid package was $8,923.
Students without need: 34 full-time freshmen who did not demonstrate need for aid received scholarships/grants; average award was $5,892. No-need awards available for academics, athletics, leadership, music/drama, state/district residency.
Scholarships offered: ***Merit:*** Academic scholarships; based on high school GPA and ACT scores. ***Athletic:*** 45 full-time freshmen received athletic scholarships; average amount $5,414.
Cumulative student debt: 77% of graduating class had student loans; average debt was $28,074.
Additional info: Audition required for music scholarship applicants.

FINANCIAL AID PROCEDURES

Forms required: FAFSA.
Dates and Deadlines: Priority date 3/1; no closing date. Applicants notified on a rolling basis starting 3/15; must reply within 2 week(s) of notification.
Transfers: No deadline.

CONTACT

Kathryn Lundin, Student Financial Services
1001 East Beltline NE, Grand Rapids, MI 49525-5897
(616) 222-1424

Davenport University

Grand Rapids, Michigan
www.davenport.edu Federal Code: 015260

4-year private university and business college in small city.
Enrollment: 9,673 undergrads, 68% part-time. 581 full-time freshmen.

BASIC COSTS (2008-2009)

Tuition and fees: $13,250.
Per-credit charge: $435.

FINANCIAL AID PICTURE (2007-2008)

Students with need: Need-based aid available for full-time and part-time students. Work study available nights, weekends, and for part-time students.
Students without need: No-need awards available for academics, alumni affiliation, athletics, leadership.

FINANCIAL AID PROCEDURES

Forms required: FAFSA.
Dates and Deadlines: Priority date 3/1; no closing date. Applicants notified on a rolling basis starting 3/1; must reply within 2 week(s) of notification.
Transfers: No deadline. Applicants notified on a rolling basis.

CONTACT

David De Boer, Executive Director of Financial Aid
6191 Kraft Avenue SE, Grand Rapids, MI 49512-5926
(866) 925-3884

Eastern Michigan University

Ypsilanti, Michigan
www.emich.edu Federal Code: 002259

4-year public university in small city.
Enrollment: 16,902 undergrads, 29% part-time. 2,366 full-time freshmen.
Selectivity: Admits 50 to 75% of applicants.

BASIC COSTS (2008-2009)

Tuition and fees: $8,069; out-of-state residents $21,464.
Per-credit charge: $230; out-of-state residents $676.
Room and board: $7,352.

FINANCIAL AID PICTURE (2007-2008)

Students with need: Out of 1,940 full-time freshmen who applied for aid, 1,514 were judged to have need. Of these, 1,469 received aid, and 176 had their full need met. Average financial aid package met 66% of need; average scholarship/grant was $3,657; average loan was $3,824. For part-time students, average financial aid package was $5,068.

Students without need: 557 full-time freshmen who did not demonstrate need for aid received scholarships/grants; average award was $2,833. No-need awards available for academics, alumni affiliation, art, athletics, leadership, minority status, music/drama, ROTC, state/district residency.
Scholarships offered: 101 full-time freshmen received athletic scholarships; average amount $10,569.

FINANCIAL AID PROCEDURES
Forms required: FAFSA.
Dates and Deadlines: Priority date 3/15; no closing date. Applicants notified on a rolling basis starting 3/1.
Transfers: No deadline. Applicants notified on a rolling basis.

CONTACT
Bernice Lindke, Vice President
400 Pierce Hall, Ypsilanti, MI 48197
(734) 487-0455

Ferris State University
Big Rapids, Michigan
www.ferris.edu Federal Code: 002260

4-year public university in large town.
Enrollment: 11,863 undergrads, 23% part-time. 2,101 full-time freshmen.

BASIC COSTS (2008-2009)
Tuition and fees: $9,162; out-of-state residents $16,062.
Per-credit charge: $300; out-of-state residents $530.
Room and board: $7,944.
Additional info: Midwest Compact states of Illinois, Indiana, Kansas, Minnesota, Missouri, Nebraska, Ohio, and Wisconsin tuition is $13,500.

FINANCIAL AID PICTURE (2008-2009)
Students with need: Average financial aid package met 84% of need; average scholarship/grant was $1,487; average loan was $3,224. For part-time students, average financial aid package was $11,075.
Students without need: No-need awards available for academics, alumni affiliation, art, athletics, leadership, minority status, music/drama, religious affiliation, ROTC.
Cumulative student debt: 71% of graduating class had student loans; average debt was $29,278.

FINANCIAL AID PROCEDURES
Forms required: FAFSA.
Dates and Deadlines: Priority date 3/1; no closing date. Applicants notified on a rolling basis starting 3/1; must reply within 3 week(s) of notification.
Transfers: Applicants notified on a rolling basis.

CONTACT
Robin Wirt, Director of Financial Aid
1201 South State Street, CSS 201, Big Rapids, MI 49307-2714
(231) 591-2110

Finlandia University
Hancock, Michigan
www.finlandia.edu Federal Code: 002322

4-year private university and liberal arts college in small town, affiliated with Evangelical Lutheran Church in America.
Enrollment: 507 undergrads, 8% part-time. 111 full-time freshmen.
Selectivity: Admits over 75% of applicants.

BASIC COSTS (2009-2010)
Tuition and fees: $18,436.
Per-credit charge: $598.
Room and board: $5,974.

FINANCIAL AID PICTURE (2008-2009)
Students with need: For part-time students, average financial aid package was $5,000.
Students without need: No-need awards available for academics, leadership, religious affiliation, state/district residency.
Cumulative student debt: 80% of graduating class had student loans; average debt was $17,483.
Additional info: Work/study program; up to $2,800 per year.

FINANCIAL AID PROCEDURES
Forms required: FAFSA, institutional form.
Dates and Deadlines: Priority date 3/1; no closing date. Applicants notified on a rolling basis starting 3/1; must reply within 2 week(s) of notification.
Transfers: Applicants notified on a rolling basis starting 2/1; must reply within 2 week(s) of notification.

CONTACT
Sandra Turnquist, Director of Financial Aid
601 Quincy Street, Hancock, MI 49930-1882
(906) 487-7261

Glen Oaks Community College
Centreville, Michigan
www.glenoaks.edu Federal Code: 002263

2-year public community college in rural community.
Enrollment: 1,700 undergrads.
Selectivity: Open admission; but selective for some programs.

BASIC COSTS (2008-2009)
Tuition and fees: $2,990.
Per-credit charge: $72.
Additional info: In-county residents pay $72 per contact hour. Students from service area counties (Branch and Cass counties in Michigan and LaGrange, Elkheart, Steuben counties in Indiana) pay $108 per contact hour. All others pay $144 per contact hour.

FINANCIAL AID PICTURE
Students with need: Need-based aid available for full-time and part-time students. Work study available nights.
Students without need: No-need awards available for academics, art, athletics, leadership, minority status, music/drama.

FINANCIAL AID PROCEDURES
Forms required: FAFSA, institutional form.
Dates and Deadlines: No deadline. Applicants notified on a rolling basis.

CONTACT
Matthew Soucy, Director of Financial Aid and Scholarship
62249 Shimmel Road, Centreville, MI 49032-9719
(269) 467-9945 ext. 250

Gogebic Community College
Ironwood, Michigan
www.gogebic.edu Federal Code: 002264

2-year public community college in small town.
Enrollment: 904 undergrads.
Selectivity: Open admission; but selective for some programs.

BASIC COSTS (2008-2009)
Tuition and fees: $3,028; out-of-district residents $3,679; out-of-state residents $4,485.
Per-credit charge: $81; out-of-district residents $102; out-of-state residents $128.
Room only: $3,680.

FINANCIAL AID PICTURE

Students with need: Need-based aid available for full-time and part-time students. Work study available nights, weekends, and for part-time students.

Students without need: No-need awards available for academics, art, athletics, job skills, leadership, music/drama, state/district residency.

FINANCIAL AID PROCEDURES

Forms required: FAFSA.

Dates and Deadlines: Priority date 5/1; no closing date. Applicants notified on a rolling basis starting 3/15; must reply within 2 week(s) of notification.

CONTACT

Sue Forbes, Director of Financial Aid
E4946 Jackson Road, Ironwood, MI 49938
(906) 932-4231 ext. 206

Grace Bible College

Grand Rapids, Michigan
www.gbcol.edu Federal Code: 002265

4-year private Bible and liberal arts college in small city, affiliated with Grace Gospel Fellowship.

Enrollment: 177 undergrads, 5% part-time. 52 full-time freshmen.

Selectivity: Admits 50 to 75% of applicants.

BASIC COSTS (2008-2009)

Tuition and fees: $13,320.

Per-credit charge: $450.

Room and board: $6,700.

FINANCIAL AID PICTURE (2007-2008)

Students with need: Out of 48 full-time freshmen who applied for aid, 41 were judged to have need. Of these, 41 received aid, and 12 had their full need met. Average financial aid package met 78% of need; average scholarship/grant was $3,875; average loan was $2,864. For part-time students, average financial aid package was $731.

Students without need: 9 full-time freshmen who did not demonstrate need for aid received scholarships/grants; average award was $4,704. No-need awards available for academics, music/drama, religious affiliation.

Cumulative student debt: 60% of graduating class had student loans; average debt was $9,181.

FINANCIAL AID PROCEDURES

Forms required: FAFSA.

Dates and Deadlines: Priority date 3/1; no closing date. Applicants notified on a rolling basis starting 5/15; must reply within 2 week(s) of notification.

Transfers: No deadline. Applicants notified on a rolling basis; must reply within 2 week(s) of notification.

CONTACT

Daniel Wait, Financial Aid Director
1011 Aldon Street SW, PO Box 910, Grand Rapids, MI 49509
(616) 261-8557

Grand Rapids Community College

Grand Rapids, Michigan
www.grcc.edu Federal Code: 002267

2-year public community college in small city.

Enrollment: 14,392 undergrads, 54% part-time. 2,393 full-time freshmen.

Selectivity: Open admission; but selective for some programs.

BASIC COSTS (2008-2009)

Tuition and fees: $2,555; out-of-district residents $5,250; out-of-state residents $7,670.

Per-credit charge: $83; out-of-district residents $173; out-of-state residents $253.

FINANCIAL AID PICTURE (2008-2009)

Students with need: Need-based aid available for full-time and part-time students. Work study available nights, weekends, and for part-time students.

Students without need: No-need awards available for academics, alumni affiliation, art, athletics, leadership, minority status, music/drama, state/district residency.

Scholarships offered: Michigan Merit Award; $2,500; based on Michigan Educational Assessment Program scores.

Additional info: Tuition reimbursement and/or child-care services for single parents and displaced homemakers who meet Perkins guidelines.

FINANCIAL AID PROCEDURES

Forms required: FAFSA.

Dates and Deadlines: Priority date 4/1; no closing date. Applicants notified on a rolling basis starting 5/1; must reply within 3 week(s) of notification.

CONTACT

Jill Nutt, Executive Director of Student Financial Services
143 Bostwick Avenue NE, Grand Rapids, MI 49503-3295
(616) 234-4030

Grand Valley State University

Allendale, Michigan
www.gvsu.edu Federal Code: 002268

4-year public university in large town.

Enrollment: 20,285 undergrads, 11% part-time. 3,884 full-time freshmen.

Selectivity: Admits over 75% of applicants.

BASIC COSTS (2008-2009)

Tuition and fees: $8,196; out-of-state residents $12,510.

Room and board: $7,224.

FINANCIAL AID PICTURE (2008-2009)

Students with need: Out of 3,279 full-time freshmen who applied for aid, 2,097 were judged to have need. Of these, 2,087 received aid, and 613 had their full need met. Average financial aid package met 83% of need; average scholarship/grant was $5,721; average loan was $4,169. For part-time students, average financial aid package was $5,553.

Students without need: 493 full-time freshmen who did not demonstrate need for aid received scholarships/grants; average award was $2,321. No-need awards available for academics, alumni affiliation, art, athletics, minority status, music/drama.

Scholarships offered: 39 full-time freshmen received athletic scholarships; average amount $6,666.

Cumulative student debt: 70% of graduating class had student loans; average debt was $21,475.

FINANCIAL AID PROCEDURES

Forms required: FAFSA.

Dates and Deadlines: Priority date 3/1; no closing date. Applicants notified on a rolling basis starting 4/1; must reply within 3 week(s) of notification.

Transfers: No deadline. Applicants notified on a rolling basis starting 3/20; must reply within 4 week(s) of notification.

CONTACT

Ed Kerestly, Director of Financial Aid
1 Campus Drive, Allendale, MI 49401-9403
(616) 331-3234

Great Lakes Christian College

Lansing, Michigan
www.glcc.edu Federal Code: 002269

4-year private Bible college in small city, affiliated with Church of Christ / Christian Church.
Enrollment: 258 undergrads.
Selectivity: Admits over 75% of applicants.

BASIC COSTS (2009-2010)

Tuition and fees: $11,980.
Per-credit charge: $360.
Room and board: $7,000.

FINANCIAL AID PICTURE (2008-2009)

Students with need: Need-based aid available for full-time and part-time students. Work study available nights, weekends, and for part-time students.
Students without need: No-need awards available for academics, alumni affiliation, music/drama.

FINANCIAL AID PROCEDURES

Forms required: FAFSA, state aid form, institutional form.
Dates and Deadlines: Priority date 8/1; no closing date. Applicants notified on a rolling basis starting 5/1; must reply within 3 week(s) of notification.
Transfers: Priority date 3/31; closing date 8/31. Applicants notified on a rolling basis; must reply within 3 week(s) of notification. FAFSA due by 6/30.

CONTACT

Tedd Kees, Director of Financial Aid
6211 West Willow Highway, Lansing, MI 48917-1299
(517) 321-0242 ext. 227

Henry Ford Community College

Dearborn, Michigan
www.hfcc.edu Federal Code: 002270

2-year public community college in small city.
Enrollment: 14,282 undergrads, 59% part-time. 1,857 full-time freshmen.
Selectivity: Open admission; but selective for some programs.

BASIC COSTS (2008-2009)

Tuition and fees: $2,412; out-of-district residents $4,062; out-of-state residents $4,212.
Per-credit charge: $65; out-of-district residents $120; out-of-state residents $125.

FINANCIAL AID PICTURE

Students with need: Work study available nights, weekends, and for part-time students.

FINANCIAL AID PROCEDURES

Forms required: FAFSA.
Dates and Deadlines: Priority date 4/1; no closing date. Applicants notified on a rolling basis starting 3/1.

CONTACT

Kevin Culler, Director of Financial Aid
5101 Evergreen Road, Dearborn, MI 48128
(313) 845-9616

Hillsdale College

Hillsdale, Michigan
www.hillsdale.edu Federal Code: 002272

4-year private liberal arts college in large town.
Enrollment: 1,378 undergrads.
Selectivity: Admits 50 to 75% of applicants.

BASIC COSTS (2009-2010)

Tuition and fees: $19,920.
Per-credit charge: $760.
Room and board: $7,750.

FINANCIAL AID PICTURE (2008-2009)

Students with need: 53% of average financial aid package awarded as scholarships/grants, 47% awarded as loans/jobs.
Students without need: No-need awards available for academics, alumni affiliation, art, athletics, leadership, music/drama, state/district residency.
Scholarships offered: Distinct Honor Scholarship: full tuition; 5 awarded. Presidential Scholarship: half tuition; 35 awarded. Trustee Scholarship: up to $8,000; 40 awarded.
Additional info: Campus employment available.

FINANCIAL AID PROCEDURES

Forms required: institutional form. CSS PROFILE required for returning students only.
Dates and Deadlines: Priority date 3/1; closing date 3/15. Applicants notified on a rolling basis starting 2/1; must reply by 5/1 or within 4 week(s) of notification.
Transfers: Priority date 2/1. Applicants notified on a rolling basis starting 2/1; must reply by 5/1 or within 4 week(s) of notification.

CONTACT

Richard Moeggenberg, Director of Financial Aid
33 East College Street, Hillsdale, MI 49242
(517) 607-2350

Hope College

Holland, Michigan
www.hope.edu Federal Code: 002273

4-year private liberal arts college in small city, affiliated with Reformed Church in America.
Enrollment: 3,153 undergrads, 2% part-time. 802 full-time freshmen.
Selectivity: Admits over 75% of applicants.

BASIC COSTS (2009-2010)

Tuition and fees: $25,660.
Room and board: $7,870.
Additional info: Tuition/fee waivers available for minority students.

FINANCIAL AID PICTURE (2008-2009)

Students with need: Out of 650 full-time freshmen who applied for aid, 488 were judged to have need. Of these, 488 received aid, and 166 had their full need met. Average financial aid package met 87% of need; average scholarship/grant was $16,696; average loan was $4,699. For part-time students, average financial aid package was $6,508.
Students without need: 260 full-time freshmen who did not demonstrate need for aid received scholarships/grants; average award was $6,714. No-need awards available for academics, art, minority status, music/drama, religious affiliation.
Scholarships offered: Merit Scholarships: $3,000-$17,000 per year. Talent Awards: $2,500; for music, art, theater, creative writing.
Cumulative student debt: 64% of graduating class had student loans; average debt was $25,889.

FINANCIAL AID PROCEDURES

Forms required: FAFSA, institutional form.
Dates and Deadlines: Priority date 3/1; no closing date. Applicants notified on a rolling basis starting 3/15.
Transfers: No deadline. Applicants notified on a rolling basis starting 3/25.

CONTACT

Phyllis Hooyman, Director of Financial Aid
69 East 10th Street, Holland, MI 49422-9000
(888) 439-8907

International Academy of Design and Technology: Detroit

Troy, Michigan
www.iadtdetroit.com/

4-year for-profit visual arts and technical college in small city.
Enrollment: 951 undergrads.
Selectivity: Open admission.

BASIC COSTS (2008-2009)

Tuition and fees: $16,620.

FINANCIAL AID PICTURE (2007-2008)

Students with need: 34% of average financial aid package awarded as scholarships/grants, 66% awarded as loans/jobs.

FINANCIAL AID PROCEDURES

Dates and Deadlines: No deadline.

CONTACT

Maureen Malane
1850 Research Drive, Troy, MI 48083

Jackson Community College

Jackson, Michigan
www.jccmi.edu Federal Code: 002274

2-year public community college in small city.
Enrollment: 6,200 undergrads.
Selectivity: Open admission; but selective for some programs.

BASIC COSTS (2008-2009)

Tuition and fees: $3,240; out-of-district residents $4,305; out-of-state residents $5,865.
Per-credit charge: $87; out-of-district residents $122; out-of-state residents $174.

FINANCIAL AID PICTURE (2008-2009)

Students with need: Need-based aid available for full-time and part-time students. Work study available nights, weekends, and for part-time students.
Students without need: No-need awards available for academics, art, leadership, music/drama, state/district residency.

FINANCIAL AID PROCEDURES

Forms required: FAFSA, institutional form.
Dates and Deadlines: Priority date 6/15; no closing date. Applicants notified on a rolling basis starting 3/1.

CONTACT

Anthony Rana
2111 Emmons Road, Jackson, MI 49201-8399
(517) 796-8436

Kalamazoo College

Kalamazoo, Michigan
www.kzoo.edu Federal Code: 002275

4-year private liberal arts college in small city.
Enrollment: 1,361 undergrads. 364 full-time freshmen.
Selectivity: Admits 50 to 75% of applicants.

BASIC COSTS (2009-2010)

Tuition and fees: $32,643.
Room and board: $7,776.

FINANCIAL AID PICTURE (2008-2009)

Students with need: Out of 267 full-time freshmen who applied for aid, 190 were judged to have need. Of these, 190 received aid, and 102 had their full need met.
Students without need: 174 full-time freshmen who did not demonstrate need for aid received scholarships/grants; average award was $10,455. No-need awards available for academics, alumni affiliation.
Scholarships offered: Honors Scholarship; $5,000 - $14,000; based on academic and co-curricular record and accomplishments; varied number awarded. Competitive Scholarships; $2,000; based on written exam in a subject area or a fine arts audition.
Additional info: Paid career development internship and senior project experiences available on campus.

FINANCIAL AID PROCEDURES

Forms required: FAFSA, institutional form. CSS PROFILE required for Early Decision applicants requesting need-based financial aid.
Dates and Deadlines: Priority date 2/15; no closing date. Applicants notified on a rolling basis starting 3/21; must reply by 5/1.
Transfers: Closing date 3/1.

CONTACT

Marian Stowers, Director of Financial Aid
Kalamazoo College Office of Admission, Kalamazoo, MI 49006-3295
(269) 337-7192

Kalamazoo Valley Community College

Kalamazoo, Michigan
www.kvcc.edu Federal Code: 006949

2-year public community college in small city.
Enrollment: 10,173 undergrads.
Selectivity: Open admission.

BASIC COSTS (2008-2009)

Tuition and fees: $2,040; out-of-district residents $3,240; out-of-state residents $4,350.
Per-credit charge: $68; out-of-district residents $108; out-of-state residents $145.

FINANCIAL AID PICTURE

Students with need: Need-based aid available for full-time and part-time students. Work study available nights, weekends, and for part-time students.
Students without need: No-need awards available for academics, athletics.

FINANCIAL AID PROCEDURES

Forms required: FAFSA, institutional form.
Dates and Deadlines: Priority date 6/1; no closing date. Applicants notified on a rolling basis starting 5/1; must reply within 2 week(s) of notification.

CONTACT

Roger Miller, Director of Financial Aid
6767 West O Avenue, Kalamazoo, MI 49003-4070
(269) 488-4340

Kellogg Community College

Battle Creek, Michigan
www.kellogg.edu Federal Code: 002276

2-year public community college in small city.
Enrollment: 4,535 undergrads, 62% part-time. 518 full-time freshmen.
Selectivity: Open admission; but selective for some programs.

BASIC COSTS (2008-2009)
Tuition and fees: $2,325; out-of-district residents $3,638; out-of-state residents $5,123.

FINANCIAL AID PICTURE (2008-2009)
Students with need: Need-based aid available for full-time and part-time students. Work study available nights.
Students without need: No-need awards available for academics, alumni affiliation, athletics.

FINANCIAL AID PROCEDURES
Forms required: FAFSA, institutional form.
Dates and Deadlines: Priority date 4/1; no closing date. Applicants notified on a rolling basis starting 4/1.
Transfers: No deadline. Applicants notified on a rolling basis.

CONTACT
Barbara Sudeikis, Director, Financial Aid
450 North Avenue, Battle Creek, MI 49017-3397
(269) 965-4123

Kendall College of Art and Design of Ferris State University
Grand Rapids, Michigan
www.kcad.edu Federal Code: 002260

4-year public visual arts college in large city.
Enrollment: 1,303 undergrads.
Selectivity: Admits 50 to 75% of applicants.

BASIC COSTS (2008-2009)
Tuition and fees: $14,412; out-of-state residents $21,390.
Additional info: Studio art courses: $582 per credit hour in-state and $873 out-of-state. General education courses: $300 per credit hour in-state and $450 out-of-state.

FINANCIAL AID PICTURE (2008-2009)
Students with need: Need-based aid available for full-time and part-time students. Work study available nights, weekends, and for part-time students.
Students without need: This college awards aid only to students with need.

FINANCIAL AID PROCEDURES
Forms required: FAFSA.
Dates and Deadlines: Priority date 2/15; no closing date. Applicants notified on a rolling basis starting 4/15.

CONTACT
Lori Deforest, Financial Aid Officer
17 Fountain Street NW, Grand Rapids, MI 49503-3002
(616) 451-2787

Kettering University
Flint, Michigan
www.kettering.edu Federal Code: 002262

4-year private university and engineering college in small city.
Enrollment: 2,134 undergrads. 441 full-time freshmen.
Selectivity: Admits 50 to 75% of applicants. GED not accepted.

BASIC COSTS (2009-2010)
Tuition and fees: $28,032.
Per-credit charge: $862.
Room and board: $6,390.

FINANCIAL AID PICTURE (2008-2009)
Students with need: Out of 413 full-time freshmen who applied for aid, 370 were judged to have need. Of these, 370 received aid. Need-based aid available for part-time students.
Students without need: 90 full-time freshmen who did not demonstrate need for aid received scholarships/grants; average award was $13,503. No-need awards available for academics, alumni affiliation, leadership, state/district residency.
Scholarships offered: Various scholarships; $20,000-$40,000 for 4 years; based on merit. Renewable scholarships; $250-$5,000 per year.

FINANCIAL AID PROCEDURES
Forms required: FAFSA.
Dates and Deadlines: Priority date 2/14; no closing date. Applicants notified on a rolling basis starting 1/15; must reply within 2 week(s) of notification.
Transfers: No deadline. Applicants notified on a rolling basis starting 2/8; must reply within 2 week(s) of notification.

CONTACT
Diane Bice, Director of Financial Aid
1700 West University Avenue, Flint, MI 48504-4898
(810) 762-7859

Kirtland Community College
Roscommon, Michigan
www.kirtland.edu Federal Code: 007171

2-year public community college in rural community.
Enrollment: 1,475 undergrads, 55% part-time. 153 full-time freshmen.
Selectivity: Open admission; but selective for some programs.

BASIC COSTS (2008-2009)
Tuition and fees: $2,865; out-of-district residents $4,800; out-of-state residents $5,805.
Per-credit charge: $78; out-of-district residents $142; out-of-state residents $176.
Additional info: Tuition/fee waivers available for minority students.

FINANCIAL AID PICTURE (2008-2009)
Students with need: Average financial aid package met 33% of need; average scholarship/grant was $2,527; average loan was $1,180. For part-time students, average financial aid package was $3,817.
Students without need: No-need awards available for academics, athletics, minority status.
Cumulative student debt: 67% of graduating class had student loans; average debt was $6,127.
Additional info: Federal, state, and institutional work-study programs available.

FINANCIAL AID PROCEDURES
Forms required: FAFSA.
Dates and Deadlines: Priority date 5/1; no closing date. Applicants notified on a rolling basis.
Transfers: No deadline.

CONTACT
Christin Horndt, Director of Financial Aid
10775 North Saint Helen Road, Roscommon, MI 48653
(989) 275-5121

Kuyper College
Grand Rapids, Michigan
www.kuyper.edu Federal Code: 002311

4-year private Bible college in large city, affiliated with Reformed.
Enrollment: 308 undergrads, 14% part-time. 64 full-time freshmen.

Selectivity: Admits over 75% of applicants.

BASIC COSTS (2008-2009)
Tuition and fees: $13,869.
Room and board: $6,100.

FINANCIAL AID PICTURE (2008-2009)
Students with need: Out of 63 full-time freshmen who applied for aid, 56 were judged to have need. Of these, 56 received aid, and 7 had their full need met. Average financial aid package met 78% of need; average scholarship/grant was $7,316; average loan was $4,047. For part-time students, average financial aid package was $9,226.
Students without need: 7 full-time freshmen who did not demonstrate need for aid received scholarships/grants; average award was $6,685. No-need awards available for academics, leadership, minority status.
Scholarships offered: Kuyper Achievement Awards: $1,000-$6,000; GPA of 3.0-4.0, ACT of 21 and above. Christian Leadership Scholarship: $1,500 renewable annually; based on Christian service activities, 3.2 cumulative GPA.
Cumulative student debt: 88% of graduating class had student loans; average debt was $19,488.

FINANCIAL AID PROCEDURES
Forms required: FAFSA, institutional form.
Dates and Deadlines: Priority date 3/1; no closing date. Applicants notified on a rolling basis starting 3/15; must reply within 2 week(s) of notification.
Transfers: No deadline. Applicants notified on a rolling basis.

CONTACT
Agnes Russell, Director of Financial Aid
3333 East Beltline Avenue Northeast, Grand Rapids, MI 49525-9749
(616) 988-3656

Lake Michigan College
Benton Harbor, Michigan
www.lakemichigancollege.edu Federal Code: 002277

2-year public community and junior college in large town.
Enrollment: 3,844 undergrads, 67% part-time. 461 full-time freshmen.
Selectivity: Open admission; but selective for some programs.

BASIC COSTS (2008-2009)
Tuition and fees: $3,105; out-of-district residents $4,170; out-of-state residents $5,190.
Per-credit charge: $73; out-of-district residents $108; out-of-state residents $142.
Additional info: Tuition/fee waivers available for adults.

FINANCIAL AID PICTURE (2007-2008)
Students with need: 96% of average financial aid package awarded as scholarships/grants, 4% awarded as loans/jobs.

FINANCIAL AID PROCEDURES
Forms required: FAFSA.
Dates and Deadlines: Priority date 3/1; no closing date. Applicants notified on a rolling basis; must reply within 2 week(s) of notification.

CONTACT
Anne Tews, Director of Financial Aid
2755 East Napier Avenue, Benton Harbor, MI 49022-1899
(269) 927-8100 ext. 5200

Lake Superior State University
Sault Ste. Marie, Michigan
www.lssu.edu Federal Code: 002293

4-year public university in small city.
Enrollment: 2,460 undergrads.
Selectivity: Admits over 75% of applicants.

BASIC COSTS (2008-2009)
Tuition and fees: $7,964; out-of-state residents $15,788.
Per-credit charge: $326; out-of-state residents $652.
Room and board: $7,567.
Additional info: Residents of Ontario pay in-state tuition. Residents of Kansas, Minnesota, Missouri, Nebraska, and North Dakota eligible for Midwest Consortium agreement rate of $489 per credit.

FINANCIAL AID PICTURE (2007-2008)
Students with need: Need-based aid available for full-time and part-time students. Work study available nights, weekends, and for part-time students.
Students without need: No-need awards available for academics, alumni affiliation, athletics, state/district residency.

FINANCIAL AID PROCEDURES
Forms required: FAFSA.
Dates and Deadlines: Priority date 3/1; no closing date. Applicants notified on a rolling basis starting 11/1; must reply within 3 week(s) of notification.
Transfers: Closing date 3/1. Applicants notified on a rolling basis starting 3/1.

CONTACT
Deborah Faust, Director of Financial Aid
650 West Easterday Avenue, Sault Ste. Marie, MI 49783-1699
(906) 635-2678

Lansing Community College
Lansing, Michigan
www.lansing.cc.mi.us Federal Code: 002278

2-year public community college in small city.
Enrollment: 14,523 undergrads, 64% part-time. 1,303 full-time freshmen.
Selectivity: Open admission; but selective for some programs.

BASIC COSTS (2008-2009)
Tuition and fees: $2,240; out-of-district residents $4,070; out-of-state residents $6,080.
Per-credit charge: $73; out-of-district residents $134; out-of-state residents $201.
Additional info: There is a $10 online course fee applied to all online courses, and separate course fees may be assessed for courses required special supplies, equipment, or travel. A $5 per billable hour facility fee is charged to students on all credit classes.

FINANCIAL AID PICTURE (2007-2008)
Students with need: Need-based aid available for full-time and part-time students. Work study available nights, weekends, and for part-time students.
Students without need: No-need awards available for academics, athletics.

FINANCIAL AID PROCEDURES
Forms required: FAFSA.
Dates and Deadlines: Priority date 7/5; no closing date. Applicants notified on a rolling basis starting 4/3.
Transfers: Priority date 7/15.

CONTACT
Stephanie Bogard, Director, Financial Aid
422 North Washington Square, Lansing, MI 48901
(517) 483-1790

Lawrence Technological University
Southfield, Michigan
www.ltu.edu Federal Code: 002279

4-year private university in small city.
Enrollment: 2,278 undergrads, 29% part-time. 367 full-time freshmen.

Selectivity: Admits 50 to 75% of applicants.

BASIC COSTS (2009-2010)
Tuition and fees: $22,958.
Per-credit charge: $755.
Room and board: $9,253.
Additional info: Tuition/fee waivers available for unemployed or children of unemployed.

FINANCIAL AID PICTURE (2007-2008)
Students with need: Out of 274 full-time freshmen who applied for aid, 217 were judged to have need. Of these, 215 received aid, and 43 had their full need met. Average financial aid package met 77% of need; average scholarship/grant was $8,761; average loan was $3,791. For part-time students, average financial aid package was $11,170.
Students without need: 42 full-time freshmen who did not demonstrate need for aid received scholarships/grants; average award was $5,012. No-need awards available for academics, alumni affiliation, art, job skills, leadership, minority status, ROTC, state/district residency.
Cumulative student debt: 70% of graduating class had student loans; average debt was $37,238.
Additional info: March 1 state deadline for Michigan Competitive Scholarship and Michigan Tuition Grant.

FINANCIAL AID PROCEDURES
Forms required: FAFSA.
Dates and Deadlines: Priority date 4/1; no closing date. Applicants notified on a rolling basis starting 3/1; must reply within 2 week(s) of notification.

CONTACT
Mark Martin, Director of Student Financial Aid
21000 West Ten Mile Road, Southfield, MI 48075-1058
(248) 204-2121

Macomb Community College
Warren, Michigan
www.macomb.edu Federal Code: 008906

2-year public community college in small city.
Enrollment: 12,901 undergrads, 62% part-time. 791 full-time freshmen.
Selectivity: Open admission; but selective for some programs.

BASIC COSTS (2008-2009)
Tuition and fees: $2,200; out-of-district residents $3,340; out-of-state residents $4,330.
Per-credit charge: $72; out-of-district residents $110; out-of-state residents $142.

FINANCIAL AID PICTURE (2007-2008)
Students with need: Need-based aid available for full-time and part-time students. Work study available nights, weekends, and for part-time students.
Students without need: No-need awards available for academics, athletics, leadership, music/drama, state/district residency.

FINANCIAL AID PROCEDURES
Forms required: FAFSA, institutional form
Dates and Deadlines: Priority date 4/15; no closing date. Applicants notified on a rolling basis starting 5/15; must reply within 2 week(s) of notification.
Transfers: Must submit financial aid transcripts from all institutions attended.

CONTACT
Judy Florian, Director of Financial Aid
14500 East Twelve Mile Road, Warren, MI 48088-3896
(586) 445-7228

Madonna University
Livonia, Michigan
www.madonna.edu Federal Code: 002282

4-year private university and liberal arts college in small city, affiliated with Roman Catholic Church.
Enrollment: 2,851 undergrads, 42% part-time. 179 full-time freshmen.
Selectivity: Admits over 75% of applicants.

BASIC COSTS (2008-2009)
Tuition and fees: $12,430.
Per-credit charge: $411.
Room and board: $6,440.
Additional info: Nursing students pay $466 per credit hour. Nonresident aliens pay $2,500 deposit.

FINANCIAL AID PICTURE (2007-2008)
Students with need: Out of 112 full-time freshmen who applied for aid, 81 were judged to have need. Of these, 81 received aid, and 21 had their full need met. Average financial aid package met 52% of need; average scholarship/grant was $4,958; average loan was $2,591. For part-time students, average financial aid package was $6,473.
Students without need: 35 full-time freshmen who did not demonstrate need for aid received scholarships/grants; average award was $2,138. No-need awards available for academics, alumni affiliation, art, athletics, leadership, minority status, music/drama, religious affiliation, state/district residency.
Scholarships offered: 29 full-time freshmen received athletic scholarships; average amount $3,826.

FINANCIAL AID PROCEDURES
Forms required: FAFSA.
Dates and Deadlines: Priority date 2/21; no closing date. Applicants notified on a rolling basis starting 4/1; must reply by 9/1 or within 2 week(s) of notification.
Transfers: No deadline. Applicants notified on a rolling basis starting 5/1; must reply within 2 week(s) of notification. Deadline for state aid is May 15.

CONTACT
Chris Ziegler, Director of Financial Aid
36600 Schoolcraft Road, Livonia, MI 48150-1176
(734) 432-5664

Marygrove College
Detroit, Michigan
www.marygrove.edu Federal Code: 002284

4-year private liberal arts college in very large city, affiliated with Roman Catholic Church.
Enrollment: 771 undergrads.
Selectivity: Admits less than 50% of applicants.

BASIC COSTS (2008-2009)
Tuition and fees: $15,520.
Per-credit charge: $538.
Room and board: $6,800.

FINANCIAL AID PICTURE (2008-2009)
Students with need: Need-based aid available for full-time and part-time students.
Students without need: This college awards aid only to students with need.

FINANCIAL AID PROCEDURES
Forms required: FAFSA, institutional form.
Dates and Deadlines: Priority date 3/15; no closing date. Applicants notified on a rolling basis starting 5/15; must reply within 2 week(s) of notification.

CONTACT
Patricia Chaplin, Director of Financial Aid
8425 West McNichols Road, Detroit, MI 48221
(313) 927-1245

Michigan Jewish Institute
Oak Park, Michigan
www.mji.edu Federal Code: 032843

4-year private business and liberal arts college in very large city, affiliated with Jewish faith.
Enrollment: 72 undergrads.
Selectivity: Open admission; but selective for some programs.

BASIC COSTS (2008-2009)
Tuition and fees: $10,500.
Per-credit charge: $350.

FINANCIAL AID PICTURE
Students with need: Work study available nights, weekends, and for part-time students.
Students without need: No-need awards available for academics.
Scholarships offered: Cooperative Computing program scholarships. Partial scholarships available for some programs.

FINANCIAL AID PROCEDURES
Transfers: Priority date 3/1; no deadline. Applicants notified on a rolling basis; must reply within 5 week(s) of notification.

CONTACT
Fran Herman, Registrar/Financial Aid Administrator
25401 Coolidge Highway, Oak Park, MI 48237
(248) 414-6900 ext. 102

Michigan State University
East Lansing, Michigan
www.msu.edu Federal Code: 002290

4-year public university in small city.
Enrollment: 35,986 undergrads, 8% part-time. 7,426 full-time freshmen.
Selectivity: Admits 50 to 75% of applicants.

BASIC COSTS (2008-2009)
Tuition and fees: $10,214; out-of-state residents $25,672.
Per-credit charge: $311; out-of-state residents $826.
Room and board: $7,026.

FINANCIAL AID PICTURE (2008-2009)
Students with need: Out of 5,286 full-time freshmen who applied for aid, 3,376 were judged to have need. Of these, 3,348 received aid, and 955 had their full need met. Average financial aid package met 74% of need; average scholarship/grant was $8,212; average loan was $3,392. For part-time students, average financial aid package was $8,477.
Students without need: This college awards aid only to students with need.
Scholarships offered: 58 full-time freshmen received athletic scholarships; average amount $16,285.
Cumulative student debt: 42% of graduating class had student loans; average debt was $19,488.

FINANCIAL AID PROCEDURES
Forms required: FAFSA.
Dates and Deadlines: No deadline. Applicants notified on a rolling basis starting 3/15; must reply within 4 week(s) of notification.

CONTACT
Richard Shipman, Director of Financial Aid
250 Administration Building, East Lansing, MI 48824
(517) 353-5940

Michigan Technological University
Houghton, Michigan
www.mtu.edu Federal Code: 002292

4-year public university in small town.
Enrollment: 5,923 undergrads, 6% part-time. 1,361 full-time freshmen.
Selectivity: Admits 50 to 75% of applicants.

BASIC COSTS (2008-2009)
Tuition and fees: $10,762; out-of-state residents $22,522.
Per-credit charge: $331; out-of-state residents $723.
Room and board: $7,738.

FINANCIAL AID PICTURE (2008-2009)
Students with need: Out of 1,167 full-time freshmen who applied for aid, 835 were judged to have need. Of these, 832 received aid, and 180 had their full need met. Average financial aid package met 72% of need; average scholarship/grant was $5,359; average loan was $3,210. For part-time students, average financial aid package was $6,106.
Students without need: 440 full-time freshmen who did not demonstrate need for aid received scholarships/grants; average award was $4,163. No-need awards available for academics, alumni affiliation, art, athletics, job skills, leadership, music/drama, ROTC, state/district residency.
Scholarships offered: 45 full-time freshmen received athletic scholarships; average amount $9,320.
Cumulative student debt: 71% of graduating class had student loans; average debt was $14,184.

FINANCIAL AID PROCEDURES
Forms required: FAFSA.
Dates and Deadlines: Priority date 2/16; no closing date. Applicants notified on a rolling basis starting 5/1.

CONTACT
Timothy Malette, Director of Financial Aid
1400 Townsend Drive, Houghton, MI 49931-1295
(906) 487-2622

Monroe County Community College
Monroe, Michigan
www.monroeccc.edu Federal Code: 002294

2-year public community college in large town.
Enrollment: 4,514 undergrads.
Selectivity: Open admission; but selective for some programs.

BASIC COSTS (2008-2009)
Tuition and fees: $2,240; out-of-district residents $3,680; out-of-state residents $4,070.
Per-credit charge: $73; out-of-district residents $121; out-of-state residents $134.
Additional info: Tuition/fee waivers available for minority students.

FINANCIAL AID PICTURE
Students with need: Need-based aid available for full-time and part-time students. Work study available nights, weekends, and for part-time students.
Students without need: No-need awards available for academics, alumni affiliation, art, leadership, music/drama, state/district residency.

FINANCIAL AID PROCEDURES
Forms required: FAFSA, institutional form.

Dates and Deadlines: Priority date 4/1; no closing date. Applicants notified on a rolling basis starting 4/1; must reply within 2 week(s) of notification.

CONTACT

Tracy Vogt, Director of Financial Aid/Placement
1555 South Raisinville Road, Monroe, MI 48161-9746
(734) 384-4135

Montcalm Community College

Sidney, Michigan
www.montcalm.edu Federal Code: 002295

2-year public community and liberal arts college in rural community.
Enrollment: 1,937 undergrads, 57% part-time. 157 full-time freshmen.
Selectivity: Open admission; but selective for some programs.

BASIC COSTS (2008-2009)

Tuition and fees: $2,385; out-of-district residents $4,005; out-of-state residents $5,295.
Per-credit charge: $74; out-of-district residents $128; out-of-state residents $171.

FINANCIAL AID PICTURE

Students with need: Need-based aid available for full-time and part-time students.
Students without need: No-need awards available for academics, state/district residency.

FINANCIAL AID PROCEDURES

Forms required: FAFSA, institutional form.
Dates and Deadlines: Priority date 2/15; no closing date. Applicants notified on a rolling basis starting 6/15; must reply within 2 week(s) of notification.
Transfers: Priority date 4/1.

CONTACT

Rebecca Powell, Director of Financial Aid
2800 College Drive, Sidney, MI 48885
(989) 328-1228

Mott Community College

Flint, Michigan
www.mcc.edu Federal Code: 002261

2-year public community college in large city.
Enrollment: 7,567 undergrads, 60% part-time. 521 full-time freshmen.
Selectivity: Open admission; but selective for some programs.

BASIC COSTS (2008-2009)

Tuition and fees: $2,801; out-of-district residents $4,004; out-of-state residents $5,336.
Per-credit charge: $85; out-of-district residents $127; out-of-state residents $169.

FINANCIAL AID PICTURE (2008-2009)

Students with need: 61% of average financial aid package awarded as scholarships/grants, 39% awarded as loans/jobs. Need-based aid available for part-time students. Work study available nights.
Students without need: No-need awards available for academics, alumni affiliation, art, athletics, leadership, minority status, music/drama, state/district residency.

FINANCIAL AID PROCEDURES

Forms required: FAFSA.
Dates and Deadlines: No deadline. Applicants notified on a rolling basis starting 5/1.
Transfers: Pell Grants adjusted for amount used at another institution.

CONTACT

Troy Boquette, Executive Director of Student Financial Services
1401 East Court Street, Flint, MI 48503-2089
(810) 762-0144

Muskegon Community College

Muskegon, Michigan
www.muskegoncc.edu Federal Code: 002297

2-year public community college in small city.
Enrollment: 4,715 undergrads.
Selectivity: Open admission; but selective for some programs.

BASIC COSTS (2008-2009)

Tuition and fees: $2,350; out-of-district residents $3,685; out-of-state residents $4,900.
Per-credit charge: $69; out-of-district residents $114; out-of-state residents $154.
Additional info: Students also assessed contact hour fees, which vary according to residency status, and course fees, which vary.

FINANCIAL AID PICTURE

Students with need: Work study available nights, weekends, and for part-time students.

FINANCIAL AID PROCEDURES

Forms required: FAFSA, institutional form.
Dates and Deadlines: Priority date 5/1; no closing date. Applicants notified on a rolling basis starting 6/1; must reply within 2 week(s) of notification.

CONTACT

Bruce Wierda, Director of Financial Aid
221 South Quarterline Road, Muskegon, MI 49442
(231) 777-0221

North Central Michigan College

Petoskey, Michigan
www.ncmich.edu Federal Code: 002299

2-year public community college in small town.
Enrollment: 2,240 undergrads.
Selectivity: Open admission; but selective for some programs.

BASIC COSTS (2008-2009)

Tuition and fees: $2,340; out-of-district residents $3,681; out-of-state residents $4,674.
Per-credit charge: $70; out-of-district residents $114; out-of-state residents $147.
Room and board: $4,432.

FINANCIAL AID PICTURE

Students with need: Need-based aid available for full-time and part-time students. Work study available nights, weekends, and for part-time students.

FINANCIAL AID PROCEDURES

Forms required: FAFSA, institutional form.
Dates and Deadlines: Closing date 4/1. Applicants notified on a rolling basis starting 4/30.

CONTACT

Virginia Panoff, Director of Financial Aid
1515 Howard Street, Petoskey, MI 49770
(231) 348-6627

Northern Michigan University

Marquette, Michigan
www.nmu.edu Federal Code: 002301

4-year public university in large town.
Enrollment: 8,240 undergrads, 7% part-time. 1,760 full-time freshmen.
Selectivity: Admits over 75% of applicants.

BASIC COSTS (2008-2009)

Tuition and fees: $7,078; out-of-state residents $11,230.
Per-credit charge: $271; out-of-state residents $444.
Room and board: $7,442.
Additional info: Excludes one-time $200 athletic fee for first time freshmen. All full-time students provided with ThinkPad or MacBook computer as part of tuition and fees. Tuition/fee waivers available for minority students.

FINANCIAL AID PICTURE (2007-2008)

Students with need: Out of 1,644 full-time freshmen who applied for aid, 1,109 were judged to have need. Of these, 1,077 received aid, and 269 had their full need met. Average financial aid package met 65% of need; average scholarship/grant was $3,940; average loan was $2,931. For part-time students, average financial aid package was $6,984.
Students without need: 148 full-time freshmen who did not demonstrate need for aid received scholarships/grants; average award was $3,160. No-need awards available for academics, art, athletics, leadership, minority status, music/drama, religious affiliation, ROTC, state/district residency.
Scholarships offered: ***Merit:*** Talent recognition awards: available in art and design, music, theater. Freshman Fellowship: $1,000 in student employment; 3.5+ GPA and ACT 24+. Dr. Edgar L. Harden Scholarship: "full ride"; 3.5+ GPA and ACT 24+. National Academic Award: $3,500; minimum 3.0+ GPA and ACT 19+; awarded to non-Michigan residents. NMU Merit Excellence Award: $2,750-$3,500; based on 3.0+ GPA and 33+ ACT. NMU Merit Award: $2,250-$3,000; 3.0+ GPA and 30-32 ACT. NMU Scholars Award: $1,250-$2,000; 3.0+ GPA and ACT 27-29. NMU Outstanding Achievement: $750-$1,500; 3.0+ GPA and 25-26 ACT. ***Athletic:*** 14 full-time freshmen received athletic scholarships; average amount $6,443.
Cumulative student debt: 61% of graduating class had student loans; average debt was $18,498.
Additional info: Audition or portfolio required for music, drama, and art scholarship applicants. Alumni Dependent Tuition Program gives resident tuition rates to nonresident dependents of NMU alumni who received master's, baccalaureate, or associate degree; renewable.

FINANCIAL AID PROCEDURES

Forms required: FAFSA.
Dates and Deadlines: Priority date 3/1; no closing date. Applicants notified on a rolling basis starting 4/1; must reply within 2 week(s) of notification.
Transfers: No deadline. Applicants notified on a rolling basis starting 4/1; must reply within 2 week(s) of notification. Merit-based transfer scholarships available.

CONTACT

Michael Rotundo, Director of Financial Aid
1401 Presque Isle Avenue, Marquette, MI 49855
(906) 227-2327

Northwestern Michigan College

Traverse City, Michigan
www.nmc.edu Federal Code: 002302

2-year public community and maritime college in large town.
Enrollment: 4,095 undergrads, 50% part-time. 679 full-time freshmen.
Selectivity: Open admission; but selective for some programs.

BASIC COSTS (2008-2009)

Tuition and fees: $2,868; out-of-district residents $4,936; out-of-state residents $6,164.
Per-credit charge: $77; out-of-district residents $142; out-of-state residents $180.
Room and board: $7,853.
Additional info: Tuition/fee waivers available for adults, minority students, unemployed or children of unemployed.

FINANCIAL AID PICTURE (2007-2008)

Students with need: Need-based aid available for full-time and part-time students. Work study available nights, weekends, and for part-time students.
Students without need: No-need awards available for academics, art, job skills, leadership, minority status, music/drama, ROTC, state/district residency.

FINANCIAL AID PROCEDURES

Forms required: FAFSA.
Dates and Deadlines: Priority date 4/1; no closing date. Applicants notified on a rolling basis starting 5/1; must reply within 2 week(s) of notification.

CONTACT

Deb Faas, Director for Financial Aid
1701 East Front Street, Traverse City, MI 49686
(231) 995-1035

Northwood University: Michigan

Midland, Michigan
www.northwood.edu Federal Code: 004072

4-year private university and business college in large town.
Enrollment: 1,946 undergrads, 3% part-time. 440 full-time freshmen.
Selectivity: Admits 50 to 75% of applicants.

BASIC COSTS (2009-2010)

Tuition and fees: $18,408.
Per-credit charge: $363.
Room and board: $7,923.

FINANCIAL AID PICTURE (2008-2009)

Students with need: Average financial aid package met 55% of need; average scholarship/grant was $6,457; average loan was $3,196. For part-time students, average financial aid package was $6,933.
Students without need: No-need awards available for academics, alumni affiliation, athletics, leadership, minority status, ROTC.
Scholarships offered: Academic scholarships; $4,000-$9,000; based on test scores and GPA; unlimited number awarded.
Cumulative student debt: 71% of graduating class had student loans; average debt was $27,554.

FINANCIAL AID PROCEDURES

Forms required: FAFSA.
Dates and Deadlines: No deadline. Applicants notified on a rolling basis starting 3/1.

CONTACT

Theresa Mieler, Financial Aid Director
4000 Whiting Drive, Midland, MI 48640
(989) 837-4230

Oakland Community College

Bloomfield Hills, Michigan
www.oaklandcc.edu Federal Code: 002303

2-year public community college in very large city.
Enrollment: 14,116 undergrads, 67% part-time. 1,179 full-time freshmen.

Selectivity: Open admission.

BASIC COSTS (2008-2009)

Tuition and fees: $1,873; out-of-district residents $3,121; out-of-state residents $4,351.

Per-credit charge: $60; out-of-district residents $102; out-of-state residents $143.

FINANCIAL AID PICTURE (2008-2009)

Students with need: Need-based aid available for full-time and part-time students.

Students without need: No-need awards available for academics, athletics.

FINANCIAL AID PROCEDURES

Forms required: FAFSA.

Dates and Deadlines: Priority date 4/15; no closing date. Applicants notified on a rolling basis starting 4/15.

Transfers: Closing date 6/30. Michigan residency required for aid to transfer students.

CONTACT

Wilma Porter, Director of Financial Assistance and Scholarships
2480 Opdyke Road, Bloomfield Hills, MI 48304-2266
(248) 341-2000

Oakland University

Rochester, Michigan
www.oakland.edu Federal Code: 002307

4-year public university in small city.

Enrollment: 13,991 undergrads, 24% part-time. 2,247 full-time freshmen.

Selectivity: Admits over 75% of applicants.

BASIC COSTS (2008-2009)

Tuition and fees: $8,055; out-of-state residents $18,803.

Room and board: $7,105.

FINANCIAL AID PICTURE (2007-2008)

Students with need: Need-based aid available for full-time and part-time students.

Students without need: No-need awards available for academics, art, athletics, leadership, music/drama, state/district residency.

Scholarships offered: Wide range of scholarships awarded on the basis of accomplishment.

FINANCIAL AID PROCEDURES

Forms required: FAFSA.

Dates and Deadlines: Priority date 2/15; no closing date. Applicants notified on a rolling basis starting 3/15.

Transfers: Closing date 4/1.

CONTACT

Cindy Hermsen, Director of Financial Aid
101 North Foundation Hall, Rochester, MI 48309-4401
(248) 370-2550

Olivet College

Olivet, Michigan
www.olivetcollege.edu Federal Code: 002308

4-year private liberal arts college in rural community, affiliated with Congregational Christian Churches and United Church of Christ.

Enrollment: 990 undergrads.

Selectivity: Admits 50 to 75% of applicants.

BASIC COSTS (2008-2009)

Tuition and fees: $19,888.

Per-credit charge: $598.

Room and board: $6,472.

FINANCIAL AID PICTURE (2007-2008)

Students with need: Need-based aid available for full-time and part-time students.

Students without need: This college awards aid only to students with need.

Scholarships offered: Scholarships: up to $2,000; for students who demonstrate history of community service and civic responsibility during high school or college. Academic merit scholarships: up to full tuition. All scholarships renewable for 4 years.

FINANCIAL AID PROCEDURES

Forms required: FAFSA.

Dates and Deadlines: No deadline. Applicants notified on a rolling basis starting 2/1; must reply within 3 week(s) of notification.

CONTACT

Mark DeRuiter, Financial Aid Director
Admissions Office, Olivet, MI 49076

Rochester College

Rochester Hills, Michigan
www.rc.edu Federal Code: 002288

4-year private liberal arts college in small city, affiliated with Church of Christ.

Enrollment: 895 undergrads.

Selectivity: Admits over 75% of applicants.

BASIC COSTS (2008-2009)

Tuition and fees: $16,610.

Per-credit charge: $488.

Room and board: $7,020.

Additional info: Tuition/fee waivers available for minority students.

FINANCIAL AID PICTURE

Students with need: Need-based aid available for full-time and part-time students. Work study available nights, weekends, and for part-time students.

Students without need: No-need awards available for academics, alumni affiliation, athletics, leadership, music/drama, state/district residency.

FINANCIAL AID PROCEDURES

Forms required: FAFSA.

Dates and Deadlines: Priority date 8/1; no closing date. Applicants notified on a rolling basis starting 6/1; must reply within 2 week(s) of notification.

CONTACT

Larry Norman, Director of Financial Aid
800 West Avon Road, Rochester Hills, MI 48307
(248) 218-2029

Sacred Heart Major Seminary

Detroit, Michigan
www.shms.org Federal Code: 002313

4-year private seminary college in very large city, affiliated with Roman Catholic Church.

Enrollment: 70 undergrads, 47% part-time. 1 full-time freshmen.

Selectivity: Admits over 75% of applicants.

BASIC COSTS (2008-2009)

Tuition and fees: $13,580.

Per-credit charge: $320.

Room and board: $7,400.

Additional info: Tuition/fee waivers available for adults.

FINANCIAL AID PICTURE (2007-2008)

Students with need: Work study available nights, weekends, and for part-time students.

Students without need: No-need awards available for academics, religious affiliation.

FINANCIAL AID PROCEDURES

Forms required: FAFSA, institutional form.

Dates and Deadlines: No deadline. Applicants notified on a rolling basis.

Transfers: No deadline. Applicants notified on a rolling basis. Must submit certified high school transcript, copy of high school diploma, copy of GED certificate showing passing score, or college transcript showing associate degree as certification of eligibility; must submit financial aid transcripts from all previous post-secondary institutions attended.

CONTACT

Jeannette Murrell, Director of Financial Aid
2701 Chicago Boulevard, Detroit, MI 48206-1799
(313) 883-8781

Saginaw Valley State University

University Center, Michigan
www.svsu.edu Federal Code: 002314

4-year public university in small city.

Enrollment: 8,018 undergrads, 17% part-time. 1,533 full-time freshmen.

Selectivity: Admits over 75% of applicants.

BASIC COSTS (2008-2009)

Tuition and fees: $6,492; out-of-state residents $14,890.

Per-credit charge: $202; out-of-state residents $482.

Room and board: $6,830.

FINANCIAL AID PICTURE (2007-2008)

Students with need: Out of 1,500 full-time freshmen who applied for aid, 1,004 were judged to have need. Of these, 986 received aid, and 236 had their full need met. Average financial aid package met 68% of need; average scholarship/grant was $3,368; average loan was $2,976. For part-time students, average financial aid package was $4,845.

Students without need: 227 full-time freshmen who did not demonstrate need for aid received scholarships/grants; average award was $3,116. No-need awards available for academics, art, athletics, leadership, minority status, music/drama.

Scholarships offered: ***Merit:*** Presidential Scholarships; tuition and selective fees up to 136 credit hours; granted to students who are first or second in high school class with minimum 24 ACT or 3.7 GPA and 28 ACT. Dean's Scholarship; $3,000 per year for four years; 3.0 GPA and 24 ACT. University Foundation Scholarship; tuition and selective fees for four courses and $1,000 to apply toward study abroad or a research project; 3.5 GPA and 24 ACT. University Scholarship; $1,000 per year for four years; 3.5 GPA. Various private scholarships also available. ***Athletic:*** 77 full-time freshmen received athletic scholarships; average amount $4,018.

Cumulative student debt: 68% of graduating class had student loans; average debt was $23,561.

FINANCIAL AID PROCEDURES

Forms required: FAFSA.

Dates and Deadlines: Priority date 2/14; no closing date. Applicants notified on a rolling basis starting 3/20; must reply within 10 week(s) of notification.

Transfers: No deadline. Applicants notified on a rolling basis; must reply within 10 week(s) of notification. Community college scholarship, private scholarships, and Transfer Dean's scholarships available.

CONTACT

Robert Lemuel, Director of Scholarships and Financial Aid
7400 Bay Road, University Center, MI 48710
(989) 964-4103

Schoolcraft College

Livonia, Michigan
www.schoolcraft.edu Federal Code: 002315

2-year public community college in small city.

Enrollment: 9,760 undergrads, 57% part-time. 1,331 full-time freshmen.

Selectivity: Open admission; but selective for some programs.

BASIC COSTS (2008-2009)

Tuition and fees: $2,380; out-of-district residents $3,400; out-of-state residents $4,990.

FINANCIAL AID PICTURE

Students with need: Need-based aid available for full-time and part-time students. Work study available nights, weekends, and for part-time students.

Students without need: No-need awards available for academics, athletics, leadership, music/drama, state/district residency.

Scholarships offered: Trustee Scholarships; $1,000-$1,200; renewable for 2nd year; based on essay, placement test, trustee application, graduation from local high school; 80 awarded.

FINANCIAL AID PROCEDURES

Forms required: FAFSA.

Dates and Deadlines: No deadline. Applicants notified on a rolling basis starting 6/1.

CONTACT

Regina Mosley, Director of Financial Aid
18600 Haggerty Road, Livonia, MI 48152-2696
(734) 462-4433

Southwestern Michigan College

Dowagiac, Michigan
www.swmich.edu Federal Code: 002317

2-year public community college in small town.

Enrollment: 2,163 undergrads, 48% part-time. 418 full-time freshmen.

Selectivity: Open admission; but selective for some programs.

BASIC COSTS (2008-2009)

Tuition and fees: $3,165; out-of-district residents $3,848; out-of-state residents $4,103.

Per-credit charge: $83; out-of-district residents $105; out-of-state residents $114.

FINANCIAL AID PICTURE (2007-2008)

Students with need: Need-based aid available for full-time and part-time students. Work study available nights, weekends, and for part-time students.

Students without need: No-need awards available for academics, art, leadership, music/drama.

FINANCIAL AID PROCEDURES

Forms required: FAFSA, institutional form.

Dates and Deadlines: Priority date 7/1; no closing date. Applicants notified on a rolling basis starting 4/1; must reply within 2 week(s) of notification.

CONTACT

Susan Fintze, Director of Financial Aid
58900 Cherry Grove Road, Dowagiac, MI 49047-9793
(269) 782-1313

Spring Arbor University

Spring Arbor, Michigan
www.arbor.edu Federal Code: 002318

4-year private university and liberal arts college in rural community, affiliated with Free Methodist Church of North America.
Enrollment: 2,615 undergrads, 25% part-time. 380 full-time freshmen.
Selectivity: Admits over 75% of applicants.

BASIC COSTS (2009-2010)

Tuition and fees: $19,790.
Per-credit charge: $485.
Room and board: $6,950.

FINANCIAL AID PICTURE (2008-2009)

Students with need: Out of 361 full-time freshmen who applied for aid, 311 were judged to have need. Of these, 311 received aid, and 240 had their full need met. Average financial aid package met 97% of need; average scholarship/grant was $11,613; average loan was $3,822. For part-time students, average financial aid package was $13,287.
Students without need: 1 full-time freshmen who did not demonstrate need for aid received scholarships/grants; average award was $2,456. No-need awards available for academics, art, athletics, minority status, music/drama, religious affiliation.
Scholarships offered: ***Merit:*** President Scholarship: $6,000; Provost Scholarship: $4,000; Faculty Scholarship: $3,000; Partnership Scholarship: $2,000; All based on high school GPA, HS rank in class, and ACT scores. National Merit Finalist: full tuition; National Merit Semifinalist: half-tuition. Trustee scholarship: $7,500; based on 29 ACT/1280 SAT. ***Athletic:*** 67 full-time freshmen received athletic scholarships; average amount $5,950.
Cumulative student debt: 84% of graduating class had student loans; average debt was $22,875.

FINANCIAL AID PROCEDURES

Forms required: FAFSA.
Dates and Deadlines: Priority date 3/1; no closing date. Applicants notified on a rolling basis starting 3/1; must reply within 2 week(s) of notification.
Transfers: No deadline. Applicants notified on a rolling basis starting 5/1; must reply within 2 week(s) of notification. Financial aid transcript required from each college previously attended.

CONTACT

Geoff Marsh, Director of Financial Aid
106 East Main Street, Spring Arbor, MI 49283-9799
(517) 750-6468

University of Detroit Mercy

Detroit, Michigan
www.udmercy.edu Federal Code: 002323

4-year private university in very large city, affiliated with Roman Catholic Church.
Enrollment: 2,995 undergrads.
Selectivity: Admits 50 to 75% of applicants.

BASIC COSTS (2008-2009)

Tuition and fees: $27,319.
Per-credit charge: $655.
Room and board: $8,250.
Additional info: Engineering and architecture students pay slightly higher tuition.

FINANCIAL AID PICTURE

Students with need: Need-based aid available for full-time and part-time students.
Students without need: No-need awards available for academics, alumni affiliation, athletics, leadership, minority status, music/drama, religious affiliation.

FINANCIAL AID PROCEDURES

Forms required: FAFSA.
Dates and Deadlines: Priority date 3/1; no closing date. Applicants notified on a rolling basis starting 3/1; must reply within 3 week(s) of notification.

CONTACT

Sandra Ross, Director of Scholarship and Financial Aid
4001 West McNichols Road, Detroit, MI 48221-3038
(313) 993-3350

University of Michigan

Ann Arbor, Michigan Federal Code: 002325
www.umich.edu CSS Code: 1839

4-year public university in small city.
Enrollment: 25,865 undergrads, 3% part-time. 5,739 full-time freshmen.
Selectivity: Admits less than 50% of applicants.

BASIC COSTS (2008-2009)

Tuition and fees: $11,037; out-of-state residents $33,069.
Per-credit charge: $423; out-of-state residents $1,341.
Room and board: $8,590.

FINANCIAL AID PICTURE (2007-2008)

Students with need: Out of 3,514 full-time freshmen who applied for aid, 2,853 were judged to have need. Of these, 2,853 received aid, and 2,568 had their full need met. Average financial aid package met 90% of need; average scholarship/grant was $7,737; average loan was $6,623. Need-based aid available for part-time students.
Students without need: 2,615 full-time freshmen who did not demonstrate need for aid received scholarships/grants; average award was $6,681. No-need awards available for academics, alumni affiliation, art, athletics, leadership, music/drama, religious affiliation, ROTC, state/district residency.
Scholarships offered: 139 full-time freshmen received athletic scholarships; average amount $27,468.
Cumulative student debt: 46% of graduating class had student loans; average debt was $25,586.

FINANCIAL AID PROCEDURES

Forms required: FAFSA, CSS PROFILE.
Dates and Deadlines: Priority date 4/30; closing date 5/30. Applicants notified on a rolling basis starting 3/15.
Transfers: Applicants notified on a rolling basis starting 3/9. Community College Scholarship available for qualified students.

CONTACT

Pamela Fowler, Executive Financial Aid Director
1220 Student Activities Building, Ann Arbor, MI 48109-1316
(734) 763-6600

University of Michigan: Dearborn

Dearborn, Michigan
www.umd.umich.edu Federal Code: 002326

4-year public university in small city.
Enrollment: 6,346 undergrads, 31% part-time. 859 full-time freshmen.
Selectivity: Admits 50 to 75% of applicants.

BASIC COSTS (2008-2009)

Tuition and fees: $8,506; out-of-state residents $18,612.

FINANCIAL AID PICTURE (2007-2008)

Students with need: Out of 550 full-time freshmen who applied for aid, 347 were judged to have need. Of these, 347 received aid, and 41 had their full need met. Average financial aid package met 41% of need; average scholarship/grant was $3,832; average loan was $2,771. Need-based aid available for part-time students.

Students without need: 512 full-time freshmen who did not demonstrate need for aid received scholarships/grants; average award was $3,123. No-need awards available for academics, alumni affiliation, athletics, job skills, leadership, minority status, ROTC.

Scholarships offered: 9 full-time freshmen received athletic scholarships; average amount $1,656.

Cumulative student debt: 53% of graduating class had student loans; average debt was $18,001.

FINANCIAL AID PROCEDURES

Forms required: FAFSA.

Dates and Deadlines: Priority date 2/15; no closing date. Applicants notified on a rolling basis starting 3/10; must reply within 3 week(s) of notification.

Transfers: Applicants notified on a rolling basis starting 4/1; must reply within 3 week(s) of notification.

CONTACT

Judy Tatum, Director of Financial Aid
4901 Evergreen Road, 1145 UC, Dearborn, MI 48128-1491
(313) 593-5000

University of Michigan: Flint

Flint, Michigan
www.umflint.edu Federal Code: 002327

4-year public university and branch campus college in small city.

Enrollment: 5,868 undergrads, 35% part-time. 587 full-time freshmen.

Selectivity: Admits over 75% of applicants.

BASIC COSTS (2008-2009)

Tuition and fees: $7,376; out-of-state residents $14,384.

Per-credit charge: $292; out-of-state residents $584.

Room and board: $6,800.

FINANCIAL AID PICTURE (2007-2008)

Students with need: Out of 460 full-time freshmen who applied for aid, 311 were judged to have need. Of these, 301 received aid, and 39 had their full need met. Average financial aid package met 68% of need; average scholarship/grant was $4,365; average loan was $3,161. For part-time students, average financial aid package was $5,408.

Students without need: 43 full-time freshmen who did not demonstrate need for aid received scholarships/grants; average award was $3,229. No-need awards available for academics, art, leadership, minority status, music/drama.

Cumulative student debt: 22% of graduating class had student loans; average debt was $24,090.

Additional info: SAT/ACT scores must be submitted for scholarship consideration.

FINANCIAL AID PROCEDURES

Forms required: FAFSA.

Dates and Deadlines: Priority date 3/1; no closing date. Applicants notified on a rolling basis starting 3/15.

Transfers: Must not be in default or owe refunds for Title IV aid.

CONTACT

Lori Vedder, Director of Financial Aid
303 East Kearsley Street, Flint, MI 48502-1950
(810) 762-3444

Walsh College of Accountancy and Business Administration

Troy, Michigan
www.walshcollege.edu Federal Code: 004071

Upper-division private business college in large city.

Enrollment: 984 undergrads, 85% part-time.

Selectivity: Open admission.

BASIC COSTS (2008-2009)

Tuition and fees: $9,070.

Per-credit charge: $294.

FINANCIAL AID PICTURE (2007-2008)

Students with need: Average financial aid package for all full-time undergraduates was $11,027; for part-time $10,333. 22% awarded as scholarships/grants, 78% awarded as loans/jobs.

Students without need: No-need awards available for academics.

Cumulative student debt: 61% of graduating class had student loans; average debt was $12,367.

FINANCIAL AID PROCEDURES

Forms required: FAFSA.

Dates and Deadlines: Priority date 3/23; no closing date.

Transfers: Priority date 3/1; no deadline. Applicants notified on a rolling basis.

CONTACT

Howard Thomas, Director, Financial Aid
PO Box 7006, Troy, MI 48007-7006
(248) 823-1285

Wayne County Community College

Detroit, Michigan
www.wcccd.edu Federal Code: 009230

2-year public community and liberal arts college in very large city.

Enrollment: 19,686 undergrads, 76% part-time. 1,250 full-time freshmen.

Selectivity: Open admission.

BASIC COSTS (2008-2009)

Tuition and fees: $2,020; out-of-district residents $2,990; out-of-state residents $3,890.

Per-credit charge: $58; out-of-district residents $90; out-of-state residents $120.

FINANCIAL AID PICTURE (2007-2008)

Students with need: 60% of average financial aid package awarded as scholarships/grants, 40% awarded as loans/jobs. Need-based aid available for part-time students. Work study available nights, weekends, and for part-time students.

Additional info: High school diploma, GED, or passing grade on ABT required for financial aid.

FINANCIAL AID PROCEDURES

Forms required: FAFSA.

Dates and Deadlines: Priority date 5/1; no closing date. Applicants notified on a rolling basis starting 5/1.

CONTACT

Myra Hawkins, Executive District Director of Financial Aid
801 West Fort Street, Detroit, MI 48226
(313) 496-2614

Wayne State University
Detroit, Michigan
www.wayne.edu Federal Code: 002329

4-year public university in very large city.
Enrollment: 19,007 undergrads, 36% part-time. 2,820 full-time freshmen.
Selectivity: Admits over 75% of applicants.

BASIC COSTS (2008-2009)
Tuition and fees: $8,109; out-of-state residents $17,379.
Per-credit charge: $239; out-of-state residents $548.
Room and board: $6,932.

FINANCIAL AID PICTURE (2007-2008)
Students with need: Out of 2,291 full-time freshmen who applied for aid, 1,904 were judged to have need. Of these, 1,890 received aid, and 209 had their full need met. Average financial aid package met 68% of need; average scholarship/grant was $4,473; average loan was $3,404. For part-time students, average financial aid package was $9,939.
Students without need: 276 full-time freshmen who did not demonstrate need for aid received scholarships/grants; average award was $5,422. No-need awards available for academics, art, athletics, leadership, music/drama.
Scholarships offered: ***Merit:*** Scholars Day award; amounts vary; invitation-only for top applicants who are admitted by 1/15; requires group interview. Presidential Scholarship; full-tuition for four years; selected from Scholars Day participants. ***Athletic:*** 26 full-time freshmen received athletic scholarships; average amount $9,808.
Cumulative student debt: 49% of graduating class had student loans; average debt was $19,618.

FINANCIAL AID PROCEDURES
Forms required: FAFSA.
Dates and Deadlines: Priority date 2/15; closing date 4/30. Applicants notified on a rolling basis starting 3/1; must reply within 2 week(s) of notification.
Transfers: No deadline. Applicants notified on a rolling basis starting 3/1; must reply within 2 week(s) of notification.

CONTACT
Al Hermsen, Director of Student Financial Aid
42 West Warren, Detroit, MI 48202
(313) 577-3378

West Shore Community College
Scottville, Michigan
www.westshore.edu Federal Code: 007950

2-year public community college in rural community.
Enrollment: 515 full-time undergrads.
Selectivity: Open admission; but selective for some programs.

BASIC COSTS (2008-2009)
Tuition and fees: $2,340; out-of-district residents $3,780; out-of-state residents $4,980.
Per-credit charge: $72; out-of-district residents $120; out-of-state residents $160.

FINANCIAL AID PICTURE (2008-2009)
Students with need: Need-based aid available for full-time and part-time students. Work study available nights, weekends, and for part-time students.

FINANCIAL AID PROCEDURES
Forms required: FAFSA.
Dates and Deadlines: Priority date 3/15; no closing date. Applicants notified on a rolling basis starting 5/15; must reply within 2 week(s) of notification.

CONTACT
Victoria Oddo, Director of Student Services
3000 North Stiles Road, Scottville, MI 49454-0277
(231) 845-6211

Western Michigan University
Kalamazoo, Michigan
www.wmich.edu Federal Code: 002330

4-year public university in small city.
Enrollment: 19,715 undergrads, 11% part-time. 3,806 full-time freshmen.
Selectivity: Admits over 75% of applicants.

BASIC COSTS (2008-2009)
Tuition and fees: $7,928; out-of-state residents $18,420.
Per-credit charge: $245; out-of-state residents $601.
Room and board: $7,565.

FINANCIAL AID PICTURE (2008-2009)
Students with need: Need-based aid available for full-time and part-time students.
Students without need: No-need awards available for academics, alumni affiliation, art, athletics, minority status, music/drama, ROTC, state/district residency.
Scholarships offered: Medallion Scholarship; $3,000-$10,000 annually; based on academic performance in high school (3.8 GPA, 25 ACT or 1130 SAT, exclusive of writing); renewable for students maintaining full-time enrollment and 3.25 GPA.

FINANCIAL AID PROCEDURES
Forms required: FAFSA.
Dates and Deadlines: Priority date 3/15; no closing date. Applicants notified on a rolling basis starting 3/15.
Transfers: No deadline. Applicants notified on a rolling basis starting 3/15.

CONTACT
Mark Delorey, Director of Financial Aid
1903 West Michigan Avenue, Kalamazoo, MI 49008-5211
(269) 387-6000

Minnesota

Academy College
Bloomington, Minnesota
www.academycollege.edu Federal Code: 013505

2-year for-profit junior and career college in large city.
Enrollment: 168 undergrads.
Selectivity: Open admission.

BASIC COSTS (2008-2009)
Additional info: Tuition ranges from $335 to $399 per credit hour depending on program.

FINANCIAL AID PICTURE (2007-2008)
Students with need: Need-based aid available for full-time and part-time students. Work study available nights, weekends, and for part-time students.

FINANCIAL AID PROCEDURES
Forms required: FAFSA, institutional form.
Dates and Deadlines: No deadline. Applicants notified on a rolling basis.

CONTACT

Mary Erickson, Director of Administration
1101 East 78th Street, Bloomington, MN 55420
(952) 851-0066

Alexandria Technical College

Alexandria, Minnesota
www.alextech.edu Federal Code: 005544

2-year public technical college in large town.
Enrollment: 1,685 undergrads.
Selectivity: Open admission; but selective for some programs.

BASIC COSTS (2008-2009)
Tuition and fees: $4,506.
Per-credit charge: $135.

FINANCIAL AID PICTURE
Students with need: Need-based aid available for full-time and part-time students.
Students without need: This college awards aid only to students with need.

FINANCIAL AID PROCEDURES
Forms required: FAFSA, institutional form.
Dates and Deadlines: Priority date 5/1; no closing date. Applicants notified on a rolling basis starting 6/30; must reply within 2 week(s) of notification.
Transfers: No deadline. Applicants notified on a rolling basis; must reply within 2 week(s) of notification.

CONTACT

Gary McFarland, Financial Aid Coordinator
1601 Jefferson Street, Alexandria, MN 56308-3799
(320) 762-4540

Anoka Technical College

Anoka, Minnesota
www.anokatech.edu Federal Code: 007350

2-year public technical college in large town.
Enrollment: 2,230 undergrads.
Selectivity: Open admission.

BASIC COSTS (2008-2009)
Tuition and fees: $4,669.
Per-credit charge: $142.
Additional info: In-state and out-of-state tuition rates are the same.

FINANCIAL AID PICTURE
Students with need: Need-based aid available for full-time and part-time students. Work study available nights.
Students without need: This college awards aid only to students with need.

FINANCIAL AID PROCEDURES
Forms required: FAFSA, institutional form.
Dates and Deadlines: No deadline. Applicants notified on a rolling basis starting 5/1.

CONTACT

Susan Rumpca, Director of Financial Aid
1355 West Highway 10, Anoka, MN 55303
(763) 576-4760

Anoka-Ramsey Community College

Coon Rapids, Minnesota
www.anokaramsey.edu Federal Code: 002332

2-year public community college in small city.
Enrollment: 6,586 undergrads.
Selectivity: Open admission; but selective for some programs.

BASIC COSTS (2008-2009)
Tuition and fees: $4,100.
Per-credit charge: $120.
Additional info: In-state and out-of-state tuition rates are the same.

FINANCIAL AID PICTURE
Students with need: Work study available nights, weekends, and for part-time students.
Students without need: This college awards aid only to students with need.

FINANCIAL AID PROCEDURES
Forms required: FAFSA, institutional form.
Dates and Deadlines: Priority date 4/1; no closing date. Applicants notified on a rolling basis; must reply within 2 week(s) of notification.

CONTACT

Karla Seymour, Financial Aid Officer
11200 Mississippi Boulevard NW, Coon Rapids, MN 55433
(763) 433-1100

Art Institutes International Minnesota

Minneapolis, Minnesota
www.artinstitutes.edu/minneapolis Federal Code: 010248

4-year for-profit culinary school and visual arts college in large city.
Enrollment: 1,872 undergrads, 27% part-time. 437 full-time freshmen.
Selectivity: Open admission.

BASIC COSTS (2008-2009)
Tuition and fees: $21,552.
Per-credit charge: $449.
Additional info: Typical full-time credit load 16 credits/quarter. Starter kits for most programs $600 to $1200. Tuition at time of enrollment locked for 4 years.

FINANCIAL AID PICTURE
Students with need: Need-based aid available for full-time students.

FINANCIAL AID PROCEDURES
Forms required: FAFSA.

CONTACT

Jakki Edwards, Director of Administrative and Financial Services
15 South Ninth Street, Minneapolis, MN 55402
(612) 332-3361

Augsburg College

Minneapolis, Minnesota
www.augsburg.edu Federal Code: 002334

4-year private liberal arts college in large city, affiliated with Evangelical Lutheran Church in America.
Enrollment: 2,919 undergrads, 17% part-time. 451 full-time freshmen.
Selectivity: Admits 50 to 75% of applicants.

BASIC COSTS (2009-2010)

Tuition and fees: $27,628.
Room and board: $7,514.

FINANCIAL AID PICTURE (2007-2008)

Students with need: Need-based aid available for full-time and part-time students.
Students without need: No-need awards available for academics, alumni affiliation, leadership, minority status, music/drama, religious affiliation.
Scholarships offered: President's Scholarships: up to full tuition annually; 3.7 GPA and ACT/SAT score 27 or higher; number awarded determined annually. Regents Scholarships: $4,000-$10,000; top 30% of class rank or test scores. Must apply before 5/1 for both scholarships.

FINANCIAL AID PROCEDURES

Forms required: FAFSA.
Dates and Deadlines: Priority date 4/15; closing date 8/1. Applicants notified on a rolling basis starting 3/1; must reply within 3 week(s) of notification.
Transfers: Priority date 7/1; closing date 8/15. Applicants notified on a rolling basis starting 3/1; must reply by 9/1.

CONTACT

Paul Terrio, Director of Enrollment Services
2211 Riverside Avenue, Minneapolis, MN 55454
(612) 330-1046

Bemidji State University

Bemidji, Minnesota
www.bemidjistate.edu Federal Code: 002336

4-year public university in large town.
Enrollment: 4,362 undergrads, 24% part-time. 718 full-time freshmen.
Selectivity: Admits over 75% of applicants.

BASIC COSTS (2008-2009)

Tuition and fees: $6,996; out-of-state residents $6,996.
Per-credit charge: $214; out-of-state residents $214.
Room and board: $6,024.
Additional info: Out-of-state students pay the same rate as in-state students. Tuition/fee waivers available for minority students.

FINANCIAL AID PICTURE (2008-2009)

Students with need: Out of 593 full-time freshmen who applied for aid, 427 were judged to have need. Of these, 421 received aid, and 149 had their full need met. Average financial aid package met 77% of need; average scholarship/grant was $5,448; average loan was $3,420. For part-time students, average financial aid package was $6,215.
Students without need: 154 full-time freshmen who did not demonstrate need for aid received scholarships/grants; average award was $8,556. No-need awards available for academics, alumni affiliation, art, athletics, music/drama.
Scholarships offered: 92 full-time freshmen received athletic scholarships; average amount $3,732.
Cumulative student debt: 67% of graduating class had student loans; average debt was $21,931

FINANCIAL AID PROCEDURES

Forms required: FAFSA, institutional form.
Dates and Deadlines: Priority date 5/15; no closing date. Applicants notified on a rolling basis starting 5/15.

CONTACT

Paul Lindseth, Director of Financial Aid
1500 Birchmont Drive NE, D-102, Bemidji, MN 56601
(218) 755-2034

Bethany Lutheran College

Mankato, Minnesota
www.blc.edu Federal Code: 002337

4-year private liberal arts college in large town, affiliated with Evangelical Lutheran Synod.
Enrollment: 610 undergrads. 174 full-time freshmen.
Selectivity: Admits over 75% of applicants.

BASIC COSTS (2008-2009)

Tuition and fees: $18,710.
Per-credit charge: $780.
Room and board: $5,800.

FINANCIAL AID PICTURE (2007-2008)

Students with need: Out of 160 full-time freshmen who applied for aid, 145 were judged to have need. Of these, 145 received aid, and 49 had their full need met. Average financial aid package met 90% of need; average scholarship/grant was $11,520; average loan was $3,819. For part-time students, average financial aid package was $11,650.
Students without need: 25 full-time freshmen who did not demonstrate need for aid received scholarships/grants; average award was $7,057. No-need awards available for academics, art, music/drama.
Cumulative student debt: 87% of graduating class had student loans; average debt was $21,876.

FINANCIAL AID PROCEDURES

Forms required: FAFSA, institutional form.
Dates and Deadlines: Priority date 4/15; no closing date. Applicants notified on a rolling basis starting 3/1; must reply within 2 week(s) of notification.
Transfers: No deadline. Applicants notified on a rolling basis starting 3/1; must reply within 2 week(s) of notification.

CONTACT

Jeffrey Younge, Financial Aid Director
700 Luther Drive, Mankato, MN 56001-4490
(507) 344-7328

Bethel University

Saint Paul, Minnesota
www.bethel.edu Federal Code: 002338

4-year private university and liberal arts college in large city, affiliated with Baptist General Conference.
Enrollment: 3,302 undergrads, 18% part-time. 572 full-time freshmen.
Selectivity: Admits over 75% of applicants.

BASIC COSTS (2009-2010)

Tuition and fees: $27,020.
Per-credit charge: $1,125.
Room and board: $7,920.
Additional info: Rate frozen as long as student continues to reside in campus housing.

FINANCIAL AID PICTURE (2007-2008)

Students with need: Out of 460 full-time freshmen who applied for aid, 387 were judged to have need. Of these, 387 received aid, and 60 had their full need met. Average financial aid package met 75% of need; average scholarship/grant was $12,159; average loan was $4,020. For part-time students, average financial aid package was $9,502.
Students without need: 154 full-time freshmen who did not demonstrate need for aid received scholarships/grants; average award was $5,119. No-need awards available for academics, alumni affiliation, art, leadership, music/drama, state/district residency.
Scholarships offered: Faculty Scholarship: $2,000-$4,900 per year. Dean's Scholarship: $5,000-$9,000 per year. President's Scholarship: $10,000-

$15,000 per year; based on academic merit or potential as signified by high school GPA, high school class rank, ACT or SAT score, and/or evidence of potential to make a significant contribution to the spiritual and social atmosphere at Bethel. Royal Scholarship: $2,000; awarded to students with family members who have previously attended Bethel University. Ministerial Scholarship: $1,000; dependent children of full-time ordained ministers or missionaries of Converge Worldwide (formerly the BGC) qualify for $1,200; those of other denominations qualify for $1,000 (both are contingent on good standing).
Cumulative student debt: 75% of graduating class had student loans; average debt was $30,747.

FINANCIAL AID PROCEDURES

Forms required: FAFSA, institutional form.
Dates and Deadlines: Priority date 4/15; no closing date. Applicants notified on a rolling basis starting 3/1; must reply by 5/1 or within 3 week(s) of notification.
Transfers: Phi Theta Kappa Scholarship ($1,000 per year) awarded to transfer students with a minimum cumulative college GPA of 3.00 and previous membership in Phi Theta Kappa academic honor society for at least one term.

CONTACT

Jeffrey Olson, Director of Financial Aid
3900 Bethel Drive, Saint Paul, MN 55112
(651) 638-6241

Capella University

Minneapolis, Minnesota
www.capella.edu Federal Code: 032673

4-year for-profit virtual university in very large city.
Enrollment: 4,103 undergrads, 78% part-time. 5 full-time freshmen.
Selectivity: Open admission; but selective for some programs.

BASIC COSTS (2008-2009)

Tuition and fees: $13,950.
Per-credit charge: $310.

FINANCIAL AID PICTURE

Students with need: Need-based aid available for full-time and part-time students.

CONTACT

Leah Harris, Financial Aid Administrator
225 South Sixth Street, 9th Floor, Minneapolis, MN 55402
(888) 227-3552

Carleton College

Northfield, Minnesota Federal Code: 002340
www.carleton.edu CSS Code: 6081

4-year private liberal arts college in large town.
Enrollment: 1,975 undergrads. 490 full-time freshmen.
Selectivity: Admits less than 50% of applicants.

BASIC COSTS (2008-2009)

Tuition and fees: $38,046.
Room and board: $9,993.

FINANCIAL AID PICTURE (2007-2008)

Students with need: Out of 378 full-time freshmen who applied for aid, 264 were judged to have need. Of these, 264 received aid, and 264 had their full need met. Average financial aid package met 100% of need; average scholarship/grant was $29,064; average loan was $3,896.
Students without need: 31 full-time freshmen who did not demonstrate need for aid received scholarships/grants; average award was $2,238. No-need awards available for academics.
Scholarships offered: National Merit, National Achievement, National Hispanic Scholars Awards: $2,000 per year; based on outstanding academic achievement and promise.
Cumulative student debt: 52% of graduating class had student loans; average debt was $20,083.
Additional info: Full financial need of all admitted applicants met through combination of work, loans, grants. Carleton Access Scholarship reduces loans for incoming students whose family income is below $75,000.

FINANCIAL AID PROCEDURES

Forms required: FAFSA, CSS PROFILE.
Dates and Deadlines: Closing date 2/15. Applicants notified by 4/1; must reply by 5/1 or within 2 week(s) of notification.
Transfers: Closing date 3/15. Applicants notified by 5/15; must reply by 6/1 or within 2 week(s) of notification.

CONTACT

Rodney Oto, Director of Student Financial Services
100 South College Street, Northfield, MN 55057
(507) 222-4138

Central Lakes College

Brainerd, Minnesota
www.clcmn.edu Federal Code: 002339

2-year public community and technical college in large town.
Enrollment: 3,087 undergrads.
Selectivity: Open admission; but selective for some programs.

BASIC COSTS (2008-2009)

Tuition and fees: $4,540.
Per-credit charge: $133.
Additional info: In-state and out-of-state tuition rates same.

FINANCIAL AID PICTURE (2007-2008)

Students with need: 44% of average financial aid package awarded as scholarships/grants, 56% awarded as loans/jobs. Need-based aid available for part-time students.

FINANCIAL AID PROCEDURES

Forms required: FAFSA, institutional form.
Dates and Deadlines: Priority date 6/1; no closing date. Applicants notified on a rolling basis starting 6/10; must reply within 2 week(s) of notification.

CONTACT

Mike Barnaby, Director of Financial Aid
501 West College Drive, Brainerd, MN 56401
(218) 855-8025

Century Community and Technical College

White Bear Lake, Minnesota
www.century.edu Federal Code: 010546

2-year public community and technical college in large town.
Enrollment: 8,548 undergrads, 52% part-time. 1,093 full-time freshmen.
Selectivity: Open admission; but selective for some programs.

BASIC COSTS (2008-2009)

Tuition and fees: $4,565.
Per-credit charge: $135.
Additional info: In-state and out-of-state tuition rates are the same.

FINANCIAL AID PICTURE (2007-2008)

Students with need: 35% of average financial aid package awarded as scholarships/grants, 65% awarded as loans/jobs. Need-based aid available for part-time students.

Students without need: This college awards aid only to students with need.

Additional info: Minnesota resident out of high school or not enrolled in college for 7 years without bachelor's or other higher degree offered cost of tuition and books for 1 course in 1 semester up to maximum of 5 credits.

FINANCIAL AID PROCEDURES

Forms required: FAFSA.

Dates and Deadlines: No deadline. Applicants notified on a rolling basis starting 5/15.

CONTACT

Lois Larson, Financial Aid Director
3300 Century Avenue North, White Bear Lake, MN 55110
(651) 779-3305

College of St. Benedict

St. Joseph, Minnesota
www.csbsju.edu Federal Code: 002341

4-year private liberal arts college for women in small town, affiliated with Roman Catholic Church.

Enrollment: 2,068 undergrads. 519 full-time freshmen.

Selectivity: Admits over 75% of applicants.

BASIC COSTS (2009-2010)

Tuition and fees: $30,136.

Per-credit charge: $1,225.

Room and board: $8,358.

FINANCIAL AID PICTURE (2008-2009)

Students with need: Out of 419 full-time freshmen who applied for aid, 340 were judged to have need. Of these, 340 received aid, and 167 had their full need met. Average financial aid package met 93% of need; average scholarship/grant was $17,550; average loan was $4,540. Need-based aid available for part-time students.

Students without need: 160 full-time freshmen who did not demonstrate need for aid received scholarships/grants; average award was $10,685. No-need awards available for academics, art, leadership, music/drama, ROTC.

Scholarships offered: Regents/Trustees Scholarship: $15,000; minimum 3.6 GPA, 30 ACT, 1980 SAT, demonstrated leadership and service, faculty interview. President's Scholarship: $10,000-$12,500. Dean's Scholarships: $3,000-$9,500; GPA, high school rank, ACT/SAT scores, leadership and service. Art, Music, and Theater Scholarships: up to $4,000; excellence in these subjects in high school; portfolio; tape; audition. Diversity Leadership Scholarships: up to $5,000; demonstrated diversity leadership and service in the area of cultural and ethnic diversity; personal statement on topic. Army ROTC and ROTC Nursing Scholarships: $28,000; demonstrated leadership potential; high school GPA, class standing, ACT/SAT scores; high achievement with broad interests and willingness to take on challenges. Phi Theta Kappa Scholarship: $1,000; member of Phi Theta Kappa (transfer students only).

FINANCIAL AID PROCEDURES

Forms required: FAFSA, institutional form.

Dates and Deadlines: Priority date 3/15; no closing date. Applicants notified on a rolling basis starting 3/15; must reply by 5/1.

CONTACT

Jane Haugen, Executive Director of Financial Aid
PO Box 7155, Collegeville, MN 56321-7155
(320) 363-5388

College of St. Catherine

St. Paul, Minnesota
www.stkate.edu Federal Code: 002342

4-year private health science and liberal arts college for women in large city, affiliated with Roman Catholic Church.

Enrollment: 3,636 undergrads, 34% part-time. 423 full-time freshmen.

Selectivity: Admits over 75% of applicants.

BASIC COSTS (2009-2010)

Tuition and fees: $27,078.

Per-credit charge: $890.

Room and board: $7,330.

FINANCIAL AID PICTURE (2007-2008)

Students with need: Need-based aid available for full-time and part-time students. Work study available nights, weekends, and for part-time students.

Students without need: No-need awards available for academics, alumni affiliation, leadership.

Scholarships offered: St. Catherine of Alexandria Merit Scholarships: $2,000-$6,000; high school seniors in top 15% of class, evidence of academic preparation, outstanding leadership abilities, involvement in extracurricular activities and community service; renewable for 3 years.

Additional info: Audition required for music scholarships.

FINANCIAL AID PROCEDURES

Forms required: FAFSA, institutional form.

Dates and Deadlines: Priority date 4/15; no closing date. Applicants notified on a rolling basis starting 3/30; must reply within 2 week(s) of notification.

CONTACT

Elizabeth Stevens, Director of Financial Aid
2004 Randolph Avenue #4-02, St. Paul, MN 55105
(651) 690-6540

College of St. Scholastica

Duluth, Minnesota
www.css.edu Federal Code: 002343

4-year private liberal arts college in small city, affiliated with Roman Catholic Church.

Enrollment: 2,138 undergrads, 2% part-time. 534 full-time freshmen.

Selectivity: Admits over 75% of applicants.

BASIC COSTS (2009-2010)

Tuition and fees: $27,284.

Per-credit charge: $844.

Room and board: $7,278.

Additional info: Tuition/fee waivers available for minority students.

FINANCIAL AID PICTURE (2008-2009)

Students with need: Average financial aid package met 78% of need; average scholarship/grant was $6,458; average loan was $3,122. For part-time students, average financial aid package was $9,994.

Students without need: No-need awards available for academics, alumni affiliation, ROTC.

Scholarships offered: Benedictine Scholarship: $4,000-$12,500 per year for up to 4 years. Opportunity Grants: $6,500. Both based on GPA, SAT/ACT score; unlimited number awarded. Divisional Merit Awards: $4,000; available to transfer students; based on major; unlimited number awarded.

Cumulative student debt: 78% of graduating class had student loans; average debt was $36,075.

FINANCIAL AID PROCEDURES

Forms required: FAFSA.

Dates and Deadlines: Priority date 3/15; no closing date. Applicants notified on a rolling basis starting 3/1; must reply by 5/1 or within 2 week(s) of notification.

CONTACT

Jon Erickson, Director of Financial Aid
1200 Kenwood Avenue, Duluth, MN 55811-4199
(218) 723-6047

College of Visual Arts

Saint Paul, Minnesota
www.cva.edu Federal Code: 007462

4-year private visual arts college in large city.
Enrollment: 186 undergrads, 3% part-time. 49 full-time freshmen.
Selectivity: Admits 50 to 75% of applicants.

BASIC COSTS (2008-2009)

Tuition and fees: $22,426.

FINANCIAL AID PICTURE (2008-2009)

Students with need: For part-time students, average financial aid package was $9,658.
Students without need: No-need awards available for academics, art.
Scholarships offered: Merit scholarship program provides annual awards ranging from $2,000 to $8,000; stipends are based on artistic and academic merit, as well as on overall strength of scholarship and admissions application; designed for prospective full-time first-year and transfer students.
Cumulative student debt: 95% of graduating class had student loans; average debt was $46,000.

FINANCIAL AID PROCEDURES

Forms required: FAFSA, institutional form.
Dates and Deadlines: Priority date 3/1; no closing date. Applicants notified on a rolling basis starting 2/15; must reply within 2 week(s) of notification.
Transfers: Priority date 4/1. Applicants notified on a rolling basis starting 3/1; must reply within 2 week(s) of notification.

CONTACT

Susan Ant, Executive Director of Enrollment
344 Summit Avenue, Saint Paul, MN 55102-2199
(651) 757-4020

Concordia College: Moorhead

Moorhead, Minnesota
www.concordiacollege.edu Federal Code: 002346

4-year private liberal arts college in small city, affiliated with Evangelical Lutheran Church in America.
Enrollment: 2,745 undergrads, 1% part-time. 825 full-time freshmen.
Selectivity: Admits over 75% of applicants.

BASIC COSTS (2009-2010)

Tuition and fees: $25,760.
Room and board: $6,276.

FINANCIAL AID PICTURE (2007-2008)

Students with need: Out of 721 full-time freshmen who applied for aid, 567 were judged to have need. Of these, 567 received aid, and 220 had their full need met. Average financial aid package met 91% of need; average scholarship/grant was $13,156; average loan was $4,046. For part-time students, average financial aid package was $17,952.
Students without need: This college awards aid only to students with need.
Scholarships offered: Concordia National Merit Scholarship: $10,000 per year for 4 years; for National Merit Scholarship finalists listing Concordia as their first choice. Soli Deo Gloria Scholarship: $12,000 per year for 4 years; based on test scores, class rank or GPA, essay and interview. Faculty Scholarships: $8,000 per year for 4 years; based on test scores, class rank or GPA, essay, and faculty interview. Excellence Scholarships: $5,000-$7,000 per year for 4 years; based on test scores, class rank or GPA, essay, and faculty interview. Performing Arts Scholarships: $1,500-$3,500 per year for 4 years; available in music drama, forensics.
Additional info: Students in ACCORD program (age 25 and older) may apply for tuition reductions for first 4 courses.

FINANCIAL AID PROCEDURES

Forms required: FAFSA, institutional form.
Dates and Deadlines: Priority date 4/15; no closing date. Applicants notified on a rolling basis starting 3/1.

CONTACT

Jane Williams, Director of Financial Aid
901 Eighth Street South, Moorhead, MN 56562-9981
(218) 299-3010

Concordia University: St. Paul

St. Paul, Minnesota
www.csp.edu Federal Code: 002347

4-year private university in large city, affiliated with Lutheran Church - Missouri Synod.
Enrollment: 1,420 undergrads, 8% part-time. 211 full-time freshmen.
Selectivity: Admits 50 to 75% of applicants.

BASIC COSTS (2009-2010)

Tuition and fees: $26,400.
Per-credit charge: $550.
Room and board: $7,250.
Additional info: Adult learners in degree completion programs have discounted tuition rates based on cost per credit. Rates vary by program.

FINANCIAL AID PICTURE (2008-2009)

Students with need: Out of 209 full-time freshmen who applied for aid, 175 were judged to have need. Of these, 175 received aid, and 37 had their full need met. Average financial aid package met 79% of need; average scholarship/grant was $15,085; average loan was $4,408. For part-time students, average financial aid package was $7,775.
Students without need: 34 full-time freshmen who did not demonstrate need for aid received scholarships/grants; average award was $9,015. No-need awards available for academics, art, athletics, minority status, music/drama, religious affiliation.
Scholarships offered: 9 full-time freshmen received athletic scholarships; average amount $10,228.
Cumulative student debt: 86% of graduating class had student loans; average debt was $33,775.
Additional info: Church districts and local congregations are major sources of aid for church-vocation students.

FINANCIAL AID PROCEDURES

Forms required: FAFSA, institutional form.
Dates and Deadlines: Priority date 5/1; no closing date. Applicants notified on a rolling basis starting 3/1; must reply within 3 week(s) of notification.
Transfers: Adult learners in degree completion programs are typically not eligible for institutional scholarships/grants because of discounted tuition rates.

CONTACT

Carolyn Chesebrough, Director of Financial Aid
275 Syndicate Street North, St. Paul, MN 55104-5494
(651) 603-6300

Crossroads College
Rochester, Minnesota
www.crossroadscollege.edu Federal Code: 002366

4-year private Bible college in small city, affiliated with Christian Church.
Enrollment: 148 undergrads, 14% part-time. 14 full-time freshmen.
Selectivity: Admits 50 to 75% of applicants.

BASIC COSTS (2009-2010)
Tuition and fees: $14,290.
Per-credit charge: $398.
Room only: $3,950.

FINANCIAL AID PICTURE (2008-2009)
Students with need: Need-based aid available for full-time and part-time students. Work study available nights.
Students without need: No-need awards available for academics, leadership, music/drama, religious affiliation.
Scholarships offered: Home-Educated Grant: $500 per semester if homeschooled for two years during high school. Travel Grant: $500 per semester for student who resides in states other than Minnesota, Iowa, Wisconsin. Crossroads Matching Grant: church funds matched up to $500 per semester; awarded to first year students.

FINANCIAL AID PROCEDURES
Forms required: FAFSA, institutional form.
Dates and Deadlines: Priority date 4/1; no closing date. Applicants notified on a rolling basis starting 2/1; must reply within 4 week(s) of notification.
Transfers: Mid-year transfer students will have financial aid calculated with the prior school term award in mind.

CONTACT
Polly Kellogg-Bradley, Director of Financial Aid
920 Mayowood Road, SW, Rochester, MN 55902
(507) 288-4563

Crown College
St. Bonifacius, Minnesota
www.crown.edu Federal Code: 002383

4-year private Bible and liberal arts college in small town, affiliated with Christian and Missionary Alliance.
Enrollment: 955 undergrads. 168 full-time freshmen.

BASIC COSTS (2009-2010)
Tuition and fees: $19,870.
Per-credit charge: $823.
Room and board: $6,986.
Additional info: Tuition/fee waivers available for minority students.

FINANCIAL AID PICTURE (2008-2009)
Students with need: Average financial aid package met 67% of need; average scholarship/grant was $5,799; average loan was $3,871. For part-time students, average financial aid package was $7,225.
Students without need: No-need awards available for academics, alumni affiliation, leadership, minority status, music/drama, religious affiliation.
Cumulative student debt: 89% of graduating class had student loans; average debt was $31,421.

FINANCIAL AID PROCEDURES
Forms required: FAFSA, institutional form.
Dates and Deadlines: Priority date 4/1; closing date 8/1. Applicants notified on a rolling basis starting 4/1; must reply within 3 week(s) of notification.
Transfers: No deadline. Applicants notified on a rolling basis; must reply within 3 week(s) of notification. Cannot have attended more than 4 years of college to receive state grant.

CONTACT
Judy Bedford, Director of Financial Aid
8700 College View Drive, St. Bonifacius, MN 55375-9001
(952) 446-4177

Dakota County Technical College
Rosemount, Minnesota
www.dctc.edu Federal Code: 010402

2-year public technical college in large town.
Enrollment: 2,393 undergrads, 38% part-time. 676 full-time freshmen.
Selectivity: Open admission; but selective for some programs.

BASIC COSTS (2008-2009)
Tuition and fees: $4,909; out-of-state residents $9,239.
Per-credit charge: $144; out-of-state residents $289.

FINANCIAL AID PICTURE
Students with need: Need-based aid available for full-time and part-time students. Work study available nights, weekends, and for part-time students.
Students without need: No-need awards available for academics, leadership.
Scholarships offered: Dakota County Techical College scholarship.

FINANCIAL AID PROCEDURES
Forms required: FAFSA.
Dates and Deadlines: No deadline. Applicants notified on a rolling basis starting 3/15.
Transfers: No deadline. FAFSA must be processed within 14 days of the first day of the semester to be considered for Minnesota State Grant for the semester.

CONTACT
Scott Roelke, Director of Scholarships and Financial Aid
1300 145th Street East, Rosemount, MN 55068
(651) 423-8299

DeVry University: Edina
Edina, Minnesota
www.devry.edu

4-year for-profit university in large town.
Enrollment: 188 undergrads, 65% part-time. 6 full-time freshmen.

BASIC COSTS (2008-2009)
Tuition and fees: $13,930.
Per-credit charge: $515.

FINANCIAL AID PICTURE (2007-2008)
Students with need: Out of 1 full-time freshmen who applied for aid, 1 were judged to have need. Of these, 1 received aid. Average financial aid package met 33% of need; average scholarship/grant was $5,910; average loan was $3,500. For part-time students, average financial aid package was $9,891.
Students without need: 1 full-time freshmen who did not demonstrate need for aid received scholarships/grants; average award was $2,820. No-need awards available for academics.

FINANCIAL AID PROCEDURES
Forms required: FAFSA.
Dates and Deadlines: No deadline. Applicants notified on a rolling basis.

CONTACT
7700 France Avenue South, Suite 575, Edina, MN 55435

Dunwoody College of Technology

Minneapolis, Minnesota
www.dunwoody.edu Federal Code: 004641

2-year private technical college in very large city.
Enrollment: 1,571 undergrads.

BASIC COSTS (2008-2009)
Tuition and fees: $13,931.
Per-credit charge: $183.

FINANCIAL AID PICTURE (2007-2008)
Students with need: Need-based aid available for full-time and part-time students.
Students without need: No-need awards available for academics.

FINANCIAL AID PROCEDURES
Forms required: FAFSA, state aid form.
Dates and Deadlines: Priority date 6/1; no closing date. Applicants notified on a rolling basis starting 2/1; must reply within 4 week(s) of notification.

CONTACT
Barb Charboneau, Director of Financial Aid
818 Dunwoody Boulevard, Minneapolis, MN 55403-1192
(612) 374-5800 ext. 3346

Fond du Lac Tribal and Community College

Cloquet, Minnesota
www.fdltcc.edu Federal Code: E00482

2-year public community college in large town.
Enrollment: 767 full-time undergrads.
Selectivity: Open admission.

BASIC COSTS (2008-2009)
Tuition and fees: $4,440; out-of-state residents $8,428.
Per-credit charge: $133; out-of-state residents $266.

FINANCIAL AID PICTURE
Students with need: Need-based aid available for full-time and part-time students.
Students without need: No-need awards available for academics.

FINANCIAL AID PROCEDURES
Forms required: FAFSA, institutional form.
Dates and Deadlines: Priority date 3/15; no closing date. Applicants notified on a rolling basis starting 4/15.

CONTACT
David Sutherland, Director of Financial Aid
2101 14th Street, Cloquet, MN 55720
(218) 879-0816

Globe University

Woodbury, Minnesota
www.globeuniversity.edu Federal Code: 004642

4-year for-profit business and health science college in small city.
Enrollment: 769 undergrads.
Selectivity: Open admission.

BASIC COSTS (2008-2009)
Tuition and fees: $17,550.
Per-credit charge: $390.

FINANCIAL AID PICTURE (2008-2009)
Students with need: Need-based aid available for full-time and part-time students.

FINANCIAL AID PROCEDURES
Forms required: FAFSA, institutional form.
Dates and Deadlines: No deadline. Applicants notified on a rolling basis starting 5/1.

CONTACT
Tina Kukowski, Director of Financial Aid
8089 Globe Drive, Woodbury, MN 55125
(651) 730-5100

Gustavus Adolphus College

St. Peter, Minnesota Federal Code: 002353
www.gustavus.edu CSS Code: 6253

4-year private liberal arts college in small town, affiliated with Evangelical Lutheran Church in America.
Enrollment: 2,515 undergrads. 631 full-time freshmen.
Selectivity: Admits 50 to 75% of applicants.

BASIC COSTS (2009-2010)
Tuition and fees: $32,080.
Room and board: $7,910.

FINANCIAL AID PICTURE (2008-2009)
Students with need: Out of 526 full-time freshmen who applied for aid, 441 were judged to have need. Of these, 441 received aid, and 200 had their full need met. Average financial aid package met 94% of need; average scholarship/grant was $9,815; average loan was $3,352.
Students without need: 189 full-time freshmen who did not demonstrate need for aid received scholarships/grants; average award was $8,095. No-need awards available for academics, alumni affiliation, art, music/drama, religious affiliation, ROTC.
Scholarships offered: Presidential Scholarship: $10,000-$14,000. National Merit finalist: $7,500; academic. Legacy Scholarship: $2,500; academic for children or siblings of alumni. Jussi Bjorling Scholarship: $1,000-$4,000; for music; 40 awarded. Anderson Theatre and Dance Scholarship: $2,000; 15 awarded. Dean's Scholarship: $1,000-$10,000; Forensic $500 - $2,000.
Cumulative student debt: 70% of graduating class had student loans; average debt was $24,297.

FINANCIAL AID PROCEDURES
Forms required: FAFSA. CSS PROFILE required of students applying for need-based assistance.
Dates and Deadlines: Priority date 2/15; closing date 4/15. Applicants notified on a rolling basis starting 12/20; must reply by 5/1 or within 2 week(s) of notification.
Transfers: Applicants notified on a rolling basis starting 12/20; must reply by 5/1 or within 2 week(s) of notification.

CONTACT
Doug Minter, Director of Student Financial Assistance
800 West College Avenue, St. Peter, MN 56082
(507) 933-7527

Hamline University

St. Paul, Minnesota
www.hamline.edu Federal Code: 002354

4-year private university and liberal arts college in very large city, affiliated with United Methodist Church.
Enrollment: 1,957 undergrads, 2% part-time. 455 full-time freshmen.
Selectivity: Admits over 75% of applicants.

BASIC COSTS (2008-2009)
Tuition and fees: $28,143.
Per-credit charge: $863.
Room and board: $7,784.
Additional info: All new students must pay $30 transcript fee.

FINANCIAL AID PICTURE (2007-2008)
Students with need: Out of 406 full-time freshmen who applied for aid, 337 were judged to have need. Of these, 336 received aid, and 77 had their full need met. Average financial aid package met 83% of need; average scholarship/grant was $14,096; average loan was $4,459. For part-time students, average financial aid package was $5,106.
Students without need: No-need awards available for academics, alumni affiliation, art, job skills, leadership, minority status, music/drama, religious affiliation, state/district residency.
Scholarships offered: Presidential Scholarship: $12,000 to full tuition; for students with excellent academic ability, strong sense of motivation. Hamline Honors Scholarship: $12,000; for students with successful academic record, involvement in school and community activities. Hamline Trustee Scholarship: $5,500; for new first-year students who have excelled academically. Departmental scholarships in biology, chemistry, French, German, music, physics, theater, creative writing: $3,000-$4,000 depending on department. National Merit Scholarship: full tuition. Diversity scholarships: $3,000. Eagle Scout or Gold Award Scholarships: amount varies. All scholarships renewable for a total of four years.
Cumulative student debt: 79% of graduating class had student loans; average debt was $31,577.

FINANCIAL AID PROCEDURES
Forms required: FAFSA.
Dates and Deadlines: Priority date 3/1; no closing date. Applicants notified on a rolling basis starting 3/1; must reply within 2 week(s) of notification.
Transfers: Priority date 4/1; no deadline. Applicants notified on a rolling basis; must reply within 2 week(s) of notification. Students who qualify for Minnesota State Grant must carry 15 semester credits to qualify for full grant each semester. If less credit is carried, grant prorated.

CONTACT
Lynette Wahl, Director of Financial Aid
1536 Hewitt Avenue, St. Paul, MN 55104-1284
(651) 523-3000

Inver Hills Community College
Inver Grove Heights, Minnesota
www.inverhills.edu Federal Code: 006935

2-year public community college in large town.
Enrollment: 4,409 undergrads, 58% part-time. 507 full-time freshmen.
Selectivity: Open admission; but selective for some programs.

BASIC COSTS (2008-2009)
Tuition and fees: $4,655.
Per-credit charge: $140.
Additional info: In-state and out-of-state tuition rates are the same.

FINANCIAL AID PICTURE (2008-2009)
Students with need: Need-based aid available for full-time and part-time students. Work study available nights, weekends, and for part-time students.
Students without need: This college awards aid only to students with need.

FINANCIAL AID PROCEDURES
Forms required: FAFSA.
Dates and Deadlines: No deadline. Applicants notified on a rolling basis starting 6/1.
Transfers: No deadline. Applicants notified on a rolling basis.

CONTACT
John Pogue, Financial Aid Officer
2500 80th Street East, Inver Grove Heights, MN 55076-3224
(651) 450-8518

Itasca Community College
Grand Rapids, Minnesota
www.itascacc.edu Federal Code: 002356

2-year public junior and liberal arts college in large town.
Enrollment: 966 undergrads, 22% part-time. 264 full-time freshmen.
Selectivity: Open admission.

BASIC COSTS (2008-2009)
Tuition and fees: $4,489; out-of-state residents $5,476.
Per-credit charge: $132; out-of-state residents $164.

FINANCIAL AID PICTURE (2007-2008)
Students with need: 60% of average financial aid package awarded as scholarships/grants, 40% awarded as loans/jobs. Need-based aid available for part-time students. Work study available nights, weekends, and for part-time students.
Students without need: No-need awards available for academics, leadership, music/drama, state/district residency.

FINANCIAL AID PROCEDURES
Forms required: FAFSA.
Dates and Deadlines: Priority date 5/1; no closing date. Applicants notified on a rolling basis starting 4/1.
Transfers: Applicants notified on a rolling basis starting 4/1.

CONTACT
Nathan Wright, Director of Financial Aid
1851 Highway 169 East, Grand Rapids, MN 55744
(218) 322-2320

Lake Superior College
Duluth, Minnesota
www.lsc.edu Federal Code: 005757

2-year public community and technical college in small city.
Enrollment: 3,516 undergrads, 37% part-time. 760 full-time freshmen.
Selectivity: Open admission; but selective for some programs.

BASIC COSTS (2008-2009)
Tuition and fees: $4,261; out-of-state residents $7,921.
Per-credit charge: $122; out-of-state residents $244.

FINANCIAL AID PICTURE (2007-2008)
Students with need: For part-time students, average financial aid package was $1,626.
Students without need: No-need awards available for academics, leadership.

FINANCIAL AID PROCEDURES
Forms required: FAFSA.
Dates and Deadlines: Priority date 5/1; no closing date. Applicants notified on a rolling basis starting 5/1.
Transfers: No deadline.

CONTACT
Sandra Olin, Director of Financial Aid
2101 Trinity Road, Duluth, MN 55811
(218) 733-7601

Leech Lake Tribal College

Cass Lake, Minnesota
www.lltc.edu Federal Code: 030964

2-year public Tribal college grounded in Anishinaabe knowledge and culture in small town.
Enrollment: 216 undergrads.
Selectivity: Open admission.

BASIC COSTS (2008-2009)
Tuition and fees: $3,980.
Per-credit charge: $125.

FINANCIAL AID PICTURE
Students with need: Need-based aid available for full-time and part-time students.
Students without need: This college awards aid only to students with need.

FINANCIAL AID PROCEDURES
Forms required: FAFSA.
Dates and Deadlines: Closing date 6/30.

CONTACT
Barbara Carlson, Director of Financial Aid
PO Box 180, Cass Lake, MN 56633
(218) 335-4224

Macalester College

St. Paul, Minnesota Federal Code: 002358
www.macalester.edu CSS Code: 6390

4-year private liberal arts college in large city, affiliated with Presbyterian Church (USA).
Enrollment: 1,871 undergrads, 1% part-time. 479 full-time freshmen.
Selectivity: Admits less than 50% of applicants.

BASIC COSTS (2008-2009)
Tuition and fees: $36,504.
Per-credit charge: $1,135.
Room and board: $8,472.

FINANCIAL AID PICTURE (2008-2009)
Students with need: Out of 359 full-time freshmen who applied for aid, 305 were judged to have need. Of these, 305 received aid, and 305 had their full need met. Average financial aid package met 100% of need; average scholarship/grant was $26,361; average loan was $2,276. For part-time students, average financial aid package was $10,431.
Students without need: 20 full-time freshmen who did not demonstrate need for aid received scholarships/grants; average award was $4,038. No-need awards available for academics, minority status.
Scholarships offered: National Merit Scholarships: $5,000; to National Merit Finalists whose first choice college is Macalester. DeWitt Wallace Distinguished Scholarships: minimum $3,000; open to National Merit semifinalists, commended students, and finalists not awarded National Merit Scholarship. DeWitt Wallace Scholarships: minimum $3,000; to selected middle-income students with need and academic records worthy of recognition. Catherine Lealtad Scholarships: minimum $3,000; to African American, Latino, and Native American students with strong high school records. Students who are National Achievement or National Hispanic Scholarship finalists with strong high school record will receive a minimum annual award of $5,000.
Additional info: College meets full need for all admitted students. Minnesota Self Loan available to qualified students.

FINANCIAL AID PROCEDURES
Forms required: FAFSA, CSS PROFILE.
Dates and Deadlines: Priority date 2/8; closing date 3/1. Applicants notified by 4/1; must reply by 5/1 or within 1 week(s) of notification.
Transfers: Applicants notified by 5/15; must reply within 2 week(s) of notification.

CONTACT
Brian Lindeman, Director of Financial Aid
1600 Grand Avenue, St. Paul, MN 55105-1899
(651) 696-6214

Martin Luther College

New Ulm, Minnesota
www.mlc-wels.edu Federal Code: 002361

4-year private college of theology and education in large town, affiliated with Wisconsin Evangelical Lutheran Synod.
Enrollment: 770 undergrads, 8% part-time. 179 full-time freshmen.

BASIC COSTS (2009-2010)
Tuition and fees: $10,660.
Per-credit charge: $220.
Room and board: $4,140.

FINANCIAL AID PICTURE (2007-2008)
Students with need: Out of 168 full-time freshmen who applied for aid, 134 were judged to have need. Of these, 134 received aid, and 40 had their full need met. Average financial aid package met 60% of need; average scholarship/grant was $4,034; average loan was $3,748. Need-based aid available for part-time students.
Students without need: 23 full-time freshmen who did not demonstrate need for aid received scholarships/grants; average award was $1,478. No-need awards available for academics, music/drama, religious affiliation.
Scholarships offered: Academic Scholarship: $500; 3.75 GPA after 6 semesters of high school or 27 ACT. Presidential Scholarship: $1,000; to student selected as high school valedictorian or ranked first in class after 7 semesters.
Cumulative student debt: 46% of graduating class had student loans; average debt was $15,151.

FINANCIAL AID PROCEDURES
Forms required: FAFSA, institutional form.
Dates and Deadlines: Priority date 4/15; closing date 9/30. Applicants notified by 3/1.

CONTACT
Gene Slettedahl, Director of Financial Aid
1995 Luther Court, New Ulm, MN 56073-3965
(507) 354-8221

Mesabi Range Community and Technical College

Virginia, Minnesota
www.mr.mnscu.edu Federal Code: 004009

2-year public community and technical college in large town.
Enrollment: 913 full-time undergrads.
Selectivity: Open admission.

BASIC COSTS (2008-2009)
Tuition and fees: $4,481; out-of-state residents $5,468.
Per-credit charge: $132; out-of-state residents $164.

FINANCIAL AID PICTURE (2008-2009)
Students with need: Need-based aid available for full-time and part-time students. Work study available nights, weekends, and for part-time students.

Students without need: No-need awards available for state/district residency.

FINANCIAL AID PROCEDURES

Forms required: FAFSA, institutional form.

Dates and Deadlines: Priority date 4/22; no closing date. Applicants notified on a rolling basis starting 5/1; must reply within 2 week(s) of notification.

CONTACT

George Walters, Director of Financial Aid
1001 Chestnut Street West, Virginia, MN 55792-3448
(218) 741-3095

Metropolitan State University

St. Paul, Minnesota
www.metrostate.edu Federal Code: 010374

4-year public university in very large city.

Enrollment: 5,880 undergrads, 63% part-time. 50 full-time freshmen.

BASIC COSTS (2008-2009)

Tuition and fees: $5,473; out-of-state residents $10,633.

Per-credit charge: $172; out-of-state residents $344.

FINANCIAL AID PICTURE (2008-2009)

Students with need: Need-based aid available for full-time and part-time students. Work study available nights, weekends, and for part-time students.

Students without need: No-need awards available for academics, leadership, minority status, state/district residency.

FINANCIAL AID PROCEDURES

Forms required: FAFSA.

Dates and Deadlines: Priority date 5/1; no closing date. Applicants notified on a rolling basis starting 5/1; must reply within 2 week(s) of notification.

CONTACT

Robert Bode, Director of Financial Aid
700 East Seventh Street, St. Paul, MN 55106-5000
(651) 793-1414

Minneapolis College of Art and Design

Minneapolis, Minnesota
www.mcad.edu Federal Code: 002365

4-year private visual arts college in very large city.

Enrollment: 678 undergrads, 4% part-time. 103 full-time freshmen.

Selectivity: Admits 50 to 75% of applicants.

BASIC COSTS (2008-2009)

Tuition and fees: $29,300.

Per-credit charge: $940.

Room only: $4,160.

Additional info: Housing costs vary; figure quoted is for double-occupancy (furnished) one-bedroom apartment. Required fees include $900 laptop computer that freshmen must purchase.

FINANCIAL AID PICTURE (2008-2009)

Students with need: Need-based aid available for full-time and part-time students.

Students without need: No-need awards available for academics, alumni affiliation, art.

Scholarships offered: Admissions Merit Scholarships: $6,000-$14,000; based on admissions file. Students admitted to the college by February 15 automatically entered into scholarship competition.

FINANCIAL AID PROCEDURES

Forms required: FAFSA.

Dates and Deadlines: Priority date 3/15; closing date 3/15. Applicants notified on a rolling basis starting 4/1; must reply by 5/1 or within 2 week(s) of notification.

Transfers: Applicants notified by 4/1; must reply by 5/1 or within 2 week(s) of notification. Transfer students apply for admission to MCAD by Feb. 15 (the scholarship priority deadline). Only students accepted by MCAD will receive an award letter. However, we encourage you to apply for admission and financial aid simultaneously. Complete the FAFSA by March 15. Be sure to include MCAD on the list of schools to receive your FAFSA analysis (MCAD code: 002365).

CONTACT

Laura Link, Director, Financial Aid Office
2501 Stevens Avenue, Minneapolis, MN 55404
(612) 874-8782

Minneapolis Community and Technical College

Minneapolis, Minnesota
www.minneapolis.edu Federal Code: 002362

2-year public community and technical college in large city.

Enrollment: 9,539 undergrads.

Selectivity: Open admission; but selective for some programs.

BASIC COSTS (2008-2009)

Tuition and fees: $4,532.

Per-credit charge: $138.

Additional info: In-state and out-of-state tuition rates are the same.

FINANCIAL AID PICTURE (2007-2008)

Students with need: Need-based aid available for full-time and part-time students. Work study available nights, weekends, and for part-time students.

Students without need: This college awards aid only to students with need.

FINANCIAL AID PROCEDURES

Forms required: FAFSA.

Dates and Deadlines: Priority date 6/1; no closing date. Applicants notified on a rolling basis starting 7/15; must reply within 2 week(s) of notification.

CONTACT

Angela Christensen, Director of Financial Aid
1501 Hennepin Avenue, Minneapolis, MN 55403-1779
(612) 659-6240

Minnesota School of Business

Minneapolis, Minnesota
www.msbcollege.edu Federal Code: 017145

4-year for-profit business and technical college in very large city.

Enrollment: 444 full-time undergrads.

BASIC COSTS (2008-2009)

Tuition and fees: $18,770.

Per-credit charge: $390.

FINANCIAL AID PICTURE (2008-2009)

Students with need: Need-based aid available for full-time and part-time students.

FINANCIAL AID PROCEDURES

Forms required: FAFSA, state aid form, institutional form.

Dates and Deadlines: No deadline. Applicants notified on a rolling basis starting 7/1; must reply within 2 week(s) of notification.

CONTACT
Financial Aid Director
1401 West 76 Street, Suite 500, Richfield, MN 55423
(612) 861-2000

Minnesota School of Business: Brooklyn Center
Brooklyn Center, Minnesota
www.msbcollege.edu Federal Code: 004646

2-year for-profit business college in large town.
Enrollment: 347 full-time undergrads.

BASIC COSTS (2008-2009)
Tuition and fees: $18,770.
Per-credit charge: $390.

FINANCIAL AID PICTURE (2008-2009)
Students with need: Need-based aid available for full-time and part-time students.
Students without need: This college awards aid only to students with need.

FINANCIAL AID PROCEDURES
Forms required: FAFSA.

CONTACT
Kari Zakariasen, Director of Financial Aid
5910 Shingle Creek Parkway, Brooklyn Center, MN 55430
(763) 566-7777

Minnesota School of Business: St. Cloud
Waite Park, Minnesota
www.msbcollege.edu

4-year for-profit virtual university in small city.
Enrollment: 953 undergrads.
Selectivity: Admits over 75% of applicants.

BASIC COSTS (2008-2009)
Tuition and fees: $18,770.
Per-credit charge: $390.

FINANCIAL AID PICTURE (2008-2009)
Students with need: Need-based aid available for full-time and part-time students.

CONTACT
Renee Cannon, Director of Financial Aid
1201 Second Street South, Waite Park, MN 55387

Minnesota State College - Southeast Technical
Winona, Minnesota
www.southeastmn.edu Federal Code: 002393

2-year public technical college in large town.
Enrollment: 1,874 undergrads, 40% part-time. 454 full-time freshmen.
Selectivity: Open admission; but selective for some programs.

BASIC COSTS (2008-2009)
Tuition and fees: $4,584; out-of-state residents $8,812.
Per-credit charge: $141; out-of-state residents $282.

FINANCIAL AID PICTURE (2007-2008)
Students with need: Need-based aid available for full-time and part-time students.
Students without need: No-need awards available for academics, leadership.

FINANCIAL AID PROCEDURES
Forms required: FAFSA, state aid form, institutional form.
Dates and Deadlines: Priority date 5/15; closing date 6/30. Applicants notified on a rolling basis; must reply within 3 week(s) of notification.
Transfers: Applicants notified on a rolling basis; must reply within 3 week(s) of notification. Mid-year transfer application forms must be accompanied by financial aid transcript.

CONTACT
Anne Dahlen, Director of Financial Aid
1250 Homer Road, Winona, MN 55987-0409
(507) 453-2710

Minnesota State Community and Technical College
Fergus Falls, Minnesota
www.minnesota.edu Federal Code: 002352

2-year public community and technical college in large town.
Enrollment: 3,228 full-time undergrads.
Selectivity: Open admission.

BASIC COSTS (2008-2009)
Tuition and fees: $4,876.
Per-credit charge: $141.
Room only: $2,450.
Additional info: Tuition/fee waivers available for adults.

FINANCIAL AID PICTURE
Students with need: Need-based aid available for full-time and part-time students. Work study available nights, weekends, and for part-time students.
Students without need: No-need awards available for academics, art, leadership, minority status, music/drama, state/district residency.
Scholarships offered: Academic and leadership scholarships: $400-$1,000 each; available to 1st and 2nd year students; over 150 awarded annually.

FINANCIAL AID PROCEDURES
Forms required: FAFSA, institutional form.
Dates and Deadlines: Priority date 6/1; no closing date. Applicants notified on a rolling basis starting 7/1.
Transfers: No deadline. Applicants notified on a rolling basis.

CONTACT
Tom Whelihan, Director of Financial Aid
1414 College Way, Fergus Falls, MN 56537-1000
(218) 736-1534

Minnesota State University: Mankato
Mankato, Minnesota
www.mnsu.edu Federal Code: 002360

4-year public university in large town.
Enrollment: 12,251 undergrads, 7% part-time. 2,344 full-time freshmen.
Selectivity: Admits 50 to 75% of applicants.

BASIC COSTS (2008-2009)
Tuition and fees: $6,263; out-of-state residents $12,508.
Per-credit charge: $219; out-of-state residents $467.
Room and board: $5,665.

FINANCIAL AID PICTURE (2007-2008)

Students with need: Out of 1,922 full-time freshmen who applied for aid, 1,215 were judged to have need. Of these, 1,215 received aid, and 502 had their full need met. Average financial aid package met 71% of need; average scholarship/grant was $4,506; average loan was $3,020. For part-time students, average financial aid package was $5,669.

Students without need: 201 full-time freshmen who did not demonstrate need for aid received scholarships/grants; average award was $2,320. No-need awards available for academics, art, athletics, leadership, minority status, music/drama.

Scholarships offered: 112 full-time freshmen received athletic scholarships; average amount $3,746.

Cumulative student debt: 74% of graduating class had student loans; average debt was $22,115.

FINANCIAL AID PROCEDURES

Forms required: FAFSA.

Dates and Deadlines: Priority date 3/15; no closing date. Applicants notified on a rolling basis starting 3/30; must reply within 2 week(s) of notification.

CONTACT

Sandra Loerts, Director of Financial Aid
122 Taylor Center, Mankato, MN 56001
(507) 389-1185

Minnesota State University: Moorhead

Moorhead, Minnesota
www.mnstate.edu Federal Code: 002367

4-year public university in small city.
Enrollment: 6,730 undergrads.
Selectivity: Admits over 75% of applicants.

BASIC COSTS (2008-2009)

Tuition and fees: $6,142.
Per-credit charge: $175.
Room and board: $5,936.
Additional info: Out-of-state students pay same rate as in-state.

FINANCIAL AID PICTURE (2008-2009)

Students with need: Need-based aid available for full-time and part-time students.

Students without need: No-need awards available for academics, art, athletics, leadership, music/drama, state/district residency.

FINANCIAL AID PROCEDURES

Forms required: FAFSA.

Dates and Deadlines: Priority date 2/15; no closing date. Applicants notified on a rolling basis starting 6/1; must reply within 2 week(s) of notification.

CONTACT

Carolyn Zehren, Director of Financial Aid and Scholarships
Owens Hall, Moorhead, MN 56563
(218) 236-2251

Minnesota West Community and Technical College

Pipestone, Minnesota
www.mnwest.edu Federal Code: 005263

2-year public community and technical college in large town.
Enrollment: 2,630 undergrads.
Selectivity: Open admission.

BASIC COSTS (2008-2009)

Tuition and fees: $4,807.
Per-credit charge: $144.
Additional info: In-state and out-of-state tuition rates are the same.

FINANCIAL AID PICTURE (2008-2009)

Students with need: 48% of average financial aid package awarded as scholarships/grants, 52% awarded as loans/jobs. Need-based aid available for part-time students. Work study available nights, weekends, and for part-time students.

FINANCIAL AID PROCEDURES

Forms required: FAFSA.

Dates and Deadlines: Priority date 6/9; no closing date. Applicants notified on a rolling basis starting 4/9; must reply within 2 week(s) of notification.

CONTACT

Marcia Rose, Financial Aid Director
1314 North Hiawatha Avenue, Pipestone, MN 56164
(800) 657-3247

National American University: St. Paul

Bloomington, Minnesota
www.national.edu Federal Code: E00640

4-year for-profit branch campus and business college in very large city.
Enrollment: 350 undergrads.
Selectivity: Open admission.

FINANCIAL AID PICTURE

Students with need: Need-based aid available for full-time and part-time students. Work study available nights, weekends, and for part-time students.

Students without need: No-need awards available for academics.

FINANCIAL AID PROCEDURES

Forms required: FAFSA.

Dates and Deadlines: Priority date 8/21; no closing date. Applicants notified on a rolling basis.

CONTACT

Auriel Collins, Financial Aid Coordinator
Mall of America West 112 West Market, Bloomington, MN 55425
(952) 883-0439

Normandale Community College

Bloomington, Minnesota
www.normandale.edu Federal Code: 007954

2-year public community college in very large city.
Enrollment: 9,482 undergrads.
Selectivity: Open admission; but selective for some programs.

BASIC COSTS (2008-2009)

Tuition and fees: $4,607.
Per-credit charge: $137.
Additional info: In-state and out-of-state tuition rates are the same.

FINANCIAL AID PICTURE (2007-2008)

Students with need: 56% of average financial aid package awarded as scholarships/grants, 44% awarded as loans/jobs. Need-based aid available for part-time students. Work study available nights, weekends, and for part-time students.

Students without need: No-need awards available for academics, leadership, music/drama, state/district residency.

FINANCIAL AID PROCEDURES

Forms required: FAFSA.

Dates and Deadlines: Priority date 4/1; no closing date. Applicants notified on a rolling basis starting 4/15.

CONTACT

Catherine Breuer, Associate Dean of Students
9700 France Avenue South, Bloomington, MN 55431
(952) 487-8202

North Hennepin Community College

Brooklyn Park, Minnesota
www.nhcc.edu Federal Code: 002370

2-year public community college in small city.
Enrollment: 6,389 undergrads, 60% part-time. 804 full-time freshmen.
Selectivity: Open admission; but selective for some programs.

BASIC COSTS (2008-2009)

Tuition and fees: $4,623.
Per-credit charge: $140.
Additional info: In-state and out-of-state tuition rates are the same.

FINANCIAL AID PICTURE (2007-2008)

Students with need: 43% of average financial aid package awarded as scholarships/grants, 57% awarded as loans/jobs. Need-based aid available for part-time students. Work study available nights, weekends, and for part-time students.
Students without need: No-need awards available for academics, art, leadership.
Additional info: Computerized financial aid application.

FINANCIAL AID PROCEDURES

Forms required: FAFSA.
Dates and Deadlines: Priority date 4/15; no closing date. Applicants notified on a rolling basis starting 6/1.
Transfers: No deadline. Applicants notified on a rolling basis.

CONTACT

Jackie Olsson, Director of Financial Aid
7411 85th Avenue North, Brooklyn Park, MN 55445
(763) 424-0702

Northland Community & Technical College

Thief River Falls, Minnesota
www.northlandcollege.edu Federal Code: 002385

2-year public community and technical college in small town.
Enrollment: 1,752 full-time undergrads.
Selectivity: Open admission.

BASIC COSTS (2008-2009)

Tuition and fees: $4,926.
Per-credit charge: $147.
Additional info: In-state and out-of-state tuition rates are the same.

FINANCIAL AID PICTURE (2007-2008)

Students with need: 34% of average financial aid package awarded as scholarships/grants, 66% awarded as loans/jobs. Need-based aid available for part-time students. Work study available nights.
Students without need: No-need awards available for academics.

FINANCIAL AID PROCEDURES

Forms required: FAFSA.
Dates and Deadlines: Priority date 5/1; no closing date. Applicants notified on a rolling basis starting 5/15.

CONTACT

Gerald Schulte, Financial Aid Director
1101 Highway One East, Thief River Falls, MN 56701
(218) 681-0946

Northwest Technical College

Bemidji, Minnesota
www.ntcmn.edu Federal Code: 005759

2-year public technical college in large town.
Enrollment: 892 undergrads, 45% part-time. 119 full-time freshmen.
Selectivity: Open admission.

BASIC COSTS (2008-2009)

Tuition and fees: $4,766.
Per-credit charge: $149.

FINANCIAL AID PICTURE (2008-2009)

Students with need: 56% of average financial aid package awarded as scholarships/grants, 44% awarded as loans/jobs. Need-based aid available for part-time students. Work study available nights.
Students without need: This college awards aid only to students with need.

FINANCIAL AID PROCEDURES

Forms required: FAFSA, institutional form.
Dates and Deadlines: Priority date 7/1; no closing date. Applicants notified on a rolling basis.

CONTACT

Paul Lindseth, Director of Financial Aid
905 Grant Avenue Southeast, Bemidji, MN 56601-4907
(218) 333-6648

Northwest Technical Institute

Eagan, Minnesota
www.nti.edu Federal Code: 008267

2-year for-profit technical college in small city.
Enrollment: 133 undergrads. 90 full-time freshmen.
Selectivity: Open admission.

BASIC COSTS (2008-2009)

Tuition and fees: $14,845.
Per-credit charge: $463.
Additional info: Tuition at time of enrollment locked for 2 years.

FINANCIAL AID PICTURE

Students with need: Need-based aid available for full-time and part-time students.

FINANCIAL AID PROCEDURES

Forms required: FAFSA, institutional form.
Dates and Deadlines: No deadline. Applicants notified on a rolling basis; must reply within 2 week(s) of notification.

CONTACT

Katherine Spear, Director of Financial Aid
950 Blue Gentian Road, Eagan, MN 55121
(952) 944-0080 ext. 101

Northwestern College

Saint Paul, Minnesota
www.nwc.edu Federal Code: 002371

4-year private Bible and liberal arts college in very large city, affiliated with nondenominational tradition.
Enrollment: 1,842 undergrads, 3% part-time. 500 full-time freshmen.
Selectivity: Admits over 75% of applicants.

BASIC COSTS (2009-2010)

Tuition and fees: $22,990.
Per-credit charge: $980.
Room and board: $7,426.
Additional info: Computer technology fee of $190. Tuition/fee waivers available for minority students.

FINANCIAL AID PICTURE (2007-2008)

Students with need: Out of 464 full-time freshmen who applied for aid, 421 were judged to have need. Of these, 421 received aid, and 56 had their full need met. Average financial aid package met 69% of need; average scholarship/grant was $11,022; average loan was $3,895. For part-time students, average financial aid package was $9,301.
Students without need: 74 full-time freshmen who did not demonstrate need for aid received scholarships/grants; average award was $5,835. No-need awards available for academics, alumni affiliation, leadership, music/drama.
Scholarships offered: Eagle Scholars Program: $11,500-$14,000 per year; ACT score of 30 or SAT score of 1320; up to 15 awarded yearly to incoming freshmen; renewable annually with successful involvement in program, including a cumulative GPA of 3.65 or higher.
Cumulative student debt: 86% of graduating class had student loans; average debt was $24,449.
Additional info: Students enrolled at least half-time in the FOCUS or Distance Education degree programs may apply for financial aid from the same Federal and state sources as traditional undergraduates. However, their expense budgets and aid are less due to lower tuition: FOCUS, $345/credit; Center for Distance Education, $260/credit.

FINANCIAL AID PROCEDURES

Forms required: FAFSA, institutional form.
Dates and Deadlines: Priority date 3/1; closing date 6/1. Applicants notified on a rolling basis starting 3/1; must reply within 2 week(s) of notification.

CONTACT

Richard Blatchley, Director of Financial Aid
3003 Snelling Avenue North, Saint Paul, MN 55113-1598
(651) 631-5212

Oak Hills Christian College

Bemidji, Minnesota
www.oakhills.edu Federal Code: 016116

4-year private Bible college in large town, affiliated with interdenominational tradition.
Enrollment: 144 undergrads, 15% part-time. 21 full-time freshmen.
Selectivity: Admits over 75% of applicants.

BASIC COSTS (2009-2010)

Tuition and fees: $13,480.
Per-credit charge: $395.
Room and board: $4,840.
Additional info: Tuition at time of enrollment locked for 4 years.

FINANCIAL AID PICTURE (2007-2008)

Students with need: Out of 21 full-time freshmen who applied for aid, 20 were judged to have need. Of these, 20 received aid, and 1 had their full need met. Average financial aid package met 55% of need; average scholarship/grant was $5,140; average loan was $3,116. For part-time students, average financial aid package was $5,287.
Students without need: 1 full-time freshmen who did not demonstrate need for aid received scholarships/grants; average award was $3,650. No-need awards available for academics, alumni affiliation.
Cumulative student debt: 100% of graduating class had student loans; average debt was $29,440.

FINANCIAL AID PROCEDURES

Forms required: FAFSA, institutional form.
Dates and Deadlines: No deadline. Applicants notified on a rolling basis starting 3/1.
Transfers: No deadline. Applicants notified on a rolling basis starting 3/1.

CONTACT

Dan Hovestol, Financial Aid Director
1600 Oak Hills Road SW, Bemidji, MN 56601-8826
(218) 751-8671 ext. 1220

Pine Technical College

Pine City, Minnesota
www.pinetech.edu Federal Code: 005535

2-year public technical college in small town.
Enrollment: 548 undergrads.
Selectivity: Open admission; but selective for some programs.

BASIC COSTS (2008-2009)

Tuition and fees: $4,341; out-of-state residents $8,196.
Per-credit charge: $129; out-of-state residents $257.

FINANCIAL AID PICTURE

Students with need: Need-based aid available for full-time and part-time students.
Students without need: No-need awards available for academics, state/district residency.

FINANCIAL AID PROCEDURES

Forms required: FAFSA, institutional form.
Dates and Deadlines: Priority date 5/5; no closing date. Applicants notified on a rolling basis starting 6/5.

CONTACT

Susan Pixley, Financial Aid Director
900 Fourth Street, SE, Pine City, MN 55063
(320) 629-5100 ext. 161

Rainy River Community College

International Falls, Minnesota
www.rrcc.mnscu.edu Federal Code: 000775

2-year public community and technical college in small town.
Enrollment: 343 undergrads. 241 full-time freshmen.
Selectivity: Open admission.

BASIC COSTS (2008-2009)

Tuition and fees: $4,517; out-of-state residents $5,504.
Per-credit charge: $132; out-of-state residents $164.
Additional info: Tuition/fee waivers available for unemployed or children of unemployed.

FINANCIAL AID PICTURE (2008-2009)

Students with need: Need-based aid available for full-time and part-time students. Work study available nights, weekends, and for part-time students.

Students without need: No-need awards available for academics, alumni affiliation, minority status, state/district residency.

Additional info: Many scholarship and employment opportunities for applicants showing little or no need.

FINANCIAL AID PROCEDURES

Forms required: FAFSA, institutional form.

Dates and Deadlines: Priority date 6/1; no closing date. Applicants notified on a rolling basis starting 5/1; must reply within 3 week(s) of notification.

CONTACT

Scott Riley, Director of Financial Aid
1501 Highway 71, International Falls, MN 56649
(218) 285-7722

Rasmussen College: Brooklyn Park

Brooklyn Park, Minnesota
www.rasmussen.edu

2-year for-profit career college in small city.

Enrollment: 913 undergrads.

Selectivity: Open admission; but selective for some programs.

FINANCIAL AID PICTURE

Students with need: Need-based aid available for full-time and part-time students.

FINANCIAL AID PROCEDURES

Forms required: FAFSA, institutional form.

Dates and Deadlines: No deadline. Applicants notified on a rolling basis.

CONTACT

Steve Yang, Director of Student Financial Services
8301 93rd Avenue North, Brooklyn Park, MN 55445

Rasmussen College: Eagan

Eagan, Minnesota
www.rasmussen.edu Federal Code: 004648

2-year for-profit career college in small city.

Enrollment: 719 undergrads.

Selectivity: Open admission; but selective for some programs.

FINANCIAL AID PICTURE (2007-2008)

Students with need: Need-based aid available for full-time and part-time students.

FINANCIAL AID PROCEDURES

Forms required: FAFSA, institutional form.

Dates and Deadlines: No deadline. Applicants notified on a rolling basis.

CONTACT

Peter Rasmussen, Director of Student Financial Services
3500 Federal Drive, Eagan, MN 55122
(651) 687-9000

Rasmussen College: Eden Prairie

Eden Prairie, Minnesota
www.rasmussen.edu Federal Code: 011686

2-year for-profit career college in small city.

Enrollment: 1,037 undergrads.

Selectivity: Open admission; but selective for some programs.

FINANCIAL AID PICTURE

Students with need: Need-based aid available for full-time and part-time students.

FINANCIAL AID PROCEDURES

Forms required: FAFSA, institutional form.

Dates and Deadlines: No deadline. Applicants notified on a rolling basis.

CONTACT

Lindsay Adams, Director of Student Financial Services
7905 Golden Triangle Drive, Suite 100, Eden Prairie, MN 55344
(952) 545-2000

Rasmussen College: Mankato

Mankato, Minnesota
www.rasmussen.edu Federal Code: 016845

2-year for-profit career college in large town.

Enrollment: 666 undergrads.

Selectivity: Open admission; but selective for some programs.

FINANCIAL AID PICTURE

Students with need: Need-based aid available for full-time and part-time students.

FINANCIAL AID PROCEDURES

Forms required: FAFSA, institutional form.

Dates and Deadlines: No deadline. Applicants notified on a rolling basis.

CONTACT

Carrie Thell, Director of Financial Aid
130 Saint Andrews Drive, Mankato, MN 56001
(507) 625-6556

Rasmussen College: St. Cloud

St. Cloud, Minnesota
www.rasmussen.edu Federal Code: 008694

2-year for-profit community and career college in small city.

Enrollment: 904 undergrads.

Selectivity: Open admission; but selective for some programs.

FINANCIAL AID PICTURE (2008-2009)

Students with need: Need-based aid available for full-time and part-time students.

FINANCIAL AID PROCEDURES

Forms required: FAFSA, institutional form.

Dates and Deadlines: No deadline. Applicants notified on a rolling basis.

CONTACT

Carole Inderrieden, Director of Student Financial Services
226 Park Avenue South, St. Cloud, MN 56301-3713
(320) 251-5600

Ridgewater College

Willmar, Minnesota
www.ridgewater.edu Federal Code: 005252

2-year public community and technical college in large town.

Enrollment: 3,676 undergrads. 798 full-time freshmen.

Selectivity: Open admission; but selective for some programs.

BASIC COSTS (2008-2009)
Tuition and fees: $4,606.
Per-credit charge: $136.
Additional info: In-state and out-of-state tuition rates are the same. Tuition/fee waivers available for adults.

FINANCIAL AID PICTURE (2008-2009)
Students with need: 33% of average financial aid package awarded as scholarships/grants, 67% awarded as loans/jobs. Need-based aid available for part-time students. Work study available nights, weekends, and for part-time students.
Additional info: Special funds are available for adult transfer students returning or continuing education after a 7-year absence from academic training. ALLISS grants provide reimbursement for one class, up to five credits for one semester.

FINANCIAL AID PROCEDURES
Forms required: FAFSA, institutional form.
Dates and Deadlines: No deadline. Applicants notified on a rolling basis.

CONTACT
Jim Rice, Director of Financial Aid
2101 15th Avenue Northwest, Willmar, MN 56201
(320) 222-7474

Riverland Community College
Austin, Minnesota
www.riverland.edu Federal Code: 002335

2-year public community and technical college in large town.
Enrollment: 3,279 undergrads, 59% part-time. 654 full-time freshmen.
Selectivity: Open admission; but selective for some programs.

BASIC COSTS (2008-2009)
Tuition and fees: $4,701.
Per-credit charge: $138.
Room and board: $2,640.
Additional info: In-state and out-of-state tuition rates are the same.

FINANCIAL AID PICTURE (2007-2008)
Students with need: Need-based aid available for part-time students.
Students without need: No-need awards available for alumni affiliation, art, job skills, leadership, music/drama, state/district residency.
Additional info: One class tuition-free for Minnesota residents over 25 who have not attended college for at least 7 years.

FINANCIAL AID PROCEDURES
Forms required: FAFSA.
Dates and Deadlines: Priority date 5/15; no closing date. Applicants notified on a rolling basis; must reply within 5 week(s) of notification.
Transfers: No deadline. Applicants notified on a rolling basis.

CONTACT
Judy Robeck, Financial Aid Director
1900 Eighth Avenue, NW, Austin, MN 55912-1407
(507) 433-0511

Rochester Community and Technical College
Rochester, Minnesota
www.roch.edu Federal Code: 002373

2-year public community and technical college in small city.
Enrollment: 3,239 full-time undergrads.
Selectivity: Open admission; but selective for some programs.

BASIC COSTS (2008-2009)
Tuition and fees: $4,820.
Per-credit charge: $138.

FINANCIAL AID PICTURE
Students with need: Need-based aid available for full-time and part-time students. Work study available nights, weekends, and for part-time students.

FINANCIAL AID PROCEDURES
Forms required: FAFSA.
Dates and Deadlines: Priority date 4/15; no closing date. Applicants notified on a rolling basis.

CONTACT
Rosemary Hicks, Director of Financial Aid
851 30th Avenue SE, Rochester, MN 55904-4999
(507) 285-7271

Saint Cloud State University
St. Cloud, Minnesota
www.stcloudstate.edu Federal Code: 002377

4-year public university in small city.
Enrollment: 13,501 undergrads, 12% part-time. 2,360 full-time freshmen.
Selectivity: Admits over 75% of applicants.

BASIC COSTS (2008-2009)
Tuition and fees: $6,147; out-of-state residents $12,474.
Per-credit charge: $180; out-of-state residents $391.
Room and board: $5,770.

FINANCIAL AID PICTURE (2008-2009)
Students with need: Out of 1,790 full-time freshmen who applied for aid, 1,249 were judged to have need. Of these, 1,249 received aid, and 818 had their full need met. Average financial aid package met 66% of need; average scholarship/grant was $5,094; average loan was $4,563. For part-time students, average financial aid package was $8,175.
Students without need: 60 full-time freshmen who did not demonstrate need for aid received scholarships/grants; average award was $1,902. No-need awards available for academics, art, athletics, leadership, music/drama.
Scholarships offered: 26 full-time freshmen received athletic scholarships; average amount $2,449.
Cumulative student debt: 70% of graduating class had student loans; average debt was $24,484.

FINANCIAL AID PROCEDURES
Forms required: FAFSA, institutional form.
Dates and Deadlines: No deadline. Applicants notified on a rolling basis starting 6/15.
Transfers: No deadline. Applicants notified on a rolling basis starting 6/15.

CONTACT
Michael Uran, Financial Aid Director
720 Fourth Avenue South, St. Cloud, MN 56301
(320) 308-2047

St. Cloud Technical College
St. Cloud, Minnesota
www.sctc.edu Federal Code: 005534

2-year public technical college in small city.
Enrollment: 3,451 undergrads, 30% part-time. 754 full-time freshmen.
Selectivity: Open admission; but selective for some programs.

BASIC COSTS (2008-2009)
Tuition and fees: $4,614.
Per-credit charge: $137.

Additional info: In-state and out-of-state tuition rates are the same.

FINANCIAL AID PICTURE (2007-2008)

Students with need: 56% of average financial aid package awarded as scholarships/grants, 44% awarded as loans/jobs. Need-based aid available for part-time students. Work study available nights, weekends, and for part-time students.

Students without need: No-need awards available for academics, leadership, state/district residency.

FINANCIAL AID PROCEDURES

Forms required: FAFSA, institutional form.

Dates and Deadlines: No deadline. Applicants notified on a rolling basis starting 6/1.

CONTACT

Anita Baugh, Financial Aid Director
1540 Northway Drive, St. Cloud, MN 56303
(320) 308-5961

St. John's University

Collegeville, Minnesota
www.csbsju.edu Federal Code: 002379

4-year private university and liberal arts college for men in rural community, affiliated with Roman Catholic Church.

Enrollment: 1,897 undergrads. 464 full-time freshmen.

Selectivity: Admits 50 to 75% of applicants.

BASIC COSTS (2009-2010)

Tuition and fees: $29,886.

Per-credit charge: $1,225.

Room and board: $7,714.

FINANCIAL AID PICTURE (2008-2009)

Students with need: Out of 356 full-time freshmen who applied for aid, 280 were judged to have need. Of these, 280 received aid, and 135 had their full need met. Average financial aid package met 95% of need; average scholarship/grant was $17,934; average loan was $4,635. For part-time students, average financial aid package was $9,850.

Students without need: 165 full-time freshmen who did not demonstrate need for aid received scholarships/grants; average award was $10,713. No-need awards available for academics, art, leadership, music/drama, ROTC.

Scholarships offered: Regents/Trustees Scholarships: $15,000; minimum 3.6 GPA, 30 ACT, 1980 SAT, demonstrated leadership and service, faculty interview. President's Scholarships: $10,500-$12,500; and Dean's Scholarships: $3,000-$9,500; GPA, high school rank, ACT/SAT scores, leadership and service. Art, Music and Theater Scholarships: up to $4,000; excellence in these subjects in high school, portfolio, tape, audition. Diversity Leadership Scholarships: up to $5,000; demonstrated diversity leadership and service in the area of cultural and ethnic diversity, personal statement on topic. Army ROTC and ROTC Nursing Scholarships: $28,000; demonstrated leadership potential, high school GPA, class standing, ACT/SAT scores, high achievement with broad interests and willingness to take on challenges. Phi Theta Kappa Scholarship: $1,000; member of Phi Theta Kappa (transfer students only).

FINANCIAL AID PROCEDURES

Forms required: FAFSA, institutional form.

Dates and Deadlines: Closing date 3/15. Applicants notified on a rolling basis starting 3/15; must reply by 5/1.

CONTACT

Stuart Perry, Director of Financial Aid
PO Box 7155, Collegeville, MN 56321-7155
(320) 363-3664

St. Mary's University of Minnesota

Winona, Minnesota
www.smumn.edu Federal Code: 002380

4-year private university in large town, affiliated with Roman Catholic Church.

Enrollment: 1,999 undergrads, 28% part-time. 404 full-time freshmen.

Selectivity: Admits 50 to 75% of applicants.

BASIC COSTS (2009-2010)

Tuition and fees: $25,570.

Per-credit charge: $840.

Room and board: $6,760.

FINANCIAL AID PICTURE (2008-2009)

Students with need: Out of 320 full-time freshmen who applied for aid, 273 were judged to have need. Of these, 271 received aid, and 52 had their full need met. Average financial aid package met 84% of need; average scholarship/grant was $15,305; average loan was $4,237. Need-based aid available for part-time students.

Students without need: 129 full-time freshmen who did not demonstrate need for aid received scholarships/grants; average award was $8,707. No-need awards available for academics, alumni affiliation, art, leadership, minority status, music/drama.

Cumulative student debt: 80% of graduating class had student loans; average debt was $33,639.

FINANCIAL AID PROCEDURES

Forms required: FAFSA.

Dates and Deadlines: Priority date 3/15; no closing date. Applicants notified on a rolling basis starting 2/1; must reply within 3 week(s) of notification.

Transfers: No deadline. Applicants notified on a rolling basis starting 2/1.

CONTACT

Jayne Wobig, Director of Financial Aid
700 Terrace Heights #2, Winona, MN 55987-1399
(507) 457-1437

St. Olaf College

Northfield, Minnesota Federal Code: 002382
www.stolaf.edu CSS Code: 6638

4-year private liberal arts college in large town, affiliated with Evangelical Lutheran Church in America.

Enrollment: 3,014 undergrads. 813 full-time freshmen.

Selectivity: Admits 50 to 75% of applicants.

BASIC COSTS (2009-2010)

Tuition and fees: $35,500.

Per-credit charge: $1,110.

Room and board: $8,200.

Additional info: Tuition/fee waivers available for adults.

FINANCIAL AID PICTURE (2008-2009)

Students with need: Out of 690 full-time freshmen who applied for aid, 519 were judged to have need. Of these, 519 received aid, and 519 had their full need met. Average financial aid package met 100% of need; average scholarship/grant was $21,424; average loan was $4,589.

Students without need: 192 full-time freshmen who did not demonstrate need for aid received scholarships/grants; average award was $10,925. No-need awards available for academics, leadership, music/drama.

Scholarships offered: Buntrock Scholarship: $12,000. Presidential Scholarship: $7,500. National Hispanic Scholar/Nat Achievement: $7,500. National Merit Scholarship: $7,500; TRiO Scholarships: $6,000. Music Scholarships: $4,000 - $7,000. Service Leadership Awards: $4,000. All are 4-year renewable; number awarded varies yearly.

Cumulative student debt: 65% of graduating class had student loans; average debt was $25,273.
Additional info: Limited number of music lesson fee waivers available for music majors, awarded on audition basis only.

FINANCIAL AID PROCEDURES
Forms required: FAFSA, CSS PROFILE.
Dates and Deadlines: Priority date 1/15; closing date 2/1. Applicants notified on a rolling basis starting 3/1; must reply by 5/1 or within 2 week(s) of notification.
Transfers: Closing date 3/1. Must reply by 5/1 or within 2 week(s) of notification.

CONTACT
Katharine Ruby, Assistant Vice President for Enrollment and Dean of Student Financial Aid
1520 St. Olaf Avenue, Northfield, MN 55057
(507) 786-3019

St. Paul College
Saint Paul, Minnesota
www.saintpaul.edu Federal Code: 005533

2-year public community and technical college in large city.
Enrollment: 5,387 undergrads, 62% part-time. 6,112 full-time freshmen.
Selectivity: Open admission; but selective for some programs.

BASIC COSTS (2008-2009)
Tuition and fees: $4,399.
Per-credit charge: $136.
Additional info: In-state and out-of-state tuition rates are the same.

FINANCIAL AID PICTURE (2008-2009)
Students with need: Need-based aid available for part-time students.
Students without need: No-need awards available for leadership.

FINANCIAL AID PROCEDURES
Forms required: FAFSA.
Dates and Deadlines: No deadline. Applicants notified on a rolling basis starting 6/1.
Transfers: Priority date 5/1; no deadline. Applicants notified on a rolling basis starting 6/1.

CONTACT
Susan Prater, Financial Aid Director
235 Marshall Avenue, Saint Paul, MN 55102-1800
(651) 846-1386

South Central College
North Mankato, Minnesota
www.southcentral.edu Federal Code: 005537

2-year public community and technical college in large town.
Enrollment: 3,424 undergrads.
Selectivity: Open admission.

BASIC COSTS (2008-2009)
Tuition and fees: $4,515.
Per-credit charge: $135.

FINANCIAL AID PICTURE (2007-2008)
Students with need: Need-based aid available for full-time and part-time students. Work study available nights.

FINANCIAL AID PROCEDURES
Forms required: FAFSA, institutional form.
Dates and Deadlines: Priority date 5/1; no closing date. Applicants notified on a rolling basis starting 6/1.
Transfers: No deadline. Applicants notified on a rolling basis starting 6/1.

CONTACT
Jayne Dinse, Financial Aid Director
1920 Lee Boulevard, North Mankato, MN 56003
(507) 389-7220

Southwest Minnesota State University
Marshall, Minnesota
www.smsu.edu Federal Code: 002375

4-year public university and liberal arts college in large town.
Enrollment: 2,600 undergrads, 15% part-time. 499 full-time freshmen.
Selectivity: Admits 50 to 75% of applicants.

BASIC COSTS (2008-2009)
Tuition and fees: $6,696.
Per-credit charge: $187.
Room and board: $5,984.

FINANCIAL AID PICTURE (2008-2009)
Students with need: Out of 391 full-time freshmen who applied for aid, 296 were judged to have need. Of these, 294 received aid, and 67 had their full need met. Average financial aid package met 59% of need; average scholarship/grant was $5,047; average loan was $3,309. For part-time students, average financial aid package was $5,047.
Students without need: 100 full-time freshmen who did not demonstrate need for aid received scholarships/grants; average award was $2,899. No-need awards available for academics, alumni affiliation, art, athletics, leadership, minority status, music/drama, state/district residency.
Scholarships offered: 61 full-time freshmen received athletic scholarships; average amount $3,330.
Cumulative student debt: 82% of graduating class had student loans; average debt was $18,003.

FINANCIAL AID PROCEDURES
Forms required: FAFSA, institutional form.
Dates and Deadlines: Priority date 3/1; no closing date. Applicants notified on a rolling basis starting 5/15.

CONTACT
David Vikander, Director of Financial Aid
1501 State Street, Marshall, MN 56258-1598
(507) 537-6281

University of Minnesota: Crookston
Crookston, Minnesota
www.UMCrookston.edu Federal Code: 004069

4-year public branch campus college in small town.
Enrollment: 1,207 undergrads, 16% part-time. 268 full-time freshmen.
Selectivity: Admits over 75% of applicants.

BASIC COSTS (2008-2009)
Tuition and fees: $9,381; out-of-state residents $9,381.
Per-credit charge: $265.
Room and board: $5,950.
Additional info: Tuition at time of enrollment locked for 4 years; tuition/fee waivers available for minority students.

FINANCIAL AID PICTURE (2008-2009)

Students with need: Out of 230 full-time freshmen who applied for aid, 177 were judged to have need. Of these, 177 received aid, and 76 had their full need met. Average financial aid package met 79% of need; average scholarship/grant was $7,248; average loan was $4,929. For part-time students, average financial aid package was $3,763.

Students without need: 50 full-time freshmen who did not demonstrate need for aid received scholarships/grants; average award was $2,393. No-need awards available for academics, athletics, leadership, minority status, ROTC.

Scholarships offered: Merit Scholarship: based on a minimum GPA of 3.25 and a minimum ACT score of 21. Presidential Scholarship: $20,000 total ($5,000 annually for four years); based on ACT score of 30 and GPA of 3.25. Chancellor Scholarship: $8,000 total ($4,000 annually for two years); based on ACT score of 27-29 and GPA of 3.25. Distinguished Scholarship: $6,000 total ($3,000 annually for two years); based on ACT score of 25-26 and 3.25 GPA. Merriam Legacy Scholarship: $4,000 total ($2,000 annually for two years); based on ACT score of 23-24 and a 3.25 GPA. Achievement Scholarship: $2,000; based on ACT score of 21-22 and 3.25 GPA.

Cumulative student debt: 84% of graduating class had student loans; average debt was $26,565.

Additional info: Tuition guarantee plan available to all students who apply for it.

FINANCIAL AID PROCEDURES

Forms required: FAFSA.

Dates and Deadlines: Priority date 2/15; no closing date. Applicants notified on a rolling basis starting 3/15.

CONTACT

Melissa Dingmann, Director of Financial Aid
2900 University Avenue, Crookston, MN 56716-5001
(218) 281-8563

University of Minnesota: Duluth

Duluth, Minnesota
www.d.umn.edu Federal Code: 002388

4-year public university in small city.

Enrollment: 9,324 undergrads.

Selectivity: Admits 50 to 75% of applicants.

BASIC COSTS (2008-2009)

Tuition and fees: $10,261; out-of-state residents $12,261.

Per-credit charge: $317; out-of-state residents $393.

Room and board: $6,078.

FINANCIAL AID PICTURE (2008-2009)

Students with need: Need-based aid available for full-time and part-time students. Work study available nights, weekends, and for part-time students.

Students without need: No-need awards available for academics, athletics, ROTC.

FINANCIAL AID PROCEDURES

Forms required: FAFSA.

Dates and Deadlines: Priority date 3/1; no closing date. Applicants notified on a rolling basis starting 3/1; must reply within 2 week(s) of notification.

CONTACT

Brenda Herzig, Director of Financial Aid
25 Solon Campus Center, Duluth, MN 55812-3000
(218) 726-8000

University of Minnesota: Morris

Morris, Minnesota
www.morris.umn.edu Federal Code: 002389

4-year public university and liberal arts college in small town.

Enrollment: 1,510 undergrads.

Selectivity: Admits 50 to 75% of applicants.

BASIC COSTS (2008-2009)

Tuition and fees: $9,996; out-of-state residents $9,996.

Per-credit charge: $317.

Room and board: $6,710.

FINANCIAL AID PICTURE (2007-2008)

Students with need: Need-based aid available for full-time and part-time students. Work study available nights, weekends, and for part-time students.

Students without need: No-need awards available for academics, alumni affiliation, leadership, minority status, music/drama.

Scholarships offered: Chancellor's Scholarship: $3,500/year for 4 years; top 5%. Dean's Scholarship: $2,500/year for 4 years; top 10%. Founder's Scholarship: $1,000/year for 4 years; top 20%. National Merit Scholarship: full tuition scholarship for 4 years. Prairie Scholars Award: full tuition/year for 4 years; Morris Scholars Award: $5,000/year for 4 years plus one-time $2,500 research or creative project stipend. President's Distinguished Scholar Award: $1,000 to $3,000/year for four years.

Additional info: Land-grant program waiving tuition for Native Americans.

FINANCIAL AID PROCEDURES

Forms required: FAFSA.

Dates and Deadlines: Priority date 3/1; no closing date. Applicants notified on a rolling basis starting 3/1; must reply within 3 week(s) of notification.

CONTACT

Jill Beauregard, Director of Financial Aid
600 East 4th Street, Morris, MN 56267
(800) 992-8863

University of Minnesota: Twin Cities

Minneapolis, Minnesota
www.umn.edu/tc Federal Code: 003969

4-year public university in very large city.

Enrollment: 28,505 undergrads, 8% part-time. 5,093 full-time freshmen.

Selectivity: Admits 50 to 75% of applicants.

BASIC COSTS (2008-2009)

Tuition and fees: $10,634; out-of-state residents $14,634.

Per-credit charge: $327; out-of-state residents $481.

Room and board: $7,280.

FINANCIAL AID PICTURE (2008-2009)

Students with need: Out of 3,970 full-time freshmen who applied for aid, 2,599 were judged to have need. Of these, 2,586 received aid, and 1,301 had their full need met. Average financial aid package met 86% of need; average scholarship/grant was $7,809; average loan was $6,273. For part-time students, average financial aid package was $7,155.

Students without need: This college awards aid only to students with need.

Cumulative student debt: 64% of graduating class had student loans; average debt was $23,811.

FINANCIAL AID PROCEDURES

Forms required: FAFSA, institutional form.

Dates and Deadlines: Priority date 3/1; no closing date. Applicants notified on a rolling basis starting 2/15.

CONTACT

Kris Wright, Director of Financial Aid
240 Williamson Hall, 231 Pillsbury Drive SE, Minneapolis, MN 55455-0115
(612) 624-1111

University of St. Thomas

Saint Paul, Minnesota
www.stthomas.edu Federal Code: 002345

4-year private university and liberal arts college in very large city, affiliated with Roman Catholic Church.
Enrollment: 6,017 undergrads, 4% part-time. 1,320 full-time freshmen.
Selectivity: Admits over 75% of applicants.

BASIC COSTS (2009-2010)
Tuition and fees: $29,467.
Room and board: $8,320.

FINANCIAL AID PICTURE (2008-2009)
Students with need: Out of 1,004 full-time freshmen who applied for aid, 750 were judged to have need. Of these, 749 received aid, and 413 had their full need met. Average financial aid package met 87% of need; average scholarship/grant was $14,344; average loan was $6,555. For part-time students, average financial aid package was $11,580.
Students without need: 558 full-time freshmen who did not demonstrate need for aid received scholarships/grants; average award was $10,504. No-need awards available for academics, music/drama, ROTC.
Cumulative student debt: 68% of graduating class had student loans; average debt was $34,869.

FINANCIAL AID PROCEDURES
Forms required: FAFSA.
Dates and Deadlines: Priority date 4/1; no closing date. Applicants notified on a rolling basis starting 3/1; must reply within 3 week(s) of notification.
Transfers: Recognition scholarship available for Minnesota community college transfer students.

CONTACT

Kris Getting, Director of Admissions and Financial Aid
2115 Summit Avenue, 32F, St. Paul, MN 55105-1096
(651) 962-6550

Vermilion Community College

Ely, Minnesota
www.vcc.edu Federal Code: 002350

2-year public community and technical college in small town.
Enrollment: 610 undergrads.
Selectivity: Open admission.

BASIC COSTS (2008-2009)
Tuition and fees: $4,511; out-of-state residents $5,498.
Per-credit charge: $132; out-of-state residents $164.
Room and board: $4,780.
Additional info: Various reciprocity agreements with some neighboring states provide tuition reduction to out-of-state students.

FINANCIAL AID PICTURE
Students with need: Need-based aid available for full-time and part-time students. Work study available nights, weekends, and for part-time students.

FINANCIAL AID PROCEDURES
Forms required: FAFSA, institutional form.
Dates and Deadlines: No deadline. Applicants notified on a rolling basis starting 4/1.

CONTACT

Kristi L'Allier, Financial Aid Director
1900 East Camp Street, Ely, MN 55731-9989
(218) 235-2153

Walden University

Minneapolis, Minnesota
www.waldenu.edu Federal Code: 025402

4-year for-profit virtual university in large city.
Enrollment: 2,466 undergrads, 93% part-time. 2 full-time freshmen.

BASIC COSTS (2008-2009)
Tuition and fees: $11,700.
Per-credit charge: $260.
Additional info: Tuition at time of enrollment locked for 4 years.

FINANCIAL AID PICTURE (2007-2008)
Students with need: Need-based aid available for full-time and part-time students.
Students without need: This college awards aid only to students with need.

FINANCIAL AID PROCEDURES
Forms required: FAFSA.
Dates and Deadlines: No deadline. Applicants notified on a rolling basis.
Transfers: No deadline. Applicants notified on a rolling basis.

CONTACT

Ernestine Whiting, National Director of Financial Aid
650 South Exeter Street, 8th Floor, Baltimore, MD 21202
(800) 444-6795

Winona State University

Winona, Minnesota
www.winona.edu Federal Code: 002394

4-year public university in large town.
Enrollment: 7,641 undergrads, 6% part-time. 1,869 full-time freshmen.
Selectivity: Admits 50 to 75% of applicants.

BASIC COSTS (2008-2009)
Tuition and fees: $6,661; out-of-state residents $11,257.
Per-credit charge: $191; out-of-state residents $345.
Room and board: $6,432.
Additional info: Fees include mandatory laptop lease for full-time students.

FINANCIAL AID PICTURE (2007-2008)
Students with need: Need-based aid available for full-time and part-time students. Work study available nights, weekends, and for part-time students.
Students without need: No-need awards available for academics, alumni affiliation, art, athletics, leadership, minority status, music/drama, ROTC, state/district residency.
Scholarships offered: Outstanding Academics Honors Award: $2,500, renewable, top 5% of class, ACT 32 or above. WSU Foundation Board Scholarship: $2,000 renewable, top 15% of class, ACT 28-31, essay/interview. Presidential Honor Scholarships: $1,500 renewable; top 15% of class, ACT 28-31; $1,000, renewable, top 10% of class, ACT 27; $750, renewable, top 15% of class, ACT 26. Resident Tuition Scholarships: $3,400, renewable, to out-of-state students, top 15% of class or ACT 25.

FINANCIAL AID PROCEDURES
Forms required: FAFSA.
Dates and Deadlines: Priority date 3/1; no closing date. Applicants notified on a rolling basis starting 5/1; must reply within 3 week(s) of notification.

CONTACT

Greg Peterson, Director of Financial Aid
Office of Admissions, Winona, MN 55987
(800) 342-5978

Mississippi

Alcorn State University

Alcorn State, Mississippi
www.alcorn.edu Federal Code: 002396

4-year public university and agricultural college in rural community.
Enrollment: 2,626 undergrads, 9% part-time. 396 full-time freshmen.
Selectivity: Admits over 75% of applicants.

BASIC COSTS (2008-2009)

Tuition and fees: $4,448; out-of-state residents $10,692.
Per-credit charge: $150; out-of-state residents $356.
Room and board: $5,168.
Additional info: 2008-09 Public institution tuition: $4498; Room and board (on-campus): $5128; Undergraduate per-credit-hour charge: $250, out-of-State: $594.

FINANCIAL AID PICTURE (2008-2009)

Students with need: Out of 396 full-time freshmen who applied for aid, 368 were judged to have need. Of these, 368 received aid, and 203 had their full need met. Average financial aid package met 82% of need; average scholarship/grant was $3,977; average loan was $3,352. For part-time students, average financial aid package was $9,302.
Students without need: 67 full-time freshmen who did not demonstrate need for aid received scholarships/grants; average award was $1,340. No-need awards available for academics, athletics, ROTC.
Scholarships offered: 42 full-time freshmen received athletic scholarships; average amount $7,390.

FINANCIAL AID PROCEDURES

Forms required: FAFSA, institutional form.
Dates and Deadlines: Priority date 4/1; no closing date. Applicants notified on a rolling basis starting 4/1; must reply within 4 week(s) of notification.

CONTACT

Juanita Russell, Director of Financial Aid
1000 ASU Drive #300, Alcorn State, MS 39096-7500
(601) 877-6190

Belhaven College

Jackson, Mississippi
www.belhaven.edu Federal Code: 002397

4-year private liberal arts college in large city, affiliated with Presbyterian Church (USA).
Enrollment: 2,152 undergrads, 6% part-time. 237 full-time freshmen.
Selectivity: Admits 50 to 75% of applicants.

BASIC COSTS (2009-2010)

Tuition and fees: $16,780.
Per-credit charge: $350.
Room and board: $6,120.

FINANCIAL AID PICTURE (2008-2009)

Students with need: Out of 165 full-time freshmen who applied for aid, 145 were judged to have need. Of these, 145 received aid, and 18 had their full need met. Average financial aid package met 63% of need; average scholarship/grant was $10,677; average loan was $2,965. For part-time students, average financial aid package was $9,243.
Students without need: 22 full-time freshmen who did not demonstrate need for aid received scholarships/grants; average award was $7,061. No-need awards available for academics, alumni affiliation, art, athletics, music/drama.
Scholarships offered: 23 full-time freshmen received athletic scholarships; average amount $6,358.
Cumulative student debt: 94% of graduating class had student loans; average debt was $23,914.

FINANCIAL AID PROCEDURES

Forms required: FAFSA.
Dates and Deadlines: Priority date 3/1; no closing date. Applicants notified on a rolling basis starting 2/1.

CONTACT

Linda Phillips, Assistant Vice President for Institutional Advancement
1500 Peachtree Street, Jackson, MS 39202
(601) 968-5933

Blue Cliff College: Gulfport

Gulfport, Mississippi
www.bluecliffcollege.com Federal Code: 035253

2-year for-profit technical college in small city.
Enrollment: 142 undergrads.
Selectivity: Open admission.

FINANCIAL AID PICTURE (2008-2009)

Students with need: Need-based aid available for full-time and part-time students.
Students without need: This college awards aid only to students with need.

FINANCIAL AID PROCEDURES

Forms required: FAFSA.

CONTACT

12251 Bernard Parkway, Gulfport, MS 39503

Blue Mountain College

Blue Mountain, Mississippi
www.bmc.edu Federal Code: 002398

4-year private liberal arts college in rural community, affiliated with Southern Baptist Convention.
Enrollment: 442 undergrads, 12% part-time. 78 full-time freshmen.
Selectivity: Admits 50 to 75% of applicants.

BASIC COSTS (2009-2010)

Tuition and fees: $8,880.
Per-credit charge: $255.
Room and board: $3,800.

FINANCIAL AID PICTURE (2007-2008)

Students with need: Average financial aid package met 81% of need; average scholarship/grant was $2,495; average loan was $5,080. For part-time students, average financial aid package was $5,899.
Students without need: No-need awards available for academics, alumni affiliation, art, athletics, leadership, music/drama, religious affiliation, state/district residency.

Scholarships offered: ACT/SAT Scholarships: varies from $1,000 to $7,000 per year; based on ACT/SAT score; number varies depending on number of applicants. Valedictorian/Salutatorian Scholarships: $1,000 to $5,000 first year; based on rank in class; unlimited number available. Child of Alumnae/Alumni: $500 first year; must be dependent of graduate; unlimited number available.
Cumulative student debt: 81% of graduating class had student loans; average debt was $15,290.

FINANCIAL AID PROCEDURES
Forms required: FAFSA, institutional form.
Dates and Deadlines: Priority date 3/1; closing date 7/31. Applicants notified on a rolling basis starting 4/1; must reply within 2 week(s) of notification.
Transfers: No deadline.

CONTACT
Michelle Hall, Director of Financial Aid
201 West Main Street, PO Box 160, Blue Mountain, MS 38610-0160
(662) 685-4771 ext. 145

Coahoma Community College
Clarksdale, Mississippi
www.coahomacc.edu Federal Code: 002401

2-year public community college in large town.
Enrollment: 2,215 undergrads.
Selectivity: Open admission; but selective for some programs.

BASIC COSTS (2008-2009)
Tuition and fees: $1,800; out-of-state residents $4,700.
Per-credit charge: $90.
Room and board: $3,514.

FINANCIAL AID PICTURE (2008-2009)
Students with need: Need-based aid available for full-time and part-time students.
Students without need: This college awards aid only to students with need.

FINANCIAL AID PROCEDURES
Forms required: FAFSA, institutional form.
Dates and Deadlines: Priority date 4/1; no closing date. Applicants notified on a rolling basis starting 7/1.
Transfers: Priority date 3/1.

CONTACT
Patricia Brooks, Director of Financial Aid
3240 Friars Point Road, Clarksdale, MS 38614-9799
(662) 627-2571

Copiah-Lincoln Community College
Wesson, Mississippi
www.colin.edu Federal Code: 002402

2-year public community college in small town.
Enrollment: 3,351 undergrads.
Selectivity: Open admission; but selective for some programs.

BASIC COSTS (2008-2009)
Tuition and fees: $1,800; out-of-state residents $3,600.
Per-credit charge: $105; out-of-state residents $180.
Room and board: $2,525.
Additional info: Housing deposit: $100.00, parking fee: $20.00.

FINANCIAL AID PICTURE (2007-2008)
Students with need: 67% of average financial aid package awarded as scholarships/grants, 33% awarded as loans/jobs. Need-based aid available for part-time students. Work study available nights, weekends, and for part-time students.
Students without need: No-need awards available for academics, art, athletics, job skills, leadership, music/drama, state/district residency.

FINANCIAL AID PROCEDURES
Forms required: FAFSA.
Dates and Deadlines: Priority date 4/1; no closing date. Applicants notified on a rolling basis starting 4/1; must reply within 2 week(s) of notification.

CONTACT
Leslie Smith, Director of Financial Aid
Box 649, Wesson, MS 39191
(601) 643-8340

Delta State University
Cleveland, Mississippi
www.deltastate.edu Federal Code: 002403

4-year public university in large town.
Enrollment: 3,212 undergrads. 398 full-time freshmen.
Selectivity: Admits less than 50% of applicants.

BASIC COSTS (2008-2009)
Tuition and fees: $4,449; out-of-state residents $11,182.
Per-credit charge: $148; out-of-state residents $373.
Room and board: $5,341.

FINANCIAL AID PICTURE (2007-2008)
Students with need: 35% of average financial aid package awarded as scholarships/grants, 65% awarded as loans/jobs. Need-based aid available for part-time students. Work study available nights, weekends, and for part-time students.
Students without need: No-need awards available for academics, alumni affiliation, art, athletics, leadership, music/drama, state/district residency.

FINANCIAL AID PROCEDURES
Forms required: FAFSA, institutional form.
Dates and Deadlines: No deadline. Applicants notified on a rolling basis starting 5/1.

CONTACT
Ann Mullins, Director of Student Financial Assistance
117 Kent Wyatt Hall, Cleveland, MS 38733
(662) 846-4670

East Central Community College
Decatur, Mississippi
www.eccc.edu Federal Code: 002404

2-year public community college in rural community.
Enrollment: 2,395 undergrads.
Selectivity: Open admission; but selective for some programs.

BASIC COSTS (2008-2009)
Tuition and fees: $1,520; out-of-state residents $3,620.
Per-credit charge: $75; out-of-state residents $162.
Room and board: $2,930.

FINANCIAL AID PICTURE (2007-2008)
Students with need: 72% of average financial aid package awarded as scholarships/grants, 28% awarded as loans/jobs.
Students without need: No-need awards available for academics, athletics, state/district residency.

FINANCIAL AID PROCEDURES

Forms required: FAFSA, institutional form.

Dates and Deadlines: No deadline. Applicants notified on a rolling basis starting 7/31; must reply within 2 week(s) of notification.

CONTACT

Brenda Carson, Director of Financial Aid
Box 129, Decatur, MS 39327
(601) 635-2111 ext. 378

East Mississippi Community College

Scooba, Mississippi
www.eastms.edu Federal Code: 002405

2-year public community college in rural community.

Enrollment: 4,184 undergrads, 33% part-time. 888 full-time freshmen.

Selectivity: Open admission; but selective for some programs.

BASIC COSTS (2008-2009)

Tuition and fees: $1,820; out-of-state residents $3,570.

Room and board: $3,000.

Additional info: $50 health fee for on-campus residents.

FINANCIAL AID PICTURE

Students with need: Need-based aid available for full-time and part-time students.

Students without need: No-need awards available for academics, art, athletics, leadership, music/drama, state/district residency.

FINANCIAL AID PROCEDURES

Forms required: FAFSA, state aid form, institutional form.

Dates and Deadlines: Priority date 4/1; no closing date. Applicants notified on a rolling basis starting 4/1; must reply within 2 week(s) of notification.

CONTACT

Jim Gibson, Financial Aid Director
Admissions Office, Scooba, MS 39358
(662) 476-5079

Hinds Community College

Raymond, Mississippi
www.hindscc.edu Federal Code: 002407

2-year public branch campus and community college in small town.

Enrollment: 10,015 undergrads.

Selectivity: Open admission; but selective for some programs.

BASIC COSTS (2008-2009)

Tuition and fees: $1,740; out-of-state residents $3,946.

Per-credit charge: $85; out-of-state residents $170.

Room and board: $2,920.

FINANCIAL AID PICTURE (2007-2008)

Students with need: Need-based aid available for full-time and part-time students.

Students without need: No-need awards available for academics, art, athletics, job skills, leadership, minority status, music/drama, state/district residency.

FINANCIAL AID PROCEDURES

Forms required: FAFSA.

Dates and Deadlines: Priority date 4/1; no closing date. Applicants notified on a rolling basis starting 5/15; must reply within 2 week(s) of notification.

Transfers: Financial aid transcripts from all previous colleges must be on file prior to award letter being released.

CONTACT

Thurman Mitchell, Director of Financial Aid, Raymond Campus
505 East Main Street, Raymond, MS 39154-1100
(601) 857-3223

Itawamba Community College

Fulton, Mississippi
www.iccms.edu Federal Code: 002409

2-year public community and technical college in small town.

Enrollment: 6,627 undergrads.

Selectivity: Open admission; but selective for some programs.

BASIC COSTS (2008-2009)

Tuition and fees: $1,630; out-of-state residents $3,380.

Per-credit charge: $85.

Room and board: $2,700.

FINANCIAL AID PICTURE (2007-2008)

Students with need: 49% of average financial aid package awarded as scholarships/grants, 51% awarded as loans/jobs. Need-based aid available for part-time students.

Students without need: No-need awards available for academics, art, athletics, leadership, music/drama, state/district residency.

FINANCIAL AID PROCEDURES

Forms required: FAFSA, institutional form.

Dates and Deadlines: Priority date 4/30; no closing date. Applicants notified on a rolling basis starting 4/15.

CONTACT

Robert Walker, Director of Financial Aid
602 West Hill Street, Fulton, MS 38843-1099
(662) 862-8222

Jackson State University

Jackson, Mississippi
www.jsums.edu Federal Code: 002410

4-year public university in small city.

Enrollment: 6,501 undergrads, 15% part-time. 951 full-time freshmen.

Selectivity: Admits 50 to 75% of applicants.

BASIC COSTS (2008-2009)

Tuition and fees: $4,634; out-of-state residents $10,978.

Per-credit charge: $154; out-of-state residents $366.

Room and board: $5,720.

FINANCIAL AID PICTURE (2007-2008)

Students with need: Need-based aid available for full-time and part-time students.

Students without need: This college awards aid only to students with need.

FINANCIAL AID PROCEDURES

Forms required: FAFSA.

Dates and Deadlines: Priority date 4/1; closing date 5/1. Applicants notified on a rolling basis starting 5/1.

CONTACT

Betty Moncure, Director, Financial Aid
1400 JR Lynch Street, Jackson, MS 39217
(601) 979-2227

Magnolia Bible College

Kosciusko, Mississippi
www.magnolia.edu Federal Code: 016788

4-year private Bible college in small town, affiliated with Church of Christ.
Enrollment: 19 undergrads.
Selectivity: Open admission; but selective for some programs.

BASIC COSTS (2008-2009)
Tuition and fees: $7,290.
Per-credit charge: $240.
Room only: $1,520.
Additional info: Reduced tuition for Attala County residents: $1,950 full-time, $65 per credit hour, $90 required fees.

FINANCIAL AID PICTURE (2008-2009)
Students with need: Need-based aid available for full-time and part-time students.
Students without need: No-need awards available for academics, leadership, religious affiliation.

FINANCIAL AID PROCEDURES
Forms required: FAFSA, institutional form.
Dates and Deadlines: Priority date 8/1; no closing date. Applicants notified on a rolling basis starting 4/15; must reply within 4 week(s) of notification.

CONTACT
Allen Coker, Financial Aid Coordinator
PO Box 1109, Kosciusko, MS 39090
(662) 289-2896 ext. 106

Meridian Community College

Meridian, Mississippi
www.meridiancc.edu Federal Code: 002413

2-year public community college in large town.
Enrollment: 3,614 undergrads.
Selectivity: Open admission; but selective for some programs.

BASIC COSTS (2008-2009)
Tuition and fees: $1,660; out-of-state residents $2,950.
Per-credit charge: $80; out-of-state residents $137.
Room and board: $3,350.

FINANCIAL AID PICTURE
Students with need: Need-based aid available for full-time and part-time students.
Students without need: No-need awards available for academics, art, athletics, leadership, music/drama, state/district residency.

FINANCIAL AID PROCEDURES
Forms required: FAFSA, institutional form.
Dates and Deadlines: Priority date 6/1; no closing date. Applicants notified on a rolling basis starting 5/15; must reply within 2 week(s) of notification.

CONTACT
Nedra Bradley, Director of Financial Aid
910 Highway 19 North, Meridian, MS 39307-5890
(601) 484-8628

Millsaps College

Jackson, Mississippi
www.millsaps.edu Federal Code: 002414

4-year private business and liberal arts college in large city, affiliated with United Methodist Church.
Enrollment: 999 undergrads, 1% part-time. 271 full-time freshmen.
Selectivity: Admits over 75% of applicants.

BASIC COSTS (2008-2009)
Tuition and fees: $24,754.
Per-credit charge: $720.
Room and board: $8,800.

FINANCIAL AID PICTURE (2008-2009)
Students with need: Out of 229 full-time freshmen who applied for aid, 175 were judged to have need. Of these, 175 received aid, and 78 had their full need met. Average financial aid package met 88% of need; average scholarship/grant was $18,510; average loan was $3,692. For part-time students, average financial aid package was $4,356.
Students without need: 95 full-time freshmen who did not demonstrate need for aid received scholarships/grants; average award was $15,141. No-need awards available for academics, art, leadership, music/drama, religious affiliation.
Cumulative student debt: 62% of graduating class had student loans; average debt was $26,576.

FINANCIAL AID PROCEDURES
Forms required: FAFSA.
Dates and Deadlines: Priority date 3/1; no closing date. Applicants notified on a rolling basis starting 3/15; must reply by 5/1 or within 2 week(s) of notification.

CONTACT
Patrick James, Director of Financial Aid
1701 North State Street, Jackson, MS 39210-0001
(601) 974-1220

Mississippi College

Clinton, Mississippi
www.mc.edu Federal Code: 002415

4-year private university in large city, affiliated with Southern Baptist Convention.
Enrollment: 3,032 undergrads, 12% part-time. 526 full-time freshmen.
Selectivity: Admits 50 to 75% of applicants.

BASIC COSTS (2009-2010)
Tuition and fees: $13,290.
Per-credit charge: $397.
Room and board: $6,020.

FINANCIAL AID PICTURE (2008-2009)
Students with need: Out of 524 full-time freshmen who applied for aid, 290 were judged to have need. Of these, 290 received aid, and 94 had their full need met. Average financial aid package met 78% of need; average scholarship/grant was $10,952; average loan was $4,802. For part-time students, average financial aid package was $12,815.
Students without need: 232 full-time freshmen who did not demonstrate need for aid received scholarships/grants; average award was $10,252. No-need awards available for academics, alumni affiliation, art, leadership, music/drama, religious affiliation.
Scholarships offered: Merit Scholarships: up to $10,000; based on various criteria including leadership, academics, church and community involvement; extensive number awarded including some specifically for transfers.

Cumulative student debt: 75% of graduating class had student loans; average debt was $24,508.
Additional info: Student reply date for institutional scholarships: May 1.

FINANCIAL AID PROCEDURES
Forms required: FAFSA, state aid form.
Dates and Deadlines: Priority date 3/1; no closing date. Applicants notified on a rolling basis starting 3/1; must reply by 5/1.
Transfers: No deadline. Applicants notified on a rolling basis.

CONTACT
Karon McMillan, Director of Financial Aid
PO Box 4026, Clinton, MS 39058
(601) 925-3212

Mississippi Delta Community College
Moorhead, Mississippi
www.msdelta.edu Federal Code: 002416

2-year public community college in rural community.
Enrollment: 3,154 undergrads.
Selectivity: Open admission; but selective for some programs.

BASIC COSTS (2008-2009)
Tuition and fees: $1,920; out-of-state residents $3,528.
Room and board: $4,390.

FINANCIAL AID PICTURE
Students with need: Need-based aid available for full-time students.
Students without need: No-need awards available for academics, athletics, state/district residency.

FINANCIAL AID PROCEDURES
Forms required: FAFSA, institutional form.
Dates and Deadlines: Priority date 8/1; no closing date. Applicants notified on a rolling basis; must reply within 2 week(s) of notification.

CONTACT
Mary Rodgers, Director of Financial Aid
Box 668, Moorhead, MS 38761
(662) 246-6263

Mississippi State University
Mississippi State, Mississippi
www.msstate.edu Federal Code: 002423

4-year public university in large town.
Enrollment: 13,204 undergrads, 9% part-time. 2,273 full-time freshmen.
Selectivity: Admits 50 to 75% of applicants.

BASIC COSTS (2008-2009)
Tuition and fees: $5,151; out-of-state residents $12,503.
Room and board: $7,333.

FINANCIAL AID PICTURE (2007-2008)
Students with need: Out of 1,565 full-time freshmen who applied for aid, 1,564 were judged to have need. Of these, 1,521 received aid, and 263 had their full need met. Average financial aid package met 64% of need; average scholarship/grant was $3,708; average loan was $3,542. For part-time students, average financial aid package was $7,613.
Students without need: 677 full-time freshmen who did not demonstrate need for aid received scholarships/grants; average award was $2,801. No-need awards available for academics, alumni affiliation, art, athletics, job skills, leadership, minority status, music/drama, ROTC, state/district residency.
Scholarships offered: ***Merit:*** Entering Freshman Scholarships: starting at $1,000 per year; based on minimum 24 ACT and 3.0 core GPA. Competitive Freshman Scholarship: covers cost of tuition, fees, room and board, books; based on a minimum 29 ACT and 3.5 core GPA. ***Athletic:*** 73 full-time freshmen received athletic scholarships; average amount $12,190.
Cumulative student debt: 40% of graduating class had student loans; average debt was $21,232.
Additional info: No institutional closing date for FAFSA.

FINANCIAL AID PROCEDURES
Forms required: FAFSA.
Dates and Deadlines: Priority date 4/1; no closing date. Applicants notified on a rolling basis starting 12/1; must reply by 5/1.
Transfers: No deadline. Applicants notified on a rolling basis.

CONTACT
Bruce Crain, Director
Box 6334, Mississippi State, MS 39762
(662) 325-2450

Mississippi University for Women
Columbus, Mississippi
www.muw.edu Federal Code: 002422

4-year public university and liberal arts college in large town.
Enrollment: 1,999 undergrads, 17% part-time. 252 full-time freshmen.
Selectivity: Admits less than 50% of applicants.

BASIC COSTS (2008-2009)
Tuition and fees: $4,423; out-of-state residents $11,688.
Per-credit charge: $184; out-of-state residents $487.
Room and board: $5,066.
Additional info: Tuition/fee waivers available for adults, minority students.

FINANCIAL AID PICTURE (2007-2008)
Students with need: Need-based aid available for full-time and part-time students. Work study available nights, weekends, and for part-time students.
Students without need: No-need awards available for academics, alumni affiliation, leadership, minority status, music/drama, ROTC, state/district residency.

FINANCIAL AID PROCEDURES
Forms required: FAFSA, state aid form.
Dates and Deadlines: Priority date 3/1; no closing date. Applicants notified on a rolling basis starting 3/15; must reply within 2 week(s) of notification.
Transfers: Closing date 4/1.

CONTACT
Dan Miller, Director of Financial Aid
1100 College St. MUW-1613, Columbus, MS 39701
(662) 329-7114

Northeast Mississippi Community College
Booneville, Mississippi
www.nemcc.edu Federal Code: 002426

2-year public community college in small town.
Enrollment: 3,297 undergrads.
Selectivity: Open admission; but selective for some programs.

BASIC COSTS (2008-2009)
Tuition and fees: $1,920; out-of-state residents $3,850.
Per-credit charge: $105; out-of-state residents $212.
Room and board: $2,984.

FINANCIAL AID PICTURE (2008-2009)
Students with need: 73% of average financial aid package awarded as scholarships/grants, 27% awarded as loans/jobs.

FINANCIAL AID PROCEDURES

Forms required: FAFSA, institutional form.
Dates and Deadlines: Priority date 4/1; closing date 6/30. Applicants notified on a rolling basis.
Transfers: No deadline.

CONTACT

Janice Prather, Director of Financial Aid
101 Cunningham Boulevard, Booneville, MS 38829

Northwest Mississippi Community College

Senatobia, Mississippi
www.northwestms.edu Federal Code: 002427

2-year public community college in small town.
Enrollment: 7,118 undergrads, 24% part-time. 2,231 full-time freshmen.
Selectivity: Open admission; but selective for some programs.

BASIC COSTS (2008-2009)

Tuition and fees: $1,700; out-of-state residents $3,700.
Per-credit charge: $80; out-of-state residents $125.
Room and board: $2,700.
Additional info: Lab fees range from $15 to $25 per course.

FINANCIAL AID PICTURE (2007-2008)

Students with need: Need-based aid available for full-time students.

FINANCIAL AID PROCEDURES

Forms required: FAFSA.
Dates and Deadlines: Priority date 4/1; no closing date. Applicants notified by 8/16.

CONTACT

Joe Boyles, Director of Financial Aid
4975 Highway 51 North, Senatobia, MS 38668
(662) 562-3271

Pearl River Community College

Poplarville, Mississippi
www.prcc.edu Federal Code: 002430

2-year public community college in small town.
Enrollment: 3,790 undergrads.
Selectivity: Open admission; but selective for some programs.

BASIC COSTS (2008-2009)

Tuition and fees: $1,806; out-of-state residents $5,511.
Per-credit charge: $90; out-of-state residents $244.
Room and board: $3,400.

FINANCIAL AID PICTURE (2007-2008)

Students with need: Need-based aid available for full-time and part-time students.
Students without need: No-need awards available for academics, alumni affiliation, athletics, leadership, music/drama, state/district residency.

FINANCIAL AID PROCEDURES

Forms required: FAFSA, institutional form.
Dates and Deadlines: Priority date 4/17; no closing date. Applicants notified on a rolling basis.

CONTACT

Valerie Horne, Director of Financial Aid
101 Highway 11 North, Poplarville, MS 39470
(601) 403-1212

Rust College

Holly Springs, Mississippi
www.rustcollege.edu Federal Code: 002433

4-year private liberal arts college in small town, affiliated with United Methodist Church.
Enrollment: 967 undergrads.
Selectivity: Admits less than 50% of applicants.

BASIC COSTS (2008-2009)

Tuition and fees: $7,000.
Per-credit charge: $300.
Room and board: $3,120.
Additional info: Tuition/fee waivers available for adults.

FINANCIAL AID PICTURE

Students with need: Need-based aid available for full-time and part-time students.
Students without need: No-need awards available for academics, leadership, music/drama, religious affiliation, state/district residency.
Scholarships offered: Honor Track: full tuition; based on top 10% of high school graduating class, GPA 3.5 and above, ACT 22 or above, SAT 1030 or above, 3 letters of recommendation, essay; 17 awarded. Presidential Scholarship: $2,000; for top 10% of high school graduating class, GPA 3.25 and above, ACT 19 and above, SAT 910 and above; 17 awarded. Academic Dean's Scholarship: for top 10% of high school graduating class, GPA 3.0 or above, ACT 17 and above, SAT 830 and above; 17 awarded. SAT scores exclusive of Writing.

FINANCIAL AID PROCEDURES

Forms required: FAFSA, state aid form, institutional form.
Dates and Deadlines: Closing date 5/1. Applicants notified on a rolling basis starting 5/1; must reply within 2 week(s) of notification.
Transfers: No deadline. Financial aid transcripts from previous schools required.

CONTACT

Helen Street, Director of Financial Aid
150 Rust Avenue, Holly Springs, MS 38635-2328
(662) 252-8000 ext. 4062

Southwest Mississippi Community College

Summit, Mississippi
www.smcc.edu Federal Code: 002436

2-year public community college in rural community.
Enrollment: 1,638 undergrads, 8% part-time. 583 full-time freshmen.
Selectivity: Open admission; but selective for some programs.

BASIC COSTS (2008-2009)

Tuition and fees: $1,800; out-of-state residents $4,500.
Per-credit charge: $75; out-of-state residents $190.
Room and board: $2,530.

FINANCIAL AID PICTURE (2008-2009)

Students with need: 99% of average financial aid package awarded as scholarships/grants, 1% awarded as loans/jobs. Need-based aid available for part-time students.

FINANCIAL AID PROCEDURES

Dates and Deadlines: No deadline. Applicants notified on a rolling basis.

CONTACT

Stacey Hodges, Director of Financial Aid
1156 College Drive, Summit, MS 39666
(601) 276-3707

Tougaloo College

Tougaloo, Mississippi
www.tougaloo.edu Federal Code: 002439

4-year private liberal arts college in large city, affiliated with United Christian Mission Society and United Church of Christ.
Enrollment: 862 undergrads, 4% part-time. 237 full-time freshmen.
Selectivity: Admits over 75% of applicants.

BASIC COSTS (2009-2010)
Tuition and fees: $9,710.
Per-credit charge: $385.
Room and board: $6,572.
Additional info: Tuition/fee waivers available for adults.

FINANCIAL AID PICTURE (2008-2009)
Students with need: Need-based aid available for full-time and part-time students.
Students without need: No-need awards available for academics, athletics, ROTC.

FINANCIAL AID PROCEDURES
Forms required: FAFSA, state aid form, institutional form.
Dates and Deadlines: Priority date 4/15; no closing date. Applicants notified on a rolling basis starting 5/1; must reply within 2 week(s) of notification.

CONTACT
Maria Thomas, Director of Financial Aid
500 West County Line Road, Tougaloo, MS 39174
(601) 977-7766

University of Mississippi

University, Mississippi
www.olemiss.edu Federal Code: 002440

4-year public university in large town.
Enrollment: 12,609 undergrads, 9% part-time. 2,437 full-time freshmen.
Selectivity: Admits over 75% of applicants.

BASIC COSTS (2008-2009)
Tuition and fees: $5,107; out-of-state residents $12,468.
Room and board: $5,914.
Additional info: Tuition/fee waivers available for minority students.

FINANCIAL AID PICTURE (2007-2008)
Students with need: Out of 1,482 full-time freshmen who applied for aid, 955 were judged to have need. Of these, 920 received aid, and 124 had their full need met. Average financial aid package met 76% of need; average scholarship/grant was $6,299; average loan was $3,809. For part-time students, average financial aid package was $1,996.
Students without need: 558 full-time freshmen who did not demonstrate need for aid received scholarships/grants; average award was $3,765. No-need awards available for academics, alumni affiliation, art, athletics, leadership, minority status, music/drama, ROTC, state/district residency.
Scholarships offered: 66 full-time freshmen received athletic scholarships; average amount $10,037.
Cumulative student debt: 39% of graduating class had student loans; average debt was $20,047.

FINANCIAL AID PROCEDURES
Forms required: FAFSA.
Dates and Deadlines: Priority date 3/15; no closing date. Applicants notified on a rolling basis starting 4/1; must reply within 3 week(s) of notification.
Transfers: No deadline. Applicants notified on a rolling basis starting 4/1; must reply within 3 week(s) of notification.

CONTACT
Laura Diven-Brown, Director of Financial Aid
145 Martindale, University, MS 38677-1848
(800) 891-4596

University of Mississippi Medical Center

Jackson, Mississippi
www.umc.edu Federal Code: 004688

Upper-division public health science college in large city.
Enrollment: 575 undergrads.
Selectivity: Open admission; but selective for some programs. GED not accepted.

BASIC COSTS (2008-2009)
Tuition and fees: $5,107; out-of-state residents $12,467.
Additional info: Tuition and fees quoted are for semester-based nursing and other health-related undergraduate programs.

FINANCIAL AID PICTURE
Students with need: Need-based aid available for full-time and part-time students.
Students without need: This college awards aid only to students with need.

FINANCIAL AID PROCEDURES
Forms required: FAFSA, state aid form, institutional form.
Dates and Deadlines: Closing date 4/1. Applicants notified by 7/15; must reply within 2 week(s) of notification.

CONTACT
Stacey Carter, Director of Student Financial Aid
2500 North State Street, Jackson, MS 39216
(601) 984-1117

University of Southern Mississippi

Hattiesburg, Mississippi
www.usm.edu Federal Code: 002441

4-year public university in small city.
Enrollment: 12,062 undergrads, 14% part-time. 1,549 full-time freshmen.
Selectivity: Admits 50 to 75% of applicants.

BASIC COSTS (2008-2009)
Tuition and fees: $5,096; out-of-state residents $12,746.
Per-credit charge: $213; out-of-state residents $532.
Room and board: $5,330.

FINANCIAL AID PICTURE (2007-2008)
Students with need: Out of 1,227 full-time freshmen who applied for aid, 947 were judged to have need. Of these, 919 received aid, and 212 had their full need met. Average financial aid package met 79% of need; average scholarship/grant was $3,698; average loan was $3,657. For part-time students, average financial aid package was $5,459.
Students without need: 231 full-time freshmen who did not demonstrate need for aid received scholarships/grants; average award was $3,831.
Scholarships offered: 82 full-time freshmen received athletic scholarships; average amount $6,700.
Cumulative student debt: 66% of graduating class had student loans; average debt was $17,350.

FINANCIAL AID PROCEDURES
Forms required: FAFSA, institutional form.
Dates and Deadlines: Priority date 3/15; no closing date.
Transfers: Merit scholarships available to community college transfer students based on college GPA.

CONTACT
David Williamson, Director of Financial Aid
118 College Drive #5166, Hattiesburg, MS 39406-0001
(601) 266-4111

William Carey University
Hattiesburg, Mississippi
www.wmcarey.edu Federal Code: 002447

4-year private university and liberal arts college in small city, affiliated with Baptist faith.
Enrollment: 1,839 undergrads, 16% part-time. 130 full-time freshmen.
Selectivity: Open admission; but selective for some programs.

BASIC COSTS (2008-2009)
Tuition and fees: $9,750.
Per-credit charge: $310.
Room and board: $3,810.

FINANCIAL AID PICTURE (2007-2008)
Students with need: Average financial aid package for all full-time undergraduates was $13,400. 21% awarded as scholarships/grants, 79% awarded as loans/jobs. Need-based aid available for part-time students. Work study available nights, weekends, and for part-time students.
Students without need: No-need awards available for academics, alumni affiliation, art, athletics, music/drama, religious affiliation.
Cumulative student debt: 85% of graduating class had student loans; average debt was $15,000.

FINANCIAL AID PROCEDURES
Forms required: FAFSA.
Dates and Deadlines: Priority date 4/1; closing date 9/1. Applicants notified on a rolling basis starting 6/1; must reply within 2 week(s) of notification.

CONTACT
William Curry, Dean of Enrollment Management & Records
498 Tuscan Avenue, Hattiesburg, MS 39401
(601) 318-6153

Missouri

Avila University
Kansas City, Missouri
www.avila.edu Federal Code: 002449

4-year private university and liberal arts college in very large city, affiliated with Roman Catholic Church.
Enrollment: 1,163 undergrads, 18% part-time. 183 full-time freshmen.
Selectivity: Admits 50 to 75% of applicants.

BASIC COSTS (2009-2010)
Tuition and fees: $20,700.
Per-credit charge: $495.
Room and board: $6,100.

FINANCIAL AID PICTURE (2007-2008)
Students with need: Out of 180 full-time freshmen who applied for aid, 178 were judged to have need. Of these, 177 received aid, and 42 had their full need met. Average financial aid package met 32% of need; average scholarship/grant was $7,293; average loan was $2,519. For part-time students, average financial aid package was $7,195.
Students without need: 82 full-time freshmen who did not demonstrate need for aid received scholarships/grants; average award was $5,107. No-need awards available for academics, alumni affiliation, art, athletics, music/drama, religious affiliation.
Scholarships offered: 35 full-time freshmen received athletic scholarships; average amount $4,622.
Additional info: Financial aid adjusted for increases in tuition based on need.

FINANCIAL AID PROCEDURES
Forms required: FAFSA, institutional form.
Dates and Deadlines: Priority date 3/1; closing date 4/1. Applicants notified on a rolling basis starting 2/1; must reply within 2 week(s) of notification.
Transfers: No deadline. Applicants notified on a rolling basis; must reply within 2 week(s) of notification. Non-need-based academic scholarship available for transfer students.

CONTACT
Director of Financial Aid
11901 Wornall Road, Kansas City, MO 64145-1007
(816) 501-3600

Baptist Bible College
Springfield, Missouri
www.gobbc.com Federal Code: 013208

4-year private Bible and seminary college in small city, affiliated with Baptist faith.
Enrollment: 489 undergrads, 13% part-time. 86 full-time freshmen.
Selectivity: Open admission.

BASIC COSTS (2009-2010)
Tuition and fees: $13,610.
Per-credit charge: $206.
Room and board: $5,400.

FINANCIAL AID PICTURE (2007-2008)
Students with need: Need-based aid available for full-time and part-time students.
Students without need: No-need awards available for academics.
Scholarships offered: Founder's Scholarship: $5,500-$9,500. Bible Scholarships: $800 per year.

FINANCIAL AID PROCEDURES
Forms required: FAFSA, institutional form.
Dates and Deadlines: Closing date 5/1. Applicants notified on a rolling basis; must reply within 2 week(s) of notification.

CONTACT
Bob Kotulski, Financial Aid Director
628 East Kearney Street, Springfield, MO 65803
(417) 268-6036

Bolivar Technical College
Bolivar, Missouri
www.bolivarcollege.org Federal Code: 035793

2-year private branch campus and technical college in small town.
Enrollment: 163 undergrads. 136 full-time freshmen.
Selectivity: Open admission; but selective for some programs.

BASIC COSTS (2008-2009)
Tuition and fees: $11,940.
Per-credit charge: $335.
Additional info: Tuition varies by program, $150-$335 per credit-hour.

FINANCIAL AID PICTURE (2007-2008)
Students with need: 65% of average financial aid package awarded as scholarships/grants, 35% awarded as loans/jobs.

FINANCIAL AID PROCEDURES

Dates and Deadlines: Priority date 4/1; no closing date.

CONTACT

Deborah George, Director of Financial Aid
PO Box 592, Bolivar, MO 65613
(417) 777-50622

Calvary Bible College and Theological Seminary

Kansas City, Missouri
www.calvary.edu Federal Code: 002450

4-year private Bible and seminary college in large city, affiliated with nondenominational tradition.

Enrollment: 230 undergrads, 23% part-time. 40 full-time freshmen.
Selectivity: Open admission; but selective for some programs.

BASIC COSTS (2009-2010)

Tuition and fees: $8,872.
Per-credit charge: $270.
Room and board: $4,400.
Additional info: Tuition/fee waivers available for minority students.

FINANCIAL AID PICTURE (2007-2008)

Students with need: 33% of average financial aid package awarded as scholarships/grants, 67% awarded as loans/jobs. Need-based aid available for part-time students.
Students without need: No-need awards available for academics, alumni affiliation, job skills, music/drama, religious affiliation, ROTC.

FINANCIAL AID PROCEDURES

Forms required: FAFSA, institutional form.
Dates and Deadlines: Priority date 3/1; closing date 4/1. Applicants notified on a rolling basis starting 5/1.
Transfers: Applicants notified on a rolling basis.

CONTACT

Ryan Lowe, Financial Aid Counselor
15800 Calvary Road, Kansas City, MO 64147
(816) 322-5152 ext. 1323

Central Christian College of the Bible

Moberly, Missouri
www.cccb.edu Federal Code: 014619

4-year private Bible college in large town, affiliated with Christian Church.
Enrollment: 398 undergrads.
Selectivity: Admits over 75% of applicants.

BASIC COSTS (2009-2010)

Additional info: Full-time students receive full scholarship for tuition only, $8,800. Room and board $5,790 for two semesters. Required fees $1,540 per semester.Off-campus students pay a $650 facilities usage fee per semester.

FINANCIAL AID PICTURE (2007-2008)

Students with need: Need-based aid available for full-time and part-time students.

FINANCIAL AID PROCEDURES

Forms required: FAFSA.
Dates and Deadlines: Priority date 3/15; closing date 4/1. Applicants notified by 5/15; must reply within 2 week(s) of notification.

CONTACT

Rhonda Dunham, Financial Aid Director
911 East Urbandale Drive, Moberly, MO 65270-1997
(888) 263-3900

Central Methodist University

Fayette, Missouri
www.centralmethodist.edu Federal Code: E00605

4-year private university and liberal arts college in small town, affiliated with United Methodist Church.
Enrollment: 1,031 undergrads, 3% part-time. 300 full-time freshmen.
Selectivity: Admits 50 to 75% of applicants.

BASIC COSTS (2009-2010)

Tuition and fees: $18,670.
Per-credit charge: $180.
Room and board: $6,240.

FINANCIAL AID PICTURE (2008-2009)

Students with need: Need-based aid available for full-time and part-time students.
Students without need: No-need awards available for academics, alumni affiliation, athletics, leadership, music/drama, religious affiliation, ROTC.

FINANCIAL AID PROCEDURES

Forms required: FAFSA.
Dates and Deadlines: Priority date 3/15; no closing date. Applicants notified on a rolling basis starting 1/30; must reply within 2 week(s) of notification.
Transfers: Institutional financial assistance based on merit is determined by college transfer GPA.

CONTACT

Linda Mackey, Director of Financial Aid
411 Central Methodist Square, Fayette, MO 65248-1198
(660) 248-6245

Chamberlain College of Nursing

St. Louis, Missouri
www.chamberlain.edu Federal Code: 006385

4-year for-profit nursing college in very large city, affiliated with United Church of Christ.
Enrollment: 2,167 undergrads.

FINANCIAL AID PICTURE

Students with need: Need-based aid available for full-time and part-time students.
Students without need: No-need awards available for academics.
Scholarships offered: Tenet Nurse Citizen Award: full tuition; based on application, essay, interview, renewable with 3.25 GPA, 1 awarded. Chancellor's Award: half tuition; for students with 24 ACT, 3.5 GPA; number awarded subject to fund availability. Merit Scholarships: up to $3,000; based on academic achievement; number awarded subject to fund availability.

FINANCIAL AID PROCEDURES

Forms required: FAFSA, institutional form.
Dates and Deadlines: No deadline. Applicants notified on a rolling basis starting 4/1; must reply within 2 week(s) of notification.
Transfers: No deadline.

CONTACT

Michelle Mohn, Financial Counselor
6150 Oakland Avenue, St. Louis, MO 63139
(314) 768-5604

College of the Ozarks
Point Lookout, Missouri
www.cofo.edu Federal Code: 002500

4-year private liberal arts college in small town, affiliated with interdenominational tradition.
Enrollment: 1,320 undergrads, 1% part-time. 274 full-time freshmen.
Selectivity: Admits less than 50% of applicants.

BASIC COSTS (2009-2010)
Room and board: $5,000.
Additional info: Cost of full-time tuition met through combination of institutional work program and federal, state, and institutional funding. Required fees: $390. Full-time students participating in work program work 15 hours per week for 16 weeks and one 40-hour work week per semester. Part-time students (commuters only) pay $295 per credit hour for tuition and additional $390 per year as required fees.

FINANCIAL AID PICTURE (2008-2009)
Students with need: Average financial aid package met 85% of need; average scholarship/grant was $10,937. For part-time students, average financial aid package was $5,452.
Students without need: No-need awards available for academics, art, athletics, leadership, music/drama, ROTC, state/district residency.
Cumulative student debt: 15% of graduating class had student loans; average debt was $4,878.

FINANCIAL AID PROCEDURES
Forms required: FAFSA.
Dates and Deadlines: Priority date 2/15; no closing date. Applicants notified by 7/1.
Transfers: No deadline. Applicants notified on a rolling basis starting 2/15.

CONTACT
Kyla McCarty, Financial Aid Director
PO Box 17, Point Lookout, MO 65726-0017
(417) 690-3290

Columbia College
Columbia, Missouri
www.ccis.edu Federal Code: 002456

4-year private liberal arts college in small city, affiliated with Christian Church (Disciples of Christ).
Enrollment: 1,101 undergrads, 18% part-time. 195 full-time freshmen.
Selectivity: Admits 50 to 75% of applicants.

BASIC COSTS (2009-2010)
Tuition and fees: $14,576.
Per-credit charge: $312.
Room and board: $5,898.

FINANCIAL AID PICTURE (2007-2008)
Students with need: Out of 100 full-time freshmen who applied for aid, 90 were judged to have need. Of these, 90 received aid, and 13 had their full need met. Average financial aid package met 69% of need; average scholarship/grant was $9,264; average loan was $3,878. For part-time students, average financial aid package was $4,663.
Students without need: 51 full-time freshmen who did not demonstrate need for aid received scholarships/grants; average award was $7,798. No-need awards available for academics, alumni affiliation, art, athletics, job skills, leadership, music/drama, religious affiliation, ROTC, state/district residency.
Scholarships offered: ***Merit:*** Columbia College Scholarship (full tuition, room/board): requires 3.5 GPA, 25 ACT or 1140 SAT, campus visit, interview, essay, letter of recommendation; renewable with 30 semester hours and 3.5 GPA. Half-tuition scholarship: minimum 3.4 GPA or GED of 2900, 24 ACT or 1110 SAT; renewable with 24 semester hours per year and 3.2 GPA for up to 3 years. ***Athletic:*** 153 full-time freshmen received athletic scholarships; average amount $7,745.
Cumulative student debt: 58% of graduating class had student loans; average debt was $17,101.

FINANCIAL AID PROCEDURES
Forms required: FAFSA.
Dates and Deadlines: No deadline. Applicants notified on a rolling basis starting 3/1.

CONTACT
Sharon Abernathy, Director of Financial Aid
1001 Rogers Street, Columbia, MO 65216
(573) 875-7360

Conception Seminary College
Conception, Missouri
www.conception.edu Federal Code: 002467

4-year private seminary college for men in rural community, affiliated with Roman Catholic Church.
Enrollment: 105 undergrads. 12 full-time freshmen.
Selectivity: Admits over 75% of applicants.

BASIC COSTS (2009-2010)
Tuition and fees: $15,786.
Per-credit charge: $180.
Room and board: $9,362.

FINANCIAL AID PICTURE
Students with need: Need-based aid available for full-time and part-time students. Work study available nights, weekends, and for part-time students.
Students without need: No-need awards available for academics.

FINANCIAL AID PROCEDURES
Forms required: FAFSA.
Dates and Deadlines: No deadline. Applicants notified on a rolling basis starting 8/1; must reply by 8/20.

CONTACT
Justin Hernandez, Financial Aid Officer
Box 502, Conception, MO 64433-0502
(660) 944-2851

Cottey College
Nevada, Missouri
www.cottey.edu Federal Code: 002458

2-year private junior and liberal arts college for women in small town.
Enrollment: 330 undergrads.

BASIC COSTS (2008-2009)
Tuition and fees: $13,900.
Room and board: $5,400.

FINANCIAL AID PICTURE (2008-2009)
Students with need: Need-based aid available for part-time students. Work study available nights, weekends, and for part-time students.
Students without need: No-need awards available for academics, alumni affiliation, art, athletics, leadership, music/drama.

FINANCIAL AID PROCEDURES
Forms required: FAFSA.

Dates and Deadlines: Priority date 3/1; no closing date. Applicants notified on a rolling basis starting 3/15; must reply by 5/1 or within 4 week(s) of notification.
Transfers: Applicants notified on a rolling basis starting 3/15; must reply within 4 week(s) of notification.

CONTACT

Sherry Pennington, Coordinator of Financial Aid
1000 West Austin Boulevard, Nevada, MO 64772
(417) 667-8181 ext. 2190

Crowder College

Neosho, Missouri
www.crowder.edu Federal Code: 002459

2-year public community and liberal arts college in small town.
Enrollment: 2,816 undergrads, 44% part-time. 466 full-time freshmen.
Selectivity: Open admission; but selective for some programs.

BASIC COSTS (2008-2009)

Tuition and fees: $2,400; out-of-district residents $3,210; out-of-state residents $4,050.
Per-credit charge: $68; out-of-district residents $95; out-of-state residents $123.
Room and board: $3,870.

FINANCIAL AID PICTURE (2007-2008)

Students with need: Need-based aid available for full-time and part-time students. Work study available nights, weekends, and for part-time students.
Students without need: This college awards aid only to students with need.

FINANCIAL AID PROCEDURES

Forms required: FAFSA, institutional form.
Dates and Deadlines: Priority date 7/1; no closing date. Applicants notified on a rolling basis starting 5/15.

CONTACT

Michelle Paul, Director of Financial Aid
601 LaClede Avenue, Neosho, MO 64850
(417) 451-3223 ext. 5434

Culver-Stockton College

Canton, Missouri
www.culver.edu Federal Code: 002460

4-year private liberal arts college in small town, affiliated with Christian Church (Disciples of Christ).
Enrollment: 771 undergrads, 4% part-time. 227 full-time freshmen.
Selectivity: Admits 50 to 75% of applicants.

BASIC COSTS (2009-2010)

Tuition and fees: $22,550.
Per-credit charge: $515.
Room and board: $7,400.

FINANCIAL AID PICTURE (2008-2009)

Students with need: Out of 207 full-time freshmen who applied for aid, 183 were judged to have need. Of these, 183 received aid, and 33 had their full need met. Average financial aid package met 81% of need; average scholarship/grant was $16,514; average loan was $4,486. For part-time students, average financial aid package was $4,905.
Students without need: 44 full-time freshmen who did not demonstrate need for aid received scholarships/grants; average award was $12,468. No-need awards available for academics, alumni affiliation, art, athletics, job skills, leadership, music/drama, religious affiliation, state/district residency.
Scholarships offered: 35 full-time freshmen received athletic scholarships; average amount $1,629.
Cumulative student debt: 92% of graduating class had student loans; average debt was $22,996.

FINANCIAL AID PROCEDURES

Forms required: FAFSA.
Dates and Deadlines: Priority date 3/1; closing date 6/1. Applicants notified on a rolling basis starting 2/15; must reply within 2 week(s) of notification.
Transfers: Must reply within 2 week(s) of notification.

CONTACT

Tina Wiseman, Director of Financial Aid
One College Hill, Canton, MO 63435-1299
(573) 288-6307

DeVry University: Kansas City

Kansas City, Missouri
www.devry.edu

4-year for-profit university in large city.
Enrollment: 945 undergrads, 47% part-time. 97 full-time freshmen.

BASIC COSTS (2008-2009)

Tuition and fees: $14,130.
Per-credit charge: $515.

FINANCIAL AID PICTURE (2007-2008)

Students with need: Need-based aid available for full-time and part-time students.
Students without need: This college awards aid only to students with need.

FINANCIAL AID PROCEDURES

Forms required: FAFSA.
Dates and Deadlines: No deadline. Applicants notified on a rolling basis.

CONTACT

Maureen Kelly, Senior Associate Director of Financial Aid
11224 Holmes Street, Kansas City, MO 64131-3626
(816) 941-0439

Drury University

Springfield, Missouri
www.drury.edu Federal Code: 002461

4-year private university and liberal arts college in large city, affiliated with United Church of Christ and Christian Church (Disciples of Christ).
Enrollment: 1,543 undergrads, 3% part-time. 334 full-time freshmen.
Selectivity: Admits 50 to 75% of applicants.

BASIC COSTS (2009-2010)

Tuition and fees: $19,158.
Per-credit charge: $620.
Room and board: $6,703.

FINANCIAL AID PICTURE (2008-2009)

Students with need: Out of 317 full-time freshmen who applied for aid, 292 were judged to have need. Of these, 292 received aid, and 263 had their full need met. Average financial aid package met 83% of need; average scholarship/grant was $6,280; average loan was $4,950. Need-based aid available for part-time students.
Students without need: 55 full-time freshmen who did not demonstrate need for aid received scholarships/grants; average award was $3,775. No-need awards available for academics, alumni affiliation, art, athletics, job skills, leadership, minority status, music/drama, religious affiliation.

Scholarships offered: ***Merit:*** Trustee Scholarship: $10,000 up to tuition, room and board; 30 awarded. Presidential Scholarship: up to $12,000 per year; 10 awarded. Dean's Scholarship: up to $8,000 a year; top 2% of high school class awarded. Leadership Scholarship: $1,000 a year. Edward Jones Minority Scholarship: $10,000; 10 awarded. Missouri A+ Scholarship: $1,000. International Baccalaureate Award: $7,000 a year. Departmental Awards: amounts and requirements vary by department. Alumni Children's: $500 yearly. Church Scholarship: $500 yearly. Bright Flight: $2,000 a year. ***Athletic:*** 32 full-time freshmen received athletic scholarships; average amount $9,280.
Cumulative student debt: 61% of graduating class had student loans; average debt was $18,384.

FINANCIAL AID PROCEDURES

Forms required: FAFSA, institutional form.
Dates and Deadlines: Closing date 3/15. Applicants notified on a rolling basis starting 3/30; must reply within 2 week(s) of notification.
Transfers: No deadline. Phi Theta Kappa Scholarship of $1,000 available.

CONTACT

Annette Avery, Director of Financial Aid
900 North Benton Avenue, Springfield, MO 65802-3712
(417) 873-7312

East Central College

Union, Missouri
www.eastcentral.edu Federal Code: 008862

2-year public community college in small town.
Enrollment: 2,396 undergrads, 37% part-time. 582 full-time freshmen.
Selectivity: Open admission; but selective for some programs.

BASIC COSTS (2008-2009)

Tuition and fees: $2,130; out-of-district residents $2,910; out-of-state residents $4,230.
Per-credit charge: $61; out-of-district residents $87; out-of-state residents $131.

FINANCIAL AID PICTURE (2007-2008)

Students with need: Need-based aid available for full-time and part-time students.
Students without need: No-need awards available for academics, alumni affiliation, art, athletics, music/drama, state/district residency.

FINANCIAL AID PROCEDURES

Forms required: FAFSA.
Dates and Deadlines: Priority date 3/1; no closing date. Applicants notified on a rolling basis starting 3/15.
Transfers: No deadline. Applicants notified on a rolling basis starting 3/15.

CONTACT

Karen Koenig-Griffin, Director of Financial Aid
1964 Prairie Dell Road, Union, MO 63084-0529
(636) 583-5195 ext. 2777

Evangel University

Springfield, Missouri
www.evangel.edu Federal Code: 002463

4-year private liberal arts college in small city, affiliated with Assemblies of God.
Enrollment: 1,718 undergrads, 7% part-time. 381 full-time freshmen.
Selectivity: Admits 50 to 75% of applicants.

BASIC COSTS (2008-2009)

Tuition and fees: $15,010.
Room and board: $5,410.

FINANCIAL AID PICTURE (2007-2008)

Students with need: Out of 321 full-time freshmen who applied for aid, 265 were judged to have need. Of these, 235 received aid, and 31 had their full need met. Average financial aid package met 54% of need; average scholarship/grant was $6,183; average loan was $3,584. For part-time students, average financial aid package was $10,353.
Students without need: This college awards aid only to students with need.
Scholarships offered: 35 full-time freshmen received athletic scholarships; average amount $5,759.

FINANCIAL AID PROCEDURES

Forms required: FAFSA.
Dates and Deadlines: Priority date 4/1; closing date 6/30. Applicants notified on a rolling basis starting 4/1; must reply within 3 week(s) of notification.

CONTACT

Dorynda Carpenter, Director of Student Financial Services
1111 North Glenstone, Springfield, MO 65802
(417) 865-2811 ext. 7300

Fontbonne University

St. Louis, Missouri
www.fontbonne.edu Federal Code: 002464

4-year private university and liberal arts college in large city, affiliated with Roman Catholic Church.
Enrollment: 2,009 undergrads, 25% part-time. 186 full-time freshmen.
Selectivity: Admits over 75% of applicants.

BASIC COSTS (2009-2010)

Tuition and fees: $19,795.
Per-credit charge: $521.
Room and board: $7,411.

FINANCIAL AID PICTURE (2007-2008)

Students with need: Out of 160 full-time freshmen who applied for aid, 139 were judged to have need. Of these, 132 received aid, and 4 had their full need met. Average financial aid package met 18% of need; average scholarship/grant was $4,265; average loan was $1,234. For part-time students, average financial aid package was $1,733.
Students without need: 59 full-time freshmen who did not demonstrate need for aid received scholarships/grants; average award was $3,708. No-need awards available for academics, alumni affiliation, art, leadership, minority status, music/drama, religious affiliation, state/district residency.
Scholarships offered: Dean's Scholarship: $6,000-$8,000; GPA, ACT, rank criteria. Alumni Scholarship: $1,000-$6,000; GPA, ACT and class rank criteria. Presidential Scholarship: up to full tuition. Campus Service Scholarship: $500-$3,000; activities, leadership. Art, theater, English, writing and computer science scholarships also available.
Cumulative student debt: 85% of graduating class had student loans; average debt was $17,500.

FINANCIAL AID PROCEDURES

Forms required: FAFSA, institutional form.
Dates and Deadlines: Closing date 4/1. Applicants notified on a rolling basis starting 2/1; must reply within 2 week(s) of notification.
Transfers: Applicants notified on a rolling basis starting 2/1; must reply within 2 week(s) of notification.

CONTACT

Nicole Moore, Director of Financial Aid
6800 Wydown Boulevard, St. Louis, MO 63105
(314) 889-1414

Goldfarb School of Nursing at Barnes-Jewish College

St. Louis, Missouri
www.barnesjewishcollege.edu Federal Code: 003689

Upper-division private nursing college in large city.
Enrollment: 511 undergrads, 47% part-time.

BASIC COSTS (2008-2009)
Tuition and fees: $13,730.
Per-credit charge: $450.

FINANCIAL AID PICTURE (2007-2008)
Students with need: 13% of average financial aid package awarded as scholarships/grants, 87% awarded as loans/jobs. Need-based aid available for part-time students.
Students without need: No-need awards available for academics, leadership.

FINANCIAL AID PROCEDURES
Forms required: FAFSA.
Dates and Deadlines: Priority date 4/1; no closing date. Applicants notified on a rolling basis.
Transfers: No deadline. Applicants notified on a rolling basis.

CONTACT
Jason Crowe, Financial Aid Director
4483 Duncan Avenue, St. Louis, MO 63110-1091
(314) 362-9250

Hannibal-LaGrange College

Hannibal, Missouri
www.hlg.edu Federal Code: 009089

4-year private liberal arts college in large town, affiliated with Southern Baptist Convention.
Enrollment: 1,005 undergrads. 199 full-time freshmen.

BASIC COSTS (2009-2010)
Tuition and fees: $15,480.
Room and board: $6,000.

FINANCIAL AID PICTURE (2008-2009)
Students with need: Need-based aid available for full-time and part-time students.
Students without need: No-need awards available for academics, art, athletics, music/drama, religious affiliation.
Additional info: Work-study opportunities vary according to on- and off-campus needs.

FINANCIAL AID PROCEDURES
Forms required: FAFSA, institutional form.
Dates and Deadlines: Closing date 7/1. Applicants notified on a rolling basis; must reply by 8/31.
Transfers: No deadline.

CONTACT
Brice Baumgardner, Director of Financial Aid
2800 Palmyra Road, Hannibal, MO 63401
(573) 629-3267

Harris-Stowe State University

St. Louis, Missouri
www.hssu.edu Federal Code: 002466

4-year public university in large city.
Enrollment: 1,799 undergrads, 27% part-time. 410 full-time freshmen.
Selectivity: Admits over 75% of applicants.

BASIC COSTS (2008-2009)
Tuition and fees: $5,340; out-of-state residents $10,092.
Per-credit charge: $164; out-of-state residents $323.

FINANCIAL AID PICTURE (2007-2008)
Students with need: Average financial aid package met 85% of need; average scholarship/grant was $3,000; average loan was $4,000. For part-time students, average financial aid package was $500.
Students without need: No-need awards available for academics, athletics, music/drama, state/district residency.
Cumulative student debt: 85% of graduating class had student loans; average debt was $12,000.

FINANCIAL AID PROCEDURES
Forms required: FAFSA, institutional form.
Dates and Deadlines: Priority date 4/1; no closing date. Must reply within 3 week(s) of notification.

CONTACT
Regina Blackshear, Director of Financial Assistance
3026 Laclede Avenue, St. Louis, MO 63103-2199
(314) 340-3500

Hickey College

St. Louis, Missouri
www.hickeycollege.edu Federal Code: 014209

4-year for-profit business and technical college in very large city.
Enrollment: 402 undergrads.
Selectivity: Open admission; but selective for some programs.

BASIC COSTS (2008-2009)
Tuition and fees: $12,520.
Room and board: $5,600.

FINANCIAL AID PICTURE
Students with need: Need-based aid available for full-time students.

FINANCIAL AID PROCEDURES
Forms required: FAFSA.
Dates and Deadlines: No deadline. Applicants notified on a rolling basis.

CONTACT
Deana Pecoroni, Director, Student Services
940 West Port Plaza, St. Louis, MO 63146
(314) 434-2212 ext. 128

Jefferson College

Hillsboro, Missouri
www.jeffco.edu Federal Code: 002468

2-year public community and technical college in rural community.
Enrollment: 4,609 undergrads, 45% part-time. 993 full-time freshmen.
Selectivity: Open admission; but selective for some programs.

BASIC COSTS (2008-2009)
Tuition and fees: $2,550; out-of-district residents $3,840; out-of-state residents $5,100.

Per-credit charge: $85; out-of-district residents $128; out-of-state residents $170.
Room only: $3,400.

FINANCIAL AID PICTURE (2007-2008)

Students with need: Out of 819 full-time freshmen who applied for aid, 529 were judged to have need. Of these, 505 received aid, and 14 had their full need met. Average financial aid package met 51% of need; average scholarship/grant was $1,806; average loan was $2,454. For part-time students, average financial aid package was $2,757.
Students without need: 17 full-time freshmen who did not demonstrate need for aid received scholarships/grants; average award was $1,204. No-need awards available for academics, art, athletics, leadership, music/drama, state/district residency.
Scholarships offered: 170 full-time freshmen received athletic scholarships; average amount $5,933.
Cumulative student debt: 36% of graduating class had student loans; average debt was $9,958.

FINANCIAL AID PROCEDURES

Forms required: FAFSA.
Dates and Deadlines: Priority date 4/1; no closing date. Applicants notified on a rolling basis starting 4/15.

CONTACT

Julie Fraser, Director of Admissions and Financial Aid
1000 Viking Drive, Hillsboro, MO 63050-2441
(636) 797-3000 ext. 212

Kansas City Art Institute

Kansas City, Missouri
www.kcai.edu Federal Code: 002473

4-year private visual arts college in large city.
Enrollment: 656 undergrads, 1% part-time. 144 full-time freshmen.
Selectivity: Admits 50 to 75% of applicants.

BASIC COSTS (2009-2010)

Tuition and fees: $28,580.
Per-credit charge: $1,190.
Room and board: $8,710.

FINANCIAL AID PICTURE (2008-2009)

Students with need: Average financial aid package met 74% of need; average scholarship/grant was $15,943; average loan was $6,014. For part-time students, average financial aid package was $18,536.
Students without need: No-need awards available for academics, art.
Cumulative student debt: 100% of graduating class had student loans; average debt was $23,375.
Additional info: February 15 and March 15 priority application dates for merit scholarships; deadline July 1.

FINANCIAL AID PROCEDURES

Forms required: FAFSA.
Dates and Deadlines: Priority date 3/15; closing date 4/1. Applicants notified on a rolling basis starting 4/1; must reply within 2 week(s) of notification.
Transfers: Applicants notified on a rolling basis starting 4/1; must reply within 2 week(s) of notification.

CONTACT

Kim Wagner, Director of Financial Aid
4415 Warwick Boulevard, Kansas City, MO 64111-1820
(816) 802-3337

Lincoln University

Jefferson City, Missouri
www.lincolnu.edu Federal Code: 002479

4-year public university and liberal arts college in large town.
Enrollment: 2,445 undergrads, 20% part-time. 546 full-time freshmen.
Selectivity: Open admission; but selective for some programs and for out-of-state students.

BASIC COSTS (2009-2010)

Tuition and fees: $6,175; out-of-state residents $10,885.
Per-credit charge: $189; out-of-state residents $346.
Room and board: $4,660.
Additional info: Students enrolled full-time must pay $233 per fall/spring semester or $96 per summer semester for health insurance if they do not provide proof of other coverage. Enrollment in the student health insurance program is required for international students.

FINANCIAL AID PICTURE (2008-2009)

Students with need: Need-based aid available for full-time students. Work study available nights, weekends, and for part-time students.
Students without need: No-need awards available for academics, art, athletics, job skills, leadership, minority status, music/drama, ROTC, state/district residency.

FINANCIAL AID PROCEDURES

Forms required: FAFSA, institutional form.
Dates and Deadlines: Priority date 3/1; no closing date. Applicants notified on a rolling basis starting 3/15; must reply within 2 week(s) of notification.
Transfers: Applicants notified on a rolling basis starting 3/15; must reply within 2 week(s) of notification.

CONTACT

Alfred Robinson, Director of Financial Aid and Student Employment
820 Chestnut Stree, B7 Young Hall, Jefferson City, MO 65102-0029
(573) 681-5363

Lindenwood University

St. Charles, Missouri
www.lindenwood.edu Federal Code: 002480

4-year private university and liberal arts college in very large city, affiliated with Presbyterian Church (USA).
Enrollment: 6,330 undergrads, 6% part-time. 1,106 full-time freshmen.
Selectivity: Admits less than 50% of applicants.

BASIC COSTS (2009-2010)

Tuition and fees: $13,300.
Per-credit charge: $370.
Room and board: $7,060.

FINANCIAL AID PICTURE (2008-2009)

Students with need: Out of 974 full-time freshmen who applied for aid, 550 were judged to have need. Of these, 550 received aid, and 193 had their full need met. Average financial aid package met 90% of need; average scholarship/grant was $2,470; average loan was $1,868. For part-time students, average financial aid package was $4,110.
Students without need: 146 full-time freshmen who did not demonstrate need for aid received scholarships/grants; average award was $4,609. No-need awards available for academics, alumni affiliation, art, job skills, leadership, music/drama, ROTC.

FINANCIAL AID PROCEDURES

Forms required: FAFSA.
Dates and Deadlines: Priority date 4/1; no closing date. Applicants notified on a rolling basis.

CONTACT
Lori Bode, Director of Financial Aid
209 South Kingshighway, St. Charles, MO 63301-1695
(636) 949-4923

Linn State Technical College
Linn, Missouri
www.linnstate.edu

2-year public technical college in small town.
Enrollment: 945 undergrads, 9% part-time. 456 full-time freshmen.
Selectivity: Open admission; but selective for some programs.

BASIC COSTS (2008-2009)
Tuition and fees: $5,370; out-of-state residents $9,750.
Per-credit charge: $146; out-of-state residents $292.
Room and board: $4,920.

FINANCIAL AID PICTURE (2007-2008)
Students with need: 59% of average financial aid package awarded as scholarships/grants, 41% awarded as loans/jobs.

FINANCIAL AID PROCEDURES
Dates and Deadlines: Priority date 3/1; no closing date.

CONTACT
Becky Whithaus, Director of Financial Aid
One Technology Drive, Linn, MO 65051
(573) 897-5145

Maryville University of Saint Louis
St. Louis, Missouri
www.maryville.edu Federal Code: 002482

4-year private university in very large city.
Enrollment: 2,818 undergrads, 39% part-time. 318 full-time freshmen.
Selectivity: Admits 50 to 75% of applicants.

BASIC COSTS (2009-2010)
Tuition and fees: $21,145.
Per-credit charge: $590.
Room and board: $8,300.

FINANCIAL AID PICTURE (2008-2009)
Students with need: Out of 281 full-time freshmen who applied for aid, 242 were judged to have need. Of these, 242 received aid, and 28 had their full need met. Average financial aid package met 78% of need; average scholarship/grant was $8,590; average loan was $2,962. For part-time students, average financial aid package was $6,589.
Students without need: 67 full-time freshmen who did not demonstrate need for aid received scholarships/grants; average award was $7,472. No-need awards available for academics, alumni affiliation, art, leadership, minority status, ROTC.
Scholarships offered: University Scholars Program: awarded to full-time freshmen with 28 ACT or 1170 SAT (exclusive of writing), high school GPA 3.5-4.0; interview required. M-PACT Award: awarded to full-time freshmen based on campus activity and impact on student life.
Cumulative student debt: 77% of graduating class had student loans; average debt was $23,155.

FINANCIAL AID PROCEDURES
Forms required: FAFSA.
Dates and Deadlines: Priority date 3/1; no closing date. Applicants notified on a rolling basis starting 3/1; must reply by 5/1 or within 2 week(s) of notification.
Transfers: No deadline. Applicants notified on a rolling basis starting 2/1. Outstanding Transfer Student Award, PTK Award, Art & Design Award scholarships available.

CONTACT
Martha Harbaugh, Director of Financial Aid
650 Maryville University Drive, St. Louis, MO 63141-7299
(314) 529-9360

Metro Business College: Jefferson City
Jefferson City, Missouri
www.metrobusinesscollege.edu Federal Code: 014710

2-year for-profit business and health science college in large town.
Enrollment: 178 undergrads, 8% part-time. 56 full-time freshmen.
Selectivity: Open admission; but selective for some programs.

BASIC COSTS (2008-2009)
Tuition and fees: $9,110.

FINANCIAL AID PICTURE
Students with need: Need-based aid available for full-time and part-time students.

FINANCIAL AID PROCEDURES
Forms required: FAFSA, institutional form.
Dates and Deadlines: No deadline. Applicants notified on a rolling basis.

CONTACT
Debbie Jenkins, Financial Aid Coordinator
1407 Southwest Boulevard, Jefferson City, MO 65109
(573) 635-6600

Metropolitan Community College: Blue River
Independence, Missouri
www.mcckc.edu Federal Code: 009140

2-year public community college in small city.
Enrollment: 2,183 undergrads, 49% part-time. 476 full-time freshmen.
Selectivity: Open admission.

BASIC COSTS (2008-2009)
Tuition and fees: $2,460; out-of-district residents $4,380; out-of-state residents $5,850.
Per-credit charge: $77; out-of-district residents $141; out-of-state residents $190.

FINANCIAL AID PICTURE (2007-2008)
Students with need: For part-time students, average financial aid package was $1,202.
Students without need: No-need awards available for academics, athletics, leadership.

FINANCIAL AID PROCEDURES
Forms required: FAFSA, institutional form.
Dates and Deadlines: Priority date 5/30; closing date 8/20. Applicants notified on a rolling basis starting 4/8.
Transfers: No deadline.

CONTACT
Cindy Butler, District Director, Student Financial Aid
3200 Broadway, Kansas City, MO 64111-2429
(816) 759-1527

Metropolitan Community College: Longview

Lee's Summit, Missouri
www.mcckc.edu Federal Code: 009140

2-year public community college in small city.
Enrollment: 4,449 undergrads, 46% part-time. 973 full-time freshmen.
Selectivity: Open admission.

BASIC COSTS (2008-2009)
Tuition and fees: $2,460; out-of-district residents $4,380; out-of-state residents $5,850.
Per-credit charge: $77; out-of-district residents $141; out-of-state residents $190.

FINANCIAL AID PICTURE (2007-2008)
Students with need: For part-time students, average financial aid package was $1,377.
Students without need: No-need awards available for academics, athletics, leadership.

FINANCIAL AID PROCEDURES
Forms required: FAFSA, institutional form.
Dates and Deadlines: Priority date 5/30; closing date 8/20. Applicants notified on a rolling basis starting 4/8.
Transfers: No deadline.

CONTACT
Cindy Butler, District Director, Student Financial Aid
500 Longview Road, Lee's Summit, MO 64081-2105
(816) 759-1527

Metropolitan Community College: Maple Woods

Kansas City, Missouri
www.mcckc.edu Federal Code: 004432

2-year public community college in large city.
Enrollment: 3,142 undergrads, 47% part-time. 637 full-time freshmen.
Selectivity: Open admission; but selective for some programs.

BASIC COSTS (2008-2009)
Tuition and fees: $2,460; out-of-district residents $4,380; out-of-state residents $5,850.
Per-credit charge: $77; out-of-district residents $141; out-of-state residents $190.

FINANCIAL AID PICTURE (2007-2008)
Students with need: For part-time students, average financial aid package was $1,288.
Students without need: No-need awards available for academics, athletics, leadership.

FINANCIAL AID PROCEDURES
Forms required: FAFSA, institutional form.
Dates and Deadlines: Priority date 5/30; no closing date. Applicants notified on a rolling basis.

CONTACT
Cindy Butler, District Director, Student Financial Aid
2601 NE Barry Road, Kansas City, MO 64156-1299
(816) 759-1527

Metropolitan Community College: Penn Valley

Kansas City, Missouri
www.mcckc.edu Federal Code: 002484

2-year public community college in large city.
Enrollment: 3,540 undergrads, 63% part-time. 366 full-time freshmen.
Selectivity: Open admission; but selective for some programs.

BASIC COSTS (2008-2009)
Tuition and fees: $2,460; out-of-district residents $4,380; out-of-state residents $5,850.
Per-credit charge: $77; out-of-district residents $141; out-of-state residents $190.

FINANCIAL AID PICTURE (2007-2008)
Students with need: For part-time students, average financial aid package was $1,622.
Students without need: No-need awards available for academics, athletics, leadership.

FINANCIAL AID PROCEDURES
Forms required: FAFSA, institutional form.
Dates and Deadlines: Priority date 5/30; no closing date. Applicants notified on a rolling basis starting 4/8.

CONTACT
Cindy Butler, District Director, Student Financial Aid
3201 Southwest Trafficway, Kansas City, MO 64111-2429
(816) 759-1527

Mineral Area College

Park Hills, Missouri
www.mineralarea.edu Federal Code: 002486

2-year public community college in small town.
Enrollment: 2,989 undergrads.
Selectivity: Open admission; but selective for some programs.

BASIC COSTS (2008-2009)
Tuition and fees: $2,490; out-of-district residents $3,240; out-of-state residents $3,960.
Per-credit charge: $83; out-of-district residents $108; out-of-state residents $132.
Room and board: $2,925.

FINANCIAL AID PICTURE (2007-2008)
Students with need: Need-based aid available for full-time and part-time students.
Students without need: No-need awards available for academics, alumni affiliation, art, athletics, leadership, music/drama, state/district residency.

FINANCIAL AID PROCEDURES
Forms required: FAFSA.
Dates and Deadlines: Priority date 4/1; no closing date. Applicants notified on a rolling basis starting 2/15; must reply within 4 week(s) of notification.

CONTACT
Denise Sebastian, Financial Aid Director
PO Box 1000, Park Hills, MO 63601-1000
(573) 518-2133

Missouri Baptist University

St. Louis, Missouri
www.mobap.edu Federal Code: 007540

4-year private university and liberal arts college in very large city, affiliated with Baptist faith.
Enrollment: 1,444 undergrads.
Selectivity: Admits 50 to 75% of applicants.

BASIC COSTS (2008-2009)

Tuition and fees: $16,872.
Per-credit charge: $560.
Room and board: $7,070.

FINANCIAL AID PICTURE (2007-2008)

Students with need: Need-based aid available for full-time and part-time students.
Students without need: No-need awards available for academics, alumni affiliation, athletics, leadership, music/drama, religious affiliation.

FINANCIAL AID PROCEDURES

Forms required: FAFSA, institutional form.
Dates and Deadlines: Priority date 4/1; no closing date. Applicants notified on a rolling basis starting 4/15; must reply within 2 week(s) of notification.
Transfers: Institutional academic scholarships available.

CONTACT

Laurie Wallace, Director of Financial Services
One College Park Drive, St. Louis, MO 63141-8698
(314) 392-2366

Missouri College

St. Louis, Missouri
www.missouricollege.com Federal Code: 009795

2-year for-profit technical college in large city.
Enrollment: 508 undergrads.
Selectivity: Open admission.

BASIC COSTS (2008-2009)

Tuition and fees: $10,650.
Additional info: Diploma programs are $345 per semester credit hour, degree programs are $365 per semester credit hour.

FINANCIAL AID PICTURE

Students with need: Need-based aid available for full-time and part-time students. Work study available nights.

FINANCIAL AID PROCEDURES

Forms required: FAFSA.
Dates and Deadlines: No deadline.

CONTACT

Jennifer Malotte, Director of Student Finance
10121 Manchester Road, St. Louis, MO 63122-1583
(314) 821-7700

Missouri Southern State University

Joplin, Missouri
www.mssu.edu Federal Code: 002488

4-year public university and liberal arts college in large town.
Enrollment: 5,189 undergrads, 26% part-time. 727 full-time freshmen.
Selectivity: Admits over 75% of applicants.

BASIC COSTS (2008-2009)

Tuition and fees: $4,816; out-of-state residents $9,106.
Per-credit charge: $143; out-of-state residents $286.
Room and board: $5,382.

FINANCIAL AID PICTURE (2008-2009)

Students with need: Out of 572 full-time freshmen who applied for aid, 445 were judged to have need. Of these, 439 received aid, and 204 had their full need met. Average financial aid package met 87% of need; average scholarship/grant was $2,108; average loan was $2,311. For part-time students, average financial aid package was $7,125.
Students without need: 177 full-time freshmen who did not demonstrate need for aid received scholarships/grants; average award was $1,583. No-need awards available for academics, art, athletics, leadership, minority status, music/drama.
Scholarships offered: 25 full-time freshmen received athletic scholarships; average amount $3,925.
Cumulative student debt: 70% of graduating class had student loans; average debt was $18,331.

FINANCIAL AID PROCEDURES

Forms required: FAFSA, institutional form.
Dates and Deadlines: Priority date 5/1; no closing date. Applicants notified on a rolling basis starting 2/15; must reply within 3 week(s) of notification.

CONTACT

James Gilbert, Director of Student Financial Aid
3950 East Newman Road, Joplin, MO 64801-1595
(417) 625-9325

Missouri State University

Springfield, Missouri
www.missouristate.edu Federal Code: 002503

4-year public university in small city.
Enrollment: 14,493 undergrads, 12% part-time. 2,452 full-time freshmen.
Selectivity: Admits 50 to 75% of applicants.

BASIC COSTS (2008-2009)

Tuition and fees: $6,256; out-of-state residents $11,536.
Per-credit charge: $186; out-of-state residents $362.
Room and board: $5,576.

FINANCIAL AID PICTURE (2008-2009)

Students with need: Out of 2,032 full-time freshmen who applied for aid, 1,372 were judged to have need. Of these, 1,325 received aid, and 291 had their full need met. Average financial aid package met 67% of need; average scholarship/grant was $5,343; average loan was $2,908. For part-time students, average financial aid package was $5,215.
Students without need: 428 full-time freshmen who did not demonstrate need for aid received scholarships/grants; average award was $4,328. No-need awards available for academics, alumni affiliation, art, athletics, job skills, leadership, minority status, music/drama, ROTC, state/district residency.
Scholarships offered: ***Merit:*** Presidential Scholarships: full tuition, room, and board; based on 30 ACT and rank in top 10% of class; 40 awarded, application deadline January 15. Board of Governors Scholarships: cover basic fees for 32 credit hours per year (plus two thirds of out of state fees for non-residents); based on 28 ACT and either top 10% class rank or 3.85 GPA; unlimited number of awards. Freshman Academic Scholarships: $2,000 per year (plus two thirds of out of state fees for non-residents); based on 26 ACT and either top 20% class rank or 3.7 GPA; unlimited number of awards. Freshman Recognition Scholarships: $1,000 per year (plus two thirds of out of state fees for non-residents); based on 24 ACT and either top 10% class rank or 3.85 GPA; unlimited number of awards. Multicultural Leadership Scholarships: cover required student fees (in-state); for students in top half of class who have demonstrated leadership in the minority community; 50

awarded; February 1 deadline. Applications must be received by March 1 to be considered for scholarships, unless otherwise noted. ***Athletic:*** 76 full-time freshmen received athletic scholarships; average amount $7,611.
Cumulative student debt: 92% of graduating class had student loans; average debt was $18,379.
Additional info: Extensive scholarship program offered to freshmen and transfer students. Out-of-state fee stipends available. Student employment service available to assist students in securing employment on campus and in community.

FINANCIAL AID PROCEDURES
Forms required: FAFSA, state aid form.
Dates and Deadlines: Priority date 5/31; no closing date. Applicants notified by 6/1.
Transfers: No deadline. Applicants notified on a rolling basis.

CONTACT
Vicki Mattocks, Director of Financial Aid
901 South National Avenue, Springfield, MO 65897
(417) 836-5262

Missouri State University: West Plains

West Plains, Missouri
www.wp.missouristate.edu Federal Code: 031060

2-year public branch campus college in large town.
Enrollment: 1,458 undergrads, 27% part-time. 407 full-time freshmen.
Selectivity: Open admission; but selective for some programs.

BASIC COSTS (2008-2009)
Tuition and fees: $3,304; out-of-state residents $6,364.
Per-credit charge: $102; out-of-state residents $204.
Room and board: $4,730.

FINANCIAL AID PICTURE (2007-2008)
Students with need: 89% of average financial aid package awarded as scholarships/grants, 11% awarded as loans/jobs. Need-based aid available for part-time students. Work study available nights, weekends, and for part-time students.
Students without need: No-need awards available for academics, athletics, state/district residency.

FINANCIAL AID PROCEDURES
Forms required: FAFSA, institutional form.
Dates and Deadlines: Priority date 3/31; no closing date. Applicants notified on a rolling basis; must reply by 4/15.

CONTACT
Matthew Morris, Director if Business and Support Services
128 Garfield Avenue, West Plains, MO 65775-2715
(417) 255-7243

Missouri Technical School

St. Louis, Missouri
www.motech.edu Federal Code: 016272

4-year for-profit engineering and technical college in very large city.
Enrollment: 114 undergrads
Selectivity: Admits over 75% of applicants.

BASIC COSTS (2008-2009)
Additional info: Tuition is $500 per credit hour. Fees are $95 per 2-month term.

FINANCIAL AID PICTURE
Students with need: Need-based aid available for full-time and part-time students.
Students without need: This college awards aid only to students with need.

FINANCIAL AID PROCEDURES
Forms required: FAFSA, institutional form.
Dates and Deadlines: No deadline. Applicants notified on a rolling basis.

CONTACT
Cindy Ann Sinnott, Financial Aid Director
1167 Corporate Lake Drive, St. Louis, MO 63132-1716
(314) 569-3600 ext. 316

Missouri University of Science and Technology

Rolla, Missouri
www.mst.edu Federal Code: 002517

4-year public university in large town.
Enrollment: 4,874 undergrads, 4% part-time. 988 full-time freshmen.
Selectivity: Admits over 75% of applicants.

BASIC COSTS (2008-2009)
Tuition and fees: $8,488; out-of-state residents $19,579.
Per-credit charge: $246; out-of-state residents $615.
Room and board: $7,035.
Additional info: Tuition/fee waivers available for minority students.

FINANCIAL AID PICTURE (2007-2008)
Students with need: Out of 799 full-time freshmen who applied for aid, 616 were judged to have need. Of these, 616 received aid, and 189 had their full need met. Average financial aid package met 46% of need; average scholarship/grant was $5,227; average loan was $3,893. For part-time students, average financial aid package was $6,869.
Students without need: 353 full-time freshmen who did not demonstrate need for aid received scholarships/grants. No-need awards available for academics, alumni affiliation, athletics, job skills, leadership, minority status, music/drama, religious affiliation, ROTC, state/district residency.
Scholarships offered: 24 full-time freshmen received athletic scholarships.

FINANCIAL AID PROCEDURES
Forms required: FAFSA.
Dates and Deadlines: Priority date 3/1; no closing date. Applicants notified on a rolling basis; must reply within 3 week(s) of notification.
Transfers: Special scholarships available to transfer students.

CONTACT
Lynn Stichnote, Director of Financial Assistance
106 Parker Hall, Rolla, MO 65409
(573) 341-4282

Missouri Valley College

Marshall, Missouri
www.moval.edu Federal Code: 002489

4-year private liberal arts college in large town, affiliated with Presbyterian Church (USA).
Enrollment: 1,400 undergrads.
Selectivity: Admits less than 50% of applicants.

BASIC COSTS (2008-2009)
Tuition and fees: $15,950.
Room and board: $6,050.

FINANCIAL AID PICTURE
Students with need: Need-based aid available for full-time and part-time students. Work study available nights, weekends, and for part-time students.

Students without need: No-need awards available for academics, state/district residency.
Scholarships offered: Talent scholarships: $1,000 to $13,000; 100 awarded for general achievement.

FINANCIAL AID PROCEDURES

Forms required: FAFSA, state aid form.
Dates and Deadlines: Priority date 3/1; no closing date. Applicants notified on a rolling basis starting 2/1; must reply within 6 week(s) of notification.
Transfers: Closing date 3/1.

CONTACT

Charles Mayfield, Director of Financial Aid
500 East College Street, Marshall, MO 65340
(660) 831-4176

Missouri Western State University

St. Joseph, Missouri
www.missouriwestern.edu Federal Code: 002490

4-year public business and liberal arts college in small city.
Enrollment: 5,000 undergrads.
Selectivity: Open admission; but selective for some programs.

BASIC COSTS (2008-2009)

Tuition and fees: $5,460; out-of-state residents $9,688.
Per-credit charge: $166; out-of-state residents $304.
Room and board: $5,868.

FINANCIAL AID PICTURE (2007-2008)

Students with need: Need-based aid available for full-time and part-time students.
Students without need: No-need awards available for academics, alumni affiliation, art, athletics, job skills, leadership, minority status, music/drama, state/district residency.
Scholarships offered: Golden Griffon Scholarship: up to $10,000 per year for 4 years; 27 ACT, top 10% of class or 3.5 GPA, evidence of involvement in extracurricular activities and community service; 2 essays and personal interview required; application deadline 2/1. President's Academic Scholarship: up to $4,000 per year; 25 ACT and either rank in the top 15% of class or 3.25 GPA required; application deadline 3/1.

FINANCIAL AID PROCEDURES

Forms required: FAFSA, institutional form.
Dates and Deadlines: Closing date 3/1. Applicants notified on a rolling basis starting 4/5; must reply within 3 week(s) of notification.
Transfers: Priority date 3/1; no deadline. Applicants notified on a rolling basis starting 4/15; must reply within 2 week(s) of notification.

CONTACT

Angela Beam, Director of Student Financial Aid
4525 Downs Drive, St. Joseph, MO 64507
(816) 271-4361

Moberly Area Community College

Moberly, Missouri
www.macc.edu Federal Code: 002491

2-year public community college in large town.
Enrollment: 3,126 undergrads, 37% part-time. 649 full-time freshmen.
Selectivity: Open admission; but selective for some programs.

BASIC COSTS (2008-2009)

Tuition and fees: $2,280; out-of-district residents $3,150; out-of-state residents $4,560.
Per-credit charge: $65; out-of-district residents $94; out-of-state residents $141.
Room only: $3,200.
Additional info: Meal plan covers 14 meals per week.

FINANCIAL AID PICTURE (2008-2009)

Students with need: 73% of average financial aid package awarded as scholarships/grants, 27% awarded as loans/jobs. Need-based aid available for part-time students. Work study available nights, weekends, and for part-time students.
Students without need: No-need awards available for academics, alumni affiliation, art, athletics, leadership, music/drama.

FINANCIAL AID PROCEDURES

Forms required: FAFSA.
Dates and Deadlines: Priority date 4/1; no closing date. Applicants notified on a rolling basis starting 4/1; must reply by 7/15 or within 2 week(s) of notification.

CONTACT

Amy Hager, Director of Financial Aid
101 College Avenue, Moberly, MO 65270-1304
(660) 263-4110 ext. 301

National American University: Kansas City

Independence, Missouri
www.national.edu

4-year for-profit university in large city.
Enrollment: 422 undergrads.
Selectivity: Open admission.

FINANCIAL AID PICTURE

Students with need: Need-based aid available for full-time and part-time students. Work study available nights, weekends, and for part-time students.
Students without need: This college awards aid only to students with need.

FINANCIAL AID PROCEDURES

Forms required: FAFSA, institutional form.
Dates and Deadlines: No deadline. Applicants notified on a rolling basis starting 6/4.

CONTACT

Katie Williams, Financial Services Advisor
3620 Arrowhead Avenue, Independence, MO 64057
(816) 412-7736

North Central Missouri College

Trenton, Missouri
www.ncmissouri.edu Federal Code: 002514

2-year public community college in small town.
Enrollment: 1,049 undergrads, 23% part-time. 295 full-time freshmen.
Selectivity: Open admission; but selective for some programs.

BASIC COSTS (2008-2009)

Tuition and fees: $2,550; out-of-district residents $3,510; out-of-state residents $4,650.
Per-credit charge: $65; out-of-district residents $97; out-of-state residents $135.
Room and board: $4,924.
Additional info: Tuition/fee waivers available for adults, minority students.

FINANCIAL AID PICTURE (2007-2008)

Students with need: Need-based aid available for full-time and part-time students.

Students without need: No-need awards available for academics, athletics, minority status, music/drama.

FINANCIAL AID PROCEDURES

Forms required: FAFSA, institutional form.

Dates and Deadlines: Priority date 3/15; no closing date. Applicants notified on a rolling basis starting 3/15.

Transfers: No deadline. Applicants notified on a rolling basis starting 4/1. Transfer students may not receive same awards after transferring since some funds campus-based.

CONTACT

Heather Turner, Financial Aid Director
1301 Main Street, Trenton, MO 64683
(660) 359-3948 ext. 402

Northwest Missouri State University

Maryville, Missouri
www.nwmissouri.edu Federal Code: 002496

4-year public university in large town.

Enrollment: 5,506 undergrads, 5% part-time. 1,519 full-time freshmen.

Selectivity: Admits over 75% of applicants.

BASIC COSTS (2009-2010)

Tuition and fees: $6,911; out-of-state residents $11,633.

Per-credit charge: $214; out-of-state residents $372.

Room and board: $6,876.

Additional info: Tuition/fees includes free laptop for full-time students and textbook rental for primary textbooks. Tuition/fee waivers available for minority students.

FINANCIAL AID PICTURE (2007-2008)

Students with need: 48% of average financial aid package awarded as scholarships/grants, 52% awarded as loans/jobs. Need-based aid available for part-time students. Work study available nights, weekends, and for part-time students.

Students without need: No-need awards available for academics, alumni affiliation, art, athletics, job skills, leadership, minority status, music/drama, state/district residency.

FINANCIAL AID PROCEDURES

Forms required: FAFSA.

Dates and Deadlines: Priority date 4/1; no closing date. Applicants notified on a rolling basis starting 3/15; must reply within 2 week(s) of notification.

Transfers: No deadline. Applicants notified on a rolling basis starting 5/10. Transfer scholarship based on academic record.

CONTACT

Del Morley, Director of Financial Assistance
800 University Drive, Maryville, MO 64468-6001
(660) 562-1363

Ozark Christian College

Joplin, Missouri
www.occ.edu Federal Code: 015569

4-year private Bible college in large town, affiliated with nondenominational tradition.

Enrollment: 602 undergrads, 12% part-time. 135 full-time freshmen.

BASIC COSTS (2008-2009)

Tuition and fees: $8,188.

Per-credit charge: $255.

Room and board: $4,170.

FINANCIAL AID PICTURE (2007-2008)

Students with need: 37% of average financial aid package awarded as scholarships/grants, 63% awarded as loans/jobs. Need-based aid available for part-time students.

Students without need: No-need awards available for academics, leadership.

FINANCIAL AID PROCEDURES

Forms required: FAFSA.

Dates and Deadlines: Priority date 4/1; no closing date. Applicants notified on a rolling basis starting 4/15; must reply within 4 week(s) of notification.

Transfers: Academic transcripts required. ACT scores may qualify student for grants or scholarships.

CONTACT

Kim Balentine, Director of Financial Aid
1111 North Main Street, Joplin, MO 64801
(417) 624-2518

Ozarks Technical Community College

Springfield, Missouri
www.otc.edu Federal Code: 030830

2-year public community and technical college in small city.

Enrollment: 9,475 undergrads.

Selectivity: Open admission; but selective for some programs.

BASIC COSTS (2008-2009)

Tuition and fees: $2,940; out-of-district residents $3,870; out-of-state residents $4,905.

Per-credit charge: $81; out-of-district residents $112; out-of-state residents $147.

FINANCIAL AID PICTURE (2007-2008)

Students with need: 58% of average financial aid package awarded as scholarships/grants, 42% awarded as loans/jobs. Need-based aid available for part-time students.

Students without need: This college awards aid only to students with need.

FINANCIAL AID PROCEDURES

Forms required: FAFSA, institutional form.

Dates and Deadlines: Closing date 3/31. Applicants notified on a rolling basis starting 5/16.

CONTACT

Jeff Ford, Director of Financial Aid
1001 East Chestnut Expressway, Springfield, MO 65802
(417) 447-6930

Park University

Parkville, Missouri
www.park.edu Federal Code: 002498

4-year private university in small town.

Enrollment: 11,080 undergrads, 90% part-time. 252 full-time freshmen.

Selectivity: Admits over 75% of applicants.

BASIC COSTS (2008-2009)

Tuition and fees: $8,190.

Per-credit charge: $273.

Room and board: $5,810.

Additional info: Tuition varies by program and hours taken.

FINANCIAL AID PICTURE (2007-2008)

Students with need: Need-based aid available for full-time and part-time students.

Students without need: No-need awards available for academics, alumni affiliation, art, athletics, job skills, leadership, minority status, music/drama, religious affiliation, ROTC.

FINANCIAL AID PROCEDURES

Forms required: FAFSA, institutional form.

Dates and Deadlines: Priority date 4/1; closing date 8/1. Applicants notified on a rolling basis starting 4/1.

Transfers: No deadline. Applicants notified by 11/1.

CONTACT

Cathy Colapietro, Associate Director of Admissions and Student Financial Services
8700 NW River Park Drive, Parkville, MO 64152
(816) 584-6290

Patricia Stevens College

St. Louis, Missouri
www.patriciastevenscollege.edu Federal Code: 008552

2-year for-profit junior and liberal arts college in very large city.

Enrollment: 105 undergrads.

Selectivity: Open admission; but selective for some programs.

BASIC COSTS (2008-2009)

Tuition and fees: $9,450.

Per-credit charge: $210.

Additional info: Use of textbooks included in tuition. Tuition at time of enrollment locked for 2 years.

FINANCIAL AID PICTURE

Students with need: Need-based aid available for full-time and part-time students.

Students without need: This college awards aid only to students with need.

FINANCIAL AID PROCEDURES

Forms required: FAFSA.

Dates and Deadlines: No deadline. Applicants notified on a rolling basis.

CONTACT

Greg Elsenrath, Financial Aid Director
330 North Fourth Street, Suite 306, St. Louis, MO 63102
(314) 421-0949 ext. 17

Ranken Technical College

St. Louis, Missouri
www.ranken.edu Federal Code: 012500

2-year private technical college in very large city.

Enrollment: 1,626 undergrads, 35% part-time. 425 full-time freshmen.

Selectivity: Open admission.

BASIC COSTS (2009-2010)

Tuition and fees: $12,498.

Per-credit charge: $515.

Additional info: Book and tool costs vary by program.

FINANCIAL AID PICTURE (2007-2008)

Students with need: 18% of average financial aid package awarded as scholarships/grants, 82% awarded as loans/jobs. Need-based aid available for part-time students. Work study available nights.

FINANCIAL AID PROCEDURES

Forms required: FAFSA.

Dates and Deadlines: No deadline. Applicants notified on a rolling basis starting 4/1.

CONTACT

Peter Murtaugh, Vice President for Finance and Administration
4431 Finney Avenue, St. Louis, MO 63113
(314) 286-4863

Research College of Nursing

Kansas City, Missouri
www.researchcollege.edu Federal Code: 006392

4-year for-profit nursing college in very large city.

Enrollment: 302 undergrads, 1% part-time. 57 full-time freshmen.

Selectivity: Admits 50 to 75% of applicants.

BASIC COSTS (2008-2009)

Tuition and fees: $24,480.

Per-credit charge: $790.

Room and board: $6,800.

FINANCIAL AID PICTURE (2008-2009)

Students with need: Need-based aid available for full-time and part-time students.

Students without need: No-need awards available for academics, alumni affiliation, leadership.

Additional info: Financial aid handled by Rockhurst University for freshmen and sophomores.

FINANCIAL AID PROCEDURES

Forms required: FAFSA, institutional form.

Dates and Deadlines: Priority date 3/15; no closing date. Applicants notified on a rolling basis starting 3/15.

Transfers: No deadline.

CONTACT

Angela Karlin, Director of Financial Aid
2525 East Meyer Boulevard, Kansas City, MO 64132-1199
(816) 995-2814

Rockhurst University

Kansas City, Missouri
www.rockhurst.edu Federal Code: 002499

4-year private business and liberal arts college in very large city, affiliated with Roman Catholic Church.

Enrollment: 1,578 undergrads, 9% part-time. 358 full-time freshmen.

Selectivity: Admits over 75% of applicants.

BASIC COSTS (2009-2010)

Tuition and fees: $25,890.

Per-credit charge: $832.

Room and board: $7,080.

FINANCIAL AID PICTURE (2008-2009)

Students with need: Out of 356 full-time freshmen who applied for aid, 330 were judged to have need. Of these, 328 received aid, and 87 had their full need met. Average financial aid package met 100% of need; average scholarship/grant was $6,626; average loan was $3,283. For part-time students, average financial aid package was $10,066.

Students without need: 21 full-time freshmen who did not demonstrate need for aid received scholarships/grants; average award was $12,415. No-need awards available for academics, alumni affiliation, art, athletics, leadership, music/drama, religious affiliation.

Scholarships offered: 33 full-time freshmen received athletic scholarships; average amount $12,017.
Additional info: Auditions, portfolios required for some scholarships.

FINANCIAL AID PROCEDURES
Forms required: FAFSA.
Dates and Deadlines: Priority date 3/1; closing date 6/30. Applicants notified on a rolling basis starting 1/30; must reply within 4 week(s) of notification.
Transfers: Must reply within 2 week(s) of notification. Scholarships awarded to qualified first-time transfers.

CONTACT
Angela Karlin, Director of Financial Aid
1100 Rockhurst Road, Kansas City, MO 64110-2561
(816) 405-4600

St. Charles Community College
Cottleville, Missouri
www.stchas.edu Federal Code: 025306

2-year public community college in small city.
Enrollment: 6,393 undergrads, 45% part-time. 1,322 full-time freshmen.
Selectivity: Open admission; but selective for some programs.

BASIC COSTS (2009-2010)
Tuition and fees: $2,400; out-of-district residents $3,540; out-of-state residents $5,250.
Per-credit charge: $80; out-of-district residents $118; out-of-state residents $175.

FINANCIAL AID PICTURE (2007-2008)
Students with need: 59% of average financial aid package awarded as scholarships/grants, 41% awarded as loans/jobs. Need-based aid available for part-time students.
Students without need: No-need awards available for academics, art, athletics, leadership, music/drama.

FINANCIAL AID PROCEDURES
Forms required: FAFSA, institutional form.
Dates and Deadlines: Priority date 7/1; no closing date. Applicants notified on a rolling basis starting 3/1.

CONTACT
Kathy Brockgreitens-Gober, Dean of Enrollment Services
4601 Mid Rivers Mall Drive, Cottleville, MO 63376
(636) 922-8270

St. Louis Christian College
Florissant, Missouri
www.slcconline.edu Federal Code: 012580

4-year private Bible college in small city, affiliated with Christian Churches/Churches of Christ affiliation.
Enrollment: 303 undergrads, 15% part-time. 39 full-time freshmen.

BASIC COSTS (2008-2009)
Room and board: $6,600.
Additional info: Full-time residential students maintaining an acceptable GPA receive full scholarships for tuition; required fees are $1300 annually. Full-time commuter students pay $148 per-credit-hour; required fees, $1300.

FINANCIAL AID PICTURE (2008-2009)
Students with need: 33% of average financial aid package awarded as scholarships/grants, 67% awarded as loans/jobs. Need-based aid available for part-time students.
Students without need: No-need awards available for academics, alumni affiliation, leadership, music/drama, religious affiliation.

Scholarships offered: President's Scholarship: full tuition; ACT score 30+; 1 available. Chancellor's Scholarships: two-thirds tuition; ACT 28+; 2 available. Dean's Scholarships: half tuition; ACT 28+; unlimited number available.

FINANCIAL AID PROCEDURES
Forms required: FAFSA, institutional form.
Dates and Deadlines: Closing date 8/1. Applicants notified on a rolling basis starting 7/20; must reply within 2 week(s) of notification.

CONTACT
Cathi Wilhoit, Financial Aid Director
1360 Grandview Drive, Florissant, MO 63033
(314) 837-6777 ext. 1101

St. Louis Community College
Saint Louis, Missouri
www.stlcc.edu Federal Code: 002469

2-year public community and junior college in large city.
Enrollment: 6,578 undergrads.
Selectivity: Open admission.

BASIC COSTS (2008-2009)
Tuition and fees: $2,490; out-of-district residents $3,690; out-of-state residents $4,740.
Per-credit charge: $83; out-of-district residents $123; out-of-state residents $158.

FINANCIAL AID PICTURE
Students with need: Need-based aid available for full-time and part-time students.
Students without need: No-need awards available for academics, art, athletics, leadership, music/drama.

FINANCIAL AID PROCEDURES
Forms required: FAFSA.
Dates and Deadlines: Priority date 4/15; no closing date. Applicants notified on a rolling basis starting 4/1.

CONTACT
Paulette Johnson, Manager of Student Financial Aid
300 South Broadway, St. Louis, MO 63102-2800
(314) 644-9117

St. Louis Community College at Meramec
St. Louis, Missouri
www.stlcc.edu Federal Code: 002471

2-year public community college in large city.
Enrollment: 24,567 undergrads.
Selectivity: Open admission; but selective for some programs.

BASIC COSTS (2008-2009)
Tuition and fees: $2,490; out-of-district residents $3,690; out-of-state residents $4,740.
Per-credit charge: $83; out-of-district residents $123; out-of-state residents $158.

FINANCIAL AID PICTURE
Students with need: Need-based aid available for full-time and part-time students.

FINANCIAL AID PROCEDURES
Forms required: FAFSA, institutional form.
Dates and Deadlines: Closing date 6/30. Applicants notified on a rolling basis starting 2/1.

CONTACT
Michael Smith, Manager of Student Aid
11333 Big Bend Boulevard, Kirkwood, MO 63122-5799
(314) 984-7500

Saint Louis University
St. Louis, Missouri
www.slu.edu Federal Code: 002506

4-year private university in very large city, affiliated with Roman Catholic Church.
Enrollment: 7,635 undergrads, 9% part-time. 1,596 full-time freshmen.
Selectivity: Admits 50 to 75% of applicants.

BASIC COSTS (2009-2010)
Tuition and fees: $31,342.
Per-credit charge: $1,080.
Room and board: $8,900.

FINANCIAL AID PICTURE (2007-2008)
Students with need: Out of 1,241 full-time freshmen who applied for aid, 995 were judged to have need. Of these, 995 received aid, and 185 had their full need met. Average financial aid package met 70% of need; average scholarship/grant was $16,092; average loan was $3,991. For part-time students, average financial aid package was $8,788.
Students without need: 538 full-time freshmen who did not demonstrate need for aid received scholarships/grants; average award was $9,857. No-need awards available for academics, art, athletics, leadership, music/drama, religious affiliation, ROTC.
Scholarships offered: ***Merit:*** Available; $3,000 to $15,000; based on high school academic achievement, test scores, leadership, and community service. Presidential scholarship applications due by 12/1. Martin Luther King Jr. scholarship applications have 2/1 priority date. ***Athletic:*** 36 full-time freshmen received athletic scholarships; average amount $11,050.
Cumulative student debt: 67% of graduating class had student loans; average debt was $29,298.
Additional info: Special assistance for TRIO eligible students applying by the priority date of 3/1; enhanced awards include guarantee of grant aid up to 80% of the cost of attendance for these students.

FINANCIAL AID PROCEDURES
Forms required: FAFSA.
Dates and Deadlines: Priority date 3/1; no closing date. Applicants notified on a rolling basis starting 3/1; must reply by 5/1 or within 4 week(s) of notification.
Transfers: No deadline. Applicants notified on a rolling basis starting 3/1; must reply by 5/1 or within 4 week(s) of notification. Students should file FAFSA by March 1 for Missouri State Funds.

CONTACT
Cari Wickliffe, Assistant Vice Provost, Student Financial Services
221 North Grand Boulevard, St. Louis, MO 63103
(314) 977-2350

St. Luke's College
Kansas City, Missouri
www.saintlukescollege.edu Federal Code: 009782

Upper-division private nursing college in large city, affiliated with Episcopal Church.
Enrollment: 118 undergrads.

BASIC COSTS (2009-2010)
Tuition and fees: $9,520.
Per-credit charge: $295.

FINANCIAL AID PICTURE (2008-2009)
Students with need: Average financial aid package for all full-time undergraduates was $12,000. 84% awarded as scholarships/grants, 16% awarded as loans/jobs. Need-based aid available for part-time students.
Cumulative student debt: 80% of graduating class had student loans; average debt was $9,827.

FINANCIAL AID PROCEDURES
Forms required: FAFSA, institutional form.
Dates and Deadlines: No deadline. Applicants notified by 5/1.

CONTACT
Marcia Shaw, Executive Director, Business Operations and Student Services
8320 Ward Parkway, Suite 300, Kansas City, MO 64114
(816) 932-2194

Southeast Missouri State University
Cape Girardeau, Missouri
www.semo.edu Federal Code: 002501

4-year public university in large town.
Enrollment: 8,632 undergrads, 19% part-time. 1,624 full-time freshmen.
Selectivity: Admits over 75% of applicants.

BASIC COSTS (2008-2009)
Tuition and fees: $6,255; out-of-state residents $10,890.
Per-credit charge: $185; out-of-state residents $339.
Room and board: $6,065.
Additional info: Tuition at time of enrollment locked for 4 years.

FINANCIAL AID PICTURE (2007-2008)
Students with need: Out of 1,317 full-time freshmen who applied for aid, 906 were judged to have need. Of these, 889 received aid, and 182 had their full need met. Average financial aid package met 69% of need; average scholarship/grant was $5,140; average loan was $3,148. For part-time students, average financial aid package was $4,710.
Students without need: 415 full-time freshmen who did not demonstrate need for aid received scholarships/grants; average award was $3,761. No-need awards available for academics, alumni affiliation, art, athletics, job skills, leadership, minority status, music/drama, ROTC, state/district residency.
Scholarships offered: 23 full-time freshmen received athletic scholarships; average amount $9,024.
Cumulative student debt: 66% of graduating class had student loans; average debt was $18,893.

FINANCIAL AID PROCEDURES
Forms required: FAFSA.
Dates and Deadlines: Priority date 3/1; no closing date. Applicants notified on a rolling basis starting 4/1; must reply within 3 week(s) of notification.
Transfers: Applicants notified on a rolling basis starting 4/1; must reply by 8/15 or within 3 week(s) of notification.

CONTACT
Karen Walker, Director of Financial Aid Services
One University Plaza, Cape Girardeau, MO 63701
(573) 651-2253

Southwest Baptist University
Bolivar, Missouri
www.sbuniv.edu Federal Code: 002502

4-year private university in small town, affiliated with Southern Baptist Convention.
Enrollment: 2,507 undergrads, 25% part-time. 473 full-time freshmen.
Selectivity: Admits 50 to 75% of applicants.

BASIC COSTS (2009-2010)
Tuition and fees: $16,530.
Room and board: $5,470.

FINANCIAL AID PICTURE (2008-2009)
Students with need: Out of 439 full-time freshmen who applied for aid, 346 were judged to have need. Of these, 343 received aid, and 125 had their full need met. Average financial aid package met 86% of need; average scholarship/grant was $5,852; average loan was $3,920. For part-time students, average financial aid package was $4,512.
Students without need: 109 full-time freshmen who did not demonstrate need for aid received scholarships/grants; average award was $7,841. No-need awards available for academics, art, athletics, minority status, music/drama, state/district residency.
Scholarships offered: 59 full-time freshmen received athletic scholarships; average amount $6,220.

FINANCIAL AID PROCEDURES
Forms required: FAFSA, institutional form.
Dates and Deadlines: Priority date 3/15; no closing date. Applicants notified on a rolling basis starting 3/1; must reply within 2 week(s) of notification.

CONTACT
Brad Gamble, Director of Financial Aid
1600 University Avenue, Bolivar, MO 65613-2597
(417) 328-1822

State Fair Community College
Sedalia, Missouri
www.sfccmo.edu Federal Code: 007628

2-year public community college in large town.
Enrollment: 2,941 undergrads.
Selectivity: Open admission; but selective for some programs.

BASIC COSTS (2008-2009)
Tuition and fees: $2,460; out-of-district residents $3,300; out-of-state residents $4,980.
Per-credit charge: $68; out-of-district residents $96; out-of-state residents $152.

FINANCIAL AID PICTURE (2007-2008)
Students with need: Need-based aid available for full-time and part-time students. Work study available nights, weekends, and for part-time students.
Students without need: This college awards aid only to students with need.

FINANCIAL AID PROCEDURES
Forms required: FAFSA.
Dates and Deadlines: Priority date 7/1; no closing date. Applicants notified on a rolling basis starting 7/15; must reply within 3 week(s) of notification.

CONTACT
John Matthews, Director of Financial Aid
3201 West 16th Street, Sedalia, MO 65301-2199
(660) 596-7295

Stephens College
Columbia, Missouri
www.stephens.edu Federal Code: 002512

4-year private liberal arts college for women in small city.
Enrollment: 923 undergrads, 17% part-time. 223 full-time freshmen.
Selectivity: Admits 50 to 75% of applicants.

BASIC COSTS (2008-2009)
Tuition and fees: $23,000.
Per-credit charge: $265.
Room and board: $8,730.

FINANCIAL AID PICTURE (2008-2009)
Students with need: Out of 197 full-time freshmen who applied for aid, 172 were judged to have need. Of these, 172 received aid, and 26 had their full need met. Average financial aid package met 77% of need; average scholarship/grant was $15,911; average loan was $2,951. For part-time students, average financial aid package was $3,185.
Students without need: 51 full-time freshmen who did not demonstrate need for aid received scholarships/grants; average award was $10,398. No-need awards available for academics, alumni affiliation, athletics, leadership, music/drama, state/district residency.
Scholarships offered: 3 full-time freshmen received athletic scholarships; average amount $4,917.
Cumulative student debt: 70% of graduating class had student loans; average debt was $21,960.

FINANCIAL AID PROCEDURES
Forms required: FAFSA.
Dates and Deadlines: Priority date 3/15; no closing date. Applicants notified on a rolling basis starting 3/1.
Transfers: Phi Theta Kappa students transferring from 2-year institutions eligible for Phi Theta Kappa scholarship.

CONTACT
Rachel Touchatt, Director of Financial Aid
1200 East Broadway, Columbia, MO 65215
(800) 876-7106

Three Rivers Community College
Poplar Bluff, Missouri
www.trcc.edu Federal Code: 004713

2-year public community college in large town.
Enrollment: 2,481 undergrads, 34% part-time. 528 full-time freshmen.
Selectivity: Open admission; but selective for some programs.

BASIC COSTS (2009-2010)
Tuition and fees: $2,505; out-of-district residents $3,765; out-of-state residents $4,605.
Per-credit charge: $70; out-of-district residents $112; out-of-state residents $140.
Room only: $3,114.
Additional info: Book rental $20 per book. Lab fees vary per course.

FINANCIAL AID PICTURE (2007-2008)
Students with need: 71% of average financial aid package awarded as scholarships/grants, 29% awarded as loans/jobs. Need-based aid available for part-time students.
Students without need: No-need awards available for academics, athletics, state/district residency.

FINANCIAL AID PROCEDURES
Forms required: FAFSA, institutional form.
Dates and Deadlines: Priority date 5/1; no closing date. Applicants notified on a rolling basis starting 6/1; must reply within 2 week(s) of notification.

CONTACT
Robert Myers, Vice President for Finance & Government Affairs
2080 Three Rivers Boulevard, Poplar Bluff, MO 63901-1308
(573) 840-9607

Truman State University
Kirksville, Missouri
www.truman.edu Federal Code: 002495

4-year public university and liberal arts college in large town.
Enrollment: 5,497 undergrads, 2% part-time. 1,405 full-time freshmen.
Selectivity: Admits over 75% of applicants.

BASIC COSTS (2008-2009)
Tuition and fees: $6,692; out-of-state residents $11,542.
Room and board: $6,290.

FINANCIAL AID PICTURE (2007-2008)
Students with need: Out of 1,124 full-time freshmen who applied for aid, 556 were judged to have need. Of these, 556 received aid, and 389 had their full need met. Average financial aid package met 85% of need; average scholarship/grant was $3,129; average loan was $3,306. Need-based aid available for part-time students.
Students without need: 832 full-time freshmen who did not demonstrate need for aid received scholarships/grants; average award was $4,535. No-need awards available for academics, alumni affiliation, art, athletics, leadership, minority status, music/drama, ROTC, state/district residency.
Scholarships offered: ***Merit:*** Pershing Scholarship: up to full tuition, room and board and up to $4,000 for study-abroad; awarded to outstanding scholars and leaders; 12 awarded. Truman Leadership Award: up to full tuition, room and board for Missouri residents; awarded for demonstrated leadership and academic achievement. International Baccalaureate Scholarship: $2,000 per academic year, awarded to students who complete the IB Diploma Programme. ***Athletic:*** 92 full-time freshmen received athletic scholarships; average amount $3,599.
Cumulative student debt: 51% of graduating class had student loans; average debt was $16,858.
Additional info: Out-of-state students whose parents work in Missouri may deduct $1 for every dollar paid in Missouri income taxes from out-of-state tuition.

FINANCIAL AID PROCEDURES
Forms required: FAFSA, institutional form.
Dates and Deadlines: Priority date 4/1; no closing date. Applicants notified on a rolling basis starting 3/1; must reply within 4 week(s) of notification.
Transfers: Applicants notified on a rolling basis starting 3/1; must reply within 4 week(s) of notification. Limited number of automatic and competitive awards offered to transfer students.

CONTACT
Kathy Elsea, Financial Aid Director
100 East Normal Street, Kirksville, MO 63501-9980
(660) 785-4130

University of Central Missouri
Warrensburg, Missouri
www.ucmo.edu Federal Code: 02454

4-year public university in large town.
Enrollment: 8,314 undergrads, 14% part-time. 1,532 full-time freshmen.
Selectivity: Admits over 75% of applicants.

BASIC COSTS (2008-2009)
Tuition and fees: $6,885; out-of-state residents $12,444.
Per-credit charge: $195; out-of-state residents $391.
Room and board: $6,320.

FINANCIAL AID PICTURE (2007-2008)
Students with need: Need-based aid available for full-time and part-time students. Work study available nights, weekends, and for part-time students.
Students without need: No-need awards available for academics, alumni affiliation, art, athletics, leadership, minority status, music/drama, ROTC, state/district residency.

FINANCIAL AID PROCEDURES
Forms required: FAFSA.
Dates and Deadlines: Priority date 3/1; no closing date. Applicants notified on a rolling basis starting 3/1; must reply within 2 week(s) of notification.
Transfers: No deadline. Must reply within 2 week(s) of notification.

CONTACT
Phil Shreves, Director, Student Financial Assistance
WDE 1400, Warrensburg, MO 64093
(660) 543-8080

University of Missouri: Columbia
Columbia, Missouri
www.missouri.edu Federal Code: 002516

4-year public university in small city.
Enrollment: 22,649 undergrads, 5% part-time. 4,904 full-time freshmen.
Selectivity: Admits over 75% of applicants.

BASIC COSTS (2008-2009)
Tuition and fees: $8,485; out-of-state residents $19,558.
Per-credit charge: $246; out-of-state residents $615.
Room and board: $8,100.

FINANCIAL AID PICTURE (2007-2008)
Students with need: Out of 3,486 full-time freshmen who applied for aid, 2,237 were judged to have need. Of these, 2,215 received aid, and 499 had their full need met. Average financial aid package met 91% of need; average scholarship/grant was $7,270; average loan was $3,723. For part-time students, average financial aid package was $10,329.
Students without need: 1,168 full-time freshmen who did not demonstrate need for aid received scholarships/grants; average award was $3,276. No-need awards available for academics, alumni affiliation, art, athletics, leadership, minority status, music/drama, ROTC, state/district residency.
Scholarships offered: 229 full-time freshmen received athletic scholarships; average amount $8,830.
Cumulative student debt: 61% of graduating class had student loans; average debt was $20,814.
Additional info: Scholarship available for international students based on success during 1st semester.

FINANCIAL AID PROCEDURES
Forms required: FAFSA.
Dates and Deadlines: Priority date 3/1; no closing date. Applicants notified on a rolling basis starting 4/1; must reply within 4 week(s) of notification.
Transfers: No deadline. Applicants notified on a rolling basis starting 4/1; must reply within 4 week(s) of notification.

CONTACT
James Brooks, Director of Student Financial Aid
230 Jesse Hall, Columbia, MO 65211
(573) 882-7506

University of Missouri: Kansas City
Kansas City, Missouri
www.umkc.edu Federal Code: 002518

4-year public university in large city.
Enrollment: 7,353 undergrads, 21% part-time. 974 full-time freshmen.
Selectivity: Admits 50 to 75% of applicants.

BASIC COSTS (2008-2009)
Tuition and fees: $8,272; out-of-state residents $19,363.
Per-credit charge: $246; out-of-state residents $614.
Room and board: $8,096.

FINANCIAL AID PICTURE (2008-2009)
Students with need: Out of 787 full-time freshmen who applied for aid, 625 were judged to have need. Of these, 615 received aid, and 84 had their full need met. Average financial aid package met 59% of need; average scholarship/grant was $7,411; average loan was $6,710. For part-time students, average financial aid package was $5,826.
Students without need: 243 full-time freshmen who did not demonstrate need for aid received scholarships/grants; average award was $4,348. No-need awards available for academics, alumni affiliation, art, athletics, leadership, minority status, music/drama, state/district residency.
Scholarships offered: 24 full-time freshmen received athletic scholarships; average amount $16,454.
Cumulative student debt: 65% of graduating class had student loans; average debt was $24,151.

FINANCIAL AID PROCEDURES
Forms required: FAFSA.
Dates and Deadlines: Priority date 3/1; no closing date. Applicants notified on a rolling basis starting 4/15; must reply within 2 week(s) of notification.

CONTACT
Jan Brandow, Director of Student Financial Aid
5100 Rockhill Road, AC120, Kansas City, MO 64110-2499
(816) 235-1154

University of Missouri: St. Louis
St. Louis, Missouri
www.umsl.edu Federal Code: 002519

4-year public university in very large city.
Enrollment: 8,681 undergrads, 35% part-time. 439 full-time freshmen.
Selectivity: Admits 50 to 75% of applicants.

BASIC COSTS (2008-2009)
Tuition and fees: $8,595; out-of-state residents $19,686.
Per-credit charge: $246; out-of-state residents $615.
Room and board: $7,782.

FINANCIAL AID PICTURE (2008-2009)
Students with need: Need-based aid available for full-time and part-time students. Work study available nights.
Students without need: No-need awards available for academics, alumni affiliation, art, athletics, music/drama, ROTC, state/district residency.
Scholarships offered: Curator's Scholarships: $3,500 renewable annually; for Missouri freshmen with high test scores and class rank; unlimited awarded. Chancellor's Scholarships: $2,500 annually; for freshmen with strong test scores and class rank; unlimited awarded. Pierre Laclede Honors College Scholarships: for freshmen and transfer students; varying amounts. Mark Twain Scholarships: $1,000 annually; for freshmen with strong test scores and class rank. National Access Scholarships: amount varies and applied to nonresident fee; for freshmen and transfer students with strong test scores and grade point average.

FINANCIAL AID PROCEDURES
Forms required: FAFSA.
Dates and Deadlines: Priority date 4/1; no closing date. Applicants notified on a rolling basis starting 4/1; must reply within 2 week(s) of notification.
Transfers: Transfer scholarships awarded on merit basis to students entering in both Fall and Spring semesters. Priority consideration given to students admitted by March 15th for Fall semester and by October 15th for the Spring semester. Students must transfer at least 45 credit hours and have minimum GPA of 3.25 to be eligible. Amounts vary, and additional criteria apply.

CONTACT
Tony Georges, Director of Student Financial Aid
One University Boulevard, St. Louis, MO 63121-4400
(314) 516-5526

Vatterott College: St. Joseph
St. Joseph, Missouri
www.vatterott-college.edu Federal Code: 026092

2-year for-profit branch campus and technical college in small city.
Enrollment: 215 undergrads.
Selectivity: Open admission.

BASIC COSTS (2008-2009)
Additional info: Program cost ranges: $10,800 to $21,000 (certificate/diploma); $24,500 to $30,600 (associate degree).

FINANCIAL AID PICTURE
Students with need: Need-based aid available for full-time and part-time students.
Scholarships offered: Make the Grade Scholarship; up to $1,000; based on high school grades.

FINANCIAL AID PROCEDURES
Forms required: FAFSA.
Dates and Deadlines: No deadline.

CONTACT
Marcia Hurley, Financial Aid Administrator
3131 Frederick Avenue, St. Joseph, MO 64506
(816) 364-5399

Washington University in St. Louis
St. Louis, Missouri Federal Code: 002520
www.wustl.edu CSS Code: 6929

4-year private university in large city.
Enrollment: 6,339 undergrads, 5% part-time. 1,417 full-time freshmen.
Selectivity: Admits less than 50% of applicants.

BASIC COSTS (2009-2010)
Tuition and fees: $38,864.
Room and board: $12,465.

FINANCIAL AID PICTURE (2008-2009)
Students with need: Out of 935 full-time freshmen who applied for aid, 543 were judged to have need. Of these, 539 received aid, and 539 had their full need met. Average financial aid package met 100% of need; average scholarship/grant was $28,345; average loan was $4,996. Need-based aid available for part-time students.
Students without need: 262 full-time freshmen who did not demonstrate need for aid received scholarships/grants; average award was $8,459. No-need awards available for academics, ROTC.
Scholarships offered: Numerous merit scholarships available ranging up to full tuition plus stipend, renewable for 4 years.

FINANCIAL AID PROCEDURES
Forms required: FAFSA, CSS PROFILE.
Dates and Deadlines: Closing date 2/15. Applicants notified by 4/1; must reply by 5/1.

CONTACT
William Witbrodt, Director of Student Financial Services
Campus Box 1089, One Brookings Drive, St. Louis, MO 63130-4899
(314) 935-5900

Webster University
St. Louis, Missouri
www.webster.edu Federal Code: 002521

4-year private university in large city.
Enrollment: 3,463 undergrads, 25% part-time. 494 full-time freshmen.
Selectivity: Admits 50 to 75% of applicants.

BASIC COSTS (2009-2010)
Tuition and fees: $21,056.
Per-credit charge: $550.
Room and board: $9,070.
Additional info: Tuition $24,556for theater conservatory students.

FINANCIAL AID PICTURE (2007-2008)
Students with need: Out of 443 full-time freshmen who applied for aid, 361 were judged to have need. Of these, 361 received aid. For part-time students, average financial aid package was $10,973.
Students without need: 129 full-time freshmen who did not demonstrate need for aid received scholarships/grants; average award was $8,217. No-need awards available for academics, art, music/drama.
Scholarships offered: Daniel Webster Scholarships: full tuition; 3.8 GPA, top 10% class rank, 29 ACT and interview; 5 awarded. Webster Academic Scholarships: from $2,000-$10,000; minimum 3.0 GPA and 23 ACT; unlimited awarded. Leadership Scholarships: $1,500; minimum 3.3 GPA and 24 ACT, resume of activities; 15 awarded.
Cumulative student debt: 56% of graduating class had student loans; average debt was $23,183.

FINANCIAL AID PROCEDURES
Forms required: FAFSA, institutional form.
Dates and Deadlines: Priority date 4/1; no closing date. Applicants notified on a rolling basis starting 2/9; must reply within 2 week(s) of notification.

CONTACT
David Garafola, Vice President, Financial
470 East Lockwood Avenue, St. Louis, MO 63119-3194
(314) 968-6992

Westminster College
Fulton, Missouri
www.westminster-mo.edu Federal Code: 002523

4-year private liberal arts college in large town, affiliated with Presbyterian Church (USA).
Enrollment: 980 undergrads. 244 full-time freshmen.
Selectivity: Admits over 75% of applicants.

BASIC COSTS (2009-2010)
Tuition and fees: $18,700.
Per-credit charge: $750.
Room and board: $7,120.
Additional info: Tuition/fee waivers available for minority students.

FINANCIAL AID PICTURE (2008-2009)
Students with need: Out of 198 full-time freshmen who applied for aid, 142 were judged to have need. Of these, 142 received aid, and 99 had their full need met. Average financial aid package met 70% of need; average scholarship/grant was $13,397; average loan was $3,154. For part-time students, average financial aid package was $10,541.
Students without need: 97 full-time freshmen who did not demonstrate need for aid received scholarships/grants; average award was $8,571. No-need awards available for academics, alumni affiliation, leadership, minority status, music/drama, religious affiliation, ROTC, state/district residency.
Scholarships offered: Churchill Scholarship: $10,000-$15,000; 29-36 ACT or 1920 SAT and 3.5 GPA. Trustee's Scholarship: $8,000-$9,000; 27-28 ACT or 1820-1910 SAT and 3.0 GPA. President's Scholarship: $6,500-$7,500; 25-26 ACT or 1700-1810 SAT and 3.0 GPA. Dean's Scholarship: $5,500-$6,500; 23-24 ACT or 1590-1690 SAT and 3.0 GPA. Founder's Award: $3,000-$4,000; 21-22 ACT or 1500-1580 SAT and 2.75 GPA.

FINANCIAL AID PROCEDURES
Forms required: FAFSA.
Dates and Deadlines: Priority date 2/15; no closing date. Applicants notified on a rolling basis starting 3/1; must reply within 3 week(s) of notification.
Transfers: Applicants notified on a rolling basis starting 3/1; must reply within 3 week(s) of notification.

CONTACT
Aimee Bristow, Director of Financial Aid
501 Westminster Avenue, Fulton, MO 65251-1299
(573) 592-5365

William Jewell College
Liberty, Missouri
www.jewell.edu Federal Code: 002524

4-year private liberal arts college in large town.
Enrollment: 1,210 undergrads, 13% part-time. 265 full-time freshmen.
Selectivity: Admits 50 to 75% of applicants.

BASIC COSTS (2009-2010)
Tuition and fees: $24,300.
Per-credit charge: $750.
Room and board: $6,700.
Additional info: Base tuition covers 12 to 18 credits per semester.

FINANCIAL AID PICTURE (2008-2009)
Students with need: Out of 244 full-time freshmen who applied for aid, 198 were judged to have need. Of these, 198 received aid, and 107 had their full need met. Average financial aid package met 93% of need; average scholarship/grant was $16,925; average loan was $4,915. Need-based aid available for part-time students.
Students without need: 47 full-time freshmen who did not demonstrate need for aid received scholarships/grants; average award was $10,394. No-need awards available for academics, alumni affiliation, art, athletics, music/drama.
Scholarships offered: ***Merit:*** Jewell Scholarship: $11,500 to full tuition; competitive academic scholarship offered annually by invitation only to qualified high school seniors; 4 full-tuition scholarships awarded annually. Oxbridge Honors Scholarship: $11,500; for students accepted into Oxbridge Honors Program. ***Athletic:*** 18 full-time freshmen received athletic scholarships; average amount $4,528.
Cumulative student debt: 73% of graduating class had student loans; average debt was $22,123.

FINANCIAL AID PROCEDURES
Forms required: FAFSA.
Dates and Deadlines: Priority date 3/1; no closing date. Applicants notified on a rolling basis starting 2/15; must reply within 1.5 week(s) of notification.
Transfers: Transfer scholarships are available for new transfer students who meet minimum requirements: 3.0 GPA and one full-time semester (15 credit hours) of transferable coursework.

CONTACT
Susan Karnes, Director, Financial Aid and Scholarship Services
500 College Hill, Liberty, MO 64068
(816) 415-5977

William Woods University
Fulton, Missouri
www.williamwoods.edu Federal Code: 002525

4-year private university and liberal arts college in large town, affiliated with Christian Church (Disciples of Christ).

Enrollment: 991 undergrads, 16% part-time. 151 full-time freshmen.

Selectivity: Admits over 75% of applicants.

BASIC COSTS (2009-2010)
Tuition and fees: $17,310.

Per-credit charge: $540.

Room and board: $6,950.

Additional info: Commuter students pay additional $50 fee per year.

FINANCIAL AID PICTURE (2008-2009)
Students with need: Out of 145 full-time freshmen who applied for aid, 140 were judged to have need. Of these, 139 received aid, and 37 had their full need met. Average financial aid package met 79% of need; average scholarship/grant was $12,245; average loan was $4,093. For part-time students, average financial aid package was $6,786.

Students without need: 11 full-time freshmen who did not demonstrate need for aid received scholarships/grants; average award was $11,011. No-need awards available for academics, alumni affiliation, art, athletics, leadership, music/drama, religious affiliation.

Scholarships offered: ***Merit:*** LEAD (Leading, Educating, Achieving and Developing) Award; $5,000 for campus residents, $2,500 for commuters; based on commitment to campus and community involvement; renewable each year if commitment has been met in previous year. ***Athletic:*** 6 full-time freshmen received athletic scholarships; average amount $4,948.

Cumulative student debt: 76% of graduating class had student loans; average debt was $17,979.

FINANCIAL AID PROCEDURES
Forms required: FAFSA, institutional form.

Dates and Deadlines: Priority date 3/1; no closing date. Applicants notified on a rolling basis starting 3/15; must reply within 2 week(s) of notification.

Transfers: No deadline. Applicants notified on a rolling basis; must reply within 2 week(s) of notification.

CONTACT
Deana Ready, Director of Financial Aid
One University Avenue, Fulton, MO 65251-2388
(573) 592-4232

Montana

Carroll College
Helena, Montana
www.carroll.edu Federal Code: 002526

4-year private liberal arts college in large town, affiliated with Roman Catholic Church.

Enrollment: 1,311 undergrads, 7% part-time. 344 full-time freshmen.

Selectivity: Admits over 75% of applicants.

BASIC COSTS (2009-2010)
Tuition and fees: $22,592.

Per-credit charge: $736.

Room and board: $7,118.

FINANCIAL AID PICTURE (2008-2009)
Students with need: Out of 338 full-time freshmen who applied for aid, 208 were judged to have need. Of these, 208 received aid, and 47 had their full need met. Average financial aid package met 83% of need; average scholarship/grant was $13,109; average loan was $4,314. For part-time students, average financial aid package was $12,608.

Students without need: 74 full-time freshmen who did not demonstrate need for aid received scholarships/grants; average award was $8,706. No-need awards available for academics, art, athletics, leadership, minority status, music/drama, religious affiliation, ROTC.

Scholarships offered: 13 full-time freshmen received athletic scholarships; average amount $4,977.

Cumulative student debt: 71% of graduating class had student loans; average debt was $25,246.

FINANCIAL AID PROCEDURES
Forms required: FAFSA.

Dates and Deadlines: Priority date 3/1; no closing date. Applicants notified on a rolling basis starting 3/1; must reply by 5/1 or within 2 week(s) of notification.

CONTACT
Janet Riis, Director of Financial Aid
1601 North Benton Avenue, Helena, MT 59625
(406) 447-5425

Chief Dull Knife College
Lame Deer, Montana
www.cdkc.edu Federal Code: 014878

2-year public junior college in rural community.

Enrollment: 119 full-time undergrads.

Selectivity: Open admission.

BASIC COSTS (2008-2009)
Tuition and fees: $2,260.

Per-credit charge: $70.

FINANCIAL AID PICTURE (2008-2009)
Students with need: Need-based aid available for full-time and part-time students. Work study available nights.

FINANCIAL AID PROCEDURES
Forms required: FAFSA, institutional form.

Dates and Deadlines: Priority date 3/1; no closing date. Applicants notified on a rolling basis; must reply within 2 week(s) of notification.

CONTACT
Michelle Three Fingers, Financial Aid Director
Box 98, Lame Deer, MT 59043
(406) 477-6215

Dawson Community College
Glendive, Montana
www.dawson.edu Federal Code: 002529

2-year public community college in small town.

Enrollment: 335 undergrads, 13% part-time. 121 full-time freshmen.

Selectivity: Open admission.

BASIC COSTS (2008-2009)
Tuition and fees: $2,736; out-of-district residents $3,843; out-of-state residents $8,499.

Per-credit charge: $52; out-of-district residents $89; out-of-state residents $244.

Room only: $2,100.

Additional info: Mandatory $600-per-semester a la carte meal plan for on-campus residents. Full-time tuition for Western Undergraduate Exchange students: $3,211 ($134 per credit hour).

FINANCIAL AID PICTURE (2007-2008)

Students with need: 56% of average financial aid package awarded as scholarships/grants, 44% awarded as loans/jobs. Work study available nights, weekends, and for part-time students.
Students without need: No-need awards available for academics, art, athletics, music/drama.

FINANCIAL AID PROCEDURES

Forms required: FAFSA.
Dates and Deadlines: Priority date 3/1; no closing date. Applicants notified on a rolling basis starting 5/15; must reply within 2 week(s) of notification.

CONTACT

Jolene Myers, Director of Admissions
300 College Drive, Glendive, MT 59330
(406) 377-9410

Flathead Valley Community College

Kalispell, Montana
www.fvcc.edu Federal Code: 006777

2-year public community college in large town.
Enrollment: 1,395 undergrads, 36% part-time. 236 full-time freshmen.
Selectivity: Open admission; but selective for some programs.

BASIC COSTS (2008-2009)

Tuition and fees: $3,472; out-of-district residents $4,844; out-of-state residents $10,612.
Per-credit charge: $124; out-of-district residents $173; out-of-state residents $379.

FINANCIAL AID PICTURE (2008-2009)

Students with need: 62% of average financial aid package awarded as scholarships/grants, 38% awarded as loans/jobs. Need-based aid available for part-time students.
Students without need: No-need awards available for academics, athletics.

FINANCIAL AID PROCEDURES

Forms required: FAFSA.
Dates and Deadlines: Priority date 3/1; no closing date. Applicants notified by 4/15; must reply within 2 week(s) of notification.

CONTACT

Cynthia Kiefer, Director of Financial Aid
777 Grandview Drive, Kalispell, MT 59901
(406) 756-3849

Fort Peck Community College

Poplar, Montana
www.fpcc.edu Federal Code: 016616

2-year public community college in small town.
Enrollment: 371 undergrads.
Selectivity: Open admission.

BASIC COSTS (2008-2009)

Tuition and fees: $1,940.
Per-credit charge: $60.
Additional info: Tuition/fee waivers available for adults, minority students.

FINANCIAL AID PICTURE

Students with need: Need-based aid available for full-time and part-time students. Work study available nights.

FINANCIAL AID PROCEDURES

Forms required: FAFSA, institutional form.
Dates and Deadlines: No deadline. Applicants notified on a rolling basis; must reply within 2 week(s) of notification.

CONTACT

Lanette Clark, Financial Aid Officer
Box 398 605 Indian, Poplar, MT 59255-0398
(406) 768-6328

Helena College of Technology of the University of Montana

Helena, Montana
www.umhelena.edu Federal Code: 007570

2-year public community and technical college in large town.
Enrollment: 908 undergrads. 196 full-time freshmen.
Selectivity: Open admission.

BASIC COSTS (2008-2009)

Tuition and fees: $3,025; out-of-state residents $8,589.
Additional info: Tuition/fee waivers available for minority students.

FINANCIAL AID PICTURE (2007-2008)

Students with need: Need-based aid available for full-time and part-time students.

FINANCIAL AID PROCEDURES

Forms required: FAFSA, institutional form.
Dates and Deadlines: Priority date 3/1; no closing date. Applicants notified on a rolling basis starting 5/1.

CONTACT

Valerie Lambert, Director of Financial Aid
1115 North Roberts Street, Helena, MT 59601-3098
(406) 444-6879

Little Big Horn College

Crow Agency, Montana
www.lbhc.cc.mt.us Federal Code: 016135

2-year private community college in rural community.
Enrollment: 265 undergrads.
Selectivity: Open admission.

BASIC COSTS (2008-2009)

Tuition and fees: $2,760.
Per-credit charge: $75.
Additional info: Tuition/fee waivers available for minority students.

FINANCIAL AID PICTURE (2008-2009)

Students with need: Need-based aid available for part-time students.

FINANCIAL AID PROCEDURES

Dates and Deadlines: No deadline. Applicants notified on a rolling basis.

CONTACT

Beverly Snell, Financial Aid Assistant
Box 370, Crow Agency, MT 59022
(406) 638-3140

Miles Community College

Miles City, Montana
www.milescc.edu/ Federal Code: 002528

2-year public community college in small town.
Enrollment: 450 undergrads, 22% part-time. 129 full-time freshmen.
Selectivity: Open admission; but selective for some programs.

BASIC COSTS (2008-2009)

Tuition and fees: $3,420; out-of-district residents $4,290; out-of-state residents $7,080.
Per-credit charge: $71; out-of-district residents $100; out-of-state residents $193.
Room and board: $4,250.

FINANCIAL AID PICTURE

Students with need: Need-based aid available for full-time and part-time students. Work study available nights, weekends, and for part-time students.
Students without need: No-need awards available for academics, athletics, leadership.
Scholarships offered: Montana residents may apply for tuition waivers and scholarships. Students must maintain 3.0 GPA and carry 15 credits. Deadline for application 03/15.

FINANCIAL AID PROCEDURES

Forms required: FAFSA.
Dates and Deadlines: Priority date 3/1; no closing date. Applicants notified on a rolling basis starting 4/15; must reply within 4 week(s) of notification.

CONTACT

Loren Lancaster, Financial Aid Officer
2715 Dickinson Street, Miles City, MT 59301
(406) 874-6208

Montana State University College of Technology: Great Falls

Great Falls, Montana
www.msugf.edu Federal Code: 009314

2-year public community and technical college in small city.
Enrollment: 1,466 undergrads. 169 full-time freshmen.
Selectivity: Open admission; but selective for some programs.

BASIC COSTS (2008-2009)

Tuition and fees: $2,999; out-of-state residents $9,151.
Additional info: Tuition/fee waivers available for minority students, unemployed or children of unemployed.

FINANCIAL AID PICTURE (2007-2008)

Students with need: Out of 139 full-time freshmen who applied for aid, 119 were judged to have need. Of these, 115 received aid, and 7 had their full need met. Average financial aid package met 61% of need; average scholarship/grant was $3,897; average loan was $2,621. For part-time students, average financial aid package was $5,125.
Cumulative student debt: 81% of graduating class had student loans; average debt was $10,025.

FINANCIAL AID PROCEDURES

Forms required: FAFSA, institutional form.
Dates and Deadlines: Priority date 3/1; no closing date. Applicants notified on a rolling basis starting 4/1; must reply within 3 week(s) of notification.
Transfers: No deadline. Applicants notified on a rolling basis; must reply within 3 week(s) of notification.

CONTACT

Leah Habel, Director of Financial Aid
2100 16th Avenue South, Great Falls, MT 59405
(406) 771-4334

Montana State University: Billings

Billings, Montana
www.msubillings.edu Federal Code: 002530

4-year public university and technical college in small city.
Enrollment: 4,100 undergrads, 27% part-time. 721 full-time freshmen.
Selectivity: Admits over 75% of applicants.

BASIC COSTS (2008-2009)

Tuition and fees: $5,172; out-of-state residents $13,980.
Room and board: $5,270.

FINANCIAL AID PICTURE (2007-2008)

Students with need: Out of 568 full-time freshmen who applied for aid, 447 were judged to have need. Of these, 420 received aid, and 20 had their full need met. Average financial aid package met 64% of need; average scholarship/grant was $3,765; average loan was $2,915. For part-time students, average financial aid package was $6,542.
Students without need: 14 full-time freshmen who did not demonstrate need for aid received scholarships/grants; average award was $1,642. No-need awards available for academics, alumni affiliation, art, athletics, job skills, leadership, minority status, music/drama, state/district residency.
Scholarships offered: 18 full-time freshmen received athletic scholarships; average amount $3,982.
Cumulative student debt: 80% of graduating class had student loans; average debt was $19,736.
Additional info: Veterans and honors fee waivers offered.

FINANCIAL AID PROCEDURES

Forms required: FAFSA.
Dates and Deadlines: Priority date 3/1; no closing date. Applicants notified on a rolling basis starting 4/1; must reply within 3 week(s) of notification.

CONTACT

Judy Chapman, Director of Financial Aid
1500 University Drive, Billings, MT 59101-0298
(406) 657-2188

Montana State University: Bozeman

Bozeman, Montana
www.montana.edu Federal Code: 002532

4-year public university in large town.
Enrollment: 10,406 undergrads, 14% part-time. 1,813 full-time freshmen.
Selectivity: Admits 50 to 75% of applicants.

BASIC COSTS (2008-2009)

Tuition and fees: $5,798; out-of-state residents $16,997.
Room and board: $7,070.
Additional info: Tuition/fee waivers available for minority students.

FINANCIAL AID PICTURE (2007-2008)

Students with need: Out of 1,237 full-time freshmen who applied for aid, 901 were judged to have need. Of these, 868 received aid, and 73 had their full need met. Average financial aid package met 76% of need; average scholarship/grant was $4,446; average loan was $3,963. For part-time students, average financial aid package was $8,660.
Students without need: 82 full-time freshmen who did not demonstrate need for aid received scholarships/grants; average award was $1,363. No-need awards available for academics, alumni affiliation, art, athletics, job

skills, leadership, minority status, music/drama, ROTC, state/district residency.
Scholarships offered: 23 full-time freshmen received athletic scholarships; average amount $5,954.
Cumulative student debt: 70% of graduating class had student loans; average debt was $21,015.

FINANCIAL AID PROCEDURES
Forms required: FAFSA.
Dates and Deadlines: Priority date 3/1; no closing date. Applicants notified on a rolling basis starting 4/1; must reply within 3 week(s) of notification.
Transfers: Priority date 7/1; no deadline.

CONTACT
Brandi Payne, Director of Financial Aid Services
PO Box 172190, Bozeman, MT 59717-2190
(406) 994-2845

Montana State University: Northern
Havre, Montana
www.msun.edu
Federal Code: 002533

4-year public university and liberal arts college in large town.
Enrollment: 878 full-time undergrads.

BASIC COSTS (2008-2009)
Tuition and fees: $4,390; out-of-state residents $15,035.
Room and board: $5,928.
Additional info: Tuition/fee waivers available for adults, minority students.

FINANCIAL AID PICTURE
Students with need: Need-based aid available for full-time and part-time students.
Students without need: No-need awards available for academics, athletics.

FINANCIAL AID PROCEDURES
Forms required: FAFSA, institutional form.
Dates and Deadlines: Priority date 4/15; no closing date. Applicants notified on a rolling basis; must reply within 2 week(s) of notification.

CONTACT
Cindy Small, Director of Financial Aid
Box 7751, Havre, MT 59501

Montana Tech of the University of Montana
Butte, Montana
www.mtech.edu
Federal Code: 002531

4-year public engineering and technical college in large town.
Enrollment: 2,086 undergrads, 9% part-time. 481 full-time freshmen.
Selectivity: Admits over 75% of applicants.

BASIC COSTS (2008-2009)
Tuition and fees: $5,713; out-of-state residents $15,352.
Room and board: $6,140.
Additional info: Tuition/fee waivers available for adults, minority students.

FINANCIAL AID PICTURE (2008-2009)
Students with need: Need-based aid available for full-time and part-time students. Work study available nights, weekends, and for part-time students.
Students without need: No-need awards available for academics, alumni affiliation, athletics, minority status, state/district residency.

FINANCIAL AID PROCEDURES
Forms required: FAFSA, institutional form.
Dates and Deadlines: Priority date 3/1; no closing date. Applicants notified on a rolling basis starting 4/1; must reply within 2 week(s) of notification.

CONTACT
Mike Richardson, Director of Financial Aid
1300 West Park Street, Butte, MT 59701-8997
(406) 496-4212

Rocky Mountain College
Billings, Montana
www.rocky.edu
Federal Code: 002534

4-year private liberal arts college in small city, affiliated with United Church of Christ, United Methodist Church, United Presbyterian Church.
Enrollment: 877 undergrads.
Selectivity: Admits 50 to 75% of applicants.

BASIC COSTS (2009-2010)
Tuition and fees: $20,016.
Per-credit charge: $820.
Room and board: $6,480.

FINANCIAL AID PICTURE (2007-2008)
Students with need: 56% of average financial aid package awarded as scholarships/grants, 44% awarded as loans/jobs. Need-based aid available for part-time students. Work study available nights, weekends, and for part-time students.
Students without need: No-need awards available for academics, alumni affiliation, art, athletics, leadership, minority status, music/drama, religious affiliation, state/district residency.

FINANCIAL AID PROCEDURES
Forms required: FAFSA, institutional form.
Dates and Deadlines: Priority date 3/1; no closing date. Applicants notified on a rolling basis starting 2/1; must reply within 4 week(s) of notification.
Transfers: No deadline. Applicants notified on a rolling basis starting 2/1; must reply within 4 week(s) of notification.

CONTACT
Lisa Browning, Vice President of Enrollment Services
1511 Poly Drive, Billings, MT 59102-1796
(406) 657-1031

Salish Kootenai College
Pablo, Montana
www.skc.edu
Federal Code: 015023

4-year private liberal arts college in rural community.
Selectivity: Open admission; but selective for some programs.

BASIC COSTS (2008-2009)
Additional info: Full-time tuition for Native American students, $2,736 ($76 per credit hour); full-time tuition for students of Native American descent, $3,384 ($94 per credit hour). Academic year required fees, $897. Tuition/fee waivers available for minority students.

FINANCIAL AID PICTURE (2007-2008)
Students with need: Need-based aid available for full-time and part-time students. Work study available nights, weekends, and for part-time students.

FINANCIAL AID PROCEDURES
Forms required: FAFSA.
Dates and Deadlines: Priority date 3/31; no closing date. Applicants notified on a rolling basis starting 7/15; must reply within 6 week(s) of notification.

CONTACT
Jackie Swain, Financial Aid Director
PO Box 70, Pablo, MT 59855
(406) 275-4855

Stone Child College

Box Elder, Montana
www.stonechild.edu Federal Code: 026109

2-year public community and junior college in rural community.
Enrollment: 213 undergrads.
Selectivity: Open admission.

BASIC COSTS (2008-2009)
Tuition and fees: $2,350.
Per-credit charge: $60.
Additional info: Students not members of Federally-recognized Native American tribe pay additional $420 in fees/year.

FINANCIAL AID PICTURE
Students with need: Need-based aid available for full-time and part-time students.
Students without need: No-need awards available for academics.
Additional info: Scholarships available to high school and GED graduates who apply for college admission during the first term after graduation.

FINANCIAL AID PROCEDURES
Forms required: FAFSA, institutional form.
Dates and Deadlines: Priority date 3/1; closing date 6/30. Applicants notified on a rolling basis.

CONTACT
Tiffany Galbavy, Financial Aid Director
RR1 Box 1082, Box Elder, MT 59521-9796
(406) 395-4313

University of Great Falls

Great Falls, Montana
www.ugf.edu Federal Code: 002527

4-year private university and liberal arts college in small city, affiliated with Roman Catholic Church.
Enrollment: 647 undergrads, 28% part-time. 112 full-time freshmen.
Selectivity: Admits over 75% of applicants.

BASIC COSTS (2009-2010)
Tuition and fees: $18,212.
Per-credit charge: $545.
Room and board: $6,610.

FINANCIAL AID PICTURE (2008-2009)
Students with need: Average financial aid package met 59% of need; average scholarship/grant was $4,730; average loan was $3,557. For part-time students, average financial aid package was $7,518.
Students without need: No-need awards available for academics, art, athletics, religious affiliation.
Scholarships offered: Freshmen scholarships: $1,000-$6,000; based on high school GPA; renewable.
Cumulative student debt: 63% of graduating class had student loans; average debt was $17,200.

FINANCIAL AID PROCEDURES
Forms required: FAFSA.
Dates and Deadlines: Priority date 5/1; no closing date. Applicants notified on a rolling basis starting 3/1; must reply within 2 week(s) of notification.

Transfers: Transfer student scholarships; $2,500-$4,000; based on college GPA; renewable.

CONTACT
Peggy Boord, Director of Financial Aid
1301 20th Street South, Great Falls, MT 59405
(406) 791-5235

University of Montana

Missoula, Montana Federal Code: 002536
www.umt.edu CSS Code: 4489

4-year public university and liberal arts college in small city.
Enrollment: 12,196 undergrads.
Selectivity: Admits over 75% of applicants.

BASIC COSTS (2008-2009)
Tuition and fees: $5,150; out-of-state residents $16,425.
Room and board: $6,258.
Additional info: Tuition/fee waivers available for minority students.

FINANCIAL AID PICTURE (2008-2009)
Students with need: 27% of average financial aid package awarded as scholarships/grants, 73% awarded as loans/jobs. Need-based aid available for part-time students. Work study available nights, weekends, and for part-time students.
Students without need: No-need awards available for academics, art, athletics, leadership, music/drama, ROTC, state/district residency.

FINANCIAL AID PROCEDURES
Forms required: FAFSA, CSS PROFILE, institutional form.
Dates and Deadlines: Priority date 2/15; no closing date. Applicants notified on a rolling basis starting 4/1; must reply by 8/1 or within 4 week(s) of notification.

CONTACT
Myron Hanson, Director of Financial Aid
Lommasson Center 103, Missoula, MT 59812
(406) 243-5373

University of Montana: Western

Dillon, Montana
www.umwestern.edu Federal Code: 002537

4-year public liberal arts and teachers college in small town.
Enrollment: 1,150 undergrads, 14% part-time. 216 full-time freshmen.
Selectivity: Open admission; but selective for some programs.

BASIC COSTS (2008-2009)
Tuition and fees: $3,675; out-of-state residents $12,491.
Room and board: $5,350.
Additional info: Tuition/fee waivers available for minority students.

FINANCIAL AID PICTURE (2007-2008)
Students with need: Need-based aid available for full-time and part-time students. Work study available nights, weekends, and for part-time students.
Students without need: No-need awards available for academics, alumni affiliation, art, athletics, leadership, minority status, state/district residency.
Additional info: Tuition and/or fee waivers for veterans, Native Americans and other minorities.

FINANCIAL AID PROCEDURES
Forms required: FAFSA.
Dates and Deadlines: Priority date 3/1; no closing date. Applicants notified on a rolling basis starting 3/1; must reply within 2 week(s) of notification.

CONTACT

Erica Jones, Director of Financial Aid
710 South Atlantic Street, Dillon, MT 59725
(406) 683-7511

CONTACT

Deb Wilke, Student Financial Aid Officer
5035 Everett Street, Lincoln, NE 68506

Nebraska

Bellevue University

Bellevue, Nebraska
www.bellevue.edu Federal Code: 002538

4-year private university and business college in large city.
Enrollment: 5,695 undergrads, 42% part-time. 34 full-time freshmen.
Selectivity: Open admission; but selective for some programs.

BASIC COSTS (2008-2009)

Tuition and fees: $6,165.
Per-credit charge: $220.
Additional info: Prices vary depending on program.

FINANCIAL AID PICTURE (2007-2008)

Students with need: Need-based aid available for full-time and part-time students. Work study available nights, weekends, and for part-time students.
Students without need: No-need awards available for academics, athletics, leadership.

FINANCIAL AID PROCEDURES

Forms required: FAFSA, institutional form.
Dates and Deadlines: Priority date 4/15; no closing date. Applicants notified on a rolling basis starting 4/15; must reply within 2 week(s) of notification.
Transfers: No deadline.

CONTACT

Jon Dotterer, Director of Financial Aid
1000 Galvin Road South, Bellevue, NE 68005-3098
(402) 557-7326

BryanLGH College of Health Sciences

Lincoln, Nebraska
www.bryanlghcollege.org/ Federal Code: 006399

4-year private health science college in large city.
Enrollment: 256 undergrads. 27 full-time freshmen.
Selectivity: Admits over 75% of applicants.

BASIC COSTS (2009-2010)

Tuition and fees: $11,400.
Per-credit charge: $380.
Additional info: Clinical Fees Nursing: $175/course; Clinical Fees Allied Health: $250/semester; Board Registry Fee estimated: $90/semester (Allied Health); ATI Testing Fee (Nursing): $60/semester.

FINANCIAL AID PICTURE (2007-2008)

Students with need: Out of 22 full-time freshmen who applied for aid, 22 were judged to have need. Of these, 22 received aid. Need-based aid available for part-time students.
Students without need: No-need awards available for academics, leadership.

FINANCIAL AID PROCEDURES

Forms required: FAFSA, institutional form.
Dates and Deadlines: Closing date 5/1. Applicants notified on a rolling basis starting 5/1; must reply within 3 week(s) of notification.

Central Community College

Grand Island, Nebraska
www.cccneb.edu Federal Code: 014468

2-year public community and technical college in large town.
Enrollment: 4,091 undergrads, 46% part-time. 756 full-time freshmen.
Selectivity: Open admission; but selective for some programs and for out-of-state students.

BASIC COSTS (2008-2009)

Tuition and fees: $2,190; out-of-state residents $3,045.
Per-credit charge: $73; out-of-state residents $106.
Room and board: $4,080.

FINANCIAL AID PICTURE

Students with need: Need-based aid available for full-time and part-time students. Work study available nights.
Students without need: No-need awards available for academics, art, athletics, job skills, leadership, music/drama.

FINANCIAL AID PROCEDURES

Forms required: FAFSA, institutional form.
Dates and Deadlines: Priority date 6/1; no closing date. Applicants notified on a rolling basis starting 3/1; must reply within 1 week(s) of notification.

CONTACT

Steve Millnitz, Financial Aid Officer
3134 West Highway 34, Grand Island, NE 68802-4903
(308) 398-7407

Chadron State College

Chadron, Nebraska
www.csc.edu Federal Code: 002539

4-year public business and liberal arts and teachers college in small town.
Enrollment: 2,050 undergrads.
Selectivity: Open admission; but selective for some programs.

BASIC COSTS (2008-2009)

Tuition and fees: $4,557; out-of-state residents $8,052.
Per-credit charge: $117; out-of-state residents $233.
Room and board: $4,654.

FINANCIAL AID PICTURE

Students with need: Need-based aid available for full-time and part-time students. Work study available nights, weekends, and for part-time students.
Students without need: No-need awards available for academics, alumni affiliation, art, athletics, leadership, minority status, music/drama, state/district residency.

FINANCIAL AID PROCEDURES

Forms required: FAFSA, institutional form.
Dates and Deadlines: Priority date 6/1; no closing date. Applicants notified on a rolling basis starting 4/1; must reply within 2 week(s) of notification.

CONTACT

Sherry Douglas, Director of Financial Aid
1000 Main Street, Chadron, NE 69337
(308) 432-6230

Clarkson College

Omaha, Nebraska
www.clarksoncollege.edu Federal Code: 009862

4-year private health science college in large city, affiliated with Episcopal Church.
Enrollment: 738 undergrads.
Selectivity: Open admission; but selective for some programs.

BASIC COSTS (2008-2009)

Tuition and fees: $13,140.
Per-credit charge: $399.
Room only: $4,400.
Additional info: Distance learning fee: $40 per credit hour.

FINANCIAL AID PICTURE (2007-2008)

Students with need: Need-based aid available for full-time and part-time students. Work study available nights, weekends, and for part-time students.
Students without need: No-need awards available for academics, alumni affiliation, minority status, religious affiliation.

FINANCIAL AID PROCEDURES

Forms required: FAFSA, institutional form.
Dates and Deadlines: Priority date 4/1; no closing date. Applicants notified on a rolling basis starting 4/13; must reply within 3 week(s) of notification.
Transfers: Priority date 3/1; no deadline. Applicants notified on a rolling basis starting 3/30.

CONTACT

Margie Harris, Director of Student Financial Services
101 South 42nd Street, Omaha, NE 68131-2739
(402) 552-2749

College of Saint Mary

Omaha, Nebraska
www.csm.edu Federal Code: 002540

4-year private nursing and liberal arts and teachers college for women in large city, affiliated with Roman Catholic Church.
Enrollment: 722 undergrads, 21% part-time. 73 full-time freshmen.
Selectivity: Admits less than 50% of applicants.

BASIC COSTS (2009-2010)

Tuition and fees: $22,260.
Per-credit charge: $720.
Room and board: $6,400.

FINANCIAL AID PICTURE (2008-2009)

Students with need: Out of 70 full-time freshmen who applied for aid, 67 were judged to have need. Of these, 67 received aid, and 11 had their full need met. Average financial aid package met 75% of need; average scholarship/grant was $14,969; average loan was $3,781. For part-time students, average financial aid package was $5,580.
Students without need: 6 full-time freshmen who did not demonstrate need for aid received scholarships/grants; average award was $8,694. No-need awards available for academics, athletics, music/drama.
Scholarships offered: 6 full-time freshmen received athletic scholarships; average amount $3,660.
Cumulative student debt: 69% of graduating class had student loans; average debt was $26,244.

FINANCIAL AID PROCEDURES

Forms required: FAFSA.
Dates and Deadlines: Priority date 3/1; no closing date. Applicants notified on a rolling basis starting 3/1; must reply within 2 week(s) of notification.
Transfers: No deadline. Applicants notified on a rolling basis starting 3/1; must reply within 2 week(s) of notification. Scholarships and need based grants available for full-time transfer students.

CONTACT

Danni Warrick, Director of Financial Aid
7000 Mercy Road, Omaha, NE 68106
(402) 399-2362

Concordia University

Seward, Nebraska
www.cune.edu Federal Code: 002541

4-year private university in small town, affiliated with Lutheran Church - Missouri Synod.
Enrollment: 1,076 undergrads, 3% part-time. 273 full-time freshmen.
Selectivity: Admits 50 to 75% of applicants.

BASIC COSTS (2009-2010)

Tuition and fees: $21,250.
Room and board: $5,520.

FINANCIAL AID PICTURE (2008-2009)

Students with need: Out of 254 full-time freshmen who applied for aid, 211 were judged to have need. Of these, 211 received aid, and 58 had their full need met. Average financial aid package met 74% of need; average scholarship/grant was $10,006; average loan was $3,223. For part-time students, average financial aid package was $4,191.
Students without need: 62 full-time freshmen who did not demonstrate need for aid received scholarships/grants; average award was $7,844. No-need awards available for academics, alumni affiliation, art, athletics, leadership, music/drama, religious affiliation.
Scholarships offered: ***Merit:*** President's scholarship: $15,000 per year; based on academic achievement. Regent's scholarship: $8,000-$11,000 per year; based on high school GPA and SAT/ACT scores. Achievement award: $3,500-$6,500 per year; based on high school GPA and SAT/ACT scores. ***Athletic:*** 33 full-time freshmen received athletic scholarships; average amount $3,789.
Cumulative student debt: 76% of graduating class had student loans; average debt was $20,393.

FINANCIAL AID PROCEDURES

Forms required: FAFSA.
Dates and Deadlines: Priority date 3/1; no closing date. Applicants notified on a rolling basis starting 3/1; must reply within 4 week(s) of notification.
Transfers: Applicants notified on a rolling basis starting 3/1; must reply within 4 week(s) of notification.

CONTACT

Gloria Hennig, Director of Financial Aid
800 North Columbia Avenue, Seward, NE 68434-1556
(800) 535-5494 ext. 7270

Creative Center

Omaha, Nebraska
www.creativecenter.edu Federal Code: 031643

4-year for-profit visual arts and career college in large city.
Enrollment: 118 undergrads, 2% part-time. 47 full-time freshmen.

BASIC COSTS (2009-2010)

Tuition and fees: $20,400.
Additional info: Tuition/fees may vary by program.

FINANCIAL AID PICTURE

Students with need: Need-based aid available for full-time and part-time students.
Students without need: No-need awards available for academics, art.
Scholarships offered: President's Award: $500. Founder's Award: $1,000. Both awards based on portfolio and high school academics. Andy Arrants

Memorial Scholarship: supply kit (approx. $500); based on submitted artwork and essay.

FINANCIAL AID PROCEDURES

Forms required: FAFSA.

Dates and Deadlines: No deadline. Applicants notified on a rolling basis starting 1/1.

Transfers: No deadline. Applicants notified on a rolling basis.

CONTACT

Sandy LaRocca, Director of Financial Aid
10850 Emmet Street, Omaha, NE 68164
(402) 898-1000 ext. 203

Creighton University

Omaha, Nebraska
www.creighton.edu Federal Code: 002542

4-year private university in very large city, affiliated with Roman Catholic Church.

Enrollment: 4,087 undergrads, 7% part-time. 986 full-time freshmen.

Selectivity: Admits over 75% of applicants.

BASIC COSTS (2009-2010)

Tuition and fees: $29,544.

Per-credit charge: $882.

Room and board: $8,814.

Additional info: Tuition/fee waivers available for minority students.

FINANCIAL AID PICTURE (2008-2009)

Students with need: Out of 765 full-time freshmen who applied for aid, 588 were judged to have need. Of these, 588 received aid, and 249 had their full need met. Average financial aid package met 92% of need; average scholarship/grant was $19,524; average loan was $6,066. Need-based aid available for part-time students.

Students without need: 345 full-time freshmen who did not demonstrate need for aid received scholarships/grants; average award was $11,988. No-need awards available for academics, alumni affiliation, art, athletics, leadership, minority status, music/drama, ROTC.

Scholarships offered: ***Merit:*** William Jennings Bryan Debate and Speech Scholarship: $4,000. Diversity Scholarship & Native American Merit Scholarship: three-quarter tuition scholarships; awarded to students who show commitment to diversity; 3.3 GPA or higher on a 4.0 scale required; applicants evaluated on academic merit, community service, school activities, leadership, and financial need. First-generation college bound students and families that earn under $60,000 encouraged to apply. Ron Hansen Scholarship in Creative Writing: $4,000. Grace Keenan Scholarship for Excellence in the Arts: $3,000; awarded to students who intend to major in visual or performing arts. Christina M. Hixson Scholarship in Business Administration: $4,500; awarded to freshman business students from high schools in CO, IA, IL, KA, MN, MO, NE, ND, SD, WI or WY with a minimum of 3.0 GPA. College of Business Administration Ethics and Social Responsibility Scholarship: $4,500; awarded to students with exceptional service accomplishments and leadership potential; 3.8 GPA and a minimum 26 ACT or 1200 SAT. Presidential Scholarship: three-quarter tuition scholarship awarded to selected applicants in the top 10% of applicant pool, based upon academics. Scott Scholarship: full tuition scholarship in the College of Business Administration; awarded to selected students in the top 10% of applicant pool; based on academics. G. Robert Muchemore Foundation Undergraduate Scholarship: full tuition scholarship; awarded to graduates of Nebraska high schools entering as freshmen; based upon academics. ***Athletic:*** 44 full-time freshmen received athletic scholarships; average amount $15,397.

FINANCIAL AID PROCEDURES

Forms required: FAFSA, institutional form.

Dates and Deadlines: Priority date 3/1; no closing date. Applicants notified on a rolling basis starting 3/15; must reply by 5/1 or within 4 week(s) of notification.

Transfers: If transferring 24 or more hours of credit, student not eligible for academic, non-need scholarships.

CONTACT

Robert Walker, Director of Financial Aid
2500 California Plaza, Omaha, NE 68178-0001
(402) 280-2731

PART III: FINANCIAL AID COLLEGE BY COLLEGE

Doane College

Crete, Nebraska
www.doane.edu Federal Code: 002544

4-year private liberal arts college in small town, affiliated with United Church of Christ.

Enrollment: 896 undergrads, 1% part-time. 248 full-time freshmen.

Selectivity: Admits over 75% of applicants.

BASIC COSTS (2009-2010)

Tuition and fees: $21,040.

Per-credit charge: $680.

Room and board: $5,970.

FINANCIAL AID PICTURE (2008-2009)

Students with need: Out of 226 full-time freshmen who applied for aid, 198 were judged to have need. Of these, 198 received aid, and 135 had their full need met. Average financial aid package met 97% of need; average scholarship/grant was $14,017; average loan was $3,891. Need-based aid available for part-time students.

Students without need: 43 full-time freshmen who did not demonstrate need for aid received scholarships/grants; average award was $12,580. No-need awards available for academics, art, athletics, music/drama.

Cumulative student debt: 86% of graduating class had student loans; average debt was $17,678.

FINANCIAL AID PROCEDURES

Forms required: FAFSA.

Dates and Deadlines: Priority date 3/1; no closing date. Applicants notified on a rolling basis starting 3/1; must reply within 2 week(s) of notification.

CONTACT

Peggy Tvrdy, Director of Financial Aid
1014 Boswell Avenue, Crete, NE 68333
(402) 826-8260

Grace University

Omaha, Nebraska
www.graceuniversity.edu Federal Code: 002547

4-year private university and Bible college in very large city, affiliated with interdenominational tradition.

Enrollment: 367 undergrads.

Selectivity: Admits 50 to 75% of applicants.

BASIC COSTS (2009-2010)

Tuition and fees: $14,930.

Per-credit charge: $390.

Room and board: $5,730.

Additional info: Tuition/fee waivers available for minority students.

FINANCIAL AID PICTURE (2008-2009)

Students with need: Need-based aid available for full-time and part-time students.

Students without need: No-need awards available for academics, alumni affiliation, music/drama.

FINANCIAL AID PROCEDURES

Forms required: FAFSA, institutional form.

Dates and Deadlines: Priority date 3/1; no closing date. Applicants notified on a rolling basis starting 3/1; must reply within 2 week(s) of notification.
Transfers: No deadline. Applicants notified on a rolling basis starting 3/1; must reply within 2 week(s) of notification.

CONTACT

Dale Brown, Director of Revenue
1311 South Ninth Street, Omaha, NE 68108-3629
(402) 449-2810

Kaplan University: Lincoln

Lincoln, Nebraska
www.kucampus.edu Federal Code: 004721

2-year for-profit branch campus college in small city.
Enrollment: 496 undergrads.
Selectivity: Open admission; but selective for some programs.

BASIC COSTS (2008-2009)

Tuition and fees: $14,070.
Additional info: Cost is for 3 terms of 12 hours each. Tuition includes books and supplies; may vary by program.

FINANCIAL AID PICTURE (2007-2008)

Students with need: Need-based aid available for full-time and part-time students. Work study available nights, weekends, and for part-time students.
Students without need: This college awards aid only to students with need.

FINANCIAL AID PROCEDURES

Forms required: FAFSA, institutional form.
Dates and Deadlines: No deadline. Applicants notified on a rolling basis starting 2/1.
Transfers: No deadline.

CONTACT

Crystal Faxon, Associate Director of Financial Aid
1821 K Street, Lincoln, NE 68508
(402) 474-5315

Kaplan University: Omaha

Omaha, Nebraska
www.khenet.kaplan.edu Federal Code: 008491

2-year for-profit career college in large city.
Enrollment: 606 undergrads, 27% part-time. 291 full-time freshmen.
Selectivity: Open admission.

BASIC COSTS (2008-2009)

Tuition and fees: $14,050.

FINANCIAL AID PICTURE

Students with need: Need-based aid available for full-time and part-time students.
Students without need: This college awards aid only to students with need.

FINANCIAL AID PROCEDURES

Forms required: FAFSA, institutional form.
Dates and Deadlines: No deadline. Applicants notified on a rolling basis.

CONTACT

Jason Jimerson, Director Of Financial Aid
5425 North 103rd. Street, Omaha, NE 68134
(402) 431-6100

Little Priest Tribal College

Winnebago, Nebraska
www.lptc.bia.edu Federal Code: 033233

2-year private community college in rural community.
Enrollment: 112 undergrads.
Selectivity: Open admission.

BASIC COSTS (2008-2009)

Tuition and fees: $2,985.
Per-credit charge: $80.

FINANCIAL AID PICTURE

Students with need: Need-based aid available for full-time and part-time students.

FINANCIAL AID PROCEDURES

Forms required: FAFSA, institutional form.
Dates and Deadlines: No deadline.

CONTACT

Billie Kitcheyan, Director of Financial Aid
PO Box 270, Winnebago, NE 68071
(402) 878-2380 ext. 125

Metropolitan Community College

Omaha, Nebraska
www.mccneb.edu Federal Code: 004432

2-year public community and technical college in large city.
Enrollment: 6,609 undergrads, 57% part-time. 864 full-time freshmen.
Selectivity: Open admission; but selective for some programs.

BASIC COSTS (2008-2009)

Tuition and fees: $2,160; out-of-state residents $3,128.
Per-credit charge: $43; out-of-state residents $65.
Room and board: $3,555.

FINANCIAL AID PICTURE (2008-2009)

Students with need: Need-based aid available for full-time and part-time students.
Students without need: No-need awards available for academics.

FINANCIAL AID PROCEDURES

Forms required: FAFSA, institutional form.
Dates and Deadlines: Priority date 3/15; no closing date. Applicants notified on a rolling basis starting 4/15.

CONTACT

Wendy Olson, Director of Financial Aid
Box 3777, Omaha, NE 68103-0777
(402) 457-2330

Mid-Plains Community College Area

North Platte, Nebraska
www.mpcc.edu Federal Code: 002557

2-year public community and technical college in large town.
Enrollment: 1,252 undergrads, 29% part-time. 255 full-time freshmen.
Selectivity: Open admission; but selective for some programs.

BASIC COSTS (2008-2009)

Tuition and fees: $2,370; out-of-state residents $2,970.
Per-credit charge: $65; out-of-state residents $85.
Room and board: $4,700.

FINANCIAL AID PICTURE (2007-2008)
Students with need: 60% of average financial aid package awarded as scholarships/grants, 40% awarded as loans/jobs. Need-based aid available for part-time students. Work study available nights.
Students without need: No-need awards available for academics, art, athletics, music/drama.

FINANCIAL AID PROCEDURES
Forms required: FAFSA, institutional form.
Dates and Deadlines: Priority date 5/1; no closing date. Applicants notified on a rolling basis starting 5/1; must reply within 3 week(s) of notification.

CONTACT
Ted Fellers, Director of Financial Aid
1101 Halligan Drive, North Platte, NE 69101
(800) 658-4348

Nebraska Christian College
Papillion, Nebraska
www.nechristian.edu Federal Code: 012976

4-year private Bible college in large town, affiliated with Christian Church/Churches of Christ.
Enrollment: 162 undergrads.

BASIC COSTS (2008-2009)
Tuition and fees: $10,400.
Per-credit charge: $300.
Room and board: $4,800.

FINANCIAL AID PICTURE (2007-2008)
Students with need: Need-based aid available for part-time students.
Students without need: No-need awards available for academics, leadership.

FINANCIAL AID PROCEDURES
Forms required: FAFSA, institutional form.
Dates and Deadlines: Priority date 6/1; no closing date. Applicants notified on a rolling basis starting 5/5.

CONTACT
Tina Larsen, Financial Aid Officer
12550 South 114th Street, Papillion, NE 68046

Nebraska College of Technical Agriculture
Curtis, Nebraska
www.ncta.unl.edu Federal Code: 007358

2-year public agricultural college in rural community.
Enrollment: 250 full-time undergrads.
Selectivity: Open admission.

BASIC COSTS (2008-2009)
Tuition and fees: $3,369; out-of-state residents $6,256.
Per-credit charge: $97; out-of-state residents $193.
Room and board: $4,309.

FINANCIAL AID PICTURE (2007-2008)
Students with need: 51% of average financial aid package awarded as scholarships/grants, 49% awarded as loans/jobs. Need-based aid available for part-time students.
Students without need: This college awards aid only to students with need.

FINANCIAL AID PROCEDURES
Forms required: FAFSA.
Dates and Deadlines: Priority date 4/1; no closing date. Applicants notified on a rolling basis starting 5/1; must reply within 2 week(s) of notification.

CONTACT
Mary Ann Mercer, Financial Aid Coordinator
404 East 7th Street, Curtis, NE 69025-0069
(308) 367-5207

Nebraska Indian Community College
Macy, Nebraska
www.thenicc.edu Federal Code: 015339

2-year public community college in rural community.
Enrollment: 94 undergrads.
Selectivity: Open admission.

BASIC COSTS (2008-2009)
Tuition and fees: $3,200.
Per-credit charge: $80.

FINANCIAL AID PICTURE
Students with need: Need-based aid available for full-time and part-time students.
Students without need: This college awards aid only to students with need.

FINANCIAL AID PROCEDURES
Forms required: FAFSA, state aid form, institutional form.
Dates and Deadlines: Priority date 7/15; no closing date. Applicants notified on a rolling basis starting 8/30; must reply within 2 week(s) of notification.

CONTACT
Veda Webster, Dean of Student Services
PO Box 428, Macy, NE 68039
(402) 837-5078 ext. 2581

Nebraska Methodist College of Nursing and Allied Health
Omaha, Nebraska
www.methodistcollege.edu Federal Code: 009937

4-year private health science and nursing college in large city, affiliated with United Methodist Church.
Enrollment: 520 undergrads, 28% part-time. 22 full-time freshmen.
Selectivity: Admits 50 to 75% of applicants.

BASIC COSTS (2009-2010)
Tuition and fees: $14,250.
Per-credit charge: $451.
Room only: $4,824.

FINANCIAL AID PICTURE (2007-2008)
Students with need: Out of 22 full-time freshmen who applied for aid, 20 were judged to have need. Of these, 20 received aid, and 2 had their full need met. Average financial aid package met 55% of need; average scholarship/grant was $5,956; average loan was $3,083. For part-time students, average financial aid package was $7,363.
Students without need: 1 full-time freshmen who did not demonstrate need for aid received scholarships/grants; average award was $6,000. No-need awards available for academics, leadership, religious affiliation, ROTC.
Scholarships offered: President's Leadership Scholarship: $8,000 per year for 4 years; 4 awarded. Dean's Scholarship: $5,000 for 4 years; 3 awarded. Excellence in Allied Health Scholarship: $5,000 per year for 2 years; 3 awarded. Horizon Scholarship: $3,000 per year; based on academic and personal merit; 45 awarded.

Cumulative student debt: 89% of graduating class had student loans; average debt was $35,422.

FINANCIAL AID PROCEDURES

Forms required: FAFSA, institutional form.

Dates and Deadlines: Priority date 5/1; no closing date. Applicants notified on a rolling basis starting 3/1; must reply within 3 week(s) of notification.

Transfers: Priority date 4/1; no deadline. Applicants notified on a rolling basis.

CONTACT

Brenda Boyd, Director of Financial Aid
720 North 87th Street, Omaha, NE 68114
(402) 354-7225

Nebraska Wesleyan University

Lincoln, Nebraska
www.nebrwesleyan.edu Federal Code: 002555

4-year private liberal arts college in small city, affiliated with United Methodist Church.

Enrollment: 1,817 undergrads, 11% part-time. 383 full-time freshmen.

Selectivity: Admits over 75% of applicants.

BASIC COSTS (2008-2009)

Tuition and fees: $21,274.

Per-credit charge: $788.

Room and board: $5,710.

Additional info: Tuition/fee waivers available for adults.

FINANCIAL AID PICTURE (2008-2009)

Students with need: Out of 334 full-time freshmen who applied for aid, 277 were judged to have need. Of these, 277 received aid, and 40 had their full need met. Average financial aid package met 73% of need; average scholarship/grant was $11,847; average loan was $4,421. For part-time students, average financial aid package was $2,812.

Students without need: 106 full-time freshmen who did not demonstrate need for aid received scholarships/grants; average award was $7,546. No-need awards available for academics, art, music/drama, religious affiliation.

Scholarships offered: Huge-NWU Scholarship: tuition, books, fees, and room and board up to $25,000; competitive; two awards per year. Board of Governors Scholar Award: $10,500; ACT 32 or SAT 1410. Wesleyan Scholar Award: $9,000; ACT 29-31 or SAT 1280-1400. Fredstrom Scholarship: $7,500; ACT 27-28 or SAT 1200-1270, or top 10% class rank. President's Scholarship: $6,000; ACT 24-26 or SAT 1090-1190 or Top 25% class rank. Recognition Scholarship: $4,500; ACT 22-23 or SAT 1010-1080 or top 33% class rank.

Cumulative student debt: 82% of graduating class had student loans; average debt was $16,458.

FINANCIAL AID PROCEDURES

Forms required: FAFSA.

Dates and Deadlines: No deadline. Applicants notified on a rolling basis starting 3/1; must reply within 4 week(s) of notification.

Transfers: No deadline. Applicants notified on a rolling basis starting 3/1; must reply within 4 week(s) of notification.

CONTACT

Thomas Ochsner, Director of Scholarships and Financial Aid
5000 St. Paul Avenue, Lincoln, NE 68504
(402) 465-2212

Northeast Community College

Norfolk, Nebraska
www.northeast.edu Federal Code: 002556

2-year public community college in large town.

Enrollment: 2,528 undergrads, 22% part-time. 730 full-time freshmen.

Selectivity: Open admission; but selective for some programs.

BASIC COSTS (2009-2010)

Tuition and fees: $2,430; out-of-state residents $2,933.

Per-credit charge: $67; out-of-state residents $84.

Room and board: $4,656.

FINANCIAL AID PICTURE (2007-2008)

Students with need: Need-based aid available for full-time and part-time students. Work study available nights, weekends, and for part-time students.

Students without need: No-need awards available for academics, athletics, music/drama.

FINANCIAL AID PROCEDURES

Forms required: FAFSA, institutional form.

Dates and Deadlines: No deadline. Applicants notified on a rolling basis; must reply within 2 week(s) of notification.

CONTACT

Stacy Dieckman, Director of Financial Aid
801 East Benjamin Avenue, Norfolk, NE 68702-0469
(402) 844-7280

Peru State College

Peru, Nebraska
www.peru.edu Federal Code: 002559

4-year public liberal arts and teachers college in rural community.

Enrollment: 1,548 undergrads.

Selectivity: Admits less than 50% of applicants.

BASIC COSTS (2008-2009)

Tuition and fees: $4,388; out-of-state residents $7,883.

Per-credit charge: $117; out-of-state residents $233.

Room and board: $5,556.

FINANCIAL AID PICTURE (2007-2008)

Students with need: Need-based aid available for full-time and part-time students.

Students without need: This college awards aid only to students with need.

FINANCIAL AID PROCEDURES

Forms required: FAFSA, institutional form.

Dates and Deadlines: Priority date 3/1; no closing date. Applicants notified on a rolling basis starting 3/1; must reply within 2 week(s) of notification.

Transfers: Must have financial aid transcripts from all previous schools sent to college.

CONTACT

Director of Financial Aid
Box 10, Peru, NE 68421-0010
(402) 872-2228

Southeast Community College

Lincoln, Nebraska
www.southeast.edu Federal Code: 007591

2-year public community college in small city.

Enrollment: 8,136 undergrads, 31% part-time. 1,619 full-time freshmen.

Selectivity: Open admission.

BASIC COSTS (2009-2010)

Tuition and fees: $2,207; out-of-state residents $2,680.

Per-credit charge: $48; out-of-state residents $59.

FINANCIAL AID PICTURE

Students with need: Need-based aid available for full-time and part-time students. Work study available nights, weekends, and for part-time students.

Students without need: No-need awards available for academics.

FINANCIAL AID PROCEDURES

Forms required: FAFSA, institutional form.

Dates and Deadlines: No deadline. Applicants notified on a rolling basis; must reply within 2 week(s) of notification.

CONTACT

Dave Sonenberg, Dean of Financial Aid
8800 O Street, Lincoln, NE 68520
(402) 437-2619

Union College

Lincoln, Nebraska
www.ucollege.edu Federal Code: 002563

4-year private liberal arts college in small city, affiliated with Seventh-day Adventists.

Enrollment: 838 undergrads, 14% part-time. 169 full-time freshmen.

Selectivity: Admits 50 to 75% of applicants.

BASIC COSTS (2008-2009)

Tuition and fees: $16,920.

Per-credit charge: $690.

Room and board: $4,680.

FINANCIAL AID PICTURE (2007-2008)

Students with need: Need-based aid available for full-time and part-time students.

Students without need: No-need awards available for academics.

Additional info: Special institutional grants offered to all freshmen and sophomores demonstrating exceptional financial need.

FINANCIAL AID PROCEDURES

Forms required: FAFSA.

Dates and Deadlines: Priority date 5/1; no closing date. Applicants notified on a rolling basis starting 4/15; must reply by 5/1 or within 3 week(s) of notification.

CONTACT

Elaina Camarena, Director of Financial Aid
3800 South 48th Street, Lincoln, NE 68506-4300
(402) 486-2505

University of Nebraska - Kearney

Kearney, Nebraska
www.unk.edu Federal Code: 002551

4-year public university in large town.

Enrollment: 4,911 undergrads, 8% part-time. 1,037 full-time freshmen.

Selectivity: Admits over 75% of applicants.

BASIC COSTS (2008-2009)

Tuition and fees: $5,426; out-of-state residents $10,001.

Per-credit charge: $146; out-of-state residents $298.

Room and board: $6,330.

FINANCIAL AID PICTURE (2008-2009)

Students with need: Need-based aid available for full-time and part-time students.

Students without need: No-need awards available for academics, alumni affiliation, art, athletics, leadership, minority status, music/drama, state/district residency.

FINANCIAL AID PROCEDURES

Forms required: FAFSA, institutional form.

Dates and Deadlines: Priority date 4/1; no closing date. Applicants notified on a rolling basis starting 3/15; must reply within 2 week(s) of notification.

CONTACT

Mary Sommers, Director of Financial Aid
905 West 25th, Kearney, NE 68849
(308) 865-8520

University of Nebraska - Lincoln

Lincoln, Nebraska
www.unl.edu Federal Code: 002565

4-year public university in small city.

Enrollment: 18,526 undergrads, 7% part-time. 4,166 full-time freshmen.

Selectivity: Admits 50 to 75% of applicants.

BASIC COSTS (2008-2009)

Tuition and fees: $6,585; out-of-state residents $17,205.

Per-credit charge: $180; out-of-state residents $534.

Room and board: $6,882.

FINANCIAL AID PICTURE (2007-2008)

Students with need: Out of 2,895 full-time freshmen who applied for aid, 1,952 were judged to have need. Of these, 1,915 received aid, and 728 had their full need met. Average financial aid package met 75% of need; average scholarship/grant was $7,219; average loan was $3,266. For part-time students, average financial aid package was $6,523.

Students without need: 606 full-time freshmen who did not demonstrate need for aid received scholarships/grants; average award was $5,049. No-need awards available for academics, alumni affiliation, art, athletics, leadership, minority status, music/drama, state/district residency.

Scholarships offered: 120 full-time freshmen received athletic scholarships; average amount $13,311.

Cumulative student debt: 61% of graduating class had student loans; average debt was $18,958.

FINANCIAL AID PROCEDURES

Forms required: FAFSA.

Dates and Deadlines: Priority date 4/15; no closing date. Applicants notified on a rolling basis starting 4/1.

Transfers: Priority application date of April 1 for scholarship consideration.

CONTACT

Craig Munier, Director of Scholarships and Financial Aid
1410 Q Street, Lincoln, NE 68588-0417
(402) 472-2030

University of Nebraska - Omaha

Omaha, Nebraska
www.unomaha.edu Federal Code: 002554

4-year public university in large city.

Enrollment: 11,069 undergrads, 21% part-time. 1,585 full-time freshmen.

Selectivity: Admits over 75% of applicants.

BASIC COSTS (2008-2009)

Tuition and fees: $5,880; out-of-state residents $15,458.

Per-credit charge: $164; out-of-state residents $483.

Room and board: $6,980.

FINANCIAL AID PICTURE (2007-2008)

Students with need: Out of 1,093 full-time freshmen who applied for aid, 731 were judged to have need. Of these, 699 received aid. For part-time students, average financial aid package was $2,183.

Students without need: 161 full-time freshmen who did not demonstrate need for aid received scholarships/grants; average award was $2,285. No-need awards available for academics, alumni affiliation, art, athletics, leadership, minority status, music/drama, ROTC, state/district residency.
Scholarships offered: 8 full-time freshmen received athletic scholarships; average amount $2,461.

FINANCIAL AID PROCEDURES
Forms required: FAFSA.
Dates and Deadlines: Priority date 3/1; no closing date. Applicants notified on a rolling basis starting 4/15; must reply within 2 week(s) of notification.

CONTACT
Randall Sell, Director of Financial Aid
6001 Dodge Street, Omaha, NE 68182-0005
(402) 554-2327

University of Nebraska Medical Center
Omaha, Nebraska
www.unmc.edu Federal Code: 006895

Upper-division public health science college in very large city.
Enrollment: 793 undergrads, 8% part-time.

BASIC COSTS (2008-2009)
Tuition and fees: $5,773; out-of-state residents $16,393.
Per-credit charge: $180; out-of-state residents $534.
Additional info: Tuition varies by program. Tuition/fee waivers available for minority students.

FINANCIAL AID PICTURE (2007-2008)
Students with need: Work study available nights, weekends, and for part-time students.

FINANCIAL AID PROCEDURES
Forms required: FAFSA, institutional form.
Dates and Deadlines: No deadline.
Transfers: Priority date 4/1; no deadline. Applicants notified on a rolling basis starting 5/1; must reply within 2 week(s) of notification.

CONTACT
Judith Walker, Director of Financial Aid
984230 Nebraska Medical Center, Omaha, NE 68198-4230
(402) 559-4199

Wayne State College
Wayne, Nebraska
www.wsc.edu Federal Code: 002566

4-year public liberal arts and teachers college in small town.
Enrollment: 2,863 undergrads, 8% part-time. 653 full-time freshmen.
Selectivity: Open admission.

BASIC COSTS (2008-2009)
Tuition and fees: $4,571; out-of-state residents $8,066.
Per-credit charge: $117; out-of-state residents $233.
Room and board: $5,054.

FINANCIAL AID PICTURE (2008-2009)
Students with need: Out of 577 full-time freshmen who applied for aid, 421 were judged to have need. Of these, 419 received aid, and 99 had their full need met. Average financial aid package met 38% of need; average scholarship/grant was $1,778; average loan was $1,624. For part-time students, average financial aid package was $3,392.
Students without need: 57 full-time freshmen who did not demonstrate need for aid received scholarships/grants; average award was $1,110. No-need awards available for academics, art, athletics, leadership, minority status, music/drama, religious affiliation, state/district residency.
Scholarships offered: 19 full-time freshmen received athletic scholarships; average amount $1,229.

FINANCIAL AID PROCEDURES
Forms required: FAFSA.
Dates and Deadlines: Priority date 4/1; no closing date. Applicants notified on a rolling basis starting 3/1; must reply within 4 week(s) of notification.

CONTACT
Kyle Rose, Director of Financial Aid
1111 Main Street, Wayne, NE 68787
(402) 375-7230

Western Nebraska Community College
Scottsbluff, Nebraska
www.wn.edu Federal Code: 002560

2-year public community college in large town.
Enrollment: 1,502 undergrads, 37% part-time. 364 full-time freshmen.
Selectivity: Open admission; but selective for some programs.

BASIC COSTS (2008-2009)
Tuition and fees: $2,370; out-of-state residents $2,730.
Per-credit charge: $66; out-of-state residents $78.
Room and board: $4,950.

FINANCIAL AID PICTURE (2008-2009)
Students with need: Out of 287 full-time freshmen who applied for aid, 230 were judged to have need. Of these, 228 received aid. Average financial aid package met 88% of need; average scholarship/grant was $4,559; average loan was $2,650. For part-time students, average financial aid package was $5,901.
Students without need: 48 full-time freshmen who did not demonstrate need for aid received scholarships/grants; average award was $876. No-need awards available for academics, art, athletics, leadership, music/drama, state/district residency.
Scholarships offered: 68 full-time freshmen received athletic scholarships; average amount $7,422.
Cumulative student debt: 31% of graduating class had student loans; average debt was $3,758.

FINANCIAL AID PROCEDURES
Forms required: FAFSA.
Dates and Deadlines: Priority date 3/1; no closing date. Applicants notified on a rolling basis starting 4/1.
Transfers: State of Nebraska limits the amount of Nebraska State Grant funds a student receives in any one year.

CONTACT
Sheila Johns, Director of Financial Aid
1601 East 27th Street, Scottsbluff, NE 69361
(308) 635-6011

York College
York, Nebraska
www.york.edu Federal Code: 002567

4-year private liberal arts and teachers college in small town, affiliated with Church of Christ.
Enrollment: 382 undergrads, 3% part-time. 110 full-time freshmen.
Selectivity: Admits 50 to 75% of applicants.

BASIC COSTS (2009-2010)

Tuition and fees: $14,000.

Per-credit charge: $390.

Room and board: $4,500.

FINANCIAL AID PICTURE (2007-2008)

Students with need: Average financial aid package met 24% of need; average scholarship/grant was $4,046; average loan was $3489.83. For part-time students, average financial aid package was $3,256.

Students without need: No-need awards available for academics, alumni affiliation, athletics, leadership, music/drama.

Cumulative student debt: 87% of graduating class had student loans; average debt was $21,290.

FINANCIAL AID PROCEDURES

Forms required: FAFSA.

Dates and Deadlines: Priority date 4/1; no closing date. Applicants notified on a rolling basis starting 3/1; must reply within 4 week(s) of notification.

Transfers: No deadline. Applicants notified on a rolling basis starting 3/1; must reply within 4 week(s) of notification.

CONTACT

Brien Alley, Director of Financial Aid
1125 East 8th Street, York, NE 68467
(402) 363-5624

Nevada

Art Institute of Las Vegas

Henderson, Nevada
www.artinstitutes.edu/lasvegas/ Federal Code: 030846

3-year for-profit culinary school and visual arts college in very large city.

Enrollment: 1,301 undergrads, 19% part-time. 241 full-time freshmen.

Selectivity: Open admission; but selective for some programs.

BASIC COSTS (2009-2010)

Tuition and fees: $22,002.

Per-credit charge: $449.

FINANCIAL AID PICTURE (2008-2009)

Students with need: Need-based aid available for full-time and part-time students. Work study available nights, weekends, and for part-time students.

Students without need: No-need awards available for academics, state/district residency.

Scholarships offered: Academic Competitiveness Grant: up to $750 the first year and up to $1,300 the second year; available to students who are receiving a Pell Grant, are full time in their first or second year of college in a degree program, who graduated from high school in 2005 or later, and who took a program of study in high school that was considered to be rigorous; each eligible student may receive 2 years of ACG; must have a 3.0 GPA at the end of the first year to receive a second year grant. C-CAP Careers Through Culinary Arts Program: approximately $36,000 - $72,000; available to students who are enrolled in a C-CAP program. CKYBER National Kitchen and Bath Association VNU Scholarship: provided for students enrolled in a NKBA (National Kitchen and Bath Association) endorsed program; GPA of 2.7 or higher; must be attending full time for the full academic year; Interior Design program students are eligible to apply. Evelyn Keedy Memorial Scholarship: $30,000 tuition; available to high school seniors who show dedication to their education and a desire for a creative career. National Art Honor Society Scholarship: first Place $20,000, second place $10,000, third place $5,000, fourth place $3,000, fifth place $2,000; high school seniors who also belong to the National Art Honor Society may apply; senior class members of the National Art Honor Society are eligible to compete.

FINANCIAL AID PROCEDURES

Dates and Deadlines: No deadline. Applicants notified on a rolling basis.

Transfers: No deadline. Applicants notified on a rolling basis.

CONTACT

Dana Sirolli, Director of Student Financial Services
2350 Corporate Circle, Henderson, NV 89074-7737
(702) 369-9944

Career College of Northern Nevada

Reno, Nevada
www.ccnn.edu Federal Code: 026215

2-year for-profit career college in large city.

Enrollment: 286 undergrads. 286 full-time freshmen.

Selectivity: Open admission.

BASIC COSTS (2008-2009)

Additional info: Tuition for associate programs ranges from $20,055 to $26,250; diploma programs, $11,655 to $15,960. Fees are $210 to $672; books range from $650 to $2,650.

FINANCIAL AID PICTURE

Students with need: Need-based aid available for full-time students.

Students without need: This college awards aid only to students with need.

FINANCIAL AID PROCEDURES

Forms required: FAFSA.

Dates and Deadlines: Closing date 5/30. Applicants notified on a rolling basis.

CONTACT

Andrea Wiggins
1195 A Corporate Boulevard, Reno, NV 89502-2331
(775) 856-2266

College of Southern Nevada

Las Vegas, Nevada
www.csn.edu Federal Code: 010362

2-year public community college in very large city.

Enrollment: 31,091 undergrads, 75% part-time. 2,020 full-time freshmen.

Selectivity: Open admission; but selective for some programs.

BASIC COSTS (2008-2009)

Tuition and fees: $1,921; out-of-state residents $7,733.

Per-credit charge: $60; out-of-state residents $120.

Additional info: Discounted tuition for residents of western states participating in Western Undergraduate Exchange: Alaska, Arizona, California, Colorado, Hawaii, Idaho, Montana, Nevada, New Mexico, North Dakota, Oregon, South Dakota, Utah, Washington, Wyoming.

FINANCIAL AID PICTURE (2007-2008)

Students with need: 68% of average financial aid package awarded as scholarships/grants, 32% awarded as loans/jobs. Work study available nights, weekends, and for part-time students.

Students without need: No-need awards available for state/district residency.

FINANCIAL AID PROCEDURES

Forms required: FAFSA.

Dates and Deadlines: Priority date 5/1; closing date 6/30. Applicants notified on a rolling basis starting 7/15; must reply within 2 week(s) of notification.

CONTACT

Peter Hurley, Financial Aid Director
6375 West Charleston Boulevard, Las Vegas, NV 89146-1164
(702) 651-4047

Great Basin College

Elko, Nevada
www.gbcnv.edu Federal Code: 006977

4-year public community and teachers college in large town.
Enrollment: 2,230 undergrads.
Selectivity: Open admission; but selective for some programs.

BASIC COSTS (2008-2009)

Tuition and fees: $1,921; out-of-state residents $7,629.
Per-credit charge: $60; out-of-state residents $123.
Room only: $3,300.
Additional info: Discounted tuition (Good Neighbor rates) available for non-resident students residing in certain counties bordering Nevada.

FINANCIAL AID PICTURE

Students with need: Need-based aid available for full-time and part-time students. Work study available nights, weekends, and for part-time students.

FINANCIAL AID PROCEDURES

Forms required: FAFSA.
Dates and Deadlines: Priority date 6/1; no closing date. Applicants notified on a rolling basis starting 7/1.
Transfers: Priority date 4/1.

CONTACT

Scott Neilsen, Director of Financial Aid
1500 College Parkway, Elko, NV 89801
(775) 753-2267

International Academy of Design and Technology: Henderson

Henderson, Nevada
www.iadtvegas.com

3-year for-profit visual arts and technical college in very large city.
Enrollment: 450 undergrads.
Selectivity: Open admission.

BASIC COSTS (2008-2009)

Tuition and fees: $16,560.
Additional info: Costs of books and supplies vary from $4,200 to $9,600 for entire program depending on course of study. Additional fees may apply.

FINANCIAL AID PICTURE (2008-2009)

Students with need: 2% of average financial aid package awarded as scholarships/grants, 98% awarded as loans/jobs.

FINANCIAL AID PROCEDURES

Dates and Deadlines: No deadline.

CONTACT

Jamehia Thibeaux, Director of Student Finance
2495 Village View Drive, Henderson, NV 89074

Las Vegas College

Las Vegas, Nevada
lasvegas-college.com Federal Code: 015804

2-year for-profit business and health science college in very large city.
Enrollment: 639 undergrads.
Selectivity: Open admission.

FINANCIAL AID PICTURE

Students with need: Need-based aid available for full-time and part-time students. Work study available nights, weekends, and for part-time students.
Students without need: This college awards aid only to students with need.

FINANCIAL AID PROCEDURES

Forms required: FAFSA.
Dates and Deadlines: Applicants notified on a rolling basis; must reply within 2 week(s) of notification.

CONTACT

Terry Farris, Director of Financial Aid
170 North Stephanie Street, Las Vegas, NV 89014

Morrison University

Reno, Nevada
www.morrison.neumont.edu Federal Code: 009948

4-year for-profit university and business college in small city.
Enrollment: 105 undergrads.
Selectivity: Open admission.

FINANCIAL AID PICTURE

Students with need: Need-based aid available for full-time students. Work study available nights.

FINANCIAL AID PROCEDURES

Forms required: FAFSA.
Dates and Deadlines: No deadline. Applicants notified on a rolling basis starting 7/1.

CONTACT

Jim Hadwick, Financial Aid Manager
10315 Professional Circle, #201, Reno, NV 89521
(775) 850-0700 ext. 110

Nevada State College

Henderson, Nevada
www.nsc.nevada.edu Federal Code: 041143

4-year public nursing and liberal arts and teachers college in large city.
Enrollment: 1,667 undergrads, 51% part-time. 142 full-time freshmen.
Selectivity: Admits over 75% of applicants.

BASIC COSTS (2008-2009)

Tuition and fees: $3,045; out-of-state residents $11,444.
Per-credit charge: $98; out-of-state residents $200.

FINANCIAL AID PICTURE (2008-2009)

Students with need: 39% of average financial aid package awarded as scholarships/grants, 61% awarded as loans/jobs. Need-based aid available for part-time students.

FINANCIAL AID PROCEDURES

Forms required: FAFSA, institutional form.
Dates and Deadlines: Priority date 3/1; closing date 6/1. Applicants notified on a rolling basis starting 5/1.

Transfers: Applicants notified on a rolling basis starting 5/1.

CONTACT

Neil Woolf, Director, Student Financial Services & Scholarships
1125 Nevada State Drive, Henderson, NV 89002
(702) 992-2150

CONTACT

John Gottardy, Director of Financial Aid, Scholarships and Student Employment
7000 Dandini Boulevard, Reno, NV 89512
(775) 673-7072

Sierra Nevada College

Incline Village, Nevada
www.sierranevada.edu Federal Code: 009192

4-year private liberal arts college in small town.
Enrollment: 354 undergrads.

BASIC COSTS (2008-2009)

Tuition and fees: $22,978.
Per-credit charge: $971.
Room and board: $8,824.

FINANCIAL AID PICTURE (2008-2009)

Students with need: Need-based aid available for full-time and part-time students.
Students without need: No-need awards available for academics, art, athletics.
Scholarships offered: Academic scholarships; $2,000-$13,000 per year; renewable.

FINANCIAL AID PROCEDURES

Forms required: FAFSA, institutional form.
Dates and Deadlines: Priority date 4/1; no closing date. Applicants notified on a rolling basis; must reply by 5/1 or within 4 week(s) of notification.
Transfers: Priority date 3/15; no deadline.

CONTACT

Nicole Ferguson, Director of Financial Aid
999 Tahoe Boulevard, Incline Village, NV 89451-4269
(775) 831-1314 ext. 7440

Truckee Meadows Community College

Reno, Nevada
www.tmcc.edu Federal Code: 010363

2-year public community and technical college in large city.
Enrollment: 10,005 undergrads, 70% part-time. 639 full-time freshmen.
Selectivity: Open admission.

BASIC COSTS (2008-2009)

Tuition and fees: $1,921; out-of-state residents $7,547.
Per-credit charge: $57.
Additional info: Discounted tuition (Good Neighbor rates) available for nonresident students residing in certain counties bordering Nevada.

FINANCIAL AID PICTURE (2007-2008)

Students with need: 60% of average financial aid package awarded as scholarships/grants, 40% awarded as loans/jobs. Work study available nights, weekends, and for part-time students.
Students without need: No-need awards available for academics, art, leadership, minority status, music/drama, state/district residency.
Additional info: Institutional grants to state residents, short-term emergency loans available. Work-study applications must reply within 10 days of notification.

FINANCIAL AID PROCEDURES

Forms required: FAFSA, institutional form.
Dates and Deadlines: Closing date 6/30. Applicants notified by 5/15.
Transfers: Priority date 3/9; no deadline. Must provide academic transcript from previous institution.

University of Nevada: Las Vegas

Las Vegas, Nevada
www.unlv.edu Federal Code: 002569

4-year public university in very large city.
Enrollment: 22,149 undergrads. 2,661 full-time freshmen.
Selectivity: Admits 50 to 75% of applicants. GED not accepted.

BASIC COSTS (2008-2009)

Tuition and fees: $4,493; out-of-state residents $15,588.
Per-credit charge: $130.
Room and board: $9,808.
Additional info: Discounted tuition (Good Neighbor rates) available for nonresident students residing in certain counties bordering Nevada. Out-of-state per-credit-hour rates: 1-6 hours, $272 per credit plus fees; 7 or more hours, $5,548 per semester plus $130 per credit and fees.

FINANCIAL AID PICTURE (2007-2008)

Students with need: Out of 1,487 full-time freshmen who applied for aid, 1,114 were judged to have need. Of these, 1,098 received aid, and 65 had their full need met. Average financial aid package met 71% of need; average scholarship/grant was $4,715. Need-based aid available for part-time students.
Students without need: No-need awards available for academics, alumni affiliation, art, athletics, job skills, leadership, minority status, music/drama, ROTC, state/district residency.
Cumulative student debt: 43% of graduating class had student loans; average debt was $18,640.
Additional info: Tuition reduction for state residents through consortium programs and for out-of-state students graduating from high schools in designated counties bordering Nevada, for military dependents residing in-state, and for dependents of children of alumni not residing in-state.

FINANCIAL AID PROCEDURES

Forms required: FAFSA, institutional form.
Dates and Deadlines: Priority date 2/1; no closing date. Applicants notified on a rolling basis starting 3/20; must reply within 2 week(s) of notification.

CONTACT

Norm Bedford, Director of Financial Aid & Scholarships
4505 Maryland Parkway Box 451021, Las Vegas, NV 89154-1021
(702) 895-3424

University of Nevada: Reno

Reno, Nevada
www.unr.edu Federal Code: 002568

4-year public university in small city.
Enrollment: 12,789 undergrads, 18% part-time. 2,226 full-time freshmen.
Selectivity: Admits over 75% of applicants. GED not accepted.

BASIC COSTS (2008-2009)

Tuition and fees: $4,561; out-of-state residents $15,656.
Per-credit charge: $134; out-of-state residents $276.
Room and board: $9,989.
Additional info: Discounted tuition (Good Neighbor rates) available for nonresident students residing in certain counties bordering Nevada. Discounted tuition also available for Western Undergraduate Exchange students.

FINANCIAL AID PICTURE (2007-2008)

Students with need: Out of 1,267 full-time freshmen who applied for aid, 784 were judged to have need. Of these, 765 received aid, and 128 had their full need met. Average financial aid package met 54% of need; average scholarship/grant was $5,324; average loan was $3,044. For part-time students, average financial aid package was $4,968.

Students without need: 1,196 full-time freshmen who did not demonstrate need for aid received scholarships/grants; average award was $2,495. No-need awards available for academics, alumni affiliation, art, athletics, music/drama.

Scholarships offered: ***Merit:*** Presidential scholarship awards: $5,000 per year; must have 3.5 unweighted GPA and 1380 SAT (exclusive of writing) or 31 ACT; must be admitted by 2/1 of year prior to enrollment and meet Nevada residency requirements. Additional scholarships: ranging from $2,500 to $5,000; based on combination of test scores and unweighted GPA. ***Athletic:*** 81 full-time freshmen received athletic scholarships; average amount $12,776.

Cumulative student debt: 36% of graduating class had student loans; average debt was $14,303.

Additional info: Reduced out-of-state tuition available for children of alumni and for non-residents from some neighboring counties in California and participants in WUE program.

FINANCIAL AID PROCEDURES

Forms required: FAFSA.

Dates and Deadlines: Priority date 2/15; no closing date. Applicants notified on a rolling basis starting 4/1; must reply within 2 week(s) of notification.

Transfers: No deadline. Applicants notified on a rolling basis; must reply within 2 week(s) of notification. Transfer GPA must be 2.0 or higher to be eligible for aid.

CONTACT

Sandy Guidry, Director, Student Financial Services
Mail Stop 120, Reno, NV 89557
(775) 784-4666

University of Southern Nevada

Henderson, Nevada
www.usn.edu Federal Code: 040653

Upper-division private university in very large city.

Enrollment: 139 undergrads.

BASIC COSTS (2008-2009)

Additional info: Tuition and fees vary by program from $26,200 to $36,200.

FINANCIAL AID PICTURE (2008-2009)

Students with need: Average financial aid package for all full-time undergraduates was $10,500. 15% awarded as scholarships/grants, 85% awarded as loans/jobs.

Students without need: No-need awards available for academics.

Cumulative student debt: 97% of graduating class had student loans; average debt was $21,000.

FINANCIAL AID PROCEDURES

Forms required: FAFSA, institutional form.

Dates and Deadlines: No deadline.

Transfers: Priority date 1/1; closing date 4/1. Applicants notified on a rolling basis starting 4/1; must reply within 2 week(s) of notification.

CONTACT

Jesse Stasher, Director of Financial Aid
11 Sunset Way, Henderson, NV 89014
(702) 968-2026

Western Nevada College

Carson City, Nevada
www.wnc.edu Federal Code: 013896

2-year public community college in small city.

Enrollment: 3,267 undergrads.

Selectivity: Open admission; but selective for some programs.

BASIC COSTS (2008-2009)

Tuition and fees: $1,921; out-of-state residents $7,647.

Per-credit charge: $60.

Additional info: Discounted tuition (Good Neighbor rates) available for non-resident students residing in certain counties bordering Nevada.

FINANCIAL AID PICTURE (2007-2008)

Students with need: 53% of average financial aid package awarded as scholarships/grants, 47% awarded as loans/jobs. Need-based aid available for part-time students. Work study available nights, weekends, and for part-time students.

Students without need: No-need awards available for academics, state/district residency.

FINANCIAL AID PROCEDURES

Forms required: FAFSA.

Dates and Deadlines: Priority date 4/1; no closing date. Applicants notified on a rolling basis.

Transfers: Maximum loan debt of $14,125 allowed. Loans received at other schools counted toward limit.

CONTACT

Lori Tiede, Director of Financial Assistance
2201 West College Parkway, Carson City, NV 89703-7399
(775) 445-3264

New Hampshire

Chester College of New England

Chester, New Hampshire
www.chestercollege.edu Federal Code: 004733

4-year private visual arts and liberal arts college in rural community.

Enrollment: 209 undergrads, 6% part-time. 62 full-time freshmen.

Selectivity: Admits less than 50% of applicants.

BASIC COSTS (2008-2009)

Tuition and fees: $16,950.

Room and board: $8,086.

Additional info: Lab fees vary per student; average cost $600.

FINANCIAL AID PICTURE (2007-2008)

Students with need: Need-based aid available for full-time and part-time students. Work study available nights, weekends, and for part-time students.

Students without need: No-need awards available for academics, art, state/district residency.

FINANCIAL AID PROCEDURES

Forms required: FAFSA, state aid form.

Dates and Deadlines: Priority date 3/15; no closing date. Applicants notified on a rolling basis starting 12/1; must reply within 2 week(s) of notification.

CONTACT

Roger Illescas, Director of Financial Aid
40 Chester Street, Chester, NH 03036
(603) 887-7404

Colby-Sawyer College

New London, New Hampshire
www.colby-sawyer.edu Federal Code: 002572

4-year private liberal arts college in small town.
Enrollment: 989 undergrads.
Selectivity: Admits over 75% of applicants.

BASIC COSTS (2008-2009)

Tuition and fees: $29,620.
Per-credit charge: $990.
Room and board: $10,340.

FINANCIAL AID PICTURE (2008-2009)

Students with need: Need-based aid available for full-time and part-time students. Work study available nights, weekends, and for part-time students.
Students without need: No-need awards available for academics, alumni affiliation, art, leadership, minority status, music/drama.

FINANCIAL AID PROCEDURES

Forms required: FAFSA.
Dates and Deadlines: Priority date 2/15; closing date 3/1. Applicants notified on a rolling basis starting 1/1; must reply by 5/1 or within 2 week(s) of notification.
Transfers: Priority date 3/1; closing date 4/15. Applicants notified on a rolling basis starting 12/15; must reply within 2 week(s) of notification.

CONTACT

Ted Craigie, Director of Financial Aid
541 Main Street, New London, NH 03257-7835
(603) 526-3717

Daniel Webster College

Nashua, New Hampshire
www.dwc.edu Federal Code: 004731

4-year private business and liberal arts college in small city.
Enrollment: 722 undergrads, 5% part-time. 256 full-time freshmen.

BASIC COSTS (2009-2010)

Tuition and fees: $28,614.
Per-credit charge: $1,098.
Room and board: $9,698.

FINANCIAL AID PICTURE (2007-2008)

Students with need: 8% of average financial aid package awarded as scholarships/grants, 92% awarded as loans/jobs. Need-based aid available for part-time students. Work study available nights, weekends, and for part-time students.
Students without need: No-need awards available for academics, alumni affiliation, leadership.
Scholarships offered: Scholarships based on GPA and test scores, leadership, guidance counselor recommendation, awarded in amounts ranging from $500 to $7,500. Alumni and other scholarships range from $500 to full tuition.

FINANCIAL AID PROCEDURES

Forms required: FAFSA, institutional form.
Dates and Deadlines: Priority date 3/1; no closing date. Applicants notified on a rolling basis starting 3/15; must reply within 2 week(s) of notification.

CONTACT

Daniel Monahan, Dean of Admissions and Financial Assistance
20 University Drive, Nashua, NH 03063
(603) 577-6590

Dartmouth College

Hanover, New Hampshire Federal Code: 002573
www.dartmouth.edu CSS Code: 3351

4-year private university and liberal arts college in large town.
Enrollment: 4,067 undergrads. 1,119 full-time freshmen.
Selectivity: Admits less than 50% of applicants.

BASIC COSTS (2009-2010)

Tuition and fees: $38,789.
Room and board: $11,295.

FINANCIAL AID PICTURE (2007-2008)

Students with need: Out of 690 full-time freshmen who applied for aid, 557 were judged to have need. Of these, 557 received aid, and 557 had their full need met. Average financial aid package met 100% of need; average scholarship/grant was $32,413; average loan was $3,341. Need-based aid available for part-time students.
Students without need: This college awards aid only to students with need.
Cumulative student debt: 52% of graduating class had student loans; average debt was $20,126.

FINANCIAL AID PROCEDURES

Forms required: FAFSA, CSS PROFILE.
Dates and Deadlines: Closing date 2/1. Applicants notified by 4/2; must reply by 5/1.
Transfers: Closing date 3/15. Applicants notified by 4/2; must reply by 5/1. Grant budget for transfer students is limited. Some admitted transfer students may not have their full needs met.

CONTACT

Virginia Hazen, Director of Financial Aid
6016 McNutt Hall, Hanover, NH 03755
(603) 646-2451

Franklin Pierce University

Rindge, New Hampshire
www.franklinpierce.edu Federal Code: 002575

4-year private university and liberal arts college in small town.
Enrollment: 2,061 undergrads, 15% part-time. 477 full-time freshmen.
Selectivity: Admits over 75% of applicants.

BASIC COSTS (2008-2009)

Tuition and fees: $28,300.
Per-credit charge: $810.
Room and board: $9,200.

FINANCIAL AID PICTURE (2008-2009)

Students with need: Need-based aid available for full-time and part-time students. Work study available nights, weekends, and for part-time students.
Students without need: No-need awards available for academics, alumni affiliation, athletics, leadership, music/drama.
Scholarships offered: Marlin Fitzwater Mass Communication: $2,000; 6 awarded. Robert Alvin Performing Arts-Theater, Music, Dance; $2,000; 2 awarded in each category. Leadership Scholarship: $2,000; 10 awarded.

FINANCIAL AID PROCEDURES

Forms required: FAFSA.
Dates and Deadlines: Closing date 3/1. Applicants notified on a rolling basis starting 3/1; must reply within 2 week(s) of notification.
Transfers: No deadline. Applicants notified on a rolling basis starting 3/1; must reply within 2 week(s) of notification.

CONTACT

Ken Ferreria, Director of Student Financial Services
40 University Drive, Rindge, NH 03461-0060
(603) 899-4180

Granite State College

Concord, New Hampshire
www.granite.edu Federal Code: 031013

4-year public liberal arts college in large town.
Enrollment: 1,174 undergrads, 54% part-time. 37 full-time freshmen.
Selectivity: Open admission.

BASIC COSTS (2008-2009)

Tuition and fees: $7,335; out-of-state residents $7,755.
Per-credit charge: $238; out-of-state residents $252.

FINANCIAL AID PICTURE (2007-2008)

Students with need: Need-based aid available for full-time and part-time students.

FINANCIAL AID PROCEDURES

Forms required: FAFSA, institutional form.
Dates and Deadlines: No deadline. Applicants notified on a rolling basis starting 4/15.
Transfers: No deadline. Applicants notified on a rolling basis starting 4/15.

CONTACT

Lisa Jo Moher, Director of Financial Aid
8 Old Suncook Road, Concord, NH 03301-7317
(603) 228-3000 ext. 322

Great Bay Community College

Stratham, New Hampshire
www.greatbay.edu Federal Code: 002583

2-year public community and technical college in small town.
Enrollment: 2,136 undergrads.
Selectivity: Open admission; but selective for some programs.

BASIC COSTS (2008-2009)

Tuition and fees: $5,400; out-of-state residents $12,150.
Per-credit charge: $175; out-of-state residents $400.
Additional info: New England Regional tuition: $262 per credit hour.

FINANCIAL AID PICTURE (2007-2008)

Students with need: Need-based aid available for full-time and part-time students. Work study available nights, weekends, and for part-time students.
Students without need: This college awards aid only to students with need.

FINANCIAL AID PROCEDURES

Forms required: FAFSA, institutional form.
Dates and Deadlines: No deadline. Applicants notified on a rolling basis; must reply within 2 week(s) of notification.
Transfers: No deadline. Applicants notified on a rolling basis; must reply within 2 week(s) of notification.

CONTACT

Lauren Hughes, Director of Financial Aid
277 Portsmouth Avenue, Stratham, NH 03885
(603) 772-1194

Hesser College

Manchester, New Hampshire
www.hesser.edu Federal Code: 004729

4-year for-profit business and junior college in small city.
Enrollment: 3,400 undergrads.
Selectivity: Open admission; but selective for some programs.

BASIC COSTS (2008-2009)

Tuition and fees: $14,220.
Per-credit charge: $478.
Room and board: $7,160.

FINANCIAL AID PICTURE

Students with need: Need-based aid available for full-time and part-time students. Work study available nights, weekends, and for part-time students.
Students without need: This college awards aid only to students with need.
Additional info: Two private loans available to assist students in paying their balance; Tree Loan, SLM Loan.

FINANCIAL AID PROCEDURES

Forms required: FAFSA, institutional form.
Dates and Deadlines: Priority date 5/1; no closing date. Applicants notified on a rolling basis starting 3/1; must reply within 3 week(s) of notification.

CONTACT

Debra Gravel, Director of Financial Aid
3 Sundial Avenue, Manchester, NH 03103
(603) 668-6660 ext. 2210

Keene State College

Keene, New Hampshire
www.keene.edu Federal Code: 002590

4-year public liberal arts and teachers college in large town.
Enrollment: 4,866 undergrads, 3% part-time. 1,301 full-time freshmen.
Selectivity: Admits 50 to 75% of applicants.

BASIC COSTS (2008-2009)

Tuition and fees: $8,778; out-of-state residents $16,628.
Per-credit charge: $275; out-of-state residents $602.
Room and board: $7,796.
Additional info: New England Regional tuition is 150% of in-state public institution tuition.

FINANCIAL AID PICTURE (2007-2008)

Students with need: Out of 1,103 full-time freshmen who applied for aid, 713 were judged to have need. Of these, 699 received aid, and 109 had their full need met. Average financial aid package met 66% of need; average scholarship/grant was $4,960; average loan was $3,644. For part-time students, average financial aid package was $5,335.
Students without need: 101 full-time freshmen who did not demonstrate need for aid received scholarships/grants; average award was $2,300. No-need awards available for academics, alumni affiliation, art, music/drama.

FINANCIAL AID PROCEDURES

Forms required: FAFSA.
Dates and Deadlines: Closing date 3/1. Applicants notified on a rolling basis; must reply within 4 week(s) of notification.
Transfers: Applicants notified on a rolling basis; must reply within 4 week(s) of notification.

CONTACT

Patricia Blodgett, Director of Financial Aid
229 Main Street, Keene, NH 03435-2604
(603) 358-2280

Magdalen College
Warner, New Hampshire
www.magdalen.edu Federal Code: 022233

4-year private liberal arts college in small town, affiliated with Roman Catholic Church.
Enrollment: 59 undergrads. 20 full-time freshmen.
Selectivity: Admits over 75% of applicants.

BASIC COSTS (2008-2009)
Tuition and fees: $12,250.
Room and board: $6,500.

FINANCIAL AID PICTURE
Students with need: Need-based aid available for full-time and part-time students.
Students without need: This college awards aid only to students with need.

FINANCIAL AID PROCEDURES
Forms required: institutional form.
Dates and Deadlines: Closing date 6/30. Applicants notified by 7/1; must reply by 7/1 or within 4 week(s) of notification.

CONTACT
Donald Regan, VP of Finance and Operations
511 Kearsarge Mountain Road, Warner, NH 03278
(603) 456-2656

Manchester Community College
Manchester, New Hampshire
www.manchestercommunitycollege.edu Federal Code: 002582

2-year public community and technical college in small city.
Enrollment: 2,174 undergrads.
Selectivity: Open admission; but selective for some programs.

BASIC COSTS (2008-2009)
Tuition and fees: $5,430; out-of-state residents $12,180.
Per-credit charge: $175; out-of-state residents $400.
Additional info: New England Regional tuition: $262 per credit hour.

FINANCIAL AID PICTURE
Students with need: Need-based aid available for full-time and part-time students. Work study available nights, weekends, and for part-time students.
Students without need: This college awards aid only to students with need.
Scholarships offered: NH high school valedictorians receive 100% tuition scholarship.
Additional info: 100% of direct educational expenses met for all financial aid applicants.

FINANCIAL AID PROCEDURES
Forms required: FAFSA, institutional form.
Dates and Deadlines: Priority date 5/1; no closing date. Applicants notified on a rolling basis starting 4/15; must reply within 2 week(s) of notification.

CONTACT
Stephanie Weldon, Financial Aid Officer
1066 Front Street, Manchester, NH 03102-8518
(603) 668-6706 ext. 352

Nashua Community College
Nashua, New Hampshire
www.nashuacc.edu Federal Code: 009236

2-year public community and technical college in small city.
Enrollment: 1,783 undergrads, 63% part-time.
Selectivity: Open admission; but selective for some programs.

BASIC COSTS (2008-2009)
Tuition and fees: $5,730; out-of-state residents $12,480.
Per-credit charge: $175; out-of-state residents $400.
Additional info: New England regional tuition: $262 per credit hour.

FINANCIAL AID PICTURE (2007-2008)
Students with need: Need-based aid available for full-time and part-time students. Work study available nights.
Students without need: This college awards aid only to students with need.

FINANCIAL AID PROCEDURES
Forms required: FAFSA.
Dates and Deadlines: Priority date 5/1; no closing date. Applicants notified on a rolling basis starting 3/1; must reply within 2 week(s) of notification.

CONTACT
Lisbeth Gonzalez, Director of Financial Aid
505 Amherst Street, Nashua, NH 03063-1026
(603) 882-6923 ext. 1528

New England College
Henniker, New Hampshire
www.nec.edu Federal Code: 002579

4-year private business and liberal arts and teachers college in small town.
Enrollment: 1,054 undergrads, 4% part-time. 298 full-time freshmen.
Selectivity: Admits over 75% of applicants.

BASIC COSTS (2009-2010)
Tuition and fees: $27,450.
Per-credit charge: $1,300.
Room and board: $9,626.
Additional info: Tuition/fee waivers available for adults.

FINANCIAL AID PICTURE (2008-2009)
Students with need: Need-based aid available for full-time and part-time students. Work study available nights, weekends, and for part-time students.
Students without need: No-need awards available for academics, alumni affiliation, art, job skills, leadership, music/drama.

FINANCIAL AID PROCEDURES
Forms required: FAFSA, institutional form.
Dates and Deadlines: Priority date 4/1; no closing date. Applicants notified on a rolling basis starting 1/12; must reply within 2 week(s) of notification.
Transfers: No deadline. Applicants notified on a rolling basis starting 1/1; must reply within 2 week(s) of notification. May 1 deadline for state grant consideration.

CONTACT
Russell Romandini, Director of Admission and Financial Aid
102 Bridge Street, Henniker, NH 03242
(603) 428-2226

NHTI-Concord's Community College

Concord, New Hampshire
www.nhti.edu Federal Code: 002581

2-year public community and technical college in large town.
Enrollment: 3,000 undergrads.
Selectivity: Open admission; but selective for some programs.

BASIC COSTS (2008-2009)
Tuition and fees: $5,760; out-of-state residents $12,510.
Per-credit charge: $175; out-of-state residents $400.
Room and board: $7,440.
Additional info: New England Regional tuition: $262 per credit hour.

FINANCIAL AID PICTURE (2008-2009)
Students with need: Need-based aid available for full-time and part-time students. Work study available nights, weekends, and for part-time students.
Students without need: This college awards aid only to students with need.
Additional info: 60% of students who apply receive some form of financial aid. State school; all financial aid need-based, primarily from federal sources. No scholarships awarded.

FINANCIAL AID PROCEDURES
Forms required: FAFSA, institutional form.
Dates and Deadlines: Priority date 5/1; no closing date. Applicants notified on a rolling basis starting 6/1; must reply within 2 week(s) of notification.
Transfers: No deadline. Applicants notified on a rolling basis.

CONTACT
Sheri Gonthier, Financial Aid Director
31 College Drive, Concord, NH 03301
(603) 271-7136

Plymouth State University

Plymouth, New Hampshire
www.plymouth.edu Federal Code: 002591

4-year public university and teachers college in small town.
Enrollment: 4,204 undergrads, 3% part-time. 1,089 full-time freshmen.
Selectivity: Admits 50 to 75% of applicants.

BASIC COSTS (2008-2009)
Tuition and fees: $8,424; out-of-state residents $16,274.
Per-credit charge: $276; out-of-state residents $602.
Room and board: $8,150.
Additional info: New England Regional tuition: 150% of in-state public institution tuition.

FINANCIAL AID PICTURE (2007-2008)
Students with need: Need-based aid available for full-time and part-time students. Work study available nights, weekends, and for part-time students.
Students without need: No-need awards available for academics, minority status, music/drama.
Scholarships offered: Presidential Scholars: $3,500; based on outstanding academic performance and overall achievement. PSU Scholars: $2,500; based on overall merit and past achievement. New Hampshire Top Scholars: $2,500; for New Hampshire residents in top 15%. Music/Theater Talent Grants: $2,500; based on talent and audition. ALANA; $2,000; for minority students based on student's admission application.

FINANCIAL AID PROCEDURES
Forms required: FAFSA.
Dates and Deadlines: Priority date 3/1; no closing date. Applicants notified on a rolling basis starting 2/15; must reply by 5/1.
Transfers: Applicants notified by 5/1.

CONTACT
June Schlabach, Director of Financial Aid
17 High Street MSC 52, Plymouth, NH 03264-1595
(603) 535-2338

River Valley Community College

Claremont, New Hampshire
www.rivervalley.edu Federal Code: 007560

2-year public technical college in large town.
Enrollment: 325 undergrads.
Selectivity: Open admission; but selective for some programs.

BASIC COSTS (2008-2009)
Tuition and fees: $5,340; out-of-state residents $12,090.
Per-credit charge: $175; out-of-state residents $400.
Additional info: New England Regional tuition: $262 per credit hour.

FINANCIAL AID PICTURE
Students with need: Need-based aid available for full-time and part-time students.
Students without need: This college awards aid only to students with need.

FINANCIAL AID PROCEDURES
Forms required: FAFSA.
Dates and Deadlines: Closing date 4/1. Applicants notified on a rolling basis; must reply within 2 week(s) of notification.

CONTACT
Julia Dower, Director of Financial Aid
One College Drive, Claremont, NH 03743-9707
(603) 542-7744

Rivier College

Nashua, New Hampshire
www.rivier.edu Federal Code: 002586

4-year private liberal arts and teachers college in small city, affiliated with Roman Catholic Church.
Enrollment: 1,402 undergrads, 28% part-time. 246 full-time freshmen.
Selectivity: Open admission; but selective for some programs.

BASIC COSTS (2008-2009)
Tuition and fees: $23,750.
Per-credit charge: $760.
Room and board: $8,673.

FINANCIAL AID PICTURE (2007-2008)
Students with need: Need-based aid available for full-time and part-time students. Work study available nights, weekends, and for part-time students.
Students without need: No-need awards available for academics, alumni affiliation, minority status.
Scholarships offered: Dean's Scholarship: $6,000 for residents, $5,000 for commuters, high school seniors with minimum 1000 SAT (exclusive of writing) and 3.0 GPA; renewable annually with minimum 2.67 GPA. Presidential Scholarship: $7,000 for residents, $6,000 for commuters, high school seniors with minimum 1150 SAT (exclusive of writing) and 3.4 GPA; renewable annually with minimum 3.0 GPA. Catholic High School Grant: $4,000 for residents, $3,000 for commuters, for students graduating from Catholic high school; renewable annually with 2.5 GPA. Honors Scholarship for honors program participants: $10,000 for residents, $2,000 for commuters. Alumni Scholarship: $2,000, for children of Rivier alumni; renewable annually with minimum 2.0 GPA. Trustee Scholarship: $8,000 for residents, $7,000 for commuters, high school seniors with minimum 1200 SAT (exclusive of writing) and 3.4

GPA; renewable annually with minimum 3.0 GPA. Founders Scholarship for National Merit Finalists: full tuition; renewable with minimum 3.0 GPA.

FINANCIAL AID PROCEDURES

Forms required: FAFSA.

Dates and Deadlines: Priority date 2/1; no closing date. Applicants notified on a rolling basis starting 3/1; must reply by 5/1 or within 2 week(s) of notification.

Transfers: Priority date 3/1. Scholarship for transfer students with minimum 3.0 GPA and 15 transferable credits.

CONTACT

Valerie Patnaude, Director of Financial Aid
420 South Main Street, Nashua, NH 03060-5086
(603) 897-8510

St. Anselm College

Manchester, New Hampshire — Federal Code: 002587
www.anselm.edu — CSS Code: 3748

4-year private nursing and liberal arts college in small city, affiliated with Roman Catholic Church.

Enrollment: 1,879 undergrads, 1% part-time. 501 full-time freshmen.

Selectivity: Admits 50 to 75% of applicants.

BASIC COSTS (2008-2009)

Tuition and fees: $29,170.

Room and board: $10,760.

Additional info: Tuition/fee waivers available for minority students.

FINANCIAL AID PICTURE (2008-2009)

Students with need: Out of 439 full-time freshmen who applied for aid, 360 were judged to have need. Of these, 360 received aid, and 83 had their full need met. Average financial aid package met 84% of need; average scholarship/grant was $16,099; average loan was $5,091. For part-time students, average financial aid package was $13,324.

Students without need: 82 full-time freshmen who did not demonstrate need for aid received scholarships/grants; average award was $13,094. No-need awards available for academics, athletics, state/district residency.

Scholarships offered: ***Merit:*** Presidential Scholarships: $3,500 to $15,000; based on grades, class rank, SAT results and extracurricular experience. ***Athletic:*** 7 full-time freshmen received athletic scholarships; average amount $29,464.

Cumulative student debt: 77% of graduating class had student loans; average debt was $35,025.

FINANCIAL AID PROCEDURES

Forms required: FAFSA, CSS PROFILE.

Dates and Deadlines: Closing date 3/15. Applicants notified on a rolling basis starting 3/10; must reply by 5/1.

Transfers: Merit scholarships not available for transfer students.

CONTACT

Elizabeth Keuffel, Director of Financial Aid
100 Saint Anselm Drive, Manchester, NH 03102-1310
(603) 641-7110

Southern New Hampshire University

Manchester, New Hampshire
www.snhu.edu — Federal Code: 002580

4-year private university in small city.

Enrollment: 2,024 undergrads, 2% part-time. 599 full-time freshmen.

Selectivity: Admits over 75% of applicants.

BASIC COSTS (2009-2010)

Tuition and fees: $26,442.

Room and board: $10,176.

FINANCIAL AID PICTURE (2008-2009)

Students with need: Need-based aid available for full-time and part-time students. Work study available nights, weekends, and for part-time students.

Students without need: No-need awards available for academics, alumni affiliation, athletics, leadership, state/district residency.

Scholarships offered: Academic scholarship: $3000-$8000; awarded to new students based on 3.0 GPA and 1000 SAT (exclusive of writing); unlimited number awarded. Presidential scholarship: 3.5 GPA and 1100 SAT (exclusive of writing).

FINANCIAL AID PROCEDURES

Forms required: FAFSA.

Dates and Deadlines: Priority date 3/15; no closing date. Applicants notified on a rolling basis starting 3/1; must reply within 3 week(s) of notification.

CONTACT

Louisa Martin, Director of Financial Aid
2500 North River Road, Manchester, NH 03106-1045
(603) 668-2211

Thomas More College of Liberal Arts

Merrimack, New Hampshire
www.thomasmorecollege.edu — Federal Code: 030431

4-year private liberal arts college in large town, affiliated with Roman Catholic Church.

Enrollment: 95 undergrads.

Selectivity: Admits less than 50% of applicants.

BASIC COSTS (2008-2009)

Tuition and fees: $13,200.

Per-credit charge: $600.

Room and board: $8,800.

FINANCIAL AID PICTURE (2008-2009)

Students with need: Need-based aid available for full-time and part-time students.

Students without need: No-need awards available for academics.

Scholarships offered: Thomas More Scholarship: full or partial tuition; based on superior academic achievement, exceptional promise or potential; several awarded. Commuter Grants: offered to full-time students within commuting distance of the college. Faith and Reason Essay Contest: half tuition for 4 years; based on essay. Summer Program Scholarship: $1,000; for students who have attended the Thomas More College Summer Program for high school students.

FINANCIAL AID PROCEDURES

Forms required: FAFSA.

Dates and Deadlines: Priority date 5/1; no closing date. Applicants notified on a rolling basis starting 5/15; must reply within 2 week(s) of notification.

CONTACT

Clint Hanson, Director of Financial Aid
Six Manchester Street, Merrimack, NH 03054-4818
(603) 880-8308 ext. 23

University of New Hampshire

Durham, New Hampshire
www.unh.edu — Federal Code: 002589

4-year public university in small town.

Enrollment: 11,845 undergrads, 2% part-time. 2,438 full-time freshmen.

Selectivity: Admits 50 to 75% of applicants.

BASIC COSTS (2008-2009)

Tuition and fees: $11,756; out-of-state residents $25,236.

Per-credit charge: $393; out-of-state residents $954.

Room and board: $8,596.

Additional info: New England Regional Student Program tuition 175% of in-state public institution tuition. College of Earth and Physical Science charges an extra $748 per year. Whittemore School of Business charges an extra $733 per year. Tuition/fee waivers available for minority students.

FINANCIAL AID PICTURE (2007-2008)

Students with need: Out of 2,030 full-time freshmen who applied for aid, 1,516 were judged to have need. Of these, 1,485 received aid, and 382 had their full need met. Average financial aid package met 84% of need; average scholarship/grant was $4,122; average loan was $2,841. For part-time students, average financial aid package was $9,815.

Students without need: 526 full-time freshmen who did not demonstrate need for aid received scholarships/grants; average award was $6,345. No-need awards available for academics, art, athletics, leadership, music/drama, ROTC.

Scholarships offered: ***Merit:*** Presidential Scholarship: half tuition. Various other awards recognizing outstanding high school achievement determined during freshmen candidate application review process; no additional application materials required. ***Athletic:*** 53 full-time freshmen received athletic scholarships; average amount $27,126.

Cumulative student debt: 75% of graduating class had student loans; average debt was $27,516.

FINANCIAL AID PROCEDURES

Forms required: FAFSA.

Dates and Deadlines: Closing date 3/1. Applicants notified on a rolling basis starting 3/1.

Transfers: Closing date 5/1. Applicants notified on a rolling basis starting 5/1.

CONTACT

Susan Allen, Director of Financial Aid
Grant House, Durham, NH 03824
(603) 862-3600

University of New Hampshire at Manchester

Manchester, New Hampshire
www.unhm.unh.edu Federal Code: 002589

4-year public university and liberal arts college in small city.

Enrollment: 792 undergrads.

Selectivity: Admits 50 to 75% of applicants.

BASIC COSTS (2008-2009)

Tuition and fees: $9,291; out-of-state residents $23,051.

Per-credit charge: $374; out-of-state residents $948.

Additional info: New England Regional Student tuition 150% of in-state public institution tuition.

FINANCIAL AID PICTURE (2008-2009)

Students with need: Work study available nights, weekends, and for part-time students.

Students without need: No-need awards available for academics, state/district residency.

FINANCIAL AID PROCEDURES

Forms required: FAFSA.

Dates and Deadlines: Closing date 3/1. Applicants notified on a rolling basis starting 4/1; must reply within 2 week(s) of notification.

Transfers: Priority date 3/1.

CONTACT

Jodi Abad, Director of Financial Aid
400 Commercial Street, Manchester, NH 03101-1113
(603) 641-4189

White Mountains Community College

Berlin, New Hampshire
www.wmcc.edu Federal Code: 005291

2-year public community and technical college in large town.

Enrollment: 666 undergrads, 49% part-time. 101 full-time freshmen.

BASIC COSTS (2008-2009)

Tuition and fees: $5,370; out-of-state residents $12,120.

Per-credit charge: $175; out-of-state residents $400.

Additional info: New England Regional tuition: $262 per credit hour.

FINANCIAL AID PICTURE

Students with need: Need-based aid available for full-time and part-time students.

Students without need: This college awards aid only to students with need.

FINANCIAL AID PROCEDURES

Forms required: FAFSA, institutional form.

Dates and Deadlines: Priority date 5/1; no closing date. Applicants notified on a rolling basis starting 5/1; must reply within 2 week(s) of notification.

CONTACT

Jacqueline Catello, Director of Financial Aid
2020 Riverside Drive, Berlin, NH 03570
(603) 752-1113

New Jersey

Atlantic Cape Community College

Mays Landing, New Jersey
www.atlantic.edu Federal Code: 002596

2-year public culinary school and community college in small town.

Enrollment: 6,578 undergrads, 46% part-time. 967 full-time freshmen.

Selectivity: Open admission; but selective for some programs.

BASIC COSTS (2008-2009)

Tuition and fees: $3,222; out-of-district residents $5,874; out-of-state residents $11,178.

Per-credit charge: $88; out of district residents $177; out-of-state residents $354.

Additional info: Tuition/fee waivers available for unemployed or children of unemployed.

FINANCIAL AID PICTURE (2007-2008)

Students with need: Out of 752 full-time freshmen who applied for aid, 644 were judged to have need. Of these, 598 received aid, and 29 had their full need met. Average financial aid package met 44% of need; average scholarship/grant was $1,903; average loan was $2,311. For part-time students, average financial aid package was $2,692.

Students without need: 5 full-time freshmen who did not demonstrate need for aid received scholarships/grants; average award was $575.

Additional info: Installment plan available for culinary arts majors. Employees of Atlantic City casinos may attend ACCC at in-county rates regardless of residence.

FINANCIAL AID PROCEDURES

Forms required: FAFSA, institutional form.

Dates and Deadlines: Priority date 5/1; no closing date. Applicants notified on a rolling basis starting 5/1.

CONTACT

Linda Desantis, Director of Financial Aid and Veterans' Affairs
5100 Black Horse Pike, Mays Landing, NJ 08330
(609) 343-5082

Bergen Community College

Paramus, New Jersey
www.bergen.edu Federal Code: 004736

2-year public community college in large town.
Enrollment: 13,389 undergrads, 40% part-time. 2,630 full-time freshmen.
Selectivity: Open admission; but selective for some programs.

BASIC COSTS (2009-2010)

Tuition and fees: $4,742; out-of-district residents $8,033; out-of-state residents $8,333.
Per-credit charge: $103; out-of-district residents $213; out-of-state residents $223.
Additional info: General Fee (15% of tuition) payable by all students each semester or session. Fee is non-refundable and based on number of credits taken.

FINANCIAL AID PICTURE (2007-2008)

Students with need: 82% of average financial aid package awarded as scholarships/grants, 18% awarded as loans/jobs.

FINANCIAL AID PROCEDURES

Forms required: FAFSA.
Dates and Deadlines: No deadline. Applicants notified on a rolling basis starting 6/1.
Transfers: Priority date 7/1.

CONTACT

Caroline Ofodile, Director of Financial Operations and Student Assistance
400 Paramus Road, Paramus, NJ 07652-1595
(201) 447-7200

Berkeley College

Woodland Park, New Jersey
www.berkeleycollege.edu Federal Code: 007502

4-year for-profit business college in large town.
Enrollment: 3,435 undergrads, 14% part-time. 802 full-time freshmen.

BASIC COSTS (2009-2010)

Tuition and fees: $19,950.
Per-credit charge: $450.
Room and board: $10,050.
Additional info: Tuition at time of enrollment locked for 4 years.

FINANCIAL AID PICTURE

Students with need: Need-based aid available for full-time students.
Students without need: No-need awards available for academics, alumni affiliation.
Additional info: Alumni scholarship examination given in November and December. Full and partial scholarships awarded.

FINANCIAL AID PROCEDURES

Forms required: FAFSA.
Dates and Deadlines: No deadline. Applicants notified on a rolling basis starting 3/1; must reply within 6 week(s) of notification.

CONTACT

Marilyn Faller, Vice President/Student Finance
44 Rifle Camp Road, Woodland Park, NJ 07424-0440
(973) 278-5400

Bloomfield College

Bloomfield, New Jersey
www.bloomfield.edu Federal Code: 002597

4-year private liberal arts and teachers college in large town, affiliated with Presbyterian Church (USA).
Enrollment: 2,002 undergrads, 21% part-time. 398 full-time freshmen.
Selectivity: Admits less than 50% of applicants.

BASIC COSTS (2008-2009)

Tuition and fees: $20,080.
Room and board: $9,500.

FINANCIAL AID PICTURE (2008-2009)

Students with need: Out of 395 full-time freshmen who applied for aid, 367 were judged to have need. Of these, 366 received aid, and 258 had their full need met. Average financial aid package met 68% of need; average scholarship/grant was $15,203; average loan was $6,888. For part-time students, average financial aid package was $12,259.
Students without need: 20 full-time freshmen who did not demonstrate need for aid received scholarships/grants; average award was $15,400. No-need awards available for academics, alumni affiliation, athletics, leadership, religious affiliation.
Scholarships offered: ***Merit:*** Trustee Scholar Award: up to $10,000; 3.2 GPA, 1100 SAT required. Presidential Scholarship: up to $8,000; 3.0 GPA and 950 SAT required. Transfer Scholarship: up to $5,000; for transfer students from 2-year colleges with 3.0 GPA. Community Service Scholarships: up to $5,000; for students with commitment to community service. Phi Theta Kappa Transfer Scholarships: $6,000; for day transfer students from 2-year colleges with 3.5 GPA who are members of Phi Theta Kappa. All required SAT scores are exclusive of Writing. ***Athletic:*** 31 full-time freshmen received athletic scholarships; average amount $16,474.
Cumulative student debt: 86% of graduating class had student loans; average debt was $23,117.

FINANCIAL AID PROCEDURES

Forms required: FAFSA.
Dates and Deadlines: Priority date 3/15; closing date 6/1. Applicants notified on a rolling basis starting 3/1; must reply within 2 week(s) of notification.
Transfers: Applicants notified on a rolling basis starting 3/1; must reply within 2 week(s) of notification.

CONTACT

Stacy Salinas, Director of Financial Aid
One Park Place, Bloomfield, NJ 07003
(973) 748-9000 ext. 212

Brookdale Community College

Lincroft, New Jersey
www.brookdalecc.edu Federal Code: 008404

2-year public community college in small city.
Enrollment: 14,642 undergrads.
Selectivity: Open admission; but selective for some programs.

BASIC COSTS (2008-2009)

Tuition and fees: $4,018; out-of-district residents $7,258; out-of-state residents $8,008.
Per-credit charge: $108; out-of-district residents $216; out-of-state residents $241.

Additional info: Tuition/fee waivers available for unemployed or children of unemployed.

FINANCIAL AID PICTURE

Students with need: Need-based aid available for full-time and part-time students.

Students without need: No-need awards available for athletics.

FINANCIAL AID PROCEDURES

Forms required: FAFSA, institutional form.

Dates and Deadlines: Priority date 5/1; no closing date. Applicants notified on a rolling basis starting 5/1; must reply within 2 week(s) of notification.

CONTACT

Michael Bennett, Director of Financial Aid
765 Newman Springs Road, Lincroft, NJ 07738
(732) 224-2361

Burlington County College

Pemberton, New Jersey
www.bcc.edu Federal Code: 007730

2-year public community college in small town.

Enrollment: 7,322 undergrads, 44% part-time. 1,659 full-time freshmen.

Selectivity: Open admission; but selective for some programs.

BASIC COSTS (2008-2009)

Tuition and fees: $2,895; out-of-district residents $3,375; out-of-state residents $5,325.

Per-credit charge: $78; out-of-district residents $94; out-of-state residents $159.

Additional info: Tuition/fee waivers available for unemployed or children of unemployed.

FINANCIAL AID PICTURE

Students with need: Need-based aid available for full-time and part-time students. Work study available nights, weekends, and for part-time students.

Students without need: This college awards aid only to students with need.

FINANCIAL AID PROCEDURES

Forms required: FAFSA.

Dates and Deadlines: No deadline. Applicants notified on a rolling basis.

CONTACT

Kris Dixon, Vice President of Student Services
601 Pemberton-Browns Mills Road, Pemberton, NJ 08068-1599
(609) 894-9311 ext. 1575

Caldwell College

Caldwell, New Jersey
www.caldwell.edu Federal Code: 002598

4-year private liberal arts college in large town, affiliated with Roman Catholic Church.

Enrollment: 1,668 undergrads.

Selectivity: Admits 50 to 75% of applicants.

BASIC COSTS (2008-2009)

Tuition and fees: $23,600.

Per-credit charge: $640.

Room and board: $9,650.

FINANCIAL AID PICTURE (2008-2009)

Students with need: Need-based aid available for full-time and part-time students. Work study available nights, weekends, and for part-time students.

Students without need: No-need awards available for academics, alumni affiliation, art, athletics, leadership, music/drama, religious affiliation.

FINANCIAL AID PROCEDURES

Forms required: FAFSA, state aid form, institutional form.

Dates and Deadlines: Priority date 4/1; no closing date. Applicants notified on a rolling basis starting 3/1; must reply within 4 week(s) of notification.

Transfers: No deadline. Applicants notified on a rolling basis; must reply within 4 week(s) of notification. Students who have filed for aid through the state previously must file FAFSA by June 1 for succeeding year.

CONTACT

Shawn O'Neil, Financial Aid Director
9 Ryerson Avenue, Caldwell, NJ 07006-6195
(973) 618-3221

Camden County College

Blackwood, New Jersey
www.camdencc.edu Federal Code: 006865

2-year public community college in large town.

Enrollment: 13,115 undergrads.

Selectivity: Open admission; but selective for some programs.

BASIC COSTS (2008-2009)

Tuition and fees: $3,210; out-of-state residents $3,330.

Per-credit charge: $88; out-of-state residents $92.

Additional info: Tuition/fee waivers available for unemployed or children of unemployed.

FINANCIAL AID PICTURE

Students with need: Need-based aid available for full-time and part-time students.

FINANCIAL AID PROCEDURES

Forms required: FAFSA, institutional form.

Dates and Deadlines: Closing date 7/1. Applicants notified on a rolling basis starting 7/1.

Transfers: Must submit financial aid transcripts from all previously attended institutions.

CONTACT

Aquila Wedington, Director of Financial Aid
Box 200, Blackwood, NJ 08012
(856) 227-7200

Centenary College

Hackettstown, New Jersey
www.centenarycollege.edu Federal Code: 002599

4-year private liberal arts college in large town, affiliated with United Methodist Church.

Enrollment: 2,283 undergrads, 8% part-time. 208 full-time freshmen.

Selectivity: Admits 50 to 75% of applicants.

BASIC COSTS (2008-2009)

Tuition and fees: $24,930.

Per-credit charge: $445.

Room and board: $8,900.

Additional info: Additional fees required for equine majors and for comprehensive learning support program.

FINANCIAL AID PICTURE (2007-2008)

Students with need: Out of 263 full-time freshmen who applied for aid, 224 were judged to have need. Of these, 223 received aid, and 59 had their full need met. Average financial aid package met 75% of need; average scholarship/grant was $13,812; average loan was $5,558. For part-time students, average financial aid package was $4,895.

Students without need: 121 full-time freshmen who did not demonstrate need for aid received scholarships/grants; average award was $8,108. No-need awards available for academics, alumni affiliation, art, leadership, minority status, music/drama, religious affiliation, state/district residency.

Scholarships offered: Academic awards: based on 2.5 GPA, 800 SAT (exclusive of Writing) or 16 ACT. Leadership awards: based on demonstrated leadership ability and potential. Equine Award. Centenary Resident Grant. Out-of-State Centenary Grant. Skylands Centenary Grant. Centenary United Methodist Scholarship.

Cumulative student debt: 86% of graduating class had student loans; average debt was $29,311.

FINANCIAL AID PROCEDURES

Forms required: FAFSA.

Dates and Deadlines: Priority date 4/1; closing date 6/1. Applicants notified on a rolling basis starting 3/1.

Transfers: Students from New Jersey colleges who have received tuition aid grants (TAG) must apply by state deadline. Students must submit financial aid transcripts from all previous institutions attended.

CONTACT

Mike Corso, Director of Financial Aid
400 Jefferson Street, Hackettstown, NJ 07840-9989
(908) 852-1400 ext. 2350

The College of New Jersey

Ewing, New Jersey
www.tcnj.edu Federal Code: 002642

4-year public liberal arts college in large town.

Enrollment: 6,194 undergrads, 2% part-time. 1,289 full-time freshmen.

Selectivity: Admits less than 50% of applicants.

BASIC COSTS (2008-2009)

Tuition and fees: $12,308; out-of-state residents $20,415.

Per-credit charge: $309; out-of-state residents $596.

Room and board: $9,612.

Additional info: Tuition/fee waivers available for unemployed or children of unemployed.

FINANCIAL AID PICTURE (2008-2009)

Students with need: Out of 1,124 full-time freshmen who applied for aid, 633 were judged to have need. Of these, 596 received aid, and 138 had their full need met. Average financial aid package met 47% of need; average scholarship/grant was $14,125; average loan was $3,285. For part-time students, average financial aid package was $3,836.

Students without need: 266 full-time freshmen who did not demonstrate need for aid received scholarships/grants; average award was $6,111. No-need awards available for academics.

Cumulative student debt: 58% of graduating class had student loans; average debt was $22,088.

Additional info: Merit scholarships available to New Jersey high school graduates based on academic distinction. Limited number of scholarships available to out-of-state students who demonstrate exceptional academic achievement in high school and on SAT.

FINANCIAL AID PROCEDURES

Forms required: FAFSA.

Dates and Deadlines: Priority date 3/1; closing date 10/1. Applicants notified on a rolling basis starting 6/1.

Transfers: No deadline.

CONTACT

Jamie Hightower, Director of Student Financial Services
Box 7718, Ewing, NJ 08628
(609) 771-2211

College of St. Elizabeth

Morristown, New Jersey
www.cse.edu Federal Code: 002600

4-year private liberal arts college for women in large town, affiliated with Roman Catholic Church.

Enrollment: 1,181 undergrads, 43% part-time. 158 full-time freshmen.

Selectivity: Admits over 75% of applicants.

BASIC COSTS (2008-2009)

Tuition and fees: $24,428.

Room and board: $10,690.

Additional info: Tuition/fee waivers available for adults.

FINANCIAL AID PICTURE (2007-2008)

Students with need: Need-based aid available for full-time and part-time students. Work study available nights, weekends, and for part-time students.

Students without need: No-need awards available for academics, alumni affiliation, art, leadership, state/district residency.

Scholarships offered: Presidential Scholarship for campus residents: full tuition. Elizabethan Scholarship: $8,000-$10,000. Seton Scholarship: $3,000-$7,000. Awards guaranteed to eligible students who apply by March 1 and enroll by May 1 for fall semester. Spring semester awards dependent upon availability of funds. International scholarships: tuition, room and board; awarded annually for fall semester only to first year students enrolled in Women's College; based on academic record, SAT scores (if submitted) and TOEFL score.

FINANCIAL AID PROCEDURES

Forms required: FAFSA.

Dates and Deadlines: Priority date 3/1; no closing date. Applicants notified on a rolling basis starting 11/15; must reply by 5/1 or within 2 week(s) of notification.

Transfers: Priority date 4/15; closing date 8/20. Scholarships available for full-time students who enroll immediately following full-time enrollment at another college. Applicants must have completed 32 credits and have 3.0 GPA. Awards range from $3,500 to half tuition. Minimum of 5 awarded annually. Preference given to applications received by June 1 for fall semester and by December 1 for spring semester. Limited number of partial scholarships awarded to international students.

CONTACT

Debra Wolff, Director of Financial Aid
2 Convent Road, Morristown, NJ 07960-6989
(973) 290-4445

County College of Morris

Randolph, New Jersey
www.ccm.edu Federal Code: 007106

2-year public community college in large town.

Enrollment: 6,922 undergrads.

Selectivity: Open admission; but selective for some programs.

BASIC COSTS (2008-2009)

Tuition and fees: $3,530; out-of-district residents $6,500; out-of-state residents $8,900.

Per-credit charge: $99; out-of-district residents $198; out-of-state residents $278.

Additional info: Tuition reciprocity agreements with neighboring counties allow some out-of-county residents to pay in-county rates. Tuition/fee waivers available for unemployed or children of unemployed.

FINANCIAL AID PICTURE

Students with need: Need-based aid available for full-time and part-time students.

Students without need: No-need awards available for athletics.

FINANCIAL AID PROCEDURES

Forms required: FAFSA.

Dates and Deadlines: Priority date 3/1; no closing date. Applicants notified on a rolling basis starting 5/1.

CONTACT

Harvey Willis, Director, Financial Aid
214 Center Grove Road, Randolph, NJ 07869-2086
(973) 328-5230

Cumberland County College

Vineland, New Jersey
www.cccnj.edu Federal Code: 002601

2-year public community college in small city.

Enrollment: 3,301 undergrads.

Selectivity: Open admission; but selective for some programs.

BASIC COSTS (2008-2009)

Tuition and fees: $3,480; out-of-district residents $6,150; out-of-state residents $11,490.

Per-credit charge: $89; out of district residents $178; out of state residents $356.

Additional info: Tuition/fee waivers available for unemployed or children of unemployed.

FINANCIAL AID PICTURE (2007-2008)

Students with need: Need-based aid available for full-time and part-time students.

Students without need: No-need awards available for academics.

FINANCIAL AID PROCEDURES

Forms required: FAFSA.

Dates and Deadlines: No deadline. Applicants notified on a rolling basis; must reply within 3 week(s) of notification.

CONTACT

Kimberly Mitchell, Director, Financial Aid
PO Box 1500, Vineland, NJ 08362-9912
(609) 691-8600

DeVry University: North Brunswick

North Brunswick, New Jersey
www.devry.edu Federal Code: 009228

4-year for-profit university in small city.

Enrollment: 1,281 undergrads, 35% part-time. 201 full-time freshmen.

BASIC COSTS (2008-2009)

Tuition and fees: $14,800.

Per-credit charge: $540.

FINANCIAL AID PICTURE (2007-2008)

Students with need: Need-based aid available for full-time and part-time students.

Students without need: This college awards aid only to students with need.

FINANCIAL AID PROCEDURES

Forms required: FAFSA.

Dates and Deadlines: No deadline. Applicants notified on a rolling basis.

CONTACT

Albert Cama, Director of Financial Aid
630 US Highway One, North Brunswick, NJ 08902-3362
(800) 333-3879

Drew University

Madison, New Jersey Federal Code: 002603
www.drew.edu CSS Code: 2193

4-year private university and liberal arts college in large town, affiliated with United Methodist Church.

Enrollment: 1,575 undergrads, 2% part-time. 390 full-time freshmen.

Selectivity: Admits 50 to 75% of applicants.

BASIC COSTS (2009-2010)

Tuition and fees: $38,017.

Per-credit charge: $1,554.

Room and board: $10,368.

FINANCIAL AID PICTURE (2007-2008)

Students with need: Average financial aid package for all full-time undergraduates was $27,675. 82% awarded as scholarships/grants, 18% awarded as loans/jobs.

Students without need: No-need awards available for academics, art, minority status, music/drama.

Cumulative student debt: 61% of graduating class had student loans; average debt was $16,640.

FINANCIAL AID PROCEDURES

Forms required: FAFSA, CSS PROFILE.

Dates and Deadlines: Closing date 2/15. Applicants notified by 3/31; must reply by 5/1.

Transfers: No deadline.

CONTACT

Mary Beth Carey, Dean of College Admissions and Financial Assistance
36 Madison Avenue, Madison, NJ 07940-4063
(973) 408-3112

Essex County College

Newark, New Jersey
www.essex.edu Federal Code: 007107

2-year public community college in large city.

Enrollment: 11,061 undergrads, 39% part-time. 2,597 full-time freshmen.

Selectivity: Open admission; but selective for some programs.

BASIC COSTS (2008-2009)

Tuition and fees: $3,765; out-of-district residents $6,615; out-of-state residents $6,615.

Per-credit charge: $95; out-of-district residents $190; out-of-state residents $190.

Additional info: Tuition/fee waivers available for unemployed or children of unemployed.

FINANCIAL AID PICTURE

Students with need: Need-based aid available for full-time and part-time students.

FINANCIAL AID PROCEDURES

Forms required: FAFSA, institutional form.

Dates and Deadlines: Priority date 6/30; no closing date. Applicants notified on a rolling basis starting 6/15; must reply within 3 week(s) of notification.

CONTACT

Mildred Cofer, Director of Financial Aid
303 University Avenue, Newark, NJ 07102
(973) 877-3000

Fairleigh Dickinson University: College at Florham

Madison, New Jersey
www.fdu.edu Federal Code: 004738

4-year private university in large town.
Enrollment: 2,410 undergrads, 6% part-time. 485 full-time freshmen.
Selectivity: Admits 50 to 75% of applicants.

BASIC COSTS (2008-2009)

Tuition and fees: $30,198.
Per-credit charge: $821.
Room and board: $10,548.

FINANCIAL AID PICTURE (2007-2008)

Students with need: Out of 421 full-time freshmen who applied for aid, 366 were judged to have need. Of these, 366 received aid. For part-time students, average financial aid package was $6,750.
Students without need: 57 full-time freshmen who did not demonstrate need for aid received scholarships/grants; average award was $8,400. No-need awards available for academics, alumni affiliation, music/drama.

FINANCIAL AID PROCEDURES

Forms required: FAFSA.
Dates and Deadlines: Priority date 2/15; no closing date. Applicants notified on a rolling basis starting 2/1; must reply by 5/1 or within 4 week(s) of notification.

CONTACT

Vincent Tunstall, University Director of Financial Aid
285 Madison Avenue, Madison, NJ 07940

Fairleigh Dickinson University: Metropolitan Campus

Teaneck, New Jersey
www.fdu.edu Federal Code: 002604

4-year private university in large town.
Enrollment: 3,415 undergrads, 37% part-time. 402 full-time freshmen.
Selectivity: Admits 50 to 75% of applicants.

BASIC COSTS (2008-2009)

Tuition and fees: $28,084.
Per-credit charge: $821.
Room and board: $10,914.

FINANCIAL AID PICTURE (2007-2008)

Students with need: Out of 330 full-time freshmen who applied for aid, 305 were judged to have need. Of these, 305 received aid. For part-time students, average financial aid package was $5,601.
Students without need: 19 full-time freshmen who did not demonstrate need for aid received scholarships/grants; average award was $7,801. No-need awards available for academics, alumni affiliation, athletics, music/drama.
Scholarships offered: 40 full-time freshmen received athletic scholarships; average amount $13,100.

FINANCIAL AID PROCEDURES

Forms required: FAFSA.
Dates and Deadlines: Priority date 2/15; no closing date. Applicants notified on a rolling basis starting 3/1; must reply by 5/1 or within 2 week(s) of notification.

CONTACT

Vincent Tunstall, University Director of Financial Aid
1000 River Road, H-DH3-10, Teaneck, NJ 07666-1996

Felician College

Lodi, New Jersey
www.felician.edu Federal Code: 002610

4-year private liberal arts college in large city, affiliated with Roman Catholic Church.
Enrollment: 1,766 undergrads, 24% part-time. 245 full-time freshmen.
Selectivity: Admits over 75% of applicants.

BASIC COSTS (2009-2010)

Tuition and fees: $25,050.
Per-credit charge: $780.
Room and board: $9,700.
Additional info: Tuition/fee waivers available for adults.

FINANCIAL AID PICTURE (2007-2008)

Students with need: Out of 210 full-time freshmen who applied for aid, 186 were judged to have need. Of these, 186 received aid, and 24 had their full need met. Average financial aid package met 10% of need; average scholarship/grant was $7,700; average loan was $3,500. Need-based aid available for part-time students.
Students without need: 44 full-time freshmen who did not demonstrate need for aid received scholarships/grants; average award was $5,900. No-need awards available for academics, alumni affiliation, athletics, religious affiliation.
Scholarships offered: 28 full-time freshmen received athletic scholarships; average amount $11,975.

FINANCIAL AID PROCEDURES

Forms required: FAFSA.
Dates and Deadlines: Priority date 6/1; no closing date. Applicants notified on a rolling basis starting 4/1; must reply within 2 week(s) of notification.

CONTACT

Marc Chalfin, Executive Vice President for Business and Finance
262 South Main Street, Lodi, NJ 07644-2198
(201) 559-6000 ext. 6010

Georgian Court University

Lakewood, New Jersey
www.georgian.edu Federal Code: 002608

4-year private university and liberal arts college for women in large town, affiliated with Roman Catholic Church.
Enrollment: 1,756 undergrads, 16% part-time. 251 full-time freshmen.
Selectivity: Admits 50 to 75% of applicants.

BASIC COSTS (2009-2010)

Tuition and fees: $24,490.
Per-credit charge: $570.
Room and board: $9,386.

FINANCIAL AID PICTURE (2008-2009)

Students with need: Out of 234 full-time freshmen who applied for aid, 212 were judged to have need. Of these, 212 received aid, and 38 had their full need met. Average financial aid package met 79% of need; average scholarship/grant was $18,289; average loan was $3,785. For part-time students, average financial aid package was $6,326.

Students without need: 38 full-time freshmen who did not demonstrate need for aid received scholarships/grants; average award was $6,456. No-need awards available for academics, alumni affiliation, art, athletics, leadership, minority status, music/drama, religious affiliation.
Scholarships offered: 7 full-time freshmen received athletic scholarships; average amount $8,399.
Cumulative student debt: 81% of graduating class had student loans; average debt was $33,620.

FINANCIAL AID PROCEDURES
Forms required: FAFSA, institutional form.
Dates and Deadlines: Priority date 3/1; no closing date. Applicants notified on a rolling basis starting 2/1; must reply within 2 week(s) of notification.
Transfers: Transfer students who have outstanding financial obligations to previous college or who are in default are not admitted before being cleared by previous college or following federal guidelines concerning defaults.

CONTACT
Carol Strauss, Director of Financial Aid
900 Lakewood Avenue, Lakewood, NJ 08701-2697
(732) 987-2258

Gloucester County College
Sewell, New Jersey
www.gccnj.edu Federal Code: 006901

2-year public community college in large town.
Enrollment: 5,698 undergrads.
Selectivity: Open admission; but selective for some programs.

BASIC COSTS (2008-2009)
Tuition and fees: $2,985; out-of-district residents $3,090; out-of-state residents $5,610.
Per-credit charge: $80; out-of-district residents $84; out-of-state residents $168.

FINANCIAL AID PICTURE (2007-2008)
Students with need: 69% of average financial aid package awarded as scholarships/grants, 31% awarded as loans/jobs. Need-based aid available for part-time students. Work study available nights.
Students without need: This college awards aid only to students with need.

FINANCIAL AID PROCEDURES
Forms required: FAFSA, institutional form.
Dates and Deadlines: Priority date 5/1; no closing date. Applicants notified on a rolling basis starting 3/20.

CONTACT
Jeffrey Williams, Financial Aid Director
1400 Tanyard Road, Sewell, NJ 08080
(856) 415-2210

Hudson County Community College
Jersey City, New Jersey
www.hccc.edu Federal Code: 012954

2-year public community college in large city.
Enrollment: 7,525 undergrads.
Selectivity: Open admission.

BASIC COSTS (2008-2009)
Tuition and fees: $3,753; out-of-district residents $6,543; out-of-state residents $9,333.
Per-credit charge: $93; out-of-district residents $186; out-of-state residents $279.

FINANCIAL AID PICTURE (2007-2008)
Students with need: Need-based aid available for full-time and part-time students.
Students without need: This college awards aid only to students with need.

FINANCIAL AID PROCEDURES
Forms required: FAFSA.
Dates and Deadlines: Priority date 7/15; no closing date. Applicants notified on a rolling basis starting 6/1; must reply within 1 week(s) of notification.
Transfers: No deadline.

CONTACT
Pamela Littles, Associate Dean of Student Financial Assistance
70 Sip Avenue, 1st Floor, Jersey City, NJ 07306
(201) 360-4200

Kean University
Union, New Jersey
www.kean.edu Federal Code: 002622

4-year public university and liberal arts college in small city.
Enrollment: 10,907 undergrads, 22% part-time. 1,418 full-time freshmen.
Selectivity: Admits 50 to 75% of applicants.

BASIC COSTS (2008-2009)
Tuition and fees: $9,179; out-of-state residents $13,661.
Per-credit charge: $200; out-of-state residents $349.
Room and board: $9,677.
Additional info: Tuition/fee waivers available for unemployed or children of unemployed.

FINANCIAL AID PICTURE (2008-2009)
Students with need: Out of 1,254 full-time freshmen who applied for aid, 952 were judged to have need. Of these, 887 received aid, and 64 had their full need met. Average financial aid package met 56% of need; average scholarship/grant was $7,210; average loan was $3,443. For part-time students, average financial aid package was $5,588.
Students without need: 51 full-time freshmen who did not demonstrate need for aid received scholarships/grants; average award was $2,905. No-need awards available for academics, alumni affiliation, art, leadership, music/drama.
Scholarships offered: Academic Merit Scholarship: $2,000; 3.25 GPA and 1200 SAT required. William Livingston Scholarship: full in-state tuition; 3.90 GPA and 1400 SAT required. Kean Scholarship: $4,000; 3.80 GPA and 1350 SAT required. Presidential Scholarship: $2,500; 3.50 GPA and 1250 SAT required. Trustee Scholarship: $3,000; 3.70 GPA and 1300 SAT required. New Jersey Center for Science and Technology Education (NJCSTE) Scholarship: full-tuition; 3.0 GPA and 1100 SAT required for students who are interested in pursuing BS/MS or BS/MA degree programs in science and technology; all applicants must be interviewed by the NJCSTE. Visual and Performing Arts Scholarship: full tuition; 3.0 GPA and portfolio review or audition required.
Cumulative student debt: 68% of graduating class had student loans; average debt was $17,723.

FINANCIAL AID PROCEDURES
Forms required: FAFSA.
Dates and Deadlines: Priority date 3/15; no closing date. Applicants notified on a rolling basis starting 3/15; must reply by 5/1.
Transfers: No deadline. Applicants notified on a rolling basis; must reply by 5/1.

CONTACT
Luis Gonzalez, Director
1000 Morris Avenue, Union, NJ 07083-0411
(908) 737-3190

Mercer County Community College

Trenton, New Jersey
www.mccc.edu Federal Code: 002641

2-year public community college in small city.
Enrollment: 8,138 undergrads.
Selectivity: Open admission.

BASIC COSTS (2008-2009)

Tuition and fees: $3,345; out-of-district residents $4,485; out-of-state residents $6,765.
Per-credit charge: $112; out-of-district residents $150; out-of-state residents $226.
Additional info: Tuition/fee waivers available for unemployed or children of unemployed.

FINANCIAL AID PICTURE (2007-2008)

Students with need: Need-based aid available for full-time and part-time students. Work study available nights.
Students without need: No-need awards available for academics, athletics, state/district residency.
Scholarships offered: MCCC Foundation Scholarship: $2,500; top 25% of high school class; 15 total awards. NJ STARS program: for top 20% of high school class.

FINANCIAL AID PROCEDURES

Forms required: FAFSA.
Dates and Deadlines: No deadline. Applicants notified on a rolling basis.

CONTACT

Reginald Page, Director of Financial Aid
Box B, Trenton, NJ 08690-1099
(609) 570-3210

Middlesex County College

Edison, New Jersey
www.middlesexcc.edu Federal Code: 002615

2-year public community college in small city.
Enrollment: 12,406 undergrads.
Selectivity: Open admission; but selective for some programs.

BASIC COSTS (2008-2009)

Tuition and fees: $3,645; out-of-district residents $6,375; out-of-state residents $6,375.
Per-credit charge: $91; out-of-district residents $182; out-of-state residents $182.
Additional info: Out-of-county and out-of-state students pay additional $915 in required fees.

FINANCIAL AID PICTURE

Students with need: Need-based aid available for full-time and part-time students.

FINANCIAL AID PROCEDURES

Forms required: FAFSA, institutional form.
Dates and Deadlines: Priority date 4/1; no closing date. Applicants notified on a rolling basis starting 5/4.

CONTACT

Gail Scott Bey, Director of Financial Aid
2600 Woodbridge Avenue, Edison, NJ 08818-3050
(732) 906-2520

Monmouth University

West Long Branch, New Jersey
www.monmouth.edu Federal Code: 002616

4-year private university in small town.
Enrollment: 4,664 undergrads, 8% part-time. 961 full-time freshmen.
Selectivity: Admits 50 to 75% of applicants.

BASIC COSTS (2009-2010)

Tuition and fees: $25,013.
Per-credit charge: $706.
Room and board: $9,554.

FINANCIAL AID PICTURE (2008-2009)

Students with need: Out of 801 full-time freshmen who applied for aid, 601 were judged to have need. Of these, 601 received aid, and 155 had their full need met. Average financial aid package met 85% of need; average scholarship/grant was $12,433; average loan was $3,696. For part-time students, average financial aid package was $6,540.
Students without need: 336 full-time freshmen who did not demonstrate need for aid received scholarships/grants; average award was $8,101. No-need awards available for academics, alumni affiliation, art, athletics, leadership.
Scholarships offered: ***Merit:*** Academic Excellence Awards; $2,000-$15,000; based on SAT scores and high school GPA; renewable annually as long as required GPA is maintained. ***Athletic:*** 29 full-time freshmen received athletic scholarships; average amount $16,622.
Cumulative student debt: 75% of graduating class had student loans; average debt was $30,853.

FINANCIAL AID PROCEDURES

Forms required: FAFSA.
Dates and Deadlines: Priority date 2/15; no closing date. Applicants notified on a rolling basis starting 2/15; must reply within 2 week(s) of notification.
Transfers: No deadline. Applicants notified on a rolling basis; must reply within 2 week(s) of notification.

CONTACT

Claire Alasio, Associate Vice President for Enrollment Management
400 Cedar Avenue, West Long Branch, NJ 07764-1898
(732) 571-3463

Montclair State University

Upper Montclair, New Jersey
www.montclair.edu Federal Code: 002617

4-year public university in large town.
Enrollment: 13,101 undergrads, 15% part-time. 2,256 full-time freshmen.
Selectivity: Admits 50 to 75% of applicants.

BASIC COSTS (2008-2009)

Tuition and fees: $9,428; out-of-state residents $17,208.
Per-credit charge: $228; out-of-state residents $487.
Room and board: $9,660.
Additional info: Tuition/fee waivers available for unemployed or children of unemployed.

FINANCIAL AID PICTURE (2008-2009)

Students with need: Out of 1,550 full-time freshmen who applied for aid, 1,156 were judged to have need. Of these, 1,077 received aid, and 23 had their full need met. Average financial aid package met 66% of need; average scholarship/grant was $7,796; average loan was $3,528. For part-time students, average financial aid package was $5,944.
Students without need: 35 full-time freshmen who did not demonstrate need for aid received scholarships/grants; average award was $4,929. No-

need awards available for academics, alumni affiliation, art, leadership, minority status, music/drama, ROTC, state/district residency.

FINANCIAL AID PROCEDURES

Forms required: FAFSA.

Dates and Deadlines: Priority date 3/1; no closing date. Applicants notified on a rolling basis starting 4/1; must reply within 2 week(s) of notification.

Transfers: Students will be eligible for financial aid beginning fall semester of the academic year for which they are admitted.

CONTACT

Frank Cuozzo, Director of Financial Aid
One Normal Avenue, Upper Montclair, NJ 07043-1624
(973) 655-4461

New Jersey City University

Jersey City, New Jersey
www.njcu.edu Federal Code: 002613

4-year public university in small city.
Enrollment: 6,068 undergrads, 28% part-time. 563 full-time freshmen.
Selectivity: Admits less than 50% of applicants.

BASIC COSTS (2008-2009)

Tuition and fees: $8,727; out-of-state residents $15,793.
Per-credit charge: $212; out-of-state residents $447.
Room and board: $8,613.

FINANCIAL AID PICTURE (2007-2008)

Students with need: Need-based aid available for full-time and part-time students.

FINANCIAL AID PROCEDURES

Forms required: FAFSA.
Dates and Deadlines: Priority date 4/15; no closing date.

CONTACT

Carmen Panlilio, Assistant Vice President for Admissions and Financial Aid
2039 Kennedy Boulevard, Jersey City, NJ 07305-1597
(201) 200-3173

New Jersey Institute of Technology

Newark, New Jersey
www.njit.edu Federal Code: 002621

4-year public university in very large city.
Enrollment: 5,213 undergrads, 17% part-time. 731 full-time freshmen.
Selectivity: Admits 50 to 75% of applicants.

BASIC COSTS (2008-2009)

Tuition and fees: $12,482; out-of-state residents $21,942.
Per-credit charge: $400; out-of-state residents $853.
Room and board: $9,206.

FINANCIAL AID PICTURE (2007-2008)

Students with need: Out of 548 full-time freshmen who applied for aid, 448 were judged to have need. Of these, 448 received aid, and 57 had their full need met. Average financial aid package met 65% of need; average scholarship/grant was $8,591; average loan was $3,529. For part-time students, average financial aid package was $6,729.

Students without need: 148 full-time freshmen who did not demonstrate need for aid received scholarships/grants; average award was $9,164. No-need awards available for academics, alumni affiliation, art, leadership, minority status, music/drama, ROTC, state/district residency.

Scholarships offered: 35 full-time freshmen received athletic scholarships; average amount $15,078.

Cumulative student debt: 1% of graduating class had student loans; average debt was $27,930.

Additional info: Extensive co-op program for all majors.

FINANCIAL AID PROCEDURES

Forms required: FAFSA.

Dates and Deadlines: Priority date 3/15; closing date 5/15. Applicants notified on a rolling basis starting 3/1; must reply within 2 week(s) of notification.

Transfers: Priority date 5/15.

CONTACT

Ivon Nunez, Director of Financial Aid
University Heights, Newark, NJ 07102
(973) 596-3478

Ocean County College

Toms River, New Jersey
www.ocean.edu Federal Code: 002624

2-year public community college in small city.
Enrollment: 8,610 undergrads.
Selectivity: Open admission; but selective for some programs.

BASIC COSTS (2008-2009)

Tuition and fees: $4,440; out-of-district residents $5,460; out-of-state residents $7,860.

Per-credit charge: $120; out-of-district residents $154; out-of-state residents $234.

Additional info: Tuition/fee waivers available for unemployed or children of unemployed.

FINANCIAL AID PICTURE (2008-2009)

Students with need: 62% of average financial aid package awarded as scholarships/grants, 38% awarded as loans/jobs. Need-based aid available for part-time students.

Students without need: This college awards aid only to students with need.

FINANCIAL AID PROCEDURES

Forms required: FAFSA.

Dates and Deadlines: Priority date 5/31; no closing date. Applicants notified on a rolling basis starting 7/15; must reply within 1 week(s) of notification.

CONTACT

Norma Betz, Director of Financial Aid
College Drive, Toms River, NJ 08754-2001
(732) 255-0400 ext. 2020

Passaic County Community College

Paterson, New Jersey Federal Code: 009994
www.pccc.edu CSS Code: 2694

2-year public community college in small city.
Enrollment: 7,902 undergrads.
Selectivity: Open admission; but selective for some programs.

BASIC COSTS (2008-2009)

Tuition and fees: $3,410; out-of-state residents $6,065.
Per-credit charge: $89; out-of-state residents $177.
Additional info: Additional course fees up to maximum of $790 per year (excluding nursing and radiography). Tuition/fee waivers available for unemployed or children of unemployed.

FINANCIAL AID PICTURE (2007-2008)

Students with need: Need-based aid available for full-time and part-time students.

Students without need: No-need awards available for academics.

Additional info: Limited scholarship funds available for low income students eligible for federal or state aid.

FINANCIAL AID PROCEDURES

Forms required: FAFSA, CSS PROFILE.

Dates and Deadlines: Priority date 8/1; no closing date. Applicants notified on a rolling basis starting 8/1; must reply within 2 week(s) of notification.

Transfers: Priority date 5/15; closing date 6/30.

CONTACT

Sharon Audet, Director of Financial Aid
One College Boulevard, Paterson, NJ 07505-1179
(973) 684-6800

Princeton University

Princeton, New Jersey
www.princeton.edu Federal Code: 002627

4-year private university in large town.

Enrollment: 4,878 undergrads. 1,250 full-time freshmen.

Selectivity: Admits less than 50% of applicants. GED not accepted.

BASIC COSTS (2009-2010)

Tuition and fees: $35,340.

Room and board: $11,680.

FINANCIAL AID PICTURE (2007-2008)

Students with need: Out of 793 full-time freshmen who applied for aid, 671 were judged to have need. Of these, 671 received aid, and 671 had their full need met. Average financial aid package met 100% of need; average scholarship/grant was $31,187.

Students without need: This college awards aid only to students with need.

Cumulative student debt: 22% of graduating class had student loans; average debt was $5,955.

Additional info: All aid need-based; all aid grant money (no loans); institution meets full demonstrated need.

FINANCIAL AID PROCEDURES

Forms required: FAFSA, institutional form.

Dates and Deadlines: Priority date 2/1; no closing date. Applicants notified by 4/1; must reply by 5/1.

CONTACT

Robin Moscato, Director of Financial Aid
Box 430, Princeton, NJ 08544-0430
(609) 258-3330

Ramapo College of New Jersey

Mahwah, New Jersey
www.ramapo.edu Federal Code: 009344

4-year public liberal arts college in large town.

Enrollment: 5,284 undergrads, 8% part-time. 909 full-time freshmen.

Selectivity: Admits less than 50% of applicants.

BASIC COSTS (2008-2009)

Tuition and fees: $10,765; out-of-state residents $17,476.

Per-credit charge: $233; out-of-state residents $433.

Room and board: $10,830.

Additional info: Tuition/fee waivers available for minority students, unemployed or children of unemployed.

FINANCIAL AID PICTURE (2007-2008)

Students with need: Out of 717 full-time freshmen who applied for aid, 476 were judged to have need. Of these, 454 received aid, and 99 had their full need met. Average financial aid package met 73% of need; average scholarship/grant was $9,966; average loan was $3,326. For part-time students, average financial aid package was $3,348.

Students without need: 63 full-time freshmen who did not demonstrate need for aid received scholarships/grants; average award was $12,591. No-need awards available for academics, state/district residency.

Cumulative student debt: 55% of graduating class had student loans; average debt was $16,041.

FINANCIAL AID PROCEDURES

Forms required: FAFSA.

Dates and Deadlines: Priority date 3/1; no closing date. Applicants notified on a rolling basis starting 4/1; must reply by 5/1 or within 2 week(s) of notification.

Transfers: No deadline. Applicants notified on a rolling basis; must reply by 5/1.

CONTACT

Mark Singer, Director of Financial Aid
505 Ramapo Valley Road, Mahwah, NJ 07430-1680
(201) 684-7549

Raritan Valley Community College

Somerville, New Jersey
www.raritanval.edu Federal Code: 007731

2-year public community college in large town.

Enrollment: 5,824 undergrads, 44% part-time. 1,166 full-time freshmen.

Selectivity: Open admission; but selective for some programs.

BASIC COSTS (2008-2009)

Tuition and fees: $3,610.

Per-credit charge: $91.

Additional info: Tuition/fee waivers available for unemployed or children of unemployed.

FINANCIAL AID PICTURE (2008-2009)

Students with need: For part-time students, average financial aid package was $2,011.

Students without need: No-need awards available for academics.

FINANCIAL AID PROCEDURES

Forms required: FAFSA.

Dates and Deadlines: No deadline. Applicants notified on a rolling basis starting 4/1.

CONTACT

Leonard Mesonas, Director of Financial Aid
PO Box 3300, Somerville, NJ 08876-1265
(908) 526-1200 ext. 8273

Richard Stockton College of New Jersey

Pomona, New Jersey
www.stockton.edu Federal Code: 009345

4-year public liberal arts college in large town.

Enrollment: 6,544 undergrads, 10% part-time. 842 full-time freshmen.

Selectivity: Admits 50 to 75% of applicants.

BASIC COSTS (2008-2009)

Tuition and fees: $9,815; out-of-state residents $14,988.

Per-credit charge: $214; out-of-state residents $387.

Room and board: $10,166.

Additional info: Tuition/fee waivers available for unemployed or children of unemployed.

FINANCIAL AID PICTURE (2008-2009)

Students with need: Out of 727 full-time freshmen who applied for aid, 554 were judged to have need. Of these, 538 received aid, and 175 had their full need met. Average financial aid package met 80% of need; average scholarship/grant was $9,341; average loan was $3,470. For part-time students, average financial aid package was $11,593.

Students without need: 94 full-time freshmen who did not demonstrate need for aid received scholarships/grants; average award was $8,459. No-need awards available for academics, art, leadership, minority status, music/drama, state/district residency.

Scholarships offered: Freshman Scholarship Program; up to full tuition, fees, and housing for 4 years; based on class rank in top 15% and 1150 SAT (exclusive of Writing).

Cumulative student debt: 66% of graduating class had student loans; average debt was $24,454.

FINANCIAL AID PROCEDURES

Forms required: FAFSA.

Dates and Deadlines: Priority date 3/1; no closing date. Applicants notified on a rolling basis starting 4/1; must reply within 2 week(s) of notification.

Transfers: No deadline. Applicants notified on a rolling basis starting 4/1; must reply within 2 week(s) of notification.

CONTACT

Jeanne Lewis, Director of Financial Aid
Jim Leeds Road, Pomona, NJ 08240-0195
(609) 652-4201

Rider University

Lawrenceville, New Jersey
www.rider.edu Federal Code: 002628

4-year private university in large town.

Enrollment: 4,606 undergrads, 14% part-time. 877 full-time freshmen.

Selectivity: Admits 50 to 75% of applicants.

BASIC COSTS (2009-2010)

Tuition and fees: $29,060.

Per-credit charge: $890.

Room and board: $10,720.

FINANCIAL AID PICTURE (2008-2009)

Students with need: Out of 752 full-time freshmen who applied for aid, 634 were judged to have need. Of these, 634 received aid, and 122 had their full need met. Average financial aid package met 73% of need; average scholarship/grant was $15,186; average loan was $3,923. For part-time students, average financial aid package was $6,594.

Students without need: 167 full-time freshmen who did not demonstrate need for aid received scholarships/grants; average award was $10,649. No-need awards available for academics, alumni affiliation, art, athletics, leadership, minority status, music/drama, state/district residency.

Scholarships offered: 52 full-time freshmen received athletic scholarships; average amount $13,850.

Cumulative student debt: 74% of graduating class had student loans; average debt was $33,156.

FINANCIAL AID PROCEDURES

Forms required: FAFSA.

Dates and Deadlines: Priority date 3/1; no closing date. Applicants notified on a rolling basis starting 3/15.

Transfers: No deadline.

CONTACT

Drew Aromando, Director of Student Financial Services
2083 Lawrenceville Road, Lawrenceville, NJ 08648-3099
(609) 896-5360

Rowan University

Glassboro, New Jersey
www.rowan.edu Federal Code: 002609

4-year public university in large town.

Enrollment: 8,910 undergrads, 12% part-time. 1,234 full-time freshmen.

Selectivity: Admits 50 to 75% of applicants.

BASIC COSTS (2008-2009)

Tuition and fees: $10,908; out-of-state residents $18,016.

Per-credit charge: $302; out-of-state residents $584.

Room and board: $9,456.

FINANCIAL AID PICTURE (2007-2008)

Students with need: Out of 1,054 full-time freshmen who applied for aid, 632 were judged to have need. Of these, 582 received aid, and 165 had their full need met. Average financial aid package met 92% of need; average scholarship/grant was $7,020; average loan was $3,182. For part-time students, average financial aid package was $4,237.

Students without need: 127 full-time freshmen who did not demonstrate need for aid received scholarships/grants; average award was $5,092. No-need awards available for academics, art, music/drama.

Scholarships offered: 487 full-time freshmen received athletic scholarships.

Cumulative student debt: 75% of graduating class had student loans; average debt was $22,746.

FINANCIAL AID PROCEDURES

Forms required: FAFSA, institutional form.

Dates and Deadlines: Closing date 3/15. Applicants notified on a rolling basis starting 5/1; must reply within 2 week(s) of notification.

CONTACT

Luis Taverez, Director of Financial Aid
Savitz Hall, 201 Mullica Hill Road, Glassboro, NJ 08028
(856) 256-4250

Rutgers, The State University of New Jersey: Camden Regional Campus

Camden, New Jersey
www.rutgers.edu Federal Code: 002629

4-year public university in small city.

Enrollment: 3,840 undergrads, 19% part-time. 475 full-time freshmen.

Selectivity: Admits 50 to 75% of applicants.

BASIC COSTS (2008-2009)

Tuition and fees: $11,358; out-of-state residents $21,306.

Per-credit charge: $299; out-of-state residents $623.

Room and board: $9,378.

Additional info: Tuition/fee waivers available for unemployed or children of unemployed.

FINANCIAL AID PICTURE (2008-2009)

Students with need: Average financial aid package met 64% of need; average scholarship/grant was $9,323; average loan was $3,269. For part-time students, average financial aid package was $5,405.

Students without need: No-need awards available for academics, alumni affiliation, art, athletics, leadership, minority status, music/drama, state/district residency.

Scholarships offered: Outstanding Scholarship Recruitment Program: $2,500-$7,500; for selected in-state resident applicants based on SAT scores

and class rank; 2,500 awarded. Carr Scholarship: $10,000; for selected minority applicants; 150 awarded. Class of 1941 Scholarship: $1,941; descendent of 1941 alumni preferred; 1 awarded. National Merit Scholarship for National Merit finalists: $1,000-$2,000; 15 or more awarded. National Achievement Scholarship for National Achievement finalists: $1,000-$2,000; 2 awarded. Rockland County-Herman T. Hopper Scholarship: out-of-state tuition; for Rockland County, New York resident; 1 awarded. Rutgers University Academic Achievement Award: $1,000; for in- and out-of-state minority students; 20 awarded. Rutgers University Alumni Federation Scholarship: $1,000; for children of Rutgers University alumni; 20 awarded. Rutgers University National Scholarship: $5,000; for out-of-state students; about 100 awarded.
Cumulative student debt: 100% of graduating class had student loans; average debt was $19,800.

FINANCIAL AID PROCEDURES

Forms required: FAFSA.
Dates and Deadlines: Priority date 3/15; no closing date. Applicants notified on a rolling basis starting 2/1; must reply within 2 week(s) of notification.

CONTACT

John Brugel, University Director of Financial Aid
406 Penn Street, Camden, NJ 08102
(856) 225-6039

Rutgers, The State University of New Jersey: New Brunswick/Piscataway Campus

Piscataway, New Jersey
www.rutgers.edu Federal Code: 002629

4-year public university in large town.
Enrollment: 27,753 undergrads, 5% part-time. 5,835 full-time freshmen.
Selectivity: Admits 50 to 75% of applicants.

BASIC COSTS (2008-2009)

Tuition and fees: $11,540; out-of-state residents $21,488.
Per-credit charge: $299; out-of-state residents $623.
Room and board: $10,232.
Additional info: Tuition and fees may vary by program. Tuition/fee waivers available for unemployed or children of unemployed.

FINANCIAL AID PICTURE (2008-2009)

Students with need: Average financial aid package met 51% of need; average scholarship/grant was $10,191; average loan was $3,466. For part-time students, average financial aid package was $6,117.
Students without need: No-need awards available for academics, alumni affiliation, art, athletics, leadership, minority status, music/drama, state/district residency.
Scholarships offered: Outstanding Scholarship Recruitment Program: $2,500-$7,500; for selected in-state resident applicants based on SAT scores and class rank; 2,500 awarded. Carr Scholarship: $10,000; for selected minority applicants; 150 awarded. Class of 1941 Scholarship: $1,941; descendent of Class of 1941 alumni preferred; 1 awarded. National Merit Scholarship: $1,000-$2,000; for National Merit finalists; 15 or more awarded. National Achievement Scholarship: $1,000-$2,000; for National Achievement finalists; 2 awarded. Rockland County-Herman T. Hopper Scholarship: out-of-state tuition; for Rockland County, New York resident; 1 awarded. Rutgers University Academic Achievement Award: $1,000; 20 awarded; for in- and out-of-state minority students. Rutgers University Alumni Federation Scholarship: $1,000; for children of Rutgers University alumni; 20 awarded. Rutgers University National Scholarship: $5,000; for out-of-state students; about 100 awards university-wide.
Cumulative student debt: 74% of graduating class had student loans; average debt was $16,300.

FINANCIAL AID PROCEDURES

Forms required: FAFSA.
Dates and Deadlines: Priority date 3/15; no closing date. Applicants notified on a rolling basis starting 2/1; must reply within 2 week(s) of notification.

CONTACT

Jean McDonald-Rash, University Director of Financial Aid
65 Davidson Road, Room 202, Piscataway, NJ 08854-8097
(732) 932-1766

Rutgers, The State University of New Jersey: Newark Regional Campus

Newark, New Jersey
www.rutgers.edu Federal Code: 002629

4-year public university in large city.
Enrollment: 6,406 undergrads, 15% part-time. 944 full-time freshmen.
Selectivity: Admits 50 to 75% of applicants.

BASIC COSTS (2008-2009)

Tuition and fees: $11,083; out-of-state residents $21,031.
Per-credit charge: $299; out-of-state residents $623.
Room and board: $10,639.
Additional info: Tuition and fees may vary by program. Tuition/fee waivers available for unemployed or children of unemployed.

FINANCIAL AID PICTURE (2008-2009)

Students with need: Average financial aid package met 64% of need; average scholarship/grant was $9,579; average loan was $3,140. For part-time students, average financial aid package was $5,349.
Students without need: No-need awards available for academics, alumni affiliation, art, athletics, leadership, minority status, music/drama, religious affiliation, state/district residency.
Scholarships offered: Outstanding Scholarship Recruitment Program: $2,500-$7,500; for selected in-state resident applicants; based on SAT scores and class rank; 2,500 awarded. Carr Scholarship: $10,000; for selected minority applicants; 150 awarded. Class of 1941 Scholarship: $1,941; descendent of Class of 1941 alumni preferred; 1 awarded. National Merit Scholarship: $1,000-$2,000; for National Merit finalists; 15 or more awarded. National Achievement Scholarship: $1,000-$2,000; for National Achievement finalists; 2 awarded. Rockland County-Herman T. Hopper Scholarship: out-of-state tuition; for Rockland County, New York resident; 1 awarded. Rutgers University Academic Achievement Award: $1,000; for in- and out-of-state minority students; 20 awarded. Rutgers University Alumni Federation Scholarship: $1,000; for children of Rutgers University alumni; 20 awarded. James Bryan Scholarship; $400; for selected in-state freshmen; 3 awarded. Rutgers University National Scholarship: $5,000; for out-of-state students; about 100 awards university-wide.
Cumulative student debt: 85% of graduating class had student loans; average debt was $17,700.

FINANCIAL AID PROCEDURES

Forms required: FAFSA.
Dates and Deadlines: Priority date 3/15; no closing date. Applicants notified on a rolling basis starting 2/1; must reply within 2 week(s) of notification.

CONTACT

John Brugel, University Director of Financial Aid
249 University Avenue, Newark, NJ 07102-1896
(973) 353-1766

Saint Peter's College

Jersey City, New Jersey
www.spc.edu Federal Code: 002638

4-year private liberal arts college in small city, affiliated with Roman Catholic Church.
Enrollment: 2,326 undergrads, 11% part-time. 544 full-time freshmen.
Selectivity: Admits 50 to 75% of applicants.

BASIC COSTS (2008-2009)

Tuition and fees: $25,666.
Per-credit charge: $839.
Room and board: $10,336.

FINANCIAL AID PICTURE (2007-2008)

Students with need: Out of 543 full-time freshmen who applied for aid, 482 were judged to have need. Of these, 472 received aid, and 81 had their full need met. Average financial aid package met 71% of need; average scholarship/grant was $18,155; average loan was $3,266. For part-time students, average financial aid package was $5,449.
Students without need: 56 full-time freshmen who did not demonstrate need for aid received scholarships/grants; average award was $15,215. No-need awards available for academics, athletics.
Scholarships offered: ***Merit:*** Academic Awards: full tuition; based on 1100 SAT (exclusive of Writing), 3.0 GPA, and in top 20% of class; 50 awarded. Incentive Awards: $500-$4,000; for selected applicants with some qualities necessary for academic awards but who are otherwise ineligible. Residential Grants: $500-$2,500 toward housing; based on academics and extracurricular activities. ***Athletic:*** 10 full-time freshmen received athletic scholarships; average amount $11,968.
Additional info: Cooperative education internships available in all majors, with average salaries exceeding $5,200.

FINANCIAL AID PROCEDURES

Forms required: FAFSA.
Dates and Deadlines: Priority date 3/15; no closing date. Applicants notified on a rolling basis starting 2/15; must reply by 5/1 or within 2 week(s) of notification.
Transfers: Student and parents (if dependent students) must be New Jersey residents for at least 1 year prior to start date. Students must complete renewal application before June 1.

CONTACT

Steve Smith, Registrar
2641 Kennedy Boulevard, Jersey City, NJ 07306
(201) 761-6060

Salem Community College

Carneys Point, New Jersey
www.salemcc.edu Federal Code: 005461

2-year public community college in small town.
Enrollment: 898 undergrads, 30% part-time. 232 full-time freshmen.
Selectivity: Open admission; but selective for some programs.

BASIC COSTS (2008-2009)

Tuition and fees: $3,515; out-of-state residents $3,815.
Per-credit charge: $87; out-of-state residents $97.
Additional info: Tuition/fee waivers available for unemployed or children of unemployed.

FINANCIAL AID PICTURE (2007-2008)

Students with need: Need-based aid available for full-time and part-time students.
Students without need: No-need awards available for academics, athletics, state/district residency.

FINANCIAL AID PROCEDURES

Forms required: FAFSA, institutional form.
Dates and Deadlines: Priority date 6/1; no closing date. Applicants notified on a rolling basis starting 4/1; must reply within 2 week(s) of notification.

CONTACT

Sharon Eastlack, Director of Financial Aid
460 Hollywood Avenue, Carneys Point, NJ 08069-2799
(856) 351-2699

Seton Hall University

South Orange, New Jersey
www.shu.edu Federal Code: 002632

4-year private university in large town, affiliated with Roman Catholic Church.
Enrollment: 4,963 undergrads, 6% part-time. 1,258 full-time freshmen.
Selectivity: Admits 50 to 75% of applicants.

BASIC COSTS (2008-2009)

Tuition and fees: $29,630.
Per-credit charge: $844.
Room and board: $11,360.
Additional info: Required fees include lease of laptop computer.

FINANCIAL AID PICTURE (2007-2008)

Students with need: Out of 1,056 full-time freshmen who applied for aid, 923 were judged to have need. Of these, 919 received aid, and 140 had their full need met. Average financial aid package met 79% of need; average scholarship/grant was $2,912; average loan was $2,033. For part-time students, average financial aid package was $8,501.
Students without need: 739 full-time freshmen who did not demonstrate need for aid received scholarships/grants; average award was $5,770. No-need awards available for academics, alumni affiliation, athletics, minority status, ROTC, state/district residency.
Scholarships offered: 55 full-time freshmen received athletic scholarships; average amount $20,901.
Cumulative student debt: 70% of graduating class had student loans; average debt was $41,378.

FINANCIAL AID PROCEDURES

Forms required: FAFSA.
Dates and Deadlines: Priority date 2/15; no closing date. Applicants notified on a rolling basis starting 3/1; must reply by 5/1 or within 4 week(s) of notification.
Transfers: Transfer academic scholarships available.

CONTACT

Lasaundra Floyd, Director of Financial Aid
400 South Orange Avenue, South Orange, NJ 07079-2680
(973) 761-9350

Somerset Christian College

Zarephath, New Jersey
www.somerset.edu Federal Code: 036663

4-year private Bible and liberal arts college in small town, affiliated with Pillar of Fire International.
Enrollment: 164 undergrads.

BASIC COSTS (2008-2009)

Tuition and fees: $11,190.
Per-credit charge: $390.

FINANCIAL AID PICTURE

Students with need: Need-based aid available for full-time and part-time students. Work study available nights.

Students without need: This college awards aid only to students with need.

FINANCIAL AID PROCEDURES

Forms required: FAFSA, state aid form.

Dates and Deadlines: No deadline. Applicants notified on a rolling basis starting 1/31.

CONTACT

Marsha Griffin, Financial Aid Administrator
10 College Way, Zarephath, NJ 08890
(800) 234-9305 ext. 1101

Stevens Institute of Technology

Hoboken, New Jersey
www.stevens.edu Federal Code: 002639

4-year private university and engineering college in small city.
Enrollment: 2,142 undergrads. 545 full-time freshmen.
Selectivity: Admits 50 to 75% of applicants. GED not accepted.

BASIC COSTS (2008-2009)

Tuition and fees: $36,800.
Per-credit charge: $1,164.
Room and board: $11,580.

FINANCIAL AID PICTURE (2008-2009)

Students with need: Need-based aid available for full-time and part-time students. Work study available nights, weekends, and for part-time students.
Students without need: No-need awards available for academics, leadership, music/drama, ROTC.
Scholarships offered: Neupauer Scholarship; full tuition; for top candidates in freshman class. Edwin A. Stevens Scholarship; $3,000-$20,000; for top candidates in freshman class. Becton Dickinson Scholarship; full tuition; for top student pursuing engineering degree. DeBaun Performing Arts Scholarship; $1,000-$5,000.

FINANCIAL AID PROCEDURES

Forms required: FAFSA.
Dates and Deadlines: Priority date 2/15; no closing date. Applicants notified on a rolling basis starting 3/30; must reply by 5/1 or within 2 week(s) of notification.
Transfers: Transfer merit scholarships, Phi Theta Kappa awards.

CONTACT

Maureen Weatherall, Vice President for University Enrollment and Academic Services
1 Castle Point on Hudson, Hoboken, NJ 07030
(201) 216-5555

Sussex County Community College

Newton, New Jersey
www.sussex.edu Federal Code: 025688

2-year public community college in small town.
Enrollment: 3,118 undergrads, 34% part-time. 773 full-time freshmen.
Selectivity: Open admission; but selective for some programs.

BASIC COSTS (2008-2009)

Tuition and fees: $3,285; out-of-state residents $5,955.
Per-credit charge: $89; out-of-state residents $178.
Additional info: Residents of Wayne, Monroe and Pike County (PA): $123 per credit hour. Tuition/fee waivers available for unemployed or children of unemployed.

FINANCIAL AID PICTURE

Students with need: Need-based aid available for full-time and part-time students.
Students without need: This college awards aid only to students with need.

FINANCIAL AID PROCEDURES

Forms required: FAFSA, institutional form.
Dates and Deadlines: Closing date 6/1. Applicants notified on a rolling basis; must reply within 2 week(s) of notification.

CONTACT

James Pegg, Director, Financial Aid
One College Hill Road, Newton, NJ 07860
(973) 300-2225

Thomas Edison State College

Trenton, New Jersey
www.tesc.edu Federal Code: 011648

4-year public liberal arts college in small city.
Enrollment: 16,797 undergrads, 100% part-time.
Selectivity: Open admission; but selective for some programs.

BASIC COSTS (2008-2009)

Tuition and fees: $4,555; out-of-state residents $6,520.
Per-credit charge: $132; out-of-state residents $175.
Additional info: Two tuition plans available-either the Comprehensive Tuition Plan: $4,555 per year (state residents and military personnel), $6,520 (out-of-state), which covers up to 36 credits per year for all credit-earning options; or the Enrolled Options Plan: $1,350 per year (state residents and military personnel), $2,445 (out-of-state) and $3,340 (international) for annual enrollment tuition and a technology services fee ($100).

FINANCIAL AID PICTURE (2007-2008)

Students with need: 17% of average financial aid package awarded as scholarships/grants, 83% awarded as loans/jobs.
Additional info: Financial aid applications should be received two months before each new term begins.

FINANCIAL AID PROCEDURES

Forms required: FAFSA, institutional form.
Dates and Deadlines: No deadline. Applicants notified on a rolling basis; must reply within 4 week(s) of notification.
Transfers: No deadline. Applicants notified on a rolling basis; must reply within 4 week(s) of notification.

CONTACT

James Owens, Director of Financial Aid
101 West State Street, Trenton, NJ 08608-1176
(609) 633-6489

Union County College

Cranford, New Jersey
www.ucc.edu Federal Code: 002643

2-year public community college in large town.
Enrollment: 10,217 undergrads, 47% part-time. 1,969 full-time freshmen.
Selectivity: Open admission; but selective for some programs.

BASIC COSTS (2008-2009)

Tuition and fees: $3,510; out-of-district residents $6,210; out-of-state residents $6,210.
Per-credit charge: $90; out-of-district residents $180; out-of-state residents $180.

Additional info: Tuition/fee waivers available for unemployed or children of unemployed.

FINANCIAL AID PICTURE (2007-2008)

Students with need: 80% of average financial aid package awarded as scholarships/grants, 20% awarded as loans/jobs. Need-based aid available for part-time students. Work study available nights, weekends, and for part-time students.

Students without need: This college awards aid only to students with need.

FINANCIAL AID PROCEDURES

Forms required: FAFSA, institutional form.

Dates and Deadlines: Priority date 5/1; no closing date. Must reply within 2 week(s) of notification.

CONTACT

Evelynn Blatt, Director of Financial Aid
1033 Springfield Avenue, Cranford, NJ 07016-1599
(908) 709-7018

University of Medicine and Dentistry of New Jersey: School of Health Related Professions

Newark, New Jersey
www.shrp.umdnj.edu

Upper-division public health science college in large city.

Enrollment: 1,450 undergrads.

BASIC COSTS (2008-2009)

Tuition and fees: $9,160; out-of-state residents $13,420.

Per-credit charge: $284; out-of-state residents $426.

FINANCIAL AID PICTURE

Students with need: Need-based aid available for full-time and part-time students.

FINANCIAL AID PROCEDURES

Forms required: FAFSA, institutional form.

CONTACT

Cheryl White, Senior Financial Aid Analyst
65 Bergen Street, Newark, NJ 07101-1709
(973) 972-4376

University of Medicine and Dentistry of New Jersey: School of Nursing

Newark, New Jersey
www.sn.umdnj.edu

4-year public nursing college in large city.

Enrollment: 850 undergrads.

BASIC COSTS (2008-2009)

Tuition and fees: $12,221; out-of-state residents $16,400

Per-credit charge: $332; out-of-state residents $471.

Additional info: Costs vary by program; costs cited are for BSN program. Additional insurance fee ($1,967) for students not covered by equivalent plan.

FINANCIAL AID PICTURE

Students with need: Need-based aid available for full-time and part-time students.

FINANCIAL AID PROCEDURES

Dates and Deadlines: Priority date 3/1; no closing date. Applicants notified on a rolling basis.

CONTACT

Elaine Varas, University Director of Financial Aid
65 Bergen Street Room 149, Newark, NJ 07101-1709
(973) 972-4376

Warren County Community College

Washington, New Jersey
www.warren.edu Federal Code: 016857

2-year public community college in small town.

Enrollment: 1,810 undergrads.

Selectivity: Open admission; but selective for some programs.

BASIC COSTS (2008-2009)

Tuition and fees: $3,443; out-of-district residents $3,743; out-of-state residents $4,343.

Per-credit charge: $91; out-of-district residents $101; out-of-state residents $121.

Additional info: Tuition/fee waivers available for unemployed or children of unemployed.

FINANCIAL AID PICTURE (2008-2009)

Students with need: Need-based aid available for full-time and part-time students. Work study available nights, weekends, and for part-time students.

Students without need: This college awards aid only to students with need.

FINANCIAL AID PROCEDURES

Forms required: FAFSA, institutional form.

Dates and Deadlines: Closing date 7/8. Applicants notified on a rolling basis; must reply within 2 week(s) of notification.

Transfers: No deadline. Applicants notified on a rolling basis.

CONTACT

Rose Lynch, Director of Financial Aid
Route 57 West, Washington, NJ 07882-4343
(908) 835-2456

William Paterson University of New Jersey

Wayne, New Jersey
www.wpunj.edu Federal Code: 002625

4-year public university and liberal arts college in large town.

Enrollment: 8,608 undergrads, 16% part-time. 1,204 full-time freshmen.

Selectivity: Admits 50 to 75% of applicants.

BASIC COSTS (2008-2009)

Tuition and fees: $10,492; out-of-state residents $17,050.

Per-credit charge: $204; out-of-state residents $418.

Room and board: $9,990.

Additional info: Tuition/fee waivers available for unemployed or children of unemployed.

FINANCIAL AID PICTURE (2008-2009)

Students with need: Average financial aid package for all full-time undergraduates was $13,667. 88% awarded as scholarships/grants, 12% awarded as loans/jobs. Need-based aid available for part-time students.

Students without need: No-need awards available for academics, alumni affiliation, music/drama.

Scholarships offered: Trustee Scholarship: full tuition for freshmen. Residential Scholarships: full tuition for freshmen and transfer. Distinguished, Academic Excellence, African American and Hispanic Students scholarships: $1,000 annually for 4 years.

FINANCIAL AID PROCEDURES
Forms required: FAFSA.
Dates and Deadlines: Priority date 4/1; no closing date. Applicants notified on a rolling basis starting 3/15.
Transfers: Must reply within 2 week(s) of notification.

CONTACT
Elizabeth Riquez, Director of Financial Aid
300 Pompton Road, Wayne, NJ 07470
(973) 720-2202

New Mexico

Art Center Design College
Albuquerque, New Mexico
www.theartcenter.edu Federal Code: 024915

4-year for-profit visual arts college in very large city.
Enrollment: 283 undergrads.

BASIC COSTS (2008-2009)
Tuition and fees: $16,320.
Additional info: Tuition at time of enrollment locked for 4 years.

FINANCIAL AID PICTURE (2008-2009)
Students with need: Work study available nights, weekends, and for part-time students.
Students without need: No-need awards available for academics.
Scholarships offered: Board of Trustees Scholarship, Transfer Student Scholarship, Scholarship for Continuing Students.

FINANCIAL AID PROCEDURES
Forms required: FAFSA.
Transfers: No deadline. Applicants notified on a rolling basis.

CONTACT
Amy Woods, Director of Student Services
5000 Marble Avenue NE, Albuquerque, NM 87119
(520) 325-0123

Central New Mexico Community College
Albuquerque, New Mexico
www.cnm.edu Federal Code: 004742

2-year public community and technical college in very large city.
Enrollment: 21,669 undergrads, 66% part-time. 2,083 full-time freshmen.
Selectivity: Open admission.

BASIC COSTS (2008-2009)
Tuition and fees: $1,064; out-of-district residents $1,304; out-of-state residents $4,880.
Per-credit charge: $41; out-of-district residents $51; out-of-state residents $200.
Additional info: In-district students do not pay tuition for technical courses, only arts and sciences courses. Non-residents pay in-state rates during summer term. Non-residents pay in-state rates for 6 or fewer credit hours during all terms.

FINANCIAL AID PICTURE (2007-2008)
Students with need: 38% of average financial aid package awarded as scholarships/grants, 62% awarded as loans/jobs. Need-based aid available for part-time students.
Students without need: No-need awards available for academics, state/district residency.

FINANCIAL AID PROCEDURES
Forms required: FAFSA.
Dates and Deadlines: Priority date 5/1; no closing date. Applicants notified on a rolling basis starting 5/1.

CONTACT
Lee Carrillo, Director of Financial Aid
525 Buena Vista SE, Albuquerque, NM 87106
(505) 224-3090

Clovis Community College
Clovis, New Mexico
www.clovis.edu Federal Code: 004743

2-year public community and junior college in large town.
Enrollment: 1,687 undergrads, 58% part-time. 167 full-time freshmen.
Selectivity: Open admission; but selective for some programs.

BASIC COSTS (2008-2009)
Tuition and fees: $808; out-of-district residents $856; out-of-state residents $1,552.
Per-credit charge: $29; out-of-district residents $31; out-of-state residents $60.

FINANCIAL AID PICTURE (2007-2008)
Students with need: 67% of average financial aid package awarded as scholarships/grants, 33% awarded as loans/jobs. Need-based aid available for part-time students. Work study available nights, weekends, and for part-time students.
Students without need: No-need awards available for academics, state/district residency.
Additional info: Public and private funds have made possible the creation of an endowment in excess of $1,000,000 to assist nursing students.

FINANCIAL AID PROCEDURES
Forms required: FAFSA.
Dates and Deadlines: Priority date 9/1; no closing date. Applicants notified on a rolling basis starting 4/15.

CONTACT
April Chavez, Director of Financial Aid
417 Schepps Boulevard, Clovis, NM 88101-8381
(575) 769-4060

Dona Ana Community College of New Mexico State University
Las Cruces, New Mexico
www.dacc.nmsu.edu Federal Code: 002657

2-year public branch campus and community college in small city.
Enrollment: 8,588 undergrads.
Selectivity: Open admission; but selective for some programs.

BASIC COSTS (2008-2009)
Tuition and fees: $1,200; out-of-district residents $1,440; out-of-state residents $3,600.
Per-credit charge: $50; out-of-district residents $60; out-of-state residents $150.
Room and board: $5,976.

FINANCIAL AID PICTURE
Students with need: Need-based aid available for full-time and part-time students.

FINANCIAL AID PROCEDURES
Forms required: FAFSA.

Dates and Deadlines: Priority date 3/1; no closing date. Applicants notified on a rolling basis starting 5/1.

CONTACT

Gladys Chairez, Financial Aid Director
MSC-3DA, Las Cruces, NM 88003-8001
(505) 527-7510

Eastern New Mexico University

Portales, New Mexico
www.enmu.edu Federal Code: 002651

4-year public university in large town.
Enrollment: 3,153 undergrads, 25% part-time. 575 full-time freshmen.
Selectivity: Admits 50 to 75% of applicants.

BASIC COSTS (2008-2009)

Tuition and fees: $3,342; out-of-state residents $8,886.
Room and board: $5,222.

FINANCIAL AID PICTURE (2008-2009)

Students with need: Average financial aid package met 35% of need; average scholarship/grant was $3,483; average loan was $3,430. For part-time students, average financial aid package was $7,085.
Students without need: No-need awards available for academics, alumni affiliation, art, athletics, leadership, music/drama, state/district residency.
Cumulative student debt: 1% of graduating class had student loans; average debt was $12,018.

FINANCIAL AID PROCEDURES

Forms required: FAFSA.
Dates and Deadlines: Priority date 3/1; no closing date. Applicants notified by 4/1; must reply within 3 week(s) of notification.
Transfers: Child care grants and non-need-based college work study limited to New Mexico residents.

CONTACT

Brent Small, Director of Financial Aid
Station Seven, Portales, NM 88130
(575) 562-2194

Eastern New Mexico University: Roswell Campus

Roswell, New Mexico
www.roswell.enmu.edu Federal Code: 002651

2-year public branch campus and community college in large town.
Enrollment: 2,249 undergrads, 56% part-time. 417 full-time freshmen.
Selectivity: Open admission; but selective for some programs.

BASIC COSTS (2008-2009)

Tuition and fees: $1,159; out-of-state residents $4,121.
Per-credit charge: $44; out-of-state residents $167.
Room and board: $7,524.

FINANCIAL AID PICTURE (2007-2008)

Students with need: Need-based aid available for full-time and part-time students. Work study available nights, weekends, and for part-time students.
Scholarships offered: New Mexico Lottery Scholarship; tuition for New Mexico residents; must attend school full-time the semester following high school graduation or GED and maintain 12 credit hours and 2.5 GPA.

FINANCIAL AID PROCEDURES

Forms required: FAFSA.
Dates and Deadlines: Priority date 4/1; no closing date. Applicants notified on a rolling basis starting 7/1; must reply within 3 week(s) of notification.
Transfers: All students receiving state aid must be New Mexico residents and enrolled in at least 6 credit hours.

CONTACT

Jessie Sjue, Director of Financial Aid
Box 6000, Roswell, NM 88202-6000
(575) 624-7152

IIA College: Albuquerque

Albuquerque, New Mexico
www.iia.edu Federal Code: 022188

2-year for-profit branch campus and career college in large city.
Enrollment: 141 undergrads.
Selectivity: Open admission; but selective for some programs.

BASIC COSTS (2009-2010)

Tuition and fees: $11,750.
Additional info: Tuition shown is an average, actual tuition and fees may vary by program.

FINANCIAL AID PICTURE

Students with need: Need-based aid available for full-time students.
Students without need: This college awards aid only to students with need.

FINANCIAL AID PROCEDURES

Forms required: FAFSA, institutional form.
Dates and Deadlines: No deadline.

CONTACT

Rich Dombrowski, Corporate Director of Financial Aid
4201 Central Avenue NW, Suite J, Albuquerque, NM 87105-1649
(602) 644-7090

Mesalands Community College

Tucumcari, New Mexico
www.mesalands.edu Federal Code: 032063

2-year public community and technical college in small town.
Enrollment: 407 undergrads, 25% part-time. 119 full-time freshmen.
Selectivity: Open admission.

BASIC COSTS (2008-2009)

Tuition and fees: $1,406; out-of-state residents $2,426.
Per-credit charge: $40; out-of-state residents $71.

FINANCIAL AID PICTURE

Students with need: Need-based aid available for full-time and part-time students. Work study available nights.
Students without need: No-need awards available for academics, athletics, leadership, minority status, music/drama, state/district residency.

FINANCIAL AID PROCEDURES

Forms required: FAFSA.
Dates and Deadlines: Priority date 4/1; no closing date. Applicants notified on a rolling basis starting 4/1; must reply within 3 week(s) of notification.

CONTACT

Amanda Hammer, Director of Financial Aid
911 South Tenth Street, Tucumcari, NM 88401
(575) 461-4413 ext. 136

Navajo Technical College

Crownpoint, New Mexico
www.navajotech.edu

2-year public community and technical college in rural community.
Enrollment: 300 full-time undergrads.
Selectivity: Open admission.

BASIC COSTS (2008-2009)

Tuition and fees: $840.
Room and board: $4,056.
Additional info: Figures quoted are for members of federally recognized tribes. Non-members pay $1680 in tuition.

FINANCIAL AID PICTURE (2007-2008)

Students with need: 96% of average financial aid package awarded as scholarships/grants, 4% awarded as loans/jobs. Need-based aid available for part-time students.
Students without need: No-need awards available for academics.

FINANCIAL AID PROCEDURES

Forms required: FAFSA, institutional form.
Dates and Deadlines: No deadline. Applicants notified on a rolling basis starting 8/5; must reply by 11/30 or within 4 week(s) of notification.
Transfers: Priority date 8/30; closing date 11/30. Applicants notified by 9/30; must reply within 4 week(s) of notification.

CONTACT

Tyrell Hardy, Financial Aid Officer
PO Box 849, Crownpoint, NM 87313
(505) 786-4309

New Mexico Highlands University

Las Vegas, New Mexico
www.nmhu.edu Federal Code: 002653

4-year public university in large town.
Enrollment: 1,984 undergrads, 24% part-time. 431 full-time freshmen.

BASIC COSTS (2008-2009)

Tuition and fees: $2,688; out-of-state residents $4,052.
Room and board: $5,364.

FINANCIAL AID PICTURE (2007-2008)

Students with need: Average financial aid package for all full-time undergraduates was $7,165. 38% awarded as scholarships/grants, 62% awarded as loans/jobs. Need-based aid available for part-time students. Work study available nights, weekends, and for part-time students.
Students without need: No-need awards available for academics, athletics, leadership, minority status, music/drama, state/district residency.
Additional info: Work study funds available on no-need basis to state residents.

FINANCIAL AID PROCEDURES

Forms required: FAFSA, institutional form.
Dates and Deadlines: Priority date 3/1; closing date 5/1. Applicants notified on a rolling basis starting 5/15; must reply within 2 week(s) of notification.
Transfers: Closing date 6/30.

CONTACT

Eileen Sedillo, Director of Financial Aid
Box 9000, Las Vegas, NM 87701
(505) 454-3318

New Mexico Institute of Mining and Technology

Socorro, New Mexico
www.nmt.edu Federal Code: 002654

4-year public engineering and liberal arts college in small town.
Enrollment: 1,173 undergrads, 5% part-time. 286 full-time freshmen.
Selectivity: Admits less than 50% of applicants.

BASIC COSTS (2008-2009)

Tuition and fees: $4,353; out-of-state residents $12,545.
Per-credit charge: $158; out-of-state residents $499.
Room and board: $5,460.

FINANCIAL AID PICTURE (2007-2008)

Students with need: Need-based aid available for full-time and part-time students.
Students without need: No-need awards available for academics, alumni affiliation, minority status, state/district residency.
Additional info: Campus research projects offer student employment based on merit.

FINANCIAL AID PROCEDURES

Forms required: FAFSA, institutional form.
Dates and Deadlines: Priority date 6/1; no closing date. Applicants notified on a rolling basis starting 4/1; must reply within 2 week(s) of notification.
Transfers: Priority date 3/1; no deadline. Applicants notified on a rolling basis starting 4/1; must reply within 2 week(s) of notification. Financial aid transcripts required from all colleges attended.

CONTACT

Annette Kaus, Director of Financial Aid
801 Leroy Place, Socorro, NM 87801
(575) 835-5333

New Mexico Junior College

Hobbs, New Mexico
www.nmjc.edu Federal Code: 002655

2-year public community and technical college in large town.
Enrollment: 2,978 undergrads.
Selectivity: Open admission; but selective for some programs.

BASIC COSTS (2008-2009)

Tuition and fees: $1,146; out-of-district residents $1,578; out-of-state residents $1,698.
Per-credit charge: $29; out-of-district residents $47; out-of-state residents $52.
Room and board: $3,800.

FINANCIAL AID PICTURE

Students with need: Need-based aid available for full-time and part-time students. Work study available nights, weekends, and for part-time students.
Students without need: No-need awards available for academics, art, athletics, leadership, music/drama.

FINANCIAL AID PROCEDURES

Forms required: FAFSA.
Dates and Deadlines: Priority date 6/1; no closing date. Applicants notified on a rolling basis; must reply within 2 week(s) of notification.

CONTACT

Laura Marquez, Director of Financial Aid
5317 Lovington Highway, Hobbs, NM 88240
(575) 392-4510

New Mexico Military Institute
Roswell, New Mexico
www.nmmi.edu Federal Code: 002656

2-year public junior and military college in large town.
Enrollment: 446 undergrads. 346 full-time freshmen.
Selectivity: Admits 50 to 75% of applicants.

BASIC COSTS (2008-2009)
Tuition and fees: $4,871; out-of-state residents $8,421.
Room and board: $3,830.

FINANCIAL AID PICTURE (2007-2008)
Students with need: 93% of average financial aid package awarded as scholarships/grants, 7% awarded as loans/jobs.
Students without need: No-need awards available for academics, alumni affiliation, athletics, ROTC, state/district residency.

FINANCIAL AID PROCEDURES
Forms required: FAFSA.
Dates and Deadlines: Priority date 4/1; no closing date. Applicants notified on a rolling basis starting 5/1; must reply within 3 week(s) of notification.
Transfers: New Mexico Scholars Program, New Mexico Success Scholarship programs available.

CONTACT
Sonya Rodriguez, Director of Admissions & Financial Aid
101 West College Boulevard, Roswell, NM 88201-5173
(575) 624-8066

New Mexico State University
Las Cruces, New Mexico
www.nmsu.edu Federal Code: 002657

4-year public university in small city.
Enrollment: 13,556 undergrads, 13% part-time. 2,336 full-time freshmen.
Selectivity: Admits over 75% of applicants.

BASIC COSTS (2008-2009)
Tuition and fees: $4,758; out-of-state residents $14,740.
Per-credit charge: $198; out-of-state residents $614.
Room and board: $5,976.

FINANCIAL AID PICTURE (2008-2009)
Students with need: Need-based aid available for full-time and part-time students.
Students without need: No-need awards available for academics, alumni affiliation, athletics, leadership, minority status, state/district residency.

FINANCIAL AID PROCEDURES
Forms required: FAFSA, institutional form.
Dates and Deadlines: No deadline. Applicants notified on a rolling basis starting 3/1.

CONTACT
Tyler Pruett, Director of Financial Aid
Box 30001, MSC 3A, Las Cruces, NM 88003-8001
(575) 646-4105

New Mexico State University at Alamogordo
Alamogordo, New Mexico
nmsu.edu/ Federal Code: 002658

2-year public branch campus college in large town.
Enrollment: 2,020 undergrads.
Selectivity: Open admission; but selective for some programs.

BASIC COSTS (2008-2009)
Tuition and fees: $1,440; out-of-district residents $1,608; out-of-state residents $4,056.
Per-credit charge: $58; out-of-district residents $65; out-of-state residents $167.

FINANCIAL AID PICTURE (2008-2009)
Students with need: Need-based aid available for full-time and part-time students.
Students without need: No-need awards available for academics, state/district residency.

FINANCIAL AID PROCEDURES
Forms required: FAFSA, institutional form.
Dates and Deadlines: Priority date 3/1; no closing date. Applicants notified by 6/1.

CONTACT
Darlene Ellinger, Financial Aid Coordinator
2400 North Scenic Drive, Alamogordo, NM 88310
(505) 439-3600

New Mexico State University at Carlsbad
Carlsbad, New Mexico
artemis.nmsu.edu/ Federal Code: 002657

2-year public branch campus and community college in large town.
Enrollment: 854 undergrads, 37% part-time. 220 full-time freshmen.
Selectivity: Open admission; but selective for some programs.

BASIC COSTS (2008-2009)
Tuition and fees: $964; out-of-district residents $1,420; out-of-state residents $2,812.
Per-credit charge: $36; out-of-district residents $55; out-of-state residents $113.

FINANCIAL AID PICTURE (2007-2008)
Students with need: 74% of average financial aid package awarded as scholarships/grants, 26% awarded as loans/jobs. Need-based aid available for part-time students.
Students without need: No-need awards available for academics, state/district residency.

FINANCIAL AID PROCEDURES
Forms required: FAFSA.
Dates and Deadlines: Priority date 3/1; no closing date. Applicants notified on a rolling basis starting 5/1; must reply within 4 week(s) of notification.

CONTACT
Judith Sears, Financial Aid Coordinator
1500 University Drive, Carlsbad, NM 88220
(575) 234-9226

New Mexico State University at Grants
Grants, New Mexico
www.grants.nmsu.edu Federal Code: 008854

2-year public branch campus and community college in small town.
Enrollment: 1,200 undergrads.
Selectivity: Open admission.

BASIC COSTS (2008-2009)
Tuition and fees: $1,320; out-of-district residents $1,440; out-of-state residents $2,904.

Per-credit charge: $55; out-of-district residents $60; out-of-state residents $121.

FINANCIAL AID PICTURE

Students with need: Need-based aid available for full-time and part-time students. Work study available nights, weekends, and for part-time students.

FINANCIAL AID PROCEDURES

Forms required: FAFSA, institutional form.

Dates and Deadlines: Priority date 3/5; no closing date. Applicants notified on a rolling basis starting 6/15; must reply by 8/28.

CONTACT

Irene Lutz, Campus Financial Officer
1500 North Third Street, Grants, NM 87020
(505) 287-7981

Northern New Mexico College

Espanola, New Mexico
www.nnmc.edu Federal Code: 005286

2-year public community and teachers college in small town.
Enrollment: 2,139 undergrads.
Selectivity: Open admission; but selective for some programs and for out-of-state students.

BASIC COSTS (2008-2009)

Tuition and fees: $1,099; out-of-state residents $2,298.
Per-credit charge: $37; out-of-state residents $87.
Room and board: $3,395.
Additional info: Upper division courses $87 per credit hour for in-state students, $367 per credit hour for out-of-state students.

FINANCIAL AID PICTURE

Students with need: Need-based aid available for full-time students.
Students without need: This college awards aid only to students with need.

FINANCIAL AID PROCEDURES

Forms required: FAFSA.
Dates and Deadlines: Priority date 3/1; no closing date. Applicants notified on a rolling basis starting 6/1; must reply within 2 week(s) of notification.

CONTACT

Alfredo Montoya, Director of Financial Aid
921 Paseo de Onate, Espanola, NM 87532
(505) 747-2128 ext. 128

St. John's College

Santa Fe, New Mexico Federal Code: 002093
www.sjcsf.edu CSS Code: 4737

4-year private liberal arts college in small city.
Enrollment: 431 undergrads, 1% part-time. 134 full-time freshmen.
Selectivity: Admits over 75% of applicants.

BASIC COSTS (2009-2010)

Tuition and fees: $41,096.
Per-credit charge: $1,165.
Room and board: $9,562.

FINANCIAL AID PICTURE (2007-2008)

Students with need: Out of 84 full-time freshmen who applied for aid, 63 were judged to have need. Of these, 63 received aid, and 58 had their full need met. Average financial aid package met 95% of need; average scholarship/grant was $24,425; average loan was $3,125. For part-time students, average financial aid package was $15,947.
Students without need: This college awards aid only to students with need.
Cumulative student debt: 45% of graduating class had student loans; average debt was $20,773.
Additional info: 100% of need met for most of those qualified to receive aid. Families receive individual attention in determining need fairly. Independent students must submit parental data. Financial aid information also required of noncustodial parent in cases of separation or divorce. Aid awarded first-come, first-served until institutional money exhausted. Apply early by February 15; after April 1 aid difficult to obtain.

FINANCIAL AID PROCEDURES

Forms required: FAFSA, CSS PROFILE.
Dates and Deadlines: Priority date 2/15; no closing date. Applicants notified on a rolling basis starting 12/10; must reply by 5/1.

CONTACT

Michael Rodriguez, Director of Financial Aid
1160 Camino Cruz Blanca, Santa Fe, NM 87505-4599
(505) 984-6058

San Juan College

Farmington, New Mexico
www.sanjuancollege.edu Federal Code: 002660

2-year public community college in large town.
Enrollment: 5,139 undergrads, 58% part-time. 577 full-time freshmen.
Selectivity: Open admission.

BASIC COSTS (2009-2010)

Tuition and fees: $768; out-of-state residents $1,680.
Per-credit charge: $32; out-of-state residents $70.

FINANCIAL AID PICTURE (2007-2008)

Students with need: 57% of average financial aid package awarded as scholarships/grants, 43% awarded as loans/jobs. Need-based aid available for part-time students. Work study available nights, weekends, and for part-time students.
Students without need: No-need awards available for academics, state/district residency.

FINANCIAL AID PROCEDURES

Forms required: FAFSA.
Dates and Deadlines: No deadline. Applicants notified on a rolling basis starting 7/1; must reply within 2 week(s) of notification.

CONTACT

Jerry McKeen, Director for Financial Aid
4601 College Boulevard, Farmington, NM 87402-4699
(505) 566-3323

Santa Fe Community College

Santa Fe, New Mexico
www.sfccnm.edu Federal Code: 016065

2-year public community college in small city.
Enrollment: 2,069 undergrads, 69% part-time. 196 full-time freshmen.
Selectivity: Open admission.

BASIC COSTS (2008-2009)

Tuition and fees: $1,113; out-of-district residents $1,434; out-of-state residents $2,469.
Per-credit charge: $32; out-of-district residents $43; out-of-state residents $78.

FINANCIAL AID PICTURE (2007-2008)

Students with need: Need-based aid available for full-time and part-time students. Work study available nights, weekends, and for part-time students.

Students without need: No-need awards available for academics, state/district residency.

FINANCIAL AID PROCEDURES

Forms required: FAFSA, institutional form.

Dates and Deadlines: Priority date 5/1; no closing date. Applicants notified on a rolling basis starting 7/15; must reply within 4 week(s) of notification.

CONTACT

Scott Whitaker, Financial Aid Director
6401 Richards Avenue, Santa Fe, NM 87508-4887
(505) 428-1268

Southwestern Indian Polytechnic Institute

Albuquerque, New Mexico
www.sipi.bia.edu Federal Code: 011185

2-year public community and technical college in large city.

Enrollment: 470 undergrads, 23% part-time. 116 full-time freshmen.

Selectivity: Open admission; but selective for some programs.

BASIC COSTS (2008-2009)

Additional info: Required fees: full-time Lodge student $280, full-time commuter $225, part-time $150. Tuition-free to Native Americans. Tuition/fee waivers available for minority students.

FINANCIAL AID PICTURE (2007-2008)

Students with need: Average financial aid package for all full-time undergraduates was $2,447. Need-based aid available for part-time students. Work study available nights, weekends, and for part-time students.

Students without need: No-need awards available for academics, leadership, minority status.

Additional info: Students with valid membership in recognized Indian tribe attend tuition-free.

FINANCIAL AID PROCEDURES

Forms required: FAFSA.

Dates and Deadlines: Closing date 3/1. Applicants notified on a rolling basis starting 9/30.

Transfers: No deadline.

CONTACT

Marilyn Pargas, Financial Aid Specialist
9169 Coors Road NW, Albuquerque, NM 87184
(505) 346-2344

University of New Mexico

Albuquerque, New Mexico
www.unm.edu Federal Code: 002663

4-year public university in very large city.

Enrollment: 18,394 undergrads, 19% part-time. 3,150 full-time freshmen.

BASIC COSTS (2008-2009)

Tuition and fees: $4,834; out-of-state residents $15,708.

Per-credit charge: $210; out-of-state residents $655.

Room and board: $7,336.

FINANCIAL AID PICTURE

Students with need: Need-based aid available for full-time and part-time students. Work study available nights, weekends, and for part-time students.

Students without need: No-need awards available for academics, alumni affiliation, art, athletics, job skills, leadership, minority status, music/drama, religious affiliation, ROTC, state/district residency.

Scholarships offered: Bridge to Success Scholarship: for first semester only while awaiting other scholarship aid; requires New Mexico residency, full-time status in degree-granting program, and acceptable GED test score and/or requisite high school GPA per sponsor. Regents' and Presidential scholarship programs have priority dates of 12/1. UNM scholars program has deadline of 2/2.

FINANCIAL AID PROCEDURES

Forms required: FAFSA.

Dates and Deadlines: Priority date 3/1; no closing date. Applicants notified on a rolling basis.

CONTACT

Kathleen O'Keefe, Director of Financial Aid
Office of Admissions, Albuquerque, NM 87196-4895
(505) 277-2041

University of the Southwest

Hobbs, New Mexico
www.usw.edu Federal Code: 013935

4-year private liberal arts and teachers college in large town.

Enrollment: 393 undergrads, 13% part-time. 86 full-time freshmen.

Selectivity: Open admission; but selective for some programs.

BASIC COSTS (2009-2010)

Tuition and fees: $12,750.

Per-credit charge: $425.

Room and board: $6,220.

FINANCIAL AID PICTURE (2008-2009)

Students with need: Need-based aid available for full-time and part-time students. Work study available nights, weekends, and for part-time students.

Students without need: No-need awards available for academics, alumni affiliation, athletics, leadership, religious affiliation, state/district residency.

FINANCIAL AID PROCEDURES

Forms required: FAFSA, institutional form.

Dates and Deadlines: Priority date 4/1; closing date 6/1. Applicants notified on a rolling basis starting 4/1; must reply within 2 week(s) of notification.

Transfers: Priority date 3/1; closing date 6/15.

CONTACT

Kerrie Mitchell, Financial Aid Officer
6610 Lovington Highway #506, Hobbs, NM 88240
(575) 392-6563

Western New Mexico University

Silver City, New Mexico
www.wnmu.edu Federal Code: 002664

4-year public university in large town.

Enrollment: 1,753 undergrads, 24% part-time. 317 full-time freshmen.

Selectivity: Open admission.

BASIC COSTS (2008-2009)

Tuition and fees: $3,430; out-of-state residents $12,718.

Room and board: $5,145.

FINANCIAL AID PICTURE (2007-2008)

Students with need: Need-based aid available for full-time and part-time students.

Students without need: No-need awards available for academics, athletics, state/district residency.

FINANCIAL AID PROCEDURES

Forms required: FAFSA, institutional form.

Dates and Deadlines: Closing date 4/1. Applicants notified on a rolling basis starting 4/1; must reply within 2 week(s) of notification.

CONTACT

Charles Kelly, Director of Financial Aid
Castorena 106, Silver City, NM 88062
(505) 538-6173

New York

Adelphi University

Garden City, New York
www.adelphi.edu Federal Code: 002666

4-year private university in large town.

Enrollment: 4,933 undergrads, 14% part-time. 944 full-time freshmen.

Selectivity: Admits 50 to 75% of applicants.

BASIC COSTS (2009-2010)

Tuition and fees: $26,230.

Per-credit charge: $780.

Room and board: $10,000.

FINANCIAL AID PICTURE (2008-2009)

Students with need: Out of 818 full-time freshmen who applied for aid, 650 were judged to have need. Of these, 625 received aid, and 17 had their full need met. Average financial aid package met 56% of need; average scholarship/grant was $5,525; average loan was $3,897. Need-based aid available for part-time students.

Students without need: 255 full-time freshmen who did not demonstrate need for aid received scholarships/grants; average award was $8,410. No-need awards available for academics, alumni affiliation, art, athletics, job skills, leadership, minority status, music/drama, religious affiliation.

Scholarships offered: ***Merit:*** Trustee Scholarship: up to full tuition; top 10% of high school class, 1350 SAT, 3.7 GPA required; 12 available. Presidential Scholarship: $12,500 to $14,500; top 10% of high school class, 1350 SAT, 3.5 GPA required; 25 available. Provost Scholarship: $10,000 to $12,000; top 15% of high school class, 1250 SAT, 3.3 GPA required; 55 available. Dean's Scholarship: $4,000 to $9,500; top 25% of high school class, 1000 SAT, 3.0 GPA required; 252 available. SAT scores listed exclusive of Writing. ***Athletic:*** 27 full-time freshmen received athletic scholarships; average amount $11,907.

FINANCIAL AID PROCEDURES

Forms required: FAFSA, state aid form.

Dates and Deadlines: Priority date 3/1; no closing date. Applicants notified on a rolling basis starting 2/15.

Transfers: No deadline.

CONTACT

Sheryl Mihopulos, Director of Financial Aid
One South Avenue, Levermore 110, Garden City, NY 11530-0701
(516) 877-3080

Adirondack Community College

Queensbury, New York
www.sunyacc.edu Federal Code: 002860

2-year public community college in large town.

Enrollment: 2,804 undergrads.

Selectivity: Open admission; but selective for some programs.

BASIC COSTS (2008-2009)

Tuition and fees: $3,357; out-of-state residents $6,487.

Per-credit charge: $131; out-of-state residents $262.

FINANCIAL AID PICTURE

Students with need: Need-based aid available for full-time and part-time students.

Students without need: This college awards aid only to students with need.

Scholarships offered: Academic Excellence Scholarship: $750 per semester for up to 4 semesters; for local high school graduates who are 1st or 2nd in class, GPA 3.5. Hill Scholarship: $500 per semester for 4 semesters; for Fort Edward High School graduate.

FINANCIAL AID PROCEDURES

Forms required: FAFSA, state aid form, institutional form.

Dates and Deadlines: Priority date 4/15; no closing date. Applicants notified on a rolling basis starting 5/1.

CONTACT

Maureen Reilly, Director of Financial Aid
640 Bay Road, Queensbury, NY 12804
(518) 743-2223

Albany College of Pharmacy and Health Sciences

Albany, New York
www.acphs.edu Federal Code: 002885

4-year private health science and pharmacy college in small city.

Enrollment: 1,098 undergrads, 1% part-time. 288 full-time freshmen.

Selectivity: Admits 50 to 75% of applicants.

BASIC COSTS (2008-2009)

Tuition and fees: $24,450.

Per-credit charge: $735.

Room and board: $7,600.

Additional info: Fees include mandatory laptop purchase.

FINANCIAL AID PICTURE (2008-2009)

Students with need: Out of 262 full-time freshmen who applied for aid, 197 were judged to have need. Of these, 193 received aid, and 31 had their full need met. Average financial aid package met 51% of need; average scholarship/grant was $8,005; average loan was $3,267. Need-based aid available for part-time students.

Students without need: 65 full-time freshmen who did not demonstrate need for aid received scholarships/grants; average award was $13,410. No-need awards available for academics, leadership.

FINANCIAL AID PROCEDURES

Forms required: FAFSA.

Dates and Deadlines: Priority date 2/1; closing date 5/1. Applicants notified on a rolling basis starting 3/20; must reply within 2 week(s) of notification.

CONTACT

Tiffany Gutierrez, Vice President, Enrollment Management
106 New Scotland Avenue, Albany, NY 12208-3492
(518) 694-7256

Alfred University

Alfred, New York
www.alfred.edu Federal Code: 002668

4-year private university in rural community.

Enrollment: 1,906 undergrads.

Selectivity: Admits over 75% of applicants.

BASIC COSTS (2009-2010)
Tuition and fees: $25,246.
Per-credit charge: $790.
Room and board: $11,174.
Additional info: Tuition info provided is for students enrolling in the College of Business or the College of Liberal Arts and Sciences. Costs for students enrolling in the School of Engineering vary by program and/or residency. Costs for students enrolling in the School of Art and Design vary by residency.

FINANCIAL AID PICTURE (2007-2008)
Students with need: 73% of average financial aid package awarded as scholarships/grants, 27% awarded as loans/jobs. Work study available nights, weekends, and for part-time students.
Students without need: No-need awards available for academics, art, leadership, music/drama.

FINANCIAL AID PROCEDURES
Forms required: FAFSA, state aid form, institutional form.
Dates and Deadlines: Closing date 3/15. Applicants notified on a rolling basis starting 2/15; must reply by 5/1 or within 2 week(s) of notification.
Transfers: Closing date 5/15. Applicants notified on a rolling basis starting 2/15; must reply by 5/1 or within 2 week(s) of notification.

CONTACT
Earl Pierce, Director of Student Financial Aid
Alumni Hall, Alfred, NY 14802-1205
(607) 871-2159

American Academy McAllister Institute of Funeral Service
New York, New York
www.funeraleducation.org Federal Code: 010813

2-year private school of mortuary science in very large city.
Enrollment: 286 undergrads.
Selectivity: Open admission.

BASIC COSTS (2009-2010)
Tuition and fees: $11,370.

FINANCIAL AID PICTURE
Students with need: Need-based aid available for full-time students.
Students without need: This college awards aid only to students with need.

FINANCIAL AID PROCEDURES
Forms required: FAFSA, state aid form.
Dates and Deadlines: Applicants notified on a rolling basis starting 7/1; must reply by 9/1 or within 3 week(s) of notification.
Transfers: Priority date 6/1.

CONTACT
Jaway Tso, Financial Aid Administrator
619 West 54th Street, New York, NY 10019-3602
(212) 220-4275

American Academy of Dramatic Arts
New York, New York
www.aada.org Federal Code: 007465

2-year private junior and performing arts college in very large city.
Enrollment: 205 undergrads. 55 full-time freshmen.
Selectivity: Admits 50 to 75% of applicants.

BASIC COSTS (2009-2010)
Tuition and fees: $27,500.

FINANCIAL AID PICTURE (2007-2008)
Students with need: Need-based aid available for full-time students.
Students without need: This college awards aid only to students with need.
Additional info: Need-based incentive grants of $200-$500 for first-year students available. Merit awards of $500-$1,500. Scholarships of $500-$3,000 available for second year. Scholarships of $500-$5,000 available for post-degree third year.

FINANCIAL AID PROCEDURES
Forms required: FAFSA, institutional form.
Dates and Deadlines: No deadline. Applicants notified on a rolling basis.

CONTACT
Roberto Lopez, Financial Aid Director
120 Madison Avenue, New York, NY 10016
(212) 686-9244 ext. 342

ASA Institute of Business and Computer Technology
Brooklyn, New York
www.asa.edu Federal Code: 030955

2-year for-profit career college in very large city.
Enrollment: 3,583 undergrads, 3% part-time. 1,286 full-time freshmen.
Selectivity: Open admission.

BASIC COSTS (2009-2010)
Tuition and fees: $11,499.
Per-credit charge: $470.

FINANCIAL AID PICTURE (2007-2008)
Students with need: 56% of average financial aid package awarded as scholarships/grants, 44% awarded as loans/jobs. Need-based aid available for part-time students. Work study available nights, weekends, and for part-time students.
Students without need: No-need awards available for academics, alumni affiliation, leadership, state/district residency.

FINANCIAL AID PROCEDURES
Forms required: FAFSA, state aid form.
Dates and Deadlines: No deadline. Applicants notified on a rolling basis starting 7/6; must reply by 10/6.
Transfers: No deadline. Applicants notified on a rolling basis starting 7/6; must reply by 10/6.

CONTACT
Victoria Shtamler, Assistant Vice President of Financial Aid
151 Lawrence Street, Brooklyn, NY 11201
(718) 532-1431

Bard College
Annandale-on-Hudson, New York Federal Code: 002671
www.bard.edu CSS Code: 2037

4-year private liberal arts college in small town, affiliated with Episcopal Church.
Enrollment: 1,826 undergrads, 3% part-time. 517 full-time freshmen.
Selectivity: Admits less than 50% of applicants.

BASIC COSTS (2009-2010)
Tuition and fees: $39,880.
Per-credit charge: $1,222.
Room and board: $11,300.

FINANCIAL AID PICTURE (2008-2009)

Students with need: Out of 335 full-time freshmen who applied for aid, 301 were judged to have need. Of these, 301 received aid, and 181 had their full need met. Average financial aid package met 89% of need; average scholarship/grant was $29,351; average loan was $3,645. For part-time students, average financial aid package was $13,247.

Students without need: 5 full-time freshmen who did not demonstrate need for aid received scholarships/grants; average award was $13,600. No-need awards available for academics.

Scholarships offered: Distinguished Scientist Scholarship: full tuition; for students intending to major in math or sciences; 10-20 awarded annually.

Cumulative student debt: 58% of graduating class had student loans; average debt was $20,201.

Additional info: Excellence and Equal Cost Program for students who graduate in top 10 of public high school class lowers fees to levels equivalent to those at home state university or college.

FINANCIAL AID PROCEDURES

Forms required: FAFSA, CSS PROFILE, state aid form.

Dates and Deadlines: Priority date 2/1; closing date 2/15. Applicants notified by 4/1; must reply by 5/1.

Transfers: Applicants notified by 4/1; must reply by 5/1.

CONTACT

Denise Ackerman, Director of Financial Aid
30 Campus Road, Annandale-on-Hudson, NY 12504-5000
(845) 758-7526

Barnard College

New York, New York — Federal Code: 002708
www.barnard.edu — CSS Code: 2038

4-year private liberal arts college for women in very large city.
Enrollment: 2,359 undergrads, 2% part-time. 574 full-time freshmen.
Selectivity: Admits less than 50% of applicants.

BASIC COSTS (2008-2009)

Tuition and fees: $37,538.
Per-credit charge: $1,200.
Room and board: $11,926.

FINANCIAL AID PICTURE (2008-2009)

Students with need: Out of 326 full-time freshmen who applied for aid, 250 were judged to have need. Of these, 250 received aid, and 250 had their full need met. Average financial aid package met 100% of need; average scholarship/grant was $33,907; average loan was $2,886. Need-based aid available for part-time students.

Students without need: This college awards aid only to students with need.

Cumulative student debt: 43% of graduating class had student loans; average debt was $15,695.

Additional info: HEOP for NY residents only; no loan. Pell eligible students: no loan for first-year students, loan reduced to $2,000 for sophomores, juniors and seniors.

FINANCIAL AID PROCEDURES

Forms required: FAFSA, CSS PROFILE.

Dates and Deadlines: Closing date 2/1. Applicants notified by 3/31; must reply by 5/1.

Transfers: Closing date 4/1. Transfers admitted in the spring are not eligible for institutional grant aid.

CONTACT

Gregory Brown, Vice President for Finance & Planning
3009 Broadway, New York, NY 10027-6598
(212) 854-2154

Berkeley College

White Plains, New York
www.berkeleycollege.edu — Federal Code: 007421

4-year for-profit business college in small city.
Enrollment: 697 undergrads, 6% part-time. 140 full-time freshmen.

BASIC COSTS (2009-2010)

Tuition and fees: $19,950.
Room only: $7,500.
Additional info: Tuition at time of enrollment locked for 4 years.

FINANCIAL AID PICTURE

Students with need: Need-based aid available for full-time students.

Students without need: No-need awards available for academics, alumni affiliation.

Additional info: Alumni scholarship examination given in November and December. Full and partial scholarships awarded.

FINANCIAL AID PROCEDURES

Forms required: FAFSA, state aid form.

Dates and Deadlines: No deadline. Applicants notified on a rolling basis starting 3/1; must reply within 6 week(s) of notification.

CONTACT

Cheryll Hope, Director, Financial Aid
99 Church Street, White Plains, NY 10601
(914) 694-1122

Berkeley College of New York City

New York, New York
www.berkeleycollege.edu — Federal Code: 008556

4-year for-profit business college in very large city.
Enrollment: 3,054 undergrads, 11% part-time. 450 full-time freshmen.

BASIC COSTS (2009-2010)

Tuition and fees: $19,950.
Additional info: Tuition at time of enrollment locked for 4 years.

FINANCIAL AID PICTURE

Students with need: Need-based aid available for full-time students.

Students without need: No-need awards available for academics, alumni affiliation.

Additional info: Alumni scholarship examination given in November and December. Full and partial scholarships awarded.

FINANCIAL AID PROCEDURES

Forms required: FAFSA.

Dates and Deadlines: No deadline. Applicants notified on a rolling basis starting 3/1; must reply within 6 week(s) of notification.

Transfers: New York State TAP Grant eligibility may be affected.

CONTACT

Marilyn Faller, VP, Student Finance
3 East 43rd Street, New York, NY 10017
(212) 986-4343

Boricua College

New York, New York
www.boricuacollege.edu — Federal Code: 013029

4-year private liberal arts college in very large city.
Enrollment: 968 undergrads. 473 full-time freshmen.
Selectivity: Admits less than 50% of applicants.

BASIC COSTS (2008-2009)

Tuition and fees: $9,000.

FINANCIAL AID PICTURE (2007-2008)

Students with need: Out of 456 full-time freshmen who applied for aid, 451 were judged to have need. Of these, 441 received aid, and 260 had their full need met. Average financial aid package met 59% of need; average scholarship/grant was $117; average loan was $2,093.

FINANCIAL AID PROCEDURES

Forms required: FAFSA, state aid form.

Dates and Deadlines: Priority date 4/30; no closing date. Applicants notified on a rolling basis; must reply within 3 week(s) of notification.

CONTACT

Rosalia Cruz, Director of Financial Aid
3755 Broadway, New York, NY 10032
(212) 694-1000 ext. 611

Broome Community College

Binghamton, New York
www.sunybroome.edu Federal Code: 002862

2-year public community college in small city.

Enrollment: 5,414 undergrads, 24% part-time. 1,192 full-time freshmen.

Selectivity: Open admission; but selective for some programs.

BASIC COSTS (2008-2009)

Tuition and fees: $3,547; out-of-state residents $6,709.

Per-credit charge: $132; out-of-state residents $264.

FINANCIAL AID PICTURE (2008-2009)

Students with need: Need-based aid available for full-time and part-time students. Work study available nights.

FINANCIAL AID PROCEDURES

Forms required: FAFSA.

Dates and Deadlines: Priority date 3/1; no closing date. Applicants notified on a rolling basis starting 3/15; must reply within 2 week(s) of notification.

CONTACT

Doug Lukasik, Director of Financial Aid
Box 1017, Binghamton, NY 13902
(607) 778-5028

Bryant & Stratton College: Albany

Albany, New York
www.bryantstratton.edu Federal Code: 004749

2-year for-profit business college in small city.

Enrollment: 686 undergrads, 32% part-time. 138 full-time freshmen.

BASIC COSTS (2008-2009)

Tuition and fees: $13,740.

Additional info: Tuition may vary depending on program.

FINANCIAL AID PICTURE (2007-2008)

Students with need: Need-based aid available for full-time and part-time students. Work study available nights, weekends, and for part-time students.

Students without need: This college awards aid only to students with need.

FINANCIAL AID PROCEDURES

Forms required: FAFSA, state aid form.

Dates and Deadlines: No deadline. Applicants notified on a rolling basis.

CONTACT

Jackie Rivers, FA Coordinator
1259 Central Avenue, Albany, NY 12205
(518) 437-1802

Bryant & Stratton College: Syracuse

Syracuse, New York
www.bryantstratton.edu Federal Code: 008276

2-year for-profit business college in small city.

Enrollment: 723 undergrads, 32% part-time. 222 full-time freshmen.

Selectivity: Open admission.

BASIC COSTS (2008-2009)

Tuition and fees: $13,775.

Per-credit charge: $458.

Additional info: Total room and board is $7,140 for triple-occupancy residence.

FINANCIAL AID PICTURE (2008-2009)

Students with need: Work study available nights, weekends, and for part-time students.

Students without need: This college awards aid only to students with need.

FINANCIAL AID PROCEDURES

Forms required: FAFSA.

Dates and Deadlines: No deadline. Applicants notified on a rolling basis starting 10/1.

Transfers: Priority date 5/1.

CONTACT

Mary Clifton, Financial Services Manager
953 James Street, Syracuse, NY 13203
(315) 472-6603

Bryant & Stratton College: Syracuse North

Liverpool, New York
www.bryantstratton.edu

2-year for-profit business college in small town.

Enrollment: 530 undergrads. 166 full-time freshmen.

Selectivity: Open admission.

BASIC COSTS (2008-2009)

Tuition and fees: $13,080.

FINANCIAL AID PICTURE (2007-2008)

Students with need: Out of 166 full-time freshmen who applied for aid, 134 were judged to have need. Of these, 134 received aid, and 125 had their full need met. Average financial aid package met 90% of need; average scholarship/grant was $9,732; average loan was $3,500. For part-time students, average financial aid package was $5,860.

Students without need: This college awards aid only to students with need.

Cumulative student debt: 94% of graduating class had student loans; average debt was $5,500.

FINANCIAL AID PROCEDURES

Forms required: FAFSA, state aid form, institutional form.

Dates and Deadlines: No deadline.

Transfers: No deadline.

CONTACT

Michelle Lee, Financial Services Manager
8687 Carling Road, Liverpool, NY 13090
(315) 652-6500

Canisius College

Buffalo, New York
www.canisius.edu Federal Code: 002681

4-year private liberal arts and teachers college in large city, affiliated with Roman Catholic Church.
Enrollment: 3,224 undergrads, 3% part-time. 807 full-time freshmen.
Selectivity: Admits over 75% of applicants.

BASIC COSTS (2009-2010)

Tuition and fees: $29,512.
Per-credit charge: $812.
Room and board: $10,556.
Additional info: Tuition/fee waivers available for minority students.

FINANCIAL AID PICTURE (2008-2009)

Students with need: Out of 719 full-time freshmen who applied for aid, 647 were judged to have need. Of these, 647 received aid, and 241 had their full need met. Average financial aid package met 88% of need; average scholarship/grant was $19,506; average loan was $3,298. Need-based aid available for part-time students.
Students without need: 140 full-time freshmen who did not demonstrate need for aid received scholarships/grants; average award was $14,649. No-need awards available for academics, alumni affiliation, art, athletics, job skills, music/drama, religious affiliation, ROTC.
Scholarships offered: ***Merit:*** Presidential Scholarships: $20,000 per year for four years. Ignatian Scholarships: $15,000 per year for four years; applicants who apply by Nov. 15 given priority consideration. Trustee's Scholarship: $12,000 per year for on-campus student, $10,000 per year for off-campus student; based on high school GPA, test scores. Dean's Scholarship: $10,000 per year for on-campus student, $8,000 per year for off-campus student; based on high school GPA, test scores. Benefactor's Scholarship: $7,000 per year for on-campus student, $5,000 per year for off-campus student; based on high school GPA, test scores. International Scholarships: international students, including Canadian students, may be eligible for academic scholarships based on academic records. ***Athletic:*** 18 full-time freshmen received athletic scholarships; average amount $19,173.
Cumulative student debt: 76% of graduating class had student loans; average debt was $30,600.

FINANCIAL AID PROCEDURES

Forms required: FAFSA, state aid form.
Dates and Deadlines: Priority date 2/15; no closing date. Applicants notified on a rolling basis starting 3/1; must reply within 2 week(s) of notification.

CONTACT

Curtis Gaume, Director of Student Financial Aid
2001 Main Street, Buffalo, NY 14208-1098
(800) 541-6348

Cayuga County Community College

Auburn, New York
www.cayuga-cc.edu Federal Code: 002861

2-year public community college in large town.
Enrollment: 2,606 undergrads, 24% part-time. 470 full-time freshmen.
Selectivity: Open admission; but selective for some programs.

BASIC COSTS (2008-2009)

Tuition and fees: $3,763; out-of-state residents $7,153.
Per-credit charge: $132; out-of-state residents $264.

FINANCIAL AID PICTURE (2007-2008)

Students with need: Need-based aid available for full-time and part-time students. Work study available nights, weekends, and for part-time students.
Students without need: This college awards aid only to students with need.

FINANCIAL AID PROCEDURES

Forms required: FAFSA, state aid form.
Dates and Deadlines: Closing date 5/1. Applicants notified on a rolling basis starting 3/15.

CONTACT

Judi Miladin, Director of Financial Aid
197 Franklin Street, Auburn, NY 13021-3099
(315) 255-1743 ext. 2470

Cazenovia College

Cazenovia, New York
www.cazenovia.edu Federal Code: 002685

4-year private liberal arts college in small town.
Enrollment: 1,062 undergrads, 8% part-time. 283 full-time freshmen.
Selectivity: Admits 50 to 75% of applicants.

BASIC COSTS (2008-2009)

Tuition and fees: $22,894.
Room and board: $9,502.

FINANCIAL AID PICTURE (2008-2009)

Students with need: Out of 259 full-time freshmen who applied for aid, 223 were judged to have need. Of these, 223 received aid, and 48 had their full need met. Average financial aid package met 78% of need; average scholarship/grant was $18,105; average loan was $3,314. Need-based aid available for part-time students.
Students without need: 38 full-time freshmen who did not demonstrate need for aid received scholarships/grants; average award was $12,245. No-need awards available for academics.

FINANCIAL AID PROCEDURES

Forms required: FAFSA, state aid form.
Dates and Deadlines: Priority date 3/15; no closing date. Applicants notified on a rolling basis starting 11/1; must reply by 5/1 or within 2 week(s) of notification.
Transfers: No deadline. Applicants notified on a rolling basis starting 11/1; must reply by 5/1 or within 2 week(s) of notification.

CONTACT

Christine Mandel, Director of Financial Aid
3 Sullivan Street, Cazenovia, NY 13035
(315) 655-7887

City University of New York: Baruch College

New York, New York
www.baruch.cuny.edu Federal Code: 007273

4-year public business and liberal arts college in very large city.
Enrollment: 12,473 undergrads, 23% part-time. 1,497 full-time freshmen.
Selectivity: Admits less than 50% of applicants.

BASIC COSTS (2008-2009)

Tuition and fees: $4,370; out-of-state residents $11,170.
Per-credit charge: $170; out-of-state residents $360.

FINANCIAL AID PICTURE (2008-2009)

Students with need: 80% of average financial aid package awarded as scholarships/grants, 20% awarded as loans/jobs. Need-based aid available for part-time students.

Students without need: No-need awards available for academics, state/district residency.

Scholarships offered: Honors college scholarships based on SAT scores and high school GPA.

FINANCIAL AID PROCEDURES

Forms required: FAFSA, state aid form.

Dates and Deadlines: Priority date 3/15; closing date 4/30. Applicants notified on a rolling basis starting 4/1; must reply by 6/1 or within 6 week(s) of notification.

Transfers: Priority date 4/1; no deadline. Applicants notified on a rolling basis; must reply within 4 week(s) of notification.

CONTACT

Nancy West, Director of Financial Aid
One Bernard Baruch Way, Box H-0720, New York, NY 10010-5585
(646) 312-1360

City University of New York: Borough of Manhattan Community College

New York, New York
www.bmcc.cuny.edu Federal Code: 002691

2-year public community college in very large city.

Enrollment: 21,118 undergrads, 35% part-time. 4,212 full-time freshmen.

Selectivity: Open admission; but selective for some programs.

BASIC COSTS (2008-2009)

Tuition and fees: $3,118; out-of-state residents $6,018.

Per-credit charge: $120; out-of-state residents $190.

FINANCIAL AID PICTURE (2007-2008)

Students with need: Out of 3,586 full-time freshmen who applied for aid, 3,342 were judged to have need. Of these, 3,145 received aid. Need-based aid available for part-time students.

Students without need: This college awards aid only to students with need.

FINANCIAL AID PROCEDURES

Forms required: FAFSA, institutional form.

Dates and Deadlines: Priority date 4/15; closing date 5/1. Applicants notified on a rolling basis starting 8/1; must reply within 2 week(s) of notification.

CONTACT

Howard Entin, Director of Financial Aid
199 Chambers Street, New York, NY 10007-1097
(212) 220-1430

City University of New York: Bronx Community College

Bronx, New York
www.bcc.cuny.edu Federal Code: 002692

2-year public community college in very large city.

Enrollment: 8,556 undergrads.

Selectivity: Open admission.

BASIC COSTS (2008-2009)

Tuition and fees: $3,104; out-of-state residents $6,004.

Per-credit charge: $120; out-of-state residents $190.

FINANCIAL AID PICTURE

Students with need: Need-based aid available for full-time and part-time students. Work study available nights, weekends, and for part-time students.

Students without need: This college awards aid only to students with need.

FINANCIAL AID PROCEDURES

Forms required: FAFSA.

Dates and Deadlines: Closing date 7/15. Applicants notified on a rolling basis starting 8/1.

CONTACT

Financial Aid Officer
2155 University Avenue, Bronx, NY 10453
(718) 289-5700

City University of New York: Brooklyn College

Brooklyn, New York
www.brooklyn.cuny.edu Federal Code: 002687

4-year public liberal arts college in very large city.

Enrollment: 12,160 undergrads, 25% part-time. 1,330 full-time freshmen.

Selectivity: Admits less than 50% of applicants.

BASIC COSTS (2008-2009)

Tuition and fees: $4,431; out-of-state residents $11,231.

Per-credit charge: $170; out-of-state residents $360.

FINANCIAL AID PICTURE (2008-2009)

Students with need: Out of 1,168 full-time freshmen who applied for aid, 1,060 were judged to have need. Of these, 1,058 received aid, and 1,040 had their full need met. Average financial aid package met 99% of need; average scholarship/grant was $3,200; average loan was $2,650. For part-time students, average financial aid package was $2,750.

Students without need: 157 full-time freshmen who did not demonstrate need for aid received scholarships/grants; average award was $1,480. No-need awards available for academics, art, leadership, music/drama, state/district residency.

Scholarships offered: Presidential Scholarship Program: for 25 freshman students for 8 tuition payments totalling $13,000. Brooklyn College Freshman Scholarships: $1,000 per year of study at Brooklyn College. Many scholarships for freshman students based on degree of study, academic merit, and community service.

Cumulative student debt: 45% of graduating class had student loans; average debt was $16,000.

FINANCIAL AID PROCEDURES

Forms required: FAFSA, state aid form.

Dates and Deadlines: Priority date 4/1; no closing date. Applicants notified on a rolling basis starting 5/1.

CONTACT

Sherwood Johnson, Director of Financial Aid
2900 Bedford Avenue, Brooklyn, NY 11210
(718) 951-5051

City University of New York: City College

New York, New York
www.ccny.cuny.edu Federal Code: 002688

4-year public university in very large city.

Enrollment: 11,494 undergrads, 23% part-time. 1,769 full-time freshmen.

Selectivity: Admits less than 50% of applicants.

BASIC COSTS (2008-2009)

Tuition and fees: $4,329; out-of-state residents $11,129.

Per-credit charge: $170; out-of-state residents $360.

Additional info: Room only on-campus; there is student housing with rates by apartment size. Tuition/fee waivers available for minority students.

FINANCIAL AID PICTURE (2007-2008)

Students with need: Out of 1,570 full-time freshmen who applied for aid, 1,555 were judged to have need. Of these, 1,500 received aid, and 1,052 had their full need met. Average financial aid package met 81% of need; average scholarship/grant was $5,822; average loan was $1,812. Need-based aid available for part-time students.

Students without need: 462 full-time freshmen who did not demonstrate need for aid received scholarships/grants; average award was $2,110. No-need awards available for academics, alumni affiliation, leadership.

Cumulative student debt: 26% of graduating class had student loans; average debt was $15,669.

FINANCIAL AID PROCEDURES

Forms required: FAFSA.

Dates and Deadlines: Priority date 4/15; no closing date. Applicants notified on a rolling basis starting 4/15.

Transfers: Priority date 3/31; no deadline. Applicants notified on a rolling basis starting 3/31.

CONTACT

Thelma Mason, Director of Financial Aid
160 Convent Avenue, New York, NY 10031
(212) 650-7000

City University of New York: College of Staten Island

Staten Island, New York
www.csi.cuny.edu Federal Code: 002698

4-year public liberal arts college in very large city.

Enrollment: 11,901 undergrads, 28% part-time. 2,281 full-time freshmen.

Selectivity: Admits over 75% of applicants.

BASIC COSTS (2008-2009)

Tuition and fees: $4,378; out-of-state residents $11,178.

Per-credit charge: $170; out-of-state residents $360.

FINANCIAL AID PICTURE (2008-2009)

Students with need: Average financial aid package met 57% of need; average scholarship/grant was $5,725; average loan was $2,924. For part-time students, average financial aid package was $4,230.

Students without need: No-need awards available for academics, art, leadership, minority status, music/drama.

FINANCIAL AID PROCEDURES

Forms required: FAFSA, state aid form.

Dates and Deadlines: Priority date 3/31; no closing date. Applicants notified on a rolling basis starting 6/1.

Transfers: Applicants notified on a rolling basis starting 5/10.

CONTACT

Philippe Marius, Director of Financial Aid
2800 Victory Boulevard 2A-104, Staten Island, NY 10314
(718) 982-2030

City University of New York: Hostos Community College

Bronx, New York
www.hostos.cuny.edu Federal Code: 008611

2-year public community college in very large city.

Enrollment: 4,715 undergrads, 37% part-time. 829 full-time freshmen.

Selectivity: Open admission; but selective for some programs.

BASIC COSTS (2008-2009)

Tuition and fees: $3,155; out-of-state residents $6,055.

Per-credit charge: $120; out-of-state residents $190.

FINANCIAL AID PICTURE

Students with need: Need-based aid available for full-time and part-time students.

FINANCIAL AID PROCEDURES

Forms required: FAFSA, state aid form, institutional form.

Dates and Deadlines: Priority date 7/1; no closing date. Applicants notified on a rolling basis; must reply within 3 week(s) of notification.

CONTACT

Joseph Alicea, Director of Financial Aid
500 Grand Concourse, Bronx, NY 10451
(718) 518-6555

City University of New York: Hunter College

New York, New York
www.hunter.cuny.edu Federal Code: 002689

4-year public liberal arts college in very large city.

Enrollment: 14,709 undergrads, 26% part-time. 1,813 full-time freshmen.

Selectivity: Admits less than 50% of applicants.

BASIC COSTS (2008-2009)

Tuition and fees: $4,399; out-of-state residents $11,199.

Per-credit charge: $170; out-of-state residents $360.

Room only: $3,726.

Additional info: Dormitory availability very limited.

FINANCIAL AID PICTURE (2007-2008)

Students with need: Out of 1,489 full-time freshmen who applied for aid, 1,005 were judged to have need. Of these, 988 received aid, and 251 had their full need met. Average financial aid package met 77% of need; average scholarship/grant was $4,361; average loan was $2,367. For part-time students, average financial aid package was $3,237.

Students without need: 310 full-time freshmen who did not demonstrate need for aid received scholarships/grants; average award was $1,870. No-need awards available for academics.

Cumulative student debt: 41% of graduating class had student loans; average debt was $7,125.

FINANCIAL AID PROCEDURES

Forms required: FAFSA, state aid form.

Dates and Deadlines: Priority date 5/1; no closing date. Applicants notified on a rolling basis starting 5/15.

CONTACT

Aristalia Rodriguez, Director of Financial Aid
695 Park Avenue, New York, NY 10065
(212) 772-4820

City University of New York: John Jay College of Criminal Justice

New York, New York
www.jjay.cuny.edu/ Federal Code: 002693

4-year public college of criminal justice and public safety in very large city.
Enrollment: 12,615 undergrads, 24% part-time. 2,414 full-time freshmen.
Selectivity: Admits 50 to 75% of applicants.

BASIC COSTS (2008-2009)
Tuition and fees: $4,329; out-of-state residents $11,129.
Per-credit charge: $170; out-of-state residents $360.

FINANCIAL AID PICTURE (2007-2008)
Students with need: Average financial aid package met 85% of need; average scholarship/grant was $2,926; average loan was $2,331. For part-time students, average financial aid package was $5,004.
Students without need: No-need awards available for academics, state/district residency.
Cumulative student debt: 46% of graduating class had student loans; average debt was $14,000.

FINANCIAL AID PROCEDURES
Forms required: FAFSA.
Dates and Deadlines: No deadline. Applicants notified on a rolling basis starting 7/15; must reply within 2 week(s) of notification.

CONTACT
Fay Williams, Director of Financial Aid
445 West 59th Street, New York, NY 10019
(212) 237-8151

City University of New York: Kingsborough Community College

Brooklyn, New York
www.kbcc.cuny.edu Federal Code: 002694

2-year public community college in very large city.
Enrollment: 11,870 undergrads, 27% part-time. 2,198 full-time freshmen.
Selectivity: Open admission.

BASIC COSTS (2008-2009)
Tuition and fees: $3,150; out-of-state residents $6,050.
Per-credit charge: $120; out-of-state residents $190.

FINANCIAL AID PICTURE
Students with need: Need-based aid available for full-time and part-time students.
Students without need: This college awards aid only to students with need.

FINANCIAL AID PROCEDURES
Forms required: FAFSA.
Dates and Deadlines: Closing date 4/30. Applicants notified on a rolling basis; must reply within 2 week(s) of notification.

CONTACT
Wayne Harewood, Director of Financial Aid
2001 Oriental Boulevard, Brooklyn, NY 11235
(718) 368-4644

City University of New York: LaGuardia Community College

Long Island City, New York
www.lagcc.cuny.edu Federal Code: 010051

2-year public community college in very large city.
Enrollment: 13,195 undergrads, 38% part-time. 3,386 full-time freshmen.
Selectivity: Open admission.

BASIC COSTS (2008-2009)
Tuition and fees: $3,142; out-of-state residents $6,042.
Per-credit charge: $120; out-of-state residents $190.

FINANCIAL AID PICTURE (2007-2008)
Students with need: Out of 2,607 full-time freshmen who applied for aid, 2,494 were judged to have need. Of these, 2,395 received aid. Average financial aid package met 48% of need; average scholarship/grant was $3,580. For part-time students, average financial aid package was $1,984.
Students without need: This college awards aid only to students with need.

FINANCIAL AID PROCEDURES
Forms required: FAFSA, state aid form, institutional form.
Dates and Deadlines: Priority date 4/15; no closing date. Applicants notified on a rolling basis starting 3/1; must reply within 4 week(s) of notification.

CONTACT
Gail Baksh-Jarrett, Director of Financial Aid
31-10 Thomson Avenue, Long Island City, NY 11101
(718) 482-7200

City University of New York: Lehman College

Bronx, New York
www.lehman.cuny.edu Federal Code: 007022

4-year public liberal arts college in very large city.
Enrollment: 8,571 undergrads, 33% part-time. 887 full-time freshmen.
Selectivity: Admits less than 50% of applicants.

BASIC COSTS (2008-2009)
Tuition and fees: $4,340; out-of-state residents $11,140.
Per-credit charge: $170; out-of-state residents $360.

FINANCIAL AID PICTURE (2007-2008)
Students with need: Out of 800 full-time freshmen who applied for aid, 800 were judged to have need. Of those, 000 received aid, and 24 had their full need met. Average financial aid package met 11% of need; average scholarship/grant was $1,579; average loan was $1,529. For part-time students, average financial aid package was $1,774.
Students without need: This college awards aid only to students with need.
Cumulative student debt: 32% of graduating class had student loans; average debt was $11,100.

FINANCIAL AID PROCEDURES
Forms required: FAFSA, state aid form.
Dates and Deadlines: No deadline. Applicants notified on a rolling basis starting 3/1.
Transfers: Applicants notified on a rolling basis starting 3/1.

CONTACT
David Martinez, Director of Financial Aid
250 Bedford Park Boulevard West, Bronx, NY 10468
(718) 960-8545

City University of New York: Medgar Evers College

Brooklyn, New York
www.mec.cuny.edu Federal Code: 010097

4-year public liberal arts college in very large city.
Enrollment: 5,710 undergrads, 35% part-time. 962 full-time freshmen.
Selectivity: Open admission; but selective for some programs.

BASIC COSTS (2008-2009)

Tuition and fees: $4,302; out-of-state residents $11,102.
Per-credit charge: $170; out-of-state residents $360.

FINANCIAL AID PICTURE (2007-2008)

Students with need: Need-based aid available for full-time and part-time students. Work study available weekends and for part-time students.
Students without need: No-need awards available for academics, leadership.

FINANCIAL AID PROCEDURES

Forms required: FAFSA, state aid form.
Dates and Deadlines: Priority date 1/2; closing date 7/31. Applicants notified on a rolling basis; must reply within 3 week(s) of notification.
Transfers: Priority date 3/1. Must reply within 2 week(s) of notification.

CONTACT

Conley James, Director of Financial Aid
1665 Bedford Avenue, Brooklyn, NY 11225-2201
(718) 270-6194

City University of New York: New York City College of Technology

Brooklyn, New York
www.citytech.cuny.edu Federal Code: 002696

4-year public technical college in very large city.
Enrollment: 13,442 undergrads, 39% part-time. 2,819 full-time freshmen.
Selectivity: Open admission; but selective for some programs.

BASIC COSTS (2008-2009)

Tuition and fees: $4,289; out-of-state residents $11,089.
Per-credit charge: $170; out-of-state residents $360.

FINANCIAL AID PICTURE (2008-2009)

Students with need: Out of 2,274 full-time freshmen who applied for aid, 2,029 were judged to have need. Of these, 1,970 received aid, and 143 had their full need met. Average financial aid package met 62% of need; average scholarship/grant was $6,250; average loan was $2,248. For part-time students, average financial aid package was $3,190.
Students without need: 40 full-time freshmen who did not demonstrate need for aid received scholarships/grants; average award was $1,250. No-need awards available for state/district residency.
Additional info: Foreign students applying for aid must have resided in New York for at least 1 year.

FINANCIAL AID PROCEDURES

Forms required: FAFSA.
Dates and Deadlines: Priority date 5/15; no closing date.

CONTACT

Sandra Higgins, Director of Financial Aid
300 Jay Street Namm G17, Brooklyn, NY 11201
(718) 260 5700

City University of New York: Queens College

Flushing, New York
www.qc.cuny.edu Federal Code: 002690

4-year public liberal arts college in very large city.
Enrollment: 14,497 undergrads, 26% part-time. 1,754 full-time freshmen.
Selectivity: Admits less than 50% of applicants.

BASIC COSTS (2008-2009)

Tuition and fees: $4,427; out-of-state residents $11,227.
Per-credit charge: $170; out-of-state residents $360.

FINANCIAL AID PICTURE (2007-2008)

Students with need: Out of 1,333 full-time freshmen who applied for aid, 1,213 were judged to have need. Of these, 970 received aid, and 247 had their full need met. Average financial aid package met 77% of need; average scholarship/grant was $1,250; average loan was $2,625. For part-time students, average financial aid package was $5,400.
Students without need: 81 full-time freshmen who did not demonstrate need for aid received scholarships/grants; average award was $773. No-need awards available for academics, athletics, music/drama, state/district residency.
Scholarships offered: ***Merit:*** CUNY Honors College; full tuition. Regents Award for Deceased or Disabled Veterans; $450 per year. Vietnam Veteran Tuition Aid Program; cost of tuition per semester. Regents Award for children of deceased police officers, firefighters, or corrections officers; $450 per year. Paul Douglas Teacher Scholarship Program; up to $5,000 per year. State Aid to Native Americans; $1,100 per year. SEEK Presidential Scholarship; Beinstock Memorial Scholarship for students with disabilities; CMP Publications Scholarship in Journalism or English; Daly Scholarship in the Physical Sciences; Foster Scholarship for women and minorities; Kupferberg Memorial Scholarship; Linakis Scholarship; Mitsui USA Scholarships; Nagdimon Scholarship; Queens College Scholarships; Weprin Memorial Scholarship in the Public Interest. ***Athletic:*** 28 full-time freshmen received athletic scholarships; average amount $4,600.

FINANCIAL AID PROCEDURES

Forms required: FAFSA, state aid form, institutional form.
Dates and Deadlines: Priority date 2/1; no closing date. Applicants notified on a rolling basis starting 3/1; must reply within 3 week(s) of notification.
Transfers: Priority date 5/1; no deadline. Applicants notified on a rolling basis.

CONTACT

Rena Smith-Kiawu, Director of Financial Aid
6530 Kissena Boulevard, Jefferson 117, Flushing, NY 11367-1597
(718) 997-5123

City University of New York: Queensborough Community College

Bayside, New York
www.qcc.cuny.edu Federal Code: 002697

2-year public community college in very large city.
Enrollment: 11,798 undergrads.
Selectivity: Open admission.

BASIC COSTS (2008-2009)

Tuition and fees: $3,136; out-of-state residents $6,036.
Per-credit charge: $120; out-of-state residents $190.

FINANCIAL AID PICTURE (2007-2008)

Students with need: Need-based aid available for full-time students.

FINANCIAL AID PROCEDURES

Forms required: FAFSA, institutional form.

Dates and Deadlines: No deadline. Applicants notified on a rolling basis starting 7/15.

CONTACT

Veronica Lukas, Director of Financial Aid
Springfield Boulevard & 56th Avenue, Bayside, NY 11364-1497
(718) 631-6262

City University of New York: York College

Jamaica, New York
www.york.cuny.edu Federal Code: 004759

4-year public liberal arts college in very large city.
Enrollment: 6,208 undergrads, 30% part-time. 1,024 full-time freshmen.

BASIC COSTS (2008-2009)

Tuition and fees: $4,312; out-of-state residents $11,112.
Per-credit charge: $170; out-of-state residents $360.

FINANCIAL AID PICTURE (2008-2009)

Students with need: Out of 838 full-time freshmen who applied for aid, 740 were judged to have need. Of these, 724 received aid. Average financial aid package met 23% of need; average scholarship/grant was $1,638; average loan was $1,329. For part-time students, average financial aid package was $2,053.
Students without need: No-need awards available for academics.
Cumulative student debt: 9% of graduating class had student loans; average debt was $9,351.

FINANCIAL AID PROCEDURES

Forms required: FAFSA.
Dates and Deadlines: Priority date 5/1; no closing date. Applicants notified on a rolling basis starting 3/1.
Transfers: No deadline. Applicants notified on a rolling basis starting 3/1.

CONTACT

Cathy Tsiapanos, Director of Financial Aid
94-20 Guy R. Brewer Boulevard, Jamaica, NY 11451-9989
(718) 262-2000 ext. 2230

Clarkson University

Potsdam, New York
www.clarkson.edu Federal Code: 002699

4-year private university in large town.
Enrollment: 2,574 undergrads. 682 full-time freshmen.
Selectivity: Admits over 75% of applicants.

BASIC COSTS (2009-2010)

Tuition and fees: $32,910.
Per-credit charge: $1,074.
Room and board: $11,118.
Additional info: Tuition/fee waivers available for minority students.

FINANCIAL AID PICTURE (2007-2008)

Students with need: Out of 574 full-time freshmen who applied for aid, 499 were judged to have need. Of these, 499 received aid, and 41 had their full need met. Average financial aid package met 86% of need; average scholarship/grant was $14,270; average loan was $5,100. Need-based aid available for part-time students.
Students without need: 75 full-time freshmen who did not demonstrate need for aid received scholarships/grants; average award was $14,529. No-need awards available for academics, alumni affiliation, leadership, minority status, ROTC.
Scholarships offered: 11 full-time freshmen received athletic scholarships; average amount $39,992.
Cumulative student debt: 84% of graduating class had student loans; average debt was $33,625.

FINANCIAL AID PROCEDURES

Forms required: FAFSA, state aid form.
Dates and Deadlines: Priority date 2/15; no closing date. Applicants notified on a rolling basis starting 3/19; must reply by 5/1 or within 2 week(s) of notification.
Transfers: Closing date 4/15. Applicants notified on a rolling basis. Presidential Scholarships, Phi Theta Kappa scholarships and Alpha Beta Gamma Awards available, in addition to state and federal programs.

CONTACT

Jennifer Wick, Director of New Student Financial Assistance
Holcroft House, Potsdam, NY 13699-5605
(800) 527-6577

Clinton Community College

Plattsburgh, New York
www.clinton.edu Federal Code: 006787

2-year public community college in large town.
Enrollment: 1,387 undergrads.
Selectivity: Open admission; but selective for some programs.

BASIC COSTS (2008-2009)

Tuition and fees: $3,684; out-of-state residents $8,784.
Per-credit charge: $141; out-of-state residents $350.

FINANCIAL AID PICTURE (2008-2009)

Students with need: Need based aid available for full-time and part-time students.
Students without need: This college awards aid only to students with need.

FINANCIAL AID PROCEDURES

Forms required: FAFSA, state aid form.
Dates and Deadlines: Priority date 6/9; no closing date. Applicants notified on a rolling basis starting 5/9; must reply within 2 week(s) of notification.

CONTACT

Karen Burnam, Director of Financial Aid
136 Clinton Point Drive, Plattsburgh, NY 12901-4297
(518) 562-4125

Cochran School of Nursing

Yonkers, New York
www.cochranschoolofnursing.us Federal Code: 006443

2-year private nursing college in small city.
Enrollment: 332 undergrads, 58% part-time.

BASIC COSTS (2009-2010)

Additional info: Tuition and required fees for full 2-year AAS program is $25,111.

FINANCIAL AID PICTURE (2008-2009)

Students with need: 74% of average financial aid package awarded as scholarships/grants, 26% awarded as loans/jobs. Need-based aid available for part-time students.
Students without need: This college awards aid only to students with need.

FINANCIAL AID PROCEDURES

Forms required: FAFSA.
Dates and Deadlines: No deadline. Applicants notified on a rolling basis.

CONTACT

Geraldine Owens, Financial Aid Officer
967 North Broadway, Yonkers, NY 10701
(914) 964-4265

Colgate University

Hamilton, New York
www.colgate.edu
Federal Code: 002701
CSS Code: 2086

4-year private liberal arts college in small town.
Enrollment: 2,806 undergrads. 738 full-time freshmen.
Selectivity: Admits less than 50% of applicants.

BASIC COSTS (2008-2009)

Tuition and fees: $39,545.
Room and board: $9,625.

FINANCIAL AID PICTURE (2007-2008)

Students with need: Out of 289 full-time freshmen who applied for aid, 235 were judged to have need. Of these, 235 received aid, and 235 had their full need met. Average financial aid package met 100% of need; average scholarship/grant was $32,574; average loan was $1,769.
Students without need: No-need awards available for athletics.
Scholarships offered: 38 full-time freshmen received athletic scholarships; average amount $36,840.
Cumulative student debt: 34% of graduating class had student loans; average debt was $20,164.

FINANCIAL AID PROCEDURES

Forms required: CSS PROFILE.
Dates and Deadlines: Closing date 1/15. Applicants notified by 4/1; must reply by 5/1 or within 2 week(s) of notification.
Transfers: Closing date 3/15. Applicants notified by 4/30; must reply by 5/15 or within 2 week(s) of notification. Financial aid for transfer students extremely limited.

CONTACT

Marcelle Tyburski, Director of Financial Aid
13 Oak Drive, Hamilton, NY 13346-1383
(315) 228-7431

College of Mount St. Vincent

Riverdale, New York
www.mountsaintvincent.edu
Federal Code: 002703

4-year private liberal arts college in very large city, affiliated with Roman Catholic Church.
Enrollment: 1,448 undergrads, 9% part-time. 375 full-time freshmen.
Selectivity: Admits 50 to 75% of applicants.

BASIC COSTS (2008-2009)

Tuition and fees: $24,600.
Per-credit charge: $700.
Room and board: $9,370.

FINANCIAL AID PICTURE (2007-2008)

Students with need: Need-based aid available for full-time students.
Students without need: No-need awards available for academics, alumni affiliation, leadership.

FINANCIAL AID PROCEDURES

Forms required: FAFSA, state aid form.
Dates and Deadlines: Priority date 3/1; no closing date. Applicants notified on a rolling basis starting 3/1; must reply by 5/1 or within 3 week(s) of notification.
Transfers: Priority date 5/15. Applicants notified on a rolling basis starting 3/1; must reply by 5/1 or within 3 week(s) of notification.

CONTACT

Monica Simotas, Director of Financial Aid
6301 Riverdale Avenue, Riverdale, NY 10471-1093
(718) 405-3289

College of New Rochelle

New Rochelle, New York
www.cnr.edu
Federal Code: 002704

4-year private nursing and liberal arts college for women in small city, affiliated with Roman Catholic Church.
Enrollment: 874 undergrads, 33% part-time. 111 full-time freshmen.
Selectivity: Admits less than 50% of applicants.

BASIC COSTS (2009-2010)

Tuition and fees: $26,426.
Per-credit charge: $861.
Room and board: $9,600.
Additional info: All incoming freshmen given laptop at no additional cost.

FINANCIAL AID PICTURE (2007-2008)

Students with need: Need-based aid available for full-time and part-time students. Work study available nights, weekends, and for part-time students.
Students without need: No-need awards available for academics, art, leadership.

FINANCIAL AID PROCEDURES

Forms required: FAFSA, institutional form.
Dates and Deadlines: Priority date 3/1; no closing date. Applicants notified on a rolling basis starting 1/1; must reply within 2 week(s) of notification.

CONTACT

Ann Pelak, Director of Financial Aid
29 Castle Place, New Rochelle, NY 10805-2339
(914) 654-5225

College of Saint Rose

Albany, New York
www.strose.edu
Federal Code: 002705

4-year private liberal arts and teachers college in small city, affiliated with Roman Catholic Church.
Enrollment: 3,051 undergrads, 7% part-time. 613 full-time freshmen.
Selectivity: Admits 50 to 75% of applicants.

BASIC COSTS (2009-2010)

Tuition and fees: $23,092.
Per-credit charge: $743.
Room and board: $9,454.

FINANCIAL AID PICTURE (2007-2008)

Students with need: Out of 582 full-time freshmen who applied for aid, 582 were judged to have need. Of these, 572 received aid, and 20 had their full need met. Average financial aid package met 49% of need; average scholarship/grant was $3,429; average loan was $1,660. For part-time students, average financial aid package was $4,924.
Students without need: 34 full-time freshmen who did not demonstrate need for aid received scholarships/grants; average award was $1,624. No-need awards available for academics, alumni affiliation, art, athletics, minority status, music/drama.
Scholarships offered: ***Merit:*** Rooney Gibbons Scholarship: $2,000 to full tuition; freshmen applicants admitted by February 1 automatically considered.

Athletic: 9 full-time freshmen received athletic scholarships; average amount $7,450.
Cumulative student debt: 84% of graduating class had student loans; average debt was $24,812.

FINANCIAL AID PROCEDURES
Forms required: FAFSA.
Dates and Deadlines: Priority date 3/1; no closing date. Applicants notified on a rolling basis starting 3/15; must reply by 5/1 or within 2 week(s) of notification.

CONTACT
Steve Dwire, Director of Financial Aid
432 Western Avenue, Albany, NY 12203
(518) 458-5424

College of Westchester
White Plains, New York
www.cw.edu Federal Code: 005208

2-year for-profit business and career college in large town.
Enrollment: 981 undergrads, 6% part-time. 388 full-time freshmen.

BASIC COSTS (2008-2009)
Tuition and fees: $19,800.
Per-credit charge: $630.
Additional info: Tuition/fee waivers available for unemployed or children of unemployed.

FINANCIAL AID PICTURE
Students with need: Need-based aid available for full-time and part-time students. Work study available nights, weekends, and for part-time students.
Students without need: No-need awards available for academics, alumni affiliation.

FINANCIAL AID PROCEDURES
Forms required: FAFSA, state aid form, institutional form.
Dates and Deadlines: No deadline. Applicants notified on a rolling basis starting 1/7; must reply within 2 week(s) of notification.

CONTACT
Dianne Pepitone, Director, Student Financial Services
325 Central Park Avenue, White Plains, NY 10602
(914) 948-4442 ext. 473

Columbia University
New York, New York Federal Code: E00485
www.columbia.edu CSS Code: 2116

4-year private university in very large city.
Enrollment: 5,667 undergrads. 1,356 full-time freshmen.
Selectivity: Admits less than 50% of applicants.

BASIC COSTS (2008-2009)
Tuition and fees: $39,326.
Room and board: $9,980.

FINANCIAL AID PICTURE (2008-2009)
Students with need: Out of 803 full-time freshmen who applied for aid, 645 were judged to have need. Of these, 645 received aid, and 645 had their full need met. Average financial aid package met 100% of need; average scholarship/grant was $33,901; average loan was $3,363.
Students without need: This college awards aid only to students with need.
Additional info: We have eliminated student loans for those receiving Columbia need-based aid and replaced them with additional University grants, and significantly reduced the parent contribution for families making less than $100,000 per year.

FINANCIAL AID PROCEDURES
Forms required: FAFSA, CSS PROFILE.
Dates and Deadlines: Closing date 3/2. Applicants notified by 4/1; must reply by 5/1.
Transfers: Closing date 4/20. Must reply within 3 week(s) of notification.

CONTACT
Office of Financial Aid
212 Hamilton Hall, MC 2807, New York, NY 10027
(212) 854-3711

Columbia University: School of General Studies
New York, New York
www.gs.columbia.edu Federal Code: E00487

4-year private university and liberal arts college in very large city.
Enrollment: 1,245 undergrads, 39% part-time. 18 full-time freshmen.
Selectivity: Admits less than 50% of applicants.

BASIC COSTS (2008-2009)
Tuition and fees: $37,958.
Per-credit charge: $1,210.
Room and board: $11,261.

FINANCIAL AID PICTURE (2008-2009)
Students with need: 61% of average financial aid package awarded as scholarships/grants, 39% awarded as loans/jobs. Need-based aid available for part-time students.
Students without need: This college awards aid only to students with need.
Scholarships offered: All applicants should submit General Studies Application for Financial Aid.

FINANCIAL AID PROCEDURES
Forms required: FAFSA, institutional form.
Dates and Deadlines: Priority date 4/15; closing date 6/1. Applicants notified on a rolling basis; must reply within 3 week(s) of notification.
Transfers: Applicants notified on a rolling basis starting 4/1; must reply within 2 week(s) of notification.

CONTACT
William Bailey, Director of Educational Financing
408 Lewisohn Hall, Mail Code 4101, New York, NY 10027
(212) 854-5410

Columbia-Greene Community College
Hudson, New York
www.sunycgcc.edu Federal Code: 006789

2-year public community college in small town.
Enrollment: 1,426 undergrads, 30% part-time. 396 full-time freshmen.
Selectivity: Open admission; but selective for some programs.

BASIC COSTS (2008-2009)
Tuition and fees: $3,496; out-of-state residents $6,712.
Per-credit charge: $134; out-of-state residents $268.

FINANCIAL AID PICTURE (2007-2008)
Students with need: 51% of average financial aid package awarded as scholarships/grants, 49% awarded as loans/jobs. Need-based aid available for part-time students. Work study available nights, weekends, and for part-time students.

Students without need: No-need awards available for academics, state/district residency.

FINANCIAL AID PROCEDURES

Forms required: FAFSA, institutional form.

Dates and Deadlines: Priority date 5/1; no closing date. Applicants notified on a rolling basis starting 7/1; must reply within 2 week(s) of notification.

CONTACT

Earl Tretheway, Director of Financial Aid
4400 Route 23, Hudson, NY 12534

Concordia College

Bronxville, New York
www.concordia-ny.edu Federal Code: 002709

4-year private liberal arts college in small town, affiliated with Lutheran Church - Missouri Synod.

Enrollment: 673 undergrads.

Selectivity: Admits 50 to 75% of applicants.

BASIC COSTS (2008-2009)

Tuition and fees: $22,930.

Room and board: $8,745.

FINANCIAL AID PICTURE

Students with need: Need-based aid available for full-time and part-time students. Work study available nights, weekends, and for part-time students.

Students without need: No-need awards available for academics, athletics, leadership, music/drama.

Scholarships offered: Fellows Scholarship: $15,000 a year; for 1800 SAT (exclusive of Writing) and 95 average. Merit Scholarships: $6,000-$9,000 for 80 average and above. Lutheran students grants available.

FINANCIAL AID PROCEDURES

Forms required: FAFSA, state aid form.

Dates and Deadlines: Priority date 4/1; no closing date. Applicants notified on a rolling basis starting 4/1; must reply by 5/1 or within 3 week(s) of notification.

CONTACT

Janice Spikereit, Director of Financial Aid
171 White Plains Road, Bronxville, NY 10708
(914) 337-9300 ext. 2146

Cooper Union for the Advancement of Science and Art

New York, New York Federal Code: 002710
www.cooper.edu CSS Code: 2097

4-year private visual arts and engineering college in very large city.

Enrollment: 898 undergrads. 206 full-time freshmen.

Selectivity: Admits less than 50% of applicants.

BASIC COSTS (2008-2009)

Tuition and fees: $34,650.

Room only: $9,900.

Additional info: Every student admitted receives full-tuition scholarship (covering tuition only) for duration of enrollment. International students assessed annual filing fee of $1,750.

FINANCIAL AID PICTURE (2007-2008)

Students with need: Out of 123 full-time freshmen who applied for aid, 61 were judged to have need. Of these, 61 received aid, and 39 had their full need met. Average financial aid package met 92% of need; average scholarship/grant was $3,249; average loan was $3,271.

Students without need: 145 full-time freshmen who did not demonstrate need for aid received scholarships/grants; average award was $33,000. No-need awards available for academics.

Cumulative student debt: 29% of graduating class had student loans; average debt was $9,900.

Additional info: All students receive full-tuition scholarships valued at approximately $33,000 per year. Students able to document need receive financial aid package that may include combination of grants, loans, work-study, internships.

FINANCIAL AID PROCEDURES

Forms required: FAFSA, CSS PROFILE.

Dates and Deadlines: Priority date 4/15; closing date 6/1. Applicants notified by 6/1; must reply by 6/30 or within 2 week(s) of notification.

Transfers: Priority date 4/1; closing date 5/1. Applicants notified by 6/1; must reply by 6/30 or within 2 week(s) of notification. Late financial aid applications processed on rolling basis.

CONTACT

Mary Ruokonen, Director of Financial Aid
30 Cooper Square, Suite 300, New York, NY 10003-7183
(212) 353-4130

Cornell University

Ithaca, New York Federal Code: 002711
www.cornell.edu CSS Code: 2098

4-year private university in large town.

Enrollment: 13,772 undergrads. 3,139 full-time freshmen.

Selectivity: Admits less than 50% of applicants.

BASIC COSTS (2009-2010)

Tuition and fees: $37,954.

Room and board: $12,160.

Additional info: Tuition amounts listed are for Endowed/Private colleges only: Architecture, Art & Planning; Arts & Sciences; Engineering; Hotel Administration. Contract/State college amounts differ and vary by residency and program.

FINANCIAL AID PICTURE (2008-2009)

Students with need: Out of 1,414 full-time freshmen who applied for aid, 1,246 were judged to have need. Of these, 1,246 received aid, and 1,246 had their full need met. Average financial aid package met 100% of need; average scholarship/grant was $26,649; average loan was $2,321.

Students without need: This college awards aid only to students with need.

Cumulative student debt: 52% of graduating class had student loans; average debt was $23,485.

Additional info: Need-based loans eliminated for undergraduates with family incomes under $60,000, and capped annually at $3,000 for incomes $60,000-$120,000.

FINANCIAL AID PROCEDURES

Forms required: FAFSA, CSS PROFILE, institutional form.

Dates and Deadlines: Closing date 1/5. Applicants notified by 4/1; must reply by 5/1.

Transfers: Priority date 2/15; closing date 3/15. Applicants notified on a rolling basis starting 3/15; must reply by 6/1 or within 2 week(s) of notification. Submit Cornell aid application forms in addition to regular required forms.

CONTACT

Thomas Keane, Director, Financial Aid and Student Employment
410 Thurston Avenue, Ithaca, NY 14850-2488
(607) 255-2000

Corning Community College
Corning, New York
www.corning-cc.edu Federal Code: 002863

2-year public community college in large town.
Enrollment: 3,189 undergrads.
Selectivity: Open admission; but selective for some programs.

BASIC COSTS (2008-2009)
Tuition and fees: $3,850; out-of-state residents $7,320.
Per-credit charge: $145; out-of-state residents $290.

FINANCIAL AID PICTURE
Students with need: Need-based aid available for full-time and part-time students. Work study available weekends and for part-time students.
Students without need: This college awards aid only to students with need.

FINANCIAL AID PROCEDURES
Forms required: FAFSA.
Dates and Deadlines: Priority date 4/1; no closing date. Applicants notified on a rolling basis starting 4/15; must reply within 2 week(s) of notification.

CONTACT
Barbara Snow, Director of Financial Aid
One Academic Drive, Corning, NY 14830
(607) 962-9011

Culinary Institute of America
Hyde Park, New York
www.ciachef.edu Federal Code: 007304

4-year private culinary school in large town.
Enrollment: 2,728 undergrads. 571 full-time freshmen.
Selectivity: Admits over 75% of applicants.

BASIC COSTS (2009-2010)
Tuition and fees: $24,630.
Room and board: $8,110.
Additional info: Room and board costs shown for typical undergraduate; costs may vary.

FINANCIAL AID PICTURE (2007-2008)
Students with need: Need-based aid available for full-time students. Work study available nights, weekends, and for part-time students.
Students without need: No-need awards available for academics, alumni affiliation, job skills, leadership, minority status.
Scholarships offered: Cream of the Crop Scholarship: up to $20,000; 10 per year; for prospective students with outstanding academic and leadership skills

FINANCIAL AID PROCEDURES
Forms required: FAFSA.
Dates and Deadlines: Priority date 12/15; no closing date. Applicants notified by 4/1; must reply by 5/1 or within 4 week(s) of notification.

CONTACT
Patricia Arcuri, Director of Financial Aid
1946 Campus Drive, Hyde Park, NY 12538-1499
(845) 451-1243

Daemen College
Amherst, New York
www.daemen.edu Federal Code: 002808

4-year private liberal arts college in small city.
Enrollment: 1,650 undergrads, 14% part-time. 406 full-time freshmen.
Selectivity: Admits 50 to 75% of applicants.

BASIC COSTS (2008-2009)
Tuition and fees: $19,870.
Per-credit charge: $645.
Room and board: $9,050.

FINANCIAL AID PICTURE (2007-2008)
Students with need: Need-based aid available for full-time and part-time students. Work study available nights, weekends, and for part-time students.
Students without need: No-need awards available for academics, art, athletics, leadership.
Scholarships offered: President's Scholarship, Dean's Scholarship, and Alumni Grant: $2,500-$10,000; renewable awards to freshmen and transfers, based on high school GPA & SAT scores. Competitive and renewable Trustee Scholarship: $17,000 (2 awards) and $14,000 (4 awards). Renewable visual arts scholarships: $5,000; 2 awards.

FINANCIAL AID PROCEDURES
Forms required: FAFSA, state aid form.
Dates and Deadlines: Priority date 2/15; no closing date. Applicants notified on a rolling basis starting 2/1; must reply within 2 week(s) of notification.

CONTACT
Jeffrey Pagano, Director of Financial Aid
4380 Main Street, Amherst, NY 14226-3592
(716) 839-8254

Davis College
Johnson City, New York
www.davisny.edu Federal Code: 015291

4-year private Bible college in large town, affiliated with nondenominational tradition.
Enrollment: 241 undergrads.

BASIC COSTS (2008-2009)
Tuition and fees: $12,250.
Per-credit charge: $375.
Room and board: $6,000.

FINANCIAL AID PICTURE (2007-2008)
Students with need: 59% of average financial aid package awarded as scholarships/grants, 41% awarded as loans/jobs.

FINANCIAL AID PROCEDURES
Forms required: FAFSA, institutional form.
Dates and Deadlines: No deadline. Applicants notified on a rolling basis.

CONTACT
Stephanie Baker, Director of Financial Aid
400 Riverside Drive, Johnson City, NY 13790
(607) 729-1581 ext. 401

Devry College of New York
Long Island City, New York
www.devry.edu Federal Code: 003099

4-year for-profit business and technical college in very large city.
Enrollment: 936 undergrads, 22% part-time. 111 full-time freshmen.

BASIC COSTS (2008-2009)
Tuition and fees: $14,800.
Per-credit charge: $540.

FINANCIAL AID PICTURE (2007-2008)
Students with need: Out of 92 full-time freshmen who applied for aid, 81 were judged to have need. Of these, 80 received aid. Average financial aid package met 43% of need; average scholarship/grant was $8,390; average loan was $6,580. For part-time students, average financial aid package was $11,659.
Students without need: This college awards aid only to students with need.
Cumulative student debt: 100% of graduating class had student loans; average debt was $29,136.

FINANCIAL AID PROCEDURES
Forms required: FAFSA.
Dates and Deadlines: No deadline. Applicants notified on a rolling basis.

CONTACT
Elvira Senese, Director, Student Finance
3020 Thomson Avenue, Long Island City, NY 11101-3051
(718) 472-2728

Dominican College of Blauvelt
Orangeburg, New York
www.dc.edu Federal Code: 002713

4-year private The College has six divisions: Allied Health, Arts & Sciences, Business, Nursing, Social Sciences, and Teacher Education. in small town.
Enrollment: 1,612 undergrads, 25% part-time. 304 full-time freshmen.
Selectivity: Admits over 75% of applicants.

BASIC COSTS (2009-2010)
Tuition and fees: $21,120.
Room and board: $9,730.

FINANCIAL AID PICTURE (2008-2009)
Students with need: Need-based aid available for full-time and part-time students. Work study available nights, weekends, and for part-time students.
Students without need: No-need awards available for academics, athletics.
Scholarships offered: All applicants considered for non-need based scholarships or grants based on high school GPA and SAT/ACT scores.
Additional info: Individual financial aid counseling available.

FINANCIAL AID PROCEDURES
Forms required: FAFSA, state aid form.
Dates and Deadlines: Priority date 2/15; no closing date. Applicants notified on a rolling basis starting 2/1.

CONTACT
Eileen Felske, Director of Financial Aid
470 Western Highway, Orangeburg, NY 10962-1210
(845) 848-7821

Dowling College
Oakdale, New York
www.dowling.edu Federal Code: 002667

4-year private liberal arts college in large town.
Enrollment: 3,288 undergrads, 36% part-time. 491 full-time freshmen.
Selectivity: Admits over 75% of applicants.

BASIC COSTS (2008-2009)
Tuition and fees: $20,310.
Per-credit charge: $636.
Room and board: $9,140.

FINANCIAL AID PICTURE (2008-2009)
Students with need: Out of 357 full-time freshmen who applied for aid, 348 were judged to have need. Of these, 348 received aid, and 1 had their full need met. Average financial aid package met 92% of need; average scholarship/grant was $3,545; average loan was $3,632. For part-time students, average financial aid package was $7,319.
Students without need: 61 full-time freshmen who did not demonstrate need for aid received scholarships/grants; average award was $5,657. No-need awards available for academics, alumni affiliation, athletics.
Scholarships offered: 46 full-time freshmen received athletic scholarships; average amount $3,130.
Cumulative student debt: 73% of graduating class had student loans; average debt was $48,161.

FINANCIAL AID PROCEDURES
Forms required: FAFSA, state aid form.
Dates and Deadlines: Priority date 4/30; no closing date. Applicants notified on a rolling basis starting 3/1.
Transfers: No deadline. Applicants notified on a rolling basis. Academic scholarships available for transfers with associate degrees.

CONTACT
Patricia Noren, Director of Student Financial Services & Bursar
150 Idle Hour Boulevard, Oakdale, NY 11769-1999
(631) 244-3368

Dutchess Community College
Poughkeepsie, New York
www.sunydutchess.edu Federal Code: 002864

2-year public community college in large town.
Enrollment: 6,434 undergrads. 1,917 full-time freshmen.
Selectivity: Open admission; but selective for some programs.

BASIC COSTS (2008-2009)
Tuition and fees: $3,292; out-of-state residents $6,167.
Per-credit charge: $120; out-of-state residents $240.

FINANCIAL AID PICTURE (2007-2008)
Students with need: 85% of average financial aid package awarded as scholarships/grants, 15% awarded as loans/jobs. Need-based aid available for part-time students.

FINANCIAL AID PROCEDURES
Forms required: FAFSA, state aid form, institutional form.
Dates and Deadlines: Priority date 5/1; no closing date. Applicants notified on a rolling basis starting 5/15; must reply within 2 week(s) of notification.

CONTACT
Susan Mead, Director of Financial Aid
53 Pendell Road, Poughkeepsie, NY 12601-1595
(845) 431-8030

D'Youville College
Buffalo, New York
www.dyc.edu Federal Code: 002712

4-year private health science and liberal arts college in large city.
Enrollment: 1,614 undergrads, 14% part-time. 164 full-time freshmen.
Selectivity: Admits over 75% of applicants.

BASIC COSTS (2008-2009)
Tuition and fees: $19,000.
Room and board: $9,300.
Additional info: Substantial tuition reduction depending on SAT scores.

FINANCIAL AID PICTURE (2007-2008)

Students with need: Out of 158 full-time freshmen who applied for aid, 141 were judged to have need. Of these, 141 received aid, and 55 had their full need met. Average financial aid package met 82% of need; average scholarship/grant was $10,465; average loan was $5,365. For part-time students, average financial aid package was $14,072.

Students without need: 18 full-time freshmen who did not demonstrate need for aid received scholarships/grants; average award was $6,253. No-need awards available for academics, leadership, religious affiliation, ROTC.

Scholarships offered: Presidential Honors Scholarship: for all students with 1100 SAT (math & verbal scores only) or 24 ACT score; covers 50% of tuition and 25% of standard double room rate in Marguerite Hall or 25% of standard rate in the apartments for full-time residents. Academic Initiative Scholarship: For students with 1000-1090 SAT (math & verbal scores only) or 21-23 ACT score and an 85 high school average. The award is for 25% of tuition and 50% of the standard double room rate in Marguerite Hall or 50% of the standard room rate in the apartments for full-time students. Achievement Scholarship: For students with 900-1090 SAT score or 19-23 ACT and an 80-84 high school average, demonstrated leadership and community service. The awards range from $1,000- $4,000. Transfer Achievement Scholarship: For students with a G.P.A. of 2.75-4.0 from previously attended institution(s). The award amounts range from $2,500-$5,000. All awards are renewable for the standard duration of the specific academic program and have GPA and other requirements.

Cumulative student debt: 71% of graduating class had student loans; average debt was $28,873.

FINANCIAL AID PROCEDURES

Forms required: FAFSA, state aid form.

Dates and Deadlines: Priority date 3/1; no closing date. Applicants notified on a rolling basis starting 4/1; must reply within 2 week(s) of notification.

Transfers: Applicants notified on a rolling basis starting 4/1; must reply within 2 week(s) of notification.

CONTACT

Lorraine Metz, Director of Financial Aid
320 Porter Avenue, Buffalo, NY 14201-1084
(716) 829-7500

Eastman School of Music of the University of Rochester

Rochester, New York
www.esm.rochester.edu Federal Code: 008124

4-year private music and performing arts college in large city.

Enrollment: 500 undergrads.

BASIC COSTS (2008-2009)

Tuition and fees: $36,100.

Per-credit charge: $1,050.

Room and board: $11,020.

FINANCIAL AID PICTURE (2007-2008)

Students with need: 78% of average financial aid package awarded as scholarships/grants, 22% awarded as loans/jobs. Need-based aid available for part-time students.

Students without need: No-need awards available for academics, alumni affiliation, job skills, leadership, minority status, music/drama, state/district residency.

Scholarships offered: All merit scholarships awarded based on admission criteria, and do not require separate application, audition, or interview.

FINANCIAL AID PROCEDURES

Forms required: FAFSA, state aid form, institutional form.

Dates and Deadlines: Closing date 2/28. Applicants notified on a rolling basis starting 3/15; must reply by 5/1 or within 2 week(s) of notification.

Transfers: No deadline. Applicants notified on a rolling basis starting 3/15; must reply by 5/1 or within 2 week(s) of notification.

CONTACT

Mary Ellen Nugent, Director of Financial Aid
26 Gibbs Street, Rochester, NY 14604-2599
(585) 274-1070

Elmira Business Institute

Elmira, New York
www.ebi-college.com Federal Code: 009043

2-year for-profit business and technical college in large town.

Enrollment: 150 undergrads.

Selectivity: Open admission.

BASIC COSTS (2008-2009)

Tuition and fees: $9,800.

Per-credit charge: $320.

Additional info: Tuition varies by program. Tuition at time of enrollment locked for 2 years.

FINANCIAL AID PICTURE (2007-2008)

Students with need: Need-based aid available for full-time and part-time students.

Students without need: This college awards aid only to students with need.

FINANCIAL AID PROCEDURES

Forms required: FAFSA, state aid form, institutional form.

Dates and Deadlines: Closing date 5/1.

CONTACT

Sue Reinbold, Financial Aid Director
303 North Main Street, Elmira, NY 14901
(607) 729-8915

Elmira Business Institute: Vestal

Vestal, New York
www.ebi-college.com Federal Code: 9043

2-year for-profit business and technical college in small city.

Enrollment: 119 undergrads.

Selectivity: Open admission.

BASIC COSTS (2008-2009)

Tuition and fees: $9,800.

Per-credit charge: $320.

Additional info: Tuition varies by program.

FINANCIAL AID PICTURE

Students with need: Need-based aid available for full-time and part-time students.

Students without need: This college awards aid only to students with need.

FINANCIAL AID PROCEDURES

Forms required: FAFSA, state aid form, institutional form.

Dates and Deadlines: No deadline. Applicants notified on a rolling basis.

CONTACT

Sue Reinbold, Administrator
4100 Vestal Road, Vestal, NY 13850

Elmira College

Elmira, New York
www.elmira.edu Federal Code: 002718

4-year private liberal arts college in large town.
Enrollment: 1,272 undergrads, 16% part-time. 316 full-time freshmen.
Selectivity: Admits 50 to 75% of applicants. GED not accepted.

BASIC COSTS (2009-2010)
Tuition and fees: $34,800.
Room and board: $10,800.

FINANCIAL AID PICTURE (2008-2009)
Students with need: Out of 265 full-time freshmen who applied for aid, 246 were judged to have need. Of these, 246 received aid, and 47 had their full need met. Average financial aid package met 80% of need; average scholarship/grant was $21,232; average loan was $3,818. Need-based aid available for part-time students.
Students without need: 67 full-time freshmen who did not demonstrate need for aid received scholarships/grants; average award was $19,846. No-need awards available for academics, leadership, ROTC, state/district residency.
Scholarships offered: Valedictorian and salutatorian: 20 anticipated awards; full and 75% tuition respectively; renewable for four years. Scholarships based on GPA, test scores, class rank, leadership: $20,000, $18,000, $15,000, $10,000 or $6,000; renewable for four years.
Cumulative student debt: 81% of graduating class had student loans; average debt was $25,233.
Additional info: Sibling Scholarship program provides 50% discounts on second immediate family member's room and board, regardless of need.

FINANCIAL AID PROCEDURES
Forms required: FAFSA, state aid form.
Dates and Deadlines: Priority date 2/1; closing date 6/30. Applicants notified on a rolling basis starting 2/1; must reply by 5/1 or within 3 week(s) of notification.
Transfers: No deadline. Applicants notified on a rolling basis starting 2/1; must reply by 5/1 or within 3 week(s) of notification. Award for enrolled U.S. citizens from outside New York State. New merit scholarship for transfer students.

CONTACT
Kathleen Cohen, Dean of Financial Aid
One Park Place, Elmira, NY 14901
(607) 735-1728

Erie Community College: City Campus

Buffalo, New York
www.ecc.edu Federal Code: 010684

2-year public community college in large city.
Enrollment: 2,894 undergrads, 21% part-time. 662 full-time freshmen.
Selectivity: Open admission; but selective for some programs.

BASIC COSTS (2008-2009)
Tuition and fees: $3,690; out-of-state residents $6,877.
Per-credit charge: $133; out-of-state residents $266.

FINANCIAL AID PICTURE
Students with need: Need-based aid available for full-time and part-time students. Work study available weekends and for part-time students.
Students without need: This college awards aid only to students with need.

FINANCIAL AID PROCEDURES
Forms required: FAFSA, state aid form.
Dates and Deadlines: Priority date 6/1; no closing date. Applicants notified on a rolling basis starting 4/1; must reply within 2 week(s) of notification.

CONTACT
Scott Weltjen, Director of Financial Aid
121 Ellicott Street, Buffalo, NY 14203-2698
(716) 851-1177

Erie Community College: North Campus

Williamsville, New York
www.ecc.edu Federal Code: 010684

2-year public community college in small city.
Enrollment: 5,461 undergrads, 24% part-time. 1,217 full-time freshmen.
Selectivity: Open admission; but selective for some programs.

BASIC COSTS (2008-2009)
Tuition and fees: $3,690; out-of-state residents $6,877.
Per-credit charge: $133; out-of-state residents $266.

FINANCIAL AID PICTURE (2007-2008)
Students with need: Need-based aid available for full-time and part-time students. Work study available weekends and for part-time students.
Students without need: This college awards aid only to students with need.

FINANCIAL AID PROCEDURES
Forms required: FAFSA, state aid form.
Dates and Deadlines: Priority date 6/1; no closing date. Applicants notified on a rolling basis starting 4/1; must reply within 2 week(s) of notification.

CONTACT
Scott Weltjen, Director of Financial Aid
6205 Main Street, Williamsville, NY 14221-7095
(716) 851-1477

Erie Community College: South Campus

Orchard Park, New York
www.ecc.edu Federal Code: 010684

2-year public community college in large town.
Enrollment: 3,289 undergrads, 21% part-time. 862 full-time freshmen.
Selectivity: Open admission; but selective for some programs.

BASIC COSTS (2008-2009)
Tuition and fees: $3,690; out-of-state residents $6,877.
Per-credit charge: $133; out-of-state residents $266.

FINANCIAL AID PICTURE
Students with need: Need-based aid available for full-time and part-time students. Work study available weekends and for part-time students.
Students without need: This college awards aid only to students with need.

FINANCIAL AID PROCEDURES
Forms required: FAFSA, state aid form.
Dates and Deadlines: Priority date 6/1; no closing date. Applicants notified on a rolling basis starting 4/1; must reply within 2 week(s) of notification.

CONTACT
Scott Weltjen, Director of Financial Aid
4041 Southwestern Boulevard, Orchard Park, NY 14127-2199
(716) 851-1677

Eugene Lang College The New School for Liberal Arts

New York, New York
www.lang.edu Federal Code: 002780

4-year private liberal arts college in very large city.
Enrollment: 1,347 undergrads, 6% part-time. 297 full-time freshmen.
Selectivity: Admits 50 to 75% of applicants.

BASIC COSTS (2009-2010)

Tuition and fees: $34,550.
Per-credit charge: $1,150.
Room and board: $16,390.

FINANCIAL AID PICTURE (2008-2009)

Students with need: Out of 187 full-time freshmen who applied for aid, 170 were judged to have need. Of these, 170 received aid, and 20 had their full need met. Average financial aid package met 80% of need; average scholarship/grant was $21,287; average loan was $8,675.
Students without need: 51 full-time freshmen who did not demonstrate need for aid received scholarships/grants; average award was $7,010. No-need awards available for academics, music/drama.
Cumulative student debt: 68% of graduating class had student loans; average debt was $21,511.

FINANCIAL AID PROCEDURES

Forms required: FAFSA.
Dates and Deadlines: No deadline. Applicants notified on a rolling basis starting 3/1; must reply within 4 week(s) of notification.
Transfers: Must reply within 4 week(s) of notification.

CONTACT

Eileen Doyle, Assistant Vice President for Financial Aid
65 West 11th Street (3rd floor), New York, NY 10011
(212) 229-8930

Excelsior College

Albany, New York
www.excelsior.edu Federal Code: 014251

4-year private virtual liberal arts college in small city.
Enrollment: 32,133 undergrads.
Selectivity: Open admission; but selective for some programs.

BASIC COSTS (2008-2009)

Additional info: Students charged $895 enrollment fee and $300 per credit hour. Because of nontraditional pricing, school does not charge set tuition based on 15 credit hours per semester.

FINANCIAL AID PICTURE (2007-2008)

Students with need: 20% of average financial aid package awarded as scholarships/grants, 80% awarded as loans/jobs. Need-based aid available for part-time students.
Students without need: This college awards aid only to students with need.
Additional info: Excelsior College is Title IV eligible for certain degree programs. College approved for all veterans educational benefit programs.

FINANCIAL AID PROCEDURES

Forms required: FAFSA, institutional form.
Dates and Deadlines: Priority date 7/1; no closing date. Applicants notified on a rolling basis starting 8/1; must reply within 2 week(s) of notification.

CONTACT

Thomas Dalton, Assistant Vice President for Enrollment Management
7 Columbia Circle, Albany, NY 12203-5159
(518) 464-8500

Fashion Institute of Technology

New York, New York
www.fitnyc.edu Federal Code: 002866

4-year public visual arts and business college in very large city.
Enrollment: 7,706 undergrads, 12% part-time. 1,104 full-time freshmen.
Selectivity: Admits less than 50% of applicants.

BASIC COSTS (2008-2009)

Tuition and fees: $3,854; out-of-state residents $10,682.
Per-credit charge: $142; out-of-state residents $427.
Room and board: $10,440.

FINANCIAL AID PICTURE (2008-2009)

Students with need: Need-based aid available for full-time and part-time students.
Students without need: This college awards aid only to students with need.

FINANCIAL AID PROCEDURES

Forms required: FAFSA, state aid form, institutional form.
Dates and Deadlines: Priority date 2/1; no closing date. Applicants notified on a rolling basis starting 4/15; must reply within 2 week(s) of notification.

CONTACT

Mina Friedmann, Director of Financial Aid
Seventh Avenue at 27th Street, New York, NY 10001-5992
(212) 217-7999

Finger Lakes Community College

Canandaigua, New York
www.flcc.edu Federal Code: 007532

2-year public community college in small town.
Enrollment: 3,941 undergrads, 21% part-time. 1,201 full-time freshmen.
Selectivity: Open admission; but selective for some programs.

BASIC COSTS (2008-2009)

Tuition and fees: $3,642; out-of-state residents $6,888.
Per-credit charge: $123; out-of-state residents $246.

FINANCIAL AID PICTURE (2007-2008)

Students with need: Out of 1,031 full-time freshmen who applied for aid, 813 were judged to have need. Of these, 811 received aid. Need-based aid available for part-time students.
Students without need: This college awards aid only to students with need.

FINANCIAL AID PROCEDURES

Forms required: FAFSA, state aid form, institutional form.
Dates and Deadlines: Priority date 4/1; no closing date. Applicants notified on a rolling basis starting 3/1; must reply within 2 week(s) of notification.

CONTACT

Susan Romano, Director, Financial Aid
4355 Lake Shore Drive, Canandaigua, NY 14424-8395
(585) 394-3500 ext. 7275

Five Towns College

Dix Hills, New York
www.ftc.edu Federal Code: 012561

4-year for-profit music and liberal arts college in large town.
Enrollment: 1,117 undergrads. 323 full-time freshmen.

BASIC COSTS (2008-2009)
Tuition and fees: $17,800.
Per-credit charge: $725.
Room and board: $11,750.

FINANCIAL AID PICTURE (2008-2009)
Students with need: Out of 200 full-time freshmen who applied for aid, 172 were judged to have need. Of these, 172 received aid, and 122 had their full need met. Average financial aid package met 48% of need; average scholarship/grant was $6,500; average loan was $3,500. For part-time students, average financial aid package was $4,000.
Students without need: 25 full-time freshmen who did not demonstrate need for aid received scholarships/grants; average award was $2,000. No-need awards available for academics, music/drama.
Cumulative student debt: 80% of graduating class had student loans; average debt was $21,000.

FINANCIAL AID PROCEDURES
Forms required: FAFSA, state aid form, institutional form.
Dates and Deadlines: Priority date 3/31; no closing date. Applicants notified on a rolling basis; must reply within 4 week(s) of notification.
Transfers: No deadline. Applicants notified on a rolling basis starting 1/1; must reply within 4 week(s) of notification.

CONTACT
Mary Venezia, Director of Financial Aid
305 North Service Road, Dix Hills, NY 11746-6055
(631) 424-7000 ext. 2113

Fordham University
Bronx, New York — Federal Code: 002722
www.fordham.edu — CSS Code: 2259

4-year private university in very large city, affiliated with Roman Catholic Church.
Enrollment: 7,882 undergrads, 7% part-time. 1,853 full-time freshmen.
Selectivity: Admits less than 50% of applicants.

BASIC COSTS (2008-2009)
Tuition and fees: $35,257.
Per-credit charge: $739.
Room and board: $12,980.

FINANCIAL AID PICTURE (2007-2008)
Students with need: Need-based aid available for full-time and part-time students.
Students without need: No-need awards available for academics, athletics, ROTC.

FINANCIAL AID PROCEDURES
Forms required: FAFSA, CSS PROFILE.
Dates and Deadlines: Closing date 2/1. Applicants notified by 3/31; must reply by 5/1 or within 2 week(s) of notification.
Transfers: Priority date 2/1; closing date 5/1.

CONTACT
Angela Van Dekker, Assistant Vice President of Student Financial Services
East 441 Fordham Road, Bronx, NY 10458
(718) 817-3800

Fulton-Montgomery Community College
Johnstown, New York
www.fmcc.suny.edu — Federal Code: 002867

2-year public community college in large town.
Enrollment: 1,887 undergrads.
Selectivity: Open admission; but selective for some programs.

BASIC COSTS (2008-2009)
Tuition and fees: $3,518; out-of-state residents $6,662.
Per-credit charge: $131; out-of-state residents $262.

FINANCIAL AID PICTURE (2007-2008)
Students with need: Need-based aid available for full-time and part-time students. Work study available nights, weekends, and for part-time students.
Students without need: No-need awards available for academics.
Scholarships offered: Academic Excellence Scholarship: $1,000 a year with limit of 2 years for residents of Fulton, Montgomery, or Hamilton or Galway Central School District. Applicants must have 3.5 cumulative GPA, submit an essay and list of extracurricular activities, and be enrolled full-time at college. Must maintain 3.3 cumulative GPA. CTW Scholarship: $1,000 a year with limit of 2 years, for Montgomery residents or applicants who attend high school in Montgomery County. Applicants must have B average. Must maintain 3.3 cumulative GPA at end of first year.

FINANCIAL AID PROCEDURES
Forms required: FAFSA, state aid form.
Dates and Deadlines: Priority date 6/1; no closing date. Applicants notified on a rolling basis starting 6/15; must reply within 2 week(s) of notification.

CONTACT
Rebecca Cozzocrea, Coordinator of Financial Aid
2805 State Highway 67, Johnstown, NY 12095
(518) 762-4651 ext. 8201

Genesee Community College
Batavia, New York
www.genesee.edu — Federal Code: 006782

2-year public community college in large town.
Enrollment: 3,903 undergrads, 24% part-time. 1,103 full-time freshmen.
Selectivity: Open admission; but selective for some programs.

BASIC COSTS (2008-2009)
Tuition and fees: $3,690; out-of-state residents $4,580.
Per-credit charge: $140; out-of-state residents $160.

FINANCIAL AID PICTURE (2007-2008)
Students with need: Need-based aid available for part-time students. Work study available nights, weekends, and for part-time students.
Cumulative student debt: 74% of graduating class had student loans; average debt was $3,116.

FINANCIAL AID PROCEDURES
Forms required: FAFSA, state aid form.
Dates and Deadlines: Priority date 3/1; closing date 5/1. Applicants notified on a rolling basis starting 4/15; must reply within 2 week(s) of notification.
Transfers: No deadline.

CONTACT
Joseph Bailey, Director of Student Financial Services
One College Road, Batavia, NY 14020-9704
(585) 345-6900

Hamilton College
Clinton, New York — Federal Code: 002728
www.hamilton.edu — CSS Code: 2286

4-year private liberal arts college in rural community.
Enrollment: 1,834 undergrads. 462 full-time freshmen.
Selectivity: Admits less than 50% of applicants.

BASIC COSTS (2009-2010)
Tuition and fees: $39,760.
Room and board: $10,100.

FINANCIAL AID PICTURE (2008-2009)

Students with need: Out of 241 full-time freshmen who applied for aid, 189 were judged to have need. Of these, 189 received aid, and 189 had their full need met. Average financial aid package met 100% of need; average scholarship/grant was $28,647; average loan was $2,714.

Students without need: This college awards aid only to students with need.

Cumulative student debt: 43% of graduating class had student loans; average debt was $18,259.

Additional info: Will meet demonstrated need of all aided applicants. Effective with the 2008-2009 academic year, incoming students were no longer awarded merit scholarships. Upperclass students that had been awarded merit scholarships previously will continue to be awarded such until their graduation.

FINANCIAL AID PROCEDURES

Forms required: FAFSA, CSS PROFILE, state aid form, institutional form.

Dates and Deadlines: Closing date 2/8. Applicants notified by 4/1; must reply by 5/1.

CONTACT

Melissa Rose, Director of Financial Aid
198 College Hill Road, Clinton, NY 13323-1293
(315) 859-4434

Hartwick College

Oneonta, New York
www.hartwick.edu Federal Code: 002729

4-year private liberal arts college in large town.

Enrollment: 1,472 undergrads, 3% part-time. 499 full-time freshmen.

Selectivity: Admits over 75% of applicants.

BASIC COSTS (2009-2010)

Tuition and fees: $33,330.

Per-credit charge: $1,085.

Room and board: $9,075.

FINANCIAL AID PICTURE (2007-2008)

Students with need: Out of 412 full-time freshmen who applied for aid, 367 were judged to have need. Of these, 367 received aid, and 45 had their full need met. Average financial aid package met 75% of need; average scholarship/grant was $18,207; average loan was $5,200. For part-time students, average financial aid package was $9,343.

Students without need: 125 full-time freshmen who did not demonstrate need for aid received scholarships/grants; average award was $9,327. No-need awards available for academics, alumni affiliation, athletics, leadership, state/district residency.

Scholarships offered: 6 full-time freshmen received athletic scholarships; average amount $17,914.

Cumulative student debt: 71% of graduating class had student loans; average debt was $24,220.

FINANCIAL AID PROCEDURES

Forms required: FAFSA.

Dates and Deadlines: Priority date 2/15; no closing date. Applicants notified by 3/15; must reply within 2 week(s) of notification.

Transfers: Priority date 8/1; no deadline. Applicants notified on a rolling basis starting 3/15; must reply within 2 week(s) of notification.

CONTACT

Melissa Allen, Director of Financial Aid
Box 4022, Oneonta, NY 13820-4022
(607) 431-4130

Helene Fuld College of Nursing

New York, New York
www.helenefuld.edu Federal Code: 015395

2-year private nursing and junior college in very large city.

Enrollment: 403 undergrads.

Selectivity: Admits over 75% of applicants.

BASIC COSTS (2008-2009)

Tuition and fees: $14,118.

Per-credit charge: $252.

FINANCIAL AID PICTURE

Students with need: Need-based aid available for full-time and part-time students.

Students without need: This college awards aid only to students with need.

FINANCIAL AID PROCEDURES

Forms required: FAFSA, state aid form.

Dates and Deadlines: No deadline. Applicants notified on a rolling basis.

CONTACT

Andrine Thomas, Financial Aid Counselor and Loan Coordinator
24 East 120th Street, New York, NY 10035
(212) 616-7253

Herkimer County Community College

Herkimer, New York
www.herkimer.edu Federal Code: 004788

2-year public community college in small town.

Enrollment: 2,653 undergrads.

Selectivity: Open admission; but selective for some programs.

BASIC COSTS (2008-2009)

Tuition and fees: $3,550; out-of-state residents $6,020.

Per-credit charge: $120; out-of-state residents $233.

Additional info: Apartment-style dorms with a la carte meal service available. Tuition/fee waivers available for unemployed or children of unemployed.

FINANCIAL AID PICTURE

Students with need: Need-based aid available for full-time and part-time students. Work study available nights, weekends, and for part-time students.

FINANCIAL AID PROCEDURES

Forms required: FAFSA, state aid form.

Dates and Deadlines: Closing date 4/1. Applicants notified on a rolling basis starting 4/1; must reply within 2 week(s) of notification.

CONTACT

Susan Tripp, Director of Financial Aid
100 Reservoir Road, Herkimer, NY 13350-1598
(315) 866-0300 ext. 8282

Hilbert College

Hamburg, New York
www.hilbert.edu Federal Code: 002735

4-year private liberal arts college in large town, affiliated with Roman Catholic Church.

Enrollment: 957 undergrads, 26% part-time. 224 full-time freshmen.

Selectivity: Admits over 75% of applicants.

BASIC COSTS (2009-2010)
Tuition and fees: $17,950.
Per-credit charge: $410.
Room and board: $7,700.
Additional info: Tuition/fee waivers available for minority students.

FINANCIAL AID PICTURE (2007-2008)
Students with need: Out of 222 full-time freshmen who applied for aid, 203 were judged to have need. Of these, 202 received aid, and 34 had their full need met. Average financial aid package met 69% of need; average scholarship/grant was $7,563; average loan was $3,773. For part-time students, average financial aid package was $6,751.
Students without need: 19 full-time freshmen who did not demonstrate need for aid received scholarships/grants; average award was $9,034. No-need awards available for academics, job skills, leadership, minority status, state/district residency.
Cumulative student debt: 93% of graduating class had student loans; average debt was $26,538.

FINANCIAL AID PROCEDURES
Forms required: FAFSA, state aid form.
Dates and Deadlines: Priority date 3/1; no closing date. Applicants notified on a rolling basis starting 3/15; must reply within 2 week(s) of notification.

CONTACT
Beverly Chudy, Director of Student Financial Aid
5200 South Park Avenue, Hamburg, NY 14075-1597
(716) 649-7900

Hobart and William Smith Colleges
Geneva, New York — Federal Code: 002731
www.hws.edu — CSS Code: 2294

4-year private liberal arts college in large town.
Enrollment: 2,069 undergrads.
Selectivity: Admits 50 to 75% of applicants.

BASIC COSTS (2008-2009)
Tuition and fees: $38,860.
Room and board: $9,686.

FINANCIAL AID PICTURE (2007-2008)
Students with need: 78% of average financial aid package awarded as scholarships/grants, 22% awarded as loans/jobs. Work study available weekends and for part-time students.
Students without need: No-need awards available for academics, art, leadership, music/drama.
Scholarships offered: Cornelius and Muriel P. Wood Scholarship and Richard Hersh Scholarship: full tuition for 4 years. Trustee Scholarship for Academic Excellence: $20,000 annually, for 4 years; based on GPA, test scores, class standing; 50 awarded. Faculty Scholarships: from $3,000-$15,000; 25-50 awarded. Phi Theta Kappa Trustee Scholarship: $2,500-$20,000 annually; for academically qualified transfer students with 2-year degree from junior or community college. Presidential Leaders Scholarship: $3,000-$12,000; based on academic excellence, leadership, personal qualities; 25-50 awarded. Arts Scholarships: $3,000-$15,000; for special talent in visual and performing arts; 15 awarded. Blackwell Medical Scholarships: full tuition for four years; MCAT waived, guaranteed seat at Upstate Medical Center at Syracuse University.

FINANCIAL AID PROCEDURES
Forms required: FAFSA, CSS PROFILE, state aid form.
Dates and Deadlines: Closing date 2/15. Applicants notified by 4/1; must reply by 5/1 or within 2 week(s) of notification.
Transfers: No deadline. Applicants notified on a rolling basis; must reply within 2 week(s) of notification.

CONTACT
Beth Turner, Director of Financial Aid Services and Office of Student Employment
629 South Main Street, Geneva, NY 14456
(315) 781-3315

Hofstra University
Hempstead, New York
www.hofstra.edu — Federal Code: 002732

4-year private university in large city.
Enrollment: 8,179 undergrads, 7% part-time. 1,730 full-time freshmen.
Selectivity: Admits 50 to 75% of applicants.

BASIC COSTS (2008-2009)
Tuition and fees: $28,630.
Per-credit charge: $845.
Room and board: $10,825.

FINANCIAL AID PICTURE (2007-2008)
Students with need: Out of 1,386 full-time freshmen who applied for aid, 1,053 were judged to have need. Of these, 1,041 received aid, and 218 had their full need met. Average financial aid package met 61% of need; average scholarship/grant was $11,185; average loan was $3,575. For part-time students, average financial aid package was $8,832.
Students without need: 387 full-time freshmen who did not demonstrate need for aid received scholarships/grants; average award was $10,611. No-need awards available for academics, art, athletics, leadership, music/drama, ROTC, state/district residency.
Scholarships offered: ***Merit:*** Hofstra's Distinguished Academic Scholar Program: full tuition; number awarded varies; for students with outstanding academic achievement. Presidential Scholarship; partial tuition; number awarded varies; for students with high academic achievement. Special financial aid funds may be available for applicants with special talents. ***Athletic:*** 20 full-time freshmen received athletic scholarships; average amount $21,266.

FINANCIAL AID PROCEDURES
Forms required: FAFSA, state aid form.
Dates and Deadlines: Priority date 2/15; no closing date. Applicants notified on a rolling basis starting 3/1; must reply by 5/1 or within 2 week(s) of notification.

CONTACT
Jessica Eads, VP for Enrollment & Dean of Admission and Financial Aid
Admissions Center, 100 Hofstra University, Hempstead, NY 11549
(516) 463-8000

Houghton College
Houghton, New York
www.houghton.edu — Federal Code: 002734

4-year private liberal arts college in rural community, affiliated with Wesleyan Church.
Enrollment: 1,330 undergrads, 4% part-time. 329 full-time freshmen.
Selectivity: Admits over 75% of applicants.

BASIC COSTS (2009-2010)
Tuition and fees: $24,440.
Per-credit charge: $1,025.
Room and board: $7,000.
Additional info: Tuition includes laptop computer, fees. Tuition/fee waivers available for minority students.

FINANCIAL AID PICTURE (2008-2009)

Students with need: Out of 291 full-time freshmen who applied for aid, 261 were judged to have need. Of these, 261 received aid, and 42 had their full need met. Average financial aid package met 82% of need; average scholarship/grant was $15,718; average loan was $4,298. For part-time students, average financial aid package was $3,730.

Students without need: 63 full-time freshmen who did not demonstrate need for aid received scholarships/grants; average award was $12,010. No-need awards available for academics, alumni affiliation, art, athletics, music/drama, religious affiliation, ROTC, state/district residency.

Scholarships offered: ***Merit:*** Excellence Scholarships: $1,250-$7,500. Chamberlain Scholarships: $10,000; Heritage Scholarships: $15,000; 6 awarded each year. Phi Theta Kappa Transfer Scholarship: $2,000. Art Scholarships: $1,000-$5,000 (based on art portfolio). Music Scholarships: $1,000-$12,500 (based on audition). ***Athletic:*** 9 full-time freshmen received athletic scholarships; average amount $7,958.

Cumulative student debt: 81% of graduating class had student loans; average debt was $30,150.

Additional info: Wesley Full Tuition Grant offered to 25 new students each year. This grant covers the balance of tuition after all state and federal aid is awarded.

FINANCIAL AID PROCEDURES

Forms required: FAFSA.

Dates and Deadlines: Priority date 3/1; no closing date. Applicants notified on a rolling basis starting 3/15; must reply by 5/1.

Transfers: No deadline. Applicants notified on a rolling basis starting 3/1; must reply by 5/1 or within 4 week(s) of notification.

CONTACT

Troy Martin, Director of Student Financial Services
1 Willard Avenue/PO Box 128, Houghton, NY 14744-0128
(585) 567-9328

Iona College

New Rochelle, New York
www.iona.edu Federal Code: 002737

4-year private business and liberal arts college in small city, affiliated with Roman Catholic Church.

Enrollment: 3,442 undergrads, 3% part-time. 922 full-time freshmen.

Selectivity: Admits 50 to 75% of applicants.

BASIC COSTS (2009-2010)

Tuition and fees: $27,500.

Per-credit charge: $850.

Room and board: $11,300.

FINANCIAL AID PICTURE (2008-2009)

Students with need: Out of 912 full-time freshmen who applied for aid, 671 were judged to have need. Of these, 669 received aid, and 166 had their full need met. Average financial aid package met 26% of need; average scholarship/grant was $4,391; average loan was $2,554. For part-time students, average financial aid package was $3,591.

Students without need: 240 full-time freshmen who did not demonstrate need for aid received scholarships/grants; average award was $11,142. No-need awards available for academics, alumni affiliation, athletics, ROTC.

Scholarships offered: 59 full-time freshmen received athletic scholarships; average amount $14,991.

Cumulative student debt: 69% of graduating class had student loans; average debt was $19,905.

FINANCIAL AID PROCEDURES

Forms required: FAFSA, state aid form, institutional form.

Dates and Deadlines: Closing date 4/15. Applicants notified on a rolling basis starting 12/20; must reply by 5/1 or within 2 week(s) of notification.

Transfers: No deadline. Applicants notified on a rolling basis; must reply within 2 week(s) of notification.

CONTACT

Mary Grant, Director of Financial Aid
715 North Avenue, New Rochelle, NY 10801-1890
(914) 633-2497

Island Drafting and Technical Institute

Amityville, New York
www.idti.edu Federal Code: 007375

2-year for-profit technical and career college in large town.

Enrollment: 139 undergrads.

Selectivity: Open admission.

BASIC COSTS (2008-2009)

Tuition and fees: $13,100.

Per-credit charge: $425.

FINANCIAL AID PICTURE

Students with need: Need-based aid available for full-time students.

Students without need: This college awards aid only to students with need.

FINANCIAL AID PROCEDURES

Dates and Deadlines: No deadline. Applicants notified on a rolling basis.

CONTACT

Daniel Greener, Financial Aid Office
128 Broadway, Amityville, NY 11701-2704
(631) 691 8733

Ithaca College

Ithaca, New York
www.ithaca.edu Federal Code: 002739

4-year private health science and liberal arts college in large town.

Enrollment: 5,968 undergrads, 1% part-time. 1,441 full-time freshmen.

Selectivity: Admits 50 to 75% of applicants.

BASIC COSTS (2009-2010)

Tuition and fees: $32,060.

Per-credit charge: $1,067.

Room and board: $11,780.

Additional info: Tuition/fee waivers available for minority students.

FINANCIAL AID PICTURE (2008-2009)

Students with need: Out of 1,202 full-time freshmen who applied for aid, 989 were judged to have need. Of these, 989 received aid, and 561 had their full need met. Average financial aid package met 91% of need; average scholarship/grant was $18,510; average loan was $5,018. For part-time students, average financial aid package was $9,254.

Students without need: 281 full-time freshmen who did not demonstrate need for aid received scholarships/grants; average award was $8,419. No-need awards available for academics, alumni affiliation, leadership, minority status, music/drama, ROTC.

Scholarships offered: President's Scholarships: $12,000-$16,000; awarded for academic achievement to approximately top 10% of applicants. Dean's Scholarships: $8,000-$9,000; awarded for academic ability to approximately top 11% to 35% of applicants. ALANA Scholarships: $4,000-$7,000 in addition to President's or Dean's Scholarship; awarded for academic achievement to 25% of applicants who represent minority groups. Flora Brown Awards: $6,000; given to those not merit eligible but deserve recognition. MLK Scholarships: $18,000; awarded to approximately 15 students annually for academic excellence and community service. Ithaca Leadership Scholarships: $7,000; demonstrated leadership and above average academic performance; approximately 30 per year. Ithaca Premier Talent Scholarships: maximum $16,000 for selected applicants majoring in music and theater; approximately 10. Park Scholar Achievement: for outstanding achievement in communications; full cost of attendance; approximately 20 per year. Ithaca College Merit Scholarship and Ithaca College National Merit Recognition Award: $2,000 scholarship plus Ithaca College President's Scholarship of $16,000; for students who designate Ithaca College as their first-choice institution to the National Merit Scholarship Corporation.

FINANCIAL AID PROCEDURES

Forms required: FAFSA.

Dates and Deadlines: Priority date 2/1; no closing date. Applicants notified on a rolling basis starting 2/15. .

Transfers: No deadline. Applicants notified on a rolling basis starting 2/15; must reply by 5/1. All need-based and merit awards available for freshmen are also available for transfers.

CONTACT

Larry Chambers, Director of Student Financial Services
953 Danby Road, Ithaca, NY 14850
(607) 274-3131

Jamestown Business College

Jamestown, New York
www.jamestownbusinesscollege.edu Federal Code: 008495

2-year for-profit business and junior college in large town.

Enrollment: 263 undergrads.

BASIC COSTS (2008-2009)

Tuition and fees: $10,200.

FINANCIAL AID PICTURE (2007-2008)

Students with need: 65% of average financial aid package awarded as scholarships/grants, 35% awarded as loans/jobs. Need-based aid available for part-time students.

Students without need: No-need awards available for academics.

FINANCIAL AID PROCEDURES

Forms required: FAFSA, state aid form..

Dates and Deadlines: No deadline. Applicants notified on a rolling basis starting 2/15.

CONTACT

Diane Sturzenbecker, Financial Aid Officer
7 Fairmount Avenue, Jamestown, NY 14702-0429
(716) 664-5100

Jamestown Community College

Jamestown, New York
www.sunyjcc.edu Federal Code: 002869

2-year public community college in large town.

Enrollment: 3,220 undergrads, 24% part-time. 991 full-time freshmen.

Selectivity: Open admission; but selective for some programs.

BASIC COSTS (2008-2009)

Tuition and fees: $4,000; out-of-state residents $7,500.

Per-credit charge: $146; out-of-state residents $264.

FINANCIAL AID PICTURE (2008-2009)

Students with need: Out of 901 full-time freshmen who applied for aid, 708 were judged to have need. Of these, 705 received aid. Need-based aid available for part-time students.

Students without need: 41 full-time freshmen who did not demonstrate need for aid received scholarships/grants; average award was $3,160. No-need awards available for academics, alumni affiliation, art, athletics, music/drama, state/district residency.

Scholarships offered: 100% resident tuition scholarship (less federal and state grants) for students who apply for admissions by 3/1 and are in the top 20% of their high school graduating class with Regents diploma if residents of Chautauqua, Cattaraugus, or Allegany counties. Guaranteed in-state tuition rate for students in Warren, Potter, McKean, Forest, Elk and Cameron counties in Pennsylvania, in top 20% of graduating class with an academic diploma.

FINANCIAL AID PROCEDURES

Forms required: FAFSA, state aid form.

Dates and Deadlines: Priority date 3/1; no closing date. Applicants notified on a rolling basis starting 4/15.

CONTACT

Laurie Vorp, Director of Financial Aid
525 Falconer Street, Jamestown, NY 14702-0020
(800) 388-8557

Jefferson Community College

Watertown, New York
www.sunyjefferson.edu Federal Code: 002870

2-year public community college in large town.

Enrollment: 2,407 undergrads.

Selectivity: Open admission; but selective for some programs.

BASIC COSTS (2008-2009)

Tuition and fees: $3,601; out-of-state residents $5,501.

Per-credit charge: $132; out-of-state residents $195.

FINANCIAL AID PICTURE (2008-2009)

Students with need: Need-based aid available for full-time and part-time students.

Students without need: This college awards aid only to students with need.

FINANCIAL AID PROCEDURES

Forms required: FAFSA, state aid form, institutional form.

Dates and Deadlines: Priority date 4/1; closing date 8/15. Applicants notified on a rolling basis starting 4/15; must reply within 2 week(s) of notification.

Transfers: No deadline.

CONTACT

James Ambrose, Director of Financial Aid
1220 Coffeen Street, Watertown, NY 13601
(315) 786-2355

Jewish Theological Seminary of America

New York, New York
www.jtsa.edu CSS Code: 2339

4-year private rabbinical and seminary college in very large city, affiliated with Jewish faith.

Enrollment: 190 undergrads, 4% part-time. 45 full-time freshmen.

Selectivity: Admits 50 to 75% of applicants. GED not accepted.

BASIC COSTS (2008-2009)

Tuition and fees: $15,000.

Per-credit charge: $750.

Room only: $9,200.

Additional info: Costs quoted paid to school only; separate costs assessed for dual-degree enrollment at Columbia University/Barnard College.

FINANCIAL AID PICTURE (2008-2009)

Students with need: Need-based aid available for full-time students.

Students without need: No-need awards available for academics, alumni affiliation, leadership.

FINANCIAL AID PROCEDURES

Forms required: FAFSA, CSS PROFILE, state aid form, institutional form.
Dates and Deadlines: Priority date 2/1; closing date 3/1. Applicants notified on a rolling basis starting 4/1; must reply within 4 week(s) of notification.

CONTACT

Linda Levine, Registrar/Director of Financial Aid
3080 Broadway, New York, NY 10027
(212) 678-8007

Juilliard School

New York, New York
www.juilliard.edu Federal Code: 002742

4-year private music and performing arts college in very large city.
Enrollment: 500 undergrads. 118 full-time freshmen.
Selectivity: Admits less than 50% of applicants.

BASIC COSTS (2008-2009)

Tuition and fees: $28,640.
Room and board: $11,250.

FINANCIAL AID PICTURE (2008-2009)

Students with need: Out of 113 full-time freshmen who applied for aid, 96 were judged to have need. Of these, 96 received aid, and 29 had their full need met. Average financial aid package met 87% of need; average scholarship/grant was $23,776; average loan was $1,980. Need-based aid available for part-time students.
Students without need: 9 full-time freshmen who did not demonstrate need for aid received scholarships/grants; average award was $15,700. No-need awards available for music/drama.
Cumulative student debt: 71% of graduating class had student loans; average debt was $26,000.

FINANCIAL AID PROCEDURES

Forms required: FAFSA, institutional form.
Dates and Deadlines: Closing date 3/1. Applicants notified by 4/1; must reply by 5/1.
Transfers: Applicants notified by 4/1; must reply by 5/1 or within 2 week(s) of notification.

CONTACT

Tina Gonzalez, Director of Financial Aid
60 Lincoln Center Plaza, New York, NY 10023-6588
(212) 799-5000 ext. 211

Keuka College

Keuka Park, New York
www.keuka.edu Federal Code: 002744

4-year private liberal arts college in rural community, affiliated with American Baptist Churches in the USA.
Enrollment: 1,483 undergrads, 19% part-time. 279 full-time freshmen.
Selectivity: Admits over 75% of applicants.

BASIC COSTS (2008-2009)

Tuition and fees: $21,760.
Per-credit charge: $705.
Room and board: $8,850.

FINANCIAL AID PICTURE (2007-2008)

Students with need: Out of 278 full-time freshmen who applied for aid, 260 were judged to have need. Of these, 260 received aid, and 61 had their full need met. Average financial aid package met 74% of need; average scholarship/grant was $12,805; average loan was $5,464. For part-time students, average financial aid package was $5,490.
Students without need: 19 full-time freshmen who did not demonstrate need for aid received scholarships/grants; average award was $13,692. No-need awards available for academics, alumni affiliation, leadership, minority status, religious affiliation.
Scholarships offered: Goals Scholarship: 1/2 tuition; 82 average and 1000 SAT or 22 ACT required. Dean's Scholarship: 1/2-full tuition; 82 average and 1000 SAT or 22 ACT required. Presidential Scholarship: full tuition; based on GPA, SAT scores, class rank. SAT scores listed are exclusive of Writing portion.
Cumulative student debt: 95% of graduating class had student loans; average debt was $16,119.

FINANCIAL AID PROCEDURES

Forms required: FAFSA.
Dates and Deadlines: Priority date 3/15; no closing date. Applicants notified on a rolling basis starting 3/1; must reply by 5/1 or within 2 week(s) of notification.

CONTACT

Jerry Hiller, Vice President of Finance and Administration
141 Cental Avenue, Keuka Park, NY 14478-0098
(315) 279-5232

King's College

New York, New York
www.tkc.edu Federal Code: 040953

4-year private liberal arts college in very large city, affiliated with nondenominational tradition.
Enrollment: 254 undergrads, 2% part-time. 68 full-time freshmen.
Selectivity: Admits over 75% of applicants.

BASIC COSTS (2009-2010)

Tuition and fees: $25,000.
Per-credit charge: $1,027.
Room only: $9,000.

FINANCIAL AID PICTURE (2008-2009)

Students with need: Out of 55 full-time freshmen who applied for aid, 44 were judged to have need. Of these, 44 received aid, and 8 had their full need met. Average financial aid package met 59% of need; average scholarship/grant was $14,938; average loan was $3,500. For part-time students, average financial aid package was $5,031.
Students without need: 22 full-time freshmen who did not demonstrate need for aid received scholarships/grants; average award was $12,545. No-need awards available for academics.
Scholarships offered: Presidential Scholarships: unlimited number; based on SAT/ACT and National Merit; $1,500 to $8,000. Founders Scholarships: 4 awards; $10,000 each; based on essay and presentation; competition held in February.
Cumulative student debt: 54% of graduating class had student loans; average debt was $9,183.

FINANCIAL AID PROCEDURES

Forms required: FAFSA.
Dates and Deadlines: Priority date 3/15; no closing date. Applicants notified on a rolling basis.

CONTACT

Anna Peters, Director of Financial Aid
350 Fifth Avenue, Lower Lobby, New York, NY 10118
(212) 659-7281

Laboratory Institute of Merchandising

New York, New York
www.limcollege.edu Federal Code: 007466

4-year for-profit college of fashion business in very large city.
Enrollment: 1,308 undergrads, 4% part-time. 302 full-time freshmen.
Selectivity: Admits 50 to 75% of applicants.

BASIC COSTS (2008-2009)

Tuition and fees: $19,825.
Per-credit charge: $600.
Room and board: $18,700.

FINANCIAL AID PICTURE (2007-2008)

Students with need: Need-based aid available for full-time and part-time students.
Students without need: This college awards aid only to students with need.

FINANCIAL AID PROCEDURES

Forms required: FAFSA, state aid form, institutional form.
Dates and Deadlines: Priority date 4/1; no closing date. Applicants notified on a rolling basis starting 2/15; must reply within 2 week(s) of notification.

CONTACT

Christopher Barto, Dean of Student Financial Services
12 East 53rd Street, New York, NY 10022
(212) 752-1530

Le Moyne College

Syracuse, New York
www.lemoyne.edu Federal Code: 002748

4-year private liberal arts college in small city, affiliated with Roman Catholic Church.
Enrollment: 2,496 undergrads, 8% part-time. 578 full-time freshmen.
Selectivity: Admits 50 to 75% of applicants.

BASIC COSTS (2009-2010)

Tuition and fees: $25,830.
Per-credit charge: $526.
Room and board: $9,990.

FINANCIAL AID PICTURE (2007-2008)

Students with need: Out of 542 full-time freshmen who applied for aid, 480 were judged to have need. Of these, 479 received aid, and 112 had their full need met. Average financial aid package met 82% of need; average scholarship/grant was $10,855; average loan was $3,807. For part-time students, average financial aid package was $5,043.
Students without need: 52 full-time freshmen who did not demonstrate need for aid received scholarships/grants; average award was $8,624. No-need awards available for academics, alumni affiliation, athletics, leadership, minority status, ROTC.
Scholarships offered: ***Merit:*** Presidential Scholarships: $19,500. Dean Scholarships: $14,500. Ignation Scholarships (Jesuit High Schools): $14,500. Leadership Scholarships: $10,000; all based on academic criteria (GPA, rank, test scores). Loyola Scholarships: $14,500; for students of color; based on academic criteria. Academic Scholarship based on college GPA and minimum number of credit completed range from $2,500 to $7,500. Phi Theta Kappa members receive an additional $2,500 per academic year. ***Athletic:*** 39 full-time freshmen received athletic scholarships; average amount $8,274.
Cumulative student debt: 84% of graduating class had student loans; average debt was $19,123.
Additional info: Parent loan program at low interest, monthly payment plans and alternative loans for students.

FINANCIAL AID PROCEDURES

Forms required: FAFSA, state aid form, institutional form.
Dates and Deadlines: Priority date 2/1; no closing date. Applicants notified by 3/15; must reply by 5/1 or within 2 week(s) of notification.
Transfers: Priority date 6/1; no deadline. Must reply by 5/1 or within 2 week(s) of notification.

CONTACT

William Cheetham, Director of Financial Aid
1419 Salt Springs Road, Syracuse, NY 13214-1301
(315) 445-4400

Long Island Business Institute

Commack, New York
www.libi.edu Federal Code: 014514

2-year for-profit business college in large town.
Enrollment: 589 undergrads, 37% part-time. 158 full-time freshmen.
Selectivity: Open admission; but selective for some programs.

BASIC COSTS (2008-2009)

Tuition and fees: $10,200.
Per-credit charge: $325.
Additional info: Tuition varies by program.

FINANCIAL AID PICTURE (2008-2009)

Students with need: Out of 141 full-time freshmen who applied for aid, 141 were judged to have need. Of these, 141 received aid. Average financial aid package met 87% of need; average scholarship/grant was $3,300; average loan was $3,000. For part-time students, average financial aid package was $1,500.
Students without need: No-need awards available for academics.

FINANCIAL AID PROCEDURES

Forms required: FAFSA, state aid form.
Dates and Deadlines: No deadline. Must reply within 2 week(s) of notification.
Transfers: No deadline.

CONTACT

Nazaret Kiregian, Director of Financial Aid
6500 Jericho Turnpike, Commack, NY 11725
(631) 499-7100 ext. 13

Long Island University: Brooklyn Campus

Brooklyn, New York
www.liu.edu Federal Code: 004779

4-year private university and liberal arts college in very large city.
Enrollment: 3,830 undergrads, 18% part-time. 759 full-time freshmen.
Selectivity: Admits over 75% of applicants.

BASIC COSTS (2008-2009)

Tuition and fees: $27,365.
Per-credit charge: $814.
Room and board: $10,040.

FINANCIAL AID PICTURE (2008-2009)

Students with need: Need-based aid available for full-time and part-time students.

FINANCIAL AID PROCEDURES

Forms required: FAFSA.

Dates and Deadlines: Priority date 3/15; no closing date. Applicants notified on a rolling basis.

CONTACT

Rose Iannicelli, Dean of Student Financial Services
1 University Plaza, Brooklyn, NY 11201
(718) 488-1037

Long Island University: C. W. Post Campus

Brookville, New York — Federal Code: 002751
www.liu.edu — CSS Code: 2070

4-year private university and liberal arts college in small town.

Enrollment: 4,925 undergrads, 13% part-time. 882 full-time freshmen.

Selectivity: Admits over 75% of applicants.

BASIC COSTS (2008-2009)

Tuition and fees: $27,400.

Per-credit charge: $814.

Room and board: $10,520.

FINANCIAL AID PICTURE (2008-2009)

Students with need: Need-based aid available for full-time and part-time students. Work study available nights, weekends, and for part-time students.

FINANCIAL AID PROCEDURES

Forms required: FAFSA, CSS PROFILE, state aid form.

Dates and Deadlines: Priority date 3/1; no closing date. Applicants notified on a rolling basis starting 3/1; must reply by 5/1.

Transfers: Applicants notified on a rolling basis starting 3/1; must reply by 5/1.

CONTACT

Karen Urdahl, Director of Financial Assistance
720 Northern Boulevard, Brookville, NY 11548-1300
(516) 299-2338

Manhattan College

Riverdale, New York
www.manhattan.edu — Federal Code: 002758

4-year private engineering and liberal arts college in very large city, affiliated with Roman Catholic Church.

Enrollment: 3,025 undergrads, 3% part-time. 726 full-time freshmen.

Selectivity: Admits 50 to 75% of applicants.

BASIC COSTS (2009-2010)

Tuition and fees: $24,680.

Room and board: $9,770.

Additional info: Program fees range from $1,000 to $1,900 depending on program.

FINANCIAL AID PICTURE (2008-2009)

Students with need: Average financial aid package met 78% of need; average scholarship/grant was $9,040; average loan was $2,472.

Students without need: This college awards aid only to students with need.

Cumulative student debt: 72% of graduating class had student loans; average debt was $28,294.

FINANCIAL AID PROCEDURES

Forms required: FAFSA.

Dates and Deadlines: Priority date 3/1; closing date 4/1. Applicants notified on a rolling basis starting 2/15; must reply by 5/1.

Transfers: Priority date 4/1; no deadline.

CONTACT

Ed Keough, Director of Student Financial Services
4513 Manhattan College Parkway, Riverdale, NY 10471
(718) 862-7100

Manhattan School of Music

New York, New York — Federal Code: 002759
www.msmnyc.edu — CSS Code: 2396

4-year private music college in very large city.

Enrollment: 422 undergrads, 1% part-time. 69 full-time freshmen.

Selectivity: Admits less than 50% of applicants.

BASIC COSTS (2009-2010)

Tuition and fees: $31,900.

Per-credit charge: $1,300.

Room and board: $14,280.

Additional info: Health fees approximately $2,300 additional unless already insured.

FINANCIAL AID PICTURE (2007-2008)

Students with need: Out of 69 full-time freshmen who applied for aid, 58 were judged to have need. Of these, 55 received aid, and 8 had their full need met. Average financial aid package met 41% of need; average scholarship/grant was $14,869; average loan was $3,833. For part-time students, average financial aid package was $12,885.

Students without need: 7 full-time freshmen who did not demonstrate need for aid received scholarships/grants; average award was $11,142. No-need awards available for academics, alumni affiliation, leadership, music/drama.

Cumulative student debt: 52% of graduating class had student loans; average debt was $16,329.

FINANCIAL AID PROCEDURES

Forms required: FAFSA, CSS PROFILE, institutional form.

Dates and Deadlines: Closing date 3/1. Applicants notified by 4/1; must reply by 5/1 or within 2 week(s) of notification.

Transfers: Applicants notified by 4/1; must reply by 5/1 or within 2 week(s) of notification. CSS PROFILE required for transfer students.

CONTACT

Amy Anderson, Associate Dean for Enrollment Management
120 Claremont Avenue, New York, NY 10027-4698
(212) 749-2802 ext. 4463

Manhattanville College

Purchase, New York
www.manhattanville.edu — Federal Code: 002760

4-year private liberal arts and teachers college in small town.

Enrollment: 1,842 undergrads, 7% part-time. 341 full-time freshmen.

Selectivity: Admits 50 to 75% of applicants.

BASIC COSTS (2009-2010)

Tuition and fees: $32,760.

Per-credit charge: $730.

Room and board: $13,500.

FINANCIAL AID PICTURE (2007-2008)

Students with need: Out of 246 full-time freshmen who applied for aid, 233 were judged to have need. Of these, 231 received aid, and 20 had their full need met. For part-time students, average financial aid package was $1,619.

Students without need: 89 full-time freshmen who did not demonstrate need for aid received scholarships/grants; average award was $16,581. No-

need awards available for academics, alumni affiliation, art, leadership, music/drama.
Additional info: Upper level students may earn additional money and academic credit through internship program.

FINANCIAL AID PROCEDURES

Forms required: FAFSA, state aid form.
Dates and Deadlines: Closing date 3/1. Applicants notified on a rolling basis starting 2/1; must reply by 5/1 or within 2 week(s) of notification.
Transfers: No deadline.

CONTACT

Maria Barlaam, Director of Financial Aid
2900 Purchase Street, Purchase, NY 10577
(914) 323-5357

Mannes College The New School for Music

New York, New York
www.mannes.edu Federal Code: 002780

4-year private music college in very large city.
Enrollment: 213 undergrads, 12% part-time. 72 full-time freshmen.
Selectivity: Admits less than 50% of applicants.

BASIC COSTS (2009-2010)

Tuition and fees: $33,600.
Per-credit charge: $1,076.
Room and board: $16,390.

FINANCIAL AID PICTURE (2008-2009)

Students with need: Out of 17 full-time freshmen who applied for aid, 16 were judged to have need. Of these, 16 received aid, and 2 had their full need met. Average financial aid package met 77% of need; average scholarship/grant was $13,798; average loan was $17,537.
Students without need: 1 full-time freshmen who did not demonstrate need for aid received scholarships/grants; average award was $11,790. No-need awards available for academics, music/drama.
Cumulative student debt: 68% of graduating class had student loans; average debt was $16,370.
Additional info: Closing date for scholarship applications 2 weeks prior to audition date.

FINANCIAL AID PROCEDURES

Forms required: FAFSA.
Dates and Deadlines: No deadline. Applicants notified on a rolling basis starting 3/1; must reply within 4 week(s) of notification.

CONTACT

Eileen Doyle, Executive Director of Undergraduate Financial Aid
150 West 85th Street, New York, NY 10024
(212) 229-8930

Maria College

Albany, New York
www.mariacollege.edu Federal Code: 002763

2-year private junior college in small city.
Enrollment: 738 undergrads.

BASIC COSTS (2008-2009)

Tuition and fees: $9,100.
Per-credit charge: $325.

FINANCIAL AID PICTURE (2008-2009)

Students with need: 48% of average financial aid package awarded as scholarships/grants, 52% awarded as loans/jobs. Need-based aid available for part-time students. Work study available nights, weekends, and for part-time students.
Students without need: This college awards aid only to students with need.

FINANCIAL AID PROCEDURES

Forms required: FAFSA, state aid form.
Dates and Deadlines: No deadline. Applicants notified on a rolling basis starting 2/1; must reply within 2 week(s) of notification.
Transfers: No deadline. Applicants notified on a rolling basis; must reply within 2 week(s) of notification.

CONTACT

Stephen Riker, Assistant Director of Financial Aid
700 New Scotland Avenue, Albany, NY 12208
(518) 438-3111 ext. 229

Marist College

Poughkeepsie, New York
www.marist.edu Federal Code: 002765

4-year private liberal arts college in small city.
Enrollment: 4,796 undergrads, 6% part-time. 1,022 full-time freshmen.
Selectivity: Admits less than 50% of applicants.

BASIC COSTS (2008-2009)

Tuition and fees: $25,596.
Per-credit charge: $585.
Room and board: $10,730.
Additional info: Tuition/fee waivers available for minority students.

FINANCIAL AID PICTURE (2008-2009)

Students with need: Out of 854 full-time freshmen who applied for aid, 616 were judged to have need. Of these, 613 received aid, and 138 had their full need met. Average financial aid package met 72% of need; average scholarship/grant was $12,662; average loan was $3,793. For part-time students, average financial aid package was $5,061.
Students without need: 294 full-time freshmen who did not demonstrate need for aid received scholarships/grants; average award was $7,159. No-need awards available for academics, athletics, music/drama, ROTC, state/district residency.
Scholarships offered: ***Merit:*** Awards vary, as much as $12,000 per recipient. ***Athletic:*** 77 full-time freshmen received athletic scholarships; average amount $11,171.
Cumulative student debt: 67% of graduating class had student loans; average debt was $23,588.

FINANCIAL AID PROCEDURES

Forms required: FAFSA, institutional form.
Dates and Deadlines: Priority date 2/15; closing date 5/1. Applicants notified on a rolling basis starting 3/15; must reply by 5/1 or within 2 week(s) of notification.
Transfers: No deadline. FAFSA should be filed as soon as possible after January 1.

CONTACT

Joseph Weglarz, Executive Director, Student Financial Services
3399 North Road, Poughkeepsie, NY 12601-1387
(845) 575-3230

Marymount Manhattan College

New York, New York
www.mmm.edu Federal Code: 002769

4-year private liberal arts college in very large city.
Enrollment: 1,897 undergrads, 12% part-time. 535 full-time freshmen.
Selectivity: Admits 50 to 75% of applicants.

BASIC COSTS (2009-2010)

Tuition and fees: $22,656.
Per-credit charge: $689.
Room and board: $12,874.

FINANCIAL AID PICTURE (2008-2009)

Students with need: Out of 436 full-time freshmen who applied for aid, 335 were judged to have need. Of these, 334 received aid, and 26 had their full need met. Average financial aid package met 50% of need; average scholarship/grant was $10,134; average loan was $2,860. For part-time students, average financial aid package was $6,256.
Students without need: 101 full-time freshmen who did not demonstrate need for aid received scholarships/grants; average award was $5,712. No-need awards available for academics, art, leadership, music/drama.
Cumulative student debt: 41% of graduating class had student loans; average debt was $16,765.
Additional info: Limited international scholarships for top applicants.

FINANCIAL AID PROCEDURES

Forms required: FAFSA.
Dates and Deadlines: Priority date 3/15; no closing date. Applicants notified on a rolling basis starting 3/15; must reply by 5/1 or within 3 week(s) of notification.
Transfers: Applicants notified by 3/1. Must submit academic and financial transcripts from previous institutions.

CONTACT

Paul Ciraulo, Executive VP for Administration and Finance
221 East 71st Street, New York, NY 10021-4597
(212) 517-0500

Medaille College

Buffalo, New York
www.medaille.edu Federal Code: 002777

4-year private liberal arts college in large city.
Enrollment: 1,669 undergrads, 2% part-time. 406 full-time freshmen.
Selectivity: Admits 50 to 75% of applicants.

BASIC COSTS (2009-2010)

Tuition and fees: $19,590.
Per-credit charge: $690.
Room and board: $9,288.
Additional info: Tuition for students admitted in Fall 2008 is $19,140; tuition for students admitted before Fall 2008 is $18,290. Tuition/fee waivers available for adults.

FINANCIAL AID PICTURE (2007-2008)

Students with need: Out of 381 full-time freshmen who applied for aid, 381 were judged to have need. Of these, 381 received aid, and 15 had their full need met. Average financial aid package met 70% of need; average scholarship/grant was $8,000; average loan was $5,000. Need-based aid available for part-time students.
Students without need: 8 full-time freshmen who did not demonstrate need for aid received scholarships/grants; average award was $8,000. No-need awards available for academics, leadership.
Scholarships offered: ***Merit:*** Available from $1,000 to $10,500. ***Athletic:*** 8 full-time freshmen received athletic scholarships.
Cumulative student debt: 90% of graduating class had student loans; average debt was $22,000.

FINANCIAL AID PROCEDURES

Forms required: FAFSA, state aid form.
Dates and Deadlines: Priority date 3/1; no closing date. Applicants notified on a rolling basis starting 3/1; must reply within 2 week(s) of notification.
Transfers: Applicants notified on a rolling basis starting 3/1.

CONTACT

Catherine Buzanski, Director of Financial Aid
18 Agassiz Circle, Buffalo, NY 14214
(716) 880-2256

Mercy College

Dobbs Ferry, New York
www.mercy.edu Federal Code: 002772

4-year private liberal arts college in large town.
Enrollment: 5,004 undergrads, 29% part-time. 702 full-time freshmen.
Selectivity: Admits 50 to 75% of applicants.

BASIC COSTS (2009-2010)

Tuition and fees: $16,490.
Per-credit charge: $672.
Room and board: $10,812.

FINANCIAL AID PICTURE (2008-2009)

Students with need: Out of 628 full-time freshmen who applied for aid, 605 were judged to have need. Of these, 557 received aid, and 2 had their full need met. Average financial aid package met 43% of need; average scholarship/grant was $9,136; average loan was $3,330. For part-time students, average financial aid package was $4,585.
Students without need: 11 full-time freshmen who did not demonstrate need for aid received scholarships/grants; average award was $4,818. No-need awards available for academics, athletics.
Scholarships offered: 12 full-time freshmen received athletic scholarships; average amount $4,034.

FINANCIAL AID PROCEDURES

Forms required: FAFSA, state aid form.
Dates and Deadlines: Priority date 2/15; no closing date. Applicants notified on a rolling basis starting 4/1; must reply within 2 week(s) of notification.
Transfers: No deadline. Applicants notified on a rolling basis starting 4/1; must reply within 2 week(s) of notification.

CONTACT

Margaret McGrail, Assistant VP for Student Financial Services
555 Broadway, Dobbs Ferry, NY 10522
(888) 464-6737

Metropolitan College of New York

New York, New York
www.metropolitan.edu Federal Code: 009769

4-year private business and liberal arts college in very large city.
Enrollment: 582 undergrads.
Selectivity: Admits less than 50% of applicants.

BASIC COSTS (2009-2010)

Tuition and fees: $16,750.
Additional info: Tuition reported is for undergraduate business program; costs for other programs may vary.

FINANCIAL AID PICTURE (2007-2008)

Students with need: Need-based aid available for full-time and part-time students.

Students without need: No-need awards available for academics.
Scholarships offered: Presidential scholarships: up to $1,300 per semester; based on academic merit; given to top 10% of accepted students each semester.
Additional info: Limited merit scholarships.

FINANCIAL AID PROCEDURES
Forms required: FAFSA, state aid form.
Dates and Deadlines: Priority date 3/15; no closing date. Applicants notified on a rolling basis.

CONTACT
Timothy James, Director of Financial Aid
431 Canal Street, New York, NY 10013-1919
(212) 343-1234 ext. 3500

Mildred Elley
Albany, New York
www.mildred-elley.edu Federal Code: 022195

2-year for-profit career college in very large city.
Enrollment: 427 undergrads.
Selectivity: Open admission; but selective for some programs.

BASIC COSTS (2008-2009)
Tuition and fees: $10,920.
Per-credit charge: $354.
Additional info: Tuition at time of enrollment locked for 2 years.

FINANCIAL AID PICTURE
Students with need: Need-based aid available for full-time and part-time students. Work study available nights.
Students without need: This college awards aid only to students with need.

FINANCIAL AID PROCEDURES
Forms required: FAFSA, state aid form.
Dates and Deadlines: No deadline.

CONTACT
Vincent Spanburgh, Director of Financial Aid Compliance
855 Central Avenue, Albany, NY 12206-1513
(518) 786-0855 ext. 228

Mohawk Valley Community College
Utica, New York
www.mvcc.edu Federal Code: 002871

2-year public community college in small city.
Enrollment: 4,857 undergrads, 21% part-time. 1,434 full-time freshmen.
Selectivity: Open admission; but selective for some programs.

BASIC COSTS (2008-2009)
Tuition and fees: $3,664; out-of-state residents $6,914.
Per-credit charge: $120; out-of-state residents $240.
Room and board: $7,500.

FINANCIAL AID PICTURE (2008-2009)
Students with need: Need-based aid available for full-time and part-time students. Work study available nights, weekends, and for part-time students.

FINANCIAL AID PROCEDURES
Forms required: FAFSA, institutional form.
Dates and Deadlines: Priority date 4/15; no closing date. Applicants notified on a rolling basis starting 3/1; must reply within 2 week(s) of notification.
Transfers: Applicants notified on a rolling basis.

CONTACT
Annette Broski, Director, Student Financial Aid
1101 Sherman Drive, Utica, NY 13501-5394
(315) 792-5415

Molloy College
Rockville Centre, New York
www.molloy.edu Federal Code: 002775

4-year private liberal arts college in large town, affiliated with Roman Catholic Church.
Enrollment: 2,817 undergrads, 25% part-time. 391 full-time freshmen.
Selectivity: Admits 50 to 75% of applicants.

BASIC COSTS (2008-2009)
Tuition and fees: $19,635.
Per-credit charge: $620.
Additional info: Tuition/fee waivers available for unemployed or children of unemployed.

FINANCIAL AID PICTURE (2008-2009)
Students with need: Out of 365 full-time freshmen who applied for aid, 297 were judged to have need. Of these, 296 received aid, and 65 had their full need met. Average financial aid package met 65% of need; average scholarship/grant was $9,660; average loan was $3,952. For part-time students, average financial aid package was $9,302.
Students without need: 42 full-time freshmen who did not demonstrate need for aid received scholarships/grants; average award was $6,694. No-need awards available for academics, art, athletics, leadership, music/drama.
Scholarships offered: ***Merit:*** Molloy Scholar Scholarship: full tuition; minimum 95 high school average and minimum 1250 SAT (exclusive of Writing) or 28 ACT; 10 awarded annually; renewable for 3.5 GPA. Dominican Academic Scholarship: $1,000 to $8,500; minimum 88 high school average and minimum 1000 SAT (exclusive of Writing); 50 awarded annually, renewable with 3.0 GPA. Community Service Awards: $1,000 to $3,000; awarded to incoming freshmen demonstrating commitment to community and school; 10 awarded annually; renewable for 2.5 GPA. ***Athletic:*** 16 full-time freshmen received athletic scholarships; average amount $7,234.

FINANCIAL AID PROCEDURES
Forms required: FAFSA, state aid form.
Dates and Deadlines: Priority date 4/15; closing date 5/1. Applicants notified on a rolling basis starting 3/1.
Transfers: All transfer applicants with a minimum of 30 credits and 3.0 GPA automatically considered for transfer scholarships ranging from $1,500-$3,000.

CONTACT
Ana Lockward, Director of Financial Aid
PO Box 5002, Rockville Centre, NY 11570
(516) 678-5000 ext. 6249

Monroe College
Bronx, New York
www.monroecollege.edu Federal Code: 004799

4-year for-profit business and health science college in very large city.
Enrollment: 6,307 undergrads, 20% part-time. 1,239 full-time freshmen.
Selectivity: Admits 50 to 75% of applicants.

BASIC COSTS (2008-2009)
Tuition and fees: $11,212.
Per-credit charge: $438.
Room and board: $7,100.

FINANCIAL AID PICTURE (2007-2008)

Students with need: Need-based aid available for full-time and part-time students. Work study available nights, weekends, and for part-time students.

Students without need: This college awards aid only to students with need.

FINANCIAL AID PROCEDURES

Forms required: FAFSA.

Dates and Deadlines: Closing date 3/31. Applicants notified on a rolling basis starting 7/1.

Transfers: No deadline. Applicants notified on a rolling basis.

CONTACT

Alex Ephrem, Senior Vice President
Monroe College Way, Bronx, NY 10468
(718) 933-6700

Monroe Community College

Rochester, New York
www.monroecc.edu Federal Code: 002872

2-year public community college in large city.

Enrollment: 16,250 undergrads, 33% part-time. 3,959 full-time freshmen.

Selectivity: Open admission; but selective for some programs.

BASIC COSTS (2008-2009)

Tuition and fees: $3,290; out-of-state residents $6,190.

Per-credit charge: $121; out-of-state residents $242.

Room only: $5,555.

FINANCIAL AID PICTURE (2007-2008)

Students with need: 50% of average financial aid package awarded as scholarships/grants, 50% awarded as loans/jobs. Need-based aid available for part-time students. Work study available nights, weekends, and for part-time students.

Students without need: This college awards aid only to students with need.

FINANCIAL AID PROCEDURES

Forms required: FAFSA, state aid form.

Dates and Deadlines: Priority date 3/30; no closing date. Applicants notified on a rolling basis starting 3/15; must reply within 2 week(s) of notification.

Transfers: No deadline. Applicants notified on a rolling basis starting 3/15; must reply within 2 week(s) of notification.

CONTACT

Jerome St. Croix, Director of Financial Aid
Office of Admissions-Monroe Community College, Rochester, NY 14692-8908
(585) 292-2050

Mount St. Mary College

Newburgh, New York
www.msmc.edu Federal Code: 002778

4 year private liberal arts college in large town, affiliated with Roman Catholic Church.

Enrollment: 2,067 undergrads, 15% part-time. 434 full-time freshmen.

Selectivity: Admits over 75% of applicants.

BASIC COSTS (2009-2010)

Tuition and fees: $21,930.

Per-credit charge: $707.

Room and board: $11,584.

FINANCIAL AID PICTURE (2008-2009)

Students with need: Out of 399 full-time freshmen who applied for aid, 327 were judged to have need. Of these, 326 received aid, and 76 had their full need met. Average financial aid package met 68% of need; average scholarship/grant was $10,524; average loan was $4,197. For part-time students, average financial aid package was $7,594.

Students without need: 86 full-time freshmen who did not demonstrate need for aid received scholarships/grants; average award was $13,082. No-need awards available for academics, ROTC.

Scholarships offered: Presidential Scholarship: approximately $12,900; renewable each year with a 3.0 GPA. Merit Grants: range from $3,000-$8,500; renewable each year with a 2.5 GPA. Both based upon acceptance into full-time, traditional program, SAT/ACT test scores, high school GPA, and high school class rank.

Cumulative student debt: 92% of graduating class had student loans; average debt was $30,412.

FINANCIAL AID PROCEDURES

Forms required: FAFSA.

Dates and Deadlines: Closing date 2/15. Applicants notified on a rolling basis starting 4/1; must reply within 2 week(s) of notification.

Transfers: Closing date 3/15. Must reply within 2 week(s) of notification.

CONTACT

Michelle Taylor, Director of Financial Aid
330 Powell Avenue, Newburgh, NY 12550
(845) 569-3194

Nassau Community College

Garden City, New York
www.ncc.edu Federal Code: 002873

2-year public community college in large town.

Enrollment: 21,631 undergrads.

Selectivity: Open admission; but selective for some programs.

BASIC COSTS (2008-2009)

Tuition and fees: $3,832; out-of-state residents $7,384.

Per-credit charge: $148; out-of-state residents $296.

FINANCIAL AID PICTURE (2007-2008)

Students with need: Need-based aid available for full-time and part-time students. Work study available nights, weekends, and for part-time students.

Students without need: No-need awards available for academics, minority status.

FINANCIAL AID PROCEDURES

Forms required: FAFSA, state aid form.

Dates and Deadlines: Priority date 6/7; no closing date. Applicants notified on a rolling basis; must reply within 1 week(s) of notification.

CONTACT

Evangeline Manjares, Dean, Financial Student Services
One Education Drive, Garden City, NY 11530
(516) 572-7396

Nazareth College

Rochester, New York
www.naz.edu Federal Code: 002779

4-year private liberal arts college in large city.

Enrollment: 2,144 undergrads, 6% part-time. 458 full-time freshmen.

Selectivity: Admits 50 to 75% of applicants.

BASIC COSTS (2009-2010)
Tuition and fees: $25,186.
Per-credit charge: $574.
Room and board: $10,304.

FINANCIAL AID PICTURE (2007-2008)
Students with need: Out of 411 full-time freshmen who applied for aid, 357 were judged to have need. Of these, 357 received aid, and 86 had their full need met. Average financial aid package met 79% of need; average scholarship/grant was $13,548; average loan was $3,694. For part-time students, average financial aid package was $11,785.
Students without need: 100 full-time freshmen who did not demonstrate need for aid received scholarships/grants; average award was $8,906. No-need awards available for academics, alumni affiliation, art, minority status, music/drama, ROTC, state/district residency.
Scholarships offered: Presidential Scholarship: $14,000 to full tuition. Dean's Scholarship: $11,000-$13,999. Founders Scholarship: $9,000-$10,999. Trustee Scholarship: $7,500-$8,999. Class of 1928 Scholarship: $1,000-$7,499. All awarded based on grades, test scores, class rank, and course load. Campus diversity, regional, art, music, and theater scholarships also available.
Cumulative student debt: 78% of graduating class had student loans; average debt was $26,711.

FINANCIAL AID PROCEDURES
Forms required: FAFSA. CSS PROFILE required of early decision applicants only.
Dates and Deadlines: Priority date 12/15; closing date 5/1. Applicants notified on a rolling basis starting 2/20; must reply by 5/1 or within 2 week(s) of notification.
Transfers: No deadline.

CONTACT
Bruce Woolley, Director of Financial Aid
4245 East Avenue, Rochester, NY 14618-3790
(585) 389-2310

New York Career Institute
New York, New York
www.nyci.com Federal Code: 014576

2-year for-profit junior college in very large city.
Enrollment: 629 undergrads, 17% part-time.
Selectivity: Open admission.

BASIC COSTS (2008-2009)
Additional info: Full-time tuition and fees for Court Reporting, Paralegal, and Medical daytime programs $11,250; for court reporting night program $10,650. Tuition for paralegal and medical evening programs $360 per credit hour.

FINANCIAL AID PICTURE
Students with need: Need-based aid available for full-time and part-time students. Work study available nights.
Students without need: This college awards aid only to students with need.

FINANCIAL AID PROCEDURES
Dates and Deadlines: No deadline. Applicants notified on a rolling basis.

CONTACT
Dennis Byrns, Financial Aid Advisor
11 Park Place, New York, NY 10007

New York Institute of Technology
Old Westbury, New York
www.nyit.edu Federal Code: 002782

4-year private university and health science college in large town.
Enrollment: 4,767 undergrads, 15% part-time. 1,492 full-time freshmen.
Selectivity: Admits over 75% of applicants.

BASIC COSTS (2009-2010)
Tuition and fees: $24,140.
Per-credit charge: $790.
Room only: $10,310.
Additional info: Room only charges apply to Manhattan campus; board charges vary on other campuses. Tuition/fee costs reported for nontechnology majors, vary for other programs. Tuition/fee waivers available for unemployed or children of unemployed.

FINANCIAL AID PICTURE (2007-2008)
Students with need: Out of 1,023 full-time freshmen who applied for aid, 860 were judged to have need. Of these, 851 received aid. For part-time students, average financial aid package was $5,739.
Students without need: 203 full-time freshmen who did not demonstrate need for aid received scholarships/grants; average award was $9,195. No-need awards available for academics, athletics.

FINANCIAL AID PROCEDURES
Forms required: FAFSA.
Dates and Deadlines: Priority date 3/1; no closing date. Applicants notified on a rolling basis starting 3/15; must reply by 5/1 or within 2 week(s) of notification.

CONTACT
Rosemary Ferrucci, Associate Dean of Financial Aid
Box 8000, Old Westbury, NY 11568
(516) 686-3835

New York School of Interior Design
New York, New York
www.nysid.edu Federal Code: 013606

4-year private visual arts college in very large city.
Enrollment: 705 undergrads, 74% part-time. 9 full-time freshmen.
Selectivity: Admits less than 50% of applicants.

BASIC COSTS (2009-2010)
Tuition and fees: $20,840.
Per-credit charge: $685.

FINANCIAL AID PICTURE (2008-2009)
Students with need: For part-time students, average financial aid package was $12,000.
Students without need: This college awards aid only to students with need.
Cumulative student debt: 60% of graduating class had student loans; average debt was $21,000.

FINANCIAL AID PROCEDURES
Forms required: FAFSA, state aid form.
Dates and Deadlines: Priority date 5/1; no closing date. Applicants notified on a rolling basis starting 2/1; must reply within 2 week(s) of notification.
Transfers: No deadline. Applicants notified on a rolling basis.

CONTACT
Nedi Goga, Financial Aid Officer
170 East 70th Street, New York, NY 10021-5110
(212) 472-1500 ext. 212

New York University

New York, New York
www.nyu.edu Federal Code: 002785

4-year private university in very large city.
Enrollment: 20,781 undergrads, 6% part-time. 4,467 full-time freshmen.
Selectivity: Admits less than 50% of applicants.

BASIC COSTS (2008-2009)

Tuition and fees: $37,372.
Per-credit charge: $1,096.
Room and board: $12,910.

FINANCIAL AID PICTURE (2008-2009)

Students with need: Out of 2,975 full-time freshmen who applied for aid, 2,371 were judged to have need. Of these, 2,361 received aid. Average financial aid package met 72% of need; average scholarship/grant was $19,391; average loan was $4,946. For part-time students, average financial aid package was $10,637.
Students without need: 232 full-time freshmen who did not demonstrate need for aid received scholarships/grants; average award was $6,920. No-need awards available for academics.
Cumulative student debt: 58% of graduating class had student loans; average debt was $34,850.
Additional info: Both need-based and merit scholarships available to first-time students. Range from $1,000 to $25,000.

FINANCIAL AID PROCEDURES

Forms required: FAFSA, state aid form.
Dates and Deadlines: Closing date 2/15. Applicants notified on a rolling basis starting 4/1; must reply by 5/1.
Transfers: Priority date 3/1; no deadline.

CONTACT

Barbara Hall, Associate Provost for Admissions and Financial Aid
665 Broadway, 11th floor, New York, NY 10012-2339
(212) 998-4444

Niagara County Community College

Sanborn, New York
www.niagaracc.suny.edu Federal Code: 002874

2-year public community college in rural community.
Enrollment: 4,583 undergrads, 25% part-time. 1,261 full-time freshmen.
Selectivity: Open admission; but selective for some programs.

BASIC COSTS (2008-2009)

Tuition and fees: $3,634; out-of-state residents $6,946.
Per-credit charge: $138; out-of-state residents $276.

FINANCIAL AID PICTURE (2007-2008)

Students with need: 53% of average financial aid package awarded as scholarships/grants, 47% awarded as loans/jobs. Need-based aid available for part-time students. Work study available nights.
Students without need: This college awards aid only to students with need.
Additional info: Assistance offered placing students in part-time employment. Students can charge books, food coupons, or $100 advance against anticipated financial aid.

FINANCIAL AID PROCEDURES

Forms required: FAFSA, state aid form.
Dates and Deadlines: Priority date 4/1; no closing date. Applicants notified on a rolling basis starting 5/1; must reply within 2 week(s) of notification.
Transfers: Must file appropriate state and federal change forms at least 4 weeks before registration date.

CONTACT

James Trimboli, Director of Financial Aid
3111 Saunders Settlement Road, Sanborn, NY 14132-9460
(716) 614-6266

Niagara University

Niagara University, New York
www.niagara.edu Federal Code: 002788

4-year private university in small city, affiliated with Roman Catholic Church.
Enrollment: 3,291 undergrads, 8% part-time. 740 full-time freshmen.
Selectivity: Admits 50 to 75% of applicants.

BASIC COSTS (2009-2010)

Tuition and fees: $24,825.
Per-credit charge: $790.
Room and board: $10,250.
Additional info: Tuition at time of enrollment locked for 4 years.

FINANCIAL AID PICTURE (2008-2009)

Students with need: Out of 735 full-time freshmen who applied for aid, 704 were judged to have need. Of these, 704 received aid, and 380 had their full need met. Average financial aid package met 79% of need; average scholarship/grant was $15,327; average loan was $4,619. For part-time students, average financial aid package was $11,406.
Students without need: 166 full-time freshmen who did not demonstrate need for aid received scholarships/grants; average award was $9,179. No-need awards available for academics, athletics, music/drama, ROTC.
Scholarships offered: 60 full-time freshmen received athletic scholarships; average amount $16,950.
Cumulative student debt: 73% of graduating class had student loans; average debt was $29,081.
Additional info: Opportunity program available for academically and economically disadvantaged students.

FINANCIAL AID PROCEDURES

Forms required: FAFSA, state aid form.
Dates and Deadlines: Priority date 2/15; no closing date. Applicants notified on a rolling basis starting 3/1; must reply within 3 week(s) of notification.
Transfers: Must reply within 3 week(s) of notification. Academic scholarship available: $9,000 per year based on minimum 3.34 GPA from transfer institution; $8,000 per year for 3.0 to 3.33 GPA; $5,500 per year for 2.5 to 2.99 GPA.

CONTACT

Maureen Salfi, Director of Financial Aid Niagara University, NY 14109
(716) 286-8686

North Country Community College

Saranac Lake, New York
www.nccc.edu Federal Code: 007111

2-year public community college in small town.
Enrollment: 1,031 undergrads.
Selectivity: Open admission; but selective for some programs.

BASIC COSTS (2008-2009)

Tuition and fees: $4,385; out-of-state residents $9,695.
Per-credit charge: $160; out-of-state residents $390.
Room and board: $8,500.

FINANCIAL AID PICTURE (2007-2008)

Students with need: Need-based aid available for full-time and part-time students. Work study available nights, weekends, and for part-time students.
Students without need: This college awards aid only to students with need.

FINANCIAL AID PROCEDURES

Forms required: FAFSA, state aid form.

Dates and Deadlines: Priority date 4/1; no closing date. Applicants notified on a rolling basis starting 4/1; must reply within 3 week(s) of notification.

CONTACT

Edwin Trathen, Vice President for Enrollment and Student Services
23 Santanoni Avenue, Saranac Lake, NY 12983
(518) 891-2915 ext. 229

Nyack College

Nyack, New York
www.nyack.edu Federal Code: 002790

4-year private liberal arts college in large town, affiliated with Christian and Missionary Alliance.

Enrollment: 1,900 undergrads.

BASIC COSTS (2009-2010)

Tuition and fees: $19,500.

Per-credit charge: $770.

Room and board: $7,900.

FINANCIAL AID PICTURE (2008-2009)

Students with need: Need-based aid available for full-time students.

Students without need: No-need awards available for academics, alumni affiliation, art, athletics, leadership, minority status, music/drama, religious affiliation, state/district residency.

FINANCIAL AID PROCEDURES

Forms required: FAFSA, state aid form.

Dates and Deadlines: Priority date 3/1; no closing date. Applicants notified on a rolling basis starting 3/1; must reply by 4/1 or within 4 week(s) of notification.

CONTACT

Dona Schepens, Financial Aid Director
1 South Boulevard, Nyack, NY 10960-3698
(845) 358-1710 ext. 791

Onondaga Community College

Syracuse, New York
www.sunyocc.edu Federal Code: 002875

2-year public community college in small city.

Enrollment: 7,539 undergrads, 25% part-time. 1,657 full-time freshmen.

Selectivity: Open admission; but selective for some programs.

BASIC COSTS (2008-2009)

Tuition and fees: $3,762; out-of-state residents $7,154.

Per-credit charge: $132; out-of-state residents $264.

FINANCIAL AID PICTURE (2007-2008)

Students with need: Need-based aid available for full-time and part-time students.

Students without need: This college awards aid only to students with need.

FINANCIAL AID PROCEDURES

Forms required: FAFSA, state aid form.

Dates and Deadlines: Priority date 2/15; no closing date. Applicants notified on a rolling basis starting 4/15; must reply within 4 week(s) of notification.

CONTACT

Lorna Roberts, Director of Financial Aid
4585 West Seneca Turnpike, Syracuse, NY 13215-4585
(315) 469-2291

Orange County Community College

Middletown, New York
www.orange.cc.ny.us Federal Code: 002876

2-year public community college in large town.

Enrollment: 6,763 undergrads.

Selectivity: Open admission; but selective for some programs.

BASIC COSTS (2008-2009)

Tuition and fees: $3,648; out-of-state residents $6,948.

Per-credit charge: $138; out-of-state residents $276.

Additional info: Tuition/fee waivers available for unemployed or children of unemployed.

FINANCIAL AID PICTURE

Students with need: Need-based aid available for full-time and part-time students.

FINANCIAL AID PROCEDURES

Forms required: FAFSA, state aid form, institutional form.

Dates and Deadlines: Priority date 5/1; no closing date. Applicants notified on a rolling basis starting 5/1; must reply within 4 week(s) of notification.

CONTACT

John Ivankovic, Director of Finacial Aid
115 South Street, Middletown, NY 10940-0115
(845) 341-4190

Pace University

New York, New York
www.pace.edu Federal Code: 002791

4-year private university in very large city.

Enrollment: 7,206 undergrads, 15% part-time. 1,615 full-time freshmen.

Selectivity: Admits 50 to 75% of applicants.

BASIC COSTS (2008-2009)

Tuition and fees: $31,364.

Per-credit charge: $879.

Room and board: $11,180.

FINANCIAL AID PICTURE (2008-2009)

Students with need: Out of 1,360 full-time freshmen who applied for aid, 1,231 were judged to have need. Of these, 1,229 received aid, and 202 had their full need met. Average financial aid package met 76% of need; average scholarship/grant was $21,866; average loan was $3,922. For part-time students, average financial aid package was $5,836.

Students without need: 383 full-time freshmen who did not demonstrate need for aid received scholarships/grants; average award was $7,468. No-need awards available for academics, athletics, music/drama.

Scholarships offered: 9 full-time freshmen received athletic scholarships; average amount $8,712.

Cumulative student debt: 69% of graduating class had student loans; average debt was $29,622.

FINANCIAL AID PROCEDURES

Forms required: FAFSA, state aid form.

Dates and Deadlines: Priority date 3/15; no closing date. Applicants notified on a rolling basis starting 2/25; must reply by 5/1 or within 3 week(s) of notification.

CONTACT

Mark Stephens, University Director, Financial Aid
1 Pace Plaza, New York, NY 10038
(212) 346-1300

Parsons The New School for Design

New York, New York
www.parsons.edu Federal Code: 002780

4-year private visual arts college in very large city.
Enrollment: 3,815 undergrads, 9% part-time. 655 full-time freshmen.
Selectivity: Admits 50 to 75% of applicants.

BASIC COSTS (2009-2010)
Tuition and fees: $36,010.
Per-credit charge: $1,202.
Room and board: $16,390.

FINANCIAL AID PICTURE (2008-2009)
Students with need: Out of 331 full-time freshmen who applied for aid, 291 were judged to have need. Of these, 291 received aid, and 29 had their full need met. Average financial aid package met 76% of need; average scholarship/grant was $16,073; average loan was $11,991. Need-based aid available for part-time students.
Students without need: 26 full-time freshmen who did not demonstrate need for aid received scholarships/grants; average award was $4,013. No-need awards available for academics, music/drama.

FINANCIAL AID PROCEDURES
Forms required: FAFSA, state aid form.
Dates and Deadlines: No deadline. Applicants notified on a rolling basis starting 3/1; must reply within 4 week(s) of notification.

CONTACT
Eileen Doyle, Assistant Provost for University Financial Aid and Enrollment Management
65 Fifth Avenue, New York, NY 10011
(212) 229-8930

Paul Smith's College

Paul Smiths, New York
www.paulsmiths.edu Federal Code: 002795

4-year private liberal arts college in rural community.
Enrollment: 927 undergrads. 302 full-time freshmen.
Selectivity: Admits over 75% of applicants.

BASIC COSTS (2009-2010)
Tuition and fees: $20,030.
Per-credit charge: $540.
Room and board: $8,940.
Additional info: Program fees range from $630 to $2,030 depending on program.

FINANCIAL AID PICTURE (2008-2009)
Students with need: Out of 285 full-time freshmen who applied for aid, 261 were judged to have need. Of these, 261 received aid, and 24 had their full need met. Average financial aid package met 69% of need; average scholarship/grant was $10,337; average loan was $2,940.
Students without need: 35 full-time freshmen who did not demonstrate need for aid received scholarships/grants; average award was $5,847. No-need awards available for academics.
Cumulative student debt: 98% of graduating class had student loans; average debt was $20,168.
Additional info: Merit aid only for international students; no financial aid application required.

FINANCIAL AID PROCEDURES
Forms required: FAFSA.
Dates and Deadlines: Priority date 3/31; no closing date. Applicants notified on a rolling basis starting 3/5; must reply within 4 week(s) of notification.
Transfers: No deadline. Applicants notified by 2/5; must reply within 4 week(s) of notification.

CONTACT
Mary Ellen Chamberlain, Director of Financial Aid
PO Box 265, Routes 30 & 86, Paul Smiths, NY 12970-0265
(518) 327-6220

Phillips Beth Israel School of Nursing

New York, New York
www.futurenursebi.org Federal Code: 006438

2-year private nursing college in very large city.
Enrollment: 285 undergrads, 86% part-time. 2 full-time freshmen.
Selectivity: Admits less than 50% of applicants.

BASIC COSTS (2009-2010)
Tuition and fees: $17,250.
Per-credit charge: $360.

FINANCIAL AID PICTURE (2008-2009)
Students with need: Out of 2 full-time freshmen who applied for aid, 2 were judged to have need. Of these, 2 received aid. Average financial aid package met 100% of need; average scholarship/grant was $3,170; average loan was $7,500. For part-time students, average financial aid package was $1,210.
Scholarships offered: Hillman Scholarship Program: full tuition, books, and uniforms; variable number awarded each year; based on academic achievement. Karpas Scholarship Program: $3,000 a year; 15 awarded; based on academic achievement.

FINANCIAL AID PROCEDURES
Forms required: FAFSA, state aid form, institutional form.
Dates and Deadlines: Closing date 6/1. Applicants notified by 8/1; must reply within 3 week(s) of notification.
Transfers: Applicants notified by 7/1; must reply within 2 week(s) of notification.

CONTACT
Wendy Chan, Financial Aid Director
776 Sixth Avenue, Fourth Floor, New York, NY 10001
(212) 614-6104

Polytechnic Institute of New York University

Brooklyn, New York Federal Code: 002796
www.poly.edu CSS Code: 2668

4-year private university in very large city.
Enrollment: 1,505 undergrads, 4% part-time. 329 full-time freshmen.
Selectivity: Admits 50 to 75% of applicants.

BASIC COSTS (2008-2009)
Tuition and fees: $32,644.
Per-credit charge: $994.
Room and board: $8,722.

FINANCIAL AID PICTURE (2007-2008)
Students with need: Out of 324 full-time freshmen who applied for aid, 237 were judged to have need. Of these, 237 received aid, and 134 had their full need met. Average financial aid package met 89% of need; average scholarship/grant was $9,964; average loan was $3,627. For part-time students, average financial aid package was $9,828.
Students without need: 87 full-time freshmen who did not demonstrate need for aid received scholarships/grants; average award was $16,583. No-need awards available for academics.

Scholarships offered: Board of Trustees Scholarships: full tuition, less any outside aid for which students are eligible; awarded to academically superior freshmen. Geiger/Fialkov Scholarships: full tuition less any outside aid for which students are eligible; awarded to superior freshmen majoring in engineering or computer science. High School Principal's Scholarship: for students nominated by high school principals in New York metropolitan region; $10,000 per year; Scholarship Committee selects recipients. Students must file FAFSA to be eligible for merit scholarships.

FINANCIAL AID PROCEDURES

Forms required: FAFSA, CSS PROFILE, state aid form, institutional form.
Dates and Deadlines: Priority date 3/1; no closing date. Applicants notified on a rolling basis starting 3/15; must reply within 2 week(s) of notification.
Transfers: Priority date 5/5; no deadline. Applicants notified on a rolling basis; must reply within 2 week(s) of notification.

CONTACT

Christine Falzerano, Director of Financial Aid
6 Metrotech Center, Brooklyn, NY 11201-2999
(718) 260-3300

Pratt Institute

Brooklyn, New York
www.pratt.edu Federal Code: 002798

4-year private university and visual arts college in very large city.
Enrollment: 3,085 undergrads, 5% part-time. 636 full-time freshmen.
Selectivity: Admits less than 50% of applicants.

BASIC COSTS (2009-2010)

Tuition and fees: $34,880.
Per-credit charge: $1,085.
Room and board: $9,756.
Additional info: All architecture students required to purchase laptop and software (discounted) during summer. All sophomore interior design majors required to purchase laptop computer. Laptop costs approximately $3,600.

FINANCIAL AID PICTURE (2008-2009)

Students with need: Out of 481 full-time freshmen who applied for aid, 407 were judged to have need. Of these, 407 received aid. Average financial aid package met 69% of need; average scholarship/grant was $8,431; average loan was $5,663. For part-time students, average financial aid package was $8,189.
Students without need: 174 full-time freshmen who did not demonstrate need for aid received scholarships/grants; average award was $7,960. No-need awards available for academics, art.
Cumulative student debt: 65% of graduating class had student loans; average debt was $27,125.

FINANCIAL AID PROCEDURES

Forms required: FAFSA, state aid form, institutional form.
Dates and Deadlines: Closing date 2/1. Applicants notified on a rolling basis starting 3/11; must reply within 2 week(s) of notification.
Transfers: Must reply by 5/1 or within 2 week(s) of notification.

CONTACT

Karen Price-Scott, Director of Financial Aid
200 Willoughby Avenue, Brooklyn, NY 11205-3817
(718) 636-3519

Rensselaer Polytechnic Institute

Troy, New York Federal Code: 002803
www.rpi.edu CSS Code: 2757

4-year private university in small city.
Enrollment: 5,367 undergrads. 1,356 full-time freshmen.
Selectivity: Admits less than 50% of applicants.

BASIC COSTS (2009-2010)

Tuition and fees: $39,165.
Per-credit charge: $1,190.
Room and board: $11,145.

FINANCIAL AID PICTURE (2008-2009)

Students with need: Out of 1,116 full-time freshmen who applied for aid, 892 were judged to have need. Of these, 892 received aid, and 643 had their full need met. Average financial aid package met 82% of need; average scholarship/grant was $23,079; average loan was $6,727.
Students without need: 436 full-time freshmen who did not demonstrate need for aid received scholarships/grants; average award was $14,085. No-need awards available for academics, alumni affiliation, art, athletics, leadership, minority status, music/drama, ROTC.
Scholarships offered: ***Merit:*** Rensselaer Medals: $15,000; awarded by participating high schools for excellence in science and mathematics. ***Athletic:*** 13 full-time freshmen received athletic scholarships; average amount $44,186.
Cumulative student debt: 70% of graduating class had student loans; average debt was $30,375.

FINANCIAL AID PROCEDURES

Forms required: FAFSA, CSS PROFILE.
Dates and Deadlines: Closing date 2/15. Applicants notified by 3/25.
Transfers: No deadline. Applicants notified on a rolling basis starting 3/31. Entering transfer students must complete two applications to apply for institutional and federal need-based aid: FAFSA and Transfer Financial Aid Application/Verification Worksheet (available upon acceptance). A number of special transfer scholarships available each year.

CONTACT

James Stevenson, Director of Financial Aid
110 Eighth Street, Troy, NY 12180-3590
(518) 276-6813

Roberts Wesleyan College

Rochester, New York
www.roberts.edu Federal Code: 002805

4-year private liberal arts college in large city, affiliated with Free Methodist Church of North America.
Enrollment: 1,339 undergrads, 8% part-time. 245 full-time freshmen.
Selectivity: Admits 50 to 75% of applicants.

BASIC COSTS (2009-2010)

Tuition and fees: $23,780.
Per-credit charge: $940.
Room and board: $8,520.

FINANCIAL AID PICTURE (2007-2008)

Students with need: Out of 223 full-time freshmen who applied for aid, 203 were judged to have need. Of these, 203 received aid, and 39 had their full need met. Average financial aid package met 81% of need; average scholarship/grant was $12,767; average loan was $5,379. For part-time students, average financial aid package was $9,266.
Students without need: 36 full-time freshmen who did not demonstrate need for aid received scholarships/grants; average award was $6,779. No-need awards available for academics, alumni affiliation, art, athletics, music/drama, religious affiliation, ROTC, state/district residency.
Scholarships offered: 7 full-time freshmen received athletic scholarships; average amount $3,906.
Additional info: Dollars for Scholars offer matching grants of up to $750.

FINANCIAL AID PROCEDURES

Forms required: FAFSA, state aid form.

Dates and Deadlines: Priority date 3/15; no closing date. Applicants notified on a rolling basis starting 3/15; must reply by 5/1 or within 2 week(s) of notification.
Transfers: Applicants notified on a rolling basis starting 3/15.

CONTACT

Stephen Field, Director of Student Financial Services
2301 Westside Drive, Rochester, NY 14624-1997
(585) 594-6150

Rochester Institute of Technology

Rochester, New York
www.rit.edu Federal Code: 002806

4-year private university in large city.
Enrollment: 13,056 undergrads, 7% part-time. 2,506 full-time freshmen.
Selectivity: Admits 50 to 75% of applicants.

BASIC COSTS (2009-2010)

Tuition and fees: $29,283.
Per-credit charge: $641.
Room and board: $9,642.
Additional info: Tuition for students matriculated full-time at the National Technical Institute for the Deaf (NTID) is $10,233. Tuition/fee waivers available for unemployed or children of unemployed.

FINANCIAL AID PICTURE (2007-2008)

Students with need: Out of 2,202 full-time freshmen who applied for aid, 1,896 were judged to have need. Of these, 1,896 received aid, and 1,570 had their full need met. Average financial aid package met 88% of need; average scholarship/grant was $13,700; average loan was $5,100. For part-time students, average financial aid package was $7,000.
Students without need: 280 full-time freshmen who did not demonstrate need for aid received scholarships/grants; average award was $7,300. No-need awards available for academics, art, leadership, ROTC.
Scholarships offered: Presidential Scholarships: $7,500 to $13,000 per year; top 10% of high school class with minimum SAT of 1860 on the three combined sections (or ACT Composite 27) or top 20% of high school class with SAT of 1950 on the three combined sections (or ACT 28).
Additional info: Most juniors and seniors participate in cooperative education program, earning an average $4,500-$6,500 per 3-month employment period through paid employment in jobs related to major.

FINANCIAL AID PROCEDURES

Forms required: FAFSA, state aid form, institutional form.
Dates and Deadlines: Priority date 3/1; no closing date. Applicants notified on a rolling basis starting 3/15; must reply by 5/1.
Transfers: Priority date 3/15. Applicants notified on a rolling basis starting 4/1; must reply by 5/1. Special merit scholarship programs available specifically for transfers with high GPA.

CONTACT

Verna Hazen, Assistant Vice President and Director of Financial Aid
60 Lomb Memorial Drive, Rochester, NY 14623-5604
(585) 475-2186

Rockland Community College

Suffern, New York
www.sunyrockland.edu Federal Code: 002877

2-year public community college in large town.
Enrollment: 6,422 undergrads.
Selectivity: Open admission.

BASIC COSTS (2008-2009)

Tuition and fees: $3,642; out-of-state residents $6,942.
Per-credit charge: $137; out-of-state residents $274.

FINANCIAL AID PICTURE (2007-2008)

Students with need: Need-based aid available for full-time and part-time students. Work study available nights, weekends, and for part-time students.
Scholarships offered: SUNY Empire State Honors Minority Scholarships: available to African American, Latino, and Native American students; 8 awarded; $1,000 per semester for 4 semesters. Jack Watson Scholarships: minimum 3.5 high school GPA or 94 average in Regents; 5 awarded; $1,163 per semester, renewable for 2nd year. Alumni Scholarships for children of alumni with 75 average; varying amounts.

FINANCIAL AID PROCEDURES

Forms required: FAFSA, institutional form.
Dates and Deadlines: Priority date 5/31; no closing date. Applicants notified on a rolling basis starting 6/1; must reply within 3 week(s) of notification.

CONTACT

Debra Brouabidi, Director of Financial Aid
145 College Road, Suffern, NY 10901
(845) 574-4000

Russell Sage College

Troy, New York
www.sage.edu/rsc Federal Code: 002810

4-year private liberal arts college for women in small city.
Enrollment: 676 undergrads, 2% part-time. 123 full-time freshmen.
Selectivity: Admits 50 to 75% of applicants.

BASIC COSTS (2009-2010)

Tuition and fees: $27,790.
Per-credit charge: $900.
Room and board: $9,670.

FINANCIAL AID PICTURE (2008-2009)

Students with need: Out of 123 full-time freshmen who applied for aid, 110 were judged to have need. Of these, 110 received aid, and 4 had their full need met. For part-time students, average financial aid package was $14,350.
Students without need: 100 full-time freshmen who did not demonstrate need for aid received scholarships/grants; average award was $9,800. No-need awards available for academics, alumni affiliation, leadership, music/drama.
Scholarships offered: Multiple awards to qualified students: Presidential and Dean's scholarship, Girl Scout scholarship, first-generation scholarship, valedictorian-salutatorian scholarship, student Sage scholarship, endowed scholarships for minority students and specific majors.
Cumulative student debt: 95% of graduating class had student loans; average debt was $29,500.

FINANCIAL AID PROCEDURES

Forms required: FAFSA, state aid form.
Dates and Deadlines: Priority date 3/1; no closing date. Applicants notified on a rolling basis starting 3/1; must reply by 5/1 or within 2 week(s) of notification.
Transfers: Phi Theta Kappa Transfer Scholarship available.

CONTACT

James Dease, Associate Vice President for Student Services
45 Ferry Street, Troy, NY 12180-4115
(518) 244-4525

Sage College of Albany

Albany, New York
www.sage.edu Federal Code: 002811

4-year private business and liberal arts college in small city.
Enrollment: 820 undergrads, 35% part-time. 65 full-time freshmen.
Selectivity: Admits 50 to 75% of applicants.

BASIC COSTS (2009-2010)

Tuition and fees: $27,790.
Per-credit charge: $900.
Room and board: $9,830.

FINANCIAL AID PICTURE (2008-2009)

Students with need: Out of 65 full-time freshmen who applied for aid, 61 were judged to have need. Of these, 61 received aid, and 2 had their full need met. For part-time students, average financial aid package was $10,450.
Students without need: 4 full-time freshmen who did not demonstrate need for aid received scholarships/grants; average award was $6,400. No-need awards available for academics, art, leadership.
Scholarships offered: Multiple awards to qualified students: Presidential and Dean's scholarships, first-generation scholarship, art scholarship, valedictorian-salutatorian scholarship, diversity leadership scholarship. Endowed scholarships available for minority students and specific majors.
Cumulative student debt: 96% of graduating class had student loans; average debt was $16,200.

FINANCIAL AID PROCEDURES

Forms required: FAFSA, state aid form.
Dates and Deadlines: Priority date 3/1; no closing date. Applicants notified on a rolling basis starting 3/1; must reply by 5/1 or within 2 week(s) of notification.
Transfers: Phi Theta Kappa transfer scholarship available.

CONTACT

James Dease, Associate Vice President for Student Services
140 New Scotland Avenue, Albany, NY 12208
(518) 292-1783

Saint Bonaventure University

St. Bonaventure, New York
www.sbu.edu Federal Code: 002817

4-year private university in large town, affiliated with Roman Catholic Church.
Enrollment: 1,892 undergrads, 1% part-time. 563 full-time freshmen.
Selectivity: Admits over 75% of applicants.

BASIC COSTS (2009-2010)

Tuition and fees: $25,785.
Per-credit charge: $745.
Room and board: $9,100.
Additional info: Tuition/fee waivers available for minority students.

FINANCIAL AID PICTURE

Students with need: Need-based aid available for full-time and part-time students. Work study available nights, weekends, and for part-time students.
Students without need: No-need awards available for academics, art, athletics, leadership, minority status, music/drama, religious affiliation, ROTC, state/district residency.

FINANCIAL AID PROCEDURES

Forms required: FAFSA, state aid form, institutional form.
Dates and Deadlines: Priority date 2/1; no closing date. Applicants notified on a rolling basis starting 4/1; must reply by 5/1 or within 3 week(s) of notification.
Transfers: Closing date 5/1.

CONTACT

Elisabeth Rankin, Director of Financial Aid
Route 417, St. Bonaventure, NY 14778-2284
(716) 375-2400

St. Elizabeth College of Nursing

Utica, New York
www.secon.edu Federal Code: 006461

2-year private nursing college in small city, affiliated with Roman Catholic Church.
Enrollment: 225 undergrads.

BASIC COSTS (2009-2010)

Tuition and fees: $12,480.
Per-credit charge: $325.

FINANCIAL AID PICTURE (2008-2009)

Students with need: Need-based aid available for full-time and part-time students.

FINANCIAL AID PROCEDURES

Forms required: FAFSA, state aid form.
Dates and Deadlines: No deadline. Applicants notified on a rolling basis starting 1/1; must reply within 2 week(s) of notification.

CONTACT

Sherry Wojnas, Director, Financial Aid
2215 Genesee Street, Utica, NY 13501
(315) 798-8206

St. Francis College

Brooklyn Heights, New York
www.stfranciscollege.edu Federal Code: 002820

4-year private liberal arts college in very large city, affiliated with Roman Catholic Church.
Enrollment: 2,344 undergrads, 12% part-time. 568 full-time freshmen.
Selectivity: Admits 50 to 75% of applicants.

BASIC COSTS (2009-2010)

Tuition and fees: $16,480.
Additional info: Tuition/fee waivers available for unemployed or children of unemployed.

FINANCIAL AID PICTURE (2008-2009)

Students with need: Need-based aid available for full-time and part-time students.
Students without need: No-need awards available for academics, athletics.
Scholarships offered: Presidential Scholarship: full tuition; minimum high school GPA 90: minimum SAT 1150. St. Francis Scholarship: $7,500; minimum high school GPA 85; minimum 1100 SAT. St. Clare Scholarship: $6,500; minimum 1100 SAT. St. Clare Scholarship: $6,500: minimum 85 high school GPA; minimum 1000 SAT. Dean's Scholarship: $3,500; minimum 1000 SAT. All scholarships renewable annually for 4-year period, provided student maintains full-time status and cumulative GPA of at least 3.0. SAT scores listed exclusive of Writing.

FINANCIAL AID PROCEDURES

Forms required: FAFSA, state aid form.
Dates and Deadlines: Priority date 2/15; no closing date. Applicants notified on a rolling basis starting 3/15; must reply within 2 week(s) of notification.

CONTACT

Joseph Cummings, Director, Student Financial Services
180 Remsen Street, Brooklyn Heights, NY 11201-9902
(718) 489-5255

St. John Fisher College

Rochester, New York
www.sjfc.edu Federal Code: 002821

4-year private liberal arts college in large town, affiliated with Roman Catholic Church.
Enrollment: 2,850 undergrads, 7% part-time. 548 full-time freshmen.
Selectivity: Admits 50 to 75% of applicants. GED not accepted.

BASIC COSTS (2009-2010)

Tuition and fees: $24,280.
Per-credit charge: $650.
Room and board: $10,090.

FINANCIAL AID PICTURE (2007-2008)

Students with need: Out of 523 full-time freshmen who applied for aid, 445 were judged to have need. Of these, 445 received aid, and 48 had their full need met. Average financial aid package met 86% of need; average scholarship/grant was $13,456; average loan was $5,278.
Students without need: 92 full-time freshmen who did not demonstrate need for aid received scholarships/grants; average award was $6,348. No-need awards available for academics, leadership.
Scholarships offered: Founders Scholarship: $8,500. Presidential Scholarship: $10,000. Trustees Scholarship: $11,000. Fisher Service Scholars Program: one-third of cost of education. First Generation Scholars Program: $5,000 to one-third of cost of education. Honors and Science Scholars: $3,000 per year ($2,500 in scholarship and $500 in the form of book voucher); laptop computer to use throughout 4 years of enrollment.
Cumulative student debt: 85% of graduating class had student loans; average debt was $29,288.

FINANCIAL AID PROCEDURES

Forms required: FAFSA, state aid form.
Dates and Deadlines: Priority date 2/15; no closing date. Applicants notified on a rolling basis starting 3/22; must reply by 5/1 or within 3 week(s) of notification.
Transfers: No deadline. Applicants notified on a rolling basis starting 3/22; must reply within 3 week(s) of notification.

CONTACT

Angela Monnat, Director of Financial Aid
3690 East Avenue, Rochester, NY 14618-3597
(585) 385-8042

St. John's University

Queens, New York
www.stjohns.edu Federal Code: 002823

4-year private university in very large city, affiliated with Roman Catholic Church.
Enrollment: 12,326 undergrads, 3% part-time. 3,154 full-time freshmen.
Selectivity: Admits less than 50% of applicants.

BASIC COSTS (2008-2009)

Tuition and fees: $28,790.
Per-credit charge: $937.
Room and board: $12,570.
Additional info: Tuition may vary by program and class year. Four-year fixed rate tuition plan available for incoming freshmen. Tuition at time of enrollment locked for 4 years.

FINANCIAL AID PICTURE (2007-2008)

Students with need: Out of 2,782 full-time freshmen who applied for aid, 2,514 were judged to have need. Of these, 2,497 received aid, and 255 had their full need met. Average financial aid package met 72% of need; average scholarship/grant was $11,390; average loan was $4,290. For part-time students, average financial aid package was $8,370.
Students without need: 199 full-time freshmen who did not demonstrate need for aid received scholarships/grants; average award was $11,756. No-need awards available for academics, alumni affiliation, art, athletics, leadership, music/drama, religious affiliation, ROTC.
Scholarships offered: 46 full-time freshmen received athletic scholarships; average amount $26,335.
Cumulative student debt: 70% of graduating class had student loans; average debt was $19,983.

FINANCIAL AID PROCEDURES

Forms required: FAFSA.
Dates and Deadlines: Priority date 2/1; no closing date. Applicants notified on a rolling basis starting 3/15; must reply within 2 week(s) of notification.
Transfers: Must reply within 2 week(s) of notification. Scholarships available if 24 credits college study completed with a minimum GPA of 3.0.

CONTACT

Jorge Rodriguez, Associate Vice President and Executive Director, Financial Aid
8000 Utopia Parkway, Queens, NY 11439
(718) 990-2000

St. Joseph's College

Brooklyn, New York
www.sjcny.edu Federal Code: 002825

4-year private liberal arts and teachers college in very large city.
Enrollment: 1,037 undergrads, 32% part-time. 120 full-time freshmen.
Selectivity: Admits 50 to 75% of applicants.

BASIC COSTS (2008-2009)

Tuition and fees: $15,963.
Per-credit charge: $505.

FINANCIAL AID PICTURE (2007-2008)

Students with need: 59% of average financial aid package awarded as scholarships/grants, 41% awarded as loans/jobs. Need-based aid available for part-time students. Work study available nights, weekends, and for part-time students.
Students without need: No-need awards available for academics, alumni affiliation, leadership.

FINANCIAL AID PROCEDURES

Forms required: FAFSA, state aid form, institutional form.
Dates and Deadlines: Priority date 2/25; no closing date. Applicants notified on a rolling basis starting 4/1; must reply by 5/1 or within 2 week(s) of notification.
Transfers: Priority date 3/15; no deadline.

CONTACT

Amy Thompson, Director of Financial Aid
245 Clinton Avenue, Brooklyn, NY 11205-3688
(718) 636-6808

St. Joseph's College of Nursing

Syracuse, New York
www.sjhsyr.org/nursing Federal Code: 006467

2-year private nursing college in small city, affiliated with Roman Catholic Church.
Enrollment: 289 undergrads, 47% part-time. 9 full-time freshmen.
Selectivity: Admits less than 50% of applicants.

BASIC COSTS (2008-2009)

Tuition and fees: $12,948.
Room only: $3,700.

Additional info: Tuition includes liberal arts component of degree taken at other institution.

FINANCIAL AID PICTURE (2007-2008)

Students with need: 20% of average financial aid package awarded as scholarships/grants, 80% awarded as loans/jobs. Need-based aid available for part-time students.

Students without need: This college awards aid only to students with need.

FINANCIAL AID PROCEDURES

Forms required: FAFSA, state aid form.

Dates and Deadlines: Priority date 3/1; no closing date. Applicants notified on a rolling basis starting 6/15.

CONTACT

Theresa Moser, Director of Financial Aid
206 Prospect Avenue, Syracuse, NY 13203
(315) 448-5040

St. Joseph's College: Suffolk Campus

Patchogue, New York
www.sjcny.edu Federal Code: E00505

4-year private branch campus and liberal arts college in large town.

Enrollment: 3,727 undergrads, 22% part-time. 495 full-time freshmen.

Selectivity: Admits over 75% of applicants.

BASIC COSTS (2008-2009)

Tuition and fees: $15,963.

Per-credit charge: $505.

FINANCIAL AID PICTURE (2007-2008)

Students with need: 53% of average financial aid package awarded as scholarships/grants, 47% awarded as loans/jobs. Need-based aid available for part-time students. Work study available nights, weekends, and for part-time students.

Students without need: No-need awards available for academics.

Scholarships offered: Board of Trustees Scholarship: full tuition less outside aid; entering freshmen with a 92 high school average and 1200 SAT. Alumni Scholarship: variable award on yearly basis to children of alumni based on need and merit. Scholastic Achievement Award: up to $8,000 per year for entering freshmen. Academic Achievement Scholarship: automatically awards up to $4,500 for 3.6 GPA or better and $3,000 for 3.3 GPA or better; to entering transfer students with 3.3 GPA or better and associate degree. SAT scores listed exclusive of Writing.

FINANCIAL AID PROCEDURES

Forms required: FAFSA, state aid form, institutional form.

Dates and Deadlines: Priority date 2/25; no closing date. Applicants notified on a rolling basis starting 3/15; must reply within 2 week(s) of notification.

Transfers: Priority date 3/15; no deadline. Applicants notified on a rolling basis starting 3/15; must reply within 2 week(s) of notification.

CONTACT

Amy Thompson, Director of Financial Aid
155 West Roe Boulevard, Patchogue, NY 11772-2603
(631) 447-3214

St. Lawrence University

Canton, New York
www.stlawu.edu Federal Code: 002829

4-year private liberal arts college in small town.

Enrollment: 2,187 undergrads. 616 full-time freshmen.

Selectivity: Admits less than 50% of applicants.

BASIC COSTS (2009-2010)

Tuition and fees: $39,765.

Room and board: $9,645.

FINANCIAL AID PICTURE (2008-2009)

Students with need: Out of 447 full-time freshmen who applied for aid, 378 were judged to have need. Of these, 377 received aid, and 209 had their full need met. Average financial aid package met 95% of need; average scholarship/grant was $26,792; average loan was $3,360.

Students without need: 117 full-time freshmen who did not demonstrate need for aid received scholarships/grants; average award was $11,488. No-need awards available for academics, alumni affiliation, athletics, minority status, ROTC, state/district residency.

Scholarships offered: ***Merit:*** Merit scholarships from $7,500 to $20,000 annually. Augsbury/North Country Scholarship: for students in some schools in northern New York and southern Ontario; nomination by counselor required. Community Service Scholarship: based on past and current service. Presidential Diversity Scholarship: for students of African American, Asian American, Hispanic American and Native American heritage. Sesquicentennial and University Scholarship: based on academic excellence, character and leadership. Vilas Scholarship: for students interested in business. ***Athletic:*** 5 full-time freshmen received athletic scholarships; average amount $45,818.

Cumulative student debt: 68% of graduating class had student loans; average debt was $29,941.

FINANCIAL AID PROCEDURES

Forms required: FAFSA.

Dates and Deadlines: Closing date 2/1. Applicants notified by 3/31; must reply by 5/1 or within 2 week(s) of notification.

Transfers: Priority date 4/1; closing date 5/1. Applicants notified on a rolling basis starting 6/1; must reply within 2 week(s) of notification.

CONTACT

Patricia Farmer, Director of Financial Aid
Payson Hall, Canton, NY 13617
(315) 229-5265

St. Thomas Aquinas College

Sparkill, New York
www.stac.edu Federal Code: 002832

4-year private liberal arts college in large town.

Enrollment: 1,429 undergrads, 6% part-time. 324 full-time freshmen.

Selectivity: Admits over 75% of applicants.

BASIC COSTS (2009-2010)

Tuition and fees: $21,170.

Per-credit charge: $665.

Room and board: $9,980.

FINANCIAL AID PICTURE (2007-2008)

Students with need: Out of 297 full-time freshmen who applied for aid, 217 were judged to have need. Of these, 214 received aid, and 28 had their full need met. Average financial aid package met 55% of need; average scholarship/grant was $9,524; average loan was $3,535. For part-time students, average financial aid package was $5,105.

Students without need: 51 full-time freshmen who did not demonstrate need for aid received scholarships/grants; average award was $7,257. No-need awards available for academics, athletics.

Scholarships offered: 10 full-time freshmen received athletic scholarships; average amount $6,250.

FINANCIAL AID PROCEDURES

Forms required: FAFSA, state aid form.

Dates and Deadlines: Priority date 2/15; no closing date. Applicants notified on a rolling basis starting 3/1; must reply by 5/1 or within 4 week(s) of notification.

Transfers: Closing date 5/1. Applicants notified on a rolling basis; must reply within 4 week(s) of notification.

CONTACT

Anna Chrissotimos, Director of Financial Aid
125 Route 340, Sparkill, NY 10976
(845) 398-4097

St. Vincent Catholic Medical Centers

Fresh Meadows, New York
www.svcmc.org/body.cfm?id=758 Federal Code: 012364

2-year private nursing college in very large city, affiliated with Roman Catholic Church.
Enrollment: 153 undergrads.

BASIC COSTS (2008-2009)

Tuition and fees: $7,020.
Per-credit charge: $468.

FINANCIAL AID PICTURE (2007-2008)

Students with need: 36% of average financial aid package awarded as scholarships/grants, 64% awarded as loans/jobs.

FINANCIAL AID PROCEDURES

Forms required: FAFSA, state aid form.
Dates and Deadlines: No deadline. Applicants notified on a rolling basis; must reply within 2 week(s) of notification.

CONTACT

Catherine Pierce, Financial Aid Coordinator
175-05 Horace Harding Expressway, Fresh Meadows, NY 11356
(718) 357-0500 ext. 124

Sarah Lawrence College

Bronxville, New York Federal Code: 002813
www.slc.edu CSS Code: 2810

4-year private liberal arts college in small city.
Enrollment: 1,309 undergrads, 3% part-time. 347 full-time freshmen.
Selectivity: Admits less than 50% of applicants.

BASIC COSTS (2008-2009)

Tuition and fees: $40,350.
Room and board: $13,716.

FINANCIAL AID PICTURE (2008-2009)

Students with need: Out of 229 full-time freshmen who applied for aid, 188 were judged to have need. Of these, 188 received aid, and 147 had their full need met. Average financial aid package met 89% of need; average scholarship/grant was $25,368; average loan was $2,349. For part-time students, average financial aid package was $23,710.
Students without need: This college awards aid only to students with need.
Cumulative student debt: [illegible]% of graduating class had student loans; average debt was $15,581.

FINANCIAL AID PROCEDURES

Forms required: FAFSA, CSS PROFILE, state aid form.
Dates and Deadlines: Closing date 2/1. Applicants notified by 4/1; must reply by 5/1.
Transfers: Closing date 3/15. Maximum institutional grant to transfer students is $27,000 a year. Loans and work study available above and beyond this grant.

CONTACT

Heather McDonnell, Director of Financial Aid
One Mead Way, Bronxville, NY 10708-5999
(914) 395-2570

Schenectady County Community College

Schenectady, New York
www.sunysccc.edu Federal Code: 006785

2-year public community college in small city.
Enrollment: 2,578 undergrads.
Selectivity: Open admission; but selective for some programs.

BASIC COSTS (2008-2009)

Tuition and fees: $3,263; out-of-state residents $6,293.
Per-credit charge: $134; out-of-state residents $260.

FINANCIAL AID PICTURE (2007-2008)

Students with need: Need-based aid available for full-time and part-time students.
Students without need: This college awards aid only to students with need.

FINANCIAL AID PROCEDURES

Forms required: FAFSA.
Dates and Deadlines: Priority date 5/1; no closing date. Applicants notified on a rolling basis starting 4/15; must reply by 8/31.

CONTACT

Brian McGarvey, Director of Financial Aid
78 Washington Avenue, Schenectady, NY 12305
(518) 381-1352

School of Visual Arts

New York, New York
www.sva.edu Federal Code: 007468

4-year for-profit visual arts college in very large city.
Enrollment: 3,402 undergrads.

BASIC COSTS (2008-2009)

Tuition and fees: $25,500.
Per-credit charge: $850.
Room only: $11,350.
Additional info: Additional fees vary by department.

FINANCIAL AID PICTURE (2008-2009)

Students with need: Need-based aid available for full-time and part-time students. Work study available nights, weekends, and for part-time students.
Students without need: No-need awards available for art.
Scholarships offered: SVA matching scholarship available to full- and part-time undergraduate and graduate students. SVA will match 25% of any outside scholarship, up to $2,500, that a student obtains.

FINANCIAL AID PROCEDURES

Forms required: FAFSA, state aid form.
Dates and Deadlines: Priority date 2/1; no closing date. Applicants notified on a rolling basis starting 2/15; must reply within 4 week(s) of notification.
Transfers: No deadline. Applicants notified on a rolling basis; must reply within 4 week(s) of notification.

CONTACT

William Berrios, Director of Financial Aid
209 East 23rd Street, New York, NY 10010-3994
(212) 592-2030

Siena College
Loudonville, New York
www.siena.edu Federal Code: 002816

4-year private liberal arts college in large town, affiliated with Roman Catholic Church.
Enrollment: 3,242 undergrads, 4% part-time. 781 full-time freshmen.
Selectivity: Admits 50 to 75% of applicants.

BASIC COSTS (2009-2010)
Tuition and fees: $25,285.
Per-credit charge: $450.
Room and board: $9,930.

FINANCIAL AID PICTURE (2007-2008)
Students with need: Out of 690 full-time freshmen who applied for aid, 564 were judged to have need. Of these, 559 received aid, and 101 had their full need met. Average financial aid package met 78% of need; average scholarship/grant was $13,180; average loan was $3,452. For part-time students, average financial aid package was $12,030.
Students without need: 105 full-time freshmen who did not demonstrate need for aid received scholarships/grants; average award was $6,995. No-need awards available for academics, athletics, leadership, minority status, ROTC, state/district residency.
Scholarships offered: 69 full-time freshmen received athletic scholarships; average amount $13,445.
Cumulative student debt: 77% of graduating class had student loans; average debt was $26,500.

FINANCIAL AID PROCEDURES
Forms required: FAFSA, state aid form.
Dates and Deadlines: Priority date 2/15; closing date 5/1. Applicants notified by 4/1; must reply by 5/1.
Transfers: Priority date 3/1.

CONTACT
Mary Lawyer, Assistant Vice President for Financial Aid
515 Loudon Road, Loudonville, NY 12211-1462
(518) 783-2427

Skidmore College
Saratoga Springs, New York Federal Code: 002814
www.skidmore.edu CSS Code: 2815

4-year private liberal arts college in large town.
Enrollment: 2,678 undergrads, 3% part-time. 652 full-time freshmen.
Selectivity: Admits less than 50% of applicants.

BASIC COSTS (2009-2010)
Tuition and fees: $40,420.
Per-credit charge: $1,320.
Room and board: $10,776.

FINANCIAL AID PICTURE (2008-2009)
Students with need: Out of 350 full-time freshmen who applied for aid, 284 were judged to have need. Of these, 284 received aid, and 244 had their full need met. Average financial aid package met 85% of need; average scholarship/grant was $29,699; average loan was $2,574.
Students without need: 3 full-time freshmen who did not demonstrate need for aid received scholarships/grants; average award was $10,000. No-need awards available for music/drama.
Scholarships offered: Porter Presidential Scholarships in Science and Mathematics: $10,000 annually; based on outstanding ability and achievement in math, science, or computer science. Filene Undergraduate Music Scholarships: $10,000 annually; based on music ability. No drama scholarships.
Cumulative student debt: 46% of graduating class had student loans; average debt was $19,163.

FINANCIAL AID PROCEDURES
Forms required: FAFSA, CSS PROFILE.
Dates and Deadlines: Closing date 1/15. Applicants notified by 4/1; must reply by 5/1.
Transfers: Priority date 4/1. Applicants notified on a rolling basis starting 4/15; must reply within 3 week(s) of notification. Some transfer students eligible for need-based grant assistance. Other transfer students eligible for grant assistance after 1 full year of enrollment or at beginning of junior year, whichever comes first.

CONTACT
Robert Shorb, Associate Dean, Director of Student Aid and Family Finance
815 North Broadway, Saratoga Springs, NY 12866
(518) 580-5750

State University of New York at Albany
Albany, New York
www.albany.edu Federal Code: 002835

4-year public university in small city.
Enrollment: 12,937 undergrads, 5% part-time. 2,514 full-time freshmen.
Selectivity: Admits 50 to 75% of applicants.

BASIC COSTS (2008-2009)
Tuition and fees: $6,078; out-of-state residents $12,338.
Per-credit charge: $181; out-of-state residents $442.
Room and board: $9,778.

FINANCIAL AID PICTURE (2007-2008)
Students with need: Out of 2,096 full-time freshmen who applied for aid, 1,370 were judged to have need. Of these, 1,342 received aid, and 213 had their full need met. Average financial aid package met 74% of need; average scholarship/grant was $5,554; average loan was $3,875. For part-time students, average financial aid package was $4,697.
Students without need: 215 full-time freshmen who did not demonstrate need for aid received scholarships/grants; average award was $3,332. No-need awards available for academics, athletics, state/district residency.
Scholarships offered: ***Merit:*** Presidential Scholarship: up to $4,000 per year for NY residents and $5,000 per year for out-of-state students; renewable; requires minimum 90 high school average and combined SAT Critical Reading and Math scores in the upper 1200s or higher. ***Athletic:*** 57 full-time freshmen received athletic scholarships; average amount $11,009.
Cumulative student debt: 70% of graduating class had student loans; average debt was $18,189.

FINANCIAL AID PROCEDURES
Forms required: FAFSA, state aid form.
Dates and Deadlines: Priority date 3/15; no closing date. Applicants notified on a rolling basis starting 3/15; must reply by 5/1.

CONTACT
Beth Post, Director of Financial Aid
Office of Undergraduate Admissions, University Hall 112, Albany, NY 12222
(518) 442-3202

State University of New York at Binghamton
Binghamton, New York
www.binghamton.edu Federal Code: 002836

4-year public university in small city.
Enrollment: 11,760 undergrads, 3% part-time. 2,438 full-time freshmen.
Selectivity: Admits less than 50% of applicants.

BASIC COSTS (2008-2009)
Tuition and fees: $6,072; out-of-state residents $12,332.
Per-credit charge: $181; out-of-state residents $442.
Room and board: $9,774.

FINANCIAL AID PICTURE (2008-2009)
Students with need: Out of 1,947 full-time freshmen who applied for aid, 1,013 were judged to have need. Of these, 1,008 received aid, and 721 had their full need met. Average financial aid package met 75% of need; average scholarship/grant was $5,092; average loan was $3,547. For part-time students, average financial aid package was $7,516.
Students without need: 50 full-time freshmen who did not demonstrate need for aid received scholarships/grants; average award was $3,113. No-need awards available for academics, art, athletics, leadership, minority status, music/drama, state/district residency.
Scholarships offered: 71 full-time freshmen received athletic scholarships; average amount $7,912.
Cumulative student debt: 54% of graduating class had student loans; average debt was $14,541.

FINANCIAL AID PROCEDURES
Forms required: FAFSA, state aid form.
Dates and Deadlines: Priority date 2/1; no closing date. Applicants notified on a rolling basis starting 4/1; must reply within 2 week(s) of notification.
Transfers: No deadline. Applicants notified on a rolling basis starting 4/1; must reply within 2 week(s) of notification.

CONTACT
Dennis Chavez, Director of Financial Aid Services
Box 6001, Binghamton, NY 13902-6001
(607) 777-2428

State University of New York at Buffalo
Buffalo, New York
www.buffalo.edu Federal Code: 002837

4-year public university in large city.
Enrollment: 18,760 undergrads, 6% part-time. 3,257 full-time freshmen.
Selectivity: Admits 50 to 75% of applicants.

BASIC COSTS (2008-2009)
Tuition and fees: $6,285; out-of-state residents $12,545.
Per-credit charge: $181; out-of-state residents $442.
Room and board: $9,552.

FINANCIAL AID PICTURE (2007-2008)
Students with need: Out of 2,572 full-time freshmen who applied for aid, 1,677 were judged to have need. Of these, 1,632 received aid, and 56 had their full need met. Average financial aid package met 68% of need; average scholarship/grant was $3,035; average loan was $3,372. For part-time students, average financial aid package was $4,640.
Students without need: 867 full-time freshmen who did not demonstrate need for aid received scholarships/grants; average award was $3,298. No-need awards available for academics, athletics, minority status, music/drama, state/district residency.
Scholarships offered: ***Merit:*** Honors program includes scholarships for high academic achievement, high SAT scores. ***Athletic:*** 34 full-time freshmen received athletic scholarships; average amount $13,402.
Cumulative student debt: 87% of graduating class had student loans; average debt was $52,591.

FINANCIAL AID PROCEDURES
Forms required: FAFSA.
Dates and Deadlines: Priority date 3/1; no closing date. Applicants notified on a rolling basis starting 2/1; must reply by 5/1.

CONTACT
Cindy Kohlman, Director of Financial Aid
12 Capen Hall, Buffalo, NY 14260-1660
(716) 645-2450

State University of New York at Farmingdale
Farmingdale, New York
www.farmingdale.edu Federal Code: 002858

4-year public technical college in large town.
Enrollment: 5,951 undergrads, 23% part-time. 1,020 full-time freshmen.
Selectivity: Admits less than 50% of applicants.

BASIC COSTS (2008-2009)
Tuition and fees: $5,375; out-of-state residents $11,635.
Per-credit charge: $181; out-of-state residents $442.
Room and board: $10,850.

FINANCIAL AID PICTURE
Students with need: Need-based aid available for full-time and part-time students.
Students without need: No-need awards available for academics.

FINANCIAL AID PROCEDURES
Forms required: FAFSA, state aid form, institutional form.
Dates and Deadlines: Priority date 4/1; no closing date. Applicants notified on a rolling basis starting 4/1.

CONTACT
Catherine Malnichuck, Director of Financial Services
2350 Broadhollow Road, Farmingdale, NY 11735-1021
(631) 420-2578

State University of New York at New Paltz
New Paltz, New York
www.newpaltz.edu Federal Code: 002846

4-year public liberal arts college in large town.
Enrollment: 6,195 undergrads, 9% part-time. 1,287 full-time freshmen.
Selectivity: Admits less than 50% of applicants.

BASIC COSTS (2008-2009)
Tuition and fees: $5,419; out-of-state residents $11,679.
Per-credit charge: $181; out-of-state residents $442.
Room and board: $8,690.

FINANCIAL AID PICTURE (2008-2009)
Students with need: Out of 1,084 full-time freshmen who applied for aid, 650 were judged to have need. Of these, 639 received aid, and 120 had their full need met. Average financial aid package met 53% of need; average scholarship/grant was $4,517; average loan was $3,245. For part-time students, average financial aid package was $4,899.
Students without need: This college awards aid only to students with need.
Cumulative student debt: 66% of graduating class had student loans; average debt was $16,798.

FINANCIAL AID PROCEDURES
Forms required: FAFSA, state aid form.
Dates and Deadlines: Priority date 3/15; no closing date. Applicants notified on a rolling basis starting 4/1; must reply within 4 week(s) of notification.
Transfers: No deadline. Applicants notified on a rolling basis starting 4/1; must reply within 4 week(s) of notification.

CONTACT

Daniel Sistarenik, Director of Financial Aid
100 Hawk Drive, New Paltz, NY 12561-2443
(845) 257-3250

State University of New York at Oswego

Oswego, New York
www.oswego.edu Federal Code: 002848

4-year public university in large town.
Enrollment: 7,095 undergrads, 6% part-time. 1,468 full-time freshmen.
Selectivity: Admits less than 50% of applicants.

BASIC COSTS (2008-2009)

Tuition and fees: $5,531; out-of-state residents $11,791.
Per-credit charge: $181; out-of-state residents $442.
Room and board: $10,170.

FINANCIAL AID PICTURE (2008-2009)

Students with need: Out of 1,319 full-time freshmen who applied for aid, 873 were judged to have need. Of these, 843 received aid, and 304 had their full need met. Average financial aid package met 87% of need; average scholarship/grant was $5,313; average loan was $5,055. For part-time students, average financial aid package was $9,103.
Students without need: 327 full-time freshmen who did not demonstrate need for aid received scholarships/grants; average award was $5,707. No-need awards available for academics, state/district residency.
Scholarships offered: Annual scholarships: $500 to $4,400 annually; based on class rank in top 15%. Additional residential scholarships for out-of-state students: $4,490 annually; requires on-campus housing.
Cumulative student debt: 84% of graduating class had student loans; average debt was $22,117.

FINANCIAL AID PROCEDURES

Forms required: FAFSA.
Dates and Deadlines: Priority date 3/1; no closing date. Applicants notified on a rolling basis starting 3/1; must reply by 5/1 or within 3 week(s) of notification.
Transfers: Transfer students entering in January need to supply financial aid transcipts from prior colleges.

CONTACT

Mark Humbert, Director of Financial Aid
229 Sheldon Hall, Oswego, NY 13126-3599
(315) 312-2248

State University of New York at Purchase

Purchase, New York
www.purchase.edu Federal Code: 006791

4-year public university in large town.
Enrollment: 3,790 undergrads, 6% part-time. 709 full-time freshmen.
Selectivity: Admits less than 50% of applicants.

BASIC COSTS (2008-2009)

Tuition and fees: $5,811; out-of-state residents $12,071.
Per-credit charge: $181; out-of-state residents $442.
Room and board: $9,908.

FINANCIAL AID PICTURE (2008-2009)

Students with need: Out of 597 full-time freshmen who applied for aid, 394 were judged to have need. Of these, 393 received aid, and 29 had their full need met. Average financial aid package met 56% of need; average scholarship/grant was $5,218; average loan was $3,501. For part-time students, average financial aid package was $10,937.
Students without need: 35 full-time freshmen who did not demonstrate need for aid received scholarships/grants; average award was $2,135. No-need awards available for academics, art, music/drama.
Cumulative student debt: 59% of graduating class had student loans; average debt was $20,209.
Additional info: All applicants automatically considered for scholarship upon review of applications, essays, auditions, and/or portfolio.

FINANCIAL AID PROCEDURES

Forms required: FAFSA, state aid form.
Dates and Deadlines: Priority date 2/1; no closing date. Applicants notified on a rolling basis starting 3/1; must reply within 2 week(s) of notification.
Transfers: Financial aid transcripts required from all previously attended institutions.

CONTACT

Corey York, Director of Financial Aid
735 Anderson Hill Road, Purchase, NY 10577-1400
(914) 251-6350

State University of New York at Stony Brook

Stony Brook, New York
www.stonybrook.edu Federal Code: 002838

4-year public university in large town.
Enrollment: 15,596 undergrads, 6% part-time. 2,762 full-time freshmen.
Selectivity: Admits less than 50% of applicants.

BASIC COSTS (2008-2009)

Tuition and fees: $5,810; out-of-state residents $12,070.
Per-credit charge: $181; out-of-state residents $442.
Room and board: $9,132.

FINANCIAL AID PICTURE (2007-2008)

Students with need: Out of 2,202 full-time freshmen who applied for aid, 1,497 were judged to have need. Of these, 1,445 received aid, and 350 had their full need met. Average financial aid package met 68% of need; average scholarship/grant was $6,626; average loan was $4,212. For part-time students, average financial aid package was $5,017.
Students without need: 377 full-time freshmen who did not demonstrate need for aid received scholarships/grants; average award was $2,571. No-need awards available for academics, alumni affiliation, art, athletics, job skills, leadership, music/drama.
Scholarships offered: 51 full-time freshmen received athletic scholarships; average amount $11,139.
Cumulative student debt: 63% of graduating class had student loans; average debt was $17,336.

FINANCIAL AID PROCEDURES

Forms required: FAFSA.
Dates and Deadlines: Priority date 3/1; no closing date. Applicants notified on a rolling basis starting 3/1; must reply by 5/1 or within 2 week(s) of notification.

CONTACT

Jacqueline Pascariello, Director Financial Aid
118 Administration Building, Stony Brook, NY 11794-1901
(631) 689-6840

State University of New York College at Brockport

Brockport, New York
www.brockport.edu Federal Code: 002841

4-year public liberal arts college in small town.
Enrollment: 6,892 undergrads, 9% part-time. 951 full-time freshmen.
Selectivity: Admits less than 50% of applicants.

BASIC COSTS (2008-2009)

Tuition and fees: $5,444; out-of-state residents $11,704.
Per-credit charge: $181; out-of-state residents $442.
Room and board: $8,630.

FINANCIAL AID PICTURE (2007-2008)

Students with need: Out of 868 full-time freshmen who applied for aid, 624 were judged to have need. Of these, 620 received aid, and 173 had their full need met. Average financial aid package met 84% of need; average scholarship/grant was $4,198; average loan was $4,340. For part-time students, average financial aid package was $4,653.
Students without need: 81 full-time freshmen who did not demonstrate need for aid received scholarships/grants; average award was $4,035. No-need awards available for academics, alumni affiliation, art, leadership, minority status, ROTC, state/district residency.
Scholarships offered: Extraordinary Academic Scholarships: $2,250 to $12,100 per year; minimum qualifications include SAT scores of 1100 (24 ACT), rank in top 25% of class, 90 average or higher. SAT score exclusive of Writing portion.
Cumulative student debt: 82% of graduating class had student loans; average debt was $24,808.

FINANCIAL AID PROCEDURES

Forms required: FAFSA.
Dates and Deadlines: Priority date 2/15; no closing date. Applicants notified on a rolling basis starting 3/15; must reply by 5/1 or within 4 week(s) of notification.

CONTACT

J. Atkinson, Assistant Vice President for Enrollment Management and Student Affairs
350 New Campus Drive, Brockport, NY 14420-2915
(585) 395-2501

State University of New York College at Buffalo

Buffalo, New York
www.buffalostate.edu Federal Code: 002842

4-year public liberal arts and teachers college in large city.
Enrollment: 9,172 undergrads, 10% part-time. 1,390 full-time freshmen.
Selectivity: Admits less than 50% of applicants.

BASIC COSTS (2008-2009)

Tuition and fees: $5,375; out-of-state residents $11,635.
Per-credit charge: $181; out-of-state residents $442.
Room and board: $9,061.
Additional info: Tuition/fee waivers available for minority students.

FINANCIAL AID PICTURE (2007-2008)

Students with need: Out of 1,220 full-time freshmen who applied for aid, 1,199 were judged to have need. Of these, 1,199 received aid, and 723 had their full need met. Average financial aid package met 71% of need; average scholarship/grant was $4,944; average loan was $3,128. For part-time students, average financial aid package was $9,814.
Students without need: This college awards aid only to students with need.
Scholarships offered: Empire Minority Scholarships; $1,000 annually for 4 years. Honors Program; $2,000 for 2 years and $1,000 for remaining 2 years.
Cumulative student debt: 69% of graduating class had student loans; average debt was $17,657.

FINANCIAL AID PROCEDURES

Forms required: FAFSA.
Dates and Deadlines: Priority date 3/15; closing date 5/1. Applicants notified on a rolling basis starting 5/1; must reply within 4 week(s) of notification.
Transfers: No deadline.

CONTACT

Kent McGowan, Director of Financial Aid
1300 Elmwood Avenue, Moot Hall, Buffalo, NY 14222-1095
(716) 878-4902

State University of New York College at Cortland

Cortland, New York
www.cortland.edu Federal Code: 002843

4-year public liberal arts and teachers college in large town.
Enrollment: 6,096 undergrads, 2% part-time. 1,196 full-time freshmen.
Selectivity: Admits less than 50% of applicants.

BASIC COSTS (2008-2009)

Tuition and fees: $5,499; out-of-state residents $11,759.
Per-credit charge: $181; out-of-state residents $442.
Room and board: $9,170.

FINANCIAL AID PICTURE (2007-2008)

Students with need: Out of 1,072 full-time freshmen who applied for aid, 673 were judged to have need. Of these, 659 received aid, and 117 had their full need met. Average financial aid package met 73% of need; average scholarship/grant was $3,043; average loan was $3,747. Need-based aid available for part-time students.
Students without need: 284 full-time freshmen who did not demonstrate need for aid received scholarships/grants; average award was $7,337. No-need awards available for academics, art, leadership, minority status, music/drama, state/district residency.

FINANCIAL AID PROCEDURES

Forms required: FAFSA, state aid form.
Dates and Deadlines: Priority date 3/1; no closing date. Applicants notified on a rolling basis starting 3/15; must reply by 5/1 or within 4 week(s) of notification.

CONTACT

Karen Gallagher, Director of Financial Aid
PO Box 2000, Cortland, NY 13045-0900
(607) 753-4717

State University of New York College at Fredonia

Fredonia, New York
www.fredonia.edu Federal Code: 002844

4-year public liberal arts college in large town.
Enrollment: 5,163 undergrads, 3% part-time. 1,187 full-time freshmen.
Selectivity: Admits 50 to 75% of applicants.

BASIC COSTS (2008-2009)

Tuition and fees: $5,588; out-of-state residents $11,848.
Per-credit charge: $181; out-of-state residents $442.
Room and board: $9,130.

FINANCIAL AID PICTURE (2008-2009)

Students with need: Out of 1,042 full-time freshmen who applied for aid, 710 were judged to have need. Of these, 705 received aid, and 185 had their full need met. Average financial aid package met 70% of need; average scholarship/grant was $3,628; average loan was $3,705. For part-time students, average financial aid package was $7,369.

Students without need: 105 full-time freshmen who did not demonstrate need for aid received scholarships/grants; average award was $1,908. No-need awards available for academics, alumni affiliation, art, athletics, leadership, minority status, music/drama.

Scholarships offered: Dean's Scholar Award: $1,000; minimum 90 high school average, 1150 SAT or 25 ACT; 100 awarded. Foundation Academic Scholarship: $1,000; minimum 90 high school average, 1100 SAT or 24 ACT; 50 awarded. President's Award of Excellence: $3,000, renewable; minimum 92 high school average, 1250 SAT or 28 ACT; 12 awarded. President's Out-of-State Scholar Award: $3,000, renewable; for non-NY residents; approximately 50 awarded.

Cumulative student debt: 88% of graduating class had student loans; average debt was $19,338.

FINANCIAL AID PROCEDURES

Forms required: FAFSA, state aid form.

Dates and Deadlines: Priority date 2/1; closing date 5/15. Applicants notified on a rolling basis starting 3/10; must reply within 4 week(s) of notification.

Transfers: Priority date 1/31. Applicants notified on a rolling basis starting 10/15. Financial aid transcripts required from prior institutions attended.

CONTACT

Daniel Tramuta, Director of Financial Aid
178 Central Avenue, Fredonia, NY 14063-1136
(716) 673-3253

State University of New York College at Geneseo

Geneseo, New York
www.geneseo.edu Federal Code: 002845

4-year public liberal arts college in small town.

Enrollment: 5,441 undergrads, 1% part-time. 1,079 full-time freshmen.

Selectivity: Admits less than 50% of applicants.

BASIC COSTS (2008-2009)

Tuition and fees: $5,658; out-of-state residents $11,918.

Per-credit charge: $181; out-of-state residents $442.

Room and board: $9,070.

FINANCIAL AID PICTURE (2008-2009)

Students with need: Out of 884 full-time freshmen who applied for aid, 392 were judged to have need. Of these, 392 received aid, and 282 had their full need met. Average financial aid package met 72% of need; average scholarship/grant was $2,090; average loan was $3,932. Need-based aid available for part-time students.

Students without need: 5 full-time freshmen who did not demonstrate need for aid received scholarships/grants; average award was $1,780. No-need awards available for academics, art, leadership, minority status, music/drama, religious affiliation, ROTC, state/district residency.

Cumulative student debt: 67% of graduating class had student loans; average debt was $18,700.

FINANCIAL AID PROCEDURES

Forms required: FAFSA, state aid form.

Dates and Deadlines: Closing date 2/15. Applicants notified on a rolling basis starting 3/15; must reply by 5/1.

CONTACT

Archie Cureton, Director of Financial Aid
1 College Circle, Geneseo, NY 14454-1471
(585) 245-5731

State University of New York College at Old Westbury

Old Westbury, New York
www.oldwestbury.edu Federal Code: 007109

4-year public business and liberal arts college in small city.

Enrollment: 3,355 undergrads, 15% part-time. 435 full-time freshmen.

Selectivity: Admits less than 50% of applicants.

BASIC COSTS (2008-2009)

Tuition and fees: $5,177; out-of-state residents $11,437.

Per-credit charge: $181; out-of-state residents $442.

Room and board: $9,032.

FINANCIAL AID PICTURE (2007-2008)

Students with need: Out of 356 full-time freshmen who applied for aid, 353 were judged to have need. Of these, 301 received aid, and 301 had their full need met. Average financial aid package met 45% of need; average scholarship/grant was $5,762; average loan was $2,088. For part-time students, average financial aid package was $2,504.

Students without need: No-need awards available for academics, alumni affiliation, state/district residency.

Cumulative student debt: 53% of graduating class had student loans; average debt was $15,374.

FINANCIAL AID PROCEDURES

Forms required: FAFSA, state aid form, institutional form.

Dates and Deadlines: Priority date 4/1; no closing date. Applicants notified on a rolling basis starting 4/15; must reply within 2 week(s) of notification.

Transfers: No deadline. Applicants notified on a rolling basis starting 4/15; must reply within 2 week(s) of notification. Financial aid transcript required.

CONTACT

Mildred O'Keefe, Director of Financial Aid
Box 307, Old Westbury, NY 11568-0307
(516) 876-3222

State University of New York College at Oneonta

Oneonta, New York
www.oneonta.edu Federal Code: 002847

4-year public liberal arts college in large town.

Enrollment: 5,508 undergrads, 2% part-time. 1,017 full-time freshmen.

Selectivity: Admits less than 50% of applicants.

BASIC COSTS (2008-2009)

Tuition and fees: $5,485; out-of-state residents $11,745.

Per-credit charge: $181; out-of-state residents $442.

Room and board: $8,106.

FINANCIAL AID PICTURE (2008-2009)

Students with need: Out of 903 full-time freshmen who applied for aid, 565 were judged to have need. Of these, 547 received aid, and 97 had their full need met. Average financial aid package met 58% of need; average scholarship/grant was $4,451; average loan was $3,494. For part-time students, average financial aid package was $5,391.

Students without need: 286 full-time freshmen who did not demonstrate need for aid received scholarships/grants; average award was $2,200. No-

need awards available for academics, alumni affiliation, leadership, minority status, music/drama, state/district residency.

Scholarships offered: Presidential Scholarships: $3,500; awarded to 149 applicants for academics, service, extracurricular activities. Deans' Scholarships: $2,000; awarded to 57 applicants based on academics. Oneonta Auxiliary Services Scholarships: $1,000; awarded to 158 applicants for academics, service, extracurricular activities. Alumni Association Board of Directors Scholarships: $1,000; awarded to 13 applicants for academics, service, extracurricular activities. Mildred Haight Memorial Scholarships: $1,000; awarded to 19 applicants for academics.

Cumulative student debt: 75% of graduating class had student loans; average debt was $19,967.

FINANCIAL AID PROCEDURES

Forms required: FAFSA, state aid form.

Dates and Deadlines: Priority date 3/15; no closing date. Applicants notified on a rolling basis starting 3/1; must reply by 5/1 or within 4 week(s) of notification.

Transfers: No deadline. Applicants notified on a rolling basis starting 3/1.

CONTACT

C. Goodhue, Director of Student Financial Aid
Admissions Office, 116 Alumni Hall, Oneonta, NY 13820-4016
(607) 436-2532

State University of New York College at Plattsburgh

Plattsburgh, New York
www.plattsburgh.edu Federal Code: 002849

4-year public liberal arts and teachers college in large town.

Enrollment: 5,602 undergrads, 5% part-time. 970 full-time freshmen.

Selectivity: Admits less than 50% of applicants.

BASIC COSTS (2008-2009)

Tuition and fees: $5,422; out-of-state residents $11,682.

Per-credit charge: $181; out-of-state residents $442.

Room and board: $8,250.

FINANCIAL AID PICTURE (2007-2008)

Students with need: Out of 806 full-time freshmen who applied for aid, 554 were judged to have need. Of these, 546 received aid, and 160 had their full need met. Average financial aid package met 84% of need; average scholarship/grant was $5,434; average loan was $4,825. For part-time students, average financial aid package was $5,916.

Students without need: 331 full-time freshmen who did not demonstrate need for aid received scholarships/grants; average award was $5,181. No-need awards available for academics, alumni affiliation, art, leadership, minority status, music/drama, ROTC, state/district residency.

Cumulative student debt: 76% of graduating class had student loans; average debt was $22,634.

FINANCIAL AID PROCEDURES

Forms required: FAFSA, state aid form.

Dates and Deadlines: Priority date 2/15; no closing date. Applicants notified on a rolling basis starting 3/15; must reply by 5/1.

Transfers: Closing date 3/1. Applicants notified by 3/31.

CONTACT

Todd Moravec, Director of Financial Aid
Kehoe Administration Building, Plattsburgh, NY 12901
(518) 564-4076

State University of New York College at Potsdam

Potsdam, New York
www.potsdam.edu Federal Code: 002850

4-year public liberal arts and teachers college in large town.

Enrollment: 3,590 undergrads, 3% part-time. 805 full-time freshmen.

Selectivity: Admits 50 to 75% of applicants.

BASIC COSTS (2008-2009)

Tuition and fees: $5,462; out-of-state residents $11,722.

Per-credit charge: $181; out-of-state residents $442.

Room and board: $8,820.

FINANCIAL AID PICTURE (2008-2009)

Students with need: Out of 725 full-time freshmen who applied for aid, 520 were judged to have need. Of these, 515 received aid, and 464 had their full need met. Average financial aid package met 90% of need; average scholarship/grant was $6,153; average loan was $3,584. For part-time students, average financial aid package was $7,790.

Students without need: 85 full-time freshmen who did not demonstrate need for aid received scholarships/grants; average award was $4,355. No-need awards available for academics, art, leadership, minority status, music/drama, ROTC.

Scholarships offered: Mt. Emmons Scholarship: covers balance of in-state tuition and mandatory fees after TAP awards, $500 book stipend, residence hall fee waiver and board; renewable with minimum 3.25 GPA; 5 awarded. Freshman Scholars Program: $1,000-$4,600; for students who show aca demic promise and potential for leadership; 1100 or higher SAT (exclusive of Writing), ACT composite of 23, or minimum 90 high school average and history of participation, leadership in extracurricular activities and community service.

Cumulative student debt: 85% of graduating class had student loans; average debt was $20,291.

Additional info: Apply early to access limited, need-based awards.

FINANCIAL AID PROCEDURES

Forms required: FAFSA, state aid form.

Dates and Deadlines: Priority date 3/1; no closing date. Applicants notified on a rolling basis starting 2/1; must reply by 5/1 or within 4 week(s) of notification.

Transfers: Transfer Scholars Program for incoming transfer students based upon outstanding academic achievement as measured by previous college GPA. $1,000-$3,000 to students with minimum cumulative GPA of 3.25 and higher. Renewable for 1 year with cumulative 3.25 GPA.

CONTACT

Susan Aldrich, Director of Financial Aid
44 Pierrepont Avenue, Potsdam, NY 13676
(315) 267-2162

State University of New York College of Agriculture and Technology at Cobleskill

Cobleskill, New York
www.cobleskill.edu Federal Code: 002856

2-year public agricultural and technical college in small town.

Enrollment: 2,588 undergrads, 3% part-time. 1,019 full-time freshmen.

Selectivity: Admits over 75% of applicants.

BASIC COSTS (2008-2009)

Tuition and fees: $5,499; out-of-state residents $11,759.

Per-credit charge: $181; out-of-state residents $442.

Room and board: $9,010.

FINANCIAL AID PICTURE (2007-2008)

Students with need: Out of 937 full-time freshmen who applied for aid, 731 were judged to have need. Of these, 710 received aid, and 111 had their full need met. Average financial aid package met 68% of need; average scholarship/grant was $4,227; average loan was $3,337. For part-time students, average financial aid package was $2,005.

Students without need: 77 full-time freshmen who did not demonstrate need for aid received scholarships/grants; average award was $1,786. No-need awards available for academics, alumni affiliation, leadership, state/district residency.

Cumulative student debt: 75% of graduating class had student loans; average debt was $22,475.

Additional info: Application deadline for scholarships March 15. Separate application required, available through admissions office.

FINANCIAL AID PROCEDURES

Forms required: FAFSA, state aid form.

Dates and Deadlines: Closing date 2/15. Applicants notified on a rolling basis; must reply within 2 week(s) of notification.

Transfers: Priority date 2/15; no deadline. Applicants notified on a rolling basis; must reply within 3 week(s) of notification.

CONTACT

Brian Smith, Director of Financial Aid
Knapp Hall, Cobleskill, NY 12043
(800) 295-8998

State University of New York College of Agriculture and Technology at Morrisville

Morrisville, New York
www.morrisville.edu Federal Code: 002859

2-year public agricultural and technical college in small town.

Enrollment: 3,125 undergrads, 9% part-time. 1,114 full-time freshmen.

Selectivity: Admits 50 to 75% of applicants.

BASIC COSTS (2008-2009)

Tuition and fees: $5,375; out-of-state residents $11,635.

Per-credit charge: $181; out-of-state residents $442.

Room and board: $8,510.

Additional info: Tuition/fee waivers available for unemployed or children of unemployed.

FINANCIAL AID PICTURE (2007-2008)

Students with need: 43% of average financial aid package awarded as scholarships/grants, 57% awarded as loans/jobs. Need-based aid available for part-time students. Work study available nights, weekends, and for part-time students.

Students without need: No-need awards available for academics.

FINANCIAL AID PROCEDURES

Forms required: FAFSA, state aid form.

Dates and Deadlines: Priority date 2/1; no closing date. Applicants notified on a rolling basis starting 3/1; must reply within 3 week(s) of notification.

Transfers: No deadline. Applicants notified on a rolling basis; must reply within 3 week(s) of notification.

CONTACT

Dacia Banks, Director of Financial Aid
PO Box 901, Morrisville, NY 13408-0901
(800) 626-5844

State University of New York College of Environmental Science and Forestry

Syracuse, New York
www.esf.edu Federal Code: 002851

4-year public university and liberal arts college in small city.

Enrollment: 1,541 undergrads, 3% part-time. 310 full-time freshmen.

Selectivity: Admits less than 50% of applicants.

BASIC COSTS (2008-2009)

Tuition and fees: $5,136; out-of-state residents $11,396.

Per-credit charge: $181; out-of-state residents $442.

Additional info: Room and board available through Syracuse University. Tuition/fee waivers available for minority students.

FINANCIAL AID PICTURE (2008-2009)

Students with need: Out of 274 full-time freshmen who applied for aid, 196 were judged to have need. Of these, 196 received aid, and 196 had their full need met. Average financial aid package met 100% of need; average scholarship/grant was $5,000; average loan was $5,500. For part-time students, average financial aid package was $8,000.

Students without need: 59 full-time freshmen who did not demonstrate need for aid received scholarships/grants; average award was $2,500. No-need awards available for academics, alumni affiliation, leadership, minority status, ROTC, state/district residency.

Cumulative student debt: 80% of graduating class had student loans; average debt was $19,000.

FINANCIAL AID PROCEDURES

Forms required: FAFSA.

Dates and Deadlines: Priority date 3/1; no closing date. Applicants notified on a rolling basis starting 3/15; must reply within 2 week(s) of notification.

Transfers: Applicants notified on a rolling basis starting 3/15; must reply within 2 week(s) of notification.

CONTACT

John View, Director of Financial Aid
106 Bray Hall, Syracuse, NY 13210
(315) 470-6670

State University of New York College of Technology at Alfred

Alfred, New York
www.alfredstate.edu Federal Code: 002854

2-year public liberal arts and technical college in rural community.

Enrollment: 3,177 undergrads, 7% part-time. 1,296 full-time freshmen.

Selectivity: Admits 50 to 75% of applicants.

BASIC COSTS (2008-2009)

Tuition and fees: $5,498; out-of-state residents $8,358.

Per-credit charge: $181; out-of-state residents $300.

Room and board: $8,660.

FINANCIAL AID PICTURE (2007-2008)

Students with need: Need-based aid available for full-time and part-time students. Work study available nights, weekends, and for part-time students.

Students without need: No-need awards available for academics, alumni affiliation, job skills, minority status.

FINANCIAL AID PROCEDURES

Forms required: FAFSA, state aid form.

Dates and Deadlines: No deadline. Applicants notified on a rolling basis starting 3/1; must reply within 3 week(s) of notification.

Transfers: No deadline. Applicants notified on a rolling basis starting 3/1; must reply within 4 week(s) of notification.

CONTACT
Jane Gilliland, Director of Student Financial Services
Huntington Administration Building, Alfred, NY 14802-1196
(607) 587-4253

State University of New York College of Technology at Canton

Canton, New York
www.canton.edu Federal Code: 002855

2-year public technical college in small town.
Enrollment: 2,647 undergrads, 13% part-time. 812 full-time freshmen.
Selectivity: Admits over 75% of applicants.

BASIC COSTS (2008-2009)
Tuition and fees: $5,514; out-of-state residents $8,374.
Per-credit charge: $181; out-of-state residents $300.
Room and board: $8,970.

FINANCIAL AID PICTURE (2007-2008)
Students with need: 66% of average financial aid package awarded as scholarships/grants, 34% awarded as loans/jobs. Need-based aid available for part-time students. Work study available nights, weekends, and for part-time students.
Students without need: No-need awards available for academics, alumni affiliation, leadership, minority status, state/district residency.

FINANCIAL AID PROCEDURES
Forms required: FAFSA, state aid form.
Dates and Deadlines: Priority date 3/15; no closing date. Applicants notified on a rolling basis starting 2/15; must reply within 4 week(s) of notification.
Transfers: Financial aid transcripts required from all previously attended schools for mid-year transfers.

CONTACT
Kerrie Cooper, Director of Financial Aid
34 Cornell Drive, Canton, NY 13617-1098
(315) 386-7616

State University of New York College of Technology at Delhi

Delhi, New York
www.delhi.edu Federal Code: 002857

2-year public liberal arts and technical college in rural community.
Enrollment: 2,751 undergrads, 9% part-time. 1,008 full-time freshmen.
Selectivity: Admits 50 to 75% of applicants.

BASIC COSTS (2008-2009)
Tuition and fees: $5,648; out-of-state residents $8,508.
Room and board: $9,204.
Additional info: Out-of-state tuition for bachelor's program: $10,610; per-credit-hour $442.

FINANCIAL AID PICTURE (2007-2008)
Students with need: 45% of average financial aid package awarded as scholarships/grants, 55% awarded as loans/jobs. Need-based aid available for part-time students.

FINANCIAL AID PROCEDURES
Forms required: FAFSA, state aid form.
Dates and Deadlines: Priority date 2/15; no closing date. Applicants notified on a rolling basis starting 3/1; must reply within 2 week(s) of notification.

CONTACT
Nancy Hughes, Financial Aid Director
2 Main Street, Delhi, NY 13753-1190
(607) 746-4000

State University of New York Downstate Medical Center

Brooklyn, New York
www.downstate.edu Federal Code: 002839

Upper-division public health science and nursing college in very large city.
Enrollment: 324 undergrads, 43% part-time.

BASIC COSTS (2008-2009)
Tuition and fees: $4,745; out-of-state residents $11,005.
Per-credit charge: $181; out-of-state residents $442.
Room only: $4,663.
Additional info: Reported room-only price is for double standard; other room-only prices vary by accommodation and can range up to $8,504.

FINANCIAL AID PICTURE (2007-2008)
Students with need: 55% of average financial aid package awarded as scholarships/grants, 45% awarded as loans/jobs. Need-based aid available for part-time students.

FINANCIAL AID PROCEDURES
Forms required: FAFSA.
Dates and Deadlines: Priority date 3/1; no closing date. Applicants notified on a rolling basis.

CONTACT
450 Clarkson Avenue, Box 60, Brooklyn, NY 11203-2098
(718) 270-2488

State University of New York Empire State College

Saratoga Springs, New York
www.esc.edu Federal Code: 010286

4-year public liberal arts college in large town.
Enrollment: 10,993 undergrads, 63% part-time. 298 full-time freshmen.
Selectivity: Admits over 75% of applicants.

BASIC COSTS (2008-2009)
Tuition and fees: $4,575; out-of-state residents $10,835.
Per-credit charge: $181; out-of-state residents $442.

FINANCIAL AID PICTURE (2007-2008)
Students with need: 36% of average financial aid package awarded as scholarships/grants, 64% awarded as loans/jobs. Need-based aid available for part-time students.
Students without need: This college awards aid only to students with need.

FINANCIAL AID PROCEDURES
Forms required: FAFSA, state aid form.
Dates and Deadlines: Priority date 4/1; no closing date. Applicants notified on a rolling basis; must reply within 3 week(s) of notification.
Transfers: No deadline. Applicants notified on a rolling basis.

CONTACT
Becky Palmieri, Director of Business Services
2 Union Avenue, Saratoga Springs, NY 12866
(518) 587-2100 ext. 2311

State University of New York Institute of Technology at Utica/Rome

Utica, New York
www.sunyit.edu Federal Code: 011678

4-year public business and nursing college in small city.
Enrollment: 1,993 undergrads, 25% part-time. 203 full-time freshmen.
Selectivity: Admits less than 50% of applicants.

BASIC COSTS (2008-2009)

Tuition and fees: $5,433; out-of-state residents $11,693.
Per-credit charge: $181; out-of-state residents $442.
Room and board: $8,320.

FINANCIAL AID PICTURE (2007-2008)

Students with need: Out of 186 full-time freshmen who applied for aid, 143 were judged to have need. Of these, 136 received aid. Need-based aid available for part-time students.
Students without need: 11 full-time freshmen who did not demonstrate need for aid received scholarships/grants; average award was $1,143. No-need awards available for academics.

FINANCIAL AID PROCEDURES

Forms required: FAFSA, state aid form.
Dates and Deadlines: Priority date 3/15; no closing date. Applicants notified on a rolling basis starting 3/17; must reply within 2 week(s) of notification.
Transfers: No deadline. Applicants notified on a rolling basis starting 3/17; must reply within 2 week(s) of notification.

CONTACT

Lisa Hoskey, Director of Financial Aid
Box 3050, Utica, NY 13504-3050
(315) 792-7210

State University of New York Maritime College

Throggs Neck, New York
www.sunymaritime.edu Federal Code: 002853

4-year public maritime college in very large city.
Enrollment: 1,432 undergrads, 6% part-time. 358 full-time freshmen.
Selectivity: Admits over 75% of applicants.

BASIC COSTS (2008-2009)

Tuition and fees: $5,426; out-of-state residents $11,686.
Per-credit charge: $181; out-of-state residents $442.
Room and board: $9,500.
Additional info: Additional required uniform charges.

FINANCIAL AID PICTURE (2007-2008)

Students with need: Out of 315 full-time freshmen who applied for aid, 198 were judged to have need. Of these, 196 received aid, and 109 had their full need met. Average financial aid package met 53% of need; average scholarship/grant was $4,958; average loan was $3,515. For part-time students, average financial aid package was $6,116.
Students without need: No-need awards available for academics, leadership, ROTC, state/district residency.
Scholarships offered: NROTC Scholarships: tuition and full room for 4 years.
Cumulative student debt: 66% of graduating class had student loans; average debt was $29,734.
Additional info: All cadets who are United States citizens, physically qualified for Merchant Marine license, and not yet 25 at time of enrollment eligible to apply for Student Incentive Payment (SIP) of $3,000 per year from Maritime Administration of the Department of Transportation. Out-of-state students who elect to participate in SIP pay in-state tuition fees.

FINANCIAL AID PROCEDURES

Forms required: FAFSA, institutional form.
Dates and Deadlines: Priority date 3/15; closing date 7/15. Applicants notified on a rolling basis starting 3/15.
Transfers: Applicants notified on a rolling basis starting 3/15. Must have minimum 2.0 cumulative GPA if degree has not yet been earned.

CONTACT

Paul Bamonte, Director of Financial Aid
6 Pennyfield Avenue, Throggs Neck, NY 10465-4198
(718) 409-7267

State University of New York Upstate Medical University

Syracuse, New York
www.upstate.edu Federal Code: 002840

Upper-division public health science and nursing college in small city.
Enrollment: 269 undergrads, 36% part-time.

BASIC COSTS (2008-2009)

Tuition and fees: $4,908; out-of-state residents $11,168.
Per-credit charge: $181; out-of-state residents $442.
Room only: $5,600.

FINANCIAL AID PICTURE (2008-2009)

Students with need: Average financial aid package for all full-time undergraduates was $10,320. 27% awarded as scholarships/grants, 73% awarded as loans/jobs. Need-based aid available for part-time students. Work study available nights, weekends, and for part-time students.
Students without need: This college awards aid only to students with need.
Cumulative student debt: 76% of graduating class had student loans; average debt was $17,650.

FINANCIAL AID PROCEDURES

Forms required: FAFSA.
Dates and Deadlines: Priority date 3/1; no closing date. Applicants notified on a rolling basis starting 6/1; must reply within 2 week(s) of notification.
Transfers: Applicants notified on a rolling basis; must reply within 2 week(s) of notification.

CONTACT

Mike Pede, Director of Financial Aid
766 Irving Avenue, Syracuse, NY 13210
(315) 464-4329

Suffolk County Community College

Selden, New York
www.sunysuffolk.edu Federal Code: 002878

2-year public community college in large town.
Enrollment: 22,839 undergrads.
Selectivity: Open admission; but selective for some programs.

BASIC COSTS (2008-2009)

Tuition and fees: $3,736; out-of-state residents $7,112.

FINANCIAL AID PICTURE (2007-2008)

Students with need: Need-based aid available for full-time and part-time students. Work study available nights, weekends, and for part-time students.
Students without need: No-need awards available for academics, art, leadership, minority status, music/drama.

FINANCIAL AID PROCEDURES

Forms required: FAFSA, state aid form.

Dates and Deadlines: Priority date 4/15; closing date 6/1. Applicants notified on a rolling basis starting 4/15; must reply within 2 week(s) of notification.
Transfers: No deadline. Applicants notified on a rolling basis starting 4/15.

CONTACT
Nancy Dunnagan, Director of Financial Aid
533 College Road, Selden, NY 11784
(631) 451-4110

Sullivan County Community College
Loch Sheldrake, New York
www.sullivan.suny.edu Federal Code: 002879

2-year public community college in small town.
Enrollment: 1,354 undergrads.
Selectivity: Open admission; but selective for some programs.

BASIC COSTS (2008-2009)
Tuition and fees: $3,904; out-of-state residents $7,432.
Per-credit charge: $138; out-of-state residents $176.

FINANCIAL AID PICTURE
Students with need: Need-based aid available for full-time and part-time students.
Additional info: 60% of students hold part-time jobs locally.

FINANCIAL AID PROCEDURES
Forms required: FAFSA.
Dates and Deadlines: Priority date 4/15; no closing date. Applicants notified on a rolling basis starting 5/15; must reply within 2 week(s) of notification.

CONTACT
James Winderl, Director of Financial Aid
112 College Road, Loch Sheldrake, NY 12759-5151
(845) 434-5750 ext. 4231

Swedish Institute
New York, New York
www.swedishinstitute.edu Federal Code: 021700

2-year for-profit health science college in very large city.
Enrollment: 575 undergrads.

BASIC COSTS (2008-2009)
Tuition and fees: $8,120.
Additional info: Students generally attend 3 semesters/year.

FINANCIAL AID PICTURE
Students with need: Need-based aid available for full-time and part-time students.
Students without need: This college awards aid only to students with need.

FINANCIAL AID PROCEDURES
Forms required: FAFSA, institutional form.
Dates and Deadlines: No deadline.

CONTACT
John Tonkinson, CFO
226 West 26th Street, 5th Floor, New York, NY 10001-6700
(212) 924-5900 ext. 124

Syracuse University
Syracuse, New York Federal Code: 002882
www.syr.edu CSS Code: 2823

4-year private university in small city.
Enrollment: 13,105 undergrads, 4% part-time. 3,168 full-time freshmen.
Selectivity: Admits 50 to 75% of applicants.

BASIC COSTS (2009-2010)
Tuition and fees: $34,926.
Per-credit charge: $1,464.
Room and board: $12,374.

FINANCIAL AID PICTURE (2008-2009)
Students with need: Out of 2,270 full-time freshmen who applied for aid, 1,862 were judged to have need. Of these, 1,862 received aid, and 1,210 had their full need met. Average financial aid package met 86% of need; average scholarship/grant was $20,750; average loan was $4,600. Need-based aid available for part-time students.
Students without need: 437 full-time freshmen who did not demonstrate need for aid received scholarships/grants; average award was $9,850. No-need awards available for academics, art, athletics, music/drama, ROTC.
Scholarships offered: 78 full-time freshmen received athletic scholarships; average amount $38,860.
Cumulative student debt: 64% of graduating class had student loans; average debt was $27,455.

FINANCIAL AID PROCEDURES
Forms required: FAFSA, CSS PROFILE.
Dates and Deadlines: Closing date 2/1. Applicants notified by 3/21; must reply by 5/1.
Transfers: Applicants notified on a rolling basis starting 3/21; must reply by 5/1 or within 2 week(s) of notification.

CONTACT
Youlonda Copeland-Morgan, Director of Scholarship and Student Aid
100 Crouse-Hinds Hall, Syracuse, NY 13244-2130
(315) 443-1513

Tompkins Cortland Community College
Dryden, New York
www.TC3.edu Federal Code: 006788

2-year public community college in small town.
Enrollment: 2,954 undergrads, 18% part-time. 885 full-time freshmen.
Selectivity: Open admission, but selective for some programs.

BASIC COSTS (2008-2009)
Tuition and fees: $4,040; out-of-state residents $7,780.
Per-credit charge: $132; out-of-state residents $274.

FINANCIAL AID PICTURE (2007-2008)
Students with need: Need-based aid available for full-time and part-time students. Work study available nights, weekends, and for part-time students.
Students without need: No-need awards available for academics.

FINANCIAL AID PROCEDURES
Forms required: FAFSA, state aid form, institutional form.
Dates and Deadlines: Priority date 4/15; no closing date. Applicants notified on a rolling basis starting 3/15; must reply within 4 week(s) of notification.

CONTACT
Michael McGraw, Director of Financial Aid
170 North Street, Dryden, NY 13053-0139
(607) 844-6581

Trocaire College

Buffalo, New York
www.trocaire.edu
Federal Code: 002812

2-year private junior college in large city, affiliated with Roman Catholic Church.
Enrollment: 1,056 undergrads.
Selectivity: Open admission; but selective for some programs.

BASIC COSTS (2008-2009)

Tuition and fees: $11,614.
Per-credit charge: $457.

FINANCIAL AID PICTURE

Students with need: Need-based aid available for full-time and part-time students.
Students without need: No-need awards available for academics, alumni affiliation.

FINANCIAL AID PROCEDURES

Forms required: FAFSA, state aid form.
Dates and Deadlines: Closing date 4/15. Applicants notified on a rolling basis starting 3/1; must reply within 2 week(s) of notification.

CONTACT

Janet McGrath, Director of Financial Aid
360 Choate Avenue, Buffalo, NY 14220
(716) 826-1200

Ulster County Community College

Stone Ridge, New York
www.sunyulster.edu
Federal Code: 002880

2-year public community college in small town.
Enrollment: 2,287 undergrads, 31% part-time. 515 full-time freshmen.
Selectivity: Open admission; but selective for some programs.

BASIC COSTS (2008-2009)

Tuition and fees: $3,951; out-of-state residents $7,371.
Per-credit charge: $130; out-of-state residents $260.

FINANCIAL AID PICTURE (2008-2009)

Students with need: Need-based aid available for full-time and part-time students.

FINANCIAL AID PROCEDURES

Forms required: FAFSA.
Dates and Deadlines: Priority date 6/1; no closing date. Applicants notified on a rolling basis starting 6/1; must reply within 2 week(s) of notification.

CONTACT

Christopher Chang, Director of Financial Aid
Cottekill Road, Stone Ridge, NY 12484
(845) 687-5058

Union College

Schenectady, New York
www.union.edu
Federal Code: 002889
CSS Code: 2920

4-year private engineering and liberal arts college in small city.
Enrollment: 2,199 undergrads. 580 full-time freshmen.
Selectivity: Admits less than 50% of applicants. GED not accepted.

BASIC COSTS (2008-2009)

Comprehensive fee: $48,552.
Additional info: Rebates offered to students living off-campus and/or not using a meal plan.

FINANCIAL AID PICTURE (2008-2009)

Students with need: Out of 296 full-time freshmen who applied for aid, 254 were judged to have need. Of these, 254 received aid, and 226 had their full need met. Average financial aid package met 99% of need; average scholarship/grant was $28,957; average loan was $3,730. Need-based aid available for part-time students.
Students without need: 82 full-time freshmen who did not demonstrate need for aid received scholarships/grants; average award was $8,106. No-need awards available for academics, ROTC.
Cumulative student debt: 52% of graduating class had student loans; average debt was $23,000.
Additional info: Cancellable loans given to eligible students who engage in public service work after graduation. Loans cancellable at rate of 20% for each year of service.

FINANCIAL AID PROCEDURES

Forms required: FAFSA, CSS PROFILE, state aid form.
Dates and Deadlines: Priority date 2/1; closing date 2/1. Applicants notified by 4/1; must reply by 5/1.
Transfers: Closing date 3/1. Financial aid applicants must submit the CSS PROFILE form and FAFSA to their respective processing agencies at least two months prior to application deadline.

CONTACT

Linda Parker, Director of Financial Aid
Grant Hall, Schenectady, NY 12308-2311
(518) 388-6123

United States Merchant Marine Academy

Kings Point, New York
www.usmma.edu
Federal Code: 002892

4-year public military and maritime college in large town.
Enrollment: 985 undergrads. 307 full-time freshmen.
Selectivity: Admits less than 50% of applicants.

BASIC COSTS (2008-2009)

Additional info: All midshipmen receive full tuition, room, board, and medical and dental expenses from the federal government. Total required freshmen fees include purchase of laptop computer, color printer, and PDA. International students pay required fees plus additional international student fee.

FINANCIAL AID PICTURE (2007-2008)

Students with need: 64% of average financial aid package awarded as scholarships/grants, 36% awarded as loans/jobs.
Additional info: Students paid by steamship companies while at sea.

FINANCIAL AID PROCEDURES

Forms required: FAFSA, institutional form.
Dates and Deadlines: Closing date 5/1. Applicants notified on a rolling basis starting 1/31.

CONTACT

Robert Johnson, Director of Admissions and Financial Aid
300 Steamboat Road, Admissions Center, Kings Point, NY 11024-1699
(516) 773-5295

United States Military Academy

West Point, New York
www.usma.edu

4-year public military college in small town.
Enrollment: 4,553 undergrads. 1,263 full-time freshmen.
Selectivity: Admits less than 50% of applicants.

BASIC COSTS (2009-2010)

Additional info: All cadets are on active duty as members of the U.S. Army and receive an annual salary of approximately $10,148. Room and board, medical, and dental care are provided by the Army. Deposit of $2,900 required for initial uniforms, books, supplies, equipment and fees. If needed, loans for deposit available from $100 to $2,900.

FINANCIAL AID PICTURE (2007-2008)

Additional info: Cadets permitted to receive scholarships, but since there are no tuition, room, or board charges, scholarships stipulated for tuition, room or board only based on need rather than merit cannot be accepted. Scholarships may be used for textbooks, uniforms, and other expenses or used dollar for dollar to offset initial $2,900 deposit.

CONTACT

646 Swift Road, West Point, NY 10996-1905

University of Rochester

Rochester, New York — Federal Code: 002894
www.rochester.edu — CSS Code: 2928

4-year private university in large city.
Enrollment: 5,178 undergrads, 2% part-time. 1,282 full-time freshmen.
Selectivity: Admits less than 50% of applicants.

BASIC COSTS (2009-2010)

Tuition and fees: $38,690.
Per-credit charge: $1,183.
Room and board: $11,200.

FINANCIAL AID PICTURE (2008-2009)

Students with need: Average financial aid package met 100% of need; average scholarship/grant was $27,021; average loan was $4,154. For part-time students, average financial aid package was $8,686.
Students without need: No-need awards available for academics, alumni affiliation, leadership, music/drama, ROTC, state/district residency.
Cumulative student debt: 55% of graduating class had student loans; average debt was $27,121.
Additional info: Alternative loans and financing information available.

FINANCIAL AID PROCEDURES

Forms required: FAFSA, CSS PROFILE, state aid form.
Dates and Deadlines: Closing date 2/1. Applicants notified by 4/1; must reply by 5/1.
Transfers: Priority date 2/1; no deadline. Must reply by 8/1.

CONTACT

Charles Puls, Associate Dean and Director of Financial Aid
300 Wilson Boulevard, Rochester, NY 14627-0251
(585) 275-3228

Utica College

Utica, New York
www.utica.edu — Federal Code: 002883

4-year private liberal arts college in small city.
Enrollment: 2,436 undergrads, 17% part-time. 543 full-time freshmen.
Selectivity: Admits 50 to 75% of applicants.

BASIC COSTS (2009-2010)

Tuition and fees: $27,284.
Per-credit charge: $840.
Room and board: $10,850.

FINANCIAL AID PICTURE (2008-2009)

Students with need: Out of 528 full-time freshmen who applied for aid, 494 were judged to have need. Of these, 492 received aid, and 67 had their full need met. Average financial aid package met 74% of need; average scholarship/grant was $10,042; average loan was $3,404. For part-time students, average financial aid package was $5,243.
Students without need: 37 full-time freshmen who did not demonstrate need for aid received scholarships/grants; average award was $11,913. No-need awards available for academics.
Cumulative student debt: 86% of graduating class had student loans; average debt was $31,899.

FINANCIAL AID PROCEDURES

Forms required: FAFSA, state aid form.
Dates and Deadlines: Priority date 2/15; no closing date. Applicants notified on a rolling basis starting 2/1; must reply by 5/1 or within 4 week(s) of notification.
Transfers: Applicants notified on a rolling basis.

CONTACT

Anita Elliot, Executive Director of Student Financial Services
1600 Burrstone Road, Utica, NY 13502-4892
(315) 792-3179

Vassar College

Poughkeepsie, New York — Federal Code: 002895
www.vassar.edu — CSS Code: 2956

4-year private liberal arts college in small city.
Enrollment: 2,343 undergrads, 1% part-time. 638 full-time freshmen.
Selectivity: Admits less than 50% of applicants.

BASIC COSTS (2009-2010)

Tuition and fees: $41,930.
Per-credit charge: $1,397.
Room and board: $9,370.

FINANCIAL AID PICTURE (2008-2009)

Students with need: Out of 438 full-time freshmen who applied for aid, 366 were judged to have need. Of these, 366 received aid, and 366 had their full need met. Average financial aid package met 100% of need; average scholarship/grant was $33,145; average loan was $1,698.
Students without need: This college awards aid only to students with need.
Cumulative student debt: 50% of graduating class had student loans; average debt was $19,910.
Additional info: No loans in the initial financial aid packages for students from families with total income used in need analysis of $60,000 or less.

FINANCIAL AID PROCEDURES

Forms required: FAFSA, CSS PROFILE, state aid form.
Dates and Deadlines: Closing date 2/1. Applicants notified by 3/30; must reply by 5/1.
Transfers: Closing date 4/1. Limited number of need-based award packages offered to transfers.

CONTACT

Michael Fraher, Director of Financial Aid
Box 10, 124 Raymond Avenue, Poughkeepsie, NY 12604-0077
(845) 437-5320

Vaughn College of Aeronautics and Technology
Flushing, New York
www.vaughn.edu Federal Code: 002665

4-year private engineering and technical college in very large city.
Enrollment: 1,071 undergrads, 24% part-time. 193 full-time freshmen.
Selectivity: Admits over 75% of applicants.

BASIC COSTS (2009-2010)
Tuition and fees: $16,700.
Per-credit charge: $550.
Room and board: $10,500.

FINANCIAL AID PICTURE (2008-2009)
Students with need: Out of 173 full-time freshmen who applied for aid, 173 were judged to have need. Of these, 173 received aid, and 60 had their full need met. Average financial aid package met 82% of need; average scholarship/grant was $1,100; average loan was $1,776. For part-time students, average financial aid package was $5,524.
Students without need: 20 full-time freshmen who did not demonstrate need for aid received scholarships/grants; average award was $2,000. No-need awards available for academics, alumni affiliation, job skills, leadership, ROTC, state/district residency.

FINANCIAL AID PROCEDURES
Forms required: FAFSA, state aid form.
Dates and Deadlines: Priority date 3/1; no closing date. Applicants notified by 4/15; must reply within 2 week(s) of notification.
Transfers: No deadline. Applicants notified on a rolling basis; must reply within 2 week(s) of notification.

CONTACT
Dorothy Martin, Director of Financial Aid
86-01 23rd Avenue, Flushing, NY 11369
(718) 429-6600

Villa Maria College of Buffalo
Buffalo, New York
www.villa.edu Federal Code: 002896

2-year private visual arts and liberal arts college in large city, affiliated with Roman Catholic Church.
Enrollment: 473 undergrads, 19% part-time. 107 full-time freshmen.
Selectivity: Open admission; but selective for some programs.

BASIC COSTS (2009-2010)
Tuition and fees: $14,870.
Per-credit charge: $485.
Additional info: Tuition/fee waivers available for unemployed or children of unemployed.

FINANCIAL AID PICTURE (2007-2008)
Students with need: Out of 100 full-time freshmen who applied for aid, 84 were judged to have need. Of these, 84 received aid, and 10 had their full need met. Average financial aid package met 88% of need; average scholarship/grant was $5,224; average loan was $3,240. For part-time students, average financial aid package was $4,926.
Students without need: 5 full-time freshmen who did not demonstrate need for aid received scholarships/grants; average award was $2,000. No-need awards available for academics, alumni affiliation, art, leadership, minority status, music/drama.
Cumulative student debt: 100% of graduating class had student loans; average debt was $47,000.

FINANCIAL AID PROCEDURES
Forms required: FAFSA.
Dates and Deadlines: No deadline. Applicants notified on a rolling basis starting 2/15; must reply within 2 week(s) of notification.
Transfers: Applicants notified on a rolling basis starting 2/15; must reply within 2 week(s) of notification.

CONTACT
Christina Horner, Director of Financial Aid and Veterans Affairs
240 Pine Ridge Road, Buffalo, NY 14225-3999
(716) 896-0700 ext. 1850

Wagner College
Staten Island, New York
www.wagner.edu Federal Code: 002899

4-year private liberal arts college in very large city, affiliated with Lutheran Church in America.
Enrollment: 1,911 undergrads, 2% part-time. 480 full-time freshmen.
Selectivity: Admits 50 to 75% of applicants.

BASIC COSTS (2009-2010)
Tuition and fees: $32,580.
Room and board: $9,700.
Additional info: Tuition/fee waivers available for unemployed or children of unemployed.

FINANCIAL AID PICTURE (2008-2009)
Students with need: Out of 384 full-time freshmen who applied for aid, 303 were judged to have need. Of these, 303 received aid, and 81 had their full need met. Average financial aid package met 74% of need; average scholarship/grant was $11,797; average loan was $4,028.
Students without need: 158 full-time freshmen who did not demonstrate need for aid received scholarships/grants; average award was $10,528. No-need awards available for academics, athletics, music/drama.
Scholarships offered: 29 full-time freshmen received athletic scholarships; average amount $20,117.
Cumulative student debt: 56% of graduating class had student loans; average debt was $34,326.

FINANCIAL AID PROCEDURES
Forms required: FAFSA, state aid form, institutional form.
Dates and Deadlines: Priority date 2/15; no closing date. Applicants notified on a rolling basis starting 3/1; must reply within 3 week(s) of notification.
Transfers: No deadline. Applicants notified on a rolling basis starting 3/1; must reply within 3 week(s) of notification.

CONTACT
Theresa Weimer, Director of Financial Aid
One Campus Road, Staten Island, NY 10301-4495
(718) 390-3183

Webb Institute
Glen Cove, New York
www.webb-institute.edu Federal Code: 002900

4-year private engineering and maritime college in large town.
Enrollment: 90 undergrads. 22 full-time freshmen.
Selectivity: Admits less than 50% of applicants. GED not accepted.

BASIC COSTS (2009-2010)
Room and board: $10,200.
Additional info: All students receive 4-year, full-tuition scholarships.

FINANCIAL AID PICTURE (2007-2008)
Students with need: Need-based aid available for full-time students.

Students without need: This college awards aid only to students with need.

FINANCIAL AID PROCEDURES

Forms required: FAFSA.

Dates and Deadlines: Closing date 7/1. Applicants notified by 8/1; must reply within 2 week(s) of notification.

CONTACT

William Murray, Director of Financial Aid
298 Crescent Beach Road, Glen Cove, NY 11542-1398
(516) 671-2213 ext. 104

Wells College

Aurora, New York
www.wells.edu Federal Code: 002901

4-year private liberal arts college in rural community.

Enrollment: 563 undergrads, 1% part-time. 155 full-time freshmen.

Selectivity: Admits 50 to 75% of applicants.

BASIC COSTS (2009-2010)

Tuition and fees: $29,680.

Per-credit charge: $790.

Room and board: $9,000.

FINANCIAL AID PICTURE (2008-2009)

Students with need: Out of 135 full-time freshmen who applied for aid, 113 were judged to have need. Of these, 113 received aid, and 30 had their full need met. Average financial aid package met 87% of need; average scholarship/grant was $14,486; average loan was $2,865. Need-based aid available for part-time students.

Students without need: 32 full-time freshmen who did not demonstrate need for aid received scholarships/grants; average award was $6,622. No-need awards available for academics, alumni affiliation, leadership.

Scholarships offered: Henry Wells Scholarship: guaranteed first-year internship or related experience and paid $3,000 internship or experiential learning program in student's upper-class years; tuition-based scholarship valued at $14,000 a year for four years. Scholarship for Leaders: $56,000 over 4 years with minimum 92 GPA; or $40,000 over 4 years with minimum 90 GPA.

Cumulative student debt: 80% of graduating class had student loans; average debt was $18,277.

FINANCIAL AID PROCEDURES

Forms required: FAFSA. CSS PROFILE required of early decision candidates only.

Dates and Deadlines: Priority date 2/15; no closing date. Applicants notified on a rolling basis starting 3/1; must reply by 5/1.

Transfers: Priority date 3/1; no deadline. Applicants notified on a rolling basis starting 3/1; must reply by 8/1.

CONTACT

Cathleen Patella, Director of Financial Aid
170 Main Street, Aurora, NY 13026
(315) 364-3289

Westchester Community College

Valhalla, New York
www.sunywcc.edu Federal Code: 002881

2-year public community college in large town.

Enrollment: 11,091 undergrads, 42% part-time. 2,042 full-time freshmen.

Selectivity: Open admission; but selective for some programs.

BASIC COSTS (2008-2009)

Tuition and fees: $3,913; out-of-state residents $9,239.

Per-credit charge: $148; out-of-state residents $370.

FINANCIAL AID PICTURE (2007-2008)

Students with need: 89% of average financial aid package awarded as scholarships/grants, 11% awarded as loans/jobs. Need-based aid available for part-time students. Work study available nights, weekends, and for part-time students.

Students without need: No-need awards available for academics.

Cumulative student debt: 13% of graduating class had student loans; average debt was $7,092.

FINANCIAL AID PROCEDURES

Forms required: FAFSA, state aid form, institutional form.

Dates and Deadlines: No deadline. Applicants notified on a rolling basis; must reply within 4 week(s) of notification.

Transfers: No deadline.

CONTACT

Eleanor Hackett, Director of Financial Aid
75 Grasslands Road, Valhalla, NY 10595
(914) 606-6773

Yeshiva Mikdash Melech

Brooklyn, New York
www.mikdashmelech.net Federal Code: 014615

5-year private rabbinical college for men in very large city, affiliated with Jewish faith.

Enrollment: 79 undergrads. 40 full-time freshmen.

Selectivity: Open admission; but selective for some programs.

BASIC COSTS (2009-2010)

Tuition and fees: $6,500.

Room and board: $3,800.

Additional info: Tuition/fee waivers available for adults.

FINANCIAL AID PICTURE (2007-2008)

Students with need: Need-based aid available for full-time and part-time students. Work study available nights.

Students without need: No-need awards available for academics, leadership, religious affiliation.

FINANCIAL AID PROCEDURES

Forms required: FAFSA.

Dates and Deadlines: No deadline. Applicants notified on a rolling basis starting 5/1.

Transfers: No deadline. Applicants notified on a rolling basis starting 5/1.

CONTACT

Samuel Ani, Financial Aid Administrator
1326 Ocean Parkway, Brooklyn, NY 11230
(718) 339-1090

North Carolina

Alamance Community College

Graham, North Carolina
www.alamancecc.edu Federal Code: 005463

2-year public community college in large town.

Enrollment: 3,740 undergrads, 64% part-time. 325 full-time freshmen.

Selectivity: Open admission; but selective for some programs.

BASIC COSTS (2008-2009)
Tuition and fees: $1,290; out-of-state residents $7,029.
Per-credit charge: $42; out-of-state residents $233.

FINANCIAL AID PICTURE (2007-2008)
Students with need: Out of 240 full-time freshmen who applied for aid, 214 were judged to have need. Of these, 190 received aid. Average financial aid package met 30% of need; average scholarship/grant was $3,000. For part-time students, average financial aid package was $1,500.
Students without need: 50 full-time freshmen who did not demonstrate need for aid received scholarships/grants; average award was $500. No-need awards available for academics, state/district residency.
Cumulative student debt: 1% of graduating class had student loans; average debt was $3,000.

FINANCIAL AID PROCEDURES
Forms required: FAFSA.
Dates and Deadlines: Priority date 5/15; no closing date. Applicants notified on a rolling basis starting 3/15; must reply within 2 week(s) of notification.
Transfers: Supplemental educational opportunity grants limited.

CONTACT
Liz Solazzo, Director of Financial Aid
Box 8000, Graham, NC 27253
(336) 506-4109

Appalachian State University
Boone, North Carolina
www.appstate.edu Federal Code: 002906

4-year public university in large town.
Enrollment: 14,373 undergrads, 5% part-time. 2,773 full-time freshmen.
Selectivity: Admits 50 to 75% of applicants. GED not accepted.

BASIC COSTS (2008-2009)
Tuition and fees: $4,275; out-of-state residents $14,334.
Room and board: $6,160.

FINANCIAL AID PICTURE (2008-2009)
Students with need: Need-based aid available for full-time and part-time students. Work study available nights, weekends, and for part-time students.
Students without need: No-need awards available for academics, alumni affiliation, art, athletics, job skills, leadership, minority status, music/drama, religious affiliation, ROTC, state/district residency.

FINANCIAL AID PROCEDURES
Forms required: FAFSA.
Dates and Deadlines: Priority date 3/15; no closing date. Applicants notified on a rolling basis starting 4/1; must reply within 3 week(s) of notification.
Transfers: No deadline. Applicants notified on a rolling basis starting 4/1; must reply within 3 week(s) of notification.

CONTACT
Esther Manogin, Director
ASU Box 32004, Boone, NC 28608
(828) 262-2190

Barton College
Wilson, North Carolina
www.barton.edu Federal Code: 002908

4-year private liberal arts college in large town, affiliated with Christian Church (Disciples of Christ).
Enrollment: 1,125 undergrads, 21% part-time. 247 full-time freshmen.
Selectivity: Admits less than 50% of applicants.

BASIC COSTS (2008-2009)
Tuition and fees: $19,938.
Per-credit charge: $785.
Room and board: $6,782.
Additional info: Tuition/fee waivers available for adults.

FINANCIAL AID PICTURE (2008-2009)
Students with need: Out of 229 full-time freshmen who applied for aid, 207 were judged to have need. Of these, 207 received aid, and 37 had their full need met. Average financial aid package met 82% of need; average scholarship/grant was $5,477; average loan was $4,361. For part-time students, average financial aid package was $6,147.
Students without need: 35 full-time freshmen who did not demonstrate need for aid received scholarships/grants; average award was $5,009. No-need awards available for academics, alumni affiliation, art, athletics, leadership, minority status, music/drama, religious affiliation, state/district residency.
Scholarships offered: 12 full-time freshmen received athletic scholarships; average amount $6,267.

FINANCIAL AID PROCEDURES
Forms required: FAFSA.
Dates and Deadlines: Priority date 4/1; no closing date. Applicants notified on a rolling basis starting 5/1; must reply within 2 week(s) of notification.

CONTACT
Shakeena White, Director of Enrollment Management
Box 5000, Wilson, NC 27893-7000
(252) 399-6323

Beaufort County Community College
Washington, North Carolina
www.beaufortccc.edu Federal Code: 008558

2-year public community college in rural community.
Enrollment: 865 full-time undergrads.
Selectivity: Open admission; but selective for some programs.

BASIC COSTS (2008-2009)
Tuition and fees: $1,408; out-of-state residents $7,530.
Per-credit charge: $42; out-of-state residents $233.
Additional info: Some programs require insurance and uniforms.

FINANCIAL AID PICTURE (2008-2009)
Students with need: Need-based aid available for full-time and part-time students.
Students without need: No-need awards available for academics.

FINANCIAL AID PROCEDURES
Forms required: FAFSA.
Dates and Deadlines: Priority date 6/1; no closing date. Applicants notified on a rolling basis starting 5/1; must reply within 2 week(s) of notification.

CONTACT
Harold Smith, Director of Financial Aid
Box 1069, Washington, NC 27889
(252) 940-6222

Belmont Abbey College
Belmont, North Carolina
www.belmontabbeycollege.edu Federal Code: 002910

4-year private liberal arts college in small town, affiliated with Roman Catholic Church.
Enrollment: 1,459 undergrads, 6% part-time. 279 full-time freshmen.
Selectivity: Admits 50 to 75% of applicants.

BASIC COSTS (2008-2009)
Tuition and fees: $21,039.
Per-credit charge: $637.
Room and board: $9,866.

FINANCIAL AID PICTURE (2008-2009)
Students with need: 50% of average financial aid package awarded as scholarships/grants, 50% awarded as loans/jobs. Need-based aid available for part-time students. Work study available nights, weekends, and for part-time students.
Students without need: No-need awards available for academics, athletics, leadership, religious affiliation, state/district residency.
Scholarships offered: Many merit scholarships offered; ranging from $500 to $20,000; based solely on academic achievement.

FINANCIAL AID PROCEDURES
Forms required: FAFSA, state aid form.
Dates and Deadlines: Priority date 4/1; no closing date. Applicants notified on a rolling basis starting 3/1; must reply within 2 week(s) of notification.

CONTACT
Anne Stevens, Director of Enrollment Management
100 Belmont - Mt. Holly Road, Belmont, NC 28012-2795
(704) 825-6665

Bennett College for Women
Greensboro, North Carolina
www.bennett.edu Federal Code: 002911

4-year private liberal arts college for women in small city, affiliated with United Methodist Church.
Enrollment: 673 undergrads, 1% part time. 192 full time freshmen.
Selectivity: Admits less than 50% of applicants.

BASIC COSTS (2009-2010)
Tuition and fees: $15,234.
Per-credit charge: $552.
Room and board: $6,736.

FINANCIAL AID PICTURE (2008-2009)
Students with need: Out of 192 full-time freshmen who applied for aid, 181 were judged to have need. Of these, 173 received aid, and 6 had their full need met. Average financial aid package met 45% of need; average scholarship/grant was $8,418; average loan was $3,170. For part-time students, average financial aid package was $4,824.
Students without need: 11 full-time freshmen who did not demonstrate need for aid received scholarships/grants; average award was $3,736. No-need awards available for state/district residency.
Cumulative student debt: 94% of graduating class had student loans; average debt was $39,810.

FINANCIAL AID PROCEDURES
Forms required: FAFSA, institutional form.
Dates and Deadlines: Closing date 4/15. Applicants notified by 7/15.

CONTACT
Keisha Ragsdale, Director of Financial Aid
900 East Washington Street, Greensboro, NC 27401-3239
(336) 517-2204

Bladen Community College
Dublin, North Carolina
www.bladencc.edu Federal Code: 007987

2-year public community college in rural community.
Enrollment: 1,323 undergrads.
Selectivity: Open admission; but selective for some programs.

BASIC COSTS (2008-2009)
Tuition and fees: $1,326; out-of-state residents $7,065.
Per-credit charge: $42; out-of-state residents $233.

FINANCIAL AID PICTURE
Students with need: Need-based aid available for full-time and part-time students. Work study available nights.

FINANCIAL AID PROCEDURES
Forms required: FAFSA.
Dates and Deadlines: Priority date 6/1; no closing date. Applicants notified on a rolling basis starting 8/1; must reply within 2 week(s) of notification.

CONTACT
Marva Dinkins, Financial Aid Director
Box 266, Dublin, NC 28332-0266
(910) 879-5562

Blue Ridge Community College
Flat Rock, North Carolina
www.blueridge.edu Federal Code: 009684

2-year public community and technical college in large town.
Enrollment: 2,146 undergrads.
Selectivity: Open admission; but selective for some programs.

BASIC COSTS (2008-2009)
Tuition and fees: $1,355; out-of-state residents $7,094.
Per-credit charge: $42; out-of-state residents $233.

FINANCIAL AID PICTURE (2007-2008)
Students with need: Need-based aid available for full-time and part-time students. Work study available nights.
Students without need: No-need awards available for academics, athletics, leadership, minority status, state/district residency.

FINANCIAL AID PROCEDURES
Forms required: FAFSA, institutional form.
Dates and Deadlines: Priority date 6/30; no closing date. Applicants notified on a rolling basis starting 2/1; must reply within 4 week(s) of notification.

CONTACT
Rita Blythe, Financial Aid Officer
180 West Campus Drive, Flat Rock, NC 28731-9624
(828) 694-1815

Brevard College
Brevard, North Carolina
www.brevard.edu Federal Code: 002912

4-year private liberal arts college in small town, affiliated with United Methodist Church.
Enrollment: 632 undergrads, 2% part-time. 183 full-time freshmen.
Selectivity: Admits less than 50% of applicants.

BASIC COSTS (2009-2010)
Tuition and fees: $20,000.
Per-credit charge: $420.
Room and board: $7,850.

FINANCIAL AID PICTURE (2008-2009)
Students with need: Need-based aid available for full-time and part-time students. Work study available nights, weekends, and for part-time students.
Students without need: No-need awards available for academics, art, athletics, job skills, leadership, minority status, music/drama, religious affiliation, state/district residency.

FINANCIAL AID PROCEDURES

Forms required: FAFSA, state aid form.

Dates and Deadlines: Priority date 4/15; no closing date. Applicants notified on a rolling basis starting 2/1; must reply within 4 week(s) of notification.

CONTACT

Lisanne Masterson, Director of Financial Aid
One Brevard College Drive, Brevard, NC 28712
(828) 884-8287

Brunswick Community College

Supply, North Carolina
www.brunswickcc.edu Federal Code: 015285

2-year public community college in small town.

Enrollment: 1,164 undergrads.

Selectivity: Open admission; but selective for some programs.

BASIC COSTS (2008-2009)

Tuition and fees: $1,442; out-of-state residents $7,564.

Per-credit charge: $42; out-of-state residents $233.

FINANCIAL AID PICTURE (2008-2009)

Students with need: Need-based aid available for full-time and part-time students. Work study available nights, weekends, and for part-time students.

Students without need: No-need awards available for academics, state/district residency.

Scholarships offered: La Dane Williamson Universal Scholarship: $1,200 per year for 2 years; must be a resident of Brunswick County for 5 years prior to application, must be a high school graduate of Brunswick County or complete GED or adult high school diploma program at Brunswick Community College, must not be eligible for Pell. Brunswick Family Scholarship: may cover total amount of tuition and fees; for Brunswick County residents of 3 years prior to application with GED or high school graduate, must not be eligible for Pell.

Additional info: Attendance required at financial aid orientation session for those receiving federal student aid.

FINANCIAL AID PROCEDURES

Forms required: FAFSA, institutional form.

Dates and Deadlines: Priority date 6/1; closing date 6/15. Applicants notified on a rolling basis starting 3/1; must reply by 6/15 or within 2 week(s) of notification.

Transfers: Priority date 6/30; no deadline.

CONTACT

Paula Almond, Coordinator of Financial Aid and Veterans Affairs
Box 30, Supply, NC 28462
(910) 755-7422

Cabarrus College of Health Sciences

Concord, North Carolina
www.cabarruscollege.edu Federal Code: 015358

4-year private health science and nursing college in small city.

Enrollment: 372 undergrads.

Selectivity: Admits less than 50% of applicants.

BASIC COSTS (2009-2010)

Tuition and fees: $9,950.

Per-credit charge: $300.

FINANCIAL AID PICTURE (2008-2009)

Students with need: 60% of average financial aid package awarded as scholarships/grants, 40% awarded as loans/jobs.

CONTACT

Valerie Richard, Director of Financial Aid
401 Medical Park Drive, Concord, NC 28025-2405
(704) 783-2445

Caldwell Community College and Technical Institute

Hudson, North Carolina
www.cccti.edu Federal Code: 004835

2-year public community and technical college in small town.

Enrollment: 3,074 undergrads, 56% part-time. 411 full-time freshmen.

Selectivity: Open admission; but selective for some programs.

BASIC COSTS (2008-2009)

Tuition and fees: $1,292; out-of-state residents $7,031.

Per-credit charge: $42; out-of-state residents $233.

FINANCIAL AID PICTURE (2008-2009)

Students with need: Need-based aid available for full-time and part-time students.

Students without need: This college awards aid only to students with need.

FINANCIAL AID PROCEDURES

Forms required: FAFSA.

Dates and Deadlines: Priority date 6/1; no closing date. Applicants notified on a rolling basis starting 6/30.

CONTACT

Eva Rader-Harmon, Director of Financial Aid
2855 Hickory Boulevard, Hudson, NC 28638-2672
(828) 726-2714

Campbell University

Buies Creek, North Carolina
www.campbell.edu Federal Code: 002913

4-year private university and liberal arts college in small town.

Enrollment: 2,906 undergrads, 5% part-time. 800 full-time freshmen.

Selectivity: Admits 50 to 75% of applicants.

BASIC COSTS (2009-2010)

Tuition and fees: $21,440.

Per-credit charge: $340.

Room and board: $7,300.

FINANCIAL AID PICTURE (2008-2009)

Students with need: Need-based aid available for full-time and part-time students. Work study available nights, weekends, and for part-time students.

Students without need: No-need awards available for academics, athletics, music/drama, religious affiliation, ROTC, state/district residency.

Scholarships offered: Presidential Scholarship: $10,000-$14,000; SAT 1725 or ACT 25 and GPA 3.4. Campbell Scholarship: $6,000-9,000; SAT 1500 or ACT 21 and GPA 3.0.

FINANCIAL AID PROCEDURES

Forms required: FAFSA.

Dates and Deadlines: Priority date 3/15; no closing date. Applicants notified on a rolling basis starting 4/15; must reply within 2 week(s) of notification.

Transfers: Priority date 3/9. Applicants notified on a rolling basis starting 4/9; must reply within 2 week(s) of notification.

CONTACT

Nancy Beasley, Director of Financial Aid
PO Box 546, Buies Creek, NC 27506
(800) 334-4111 ext. 1310

Cape Fear Community College

Wilmington, North Carolina
www.cfcc.edu Federal Code: 005320

2-year public community college in small city.
Enrollment: 6,799 undergrads, 46% part-time. 956 full-time freshmen.
Selectivity: Open admission; but selective for some programs.

BASIC COSTS (2008-2009)
Tuition and fees: $1,491; out-of-state residents $7,603.
Per-credit charge: $42; out-of-state residents $233.

FINANCIAL AID PICTURE (2007-2008)
Students with need: 70% of average financial aid package awarded as scholarships/grants, 30% awarded as loans/jobs. Need-based aid available for part-time students. Work study available nights.
Students without need: No-need awards available for academics, athletics, job skills, leadership, music/drama, religious affiliation.

FINANCIAL AID PROCEDURES
Forms required: FAFSA.
Dates and Deadlines: Priority date 6/1; no closing date. Applicants notified on a rolling basis starting 4/1; must reply within 2 week(s) of notification.

CONTACT
Jo-Ann Craig, Director of Financial Aid
411 North Front Street, Wilmington, NC 28401-3910
(910) 362-7055

Carolina Christian College

Winston-Salem, North Carolina
www.carolina.edu

4-year private Bible college in large city, affiliated with Church of Christ.
Enrollment: 24 undergrads, 8% part-time.
Selectivity: Open admission.

BASIC COSTS (2008-2009)
Tuition and fees: $4,700.
Per-credit charge: $125.

FINANCIAL AID PICTURE (2008-2009)
Students with need: Need-based aid available for full-time and part-time students.

FINANCIAL AID PROCEDURES
Forms required: FAFSA.
Dates and Deadlines: No deadline. Applicants notified on a rolling basis.
Transfers: No deadline. Applicants notified on a rolling basis.

CONTACT
LaTanya Lucas, Director of Financial Aid
Box 777, Winston-Salem, NC 27105
(336) 744-0900 ext. 103

Carolinas College of Health Sciences

Charlotte, North Carolina
www.carolinascollege.edu Federal Code: 031042

2-year public health science and junior college in very large city.
Enrollment: 528 undergrads.
Selectivity: Open admission; but selective for some programs.

BASIC COSTS (2008-2009)
Tuition and fees: $6,895.
Per-credit charge: $210.
Additional info: Tuition varies by program.

FINANCIAL AID PICTURE (2007-2008)
Students with need: Need-based aid available for full-time and part-time students.
Students without need: No-need awards available for academics.

FINANCIAL AID PROCEDURES
Forms required: FAFSA, institutional form.
Dates and Deadlines: Priority date 5/1; no closing date. Applicants notified on a rolling basis starting 5/1.

CONTACT
Jill Powell, Financial Aid Officer
PO Box 32861, Charlotte, NC 28232
(704) 355-8894

Carteret Community College

Morehead City, North Carolina
www.carteret.edu Federal Code: 008081

2-year public community and technical college in small town.
Enrollment: 1,418 undergrads, 55% part-time. 135 full-time freshmen.
Selectivity: Open admission; but selective for some programs.

BASIC COSTS (2008-2009)
Tuition and fees: $1,395; out-of-state residents $7,517.
Per-credit charge: $42; out-of-state residents $233.

FINANCIAL AID PICTURE (2007-2008)
Students with need: 75% of average financial aid package awarded as scholarships/grants, 25% awarded as loans/jobs. Need-based aid available for part-time students.
Students without need: No-need awards available for academics, leadership, minority status, state/district residency.
Additional info: Institutional student loan program administered by college. Student may charge up to $600 for books, supplies and tuition per quarter. Repayment due by 11th week of semester.

FINANCIAL AID PROCEDURES
Forms required: FAFSA, institutional form.
Dates and Deadlines: No deadline. Applicants notified on a rolling basis starting 7/1; must reply within 2 week(s) of notification.

CONTACT
Brenda Long, Financial Aid Officer
3505 Arendell Street, Morehead City, NC 28557-2989
(252) 222-6297

Catawba College

Salisbury, North Carolina
www.catawba.edu Federal Code: 002914

4-year private liberal arts college in large town, affiliated with United Church of Christ.
Enrollment: 1,225 undergrads, 5% part-time. 266 full-time freshmen.
Selectivity: Admits 50 to 75% of applicants.

BASIC COSTS (2009-2010)
Tuition and fees: $23,740.
Per-credit charge: $620.
Room and board: $8,200.

FINANCIAL AID PICTURE (2007-2008)

Students with need: Out of 234 full-time freshmen who applied for aid, 199 were judged to have need. Of these, 199 received aid, and 61 had their full need met. Average financial aid package met 89% of need; average scholarship/grant was $5,105; average loan was $4,436. For part-time students, average financial aid package was $9,166.

Students without need: 37 full-time freshmen who did not demonstrate need for aid received scholarships/grants; average award was $11,431. No-need awards available for academics, athletics, music/drama, state/district residency.

Scholarships offered: 79 full-time freshmen received athletic scholarships; average amount $6,778.

Cumulative student debt: 76% of graduating class had student loans; average debt was $21,892.

FINANCIAL AID PROCEDURES

Forms required: FAFSA, state aid form.

Dates and Deadlines: Priority date 3/15; no closing date. Applicants notified on a rolling basis starting 11/1; must reply within 2 week(s) of notification.

CONTACT

Melanie McCulloh, Director of Scholarships and Financial Assistance
2300 West Innes Street, Salisbury, NC 28144-2488
(704) 637-4416

Catawba Valley Community College

Hickory, North Carolina
www.cvcc.edu Federal Code: 005318

2-year public community college in large town.

Enrollment: 3,740 undergrads, 58% part-time. 507 full-time freshmen.

Selectivity: Open admission; but selective for some programs.

BASIC COSTS (2008-2009)

Tuition and fees: $1,366; out-of-state residents $7,488.

Per-credit charge: $42; out-of-state residents $233.

Additional info: Tuition/fee waivers available for unemployed or children of unemployed.

FINANCIAL AID PICTURE (2007-2008)

Students with need: Out of 444 full-time freshmen who applied for aid, 292 were judged to have need. Of these, 247 received aid, and 1 had their full need met. Need-based aid available for part-time students.

Students without need: 251 full-time freshmen who did not demonstrate need for aid received scholarships/grants; average award was $2,323. No-need awards available for academics, leadership, music/drama.

FINANCIAL AID PROCEDURES

Forms required: FAFSA.

Dates and Deadlines: Closing date 3/15. Applicants notified on a rolling basis starting 5/15.

CONTACT

Debbie Barger, Director of Scholarships and Financial Aid
2550 Highway 70 SE, Hickory, NC 28602
(828) 327-7000 ext. 4214

Central Carolina Community College

Sanford, North Carolina
www.cccc.edu Federal Code: 005449

2-year public community college in large town.

Enrollment: 3,934 undergrads.

Selectivity: Open admission; but selective for some programs.

BASIC COSTS (2008-2009)

Tuition and fees: $1,348; out-of-state residents $7,087.

Per-credit charge: $42; out-of-state residents $233.

FINANCIAL AID PICTURE

Students with need: Need-based aid available for full-time and part-time students. Work study available nights.

Students without need: No-need awards available for academics.

FINANCIAL AID PROCEDURES

Forms required: FAFSA, institutional form.

Dates and Deadlines: Priority date 3/15; closing date 5/1. Applicants notified on a rolling basis starting 7/1; must reply within 2 week(s) of notification.

Transfers: No deadline.

CONTACT

Theresa Phelps, Director of Financial Aid
1105 Kelly Drive, Sanford, NC 27330
(919) 718-7229

Central Piedmont Community College

Charlotte, North Carolina
www.cpcc.edu Federal Code: 002915

2-year public community college in very large city.

Enrollment: 15,380 undergrads, 58% part-time. 1,470 full-time freshmen.

Selectivity: Open admission; but selective for some programs.

BASIC COSTS (2008-2009)

Tuition and fees: $1,458; out-of-state residents $7,197.

Per-credit charge: $42; out-of-state residents $233.

FINANCIAL AID PICTURE

Students with need: Need-based aid available for full-time and part-time students.

Students without need: No-need awards available for academics, minority status.

FINANCIAL AID PROCEDURES

Forms required: FAFSA.

Dates and Deadlines: Priority date 4/1; closing date 6/1. Applicants notified on a rolling basis.

CONTACT

Debbie Brooks, Director, Student Financial Aid
Box 35009, Charlotte, NC 28235-5009
(704) 330-6942

Chowan University

Murfreesboro, North Carolina
www.chowan.edu Federal Code: 002916

4-year private university and liberal arts college in rural community, affiliated with Southern Baptist Convention.

Enrollment: 897 undergrads.

BASIC COSTS (2009-2010)

Tuition and fees: $19,065.

Per-credit charge: $325.

Room and board: $7,310.

FINANCIAL AID PICTURE (2007-2008)

Students with need: Need-based aid available for full-time and part-time students. Work study available nights, weekends, and for part-time students.

Students without need: No-need awards available for academics, athletics, leadership, music/drama, religious affiliation, state/district residency.

Scholarships offered: Scholarship program for students serving as student body president who qualify for admission; full tuition.

FINANCIAL AID PROCEDURES

Forms required: FAFSA.

Dates and Deadlines: Priority date 3/1; no closing date. Applicants notified on a rolling basis starting 3/1; must reply within 2 week(s) of notification.

CONTACT

Stephanie Harrell, Director of Financial Aid
One University Place, Murfreesboro, NC 27855-9901
(252) 398-1229

Coastal Carolina Community College

Jacksonville, North Carolina
www.coastalcarolina.edu Federal Code: 005316

2-year public community college in large town.

Enrollment: 3,913 undergrads, 52% part-time. 487 full-time freshmen.

Selectivity: Open admission; but selective for some programs.

BASIC COSTS (2008-2009)

Tuition and fees: $1,290; out-of-state residents $7,029.

Per-credit charge: $42; out-of-state residents $233.

FINANCIAL AID PICTURE (2007-2008)

Students with need: Need-based aid available for full-time and part-time students. Work study available nights, weekends, and for part-time students.

Students without need: No-need awards available for academics, state/district residency.

FINANCIAL AID PROCEDURES

Forms required: FAFSA, institutional form.

Dates and Deadlines: Priority date 5/15; no closing date. Applicants notified on a rolling basis starting 5/15; must reply within 2 week(s) of notification.

CONTACT

Lyon Tammy, Director for Financial Aid Services
444 Western Boulevard, Jacksonville, NC 28546-6877

College of the Albemarle

Elizabeth City, North Carolina
www.albemarle.cc.nc.us Federal Code: 002917

2-year public branch campus and community college in large town.

Enrollment: 1,795 undergrads.

Selectivity: Open admission; but selective for some programs.

BASIC COSTS (2008-2009)

Tuition and fees: $1,414; out-of-state residents $7,535.

Per-credit charge: $42; out-of-state residents $233.

FINANCIAL AID PICTURE (2007-2008)

Students with need: Need-based aid available for full-time and part-time students.

Students without need: No-need awards available for academics, art, leadership, minority status, music/drama, state/district residency.

Additional info: Separate application must be submitted for COA Private Scholarships.

FINANCIAL AID PROCEDURES

Forms required: FAFSA.

Dates and Deadlines: Priority date 3/15; no closing date. Applicants notified on a rolling basis starting 5/1; must reply within 2 week(s) of notification.

CONTACT

Angie Dawson, Director of Scholarships and Student Aid
1208 North Road Street, Elizabeth City, NC 27906-2327
(252) 335-0821 ext. 2355

Davidson College

Davidson, North Carolina Federal Code: 002918
www.davidson.edu CSS Code: 5150

4-year private liberal arts college in small town, affiliated with Presbyterian Church (USA).

Enrollment: 1,661 undergrads. 465 full-time freshmen.

Selectivity: Admits less than 50% of applicants. GED not accepted.

BASIC COSTS (2008-2009)

Tuition and fees: $33,479.

Room and board: $9,471.

FINANCIAL AID PICTURE (2007-2008)

Students with need: Out of 243 full-time freshmen who applied for aid, 159 were judged to have need. Of these, 155 received aid, and 155 had their full need met. Average financial aid package met 100% of need; average scholarship/grant was $20,793; average loan was $2,208. Need-based aid available for part-time students.

Students without need: 48 full-time freshmen who did not demonstrate need for aid received scholarships/grants; average award was $16,610. No-need awards available for academics, art, athletics, leadership, minority status, music/drama, ROTC.

Scholarships offered: ***Merit:*** Thompson S./Sarah S. Baker Scholarships: comprehensive fees; for first-time students with highest achievements; 3 awarded. John Montgomery Belk Scholarship: comprehensive fees; for Southeast applicants with highest achievements; 6 awarded. Amos Norris Scholarship: full cost; for first-time student athlete; 1 awarded. William Holt Terry Scholarships: full tuition; for first-year students with leadership skills and personal qualities, 2 awarded. John I. Smith Scholars Programs: full tuition; for first-year students with leadership, academic excellence, and commitment to community service; 2 awarded. ***Athletic:*** 49 full-time freshmen received athletic scholarships; average amount $14,690.

Cumulative student debt: 33% of graduating class had student loans; average debt was $25,025.

Additional info: The college has increased the money it provides for grants in financial aid packages and eliminated mandatory loans.

FINANCIAL AID PROCEDURES

Forms required: FAFSA, CSS PROFILE.

Dates and Deadlines: Closing date 2/15. Applicants notified by 4/1; must reply by 5/1.

Transfers: Priority date 2/15; closing date 3/15.

CONTACT

David Gelinas, Director of Financial Aid
Box 7156, Davidson, NC 28035-7156
(704) 894-2232

Davidson County Community College

Lexington, North Carolina
www.davidsonccc.edu Federal Code: 002919

2-year public community college in large town.

Enrollment: 2,912 undergrads.

Selectivity: Open admission; but selective for some programs.

BASIC COSTS (2008-2009)

Tuition and fees: $1,370; out-of-state residents $7,109.

Per-credit charge: $42; out-of-state residents $233.

FINANCIAL AID PICTURE (2007-2008)
Students with need: Need-based aid available for full-time and part-time students.
Students without need: No-need awards available for academics, leadership.

FINANCIAL AID PROCEDURES
Forms required: FAFSA, institutional form.
Dates and Deadlines: Closing date 3/31. Applicants notified on a rolling basis starting 7/1; must reply within 2 week(s) of notification.

CONTACT
Anita Pennix, Director, Financial Aid
PO Box 1287, Lexington, NC 27293-1287
(336) 249-8186 ext. 237

Duke University
Durham, North Carolina
www.duke.edu
Federal Code: 002920
CSS Code: 5156

4-year private university in small city, affiliated with United Methodist Church.
Enrollment: 6,352 undergrads. 1,699 full-time freshmen.
Selectivity: Admits less than 50% of applicants. GED not accepted.

BASIC COSTS (2009-2010)
Tuition and fees: $38,741.
Per-credit charge: $1,171.
Room and board: $11,154.

FINANCIAL AID PICTURE
Students with need: Need-based aid available for full-time students.
Students without need: No-need awards available for academics, alumni affiliation, art, athletics, leadership, minority status, religious affiliation, ROTC, state/district residency.

FINANCIAL AID PROCEDURES
Forms required: FAFSA, CSS PROFILE.
Dates and Deadlines: Closing date 3/1. Applicants notified by 4/1; must reply by 5/1 or within 4 week(s) of notification.

CONTACT
Alison Rabil, Director of Financial Aid
2138 Campus Drive, Durham, NC 27708
(919) 684-6225

Durham Technical Community College
Durham, North Carolina
www.durhamtech.edu
Federal Code: 005448

2-year public community and technical college in small city.
Enrollment: 3,050 undergrads.
Selectivity: Open admission; but selective for some programs.

BASIC COSTS (2008-2009)
Tuition and fees: $1,340; out-of-state residents $7,079.
Per-credit charge: $42; out-of-state residents $233.

FINANCIAL AID PICTURE
Students with need: Need-based aid available for full-time and part-time students. Work study available nights.
Students without need: No-need awards available for academics, minority status, state/district residency.
Additional info: Special funds available to single parents for tuition, fees, books, supplies and child care expenses.

FINANCIAL AID PROCEDURES
Forms required: FAFSA.
Dates and Deadlines: Applicants notified on a rolling basis starting 1/31; must reply within 3 week(s) of notification.

CONTACT
Cameron Murray, Director of Financial Aid
1637 Lawson Street, Durham, NC 27703
(919) 686-3661

East Carolina University
Greenville, North Carolina
www.ecu.edu
Federal Code: 002923

4-year public university in small city.
Enrollment: 20,717 undergrads, 12% part-time. 4,522 full-time freshmen.
Selectivity: Admits 50 to 75% of applicants.

BASIC COSTS (2008-2009)
Tuition and fees: $4,406; out-of-state residents $14,920.
Room and board: $7,630.

FINANCIAL AID PICTURE (2008-2009)
Students with need: Need-based aid available for full-time and part-time students.
Students without need: No-need awards available for academics, alumni affiliation, art, athletics, minority status, ROTC.

FINANCIAL AID PROCEDURES
Forms required: FAFSA.
Dates and Deadlines: Priority date 4/15; no closing date. Applicants notified on a rolling basis starting 3/15; must reply within 3 week(s) of notification.

CONTACT
Julie Poorman, Director of Student Financial Aid
Office of Undergraduate Admissions, Greenville, NC 27858-4353
(252) 328-6610

Edgecombe Community College
Tarboro, North Carolina
www.edgecombe.edu
Federal Code: 008855

2-year public community college in large town.
Enrollment: 2,579 undergrads.
Selectivity: Open admission; but selective for some programs.

BASIC COSTS (2008-2009)
Tuition and fees: $1,284; out-of-state residents $7,023.
Per-credit charge: $42; out-of-state residents $220.

FINANCIAL AID PICTURE (2008-2009)
Students with need: 79% of average financial aid package awarded as scholarships/grants, 21% awarded as loans/jobs. Need-based aid available for part-time students.
Students without need: This college awards aid only to students with need.

FINANCIAL AID PROCEDURES
Forms required: FAFSA, institutional form.
Dates and Deadlines: No deadline. Applicants notified on a rolling basis starting 8/15; must reply within 3 week(s) of notification.
Transfers: No deadline.

CONTACT
Henry Anderson, Director of Financial Aid
2009 West Wilson Street, Tarboro, NC 27886
(252) 823-5166 ext. 258

Elizabeth City State University

Elizabeth City, North Carolina
www.ecsu.edu Federal Code: 002926

4-year public liberal arts college in large town.
Enrollment: 3,097 undergrads.
Selectivity: Admits less than 50% of applicants.

BASIC COSTS (2008-2009)

Tuition and fees: $2,914; out-of-state residents $11,928.
Room and board: $5,159.

FINANCIAL AID PICTURE

Students with need: Need-based aid available for full-time students. Work study available nights, weekends, and for part-time students.
Students without need: No-need awards available for academics, athletics, minority status, ROTC, state/district residency.

FINANCIAL AID PROCEDURES

Forms required: FAFSA.
Dates and Deadlines: Priority date 3/1; closing date 3/15. Applicants notified on a rolling basis starting 6/1; must reply within 3 week(s) of notification.
Transfers: Closing date 8/1. Applicants notified on a rolling basis starting 6/1; must reply within 3 week(s) of notification.

CONTACT

Kenneth Wilson, Associate Director of Financial Aid
1704 Weeksville Road, Campus Box 901, Elizabeth City, NC 27909
(252) 335-3283

Elon University

Elon, North Carolina Federal Code: 002927
www.elon.edu CSS Code: 5183

4-year private university and liberal arts college in large town, affiliated with United Church of Christ.
Enrollment: 4,992 undergrads, 2% part-time. 1,291 full-time freshmen.
Selectivity: Admits less than 50% of applicants.

BASIC COSTS (2008-2009)

Tuition and fees: $24,076.
Per-credit charge: $746.
Room and board: $7,770.

FINANCIAL AID PICTURE (2008-2009)

Students with need: Out of 704 full-time freshmen who applied for aid, 405 were judged to have need. Of these, 405 received aid. Average financial aid package met 77% of need; average scholarship/grant was $10,090; average loan was $3,382. Need-based aid available for part-time students.
Students without need: 381 full-time freshmen who did not demonstrate need for aid received scholarships/grants; average award was $5,253. No-need awards available for academics, art, athletics, leadership, music/drama, ROTC, state/district residency.
Scholarships offered: ***Merit:*** Presidential Scholarships: $1,000-$4,500 annually; based on academic credentials. Fellows Programs (Communications, Science, Jefferson-Pilot Business, Honors, Isabella Cannon Leadership): $2,500-$8,000 annually; based on merit. North Carolina Teaching Fellows: $13,000 annually. Engineering Scholarships: $3,000 annually. Performing Arts Scholarships: $500-$6,000; talent-based. Music Scholarships: $500-$5,000; talent and need-based. ***Athletic:*** 59 full-time freshmen received athletic scholarships; average amount $21,110.
Cumulative student debt: 45% of graduating class had student loans; average debt was $23,392.

FINANCIAL AID PROCEDURES

Forms required: FAFSA, CSS PROFILE, institutional form.
Dates and Deadlines: Priority date 2/15; no closing date. Applicants notified on a rolling basis starting 3/30.

CONTACT

Pat Murphy, Director of Financial Planning
2700 Campus Box, Elon, NC 27244-2010
(336) 278-7640

Fayetteville State University

Fayetteville, North Carolina
www.uncfsu.edu Federal Code: 002928

4-year public university in small city.
Enrollment: 5,608 undergrads.

BASIC COSTS (2008-2009)

Tuition and fees: $3,301; out-of-state residents $13,483.
Room and board: $5,010.
Additional info: Application fees-$25, Orientation fees-$45, Car registration-$45, Ins.-$378, Room breakage Deposit-$125, Bronco card-$24, Late registration fee-$20.

FINANCIAL AID PICTURE

Students with need: Need-based aid available for full-time and part-time students. Work study available nights, weekends, and for part-time students.
Students without need: No-need awards available for academics, alumni affiliation, athletics, music/drama, ROTC, state/district residency.

FINANCIAL AID PROCEDURES

Forms required: FAFSA.
Dates and Deadlines: Priority date 3/1; closing date 4/1. Applicants notified on a rolling basis starting 4/15; must reply within 2 week(s) of notification.

CONTACT

Kamesia Ewing, Director of Financial Aid
1200 Murchison Road, Fayetteville, NC 28301-4298
(910) 672-1325

Fayetteville Technical Community College

Fayetteville, North Carolina
www.faytechcc.edu Federal Code: 007640

2-year public community and technical college in large city.
Enrollment: 8,195 undergrads, 63% part-time. 835 full-time freshmen.
Selectivity: Open admission; but selective for some programs

BASIC COSTS (2008-2009)

Tuition and fees: $1,404; out-of-state residents $7,586.
Per-credit charge: $42; out-of-state residents $233.

FINANCIAL AID PICTURE (2007-2008)

Students with need: 53% of average financial aid package awarded as scholarships/grants, 47% awarded as loans/jobs. Need-based aid available for part-time students.

FINANCIAL AID PROCEDURES

Forms required: FAFSA.
Dates and Deadlines: Priority date 6/1; closing date 7/15. Applicants notified on a rolling basis starting 4/1.

CONTACT

Eleanor Van Valkenburg, Director of Student Financial Aid Services
PO Box 35236, Fayetteville, NC 28303-0236
(910) 678-5242

Forsyth Technical Community College

Winston-Salem, North Carolina
www.forsythtech.edu Federal Code: 005317

2-year public community and technical college in small city.
Enrollment: 6,749 undergrads, 53% part-time. 943 full-time freshmen.
Selectivity: Open admission; but selective for some programs.

BASIC COSTS (2008-2009)

Tuition and fees: $1,476; out-of-state residents $7,598.
Per-credit charge: $42; out-of-state residents $233.

FINANCIAL AID PICTURE (2007-2008)

Students with need: Need-based aid available for full-time and part-time students. Work study available nights.
Students without need: No-need awards available for academics, state/district residency.
Additional info: Apply for aid as close to January 1 as possible for best consideration.

FINANCIAL AID PROCEDURES

Forms required: FAFSA, institutional form.
Dates and Deadlines: Priority date 6/1; no closing date. Applicants notified on a rolling basis starting 7/1; must reply within 2 week(s) of notification.
Transfers: No deadline. Mid-year transfer students must submit a financial aid transcript from previous college in order for financial aid office to award any Federal Pell Grant funds to eligible students.

CONTACT

Ricky Hodges, Director of Student Financial Services
2100 Silas Creek Parkway, Winston-Salem, NC 27103

Gardner-Webb University

Boiling Springs, North Carolina
www.gardner-webb.edu Federal Code: 002929

4-year private university and liberal arts college in small town, affiliated with Southern Baptist Convention.
Enrollment: 2,600 undergrads, 17% part-time. 441 full-time freshmen.
Selectivity: Admits 50 to 75% of applicants.

BASIC COSTS (2009-2010)

Tuition and fees: $21,170.
Per-credit charge: $345.
Room and board: $6,810.

FINANCIAL AID PICTURE (2007-2008)

Students with need: Out of 359 full-time freshmen who applied for aid, 285 were judged to have need. Of these, 285 received aid, and 84 had their full need met. Average financial aid package met 60% of need; average scholarship/grant was $7,375; average loan was $4,109. Need-based aid available for part-time students.
Students without need: 96 full-time freshmen who did not demonstrate need for aid received scholarships/grants; average award was $6,039. No-need awards available for academics, athletics, leadership, music/drama, religious affiliation, ROTC, state/district residency.
Scholarships offered: 38 full-time freshmen received athletic scholarships; average amount $12,199.

FINANCIAL AID PROCEDURES

Forms required: FAFSA, state aid form.
Dates and Deadlines: Priority date 3/15; no closing date. Applicants notified on a rolling basis starting 3/1; must reply within 2 week(s) of notification.
Transfers: No deadline. Applicants notified on a rolling basis.

CONTACT

Debra Hintz, Director of Financial Planning
Box 817, Boiling Springs, NC 28017
(704) 406-4243

Gaston College

Dallas, North Carolina
www.gaston.cc.nc.us Federal Code: 002973

2-year public community college in small town.
Enrollment: 2,040 full-time undergrads.
Selectivity: Open admission; but selective for some programs.

BASIC COSTS (2008-2009)

Tuition and fees: $1,300; out-of-state residents $7,039.
Per-credit charge: $42; out-of-state residents $233.

FINANCIAL AID PICTURE

Students with need: Need-based aid available for full-time students.
Students without need: No-need awards available for academics, state/district residency.
Scholarships offered: Academic Scholarship: over 30 available, $1,100, GPA of 3.0 or better. Careers Scholarship: 10 available, $1,100 each, must pursue career in specified engineering technologies or industrial technologies major and have GPA of 3.0 or better.
Additional info: Grants/scholarships available for women pursuing nontraditional roles.

FINANCIAL AID PROCEDURES

Forms required: FAFSA, institutional form.
Dates and Deadlines: Priority date 3/15; no closing date. Applicants notified on a rolling basis.

CONTACT

Peggy Oates, Director of Financial Aid and Veterans Affairs
201 Highway 321 South, Dallas, NC 28034-1499
(704) 922-6227

Greensboro College

Greensboro, North Carolina
www.greensborocollege.edu Federal Code: 002930

4-year private liberal arts college in large city, affiliated with United Methodist Church.
Enrollment: 1,043 undergrads, 15% part-time. 212 full-time freshmen.
Selectivity: Admits 50 to 75% of applicants.

BASIC COSTS (2009-2010)

Tuition and fees: $23,346.
Per-credit charge: $635.
Room and board: $8,721.

FINANCIAL AID PICTURE (2008-2009)

Students with need: Need-based aid available for full-time and part-time students. Work study available nights, weekends, and for part-time students.
Students without need: No-need awards available for academics, alumni affiliation, art, leadership, music/drama, religious affiliation, state/district residency.
Scholarships offered: Presidential Scholarships: full tuition, fees, room, and board; number of awards vary.

FINANCIAL AID PROCEDURES

Forms required: FAFSA, state aid form, institutional form.
Dates and Deadlines: Priority date 4/15; no closing date. Applicants notified on a rolling basis starting 2/1; must reply within 2 week(s) of notification.
Transfers: Closing date 4/15. Must reply within 4 week(s) of notification.

CONTACT
Dawn Young, Director of Financial Aid
815 West Market Street, Greensboro, NC 27401-1875
(336) 272-7102 ext. 217

Guilford College
Greensboro, North Carolina
www.guilford.edu Federal Code: 002931

4-year private liberal arts college in small city, affiliated with Society of Friends (Quaker).
Enrollment: 2,641 undergrads, 16% part-time. 451 full-time freshmen.
Selectivity: Admits 50 to 75% of applicants.

BASIC COSTS (2008-2009)
Tuition and fees: $26,030.
Per-credit charge: $795.
Room and board: $7,140.
Additional info: Parking fee $70, required athletic insurance $183. Tuition/fee waivers available for adults.

FINANCIAL AID PICTURE (2007-2008)
Students with need: Out of 341 full-time freshmen who applied for aid, 271 were judged to have need. Of these, 271 received aid, and 162 had their full need met. Need-based aid available for part-time students.
Students without need: 153 full-time freshmen who did not demonstrate need for aid received scholarships/grants; average award was $8,692. No-need awards available for academics.
Scholarships offered: Honors Scholarship: $7,500 to full tuition. Presidential Scholarship: $5,000. Incentive grants: $3,000; based on participation or leadership in school or community activities. Quaker Leadership Scholarships: $3,000; candidates must be active members of the Religious Society of Friends.
Cumulative student debt: 66% of graduating class had student loans; average debt was $22,780.

FINANCIAL AID PROCEDURES
Forms required: FAFSA.
Dates and Deadlines: Priority date 3/1; no closing date. Applicants notified on a rolling basis starting 2/15; must reply within 2 week(s) of notification.

CONTACT
Dianne Harrison, Director of Financial Aid
Admissions, New Garden Hall, Greensboro, NC 27410-4108
(336) 316-2354

Guilford Technical Community College
Jamestown, North Carolina
www.gtcc.edu Federal Code: 004838

2-year public community college in large city.
Enrollment: 7,501 undergrads.
Selectivity: Open admission; but selective for some programs.

BASIC COSTS (2008-2009)
Tuition and fees: $1,417; out-of-state residents $7,156.
Per-credit charge: $42; out-of-state residents $233.

FINANCIAL AID PICTURE (2007-2008)
Students with need: 67% of average financial aid package awarded as scholarships/grants, 33% awarded as loans/jobs. Need-based aid available for part-time students.

FINANCIAL AID PROCEDURES
Forms required: FAFSA.
Dates and Deadlines: Priority date 3/15; no closing date. Applicants notified on a rolling basis starting 7/1; must reply within 2 week(s) of notification.

CONTACT
Lisa Koretoff, Director of Financial Aid
PO Box 309, Jamestown, NC 27282
(336) 334-4822 ext. 5352

Halifax Community College
Weldon, North Carolina
www.hcc.cc.nc.us Federal Code: 007986

2-year public community college in small town.
Enrollment: 974 undergrads.
Selectivity: Open admission; but selective for some programs.

BASIC COSTS (2008-2009)
Tuition and fees: $1,462; out-of-state residents $7,584.
Per-credit charge: $42; out-of-state residents $233.

FINANCIAL AID PICTURE (2007-2008)
Students with need: Need-based aid available for full-time students.

FINANCIAL AID PROCEDURES
Dates and Deadlines: Priority date 6/1; no closing date. Applicants notified on a rolling basis starting 8/1; must reply within 2 week(s) of notification.

CONTACT
Tara Keeter, Director, Financial Aid
Drawer 809, Weldon, NC 27890
(252) 536-7223

Haywood Community College
Clyde, North Carolina
www.haywood.edu Federal Code: 008083

2-year public community and technical college in rural community.
Enrollment: 1,453 undergrads.
Selectivity: Open admission; but selective for some programs.

BASIC COSTS (2008-2009)
Tuition and fees: $1,394; out-of-state residents $7,516.
Per-credit charge: $42; out-of-state residents $233.

FINANCIAL AID PICTURE (2007-2008)
Students with need. Need-based aid available for full-time and part-time students.
Students without need: No-need awards available for academics.
Additional info: Complete FAFSA by priority filing date for consideration for institutional scholarships.

FINANCIAL AID PROCEDURES
Forms required: FAFSA, institutional form.
Dates and Deadlines: Priority date 4/1; no closing date. Applicants notified on a rolling basis starting 4/15; must reply within 2 week(s) of notification.

CONTACT
Kathy Lovedahl, Coordinator Financial Aid
185 Freelander Drive, Clyde, NC 28721-9454
(828) 627-4506

High Point University

High Point, North Carolina
www.highpoint.edu Federal Code: 002933

4-year private university and liberal arts college in small city, affiliated with United Methodist Church.
Enrollment: 3,046 undergrads, 8% part-time. 882 full-time freshmen.
Selectivity: Admits 50 to 75% of applicants.

BASIC COSTS (2009-2010)

Per-credit charge: $636.
Comprehensive fee: $34,000.

FINANCIAL AID PICTURE (2007-2008)

Students with need: Need-based aid available for full-time and part-time students. Work study available nights, weekends, and for part-time students.
Students without need: No-need awards available for academics, alumni affiliation, art, athletics, leadership, music/drama, religious affiliation, state/district residency.
Scholarships offered: Awarded annually to qualified freshmen: Keller Scholarship: $24,000. University Fellowship: $20,000. Presidential Fellowship: $15,000. Presidential Scholarship: $9,000. Leadership Fellowship: $7,000. Leadership Scholarship: $5,000. All scholarships based on merit. Application and interview required.

FINANCIAL AID PROCEDURES

Forms required: FAFSA, state aid form.
Dates and Deadlines: Priority date 3/1; no closing date. Applicants notified on a rolling basis starting 4/1; must reply within 3 week(s) of notification.
Transfers: No deadline. Applicants notified on a rolling basis starting 5/1; must reply within 3 week(s) of notification.

CONTACT

Julie Setzer, Director of Student Financial Services
833 Montlieu Avenue, High Point, NC 27262-3598
(336) 841-9166

Isothermal Community College

Spindale, North Carolina
www.isothermal.edu Federal Code: 002934

2-year public community college in small town.
Enrollment: 1,652 undergrads, 41% part-time. 222 full-time freshmen.
Selectivity: Open admission.

BASIC COSTS (2008-2009)

Tuition and fees: $1,298; out-of-state residents $7,037.
Per-credit charge: $42; out-of-state residents $233.

FINANCIAL AID PICTURE (2007-2008)

Students with need: Need-based aid available for full-time and part-time students. Work study available nights.
Students without need: No-need awards available for academics, job skills, leadership, minority status, music/drama, state/district residency.

FINANCIAL AID PROCEDURES

Forms required: FAFSA, institutional form.
Dates and Deadlines: Priority date 5/31; no closing date. Applicants notified on a rolling basis starting 4/30; must reply within 4 week(s) of notification.

CONTACT

Jeffery Boyle, Director of Financial Aid
PO Box 804, Spindale, NC 28160-0804
(828) 286-3636 ext. 468

James Sprunt Community College

Kenansville, North Carolina
www.jamessprunt.edu Federal Code: 007687

2-year public community college in rural community.
Enrollment: 926 undergrads, 41% part-time. 157 full-time freshmen.
Selectivity: Open admission; but selective for some programs.

BASIC COSTS (2008-2009)

Tuition and fees: $1,414; out-of-state residents $7,536.
Per-credit charge: $42; out-of-state residents $233.

FINANCIAL AID PICTURE (2007-2008)

Students with need: Out of 59 full-time freshmen who applied for aid, 59 were judged to have need. Of these, 59 received aid. Average financial aid package met 60% of need; average scholarship/grant was $2,500; average loan was $3,000. For part-time students, average financial aid package was $1,889.
Students without need: This college awards aid only to students with need.

FINANCIAL AID PROCEDURES

Forms required: FAFSA, state aid form, institutional form.
Dates and Deadlines: Priority date 6/1; no closing date. Applicants notified on a rolling basis starting 7/15; must reply within 2 week(s) of notification.

CONTACT

Connie Taylor, Financial Aid Officer
PO Box 398, Kenansville, NC 28349-0398
(910) 296-2503

John Wesley College

High Point, North Carolina
www.johnwesley.edu Federal Code: 013819

4-year private Bible college in small city, affiliated with interdenominational tradition.
Enrollment: 78 undergrads.

BASIC COSTS (2008-2009)

Tuition and fees: $10,730.
Per-credit charge: $375.
Room only: $2,344.

FINANCIAL AID PICTURE (2007-2008)

Students with need: Need-based aid available for full-time and part-time students. Work study available nights, weekends, and for part-time students.
Scholarships offered: Early Acceptance; $100. Academic Honor; 10% of tuition.
Additional info: Early Acceptance Scholarships, Academic Honor Scholarships, Married Student Credit and Minister/Missionary Dependent Scholarship available.

FINANCIAL AID PROCEDURES

Forms required: FAFSA.
Dates and Deadlines: Priority date 3/15; no closing date. Applicants notified on a rolling basis starting 6/1; must reply within 3 week(s) of notification.
Transfers: Closing date 3/15.

CONTACT

Shirley Carter, Director of Financial Aid
2314 North Centennial, High Point, NC 27265-3197
(336) 889-2262 ext. 129

Johnson & Wales University: Charlotte

Charlotte, North Carolina
www.jwu.edu

4-year private university in very large city.
Enrollment: 2,436 undergrads, 2% part-time. 633 full-time freshmen.
Selectivity: Admits 50 to 75% of applicants.

BASIC COSTS (2009-2010)

Tuition and fees: $23,490.
Room and board: $9,249.

FINANCIAL AID PICTURE (2008-2009)

Students with need: Out of 626 full-time freshmen who applied for aid, 521 were judged to have need. Of these, 521 received aid, and 35 had their full need met. Average financial aid package met 66% of need; average scholarship/grant was $8,733; average loan was $3,314. For part-time students, average financial aid package was $8,476.
Students without need: 93 full-time freshmen who did not demonstrate need for aid received scholarships/grants; average award was $4,405. No-need awards available for academics, alumni affiliation, job skills, leadership, state/district residency.
Cumulative student debt: 85% of graduating class had student loans; average debt was $27,500.

FINANCIAL AID PROCEDURES

Forms required: FAFSA.
Dates and Deadlines: No deadline. Applicants notified on a rolling basis starting 3/1.
Transfers: No deadline. Applicants notified on a rolling basis.

CONTACT

Director of Financial Aid
801 West Trade Street, Charlotte, NC 28202
(800) 342-5598

Johnson C. Smith University

Charlotte, North Carolina
www.jcsu.edu Federal Code: 002936

4-year private university and liberal arts college in very large city.
Enrollment: 1,571 undergrads, 2% part-time. 501 full-time freshmen.
Selectivity: Admits less than 50% of applicants.

BASIC COSTS (2008-2009)

Tuition and fees: $15,754.
Per-credit charge: $361.
Room and board: $6,132.

FINANCIAL AID PICTURE (2007-2008)

Students with need: Out of 431 full-time freshmen who applied for aid, 405 were judged to have need. Of these, 405 received aid, and 2 had their full need met. Average financial aid package met 59% of need; average scholarship/grant was $4,493; average loan was $3,500. Need-based aid available for part-time students.
Students without need: No-need awards available for academics, athletics, ROTC, state/district residency.
Scholarships offered: 1 full-time freshmen received athletic scholarships; average amount $21,886.
Cumulative student debt: 84% of graduating class had student loans; average debt was $34,308.

FINANCIAL AID PROCEDURES

Forms required: FAFSA.
Dates and Deadlines: Priority date 3/1; no closing date. Applicants notified on a rolling basis starting 3/1; must reply within 2 week(s) of notification.
Transfers: No deadline. Applicants notified on a rolling basis starting 4/1; must reply within 2 week(s) of notification.

CONTACT

Keisha Ramey, Associate Director
100 Beatties Ford Road, Charlotte, NC 28216-5398
(704) 378-1035

Johnston Community College

Smithfield, North Carolina
www.johnstoncc.edu Federal Code: 009336

2-year public community and technical college in large town.
Enrollment: 4,178 undergrads. 723 full-time freshmen.
Selectivity: Open admission; but selective for some programs.

BASIC COSTS (2008-2009)

Tuition and fees: $1,441; out-of-state residents $7,563.
Per-credit charge: $42; out-of-state residents $233.

FINANCIAL AID PICTURE (2007-2008)

Students with need: Need-based aid available for full-time and part-time students.
Students without need: This college awards aid only to students with need.

FINANCIAL AID PROCEDURES

Forms required: FAFSA, institutional form.
Dates and Deadlines: Priority date 5/31; no closing date. Applicants notified on a rolling basis starting 6/1; must reply within 2 week(s) of notification.

CONTACT

Betty Woodall, Financial Aid Director
PO Box 2350, Smithfield, NC 27577
(919) 209-2036

Lees-McRae College

Banner Elk, North Carolina
www.lmc.edu Federal Code: 002923

4-year private liberal arts college in rural community, affiliated with Presbyterian Church (USA).
Enrollment: 948 undergrads. 229 full-time freshmen.
Selectivity: Admits 50 to 75% of applicants.

BASIC COSTS (2009-2010)

Tuition and fees: $21,625.
Per-credit charge: $600.
Room and board: $7,400.

FINANCIAL AID PICTURE (2008-2009)

Students with need: Out of 190 full-time freshmen who applied for aid, 164 were judged to have need. Of these, 164 received aid, and 7 had their full need met. Average financial aid package met 76% of need; average scholarship/grant was $9,200; average loan was $3,500. Need-based aid available for part-time students.
Students without need: 26 full-time freshmen who did not demonstrate need for aid received scholarships/grants; average award was $4,500. No-need awards available for academics, alumni affiliation, art, athletics, leadership, music/drama, religious affiliation, state/district residency.
Scholarships offered: 11 full-time freshmen received athletic scholarships; average amount $4,000.

FINANCIAL AID PROCEDURES

Forms required: FAFSA, state aid form.
Dates and Deadlines: Priority date 3/15; no closing date. Applicants notified on a rolling basis starting 2/15; must reply within 2 week(s) of notification.

CONTACT
Cathy Shell, Director of Financial Aid
Box 128, Banner Elk, NC 28604
(828) 898-8740

Lenoir Community College
Kinston, North Carolina
www.lenoircc.edu Federal Code: 002940

2-year public community college in large town.
Enrollment: 2,967 undergrads.
Selectivity: Open admission; but selective for some programs.

BASIC COSTS (2008-2009)
Tuition and fees: $1,447; out-of-state residents $7,569.
Per-credit charge: $42; out-of-state residents $233.

FINANCIAL AID PICTURE
Students with need: Need-based aid available for full-time and part-time students. Work study available nights.
Students without need: No-need awards available for academics, athletics, leadership, state/district residency.

FINANCIAL AID PROCEDURES
Forms required: institutional form.
Dates and Deadlines: Priority date 7/1; closing date 8/15. Applicants notified on a rolling basis starting 8/1; must reply within 2 week(s) of notification.

CONTACT
Reekita Brunton, Director of Student Financial Aid
Box 188, Kinston, NC 28502-0188
(252) 527-6223

Lenoir-Rhyne University
Hickory, North Carolina
www.lr.edu Federal Code: 002941

4-year private liberal arts college in large town, affiliated with Evangelical Lutheran Church in America.
Enrollment: 1,347 undergrads, 5% part-time. 346 full-time freshmen.
Selectivity: Admits over 75% of applicants.

BASIC COSTS (2009-2010)
Tuition and fees: $24,200.
Per-credit charge: $1,000.
Room and board: $8,540.
Additional info: Tuition/fee waivers available for minority students.

FINANCIAL AID PICTURE (2007-2008)
Students with need: Need-based aid available for full-time and part-time students. Work study available nights, weekends, and for part-time students.
Students without need: No-need awards available for academics, athletics, job skills, leadership, minority status, music/drama, ROTC, state/district residency.

FINANCIAL AID PROCEDURES
Forms required: FAFSA, state aid form.
Dates and Deadlines: Priority date 3/1; closing date 8/1. Applicants notified on a rolling basis starting 3/1; must reply within 2 week(s) of notification.

CONTACT
Division of Enrollment Management
PO Box 7227, Hickory, NC 28603
(800) 277-05721

Livingstone College
Salisbury, North Carolina
www.livingstone.edu Federal Code: 002942

4-year private liberal arts college in large town, affiliated with African Methodist Episcopal Zion Church.
Enrollment: 994 undergrads.
Selectivity: Admits 50 to 75% of applicants.

BASIC COSTS (2008-2009)
Tuition and fees: $12,915.
Per-credit charge: $526.
Room and board: $6,040.

FINANCIAL AID PICTURE (2007-2008)
Students with need: Need-based aid available for full-time and part-time students. Work study available nights, weekends, and for part-time students.
Students without need: No-need awards available for academics, alumni affiliation, athletics, leadership, music/drama, religious affiliation, ROTC, state/district residency.

FINANCIAL AID PROCEDURES
Forms required: FAFSA, state aid form.
Dates and Deadlines: Priority date 3/15; closing date 6/30. Applicants notified by 5/1; must reply within 4 week(s) of notification.

CONTACT
Sherri Jefferson, Director of Financial Aid
701 West Monroe Street, Salisbury, NC 28144-5213
(704) 216-6273

Louisburg College
Louisburg, North Carolina
www.louisburg.edu Federal Code: 002943

2-year private junior college in small town, affiliated with United Methodist Church.
Enrollment: 586 undergrads.
Selectivity: Admits 50 to 75% of applicants.

BASIC COSTS (2009-2010)
Tuition and fees: $13,915.
Per-credit charge: $1,010.
Room and board: $8,632.
Additional info: Book rental fees are included in the tuition charges.

FINANCIAL AID PICTURE (2007-2008)
Students with need: 50% of average financial aid package awarded as scholarships/grants, 50% awarded as loans/jobs. Work study available nights, weekends, and for part-time students.
Additional info: Job location and development program helps students obtain work in the community.

FINANCIAL AID PROCEDURES
Forms required: FAFSA, institutional form.
Dates and Deadlines: Priority date 3/1; no closing date. Applicants notified on a rolling basis starting 3/15.

CONTACT
Sean Van Pallandt, Director of Financial Aid
501 North Main Street, Louisburg, NC 27549
(919) 497-3203

Mars Hill College

Mars Hill, North Carolina
www.mhc.edu Federal Code: 002944

4-year private liberal arts college in small town, affiliated with Baptist faith.
Enrollment: 1,203 undergrads, 6% part-time. 297 full-time freshmen.
Selectivity: Admits 50 to 75% of applicants.

BASIC COSTS (2008-2009)
Tuition and fees: $19,894.
Per-credit charge: $660.
Room and board: $6,891.

FINANCIAL AID PICTURE (2008-2009)
Students with need: Need-based aid available for full-time and part-time students. Work study available nights.
Students without need: No-need awards available for academics, art, athletics, religious affiliation, state/district residency.
Scholarships offered: Awards based on merit, SAT/ACT scores, and GPA. Money available for four years, requiring minimum GPA.

FINANCIAL AID PROCEDURES
Forms required: FAFSA, state aid form, institutional form.
Dates and Deadlines: No deadline. Applicants notified on a rolling basis; must reply within 2 week(s) of notification.

CONTACT
Amanda Willis, Director of Financial Aid
Blackwell Hall, Box 370, Mars Hill, NC 28754
(828) 689-1123

Martin Community College

Williamston, North Carolina
www.martincc.edu Federal Code: 007988

2-year public community and technical college in small town.
Enrollment: 689 undergrads, 52% part-time. 70 full-time freshmen.
Selectivity: Open admission; but selective for some programs.

BASIC COSTS (2008-2009)
Tuition and fees: $1,298; out-of-state residents $7,037.
Per-credit charge: $42; out-of-state residents $233.

FINANCIAL AID PICTURE
Students with need: Need-based aid available for full-time and part-time students. Work study available nights.
Students without need: No-need awards available for academics.

FINANCIAL AID PROCEDURES
Forms required: FAFSA.
Dates and Deadlines: No deadline. Applicants notified on a rolling basis starting 5/1.

CONTACT
Michelle Lane, Director of Financial Aid
1161 Kehukee Park Road, Williamston, NC 27892-9988
(252) 792-1521 ext. 244

Mayland Community College

Spruce Pine, North Carolina
www.mayland.edu Federal Code: 011197

2-year public community college in rural community.
Enrollment: 1,551 undergrads.
Selectivity: Open admission; but selective for some programs.

BASIC COSTS (2008-2009)
Tuition and fees: $1,560; out-of-state residents $7,682.
Per-credit charge: $42; out-of-state residents $233.

FINANCIAL AID PICTURE (2008-2009)
Students with need: Need-based aid available for full-time and part-time students.

FINANCIAL AID PROCEDURES
Forms required: FAFSA, institutional form.
Dates and Deadlines: Priority date 3/15; no closing date. Applicants notified on a rolling basis starting 6/15.

CONTACT
Pamela Ellis, Director of Financial Aid
Box 547, Spruce Pine, NC 28777
(828) 765-7351

McDowell Technical Community College

Marion, North Carolina
www.mcdowelltech.edu Federal Code: 008085

2-year public community and technical college in small town.
Enrollment: 1,004 undergrads.
Selectivity: Open admission; but selective for some programs.

BASIC COSTS (2008-2009)
Tuition and fees: $1,400; out-of-state residents $7,522.
Per-credit charge: $42; out-of-state residents $233.

FINANCIAL AID PICTURE (2007-2008)
Students with need: Need-based aid available for full-time and part-time students. Work study available nights.
Students without need: This college awards aid only to students with need.

FINANCIAL AID PROCEDURES
Forms required: FAFSA, institutional form.
Dates and Deadlines: Priority date 3/15; no closing date. Applicants notified on a rolling basis starting 7/1.

CONTACT
Kim Shuford, Director of Financial Aid
54 College Drive, Marion, NC 28752
(828) 652-0602

Meredith College

Raleigh, North Carolina
www.meredith.edu Federal Code: 002945

4-year private liberal arts college for women in large city.
Enrollment: 1,901 undergrads, 9% part-time. 397 full-time freshmen.
Selectivity: Admits 50 to 75% of applicants. GED not accepted.

BASIC COSTS (2008-2009)
Tuition and fees: $23,550.
Per-credit charge: $615.
Room and board: $6,740.
Additional info: Tuition includes a new laptop computer for each full-time freshman, which will be replaced with a new laptop during her junior year. Upon graduation from Meredith, the laptop remains the property of the student.

FINANCIAL AID PICTURE (2008-2009)
Students with need: Need-based aid available for full-time and part-time students.

Students without need: No-need awards available for academics, art, leadership, minority status, music/drama, religious affiliation, state/district residency.

Scholarships offered: Presidential Scholarships: tuition plus a stipend for study abroad; based on superior academic ability and achievement; 3-5 awarded. Talent Scholarships: varying amounts; available for students planning to major in art, music, interior design and computer science/ mathematics/pre-engineering and based on on-campus competition. Teaching Fellows Scholarship: $6,500 per year to match a similar stipend from the State; study abroad opportunity, based on state-wide competition; approximately 25 awarded.

FINANCIAL AID PROCEDURES

Forms required: FAFSA.

Dates and Deadlines: Priority date 2/15; no closing date. Applicants notified on a rolling basis starting 3/15; must reply by 5/1 or within 2 week(s) of notification.

CONTACT

Kevin Michaelsen, Director of Financial Assistance
3800 Hillsborough Street, Raleigh, NC 27607-5298
(919) 760-8565

Methodist University

Fayetteville, North Carolina
www.methodist.edu Federal Code: 002946

4-year private liberal arts college in small city; affiliated with United Methodist Church.

Enrollment: 1,929 undergrads, 15% part-time. 439 full-time freshmen.

Selectivity: Admits 50 to 75% of applicants.

BASIC COSTS (2009-2010)

Tuition and fees: $23,038.

Per-credit charge: $715.

Room and board: $8,400.

Additional info: Professional golf management, professional tennis management, and music students have additional fees.

FINANCIAL AID PICTURE (2007-2008)

Students with need: Need-based aid available for full-time and part-time students. Work study available nights, weekends, and for part-time students.

Students without need: No-need awards available for academics, alumni affiliation, leadership, music/drama, religious affiliation, ROTC, state/district residency.

Scholarships offered: Presidential Scholarship: $5,250-$17,000/yr; 3.1+ GPA, 1000+ SAT or 22+ ACT. Merit scholarship: $3,250-$4,250; residential freshmen; 2.9+ GPA, 900+ SAT or 19+ ACT; leadership. SAT scores exclusive of Writing.

FINANCIAL AID PROCEDURES

Forms required: FAFSA.

Dates and Deadlines: Priority date 5/1; closing date 7/1. Applicants notified on a rolling basis starting 3/1; must reply within 2 week(s) of notification.

Transfers: No deadline. Applicants notified on a rolling basis; must reply within 2 week(s) of notification.

CONTACT

Bonnie Adamson, Director of Financial Aid
5400 Ramsey Street, Fayetteville, NC 28311-1498
(910) 630-7192

Miller-Motte Technical College

Wilmington, North Carolina
www.miller-motte.edu Federal Code: E00896

4-year for-profit business and technical college in small city.

Enrollment: 747 undergrads.

Selectivity: Open admission; but selective for some programs.

BASIC COSTS (2008-2009)

Tuition and fees: $10,890.

Per-credit charge: $220.

Additional info: Tuition at time of enrollment locked for 4 years.

FINANCIAL AID PICTURE (2007-2008)

Students with need: Need-based aid available for full-time and part-time students. Work study available nights, weekends, and for part-time students.

Students without need: This college awards aid only to students with need.

FINANCIAL AID PROCEDURES

Forms required: FAFSA, institutional form.

Dates and Deadlines: No deadline.

CONTACT

Michele Carroll, Financial Aid Officer
5000 Market Street, Wilmington, NC 28405
(910) 392-4660

Mitchell Community College

Statesville, North Carolina
www.mitchellcc.edu Federal Code: 002947

2-year public community college in large town.

Enrollment: 2,982 undergrads.

Selectivity: Open admission; but selective for some programs.

BASIC COSTS (2008-2009)

Tuition and fees: $1,328; out-of-state residents $7,067.

Per-credit charge: $42; out-of-state residents $233.

FINANCIAL AID PICTURE

Students with need: Need-based aid available for full-time and part-time students.

FINANCIAL AID PROCEDURES

Forms required: FAFSA, institutional form.

Dates and Deadlines: No deadline. Applicants notified on a rolling basis starting 3/1; must reply within 2 week(s) of notification.

Transfers: Students are monitored through NSLDS's Transfer Monitoring List.

CONTACT

Candace Cooper, Financial Aid Officer
500 West Broad Street, Statesville, NC 28677
(704) 878-3256

Montgomery Community College

Troy, North Carolina
www.montgomery.edu Federal Code: 008087

2-year public community college in small town.

Enrollment: 732 undergrads, 44% part-time. 79 full-time freshmen.

Selectivity: Open admission; but selective for some programs.

BASIC COSTS (2008-2009)

Tuition and fees: $1,410; out-of-state residents $7,532.

Per-credit charge: $42; out-of-state residents $233.

FINANCIAL AID PICTURE

Students with need: Need-based aid available for full-time and part-time students. Work study available nights.

Students without need: No-need awards available for academics, minority status, state/district residency.

FINANCIAL AID PROCEDURES

Forms required: FAFSA, institutional form.

Dates and Deadlines: Priority date 7/15; no closing date. Applicants notified on a rolling basis starting 6/1.

CONTACT

Doni Cody, Director of Financial Aid
1011 Page Street, Troy, NC 27371-0787
(910) 576-6222 ext. 519

Montreat College

Montreat, North Carolina
www.montreat.edu Federal Code: 002948

4-year private liberal arts college in small town, affiliated with Presbyterian Church Reformed and Independent.

Enrollment: 932 undergrads, 1% part-time. 148 full-time freshmen.

Selectivity: Open admission; but selective for some programs.

BASIC COSTS (2009-2010)

Tuition and fees: $20,576.

Room and board: $6,541.

FINANCIAL AID PICTURE (2007-2008)

Students with need: Out of 148 full-time freshmen who applied for aid, 129 were judged to have need. Of these, 129 received aid, and 22 had their full need met. Average financial aid package met 62% of need; average scholarship/grant was $9,660; average loan was $3,167. For part-time students, average financial aid package was $13,192.

Students without need: 14 full-time freshmen who did not demonstrate need for aid received scholarships/grants; average award was $4,625. No-need awards available for academics, alumni affiliation, athletics, leadership, music/drama, religious affiliation, state/district residency.

Scholarships offered: 8 full-time freshmen received athletic scholarships; average amount $3,281.

FINANCIAL AID PROCEDURES

Forms required: FAFSA, state aid form, institutional form.

Dates and Deadlines: Priority date 3/15; no closing date. Applicants notified on a rolling basis starting 1/15; must reply within 2 week(s) of notification.

Transfers: Priority date 4/1; no deadline. Applicants notified on a rolling basis starting 1/15; must reply within 2 week(s) of notification.

CONTACT

Beth Pocock, Director of Financial Aid
Box 1267, Montreat, NC 28757-1267
(800) 545-4656

Mount Olive College

Mount Olive, North Carolina
www.moc.edu Federal Code: 002949

4-year private liberal arts college in small town, affiliated with Free Will Baptists.

Enrollment: 3,390 undergrads, 23% part-time. 300 full-time freshmen.

Selectivity: Open admission; but selective for some programs.

BASIC COSTS (2009-2010)

Tuition and fees: $13,776.

Per-credit charge: $310.

Room and board: $5,540.

FINANCIAL AID PICTURE (2007-2008)

Students with need: Average financial aid package met 69% of need; average scholarship/grant was $7,196; average loan was $2,492. For part-time students, average financial aid package was $6,488.

Students without need: No-need awards available for academics, art, athletics, leadership, music/drama, religious affiliation.

Scholarships offered: 9 full-time freshmen received athletic scholarships; average amount $4,493.

Cumulative student debt: 94% of graduating class had student loans; average debt was $13,854.

FINANCIAL AID PROCEDURES

Forms required: FAFSA, state aid form.

Dates and Deadlines: No deadline. Applicants notified on a rolling basis starting 2/14; must reply within 2 week(s) of notification.

Transfers: Special scholarship program available for transfers from North Carolina community colleges.

CONTACT

Karen Statler, Director of Financial Aid
634 Henderson Street, Mount Olive, NC 28365
(919) 658-7164

Nash Community College

Rocky Mount, North Carolina
www.nashcc.edu Federal Code: 008557

2-year public community college in small city.

Enrollment: 2,991 undergrads.

Selectivity: Open admission; but selective for some programs.

BASIC COSTS (2008-2009)

Tuition and fees: $1,380; out-of-state residents $7,119.

Per-credit charge: $42; out-of-state residents $233.

FINANCIAL AID PICTURE

Students with need: Need-based aid available for full-time and part-time students.

Students without need: No-need awards available for academics.

FINANCIAL AID PROCEDURES

Forms required: FAFSA, institutional form.

Dates and Deadlines: Priority date 6/30; no closing date. Applicants notified on a rolling basis starting 7/15.

CONTACT

Tammy Lester, Financial Aid Officer
Box 7488, Rocky Mount, NC 27804-0488
(252) 451-8371

North Carolina Agricultural and Technical State University

Greensboro, North Carolina
www.ncat.edu Federal Code: 002905

4-year public university in small city.

Enrollment: 8,632 undergrads, 9% part-time. 1,592 full-time freshmen.

Selectivity: Admits 50 to 75% of applicants.

BASIC COSTS (2008-2009)

Tuition and fees: $3,593; out-of-state residents $13,035.

Room and board: $5,336.

FINANCIAL AID PICTURE (2008-2009)

Students with need: Need-based aid available for full-time and part-time students.

Students without need: No-need awards available for academics, athletics, music/drama, ROTC.

FINANCIAL AID PROCEDURES

Forms required: FAFSA.

Dates and Deadlines: Priority date 3/15; no closing date. Applicants notified on a rolling basis starting 4/1; must reply within 2 week(s) of notification.

CONTACT

Sherri Avent, Director of Student Financial Aid
Webb Hall, Greensboro, NC 27411-0001
(800) 443-0835

North Carolina Central University

Durham, North Carolina
www.nccu.edu Federal Code: 002950

4-year public university in small city.
Enrollment: 5,497 undergrads.
Selectivity: Admits 50 to 75% of applicants.

BASIC COSTS (2008-2009)

Tuition and fees: $3,751; out-of-state residents $13,495.
Room and board: $5,743.

FINANCIAL AID PICTURE

Students with need: Need-based aid available for full-time and part-time students.

Students without need: No-need awards available for academics, alumni affiliation, athletics, minority status, music/drama, state/district residency.

Additional info: Departmental grants based on need plus other available criteria.

FINANCIAL AID PROCEDURES

Forms required: FAFSA.

Dates and Deadlines: Priority date 4/1; no closing date. Applicants notified by 5/1; must reply within 2 week(s) of notification.

CONTACT

Sharon Oliver, Director of Student Financial Aid
PO Box 19717, Durham, NC 27707
(919) 530-6180

North Carolina State University

Raleigh, North Carolina
www.ncsu.edu Federal Code: 002972

4-year public university in large city.
Enrollment: 22,839 undergrads, 7% part-time. 4,818 full-time freshmen.
Selectivity: Admits 50 to 75% of applicants. GED not accepted.

BASIC COSTS (2008-2009)

Tuition and fees: $5,274; out-of-state residents $17,572.
Room and board: $7,982.

FINANCIAL AID PICTURE (2008-2009)

Students with need: Out of 3,364 full-time freshmen who applied for aid, 2,038 were judged to have need. Of these, 2,019 received aid, and 1,189 had their full need met. Average financial aid package met 90% of need; average scholarship/grant was $9,282; average loan was $2,427. For part-time students, average financial aid package was $6,485.

Students without need: 201 full-time freshmen who did not demonstrate need for aid received scholarships/grants; average award was $5,946. No-need awards available for academics, alumni affiliation, athletics, leadership, ROTC, state/district residency.

Scholarships offered: ***Merit:*** Park Scholarships: 4 year scholarship that covers almost all expenses; approximately 50 awarded each year. Caldwell scholarships: awarded at end of freshmen year for 3 years covering most expenses. ***Athletic:*** 72 full-time freshmen received athletic scholarships; average amount $9,682.

Cumulative student debt: 49% of graduating class had student loans; average debt was $14,996.

Additional info: Freshman Merit Scholarships; students submitting complete admissions application by the November 1 Early Action deadline automatically considered, additional information may be required after initial review.

FINANCIAL AID PROCEDURES

Forms required: FAFSA, institutional form. CSS PROFILE recommended for early scholarship consideration.

Dates and Deadlines: Priority date 3/1; no closing date. Applicants notified on a rolling basis starting 4/1.

CONTACT

Julia Mallette, Associate Vice Provost and Director of Scholarships and Financial Aid
203 Peele Hall, Box 7103, Raleigh, NC 27695-7103
(919) 515-2421

North Carolina Wesleyan College

Rocky Mount, North Carolina
www.ncwc.edu Federal Code: 002951

4-year private liberal arts college in small city, affiliated with United Methodist Church.
Enrollment: 1,318 undergrads, 21% part-time. 278 full-time freshmen.
Selectivity: Admits 50 to 75% of applicants.

BASIC COSTS (2008-2009)

Tuition and fees: $20,790.
Per-credit charge: $300.
Room and board: $7,380.

FINANCIAL AID PICTURE (2007-2008)

Students with need: Need-based aid available for full-time and part-time students.

Students without need: This college awards aid only to students with need.

Additional info: Scholarships based on GPA. Various scholarship and leadership awards available.

FINANCIAL AID PROCEDURES

Forms required: FAFSA.

Dates and Deadlines: Priority date 3/1; no closing date. Applicants notified on a rolling basis starting 1/1; must reply within 2 week(s) of notification.

Transfers: No deadline. Applicants notified on a rolling basis; must reply within 2 week(s) of notification.

CONTACT

Deana Summerlin, Director of Financial Aid
3400 North Wesleyan Boulevard, Rocky Mount, NC 27804
(252) 985-5295

Pamlico Community College

Grantsboro, North Carolina
www.pamlicocc.edu Federal Code: 007031

2-year public community college in rural community.
Enrollment: 471 undergrads.
Selectivity: Open admission.

BASIC COSTS (2008-2009)

Tuition and fees: $1,295; out-of-state residents $7,034.

Per-credit charge: $42; out-of-state residents $233.

FINANCIAL AID PICTURE (2008-2009)

Students with need: 99% of average financial aid package awarded as scholarships/grants, 1% awarded as loans/jobs.

Additional info: Jobs Training Partner Act and Displaced Homemaker Programs cover tuition, books, fees.

FINANCIAL AID PROCEDURES

Forms required: FAFSA.

Dates and Deadlines: Priority date 3/15; no closing date. Applicants notified on a rolling basis.

CONTACT

Kris Patterson, Financial Aid Officer
PO Box 185, Grantsboro, NC 28529
(252) 249-1851 ext. 3021

Peace College

Raleigh, North Carolina
www.peace.edu Federal Code: 002953

4-year private liberal arts college for women in large city, affiliated with Presbyterian Church (USA).

Enrollment: 665 undergrads, 4% part-time. 185 full-time freshmen.

Selectivity: Admits 50 to 75% of applicants.

BASIC COSTS (2009-2010)

Tuition and fees: $22,993.

Per-credit charge: $600.

Room and board: $7,820.

FINANCIAL AID PICTURE (2008-2009)

Students with need: Out of 158 full-time freshmen who applied for aid, 143 were judged to have need. Of these, 143 received aid, and 23 had their full need met. Average financial aid package met 78% of need; average scholarship/grant was $17,208; average loan was $3,103. For part-time students, average financial aid package was $8,014.

Students without need: 54 full-time freshmen who did not demonstrate need for aid received scholarships/grants; average award was $7,244. No-need awards available for academics, art, music/drama, state/district residency.

Cumulative student debt: 80% of graduating class had student loans; average debt was $29,025.

FINANCIAL AID PROCEDURES

Forms required: FAFSA.

Dates and Deadlines: Priority date 3/15; no closing date. Applicants notified on a rolling basis starting 3/1; must reply within 4 week(s) of notification.

Transfers: Priority date 3/1; no deadline. Applicants notified on a rolling basis starting 2/28; must reply within 4 week(s) of notification. Transfer merit scholarships available.

CONTACT

Angela Kirkley, Director of Financial Aid
15 East Peace Street, Raleigh, NC 27604-1194
(919) 508-2249

Pfeiffer University

Misenheimer, North Carolina
www.pfeiffer.edu Federal Code: 002955

4-year private university and liberal arts college in rural community, affiliated with United Methodist Church.

Enrollment: 1,089 undergrads, 13% part-time. 194 full-time freshmen.

Selectivity: Admits 50 to 75% of applicants.

BASIC COSTS (2008-2009)

Tuition and fees: $18,570.

Per-credit charge: $425.

Room and board: $7,360.

FINANCIAL AID PICTURE (2007-2008)

Students with need: Out of 190 full-time freshmen who applied for aid, 155 were judged to have need. Of these, 155 received aid, and 45 had their full need met. Average financial aid package met 80% of need; average scholarship/grant was $11,529; average loan was $2,959. For part-time students, average financial aid package was $7,080.

Students without need: 41 full-time freshmen who did not demonstrate need for aid received scholarships/grants; average award was $5,730. No-need awards available for academics, alumni affiliation, athletics, leadership, music/drama, religious affiliation, state/district residency.

Scholarships offered: ***Merit:*** Honor, Presidential, University, and Legacy Scholarships - from $3,500 to full tuition per year. ***Athletic:*** 42 full-time freshmen received athletic scholarships; average amount $4,592.

Cumulative student debt: 87% of graduating class had student loans; average debt was $21,000.

FINANCIAL AID PROCEDURES

Forms required: FAFSA, state aid form.

Dates and Deadlines: Priority date 5/1; no closing date. Applicants notified on a rolling basis starting 3/1; must reply within 2 week(s) of notification.

Transfers: Priority date 3/15.

CONTACT

Amy Brown, Director of Financial Aid
Box 960, Misenheimer, NC 28109
(704) 463-1360 ext. 2070

Piedmont Baptist College

Winston-Salem, North Carolina
www.pbc.edu Federal Code: 002956

4-year private Bible and seminary college in small city, affiliated with Baptist faith.

Enrollment: 273 undergrads, 27% part-time. 50 full-time freshmen.

BASIC COSTS (2009-2010)

Tuition and fees: $11,565.

Per-credit charge: $346.

Room and board: $5,760.

FINANCIAL AID PICTURE

Students with need: Need-based aid available for full-time and part-time students. Work study available nights, weekends, and for part-time students.

FINANCIAL AID PROCEDURES

Forms required: institutional form.

Dates and Deadlines: No deadline. Applicants notified on a rolling basis starting 3/1.

CONTACT

Ronnie Mathis, Financial Aid Officer
420 South Boad Street, Winston-Salem, NC 27101-5133
(336) 714-7987

Pitt Community College
Greenville, North Carolina
www.pittcc.edu Federal Code: 004062

2-year public community and technical college in small city.
Enrollment: 5,813 undergrads.
Selectivity: Open admission; but selective for some programs.

BASIC COSTS (2008-2009)
Tuition and fees: $1,430; out-of-state residents $7,552.
Per-credit charge: $42; out-of-state residents $233.

FINANCIAL AID PICTURE (2007-2008)
Students with need: 69% of average financial aid package awarded as scholarships/grants, 31% awarded as loans/jobs. Need-based aid available for part-time students. Work study available nights.
Students without need: No-need awards available for academics, athletics, ROTC.

FINANCIAL AID PROCEDURES
Forms required: FAFSA.
Dates and Deadlines: Priority date 3/15; no closing date. Applicants notified on a rolling basis starting 2/1.

CONTACT
Lisa Reichstein, Financial Aid Director
PO Drawer 7007, Greenville, NC 27835-7007
(252) 321-4339

Queens University of Charlotte
Charlotte, North Carolina
www.queens.edu Federal Code: 002957

4-year private university in very large city, affiliated with Presbyterian Church (USA).
Enrollment: 1,718 undergrads, 31% part-time. 307 full-time freshmen.
Selectivity: Admits over 75% of applicants.

BASIC COSTS (2008-2009)
Tuition and fees: $22,068.
Per-credit charge: $335.
Room and board: $7,882.

FINANCIAL AID PICTURE (2008-2009)
Students with need: Out of 238 full-time freshmen who applied for aid, 195 were judged to have need. Of these, 195 received aid, and 76 had their full need met. Average financial aid package met 81% of need; average scholarship/grant was $14,560; average loan was $3,084. For part-time students, average financial aid package was $5,688.
Students without need: 65 full-time freshmen who did not demonstrate need for aid received scholarships/grants; average award was $9,473.
Scholarships offered: ***Merit:*** Presidential Scholarships: full tuition; based on special application/recommendations; deadline 12/15; 12 awarded. ***Athletic:*** 33 full-time freshmen received athletic scholarships; average amount $5,692.
Cumulative student debt: 85% of graduating class had student loans; average debt was $22,520.

FINANCIAL AID PROCEDURES
Forms required: FAFSA, state aid form.
Dates and Deadlines: Priority date 3/1; no closing date. Applicants notified on a rolling basis starting 3/15; must reply by 5/1 or within 3 week(s) of notification.
Transfers: No deadline. Applicants notified on a rolling basis starting 3/15; must reply by 5/1 or within 3 week(s) of notification.

CONTACT
Eileen Dills, Associate Vice President of Student Financial Services
1900 Selwyn Ave, Charlotte, NC 28274
(704) 337-2225

Randolph Community College
Asheboro, North Carolina
www.randolph.edu Federal Code: 005447

2-year public community and technical college in large town.
Enrollment: 3,177 undergrads.
Selectivity: Open admission; but selective for some programs.

BASIC COSTS (2008-2009)
Tuition and fees: $1,320; out-of-state residents $7,059.
Per-credit charge: $42; out-of-state residents $233.

FINANCIAL AID PICTURE (2007-2008)
Students with need: Work study available nights.
Students without need: No-need awards available for academics, leadership, minority status, state/district residency.

FINANCIAL AID PROCEDURES
Forms required: FAFSA.
Dates and Deadlines: No deadline. Applicants notified on a rolling basis.
Transfers: No deadline.

CONTACT
Chad Williams, Director of Financial Aid
PO Box 1009, Asheboro, NC 27204-1009
(336) 633-0222

Richmond Community College
Hamlet, North Carolina
www.richmondcc.edu Federal Code: 005464

2-year public community college in small town.
Enrollment: 1,700 undergrads.
Selectivity: Open admission; but selective for some programs.

BASIC COSTS (2008-2009)
Tuition and fees: $1,422; out-of-state residents $7,544.
Per-credit charge: $42; out-of-state residents $233.

FINANCIAL AID PICTURE
Students with need: Need-based aid available for full-time and part-time students. Work study available nights.
Students without need: No-need awards available for academics, leadership.

FINANCIAL AID PROCEDURES
Forms required: FAFSA, institutional form.
Dates and Deadlines: No deadline. Applicants notified on a rolling basis starting 7/8; must reply within 2 week(s) of notification.

CONTACT
Beth McQueen, Director of Financial Aid
Box 1189, Hamlet, NC 28345
(910) 410-1726

Roanoke Bible College
Elizabeth City, North Carolina
www.roanokebible.edu Federal Code: 014101

4-year private Bible college in large town, affiliated with Church of Christ.
Enrollment: 166 undergrads. 34 full-time freshmen.

Selectivity: Admits 50 to 75% of applicants.

BASIC COSTS (2009-2010)

Tuition and fees: $9,700.
Per-credit charge: $310.
Room and board: $6,790.

FINANCIAL AID PICTURE (2007-2008)

Students with need: Out of 33 full-time freshmen who applied for aid, 31 were judged to have need. Of these, 31 received aid, and 4 had their full need met. Average financial aid package met 78% of need; average scholarship/grant was $3,390; average loan was $2,625. For part-time students, average financial aid package was $3,892.
Students without need: 2 full-time freshmen who did not demonstrate need for aid received scholarships/grants; average award was $1,305. No-need awards available for academics, alumni affiliation, leadership, music/drama, religious affiliation.
Scholarships offered: Full tuition and half tuition available, based on demonstration of exceptional academic ability.
Cumulative student debt: 80% of graduating class had student loans; average debt was $21,314.

FINANCIAL AID PROCEDURES

Forms required: FAFSA, institutional form.
Dates and Deadlines: Priority date 3/15; no closing date. Applicants notified on a rolling basis starting 4/1; must reply within 2 week(s) of notification.
Transfers: Priority date 3/1; no deadline. Must reply within 2 week(s) of notification.

CONTACT

Lisa Pipkin, Financial Aid Administrator
715 North Poindexter Street, Elizabeth City, NC 27909
(252) 334-2020

Roanoke-Chowan Community College

Ahoskie, North Carolina
www.roanokechowan.edu Federal Code: 008613

2-year public community college in small town.
Enrollment: 998 undergrads.
Selectivity: Open admission; but selective for out-of-state students.

BASIC COSTS (2008-2009)

Tuition and fees: $1,445; out-of-state residents $7,567.
Per-credit charge: $42; out-of-state residents $233.

FINANCIAL AID PICTURE (2007-2008)

Students with need: Need-based aid available for part-time students.
Students without need: No-need awards available for academics.

FINANCIAL AID PROCEDURES

Forms required: FAFSA.
Dates and Deadlines: Priority date 3/15; no closing date. Applicants notified on a rolling basis starting 7/1.

CONTACT

Tricia Sawyer, Financial Aid Director
109 Community College Road, Ahoskie, NC 27910-9522
(252) 862-1320

Robeson Community College

Lumberton, North Carolina
www.robeson.edu Federal Code: 008612

2-year public community college in large town.
Enrollment: 2,289 undergrads.
Selectivity: Open admission; but selective for some programs.

BASIC COSTS (2008-2009)

Tuition and fees: $1,324; out-of-state residents $7,526.
Per-credit charge: $42; out-of-state residents $233.

FINANCIAL AID PICTURE (2007-2008)

Students with need: 99% of average financial aid package awarded as scholarships/grants, 1% awarded as loans/jobs. Need-based aid available for part-time students.

FINANCIAL AID PROCEDURES

Forms required: FAFSA.
Dates and Deadlines: Priority date 5/15; no closing date. Applicants notified on a rolling basis starting 7/31.

CONTACT

Anna Maynor, Director of Financial Aid
PO Box 1420, Lumberton, NC 28359
(910) 272-3352

Rockingham Community College

Wentworth, North Carolina
www.rockinghamcc.edu Federal Code: 002958

2-year public community college in rural community.
Enrollment: 1,812 undergrads, 50% part-time. 281 full-time freshmen.
Selectivity: Open admission; but selective for some programs.

BASIC COSTS (2008-2009)

Tuition and fees: $1,440; out-of-state residents $7,561.
Per-credit charge: $42; out-of-state residents $233.

FINANCIAL AID PICTURE (2007-2008)

Students with need: Need-based aid available for full-time and part-time students.
Students without need: No-need awards available for academics, art, job skills, leadership, minority status, state/district residency.

FINANCIAL AID PROCEDURES

Forms required: FAFSA, institutional form.
Dates and Deadlines: Priority date 3/15; no closing date. Applicants notified on a rolling basis starting 5/30; must reply within 2 week(s) of notification.

CONTACT

Coe Trent, Director of Financial Aid
Box 38, Wentworth, NC 27375-0038
(336) 342-4261 ext. 2204

Rowan-Cabarrus Community College

Salisbury, North Carolina
www.rowancabarrus.edu Federal Code: 005754

2-year public community and technical college in large town.
Enrollment: 5,876 undergrads.
Selectivity: Open admission; but selective for some programs.

BASIC COSTS (2008-2009)

Tuition and fees: $1,324; out-of-state residents $7,063.
Per-credit charge: $42; out-of-state residents $230.

FINANCIAL AID PICTURE (2008-2009)

Students with need: Need-based aid available for full-time and part-time students. Work study available nights.
Students without need: No-need awards available for academics, job skills, state/district residency.

FINANCIAL AID PROCEDURES

Forms required: FAFSA.

Dates and Deadlines: Priority date 3/15; closing date 8/1. Applicants notified on a rolling basis starting 5/1; must reply within 3 week(s) of notification.
Transfers: No deadline.

CONTACT

Lisa Ledbetter, Director, Financial Aid
Box 1595, Salisbury, NC 28145
(704) 637-0760 ext. 273

St. Andrews Presbyterian College

Laurinburg, North Carolina
www.sapc.edu Federal Code: 002967

4-year private liberal arts college in large town, affiliated with Presbyterian Church (USA).
Enrollment: 603 undergrads, 4% part-time. 220 full-time freshmen.
Selectivity: Admits over 75% of applicants.

BASIC COSTS (2009-2010)

Tuition and fees: $21,190.
Per-credit charge: $450.
Room and board: $8,762.
Additional info: Private living, lab fees, and equestrian fees additional.

FINANCIAL AID PICTURE (2007-2008)

Students with need: Out of 187 full-time freshmen who applied for aid, 149 were judged to have need. Of these, 149 received aid, and 52 had their full need met. Average financial aid package met 77% of need; average scholarship/grant was $10,974; average loan was $3,473. For part-time students, average financial aid package was $6,951.
Students without need: 67 full-time freshmen who did not demonstrate need for aid received scholarships/grants; average award was $10,881. No-need awards available for academics, alumni affiliation, art, athletics, leadership, music/drama.
Scholarships offered: 46 full-time freshmen received athletic scholarships; average amount $3,559.
Cumulative student debt: 73% of graduating class had student loans; average debt was $17,342.

FINANCIAL AID PROCEDURES

Forms required: FAFSA, state aid form.
Dates and Deadlines: Priority date 5/1; no closing date. Applicants notified on a rolling basis starting 10/1; must reply within 2 week(s) of notification.
Transfers: No deadline. Applicants notified on a rolling basis starting 10/1; must reply within 2 week(s) of notification.

CONTACT

Kim Driggers, Director, Financial Aid
1700 Dogwood Mile, Laurinburg, NC 28352
(910) 277-5560

St. Augustine's College

Raleigh, North Carolina
www.st-aug.edu Federal Code: 002968

4-year private liberal arts college in large city, affiliated with Episcopal Church.
Enrollment: 1,417 undergrads.
Selectivity: Admits 50 to 75% of applicants.

BASIC COSTS (2008-2009)

Tuition and fees: $14,124.
Per-credit charge: $440.
Room and board: $6,652.

FINANCIAL AID PICTURE (2008-2009)

Students with need: 65% of average financial aid package awarded as scholarships/grants, 35% awarded as loans/jobs. Need-based aid available for part-time students.
Students without need: No-need awards available for academics, art, athletics, leadership, minority status, music/drama, religious affiliation, ROTC, state/district residency.
Scholarships offered: Institutional Merit Scholarships based on high school record, evidence of leadership, and SAT score.

FINANCIAL AID PROCEDURES

Forms required: FAFSA, institutional form.
Dates and Deadlines: Closing date 3/15. Applicants notified on a rolling basis starting 5/1; must reply within 2 week(s) of notification.
Transfers: All transfer students must submit a financial aid transcript.

CONTACT

Nadine Ford, Director of Financial Aid
1315 Oakwood Avenue, Raleigh, NC 27610-2298
(919) 516-4131

Salem College

Winston-Salem, North Carolina
www.salem.edu Federal Code: 002960

4-year private liberal arts college for women in small city, affiliated with Moravian Church in America.
Enrollment: 699 undergrads, 18% part-time. 121 full-time freshmen.
Selectivity: Admits 50 to 75% of applicants.

BASIC COSTS (2009-2010)

Tuition and fees: $21,380.
Room and board: $11,210.
Additional info: Traditional-age students must enroll full-time. Students registering through the Fleer Center for Adult Education pay $1,045 tuition per course. Graduate students pay $294 per credit hour. Tuition/fee waivers available for adults.

FINANCIAL AID PICTURE (2007-2008)

Students with need: 73% of average financial aid package awarded as scholarships/grants, 27% awarded as loans/jobs. Need-based aid available for part-time students. Work study available nights, weekends, and for part-time students.
Students without need: No-need awards available for academics, alumni affiliation, leadership, minority status, music/drama, state/district residency.
Cumulative student debt: 70% of graduating class had student loans; average debt was $17,125.

FINANCIAL AID PROCEDURES

Forms required: FAFSA.
Dates and Deadlines: Priority date 3/1; no closing date. Applicants notified on a rolling basis starting 3/1; must reply by 5/1 or within 2 week(s) of notification.

CONTACT

Jerry Donna, Director of Financial Aid
601 South Church Street, Winston-Salem, NC 27108
(336) 721-2808

Sampson Community College

Clinton, North Carolina
www.sampsoncc.edu Federal Code: 007892

2-year public community college in small town.
Enrollment: 1,278 undergrads, 58% part-time. 288 full-time freshmen.
Selectivity: Open admission; but selective for some programs.

BASIC COSTS (2008-2009)
Tuition and fees: $1,421; out-of-state residents $7,543.
Per-credit charge: $42; out-of-state residents $233.

FINANCIAL AID PICTURE
Students with need: Need-based aid available for full-time and part-time students.
Students without need: No-need awards available for academics, state/district residency.
Additional info: Short-term loans available to students waiting for federal aid to be approved. Covers tuition, fees and books only.

FINANCIAL AID PROCEDURES
Forms required: FAFSA.
Dates and Deadlines: Priority date 7/1; no closing date. Applicants notified on a rolling basis starting 7/15; must reply within 2 week(s) of notification.

CONTACT
Judye Tart, Director of Financial Aid
PO Box 318, Clinton, NC 28329
(910) 592-8084 ext. 2024

Sandhills Community College
Pinehurst, North Carolina
www.sandhills.edu Federal Code: 002961

2-year public community college in large town.
Enrollment: 3,947 undergrads.
Selectivity: Open admission; but selective for some programs.

BASIC COSTS (2008-2009)
Tuition and fees: $1,330; out-of-state residents $7,069.
Per-credit charge: $42; out-of-state residents $233.

FINANCIAL AID PICTURE (2007-2008)
Students with need: 82% of average financial aid package awarded as scholarships/grants, 18% awarded as loans/jobs. Need-based aid available for part-time students.
Students without need: No-need awards available for academics.
Scholarships offered: Sandhills Scholars; upper 15% of graduating class; 11 awarded.
Additional info: Scholarships available, limited loan capability.

FINANCIAL AID PROCEDURES
Forms required: FAFSA.
Dates and Deadlines: Priority date 6/1; no closing date. Applicants notified on a rolling basis starting 2/1; must reply by 8/1 or within 4 week(s) of notification.

CONTACT
Heather Willett, Director of Financial Aid
3395 Airport Road, Pinehurst, NC 28374
(910) 695-3743

Shaw University
Raleigh, North Carolina
www.shawuniversity.edu Federal Code: 002962

4-year private university and liberal arts college in large city, affiliated with Baptist faith.
Enrollment: 2,453 undergrads.

BASIC COSTS (2008-2009)
Tuition and fees: $11,696.
Per-credit charge: $389.
Room and board: $7,200.

FINANCIAL AID PICTURE (2007-2008)
Students with need: Need-based aid available for full-time and part-time students. Work study available nights, weekends, and for part-time students.
Students without need: No-need awards available for academics, alumni affiliation, art, athletics, music/drama, religious affiliation.
Scholarships offered: Presidential Scholarship, based on GPA and SAT.

FINANCIAL AID PROCEDURES
Forms required: FAFSA.
Dates and Deadlines: Priority date 3/1; no closing date. Applicants notified on a rolling basis starting 3/15; must reply within 2 week(s) of notification.

CONTACT
Rochelle King, Director of Financial Aid
118 East South Street, Raleigh, NC 27601
(919) 546-8240

South College
Asheville, North Carolina
www.southcollegenc.edu Federal Code: 010264

2-year for-profit health science and technical college in small city.
Enrollment: 141 undergrads.
Selectivity: Open admission; but selective for some programs.

BASIC COSTS (2008-2009)
Tuition and fees: $13,200.
Per-credit charge: $350.

FINANCIAL AID PICTURE (2007-2008)
Students with need: 40% of average financial aid package awarded as scholarships/grants, 60% awarded as loans/jobs. Need-based aid available for part-time students.

FINANCIAL AID PROCEDURES
Forms required: FAFSA.
Dates and Deadlines: No deadline. Applicants notified on a rolling basis.

CONTACT
Julia Dennis, Financial Aid Director
29 Turtle Creek Drive, Asheville, NC 28803
(828) 277-5521

South Piedmont Community College
Polkton, North Carolina
www.spcc.edu Federal Code: 007985

2-year public community college in small city.
Enrollment: 2,310 undergrads.
Selectivity: Open admission; but selective for some programs.

BASIC COSTS (2008-2009)
Tuition and fees: $1,372; out-of-state residents $7,111.
Per-credit charge: $56; out-of-state residents $248.

FINANCIAL AID PICTURE (2008-2009)
Students with need: 98% of average financial aid package awarded as scholarships/grants, 2% awarded as loans/jobs. Need-based aid available for part-time students. Work study available nights, weekends, and for part-time students.
Additional info: Small amount of nonfederal scholarship aid available.

FINANCIAL AID PROCEDURES
Forms required: FAFSA.
Dates and Deadlines: No deadline. Applicants notified on a rolling basis.

CONTACT

Vickie Cameron, Director of Financial Aid
PO Box 126, Polkton, NC 28135
(704) 272-5325

Southeastern Community College

Whiteville, North Carolina
www.sccnc.edu Federal Code: 002964

2-year public community college in small town.
Enrollment: 1,630 undergrads.
Selectivity: Open admission; but selective for some programs.

BASIC COSTS (2008-2009)

Tuition and fees: $1,329; out-of-state residents $7,068.
Per-credit charge: $42; out-of-state residents $233.

FINANCIAL AID PICTURE (2007-2008)

Students with need: Need-based aid available for full-time and part-time students.
Students without need: No-need awards available for academics, athletics, leadership, music/drama, state/district residency.

FINANCIAL AID PROCEDURES

Forms required: FAFSA.
Dates and Deadlines: Priority date 4/1; no closing date. Applicants notified on a rolling basis starting 6/1; must reply within 2 week(s) of notification.

CONTACT

Glenn Hanson, Director of Financial Aid
4564 Chadbourn Highway, Whiteville, NC 28472-0151
(910) 642-7141 ext. 214

Southwestern Community College

Sylva, North Carolina
www.southwesterncc.edu Federal Code: 008466

2-year public community college in rural community.
Enrollment: 900 full-time undergrads.
Selectivity: Open admission; but selective for some programs.

BASIC COSTS (2008-2009)

Tuition and fees: $1,324; out-of-state residents $7,063.
Per-credit charge: $42; out-of-state residents $233.

FINANCIAL AID PICTURE

Students with need: Need-based aid available for full-time and part-time students.

FINANCIAL AID PROCEDURES

Forms required: FAFSA.
Dates and Deadlines: Priority date 4/30; no closing date. Applicants notified on a rolling basis starting 5/1; must reply within 2 week(s) of notification.

CONTACT

Melody Lawrence, Director of Financial Aid
447 College Drive, Sylva, NC 28779
(828) 586-4091 ext. 224

Stanly Community College

Albemarle, North Carolina
www.stanly.edu Federal Code: 011194

2-year public community college in large town.
Enrollment: 3,090 undergrads.
Selectivity: Open admission; but selective for some programs.

BASIC COSTS (2008-2009)

Tuition and fees: $1,376; out-of-state residents $7,115.
Per-credit charge: $42; out-of-state residents $233.

FINANCIAL AID PICTURE (2007-2008)

Students with need: Need-based aid available for full-time and part-time students.
Students without need: This college awards aid only to students with need.

FINANCIAL AID PROCEDURES

Forms required: FAFSA, institutional form.
Dates and Deadlines: Closing date 4/15. Applicants notified on a rolling basis starting 6/1; must reply within 2 week(s) of notification.
Transfers: No deadline. Applicants notified on a rolling basis.

CONTACT

Petra Fields, Director of Financial Aid
141 College Drive, Albemarle, NC 28001
(704) 991-0231

Surry Community College

Dobson, North Carolina
www.surry.edu Federal Code: 002970

2-year public community college in rural community.
Enrollment: 1,578 full-time undergrads.
Selectivity: Open admission; but selective for some programs.

BASIC COSTS (2008-2009)

Tuition and fees: $1,420; out-of-state residents $7,542.
Per-credit charge: $42; out-of-state residents $233.

FINANCIAL AID PICTURE (2007-2008)

Students with need: Need-based aid available for full-time and part-time students. Work study available nights.
Students without need: No-need awards available for academics.

FINANCIAL AID PROCEDURES

Forms required: FAFSA, institutional form.
Dates and Deadlines: Priority date 5/1; no closing date. Applicants notified on a rolling basis starting 6/1; must reply within 2 week(s) of notification.
Transfers: Priority date 6/1.

CONTACT

Andrea Simpson, Financial Aid Director
630 South Main Street, Dobson, NC 27017
(336) 386-3263

Tri-County Community College

Murphy, North Carolina
www.tricountycc.edu Federal Code: 009430

2-year public community college in rural community.
Enrollment: 648 undergrads, 35% part-time. 421 full-time freshmen.
Selectivity: Open admission.

BASIC COSTS (2008-2009)

Tuition and fees: $1,319; out-of-state residents $7,058.
Per-credit charge: $42; out-of-state residents $233.

FINANCIAL AID PICTURE (2007-2008)

Students with need: Out of 400 full-time freshmen who applied for aid, 350 were judged to have need. Of these, 350 received aid. Average financial aid package met 50% of need; average scholarship/grant was $2,500. For part-time students, average financial aid package was $1,800.

Students without need: This college awards aid only to students with need.

FINANCIAL AID PROCEDURES

Forms required: FAFSA.

Dates and Deadlines: Priority date 6/30; no closing date. Applicants notified on a rolling basis starting 6/1; must reply within 4 week(s) of notification.

CONTACT

Diane Owl, Financial Aid Officer
4600 Highway 64 East, Murphy, NC 28906
(828) 837-6810

University of North Carolina at Asheville

Asheville, North Carolina
www.unca.edu Federal Code: 002907

4-year public university and liberal arts college in small city.

Enrollment: 3,150 undergrads, 11% part-time, 572 full-time freshmen.

Selectivity: Admits 50 to 75% of applicants. GED not accepted.

BASIC COSTS (2008-2009)

Tuition and fees: $4,255; out-of-state residents $15,585.

Room and board: $6,620.

FINANCIAL AID PICTURE (2007-2008)

Students with need: Out of 405 full-time freshmen who applied for aid, 215 were judged to have need. Of these, 215 received aid, and 81 had their full need met. Average financial aid package met 79% of need; average scholarship/grant was $4,554; average loan was $3,004. For part-time students, average financial aid package was $7,305.

Students without need: 41 full-time freshmen who did not demonstrate need for aid received scholarships/grants; average award was $3,790. No-need awards available for academics, alumni affiliation, art, athletics, job skills, leadership, minority status, music/drama, state/district residency.

Scholarships offered: ***Merit:*** North Carolina Teaching Fellows program: $6,500 per year; for outstanding North Carolina high school students with desire and talent to become teachers. University Laurels Program: $500 to full in-state tuition and fees; essay, list of co-curricular activities and participation in Laurels Interview Day. Leadership Scholarship: $1,000, renewable; solid academic record and leadership ability. ***Athletic:*** 21 full-time freshmen received athletic scholarships; average amount $5,535.

Cumulative student debt: 50% of graduating class had student loans; average debt was $14,685.

FINANCIAL AID PROCEDURES

Forms required: FAFSA.

Dates and Deadlines: Priority date 3/1; no closing date. Applicants notified on a rolling basis starting 3/15.

CONTACT

Pat McClellan, Dean of Academic Administration
CPO#1320, UNCA, Asheville, NC 28804-8510
(828) 251-6535

University of North Carolina at Chapel Hill

Chapel Hill, North Carolina Federal Code: 002974
www.unc.edu CSS Code: 5816

4-year public university in large town.

Enrollment: 17,422 undergrads, 2% part-time. 3,852 full-time freshmen.

Selectivity: Admits less than 50% of applicants. GED not accepted.

BASIC COSTS (2008-2009)

Tuition and fees: $5,397; out-of-state residents $22,295.

Room and board: $7,334.

Additional info: Fees may be higher for dental programs.

FINANCIAL AID PICTURE (2007-2008)

Students with need: Need-based aid available for full-time and part-time students.

Students without need: No-need awards available for academics, alumni affiliation, art, athletics, leadership, music/drama, religious affiliation, state/district residency.

Scholarships offered: Morehead Scholarships: full tuition and expenses; based on academic merit, leadership, athletics, moral character; approximately 50 awarded, in-state and out-of-state. Robertson Scholarships: full tuition and expenses; based on academic merit, leadership, community service; 15 to 18 awarded to both in-state and out-of-state residents. Carolina Scholars: $7,500 for in-state residents; cost of tuition, fees, room and board for non-NC residents; based on academic merit, leadership, residency specifications; 30-40 awarded with majority going to in-state residents. Pogue Scholarships: $7,500 for NC residents; cost of tuition, fees, room and board for non-NC residents; based on academic merit, leadership, involvement and interest in issues of diversity; 22 in-state, 5 out-of-state scholarships awarded. College Fellows Awards: $2,500; based on academic merit, leadership; North Carolina residency; 15-200 awarded. Other academic scholarships: $2,500, full cost; based on academic merit, leadership, North Carolina residency; approximately 75 awarded. As a result of legislation passed in 2005, non-residents receiving "full" academic scholarships are eligible for North Carolina residency status for tuition purposes.

Additional info: Carolina meets 100% of all need documented for both resident and non-resident undergraduates who quality for need based aid, with a favorable mix of approximately 2/3 grants and scholarships and 1/3 loans and work study.

FINANCIAL AID PROCEDURES

Forms required: FAFSA, CSS PROFILE.

Dates and Deadlines: Priority date 3/1; no closing date. Applicants notified on a rolling basis starting 3/15; must reply by 5/1.

CONTACT

Shirley Ort, Director for Office of Student Aid/Associate Provost
Jackson Hall CB #2200, Chapel Hill, NC 27599-2200
(919) 962-8396

University of North Carolina at Charlotte

Charlotte, North Carolina
www.uncc.edu Federal Code: 002975

4-year public university in very large city.

Enrollment: 18,216 undergrads, 15% part-time. 2,934 full-time freshmen.

Selectivity: Admits over 75% of applicants.

BASIC COSTS (2008-2009)

Tuition and fees: $4,279; out-of-state residents $14,691.

Room and board: $6,800.

FINANCIAL AID PICTURE (2007-2008)

Students with need: Out of 2,092 full-time freshmen who applied for aid, 1,390 were judged to have need. Of these, 1,354 received aid, and 140 had their full need met. Average financial aid package met 73% of need; average scholarship/grant was $5,065; average loan was $3,108. For part-time students, average financial aid package was $5,383.

Students without need: 51 full-time freshmen who did not demonstrate need for aid received scholarships/grants; average award was $2,757. No-need awards available for academics, athletics, leadership, music/drama.

Scholarships offered: 71 full-time freshmen received athletic scholarships; average amount $10,990.

Cumulative student debt: 45% of graduating class had student loans; average debt was $16,663.

FINANCIAL AID PROCEDURES

Forms required: FAFSA.

Dates and Deadlines: Priority date 4/1; no closing date. Applicants notified on a rolling basis starting 4/1; must reply within 3 week(s) of notification.

CONTACT

Anthony Carter, Director of Student Financial Aid
9201 University City Boulevard, Charlotte, NC 28223-0001
(704) 687-2461

University of North Carolina at Greensboro

Greensboro, North Carolina
www.uncg.edu Federal Code: 002976

4-year public university in small city.

Enrollment: 13,545 undergrads, 12% part-time. 2,472 full-time freshmen.

Selectivity: Admits 50 to 75% of applicants. GED not accepted.

BASIC COSTS (2008-2009)

Tuition and fees: $4,135; out-of-state residents $15,629.

Per-credit charge: $313; out-of-state residents $1,750.

Room and board: $6,188.

FINANCIAL AID PICTURE (2008-2009)

Students with need: Out of 1,997 full-time freshmen who applied for aid, 1,835 were judged to have need. Of these, 1,832 received aid, and 1,319 had their full need met. Average financial aid package met 64% of need; average scholarship/grant was $8,512; average loan was $2,586. For part-time students, average financial aid package was $8,465.

Students without need: 153 full-time freshmen who did not demonstrate need for aid received scholarships/grants; average award was $2,447. No-need awards available for academics, alumni affiliation, art, athletics, leadership, music/drama, state/district residency.

Scholarships offered: 30 full-time freshmen received athletic scholarships; average amount $7,851.

Cumulative student debt: 65% of graduating class had student loans; average debt was $16,326.

FINANCIAL AID PROCEDURES

Forms required: FAFSA.

Dates and Deadlines: Priority date 3/1; no closing date. Applicants notified on a rolling basis starting 3/15; must reply within 3 week(s) of notification.

CONTACT

Deborah Tollefson, Director of Financial Aid
1400 Spring Garden Street, Greensboro, NC 27402-6170
(336) 334-5702

University of North Carolina at Pembroke

Pembroke, North Carolina
www.uncp.edu Federal Code: 002954

4-year public university and liberal arts college in small town.

Enrollment: 5,280 undergrads, 19% part-time. 1,057 full-time freshmen.

Selectivity: Admits over 75% of applicants.

BASIC COSTS (2008-2009)

Tuition and fees: $3,608; out-of-state residents $12,868.

Room and board: $6,190.

FINANCIAL AID PICTURE (2008-2009)

Students with need: Out of 969 full-time freshmen who applied for aid, 755 were judged to have need. Of these, 742 received aid, and 74 had their full need met. Average financial aid package met 76% of need; average scholarship/grant was $5,928; average loan was $3,195. For part-time students, average financial aid package was $5,002.

Students without need: 4 full-time freshmen who did not demonstrate need for aid received scholarships/grants; average award was $987. No-need awards available for academics, alumni affiliation, art, athletics, music/drama, state/district residency.

FINANCIAL AID PROCEDURES

Forms required: FAFSA.

Dates and Deadlines: Priority date 3/15; no closing date. Applicants notified on a rolling basis starting 4/15; must reply within 2 week(s) of notification.

CONTACT

Alvin Blackmon, Director of Financial Aid
Box 1510, Pembroke, NC 28372
(910) 521-6255

University of North Carolina at Wilmington

Wilmington, North Carolina
www.uncw.edu Federal Code: 002984

4-year public university in small city.

Enrollment: 10,625 undergrads, 7% part-time. 2,069 full-time freshmen.

Selectivity: Admits 50 to 75% of applicants.

BASIC COSTS (2008-2009)

Tuition and fees: $4,527; out-of-state residents $14,694.

Room and board: $7,280.

FINANCIAL AID PICTURE (2008-2009)

Students with need: Out of 1,012 full-time freshmen who applied for aid, 554 were judged to have need. Of these, 545 received aid, and 367 had their full need met. Average financial aid package met 88% of need; average scholarship/grant was $3,763; average loan was $2,792. Need-based aid available for part-time students.

Students without need: 50 full-time freshmen who did not demonstrate need for aid received scholarships/grants; average award was $1,355. No-need awards available for academics, athletics, leadership, minority status, music/drama, state/district residency.

Scholarships offered: 37 full-time freshmen received athletic scholarships; average amount $5,575.

FINANCIAL AID PROCEDURES

Forms required: FAFSA, institutional form.

Dates and Deadlines: Priority date 3/15; no closing date. Applicants notified on a rolling basis starting 4/1; must reply within 3 week(s) of notification.

CONTACT

Emily Bliss, Director of Financial Aid and Veteran Services
601 South College Road, Wilmington, NC 28403-5904
(910) 962-3177

University of North Carolina School of the Arts

Winston-Salem, North Carolina
www.ncarts.edu Federal Code: 003981

4-year public visual arts and performing arts college in small city.

Enrollment: 765 undergrads. 182 full-time freshmen.

Selectivity: Admits less than 50% of applicants.

BASIC COSTS (2008-2009)

Tuition and fees: $5,216; out-of-state residents $17,096.

Room and board: $6,831.

Additional info: Required fees may vary by program.

FINANCIAL AID PICTURE (2007-2008)

Students with need: 50% of average financial aid package awarded as scholarships/grants, 50% awarded as loans/jobs. Need-based aid available for part-time students. Work study available nights, weekends, and for part-time students.

Students without need: No-need awards available for academics, art, leadership, music/drama, state/district residency.

FINANCIAL AID PROCEDURES

Forms required: FAFSA.

Dates and Deadlines: Priority date 3/1; no closing date. Applicants notified on a rolling basis starting 4/1; must reply within 2 week(s) of notification.

CONTACT

Jane Kamiab, Director of Financial Aid
1533 South Main Street, Winston-Salem, NC 27127-2188
(336) 770-3297

Vance-Granville Community College

Henderson, North Carolina
www.vgcc.edu Federal Code: 009903

2-year public community college in large town.

Enrollment: 3,948 undergrads.

Selectivity: Open admission; but selective for some programs.

BASIC COSTS (2008-2009)

Tuition and fees: $1,408; out-of-state residents $7,530.

Per-credit charge: $42; out-of-state residents $233.

FINANCIAL AID PICTURE (2007-2008)

Students with need: Need-based aid available for full-time and part-time students.

Students without need: No-need awards available for academics.

FINANCIAL AID PROCEDURES

Forms required: FAFSA.

Dates and Deadlines: Closing date 3/15. Applicants notified on a rolling basis starting 5/1; must reply within 2 week(s) of notification.

CONTACT

Frank Clark, Financial Aid Officer
Box 917, Henderson, NC 27536
(252) 492-2061

Wake Forest University

Winston-Salem, North Carolina Federal Code: 002978
www.wfu.edu CSS Code: 5885

4-year private university in small city.

Enrollment: 4,466 undergrads, 2% part-time. 1,199 full-time freshmen.

Selectivity: Admits less than 50% of applicants.

BASIC COSTS (2008-2009)

Tuition and fees: $36,975.

Per-credit charge: $1,517.

Room and board: $9,945.

Additional info: Tuition covers cost of an IBM Thinkpad computer and inkjet printer for freshmen.

FINANCIAL AID PICTURE (2008-2009)

Students with need: Out of 430 full-time freshmen who applied for aid, 344 were judged to have need. Of these, 338 received aid, and 295 had their full need met. Average financial aid package met 99% of need; average scholarship/grant was $23,682; average loan was $6,536. For part-time students, average financial aid package was $24,503.

Students without need: 78 full-time freshmen who did not demonstrate need for aid received scholarships/grants; average award was $14,742. No-need awards available for academics, alumni affiliation, art, athletics, leadership, music/drama, religious affiliation, ROTC, state/district residency.

Scholarships offered: ***Merit:*** Reynolds Scholarship: full tuition, room and board, books, fees for 4 years, also provides for summer study; 6 awarded. Joseph G. Gordon Scholarship: full tuition for 4 years; for underrepresented students with exceptional promise and leadership; 7 awarded. Carswell Scholarship: based on intellect and leadership; between 3/4 and full tuition for 4 years, including summer grant for travel and study projects; 10-12 awarded. Presidential Scholarship: for students gifted in areas such as writing, studio art, music theater, debate, leadership, dance, entrepreneurship, and community service; 20 awarded. Poteat Scholarship: $12,100; for North Carolina residents who are active members of a Baptist Church in North Carolina, must make an active contribution to church and society; 18 awarded. ***Athletic:*** 68 full-time freshmen received athletic scholarships; average amount $36,754.

Cumulative student debt: 38% of graduating class had student loans; average debt was $24,827.

Additional info: In fall 2008, freshmen with an annual family income of less than $40,000 will have their student loans capped at $4,000 per year during their college years. Other financial aid to the students will come from grant and scholarship increases and work-study opportunities.

FINANCIAL AID PROCEDURES

Forms required: FAFSA, CSS PROFILE, state aid form.

Dates and Deadlines: Priority date 2/1; closing date 3/1. Applicants notified on a rolling basis starting 4/1; must reply by 5/1 or within 4 week(s) of notification.

CONTACT

William Wells, Director of Financial Aid
PO Box 7305, Winston-Salem, NC 27109-7305
(336) 758-5154

Wake Technical Community College

Raleigh, North Carolina
www.waketech.edu Federal Code: 004844

2-year public community and technical college in small city

Enrollment: 13,775 undergrads.

Selectivity: Open admission; but selective for some programs.

BASIC COSTS (2008-2009)

Tuition and fees: $1,320; out-of-state residents $7,059.

Per-credit charge: $42; out-of-state residents $233.

FINANCIAL AID PICTURE

Students with need: Need-based aid available for full-time and part-time students.

Students without need: No-need awards available for academics, job skills, leadership, state/district residency.

FINANCIAL AID PROCEDURES

Forms required: FAFSA, institutional form.

Dates and Deadlines: Priority date 3/15; no closing date. Applicants notified on a rolling basis starting 4/1; must reply within 2 week(s) of notification.

Transfers: Child care grant and NCCCS Grant and Loan Program available.

CONTACT

Regina Huggins, Financial Aid Director
9101 Fayetteville Road, Raleigh, NC 27603
(919) 866-5410

Warren Wilson College

Asheville, North Carolina
www.warren-wilson.edu Federal Code: 002979

4-year private liberal arts college in small city, affiliated with Presbyterian Church (USA).

Enrollment: 955 undergrads.

BASIC COSTS (2009-2010)

Tuition and fees: $24,196.
Per-credit charge: $996.
Room and board: $7,770.
Additional info: All resident students required to work 15 hours per week in college's work program. $3,480 earnings credited toward tuition costs.

FINANCIAL AID PICTURE (2008-2009)

Students with need: Need-based aid available for full-time and part-time students.
Students without need: No-need awards available for academics, art, job skills, leadership, religious affiliation, state/district residency.
Scholarships offered: Wilson Honor: 1 awarded; $5,000 annually. Warner Honor: 2 awarded; $4,000 annually. Transfer Honor: 2 awarded; $2,000 annually. Sutton Honor: 20 awarded; $1,000 annually. Work Scholarship: 2 awarded; $1,500 annually. Service Scholarship: 2 awarded; $1,500 annually. National Merit: unlimited numbers awarded; $4,000 annually. Valedictorian/ Salutatorian Scholarship: 10 awarded; $2,000 annually. North Carolina Presidential Scholarship: 30 awarded; $1,000 annually. All renewable with 3.0 cumulative GPA and successful completion of a minimum of 12 credit hours each semester.

FINANCIAL AID PROCEDURES

Forms required: FAFSA, state aid form, institutional form.
Dates and Deadlines: Priority date 4/1; no closing date. Applicants notified on a rolling basis starting 3/1; must reply within 3 week(s) of notification.
Transfers: No deadline. Applicants notified on a rolling basis starting 3/1; must reply within 3 week(s) of notification.

CONTACT

Kathy Pack, Director of Financial Aid
Office of Admission, Asheville, NC 28815-9000
(828) 771-2082

Wayne Community College

Goldsboro, North Carolina
www.waynecc.edu Federal Code: 008216

2-year public community college in large town.
Enrollment: 2,885 undergrads.
Selectivity: Open admission; but selective for some programs.

BASIC COSTS (2008-2009)

Tuition and fees: $1,324; out-of-state residents $7,063.
Per-credit charge: $42; out-of-state residents $233.

FINANCIAL AID PICTURE (2007-2008)

Students with need: Need-based aid available for full-time and part-time students. Work study available nights.
Students without need: No-need awards available for academics, job skills.

FINANCIAL AID PROCEDURES

Forms required: FAFSA, institutional form.
Dates and Deadlines: Priority date 3/15; no closing date. Applicants notified on a rolling basis starting 6/1; must reply within 2 week(s) of notification.

CONTACT

Karen Statler, Financial Aid Director
PO Box 8002, Goldsboro, NC 27533-8002
(919) 735-5151

Western Carolina University

Cullowhee, North Carolina
www.wcu.edu Federal Code: 002981

4-year public university in small town.
Enrollment: 6,896 undergrads, 16% part-time. 1,221 full-time freshmen.
Selectivity: Admits 50 to 75% of applicants.

BASIC COSTS (2008-2009)

Tuition and fees: $4,413; out-of-state residents $13,996.
Room and board: $5,626.

FINANCIAL AID PICTURE (2008-2009)

Students with need: Out of 972 full-time freshmen who applied for aid, 670 were judged to have need. Of these, 662 received aid, and 380 had their full need met. Average financial aid package met 87% of need; average scholarship/grant was $7,868; average loan was $3,644. For part-time students, average financial aid package was $4,527.
Students without need: 97 full-time freshmen who did not demonstrate need for aid received scholarships/grants; average award was $2,059. No-need awards available for academics, art, athletics, leadership, music/drama, state/district residency.
Scholarships offered: ***Merit:*** WCU awards merit-based scholarships each year to students that demonstrate excellent academic, athletic, artistic, professional, cultural and/or civic achievement. The number and amount of awards vary. ***Athletic:*** 67 full-time freshmen received athletic scholarships; average amount $8,984.
Cumulative student debt: 59% of graduating class had student loans; average debt was $13,354.

FINANCIAL AID PROCEDURES

Forms required: FAFSA, institutional form.
Dates and Deadlines: Priority date 3/31; no closing date. Applicants notified on a rolling basis starting 4/1.

CONTACT

Trina Orr, Director of Student Financial Aid
102 Camp Building, Cullowhee, NC 28723
(828) 227-7290

Western Piedmont Community College

Morganton, North Carolina
www.wpcc.edu Federal Code: 002982

2-year public community college in large town.
Enrollment: 2,030 undergrads.
Selectivity: Open admission; but selective for some programs.

BASIC COSTS (2008-2009)

Tuition and fees: $1,287; out-of-state residents $7,026.
Per-credit charge: $42; out-of-state residents $233.

FINANCIAL AID PICTURE (2007-2008)

Students with need: Need-based aid available for full-time and part-time students.
Students without need: No-need awards available for academics.

FINANCIAL AID PROCEDURES

Forms required: FAFSA.

Dates and Deadlines: Priority date 6/1; no closing date. Applicants notified on a rolling basis starting 6/15; must reply within 2 week(s) of notification.

CONTACT

Keith Conley, Director of Financial Aid
1001 Burkemont Avenue, Morganton, NC 28655-4504
(828) 438-6042

Wilkes Community College

Wilkesboro, North Carolina
www.wilkescc.edu Federal Code: 002983

2-year public community college in small town.
Enrollment: 2,060 undergrads.
Selectivity: Open admission; but selective for some programs.

BASIC COSTS (2008-2009)

Tuition and fees: $1,340; out-of-state residents $7,079.
Per-credit charge: $42; out-of-state residents $233.

FINANCIAL AID PICTURE (2007-2008)

Students with need: Need-based aid available for full-time and part-time students. Work study available nights.
Students without need: No-need awards available for academics, art, job skills, leadership, minority status, music/drama, state/district residency.

FINANCIAL AID PROCEDURES

Forms required: FAFSA.
Dates and Deadlines: Priority date 5/1; no closing date. Applicants notified on a rolling basis starting 4/1; must reply by 8/1.
Transfers: No deadline.

CONTACT

Vickie Call, Director of Financial Aid
1328 South Collegiate Drive, Wilkesboro, NC 28697-0120
(336) 838-6146

Wilson Community College

Wilson, North Carolina
www.wilsoncc.edu Federal Code: 004845

2-year public community college in large town.
Enrollment: 1,483 undergrads, 54% part-time. 196 full-time freshmen.
Selectivity: Open admission; but selective for some programs.

BASIC COSTS (2008-2009)

Tuition and fees: $1,408; out-of-state residents $7,530.
Per-credit charge: $42; out-of-state residents $233.

FINANCIAL AID PICTURE

Students with need: Need-based aid available for full-time and part-time students.
Students without need: No-need awards available for academics.

FINANCIAL AID PROCEDURES

Forms required: FAFSA, institutional form.
Dates and Deadlines: Priority date 3/15; no closing date. Applicants notified on a rolling basis.

CONTACT

Rex Bissette, Director of Financial Aid and Veterans Affairs
Box 4305, Wilson, NC 27893-0305
(252) 246-1274

Wingate University

Wingate, North Carolina
www.wingate.edu Federal Code: 002985

4-year private university and liberal arts college in small town, affiliated with Baptist faith.
Enrollment: 1,440 undergrads, 3% part-time. 431 full-time freshmen.
Selectivity: Open admission; but selective for some programs.

BASIC COSTS (2008-2009)

Tuition and fees: $19,350.
Per-credit charge: $610.
Room and board: $7,700.
Additional info: Some music and art courses carry a fee.

FINANCIAL AID PICTURE (2008-2009)

Students with need: Need-based aid available for full-time and part-time students. Work study available nights, weekends, and for part-time students.
Students without need: No-need awards available for academics, alumni affiliation, art, athletics, music/drama, state/district residency.
Additional info: Institutional aid may not be available after June 1.

FINANCIAL AID PROCEDURES

Forms required: FAFSA.
Dates and Deadlines: Priority date 5/1; no closing date. Applicants notified on a rolling basis starting 3/1; must reply within 2 week(s) of notification.
Transfers: Priority date 3/1; no deadline. Applicants notified on a rolling basis; must reply within 2 week(s) of notification. Must submit financial aid transcripts from previous colleges attended.

CONTACT

Teresa Williams, Director of Financial Planning
Campus Box 3059, Wingate, NC 28174-0157
(704) 233-8209

Winston-Salem State University

Winston-Salem, North Carolina
www.wssu.edu Federal Code: 002986

4-year public university and health science college in small city.
Enrollment: 5,948 undergrads.
Selectivity: Admits 50 to 75% of applicants.

BASIC COSTS (2008-2009)

Tuition and fees: $3,389; out-of-state residents $12,029.
Room and board: $5,942.

FINANCIAL AID PICTURE (2007-2008)

Students with need: 57% of average financial aid package awarded as scholarships/grants, 43% awarded as loans/jobs.
Students without need: No-need awards available for academics, athletics, ROTC, state/district residency.

FINANCIAL AID PROCEDURES

Forms required: FAFSA.
Dates and Deadlines: Priority date 5/1; no closing date. Applicants notified by 5/15; must reply within 2 week(s) of notification.
Transfers: Closing date 3/15. Applicants notified on a rolling basis.

CONTACT

Tomikia Legrande, Director of Financial Aid
601 Martin Luther King Jr Drive, Winston-Salem, NC 27110
(336) 750-3280

North Dakota

Bismarck State College

Bismarck, North Dakota
www.bismarckstate.edu Federal Code: 002988

2-year public community college in small city.
Enrollment: 3,788 undergrads, 34% part-time. 807 full-time freshmen.
Selectivity: Open admission; but selective for some programs.

BASIC COSTS (2008-2009)

Tuition and fees: $3,933; out-of-state residents $9,551.
Per-credit charge: $112; out-of-state residents $299.
Room and board: $4,525.
Additional info: Full-time annual tuition for residents of Minnesota: $4,075. Full-time annual tuition for residents of South Dakota, Montana, Manitoba, Saskatchewan: $4,205. Tuition/fee waivers available for minority students.

FINANCIAL AID PICTURE

Students with need: Need-based aid available for full-time and part-time students. Work study available nights, weekends, and for part-time students.
Students without need: This college awards aid only to students with need.
Scholarships offered: Academic Scholarship; $900; for students enrolled in 15 credit hours who maintain 3.0 GPA; 79 awarded.

FINANCIAL AID PROCEDURES

Forms required: FAFSA.
Dates and Deadlines: Priority date 3/15; no closing date. Applicants notified on a rolling basis starting 6/1; must reply within 3 week(s) of notification.
Transfers: Financial aid based on funds available.

CONTACT

Jeffrey Jacobs, Director of Financial Aid
PO Box 5587, Bismarck, ND 58506-5587
(701) 224-5494

Cankdeska Cikana Community College

Fort Totten, North Dakota
www.littlehoop.edu Federal Code: 015793

2-year public community college in rural community.
Enrollment: 181 undergrads.
Selectivity: Open admission.

BASIC COSTS (2008-2009)

Tuition and fees: $3,040.
Per-credit charge: $98.

FINANCIAL AID PICTURE (2007-2008)

Students with need: Need-based aid available for full-time and part-time students.
Students without need: This college awards aid only to students with need.

FINANCIAL AID PROCEDURES

Forms required: FAFSA, institutional form.
Dates and Deadlines: Closing date 8/20. Applicants notified on a rolling basis.

CONTACT

Kristi Black, Director of Financial Aid
Box 269, Fort Totten, ND 58335
(701) 766-1341

Dickinson State University

Dickinson, North Dakota
www.dsu.nodak.edu Federal Code: 002989

4-year public university in large town.
Enrollment: 2,730 undergrads, 31% part-time. 335 full-time freshmen.
Selectivity: Open admission; but selective for some programs.

BASIC COSTS (2008-2009)

Tuition and fees: $5,084; out-of-state residents $11,796.
Room and board: $4,280.
Additional info: Tuition for Minnesota residents: $4,197. Tuition for South Dakota, Montana, Manitoba, Saskatchewan residents: $5,024. Tuition/fee waivers available for minority students.

FINANCIAL AID PICTURE (2007-2008)

Students with need: 23% of average financial aid package awarded as scholarships/grants, 77% awarded as loans/jobs. Need-based aid available for part-time students. Work study available nights, weekends, and for part-time students.
Students without need: No-need awards available for academics, alumni affiliation, art, athletics, job skills, leadership, minority status, music/drama, religious affiliation, state/district residency.
Additional info: Scholarships available to new students, priority deadline December 1.

FINANCIAL AID PROCEDURES

Forms required: FAFSA.
Dates and Deadlines: Priority date 3/15; no closing date. Must reply within 2 week(s) of notification.

CONTACT

Sandy Klein, Director of Financial Aid
291 Campus Drive, Dickinson, ND 58601-4896
(701) 483-2371

Fort Berthold Community College

New Town, North Dakota
www.fbcc.bia.edu Federal Code: 015536

2-year public community college in small town.
Enrollment: 133 undergrads, 32% part-time. 30 full-time freshmen.
Selectivity: Open admission.

BASIC COSTS (2008-2009)

Tuition and fees: $3,340.
Per-credit charge: $110.

FINANCIAL AID PICTURE (2007-2008)

Students with need: Out of 30 full-time freshmen who applied for aid, 30 were judged to have need. Of these, 30 received aid.

FINANCIAL AID PROCEDURES

Transfers: No deadline. Applicants notified on a rolling basis.

CONTACT

Mariam Fixico, Director of Financial Aid
Box 490, New Town, ND 58763

Jamestown College

Jamestown, North Dakota
www.jc.edu Federal Code: 002990

4-year private liberal arts college in large town, affiliated with Presbyterian Church (USA).
Enrollment: 990 undergrads, 5% part-time. 280 full-time freshmen.

Selectivity: Admits 50 to 75% of applicants.

BASIC COSTS (2009-2010)

Tuition and fees: $16,006.
Per-credit charge: $380.
Room and board: $5,156.

FINANCIAL AID PICTURE (2008-2009)

Students with need: Out of 243 full-time freshmen who applied for aid, 188 were judged to have need. Of these, 187 received aid, and 49 had their full need met. Average financial aid package met 85% of need; average scholarship/grant was $9,840; average loan was $3,794. For part-time students, average financial aid package was $2,014.
Students without need: 91 full-time freshmen who did not demonstrate need for aid received scholarships/grants; average award was $9,161. No-need awards available for academics, alumni affiliation, art, athletics, leadership, music/drama, religious affiliation.
Scholarships offered: ***Merit:*** Wilson Scholarships: full tuition; for academic merit and leadership. Presidential Scholarships: $10,000 annually; for academic merit and leadership.Arnold Chemistry Scholarships: $2,500 annually; for chemistry majors. ***Athletic:*** 70 full-time freshmen received athletic scholarships; average amount $2,922.
Cumulative student debt: 87% of graduating class had student loans; average debt was $25,975.
Additional info: FAFSA must be received by March 15th for North Dakota residents to be considered for North Dakota state grants.

FINANCIAL AID PROCEDURES

Forms required: FAFSA.
Dates and Deadlines: Priority date 3/15; no closing date. Applicants notified on a rolling basis starting 2/1.
Transfers: No deadline. Applicants notified on a rolling basis; must reply within 2 week(s) of notification.

CONTACT

Margery Michael, Director of Financial Aid
6081 College Lane, Jamestown, ND 58405
(701) 252-3467 ext. 5556

Lake Region State College

Devils Lake, North Dakota
www.lrsc.edu Federal Code: 002991

2-year public community and technical college in small town.
Enrollment: 627 undergrads, 34% part-time.
Selectivity: Open admission; but selective for some programs.

BASIC COSTS (2008-2009)

Tuition and fees: $3,908; out-of-state residents $3,908.
Per-credit charge: $128; out-of-state residents $122.
Room and board: $4,608.
Additional info: Tuition/fee waivers available for minority students.

FINANCIAL AID PICTURE (2008-2009)

Students with need: Average financial aid package met 76% of need; average scholarship/grant was $3,290; average loan was $2,873. For part-time students, average financial aid package was $3,291.
Students without need: No-need awards available for academics, athletics, leadership, minority status, music/drama.
Cumulative student debt: 72% of graduating class had student loans; average debt was $9,226.

FINANCIAL AID PROCEDURES

Forms required: FAFSA.
Dates and Deadlines: Priority date 3/15; no closing date. Applicants notified on a rolling basis starting 5/15; must reply within 2 week(s) of notification.
Transfers: No deadline. Applicants notified on a rolling basis starting 5/1; must reply within 4 week(s) of notification.

CONTACT

Katie Nettell, Director of Financial Aid
1801 College Drive North, Devils Lake, ND 58301-1598
(701) 662-1516

Mayville State University

Mayville, North Dakota
www.mayvillestate.edu Federal Code: 002993

4-year public business and teachers college in small town.
Enrollment: 789 undergrads, 43% part-time. 87 full-time freshmen.
Selectivity: Open admission; but selective for some programs.

BASIC COSTS (2008-2009)

Tuition and fees: $5,654; out-of-state residents $7,646.
Per-credit charge: $166; out-of-state residents $249.
Room and board: $4,272.
Additional info: Full-time tuition for South Dakota, Montana, Kansas, Michigan, Missouri, Nebraska, Manitoba, and Saskatchewan residents: $4,981. Full-time tuition for Minnesota residents: $4,242. All other states and Canadian provinces: $5,977. Tuition/fee waivers available for minority students.

FINANCIAL AID PICTURE (2008-2009)

Students with need: Out of 86 full-time freshmen who applied for aid, 79 were judged to have need. Of these, 79 received aid, and 40 had their full need met. Average financial aid package met 100% of need; average scholarship/grant was $2,815; average loan was $2,591. For part-time students, average financial aid package was $4,956.
Students without need: 59 full-time freshmen who did not demonstrate need for aid received scholarships/grants; average award was $1,005. No-need awards available for academics, athletics, leadership, minority status, music/drama, state/district residency.
Scholarships offered: ***Merit:*** Non-resident academic scholarship; $500-2,000 per year; based on academic criteria of students from select states. ***Athletic:*** 19 full-time freshmen received athletic scholarships; average amount $1,205.
Cumulative student debt: 89% of graduating class had student loans; average debt was $19,338.

FINANCIAL AID PROCEDURES

Forms required: FAFSA.
Dates and Deadlines: Priority date 2/15; no closing date. Applicants notified on a rolling basis starting 5/1; must reply within 2 week(s) of notification.

CONTACT

Shirley Hanson, Director of Financial Aid
330 Third Street, NE, Mayville, ND 58257-1299
(701) 788-4767

Medcenter One College of Nursing

Bismarck, North Dakota
www.medcenterone.com/collegeofnursing
Federal Code: 009354

Upper-division private nursing college in small city.
Enrollment: 91 undergrads, 2% part-time.

BASIC COSTS (2008-2009)

Tuition and fees: $10,017.
Per-credit charge: $386.

FINANCIAL AID PICTURE (2007-2008)

Students with need: Average financial aid package for all full-time undergraduates was $10,435; for part-time $8,302. 46% awarded as scholarships/grants, 54% awarded as loans/jobs. Work study available weekends and for part-time students.

FINANCIAL AID PROCEDURES

Dates and Deadlines: No deadline.
Transfers: Priority date 3/1; no deadline. Applicants notified on a rolling basis starting 6/1; must reply within 2 week(s) of notification.

CONTACT

Janell Thomas, Director/Registrar
512 North 7th Street, Bismarck, ND 58501-4425
(701) 323-6270

Minot State University

Minot, North Dakota
www.minotstateu.edu Federal Code: 002994

4-year public university and liberal arts college in large town.
Enrollment: 3,172 undergrads, 29% part-time. 457 full-time freshmen.
Selectivity: Admits 50 to 75% of applicants.

BASIC COSTS (2008-2009)

Tuition and fees: $5,043; out-of-state residents $12,022.
Per-credit charge: $174; out-of-state residents $465.
Room and board: $4,450.
Additional info: Tuition/fee waivers available for minority students.

FINANCIAL AID PICTURE (2007-2008)

Students with need: Out of 401 full-time freshmen who applied for aid, 259 were judged to have need. Of these, 258 received aid, and 258 had their full need met. Average financial aid package met 85% of need; average scholarship/grant was $3,216; average loan was $3,170. For part-time students, average financial aid package was $5,633.
Students without need: 107 full-time freshmen who did not demonstrate need for aid received scholarships/grants; average award was $936. No-need awards available for academics, alumni affiliation, art, athletics, minority status, music/drama, state/district residency.
Scholarships offered: 20 full-time freshmen received athletic scholarships; average amount $923.
Cumulative student debt: 97% of graduating class had student loans; average debt was $17,296.
Additional info: Scholarship application deadline is 2/15.

FINANCIAL AID PROCEDURES

Forms required: FAFSA, institutional form.
Dates and Deadlines: Priority date 3/15; no closing date. Applicants notified on a rolling basis starting 5/1; must reply within 2 week(s) of notification.
Transfers: No deadline. Applicants notified by 5/1; must reply within 2 week(s) of notification.

CONTACT

Dale Gehring, Director of Financial Aid
500 University Avenue West, Minot, ND 58707-5002
(701) 858-3375

Minot State University: Bottineau Campus

Bottineau, North Dakota
www.msub.edu Federal Code: 002995

2-year public branch campus and junior college in small town.
Enrollment: 638 undergrads.
Selectivity: Open admission.

BASIC COSTS (2008-2009)

Tuition and fees: $3,802; out-of-state residents $5,362.
Room and board: $4,122.
Additional info: Tuition/fee waivers available for minority students.

FINANCIAL AID PICTURE

Students with need: Need-based aid available for full-time and part-time students. Work study available nights, weekends, and for part-time students.
Students without need: No-need awards available for academics, alumni affiliation, athletics, music/drama.

FINANCIAL AID PROCEDURES

Forms required: FAFSA.
Dates and Deadlines: Priority date 4/15; no closing date. Applicants notified on a rolling basis starting 6/1; must reply within 2 week(s) of notification.

CONTACT

Kim Gourneau, Financial Aid Officer
105 Simrall Boulevard, Bottineau, ND 58318-1198
(701) 228-5437

North Dakota State College of Science

Wahpeton, North Dakota
www.ndscs.nodak.edu Federal Code: 002996

2-year public junior and technical college in small town.
Enrollment: 2,545 undergrads. 563 full-time freshmen.
Selectivity: Open admission; but selective for some programs.

BASIC COSTS (2008-2009)

Tuition and fees: $3,888; out-of-state residents $9,512.
Per-credit charge: $112; out-of-state residents $299.
Room and board: $4,598.
Additional info: Full-time tuition for Minnesota residents: $4,075. Full-time tuition for South Dakota, Montana, Saskatchewan, Manitoba residents: $4,209. Tuition/fee waivers available for minority students.

FINANCIAL AID PICTURE (2008-2009)

Students with need: Need-based aid available for full-time and part-time students. Work study available nights, weekends, and for part-time students.
Students without need: No-need awards available for academics, athletics, job skills, music/drama, state/district residency.

FINANCIAL AID PROCEDURES

Forms required: FAFSA, institutional form.
Dates and Deadlines: Priority date 4/15; no closing date. Applicants notified on a rolling basis starting 6/1; must reply within 2 week(s) of notification.
Transfers: Priority date 3/15; no deadline. Must reply within 2 week(s) of notification.

CONTACT

Shelly Blome, Director of Financial Aid
800 North 6th Street, Wahpeton, ND 58076
(701) 671-2207

North Dakota State University

Fargo, North Dakota
www.ndsu.edu Federal Code: 002997

4-year public university in small city.
Enrollment: 10,799 undergrads, 7% part-time. 2,300 full-time freshmen.
Selectivity: Admits over 75% of applicants.

BASIC COSTS (2008-2009)

Tuition and fees: $6,226; out-of-state residents $15,015.
Per-credit charge: $219; out-of-state residents $585.
Room and board: $6,220.
Additional info: Tuition for South Dakota, Montana, Manitoba, Saskatchewan residents: $7,895. Tuition/fee waivers available for minority students.

FINANCIAL AID PICTURE (2007-2008)
Students with need: Out of 2,037 full-time freshmen who applied for aid, 1,365 were judged to have need. Of these, 1,336 received aid, and 355 had their full need met. Average financial aid package met 38% of need; average scholarship/grant was $3,729; average loan was $3,853. For part-time students, average financial aid package was $6,296.
Students without need: 572 full-time freshmen who did not demonstrate need for aid received scholarships/grants; average award was $1,692. No-need awards available for academics, alumni affiliation, art, athletics, leadership, minority status, music/drama, ROTC, state/district residency.
Scholarships offered: ***Merit:*** New Student Scholarships: vary in amount awarded; based on 25 ACT or 1200 SAT (exclusive of writing) and 3.5 GPA. ***Athletic:*** 68 full-time freshmen received athletic scholarships; average amount $8,487.

FINANCIAL AID PROCEDURES
Forms required: FAFSA.
Dates and Deadlines: Closing date 3/15. Applicants notified on a rolling basis starting 3/15.
Transfers: Priority date 3/15.

CONTACT
Jeanne Enebo, Director of Student Financial Services
Ceres Hall 124, Fargo, ND 58105-5454
(701) 231-7533

Rasmussen College: Bismarck
Bismarck, North Dakota
www.rasmussen.edu

2-year for-profit career college in small city.
Enrollment: 400 undergrads.
Selectivity: Open admission.

BASIC COSTS (2008-2009)
Tuition and fees: $15,750.
Per-credit charge: $350.

FINANCIAL AID PICTURE
Students with need: Need-based aid available for full-time and part-time students.

FINANCIAL AID PROCEDURES
Forms required: FAFSA, institutional form.
Dates and Deadlines: No deadline. Applicants notified on a rolling basis.

CONTACT
Eric Wingenbach, Director of Student Financial Services
1701 East Century Avenue, Bismarck, ND 58503
(701) 530-9600

Rasmussen College: Fargo
Fargo, North Dakota
www.rasmussen.edu Federal Code: 004846

4-year for-profit career college in small city.
Enrollment: 505 full-time undergrads.
Selectivity: Open admission; but selective for some programs.

BASIC COSTS (2008-2009)
Tuition and fees: $16,800.

FINANCIAL AID PICTURE (2007-2008)
Students with need: Need-based aid available for full-time and part-time students.

FINANCIAL AID PROCEDURES
Forms required: FAFSA, institutional form.
Dates and Deadlines: No deadline. Applicants notified on a rolling basis.

CONTACT
Crystal Vold, Director of Student Financial Services
4012 19th Avenue SW, Fargo, ND 58103
(701) 277-3889

Sitting Bull College
Fort Yates, North Dakota
www.sittingbull.edu Federal Code: 014993

2-year public community college in small town.
Enrollment: 310 undergrads.
Selectivity: Open admission.

BASIC COSTS (2008-2009)
Tuition and fees: $3,140.
Per-credit charge: $100.

FINANCIAL AID PICTURE (2007-2008)
Students with need: Need-based aid available for full-time and part-time students.

FINANCIAL AID PROCEDURES
Forms required: FAFSA, institutional form.
Dates and Deadlines: Priority date 5/1; no closing date. Applicants notified on a rolling basis starting 7/15; must reply within 6 week(s) of notification.

CONTACT
Donna Seaboy, Financial Aid Director
1341 92nd Street, Fort Yates, ND 58538
(701) 854-8013

Turtle Mountain Community College
Belcourt, North Dakota
www.tm.edu Federal Code: 009450

2-year public community college in rural community.
Enrollment: 604 undergrads.
Selectivity: Open admission; but selective for some programs.

BASIC COSTS (2008-2009)
Tuition and fees: $2,000.
Room and board: $3,664.
Additional info: Room and board for dependent students $3,664, for independent students $6,374.

FINANCIAL AID PICTURE (2007-2008)
Students with need: 99% of average financial aid package awarded as scholarships/grants, 1% awarded as loans/jobs.

FINANCIAL AID PROCEDURES
Forms required: FAFSA.
Dates and Deadlines: Priority date 4/15; closing date 5/1.

CONTACT
Wanda Laduce, Financial Aid Director
PO Box 340, Belcourt, ND 58316
(701) 477-7862

United Tribes Technical College

Bismarck, North Dakota
www.uttc.edu Federal Code: 014470

2-year private technical college in small city.
Enrollment: 363 undergrads.
Selectivity: Open admission; but selective for some programs.

BASIC COSTS (2008-2009)

Tuition and fees: $3,115.
Per-credit charge: $88.
Room and board: $3,000.
Additional info: Tuition/fee waivers available for adults, minority students.

FINANCIAL AID PICTURE (2008-2009)

Students with need: Need-based aid available for full-time and part-time students. Work study available nights, weekends, and for part-time students.

FINANCIAL AID PROCEDURES

Forms required: FAFSA.
Dates and Deadlines: Priority date 5/29; no closing date. Applicants notified on a rolling basis starting 5/29; must reply within 2 week(s) of notification.

CONTACT

Nathan Stratton, Financial Aid Director
3315 University Drive, Bismarck, ND 58504
(701) 255-3285 ext. 1211

University of Mary

Bismarck, North Dakota
www.umary.edu Federal Code: 002992

4-year private university in small city, affiliated with Roman Catholic Church.
Enrollment: 2,052 undergrads, 20% part-time. 367 full-time freshmen.
Selectivity: Admits over 75% of applicants.

BASIC COSTS (2009-2010)

Tuition and fees: $12,584.
Per-credit charge: $390.
Room and board: $4,940.

FINANCIAL AID PICTURE (2007-2008)

Students with need: Out of 336 full-time freshmen who applied for aid, 270 were judged to have need. Of these, 270 received aid. Need-based aid available for part-time students.
Students without need: 258 full-time freshmen who did not demonstrate need for aid received scholarships/grants; average award was $4,134. No-need awards available for academics, athletics, leadership, music/drama, state/district residency.
Scholarships offered: ***Merit:*** Awards given to high percentage of new freshmen; scholarship competition days held annually with awards ranging from $3,500 to 100% of tuition; athletic, music, speech, drama and leadership scholarships also offered. ***Athletic:*** 43 full-time freshmen received athletic scholarships; average amount $5,119.

FINANCIAL AID PROCEDURES

Forms required: FAFSA.
Dates and Deadlines: Priority date 3/15; no closing date. Must reply within 2 week(s) of notification.
Transfers: Priority date 5/1; no deadline. Applicants notified on a rolling basis starting 5/1; must reply within 2 week(s) of notification.

CONTACT

Brenda Zastophil, Director of Student Financial Aid
7500 University Drive, Bismarck, ND 58504-9652
(701) 355-8244 ext. 283

University of North Dakota

Grand Forks, North Dakota
www.und.edu Federal Code: 003005

4-year public university in small city.
Enrollment: 10,129 undergrads, 14% part-time. 1,828 full-time freshmen.
Selectivity: Admits over 75% of applicants.

BASIC COSTS (2008-2009)

Tuition and fees: $6,513; out-of-state residents $15,325.
Per-credit charge: $220; out-of-state residents $587.
Room and board: $5,735.
Additional info: Tuition for South Dakota, Montana, Saskatchewan, Manitoba residents: $7,914. Tuition/fee waivers available for minority students.

FINANCIAL AID PICTURE (2007-2008)

Students with need: Out of 1,577 full-time freshmen who applied for aid, 1,105 were judged to have need. Of these, 1,085 received aid, and 292 had their full need met. Average financial aid package met 37% of need; average scholarship/grant was $3,267; average loan was $4,512. For part-time students, average financial aid package was $6,106.
Students without need: 510 full-time freshmen who did not demonstrate need for aid received scholarships/grants; average award was $1,035. No-need awards available for academics, alumni affiliation, art, athletics, job skills, leadership, music/drama, religious affiliation, ROTC.
Scholarships offered: ***Merit:*** 15 freshmen will receive $2,500 a year for 4 years; they are either National Merit Finalists listing UND as first choice and in top 10% of graduating class, or in top 10% and have minimum composite of 32 on the ACT. 55 scholarships of $2,000/yr for 4 years provided to students in top 10% of graduating class who are National Merit Semifinalists or have ACT composite of 29-31. 40 students with ACT of 27-28 and in upper 10% of graduating class will receive $1,000 for their freshman year. ***Athletic:*** 49 full-time freshmen received athletic scholarships; average amount $5,672.
Cumulative student debt: 65% of graduating class had student loans; average debt was $21,330.

FINANCIAL AID PROCEDURES

Forms required: FAFSA.
Dates and Deadlines: Priority date 3/15; no closing date. Applicants notified on a rolling basis starting 5/15; must reply within 4 week(s) of notification.

CONTACT

Robin Holden, Director of Student Financial Aid
Twamley Hall Room 205 264 Centennial Drive Stop 8357, Grand Forks, ND 58202-8357
(701) 777-3121

Valley City State University

Valley City, North Dakota
www.vcsu.edu Federal Code: 003008

4-year public liberal arts and teachers college in small town.
Enrollment: 900 undergrads, 25% part-time. 160 full-time freshmen.
Selectivity: Admits over 75% of applicants.

BASIC COSTS (2008-2009)

Tuition and fees: $5,781; out-of-state residents $12,691.
Per-credit charge: $138; out-of-state residents $368.
Room and board: $4,248.
Additional info: Full-time tuition for South Dakota, Montana, Manitoba, Saskatchewan residents: $5,172. Full-time tuition for WUE students: $6,209. Tuition/fee waivers available for minority students.

FINANCIAL AID PICTURE (2008-2009)
Students with need: Out of 160 full-time freshmen who applied for aid, 134 were judged to have need. Of these, 134 received aid, and 55 had their full need met. Average financial aid package met 86% of need; average scholarship/grant was $3,364; average loan was $2,614. For part-time students, average financial aid package was $5,285.
Students without need: 110 full-time freshmen who did not demonstrate need for aid received scholarships/grants; average award was $2,355. No-need awards available for academics, alumni affiliation, athletics, leadership, minority status, music/drama.
Scholarships offered: ***Merit:*** Presidents Scholarship: $2,500 per year for 4 years. Meredith Scholarship: $3,000 per year for 4 years; science or math students only. McCready Scholarship: tuition and books for 4 years. ***Athletic:*** 18 full-time freshmen received athletic scholarships; average amount $972.
Cumulative student debt: 83% of graduating class had student loans; average debt was $20,469.

FINANCIAL AID PROCEDURES
Forms required: FAFSA.
Dates and Deadlines: Priority date 3/15; no closing date. Applicants notified on a rolling basis starting 2/1; must reply within 4 week(s) of notification.

CONTACT
Betty Schumacher, Director of Financial Aid
101 College Street SW, Valley City, ND 58072-4098
(701) 845-7412

Williston State College
Williston, North Dakota
www.wsc.nodak.edu Federal Code: 003007

2-year public junior college in large town.
Enrollment: 399 undergrads. 135 full-time freshmen.
Selectivity: Open admission; but selective for some programs.

BASIC COSTS (2008-2009)
Tuition and fees: $3,378; out-of-state residents $4,687.
Per-credit charge: $101; out-of-state residents $151.
Room and board: $3,218.
Additional info: Tuition for Minnesota residents: $3,532. Tuition for South Dakota, Montana, and Canadian residents: $2,618. Tuition/fee waivers available for minority students.

FINANCIAL AID PICTURE (2007-2008)
Students with need: Out of 124 full-time freshmen who applied for aid, 106 were judged to have need. Of these, 103 received aid, and 28 had their full need met. Average financial aid package met 96% of need; average scholarship/grant was $3,065; average loan was $3,260. For part-time students, average financial aid package was $4,452.
Students without need: 62 full-time freshmen who did not demonstrate need for aid received scholarships/grants; average award was $1,317. No-need awards available for academics, athletics, music/drama.
Scholarships offered: 8 full-time freshmen received athletic scholarships; average amount $3,583.
Cumulative student debt: 81% of graduating class had student loans; average debt was $7,929.

FINANCIAL AID PROCEDURES
Forms required: FAFSA.
Dates and Deadlines: Priority date 3/15; no closing date. Applicants notified on a rolling basis starting 5/15.

CONTACT
Lynn Hagen-Aaberg, Financial Aid Director
1410 University Avenue, Williston, ND 58802-1326
(701) 774-4244

Ohio

Antioch University McGregor
Yellow Springs, Ohio
www.mcgregor.edu Federal Code: E00553

4-year private university and branch campus and liberal arts college in small town.
Enrollment: 160 undergrads, 58% part-time.

BASIC COSTS (2009-2010)
Tuition and fees: $15,720.
Per-credit charge: $315.

FINANCIAL AID PICTURE (2007-2008)
Students with need: Need-based aid available for full-time and part-time students.

FINANCIAL AID PROCEDURES
Dates and Deadlines: No deadline. Applicants notified on a rolling basis.

CONTACT
Kathy John, Director of Financial Aid
900 Dayton Street, Yellow Springs, OH 45387
(937) 769-1840

Art Academy of Cincinnati
Cincinnati, Ohio
www.artacademy.edu Federal Code: 003011

4-year private visual arts college in large city.
Enrollment: 159 undergrads, 4% part-time. 47 full-time freshmen.
Selectivity: Admits less than 50% of applicants.

BASIC COSTS (2008-2009)
Tuition and fees: $21,300.
Per-credit charge: $875.
Room and board: $6,800.

FINANCIAL AID PICTURE
Students with need: Need-based aid available for full-time and part-time students.
Students without need: No-need awards available for academics, art.
Scholarships offered: Annual scholarships awarded to entering and transfer students and to continuing students based on portfolio competition.

FINANCIAL AID PROCEDURES
Forms required: FAFSA.
Dates and Deadlines: Priority date 4/1; no closing date. Applicants notified on a rolling basis starting 3/1.

CONTACT
Karen Geiger, Financial Aid Director
1212 Jackson Street, Cincinnati, OH 45202
(513) 562-8751

Art Institute of Cincinnati
Cincinnati, Ohio
www.aic-arts.edu Federal Code: 014804

2-year for-profit visual arts college in large city.
Enrollment: 70 undergrads.

BASIC COSTS (2008-2009)

Tuition and fees: $14,047.
Additional info: Total program cost $40,221 (8 quarters). Tuition at time of enrollment locked for 2 years.

FINANCIAL AID PICTURE (2007-2008)

Students with need: Need-based aid available for full-time students.
Students without need: No-need awards available for academics, art.

FINANCIAL AID PROCEDURES

Forms required: FAFSA.
Dates and Deadlines: No deadline. Applicants notified on a rolling basis starting 9/1; must reply within 1 week(s) of notification.
Transfers: No deadline. Applicants notified on a rolling basis; must reply within 4 week(s) of notification.

CONTACT

Gary Lay, Financial Aid Director
1171 East Kemper Road, Cincinnati, OH 45246
(513) 751-1206

Ashland University

Ashland, Ohio
www.ashland.edu Federal Code: 003012

4-year private university and liberal arts college in large town, affiliated with Brethren Church.
Enrollment: 2,594 undergrads, 9% part-time. 562 full-time freshmen.
Selectivity: Admits over 75% of applicants.

BASIC COSTS (2008-2009)

Tuition and fees: $24,342.
Per-credit charge: $723.
Room and board: $8,876.
Additional info: Tuition/fee waivers available for minority students.

FINANCIAL AID PICTURE (2008-2009)

Students with need: Out of 553 full-time freshmen who applied for aid, 499 were judged to have need. Of these, 499 received aid. Average financial aid package met 90% of need; average scholarship/grant was $17,268; average loan was $4,244. For part-time students, average financial aid package was $10,626.
Students without need: 30 full-time freshmen who did not demonstrate need for aid received scholarships/grants; average award was $6,952. No-need awards available for academics, alumni affiliation, art, athletics, job skills, leadership, minority status, music/drama, religious affiliation.
Scholarships offered: ***Merit:*** Presidential Scholarships; $10,000 based on 3.75 GPA and 27 ACT or 1200 SAT; $9,000 based on 3.5-3.74 GPA and 25-26 ACT or 1130-1190 SAT; $8,000 based on 3.25-3.49 GPA and 23-24 ACT or 1050-1120 SAT. Director's Scholarships; $6,000; based on 3.0 GPA, 21 ACT or 970 SAT. SAT scores exclusive of Writing. ***Athletic:*** 15 full-time freshmen received athletic scholarships; average amount $9,915.

FINANCIAL AID PROCEDURES

Forms required: FAFSA, institutional form.
Dates and Deadlines: Priority date 3/15; no closing date. Applicants notified on a rolling basis starting 3/15; must reply within 5 week(s) of notification.
Transfers: Applicants notified on a rolling basis starting 3/1; must reply within 3 week(s) of notification. Awards for students transferring in 15 credits or more will be based on the student's college transfer GPA while awards for students transferring fewer than 15 credits will be based on the student's high school GPA and ACT/SAT score.

CONTACT

Stephen Howell, Director of Financial Aid
401 College Avenue, Ashland, OH 44805-9981
(419) 289-5002

Baldwin-Wallace College

Berea, Ohio
www.bw.edu Federal Code: 003014

4-year private liberal arts college in large town, affiliated with United Methodist Church.
Enrollment: 3,535 undergrads, 12% part-time. 738 full-time freshmen.
Selectivity: Admits 50 to 75% of applicants.

BASIC COSTS (2009-2010)

Tuition and fees: $24,230.
Per-credit charge: $770.
Room and board: $7,960.
Additional info: Conservatory tuition is higher. Tuition/fee waivers available for minority students.

FINANCIAL AID PICTURE (2008-2009)

Students with need: Out of 668 full-time freshmen who applied for aid, 586 were judged to have need. Of these, 586 received aid, and 332 had their full need met. Average financial aid package met 93% of need; average scholarship/grant was $14,522; average loan was $4,389. For part-time students, average financial aid package was $5,584.
Students without need: 106 full-time freshmen who did not demonstrate need for aid received scholarships/grants; average award was $9,340. No-need awards available for academics, alumni affiliation, leadership, minority status, music/drama, religious affiliation.
Scholarships offered: Presidential Scholarship; $13,000; 27 ACT/1220 SAT and 3.9 GPA or 27 ACT/1220 SAT and rank in top 5% required. Trustees Scholarship; $10,000; 25 ACT/1140 SAT and 3.7 GPA or 25 ACT/1140 SAT and rank of top 15% required. Dean's Scholarship; $7,500; 23 ACT/1060 SAT and 3.4 GPA or 23 ACT/1060 SAT and rank in the top 25% required. All SAT scores exclusive of Writing section. Heritage Award; $1,000-$4,000; based upon overall quality of admission application; available to selected underrepresented and underserved students. Scholars Award; up to $7,500; based on excellent academic achievement; available to those who have not received other merit-based scholarship. Griffiths Scholarship; $1,000-$8,000; based upon performance review and admission application; available to talented conservatory students. Director's Conservatory Talent Award; $1,000-$8,000; based upon performance review and admission application; available to talented conservatory students. Ministerial Award; up to 50% tuition award, in combination with any other award; based on status as child of United Methodist minister parents. Combined total university awards cannot exceed 75% of tuition.
Cumulative student debt: 82% of graduating class had student loans; average debt was $19,586.

FINANCIAL AID PROCEDURES

Forms required: FAFSA.
Dates and Deadlines: Priority date 5/1; closing date 9/1. Applicants notified on a rolling basis starting 2/14.
Transfers: Priority date 7/1; closing date 9/15. Applicants notified on a rolling basis starting 5/1.

CONTACT

George Rolleston, Director of Financial Aid
275 Eastland Road, Berea, OH 44017-2088
(440) 826-2108

Belmont Technical College

St. Clairsville, Ohio
www.btc.edu Federal Code: 009941

2-year public community and technical college in small town.
Enrollment: 1,798 undergrads.
Selectivity: Open admission; but selective for some programs.

BASIC COSTS (2008-2009)
Tuition and fees: $3,784; out-of-state residents $6,585.
Per-credit charge: $61; out-of-state residents $123.
Additional info: Tuition/fee waivers available for unemployed or children of unemployed.

FINANCIAL AID PICTURE (2007-2008)
Students with need: Need-based aid available for full-time and part-time students.
Students without need: No-need awards available for state/district residency.

FINANCIAL AID PROCEDURES
Forms required: FAFSA.
Dates and Deadlines: No deadline. Applicants notified on a rolling basis starting 6/1; must reply within 2 week(s) of notification.

CONTACT
Jody Peeler, Associate Dean of Financial Aid
120 Fox Shannon Place, St. Clairsville, OH 43950
(740) 695-9500 ext. 1029

Bluffton University
Bluffton, Ohio
www.bluffton.edu Federal Code: 003016

4-year private liberal arts college in small town, affiliated with Mennonite Church.
Enrollment: 957 undergrads, 3% part-time. 272 full-time freshmen.
Selectivity: Admits 50 to 75% of applicants.

BASIC COSTS (2009-2010)
Tuition and fees: $24,044.
Per-credit charge: $983.
Room and board: $7,970.
Additional info: Tuition/fee waivers available for minority students.

FINANCIAL AID PICTURE (2008-2009)
Students with need: Out of 261 full-time freshmen who applied for aid, 242 were judged to have need. Of these, 242 received aid, and 165 had their full need met. Average financial aid package met 97% of need; average scholarship/grant was $16,137; average loan was $4,682. For part-time students, average financial aid package was $12,389.
Students without need: 25 full-time freshmen who did not demonstrate need for aid received scholarships/grants; average award was $8,779. No-need awards available for academics, art, job skills, leadership, minority status, music/drama, state/district residency.
Scholarships offered: Academic distinction scholarship; tuition equalization scholarship plus $1,000; 3.5 GPA, 25 ACT or 1140 SAT required. Academic honors scholarship; tuition equalization scholarship plus $2,000; 27 ACT or 1220 SAT required. SAT scores exclusive of Writing. Tuition equalization is difference between tuition and fees at Bluffton and average tuition and fees at selected 4-year public institutions in Ohio during previous year.
Cumulative student debt: 86% of graduating class had student loans; average debt was $27,701.

FINANCIAL AID PROCEDURES
Forms required: FAFSA.
Dates and Deadlines: Priority date 6/1; closing date 10/1. Applicants notified on a rolling basis starting 3/1; must reply within 3 week(s) of notification.
Transfers: Institutional non-need-based aid for transfer students awarded based on test scores in combination with work at previous institutions and high school academic performance.

CONTACT
Mary Cannon, Director of Financial Aid
1 University Drive, Bluffton, OH 45817-2104
(419) 358-3266

Bohecker College
Ravenna, Ohio
www.boheckers.com Federal Code: 016270

2-year for-profit business college in large town.
Enrollment: 450 undergrads.
Selectivity: Admits over 75% of applicants.

BASIC COSTS (2008-2009)
Tuition and fees: $8,868.

FINANCIAL AID PICTURE
Students with need: Need-based aid available for full-time and part-time students.
Students without need: This college awards aid only to students with need.

FINANCIAL AID PROCEDURES
Forms required: FAFSA.
Dates and Deadlines: Applicants notified on a rolling basis.

CONTACT
Trudy Young, Financial Aid Director
326 East Main Street, Ravenna, OH 44266
(330) 297-7319

Bowling Green State University
Bowling Green, Ohio
www.bgsu.edu Federal Code: 003018

4-year public university in large town.
Enrollment: 14,596 undergrads, 6% part-time. 3,233 full-time freshmen.
Selectivity: Admits over 75% of applicants.

BASIC COSTS (2008-2009)
Tuition and fees: $9,060; out-of-state residents $16,368.
Per-credit charge: $380; out-of-state residents $729.
Room and board: $7,220.

FINANCIAL AID PICTURE (2007-2008)
Students with need: Out of 3,000 full-time freshmen who applied for aid, 2,231 were judged to have need. Of these, 2,163 received aid, and 313 had their full need met. Average financial aid package met 73% of need; average scholarship/grant was $6,213; average loan was $6,365. For part-time students, average financial aid package was $9,209.
Students without need: 310 full-time freshmen who did not demonstrate need for aid received scholarships/grants; average award was $4,011. No-need awards available for academics, alumni affiliation, art, athletics, leadership, minority status, music/drama, ROTC, state/district residency.
Scholarships offered: 82 full-time freshmen received athletic scholarships; average amount $15,531.
Cumulative student debt: 70% of graduating class had student loans; average debt was $26,860.

FINANCIAL AID PROCEDURES
Forms required: FAFSA.
Dates and Deadlines: No deadline. Applicants notified on a rolling basis starting 4/15; must reply within 3 week(s) of notification.

CONTACT
Gregory Guzman, Director
110 McFall Center, Bowling Green, OH 43403-0085
(419) 372-2651

Bowling Green State University: Firelands College

Huron, Ohio
www.firelands.bgsu.edu Federal Code: 003018

2-year public branch campus college in small town.
Enrollment: 1,697 undergrads.
Selectivity: Open admission.

BASIC COSTS (2008-2009)

Tuition and fees: $4,228; out-of-state residents $11,536.

FINANCIAL AID PICTURE (2007-2008)

Students with need: Need-based aid available for full-time and part-time students.
Students without need: This college awards aid only to students with need.
Scholarships offered: FOCUS Scholarship (Firelands Opportunities in College for Under-represented Students); full tuition; for historically under-represented students in all Firelands majors; 4-6 awards annually.
Additional info: Scholarship application deadline May 1. Technology computer loan program available. Based on need, students may receive computer on semester by semester loan basis.

FINANCIAL AID PROCEDURES

Forms required: FAFSA.
Dates and Deadlines: Priority date 3/1; no closing date. Applicants notified on a rolling basis starting 4/15; must reply within 2 week(s) of notification.

CONTACT

Debralee Divers, Director of Admissions and Financial Aid
One University Drive, Huron, OH 44839
(419) 433-5560

Bryant & Stratton College: Cleveland

Cleveland, Ohio
www.bryantstratton.edu Federal Code: 022744

2-year for-profit technical college in very large city.
Enrollment: 712 undergrads.
Selectivity: Open admission.

BASIC COSTS (2008-2009)

Tuition and fees: $13,775.
Per-credit charge: $458.

FINANCIAL AID PICTURE (2007-2008)

Students with need: Need-based aid available for full-time and part-time students. Work study available nights.
Students without need: No-need awards available for academics.

FINANCIAL AID PROCEDURES

Forms required: FAFSA, institutional form.
Dates and Deadlines: No deadline. Applicants notified on a rolling basis starting 5/1; must reply within 2 week(s) of notification.
Transfers: No deadline. By state regulation, Ohio Institutional Grant can be awarded only 3 times a fiscal year.

CONTACT

Donna McCullough, Director of Financial Services
1700 East 13th Street, Cleveland, OH 44114-3203
(216) 771-1700

Bryant & Stratton College: Eastlake

Eastlake, Ohio
www.bryantstratton.edu Federal Code: 022744

4-year for-profit business college in small town.
Enrollment: 709 undergrads.
Selectivity: Open admission.

BASIC COSTS (2008-2009)

Tuition and fees: $15,230.

FINANCIAL AID PICTURE (2007-2008)

Students with need: Need-based aid available for full-time and part-time students.
Students without need: No-need awards available for academics.

FINANCIAL AID PROCEDURES

Forms required: FAFSA.
Dates and Deadlines: No deadline. Applicants notified on a rolling basis.

CONTACT

Lisa Patterson, Financial Aid Manager
35350 Curtis Boulevard, Eastlake, OH 44095
(440) 510-1112

Capital University

Columbus, Ohio
www.capital.edu Federal Code: 003023

4-year private university in very large city, affiliated with Evangelical Lutheran Church in America.
Enrollment: 2,552 undergrads, 9% part-time. 629 full-time freshmen.
Selectivity: Admits over 75% of applicants.

BASIC COSTS (2008-2009)

Tuition and fees: $27,680.
Per-credit charge: $925.
Room and board: $7,150.

FINANCIAL AID PICTURE (2007-2008)

Students with need: Out of 579 full-time freshmen who applied for aid, 518 were judged to have need. Of these, 518 received aid, and 136 had their full need met. Average financial aid package met 23% of need; average scholarship/grant was $6,317; average loan was $2,820. For part-time students, average financial aid package was $20,993.
Students without need: 111 full-time freshmen who did not demonstrate need for aid received scholarships/grants; average award was $12,143. No-need awards available for academics, alumni affiliation, art, minority status, music/drama, religious affiliation, ROTC, state/district residency.
Scholarships offered: Scholarships and grants from $1,000 to full tuition available.
Cumulative student debt: 85% of graduating class had student loans; average debt was $23,550.

FINANCIAL AID PROCEDURES

Forms required: FAFSA.
Dates and Deadlines: Priority date 2/28; no closing date. Applicants notified on a rolling basis starting 3/1; must reply by 5/1.
Transfers: Priority date 7/15.

CONTACT

Pamela Varda, Director of Financial Aid
1 College and Main, Columbus, OH 43209-2394
(614) 236-6511

Case Western Reserve University

Cleveland, Ohio
www.case.edu Federal Code: E00077

4-year private university in very large city.
Enrollment: 4,267 undergrads, 2% part-time. 1,026 full-time freshmen.
Selectivity: Admits 50 to 75% of applicants.

BASIC COSTS (2009-2010)

Tuition and fees: $36,238.
Per-credit charge: $1,496.
Room and board: $10,890.

FINANCIAL AID PICTURE (2008-2009)

Students with need: Out of 912 full-time freshmen who applied for aid, 761 were judged to have need. Of these, 730 received aid, and 658 had their full need met. Average financial aid package met 88% of need; average scholarship/grant was $23,465; average loan was $6,898. Need-based aid available for part-time students.
Students without need: 189 full-time freshmen who did not demonstrate need for aid received scholarships/grants; average award was $20,329. No-need awards available for academics, art, leadership, music/drama.

FINANCIAL AID PROCEDURES

Forms required: FAFSA, institutional form.
Dates and Deadlines: Priority date 2/1; no closing date. Applicants notified on a rolling basis starting 2/15; must reply by 5/1 or within 2 week(s) of notification.
Transfers: Priority date 5/15.

CONTACT

Donald Chenelle, Director of University Financial Aid
Wolstein Hall, Cleveland, OH 44106 7055
(216) 368-4530

Cedarville University

Cedarville, Ohio
www.cedarville.edu Federal Code: 003025

4-year private university and liberal arts college in small town, affiliated with Baptist faith.
Enrollment: 2,940 undergrads, 2% part-time. 867 full-time freshmen.

BASIC COSTS (2008-2009)

Tuition and fees: $20,992.
Per-credit charge: $656.
Room and board: $5,010.

FINANCIAL AID PICTURE (2007-2008)

Students with need: Out of 701 full-time freshmen who applied for aid, 558 were judged to have need. Of these, 554 received aid, and 280 had their full need met. Average financial aid package met 31% of need; average scholarship/grant was $2,801; average loan was $3,178. For part-time students, average financial aid package was $12,369.
Students without need: 215 full-time freshmen who did not demonstrate need for aid received scholarships/grants; average award was $9,149. No-need awards available for academics, alumni affiliation, athletics, leadership, minority status, music/drama, ROTC, state/district residency.
Scholarships offered: 49 full-time freshmen received athletic scholarships; average amount $2,539.
Cumulative student debt: 66% of graduating class had student loans; average debt was $23,151.

FINANCIAL AID PROCEDURES

Forms required: FAFSA.
Dates and Deadlines: Priority date 3/1; no closing date. Applicants notified on a rolling basis starting 3/1; must reply within 4 week(s) of notification.
Transfers: No deadline. Applicants notified on a rolling basis starting 2/1.

CONTACT

Fred Merritt, Director of Financial Aid
251 North Main Street, Cedarville, OH 45314
(937) 766-7866

Central Ohio Technical College

Newark, Ohio
www.cotc.edu Federal Code: 011046

2-year public technical college in large town.
Enrollment: 3,110 undergrads.
Selectivity: Open admission; but selective for some programs.

BASIC COSTS (2008-2009)

Tuition and fees: $3,600; out-of-state residents $6,300.
Per-credit charge: $76; out-of-state residents $151.

FINANCIAL AID PICTURE (2007-2008)

Students with need: Need-based aid available for full-time and part-time students. Work study available nights, weekends, and for part-time students.
Students without need: No-need awards available for academics.
Scholarships offered: Presidential Achievement Award; $1,800 annually; based on 3.0 GPA; 5 awarded. Minority Achievement Award; $850 annually; based on 2.5 GPA; 2 awarded.

FINANCIAL AID PROCEDURES

Forms required: FAFSA.
Dates and Deadlines: Priority date 3/1; no closing date. Applicants notified on a rolling basis starting 5/1; must reply within 3 week(s) of notification.

CONTACT

Faith Phillips, Director of Financial Aid
1179 University Drive, Newark, OH 43055
(740) 366-9435

Central State University

Wilberforce, Ohio
www.centralstate.edu Federal Code: 003026

4-year public university and liberal arts college in rural community.
Enrollment: 2,107 undergrads, 7% part-time. 646 full-time freshmen.
Selectivity: Admits less than 50% of applicants.

BASIC COSTS (2008-2009)

Tuition and fees: $5,294; out-of-state residents $11,462.
Room and board: $7,402.

FINANCIAL AID PICTURE (2008-2009)

Students with need: Need-based aid available for full-time and part-time students. Work study available nights, weekends, and for part-time students.
Students without need: No-need awards available for academics, alumni affiliation, art, athletics, leadership, music/drama, religious affiliation, ROTC.

FINANCIAL AID PROCEDURES

Forms required: FAFSA, institutional form.
Dates and Deadlines: Priority date 2/15; no closing date. Applicants notified on a rolling basis starting 5/1.
Transfers: No deadline.

CONTACT

Phyllis Jeffers-Coly, Dean, Student Enrollment Services
PO Box 1004, Wilberforce, OH 45384-1004
(937) 376-6579

Chatfield College
St. Martin, Ohio
www.chatfield.edu Federal Code: 010880

2-year private liberal arts college in rural community, affiliated with Roman Catholic Church.
Enrollment: 248 undergrads, 42% part-time. 56 full-time freshmen.
Selectivity: Open admission.

BASIC COSTS (2008-2009)
Tuition and fees: $9,190.

FINANCIAL AID PICTURE
Students with need: Need-based aid available for full-time and part-time students.
Students without need: No-need awards available for academics, leadership.
Additional info: Institutional grants/scholarships given primarily to first-year students to reduce debt load during initial year.

FINANCIAL AID PROCEDURES
Forms required: FAFSA, institutional form.
Dates and Deadlines: Priority date 5/1; closing date 8/3. Applicants notified on a rolling basis starting 4/1; must reply within 2 week(s) of notification.

CONTACT
Zana Smith, Student Financial Services Officer
20918 State Route 251, St. Martin, OH 45118
(513) 875-3344

Cincinnati Christian University
Cincinnati, Ohio
www.ccuniversity.edu Federal Code: 003029

4-year private university in very large city, affiliated with Church of Christ/Christian Church.
Enrollment: 800 undergrads, 18% part-time. 241 full-time freshmen.
Selectivity: Admits over 75% of applicants.

BASIC COSTS (2008-2009)
Tuition and fees: $12,143.
Per-credit charge: $368.
Room and board: $6,350.

FINANCIAL AID PICTURE (2007-2008)
Students with need: Out of 152 full-time freshmen who applied for aid, 126 were judged to have need. Of these, 123 received aid, and 25 had their full need met. Average financial aid package met 52% of need; average scholarship/grant was $4,838; average loan was $3,830. For part-time students, average financial aid package was $6,507.
Students without need: 62 full-time freshmen who did not demonstrate need for aid received scholarships/grants; average award was $2,269. No-need awards available for academics, athletics, leadership, music/drama, religious affiliation, state/district residency.

FINANCIAL AID PROCEDURES
Forms required: FAFSA.
Dates and Deadlines: Priority date 3/1; no closing date. Applicants notified on a rolling basis starting 4/1; must reply within 2 week(s) of notification.
Transfers: No deadline.

CONTACT
Michael Gibboney, Financial Aid Director
2700 Glenway Avenue, Cincinnati, OH 45204-3200
(513) 244-8100 ext. 8450

Cincinnati College of Mortuary Science
Cincinnati, Ohio
www.ccms.edu Federal Code: 010906

4-year private school of mortuary science in large city.
Enrollment: 100 undergrads.
Selectivity: Open admission.

BASIC COSTS (2008-2009)
Tuition and fees: $8,775.
Per-credit charge: $195.
Additional info: Tuition for 4-qtr. A.A.S. $14,625; 5-qtr. B.M.S. $17,550; 6-qtr. A.A.S. $19,695. Books and supplies for 4 quarter students $1,400; 6 quarter students $1,800; 5th quarter only $100.

FINANCIAL AID PICTURE (2008-2009)
Students with need: 24% of average financial aid package awarded as scholarships/grants, 76% awarded as loans/jobs. Need-based aid available for part-time students.
Students without need: This college awards aid only to students with need.

FINANCIAL AID PROCEDURES
Forms required: FAFSA.
Dates and Deadlines: Priority date 7/1; no closing date. Applicants notified on a rolling basis starting 3/1; must reply within 2 week(s) of notification.

CONTACT
Gail Warnemunde, Financial Aid Director
645 West North Bend Road, Cincinnati, OH 45224-1428
(513) 618-1926

Cincinnati State Technical and Community College
Cincinnati, Ohio
www.cincinnatistate.edu Federal Code: 010345

2-year public community and technical college in large city.
Enrollment: 7,325 undergrads, 55% part-time. 1,369 full-time freshmen.
Selectivity: Open admission; but selective for some programs.

BASIC COSTS (2008-2009)
Tuition and fees: $3,867; out-of-state residents $7,476.
Per-credit charge: $80; out-of-state residents $160.

FINANCIAL AID PICTURE (2007-2008)
Students with need: 54% of average financial aid package awarded as scholarships/grants, 46% awarded as loans/jobs. Need-based aid available for part-time students. Work study available nights, weekends, and for part-time students.
Students without need: No-need awards available for academics, athletics, state/district residency.

FINANCIAL AID PROCEDURES
Forms required: FAFSA.
Dates and Deadlines: Priority date 2/15; no closing date. Applicants notified on a rolling basis starting 3/15; must reply within 4 week(s) of notification.

CONTACT
Dawn Smith, Director of Student Financial Aid/Scholarships
3520 Central Parkway, Cincinnati, OH 45223-2690
(513) 569-1530

Clark State Community College
Springfield, Ohio
www.clarkstate.edu Federal Code: 004852

2-year public community college in small city.
Enrollment: 1,250 full-time undergrads.
Selectivity: Open admission; but selective for some programs.

BASIC COSTS (2008-2009)
Tuition and fees: $3,485; out-of-state residents $6,432.
Per-credit charge: $66; out-of-state residents $131.

FINANCIAL AID PICTURE
Students with need: Work study available nights, weekends, and for part-time students.

FINANCIAL AID PROCEDURES
Forms required: FAFSA.
Dates and Deadlines: Priority date 6/15; no closing date. Applicants notified on a rolling basis.

CONTACT
Kathy Klay, Director of Financial Aid
Box 570, Springfield, OH 45501-0570
(937) 328-6034

Cleveland Institute of Art
Cleveland, Ohio
www.cia.edu Federal Code: 003982

4-year private visual arts college in very large city.
Enrollment: 492 undergrads, 1% part-time. 101 full-time freshmen.
Selectivity: Admits over 75% of applicants.

BASIC COSTS (2009-2010)
Tuition and fees: $31,904.
Per-credit charge: $1,250.
Room and board: $10,536.

FINANCIAL AID PICTURE (2008-2009)
Students with need: Out of 93 full-time freshmen who applied for aid, 86 were judged to have need. Of these, 86 received aid, and 14 had their full need met. Average financial aid package met 71% of need; average scholarship/grant was $17,599; average loan was $4,707. For part-time students, average financial aid package was $10,500.
Students without need: 15 full-time freshmen who did not demonstrate need for aid received scholarships/grants; average award was $11,714. No-need awards available for academics, art.

FINANCIAL AID PROCEDURES
Forms required: FAFSA, institutional form.
Dates and Deadlines: Priority date 3/15; no closing date. Applicants notified on a rolling basis starting 3/16; must reply within 4 week(s) of notification.

CONTACT
Sheila Cowman, Director of Admissions and Financial Aid
11141 East Boulevard, Cleveland, OH 44106-1710
(216) 421-7425

Cleveland Institute of Electronics
Cleveland, Ohio
www.cie-wc.edu Federal Code: 015382

2-year for-profit technical college in very large city.
Enrollment: 1,856 undergrads.
Selectivity: Open admission.

BASIC COSTS (2008-2009)
Tuition and fees: $3,770.
Additional info: Associate degree tuition $1,885 per 6-month term.

FINANCIAL AID PICTURE (2008-2009)
Students with need: Need-based aid available for full-time students.
Students without need: This college awards aid only to students with need.

FINANCIAL AID PROCEDURES
Forms required: FAFSA.
Dates and Deadlines: No deadline.

CONTACT
Scott Meyer, Director of Financial Aid
1776 East 17th Street, Cleveland, OH 44114-3679
(216) 781-9400

Cleveland Institute of Music
Cleveland, Ohio
www.cim.edu Federal Code: 003031

4-year private music college in very large city.
Enrollment: 230 undergrads.

BASIC COSTS (2009-2010)
Tuition and fees: $36,674.
Per-credit charge: $1,406.
Room and board: $10,567.

FINANCIAL AID PICTURE (2007-2008)
Students with need: Need-based aid available for full-time and part-time students.
Students without need: No-need awards available for academics, music/drama.

FINANCIAL AID PROCEDURES
Forms required: FAFSA, institutional form.
Dates and Deadlines: Priority date 2/15; no closing date. Applicants notified on a rolling basis starting 4/1; must reply by 5/1 or within 2 week(s) of notification.
Transfers: Applicants notified on a rolling basis starting 4/1; must reply by 5/1 or within 2 week(s) of notification.

CONTACT
Kristie Gripp, Director of Financial Aid
11021 East Boulevard, Cleveland, OH 44106
(216) 795 3192

Cleveland State University
Cleveland, Ohio
www.csuohio.edu Federal Code: 003032

4-year public university in very large city.
Enrollment: 9,375 undergrads, 25% part-time. 1,016 full-time freshmen.
Selectivity: Admits 50 to 75% of applicants.

BASIC COSTS (2009-2010)
Tuition and fees: $7,970; out-of-state residents $10,774.
Per-credit charge: $330; out-of-state residents $444.
Room and board: $8,700.

FINANCIAL AID PICTURE (2008-2009)

Students with need: Out of 723 full-time freshmen who applied for aid, 642 were judged to have need. Of these, 626 received aid, and 52 had their full need met. Average financial aid package met 48% of need; average scholarship/grant was $5,994; average loan was $3,270. For part-time students, average financial aid package was $6,231.
Students without need: 100 full-time freshmen who did not demonstrate need for aid received scholarships/grants; average award was $7,954. No-need awards available for academics, alumni affiliation, art, athletics, leadership, minority status, music/drama, religious affiliation, ROTC.
Scholarships offered: 36 full-time freshmen received athletic scholarships; average amount $9,701.

FINANCIAL AID PROCEDURES

Forms required: FAFSA.
Dates and Deadlines: Priority date 2/15; no closing date. Applicants notified on a rolling basis starting 3/15; must reply within 4 week(s) of notification.

CONTACT

Rachel Schmidt, Director of Financial Aid
2121 Euclid Avenue, Cleveland, OH 44115-2214
(888) 278-6446

College of Mount St. Joseph

Cincinnati, Ohio
www.msj.edu Federal Code: 003033

4-year private liberal arts college in very large city, affiliated with Roman Catholic Church.
Enrollment: 1,817 undergrads, 27% part-time. 300 full-time freshmen.
Selectivity: Admits 50 to 75% of applicants.

BASIC COSTS (2009-2010)

Tuition and fees: $22,800.
Per-credit charge: $465.
Room and board: $7,152.

FINANCIAL AID PICTURE (2008-2009)

Students with need: Out of 282 full-time freshmen who applied for aid, 247 were judged to have need. Of these, 247 received aid, and 40 had their full need met. Average financial aid package met 84% of need; average scholarship/grant was $13,901; average loan was $3,908. For part-time students, average financial aid package was $7,230.
Students without need: 52 full-time freshmen who did not demonstrate need for aid received scholarships/grants; average award was $6,020. No-need awards available for academics, art, leadership, music/drama, ROTC, state/district residency.
Scholarships offered: Presidential Scholarship; $11,000; 26-36 ACT or 1170 SAT. Trustee Scholarship; $10,000; 24-25 ACT or 1090 SAT. Dean's Scholarship; $9,000; 22-23 ACT or 1020 SAT. Merit Award; $7,500; 20-21 ACT or 940 SAT. Challenge Award; $3,500 per semester; 18-19 ACT or 860 SAT. Director's Award; $3,500 per semester; 21 ACT or 990 SAT and 2.75 high school GPA. Transfer Scholarship; $5,000; 3.0 college GPA with at least 24 hours earned. All SAT scores exclusive of Writing.
Cumulative student debt: 81% of graduating class had student loans; average debt was $29,438.

FINANCIAL AID PROCEDURES

Forms required: FAFSA.
Dates and Deadlines: Priority date 3/1; no closing date. Applicants notified on a rolling basis starting 2/15; must reply by 5/1 or within 4 week(s) of notification.
Transfers: Applicants notified on a rolling basis starting 2/15; must reply within 4 week(s) of notification.

CONTACT

Kathryn Kelly, Director of Student Administrative Services
5701 Delhi Road, Cincinnati, OH 45233-1670
(513) 244-4418

College of Wooster

Wooster, Ohio Federal Code: 003037
www.wooster.edu CSS Code: 1134

4-year private liberal arts college in large town.
Enrollment: 1,868 undergrads. 514 full-time freshmen.
Selectivity: Admits over 75% of applicants.

BASIC COSTS (2008-2009)

Tuition and fees: $33,770.
Room and board: $8,650.

FINANCIAL AID PICTURE (2008-2009)

Students with need: Out of 388 full-time freshmen who applied for aid, 318 were judged to have need. Of these, 318 received aid, and 170 had their full need met. Average financial aid package met 92% of need; average scholarship/grant was $22,343; average loan was $4,495. For part-time students, average financial aid package was $2,750.
Students without need: 170 full-time freshmen who did not demonstrate need for aid received scholarships/grants; average award was $15,935. No-need awards available for academics, minority status, music/drama, religious affiliation, state/district residency.
Cumulative student debt: 63% of graduating class had student loans; average debt was $29,815.

FINANCIAL AID PROCEDURES

Forms required: FAFSA, institutional form. Either CSS PROFILE or institution application from prospectives.
Dates and Deadlines: Priority date 2/15; no closing date. Applicants notified by 4/1; must reply by 5/1.

CONTACT

David Miller, Director of Financial Aid
847 College Avenue, Wooster, OH 44691-2363
(330) 263-2317

Columbus College of Art and Design

Columbus, Ohio
www.ccad.edu Federal Code: 003039

4-year private visual arts college in very large city.
Enrollment: 1,391 undergrads, 5% part-time. 168 full-time freshmen.
Selectivity: Admits 50 to 75% of applicants.

BASIC COSTS (2008-2009)

Tuition and fees: $23,564.
Per-credit charge: $955.
Room and board: $6,750.

FINANCIAL AID PICTURE (2008-2009)

Students with need: Average financial aid package met 65% of need; average scholarship/grant was $13,620; average loan was $5,085. For part-time students, average financial aid package was $13,439.
Students without need: No-need awards available for academics, art, ROTC, state/district residency.

FINANCIAL AID PROCEDURES

Forms required: FAFSA.
Dates and Deadlines: Priority date 3/2; closing date 6/4. Applicants notified on a rolling basis starting 3/15; must reply within 2 week(s) of notification.

CONTACT

Anna Marie Schofield, Director of Financial Aid
107 North Ninth Street, Columbus, OH 43215-3875
(614) 222-3274

Columbus State Community College

Columbus, Ohio
www.cscc.edu Federal Code: 006867

2-year public community and technical college in very large city.
Enrollment: 13,060 undergrads.
Selectivity: Open admission; but selective for some programs.

BASIC COSTS (2008-2009)

Tuition and fees: $3,555; out-of-state residents $7,875.
Per-credit charge: $70; out-of-state residents $166.

FINANCIAL AID PICTURE

Students with need: Need-based aid available for full-time and part-time students. Work study available nights, weekends, and for part-time students.
Students without need: No-need awards available for athletics, state/district residency.

FINANCIAL AID PROCEDURES

Forms required: FAFSA.
Dates and Deadlines: Priority date 7/24; no closing date. Applicants notified on a rolling basis starting 4/1.

CONTACT

David Metz, Director of Financial Aid
550 East Spring Street, Columbus, OH 43216-1609
(614) 287-2648

Cuyahoga Community College: Metropolitan Campus

Cleveland, Ohio
www.tri-c.edu Federal Code: 003040

2-year public community college in very large city.
Enrollment: 10,339 undergrads, 54% part-time. 1,486 full-time freshmen.
Selectivity: Open admission; but selective for some programs.

BASIC COSTS (2008-2009)

Tuition and fees: $2,416; out-of-district residents $3,194; out-of-state residents $6,541.
Per-credit charge: $73; out-of-district residents $99; out-of-state residents $210.

FINANCIAL AID PICTURE (2008-2009)

Students with need: Average financial aid package met 100% of need; average scholarship/grant was $5,987; average loan was $2,931. For part-time students, average financial aid package was $5,275.
Students without need: No-need awards available for academics, art, athletics, leadership, minority status, music/drama.
Cumulative student debt: 20% of graduating class had student loans; average debt was $8,063.

FINANCIAL AID PROCEDURES

Forms required: FAFSA, institutional form.
Dates and Deadlines: No deadline. Applicants notified on a rolling basis starting 5/8.
Transfers: Priority date 5/8.

CONTACT

Angela Johnson, Campus Director
2900 Community College Avenue, Cleveland, OH 44115-2878
(216) 987-4100

Davis College

Toledo, Ohio
www.daviscollege.edu Federal Code: 004855

2-year for-profit junior college in large city.
Enrollment: 477 undergrads, 57% part-time. 28 full-time freshmen.
Selectivity: Admits over 75% of applicants.

BASIC COSTS (2008-2009)

Tuition and fees: $11,145.
Per-credit charge: $237.

FINANCIAL AID PICTURE (2007-2008)

Students with need: Out of 28 full-time freshmen who applied for aid, 28 were judged to have need. Of these, 27 received aid, and 22 had their full need met. Average financial aid package met 89% of need. Need-based aid available for part-time students.
Students without need: This college awards aid only to students with need.

FINANCIAL AID PROCEDURES

Forms required: FAFSA.
Dates and Deadlines: No deadline. Applicants notified on a rolling basis.

CONTACT

Kelly Parker, Director of Financial Aid
4747 Monroe Street, Toledo, OH 43623
(419) 473-2700

Defiance College

Defiance, Ohio
www.defiance.edu Federal Code: 003041

4-year private liberal arts college in large town, affiliated with United Church of Christ.
Enrollment: 891 undergrads, 19% part-time. 218 full-time freshmen.
Selectivity: Admits 50 to 75% of applicants.

BASIC COSTS (2009-2010)

Tuition and fees: $22,895.
Per-credit charge: $360.
Room and board: $7,750.
Additional info: Tuition/fee waivers available for adults.

FINANCIAL AID PICTURE (2007-2008)

Students with need: Need-based aid available for full-time and part-time students. Work study available nights, weekends, and for part-time students.
Students without need: No-need awards available for academics, leadership.
Scholarships offered: Presidential Scholar Program; $11,000-full tuition; based on 3.5 GPA, 27 ACT/1210 SAT, and interview. Pilgrim Scholar Program; $10,000-$15,000; based on 3.2 GPA, 24 ACT/1090 SAT, and interview. Achievement Scholar Program; $9,000-$12,000; based on 2,8 GPA, 21 ACT/980 SAT, and interview. Defiance College Scholarship; $4,000-$10,000; based on 2.5-4.0 GPA and 18-36 ACT/850-1600 SAT. Citizen Leader Award; $2,000; awarded to students with demonstrated record of service in their communities; application and interview required. Lillian Rae Dunlap Award; $1,000; minimum 2.25 GPA; recognizes and rewards the achievements of under-represented student population.

FINANCIAL AID PROCEDURES

Forms required: FAFSA.
Dates and Deadlines: Priority date 3/1; no closing date. Applicants notified on a rolling basis starting 3/15; must reply within 3 week(s) of notification.

CONTACT
Amy Francis, Director of Financial Aid
701 North Clinton Street, Defiance, OH 43512-1695
(419) 782-458

Denison University
Granville, Ohio
www.denison.edu Federal Code: 003042

4-year private liberal arts college in small town.
Enrollment: 2,180 undergrads. 605 full-time freshmen.
Selectivity: Admits less than 50% of applicants.

BASIC COSTS (2009-2010)
Tuition and fees: $36,560.
Per-credit charge: $1,115.
Room and board: $9,160.
Additional info: Tuition/fee waivers available for adults.

FINANCIAL AID PICTURE (2008-2009)
Students with need: Out of 373 full-time freshmen who applied for aid, 290 were judged to have need. Of these, 290 received aid, and 232 had their full need met. Average financial aid package met 97% of need; average scholarship/grant was $26,212; average loan was $3,734. Need-based aid available for part-time students.
Students without need: 282 full-time freshmen who did not demonstrate need for aid received scholarships/grants; average award was $15,486. No-need awards available for academics, art, leadership, music/drama, state/district residency.

FINANCIAL AID PROCEDURES
Forms required: FAFSA.
Dates and Deadlines: Priority date 2/15; no closing date. Applicants notified by 3/30; must reply by 5/1 or within 2 week(s) of notification.

CONTACT
Nancy Hoover, Director of Financial Aid and Student Employment
Box H, Granville, OH 43023
(740) 587-6279

DeVry University: Columbus
Columbus, Ohio
www.devry.edu Federal Code: 003099

4-year for-profit university in very large city.
Enrollment: 2,520 undergrads, 41% part-time. 335 full-time freshmen.

BASIC COSTS (2008-2009)
Tuition and fees: $14,130.
Per-credit charge: $515.

FINANCIAL AID PICTURE (2007-2008)
Students with need: Need-based aid available for full-time and part-time students.
Students without need: This college awards aid only to students with need.

FINANCIAL AID PROCEDURES
Forms required: FAFSA.
Dates and Deadlines: No deadline. Applicants notified on a rolling basis.

CONTACT
Cynthia Price, Director of Financial Aid
1350 Alum Creek Drive, Columbus, OH 43209-2705
(614) 253-7291

Edison State Community College
Piqua, Ohio
www.edisonohio.edu Federal Code: 012750

2-year public community college in large town.
Enrollment: 2,249 undergrads, 57% part-time. 363 full-time freshmen.
Selectivity: Open admission; but selective for some programs.

BASIC COSTS (2008-2009)
Tuition and fees: $3,450; out-of-state residents $6,420.
Per-credit charge: $99; out-of-state residents $198.

FINANCIAL AID PICTURE
Students with need: Need-based aid available for full-time and part-time students. Work study available nights, weekends, and for part-time students.
Students without need: No-need awards available for academics, art, athletics.

FINANCIAL AID PROCEDURES
Forms required: FAFSA, institutional form.
Dates and Deadlines: Priority date 5/2; no closing date. Applicants notified on a rolling basis starting 5/15.

CONTACT
Kathi Richards, Director of Student Financial Aid
1973 Edison Drive, Piqua, OH 45356-9253
(937) 778-7910

ETI Technical College of Niles
Niles, Ohio
www.eticollege.edu Federal Code: 030790

2-year for-profit technical college in large city.
Enrollment: 188 undergrads, 12% part-time. 86 full-time freshmen.
Selectivity: Open admission; but selective for some programs.

BASIC COSTS (2008-2009)
Tuition and fees: $7,600.
Per-credit charge: $236.
Additional info: Full-time tuition varies by program: $7114-$7,632. Tuition at time of enrollment locked for 2 years.

FINANCIAL AID PICTURE (2008-2009)
Students with need: Average financial aid package for all full-time undergraduates was $8,800. 32% awarded as scholarships/grants, 68% awarded as loans/jobs. Need-based aid available for part-time students.

FINANCIAL AID PROCEDURES
Forms required: FAFSA.
Dates and Deadlines: No deadline. Applicants notified on a rolling basis; must reply within 16 week(s) of notification.
Transfers: No deadline.

CONTACT
Kay Madigan, Financial Aid Director
2076 Youngstown Warren Road, Niles, OH 44446-4398
(330) 652-9919

Franciscan University of Steubenville
Steubenville, Ohio
www.franciscan.edu Federal Code: 003036

4-year private university in large town, affiliated with Roman Catholic Church.
Enrollment: 2,002 undergrads.
Selectivity: Admits 50 to 75% of applicants.

BASIC COSTS (2009-2010)
Tuition and fees: $19,650.
Per-credit charge: $645.
Room and board: $6,750.

FINANCIAL AID PICTURE (2007-2008)
Students with need: 44% of average financial aid package awarded as scholarships/grants, 56% awarded as loans/jobs. Need-based aid available for part-time students. Work study available nights, weekends, and for part-time students.
Students without need: No-need awards available for academics, leadership, religious affiliation.

FINANCIAL AID PROCEDURES
Forms required: FAFSA.
Dates and Deadlines: No deadline. Applicants notified on a rolling basis starting 3/15; must reply within 3 week(s) of notification.
Transfers: Closing date 8/1.

CONTACT
John Herrmann, Director of Student Financial Services
1235 University Boulevard, Steubenville, OH 43952-1763
(740) 283-6211

Franklin University
Columbus, Ohio
www.franklin.edu Federal Code: 003046

4-year private university and business college in very large city.
Enrollment: 7,688 undergrads.
Selectivity: Open admission; but selective for some programs.

BASIC COSTS (2008-2009)
Tuition and fees: $8,400.
Per-credit charge: $280.

FINANCIAL AID PICTURE (2007-2008)
Students with need: Need-based aid available for full-time and part-time students.
Students without need: No-need awards available for academics, leadership, minority status.

FINANCIAL AID PROCEDURES
Forms required: FAFSA.
Dates and Deadlines: Priority date 6/15; no closing date. Applicants notified on a rolling basis; must reply within 2 week(s) of notification.
Transfers: One scholarship specifically for transfer students: Transfer Achievement.

CONTACT
Goldie Langley, Director of Financial Aid
201 South Grant Avenue, Columbus, OH 43215-5399
(614) 797-4700

Gallipolis Career College
Gallipolis, Ohio
www.gallipoliscareercollege.com Federal Code: 030079

2-year for-profit business and technical college in small town.
Enrollment: 147 undergrads.
Selectivity: Open admission.

BASIC COSTS (2008-2009)
Tuition and fees: $9,650.
Per-credit charge: $200.

FINANCIAL AID PICTURE (2007-2008)
Students with need: 67% of average financial aid package awarded as scholarships/grants, 33% awarded as loans/jobs. Need-based aid available for part-time students.
Students without need: This college awards aid only to students with need.

FINANCIAL AID PROCEDURES
Forms required: FAFSA, institutional form.
Dates and Deadlines: No deadline.

CONTACT
Jeanette Shirey, Financial Aid Administrator
1176 Jackson Pike, Suite 312, Gallipolis, OH 45631
(740) 446-4367

God's Bible School and College
Cincinnati, Ohio
www.gbs.edu Federal Code: 015691

4-year private Bible college in large city, affiliated with interdenominational tradition.
Enrollment: 278 undergrads.
Selectivity: Open admission.

BASIC COSTS (2009-2010)
Tuition and fees: $5,580.
Per-credit charge: $185.
Room and board: $3,450.

FINANCIAL AID PICTURE (2008-2009)
Students with need: 71% of average financial aid package awarded as scholarships/grants, 29% awarded as loans/jobs. Need-based aid available for part-time students.
Students without need: No-need awards available for academics, leadership, music/drama, religious affiliation.
Additional info: Institutional work scholarships available.

FINANCIAL AID PROCEDURES
Forms required: FAFSA.
Dates and Deadlines: Priority date 4/30; no closing date. Applicants notified on a rolling basis.

CONTACT
Stephen Buckland, Director of Financial Aid
1810 Young Street, Cincinnati, OH 45202-6838
(513) 721-7944 ext. 205

Heidelberg University
Tiffin, Ohio
www.heidelberg.edu Federal Code: 003048

4-year private liberal arts college in large town, affiliated with United Church of Christ.
Enrollment: 1,255 undergrads, 5% part-time. 390 full-time freshmen.
Selectivity: Admits 50 to 75% of applicants.

BASIC COSTS (2009-2010)
Tuition and fees: $21,330.
Per-credit charge: $595.
Room and board: $8,138.

FINANCIAL AID PICTURE (2008-2009)

Students with need: Out of 368 full-time freshmen who applied for aid, 328 were judged to have need. Of these, 328 received aid, and 90 had their full need met. Average financial aid package met 84% of need; average scholarship/grant was $13,019; average loan was $4,079. Need-based aid available for part-time students.

Students without need: 30 full-time freshmen who did not demonstrate need for aid received scholarships/grants; average award was $8,833. No-need awards available for academics, music/drama, religious affiliation, state/district residency.

Cumulative student debt: 74% of graduating class had student loans; average debt was $30,589.

FINANCIAL AID PROCEDURES

Forms required: FAFSA.

Dates and Deadlines: Priority date 3/1; no closing date. Applicants notified on a rolling basis starting 3/15; must reply by 5/1 or within 2 week(s) of notification.

CONTACT

Juli Weininger, Director of Financial Aid
310 East Market Street, Tiffin, OH 44883-2462
(419) 448-2293

Hiram College

Hiram, Ohio
www.hiram.edu Federal Code: 003049

4-year private liberal arts college in rural community, affiliated with Christian Church (Disciples of Christ).

Enrollment: 1,313 undergrads, 14% part-time. 331 full-time freshmen.

Selectivity: Admits over 75% of applicants.

BASIC COSTS (2009-2010)

Tuition and fees: $27,135.

Room and board: $9,010.

Additional info: Tuition at time of enrollment locked for 4 years.

FINANCIAL AID PICTURE (2008-2009)

Students with need: 52% of average financial aid package awarded as scholarships/grants, 48% awarded as loans/jobs. Need-based aid available for part-time students. Work study available nights, weekends, and for part-time students.

Students without need: No-need awards available for academics, alumni affiliation, music/drama, religious affiliation, state/district residency.

Cumulative student debt: 78% of graduating class had student loans; average debt was $21,247.

FINANCIAL AID PROCEDURES

Forms required: FAFSA.

Dates and Deadlines: Priority date 2/15; no closing date. Applicants notified on a rolling basis starting 2/15; must reply by 5/1 or within 2 week(s) of notification.

Transfers: Transfer merit scholarships available. Phi Theta Kappa scholarships available.

CONTACT

Andrea Caputo, Director of Student Financial Aid
Teachout Price Hall, Hiram, OH 44234
(330) 569-5107

Hocking College

Nelsonville, Ohio
www.hocking.edu Federal Code: 007598

2-year public technical college in small town.

Enrollment: 4,235 undergrads, 24% part-time. 1,233 full-time freshmen.

Selectivity: Open admission; but selective for some programs.

BASIC COSTS (2008-2009)

Tuition and fees: $3,546; out-of-state residents $7,092.

Per-credit charge: $68; out-of-state residents $167.

FINANCIAL AID PICTURE (2007-2008)

Students with need: Out of 1,094 full-time freshmen who applied for aid, 892 were judged to have need. Of these, 892 received aid. Need-based aid available for part-time students.

Students without need: 49 full-time freshmen who did not demonstrate need for aid received scholarships/grants; average award was $524. No-need awards available for academics, minority status, state/district residency.

FINANCIAL AID PROCEDURES

Forms required: FAFSA, institutional form.

Dates and Deadlines: Priority date 2/28; no closing date. Applicants notified on a rolling basis starting 4/15.

Transfers: Non-entitlement aid awarded on first-come, first-serve basis.

CONTACT

Roger Springer, Financial Services Director
3301 Hocking Parkway, Nelsonville, OH 45764-9704
(740) 753-7080

International College of Broadcasting

Dayton, Ohio
www.icbcollege.com Federal Code: 013132

2-year for-profit technical college in small city.

Enrollment: 105 undergrads.

Selectivity: Open admission.

BASIC COSTS (2008-2009)

Tuition and fees: $10,395.

Per-credit charge: $362.

FINANCIAL AID PICTURE

Students with need: Need-based aid available for full-time and part-time students.

FINANCIAL AID PROCEDURES

Forms required: FAFSA.

Dates and Deadlines: No deadline. Applicants notified on a rolling basis starting 11/1.

CONTACT

Zena Williams, Financial Aid Director
6 South Smithville Road, Dayton, OH 45431
(937) 258-8251 ext. 203

James A. Rhodes State College

Lima, Ohio
www.rhodesstate.edu Federal Code: 010027

2-year public nursing and technical college in large town.

Enrollment: 3,369 undergrads, 42% part-time.

Selectivity: Open admission; but selective for some programs.

BASIC COSTS (2008-2009)

Tuition and fees: $4,229; out-of-state residents $8,382.
Per-credit charge: $76; out-of-state residents $168.

FINANCIAL AID PICTURE (2007-2008)

Students with need: Need-based aid available for full-time and part-time students. Work study available nights, weekends, and for part-time students.
Students without need: No-need awards available for academics.

FINANCIAL AID PROCEDURES

Forms required: FAFSA.
Dates and Deadlines: Priority date 2/15; no closing date. Applicants notified on a rolling basis starting 5/1; must reply within 2 week(s) of notification.

CONTACT

Cathy Kohli, Director of Financial Aid
4240 Campus Drive, PS 148, Lima, OH 45804-3597
(419) 995-8800

Jefferson Community College

Steubenville, Ohio
www.jcc.edu Federal Code: 007275

2-year public community and technical college in large town.
Enrollment: 1,597 undergrads, 44% part-time. 287 full-time freshmen.
Selectivity: Open admission; but selective for some programs.

BASIC COSTS (2008-2009)

Tuition and fees: $2,700; out-of-district residents $2,880; out-of-state residents $3,690.
Per-credit charge: $90; out-of-district residents $93; out-of-state residents $120.
Additional info: Residents of 5 neighboring West Virginia counties eligible for in-state, out-of-district tuition rates.

FINANCIAL AID PICTURE

Students with need: Need-based aid available for full-time and part-time students. Work study available nights, weekends, and for part-time students.
Students without need: This college awards aid only to students with need.
Scholarships offered: Horizon Grant; two-year tuition scholarship; awarded to all students graduating from a Jefferson County high school with 2.5 GPA; student must enroll full-time for fall semester immediately following high school graduation.

FINANCIAL AID PROCEDURES

Forms required: FAFSA, institutional form.
Dates and Deadlines: Priority date 7/1; no closing date. Applicants notified on a rolling basis starting 6/15.

CONTACT

Kelly Wilson, Director of Student Information and Financial Aid
4000 Sunset Boulevard, Steubenville, OH 43952
(740) 264-5591 ext. 135

John Carroll University

University Heights, Ohio
www.jcu.edu Federal Code: 003050

4-year private university and liberal arts college in large town, affiliated with Roman Catholic Church.
Enrollment: 3,081 undergrads, 2% part-time. 792 full-time freshmen.
Selectivity: Admits over 75% of applicants.

BASIC COSTS (2009-2010)

Tuition and fees: $28,840.
Per-credit charge: $846.
Room and board: $8,330.

FINANCIAL AID PICTURE (2008-2009)

Students with need: Out of 695 full-time freshmen who applied for aid, 584 were judged to have need. Of these, 584 received aid, and 128 had their full need met. Average financial aid package met 90% of need; average scholarship/grant was $19,700; average loan was $3,171. For part-time students, average financial aid package was $10,840.
Students without need: 191 full-time freshmen who did not demonstrate need for aid received scholarships/grants; average award was $9,592. No-need awards available for academics, alumni affiliation, leadership, minority status, ROTC, state/district residency.
Scholarships offered: Presidential Leadership awards, Arrupe Scholarships and Magis Scholarships; all range from 1/4 to full tuition; based on academic background, leadership and service. Castellano Scholarship; full tuition; awarded each year to a student who will study Latin or Greek. Mastin Scholarship; offered to 3 students each year who will study natural sciences or math. Ignatian Mission Scholarship; offered each year to graduates of Jesuit high schools.
Cumulative student debt: 75% of graduating class had student loans; average debt was $19,079.
Additional info: Institutional form for need analysis required from upperclassmen and transfer students only.

FINANCIAL AID PROCEDURES

Forms required: FAFSA.
Dates and Deadlines: Priority date 2/15; closing date 3/15. Applicants notified on a rolling basis starting 2/15; must reply by 5/1 or within 4 week(s) of notification.
Transfers: Renewable scholarships for students transferring from local community colleges.

CONTACT

Patrick Prosser, Director of Financial Aid
20700 North Park Boulevard, University Heights, OH 44118-4581
(216) 397-4248

Kent State University

Kent, Ohio
www.kent.edu Federal Code: 003051

4-year public university in large town.
Enrollment: 17,660 undergrads, 11% part-time. 3,739 full-time freshmen.
Selectivity: Admits 50 to 75% of applicants.

BASIC COSTS (2008-2009)

Tuition and fees: $8,430; out-of-state residents $15,862.
Per-credit charge: $384; out-of-state residents $722.
Room and board: $7,200.

FINANCIAL AID PICTURE (2008-2009)

Students with need: Out of 3,102 full-time freshmen who applied for aid, 2,478 were judged to have need. Of these, 2,478 received aid, and 1,386 had their full need met. Average financial aid package met 65% of need; average scholarship/grant was $5,676; average loan was $3,553. For part-time students, average financial aid package was $5,598.
Students without need: 677 full-time freshmen who did not demonstrate need for aid received scholarships/grants; average award was $3,628. No-need awards available for academics, alumni affiliation, art, athletics, leadership, minority status, music/drama, ROTC, state/district residency.
Scholarships offered: ***Merit:*** Trustee Scholarship; $1,000-$2,500 annually; based on 3.25 GPA, ACT scores, leadership activities; 500 available. ***Athletic:*** 38 full-time freshmen received athletic scholarships; average amount $14,127.
Cumulative student debt: 71% of graduating class had student loans; average debt was $23,957.

Additional info: Participant in US Department of Education's Quality Assurance Program and Experimental Sites Program.

FINANCIAL AID PROCEDURES

Forms required: FAFSA.

Dates and Deadlines: Priority date 3/1; no closing date. Applicants notified on a rolling basis starting 3/15; must reply within 2 week(s) of notification.

CONTACT

Mark Evans, Director of Student Financial Aid
PO Box 5190, Kent, OH 44242-0001
(330) 672-2972

Kent State University: Ashtabula

Ashtabula, Ohio
www.ashtabula.kent.edu Federal Code: 003051

2-year public branch campus college in large town.
Enrollment: 1,488 undergrads, 44% part-time. 205 full-time freshmen.
Selectivity: Open admission; but selective for some programs.

BASIC COSTS (2008-2009)

Tuition and fees: $4,770; out-of-state residents $12,202.
Per-credit charge: $217; out-of-state residents $555.

FINANCIAL AID PICTURE (2008-2009)

Students with need: Out of 188 full-time freshmen who applied for aid, 169 were judged to have need. Of these, 169 received aid, and 81 had their full need met. Average financial aid package met 49% of need; average scholarship/grant was $5,511; average loan was $2,786. For part-time students, average financial aid package was $5,828.
Students without need: 5 full-time freshmen who did not demonstrate need for aid received scholarships/grants; average award was $2,160. No-need awards available for academics, alumni affiliation, art, athletics, job skills, leadership, minority status, music/drama, ROTC, state/district residency.
Cumulative student debt: 75% of graduating class had student loans; average debt was $17,643.

FINANCIAL AID PROCEDURES

Forms required: FAFSA.

Dates and Deadlines: Priority date 3/1; no closing date. Applicants notified on a rolling basis starting 3/15; must reply within 2 week(s) of notification.

CONTACT

Robyn Gifford, Academic Advisor
3325 West I3th Street, Ashtabula, OH 44004
(440) 964-3322

Kent State University: East Liverpool

East Liverpool, Ohio
www.kenteliv.kent.edu Federal Code: 003051

2-year public branch campus college in large town.
Enrollment: 835 undergrads, 44% part-time. 98 full-time freshmen.
Selectivity: Open admission; but selective for some programs.

BASIC COSTS (2008-2009)

Tuition and fees: $4,770; out-of-state residents $12,202.
Per-credit charge: $217; out-of-state residents $555.

FINANCIAL AID PICTURE (2008-2009)

Students with need: Out of 88 full-time freshmen who applied for aid, 76 were judged to have need. Of these, 76 received aid, and 23 had their full need met. Average financial aid package met 49% of need; average scholarship/grant was $5,936; average loan was $2,899. For part-time students, average financial aid package was $5,714.
Students without need: 6 full-time freshmen who did not demonstrate need for aid received scholarships/grants; average award was $2,340. No-need awards available for academics, alumni affiliation, art, athletics, leadership, minority status, music/drama, ROTC, state/district residency.
Cumulative student debt: 83% of graduating class had student loans; average debt was $19,911.

FINANCIAL AID PROCEDURES

Forms required: FAFSA.

Dates and Deadlines: Priority date 3/1; no closing date. Applicants notified on a rolling basis starting 3/15; must reply within 2 week(s) of notification.

CONTACT

Beth Allison-Christy, Administrative Assistant
400 East Fourth Street, East Liverpool, OH 43920
(330) 385-3805

Kent State University: Geauga

Burton, Ohio
www.geauga.kent.edu Federal Code: 003059

2-year public branch campus college in rural community.
Enrollment: 1,337 undergrads, 42% part-time. 125 full-time freshmen.
Selectivity: Open admission; but selective for some programs.

BASIC COSTS (2008-2009)

Tuition and fees: $4,770; out-of-state residents $12,202.
Per-credit charge: $217; out-of-state residents $555.

FINANCIAL AID PICTURE (2008-2009)

Students with need: Out of 97 full-time freshmen who applied for aid, 78 were judged to have need. Of these, 78 received aid, and 34 had their full need met. Average financial aid package met 47% of need; average scholarship/grant was $4,588; average loan was $2,851. For part-time students, average financial aid package was $5,072.
Students without need: 2 full-time freshmen who did not demonstrate need for aid received scholarships/grants; average award was $1,750. No-need awards available for academics, alumni affiliation, art, athletics, leadership, minority status, music/drama, ROTC, state/district residency.
Cumulative student debt: 62% of graduating class had student loans; average debt was $25,901.

FINANCIAL AID PROCEDURES

Forms required: FAFSA.

Dates and Deadlines: Priority date 3/1; no closing date. Must reply within 2 week(s) of notification.

CONTACT

Donna Holcomb, Financial Aid Advisor
Office of Admissions, Burton, OH 44021
(440) 834-8846

Kent State University: Salem

Salem, Ohio
www.salem.kent.edu Federal Code: 003061

2-year public branch campus college in large town.
Enrollment: 1,201 undergrads, 30% part-time. 167 full-time freshmen.
Selectivity: Open admission; but selective for some programs.

BASIC COSTS (2008-2009)

Tuition and fees: $4,770; out-of-state residents $12,202.
Per-credit charge: $217; out-of-state residents $555.

FINANCIAL AID PICTURE (2008-2009)

Students with need: Out of 145 full-time freshmen who applied for aid, 119 were judged to have need. Of these, 119 received aid, and 49 had their full need met. Average financial aid package met 51% of need; average scholarship/grant was $5,096; average loan was $2,899. For part-time students, average financial aid package was $5,397.

Students without need: No-need awards available for academics, alumni affiliation, art, athletics, leadership, minority status, music/drama, ROTC.

FINANCIAL AID PROCEDURES

Forms required: FAFSA.

Dates and Deadlines: Priority date 3/1; no closing date. Applicants notified on a rolling basis starting 3/15; must reply within 2 week(s) of notification.

Transfers: Priority date 2/15.

CONTACT

Juddy Heisler, Administrative Clerk
2491 State Route 45 South, Salem, OH 44460
(330) 332-0361

Kent State University: Stark

Canton, Ohio
www.stark.kent.edu Federal Code: 003054

2-year public branch campus college in small city.

Enrollment: 3,601 undergrads, 30% part-time. 625 full-time freshmen.

Selectivity: Open admission; but selective for some programs.

BASIC COSTS (2008-2009)

Tuition and fees: $4,770; out-of-state residents $12,202.

Per-credit charge: $217; out-of-state residents $555.

FINANCIAL AID PICTURE (2008-2009)

Students with need: Out of 479 full-time freshmen who applied for aid, 395 were judged to have need. Of these, 395 received aid, and 176 had their full need met. Average financial aid package met 49% of need; average scholarship/grant was $4,578; average loan was $2,717. For part-time students, average financial aid package was $5,307.

Students without need: 19 full-time freshmen who did not demonstrate need for aid received scholarships/grants; average award was $2,338. No-need awards available for academics, alumni affiliation, art, athletics, leadership, minority status, music/drama, ROTC, state/district residency.

Cumulative student debt: 68% of graduating class had student loans; average debt was $21,779.

FINANCIAL AID PROCEDURES

Forms required: FAFSA.

Dates and Deadlines: Priority date 3/1; no closing date. Applicants notified on a rolling basis starting 3/15; must reply within 2 week(s) of notification.

CONTACT

Nina Antram, Financial Aid Officer
6000 Frank Avenue NW, Canton, OH 44720-7599
(330) 535-3377

Kent State University: Trumbull

Warren, Ohio
www.trumbull.kent.edu Federal Code: 003051

2-year public branch campus college in small city.

Enrollment: 1,883 undergrads, 38% part-time. 251 full-time freshmen.

Selectivity: Open admission; but selective for some programs.

BASIC COSTS (2008-2009)

Tuition and fees: $4,770; out-of-state residents $12,202.

Per-credit charge: $217; out-of-state residents $555.

FINANCIAL AID PICTURE (2008-2009)

Students with need: Out of 209 full-time freshmen who applied for aid, 180 were judged to have need. Of these, 180 received aid, and 86 had their full need met. Average financial aid package met 50% of need; average scholarship/grant was $5,279; average loan was $3,010. For part-time students, average financial aid package was $5,340.

Students without need: 3 full-time freshmen who did not demonstrate need for aid received scholarships/grants; average award was $1,333. No-need awards available for academics, alumni affiliation, art, athletics, leadership, minority status, music/drama, ROTC, state/district residency.

Cumulative student debt: 67% of graduating class had student loans; average debt was $20,835.

FINANCIAL AID PROCEDURES

Forms required: FAFSA.

Dates and Deadlines: Priority date 3/1; no closing date. Applicants notified on a rolling basis starting 3/15; must reply within 2 week(s) of notification.

CONTACT

Sarah Helmick, Financial Aid Advisor
4314 Mahoning Avenue, NW, Warren, OH 44483-1998
(330) 847-0571

Kent State University: Tuscarawas

New Philadelphia, Ohio
www.tusc.kent.edu Federal Code: 003051

2-year public branch campus college in large town.

Enrollment: 1,773 undergrads, 38% part-time. 293 full-time freshmen.

Selectivity: Open admission; but selective for some programs and for out-of-state students.

BASIC COSTS (2008-2009)

Tuition and fees: $4,770; out-of-state residents $12,202.

Per-credit charge: $217; out-of-state residents $555.

FINANCIAL AID PICTURE (2008-2009)

Students with need: Out of 241 full-time freshmen who applied for aid, 218 were judged to have need. Of these, 218 received aid, and 95 had their full need met. Average financial aid package met 49% of need; average scholarship/grant was $4,891; average loan was $2,881. For part-time students, average financial aid package was $5,470.

Students without need: 4 full-time freshmen who did not demonstrate need for aid received scholarships/grants; average award was $588. No-need awards available for academics, alumni affiliation, art, athletics, leadership, minority status, music/drama, ROTC.

Cumulative student debt: 74% of graduating class had student loans; average debt was $17,258.

FINANCIAL AID PROCEDURES

Forms required: FAFSA.

Dates and Deadlines: Closing date 3/1. Applicants notified on a rolling basis starting 3/15; must reply within 2 week(s) of notification.

Transfers: Financial aid transcripts from all previous institutions required.

CONTACT

Dawn Plug, Financial Aid Coordinator
330 University Drive Northeast, New Philadelphia, OH 44663-9403
(330) 330 3301 ext. 47474

Kenyon College

Gambier, Ohio Federal Code: 003065
www.kenyon.edu CSS Code: 1370

4-year private liberal arts college in rural community.

Enrollment: 1,635 undergrads. 454 full-time freshmen.

Selectivity: Admits less than 50% of applicants.

BASIC COSTS (2009-2010)

Tuition and fees: $40,980.
Room and board: $7,260.

FINANCIAL AID PICTURE (2008-2009)

Students with need: Out of 270 full-time freshmen who applied for aid, 189 were judged to have need. Of these, 189 received aid, and 95 had their full need met. Average financial aid package met 98% of need; average scholarship/grant was $28,512; average loan was $3,067.
Students without need: 125 full-time freshmen who did not demonstrate need for aid received scholarships/grants; average award was $9,615. No-need awards available for academics, leadership, minority status.
Scholarships offered: Honor Scholarships, Science Scholarships, Trustee Opportunity Scholarships; averages around $16,000 a year; competitively based on excellence in academic achievement, extracurricular leadership, and community involvement. Distinguished Academic Scholarships; $2,000-$10,000; based on academic accomplishment, standardized test results, and extracurricular achievement. Scholarships for National Merit finalists available.
Cumulative student debt: 66% of graduating class had student loans; average debt was $19,462.

FINANCIAL AID PROCEDURES

Forms required: FAFSA, CSS PROFILE.
Dates and Deadlines: Closing date 2/15. Applicants notified by 4/1; must reply by 5/1.
Transfers: Closing date 4/15. Applicants notified by 5/15; must reply by 6/1.

CONTACT

Craig Daugherty, Director of Financial Aid
Ransom Hall, Gambier, OH 43022
(740) 427-5430

Kettering College of Medical Arts

Kettering, Ohio
www.kcma.edu Federal Code: 007035

4-year private health science and nursing college in large city, affiliated with Seventh-day Adventists.
Enrollment: 761 undergrads.
Selectivity: Admits 50 to 75% of applicants.

BASIC COSTS (2008-2009)

Tuition and fees: $9,690.
Per-credit charge: $315.
Room only: $2,900.
Additional info: Tuition and fees may vary by program.

FINANCIAL AID PICTURE

Students with need: Need-based aid available for full-time and part-time students.
Students without need: No-need awards available for academics.

FINANCIAL AID PROCEDURES

Forms required: FAFSA, institutional form.
Dates and Deadlines: Priority date 3/31; no closing date. Applicants notified on a rolling basis starting 5/15; must reply within 3 week(s) of notification.

CONTACT

Kim Snell, Director of Student Finance
3737 Southern Boulevard, Kettering, OH 45429-1299
(937) 296-7210

Lake Erie College

Painesville, Ohio
www.lec.edu Federal Code: 003066

4-year private liberal arts college in large town.
Enrollment: 728 undergrads.
Selectivity: Admits 50 to 75% of applicants.

BASIC COSTS (2008-2009)

Tuition and fees: $25,220.
Per-credit charge: $560.
Room and board: $7,650.
Additional info: Equestrian fee $880 per course.

FINANCIAL AID PICTURE (2007-2008)

Students with need: Need-based aid available for full-time and part-time students. Work study available nights, weekends, and for part-time students.
Students without need: No-need awards available for academics, art, leadership, music/drama, state/district residency.
Additional info: Twins' scholarship, sibling discount.

FINANCIAL AID PROCEDURES

Forms required: FAFSA.
Dates and Deadlines: No deadline. Applicants notified on a rolling basis; must reply within 2 week(s) of notification.
Transfers: No deadline.

CONTACT

Patricia Pangonis, Director of Financial Aid
391 West Washington Street, Painesville, OH 44077-3389
(440) 375-7100

Lakeland Community College

Kirtland, Ohio
www.lakelandcc.edu Federal Code: 006804

2-year public community college in large town.
Enrollment: 8,924 undergrads.
Selectivity: Open admission; but selective for some programs.

BASIC COSTS (2008-2009)

Tuition and fees: $2,726; out-of-district residents $3,333; out-of-state residents $7,095.
Per-credit charge: $79; out-of-district residents $99; out-of-state residents $225.

FINANCIAL AID PICTURE (2007-2008)

Students with need: 41% of average financial aid package awarded as scholarships/grants, 59% awarded as loans/jobs. Need-based aid available for part-time students. Work study available nights, weekends, and for part-time students.
Students without need: No-need awards available for academics, art, athletics, job skills, leadership, minority status, music/drama, state/district residency.
Additional info: Loans available for tuition and books.

FINANCIAL AID PROCEDURES

Forms required: FAFSA, institutional form.
Dates and Deadlines: Priority date 3/1; no closing date. Applicants notified on a rolling basis starting 5/1.
Transfers: Ohio Instructional Grant Transfer Form.

CONTACT

Melissa Amspaugh, Director of Financial Aid
7700 Clocktower Drive, Kirtland, OH 44094-5198
(440) 525-7070

Laura and Alvin Siegal College of Judaic Studies

Cleveland, Ohio
www.siegalcollege.edu Federal Code: 012838

4-year private liberal arts and teachers college in large town, affiliated with Jewish faith.
Enrollment: 11 undergrads.
Selectivity: Admits 50 to 75% of applicants.

BASIC COSTS (2008-2009)

Tuition and fees: $15,775.
Per-credit charge: $525.
Additional info: Tuition/fee waivers available for adults.

FINANCIAL AID PICTURE (2008-2009)

Students with need: Need-based aid available for full-time and part-time students.

FINANCIAL AID PROCEDURES

Forms required: institutional form.
Dates and Deadlines: No deadline. Applicants notified on a rolling basis.

CONTACT

Ruth Kronick, Director of Student Services
26500 Shaker Boulevard, Cleveland, OH 44122
(216) 464-4050 ext. 101

Lourdes College

Sylvania, Ohio
www.lourdes.edu Federal Code: 003069

4-year private liberal arts college in large town, affiliated with Roman Catholic Church.
Enrollment: 1,744 undergrads, 45% part-time. 113 full-time freshmen.
Selectivity: Admits over 75% of applicants.

BASIC COSTS (2009-2010)

Tuition and fees: $15,300.
Per-credit charge: $448.

FINANCIAL AID PICTURE (2008-2009)

Students with need: Out of 96 full-time freshmen who applied for aid, 73 were judged to have need. Of these, 73 received aid. For part-time students, average financial aid package was $5,981.
Students without need: No-need awards available for academics, art, minority status, state/district residency.

FINANCIAL AID PROCEDURES

Forms required: FAFSA
Dates and Deadlines: Priority date 3/1; no closing date. Applicants notified on a rolling basis starting 3/1; must reply within 4 week(s) of notification.

CONTACT

Denise McCluskey, Director of Financial Aid
6832 Convent Boulevard, Sylvania, OH 43560-2898
(419) 824-3732

Malone University

Canton, Ohio
www.malone.edu Federal Code: 003072

4-year private university in small city, affiliated with Evangelical Friends Church-Eastern Region.
Enrollment: 1,929 undergrads, 10% part-time. 389 full-time freshmen.
Selectivity: Admits 50 to 75% of applicants.

BASIC COSTS (2009-2010)

Tuition and fees: $21,080.
Per-credit charge: $370.
Room and board: $7,100.

FINANCIAL AID PICTURE (2008-2009)

Students with need: Out of 362 full-time freshmen who applied for aid, 329 were judged to have need. Of these, 329 received aid, and 59 had their full need met. Average financial aid package met 77% of need; average scholarship/grant was $12,614; average loan was $4,111. For part-time students, average financial aid package was $5,948.
Students without need: 40 full-time freshmen who did not demonstrate need for aid received scholarships/grants; average award was $6,522. No-need awards available for academics, alumni affiliation, athletics, leadership, music/drama, religious affiliation.
Scholarships offered: 14 full-time freshmen received athletic scholarships; average amount $6,596.
Cumulative student debt: 84% of graduating class had student loans; average debt was $24,539.
Additional info: Prepayment discounts and employer deferred payments available for students in adult degree-completion programs. Employer deferred payment plan is available for traditional undergraduate students.

FINANCIAL AID PROCEDURES

Forms required: FAFSA.
Dates and Deadlines: Priority date 3/1; closing date 7/31. Applicants notified on a rolling basis starting 3/1; must reply within 2 week(s) of notification.

CONTACT

Pamela Pustay, Director of Financial Aid
2600 Cleveland Avenue NW, Canton, OH 44709-3897
(330) 471-8100 ext. 8159

Marietta College

Marietta, Ohio
www.marietta.edu Federal Code: 003073

4-year private liberal arts college in large town.
Enrollment: 1,438 undergrads, 3% part-time. 385 full-time freshmen.
Selectivity: Admits over 75% of applicants.

BASIC COSTS (2008-2009)

Tuition and fees: $26,080.
Room and board: $7,764.

FINANCIAL AID PICTURE (2008-2009)

Students with need: Out of 371 full-time freshmen who applied for aid, 324 were judged to have need. Of these, 324 received aid, and 114 had their full need met. Average financial aid package met 91% of need; average scholarship/grant was $14,366; average loan was $3,954. For part-time students, average financial aid package was $7,906.
Students without need: 84 full-time freshmen who did not demonstrate need for aid received scholarships/grants; average award was $12,318. No-need awards available for academics, alumni affiliation, art, leadership, minority status, music/drama, state/district residency.
Scholarships offered: McCoy Scholarship; full tuition, room/board. Trustees' Scholarships; full tuition; up to 10 awarded. President's Scholarship, half tuition; up to 20 awarded. Dean's Awards; $6,000-$10,000. Rickey Physics Scholarships; $18,000. Charles Sumner Harrison Awards; $5,000; for multicultural students and leaders. Fine Arts Awards; $1,000-$3,000; audition/portfolio required. All scholarships renewable for four years.
Additional info: Auditions/portfolios for art, creative writing, music and theater required for competitive fine art scholarships.

FINANCIAL AID PROCEDURES

Forms required: FAFSA, institutional form.

Dates and Deadlines: Priority date 3/1; closing date 4/15. Applicants notified on a rolling basis starting 3/15; must reply by 5/1 or within 2 week(s) of notification.
Transfers: Priority date 4/15; closing date 6/15. Applicants notified on a rolling basis starting 4/1; must reply by 6/30 or within 2 week(s) of notification.

CONTACT
Kevin Lamb, Director of Student Financial Services
215 Fifth Street, Marietta, OH 45750-4005
(740) 376-4712

Marion Technical College
Marion, Ohio
www.mtc.edu Federal Code: 010736

2-year public technical college in large town.
Enrollment: 1,079 full-time undergrads.
Selectivity: Open admission; but selective for some programs.

BASIC COSTS (2008-2009)
Tuition and fees: $3,660; out-of-state residents $5,568.
Per-credit charge: $83; out-of-state residents $237.

FINANCIAL AID PICTURE (2008-2009)
Students with need: Need-based aid available for full-time and part-time students.
Students without need: No-need awards available for academics, leadership, minority status.
Scholarships offered: Foundation Scholarship; first year full tuition; for applicants in top 5% of class. President's Scholarship; $1,200; for applicants in top 50% of class. Tech Prep Scholarship; $1,200; for graduates of Tech Prep program. All scholarships require 2.5 GPA and successful completion of proficiency exams.

FINANCIAL AID PROCEDURES
Forms required: FAFSA, institutional form.
Dates and Deadlines: Closing date 6/1. Applicants notified on a rolling basis.
Transfers: No deadline. Applicants notified on a rolling basis.

CONTACT
Deb Langdon, Financial Aid Coordinator
1467 Mount Vernon Avenue, Marion, OH 43302-5694
(740) 389-4636 ext. 334

MedCentral College of Nursing
Mansfield, Ohio
www.medcentral.edu Federal Code: 035864

4-year private nursing college in small city.
Enrollment: 391 undergrads.
Selectivity: Admits 50 to 75% of applicants.

BASIC COSTS (2008-2009)
Tuition and fees: $11,420.
Per-credit charge: $375.
Room only: $5,130.

FINANCIAL AID PICTURE (2007-2008)
Students with need: 41% of average financial aid package awarded as scholarships/grants, 59% awarded as loans/jobs. Need-based aid available for part-time students. Work study available nights, weekends, and for part-time students.
Students without need: No-need awards available for academics, leadership.

FINANCIAL AID PROCEDURES
Forms required: FAFSA, institutional form.
Dates and Deadlines: Priority date 4/2; closing date 9/15. Applicants notified on a rolling basis starting 4/1; must reply by 5/1 or within 2 week(s) of notification.
Transfers: Closing date 4/1. Applicants notified on a rolling basis starting 3/15; must reply by 5/1 or within 2 week(s) of notification.

CONTACT
Allen Wright, Director of Financial Aid
335 Glessner Avenue, Mansfield, OH 44903-2265
(419) 520-2600

Mercy College of Northwest Ohio
Toledo, Ohio
www.mercycollege.edu Federal Code: 030970

4-year private health science and nursing college in large city, affiliated with Roman Catholic Church.
Enrollment: 921 undergrads, 51% part-time. 64 full-time freshmen.
Selectivity: Admits 50 to 75% of applicants.

BASIC COSTS (2009-2010)
Tuition and fees: $9,500.
Per-credit charge: $295.

FINANCIAL AID PICTURE (2007-2008)
Students with need: Average financial aid package met 37% of need; average scholarship/grant was $3,604; average loan was $2,969. For part-time students, average financial aid package was $6,025.
Students without need: No-need awards available for academics, alumni affiliation, leadership, religious affiliation, state/district residency.
Cumulative student debt: 50% of graduating class had student loans; average debt was $8,562.

FINANCIAL AID PROCEDURES
Forms required: FAFSA.
Dates and Deadlines: Priority date 3/1; no closing date. Applicants notified on a rolling basis starting 3/1; must reply within 2 week(s) of notification.

CONTACT
Julie Leslie, Financial Aid Director
2221 Madison Avenue, Toledo, OH 43604
(419) 251-1598

Miami University: Hamilton Campus
Hamilton, Ohio
www.ham.muohio.edu Federal Code: 003077

2-year public branch campus college in small city.
Enrollment: 3,491 undergrads, 22% part-time. 703 full-time freshmen.
Selectivity: Open admission; but selective for some programs.

BASIC COSTS (2008-2009)
Tuition and fees: $4,314; out-of-state residents $17,945.
Per-credit charge: $180; out-of-state residents $748.

FINANCIAL AID PICTURE (2008-2009)
Students with need: Need-based aid available for full-time and part-time students. Work study available nights, weekends, and for part-time students.
Students without need: No-need awards available for academics, athletics, leadership, minority status, state/district residency.
Additional info: Special gift funds for needy, multicultural students who enter with appropriate academic record. Separate application required for scholarships; closing date January 31.

FINANCIAL AID PROCEDURES
Forms required: FAFSA.

Dates and Deadlines: Priority date 2/15; no closing date. Applicants notified on a rolling basis starting 4/1.
Transfers: Transfer students must complete one semester at Miami University to be considered for scholarships.

CONTACT
Ann Alfers, Financial Aid Coordinator
1601 University Boulevard, Hamilton, OH 45011-3399
(513) 785-3123

Miami University: Middletown Campus
Middletown, Ohio
www.mid.muohio.edu Federal Code: 003077

2-year public branch campus and community college in large town.
Enrollment: 2,400 undergrads.
Selectivity: Open admission; but selective for some programs.

BASIC COSTS (2008-2009)
Tuition and fees: $4,314; out-of-state residents $17,945.
Per-credit charge: $180; out-of-state residents $748.
Additional info: Students paying by the credit hour pay $15.25 general fee per credit hour.

FINANCIAL AID PICTURE
Students with need: Need-based aid available for full-time and part-time students.
Students without need: This college awards aid only to students with need.

FINANCIAL AID PROCEDURES
Forms required: FAFSA.
Dates and Deadlines: Priority date 2/15; no closing date. Applicants notified on a rolling basis.
Transfers: Applicants must file by February 15 to be considered for campus-based aid or alumni scholarships.

CONTACT
Stacey Adams, Director of Admissions and Financial Aid
4200 East University Boulevard, Middletown, OH 45042
(513) 727-3346

Miami University: Oxford Campus
Oxford, Ohio
www.muohio.edu Federal Code: 003077

4-year public university in large town.
Enrollment: 14,699 undergrads, 2% part-time. 3,571 full-time freshmen.
Selectivity: Admits over 75% of applicants.

BASIC COSTS (2008-2009)
Tuition and fees: $11,887; out-of-state residents $25,771.
Per-credit charge: $412; out-of-state residents $1,054.
Room and board: $8,998.
Additional info: Reported in-state tuition represents maximum range that freshmen will be charged.

FINANCIAL AID PICTURE (2008-2009)
Students with need: Out of 2,538 full-time freshmen who applied for aid, 1,505 were judged to have need. Of these, 1,492 received aid, and 603 had their full need met. Average financial aid package met 77% of need; average scholarship/grant was $6,716; average loan was $5,571. For part-time students, average financial aid package was $8,170.
Students without need: 697 full-time freshmen who did not demonstrate need for aid received scholarships/grants; average award was $3,785. No-need awards available for academics, art, athletics, leadership, minority status, music/drama, ROTC, state/district residency.
Scholarships offered: ***Merit:*** Ohio Resident Scholarship; approximately $4,700; all full-time students who are Ohio residents are eligible. Ohio Leader Scholarship; $9,150-$11,900 depending on need; all full-time students who are Ohio residents are eligible. ***Athletic:*** 72 full-time freshmen received athletic scholarships; average amount $23,384.
Cumulative student debt: 51% of graduating class had student loans; average debt was $26,798.

FINANCIAL AID PROCEDURES
Forms required: FAFSA.
Dates and Deadlines: Priority date 2/15; no closing date. Applicants notified on a rolling basis starting 3/20; must reply by 5/1 or within 3 week(s) of notification.
Transfers: Institutional merit scholarships not available to transfer students during first year of enrollment.

CONTACT
Chuck Knepfle, Director of Student Financial Assistance
301 South Campus Avenue, Oxford, OH 45056
(513) 529-8734

Miami-Jacobs Career College
Dayton, Ohio
www.miamijacobs.edu Federal Code: 003076

2-year for-profit junior college in small city.
Enrollment: 248 undergrads.
Selectivity: Admits 50 to 75% of applicants.

BASIC COSTS (2008-2009)
Tuition and fees: $11,010.
Per-credit charge: $305.

FINANCIAL AID PICTURE
Students with need: Need-based aid available for full-time and part-time students.
Students without need: This college awards aid only to students with need.

FINANCIAL AID PROCEDURES
Forms required: FAFSA, institutional form.
Dates and Deadlines: No deadline. Applicants notified on a rolling basis.

CONTACT
Marcia Byrd, Director of Financial Aid
110 North Patterson Boulevard, Dayton, OH 45402
(937) 461-5174

Mount Carmel College of Nursing
Columbus, Ohio
www.mccn.edu Federal Code: 030719

4-year private nursing college in very large city, affiliated with Roman Catholic Church.
Enrollment: 690 undergrads.
Selectivity: Admits 50 to 75% of applicants.

BASIC COSTS (2009-2010)
Tuition and fees: $8,897.
Per-credit charge: $314.

FINANCIAL AID PICTURE (2008-2009)
Students with need: 26% of average financial aid package awarded as scholarships/grants, 74% awarded as loans/jobs.

FINANCIAL AID PROCEDURES

Forms required: FAFSA, institutional form.

Dates and Deadlines: Priority date 3/1; no closing date. Applicants notified on a rolling basis.

CONTACT

Alyncia Bowen, Financial Aid Director
127 South Davis Avenue, Columbus, OH 43222-1589
(614) 234-5800

Mount Union College

Alliance, Ohio
www.muc.edu Federal Code: 003083

4-year private liberal arts college in large town, affiliated with United Methodist Church.

Enrollment: 2,203 undergrads, 3% part-time. 727 full-time freshmen.

Selectivity: Admits over 75% of applicants.

BASIC COSTS (2009-2010)

Tuition and fees: $24,130.

Per-credit charge: $995.

Room and board: $7,420.

Additional info: Tuition/fee waivers available for minority students.

FINANCIAL AID PICTURE (2007-2008)

Students with need: Out of 547 full-time freshmen who applied for aid, 480 were judged to have need. Of these, 479 received aid, and 107 had their full need met. Average financial aid package met 83% of need; average scholarship/grant was $13,776; average loan was $5,071. For part-time students, average financial aid package was $17,503.

Students without need: 102 full-time freshmen who did not demonstrate need for aid received scholarships/grants; average award was $6,372. No-need awards available for academics, alumni affiliation, art, job skills, leadership, music/drama, religious affiliation, ROTC, state/district residency.

Cumulative student debt: 86% of graduating class had student loans; average debt was $29,348.

FINANCIAL AID PROCEDURES

Forms required: FAFSA.

Dates and Deadlines: Priority date 4/1; no closing date. Applicants notified on a rolling basis starting 3/15; must reply within 4 week(s) of notification.

Transfers: No deadline. Applicants notified on a rolling basis; must reply within 4 week(s) of notification.

CONTACT

Emily Swain, Director of Student Financial Services
1972 Clark Avenue, Alliance, OH 44601-3993
(330) 823-2674

Mount Vernon Nazarene University

Mount Vernon, Ohio
www.mvnu.edu Federal Code: 007085

4-year private university in large town, affiliated with Church of the Nazarene.

Enrollment: 1,984 undergrads, 9% part-time. 368 full-time freshmen.

Selectivity: Admits over 75% of applicants.

BASIC COSTS (2009-2010)

Tuition and fees: $20,580.

Per-credit charge: $713.

Room and board: $5,890.

FINANCIAL AID PICTURE (2008-2009)

Students with need: Out of 368 full-time freshmen who applied for aid, 335 were judged to have need. Of these, 335 received aid, and 47 had their full need met. Average financial aid package met 68% of need; average scholarship/grant was $9,983; average loan was $3,882. For part-time students, average financial aid package was $8,021.

Students without need: 23 full-time freshmen who did not demonstrate need for aid received scholarships/grants; average award was $6,532. No-need awards available for academics, athletics, minority status, music/drama, religious affiliation, state/district residency.

Scholarships offered: ***Merit:*** Academic scholarships; $3,000-$15,000; for first time students based on combination of ACT/SAT and GPA. ***Athletic:*** 22 full-time freshmen received athletic scholarships; average amount $3,549.

Cumulative student debt: 87% of graduating class had student loans; average debt was $32,791.

FINANCIAL AID PROCEDURES

Forms required: FAFSA, institutional form.

Dates and Deadlines: Priority date 3/15; no closing date. Applicants notified on a rolling basis starting 2/28; must reply within 2 week(s) of notification.

Transfers: No deadline. Applicants notified on a rolling basis starting 9/1; must reply within 2 week(s) of notification. Filing deadline for Ohio financial aid is October 1st.

CONTACT

Michelle Saigh, Director of Financial Aid
800 Martinsburg Road, Mount Vernon, OH 43050
(740) 397-9000 ext. 4520

Muskingum College

New Concord, Ohio
www.muskingum.edu Federal Code: 003084

4-year private liberal arts college in small town, affiliated with Presbyterian Church (USA).

Enrollment: 1,664 undergrads, 7% part-time. 482 full-time freshmen.

Selectivity: Admits over 75% of applicants.

BASIC COSTS (2009-2010)

Tuition and fees: $19,990.

Per-credit charge: $405.

Room and board: $7,740.

Additional info: Tuition/fee waivers available for minority students.

FINANCIAL AID PICTURE (2008-2009)

Students with need: Need-based aid available for full-time and part-time students.

Students without need: No-need awards available for academics, alumni affiliation, art, leadership, minority status, music/drama, religious affiliation, state/district residency.

Additional info: Scholarship priority date February 1.

FINANCIAL AID PROCEDURES

Forms required: FAFSA.

Dates and Deadlines: Priority date 3/15; closing date 8/1. Applicants notified on a rolling basis starting 3/1; must reply by 5/1 or within 2 week(s) of notification.

CONTACT

Jeff Zellers, Vice President of Enrollment
163 Stormont Street, New Concord, OH 43762-1199
(740) 826-8139

North Central State College

Mansfield, Ohio
www.ncstatecollege.edu Federal Code: 005313

2-year public technical college in small city.
Enrollment: 3,250 undergrads.
Selectivity: Open admission; but selective for some programs.

BASIC COSTS (2008-2009)
Tuition and fees: $3,634; out-of-state residents $6,694.
Per-credit charge: $68; out-of-state residents $136.

FINANCIAL AID PICTURE
Students with need: Need-based aid available for full-time and part-time students.
Students without need: This college awards aid only to students with need.

FINANCIAL AID PROCEDURES
Forms required: FAFSA.
Dates and Deadlines: Priority date 4/1; no closing date. Applicants notified on a rolling basis starting 5/30; must reply within 1 week(s) of notification.

CONTACT
Doris Smith, Assistant Dean of Financial Aid
2441 Kenwood Circle, PO Box 698, Mansfield, OH 44901-0698
(419) 755-4899

Northwest State Community College

Archbold, Ohio
www.northweststate.edu Federal Code: 008677

2-year public community and technical college in small town.
Enrollment: 1,840 undergrads.
Selectivity: Open admission; but selective for some programs.

BASIC COSTS (2008-2009)
Tuition and fees: $4,140; out-of-state residents $7,410.
Per-credit charge: $130; out-of-state residents $239.

FINANCIAL AID PICTURE
Students with need: Need-based aid available for full-time and part-time students.
Students without need: No-need awards available for academics.

FINANCIAL AID PROCEDURES
Forms required: FAFSA, institutional form.
Dates and Deadlines: Priority date 6/1; no closing date. Applicants notified on a rolling basis starting 4/1.

CONTACT
Amy Francis, Financial Aid Officer
22600 State Route 34, Archbold, OH 43502
(419) 267-5511 ext. 326

Notre Dame College

Cleveland, Ohio
www.notredamecollege.edu Federal Code: 003085

4-year private liberal arts college in very large city, affiliated with Roman Catholic Church.
Enrollment: 1,803 undergrads.
Selectivity: Admits less than 50% of applicants.

BASIC COSTS (2008-2009)
Tuition and fees: $22,096.
Per-credit charge: $446.
Room and board: $7,372.

FINANCIAL AID PICTURE
Students with need: Need-based aid available for full-time students.
Students without need: No-need awards available for academics, state/district residency.
Scholarships offered: Merit Scholarships; $2,500-$7,500; based on GPA and ACT or SAT scores. Presidential Scholarships; $3,000 awarded in addition to Merit Scholarships; based on 3.9 GPA and 27 ACT or 1210 SAT (exclusive of writing).

FINANCIAL AID PROCEDURES
Forms required: FAFSA.
Dates and Deadlines: Closing date 5/1. Applicants notified on a rolling basis starting 1/1; must reply within 2 week(s) of notification.

CONTACT
Mary McCrystal, Director of Student Financial Assistance
4545 College Road, Cleveland, OH 44121-4293
(216) 373-5263

Oberlin College

Oberlin, Ohio Federal Code: 003086
www.oberlin.edu CSS Code: 1587

4-year private music and liberal arts college in small town.
Enrollment: 2,839 undergrads, 2% part-time. 755 full-time freshmen.
Selectivity: Admits less than 50% of applicants.

BASIC COSTS (2008-2009)
Tuition and fees: $36,282.
Per-credit charge: $1,500.
Room and board: $9,280.

FINANCIAL AID PICTURE (2008-2009)
Students with need: Out of 452 full-time freshmen who applied for aid, 399 were judged to have need. Of these, 399 received aid, and 399 had their full need met. Average financial aid package met 100% of need; average scholarship/grant was $27,323; average loan was $2,754. For part-time students, average financial aid package was $29,394.
Students without need: 244 full-time freshmen who did not demonstrate need for aid received scholarships/grants; average award was $11,019. No-need awards available for academics, music/drama.
Scholarships offered: Bonner Scholarship; based on community service. John Frederick Oberlin Scholarship; based on academic merit. Stern Scholarship; based on excellence in sciences. Mary Elizabeth Johnston Scholarship; based on academic merit; available to Ohio residents only. Dean's Scholarship; available to Conservatory of Music students.

FINANCIAL AID PROCEDURES
Forms required: FAFSA, CSS PROFILE, institutional form.
Dates and Deadlines: Priority date 1/15; closing date 2/1. Applicants notified by 4/1; must reply by 5/1 or within 2 week(s) of notification.
Transfers: Closing date 3/1. Limited scholarship funding available for transfer students.

CONTACT
Robert Reddy, Director of Financial Aid
Carnegie Building, 101 North Professor Street, Oberlin, OH 44074
(440) 775-8142

Ohio Christian University
Circleville, Ohio
www.ohiochristian.edu Federal Code: 003030

4-year private Bible college in large town, affiliated with Churches of Christ in Christian Union.
Enrollment: 769 undergrads, 13% part-time. 246 full-time freshmen.
Selectivity: Admits over 75% of applicants.

BASIC COSTS (2009-2010)
Tuition and fees: $15,050.
Per-credit charge: $550.
Room and board: $5,990.
Additional info: Tuition/fee waivers available for minority students.

FINANCIAL AID PICTURE (2007-2008)
Students with need: Out of 238 full-time freshmen who applied for aid, 190 were judged to have need. Of these, 188 received aid, and 124 had their full need met. Average financial aid package met 75% of need; average scholarship/grant was $3,000; average loan was $2,660. For part-time students, average financial aid package was $6,000.
Students without need: This college awards aid only to students with need.
Cumulative student debt: 90% of graduating class had student loans; average debt was $26,000.
Additional info: Religious affiliation tuition discount.

FINANCIAL AID PROCEDURES
Forms required: FAFSA, institutional form.
Dates and Deadlines: Priority date 5/7; no closing date. Applicants notified on a rolling basis starting 5/1; must reply within 2 week(s) of notification.
Transfers: Closing date 3/1. Applicants notified on a rolling basis; must reply within 2 week(s) of notification.

CONTACT
Mike Fracassa, Director of Financial Aid
1476 Lancaster Pike, Circleville, OH 43113
(800) 701-0222

Ohio Dominican University
Columbus, Ohio
www.ohiodominican.edu Federal Code: 003035

4-year private university and liberal arts college in very large city, affiliated with Roman Catholic Church.
Enrollment: 2,106 undergrads, 25% part-time. 358 full-time freshmen.
Selectivity: Admits 50 to 75% of applicants.

BASIC COSTS (2009-2010)
Tuition and fees: $24,200.
Per-credit charge: $488.
Room and board: $7,900.

FINANCIAL AID PICTURE
Students with need: Need-based aid available for full-time and part-time students. Work study available nights, weekends, and for part-time students.
Students without need: No-need awards available for academics, athletics, state/district residency.

FINANCIAL AID PROCEDURES
Forms required: FAFSA.
Dates and Deadlines: Priority date 4/1; no closing date. Applicants notified on a rolling basis starting 3/1; must reply within 2 week(s) of notification.

CONTACT
Laura Meek, Director of Financial Aid
1216 Sunbury Road, Columbus, OH 43219
(614) 251-4778

Ohio Institute of Photography and Technology
Dayton, Ohio
www.oipt.com Federal Code: 020520

2-year for-profit technical college in very large city.
Enrollment: 813 undergrads, 9% part-time. 120 full-time freshmen.
Selectivity: Open admission; but selective for some programs.

BASIC COSTS (2008-2009)
Tuition and fees: $21,093.
Additional info: Tuition listed reflects the Photographic Technology program. Tuition varies by program.

FINANCIAL AID PICTURE
Students with need: Need-based aid available for full-time and part-time students.

FINANCIAL AID PROCEDURES
Forms required: FAFSA, institutional form.
Dates and Deadlines: No deadline. Applicants notified on a rolling basis starting 3/1.

CONTACT
Director of Financial Aid
2029 Edgefield Road, Dayton, OH 45439
(937) 294-6155

Ohio Northern University
Ada, Ohio
www.onu.edu Federal Code: 003089

4-year private university in small town, affiliated with United Methodist Church.
Enrollment: 2,591 undergrads, 2% part-time. 749 full-time freshmen.
Selectivity: Admits over 75% of applicants.

BASIC COSTS (2008-2009)
Tuition and fees: $30,765.
Room and board: $7,890.
Additional info: Tuition/fee waivers available for minority students.

FINANCIAL AID PICTURE (2008-2009)
Students with need: Need-based aid available for full-time and part-time students. Work study available nights, weekends, and for part-time students.
Students without need: No-need awards available for academics, alumni affiliation, art, leadership, music/drama, ROTC, state/district residency.
Scholarships offered: Presidential Scholarship; up to $25,000; based on 3.5 GPA, 30 ACT or 1320 SAT, and on-campus competition. Trustees Scholarship; up to $22,000; based on 3.5 GPA, 28 ACT or 1240 SAT, and on-campus competition. Academic Honors Scholarship; up to $20,000; based on 3.3 GPA, 26 ACT or 1170 SAT, and on-campus competition. Distinguished Achievement Scholarship; up to $16,000; based on 3.2 GPA, 24 ACT or 1090 SAT, on-campus competition, and leadership activities. Deans Scholarship; $6,000 to $12,000; based on 3.3 GPA and 25 ACT or 1130 SAT. Criteria listed is for Colleges of Arts & Sciences, Business Administration and Engineering. College of Pharmacy has slightly higher credentials. SAT scores exclusive of Writing.

FINANCIAL AID PROCEDURES
Forms required: FAFSA, institutional form.
Dates and Deadlines: Priority date 4/15; closing date 6/1. Applicants notified on a rolling basis starting 2/15; must reply within 2 week(s) of notification.

CONTACT
Melanie Weaver, Director of Financial Aid
525 South Main Street, Ada, OH 45810
(419) 772-2272

Ohio State University Agricultural Technical Institute

Wooster, Ohio
www.ati.osu.edu Federal Code: 003090

2-year public agricultural and branch campus college in large town.
Enrollment: 782 undergrads. 375 full-time freshmen.
Selectivity: Open admission; but selective for out-of-state students.

BASIC COSTS (2008-2009)
Tuition and fees: $5,859; out-of-state residents $19,098.

FINANCIAL AID PICTURE (2008-2009)
Students with need: Need-based aid available for full-time and part-time students. Work study available nights, weekends, and for part-time students.
Students without need: This college awards aid only to students with need.

FINANCIAL AID PROCEDURES
Forms required: FAFSA.
Dates and Deadlines: Priority date 3/1; no closing date. Applicants notified on a rolling basis starting 5/1; must reply within 4 week(s) of notification.
Transfers: Priority date 1/1; closing date 3/1.

CONTACT
Barbara LaMoreaux, Coordinator, Financial Aid
1328 Dover Road, Wooster, OH 44691

Ohio State University: Columbus Campus

Columbus, Ohio
www.osu.edu Federal Code: 003090

4-year public university in very large city.
Enrollment: 38,719 undergrads, 6% part-time. 6,153 full-time freshmen.
Selectivity: Admits 50 to 75% of applicants.

BASIC COSTS (2008-2009)
Tuition and fees: $8,679; out-of-state residents $21,918.
Room and board: $7,755.

FINANCIAL AID PICTURE (2008-2009)
Students with need: Out of 4,880 full-time freshmen who applied for aid, 3,117 were judged to have need. Of these, 3,115 received aid, and 931 had their full need met. Average financial aid package met 69% of need; average scholarship/grant was $7,667; average loan was $3,248. For part-time students, average financial aid package was $8,504.
Students without need: 1,954 full-time freshmen who did not demonstrate need for aid received scholarships/grants; average award was $4,223. No-need awards available for academics, alumni affiliation, art, athletics, job skills, leadership, minority status, music/drama, ROTC, state/district residency.
Scholarships offered: 103 full-time freshmen received athletic scholarships; average amount $15,524.
Cumulative student debt: 57% of graduating class had student loans; average debt was $21,413.

FINANCIAL AID PROCEDURES
Forms required: FAFSA.
Dates and Deadlines: Priority date 2/15; no closing date. Must reply by 5/1 or within 4 week(s) of notification.
Transfers: Priority date 6/25. Applicants notified by 5/29; must reply within 4 week(s) of notification.

CONTACT
110 Enarson Hall, Columbus, OH 43210
(614) 292-0300

Ohio State University: Lima Campus

Lima, Ohio
www.lima.ohio-state.edu Federal Code: 003090

4-year public branch campus college in large town.
Enrollment: 1,268 undergrads, 10% part-time. 490 full-time freshmen.
Selectivity: Open admission; but selective for out-of-state students.

BASIC COSTS (2008-2009)
Tuition and fees: $5,664; out-of-state residents $18,903.

FINANCIAL AID PICTURE (2008-2009)
Students with need: Out of 442 full-time freshmen who applied for aid, 339 were judged to have need. Of these, 335 received aid, and 35 had their full need met. Average financial aid package met 58% of need; average scholarship/grant was $3,787; average loan was $3,344. For part-time students, average financial aid package was $7,532.
Students without need: 99 full-time freshmen who did not demonstrate need for aid received scholarships/grants; average award was $770. No-need awards available for academics, alumni affiliation, art, athletics, job skills, leadership, minority status, music/drama, religious affiliation, ROTC, state/district residency.

FINANCIAL AID PROCEDURES
Forms required: FAFSA.
Dates and Deadlines: Priority date 3/1; no closing date. Applicants notified on a rolling basis starting 4/1; must reply within 4 week(s) of notification.
Transfers: Priority date 6/25. Applicants notified on a rolling basis starting 5/29; must reply within 4 week(s) of notification.

CONTACT
Bryan Albright, Coordinator, Financial Aid
4240 Campus Drive, Lima, OH 45804-3596
(419) 995-8147

Ohio State University: Mansfield Campus

Mansfield, Ohio
www.mansfield.ohio-state.edu Federal Code: 003090

4-year public branch campus college in small city.
Enrollment: 1,143 undergrads, 13% part-time. 490 full-time freshmen.
Selectivity: Open admission; but selective for out-of-state students.

BASIC COSTS (2008-2009)
Tuition and fees: $5,664; out-of-state residents $18,903.
Room and board: $4,440.

FINANCIAL AID PICTURE (2008-2009)
Students with need: Out of 395 full-time freshmen who applied for aid, 320 were judged to have need. Of these, 327 received aid, and 38 had their full need met. Average financial aid package met 61% of need; average scholarship/grant was $4,866; average loan was $3,331. For part-time students, average financial aid package was $9,084.
Students without need: 48 full-time freshmen who did not demonstrate need for aid received scholarships/grants; average award was $1,677. No-need awards available for academics, alumni affiliation, art, athletics, job skills, leadership, minority status, music/drama, ROTC, state/district residency.

FINANCIAL AID PROCEDURES

Forms required: FAFSA.
Dates and Deadlines: Priority date 3/1; no closing date. Applicants notified on a rolling basis starting 4/5; must reply within 4 week(s) of notification.
Transfers: Priority date 6/25. Applicants notified on a rolling basis starting 5/29; must reply within 4 week(s) of notification.

CONTACT

Director, Student Financial Aid
1680 University Drive, Mansfield, OH 44906
(419) 755-4011

Ohio State University: Marion Campus

Marion, Ohio
www.marion.ohio-state.edu Federal Code: 003090

4-year public branch campus college in large town.
Enrollment: 1,507 undergrads, 12% part-time. 529 full-time freshmen.
Selectivity: Open admission; but selective for out-of-state students.

BASIC COSTS (2008-2009)

Tuition and fees: $5,664; out-of-state residents $18,903.

FINANCIAL AID PICTURE (2008-2009)

Students with need: Out of 425 full-time freshmen who applied for aid, 333 were judged to have need. Of these, 333 received aid, and 52 had their full need met. Average financial aid package met 63% of need; average scholarship/grant was $4,425; average loan was $3,247. For part-time students, average financial aid package was $7,688.
Students without need: 66 full-time freshmen who did not demonstrate need for aid received scholarships/grants; average award was $1,589. No-need awards available for academics, alumni affiliation, art, athletics, job skills, leadership, minority status, music/drama, ROTC, state/district residency.

FINANCIAL AID PROCEDURES

Forms required: FAFSA.
Dates and Deadlines: Priority date 3/1; no closing date. Applicants notified on a rolling basis starting 5/1; must reply within 4 week(s) of notification.
Transfers: Priority date 6/25. Applicants notified by 5/29; must reply within 4 week(s) of notification.

CONTACT

Matt Moreau, Coordinator of Admissions
1465 Mount Vernon Avenue, Marion, OH 43302
(740) 389-6786 ext. 6273

Ohio State University: Newark Campus

Newark, Ohio
www.newark.osu.edu Federal Code: 003095

4-year public branch campus college in large town.
Enrollment: 2,259 undergrads, 10% part-time. 1,067 full-time freshmen.
Selectivity: Open admission; but selective for out-of-state students.

BASIC COSTS (2008-2009)

Tuition and fees: $5,664; out-of-state residents $18,903.
Room only: $5,475.

FINANCIAL AID PICTURE (2008-2009)

Students with need: Out of 880 full-time freshmen who applied for aid, 669 were judged to have need. Of these, 668 received aid, and 89 had their full need met. Average financial aid package met 59% of need; average scholarship/grant was $5,149; average loan was $3,272. For part-time students, average financial aid package was $7,374.
Students without need: 9 full-time freshmen who did not demonstrate need for aid received scholarships/grants; average award was $3,050. No-need awards available for academics, alumni affiliation, art, athletics, job skills, leadership, minority status, music/drama, ROTC, state/district residency.

FINANCIAL AID PROCEDURES

Forms required: FAFSA.
Dates and Deadlines: Priority date 3/1; no closing date. Applicants notified on a rolling basis starting 5/1; must reply within 4 week(s) of notification.
Transfers: Priority date 6/25. Applicants notified by 5/29; must reply within 4 week(s) of notification.

CONTACT

1179 University Drive, Newark, OH 43055
(740) 366-9435

Ohio Technical College

Cleveland, Ohio
www.ohiotechnicalcollege.com Federal Code: 011745

2-year for-profit technical college in very large city.
Enrollment: 801 undergrads.

BASIC COSTS (2008-2009)

Additional info: Tuition for full associate programs range from $25,000 to $29,400; full diploma programs range from $18,400 to $26,280; full certificate programs range from $2,700 to $4,500. Fees are $100.

FINANCIAL AID PICTURE (2007-2008)

Students with need: 35% of average financial aid package awarded as scholarships/grants, 65% awarded as loans/jobs.

FINANCIAL AID PROCEDURES

Dates and Deadlines: No deadline.

CONTACT

Jennifer Tucker, Director of Financial Aid
1374 East 51st Street, Cleveland, OH 44103-1269

Ohio University

Athens, Ohio
www.ohio.edu Federal Code: 003100

4-year public university in large town.
Enrollment: 17,085 undergrads, 5% part-time. 3,924 full-time freshmen.
Selectivity: Admits over 75% of applicants.

BASIC COSTS (2008-2009)

Tuition and fees: $8,907; out-of-state residents $17,871.
Per-credit charge: $283; out-of-state residents $578.
Room and board: $8,906.

FINANCIAL AID PICTURE (2008-2009)

Students with need: Out of 3,513 full-time freshmen who applied for aid, 2,194 were judged to have need. Of these, 2,147 received aid, and 340 had their full need met. Average financial aid package met 58% of need; average scholarship/grant was $6,141; average loan was $3,423. For part-time students, average financial aid package was $6,482.
Students without need: 693 full-time freshmen who did not demonstrate need for aid received scholarships/grants; average award was $3,921. No-need awards available for academics, art, athletics, minority status, music/drama, religious affiliation, ROTC.
Scholarships offered: 77 full-time freshmen received athletic scholarships; average amount $15,485.
Cumulative student debt: 66% of graduating class had student loans; average debt was $23,041.

FINANCIAL AID PROCEDURES

Forms required: FAFSA.

Dates and Deadlines: Priority date 3/15; closing date 4/1. Applicants notified on a rolling basis starting 4/1; must reply within 3 week(s) of notification.

CONTACT

Sondra Williams, Director, Student Financial Aid and Scholarships
120 Chubb Hall, Athens, OH 45701-2979
(740) 593-4141

Ohio University: Chillicothe Campus

Chillicothe, Ohio
www.chillicothe.ohiou.edu Federal Code: 003102

4-year public branch campus college in large town.

Enrollment: 1,855 undergrads.

Selectivity: Open admission; but selective for some programs.

BASIC COSTS (2008-2009)

Tuition and fees: $4,581; out-of-state residents $8,904.

Per-credit charge: $139; out-of-state residents $270.

FINANCIAL AID PICTURE

Students with need: Need-based aid available for full-time and part-time students.

FINANCIAL AID PROCEDURES

Forms required: FAFSA.

Dates and Deadlines: No deadline. Applicants notified on a rolling basis.

CONTACT

Dennis Bothel, Coordinator of Academic Advising
101 University Drive, Chillicothe, OH 45601
(740) 774-7228

Ohio University: Eastern Campus

St. Clairsville, Ohio
www.eastern.ohiou.edu Federal Code: 003101

4-year public branch campus college in small town.

Enrollment: 774 undergrads.

Selectivity: Open admission; but selective for some programs.

BASIC COSTS (2008-2009)

Tuition and fees: $4,395; out-of-state residents $5,715.

Per-credit charge: $134; out-of-state residents $174.

FINANCIAL AID PICTURE (2007-2008)

Students with need: Need-based aid available for full-time and part-time students.

Students without need: No-need awards available for academics, alumni affiliation, minority status.

FINANCIAL AID PROCEDURES

Forms required: FAFSA.

Dates and Deadlines: Priority date 3/15; no closing date. Applicants notified by 5/15.

Transfers: Priority date 3/1; closing date 5/1.

CONTACT

Kevin Chenoweth, Student Services Manager
45425 National Road West, St. Clairsville, OH 43950-9724
(740) 695-1720 ext. 209

Ohio University: Lancaster Campus

Lancaster, Ohio
www.lancaster.ohiou.edu Federal Code: 003104

4-year public branch campus college in large town.

Enrollment: 1,632 undergrads.

Selectivity: Open admission; but selective for some programs.

BASIC COSTS (2008-2009)

Tuition and fees: $4,581; out-of-state residents $8,904.

Per-credit charge: $139; out-of-state residents $270.

FINANCIAL AID PICTURE

Students with need: Need-based aid available for full-time and part-time students.

Additional info: Scholarship application deadline April 1.

FINANCIAL AID PROCEDURES

Forms required: FAFSA.

Dates and Deadlines: Priority date 2/15; no closing date. Applicants notified on a rolling basis; must reply within 2 week(s) of notification.

CONTACT

Pat Fox, Coordinator, Financial Aid
1570 Granville Pike, Lancaster, OH 43130
(740) 654-6711 ext. 209

Ohio University: Southern Campus at Ironton

Ironton, Ohio
www.southern.ohiou.edu Federal Code: 003103

4-year public branch campus college in large town.

Enrollment: 1,166 full-time undergrads.

Selectivity: Open admission.

BASIC COSTS (2008-2009)

Tuition and fees: $4,395; out-of-state residents $5,715.

Per-credit charge: $134; out-of-state residents $174.

FINANCIAL AID PICTURE

Students with need: Need-based aid available for full-time and part-time students.

Students without need: No-need awards available for academics, state/district residency.

FINANCIAL AID PROCEDURES

Forms required: FAFSA.

Dates and Deadlines: Priority date 3/15; no closing date. Applicants notified on a rolling basis starting 4/1.

CONTACT

Jacki Adkins, Coordinator of Financial Aid and Scholarships
1804 Liberty Avenue, Ironton, OH 45638
(740) 533-4600

Ohio Valley College of Technology

East Liverpool, Ohio
www.ovct.edu Federal Code: 016261

2-year for-profit business and technical college in large town.

Enrollment: 147 undergrads, 10% part-time. 42 full-time freshmen.

BASIC COSTS (2008-2009)

Tuition and fees: $8,185.

FINANCIAL AID PICTURE

Students with need: Need-based aid available for full-time and part-time students.

Students without need: This college awards aid only to students with need.

FINANCIAL AID PROCEDURES

Forms required: FAFSA.

Dates and Deadlines: Priority date 10/1; no closing date. Applicants notified on a rolling basis; must reply within 6 week(s) of notification.

CONTACT

Mary Galeno, Financial Aid Officer
16808 St. Clair Avenue, PO Box 7000, East Liverpool, OH 43920
(330) 385-1070

Ohio Wesleyan University

Delaware, Ohio
www.owu.edu Federal Code: 003109

4-year private liberal arts college in large town, affiliated with United Methodist Church.

Enrollment: 1,947 undergrads. 577 full-time freshmen.

Selectivity: Admits 50 to 75% of applicants.

BASIC COSTS (2009-2010)

Tuition and fees: $35,030.

Room and board: $9,224.

FINANCIAL AID PICTURE (2008-2009)

Students with need: Out of 461 full-time freshmen who applied for aid, 363 were judged to have need. Of these, 363 received aid, and 118 had their full need met. Average financial aid package met 88% of need; average scholarship/grant was $21,924; average loan was $5,380. For part-time students, average financial aid package was $18,574.

Students without need: 198 full-time freshmen who did not demonstrate need for aid received scholarships/grants; average award was $15,031. No-need awards available for academics, alumni affiliation, art, leadership, minority status, music/drama, religious affiliation, state/district residency.

Scholarships offered: Presidential scholarships; full tuition; 25 awarded. Trustee scholarships; 75% of tuition; 40 awarded. Faculty scholarships; 50% of tuition; 140 awarded.

Cumulative student debt: 77% of graduating class had student loans; average debt was $26,704.

FINANCIAL AID PROCEDURES

Forms required: FAFSA, institutional form.

Dates and Deadlines: Priority date 3/1; closing date 5/1. Applicants notified on a rolling basis starting 2/15; must reply by 5/1 or within 2 week(s) of notification.

Transfers: Must reply within 2 week(s) of notification.

CONTACT

Lee Harrell, Assistant Vice President of Admission and Financial Aid
75 South Sandusky Street, Delaware, OH 43015-2398
(740) 368-3050

Otterbein College

Westerville, Ohio
www.otterbein.edu Federal Code: 003110

4-year private liberal arts college in large town, affiliated with United Methodist Church.

Enrollment: 2,748 undergrads.

Selectivity: Admits over 75% of applicants.

BASIC COSTS (2008-2009)

Tuition and fees: $26,319.

Per-credit charge: $315.

Room and board: $7,461.

Additional info: Tuition/fee waivers available for adults, minority students.

FINANCIAL AID PICTURE

Students with need: Work study available nights, weekends, and for part-time students.

Students without need: No-need awards available for academics, alumni affiliation, art, leadership, minority status, music/drama, state/district residency.

FINANCIAL AID PROCEDURES

Forms required: FAFSA.

Dates and Deadlines: Priority date 4/1; no closing date. Applicants notified on a rolling basis starting 2/15.

Transfers: Transfer students must complete appropriate state grant transfer paperwork.

CONTACT

Thomas Yarnell, Director of Financial Aid
One Otterbein College, Westerville, OH 43081
(614) 823-1502

Owens Community College: Toledo

Toledo, Ohio
www.owens.edu Federal Code: 005753

2-year public community college in large city.

Enrollment: 9,636 undergrads, 52% part-time. 2,258 full-time freshmen.

Selectivity: Open admission; but selective for some programs.

BASIC COSTS (2008-2009)

Tuition and fees: $2,972; out-of-state residents $5,552.

Per-credit charge: $108; out-of-state residents $323.

FINANCIAL AID PICTURE (2008-2009)

Students with need: For part-time students, average financial aid package was $5,676.

Students without need: No-need awards available for academics, alumni affiliation, athletics, leadership, state/district residency.

Additional info: Other types of financial aid available: federal family education loan program, private foundation loan (SCHELL).

FINANCIAL AID PROCEDURES

Forms required: FAFSA.

Dates and Deadlines: Priority date 3/31; no closing date. Applicants notified by 2/7.

CONTACT

Betsy Johnson, Director of Financial Aid
PO Box 10000, Toledo, OH 43699-1947
(567) 661-7343

Pontifical College Josephinum

Columbus, Ohio
www.pcj.edu Federal Code: 003113

4-year private liberal arts and seminary college for men in very large city, affiliated with Roman Catholic Church.

Enrollment: 164 undergrads.

Selectivity: Admits over 75% of applicants.

BASIC COSTS (2009-2010)

Tuition and fees: $17,417.

Per-credit charge: $650.

Room and board: $7,908.

FINANCIAL AID PICTURE (2007-2008)

Students with need: Need-based aid available for full-time and part-time students. Work study available nights, weekends, and for part-time students.
Students without need: This college awards aid only to students with need.

FINANCIAL AID PROCEDURES

Forms required: FAFSA, institutional form.
Dates and Deadlines: Priority date 9/2; no closing date. Applicants notified on a rolling basis starting 8/15; must reply within 2 week(s) of notification.

CONTACT

Marky Leichtnam, Director of Financial Aid
7625 North High Street, Columbus, OH 43235-1499
(614) 985-2212

School of Advertising Art

Kettering, Ohio
www.saacollege.com Federal Code: 017160

2-year for-profit visual arts and technical college in small city.
Enrollment: 143 undergrads.

BASIC COSTS (2009-2010)

Tuition and fees: $24,433.
Per-credit charge: $350.

FINANCIAL AID PICTURE (2007-2008)

Students with need: 2% of average financial aid package awarded as scholarships/grants, 98% awarded as loans/jobs.
Students without need: No-need awards available for academics, art, leadership.

FINANCIAL AID PROCEDURES

Forms required: FAFSA.
Dates and Deadlines: No deadline. Applicants notified on a rolling basis starting 4/1; must reply by 7/1 or within 1 week(s) of notification.
Transfers: No deadline. Applicants notified on a rolling basis starting 4/1; must reply by 7/1 or within 1 week(s) of notification.

CONTACT

Tamara Arment, Financial Aid Director
1725 East David Road, Kettering, OH 45440-1612
(937) 294-0592 ext. 104

Shawnee State University

Portsmouth, Ohio
www.shawnee.edu Federal Code: 009942

4-year public university in large town.
Enrollment: 2,919 undergrads, 17% part-time. 596 full-time freshmen.
Selectivity: Open admission; but selective for some programs.

BASIC COSTS (2008-2009)

Tuition and fees: $5,832; out-of-state residents $10,176.
Per-credit charge: $216; out-of-state residents $397.
Room and board: $7,670.

FINANCIAL AID PICTURE

Students with need: Need-based aid available for full-time and part-time students.
Students without need: No-need awards available for academics.
Additional info: ACT recommended for scholarship applicants.

FINANCIAL AID PROCEDURES

Forms required: FAFSA, institutional form.
Dates and Deadlines: Priority date 6/15; no closing date. Applicants notified on a rolling basis starting 5/1; must reply within 4 week(s) of notification.

CONTACT

Barbara Bradbury, Financial Aid Director
940 Second Street, Portsmouth, OH 45662
(740) 351-4243

Sinclair Community College

Dayton, Ohio
www.sinclair.edu Federal Code: 003119

2-year public community college in small city.
Enrollment: 19,053 undergrads, 57% part-time. 2,351 full-time freshmen.
Selectivity: Open admission; but selective for some programs.

BASIC COSTS (2008-2009)

Tuition and fees: $2,026; out-of-district residents $3,308; out-of-state residents $6,526.
Per-credit charge: $42; out-of-district residents $70; out-of-state residents $142.

FINANCIAL AID PICTURE (2008-2009)

Students with need: Need-based aid available for full-time and part-time students. Work study available nights, weekends, and for part-time students.
Students without need: No-need awards available for academics, athletics, state/district residency.

FINANCIAL AID PROCEDURES

Forms required: FAFSA, institutional form.
Dates and Deadlines: Priority date 5/1; closing date 8/1. Applicants notified on a rolling basis.
Transfers: No deadline.

CONTACT

Carlyn Bozeman, Director of Financial Aid and Scholarships
444 West Third Street, Dayton, OH 45402-1460
(937) 512-3000

Southern State Community College

Hillsboro, Ohio
www.sscc.edu Federal Code: 012870

2-year public community college in small town.
Enrollment: 2,584 undergrads, 44% part-time. 511 full-time freshmen.
Selectivity: Open admission; but selective for some programs.

BASIC COSTS (2008-2009)

Tuition and fees: $3,390; out-of-state residents $6,528.
Per-credit charge: $81; out-of-state residents $162.

FINANCIAL AID PICTURE (2007-2008)

Students with need: 57% of average financial aid package awarded as scholarships/grants, 43% awarded as loans/jobs. Need-based aid available for part-time students.
Students without need: No-need awards available for academics, art, athletics, music/drama.

FINANCIAL AID PROCEDURES

Forms required: FAFSA, institutional form.
Dates and Deadlines: Priority date 7/1; closing date 9/1. Applicants notified by 4/15; must reply within 2 week(s) of notification.
Transfers: No deadline.

CONTACT
Janeen Deatley, Financial Aid Director
100 Hobart Drive, Hillsboro, OH 45133
(937) 393-3431 ext. 2610

Southwestern College: Dayton

Dayton, Ohio
www.swcollege.net Federal Code: 030161

2-year for-profit business college in small city.
Enrollment: 800 undergrads.
Selectivity: Open admission.

BASIC COSTS (2008-2009)
Tuition and fees: $10,000.

FINANCIAL AID PICTURE
Students with need: Need-based aid available for full-time and part-time students.
Students without need: This college awards aid only to students with need.

FINANCIAL AID PROCEDURES
Forms required: FAFSA.
Dates and Deadlines: No deadline.

CONTACT
Abby Wilkins, Director of Financial Aid
111 West 1st Street, Dayton, OH 45402

Southwestern College: Tri-County

Cincinnati, Ohio
www.swcollege.net Federal Code: 012128

2-year for-profit career college in small city.
Enrollment: 668 undergrads.
Selectivity: Open admission.

BASIC COSTS (2009-2010)
Tuition and fees: $11,400.

FINANCIAL AID PICTURE (2007-2008)
Students with need: Need-based aid available for full-time students.
Students without need: This college awards aid only to students with need.

FINANCIAL AID PROCEDURES
Forms required: FAFSA, state aid form.
Dates and Deadlines: No deadline.

CONTACT
Jill Matosky, Financial Aid Director
149 Northland Boulevard, Cincinnati, OH 45246
(513) 874-0432

Southwestern College: Vine Street Campus

Cincinnati, Ohio
www.swcollege.net Federal Code: 012128

2-year for-profit business and health science college in large city.
Enrollment: 420 undergrads.
Selectivity: Open admission.

BASIC COSTS (2009-2010)
Tuition and fees: $10,600.
Per-credit charge: $275.

FINANCIAL AID PICTURE
Students with need: Need-based aid available for full-time and part-time students.
Students without need: This college awards aid only to students with need.

FINANCIAL AID PROCEDURES
Forms required: FAFSA.

CONTACT
Charlene Williams, Financial Aid Director
632 Vine Street, Cincinnati, OH 45202
(513) 421-3212

Stark State College of Technology

North Canton, Ohio
www.starkstate.edu Federal Code: 011141

2-year public technical college in small city.
Enrollment: 9,395 undergrads.
Selectivity: Open admission; but selective for some programs.

BASIC COSTS (2008-2009)
Tuition and fees: $3,810; out-of-state residents $5,610.
Per-credit charge: $103; out-of-state residents $163.

FINANCIAL AID PICTURE
Students with need: Need-based aid available for full-time and part-time students. Work study available nights, weekends, and for part-time students.
Students without need: This college awards aid only to students with need.

FINANCIAL AID PROCEDURES
Forms required: FAFSA, institutional form.
Dates and Deadlines: Priority date 5/1; no closing date. Applicants notified on a rolling basis starting 4/1; must reply within 4 week(s) of notification.

CONTACT
Amy Baker, Director of Financial Aid
6200 Frank Avenue NW, North Canton, OH 44720
(330) 494-6170

Stautzenberger College

Maumee, Ohio
www.sctoday.edu Federal Code: 004866

2-year for-profit business and technical college in large city.
Enrollment: 850 undergrads.
Selectivity: Open admission.

BASIC COSTS (2008-2009)
Additional info: Tuition ranges from $210 to $375 per credit hour; required fees, $270.

FINANCIAL AID PICTURE
Students with need: Need-based aid available for full-time and part-time students.
Students without need: This college awards aid only to students with need.

FINANCIAL AID PROCEDURES
Forms required: FAFSA.
Dates and Deadlines: No deadline. Applicants notified on a rolling basis.

CONTACT

Mari Huffman, Financial Aid Director
1796 Indian Wood Circle, Maumee, OH 43537
(419) 866-0261

Stautzenberger College: Strongsville

Brecksville, Ohio
www.LearnWhatYouLove.com

2-year for-profit career college in large town.
Enrollment: 399 undergrads.
Selectivity: Open admission.

BASIC COSTS (2008-2009)

Tuition and fees: $9,540.
Per-credit charge: $210.

FINANCIAL AID PICTURE (2007-2008)

Students with need: 41% of average financial aid package awarded as scholarships/grants, 59% awarded as loans/jobs. Need-based aid available for part-time students.
Students without need: This college awards aid only to students with need.

FINANCIAL AID PROCEDURES

Forms required: FAFSA.
Dates and Deadlines: No deadline. Applicants notified on a rolling basis.
Transfers: No deadline. Applicants notified on a rolling basis.

CONTACT

Mari Huffman, Director of Financial Aid
8001 Katherine Boulevard, Brecksville, OH 44141

Technology Education College

Columbus, Ohio
www.teccollege.com Federal Code: 011005

2-year for-profit health science and technical and career college in very large city.
Enrollment: 250 undergrads.
Selectivity: Open admission.

BASIC COSTS (2008-2009)

Additional info: Tuition varies per program, but averages $11,952 per academic year.

FINANCIAL AID PICTURE

Students with need: Need-based aid available for full-time and part-time students. Work study available nights.
Students without need: This college awards aid only to students with need.

FINANCIAL AID PROCEDURES

Forms required: FAFSA, institutional form.
Dates and Deadlines: No deadline. Applicants notified on a rolling basis.

CONTACT

Nicole Morgan, Director of Financial Aid
2745 Winchester Pike, Columbus, OH 43232
(614) 456-4600

Terra State Community College

Fremont, Ohio
www.terra.edu Federal Code: 008278

2-year public community and technical college in large town.
Enrollment: 2,464 undergrads.
Selectivity: Open admission.

BASIC COSTS (2008-2009)

Tuition and fees: $3,610; out-of-state residents $5,657.
Per-credit charge: $108; out-of-state residents $176.

FINANCIAL AID PICTURE

Students with need: Need-based aid available for full-time and part-time students.
Students without need: No-need awards available for academics.

FINANCIAL AID PROCEDURES

Forms required: FAFSA, institutional form.
Dates and Deadlines: Priority date 5/1; no closing date. Applicants notified on a rolling basis starting 5/15.

CONTACT

Dale Stearns, Director of Financial Aid
2830 Napoleon Road, Fremont, OH 43420-9600
(419) 559-2344

Tiffin University

Tiffin, Ohio
www.tiffin.edu Federal Code: 003121

4-year private university and business college in large town.
Enrollment: 1,716 undergrads, 9% part-time. 408 full-time freshmen.
Selectivity: Admits 50 to 75% of applicants.

BASIC COSTS (2009-2010)

Tuition and fees: $17,730.
Per-credit charge: $591.
Room and board: $7,985.

FINANCIAL AID PICTURE (2008-2009)

Students with need: Out of 405 full-time freshmen who applied for aid, 363 were judged to have need. Of these, 363 received aid, and 41 had their full need met. Average financial aid package met 11% of need; average scholarship/grant was $5,720; average loan was $3,375. For part-time students, average financial aid package was $3,942.
Students without need: 26 full-time freshmen who did not demonstrate need for aid received scholarships/grants, average award was $7,231. No-need awards available for academics, alumni affiliation, athletics, leadership, music/drama, state/district residency.
Scholarships offered: 7 full-time freshmen received athletic scholarships; average amount $7,250.
Cumulative student debt: 95% of graduating class had student loans; average debt was $26,010.

FINANCIAL AID PROCEDURES

Forms required: FAFSA.
Dates and Deadlines: No deadline. Applicants notified on a rolling basis starting 1/15; must reply within 2 week(s) of notification.
Transfers: No deadline.

CONTACT

Cindy Little, Director of Financial Aid
155 Miami Street, Tiffin, OH 44883
(800) 968-6446 ext. 3279

Trumbull Business College

Warren, Ohio
www.tbc-trumbullbusiness.com Federal Code: 013585

2-year for-profit business college in large town.
Enrollment: 322 undergrads.
Selectivity: Open admission.

BASIC COSTS (2008-2009)

Tuition and fees: $12,171.
Per-credit charge: $252.

FINANCIAL AID PICTURE

Students with need: Need-based aid available for full-time and part-time students.

FINANCIAL AID PROCEDURES

Forms required: FAFSA.

CONTACT

Florence Henning, Financial Assistance Director
3200 Ridge Road, Warren, OH 44484
(330) 369-3200 ext. 12

Union Institute & University

Cincinnati, Ohio
www.tui.edu Federal Code: 010923

4-year private university in very large city.
Enrollment: 916 undergrads, 33% part-time. 20 full-time freshmen.

BASIC COSTS (2008-2009)

Tuition and fees: $10,528.
Per-credit charge: $434.

FINANCIAL AID PICTURE (2007-2008)

Students with need: Need-based aid available for full-time and part-time students.
Students without need: No-need awards available for academics, state/district residency.

FINANCIAL AID PROCEDURES

Forms required: FAFSA, institutional form.
Dates and Deadlines: No deadline. Must reply within 4 week(s) of notification.

CONTACT

Victoria Walker, Director of Financial Aid
440 East McMillan Street, Cincinnati, OH 45206
(800) 486-3116

University of Akron

Akron, Ohio
www.uakron.edu Federal Code: 003123

4-year public university in small city.
Enrollment: 18,521 undergrads, 19% part-time. 3,917 full-time freshmen.
Selectivity: Admits 50 to 75% of applicants.

BASIC COSTS (2008-2009)

Tuition and fees: $8,612; out-of-state residents $17,861.
Per-credit charge: $301; out-of-state residents $609.
Room and board: $8,311.

FINANCIAL AID PICTURE (2007-2008)

Students with need: Out of 3,263 full-time freshmen who applied for aid, 2,650 were judged to have need. Of these, 2,650 received aid, and 230 had their full need met. Average financial aid package met 50% of need; average scholarship/grant was $4,956; average loan was $3,371. For part-time students, average financial aid package was $5,071.
Students without need: 352 full-time freshmen who did not demonstrate need for aid received scholarships/grants; average award was $3,533. No-need awards available for academics, art, athletics, leadership, music/drama, ROTC, state/district residency.
Scholarships offered: ***Merit:*** Scholarships for Excellence; $6,000 per year; based on 3.8 GPA, 30 ACT, 1320 SAT (exclusive of Writing); deadline February 1. Presidential Scholarships; $3,000 per year; based on 3.8 GPA, 27 ACT, 1200 SAT. Honors Scholarships; $1,500-$3,000 per year; based on top 10% of class, 3.5 GPA; deadline December 31. Jim and Vanita Oeschlager Leadership Award; $1,000-$17,000 per year; based on leadership and service. Academic Scholarship; $500-$1,500 per year; based on upper 30% of high school class, 21 ACT, 3.0 GPA. Akron Advantage Award; non-resident surcharge reduction of 60% or 100%; for students who meet academic criteria from 49 states outside of Ohio plus U.S. territories. ***Athletic:*** 31 full-time freshmen received athletic scholarships; average amount $8,796.
Cumulative student debt: 63% of graduating class had student loans; average debt was $17,450.

FINANCIAL AID PROCEDURES

Forms required: FAFSA, institutional form.
Dates and Deadlines: Priority date 2/1; no closing date. Applicants notified on a rolling basis starting 4/1; must reply within 2 week(s) of notification.
Transfers: Priority date 3/1; no deadline. Applicants notified on a rolling basis starting 6/15; must reply within 2 week(s) of notification.

CONTACT

Douglas McNutt, Director, Student Financial Aid
The University of Akron, Akron, OH 44325-2001
(330) 972-7032

University of Akron: Wayne College

Orrville, Ohio
www.wayne.uakron.edu Federal Code: 003123

2-year public branch campus and junior college in small town.
Enrollment: 1,700 undergrads.
Selectivity: Open admission.

BASIC COSTS (2008-2009)

Tuition and fees: $5,331; out-of-state residents $12,854.

FINANCIAL AID PICTURE

Students with need: Need-based aid available for full-time and part-time students. Work study available nights, weekends, and for part-time students.
Students without need: No-need awards available for academics, art, athletics, leadership, minority status, music/drama, state/district residency.
Additional info: All financial aid processed through University of Akron.

FINANCIAL AID PROCEDURES

Forms required: FAFSA, institutional form.
Dates and Deadlines: Closing date 3/15. Applicants notified on a rolling basis starting 4/15.

CONTACT

Theresa Mountel, Financial Aid Counselor
1901 Smucker Road, Orrville, OH 44667-9758
(330) 684-8900

University of Cincinnati

Cincinnati, Ohio
www.uc.edu Federal Code: 003125

4-year public university in large city.
Enrollment: 20,183 undergrads, 15% part-time. 3,679 full-time freshmen.
Selectivity: Admits 50 to 75% of applicants.

BASIC COSTS (2008-2009)

Tuition and fees: $9,399; out-of-state residents $23,922.
Per-credit charge: $262; out-of-state residents $665.
Room and board: $9,240.

FINANCIAL AID PICTURE (2008-2009)

Students with need: Need-based aid available for full-time and part-time students. Work study available nights, weekends, and for part-time students.
Students without need: No-need awards available for academics, alumni affiliation, art, athletics, leadership, minority status, music/drama, ROTC, state/district residency.

FINANCIAL AID PROCEDURES

Forms required: FAFSA.
Dates and Deadlines: No deadline. Applicants notified on a rolling basis starting 3/10; must reply within 2 week(s) of notification.

CONTACT

Connie Williams, Director, Financial Aid
PO Box 210091, Cincinnati, OH 45221-0091
(513) 556-6982

University of Cincinnati: Clermont College

Batavia, Ohio
www.ucclermont.edu Federal Code: 003125

2-year public branch campus college in small town.
Enrollment: 2,886 undergrads, 34% part-time. 654 full-time freshmen.
Selectivity: Open admission; but selective for some programs.

BASIC COSTS (2008-2009)

Tuition and fees: $4,542; out-of-state residents $11,394.
Per-credit charge: $127; out-of-state residents $317.

FINANCIAL AID PICTURE (2008-2009)

Students with need: Need-based aid available for full-time and part-time students. Work study available nights, weekends, and for part-time students.
Students without need: No-need awards available for academics, state/district residency
Additional info: All financial aid applications and awards administered through Uptown campus except in-house loans and scholarships.

FINANCIAL AID PROCEDURES

Forms required: FAFSA.
Dates and Deadlines: No deadline. Applicants notified on a rolling basis.

CONTACT

Jessica Max, University Services Associate
4200 Clermont College Drive, Batavia, OH 45103
(513) 732-5202

University of Cincinnati: Raymond Walters College

Cincinnati, Ohio
www.rwc.uc.edu Federal Code: 003125

2-year public branch campus college in large city.
Enrollment: 3,859 undergrads.
Selectivity: Open admission; but selective for some programs.

BASIC COSTS (2008-2009)

Tuition and fees: $5,232; out-of-state residents $13,566.
Per-credit charge: $146; out-of-state residents $377.

FINANCIAL AID PICTURE

Students with need: Need-based aid available for full-time and part-time students.
Students without need: This college awards aid only to students with need.
Scholarships offered: Dean's scholarships; $1,500; based on 2.5 GPA, tech prep program participation, 2-page essay; 10 available. Cincinnatus Scholarship Competition; $1,500-full tuition, room, board and books; must have 26 ACT or be in top 5% of high school class to qualify to compete.
Additional info: All financial aid applications and awards administered through main campus.

FINANCIAL AID PROCEDURES

Forms required: FAFSA.
Dates and Deadlines: Priority date 3/15; no closing date. Applicants notified on a rolling basis starting 3/15; must reply within 2 week(s) of notification.

CONTACT

Chris Powers, Director of Enrollment Management
9555 Plainfield Road, Cincinnati, OH 45236-1096
(513) 745-5740

University of Dayton

Dayton, Ohio
www.udayton.edu Federal Code: 003127

4-year private university in small city, affiliated with Roman Catholic Church.
Enrollment: 7,420 undergrads, 4% part-time. 1,773 full-time freshmen.
Selectivity: Admits 50 to 75% of applicants.

BASIC COSTS (2009-2010)

Tuition and fees: $28,690.
Per-credit charge: $917.
Room and board: $8,290.
Additional info: $1,299 additional cost to all new incoming students for purchase of computer from university. International students pay additional $75 per month for health and accident insurance. Engineering majors required to pay additional $870 per semester in fees. Tuition/fee waivers available for adults.

FINANCIAL AID PICTURE (2007-2008)

Students with need: Out of 1,380 full-time freshmen who applied for aid, 1,040 were judged to have need. Of these, 1,036 received aid. Average financial aid package met 95% of need; average scholarship/grant was $12,448; average loan was $6,077. For part-time students, average financial aid package was $5,270.
Students without need: 852 full-time freshmen who did not demonstrate need for aid received scholarships/grants; average award was $6,832. No-need awards available for academics, alumni affiliation, art, athletics, leadership, music/drama, ROTC, state/district residency.
Scholarships offered: ***Merit:*** Berry Scholarships; up to full tuition; based on GPA, ACT/SAT scores, service and leadership. Marianist Heritage Awards; $1,000 to full tuition; available to all graduates of Marianist high schools who

meet academic criteria. Music talent awards; $1,000 to $5,000; based on auditions. President's Scholarship; $1,000 to $10,000; based on GPA, ACT/SAT scores, service and leadership. Visual arts awards; amounts vary; based on student portfolios. Chaminade Scholarships; $2,500; for students accepted to the Chaminade Scholars Program. National Merit Scholarships; $1,000 to $2,000; available to all students who are selected by the National Merit Scholarship Corporation and select UD as their first choice. Army ROTC awards; supplements U.S. Army ROTC awards with scholarship incentives. ***Athletic:*** 23 full-time freshmen received athletic scholarships; average amount $14,321.

Cumulative student debt: 59% of graduating class had student loans; average debt was $19,162.

FINANCIAL AID PROCEDURES

Forms required: FAFSA.

Dates and Deadlines: Priority date 3/31; no closing date. Applicants notified on a rolling basis starting 3/1; must reply by 5/1 or within 3 week(s) of notification.

Transfers: Priority date 6/1; no deadline. Applicants notified on a rolling basis starting 2/25; must reply within 2 week(s) of notification. Students must submit FAFSA prior to October 1 each year for consideration for state funds.

CONTACT

Kathy Harmon, Director of Financial Aid
300 College Park, Dayton, OH 45469-1300
(937) 229-4311

University of Findlay

Findlay, Ohio
www.findlay.edu Federal Code: 003045

4-year private university and health science college in large town, affiliated with Church of God.

Enrollment: 3,011 undergrads, 11% part-time. 617 full-time freshmen.

Selectivity: Admits 50 to 75% of applicants.

BASIC COSTS (2009-2010)

Tuition and fees: $25,774.

Per-credit charge: $552.

Room and board: $8,554.

Additional info: Pre-veterinary and equestrian students pay higher tuition in years one and two; pharmacy students pay higher tuition throughout the program.

FINANCIAL AID PICTURE (2007-2008)

Students with need: Average financial aid package met 71% of need; average scholarship/grant was $11,972; average loan was $3,029.

Students without need: No-need awards available for academics, alumni affiliation, athletics, music/drama, state/district residency.

Scholarships offered: Full tuition available to select valedictorian/salutatorians. Automatic academic awards available based on GPA, test scores.

Cumulative student debt: 89% of graduating class had student loans; average debt was $326,000.

FINANCIAL AID PROCEDURES

Forms required: FAFSA.

Dates and Deadlines: Priority date 8/1; closing date 9/1. Applicants notified on a rolling basis starting 3/1; must reply within 2 week(s) of notification.

CONTACT

Arman Habegger, Director of Financial Aid
1000 North Main Street, Findlay, OH 45840-3653
(419) 434-4791

University of Northwestern Ohio

Lima, Ohio
www.unoh.edu Federal Code: 004861

2-year private business and technical college in large town.

Enrollment: 3,616 undergrads.

BASIC COSTS (2008-2009)

Tuition and fees: $9,063.

Per-credit charge: $195.

Room only: $2,700.

Additional info: $245 per credit hour charge for virtual classes. Tuition/fee waivers available for minority students.

FINANCIAL AID PICTURE (2007-2008)

Students with need: 36% of average financial aid package awarded as scholarships/grants, 64% awarded as loans/jobs. Need-based aid available for part-time students. Work study available nights.

Students without need: No-need awards available for academics, job skills, minority status.

FINANCIAL AID PROCEDURES

Forms required: FAFSA.

Dates and Deadlines: Priority date 4/1; no closing date. Applicants notified on a rolling basis starting 4/30; must reply within 2 week(s) of notification.

Transfers: No deadline. Applicants notified on a rolling basis.

CONTACT

Wendell Schick, Director of Financial Aid
1441 North Cable Road, Lima, OH 45805
(419) 227-3141

University of Rio Grande

Rio Grande, Ohio
www.rio.edu Federal Code: 003116

4-year private community and liberal arts college in rural community.

Enrollment: 1,484 undergrads, 17% part-time. 342 full-time freshmen.

Selectivity: Open admission; but selective for some programs.

BASIC COSTS (2008-2009)

Tuition and fees: $18,260.

Room and board: $7,000.

Additional info: Tuition reported is for private university sector of institution. Public community college in-state in-district tuition: $2,880 ($96 per credit hour); in-state out-of-district, $3,450 ($115 per credit hour). All public community college undergraduates pay $632 in required fees. Out-of-state community college students charged private tuition rate.

FINANCIAL AID PICTURE (2007-2008)

Students with need: Out of 313 full-time freshmen who applied for aid, 251 were judged to have need. Of these, 241 received aid, and 49 had their full need met. Average financial aid package met 55% of need; average scholarship/grant was $2,655; average loan was $1,595. For part-time students, average financial aid package was $9,210.

Students without need: No-need awards available for academics, alumni affiliation, athletics, leadership, music/drama, state/district residency.

FINANCIAL AID PROCEDURES

Forms required: FAFSA, institutional form.

Dates and Deadlines: Priority date 3/15; no closing date. Applicants notified on a rolling basis starting 1/15; must reply within 3 week(s) of notification.

CONTACT

Dawn Knepper, Financial Aid Director
218 North College Avenue, Rio Grande, OH 45674
(740) 245-7218

University of Toledo

Toledo, Ohio
www.utoledo.edu Federal Code: 003131

4-year public university in large city.
Enrollment: 16,737 undergrads, 16% part-time. 3,943 full-time freshmen.
Selectivity: Open admission; but selective for some programs and for out-of-state students.

BASIC COSTS (2008-2009)

Tuition and fees: $7,926; out-of-state residents $16,738.
Per-credit charge: $284; out-of-state residents $651.
Room and board: $8,814.

FINANCIAL AID PICTURE (2008-2009)

Students with need: Out of 3,368 full-time freshmen who applied for aid, 2,482 were judged to have need. Of these, 2,481 received aid, and 503 had their full need met. Average financial aid package met 66% of need; average scholarship/grant was $6,536; average loan was $3,604. For part-time students, average financial aid package was $6,869.
Students without need: 1,302 full-time freshmen who did not demonstrate need for aid received scholarships/grants; average award was $3,773. No-need awards available for academics, alumni affiliation, art, athletics, leadership, minority status, music/drama, ROTC, state/district residency.
Scholarships offered: ***Merit:*** Freshman merit scholarships; $100 to $4,500; 400 awarded. ***Athletic:*** 54 full-time freshmen received athletic scholarships; average amount $14,710.
Cumulative student debt: 69% of graduating class had student loans; average debt was $25,711.
Additional info: March priority date for federal aid. Students encouraged to apply as early as December for priority consideration for institutional aid.

FINANCIAL AID PROCEDURES

Forms required: FAFSA.
Dates and Deadlines: Priority date 3/1; no closing date. Applicants notified on a rolling basis starting 3/1; must reply within 8 week(s) of notification.

CONTACT

Carolyn Baumgartner, Director of Financial Aid
2801 West Bancroft Street, Toledo, OH 43606-3398
(419) 530-2800

Urbana University

Urbana, Ohio
www.urbana.edu Federal Code: 003133

4-year private liberal arts college in large town.
Enrollment: 829 full-time undergrads.

BASIC COSTS (2008-2009)

Tuition and fees: $19,864.
Per-credit charge: $390.
Room and board: $7,570.

FINANCIAL AID PICTURE (2008-2009)

Students with need: Need-based aid available for full-time and part-time students. Work study available nights, weekends, and for part-time students.
Students without need: No-need awards available for academics, alumni affiliation, athletics, music/drama.
Scholarships offered: All regularly accepted students receive cash scholarship for academics, music, or athletics.

FINANCIAL AID PROCEDURES

Forms required: FAFSA.
Dates and Deadlines: Closing date 4/1. Applicants notified on a rolling basis starting 3/1; must reply within 4 week(s) of notification.
Transfers: No deadline.

CONTACT

Amy Barnhart, Director of Financial Aid
579 College Way, Urbana, OH 43078
(937) 484-1355

Ursuline College

Pepper Pike, Ohio
www.ursuline.edu Federal Code: 003134

4-year private liberal arts college for women in small town, affiliated with Roman Catholic Church.
Enrollment: 1,093 undergrads, 32% part-time. 110 full-time freshmen.
Selectivity: Admits less than 50% of applicants.

BASIC COSTS (2008-2009)

Tuition and fees: $22,060.
Per-credit charge: $728.
Room and board: $7,352.

FINANCIAL AID PICTURE (2007-2008)

Students with need: Out of 96 full-time freshmen who applied for aid, 86 were judged to have need. Of these, 86 received aid, and 18 had their full need met. Average financial aid package met 87% of need; average scholarship/grant was $13,674; average loan was $4,615. For part-time students, average financial aid package was $8,773.
Students without need: 23 full-time freshmen who did not demonstrate need for aid received scholarships/grants; average award was $8,343. No-need awards available for academics, art, athletics, leadership, religious affiliation, ROTC.
Scholarships offered: ***Merit:*** Ursuline Scholarship; $5,000 to $7,000 renewable. Ursuline Award; $1,500 to $3,500 renewable. Presidential Scholarship; $11,000 renewable. Dean's Scholarship; $9,000 renewable. Unlimited number available for each. ***Athletic:*** 6 full-time freshmen received athletic scholarships; average amount $3,879.
Cumulative student debt: 42% of graduating class had student loans; average debt was $24,150.

FINANCIAL AID PROCEDURES

Forms required: FAFSA.
Dates and Deadlines: Priority date 3/15; no closing date. Applicants notified on a rolling basis starting 3/1; must reply within 2 week(s) of notification.

CONTACT

Mary Lynn Perri, Director of Financial Aid
2550 Lander Road, Pepper Pike, OH 44124-4398
(440) 646-8309

Vatterott College: Cleveland

Broadview Heights, Ohio
www.vatterott-college.edu

2-year for-profit technical college in large town.
Enrollment: 243 undergrads.
Selectivity: Open admission.

BASIC COSTS (2008-2009)

Additional info: Program cost ranges: $18,400 to $19,600 (certificate/diploma); $32,250 (associate degree).

FINANCIAL AID PICTURE (2008-2009)

Students with need: 35% of average financial aid package awarded as scholarships/grants, 65% awarded as loans/jobs.

FINANCIAL AID PROCEDURES

Dates and Deadlines: No deadline.

CONTACT

Linda Sullivan, Director of Financial Aid
5025 East Royalton Road, Broadview Heights, OH 44147

Virginia Marti College of Art and Design

Lakewood, Ohio
www.vmcad.edu Federal Code: 012896

2-year for-profit visual arts and business college in large city.
Enrollment: 260 undergrads.

BASIC COSTS (2008-2009)

Tuition and fees: $19,215.
Per-credit charge: $345.
Additional info: Tuition at time of enrollment locked for 2 years.

FINANCIAL AID PICTURE

Students with need: Need-based aid available for full-time students.
Students without need: This college awards aid only to students with need.

FINANCIAL AID PROCEDURES

Forms required: FAFSA.
Dates and Deadlines: No deadline. Applicants notified on a rolling basis.

CONTACT

Jennifer Minkiewicz, Financial Aid Officer
11724 Detroit Avenue, Lakewood, OH 44107

Walsh University

North Canton, Ohio
www.walsh.edu Federal Code: 003135

4-year private university and liberal arts college in small city, affiliated with Roman Catholic Church.
Enrollment: 2,291 undergrads, 19% part-time. 516 full-time freshmen.
Selectivity: Admits over 75% of applicants.

BASIC COSTS (2008-2009)

Tuition and fees: $20,050.
Per-credit charge: $640.
Room and board: $7,760.

FINANCIAL AID PICTURE (2008-2009)

Students with need: Out of 513 full-time freshmen who applied for aid, 451 were judged to have need. Of these, 451 received aid, and 243 had their full need met. Average financial aid package met 73% of need; average scholarship/grant was $4,008; average loan was $2,816. For part-time students, average financial aid package was $6,604.
Students without need: 87 full-time freshmen who did not demonstrate need for aid received scholarships/grants; average award was $6,114. No-need awards available for academics, alumni affiliation, athletics, music/drama, religious affiliation, state/district residency.
Scholarships offered: ***Merit:*** $1,000 for incoming freshmen who have graduated from Catholic high school. ***Athletic:*** 163 full-time freshmen received athletic scholarships; average amount $3,898.
Cumulative student debt: 98% of graduating class had student loans; average debt was $21,352.

FINANCIAL AID PROCEDURES

Forms required: FAFSA, institutional form.
Dates and Deadlines: Priority date 3/15; no closing date. Applicants notified on a rolling basis starting 2/15.
Transfers: No deadline. Applicants notified on a rolling basis starting 3/15.

CONTACT

Holly Van Gilder, Financial Aid Director
2020 East Maple Street NW, North Canton, OH 44720-3396
(330) 490-7146

Wilberforce University

Wilberforce, Ohio
www.wilberforce.edu Federal Code: 003141

4-year private liberal arts college in rural community, affiliated with African Methodist Episcopal Church.
Enrollment: 807 undergrads.
Selectivity: Admits 50 to 75% of applicants.

BASIC COSTS (2008-2009)

Tuition and fees: $11,560.
Per-credit charge: $438.
Room and board: $5,320.

FINANCIAL AID PICTURE

Students with need: Need-based aid available for full-time and part-time students.

FINANCIAL AID PROCEDURES

Forms required: FAFSA, institutional form.
Dates and Deadlines: Priority date 3/15; closing date 6/1. Applicants notified on a rolling basis starting 3/15; must reply within 2 week(s) of notification.

CONTACT

Shelline Perry, Director for Financial Aid
1055 North Bickett Road, Wilberforce, OH 45384-1001
(937) 708-5727

Wilmington College

Wilmington, Ohio
www.wilmington.edu Federal Code: 003142

4-year private liberal arts college in large town, affiliated with Society of Friends (Quaker).
Enrollment: 1,440 undergrads, 17% part-time. 347 full-time freshmen.
Selectivity: Admits over 75% of applicants.

BASIC COSTS (2008-2009)

Tuition and fees: $23,372.
Per-credit charge: $425.
Room and board: $8,010.

FINANCIAL AID PICTURE

Students with need: Need-based aid available for full-time and part-time students.
Students without need: No-need awards available for academics, alumni affiliation, religious affiliation, state/district residency.

FINANCIAL AID PROCEDURES

Forms required: FAFSA.
Dates and Deadlines: Priority date 3/31; closing date 6/1. Applicants notified on a rolling basis starting 3/1; must reply by 5/1 or within 2 week(s) of notification.

CONTACT

Cheryl Loualen, Director of Financial Aid
Box 1325 Pyle Center, Wilmington, OH 45177
(937) 382-6661 ext. 249

Wittenberg University

Springfield, Ohio
www.wittenberg.edu Federal Code: 003143

4-year private liberal arts college in small city, affiliated with Evangelical Lutheran Church in America.
Enrollment: 1,811 undergrads, 1% part-time. 510 full-time freshmen.
Selectivity: Admits 50 to 75% of applicants.

BASIC COSTS (2009-2010)

Tuition and fees: $34,190.
Per-credit charge: $1,130.
Room and board: $8,772.

FINANCIAL AID PICTURE (2007-2008)

Students with need: Need-based aid available for full-time students. Work study available nights, weekends, and for part-time students.
Students without need: This college awards aid only to students with need.
Scholarships offered: Smith Family Scholar Award; full tuition; renewable; based on academic achievement and other qualities. University Scholar Award; half tuition; renewable; based on academic achievement and other qualities. Broadwell Chinn Scholarship; half tuition; renewable; based on minority status, academic achievement, and other qualities.
Additional info: Auditions required from applicants for music, theater, and dance scholarships. Portfolio required of applicants for art scholarships.

FINANCIAL AID PROCEDURES

Forms required: FAFSA.
Dates and Deadlines: Priority date 3/15; no closing date. Applicants notified on a rolling basis starting 3/1; must reply by 5/1 or within 2 week(s) of notification.
Transfers: Priority date 5/15.

CONTACT

Jonathan Green, Director of Financial Aid
Ward Street and North Wittenberg, Springfield, OH 45501-0720
(937) 327-7321

Wright State University

Dayton, Ohio
www.wright.edu Federal Code: 003078

4-year public university in small city.
Enrollment: 12,326 undergrads, 12% part-time. 2,352 full-time freshmen.
Selectivity: Admits over 75% of applicants.

BASIC COSTS (2008-2009)

Tuition and fees: $7,278; out-of-state residents $14,004.
Per-credit charge: $219; out-of-state residents $425.
Room and board: $7,180.

FINANCIAL AID PICTURE (2007-2008)

Students with need: Out of 1,926 full-time freshmen who applied for aid, 1,569 were judged to have need. Of these, 1,562 received aid, and 283 had their full need met. Average financial aid package met 62% of need; average scholarship/grant was $4,362; average loan was $3,602. For part-time students, average financial aid package was $6,961.
Students without need: 270 full-time freshmen who did not demonstrate need for aid received scholarships/grants; average award was $3,136. Noneed awards available for academics, alumni affiliation, art, athletics, leadership, minority status, music/drama, ROTC.
Scholarships offered: 35 full-time freshmen received athletic scholarships; average amount $10,216.
Cumulative student debt: 71% of graduating class had student loans; average debt was $22,829.

FINANCIAL AID PROCEDURES

Forms required: FAFSA.
Dates and Deadlines: Priority date 2/15; no closing date. Applicants notified on a rolling basis starting 3/15.

CONTACT

Willie Boyd, Director of Financial Aid
3640 Colonel Glenn Highway, Dayton, OH 45435
(937) 775-5727

Wright State University: Lake Campus

Celina, Ohio
www.wright.edu/lake Federal Code: 003078

2-year public branch campus college in small town.
Enrollment: 653 undergrads, 23% part-time. 125 full-time freshmen.
Selectivity: Open admission; but selective for some programs.

BASIC COSTS (2008-2009)

Tuition and fees: $4,893; out-of-state residents $11,619.
Per-credit charge: $148; out-of-state residents $354.
Additional info: Tuition at time of enrollment locked for 2 years.

FINANCIAL AID PICTURE (2007-2008)

Students with need: Out of 99 full-time freshmen who applied for aid, 81 were judged to have need. Of these, 80 received aid, and 18 had their full need met. Average financial aid package met 64% of need; average scholarship/grant was $3,932; average loan was $3,215. For part-time students, average financial aid package was $5,809.
Students without need: 17 full-time freshmen who did not demonstrate need for aid received scholarships/grants; average award was $2,840. Noneed awards available for academics, alumni affiliation, art, athletics, leadership, minority status, music/drama, ROTC.

FINANCIAL AID PROCEDURES

Forms required: FAFSA.
Dates and Deadlines: Priority date 2/15; no closing date. Applicants notified on a rolling basis starting 3/15.

CONTACT

B.J. Hobler, Registrar
7600 State Route 703, Celina, OH 45822-2952
(419) 586-0336

Xavier University

Cincinnati, Ohio
www.xavier.edu Federal Code: 003144

4-year private university in large city, affiliated with Roman Catholic Church.
Enrollment: 3,780 undergrads, 10% part-time. 860 full-time freshmen.
Selectivity: Admits over 75% of applicants.

BASIC COSTS (2009-2010)

Tuition and fees: $28,570.
Per-credit charge: $550.
Room and board: $9,530.
Additional info: Tuition/fee waivers available for adults, unemployed or children of unemployed.

FINANCIAL AID PICTURE (2008-2009)

Students with need: Out of 676 full-time freshmen who applied for aid, 531 were judged to have need. Of these, 530 received aid, and 146 had their full need met. Average financial aid package met 78% of need; average scholarship/grant was $11,289; average loan was $4,470. For part-time students, average financial aid package was $5,832.

Students without need: 226 full-time freshmen who did not demonstrate need for aid received scholarships/grants; average award was $9,922. No-need awards available for academics, alumni affiliation, art, athletics, leadership, music/drama, religious affiliation.
Scholarships offered: ***Merit:*** Saint Francis Xavier Scholarship; full tuition; based on leadership, talent and highest academic achievement, competitive; 10 awarded. Community Engaged Fellowship; $18,000; 10 awarded. Chancellor Scholarship; $17,000; based on leadership, talent, and highest academic achievement; number of award varies. Trustee Scholarship; $15,000; based on academic achievement; number of award varies. Schawe Scholarship; $15,000; based on academic achievement; number of award varies. Presidential Scholarship; $13,000; based on academic achievement; number of award varies. Honor Award; $10,000; based on academic achievement; number of award varies. Buschmann Award; $8,000; based on academic leadership and service records; number of award varies. Leadership Award; $5,000; number of award varies. ***Athletic:*** 38 full-time freshmen received athletic scholarships; average amount $12,057.
Cumulative student debt: 68% of graduating class had student loans; average debt was $22,879.

FINANCIAL AID PROCEDURES

Forms required: FAFSA.
Dates and Deadlines: Priority date 2/15; no closing date. Applicants notified on a rolling basis starting 2/15; must reply by 5/1.
Transfers: No deadline. Applicants notified on a rolling basis starting 3/1; must reply by 5/1.

CONTACT

Paul Calme, Director of Financial Aid
3800 Victory Parkway, Cincinnati, OH 45207-5311
(513) 745-3142

Youngstown State University

Youngstown, Ohio
www.ysu.edu Federal Code: 003145

4-year public university in small city.
Enrollment: 12,090 undergrads, 19% part-time. 2,082 full-time freshmen.
Selectivity: Open admission; but selective for some programs and for out-of-state students.

BASIC COSTS (2008-2009)

Tuition and fees: $6,721; out-of-state residents $12,394.
Room and board: $7,090.
Additional info: Residents of any out-of-state area within 100 miles of campus are charged $9,414 yearly tuition. Per credit hour charge is $392.

FINANCIAL AID PICTURE (2007-2008)

Students with need: 33% of average financial aid package awarded as scholarships/grants, 67% awarded as loans/jobs. Need-based aid available for part-time students.
Students without need: No-need awards available for academics, alumni affiliation, athletics, ROTC, state/district residency.

FINANCIAL AID PROCEDURES

Forms required: FAFSA, institutional form.
Dates and Deadlines: Priority date 2/15; no closing date. Applicants notified on a rolling basis starting 5/30; must reply within 2 week(s) of notification.

CONTACT

Elaine Ruse, Director of Scholarships and Financial Aid
One University Plaza, Youngstown, OH 44555-0001
(330) 941-3505

Zane State College

Zanesville, Ohio
www.zanestate.edu Federal Code: 008133

2-year public technical college in large town.
Enrollment: 1,942 undergrads, 40% part-time. 226 full-time freshmen.
Selectivity: Open admission; but selective for some programs.

BASIC COSTS (2008-2009)

Tuition and fees: $3,825; out-of-state residents $7,650.
Per-credit charge: $75; out-of-state residents $160.

FINANCIAL AID PICTURE

Students with need: Need-based aid available for full-time and part-time students.

FINANCIAL AID PROCEDURES

Forms required: FAFSA.
Dates and Deadlines: Priority date 5/1; closing date 7/15. Must reply by 9/1.

CONTACT

Amanda McPherson, Financial Aid Director
1555 Newark Road, Zanesville, OH 43701-2626
(740) 454-2501 ext. 1275

Oklahoma

Bacone College

Muskogee, Oklahoma
www.bacone.edu Federal Code: 003147

4-year private liberal arts college in large town, affiliated with American Baptist Churches in the USA.
Enrollment: 928 undergrads, 12% part-time. 96 full-time freshmen.
Selectivity: Admits 50 to 75% of applicants.

BASIC COSTS (2009-2010)

Tuition and fees: $11,700.
Per-credit charge: $431.
Room and board: $8,000.

FINANCIAL AID PICTURE (2008-2009)

Students with need: Need-based aid available for full-time and part-time students. Work study available nights, weekends, and for part-time students.
Students without need: This college awards aid only to students with need.

FINANCIAL AID PROCEDURES

Forms required: FAFSA.
Dates and Deadlines: Priority date 3/31; no closing date. Applicants notified on a rolling basis starting 4/1; must reply within 2 week(s) of notification.
Transfers: No deadline. Applicants notified on a rolling basis.

CONTACT

Kathye Watson, Director of Financial Aid
2299 Old Bacone Road, Muskogee, OK 74403
(918) 781-7340

Cameron University

Lawton, Oklahoma
www.cameron.edu Federal Code: 003150

4-year public university and liberal arts college in small city.
Enrollment: 4,700 undergrads, 32% part-time. 701 full-time freshmen.

Selectivity: Admits over 75% of applicants.

BASIC COSTS (2008-2009)

Tuition and fees: $4,110; out-of-state residents $9,975.

Per-credit charge: $94; out-of-state residents $289.

Room and board: $3,560.

FINANCIAL AID PICTURE (2007-2008)

Students with need: Out of 498 full-time freshmen who applied for aid, 443 were judged to have need. Of these, 385 received aid, and 315 had their full need met. Average financial aid package met 85% of need; average scholarship/grant was $3,500; average loan was $1,000. For part-time students, average financial aid package was $7,458.

Students without need: 105 full-time freshmen who did not demonstrate need for aid received scholarships/grants; average award was $500. No-need awards available for academics, alumni affiliation, art, athletics, leadership, music/drama, ROTC.

Scholarships offered: 17 full-time freshmen received athletic scholarships; average amount $1,500.

Cumulative student debt: 30% of graduating class had student loans; average debt was $6,300.

FINANCIAL AID PROCEDURES

Forms required: FAFSA.

Dates and Deadlines: Priority date 5/1; no closing date. Applicants notified on a rolling basis starting 4/1; must reply by 8/7 or within 2 week(s) of notification.

Transfers: Priority date 6/1; no deadline. Applicants notified on a rolling basis starting 6/1. Academic transcripts required.

CONTACT

Carol Claiborne, Director of Financial Assistance
2800 West Gore Boulevard, Lawton, OK 73505-6377
(580) 581-2293

Carl Albert State College

Poteau, Oklahoma
www.carlalbert.edu Federal Code: 003176

2-year public community and junior college in large town.

Enrollment: 2,480 undergrads.

Selectivity: Open admission; but selective for some programs.

BASIC COSTS (2008-2009)

Tuition and fees: $2,250; out-of-state residents $5,220.

Per-credit charge: $51; out-of-state residents $150.

Room and board: $3,384.

Additional info: Tuition/fee waivers available for minority students.

FINANCIAL AID PICTURE

Students with need: Need-based aid available for full-time and part-time students. Work study available nights.

Students without need: This college awards aid only to students with need.

FINANCIAL AID PROCEDURES

Forms required: FAFSA, institutional form.

Dates and Deadlines: No deadline. Applicants notified on a rolling basis.

CONTACT

Robin Benson, Director of Financial Aid
1507 South McKenna, Poteau, OK 74953-5208
(918) 647-1343

Connors State College

Warner, Oklahoma
www.connorsstate.edu Federal Code: 003153

2-year public community and junior college in rural community.

Enrollment: 1,747 undergrads, 30% part-time. 465 full-time freshmen.

Selectivity: Open admission; but selective for some programs.

BASIC COSTS (2008-2009)

Tuition and fees: $2,598; out-of-state residents $6,225.

Per-credit charge: $66; out-of-state residents $187.

Room and board: $6,692.

Additional info: Apartment-style housing.

FINANCIAL AID PICTURE (2008-2009)

Students with need: Need-based aid available for full-time and part-time students.

Students without need: No-need awards available for academics, alumni affiliation, athletics, leadership, state/district residency.

FINANCIAL AID PROCEDURES

Forms required: FAFSA, institutional form.

Dates and Deadlines: Priority date 2/28; closing date 5/1. Applicants notified on a rolling basis starting 4/1; must reply within 2 week(s) of notification.

CONTACT

Wanda Fuller, Director of Financial Aid
RR 1, Box 1000, Warner, OK 74469-9700
(918) 463-6220

East Central University

Ada, Oklahoma
www.ecok.edu Federal Code: 003154

4-year public university in large town.

Enrollment: 2,850 full-time undergrads.

Selectivity: Admits over 75% of applicants.

BASIC COSTS (2008-2009)

Tuition and fees: $4,221; out-of-state residents $10,236.

Per-credit charge: $112; out-of-state residents $290.

Room and board: $4,080.

FINANCIAL AID PICTURE (2008-2009)

Students with need: Need-based aid available for full-time and part-time students. Work study available nights, weekends, and for part-time students.

Students without need: No-need awards available for academics, athletics.

FINANCIAL AID PROCEDURES

Forms required: FAFSA.

Dates and Deadlines: Closing date 3/1. Applicants notified on a rolling basis starting 4/15; must reply within 2 week(s) of notification.

CONTACT

Marcia Carter, Director of Student Financial Aid
PMBJ8, 1100 East 14th Street, Ada, OK 74820
(580) 559-5243

Eastern Oklahoma State College

Wilburton, Oklahoma
www.eosc.edu Federal Code: 003155

2-year public community college in small town.

Enrollment: 1,589 undergrads.

Selectivity: Open admission; but selective for some programs.

BASIC COSTS (2008-2009)
Tuition and fees: $2,835; out-of-state residents $6,452.
Per-credit charge: $68; out-of-state residents $189.
Room and board: $4,624.
Additional info: Tuition/fee waivers available for minority students, unemployed or children of unemployed.

FINANCIAL AID PICTURE (2007-2008)
Students with need: 70% of average financial aid package awarded as scholarships/grants, 30% awarded as loans/jobs. Need-based aid available for part-time students.
Students without need: This college awards aid only to students with need.

FINANCIAL AID PROCEDURES
Forms required: FAFSA, institutional form.
Dates and Deadlines: Priority date 3/1; no closing date. Applicants notified on a rolling basis starting 5/1; must reply within 2 week(s) of notification.
Transfers: Priority date 4/30.

CONTACT
Mimi Kelley, Director of Financial Aid
1301 West Main Street, Wilburton, OK 74578-4999
(918) 465-2361 ext. 207

Langston University
Langston, Oklahoma Federal Code: 003157
www.lunet.edu CSS Code: 6361

4-year public university and liberal arts college in rural community.
Enrollment: 2,441 undergrads, 16% part-time. 552 full-time freshmen.
Selectivity: Admits less than 50% of applicants.

BASIC COSTS (2008-2009)
Tuition and fees: $3,827; out-of-state residents $9,407.
Per-credit charge: $88; out-of-state residents $274.
Room and board: $6,890.
Additional info: Housing is apartment-style. Tuition at time of enrollment locked for 4 years.

FINANCIAL AID PICTURE (2007-2008)
Students with need: Need-based aid available for full-time and part-time students.
Students without need: This college awards aid only to students with need.

FINANCIAL AID PROCEDURES
Forms required: CSS PROFILE, state aid form.
Dates and Deadlines: Priority date 3/1; closing date 5/1. Applicants notified on a rolling basis starting 7/15; must reply within 2 week(s) of notification.

CONTACT
Linda Morris, Financial Aid Director
Box 728, Langston, OK 73050

Mid-America Christian University
Oklahoma City, Oklahoma
www.macu.edu Federal Code: 006942

4-year private university and liberal arts college in very large city, affiliated with Church of God.
Enrollment: 758 undergrads.
Selectivity: Open admission.

BASIC COSTS (2009-2010)
Tuition and fees: $13,480.
Per-credit charge: $520.
Room and board: $5,560.

FINANCIAL AID PICTURE (2008-2009)
Students with need: Need-based aid available for full-time and part-time students.
Students without need: No-need awards available for academics, leadership, minority status, music/drama.

FINANCIAL AID PROCEDURES
Forms required: FAFSA.
Dates and Deadlines: Priority date 5/1; no closing date. Applicants notified on a rolling basis starting 5/1.

CONTACT
James Menefee, Director of Student Financial Services
3500 SW 119th Street, Oklahoma City, OK 73170
(405) 692-3182

Northeastern Oklahoma Agricultural and Mechanical College
Miami, Oklahoma
www.neo.edu Federal Code: 316000

2-year public community and junior college in large town.
Enrollment: 1,698 undergrads, 21% part-time. 603 full-time freshmen.
Selectivity: Open admission.

BASIC COSTS (2008-2009)
Tuition and fees: $2,442; out-of-state residents $6,263.
Per-credit charge: $58; out-of-state residents $185.
Room and board: $3,858.

FINANCIAL AID PICTURE (2007-2008)
Students with need: Need-based aid available for full-time and part-time students. Work study available nights, weekends, and for part-time students.
Students without need: No-need awards available for academics, art, athletics, leadership, music/drama, state/district residency.

FINANCIAL AID PROCEDURES
Forms required: FAFSA.
Dates and Deadlines: Priority date 4/1; no closing date. Applicants notified on a rolling basis starting 4/1; must reply by 8/30 or within 2 week(s) of notification.
Transfers: No deadline. Applicants notified on a rolling basis starting 4/1; must reply within 2 week(s) of notification.

CONTACT
Tammy Higgins, Director of Financial Aid
200 I Street Northeast, Miami, OK 74354-6497
(918) 540-6235

Northeastern State University
Tahlequah, Oklahoma
www.nsuok.edu Federal Code: 003161

4-year public university in large town.
Enrollment: 7,727 undergrads, 27% part-time. 953 full-time freshmen.
Selectivity: Admits 50 to 75% of applicants.

BASIC COSTS (2008-2009)
Tuition and fees: $4,155; out-of-state residents $10,245.
Per-credit charge: $107; out-of-state residents $310.
Room and board: $4,784.
Additional info: Tuition at time of enrollment locked for 4 years; tuition/fee waivers available for adults, minority students.

FINANCIAL AID PICTURE (2008-2009)
Students with need: Out of 824 full-time freshmen who applied for aid, 615 were judged to have need. Of these, 587 received aid, and 405 had their full need met. Average financial aid package met 69% of need; average scholarship/grant was $4,710; average loan was $2,032. For part-time students, average financial aid package was $5,722.
Students without need: 286 full-time freshmen who did not demonstrate need for aid received scholarships/grants; average award was $1,022. No-need awards available for academics, alumni affiliation, art, athletics, job skills, leadership, minority status, music/drama, religious affiliation, ROTC, state/district residency.
Scholarships offered: ***Merit:*** Honors Program; $2,900 per year with 28 ACT or up to $7,426 per year with 30 ACT; determined primarily by ACT and 3.8 high school GPA. ***Athletic:*** 48 full-time freshmen received athletic scholarships; average amount $3,096.
Cumulative student debt: 64% of graduating class had student loans; average debt was $18,573.
Additional info: Participates in off-campus job location & development program to assist students with off-campus employers to earn money for college expenses.

FINANCIAL AID PROCEDURES
Forms required: FAFSA, institutional form.
Dates and Deadlines: Priority date 3/15; no closing date. Applicants notified on a rolling basis starting 3/15.
Transfers: Priority date 12/15; no deadline. State grant deadline is April 15.

CONTACT
Teri Cochran, Director of Student Financial Services
600 North Grand Avenue, Tahlequah, OK 74464-2399
(918) 444-3456

Northern Oklahoma College
Tonkawa, Oklahoma
www.north-ok.edu Federal Code: 003162

2-year public community college in small town.
Enrollment: 3,804 undergrads.
Selectivity: Open admission; but selective for out-of-state students.

BASIC COSTS (2008-2009)
Tuition and fees: $2,303; out-of-state residents $5,813.
Per-credit charge: $53; out-of-state residents $170.
Room and board: $3,790.
Additional info: Tuition/fee waivers available for adults, minority students, unemployed or children of unemployed.

FINANCIAL AID PICTURE
Students with need: Need-based aid available for full-time and part-time students.

FINANCIAL AID PROCEDURES
Forms required: FAFSA, institutional form.
Dates and Deadlines: Priority date 6/1; no closing date. Applicants notified on a rolling basis starting 4/1.

CONTACT
Linda Brown, Director of Financial Aid
Box 310, Tonkawa, OK 74653-0310
(580) 628-6240

Northwestern Oklahoma State University
Alva, Oklahoma
www.nwosu.edu Federal Code: 003163

4-year public university and teachers college in small town.
Enrollment: 1,747 undergrads, 28% part-time. 265 full-time freshmen.
Selectivity: Admits over 75% of applicants.

BASIC COSTS (2008-2009)
Tuition and fees: $4,110; out-of-state residents $10,140.
Per-credit charge: $116; out-of-state residents $317.
Room and board: $3,560.

FINANCIAL AID PICTURE (2007-2008)
Students with need: Need-based aid available for full-time and part-time students. Work study available nights, weekends, and for part-time students.
Students without need: No-need awards available for academics, alumni affiliation, art, athletics, leadership, music/drama.

FINANCIAL AID PROCEDURES
Forms required: FAFSA.
Dates and Deadlines: No deadline. Applicants notified on a rolling basis starting 5/1.

CONTACT
Irala Magee, Director of Financial Aid
709 Oklahoma Boulevard, Alva, OK 73717-2799
(580) 327-8542

Oklahoma Baptist University
Shawnee, Oklahoma
www.okbu.edu Federal Code: 003164

4-year private university and liberal arts college in large town, affiliated with Southern Baptist Convention.
Enrollment: 1,425 undergrads.
Selectivity: Admits 50 to 75% of applicants.

BASIC COSTS (2009-2010)
Tuition and fees: $17,624.
Room and board: $5,510.

FINANCIAL AID PICTURE (2007-2008)
Students with need: Need-based aid available for full-time and part-time students. Work study available nights, weekends, and for part-time students.
Students without need: No-need awards available for academics, alumni affiliation, art, athletics, job skills, leadership, music/drama, religious affiliation, ROTC, state/district residency.
Scholarships offered: Prichard Church Vocation Scholarship; $1,800; offered to all students preparing for vocational ministry associated with Southern Baptist Convention. Missionary Kid (MK) Scholarship; minimum $5,000 per year; for children of Southern Baptist missionaries. OBU Bison Grants; amount varies; based on award package and need.

FINANCIAL AID PROCEDURES
Forms required: FAFSA, institutional form.
Dates and Deadlines: Priority date 3/1; no closing date. Applicants notified on a rolling basis starting 3/1; must reply by 5/1 or within 2 week(s) of notification.
Transfers: Priority date 4/1; no deadline. Applicants notified on a rolling basis starting 3/1; must reply within 2 week(s) of notification. Transfers receive 1 semester of financial aid on probationary basis. During probation semester, must complete 12 hours with at least 2.0 GPA in order to receive financial aid in subsequent semesters.

CONTACT

Jonna Raney, Director of Student Financial Services
500 West University, Shawnee, OK 74804
(405) 878-2016

Oklahoma Christian University

Oklahoma City, Oklahoma
www.oc.edu Federal Code: 003165

4-year private liberal arts college in very large city, affiliated with Church of Christ.
Enrollment: 1,904 undergrads. 455 full-time freshmen.
Selectivity: Admits less than 50% of applicants.

BASIC COSTS (2008-2009)

Tuition and fees: $16,566.
Per-credit charge: $612.
Room and board: $6,390.

FINANCIAL AID PICTURE (2007-2008)

Students with need: Need-based aid available for full-time and part-time students. Work study available nights, weekends, and for part-time students.
Students without need: No-need awards available for academics, art, athletics, leadership, music/drama, religious affiliation, ROTC.
Scholarships offered: Academic merit scholarships available.

FINANCIAL AID PROCEDURES

Forms required: FAFSA.
Dates and Deadlines: Priority date 3/15; closing date 8/31. Applicants notified on a rolling basis starting 1/15; must reply within 4 week(s) of notification.
Transfers: Applicants notified on a rolling basis starting 1/15; must reply within 4 week(s) of notification. Will award based on unofficial transcript. Must have all official transcripts before awards will be disbursed.

CONTACT

Clint LaRue, Director, Student Financial Services
Box 11000, Oklahoma City, OK 73136-1100
(405) 425-5190

Oklahoma City Community College

Oklahoma City, Oklahoma
www.occc.edu Federal Code: 010391

2-year public community college in large city.
Enrollment: 11,027 undergrads, 62% part-time. 1,155 full-time freshmen.
Selectivity: Open admission; but selective for some programs.

BASIC COSTS (2008-2009)

Tuition and fees: $2,521; out-of-state residents $6,721.
Per-credit charge: $61; out-of-state residents $201.
Additional info: Tuition/fee waivers available for adults.

FINANCIAL AID PICTURE (2007-2008)

Students with need: Out of 392 full-time freshmen who applied for aid, 327 were judged to have need. Of these, 327 received aid. Average financial aid package met 63% of need; average scholarship/grant was $2,288; average loan was $2,250. For part-time students, average financial aid package was $4,478.
Students without need: 68 full-time freshmen who did not demonstrate need for aid received scholarships/grants; average award was $848. No-need awards available for academics, alumni affiliation, art, leadership, music/drama, state/district residency.

FINANCIAL AID PROCEDURES

Forms required: FAFSA.
Dates and Deadlines: Priority date 4/15; no closing date. Applicants notified on a rolling basis starting 2/15.
Transfers: Applicants notified on a rolling basis starting 2/15. Those with previous degrees or over 90 credit hours attempted must appeal for eligibility for federally funded financial assistance.

CONTACT

Harold Case, Director of Financial Aid
7777 South May Avenue, Oklahoma City, OK 73159
(405) 682-7525

Oklahoma City University

Oklahoma City, Oklahoma
www.okcu.edu Federal Code: 003166

4-year private university and liberal arts college in very large city, affiliated with United Methodist Church.
Enrollment: 2,190 undergrads, 17% part-time. 348 full-time freshmen.
Selectivity: Admits over 75% of applicants.

BASIC COSTS (2008-2009)

Tuition and fees: $23,400.
Per-credit charge: $730.
Room and board: $7,056.

FINANCIAL AID PICTURE (2007-2008)

Students with need: Out of 303 full-time freshmen who applied for aid, 238 were judged to have need. Of these, 237 received aid, and 53 had their full need met. Average financial aid package met 72% of need; average scholarship/grant was $15,669; average loan was $3,651. For part-time students, average financial aid package was $9,979.
Students without need: 57 full-time freshmen who did not demonstrate need for aid received scholarships/grants; average award was $11,233. No-need awards available for academics, art, athletics, job skills, leadership, music/drama, religious affiliation, ROTC.
Scholarships offered: 23 full-time freshmen received athletic scholarships; average amount $6,517.

FINANCIAL AID PROCEDURES

Forms required: FAFSA, institutional form.
Dates and Deadlines: Priority date 3/1; closing date 6/30. Applicants notified on a rolling basis starting 2/24; must reply within 2 week(s) of notification.
Transfers: Applicants notified on a rolling basis starting 2/24; must reply within 2 week(s) of notification. Financial aid transcripts required from all previously attended institutions whether or not financial aid was received.

CONTACT

Denise Flis, Director of Financial Aid
2501 North Blackwelder Avenue, Oklahoma City, OK 73106-1493
(405) 208-5211

Oklahoma Panhandle State University

Goodwell, Oklahoma
www.opsu.edu Federal Code: 003174

4-year public agricultural and liberal arts college in rural community.
Enrollment: 1,124 undergrads, 13% part-time. 278 full-time freshmen.
Selectivity: Admits over 75% of applicants.

BASIC COSTS (2008-2009)

Tuition and fees: $4,202; out-of-state residents $9,542.
Per-credit charge: $91; out-of-state residents $269.
Room and board: $3,270.

FINANCIAL AID PICTURE (2007-2008)

Students with need: Need-based aid available for full-time and part-time students.

Students without need: This college awards aid only to students with need.

FINANCIAL AID PROCEDURES

Forms required: FAFSA, institutional form.

Dates and Deadlines: Priority date 3/15; no closing date. Applicants notified by 5/1.

Transfers: No deadline. Applicants notified on a rolling basis.

CONTACT

Mel Riley, Director of Financial Aid
OPSU Admissions, Goodwell, OK 73939-0430
(580) 349-1582

Oklahoma State University

Stillwater, Oklahoma
www.osu.okstate.edu Federal Code: 003170

4-year public university in small city.

Enrollment: 17,701 undergrads, 13% part-time. 3,103 full-time freshmen.

Selectivity: Admits over 75% of applicants.

BASIC COSTS (2008-2009)

Tuition and fees: $6,887; out-of-state residents $17,241.

Per-credit charge: $131; out-of-state residents $477.

Room and board: $6,358.

FINANCIAL AID PICTURE (2007-2008)

Students with need: Out of 2,050 full-time freshmen who applied for aid, 1,489 were judged to have need. Of these, 1,454 received aid, and 247 had their full need met. Average financial aid package met 72% of need; average scholarship/grant was $5,687; average loan was $3,158. For part-time students, average financial aid package was $5,709.

Students without need: 921 full-time freshmen who did not demonstrate need for aid received scholarships/grants; average award was $3,899. No-need awards available for academics, alumni affiliation, art, athletics, leadership, minority status, music/drama, ROTC, state/district residency.

Scholarships offered: 42 full-time freshmen received athletic scholarships; average amount $10,566.

Cumulative student debt: 55% of graduating class had student loans; average debt was $18,989.

FINANCIAL AID PROCEDURES

Forms required: FAFSA.

Dates and Deadlines: No deadline. Applicants notified on a rolling basis starting 10/1; must reply within 4 week(s) of notification.

CONTACT

Charles Bruce, Senior Director of Scholarships & Financial Aid
219 Student Union, Stillwater, OK 74078
(405) 744-6604

Oklahoma State University Institute of Technology: Okmulgee

Okmulgee, Oklahoma
www.osuit.edu Federal Code: 003172

2-year public branch campus and technical college in large town.

Enrollment: 2,100 undergrads.

Selectivity: Open admission; but selective for some programs.

BASIC COSTS (2008-2009)

Tuition and fees: $3,705; out-of-state residents $9,015.

Per-credit charge: $92; out-of-state residents $269.

Room and board: $5,180.

FINANCIAL AID PICTURE (2007-2008)

Students with need: Need-based aid available for full-time and part-time students. Work study available nights, weekends, and for part-time students.

FINANCIAL AID PROCEDURES

Forms required: FAFSA, institutional form.

Dates and Deadlines: Priority date 4/1; no closing date. Applicants notified on a rolling basis.

Transfers: Requirement of financial aid transcript from any institution(s) attended during transferring academic year.

CONTACT

Mary Bledsoe, Director of Student Financial Services
1801 East Fourth Street, Okmulgee, OK 74447-3901
(918) 293-5290

Oklahoma State University: Oklahoma City

Oklahoma City, Oklahoma
www.osuokc.edu Federal Code: 009647

2-year public branch campus and technical college in very large city.

Enrollment: 5,742 undergrads.

Selectivity: Open admission; but selective for some programs.

BASIC COSTS (2008-2009)

Tuition and fees: $2,930; out-of-state residents $7,790.

Per-credit charge: $76; out-of-state residents $238.

Additional info: Tuition/fee waivers available for adults, minority students.

FINANCIAL AID PICTURE (2007-2008)

Students with need: Need-based aid available for full-time and part-time students.

Students without need: This college awards aid only to students with need.

FINANCIAL AID PROCEDURES

Forms required: FAFSA.

Dates and Deadlines: Priority date 7/15; no closing date. Applicants notified on a rolling basis starting 8/1; must reply within 2 week(s) of notification.

CONTACT

Bessie Carter, Director of Financial Aid
900 North Portland, Oklahoma City, OK 73107-6195
(405) 945-8646

Oklahoma Wesleyan University

Bartlesville, Oklahoma
www.okwu.edu Federal Code: 003151

4-year private university and liberal arts college in large town, affiliated with Wesleyan Church.

Enrollment: 1,015 undergrads.

Selectivity: Admits less than 50% of applicants.

BASIC COSTS (2009-2010)

Tuition and fees: $17,770.

Per-credit charge: $700.

Room and board: $6,288.

FINANCIAL AID PICTURE (2008-2009)

Students with need: 21% of average financial aid package awarded as scholarships/grants, 79% awarded as loans/jobs. Need-based aid available for part-time students. Work study available nights.

Students without need: No-need awards available for academics, alumni affiliation, athletics, leadership, music/drama, religious affiliation, state/district residency.

FINANCIAL AID PROCEDURES

Forms required: FAFSA, institutional form.

Dates and Deadlines: Priority date 4/1; no closing date. Applicants notified on a rolling basis starting 4/1; must reply by 5/1 or within 2 week(s) of notification.

Transfers: Priority date 3/1; closing date 8/1. Applicants notified on a rolling basis; must reply within 2 week(s) of notification.

CONTACT

Lee Kanakis, Director of Student Financial Services
2201 Silver Lake Road, Bartlesville, OK 74006
(918) 335-6282

Oral Roberts University

Tulsa, Oklahoma
www.oru.edu Federal Code: 003985

4-year private university and liberal arts college in large city, affiliated with nondenominational tradition.

Enrollment: 2,558 undergrads, 9% part-time. 598 full-time freshmen.

Selectivity: Admits 50 to 75% of applicants.

BASIC COSTS (2009-2010)

Tuition and fees: $19,106.

Per-credit charge: $772.

Room and board: $7,916.

FINANCIAL AID PICTURE (2007-2008)

Students with need: Average financial aid package met 86% of need; average scholarship/grant was $9,759; average loan was $6,534. For part-time students, average financial aid package was $6,289.

Students without need: 152 full-time freshmen who did not demonstrate need for aid received scholarships/grants; average award was $6,871. No-need awards available for academics, alumni affiliation, art, athletics, leadership, music/drama.

Scholarships offered: 16 full-time freshmen received athletic scholarships; average amount $19,354.

Cumulative student debt: 67% of graduating class had student loans; average debt was $34,555.

FINANCIAL AID PROCEDURES

Forms required: FAFSA.

Dates and Deadlines: Priority date 3/15; no closing date. Must reply by 7/15.

Transfers: Priority date 3/30. Applicants notified on a rolling basis starting 4/1. Transfer applicants eligible for some scholarships.

CONTACT

Shannon Panthin, Director of Financial Aid
7777 South Lewis Avenue, Tulsa, OK 74171
(918) 495-6510

Platt College: Oklahoma City Central

Oklahoma City, Oklahoma
www.plattcollege.org Federal Code: 023068

2-year for-profit branch campus and health science college in small city.

Enrollment: 200 undergrads.

Selectivity: Open admission; but selective for some programs.

BASIC COSTS (2008-2009)

Additional info: Tuition varies by program. Full-time tuition ranges from $10,200 to $23,600. Required fees $100.

FINANCIAL AID PICTURE

Students with need: Need-based aid available for full-time students.

FINANCIAL AID PROCEDURES

Forms required: FAFSA.

CONTACT

Amy Hocker, Financial Aid Director
309 South Ann Arbor, Oklahoma City, OK 73128
(405) 946-7799

Platt College: Tulsa

Tulsa, Oklahoma
www.plattcollege.org Federal Code: 016312

2-year for-profit health science college in large city.

Enrollment: 75 undergrads.

Selectivity: Open admission; but selective for some programs.

BASIC COSTS (2008-2009)

Additional info: Tuition varies by program. Full-time tuition ranges from $10,300 to $23,600, depending on program. Required fees $100.

FINANCIAL AID PICTURE

Students with need: Need-based aid available for full-time and part-time students.

Students without need: This college awards aid only to students with need.

FINANCIAL AID PROCEDURES

Forms required: FAFSA.

Dates and Deadlines: No deadline.

CONTACT

Linda Bates, Director of Compliance-Financial Services
3801 South Sheridan, Tulsa, OK 74145-1132
(918) 663-9000

Redlands Community College

El Reno, Oklahoma
www.redlandscc.edu Federal Code: 003156

2-year public community college in large town.

Enrollment: 2,463 undergrads, 64% part-time. 541 full-time freshmen.

Selectivity: Open admission; but selective for some programs.

BASIC COSTS (2008-2009)

Tuition and fees: $2,903; out-of-state residents $5,153.

Per-credit charge: $97; out-of-state residents $172.

Additional info: Tuition/fee waivers available for adults.

FINANCIAL AID PICTURE (2007-2008)

Students with need: Average financial aid package met 95% of need; average scholarship/grant was $3,197; average loan was $2,765. For part-time students, average financial aid package was $2,375.

Students without need: No-need awards available for academics, athletics, leadership.

FINANCIAL AID PROCEDURES

Forms required: FAFSA.

Dates and Deadlines: Priority date 7/1; no closing date. Applicants notified on a rolling basis starting 6/1; must reply within 6 week(s) of notification.

Transfers: No deadline. Applicants notified on a rolling basis; must reply within 6 week(s) of notification.

CONTACT

Karen Jeffers, Director of Financial Aid
1300 South Country Club Road, El Reno, OK 73036
(866) 415-6367 ext. 1442

Rogers State University

Claremore, Oklahoma
www.rsu.edu Federal Code: 003168

4-year public university in large town.
Enrollment: 3,788 undergrads, 40% part-time. 628 full-time freshmen.
Selectivity: Admits 50 to 75% of applicants.

BASIC COSTS (2008-2009)

Tuition and fees: $4,277; out-of-state residents $9,734.
Per-credit charge: $91; out-of-state residents $273.
Room and board: $7,095.

FINANCIAL AID PICTURE (2008-2009)

Students with need: Out of 538 full-time freshmen who applied for aid, 396 were judged to have need. Of these, 388 received aid, and 24 had their full need met. Average financial aid package met 61% of need; average scholarship/grant was $1,852; average loan was $1,051. For part-time students, average financial aid package was $2,806.
Students without need: 108 full-time freshmen who did not demonstrate need for aid received scholarships/grants; average award was $1,275. No-need awards available for academics, athletics, leadership, music/drama.
Scholarships offered: 24 full-time freshmen received athletic scholarships; average amount $795.

FINANCIAL AID PROCEDURES

Forms required: FAFSA, institutional form.
Dates and Deadlines: Priority date 6/1; no closing date. Applicants notified on a rolling basis starting 4/1; must reply within 3 week(s) of notification.
Transfers: No deadline. Applicants notified on a rolling basis starting 4/7; must reply within 3 week(s) of notification.

CONTACT

David Barron, Director, Financial Aid
1701 West Will Rogers Boulevard, Claremore, OK 74017
(918) 343-7555

Rose State College

Midwest City, Oklahoma
www.rose.edu Federal Code: 009185

2-year public community college in small city.
Enrollment: 6,581 undergrads, 59% part-time. 795 full-time freshmen.
Selectivity: Open admission; but selective for some programs.

BASIC COSTS (2008-2009)

Tuition and fees: $2,534; out-of-state residents $7,394.
Per-credit charge: $65; out-of-state residents $227.

FINANCIAL AID PICTURE (2007-2008)

Students with need: 43% of average financial aid package awarded as scholarships/grants, 57% awarded as loans/jobs. Need-based aid available for part-time students. Work study available nights, weekends, and for part-time students.
Students without need: No-need awards available for academics, athletics.

FINANCIAL AID PROCEDURES

Forms required: FAFSA.
Dates and Deadlines: Priority date 6/1; no closing date. Applicants notified on a rolling basis starting 3/1; must reply within 4 week(s) of notification.

CONTACT

Steven Daffer, Director of Financial Aid
6420 SE 15th Street, Midwest City, OK 73110
(405) 733-7424

St. Gregory's University

Shawnee, Oklahoma
www.stgregorys.edu Federal Code: 003183

4-year private university and liberal arts college in large town, affiliated with Roman Catholic Church.
Enrollment: 700 undergrads, 58% part-time. 104 full-time freshmen.
Selectivity: Admits over 75% of applicants.

BASIC COSTS (2008-2009)

Tuition and fees: $15,560.
Per-credit charge: $490.
Room and board: $6,288.
Additional info: Tuition/fee waivers available for adults.

FINANCIAL AID PICTURE (2007-2008)

Students with need: Need-based aid available for full-time and part-time students. Work study available nights, weekends, and for part-time students.
Students without need: No-need awards available for academics, alumni affiliation, art, athletics, job skills, leadership, music/drama, religious affiliation.
Scholarships offered: Leadership Scholarship; $500-$2,000. Academic Scholarship; $500-$5,100. Need-based scholarship; $500 $1,500.

FINANCIAL AID PROCEDURES

Forms required: FAFSA, institutional form.
Dates and Deadlines: Priority date 4/1; no closing date. Applicants notified on a rolling basis starting 2/15; must reply within 3 week(s) of notification.
Transfers: No deadline. Applicants notified on a rolling basis.

CONTACT

Debra Gambill, Director of Financial Aid
1900 West MacArthur Drive, Shawnee, OK 74804
(405) 878-5412

Seminole State College

Seminole, Oklahoma
www.ssc.cc.ok.us Federal Code: 003178

2-year public community and junior college in small town.
Enrollment: 1,400 full-time undergrads.
Selectivity: Open admission; but selective for some programs.

BASIC COSTS (2008-2009)

Tuition and fees: $2,849; out-of-state residents $6,665.
Per-credit charge: $58; out-of-state residents $185.
Room and board: $5,850.

FINANCIAL AID PICTURE (2008-2009)

Students with need: Need-based aid available for full-time students.
Students without need: No-need awards available for academics, athletics, state/district residency.

FINANCIAL AID PROCEDURES

Forms required: FAFSA, institutional form.
Dates and Deadlines: Priority date 7/15; no closing date. Applicants notified on a rolling basis starting 3/1; must reply within 4 week(s) of notification.

CONTACT
Chris Lindley, Director of Enrollment Management
2701 Boren Boulevard, Seminole, OK 74868
(405) 382-9247

Southeastern Oklahoma State University
Durant, Oklahoma
www.sosu.edu Federal Code: 003179

4-year public liberal arts and teachers college in large town.
Enrollment: 3,465 undergrads, 21% part-time. 521 full-time freshmen.
Selectivity: Admits over 75% of applicants.

BASIC COSTS (2008-2009)
Tuition and fees: $4,316; out-of-state residents $10,687.
Per-credit charge: $121; out-of-state residents $334.
Room and board: $4,650.
Additional info: Tuition/fee waivers available for minority students.

FINANCIAL AID PICTURE (2007-2008)
Students with need: Out of 434 full-time freshmen who applied for aid, 407 were judged to have need. Of these, 398 received aid, and 173 had their full need met. Average financial aid package met 64% of need; average scholarship/grant was $1,055; average loan was $1,199. For part-time students, average financial aid package was $981.
Students without need: 2 full-time freshmen who did not demonstrate need for aid received scholarships/grants; average award was $1,156. No-need awards available for academics, alumni affiliation, art, athletics, job skills, leadership, minority status, music/drama, state/district residency.
Scholarships offered: 52 full-time freshmen received athletic scholarships; average amount $1,467.
Cumulative student debt: 37% of graduating class had student loans; average debt was $6,852.

FINANCIAL AID PROCEDURES
Forms required: FAFSA, institutional form.
Dates and Deadlines: Priority date 3/1; no closing date. Applicants notified on a rolling basis starting 4/15; must reply within 2 week(s) of notification.

CONTACT
Sherry Hudson, Director of Student Financial Aid
1405 North Fourth Avenue, PMB 4225, Durant, OK 74701-0607
(580) 745-2186

Southern Nazarene University
Bethany, Oklahoma
www.snu.edu Federal Code: 003149

4-year private university and liberal arts college in large town, affiliated with Church of the Nazarene.
Enrollment: 1,611 undergrads, 3% part-time. 268 full-time freshmen.
Selectivity: Open admission.

BASIC COSTS (2008-2009)
Tuition and fees: $17,224.
Per-credit charge: $540.
Room and board: $5,772.

FINANCIAL AID PICTURE (2007-2008)
Students with need: 45% of average financial aid package awarded as scholarships/grants, 55% awarded as loans/jobs.
Students without need: No-need awards available for academics, athletics, ROTC, state/district residency.

FINANCIAL AID PROCEDURES
Forms required: FAFSA, institutional form.
Dates and Deadlines: Priority date 3/1; no closing date. Applicants notified on a rolling basis starting 5/1; must reply within 2 week(s) of notification.

CONTACT
Diana Lee, Director of Financial Assistance
6729 NW 39th Expressway, Bethany, OK 73008
(405) 491-6310

Southwestern Christian University
Bethany, Oklahoma
www.swcu.edu Federal Code: 003180

4-year private liberal arts college in large town, affiliated with Pentecostal Holiness Church.
Enrollment: 190 undergrads.

BASIC COSTS (2009-2010)
Tuition and fees: $10,700.
Per-credit charge: $325.
Room and board: $4,800.
Additional info: Adult education program $350 per credit hour.

FINANCIAL AID PICTURE (2008-2009)
Students with need: Need-based aid available for full-time and part-time students. Work study available nights, weekends, and for part-time students.
Students without need: No-need awards available for academics, alumni affiliation, leadership, music/drama, religious affiliation.

FINANCIAL AID PROCEDURES
Forms required: FAFSA.
Dates and Deadlines: Priority date 8/1; no closing date. Applicants notified on a rolling basis starting 5/1; must reply within 2 week(s) of notification.

CONTACT
Daniel Watkins, Director of Financial Aid
Box 340, Bethany, OK 73008
(405) 789-7661 ext. 3456

Southwestern Oklahoma State University
Weatherford, Oklahoma
www.swosu.edu Federal Code: 003181

4-year public university in large town.
Enrollment: 4,059 undergrads, 12% part-time. 885 full-time freshmen.
Selectivity: Admits over 75% of applicants.

BASIC COSTS (2008-2009)
Tuition and fees: $4,110; out-of-state residents $9,450.
Per-credit charge: $112; out-of-state residents $290.
Room and board: $3,900.

FINANCIAL AID PICTURE (2008-2009)
Students with need: Out of 679 full-time freshmen who applied for aid, 513 were judged to have need. Of these, 505 received aid, and 79 had their full need met. Average financial aid package met 90% of need; average scholarship/grant was $1,155; average loan was $1,351. For part-time students, average financial aid package was $3,637.
Students without need: 173 full-time freshmen who did not demonstrate need for aid received scholarships/grants; average award was $415. No-need awards available for academics, alumni affiliation, art, athletics, job skills, leadership, music/drama, state/district residency.
Scholarships offered: 72 full-time freshmen received athletic scholarships; average amount $974.

FINANCIAL AID PROCEDURES
Forms required: FAFSA, institutional form.

Dates and Deadlines: Priority date 3/1; no closing date. Applicants notified on a rolling basis starting 1/1.

CONTACT

Jerome Wichert, Director of Student Financial Services
100 Campus Drive, Weatherford, OK 73096
(508) 774-3786

Spartan College of Aeronautics and Technology

Tulsa, Oklahoma
www.spartan.edu Federal Code: 007678

4-year for-profit technical college in large city.
Enrollment: 1,239 undergrads.
Selectivity: Admits less than 50% of applicants.

BASIC COSTS (2009-2010)

Tuition and fees: $15,345.
Additional info: Tuition at time of enrollment locked for 4 years.

FINANCIAL AID PICTURE (2007-2008)

Students with need: Need-based aid available for full-time and part-time students. Work study available nights, weekends, and for part-time students.

FINANCIAL AID PROCEDURES

Forms required: FAFSA, institutional form.
Dates and Deadlines: No deadline. Applicants notified on a rolling basis starting 2/1; must reply within 2 week(s) of notification.
Transfers: No deadline. Applicants notified on a rolling basis; must reply within 2 week(s) of notification.

CONTACT

Christina Foster, Director of Financial Aid
Box 582833, Tulsa, OK 74158-2833
(918) 836-6886

Tulsa Community College

Tulsa, Oklahoma
www.tulsacc.edu Federal Code: 009763

2-year public community college in large city.
Enrollment: 12,162 undergrads.
Selectivity: Open admission; but selective for some programs.

BASIC COSTS (2008-2009)

Tuition and fees: $2,709; out-of-state residents $7,376.
Per-credit charge: $62; out-of-state residents $218.
Additional info: Tuition/fee waivers available for minority students.

FINANCIAL AID PICTURE

Students with need: Need-based aid available for full-time and part-time students. Work study available nights, weekends, and for part-time students.
Students without need: No-need awards available for academics, art, leadership, music/drama, state/district residency.

FINANCIAL AID PROCEDURES

Forms required: FAFSA, institutional form.
Dates and Deadlines: Priority date 8/1; no closing date. Applicants notified on a rolling basis starting 4/1; must reply within 2 week(s) of notification.

CONTACT

Matt Short, Director of Student Financial Services
6111 East Skelly Drive, Tulsa, OK 74135
(918) 595-7155

Tulsa Welding School

Tulsa, Oklahoma
www.weldingschool.com Federal Code: 015733

2-year for-profit technical college in very large city.
Enrollment: 730 undergrads.
Selectivity: Open admission.

BASIC COSTS (2008-2009)

Additional info: Tuition and fees vary by program from $8,355 to $14,690.

FINANCIAL AID PICTURE

Students with need: Need-based aid available for full-time students.
Students without need: This college awards aid only to students with need.

FINANCIAL AID PROCEDURES

Forms required: FAFSA.

CONTACT

Ava Edens, Financial Aid Director
2545 East 11th Street, Tulsa, OK 74104-3909
(918) 587-6789

University of Central Oklahoma

Edmond, Oklahoma
www.uco.edu Federal Code: 003152

4-year public university in small city.
Enrollment: 14,019 undergrads, 31% part-time. 1,815 full-time freshmen.
Selectivity: Admits 50 to 75% of applicants.

BASIC COSTS (2008-2009)

Tuition and fees: $4,223; out-of-state residents $10,652.
Per-credit charge: $123; out-of-state residents $337.
Room and board: $5,623.
Additional info: Tuition/fee waivers available for minority students.

FINANCIAL AID PICTURE (2007-2008)

Students with need: Out of 1,079 full-time freshmen who applied for aid, 771 were judged to have need. Of these, 691 received aid, and 57 had their full need met. Average financial aid package met 67% of need; average scholarship/grant was $7,524; average loan was $2,942. For part-time students, average financial aid package was $4,976.
Students without need: 213 full-time freshmen who did not demonstrate need for aid received scholarships/grants; average award was $2,767. No-need awards available for academics, alumni affiliation, art, athletics, leadership, minority status, music/drama, ROTC, state/district residency.
Scholarships offered: 45 full-time freshmen received athletic scholarships; average amount $3,045.
Cumulative student debt: 48% of graduating class had student loans; average debt was $17,385.

FINANCIAL AID PROCEDURES

Forms required: FAFSA, institutional form.
Dates and Deadlines: Priority date 5/31; no closing date. Applicants notified on a rolling basis starting 5/1; must reply by 6/30 or within 4 week(s) of notification.
Transfers: No deadline. Applicants notified on a rolling basis starting 5/1; must reply by 6/30 or within 4 week(s) of notification.

CONTACT

Sheila McGill, Director of Financial Aid
100 North University Drive, Edmond, OK 73034-0151
(405) 974-3334

University of Oklahoma

Norman, Oklahoma
www.ou.edu Federal Code: 003184

4-year public university in small city.
Enrollment: 20,350 undergrads, 13% part-time. 3,482 full-time freshmen.
Selectivity: Admits over 75% of applicants.

BASIC COSTS (2008-2009)

Tuition and fees: $7,423; out-of-state residents $17,404.
Per-credit charge: $118; out-of-state residents $451.
Room and board: $7,376.
Additional info: Computer course fees and other college level fees vary by college. Tuition/fee waivers available for minority students.

FINANCIAL AID PICTURE (2007-2008)

Students with need: Out of 2,405 full-time freshmen who applied for aid, 2,303 were judged to have need. Of these, 2,303 received aid, and 1,175 had their full need met. Average financial aid package met 93% of need; average scholarship/grant was $5,004; average loan was $3,732. For part-time students, average financial aid package was $7,104.
Students without need: 434 full-time freshmen who did not demonstrate need for aid received scholarships/grants; average award was $1,124. No-need awards available for academics, alumni affiliation, art, athletics, leadership, music/drama, religious affiliation, ROTC.
Scholarships offered: ***Merit:*** Presidents Leadership Class; $1,000 in-state, $4,700 out-of-state; 100 awarded. Scholar's Program; $1,500-$2,500 in-state and $2,500-$5,000 out-of-state; based on academic merit. ***Athletic:*** 49 full-time freshmen received athletic scholarships; average amount $15,156.
Cumulative student debt: 46% of graduating class had student loans; average debt was $20,341.
Additional info: Institutional loans are available for early applicants who do not qualify for federal or state need-based aid.

FINANCIAL AID PROCEDURES

Forms required: FAFSA.
Dates and Deadlines: Priority date 3/1; no closing date. Applicants notified on a rolling basis starting 3/15; must reply within 6 week(s) of notification.
Transfers: Applicants notified on a rolling basis starting 3/1; must reply within 6 week(s) of notification. Transfer leadership resident tuition waiver and transfer academic excellence tuition waiver available.

CONTACT

Caryn Pacheco, Director of Financial Aid
550 Parrington Oval, L-1, Norman, OK 73019-3032
(405) 325-5505

University of Science and Arts of Oklahoma

Chickasha, Oklahoma
www.usao.edu Federal Code: 003167

4-year public university and liberal arts college in large town.
Enrollment: 1,041 undergrads, 10% part-time. 221 full-time freshmen.
Selectivity: Admits over 75% of applicants.

BASIC COSTS (2008-2009)

Tuition and fees: $4,440; out-of-state residents $10,560.
Per-credit charge: $109; out-of-state residents $313.
Room and board: $4,860.
Additional info: Tuition at time of enrollment locked for 4 years.

FINANCIAL AID PICTURE (2008-2009)

Students with need: Out of 165 full-time freshmen who applied for aid, 127 were judged to have need. Of these, 127 received aid, and 33 had their full need met. Average financial aid package met 74% of need; average scholarship/grant was $6,861; average loan was $2,671. For part-time students, average financial aid package was $5,533.
Students without need: 53 full-time freshmen who did not demonstrate need for aid received scholarships/grants; average award was $4,867. No-need awards available for academics, art, athletics, leadership, music/drama, state/district residency.
Scholarships offered: 24 full-time freshmen received athletic scholarships; average amount $7,133.
Cumulative student debt: 59% of graduating class had student loans; average debt was $15,905.

FINANCIAL AID PROCEDURES

Forms required: FAFSA, institutional form.
Dates and Deadlines: Priority date 3/15; no closing date. Applicants notified on a rolling basis starting 3/15; must reply within 4 week(s) of notification.
Transfers: No deadline. Applicants notified on a rolling basis starting 3/15; must reply within 4 week(s) of notification.

CONTACT

Nancy Moats, Director of Financial Aid
1727 West Alabama, Chickasha, OK 73018-5322
(405) 574-1240

University of Tulsa

Tulsa, Oklahoma
www.utulsa.edu Federal Code: 003185

4-year private university in large city, affiliated with Presbyterian Church (USA).
Enrollment: 2,981 undergrads, 4% part-time. 653 full-time freshmen.
Selectivity: Admits less than 50% of applicants.

BASIC COSTS (2009-2010)

Tuition and fees: $26,812.
Per-credit charge: $959.
Room and board: $8,544.
Additional info: A one-time $425 fee is charged first-time students for orientation, lifetime transcripts, course drop/add transactions, and graduation/commencement.

FINANCIAL AID PICTURE (2007-2008)

Students with need: Out of 591 full-time freshmen who applied for aid, 287 were judged to have need. Of these, 287 received aid, and 138 had their full need met. Average financial aid package met 88% of need; average scholarship/grant was $5,332; average loan was $5,486. For part-time students, average financial aid package was $14,023.
Students without need: 256 full-time freshmen who did not demonstrate need for aid received scholarships/grants; average award was $11,224. No-need awards available for academics, alumni affiliation, art, athletics, leadership, minority status, music/drama, religious affiliation.
Scholarships offered: 67 full-time freshmen received athletic scholarships; average amount $21,447.
Cumulative student debt: 36% of graduating class had student loans; average debt was $28,364.

FINANCIAL AID PROCEDURES

Forms required: FAFSA, institutional form.
Dates and Deadlines: Priority date 4/1; no closing date. Applicants notified on a rolling basis starting 3/1; must reply by 5/1 or within 2 week(s) of notification.
Transfers: Priority date 5/1. Applicants notified on a rolling basis starting 3/1; must reply by 5/1 or within 2 week(s) of notification.

CONTACT

Vicki Hendrickson, Director of Student Financial Services
800 South Tucker Drive, Tulsa, OK 74104-3189
(918) 631-2526

Vatterott College

Oklahoma City, Oklahoma
www.vatterott-college.com Federal Code: 020693

2-year for-profit technical and career college in very large city.
Enrollment: 260 undergrads.
Selectivity: Open admission.

BASIC COSTS (2008-2009)

Additional info: Program cost ranges: $17,200 to $22,000 (certificate/diploma); $24,250 to $32,050 (associate degree).

FINANCIAL AID PICTURE (2007-2008)

Students with need: Need-based aid available for full-time students.
Students without need: This college awards aid only to students with need.

FINANCIAL AID PROCEDURES

Forms required: FAFSA.
Dates and Deadlines: No deadline.

CONTACT

Janice Stepp, Director of Financial Aid
4621 NW 23rd Street, Oklahoma City, OK 73127
(405) 945-0088

Western Oklahoma State College

Altus, Oklahoma
www.wosc.edu Federal Code: 003146

2-year public community college in large town.
Enrollment: 720 full-time undergrads.
Selectivity: Open admission.

BASIC COSTS (2008-2009)

Tuition and fees: $2,684; out-of-state residents $6,164.
Per-credit charge: $57; out-of-state residents $173.
Room and board: $3,750.

FINANCIAL AID PICTURE (2007-2008)

Students with need: Need-based aid available for full-time and part-time students. Work study available nights, weekends, and for part-time students.
Students without need: No-need awards available for academics, alumni affiliation, art, athletics, leadership, music/drama, state/district residency.

FINANCIAL AID PROCEDURES

Forms required: FAFSA, institutional form.
Dates and Deadlines: Priority date 3/1; no closing date. Applicants notified on a rolling basis; must reply within 3 week(s) of notification.

CONTACT

Myrna Cross, Director of Financial Aid/Veterans' Affairs
2801 North Main Street, Altus, OK 73521
(580) 477-7709

Oregon

Art Institute of Portland

Portland, Oregon
www.aipd.artinstitutes.edu Federal Code: 007819

4-year for-profit visual arts and liberal arts college in large city.
Enrollment: 1,776 undergrads.
Selectivity: Admits 50 to 75% of applicants.

BASIC COSTS (2008-2009)

Tuition and fees: $19,395.
Per-credit charge: $431.
Room only: $8,274.

FINANCIAL AID PICTURE (2008-2009)

Students with need: 31% of average financial aid package awarded as scholarships/grants, 69% awarded as loans/jobs. Need-based aid available for part-time students. Work study available nights, weekends, and for part-time students.
Students without need: No-need awards available for art.
Additional info: Applicants encouraged to apply early for financial aid. Scholarship deadlines range from January 1 to March 1.

FINANCIAL AID PROCEDURES

Forms required: FAFSA.
Dates and Deadlines: Priority date 3/1; no closing date. Applicants notified on a rolling basis starting 1/1; must reply within 5 week(s) of notification.
Transfers: No deadline. Applicants notified on a rolling basis starting 1/1.

CONTACT

Mickey Jacobson, Director of Student Financial Services
1122 Northwest Davis Street, Portland, OR 97209-2911
(503) 382-4784

Blue Mountain Community College

Pendleton, Oregon
www.bluecc.edu Federal Code: 003186

2-year public community college in large town.
Enrollment: 700 full-time undergrads.
Selectivity: Open admission; but selective for some programs.

BASIC COSTS (2008-2009)

Tuition and fees: $3,417; out-of-state residents $9,357.
Per-credit charge: $66; out-of-state residents $198.
Additional info: Washington, Idaho, Nevada, Montana, and California state residents pay in-state tuition.

FINANCIAL AID PICTURE

Students with need: Need-based aid available for full-time and part-time students. Work study available nights, weekends, and for part-time students.
Students without need: No-need awards available for athletics, music/drama.

FINANCIAL AID PROCEDURES

Forms required: FAFSA.
Dates and Deadlines: Priority date 3/30; no closing date. Applicants notified on a rolling basis starting 4/1; must reply within 2 week(s) of notification.

CONTACT

Karen Graybeal, Director of Financial Aid
2411 Northwest Carden Avenue, Pendleton, OR 97801
(541) 278-5790

Central Oregon Community College
Bend, Oregon
www.cocc.edu Federal Code: 003188

2-year public community college in small city.
Enrollment: 4,430 undergrads, 53% part-time. 492 full-time freshmen.
Selectivity: Open admission; but selective for some programs.

BASIC COSTS (2009-2010)
Tuition and fees: $2,958; out-of-district residents $3,993; out-of-state residents $8,088.
Per-credit charge: $63; out-of-district residents $86; out-of-state residents $176.
Room and board: $7,326.
Additional info: Residents of WA, ID, NV and CA pay the in-state, out-of-district tuition. Emergency Medical Services, Aviation, Nursing, Culinary and Massage Therapy programs carry additional fees.

FINANCIAL AID PICTURE (2008-2009)
Students with need: Out of 369 full-time freshmen who applied for aid, 301 were judged to have need. Of these, 291 received aid, and 77 had their full need met. Average financial aid package met 83% of need; average scholarship/grant was $5,701; average loan was $3,221. For part time students, average financial aid package was $6,748.
Students without need: 6 full-time freshmen who did not demonstrate need for aid received scholarships/grants; average award was $2,700. No-need awards available for academics, state/district residency.
Additional info: Institution-sponsored short-term loans. Extensive part-time student employment.

FINANCIAL AID PROCEDURES
Forms required: FAFSA.
Dates and Deadlines: No deadline. Applicants notified on a rolling basis starting 3/30; must reply within 4 week(s) of notification.

CONTACT
Kevin Multop, Director of Financial Aid
2600 Northwest College Way, Bend, OR 97701-5998
(541) 383-7260

Chemeketa Community College
Salem, Oregon
www.chemeketa.edu Federal Code: 003218

2-year public community and junior college in small city.
Enrollment: 8,016 undergrads.
Selectivity: Open admission; but selective for some programs.

BASIC COSTS (2008-2009)
Tuition and fees: $3,038; out-of-state residents $9,698.
Per-credit charge: $61; out-of-state residents $209.
Additional info: International students have additional required fees. Individual courses may have extra fees.

FINANCIAL AID PICTURE (2007-2008)
Students with need: Need-based aid available for full-time and part-time students. Work study available nights, weekends, and for part-time students.
Students without need: This college awards aid only to students with need.

FINANCIAL AID PROCEDURES
Forms required: FAFSA.
Dates and Deadlines: Priority date 4/1; no closing date. Applicants notified on a rolling basis starting 6/30; must reply within 2 week(s) of notification.
Transfers: Priority date 6/30; no deadline. Applicants notified on a rolling basis; must reply within 4 week(s) of notification.

CONTACT
Kathy Campbell, Financial Aid Director
Admissions Office, Salem, OR 97305-1453
(503) 399-5018

Clackamas Community College
Oregon City, Oregon
www.clackamas.edu Federal Code: 004878

2-year public community college in small city.
Enrollment: 2,135 full-time undergrads.
Selectivity: Open admission; but selective for some programs.

BASIC COSTS (2008-2009)
Tuition and fees: $3,015; out-of-state residents $9,360.
Per-credit charge: $62; out-of-state residents $203.
Additional info: In-state tuition applies to residents of Oregon, Washington, Idaho, Nevada and California.

FINANCIAL AID PICTURE (2007-2008)
Students with need: Need-based aid available for full-time and part-time students. Work study available nights, weekends, and for part-time students.
Students without need: No-need awards available for academics, art, athletics, leadership, music/drama.
Additional info: Institutional tuition rebate guarantee. Frozen tuition rates for new fall students who graduate within 3 years. Any tuition increase levied by college during those 3 years will be refunded to student upon graduation.

FINANCIAL AID PROCEDURES
Forms required: FAFSA, institutional form.
Dates and Deadlines: Priority date 4/10; no closing date. Applicants notified on a rolling basis starting 3/15; must reply within 3 week(s) of notification.
Transfers: No deadline. Applicants notified on a rolling basis.

CONTACT
Fayne Griffiths, Director, Student Financial Services
19600 Molalla Avenue, Oregon City, OR 97045
(503) 657-6958 ext. 2745

Clatsop Community College
Astoria, Oregon
www.clatsopcollege.com Federal Code: 003189

2-year public community college in large town.
Enrollment: 634 undergrads.
Selectivity: Open admission; but selective for some programs.

BASIC COSTS (2008-2009)
Tuition and fees: $3,150; out-of-state residents $6,030.
Per-credit charge: $64; out-of-state residents $128.

FINANCIAL AID PICTURE (2007-2008)
Students with need: Need-based aid available for full-time and part-time students.
Students without need: No-need awards available for academics.
Scholarships offered: Rochester scholarships; $3,000-$5,000; awarded to math or science majors with 3.0 GPA; 3 reference letters required; number awarded varies yearly.

FINANCIAL AID PROCEDURES
Forms required: FAFSA, institutional form.
Dates and Deadlines: Priority date 5/1; no closing date. Applicants notified on a rolling basis starting 2/1.
Transfers: Students who apply after July 1 may only be eligible for Pell Grants and loans depending on availability of funds. Reply deadline 1 week before start of classes.

CONTACT
Sharon Boring, Director of Financial Aid
1653 Jerome Avenue, Astoria, OR 97103
(503) 338-2412

Concordia University
Portland, Oregon
www.cu-portland.edu Federal Code: 003191

4-year private liberal arts and teachers college in very large city, affiliated with Lutheran Church - Missouri Synod.
Enrollment: 995 undergrads, 12% part-time. 160 full-time freshmen.
Selectivity: Admits 50 to 75% of applicants.

BASIC COSTS (2008-2009)
Tuition and fees: $22,100.
Per-credit charge: $680.
Room and board: $6,400.
Additional info: Tuition/fee waivers available for adults.

FINANCIAL AID PICTURE (2008-2009)
Students with need: Need-based aid available for full-time and part-time students. Work study available nights, weekends, and for part-time students.
Students without need: No-need awards available for academics, athletics, leadership, music/drama, religious affiliation.
Scholarships offered: President's Scholarship; $8,000; based on academic index. Regent's Scholarship; $6,000; calculated from GPA and ACT/SAT score. University Award; $4,500; calculated from GPA and ACT/SAT score. Dean's Award; $5,000; based on academic index. Honors Scholarship; 50% tuition.

FINANCIAL AID PROCEDURES
Forms required: FAFSA.
Dates and Deadlines: No deadline. Applicants notified on a rolling basis starting 3/15; must reply by 5/1 or within 3 week(s) of notification.
Transfers: No deadline. Applicants notified on a rolling basis.

CONTACT
Rhoda Reseburg, Financial Aid Director
2811 Northeast Holman Street, Portland, OR 97211-6099
(503) 280-8514

Corban College
Salem, Oregon
www.corban.edu Federal Code: 001339

4-year private liberal arts college in small city, affiliated with Baptist faith.
Enrollment: 812 undergrads, 9% part-time. 175 full-time freshmen.
Selectivity: Admits over 75% of applicants.

BASIC COSTS (2009-2010)
Tuition and fees: $23,202.
Per-credit charge: $955.
Room and board: $8,068.

FINANCIAL AID PICTURE (2007-2008)
Students with need: Out of 159 full-time freshmen who applied for aid, 141 were judged to have need. Of these, 141 received aid, and 26 had their full need met. Average financial aid package met 65% of need; average scholarship/grant was $12,878; average loan was $3,588. For part-time students, average financial aid package was $10,564.
Students without need: 29 full-time freshmen who did not demonstrate need for aid received scholarships/grants; average award was $4,254. No-need awards available for academics, alumni affiliation, athletics, leadership, music/drama, ROTC.
Scholarships offered: 14 full-time freshmen received athletic scholarships; average amount $5,514.
Cumulative student debt: 85% of graduating class had student loans; average debt was $28,347.

FINANCIAL AID PROCEDURES
Forms required: FAFSA.
Dates and Deadlines: Priority date 2/15; no closing date. Applicants notified on a rolling basis starting 3/1.

CONTACT
Nathan Warthan, Director of Financial Aid
5000 Deer Park Drive SE, Salem, OR 97317-9392
(503) 375-7006

DeVry University: Portland
Portland, Oregon
www.devry.edu

4-year for-profit university in very large city.
Enrollment: 101 undergrads, 46% part-time. 4 full-time freshmen.

BASIC COSTS (2008-2009)
Tuition and fees: $13,930.
Per-credit charge: $515.

FINANCIAL AID PICTURE (2007-2008)
Students with need: Out of 3 full-time freshmen who applied for aid, 3 were judged to have need. Of these, 3 received aid. Average financial aid package met 25% of need; average scholarship/grant was $2,430; average loan was $3,916. For part-time students, average financial aid package was $9,993.
Students without need: No-need awards available for academics.

FINANCIAL AID PROCEDURES
Forms required: FAFSA.
Dates and Deadlines: No deadline. Applicants notified on a rolling basis.

CONTACT
Director of Financial Aid
Peterkort Center II, Portland, OR 97225
(503) 296-7468

Eastern Oregon University
La Grande, Oregon
www.eou.edu Federal Code: 003193

4-year public university and liberal arts college in large town.
Enrollment: 2,823 undergrads, 37% part-time. 312 full-time freshmen.
Selectivity: Admits less than 50% of applicants.

BASIC COSTS (2008-2009)
Tuition and fees: $6,240; out-of-state residents $6,240.
Room and board: $9,100.

FINANCIAL AID PICTURE (2008-2009)
Students with need: Out of 278 full-time freshmen who applied for aid, 228 were judged to have need. Of these, 227 received aid, and 96 had their full need met. Average financial aid package met 40% of need; average scholarship/grant was $5,520; average loan was $2,166. For part-time students, average financial aid package was $7,737.
Students without need: 12 full-time freshmen who did not demonstrate need for aid received scholarships/grants; average award was $1,154. No-need awards available for academics, art, leadership, minority status, music/drama, state/district residency.
Scholarships offered: ***Merit:*** University Scholars Scholarships; full-tuition; based on personal essay, recommendations, GPA, activities and awards.

Athletic: 64 full-time freshmen received athletic scholarships; average amount $1,904.
Cumulative student debt: 75% of graduating class had student loans; average debt was $21,415.

FINANCIAL AID PROCEDURES

Forms required: FAFSA.
Dates and Deadlines: Priority date 3/1; no closing date. Applicants notified on a rolling basis starting 4/1; must reply within 4 week(s) of notification.
Transfers: No deadline. Applicants notified on a rolling basis.

CONTACT

Carolyn Prescott, Director of Financial Aid
One University Boulevard, La Grande, OR 97850
(541) 962-3550

Eugene Bible College

Eugene, Oregon
www.ebc.edu Federal Code: 015167

4-year private Bible college in small city, affiliated with Open Bible Standard Churches.
Enrollment: 103 undergrads, 20% part-time. 29 full-time freshmen.
Selectivity: Admits 50 to 75% of applicants.

BASIC COSTS (2009-2010)

Tuition and fees: $10,958.
Per-credit charge: $275.
Room and board: $5,670.

FINANCIAL AID PICTURE (2007-2008)

Students with need: 92% of average financial aid package awarded as scholarships/grants, 8% awarded as loans/jobs. Need-based aid available for part-time students. Work study available nights, weekends, and for part-time students.
Students without need: No-need awards available for academics, athletics, leadership, religious affiliation.
Scholarships offered: Honors award; $300; 3.7 GPA required.
Additional info: Some early acceptance awards possible for those admitted by May 15. Distance awards to those coming from over 1,000 miles away. Some awards for husbands and wives enrolled at same time.

FINANCIAL AID PROCEDURES

Forms required: FAFSA.
Dates and Deadlines: Priority date 5/1; closing date 9/1. Applicants notified on a rolling basis starting 7/15; must reply within 4 week(s) of notification.
Transfers: No deadline.

CONTACT

Aaron Denbo, Director of Financial Aid
2155 Bailey Hill Road, Eugene, OR 97405
(800) 322-2638

George Fox University

Newberg, Oregon
www.georgefox.edu Federal Code: 003194

4-year private university and seminary college in large town, affiliated with Society of Friends (Quaker).
Enrollment: 1,962 undergrads, 14% part-time. 390 full-time freshmen.
Selectivity: Admits over 75% of applicants.

BASIC COSTS (2009-2010)

Tuition and fees: $26,180.
Per-credit charge: $780.
Room and board: $8,320.

Additional info: Tuition/fee waivers available for minority students.

FINANCIAL AID PICTURE (2008-2009)

Students with need: Out of 351 full-time freshmen who applied for aid, 314 were judged to have need. Of these, 314 received aid, and 138 had their full need met. Average financial aid package met 89% of need; average scholarship/grant was $9,095; average loan was $3,402. For part-time students, average financial aid package was $9,925.
Students without need: 69 full-time freshmen who did not demonstrate need for aid received scholarships/grants; average award was $786. No-need awards available for academics, alumni affiliation, art, job skills, leadership, minority status, music/drama, religious affiliation.
Scholarships offered: Academic merit awards; $2,500-$10,000 per year; based on GPA, SAT/ACT scores and rigor of high school curriculum; renewable based on academic performance.
Additional info: Audition required for music and drama scholarships.

FINANCIAL AID PROCEDURES

Forms required: FAFSA, state aid form.
Dates and Deadlines: Priority date 2/1; no closing date. Applicants notified on a rolling basis starting 3/1; must reply within 6 week(s) of notification.

CONTACT

Rob Clarke, Executive Director of Student Financial Services
414 North Meridian Street, Newberg, OR 97132-2697
(503) 554-2290

Lane Community College

Eugene, Oregon
www.lanecc.edu Federal Code: 003196

2-year public community college in small city.
Enrollment: 7,574 undergrads.
Selectivity: Open admission; but selective for some programs.

BASIC COSTS (2008-2009)

Tuition and fees: $3,729; out-of-state residents $12,031.
Per-credit charge: $76; out-of-state residents $260.

FINANCIAL AID PICTURE (2007-2008)

Students with need: 63% of average financial aid package awarded as scholarships/grants, 37% awarded as loans/jobs. Need-based aid available for part-time students. Work study available nights, weekends, and for part-time students.
Students without need: No-need awards available for art, athletics, minority status, music/drama.

FINANCIAL AID PROCEDURES

Forms required: FAFSA.
Dates and Deadlines: Closing date 2/15. Applicants notified on a rolling basis starting 6/1; must reply within 2 week(s) of notification.

CONTACT

Burt Logan, Director of Financial Aid
4000 East 30th Avenue, Eugene, OR 97405
(541) 463-3100

Lewis & Clark College

Portland, Oregon Federal Code: 003197
www.lclark.edu CSS Code: 4384

4-year private liberal arts college in very large city.
Enrollment: 1,921 undergrads, 1% part-time. 533 full-time freshmen.
Selectivity: Admits 50 to 75% of applicants.

BASIC COSTS (2009-2010)

Tuition and fees: $35,233.
Per-credit charge: $1,750.
Room and board: $9,006.

FINANCIAL AID PICTURE (2008-2009)

Students with need: Out of 378 full-time freshmen who applied for aid, 275 were judged to have need. Of these, 275 received aid, and 101 had their full need met. Average financial aid package met 88% of need; average scholarship/grant was $17,363; average loan was $4,342. For part-time students, average financial aid package was $15,625.
Students without need: 103 full-time freshmen who did not demonstrate need for aid received scholarships/grants; average award was $7,014. No-need awards available for academics, leadership, music/drama.
Scholarships offered: Neely Scholarship; full tuition; up to 10 awards. Trustee Scholarship; half tuition; up to 15 awards. Dean's Scholarships; one quarter tuition. Music scholarships; $2,525-$8,425; by audition. Forensic scholarships; $2,525-$8,425; separate application required. Leadership and service awards; one quarter tuition.
Cumulative student debt: 57% of graduating class had student loans; average debt was $20,611.

FINANCIAL AID PROCEDURES

Forms required: FAFSA, CSS PROFILE.
Dates and Deadlines: Priority date 2/15; no closing date. Applicants notified on a rolling basis starting 3/1.
Transfers: Transfers eligible for merit-based Dean's scholarships of up to $10,000, not eligible for Neely or Trustee scholarships. Financial aid transcript form from previous institutions required.

CONTACT

Glendi Gaddis, Director of Student Financial Services
0615 SW Palatine Hill Road, Portland, OR 97219-7899
(503) 768-7090

Linfield College

McMinnville, Oregon
www.linfield.edu Federal Code: 003198

4-year private liberal arts college in large town, affiliated with American Baptist Churches in the USA.
Enrollment: 1,678 undergrads, 1% part-time. 478 full-time freshmen.
Selectivity: Admits over 75% of applicants.

BASIC COSTS (2009-2010)

Tuition and fees: $29,034.
Per-credit charge: $895.
Room and board: $8,280.

FINANCIAL AID PICTURE (2008-2009)

Students with need: Out of 327 full-time freshmen who applied for aid, 327 were judged to have need. Of these, 327 received aid, and 126 had their full need met. Average financial aid package met 87% of need; average scholarship/grant was $6,269; average loan was $3,870. For part-time students, average financial aid package was $17,940.
Students without need: 110 full-time freshmen who did not demonstrate need for aid received scholarships/grants; average award was $10,226. No-need awards available for academics, music/drama.
Scholarships offered: National Merit Scholarship; half- to full-tuition; for National Merit Finalists who list Linfield as first choice. Trustee Scholarships; $11,300 to $16,900; based on academic record and 3.75 GPA. Faculty Scholarships; $7,700 to $11,000; based on academic record and 3.4 GPA. Linfield Competitive Scholarships; $10,000-$16,000; separate application required. Music Achievement Awards; $1,500-$2,500; audition or recorded performance required, must intend to major or minor in music. Leadership/ Service Scholarship; up to $3,000; based on high levels of leadership, initiative, and service to others through student government, school activities, community organizations, and church or social service agencies; separate application required; up to 5 awarded. Academic All-Star Scholarships; $2,500 for 1st place, $1,500 for 2nd or 3rd place; supplements other competition-based scholarships.
Cumulative student debt: 72% of graduating class had student loans; average debt was $27,140.

FINANCIAL AID PROCEDURES

Forms required: FAFSA.
Dates and Deadlines: Priority date 2/1; no closing date. Applicants notified by 4/1; must reply by 5/1.
Transfers: Priority date 2/15. Transfer Scholarships; $5,000-$10,000; for students who have attended 2- or 4-year accredited colleges full-time and have 3.25 GPA. Phi Theta Kappa Scholarships; $2,000; up to 10 awarded each year to members of Phi Theta Kappa; 3.25 GPA in transferable courses required.

CONTACT

Crisanne Werner, Director of Financial Aid
900 Southeast Baker Street, McMinnville, OR 97218-6894
(503) 883-2225

Linn-Benton Community College

Albany, Oregon
www.linnbenton.edu Federal Code: 006938

2-year public community college in large town.
Enrollment: 5,079 undergrads, 47% part-time. 933 full-time freshmen.
Selectivity: Open admission; but selective for some programs.

BASIC COSTS (2008-2009)

Tuition and fees: $3,112; out-of-state residents $7,657.
Per-credit charge: $65; out-of-state residents $166.
Additional info: Tuition/fee waivers available for unemployed or children of unemployed.

FINANCIAL AID PICTURE (2007-2008)

Students with need: Out of 646 full-time freshmen who applied for aid, 538 were judged to have need. Of these, 511 received aid, and 68 had their full need met. Average financial aid package met 60% of need; average scholarship/grant was $4,172; average loan was $2,799. For part-time students, average financial aid package was $4,932.
Students without need: 102 full-time freshmen who did not demonstrate need for aid received scholarships/grants; average award was $1,856. No-need awards available for academics, art, job skills, leadership, music/drama, state/district residency.
Scholarships offered: 6 full-time freshmen received athletic scholarships; average amount $1,711.
Cumulative student debt: 43% of graduating class had student loans; average debt was $9,619.

FINANCIAL AID PROCEDURES

Forms required: FAFSA.
Dates and Deadlines: Priority date 4/1; no closing date. Applicants notified on a rolling basis starting 4/15; must reply within 2 week(s) of notification.

CONTACT

Danny Aynes
6500 SW Pacific Boulevard, Albany, OR 97321-3779
(541) 917-4850

Marylhurst University
Marylhurst, Oregon
www.marylhurst.edu Federal Code: 003199

4-year private university and liberal arts college in large town, affiliated with Roman Catholic Church.
Enrollment: 870 undergrads, 74% part-time. 23 full-time freshmen.
Selectivity: Open admission; but selective for some programs.

BASIC COSTS (2008-2009)
Tuition and fees: $16,200.
Per-credit charge: $349.

FINANCIAL AID PICTURE (2007-2008)
Students with need: Out of 6 full-time freshmen who applied for aid, 4 were judged to have need. Of these, 4 received aid. Average financial aid package met 43% of need; average scholarship/grant was $7,010; average loan was $4,791. For part-time students, average financial aid package was $7,996.
Students without need: 6 full-time freshmen who did not demonstrate need for aid received scholarships/grants; average award was $343. No-need awards available for academics.
Cumulative student debt: 80% of graduating class had student loans; average debt was $20,275.

FINANCIAL AID PROCEDURES
Forms required: FAFSA, institutional form.
Dates and Deadlines: Priority date 6/1; no closing date. Applicants notified on a rolling basis starting 5/1.
Transfers: No deadline. Applicants notified on a rolling basis starting 5/1.

CONTACT
Tracy Reisinger, Director of Financial Aid
PO Box 261, Marylhurst, OR 97036-0261
(503) 699-6253

Mt. Hood Community College
Gresham, Oregon
www.mhcc.cc.or.us Federal Code: 003204

2-year public community college in small city.
Enrollment: 7,245 undergrads, 57% part-time. 1,011 full-time freshmen.
Selectivity: Open admission; but selective for some programs.

BASIC COSTS (2009-2010)
Tuition and fees: $3,673; out-of-state residents $9,991.
Per-credit charge: $69; out-of-state residents $209.

FINANCIAL AID PICTURE (2007-2008)
Students with need: Need-based aid available for full-time and part-time students.
Students without need: No-need awards available for academics.

FINANCIAL AID PROCEDURES
Forms required: FAFSA, institutional form.
Dates and Deadlines: No deadline. Applicants notified on a rolling basis starting 2/15; must reply within 4 week(s) of notification.

CONTACT
Patricia Martin, Associate Dean, Enrollment Services
26000 Southeast Stark Street, Gresham, OR 97030
(503) 491-7265

Multnomah University
Portland, Oregon
www.multnomah.edu Federal Code: 003206

4-year private Bible and seminary college in very large city, affiliated with interdenominational tradition.
Enrollment: 582 undergrads, 12% part-time. 60 full-time freshmen.
Selectivity: Admits 50 to 75% of applicants.

BASIC COSTS (2008-2009)
Tuition and fees: $14,100.
Per-credit charge: $470.
Room and board: $5,840.
Additional info: Cost of health insurance if student is not covered is $1,200.

FINANCIAL AID PICTURE (2007-2008)
Students with need: Out of 60 full-time freshmen who applied for aid, 49 were judged to have need. Of these, 48 received aid, and 4 had their full need met. Average financial aid package met 51% of need; average scholarship/grant was $4,979; average loan was $2,709. For part-time students, average financial aid package was $6,984.
Students without need: 2 full-time freshmen who did not demonstrate need for aid received scholarships/grants; average award was $1,400. No-need awards available for academics.
Cumulative student debt: 96% of graduating class had student loans; average debt was $21,390.

FINANCIAL AID PROCEDURES
Forms required: FAFSA, institutional form.
Dates and Deadlines: Priority date 3/1; closing date 8/1. Applicants notified on a rolling basis starting 4/1; must reply within 3 week(s) of notification.

CONTACT
Mary McGlothlan, Director of Financial Aid
8435 Northeast Glisan Street, Portland, OR 97220-5898
(503) 251-5336

Northwest Christian University
Eugene, Oregon
www.northwestchristian.edu Federal Code: 003208

4-year private university in small city, affiliated with Christian Church (Disciples of Christ).
Enrollment: 429 undergrads, 28% part-time. 77 full-time freshmen.
Selectivity: Admits over 75% of applicants.

BASIC COSTS (2009-2010)
Tuition and fees: $22,900.
Per-credit charge: $770.
Room and board: $6,800.

FINANCIAL AID PICTURE (2008-2009)
Students with need: Out of 75 full-time freshmen who applied for aid, 70 were judged to have need. Of these, 70 received aid, and 15 had their full need met. Average financial aid package met 79% of need; average scholarship/grant was $13,962; average loan was $2,385. For part-time students, average financial aid package was $10,979.
Students without need: 6 full-time freshmen who did not demonstrate need for aid received scholarships/grants; average award was $6,785. No-need awards available for academics, athletics, leadership, music/drama, religious affiliation.
Scholarships offered: ***Merit:*** Academic scholarships; $2,000-$12,000; GPA/SAT or ACT scores; not limited. Leadership bonuses; $500-$3,000; school, community, church leadership roles; not limited. ***Athletic:*** 7 full-time freshmen received athletic scholarships; average amount $1,998.

Cumulative student debt: 90% of graduating class had student loans; average debt was $19,843.

FINANCIAL AID PROCEDURES

Forms required: FAFSA.

Dates and Deadlines: Priority date 3/1; no closing date. Applicants notified on a rolling basis starting 3/1; must reply within 2 week(s) of notification.

Transfers: No deadline. Applicants notified on a rolling basis.

CONTACT

David Haggard, Director of Financial Aid
828 East 11th Avenue, Eugene, OR 97401-3745
(541) 684-7211

Oregon College of Art & Craft

Portland, Oregon
www.ocac.edu Federal Code: 030073

4-year private visual arts college in very large city.

Enrollment: 115 undergrads, 19% part-time. 3 full-time freshmen.

Selectivity: Admits over 75% of applicants.

BASIC COSTS (2008-2009)

Tuition and fees: $20,416.

Per-credit charge: $822.

Room and board: $1,800.

Additional info: Fees vary by area of concentration.

FINANCIAL AID PICTURE (2008-2009)

Students with need: Average financial aid package met 56% of need; average scholarship/grant was $2,281; average loan was $3,500. For part-time students, average financial aid package was $11,492.

Students without need: No-need awards available for academics, art.

Cumulative student debt: 100% of graduating class had student loans; average debt was $31,000.

FINANCIAL AID PROCEDURES

Forms required: FAFSA.

Dates and Deadlines: Priority date 3/1; no closing date. Applicants notified on a rolling basis starting 3/15.

CONTACT

Lisa Newman, Financial Aid Officer
8245 SW Barnes Road, Portland, OR 97225-6349
(503) 297-5544 ext. 124

Oregon Health & Science University

Portland, Oregon
www.ohsu.edu Federal Code: 004883

3-year public university and health science college in very large city.

Enrollment: 604 undergrads.

BASIC COSTS (2008-2009)

Tuition and fees: $18,341; out-of-state residents $29,321.

Per-credit charge: $289; out-of-state residents $533.

Additional info: Tuition shown is for undergraduate nursing program; costs for other programs vary.

FINANCIAL AID PICTURE (2008-2009)

Students with need: Average financial aid package for all full-time undergraduates was $12,085; for part-time $7,966. 20% awarded as scholarships/grants, 80% awarded as loans/jobs. Work study available nights, weekends, and for part-time students.

Students without need: No-need awards available for academics, minority status, state/district residency.

FINANCIAL AID PROCEDURES

Dates and Deadlines: Priority date 3/1; no closing date.

Transfers: No deadline. Applicants notified on a rolling basis starting 5/10; must reply within 4 week(s) of notification.

CONTACT

Cherie Honnell, Director of Financial Aid/Registrar
3181 SW Sam Jackson Park Road, Portland, OR 97239
(503) 494-7800

Oregon Institute of Technology

Klamath Falls, Oregon
www.oit.edu Federal Code: 003211

4-year public career college in small city.

Enrollment: 2,603 undergrads. 210 full-time freshmen.

Selectivity: Admits over 75% of applicants.

BASIC COSTS (2008-2009)

Tuition and fees: $6,297; out-of-state residents $16,692.

Per-credit charge: $108; out-of-state residents $339.

Room and board: $7,132.

Additional info: Tuition/fee waivers available for minority students.

FINANCIAL AID PICTURE (2007-2008)

Students with need: Out of 210 full-time freshmen who applied for aid, 182 were judged to have need. Of these, 178 received aid, and 65 had their full need met. Average financial aid package met 22% of need; average scholarship/grant was $3,034; average loan was $2,456. For part-time students, average financial aid package was $4,599.

Students without need: No-need awards available for academics, athletics, leadership, minority status.

Scholarships offered: 3 full-time freshmen received athletic scholarships; average amount $1,549.

FINANCIAL AID PROCEDURES

Forms required: FAFSA.

Dates and Deadlines: Priority date 3/1; no closing date. Applicants notified on a rolling basis starting 4/1; must reply within 3 week(s) of notification.

Transfers: Closing date 2/1.

CONTACT

Tracey Lehman, Director of Financial Aid
3201 Campus Drive, Klamath Falls, OR 97601
(541) 885-1280

Oregon State University

Corvallis, Oregon
www.oregonstate.edu Federal Code: 003210

4-year public university in small city.

Enrollment: 15,907 undergrads, 12% part-time. 2,948 full-time freshmen.

Selectivity: Admits over 75% of applicants.

BASIC COSTS (2008-2009)

Tuition and fees: $6,187; out-of-state residents $18,823.

Per-credit charge: $128; out-of-state residents $479.

Room and board: $8,208.

FINANCIAL AID PICTURE (2008-2009)

Students with need: Out of 2,288 full-time freshmen who applied for aid, 1,449 were judged to have need. Of these, 1,411 received aid, and 261 had their full need met. Average financial aid package met 63% of need; average scholarship/grant was $2,738; average loan was $3,278. For part-time students, average financial aid package was $7,747.

Students without need: No-need awards available for academics, athletics, job skills, leadership, minority status, ROTC, state/district residency.
Scholarships offered: 64 full-time freshmen received athletic scholarships; average amount $17,006.

FINANCIAL AID PROCEDURES

Forms required: FAFSA.
Dates and Deadlines: Priority date 2/1; closing date 5/1. Applicants notified on a rolling basis starting 4/1; must reply within 4 week(s) of notification.
Transfers: Priority date 3/1; no deadline.

CONTACT

Emilio Vejil, Director of Financial Aid
104 Kerr Administration Building, Corvallis, OR 97331-2130
(541) 731-2241

Pacific Northwest College of Art

Portland, Oregon
www.pnca.edu Federal Code: 003207

4-year private visual arts college in large city.
Enrollment: 477 undergrads, 8% part-time. 92 full-time freshmen.
Selectivity: Admits 50 to 75% of applicants.

BASIC COSTS (2009-2010)

Tuition and fees: $23,304.
Per-credit charge: $930.
Additional info: Off-campus housing available, approximately one mile from campus. Cost is $4,090.

FINANCIAL AID PICTURE (2008-2009)

Students with need: Need-based aid available for full-time and part-time students. Work study available nights, weekends, and for part-time students.
Students without need: No-need awards available for academics, art.
Scholarships offered: Leta Kennedy Student Scholarships; $10,000; based on artistic merit. Dorothy Lemelson Scholarship; cost of attendance; based on artistic and academic merit; renewable up to 4 years; 1 awarded. Other renewable scholarships available.

FINANCIAL AID PROCEDURES

Forms required: FAFSA.
Dates and Deadlines: Priority date 3/1; no closing date. Applicants notified on a rolling basis starting 4/1; must reply by 5/1 or within 4 week(s) of notification.
Transfers: No deadline. Applicants notified on a rolling basis starting 4/1; must reply by 5/1 or within 4 week(s) of notification.

CONTACT

Heidi Locke, Director of Financial Aid
1241 NW Johnson Street, Portland, OR 97209
(503) 821-8972

Pacific University

Forest Grove, Oregon
www.pacificu.edu Federal Code: 003212

4-year private university in large town, affiliated with United Church of Christ.
Enrollment: 1,451 undergrads, 3% part-time. 345 full-time freshmen.
Selectivity: Admits over 75% of applicants.

BASIC COSTS (2008-2009)

Tuition and fees: $28,270.
Per-credit charge: $1,150.
Room and board: $7,482.

FINANCIAL AID PICTURE (2008-2009)

Students with need: Out of 310 full-time freshmen who applied for aid, 255 were judged to have need. Of these, 255 received aid, and 91 had their full need met. Average financial aid package met 88% of need; average scholarship/grant was $14,223; average loan was $7,789. For part-time students, average financial aid package was $15,172.
Students without need: 82 full-time freshmen who did not demonstrate need for aid received scholarships/grants; average award was $11,740. No-need awards available for academics, alumni affiliation, art, music/drama.
Scholarships offered: Honors Scholarship; $9,000. Presidential Scholarship; $8,000. Trustee Scholarship; $7,500. University Scholarship; $6,500. Pacesetters Scholarship; $1,000 to $3,000. Music and Forensics Talent Awards; $1,000 to $3,000. Number of awards varies.
Cumulative student debt: 78% of graduating class had student loans; average debt was $24,485.

FINANCIAL AID PROCEDURES

Forms required: FAFSA.
Dates and Deadlines: Priority date 3/1; no closing date. Applicants notified on a rolling basis starting 3/1.

CONTACT

Michael Johnson, Director of Financial Aid
2043 College Way, Forest Grove, OR 97116-1797
(503) 352-2222

Pioneer Pacific College

Wilsonville, Oregon
www.pioneerpacific.edu Federal Code: 016520

2-year for-profit career college in large town.
Enrollment: 364 undergrads, 32% part-time. 180 full-time freshmen.
Selectivity: Open admission; but selective for some programs.

BASIC COSTS (2009-2010)

Tuition and fees: $10,993.
Per-credit charge: $420.
Additional info: Costs vary by program from $7,840 to $27,835. Certain programs have additional lab fees. Tuition at time of enrollment locked for 2 years.

FINANCIAL AID PICTURE

Students with need: Need-based aid available for full-time and part-time students.
Students without need: This college awards aid only to students with need.
Scholarships offered: High school scholarship program and community scholarship program available.

FINANCIAL AID PROCEDURES

Forms required: FAFSA.
Dates and Deadlines: No deadline. Applicants notified on a rolling basis starting 2/27.

CONTACT

Michael Hargrave, Executive Director of Financial Aid
27501 Southwest Parkway Avenue, Wilsonville, OR 97070
(503) 654-8000

Portland Community College

Portland, Oregon
www.pcc.edu Federal Code: 003213

2-year public community college in very large city.
Enrollment: 26,436 undergrads.
Selectivity: Open admission; but selective for some programs.

BASIC COSTS (2008-2009)

Tuition and fees: $3,425; out-of-state residents $9,185.
Per-credit charge: $70; out-of-state residents $198.

FINANCIAL AID PICTURE (2007-2008)

Students with need: 36% of average financial aid package awarded as scholarships/grants, 64% awarded as loans/jobs. Need-based aid available for part-time students. Work study available nights, weekends, and for part-time students.
Students without need: This college awards aid only to students with need.

FINANCIAL AID PROCEDURES

Forms required: FAFSA.
Dates and Deadlines: Priority date 3/1; no closing date. Applicants notified on a rolling basis starting 6/1; must reply within 3 week(s) of notification.

CONTACT

Corbett Gottfried, Director of Financial Aid
Box 19000, Portland, OR 97280-0990
(503) 977-4934

Portland State University

Portland, Oregon
www.pdx.edu Federal Code: 003216

4-year public university in very large city.
Enrollment: 17,930 undergrads, 30% part-time. 1,567 full-time freshmen.
Selectivity: Admits over 75% of applicants.

BASIC COSTS (2008-2009)

Tuition and fees: $6,147; out-of-state residents $18,837.
Per-credit charge: $109; out-of-state residents $391.
Room and board: $9,486.

FINANCIAL AID PICTURE (2008-2009)

Students with need: Need-based aid available for full-time and part-time students. Work study available nights, weekends, and for part-time students.
Students without need: No-need awards available for academics, art, athletics, music/drama, state/district residency.

FINANCIAL AID PROCEDURES

Forms required: FAFSA.
Dates and Deadlines: Priority date 2/28; no closing date. Applicants notified on a rolling basis; must reply within 4 week(s) of notification.

CONTACT

Phillip Rodgers, Director of Financial Aid
PO Box 751-ADM, Portland, OR 97207-0751
(800) 547-8887

Reed College

Portland, Oregon Federal Code: 003217
www.reed.edu CSS Code: 4654

4-year private liberal arts college in very large city.
Enrollment: 1,408 undergrads. 330 full-time freshmen.
Selectivity: Admits less than 50% of applicants.

BASIC COSTS (2009-2010)

Tuition and fees: $39,700.
Per-credit charge: $1,675.
Room and board: $10,250.

FINANCIAL AID PICTURE (2008-2009)

Students with need: Out of 213 full-time freshmen who applied for aid, 169 were judged to have need. Of these, 169 received aid, and 165 had their full need met. Average financial aid package met 100% of need; average scholarship/grant was $31,668; average loan was $3,043.
Students without need: This college awards aid only to students with need.
Cumulative student debt: 53% of graduating class had student loans; average debt was $17,296.
Additional info: College meets demonstrated need of continuing students who have attended Reed minimum of 2 semesters, who file financial aid applications on time, and who maintain satisfactory academic progress. Institutional aid consideration is for total of 8 semesters.

FINANCIAL AID PROCEDURES

Forms required: FAFSA, CSS PROFILE, institutional form.
Dates and Deadlines: Closing date 1/15. Applicants notified by 4/1; must reply by 5/1 or within 2 week(s) of notification.
Transfers: Must reply by 6/1.

CONTACT

Leslie Limper, Director of Financial Aid
3203 SE Woodstock Boulevard, Portland, OR 97202-8199
(800) 547-4750

Rogue Community College

Grants Pass, Oregon
www.roguecc.edu Federal Code: 010071

2-year public community college in large town.
Enrollment: 3,232 undergrads, 57% part-time. 279 full-time freshmen.
Selectivity: Open admission; but selective for some programs.

BASIC COSTS (2008-2009)

Tuition and fees: $3,390; out-of-state residents $4,065.
Per-credit charge: $68; out-of-state residents $83.
Additional info: Washington, Idaho, Nevada, and California residents pay in-state tuition. Tuition/fee waivers available for unemployed or children of unemployed.

FINANCIAL AID PICTURE (2007-2008)

Students with need: Out of 209 full-time freshmen who applied for aid, 160 were judged to have need. Of these, 160 received aid, and 18 had their full need met. Average financial aid package met 78% of need; average scholarship/grant was $3,495; average loan was $2,469. For part-time students, average financial aid package was $6,838.
Students without need: 25 full-time freshmen who did not demonstrate need for aid received scholarships/grants; average award was $1,386.

FINANCIAL AID PROCEDURES

Forms required: FAFSA, institutional form.
Dates and Deadlines: Priority date 5/1; no closing date. Applicants notified on a rolling basis; must reply within 2 week(s) of notification.

CONTACT

Anna Manley, Director of Financial Aid
3345 Redwood Highway, Grants Pass, OR 97527
(541) 956-7501 ext. 1

Southern Oregon University

Ashland, Oregon
www.sou.edu Federal Code: 003219

4-year public university and liberal arts college in large town.
Enrollment: 4,084 undergrads, 20% part-time. 646 full-time freshmen.
Selectivity: Admits over 75% of applicants.

BASIC COSTS (2008-2009)
Tuition and fees: $5,718; out-of-state residents $18,264.
Room and board: $7,875.
Additional info: Tuition/fee waivers available for minority students.

FINANCIAL AID PICTURE (2008-2009)
Students with need: Need-based aid available for full-time and part-time students. Work study available nights, weekends, and for part-time students.
Students without need: No-need awards available for academics, alumni affiliation, art, athletics, leadership, minority status, music/drama, religious affiliation, state/district residency.

FINANCIAL AID PROCEDURES
Forms required: FAFSA.
Dates and Deadlines: No deadline. Applicants notified on a rolling basis starting 3/1; must reply within 2 week(s) of notification.

CONTACT
Diana Watson-Paul, Associate Director of Financial Aid
1250 Siskiyou Boulevard, Ashland, OR 97520-5032
(541) 552-6600

Southwestern Oregon Community College
Coos Bay, Oregon
www.socc.edu Federal Code: 003220

2-year public culinary school and community college in large town.
Enrollment: 1,600 undergrads.
Selectivity: Open admission; but selective for some programs.

BASIC COSTS (2008-2009)
Tuition and fees: $3,660.
Per-credit charge: $62.
Room and board: $6,160.
Additional info: Tuition/fee waivers available for adults, unemployed or children of unemployed.

FINANCIAL AID PICTURE (2007-2008)
Students with need: Need-based aid available for full-time and part-time students.
Students without need: No-need awards available for art, athletics, leadership, music/drama.

FINANCIAL AID PROCEDURES
Forms required: FAFSA.
Dates and Deadlines: Priority date 2/28; closing date 6/30. Applicants notified on a rolling basis starting 5/1; must reply within 3 week(s) of notification.

CONTACT
Avena Singh, Director of Financial Aid
1988 Newmark Avenue, Coos Bay, OR 97420-2956
(541) 888-7337

Treasure Valley Community College
Ontario, Oregon
www.tvcc.cc Federal Code: 003221

2-year public community college in small town.
Enrollment: 2,122 undergrads, 44% part-time. 829 full-time freshmen.
Selectivity: Open admission; but selective for some programs.

BASIC COSTS (2008-2009)
Tuition and fees: $3,600; out-of-state residents $4,050.
Per-credit charge: $68; out-of-state residents $78.
Room and board: $6,660.

FINANCIAL AID PICTURE (2007-2008)
Students with need: Out of 829 full-time freshmen who applied for aid, 655 were judged to have need. Of these, 525 received aid, and 19 had their full need met. Average financial aid package met 34% of need; average scholarship/grant was $3,637; average loan was $2,511. For part-time students, average financial aid package was $4,438.
Students without need: No-need awards available for academics, athletics, leadership, music/drama, state/district residency.
Scholarships offered: 14 full-time freshmen received athletic scholarships; average amount $1,721.
Cumulative student debt: 87% of graduating class had student loans; average debt was $10,090.

FINANCIAL AID PROCEDURES
Forms required: FAFSA.
Dates and Deadlines: Priority date 4/1; no closing date. Applicants notified on a rolling basis starting 5/1.
Transfers: No deadline. Applicants notified on a rolling basis.

CONTACT
Jonathan Gillen, Comptroller
650 College Boulevard, Ontario, OR 97914
(541) 881-8822 ext. 233

Umpqua Community College
Roseburg, Oregon
www.umpqua.edu Federal Code: 003222

2-year public community college in large town.
Enrollment: 1,444 undergrads, 41% part-time. 267 full-time freshmen.
Selectivity: Open admission; but selective for some programs.

BASIC COSTS (2009-2010)
Tuition and fees: $3,195; out-of-state residents $8,775.
Per-credit charge: $63; out-of-state residents $186.

FINANCIAL AID PICTURE (2007-2008)
Students with need: Out of 230 full-time freshmen who applied for aid, 106 were judged to have need. Of these, 103 received aid. Need-based aid available for part-time students.
Students without need: No-need awards available for academics, athletics.

FINANCIAL AID PROCEDURES
Forms required: FAFSA.
Dates and Deadlines: Priority date 3/1; no closing date. Applicants notified on a rolling basis starting 5/1; must reply within 2 week(s) of notification.

CONTACT
Laurie Spangenberg, Director of Financial Aid
1140 College Road, Roseburg, OR 97470-0226
(541) 440-4602

University of Oregon
Eugene, Oregon
www.uoregon.edu Federal Code: 003223

4-year public university in small city.
Enrollment: 17,356 undergrads, 7% part-time. 4,193 full-time freshmen.
Selectivity: Admits over 75% of applicants.

BASIC COSTS (2008-2009)
Tuition and fees: $6,435; out-of-state residents $19,992.
Room and board: $8,478.
Additional info: Additional program-specific fees may apply.

FINANCIAL AID PICTURE (2008-2009)

Students with need: Out of 2,687 full-time freshmen who applied for aid, 1,559 were judged to have need. Of these, 1,429 received aid, and 270 had their full need met. Average financial aid package met 55% of need; average scholarship/grant was $6,114; average loan was $3,755. For part-time students, average financial aid package was $7,837.

Students without need: 493 full-time freshmen who did not demonstrate need for aid received scholarships/grants; average award was $2,457. No-need awards available for academics, athletics, leadership, minority status, music/drama, ROTC, state/district residency.

Scholarships offered: Presidential Scholarship; up to $6,000 for up to 4 years; merit-based for Oregon residents. National Merit Scholarship; $2,000 for up to 4 years. Staton Scholarship; $5,000 for up to 4 years; based on extraordinary financial need. Laurel Award; amounts vary; competitive merit award. General University Scholarship; up to $2,700; merit-based. Dean's Scholarship; up to $6,000 for up to 12 terms; merit-based. Diversity-Building Scholarship; amounts determined by committee; for ethnic minority, first generation, or non-traditional students.

Cumulative student debt: 55% of graduating class had student loans; average debt was $18,805.

FINANCIAL AID PROCEDURES

Forms required: FAFSA.

Dates and Deadlines: Closing date 2/1. Applicants notified on a rolling basis starting 4/15; must reply within 4 week(s) of notification.

CONTACT

Elizabeth Bickford, Director, Financial Aid and Scholarships
1217 University of Oregon, Eugene, OR 97403-1217
(541) 346-3221

University of Portland

Portland, Oregon
www.up.edu Federal Code: 003224

4-year private university in large city, affiliated with Roman Catholic Church.

Enrollment: 2,997 undergrads, 2% part-time. 791 full-time freshmen.

Selectivity: Admits over 75% of applicants.

BASIC COSTS (2009-2010)

Tuition and fees: $30,940.

Per-credit charge: $970.

Room and board: $9,115.

FINANCIAL AID PICTURE (2008-2009)

Students with need: Out of 672 full-time freshmen who applied for aid, 479 were judged to have need. Of these, 479 received aid, and 86 had their full need met. Average financial aid package met 93% of need; average scholarship/grant was $17,548; average loan was $3,896. For part-time students, average financial aid package was $17,484.

Students without need: 257 full-time freshmen who did not demonstrate need for aid received scholarships/grants; average award was $20,465. No-need awards available for academics, alumni affiliation, athletics, music/drama, religious affiliation, ROTC.

Scholarships offered: ***Merit:*** President's Scholarship; up to $10,000; based on academic excellence, school and community involvement, and other factors. Holy Cross Scholarship; up to $6,000; based on academic excellence, school and community involvement, and other factors. Arthur A. Schulte Scholarship, up to $6,000. ***Athletic:*** 37 full-time freshmen received athletic scholarships; average amount $27,373.

Cumulative student debt: 63% of graduating class had student loans; average debt was $22,787.

FINANCIAL AID PROCEDURES

Forms required: FAFSA.

Dates and Deadlines: Priority date 3/1; no closing date. Applicants notified on a rolling basis starting 3/15; must reply within 3 week(s) of notification.

CONTACT

Janet Turner, Director of Financial Aid
5000 North Willamette Boulevard, Portland, OR 97203-5798
(503) 943-7311

Warner Pacific College

Portland, Oregon
www.warnerpacific.edu Federal Code: 003225

4-year private liberal arts college in very large city, affiliated with Church of God.

Enrollment: 874 undergrads, 2% part-time. 81 full-time freshmen.

Selectivity: Admits less than 50% of applicants.

BASIC COSTS (2009-2010)

Tuition and fees: $17,110.

Room and board: $6,646.

Additional info: Per-credit-hour charge: 1-5 credits, $475; 6-11 credits, $750.

FINANCIAL AID PICTURE (2007-2008)

Students with need: Out of 78 full-time freshmen who applied for aid, 72 were judged to have need. Of these, 72 received aid, and 10 had their full need met. Average financial aid package met 75% of need; average scholarship/grant was $6,472; average loan was $3,998. For part-time students, average financial aid package was $20,284.

Students without need: 5 full-time freshmen who did not demonstrate need for aid received scholarships/grants; average award was $5,200. No-need awards available for academics, alumni affiliation, athletics, leadership, minority status, music/drama, religious affiliation.

Scholarships offered: 28 full-time freshmen received athletic scholarships; average amount $4,013.

FINANCIAL AID PROCEDURES

Forms required: FAFSA.

Dates and Deadlines: Priority date 3/1; closing date 8/30. Applicants notified on a rolling basis starting 3/1; must reply within 4 week(s) of notification.

Transfers: No deadline. Applicants notified on a rolling basis starting 3/1; must reply within 2 week(s) of notification.

CONTACT

Cynthia Pollard, Director of Financial Aid
2219 SE 68th Avenue, Portland, OR 97215-4026
(503) 517-1017

Western Oregon University

Monmouth, Oregon
www.wou.edu Federal Code: 003209

4-year public liberal arts and teachers college in small town.

Enrollment: 4,703 undergrads, 15% part-time. 868 full-time freshmen.

Selectivity: Admits less than 50% of applicants.

BASIC COSTS (2008-2009)

Tuition and fees: $6,318; out-of-state residents $16,893.

Room and board: $7,710.

Additional info: Resident tuition reflects a four-year tuition commitment. Tuition at time of enrollment locked for 4 years; tuition/fee waivers available for minority students.

FINANCIAL AID PICTURE (2008-2009)

Students with need: Average financial aid package met 70% of need; average scholarship/grant was $6,539; average loan was $3,390. For part-time students, average financial aid package was $7,231.

Students without need: No-need awards available for academics, alumni affiliation, art, athletics, leadership, music/drama.

Cumulative student debt: 61% of graduating class had student loans; average debt was $22,037.

FINANCIAL AID PROCEDURES

Forms required: FAFSA.

Dates and Deadlines: Priority date 3/1; no closing date. Applicants notified on a rolling basis starting 2/28; must reply within 3 week(s) of notification.

CONTACT

Donna Fossum, Director of Financial Aid
345 North Monmouth Avenue, Monmouth, OR 97361
(503) 838-8475

Willamette University

Salem, Oregon
www.willamette.edu Federal Code: 003227

4-year private university and liberal arts college in small city, affiliated with United Methodist Church.

Enrollment: 1,758 undergrads, 1% part-time. 482 full-time freshmen.

Selectivity: Admits over 75% of applicants.

BASIC COSTS (2009-2010)

Tuition and fees: $35,610.

Room and board: $8,350.

FINANCIAL AID PICTURE (2008-2009)

Students with need: Out of 371 full-time freshmen who applied for aid, 278 were judged to have need. Of these, 278 received aid, and 69 had their full need met. Average financial aid package met 93% of need; average scholarship/grant was $21,412; average loan was $4,430. For part-time students, average financial aid package was $12,521.

Students without need: 187 full-time freshmen who did not demonstrate need for aid received scholarships/grants; average award was $11,728. No-need awards available for academics, alumni affiliation, leadership, minority status, music/drama, religious affiliation.

Scholarships offered: Academic merit awards; $5,000-$15,000; based on superior academic achievement and promise. Music, forensics, theater scholarships; average $3,000-$5,000; based on talent. Mark O. Hatfield Scholarship; full tuition; based on excellent academic record and demonstrated commitment to service leadership.

Cumulative student debt: 63% of graduating class had student loans; average debt was $24,465.

FINANCIAL AID PROCEDURES

Forms required: FAFSA. CSS PROFILE recommended of early action applicants.

Dates and Deadlines: Closing date 2/1. Applicants notified by 4/1; must reply by 5/1 or within 2 week(s) of notification.

Transfers: Applicants notified by 4/15.

CONTACT

Patricia Hoban, Director of Financial Aid
900 State Street, Salem, OR 97301-3922
(503) 370-6273

Pennsylvania

Albright College

Reading, Pennsylvania
www.albright.edu Federal Code: 003229

4-year private liberal arts college in small city, affiliated with United Methodist Church.

Enrollment: 2,209 undergrads. 509 full-time freshmen.

Selectivity: Admits 50 to 75% of applicants.

BASIC COSTS (2009-2010)

Tuition and fees: $31,600.

Per-credit charge: $969.

Room and board: $8,770.

Additional info: Tuition/fee waivers available for minority students.

FINANCIAL AID PICTURE (2008-2009)

Students with need: Average financial aid package met 78% of need; average scholarship/grant was $17,832; average loan was $4,990. For part-time students, average financial aid package was $3,931.

Students without need: 66 full-time freshmen who did not demonstrate need for aid received scholarships/grants; average award was $11,424. No-need awards available for academics, alumni affiliation, art, leadership, minority status, music/drama, religious affiliation.

Cumulative student debt: 83% of graduating class had student loans; average debt was $31,720.

FINANCIAL AID PROCEDURES

Forms required: FAFSA.

Dates and Deadlines: Priority date 3/1; no closing date. Applicants notified on a rolling basis starting 2/15; must reply by 5/1 or within 2 week(s) of notification.

Transfers: Priority date 6/1; no deadline. Applicants notified on a rolling basis starting 2/15; must reply within 2 week(s) of notification.

CONTACT

Mary Duffy, Director of Financial Aid
13th & Bern Streets, Reading, PA 19612-5234
(610) 921-7515

Allegheny College

Meadville, Pennsylvania
www.allegheny.edu Federal Code: 003230

4-year private liberal arts college in large town, affiliated with United Methodist Church.

Enrollment: 2,099 undergrads, 1% part-time. 562 full-time freshmen.

Selectivity: Admits 50 to 75% of applicants.

BASIC COSTS (2009-2010)

Tuition and fees: $33,560.

Per-credit charge: $1,385.

Room and board: $8,440.

FINANCIAL AID PICTURE (2008-2009)

Students with need: Out of 468 full-time freshmen who applied for aid, 389 were judged to have need. Of these, 389 received aid, and 205 had their full need met. Average financial aid package met 95% of need; average scholarship/grant was $20,833; average loan was $4,662. For part-time students, average financial aid package was $3,512.

Students without need: 161 full-time freshmen who did not demonstrate need for aid received scholarships/grants; average award was $10,643. No-need awards available for academics, leadership, minority status, state/district residency.

Scholarships offered: Trustee Scholarships; up to $20,000 per year.

FINANCIAL AID PROCEDURES

Forms required: FAFSA.

Dates and Deadlines: Priority date 2/15; no closing date. Applicants notified on a rolling basis starting 3/1; must reply by 5/1 or within 4 week(s) of notification.

Transfers: Priority date 6/1; no deadline. Applicants notified on a rolling basis; must reply within 3 week(s) of notification. Trustee Scholarships; up to $12,500; available for entering transfer students.

CONTACT
Sheryle Proper, Director of Financial Aid
Box 5, 520 North Main Street, Meadville, PA 16335
(800) 835-7780

Alvernia University
Reading, Pennsylvania
www.alvernia.edu Federal Code: 003233

4-year private university and liberal arts college in small city, affiliated with Roman Catholic Church.
Enrollment: 1,918 undergrads, 18% part-time. 306 full-time freshmen.
Selectivity: Admits over 75% of applicants.

BASIC COSTS (2009-2010)
Tuition and fees: $24,350.
Per-credit charge: $660.
Room and board: $9,212.
Additional info: Tuition/fee waivers available for minority students.

FINANCIAL AID PICTURE (2007-2008)
Students with need: Out of 288 full-time freshmen who applied for aid, 268 were judged to have need. Of these, 233 received aid, and 54 had their full need met. Average financial aid package met 57% of need; average scholarship/grant was $10,437; average loan was $5,173. For part-time students, average financial aid package was $14,187.
Students without need: 32 full-time freshmen who did not demonstrate need for aid received scholarships/grants; average award was $4,778. No-need awards available for academics, state/district residency.
Cumulative student debt: 98% of graduating class had student loans; average debt was $30,763.

FINANCIAL AID PROCEDURES
Forms required: FAFSA, state aid form.
Dates and Deadlines: Priority date 5/1; no closing date. Applicants notified on a rolling basis starting 2/20; must reply within 2 week(s) of notification.
Transfers: Priority date 5/8; no deadline. Applicants notified on a rolling basis starting 2/20; must reply within 2 week(s) of notification.

CONTACT
Rachel Gordon, Director of Financial Aid
400 St. Bernardine Street, Reading, PA 19607-1799
(610) 796-8356

Antonelli Institute of Art and Photography
Erdenheim, Pennsylvania
www.antonelli.edu Federal Code: 007430

2-year for-profit visual arts and junior college in large town.
Enrollment: 219 undergrads. 115 full-time freshmen.
Selectivity: Admits 50 to 75% of applicants.

BASIC COSTS (2008-2009)
Tuition and fees: $19,325.
Per-credit charge: $640.
Room only: $7,500
Additional info: Annual tuition for graphic design/commercial art students is $17,200; for photography students $19,200.

FINANCIAL AID PICTURE (2007-2008)
Students with need: Average financial aid package met 42% of need; average scholarship/grant was $6,200; average loan was $3,500. For part-time students, average financial aid package was $2,050.
Students without need: This college awards aid only to students with need.
Cumulative student debt: 91% of graduating class had student loans; average debt was $10,390.

FINANCIAL AID PROCEDURES
Forms required: FAFSA.
Dates and Deadlines: No deadline. Applicants notified on a rolling basis; must reply within 2 week(s) of notification.
Transfers: Priority date 3/15; closing date 8/1.

CONTACT
Eugene Awot, Director of Financial Aid
300 Montgomery Avenue, Erdenheim, PA 19038-8242
(215) 836-2222

Arcadia University
Glenside, Pennsylvania
www.arcadia.edu Federal Code: 003235

4-year private university in large town, affiliated with Presbyterian Church (USA).
Enrollment: 2,143 undergrads, 7% part-time. 593 full-time freshmen.
Selectivity: Admits 50 to 75% of applicants.

BASIC COSTS (2008-2009)
Tuition and fees: $29,700.
Per-credit charge: $490.
Room and board: $10,280.

FINANCIAL AID PICTURE (2008-2009)
Students with need: Need-based aid available for full-time and part-time students. Work study available nights, weekends, and for part-time students.
Students without need: No-need awards available for academics, alumni affiliation, art, leadership, music/drama.
Scholarships offered: Distinguished Scholarships: $13,500 to $18,000; granted to full-time students based on grades, test scores, coursework taken, high school rank and involvement. Arcadia University Achievement Awards: $1,000-$13,000; granted to full-time students who have demonstrated outstanding leadership, exceptional community and/or volunteer service or special talents. Landman Scholarship: full tuition; based on academic excellence, outstanding leadership, and community and volunteer service. Writing Achievement Awards: offered to those who score among the highest in the applicant pool annually on SAT or ACT Writing Sections.

FINANCIAL AID PROCEDURES
Forms required: FAFSA, institutional form.
Dates and Deadlines: Priority date 3/1; no closing date. Applicants notified on a rolling basis starting 2/15; must reply by 5/1.
Transfers: Applicants notified on a rolling basis starting 2/15; must reply by 5/1.

CONTACT
Holly Kirkpatrick, Director of Enrollment Management and Director of Financial Aid
450 South Easton Road, Glenside, PA 19038-3295
(215) 572-2980

Art Institute of Philadelphia
Philadelphia, Pennsylvania
www.artinstitutes.edu/Philadelphia Federal Code: 008350

4-year for-profit visual arts college in very large city.
Enrollment: 3,602 undergrads.

FINANCIAL AID PICTURE
Students with need: Need-based aid available for full-time and part-time students. Work study available nights, weekends, and for part-time students.
Additional info: Institute-sponsored scholarships available.

FINANCIAL AID PROCEDURES

Forms required: FAFSA, institutional form.

Dates and Deadlines: No deadline. Applicants notified on a rolling basis starting 3/1; must reply within 2 week(s) of notification.

Transfers: No deadline. Transfer students applying for financial aid must meet standards for satisfactory academic progress as defined by State Grant Program.

CONTACT

Felicia Bryant, Director of Student Financial Services
1622 Chestnut Street, Philadelphia, PA 19103-5198
(215) 567-7080 ext. 6392

Baptist Bible College of Pennsylvania

Clarks Summit, Pennsylvania
www.bbc.edu Federal Code: 002670

4-year private Bible and seminary college in small city, affiliated with Baptist faith.

Enrollment: 549 undergrads.

Selectivity: Admits 50 to 75% of applicants.

BASIC COSTS (2008-2009)

Tuition and fees: $15,840.

Per-credit charge: $615.

Room and board: $5,900.

FINANCIAL AID PICTURE (2007-2008)

Students with need: Need-based aid available for part-time students. Work study available nights, weekends, and for part-time students.

Students without need: No-need awards available for academics, leadership, music/drama, religious affiliation.

FINANCIAL AID PROCEDURES

Forms required: FAFSA, institutional form.

Dates and Deadlines: Closing date 5/1. Applicants notified on a rolling basis starting 4/1.

CONTACT

David Weinerth, Director of Student Financial Services
538 Venard Road, Clarks Summit, PA 18411-1297
(570) 585-9215

Berks Technical Institute

Wyomissing, Pennsylvania
www.berks.edu Federal Code: 017149

2-year for-profit business and technical college in small city.

Enrollment: 566 undergrads.

BASIC COSTS (2008-2009)

Additional info: Approximate cost for diploma program, $9,600 to $17,000; for degree program, $21,000 to $30,000.

FINANCIAL AID PICTURE

Students with need: Need-based aid available for full-time and part-time students.

Students without need: This college awards aid only to students with need.

FINANCIAL AID PROCEDURES

Forms required: FAFSA, state aid form.

Dates and Deadlines: No deadline. Applicants notified on a rolling basis; must reply within 2 week(s) of notification.

Transfers: Deadline for first-time financial aid applicants is August 1. Deadline for renewal applicants is May 1.

CONTACT

Valerie Wessner, Financial Aid Director
2205 Ridgewood Road, Wyomissing, PA 19610
(610) 372-1722

Bloomsburg University of Pennsylvania

Bloomsburg, Pennsylvania
www.bloomu.edu Federal Code: 003315

4-year public university and liberal arts college in large town.

Enrollment: 7,840 undergrads, 4% part-time. 1,805 full-time freshmen.

Selectivity: Admits 50 to 75% of applicants.

BASIC COSTS (2008-2009)

Tuition and fees: $6,848; out-of-state residents $14,886.

Per-credit charge: $223; out-of-state residents $558.

Room and board: $6,292.

Additional info: Tuition/fee waivers available for minority students.

FINANCIAL AID PICTURE (2008-2009)

Students with need: Out of 1,619 full-time freshmen who applied for aid, 1,538 were judged to have need. Of these, 1,375 received aid, and 1,238 had their full need met. Average financial aid package met 69% of need; average scholarship/grant was $5,852; average loan was $3,296. For part-time students, average financial aid package was $7,043.

Students without need: 49 full-time freshmen who did not demonstrate need for aid received scholarships/grants; average award was $2,044. No-need awards available for academics, art, athletics, job skills, leadership, minority status, music/drama, ROTC, state/district residency.

Scholarships offered: 72 full-time freshmen received athletic scholarships; average amount $2,802.

Cumulative student debt: 71% of graduating class had student loans; average debt was $19,645.

FINANCIAL AID PROCEDURES

Forms required: FAFSA.

Dates and Deadlines: Priority date 3/15; no closing date. Applicants notified on a rolling basis starting 4/1.

Transfers: Evaluation of transfer credits must be completed before financial aid can be finalized.

CONTACT

Thomas Lyons, Director of Financial Aid
104 Student Service Center, Bloomsburg, PA 17815
(570) 389-4297

Bryn Athyn College of the New Church

Bryn Athyn, Pennsylvania
www.brynathyn.edu Federal Code: 003228

4-year private liberal arts college in small town, affiliated with General Church of the New Jerusalem (Swedenborgian).

Enrollment: 141 undergrads, 4% part-time. 43 full-time freshmen.

Selectivity: Admits over 75% of applicants.

BASIC COSTS (2009-2010)

Tuition and fees: $11,991.

Per-credit charge: $375.

Room and board: $6,300.

FINANCIAL AID PICTURE (2008-2009)

Students with need: 83% of average financial aid package awarded as scholarships/grants, 17% awarded as loans/jobs. Need-based aid available for part-time students.

Students without need: No-need awards available for academics, leadership, religious affiliation.

FINANCIAL AID PROCEDURES
Forms required: FAFSA, institutional form.
Dates and Deadlines: Closing date 6/1. Applicants notified on a rolling basis starting 4/30; must reply by 9/30.
Transfers: No deadline. Applicants notified on a rolling basis starting 7/1; must reply within 6 week(s) of notification.

CONTACT
Wendy Cooper, Associate Director of Financial Aid
PO Box 717, Bryn Athyn, PA 19009-0717
(267) 502-2630

Bryn Mawr College
Bryn Mawr, Pennsylvania — Federal Code: 003237
www.brynmawr.edu — CSS Code: 2049

4-year private liberal arts college for women in very large city.
Enrollment: 1,274 undergrads, 1% part-time. 366 full-time freshmen.
Selectivity: Admits less than 50% of applicants.

BASIC COSTS (2009-2010)
Tuition and fees: $38,034.
Room and board: $12,000.

FINANCIAL AID PICTURE (2008-2009)
Students with need: Out of 231 full-time freshmen who applied for aid, 175 were judged to have need. Of these, 175 received aid, and 175 had their full need met. Average financial aid package met 100% of need; average scholarship/grant was $28,170; average loan was $4,496. Need-based aid available for part-time students.
Students without need: This college awards aid only to students with need.
Cumulative student debt: 54% of graduating class had student loans; average debt was $20,019.

FINANCIAL AID PROCEDURES
Forms required: FAFSA, CSS PROFILE.
Dates and Deadlines: Priority date 2/5; closing date 3/1. Applicants notified by 3/23; must reply by 5/1.
Transfers: Closing date 3/15. Must reply by 5/1.

CONTACT
Ethel Desmarais, Director of Financial Aid
101 North Merion Avenue, Bryn Mawr, PA 19010-2899
(610) 526-5245

Bucknell University
Lewisburg, Pennsylvania — Federal Code: 003238
www.bucknell.edu — CSS Code: 2050

4-year private university in small town.
Enrollment: 3,560 undergrads. 957 full-time freshmen.
Selectivity: Admits less than 50% of applicants.

BASIC COSTS (2009-2010)
Tuition and fees: $40,816.
Room and board: $9,504.

FINANCIAL AID PICTURE (2008-2009)
Students with need: Out of 473 full-time freshmen who applied for aid, 399 were judged to have need. Of these, 399 received aid, and 389 had their full need met. Average financial aid package met 95% of need; average scholarship/grant was $22,400; average loan was $4,500.
Students without need: 40 full-time freshmen who did not demonstrate need for aid received scholarships/grants; average award was $8,388. No-need awards available for academics, art, athletics, leadership, music/drama, ROTC.
Scholarships offered: ***Merit:*** Scholarships available to a limited number of students who have demonstrated exceptional achievements in academics, art and performing arts, music, and athletics. ***Athletic:*** 21 full-time freshmen received athletic scholarships; average amount $8,524.
Cumulative student debt: 61% of graduating class had student loans; average debt was $18,500.

FINANCIAL AID PROCEDURES
Forms required: FAFSA, CSS PROFILE.
Dates and Deadlines: Closing date 1/1. Applicants notified by 4/1; must reply by 5/1.
Transfers: Closing date 3/15. Applicants notified by 5/1; must reply by 6/1. Aid restricted to 2-year college graduates.

CONTACT
Andrea Stauffer, Director of Financial Aid
Freas Hall, Lewisburg, PA 17837-9988
(570) 577-1331

Bucks County Community College
Newtown, Pennsylvania
www.bucks.edu — Federal Code: 003239

2-year public community college in large town.
Enrollment: 10,084 undergrads.
Selectivity: Open admission; but selective for some programs.

BASIC COSTS (2008-2009)
Tuition and fees: $3,584; out-of-district residents $6,734; out-of-state residents $9,884.
Per-credit charge: $95; out-of-district residents $190; out-of-state residents $285.

FINANCIAL AID PICTURE (2008-2009)
Students with need: 69% of average financial aid package awarded as scholarships/grants, 31% awarded as loans/jobs. Need-based aid available for part-time students. Work study available nights, weekends, and for part-time students.
Students without need: No-need awards available for academics.

FINANCIAL AID PROCEDURES
Forms required: FAFSA.
Dates and Deadlines: Closing date 5/1. Applicants notified on a rolling basis starting 6/1; must reply within 2 week(s) of notification.
Transfers: Applicants notified on a rolling basis starting 6/1; must reply within 2 week(s) of notification.

CONTACT
Donna Wilkoski, Director of Financial Aid
275 Swamp Road, Newtown, PA 18940
(215) 968-8200

Butler County Community College
Butler, Pennsylvania
www.bc3.edu — Federal Code: 003240

2-year public community college in large town.
Enrollment: 3,837 undergrads, 48% part-time.
Selectivity: Open admission; but selective for some programs.

BASIC COSTS (2008-2009)
Tuition and fees: $2,790; out-of-district residents $4,980; out-of-state residents $7,170.

Per-credit charge: $73; out-of-district residents $146; out-of-state residents $219.

FINANCIAL AID PICTURE (2007-2008)

Students with need: 48% of average financial aid package awarded as scholarships/grants, 52% awarded as loans/jobs. Need-based aid available for part-time students.
Students without need: No-need awards available for academics, state/district residency.

FINANCIAL AID PROCEDURES

Forms required: FAFSA.
Dates and Deadlines: Priority date 4/15; no closing date. Applicants notified on a rolling basis starting 5/1; must reply within 2 week(s) of notification.

CONTACT

Julianne Louttit, Director of Financial Aid
PO Box 1203, Butler, PA 16003-1203
(724) 287-8711 ext. 8329

Cabrini College

Radnor, Pennsylvania
www.cabrini.edu Federal Code: 003241

4-year private liberal arts college in large town, affiliated with Roman Catholic Church.
Enrollment: 1,807 undergrads, 7% part-time. 503 full-time freshmen.
Selectivity: Admits 50 to 75% of applicants.

BASIC COSTS (2008-2009)

Tuition and fees: $30,010.
Room and board: $10,890.

FINANCIAL AID PICTURE (2008-2009)

Students with need: Need-based aid available for full-time and part-time students. Work study available nights, weekends, and for part-time students.
Students without need: No-need awards available for academics, alumni affiliation.

FINANCIAL AID PROCEDURES

Forms required: FAFSA.
Dates and Deadlines: Closing date 4/1. Applicants notified on a rolling basis starting 3/1.
Transfers: Achievement scholarships available.

CONTACT

Michael Colahan, Financial Aid Director
610 King of Prussia Road, Radnor, PA 19087-3698
(610) 902-8420

California University of Pennsylvania

California, Pennsylvania
www.cup.edu Federal Code: 003316

4-year public university in small town.
Enrollment: 6,872 undergrads.
Selectivity: Admits 50 to 75% of applicants.

BASIC COSTS (2008-2009)

Tuition and fees: $7,315; out-of-state residents $10,531.
Per-credit charge: $223; out-of-state residents $357.
Room and board: $8,886.
Additional info: Tuition/fee waivers available for adults, minority students.

FINANCIAL AID PICTURE (2007-2008)

Students with need: Need-based aid available for full-time and part-time students. Work study available nights, weekends, and for part-time students.
Students without need: No-need awards available for academics, alumni affiliation, art, athletics, leadership, minority status, music/drama, religious affiliation, ROTC, state/district residency.

FINANCIAL AID PROCEDURES

Forms required: FAFSA, state aid form.
Dates and Deadlines: Priority date 5/1; no closing date. Applicants notified on a rolling basis starting 4/1; must reply within 3 week(s) of notification.

CONTACT

Robert Thorn, Director of Financial Aid
250 University Avenue, California, PA 15419-1394
(724) 938-4415

Cambria-Rowe Business College

Johnstown, Pennsylvania
www.crbc.net Federal Code: 004889

2-year for-profit business college in small city.
Enrollment: 186 undergrads.

BASIC COSTS (2008-2009)

Tuition and fees: $9,500.
Additional info: Depending on choice of laptop, fees could be as much as $1,140.

FINANCIAL AID PICTURE

Students with need: Need-based aid available for full-time and part-time students.
Students without need: No-need awards available for academics, leadership.
Scholarships offered: Presidential Grant (3 awarded) 50% tuition; FBLA Scholarship (2 awarded) $3,000.

FINANCIAL AID PROCEDURES

Forms required: FAFSA, state aid form.
Dates and Deadlines: Closing date 8/1. Applicants notified on a rolling basis.
Transfers: Closing date 5/1.

CONTACT

Judy Miller, Financial Aid Advisor
221 Central Avenue, Johnstown, PA 15902
(814) 536-5168

Cambria-Rowe Business College: Indiana

Indiana, Pennsylvania
www.crbc.net Federal Code: 004889

2-year for-profit business and technical college in small town.
Enrollment: 108 undergrads, 3% part-time. 40 full-time freshmen.
Selectivity: Admits over 75% of applicants.

BASIC COSTS (2009-2010)

Tuition and fees: $9,840.
Per-credit charge: $265.
Additional info: Depending on choice of laptop, fees could be as much as $1,140.

FINANCIAL AID PICTURE

Students with need: Need-based aid available for full-time and part-time students.

FINANCIAL AID PROCEDURES

Forms required: FAFSA.
Dates and Deadlines: No deadline. Applicants notified on a rolling basis.

CONTACT
Judy Miller, Financial Aid Officer
422 South 13th Street, Indiana, PA 15701
(814) 536-5168

Carlow University
Pittsburgh, Pennsylvania
www.carlow.edu Federal Code: 003303

4-year private university and liberal arts college for women in large city, affiliated with Roman Catholic Church.
Enrollment: 1,502 undergrads, 24% part-time. 232 full-time freshmen.
Selectivity: Admits 50 to 75% of applicants.

BASIC COSTS (2009-2010)
Tuition and fees: $21,720.
Per-credit charge: $682.
Room and board: $8,552.
Additional info: Undergraduate adult students pay $520 per credit hour. Tuition/fee waivers available for unemployed or children of unemployed.

FINANCIAL AID PICTURE (2007-2008)
Students with need: 57% of average financial aid package awarded as scholarships/grants, 43% awarded as loans/jobs. Need-based aid available for part-time students. Work study available nights, weekends, and for part-time students.
Students without need: No-need awards available for academics, alumni affiliation, athletics, leadership.
Scholarships offered: Full tuition scholarship: 3.75 GPA, 1300 SAT required. Half tuition scholarship: 3.5 GPA, 1200 SAT required. Presidential scholarship: $5,000 to $10,000; 3.25 GPA, 1000 SAT required. Valedictorian scholarship: $10,000. McAuley scholarship: $2,500; 3.25 GPA, 930 SAT required; one per Catholic high school in diocese of Pittsburgh, Johnston/Altoona and Greensburg. Legacy scholarship: $2,500; to children or grandchildren of alumnae. Dean's Recognition scholarship: $4,000; 3.00 GPA and 930 SAT required. Sister Maurice Whalen scholarship: to those who submit projects to Pittsburgh Regional Science and Engineering Fair, also requires 3.25 GPA and 1000 SAT. Rose Marie Beard Women of Spirit Honors Scholarship: $4,000 for first year; 3.5 GPA, 1100 SAT, rank in top 15% of high school class, evidence of significant leadership required. All SAT scores exclusive of Writing.

FINANCIAL AID PROCEDURES
Forms required: FAFSA.
Dates and Deadlines: Priority date 4/1; no closing date. Applicants notified on a rolling basis starting 2/15; must reply within 4 week(s) of notification.
Transfers: No deadline. Must reply within 4 week(s) of notification.

CONTACT
Natalie Wilson, Director of Financial Aid
3333 Fifth Avenue, Pittsburgh, PA 15213-3165
(412) 578-6058

Carnegie Mellon University
Pittsburgh, Pennsylvania
www.cmu.edu Federal Code: 003242

4-year private university in large city.
Enrollment: 5,892 undergrads, 2% part-time. 1,465 full-time freshmen.
Selectivity: Admits less than 50% of applicants.

BASIC COSTS (2009-2010)
Tuition and fees: $40,920.
Room and board: $10,340.

FINANCIAL AID PICTURE (2008-2009)
Students with need: Out of 1,008 full-time freshmen who applied for aid, 757 were judged to have need. Of these, 753 received aid, and 270 had their full need met. Average financial aid package met 84% of need; average scholarship/grant was $23,539; average loan was $3,775. For part-time students, average financial aid package was $22,006.
Students without need: 149 full-time freshmen who did not demonstrate need for aid received scholarships/grants; average award was $10,712. No-need awards available for academics, art, leadership, minority status, music/drama, state/district residency.
Cumulative student debt: 50% of graduating class had student loans; average debt was $30,533.
Additional info: Early need analysis offered; merit awards available. Students notified within week to 10 days of receipt of financial aid application.

FINANCIAL AID PROCEDURES
Forms required: FAFSA, institutional form.
Dates and Deadlines: Priority date 2/15; no closing date. Applicants notified by 3/15.
Transfers: Students applying for spring transfer must file FAFSA by 11/1 and are notified of award 12/15 or soon after. College of Fine Arts applicants applying for fall transfer must file FAFSA by 2/15 and are notified of award by 4/15. All other applicants for fall transfer must submit FAFSA by 5/1 and are notified of award during the month of June.

CONTACT
Linda Anderson, Director of Student Financial Aid
5000 Forbes Avenue, Pittsburgh, PA 15213-3890
(412) 268-8186

Cedar Crest College
Allentown, Pennsylvania
www.cedarcrest.edu Federal Code: 003243

4-year private liberal arts college for women in small city.
Enrollment: 1,653 undergrads, 42% part-time. 194 full-time freshmen.
Selectivity: Admits 50 to 75% of applicants.

BASIC COSTS (2008-2009)
Tuition and fees: $26,668.
Per-credit charge: $889.
Room and board: $9,009.
Additional info: On-campus students pay $300 resident communication fee; continuing education program's average per-credit-hour cost, $570.

FINANCIAL AID PICTURE (2008-2009)
Students with need: Out of 189 full-time freshmen who applied for aid, 169 were judged to have need. Of these, 169 received aid, and 17 had their full need met. Average financial aid package met 79% of need; average scholarship/grant was $17,395; average loan was $3,879. For part-time students, average financial aid package was $6,241.
Students without need: 24 full-time freshmen who did not demonstrate need for aid received scholarships/grants; average award was $10,041. No-need awards available for academics, alumni affiliation, art, leadership, music/drama.
Scholarships offered: Presidential Scholarship; up to half tuition; for freshmen with SAT scores over 1150 and in top 10% of class; renewable for four years with GPA of 3.0. 1867 Award, one-third of tuition; renewable for four years with GPA of 3.0; for freshmen with SAT of 1100 and in top 25% of class. Girl Scout Gold Awards; $1,000 per year; for recipients of the Girl Scout Gold Award. Art, Dance, and Performing Arts Scholarships; $1,500 per year; based on portfolio review, audition, and commitment to the creative process. Governor's School of Excellence Award; $1,000 per year; for graduates of Governor's Schools of Excellence. Hugh O'Brian Youth (HOBY) Awards; $1,000 per year; for freshmen who are HOBY alumnae. SAT scores exclusive of Writing portion.

Cumulative student debt: 92% of graduating class had student loans; average debt was $33,050.

FINANCIAL AID PROCEDURES

Forms required: FAFSA.

Dates and Deadlines: Priority date 5/1; no closing date. Applicants notified on a rolling basis starting 1/1; must reply within 2 week(s) of notification.

Transfers: Certain academic scholarships are available for transfers only, such as the Phi Theta Kappa Scholarship, Lifelong Learning Transfer Scholarship and Traditional Transfer Scholarship.

CONTACT

Lori Williams, Director of Student Financial Services
100 College Drive, Allentown, PA 18104-6196
(610) 740-3785

Central Pennsylvania College

Summerdale, Pennsylvania
www.centralpenn.edu Federal Code: 004890

4-year for-profit business and technical college in rural community.

Enrollment: 1,086 undergrads, 43% part-time. 102 full-time freshmen.

Selectivity: Open admission; but selective for some programs.

BASIC COSTS (2008-2009)

Tuition and fees: $16,425.
Per-credit charge: $350.
Room and board: $6,015.

FINANCIAL AID PICTURE

Students with need: Need-based aid available for full-time and part-time students.

Students without need: No-need awards available for academics, alumni affiliation, job skills, leadership, minority status, state/district residency.

FINANCIAL AID PROCEDURES

Forms required: FAFSA, state aid form, institutional form.

Dates and Deadlines: Priority date 3/15; no closing date. Applicants notified on a rolling basis starting 2/1; must reply within 2 week(s) of notification.

CONTACT

Kathy Shepard, Financial Aid Director
College Hill & Valley Roads, Summerdale, PA 17093-0309
(717) 728-2261

Chatham University

Pittsburgh, Pennsylvania
www.chatham.edu Federal Code: 003244

4-year private university and liberal arts college for women in large city.

Enrollment: 763 undergrads, 11% part-time. 176 full-time freshmen.

Selectivity: Admits 50 to 75% of applicants.

BASIC COSTS (2008-2009)

Tuition and fees: $27,496.
Per-credit charge: $642.
Room and board: $8,286.
Additional info: Required fees ($1,020) cover technology fee, which includes cost of HP tablet computer (required for all first-time first-year students) and the campus fee.

FINANCIAL AID PICTURE (2008-2009)

Students with need: Out of 141 full-time freshmen who applied for aid, 130 were judged to have need. Of these, 130 received aid. Average financial aid package met 81% of need; average scholarship/grant was $4,391; average loan was $5,205. For part-time students, average financial aid package was $5,312.

Students without need: 33 full-time freshmen who did not demonstrate need for aid received scholarships/grants; average award was $13,727. No-need awards available for academics, alumni affiliation, leadership, music/drama, state/district residency.

Scholarships offered: Presidential Scholarship; up to $12,000. Trustee Scholarship; up to $9,000. Founders' Scholarship; up to $7,000. All based on academic excellence and renewable annually based on GPA of 2.8 or higher.

FINANCIAL AID PROCEDURES

Forms required: FAFSA.

Dates and Deadlines: Priority date 5/1; no closing date. Applicants notified on a rolling basis starting 2/15; must reply by 5/1 or within 2 week(s) of notification.

Transfers: Special scholarships are available for transfer students.

CONTACT

Jennifer Burns, Director of Financial Aid
Woodland Road, Pittsburgh, PA 15232
(412) 365-1777

Chestnut Hill College

Philadelphia, Pennsylvania
www.chc.edu Federal Code: 003245

4-year private liberal arts college in very large city, affiliated with Roman Catholic Church.

Enrollment: 1,277 undergrads, 20% part-time. 201 full-time freshmen.

Selectivity: Admits 50 to 75% of applicants.

BASIC COSTS (2009-2010)

Tuition and fees: $27,100.
Per-credit charge: $575.
Room and board: $8,800.

FINANCIAL AID PICTURE (2008-2009)

Students with need: Out of 180 full-time freshmen who applied for aid, 163 were judged to have need. Of these, 161 received aid, and 26 had their full need met. Average financial aid package met 72% of need; average scholarship/grant was $15,170; average loan was $3,736. For part-time students, average financial aid package was $6,582.

Students without need: 22 full-time freshmen who did not demonstrate need for aid received scholarships/grants; average award was $10,813. No-need awards available for academics, alumni affiliation, athletics, leadership, religious affiliation.

Scholarships offered: ***Merit:*** Full-tuition and partial-tuition awards; based on academics. ***Athletic:*** 15 full-time freshmen received athletic scholarships; average amount $4,285.

Additional info: Application priority date 1/15 for merit-based scholarships.

FINANCIAL AID PROCEDURES

Forms required: FAFSA.

Dates and Deadlines: Closing date 4/15. Applicants notified on a rolling basis starting 1/31; must reply by 5/1 or within 3 week(s) of notification.

CONTACT

Nicholas Flocco, Director of Financial Aid
9601 Germantown Avenue, Philadelphia, PA 19118-2693
(215) 248-7182

Cheyney University of Pennsylvania

Cheyney, Pennsylvania
www.cheyney.edu Federal Code: 003317

4-year public university in small town.

Enrollment: 1,315 undergrads, 7% part-time. 280 full-time freshmen.

Selectivity: Admits less than 50% of applicants.

BASIC COSTS (2008-2009)

Tuition and fees: $7,089; out-of-state residents $15,127.
Per-credit charge: $223; out-of-state residents $558.
Room and board: $7,156.
Additional info: Tuition for residents of MD, NY, NJ and DE is $10,716. Tuition/fee waivers available for minority students.

FINANCIAL AID PICTURE

Students with need: Need-based aid available for full-time and part-time students.
Students without need: No-need awards available for academics, athletics.

FINANCIAL AID PROCEDURES

Forms required: FAFSA.
Dates and Deadlines: Priority date 3/15; no closing date. Applicants notified on a rolling basis starting 4/1; must reply within 2 week(s) of notification.

CONTACT

Harold Johnson, Director of Financial Aid
1837 University Circle, Cheyney, PA 19319-0019
(610) 399-2302

Clarion University of Pennsylvania

Clarion, Pennsylvania
www.clarion.edu Federal Code: 003318

4-year public business and teachers college in small town.
Enrollment: 5,724 undergrads, 11% part-time. 1,390 full-time freshmen.
Selectivity: Admits 50 to 75% of applicants.

BASIC COSTS (2008-2009)

Tuition and fees: $7,104; out-of-state residents $12,462.
Per-credit charge: $223; out-of-state residents $447.
Room and board: $6,068.
Additional info: Tuition for incoming out-of-state residents with SAT of 1100 or higher and at least a 3.5 GPA or the top 20% of their graduating class is $7,766.

FINANCIAL AID PICTURE (2007-2008)

Students with need: Out of 1,274 full-time freshmen who applied for aid, 1,025 were judged to have need. Of these, 993 received aid, and 142 had their full need met. Average financial aid package met 68% of need; average scholarship/grant was $5,676; average loan was $3,253. For part-time students, average financial aid package was $3,969.
Students without need: 79 full-time freshmen who did not demonstrate need for aid received scholarships/grants; average award was $2,517. No-need awards available for academics, art, athletics, leadership, minority status, music/drama, state/district residency.
Scholarships offered: 62 full-time freshmen received athletic scholarships; average amount $2,332.

FINANCIAL AID PROCEDURES

Forms required: FAFSA.
Dates and Deadlines: Closing date 4/15. Applicants notified on a rolling basis starting 3/1.

CONTACT

Kenneth Grugel, Director of Financial Aid
840 Wood Street, Clarion, PA 16214
(814) 226-2315

Commonwealth Technical Institute

Johnstown, Pennsylvania
www.hgac.org

2-year private technical college in small city.
Enrollment: 74 undergrads.
Selectivity: Open admission.

BASIC COSTS (2009-2010)

Tuition and fees: $11,224.
Room and board: $9,516.

FINANCIAL AID PICTURE (2007-2008)

Students with need: Need-based aid available for full-time and part-time students. Work study available nights, weekends, and for part-time students.
Students without need: This college awards aid only to students with need.

FINANCIAL AID PROCEDURES

Forms required: FAFSA.
Dates and Deadlines: No deadline. Applicants notified on a rolling basis.

CONTACT

Ann Yurcisin, Financial Aid Director
727 Goucher Street, Johnstown, PA 15905-3902
(814) 255-8351

Community College of Allegheny County

Pittsburgh, Pennsylvania
www.ccac.edu

2-year public community college in very large city.
Enrollment: 17,406 undergrads.
Selectivity: Open admission; but selective for some programs.

BASIC COSTS (2008-2009)

Tuition and fees: $2,819; out-of-district residents $5,399; out-of-state residents $7,949.
Per-credit charge: $85; out-of-district residents $171; out-of-state residents $256.
Additional info: If county does not have community college, tuition is $2,970 per year. Nursing and allied health courses subject to additional fees.

FINANCIAL AID PICTURE (2007-2008)

Students with need: Need-based aid available for full-time and part-time students. Work study available nights, weekends, and for part-time students.
Students without need: No-need awards available for academics, minority status.

FINANCIAL AID PROCEDURES

Forms required: FAFSA.
Dates and Deadlines: Priority date 5/1; no closing date. Applicants notified on a rolling basis starting 5/1.

CONTACT

Margaret Barton, Director of Financial Aid
800 Allegheny Avenue, Pittsburgh, PA 15233
(412) 323-2323

Community College of Beaver County

Monaca, Pennsylvania
www.ccbc.edu Federal Code: 006807

2-year public community college in small town.
Enrollment: 1,859 undergrads.
Selectivity: Open admission; but selective for some programs.

BASIC COSTS (2008-2009)
Tuition and fees: $3,255; out-of-district residents $6,300; out-of-state residents $9,345.
Per-credit charge: $87; out-of-district residents $173; out-of-state residents $260.
Additional info: Academic enhancement fees, ranging from $25 to $600 per course, apply in programs requiring specialized technology and equipment; $10 per-credit-hour fee for courses that include a lab.

FINANCIAL AID PICTURE (2007-2008)
Students with need: Need-based aid available for full-time and part-time students. Work study available nights, weekends, and for part-time students.
Students without need: No-need awards available for academics, athletics, state/district residency.
Scholarships offered: Academic Excellence Scholarship; full tuition.

FINANCIAL AID PROCEDURES
Forms required: FAFSA, state aid form, institutional form.
Dates and Deadlines: Priority date 5/1; closing date 7/1. Applicants notified on a rolling basis starting 8/5; must reply within 2 week(s) of notification.
Transfers: Priority date 5/6.

CONTACT
Doug Mailer, Director of Financial Aid
One Campus Drive, Monaca, PA 15061-2588
(724) 775-8561 ext. 260

Community College of Philadelphia
Philadelphia, Pennsylvania
www.ccp.edu Federal Code: 003249

2-year public community college in very large city.
Enrollment: 17,327 undergrads, 67% part-time. 1,711 full-time freshmen.
Selectivity: Open admission; but selective for some programs.

BASIC COSTS (2008-2009)
Tuition and fees: $4,410; out-of-district residents $8,160; out-of-state residents $11,910.
Per-credit charge: $115; out-of-district residents $230; out-of-state residents $345.

FINANCIAL AID PICTURE (2007-2008)
Students with need: 54% of average financial aid package awarded as scholarships/grants, 46% awarded as loans/jobs. Need-based aid available for part-time students. Work study available nights, weekends, and for part-time students.
Students without need: This college awards aid only to students with need.

FINANCIAL AID PROCEDURES
Forms required: FAFSA, institutional form.
Dates and Deadlines: Closing date 5/1. Applicants notified on a rolling basis.
Transfers: No deadline.

CONTACT
Gim Lim, Director of Financial Aid
1700 Spring Garden Street, Philadelphia, PA 19130-3991
(215) 751-8270

Consolidated School of Business: Lancaster
Lancaster, Pennsylvania
www.csb.edu Federal Code: 030299

2-year for-profit business college in small city.
Enrollment: 156 undergrads.
Selectivity: Open admission.

BASIC COSTS (2008-2009)
Tuition and fees: $11,500.

FINANCIAL AID PICTURE
Students with need: Need-based aid available for full-time and part-time students.

FINANCIAL AID PROCEDURES
Forms required: FAFSA, state aid form.
Dates and Deadlines: No deadline. Applicants notified on a rolling basis.

CONTACT
William Hoyt, Director of Financial Aid
2124 Ambassador Circle, Lancaster, PA 17603
(717) 394-6211

Consolidated School of Business: York
York, Pennsylvania
www.csb.edu Federal Code: 022896

2-year for-profit business college in small city.
Enrollment: 112 undergrads.
Selectivity: Open admission.

BASIC COSTS (2008-2009)
Tuition and fees: $11,850.

FINANCIAL AID PICTURE
Students with need: Need-based aid available for full-time and part-time students.

FINANCIAL AID PROCEDURES
Forms required: FAFSA, state aid form.
Dates and Deadlines: No deadline. Applicants notified on a rolling basis.

CONTACT
William Hoyt, Director of Financial Aid
York City Business and Industry Park, York, PA 17404
(717) 764-9550

Curtis Institute of Music
Philadelphia, Pennsylvania
www.curtis.edu Federal Code: 003251

4-year private music college in very large city.
Enrollment: 132 undergrads. 10 full-time freshmen.
Selectivity: Admits less than 50% of applicants.

BASIC COSTS (2009-2010)
Additional info: All students awarded a full-tuition scholarship. Bachelor of Music students pay $2,290 (required fees) and $17,910 (additional expenses), which covers supplies, off-campus room/board, and miscellaneous expenses for the academic year. Students required to have adequate health insurance coverage.

FINANCIAL AID PICTURE (2008-2009)
Students with need: Average financial aid package met 80% of need; average scholarship/grant was $7,016; average loan was $3,832. Need-based aid available for part-time students.
Students without need: This college awards aid only to students with need.
Cumulative student debt: 70% of graduating class had student loans; average debt was $20,000.
Additional info: All admitted students receive a full tuition scholarship. The estimated value of this scholarship is $33,500.

FINANCIAL AID PROCEDURES

Forms required: FAFSA, institutional form.

Dates and Deadlines: Priority date 3/1; no closing date. Applicants notified by 4/1; must reply by 5/1 or within 2 week(s) of notification.

CONTACT

Richard Woodland, Director of Student Services and Financial Assistance
1726 Locust Street, Philadelphia, PA 19103-6187
(215) 717-3188

Dean Institute of Technology

Pittsburgh, Pennsylvania
www.deantech.edu Federal Code: 009186

2-year for-profit technical college in large city.

Enrollment: 205 undergrads, 33% part-time. 33 full-time freshmen.

Selectivity: Open admission.

BASIC COSTS (2009-2010)

Tuition and fees: $19,350.

Per-credit charge: $215.

FINANCIAL AID PICTURE

Students with need: Need-based aid available for full-time and part-time students.

FINANCIAL AID PROCEDURES

Forms required: FAFSA.

Dates and Deadlines: Closing date 8/1. Applicants notified on a rolling basis; must reply within 8 week(s) of notification.

CONTACT

Nancy Grom, Director of Financial Aid
1501 West Liberty Avenue, Pittsburgh, PA 15226
(412) 531-4433 ext. 121

Delaware Valley College

Doylestown, Pennsylvania
www.delval.edu Federal Code: 003252

4-year private agricultural and liberal arts college in large town.

Enrollment: 1,798 undergrads, 9% part-time. 430 full-time freshmen.

Selectivity: Admits 50 to 75% of applicants.

BASIC COSTS (2008-2009)

Tuition and fees: $27,078.

Per-credit charge: $681.

Room and board: $9,502.

Additional info: Tuition/fee waivers available for adults.

FINANCIAL AID PICTURE (2007-2008)

Students with need: Out of 385 full-time freshmen who applied for aid, 333 were judged to have need. Of these, 333 received aid, and 66 had their full need met. Average financial aid package met 69% of need; average scholarship/grant was $14,578; average loan was $3,240. For part-time students, average financial aid package was $3,592.

Students without need: 84 full-time freshmen who did not demonstrate need for aid received scholarships/grants; average award was $10,378. No-need awards available for academics, alumni affiliation, music/drama.

Cumulative student debt: 56% of graduating class had student loans; average debt was $28,292.

FINANCIAL AID PROCEDURES

Forms required: FAFSA.

Dates and Deadlines: Priority date 4/1; no closing date. Applicants notified on a rolling basis starting 2/1; must reply by 5/1.

Transfers: No deadline. Applicants notified on a rolling basis; must reply by 4/1.

CONTACT

Robert Sauer, Director of Financial Aid
700 East Butler Avenue, Doylestown, PA 18901-2697
(215) 489-2272

DeSales University

Center Valley, Pennsylvania
www.desales.edu Federal Code: 003986

4-year private university in small town, affiliated with Roman Catholic Church.

Enrollment: 2,389 undergrads, 24% part-time. 402 full-time freshmen.

Selectivity: Admits 50 to 75% of applicants.

BASIC COSTS (2009-2010)

Tuition and fees: $27,000.

Room and board: $9,750.

FINANCIAL AID PICTURE (2008-2009)

Students with need: Average financial aid package met 65% of need; average scholarship/grant was $9,146; average loan was $3,322. For part-time students, average financial aid package was $1,835.

Students without need: No-need awards available for academics, leadership, music/drama.

Scholarships offered: Presidential Scholarships; full tuition; top 5% of class and 1300 SAT. Trustee Scholarships; from $6,000; top 15% of class, minimum 1200 SAT. DeSales Scholarships; $4,000; top 25% of class, minimum 1100 SAT. All SAT scores exclusive of writing.

Cumulative student debt: 82% of graduating class had student loans; average debt was $24,720.

FINANCIAL AID PROCEDURES

Forms required: FAFSA, state aid form.

Dates and Deadlines: Priority date 2/1; closing date 5/1. Applicants notified on a rolling basis starting 2/15; must reply by 5/1 or within 2 week(s) of notification.

Transfers: No deadline. Transfer scholarships require 3.0 GPA, 8 completed courses. Transfer Opportunity Program (TOP), a grant equal to tuition at participating community college, requires associate degree to qualify.

CONTACT

Joyce Farmer, Director of Financial Aid
2755 Station Avenue, Center Valley, PA 18034-9568
(610) 282-1100 ext. 1287

DeVry University: Fort Washington

Fort Washington, Pennsylvania
www.devry.edu

4-year for-profit university in large town.

Enrollment: 889 undergrads, 49% part-time. 94 full-time freshmen.

BASIC COSTS (2008-2009)

Tuition and fees: $14,800.

Per-credit charge: $540.

FINANCIAL AID PICTURE (2007-2008)

Students with need: Out of 79 full-time freshmen who applied for aid, 76 were judged to have need. Of these, 74 received aid. Average financial aid package met 34% of need; average scholarship/grant was $7,020; average loan was $5,757. For part-time students, average financial aid package was $9,548.

Students without need: This college awards aid only to students with need.

Cumulative student debt: 50% of graduating class had student loans; average debt was $15,638.

FINANCIAL AID PROCEDURES

Forms required: FAFSA.
Dates and Deadlines: No deadline. Applicants notified on a rolling basis.

CONTACT

Citristal Claiborne, Director of Financial Aid
1140 Virginia Drive, Fort Washington, PA 19034-3204
(215) 591-5724

Dickinson College

Carlisle, Pennsylvania — Federal Code: 003253
www.dickinson.edu — CSS Code: 2186

4-year private liberal arts college in large town.
Enrollment: 2,364 undergrads. 613 full-time freshmen.
Selectivity: Admits less than 50% of applicants.

BASIC COSTS (2009-2010)

Tuition and fees: $40,139.
Per-credit charge: $1,244.
Room and board: $10,080.

FINANCIAL AID PICTURE (2008-2009)

Students with need: Out of 392 full-time freshmen who applied for aid, 307 were judged to have need. Of these, 305 received aid, and 266 had their full need met. Average financial aid package met 98% of need; average scholarship/grant was $26,387; average loan was $3,887. For part-time students, average financial aid package was $15,200.
Students without need: 55 full-time freshmen who did not demonstrate need for aid received scholarships/grants; average award was $12,965. No-need awards available for academics, leadership, ROTC.
Scholarships offered: John Dickinson and Benjamin Rush Scholarships; awarded to most academically competitive students. Additional Engage the World Fellowship for selected John Dickinson Scholarship winners. John Montgomery Scholarship; awarded to first-year students who possess strong credentials, talent in the arts, or competency in 2 foreign languages in addition to English. Scholars must also demonstrate strong leadership in high school and community.
Cumulative student debt: 53% of graduating class had student loans; average debt was $21,924.

FINANCIAL AID PROCEDURES

Forms required: FAFSA, CSS PROFILE, state aid form.
Dates and Deadlines: Closing date 2/1. Applicants notified by 3/31; must reply by 5/1 or within 2 week(s) of notification.
Transfers: Closing date 4/1. Applicants notified on a rolling basis starting 5/1; must reply within 2 week(s) of notification.

CONTACT

Judith Carter, Director of Financial Aid
PO Box 1773, Carlisle, PA 17013-2896
(717) 245-1308

Douglas Education Center

Monessen, Pennsylvania
www.douglas-school.com — Federal Code: 013957

2-year for-profit visual arts and business college in small town.
Enrollment: 285 undergrads.
Selectivity: Open admission.

BASIC COSTS (2008-2009)

Additional info: All-inclusive associate, certificate and diploma programs in art, business, cosmetology and medical fields available from $3,290 to $39,825. Books and supplies range from $190 to $2,240.

FINANCIAL AID PICTURE (2008-2009)

Students with need: Need-based aid available for full-time and part-time students. Work study available nights, weekends, and for part-time students.
Students without need: This college awards aid only to students with need.

FINANCIAL AID PROCEDURES

Dates and Deadlines: No deadline. Applicants notified on a rolling basis.

CONTACT

Alison Pfender, Director of Financial Aid
130 Seventh Street, Monessen, PA 15062
(724) 684-3684 ext. 101

Drexel University

Philadelphia, Pennsylvania
www.drexel.edu — Federal Code: 003256

5-year private university in very large city.
Enrollment: 13,139 undergrads, 17% part-time. 2,430 full-time freshmen.
Selectivity: Admits 50 to 75% of applicants.

BASIC COSTS (2009-2010)

Tuition and fees: $31,835.
Per-credit charge: $820.
Room and board: $12,680.
Additional info: Tuition listed is for 5-year program with co-op quarter terms.

FINANCIAL AID PICTURE (2008-2009)

Students with need: Need-based aid available for full-time students.
Students without need: No-need awards available for academics, alumni affiliation, art, athletics, leadership, music/drama, ROTC.

FINANCIAL AID PROCEDURES

Forms required: FAFSA.
Dates and Deadlines: Closing date 3/1. Applicants notified on a rolling basis starting 3/15.
Transfers: Priority date 3/2. Scholarships available in amounts up to $8,000. 3.2 GPA and 30 credit hours at time of application required for eligibility.

CONTACT

Helen Gourousis, Director of Financial Aid
3141 Chestnut Street, Philadelphia, PA 19104-2875
(215) 895-2537

DuBois Business College

DuBois, Pennsylvania
www.dbcollege.com — Federal Code: 004893

2-year for-profit business and technical college in large town.
Enrollment: 254 undergrads.
Selectivity: Open admission.

BASIC COSTS (2008-2009)

Tuition and fees: $9,450.
Per-credit charge: $194.

FINANCIAL AID PICTURE

Students with need: Need-based aid available for full-time students.

FINANCIAL AID PROCEDURES

Forms required: FAFSA.
Dates and Deadlines: Closing date 8/1. Applicants notified on a rolling basis.

CONTACT

Karen Alderton, Financial Aid Director
One Beaver Drive, DuBois, PA 15801
(814) 371-6920

Duquesne University

Pittsburgh, Pennsylvania
www.duq.edu Federal Code: 003258

4-year private university in large city, affiliated with Roman Catholic Church.
Enrollment: 5,616 undergrads, 4% part-time. 1,354 full-time freshmen.
Selectivity: Admits over 75% of applicants.

BASIC COSTS (2008-2009)

Tuition and fees: $25,475.
Per-credit charge: $765.
Room and board: $8,888.

FINANCIAL AID PICTURE (2007-2008)

Students with need: Out of 1,200 full-time freshmen who applied for aid, 961 were judged to have need. Of these, 961 received aid, and 690 had their full need met. Average financial aid package met 89% of need; average scholarship/grant was $12,428; average loan was $4,331. For part-time students, average financial aid package was $10,038.
Students without need: 358 full-time freshmen who did not demonstrate need for aid received scholarships/grants; average award was $7,195. No-need awards available for academics, athletics, music/drama, ROTC.
Scholarships offered: ***Merit:*** Competitive scholarships available for academically and/or artistically talented students. ***Athletic:*** 99 full-time freshmen received athletic scholarships; average amount $12,241.
Cumulative student debt: 80% of graduating class had student loans; average debt was $29,616.

FINANCIAL AID PROCEDURES

Forms required: FAFSA, institutional form.
Dates and Deadlines: Closing date 5/1. Applicants notified on a rolling basis starting 3/1; must reply by 5/1 or within 3 week(s) of notification.
Transfers: No deadline. Must reply within 3 week(s) of notification.

CONTACT

Richard Esposito, Director of Financial Aid
600 Forbes Avenue, Administration Building, Pittsburgh, PA 15282-0201
(412) 396-6607

East Stroudsburg University of Pennsylvania

East Stroudsburg, Pennsylvania
www4.esu.edu Federal Code: 003320

4-year public university in large town.
Enrollment: 5,995 undergrads, 7% part-time. 1,270 full-time freshmen.
Selectivity: Admits 50 to 75% of applicants.

BASIC COSTS (2008-2009)

Tuition and fees: $7,089; out-of-state residents $15,127.
Per-credit charge: $223; out-of-state residents $558.
Room and board: $6,148.
Additional info: Tuition for incoming out of state residents who are high achieving science and technology majors (biology, chemistry, computer science, mathematics, and physics) is $8,038.

FINANCIAL AID PICTURE (2007-2008)

Students with need: Out of 933 full-time freshmen who applied for aid, 666 were judged to have need. Of these, 592 received aid, and 402 had their full need met. Average financial aid package met 81% of need; average scholarship/grant was $4,372; average loan was $3,279. For part-time students, average financial aid package was $4,479.
Students without need: 244 full-time freshmen who did not demonstrate need for aid received scholarships/grants; average award was $8,308. No-need awards available for academics, alumni affiliation, art, athletics, leadership, minority status, music/drama, religious affiliation, state/district residency.
Scholarships offered: 66 full-time freshmen received athletic scholarships; average amount $2,359.
Cumulative student debt: 75% of graduating class had student loans; average debt was $22,880.

FINANCIAL AID PROCEDURES

Forms required: FAFSA.
Dates and Deadlines: Closing date 3/1. Applicants notified by 4/1; must reply by 5/1.

CONTACT

Phyllis Swinson, Associate Director of Financial Aid
200 Prospect Street, East Stroudsburg, PA 18301-2999
(570) 422-2800

Edinboro University of Pennsylvania

Edinboro, Pennsylvania
www.edinboro.edu Federal Code: 003321

4-year public university and teachers college in small town.
Enrollment: 5,928 undergrads, 10% part-time. 1,219 full-time freshmen.
Selectivity: Admits 50 to 75% of applicants.

BASIC COSTS (2008-2009)

Tuition and fees: $7,042; out-of-state residents $9,722.
Per-credit charge: $223; out-of-state residents $335.
Room and board: $6,734.

FINANCIAL AID PICTURE (2007-2008)

Students with need: Out of 1,214 full-time freshmen who applied for aid, 1,034 were judged to have need. Of these, 1,004 received aid, and 48 had their full need met. Average financial aid package met 49% of need; average scholarship/grant was $4,076; average loan was $2,909. For part-time students, average financial aid package was $4,133.
Students without need: 48 full-time freshmen who did not demonstrate need for aid received scholarships/grants; average award was $2,400. No-need awards available for academics, alumni affiliation, art, athletics, job skills, leadership, minority status, music/drama, religious affiliation, ROTC, state/district residency.
Scholarships offered: 39 full-time freshmen received athletic scholarships; average amount $1,865.
Cumulative student debt: 51% of graduating class had student loans; average debt was $11,237.

FINANCIAL AID PROCEDURES

Forms required: FAFSA.
Dates and Deadlines: Priority date 3/15; closing date 5/1. Applicants notified on a rolling basis starting 3/20; must reply within 2 week(s) of notification.

CONTACT

Dorothy Body, Assistant Vice President for Student Financial Support and Services
200 East Normal Street, Edinboro, PA 16444
(888) 611-2680

Elizabethtown College

Elizabethtown, Pennsylvania
www.etown.edu Federal Code: 003262

4-year private liberal arts college in large town, affiliated with Church of the Brethren.
Enrollment: 2,178 undergrads, 16% part-time. 525 full-time freshmen.
Selectivity: Admits 50 to 75% of applicants.

BASIC COSTS (2009-2010)

Tuition and fees: $31,800.
Per-credit charge: $770.
Room and board: $8,150.

FINANCIAL AID PICTURE (2008-2009)

Students with need: Out of 456 full-time freshmen who applied for aid, 387 were judged to have need. Of these, 387 received aid, and 79 had their full need met. Average financial aid package met 83% of need; average scholarship/grant was $17,932; average loan was $3,557. Need-based aid available for part-time students.
Students without need: 111 full-time freshmen who did not demonstrate need for aid received scholarships/grants; average award was $12,503. No-need awards available for academics, art, music/drama, religious affiliation.
Scholarships offered: Presidential Scholarships; up to $16,000 annually; top 2% of class and minimum 1300 SAT score. Provost Scholarships; up to $13,500 annually; top 10% of class with minimum 1150 SAT; unlimited number awarded. Dean's Scholarships; up to $11,000 annually; for students with very strong academic achievement who do not qualify for other merit awards; unlimited number awarded. Music scholarships; $1,000-$4,000; based on audition. SAT scores exclusive of Writing portion.

FINANCIAL AID PROCEDURES

Forms required: FAFSA, institutional form.
Dates and Deadlines: Priority date 3/15; no closing date. Applicants notified on a rolling basis starting 3/1; must reply by 5/1 or within 2 week(s) of notification.

CONTACT

Elizabeth McCloud, Director of Financial Aid
One Alpha Drive, Elizabethtown, PA 17022-2298
(717) 361-1404

Franklin & Marshall College

Lancaster, Pennsylvania Federal Code: 003265
www.fandm.edu CSS Code: 2261

4-year private liberal arts college in small city.
Enrollment: 2,118 undergrads. 588 full-time freshmen.
Selectivity: Admits less than 50% of applicants.

BASIC COSTS (2009-2010)

Tuition and fees: $39,980.
Room and board: $10,430.

FINANCIAL AID PICTURE (2008-2009)

Students with need: Need-based aid available for full-time students.
Students without need: No-need awards available for academics, art, leadership, music/drama.
Scholarships offered: John Marshall Scholarships; $12,500 awarded annually; independent initiative in intellectual or service areas considered. National Merit Recognition; $18,000 renewable annually. Presidential Scholarships; $7,500 annually. All based on academic performance, class rank. Klein Scholarship; $5,000; awarded based on academic and community achievement. Gray Scholarship; awarded to outstanding applicants of African-, Latino-, and Asian-American descent; minimizes loans.

FINANCIAL AID PROCEDURES

Forms required: FAFSA, CSS PROFILE, institutional form.
Dates and Deadlines: Priority date 2/1; closing date 3/1. Applicants notified by 3/15; must reply by 5/1.
Transfers: Closing date 2/1.

CONTACT

Clarke Paine, Director of Student Aid
PO Box 3003, Lancaster, PA 17604-3003
(717) 291-3991

Gannon University

Erie, Pennsylvania
www.gannon.edu Federal Code: 003266

4-year private university in small city, affiliated with Roman Catholic Church.
Enrollment: 2,495 undergrads, 6% part-time. 624 full-time freshmen.
Selectivity: Admits over 75% of applicants.

BASIC COSTS (2008-2009)

Tuition and fees: $22,662.
Per-credit charge: $685.
Room and board: $8,710.
Additional info: Tuition/fee waivers available for adults, unemployed or children of unemployed.

FINANCIAL AID PICTURE (2008-2009)

Students with need: Out of 601 full-time freshmen who applied for aid, 526 were judged to have need. Of these, 525 received aid, and 184 had their full need met. Average financial aid package met 77% of need; average scholarship/grant was $13,599; average loan was $3,347. For part-time students, average financial aid package was $5,336.
Students without need: 89 full-time freshmen who did not demonstrate need for aid received scholarships/grants; average award was $7,953. No-need awards available for academics, athletics, leadership, music/drama, religious affiliation, ROTC.
Scholarships offered: ***Merit:*** Academic Awards; $1,000 to full tuition; based on high school rank, GPA, and test scores. Leadership Awards; $1,000-$1,500; based on leadership and activities. Diocesan Scholarship; $1,000 Parish Grant; for students that belong to a parish within the Diocese of Erie. Diocesan High School Grant; $1,500; for students who attended a Catholic high school within the Diocese of Erie. Catholic High School Grant; $1,000; for any student who attended a Catholic high school outside of the Diocese of Erie. Athletic scholarships; $1,000 to full tuition, room and board. ***Athletic:*** 18 full-time freshmen received athletic scholarships; average amount $16,514.
Cumulative student debt: 91% of graduating class had student loans; average debt was $26,170.

FINANCIAL AID PROCEDURES

Forms required: FAFSA, institutional form.
Dates and Deadlines: Priority date 3/15; no closing date. Applicants notified on a rolling basis starting 11/1; must reply by 5/1 or within 4 week(s) of notification.

CONTACT

Sharon Krahe, Director of Financial Aid
109 University Square, Erie, PA 16541-0001
(814) 871-7337

Geneva College

Beaver Falls, Pennsylvania
www.geneva.edu Federal Code: 003267

4-year private liberal arts college in large town, affiliated with Reformed Presbyterian Church of North America.
Enrollment: 1,381 undergrads, 2% part-time. 380 full-time freshmen.
Selectivity: Admits over 75% of applicants.

BASIC COSTS (2008-2009)

Tuition and fees: $20,400.
Per-credit charge: $680.
Room and board: $7,450.
Additional info: Tuition/fee waivers available for minority students.

FINANCIAL AID PICTURE (2008-2009)

Students with need: Out of 354 full-time freshmen who applied for aid, 318 were judged to have need. Of these, 318 received aid, and 58 had their full need met. Average financial aid package met 81% of need; average scholarship/grant was $13,070; average loan was $3,791. For part-time students, average financial aid package was $14,519.
Students without need: 50 full-time freshmen who did not demonstrate need for aid received scholarships/grants; average award was $6,292. No-need awards available for academics, music/drama, religious affiliation.
Scholarships offered: Academic scholarships, scholarships for National Merit finalists and semifinalists, grants for members of controlling church and other denominations identified by the college.
Cumulative student debt: 96% of graduating class had student loans; average debt was $29,827.

FINANCIAL AID PROCEDURES

Forms required: FAFSA.
Dates and Deadlines: Priority date 3/15; no closing date. Applicants notified on a rolling basis starting 3/1; must reply by 5/1 or within 4 week(s) of notification.
Transfers: Applicants notified on a rolling basis starting 3/1.

CONTACT

Steven Bell, Director of Financial Aid
3200 College Avenue, Beaver Falls, PA 15010
(724) 847-6530

Gettysburg College

Gettysburg, Pennsylvania Federal Code: 003268
www.gettysburg.edu CSS Code: 2275

4-year private liberal arts college in large town.
Enrollment: 2,457 undergrads. 714 full-time freshmen.
Selectivity: Admits less than 50% of applicants.

BASIC COSTS (2009-2010)

Tuition and fees: $39,200.
Room and board: $9,360.

FINANCIAL AID PICTURE (2008-2009)

Students with need: Out of 483 full-time freshmen who applied for aid, 388 were judged to have need. Of these, 388 received aid, and 374 had their full need met. Average financial aid package met 100% of need; average scholarship/grant was $25,221; average loan was $3,758.
Students without need: 108 full-time freshmen who did not demonstrate need for aid received scholarships/grants; average award was $10,259. No-need awards available for academics, music/drama.
Scholarships offered: Presidential, Dean's, and Founders Scholarships; based on high school class rank and standardized test scores; number awarded varies. Wagnild Scholarship and Sunderman Scholarships for music talent; audition required.
Cumulative student debt: 66% of graduating class had student loans; average debt was $23,992.

FINANCIAL AID PROCEDURES

Forms required: FAFSA, CSS PROFILE.
Dates and Deadlines: Closing date 2/15. Applicants notified by 3/26; must reply by 5/1.
Transfers: Priority date 4/15. Must reply within 2 week(s) of notification.

CONTACT

Christina Gormley, Director of Financial Aid
300 North Washington Street, Gettysburg, PA 17325-1484
(717) 337-6611

Grove City College

Grove City, Pennsylvania
www.gcc.edu Federal Code: G03269

4-year private liberal arts college in small town, affiliated with Presbyterian Church (USA).
Enrollment: 2,480 undergrads. 621 full-time freshmen.
Selectivity: Admits 50 to 75% of applicants.

BASIC COSTS (2009-2010)

Tuition and fees: $12,590.
Room and board: $6,824.
Additional info: Tuition includes cost of tablet PC and printer.

FINANCIAL AID PICTURE (2008-2009)

Students with need: Out of 356 full-time freshmen who applied for aid, 250 were judged to have need. Of these, 246 received aid, and 29 had their full need met. Average financial aid package met 60% of need; average scholarship/grant was $6,371.
Students without need: 54 full-time freshmen who did not demonstrate need for aid received scholarships/grants; average award was $2,583. No-need awards available for academics, leadership, minority status.
Scholarships offered: Trustee Scholarships; $5,000; issued to a select group of accepted students who meet academic requirements; 24 awarded. Presidential Scholarships; $500; for all valedictorians in class of 30 or more, salutatorians in class of 100 or more, and National Merit Finalists. Engineering Scholarships; $2,500; 4 awarded.
Additional info: Institutional aid applications required for institutional scholarships, loans, and student employment.

FINANCIAL AID PROCEDURES

Forms required: institutional form.
Dates and Deadlines: Closing date 4/15. Applicants notified on a rolling basis starting 3/15; must reply by 5/1.
Transfers: Closing date 12/15. Applicants notified on a rolling basis; must reply within 2 week(s) of notification. Financial aid form must be submitted with transfer enrollment application.

CONTACT

Thomas Ball, Director of Financial Aid
100 Campus Drive, Grove City, PA 16127-2104
(724) 458-3300

Gwynedd-Mercy College

Gwynedd Valley, Pennsylvania
www.gmc.edu Federal Code: 003270

4-year private health science and liberal arts college in large town, affiliated with Roman Catholic Church.
Enrollment: 1,963 undergrads, 26% part-time. 290 full-time freshmen.
Selectivity: Admits 50 to 75% of applicants.

BASIC COSTS (2009-2010)
Tuition and fees: $24,180.
Per-credit charge: $500.
Room and board: $9,330.
Additional info: Tuition and fees for nursing and allied health programs $25,230 for full-time, and $600 per credit hour for part-time.

FINANCIAL AID PICTURE (2007-2008)
Students with need: Out of 264 full-time freshmen who applied for aid, 211 were judged to have need. Of these, 211 received aid, and 42 had their full need met. Average financial aid package met 75% of need; average scholarship/grant was $12,370; average loan was $3,225. Need-based aid available for part-time students.
Students without need: 61 full-time freshmen who did not demonstrate need for aid received scholarships/grants; average award was $13,725. No-need awards available for academics, leadership.
Scholarships offered: Presidential scholarship; $10,000; must have 1200 SAT and be in top 30% of class, essay required; 2/15 deadline. Connelly Scholarship; $6,000-$7,000; must have 1100 SAT and be in top 50% of class. Mother Mary Bernard Scholarship; $4,500-$5,000; must have 1000 SAT, be in top 50% of class, and have documented leadership experience. Yearly scholarship for Catholic school graduates; $2,000 (tuition incentive grant). All SAT scores exclusive of Writing.
Cumulative student debt: 88% of graduating class had student loans; average debt was $20,636.

FINANCIAL AID PROCEDURES
Forms required: FAFSA, institutional form.
Dates and Deadlines: Priority date 3/1; closing date 7/15. Applicants notified on a rolling basis starting 2/15; must reply by 5/1 or within 2 week(s) of notification.
Transfers: Priority date 3/15.

CONTACT
Barbara Kaufmann, Director of Student Financial Aid
1325 Sumneytown Pike, Gwynedd Valley, PA 19437-0901
(215) 646-7300 ext. 483

Harcum College
Bryn Mawr, Pennsylvania
www.harcum.edu Federal Code: 003272

2-year private junior college in large town.
Enrollment: 949 undergrads.

BASIC COSTS (2008-2009)
Tuition and fees: $17,510.
Per-credit charge: $550.
Room and board: $7,680.

FINANCIAL AID PICTURE (2008-2009)
Students with need: 50% of average financial aid package awarded as scholarships/grants, 50% awarded as loans/jobs. Need-based aid available for part-time students. Work study available nights, weekends, and for part-time students.
Students without need: No-need awards available for academics, leadership.
Scholarships offered: Scholarships available based on academic achievement.

FINANCIAL AID PROCEDURES
Forms required: FAFSA, institutional form.
Dates and Deadlines: Priority date 4/15; closing date 5/1. Applicants notified on a rolling basis starting 3/1; must reply within 3 week(s) of notification.
Transfers: Priority date 3/15.

CONTACT
Eli Moinester, Director of Financial Aid
750 Montgomery Avenue, Bryn Mawr, PA 19010-3476
(610) 526-6098

Harrisburg Area Community College
Harrisburg, Pennsylvania
www.hacc.edu Federal Code: 003273

2-year public community college in small city.
Enrollment: 11,703 undergrads, 66% part-time. 1,889 full-time freshmen.
Selectivity: Open admission; but selective for some programs.

BASIC COSTS (2009-2010)
Tuition and fees: $3,960; out-of-district residents $6,510; out-of-state residents $9,360.
Per-credit charge: $97; out-of-district residents $178; out-of-state residents $268.

FINANCIAL AID PICTURE (2007-2008)
Students with need: Out of 1,456 full-time freshmen who applied for aid, 1,020 were judged to have need. Of these, 949 received aid, and 54 had their full need met. Average financial aid package met 51% of need; average scholarship/grant was $1,826; average loan was $2,906. For part-time students, average financial aid package was $4,446.
Students without need: 1 full-time freshmen who did not demonstrate need for aid received scholarships/grants; average award was $1,000. No-need awards available for academics.
Additional info: Federal work study community service positions available.

FINANCIAL AID PROCEDURES
Forms required: FAFSA, institutional form.
Dates and Deadlines: Priority date 3/15; no closing date. Applicants notified on a rolling basis starting 6/1.
Transfers: PHEAA state grants require separate academic progress review by financial aid staff.

CONTACT
Robert Fryer, Director of Financial Aid
One HACC Drive, Cooper 206, Harrisburg, PA 17110-2999
(717) 780-2330

Harrisburg University of Science and Technology
Harrisburg, Pennsylvania
www.HarrisburgU.net Federal Code: 039483

4-year private university in small city.
Enrollment: 157 undergrads, 16% part-time. 33 full-time freshmen.

BASIC COSTS (2009-2010)
Tuition and fees: $18,000.
Per-credit charge: $800.
Additional info: Laptop required. Estimated Cost: $1,200.

FINANCIAL AID PICTURE (2007-2008)
Students with need: Out of 33 full-time freshmen who applied for aid, 28 were judged to have need. Of these, 28 received aid. Average financial aid package met 85% of need; average scholarship/grant was $3,000; average loan was $3,500. Need-based aid available for part-time students.
Students without need: 2 full-time freshmen who did not demonstrate need for aid received scholarships/grants; average award was $4,000. No-need awards available for academics, leadership, state/district residency.
Scholarships offered: Various scholarships; $1,000-$18,000, depending on specific criteria.

Cumulative student debt: 92% of graduating class had student loans; average debt was $20,000.

FINANCIAL AID PROCEDURES

Forms required: FAFSA.

Dates and Deadlines: No deadline. Applicants notified on a rolling basis; must reply within 2 week(s) of notification.

Transfers: Priority date 5/1; no deadline. Applicants notified on a rolling basis; must reply within 4 week(s) of notification.

CONTACT

Vincent Frank, Director of Financial Aid
326 Market Street, Harrisburg, PA 17101-2208
(717) 901-5115

Haverford College

Haverford, Pennsylvania Federal Code: 003274
www.haverford.edu CSS Code: 2289

4-year private liberal arts college in large town.

Enrollment: 1,169 undergrads. 327 full-time freshmen.

Selectivity: Admits less than 50% of applicants.

BASIC COSTS (2009-2010)

Tuition and fees: $39,085.

Room and board: $11,890.

FINANCIAL AID PICTURE (2008-2009)

Students with need: Out of 208 full-time freshmen who applied for aid, 169 were judged to have need. Of these, 169 received aid, and 169 had their full need met. Average financial aid package met 100% of need; average scholarship/grant was $31,983; average loan was $539.

Students without need: This college awards aid only to students with need.

Cumulative student debt: 41% of graduating class had student loans; average debt was $17,125.

FINANCIAL AID PROCEDURES

Forms required: FAFSA, CSS PROFILE, state aid form.

Dates and Deadlines: Closing date 1/31. Applicants notified by 4/8; must reply by 5/1.

Transfers: Closing date 3/1.

CONTACT

David Hoy, Director of Financial Aid
370 Lancaster Avenue, Haverford, PA 19041-1392
(610) 896-1350

Holy Family University

Philadelphia, Pennsylvania
www.holyfamily.edu Federal Code: 003275

4-year private university and liberal arts college in very large city, affiliated with Roman Catholic Church.

Enrollment: 2,184 undergrads, 28% part-time. 404 full-time freshmen.

Selectivity: Admits 50 to 75% of applicants.

BASIC COSTS (2009-2010)

Tuition and fees: $22,460.

Per-credit charge: $470.

Room and board: $9,900.

FINANCIAL AID PICTURE (2007-2008)

Students with need: Average financial aid package met 90% of need. Need-based aid available for part-time students.

Students without need: 98 full-time freshmen who did not demonstrate need for aid received scholarships/grants; average award was $8,800. No-need awards available for academics, alumni affiliation, athletics.

Scholarships offered: 98 full-time freshmen received athletic scholarships; average amount $6,500.

Cumulative student debt: 85% of graduating class had student loans; average debt was $18,500.

FINANCIAL AID PROCEDURES

Forms required: FAFSA, institutional form.

Dates and Deadlines: Priority date 3/1; no closing date. Applicants notified on a rolling basis starting 3/15; must reply within 2 week(s) of notification.

Transfers: Priority date 4/1; closing date 5/1. Applicants notified on a rolling basis starting 5/1; must reply within 3 week(s) of notification.

CONTACT

Janice Hetrick, Director of Financial Aid
9801 Frankford Avenue, Philadelphia, PA 19114-2009
(215) 637-5538

Hussian School of Art

Philadelphia, Pennsylvania
www.hussianart.edu Federal Code: 007469

2-year for-profit visual arts and technical college in very large city.

Enrollment: 136 undergrads. 51 full-time freshmen.

Selectivity: Admits over 75% of applicants.

BASIC COSTS (2009-2010)

Tuition and fees: $12,550.

Additional info: Supply costs estimated at $375 for required Freshman Supply Kit; consumable supply estimate at $350 additional for the freshman year.

FINANCIAL AID PICTURE (2007-2008)

Students with need: Need-based aid available for full-time students.

FINANCIAL AID PROCEDURES

Forms required: FAFSA, state aid form, institutional form.

Dates and Deadlines: No deadline. Applicants notified on a rolling basis starting 2/15; must reply within 3 week(s) of notification.

Transfers: Priority date 3/15; no deadline. Applicants notified on a rolling basis starting 4/1.

CONTACT

Susan Cohen, Financial Aid Director
The Bourse, Suite 300, 111 South Independence Mall East, Philadelphia, PA 19106
(215) 574-9600 ext. 206

Immaculata University

Immaculata, Pennsylvania
www.immaculata.edu Federal Code: 003276

4-year private university and liberal arts college in large town, affiliated with Roman Catholic Church.

Enrollment: 2,776 undergrads, 61% part-time. 239 full-time freshmen.

Selectivity: Admits over 75% of applicants.

BASIC COSTS (2009-2010)

Tuition and fees: $26,540.

Per-credit charge: $420.

Room and board: $10,920.

Additional info: Tuition at time of enrollment locked for 4 years.

FINANCIAL AID PICTURE (2008-2009)

Students with need: Need-based aid available for full-time and part-time students. Work study available nights, weekends, and for part-time students.

Students without need: No-need awards available for academics, alumni affiliation, art, job skills, leadership, minority status, music/drama, religious affiliation, state/district residency.

FINANCIAL AID PROCEDURES

Forms required: FAFSA.

Dates and Deadlines: Priority date 2/15; closing date 4/15. Applicants notified on a rolling basis starting 2/1; must reply within 2 week(s) of notification.

Transfers: No deadline. Applicants notified on a rolling basis starting 1/1; must reply within 2 week(s) of notification.

CONTACT

Robert Forest, Director of Financial Aid
PO Box 642, Immaculata, PA 19345-0642
(610) 647-4400 ext. 3026

Indiana University of Pennsylvania

Indiana, Pennsylvania
www.iup.edu Federal Code: 003277

4-year public university in large town.

Enrollment: 11,565 undergrads, 5% part-time. 2,532 full-time freshmen.

Selectivity: Admits 50 to 75% of applicants.

BASIC COSTS (2008-2009)

Tuition and fees: $6,958; out-of-state residents $14,996.

Per-credit charge: $223; out-of-state residents $558.

Room and board: $5,578.

Additional info: Additional fees of $92 for out-of-state students. Tuition is $8,038 for students in any of these categories: OH, VA, WV, IN and MI residents; branch campus students from any state; out-of-state students with high school GPA of at least 3.0; any transfer student with GPA of at least 3.0.

FINANCIAL AID PICTURE (2007-2008)

Students with need: Average financial aid package met 83% of need; average scholarship/grant was $5,285; average loan was $3,779. For part-time students, average financial aid package was $6,734.

Students without need: 110 full-time freshmen who did not demonstrate need for aid received scholarships/grants; average award was $2,422. No-need awards available for academics, alumni affiliation, art, athletics, job skills, leadership, music/drama, ROTC, state/district residency.

Scholarships offered: 62 full-time freshmen received athletic scholarships; average amount $2,728.

Cumulative student debt: 82% of graduating class had student loans; average debt was $23,265.

FINANCIAL AID PROCEDURES

Forms required: FAFSA.

Dates and Deadlines: Priority date 4/15; no closing date. Applicants notified on a rolling basis starting 3/15.

Transfers: Must reply within 2 week(s) of notification.

CONTACT

Patricia McCarthy, Director of Financial Aid
117 John Sutton Hall, 1011 South Drive, Indiana, PA 15705-1088
(724) 357-2218

JNA Institute of Culinary Arts

Philadelphia, Pennsylvania
www.culinaryarts.com Federal Code: 031033

2-year for-profit technical college in very large city.

Enrollment: 60 undergrads.

Selectivity: Open admission.

BASIC COSTS (2008-2009)

Additional info: Tuition for 15-month associate program, $17,000; 6-month professional cooking diploma program, $8,500. Required fees $75 for both programs. Books and supplies are $225 for the diploma program and $1,050 for the associate program.

FINANCIAL AID PICTURE

Students with need: Need-based aid available for full-time students.

FINANCIAL AID PROCEDURES

Forms required: FAFSA.

CONTACT

Gerald Connor, Financial Aid Director
1212 South Broad Street, Philadelphia, PA 19146
(215) 468-8800

Johnson College

Scranton, Pennsylvania
www.johnson.edu Federal Code: 014734

2-year private technical college in small city.

Enrollment: 394 undergrads.

Selectivity: Open admission; but selective for some programs.

BASIC COSTS (2008-2009)

Tuition and fees: $14,530.

Per-credit charge: $375.

Room only: $3,612.

FINANCIAL AID PICTURE

Students with need: Need-based aid available for full-time and part-time students. Work study available nights, weekends, and for part-time students.

Students without need: No-need awards available for academics.

FINANCIAL AID PROCEDURES

Forms required: FAFSA, institutional form.

Dates and Deadlines: Priority date 4/28; no closing date. Applicants notified on a rolling basis starting 4/15; must reply within 2 week(s) of notification.

Transfers: Priority date 5/1.

CONTACT

Ed Moyer, Director of Financial Aid
3427 North Main Avenue, Scranton, PA 18508
(570) 342-6404 ext. 126

Juniata College

Huntingdon, Pennsylvania
www.juniata.edu Federal Code: 003279

4-year private liberal arts college in small town.

Enrollment: 1,402 undergrads. 460 full-time freshmen.

Selectivity: Admits 50 to 75% of applicants.

BASIC COSTS (2009-2010)

Tuition and fees: $31,550.

Per-credit charge: $1,285.

Room and board: $8,650.

Additional info: Tuition/fee waivers available for adults.

FINANCIAL AID PICTURE (2008-2009)

Students with need: Out of 386 full-time freshmen who applied for aid, 328 were judged to have need. Of these, 328 received aid, and 103 had their full need met. Average financial aid package met 87% of need; average scholarship/grant was $18,469; average loan was $3,822. Need-based aid available for part-time students.

Students without need: 131 full-time freshmen who did not demonstrate need for aid received scholarships/grants; average award was $16,761. No-need awards available for academics, art.
Scholarships offered: Ron & Ann Wertz Arts Scholarship, Environmental Responsibility Scholarship, Richard M. Simpson Leadership Scholarship, J. Omar Good Service & Peacemaking Scholarship; full tuition; nominated by alumni, 1 awarded for each. Burkholder Scholarship; full tuition, room and board; 1 awarded. Friendship Scholarship; $2,000; awarded to international student. Calvert Ellis Scholarships; $15,000; based on high school GPA or SAT scores. Area Residents Scholarships; half tuition; for area residents. Ray Day Scholarship; up to $5,000; for a minority student. John & Irene Dale Scholarship; $3,000; for information technology student. Heritage Scholarships; up to $8,000; for minority students with demonstrated commitment to leadership, community service and diversity. John Stauffer Scholarships; 4 full tuition for National Merit or National Achievement finalist status. Quinter Scholarships; $16,000; based upon GPA and SAT. Presidential Scholarships; $12,000; based upon GPA and SAT. Transfer Scholarships; up to $9,000; based upon credits completed and GPA. Eagles Abroad Scholarships; international experience plus $3,000, based upon commitment to international experience in France, Germany, Mexico, Spain, or Russia.
Cumulative student debt: 85% of graduating class had student loans; average debt was $21,343.

FINANCIAL AID PROCEDURES
Forms required: FAFSA.
Dates and Deadlines: Closing date 3/1. Applicants notified on a rolling basis starting 2/21; must reply by 5/1.

CONTACT
Valerie Rennell, Director of Student Financial Planning
1700 Moore Street, Huntingdon, PA 16652-2196
(814) 641-3142

Kaplan Career Institute: Pittsburgh
Pittsburgh, Pennsylvania
www.icmschool.com Federal Code: 007436

2-year for-profit business and health science college in large city.
Enrollment: 827 undergrads.

BASIC COSTS (2008-2009)
Tuition and fees: $17,080.
Additional info: Tuition costs include books and supplies.

FINANCIAL AID PICTURE
Students with need: Need-based aid available for full-time and part-time students. Work study available nights.
Students without need: This college awards aid only to students with need.

FINANCIAL AID PROCEDURES
Forms required: FAFSA, state aid form, institutional form.
Dates and Deadlines: Closing date 4/30. Applicants notified on a rolling basis.

CONTACT
Christopher Fox, Director of Financial Aid
10 Wood Street, Pittsburgh, PA 15222
(412) 261-2647 ext. 205

Keystone College
La Plume, Pennsylvania
www.keystone.edu Federal Code: 003280

4-year private junior and liberal arts college in small town.
Enrollment: 1,687 undergrads, 23% part-time. 361 full-time freshmen.
Selectivity: Admits over 75% of applicants.

BASIC COSTS (2009-2010)
Tuition and fees: $18,420.
Per-credit charge: $390.
Room and board: $8,760.
Additional info: Tuition/fee waivers available for adults.

FINANCIAL AID PICTURE (2007-2008)
Students with need: Average financial aid package met 71% of need; average scholarship/grant was $15,158; average loan was $2,625. For part-time students, average financial aid package was $3,700.
Students without need: 48 full-time freshmen who did not demonstrate need for aid received scholarships/grants; average award was $8,000. No-need awards available for academics, leadership, ROTC.
Scholarships offered: Academic Excellence Scholarship: one-half tuition up to full tuition; for all full-time, first-time students in the top 5% of their class with SAT scores of 1100 or above (exclusive of Writing). Presidential Scholarship: up to $7,000 each year; based on class rank and SAT/ACT scores. Trustee Scholarship: up to $6,000 each year; based on class rank and SAT/ACT scores. Leadership Award: up to $5,000 each year; students demonstrating non-athletic leadership skills in high school.
Cumulative student debt: 82% of graduating class had student loans; average debt was $22,075.

FINANCIAL AID PROCEDURES
Forms required: FAFSA, state aid form.
Dates and Deadlines: Priority date 5/1; no closing date. Applicants notified on a rolling basis starting 2/2; must reply within 2 week(s) of notification.
Transfers: No deadline. Applicants notified on a rolling basis starting 2/2; must reply within 3 week(s) of notification.

CONTACT
Ginger Kline, Director of Financial Assistance & Planning
One College Green, La Plume, PA 18440-1099
(570) 945-8967

Keystone Technical Institute
Harrisburg, Pennsylvania
www.kti.edu Federal Code: 022342

2-year for-profit health science and technical college in small city.
Enrollment: 57 undergrads.

BASIC COSTS (2008-2009)
Additional info: Tuition and fees vary by program.

FINANCIAL AID PICTURE
Students with need: Need-based aid available for full-time and part-time students. Work study available nights.
Students without need: This college awards aid only to students with need.
Scholarships offered: Half-tuition scholarships; 13 available to degree-seeking students.

FINANCIAL AID PROCEDURES
Forms required: FAFSA, state aid form.
Dates and Deadlines: Priority date 8/1; no closing date. Applicants notified on a rolling basis.
Transfers: State grant deadline for first-time recipients August 1. Renewal application deadline May 1.

CONTACT
Tracy Stewart, Financial Aid Coordinator
2301 Academy Drive, Harrisburg, PA 17112-1012
(717) 545-4747

King's College
Wilkes-Barre, Pennsylvania
www.kings.edu Federal Code: 003282

4-year private business and liberal arts college in small city, affiliated with Roman Catholic Church.
Enrollment: 2,070 undergrads, 4% part-time. 560 full-time freshmen.
Selectivity: Admits over 75% of applicants.

BASIC COSTS (2009-2010)
Tuition and fees: $25,644.
Per-credit charge: $495.
Room and board: $9,838.

FINANCIAL AID PICTURE (2008-2009)
Students with need: Out of 528 full-time freshmen who applied for aid, 452 were judged to have need. Of these, 452 received aid, and 87 had their full need met. Average financial aid package met 79% of need; average scholarship/grant was $13,487; average loan was $4,046. For part-time students, average financial aid package was $8,272.
Students without need: 104 full-time freshmen who did not demonstrate need for aid received scholarships/grants; average award was $9,864. No-need awards available for academics, leadership, ROTC.
Cumulative student debt: 86% of graduating class had student loans; average debt was $28,145.
Additional info: Any minority student with financial need may receive some aid in the form of a diversity scholarship.

FINANCIAL AID PROCEDURES
Forms required: FAFSA, institutional form.
Dates and Deadlines: Priority date 2/15; no closing date. Applicants notified on a rolling basis starting 3/1; must reply within 2 week(s) of notification.
Transfers: Priority date 2/1; no deadline. Applicants notified on a rolling basis; must reply by 5/1 or within 2 week(s) of notification.

CONTACT
Ellen McGuire, Director of Financial Aid
133 North River Street, Wilkes-Barre, PA 18711
(570) 208-5868

Kutztown University of Pennsylvania
Kutztown, Pennsylvania
www.kutztown.edu Federal Code: 003322

4-year public university in small town.
Enrollment: 8,813 undergrads, 5% part-time. 1,927 full-time freshmen.
Selectivity: Admits 50 to 75% of applicants.

BASIC COSTS (2008-2009)
Tuition and fees: $7,126; out-of-state residents $15,164.
Per-credit charge: $223; out-of-state residents $558.
Room and board: $7,330.

FINANCIAL AID PICTURE (2007-2008)
Students with need: Out of 1,713 full-time freshmen who applied for aid, 1,212 were judged to have need. Of these, 1,170 received aid, and 872 had their full need met. Average financial aid package met 58% of need; average scholarship/grant was $5,390; average loan was $3,265. For part-time students, average financial aid package was $5,786.
Students without need: 80 full-time freshmen who did not demonstrate need for aid received scholarships/grants; average award was $2,392. No-need awards available for academics, art, athletics, leadership, minority status, music/drama.
Scholarships offered: 31 full-time freshmen received athletic scholarships; average amount $1,924.
Cumulative student debt: 84% of graduating class had student loans; average debt was $17,881.

FINANCIAL AID PROCEDURES
Forms required: FAFSA.
Dates and Deadlines: Priority date 2/15; no closing date. Applicants notified on a rolling basis starting 3/30; must reply by 5/1 or within 4 week(s) of notification.

CONTACT
Bernard McCree, Director of Financial Aid
Admissions Office, Kutztown, PA 19530-0730
(610) 683-4077

La Roche College
Pittsburgh, Pennsylvania
www.laroche.edu Federal Code: 003987

4-year private liberal arts college in large city, affiliated with Roman Catholic Church.
Enrollment: 1,228 undergrads, 13% part-time. 227 full-time freshmen.
Selectivity: Admits 50 to 75% of applicants.

BASIC COSTS (2009-2010)
Tuition and fees: $21,638.
Room and board: $8,756.

FINANCIAL AID PICTURE (2008-2009)
Students with need: Out of 217 full-time freshmen who applied for aid, 213 were judged to have need. Of these, 213 received aid. Average financial aid package met 92% of need; average scholarship/grant was $2,581; average loan was $3,222. For part-time students, average financial aid package was $7,067.
Students without need: 43 full-time freshmen who did not demonstrate need for aid received scholarships/grants; average award was $7,692. No-need awards available for academics.
Cumulative student debt: 86% of graduating class had student loans; average debt was $34,189.

FINANCIAL AID PROCEDURES
Forms required: FAFSA.
Dates and Deadlines: Priority date 2/15; closing date 5/1. Applicants notified on a rolling basis starting 2/15; must reply within 2 week(s) of notification.

CONTACT
Sharon Platt, Director of Financial Aid
9000 Babcock Boulevard, Pittsburgh, PA 15237
(412) 536-1120

La Salle University
Philadelphia, Pennsylvania
www.lasalle.edu Federal Code: 003287

4-year private university and liberal arts college in very large city, affiliated with Roman Catholic Church.
Enrollment: 4,151 undergrads, 25% part-time. 847 full-time freshmen.
Selectivity: Admits 50 to 75% of applicants.

BASIC COSTS (2009-2010)
Tuition and fees: $32,700.
Room and board: $10,850.

FINANCIAL AID PICTURE (2008-2009)

Students with need: Out of 772 full-time freshmen who applied for aid, 679 were judged to have need. Of these, 679 received aid, and 152 had their full need met. Average financial aid package met 76% of need; average scholarship/grant was $17,476; average loan was $3,853. For part-time students, average financial aid package was $7,077.

Students without need: 150 full-time freshmen who did not demonstrate need for aid received scholarships/grants; average award was $11,374. No-need awards available for academics, athletics, ROTC.

Scholarships offered: ***Merit:*** Christian Brothers Scholarship; full tuition; based on academics and extracurricular leadership. Community Service Scholarship; half tuition; based on involvement in community service and academics. ***Athletic:*** 41 full-time freshmen received athletic scholarships; average amount $12,134.

Cumulative student debt: 78% of graduating class had student loans; average debt was $37,831.

FINANCIAL AID PROCEDURES

Forms required: FAFSA.

Dates and Deadlines: Priority date 2/15; no closing date. Applicants notified on a rolling basis starting 3/15; must reply by 5/1 or within 2 week(s) of notification.

Transfers: Applicants notified on a rolling basis starting 3/15; must reply by 5/1 or within 2 week(s) of notification.

CONTACT

Michael Wisnieski, Director of Financial Aid
1900 West Olney Avenue, Philadelphia, PA 19141-1199
(215) 951-1070

Lackawanna College

Scranton, Pennsylvania
www.lackawanna.edu Federal Code: 003283

2-year private junior college in small city.

Enrollment: 1,322 undergrads, 23% part-time. 511 full-time freshmen.

Selectivity: Open admission.

BASIC COSTS (2008-2009)

Tuition and fees: $10,560.

Per-credit charge: $350.

Room and board: $6,800.

FINANCIAL AID PICTURE (2008-2009)

Students with need: Average financial aid package met 55% of need; average scholarship/grant was $5,867; average loan was $3,379. For part-time students, average financial aid package was $5,916.

Students without need: No-need awards available for academics, athletics, leadership.

Cumulative student debt: 93% of graduating class had student loans; average debt was $13,574.

FINANCIAL AID PROCEDURES

Forms required: FAFSA, state aid form, institutional form.

Dates and Deadlines: Priority date 5/1; no closing date. Applicants notified on a rolling basis starting 5/1.

Transfers: No deadline. Applicants notified on a rolling basis.

CONTACT

Babara Hapeman, Director of Financial Aid
501 Vine Street, Scranton, PA 18509
(570) 961-7859

Lafayette College

Easton, Pennsylvania Federal Code: 003284
www.lafayette.edu CSS Code: 2361

4-year private engineering and liberal arts college in large town, affiliated with Presbyterian Church (USA).

Enrollment: 2,352 undergrads, 1% part-time. 592 full-time freshmen.

Selectivity: Admits less than 50% of applicants.

BASIC COSTS (2009-2010)

Tuition and fees: $38,490.

Per-credit charge: $421.

Room and board: $11,799.

FINANCIAL AID PICTURE (2007-2008)

Students with need: Out of 403 full-time freshmen who applied for aid, 331 were judged to have need. Of these, 306 received aid, and 306 had their full need met. Average financial aid package met 100% of need; average scholarship/grant was $26,383; average loan was $3,984. Need-based aid available for part-time students.

Students without need: 39 full-time freshmen who did not demonstrate need for aid received scholarships/grants; average award was $11,490. No-need awards available for academics, athletics, leadership, ROTC.

Scholarships offered: ***Merit:*** Marquis Scholarships; $16,000; based on academic merit. Trustee Scholarship; $8,000; based on academic merit; awarded to 15% of each entering class. ***Athletic:*** 15 full-time freshmen received athletic scholarships; average amount $29,229.

Cumulative student debt: 54% of graduating class had student loans; average debt was $18,747.

Additional info: Parent loans, up to $7,500 annually, available with college absorbing interest while student is enrolled. Family has 8 years after graduation to repay. Not limited to those demonstrating need.

FINANCIAL AID PROCEDURES

Forms required: FAFSA, CSS PROFILE.

Dates and Deadlines: Priority date 2/15; closing date 3/15. Applicants notified by 4/1; must reply by 5/1.

Transfers: Closing date 5/1.

CONTACT

Arlina DeNardo, Director of Student Financial Aid
118 Markle Hall, Easton, PA 18042
(610) 330-5055

Lancaster Bible College

Lancaster, Pennsylvania
www.lbc.edu Federal Code: 003285

4-year private Bible college in small city, affiliated with nondenominational tradition.

Enrollment: 659 undergrads, 20% part-time. 118 full-time freshmen.

Selectivity: Admits 50 to 75% of applicants.

BASIC COSTS (2008-2009)

Tuition and fees: $15,290.

Per-credit charge: $495.

Room and board: $6,510.

FINANCIAL AID PICTURE (2007-2008)

Students with need: Need-based aid available for full-time and part-time students. Work study available nights, weekends, and for part-time students.

Students without need: No-need awards available for academics, alumni affiliation, leadership, music/drama, state/district residency.

Scholarships offered: Child of Full-time Christian Worker Scholarship; 50% reduction in tuition, room and board; available to dependent students where major wage earner or head of household is in full-time Christian work.

FINANCIAL AID PROCEDURES

Forms required: FAFSA, state aid form.

Dates and Deadlines: Priority date 5/1; no closing date. Applicants notified on a rolling basis starting 3/15; must reply within 3 week(s) of notification.

CONTACT

Karen Fox, Director of Financial Aid
901 Eden Road, Lancaster, PA 17601-5036
(717) 560-8254

Laurel Business Institute

Uniontown, Pennsylvania
www.laurel.edu Federal Code: 017118

2-year for-profit technical and career college in large town.

Enrollment: 316 undergrads, 2% part-time. 110 full-time freshmen.

Selectivity: Admits over 75% of applicants.

BASIC COSTS (2008-2009)

Tuition and fees: $8,055.

Per-credit charge: $225.

FINANCIAL AID PICTURE (2008-2009)

Students with need: Need-based aid available for full-time and part-time students.

Students without need: This college awards aid only to students with need.

Scholarships offered: One full tuition, several half tuition (including GED scholarships); based on high school transcripts or GED scores, letters of reference, and personal interview.

FINANCIAL AID PROCEDURES

Forms required: FAFSA, institutional form.

Dates and Deadlines: Closing date 8/1. Applicants notified on a rolling basis; must reply within 4 week(s) of notification.

Transfers: No deadline. Must reply within 4 week(s) of notification.

CONTACT

Stephanie Migyanko, Director of Financial Aid
11 East Penn Street, Uniontown, PA 15401
(724) 439-4900

Lebanon Valley College

Annville, Pennsylvania
www.lvc.edu Federal Code: 003288

4-year private liberal arts college in small town, affiliated with United Methodist Church.

Enrollment: 1,655 undergrads, 4% part-time. 396 full-time freshmen.

Selectivity: Admits 50 to 75% of applicants.

BASIC COSTS (2008-2009)

Tuition and fees: $29,350.

Per-credit charge: $480.

Room and board: $7,760.

Additional info: Tuition/fee waivers available for minority students.

FINANCIAL AID PICTURE (2008-2009)

Students with need: Out of 371 full-time freshmen who applied for aid, 316 were judged to have need. Of these, 316 received aid, and 99 had their full need met. Average financial aid package met 86% of need; average scholarship/grant was $17,604; average loan was $4,566. For part-time students, average financial aid package was $2,130.

Students without need: 66 full-time freshmen who did not demonstrate need for aid received scholarships/grants; average award was $11,871. No-need awards available for academics, alumni affiliation, music/drama.

Scholarships offered: Vickroy Scholarship; half tuition; automatic for admitted applicants in top 10% of graduating class. Leadership scholarship; one-third tuition; automatic for admitted applicants in top 20% of graduating class. Achievement Scholarship; one-quarter tuition; automatic for admitted applicants in top 30% of graduating class.

Cumulative student debt: 81% of graduating class had student loans; average debt was $32,437.

FINANCIAL AID PROCEDURES

Forms required: FAFSA, institutional form.

Dates and Deadlines: Priority date 3/1; no closing date. Applicants notified on a rolling basis starting 3/1; must reply by 5/1 or within 2 week(s) of notification.

Transfers: Must reply by 5/1 or within 2 week(s) of notification. Students transferring 15 or fewer credits are considered for scholarships on the same basis as high school seniors. Students transferring 16 or more credits are considered for scholarships based on their college academic performance and program.

CONTACT

Kendra Feigert, Director of Financial Aid
101 North College Avenue, Annville, PA 17003-1400
(717) 867-6181

Lehigh Carbon Community College

Schnecksville, Pennsylvania
www.lccc.edu Federal Code: 006810

2-year public community college in small town.

Enrollment: 6,280 undergrads, 54% part-time. 1,139 full-time freshmen.

Selectivity: Open admission; but selective for some programs.

BASIC COSTS (2009-2010)

Tuition and fees: $2,976; out-of-district residents $5,712; out-of-state residents $8,448.

Per-credit charge: $85; out-of-district residents $179; out-of-state residents $273.

FINANCIAL AID PICTURE (2007-2008)

Students with need: Need-based aid available for full-time and part-time students. Work study available nights.

Students without need: No-need awards available for academics, state/district residency.

FINANCIAL AID PROCEDURES

Forms required: FAFSA.

Dates and Deadlines: No deadline. Applicants notified on a rolling basis starting 5/5; must reply within 2 week(s) of notification.

Transfers: No deadline. Applicants notified on a rolling basis.

CONTACT

Marian Snyder, Director of Financial Aid
4525 Education Park Drive, Schnecksville, PA 18078
(610) 799-1133

Lehigh University

Bethlehem, Pennsylvania Federal Code: 003289
www.lehigh.edu CSS Code: 2365

4-year private university in small city.

Enrollment: 4,856 undergrads, 1% part-time. 1,205 full-time freshmen.

Selectivity: Admits less than 50% of applicants.

BASIC COSTS (2009-2010)

Tuition and fees: $38,630.

Per-credit charge: $1,600.

Room and board: $10,200.

FINANCIAL AID PICTURE (2008-2009)

Students with need: Out of 758 full-time freshmen who applied for aid, 522 were judged to have need. Of these, 522 received aid, and 271 had their full need met. Average financial aid package met 96% of need; average scholarship/grant was $27,552; average loan was $3,420. For part-time students, average financial aid package was $17,611.

Students without need: 83 full-time freshmen who did not demonstrate need for aid received scholarships/grants; average award was $11,110. No-need awards available for academics, art, athletics, leadership, music/drama, ROTC.

Scholarships offered: ***Merit:*** Asa Packer Scholarships; $15,000; for exceptional academic and leadership skills. Dean's Scholarships; $10,000; for academic excellence and leadership skills. Baker Scholarship; $2,500; for excellence in music or theater and superior academic record. Choral Arts Scholarships; $2,500; for singing talent. ***Athletic:*** 13 full-time freshmen received athletic scholarships; average amount $32,063.

Cumulative student debt: 58% of graduating class had student loans; average debt was $29,756.

Additional info: Loans eliminated for students eligible for financial aid and whose family income is less than $50,000.

FINANCIAL AID PROCEDURES

Forms required: FAFSA, CSS PROFILE.

Dates and Deadlines: Closing date 2/15. Applicants notified by 3/30; must reply by 5/1 or within 3 week(s) of notification.

Transfers: Closing date 3/1. Applicants notified on a rolling basis starting 5/15; must reply within 3 week(s) of notification.

CONTACT

Linda Bell, Director of Financial Aid
27 Memorial Drive West, Bethlehem, PA 18015-3094
(610) 758-3181

Lincoln University

Lincoln University, Pennsylvania
www.lincoln.edu Federal Code: 003290

4-year public university and liberal arts college in small town.

Enrollment: 1,966 undergrads, 2% part-time. 531 full-time freshmen.

Selectivity: Admits less than 50% of applicants.

BASIC COSTS (2008-2009)

Tuition and fees: $8,240; out-of-state residents $12,846.

Per-credit charge: $238; out-of-state residents $404.

Room and board: $7,850.

Additional info: Out-of-state students pay additional $612 in fees, which are included in out-of-state tuition figure.

FINANCIAL AID PICTURE (2008-2009)

Students with need: Need-based aid available for full-time and part-time students. Work study available nights, weekends, and for part-time students.

Students without need: No-need awards available for academics, alumni affiliation, leadership, music/drama.

FINANCIAL AID PROCEDURES

Forms required: FAFSA.

Dates and Deadlines: Closing date 5/1. Applicants notified on a rolling basis starting 4/1; must reply within 3 week(s) of notification.

CONTACT

Thelma Ross, Director of Financial Aid
1570 Baltimore Pike, Lincoln University, PA 19352-0999
(800) 561-2606

Lock Haven University of Pennsylvania

Lock Haven, Pennsylvania
www.lhup.edu Federal Code: 003323

4-year public university and liberal arts college in small town.

Enrollment: 4,817 undergrads, 6% part-time. 1,273 full-time freshmen.

Selectivity: Admits 50 to 75% of applicants.

BASIC COSTS (2008-2009)

Tuition and fees: $6,917; out-of-state residents $12,955.

Per-credit charge: $223; out-of-state residents $475.

Room and board: $6,448.

Additional info: All freshman students are required to have a laptop computer for use in the classroom. Computers can be purchased through the university; cost of computer is not included in mandatory fees. The university has a small number of laptops available to students who cannot afford to make such a purchase. Tuition/fee waivers available for minority students.

FINANCIAL AID PICTURE (2008-2009)

Students with need: Out of 1,246 full-time freshmen who applied for aid, 971 were judged to have need. Of these, 971 received aid, and 437 had their full need met. Average financial aid package met 73% of need; average scholarship/grant was $4,634; average loan was $3,500. For part-time students, average financial aid package was $2,200.

Students without need: 48 full-time freshmen who did not demonstrate need for aid received scholarships/grants; average award was $1,245. No-need awards available for academics, art, athletics, leadership, minority status, music/drama, ROTC, state/district residency.

Scholarships offered: 50 full-time freshmen received athletic scholarships; average amount $2,301.

Cumulative student debt: 85% of graduating class had student loans; average debt was $22,585.

FINANCIAL AID PROCEDURES

Forms required: FAFSA.

Dates and Deadlines: Closing date 3/15. Applicants notified on a rolling basis starting 4/1; must reply within 2 week(s) of notification.

Transfers: Priority date 4/1.

CONTACT

James Theeuwes, Director of Student Financial Services
Akeley Hall, Lock Haven, PA 17745
(877) 405-3057

Luzerne County Community College

Nanticoke, Pennsylvania
www.luzerne.edu Federal Code: 006811

2-year public community college in large town.

Enrollment: 6,188 undergrads, 47% part-time. 1,199 full-time freshmen.

Selectivity: Open admission; but selective for some programs.

BASIC COSTS (2008-2009)

Tuition and fees: $2,940; out-of-district residents $5,640; out-of-state residents $8,340.

Per-credit charge: $80; out-of-district residents $160; out-of-state residents $240.

FINANCIAL AID PICTURE (2007-2008)

Students with need: 49% of average financial aid package awarded as scholarships/grants, 51% awarded as loans/jobs. Need-based aid available for part-time students.

FINANCIAL AID PROCEDURES

Forms required: FAFSA, institutional form.

Dates and Deadlines: Priority date 4/15; no closing date. Applicants notified on a rolling basis starting 7/1.

CONTACT
Mary Kosin, Director of Financial Aid
1333 South Prospect Street, Nanticoke, PA 18634-3899
(570) 740-0395

Lycoming College
Williamsport, Pennsylvania
www.lycoming.edu Federal Code: 003293

4-year private liberal arts college in small city, affiliated with United Methodist Church.
Enrollment: 1,325 undergrads. 340 full-time freshmen.
Selectivity: Admits 50 to 75% of applicants.

BASIC COSTS (2008-2009)
Tuition and fees: $28,764.
Per-credit charge: $882.
Room and board: $7,672.
Additional info: Tuition/fee waivers available for minority students.

FINANCIAL AID PICTURE (2008-2009)
Students with need: Out of 325 full-time freshmen who applied for aid, 289 were judged to have need. Of these, 289 received aid, and 62 had their full need met. Average financial aid package met 82% of need; average scholarship/grant was $18,116; average loan was $4,274. For part-time students, average financial aid package was $4,590.
Students without need: 47 full-time freshmen who did not demonstrate need for aid received scholarships/grants; average award was $10,801. No-need awards available for academics, art, leadership, minority status, music/drama.
Cumulative student debt: 85% of graduating class had student loans; average debt was $27,179.

FINANCIAL AID PROCEDURES
Forms required: FAFSA, institutional form.
Dates and Deadlines: Priority date 3/1; no closing date. Applicants notified on a rolling basis starting 3/1; must reply by 5/1.
Transfers: No deadline.

CONTACT
James Spencer, Dean of Admissions and Financial Aid
700 College Place, Williamsport, PA 17701
(570) 321-4026

Manor College
Jenkintown, Pennsylvania
www.manor.edu Federal Code: 003294

2-year private junior college in small town, affiliated with Ukrainian Catholic Church.
Enrollment: 802 undergrads, 43% part-time. 132 full-time freshmen.
Selectivity: Admits less than 50% of applicants.

BASIC COSTS (2008-2009)
Tuition and fees: $12,156.
Per-credit charge: $255.
Room and board: $5,772.
Additional info: Tuition for allied health program: $12,328; $348 per credit hour.

FINANCIAL AID PICTURE (2008-2009)
Students with need: Average financial aid package met 32% of need; average scholarship/grant was $4,850; average loan was $3,520. For part-time students, average financial aid package was $4,680.
Students without need: No-need awards available for academics, alumni affiliation, art.
Scholarships offered: Basilian Scholarship; for every freshman with A or B high school average and minimum 900 SAT (exclusive of writing).
Cumulative student debt: 97% of graduating class had student loans; average debt was $8,000.

FINANCIAL AID PROCEDURES
Forms required: FAFSA.
Dates and Deadlines: Priority date 4/1; no closing date. Applicants notified on a rolling basis starting 3/1; must reply within 2 week(s) of notification.
Transfers: No deadline. Applicants notified on a rolling basis starting 12/1; must reply within 2 week(s) of notification.

CONTACT
Peter Lysionek, Director of Financial Aid
700 Fox Chase Road, Jenkintown, PA 19046-3319
(215) 884-6051

Mansfield University of Pennsylvania
Mansfield, Pennsylvania
www.mansfield.edu Federal Code: 003324

4-year public university and liberal arts college in small town.
Enrollment: 2,877 undergrads, 7% part-time. 662 full-time freshmen.
Selectivity: Admits 50 to 75% of applicants.

BASIC COSTS (2008-2009)
Tuition and fees: $7,359; out-of-state residents $15,397.
Per-credit charge: $223; out-of-state residents $558.
Room and board: $6,672.
Additional info: Tuition for NY residents is $8,842; per-credit-hour charge for NY residents is $368.

FINANCIAL AID PICTURE (2007-2008)
Students with need: Need-based aid available for full-time and part-time students. Work study available nights, weekends, and for part-time students.
Students without need: No-need awards available for academics, art, athletics, leadership, music/drama, state/district residency.

FINANCIAL AID PROCEDURES
Forms required: FAFSA, institutional form.
Dates and Deadlines: Priority date 3/15; no closing date. Applicants notified on a rolling basis starting 3/15; must reply within 2 week(s) of notification.

CONTACT
Barbara Schmitt, Director of Financial Aid
South Hall, Mansfield, PA 16933
(570) 662-4129

Marywood University
Scranton, Pennsylvania
www.marywood.edu Federal Code: 003296

4-year private university in small city, affiliated with Roman Catholic Church.
Enrollment: 2,039 undergrads, 5% part-time. 422 full-time freshmen.
Selectivity: Admits over 75% of applicants.

BASIC COSTS (2009-2010)
Tuition and fees: $26,270.
Room and board: $11,498.

FINANCIAL AID PICTURE (2008-2009)
Students with need: Out of 394 full-time freshmen who applied for aid, 345 were judged to have need. Of these, 344 received aid, and 84 had their full need met. Average financial aid package met 80% of need; average scholarship/grant was $15,206; average loan was $3,661. For part-time students, average financial aid package was $7,728.

Students without need: 73 full-time freshmen who did not demonstrate need for aid received scholarships/grants; average award was $11,038. No-need awards available for academics, alumni affiliation, art, leadership, music/drama, ROTC.
Cumulative student debt: 98% of graduating class had student loans; average debt was $35,900.

FINANCIAL AID PROCEDURES
Forms required: FAFSA.
Dates and Deadlines: Priority date 2/15; no closing date. Applicants notified on a rolling basis starting 2/15; must reply by 5/1 or within 3 week(s) of notification.
Transfers: No deadline. Applicants notified on a rolling basis starting 3/1; must reply by 5/1 or within 3 week(s) of notification.

CONTACT
Stanley Skrutski, Director of Financial Aid
2300 Adams Avenue, Scranton, PA 18509-1598
(570) 348-6225

Mercyhurst College
Erie, Pennsylvania
www.mercyhurst.edu Federal Code: 003297

4-year private liberal arts college in small city, affiliated with Roman Catholic Church.
Enrollment: 3,842 undergrads, 12% part-time. 642 full-time freshmen.
Selectivity: Admits 50 to 75% of applicants.

BASIC COSTS (2009-2010)
Tuition and fees: $24,351.
Per-credit charge: $758.
Room and board: $8,607.
Additional info: Tuition/fee waivers available for adults, minority students, unemployed or children of unemployed.

FINANCIAL AID PICTURE (2008-2009)
Students with need: Need-based aid available for full-time and part-time students. Work study available nights, weekends, and for part-time students.
Students without need: No-need awards available for academics, alumni affiliation, art, athletics, leadership, minority status, music/drama, religious affiliation, ROTC.

FINANCIAL AID PROCEDURES
Forms required: FAFSA.
Dates and Deadlines: Priority date 3/1; no closing date. Applicants notified on a rolling basis starting 2/15; must reply by 5/1 or within 2 week(s) of notification.
Transfers: No deadline. Applicants notified on a rolling basis; must reply within 2 week(s) of notification.

CONTACT
Ann Jelinek, Director of Student Financial Services
501 East 38th Street, Erie, PA 16546-0001
(814) 824-2288

Messiah College
Grantham, Pennsylvania
www.messiah.edu Federal Code: 003298

4-year private liberal arts college in small town, affiliated with interdenominational tradition.
Enrollment: 2,763 undergrads, 1% part-time. 711 full-time freshmen.
Selectivity: Admits 50 to 75% of applicants.

BASIC COSTS (2009-2010)
Tuition and fees: $26,700.
Per-credit charge: $1,080.
Room and board: $7,880.
Additional info: Tuition/fee waivers available for adults.

FINANCIAL AID PICTURE (2008-2009)
Students with need: Out of 612 full-time freshmen who applied for aid, 510 were judged to have need. Of these, 510 received aid, and 126 had their full need met. Average financial aid package met 75% of need; average scholarship/grant was $13,204; average loan was $3,640. For part-time students, average financial aid package was $9,284.
Students without need: 197 full-time freshmen who did not demonstrate need for aid received scholarships/grants; average award was $9,582. No-need awards available for academics, art, leadership, music/drama, religious affiliation.

FINANCIAL AID PROCEDURES
Forms required: FAFSA.
Dates and Deadlines: Priority date 4/1; no closing date. Applicants notified on a rolling basis starting 3/15; must reply by 5/1 or within 4 week(s) of notification.

CONTACT
Greg Gearhart, Director of Financial Aid
PO Box 3005, Grantham, PA 17027-0800
(717) 691-6007

Metropolitan Career Center Computer Technology Institute
Philadelphia, Pennsylvania
www.careersinit.org

2-year private technical college in very large city.
Enrollment: 174 undergrads.

BASIC COSTS (2008-2009)
Additional info: Full program cost is $18,050 and includes all fees and supplies.

FINANCIAL AID PICTURE (2007-2008)
Students with need: 60% of average financial aid package awarded as scholarships/grants, 40% awarded as loans/jobs.

FINANCIAL AID PROCEDURES
Dates and Deadlines: No deadline.

CONTACT
Florine Lewis, Financial Aid Administrator
100 South Broad Street, Suite 830, Philadelphia, PA 19110

Millersville University of Pennsylvania
Millersville, Pennsylvania
www.millersville.edu Federal Code: 003325

4-year public university and liberal arts college in small town.
Enrollment: 7,098 undergrads, 8% part-time. 1,326 full-time freshmen.
Selectivity: Admits 50 to 75% of applicants.

BASIC COSTS (2008-2009)
Tuition and fees: $6,866; out-of-state residents $14,904.
Per-credit charge: $223; out-of-state residents $558.
Room and board: $7,308.

FINANCIAL AID PICTURE (2007-2008)

Students with need: Out of 1,152 full-time freshmen who applied for aid, 784 were judged to have need. Of these, 758 received aid, and 98 had their full need met. Average financial aid package met 76% of need; average scholarship/grant was $5,320; average loan was $3,271. For part-time students, average financial aid package was $5,641.

Students without need: 24 full-time freshmen who did not demonstrate need for aid received scholarships/grants; average award was $2,262. No-need awards available for academics, athletics, minority status.

Scholarships offered: 20 full-time freshmen received athletic scholarships; average amount $1,360.

Cumulative student debt: 66% of graduating class had student loans; average debt was $20,931.

FINANCIAL AID PROCEDURES

Forms required: FAFSA.

Dates and Deadlines: Closing date 3/15. Applicants notified on a rolling basis starting 3/19; must reply within 2 week(s) of notification.

Transfers: No deadline. Applicants notified on a rolling basis.

CONTACT

Dwight Horsey, Director of Financial Aid
PO Box 1002, Millersville, PA 17551-0302
(717) 872-3026

Misericordia University

Dallas, Pennsylvania
www.misericordia.edu Federal Code: 003247

4-year private health science and liberal arts college in large town, affiliated with Roman Catholic Church.

Enrollment: 2,120 undergrads, 26% part-time. 378 full-time freshmen.

Selectivity: Admits 50 to 75% of applicants.

BASIC COSTS (2009-2010)

Tuition and fees: $24,050.

Per-credit charge: $450.

Room and board: $10,050.

Additional info: Tuition/fee waivers available for adults.

FINANCIAL AID PICTURE (2008-2009)

Students with need: Out of 359 full-time freshmen who applied for aid, 319 were judged to have need. Of these, 319 received aid, and 49 had their full need met. Average financial aid package met 73% of need; average scholarship/grant was $12,295; average loan was $5,385. For part-time students, average financial aid package was $3,774.

Students without need: 38 full-time freshmen who did not demonstrate need for aid received scholarships/grants; average award was $6,700. No-need awards available for academics, alumni affiliation, leadership, minority status, state/district residency.

Scholarships offered: McAuley Award; $1,000-$5,000 per year; based on out-of-classroom activities. Partnership Scholarship; $2,500 per year; for students interested in specific careers. Academic Scholarship; $2,000-$15,000 per year; based on academic abilities.

Cumulative student debt: 76% of graduating class had student loans; average debt was $20,345.

FINANCIAL AID PROCEDURES

Forms required: FAFSA, institutional form.

Dates and Deadlines: Priority date 3/1; closing date 5/1. Applicants notified on a rolling basis starting 3/15; must reply by 5/1.

Transfers: No deadline. Applicants notified on a rolling basis starting 3/15.

CONTACT

Jane Dessoye, Executive Director of Enrollment Management
301 Lake Street, Dallas, PA 18612-1098
(570) 674-6280

Montgomery County Community College

Blue Bell, Pennsylvania
www.mc3.edu Federal Code: 004452

2-year public community college in large town.

Enrollment: 12,142 undergrads, 54% part-time. 2,355 full-time freshmen.

Selectivity: Open admission; but selective for some programs.

BASIC COSTS (2009-2010)

Tuition and fees: $3,270; out-of-district residents $6,240; out-of-state residents $9,210.

Per-credit charge: $89; out-of-district residents $178; out-of-state residents $267.

FINANCIAL AID PICTURE (2007-2008)

Students with need: Out of 1,052 full-time freshmen who applied for aid, 828 were judged to have need. Of these, 697 received aid, and 55 had their full need met. Average financial aid package met 15% of need; average scholarship/grant was $2,037; average loan was $1,637. For part-time students, average financial aid package was $3,344.

Students without need: 170 full-time freshmen who did not demonstrate need for aid received scholarships/grants; average award was $2,628. No-need awards available for academics.

FINANCIAL AID PROCEDURES

Forms required: FAFSA.

Dates and Deadlines: Priority date 5/1; no closing date. Applicants notified on a rolling basis starting 2/1.

Transfers: No deadline.

CONTACT

Cindy Haney, Director of Financial Aid
340 DeKalb Pike, Blue Bell, PA 19422
(215) 641-6566

Moore College of Art and Design

Philadelphia, Pennsylvania
www.moore.edu Federal Code: 003300

4-year private visual arts college for women in very large city.

Enrollment: 525 undergrads, 6% part-time. 107 full-time freshmen.

Selectivity: Admits 50 to 75% of applicants.

BASIC COSTS (2008-2009)

Tuition and fees: $27,718.

Room and board: $10,501.

FINANCIAL AID PICTURE (2008-2009)

Students with need: Need-based aid available for full-time and part-time students.

Students without need: No-need awards available for academics, art, leadership.

FINANCIAL AID PROCEDURES

Forms required: FAFSA.

Dates and Deadlines: Priority date 3/1; closing date 5/1. Applicants notified on a rolling basis starting 2/15; must reply within 2 week(s) of notification.

Transfers: Priority date 5/1; no deadline.

CONTACT

Kristina Fripps, Director of Financial Aid
The Parkway at 20th Street, Philadelphia, PA 19103-1179
(215) 568-4515

Moravian College

Bethlehem, Pennsylvania Federal Code: 003301
www.moravian.edu CSS Code: 2418

4-year private liberal arts college in small city, affiliated with Moravian Church in America.

Enrollment: 1,668 undergrads, 6% part-time. 387 full-time freshmen.

Selectivity: Admits 50 to 75% of applicants.

BASIC COSTS (2008-2009)

Tuition and fees: $30,062.

Per-credit charge: $821.

Room and board: $8,312.

FINANCIAL AID PICTURE (2008-2009)

Students with need: Out of 341 full-time freshmen who applied for aid, 292 were judged to have need. Of these, 291 received aid, and 43 had their full need met. Average financial aid package met 81% of need; average scholarship/grant was $17,213; average loan was $4,025. For part-time students, average financial aid package was $9,002.

Students without need: 70 full-time freshmen who did not demonstrate need for aid received scholarships/grants; average award was $9,541. No-need awards available for academics, alumni affiliation, leadership, minority status, music/drama, religious affiliation, ROTC.

Scholarships offered: Comenius Scholarship; $10,000 to full tuition; top 10% of high school class and minimum 1850 SAT required. Founders Scholarship; $4,000-$8,000; for top 25% or 1700 SAT. Trustee Scholarship; $6,000-$10,000; must be National Honor Society member, in top 20% of class. All scholarships require at least 500 on each section of SAT. Other scholarships available based on interest in the sciences, leadership and interest in promoting diversity and/or challenging circumstances in attending college.

FINANCIAL AID PROCEDURES

Forms required: FAFSA, CSS PROFILE.

Dates and Deadlines: Priority date 2/14; closing date 3/15. Applicants notified on a rolling basis starting 4/1; must reply by 5/1 or within 2 week(s) of notification.

Transfers: Priority date 3/15; closing date 5/1. Applicants notified on a rolling basis starting 4/1.

CONTACT

Stephen Cassel, Director of Financial Aid
1200 Main Street, Bethlehem, PA 18018
(610) 861-1330

Mount Aloysius College

Cresson, Pennsylvania
www.mtaloy.edu Federal Code: 003302

4-year private liberal arts college in small town, affiliated with Roman Catholic Church.

Enrollment: 1,523 undergrads, 25% part-time. 326 full-time freshmen.

Selectivity: Admits 50 to 75% of applicants.

BASIC COSTS (2009-2010)

Tuition and fees: $17,280.

Per-credit charge: $480.

Room and board: $7,300.

Additional info: Tuition/fee waivers available for unemployed or children of unemployed.

FINANCIAL AID PICTURE (2007-2008)

Students with need: Out of 326 full-time freshmen who applied for aid, 301 were judged to have need. Of these, 301 received aid. Average financial aid package met 25% of need; average scholarship/grant was $2,242; average loan was $3,210. For part-time students, average financial aid package was $4,500.

Students without need: 25 full-time freshmen who did not demonstrate need for aid received scholarships/grants. No-need awards available for academics, art, leadership, music/drama, religious affiliation.

FINANCIAL AID PROCEDURES

Forms required: FAFSA.

Dates and Deadlines: Priority date 4/1; no closing date. Applicants notified on a rolling basis starting 3/15; must reply within 4 week(s) of notification.

Transfers: No deadline.

CONTACT

Stacy Schenk, Director of Financial Aid
7373 Admiral Peary Highway, Cresson, PA 16630
(814) 886-6357

Muhlenberg College

Allentown, Pennsylvania Federal Code: 003304
www.muhlenberg.edu CSS Code: 2424

4-year private liberal arts college in small city, affiliated with Evangelical Lutheran Church in America.

Enrollment: 2,372 undergrads, 4% part-time. 597 full-time freshmen.

Selectivity: Admits less than 50% of applicants.

BASIC COSTS (2009-2010)

Tuition and fees: $36,990.

Room and board: $8,440.

FINANCIAL AID PICTURE (2008-2009)

Students with need: Out of 390 full-time freshmen who applied for aid, 278 were judged to have need. Of these, 273 received aid, and 255 had their full need met. Average financial aid package met 92% of need; average scholarship/grant was $20,683; average loan was $3,326. For part-time students, average financial aid package was $6,175.

Students without need: 205 full-time freshmen who did not demonstrate need for aid received scholarships/grants; average award was $12,629. No-need awards available for academics, art, leadership, music/drama.

Cumulative student debt: 82% of graduating class had student loans; average debt was $18,542.

FINANCIAL AID PROCEDURES

Forms required: FAFSA, CSS PROFILE, institutional form.

Dates and Deadlines: Closing date 2/15. Applicants notified by 4/1; must reply by 5/1.

Transfers: Closing date 4/15. Transfers awarded aid on a funds-available basis after returning students and freshmen have been served.

CONTACT

Gregory Mitton, Director of Financial Aid
2400 Chew Street, Allentown, PA 18104
(484) 664-3175

Neumann College

Aston, Pennsylvania
www.neumann.edu Federal Code: 003988

4-year private liberal arts college in large town, affiliated with Roman Catholic Church.

Enrollment: 2,484 undergrads, 18% part-time. 539 full-time freshmen.

Selectivity: Admits over 75% of applicants.

BASIC COSTS (2009-2010)
Tuition and fees: $21,360.
Per-credit charge: $470.
Room and board: $9,718.

FINANCIAL AID PICTURE (2007-2008)
Students with need: Out of 487 full-time freshmen who applied for aid, 487 were judged to have need. Of these, 487 received aid, and 322 had their full need met.
Students without need: This college awards aid only to students with need.

FINANCIAL AID PROCEDURES
Forms required: FAFSA.
Dates and Deadlines: No deadline. Applicants notified on a rolling basis; must reply within 2 week(s) of notification.
Transfers: Priority date 3/7; closing date 6/1. Must reply within 2 week(s) of notification.

CONTACT
Katharine Markert, Director of Financial Aid
One Neumann Drive, Aston, PA 19014-1298
(610) 558-5520

New Castle School of Trades

Pulaski, Pennsylvania
www.ncstrades.com Federal Code: 007780

2-year for-profit technical college in rural community.
Enrollment: 385 undergrads.

BASIC COSTS (2008-2009)
Additional info: Tuition varies by program from $4,838 to $16,950. Costs include fees. Books and tool expenses up to $2,672.

FINANCIAL AID PICTURE (2007-2008)
Students with need: Need-based aid available for full-time and part-time students.

CONTACT
Trudy Sotter, Financial Aid
4164 US 422, Pulaski, PA 16143-9721
(724) 964-8811

Newport Business Institute: Lower Burrell

Lower Burrell, Pennsylvania
www.nbi.edu Federal Code: 004901

2-year for-profit business college in small town.
Enrollment: 61 undergrads.
Selectivity: Open admission.

BASIC COSTS (2008-2009)
Tuition and fees: $10,950.

FINANCIAL AID PICTURE
Students with need: Need-based aid available for full-time and part-time students.
Students without need: No-need awards available for academics, leadership.

FINANCIAL AID PROCEDURES
Forms required: FAFSA, state aid form.
Dates and Deadlines: No deadline. Applicants notified on a rolling basis starting 5/1.

CONTACT
Rosemary Leipertz, Director of Financial Aid
945 Greensburg Road, Lower Burrell, PA 15068
(724) 339-7542

Northampton Community College

Bethlehem, Pennsylvania
www.northampton.edu Federal Code: 007191

2-year public community college in small city.
Enrollment: 10,032 undergrads, 55% part-time. 1,714 full-time freshmen.
Selectivity: Open admission; but selective for some programs.

BASIC COSTS (2008-2009)
Tuition and fees: $3,090; out-of-district residents $5,340; out-of-state residents $7,590.
Per-credit charge: $75; out-of-district residents $150; out-of-state residents $225.
Room and board: $6,658.
Additional info: Tuition/fee waivers available for unemployed or children of unemployed.

FINANCIAL AID PICTURE (2008-2009)
Students with need: Average financial aid package for all full-time undergraduates was $3,530; for part-time $1,834. 71% awarded as scholarships/grants, 29% awarded as loans/jobs. Work study available nights, weekends, and for part-time students.
Students without need: No-need awards available for academics, alumni affiliation, art, leadership, minority status, music/drama.

FINANCIAL AID PROCEDURES
Forms required: FAFSA, institutional form.
Dates and Deadlines: Priority date 3/31; no closing date. Applicants notified on a rolling basis starting 6/1; must reply within 2 week(s) of notification.

CONTACT
Cindy King, Director of Financial Aid
3835 Green Pond Road, Bethlehem, PA 18020
(610) 861-5510

Oakbridge Academy of Arts

Lower Burrell, Pennsylvania
www.oaa.edu Federal Code: 015063

2-year for-profit visual arts college in large town.
Enrollment: 49 undergrads. 24 full-time freshmen.
Selectivity: Open admission.

BASIC COSTS (2008-2009)
Tuition and fees: $10,650.

FINANCIAL AID PICTURE
Students with need: Need-based aid available for full-time and part-time students.
Students without need: This college awards aid only to students with need.
Scholarships offered: Jeanne H. Mullen art scholarship; half tuition; based on portfolio; 2 awarded per year.

FINANCIAL AID PROCEDURES
Forms required: FAFSA, state aid form.
Dates and Deadlines: Closing date 5/1. Applicants notified on a rolling basis; must reply by 5/1.

CONTACT

Rosemary Leipertz, Financial Aid Director
1250 Greensburg Road, Lower Burrell, PA 15068
(724) 335-5336

Orleans Technical Institute - Center City Campus

Philadelphia, Pennsylvania
www.orleanstech.edu

2-year private technical and career college in very large city.
Enrollment: 82 full-time undergrads.
Selectivity: Open admission.

BASIC COSTS (2008-2009)

Additional info: Tuition for full associate program (3 years, including internship) is $33,000.

FINANCIAL AID PICTURE

Students with need: Need-based aid available for full-time and part-time students.

FINANCIAL AID PROCEDURES

Forms required: FAFSA, institutional form.
Dates and Deadlines: No deadline. Applicants notified on a rolling basis.

CONTACT

Latanya Byrd, Financial Aid Director
2770 Red Lion Road, Philadelphia, PA 19114
(215) 728-4702

Peirce College

Philadelphia, Pennsylvania
www.peirce.edu Federal Code: 003309

4-year private business and technical college in very large city.
Enrollment: 2,033 undergrads, 61% part-time. 9 full-time freshmen.
Selectivity: Open admission.

BASIC COSTS (2008-2009)

Tuition and fees: $14,350.
Per-credit charge: $445.

FINANCIAL AID PICTURE (2007-2008)

Students with need: Out of 6 full-time freshmen who applied for aid, 6 were judged to have need. Of these, 6 received aid. Average financial aid package met 46% of need; average scholarship/grant was $4,761; average loan was $3,908. For part-time students, average financial aid package was $5,933.
Students without need: No-need awards available for alumni affiliation, leadership.
Cumulative student debt: 85% of graduating class had student loans; average debt was $18,724.
Additional info: Tuition discounts available for US students serving in US military and in protect-and-serve fields.

FINANCIAL AID PROCEDURES

Forms required: FAFSA.
Dates and Deadlines: Priority date 5/1; no closing date. Applicants notified on a rolling basis; must reply within 3 week(s) of notification.

CONTACT

Lisa Gargiulo, Manager, Student Financial Services
1420 Pine Street, Philadelphia, PA 19102-4699
(888) 467-3472 ext. 9370

Penn State Abington

Abington, Pennsylvania
www.abington.psu.edu Federal Code: 003329

4-year public branch campus college in small city.
Enrollment: 2,857 undergrads, 11% part-time. 864 full-time freshmen.
Selectivity: Admits over 75% of applicants.

BASIC COSTS (2008-2009)

Tuition and fees: $11,800; out-of-state residents $17,590.
Per-credit charge: $445; out-of-state residents $700.

FINANCIAL AID PICTURE (2007-2008)

Students with need: Out of 746 full-time freshmen who applied for aid, 560 were judged to have need. Of these, 544 received aid, and 27 had their full need met. Average financial aid package met 67% of need; average scholarship/grant was $6,519; average loan was $3,183. For part-time students, average financial aid package was $5,935.
Students without need: 50 full-time freshmen who did not demonstrate need for aid received scholarships/grants; average award was $1,466. No-need awards available for academics, alumni affiliation, athletics, ROTC.
Cumulative student debt: 69% of graduating class had student loans; average debt was $26,800.

FINANCIAL AID PROCEDURES

Forms required: FAFSA.
Dates and Deadlines: Priority date 2/15; no closing date. Applicants notified on a rolling basis starting 3/1.
Transfers: Closing date 5/1. Schools required to obtain student aid information through National Student Loan Data System (NSLDS).

CONTACT

Anna Griswold, Assistant Vice Provost for Student Aid
201 Shields Building, University Park, PA 16802-1294
(814) 865-6301

Penn State Altoona

Altoona, Pennsylvania
www.aa.psu.edu Federal Code: 003329

4-year public branch campus college in small city.
Enrollment: 3,870 undergrads, 5% part-time. 1,483 full-time freshmen.
Selectivity: Admits 50 to 75% of applicants.

BASIC COSTS (2008-2009)

Tuition and fees: $12,182; out-of-state residents $18,270.
Per-credit charge: $479; out-of-state residents $732.
Room and board: $8,270.

FINANCIAL AID PICTURE (2007-2008)

Students with need: Out of 1,221 full-time freshmen who applied for aid, 936 were judged to have need. Of these, 902 received aid, and 36 had their full need met. Average financial aid package met 59% of need; average scholarship/grant was $5,676; average loan was $3,553. For part-time students, average financial aid package was $6,395.
Students without need: 34 full-time freshmen who did not demonstrate need for aid received scholarships/grants; average award was $894. No-need awards available for academics, alumni affiliation, athletics, ROTC.
Cumulative student debt: 69% of graduating class had student loans; average debt was $26,800.

FINANCIAL AID PROCEDURES

Forms required: FAFSA.
Dates and Deadlines: Priority date 2/15; no closing date. Applicants notified on a rolling basis starting 3/1.
Transfers: Closing date 5/1. Schools required to obtain student aid information through National Student Loan Data System (NSLDS).

CONTACT

Anna Griswold, Assistant Vice Provost for Student Aid
201 Shields Building, University Park, PA 16802-1294
(814) 865-6301

Penn State Beaver

Monaca, Pennsylvania
www.br.psu.edu Federal Code: 003329

4-year public branch campus college in small town.
Enrollment: 711 undergrads, 5% part-time. 300 full-time freshmen.
Selectivity: Admits over 75% of applicants.

BASIC COSTS (2008-2009)

Tuition and fees: $11,800; out-of-state residents $17,590.
Per-credit charge: $445; out-of-state residents $700.
Room and board: $8,270.

FINANCIAL AID PICTURE (2007-2008)

Students with need: Out of 257 full-time freshmen who applied for aid, 204 were judged to have need. Of these, 199 received aid, and 12 had their full need met. Average financial aid package met 64% of need; average scholarship/grant was $6,024; average loan was $3,310. For part-time students, average financial aid package was $6,081.
Students without need: 29 full-time freshmen who did not demonstrate need for aid received scholarships/grants; average award was $2,155. No-need awards available for academics, alumni affiliation, athletics, ROTC.
Cumulative student debt: 69% of graduating class had student loans; average debt was $26,800.

FINANCIAL AID PROCEDURES

Forms required: FAFSA.
Dates and Deadlines: Priority date 2/15; no closing date. Applicants notified on a rolling basis starting 3/1.
Transfers: Closing date 5/1. Schools required to obtain student aid information through National Student Loan Data System (NSLDS).

CONTACT

Anna Griswold, Assistant Vice Provost for Student Aid
201 Shields Building, University Park, PA 16802-1294
(814) 865-6301

Penn State Berks

Reading, Pennsylvania
www.bk.psu.edu Federal Code: 003329

4-year public branch campus college in small city.
Enrollment: 2,576 undergrads, 7% part-time. 919 full-time freshmen.
Selectivity: Admits over 75% of applicants.

BASIC COSTS (2008-2009)

Tuition and fees: $12,282; out-of-state residents $18,370.
Per-credit charge: $479; out-of-state residents $732.
Room and board: $8,990.

FINANCIAL AID PICTURE (2007-2008)

Students with need: Out of 754 full-time freshmen who applied for aid, 552 were judged to have need. Of these, 530 received aid, and 24 had their full need met. Average financial aid package met 58% of need; average scholarship/grant was $5,493; average loan was $3,392. For part-time students, average financial aid package was $5,889.
Students without need: 14 full-time freshmen who did not demonstrate need for aid received scholarships/grants; average award was $1,242. No-need awards available for academics, alumni affiliation, athletics, ROTC.
Cumulative student debt: 69% of graduating class had student loans; average debt was $26,800.

FINANCIAL AID PROCEDURES

Forms required: FAFSA.
Dates and Deadlines: Priority date 2/15; no closing date. Applicants notified on a rolling basis starting 3/1.
Transfers: Closing date 5/1. Schools required to obtain student aid information through National Student Loan Data System (NSLDS).

CONTACT

Anna Griswold, Assistant Vice Provost for Student Aid
201 Shields Building, University Park, PA 16802-1294
(814) 865-6301

Penn State Brandywine

Media, Pennsylvania
www.de.psu.edu Federal Code: 006922

4-year public branch campus college in small town.
Enrollment: 1,439 undergrads, 9% part-time. 425 full-time freshmen.
Selectivity: Admits over 75% of applicants.

BASIC COSTS (2008-2009)

Tuition and fees: $11,700; out-of-state residents $17,490.
Per-credit charge: $445; out-of-state residents $700.

FINANCIAL AID PICTURE (2007-2008)

Students with need: Out of 346 full-time freshmen who applied for aid, 246 were judged to have need. Of these, 240 received aid, and 12 had their full need met. Average financial aid package met 66% of need; average scholarship/grant was $5,542; average loan was $3,131. For part-time students, average financial aid package was $5,806.
Students without need: 66 full-time freshmen who did not demonstrate need for aid received scholarships/grants; average award was $2,722. No-need awards available for academics, alumni affiliation, athletics, ROTC.
Cumulative student debt: 69% of graduating class had student loans; average debt was $26,800.

FINANCIAL AID PROCEDURES

Forms required: FAFSA.
Dates and Deadlines: Priority date 2/15; no closing date. Applicants notified on a rolling basis starting 3/1.
Transfers: Closing date 5/1. Schools required to obtain student aid information through National Student Loan Data System (NSLDS).

CONTACT

Anna Griswold, Assistant Vice Provost for Student Aid
201 Shields Building, University Park, PA 16802-1294
(814) 865-6301

Penn State DuBois

DuBois, Pennsylvania
www.ds.psu.edu Federal Code: 003335

4-year public branch campus college in small town.
Enrollment: 769 undergrads, 15% part-time. 220 full-time freshmen.
Selectivity: Admits over 75% of applicants.

BASIC COSTS (2008-2009)

Tuition and fees: $11,680; out-of-state residents $17,470.
Per-credit charge: $445; out-of-state residents $700.

FINANCIAL AID PICTURE (2007-2008)

Students with need: Out of 204 full-time freshmen who applied for aid, 189 were judged to have need. Of these, 187 received aid, and 14 had their full need met. Average financial aid package met 66% of need; average scholarship/grant was $5,908; average loan was $3,252. For part-time students, average financial aid package was $6,679.

Students without need: 2 full-time freshmen who did not demonstrate need for aid received scholarships/grants; average award was $2,125. No-need awards available for academics, alumni affiliation, athletics, ROTC.
Cumulative student debt: 69% of graduating class had student loans; average debt was $26,800.

FINANCIAL AID PROCEDURES
Forms required: FAFSA.
Dates and Deadlines: Priority date 2/15; no closing date. Applicants notified on a rolling basis starting 3/1.
Transfers: Closing date 5/1. Schools required to obtain student aid information through National Student Loan Data System (NSLDS).

CONTACT
Anna Griswold, Assistant Vice Provost for Student Aid
201 Shields Building, University Park, PA 16802-1294
(814) 865-6301

Penn State Erie, The Behrend College
Erie, Pennsylvania
www.pserie.psu.edu Federal Code: 003329

4-year public branch campus college in small city.
Enrollment: 4,029 undergrads, 4% part-time. 1,155 full-time freshmen.
Selectivity: Admits over 75% of applicants.

BASIC COSTS (2008-2009)
Tuition and fees: $12,282; out-of-state residents $18,370.
Per-credit charge: $479; out-of-state residents $732.
Room and board: $8,270.

FINANCIAL AID PICTURE (2007-2008)
Students with need: Out of 1,026 full-time freshmen who applied for aid, 843 were judged to have need. Of these, 819 received aid, and 39 had their full need met. Average financial aid package met 62% of need; average scholarship/grant was $5,822; average loan was $3,712. For part-time students, average financial aid package was $5,917.
Students without need: 24 full-time freshmen who did not demonstrate need for aid received scholarships/grants; average award was $1,747. No-need awards available for academics, alumni affiliation, athletics, ROTC.
Cumulative student debt: 69% of graduating class had student loans; average debt was $26,800.

FINANCIAL AID PROCEDURES
Forms required: FAFSA.
Dates and Deadlines: Priority date 2/15; no closing date. Applicants notified on a rolling basis starting 3/1.
Transfers: Closing date 5/1. Schools required to obtain student aid information through National Student Loan Data System (NSLDS).

CONTACT
Anna Griswold, Assistant Vice Provost for Student Aid
201 Shields Building, University Park, PA 16801-1294
(814) 865-6301

Penn State Fayette, The Eberly Campus
Uniontown, Pennsylvania
www.fe.psu.edu Federal Code: 003329

4-year public branch campus college in large town.
Enrollment: 899 undergrads, 19% part-time. 236 full-time freshmen.
Selectivity: Admits over 75% of applicants.

BASIC COSTS (2008-2009)
Tuition and fees: $11,700; out-of-state residents $17,490.
Per-credit charge: $445; out-of-state residents $700.

FINANCIAL AID PICTURE (2007-2008)
Students with need: Out of 224 full-time freshmen who applied for aid, 195 were judged to have need. Of these, 194 received aid, and 18 had their full need met. Average financial aid package met 68% of need; average scholarship/grant was $5,724; average loan was $3,362. For part-time students, average financial aid package was $7,919.
Students without need: 17 full-time freshmen who did not demonstrate need for aid received scholarships/grants; average award was $2,164. No-need awards available for academics, alumni affiliation, athletics, ROTC.
Cumulative student debt: 69% of graduating class had student loans; average debt was $26,800.

FINANCIAL AID PROCEDURES
Forms required: FAFSA.
Dates and Deadlines: Priority date 2/15; no closing date. Applicants notified on a rolling basis starting 3/1.
Transfers: Closing date 5/1. Schools required to obtain student aid information through National Student Loan Data System (NSLDS).

CONTACT
Anna Griswold, Assistant Vice Provost for Student Aid
201 Shields Building, University Park, PA 16802-1294
(814) 865-6301

Penn State Greater Allegheny
McKeesport, Pennsylvania
www.mk.psu.edu Federal Code: 003329

4-year public branch campus college in large town.
Enrollment: 643 undergrads, 6% part-time. 269 full-time freshmen.
Selectivity: Admits over 75% of applicants.

BASIC COSTS (2008-2009)
Tuition and fees: $11,800; out-of-state residents $17,590.
Per-credit charge: $445; out-of-state residents $700.
Room and board: $8,270.

FINANCIAL AID PICTURE (2007-2008)
Students with need: Out of 247 full-time freshmen who applied for aid, 214 were judged to have need. Of these, 211 received aid, and 11 had their full need met. Average financial aid package met 65% of need; average scholarship/grant was $6,037; average loan was $3,357. For part-time students, average financial aid package was $5,451.
Students without need: 20 full-time freshmen who did not demonstrate need for aid received scholarships/grants; average award was $2,899. No-need awards available for academics, alumni affiliation, athletics, ROTC.
Cumulative student debt: 69% of graduating class had student loans; average debt was $26,800.

FINANCIAL AID PROCEDURES
Forms required: FAFSA.
Dates and Deadlines: Priority date 2/15; no closing date. Applicants notified on a rolling basis starting 3/1.
Transfers: Closing date 5/1. Schools required to obtain student aid information through National Student Loan Data System (NSLDS).

CONTACT
Anna Griswold, Assistant Vice Provost for Student Aid
201 Shields Building, University Park, PA 16802-1294
(814) 865-6301

Penn State Harrisburg

Middletown, Pennsylvania
www.hbg.psu.edu Federal Code: 003329

4-year public branch campus college in small town.
Enrollment: 2,420 undergrads, 16% part-time. 418 full-time freshmen.
Selectivity: Admits 50 to 75% of applicants.

BASIC COSTS (2008-2009)

Tuition and fees: $12,282; out-of-state residents $18,370.
Per-credit charge: $479; out-of-state residents $732.
Room and board: $9,380.

FINANCIAL AID PICTURE (2007-2008)

Students with need: Out of 348 full-time freshmen who applied for aid, 247 were judged to have need. Of these, 237 received aid, and 17 had their full need met. Average financial aid package met 55% of need; average scholarship/grant was $6,129; average loan was $3,578. For part-time students, average financial aid package was $6,594.
Students without need: 4 full-time freshmen who did not demonstrate need for aid received scholarships/grants; average award was $2,425. No-need awards available for academics, alumni affiliation, athletics, ROTC.
Cumulative student debt: 69% of graduating class had student loans; average debt was $26,800.

FINANCIAL AID PROCEDURES

Forms required: FAFSA.
Dates and Deadlines: Priority date 2/15; no closing date. Applicants notified on a rolling basis starting 3/1.
Transfers: Closing date 5/1. Schools required to obtain student aid information through National Student Loan Data System (NSLDS).

CONTACT

Anna Griswold, Assistant Vice Provost for Student Aid
201 Shields Building, University Park, PA 16802-1294
(814) 865-6301

Penn State Hazleton

Hazleton, Pennsylvania
www.hn.psu.edu Federal Code: 003338

4-year public branch campus college in large town.
Enrollment: 1,186 undergrads, 3% part-time. 566 full-time freshmen.
Selectivity: Admits over 75% of applicants.

BASIC COSTS (2008-2009)

Tuition and fees: $11,600; out-of-state residents $17,390.
Per-credit charge: $445; out-of-state residents $700.
Room and board: $8,270.

FINANCIAL AID PICTURE (2007-2008)

Students with need: Out of 507 full-time freshmen who applied for aid, 408 were judged to have need. Of these, 394 received aid, and 18 had their full need met. Average financial aid package met 61% of need; average scholarship/grant was $5,607; average loan was $3,340. For part-time students, average financial aid package was $5,123.
Students without need: 50 full-time freshmen who did not demonstrate need for aid received scholarships/grants; average award was $2,579. No-need awards available for academics, alumni affiliation, athletics, ROTC.
Cumulative student debt: 69% of graduating class had student loans; average debt was $26,800.

FINANCIAL AID PROCEDURES

Forms required: FAFSA.
Dates and Deadlines: Priority date 2/15; no closing date. Applicants notified on a rolling basis starting 3/1.
Transfers: Closing date 5/1. Schools required to obtain student aid information through National Student Loan Data System (NSLDS).

CONTACT

Anna Griswold, Assistant Vice Provost for Student Aid
201 Shields Building, University Park, PA 16802-1294
(814) 865-6301

Penn State Lehigh Valley

Fogelsville, Pennsylvania
www.lv.psu.edu Federal Code: 003329

4-year public branch campus college in rural community.
Enrollment: 676 undergrads, 13% part-time. 239 full-time freshmen.
Selectivity: Admits over 75% of applicants.

BASIC COSTS (2008-2009)

Tuition and fees: $11,750; out-of-state residents $17,540.
Per-credit charge: $445; out-of-state residents $700.

FINANCIAL AID PICTURE (2007-2008)

Students with need: Out of 201 full-time freshmen who applied for aid, 149 were judged to have need. Of these, 141 received aid, and 13 had their full need met. Average financial aid package met 63% of need; average scholarship/grant was $5,936; average loan was $3,537. For part-time students, average financial aid package was $7,907.
Students without need: 20 full-time freshmen who did not demonstrate need for aid received scholarships/grants; average award was $2,327. No-need awards available for academics, alumni affiliation, athletics, ROTC.
Cumulative student debt: 69% of graduating class had student loans; average debt was $26,800.

FINANCIAL AID PROCEDURES

Forms required: FAFSA.
Dates and Deadlines: Priority date 2/15; no closing date. Applicants notified on a rolling basis starting 3/1.
Transfers: Closing date 5/1. Schools required to obtain student aid information through National Student Loan Data System (NSLDS).

CONTACT

Anna Griswold, Assistant Vice Provost for Student Aid
201 Shields Building, University Park, PA 16802-1294
(814) 865-6301

Penn State Mont Alto

Mont Alto, Pennsylvania
www.ma.psu.edu Federal Code: 003340

4-year public branch campus college in rural community.
Enrollment: 1,025 undergrads, 22% part-time. 353 full-time freshmen.
Selectivity: Admits over 75% of applicants.

BASIC COSTS (2008-2009)

Tuition and fees: $11,800; out-of-state residents $17,590.
Per-credit charge: $445; out-of-state residents $700.
Room and board: $8,270.

FINANCIAL AID PICTURE (2007-2008)

Students with need: Out of 309 full-time freshmen who applied for aid, 241 were judged to have need. Of these, 238 received aid, and 23 had their full need met. Average financial aid package met 61% of need; average scholarship/grant was $4,650; average loan was $3,387. For part-time students, average financial aid package was $6,875.
Students without need: 32 full-time freshmen who did not demonstrate need for aid received scholarships/grants; average award was $3,004. No-need awards available for academics, alumni affiliation, athletics, ROTC.

Cumulative student debt: 69% of graduating class had student loans; average debt was $26,800.

FINANCIAL AID PROCEDURES

Forms required: FAFSA.

Dates and Deadlines: Priority date 2/15; no closing date. Applicants notified on a rolling basis starting 3/1.

Transfers: Closing date 5/1. Schools required to obtain student aid information through National Student Loan Data System (NSLDS).

CONTACT

Anna Griswold, Assistant Vice Provost for Student Aid
201 Shields Building, University Park, PA 16802-1294
(814) 865-6301

Penn State New Kensington

New Kensington, Pennsylvania
www.nk.psu.edu Federal Code: 003329

4-year public branch campus college in large town.

Enrollment: 707 undergrads, 18% part-time. 204 full-time freshmen.

Selectivity: Admits over 75% of applicants.

BASIC COSTS (2008-2009)

Tuition and fees: $11,700; out-of-state residents $17,490.

Per-credit charge: $445; out-of-state residents $700.

FINANCIAL AID PICTURE (2007-2008)

Students with need: Out of 190 full-time freshmen who applied for aid, 152 were judged to have need. Of these, 149 received aid, and 14 had their full need met. Average financial aid package met 65% of need; average scholarship/grant was $4,987; average loan was $3,067. For part-time students, average financial aid package was $6,714.

Students without need: 22 full-time freshmen who did not demonstrate need for aid received scholarships/grants; average award was $2,273. No-need awards available for academics, alumni affiliation, athletics, ROTC.

Cumulative student debt: 69% of graduating class had student loans; average debt was $26,800.

FINANCIAL AID PROCEDURES

Forms required: FAFSA.

Dates and Deadlines: Priority date 2/15; no closing date. Applicants notified on a rolling basis starting 3/1.

Transfers: Closing date 5/1. Schools required to obtain student aid information through National Student Loan Data System (NSLDS).

CONTACT

Anna Griswold, Assistant Vice Provost for Student Aid
201 Shields Building, University Park, PA 16802-1294
(814) 865-6301

Penn State Schuylkill

Schuylkill Haven, Pennsylvania
www.sl.psu.edu Federal Code: 003343

4-year public branch campus college in small town.

Enrollment: 905 undergrads, 9% part-time. 333 full-time freshmen.

Selectivity: Admits over 75% of applicants.

BASIC COSTS (2008-2009)

Tuition and fees: $11,700; out-of-state residents $17,490.

Per-credit charge: $445; out-of-state residents $700.

FINANCIAL AID PICTURE (2007-2008)

Students with need: Out of 315 full-time freshmen who applied for aid, 270 were judged to have need. Of these, 267 received aid, and 15 had their full need met. Average financial aid package met 59% of need; average scholarship/grant was $6,478; average loan was $3,448. For part-time students, average financial aid package was $5,790.

Students without need: 12 full-time freshmen who did not demonstrate need for aid received scholarships/grants; average award was $1,893. No-need awards available for academics, alumni affiliation, athletics, ROTC.

Cumulative student debt: 69% of graduating class had student loans; average debt was $26,800.

FINANCIAL AID PROCEDURES

Forms required: FAFSA.

Dates and Deadlines: Priority date 2/15; no closing date. Applicants notified on a rolling basis starting 3/1.

Transfers: Closing date 5/1. Schools required to obtain student aid information through National Student Loan Data System (NSLDS).

CONTACT

Anna Griswold, Assistant Vice Provost for Student Aid
201 Shields Building, University Park, PA 16802-1294
(814) 865-6301

Penn State Shenango

Sharon, Pennsylvania
www.shenango.psu.edu Federal Code: 003329

4-year public branch campus college in large town.

Enrollment: 641 undergrads, 28% part-time. 134 full-time freshmen.

Selectivity: Admits over 75% of applicants.

BASIC COSTS (2008-2009)

Tuition and fees: $11,600; out-of-state residents $17,390.

Per-credit charge: $445; out-of-state residents $700.

FINANCIAL AID PICTURE (2007-2008)

Students with need: Out of 125 full-time freshmen who applied for aid, 111 were judged to have need. Of these, 111 received aid, and 6 had their full need met. Average financial aid package met 64% of need; average scholarship/grant was $5,651; average loan was $3,405. For part-time students, average financial aid package was $7,037.

Students without need: 12 full-time freshmen who did not demonstrate need for aid received scholarships/grants; average award was $2,092. No-need awards available for academics, alumni affiliation, athletics, ROTC.

Cumulative student debt: 69% of graduating class had student loans; average debt was $26,800.

FINANCIAL AID PROCEDURES

Forms required: FAFSA.

Dates and Deadlines: Priority date 2/15; no closing date. Applicants notified on a rolling basis starting 3/1.

Transfers: Closing date 5/1. Schools required to obtain student aid information through National Student Loan Data System (NSLDS).

CONTACT

Anna Griswold, Assistant Vice Provost for Student Aid
201 Shields Building, University Park, PA 16802-1294
(814) 865-6301

Penn State University Park

University Park, Pennsylvania
www.psu.edu Federal Code: 003329

4-year public university in large town.

Enrollment: 37,171 undergrads, 2% part-time. 6,483 full-time freshmen.

Selectivity: Admits 50 to 75% of applicants.

BASIC COSTS (2008-2009)

Tuition and fees: $13,706; out-of-state residents $24,940.
Per-credit charge: $542; out-of-state residents $1,010.
Room and board: $8,270.

FINANCIAL AID PICTURE (2007-2008)

Students with need: Out of 4,805 full-time freshmen who applied for aid, 3,110 were judged to have need. Of these, 2,929 received aid, and 242 had their full need met. Average financial aid package met 61% of need; average scholarship/grant was $6,266; average loan was $3,492. For part-time students, average financial aid package was $7,203.
Students without need: 410 full-time freshmen who did not demonstrate need for aid received scholarships/grants; average award was $3,878. No-need awards available for academics, alumni affiliation, athletics, ROTC.
Scholarships offered: 120 full-time freshmen received athletic scholarships; average amount $18,020.
Cumulative student debt: 69% of graduating class had student loans; average debt was $26,800.

FINANCIAL AID PROCEDURES

Forms required: FAFSA.
Dates and Deadlines: Priority date 2/15; no closing date. Applicants notified on a rolling basis starting 3/1.
Transfers: Closing date 5/1. Schools required to obtain student aid information through National Student Loan Data System (NSLDS).

CONTACT

Anna Griswold, Assistant Vice Provost for Student Aid
201 Shields Building, University Park, PA 16802-1294
(814) 865-6301

Penn State Wilkes-Barre

Lehman, Pennsylvania
www.wb.psu.edu Federal Code: 003329

4-year public branch campus college in small city.
Enrollment: 534 undergrads, 9% part-time. 173 full-time freshmen.
Selectivity: Admits over 75% of applicants.

BASIC COSTS (2008-2009)

Tuition and fees: $11,700; out-of-state residents $17,490.
Per-credit charge: $445; out-of-state residents $700.

FINANCIAL AID PICTURE (2007-2008)

Students with need: Out of 165 full-time freshmen who applied for aid, 125 were judged to have need. Of these, 124 received aid, and 8 had their full need met. Average financial aid package met 64% of need; average scholarship/grant was $5,458; average loan was $3,042. For part-time students, average financial aid package was $5,300.
Students without need: 25 full-time freshmen who did not demonstrate need for aid received scholarships/grants; average award was $2,925. No-need awards available for academics, alumni affiliation, athletics, ROTC.
Cumulative student debt: 69% of graduating class had student loans; average debt was $26,800.

FINANCIAL AID PROCEDURES

Forms required: FAFSA.
Dates and Deadlines: Priority date 2/15; no closing date. Applicants notified on a rolling basis starting 3/1.
Transfers: Closing date 5/1. Schools required to obtain student aid information through National Student Loan Data System (NSLDS).

CONTACT

Anna Griswold, Assistant Vice Provost for Student Aid
201 Shields Building, University Park, PA 16802-1294
(814) 865-6301

Penn State Worthington Scranton

Dunmore, Pennsylvania
www.sn.psu.edu Federal Code: 003344

4-year public branch campus college in large town.
Enrollment: 1,222 undergrads, 16% part-time. 294 full-time freshmen.
Selectivity: Admits over 75% of applicants.

BASIC COSTS (2008-2009)

Tuition and fees: $11,660; out-of-state residents $17,450.
Per-credit charge: $445; out-of-state residents $700.

FINANCIAL AID PICTURE (2007-2008)

Students with need: Out of 275 full-time freshmen who applied for aid, 226 were judged to have need. Of these, 221 received aid, and 16 had their full need met. Average financial aid package met 65% of need; average scholarship/grant was $5,185; average loan was $3,220. For part-time students, average financial aid package was $6,357.
Students without need: 24 full-time freshmen who did not demonstrate need for aid received scholarships/grants; average award was $2,715. No-need awards available for academics, alumni affiliation, athletics, ROTC.
Cumulative student debt: 69% of graduating class had student loans; average debt was $26,800.

FINANCIAL AID PROCEDURES

Forms required: FAFSA.
Dates and Deadlines: Priority date 2/15; no closing date. Applicants notified on a rolling basis starting 3/1.
Transfers: Closing date 5/1. Schools required to obtain student aid information through National Student Loan Data System (NSLDS).

CONTACT

Anna Griswold, Assistant Vice Provost for Student Aid
201 Shields Building, University Park, PA 16802-1294
(814) 865-6301

Penn State York

York, Pennsylvania
www.yk.psu.edu Federal Code: 003347

4-year public branch campus college in large town.
Enrollment: 1,149 undergrads, 24% part-time. 321 full-time freshmen.
Selectivity: Admits over 75% of applicants.

BASIC COSTS (2008-2009)

Tuition and fees: $11,660; out-of-state residents $17,450.
Per-credit charge: $445; out-of-state residents $700.

FINANCIAL AID PICTURE (2007-2008)

Students with need: Out of 274 full-time freshmen who applied for aid, 205 were judged to have need. Of these, 200 received aid, and 12 had their full need met. Average financial aid package met 58% of need; average scholarship/grant was $4,878; average loan was $3,200. For part-time students, average financial aid package was $6,972.
Students without need: 31 full-time freshmen who did not demonstrate need for aid received scholarships/grants; average award was $2,834. No-need awards available for academics, alumni affiliation, athletics, ROTC.
Cumulative student debt: 69% of graduating class had student loans; average debt was $26,800.

FINANCIAL AID PROCEDURES

Forms required: FAFSA.
Dates and Deadlines: Priority date 2/15; no closing date. Applicants notified on a rolling basis starting 3/1.
Transfers: Closing date 5/1. Schools required to obtain student aid information through National Student Loan Data System (NSLDS).

CONTACT

Anna Griswold, Assistant Vice Provost for Student Aid
201 Shields Building, University Park, PA 16802-1294
(814) 865-6301

Pennsylvania College of Technology

Williamsport, Pennsylvania
www.pct.edu Federal Code: 003395

4-year public technical college in small city.
Enrollment: 6,427 undergrads, 13% part-time. 1,435 full-time freshmen.
Selectivity: Open admission; but selective for some programs.

BASIC COSTS (2008-2009)

Tuition and fees: $11,790; out-of-state residents $14,820.
Per-credit charge: $334; out-of-state residents $435.
Room and board: $8,250.

FINANCIAL AID PICTURE (2007-2008)

Students with need: Need-based aid available for full-time and part-time students. Work study available nights, weekends, and for part-time students.
Students without need: No-need awards available for academics, alumni affiliation.

FINANCIAL AID PROCEDURES

Forms required: FAFSA, institutional form.
Dates and Deadlines: Priority date 4/1; no closing date. Applicants notified on a rolling basis starting 6/1; must reply by 7/1 or within 4 week(s) of notification.

CONTACT

Candace Baran, Director of Financial Aid
One College Avenue, Williamsport, PA 17701
(570) 327-4766

Pennsylvania Culinary Institute

Pittsburgh, Pennsylvania
www.paculinary.com Federal Code: 030068

2-year for-profit culinary school and technical college in large city.
Enrollment: 1,092 full-time undergrads.

BASIC COSTS (2008-2009)

Additional info: Total costs vary by program: Culinary Arts $41,885; Patisserie & Baking $37,485; Hospitality & Restaurant Management $35,518.

FINANCIAL AID PICTURE (2008-2009)

Students with need: Need-based aid available for full-time students.
Students without need: This college awards aid only to students with need.

FINANCIAL AID PROCEDURES

Forms required: FAFSA, institutional form.
Dates and Deadlines: No deadline. Applicants notified on a rolling basis.

CONTACT

Paul Steele, Director of Student Finance
717 Liberty Avenue, Pittsburgh, PA 15222
(412) 566-2433

Pennsylvania Highlands Community College

Johnstown, Pennsylvania
www.pennhighlands.edu Federal Code: 031804

2-year public community college in large town.
Enrollment: 972 undergrads, 32% part-time. 206 full-time freshmen.
Selectivity: Open admission.

BASIC COSTS (2008-2009)

Tuition and fees: $3,270; out-of-district residents $5,860; out-of-state residents $8,450.
Per-credit charge: $86; out-of-district residents $172; out-of-state residents $258.
Additional info: Students in Blair, Bedford and Somerset counties pay tuition of $3,890 per year. Students outside Cambria County pay additional fee of $210 per year.

FINANCIAL AID PICTURE

Students with need: Need-based aid available for full-time and part-time students. Work study available nights.
Students without need: No-need awards available for academics, state/district residency.

FINANCIAL AID PROCEDURES

Forms required: FAFSA.
Dates and Deadlines: Closing date 4/1. Applicants notified on a rolling basis; must reply by 8/1.

CONTACT

Brenda Coughenour, Director of Financial Aid
101 Community College Way, Johnstown, PA 15904
(814) 262-6454

Pennsylvania Institute of Technology

Media, Pennsylvania
www.pit.edu Federal Code: 010998

2-year private technical college in small town.
Enrollment: 768 undergrads, 24% part-time. 249 full-time freshmen.
Selectivity: Open admission; but selective for some programs.

BASIC COSTS (2009-2010)

Tuition and fees: $10,350.
Per-credit charge: $315.

FINANCIAL AID PICTURE

Students with need: Need-based aid available for full-time and part-time students. Work study available nights, weekends, and for part-time students.
Students without need: No-need awards available for academics, leadership.
Scholarships offered: Presidential Scholarship; half tuition; for current high school graduates; SAT scores required.

FINANCIAL AID PROCEDURES

Forms required: FAFSA, institutional form.
Dates and Deadlines: Closing date 8/1. Applicants notified on a rolling basis starting 7/1.
Transfers: No deadline.

CONTACT

Crystal Donnelly, Director of Financial Aid
800 Manchester Avenue, Media, PA 19063-4098
(610) 892-1536

Philadelphia Biblical University

Langhorne, Pennsylvania
www.pbu.edu Federal Code: 003351

4-year private university and Bible college in small town, affiliated with Protestant Evangelical tradition.
Enrollment: 1,049 undergrads, 6% part-time. 185 full-time freshmen.
Selectivity: Admits over 75% of applicants.

BASIC COSTS (2009-2010)

Tuition and fees: $19,272.
Per-credit charge: $560.
Room and board: $7,650.

FINANCIAL AID PICTURE (2008-2009)

Students with need: Out of 151 full-time freshmen who applied for aid, 137 were judged to have need. Of these, 136 received aid, and 24 had their full need met. Average financial aid package met 71% of need; average scholarship/grant was $10,474; average loan was $4,000. For part-time students, average financial aid package was $6,394.
Students without need: 15 full-time freshmen who did not demonstrate need for aid received scholarships/grants; average award was $9,093. No-need awards available for academics, leadership, minority status.
Cumulative student debt: 90% of graduating class had student loans; average debt was $26,475.

FINANCIAL AID PROCEDURES

Forms required: FAFSA.
Dates and Deadlines: Priority date 3/1; no closing date. Applicants notified on a rolling basis starting 2/15.

CONTACT

Director of Financial Aid
200 Manor Avenue, Langhorne, PA 19047-2990
(215) 702-4246

Philadelphia University

Philadelphia, Pennsylvania
www.philau.edu Federal Code: 003354

4-year private university in very large city.
Enrollment: 2,768 undergrads, 6% part-time. 731 full-time freshmen.
Selectivity: Admits 50 to 75% of applicants.

BASIC COSTS (2009-2010)

Tuition and fees: $27,498.
Per-credit charge: $486.
Room and board: $9,182.

FINANCIAL AID PICTURE (2008-2009)

Students with need: Out of 635 full-time freshmen who applied for aid, 546 were judged to have need. Of these, 546 received aid, and 65 had their full need met. Average financial aid package met 73% of need; average scholarship/grant was $14,673; average loan was $3,853. For part-time students, average financial aid package was $6,354.
Students without need: 174 full-time freshmen who did not demonstrate need for aid received scholarships/grants; average award was $6,445. No-need awards available for academics, athletics.
Scholarships offered: 21 full-time freshmen received athletic scholarships; average amount $9,365.
Cumulative student debt: 75% of graduating class had student loans; average debt was $30,062.

FINANCIAL AID PROCEDURES

Forms required: FAFSA.
Dates and Deadlines: Closing date 4/15. Applicants notified on a rolling basis starting 2/10; must reply by 5/1.

CONTACT

Lisa Cooper, Director of Financial Aid
School House Lane and Henry Avenue, Philadelphia, PA 19144-5497
(215) 951-2940

Pittsburgh Institute of Aeronautics

Pittsburgh, Pennsylvania
www.pia.edu Federal Code: 005310

2-year private technical college in large city.
Enrollment: 249 undergrads.
Selectivity: Open admission.

BASIC COSTS (2009-2010)

Tuition and fees: $14,705.

FINANCIAL AID PICTURE

Students with need: Need-based aid available for full-time students.

FINANCIAL AID PROCEDURES

Forms required: FAFSA.
Dates and Deadlines: Priority date 5/1; no closing date. Applicants notified on a rolling basis.
Transfers: No deadline. Applicants notified on a rolling basis.

CONTACT

Donata Clark, Financial Aid Officer
Box 10897, Pittsburgh, PA 15236-0897
(412) 346-2100

Pittsburgh Institute of Mortuary Science

Pittsburgh, Pennsylvania
www.pims.edu Federal Code: 010814

2-year private technical college in large city.
Enrollment: 85 full-time undergrads.
Selectivity: Open admission.

BASIC COSTS (2008-2009)

Tuition and fees: $14,780.

FINANCIAL AID PICTURE (2007-2008)

Students with need: Need-based aid available for full-time and part-time students.

FINANCIAL AID PROCEDURES

Forms required: FAFSA.
Dates and Deadlines: No deadline. Applicants notified on a rolling basis.

CONTACT

Karen Rocco, Financial Aid Officer
5808 Baum Boulevard, Pittsburgh, PA 15206-3706
(412) 362-8500

Pittsburgh Technical Institute

Oakdale, Pennsylvania
www.pti.edu Federal Code: 007437

2-year for-profit technical and career college in large town.
Enrollment: 2,072 undergrads. 1,013 full-time freshmen.
Selectivity: Open admission; but selective for some programs.

BASIC COSTS (2008-2009)

Additional info: Tuition and supply costs vary by program. Tuition does not increase if student maintains continuous and consistent enrollment. Tuition at time of enrollment locked for 2 years.

FINANCIAL AID PICTURE (2007-2008)

Students with need: 53% of average financial aid package awarded as scholarships/grants, 47% awarded as loans/jobs. Need-based aid available for part-time students.

FINANCIAL AID PROCEDURES

Forms required: FAFSA, state aid form, institutional form.
Dates and Deadlines: No deadline. Applicants notified on a rolling basis.
Transfers: Applicants notified on a rolling basis.

CONTACT

Mark Scott, Senior Vice President of Academic Affairs
1111 McKee Road, Oakdale, PA 15071-3205
(412) 809-5250

PJA School

Upper Darby, Pennsylvania
www.pjaschool.com Federal Code: 023013

2-year for-profit business and career college in very large city.
Enrollment: 250 undergrads.

BASIC COSTS (2008-2009)

Tuition and fees: $10,830.
Additional info: Books and materials included in cost of tuition. Tuition at time of enrollment locked for 2 years.

FINANCIAL AID PICTURE

Students with need: Need-based aid available for full-time and part-time students.
Students without need: This college awards aid only to students with need.
Additional info: Interest-free payment plan available.

FINANCIAL AID PROCEDURES

Forms required: FAFSA, institutional form.
Dates and Deadlines: No deadline. Applicants notified on a rolling basis.

CONTACT

Yolina Reynolds, Director of Financial Aid
7900 West Chester Pike, Upper Darby, PA 19082
(610) 789-6700

Point Park University

Pittsburgh, Pennsylvania
www.pointpark.edu Federal Code: 003357

4-year private university in large city.
Enrollment: 3,241 undergrads, 21% part-time. 456 full-time freshmen.
Selectivity: Admits 50 to 75% of applicants.

BASIC COSTS (2008-2009)

Tuition and fees: $20,570.
Per-credit charge: $552.
Room and board: $8,940.
Additional info: Tuition/fee waivers available for adults.

FINANCIAL AID PICTURE (2007-2008)

Students with need: Out of 429 full-time freshmen who applied for aid, 355 were judged to have need. Of these, 355 received aid, and 85 had their full need met. Average financial aid package met 68% of need; average scholarship/grant was $8,684; average loan was $5,229. For part-time students, average financial aid package was $9,148.
Students without need: 187 full-time freshmen who did not demonstrate need for aid received scholarships/grants; average award was $3,768. No-need awards available for academics, alumni affiliation, art, athletics, leadership, music/drama.
Scholarships offered: 14 full-time freshmen received athletic scholarships; average amount $6,038.
Cumulative student debt: 73% of graduating class had student loans; average debt was $30,385.

FINANCIAL AID PROCEDURES

Forms required: FAFSA.
Dates and Deadlines: Priority date 4/15; no closing date. Applicants notified on a rolling basis starting 2/16; must reply by 8/30 or within 2 week(s) of notification.

CONTACT

Sandra Cronin, Director of Financial Aid
201 Wood Street, Pittsburgh, PA 15222-1984
(412) 392-3935

Reading Area Community College

Reading, Pennsylvania
www.racc.edu Federal Code: 010388

2-year public community college in small city.
Enrollment: 4,250 undergrads.
Selectivity: Open admission; but selective for some programs.

BASIC COSTS (2008-2009)

Tuition and fees: $3,510; out-of-district residents $5,730; out-of-state residents $7,950.
Per-credit charge: $74; out-of-district residents $148; out-of-state residents $222.

FINANCIAL AID PICTURE (2007-2008)

Students with need: 44% of average financial aid package awarded as scholarships/grants, 56% awarded as loans/jobs.

FINANCIAL AID PROCEDURES

Forms required: FAFSA, institutional form.
Dates and Deadlines: Priority date 7/1; no closing date. Applicants notified on a rolling basis starting 4/15; must reply within 2 week(s) of notification.

CONTACT

Benjamin Rosenberger, Financial Aid Coordinator
10 South Second Street, Reading, PA 19603-1706
(610) 372-4721

Restaurant School at Walnut Hill College

Philadelphia, Pennsylvania
www.walnuthillcollege.edu Federal Code: 015499

4-year for-profit culinary school and business college in very large city.
Enrollment: 543 undergrads.
Selectivity: Admits 50 to 75% of applicants.

FINANCIAL AID PICTURE (2008-2009)

Students with need: 27% of average financial aid package awarded as scholarships/grants, 73% awarded as loans/jobs.

FINANCIAL AID PROCEDURES

Dates and Deadlines: No deadline.

CONTACT

Rhonda Moore, Associate Director of Financial Aid
4207 Walnut Street, Philadelphia, PA 19104

Robert Morris University

Moon Township, Pennsylvania
www.rmu.edu Federal Code: 001746

4-year private university in large town.
Enrollment: 3,681 undergrads, 15% part-time. 646 full-time freshmen.
Selectivity: Admits 50 to 75% of applicants.

BASIC COSTS (2009-2010)
Tuition and fees: $20,660.
Per-credit charge: $665.
Room and board: $10,370.

FINANCIAL AID PICTURE (2008-2009)
Students with need: Out of 594 full-time freshmen who applied for aid, 517 were judged to have need. Of these, 517 received aid, and 118 had their full need met. Average financial aid package met 77% of need; average scholarship/grant was $11,744; average loan was $4,444. For part-time students, average financial aid package was $6,488.
Students without need: 122 full-time freshmen who did not demonstrate need for aid received scholarships/grants; average award was $13,236. No-need awards available for academics, athletics.
Scholarships offered: 21 full-time freshmen received athletic scholarships; average amount $11,112.
Cumulative student debt: 79% of graduating class had student loans; average debt was $31,049.

FINANCIAL AID PROCEDURES
Forms required: FAFSA.
Dates and Deadlines: No deadline. Applicants notified on a rolling basis starting 3/15.

CONTACT
Stephanie Hendershot, Director of Financial Aid
6001 University Boulevard, Moon Township, PA 15108-1189
(412) 262-8677

Rosedale Technical Institute

Pittsburgh, Pennsylvania
www.rosedaletech.org Federal Code: 012050

2-year private technical and career college in large city.
Enrollment: 227 undergrads.

BASIC COSTS (2008-2009)
Tuition and fees: $11,610.

FINANCIAL AID PICTURE
Students with need: Need-based aid available for full-time students.

FINANCIAL AID PROCEDURES
Forms required: FAFSA.
Dates and Deadlines: Closing date 8/1.

CONTACT
Kathleen Stein, Director of Financial Aid
215 Beecham Drive, Pittsburgh, PA 15205-9791
(412) 521-6200

Rosemont College

Rosemont, Pennsylvania
www.rosemont.edu Federal Code: 003360

4-year private liberal arts college in small town, affiliated with Roman Catholic Church.
Enrollment: 506 undergrads, 23% part-time. 126 full-time freshmen.
Selectivity: Admits 50 to 75% of applicants.

BASIC COSTS (2008-2009)
Tuition and fees: $24,810.
Per-credit charge: $900.
Room and board: $9,980.

FINANCIAL AID PICTURE (2008-2009)
Students with need: Out of 125 full-time freshmen who applied for aid, 111 were judged to have need. Of these, 111 received aid, and 14 had their full need met. Average financial aid package met 75% of need; average scholarship/grant was $20,209; average loan was $3,555. For part-time students, average financial aid package was $8,209.
Students without need: 16 full-time freshmen who did not demonstrate need for aid received scholarships/grants; average award was $10,468. No-need awards available for academics, art, leadership, religious affiliation.
Cumulative student debt: 86% of graduating class had student loans; average debt was $21,807.

FINANCIAL AID PROCEDURES
Forms required: FAFSA.
Dates and Deadlines: Priority date 2/15; no closing date. Applicants notified on a rolling basis starting 2/15; must reply within 4 week(s) of notification.
Transfers: No deadline. Applicants notified on a rolling basis starting 2/15; must reply within 4 week(s) of notification.

CONTACT
Melissa Walsh, Director of Financial Aid
1400 Montgomery Avenue, Rosemont, PA 19010-1699
(610) 527-0200 ext. 2220

St. Charles Borromeo Seminary - Overbrook

Wynnewood, Pennsylvania
www.scs.edu Federal Code: 016229

4-year private seminary college for men in large town, affiliated with Roman Catholic Church.
Enrollment: 52 undergrads. 6 full-time freshmen.
Selectivity: Admits over 75% of applicants.

BASIC COSTS (2008-2009)
Tuition and fees: $13,306.
Room and board: $8,931.

FINANCIAL AID PICTURE (2008-2009)
Students with need: Out of 5 full-time freshmen who applied for aid, 3 were judged to have need. Of these, 3 received aid, and 2 had their full need met. Average financial aid package met 30% of need; average scholarship/grant was $2,521; average loan was $3,500. Need-based aid available for part-time students.
Students without need: 2 full-time freshmen who did not demonstrate need for aid received scholarships/grants; average award was $13,678. No-need awards available for religious affiliation.

FINANCIAL AID PROCEDURES
Forms required: FAFSA, institutional form.
Dates and Deadlines: No deadline. Applicants notified on a rolling basis starting 6/1; must reply within 4 week(s) of notification.

CONTACT
Bonnie Behm, Financial Aid Coordinator
100 East Wynnewood Road, Wynnewood, PA 19096
(610) 785-6582

St. Francis University

Loretto, Pennsylvania
www.francis.edu Federal Code: 003366

4-year private university and liberal arts college in rural community, affiliated with Roman Catholic Church.
Enrollment: 1,571 undergrads, 6% part-time. 394 full-time freshmen.
Selectivity: Admits over 75% of applicants.

BASIC COSTS (2008-2009)

Tuition and fees: $24,840.
Per-credit charge: $743.
Room and board: $8,422.
Additional info: Tuition/fee waivers available for adults.

FINANCIAL AID PICTURE (2007-2008)

Students with need: Out of 372 full-time freshmen who applied for aid, 326 were judged to have need. Of these, 319 received aid, and 55 had their full need met. Average financial aid package met 66% of need; average scholarship/grant was $13,069; average loan was $2,775. For part-time students, average financial aid package was $19,186.
Students without need: 61 full-time freshmen who did not demonstrate need for aid received scholarships/grants; average award was $12,684. No-need awards available for academics, alumni affiliation, athletics, music/drama, religious affiliation.
Scholarships offered: 38 full-time freshmen received athletic scholarships; average amount $8,976.
Cumulative student debt: 86% of graduating class had student loans; average debt was $18,762.

FINANCIAL AID PROCEDURES

Forms required: FAFSA.
Dates and Deadlines: Priority date 5/1; no closing date. Applicants notified on a rolling basis starting 3/1.
Transfers: No deadline. Applicants notified on a rolling basis. Associate degree transfer scholarship based on academic achievement. Returning adult student scholarships available to qualifying transfers after one semester.

CONTACT

Jamie Kosh, Director of Financial Aid
Box 600, Loretto, PA 15940

Saint Joseph's University

Philadelphia, Pennsylvania
www.sju.edu Federal Code: 003367

4-year private university in very large city, affiliated with Roman Catholic Church.
Enrollment: 5,161 undergrads, 13% part-time. 1,475 full-time freshmen.
Selectivity: Admits over 75% of applicants. GED not accepted.

BASIC COSTS (2009-2010)

Tuition and fees: $34,090.
Room and board: $11,575.

FINANCIAL AID PICTURE (2008-2009)

Students with need: Out of 1,074 full-time freshmen who applied for aid, 793 were judged to have need. Of these, 793 received aid, and 181 had their full need met. Average financial aid package met 83% of need; average scholarship/grant was $14,746; average loan was $3,685. Need-based aid available for part-time students.
Students without need: 532 full-time freshmen who did not demonstrate need for aid received scholarships/grants; average award was $10,464. No-need awards available for academics, art, athletics, minority status, music/drama, ROTC.
Scholarships offered: 38 full-time freshmen received athletic scholarships; average amount $14,372.

FINANCIAL AID PROCEDURES

Forms required: FAFSA.
Dates and Deadlines: Priority date 2/15; no closing date. Applicants notified on a rolling basis starting 3/1; must reply by 5/1.
Transfers: Financial aid for transfers subject to availability of funds.

CONTACT

Eileen Tucker, Director of Financial Aid
5600 City Avenue, Philadelphia, PA 19131
(610) 660-1556

St. Vincent College

Latrobe, Pennsylvania
www.stvincent.edu Federal Code: 003368

4-year private liberal arts college in large town, affiliated with Roman Catholic Church.
Enrollment: 1,676 undergrads, 2% part-time. 443 full-time freshmen.
Selectivity: Admits 50 to 75% of applicants.

BASIC COSTS (2009-2010)

Tuition and fees: $26,146.
Per-credit charge: $793.
Room and board: $8,184.

FINANCIAL AID PICTURE (2008-2009)

Students with need: Out of 440 full-time freshmen who applied for aid, 359 were judged to have need. Of these, 359 received aid, and 92 had their full need met. Average financial aid package met 87% of need; average scholarship/grant was $15,630; average loan was $4,208. For part-time students, average financial aid package was $8,384.
Students without need: 84 full-time freshmen who did not demonstrate need for aid received scholarships/grants; average award was $14,600. No-need awards available for academics, alumni affiliation, leadership, minority status, music/drama, religious affiliation.
Scholarships offered: Academic Merit Scholarship: $5,000 to $14,000, based on high school GPA, class rank, and SAT scores. Leadership Merit Grant: $500 to $3,000, based on extracurricular activities and recommendations. Competitive scholarships from $4,000 to full tuition.
Cumulative student debt: 79% of graduating class had student loans; average debt was $30,264.

FINANCIAL AID PROCEDURES

Forms required: FAFSA, state aid form.
Dates and Deadlines: Priority date 3/1; closing date 5/1. Applicants notified on a rolling basis starting 3/1; must reply within 2 week(s) of notification.
Transfers: Applicants notified on a rolling basis starting 3/1; must reply within 2 week(s) of notification.

CONTACT

Kimberly Woodley, Director of Financial Aid
300 Fraser Purchase Road, Latrobe, PA 15650-2690
(800) 782-5549

Seton Hill University

Greensburg, Pennsylvania
www.setonhill.edu Federal Code: 003362

4-year private university and liberal arts college in large town, affiliated with Roman Catholic Church.
Enrollment: 1,480 undergrads, 10% part-time. 371 full-time freshmen.
Selectivity: Admits 50 to 75% of applicants.

BASIC COSTS (2009-2010)

Tuition and fees: $26,622.
Per-credit charge: $705.

Room and board: $8,550.
Additional info: Tuition/fee waivers available for adults.

FINANCIAL AID PICTURE (2008-2009)

Students with need: Out of 337 full-time freshmen who applied for aid, 300 were judged to have need. Of these, 299 received aid, and 52 had their full need met. Average financial aid package met 80% of need; average scholarship/grant was $17,828; average loan was $5,133. For part-time students, average financial aid package was $11,285.
Students without need: 56 full-time freshmen who did not demonstrate need for aid received scholarships/grants; average award was $15,705. No-need awards available for academics, alumni affiliation, art, athletics, leadership, minority status, music/drama, state/district residency.
Scholarships offered: ***Merit:*** Presidential Scholarships; up to one-half of tuition per academic year; given to top 10%, 20%, and 30% of high school class. Other scholarships include those for valedictorians, academic performance, special talents. ***Athletic:*** 24 full-time freshmen received athletic scholarships; average amount $11,074.
Cumulative student debt: 97% of graduating class had student loans; average debt was $27,120.

FINANCIAL AID PROCEDURES

Forms required: FAFSA, state aid form, institutional form.
Dates and Deadlines: Priority date 5/1; no closing date. Applicants notified on a rolling basis starting 11/15; must reply by 5/1 or within 2 week(s) of notification.
Transfers: Priority date 8/1; closing date 8/15. Applicants notified on a rolling basis starting 1/1; must reply within 2 week(s) of notification. Scholarship available for full-time transfer students with 3.5 GPA.

CONTACT

Maryann Dudas, Director of Financial Aid
1 Seton Hill Drive, Greensburg, PA 15601
(724) 838-4293

Shippensburg University of Pennsylvania

Shippensburg, Pennsylvania
www.ship.edu Federal Code: 003326

4-year public university in small town.
Enrollment: 6,634 undergrads, 4% part-time. 1,718 full-time freshmen.
Selectivity: Admits 50 to 75% of applicants.

BASIC COSTS (2008-2009)

Tuition and fees: $7,099; out-of-state residents $15,137.
Per-credit charge: $223; out-of-state residents $558.
Room and board: $6,604.

FINANCIAL AID PICTURE (2008-2009)

Students with need: Out of 1,476 full-time freshmen who applied for aid, 961 were judged to have need. Of these, 901 received aid, and 163 had their full need met. Average financial aid package met 68% of need; average scholarship/grant was $5,264; average loan was $3,244. For part-time students, average financial aid package was $5,422.
Students without need: 151 full-time freshmen who did not demonstrate need for aid received scholarships/grants; average award was $2,985. No-need awards available for academics, athletics.
Scholarships offered: 81 full-time freshmen received athletic scholarships; average amount $2,384.
Cumulative student debt: 72% of graduating class had student loans; average debt was $20,148.

FINANCIAL AID PROCEDURES

Forms required: FAFSA.
Dates and Deadlines: Priority date 3/15; no closing date. Applicants notified on a rolling basis; must reply within 2 week(s) of notification.
Transfers: No deadline. Applicants notified on a rolling basis.

CONTACT

Peter D'Annibale, Director of Financial Aid
1871 Old Main Drive, Shippensburg, PA 17257-2299
(717) 477-1131

Slippery Rock University of Pennsylvania

Slippery Rock, Pennsylvania
www.sru.edu Federal Code: 003327

4-year public university in rural community.
Enrollment: 7,620 undergrads, 6% part-time. 1,546 full-time freshmen.
Selectivity: Admits 50 to 75% of applicants.

BASIC COSTS (2008-2009)

Tuition and fees: $6,934; out-of-state residents $9,614.
Per-credit charge: $223; out-of-state residents $558.
Room and board: $8,066.
Additional info: Tuition for out-of-state students with at least 3.0 GPA is $8,038; all out-of-state undergraduates pay an additional $92 in required fees.

FINANCIAL AID PICTURE (2008-2009)

Students with need: Out of 1,437 full-time freshmen who applied for aid, 1,022 were judged to have need. Of these, 1,004 received aid, and 509 had their full need met. Average financial aid package met 64% of need; average scholarship/grant was $3,106; average loan was $3,172. For part-time students, average financial aid package was $5,697.
Students without need: 357 full-time freshmen who did not demonstrate need for aid received scholarships/grants; average award was $6,678. No-need awards available for academics, alumni affiliation, art, athletics, job skills, leadership, minority status, music/drama, ROTC, state/district residency.
Scholarships offered: 64 full-time freshmen received athletic scholarships; average amount $3,090.
Cumulative student debt: 82% of graduating class had student loans; average debt was $22,940.
Additional info: May 1 closing date for Pennsylvania state grants.

FINANCIAL AID PROCEDURES

Forms required: FAFSA.
Dates and Deadlines: Priority date 5/1; no closing date. Applicants notified on a rolling basis starting 3/15.

CONTACT

Patricia Hladio, Director of Financial Aid
1 Morrow Way, Slippery Rock, PA 16057-1383
(724) 738-2044

South Hills School of Business & Technology

State College, Pennsylvania
www.southhills.edu Federal Code: 013263

2-year for-profit business and technical college in large town.
Enrollment: 652 undergrads, 9% part-time. 313 full-time freshmen.
Selectivity: Open admission; but selective for some programs.

BASIC COSTS (2009-2010)

Tuition and fees: $13,573.
Per-credit charge: $356.

FINANCIAL AID PICTURE (2008-2009)

Students with need: Need-based aid available for part-time students.
Students without need: This college awards aid only to students with need.
Cumulative student debt: 89% of graduating class had student loans; average debt was $23,000.

FINANCIAL AID PROCEDURES

Forms required: FAFSA.

Dates and Deadlines: Closing date 6/30. Applicants notified on a rolling basis starting 7/5.

Transfers: No deadline.

CONTACT

Harriet Arndt, Financial Aid Director
480 Waupelani Drive, State College, PA 16801-4516
(814) 234-7755

South Hills School of Business & Technology: Altoona

Altoona, Pennsylvania
www.southhills.edu Federal Code: 010281

2-year for-profit business and technical college in small city.

Enrollment: 125 undergrads.

Selectivity: Open admission; but selective for some programs.

BASIC COSTS (2009-2010)

Tuition and fees: $13,623.

Per-credit charge: $374.

FINANCIAL AID PICTURE

Students with need: Need-based aid available for full-time and part-time students.

Students without need: This college awards aid only to students with need.

FINANCIAL AID PROCEDURES

Forms required: FAFSA.

Dates and Deadlines: Closing date 6/30. Applicants notified on a rolling basis starting 7/1.

Transfers: No deadline.

CONTACT

Joan Grassi, Financial Aid Counselor
508 58th Street, Altoona, PA 16602
(814) 944-6134 ext. 3052

Susquehanna University

Selinsgrove, Pennsylvania Federal Code: 003369
www.susqu.edu CSS Code: 2820

4-year private university and liberal arts college in small town, affiliated with Evangelical Lutheran Church in America.

Enrollment: 2,066 undergrads, 1% part-time. 616 full-time freshmen.

Selectivity: Admits 50 to 75% of applicants.

BASIC COSTS (2009-2010)

Tuition and fees: $32,450.

Per-credit charge: $1,015.

Room and board: $8,800.

FINANCIAL AID PICTURE (2008-2009)

Students with need: Out of 508 full-time freshmen who applied for aid, 417 were judged to have need. Of these, 417 received aid, and 178 had their full need met. Average financial aid package met 82% of need; average scholarship/grant was $19,812; average loan was $3,711. For part-time students, average financial aid package was $21,551.

Students without need: 177 full-time freshmen who did not demonstrate need for aid received scholarships/grants; average award was $9,665. No-need awards available for academics, alumni affiliation, leadership, minority status, music/drama, ROTC.

Scholarships offered: Scholarships; $1,000 to $16,000; renewable annually; based on outstanding academic achievement, personal accomplishment, and/or musical talent. Alumni scholarships; $2,500; for 5 new legacy students with best academic records. Annual scholarships; $2,000; to dependent children of ordained Lutheran clergy.

Additional info: Graduated pay scale for federal work-study program.

FINANCIAL AID PROCEDURES

Forms required: FAFSA, CSS PROFILE.

Dates and Deadlines: Priority date 3/1; closing date 5/1. Applicants notified by 3/1; must reply by 5/1.

Transfers: Priority date 5/1; closing date 7/1. Transfer students eligible for financial aid and scholarship consideration.

CONTACT

Helen Nunn, Director of Financial Aid
514 University Avenue, Selinsgrove, PA 17870-1164
(570) 372-4450

Swarthmore College

Swarthmore, Pennsylvania Federal Code: 003370
www.swarthmore.edu CSS Code: 2821

4-year private liberal arts college in small town.

Enrollment: 1,477 undergrads. 372 full-time freshmen.

Selectivity: Admits less than 50% of applicants.

BASIC COSTS (2008-2009)

Tuition and fees: $36,490.

Room and board: $11,314.

FINANCIAL AID PICTURE (2008-2009)

Students with need: Out of 242 full-time freshmen who applied for aid, 181 were judged to have need. Of these, 181 received aid, and 181 had their full need met. Average financial aid package met 100% of need; average scholarship/grant was $33,328.

Students without need: 1 full-time freshmen who did not demonstrate need for aid received scholarships/grants; average award was $36,154. No-need awards available for academics, leadership, state/district residency.

Additional info: 100% of demonstrated financial need met for all admitted students.

FINANCIAL AID PROCEDURES

Forms required: FAFSA, CSS PROFILE, state aid form, institutional form.

Dates and Deadlines: Closing date 2/15. Applicants notified by 4/1; must reply by 5/1.

Transfers: Closing date 4/1. Applicants notified by 5/15. No aid consideration is presently possible for foreign national transfer applicants.

CONTACT

Laura Talbot, Director of Financial Aid
500 College Avenue, Swarthmore, PA 19081
(610) 328-8358

Talmudical Yeshiva of Philadelphia

Philadelphia, Pennsylvania Federal Code: 012523

4-year private rabbinical college for men in very large city, affiliated with Jewish faith.

Enrollment: 112 undergrads. 35 full-time freshmen.

Selectivity: Admits over 75% of applicants.

BASIC COSTS (2008-2009)

Tuition and fees: $7,300.

Room and board: $6,000.

FINANCIAL AID PICTURE (2007-2008)

Students with need: Out of 22 full-time freshmen who applied for aid, 22 were judged to have need. Of these, 22 received aid.

Students without need: This college awards aid only to students with need.

FINANCIAL AID PROCEDURES

Forms required: FAFSA, institutional form.

Dates and Deadlines: Priority date 8/1; closing date 5/1. Applicants notified on a rolling basis starting 3/15; must reply within 2 week(s) of notification.

CONTACT

Chaya Hoberman, Financial Aid Officer
6063 Drexel Road, Philadelphia, PA 19131
(215) 477-1000

Temple University

Philadelphia, Pennsylvania
www.temple.edu Federal Code: 003371

4-year public university in very large city.

Enrollment: 25,598 undergrads, 11% part-time. 4,066 full-time freshmen.

Selectivity: Admits 50 to 75% of applicants.

BASIC COSTS (2008-2009)

Tuition and fees: $11,448; out-of-state residents $20,468.

Per-credit charge: $420; out-of-state residents $707.

Room and board: $8,884.

FINANCIAL AID PICTURE (2007-2008)

Students with need: Out of 4,058 full-time freshmen who applied for aid, 2,962 were judged to have need. Of these, 2,910 received aid, and 991 had their full need met. Average financial aid package met 87% of need; average scholarship/grant was $5,617; average loan was $3,328. For part-time students, average financial aid package was $8,289.

Students without need: 693 full-time freshmen who did not demonstrate need for aid received scholarships/grants; average award was $7,485. No-need awards available for academics, art, athletics, music/drama, ROTC.

Scholarships offered: 25 full-time freshmen received athletic scholarships; average amount $13,446.

Cumulative student debt: 73% of graduating class had student loans; average debt was $29,809.

FINANCIAL AID PROCEDURES

Forms required: FAFSA.

Dates and Deadlines: Closing date 3/1. Applicants notified on a rolling basis starting 2/15; must reply by 5/1 or within 3 week(s) of notification.

Transfers: Priority date 3/1; no deadline. Must reply within 2 week(s) of notification.

CONTACT

John Morris, Director, Student Financial Services
103 Conwell Hall, Philadelphia, PA 19122-6096
(215) 204-2244

Thiel College

Greenville, Pennsylvania
www.thiel.edu Federal Code: 003376

4-year private liberal arts college in small town, affiliated with Evangelical Lutheran Church in America.

Enrollment: 1,091 undergrads, 2% part-time. 317 full-time freshmen.

Selectivity: Admits 50 to 75% of applicants.

BASIC COSTS (2009-2010)

Tuition and fees: $22,448.

Per-credit charge: $670.

Room and board: $8,790.

FINANCIAL AID PICTURE (2008-2009)

Students with need: Out of 281 full-time freshmen who applied for aid, 267 were judged to have need. Of these, 267 received aid, and 31 had their full need met. Average financial aid package met 75% of need; average scholarship/grant was $14,779; average loan was $5,719. For part-time students, average financial aid package was $7,521.

Students without need: 32 full-time freshmen who did not demonstrate need for aid received scholarships/grants; average award was $11,272. No-need awards available for academics, alumni affiliation, leadership, music/drama, religious affiliation, state/district residency.

FINANCIAL AID PROCEDURES

Forms required: FAFSA, state aid form.

Dates and Deadlines: Priority date 3/15; no closing date. Applicants notified on a rolling basis starting 2/15; must reply within 2 week(s) of notification.

Transfers: Priority date 6/1. Applicants notified on a rolling basis starting 2/1; must reply within 2 week(s) of notification.

CONTACT

Scott Hartle, Vice President Financial Services
75 College Avenue, Greenville, PA 16125-2181
(724) 589-2250

Thomas Jefferson University: College of Health Professions

Philadelphia, Pennsylvania
www.jefferson.edu/jchp Federal Code: 012393

Upper-division private health science and nursing college in very large city.

Enrollment: 893 undergrads, 16% part-time.

BASIC COSTS (2008-2009)

Tuition and fees: $24,514.

Per-credit charge: $797.

FINANCIAL AID PICTURE (2007-2008)

Students with need: Need-based aid available for full-time students.

Students without need: No-need awards available for academics, leadership, state/district residency.

Scholarships offered: Range of merit-based scholarships available for selected applicants.

FINANCIAL AID PROCEDURES

Forms required: FAFSA, institutional form.

Dates and Deadlines: Priority date 5/1; no closing date. Applicants notified on a rolling basis starting 4/1; must reply within 2 week(s) of notification.

Transfers: Applicants notified on a rolling basis starting 11/15; must reply within 2 week(s) of notification.

CONTACT

Susan McFadden, University Director of Financial Aid
130 South Ninth Street, Edison Building, Suite 100, Philadelphia, PA 19107
(215) 955-2867

Triangle Tech: Bethlehem

Bethlehem, Pennsylvania
www.triangle-tech.edu Federal Code: 014895

2-year for-profit branch campus and technical college in small city.

Enrollment: 98 undergrads. 151 full-time freshmen.

Selectivity: Open admission.

BASIC COSTS (2008-2009)

Tuition and fees: $13,547.

Per-credit charge: $367.

FINANCIAL AID PICTURE (2007-2008)

Students with need: Out of 142 full-time freshmen who applied for aid, 131 were judged to have need. Of these, 131 received aid. Average financial aid package met 35% of need; average scholarship/grant was $4,609; average loan was $1,997. Need-based aid available for part-time students.

Students without need: 1 full-time freshmen who did not demonstrate need for aid received scholarships/grants; average award was $1,497.

Cumulative student debt: 72% of graduating class had student loans; average debt was $10,000.

FINANCIAL AID PROCEDURES

Forms required: FAFSA.

Dates and Deadlines: No deadline. Applicants notified on a rolling basis.

CONTACT

Catherine Waxter, Director of Financial Aid
31 South Commerce Way, Lehigh Valley Industrial Park IV, Bethlehem, PA 18017
(610) 691-1300

Triangle Tech: DuBois

DuBois, Pennsylvania
www.triangle-tech.edu Federal Code: 021744

2-year for-profit technical college in large town.

Enrollment: 236 undergrads. 140 full-time freshmen.

Selectivity: Open admission.

BASIC COSTS (2008-2009)

Tuition and fees: $13,605.

Per-credit charge: $367.

FINANCIAL AID PICTURE (2007-2008)

Students with need: Out of 136 full-time freshmen who applied for aid, 136 were judged to have need. Of these, 136 received aid. Average financial aid package met 100% of need; average scholarship/grant was $3,375; average loan was $2,825. Need-based aid available for part-time students.

Students without need: This college awards aid only to students with need.

FINANCIAL AID PROCEDURES

Forms required: FAFSA, state aid form, institutional form.

Dates and Deadlines: No deadline. Applicants notified on a rolling basis.

CONTACT

Catherine Waxter, Corporate Director of Financial Aid
PO Box 551, DuBois, PA 15801-0551
(724) 832-1050

Triangle Tech: Erie

Erie, Pennsylvania
www.triangle-tech.edu Federal Code: 014417

2-year for-profit technical college in small city.

Enrollment: 144 undergrads. 42 full-time freshmen.

Selectivity: Open admission.

BASIC COSTS (2008-2009)

Tuition and fees: $13,497.

Per-credit charge: $367.

FINANCIAL AID PICTURE (2007-2008)

Students with need: 44% of average financial aid package awarded as scholarships/grants, 56% awarded as loans/jobs. Need-based aid available for part-time students.

FINANCIAL AID PROCEDURES

Forms required: FAFSA.

Dates and Deadlines: Applicants notified on a rolling basis.

CONTACT

Cathy Waxter, Corporate Director of Financial Aid
2000 Liberty Street, Erie, PA 16502-2594
(724) 832-1050

Triangle Tech: Greensburg

Greensburg, Pennsylvania
www.triangle-tech.edu Federal Code: 014895

2-year for-profit technical college in large town.

Enrollment: 209 undergrads. 322 full-time freshmen.

Selectivity: Open admission.

BASIC COSTS (2008-2009)

Tuition and fees: $13,478.

Per-credit charge: $367.

Additional info: Tuition at time of enrollment locked for 2 years.

FINANCIAL AID PICTURE (2007-2008)

Students with need: Out of 318 full-time freshmen who applied for aid, 318 were judged to have need. Of these, 318 received aid, and 114 had their full need met. Average financial aid package met 35% of need; average scholarship/grant was $8,721; average loan was $4,363. Need-based aid available for part-time students.

Scholarships offered: 5 full-time freshmen received athletic scholarships; average amount $3,583.

Cumulative student debt: 56% of graduating class had student loans; average debt was $6,576.

FINANCIAL AID PROCEDURES

Forms required: FAFSA, institutional form.

Dates and Deadlines: No deadline. Applicants notified on a rolling basis starting 1/1.

Transfers: No deadline.

CONTACT

Catherine Waxter, Director of Financial Aid
222 East Pittsburgh Street, Suite A, Greensburg, PA 15601-3304
(724) 832-1050

Triangle Tech: Pittsburgh

Pittsburgh, Pennsylvania
www.triangle-tech.edu Federal Code: 007839

2-year for-profit technical college in large city.

Enrollment: 247 undergrads. 386 full-time freshmen.

Selectivity: Open admission; but selective for some programs.

BASIC COSTS (2008-2009)

Tuition and fees: $13,558.

Per-credit charge: $367.

FINANCIAL AID PICTURE (2007-2008)

Students with need: Out of 377 full-time freshmen who applied for aid, 377 were judged to have need. Of these, 377 received aid, and 119 had their full need met. Average financial aid package met 32% of need; average scholarship/grant was $5,839; average loan was $4,890. Need-based aid available for part-time students.

Students without need: No-need awards available for academics, state/district residency.
Scholarships offered: 6 full-time freshmen received athletic scholarships; average amount $4,061.
Cumulative student debt: 62% of graduating class had student loans; average debt was $7,232.

FINANCIAL AID PROCEDURES

Forms required: FAFSA, institutional form.
Dates and Deadlines: No deadline. Applicants notified on a rolling basis.
Transfers: No deadline.

CONTACT

Cathy Waxter, Corporate Director of Financial Aid
1940 Perrysville Avenue, Pittsburgh, PA 15214-3897
(412) 359-1000

Triangle Tech: Sunbury

Sunbury, Pennsylvania
www.triangle-tech.edu

2-year for-profit technical college in large town.
Enrollment: 111 undergrads. 70 full-time freshmen.

BASIC COSTS (2008-2009)

Tuition and fees: $13,670.
Per-credit charge: $367.

FINANCIAL AID PICTURE (2007-2008)

Students with need: Out of 68 full-time freshmen who applied for aid, 68 were judged to have need. Of these, 68 received aid. Average financial aid package met 96% of need; average scholarship/grant was $4,846; average loan was $3,414.

FINANCIAL AID PROCEDURES

Forms required: FAFSA, institutional form.
Dates and Deadlines: No deadline.

CONTACT

Cathy Waxter, Director of Financial Aid
191 Performance Road, Sunbury, PA 17801

University of Pennsylvania

Philadelphia, Pennsylvania Federal Code: 003378
www.upenn.edu CSS Code: 2926

4-year private university in very large city.
Enrollment: 9,756 undergrads, 2% part-time. 2,400 full-time freshmen.
Selectivity: Admits less than 50% of applicants.

BASIC COSTS (2009-2010)

Tuition and fees: $38,970.
Room and board: $11,016.

FINANCIAL AID PICTURE (2007-2008)

Students with need: Out of 1,243 full-time freshmen who applied for aid, 923 were judged to have need. Of these, 923 received aid, and 923 had their full need met. Average financial aid package met 100% of need; average scholarship/grant was $29,284; average loan was $1,912. Need-based aid available for part-time students.
Students without need: This college awards aid only to students with need.
Cumulative student debt: 41% of graduating class had student loans; average debt was $19,085.

FINANCIAL AID PROCEDURES

Forms required: FAFSA, CSS PROFILE, institutional form.
Dates and Deadlines: Priority date 2/15; no closing date. Applicants notified by 4/1; must reply by 5/1.
Transfers: Closing date 3/15. Applicants notified on a rolling basis starting 5/15; must reply within 4 week(s) of notification.

CONTACT

William Schilling, Director of Financial Aid
1 College Hall, Philadelphia, PA 19104
(215) 898-1988

University of Pittsburgh

Pittsburgh, Pennsylvania
www.pitt.edu Federal Code: 008815

4-year public university in large city.
Enrollment: 17,054 undergrads, 6% part-time. 3,554 full-time freshmen.
Selectivity: Admits 50 to 75% of applicants. GED not accepted.

BASIC COSTS (2008-2009)

Tuition and fees: $13,642; out-of-state residents $23,290.
Per-credit charge: $534; out-of-state residents $936.
Room and board: $8,600.

FINANCIAL AID PICTURE (2008-2009)

Students with need: Out of 2,792 full-time freshmen who applied for aid, 1,900 were judged to have need. Of these, 1,861 received aid, and 793 had their full need met. Average financial aid package met 82% of need; average scholarship/grant was $9,170; average loan was $5,356. Need-based aid available for part-time students.
Students without need: 294 full-time freshmen who did not demonstrate need for aid received scholarships/grants; average award was $13,504. No-need awards available for academics, athletics.
Scholarships offered: ***Merit:*** Academic Scholarships; $1,000 to full tuition, room and board; renewable up to 4 years with 3.0 GPA. ***Athletic:*** 43 full-time freshmen received athletic scholarships; average amount $19,962.

FINANCIAL AID PROCEDURES

Forms required: FAFSA.
Dates and Deadlines: Priority date 3/1; no closing date. Applicants notified on a rolling basis starting 3/15.
Transfers: Priority date 5/1; no deadline. Applicants notified on a rolling basis. Transfer students not eligible for freshman scholarships.

CONTACT

Betsy Porter, Director, Office of Admissions and Financial Aid
4227 Fifth Avenue, 1st Floor, Alumni Hall, Pittsburgh, PA 15260
(412) 624-7488

University of Pittsburgh at Bradford

Bradford, Pennsylvania
www.upb.pitt.edu Federal Code: 003380

4-year public university in large town.
Enrollment: 1,456 undergrads, 9% part-time. 375 full-time freshmen.
Selectivity: Admits 50 to 75% of applicants.

BASIC COSTS (2008-2009)

Tuition and fees: $11,722; out-of-state residents $21,282.
Per-credit charge: $458; out-of-state residents $857.
Room and board: $7,050.

FINANCIAL AID PICTURE (2008-2009)

Students with need: Out of 355 full-time freshmen who applied for aid, 304 were judged to have need. Of these, 304 received aid, and 139 had their full need met. Average financial aid package met 89% of need; average scholarship/grant was $8,782; average loan was $3,245. For part-time students, average financial aid package was $6,503.

Students without need: 11 full-time freshmen who did not demonstrate need for aid received scholarships/grants; average award was $7,125. No-need awards available for academics, alumni affiliation, ROTC, state/district residency.

Scholarships offered: Panther Scholarship; for full-time on-campus residents or students who commute from Cameron, Elk, Forest, McKean, Potter, or Warren counties. Valedictorian/Salutatorian Scholarship; for Pennsylvania students. International Student Scholarship; for international students who plan to enroll full-time and reside on campus.

Cumulative student debt: 92% of graduating class had student loans; average debt was $26,463.

FINANCIAL AID PROCEDURES

Forms required: FAFSA.

Dates and Deadlines: Priority date 3/1; no closing date. Applicants notified on a rolling basis starting 4/1; must reply within 2 week(s) of notification.

Transfers: No deadline. Applicants notified on a rolling basis starting 4/1; must reply within 2 week(s) of notification. Transfers must meet academic policy guidelines.

CONTACT

Melissa Ibanez, Director of Financial Aid
300 Campus Drive, Bradford, PA 16701
(814) 362-7550

University of Pittsburgh at Greensburg

Greensburg, Pennsylvania
www.upg.pitt.edu Federal Code: 003381

4-year public branch campus and liberal arts college in large town.

Enrollment: 1,807 undergrads, 7% part-time. 460 full-time freshmen.

Selectivity: Admits 50 to 75% of applicants.

BASIC COSTS (2008-2009)

Tuition and fees: $11,782; out-of-state residents $21,342.

Per-credit charge: $458; out-of-state residents $857.

Room and board: $7,530.

FINANCIAL AID PICTURE (2008-2009)

Students with need: Out of 406 full-time freshmen who applied for aid, 342 were judged to have need. Of these, 340 received aid, and 45 had their full need met. Average financial aid package met 53% of need; average scholarship/grant was $6,177; average loan was $3,592. For part-time students, average financial aid package was $6,679.

Students without need: 36 full-time freshmen who did not demonstrate need for aid received scholarships/grants; average award was $1,526. No-need awards available for academics, leadership, minority status.

Cumulative student debt: 80% of graduating class had student loans; average debt was $21,468.

FINANCIAL AID PROCEDURES

Forms required: FAFSA, state aid form.

Dates and Deadlines: Priority date 2/15; no closing date. Applicants notified on a rolling basis starting 3/15; must reply within 3 week(s) of notification.

Transfers: No deadline.

CONTACT

Brandi Darr, Director of Financial Aid
150 Finoli Drive, Greensburg, PA 15601
(724) 836-9881

University of Pittsburgh at Johnstown

Johnstown, Pennsylvania
www.upj.pitt.edu Federal Code: 008815

4-year public engineering and liberal arts college in small city.

Enrollment: 3,024 undergrads, 5% part-time. 832 full-time freshmen.

Selectivity: Admits over 75% of applicants.

BASIC COSTS (2008-2009)

Tuition and fees: $11,754; out-of-state residents $21,314.

Per-credit charge: $458; out-of-state residents $857.

Room and board: $6,860.

FINANCIAL AID PICTURE (2008-2009)

Students with need: Out of 716 full-time freshmen who applied for aid, 712 were judged to have need. Of these, 589 received aid, and 53 had their full need met. Average financial aid package met 56% of need; average scholarship/grant was $5,321; average loan was $3,602. For part-time students, average financial aid package was $582.

Students without need: 37 full-time freshmen who did not demonstrate need for aid received scholarships/grants; average award was $3,626. No-need awards available for academics, athletics, leadership, minority status, state/district residency.

Scholarships offered: ***Merit:*** President's Scholarships and Leadership Scholarships; $1,500 to full tuition yearly; renewable; 1220 SAT (exclusive of Writing), 3.8 GPA, and top 10% of graduating class required; priority given to those who apply by 12/01. ***Athletic:*** 24 full-time freshmen received athletic scholarships; average amount $6,531.

Cumulative student debt: 86% of graduating class had student loans; average debt was $23,295.

FINANCIAL AID PROCEDURES

Forms required: FAFSA, state aid form.

Dates and Deadlines: Priority date 4/1; no closing date. Applicants notified on a rolling basis starting 3/15; must reply within 2 week(s) of notification.

CONTACT

Jeanine Lawn, Director of Financial Aid
450 Schoolhouse Road, 157 Blackington Hall, Johnstown, PA 15904-1200
(800) 881-5544

University of Pittsburgh at Titusville

Titusville, Pennsylvania
www.upt.pitt.edu Federal Code: 008815

2-year public branch campus and liberal arts college in small town.

Enrollment: 537 undergrads, 20% part-time. 192 full-time freshmen.

Selectivity: Admits over 75% of applicants.

BASIC COSTS (2008-2009)

Tuition and fees: $10,430; out-of-state residents $19,050.

Per-credit charge: $404; out-of-state residents $763.

Room and board: $8,076.

Additional info: Tuition/fee waivers available for adults.

FINANCIAL AID PICTURE (2008-2009)

Students with need: Average financial aid package met 78% of need; average scholarship/grant was $10,500; average loan was $3,500. For part-time students, average financial aid package was $9,100.

Students without need: No-need awards available for academics, athletics, state/district residency.

Scholarships offered: Science scholarships; $2,000; awarded to top 5 students with science as a major; renewable with 3.0 GPA and continued science major. Presidential scholarships; $2,500; awarded based on high school academic record; 6 awarded.

FINANCIAL AID PROCEDURES

Forms required: FAFSA.

Dates and Deadlines: Priority date 3/1; no closing date. Applicants notified on a rolling basis; must reply within 2 week(s) of notification.

Transfers: No deadline. Applicants notified on a rolling basis starting 4/1; must reply within 2 week(s) of notification. Pennsylvania residents must apply by 5/1 for PHEAA. Transfer students must have completed 24 credits to renew. Information retrieved from NSLDS is utilized to determine transfer student eligibility for financial aid.

CONTACT

Sue Bloom, Director of Financial Aid
UPT Admissions Office, Titusville, PA 16354-0287
(814) 827-4495

University of Scranton

Scranton, Pennsylvania
www.scranton.edu Federal Code: 003384

4-year private university and liberal arts college in small city, affiliated with Roman Catholic Church.

Enrollment: 4,010 undergrads, 4% part-time. 961 full-time freshmen.

Selectivity: Admits 50 to 75% of applicants.

BASIC COSTS (2009-2010)

Tuition and fees: $33,124.
Per-credit charge: $846.
Room and board: $11,440.

FINANCIAL AID PICTURE (2008-2009)

Students with need: Need-based aid available for full-time and part-time students. Work study available nights, weekends, and for part-time students.

Students without need: No-need awards available for academics, minority status, ROTC.

FINANCIAL AID PROCEDURES

Forms required: FAFSA.

Dates and Deadlines: Priority date 2/15; no closing date. Applicants notified on a rolling basis starting 3/1; must reply by 5/1 or within 2 week(s) of notification.

Transfers: Institutional grants available based on financial need.

CONTACT

William Burke, Director of Financial Aid
800 Linden Street, Scranton, PA 18510-4699
(570) 941-7700

University of the Arts

Philadelphia, Pennsylvania
www.uarts.edu Federal Code: 003350

4-year private visual arts and performing arts college in very large city.

Enrollment: 2,167 undergrads, 1% part-time. 549 full-time freshmen.

BASIC COSTS (2008-2009)

Tuition and fees: $30,600.
Per-credit charge: $1,230.
Room only: $8,712.

FINANCIAL AID PICTURE

Students with need: Need-based aid available for full-time and part-time students. Work study available nights, weekends, and for part-time students.

Students without need: No-need awards available for academics, art, music/drama.

Scholarships offered: Merit awards; available to students who demonstrate exceptional talent and academic abilities.

FINANCIAL AID PROCEDURES

Forms required: FAFSA.

Dates and Deadlines: Priority date 3/1; no closing date. Applicants notified on a rolling basis starting 3/15; must reply within 2 week(s) of notification.

Transfers: Undergraduate transfers not eligible for federal, state, or university aid if 4-year degree previously conferred.

CONTACT

Chris Pesotski, Director, Financial Aid
320 South Broad Street, Philadelphia, PA 19102
(215) 717-6170

University of the Sciences in Philadelphia

Philadelphia, Pennsylvania
www.usp.edu Federal Code: 003353

4-year private health science and pharmacy college in very large city.

Enrollment: 2,063 undergrads, 1% part-time. 535 full-time freshmen.

Selectivity: Admits 50 to 75% of applicants.

BASIC COSTS (2008-2009)

Tuition and fees: $28,506.
Per-credit charge: $1,130.
Room and board: $11,146.

FINANCIAL AID PICTURE (2007-2008)

Students with need: Out of 490 full-time freshmen who applied for aid, 490 were judged to have need. Of these, 490 received aid, and 283 had their full need met. Average financial aid package met 78% of need; average scholarship/grant was $9,954; average loan was $3,600. For part-time students, average financial aid package was $8,250.

Students without need: 42 full-time freshmen who did not demonstrate need for aid received scholarships/grants; average award was $8,263. No-need awards available for academics, athletics.

Scholarships offered: 2 full-time freshmen received athletic scholarships; average amount $2,500.

FINANCIAL AID PROCEDURES

Forms required: FAFSA.

Dates and Deadlines: Closing date 3/15. Applicants notified on a rolling basis starting 1/15; must reply by 5/1 or within 2 week(s) of notification.

CONTACT

Paula Lehrberger, Director of Financial Aid
600 South 43rd Street, Philadelphia, PA 19104-4495
(215) 596-8894

Ursinus College

Collegeville, Pennsylvania Federal Code: 003385
www.ursinus.edu CSS Code: 2931

4-year private liberal arts college in small town.

Enrollment: 1,655 undergrads. 543 full-time freshmen.

Selectivity: Admits 50 to 75% of applicants.

BASIC COSTS (2008-2009)

Tuition and fees: $36,910.
Per-credit charge: $1,148.
Room and board: $8,800.

FINANCIAL AID PICTURE (2008-2009)

Students with need: Average financial aid package met 84% of need; average scholarship/grant was $22,007; average loan was $3,832.

Students without need: No-need awards available for academics, alumni affiliation, art, leadership, music/drama.

Cumulative student debt: 75% of graduating class had student loans; average debt was $21,171.

FINANCIAL AID PROCEDURES

Forms required: FAFSA, CSS PROFILE, institutional form.
Dates and Deadlines: Closing date 2/15. Applicants notified by 4/1; must reply by 5/1 or within 2 week(s) of notification.
Transfers: Closing date 8/1.

CONTACT

Suzanne Sparrow, Director of Student Financial Services
PO Box 1000, Collegeville, PA 19426-1000
(610) 409-3600

Valley Forge Christian College

Phoenixville, Pennsylvania
www.vfcc.edu Federal Code: 003306

4-year private liberal arts college in large town, affiliated with Assemblies of God.
Enrollment: 969 undergrads, 16% part-time. 266 full-time freshmen.
Selectivity: Admits over 75% of applicants.

BASIC COSTS (2009-2010)

Tuition and fees: $14,232.
Per-credit charge: $513.
Room and board: $6,896.

FINANCIAL AID PICTURE (2007-2008)

Students with need: Out of 170 full-time freshmen who applied for aid, 149 were judged to have need. Of these, 147 received aid, and 14 had their full need met. Average financial aid package met 52% of need; average scholarship/grant was $6,059; average loan was $3,187. For part-time students, average financial aid package was $6,615.
Students without need: 107 full-time freshmen who did not demonstrate need for aid received scholarships/grants; average award was $4,566. No-need awards available for academics, leadership, music/drama, religious affiliation, state/district residency.
Scholarships offered: Trustee's Scholarship, President's Scholarship, Dean's Scholarship, Professor's Scholarship; ranging from full tuition (minimum 3.5 GPA, 1300 SAT or 29 ACT, and upper 10% class rank) to $1,000-$5,000 (minimum 3.3 GPA and 1030 SAT or 22 ACT); application required for awards; renewable with 3.5 GPA. SAT scores exclusive of Writing.
Cumulative student debt: 98% of graduating class had student loans; average debt was $32,505.

FINANCIAL AID PROCEDURES

Forms required: FAFSA.
Dates and Deadlines: Priority date 5/1; no closing date. Applicants notified on a rolling basis starting 3/15; must reply within 3 week(s) of notification.

CONTACT

Evie Meyer, Director of Financial Aid
1401 Charlestown Road, Phoenixville, PA 19460
(610) 917-1475

Valley Forge Military Academy & College

Wayne, Pennsylvania
www.vfmac.edu Federal Code: 003386

2-year private junior and military college in small city.
Enrollment: 217 undergrads.

BASIC COSTS (2008-2009)

Tuition and fees: $26,441.
Room and board: $8,535.

FINANCIAL AID PICTURE (2007-2008)

Students with need: Need-based aid available for full-time students. Work study available nights, weekends, and for part-time students.
Students without need: No-need awards available for academics, alumni affiliation, athletics, music/drama, ROTC, state/district residency.
Additional info: Students enrolled in advanced military science program can receive up to $5,000 from the Army. In addition, competitively awarded ROTC scholarships pay average of another $14,100 per school year for direct educational expenses.

FINANCIAL AID PROCEDURES

Forms required: FAFSA, institutional form.
Dates and Deadlines: Closing date 5/1. Applicants notified on a rolling basis starting 5/15; must reply within 2 week(s) of notification.
Transfers: Must submit financial aid transcripts from all previously attended colleges, even if aid was not received.

CONTACT

Donna Speranza, Financial Aid Director
1001 Eagle Road, Wayne, PA 19087
(610) 989-1300 ext. 1306

Vet Tech Institute

Pittsburgh, Pennsylvania
www.vettechinstitute.edu Federal Code: 008568

2-year for-profit health science and technical college in large city.
Enrollment: 320 undergrads.

BASIC COSTS (2008-2009)

Tuition and fees: $29,250.
Additional info: Tuition at time of enrollment locked for 2 years.

FINANCIAL AID PICTURE

Students with need: Work study available nights.
Students without need: No-need awards available for academics.
Scholarships offered: $1,000 scholarships; 5 offered to commuters. $2,000 scholarships; 2 offered to students not living at home. Awarded based on results of examination given at school in November and March.

FINANCIAL AID PROCEDURES

Forms required: FAFSA, state aid form.
Dates and Deadlines: No deadline. Applicants notified on a rolling basis.

CONTACT

Donna Durr, Financial Aid Director
125 Seventh Street, Pittsburgh, PA 15222-3400
(800) 570-0693

Villanova University

Villanova, Pennsylvania
www.villanova.edu Federal Code: 003388

4-year private university in large town, affiliated with Roman Catholic Church.
Enrollment: 6,884 undergrads, 4% part-time. 1,604 full-time freshmen.
Selectivity: Admits less than 50% of applicants.

BASIC COSTS (2009-2010)

Tuition and fees: $37,655.
Per-credit charge: $1,540.
Room and board: $10,070.
Additional info: Full-time tuition includes laptop for all students.

FINANCIAL AID PICTURE (2008-2009)

Students with need: Out of 1,045 full-time freshmen who applied for aid, 755 were judged to have need. Of these, 748 received aid, and 177 had their full need met. Average financial aid package met 84% of need; average scholarship/grant was $23,198; average loan was $3,692. For part-time students, average financial aid package was $14,364.

Students without need: 102 full-time freshmen who did not demonstrate need for aid received scholarships/grants; average award was $9,274. No-need awards available for academics, alumni affiliation, athletics, leadership, minority status, religious affiliation, ROTC.

Scholarships offered: 38 full-time freshmen received athletic scholarships; average amount $35,172.

FINANCIAL AID PROCEDURES

Forms required: FAFSA, institutional form.

Dates and Deadlines: Closing date 2/7. Applicants notified by 4/1; must reply by 5/1 or within 2 week(s) of notification.

Transfers: Closing date 7/15. Applicants notified on a rolling basis starting 5/1; must reply within 2 week(s) of notification.

CONTACT

Bonnie Lee Behm, Director of Financial Assistance
800 Lancaster Avenue, Villanova, PA 19085-1672
(610) 519-4010

Washington & Jefferson College

Washington, Pennsylvania
www.washjeff.edu Federal Code: 003389

4-year private liberal arts college in large town.

Enrollment: 1,488 undergrads, 1% part-time. 399 full-time freshmen.

Selectivity: Admits less than 50% of applicants.

BASIC COSTS (2009-2010)

Tuition and fees: $32,895.

Per-credit charge: $815.

Room and board: $9,110.

FINANCIAL AID PICTURE (2008-2009)

Students with need: Out of 348 full-time freshmen who applied for aid, 299 were judged to have need. Of these, 299 received aid, and 46 had their full need met. Average financial aid package met 80% of need; average scholarship/grant was $16,433; average loan was $3,934. For part-time students, average financial aid package was $6,623.

Students without need: 94 full-time freshmen who did not demonstrate need for aid received scholarships/grants; average award was $11,090. No-need awards available for academics, alumni affiliation.

Scholarships offered: Presidential Scholarship; based on distinguished academic performance. Scholars Award; based on distinguished academic performance. Joseph Hardy Sr. Scholarship; for students in entrepreneurial studies program. Dean's Award; based on academic performance in high school, distinguished achievement outside the classroom, and good citizenship. Challenge Grant; for students who show academic promise. Alumni Scholarship; for students whose father and/or mother are alumni.

Cumulative student debt: 75% of graduating class had student loans; average debt was $20,000.

FINANCIAL AID PROCEDURES

Forms required: FAFSA.

Dates and Deadlines: Priority date 2/15; no closing date. Applicants notified on a rolling basis starting 3/1; must reply by 5/1.

Transfers: Must reply within 2 week(s) of notification. Students should complete the FAFSA as soon as possible. Financial aid awards will be made when FAFSA has been received and the student has been accepted for admission. For students selected for verification, these awards are estimated until the required tax documentation has been received and reviewed.

CONTACT

Michelle Vettorel, Director of Financial Aid
60 South Lincoln Street, Washington, PA 15301
(724) 223-6019

Waynesburg University

Waynesburg, Pennsylvania
www.waynesburg.edu Federal Code: 003391

4-year private liberal arts college in small town, affiliated with Presbyterian Church (USA).

Enrollment: 1,640 undergrads, 4% part-time. 380 full-time freshmen.

Selectivity: Admits over 75% of applicants.

BASIC COSTS (2009-2010)

Tuition and fees: $17,760.

Per-credit charge: $730.

Room and board: $7,370.

FINANCIAL AID PICTURE (2008-2009)

Students with need: Average financial aid package met 82% of need; average scholarship/grant was $10,892; average loan was $3,747. For part-time students, average financial aid package was $5,523.

Students without need: No-need awards available for academics, alumni affiliation, job skills, leadership, religious affiliation, state/district residency.

Scholarships offered: A.B. Miller Scholarship; $8,000. Presidential Honor Scholarship; $6,000. Honor Scholarship; $4,000. College Leadership Program; $1,000-$1,900.

Cumulative student debt: 85% of graduating class had student loans; average debt was $19,000.

FINANCIAL AID PROCEDURES

Forms required: FAFSA, state aid form.

Dates and Deadlines: Priority date 3/15; no closing date. Applicants notified on a rolling basis starting 2/15; must reply within 2 week(s) of notification.

Transfers: No deadline. Applicants notified on a rolling basis; must reply within 2 week(s) of notification.

CONTACT

Matthew Stokan, Director of Financial Aid
51 West College Street, Waynesburg, PA 15370-1222
(724) 852-3208

West Chester University of Pennsylvania

West Chester, Pennsylvania
www.wcupa.edu Federal Code: 003328

4-year public university in large town.

Enrollment: 11,127 undergrads, 8% part-time. 1,957 full-time freshmen.

Selectivity: Admits less than 50% of applicants.

BASIC COSTS (2008-2009)

Tuition and fees: $6,737; out-of-state residents $14,775.

Per-credit charge: $223; out-of-state residents $558.

Room and board: $6,874.

FINANCIAL AID PICTURE (2007-2008)

Students with need: Out of 1,650 full-time freshmen who applied for aid, 1,039 were judged to have need. Of these, 976 received aid, and 378 had their full need met. Average financial aid package met 61% of need; average scholarship/grant was $5,251; average loan was $3,523. For part-time students, average financial aid package was $7,269.

Students without need: 110 full-time freshmen who did not demonstrate need for aid received scholarships/grants; average award was $2,383.

Scholarships offered: 21 full-time freshmen received athletic scholarships; average amount $2,467.

Cumulative student debt: 65% of graduating class had student loans; average debt was $25,179.

FINANCIAL AID PROCEDURES

Forms required: FAFSA.

Dates and Deadlines: Priority date 3/1; no closing date. Must reply within 4 week(s) of notification.

CONTACT

Dana Parker, Director of Financial Aid
Messikomer Hall, West Chester, PA 19383
(610) 436-2627

Westminster College

New Wilmington, Pennsylvania
www.westminster.edu Federal Code: 003392

4-year private liberal arts college in small town, affiliated with Presbyterian Church (USA).

Enrollment: 1,408 undergrads.

Selectivity: Admits 50 to 75% of applicants.

BASIC COSTS (2008-2009)

Tuition and fees: $28,100.

Per-credit charge: $820.

Room and board: $8,100.

Additional info: Tuition/fee waivers available for adults.

FINANCIAL AID PICTURE (2008-2009)

Students with need: Need-based aid available for full-time and part-time students.

Students without need: No-need awards available for academics, athletics.

FINANCIAL AID PROCEDURES

Forms required: FAFSA, institutional form.

Dates and Deadlines: Closing date 5/1. Applicants notified on a rolling basis starting 11/1; must reply by 5/1 or within 3 week(s) of notification.

CONTACT

Cheryl Gerber, Director of Financial Aid
Admissions, Westminster College, New Wilmington, PA 16172-0001
(724) 946-7102

Westmoreland County Community College

Youngwood, Pennsylvania
www.wccc.edu Federal Code: 010176

2-year public community college in small town.

Enrollment: 5,584 undergrads, 48% part-time. 1,198 full-time freshmen.

Selectivity: Open admission; but selective for some programs.

BASIC COSTS (2008-2009)

Tuition and fees: $2,580; out-of-district residents $4,860; out-of-state residents $7,140.

Per-credit charge: $76; out-of-district residents $152; out-of-state residents $228.

FINANCIAL AID PICTURE

Students with need: Need-based aid available for full-time and part-time students. Work study available nights.

Students without need: No-need awards available for academics.

FINANCIAL AID PROCEDURES

Forms required: FAFSA, institutional form.

Dates and Deadlines: No deadline. Applicants notified on a rolling basis starting 5/1.

CONTACT

Gary Means, Director of Financial Aid
145 Pavilion Lane, Youngwood, PA 15697
(724) 925-4063

Widener University

Chester, Pennsylvania
www.widener.edu Federal Code: 003313

4-year private university in large town.

Enrollment: 3,206 undergrads, 17% part-time. 718 full-time freshmen.

Selectivity: Admits 50 to 75% of applicants.

BASIC COSTS (2009-2010)

Tuition and fees: $31,840.

Per-credit charge: $1,045.

Room and board: $11,270.

Additional info: $1,050 additional fee for engineering students; $230 additional fee for junior/senior nursing students.

FINANCIAL AID PICTURE (2008-2009)

Students with need: Out of 648 full-time freshmen who applied for aid, 587 were judged to have need. Of these, 587 received aid, and 91 had their full need met. Average financial aid package met 80% of need; average scholarship/grant was $10,523; average loan was $4,370. For part-time students, average financial aid package was $9,133.

Students without need: 101 full-time freshmen who did not demonstrate need for aid received scholarships/grants; average award was $12,043. No-need awards available for academics, leadership, music/drama, ROTC.

Scholarships offered: Academic Scholarships; $4,000 to full tuition; based on SAT and GPA; renewable. Music, leadership, and community service scholarships; based on performance evaluations.

Cumulative student debt: 93% of graduating class had student loans; average debt was $36,398.

FINANCIAL AID PROCEDURES

Forms required: FAFSA.

Dates and Deadlines: Priority date 2/15; no closing date. Applicants notified on a rolling basis starting 3/15; must reply within 4 week(s) of notification.

Transfers: Transfer scholarships; $2,500 to $10,000; based on GPA and minimum of 24 transferable credits.

CONTACT

Thomas Malloy, Director of Financial Aid
One University Place, Chester, PA 19013
(610) 499-4174

Wilkes University

Wilkes-Barre, Pennsylvania
www.wilkes.edu Federal Code: 003394

4-year private university in small city.

Enrollment: 2,211 undergrads, 6% part-time. 561 full-time freshmen.

Selectivity: Admits over 75% of applicants.

BASIC COSTS (2008-2009)

Tuition and fees: $25,170.

Per-credit charge: $660.

Room and board: $10,780.

FINANCIAL AID PICTURE (2008-2009)

Students with need: Need-based aid available for full-time and part-time students.

Students without need: No-need awards available for academics, leadership, minority status, music/drama.

FINANCIAL AID PROCEDURES

Forms required: FAFSA.

Dates and Deadlines: Priority date 3/1; no closing date. Applicants notified on a rolling basis starting 3/1.

CONTACT

Michael Frantz, Vice President of Enrollment Services
84 West South Street, Wilkes-Barre, PA 18766
(570) 408-2000

Wilson College

Chambersburg, Pennsylvania
www.wilson.edu Federal Code: 003396

4-year private liberal arts college for women in large town, affiliated with Presbyterian Church (USA).

Enrollment: 497 undergrads, 36% part-time. 87 full-time freshmen.

Selectivity: Admits 50 to 75% of applicants.

BASIC COSTS (2008-2009)

Tuition and fees: $25,900.

Room and board: $8,630.

FINANCIAL AID PICTURE (2008-2009)

Students with need: Need-based aid available for full-time and part-time students. Work study available nights, weekends, and for part-time students.

Students without need: No-need awards available for academics, alumni affiliation, religious affiliation, state/district residency.

Scholarships offered: Scholarships; for full-time students who are members of Presbyterian Church, USA. Curran Scholarships; awarded to incoming students with significant community service.

FINANCIAL AID PROCEDURES

Forms required: FAFSA, state aid form, institutional form.

Dates and Deadlines: Priority date 4/30; no closing date. Applicants notified on a rolling basis starting 2/15.

Transfers: Tuition scholarships available to transfer articulation students who hold associate degrees from Harrisburg Area Community College, Hagerstown Community College, Central Penn College, Luzerne County Community College, Lehigh Carbon Community College, Harcum College, Frederick Community College, Howard Community College, Cottey College; transfer merit scholarships for students with 3.0 GPA; Phi Theta Kappa scholarship.

CONTACT

Linda Brittain, Associate Dean of Enrollment and Director of Financial Aid
1015 Philadelphia Avenue, Chambersburg, PA 17201-1285
(717) 262-2016

York College of Pennsylvania

York, Pennsylvania
www.ycp.edu Federal Code: 003399

4-year private liberal arts college in small city.

Enrollment: 5,126 undergrads, 10% part-time. 1,092 full-time freshmen.

Selectivity: Admits 50 to 75% of applicants.

BASIC COSTS (2009-2010)

Tuition and fees: $14,460.

Per-credit charge: $405.

Room and board: $8,080.

FINANCIAL AID PICTURE (2008-2009)

Students with need: Out of 950 full-time freshmen who applied for aid, 625 were judged to have need. Of these, 615 received aid, and 171 had their full need met. Average financial aid package met 73% of need; average scholarship/grant was $5,103; average loan was $5,248. For part-time students, average financial aid package was $5,946.

Students without need: 219 full-time freshmen who did not demonstrate need for aid received scholarships/grants; average award was $2,988. No-need awards available for academics, alumni affiliation, music/drama.

Scholarships offered: Trustee Scholarships; full tuition; for students with top 20% class rank and 1210 SAT or 29 ACT; 10 awarded. Valedictorian and Salutatorian Scholarships; half tuition; for students who are valedictorians or salutatorians and have 1150 SAT or 26 ACT; unlimited number awarded. Dean's Academic Scholarships; one-third tuition; for students with top 40% class rank and 1150 SAT or 26 ACT. SAT scores exclusive of Writing portion.

Cumulative student debt: 69% of graduating class had student loans; average debt was $20,625.

FINANCIAL AID PROCEDURES

Forms required: FAFSA.

Dates and Deadlines: No deadline. Applicants notified on a rolling basis starting 3/1; must reply within 4 week(s) of notification.

Transfers: No deadline. Applicants notified on a rolling basis starting 3/9. Transfer Merit Scholarship; $2,000 ($1,000 per semester) for entering transfer students with minimum 3.5 GPA.

CONTACT

Calvin Williams, Director of Financial Aid
441 Country Club Road, York, PA 17403-3651
(717) 849-1682

Yorktowne Business Institute

York, Pennsylvania
www.ybi.edu Federal Code: 014766

2-year for-profit business and health science college in small city.

Enrollment: 250 undergrads.

Selectivity: Open admission; but selective for some programs.

BASIC COSTS (2008-2009)

Additional info: Tuition $18,750 for business and medical programs, $28,470 for culinary program. Fees vary and are charged on a per term basis.

FINANCIAL AID PICTURE

Students with need: Need-based aid available for full-time and part-time students.

FINANCIAL AID PROCEDURES

Forms required: FAFSA, state aid form.

Dates and Deadlines: Priority date 5/1; no closing date.

CONTACT

Deborah Bostick, Financial Aid Director
West 7th Avenue, York, PA 17404-2034
(717) 846-5000 ext. 130

Puerto Rico

Atlantic College

Guaynabo, Puerto Rico
www.atlanticcollege.edu Federal Code: 016871

4-year private liberal arts college in small city.

Selectivity: Open admission.

BASIC COSTS (2008-2009)
Tuition and fees: $6,175.
Per-credit charge: $125.
Additional info: Tuition at time of enrollment locked for 4 years.

FINANCIAL AID PICTURE
Students with need: Need-based aid available for full-time and part-time students. Work study available nights.
Students without need: This college awards aid only to students with need.

FINANCIAL AID PROCEDURES
Forms required: FAFSA, institutional form.
Dates and Deadlines: Closing date 6/30. Applicants notified on a rolling basis starting 4/1; must reply within 2 week(s) of notification.
Transfers: Priority date 1/7; closing date 6/7.

CONTACT
Janice Rivera, Director of Financial Aid
PO Box 3918, Guaynabo, PR 00970
(787) 789-4251

Bayamon Central University
Bayamon, Puerto Rico
www.ucb.edu.pr Federal Code: 010015

4-year private university in large city, affiliated with Roman Catholic Church.
Selectivity: Admits less than 50% of applicants.

BASIC COSTS (2008-2009)
Tuition and fees: $7,250.

FINANCIAL AID PICTURE (2008-2009)
Students with need: Need-based aid available for full time and part-time students. Work study available nights.
Students without need: This college awards aid only to students with need.

FINANCIAL AID PROCEDURES
Forms required: FAFSA, institutional form.
Dates and Deadlines: Priority date 5/31; closing date 7/2.
Transfers: Closing date 5/30.

CONTACT
Velma Aponte, Director of Financial Aid Office
PO Box 1725, Bayamon, PR 00960-1725
(787) 786-3030 ext. 2116

Caribbean University
Bayamon, Puerto Rico
www.caribbean.edu Federal Code: 012525

4-year private health science and liberal arts college in large city.
Enrollment: 4,600 undergrads.

BASIC COSTS (2009-2010)
Tuition and fees: $4,520.
Additional info: Annual full-time tuition for engineering program: $3,960; per-credit-hour charge: $165.

FINANCIAL AID PICTURE (2007-2008)
Students with need: 65% of average financial aid package awarded as scholarships/grants, 35% awarded as loans/jobs. Need-based aid available for part-time students. Work study available nights, weekends, and for part-time students.
Students without need: This college awards aid only to students with need.
Cumulative student debt: 10% of graduating class had student loans; average debt was $3,000.

FINANCIAL AID PROCEDURES
Forms required: FAFSA.
Dates and Deadlines: Priority date 5/30; no closing date. Applicants notified on a rolling basis starting 7/30; must reply within 2 week(s) of notification.
Transfers: Closing date 5/30. Applicants notified on a rolling basis.

CONTACT
Edwin Sanchez, Financial Aid Director
PO Box 493, Bayamon, PR 00960-0493
(787) 780-0070 ext. 1125

Carlos Albizu University: San Juan
San Juan, Puerto Rico
www.albizu.edu Federal Code: 010724

Upper-division private university in large town.
Enrollment: 181 undergrads.

BASIC COSTS (2009-2010)
Tuition and fees: $5,123.
Per-credit charge: $160.

FINANCIAL AID PICTURE (2007-2008)
Students with need: 71% of average financial aid package awarded as scholarships/grants, 29% awarded as loans/jobs.

FINANCIAL AID PROCEDURES
Dates and Deadlines: Priority date 3/20; no closing date.

CONTACT
Doris Quero-Mendez, Financial Aid Director
151 Tanca Street, San Juan, PR 00902-3711
(787) 725-6500 ext. 1515

Colegio Pentecostal Mizpa
San Juan, Puerto Rico
www.colmizpa.edu Federal Code: 035313

4-year private Bible college in very large city, affiliated with Pentecostal Holiness Church.
Enrollment: 237 undergrads, 62% part-time. 7 full-time freshmen.
Selectivity: Admits over 75% of applicants.

FINANCIAL AID PICTURE (2007-2008)
Students with need: Need-based aid available for part-time students.
Students without need: This college awards aid only to students with need.

FINANCIAL AID PROCEDURES
Forms required: FAFSA.
Dates and Deadlines: No deadline.
Transfers: Applicants notified by 8/30.

CONTACT
Elisamuel Rodriguez, Administrative Dean
PO Box 20966, San Juan, PR 00928-0966

Columbia Centro Universitario: Caguas
Caguas, Puerto Rico
www.columbiaco.edu Federal Code: 013517

4-year for-profit business and technical college in small city.
Enrollment: 999 undergrads, 53% part-time. 147 full-time freshmen.

Selectivity: Open admission; but selective for some programs.

BASIC COSTS (2008-2009)
Tuition and fees: $4,360.
Per-credit charge: $160.

FINANCIAL AID PICTURE (2007-2008)
Students with need: Average financial aid package for all full-time undergraduates was $5,231; for part-time $5,231.
Students without need: This college awards aid only to students with need.

CONTACT
Virginia Guang, Financial Aid Administrator
PO Box 8517, Caguas, PR 00726
(787) 743-4041 ext. 223

Columbia Centro Universitario: Yauco
Yauco, Puerto Rico
www.columbiaco.edu Federal Code: 008902

2-year for-profit business and nursing college in large town.
Enrollment: 544 undergrads, 36% part-time. 120 full-time freshmen.
Selectivity: Open admission; but selective for some programs.

BASIC COSTS (2008-2009)
Tuition and fees: $4,360.
Per-credit charge: $160.

FINANCIAL AID PICTURE (2007-2008)
Students with need: 53% of average financial aid package awarded as scholarships/grants, 47% awarded as loans/jobs. Need-based aid available for part-time students. Work study available weekends and for part-time students.
Students without need: This college awards aid only to students with need.

FINANCIAL AID PROCEDURES
Forms required: FAFSA, institutional form.

CONTACT
Edwin Vargas, Director of Financial Aid
Box 3062, Yauco, PR 00698-3062

Conservatory of Music of Puerto Rico
San Juan, Puerto Rico
www.cmpr.edu Federal Code: 010819

4-year public music college in large city.
Enrollment: 402 undergrads, 25% part-time. 92 full-time freshmen.
Selectivity: Admits 50 to 75% of applicants.

BASIC COSTS (2008-2009)
Tuition and fees: $2,750.
Per-credit charge: $75.

FINANCIAL AID PICTURE (2007-2008)
Students with need: Out of 55 full-time freshmen who applied for aid, 55 were judged to have need. Of these, 55 received aid, and 29 had their full need met. Average financial aid package met 52% of need; average scholarship/grant was $3,096; average loan was $2,625. Need-based aid available for part-time students.
Students without need: This college awards aid only to students with need.

FINANCIAL AID PROCEDURES
Forms required: FAFSA, institutional form.
Dates and Deadlines: Priority date 12/15; no closing date. Applicants notified on a rolling basis starting 4/30.
Transfers: Closing date 4/15.

CONTACT
Jorge Medina, Financial Aid Officer
Rafael Lamar #350 Esq. Roosevelt, San Juan, PR 00918-2199
(787) 751-0160 ext. 231

Escuela de Artes Plasticas de Puerto Rico
San Juan, Puerto Rico
www.eap.edu Federal Code: 017345

4-year public visual arts college in large city.
Enrollment: 512 undergrads, 33% part-time. 69 full-time freshmen.
Selectivity: Admits 50 to 75% of applicants.

BASIC COSTS (2008-2009)
Tuition and fees: $2,611.
Per-credit charge: $80.

FINANCIAL AID PICTURE (2007-2008)
Students with need: 99% of average financial aid package awarded as scholarships/grants, 1% awarded as loans/jobs. Need-based aid available for part-time students. Work study available weekends and for part-time students.
Students without need: This college awards aid only to students with need.

FINANCIAL AID PROCEDURES
Forms required: FAFSA, institutional form.
Dates and Deadlines: Priority date 4/25; closing date 5/23. Applicants notified by 7/11.

CONTACT
Alfred Melendez, Director of Financial Aid
PO Box 9021112, San Juan, PR 00902-1112

Huertas Junior College
Caguas, Puerto Rico
www.huertas.edu Federal Code: 014105

2-year for-profit junior and technical college in small city.
Enrollment: 1,774 undergrads, 17% part-time. 373 full-time freshmen.
Selectivity: Open admission.

BASIC COSTS (2008-2009)
Additional info: Tuition at time of enrollment locked for 2 years.

FINANCIAL AID PICTURE (2008-2009)
Students with need: Out of 373 full-time freshmen who applied for aid, 316 were judged to have need. Of these, 316 received aid. Need-based aid available for part-time students.
Students without need: This college awards aid only to students with need.

FINANCIAL AID PROCEDURES
Forms required: FAFSA, institutional form.
Dates and Deadlines: No deadline. Applicants notified on a rolling basis.

CONTACT
Wanda Ortiz, Financial Aid Director
PO Box 8429, Caguas, PR 00726
(787) 746-1400

Humacao Community College

Humacao, Puerto Rico Federal Code: 014952

2-year private business and community college in small city.
Enrollment: 769 undergrads, 25% part-time. 218 full-time freshmen.
Selectivity: Open admission.

BASIC COSTS (2009-2010)

Tuition and fees: $4,602.
Per-credit charge: $108.

FINANCIAL AID PICTURE (2007-2008)

Students with need: 98% of average financial aid package awarded as scholarships/grants, 2% awarded as loans/jobs. Need-based aid available for part-time students. Work study available nights.
Students without need: This college awards aid only to students with need.

FINANCIAL AID PROCEDURES

Forms required: FAFSA, state aid form, institutional form.
Dates and Deadlines: Priority date 1/1; closing date 6/30. Applicants notified on a rolling basis starting 3/4.
Transfers: No deadline.

CONTACT

Esther Figueroa, Financial Aid Director
PO Box 9139, Humacao, PR 00792-9139
(787) 852-1430 ext. 28

Inter American University of Puerto Rico: Aguadilla Campus

Aguadilla, Puerto Rico
www.aguadilla.inter.edu Federal Code: 003939

4-year private university and liberal arts college in small city.
Enrollment: 4,224 undergrads, 17% part-time. 637 full-time freshmen.
Selectivity: Open admission; but selective for some programs.

BASIC COSTS (2009-2010)

Tuition and fees: $5,308.
Per-credit charge: $161.
Additional info: Tuition at time of enrollment locked for 4 years.

FINANCIAL AID PICTURE

Students with need: Need-based aid available for full-time and part-time students. Work study available nights, weekends, and for part-time students.
Students without need: No-need awards available for academics.

FINANCIAL AID PROCEDURES

Forms required: FAFSA.
Dates and Deadlines: Closing date 4/30. Applicants notified by 6/15; must reply by 8/8.
Transfers: No deadline.

CONTACT

Gloria Cortes, Director of Financial Aid
Box 20000, Aguadilla, PR 00605
(787) 891-0925 ext. 2110

Inter American University of Puerto Rico: Arecibo Campus

Arecibo, Puerto Rico
www.arecibo.inter.edu Federal Code: 005026

4-year private liberal arts college in small city.
Enrollment: 4,454 undergrads.
Selectivity: Admits over 75% of applicants.

BASIC COSTS (2008-2009)

Tuition and fees: $5,382.
Per-credit charge: $154.

FINANCIAL AID PICTURE (2007-2008)

Students with need: 66% of average financial aid package awarded as scholarships/grants, 34% awarded as loans/jobs. Need-based aid available for part-time students. Work study available nights, weekends, and for part-time students.
Students without need: No-need awards available for academics, athletics.

FINANCIAL AID PROCEDURES

Forms required: FAFSA, institutional form.
Dates and Deadlines: Priority date 5/1; no closing date. Applicants notified on a rolling basis.

CONTACT

Ramon de Jesus, Director of Financial Aid
PO Box 4050, Arecibo, PR 00614-4050
(787) 878-5475 ext. 2275

Inter American University of Puerto Rico: Bayamon Campus

Bayamon, Puerto Rico
bc.inter.edu Federal Code: 003938

4-year private university and engineering college in small city.
Enrollment: 5,114 undergrads, 16% part-time. 1,234 full-time freshmen.
Selectivity: Admits less than 50% of applicants.

BASIC COSTS (2008-2009)

Tuition and fees: $5,382.
Per-credit charge: $154.

FINANCIAL AID PICTURE (2008-2009)

Students with need: Out of 1,213 full-time freshmen who applied for aid, 1,192 were judged to have need. Of these, 974 received aid. Average financial aid package met 2% of need; average scholarship/grant was $233; average loan was $242. For part-time students, average financial aid package was $139.
Students without need: This college awards aid only to students with need.
Scholarships offered: 5 full-time freshmen received athletic scholarships; average amount $310.

FINANCIAL AID PROCEDURES

Forms required: FAFSA.
Dates and Deadlines: Priority date 6/30; no closing date. Applicants notified on a rolling basis starting 5/10.

CONTACT

Hector Vargas, Interim Director of Financial Aid
500 Dr. John Will Harris Road, Bayamon, PR 00957
(787) 279-1912 ext. 2025

Inter American University of Puerto Rico: Fajardo Campus

Fajardo, Puerto Rico
fajardo.inter.edu Federal Code: 010763

4-year private university and branch campus college in large town.
Enrollment: 2,130 undergrads.
Selectivity: Admits less than 50% of applicants.

BASIC COSTS (2008-2009)

Tuition and fees: $5,382.
Per-credit charge: $154.

FINANCIAL AID PICTURE (2007-2008)

Students with need: 81% of average financial aid package awarded as scholarships/grants, 19% awarded as loans/jobs.

FINANCIAL AID PROCEDURES

Forms required: FAFSA, institutional form.
Dates and Deadlines: Closing date 4/30. Applicants notified on a rolling basis.
Transfers: Closing date 4/9.

CONTACT

Lydia Santiago, Dean of Administration
Call Box 70003, Fajardo, PR 00738-7003
(787) 863-2390 ext. 2309

Inter American University of Puerto Rico: Metropolitan Campus

San Juan, Puerto Rico
www.metro.inter.edu Federal Code: 003938

4-year private branch campus college in large city.
Enrollment: 6,821 undergrads, 40% part-time. 622 full-time freshmen.
Selectivity: Admits less than 50% of applicants.

BASIC COSTS (2008-2009)

Tuition and fees: $5,382.
Per-credit charge: $154.

FINANCIAL AID PICTURE (2008-2009)

Students with need: Average financial aid package met 1% of need; average scholarship/grant was $39; average loan was $123. For part-time students, average financial aid package was $510.

FINANCIAL AID PROCEDURES

Forms required: FAFSA.
Dates and Deadlines: Closing date 4/30. Applicants notified on a rolling basis.

CONTACT

Glenda Diaz, Director of Financial Aid
Box 191293, San Juan, PR 00919-1293
(787) 250-1912 ext. 2185

Inter American University of Puerto Rico: Guayama Campus

Guayama, Puerto Rico
www.guayama.inter.edu Federal Code: 010764

4-year private university in large town.
Enrollment: 2,157 undergrads, 33% part-time. 356 full-time freshmen.
Selectivity: Admits 50 to 75% of applicants.

BASIC COSTS (2008-2009)

Tuition and fees: $5,332.
Per-credit charge: $154.

FINANCIAL AID PICTURE (2008-2009)

Students with need: Average financial aid package met 1% of need; average scholarship/grant was $70; average loan was $168. For part-time students, average financial aid package was $209.
Students without need: This college awards aid only to students with need.

FINANCIAL AID PROCEDURES

Forms required: FAFSA, institutional form.
Dates and Deadlines: Closing date 4/29. Applicants notified by 6/15; must reply by 7/30.
Transfers: No deadline.

CONTACT

Jose Vechini-Rodriguez, Director of Financial Aid
PO Box 10004, Guayama, PR 00785
(787) 864-2222 ext. 2206

Inter American University of Puerto Rico: Ponce Campus

Mercedita, Puerto Rico
ponce.inter.edu Federal Code: 005029

4-year private university in large town.
Enrollment: 5,673 undergrads, 39% part-time. 471 full-time freshmen.
Selectivity: Admits 50 to 75% of applicants.

BASIC COSTS (2008-2009)

Tuition and fees: $5,382.
Per-credit charge: $154.

FINANCIAL AID PICTURE (2008-2009)

Students with need: Average financial aid package met 3% of need; average scholarship/grant was $303; average loan was $415. For part-time students, average financial aid package was $271.
Students without need: This college awards aid only to students with need.
Scholarships offered: Scholarship program for first-time freshmen with a high school academic index of 3.0 or higher.

FINANCIAL AID PROCEDURES

Forms required: FAFSA.
Dates and Deadlines: No deadline.

CONTACT

Juan Portalatin, Director of Financial Aid
104 Turpo Industrial Park Road #1, Mercedita, PR 00715-1602
(787) 841-0102

Inter American University of Puerto Rico: San German Campus

San German, Puerto Rico
www.sg.inter.edu Federal Code: 00714

4-year private university in large town.
Enrollment: 4,798 undergrads, 27% part-time. 1,091 full-time freshmen.
Selectivity: Admits over 75% of applicants.

BASIC COSTS (2008-2009)

Tuition and fees: $5,382.
Per-credit charge: $154.
Room and board: $2,500.
Additional info: Tuition at time of enrollment locked for 4 years.

FINANCIAL AID PICTURE (2007-2008)

Students with need: Out of 1,044 full-time freshmen who applied for aid, 1,024 were judged to have need. Of these, 758 received aid, and 2 had their full need met. Average financial aid package met 3% of need; average scholarship/grant was $310; average loan was $398. For part-time students, average financial aid package was $250.
Students without need: No-need awards available for academics, athletics.
Scholarships offered: 35 full-time freshmen received athletic scholarships; average amount $779.

FINANCIAL AID PROCEDURES

Forms required: FAFSA, institutional form.
Dates and Deadlines: Closing date 5/14. Applicants notified on a rolling basis; must reply by 8/1.

CONTACT

Maria Lugo, Director of Financial Aid
Box 5100, San German, PR 00683-9801
(787) 264-1912

National College of Business and Technology: Arecibo

Arecibo, Puerto Rico
www.nationalcollegepr.edu Federal Code: 015953

3-year for-profit business and technical college in small city.
Enrollment: 2,014 undergrads. 690 full-time freshmen.
Selectivity: Admits 50 to 75% of applicants.

BASIC COSTS (2009-2010)

Tuition and fees: $7,260.
Per-credit charge: $165.

FINANCIAL AID PICTURE (2007-2008)

Students with need: Out of 646 full time freshmen who applied for aid, 646 were judged to have need. Of these, 636 received aid, and 1 had their full need met. Average financial aid package met 3% of need; average scholarship/grant was $2,946; average loan was $583. For part-time students, average financial aid package was $2,249.
Students without need: This college awards aid only to students with need.

FINANCIAL AID PROCEDURES

Forms required: FAFSA.
Dates and Deadlines: Priority date 12/31; closing date 4/29. Applicants notified on a rolling basis starting 5/2; must reply by 5/15 or within 2 week(s) of notification.

CONTACT

Desi Lopez-Padilla, Vice President of Compliance
PO Box 4035, MSC 452, Arecibo, PR 00614
(787) 780-5134 ext. 4020

National College of Business and Technology: Bayamon

Bayamon, Puerto Rico
www.nationalcollegepr.edu Federal Code: 015953

3-year for-profit business and technical college in small city.
Enrollment: 2,443 undergrads. 1,157 full-time freshmen.
Selectivity: Open admission; but selective for some programs.

BASIC COSTS (2009-2010)

Tuition and fees: $7,260.
Per-credit charge: $165.

FINANCIAL AID PICTURE (2007-2008)

Students with need: Out of 1,101 full-time freshmen who applied for aid, 1,101 were judged to have need. Of these, 1,071 received aid, and 3 had their full need met. Average financial aid package met 2% of need; average scholarship/grant was $2,946; average loan was $583. For part-time students, average financial aid package was $2,249.
Students without need: This college awards aid only to students with need.

FINANCIAL AID PROCEDURES

Forms required: FAFSA.
Dates and Deadlines: Priority date 12/31; closing date 4/29. Applicants notified on a rolling basis starting 5/2; must reply by 5/15 or within 2 week(s) of notification.
Transfers: No deadline.

CONTACT

Desi Lopez, Vice President of Compliance
PO Box 2036, Bayamon, PR 00960
(787) 780-5134 ext. 4134

National College of Business and Technology: Rio Grande

Rio Grande, Puerto Rico
www.nationalcollegepr.edu Federal Code: E01213

3-year for-profit business and technical college in small town.
Enrollment: 1,505 undergrads. 767 full-time freshmen.
Selectivity: Admits 50 to 75% of applicants.

BASIC COSTS (2009-2010)

Tuition and fees: $7,260.
Per-credit charge: $165.

FINANCIAL AID PICTURE (2007-2008)

Students with need: Out of 738 full-time freshmen who applied for aid, 738 were judged to have need. Of these, 702 received aid. Average financial aid package met 3% of need; average scholarship/grant was $2,946; average loan was $583. For part-time students, average financial aid package was $2,249.
Students without need: This college awards aid only to students with need.

FINANCIAL AID PROCEDURES

Forms required: FAFSA.
Dates and Deadlines: Must reply by 5/15 or within 2 week(s) of notification.
Transfers: No deadline.

CONTACT

Desi Lopez, Vice President of Compliance
PO Box 3064, Rio Grande, PR 00745
(787) 780-5134 ext. 4134

Pontifical Catholic University of Puerto Rico

Ponce, Puerto Rico
www.pucpr.edu Federal Code: 003936

4-year private university in small city, affiliated with Roman Catholic Church.
Enrollment: 5,246 undergrads.
Selectivity: Admits over 75% of applicants.

BASIC COSTS (2008-2009)
Tuition and fees: $5,478.
Per-credit charge: $155.
Room only: $1,275.

FINANCIAL AID PICTURE (2008-2009)
Students with need: Need-based aid available for full-time and part-time students. Work study available nights, weekends, and for part-time students.
Students without need: No-need awards available for academics, athletics.

FINANCIAL AID PROCEDURES
Forms required: FAFSA, institutional form.
Dates and Deadlines: Priority date 5/1; no closing date. Applicants notified by 6/15; must reply within 4 week(s) of notification.
Transfers: Priority date 5/8. Distribution of awards based on availability of funds when application received.

CONTACT
Rosalia Martinez, Director of Financial Aid
2250 Las Americas Avenue, Suite 284, Ponce, PR 00717-9777
(787) 651-2000 ext. 1054

Turabo University

Gurabo, Puerto Rico
www.suagm.edu/ut Federal Code: 011719

4-year private university and liberal arts college in small city.
Enrollment: 13,056 undergrads, 21% part-time. 2,124 full-time freshmen.
Selectivity: Open admission; but selective for some programs.

BASIC COSTS (2008-2009)
Tuition and fees: $4,584.
Room and board: $6,735.

FINANCIAL AID PICTURE (2008-2009)
Students with need: Need-based aid available for full-time and part-time students.
Students without need: This college awards aid only to students with need.

FINANCIAL AID PROCEDURES
Forms required: FAFSA.
Dates and Deadlines: Priority date 5/30; no closing date. Applicants notified by 8/30.

CONTACT
Carmen Rivera-Lopez, Admissions and Financial Aid Director
PO Box 3030, Gurabo, PR 00778
(787) 743-797 ext. 4350

Universidad Adventista de las Antillas

Mayaguez, Puerto Rico
www.uaa.edu Federal Code: 005019

4-year private university and liberal arts college in small city, affiliated with Seventh-day Adventists.
Enrollment: 883 undergrads, 10% part-time.
Selectivity: Open admission; but selective for some programs.

BASIC COSTS (2008-2009)
Tuition and fees: $9,922.
Room and board: $3,300.
Additional info: Tuition for nonresident aliens is the sum of private tuition ($4,408 per semester) and the Form I-20 deposit ($4,000 only in the first year); after the first year, these students receive credit refund at registration ($500 per semester). An average of $150 per semester is included in tuition for lab expenses.

FINANCIAL AID PICTURE (2008-2009)
Students with need: Need-based aid available for full-time and part-time students.

FINANCIAL AID PROCEDURES
Forms required: FAFSA, institutional form.
Dates and Deadlines: No deadline. Applicants notified on a rolling basis starting 8/15; must reply within 3 week(s) of notification.

CONTACT
Awilda Matos, Director of Financial Aid
PO Box 118, Mayaguez, PR 00681-0118
(787) 834-9595 ext. 2200

Universidad del Este

Carolina, Puerto Rico
www.suagm.edu/une Federal Code: 011718

4-year private university and liberal arts college in small city.
Enrollment: 11,920 undergrads, 31% part-time. 1,860 full-time freshmen.
Selectivity: Open admission; but selective for some programs.

BASIC COSTS (2008-2009)
Tuition and fees: $4,584.
Room and board: $6,735.

FINANCIAL AID PICTURE (2008-2009)
Students with need: Need-based aid available for full-time and part-time students.
Students without need: No-need awards available for academics, athletics.

FINANCIAL AID PROCEDURES
Forms required: FAFSA, state aid form, institutional form.
Dates and Deadlines: Priority date 5/30; no closing date. Applicants notified by 7/30.

CONTACT
Clotilde Santiago, Admissions and Financial Aid Director
PO Box 2010, Carolina, PR 00984-2010
(787) 257-7373 ext. 3401

Universidad Metropolitana

Rio Piedras, Puerto Rico
www.suagm.edu/umet Federal Code: 025875

4-year private university and liberal arts college in large city.
Enrollment: 9,797 undergrads, 20% part-time. 1,692 full-time freshmen.
Selectivity: Admits 50 to 75% of applicants.

BASIC COSTS (2008-2009)
Tuition and fees: $4,584.
Room and board: $6,735.

FINANCIAL AID PICTURE
Students with need: Need-based aid available for full-time and part-time students. Work study available nights.

Students without need: This college awards aid only to students with need.

FINANCIAL AID PROCEDURES

Forms required: FAFSA.

Dates and Deadlines: Priority date 5/30; no closing date. Applicants notified by 7/30.

CONTACT

Julio Rodriguez, Admissions and Financial Aid Director
Apartado 21150, San Juan, PR 00928
(787) 766-1717 ext. 6587

Universidad Politecnica de Puerto Rico

Hato Rey, Puerto Rico
www.pupr.edu Federal Code: 014055

5-year private university and engineering college in large city.

Enrollment: 5,133 undergrads.

Selectivity: Admits over 75% of applicants.

BASIC COSTS (2008-2009)

Tuition and fees: $6,393.

Room and board: $5,886.

FINANCIAL AID PICTURE (2007-2008)

Students with need: Need-based aid available for full-time and part-time students.

Students without need: No-need awards available for academics, music/drama.

FINANCIAL AID PROCEDURES

Forms required: FAFSA.

Dates and Deadlines: Priority date 5/15; closing date 6/30. Applicants notified by 7/15.

CONTACT

Carmen Ortiz, Director of Financial Aid
PO Box 192017, San Juan, PR 00919-2017
(787) 622-8000 ext. 249

University College of San Juan

San Juan, Puerto Rico
www.cunisanjuan.edu Federal Code: 010567

4-year public community and technical college in very large city.

Enrollment: 1,355 undergrads.

Selectivity: Admits over 75% of applicants.

BASIC COSTS (2008-2009)

Tuition and fees: $3,150.

Per-credit charge: $85.

Additional info: Tuition at time of enrollment locked for 4 years.

FINANCIAL AID PICTURE (2007-2008)

Students with need: Need-based aid available for full-time and part-time students.

Students without need: This college awards aid only to students with need.

FINANCIAL AID PROCEDURES

Forms required: FAFSA, institutional form.

Dates and Deadlines: Closing date 9/30. Applicants notified by 10/30.

Transfers: Financial aid transcripts.

CONTACT

Gloria Mirabal, Director of Financial Aid
180 Jose R. Oliver Avenue, San Juan, PR 00918
(787) 250-7111 ext. 2287

University of Puerto Rico: Aguadilla

Aguadilla, Puerto Rico
www.uprag.edu Federal Code: 012123

4-year public liberal arts and technical college in small city.

Enrollment: 2,934 undergrads, 9% part-time. 723 full-time freshmen.

Selectivity: Admits over 75% of applicants.

BASIC COSTS (2008-2009)

Tuition and fees: $1,752; out-of-state residents $4,077.

Per-credit charge: $47.

FINANCIAL AID PICTURE (2007-2008)

Students with need: 83% of average financial aid package awarded as scholarships/grants, 17% awarded as loans/jobs. Need-based aid available for part-time students.

Students without need: This college awards aid only to students with need.

FINANCIAL AID PROCEDURES

Forms required: FAFSA, institutional form.

Dates and Deadlines: Closing date 5/6. Applicants notified on a rolling basis starting 4/1; must reply within 1 week(s) of notification.

Transfers: No deadline.

CONTACT

Doris Roman, Financial Aid Director
Box 6150, Aguadilla, PR 00604-6150
(787) 890-0109

University of Puerto Rico: Arecibo

Arecibo, Puerto Rico
www.upra.edu Federal Code: 007228

4-year public university in small city.

BASIC COSTS (2008-2009)

Tuition and fees: $1,752; out-of-state residents $4,077.

Per-credit charge: $47.

FINANCIAL AID PICTURE (2007-2008)

Students with need: Need-based aid available for full-time and part-time students.

Students without need: This college awards aid only to students with need.

FINANCIAL AID PROCEDURES

Forms required: FAFSA, institutional form.

Dates and Deadlines: Closing date 4/27.

Transfers: Closing date 5/25.

CONTACT

Myrta Ortiz, Financial Aid Officer
PO Box 4010, Arecibo, PR 00614-4010
(787) 815-0000 ext. 4501

University of Puerto Rico: Carolina Regional College

Carolina, Puerto Rico
www.uprc.edu Federal Code: 003942

4-year public university in small city.
Enrollment: 4,154 undergrads, 24% part-time. 741 full-time freshmen.
Selectivity: Admits less than 50% of applicants.

BASIC COSTS (2008-2009)

Tuition and fees: $2,910; out-of-state residents $4,248.
Per-credit charge: $47.

FINANCIAL AID PICTURE (2007-2008)

Students with need: Out of 741 full-time freshmen who applied for aid, 741 were judged to have need. Of these, 741 received aid, and 3 had their full need met. Average financial aid package met 42% of need; average scholarship/grant was $393. For part-time students, average financial aid package was $3,067.
Students without need: This college awards aid only to students with need.

FINANCIAL AID PROCEDURES

Forms required: FAFSA, state aid form, institutional form.
Dates and Deadlines: Closing date 6/30. Applicants notified on a rolling basis starting 6/10.

CONTACT

Santa Castro, Financial Aid Officer/Director
PO Box 4800, Carolina, PR 00984-4800
(787) 769-0188

University of Puerto Rico: Cayey University College

Cayey, Puerto Rico
www.cayey.upr.edu Federal Code: 007206

4-year public liberal arts and teachers college in large town.
Enrollment: 3,691 undergrads, 10% part-time. 813 full-time freshmen.
Selectivity: Admits less than 50% of applicants.

BASIC COSTS (2008-2009)

Tuition and fees: $1,752; out-of-state residents $4,077.
Per-credit charge: $47.
Additional info: Tuition at time of enrollment locked for 4 years.

FINANCIAL AID PICTURE (2008-2009)

Students with need: Need-based aid available for full-time and part-time students. Work study available nights, weekends, and for part-time students.
Students without need: This college awards aid only to students with need.

FINANCIAL AID PROCEDURES

Forms required: FAFSA.
Dates and Deadlines: Closing date 6/30. Applicants notified by 7/30.
Transfers: Priority date 1/30; closing date 2/28.

CONTACT

James Rivera, Director of Financial Aid
Oficina de Admisiones UPR- Cayey, Cayey, PR 00736
(787) 738-2161 ext. 2061

University of Puerto Rico: Humacao

Humacao, Puerto Rico
www.uprh.edu Federal Code: 003942

4-year public university and liberal arts college in small city.
Enrollment: 4,500 undergrads, 8% part-time. 1,134 full-time freshmen.
Selectivity: Admits less than 50% of applicants.

BASIC COSTS (2008-2009)

Tuition and fees: $1,752; out-of-state residents $4,077.
Per-credit charge: $47.

FINANCIAL AID PICTURE (2008-2009)

Students with need: Need-based aid available for full-time and part-time students.
Students without need: No-need awards available for academics, athletics, music/drama.

FINANCIAL AID PROCEDURES

Forms required: FAFSA, institutional form.
Dates and Deadlines: Closing date 7/31. Applicants notified by 9/30.

CONTACT

Mariolga Rotger, Director of Financial Aid
100 Road 908 CUH Station, Humacao, PR 00791
(787) 850-9342

University of Puerto Rico: Mayaguez

Mayaguez, Puerto Rico
www.uprm.edu Federal Code: 003944

5-year public university in small city.
Enrollment: 12,011 undergrads, 6% part-time. 2,558 full-time freshmen.
Selectivity: Admits over 75% of applicants.

BASIC COSTS (2008-2009)

Tuition and fees: $1,752; out-of-state residents $4,077.
Per-credit charge: $47.

FINANCIAL AID PICTURE (2007-2008)

Students with need: Out of 1,764 full-time freshmen who applied for aid, 1,634 were judged to have need. Of these, 1,634 received aid. Average financial aid package met 65% of need; average scholarship/grant was $4,553; average loan was $3,500. For part-time students, average financial aid package was $739.
Students without need: This college awards aid only to students with need.
Cumulative student debt: 55% of graduating class had student loans; average debt was $12,000.

FINANCIAL AID PROCEDURES

Forms required: FAFSA, institutional form.
Dates and Deadlines: Priority date 1/30; closing date 6/30. Applicants notified on a rolling basis starting 5/30.
Transfers: Deadline according to admission date.

CONTACT

Ana Rodriguez, Director of Financial Aid
Admissions Office, Mayaguez, PR 00681-9021
(787) 265-1920

University of Puerto Rico: Medical Sciences

San Juan, Puerto Rico
www.rcm.upr.edu Federal Code: 003945

4-year public university in large city.
Enrollment: 462 undergrads, 13% part-time.

BASIC COSTS (2008-2009)
Tuition and fees: $1,752; out-of-state residents $4,077.
Per-credit charge: $47.

FINANCIAL AID PICTURE (2008-2009)
Students with need: Need-based aid available for full-time and part-time students. Work study available nights, weekends, and for part-time students.
Students without need: This college awards aid only to students with need.

FINANCIAL AID PROCEDURES
Forms required: FAFSA, institutional form.
Dates and Deadlines: Priority date 4/30; closing date 6/15. Applicants notified on a rolling basis starting 8/1; must reply within 2 week(s) of notification.

CONTACT
Zoraida Figueroa, Director of Financial Aid
PO Box 365067, San Juan, PR 00936-5067
(787) 758-2525 ext. 3205

University of Puerto Rico: Ponce

Ponce, Puerto Rico
www.uprp.edu Federal Code: 009652

4-year public university and branch campus college in small city.
Enrollment: 3,232 undergrads, 12% part-time. 880 full-time freshmen.
Selectivity: Admits less than 50% of applicants.

BASIC COSTS (2008-2009)
Tuition and fees: $1,752; out-of-state residents $4,077.
Per-credit charge: $47.

FINANCIAL AID PICTURE (2007-2008)
Students with need: 86% of average financial aid package awarded as scholarships/grants, 14% awarded as loans/jobs.
Students without need: This college awards aid only to students with need.

FINANCIAL AID PROCEDURES
Forms required: FAFSA, institutional form.
Dates and Deadlines: Closing date 5/30.

CONTACT
Carmelo Vega, Financial Aid Officer
Box 7186, Ponce, PR 00732
(787) 844-8181 ext. 2555

University of Puerto Rico: Rio Piedras

San Juan, Puerto Rico
www.uprrp.edu Federal Code: 007108

4-year public university in large city.
Enrollment: 15,177 undergrads, 15% part-time. 2,769 full-time freshmen.
Selectivity: Admits less than 50% of applicants.

BASIC COSTS (2008-2009)
Tuition and fees: $1,752; out-of-state residents $4,077.
Per-credit charge: $47.
Room and board: $8,180.

FINANCIAL AID PICTURE (2008-2009)
Students with need: Need-based aid available for full-time and part-time students.
Students without need: This college awards aid only to students with need.
Additional info: Tuition waived for honor students, athletes, members of chorus, and others with special talents.

FINANCIAL AID PROCEDURES
Forms required: FAFSA.

CONTACT
Luz Santiago, Director of Financial Aid
Box 23344, San Juan, PR 00931-3344

University of Puerto Rico: Utuado

Utuado, Puerto Rico
www.uprutuado.edu Federal Code: 010922

4-year public agricultural college in large town.
Enrollment: 1,596 undergrads.
Selectivity: GED not accepted.

BASIC COSTS (2008-2009)
Tuition and fees: $1,752; out-of-state residents $4,077.
Per-credit charge: $47.

FINANCIAL AID PICTURE
Students with need: Need-based aid available for full-time and part-time students. Work study available nights.
Students without need: This college awards aid only to students with need.

FINANCIAL AID PROCEDURES
Forms required: FAFSA.
Dates and Deadlines: Priority date 5/31; no closing date. Applicants notified on a rolling basis starting 9/30; must reply within 4 week(s) of notification.
Transfers: Priority date 5/30; closing date 6/15. Closing date for Pell Grant applicants March 31.

CONTACT
Edgar Salva, Financial Assistance Officer
PO Box 2500, Utuado, PR 00641
(787) 894-2828 ext. 2603

University of the Sacred Heart

Santurce, Puerto Rico
www.sagrado.edu Federal Code: 003937

4-year private university and liberal arts college in large city, affiliated with Roman Catholic Church.
Enrollment: 4,552 undergrads, 18% part-time. 750 full-time freshmen.

BASIC COSTS (2008-2009)
Tuition and fees: $5,820.
Per-credit charge: $165.
Room only: $2,400.

FINANCIAL AID PICTURE
Students with need: Need-based aid available for full-time and part-time students.
Students without need: No-need awards available for academics, athletics.

FINANCIAL AID PROCEDURES
Forms required: FAFSA, institutional form.

Dates and Deadlines: Priority date 4/30; closing date 5/30. Applicants notified on a rolling basis starting 6/15; must reply by 8/30.
Transfers: No deadline.

CONTACT

Luis Diaz, Director of Financial Aid
Universidad del Sagrado Corazon Oficina de Nuevo Ingreso, San Juan, PR 00914-0383

Rhode Island

Brown University

Providence, Rhode Island — Federal Code: 003401
www.brown.edu — CSS Code: 3094

4-year private university and liberal arts college in small city.
Enrollment: 5,874 undergrads. 1,548 full-time freshmen.
Selectivity: Admits less than 50% of applicants. GED not accepted.

BASIC COSTS (2008-2009)

Tuition and fees: $37,718.
Room and board: $10,022.

FINANCIAL AID PICTURE (2008-2009)

Students with need: Out of 918 full-time freshmen who applied for aid, 685 were judged to have need. Of these, 685 received aid, and 685 had their full need met. Average financial aid package met 100% of need; average scholarship/grant was $30,375; average loan was $2,234. Need-based aid available for part-time students.
Students without need: This college awards aid only to students with need.
Cumulative student debt: 44% of graduating class had student loans; average debt was $19,390.

FINANCIAL AID PROCEDURES

Forms required: FAFSA, CSS PROFILE.
Dates and Deadlines: Closing date 2/1. Applicants notified by 4/1; must reply by 5/1.
Transfers: Closing date 4/15.

CONTACT

James Tilton, Director of Financial Aid
45 Prospect Street, Providence, RI 02912
(401) 863-2721

Bryant University

Smithfield, Rhode Island
www.bryant.edu — Federal Code: 003402

4-year private business and liberal arts college in large town.
Enrollment: 3,474 undergrads, 4% part-time. 849 full-time freshmen.
Selectivity: Admits less than 50% of applicants.

BASIC COSTS (2008-2009)

Tuition and fees: $30,871.
Per-credit charge: $345.
Room and board: $11,251.
Additional info: Tuition includes cost of laptop computer. $800 nonrefundable enrollment commitment deposit is required of both residents and commuters.

FINANCIAL AID PICTURE (2007-2008)

Students with need: Out of 668 full-time freshmen who applied for aid, 567 were judged to have need. Of these, 567 received aid, and 76 had their full need met. Average financial aid package met 70% of need; average scholarship/grant was $11,010; average loan was $4,459. For part-time students, average financial aid package was $5,063.
Students without need: 138 full-time freshmen who did not demonstrate need for aid received scholarships/grants; average award was $12,892. No-need awards available for academics, athletics, minority status, ROTC.
Scholarships offered: 20 full-time freshmen received athletic scholarships; average amount $7,175.
Cumulative student debt: 73% of graduating class had student loans; average debt was $33,461.

FINANCIAL AID PROCEDURES

Forms required: FAFSA.
Dates and Deadlines: Closing date 2/15. Applicants notified by 3/24; must reply by 5/1.
Transfers: Closing date 4/1.

CONTACT

John Canning, Director of Financial Aid
1150 Douglas Pike, Smithfield, RI 02917
(401) 232-6020

Community College of Rhode Island

Warwick, Rhode Island
www.ccri.edu — Federal Code: 004916

2-year public community college in small city.
Enrollment: 16,007 undergrads, 60% part-time. 2,316 full-time freshmen.
Selectivity: Open admission; but selective for some programs.

BASIC COSTS (2008-2009)

Tuition and fees: $3,090; out-of-state residents $8,216.
Per-credit charge: $128; out-of-state residents $378.
Additional info: Tuition/fee waivers available for unemployed or children of unemployed.

FINANCIAL AID PICTURE

Students with need: Need-based aid available for full-time and part-time students. Work study available nights, weekends, and for part-time students.
Students without need: No-need awards available for athletics.

FINANCIAL AID PROCEDURES

Forms required: FAFSA, institutional form.
Dates and Deadlines: Priority date 3/1; no closing date. Applicants notified on a rolling basis starting 5/1; must reply within 2 week(s) of notification.

CONTACT

Christine Jenkins, Associate Dean of Enrollment Services
400 East Avenue, Warwick, RI 02886-1807
(401) 455-6006

Johnson & Wales University: Providence

Providence, Rhode Island
www.jwu.edu — Federal Code: 003404

4-year private university in small city.
Enrollment: 9,395 undergrads, 9% part-time. 2,488 full-time freshmen.
Selectivity: Admits 50 to 75% of applicants.

BASIC COSTS (2009-2010)

Tuition and fees: $23,490.

Additional info: Freshman required fees include $265 orientation fee. Weekend meal plan available for $1,026. Tuition at time of enrollment locked for 4 years.

FINANCIAL AID PICTURE (2008-2009)

Students with need: Out of 2,364 full-time freshmen who applied for aid, 1,786 were judged to have need. Of these, 1,778 received aid, and 147 had their full need met. Average financial aid package met 66% of need; average scholarship/grant was $7,848; average loan was $3,272. For part-time students, average financial aid package was $6,888.

Students without need: 494 full-time freshmen who did not demonstrate need for aid received scholarships/grants; average award was $4,878. No-need awards available for academics, alumni affiliation, job skills, leadership, state/district residency.

Cumulative student debt: 82% of graduating class had student loans; average debt was $28,195.

FINANCIAL AID PROCEDURES

Forms required: FAFSA.

Dates and Deadlines: No deadline. Applicants notified on a rolling basis starting 3/1; must reply within 2 week(s) of notification.

Transfers: Transfer scholarships available.

CONTACT

Lynn Robinson, Director of Financial Aid
8 Abbott Park Place, Providence, RI 02903-3703
(800) 342-5598 ext. 4648

New England Institute of Technology

Warwick, Rhode Island
www.neit.edu Federal Code: 007845

4-year private technical college in small city.

Enrollment: 3,134 undergrads.

Selectivity: Open admission.

BASIC COSTS (2009-2010)

Tuition and fees: $18,140.

Per-credit charge: $390.

Additional info: Tuition at time of enrollment locked for 4 years.

FINANCIAL AID PICTURE

Students with need: Need-based aid available for full-time and part-time students. Work study available nights, weekends, and for part-time students.

Students without need: No-need awards available for academics.

Additional info: Tuition at time of first enrollment guaranteed all students for 2 years.

FINANCIAL AID PROCEDURES

Forms required: FAFSA, institutional form.

Dates and Deadlines: Priority date 6/1; no closing date. Applicants notified on a rolling basis starting 6/15.

CONTACT

Larry Blair, Director of Financial Aid
2500 Post Road, Warwick, RI 02886-2286
(401) 467-7744

Providence College

Providence, Rhode Island Federal Code: 003406
www.providence.edu CSS Code: 3693

4-year private liberal arts college in small city, affiliated with Roman Catholic Church.

Enrollment: 3,931 undergrads. 968 full-time freshmen.

Selectivity: Admits less than 50% of applicants. GED not accepted.

BASIC COSTS (2008-2009)

Tuition and fees: $31,379.

Per-credit charge: $1,027.

Room and board: $10,810.

Additional info: Tuition/fee waivers available for minority students.

FINANCIAL AID PICTURE (2008-2009)

Students with need: Out of 730 full-time freshmen who applied for aid, 501 were judged to have need. Of these, 501 received aid, and 198 had their full need met. Average financial aid package met 76% of need; average scholarship/grant was $15,100; average loan was $4,135. For part-time students, average financial aid package was $4,800.

Students without need: 93 full-time freshmen who did not demonstrate need for aid received scholarships/grants; average award was $21,895. No-need awards available for academics, athletics, minority status, ROTC.

Scholarships offered: 35 full-time freshmen received athletic scholarships; average amount $26,220.

Cumulative student debt: 64% of graduating class had student loans; average debt was $33,297.

FINANCIAL AID PROCEDURES

Forms required: FAFSA, CSS PROFILE.

Dates and Deadlines: Closing date 2/1. Applicants notified by 4/1; must reply by 5/1.

Transfers: Closing date 4/15. Applicants notified by 6/30.

CONTACT

Sandra Oliveira, Director of Financial Aid
Harkins Hall 222, 1 Cunningham Square, Providence, RI 02918-0001
(401) 865-2286

Rhode Island College

Providence, Rhode Island
www.ric.edu Federal Code: 003407

4-year public liberal arts college in small city.

Enrollment: 7,192 undergrads, 25% part-time. 1,152 full-time freshmen.

Selectivity: Admits 50 to 75% of applicants.

BASIC COSTS (2008-2009)

Tuition and fees: $5,771; out-of-state residents $14,482.

Per-credit charge: $208; out-of-state residents $570.

Room and board: $8,390.

Additional info: Permanent residents of Massachusetts communities within a 20-mile radius of Providence are eligible for Rhode Island's in-state tuition plus 50% of the in-state rate. Tuition/fee waivers available for unemployed or children of unemployed.

FINANCIAL AID PICTURE (2008-2009)

Students with need: Out of 971 full-time freshmen who applied for aid, 683 were judged to have need. Of these, 673 received aid, and 127 had their full need met. Average financial aid package met 27% of need; average scholarship/grant was $6,485; average loan was $3,221. For part-time students, average financial aid package was $5,670.

Students without need: 60 full-time freshmen who did not demonstrate need for aid received scholarships/grants; average award was $2,009. No-need awards available for academics, alumni affiliation, art, music/drama.

Scholarships offered: Presidential Scholarships; $2,000 per year; for entering freshmen in the top 30% of class with minimum combined SAT score of 1100 (exclusive of Writing) who apply for admission by Dec 15; approximately 100 awards available to each entering class.

Cumulative student debt: 74% of graduating class had student loans; average debt was $15,841.

FINANCIAL AID PROCEDURES

Forms required: FAFSA, institutional form.

Dates and Deadlines: Priority date 3/1; no closing date. Applicants notified on a rolling basis starting 3/15; must reply within 3 week(s) of notification.
Transfers: Priority date 5/15. Applicants notified on a rolling basis starting 3/15; must reply by 5/1 or within 3 week(s) of notification.

CONTACT

James Hanbury, Director of Financial Aid
600 Mount Pleasant Avenue, Providence, RI 02908
(401) 456-8033

Rhode Island School of Design

Providence, Rhode Island — Federal Code: 003409
www.risd.edu — CSS Code: 3726

4-year private visual arts college in small city.
Enrollment: 1,926 undergrads.
Selectivity: Admits less than 50% of applicants.

BASIC COSTS (2009-2010)

Tuition and fees: $36,659.
Per-credit charge: $1,205.
Room and board: $10,846.

FINANCIAL AID PICTURE (2007-2008)

Students with need: Need-based aid available for full-time students. Work study available nights, weekends, and for part-time students.

FINANCIAL AID PROCEDURES

Forms required: FAFSA, CSS PROFILE.
Dates and Deadlines: Closing date 2/15. Applicants notified by 4/1; must reply by 5/1.
Transfers: Closing date 3/15. Applicants notified by 4/25; must reply by 5/22. Transfer students with previous undergraduate degree not eligible for scholarship aid.

CONTACT

Director of Financial Aid
Two College Street, Providence, RI 02903-2791
(401) 454-6661

Roger Williams University

Bristol, Rhode Island — Federal Code: 003410
www.rwu.edu — CSS Code: 3729

4-year private university and liberal arts college in large town.
Enrollment: 4,297 undergrads, 13% part-time. 954 full-time freshmen.
Selectivity: Admits 50 to 75% of applicants.

BASIC COSTS (2008-2009)

Tuition and fees: $27,718.
Per-credit charge: $1,082.
Room and board: $11,880.
Additional info: Tuition differential for architecture program.

FINANCIAL AID PICTURE (2008-2009)

Students with need: Out of 724 full-time freshmen who applied for aid, 547 were judged to have need. Of these, 543 received aid, and 20 had their full need met. Average financial aid package met 88% of need; average scholarship/grant was $5,769; average loan was $3,834. For part-time students, average financial aid package was $5,937.
Students without need: 159 full-time freshmen who did not demonstrate need for aid received scholarships/grants; average award was $7,315. No-need awards available for academics, ROTC.
Cumulative student debt: 79% of graduating class had student loans; average debt was $30,874.

FINANCIAL AID PROCEDURES

Forms required: FAFSA, CSS PROFILE.
Dates and Deadlines: Priority date 1/1; closing date 2/1. Applicants notified on a rolling basis starting 3/20; must reply by 5/1.
Transfers: Must reply by 5/1.

CONTACT

Tracy DaCosta, Assistant VP of Enrollment Management & Retention
1 Old Ferry Rd, Bristol, RI 02809-2921
(401) 254-3100

Salve Regina University

Newport, Rhode Island — Federal Code: 003411
www.salve.edu — CSS Code: 3759

4-year private university and liberal arts college in large town, affiliated with Roman Catholic Church.
Enrollment: 2,078 undergrads, 4% part-time. 556 full-time freshmen.
Selectivity: Admits 50 to 75% of applicants.

BASIC COSTS (2008-2009)

Tuition and fees: $31,500.
Per-credit charge: $965.
Room and board: $10,700.
Additional info: Required fees include a one-time laptop fee of $2,350 for all first-year students.

FINANCIAL AID PICTURE (2008-2009)

Students with need: Need-based aid available for full-time and part-time students. Work study available nights, weekends, and for part-time students.
Students without need: No-need awards available for academics, ROTC.

FINANCIAL AID PROCEDURES

Forms required: FAFSA, CSS PROFILE.
Dates and Deadlines: Priority date 3/1; no closing date. Applicants notified by 4/1; must reply by 4/15 or within 2 week(s) of notification.
Transfers: Closing date 2/1. Applicants notified by 3/1; must reply by 5/1 or within 2 week(s) of notification. Must provide financial aid transcripts from previous institutions attended.

CONTACT

Aida Mirante, Director of Financial Aid
100 Ochre Point Avenue, Newport, RI 02840-4192
(401) 341-2901

University of Rhode Island

Kingston, Rhode Island
www.uri.edu — Federal Code: 003414

4-year public university in small town.
Enrollment: 12,520 undergrads, 11% part-time. 2,986 full-time freshmen.
Selectivity: Admits over 75% of applicants.

BASIC COSTS (2008-2009)

Tuition and fees: $8,678; out-of-state residents $24,776.
Per-credit charge: $311; out-of-state residents $981.
Room and board: $8,828.
Additional info: Tuition/fee waivers available for unemployed or children of unemployed.

FINANCIAL AID PICTURE (2008-2009)

Students with need: Out of 2,485 full-time freshmen who applied for aid, 1,958 were judged to have need. Of these, 1,591 received aid, and 1,235 had their full need met. Average financial aid package met 57% of need; average scholarship/grant was $6,563; average loan was $5,905. For part-time students, average financial aid package was $8,077.

Students without need: 150 full-time freshmen who did not demonstrate need for aid received scholarships/grants; average award was $3,931. No-need awards available for academics, alumni affiliation, art, athletics, music/drama, ROTC.
Scholarships offered: 5 full-time freshmen received athletic scholarships; average amount $1,400.
Cumulative student debt: 71% of graduating class had student loans; average debt was $22,500.

FINANCIAL AID PROCEDURES
Forms required: FAFSA.
Dates and Deadlines: Priority date 3/1; no closing date. Applicants notified on a rolling basis starting 3/31; must reply by 5/1.
Transfers: No deadline. Applicants notified on a rolling basis starting 4/1; must reply within 2 week(s) of notification.

CONTACT
Bonnie Saccucci, Senior Associate Director of Enrollment Services
14 Upper College Road, Kingston, RI 02881-1322
(401) 874-9500

South Carolina

Aiken Technical College
Aiken, South Carolina
www.atc.edu Federal Code: 010056

2-year public community and technical college in small city.
Enrollment: 2,655 undergrads.
Selectivity: Open admission; but selective for some programs.

BASIC COSTS (2008-2009)
Tuition and fees: $3,356; out-of-district residents $3,716; out-of-state residents $9,644.

FINANCIAL AID PICTURE (2007-2008)
Students with need: Need-based aid available for full-time and part-time students. Work study available nights, weekends, and for part-time students.
Students without need: No-need awards available for academics, athletics, leadership, minority status, state/district residency.
Scholarships offered: Vernon Ford Scholarships: $1,000 annually; for candidates with minimum GPA of 3.0; 8 awarded annually. N. Augusta 2000: $2,000 annually; 2 awarded. Wachenhut Criminal Justice Scholarship: $1,000; 1 awarded. Presidential: $10,000 annually; 10 awarded.

FINANCIAL AID PROCEDURES
Forms required: FAFSA.
Dates and Deadlines: Priority date 5/1; closing date 6/30. Applicants notified on a rolling basis starting 4/1; must reply within 2 week(s) of notification.
Transfers: Applicants notified on a rolling basis; must reply within 2 week(s) of notification.

CONTACT
Amanda Chittum, Director of Financial Aid
PO Drawer 696, Aiken, SC 29802
(803) 593-9954 ext. 1261

Allen University
Columbia, South Carolina
www.allenuniversity.edu Federal Code: 003417

4-year private university and liberal arts college in large city, affiliated with African Methodist Episcopal Church.
Enrollment: 727 undergrads, 1% part-time. 326 full-time freshmen.
Selectivity: Open admission.

BASIC COSTS (2008-2009)
Tuition and fees: $9,884.
Room and board: $5,240.

FINANCIAL AID PICTURE (2008-2009)
Students with need: Need-based aid available for full-time and part-time students.
Students without need: No-need awards available for academics, athletics, music/drama, ROTC.

FINANCIAL AID PROCEDURES
Forms required: FAFSA.
Dates and Deadlines: Priority date 4/15; closing date 7/20. Applicants notified on a rolling basis starting 4/1; must reply within 2 week(s) of notification.
Transfers: No deadline.

CONTACT
1530 Harden Street, Columbia, SC 29204

Anderson University
Anderson, South Carolina
www.andersonuniversity.edu Federal Code: 003418

4-year private liberal arts and teachers college in large town, affiliated with Southern Baptist Convention.
Enrollment: 1,971 undergrads, 24% part-time. 402 full-time freshmen.
Selectivity: Admits over 75% of applicants.

BASIC COSTS (2009-2010)
Tuition and fees: $19,212.
Per-credit charge: $500.
Room and board: $7,600.
Additional info: Tuition/fee waivers available for adults.

FINANCIAL AID PICTURE
Students with need: Need-based aid available for full-time and part-time students. Work study available nights, weekends, and for part-time students.
Students without need: No-need awards available for academics, alumni affiliation, art, athletics, leadership, minority status, music/drama, religious affiliation, state/district residency.

FINANCIAL AID PROCEDURES
Forms required: FAFSA.
Dates and Deadlines: Priority date 3/1; closing date 6/30. Applicants notified on a rolling basis starting 3/15; must reply within 2 week(s) of notification.

CONTACT
Becky Pressley, Director of Financial Aid
316 Boulevard, Anderson, SC 29621-4002
(864) 231-2070

Benedict College
Columbia, South Carolina
www.benedict.edu Federal Code: 003420

4-year private liberal arts college in very large city, affiliated with American Baptist Churches in the USA.
Enrollment: 2,883 undergrads, 4% part-time. 888 full-time freshmen.
Selectivity: Open admission.

BASIC COSTS (2008-2009)
Tuition and fees: $14,570.
Per-credit charge: $436.
Room and board: $6,702.

FINANCIAL AID PICTURE
Students with need: Need-based aid available for full-time and part-time students.

FINANCIAL AID PROCEDURES
Forms required: FAFSA.
Dates and Deadlines: Priority date 4/15; no closing date. Applicants notified on a rolling basis starting 4/15.

CONTACT
Sul Black, Director of Financial Aid
1600 Harden Street, Columbia, SC 29204
(803) 253-5105

Central Carolina Technical College
Sumter, South Carolina
www.cctech.edu Federal Code: 003995

2-year public community and technical college in large town.
Enrollment: 2,924 undergrads, 65% part-time. 308 full-time freshmen.
Selectivity: Open admission; but selective for some programs.

BASIC COSTS (2008-2009)
Tuition and fees: $3,020; out-of-district residents $3,548; out-of-state residents $5,372.

FINANCIAL AID PICTURE (2007-2008)
Students with need: Need-based aid available for full-time and part-time students. Work study available nights.
Students without need: This college awards aid only to students with need.

FINANCIAL AID PROCEDURES
Forms required: FAFSA, state aid form.
Dates and Deadlines: Priority date 4/1; no closing date. Applicants notified on a rolling basis; must reply within 2 week(s) of notification.

CONTACT
Sarah Dowd, Director of Financial Aid
506 North Guignard Drive, Sumter, SC 29150-2499
(803) 778-7831

Charleston Southern University
Charleston, South Carolina
www.csuniv.edu Federal Code: 003419

4-year private university and liberal arts college in large city, affiliated with Southern Baptist Convention.
Enrollment: 2,761 undergrads.
Selectivity: Admits 50 to 75% of applicants.

BASIC COSTS (2008-2009)
Tuition and fees: $18,678.
Per-credit charge: $360.
Room and board: $7,178.

FINANCIAL AID PICTURE (2007-2008)
Students with need: Need-based aid available for full-time and part-time students. Work study available nights, weekends, and for part-time students.
Students without need: No-need awards available for academics, athletics, religious affiliation, ROTC.

FINANCIAL AID PROCEDURES
Forms required: FAFSA, state aid form.
Dates and Deadlines: Priority date 4/15; no closing date. Applicants notified on a rolling basis starting 3/1; must reply within 2 week(s) of notification.

CONTACT
Pam Hester, Director of Financial Aid
9200 University Boulevard, Charleston, SC 29423-8087
(843) 863-7050

The Citadel
Charleston, South Carolina
www.citadel.edu Federal Code: 003423

4-year public military college in large city.
Enrollment: 2,241 undergrads, 3% part-time. 606 full-time freshmen.
Selectivity: Admits over 75% of applicants.

BASIC COSTS (2008-2009)
Tuition and fees: $8,428; out-of-state residents $21,031.
Per-credit charge: $277; out-of-state residents $486.
Room and board: $5,750.
Additional info: Students in Corps of Cadets required to pay $1,089 in fees which include laundry and dry cleaning charges and infirmary fees. Freshmen also pay $5,630 deposit and upperclassmen pay $1,750 deposit for uniforms, books, and supplies.

FINANCIAL AID PICTURE (2008-2009)
Students with need: Out of 475 full-time freshmen who applied for aid, 339 were judged to have need. Of these, 327 received aid, and 143 had their full need met. Average financial aid package met 71% of need; average scholarship/grant was $15,220; average loan was $3,453. For part-time students, average financial aid package was $5,377.
Students without need: 41 full-time freshmen who did not demonstrate need for aid received scholarships/grants; average award was $12,143. No-need awards available for academics, athletics, leadership, ROTC, state/district residency.
Scholarships offered: 28 full-time freshmen received athletic scholarships; average amount $25,067.
Cumulative student debt: 41% of graduating class had student loans; average debt was $15,991.

FINANCIAL AID PROCEDURES
Forms required: FAFSA.
Dates and Deadlines: Priority date 2/28; no closing date. Applicants notified on a rolling basis starting 4/1; must reply by 5/1 or within 2 week(s) of notification.
Transfers: No deadline.

CONTACT
Henry Fuller, Director of Financial Aid
171 Moultrie Street, Charleston, SC 29409
(843) 953-5187

Claflin University
Orangeburg, South Carolina
www.claflin.edu Federal Code: 003424

4-year private liberal arts college in large town, affiliated with United Methodist Church.
Enrollment: 1,657 undergrads, 2% part-time. 465 full-time freshmen.
Selectivity: Admits less than 50% of applicants.

BASIC COSTS (2008-2009)
Tuition and fees: $12,768.
Room and board: $6,806.

FINANCIAL AID PICTURE (2008-2009)

Students with need: Out of 432 full-time freshmen who applied for aid, 415 were judged to have need. Of these, 415 received aid, and 51 had their full need met. Average financial aid package met 73% of need; average scholarship/grant was $12,640; average loan was $6,871.

Cumulative student debt: 89% of graduating class had student loans; average debt was $3,403.

FINANCIAL AID PROCEDURES

Forms required: FAFSA, institutional form.

Dates and Deadlines: Priority date 4/15; no closing date. Applicants notified on a rolling basis starting 5/15; must reply within 2 week(s) of notification.

Transfers: No deadline. Applicants notified on a rolling basis.

CONTACT

Terria Williams, Director of Financial Aid
400 Magnolia Street, Orangeburg, SC 29115
(803) 535-5334

Clemson University

Clemson, South Carolina
www.clemson.edu Federal Code: 003425

4-year public university and agricultural college in large town.

Enrollment: 14,624 undergrads, 6% part-time. 2,735 full-time freshmen.

Selectivity: Admits 50 to 75% of applicants.

BASIC COSTS (2008-2009)

Tuition and fees: $11,108; out-of-state residents $24,130.

Room and board: $6,556.

Additional info: Laptop computer required of all entering new students. This cost has been estimated at $1600.

FINANCIAL AID PICTURE (2007-2008)

Students with need: Out of 1,800 full-time freshmen who applied for aid, 1,240 were judged to have need. Of these, 1,213 received aid, and 410 had their full need met. Average financial aid package met 74% of need; average scholarship/grant was $4,416; average loan was $3,696. For part-time students, average financial aid package was $7,975.

Students without need: 624 full-time freshmen who did not demonstrate need for aid received scholarships/grants; average award was $2,609. No-need awards available for academics, art, athletics, leadership, minority status, music/drama, ROTC, state/district residency.

Scholarships offered: 82 full-time freshmen received athletic scholarships; average amount $12,072.

Cumulative student debt: 49% of graduating class had student loans; average debt was $17,556.

FINANCIAL AID PROCEDURES

Forms required: FAFSA.

Dates and Deadlines: Priority date 4/1; no closing date. Applicants notified on a rolling basis starting 4/1; must reply within 3 week(s) of notification.

Transfers: Transfer students must earn 12 semester hours before being considered for institutional scholarship.

CONTACT

Marvin Carmichael, Director of Student Financial Aid
105 Sikes Hall, Clemson, SC 29634-5124
(864) 656-2280

Coastal Carolina University

Conway, South Carolina
www.coastal.edu Federal Code: 003451

4-year public university in small city.

Enrollment: 7,322 undergrads, 6% part-time. 1,649 full-time freshmen.

Selectivity: Admits 50 to 75% of applicants.

BASIC COSTS (2008-2009)

Tuition and fees: $8,650; out-of-state residents $18,090.

Per-credit charge: $360; out-of-state residents $754.

Room and board: $7,080.

FINANCIAL AID PICTURE (2007-2008)

Students with need: Out of 1,382 full-time freshmen who applied for aid, 1,006 were judged to have need. Of these, 984 received aid, and 159 had their full need met. Average financial aid package met 53% of need; average scholarship/grant was $4,016; average loan was $6,861. For part-time students, average financial aid package was $4,675.

Students without need: 366 full-time freshmen who did not demonstrate need for aid received scholarships/grants; average award was $9,800. No-need awards available for academics, art, athletics, leadership, music/drama, state/district residency.

Scholarships offered: 99 full-time freshmen received athletic scholarships; average amount $7,659.

Cumulative student debt: 67% of graduating class had student loans; average debt was $24,856.

FINANCIAL AID PROCEDURES

Forms required: FAFSA.

Dates and Deadlines: Priority date 3/1; no closing date. Applicants notified on a rolling basis starting 3/1; must reply by 5/15.

Transfers: No deadline. Applicants notified on a rolling basis; must reply within 4 week(s) of notification.

CONTACT

Dawn Hitchcock, Director of Financial Aid
PO Box 261954, Conway, SC 29528-6054
(843) 349-2313

College of Charleston

Charleston, South Carolina
www.cofc.edu Federal Code: 003428

4-year public liberal arts college in large city.

Enrollment: 9,415 undergrads, 5% part-time. 2,062 full-time freshmen.

Selectivity: Admits 50 to 75% of applicants.

BASIC COSTS (2008-2009)

Tuition and fees: $8,400; out-of-state residents $20,418.

Per-credit charge: $350; out-of-state residents $851.

Room and board: $8,999.

FINANCIAL AID PICTURE (2007-2008)

Students with need: Out of 1,257 full-time freshmen who applied for aid, 829 were judged to have need. Of these, 796 received aid, and 232 had their full need met. Average financial aid package met 65% of need; average scholarship/grant was $2,815; average loan was $3,424. For part-time students, average financial aid package was $8,827.

Students without need: 233 full-time freshmen who did not demonstrate need for aid received scholarships/grants; average award was $4,944. No-need awards available for academics, alumni affiliation, art, athletics, music/drama.

Scholarships offered: ***Merit:*** Foundation Scholarships: from $1,000-$4,000 annually for up to 4 years, based on high school performance, test scores, and leadership qualities, no additional application required. ***Athletic:*** 33 full-time freshmen received athletic scholarships; average amount $14,214.

Cumulative student debt: 46% of graduating class had student loans; average debt was $17,118.

FINANCIAL AID PROCEDURES

Forms required: FAFSA.

Dates and Deadlines: Priority date 3/15; no closing date. Applicants notified on a rolling basis starting 4/10; must reply within 8 week(s) of notification.

Transfers: No aid available to transfer students who enroll for first time in summer school.

CONTACT

Donald Griggs, Director of Financial Assistance and Veterans Affairs
Office of Admissions and Adult Student Services, Charleston, SC 29424-0001
(843) 953-5540

Columbia College

Columbia, South Carolina
www.columbiacollegesc.edu Federal Code: 003430

4-year private liberal arts college for women in large city, affiliated with United Methodist Church.
Enrollment: 1,225 undergrads, 21% part-time. 3,868 full-time freshmen.
Selectivity: Admits over 75% of applicants.

BASIC COSTS (2008-2009)

Tuition and fees: $23,030.
Per-credit charge: $607.
Room and board: $6,450.

FINANCIAL AID PICTURE (2007-2008)

Students with need: Out of 2,174 full-time freshmen who applied for aid, 1,187 were judged to have need. Of these, 1,089 received aid, and 188 had their full need met. Average financial aid package met 55% of need; average scholarship/grant was $14,391; average loan was $3,066. For part-time students, average financial aid package was $6,096.
Students without need: 362 full-time freshmen who did not demonstrate need for aid received scholarships/grants; average award was $10,186. No-need awards available for academics, alumni affiliation, art, athletics, leadership, music/drama.
Scholarships offered: ***Merit:*** Founders Scholarship: full tuition. Presidential Scholarships: $10,000 annually. Trustees Scholarships: $8,000 annually. ***Athletic:*** 19 full-time freshmen received athletic scholarships; average amount $6,379.
Cumulative student debt: 94% of graduating class had student loans; average debt was $14,418.

FINANCIAL AID PROCEDURES

Forms required: FAFSA.
Dates and Deadlines: Priority date 4/1; no closing date. Applicants notified on a rolling basis starting 3/15; must reply within 2 week(s) of notification.
Transfers: Priority date 4/15. Must meet institutional standards of satisfactory academic progress.

CONTACT

Donna Quick, Director of Financial Aid
1301 Columbia College Drive, Columbia, SC 29203
(803) 786-3612

Columbia International University

Columbia, South Carolina
www.ciu.edu Federal Code: 003429

4-year private university and Bible college in small city, affiliated with multidenominational/evangelical churches.
Enrollment: 455 undergrads.
Selectivity: Admits over 75% of applicants.

BASIC COSTS (2008-2009)

Tuition and fees: $16,270.
Per-credit charge: $660.
Room and board: $5,800.
Additional info: Tuition/fee waivers available for minority students.

FINANCIAL AID PICTURE (2008-2009)

Students with need: Need-based aid available for full-time and part-time students. Work study available nights, weekends, and for part-time students.
Students without need: No-need awards available for academics, leadership, state/district residency.
Additional info: Spouse scholarship program; special short quarter scholarships for missionaries on furlough.

FINANCIAL AID PROCEDURES

Forms required: FAFSA, institutional form.
Dates and Deadlines: Priority date 1/31; no closing date. Applicants notified on a rolling basis starting 12/18; must reply within 4 week(s) of notification.
Transfers: FAFSA must be processed by June 30 for state need-based aid. State aid requires 1-year residency prior to award in most cases. Non-need-based state aid requires graduation from state high school.

CONTACT

Bob Patton, Director of Financial Aid
PO Box 3122, Columbia, SC 29230-3122
(803) 777-2227 ext. 5036

Converse College

Spartanburg, South Carolina
www.converse.edu Federal Code: 003431

4-year private music and liberal arts college for women in small city.
Enrollment: 725 undergrads, 12% part-time. 162 full-time freshmen.
Selectivity: Admits 50 to 75% of applicants.

BASIC COSTS (2008-2009)

Tuition and fees: $24,500.
Per-credit charge: $775.
Room and board: $7,550.
Additional info: Special fees for laboratory, studio art, computer programming, and other courses requiring special materials.

FINANCIAL AID PICTURE (2008-2009)

Students with need: Out of 145 full-time freshmen who applied for aid, 129 were judged to have need. Of these, 129 received aid, and 47 had their full need met. Average financial aid package met 89% of need; average scholarship/grant was $20,454; average loan was $4,509. For part-time students, average financial aid package was $7,056.
Students without need: 37 full-time freshmen who did not demonstrate need for aid received scholarships/grants; average award was $19,324. No-need awards available for academics, alumni affiliation, art, athletics, leadership, music/drama, ROTC, state/district residency.
Scholarships offered: 10 full-time freshmen received athletic scholarships; average amount $10,720.
Cumulative student debt: 67% of graduating class had student loans; average debt was $22,340.

FINANCIAL AID PROCEDURES

Forms required: FAFSA.
Dates and Deadlines: Closing date 3/15. Applicants notified on a rolling basis starting 3/1; must reply by 5/1 or within 2 week(s) of notification.

CONTACT

Margaret Collins, Director of Scholarships and Financial Assistance
580 East Main Street, Spartanburg, SC 29302-0006
(864) 596-9019

Denmark Technical College

Denmark, South Carolina
www.denmarktech.edu Federal Code: 005363

2-year public technical college in small town.
Enrollment: 1,400 undergrads.
Selectivity: Open admission.

BASIC COSTS (2008-2009)

Tuition and fees: $2,378; out-of-state residents $4,466.
Room and board: $3,386.

FINANCIAL AID PICTURE

Students with need: Need-based aid available for full-time and part-time students.

FINANCIAL AID PROCEDURES

Forms required: FAFSA.
Dates and Deadlines: No deadline. Applicants notified on a rolling basis starting 6/1; must reply within 2 week(s) of notification.

CONTACT

Kelvin Bonnett, Assistant Director of Financial Aid
1126 Solomon Blatt Boulevard, Denmark, SC 29042
(803) 793-5161

Erskine College

Due West, South Carolina
www.erskine.edu Federal Code: 003432

4-year private liberal arts and seminary college in rural community, affiliated with Associate Reformed Presbyterian Church.
Enrollment: 563 undergrads. 185 full-time freshmen.
Selectivity: Admits 50 to 75% of applicants.

BASIC COSTS (2009-2010)

Tuition and fees: $24,645.
Per-credit charge: $852.
Room and board: $8,325.

FINANCIAL AID PICTURE (2007-2008)

Students with need: Out of 155 full-time freshmen who applied for aid, 149 were judged to have need. Of these, 149 received aid, and 119 had their full need met. Need-based aid available for part-time students.
Students without need: 24 full-time freshmen who did not demonstrate need for aid received scholarships/grants. No-need awards available for academics, alumni affiliation, art, athletics, leadership, minority status, music/drama, religious affiliation, state/district residency.
Cumulative student debt: 82% of graduating class had student loans; average debt was $14,756.
Additional info: Filing deadline 5/1 for institutional form, 6/30 for state form.

FINANCIAL AID PROCEDURES

Forms required: FAFSA, state aid form, institutional form.
Dates and Deadlines: Priority date 4/1; no closing date. Applicants notified on a rolling basis starting 12/15; must reply within 2 week(s) of notification.
Transfers: Closing date 5/1. South Carolina residents must have earned 24 hours in previous year to receive SC tuition grant and 30 hours plus 3.0 GPA to receive the Life Scholarship.

CONTACT

Allison Sullivan, Director of Financial Aid
PO Box 338, Due West, SC 29639-0176
(864) 379-8832

Florence-Darlington Technical College

Florence, South Carolina
www.fdtc.edu Federal Code: 003990

2-year public community and technical college in small city.
Enrollment: 4,505 undergrads.
Selectivity: Open admission; but selective for some programs.

BASIC COSTS (2008-2009)

Tuition and fees: $3,190; out-of-district residents $3,452; out-of-state residents $5,286.

FINANCIAL AID PICTURE (2007-2008)

Students with need: 79% of average financial aid package awarded as scholarships/grants, 21% awarded as loans/jobs. Need-based aid available for part-time students.
Students without need: No-need awards available for academics.

FINANCIAL AID PROCEDURES

Forms required: FAFSA.
Dates and Deadlines: Priority date 5/1; no closing date. Applicants notified on a rolling basis starting 7/1; must reply within 2 week(s) of notification.

CONTACT

Joseph Durant, Director of Financial Assistance
PO Box 100548, Florence, SC 29501-0548
(843) 661-8085

Forrest Junior College

Anderson, South Carolina
www.forrestcollege.edu Federal Code: 004924

2-year for-profit business and junior college in large town.
Enrollment: 98 undergrads, 10% part-time. 7 full-time freshmen.
Selectivity: Open admission; but selective for some programs.

BASIC COSTS (2008-2009)

Tuition and fees: $9,290.
Per-credit charge: $197.

FINANCIAL AID PICTURE (2008-2009)

Students with need: Need-based aid available for full-time and part-time students. Work study available nights, weekends, and for part-time students.
Students without need: This college awards aid only to students with need.

FINANCIAL AID PROCEDURES

Forms required: FAFSA.
Dates and Deadlines: No deadline. Applicants notified on a rolling basis starting 4/30; must reply by 5/31 or within 4 week(s) of notification.

CONTACT

Kathy Montgomery, Director of Financial Aid
601 East River Street, Anderson, SC 29624
(864) 225-7653

Francis Marion University

Florence, South Carolina
www.fmarion.edu Federal Code: 009226

4-year public university and liberal arts college in small city.
Enrollment: 3,185 undergrads, 4% part-time. 677 full-time freshmen.
Selectivity: Admits 50 to 75% of applicants.

BASIC COSTS (2008-2009)

Tuition and fees: $7,632; out-of-state residents $14,979.

Per-credit charge: $367; out-of-state residents $735.

Room and board: $6,024.

FINANCIAL AID PICTURE (2008-2009)

Students with need: Out of 582 full-time freshmen who applied for aid, 517 were judged to have need. Of these, 501 received aid. Need-based aid available for part-time students.

Students without need: No-need awards available for academics, music/drama.

Cumulative student debt: 75% of graduating class had student loans; average debt was $23,487.

FINANCIAL AID PROCEDURES

Forms required: FAFSA.

Dates and Deadlines: Priority date 3/1; no closing date. Applicants notified on a rolling basis starting 4/15.

Transfers: Institutional scholarships available after 1 semester completed in residence.

CONTACT

Kim Ellisor, Director of Financial Assistance
PO Box 100547, Florence, SC 29502-0547
(843) 661-1190

Furman University

Greenville, South Carolina — Federal Code: 003434
www.furman.edu — CSS Code: 5222

4-year private liberal arts college in small city.

Enrollment: 2,771 undergrads, 4% part-time. 753 full-time freshmen.

Selectivity: Admits 50 to 75% of applicants.

BASIC COSTS (2009-2010)

Tuition and fees: $36,656.

Per-credit charge: $1,134.

Room and board: $9,170.

FINANCIAL AID PICTURE (2008-2009)

Students with need: Out of 456 full-time freshmen who applied for aid, 315 were judged to have need. Of these, 315 received aid, and 124 had their full need met. Average financial aid package met 85% of need; average scholarship/grant was $23,709; average loan was $4,102. For part-time students, average financial aid package was $5,666.

Students without need: 222 full-time freshmen who did not demonstrate need for aid received scholarships/grants; average award was $15,360. No-need awards available for academics, alumni affiliation, art, athletics, leadership, music/drama, religious affiliation, ROTC, state/district residency.

Scholarships offered: 67 full-time freshmen received athletic scholarships; average amount $27,529.

Cumulative student debt: 45% of graduating class had student loans; average debt was $24,325.

Additional info: 5-point comprehensive education financing plan includes financial aid packaging, money management counseling, debt management counseling, outside scholarship coordination, summer job-match program.

FINANCIAL AID PROCEDURES

Forms required: FAFSA, CSS PROFILE, state aid form, institutional form.

Dates and Deadlines: Closing date 1/15. Applicants notified by 3/15; must reply by 5/1.

Transfers: Closing date 6/1. For South Carolina Tuition Grant, must have earned 24 credits in previous year. For Life Scholarship, must have 3.0 cumulative GPA and 30 credits earned.

CONTACT

Forrest Stuart, Director of Financial Aid
3300 Poinsett Highway, Greenville, SC 29613
(864) 294-2204

Greenville Technical College

Greenville, South Carolina
www.gvltec.edu — Federal Code: 003991

2-year public community and technical college in large city.

Enrollment: 12,848 undergrads, 52% part-time. 1,886 full-time freshmen.

Selectivity: Open admission; but selective for some programs.

BASIC COSTS (2008-2009)

Tuition and fees: $3,396; out-of-district residents $3,680; out-of-state residents $6,912.

FINANCIAL AID PICTURE (2007-2008)

Students with need: 32% of average financial aid package awarded as scholarships/grants, 68% awarded as loans/jobs. Need-based aid available for part-time students. Work study available nights, weekends, and for part-time students.

Students without need: No-need awards available for academics, state/district residency.

FINANCIAL AID PROCEDURES

Forms required: FAFSA.

Dates and Deadlines: Priority date 5/1; no closing date. Applicants notified on a rolling basis starting 6/15; must reply within 2 week(s) of notification.

Transfers: No deadline. Applicants notified on a rolling basis starting 12/1; must reply within 2 week(s) of notification.

CONTACT

Janie Reid, Financial Aid Director
PO Box 5616, Greenville, SC 29606-5616
(864) 250-8128

Horry-Georgetown Technical College

Conway, South Carolina
www.hgtc.edu — Federal Code: 004925

2-year public community and technical college in large town.

Enrollment: 5,603 undergrads, 59% part-time. 674 full-time freshmen.

Selectivity: Open admission; but selective for some programs.

BASIC COSTS (2008-2009)

Tuition and fees: $3,194; out-of-district residents $4,026; out-of-state residents $5,034.

FINANCIAL AID PICTURE (2008-2009)

Students with need: 59% of average financial aid package awarded as scholarships/grants, 41% awarded as loans/jobs. Need-based aid available for part-time students.

Students without need: No-need awards available for academics, state/district residency.

Additional info: Participates in South Carolina lottery tuition assistance program. Full-time technical college students who are state residents receive assistance for tuition not covered by federal or need-based grants.

FINANCIAL AID PROCEDURES

Forms required: FAFSA.

Dates and Deadlines: Priority date 4/1; closing date 6/30. Applicants notified on a rolling basis starting 4/1.

CONTACT
Susan Thompson, Director of Financial Aid and Veterans Affairs
PO Box 261966, Conway, SC 29528
(843) 349-5251

Lander University
Greenwood, South Carolina
www.lander.edu Federal Code: 003435

4-year public liberal arts and teachers college in large town.
Enrollment: 2,493 undergrads, 9% part-time. 554 full-time freshmen.
Selectivity: Admits less than 50% of applicants.

BASIC COSTS (2008-2009)
Tuition and fees: $8,540; out-of-state residents $16,000.
Per-credit charge: $349; out-of-state residents $660.
Room and board: $6,642.

FINANCIAL AID PICTURE (2007-2008)
Students with need: Need-based aid available for full-time and part-time students. Work study available weekends and for part-time students.
Students without need: No-need awards available for academics, art, athletics, leadership, music/drama.

FINANCIAL AID PROCEDURES
Forms required: FAFSA.
Dates and Deadlines: Priority date 4/15; no closing date. Applicants notified on a rolling basis starting 4/15; must reply within 4 week(s) of notification.

CONTACT
Fred Hardin, Director of Financial Aid
Stanley Avenue, Greenwood, SC 29649-2099
(864) 388-8340

Limestone College
Gaffney, South Carolina
www.limestone.edu Federal Code: 003436

4-year private liberal arts college in large town.
Enrollment: 742 undergrads, 2% part-time. 171 full-time freshmen.
Selectivity: Admits 50 to 75% of applicants.

BASIC COSTS (2009-2010)
Tuition and fees: $18,300.
Per-credit charge: $762.
Room and board: $6,800.

FINANCIAL AID PICTURE (2008-2009)
Students with need: Average financial aid package met 68% of need; average scholarship/grant was $12,036; average loan was $3,022. For part-time students, average financial aid package was $8,721.
Students without need: No-need awards available for academics, alumni affiliation, art, athletics, job skills, leadership, music/drama, religious affiliation, ROTC, state/district residency.
Scholarships offered: Presidential Scholarship: full tuition; SAT above 1300, GPA 3.5 or above; 1 available. Academic Dean Scholarships: partial tuition, based on academic achievement (GPA 3.0 or above). Founders Scholarships: partial tuition; GPA 2.75 or above. R.S. Campbell Scholarship: SAT above 1100, GPA 3.25 or above; 1 available. Leadership Scholarship: partial tuition; based on evidence of student leadership. Drada Hoover Scholarship: SAT 1200 or higher; GPA 3.5; top 10% of graduating class. SAT scores exclusive of Writing.
Cumulative student debt: 89% of graduating class had student loans; average debt was $22,416.

FINANCIAL AID PROCEDURES
Forms required: FAFSA.
Dates and Deadlines: Priority date 2/1; no closing date. Applicants notified on a rolling basis starting 1/15; must reply within 3 week(s) of notification.
Transfers: Priority date 5/1; no deadline. Applicants notified on a rolling basis; must reply within 3 week(s) of notification.

CONTACT
Bobby Greer, Director of Financial Aid
1115 College Drive, Gaffney, SC 29340-3799
(800) 795-7151 ext. 8231

Medical University of South Carolina
Charleston, South Carolina
www.musc.edu Federal Code: 003438

Upper-division public university in large city.
Enrollment: 316 undergrads.

BASIC COSTS (2008-2009)
Additional info: Tuition/fee waivers available for adults, minority students.

FINANCIAL AID PICTURE (2007-2008)
Students with need: Need-based aid available for full-time and part-time students.
Students without need: No-need awards available for academics, alumni affiliation, minority status, state/district residency.

FINANCIAL AID PROCEDURES
Forms required: FAFSA, institutional form.
Dates and Deadlines: Priority date 3/10; no closing date. Applicants notified on a rolling basis starting 4/21.

CONTACT
Cecile Kamath, Director, Student Financial Aid
41 Bee Street, Charleston, SC 29425
(843) 792-2536

Midlands Technical College
Columbia, South Carolina
www.midlandstech.edu Federal Code: 003993

2-year public technical college in large city.
Enrollment: 10,706 undergrads, 52% part-time. 1,558 full-time freshmen.
Selectivity: Open admission; but selective for some programs.

BASIC COSTS (2008-2009)
Tuition and fees: $3,360; out-of-district residents $4,176; out-of-state residents $9,840.

FINANCIAL AID PICTURE (2007-2008)
Students with need: Average financial aid package met 65% of need; average scholarship/grant was $3,896; average loan was $3,087. For part-time students, average financial aid package was $3,776.

FINANCIAL AID PROCEDURES
Forms required: FAFSA.
Dates and Deadlines: Priority date 4/15; no closing date. Applicants notified on a rolling basis; must reply within 2 week(s) of notification.

CONTACT
Michele Bowles, Director of Student Financial Services
PO Box 2408, Columbia, SC 29202
(803) 738-7792

Miller-Motte Technical College
North Charleston, South Carolina
www.miller-motte.net

2-year for-profit branch campus and technical college in small city.
Enrollment: 745 undergrads.
Selectivity: Open admission.

BASIC COSTS (2008-2009)
Tuition and fees: $10,575.
Per-credit charge: $235.
Additional info: Fees vary according to programs from $6-$27 per credit hour.

FINANCIAL AID PICTURE (2007-2008)
Students with need: 27% of average financial aid package awarded as scholarships/grants, 73% awarded as loans/jobs.

FINANCIAL AID PROCEDURES
Forms required: FAFSA, institutional form.
Dates and Deadlines: Applicants notified on a rolling basis.

CONTACT
Roxanne Porter, Financial Aid Director
8085 Rivers Avenue, Suite E, North Charleston, SC 29406
(843) 574-0101

Morris College
Sumter, South Carolina
www.morris.edu Federal Code: 218399

4-year private liberal arts college in large town, affiliated with Baptist faith.
Enrollment: 920 undergrads, 3% part-time. 295 full-time freshmen.
Selectivity: Admits over 75% of applicants.

BASIC COSTS (2009-2010)
Tuition and fees: $9,901.
Per-credit charge: $401.
Room and board: $4,386.

FINANCIAL AID PICTURE (2007-2008)
Students with need: Out of 295 full-time freshmen who applied for aid, 285 were judged to have need. Of these, 285 received aid, and 20 had their full need met. Average financial aid package met 85% of need; average scholarship/grant was $4,310; average loan was $3,500. For part-time students, average financial aid package was $6,750.
Students without need: This college awards aid only to students with need.
Scholarships offered: Presidential Scholarship: $750-$2,500; must have been admitted and rank in the first quarter of high school graduating class; larger awards available to salutatorians ($2,000) and valedictorians ($2,500); awards renewable up to 4 years if student maintains B average and excellent citizenship record. Luns C. Richardson Endowed Scholarship: $4,500; first-time freshman student who has been admitted, completed academic (college prep) curriculum with GPA of 3.5 or better, has exceptional letters of recommendation from at least 2 classroom teachers and one guidance counselor, principal, or assistant principal, and plans to enroll as full-time student for 4 consecutive years.

FINANCIAL AID PROCEDURES
Forms required: FAFSA, institutional form.
Dates and Deadlines: Priority date 3/30; no closing date. Applicants notified on a rolling basis starting 6/1; must reply within 2 week(s) of notification.
Transfers: Must reply within 2 week(s) of notification.

CONTACT
Sandra Gibson, Financial Aid Officer
100 West College Street, Sumter, SC 29150-3599
(803) 934-3238

Newberry College
Newberry, South Carolina
www.newberry.edu Federal Code: 003440

4-year private liberal arts college in small city, affiliated with Evangelical Lutheran Church in America.
Enrollment: 964 undergrads, 1% part-time. 297 full-time freshmen.
Selectivity: Admits over 75% of applicants.

BASIC COSTS (2009-2010)
Tuition and fees: $21,470.
Per-credit charge: $500.
Room and board: $7,750.

FINANCIAL AID PICTURE (2007-2008)
Students with need: 71% of average financial aid package awarded as scholarships/grants, 29% awarded as loans/jobs. Need-based aid available for part-time students. Work study available nights, weekends, and for part-time students.
Students without need: No-need awards available for academics, alumni affiliation, athletics, leadership, music/drama, religious affiliation, ROTC, state/district residency.

FINANCIAL AID PROCEDURES
Forms required: FAFSA, institutional form.
Dates and Deadlines: Priority date 3/15; no closing date. Applicants notified on a rolling basis starting 3/1; must reply by 5/1 or within 2 week(s) of notification.

CONTACT
Missy Lutz, Director of Financial Aid
2100 College Street, Newberry, SC 29108
(803) 321-5128

North Greenville University
Tigerville, South Carolina
www.ngu.edu Federal Code: 003441

4-year private liberal arts college in rural community, affiliated with Southern Baptist Convention.
Enrollment: 1,916 undergrads, 4% part-time. 512 full-time freshmen.
Selectivity: Admits 50 to 75% of applicants.

BASIC COSTS (2009-2010)
Tuition and fees: $12,264.
Per-credit charge: $210.
Room and board: $7,056.

FINANCIAL AID PICTURE
Students with need: Need-based aid available for full-time and part-time students.
Students without need: This college awards aid only to students with need.

FINANCIAL AID PROCEDURES
Forms required: FAFSA.
Dates and Deadlines: Priority date 6/1; closing date 6/30. Applicants notified on a rolling basis starting 8/1; must reply within 2 week(s) of notification.
Transfers: No deadline.

CONTACT

Mike Jordan, Director of Financial Aid
PO Box 1892, Tigerville, SC 29688-1892
(864) 977-7050

Orangeburg-Calhoun Technical College

Orangeburg, South Carolina
www.octech.edu Federal Code: 006815

2-year public community and technical college in large town.
Enrollment: 2,290 undergrads.
Selectivity: Open admission; but selective for some programs.

BASIC COSTS (2008-2009)

Tuition and fees: $3,078; out-of-district residents $3,798; out-of-state residents $4,518.

FINANCIAL AID PICTURE

Students with need: Need-based aid available for full-time and part-time students.
Students without need: This college awards aid only to students with need.
Scholarships offered: College Foundation Scholarship: full academic tuition; for high school valedictorians and salutatorians.

FINANCIAL AID PROCEDURES

Forms required: FAFSA, institutional form.
Dates and Deadlines: Priority date 6/4; no closing date. Applicants notified on a rolling basis starting 5/1; must reply within 2 week(s) of notification.
Transfers: Priority date 6/1. Financial aid transcripts required of mid-year transfers prior to disbursement of aid.

CONTACT

Caroline Thornton, Director of Institutional Research
3250 St. Matthews Road, Orangeburg, SC 29118-8222
(803) 535-1249

Piedmont Technical College

Greenwood, South Carolina
www.ptc.edu Federal Code: 003992

2-year public community and technical college in small city.
Enrollment: 3,960 undergrads.
Selectivity: Open admission; but selective for some programs.

BASIC COSTS (2008-2009)

Tuition and fees: $3,126; out of district residents $3,534; out of state residents $4,734.
Additional info: In Service Area, not fully supporting tuition, $3,288.

FINANCIAL AID PICTURE

Students with need: Need-based aid available for full-time and part-time students. Work study available nights, weekends, and for part-time students.
Students without need: This college awards aid only to students with need.

FINANCIAL AID PROCEDURES

Forms required: FAFSA.
Dates and Deadlines: Priority date 5/1; no closing date. Applicants notified on a rolling basis starting 6/1; must reply within 2 week(s) of notification.

CONTACT

Deborah Williams, Director of Financial Aid
PO Box 1467, Greenwood, SC 29648
(864) 941-8365

Presbyterian College

Clinton, South Carolina
www.presby.edu Federal Code: 003445

4-year private liberal arts college in small town, affiliated with Presbyterian Church (USA).
Enrollment: 1,140 undergrads, 1% part-time. 323 full-time freshmen.
Selectivity: Admits 50 to 75% of applicants.

BASIC COSTS (2009-2010)

Tuition and fees: $28,880.
Per-credit charge: $1,102.
Room and board: $8,345.

FINANCIAL AID PICTURE (2008-2009)

Students with need: Need-based aid available for full-time and part-time students.
Students without need: No-need awards available for academics, alumni affiliation, athletics, job skills, leadership, minority status, music/drama, religious affiliation, ROTC.
Scholarships offered: Academic and leadership scholarships, applications by December 5; number and amounts awarded vary; music awards based on audition.

FINANCIAL AID PROCEDURES

Forms required: FAFSA.
Dates and Deadlines: Priority date 3/15; closing date 6/30. Applicants notified on a rolling basis starting 4/1; must reply by 5/1.

CONTACT

Jeffrey Holliday, Director of Financial Aid
503 South Broad Street, Clinton, SC 29325
(864) 833-8290

South University: Columbia

Columbia, South Carolina
www.southuniversity.edu Federal Code: 004922

4-year for-profit university in small city.
Enrollment: 774 undergrads, 35% part-time. 31 full-time freshmen.
Selectivity: Open admission; but selective for some programs.

BASIC COSTS (2008-2009)

Tuition and fees: $13,035.
Per-credit charge: $295.

FINANCIAL AID PICTURE

Students with need: Need-based aid available for full-time and part-time students.
Students without need: This college awards aid only to students with need.

FINANCIAL AID PROCEDURES

Forms required: FAFSA.
Dates and Deadlines: Priority date 5/30; no closing date. Applicants notified on a rolling basis starting 5/30.

CONTACT

Walter Haversat, Financial Aid Director
9 Science Court, Columbia, SC 29203
(803) 799-9082

Southern Wesleyan University

Central, South Carolina
www.swu.edu Federal Code: 003422

4-year private university and liberal arts college in small town, affiliated with Wesleyan Church.
Enrollment: 1,616 undergrads. 142 full-time freshmen.
Selectivity: Admits over 75% of applicants.

BASIC COSTS (2009-2010)

Tuition and fees: $18,700.
Room and board: $7,800.

FINANCIAL AID PICTURE (2008-2009)

Students with need: Average financial aid package met 75% of need; average scholarship/grant was $12,621; average loan was $3,145. For part-time students, average financial aid package was $5,969.
Students without need: No-need awards available for academics, athletics, music/drama.
Cumulative student debt: 86% of graduating class had student loans; average debt was $24,435.

FINANCIAL AID PROCEDURES

Forms required: FAFSA, institutional form.
Dates and Deadlines: Priority date 3/31; closing date 6/30. Applicants notified on a rolling basis starting 2/1; must reply within 2 week(s) of notification.
Transfers: Priority date 4/1. Applicants notified on a rolling basis starting 2/1; must reply within 2 week(s) of notification.

CONTACT

Jeff Dennis, Financial Aid Director
PO Box 1020, Central, SC 29630-1020
(800) 289-1292

Spartanburg Community College

Spartanburg, South Carolina
www.sccsc.edu Federal Code: 003994

2-year public community and technical college in small city.
Enrollment: 4,678 undergrads.
Selectivity: Open admission; but selective for some programs.

BASIC COSTS (2008-2009)

Tuition and fees: $3,314; out-of-district residents $4,134; out-of-state residents $7,048.

FINANCIAL AID PICTURE (2007-2008)

Students with need: 98% of average financial aid package awarded as scholarships/grants, 2% awarded as loans/jobs. Need-based aid available for part-time students.
Additional info: Participates in South Carolina lottery tuition assistance program. Full-time technical college students who are state residents receive assistance for tuition not covered by federal or need-based grants.

FINANCIAL AID PROCEDURES

Forms required: FAFSA.
Dates and Deadlines: Priority date 2/28; closing date 5/1. Applicants notified on a rolling basis starting 5/1.
Transfers: No deadline. Applicants notified on a rolling basis starting 8/15.

CONTACT

Nancy Garmroth, Director of Financial Aid
Box 4386, Spartanburg, SC 29305-4386
(864) 592-4810

Spartanburg Methodist College

Spartanburg, South Carolina
www.smcsc.edu Federal Code: 003447

2-year private junior and liberal arts college in small city, affiliated with United Methodist Church.
Enrollment: 727 undergrads, 2% part-time. 444 full-time freshmen.
Selectivity: Admits 50 to 75% of applicants.

BASIC COSTS (2008-2009)

Tuition and fees: $11,731.
Per-credit charge: $312.
Room and board: $6,741.
Additional info: Tuition/fee waivers available for adults, unemployed or children of unemployed.

FINANCIAL AID PICTURE (2008-2009)

Students with need: Need-based aid available for full-time and part-time students. Work study available nights, weekends, and for part-time students.
Students without need: No-need awards available for academics, athletics, job skills, leadership, music/drama, religious affiliation, state/district residency.
Scholarships offered: Milliken Scholars: $4,100. Camak Scholars: $3,500. Trustee Scholars: $3,000. Presidential Scholars: $2,400.

FINANCIAL AID PROCEDURES

Forms required: FAFSA.
Dates and Deadlines: Priority date 6/30; closing date 8/22. Applicants notified on a rolling basis starting 3/1; must reply within 2 week(s) of notification.
Transfers: No deadline. Applicants notified on a rolling basis starting 3/1; must reply within 2 week(s) of notification. To be eligible for financial aid, full time students must pass the equivalent of 12 hours.

CONTACT

Kendra Burnette, Director of Financial Aid
1000 Powell Mill Road, Spartanburg, SC 29301-5899
(864) 587-4298

Technical College of the Lowcountry

Beaufort, South Carolina
www.tcl.edu Federal Code: 009910

2-year public community and technical college in small town.
Enrollment: 1,900 undergrads.
Selectivity: Open admission; but selective for some programs.

BASIC COSTS (2008-2009)

Tuition and fees: $3,270; out-of-state residents $7,082.

FINANCIAL AID PICTURE

Students with need: Need-based aid available for full-time and part-time students.
Students without need: This college awards aid only to students with need.
Additional info: State lottery aid may be available to South Carolina residents who take 6 credit hours or more.

FINANCIAL AID PROCEDURES

Forms required: FAFSA.
Dates and Deadlines: No deadline.

CONTACT

Cleo Martin, Coordinator of Financial Aid
921 South Ribaut Road, Beaufort, SC 29901-1288
(843) 525-8337

Tri-County Technical College

Pendleton, South Carolina
www.tctc.edu Federal Code: 004926

2-year public community and technical college in small town.
Enrollment: 5,730 undergrads.
Selectivity: Open admission; but selective for some programs.

BASIC COSTS (2008-2009)

Tuition and fees: $3,060; out-of-district residents $3,384; out-of-state residents $6,786.

FINANCIAL AID PICTURE

Students with need: Need-based aid available for full-time and part-time students. Work study available nights.
Students without need: No-need awards available for academics, state/district residency.
Scholarships offered: General and departmental scholarships: more than 125 awarded; some with special qualification criteria, such as student's career field or place of residency.
Additional info: Deadline for application to institutional scholarships April 2.

FINANCIAL AID PROCEDURES

Forms required: FAFSA.
Dates and Deadlines: Priority date 6/30; no closing date. Applicants notified on a rolling basis starting 6/15; must reply within 2 week(s) of notification.
Transfers: Priority date 5/1; no deadline. Applicants notified on a rolling basis starting 6/1.

CONTACT

Bill Whitlock, Director of Financial Aid
Box 587, Pendleton, SC 29670
(864) 646-8361

Trident Technical College

Charleston, South Carolina
www.tridenttech.edu Federal Code: 004920

2-year public community and technical college in large city.
Enrollment: 11,840 undergrads, 54% part-time. 1,611 full-time freshmen.
Selectivity: Open admission; but selective for some programs.

BASIC COSTS (2008-2009)

Tuition and fees: $3,330; out-of-district residents $3,696; out-of-state residents $6,380.

FINANCIAL AID PICTURE

Students with need: Need-based aid available for full-time and part-time students. Work study available nights, weekends, and for part-time students.

FINANCIAL AID PROCEDURES

Forms required: FAFSA.
Dates and Deadlines: No deadline. Applicants notified on a rolling basis; must reply within 6 week(s) of notification.
Transfers: No deadline. Applicants notified on a rolling basis; must reply within 6 week(s) of notification.

CONTACT

Ellen Green, Director of Financial Aid/Veterans Assistance
Box 118067, AM-M, Charleston, SC 29423-8067
(843) 574-6147

University of South Carolina

Columbia, South Carolina
www.sc.edu Federal Code: 003448

4-year public university in small city.
Enrollment: 19,458 undergrads, 7% part-time. 3,658 full-time freshmen.
Selectivity: Admits 50 to 75% of applicants.

BASIC COSTS (2008-2009)

Tuition and fees: $8,838; out-of-state residents $22,908.
Per-credit charge: $395; out-of-state residents $1,029.
Room and board: $6,652.
Additional info: Health professions (pharmacy, health, nursing), law and medical professions have higher undergraduate and graduate fees.

FINANCIAL AID PICTURE (2008-2009)

Students with need: Out of 2,541 full-time freshmen who applied for aid, 1,528 were judged to have need. Of these, 1,522 received aid, and 481 had their full need met. Average financial aid package met 75% of need; average scholarship/grant was $4,368; average loan was $2,401. For part-time students, average financial aid package was $7,429.
Students without need: 1,729 full-time freshmen who did not demonstrate need for aid received scholarships/grants; average award was $6,382. No-need awards available for academics, alumni affiliation, art, athletics, job skills, leadership, minority status, music/drama, religious affiliation, ROTC, state/district residency.
Scholarships offered: 122 full-time freshmen received athletic scholarships; average amount $9,423.
Cumulative student debt: 45% of graduating class had student loans; average debt was $21,315.

FINANCIAL AID PROCEDURES

Forms required: FAFSA.
Dates and Deadlines: Priority date 4/1; no closing date. Applicants notified on a rolling basis starting 4/1.

CONTACT

Edgar Miller, Director of Financial Aid and Scholarships
Office of Undergraduate Admissions, Columbia, SC 29208
(803) 777-8134

University of South Carolina at Aiken

Aiken, South Carolina
www.usca.edu Federal Code: 003449

4-year public university and liberal arts college in large town.
Enrollment: 2,813 undergrads, 15% part-time. 584 full-time freshmen.
Selectivity: Admits less than 50% of applicants.

BASIC COSTS (2008-2009)

Tuition and fees: $7,582; out-of-state residents $14,946.
Per-credit charge: $318; out-of-state residents $631.
Room and board: $6,250.

FINANCIAL AID PICTURE (2007-2008)

Students with need: Out of 520 full-time freshmen who applied for aid, 281 were judged to have need. Of these, 237 received aid, and 72 had their full need met. Average financial aid package met 81% of need; average scholarship/grant was $1,310; average loan was $3,330. For part-time students, average financial aid package was $6,713.
Students without need: 23 full-time freshmen who did not demonstrate need for aid received scholarships/grants; average award was $1,550. No-need awards available for academics, alumni affiliation, art, athletics, leadership, minority status, music/drama, state/district residency.
Scholarships offered: 46 full-time freshmen received athletic scholarships; average amount $2,962.

Cumulative student debt: 47% of graduating class had student loans; average debt was $24,668.

FINANCIAL AID PROCEDURES

Forms required: FAFSA.
Dates and Deadlines: Priority date 3/15; no closing date. Applicants notified on a rolling basis starting 11/1; must reply within 2 week(s) of notification.
Transfers: Financial aid transcripts from previous institutions required.

CONTACT

Glenn Shumpert, Director of Financial Aid
471 University Parkway, Aiken, SC 29801-6399
(803) 641-3476

University of South Carolina at Beaufort

Bluffton, South Carolina
www.uscb.edu Federal Code: 003450

4-year public university and liberal arts college in large town.
Enrollment: 1,313 undergrads, 25% part-time. 282 full-time freshmen.

BASIC COSTS (2008-2009)

Tuition and fees: $7,134; out-of-state residents $14,710.
Per-credit charge: $278; out-of-state residents $593.

FINANCIAL AID PICTURE (2008-2009)

Students with need: Need-based aid available for full-time and part-time students. Work study available nights, weekends, and for part-time students.
Students without need: No-need awards available for academics, state/district residency.

FINANCIAL AID PROCEDURES

Forms required: FAFSA.
Dates and Deadlines: Priority date 4/15; no closing date. Applicants notified on a rolling basis starting 5/31; must reply within 2 week(s) of notification.

CONTACT

Patricia Greene, Director and VA Coordinator of Financial Aid
One University Boulevard, Bluffton, SC 29909
(843) 521-3104

University of South Carolina at Sumter

Sumter, South Carolina
www.uscsumter.edu Federal Code: 003426

2-year public branch campus college in small city.
Enrollment: 870 undergrads, 25% part-time. 223 full-time freshmen.

BASIC COSTS (2008-2009)

Tuition and fees: $5,264; out-of-state residents $12,680.
Per-credit charge: $206; out-of-state residents $515.

FINANCIAL AID PICTURE (2008-2009)

Students with need: Need-based aid available for full-time and part-time students. Work study available nights, weekends, and for part-time students.
Students without need: This college awards aid only to students with need.

FINANCIAL AID PROCEDURES

Forms required: FAFSA.
Dates and Deadlines: Priority date 4/15; no closing date. Applicants notified on a rolling basis starting 4/16; must reply within 2 week(s) of notification.

CONTACT

Sue Sims, Financial Aid Director
200 Miller Road, Sumter, SC 29150-2498
(803) 938-3766

University of South Carolina at Union

Union, South Carolina
uscunion.sc.edu Federal Code: 004927

2-year public branch campus college in small town.
Enrollment: 250 undergrads.

BASIC COSTS (2008-2009)

Tuition and fees: $5,264; out-of-state residents $12,680.
Per-credit charge: $206; out-of-state residents $515.

FINANCIAL AID PICTURE

Students with need: Work study available nights, weekends, and for part-time students.
Students without need: This college awards aid only to students with need.

FINANCIAL AID PROCEDURES

Forms required: FAFSA.
Dates and Deadlines: Priority date 4/15; no closing date. Applicants notified on a rolling basis starting 7/15; must reply within 2 week(s) of notification.

CONTACT

Bobby Holcombe, Financial Aid Director
PO Drawer 729, Union, SC 29379
(864) 429-8728

University of South Carolina Upstate

Spartanburg, South Carolina
www.uscupstate.edu Federal Code: 006951

4-year public university in small city.
Enrollment: 4,754 undergrads, 13% part-time. 805 full-time freshmen.
Selectivity: Admits 50 to 75% of applicants.

BASIC COSTS (2008-2009)

Tuition and fees: $8,512; out-of-state residents $16,854.
Per-credit charge: $345; out-of-state residents $699.
Room and board: $6,400.

FINANCIAL AID PICTURE (2007-2008)

Students with need: Out of 666 full-time freshmen who applied for aid, 503 were judged to have need. Of these, 500 received aid, and 121 had their full need met. Average financial aid package met 67% of need; average scholarship/grant was $4,139; average loan was $3,064. For part-time students, average financial aid package was $5,384.
Students without need: 19 full-time freshmen who did not demonstrate need for aid received scholarships/grants; average award was $2,103. No-need awards available for academics, athletics, minority status, ROTC, state/district residency.
Scholarships offered: 124 full-time freshmen received athletic scholarships; average amount $7,329.
Cumulative student debt: 72% of graduating class had student loans; average debt was $19,005.
Additional info: Out-of-state students who are recipients of financial aid may qualify for out-of-state fee waiver. Educational benefits available to veterans and children of deceased/disabled veterans.

FINANCIAL AID PROCEDURES

Forms required: FAFSA, institutional form.
Dates and Deadlines: Priority date 3/1; closing date 7/15. Applicants notified on a rolling basis starting 5/1; must reply within 2 week(s) of notification.
Transfers: Students eligible for financial assistance for total of 5 years or 10 full-time semesters at all post-secondary institutions attended for the bachelor's degree, and 5 full-time semesters of enrollment for associate's degree in nursing.

CONTACT
Kim Jenerette, Director of Financial Aid and Scholarships
800 University Way, Spartanburg, SC 29303
(864) 503-5340

University of South Carolina: Salkehatchie Regional Campus

Allendale, South Carolina
uscsalkehatchie.sc.edu Federal Code: 003454

2-year public branch campus college in rural community.
Enrollment: 700 undergrads.

BASIC COSTS (2008-2009)
Tuition and fees: $5,264; out-of-state residents $12,680.
Per-credit charge: $206; out-of-state residents $515.

FINANCIAL AID PICTURE (2007-2008)
Students with need: Need-based aid available for full-time and part-time students. Work study available nights, weekends, and for part-time students.
Students without need: No-need awards available for academics.

FINANCIAL AID PROCEDURES
Forms required: FAFSA.
Dates and Deadlines: Priority date 4/30; no closing date. Applicants notified on a rolling basis starting 6/1.

CONTACT
Julie Hadwin, Director of Financial Aid
PO Box 617, Allendale, SC 29810
(803) 584-3446

Williamsburg Technical College

Kingstree, South Carolina
www.wiltech.edu Federal Code: 009322

2-year public community and technical college in small town.
Enrollment: 588 undergrads.
Selectivity: Open admission.

BASIC COSTS (2008-2009)
Tuition and fees: $2,942; out-of-district residents $3,062; out-of-state residents $5,642.

FINANCIAL AID PICTURE
Students with need: Need-based aid available for full-time and part-time students. Work study available nights, weekends, and for part-time students.
Students without need: No-need awards available for academics, leadership, minority status, state/district residency.
Additional info: Tuition waivers for children of war veterans.

FINANCIAL AID PROCEDURES
Forms required: FAFSA.
Dates and Deadlines: Priority date 4/15; no closing date. Applicants notified on a rolling basis starting 7/1; must reply within 4 week(s) of notification.

CONTACT
Jean Boos, Director of Financial Aid
601 Martin Luther King Jr. Avenue, Kingstree, SC 29556-4197
(843) 355-4166

Winthrop University

Rock Hill, South Carolina
www.winthrop.edu Federal Code: 003456

4-year public university in small city.
Enrollment: 4,801 undergrads, 7% part-time. 1,075 full-time freshmen.
Selectivity: Admits 50 to 75% of applicants.

BASIC COSTS (2008-2009)
Tuition and fees: $11,060; out-of-state residents $20,610.
Per-credit charge: $460; out-of-state residents $858.
Room and board: $6,140.

FINANCIAL AID PICTURE (2007-2008)
Students with need: 61% of average financial aid package awarded as scholarships/grants, 39% awarded as loans/jobs. Need-based aid available for part-time students.
Students without need: No-need awards available for academics, art, athletics, music/drama, state/district residency.
Additional info: Academic scholarships from $1,500 to full tuition and board awarded to approximately one-third of entering freshman class each year.

FINANCIAL AID PROCEDURES
Forms required: FAFSA.
Dates and Deadlines: Priority date 3/1; no closing date. Applicants notified on a rolling basis starting 4/1; must reply within 2 week(s) of notification.
Transfers: Transfer students are not eligible for academic scholarship their first year.

CONTACT
Betty Whalen, Director, Financial Resource Center
701 Oakland Avenue, Rock Hill, SC 29733
(803) 323-2189

Wofford College

Spartanburg, South Carolina
www.wofford.edu Federal Code: 003457

4-year private liberal arts college in small city, affiliated with United Methodist Church.
Enrollment: 1,377 undergrads, 1% part-time. 415 full-time freshmen.
Selectivity: Admits 50 to 75% of applicants.

BASIC COSTS (2009-2010)
Tuition and fees: $30,280.
Per-credit charge: $1,195.
Room and board: $8,480.

FINANCIAL AID PICTURE (2008-2009)
Students with need: Out of 293 full-time freshmen who applied for aid, 216 were judged to have need. Of these, 216 received aid, and 117 had their full need met. Average financial aid package met 88% of need; average scholarship/grant was $25,295; average loan was $3,655. For part-time students, average financial aid package was $10,190.
Students without need: 96 full-time freshmen who did not demonstrate need for aid received scholarships/grants; average award was $13,011. No-need awards available for academics, athletics, leadership, music/drama, religious affiliation, ROTC, state/district residency.
Scholarships offered: 41 full-time freshmen received athletic scholarships; average amount $14,960.
Cumulative student debt: 50% of graduating class had student loans; average debt was $17,831.

FINANCIAL AID PROCEDURES
Forms required: FAFSA.
Dates and Deadlines: Priority date 3/15; no closing date. Applicants notified on a rolling basis starting 3/31; must reply by 5/1.

CONTACT
Kay Walton, Director of Financial Aid
429 North Church Street, Spartanburg, SC 29303-3663
(864) 597-4149

York Technical College
Rock Hill, South Carolina
www.yorktech.com Federal Code: 003996

2-year public community and technical college in large town.
Enrollment: 4,248 undergrads.
Selectivity: Open admission; but selective for some programs.

BASIC COSTS (2008-2009)
Tuition and fees: $3,244; out-of-district residents $3,592; out-of-state residents $7,288.

FINANCIAL AID PICTURE (2007-2008)
Students with need: Need-based aid available for full-time and part-time students. Work study available nights.
Students without need: No-need awards available for academics, leadership, state/district residency.

FINANCIAL AID PROCEDURES
Forms required: FAFSA.
Dates and Deadlines: Priority date 6/1; no closing date. Applicants notified on a rolling basis starting 3/1.
Transfers: No deadline. Applicants notified on a rolling basis starting 3/1.

CONTACT
Angela Fowler, Financial Aid Department Manager
452 South Anderson Road, Rock Hill, SC 29730
(803) 327-8005

South Dakota

Augustana College
Sioux Falls, South Dakota
www.augie.edu Federal Code: 003458

4-year private liberal arts college in small city, affiliated with Evangelical Lutheran Church in America.
Enrollment: 1,701 undergrads, 4% part-time. 427 full-time freshmen.
Selectivity: Admits over 75% of applicants.

BASIC COSTS (2009-2010)
Tuition and fees: $23,550.
Room and board: $6,188.
Additional info: Tuition/fee waivers available for minority students.

FINANCIAL AID PICTURE (2008-2009)
Students with need: Need-based aid available for full-time and part-time students. Work study available nights, weekends, and for part-time students.
Students without need: No-need awards available for academics, alumni affiliation, art, athletics, leadership, minority status, music/drama, religious affiliation, state/district residency.
Scholarships offered: Distinguished Scholars Scholarships: Trustees and Presidential Scholarships for students with a 27 ACT or above and 3.5 GPA and above; ProMusica scholarships, ProDramatis scholarships, ProArtis Scholarships; Fryxell Scholarships for journalism/english majors;.

FINANCIAL AID PROCEDURES
Forms required: FAFSA.
Dates and Deadlines: Priority date 3/1; no closing date. Applicants notified on a rolling basis starting 3/15; must reply within 3 week(s) of notification.
Transfers: No deadline. Applicants notified on a rolling basis starting 4/1; must reply within 3 week(s) of notification.

CONTACT
Brenda Murtha, Director of Financial Aid
2001 South Summit Avenue, Sioux Falls, SD 57197-9990
(605) 274-5216

Black Hills State University
Spearfish, South Dakota
www.bhsu.edu Federal Code: 003459

4-year public liberal arts and teachers college in large town.
Enrollment: 3,139 undergrads, 20% part-time. 547 full-time freshmen.
Selectivity: Admits over 75% of applicants.

BASIC COSTS (2008-2009)
Tuition and fees: $5,877; out-of-state residents $7,197.
Per-credit charge: $88; out-of-state residents $132.
Room and board: $5,438.
Additional info: Reciprocity agreements reduce tuition for some out-of-state students .

FINANCIAL AID PICTURE (2007-2008)
Students with need: Need-based aid available for full-time and part-time students.
Students without need: This college awards aid only to students with need.

FINANCIAL AID PROCEDURES
Forms required: FAFSA.
Dates and Deadlines: Closing date 2/15. Applicants notified on a rolling basis starting 5/15; must reply within 3 week(s) of notification.

CONTACT
Deb Henriksen, Director of Financial Aid
University Street Box 9502, Spearfish, SD 57799-9502
(605) 642-6581

Dakota State University
Madison, South Dakota
www.dsu.edu Federal Code: 003463

4-year public university in small town.
Enrollment: 1,450 undergrads, 24% part-time. 244 full-time freshmen.
Selectivity: Admits over 75% of applicants.

BASIC COSTS (2008-2009)
Tuition and fees: $6,497; out-of-state residents $7,817.
Per-credit charge: $88; out-of-state residents $132.
Room and board: $4,681.
Additional info: Reciprocity agreements reduce tuition for some out-of-state students.

FINANCIAL AID PICTURE (2007-2008)
Students with need: Out of 225 full-time freshmen who applied for aid, 169 were judged to have need. Of these, 169 received aid, and 35 had their full need met. Average financial aid package met 85% of need; average scholarship/grant was $3,317; average loan was $4,028. For part-time students, average financial aid package was $5,514.
Students without need: 51 full-time freshmen who did not demonstrate need for aid received scholarships/grants; average award was $5,517. No-need awards available for academics, alumni affiliation, art, athletics, leadership, minority status, music/drama, state/district residency.
Scholarships offered: 42 full-time freshmen received athletic scholarships; average amount $1,574.

Cumulative student debt: 92% of graduating class had student loans; average debt was $21,189.
Additional info: Application deadline for grants and scholarships March 1. No deadline for loan and job applications.

FINANCIAL AID PROCEDURES

Forms required: FAFSA.
Dates and Deadlines: Priority date 3/1; no closing date. Applicants notified on a rolling basis starting 4/1; must reply within 2 week(s) of notification.
Transfers: No deadline. Applicants notified on a rolling basis starting 4/1; must reply within 2 week(s) of notification.

CONTACT

Denise Grayson, Financial Aid Director
820 North Washington Avenue, Madison, SD 57042
(605) 256-5152

Dakota Wesleyan University

Mitchell, South Dakota
www.dwu.edu Federal Code: 003461

4-year private university and liberal arts college in large town, affiliated with United Methodist Church.
Enrollment: 682 undergrads, 7% part-time. 166 full-time freshmen.
Selectivity: Open admission; but selective for some programs.

BASIC COSTS (2009-2010)

Tuition and fees: $1,900.
Room and board: $5,870.

FINANCIAL AID PICTURE (2008-2009)

Students with need: Out of 150 full-time freshmen who applied for aid, 139 were judged to have need. Of these, 139 received aid, and 52 had their full need met. Average financial aid package met 60% of need. Need-based aid available for part-time students.
Students without need: 24 full-time freshmen who did not demonstrate need for aid received scholarships/grants; average award was $10,700. No-need awards available for academics, alumni affiliation, art, athletics, leadership, minority status, music/drama, religious affiliation.
Scholarships offered: 17 full-time freshmen received athletic scholarships; average amount $3,500.
Cumulative student debt: 94% of graduating class had student loans; average debt was $36,000.

FINANCIAL AID PROCEDURES

Forms required: FAFSA.
Dates and Deadlines: Priority date 4/15; no closing date. Applicants notified on a rolling basis starting 3/1; must reply within 2 week(s) of notification.
Transfers: No deadline. Applicants notified on a rolling basis; must reply within 2 week(s) of notification.

CONTACT

Kristy O'Kief, Director of Financial Aid
1200 West University Avenue, Mitchell, SD 57301-4398
(605) 995-2650

Kilian Community College

Sioux Falls, South Dakota
www.kilian.edu Federal Code: 015000

2-year private community college in small city.
Enrollment: 286 undergrads, 83% part-time. 20 full-time freshmen.
Selectivity: Open admission.

BASIC COSTS (2008-2009)

Tuition and fees: $8,469.
Per-credit charge: $229.

FINANCIAL AID PICTURE (2007-2008)

Students with need: Out of 17 full-time freshmen who applied for aid, 17 were judged to have need. Of these, 17 received aid. For part-time students, average financial aid package was $1,874.
Students without need: No-need awards available for academics, leadership, minority status.

FINANCIAL AID PROCEDURES

Forms required: FAFSA, institutional form.
Dates and Deadlines: No deadline. Applicants notified on a rolling basis starting 7/1; must reply within 2 week(s) of notification.
Transfers: No deadline. Applicants notified on a rolling basis starting 7/1; must reply within 2 week(s) of notification.

CONTACT

Patti Klinkhammer, Director of Financial Aid
300 East 6th Street, Sioux Falls, SD 57103-7020
(605) 221-3100

Lake Area Technical Institute

Watertown, South Dakota
www.lakeareatech.edu Federal Code: 005309

2-year public technical college in large town.
Enrollment: 1,259 undergrads.
Selectivity: Open admission; but selective for some programs.

BASIC COSTS (2008-2009)

Additional info: Approximate program costs $4,000 - $7,000 per year, depending on course of study; includes tuition, books and supplies.

FINANCIAL AID PICTURE

Students with need: Need-based aid available for full-time and part-time students.
Students without need: This college awards aid only to students with need.

FINANCIAL AID PROCEDURES

Forms required: FAFSA.
Dates and Deadlines: Priority date 4/15; no closing date. Applicants notified on a rolling basis starting 5/1.

CONTACT

Marlene Seeklander, Financial Aid Director
PO Box 730, Watertown, SD 57201
(605) 882-5284

Mitchell Technical Institute

Mitchell, South Dakota
www.mitchelltech.com Federal Code: 008284

2-year public culinary school and technical college in large town.
Enrollment: 633 undergrads, 3% part-time. 340 full-time freshmen.
Selectivity: Open admission; but selective for some programs.

BASIC COSTS (2009-2010)

Tuition and fees: $4,600.

FINANCIAL AID PICTURE (2007-2008)

Students with need: Need-based aid available for full-time and part-time students.

FINANCIAL AID PROCEDURES

Forms required: FAFSA.

Dates and Deadlines: No deadline. Applicants notified on a rolling basis; must reply within 3 week(s) of notification.

CONTACT

Grant Uecker, Financial Aid Coordinator
821 North Capital Street, Mitchell, SD 57301
(605) 995-3052 ext. 2315

Mount Marty College

Yankton, South Dakota
www.mtmc.edu Federal Code: 003465

4-year private liberal arts college in large town, affiliated with Roman Catholic Church.
Enrollment: 825 undergrads, 28% part-time. 139 full-time freshmen.
Selectivity: Open admission; but selective for some programs.

BASIC COSTS (2009-2010)

Tuition and fees: $18,908.
Per-credit charge: $657.
Room and board: $5,366.

FINANCIAL AID PICTURE (2008-2009)

Students with need: Need-based aid available for full-time and part-time students. Work study available nights, weekends, and for part-time students.
Students without need: No-need awards available for academics, art, athletics, leadership, music/drama, religious affiliation.
Additional info: Prestige scholarships application deadline 2/1.

FINANCIAL AID PROCEDURES

Forms required: FAFSA, institutional form.
Dates and Deadlines: Priority date 3/1; no closing date. Applicants notified on a rolling basis starting 3/15; must reply within 2 week(s) of notification.
Transfers: No deadline. Applicants notified on a rolling basis; must reply within 2 week(s) of notification.

CONTACT

Kenneth Kocer, Director of Financial Assistance
1105 West Eighth Street, Yankton, SD 57078
(605) 668-1589

National American University: Rapid City

Rapid City, South Dakota
www.national.edu Federal Code: 004057

4-year for-profit business and technical college in small city.
Enrollment: 475 undergrads.
Selectivity: Open admission; but selective for some programs.

BASIC COSTS (2008-2009)

Additional info: Tuition/fee waivers available for unemployed or children of unemployed.

FINANCIAL AID PICTURE

Students with need: Need-based aid available for full-time and part-time students. Work study available nights, weekends, and for part-time students.
Students without need: This college awards aid only to students with need.

FINANCIAL AID PROCEDURES

Forms required: FAFSA, institutional form.
Dates and Deadlines: No deadline. Applicants notified on a rolling basis; must reply within 4 week(s) of notification.

CONTACT

Cheryl Bullinger, Director of Financial Aid
321 Kansas City Street, Rapid City, SD 57701

Northern State University

Aberdeen, South Dakota
www.northern.edu Federal Code: 003466

4-year public university and liberal arts college in large town.
Enrollment: 1,946 undergrads, 11% part-time. 389 full-time freshmen.
Selectivity: Admits over 75% of applicants.

BASIC COSTS (2008-2009)

Tuition and fees: $5,712; out-of-state residents $7,032.
Per-credit charge: $88; out-of-state residents $132.
Room and board: $4,486.
Additional info: Reciprocity agreements reduce tuition for some out-of-state students.

FINANCIAL AID PICTURE (2008-2009)

Students with need: Need-based aid available for full-time and part-time students. Work study available nights, weekends, and for part-time students.
Students without need: No-need awards available for academics, art, athletics, leadership, minority status, music/drama, state/district residency.

FINANCIAL AID PROCEDURES

Forms required: FAFSA.
Dates and Deadlines: Priority date 3/1; no closing date. Applicants notified on a rolling basis starting 5/1; must reply within 2 week(s) of notification.
Transfers: Applicants notified by 4/15; must reply within 2 week(s) of notification. Financial aid transcript(s) required from all schools previously attended.

CONTACT

Sharon Kienow, Director of Student Financial Assistance
1200 South Jay Street, Aberdeen, SD 57401-7198
(605) 626-2640

Oglala Lakota College

Kyle, South Dakota
www.olc.edu Federal Code: 014659

4-year public liberal arts and teachers college in small town.
Enrollment: 1,551 undergrads, 50% part-time. 154 full-time freshmen.
Selectivity: Open admission.

BASIC COSTS (2009-2010)

Tuition and fees: $2,900.
Additional info: Above rates for Native Americans. Non-Native American students pay tuition rate of $2,940 and $98 per credit hour.

FINANCIAL AID PICTURE (2007-2008)

Students with need: 99% of average financial aid package awarded as scholarships/grants, 1% awarded as loans/jobs.
Additional info: Deadline for applications for Bureau of Indian Affairs Higher Education Grants, is March 15; applicants notified early summer.

FINANCIAL AID PROCEDURES

Dates and Deadlines: No deadline. Applicants notified on a rolling basis.

CONTACT

Billi Hornbeck, Financial Aid Director
Box 490, Kyle, SD 57752-0490
(605) 455-6037

Presentation College

Aberdeen, South Dakota
www.presentation.edu Federal Code: 003467

4-year private business and health science college in large town, affiliated with Roman Catholic Church.
Enrollment: 504 undergrads.
Selectivity: Admits 50 to 75% of applicants.

BASIC COSTS (2008-2009)

Tuition and fees: $13,951.
Per-credit charge: $504.
Room and board: $4,875.

FINANCIAL AID PICTURE (2008-2009)

Students with need: Need-based aid available for full-time and part-time students. Work study available nights, weekends, and for part-time students.

FINANCIAL AID PROCEDURES

Forms required: FAFSA.
Dates and Deadlines: Priority date 4/1; no closing date. Applicants notified on a rolling basis starting 5/1; must reply within 2 week(s) of notification.

CONTACT

Val Weisser, Financial Aid Director
1500 North Main Street, Aberdeen, SD 57401
(605) 229-8429

South Dakota School of Mines and Technology

Rapid City, South Dakota
www.sdsmt.edu Federal Code: 003470

4-year public university and engineering college in small city.
Enrollment: 1,564 undergrads, 12% part-time. 345 full-time freshmen.
Selectivity: Admits over 75% of applicants.

BASIC COSTS (2008-2009)

Tuition and fees: $6,040; out-of-state residents $7,360.
Per-credit charge: $88; out-of-state residents $132.
Room and board: $4,400.
Additional info: Reciprocity agreements reduce tuition for some out-of-state students.

FINANCIAL AID PICTURE (2007-2008)

Students with need: Out of 328 full-time freshmen who applied for aid, 188 were judged to have need. Of these, 187 received aid, and 51 had their full need met. Average financial aid package met 76% of need; average scholarship/grant was $3,510; average loan was $2,993. For part-time students, average financial aid package was $6,590.
Students without need: 90 full-time freshmen who did not demonstrate need for aid received scholarships/grants; average award was $2,979. No-need awards available for academics, athletics, leadership, ROTC.
Scholarships offered: ***Merit:*** Presidential Scholarship: $100 to $5,000; 5 awarded. Surbeck Scholars: $7,000; 2 awarded. All based on ACT/SAT scores, high school GPA, and class rank. Number of awards may vary from year to year depending on availability of funding. ***Athletic:*** 24 full-time freshmen received athletic scholarships; average amount $3,338.
Additional info: Closing date for scholarship applications February 1.

FINANCIAL AID PROCEDURES

Forms required: FAFSA.
Dates and Deadlines: Priority date 3/15; no closing date. Applicants notified on a rolling basis starting 5/1; must reply within 3 week(s) of notification.

CONTACT

David Martin, Director of Financial Aid
501 East St. Joseph Street, Rapid City, SD 57701
(605) 394-2274

South Dakota State University

Brookings, South Dakota
www.sdstate.edu Federal Code: 003471

4-year public university in large town.
Enrollment: 9,516 undergrads, 13% part-time. 2,009 full-time freshmen.
Selectivity: Admits over 75% of applicants.

BASIC COSTS (2008-2009)

Tuition and fees: $5,786; out-of-state residents $7,128.
Per-credit charge: $88; out-of-state residents $132.
Room and board: $5,423.
Additional info: Reduced out-of-state tuition for Minnesota students.

FINANCIAL AID PICTURE (2008-2009)

Students with need: Out of 1,692 full-time freshmen who applied for aid, 1,421 were judged to have need. Of these, 1,421 received aid, and 1,123 had their full need met. Average financial aid package met 89% of need; average scholarship/grant was $4,144; average loan was $4,432. Need-based aid available for part-time students.
Students without need: 481 full-time freshmen who did not demonstrate need for aid received scholarships/grants; average award was $1,641. No-need awards available for academics, art, athletics, job skills, leadership, minority status, music/drama, ROTC, state/district residency.
Scholarships offered: ***Merit:*** Academic scholarships for first-year freshmen: $500-$7,000; based on academic performance in high school; 1,420 awarded. Minimum academic scholarship for new first-year students: $1,000; based on ACT 24+; renewable. ***Athletic:*** 124 full-time freshmen received athletic scholarships; average amount $5,722.
Cumulative student debt: 82% of graduating class had student loans; average debt was $21,044.

FINANCIAL AID PROCEDURES

Forms required: FAFSA.
Dates and Deadlines: Priority date 3/11; no closing date. Applicants notified on a rolling basis starting 4/1; must reply within 3 week(s) of notification.
Transfers: No deadline. Applicants notified on a rolling basis starting 4/1; must reply within 3 week(s) of notification.

CONTACT

Jay Larsen, Director of Financial Aid
Box 2201 SAD 200, Brookings, SD 57007-0649
(605) 688-4695

Southeast Technical Institute

Sioux Falls, South Dakota
www.southeasttech.edu Federal Code: 008285

2-year public technical college in small city.
Enrollment: 2,093 undergrads, 21% part-time. 542 full-time freshmen.
Selectivity: Open admission; but selective for some programs.

BASIC COSTS (2008-2009)

Tuition and fees: $3,817.
Per-credit charge: $78.
Additional info: $450 per semester laptop fee required for some students. Students able to keep laptop after paying for 4 semesters of the lease.

FINANCIAL AID PICTURE

Students with need: Need-based aid available for full-time and part-time students.

Students without need: This college awards aid only to students with need.

FINANCIAL AID PROCEDURES

Forms required: FAFSA.

Dates and Deadlines: Priority date 5/1; no closing date. Applicants notified on a rolling basis starting 5/1; must reply within 3 week(s) of notification.

CONTACT

Lynette Grabowska, Financial Aid Officer
2320 North Career Avenue, Sioux Falls, SD 57107
(605) 367-7867

University of Sioux Falls

Sioux Falls, South Dakota
www.usiouxfalls.edu Federal Code: 003469

4-year private university and liberal arts college in small city, affiliated with American Baptist Churches in the USA.

Enrollment: 1,243 undergrads, 19% part-time. 286 full-time freshmen.

Selectivity: Admits over 75% of applicants.

BASIC COSTS (2009-2010)

Tuition and fees: $20,290.

Per-credit charge: $280.

Room and board: $5,920.

Additional info: Tuition/fee waivers available for adults.

FINANCIAL AID PICTURE (2007-2008)

Students with need: 64% of average financial aid package awarded as scholarships/grants, 36% awarded as loans/jobs. Need-based aid available for part-time students. Work study available nights, weekends, and for part-time students.

Students without need: No-need awards available for academics, alumni affiliation, art, athletics, job skills, leadership, music/drama, religious affiliation, state/district residency.

FINANCIAL AID PROCEDURES

Forms required: FAFSA.

Dates and Deadlines: Priority date 3/1; no closing date. Applicants notified on a rolling basis starting 3/1; must reply within 2 week(s) of notification.

CONTACT

Laura Olson, Director of Financial Aid
1101 West 22nd Street, Sioux Falls, SD 57105-1699
(605) 331-6623

University of South Dakota

Vermillion, South Dakota
www.usd.edu Federal Code: 003474

4-year public university in large town.

Enrollment: 6,036 undergrads, 27% part-time. 1,025 full-time freshmen.

Selectivity: Admits over 75% of applicants.

BASIC COSTS (2008-2009)

Tuition and fees: $5,828; out-of-state residents $7,148.

Per-credit charge: $88; out-of-state residents $132.

Room and board: $5,442.

Additional info: Reciprocity agreement in place for Minnesota residents. Reduced tuition for Iowa residents.

FINANCIAL AID PICTURE (2007-2008)

Students with need: Out of 900 full-time freshmen who applied for aid, 601 were judged to have need. Of these, 521 received aid, and 438 had their full need met. Average financial aid package met 76% of need; average scholarship/grant was $4,189; average loan was $3,408. For part-time students, average financial aid package was $5,807.

Students without need: 297 full-time freshmen who did not demonstrate need for aid received scholarships/grants; average award was $3,598. No-need awards available for academics, art, athletics, leadership, minority status, music/drama, ROTC.

Scholarships offered: 60 full-time freshmen received athletic scholarships; average amount $4,725.

FINANCIAL AID PROCEDURES

Forms required: FAFSA.

Dates and Deadlines: Priority date 3/15; no closing date. Applicants notified on a rolling basis starting 5/5.

CONTACT

Julie Pier, Director of Student Financial Aid
414 East Clark Street, Vermillion, SD 57069-2390
(605) 677-5446

Western Dakota Technical Institute

Rapid City, South Dakota
www.wdt.edu Federal Code: 010170

2-year public technical college in small city.

Enrollment: 924 undergrads.

Selectivity: Open admission; but selective for some programs.

BASIC COSTS (2008-2009)

Tuition and fees: $3,885.

Per-credit charge: $78.

Additional info: Total program cost ranges from $4,850- $13,150 depending on course of study.

FINANCIAL AID PICTURE

Students with need: Need-based aid available for full-time and part-time students. Work study available nights, weekends, and for part-time students.

FINANCIAL AID PROCEDURES

Forms required: FAFSA.

Dates and Deadlines: Priority date 4/20; no closing date. Applicants notified on a rolling basis starting 6/30; must reply within 2 week(s) of notification.

CONTACT

Starla Russell, Manager of Financial Aid
800 Mickelson Drive, Rapid City, SD 57703
(605) 394-4034

Tennessee

Aquinas College

Nashville, Tennessee
www.aquinascollege.edu Federal Code: 003477

4-year private nursing and liberal arts college in very large city, affiliated with Roman Catholic Church.

Enrollment: 821 undergrads.

Selectivity: Admits 50 to 75% of applicants.

BASIC COSTS (2009-2010)

Tuition and fees: $16,930.

Per-credit charge: $556.

Additional info: Additional $50 per-credit hour for nursing classes. Additional required fees for nursing and teacher education programs.

FINANCIAL AID PICTURE (2008-2009)

Students with need: Need-based aid available for full-time and part-time students. Work study available nights.

Students without need: No-need awards available for academics, alumni affiliation, leadership, religious affiliation.

FINANCIAL AID PROCEDURES

Forms required: FAFSA.

Dates and Deadlines: Priority date 3/1; no closing date. Applicants notified on a rolling basis starting 3/1; must reply within 2 week(s) of notification.

Transfers: No deadline. Applicants notified on a rolling basis; must reply within 2 week(s) of notification.

CONTACT

Kylie Pruitt, Director of Financial Aid
4210 Harding Road, Nashville, TN 37205-2086
(615) 297-7545 ext. 442

Austin Peay State University

Clarksville, Tennessee
www.apsu.edu Federal Code: 003478

4-year public university and liberal arts college in small city.

Enrollment: 8,403 undergrads, 23% part-time. 1,326 full-time freshmen.

Selectivity: Admits over 75% of applicants.

BASIC COSTS (2008-2009)

Tuition and fees: $5,526; out-of-state residents $16,418.

Per-credit charge: $189; out-of-state residents $662.

Room and board: $5,870.

FINANCIAL AID PICTURE (2007-2008)

Students with need: 47% of average financial aid package awarded as scholarships/grants, 53% awarded as loans/jobs. Need-based aid available for part-time students. Work study available nights, weekends, and for part-time students.

Students without need: No-need awards available for academics, art, athletics, leadership, music/drama, ROTC, state/district residency.

FINANCIAL AID PROCEDURES

Forms required: FAFSA.

Dates and Deadlines: Priority date 3/1; no closing date. Applicants notified on a rolling basis starting 5/1.

CONTACT

Donna Price, Director of Financial Aid
PO Box 4548, Clarksville, TN 37044
(931) 221-7907

Baptist College of Health Sciences

Memphis, Tennessee
www.bchs.edu Federal Code: 034403

4-year private health science and nursing college in very large city, affiliated with Baptist faith.

Enrollment: 928 undergrads, 40% part-time. 51 full-time freshmen.

Selectivity: Admits less than 50% of applicants. GED not accepted.

BASIC COSTS (2008-2009)

Tuition and fees: $9,070.

Per-credit charge: $274.

FINANCIAL AID PICTURE (2007-2008)

Students with need: 41% of average financial aid package awarded as scholarships/grants, 59% awarded as loans/jobs.

CONTACT

Rex Thompson, Vice President, Business and Financial Services
1003 Monroe Avenue, Memphis, TN 38104
(901) 572-2446

Belmont University

Nashville, Tennessee
www.belmont.edu Federal Code: 003479

4-year private university in very large city.

Enrollment: 4,131 undergrads, 7% part-time. 808 full-time freshmen.

Selectivity: Admits 50 to 75% of applicants.

BASIC COSTS (2009-2010)

Tuition and fees: $22,360.

Per-credit charge: $820.

Room and board: $8,590.

FINANCIAL AID PICTURE (2007-2008)

Students with need: Out of 704 full-time freshmen who applied for aid, 391 were judged to have need. Of these, 391 received aid, and 111 had their full need met. Average financial aid package met 78% of need; average scholarship/grant was $4,678; average loan was $3,377. For part-time students, average financial aid package was $4,598.

Students without need: 147 full-time freshmen who did not demonstrate need for aid received scholarships/grants; average award was $5,047. No-need awards available for academics, art, athletics, leadership, music/drama, religious affiliation, state/district residency.

Scholarships offered: 26 full-time freshmen received athletic scholarships; average amount $18,216.

Cumulative student debt: 50% of graduating class had student loans; average debt was $14,319.

FINANCIAL AID PROCEDURES

Forms required: FAFSA.

Dates and Deadlines: Priority date 3/1; no closing date. Applicants notified on a rolling basis starting 3/15; must reply by 5/1 or within 2 week(s) of notification.

Transfers: Applicants notified on a rolling basis starting 3/1; must reply by 5/1 or within 2 week(s) of notification. Scholarships available.

CONTACT

Paula Gill, Director of Student Financial Services
1900 Belmont Boulevard, Nashville, TN 37212-3757
(615) 460-6403

Bethel College

McKenzie, Tennessee
www.bethel-college.edu Federal Code: 003480

4-year private liberal arts college in small town, affiliated with Presbyterian Church (USA).

Enrollment: 2,126 undergrads, 17% part-time. 259 full-time freshmen.

Selectivity: Admits 50 to 75% of applicants.

BASIC COSTS (2009-2010)

Tuition and fees: $12,242.

Per-credit charge: $358.

Room and board: $6,926.

FINANCIAL AID PICTURE (2008-2009)

Students with need: 55% of average financial aid package awarded as scholarships/grants, 45% awarded as loans/jobs. Need-based aid available for part-time students. Work study available nights, weekends, and for part-time students.

Students without need: No-need awards available for academics, athletics, music/drama, religious affiliation, state/district residency.

FINANCIAL AID PROCEDURES

Forms required: FAFSA, institutional form.

Dates and Deadlines: Priority date 3/3; closing date 6/30. Applicants notified on a rolling basis starting 3/1.

Transfers: Financial aid transcripts from previously attended institutions required.

CONTACT

Laura Bateman, Director of Financial Aid
325 Cherry Avenue, McKenzie, TN 38201
(731) 352-4021

Carson-Newman College

Jefferson City, Tennessee
www.cn.edu Federal Code: 003481

4-year private liberal arts college in small town, affiliated with Southern Baptist Convention.

Enrollment: 1,808 undergrads, 6% part-time. 444 full-time freshmen.

Selectivity: Admits 50 to 75% of applicants.

BASIC COSTS (2009-2010)

Tuition and fees: $18,702.

Per-credit charge: $745.

Room and board: $5,608.

Additional info: Tuition/fee waivers available for adults, minority students.

FINANCIAL AID PICTURE (2008-2009)

Students with need: Out of 426 full-time freshmen who applied for aid, 353 were judged to have need. Of these, 353 received aid, and 93 had their full need met. Average financial aid package met 79% of need; average scholarship/grant was $12,838; average loan was $2,757. For part-time students, average financial aid package was $9,792.

Students without need: 80 full-time freshmen who did not demonstrate need for aid received scholarships/grants; average award was $6,960. No-need awards available for academics, art, athletics, leadership, minority status, music/drama, religious affiliation, ROTC.

Scholarships offered: 23 full-time freshmen received athletic scholarships; average amount $9,280.

FINANCIAL AID PROCEDURES

Forms required: FAFSA, institutional form.

Dates and Deadlines: Priority date 4/1; no closing date. Applicants notified on a rolling basis starting 2/1; must reply within 2 week(s) of notification.

CONTACT

Danette Seale, Director of Financial Aid
1646 Russell Avenue, Jefferson City, TN 37760
(865) 471-3247

Chattanooga State Technical Community College

Chattanooga, Tennessee
www.chattanoogastate.edu Federal Code: 003998

2-year public community and technical college in small city.

Enrollment: 6,759 undergrads.

Selectivity: Open admission; but selective for some programs.

BASIC COSTS (2008-2009)

Tuition and fees: $2,797; out-of-state residents $10,297.

Per-credit charge: $107; out-of-state residents $431.

FINANCIAL AID PICTURE (2008-2009)

Students with need: Need-based aid available for full-time and part-time students. Work study available nights, weekends, and for part-time students.

Students without need: No-need awards available for state/district residency.

FINANCIAL AID PROCEDURES

Forms required: FAFSA.

Dates and Deadlines: Priority date 4/1; no closing date. Applicants notified on a rolling basis starting 4/1; must reply within 2 week(s) of notification.

CONTACT

Jeanne Hinchee, Director of Financial Aid
4501 Amnicola Highway, Chattanooga, TN 37406
(423) 697-4402

Christian Brothers University

Memphis, Tennessee
www.cbu.edu Federal Code: 003482

4-year private university in very large city, affiliated with Roman Catholic Church.

Enrollment: 1,404 undergrads, 14% part-time. 321 full-time freshmen.

Selectivity: Admits 50 to 75% of applicants.

BASIC COSTS (2009-2010)

Tuition and fees: $23,730.

Per-credit charge: $740.

Room and board: $6,320.

Additional info: Tuition/fee waivers available for adults.

FINANCIAL AID PICTURE (2007-2008)

Students with need: Out of 296 full-time freshmen who applied for aid, 229 were judged to have need. Of these, 229 received aid, and 64 had their full need met. Average financial aid package met 93% of need; average scholarship/grant was $6,626; average loan was $3,271. For part-time students, average financial aid package was $6,487.

Students without need: 76 full-time freshmen who did not demonstrate need for aid received scholarships/grants; average award was $8,032. No-need awards available for academics, alumni affiliation, athletics, music/drama, state/district residency.

Scholarships offered: 36 full-time freshmen received athletic scholarships; average amount $6,757.

Additional info: ROTC scholarships available to qualified applicants.

FINANCIAL AID PROCEDURES

Forms required: FAFSA.

Dates and Deadlines: Priority date 2/15; no closing date. Applicants notified on a rolling basis starting 3/1; must reply within 2 week(s) of notification.

CONTACT

Jim Shannon, Director of Student Financial Resources
650 East Parkway South, Memphis, TN 38104-5519
(901) 321-3305

Cleveland State Community College

Cleveland, Tennessee
www.clevelandstatecc.edu Federal Code: 003999

2-year public community college in small city.

Enrollment: 2,273 undergrads, 39% part-time. 478 full-time freshmen.

Selectivity: Open admission; but selective for some programs.

BASIC COSTS (2008-2009)
Tuition and fees: $2,769; out-of-state residents $10,269.
Per-credit charge: $107; out-of-state residents $431.

FINANCIAL AID PICTURE (2007-2008)
Students with need: Out of 448 full-time freshmen who applied for aid, 280 were judged to have need. Of these, 269 received aid, and 54 had their full need met. Average financial aid package met 77% of need; average scholarship/grant was $4,247; average loan was $2,679. For part-time students, average financial aid package was $3,640.
Students without need: 115 full-time freshmen who did not demonstrate need for aid received scholarships/grants; average award was $3,169. No-need awards available for athletics, minority status.
Scholarships offered: 9 full-time freshmen received athletic scholarships; average amount $2,283.

FINANCIAL AID PROCEDURES
Forms required: FAFSA, institutional form.
Dates and Deadlines: Priority date 6/15; no closing date. Applicants notified on a rolling basis starting 7/1; must reply within 2 week(s) of notification.

CONTACT
Geraldine Parks, Director of Financial Aid
3535 Adkisson Drive, Cleveland, TN 37320-3570
(423) 478-6215

Columbia State Community College
Columbia, Tennessee
www.columbiastate.edu Federal Code: 003483

2-year public community college in large town.
Enrollment: 4,828 undergrads.
Selectivity: Open admission; but selective for some programs.

BASIC COSTS (2008-2009)
Tuition and fees: $2,747; out-of-state residents $10,247.
Per-credit charge: $107; out-of-state residents $431.

FINANCIAL AID PICTURE
Students with need: Need-based aid available for full-time and part-time students.
Students without need: No-need awards available for academics, athletics, state/district residency.

FINANCIAL AID PROCEDURES
Forms required: FAFSA, institutional form.
Dates and Deadlines: Closing date 3/15. Applicants notified on a rolling basis starting 5/15; must reply within 2 week(s) of notification.

CONTACT
Pauletta Burns, Director, Financial Assistance
1665 Hampshire Pike, Columbia, TN 38401
(931) 540-2583

Crichton College
Memphis, Tennessee
www.crichton.edu Federal Code: 009982

4-year private liberal arts college in very large city, affiliated with nondenominational tradition.
Enrollment: 912 undergrads, 21% part-time. 91 full-time freshmen.
Selectivity: Admits less than 50% of applicants.

BASIC COSTS (2008-2009)
Tuition and fees: $12,120.
Per-credit charge: $481.
Room and board: $8,332.

FINANCIAL AID PICTURE (2007-2008)
Students with need: For part-time students, average financial aid package was $4,634.
Students without need: No-need awards available for academics, alumni affiliation, athletics, leadership, music/drama, religious affiliation.
Scholarships offered: Academic scholarships awarded based on student?s academic information, including applicant?s cumulative unweighted high school GPA and ACT or SAT test scores. Presidential Award - Potential Award Amount: $6,000 per year for four years Excellence Award - Potential Award Amount: $4,000 per year for four years Meritorious Award - Potential Award Amount: $2,000 per year for four years.

FINANCIAL AID PROCEDURES
Forms required: FAFSA, institutional form.
Dates and Deadlines: Priority date 3/15; no closing date. Applicants notified on a rolling basis starting 3/1; must reply within 2 week(s) of notification.
Transfers: No deadline. Applicants notified on a rolling basis; must reply within 2 week(s) of notification.

CONTACT
Melanie Johnson, Director of Student Finance
255 North Highland, Memphis, TN 38111-1375
(901) 320-9787

Cumberland University
Lebanon, Tennessee
www.cumberland.edu Federal Code: 003485

4-year private university and liberal arts college in large town.
Enrollment: 998 undergrads, 10% part-time. 195 full-time freshmen.
Selectivity: Admits 50 to 75% of applicants.

BASIC COSTS (2009-2010)
Tuition and fees: $17,430.
Per-credit charge: $690.
Room and board: $6,350.

FINANCIAL AID PICTURE (2008-2009)
Students with need: Need-based aid available for full-time and part-time students.
Students without need: No-need awards available for academics, art, athletics, music/drama.

FINANCIAL AID PROCEDURES
Forms required: FAFSA, institutional form.
Dates and Deadlines: Priority date 2/1; no closing date. Applicants notified on a rolling basis starting 5/1; must reply within 2 week(s) of notification.
Transfers: Priority date 2/15. Applicants notified on a rolling basis starting 5/1.

CONTACT
Judy Jordan, Vice President of Fiscal Affairs
One Cumberland Square, Lebanon, TN 37087
(615) 444-2562 ext. 1222

Dyersburg State Community College
Dyersburg, Tennessee
www.dscc.edu Federal Code: 006835

2-year public community college in large town.
Enrollment: 2,170 undergrads, 41% part-time. 530 full-time freshmen.
Selectivity: Open admission; but selective for some programs.

BASIC COSTS (2008-2009)
Tuition and fees: $2,777; out-of-state residents $10,277.
Per-credit charge: $107; out-of-state residents $431.

FINANCIAL AID PICTURE (2007-2008)
Students with need: Need-based aid available for full-time and part-time students. Work study available nights.
Students without need: No-need awards available for academics, alumni affiliation, athletics, job skills, leadership, minority status, music/drama, state/district residency.

FINANCIAL AID PROCEDURES
Forms required: FAFSA.
Dates and Deadlines: Priority date 3/1; no closing date. Applicants notified on a rolling basis starting 3/1; must reply within 2 week(s) of notification.

CONTACT
Sandra Rockett, Director of Financial Aid
1510 Lake Road, Dyersburg, TN 38024
(731) 286-3238

East Tennessee State University
Johnson City, Tennessee
www.etsu.edu Federal Code: 003487

4-year public university in small city.
Enrollment: 10,654 undergrads.
Selectivity: Admits over 75% of applicants.

BASIC COSTS (2008-2009)
Tuition and fees: $5,201; out-of-state residents $16,093.
Per-credit charge: $189; out-of-state residents $662.
Room and board: $5,278.

FINANCIAL AID PICTURE (2008-2009)
Students with need: Need-based aid available for full-time and part-time students. Work study available nights, weekends, and for part-time students.
Students without need: No-need awards available for academics, alumni affiliation, art, athletics, job skills, leadership, minority status, music/drama, religious affiliation, ROTC, state/district residency.
Additional info: Housing costs payable by installment.

FINANCIAL AID PROCEDURES
Forms required: FAFSA.
Dates and Deadlines: Priority date 4/15; no closing date. Applicants notified on a rolling basis starting 4/15; must reply within 2 week(s) of notification.

CONTACT
Margaret Miller, Director of Financial Aid
ETSU Box 70731, Johnson City, TN 37614
(423) 439-4300

Fisk University
Nashville, Tennessee
www.fisk.edu Federal Code: 003490

4-year private liberal arts college in very large city, affiliated with United Church of Christ.
Enrollment: 683 undergrads, 4% part-time. 113 full-time freshmen.
Selectivity: Admits 50 to 75% of applicants.

BASIC COSTS (2009-2010)
Tuition and fees: $17,000.
Per-credit charge: $660.
Room and board: $8,120.

FINANCIAL AID PICTURE (2008-2009)
Students with need: Need-based aid available for full-time and part-time students.
Students without need: This college awards aid only to students with need.

FINANCIAL AID PROCEDURES
Forms required: FAFSA.
Dates and Deadlines: Priority date 3/1; closing date 7/1. Applicants notified on a rolling basis starting 4/1; must reply within 2 week(s) of notification.

CONTACT
Russelle Keese, Director of Financial Aid
1000 17th Avenue North, Nashville, TN 37208-3051
(615) 329-8585

Free Will Baptist Bible College
Nashville, Tennessee
www.fwbbc.edu Federal Code: 030018

4-year private Bible and teachers college in very large city, affiliated with Free Will Baptists.
Enrollment: 269 undergrads, 22% part-time. 63 full-time freshmen.
Selectivity: Open admission.

BASIC COSTS (2008-2009)
Tuition and fees: $13,086.
Per-credit charge: $409.
Room and board: $5,358.

FINANCIAL AID PICTURE (2007-2008)
Students with need: 34% of average financial aid package awarded as scholarships/grants, 66% awarded as loans/jobs. Need-based aid available for part-time students. Work study available nights, weekends, and for part-time students.
Students without need: No-need awards available for academics, art, music/drama.
Scholarships offered: Presidential Honors Scholarship: $1,000 per semester, renewable for 8 semesters; high school GPA 3.5+, and ACT 29+, must maintain college GPA 3.25; awarded to four students yearly.

FINANCIAL AID PROCEDURES
Forms required: FAFSA, institutional form.
Dates and Deadlines: Priority date 4/15; no closing date. Applicants notified on a rolling basis starting 7/1; must reply within 2 week(s) of notification.
Transfers: No deadline.

CONTACT
Jeff Caudill, Director of Enrollment Services
3606 West End Avenue, Nashville, TN 37205-2403
(615) 844-5000 ext. 5249

Freed-Hardeman University
Henderson, Tennessee
www.fhu.edu Federal Code: 003492

4-year private university and liberal arts college in small town, affiliated with Church of Christ.
Enrollment: 1,534 undergrads, 8% part-time. 405 full-time freshmen.
Selectivity: Admits 50 to 75% of applicants.

BASIC COSTS (2009-2010)
Tuition and fees: $14,300.
Per-credit charge: $402.
Room and board: $7,090.
Additional info: Tuition/fee waivers available for minority students.

FINANCIAL AID PICTURE (2008-2009)
Students with need: Need-based aid available for full-time and part-time students. Work study available nights, weekends, and for part-time students.
Students without need: No-need awards available for academics, art, athletics, leadership, minority status, music/drama, state/district residency.

FINANCIAL AID PROCEDURES

Forms required: FAFSA.
Dates and Deadlines: Priority date 3/1; no closing date. Applicants notified on a rolling basis starting 3/1; must reply within 4 week(s) of notification.

CONTACT

Larry Cyr, Director of Financial Aid
158 East Main Street, Henderson, TN 38340
(731) 989-6662

International Academy of Design and Technology: Nashville

Nashville, Tennessee
www.iadtnashville.com

4-year for-profit branch campus and visual arts college in very large city.
Enrollment: 643 undergrads.
Selectivity: Open admission.

BASIC COSTS (2008-2009)

Tuition and fees: $15,875.

FINANCIAL AID PICTURE (2008-2009)

Students with need: 32% of average financial aid package awarded as scholarships/grants, 68% awarded as loans/jobs.

FINANCIAL AID PROCEDURES

Dates and Deadlines: No deadline.

CONTACT

Lisa Kennicott, Director of Financial Aid
1 Bridgestone Park, Nashville, TN 37214

Jackson State Community College

Jackson, Tennessee
www.jscc.edu Federal Code: 004937

2-year public community college in small city.
Enrollment: 4,381 undergrads, 51% part-time. 920 full-time freshmen.
Selectivity: Open admission; but selective for some programs.

BASIC COSTS (2008-2009)

Tuition and fees: $2,759; out-of-state residents $10,259.
Per-credit charge: $107; out-of-state residents $431.
Additional info: Tuition/fee waivers available for adults, minority students.

FINANCIAL AID PICTURE (2007-2008)

Students with need: Out of 683 full-time freshmen who applied for aid, 542 were judged to have need. Of these, 523 received aid, and 36 had their full need met. Average financial aid package met 82% of need; average scholarship/grant was $3,438; average loan was $3,150. For part-time students, average financial aid package was $2,080.
Students without need: 106 full-time freshmen who did not demonstrate need for aid received scholarships/grants; average award was $2,424. No-need awards available for academics, art, athletics, job skills, leadership, minority status, music/drama
Scholarships offered: 29 full-time freshmen received athletic scholarships; average amount $1,969.
Cumulative student debt: 2% of graduating class had student loans; average debt was $2,894.

FINANCIAL AID PROCEDURES

Forms required: FAFSA, institutional form.
Dates and Deadlines: Priority date 3/15; no closing date. Applicants notified on a rolling basis starting 6/1; must reply within 2 week(s) of notification.

CONTACT

Dewana Latimer, Director of Financial Aid
2046 North Parkway, Jackson, TN 38301-3797
(731) 425-2605

Johnson Bible College

Knoxville, Tennessee
www.jbc.edu Federal Code: 003495

4-year private Bible college in large city, affiliated with Christian Church.
Enrollment: 664 undergrads, 3% part-time. 119 full-time freshmen.

BASIC COSTS (2009-2010)

Tuition and fees: $8,610.
Room and board: $5,350.
Additional info: Part-time students pay mandatory fee of $35 per credit hour. Tuition/fee waivers available for minority students.

FINANCIAL AID PICTURE (2008-2009)

Students with need: Need-based aid available for full-time and part-time students. Work study available nights, weekends, and for part-time students.
Students without need: No-need awards available for academics, leadership, minority status, music/drama, religious affiliation, state/district residency.

FINANCIAL AID PROCEDURES

Forms required: FAFSA, institutional form.
Dates and Deadlines: Priority date 5/1; closing date 8/1. Applicants notified on a rolling basis starting 4/30; must reply within 2 week(s) of notification.
Transfers: No deadline.

CONTACT

Janette Overton, Financial Aid Director
7900 Johnson Drive, Knoxville, TN 37998-0001
(865) 251-2303

King College

Bristol, Tennessee
www.king.edu Federal Code: 003496

4-year private nursing and liberal arts college in large town, affiliated with Presbyterian Church (USA).
Enrollment: 1,320 undergrads, 2% part-time. 184 full-time freshmen.
Selectivity: Admits 50 to 75% of applicants.

BASIC COSTS (2009-2010)

Tuition and fees: $21,880.
Room and board: $7,418.

FINANCIAL AID PICTURE (2008-2009)

Students with need: Out of 173 full-time freshmen who applied for aid, 147 were judged to have need. Of these, 147 received aid, and 31 had their full need met. Average financial aid package met 84% of need; average scholarship/grant was $16,000; average loan was $4,239. For part-time students, average financial aid package was $9,568.
Students without need: 29 full-time freshmen who did not demonstrate need for aid received scholarships/grants; average award was $11,177. No-need awards available for academics, art, athletics, music/drama.
Scholarships offered: 26 full-time freshmen received athletic scholarships; average amount $7,877.
Cumulative student debt: 98% of graduating class had student loans; average debt was $15,019.

FINANCIAL AID PROCEDURES

Forms required: FAFSA.

Dates and Deadlines: Priority date 3/1; no closing date. Applicants notified on a rolling basis starting 4/1; must reply within 2 week(s) of notification.

CONTACT

Brenda Clark, Financial Aid Director
1350 King College Road, Bristol, TN 37620-2699
(423) 652-4725

Lambuth University

Jackson, Tennessee
www.lambuth.edu Federal Code: 003498

4-year private university and liberal arts college in small city, affiliated with United Methodist Church.

Enrollment: 765 undergrads, 2% part-time. 205 full-time freshmen.

Selectivity: Admits 50 to 75% of applicants.

BASIC COSTS (2009-2010)

Tuition and fees: $18,570.

Per-credit charge: $750.

Room and board: $8,015.

Additional info: Tuition/fee waivers available for adults.

FINANCIAL AID PICTURE (2008-2009)

Students with need: Out of 204 full-time freshmen who applied for aid, 166 were judged to have need. Of these, 164 received aid, and 86 had their full need met. Average financial aid package met 77% of need; average scholarship/grant was $13,752; average loan was $3,909. Need-based aid available for part-time students.

Students without need: 30 full-time freshmen who did not demonstrate need for aid received scholarships/grants; average award was $10,713. No-need awards available for academics, alumni affiliation, art, athletics, job skills, leadership, music/drama, religious affiliation, state/district residency.

Scholarships offered: ***Merit:*** Hyde Scholarships; full tuition, require admission acceptance deadline of February 1, ACT of 30 or higher, GPA, of 3.5 or higher, 2 awarded. ***Athletic:*** 18 full-time freshmen received athletic scholarships; average amount $9,624.

Cumulative student debt: 66% of graduating class had student loans; average debt was $19,950.

Additional info: Part-time students eligible for federal and state aid, but not institutional aid.

FINANCIAL AID PROCEDURES

Forms required: FAFSA.

Dates and Deadlines: Priority date 2/15; no closing date. Applicants notified on a rolling basis starting 3/1; must reply by 5/1 or within 2 week(s) of notification.

Transfers: Applicants notified on a rolling basis starting 3/1; must reply by 5/1 or within 2 week(s) of notification.

CONTACT

Karen Myers, Director of Financial Aid
705 Lambuth Boulevard, Jackson, TN 38301-5296
(731) 425-3332

Lane College

Jackson, Tennessee
www.lanecollege.edu Federal Code: 003499

4-year private liberal arts college in small city, affiliated with Christian Methodist Episcopal Church.

Enrollment: 1,982 undergrads, 2% part-time. 625 full-time freshmen.

Selectivity: Admits less than 50% of applicants.

BASIC COSTS (2008-2009)

Tuition and fees: $7,770.

Room and board: $5,250.

FINANCIAL AID PICTURE (2007-2008)

Students with need: Out of 588 full-time freshmen who applied for aid, 540 were judged to have need. Of these, 481 received aid, and 5 had their full need met. Average financial aid package met 1% of need; average scholarship/grant was $879. Need-based aid available for part-time students.

Students without need: 48 full-time freshmen who did not demonstrate need for aid received scholarships/grants; average award was $879. No-need awards available for academics, athletics, religious affiliation.

Scholarships offered: 48 full-time freshmen received athletic scholarships; average amount $858.

FINANCIAL AID PROCEDURES

Forms required: FAFSA.

Dates and Deadlines: Priority date 3/1; no closing date. Applicants notified on a rolling basis starting 3/31; must reply within 2 week(s) of notification.

Transfers: No deadline. Applicants notified on a rolling basis; must reply within 2 week(s) of notification.

CONTACT

Tony Calhoun, Director of Financial Aid
545 Lane Avenue, Jackson, TN 38301-4598
(731) 426-7537

Lee University

Cleveland, Tennessee
www.leeuniversity.edu Federal Code: 003500

4-year private university and liberal arts college in large town, affiliated with Church of God.

Enrollment: 3,689 undergrads, 9% part-time. 848 full-time freshmen.

Selectivity: Admits 50 to 75% of applicants.

BASIC COSTS (2009-2010)

Tuition and fees: $11,660.

Per-credit charge: $463.

Room and board: $5,650.

FINANCIAL AID PICTURE (2008-2009)

Students with need: Out of 702 full-time freshmen who applied for aid, 539 were judged to have need. Of these, 522 received aid, and 175 had their full need met. Average financial aid package met 65% of need; average scholarship/grant was $7,968; average loan was $3,701. For part-time students, average financial aid package was $5,069.

Students without need: 231 full-time freshmen who did not demonstrate need for aid received scholarships/grants; average award was $10,324. No-need awards available for academics, alumni affiliation, athletics, leadership, minority status, music/drama, religious affiliation, state/district residency.

Scholarships offered: 28 full-time freshmen received athletic scholarships; average amount $6,901.

Cumulative student debt: 67% of graduating class had student loans; average debt was $33,109.

FINANCIAL AID PROCEDURES

Forms required: FAFSA.

Dates and Deadlines: Priority date 3/15; no closing date. Applicants notified on a rolling basis starting 2/1; must reply within 3 week(s) of notification.

CONTACT

Michael Ellis, Director of Student Financial Aid
1120 North Ocoee Street, Cleveland, TN 37320-3450
(423) 614-8304

LeMoyne-Owen College

Memphis, Tennessee
www.loc.edu Federal Code: 003501

4-year private liberal arts college in very large city, affiliated with United Church of Christ and Tennessee Baptist Convention.
Enrollment: 658 undergrads.
Selectivity: Admits less than 50% of applicants.

BASIC COSTS (2008-2009)
Tuition and fees: $10,318.
Room and board: $4,852.

FINANCIAL AID PICTURE (2007-2008)
Students with need: Need-based aid available for full-time and part-time students.
Students without need: No-need awards available for academics, athletics, music/drama.

FINANCIAL AID PROCEDURES
Forms required: FAFSA.
Dates and Deadlines: Priority date 4/15; no closing date. Applicants notified on a rolling basis starting 4/1.
Transfers: No deadline. Applicants notified on a rolling basis starting 4/1.

CONTACT
Ledell Conard, Financial Aid Director
807 Walker Avenue, Memphis, TN 38126
(901) 435-1550

Lincoln Memorial University

Harrogate, Tennessee
www.lmunet.edu Federal Code: 003502

4-year private university and liberal arts college in small town.
Enrollment: 1,336 undergrads, 14% part-time. 255 full-time freshmen.

BASIC COSTS (2008-2009)
Tuition and fees: $15,120.
Per-credit charge: $630.
Room and board: $5,580.

FINANCIAL AID PICTURE
Students with need: Need-based aid available for full-time and part-time students.
Students without need: No-need awards available for academics, athletics, music/drama, state/district residency.

FINANCIAL AID PROCEDURES
Forms required: FAFSA.
Dates and Deadlines: Priority date 4/1; no closing date. Applicants notified on a rolling basis starting 4/15; must reply within 3 week(s) of notification.

CONTACT
Bryan Erslan, Director of Financial Aid
6965 Cumberland Gap Parkway, Harrogate, TN 37752-1901
(423) 869-6336

Lipscomb University

Nashville, Tennessee
www.lipscomb.edu Federal Code: 003486

4-year private Bible and liberal arts college in very large city, affiliated with Church of Christ.
Enrollment: 2,384 undergrads, 7% part-time. 657 full-time freshmen.
Selectivity: Admits 50 to 75% of applicants.

BASIC COSTS (2009-2010)
Tuition and fees: $20,390.
Per-credit charge: $775.
Room and board: $7,850.

FINANCIAL AID PICTURE (2008-2009)
Students with need: Out of 652 full-time freshmen who applied for aid, 402 were judged to have need. Of these, 402 received aid, and 115 had their full need met. Average financial aid package met 65% of need; average scholarship/grant was $5,568; average loan was $3,638. For part-time students, average financial aid package was $11,593.
Students without need: 166 full-time freshmen who did not demonstrate need for aid received scholarships/grants; average award was $5,882. No-need awards available for academics, alumni affiliation, art, athletics, leadership, minority status, music/drama, religious affiliation, state/district residency.
Scholarships offered: 130 full-time freshmen received athletic scholarships; average amount $11,667.

FINANCIAL AID PROCEDURES
Forms required: FAFSA.
Dates and Deadlines: Priority date 3/1; no closing date. Applicants notified on a rolling basis starting 2/15.

CONTACT
Karita Waters, Director of Financial Aid
One University Park Drive, Nashville, TN 37204-3951
(615) 966-1791

Martin Methodist College

Pulaski, Tennessee
www.martinmethodist.edu Federal Code: 003504

4-year private liberal arts college in small town, affiliated with United Methodist Church.
Enrollment: 892 undergrads, 18% part-time. 205 full-time freshmen.
Selectivity: Open admission; but selective for some programs.

BASIC COSTS (2008-2009)
Tuition and fees: $17,626.
Per-credit charge: $718.
Room and board: $6,800.

FINANCIAL AID PICTURE (2007-2008)
Students with need: Need-based aid available for full-time and part-time students. Work study available nights, weekends, and for part-time students.
Students without need: No-need awards available for academics, art, athletics, leadership, music/drama, religious affiliation, state/district residency.
Scholarships offered: Two full academic scholarships per year awarded through interview and essay competition.

FINANCIAL AID PROCEDURES
Forms required: FAFSA, institutional form.
Dates and Deadlines: No deadline. Applicants notified on a rolling basis starting 3/1; must reply within 2 week(s) of notification.
Transfers: Closing date 9/13.

CONTACT
Emma Hiubb, Director of Financial Aid
433 West Madison, Pulaski, TN 38478-2799
(931) 363-9804

Maryville College

Maryville, Tennessee
www.maryvillecollege.edu Federal Code: 003505

4-year private liberal arts college in small city, affiliated with Presbyterian Church (USA).
Enrollment: 1,114 undergrads, 2% part-time. 297 full-time freshmen.
Selectivity: Admits over 75% of applicants.

BASIC COSTS (2009-2010)

Tuition and fees: $27,971.
Per-credit charge: $1,137.
Room and board: $8,560.

FINANCIAL AID PICTURE (2008-2009)

Students with need: Out of 259 full-time freshmen who applied for aid, 259 were judged to have need. Of these, 259 received aid, and 171 had their full need met. Average financial aid package met 91% of need; average scholarship/grant was $20,692; average loan was $3,158. For part-time students, average financial aid package was $6,983.
Students without need: 39 full-time freshmen who did not demonstrate need for aid received scholarships/grants; average award was $14,417. No-need awards available for academics, art, leadership, minority status, music/drama, religious affiliation, state/district residency.
Scholarships offered: Presidential Scholarship; full tuition; awarded for leadership and academic ability. Dean's Scholarship; consisting of a large portion of tuition awarded to selected entering freshman with 3.5 GPA.
Cumulative student debt: 92% of graduating class had student loans; average debt was $13,929.

FINANCIAL AID PROCEDURES

Forms required: FAFSA.
Dates and Deadlines: Priority date 3/1; no closing date. Applicants notified on a rolling basis starting 3/15; must reply within 4 week(s) of notification.

CONTACT

Richard Brand, Director of Financial Aid
502 East Lamar Alexander Parkway, Maryville, TN 37804-5907
(865) 981-8100

Memphis College of Art

Memphis, Tennessee
www.mca.edu Federal Code: 003507

4-year private visual arts college in very large city.
Enrollment: 320 undergrads, 6% part-time. 102 full-time freshmen.
Selectivity: Admits 50 to 75% of applicants.

BASIC COSTS (2008-2009)

Tuition and fees: $21,560.
Per-credit charge: $915.
Room and board: $7,600.

FINANCIAL AID PICTURE (2008-2009)

Students with need: Need-based aid available for full-time and part-time students. Work study available nights.
Students without need: No-need awards available for academics, art.
Scholarships offered: Tuition scholarships ranging from $2,500 up to full tuition based on merit.
Additional info: Students considered for institutional resources through admissions application process.

FINANCIAL AID PROCEDURES

Forms required: FAFSA.
Dates and Deadlines: Priority date 3/1; no closing date. Applicants notified on a rolling basis starting 3/15; must reply within 3 week(s) of notification.
Transfers: Priority date 8/1. Applicants notified on a rolling basis; must reply within 3 week(s) of notification. Grants of $1,000 awarded to students who attended accredited junior or community college earning at least 60 credit hours.

CONTACT

Lynn Holladay, Director of Financial Aid
1930 Poplar Avenue, Memphis, TN 38104-2764
(901) 272-5136

Middle Tennessee State University

Murfreesboro, Tennessee
www.mtsu.edu Federal Code: 003510

4-year public university in small city.
Enrollment: 21,252 undergrads, 15% part-time. 3,385 full-time freshmen.
Selectivity: Admits 50 to 75% of applicants.

BASIC COSTS (2008-2009)

Tuition and fees: $5,700; out-of-state residents $16,592.
Per-credit charge: $189; out-of-state residents $662.
Room and board: $6,453.

FINANCIAL AID PICTURE (2008-2009)

Students with need: Need-based aid available for full-time and part-time students. Work study available nights, weekends, and for part-time students.
Students without need: No-need awards available for academics, alumni affiliation, art, athletics, job skills, leadership, minority status, music/drama, religious affiliation, ROTC, state/district residency.
Additional info: Application filing deadline for scholarships February 15.

FINANCIAL AID PROCEDURES

Forms required: FAFSA.
Dates and Deadlines: Priority date 5/1; no closing date. Applicants notified on a rolling basis starting 4/15; must reply within 2 week(s) of notification.

CONTACT

David Hutton, Director of Student Financial Aid
1301 East Main Street, Murfreesboro, TN 37132
(615) 898-2830

Miller-Motte Technical College: Clarksville

Clarksville, Tennessee
www.miller-motte.com Federal Code: 026142

2-year for-profit business and health science college in small city.
Enrollment: 558 undergrads.
Selectivity: Open admission; but selective for some programs.

BASIC COSTS (2008-2009)

Tuition and fees: $11,170.
Per-credit charge: $231.
Additional info: Required fees vary by program.

FINANCIAL AID PICTURE

Students with need: Need-based aid available for full-time and part-time students. Work study available nights, weekends, and for part-time students.
Students without need: This college awards aid only to students with need.

FINANCIAL AID PROCEDURES

Forms required: FAFSA, institutional form.
Dates and Deadlines: No deadline. Applicants notified on a rolling basis.
Transfers: No deadline.

CONTACT

Amy Flowers, Financial Aid Director
1820 Business Park Drive, Clarksville, TN 37040
(931) 553-0071

Milligan College

Milligan College, Utah
www.milligan.edu Federal Code: 003511

4-year private liberal arts college in small city, affiliated with Christian Churches/ Churches of Christ.
Enrollment: 837 undergrads, 3% part-time. 200 full-time freshmen.
Selectivity: Admits 50 to 75% of applicants.

BASIC COSTS (2008-2009)

Tuition and fees: $20,560.
Per-credit charge: $545.
Room and board: $5,850.

FINANCIAL AID PICTURE (2008-2009)

Students with need: Average financial aid package met 85% of need; average scholarship/grant was $13,884; average loan was $3,348. For part-time students, average financial aid package was $11,334.
Students without need: No-need awards available for academics, alumni affiliation, art, athletics, job skills, minority status, music/drama, religious affiliation, state/district residency.
Cumulative student debt: 72% of graduating class had student loans; average debt was $15,591.

FINANCIAL AID PROCEDURES

Forms required: FAFSA.
Dates and Deadlines: Priority date 3/1; no closing date. Applicants notified on a rolling basis starting 3/15; must reply within 2 week(s) of notification.

CONTACT

Diane Keasling, Coordinator of Financial Aid
Box 210, Milligan College, TN 37682
(800) 447-4880

Motlow State Community College

Lynchburg, Tennessee
www.mscc.cc.tn.us Federal Code: 006836

2-year public community college in rural community.
Enrollment: 3,741 undergrads, 37% part-time. 1,066 full-time freshmen.
Selectivity: Open admission; but selective for some programs.

BASIC COSTS (2008-2009)

Tuition and fees: $2,765; out-of-state residents $10,265.
Per-credit charge: $107; out-of-state residents $431.

FINANCIAL AID PICTURE (2007-2008)

Students with need: Need-based aid available for full-time and part-time students.
Students without need: No-need awards available for academics, alumni affiliation, art, athletics, leadership, state/district residency.

FINANCIAL AID PROCEDURES

Forms required: FAFSA.
Dates and Deadlines: No deadline. Applicants notified on a rolling basis starting 3/15.

CONTACT

Joe Myers, Director of Financial Aid and Scholarships
Box 8500, Lynchburg, TN 37352-8500
(931) 393-1553

Nashville Auto-Diesel College

Nashville, Tennessee
www.nadcedu.com Federal Code: 007440

1-year for-profit technical college in large city.
Enrollment: 2,956 undergrads.

BASIC COSTS (2008-2009)

Tuition and fees: $14,195.
Room and board: $5,502.
Additional info: Full program costs range from $21,400 to $32,600 for diploma programs; $27,400 to $34,900 for associate programs.

FINANCIAL AID PICTURE

Students with need: Need-based aid available for full-time students. Work study available nights, weekends, and for part-time students.
Students without need: This college awards aid only to students with need.

FINANCIAL AID PROCEDURES

Forms required: FAFSA, state aid form.
Dates and Deadlines: No deadline. Applicants notified on a rolling basis.

CONTACT

Jamie Cortinas, Director of Financial Aid
1524 Gallatin Road, Nashville, TN 37206
(615) 650-8202

Nashville State Community College

Nashville, Tennessee
www.nscc.edu Federal Code: 007534

2-year public community and technical college in very large city.
Enrollment: 7,716 undergrads.
Selectivity: Open admission; but selective for some programs.

BASIC COSTS (2008-2009)

Tuition and fees: $2,731; out-of-state residents $10,231.
Per-credit charge: $107; out-of-state residents $431.

FINANCIAL AID PICTURE (2008-2009)

Students with need: Need-based aid available for full-time and part-time students. Work study available nights, weekends, and for part-time students.
Students without need: No-need awards available for academics, minority status.

FINANCIAL AID PROCEDURES

Forms required: FAFSA, institutional form.
Dates and Deadlines: Priority date 3/1; no closing date. Applicants notified on a rolling basis starting 6/1; must reply within 2 week(s) of notification.

CONTACT

Stephen White, Director of Financial Aid
120 White Bridge Road, Nashville, TN 37209-4515
(615) 353-3250

National College: Bristol

Bristol, Tennessee
www.ncbt.edu Federal Code: 003726

2-year for-profit business college in large town.
Enrollment: 300 undergrads.
Selectivity: Open admission.

BASIC COSTS (2008-2009)
Tuition and fees: $9,585.
Per-credit charge: $212.

FINANCIAL AID PICTURE
Students with need: Need-based aid available for full-time and part-time students.
Students without need: This college awards aid only to students with need.

FINANCIAL AID PROCEDURES
Forms required: FAFSA.
Dates and Deadlines: No deadline. Applicants notified on a rolling basis starting 9/1.

CONTACT
Pamela Cotton, Director of Financial Aid and Compliance Officer
1328 Highway 11W, Bristol, TN 37620

National College: Nashville
Nashville, Tennessee
www.ncbt.edu Federal Code: 003726

2-year for-profit business and technical college in large city.
Enrollment: 298 undergrads.
Selectivity: Open admission.

BASIC COSTS (2008-2009)
Tuition and fees: $9,540.
Per-credit charge: $212.

FINANCIAL AID PICTURE
Students with need: Need-based aid available for full-time and part-time students.
Students without need: This college awards aid only to students with need.

FINANCIAL AID PROCEDURES
Forms required: FAFSA.
Dates and Deadlines: No deadline.

CONTACT
Pamela Cotton, Director of Financial Aid and Compliance Officer
PO Box 6400, Roanoke, VA 24017
(615) 333-3344

Nossi College of Art
Goodlettsville, Tennessee
www.nossi.com Federal Code: 017347

2-year private visual arts and technical college in large town.
Enrollment: 425 undergrads.
Selectivity: Admits over 75% of applicants.

BASIC COSTS (2008-2009)
Additional info: Tuition for first year (3 semesters) $10,500; required fees $240.

FINANCIAL AID PICTURE
Students with need: Need-based aid available for full-time and part-time students.

CONTACT
Mary Kidd, Financial Aid Director
907 Rivergate Parkway, Building E-6, Goodlettsville, TN 37072
(615) 851-1088

O'More College of Design
Franklin, Tennessee
www.omorecollege.edu Federal Code: 014663

4-year private visual arts college in large town.
Enrollment: 200 undergrads.
Selectivity: Admits less than 50% of applicants.

BASIC COSTS (2008-2009)
Tuition and fees: $17,280.

FINANCIAL AID PICTURE (2008-2009)
Students with need: 52% of average financial aid package awarded as scholarships/grants, 48% awarded as loans/jobs. Need-based aid available for part-time students.
Students without need: This college awards aid only to students with need.
Scholarships offered: Academic scholarships available.

FINANCIAL AID PROCEDURES
Forms required: FAFSA.
Dates and Deadlines: Priority date 4/1; no closing date. Applicants notified on a rolling basis starting 8/1.
Transfers: Priority date 5/5; no deadline.

CONTACT
Jerry Masterson, Financial Aid Director
423 South Margin Street, Franklin, TN 37064-0908
(615) 794-4254 ext. 238

Pellissippi State Technical Community College
Knoxville, Tennessee
www.pstcc.edu Federal Code: 012693

2-year public community and technical college in small city.
Enrollment: 8,742 undergrads.
Selectivity: Open admission.

BASIC COSTS (2008-2009)
Tuition and fees: $2,799; out-of-state residents $10,299.
Per-credit charge: $107; out-of-state residents $431.

FINANCIAL AID PICTURE (2008-2009)
Students with need: Need-based aid available for full-time and part-time students. Work study available nights, weekends, and for part-time students.
Students without need: No-need awards available for academics, art, minority status, music/drama.

FINANCIAL AID PROCEDURES
Forms required: FAFSA.
Dates and Deadlines: Priority date 5/1; no closing date. Applicants notified on a rolling basis starting 7/15; must reply within 2 week(s) of notification.

CONTACT
Paul McKinney, Director of Financial Aid
Box 22990, Knoxville, TN 37933-0990
(423) 694-6565

Remington College: Memphis
Memphis, Tennessee
www.remingtoncollege.edu

2-year for-profit business and technical college in very large city.
Enrollment: 450 undergrads.

BASIC COSTS (2008-2009)
Additional info: Costs of entire programs leading to certificate, associate degree, bachelor's degree range from $13,500 to $37,000; includes books and supplies.

FINANCIAL AID PICTURE
Students with need: Need-based aid available for full-time and part-time students.
Students without need: This college awards aid only to students with need.

FINANCIAL AID PROCEDURES
Forms required: FAFSA, institutional form.
Dates and Deadlines: No deadline. Applicants notified on a rolling basis; must reply within 2 week(s) of notification.

CONTACT
Jimmy Bessinger, Director of Financial Services
2710 Nonconnah Boulevard, Memphis, TN 38132

Rhodes College
Memphis, Tennessee — Federal Code: 003519
www.rhodes.edu — CSS Code: 1730

4-year private liberal arts college in very large city, affiliated with Presbyterian Church (USA).
Enrollment: 1,649 undergrads. 477 full-time freshmen.
Selectivity: Admits less than 50% of applicants.

BASIC COSTS (2008-2009)
Tuition and fees: $32,446
Room and board: $7,842.

FINANCIAL AID PICTURE (2008-2009)
Students with need: Average financial aid package met 89% of need; average scholarship/grant was $19,705; average loan was $2,424.
Students without need: No-need awards available for academics, art, minority status, music/drama, religious affiliation.
Cumulative student debt: 46% of graduating class had student loans; average debt was $26,064.
Additional info: Auditions required for theater and music achievement awards and art achievement awards. Interviews recommended for merit scholarships.

FINANCIAL AID PROCEDURES
Forms required: FAFSA, CSS PROFILE.
Dates and Deadlines: Closing date 3/1. Must reply by 5/1.

CONTACT
Art Weeden, Director of Financial Aid
2000 North Parkway, Memphis, TN 38112
(901) 843-3810

Roane State Community College
Harriman, Tennessee
www.roanestate.edu — Federal Code: 009914

2-year public community and junior college in small town.
Enrollment: 4,417 undergrads, 37% part-time. 903 full-time freshmen.
Selectivity: Open admission; but selective for some programs.

BASIC COSTS (2008-2009)
Tuition and fees: $2,788; out-of-state residents $10,288.
Per-credit charge: $107; out-of-state residents $431.

FINANCIAL AID PICTURE (2007-2008)
Students with need: Need-based aid available for full-time and part-time students. Work study available nights, weekends, and for part-time students.
Students without need: No-need awards available for academics, art, athletics, leadership, music/drama, state/district residency.

FINANCIAL AID PROCEDURES
Forms required: FAFSA, institutional form.
Dates and Deadlines: Priority date 4/1; no closing date. Applicants notified on a rolling basis starting 5/1.

CONTACT
Joy Goldberg, Assistant Vice President of Financial Aid
276 Patton Lane, Harriman, TN 37748
(865) 882-4545

South College
Knoxville, Tennessee
www.southcollegetn.edu — Federal Code: 004938

4-year for-profit liberal arts college in small city.
Enrollment: 725 undergrads.

BASIC COSTS (2008-2009)
Tuition and fees: $14,925.
Additional info: Reported annual costs are for programs in physical therapy assistance, radiography, health science. Costs of other programs vary by program.

FINANCIAL AID PICTURE (2007-2008)
Students with need: Need-based aid available for full-time and part-time students.
Students without need: This college awards aid only to students with need.

FINANCIAL AID PROCEDURES
Forms required: FAFSA, institutional form.
Dates and Deadlines: No deadline. Applicants notified on a rolling basis.

CONTACT
Larry Broadwater, Financial Aid Director
3904 Lonas Drive, Knoxville, TN 37909
(865) 251-1800

Southern Adventist University
Collegedale, Tennessee
www.southern.edu — Federal Code: 003518

4-year private university and liberal arts college in small town, affiliated with Seventh-day Adventists.
Enrollment: 2,430 undergrads.
Selectivity: Admits 50 to 75% of applicants.

BASIC COSTS (2009-2010)
Tuition and fees: $17,112.
Per-credit charge: $692.
Room and board: $5,080.

FINANCIAL AID PICTURE (2008-2009)
Students with need: Average financial aid package met 85% of need; average scholarship/grant was $10,115; average loan was $4,688. For part-time students, average financial aid package was $16,042.
Students without need: No-need awards available for academics, alumni affiliation, art, leadership, music/drama.
Scholarships offered: Freshman scholarship based on combination of high school GPA, ACT/SAT scores, leadership positions held.

Cumulative student debt: 61% of graduating class had student loans; average debt was $18,846.

FINANCIAL AID PROCEDURES

Forms required: FAFSA, state aid form.
Dates and Deadlines: Priority date 3/1; no closing date. Applicants notified on a rolling basis starting 2/15; must reply within 2 week(s) of notification.
Transfers: No deadline. Applicants notified on a rolling basis.

CONTACT

Marc Grundy, Associate VP for Enrollment Services
Box 370, Collegedale, TN 37315-0370
(423) 236-2835

Southwest Tennessee Community College

Memphis, Tennessee
www.southwest.tn.edu Federal Code: 010439

2-year public community college in very large city.
Enrollment: 10,464 undergrads, 51% part-time. 1,518 full-time freshmen.
Selectivity: Open admission; but selective for some programs.

BASIC COSTS (2008-2009)

Tuition and fees: $2,791; out-of-state residents $10,291.
Per-credit charge: $107; out-of-state residents $431.
Additional info: Tuition/fee waivers available for minority students.

FINANCIAL AID PICTURE

Students with need: Need-based aid available for full-time and part-time students. Work study available nights, weekends, and for part-time students.
Students without need: This college awards aid only to students with need.
Additional info: State grants available to eligible students who apply by 4/1.

FINANCIAL AID PROCEDURES

Forms required: FAFSA.
Dates and Deadlines: Priority date 3/15; no closing date. Applicants notified on a rolling basis starting 6/1; must reply within 4 week(s) of notification.
Transfers: Priority date 4/15.

CONTACT

Tina Studaway, Director Financial Aid
PO Box 780, Memphis, TN 38101-0780
(901) 333-5956

Tennessee State University

Nashville, Tennessee
www.tnstate.edu Federal Code: 003522

4-year public university in very large city.
Enrollment: 6,284 undergrads, 19% part-time. 1,018 full-time freshmen.
Selectivity: Admits 50 to 75% of applicants.

BASIC COSTS (2008-2009)

Tuition and fees: $5,102; out-of-state residents $15,994.
Per-credit charge: $189; out-of-state residents $662.
Room and board: $5,282.
Additional info: Tuition/fee waivers available for minority students.

FINANCIAL AID PICTURE (2007-2008)

Students with need: Need-based aid available for full-time students.
Students without need: No-need awards available for academics.

FINANCIAL AID PROCEDURES

Forms required: FAFSA.
Dates and Deadlines: Priority date 4/1; no closing date. Applicants notified on a rolling basis starting 4/15; must reply within 3 week(s) of notification.

CONTACT

Cynthia Brooks, Vice President of Finance/Accounting
3500 John A. Merritt Boulevard, Nashville, TN 37209-1561
(615) 963-5701

Tennessee Technological University

Cookeville, Tennessee
www.tntech.edu Federal Code: 003523

4-year public university in large town.
Enrollment: 8,102 undergrads, 8% part-time. 1,661 full-time freshmen.
Selectivity: Admits over 75% of applicants.

BASIC COSTS (2008-2009)

Tuition and fees: $5,244; out-of-state residents $16,136.
Per-credit charge: $189; out-of-state residents $662.
Room and board: $6,634.
Additional info: Tuition/fee waivers available for minority students.

FINANCIAL AID PICTURE (2007-2008)

Students with need: Need-based aid available for full-time and part-time students. Work study available nights, weekends, and for part-time students.
Students without need: No-need awards available for academics, alumni affiliation, art, athletics, leadership, minority status, music/drama, ROTC, state/district residency.
Scholarships offered: Presidential Scholarship; $4,000 renewable annually. Awarded to National Merit Finalists.
Additional info: Tuition and/or fee waivers available for children of Tennessee public school teachers.

FINANCIAL AID PROCEDURES

Forms required: FAFSA.
Dates and Deadlines: Priority date 3/15; no closing date. Applicants notified on a rolling basis starting 3/15; must reply within 2 week(s) of notification.
Transfers: No deadline. Applicants notified on a rolling basis starting 6/1; must reply within 2 week(s) of notification.

CONTACT

Lester McKenzie, Director of Student Financial Aid
Office of Admissions, Cookeville, TN 38505-0001
(931) 372-3073

Tennessee Temple University

Chattanooga, Tennessee
www.tntemple.edu Federal Code: 003524

4-year private university and Bible college in small city, affiliated with Baptist faith.
Enrollment: 505 undergrads.
Selectivity: Admits less than 50% of applicants.

BASIC COSTS (2008-2009)

Tuition and fees: $10,662.
Room and board: $5,930.

FINANCIAL AID PICTURE

Students with need: Need-based aid available for full-time and part-time students. Work study available nights, weekends, and for part-time students.
Students without need: No-need awards available for academics, alumni affiliation, athletics, leadership, music/drama, state/district residency.

FINANCIAL AID PROCEDURES

Forms required: FAFSA.
Dates and Deadlines: Priority date 3/31; no closing date. Applicants notified on a rolling basis starting 2/15; must reply within 2 week(s) of notification.

CONTACT

Heather Smith, Assistant Director of Financial Aid
1815 Union Avenue, Chattanooga, TN 37404
(423) 493-4207

Tennessee Wesleyan College

Athens, Tennessee
www.twcnet.edu Federal Code: 003525

4-year private liberal arts and teachers college in large town, affiliated with United Methodist Church.

Enrollment: 979 undergrads, 14% part-time. 471 full-time freshmen.

Selectivity: Admits over 75% of applicants.

BASIC COSTS (2009-2010)

Tuition and fees: $18,600.

Room and board: $6,100.

Additional info: Tuition/fee waivers available for minority students.

FINANCIAL AID PICTURE (2007-2008)

Students with need: Out of 374 full-time freshmen who applied for aid, 309 were judged to have need. Of these, 305 received aid, and 79 had their full need met. Average financial aid package met 75% of need; average scholarship/grant was $12,625; average loan was $3,205. Need-based aid available for part-time students.

Students without need: 60 full-time freshmen who did not demonstrate need for aid received scholarships/grants; average award was $9,186. No-need awards available for academics, alumni affiliation, athletics, job skills, minority status, music/drama, religious affiliation.

Scholarships offered: 52 full-time freshmen received athletic scholarships; average amount $7,244.

Cumulative student debt: 60% of graduating class had student loans; average debt was $9,067.

FINANCIAL AID PROCEDURES

Forms required: FAFSA, institutional form.

Dates and Deadlines: No deadline. Applicants notified on a rolling basis starting 2/15; must reply within 2 week(s) of notification.

CONTACT

Bob Perry, Director of Financial Aid
204 East College Street, Athens, TN 37371-0040
(423) 746-5215

Trevecca Nazarene University

Nashville, Tennessee
www.trevecca.edu Federal Code: 003526

4-year private university and liberal arts college in very large city, affiliated with Church of the Nazarene.

Enrollment: 1,182 undergrads, 7% part-time. 218 full-time freshmen.

Selectivity: Admits 50 to 75% of applicants.

BASIC COSTS (2009-2010)

Tuition and fees: $16,776.

Room and board: $7,348.

FINANCIAL AID PICTURE (2007-2008)

Students with need: 34% of average financial aid package awarded as scholarships/grants, 66% awarded as loans/jobs.

Students without need: No-need awards available for academics, alumni affiliation, athletics, leadership, minority status, religious affiliation.

FINANCIAL AID PROCEDURES

Forms required: FAFSA.

Dates and Deadlines: Priority date 3/1; no closing date. Applicants notified on a rolling basis starting 3/1.

CONTACT

Eddie White, Assistant Director of Financial Aid
333 Murfreesboro Road, Nashville, TN 37210
(615) 248-1242

Tusculum College

Greeneville, Tennessee
www.tusculum.edu Federal Code: 003527

4-year private liberal arts college in large town, affiliated with Presbyterian Church (USA).

Enrollment: 2,070 undergrads, 1% part-time. 352 full-time freshmen.

Selectivity: Admits 50 to 75% of applicants.

BASIC COSTS (2008-2009)

Tuition and fees: $18,870.

Room and board: $7,120.

FINANCIAL AID PICTURE

Students with need: Need-based aid available for full-time and part-time students. Work study available nights, weekends, and for part-time students.

Students without need: No-need awards available for academics, athletics, leadership, religious affiliation, state/district residency.

FINANCIAL AID PROCEDURES

Forms required: FAFSA.

Dates and Deadlines: Closing date 2/15. Applicants notified on a rolling basis starting 3/1; must reply within 3 week(s) of notification.

CONTACT

Karen Chapman, Director of Financial Aid
60 Shiloh Road, Greeneville, TN 37743
(423) 636-7376

Union University

Jackson, Tennessee
www.uu.edu Federal Code: 003528

4-year private university and liberal arts college in small city, affiliated with Southern Baptist Convention.

Enrollment: 2,275 undergrads, 11% part-time. 437 full-time freshmen.

Selectivity: Admits over 75% of applicants.

BASIC COSTS (2009-2010)

Tuition and fees: $20,940.

Per-credit charge: $690.

Room and board: $6,930.

Additional info: Tuition/fee waivers available for minority students.

FINANCIAL AID PICTURE (2008-2009)

Students with need: Average financial aid package met 80% of need; average scholarship/grant was $5,503; average loan was $3,754. For part-time students, average financial aid package was $1,212.

Students without need: No-need awards available for academics, alumni affiliation, art, athletics, leadership, minority status, music/drama, religious affiliation, state/district residency.

FINANCIAL AID PROCEDURES

Forms required: FAFSA, institutional form.

Dates and Deadlines: Priority date 2/15; closing date 3/1. Applicants notified on a rolling basis starting 2/15; must reply by 5/1 or within 2 week(s) of notification.

CONTACT

John Brandt, Director of Student Financial Planning
1050 Union University Drive, Jackson, TN 38305-3697
(731) 661-5015

University of Memphis

Memphis, Tennessee
www.memphis.edu Federal Code: 003509

4-year public university in very large city.
Enrollment: 15,116 undergrads, 22% part-time. 1,945 full-time freshmen.
Selectivity: Admits 50 to 75% of applicants.

BASIC COSTS (2008-2009)

Tuition and fees: $6,128; out-of-state residents $17,714.
Per-credit charge: $210; out-of-state residents $485.
Room and board: $5,660.
Additional info: Tuition/fee waivers available for adults, minority students.

FINANCIAL AID PICTURE (2008-2009)

Students with need: Out of 1,849 full-time freshmen who applied for aid, 1,354 were judged to have need. Of these, 1,135 received aid, and 98 had their full need met. Average financial aid package met 79% of need; average scholarship/grant was $5,759; average loan was $1,667. For part-time students, average financial aid package was $5,039.
Students without need: 914 full-time freshmen who did not demonstrate need for aid received scholarships/grants; average award was $8,236. No-need awards available for academics, alumni affiliation, art, athletics, leadership, minority status, music/drama, ROTC, state/district residency.
Scholarships offered: 73 full-time freshmen received athletic scholarships; average amount $12,734.
Cumulative student debt: 22% of graduating class had student loans; average debt was $21,265.

FINANCIAL AID PROCEDURES

Forms required: FAFSA.
Dates and Deadlines: Priority date 3/1; closing date 6/1. Applicants notified on a rolling basis starting 3/1; must reply within 2 week(s) of notification.

CONTACT

Richard Ritzman, Director of Student Financial Aid
101 Wilder Tower, Memphis, TN 38152
(901) 678-4825

University of Tennessee Health Science Center

Memphis, Tennessee
www.utmem.edu Federal Code: 353006

Upper-division public university and health science college in very large city.
Enrollment: 289 undergrads, 20% part-time.

BASIC COSTS (2008-2009)

Tuition and fees: $5,652; out-of-state residents $12,902.
Additional info: Above cost are for bachelor's program in nursing. Other programs vary by cost. Tuition/fee waivers available for minority students.

FINANCIAL AID PICTURE (2008-2009)

Students with need: Average financial aid package for all full-time undergraduates was $10,230; for part-time $11,765. 7% awarded as scholarships/grants, 93% awarded as loans/jobs. Work study available nights, weekends, and for part-time students.
Students without need: No-need awards available for academics, leadership, minority status, state/district residency.
Cumulative student debt: 98% of graduating class had student loans; average debt was $20,000.

Additional info: Scholarships available to defray out-of-state portion of fees charged to out-of-state minority students.

FINANCIAL AID PROCEDURES

Forms required: FAFSA.
Dates and Deadlines: Priority date 2/28; no closing date. Applicants notified on a rolling basis starting 5/1; must reply within 2 week(s) of notification.
Transfers: No deadline. Applicants notified on a rolling basis starting 5/1; must reply within 2 week(s) of notification.

CONTACT

Felicia Christian, Director of Financial Aid
800 Madison Avenue, Memphis, TN 38163
(901) 448-5568

University of Tennessee: Chattanooga

Chattanooga, Tennessee
www.utc.edu Federal Code: 003529

4-year public university in large city.
Enrollment: 8,232 undergrads, 11% part-time. 2,028 full-time freshmen.
Selectivity: Admits over 75% of applicants.

BASIC COSTS (2008-2009)

Tuition and fees: $5,310; out-of-state residents $15,870.
Per-credit charge: $176; out-of-state residents $770.
Room and board: $6,983.

FINANCIAL AID PICTURE (2008-2009)

Students with need: Out of 1,974 full-time freshmen who applied for aid, 1,181 were judged to have need. Of these, 1,168 received aid, and 729 had their full need met. Average financial aid package met 86% of need; average scholarship/grant was $4,270; average loan was $3,803. For part-time students, average financial aid package was $4,188.
Students without need: 388 full-time freshmen who did not demonstrate need for aid received scholarships/grants; average award was $3,001. No-need awards available for academics, alumni affiliation, art, athletics, job skills, leadership, minority status, music/drama, religious affiliation, ROTC, state/district residency.
Scholarships offered: 41 full-time freshmen received athletic scholarships; average amount $10,235.
Cumulative student debt: 64% of graduating class had student loans; average debt was $19,344.

FINANCIAL AID PROCEDURES

Forms required: FAFSA, institutional form.
Dates and Deadlines: Priority date 4/1; no closing date. Applicants notified on a rolling basis starting 3/1; must reply within 6 week(s) of notification.
Transfers: Applicants notified on a rolling basis starting 3/1; must reply within 6 week(s) of notification.

CONTACT

Rexann Bumpus, Director of Financial Aid
615 McCallie Avenue, Chattanooga, TN 37403
(423) 425-4677

University of Tennessee: Knoxville

Knoxville, Tennessee
www.utk.edu Federal Code: 003530

4-year public university in large city.
Enrollment: 21,378 undergrads, 5% part-time. 4,200 full-time freshmen.
Selectivity: Admits 50 to 75% of applicants.

BASIC COSTS (2008-2009)

Tuition and fees: $6,250; out-of-state residents $18,908.
Per-credit charge: $227; out-of-state residents $755.
Room and board: $6,888.
Additional info: Out-of-state students pay additional required fees of $300.

FINANCIAL AID PICTURE (2008-2009)

Students with need: Out of 3,966 full-time freshmen who applied for aid, 1,990 were judged to have need. Of these, 1,967 received aid, and 767 had their full need met. Average financial aid package met 79% of need; average scholarship/grant was $2,746; average loan was $3,708. For part-time students, average financial aid package was $8,460.
Students without need: This college awards aid only to students with need.
Scholarships offered: ***Merit:*** Academic College Scholarship Application part of financial aid forms, must be completed by all students. ***Athletic:*** 92 full-time freshmen received athletic scholarships; average amount $15,359.
Cumulative student debt: 51% of graduating class had student loans; average debt was $24,690.
Additional info: Application priority date for scholarships 2/1.

FINANCIAL AID PROCEDURES

Forms required: FAFSA.
Dates and Deadlines: Priority date 3/1; no closing date. Applicants notified on a rolling basis starting 3/15; must reply within 3 week(s) of notification.
Transfers: Transfer students must provide financial aid transcripts from all colleges previously attended regardless of whether any aid was received.

CONTACT

Jeff Gerkin, Director of Financial Aid
320 Student Services Building, Knoxville, TN 37996-0230
(865) 974-3131

University of Tennessee: Martin

Martin, Tennessee
www.utm.edu Federal Code: 003531

4-year public university in small town.
Enrollment: 6,090 undergrads, 10% part-time. 1,359 full-time freshmen.
Selectivity: Admits over 75% of applicants.

BASIC COSTS (2008-2009)

Tuition and fees: $5,255; out-of-state residents $15,897.
Per-credit charge: $184; out-of-state residents $628.
Room and board: $4,606.

FINANCIAL AID PICTURE (2008-2009)

Students with need: Out of 1,320 full-time freshmen who applied for aid, 909 were judged to have need. Of these, 902 received aid, and 423 had their full need met. Average financial aid package met 83% of need; average scholarship/grant was $5,774; average loan was $2,693. For part-time students, average financial aid package was $8,086.
Students without need: This college awards aid only to students with need.
Scholarships offered: 27 full-time freshmen received athletic scholarships; average amount $10,893.
Cumulative student debt: 45% of graduating class had student loans; average debt was $23,412.

FINANCIAL AID PROCEDURES

Forms required: FAFSA.
Dates and Deadlines: Priority date 3/1; no closing date. Applicants notified on a rolling basis starting 4/1.

CONTACT

Sandy Neel, Director of Student Financial Assistance
200 Hall Moody Administration Building, Martin, TN 38238
(731) 881-7040

University of the South

Sewanee, Tennessee
www.sewanee.edu Federal Code: 003534

4-year private university in rural community, affiliated with Episcopal Church.
Enrollment: 1,464 undergrads. 410 full-time freshmen.
Selectivity: Admits 50 to 75% of applicants. GED not accepted.

BASIC COSTS (2009-2010)

Tuition and fees: $34,172.
Per-credit charge: $1,230.
Room and board: $9,760.

FINANCIAL AID PICTURE (2008-2009)

Students with need: Out of 234 full-time freshmen who applied for aid, 161 were judged to have need. Of these, 160 received aid, and 133 had their full need met. Average financial aid package met 98% of need; average scholarship/grant was $25,676; average loan was $3,759.
Students without need: 95 full-time freshmen who did not demonstrate need for aid received scholarships/grants; average award was $17,281. No-need awards available for academics, minority status, religious affiliation.
Scholarships offered: Benedict Scholars Program for exceptional freshmen; 3 full cost scholarships. Wilkins Scholarships for outstanding incoming freshmen; half tuition, 25 awarded.
Cumulative student debt: 45% of graduating class had student loans; average debt was $15,885.

FINANCIAL AID PROCEDURES

Forms required: FAFSA, institutional form.
Dates and Deadlines: Priority date 3/1; no closing date. Applicants notified by 4/1; must reply within 4 week(s) of notification.

CONTACT

Beth Crager, Director of Financial Aid
Office of Admission, Sewanee, TN 37383-1000
(931) 598-1312

Vanderbilt University

Nashville, Tennessee Federal Code: 003535
www.vanderbilt.edu CSS Code: 1871

4-year private university in very large city.
Enrollment: 6,598 undergrads. 1,569 full-time freshmen.
Selectivity: Admits less than 50% of applicants.

BASIC COSTS (2008-2009)

Tuition and fees: $37,005.
Room and board: $12,028.

FINANCIAL AID PICTURE (2008-2009)

Students with need: Out of 788 full-time freshmen who applied for aid, 660 were judged to have need. Of these, 659 received aid, and 653 had their full need met. Average financial aid package met 100% of need; average scholarship/grant was $31,711; average loan was $2,899.
Students without need: 208 full-time freshmen who did not demonstrate need for aid received scholarships/grants; average award was $12,359. No-need awards available for academics, athletics, leadership, minority status, music/drama, ROTC, state/district residency.
Scholarships offered: 34 full-time freshmen received athletic scholarships; average amount $32,294.
Cumulative student debt: 38% of graduating class had student loans; average debt was $19,839.
Additional info: Financial aid packages for incoming students do not include need-based loans. Need-based loans replaced with increased amounts of scholarship and/or grant assistance.

FINANCIAL AID PROCEDURES

Forms required: FAFSA, CSS PROFILE.

Dates and Deadlines: Priority date 2/1; no closing date. Applicants notified on a rolling basis starting 4/1; must reply by 5/1.

Transfers: Priority date 4/15.

CONTACT

David Mohning, Director of Student Financial Aid
2305 West End Avenue, Nashville, TN 37203-1727
(615) 322-3591

Volunteer State Community College

Gallatin, Tennessee
www.volstate.edu Federal Code: 009912

2-year public community and junior college in small city.

Enrollment: 5,667 undergrads, 40% part-time. 1,193 full-time freshmen.

Selectivity: Open admission; but selective for some programs.

BASIC COSTS (2008-2009)

Tuition and fees: $2,767; out-of-state residents $10,267.

Per-credit charge: $107; out-of-state residents $431.

Additional info: Tuition/fee waivers available for minority students.

FINANCIAL AID PICTURE (2007-2008)

Students with need: Need-based aid available for full-time and part-time students.

Students without need: No-need awards available for academics, art, athletics, leadership, minority status, music/drama, religious affiliation, state/district residency.

FINANCIAL AID PROCEDURES

Forms required: FAFSA, institutional form.

Dates and Deadlines: Priority date 4/15; no closing date. Applicants notified on a rolling basis; must reply within 2 week(s) of notification.

Transfers: No deadline. Applicants notified on a rolling basis; must reply within 2 week(s) of notification.

CONTACT

Sue Pedigo, Director of Financial Aid
1480 Nashville Pike, Gallatin, TN 37066
(615) 452-8600 ext. 3456

Walters State Community College

Morristown, Tennessee
www.ws.edu Federal Code: 008863

2-year public culinary school and community college in small city.

Enrollment: 4,526 undergrads, 34% part-time. 1,209 full-time freshmen.

Selectivity: Open admission; but selective for some programs.

BASIC COSTS (2008-2009)

Tuition and fees: $2,775; out-of-state residents $10,275.

Per-credit charge: $107; out-of-state residents $431.

Additional info: Tuition/fee waivers available for minority students.

FINANCIAL AID PICTURE (2007-2008)

Students with need: Out of 948 full-time freshmen who applied for aid, 644 were judged to have need. Of these, 615 received aid, and 139 had their full need met. Average financial aid package met 78% of need; average scholarship/grant was $3,874; average loan was $2,329. For part-time students, average financial aid package was $3,126.

Students without need: 235 full-time freshmen who did not demonstrate need for aid received scholarships/grants; average award was $2,644. No-need awards available for academics, athletics, minority status, music/drama, state/district residency.

Scholarships offered: 29 full-time freshmen received athletic scholarships; average amount $1,361.

Cumulative student debt: 65% of graduating class had student loans; average debt was $6,654.

FINANCIAL AID PROCEDURES

Forms required: FAFSA.

Dates and Deadlines: Priority date 5/1; no closing date. Applicants notified on a rolling basis.

Transfers: No deadline. Applicants notified on a rolling basis.

CONTACT

Linda Mason, Director of Financial Aid
500 South Davy Crockett Parkway, Morristown, TN 37813-6899
(423) 585-6811

Texas

Abilene Christian University

Abilene, Texas
www.acu.edu Federal Code: 003537

4-year private university in small city, affiliated with Church of Christ.

Enrollment: 3,845 undergrads, 6% part-time. 887 full-time freshmen.

Selectivity: Admits less than 50% of applicants.

BASIC COSTS (2008-2009)

Tuition and fees: $18,855.

Per-credit charge: $596.

Room and board: $7,236.

FINANCIAL AID PICTURE (2007-2008)

Students with need: Out of 753 full-time freshmen who applied for aid, 596 were judged to have need. Of these, 596 received aid, and 161 had their full need met. Average financial aid package met 76% of need; average scholarship/grant was $10,998; average loan was $3,378. For part-time students, average financial aid package was $5,336.

Students without need: 126 full-time freshmen who did not demonstrate need for aid received scholarships/grants; average award was $6,372. No-need awards available for academics, art, athletics, leadership, minority status, music/drama, religious affiliation, state/district residency.

Scholarships offered: ***Merit:*** Presidential Scholarship: half or full tuition; based on interview, ACT or SAT scores. Heritage Award: $1,000 per year; based on Church of Christ, ACT or SAT scores. Transfer Scholarship: $1,000-$2,000; based on GPA. ***Athletic:*** 56 full-time freshmen received athletic scholarships; average amount $9,199.

Cumulative student debt: 71% of graduating class had student loans; average debt was $31,402.

Additional info: Early estimate service available.

FINANCIAL AID PROCEDURES

Forms required: FAFSA, institutional form.

Dates and Deadlines: Priority date 3/1; no closing date. Applicants notified on a rolling basis starting 4/1.

CONTACT

Michael Lewis, Director of Student Financial Services
ACU Box 29000, Abilene, TX 79699
(325) 674-6850

Alvin Community College
Alvin, Texas
www.alvincollege.edu Federal Code: 003539

2-year public community and liberal arts college in large town.
Enrollment: 2,817 undergrads.
Selectivity: Open admission; but selective for some programs.

BASIC COSTS (2009-2010)
Tuition and fees: $1,216; out-of-district residents $2,056; out-of-state residents $3,616.
Per-credit charge: $30; out-of-district residents $58; out-of-state residents $110.

FINANCIAL AID PICTURE
Students with need: Need-based aid available for full-time and part-time students. Work study available nights, weekends, and for part-time students.
Students without need: This college awards aid only to students with need.

FINANCIAL AID PROCEDURES
Forms required: FAFSA.
Dates and Deadlines: Priority date 6/30; no closing date. Applicants notified on a rolling basis; must reply within 2 week(s) of notification.

CONTACT
Dora Sims, Director of Student Financial Aid and Placement
3110 Mustang Road, Alvin, TX 77511-4898
(281) 756-3524

Angelina College
Lufkin, Texas
www.angelina.edu Federal Code: 006661

2-year public community college in large town.
Enrollment: 4,934 undergrads, 65% part-time. 1,190 full-time freshmen.
Selectivity: Open admission; but selective for some programs.

BASIC COSTS (2008-2009)
Tuition and fees: $1,200; out-of-district residents $1,800; out-of-state residents $2,550.
Per-credit charge: $33; out-of-district residents $53; out-of-state residents $78.
Room and board: $5,550.
Additional info: Students taking 1-3 credits pay higher per-credit-hour charge.

FINANCIAL AID PICTURE (2007-2008)
Students with need: Out of 983 full-time freshmen who applied for aid, 918 were judged to have need. Of these, 888 received aid, and 29 had their full need met. Average financial aid package met 69% of need; average scholarship/grant was $2,404. For part-time students, average financial aid package was $1,796.
Students without need: This college awards aid only to students with need.
Scholarships offered: 21 full-time freshmen received athletic scholarships; average amount $5,501.

FINANCIAL AID PROCEDURES
Forms required: FAFSA, institutional form.
Dates and Deadlines: Priority date 7/15; no closing date. Applicants notified on a rolling basis starting 7/15.

CONTACT
Susan Jones, Director of Financial Aid
PO Box 1768, Lufkin, TX 75902-1768
(936) 633-5291

Angelo State University
San Angelo, Texas
www.angelo.edu Federal Code: 003541

4-year public university in small city.
Enrollment: 5,512 undergrads, 14% part-time. 1,481 full-time freshmen.
Selectivity: Admits over 75% of applicants.

BASIC COSTS (2008-2009)
Tuition and fees: $5,411; out-of-state residents $13,841.
Per-credit charge: $132; out-of-state residents $413.
Room and board: $6,612.
Additional info: Fifty percent of freshmen dorms are private rooms and higher rates apply.

FINANCIAL AID PICTURE (2007-2008)
Students with need: Out of 1,240 full-time freshmen who applied for aid, 974 were judged to have need. Of these, 941 received aid. For part-time students, average financial aid package was $2,123.
Students without need: 226 full-time freshmen who did not demonstrate need for aid received scholarships/grants. No-need awards available for academics, athletics, leadership, music/drama, ROTC, state/district residency.
Scholarships offered: ***Merit:*** Carr Academic Scholarship program: average award of $3,200 per year for freshmen; one of every six ASU students receives a Carr Scholarship. Special Academic Scholarships available for undergraduates majoring in chemistry/biochemistry, math, physics, French or German. ***Athletic:*** 45 full-time freshmen received athletic scholarships; average amount $3,137.
Cumulative student debt: 60% of graduating class had student loans; average debt was $11,306.
Additional info: The Blue and Gold Guarantee provides full tuition and mandatory fees for first-time Texas resident freshmen from families with adjusted gross income of $40,000 or less. Must be Pell eligible.

FINANCIAL AID PROCEDURES
Forms required: FAFSA.
Dates and Deadlines: Priority date 4/1; no closing date. Applicants notified on a rolling basis starting 4/1; must reply within 4 week(s) of notification.
Transfers: No deadline. Applicants notified on a rolling basis starting 4/1; must reply within 5 week(s) of notification.

CONTACT
Lyn Wheeler, Director of Financial Aid
ASU Station #11014, San Angelo, TX 76909-1014
(800) 946-8627

Arlington Baptist College
Arlington, Texas
www.abconline.edu Federal Code: 014305

4-year private Bible and teachers college in very large city, affiliated with Baptist faith.
Enrollment: 138 undergrads, 22% part-time. 17 full-time freshmen.
Selectivity: Open admission.

BASIC COSTS (2008-2009)
Tuition and fees: $6,740.
Per-credit charge: $200.
Room and board: $4,200.

FINANCIAL AID PICTURE (2007-2008)
Students with need: Out of 15 full-time freshmen who applied for aid, 15 were judged to have need. Of these, 15 received aid, and 15 had their full need met. Average financial aid package met 80% of need; average scholarship/grant was $1,537; average loan was $2,223. For part-time students, average financial aid package was $4,640.

Students without need: This college awards aid only to students with need.
Cumulative student debt: 70% of graduating class had student loans; average debt was $9,500.

FINANCIAL AID PROCEDURES

Forms required: FAFSA.
Dates and Deadlines: Closing date 8/15. Applicants notified on a rolling basis.

CONTACT

David Clogston, Business Manager
3001 West Division, Arlington, TX 76012
(817) 461-8741 ext. 114

Art Institute of Dallas

Dallas, Texas
www.aid.edu Federal Code: 017360

4-year for-profit visual arts college in very large city.
Enrollment: 1,897 undergrads.
Selectivity: Open admission; but selective for some programs.

BASIC COSTS (2008-2009)

Additional info: Total program costs vary by program: bachelor's programs $84,012-$88,530; associate programs $49,332-$52,075.

FINANCIAL AID PICTURE

Students with need: Need-based aid available for full-time students.

FINANCIAL AID PROCEDURES

Forms required: FAFSA.
Dates and Deadlines: Applicants notified on a rolling basis.

CONTACT

Two North Park, 8080 Park Lane, Dallas, TX 75231
(214) 692-8080

Austin College

Sherman, Texas
www.austincollege.edu Federal Code: 003543

4-year private liberal arts and teachers college in small city, affiliated with Presbyterian Church (USA).
Enrollment: 1,253 undergrads. 319 full-time freshmen.
Selectivity: Admits over 75% of applicants.

BASIC COSTS (2009-2010)

Tuition and fees: $27,875.
Per-credit charge: $1,004.
Room and board: $9,090.

FINANCIAL AID PICTURE (2008-2009)

Students with need: Out of 253 full-time freshmen who applied for aid, 204 were judged to have need. Of these, 204 received aid, and 204 had their full need met. Average financial aid package met 99% of need; average scholarship/grant was $19,197; average loan was $5,130. Need-based aid available for part-time students.
Students without need: 111 full-time freshmen who did not demonstrate need for aid received scholarships/grants; average award was $13,653. No-need awards available for academics, alumni affiliation, art, leadership, music/drama, religious affiliation, state/district residency.

FINANCIAL AID PROCEDURES

Forms required: FAFSA.
Dates and Deadlines: Priority date 4/1; no closing date. Applicants notified on a rolling basis starting 3/1; must reply by 5/1.
Transfers: Applicants notified on a rolling basis starting 3/1; must reply by 5/1.

CONTACT

Laurie Coulter, Executive Director of Financial Aid
900 North Grand Avenue, Suite 6N, Sherman, TX 75090-4400
(903) 813-2900

Austin Community College

Austin, Texas
www.austincc.edu Federal Code: 012015

2-year public community college in very large city.
Enrollment: 25,980 undergrads. 602 full-time freshmen.
Selectivity: Open admission; but selective for some programs.

BASIC COSTS (2008-2009)

Tuition and fees: $1,608; out-of-district residents $4,248; out-of-state residents $8,988.
Per-credit charge: $39; out-of-district residents $127; out-of-state residents $285.

FINANCIAL AID PICTURE (2007-2008)

Students with need: Out of 565 full-time freshmen who applied for aid, 494 were judged to have need. Of these, 494 received aid. Need-based aid available for part-time students.

FINANCIAL AID PROCEDURES

Forms required: FAFSA, institutional form.
Dates and Deadlines: Closing date 4/1. Applicants notified on a rolling basis starting 6/1; must reply within 2 week(s) of notification.

CONTACT

Terry Bazan, Director, Financial Assistance
PO Box 15306, Austin, TX 78681-5306
(512) 223-7550

Austin Graduate School of Theology

Austin, Texas
www.austingrad.edu Federal Code: 017322

Upper-division private Bible and seminary college in large city, affiliated with Church of Christ.
Enrollment: 22 undergrads, 91% part-time.

BASIC COSTS (2008-2009)

Tuition and fees: $7,500.
Per-credit charge: $250.

FINANCIAL AID PICTURE (2007-2008)

Students with need: 62% of average financial aid package awarded as scholarships/grants, 38% awarded as loans/jobs. Need-based aid available for part-time students. Work study available nights.
Students without need: No-need awards available for academics, leadership.
Additional info: Generous scholarships for students taking at least 12 hours. Federal work study program available. Institutional work study program (need-based) available.

FINANCIAL AID PROCEDURES

Forms required: FAFSA, institutional form.
Dates and Deadlines: Priority date 7/1; closing date 8/1.
Transfers: No deadline.

CONTACT
Dave Arthur, Vice President
7640 Guadalupe Street, Austin, TX 78752-1333
(512) 476-2772

Baylor University
Waco, Texas
www.baylor.edu Federal Code: 003545

4-year private university in small city, affiliated with Baptist faith.
Enrollment: 12,105 undergrads, 2% part-time. 3,056 full-time freshmen.
Selectivity: Admits 50 to 75% of applicants.

BASIC COSTS (2009-2010)
Tuition and fees: $27,910.
Per-credit charge: $1,055.
Room and board: $7,971.
Additional info: Cited cost includes room rate of $4,240 per year for community bath and 16-meal plan. Other room types are higher.

FINANCIAL AID PICTURE (2008-2009)
Students with need: Out of 2,130 full-time freshmen who applied for aid, 1,670 were judged to have need. Of these, 1,669 received aid, and 225 had their full need met. Average financial aid package met 69% of need; average scholarship/grant was $15,395; average loan was $2,636. For part-time students, average financial aid package was $9,300.
Students without need: 1,143 full-time freshmen who did not demonstrate need for aid received scholarships/grants; average award was $7,991. No-need awards available for academics, art, athletics, job skills, leadership, music/drama, ROTC.
Scholarships offered: ***Merit:*** Regent's Scholarship: full tuition; limited to National Merit finalists who list Baylor as first choice; unlimited number. President's Scholarship: $40,000 to $58,000 divided over 4 years. Provost's Baylor Scholarship: $32,000 to $40,000 divided over 4 years. Dean's Scholarship: $10,000 to $22,000 divided over 4 years. There are a limited number of all awarded based on admission date, high school rank and SAT/ACT scores. ***Athletic:*** 73 full-time freshmen received athletic scholarships; average amount $21,548.

FINANCIAL AID PROCEDURES
Forms required: FAFSA.
Dates and Deadlines: Priority date 1/15; closing date 8/15. Applicants notified on a rolling basis starting 3/1; must reply by 5/1 or within 2 week(s) of notification.
Transfers: Must reply by 5/1 or within 2 week(s) of notification.

CONTACT
Jackie Diaz, Assistant Vice President
One Bear Place #97056, Waco, TX 76798-7056
(800) 229-5678

Blinn College
Brenham, Texas
www.blinn.edu Federal Code: 003549

2-year public community college in large town.
Enrollment: 13,040 undergrads, 40% part-time. 2,488 full-time freshmen.
Selectivity: Open admission; but selective for some programs.

BASIC COSTS (2008-2009)
Tuition and fees: $1,890; out-of-district residents $2,760; out-of-state residents $5,040.
Per-credit charge: $35; out-of-district residents $64; out-of-state residents $140.
Room and board: $4,940.

FINANCIAL AID PICTURE (2008-2009)
Students with need: Need-based aid available for full-time and part-time students.

FINANCIAL AID PROCEDURES
Forms required: FAFSA, institutional form.
Dates and Deadlines: Priority date 6/1; no closing date. Applicants notified on a rolling basis starting 7/1.

CONTACT
Tracy Lutkenhaus, Director of Financial Aid
902 College Avenue, Brenham, TX 77833
(979) 830-4144

Bradford School of Business
Houston, Texas
www.bradfordschoolhouston.edu

2-year for-profit technical college in very large city.
Enrollment: 53 undergrads.

BASIC COSTS (2008-2009)
Tuition and fees: $13,800.
Additional info: Lab fees vary depending upon program selected.

FINANCIAL AID PICTURE
Students with need: Need-based aid available for full-time students.

CONTACT
4669 Southwest Freeway, Houston, TX 77027

Brazosport College
Lake Jackson, Texas
www.brazosport.edu Federal Code: 007287

2-year public community college in large town.
Enrollment: 3,883 undergrads.
Selectivity: Open admission; but selective for some programs.

BASIC COSTS (2008-2009)
Tuition and fees: $1,392; out-of-district residents $2,022; out-of-state residents $3,432.
Per-credit charge: $31; out-of-district residents $52; out-of-state residents $99.

FINANCIAL AID PICTURE (2007-2008)
Students with need: 85% of average financial aid package awarded as scholarships/grants, 15% awarded as loans/jobs. Need-based aid available for part-time students.
Students without need: No-need awards available for academics, art, job skills, leadership, music/drama, state/district residency.

FINANCIAL AID PROCEDURES
Forms required: FAFSA, institutional form.
Dates and Deadlines: Priority date 7/1; no closing date. Applicants notified on a rolling basis starting 5/1.

CONTACT
Kay Wright, Director of Financial Aid
500 College Drive, Lake Jackson, TX 77566
(979) 230-3377

Cedar Valley College

Lancaster, Texas
www.cedarvalleycollege.edu Federal Code: 014035

2-year public community college in large town.
Enrollment: 4,400 undergrads.
Selectivity: Open admission.

BASIC COSTS (2008-2009)

Tuition and fees: $1,170; out-of-district residents $2,160; out-of-state residents $3,450.
Per-credit charge: $39; out-of-district residents $72.

FINANCIAL AID PICTURE

Students with need: Need-based aid available for full-time students.

FINANCIAL AID PROCEDURES

Forms required: FAFSA.
Dates and Deadlines: Priority date 5/1; no closing date. Applicants notified on a rolling basis.

CONTACT

DeCha Reid, Director of Financial Aid
3030 North Dallas Avenue, Lancaster, TX 75134
(972) 860-8280

Central Texas College

Killeen, Texas
www.ctcd.edu Federal Code: 004003

2-year public community and technical college in small city.
Enrollment: 18,488 undergrads.
Selectivity: Open admission; but selective for some programs.

BASIC COSTS (2008-2009)

Tuition and fees: $1,380; out-of-district residents $1,680; out-of-state residents $4,140.
Per-credit charge: $36; out-of-district residents $46; out-of-state residents $130.
Room and board: $3,300.

FINANCIAL AID PICTURE

Students with need: Need-based aid available for full-time and part-time students. Work study available nights, weekends, and for part-time students.
Students without need: This college awards aid only to students with need.

FINANCIAL AID PROCEDURES

Forms required: FAFSA, institutional form.
Dates and Deadlines: Closing date 7/1. Applicants notified on a rolling basis starting 3/1; must reply within 4 week(s) of notification.

CONTACT

Annabelle Smith, Director of Student Financial Aid
Box 1800, Killeen, TX 76540
(254) 526-1508

Clarendon College

Clarendon, Texas
www.clarendoncollege.edu Federal Code: 003554

2-year public community college in rural community.
Enrollment: 1,151 undergrads, 53% part-time. 230 full-time freshmen.
Selectivity: Open admission; but selective for some programs.

BASIC COSTS (2008-2009)

Tuition and fees: $2,370; out-of-district residents $2,940; out-of-state residents $3,510.
Room and board: $3,450.

FINANCIAL AID PICTURE (2007-2008)

Students with need: Average financial aid package for all full-time undergraduates was $8,280; for part-time $5,655. 48% awarded as scholarships/grants, 52% awarded as loans/jobs. Work study available nights, weekends, and for part-time students.
Students without need: No-need awards available for academics, art, athletics, leadership, music/drama, state/district residency.
Scholarships offered: Named and endowed scholarships available based on academic achievement, need, and/or other requirements as stipulated by the scholarship donor.

FINANCIAL AID PROCEDURES

Forms required: FAFSA, institutional form.
Dates and Deadlines: Priority date 8/1; no closing date. Applicants notified on a rolling basis starting 5/15; must reply by 8/15 or within 2 week(s) of notification.
Transfers: No deadline. Applicants notified on a rolling basis starting 11/15; must reply within 4 week(s) of notification.

CONTACT

Reagan Silva, Director of Financial Aid
PO Box 968, Clarendon, TX 79226
(806) 874-3571 ext. 112

Coastal Bend College

Beeville, Texas
www.coastalbend.edu Federal Code: 003546

2-year public community college in large town.
Enrollment: 3,450 undergrads, 59% part-time. 508 full-time freshmen.
Selectivity: Open admission; but selective for some programs.

BASIC COSTS (2008-2009)

Tuition and fees: $1,820; out-of-district residents $3,590; out-of-state residents $4,040.
Room only: $1,560.
Additional info: Meal ticket (a la carte) food service available.

FINANCIAL AID PICTURE (2007-2008)

Students with need: Need-based aid available for full-time and part-time students.
Students without need: No-need awards available for academics, leadership.

FINANCIAL AID PROCEDURES

Forms required: FAFSA, institutional form.
Dates and Deadlines: Priority date 4/1; no closing date. Applicants notified on a rolling basis starting 5/1; must reply within 2 week(s) of notification.
Transfers: No deadline. Applicants notified on a rolling basis.

CONTACT

Nora Morales, Director of Financial Aid
3800 Charco Road, Beeville, TX 78102
(361) 354-2238

College of Saint Thomas More

Fort Worth, Texas
www.cstm.edu Federal Code: 031894

4-year private liberal arts college in very large city, affiliated with Roman Catholic Church.
Enrollment: 31 undergrads, 35% part-time. 3 full-time freshmen.
Selectivity: Admits over 75% of applicants.

BASIC COSTS (2008-2009)

Tuition and fees: $12,150.
Per-credit charge: $400.
Room only: $4,050.
Additional info: Student housing includes use of private kitchen.

FINANCIAL AID PICTURE (2007-2008)

Students with need: 70% of average financial aid package awarded as scholarships/grants, 30% awarded as loans/jobs. Need-based aid available for part-time students. Work study available nights, weekends, and for part-time students.
Students without need: No-need awards available for academics.

FINANCIAL AID PROCEDURES

Forms required: FAFSA.
Dates and Deadlines: Closing date 7/1. Applicants notified on a rolling basis starting 1/1.

CONTACT

Corky Swanson, Financial Aid Department
3020 Lubbock Avenue, Fort Worth, TX 76109
(817) 673-1934

College of the Mainland

Texas City, Texas
www.com.edu Federal Code: 007096

2-year public community and technical college in large town.
Enrollment: 3,561 undergrads.
Selectivity: Open admission; but selective for some programs.

BASIC COSTS (2008-2009)

Tuition and fees: $1,282; out-of-district residents $2,302; out-of-state residents $3,262.

FINANCIAL AID PICTURE

Students with need: Need-based aid available for full-time and part-time students. Work study available nights, weekends, and for part-time students.
Students without need: This college awards aid only to students with need.

FINANCIAL AID PROCEDURES

Forms required: FAFSA, institutional form.
Dates and Deadlines: No deadline. Applicants notified on a rolling basis.
Transfers: Priority date 8/1.

CONTACT

Becky Miles, Director, Student Financial Services
1200 Amburn Road, Texas City, TX 77591
(409) 938-1211 ext. 274

Collin County Community College District

Plano, Texas
www.ccccd.edu Federal Code: 016792

2-year public community college in large city.
Enrollment: 20,695 undergrads, 59% part-time. 2,768 full-time freshmen.
Selectivity: Open admission; but selective for some programs.

BASIC COSTS (2008-2009)

Tuition and fees: $1,114; out-of-district residents $1,534; out-of-state residents $3,184.
Per-credit charge: $37; out-of-district residents $51; out-of-state residents $106.

FINANCIAL AID PICTURE (2007-2008)

Students with need: Out of 984 full-time freshmen who applied for aid, 802 were judged to have need. Of these, 642 received aid, and 128 had their full need met. Average financial aid package met 32% of need; average scholarship/grant was $3,650; average loan was $2,773. For part-time students, average financial aid package was $3,216.
Students without need: 30 full-time freshmen who did not demonstrate need for aid received scholarships/grants; average award was $1,042. No-need awards available for academics, art, athletics, music/drama.
Scholarships offered: 20 full-time freshmen received athletic scholarships; average amount $4,906.
Cumulative student debt: 11% of graduating class had student loans; average debt was $5,906.

FINANCIAL AID PROCEDURES

Forms required: FAFSA, institutional form.
Dates and Deadlines: Priority date 6/1; closing date 6/30. Applicants notified on a rolling basis starting 5/1; must reply within 2 week(s) of notification.
Transfers: Applicants must have cumulative GPA of 2.0 and less than 90 transferable credit hours.

CONTACT

Debra Wilkison, Director of Financial Aid
2800 East Spring Creek Parkway, Plano, TX 75074
(972) 881-5760

Commonwealth Institute of Funeral Service

Houston, Texas
www.commonwealthinst.org Federal Code: 003556

2-year private school of mortuary science in very large city.
Enrollment: 97 undergrads.

BASIC COSTS (2008-2009)

Tuition and fees: $6,290.
Per-credit charge: $143.

FINANCIAL AID PICTURE

Students with need: Need-based aid available for full-time and part-time students.
Students without need: This college awards aid only to students with need.
Scholarships offered: Scholarship awards: $250-$500 based on funds available; recipients selected on academic achievement, leadership and professional promise, as well as any stipulations by the donor, by a committee of Commonwealth Institute graduate employers, alumni, and benefactors.

FINANCIAL AID PROCEDURES

Forms required: FAFSA.

Dates and Deadlines: Priority date 7/20; no closing date. Applicants notified on a rolling basis starting 7/12.

CONTACT

Dennis Christie, Director of Financial Aid
415 Barren Springs Drive, Houston, TX 77090-5913
(281) 873-0262

Concordia University Texas

Austin, Texas
www.concordia.edu Federal Code: 003557

4-year private university and liberal arts college in very large city, affiliated with Lutheran Church - Missouri Synod.
Enrollment: 1,169 undergrads, 23% part-time. 138 full-time freshmen.
Selectivity: Admits 50 to 75% of applicants.

BASIC COSTS (2008-2009)

Tuition and fees: $20,490.
Per-credit charge: $670.
Room and board: $7,800.
Additional info: Tuition/fee waivers available for adults.

FINANCIAL AID PICTURE (2007-2008)

Students with need: Out of 82 full-time freshmen who applied for aid, 59 were judged to have need. Of these, 56 received aid, and 13 had their full need met. Average financial aid package met 79% of need; average scholarship/grant was $10,644; average loan was $5,626. For part-time students, average financial aid package was $11,788.
Students without need: 16 full-time freshmen who did not demonstrate need for aid received scholarships/grants; average award was $7,696. No-need awards available for academics, alumni affiliation, leadership, music/drama, religious affiliation.
Cumulative student debt: 66% of graduating class had student loans; average debt was $21,427.

FINANCIAL AID PROCEDURES

Forms required: FAFSA, institutional form.
Dates and Deadlines: No deadline. Applicants notified on a rolling basis starting 2/15; must reply within 2 week(s) of notification.
Transfers: Financial aid transcripts from all previously attended trade/technical schools and colleges/universities required.

CONTACT

Cathy Schryer, Director of Financial Assistance
11400 Concordia University Drive, Austin, TX 78726
(512) 486-1283

Dallas Baptist University

Dallas, Texas
www.dbu.edu Federal Code: 003560

4-year private university in very large city, affiliated with Baptist faith.
Enrollment: 3,575 undergrads, 38% part-time. 348 full-time freshmen.
Selectivity: Admits less than 50% of applicants.

BASIC COSTS (2008-2009)

Tuition and fees: $16,440.
Per-credit charge: $548.
Room and board: $5,409.

FINANCIAL AID PICTURE (2008-2009)

Students with need: Out of 335 full-time freshmen who applied for aid, 217 were judged to have need. Of these, 216 received aid, and 129 had their full need met. Average financial aid package met 86% of need; average scholarship/grant was $3,046; average loan was $3,023. For part-time students, average financial aid package was $4,921.
Students without need: 92 full-time freshmen who did not demonstrate need for aid received scholarships/grants; average award was $7,617. No-need awards available for academics, athletics, job skills, leadership, music/drama, religious affiliation.
Scholarships offered: 30 full-time freshmen received athletic scholarships; average amount $9,736.
Cumulative student debt: 51% of graduating class had student loans; average debt was $16,354.

FINANCIAL AID PROCEDURES

Forms required: FAFSA, institutional form.
Dates and Deadlines: Priority date 3/6; closing date 5/1. Applicants notified on a rolling basis starting 2/1.
Transfers: Priority date 3/17; no deadline. Applicants notified on a rolling basis.

CONTACT

Donald Zackary, Director of Financial Aid
3000 Mountain Creek Parkway, Dallas, TX 75211-9299
(214) 333-5363

Dallas Christian College

Dallas, Texas
www.dallas.edu Federal Code: 006941

4-year private Bible college in very large city, affiliated with nondenominational tradition.
Enrollment: 301 undergrads, 37% part-time. 30 full-time freshmen.
Selectivity: Admits less than 50% of applicants.

BASIC COSTS (2008-2009)

Tuition and fees: $10,170.
Per-credit charge: $319.
Room and board: $6,250.

FINANCIAL AID PICTURE (2008-2009)

Students with need: Need-based aid available for full-time and part-time students.
Students without need: No-need awards available for leadership, music/drama.

FINANCIAL AID PROCEDURES

Forms required: FAFSA, institutional form.
Dates and Deadlines: Closing date 4/15. Applicants notified on a rolling basis; must reply within 2 week(s) of notification.

CONTACT

Mark Stanley, Executive Vice President
2700 Christian Parkway, Dallas, TX 75234-7299
(972) 241-3371 ext. 158

Del Mar College

Corpus Christi, Texas
www.delmar.edu Federal Code: 003563

2-year public community college in large city.
Enrollment: 11,310 undergrads, 71% part-time. 796 full-time freshmen.
Selectivity: Open admission; but selective for some programs.

BASIC COSTS (2008-2009)

Tuition and fees: $2,124; out-of-district residents $5,124; out-of-state residents $6,234.

Per-credit charge: $37; out-of-district residents $137; out-of-state residents $174.

FINANCIAL AID PICTURE (2007-2008)

Students with need: 75% of average financial aid package awarded as scholarships/grants, 25% awarded as loans/jobs. Need-based aid available for part-time students. Work study available nights, weekends, and for part-time students.

Students without need: This college awards aid only to students with need.

FINANCIAL AID PROCEDURES

Forms required: FAFSA.

Dates and Deadlines: Priority date 5/1; no closing date. Applicants notified on a rolling basis starting 7/1; must reply within 2 week(s) of notification.

CONTACT

Enrique Garcia, Assistant Dean of Financial Aid and Retention Services
101 Baldwin Boulevard, Corpus Christi, TX 78404-3897
(361) 698-1293

DeVry University: Houston

Houston, Texas
www.devry.edu

4-year for-profit university in very large city.

Enrollment: 1,095 undergrads, 48% part-time. 138 full-time freshmen.

BASIC COSTS (2008-2009)

Tuition and fees: $14,130.

Per-credit charge: $515.

FINANCIAL AID PICTURE (2007-2008)

Students with need: Out of 105 full-time freshmen who applied for aid, 100 were judged to have need. Of these, 100 received aid, and 3 had their full need met. Average financial aid package met 42% of need; average scholarship/grant was $5,431; average loan was $6,882. For part-time students, average financial aid package was $10,172.

Students without need: 9 full-time freshmen who did not demonstrate need for aid received scholarships/grants; average award was $13,352. No-need awards available for academics.

Cumulative student debt: 100% of graduating class had student loans; average debt was $30,068.

FINANCIAL AID PROCEDURES

Forms required: FAFSA.

Dates and Deadlines: No deadline. Applicants notified on a rolling basis.

CONTACT

11125 Equity Drive, Houston, TX 77041-8217
(713) 973-3000

DeVry University: Irving

Dallas, Texas
www.devry.edu Federal Code: 010139

4-year for-profit university in small city.

Enrollment: 1,582 undergrads, 54% part-time. 174 full-time freshmen.

BASIC COSTS (2008-2009)

Tuition and fees: $14,130.

Per-credit charge: $515.

FINANCIAL AID PICTURE (2007-2008)

Students with need: Out of 130 full-time freshmen who applied for aid, 126 were judged to have need. Of these, 122 received aid, and 2 had their full need met. Average financial aid package met 39% of need; average scholarship/grant was $5,371; average loan was $7,845. For part-time students, average financial aid package was $10,507.

Students without need: This college awards aid only to students with need.

Cumulative student debt: 60% of graduating class had student loans; average debt was $31,895.

FINANCIAL AID PROCEDURES

Forms required: FAFSA.

Dates and Deadlines: No deadline. Applicants notified on a rolling basis.

CONTACT

Nga Phan, Director, Financial Aid
4800 Regent Boulevard, Dallas, TX 75063-2439
(972) 929-9740

East Texas Baptist University

Marshall, Texas
www.etbu.edu Federal Code: 003564

4-year private university and liberal arts college in large town, affiliated with Baptist faith.

Enrollment: 1,134 undergrads, 4% part-time. 312 full-time freshmen.

Selectivity: Admits 50 to 75% of applicants.

BASIC COSTS (2009-2010)

Tuition and fees: $17,180.

Per-credit charge: $600.

Room and board: $5,164.

Additional info: Tuition at time of enrollment locked for 4 years.

FINANCIAL AID PICTURE (2007-2008)

Students with need: Out of 294 full-time freshmen who applied for aid, 252 were judged to have need. Of these, 252 received aid, and 46 had their full need met. Average financial aid package met 61% of need; average scholarship/grant was $7,156; average loan was $2,966. For part-time students, average financial aid package was $5,475.

Students without need: 60 full-time freshmen who did not demonstrate need for aid received scholarships/grants; average award was $5,858. No-need awards available for academics, alumni affiliation, leadership, music/drama, religious affiliation.

Scholarships offered: For freshmen or students transferring less than 24 hours, based on ACT/SAT (Critical Reading and Math) and recalculated high school GPA: Presidential Scholarship; $7,000. Honor Scholarship; $6,000. Dean Scholarship; $5,000. Achievement Grant; $2,400. For transfer students: Transfer Honor Scholarship; $6,000. Transfer Dean Scholarship; $5,000. Transfer Achievement Grant; $2,400. All amounts are per academic year.

FINANCIAL AID PROCEDURES

Forms required: FAFSA, institutional form.

Dates and Deadlines: Priority date 0/1; no closing date. Applicants notified on a rolling basis starting 1/15; must reply within 3 week(s) of notification.

Transfers: No deadline. Applicants notified on a rolling basis starting 2/1; must reply within 3 week(s) of notification.

CONTACT

Tommy Young, Director of Financial Aid
1209 North Grove, Marshall, TX 75670-1498
(903) 923-2138

Eastfield College

Mesquite, Texas
www.efc.dcccd.edu Federal Code: 008510

2-year public community and liberal arts college in small city.
Enrollment: 10,025 undergrads, 76% part-time. 565 full-time freshmen.
Selectivity: Open admission.

BASIC COSTS (2008-2009)

Tuition and fees: $1,170; out-of-district residents $2,160; out-of-state residents $3,450.
Per-credit charge: $39; out-of-district residents $72.

FINANCIAL AID PICTURE

Students with need: Need-based aid available for full-time and part-time students. Work study available nights, weekends, and for part-time students.
Scholarships offered: Lecroy Scholars Program: $600 per semester; based on demonstrated church, community, or academic leadership and 3.0 GPA; requires enrollment in at least 12 credit hours; 5-10 awarded. Erin Tierney Kramp Encouragement Program: $600 per semester; based on demonstrated courage in the face of adversity, moral character, leadership, and high academic standards; requires enrollment in 8 hours for awarding semester, and maintenance of high academic standards; 2 awarded.

FINANCIAL AID PROCEDURES

Forms required: FAFSA, institutional form.
Dates and Deadlines: Priority date 5/1; no closing date. Applicants notified on a rolling basis starting 4/15.

CONTACT

Dana Mingo, Dean of Financial Aid
3737 Motley Drive, Mesquite, TX 75150
(972) 860-8385

El Centro College

Dallas, Texas
www.elcentrocollege.edu Federal Code: 004453

2-year public community college in very large city.
Enrollment: 5,984 undergrads, 77% part-time. 273 full-time freshmen.
Selectivity: Open admission; but selective for some programs.

BASIC COSTS (2008-2009)

Tuition and fees: $1,170; out-of-district residents $2,160; out-of-state residents $3,450.
Per-credit charge: $39; out-of-district residents $72.
Additional info: Tuition/fee waivers available for minority students, unemployed or children of unemployed.

FINANCIAL AID PICTURE

Students with need: Need-based aid available for full-time and part-time students.
Additional info: Interview required for financial aid applicants.

FINANCIAL AID PROCEDURES

Forms required: FAFSA.
Dates and Deadlines: Priority date 5/1; no closing date. Applicants notified on a rolling basis; must reply within 2 week(s) of notification.
Transfers: Financial aid transcript may be required from previous institutions attended.

CONTACT

John Wells, Director of Financial Aid
801 Main Street, Dallas, TX 75202
(214) 860-2099

El Paso Community College

El Paso, Texas
www.epcc.edu Federal Code: 010387

2-year public community college in very large city.
Enrollment: 23,350 undergrads.
Selectivity: Open admission; but selective for some programs.

BASIC COSTS (2008-2009)

Tuition and fees: $1,700; out-of-state residents $2,442.
Per-credit charge: $47; out-of-state residents $71.
Additional info: Per-credit-hour costs listed are for each additional credit-hour beyond one credit-hour for in-state students, and beyond six credit-hours for out-of-state students.

FINANCIAL AID PICTURE (2007-2008)

Students with need: 90% of average financial aid package awarded as scholarships/grants, 10% awarded as loans/jobs. Work study available nights, weekends, and for part-time students.
Students without need: No-need awards available for academics, athletics.

FINANCIAL AID PROCEDURES

Forms required: FAFSA, institutional form.
Dates and Deadlines: Priority date 5/1; no closing date. Applicants notified on a rolling basis starting 7/1; must reply within 2 week(s) of notification.

CONTACT

Linda Gonzalez-Hensgen, Director of Student Financial Services
Box 20500, El Paso, TX 79998
(915) 831-2566

Frank Phillips College

Borger, Texas
www.fpctx.edu Federal Code: 003568

2-year public community and junior college in large town.
Enrollment: 755 undergrads, 32% part-time. 158 full-time freshmen.
Selectivity: Open admission.

BASIC COSTS (2008-2009)

Tuition and fees: $2,333; out-of-district residents $2,963; out-of-state residents $3,173.
Per-credit charge: $64; out-of-district residents $106; out-of-state residents $120.
Room and board: $4,150

FINANCIAL AID PICTURE (2007-2008)

Students with need: Need-based aid available for full-time and part-time students. Work study available nights, weekends, and for part-time students.
Students without need: No-need awards available for academics, athletics, music/drama, state/district residency.
Scholarships offered: Various scholarships available including BEDC, Presidential, Dean's, Access, Opportunity, and Re-entering Adult Learner.
Additional info: Some Texas fire department and police department personnel, active duty military personnel, children of military missing in action may qualify for reduced or waived tuition. Out-of-state tuition waived for students living in Oklahoma counties adjacent to Texas.

FINANCIAL AID PROCEDURES

Forms required: FAFSA, institutional form.
Dates and Deadlines: No deadline. Applicants notified on a rolling basis; must reply within 2 week(s) of notification.
Transfers: No deadline. Applicants notified on a rolling basis.

CONTACT
Beverly Fields, Director of Financial Services
Box 5118, Borger, TX 79008-5118
(806) 457-4200 ext. 718

Galveston College
Galveston, Texas
www.gc.edu Federal Code: 004972

2-year public community college in small city.
Enrollment: 1,790 undergrads, 73% part-time. 131 full-time freshmen.
Selectivity: Open admission; but selective for some programs.

BASIC COSTS (2008-2009)
Tuition and fees: $1,414; out-of-state residents $2,314.
Per-credit charge: $30; out-of-state residents $60.

FINANCIAL AID PICTURE (2007-2008)
Students with need: Need-based aid available for full-time and part-time students.
Students without need: This college awards aid only to students with need.

FINANCIAL AID PROCEDURES
Forms required: FAFSA.
Dates and Deadlines: Priority date 6/9; no closing date. Applicants notified on a rolling basis starting 6/1.

CONTACT
Ron Crumedy, Financial Aid Manager
4015 Avenue Q, Galveston, TX 77550-7447
(409) 944-1235

Hallmark College of Aeronautics
San Antonio, Texas
www.hallmarkcollege.edu Federal Code: 010509

2-year for-profit technical and career college in very large city.
Enrollment: 166 undergrads. 166 full-time freshmen.

BASIC COSTS (2008-2009)
Additional info: Tuition for combined associate program in airframe technology or powerplant technology: $29,400. Costs include books, equipment and supplies. Registration fee: $100. Course fees vary. International students pay additional 8%. Tuition at time of enrollment locked for 2 years.

FINANCIAL AID PICTURE
Students with need: Need-based aid available for full-time students.

FINANCIAL AID PROCEDURES
Forms required: FAFSA.
Dates and Deadlines: No deadline. Applicants notified on a rolling basis.

CONTACT
Grace Calixto, Director of Financial Planning
8901 Wetmore Road, San Antonio, TX 78230
(210) 690-9000

Hallmark College of Technology
San Antonio, Texas
www.hallmarkcollege.edu Federal Code: 010509

2-year for-profit technical and career college in very large city.
Enrollment: 438 undergrads. 438 full-time freshmen.

BASIC COSTS (2008-2009)
Additional info: Costs for associate programs range from $19,566 to $30,800; additional registration fee $110 for all programs. Tuition at time of enrollment locked for 2 years.

FINANCIAL AID PICTURE
Students with need: Need-based aid available for full-time students.

FINANCIAL AID PROCEDURES
Forms required: FAFSA.
Dates and Deadlines: No deadline. Applicants notified on a rolling basis.

CONTACT
Grace Calixto, Director of Financial Planning
Hallmark College, San Antonio, TX 78230-1737
(210) 690-9000 ext. 212

Hardin-Simmons University
Abilene, Texas
www.hsutx.edu Federal Code: 003571

4-year private university in small city, affiliated with Baptist faith.
Enrollment: 1,914 undergrads, 9% part-time. 471 full-time freshmen.
Selectivity: Admits less than 50% of applicants.

BASIC COSTS (2009-2010)
Tuition and fees: $19,790.
Per-credit charge: $625.
Room and board: $5,788.
Additional info: Tuition at time of enrollment locked for 4 years.

FINANCIAL AID PICTURE (2008-2009)
Students with need: Out of 463 full-time freshmen who applied for aid, 322 were judged to have need. Of these, 322 received aid, and 96 had their full need met. Average financial aid package met 65% of need; average scholarship/grant was $5,814; average loan was $3,132. For part-time students, average financial aid package was $8,692.
Students without need: 68 full-time freshmen who did not demonstrate need for aid received scholarships/grants; average award was $4,031. No-need awards available for academics, art, job skills, leadership, music/drama, religious affiliation.
Cumulative student debt: 78% of graduating class had student loans; average debt was $33,475.

FINANCIAL AID PROCEDURES
Forms required: FAFSA.
Dates and Deadlines: Priority date 3/1; no closing date. Applicants notified on a rolling basis starting 2/1; must reply within 2 week(s) of notification.

CONTACT
Jim Jones, Director of Financial Aid and Scholarships
PO Box 16050, Abilene, TX 79698-0001
(325) 670-1206

Hill College
Hillsboro, Texas
www.hillcollege.edu Federal Code: 003573

2-year public community and junior college in small town.
Enrollment: 3,712 undergrads.
Selectivity: Open admission; but selective for some programs.

BASIC COSTS (2008-2009)
Tuition and fees: $1,620; out-of-district residents $2,100; out-of-state residents $2,500.
Room and board: $2,950.

FINANCIAL AID PICTURE (2008-2009)

Students with need: Need-based aid available for full-time and part-time students.

Students without need: No-need awards available for academics, athletics, music/drama.

FINANCIAL AID PROCEDURES

Forms required: FAFSA, institutional form.

Dates and Deadlines: Closing date 7/1. Applicants notified on a rolling basis.

CONTACT

Susan Russell, Director of Student Financial Aid
Box 619, Hillsboro, TX 76645
(254) 582-2555 ext. 285

Houston Baptist University

Houston, Texas
www.hbu.edu Federal Code: 003576

4-year private university and liberal arts college in very large city, affiliated with Baptist faith.

Enrollment: 2,177 undergrads, 13% part-time. 556 full-time freshmen.

Selectivity: Admits less than 50% of applicants.

BASIC COSTS (2009-2010)

Tuition and fees: $20,830.

Per-credit charge: $744.

Room and board: $6,975.

Additional info: Tuition is flat rate for fall and spring for undergraduates taking 12-18 hours per semester. Tuition at time of enrollment locked for 4 years.

FINANCIAL AID PICTURE (2008-2009)

Students with need: Out of 451 full-time freshmen who applied for aid, 393 were judged to have need. Of these, 392 received aid, and 77 had their full need met. Average financial aid package met 75% of need; average scholarship/grant was $5,765; average loan was $3,622. For part-time students, average financial aid package was $14,100.

Students without need: 156 full-time freshmen who did not demonstrate need for aid received scholarships/grants; average award was $7,722. No-need awards available for academics, alumni affiliation, art, athletics, music/drama, religious affiliation, ROTC.

Scholarships offered: ***Merit:*** Endowed Academic Scholarship: full or three-quarters tuition for four years; limited number available; for new freshmen with 1300 SAT or 30 ACT. Founders Academic Scholarship: minimum 1250 SAT or 28 ACT required for freshmen, 3.75 GPA on 30 or more semester hours required for transfers. Presidential Academic Scholarship: $4,300 per year, renewable; 1175 SAT or 26 ACT required for freshmen, 3.5 GPA required for transfers. Legacy Grant: $2,700 per year; renewable; 1100 SAT or 24 ACT required for freshmen, 3.25 GPA required for transfers. All SAT scores are exclusive of Writing. Valedictorian Scholarship: $1,500 per year; renewable; for valedictorians from Texas high schools. Ministerial Dependents Grant: $4,300 per year; for dependent children of ordained/licensed Southern Baptist ministers and missionaries. Grants-In-Aid: awards vary; for students who contribute special abilities or services to the University; awarded in music, art, athletics and nursing. Church Matching Award: awards vary. ***Athletic:*** 42 full-time freshmen received athletic scholarships; average amount $16,904.

FINANCIAL AID PROCEDURES

Forms required: FAFSA.

Dates and Deadlines: Priority date 3/1; closing date 4/15. Applicants notified on a rolling basis starting 3/10.

CONTACT

Debora Burnett, Director of Financial Services
7502 Fondren Road, Houston, TX 77074-3298
(281) 649-3471

Houston Community College System

Houston, Texas
www.hccs.edu Federal Code: 010422

2-year public community college in very large city.

Enrollment: 32,836 undergrads, 66% part-time. 3,106 full-time freshmen.

Selectivity: Open admission; but selective for some programs.

BASIC COSTS (2008-2009)

Tuition and fees: $1,674; out-of-district residents $3,294; out-of-state residents $3,894.

FINANCIAL AID PICTURE (2007-2008)

Students with need: Need-based aid available for full-time and part-time students. Work study available nights, weekends, and for part-time students.

FINANCIAL AID PROCEDURES

Dates and Deadlines: No deadline. Applicants notified on a rolling basis starting 6/1; must reply within 2 week(s) of notification.

CONTACT

Avis Horde, Director of Financial Aid
3100 Main, Houston, TX 77266-7517
(713) 718-8550

Howard College

Big Spring, Texas
www.howardcollege.edu Federal Code: 003574

2-year public community college in large town.

Enrollment: 3,415 undergrads, 65% part-time. 332 full-time freshmen.

Selectivity: Open admission; but selective for some programs.

BASIC COSTS (2008-2009)

Tuition and fees: $1,712; out-of-district residents $2,132; out-of-state residents $2,832.

Room and board: $3,600.

FINANCIAL AID PICTURE

Students with need: Need-based aid available for full-time and part-time students.

Students without need: No-need awards available for academics, art, athletics, leadership, music/drama.

FINANCIAL AID PROCEDURES

Forms required: FAFSA, institutional form.

Dates and Deadlines: Priority date 4/1; no closing date. Applicants notified on a rolling basis starting 7/15; must reply within 2 week(s) of notification.

CONTACT

Rebecca Villanueva, Director of Financial Aid
1001 Birdwell Lane, Big Spring, TX 79720
(432) 264-5083

Howard Payne University

Brownwood, Texas
www.hputx.edu Federal Code: 003575

4-year private liberal arts and teachers college in large town, affiliated with Baptist faith.

Enrollment: 1,173 undergrads, 11% part-time. 256 full-time freshmen.

Selectivity: Admits 50 to 75% of applicants.

BASIC COSTS (2008-2009)

Tuition and fees: $17,400.
Per-credit charge: $510.
Room and board: $5,051.

FINANCIAL AID PICTURE (2007-2008)

Students with need: Out of 227 full-time freshmen who applied for aid, 201 were judged to have need. Of these, 201 received aid, and 49 had their full need met. Average financial aid package met 80% of need; average scholarship/grant was $9,156; average loan was $2,794. For part-time students, average financial aid package was $6,111.
Students without need: 39 full-time freshmen who did not demonstrate need for aid received scholarships/grants; average award was $4,781. No-need awards available for academics, alumni affiliation, art, music/drama.
Scholarships offered: Merit-based scholarship available to all approved home school applicants, $5,000 annually ($20,000 over 4 years).
Cumulative student debt: 76% of graduating class had student loans; average debt was $23,100.

FINANCIAL AID PROCEDURES

Forms required: FAFSA, state aid form, institutional form.
Dates and Deadlines: Priority date 3/15; no closing date. Applicants notified on a rolling basis starting 2/1; must reply within 2 week(s) of notification.

CONTACT

Glenda Huff, Director of Student Financial Aid
1000 Fisk Street, Brownwood, TX 76801-2794
(325) 649-8015

Huston-Tillotson University

Austin, Texas
www.htu.edu Federal Code: 003577

4-year private business and liberal arts college in very large city, affiliated with United Church of Christ and United Methodist Church.
Enrollment: 721 undergrads, 6% part-time. 179 full-time freshmen.
Selectivity: Admits 50 to 75% of applicants.

BASIC COSTS (2008-2009)

Tuition and fees: $11,184.
Per-credit charge: $315.
Room and board: $6,400.

FINANCIAL AID PICTURE (2007-2008)

Students with need: Need-based aid available for full-time and part-time students. Work study available nights, weekends, and for part-time students.
Students without need: No-need awards available for academics, alumni affiliation, art, athletics, job skills, leadership, minority status, music/drama, religious affiliation, state/district residency.

FINANCIAL AID PROCEDURES

Forms required: FAFSA, institutional form.
Dates and Deadlines: Priority date 3/15; no closing date. Applicants notified on a rolling basis starting 4/1; must reply within 4 week(s) of notification.
Transfers: No deadline.

CONTACT

Antonio Holloway, Director of Financial Aid
900 Chicon Street, Austin, TX 78702-2795
(512) 505-3031

Jacksonville College

Jacksonville, Texas
www.jacksonville-college.edu Federal Code: 003579

2-year private junior and liberal arts college in large town, affiliated with Baptist faith.
Enrollment: 275 undergrads.
Selectivity: Open admission.

BASIC COSTS (2009-2010)

Tuition and fees: $6,896.
Per-credit charge: $210.
Room and board: $3,014.

FINANCIAL AID PICTURE (2008-2009)

Students with need: Need-based aid available for full-time and part-time students.
Students without need: No-need awards available for academics, athletics, leadership, music/drama, religious affiliation, state/district residency.

FINANCIAL AID PROCEDURES

Forms required: FAFSA, state aid form, institutional form.
Dates and Deadlines: Priority date 8/1; no closing date. Applicants notified on a rolling basis.
Transfers: No deadline. Applicants notified on a rolling basis.

CONTACT

Don Compton, Financial Aid Officer
105 B.J. Albritton Drive, Jacksonville, TX 75766-4759
(903) 586-2518 ext. 7135

Jarvis Christian College

Hawkins, Texas
www.jarvis.edu Federal Code: 003637

4-year private liberal arts and teachers college in rural community, affiliated with Christian Church (Disciples of Christ).
Enrollment: 695 undergrads. 144 full-time freshmen.
Selectivity: Open admission.

BASIC COSTS (2009-2010)

Tuition and fees: $8,208.
Room and board: $5,078.

FINANCIAL AID PICTURE (2007-2008)

Students with need: Out of 144 full-time freshmen who applied for aid, 144 were judged to have need. Of these, 144 received aid, and 132 had their full need met. Need-based aid available for part-time students.
Students without need: This college awards aid only to students with need.
Scholarships offered: 15 full-time freshmen received athletic scholarships.
Additional info: High school transcript required for scholarship consideration.

FINANCIAL AID PROCEDURES

Forms required: FAFSA, state aid form.
Dates and Deadlines: Priority date 6/30; closing date 1/3. Applicants notified on a rolling basis starting 5/1; must reply within 2 week(s) of notification.
Transfers: Priority date 4/15; no deadline. Applicants notified on a rolling basis starting 7/1; must reply within 2 week(s) of notification.

CONTACT

Harriett Harris, Director of Admission and Financial Aid
PO Box 1470, Hawkins, TX 75765-1470
(903) 769-5741

Kilgore College
Kilgore, Texas
www.kilgore.edu Federal Code: 003580

2-year public community college in large town.
Enrollment: 5,513 undergrads, 52% part-time. 888 full-time freshmen.
Selectivity: Open admission; but selective for some programs.

BASIC COSTS (2008-2009)
Tuition and fees: $1,320; out-of-district residents $2,790; out-of-state residents $3,810.
Per-credit charge: $22; out-of-district residents $71; out-of-state residents $105.
Room and board: $3,630.
Additional info: Tuition/fee waivers available for unemployed or children of unemployed.

FINANCIAL AID PICTURE (2007-2008)
Students with need: Need-based aid available for full-time and part-time students.
Students without need: No-need awards available for academics, alumni affiliation, art, athletics, job skills, leadership, music/drama, state/district residency.
Scholarships offered: Presidential Scholarships: tuition, fees and books for 4 semesters; ACT 25 or top 10% of senior class; 20 available; renewable at 2.5 GPA.
Additional info: State of Texas grants and loans available for honor graduates with unmet needs and for non-traditional students.

FINANCIAL AID PROCEDURES
Forms required: FAFSA, state aid form, institutional form.
Dates and Deadlines: Priority date 6/1; closing date 7/15. Applicants notified on a rolling basis starting 3/1; must reply within 2 week(s) of notification.
Transfers: No deadline. Transfer students must submit financial aid transcript from previous school plus all appropriate internal aid forms and show proof of high school graduation or GED.

CONTACT
Annette Morgan, Director of Financial Aid
1100 Broadway, Kilgore, TX 75662-3299
(903) 983-8183

Lamar Institute of Technology
Beaumont, Texas
www.lit.edu Federal Code: 036273

2-year public technical college in small city.
Enrollment: 2,718 undergrads.
Selectivity: Open admission; but selective for some programs.

BASIC COSTS (2008-2009)
Tuition and fees: $3,810; out-of-state residents $12,090.
Per-credit charge: $86; out-of-state residents $362.

FINANCIAL AID PICTURE (2008-2009)
Students with need: 67% of average financial aid package awarded as scholarships/grants, 33% awarded as loans/jobs.

FINANCIAL AID PROCEDURES
Dates and Deadlines: Priority date 4/1; no closing date.

CONTACT
Lisa Schroeder, Director, Student Financial Aid
PO Box 10043, Beaumont, TX 77705
(409) 880-2137

Lamar State College at Orange
Orange, Texas
www.lsco.edu Federal Code: 016748

2-year public junior and liberal arts college in small city.
Enrollment: 1,823 undergrads, 44% part-time. 321 full-time freshmen.
Selectivity: Open admission; but selective for some programs.

BASIC COSTS (2008-2009)
Tuition and fees: $3,400; out-of-state residents $11,830.
Per-credit charge: $84; out-of-state residents $365.

FINANCIAL AID PICTURE (2007-2008)
Students with need: Need-based aid available for full-time and part-time students.
Students without need: This college awards aid only to students with need.

FINANCIAL AID PROCEDURES
Forms required: FAFSA, institutional form.
Dates and Deadlines: Priority date 4/1; no closing date. Applicants notified on a rolling basis starting 5/15; must reply within 2 week(s) of notification.

CONTACT
Kerry Olson, Director of Financial Aid
410 Front Street, Orange, TX 77630
(409) 882-3317

Lamar State College at Port Arthur
Port Arthur, Texas
www.lamarpa.edu Federal Code: 016666

2-year public community and technical college in small city.
Enrollment: 1,985 undergrads.
Selectivity: Open admission; but selective for some programs.

BASIC COSTS (2008-2009)
Tuition and fees: $4,117; out-of-state residents $12,547.

FINANCIAL AID PICTURE
Students with need: Need-based aid available for full-time and part-time students. Work study available nights, weekends, and for part-time students.
Students without need: This college awards aid only to students with need.

FINANCIAL AID PROCEDURES
Forms required: FAFSA, institutional form.
Dates and Deadlines: Priority date 4/1; no closing date. Applicants notified on a rolling basis starting 4/15; must reply within 2 week(s) of notification.

CONTACT
Diane Hargett, Director of Financial Aid
Box 310, Port Arthur, TX 77641-0310
(409) 984-6203

Lamar University
Beaumont, Texas
www.lamar.edu Federal Code: 003581

4-year public university in small city.
Enrollment: 8,429 undergrads, 25% part-time. 1,382 full-time freshmen.
Selectivity: Admits over 75% of applicants.

BASIC COSTS (2008-2009)
Tuition and fees: $6,014; out-of-state residents $14,444.
Per-credit charge: $145; out-of-state residents $426.

Room and board: $6,290.

FINANCIAL AID PICTURE (2008-2009)

Students with need: Out of 1,009 full-time freshmen who applied for aid, 636 were judged to have need. Of these, 636 received aid, and 109 had their full need met. Average financial aid package met 51% of need. For part-time students, average financial aid package was $10,650.

Students without need: This college awards aid only to students with need.

FINANCIAL AID PROCEDURES

Forms required: FAFSA, institutional form.

Dates and Deadlines: Priority date 4/1; no closing date. Applicants notified on a rolling basis starting 4/1; must reply within 2 week(s) of notification.

CONTACT

Jill Rowley, Director of Financial Aid
Box 10009, Beaumont, TX 77705
(409) 880-8450

Lee College

Baytown, Texas
www.lee.edu Federal Code: 003583

2-year public community college in small city.

Enrollment: 5,841 undergrads.

Selectivity: Open admission; but selective for some programs.

BASIC COSTS (2008-2009)

Tuition and fees: $1,302; out-of-district residents $2,052; out-of-state residents $3,102.

Per-credit charge: $25; out-of-district residents $50; out-of-state residents $85.

FINANCIAL AID PICTURE

Students with need: Need-based aid available for full-time and part-time students.

Students without need: No-need awards available for academics, art, athletics, job skills, music/drama.

FINANCIAL AID PROCEDURES

Forms required: FAFSA.

Dates and Deadlines: Priority date 4/1; no closing date. Applicants notified on a rolling basis starting 6/1.

CONTACT

Sharon Mullins, Financial Aid Officer
Box 818, Baytown, TX 77522
(281) 425-6362

LeTourneau University

Longview, Texas
www.letu.edu Federal Code: 003584

4-year private university in small city, affiliated with nondenominational tradition.

Enrollment: 3,296 undergrads, 8% part-time. 341 full-time freshmen.

Selectivity: Admits 50 to 75% of applicants.

BASIC COSTS (2008-2009)

Tuition and fees: $19,140.

Room and board: $7,500.

Additional info: Tuition for 1-6 hours is $344 per credit, for 7-11 hours is $756 per credit.

FINANCIAL AID PICTURE (2007-2008)

Students with need: Need-based aid available for full-time and part-time students. Work study available nights, weekends, and for part-time students.

Students without need: No-need awards available for academics, leadership.

Scholarships offered: Freshmen scholarships: Honors Scholarship, $6,000 per year; Dean's Scholarship: $8,000 per year; Presidential: $9,000 per year; based on SAT and/or ACT scores and cumulative high school GPA.

FINANCIAL AID PROCEDURES

Forms required: FAFSA.

Dates and Deadlines: Priority date 2/15; no closing date. Applicants notified on a rolling basis starting 3/1; must reply within 3 week(s) of notification.

CONTACT

Delinda Hall, Senior Director of Enrollment Services and Financial Aid
PO Box 7001, Longview, TX 75607-7001
(903) 233-4350

Lon Morris College

Jacksonville, Texas
www.lonmorris.edu Federal Code: 003585

2-year private junior and liberal arts college in large town, affiliated with United Methodist Church.

Enrollment: 340 undergrads.

BASIC COSTS (2008-2009)

Tuition and fees: $13,500.

Room and board: $6,130.

FINANCIAL AID PICTURE (2008-2009)

Students with need: Need-based aid available for full-time and part-time students. Work study available nights, weekends, and for part-time students.

Students without need: This college awards aid only to students with need.

FINANCIAL AID PROCEDURES

Forms required: FAFSA, state aid form, institutional form.

Dates and Deadlines: Priority date 5/1; no closing date. Applicants notified on a rolling basis starting 2/15; must reply within 2 week(s) of notification.

CONTACT

Kris Marquis, Financial Aid Director
800 College Avenue, Jacksonville, TX 75766
(903) 589-4061

Lone Star College System

The Woodlands, Texas
www.nhmccd.edu Federal Code: 011145

2-year public community college in very large city.

Enrollment: 51,718 undergrads.

Selectivity: Open admission; but selective for some programs.

BASIC COSTS (2008-2009)

Tuition and fees: $1,360; out-of-district residents $2,860; out-of-state residents $3,310.

Per-credit charge: $36; out-of-district residents $86; out-of-state residents $101.

FINANCIAL AID PICTURE (2007-2008)

Students with need: Need-based aid available for full-time and part-time students. Work study available nights, weekends, and for part-time students.

Students without need: No-need awards available for academics.

FINANCIAL AID PROCEDURES

Forms required: FAFSA, institutional form.

Dates and Deadlines: Priority date 4/1; no closing date. Applicants notified on a rolling basis starting 4/1.

CONTACT

Jason Kot, District Director of Financial Aid
5000 Research Forest Drive, The Woodlands, TX 77381-4356
(832) 813-6607

Lubbock Christian University

Lubbock, Texas
www.lcu.edu Federal Code: 003586

4-year private university and liberal arts college in small city, affiliated with Church of Christ.

Enrollment: 1,564 undergrads, 18% part-time. 305 full-time freshmen.

Selectivity: Admits 50 to 75% of applicants.

BASIC COSTS (2009-2010)

Tuition and fees: $15,280.

Per-credit charge: $470.

Room and board: $4,956.

FINANCIAL AID PICTURE (2007-2008)

Students with need: Out of 222 full-time freshmen who applied for aid, 192 were judged to have need. Of these, 192 received aid, and 24 had their full need met. Average financial aid package met 74% of need; average scholarship/grant was $7,949; average loan was $3,465. For part-time students, average financial aid package was $6,027.

Students without need: 53 full-time freshmen who did not demonstrate need for aid received scholarships/grants; average award was $9,124. No-need awards available for academics, athletics, job skills, leadership, music/drama.

Scholarships offered: 24 full-time freshmen received athletic scholarships; average amount $5,237.

Cumulative student debt: 81% of graduating class had student loans; average debt was $25,352.

FINANCIAL AID PROCEDURES

Forms required: FAFSA, institutional form.

Dates and Deadlines: Priority date 6/1; no closing date. Applicants notified on a rolling basis starting 3/1.

Transfers: No deadline. Applicants notified on a rolling basis.

CONTACT

Amy Hardesty, Director, Financial Assistance
5601 19th Street, Lubbock, TX 79407
(806) 720-7176

McLennan Community College

Waco, Texas
www.mclennan.edu Federal Code: 003590

2-year public community and junior college in small city.

Enrollment: 7,899 undergrads.

Selectivity: Open admission; but selective for some programs.

BASIC COSTS (2008-2009)

Tuition and fees: $2,100; out-of-district residents $2,460; out-of-state residents $3,900.

Per-credit charge: $61; out-of-district residents $73; out-of-state residents $121.

FINANCIAL AID PICTURE (2007-2008)

Students with need: 57% of average financial aid package awarded as scholarships/grants, 43% awarded as loans/jobs. Need-based aid available for part-time students.

Students without need: No-need awards available for athletics.

Scholarships offered: Academic scholarship: awarded to individuals selected for Tartan scholar's program.

FINANCIAL AID PROCEDURES

Forms required: FAFSA.

Dates and Deadlines: Priority date 6/1; no closing date. Applicants notified on a rolling basis starting 5/1.

CONTACT

James Kubacak, Director of Financial Aid
1400 College Drive, Waco, TX 76708
(254) 299-8698

McMurry University

Abilene, Texas
www.mcm.edu Federal Code: 003591

4-year private university and liberal arts college in small city, affiliated with United Methodist Church.

Enrollment: 1,383 undergrads, 13% part-time. 332 full-time freshmen.

Selectivity: Admits 50 to 75% of applicants.

BASIC COSTS (2008-2009)

Tuition and fees: $18,135.

Per-credit charge: $535.

Room and board: $6,657.

FINANCIAL AID PICTURE (2008-2009)

Students with need: Out of 313 full-time freshmen who applied for aid, 282 were judged to have need. Of these, 282 received aid, and 55 had their full need met. Average financial aid package met 92% of need; average scholarship/grant was $11,389; average loan was $3,165. For part-time students, average financial aid package was $6,326.

Students without need: 300 full-time freshmen who did not demonstrate need for aid received scholarships/grants; average award was $6,650. No-need awards available for academics, alumni affiliation, art, music/drama, religious affiliation.

Cumulative student debt: 83% of graduating class had student loans; average debt was $25,338.

FINANCIAL AID PROCEDURES

Forms required: FAFSA.

Dates and Deadlines: Priority date 3/15; no closing date. Applicants notified on a rolling basis starting 2/1; must reply within 3 week(s) of notification.

Transfers: No deadline. Applicants notified on a rolling basis starting 2/1; must reply by 6/30.

CONTACT

Rachel Atkins, Director of Financial Aid
South 14th and Sayles Boulevard, Abilene, TX 79697-0001
(325) 793-4713

Midland College

Midland, Texas
www.midland.edu Federal Code: 009797

2-year public community college in small city.

Enrollment: 3,509 undergrads.

Selectivity: Open admission; but selective for some programs.

BASIC COSTS (2008-2009)
Tuition and fees: $1,710; out-of-district residents $2,310; out-of-state residents $3,240.
Per-credit charge: $43; out-of-district residents $63; out-of-state residents $94.
Room and board: $3,900.
Additional info: Additional $48 charge per credit hour for baccalaureate program.

FINANCIAL AID PICTURE (2007-2008)
Students with need: 92% of average financial aid package awarded as scholarships/grants, 8% awarded as loans/jobs. Need-based aid available for part-time students.
Students without need: No-need awards available for academics, athletics, minority status, music/drama, state/district residency.
Scholarships offered: Abell-Hangar Foundations Scholarships: varying amounts; renewable; available for full-time or part-time study to any Midland High, Midland Lee, or Greenwood High School graduate.

FINANCIAL AID PROCEDURES
Forms required: FAFSA.
Dates and Deadlines: Priority date 4/2; closing date 6/1. Applicants notified on a rolling basis starting 5/15; must reply within 2 week(s) of notification.
Transfers: No deadline.

CONTACT
Latisha Williams, Director of Financial Aid
3600 North Garfield, Midland, TX 79705
(432) 685-4733

Midwestern State University
Wichita Falls, Texas
www.mwsu.edu Federal Code: 003592

4-year public university and liberal arts college in small city.
Enrollment: 5,360 undergrads, 26% part-time. 685 full-time freshmen.
Selectivity: Admits 50 to 75% of applicants.

BASIC COSTS (2008-2009)
Tuition and fees: $5,918; out-of-state residents $6,818.
Per-credit charge: $50; out-of-state residents $80.
Room and board: $5,600.

FINANCIAL AID PICTURE (2008-2009)
Students with need: Out of 453 full-time freshmen who applied for aid, 301 were judged to have need. Of these, 300 received aid, and 93 had their full need met. Average financial aid package met 75% of need; average scholarship/grant was $6,178; average loan was $5,783. For part-time students, average financial aid package was $5,364.
Students without need: 122 full-time freshmen who did not demonstrate need for aid received scholarships/grants; average award was $2,652. No-need awards available for academics, alumni affiliation, art, athletics, leadership, music/drama.
Scholarships offered: 22 full-time freshmen received athletic scholarships; average amount $4,290.
Cumulative student debt: 59% of graduating class had student loans; average debt was $19,645.
Additional info: Employees offered educational incentive plan in which tuition reimbursed provided employee meets stated criteria. Additionally, dependents and children of faculty and staff may receive scholarship to defer local tuition and fees.

FINANCIAL AID PROCEDURES
Forms required: FAFSA.
Dates and Deadlines: Priority date 5/1; no closing date. Applicants notified on a rolling basis starting 4/1; must reply within 4 week(s) of notification.
Transfers: No deadline. Applicants notified on a rolling basis starting 3/15.

CONTACT
Kathy Pennartz, Director of Financial Aid
3410 Taft Boulevard, Wichita Falls, TX 76308-2099
(940) 397-4119

North Central Texas College
Gainesville, Texas
www.nctc.edu Federal Code: 003558

2-year public community college in large town.
Enrollment: 7,444 undergrads.
Selectivity: Open admission; but selective for some programs.

BASIC COSTS (2008-2009)
Tuition and fees: $1,350; out-of-district residents $2,310; out-of-state residents $3,450.
Per-credit charge: $35; out-of-district residents $67; out-of-state residents $105.
Room and board: $3,528.

FINANCIAL AID PICTURE
Students with need: Need-based aid available for full-time and part-time students. Work study available nights.
Students without need: This college awards aid only to students with need.

FINANCIAL AID PROCEDURES
Forms required: FAFSA.
Dates and Deadlines: Priority date 5/1; no closing date. Applicants notified on a rolling basis starting 6/1; must reply within 4 week(s) of notification.

CONTACT
Ashley Tatum, Director of Financial Aid
1525 West California Street, Gainesville, TX 76240

North Lake College
Irving, Texas
www.northlakecollege.edu Federal Code: 014036

2-year public community and liberal arts college in small city.
Enrollment: 7,985 undergrads.
Selectivity: Open admission.

BASIC COSTS (2008-2009)
Tuition and fees: $1,170; out-of-district residents $2,160; out-of-state residents $3,450.
Per-credit charge: $39; out-of-district residents $72.

FINANCIAL AID PICTURE
Students with need: Need-based aid available for full-time and part-time students.
Students without need: No-need awards available for academics, minority status, state/district residency.

FINANCIAL AID PROCEDURES
Forms required: FAFSA, state aid form.
Dates and Deadlines: Priority date 3/1; closing date 5/1. Applicants notified on a rolling basis starting 7/1.
Transfers: Applicants notified on a rolling basis starting 8/1.

CONTACT
Paul Felix, Director of Financial Aid
5001 North MacArthur Boulevard, Irving, TX 75038-3899
(972) 273-3321

Northwest Vista College

San Antonio, Texas
www.accd.edu/nvc Federal Code: 033723

2-year public community college in very large city.
Enrollment: 11,961 undergrads.
Selectivity: Open admission.

BASIC COSTS (2008-2009)

Tuition and fees: $1,772; out-of-district residents $3,092; out-of-state residents $5,732.

FINANCIAL AID PICTURE

Students with need: Need-based aid available for full-time and part-time students. Work study available nights, weekends, and for part-time students.
Students without need: No-need awards available for academics, leadership.

FINANCIAL AID PROCEDURES

Forms required: FAFSA.
Dates and Deadlines: Priority date 4/1; no closing date. Applicants notified on a rolling basis starting 5/15; must reply within 2 week(s) of notification.

CONTACT

Noe Ortiz, Financial Aid Director
3535 North Ellison Drive, San Antonio, TX 78251-4217
(210) 486-4168

Northwood University: Texas

Cedar Hill, Texas
www.northwood.edu Federal Code: 013040

4-year private university and business college in large town.
Enrollment: 461 undergrads, 5% part-time. 89 full-time freshmen.
Selectivity: Admits 50 to 75% of applicants.

BASIC COSTS (2008-2009)

Tuition and fees: $18,468.
Per-credit charge: $346.
Room and board: $7,506.

FINANCIAL AID PICTURE (2008-2009)

Students with need: Out of 80 full-time freshmen who applied for aid, 73 were judged to have need. Of these, 73 received aid, and 13 had their full need met. Average financial aid package met 64% of need; average scholarship/grant was $6,098; average loan was $3,344. For part-time students, average financial aid package was $6,370.
Students without need: 7 full-time freshmen who did not demonstrate need for aid received scholarships/grants; average award was $6,000. No-need awards available for academics, alumni affiliation, athletics, leadership, minority status, state/district residency.
Scholarships offered: ***Merit:*** Academic Scholarships: $4,000-$9,000; based on test scores and GPA; unlimited number awarded. ***Athletic:*** 5 full-time freshmen received athletic scholarships; average amount $4,200.
Cumulative student debt: 83% of graduating class had student loans; average debt was $22,820.

FINANCIAL AID PROCEDURES

Forms required: FAFSA.
Dates and Deadlines: No deadline. Applicants notified on a rolling basis starting 3/1.
Transfers: No deadline. Applicants notified on a rolling basis.

CONTACT

Lisa Seals, Director of Financial Aid
1114 West FM 1382, Cedar Hill, TX 75104
(972) 293-5430

Odessa College

Odessa, Texas
www.odessa.edu Federal Code: 003596

2-year public community college in small city.
Enrollment: 3,177 undergrads, 66% part-time. 383 full-time freshmen.
Selectivity: Open admission; but selective for some programs.

BASIC COSTS (2009-2010)

Tuition and fees: $1,740; out-of-district residents $2,340; out-of-state residents $3,240.
Room and board: $4,687.

FINANCIAL AID PICTURE (2007-2008)

Students with need: Need-based aid available for full-time and part-time students. Work study available nights.
Students without need: No-need awards available for academics, athletics, music/drama.

FINANCIAL AID PROCEDURES

Forms required: FAFSA.
Dates and Deadlines: Priority date 5/1; no closing date. Applicants notified on a rolling basis starting 6/15.

CONTACT

Dee Nesmith, Director of Student Financial Aid
201 West University, Odessa, TX 79764-7127
(432) 335-6429

Our Lady of the Lake University of San Antonio

San Antonio, Texas
www.ollusa.edu Federal Code: 003598

4-year private university in very large city, affiliated with Roman Catholic Church.
Enrollment: 1,546 undergrads, 26% part-time. 306 full-time freshmen.
Selectivity: Admits 50 to 75% of applicants.

BASIC COSTS (2009-2010)

Tuition and fees: $20,824.
Per-credit charge: $659.
Room and board: $6,541.

FINANCIAL AID PICTURE (2008-2009)

Students with need: 47% of average financial aid package awarded as scholarships/grants, 53% awarded as loans/jobs. Need-based aid available for part-time students. Work study available nights, weekends, and for part-time students.
Students without need: No-need awards available for academics, alumni affiliation, art, music/drama.
Scholarships offered: General academic scholarship: $1,205 awarded yearly, renewable. Art/fine arts and music: 4 awarded yearly, renewable. Children of faculty/staff: 60 awarded yearly, renewable. All based on GPA scores and high school record.

FINANCIAL AID PROCEDURES

Forms required: FAFSA.
Dates and Deadlines: Priority date 2/28; no closing date. Applicants notified on a rolling basis starting 4/1; must reply within 2 week(s) of notification.

CONTACT

Michael Fuller, Director of Financial Aid
411 Southwest 24th Street, San Antonio, TX 78207-4689
(210) 434-6711 ext. 2541

Palo Alto College
San Antonio, Texas
www.accd.edu/pac Federal Code: 016615

2-year public community college in very large city.
Enrollment: 7,880 undergrads.
Selectivity: Open admission.

BASIC COSTS (2008-2009)
Tuition and fees: $1,802; out-of-district residents $3,122; out-of-state residents $5,762.

FINANCIAL AID PICTURE (2007-2008)
Students with need: 81% of average financial aid package awarded as scholarships/grants, 19% awarded as loans/jobs. Need-based aid available for part-time students.
Students without need: This college awards aid only to students with need.
Scholarships offered: Alamo Community College District Scholarship: $1,000; 50 awarded.

FINANCIAL AID PROCEDURES
Forms required: FAFSA, state aid form.
Dates and Deadlines: Priority date 4/1; closing date 6/1. Applicants notified on a rolling basis starting 5/31.

CONTACT
Lamar Duarte, Director of Financial Aid
1400 West Villaret Boulevard, San Antonio, TX 78224-2499
(210) 921-5316

Panola College
Carthage, Texas
www.panola.edu Federal Code: 003600

2-year public community and junior college in small town.
Enrollment: 1,985 undergrads, 52% part-time. 318 full-time freshmen.
Selectivity: Open admission; but selective for some programs.

BASIC COSTS (2008-2009)
Tuition and fees: $1,620; out-of-district residents $2,490; out-of-state residents $3,210.
Room and board: $4,160.

FINANCIAL AID PICTURE (2007-2008)
Students with need: 96% of average financial aid package awarded as scholarships/grants, 4% awarded as loans/jobs. Need-based aid available for part-time students. Work study available nights, weekends, and for part-time students.
Students without need: No-need awards available for academics, alumni affiliation, art, athletics, leadership, music/drama.
Scholarships offered: Several departmental and organization-sponsored scholarships, Presidential scholarship, Dean's scholarship.

FINANCIAL AID PROCEDURES
Forms required: FAFSA, institutional form.
Dates and Deadlines: Priority date 6/1; no closing date. Applicants notified on a rolling basis starting 6/1.
Transfers: No deadline. Applicants notified on a rolling basis.

CONTACT
Denise Welch, Director of Financial Aid
1109 West Panola Street, Carthage, TX 75633
(903) 693-2039

Paris Junior College
Paris, Texas
www.parisjc.edu Federal Code: 003601

2-year public community and junior college in large town.
Enrollment: 4,733 undergrads, 60% part-time. 648 full-time freshmen.
Selectivity: Open admission; but selective for some programs.

BASIC COSTS (2008-2009)
Tuition and fees: $1,350; out-of-district residents $2,250; out-of-state residents $3,450.
Room and board: $4,132.

FINANCIAL AID PICTURE (2007-2008)
Students with need: Need-based aid available for full-time and part-time students.
Students without need: No-need awards available for athletics, music/drama.

FINANCIAL AID PROCEDURES
Forms required: FAFSA.
Dates and Deadlines: No deadline. Applicants notified on a rolling basis starting 6/1.

CONTACT
Linda Slawson, Director of Financial Aid
2400 Clarksville Street, Paris, TX 75460
(903) 782-0256

Prairie View A&M University
Prairie View, Texas
www.pvamu.edu Federal Code: 003630

4-year public university in small town.
Enrollment: 6,178 undergrads, 8% part-time. 1,291 full-time freshmen.
Selectivity: Admits 50 to 75% of applicants.

BASIC COSTS (2009-2010)
Tuition and fees: $7,199; out-of-state residents $15,689.
Room and board: $7,445.

FINANCIAL AID PICTURE (2008-2009)
Students with need: 53% of average financial aid package awarded as scholarships/grants, 47% awarded as loans/jobs. Need-based aid available for part-time students. Work study available nights, weekends, and for part-time students.
Students without need: No-need awards available for academics, athletics, ROTC.

FINANCIAL AID PROCEDURES
Forms required: FAFSA, institutional form.
Dates and Deadlines: Closing date 3/15. Applicants notified by 6/1; must reply by 8/1.
Transfers: Closing date 3/1. Minimum 2.0 GPA from all colleges attended required to be considered for financial aid.

CONTACT
Carlos Clark, Director of Financial Aid
PO Box 519, MS 1009, Prairie View, TX 77446-0519

Ranger College
Ranger, Texas
www.rangercollege.edu Federal Code: 003603

2-year public junior college in rural community.
Enrollment: 776 undergrads.

Selectivity: Open admission; but selective for some programs.

BASIC COSTS (2008-2009)

Tuition and fees: $2,252; out-of-state residents $2,432.
Room and board: $3,452.

FINANCIAL AID PICTURE (2007-2008)

Students with need: Need-based aid available for full-time and part-time students.
Students without need: This college awards aid only to students with need.

FINANCIAL AID PROCEDURES

Forms required: FAFSA.
Dates and Deadlines: Priority date 6/1; closing date 7/24. Applicants notified on a rolling basis; must reply within 2 week(s) of notification.
Transfers: Applicants notified on a rolling basis; must reply within 2 week(s) of notification.

CONTACT

Sharon King, Financial Aid Director
1100 College Circle, Ranger, TX 76470
(254) 647-3234 ext. 117

Rice University

Houston, Texas — Federal Code: 003604
www.rice.edu — CSS Code: 6609

4-year private university in very large city.
Enrollment: 3,102 undergrads, 1% part-time. 789 full-time freshmen.
Selectivity: Admits less than 50% of applicants.

BASIC COSTS (2009-2010)

Tuition and fees: $32,105.
Per-credit charge: $1,310.
Room and board: $11,230.

FINANCIAL AID PICTURE (2008-2009)

Students with need: Out of 679 full-time freshmen who applied for aid, 275 were judged to have need. Of these, 275 received aid, and 275 had their full need met. Average financial aid package met 100% of need; average scholarship/grant was $28,392; average loan was $896. Need-based aid available for part-time students.
Students without need: 93 full-time freshmen who did not demonstrate need for aid received scholarships/grants; average award was $9,589. No-need awards available for academics, art, athletics, leadership, minority status, music/drama, ROTC, state/district residency.
Scholarships offered: 56 full-time freshmen received athletic scholarships; average amount $16,276.
Cumulative student debt: 42% of graduating class had student loans; average debt was $11,108.

FINANCIAL AID PROCEDURES

Forms required: FAFSA, CSS PROFILE.
Dates and Deadlines: Priority date 3/1; no closing date. Applicants notified by 4/1; must reply by 5/1.
Transfers: Priority date 4/1.

CONTACT

Anne Walker, Director of Student Financial Services
6100 Main Street, Houston, TX 77251-1892
(713) 348-4958

Richland College

Dallas, Texas
www.rlc.dcccd.edu — Federal Code: 008504

2-year public community college in very large city.
Enrollment: 12,177 undergrads.
Selectivity: Open admission.

BASIC COSTS (2008-2009)

Tuition and fees: $1,170; out-of-district residents $2,160; out-of-state residents $3,450.
Per-credit charge: $39; out-of-district residents $72.

FINANCIAL AID PICTURE (2008-2009)

Students with need: 68% of average financial aid package awarded as scholarships/grants, 32% awarded as loans/jobs. Need-based aid available for part-time students. Work study available nights.
Students without need: No-need awards available for art, leadership, music/drama.

FINANCIAL AID PROCEDURES

Forms required: FAFSA.
Dates and Deadlines: Priority date 5/2; closing date 7/31. Applicants notified on a rolling basis starting 6/1; must reply within 2 week(s) of notification.

CONTACT

Michael Williams, Director of Financial Aid
12800 Abrams Road, Dallas, TX 75243-2199
(972) 238-6188

St. Edward's University

Austin, Texas
www.gotostedwards.com — Federal Code: 003621

4-year private university and liberal arts college in very large city, affiliated with Roman Catholic Church.
Enrollment: 4,341 undergrads, 21% part-time. 742 full-time freshmen.
Selectivity: Admits 50 to 75% of applicants.

BASIC COSTS (2009-2010)

Tuition and fees: $24,440.
Per-credit charge: $805.
Room and board: $8,496.

FINANCIAL AID PICTURE (2008-2009)

Students with need: Out of 586 full-time freshmen who applied for aid, 475 were judged to have need. Of these, 475 received aid, and 76 had their full need met. Average financial aid package met 75% of need; average scholarship/grant was $12,160; average loan was $3,232. For part-time students, average financial aid package was $6,241.
Students without need: 75 full-time freshmen who did not demonstrate need for aid received scholarships/grants; average award was $7,920. No-need awards available for academics, art, athletics, leadership, music/drama, state/district residency.
Scholarships offered: ***Merit:*** Trustees' Scholar Award: $9,000 per year; have minimum 1200 SAT; be in top 20% of class. Holy Cross Scholar Award: full tuition; have minimum 1250 SAT; be in top 10% of class; show superior leadership and service. Academic Scholar Award: $5,000 per year; have minimum 1100 SAT; be in top 25% of class. All SAT scores exclusive of Writing. ***Athletic:*** 34 full-time freshmen received athletic scholarships; average amount $14,707.
Cumulative student debt: 72% of graduating class had student loans; average debt was $27,093.

FINANCIAL AID PROCEDURES

Forms required: FAFSA.

Dates and Deadlines: Priority date 3/1; closing date 4/15. Applicants notified on a rolling basis starting 1/15; must reply by 5/1 or within 2 week(s) of notification.
Transfers: Must reply by 5/1 or within 2 week(s) of notification.

CONTACT
Doris Constantine, Associate VP and Director of Student Financial Services
3001 South Congress Avenue, Austin, TX 78704-6489
(512) 448-8520

St. Mary's University
San Antonio, Texas
www.stmarytx.edu Federal Code: 003623

4-year private university in very large city, affiliated with Roman Catholic Church.
Enrollment: 2,360 undergrads, 7% part-time. 565 full-time freshmen.
Selectivity: Admits 50 to 75% of applicants.

BASIC COSTS (2008-2009)
Tuition and fees: $21,156.
Per-credit charge: $640.
Room and board: $6,892.
Additional info: Notebook computer $1,000.

FINANCIAL AID PICTURE (2007-2008)
Students with need: Out of 508 full-time freshmen who applied for aid, 445 were judged to have need. Of these, 445 received aid, and 39 had their full need met. Average financial aid package met 83% of need; average scholarship/grant was $15,952; average loan was $4,315. For part-time students, average financial aid package was $12,567.
Students without need: 118 full-time freshmen who did not demonstrate need for aid received scholarships/grants; average award was $10,210. No-need awards available for academics, alumni affiliation, athletics, leadership, music/drama, ROTC.
Scholarships offered: 32 full-time freshmen received athletic scholarships; average amount $8,564.
Cumulative student debt: 86% of graduating class had student loans; average debt was $22,000.

FINANCIAL AID PROCEDURES
Forms required: FAFSA.
Dates and Deadlines: Priority date 2/15; no closing date. Applicants notified on a rolling basis starting 3/1; must reply by 5/1 or within 2 week(s) of notification.

CONTACT
David Krause, Director of Financial Assistance
One Camino Santa Maria, San Antonio, TX 78228-8503
(210) 436-3141

St. Philip's College
San Antonio, Texas
www.accd.edu/spc Federal Code: 003608

2-year public community college in very large city.
Enrollment: 7,617 undergrads, 63% part-time. 851 full-time freshmen.
Selectivity: Open admission; but selective for some programs.

BASIC COSTS (2008-2009)
Tuition and fees: $1,802; out-of-district residents $3,122; out-of-state residents $5,762.
Per-credit charge: $51; out-of-district residents $95; out-of-state residents $183.

FINANCIAL AID PICTURE (2007-2008)
Students with need: 70% of average financial aid package awarded as scholarships/grants, 30% awarded as loans/jobs. Need-based aid available for part-time students. Work study available nights, weekends, and for part-time students.
Students without need: This college awards aid only to students with need.

FINANCIAL AID PROCEDURES
Forms required: FAFSA.
Dates and Deadlines: No deadline.

CONTACT
Diego Bernal, Director of Financial Aid
1801 Martin Luther King Drive, San Antonio, TX 78203
(210) 486-2275

Sam Houston State University
Huntsville, Texas
www.shsu.edu Federal Code: 003606

4-year public university in large town.
Enrollment: 14,303 undergrads, 16% part-time. 2,090 full-time freshmen.
Selectivity: Admits 50 to 75% of applicants.

BASIC COSTS (2008-2009)
Tuition and fees: $5,910; out-of-state residents $14,250.
Per-credit charge: $148; out-of-state residents $429.
Room and board: $6,046.

FINANCIAL AID PICTURE (2007-2008)
Students with need: 47% of average financial aid package awarded as scholarships/grants, 53% awarded as loans/jobs. Need-based aid available for part-time students.
Students without need: No-need awards available for academics, athletics, ROTC.

FINANCIAL AID PROCEDURES
Forms required: FAFSA, institutional form.
Dates and Deadlines: Priority date 3/31; closing date 5/31. Applicants notified on a rolling basis starting 5/1; must reply within 4 week(s) of notification.

CONTACT
Randal Lewis, Vice President for Finance & Operations
Box 2418, Huntsville, TX 77341-2418
(936) 294-1774

San Antonio College
San Antonio, Texas
www.accd.edu/sac Federal Code: 009163

2-year public community college in very large city.
Enrollment: 21,766 undergrads.
Selectivity: Open admission; but selective for some programs.

BASIC COSTS (2008-2009)
Tuition and fees: $1,666; out-of-district residents $2,986; out-of-state residents $5,626.
Per-credit charge: $51; out-of-district residents $95; out-of-state residents $183.

FINANCIAL AID PICTURE (2007-2008)
Students with need: Need-based aid available for full-time and part-time students. Work study available nights, weekends, and for part-time students.
Students without need: This college awards aid only to students with need.

Additional info: Leveraging Educational Assistance Partnership (LEAP), public student incentive grant, towards excellence access and success grants (Texas and Texas II grants) available.

FINANCIAL AID PROCEDURES

Forms required: FAFSA.

Dates and Deadlines: Priority date 3/1; no closing date. Applicants notified by 7/1.

CONTACT

Tom Campos, Director of Student Financial Services
1300 San Pedro Avenue, San Antonio, TX 78212-4299
(210) 486-0600

San Jacinto College

Pasadena, Texas
www.sanjac.edu

2-year public community and technical college in very large city.

Enrollment: 24,635 undergrads, 61% part-time. 4,043 full-time freshmen.

Selectivity: Open admission; but selective for some programs.

BASIC COSTS (2009-2010)

Tuition and fees: $1,376; out-of-district residents $2,176; out-of-state residents $3,776.

Per-credit charge: $33; out-of-district residents $58; out-of-state residents $108.

FINANCIAL AID PICTURE (2007-2008)

Students with need: Out of 1,817 full-time freshmen who applied for aid, 1,615 were judged to have need. Of these, 916 received aid, and 8 had their full need met. For part-time students, average financial aid package was $1,512.

Students without need: This college awards aid only to students with need.

Scholarships offered: 37 full-time freshmen received athletic scholarships; average amount $2,493.

FINANCIAL AID PROCEDURES

Forms required: FAFSA, institutional form.

Dates and Deadlines: Priority date 7/1; no closing date. Applicants notified on a rolling basis starting 4/1; must reply within 4 week(s) of notification.

Transfers: Applicants notified on a rolling basis starting 4/1; must reply within 4 week(s) of notification.

CONTACT

Robert Merino, Director of Financial Aid
8060 Spencer Highway, Pasadena, TX 77505-5999
(281) 998-6150

Schreiner University

Kerrville, Texas
www.schreiner.edu Federal Code: 003610

4-year private liberal arts college in large town, affiliated with Presbyterian Church (USA).

Enrollment: 940 undergrads, 4% part-time. 283 full-time freshmen.

Selectivity: Admits 50 to 75% of applicants.

BASIC COSTS (2009-2010)

Tuition and fees: $18,731.

Per-credit charge: $774.

Room and board: $8,376.

FINANCIAL AID PICTURE (2007-2008)

Students with need: Out of 245 full-time freshmen who applied for aid, 202 were judged to have need. Of these, 202 received aid, and 40 had their full need met. Average financial aid package met 71% of need; average scholarship/grant was $10,133; average loan was $2,768. For part-time students, average financial aid package was $9,669.

Students without need: 68 full-time freshmen who did not demonstrate need for aid received scholarships/grants; average award was $6,289. No-need awards available for academics, art, leadership, music/drama, religious affiliation.

Scholarships offered: Awards for students with exceptional academic achievement and leadership abilities; partial and full tuition; 3.5 GPA and 1100 SAT (exclusive of Writing) or 24 ACT; 66 awarded after participation in the Schreiner Scholars program.

Cumulative student debt: 84% of graduating class had student loans; average debt was $7,562.

FINANCIAL AID PROCEDURES

Forms required: FAFSA.

Dates and Deadlines: No deadline. Applicants notified on a rolling basis starting 2/8; must reply within 2 week(s) of notification.

Transfers: Priority date 4/15; no deadline.

CONTACT

Toni Bryant, Director of Financial Aid
2100 Memorial Boulevard, Kerrville, TX 78028-5697
(830) 896-5411

South Plains College

Levelland, Texas
www.southplainscollege.edu Federal Code: 003611

2-year public community and junior college in large town.

Enrollment: 6,970 undergrads, 39% part-time. 1,117 full-time freshmen.

Selectivity: Open admission; but selective for some programs.

BASIC COSTS (2008-2009)

Tuition and fees: $1,892; out-of-district residents $2,552; out-of-state residents $3,032.

Room and board: $3,200.

FINANCIAL AID PICTURE

Students with need: Need-based aid available for full-time and part-time students.

Students without need: No-need awards available for academics, art, athletics, leadership, music/drama, state/district residency.

FINANCIAL AID PROCEDURES

Forms required: FAFSA.

Dates and Deadlines: Priority date 6/1; no closing date. Applicants notified on a rolling basis starting 6/30; must reply within 2 week(s) of notification.

CONTACT

Jim Ann Batenhorst, Director of Financial Aid
1401 South College Avenue, Levelland, TX 79336
(806) 894-9611

South Texas College

McAllen, Texas
www.southtexascollege.edu Federal Code: 031034

2-year public community and technical college in small city.

Enrollment: 21,425 undergrads, 67% part-time. 1,570 full-time freshmen.

Selectivity: Open admission; but selective for some programs.

BASIC COSTS (2008-2009)

Tuition and fees: $2,510; out-of-district residents $3,023; out-of-state residents $6,800.

FINANCIAL AID PICTURE (2007-2008)

Students with need: 99% of average financial aid package awarded as scholarships/grants, 1% awarded as loans/jobs. Need-based aid available for part-time students. Work study available nights, weekends, and for part-time students.

Students without need: This college awards aid only to students with need.

FINANCIAL AID PROCEDURES

Forms required: FAFSA.

Dates and Deadlines: Priority date 3/1; no closing date. Applicants notified on a rolling basis starting 4/15.

CONTACT

Miguel Carranza, Director of Financial Aid
3201 West Pecan Boulevard, McAllen, TX 78502
(956) 872-8375

Southern Methodist University

Dallas, Texas
www.smu.edu
Federal Code: 003613
CSS Code: 6660

4-year private university in large town, affiliated with United Methodist Church.

Enrollment: 6,172 undergrads, 4% part-time. 1,398 full-time freshmen.

Selectivity: Admits less than 50% of applicants. GED not accepted.

BASIC COSTS (2009-2010)

Tuition and fees: $35,160.

Per-credit charge: $1,304.

Room and board: $12,445.

FINANCIAL AID PICTURE (2008-2009)

Students with need: Out of 638 full-time freshmen who applied for aid, 445 were judged to have need. Of these, 445 received aid, and 185 had their full need met. Average financial aid package met 88% of need; average scholarship/grant was $17,383; average loan was $2,481. For part-time students, average financial aid package was $9,700.

Students without need: 580 full-time freshmen who did not demonstrate need for aid received scholarships/grants; average award was $12,633. No-need awards available for academics, art, athletics, leadership, music/drama, religious affiliation, ROTC, state/district residency.

Scholarships offered: 70 full-time freshmen received athletic scholarships; average amount $36,895.

Cumulative student debt: 33% of graduating class had student loans; average debt was $16,756.

FINANCIAL AID PROCEDURES

Forms required: FAFSA, CSS PROFILE.

Dates and Deadlines: Priority date 2/15; no closing date. Applicants notified on a rolling basis starting 3/15.

Transfers: Priority date 4/1. Merit scholarships available for community college and senior institution honor transfers. Students entering without scholarship aid will receive need-based aid up to cost of tuition.

CONTACT

Marc Peterson, Executive Director of Enrollment Services
PO Box 750181, Dallas, TX 75275-0181
(214) 768-2068

Southwest Institute of Technology

Austin, Texas
www.switaustin.com
Federal Code: 020936

2-year for-profit technical college in large city.

Enrollment: 32 undergrads.

Selectivity: Open admission.

BASIC COSTS (2008-2009)

Tuition and fees: $19,419.

Per-credit charge: $325.

FINANCIAL AID PICTURE (2008-2009)

Students with need: Need-based aid available for full-time students. Work study available nights, weekends, and for part-time students.

Students without need: This college awards aid only to students with need.

FINANCIAL AID PROCEDURES

Forms required: FAFSA, institutional form.

Dates and Deadlines: No deadline.

CONTACT

Lisa Ruszczyk, Corporate Financial Aid Director
5424 Highway 290 West, Suite 200, Austin, TX 78735
(512) 892-2640

Southwest Texas Junior College

Uvalde, Texas
www.swtjc.edu
Federal Code: 003614

2-year public community and junior college in large town.

Enrollment: 1,899 full-time undergrads.

Selectivity: Open admission.

BASIC COSTS (2008-2009)

Tuition and fees: $1,931; out-of-district residents $2,816; out-of-state residents $3,341.

Per-credit charge: $43; out-of-district residents $73; out-of-state residents $90.

Room and board: $3,100.

Additional info: Additional fees for off-campus classes may apply.

FINANCIAL AID PICTURE

Students with need: Need-based aid available for full-time and part-time students.

FINANCIAL AID PROCEDURES

Forms required: FAFSA.

Dates and Deadlines: Priority date 6/15; no closing date. Applicants notified on a rolling basis starting 5/1; must reply within 2 week(s) of notification.

CONTACT

Ana Almaraz, Director of Financial Aid
Garner Field Road, Uvalde, TX 78801
(830) 278-4401

Southwestern Adventist University

Keene, Texas
www.swau.edu
Federal Code: 003619

4-year private university and liberal arts college in small town, affiliated with Seventh-day Adventists.

Enrollment: 728 undergrads.

Selectivity: Admits less than 50% of applicants.

BASIC COSTS (2008-2009)
Tuition and fees: $15,236.
Per-credit charge: $619.
Room and board: $6,742.

FINANCIAL AID PICTURE
Students with need: Need-based aid available for full-time and part-time students.
Students without need: No-need awards available for academics, leadership, music/drama.

FINANCIAL AID PROCEDURES
Forms required: FAFSA, institutional form.
Dates and Deadlines: Priority date 3/15; no closing date. Applicants notified on a rolling basis starting 4/15.

CONTACT
Patricia Norwood, Assistant Vice President for Financial Administration, Student Finance
Box 567, Keene, TX 76059
(817) 202-6262

Southwestern Assemblies of God University
Waxahachie, Texas
www.sagu.edu Federal Code: 003616

4-year private university and Bible college in large town, affiliated with Assemblies of God.
Enrollment: 1,545 undergrads, 23% part-time. 256 full-time freshmen.

BASIC COSTS (2008-2009)
Tuition and fees: $12,850.
Per-credit charge: $399.
Room and board: $5,282.

FINANCIAL AID PICTURE (2007-2008)
Students with need: Out of 207 full-time freshmen who applied for aid, 182 were judged to have need. Of these, 182 received aid, and 17 had their full need met. Average financial aid package met 59% of need; average scholarship/grant was $7,151; average loan was $3,549. For part-time students, average financial aid package was $8,407.
Students without need: 50 full-time freshmen who did not demonstrate need for aid received scholarships/grants; average award was $2,871.
Scholarships offered: 11 full-time freshmen received athletic scholarships; average amount $4,344.

FINANCIAL AID PROCEDURES
Forms required: FAFSA.
Dates and Deadlines: Priority date 3/1; closing date 6/1. Applicants notified on a rolling basis starting 6/1; must reply within 2 week(s) of notification.

CONTACT
Karen Lazarz, Director of Financial Aid
1200 Sycamore Street, Waxahachie, TX 75165
(972) 825-4730

Southwestern University
Georgetown, Texas
www.southwestern.edu Federal Code: 003620

4-year private liberal arts college in large town, affiliated with United Methodist Church.
Enrollment: 1,259 undergrads, 1% part-time. 349 full-time freshmen.
Selectivity: Admits 50 to 75% of applicants.

BASIC COSTS (2009-2010)
Tuition and fees: $30,220.
Per-credit charge: $1,255.
Room and board: $9,502.

FINANCIAL AID PICTURE (2008-2009)
Students with need: Out of 265 full-time freshmen who applied for aid, 205 were judged to have need. Of these, 202 received aid, and 66 had their full need met. Average financial aid package met 87% of need; average scholarship/grant was $20,783; average loan was $4,951. For part-time students, average financial aid package was $9,462.
Students without need: 112 full-time freshmen who did not demonstrate need for aid received scholarships/grants; average award was $11,733. No-need awards available for academics, art, minority status, music/drama, religious affiliation.
Scholarships offered: Academic Merit Scholarships: $2,000 to $19,000 per year. Brown Scholarships: full tuition, room and board. National Merit Finalist Awards: $2,000 per year. Fine Arts Scholarships: $3,500 to $10,000 per year; for students majoring in art, music or theater; based on talent, auditions or portfolio review. Music Performance Awards: up to $2,500; based on talent and awarded to non-fine arts majors who wish to participate in university ensemble. Dixon Scholarship: $5,000 per year or full tuition; awarded to high-achieving African-American, Hispanic, and Native American students. Beneficiary Grants: $6,000 per year; awarded to dependents of United Methodist clergy. Preministerial Scholarships: $3,000 per year; to students interested in full-time ministry careers.
Cumulative student debt: 43% of graduating class had student loans; average debt was $23,601.

FINANCIAL AID PROCEDURES
Forms required: FAFSA.
Dates and Deadlines: Priority date 3/1; no closing date. Applicants notified on a rolling basis starting 3/1; must reply by 5/1 or within 2 week(s) of notification.
Transfers: Closing date 5/15.

CONTACT
James Gaeta, Director of Financial Aid
1001 East University Avenue, Georgetown, TX 78626
(512) 863-1259

Stephen F. Austin State University
Nacogdoches, Texas
www.sfasu.edu Federal Code: 003624

4-year public university in large town.
Enrollment: 10,404 undergrads, 13% part-time. 2,028 full-time freshmen.
Selectivity: Admits 50 to 75% of applicants.

BASIC COSTS (2009-2010)
Tuition and fees: $6,432; out-of-state residents $14,862.
Per-credit charge: $156; out-of-state residents $437.
Room and board: $7,022.

FINANCIAL AID PICTURE (2007-2008)
Students with need: Out of 1,570 full-time freshmen who applied for aid, 1,148 were judged to have need. Of these, 1,132 received aid, and 786 had their full need met. Average financial aid package met 87% of need; average scholarship/grant was $3,186; average loan was $3,115. For part-time students, average financial aid package was $8,814.
Students without need: 116 full-time freshmen who did not demonstrate need for aid received scholarships/grants; average award was $3,514. No-need awards available for academics, alumni affiliation, athletics, leadership, music/drama, state/district residency.
Scholarships offered: ***Merit:*** Academic Excellence Scholarship Program: $2,000 per year; rank in top 10% of high school class or top quartile class with 1100 SAT (exclusive of Writing) or 24 ACT; renewable with 3.5 GPA.

Dugas Full Support Scholarships: $4,000 per semester; active member of School of Honors; 3 awarded. University Scholars Program awards: $1,000 per semester; minimum 1220 SAT, 27 ACT, 3.0 GPA maintenance; up to 11 awarded. Student Foundation Association Leadership Scholarship: amounts vary; demonstrated leadership capabilities and academic achievement throughout high school career; 1 awarded. ***Athletic:*** 70 full-time freshmen received athletic scholarships; average amount $7,837.

Cumulative student debt: 67% of graduating class had student loans; average debt was $15,652.

FINANCIAL AID PROCEDURES

Forms required: FAFSA, institutional form.

Dates and Deadlines: Priority date 4/1; no closing date. Applicants notified on a rolling basis starting 4/10; must reply within 3 week(s) of notification.

CONTACT

Mike O'Rear, Director of Financial Aid
Box 13051, SFA Station, Nacogdoches, TX 75962-3051
(936) 468-2403

Sul Ross State University

Alpine, Texas
www.sulross.edu Federal Code: 003625

4-year public university in small town.

Enrollment: 1,978 undergrads, 35% part-time. 310 full-time freshmen.

BASIC COSTS (2008-2009)

Tuition and fees: $5,058; out-of-state residents $13,398.

Per-credit charge: $116; out-of-state residents $394.

Room and board: $6,190.

FINANCIAL AID PICTURE

Students with need: Need-based aid available for full-time and part-time students.

Students without need: No-need awards available for academics, alumni affiliation, leadership.

FINANCIAL AID PROCEDURES

Forms required: FAFSA, institutional form.

Dates and Deadlines: Priority date 5/1; no closing date. Applicants notified on a rolling basis starting 5/1; must reply within 2 week(s) of notification.

CONTACT

Rowena Gallego, Director Student Financial Assistance
Box C-114, Alpine, TX 79832
(432) 837-8055

Tarleton State University

Stephenville, Texas
www.tarleton.edu Federal Code: 003631

4-year public university in large town.

Enrollment: 7,860 undergrads, 25% part-time. 1,206 full-time freshmen.

Selectivity: Admits 50 to 75% of applicants.

BASIC COSTS (2008-2009)

Tuition and fees: $5,565; out-of-state residents $13,995.

Per-credit charge: $139; out-of-state residents $420.

Room and board: $6,984.

Additional info: Freshmen pay additional $100 first-year experience fee, first semester only. All undergraduates: distance learning fee additional $40 per credit hour.

FINANCIAL AID PICTURE (2007-2008)

Students with need: Out of 963 full-time freshmen who applied for aid, 849 were judged to have need. Of these, 625 received aid, and 569 had their full need met. Average financial aid package met 76% of need; average scholarship/grant was $4,278; average loan was $2,969. For part-time students, average financial aid package was $6,750.

Students without need: 336 full-time freshmen who did not demonstrate need for aid received scholarships/grants; average award was $4,716. No-need awards available for academics, alumni affiliation, art, athletics, leadership, music/drama, ROTC.

Scholarships offered: 66 full-time freshmen received athletic scholarships; average amount $3,889.

Cumulative student debt: 55% of graduating class had student loans; average debt was $17,239.

FINANCIAL AID PROCEDURES

Forms required: FAFSA.

Dates and Deadlines: Priority date 4/1; closing date 10/15. Applicants notified on a rolling basis starting 2/1; must reply within 2 week(s) of notification.

Transfers: No deadline.

CONTACT

Betty Murray, Director, Student Financial Aid
Box T-0030, Stephenville, TX 76402
(254) 968-9070

Tarrant County College

Fort Worth, Texas
www.tccd.edu Federal Code: 003626

2-year public community and liberal arts college in very large city.

Enrollment: 39,597 undergrads.

Selectivity: Open admission; but selective for some programs.

BASIC COSTS (2009-2010)

Tuition and fees: $1,500; out-of-district residents $2,190; out-of-state residents $4,950.

Per-credit charge: $50; out-of-district residents $73; out-of-state residents $165.

FINANCIAL AID PICTURE (2007-2008)

Students with need: Need-based aid available for part-time students.

Students without need: No-need awards available for academics.

FINANCIAL AID PROCEDURES

Forms required: FAFSA, institutional form.

Dates and Deadlines: Priority date 5/1; no closing date. Applicants notified on a rolling basis starting 5/1; must reply within 2 week(s) of notification.

CONTACT

David Ximenez, District Director of Financial Aid
1500 Houston Street, Fort Worth, TX 76102-6599
(817) 515-4243

Temple College

Temple, Texas
www.templejc.edu Federal Code: 003627

2-year public community college in small city.

Enrollment: 4,970 undergrads, 61% part-time. 415 full-time freshmen.

Selectivity: Open admission; but selective for some programs.

BASIC COSTS (2008-2009)

Tuition and fees: $2,100; out-of-district residents $3,300; out-of-state residents $5,280.

Per-credit charge: $70; out-of-district residents $110; out-of-state residents $176.

FINANCIAL AID PICTURE (2007-2008)

Students with need: Need-based aid available for full-time and part-time students. Work study available nights.

Students without need: This college awards aid only to students with need.

FINANCIAL AID PROCEDURES

Forms required: FAFSA.

Dates and Deadlines: Priority date 6/1; no closing date. Applicants notified on a rolling basis starting 5/1; must reply within 4 week(s) of notification.

CONTACT

Federico Pena, Director of Financial Aid
2600 South First Street, Temple, TX 76504-7435
(254) 298-8321

Texarkana College

Texarkana, Texas
www.texarkanacollege.edu Federal Code: 003628

2-year public community college in small city.
Enrollment: 4,654 undergrads.
Selectivity: Open admission.

BASIC COSTS (2008-2009)

Tuition and fees: $1,110; out-of-district residents $1,770; out-of-state residents $2,270.

Per-credit charge: $34; out-of-district residents $56; out-of-state residents $73.

Additional info: Arkansas and Oklahoma residents pay out-of-district rates.

FINANCIAL AID PICTURE

Students with need: Need-based aid available for full-time and part-time students. Work study available nights, weekends, and for part-time students.

Students without need: No-need awards available for academics, athletics.

FINANCIAL AID PROCEDURES

Forms required: FAFSA, institutional form.

Dates and Deadlines: Priority date 6/1; no closing date. Applicants notified on a rolling basis starting 3/1.

CONTACT

Robin Thomas, Director of Financial Aid
2500 North Robison Road, Texarkana, TX 75599
(903) 832-5565 ext. 3214

Texas A&M International University

Laredo, Texas
www.tamiu.edu Federal Code: 009651

4-year public university in small city.
Enrollment: 4,734 undergrads.
Selectivity: Admits 50 to 75% of applicants.

BASIC COSTS (2008-2009)

Tuition and fees: $5,417; out-of-state residents $13,757.
Per-credit charge: $130; out-of-state residents $408.
Room and board: $6,750.

FINANCIAL AID PICTURE (2007-2008)

Students with need: 62% of average financial aid package awarded as scholarships/grants, 38% awarded as loans/jobs. Need-based aid available for part-time students. Work study available nights.

Students without need: No-need awards available for academics.

FINANCIAL AID PROCEDURES

Forms required: FAFSA, institutional form.

Dates and Deadlines: Priority date 3/15; no closing date. Applicants notified on a rolling basis starting 7/15; must reply within 2 week(s) of notification.

CONTACT

Laura Elizondo, Director of Financial Aid
5201 University Boulevard, Laredo, TX 78041-1900
(956) 326-2225

Texas A&M University

College Station, Texas
www.tamu.edu Federal Code: 003632

4-year public university in small city.
Enrollment: 38,341 undergrads, 8% part-time. 7,581 full-time freshmen.
Selectivity: Admits 50 to 75% of applicants.

BASIC COSTS (2008-2009)

Tuition and fees: $7,844; out-of-state residents $22,184.
Per-credit charge: $163; out-of-state residents $641.
Room and board: $8,000.

FINANCIAL AID PICTURE (2007-2008)

Students with need: Out of 4,843 full-time freshmen who applied for aid, 2,874 were judged to have need. Of these, 2,815 received aid, and 1,470 had their full need met. Average financial aid package met 89% of need; average scholarship/grant was $9,951; average loan was $3,874. For part-time students, average financial aid package was $9,095.

Students without need: 1,034 full-time freshmen who did not demonstrate need for aid received scholarships/grants; average award was $3,894. No-need awards available for academics, alumni affiliation, art, athletics, job skills, leadership, music/drama, ROTC, state/district residency.

Scholarships offered: 55 full-time freshmen received athletic scholarships; average amount $10,037.

Cumulative student debt: 54% of graduating class had student loans; average debt was $19,940.

Additional info: Short-term loans available. Out-of-state students awarded academic scholarships of $1,000 or more are eligible for waiver of out-of-state tuition.

FINANCIAL AID PROCEDURES

Forms required: FAFSA.

Dates and Deadlines: Priority date 3/31; no closing date. Applicants notified on a rolling basis starting 3/15; must reply within 4 week(s) of notification.

Transfers: Must provide previous financial aid transcript.

CONTACT

Joseph Pettibon, Assistant Provost - Student Financial Aid
PO Box 30014, College Station, TX 77842-3014
(979) 845-3236

Texas A&M University-Baylor College of Dentistry

Dallas, Texas
www.bcd.tamhsc.edu Federal Code: 004948

Upper-division public health science college in very large city.
Enrollment: 61 undergrads.

BASIC COSTS (2008-2009)

Tuition and fees: $5,660; out-of-state residents $15,495.
Per-credit charge: $109; out-of-state residents $390.

FINANCIAL AID PICTURE (2007-2008)

Students with need: Average financial aid package for all full-time undergraduates was $7,993. 50% awarded as scholarships/grants, 50% awarded as loans/jobs. Need-based aid available for part-time students.

Students without need: No-need awards available for academics.

FINANCIAL AID PROCEDURES

Forms required: FAFSA, institutional form.

Dates and Deadlines: Priority date 3/15; no closing date. Applicants notified on a rolling basis starting 6/1; must reply within 2 week(s) of notification.

CONTACT

Kay Egbert, Director of Student Aid
PO Box 660677, Dallas, TX 75266-0677

Texas A&M University-Commerce

Commerce, Texas
www.tamu-commerce.edu Federal Code: 003565

4-year public university in small town.

Enrollment: 4,990 undergrads, 27% part-time. 568 full-time freshmen.

Selectivity: Admits 50 to 75% of applicants.

BASIC COSTS (2008-2009)

Tuition and fees: $5,130; out-of-state residents $13,380.

Room and board: $6,650.

FINANCIAL AID PICTURE (2007-2008)

Students with need: Out of 474 full-time freshmen who applied for aid, 354 were judged to have need. Of these, 351 received aid, and 98 had their full need met. Average financial aid package met 65% of need; average scholarship/grant was $6,012; average loan was $2,122. Need-based aid available for part-time students.

Students without need: 122 full-time freshmen who did not demonstrate need for aid received scholarships/grants; average award was $1,978. No-need awards available for academics, art, athletics, leadership, music/drama.

Cumulative student debt: 69% of graduating class had student loans; average debt was $19,032.

Additional info: Work-study also available for full-time students.

FINANCIAL AID PROCEDURES

Forms required: FAFSA.

Dates and Deadlines: Priority date 4/1; no closing date. Applicants notified on a rolling basis starting 4/1; must reply within 2 week(s) of notification.

CONTACT

Dolly Lasater, Director of Financial Aid
Box 3011, Commerce, TX 75429-3011
(903) 886-5091

Texas A&M University-Corpus Christi

Corpus Christi, Texas
www.tamucc.edu Federal Code: 011161

4-year public university in large city.

Enrollment: 7,249 undergrads, 21% part-time. 1,208 full-time freshmen.

Selectivity: Admits 50 to 75% of applicants.

BASIC COSTS (2008-2009)

Tuition and fees: $5,737; out-of-state residents $14,167.

Room and board: $8,709.

FINANCIAL AID PICTURE (2007-2008)

Students with need: 43% of average financial aid package awarded as scholarships/grants, 57% awarded as loans/jobs. Need-based aid available for part-time students.

Students without need: No-need awards available for academics, art, athletics, music/drama.

FINANCIAL AID PROCEDURES

Forms required: FAFSA, institutional form.

Dates and Deadlines: Closing date 4/1. Applicants notified on a rolling basis starting 5/1; must reply within 2 week(s) of notification.

CONTACT

Jeannie Gage, Financial Assistance Director
6300 Ocean Drive, Corpus Christi, TX 78412
(361) 825-2338

Texas A&M University-Galveston

Galveston, Texas
www.tamug.edu Federal Code: 003632

4-year public university and branch campus college in small city.

Enrollment: 1,566 undergrads, 10% part-time. 438 full-time freshmen.

Selectivity: Admits over 75% of applicants.

BASIC COSTS (2008-2009)

Tuition and fees: $6,528; out-of-state residents $14,958.

Per-credit charge: $167; out-of-state residents $448.

Room and board: $5,758.

FINANCIAL AID PICTURE (2007-2008)

Students with need: Out of 272 full-time freshmen who applied for aid, 233 were judged to have need. Of these, 219 received aid, and 44 had their full need met. Average financial aid package met 14% of need; average scholarship/grant was $4,898; average loan was $2,789. For part-time students, average financial aid package was $8,395.

Students without need: 15 full-time freshmen who did not demonstrate need for aid received scholarships/grants; average award was $4,607. No-need awards available for academics, state/district residency.

Cumulative student debt: 86% of graduating class had student loans; average debt was $11,055.

FINANCIAL AID PROCEDURES

Forms required: FAFSA.

Dates and Deadlines: Priority date 4/1; no closing date. Applicants notified on a rolling basis starting 3/15; must reply within 3 week(s) of notification.

CONTACT

Dennis Carlton, Director of Financial Aid
PO Box 1675, Galveston, TX 77553-1675
(409) 740-4500

Texas A&M University-Kingsville

Kingsville, Texas
www.tamuk.edu Federal Code: 003639

4-year public university in large town.

Enrollment: 5,512 undergrads.

Selectivity: Open admission; but selective for some programs.

BASIC COSTS (2008-2009)

Tuition and fees: $5,424; out-of-state residents $13,854.

Room and board: $4,874.

FINANCIAL AID PICTURE

Students with need: Need-based aid available for full-time students.

Students without need: No-need awards available for academics, leadership.

FINANCIAL AID PROCEDURES

Forms required: FAFSA.

Dates and Deadlines: Applicants notified on a rolling basis.

CONTACT

William Saenz, Financial Aid Officer
MSC 105, Kingsville, TX 78363-8201
(361) 593-3911

Texas A&M University-Texarkana

Texarkana, Texas
www.tamut.edu Federal Code: 031703

Upper-division public university in small city.

Enrollment: 1,030 undergrads, 61% part-time.

BASIC COSTS (2008-2009)

Tuition and fees: $4,235; out-of-state residents $12,665.

FINANCIAL AID PICTURE (2008-2009)

Students with need: 57% of average financial aid package awarded as scholarships/grants, 43% awarded as loans/jobs. Need-based aid available for part-time students. Work study available nights, weekends, and for part-time students.

Students without need: No-need awards available for academics, leadership, state/district residency.

FINANCIAL AID PROCEDURES

Dates and Deadlines: Priority date 5/1; closing date 11/1.

Transfers: Applicants notified on a rolling basis; must reply within 10 week(s) of notification. Must have completed minimum of 54 semester hours of transferable college credit to apply for financial aid. Notified applicants must reply within 45 days from date of award letter. Exceptions made on individual basis. April 1 financial aid deadline for scholarships.

CONTACT

Marilyn Raney, Director of Financial Aid
2600 North Robinson Road, Texarkana, TX 75505-5518
(903) 233-3060

Texas Christian University

Fort Worth, Texas
www.tcu.edu Federal Code: 003636

4-year private university in very large city, affiliated with Christian Church (Disciples of Christ).

Enrollment: 7,369 undergrads, 4% part-time. 1,630 full-time freshmen.

Selectivity: Admits 50 to 75% of applicants. GED not accepted.

BASIC COSTS (2009-2010)

Tuition and fees: $28,298.

Per-credit charge: $1,190.

Room and board: $9,800.

Additional info: Tuition/fee waivers available for adults, minority students.

FINANCIAL AID PICTURE (2008-2009)

Students with need: Out of 764 full-time freshmen who applied for aid, 555 were judged to have need. Of these, 553 received aid, and 195 had their full need met. Average financial aid package met 75% of need; average scholarship/grant was $16,065; average loan was $3,885. For part-time students, average financial aid package was $12,588.

Students without need: 412 full-time freshmen who did not demonstrate need for aid received scholarships/grants; average award was $10,071. No-need awards available for academics, alumni affiliation, art, minority status, music/drama, religious affiliation, ROTC, state/district residency.

Scholarships offered: 62 full-time freshmen received athletic scholarships; average amount $24,033.

Cumulative student debt: 59% of graduating class had student loans; average debt was $26,503.

FINANCIAL AID PROCEDURES

Forms required: FAFSA.

Dates and Deadlines: Closing date 5/1. Applicants notified on a rolling basis starting 3/15; must reply by 5/1 or within 2 week(s) of notification.

Transfers: Priority date 6/1. Must reply by 5/1.

CONTACT

Michael Scott, Director of Scholarships and Student Financial Aid
TCU Box 297013, Fort Worth, TX 76129
(817) 257-7858

Texas College

Tyler, Texas
www.texascollege.edu Federal Code: 003638

4-year private liberal arts college in small city, affiliated with Christian Methodist Episcopal Church.

Enrollment: 705 undergrads, 6% part-time. 183 full-time freshmen.

Selectivity: Open admission.

BASIC COSTS (2009-2010)

Tuition and fees: $9,228.

Per-credit charge: $333.

Room and board: $6,600.

FINANCIAL AID PICTURE (2007-2008)

Students with need: Need-based aid available for full-time and part-time students.

FINANCIAL AID PROCEDURES

Dates and Deadlines: Priority date 6/1; no closing date.

CONTACT

Cecelia Jones, Director of Financial Aid
2404 North Grand Avenue, Tyler, TX 75712-4500
(903) 593-8311 ext. 2208

Texas Lutheran University

Seguin, Texas
www.tlu.edu Federal Code: 003641

4-year private university and liberal arts college in large town, affiliated with Evangelical Lutheran Church in America.

Enrollment: 1,400 undergrads, 3% part-time. 396 full-time freshmen.

Selectivity: Admits 50 to 75% of applicants.

BASIC COSTS (2009-2010)

Tuition and fees: $21,910.

Per-credit charge: $700.

Room and board: $6,870.

FINANCIAL AID PICTURE (2008-2009)

Students with need: Out of 391 full-time freshmen who applied for aid, 302 were judged to have need. Of these, 302 received aid, and 138 had their full need met. Average financial aid package met 46% of need; average scholarship/grant was $13,912; average loan was $4,109. For part-time students, average financial aid package was $7,481.

Students without need: No-need awards available for academics, alumni affiliation, leadership, music/drama, religious affiliation.

Scholarships offered: Pacesetter Award for College Excellence: up to $14,000 per year; 3.5 GPA and SAT/ACT 1250/28 or rank in top 10% of class with minimum 1100/24 SAT/ACT score, must be accepted by specific date and be invited to participate in on-campus Pacesetter event. Academic Excellence Award: up to $7,000 per year; minimum articulated high school GPA of 3.25 and either SAT/ACT 1150/25 or rank in top 15% of class; awarded automatically upon acceptance to TLU. All SAT scores exclusive of Writing.

FINANCIAL AID PROCEDURES

Forms required: FAFSA.
Dates and Deadlines: Priority date 3/1; no closing date. Applicants notified on a rolling basis starting 3/1; must reply within 2 week(s) of notification.
Transfers: No deadline. Applicants notified on a rolling basis; must reply within 2 week(s) of notification.

CONTACT

Cathleen Wright, Director Financial Aid
1000 West Court Street, Seguin, TX 78155-5999
(830) 372-8075

Texas Southern University

Houston, Texas
www.tsu.edu Federal Code: 003642

4-year public university in very large city.
Enrollment: 7,132 undergrads, 19% part-time. 1,271 full-time freshmen.
Selectivity: Open admission; but selective for some programs.

BASIC COSTS (2008-2009)

Tuition and fees: $6,401; out-of-state residents $14,831.
Per-credit charge: $100; out-of-state residents $331.
Additional info: Tuition/fee waivers available for minority students.

FINANCIAL AID PICTURE (2007-2008)

Students with need: Need-based aid available for full-time and part-time students. Work study available nights, weekends, and for part-time students.
Students without need: This college awards aid only to students with need.

FINANCIAL AID PROCEDURES

Forms required: FAFSA.
Dates and Deadlines: Priority date 5/1; no closing date. Applicants notified on a rolling basis starting 6/1.
Transfers: Priority date 4/1; closing date 8/30.

CONTACT

Albert Tezeno, Director of Financial Aid
3100 Cleburne Street, Houston, TX 77004
(713) 313-7802

Texas State Technical College: Harlingen

Harlingen, Texas
www.harlingen.tstc.edu Federal Code: 009225

2-year public technical college in small city.
Enrollment: 1,703 undergrads.
Selectivity: Open admission; but selective for some programs.

BASIC COSTS (2008-2009)

Tuition and fees: $2,870; out-of-state residents $6,400.
Per-credit charge: $66; out-of-state residents $185.
Room and board: $3,160.

FINANCIAL AID PICTURE (2008-2009)

Students with need: Need-based aid available for full-time and part-time students.

FINANCIAL AID PROCEDURES

Forms required: FAFSA, institutional form.
Dates and Deadlines: Closing date 4/30. Applicants notified on a rolling basis starting 6/30; must reply within 2 week(s) of notification.

CONTACT

Teri Zamora, Vice President of Financial Services
1902 North Loop 499, Harlingen, TX 78550-3697
(956) 364-4337

Texas State Technical College: Waco

Waco, Texas
www.waco.tstc.edu Federal Code: 003634

2-year public technical college in small city.
Enrollment: 5,224 undergrads.
Selectivity: Open admission.

BASIC COSTS (2008-2009)

Tuition and fees: $2,834; out-of-state residents $6,404.
Per-credit charge: $66; out-of-state residents $185.
Room and board: $4,800.

FINANCIAL AID PICTURE (2007-2008)

Students with need: 54% of average financial aid package awarded as scholarships/grants, 46% awarded as loans/jobs. Need-based aid available for part-time students.
Students without need: This college awards aid only to students with need.

FINANCIAL AID PROCEDURES

Forms required: FAFSA.
Dates and Deadlines: Priority date 6/1; no closing date. Applicants notified on a rolling basis starting 5/15.
Transfers: No deadline. Applicants notified on a rolling basis.

CONTACT

Jackie Adler, Director, Financial Aid
3801 Campus Drive, Waco, TX 76705
(254) 867-4814

Texas State Technical College: West Texas

Sweetwater, Texas
www.westtexas.tstc.edu Federal Code: 009932

2-year public technical college in large town.
Enrollment: 1,071 undergrads.
Selectivity: Open admission; but selective for some programs.

BASIC COSTS (2008-2009)

Tuition and fees: $2,830; out-of-state residents $6,400.
Per-credit charge: $66; out-of-state residents $185.
Room and board: $4,250.

FINANCIAL AID PICTURE (2007-2008)

Students with need: Need-based aid available for full-time and part-time students. Work study available nights, weekends, and for part-time students.
Students without need: No-need awards available for academics, leadership.

FINANCIAL AID PROCEDURES

Forms required: FAFSA, institutional form.
Dates and Deadlines: Priority date 5/1; no closing date. Applicants notified on a rolling basis starting 7/1.
Transfers: No deadline. Applicants notified on a rolling basis starting 7/1; must reply by 8/20.

CONTACT
Kevin Shipp, Associate Vice President of Student Accounting
300 Homer K Taylor Drive, Sweetwater, TX 79556
(325) 235-7378

Texas State University: San Marcos
San Marcos, Texas
www.txstate.edu Federal Code: 003615

4-year public university in large town.
Enrollment: 24,810 undergrads, 19% part-time. 3,182 full-time freshmen.
Selectivity: Admits 50 to 75% of applicants.

BASIC COSTS (2008-2009)
Tuition and fees: $6,994; out-of-state residents $15,424.
Per-credit charge: $170; out-of-state residents $451.
Room and board: $6,012.

FINANCIAL AID PICTURE (2008-2009)
Students with need: Out of 2,229 full-time freshmen who applied for aid, 1,538 were judged to have need. Of these, 1,468 received aid, and 135 had their full need met. Average financial aid package met 70% of need; average scholarship/grant was $6,280; average loan was $3,173. For part-time students, average financial aid package was $10,818.
Students without need: 171 full-time freshmen who did not demonstrate need for aid received scholarships/grants; average award was $2,217. No-need awards available for academics, art, athletics, leadership, music/drama, ROTC, state/district residency.
Scholarships offered: ***Merit:*** Terry Foundation Scholarship: $12,500; 16 awarded. McCoy Scholarship of Excellence: $8,000; number awarded varies. McCoy Scholarship of Distinction: $5,000; number varies. University Scholars: $3,000; 8 awarded. Lone Star Scholarship: $2,500; 10 awarded. ***Athletic:*** 52 full-time freshmen received athletic scholarships; average amount $6,712.
Cumulative student debt: 57% of graduating class had student loans; average debt was $17,994.
Additional info: To be eligible for the Bobcat Promise program you must be an entering first-time freshmen (transfer students are not eligible), be a Texas resident, have a family adjusted gross income of $25,000 or less, be enrolled full-time and complete at least 30 credit hours during each academic year (fall and spring semester), and submit a completed FAFSA no later than April 1.

FINANCIAL AID PROCEDURES
Forms required: FAFSA.
Dates and Deadlines: Priority date 4/1; no closing date. Applicants notified on a rolling basis starting 5/1; must reply within 3 week(s) of notification.

CONTACT
Mariko Gomez, Director of Financial Aid & Scholarship Office
429 North Guadalupe Street, San Marcos, TX 78666-5709
(512) 245-2315

Texas Tech University
Lubbock, Texas
www.ttu.edu Federal Code: 003644

4-year public university in small city.
Enrollment: 23,080 undergrads, 8% part-time. 4,338 full-time freshmen.
Selectivity: Admits 50 to 75% of applicants.

BASIC COSTS (2008-2009)
Tuition and fees: $6,783; out-of-state residents $15,213.
Per-credit charge: $144; out-of-state residents $425.
Room and board: $7,310.
Additional info: Students from adjacent counties in New Mexico and Oklahoma pay in-state tuition rates; students from all other counties in New Mexico and Oklahoma pay reduced out-of-state tuition rates.

FINANCIAL AID PICTURE (2007-2008)
Students with need: Need-based aid available for full-time and part-time students.
Students without need: No-need awards available for academics, art, athletics, job skills, leadership, music/drama, ROTC.
Scholarships offered: Presidential Plus Scholarship: $12,700 per year for up to 5 years; awarded to National Merit Finalists who select Texas Tech as school of choice. Presidential Endowed Scholarship: $6,000 per year for up to 5 years; top 10% of high school graduating class and SAT 1400 or ACT 31. Honors Endowed Scholarship: $4,000 per year up to 5 years; top 10% of high school graduating class and SAT 1300 or ACT 29. University Scholars Scholarship: $2,500 per year up to 4 years; top 10% of high school graduating class and SAT 1250 or ACT 28.

FINANCIAL AID PROCEDURES
Forms required: FAFSA.
Dates and Deadlines: Priority date 4/15; no closing date. Applicants notified on a rolling basis; must reply within 2 week(s) of notification.

CONTACT
Becky Wilson, Director of Financial Aid
Box 45005, Lubbock, TX 79409-5005
(806) 742-3681

Texas Tech University Health Sciences Center
Lubbock, Texas
www.ttuhsc.edu Federal Code: 010674

Upper-division public university in small city.
Enrollment: 723 undergrads, 12% part-time.

BASIC COSTS (2008-2009)
Additional info: Tuition and fees vary for each of the programs within the five schools: Allied Health, Medicine, Nursing, Pharmacy and the Graduate School of Biomedical Sciences.

FINANCIAL AID PICTURE (2007-2008)
Students with need: 39% of average financial aid package awarded as scholarships/grants, 61% awarded as loans/jobs. Need-based aid available for part-time students.
Students without need: No-need awards available for academics.

FINANCIAL AID PROCEDURES
Transfers: No deadline. Applicants notified on a rolling basis.

CONTACT
Marcus Wilson, Director, Financial Aid
3601 Fourth Street, Lubbock, TX 79430

Texas Wesleyan University
Fort Worth, Texas
www.txwes.edu Federal Code: 003645

4-year private university in large city, affiliated with United Methodist Church.
Enrollment: 1,488 undergrads, 24% part-time. 191 full-time freshmen.
Selectivity: Admits 50 to 75% of applicants.

BASIC COSTS (2009-2010)
Tuition and fees: $17,760.
Per-credit charge: $546.
Room and board: $6,656.

FINANCIAL AID PICTURE (2007-2008)

Students with need: Out of 169 full-time freshmen who applied for aid, 147 were judged to have need. Of these, 147 received aid, and 30 had their full need met. Average financial aid package met 59% of need; average scholarship/grant was $9,011; average loan was $2,500. For part-time students, average financial aid package was $6,201.

Students without need: This college awards aid only to students with need.

Scholarships offered: 11 full-time freshmen received athletic scholarships; average amount $8,787.

FINANCIAL AID PROCEDURES

Forms required: FAFSA.

Dates and Deadlines: Priority date 3/15; no closing date. Applicants notified on a rolling basis starting 3/15.

CONTACT

Shanna Hollis, Financial Aid Director
1201 Wesleyan Street, Fort Worth, TX 76105-1536
(817) 531-4420

Texas Woman's University

Denton, Texas
www.twu.edu Federal Code: 003646

4-year public university in small city.

Enrollment: 7,389 undergrads, 31% part-time. 778 full-time freshmen.

Selectivity: Admits 50 to 75% of applicants.

BASIC COSTS (2008-2009)

Tuition and fees: $6,540; out-of-state residents $14,880.

Per-credit charge: $143; out-of-state residents $421.

Room and board: $5,846.

FINANCIAL AID PICTURE (2008-2009)

Students with need: Need-based aid available for full-time and part-time students. Work study available nights, weekends, and for part-time students.

Scholarships offered: Chancellor's Endowed Scholarship: full tuition and fees, room and board; based on high school valedictorian status, extracurricular activities, SAT score; 2 awarded. Presidential Scholarship: full tuition and fees; awarded to valedictorian or salutatorian. Honors Scholarship: $1,500 annually up to 4 years; based on admission to honors program and SAT score. New Freshman Scholarship: $1,500 annually up to 4 years; based on SAT/ACT score, class rank and GPA. Transfer Student Scholarship: $1,500 annually up to 4 years; based on GPA, must have completed at least 12 credit hours. New Student Scholarship: $1,800 annually up to 4 years; based on high school rank, ACT/SAT score; 150 awarded.

FINANCIAL AID PROCEDURES

Forms required: FAFSA, institutional form.

Dates and Deadlines: Priority date 4/1; no closing date. Applicants notified on a rolling basis starting 3/1; must reply within 2 week(s) of notification.

CONTACT

Governor Jackson, Director of Financial Aid
Box 425589, Denton, TX 76204-5589
(940) 898-3064

Trinity University

San Antonio, Texas
www.trinity.edu Federal Code: 003647

4-year private liberal arts college in very large city, affiliated with Presbyterian Church (USA).

Enrollment: 2,475 undergrads, 1% part-time. 655 full-time freshmen.

Selectivity: Admits 50 to 75% of applicants.

BASIC COSTS (2009-2010)

Tuition and fees: $29,317.

Per-credit charge: $1,178.

Room and board: $8,895.

FINANCIAL AID PICTURE (2008-2009)

Students with need: Out of 394 full-time freshmen who applied for aid, 263 were judged to have need. Of these, 263 received aid, and 129 had their full need met. Average financial aid package met 95% of need; average scholarship/grant was $17,299; average loan was $4,746. For part-time students, average financial aid package was $8,649.

Students without need: 293 full-time freshmen who did not demonstrate need for aid received scholarships/grants; average award was $11,999. No-need awards available for academics, leadership, music/drama.

FINANCIAL AID PROCEDURES

Forms required: FAFSA.

Dates and Deadlines: Priority date 2/1; closing date 4/1. Must reply by 5/1 or within 4 week(s) of notification.

Transfers: Priority date 5/1; no deadline.

CONTACT

Sean Smith, Director of Financial Aid
One Trinity Place, San Antonio, TX 78212-7200
(210) 999-8315

Tyler Junior College

Tyler, Texas
www.tjc.edu Federal Code: 003648

2-year public junior college in small city.

Enrollment: 9,685 undergrads.

Selectivity: Open admission; but selective for some programs.

BASIC COSTS (2008-2009)

Tuition and fees: $1,730; out-of-district residents $2,780; out-of-state residents $3,530.

Per-credit charge: $23; out-of-district residents $58; out-of-state residents $93.

Room and board: $4,150.

FINANCIAL AID PICTURE (2008-2009)

Students with need: Need-based aid available for full-time and part-time students.

Students without need: No-need awards available for academics, alumni affiliation, art, athletics, leadership, music/drama.

FINANCIAL AID PROCEDURES

Forms required: FAFSA, institutional form.

Dates and Deadlines: Priority date 6/1; no closing date. Applicants notified on a rolling basis starting 3/1; must reply within 2 week(s) of notification.

Transfers: Financial aid transcript required if student enrolled same year elsewhere.

CONTACT

Devon Wiggins, Director of Student Financial Aid and Scholarship
Box 9020, Tyler, TX 75711-9020
(903) 510-2385

University of Dallas

Irving, Texas
www.udallas.edu Federal Code: 003651

4-year private university and liberal arts college in small city, affiliated with Roman Catholic Church.

Enrollment: 1,289 undergrads, 2% part-time. 363 full-time freshmen.

Selectivity: Admits over 75% of applicants.

BASIC COSTS (2009-2010)
Tuition and fees: $26,294.
Per-credit charge: $1,034.
Room and board: $8,220.

FINANCIAL AID PICTURE (2007-2008)
Students with need: Out of 292 full-time freshmen who applied for aid, 237 were judged to have need. Of these, 237 received aid, and 68 had their full need met. Average financial aid package met 84% of need; average scholarship/grant was $15,925; average loan was $4,325. For part-time students, average financial aid package was $10,820.
Students without need: 122 full-time freshmen who did not demonstrate need for aid received scholarships/grants; average award was $10,955. No-need awards available for academics, art, leadership, music/drama.
Cumulative student debt: 70% of graduating class had student loans; average debt was $24,000.

FINANCIAL AID PROCEDURES
Forms required: FAFSA.
Dates and Deadlines: Priority date 3/1; closing date 7/1. Applicants notified on a rolling basis starting 3/1; must reply by 5/1 or within 2 week(s) of notification.
Transfers: Priority date 4/1; closing date 7/15. Must reply by 5/1 or within 2 week(s) of notification.

CONTACT
Laurie Rosenkrantz, Assistant Dean of Financial Aid and Enrollment
1845 East Northgate Drive, Irving, TX 75062-4736
(972) 721-5266

University of Houston
Houston, Texas
www.uh.edu Federal Code: 003652

4-year public university in very large city.
Enrollment: 27,602 undergrads, 26% part-time. 3,486 full-time freshmen.
Selectivity: Admits over 75% of applicants.

BASIC COSTS (2008-2009)
Tuition and fees: $8,167; out-of-state residents $16,597.
Per-credit charge: $174; out-of-state residents $455.
Room and board: $6,935.

FINANCIAL AID PICTURE (2008-2009)
Students with need: Out of 2,546 full-time freshmen who applied for aid, 2,091 were judged to have need. Of these, 2,007 received aid, and 551 had their full need met. Average financial aid package met 74% of need; average scholarship/grant was $7,481; average loan was $5,031. For part-time students, average financial aid package was $9,612.
Students without need: 182 full-time freshmen who did not demonstrate need for aid received scholarships/grants; average award was $4,603. No-need awards available for academics, alumni affiliation, art, athletics, job skills, leadership, music/drama, ROTC, state/district residency.
Scholarships offered: 27 full-time freshmen received athletic scholarships; average amount $3,333.

FINANCIAL AID PROCEDURES
Forms required: FAFSA.
Dates and Deadlines: Priority date 4/1; no closing date. Applicants notified on a rolling basis starting 5/1; must reply within 4 week(s) of notification.
Transfers: Closing date 4/1. Applicants notified by 4/1; must reply by 7/1.

CONTACT
Sal Loria, Executive Director
122 E. Cullen Building, Houston, TX 77204-2023
(713) 743-1010

University of Houston-Clear Lake
Houston, Texas
www.uhcl.edu Federal Code: 011711

Upper-division public university in very large city.
Enrollment: 3,912 undergrads, 51% part-time.

BASIC COSTS (2008-2009)
Tuition and fees: $5,532; out-of-state residents $14,442.
Room only: $10,308.

FINANCIAL AID PICTURE (2007-2008)
Students with need: Average financial aid package for all full-time undergraduates was $6,440; for part-time $5,422. 41% awarded as scholarships/grants, 59% awarded as loans/jobs. Work study available nights, weekends, and for part-time students.
Students without need: No-need awards available for state/district residency.
Cumulative student debt: 63% of graduating class had student loans; average debt was $18,572.

FINANCIAL AID PROCEDURES
Forms required: FAFSA, institutional form.
Dates and Deadlines: Priority date 4/1; no closing date. Applicants notified on a rolling basis starting 6/4; must reply within 4 week(s) of notification.
Transfers: No deadline. Applicants notified on a rolling basis starting 5/15; must reply within 4 week(s) of notification.

CONTACT
Lynda McKendree, Director, Financial Aid/Veterans Affairs
2700 Bay Area Boulevard, Houston, TX 77058-1098
(281) 283-2481

University of Houston-Downtown
Houston, Texas
www.uhd.edu Federal Code: 003612

4-year public university in very large city.
Enrollment: 12,134 undergrads, 52% part-time. 699 full-time freshmen.
Selectivity: Open admission.

BASIC COSTS (2008-2009)
Tuition and fees: $5,000; out-of-state residents $13,430.
Per-credit charge: $135; out-of-state residents $416.

FINANCIAL AID PICTURE (2008-2009)
Students with need: Out of 566 full-time freshmen who applied for aid, 526 were judged to have need. Of these, 514 received aid, and 18 had their full need met. Average financial aid package met 59% of need; average scholarship/grant was $7,134; average loan was $3,254. For part-time students, average financial aid package was $6,745.
Students without need: 212 full-time freshmen who did not demonstrate need for aid received scholarships/grants; average award was $2,431. No-need awards available for academics, leadership.
Cumulative student debt: 76% of graduating class had student loans; average debt was $14,771.

FINANCIAL AID PROCEDURES
Forms required: FAFSA.
Dates and Deadlines: Priority date 4/1; no closing date. Applicants notified on a rolling basis starting 4/15; must reply within 4 week(s) of notification.
Transfers: No deadline. Applicants notified on a rolling basis starting 4/15; must reply within 4 week(s) of notification.

CONTACT

LaTasha Goudeau, Director of Scholarships and Financial Aid
One Main Street, Suite 350-S, Houston, TX 77002
(713) 221-8041

University of Houston-Victoria

Victoria, Texas
www.uhv.edu Federal Code: 013231

Upper-division public university in small city.
Enrollment: 1,569 undergrads, 63% part-time.

BASIC COSTS (2008-2009)

Tuition and fees: $5,220; out-of-state residents $13,650.
Per-credit charge: $137; out-of-state residents $418.

FINANCIAL AID PICTURE (2007-2008)

Students with need: Need-based aid available for full-time and part-time students. Work study available weekends and for part-time students.
Students without need: No-need awards available for academics, athletics, leadership, state/district residency.
Additional info: Short-term loans available at registration.

FINANCIAL AID PROCEDURES

Forms required: FAFSA.
Dates and Deadlines: No deadline. Applicants notified on a rolling basis; must reply within 3 week(s) of notification.
Transfers: No deadline. Applicants notified on a rolling basis; must reply within 3 week(s) of notification.

CONTACT

Carolyn Mallory, Financial Aid Director
3007 North Ben Wilson, Victoria, TX 77901-4450
(361) 570-4131

University of Mary Hardin-Baylor

Belton, Texas
www.umhb.edu Federal Code: 003588

4-year private university in large town, affiliated with Baptist faith.
Enrollment: 2,502 undergrads, 12% part-time. 474 full-time freshmen.
Selectivity: Admits less than 50% of applicants.

BASIC COSTS (2009-2010)

Tuition and fees: $20,650.
Per-credit charge: $610.
Room and board: $5,350.
Additional info: Tuition/fee waivers available for minority students.

FINANCIAL AID PICTURE (2008-2009)

Students with need: Out of 393 full-time freshmen who applied for aid, 312 were judged to have need. Of these, 312 received aid, and 46 had their full need met. Average financial aid package met 64% of need; average scholarship/grant was $8,888; average loan was $3,911. For part-time students, average financial aid package was $7,528.
Students without need: 59 full-time freshmen who did not demonstrate need for aid received scholarships/grants; average award was $8,183. No-need awards available for academics, art, leadership, music/drama, religious affiliation.

FINANCIAL AID PROCEDURES

Forms required: FAFSA.
Dates and Deadlines: Priority date 3/1; no closing date. Applicants notified on a rolling basis starting 2/1; must reply within 2 week(s) of notification.
Transfers: No deadline. Applicants notified on a rolling basis starting 11/1; must reply within 2 week(s) of notification.

CONTACT

Ron Brown, Associate VP for Enrollment Management/Director of Financial Aid
900 College Street, Belton, TX 76513
(254) 295-4517

University of North Texas

Denton, Texas
www.unt.edu Federal Code: 003594

4-year public university and liberal arts college in small city.
Enrollment: 27,779 undergrads, 22% part-time. 3,502 full-time freshmen.
Selectivity: Admits 50 to 75% of applicants.

BASIC COSTS (2008-2009)

Tuition and fees: $6,767; out-of-state residents $15,107.
Per-credit charge: $161; out-of-state residents $439.
Room and board: $6,026.

FINANCIAL AID PICTURE (2007-2008)

Students with need: Out of 2,414 full-time freshmen who applied for aid, 1,578 were judged to have need. Of these, 1,553 received aid, and 483 had their full need met. Average financial aid package met 79% of need; average scholarship/grant was $5,830; average loan was $2,815. For part-time students, average financial aid package was $7,617.
Students without need: 412 full-time freshmen who did not demonstrate need for aid received scholarships/grants; average award was $3,679. No-need awards available for academics.
Scholarships offered: 40 full-time freshmen received athletic scholarships; average amount $11,203.

FINANCIAL AID PROCEDURES

Forms required: FAFSA.
Dates and Deadlines: Priority date 4/15; no closing date. Applicants notified on a rolling basis starting 4/1.

CONTACT

Carolyn Cunningham, Director of Financial Aid
1401 West Prairie, Suite 309, Denton, TX 76203-5017
(940) 565-2302

University of St. Thomas

Houston, Texas
www.stthom.edu Federal Code: 003654

4-year private university and liberal arts college in very large city, affiliated with Roman Catholic Church.
Enrollment: 1,657 undergrads, 23% part-time. 292 full-time freshmen.
Selectivity: Admits over 75% of applicants.

BASIC COSTS (2009-2010)

Tuition and fees: $21,830.
Per-credit charge: $717.
Room and board: $7,700.

FINANCIAL AID PICTURE (2008-2009)

Students with need: Out of 205 full-time freshmen who applied for aid, 162 were judged to have need. Of these, 160 received aid, and 21 had their full need met. Average financial aid package met 78% of need; average scholarship/grant was $13,251; average loan was $3,521. For part-time students, average financial aid package was $7,338.
Students without need: 90 full-time freshmen who did not demonstrate need for aid received scholarships/grants; average award was $9,277. No-need awards available for academics, athletics.
Cumulative student debt: 69% of graduating class had student loans; average debt was $21,943.

FINANCIAL AID PROCEDURES

Forms required: FAFSA.

Dates and Deadlines: No deadline. Applicants notified on a rolling basis starting 3/22; must reply within 2 week(s) of notification.

CONTACT

Scott Moore, Dean of Scholarships and Financial Aid
3800 Montrose Boulevard, Houston, TX 77006-4626
(713) 942-3465

University of Texas at Arlington

Arlington, Texas
www.uta.edu Federal Code: 003656

4-year public university in large city.
Enrollment: 18,586 undergrads, 30% part-time. 1,983 full-time freshmen.
Selectivity: Admits over 75% of applicants. GED not accepted.

BASIC COSTS (2008-2009)

Tuition and fees: $7,780; out-of-state residents $16,210.
Room and board: $5,916.

FINANCIAL AID PICTURE (2008-2009)

Students with need: Need-based aid available for full-time and part-time students. Work study available nights, weekends, and for part-time students.
Scholarships offered: Academic Scholarships: $1,000-$4,000 per year, renewable; based on minimum SAT 1050 (exclusive of Writing) or ACT 22, top 25% of high school class.

FINANCIAL AID PROCEDURES

Forms required: FAFSA.
Dates and Deadlines: Priority date 5/15; no closing date. Applicants notified on a rolling basis starting 4/1; must reply within 3 week(s) of notification.
Transfers: Must reply within 3 week(s) of notification. To receive Texas grant or Texas B on Time loan, student must have either received Texas grant at prior school or completed associates degree at prior school.

CONTACT

Karen Krause, Director of Financial Aid
Box 19111, Arlington, TX 76019
(817) 272-3561

University of Texas at Austin

Austin, Texas
www.utexas.edu Federal Code: 003658

4-year public university in very large city.
Enrollment: 36,711 undergrads, 6% part-time. 6,679 full-time freshmen.
Selectivity: Admits less than 50% of applicants.

BASIC COSTS (2008-2009)

Tuition and fees: $8,532; out-of-state residents $27,760.
Room and board: $9,246.

FINANCIAL AID PICTURE (2008-2009)

Students with need: Out of 4,800 full-time freshmen who applied for aid, 4,000 were judged to have need. Of these, 4,000 received aid, and 2,600 had their full need met. Average financial aid package met 82% of need; average scholarship/grant was $6,500; average loan was $3,900. Need-based aid available for part-time students.
Students without need: 1,250 full-time freshmen who did not demonstrate need for aid received scholarships/grants. No-need awards available for academics, art, athletics, leadership, music/drama, ROTC, state/district residency.
Cumulative student debt: 42% of graduating class had student loans; average debt was $17,000.
Additional info: In general, Texas resident students from families earning less than $40,000 will be awarded grant/scholarship aid (from federal, state, institutional and private sources) to cover tuition costs.

FINANCIAL AID PROCEDURES

Forms required: FAFSA.
Dates and Deadlines: Priority date 4/1; no closing date. Applicants notified on a rolling basis starting 3/15.

CONTACT

Thomas Melecki, Director of Student Financial Services
PO Box 8058, Austin, TX 78713-8058
(512) 475-6282

University of Texas at Brownsville - Texas Southmost College

Brownsville, Texas
www.utb.edu Federal Code: 030646

4-year public university and community college in small city.
Enrollment: 10,145 undergrads, 47% part-time. 1,381 full-time freshmen.
Selectivity: Open admission; but selective for some programs.

BASIC COSTS (2008-2009)

Tuition and fees: $5,258; out-of-state residents $13,688.
Per-credit charge: $128; out-of-state residents $409.

FINANCIAL AID PICTURE (2007-2008)

Students with need: 59% of average financial aid package awarded as scholarships/grants, 41% awarded as loans/jobs. Need-based aid available for part-time students.

FINANCIAL AID PROCEDURES

Forms required: FAFSA.
Dates and Deadlines: Priority date 3/1; closing date 8/15. Applicants notified on a rolling basis; must reply within 4 week(s) of notification.

CONTACT

Mari Chapa, Director of Financial Aid
80 Fort Brown, Brownsville, TX 78520
(956) 882-8277

University of Texas at Dallas

Richardson, Texas
www.utdallas.edu Federal Code: 009741

4-year public university in very large city.
Enrollment: 9,202 undergrads, 25% part-time. 1,091 full-time freshmen.
Selectivity: Admits 50 to 75% of applicants.

BASIC COSTS (2008-2009)

Tuition and fees: $9,850; out-of-state residents $21,000.
Per-credit charge: $328; out-of-state residents $700.
Room and board: $6,828.

FINANCIAL AID PICTURE (2008-2009)

Students with need: Out of 612 full-time freshmen who applied for aid, 495 were judged to have need. Of these, 495 received aid, and 220 had their full need met. Average financial aid package met 81% of need; average scholarship/grant was $7,336; average loan was $3,228. For part-time students, average financial aid package was $6,970.
Students without need: 352 full-time freshmen who did not demonstrate need for aid received scholarships/grants; average award was $9,926. No-need awards available for academics.
Scholarships offered: Eugene McDermott Scholars Program Awards: full tuition and fees plus domestic and international travel costs for enhancement

of scholar's education; based on being in top 10% of high school class, high scores on entrance exams, evidence of leadership abilities; 20 awarded.

FINANCIAL AID PROCEDURES

Forms required: FAFSA.

Dates and Deadlines: Priority date 3/31; closing date 4/12. Applicants notified on a rolling basis starting 3/1; must reply within 2 week(s) of notification.

Transfers: Priority date 4/1.

CONTACT

Karen Jarrell, Assistant VP of Financial Aid
Office of Enrollment Services, Richardson, TX 75083-0688
(972) 883-2941

University of Texas at El Paso

El Paso, Texas
www.utep.edu Federal Code: 003661

4-year public university in very large city.

Enrollment: 16,976 undergrads.

Selectivity: Admits over 75% of applicants.

BASIC COSTS (2008-2009)

Tuition and fees: $5,924; out-of-state residents $14,354.

Per-credit charge: $152; out-of-state residents $433.

Room only: $4,365.

Additional info: Mexican citizens who show need may qualify for in-state tuition. Reported room-only cost based on double-occupancy apartment at $485 per month for nine months. Optional a la carte meal plan.

FINANCIAL AID PICTURE (2007-2008)

Students with need: 43% of average financial aid package awarded as scholarships/grants, 57% awarded as loans/jobs. Need-based aid available for part-time students.

Students without need: No-need awards available for academics, alumni affiliation, art, athletics, job skills, leadership, minority status, music/drama, religious affiliation, ROTC, state/district residency.

Additional info: Emergency loans available.

FINANCIAL AID PROCEDURES

Forms required: FAFSA, institutional form.

Dates and Deadlines: Closing date 3/15. Applicants notified by 6/30; must reply within 2 week(s) of notification.

Transfers: No deadline.

CONTACT

Raul Lerma, Director of Financial Aid
500 West University Avenue, El Paso, TX 79968-0510
(915) 747-5204

University of Texas at San Antonio

San Antonio, Texas
www.utsa.edu Federal Code: 010115

4-year public university in very large city.

Enrollment: 24,308 undergrads, 20% part-time. 4,836 full-time freshmen.

Selectivity: Admits over 75% of applicants.

BASIC COSTS (2008-2009)

Tuition and fees: $7,100; out-of-state residents $15,530.

Per-credit charge: $160; out-of-state residents $441.

Room and board: $7,821.

FINANCIAL AID PICTURE (2007-2008)

Students with need: Out of 3,638 full-time freshmen who applied for aid, 2,510 were judged to have need. Of these, 2,387 received aid, and 656 had their full need met. Average financial aid package met 60% of need; average scholarship/grant was $6,317; average loan was $3,176. For part-time students, average financial aid package was $5,082.

Students without need: 319 full-time freshmen who did not demonstrate need for aid received scholarships/grants; average award was $1,505. No-need awards available for academics, alumni affiliation, art, athletics, job skills, leadership, music/drama, ROTC, state/district residency.

Scholarships offered: 75 full-time freshmen received athletic scholarships; average amount $5,843.

Cumulative student debt: 67% of graduating class had student loans; average debt was $20,083.

FINANCIAL AID PROCEDURES

Forms required: FAFSA, institutional form.

Dates and Deadlines: Priority date 3/31; no closing date. Applicants notified on a rolling basis starting 4/1; must reply within 4 week(s) of notification.

Transfers: No deadline. Applicants notified on a rolling basis starting 4/1; must reply within 4 week(s) of notification.

CONTACT

Lisa Blazer, Assistant Vice President of Financial Aid
One UTSA Circle, San Antonio, TX 78249-0617
(210) 458-7828

University of Texas at Tyler

Tyler, Texas
www.uttyler.edu Federal Code: 011163

4-year public university in small city.

Enrollment: 4,958 undergrads, 23% part-time. 584 full-time freshmen.

Selectivity: Admits over 75% of applicants.

BASIC COSTS (2008-2009)

Tuition and fees: $5,742; out-of-state residents $14,172.

Per-credit charge: $50; out-of-state residents $331.

Room and board: $7,510.

FINANCIAL AID PICTURE (2007-2008)

Students with need: Need-based aid available for full-time and part-time students.

Students without need: No-need awards available for academics, art, music/drama.

Additional info: Apply early for all programs.

FINANCIAL AID PROCEDURES

Forms required: FAFSA, institutional form.

Dates and Deadlines: Priority date 4/1; no closing date. Applicants notified on a rolling basis starting 4/15; must reply within 2 week(s) of notification.

CONTACT

Candice Lindsey, Associate Dean for Enrollment Management and Financial Aid
3900 University Boulevard, Tyler, TX 75799
(903) 566-7180

University of Texas Medical Branch at Galveston

Galveston, Texas
www.utmb.edu Federal Code: 013976

Upper-division public health science and nursing college in small city.

Enrollment: 470 undergrads, 43% part-time.

BASIC COSTS (2008-2009)
Tuition and fees: $5,443; out-of-state residents $13,873.
Per-credit charge: $156; out-of-state residents $437.
Additional info: Tuition and fees vary by program.

FINANCIAL AID PICTURE (2007-2008)
Students with need: Need-based aid available for full-time and part-time students. Work study available nights, weekends, and for part-time students.
Students without need: No-need awards available for academics, minority status, state/district residency.

FINANCIAL AID PROCEDURES
Forms required: FAFSA.
Dates and Deadlines: No deadline. Applicants notified on a rolling basis; must reply within 4 week(s) of notification.

CONTACT
301 University Boulevard, Galveston, TX 77555-1305
(409) 772-1215

University of Texas of the Permian Basin
Odessa, Texas
www.utpb.edu Federal Code: 009930

4-year public university in small city.
Enrollment: 2,489 undergrads, 26% part-time. 354 full-time freshmen.
Selectivity: Admits over 75% of applicants.

BASIC COSTS (2008-2009)
Tuition and fees: $4,934; out-of-state residents $13,364.
Additional info: New Mexico residents living in areas contiguous to Texas border pay in-district rate.

FINANCIAL AID PICTURE (2007-2008)
Students with need: Out of 267 full-time freshmen who applied for aid, 201 were judged to have need. Of these, 201 received aid, and 2 had their full need met. Average financial aid package met 69% of need; average scholarship/grant was $5,161; average loan was $2,605. For part-time students, average financial aid package was $6,039.
Students without need: 139 full-time freshmen who did not demonstrate need for aid received scholarships/grants; average award was $1,981. No-need awards available for academics, art, athletics, music/drama.
Scholarships offered: 28 full-time freshmen received athletic scholarships; average amount $1,971.
Cumulative student debt: 58% of graduating class had student loans; average debt was $15,459.

FINANCIAL AID PROCEDURES
Forms required: FAFSA.
Dates and Deadlines: Priority date 5/1; closing date 7/15. Applicants notified on a rolling basis starting 6/1; must reply within 2 week(s) of notification.

CONTACT
Robert Vasquez, Director of Financial Aid
4901 East University, Odessa, TX 79762
(432) 552-2620

University of Texas Southwestern Medical Center at Dallas
Dallas, Texas
www.utsouthwestern.edu Federal Code: 010019

Upper-division public university and health science college in very large city.
Enrollment: 103 undergrads, 8% part-time.

BASIC COSTS (2008-2009)
Tuition and fees: $4,190; out-of-state residents $12,530.
Additional info: Tuition and fees are based on Allied Health program.

FINANCIAL AID PICTURE (2008-2009)
Students with need: Average financial aid package for all full-time undergraduates was $16,150. 22% awarded as scholarships/grants, 78% awarded as loans/jobs. Need-based aid available for part-time students. Work study available nights, weekends, and for part-time students.

FINANCIAL AID PROCEDURES
Dates and Deadlines: No deadline. Must reply within 2 week(s) of notification.
Transfers: Priority date 3/1. Applicants notified on a rolling basis starting 4/1; must reply within 3 week(s) of notification.

CONTACT
Charles Kettlewell, Registrar and Director of Financial Aid
5323 Harry Hines Boulevard, Dallas, TX 75390-9162
(214) 648-3611

University of Texas: Pan American
Edinburg, Texas
www.utpa.edu Federal Code: 003599

4-year public university in small city.
Enrollment: 15,064 undergrads, 25% part-time. 2,527 full-time freshmen.
Selectivity: Admits over 75% of applicants.

BASIC COSTS (2008-2009)
Tuition and fees: $5,125; out-of-state residents $13,555.
Per-credit charge: $138; out-of-state residents $419.
Room and board: $4,900.
Additional info: Mexican citizens may be eligible for in-state tuition rates.

FINANCIAL AID PICTURE (2007-2008)
Students with need: Out of 2,109 full-time freshmen who applied for aid, 2,022 were judged to have need. Of these, 1,984 received aid, and 152 had their full need met. Average financial aid package met 72% of need; average scholarship/grant was $9,057; average loan was $1,868. For part-time students, average financial aid package was $6,818.
Students without need: 123 full-time freshmen who did not demonstrate need for aid received scholarships/grants; average award was $5,484. No-need awards available for academics, alumni affiliation, art, athletics, leadership, music/drama, ROTC, state/district residency.
Scholarships offered: 17 full-time freshmen received athletic scholarships; average amount $8,230.
Cumulative student debt: 64% of graduating class had student loans; average debt was $12,302.

FINANCIAL AID PROCEDURES
Forms required: FAFSA.
Dates and Deadlines: Closing date 3/1. Applicants notified on a rolling basis starting 3/15; must reply within 2 week(s) of notification.
Transfers: Priority date 3/1; no deadline. Applicants notified on a rolling basis; must reply within 2 week(s) of notification.

CONTACT
Elaine Rivera, Executive Director of Student Financial Services
1201 West University Drive, Edinburg, TX 78541-2999
(956) 381-2501

University of the Incarnate Word

San Antonio, Texas
www.uiw.edu Federal Code: 003578

4-year private university and liberal arts college in very large city, affiliated with Roman Catholic Church.

Enrollment: 5,071 undergrads, 35% part-time. 884 full-time freshmen.
Selectivity: Admits 50 to 75% of applicants.

BASIC COSTS (2009-2010)

Tuition and fees: $21,290.
Per-credit charge: $675.
Room and board: $8,780.

FINANCIAL AID PICTURE (2008-2009)

Students with need: Out of 868 full-time freshmen who applied for aid, 685 were judged to have need. Of these, 685 received aid, and 229 had their full need met. Average financial aid package met 65% of need; average scholarship/grant was $7,132; average loan was $3,550. For part-time students, average financial aid package was $6,889.
Students without need: 178 full-time freshmen who did not demonstrate need for aid received scholarships/grants; average award was $6,391. No-need awards available for academics, alumni affiliation, art, athletics, leadership, music/drama, religious affiliation, ROTC, state/district residency.
Scholarships offered: 31 full-time freshmen received athletic scholarships; average amount $13,439.
Cumulative student debt: 86% of graduating class had student loans; average debt was $39,985.
Additional info: Students encouraged to pursue outside scholarship programs.

FINANCIAL AID PROCEDURES

Forms required: FAFSA.
Dates and Deadlines: Priority date 4/1; no closing date. Applicants notified on a rolling basis starting 2/15; must reply within 2 week(s) of notification.

CONTACT

Amy Carcanagues, Director of Financial Assistance
4301 Broadway, San Antonio, TX 78209-6397
(210) 829-6008

Wade College

Dallas, Texas
www.wadecollege.edu Federal Code: 010130

2-year for-profit junior and career college in very large city.
Enrollment: 242 undergrads.
Selectivity: Open admission.

BASIC COSTS (2008-2009)

Tuition and fees: $9,390.
Room only: $4,000.
Additional info: Tuition at time of enrollment locked for 2 years.

FINANCIAL AID PICTURE (2007-2008)

Students with need: Need-based aid available for full-time and part-time students. Work study available nights, weekends, and for part-time students.
Students without need: This college awards aid only to students with need.

FINANCIAL AID PROCEDURES

Forms required: FAFSA.
Dates and Deadlines: No deadline. Applicants notified on a rolling basis; must reply within 4 week(s) of notification.

CONTACT

Lisa Hoover, Director of Financial Aid
Dallas Market Center, PO Box 421149, Dallas, TX 75342
(214) 637-3530

Wayland Baptist University

Plainview, Texas
www.wbu.edu Federal Code: 003663

4-year private university and liberal arts college in large town, affiliated with Southern Baptist Convention.
Enrollment: 891 undergrads, 14% part-time. 199 full-time freshmen.
Selectivity: Admits over 75% of applicants.

BASIC COSTS (2008-2009)

Tuition and fees: $12,000.
Per-credit charge: $380.
Room and board: $3,691.

FINANCIAL AID PICTURE (2008-2009)

Students with need: Out of 161 full-time freshmen who applied for aid, 156 were judged to have need. Of these, 150 received aid, and 28 had their full need met. Average financial aid package met 68% of need; average scholarship/grant was $6,286; average loan was $2,846. For part-time students, average financial aid package was $5,998.
Students without need: 43 full-time freshmen who did not demonstrate need for aid received scholarships/grants; average award was $9,395. No-need awards available for academics, alumni affiliation, art, athletics, job skills, leadership, minority status, music/drama, religious affiliation, state/district residency.
Scholarships offered: 19 full-time freshmen received athletic scholarships; average amount $8,532.
Cumulative student debt: 63% of graduating class had student loans; average debt was $21,575.

FINANCIAL AID PROCEDURES

Forms required: FAFSA, institutional form.
Dates and Deadlines: Priority date 5/1; no closing date. Applicants notified on a rolling basis starting 2/15; must reply within 3 week(s) of notification.
Transfers: No deadline. Applicants notified on a rolling basis.

CONTACT

Karen LaQuey, Director of Financial Aid
1900 West Seventh Street, CMB #712, Plainview, TX 79072
(806) 291-3520

Weatherford College

Weatherford, Texas
www.wc.edu Federal Code: 003664

2-year public community college in large town.
Enrollment: 4,396 undergrads, 51% part-time. 738 full-time freshmen.
Selectivity: Open admission; but selective for some programs.

BASIC COSTS (2008-2009)

Tuition and fees: $1,770; out-of-district residents $2,550; out-of-state residents $3,930.
Per-credit charge: $59; out-of-district residents $85; out-of-state residents $131.
Room and board: $7,180.

FINANCIAL AID PICTURE

Students with need: Work study available nights, weekends, and for part-time students.
Students without need: This college awards aid only to students with need.

FINANCIAL AID PROCEDURES

Forms required: FAFSA.

Dates and Deadlines: Priority date 7/3; no closing date. Applicants notified on a rolling basis; must reply within 2 week(s) of notification.

CONTACT

Kathy Bassham, Director of Student Financial Aid
225 College Park Drive, Weatherford, TX 76086
(817) 598-6295

West Texas A&M University

Canyon, Texas
www.wtamu.edu Federal Code: 003665

4-year public university in large town.

Enrollment: 6,051 undergrads, 23% part-time. 1,149 full-time freshmen.

BASIC COSTS (2008-2009)

Tuition and fees: $5,312; out-of-state residents $13,652.

Per-credit charge: $120; out-of-state residents $328.

Room and board: $5,710.

Additional info: Out-of-district students from border counties pay in-state tuition. Tuition reduction plan available to students from border states.

FINANCIAL AID PICTURE (2008-2009)

Students with need: Need-based aid available for full-time and part-time students. Work study available nights, weekends, and for part-time students.

Students without need: No-need awards available for academics, art, athletics, leadership, music/drama, state/district residency.

Additional info: Scholarship deadline February 1.

FINANCIAL AID PROCEDURES

Forms required: FAFSA.

Dates and Deadlines: Priority date 4/15; no closing date. Applicants notified on a rolling basis starting 3/1; must reply within 2 week(s) of notification.

Transfers: No deadline. Applicants notified on a rolling basis; must reply within 2 week(s) of notification. Must provide financial aid transcripts through last semester of attendance. All academic transcripts must be on file.

CONTACT

Jim Reed, Director of Financial Aid
2501 Fourth Avenue, WTAMU Box 60907, Canyon, TX 79016-0001
(806) 651-2055

Western Technical College

El Paso, Texas
www.wtc-ep.edu Federal Code: 014535

2-year for-profit technical college in very large city.

Enrollment: 268 undergrads.

Selectivity: Open admission; but selective for some programs.

FINANCIAL AID PICTURE

Students with need: Need-based aid available for full-time and part-time students.

Students without need: This college awards aid only to students with need.

FINANCIAL AID PROCEDURES

Forms required: FAFSA.

Dates and Deadlines: No deadline. Applicants notified on a rolling basis.

CONTACT

Jennifer Phillips, Financial Aid Director
9624 Plaza Circle, El Paso, TX 79927
(915) 532-3737 ext. 105

Western Texas College

Snyder, Texas
www.wtc.edu Federal Code: 009549

2-year public community and junior college in large town.

Enrollment: 2,002 undergrads.

Selectivity: Open admission; but selective for some programs.

BASIC COSTS (2008-2009)

Tuition and fees: $1,980; out-of-district residents $2,420; out-of-state residents $3,150.

Per-credit charge: $39; out-of-district residents $58; out-of-state residents $83.

Room and board: $4,900.

FINANCIAL AID PICTURE (2008-2009)

Students with need: Need-based aid available for full-time and part-time students. Work study available nights, weekends, and for part-time students.

Students without need: No-need awards available for academics, art, athletics, leadership, music/drama, state/district residency.

FINANCIAL AID PROCEDURES

Forms required: FAFSA, institutional form.

Dates and Deadlines: Closing date 8/1. Applicants notified on a rolling basis starting 5/1; must reply within 2 week(s) of notification.

CONTACT

Kathy Hall, Director of Student Financial Aid
6200 College Avenue, Snyder, TX 79549
(325) 573-8511 ext. 309

Westwood College: Houston South

Houston, Texas
www.westwood.edu Federal Code: 007548

2-year for-profit technical college in very large city.

Enrollment: 440 undergrads.

BASIC COSTS (2008-2009)

Additional info: Cost per term differs by program and ranges from $3,088-$4,609. One-time cost of toolkits $100-$490.

FINANCIAL AID PICTURE (2007-2008)

Students with need: Need-based aid available for full-time and part-time students.

FINANCIAL AID PROCEDURES

Forms required: FAFSA, institutional form.

Dates and Deadlines: No deadline.

CONTACT

Sharon Richard, Assistant Director of Student Finance
7322 Southwest Freeway, Houston, TX 77074
(713) 777-4779 ext. 13131

Wharton County Junior College

Wharton, Texas
www.wcjc.edu Federal Code: 003668

2-year public junior college in small town.

Enrollment: 6,115 undergrads, 57% part-time. 996 full-time freshmen.

Selectivity: Open admission; but selective for some programs.

BASIC COSTS (2009-2010)

Tuition and fees: $1,620; out-of-state residents $2,580.

Per-credit charge: $32; out-of-state residents $64.

Room and board: $3,550.
Additional info: Annual out-of-district fees $1,560.

FINANCIAL AID PICTURE

Students with need: Need-based aid available for full-time and part-time students.
Students without need: No-need awards available for academics, athletics, music/drama.

FINANCIAL AID PROCEDURES

Forms required: FAFSA.
Dates and Deadlines: Closing date 6/1. Applicants notified on a rolling basis starting 8/1; must reply by 8/15.

CONTACT

Richard Hyde, Director of Financial Aid
911 Boling Highway, Wharton, TX 77488-0080
(979) 532-4560 ext. 6345

Wiley College

Marshall, Texas
www.wileyc.edu Federal Code: 003669

4-year private liberal arts college in large town, affiliated with United Methodist Church.
Enrollment: 947 undergrads.
Selectivity: Open admission; but selective for some programs.

BASIC COSTS (2008-2009)

Tuition and fees: $9,970.
Per-credit charge: $269.
Room and board: $5,620.
Additional info: Reported tuition includes cost of books.

FINANCIAL AID PICTURE

Students with need: Need-based aid available for full-time and part-time students.
Students without need: This college awards aid only to students with need.

FINANCIAL AID PROCEDURES

Forms required: FAFSA, institutional form.
Dates and Deadlines: No deadline. Applicants notified on a rolling basis.

CONTACT

Eric King, Director of Financial Aid
711 Wiley Avenue, Marshall, TX 75670
(903) 927-3217

Utah

Brigham Young University

Provo, Utah
www.byu.edu Federal Code: 003670

4-year private university in small city, affiliated with Church of Jesus Christ of Latter-day Saints.
Enrollment: 30,912 undergrads, 9% part-time. 5,905 full-time freshmen.
Selectivity: Admits 50 to 75% of applicants.

BASIC COSTS (2009-2010)

Tuition and fees: $4,290.
Per-credit charge: $220.
Room and board: $6,840.
Additional info: Tuition is $8,580 for nonmembers of The Church of Jesus Christ of Latter-day Saints. Undergraduate per-credit-hour charge $440 for nonmembers.

FINANCIAL AID PICTURE (2008-2009)

Students with need: Out of 1,975 full-time freshmen who applied for aid, 1,238 were judged to have need. Of these, 1,021 received aid. Average financial aid package met 24% of need; average scholarship/grant was $1,770; average loan was $1,046. For part-time students, average financial aid package was $4,138.
Students without need: No-need awards available for academics, art, athletics, leadership, minority status, music/drama, religious affiliation, ROTC, state/district residency.
Cumulative student debt: 35% of graduating class had student loans; average debt was $13,926.
Additional info: Students notified of scholarships on or about April 20.

FINANCIAL AID PROCEDURES

Forms required: FAFSA.
Dates and Deadlines: Priority date 4/15; no closing date. Applicants notified on a rolling basis starting 4/1.
Transfers: Must provide financial aid transcript.

CONTACT

Paul Conrad, Director of Financial Aid
A-41ASB, BYU, Provo, UT 84602
(801) 422-4104

College of Eastern Utah

Price, Utah
www.ceu.edu Federal Code: 003676

2-year public community college in small town.
Enrollment: 1,100 full-time undergrads.
Selectivity: Open admission; but selective for some programs.

BASIC COSTS (2008-2009)

Tuition and fees: $2,242; out-of-state residents $4,142.
Room and board: $4,120.

FINANCIAL AID PICTURE

Students with need: Need-based aid available for full-time and part-time students. Work study available nights, weekends, and for part-time students.
Students without need: No-need awards available for academics, art, athletics, leadership, minority status, music/drama, religious affiliation, state/district residency.

FINANCIAL AID PROCEDURES

Forms required: FAFSA, institutional form.
Dates and Deadlines: Priority date 2/1; no closing date. Applicants notified on a rolling basis starting 3/15; must reply within 2 week(s) of notification.

CONTACT

Kim Booth, Financial Aid Director
451 East 400 North, Price, UT 84501
(435) 613-5207

Dixie State College of Utah

St. George, Utah
new.dixie.edu Federal Code: 003671

4-year public liberal arts college in small city.
Enrollment: 5,193 undergrads, 35% part-time. 991 full-time freshmen.
Selectivity: Open admission; but selective for some programs.

BASIC COSTS (2008-2009)

Tuition and fees: $2,893; out-of-state residents $10,063.

Room and board: $3,498.

FINANCIAL AID PICTURE (2007-2008)

Students with need: Out of 522 full-time freshmen who applied for aid, 420 were judged to have need. Of these, 406 received aid, and 45 had their full need met. Average financial aid package met 44% of need; average scholarship/grant was $3,994; average loan was $2,838. For part-time students, average financial aid package was $3,786.

Students without need: 452 full-time freshmen who did not demonstrate need for aid received scholarships/grants; average award was $1,738. No-need awards available for academics, alumni affiliation, art, athletics, leadership, minority status, music/drama, religious affiliation.

Scholarships offered: 48 full-time freshmen received athletic scholarships; average amount $3,852.

Cumulative student debt: 36% of graduating class had student loans; average debt was $12,571.

Additional info: SunFirst Bank Scholarship for communications students; Daniels Fund Scholarship for non-traditional students based on need.

FINANCIAL AID PROCEDURES

Forms required: FAFSA.

Dates and Deadlines: Priority date 3/1; closing date 5/1. Applicants notified on a rolling basis starting 3/1; must reply within 2 week(s) of notification.

CONTACT

JD Robertson, Director of Financial Aid
225 South 700 East, St. George, UT 84770-3876
(435) 652-7575

LDS Business College

Salt Lake City, Utah
www.ldsbc.edu Federal Code: 003672

2-year private business and junior college in small city, affiliated with Church of Jesus Christ of Latter-day Saints.

Enrollment: 1,373 undergrads, 26% part-time. 247 full-time freshmen.

Selectivity: Open admission.

BASIC COSTS (2009-2010)

Tuition and fees: $2,800.

Per-credit charge: $117.

Additional info: Students not members of The Church of Jesus Christ of Latter-day Saints pay tuition of $5,600 per academic year, $235 per-credit-hour.

FINANCIAL AID PICTURE (2007-2008)

Students with need: Need-based aid available for full-time and part-time students.

Students without need: No-need awards available for academics, leadership.

Scholarships offered: Service scholarships; half-tuition for one semester; for Church of Jesus Christ of Latter-day Saints missionaries who have returned from mission within past year.

FINANCIAL AID PROCEDURES

Forms required: FAFSA.

Dates and Deadlines: Priority date 7/1; no closing date. Applicants notified on a rolling basis starting 3/1; must reply within 3 week(s) of notification.

CONTACT

Doug Horne, Financial Aid Administrator
95 North 300 West, Salt Lake City, UT 84101-3500
(801) 524-8110

Salt Lake Community College

Salt Lake City, Utah
www.slcc.edu Federal Code: 005220

2-year public community and technical college in very large city.

Enrollment: 27,916 undergrads.

Selectivity: Open admission; but selective for some programs.

BASIC COSTS (2008-2009)

Tuition and fees: $2,660; out-of-state residents $8,374.

Additional info: Tuition/fee waivers available for adults, minority students.

FINANCIAL AID PICTURE (2007-2008)

Students with need: Need-based aid available for full-time and part-time students. Work study available nights, weekends, and for part-time students.

Students without need: No-need awards available for academics, alumni affiliation, art, athletics, leadership, minority status, music/drama.

FINANCIAL AID PROCEDURES

Forms required: FAFSA, institutional form.

Dates and Deadlines: Priority date 5/1; no closing date. Applicants notified on a rolling basis starting 5/1; must reply within 4 week(s) of notification.

CONTACT

Cristi Millard, Director of Financial Aid
4600 South Redwood Road, Salt Lake City, UT 84130-0808
(801) 957-4410

Snow College

Ephraim, Utah
www.snow.edu Federal Code: 003679

2-year public community and junior college in small town.

Enrollment: 3,798 undergrads, 40% part-time. 1,196 full-time freshmen.

Selectivity: Open admission.

BASIC COSTS (2008-2009)

Tuition and fees: $2,346; out-of-state residents $8,228.

Room and board: $3,000.

FINANCIAL AID PICTURE (2007-2008)

Students with need: Out of 431 full-time freshmen who applied for aid, 253 were judged to have need. Of these, 253 received aid, and 5 had their full need met. For part-time students, average financial aid package was $2,616.

Students without need: 13 full-time freshmen who did not demonstrate need for aid received scholarships/grants; average award was $811. No-need awards available for academics, alumni affiliation, athletics, leadership, music/drama, state/district residency.

Scholarships offered: 99 full-time freshmen received athletic scholarships; average amount $700.

FINANCIAL AID PROCEDURES

Forms required: FAFSA, institutional form.

Dates and Deadlines: Priority date 3/1; closing date 7/15. Applicants notified on a rolling basis starting 8/1; must reply within 1 week(s) of notification.

Transfers: Priority date 3/15; closing date 6/15. Applicants notified on a rolling basis. F.A.T. required for mid-year transfers.

CONTACT

Jack Dalene, Director of Financial Aid
150 East College Avenue, Ephraim, UT 84627
(435) 283-7132

Southern Utah University

Cedar City, Utah
www.suu.edu Federal Code: 003678

4-year public university in large town.
Enrollment: 5,434 undergrads, 12% part-time. 1,163 full-time freshmen.
Selectivity: Admits 50 to 75% of applicants.

BASIC COSTS (2008-2009)

Tuition and fees: $4,028; out-of-state residents $12,086.
Room and board: $5,238.

FINANCIAL AID PICTURE (2007-2008)

Students with need: Out of 743 full-time freshmen who applied for aid, 591 were judged to have need. Of these, 586 received aid, and 76 had their full need met. Average financial aid package met 64% of need; average scholarship/grant was $4,450; average loan was $3,141. For part-time students, average financial aid package was $3,844.
Students without need: 562 full-time freshmen who did not demonstrate need for aid received scholarships/grants; average award was $5,140. No-need awards available for academics, alumni affiliation, art, athletics, job skills, leadership, minority status, music/drama, state/district residency.
Scholarships offered: 78 full-time freshmen received athletic scholarships; average amount $5,223.
Cumulative student debt: 45% of graduating class had student loans; average debt was $8,719.

FINANCIAL AID PROCEDURES

Forms required: FAFSA, institutional form.
Dates and Deadlines: No deadline. Applicants notified on a rolling basis starting 11/1.

CONTACT

Paul Morris, Director of Financial Aid
351 West Center Street, Cedar City, UT 84720
(435) 586-7735

University of Utah

Salt Lake City, Utah
www.utah.edu Federal Code: 003675

4-year public university in very large city.
Enrollment: 20,475 undergrads, 30% part-time. 2,320 full-time freshmen.
Selectivity: Admits over 75% of applicants.

BASIC COSTS (2008-2009)

Tuition and fees: $5,285; out-of-state residents $16,601.
Room and board: $5,972.

FINANCIAL AID PICTURE (2008-2009)

Students with need: Out of 1,033 full-time freshmen who applied for aid, 715 were judged to have need. Of these, 707 received aid, and 145 had their full need met. Average financial aid package met 57% of need; average scholarship/grant was $5,896; average loan was $4,050. For part-time students, average financial aid package was $7,146.
Students without need: 204 full-time freshmen who did not demonstrate need for aid received scholarships/grants; average award was $5,347. No-need awards available for academics, alumni affiliation, art, athletics, leadership, minority status, music/drama, ROTC, state/district residency.
Scholarships offered: 5 full-time freshmen received athletic scholarships; average amount $18,524.
Cumulative student debt: 40% of graduating class had student loans; average debt was $11,749.

FINANCIAL AID PROCEDURES

Forms required: FAFSA, institutional form.
Dates and Deadlines: Closing date 3/15. Applicants notified on a rolling basis starting 4/15; must reply within 6 week(s) of notification.
Transfers: Priority date 2/15; no deadline. Applicants notified on a rolling basis starting 4/15; must reply within 6 week(s) of notification.

CONTACT

John Curl, Director of Financial Aid and Scholarship
201 South 1460 East, Room 250 S, Salt Lake City, UT 84112-9057
(801) 581-6211

Utah Career College

West Jordan, Utah
www.utahcollege.edu Federal Code: 011166

2-year for-profit technical and career college in small city.
Enrollment: 603 undergrads.
Selectivity: Open admission; but selective for some programs.

BASIC COSTS (2008-2009)

Tuition and fees: $16,200.
Per-credit charge: $360.
Additional info: Nursing program courses $458 per credit hour.

FINANCIAL AID PICTURE (2008-2009)

Students with need: Need-based aid available for full-time and part-time students.
Students without need: This college awards aid only to students with need.

FINANCIAL AID PROCEDURES

Forms required: FAFSA, institutional form.
Dates and Deadlines: No deadline. Applicants notified on a rolling basis starting 7/1; must reply within 2 week(s) of notification.

CONTACT

Nicole Whitesides, Director of Financial Aid
1902 West 7800 South, West Jordan, UT 84088
(801) 304-4224

Utah State University

Logan, Utah
www.usu.edu Federal Code: 003677

4-year public university in small city.
Enrollment: 13,251 undergrads, 16% part-time. 2,549 full-time freshmen.
Selectivity: Admits over 75% of applicants.

BASIC COSTS (2008-2009)

Tuition and fees: $4,445; out-of-state residents $12,951.
Room and board: $4,650.

FINANCIAL AID PICTURE (2008-2009)

Students with need: Out of 1,211 full-time freshmen who applied for aid, 872 were judged to have need. Of these, 854 received aid, and 180 had their full need met. Average financial aid package met 68% of need; average scholarship/grant was $3,850; average loan was $3,300. For part-time students, average financial aid package was $5,930.
Students without need: 136 full-time freshmen who did not demonstrate need for aid received scholarships/grants; average award was $2,630. No-need awards available for academics, alumni affiliation, art, athletics, leadership, minority status, music/drama, religious affiliation, ROTC.
Scholarships offered: 51 full-time freshmen received athletic scholarships; average amount $12,700.

FINANCIAL AID PROCEDURES

Forms required: FAFSA.

Dates and Deadlines: No deadline. Applicants notified on a rolling basis starting 4/1; must reply within 4 week(s) of notification.

CONTACT

Steve Sharp, Director of Financial Aid
0160 Old Main Hill, Logan, UT 84322-0160
(435) 797-0173

Utah Valley University

Orem, Utah
www.uvu.edu Federal Code: 004027

4-year public university and technical college in small city.
Enrollment: 21,857 undergrads, 43% part-time. 2,430 full-time freshmen.
Selectivity: Open admission.

BASIC COSTS (2008-2009)

Tuition and fees: $3,752; out-of-state residents $11,514.

FINANCIAL AID PICTURE (2008-2009)

Students with need: Out of 1,161 full-time freshmen who applied for aid, 1,003 were judged to have need. Of these, 888 received aid, and 34 had their full need met. Average financial aid package met 64% of need; average scholarship/grant was $4,104; average loan was $3,397. For part-time students, average financial aid package was $5,653.
Students without need: 11 full-time freshmen who did not demonstrate need for aid received scholarships/grants; average award was $3,709. No-need awards available for academics, alumni affiliation, art, athletics, job skills, leadership, minority status, music/drama, religious affiliation, ROTC, state/district residency.
Scholarships offered: 38 full-time freshmen received athletic scholarships; average amount $8,694.
Cumulative student debt: 66% of graduating class had student loans; average debt was $13,714.

FINANCIAL AID PROCEDURES

Forms required: FAFSA, institutional form.
Dates and Deadlines: Priority date 5/1; no closing date. Applicants notified on a rolling basis starting 5/15; must reply within 2 week(s) of notification.
Transfers: No deadline.

CONTACT

Michael Francis, Assistant Vice President for Finance and Controller
800 West University Parkway, Orem, UT 84058-5999
(801) 863-8442

Weber State University

Ogden, Utah
www.weber.edu Federal Code: 003680

4-year public university in small city.
Enrollment: 16,831 undergrads, 44% part-time. 1,507 full-time freshmen.
Selectivity: Open admission; but selective for some programs.

BASIC COSTS (2008-2009)

Tuition and fees: $3,850; out-of-state residents $11,157.
Room and board: $7,578.

FINANCIAL AID PICTURE (2007-2008)

Students with need: Out of 648 full-time freshmen who applied for aid, 540 were judged to have need. Of these, 474 received aid, and 14 had their full need met. Average financial aid package met 41% of need; average scholarship/grant was $3,121; average loan was $2,906. For part-time students, average financial aid package was $4,034.
Students without need: This college awards aid only to students with need.
Scholarships offered: 91 full-time freshmen received athletic scholarships; average amount $7,499.

FINANCIAL AID PROCEDURES

Forms required: FAFSA, institutional form.
Dates and Deadlines: Priority date 3/1; no closing date. Applicants notified on a rolling basis starting 3/15; must reply within 2 week(s) of notification.

CONTACT

Jeb Spencer, Director of Financial Aid
1137 University Circle, Ogden, UT 84408-1137
(801) 626-7569

Westminster College

Salt Lake City, Utah
www.westminstercollege.edu Federal Code: 003681

4-year private liberal arts college in very large city.
Enrollment: 2,104 undergrads, 8% part-time. 444 full-time freshmen.
Selectivity: Admits over 75% of applicants.

BASIC COSTS (2009-2010)

Tuition and fees: $24,996.
Per-credit charge: $1,024.
Room and board: $7,006.

FINANCIAL AID PICTURE (2008-2009)

Students with need: Out of 316 full-time freshmen who applied for aid, 242 were judged to have need. Of these, 242 received aid, and 90 had their full need met. Average financial aid package met 87% of need; average scholarship/grant was $14,306; average loan was $4,077. For part-time students, average financial aid package was $10,811.
Students without need: 186 full-time freshmen who did not demonstrate need for aid received scholarships/grants; average award was $10,202. No-need awards available for academics, alumni affiliation, art, athletics, leadership, minority status, music/drama, religious affiliation, ROTC.
Scholarships offered: 6 full-time freshmen received athletic scholarships; average amount $3,417.
Cumulative student debt: 66% of graduating class had student loans; average debt was $18,548.

FINANCIAL AID PROCEDURES

Forms required: FAFSA.
Dates and Deadlines: Priority date 4/15; no closing date. Applicants notified on a rolling basis starting 3/15; must reply by 5/1 or within 3 week(s) of notification.
Transfers: Full-time transfer students with 3.0 GPA eligible for work study, loans, scholarships and grants which range from $3,000-$8,000 per year.

CONTACT

Elizabeth Key, Director of Financial Aid
1840 South 1300 East, Salt Lake City, UT 84105
(801) 832-2500

Vermont

Bennington College

Bennington, Vermont Federal Code: 003682
www.bennington.edu CSS Code: 3080

4-year private liberal arts college in large town.
Enrollment: 618 undergrads, 1% part-time. 190 full-time freshmen.
Selectivity: Admits 50 to 75% of applicants.

BASIC COSTS (2009-2010)

Tuition and fees: $39,760.

Per-credit charge: $1,290.

Room and board: $11,100.

FINANCIAL AID PICTURE (2008-2009)

Students with need: Out of 135 full-time freshmen who applied for aid, 118 were judged to have need. Of these, 115 received aid, and 16 had their full need met. Average financial aid package met 80% of need; average scholarship/grant was $26,395; average loan was $2,980. For part-time students, average financial aid package was $11,747.

Students without need: 10 full-time freshmen who did not demonstrate need for aid received scholarships/grants; average award was $9,750. No-need awards available for academics.

Cumulative student debt: 68% of graduating class had student loans; average debt was $25,957.

Additional info: All applicants for undergraduate admission considered for scholarships based on quality of overall application.

FINANCIAL AID PROCEDURES

Forms required: FAFSA, institutional form. CSS PROFILE required of early decision applicants only.

Dates and Deadlines: Priority date 3/1; no closing date. Applicants notified by 4/1; must reply by 5/1 or within 2 week(s) of notification.

Transfers: Priority date 3/15; closing date 8/1. Applicants notified on a rolling basis starting 5/1; must reply by 6/1 or within 2 week(s) of notification.

CONTACT

Meg Woolmington, Director of Financial Aid
One College Drive, Bennington, VT 05201-6003
(802) 440-4325

Burlington College

Burlington, Vermont
www.burlington.edu Federal Code: 012183

4-year private liberal arts college in small city.

Enrollment: 157 undergrads, 31% part-time. 20 full-time freshmen.

Selectivity: Admits 50 to 75% of applicants.

BASIC COSTS (2008-2009)

Tuition and fees: $19,640.

Per-credit charge: $650.

Room only: $6,095.

FINANCIAL AID PICTURE (2008-2009)

Students with need: Average financial aid package met 56% of need; average scholarship/grant was $6,496; average loan was $4,786. For part-time students, average financial aid package was $8,415.

Students without need: No-need awards available for academics, leadership.

Cumulative student debt: 71% of graduating class had student loans; average debt was $28,888.

FINANCIAL AID PROCEDURES

Forms required: FAFSA, state aid form.

Dates and Deadlines: No deadline. Applicants notified on a rolling basis starting 3/15.

Transfers: No deadline. Applicants notified on a rolling basis.

CONTACT

Lindy Walsh, Financial Aid Coordinator
95 North Avenue, Burlington, VT 05401
(802) 862-9616 ext. 110

Castleton State College

Castleton, Vermont
www.castleton.edu Federal Code: 003683

4-year public liberal arts college in small town.

Enrollment: 1,891 undergrads, 8% part-time. 463 full-time freshmen.

Selectivity: Admits 50 to 75% of applicants.

BASIC COSTS (2008-2009)

Tuition and fees: $8,284; out-of-state residents $16,948.

Per-credit charge: $312; out-of-state residents $673.

Room and board: $7,510.

Additional info: New England Board of Higher Education rate for students from other New England states: 150% of Vermont resident tuition. Available to degree candidates in academic areas not offered by educational institutions in their home states.

FINANCIAL AID PICTURE (2007-2008)

Students with need: Need-based aid available for full-time and part-time students.

Students without need: No-need awards available for academics, alumni affiliation, art, leadership, music/drama, state/district residency.

FINANCIAL AID PROCEDURES

Forms required: FAFSA.

Dates and Deadlines: Priority date 2/15; no closing date. Applicants notified on a rolling basis starting 1/1; must reply by 5/1 or within 2 week(s) of notification.

CONTACT

Kathy O'Meara, Financial Aid Director
Seminary Street, Castleton, VT 05735
(802) 468-1286

Champlain College

Burlington, Vermont
www.champlain.edu Federal Code: 003684

4-year private business and liberal arts college in small city.

Enrollment: 2,618 undergrads, 20% part-time. 608 full-time freshmen.

Selectivity: Admits 50 to 75% of applicants.

BASIC COSTS (2009-2010)

Tuition and fees: $25,900.

Per-credit charge: $1,075.

Room and board: $11,670.

FINANCIAL AID PICTURE (2008-2009)

Students with need: Need-based aid available for part-time students. Work study available nights, weekends, and for part-time students.

Students without need: No-need awards available for academics, leadership.

FINANCIAL AID PROCEDURES

Forms required: FAFSA.

Dates and Deadlines: Closing date 3/1. Applicants notified by 3/19; must reply by 5/1.

Transfers: Closing date 5/1. Applicants notified on a rolling basis starting 5/1; must reply within 2 week(s) of notification.

CONTACT

Donna Stevens, Director of Financial Aid
163 South Willard Street, Burlington, VT 05402-0670
(802) 860-2730

College of St. Joseph in Vermont

Rutland, Vermont
www.csj.edu Federal Code: 003685

4-year private liberal arts and teachers college in large town, affiliated with Roman Catholic Church.
Enrollment: 202 undergrads, 24% part-time. 43 full-time freshmen.
Selectivity: Admits over 75% of applicants.

BASIC COSTS (2008-2009)

Tuition and fees: $16,790.
Per-credit charge: $250.
Room and board: $8,150.

FINANCIAL AID PICTURE (2008-2009)

Students with need: Average financial aid package met 77% of need; average scholarship/grant was $11,115; average loan was $3,876. For part-time students, average financial aid package was $5,329.
Students without need: No-need awards available for academics.
Cumulative student debt: 95% of graduating class had student loans; average debt was $40,224.
Additional info: Instructors at local Catholic schools are granted a tuition reduction.

FINANCIAL AID PROCEDURES

Forms required: FAFSA, institutional form.
Dates and Deadlines: Priority date 3/1; no closing date. Applicants notified on a rolling basis starting 3/15.
Transfers: No deadline. Applicants notified on a rolling basis.

CONTACT

Julie Rosmus, Financial Aid Director
71 Clement Road, Rutland, VT 05701-3899
(802) 773-5900 ext. 3274

Community College of Vermont

Waterbury, Vermont
www.ccv.edu Federal Code: 011167

2-year public community and liberal arts college in small town.
Enrollment: 3,869 undergrads.
Selectivity: Open admission.

BASIC COSTS (2008-2009)

Tuition and fees: $5,830; out-of-state residents $11,560.
Per-credit charge: $191; out-of-state residents $382.
Additional info: New England Board of Higher Education rate for students from other New England states: 150% of Vermont resident tuition. Available to degree candidates in academic areas not offered by educational institutions in their home states.

FINANCIAL AID PICTURE (2008-2009)

Students with need: Need-based aid available for full-time and part-time students. Work study available nights.
Students without need: This college awards aid only to students with need.

FINANCIAL AID PROCEDURES

Forms required: FAFSA, state aid form, institutional form.
Dates and Deadlines: No deadline. Applicants notified on a rolling basis starting 9/1; must reply within 3 week(s) of notification.

CONTACT

Pam Chisholm, Director for Financial Aid
PO BOX 120, Waterbury, VT 05676-0120
(802) 241-3535

Goddard College

Plainfield, Vermont
www.goddard.edu Federal Code: 003686

4-year private liberal arts college in rural community.
Enrollment: 243 undergrads. 9 full-time freshmen.
Selectivity: Admits over 75% of applicants.

BASIC COSTS (2008-2009)

Additional info: Annual tuition for distance learning Bachelor of Arts is $11,504, for Bachelor of Arts in Writing $12,554. Students attend one week on campus each semester; room and board is $1,088.

FINANCIAL AID PICTURE (2007-2008)

Students with need: Out of 9 full-time freshmen who applied for aid, 8 were judged to have need. Of these, 8 received aid, and 1 had their full need met. Average financial aid package met 40% of need; average scholarship/grant was $4,376; average loan was $4,232.
Students without need: No-need awards available for academics, art, job skills, leadership, music/drama, state/district residency.
Cumulative student debt: 79% of graduating class had student loans; average debt was $21,639.

FINANCIAL AID PROCEDURES

Forms required: FAFSA.
Dates and Deadlines: No deadline. Applicants notified on a rolling basis starting 4/15; must reply within 4 week(s) of notification.
Transfers: No deadline. Applicants notified on a rolling basis.

CONTACT

Beverly Jene, Director of Financial Aid
Goddard College Admissions, Plainfield, VT 05667
(800) 468-4888

Green Mountain College

Poultney, Vermont
www.greenmtn.edu Federal Code: 003687

4-year private liberal arts college in small town, affiliated with United Methodist Church.
Enrollment: 767 undergrads, 2% part-time. 219 full-time freshmen.
Selectivity: Admits 50 to 75% of applicants.

BASIC COSTS (2008-2009)

Tuition and fees: $25,838.
Per-credit charge: $832.
Room and board: $9,522.

FINANCIAL AID PICTURE (2008-2009)

Students with need: Out of 179 full-time freshmen who applied for aid, 150 were judged to have need. Of these, 150 received aid, and 19 had their full need met. Average financial aid package met 68% of need; average scholarship/grant was $14,969; average loan was $3,942. For part-time students, average financial aid package was $17,514.
Students without need: 44 full-time freshmen who did not demonstrate need for aid received scholarships/grants; average award was $12,713. No-need awards available for academics, alumni affiliation, art, leadership, music/drama, religious affiliation.
Scholarships offered: Scholarships for art, performing arts, environmental service, leadership, service: range from $1,000 to $7,000; renewable annually. Make A Difference Scholarship: full tuition; room and board fees; based on merit.
Cumulative student debt: 78% of graduating class had student loans; average debt was $32,448.
Additional info: Service/recognition awards available to all students.

FINANCIAL AID PROCEDURES

Forms required: FAFSA. CSS PROFILE is recommended to receive an earlier financial aid package.

Dates and Deadlines: Priority date 3/1; no closing date. Applicants notified on a rolling basis starting 11/1; must reply by 5/1 or within 4 week(s) of notification.

Transfers: No deadline. Applicants notified on a rolling basis; must reply by 5/1 or within 4 week(s) of notification.

CONTACT

Wendy Ellis, Director of Financial Aid
One Brennan Circle, Poultney, VT 05764
(802) 287-8210

Johnson State College

Johnson, Vermont
www.jsc.edu Federal Code: 003688

4-year public liberal arts college in rural community.

Enrollment: 1,520 undergrads, 31% part-time. 273 full-time freshmen.

Selectivity: Admits over 75% of applicants.

BASIC COSTS (2008-2009)

Tuition and fees: $8,184; out-of-state residents $16,848.

Per-credit charge: $312; out-of-state residents $673.

Room and board: $7,510.

Additional info: New England Board of Higher Education rate for students from other New England states: 150% of Vermont resident tuition. Available to degree candidates in academic areas not offered by educational institutions in their home states.

FINANCIAL AID PICTURE (2008-2009)

Students with need: Need-based aid available for full-time and part-time students.

Students without need: No-need awards available for academics.

FINANCIAL AID PROCEDURES

Forms required: FAFSA, state aid form.

Dates and Deadlines: Priority date 3/1; no closing date. Applicants notified on a rolling basis starting 4/1; must reply within 3 week(s) of notification.

Transfers: Financial aid transcripts from previously attended colleges required.

CONTACT

Lisa Cummings, Director of Financial Aid
337 College Hill, Johnson, VT 05656
(800) 635-2356

Landmark College

Putney, Vermont
www.landmark.edu Federal Code: 017157

2-year private liberal arts college in small town.

Enrollment: 486 undergrads. 131 full-time freshmen.

Selectivity: Admits over 75% of applicants.

BASIC COSTS (2009-2010)

Tuition and fees: $45,800.

Room and board: $8,100.

Additional info: Notebook computer and software required; approximate cost through school $1,500.

FINANCIAL AID PICTURE (2008-2009)

Students with need: Average financial aid package for all full-time undergraduates was $15,500. 74% awarded as scholarships/grants, 26% awarded as loans/jobs. Need-based aid available for part-time students. Work study available nights, weekends, and for part-time students.

Students without need: No-need awards available for academics, art, leadership, minority status, music/drama.

Cumulative student debt: 75% of graduating class had student loans; average debt was $4,372.

Additional info: Students encouraged to apply to their state departments of vocational rehabilitation for additional financial assistance.

FINANCIAL AID PROCEDURES

Forms required: FAFSA.

Dates and Deadlines: Priority date 3/15; no closing date. Applicants notified on a rolling basis starting 4/15; must reply within 2 week(s) of notification.

Transfers: No deadline. Applicants notified on a rolling basis; must reply within 2 week(s) of notification.

CONTACT

Cathy Mullins, Director of Financial Aid
River Road South, Putney, VT 05346
(802) 387-6736

Lyndon State College

Lyndonville, Vermont
www.lyndonstate.edu Federal Code: 003689

4-year public liberal arts and teachers college in small town.

Enrollment: 1,391 undergrads.

BASIC COSTS (2008-2009)

Tuition and fees: $8,284; out-of-state residents $16,948.

Per-credit charge: $312; out-of-state residents $673.

Room and board: $7,510.

Additional info: New England Board of Higher Education rate for students from other New England states: 150% of Vermont resident tuition. Available to degree candidates in academic areas not offered by educational institutions in their home states. Tuition/fee waivers available for unemployed or children of unemployed.

FINANCIAL AID PICTURE (2007-2008)

Students with need: Need-based aid available for full-time and part-time students. Work study available nights, weekends, and for part-time students.

Students without need: No-need awards available for academics, leadership.

FINANCIAL AID PROCEDURES

Forms required: FAFSA.

Dates and Deadlines: Priority date 2/1; no closing date. Applicants notified on a rolling basis starting 4/1; must reply within 2 week(s) of notification.

CONTACT

Tanya Bradley, Director of Financial Aid
1001 College Road, Lyndonville, VT 05851
(802) 626-6218

Marlboro College

Marlboro, Vermont
www.marlboro.edu Federal Code: 003690

4-year private liberal arts college in rural community.

Enrollment: 328 undergrads, 2% part-time. 77 full-time freshmen.

Selectivity: Admits 50 to 75% of applicants.

BASIC COSTS (2009-2010)
Tuition and fees: $33,660.
Room and board: $9,220.

FINANCIAL AID PICTURE (2008-2009)
Students with need: 66% of average financial aid package awarded as scholarships/grants, 34% awarded as loans/jobs. Need-based aid available for part-time students.
Students without need: No-need awards available for academics, leadership.

FINANCIAL AID PROCEDURES
Forms required: FAFSA.
Dates and Deadlines: Closing date 3/1. Applicants notified on a rolling basis starting 2/15; must reply by 5/1 or within 2 week(s) of notification.

CONTACT
Doug Swartz, Dean of Enrollment and Financial Aid
PO Box A, Marlboro, VT 05344-0300
(802) 258-9237

Middlebury College
Middlebury, Vermont — Federal Code: 003691
www.middlebury.edu — CSS Code: 3526

4-year private liberal arts college in small town.
Enrollment: 2,422 undergrads. 644 full-time freshmen.
Selectivity: Admits less than 50% of applicants.

BASIC COSTS (2009-2010)
Comprehensive fee: $50,780.

FINANCIAL AID PICTURE (2007-2008)
Students with need: Out of 390 full-time freshmen who applied for aid, 308 were judged to have need. Of these, 308 received aid, and 308 had their full need met. Average financial aid package met 100% of need; average scholarship/grant was $31,446; average loan was $3,231. Need-based aid available for part-time students.
Students without need: This college awards aid only to students with need.
Cumulative student debt: 36% of graduating class had student loans; average debt was $19,981.
Additional info: College maintains need-blind admissions policy and meets full demonstrated financial need of students who qualify for admission, to degree resources permit.

FINANCIAL AID PROCEDURES
Forms required: FAFSA, CSS PROFILE, institutional form.
Dates and Deadlines: Priority date 11/15; closing date 2/1. Applicants notified by 4/1; must reply by 5/1.
Transfers: Closing date 3/1. Applicants notified by 4/15.

CONTACT
Kim Downs, Director of Student Financial Services
The Emma Willard House, Middlebury, VT 05753-6002
(802) 443-5158

New England Culinary Institute
Montpelier, Vermont
www.neci.edu — Federal Code: 022540

2-year for-profit culinary school in small town.
Enrollment: 628 undergrads.

BASIC COSTS (2008-2009)
Tuition and fees: $25,681.
Room and board: $8,776.
Additional info: Costs vary with program. Required fees include books, knife kit, library and room deposit.

FINANCIAL AID PICTURE (2008-2009)
Students with need: Need-based aid available for full-time students. Work study available nights, weekends, and for part-time students.
Students without need: No-need awards available for academics, alumni affiliation, job skills.
Scholarships offered: Next Generation Scholarship: $1,000 awarded to students recommended by alumni. James Beard Foundation: $1,000-$2,000 awarded. Massachusetts Restaurant Association: up to $2,500 awarded. National Restaurant Association: up to $2,000 awarded.

FINANCIAL AID PROCEDURES
Forms required: FAFSA, state aid form.
Dates and Deadlines: No deadline. Applicants notified on a rolling basis.
Transfers: No deadline. Applicants notified on a rolling basis.

CONTACT
Heather Hansen, Financial Planner
56 College Street, Montpelier, VT 05602
(877) 223-6324

Norwich University
Northfield, Vermont — Federal Code: 003692
www.norwich.edu — CSS Code: 3669

4-year private university and military college in small town.
Enrollment: 2,148 undergrads.

BASIC COSTS (2009-2010)
Tuition and fees: $27,370.
Per-credit charge: $761.
Room and board: $9,484.
Additional info: Military students pay an additional $1,550 per year for cadet uniform for first and second years.

FINANCIAL AID PICTURE
Students with need: Need-based aid available for full-time and part-time students.
Students without need: No-need awards available for academics, leadership, music/drama, ROTC.
Additional info: Winners of ROTC scholarships receive full room and board; must maintain 2.75 GPA. Renewable up to 4 years.

FINANCIAL AID PROCEDURES
Forms required: FAFSA, CSS PROFILE, institutional form.
Dates and Deadlines: Priority date 3/1; no closing date. Applicants notified on a rolling basis starting 12/15.

CONTACT
Tracey Mingo, Director of Financial Aid
158 Harmon Drive, Northfield, VT 05663
(802) 485-2015

St. Michael's College
Colchester, Vermont
www.smcvt.edu — Federal Code: 003694

4-year private liberal arts college in large town, affiliated with Roman Catholic Church.
Enrollment: 1,980 undergrads, 1% part-time. 543 full-time freshmen.
Selectivity: Admits 50 to 75% of applicants.

BASIC COSTS (2009-2010)
Tuition and fees: $33,215.
Per-credit charge: $1,100.

Room and board: $8,280.

FINANCIAL AID PICTURE (2008-2009)

Students with need: Out of 414 full-time freshmen who applied for aid, 319 were judged to have need. Of these, 319 received aid, and 101 had their full need met. Average financial aid package met 76% of need; average scholarship/grant was $14,273; average loan was $4,658. Need-based aid available for part-time students.

Students without need: 176 full-time freshmen who did not demonstrate need for aid received scholarships/grants; average award was $7,046. No-need awards available for academics, athletics, ROTC.

Scholarships offered: 5 full-time freshmen received athletic scholarships; average amount $39,900.

Cumulative student debt: 74% of graduating class had student loans; average debt was $26,044.

FINANCIAL AID PROCEDURES

Forms required: FAFSA.

Dates and Deadlines: Priority date 3/15; no closing date. Applicants notified on a rolling basis starting 2/1; must reply by 5/1 or within 2 week(s) of notification.

CONTACT

Daniel Couture, Director of Student Financial Services
One Winooski Park, Colchester, VT 05439
(802) 654-3244

Southern Vermont College

Bennington, Vermont
www.svc.edu Federal Code: 003693

4-year private liberal arts college in large town.

Enrollment: 444 undergrads, 13% part-time. 131 full-time freshmen.

Selectivity: Admits 50 to 75% of applicants.

BASIC COSTS (2008-2009)

Tuition and fees: $18,160.

Per-credit charge: $575.

Room and board: $8,500.

Additional info: Health insurance, if applicable, $650 per year.

FINANCIAL AID PICTURE (2008-2009)

Students with need: Need-based aid available for full-time and part-time students. Work study available nights, weekends, and for part-time students.

Students without need: No-need awards available for academics, leadership.

Cumulative student debt: 96% of graduating class had student loans; average debt was $7,924.

FINANCIAL AID PROCEDURES

Forms required: FAFSA, state aid form.

Dates and Deadlines: No deadline. Applicants notified on a rolling basis.

CONTACT

Joel Phelps, Director of Financial Aid Services
982 Mansion Drive, Bennington, VT 05201
(802) 447-6306

Sterling College

Craftsbury Common, Vermont
www.sterlingcollege.edu Federal Code: 014991

4-year private liberal arts college in rural community.

Enrollment: 98 undergrads, 4% part-time. 27 full-time freshmen.

Selectivity: Admits over 75% of applicants.

BASIC COSTS (2009-2010)

Tuition and fees: $23,621.

Per-credit charge: $690.

Room and board: $7,554.

Additional info: Students receive $1600 tuition and book credit in exchange for work done on campus.

FINANCIAL AID PICTURE (2008-2009)

Students with need: Need-based aid available for full-time and part-time students. Work study available nights, weekends, and for part-time students.

Students without need: No-need awards available for academics, leadership, state/district residency.

Scholarships offered: Achievement Scholarships: $700-$1,200; demonstration of a significant life achievement. Vermont Scholarship: $1,000-$2,000; for Vermont residents. Bounder Scholarship: $500; applicants who live west of the Mississippi or in the Deep South. Presidential Scholarship: $500-$5,000; applicants who have performed well academically, pursued some degree of activity in environmental, outdoor leadership, or resource management. SCA Award: $1,000; alumni of Student Conservation Association. Transfer Award: $1,000; transfer students for transfer costs. Environmental Steward Scholarship: full-tuition; awarded to student who has displayed exceptional commitment to environment. Vermont Youth Conservation Corps Award: $1,000; awarded to alumni of VYCC.

FINANCIAL AID PROCEDURES

Forms required: FAFSA, state aid form, institutional form.

Dates and Deadlines: Priority date 3/15; no closing date. Applicants notified on a rolling basis starting 2/1; must reply by 5/1 or within 2 week(s) of notification.

CONTACT

Edward Houston, Director of Financial Aid
PO Box 72, Craftsbury Common, VT 05827-0072
(800) 648-3591 ext. 3

University of Vermont

Burlington, Vermont
www.uvm.edu Federal Code: 003696

4-year public university in large town.

Enrollment: 9,867 undergrads, 4% part-time. 2,432 full-time freshmen.

Selectivity: Admits 50 to 75% of applicants.

BASIC COSTS (2008-2009)

Tuition and fees: $12,844; out-of-state residents $29,682.

Per-credit charge: $460; out-of-state residents $1,162.

Room and board: $8,534.

FINANCIAL AID PICTURE (2007-2008)

Students with need: Out of 1,753 full-time freshmen who applied for aid, 1,297 were judged to have need. Of these, 1,295 received aid, and 347 had their full need met. Average financial aid package met 81% of need; average scholarship/grant was $12,311; average loan was $5,760. For part-time students, average financial aid package was $8,583.

Students without need: 754 full-time freshmen who did not demonstrate need for aid received scholarships/grants; average award was $1,920. No-need awards available for academics, art, athletics, ROTC.

Scholarships offered: 43 full-time freshmen received athletic scholarships; average amount $16,927.

Cumulative student debt: 60% of graduating class had student loans; average debt was $25,599.

FINANCIAL AID PROCEDURES

Forms required: FAFSA.

Dates and Deadlines: Priority date 2/10; no closing date. Applicants notified on a rolling basis starting 3/15; must reply within 4 week(s) of notification.

Transfers: No deadline. Applicants notified on a rolling basis starting 3/15; must reply within 4 week(s) of notification. Merit-based scholarships not available to transfer students.

CONTACT

Cecilia Dry, Assistant Controller and Director Student Financial Services
194 South Prospect Street, Burlington, VT 05401-3596
(802) 656-5700

Vermont Technical College

Randolph Center, Vermont
www.vtc.edu Federal Code: 003698

4-year public technical college in small town.
Enrollment: 1,454 undergrads, 16% part-time. 284 full-time freshmen.
Selectivity: Admits 50 to 75% of applicants.

BASIC COSTS (2008-2009)

Tuition and fees: $9,984; out-of-state residents $18,408.
Per-credit charge: $387; out-of-state residents $738.
Room and board: $7,510.
Additional info: New England Board of Higher Education rate for students from other New England states: 150% of Vermont resident tuition. Available to degree candidates in academic areas not offered by educational institutions in their home states.

FINANCIAL AID PICTURE (2007-2008)

Students with need: Out of 260 full-time freshmen who applied for aid, 225 were judged to have need. Of these, 224 received aid, and 40 had their full need met. Average financial aid package met 72% of need; average scholarship/grant was $5,305; average loan was $2,840. For part-time students, average financial aid package was $6,715.
Students without need: 3 full-time freshmen who did not demonstrate need for aid received scholarships/grants; average award was $700. No-need awards available for academics.
Scholarships offered: Presidential Scholarship: $5,000; awarded to 5 nonresidents. Scholars program: full tuition for 2 years (excluding room and board); awarded to 4 Vermont students.
Cumulative student debt: 80% of graduating class had student loans; average debt was $25,600.

FINANCIAL AID PROCEDURES

Forms required: FAFSA.
Dates and Deadlines: Priority date 3/1; no closing date. Applicants notified on a rolling basis starting 3/15; must reply within 2 week(s) of notification.

CONTACT

Cathy McCullough, Director of Financial Aid
PO Box 500, Randolph Center, VT 05061-0500
(800) 965-8790

Virginia

Art Institute of Washington

Arlington, Virginia
www.aiw.artinstitutes.edu Federal Code: 009270

4-year for-profit culinary school and visual arts college in small city.
Enrollment: 914 undergrads. 573 full-time freshmen.

BASIC COSTS (2008-2009)

Tuition and fees: $21,744.
Room only: $9,246.

FINANCIAL AID PICTURE

Students with need: Need-based aid available for part-time students.

FINANCIAL AID PROCEDURES

Forms required: FAFSA, institutional form.

CONTACT

Sam Miller, Director of Student Financial Services
1820 North Fort Myer Drive, Arlington, VA 22209-1802
(703) 358-9550

Averett University

Danville, Virginia
www.averett.edu Federal Code: 003702

4-year private university and liberal arts college in small city.
Enrollment: 774 undergrads, 3% part-time. 243 full-time freshmen.
Selectivity: Admits over 75% of applicants.

BASIC COSTS (2008-2009)

Tuition and fees: $21,300.
Room and board: $7,390.

FINANCIAL AID PICTURE (2007-2008)

Students with need: Out of 228 full-time freshmen who applied for aid, 207 were judged to have need. Of these, 206 received aid, and 30 had their full need met. Average financial aid package met 76% of need; average scholarship/grant was $10,326; average loan was $4,966. For part-time students, average financial aid package was $11,400.
Students without need: 36 full-time freshmen who did not demonstrate need for aid received scholarships/grants; average award was $10,952. No-need awards available for academics, alumni affiliation, art, leadership, minority status, music/drama, state/district residency.
Cumulative student debt: 67% of graduating class had student loans; average debt was $30,943.

FINANCIAL AID PROCEDURES

Forms required: FAFSA, state aid form.
Dates and Deadlines: Priority date 4/1; no closing date. Applicants notified on a rolling basis starting 2/15; must reply within 2 week(s) of notification.
Transfers: No deadline. Applicants notified on a rolling basis starting 2/15; must reply within 2 week(s) of notification.

CONTACT

Carl Bradsher, Dean of Financial Assistance
420 West Main Street, Danville, VA 24541
(434) 791-5890

Blue Ridge Community College

Weyers Cave, Virginia
www.brcc.edu Federal Code: 006819

2-year public community college in rural community.
Enrollment: 4,466 undergrads.
Selectivity: Open admission; but selective for some programs.

BASIC COSTS (2008-2009)

Tuition and fees: $2,678; out-of-state residents $7,842.
Per-credit charge: $82; out-of-state residents $264.
Additional info: Out of state students pay an additional $90 capital outlay fee.

FINANCIAL AID PICTURE (2007-2008)

Students with need: Need-based aid available for full-time and part-time students.
Students without need: No-need awards available for academics, job skills, leadership, minority status.

FINANCIAL AID PROCEDURES

Forms required: FAFSA, institutional form.

Dates and Deadlines: Priority date 5/1; no closing date. Applicants notified on a rolling basis starting 5/30; must reply within 2 week(s) of notification.

CONTACT

Robert Clemmer, Financial Aid Officer
Box 80, Weyers Cave, VA 24486-9989
(540) 234-9261 ext. 2223

Bluefield College

Bluefield, Virginia
www.bluefield.edu Federal Code: 003703

4-year private liberal arts college in small town, affiliated with Baptist faith.

Enrollment: 730 undergrads, 17% part-time. 80 full-time freshmen.

Selectivity: Admits 50 to 75% of applicants.

BASIC COSTS (2009-2010)

Tuition and fees: $17,900.

Per-credit charge: $520.

Room and board: $6,826.

Additional info: Tuition/fee waivers available for adults.

FINANCIAL AID PICTURE (2008-2009)

Students with need: Average financial aid package met 82% of need; average scholarship/grant was $11,959; average loan was $3,110. For part-time students, average financial aid package was $7,267.

Students without need: No-need awards available for academics, alumni affiliation, art, athletics, music/drama, religious affiliation, state/district residency.

Cumulative student debt: 84% of graduating class had student loans; average debt was $16,781.

FINANCIAL AID PROCEDURES

Forms required: FAFSA, state aid form.

Dates and Deadlines: Priority date 3/15; no closing date. Applicants notified on a rolling basis starting 3/1; must reply within 3 week(s) of notification.

Transfers: No deadline. Applicants notified on a rolling basis starting 3/1; must reply within 3 week(s) of notification.

CONTACT

Sheila Nelson-Hensley, Director of Financial Aid
3000 College Drive, Bluefield, VA 24605
(276) 326-4215

Bridgewater College

Bridgewater, Virginia
www.bridgewater.edu Federal Code: 003704

4-year private liberal arts college in small town, affiliated with Church of the Brethren.

Enrollment: 1,490 undergrads, 1% part-time. 488 full-time freshmen.

Selectivity: Admits over 75% of applicants.

BASIC COSTS (2009-2010)

Tuition and fees: $24,500.

Per-credit charge: $825.

Room and board: $9,900.

Additional info: Tuition/fee waivers available for minority students.

FINANCIAL AID PICTURE (2008-2009)

Students with need: Out of 451 full-time freshmen who applied for aid, 378 were judged to have need. Of these, 378 received aid, and 67 had their full need met. Average financial aid package met 77% of need; average scholarship/grant was $17,739; average loan was $4,575. For part-time students, average financial aid package was $4,162.

Students without need: 109 full-time freshmen who did not demonstrate need for aid received scholarships/grants; average award was $10,922. No-need awards available for academics, music/drama, religious affiliation.

Scholarships offered: President's Merit & ACE scholarships: $9,000 to full tuition; based on an applicant's performance in high school, ACT or SAT scores, class rank, and other factors from the applicant's record.

Cumulative student debt: 71% of graduating class had student loans; average debt was $29,519.

FINANCIAL AID PROCEDURES

Forms required: FAFSA, state aid form.

Dates and Deadlines: Priority date 3/1; no closing date. Applicants notified on a rolling basis starting 3/16; must reply within 2 week(s) of notification.

CONTACT

Scott Morrison, Director of Financial Aid
402 East College Street, Bridgewater, VA 22812-1599
(540) 828-5377

Bryant & Stratton College: Richmond

Richmond, Virginia
www.bryantstratton.edu Federal Code: 010061

2-year for-profit career college in small city.

Enrollment: 572 undergrads, 49% part-time. 171 full-time freshmen.

Selectivity: Open admission; but selective for some programs.

BASIC COSTS (2008-2009)

Tuition and fees: $13,775.

Additional info: Annual tuition for bachelor's degree may vary by program.

FINANCIAL AID PICTURE (2007-2008)

Students with need: 33% of average financial aid package awarded as scholarships/grants, 67% awarded as loans/jobs. Need-based aid available for part-time students.

Students without need: This college awards aid only to students with need.

FINANCIAL AID PROCEDURES

Forms required: FAFSA.

Dates and Deadlines: No deadline.

Transfers: No deadline.

CONTACT

Dita Terry, Business Office Director
8141 Hull Street Road, Richmond, VA 23235
(804) 745-2444

Bryant & Stratton College: Virginia Beach

Virginia Beach, Virginia
www.bryantstratton.edu Federal Code: 002678

2-year for-profit business and junior college in large city.

Enrollment: 567 undergrads, 54% part-time. 97 full-time freshmen.

Selectivity: Open admission.

BASIC COSTS (2008-2009)

Tuition and fees: $13,775.

Per-credit charge: $458.

FINANCIAL AID PICTURE (2008-2009)

Students with need: Need-based aid available for full-time and part-time students. Work study available nights.

FINANCIAL AID PROCEDURES

Forms required: FAFSA.

Dates and Deadlines: No deadline. Applicants notified on a rolling basis.

CONTACT

Bethann Verbal, Director of Financial Aid
301 Centre Pointe Drive, Virginia Beach, VA 23462-4417
(757) 499-7900

Centura College: Norfolk

Norfolk, Virginia Federal Code: 016418

2-year for-profit branch campus and career college in large city.

Enrollment: 370 full-time undergrads.

Selectivity: Open admission.

BASIC COSTS (2008-2009)

Tuition and fees: $11,060.

Additional info: Annual tuition and fees reported are representative and will vary depending on program.

FINANCIAL AID PICTURE (2008-2009)

Students with need: 24% of average financial aid package awarded as scholarships/grants, 76% awarded as loans/jobs.

CONTACT

Shakema Farmer, Financial Aid Manager
7020 North Military Highway, Norfolk, VA 23518-4202
(757) 853-2121

Christendom College

Front Royal, Virginia
www.christendom.edu

4-year private liberal arts college in large town, affiliated with Roman Catholic Church.

Enrollment: 421 undergrads, 1% part-time. 123 full-time freshmen.

Selectivity: Admits over 75% of applicants.

BASIC COSTS (2009-2010)

Tuition and fees: $18,570.

Room and board: $7,390.

FINANCIAL AID PICTURE (2008-2009)

Students with need: Out of 76 full-time freshmen who applied for aid, 61 were judged to have need. Of these, 61 received aid, and 61 had their full need met. Average financial aid package met 90% of need; average scholarship/grant was $6,565; average loan was $5,719.

Students without need: 36 full-time freshmen who did not demonstrate need for aid received scholarships/grants; average award was $7,570. No-need awards available for academics, alumni affiliation.

Cumulative student debt: 60% of graduating class had student loans; average debt was $22,000.

Additional info: Christendom accepts no direct federal aid, nor does it participate in indirect programs of federal aid.

FINANCIAL AID PROCEDURES

Forms required: institutional form.

Dates and Deadlines: Priority date 4/1; closing date 6/1. Applicants notified on a rolling basis starting 2/1; must reply within 4 week(s) of notification.

CONTACT

Alisa Polk, Financial Aid Officer
134 Christendom Drive, Front Royal, VA 22630
(800) 877-5456

Christopher Newport University

Newport News, Virginia
www.cnu.edu Federal Code: 003706

4-year public university and liberal arts college in small city.

Enrollment: 4,746 undergrads, 3% part-time. 1,137 full-time freshmen.

Selectivity: Admits 50 to 75% of applicants.

BASIC COSTS (2008-2009)

Tuition and fees: $7,550; out-of-state residents $14,932.

Per-credit charge: $315; out-of-state residents $613.

Room and board: $8,900.

FINANCIAL AID PICTURE (2008-2009)

Students with need: Out of 822 full-time freshmen who applied for aid, 468 were judged to have need. Of these, 460 received aid, and 118 had their full need met. Average financial aid package met 75% of need; average scholarship/grant was $5,096; average loan was $3,100. For part-time students, average financial aid package was $5,419.

Students without need: 116 full-time freshmen who did not demonstrate need for aid received scholarships/grants; average award was $1,925. No-need awards available for academics, art, leadership, music/drama, state/district residency.

Cumulative student debt: 57% of graduating class had student loans; average debt was $17,752.

FINANCIAL AID PROCEDURES

Forms required: FAFSA.

Dates and Deadlines: Priority date 3/1; no closing date. Applicants notified on a rolling basis starting 2/21; must reply within 3 week(s) of notification.

Transfers: No deadline. Applicants notified on a rolling basis starting 3/1; must reply within 2 week(s) of notification.

CONTACT

Mary Wigginton, Director of Financial Aid
1 University Place, Newport News, VA 23606-2998
(757) 594-7170

College of William and Mary

Williamsburg, Virginia
www.wm.edu Federal Code: 003705

4-year public university in large town.

Enrollment: 5,811 undergrads, 1% part-time. 1,386 full-time freshmen.

Selectivity: Admits less than 50% of applicants.

BASIC COSTS (2008-2009)

Tuition and fees: $10,246; out-of-state residents $29,116.

Per-credit charge: $225; out-of-state residents $840.

Room and board: $8,030.

FINANCIAL AID PICTURE (2008-2009)

Students with need: Out of 814 full-time freshmen who applied for aid, 393 were judged to have need. Of these, 393 received aid, and 168 had their full need met. Average financial aid package met 82% of need; average scholarship/grant was $13,088; average loan was $2,690. For part-time students, average financial aid package was $9,000.

Students without need: 32 full-time freshmen who did not demonstrate need for aid received scholarships/grants; average award was $7,396. No-need awards available for academics, athletics, leadership, ROTC.

Scholarships offered: 60 full-time freshmen received athletic scholarships; average amount $16,780.
Cumulative student debt: 39% of graduating class had student loans; average debt was $12,859.

FINANCIAL AID PROCEDURES
Forms required: FAFSA.
Dates and Deadlines: Priority date 2/15; no closing date. Applicants notified on a rolling basis starting 3/15; must reply by 5/1 or within 2 week(s) of notification.

CONTACT
Edward Irish, Director of Student Financial Aid
PO Box 8795, Williamsburg, VA 23187-8795
(757) 221-2420

Dabney S. Lancaster Community College
Clifton Forge, Virginia
www.dslcc.edu Federal Code: 004996

2-year public community college in small town.
Enrollment: 529 undergrads, 40% part-time. 142 full-time freshmen.
Selectivity: Open admission; but selective for some programs.

BASIC COSTS (2008-2009)
Tuition and fees: $2,636; out-of-state residents $7,800.
Per-credit charge: $82; out-of-state residents $254.
Additional info: Out of state students pay an additional $90 capital outlay fee.

FINANCIAL AID PICTURE
Students with need: Need-based aid available for full-time and part-time students.
Students without need: This college awards aid only to students with need.

FINANCIAL AID PROCEDURES
Forms required: FAFSA, institutional form.
Dates and Deadlines: Priority date 3/15; no closing date. Applicants notified on a rolling basis starting 4/15; must reply within 2 week(s) of notification.

CONTACT
Sandra Haverlack, Coordinator of Financial Aid and Veterans Affairs
Box 1000, Clifton Forge, VA 24422
(540) 863-2822

Danville Community College
Danville, Virginia
www.dcc.vccs.edu Federal Code: 003758

2-year public community college in small city.
Enrollment: 2,106 undergrads.
Selectivity: Open admission; but selective for some programs.

BASIC COSTS (2008-2009)
Tuition and fees: $2,617; out-of-state residents $7,781.
Per-credit charge: $82; out-of-state residents $254.
Additional info: Out of state students pay an additional $90 capital outlay fee.

FINANCIAL AID PICTURE (2007-2008)
Students with need: Need-based aid available for full-time and part-time students.
Students without need: This college awards aid only to students with need.
Scholarships offered: Educational Foundation Scholarship: $250 to $1,500; based on separate application; deadline mid-March prior to award year.

FINANCIAL AID PROCEDURES
Forms required: FAFSA.
Dates and Deadlines: Priority date 6/1; no closing date. Applicants notified on a rolling basis starting 5/1; must reply within 2 week(s) of notification.
Transfers: Limited aid available to transfer students admitted in spring semester.

CONTACT
Mary Gore, Assistant Coordinator of Financial Aid
1008 South Main Street, Danville, VA 24541
(434) 797-8439

DeVry University: Arlington
Arlington, Virginia
www.devry.edu

4-year for-profit university in very large city.
Enrollment: 593 undergrads, 46% part-time. 97 full-time freshmen.

BASIC COSTS (2008-2009)
Tuition and fees: $14,390.
Per-credit charge: $525.

FINANCIAL AID PICTURE (2007-2008)
Students with need: Need-based aid available for full-time and part-time students.
Students without need: This college awards aid only to students with need.

FINANCIAL AID PROCEDURES
Forms required: FAFSA.
Dates and Deadlines: No deadline. Applicants notified on a rolling basis.

CONTACT
Roberta McDevitt, Director of Student Finance
2450 Crystal Drive, Arlington, VA 22202
(703) 414-4000

Eastern Mennonite University
Harrisonburg, Virginia
www.emu.edu Federal Code: 003708

4-year private university and liberal arts college in large town, affiliated with Mennonite Church.
Enrollment: 951 undergrads, 1% part-time. 183 full-time freshmen.
Selectivity: Admits 50 to 75% of applicants.

BASIC COSTS (2008-2009)
Tuition and fees: $23,180.
Room and board: $7,200.

FINANCIAL AID PICTURE (2008-2009)
Students with need: Need-based aid available for full-time and part-time students. Work study available nights, weekends, and for part-time students.
Students without need: No-need awards available for academics, alumni affiliation, art, leadership, religious affiliation, state/district residency.
Scholarships offered: President's Scholarship: GPA of 3.9 or higher. Academic Achievement Scholarship: minimum 3.2 GPA. University Grant: minimum 2.5 GPA; minimum SAT score of 920 (exclusive of Writing) or ACT score of 20 required for all scholarships. Amounts based on GPA and test scores; no limit on number of awards. Full-tuition scholarships available for 2 honors program applicants with highest test scores and GPA; half tuition scholarships available for next 10 candidates.

FINANCIAL AID PROCEDURES
Forms required: FAFSA, state aid form.

Dates and Deadlines: Priority date 3/1; no closing date. Applicants notified on a rolling basis starting 3/1; must reply within 4 week(s) of notification.
Transfers: No deadline. Applicants notified on a rolling basis starting 3/1; must reply within 4 week(s) of notification.

CONTACT

Michele Hensley, Director of Financial Assistance
1200 Park Road, Harrisonburg, VA 22802-2462
(540) 432-4137

Eastern Shore Community College

Melfa, Virginia
www.es.vccs.edu Federal Code: 003748

2-year public community college in rural community.
Enrollment: 582 undergrads.
Selectivity: Open admission.

BASIC COSTS (2008-2009)

Tuition and fees: $2,645; out-of-state residents $7,809.
Per-credit charge: $82; out-of-state residents $254.
Additional info: Out of state students pay an additional $90 capital outlay fee.

FINANCIAL AID PICTURE

Students with need: Need-based aid available for full-time and part-time students.
Students without need: This college awards aid only to students with need.
Additional info: ESCC is a member of the Servicemembers Opportunity Colleges (SOC) program. This is a world-wide network of colleges and universities working with the Armed Forces dedicated to helping service people and their families get college degrees.

FINANCIAL AID PROCEDURES

Forms required: FAFSA.
Dates and Deadlines: Priority date 5/1; no closing date. Applicants notified on a rolling basis starting 6/1; must reply within 2 week(s) of notification.

CONTACT

P Smith, Chief Financial Aid Officer
29300 Lankford Highway, Melfa, VA 23410-9755
(757) 789-1732

ECPI College of Technology: Virginia Beach

Virginia Beach, Virginia
www.ecpi.edu Federal Code: 010198

4-year for-profit health science and technical college in very large city.
Enrollment: 6,000 undergrads.

BASIC COSTS (2008-2009)

Tuition and fees: $10,650.
Per-credit charge: $272.

FINANCIAL AID PICTURE

Students with need: Need-based aid available for full-time and part-time students. Work study available nights.
Students without need: No-need awards available for academics.

FINANCIAL AID PROCEDURES

Forms required: institutional form.
Dates and Deadlines: No deadline. Applicants notified on a rolling basis.

CONTACT

Kathi Turner, Director of Financial Aid
5555 Greenwich Road, Suite 300, Virginia Beach, VA 23462-6542
(757) 671-7171 ext. 311

ECPI Technical College: Roanoke

Roanoke, Virginia
www.ecpitech.edu Federal Code: 017205

2-year for-profit technical college in small city.
Enrollment: 347 undergrads.

BASIC COSTS (2008-2009)

Tuition and fees: $10,650.

FINANCIAL AID PICTURE

Students with need: Need-based aid available for full-time and part-time students.

FINANCIAL AID PROCEDURES

Forms required: FAFSA.
Dates and Deadlines: No deadline. Applicants notified on a rolling basis.

CONTACT

Carol Rouch, Director of Financial Aid
5234 Airport Road, Roanoke, VA 24012
(540) 563-8080

Emory & Henry College

Emory, Virginia
www.ehc.edu Federal Code: 003709

4-year private liberal arts college in rural community, affiliated with United Methodist Church.
Enrollment: 886 undergrads, 2% part-time. 241 full-time freshmen.
Selectivity: Admits 50 to 75% of applicants.

BASIC COSTS (2008-2009)

Tuition and fees: $23,860.
Per-credit charge: $985.
Room and board: $7,980.

FINANCIAL AID PICTURE (2008-2009)

Students with need: Out of 226 full-time freshmen who applied for aid, 198 were judged to have need. Of these, 198 received aid, and 53 had their full need met. Average financial aid package met 90% of need; average scholarship/grant was $20,518; average loan was $3,436. For part-time students, average financial aid package was $15,339.
Students without need: 28 full-time freshmen who did not demonstrate need for aid received scholarships/grants; average award was $12,045. No-need awards available for academics, art, music/drama, religious affiliation, state/district residency.
Cumulative student debt: 61% of graduating class had student loans; average debt was $19,744.
Additional info: Virginia residents eligible for additional in-state tuition grants.

FINANCIAL AID PROCEDURES

Forms required: FAFSA, state aid form.
Dates and Deadlines: Priority date 4/15; no closing date. Applicants notified on a rolling basis starting 3/1; must reply by 6/15.
Transfers: Priority date 4/1; closing date 5/15. Applicants notified on a rolling basis starting 2/15; must reply by 6/15 or within 4 week(s) of notification. Financial aid based on academic credits accepted for transfer.

CONTACT
Margaret Murphy, Director of Financial Aid and Student Services
Box 10, Emory, VA 24327
(276) 944-6115

Ferrum College
Ferrum, Virginia
www.ferrum.edu

4-year private liberal arts college in rural community, affiliated with United Methodist Church.
Enrollment: 1,367 undergrads, 1% part-time. 587 full-time freshmen.
Selectivity: Admits over 75% of applicants.

BASIC COSTS (2008-2009)
Tuition and fees: $22,545.
Per-credit charge: $450.
Room and board: $7,300.

FINANCIAL AID PICTURE (2008-2009)
Students with need: Out of 568 full-time freshmen who applied for aid, 509 were judged to have need. Of these, 509 received aid. Average financial aid package met 98% of need; average scholarship/grant was $11,542; average loan was $3,228. For part-time students, average financial aid package was $7,489.
Students without need: 67 full-time freshmen who did not demonstrate need for aid received scholarships/grants; average award was $6,221. No-need awards available for academics, leadership, religious affiliation, state/district residency.
Scholarships offered: Ferrum Scholarship: $5,000-$10,000; high school GPA must be 3.0 or higher and SAT score must be 1500 or higher. Ferrum Merit Grant: $1,000-$7,000; high school GPA must be 2.0 or higher and SAT score must be in the range of 1050.
Cumulative student debt: 86% of graduating class had student loans; average debt was $24,288.

FINANCIAL AID PROCEDURES
Forms required: FAFSA, state aid form.
Dates and Deadlines: Priority date 3/1; no closing date. Applicants notified on a rolling basis starting 1/10.

CONTACT
Heather Hollandsworth, Director of Financial Aid
Spilman-Daniel House, Ferrum, VA 24088
(540) 365-4282

George Mason University
Fairfax, Virginia
www.gmu.edu Federal Code: 003749

4-year public university in large town.
Enrollment: 18,240 undergrads, 22% part-time. 2,175 full-time freshmen.
Selectivity: Admits 50 to 75% of applicants.

BASIC COSTS (2008-2009)
Tuition and fees: $7,512; out-of-state residents $22,476.
Per-credit charge: $230; out-of-state residents $854.
Room and board: $7,360.

FINANCIAL AID PICTURE (2007-2008)
Students with need: Out of 1,460 full-time freshmen who applied for aid, 931 were judged to have need. Of these, 889 received aid, and 153 had their full need met. Average financial aid package met 71% of need; average scholarship/grant was $5,835; average loan was $3,393. For part-time students, average financial aid package was $6,059.
Students without need: 81 full-time freshmen who did not demonstrate need for aid received scholarships/grants; average award was $6,137. No-need awards available for academics, athletics, minority status, music/drama, ROTC, state/district residency.
Scholarships offered: 51 full-time freshmen received athletic scholarships; average amount $12,915.
Cumulative student debt: 54% of graduating class had student loans; average debt was $18,547.

FINANCIAL AID PROCEDURES
Forms required: FAFSA.
Dates and Deadlines: Priority date 3/1; no closing date. Applicants notified on a rolling basis starting 4/1; must reply within 3 week(s) of notification.

CONTACT
Jevita de Freitas, Director, Student Financial Aid
4400 University Drive, MSN 3A4, Fairfax, VA 22030-4444

Germanna Community College
Locust Grove, Virginia
www.germanna.edu Federal Code: 008660

2-year public community college in rural community.
Enrollment: 4,157 undergrads.
Selectivity: Open admission; but selective for some programs.

BASIC COSTS (2008-2009)
Tuition and fees: $2,638; out-of-state residents $7,802.
Per-credit charge: $82; out-of-state residents $254.
Additional info: An indirect cost fee of $31 per credit hour is charged to all out-of-state distance learning students.

FINANCIAL AID PICTURE (2007-2008)
Students with need: Need-based aid available for full-time and part-time students.
Students without need: No-need awards available for academics.

FINANCIAL AID PROCEDURES
Forms required: FAFSA.
Dates and Deadlines: Priority date 4/1; no closing date. Applicants notified on a rolling basis starting 5/15; must reply within 2 week(s) of notification.

CONTACT
Michael Farris, Financial Aid Coordinator
2130 Germanna Highway, Locust Grove, VA 22508-2102
(540) 423-9124

Hampden-Sydney College
Hampden-Sydney, Virginia Federal Code: 003713
www.hsc.edu CSS Code: 5291

4-year private liberal arts college for men in rural community, affiliated with Presbyterian Church (USA).
Enrollment: 1,120 undergrads. 314 full-time freshmen.
Selectivity: Admits 50 to 75% of applicants.

BASIC COSTS (2008-2009)
Tuition and fees: $29,366.
Room and board: $9,228.

FINANCIAL AID PICTURE (2008-2009)
Students with need: Out of 216 full-time freshmen who applied for aid, 168 were judged to have need. Of these, 167 received aid, and 58 had their full need met. Average financial aid package met 85% of need; average scholarship/grant was $18,714; average loan was $3,847. Need-based aid available for part-time students.

Students without need: 159 full-time freshmen who did not demonstrate need for aid received scholarships/grants; average award was $18,223. No-need awards available for academics, leadership, religious affiliation, ROTC, state/district residency.

Scholarships offered: Allan Scholarship: $20,000 annually. Venable Scholarship: $16,000 annually. Patrick Henry Scholarship: $12,000 annually. Achievement Awards: range from $2,000-$10,000 annually. All based on academic ability.

FINANCIAL AID PROCEDURES

Forms required: FAFSA, CSS PROFILE, state aid form.

Dates and Deadlines: Priority date 3/1; no closing date. Applicants notified on a rolling basis starting 2/1; must reply by 5/1 or within 2 week(s) of notification.

Transfers: No deadline. Applicants notified on a rolling basis; must reply within 2 week(s) of notification.

CONTACT

Keith Wellings, Director of Financial Aid
Box 667, Hampden-Sydney, VA 23943
(434) 223-6119

Hampton University

Hampton, Virginia
www.hamptonu.edu Federal Code: 003714

4-year private university in small city.

Enrollment: 4,689 undergrads, 5% part-time. 1,191 full-time freshmen.

BASIC COSTS (2008-2009)

Tuition and fees: $16,392.

Per-credit charge: $370.

Room and board: $7,440.

FINANCIAL AID PICTURE (2008-2009)

Students with need: Need-based aid available for full-time and part-time students. Work study available nights, weekends, and for part-time students.

Students without need: No-need awards available for academics, athletics, leadership, music/drama, ROTC.

FINANCIAL AID PROCEDURES

Forms required: FAFSA.

Dates and Deadlines: Priority date 3/1; no closing date. Applicants notified on a rolling basis starting 4/15; must reply within 2 week(s) of notification.

CONTACT

Marcia Boyd, Financial Aid Director
Office of Admissions, Hampton, VA 23668
(757) 727-5332

Hollins University

Roanoke, Virginia
www.hollins.edu Federal Code: 003715

4-year private university and liberal arts college for women in small city.

Enrollment: 785 undergrads, 5% part-time. 209 full-time freshmen.

Selectivity: Admits over 75% of applicants.

BASIC COSTS (2009-2010)

Tuition and fees: $28,280.

Room and board: $10,040.

FINANCIAL AID PICTURE (2008-2009)

Students with need: Need-based aid available for full-time and part-time students. Work study available nights, weekends, and for part-time students.

Students without need: No-need awards available for academics, alumni affiliation, art, leadership, music/drama, state/district residency.

Scholarships offered: Scholar Awards: $5,000 full tuition; academic merit. Founder's Awards: $1,500-$7,000; organizational involvement. Creative Talent Awards: $1,500-$7,000; distinguished achievement or outstanding involvement in art, photography/film, creative writing, music, dance or theater.

FINANCIAL AID PROCEDURES

Forms required: FAFSA, state aid form.

Dates and Deadlines: Priority date 2/15; no closing date. Applicants notified on a rolling basis starting 3/1; must reply by 5/1.

Transfers: Priority date 7/1; closing date 7/15.

CONTACT

Ken Flick, Director of Scholarships and Financial Assistance
PO Box 9707, Roanoke, VA 24020-1707
(540) 362-6332

J. Sargeant Reynolds Community College

Richmond, Virginia
www.reynolds.edu Federal Code: 003759

2-year public community college in very large city.

Enrollment: 8,750 undergrads.

Selectivity: Open admission; but selective for some programs.

BASIC COSTS (2008-2009)

Tuition and fees: $2,810; out-of-state residents $7,974.

Per-credit charge: $82; out-of-state residents $254.

Additional info: Out-of-state students pay additional $90 capital outlay fee.

FINANCIAL AID PICTURE

Students with need: Need-based aid available for full-time and part-time students. Work study available nights, weekends, and for part-time students.

Students without need: No-need awards available for academics.

Scholarships offered: Local Board Scholarship: full tuition; high school students with minimum 3.0 GPA; 23 awarded. Eric and Jeanette Lipman Endowed Scholarship: based on academic excellence; number and amount awarded varies. Central Fidelity Bank Scholarship: $1,500; first-year students; minimum 2.5 cumulative GPA; 2 awarded.

FINANCIAL AID PROCEDURES

Forms required: FAFSA.

Dates and Deadlines: Priority date 6/30; no closing date. Applicants notified on a rolling basis starting 7/15; must reply within 2 week(s) of notification.

CONTACT

Keisha Pope, Director of Financial Aid
Box 85622, Richmond, VA 23285-5622
(804) 523-5137

James Madison University

Harrisonburg, Virginia
www.jmu.edu Federal Code: 003721

4-year public university in large town.

Enrollment: 16,648 undergrads, 3% part-time. 3,956 full-time freshmen.

Selectivity: Admits 50 to 75% of applicants.

BASIC COSTS (2008-2009)

Tuition and fees: $6,964; out-of-state residents $18,458.

Per-credit charge: $118; out-of-state residents $497.

Room and board: $7,458.

FINANCIAL AID PICTURE (2008-2009)

Students with need: Out of 2,916 full-time freshmen who applied for aid, 1,447 were judged to have need. Of these, 1,214 received aid, and 1,189 had their full need met. Average financial aid package met 45% of need; average scholarship/grant was $7,046; average loan was $3,488. For part-time students, average financial aid package was $8,511.

Students without need: 161 full-time freshmen who did not demonstrate need for aid received scholarships/grants; average award was $2,032. No-need awards available for academics, alumni affiliation, art, athletics, leadership, minority status, music/drama, state/district residency.

Scholarships offered: 82 full-time freshmen received athletic scholarships; average amount $14,746.

Cumulative student debt: 46% of graduating class had student loans; average debt was $17,395.

FINANCIAL AID PROCEDURES

Forms required: FAFSA.

Dates and Deadlines: Priority date 3/1; no closing date. Applicants notified on a rolling basis starting 4/1; must reply within 4 week(s) of notification.

Transfers: Closing date 3/1. Applicants notified on a rolling basis starting 4/1; must reply within 4 week(s) of notification.

CONTACT

Lisa Turner, Director of Financial Aid and Scholarships
Sonner Hall, MSC 0101, Harrisonburg, VA 22807
(540) 568-7820

Jefferson College of Health Sciences

Roanoke, Virginia
www.jchs.edu Federal Code: 009893

4-year private health science and nursing college in large city.

Enrollment: 899 undergrads, 31% part-time. 86 full-time freshmen.

Selectivity: Admits less than 50% of applicants.

BASIC COSTS (2008-2009)

Tuition and fees: $16,275.

Per-credit charge: $470.

Room and board: $7,010.

FINANCIAL AID PICTURE (2007-2008)

Students with need: Out of 80 full-time freshmen who applied for aid, 71 were judged to have need. Of these, 71 received aid, and 42 had their full need met. Average financial aid package met 40% of need; average scholarship/grant was $3,213; average loan was $3,626. For part-time students, average financial aid package was $6,527.

Students without need: 13 full-time freshmen who did not demonstrate need for aid received scholarships/grants; average award was $6,880. No-need awards available for academics.

FINANCIAL AID PROCEDURES

Forms required: FAFSA, institutional form.

Dates and Deadlines: No deadline. Applicants notified on a rolling basis; must reply within 2 week(s) of notification.

CONTACT

Deborah Johnson, Financial Aid Officer
Box 13186, Roanoke, VA 24031-3186
(540) 985-8483

John Tyler Community College

Chester, Virginia
www.jtcc.edu Federal Code: 004004

2-year public community college in small city.

Enrollment: 4,989 undergrads, 60% part-time. 446 full-time freshmen.

Selectivity: Open admission; but selective for some programs.

BASIC COSTS (2008-2009)

Tuition and fees: $2,635; out-of-state residents $7,799.

Per-credit charge: $82; out-of-state residents $254.

Additional info: Out-of-state students pay additional $90 capital outlay fee.

FINANCIAL AID PICTURE (2007-2008)

Students with need: Need-based aid available for full-time and part-time students. Work study available nights, weekends, and for part-time students.

Students without need: No-need awards available for academics, state/district residency.

FINANCIAL AID PROCEDURES

Forms required: FAFSA.

Dates and Deadlines: Priority date 5/15; closing date 7/15. Applicants notified on a rolling basis starting 6/15.

CONTACT

Fred Taylor, Vice President for Finance and Administration
13101 Jefferson Davis Highway, Chester, VA 23831-5316
(804) 706-5016

Liberty University

Lynchburg, Virginia
www.liberty.edu Federal Code: 010392

4-year private university in small city, affiliated with Baptist faith.

Enrollment: 21,506 undergrads, 32% part-time. 2,481 full-time freshmen.

Selectivity: Admits over 75% of applicants.

BASIC COSTS (2009-2010)

Tuition and fees: $17,742.

Per-credit charge: $550.

Room and board: $5,996.

FINANCIAL AID PICTURE (2008-2009)

Students with need: Need-based aid available for full-time and part-time students.

Students without need: No-need awards available for academics, alumni affiliation, athletics, leadership, music/drama, religious affiliation, ROTC, state/district residency.

Scholarships offered: Liberty Academic Achievement Scholarship: based on combination of high school grades and standardized test scores. Students may qualify for up to $6,000. Additional $3,500 could be applied if student is also accepted into the Honors Program.

FINANCIAL AID PROCEDURES

Forms required: FAFSA, state aid form.

Dates and Deadlines: Closing date 3/1. Applicants notified on a rolling basis starting 3/15; must reply within 3 week(s) of notification.

Transfers: Applicants notified on a rolling basis starting 3/15; must reply within 3 week(s) of notification.

CONTACT

Robert Ritz, Director of Student Financial Aid
1971 University Boulevard, Lynchburg, VA 24502
(434) 582-2270

Longwood University

Farmville, Virginia
www.longwood.edu Federal Code: 003719

4-year public university in small town.

Enrollment: 3,971 undergrads, 4% part-time. 954 full-time freshmen.

Selectivity: Admits 50 to 75% of applicants.

BASIC COSTS (2008-2009)
Tuition and fees: $8,502; out-of-state residents $17,114.
Room and board: $6,856.
Additional info: Required laptop computer for first-year students $1,700.

FINANCIAL AID PICTURE (2007-2008)
Students with need: Out of 579 full-time freshmen who applied for aid, 434 were judged to have need. Of these, 434 received aid, and 59 had their full need met. Average financial aid package met 64% of need; average scholarship/grant was $5,201; average loan was $3,297. For part-time students, average financial aid package was $5,435.
Students without need: 16 full-time freshmen who did not demonstrate need for aid received scholarships/grants; average award was $3,729. No-need awards available for academics, alumni affiliation, art, athletics, leadership, music/drama, ROTC, state/district residency.
Scholarships offered: ***Merit:*** Longwood Scholars: $2,200. Hull Scholarship: $5,000. Citizen Scholars: $5,500. All awards based on high school GPA and test scores. ***Athletic:*** 10 full-time freshmen received athletic scholarships; average amount $8,244.
Cumulative student debt: 63% of graduating class had student loans; average debt was $14,934.

FINANCIAL AID PROCEDURES
Forms required: FAFSA.
Dates and Deadlines: Priority date 3/1; no closing date. Applicants notified on a rolling basis starting 4/1; must reply within 4 week(s) of notification.
Transfers: Applicants notified by 4/1; must reply by 5/1.

CONTACT
Karen Schinabeck, Director of Financial Aid
201 High Street, Farmville, VA 23909-1898
(434) 395-2077

Lord Fairfax Community College
Middletown, Virginia
www.lfcc.edu Federal Code: 008659

2-year public community college in small town.
Enrollment: 3,827 undergrads.
Selectivity: Open admission.

BASIC COSTS (2008-2009)
Tuition and fees: $2,647; out-of-state residents $7,811.
Per-credit charge: $82; out-of-state residents $254.
Additional info: Out-of-state students pay an additional $90 capital outlay fee.

FINANCIAL AID PICTURE (2007-2008)
Students with need: Need-based aid available for part-time students.
Students without need: This college awards aid only to students with need.

FINANCIAL AID PROCEDURES
Forms required: FAFSA.
Dates and Deadlines: Priority date 5/1; no closing date. Applicants notified on a rolling basis starting 6/1.

CONTACT
Aaron Whitacre, Coordinator of Financial Aid and Veterans Affairs
173 Skirmisher Lane, Middletown, VA 22645
(540) 868-7274

Lynchburg College
Lynchburg, Virginia
www.lynchburg.edu Federal Code: 003720

4-year private liberal arts college in small city, affiliated with Christian Church (Disciples of Christ).
Enrollment: 2,091 undergrads, 4% part-time. 594 full-time freshmen.
Selectivity: Admits 50 to 75% of applicants.

BASIC COSTS (2009-2010)
Tuition and fees: $28,105.
Per-credit charge: $375.
Room and board: $7,570.
Additional info: Tuition/fee waivers available for adults.

FINANCIAL AID PICTURE (2008-2009)
Students with need: Out of 479 full-time freshmen who applied for aid, 382 were judged to have need. Of these, 382 received aid, and 89 had their full need met. Average financial aid package met 82% of need; average scholarship/grant was $16,846; average loan was $2,889. For part-time students, average financial aid package was $6,467.
Students without need: 171 full-time freshmen who did not demonstrate need for aid received scholarships/grants; average award was $9,833. No-need awards available for academics, leadership, music/drama, religious affiliation.
Cumulative student debt: 69% of graduating class had student loans; average debt was $26,915.

FINANCIAL AID PROCEDURES
Forms required: FAFSA, state aid form.
Dates and Deadlines: Priority date 3/1; no closing date. Applicants notified on a rolling basis starting 3/15; must reply by 5/1 or within 2 week(s) of notification.
Transfers: Priority date 7/1; no deadline. Applicants notified on a rolling basis starting 3/5; must reply within 2 week(s) of notification.

CONTACT
Michelle Davis, Director of Financial Aid
1501 Lakeside Drive, Lynchburg, VA 24501-3199
(434) 544-8228

Mary Baldwin College
Staunton, Virginia
www.mbc.edu Federal Code: 003723

4-year private liberal arts college for women in large town, affiliated with Presbyterian Church (USA).
Enrollment: 1,390 undergrads, 26% part-time. 246 full-time freshmen.
Selectivity: Admits 50 to 75% of applicants.

BASIC COSTS (2008-2009)
Tuition and fees: $23,645.
Per-credit charge: $400.
Room and board: $6,730.

FINANCIAL AID PICTURE (2007-2008)
Students with need: Out of 223 full-time freshmen who applied for aid, 197 were judged to have need. Of these, 197 received aid, and 111 had their full need met. Average financial aid package met 91% of need; average scholarship/grant was $11,175; average loan was $2,548. For part-time students, average financial aid package was $8,710.
Students without need: 49 full-time freshmen who did not demonstrate need for aid received scholarships/grants; average award was $15,719. No-need awards available for academics, leadership, state/district residency.
Cumulative student debt: 78% of graduating class had student loans; average debt was $20,548.

FINANCIAL AID PROCEDURES

Forms required: FAFSA, state aid form.
Dates and Deadlines: Priority date 5/15; no closing date. Applicants notified on a rolling basis starting 2/1; must reply by 5/1.
Transfers: No deadline. Applicants notified on a rolling basis starting 2/1; must reply by 5/1.

CONTACT

Lisa Branson, Associate Vice President for Enrollment Management
Office of Admissions, Staunton, VA 24401
(540) 887-7022

Marymount University

Arlington, Virginia
www.marymount.edu Federal Code: 003724

4-year private university in small city, affiliated with Roman Catholic Church.
Enrollment: 2,162 undergrads, 14% part-time. 404 full-time freshmen.
Selectivity: Admits over 75% of applicants.

BASIC COSTS (2009-2010)

Tuition and fees: $22,620.
Per-credit charge: $725.
Room and board: $9,745.

FINANCIAL AID PICTURE (2008-2009)

Students with need: Out of 332 full-time freshmen who applied for aid, 271 were judged to have need. Of these, 270 received aid, and 47 had their full need met. Average financial aid package met 72% of need; average scholarship/grant was $5,108; average loan was $3,612. For part-time students, average financial aid package was $6,932.
Students without need: 118 full-time freshmen who did not demonstrate need for aid received scholarships/grants; average award was $9,765. No-need awards available for academics, alumni affiliation, leadership, ROTC, state/district residency.
Scholarships offered: Freshman Academic Scholarship: Guaranteed for full-time freshman with cumulative high school GPA of 3.3 or better and combined SAT score (exclusive of Writing) of 1100 or higher; renewable for four years for students who maintain academic eligibility.
Cumulative student debt: 78% of graduating class had student loans; average debt was $22,993.

FINANCIAL AID PROCEDURES

Forms required: FAFSA.
Dates and Deadlines: Priority date 3/1; no closing date. Applicants notified on a rolling basis starting 3/15; must reply within 2 week(s) of notification.
Transfers: No deadline. Applicants notified on a rolling basis starting 3/15; must reply within 2 week(s) of notification. Academic scholarships available; apply by May 1

CONTACT

Debbie Raines, Director of Financial Aid
2807 North Glebe Road, Arlington, VA 22207-4299
(703) 284-1530

Miller Motte Technical College: Lynchburg

Lynchburg, Virginia
www.miller-motte.com Federal Code: 004992

2-year for-profit technical college in small city.
Enrollment: 335 undergrads.
Selectivity: Open admission.

BASIC COSTS (2008-2009)

Tuition and fees: $6,750.
Per-credit charge: $225.

FINANCIAL AID PICTURE

Students with need: Need-based aid available for full-time and part-time students. Work study available nights.
Students without need: This college awards aid only to students with need.

FINANCIAL AID PROCEDURES

Forms required: FAFSA.
Dates and Deadlines: No deadline. Applicants notified on a rolling basis.

CONTACT

Allison Connors, Director of Financial Aid
1011 Creekside Lane, Lynchburg, VA 24502
(434) 239-5222

Mountain Empire Community College

Big Stone Gap, Virginia
www.mecc.edu Federal Code: 009629

2-year public community college in small town.
Enrollment: 1,983 undergrads.
Selectivity: Open admission; but selective for some programs.

BASIC COSTS (2008-2009)

Tuition and fees: $2,675; out-of-state residents $7,839.
Per-credit charge: $82; out-of-state residents $254.
Additional info: Out-of-state students pay additional $90 capital outlay fee.

FINANCIAL AID PICTURE (2007-2008)

Students with need: Need-based aid available for full-time and part-time students.
Students without need: No-need awards available for academics, state/district residency.
Scholarships offered: Presidential Honor Scholarship: full tuition; for valedictorian or salutatorian. Dean's Academic Honor Award: $500-$1,000; for top 10 in graduating class.
Additional info: The college does not participate in loan programs. All financial aid is in form of grants, scholarships, or work study.

FINANCIAL AID PROCEDURES

Forms required: FAFSA.
Dates and Deadlines: Priority date 5/1; no closing date. Applicants notified on a rolling basis starting 1/1.

CONTACT

Director of Enrollment Services
3441 Mountain Empire Road, Big Stone Gap, VA 24219
(276) 523-2400 ext. 470

National College: Bluefield

Bluefield, Virginia
www.ncbt.edu Federal Code: 003726

2-year for-profit business college in small city.
Enrollment: 194 undergrads.
Selectivity: Open admission.

BASIC COSTS (2008-2009)

Tuition and fees: $9,585.
Per-credit charge: $212.

FINANCIAL AID PICTURE

Students with need: Need-based aid available for full-time and part-time students.

Students without need: This college awards aid only to students with need.

FINANCIAL AID PROCEDURES

Forms required: FAFSA.

Dates and Deadlines: No deadline. Applicants notified on a rolling basis starting 9/1.

CONTACT

Pamela Cotton, Director of Financial Aid and Compliance Officer
PO Box 6400, Roanoke, VA 24017
(540) 986-1800

National College: Charlottesville

Charlottesville, Virginia
www.ncbt.edu Federal Code: 003726

2-year for-profit business college in small city.
Enrollment: 199 undergrads.
Selectivity: Open admission.

BASIC COSTS (2008-2009)

Tuition and fees: $9,585.
Per-credit charge: $212.

FINANCIAL AID PICTURE

Students with need: Need-based aid available for full-time and part-time students.

Students without need: This college awards aid only to students with need.

FINANCIAL AID PROCEDURES

Forms required: FAFSA.

Dates and Deadlines: No deadline. Applicants notified on a rolling basis.

CONTACT

Pamela Cotton, Director of Financial Aid and Compliance Officer
PO Box 6400, Roanoke, VA 24017
(540) 986-1800

National College: Danville

Danville, Virginia
www.ncbt.edu Federal Code: 003726

2-year for-profit branch campus and business college in small city.
Enrollment: 343 undergrads.
Selectivity: Open admission.

BASIC COSTS (2008-2009)

Tuition and fees: $9,585.
Per-credit charge: $212.

FINANCIAL AID PICTURE

Students with need: Need-based aid available for full-time and part-time students.

Students without need: This college awards aid only to students with need.

FINANCIAL AID PROCEDURES

Forms required: FAFSA.

Dates and Deadlines: No deadline. Applicants notified on a rolling basis starting 9/1.

CONTACT

Pamela Cotton, Director of Financial Aid and Compliance Officer
PO Box 6400, Roanoke, VA 24017
(540) 986-1800

National College: Harrisonburg

Harrisonburg, Virginia
www.national-college.edu Federal Code: 003726

2-year for-profit business college in large town.
Enrollment: 352 undergrads.
Selectivity: Open admission.

BASIC COSTS (2008-2009)

Tuition and fees: $9,585.
Per-credit charge: $212.

FINANCIAL AID PICTURE

Students with need: Need-based aid available for full-time and part-time students.

Students without need: This college awards aid only to students with need.

FINANCIAL AID PROCEDURES

Forms required: FAFSA.

Dates and Deadlines: No deadline. Applicants notified on a rolling basis starting 9/1.

CONTACT

Pamela Cotton, Director of Financial Aid and Compliance Officer
PO Box 6400, Roanoke, VA 24017
(540) 986-1800

National College: Lynchburg

Lynchburg, Virginia
www.national-college.edu Federal Code: 010489

2-year for-profit business college in small city.
Enrollment: 302 undergrads.
Selectivity: Open admission.

BASIC COSTS (2008-2009)

Tuition and fees: $9,585.
Per-credit charge: $212.

FINANCIAL AID PICTURE

Students with need: Need-based aid available for full-time and part-time students.

Students without need: This college awards aid only to students with need.

FINANCIAL AID PROCEDURES

Forms required: FAFSA.

Dates and Deadlines: No deadline. Applicants notified on a rolling basis starting 9/1.

CONTACT

Pamela Cotton, Director of Financial Aid and Compliance Officer
PO Box 6400, Roanoke, VA 24017
(540) 986-1000

National College: Martinsville

Martinsville, Virginia
www.national-college.edu Federal Code: 003726

2-year private business and junior college in small city.
Enrollment: 382 undergrads.
Selectivity: Open admission.

BASIC COSTS (2008-2009)
Tuition and fees: $9,585.
Per-credit charge: $212.

FINANCIAL AID PICTURE
Students with need: Need-based aid available for full-time and part-time students.
Students without need: This college awards aid only to students with need.

FINANCIAL AID PROCEDURES
Forms required: FAFSA.
Dates and Deadlines: No deadline. Applicants notified on a rolling basis.

CONTACT
Pamela Cotton, Director of Financial Aid and Compliance Officer
PO Box 6400, Roanoke, VA 24017
(540) 986-1800

National College: Roanoke Valley

Roanoke, Virginia
www.national-college.edu Federal Code: 003726

4-year for-profit business college in large city.
Enrollment: 615 undergrads.
Selectivity: Open admission.

BASIC COSTS (2008-2009)
Tuition and fees: $9,585.
Per-credit charge: $212.

FINANCIAL AID PICTURE
Students with need: Need-based aid available for full-time and part-time students.
Students without need: This college awards aid only to students with need.

FINANCIAL AID PROCEDURES
Forms required: FAFSA.
Dates and Deadlines: No deadline. Applicants notified on a rolling basis.

CONTACT
Pamela Cotton, Director of Financial Aid and Compliance Officer
PO Box 6400, Roanoke, VA 24017-0400
(540) 986-1800

New River Community College

Dublin, Virginia
www.nr.edu Federal Code: 005223

2-year public community college in rural community.
Enrollment: 2,889 undergrads.
Selectivity: Open admission.

BASIC COSTS (2008-2009)
Tuition and fees: $2,647; out-of-state residents $7,811.
Per-credit charge: $82; out-of-state residents $254.
Additional info: Out-of-state students pay additional $90 capital outlay fee.

FINANCIAL AID PICTURE (2007-2008)
Students with need: 12% of average financial aid package awarded as scholarships/grants, 88% awarded as loans/jobs. Need-based aid available for part-time students.

FINANCIAL AID PROCEDURES
Forms required: FAFSA, institutional form.
Dates and Deadlines: Priority date 4/15; no closing date. Applicants notified on a rolling basis starting 6/1.

CONTACT
Joseph Sheffey, Coordinator of Financial Aid
Drawer 1127, Dublin, VA 24084
(540) 674-3615

Norfolk State University

Norfolk, Virginia
www.nsu.edu Federal Code: 003765

4-year public university in small city.
Enrollment: 5,582 undergrads, 16% part-time. 1,143 full-time freshmen.

BASIC COSTS (2008-2009)
Tuition and fees: $5,560; out-of-state residents $16,807.
Per-credit charge: $247; out-of-state residents $622.
Room and board: $7,116.

FINANCIAL AID PICTURE (2008-2009)
Students with need: Need-based aid available for full-time and part-time students.
Students without need: No-need awards available for academics, alumni affiliation, athletics, leadership, music/drama, ROTC, state/district residency.

FINANCIAL AID PROCEDURES
Forms required: FAFSA.
Dates and Deadlines: Priority date 5/31; no closing date. Applicants notified on a rolling basis starting 4/1; must reply within 2 week(s) of notification.

CONTACT
Kevin Burns, Director of Student Financial Services
700 Park Avenue, Norfolk, VA 23504
(757) 823-8381

Old Dominion University

Norfolk, Virginia
www.odu.edu Federal Code: 003728

4-year public university in small city.
Enrollment: 16,971 undergrads, 25% part-time. 2,701 full-time freshmen.
Selectivity: Admits 50 to 75% of applicants.

BASIC COSTS (2008-2009)
Tuition and fees: $6,918; out-of-state residents $18,588.
Per-credit charge: $224; out-of-state residents $613.
Room and board: $7,100.

FINANCIAL AID PICTURE (2008-2009)
Students with need: Out of 2,105 full-time freshmen who applied for aid 1,849 were judged to have need. Of these, 1,689 received aid, and 1,078 had their full need met. Average financial aid package met 85% of need; average scholarship/grant was $4,578; average loan was $3,370. For part-time students, average financial aid package was $5,303.
Students without need: 110 full-time freshmen who did not demonstrate need for aid received scholarships/grants; average award was $3,422. No-need awards available for academics, alumni affiliation, art, athletics, leadership, music/drama, ROTC, state/district residency.

Scholarships offered: 91 full-time freshmen received athletic scholarships; average amount $13,198.
Cumulative student debt: 82% of graduating class had student loans; average debt was $17,250.

FINANCIAL AID PROCEDURES
Forms required: FAFSA.
Dates and Deadlines: Priority date 2/15; closing date 3/15. Applicants notified on a rolling basis starting 2/1; must reply within 2 week(s) of notification.
Transfers: Applicants notified on a rolling basis starting 2/1; must reply within 2 week(s) of notification.

CONTACT
Veronica Finch, Director of Financial Aid
108 Rollins Hall, 5115 Hampton Boulevard, Norfolk, VA 23529
(757) 683-3683

Patrick Henry College
Purcellville, Virginia Federal Code: 039513
www.phc.edu CSS Code: 2804

4-year private liberal arts college in small town, affiliated with nondenominational Christian.
Enrollment: 327 undergrads, 7% part-time.

BASIC COSTS (2008-2009)
Tuition and fees: $18,500.
Room and board: $6,600.

FINANCIAL AID PICTURE (2008-2009)
Students with need: Average financial aid package for all full-time undergraduates was $7,266. 29% awarded as scholarships/grants, 71% awarded as loans/jobs.
Students without need: No-need awards available for academics, leadership, music/drama, state/district residency.

FINANCIAL AID PROCEDURES
Forms required: institutional form. Required for students seeking need-based aid.
Dates and Deadlines: Priority date 2/1; closing date 6/15. Applicants notified on a rolling basis starting 4/1; must reply by 5/1.

CONTACT
Mark Richard, Financial Aid Administrator
One Patrick Henry Circle, Purcellville, VA 20132-3197
(540) 338-1776 ext. 8780

Patrick Henry Community College
Martinsville, Virginia
www.ph.vccs.edu Federal Code: 003751

2-year public community college in large town.
Enrollment: 2,948 undergrads.
Selectivity: Open admission.

BASIC COSTS (2008-2009)
Tuition and fees: $2,640; out-of-state residents $7,804.
Per-credit charge: $82; out-of-state residents $254.
Additional info: Out-of-state students pay additional $90 capital outlay fee.

FINANCIAL AID PICTURE
Students with need: Need-based aid available for full-time and part-time students.

FINANCIAL AID PROCEDURES
Forms required: FAFSA.
Dates and Deadlines: Priority date 6/1; no closing date. Applicants notified on a rolling basis starting 6/15.

CONTACT
Joe Philpott, Financial Aid
Box 5311, Martinsville, VA 24115-5311
(276) 656-0317

Paul D. Camp Community College
Franklin, Virginia
www.pc.vccs.edu Federal Code: 009159

2-year public community college in small town.
Enrollment: 746 undergrads.
Selectivity: Open admission; but selective for some programs.

BASIC COSTS (2008-2009)
Tuition and fees: $2,585; out-of-state residents $7,749.
Per-credit charge: $82; out-of-state residents $254.
Additional info: Out-of-state students pay additional $90 capital outlay fee.

FINANCIAL AID PICTURE
Students with need: Need-based aid available for full-time and part-time students. Work study available nights.

FINANCIAL AID PROCEDURES
Forms required: FAFSA.
Dates and Deadlines: Priority date 6/1; no closing date. Applicants notified on a rolling basis starting 8/1; must reply within 2 week(s) of notification.

CONTACT
Teresa King, Financial Aid Coordinator
100 North College Drive, Franklin, VA 23851-0737
(757) 925-6307

Piedmont Virginia Community College
Charlottesville, Virginia
www.pvcc.edu Federal Code: 009928

2-year public community college in large town.
Enrollment: 3,138 undergrads.
Selectivity: Open admission; but selective for some programs.

BASIC COSTS (2008-2009)
Tuition and fees: $2,645; out-of-state residents $7,829.
Per-credit charge: $82; out-of-state residents $254.
Additional info: Out-of-state students pay additional $90 capital outlay fee.

FINANCIAL AID PICTURE (2007-2008)
Students with need: Need-based aid available for full-time and part-time students. Work study available nights, weekends, and for part-time students.
Students without need: No-need awards available for academics.

FINANCIAL AID PROCEDURES
Forms required: FAFSA.
Dates and Deadlines: No deadline. Applicants notified on a rolling basis starting 4/1.
Transfers: Must meet Satisfactory Academic Progress standards.

CONTACT
Carol Larson, Director of Financial Aid
501 College Drive, Charlottesville, VA 22902-7589
(434) 961-6545

Radford University

Radford, Virginia
www.radford.edu Federal Code: 003732

4-year public university in large town.
Enrollment: 8,107 undergrads, 4% part-time. 1,841 full-time freshmen.
Selectivity: Admits 50 to 75% of applicants.

BASIC COSTS (2008-2009)

Tuition and fees: $6,536; out-of-state residents $15,550.
Per-credit charge: $174; out-of-state residents $550.
Room and board: $6,716.

FINANCIAL AID PICTURE (2007-2008)

Students with need: Out of 1,144 full-time freshmen who applied for aid, 645 were judged to have need. Of these, 613 received aid, and 201 had their full need met. Average financial aid package met 78% of need; average scholarship/grant was $6,025; average loan was $3,119. For part-time students, average financial aid package was $7,431.
Students without need: 70 full-time freshmen who did not demonstrate need for aid received scholarships/grants; average award was $4,911. No-need awards available for academics, art, athletics, leadership, music/drama, ROTC.
Scholarships offered: 50 full-time freshmen received athletic scholarships; average amount $9,228.
Cumulative student debt: 94% of graduating class had student loans; average debt was $19,465.
Additional info: Student's need and grades considered. Top consideration given to those with greatest need and who apply by deadline.

FINANCIAL AID PROCEDURES

Forms required: FAFSA.
Dates and Deadlines: Priority date 3/1; no closing date. Applicants notified on a rolling basis starting 4/15; must reply within 4 week(s) of notification.

CONTACT

Barbara Porter, Director of Financial Aid
209 Martin Hall, Radford, VA 24142
(540) 831-5408

Randolph College

Lynchburg, Virginia
www.randolphcollege.edu Federal Code: 003734

4-year private liberal arts college in small city, affiliated with United Methodist Church.
Enrollment: 549 undergrads, 1% part-time. 144 full-time freshmen.
Selectivity: Admits over 75% of applicants.

BASIC COSTS (2008-2009)

Tuition and fees: $27,890.
Per-credit charge: $1,120.
Room and board: $9,310.
Additional info: Room and board charges include free use of laundry facilities. Tuition/fee waivers available for adults.

FINANCIAL AID PICTURE (2008-2009)

Students with need: Out of 133 full-time freshmen who applied for aid, 111 were judged to have need. Of these, 110 received aid, and 31 had their full need met. Average financial aid package met 85% of need; average scholarship/grant was $16,917; average loan was $6,653. For part-time students, average financial aid package was $21,612.
Students without need: 36 full-time freshmen who did not demonstrate need for aid received scholarships/grants; average award was $13,228. No-need awards available for academics, alumni affiliation, art, leadership, minority status, music/drama, religious affiliation, state/district residency.
Scholarships offered: College offers approximately $2 million annually in renewable scholarships to incoming first-year students. Grants range up to full tuition. Applications submitted by December 1 receive priority consideration for Presidential Scholarships; applications submitted by February 1 receive priority consideration for other merit awards and need-based awards. Awards include Gottwald Scholarship: full tuition plus travel stipend; based on academic profile; approximately 3 awarded in each class. Presidential Scholars: $17,500; renewable annually; based on academic profile.
Cumulative student debt: 75% of graduating class had student loans; average debt was $27,218.

FINANCIAL AID PROCEDURES

Forms required: FAFSA, state aid form.
Dates and Deadlines: Priority date 3/1; no closing date. Applicants notified on a rolling basis starting 3/1; must reply by 5/1 or within 2 week(s) of notification.
Transfers: Applicants notified on a rolling basis starting 3/1; must reply by 5/1 or within 2 week(s) of notification.

CONTACT

Kay Mattox, Director of Student Financial Services
2500 Rivermont Avenue, Lynchburg, VA 24503-1555
(434) 947-8128

Randolph-Macon College

Ashland, Virginia
www.rmc.edu Federal Code: 003733

4-year private liberal arts college in small town, affiliated with United Methodist Church.
Enrollment: 1,178 undergrads, 1% part-time. 362 full-time freshmen.
Selectivity: Admits 50 to 75% of applicants.

BASIC COSTS (2009-2010)

Tuition and fees: $29,182.
Per-credit charge: $1,052.
Room and board: $8,891.

FINANCIAL AID PICTURE (2008-2009)

Students with need: Out of 249 full-time freshmen who applied for aid, 240 were judged to have need. Of these, 240 received aid, and 72 had their full need met. Average financial aid package met 85% of need; average scholarship/grant was $18,143; average loan was $4,385. For part-time students, average financial aid package was $12,100.
Students without need: 122 full-time freshmen who did not demonstrate need for aid received scholarships/grants; average award was $16,319. No-need awards available for academics, alumni affiliation, minority status, religious affiliation, state/district residency.
Scholarships offered: Randolph-Macon's Presidential Scholars Program: $7,500 up to $20,000 per year; academic awards.
Cumulative student debt: 72% of graduating class had student loans; average debt was $23,564.

FINANCIAL AID PROCEDURES

Forms required: FAFSA, state aid form.
Dates and Deadlines: Priority date 2/1; closing date 3/1. Applicants notified by 3/15; must reply by 5/1 or within 2 week(s) of notification.
Transfers: Applicants notified by 3/15; must reply by 5/1 or within 2 week(s) of notification.

CONTACT

Mary Neal, Director of Financial Aid
PO Box 5005, Ashland, VA 23005-5505
(804) 752-7529

Rappahannock Community College

Glenns, Virginia
www.rappahannock.edu Federal Code: 009160

2-year public community college in rural community.
Enrollment: 1,612 undergrads.
Selectivity: Open admission.

BASIC COSTS (2008-2009)

Tuition and fees: $2,615; out-of-state residents $7,779.
Per-credit charge: $82; out-of-state residents $254.
Additional info: Out-of-state students pay additional $90 capital outlay fee.

FINANCIAL AID PICTURE

Students with need: Need-based aid available for full-time and part-time students.

FINANCIAL AID PROCEDURES

Forms required: FAFSA, institutional form.
Dates and Deadlines: Priority date 5/15; no closing date. Applicants notified on a rolling basis starting 6/30.

CONTACT

Carolyn Ward, Director of Financial Aid
12745 College Drive, Glenns, VA 23149-2616
(804) 758-6737

Regent University

Virginia Beach, Virginia
www.regent.edu Federal Code: 030913

4-year private university in large city, affiliated with interdenominational tradition.
Enrollment: 1,458 undergrads, 43% part-time. 121 full-time freshmen.
Selectivity: Admits over 75% of applicants.

BASIC COSTS (2009-2010)

Tuition and fees: $13,950.
Per-credit charge: $460.
Room only: $5,625.

FINANCIAL AID PICTURE (2007-2008)

Students with need: Average financial aid package met 49% of need; average scholarship/grant was $5,253; average loan was $2,178. For part-time students, average financial aid package was $5,889.
Students without need: No-need awards available for academics, leadership.
Cumulative student debt: 65% of graduating class had student loans; average debt was $25,170.

FINANCIAL AID PROCEDURES

Forms required: FAFSA, state aid form, institutional form.
Dates and Deadlines: Priority date 3/15; no closing date. Applicants notified on a rolling basis starting 3/1; must reply within 2 week(s) of notification.
Transfers: Closing date 8/1. Applicants notified on a rolling basis starting 3/15; must reply within 2 week(s) of notification. Must be able to determine number of transfer credits before full award package is offered. Student should submit all academic transcripts in a timely manner to ensure transfer articulation occurs in a timely manner.

CONTACT

Joe Dobrota, Director of Central Financial Aid
1000 Regent University Drive, SC 218, Virginia Beach, VA 23464-9800
(757) 352-4125

Richard Bland College

Petersburg, Virginia
www.rbc.edu Federal Code: 003707

2-year public junior and liberal arts college in small city.
Enrollment: 1,310 undergrads, 23% part-time. 567 full-time freshmen.
Selectivity: Admits over 75% of applicants.

BASIC COSTS (2008-2009)

Tuition and fees: $3,048; out-of-state residents $11,638.
Per-credit charge: $100; out-of-state residents $456.
Room only: $8,400.

FINANCIAL AID PICTURE (2007-2008)

Students with need: Need-based aid available for full-time and part-time students.
Students without need: No-need awards available for academics.
Scholarships offered: Presidential Scholarships: average $1,000; for full-time first-time Virginia residents; based on minimum 3.5 high school GPA.

FINANCIAL AID PROCEDURES

Forms required: FAFSA, institutional form.
Dates and Deadlines: Priority date 5/1; no closing date. Applicants notified by 6/1; must reply within 2 week(s) of notification.

CONTACT

J Hart, Coordinator of Financial Aid
11301 Johnson Road, Petersburg, VA 23805
(804) 862-6223

Roanoke College

Salem, Virginia
www.roanoke.edu Federal Code: 003736

4-year private liberal arts college in large town, affiliated with Evangelical Lutheran Church in America.
Enrollment: 1,947 undergrads, 2% part-time. 529 full-time freshmen.
Selectivity: Admits 50 to 75% of applicants.

BASIC COSTS (2008-2009)

Tuition and fees: $27,935.
Room and board: $9,285.
Additional info: Tuition/fee waivers available for adults.

FINANCIAL AID PICTURE (2008-2009)

Students with need: Out of 411 full-time freshmen who applied for aid, 335 were judged to have need. Of these, 335 received aid, and 117 had their full need met. Average financial aid package met 89% of need; average scholarship/grant was $19,390; average loan was $3,958. For part-time students, average financial aid package was $4,392.
Students without need: 181 full-time freshmen who did not demonstrate need for aid received scholarships/grants; average award was $11,010. No-need awards available for academics, minority status, music/drama, religious affiliation.
Scholarships offered: William Beard Scholarship: up to 3 awarded; full tuition, room and board. The David Bittle Scholarship: up to 12 awarded; full tuition. The Christopher Baughman Scholarship: up to 50 awarded; valued at $4,500 per year and added to previously awarded college scholarships.
Cumulative student debt: 68% of graduating class had student loans; average debt was $25,498.

FINANCIAL AID PROCEDURES

Forms required: FAFSA, state aid form.
Dates and Deadlines: Priority date 3/1; no closing date. Applicants notified on a rolling basis starting 11/1; must reply within 2 week(s) of notification.

CONTACT

Thomas Blair, Director of Financial Aid
221 College Lane, Salem, VA 24153-3794
(540) 375-2235

St. Paul's College

Lawrenceville, Virginia
www.saintpauls.edu Federal Code: 003739

4-year private liberal arts college in small town, affiliated with Episcopal Church.
Enrollment: 642 undergrads, 3% part-time. 199 full-time freshmen.
Selectivity: Admits over 75% of applicants.

BASIC COSTS (2008-2009)

Tuition and fees: $13,210.
Per-credit charge: $495.
Room and board: $6,640.
Additional info: Tuition/fee waivers available for minority students.

FINANCIAL AID PICTURE (2007-2008)

Students with need: Work study available nights, weekends, and for part-time students.
Students without need: No-need awards available for academics, athletics, leadership, ROTC.

FINANCIAL AID PROCEDURES

Forms required: FAFSA, state aid form.
Dates and Deadlines: No deadline. Applicants notified on a rolling basis starting 1/15; must reply by 7/1 or within 4 week(s) of notification.
Transfers: No deadline. Applicants notified on a rolling basis; must reply within 2 week(s) of notification.

CONTACT

Karen Lyons, Assistant Director of Financial Aid
115 College Drive, Lawrenceville, VA 23868
(434) 848-6496

Shenandoah University

Winchester, Virginia
www.su.edu Federal Code: 003737

4-year private university in small city, affiliated with United Methodist Church.
Enrollment: 1,671 undergrads, 5% part-time. 399 full-time freshmen.
Selectivity: Admits over 75% of applicants.

BASIC COSTS (2009-2010)

Tuition and fees: $24,150.
Per-credit charge: $695.
Room and board: $8,600.

FINANCIAL AID PICTURE (2008-2009)

Students with need: Out of 336 full-time freshmen who applied for aid, 336 were judged to have need. Of these, 336 received aid, and 40 had their full need met. Average financial aid package met 86% of need; average scholarship/grant was $8,000; average loan was $3,500. Need-based aid available for part-time students.
Students without need: 48 full-time freshmen who did not demonstrate need for aid received scholarships/grants; average award was $6,000. No-need awards available for academics, job skills, music/drama, religious affiliation, state/district residency.
Cumulative student debt: 85% of graduating class had student loans; average debt was $54,000.

FINANCIAL AID PROCEDURES

Forms required: FAFSA, state aid form.
Dates and Deadlines: Closing date 3/15. Applicants notified on a rolling basis starting 3/15; must reply within 2 week(s) of notification.
Transfers: Priority date 3/15. Applicants notified on a rolling basis starting 3/15.

CONTACT

Nancy Bragg, Director of Financial Aid
1460 University Drive, Winchester, VA 22601-5195
(540) 665-4538

Southside Virginia Community College

Alberta, Virginia
www.sv.vccs.edu Federal Code: 008661

2-year public community college in rural community.
Enrollment: 2,661 undergrads.
Selectivity: Open admission; but selective for some programs.

BASIC COSTS (2008-2009)

Tuition and fees: $2,660; out-of-state residents $7,824.
Per-credit charge: $82; out-of-state residents $254.
Additional info: Out-of-state students pay additional $90 capital outlay fee.

FINANCIAL AID PICTURE (2007-2008)

Students with need: 98% of average financial aid package awarded as scholarships/grants, 2% awarded as loans/jobs. Need-based aid available for part-time students. Work study available nights.
Students without need: No-need awards available for academics.
Scholarships offered: Guaranteed Academic Merit Award: $1,500, for high school graduates within college's service area with 3.0 GPA who do not receive at least $1,500 in need-based aid.

FINANCIAL AID PROCEDURES

Forms required: FAFSA.
Dates and Deadlines: Priority date 6/1; closing date 8/1. Applicants notified on a rolling basis starting 6/15.
Transfers: State aid limited to in-state residents.

CONTACT

Sally Tharrington, Director of Financial Aid
109 Campus Drive, Alberta, VA 23821
(434) 736-2026

Southwest Virginia Community College

Richlands, Virginia
www.sw.edu Federal Code: 007260

2-year public community college in small town.
Enrollment: 2,494 undergrads, 49% part-time. 482 full-time freshmen.
Selectivity: Open admission; but selective for some programs.

BASIC COSTS (2008-2009)

Tuition and fees: $2,630; out-of-state residents $7,794.
Per-credit charge: $82; out-of-state residents $254.
Additional info: Out of state students pay an additional $90 capital outlay fee.

FINANCIAL AID PICTURE (2008-2009)

Students with need: Need-based aid available for part-time students.
Students without need: This college awards aid only to students with need.

FINANCIAL AID PROCEDURES

Forms required: FAFSA, institutional form.
Dates and Deadlines: Priority date 5/30; no closing date. Applicants notified on a rolling basis starting 7/1.

CONTACT
Rod Moore, Associate Vice President of Student Development Services
PO Box SVCC, Richlands, VA 24641-1101
(276) 964-7290

Sweet Briar College
Sweet Briar, Virginia
www.sbc.edu Federal Code: 003742

4-year private liberal arts college for women in rural community.
Enrollment: 647 undergrads, 1% part-time. 194 full-time freshmen.
Selectivity: Admits over 75% of applicants.

BASIC COSTS (2008-2009)
Tuition and fees: $26,995.
Per-credit charge: $890.
Room and board: $10,160.
Additional info: Tuition/fee waivers available for adults.

FINANCIAL AID PICTURE (2008-2009)
Students with need: Out of 152 full-time freshmen who applied for aid, 127 were judged to have need. Of these, 127 received aid, and 104 had their full need met. Average financial aid package met 71% of need; average scholarship/grant was $13,427; average loan was $4,295. For part-time students, average financial aid package was $8,264.
Students without need: 64 full-time freshmen who did not demonstrate need for aid received scholarships/grants; average award was $11,977. No-need awards available for academics, art, leadership, music/drama, state/district residency.
Scholarships offered: Founders and Prothro Scholarships: up to $15,000. Commonwealth Scholarships: up to $13,000. Betty Bean Black Scholarships: up to $12,000. Sweet Briar Scholarships: up to $9,000; for students with special talents in specific area. All awards based on academic qualifications; renewable annually with specified GPA.
Cumulative student debt: 50% of graduating class had student loans; average debt was $20,118.

FINANCIAL AID PROCEDURES
Forms required: FAFSA.
Dates and Deadlines: Priority date 2/15; no closing date. Applicants notified on a rolling basis starting 3/1; must reply by 5/1 or within 2 week(s) of notification.
Transfers: Closing date 7/15.

CONTACT
Bobbi Carpenter, Director of Financial Aid
PO Box B, Sweet Briar, VA 24595

Thomas Nelson Community College
Hampton, Virginia
www.tncc.edu Federal Code: 006871

2-year public community college in small city..
Enrollment: 7,571 undergrads.
Selectivity: Open admission; but selective for some programs.

BASIC COSTS (2008-2009)
Tuition and fees: $2,626; out-of-state residents $7,790.
Per-credit charge: $82; out-of-state residents $264.
Additional info: Out-of-state students pay additional $90 capital outlay fee.

FINANCIAL AID PICTURE (2008-2009)
Students with need: Need-based aid available for full-time and part-time students. Work study available nights.

FINANCIAL AID PROCEDURES
Forms required: FAFSA, institutional form.
Dates and Deadlines: Priority date 5/1; no closing date. Applicants notified on a rolling basis starting 6/1; must reply within 2 week(s) of notification.
Transfers: Priority date 5/8; no deadline. Applicants notified on a rolling basis; must reply within 2 week(s) of notification.

CONTACT
Kathryn Anderson, Director of Financial Aid, Veterans Affairs, and Scholarships
Box 9407, Hampton, VA 23670
(757) 825-2848

Tidewater Community College
Norfolk, Virginia
www.tcc.vccs.edu Federal Code: 003712

2-year public community college in large city.
Enrollment: 22,852 undergrads.
Selectivity: Open admission; but selective for some programs.

BASIC COSTS (2008-2009)
Tuition and fees: $2,846; out-of-state residents $8,010.
Per-credit charge: $82; out-of-state residents $254.
Additional info: Out-of-state students pay additional $90 capital outlay fee.

FINANCIAL AID PICTURE (2007-2008)
Students with need: Need-based aid available for full-time and part-time students.
Students without need: This college awards aid only to students with need.

FINANCIAL AID PROCEDURES
Forms required: FAFSA.
Dates and Deadlines: Priority date 4/1; no closing date. Applicants notified on a rolling basis starting 4/1.

CONTACT
Norma Ferki, Director of Financial Aid
7000 College Drive/Portsmouth Campus, Portsmouth, VA 23703
(757) 822-1360

University of Mary Washington
Fredericksburg, Virginia
www.umw.edu Federal Code: 003746

4-year public university and liberal arts college in small city.
Enrollment: 4,070 undergrads, 12% part-time. 848 full-time freshmen.
Selectivity: Admits 50 to 75% of applicants.

BASIC COSTS (2008-2009)
Tuition and fees: $6,694; out-of-state residents $17,861.
Per-credit charge: $237; out-of-state residents $702.
Room and board: $7,846.

FINANCIAL AID PICTURE (2008-2009)
Students with need: Out of 590 full-time freshmen who applied for aid, 250 were judged to have need. Of these, 220 received aid, and 30 had their full need met. Average financial aid package met 50% of need; average scholarship/grant was $5,600; average loan was $2,600. For part-time students, average financial aid package was $8,200.
Students without need: 75 full-time freshmen who did not demonstrate need for aid received scholarships/grants; average award was $1,450. No-need awards available for academics, alumni affiliation, art, leadership, music/drama, state/district residency.

Scholarships offered: Scholastic Excellence Award: from $500 to $6,000; honors admissions automatically considered. Two Virginia residents will receive tuition, fees, room and board up to $10,000. One non-Virginia award for tuition, fees, room and board. All scholarships renewable.
Cumulative student debt: 57% of graduating class had student loans; average debt was $16,000.

FINANCIAL AID PROCEDURES

Forms required: FAFSA, institutional form.
Dates and Deadlines: Priority date 3/1; closing date 5/31. Applicants notified by 4/15; must reply by 5/1 or within 2 week(s) of notification.

CONTACT

Deborah Harber, Senior Associate Dean for Financial Aid
1301 College Avenue, Fredericksburg, VA 22401-5300
(540) 654-2468

University of Richmond

University of Richmond, Virginia
www.richmond.edu Federal Code: 003744

4-year private university and liberal arts college in very large city.
Enrollment: 2,689 undergrads, 1% part-time. 737 full-time freshmen.
Selectivity: Admits less than 50% of applicants.

BASIC COSTS (2009-2010)

Tuition and fees: $40,010.
Per-credit charge: $2,000.
Room and board: $8,480.

FINANCIAL AID PICTURE (2008-2009)

Students with need: Out of 412 full-time freshmen who applied for aid, 308 were judged to have need. Of these, 308 received aid, and 299 had their full need met. Average financial aid package met 100% of need; average scholarship/grant was $31,626; average loan was $2,961. For part-time students, average financial aid package was $13,678.
Students without need: 49 full-time freshmen who did not demonstrate need for aid received scholarships/grants; average award was $32,724. No-need awards available for academics, art, athletics, leadership, minority status, music/drama, ROTC.
Scholarships offered: ***Merit:*** Richmond Scholars program: full tuition scholarships; up to 50 entering freshmen. Presidential Scholarships: up to $15,000. ***Athletic:*** 46 full-time freshmen received athletic scholarships; average amount $29,515.
Cumulative student debt: 43% of graduating class had student loans; average debt was $20,915.
Additional info: VA residents whose family income is $40,000 or less and who qualify for need-based aid will receive grant assistance equal to full tuition, room and board. Early decision: Financial aid package estimated using historical data; applicant still required to submit all financial aid forms.

FINANCIAL AID PROCEDURES

Forms required: FAFSA, institutional form.
Dates and Deadlines: Closing date 2/15. Applicants notified by 4/1; must reply within 4 week(s) of notification.

CONTACT

Cindy Deffenbaugh, Director of Student Financial Aid
28 Westhampton Way, University of Richmond, VA 23173
(804) 289-8438

University of Virginia

Charlottesville, Virginia
www.virginia.edu Federal Code: 003745

4-year public university in small city.
Enrollment: 13,869 undergrads, 2% part-time. 3,252 full-time freshmen.
Selectivity: Admits less than 50% of applicants.

BASIC COSTS (2008-2009)

Tuition and fees: $9,505; out-of-state residents $29,798.
Room and board: $7,820.

FINANCIAL AID PICTURE (2008-2009)

Students with need: Out of 1,972 full-time freshmen who applied for aid, 875 were judged to have need. Of these, 875 received aid, and 875 had their full need met. Average financial aid package met 100% of need; average scholarship/grant was $13,449; average loan was $4,331. For part-time students, average financial aid package was $15,035.
Students without need: 429 full-time freshmen who did not demonstrate need for aid received scholarships/grants; average award was $9,124. No-need awards available for academics, athletics, leadership, minority status, music/drama, state/district residency.
Scholarships offered: 124 full-time freshmen received athletic scholarships; average amount $20,096.
Cumulative student debt: 33% of graduating class had student loans; average debt was $19,016.

FINANCIAL AID PROCEDURES

Forms required: FAFSA, institutional form.
Dates and Deadlines: Priority date 3/1; no closing date. Applicants notified by 4/1; must reply by 5/1.

CONTACT

Yvonne Hubbard, Director Student Financial Services
Box 400160, Charlottesville, VA 22904-4160
(434) 982-6000

University of Virginia's College at Wise

Wise, Virginia
www.uvawise.edu Federal Code: 003747

4-year public liberal arts college in small town.
Enrollment: 1,612 undergrads, 11% part-time. 425 full-time freshmen.
Selectivity: Admits over 75% of applicants.

BASIC COSTS (2008-2009)

Tuition and fees: $6,439; out-of-state residents $18,213.
Per-credit charge: $144; out-of-state residents $629.
Room and board: $7,350.

FINANCIAL AID PICTURE (2008-2009)

Students with need: Out of 349 full-time freshmen who applied for aid, 272 were judged to have need. Of these, 272 received aid, and 258 had their full need met. Average financial aid package met 94% of need; average scholarship/grant was $5,837; average loan was $2,180. For part-time students, average financial aid package was $4,845.
Students without need: 128 full-time freshmen who did not demonstrate need for aid received scholarships/grants; average award was $2,505. No-need awards available for academics, alumni affiliation, art, athletics, job skills, leadership, music/drama, religious affiliation, state/district residency.
Scholarships offered: 43 full-time freshmen received athletic scholarships; average amount $1,593.
Cumulative student debt: 59% of graduating class had student loans; average debt was $10,252.

FINANCIAL AID PROCEDURES

Forms required: FAFSA.

Dates and Deadlines: Priority date 4/1; no closing date. Applicants notified on a rolling basis starting 2/15; must reply within 4 week(s) of notification.

CONTACT

Bill Wendle, Director of Financial Aid
1 College Avenue, Wise, VA 24293-4412
(276) 328-0139

Virginia Commonwealth University

Richmond, Virginia
www.vcu.edu Federal Code: 003735

4-year public university in small city.
Enrollment: 20,993 undergrads, 13% part-time. 3,694 full-time freshmen.
Selectivity: Admits 50 to 75% of applicants.

BASIC COSTS (2008-2009)

Tuition and fees: $6,779; out-of-state residents $19,556.
Per-credit charge: $209; out-of-state residents $741.
Room and board: $7,914.

FINANCIAL AID PICTURE (2007-2008)

Students with need: Out of 2,526 full-time freshmen who applied for aid, 1,713 were judged to have need. Of these, 1,713 received aid, and 187 had their full need met. Average financial aid package met 69% of need; average scholarship/grant was $5,166. For part-time students, average financial aid package was $6,213.
Students without need: 204 full-time freshmen who did not demonstrate need for aid received scholarships/grants; average award was $4,000. No-need awards available for academics, alumni affiliation, art, athletics, leadership, music/drama.
Scholarships offered: ***Merit:*** Academic Achievement, Access Grant, and Transfer Achievement Scholarships from $1,000 to $1,500 awarded to VA residents based on need, merit, income level or transfer status. ***Athletic:*** 11 full-time freshmen received athletic scholarships; average amount $8,104.

FINANCIAL AID PROCEDURES

Forms required: FAFSA.
Dates and Deadlines: Priority date 3/1; no closing date. Applicants notified on a rolling basis starting 4/1; must reply within 2 week(s) of notification.
Transfers: Applicants notified by 4/1; must reply within 2 week(s) of notification.

CONTACT

Susan Kadir, Director of Financial Aid
Box 842526, Richmond, VA 23284-2526
(804) 828-6669

Virginia Highlands Community College

Abingdon, Virginia
www.vhcc.edu Federal Code: 007099

2-year public community college in small town.
Enrollment: 2,650 undergrads.
Selectivity: Open admission; but selective for some programs.

BASIC COSTS (2008-2009)

Tuition and fees: $2,675; out-of-state residents $7,839.
Per-credit charge: $82; out-of-state residents $254.
Additional info: Out-of-state students pay additional $90 capital outlay fee.

FINANCIAL AID PICTURE (2007-2008)

Students with need: 90% of average financial aid package awarded as scholarships/grants, 10% awarded as loans/jobs.

FINANCIAL AID PROCEDURES

Forms required: FAFSA, institutional form.
Dates and Deadlines: No deadline. Applicants notified on a rolling basis starting 5/1.

CONTACT

David Matlock, Director of Admissions, Records and Financial Aid
PO Box 828, Abingdon, VA 24212-0828
(276) 739-2412

Virginia Intermont College

Bristol, Virginia
www.vic.edu Federal Code: 003752

4-year private liberal arts college in small city, affiliated with Baptist faith.
Enrollment: 549 undergrads. 100 full-time freshmen.
Selectivity: Admits 50 to 75% of applicants.

BASIC COSTS (2009-2010)

Tuition and fees: $23,373.
Per-credit charge: $220.
Room and board: $7,324.

FINANCIAL AID PICTURE (2007-2008)

Students with need: Out of 70 full-time freshmen who applied for aid, 59 were judged to have need. Of these, 59 received aid, and 10 had their full need met. Average financial aid package met 58% of need; average scholarship/grant was $9,413; average loan was $3,247. For part-time students, average financial aid package was $3,329.
Students without need: 36 full-time freshmen who did not demonstrate need for aid received scholarships/grants; average award was $5,955. No-need awards available for art, athletics, music/drama, religious affiliation, state/district residency.
Scholarships offered: 9 full-time freshmen received athletic scholarships; average amount $7,228.

FINANCIAL AID PROCEDURES

Forms required: FAFSA, state aid form.
Dates and Deadlines: Priority date 3/1; closing date 6/1. Applicants notified on a rolling basis starting 2/15; must reply within 3 week(s) of notification.
Transfers: Priority date 2/15; no deadline. Applicants notified on a rolling basis starting 1/1; must reply within 3 week(s) of notification. Limited to certain number of units of state aid.

CONTACT

Denise Posey, Financial Aid Director
1013 Moore Street, Bristol, VA 24201
(276) 466-7871

Virginia Military Institute

Lexington, Virginia
www.vmi.edu Federal Code: 003753

4-year public liberal arts and military college in small town.
Enrollment: 1,428 undergrads. 419 full-time freshmen.
Selectivity: Admits 50 to 75% of applicants. GED not accepted.

BASIC COSTS (2008-2009)

Tuition and fees: $10,556; out-of-state residents $27,454.
Per-credit charge: $164; out-of-state residents $551.
Room and board: $6,444.

FINANCIAL AID PICTURE (2007-2008)

Students with need: Out of 283 full-time freshmen who applied for aid, 195 were judged to have need. Of these, 195 received aid, and 108 had their full need met. Average financial aid package met 91% of need; average scholarship/grant was $8,398; average loan was $3,358.

Students without need: 60 full-time freshmen who did not demonstrate need for aid received scholarships/grants; average award was $6,185. No-need awards available for academics, athletics, leadership, music/drama, ROTC.

Scholarships offered: ***Merit:*** Institute Scholarship: up to $19,830; 10-12 awarded; for superior academic performance, demonstrated character and leadership, extracurricular activities, 3.7 high school GPA, minimum 1250 SAT (exclusive of Writing) or 27 ACT, rank in top 5% of class. ***Athletic:*** 46 full-time freshmen received athletic scholarships; average amount $14,331.

Cumulative student debt: 52% of graduating class had student loans; average debt was $19,114.

FINANCIAL AID PROCEDURES

Forms required: FAFSA, institutional form.

Dates and Deadlines: Priority date 3/1; no closing date. Applicants notified on a rolling basis starting 3/15; must reply by 5/1.

CONTACT

Timothy Golden, Director of Financial Aid
VMI Office of Admissions, Lexington, VA 24450-9967
(540) 464-7208

Virginia Polytechnic Institute and State University

Blacksburg, Virginia
www.vt.edu Federal Code: 003754

4-year public university in large town.

Enrollment: 23,447 undergrads, 2% part-time. 5,119 full-time freshmen.

Selectivity: Admits 50 to 75% of applicants.

BASIC COSTS (2008-2009)

Tuition and fees: $8,198; out-of-state residents $20,655.

Per-credit charge: $264; out-of-state residents $783.

Room and board: $5,476.

FINANCIAL AID PICTURE (2007-2008)

Students with need: Out of 3,687 full-time freshmen who applied for aid, 2,211 were judged to have need. Of these, 1,819 received aid, and 334 had their full need met. Average financial aid package met 64% of need; average scholarship/grant was $6,924; average loan was $3,917. Need-based aid available for part-time students.

Students without need: 600 full-time freshmen who did not demonstrate need for aid received scholarships/grants; average award was $2,562. No-need awards available for art, athletics, ROTC.

Scholarships offered: 114 full-time freshmen received athletic scholarships; average amount $10,078.

Cumulative student debt: 52% of graduating class had student loans; average debt was $21,678.

FINANCIAL AID PROCEDURES

Forms required: FAFSA.

Dates and Deadlines: Priority date 3/11; no closing date. Applicants notified on a rolling basis starting 3/30; must reply by 5/1 or within 4 week(s) of notification.

Transfers: Priority date 2/1; closing date 3/11. Based on family EFC per FAFSA and available resources.

CONTACT

Barry Simmons, Director of Financial Aid
201 Burruss Hall, Blacksburg, VA 24061-0202
(540) 231-9555

Virginia State University

Petersburg, Virginia
www.vsu.edu Federal Code: 003764

4-year public university in large town.

Enrollment: 4,420 undergrads, 7% part-time. 1,286 full-time freshmen.

Selectivity: Admits 50 to 75% of applicants.

BASIC COSTS (2008-2009)

Tuition and fees: $5,903; out-of-state residents $14,018.

Per-credit charge: $197; out-of-state residents $468.

Room and board: $7,710.

Additional info: Out of state students pay an additional fee.

FINANCIAL AID PICTURE (2007-2008)

Students with need: Need-based aid available for full-time and part-time students. Work study available nights, weekends, and for part-time students.

Students without need: No-need awards available for academics, alumni affiliation, art, athletics, job skills, leadership, music/drama, religious affiliation, ROTC.

Scholarships offered: Presidential Scholarships: 3.2 GPA, SAT 1100 or ACT 24; $7,000. Provost's Scholarships: 3.0 GPA, SAT 1000 or ACT 21; $3,500. SAT exclusive of Writing. Fine and Performing Arts Scholarships: outstanding talent in music or fine arts, audition or portfolio may be required, recommendation required; $1,500. Math, Science, and Technology Scholarships: 3.0 GPA, above average ability in math, science, or technology, recommendation and essay required; $1,500.

Additional info: Strongly recommend that students apply for scholarship assistance through federal, state, local and private agencies.

FINANCIAL AID PROCEDURES

Forms required: FAFSA, institutional form.

Dates and Deadlines: Priority date 3/31; closing date 5/1. Applicants notified on a rolling basis starting 5/1; must reply within 2 week(s) of notification.

Transfers: Priority date 3/1.

CONTACT

Henry Debose, Director of Financial Aid
One Hayden Drive, Petersburg, VA 23806
(804) 524-5990

Virginia Union University

Richmond, Virginia
www.vuu.edu Federal Code: 003766

4-year private university and liberal arts college in small city, affiliated with Baptist faith.

Enrollment: 1,073 undergrads, 3% part-time. 352 full-time freshmen.

Selectivity: Admits 50 to 75% of applicants.

BASIC COSTS (2009-2010)

Tuition and fees: $13,662.

Room and board: $6,328.

FINANCIAL AID PICTURE (2008-2009)

Students with need: Need-based aid available for full-time and part-time students. Work study available nights, weekends, and for part-time students.

Students without need: No-need awards available for academics, athletics, ROTC, state/district residency.

FINANCIAL AID PROCEDURES

Forms required: FAFSA.

Dates and Deadlines: Priority date 4/27; no closing date. Applicants notified on a rolling basis starting 5/1; must reply within 2 week(s) of notification.

Transfers: No deadline. Student must submit a financial aid transcript from all prior schools attended before receiving aid.

CONTACT
Donna Mack-Tatum, Director of Financial Aid
1500 North Lombardy Street, Richmond, VA 23220
(804) 257-5882

Virginia Wesleyan College
Norfolk, Virginia
www.vwc.edu Federal Code: 003767

4-year private liberal arts college in large city, affiliated with United Methodist Church.
Enrollment: 1,326 undergrads, 13% part-time. 362 full-time freshmen.
Selectivity: Admits over 75% of applicants.

BASIC COSTS (2008-2009)
Tuition and fees: $26,438.
Per-credit charge: $1,081.
Room and board: $7,100.
Additional info: Tuition/fee waivers available for adults.

FINANCIAL AID PICTURE (2007-2008)
Students with need: Out of 327 full-time freshmen who applied for aid, 286 were judged to have need. Of these, 286 received aid, and 47 had their full need met. Average financial aid package met 77% of need; average scholarship/grant was $4,005; average loan was $3,950. For part-time students, average financial aid package was $3,283.
Students without need: 71 full-time freshmen who did not demonstrate need for aid received scholarships/grants; average award was $8,059. No-need awards available for academics, alumni affiliation, leadership, religious affiliation, ROTC, state/district residency.
Cumulative student debt: 71% of graduating class had student loans; average debt was $25,740.

FINANCIAL AID PROCEDURES
Forms required: FAFSA, state aid form.
Dates and Deadlines: Priority date 3/1; no closing date. Applicants notified on a rolling basis starting 2/15; must reply by 5/1 or within 2 week(s) of notification.
Transfers: Applicants notified on a rolling basis starting 2/15; must reply by 5/1 or within 2 week(s) of notification. 4-semester maximum of special aid available for students who graduated with 3.0 GPA and earned an associate degree from local community college. Must enroll full time and maintain 2.5 GPA minimum.

CONTACT
Angie Hawkins, Director of Financial Aid
1584 Wesleyan Drive, Norfolk, VA 23502-5599
(757) 455-3345

Virginia Western Community College
Roanoke, Virginia
www.virginiawestern.edu Federal Code: 003760

2-year public community college in small city.
Enrollment: 4,665 undergrads.
Selectivity: Open admission; but selective for some programs.

BASIC COSTS (2008-2009)
Tuition and fees: $2,663; out-of-state residents $7,827.
Per-credit charge: $82; out-of-state residents $254.
Additional info: Out-of-state students pay additional $90 capital outlay fee.

FINANCIAL AID PICTURE
Students with need: Need-based aid available for full-time and part-time students.
Students without need: No-need awards available for academics, state/district residency.

FINANCIAL AID PROCEDURES
Forms required: FAFSA.
Dates and Deadlines: No deadline. Applicants notified on a rolling basis starting 4/1.
Transfers: No deadline. Applicants notified on a rolling basis.

CONTACT
Shawn Thomas, Financial Aid Officer
Box 14007, Roanoke, VA 24038
(540) 857-7331

Washington and Lee University
Lexington, Virginia Federal Code: 003768
www.wlu.edu CSS Code: 5887

4-year private university and liberal arts college in small town.
Enrollment: 1,749 undergrads. 454 full-time freshmen.
Selectivity: Admits less than 50% of applicants.

BASIC COSTS (2008-2009)
Tuition and fees: $37,412.
Room and board: $9,400.

FINANCIAL AID PICTURE (2008-2009)
Students with need: Out of 244 full-time freshmen who applied for aid, 177 were judged to have need. Of these, 177 received aid, and 160 had their full need met. Average financial aid package met 99% of need; average scholarship/grant was $27,989; average loan was $3,101. Need-based aid available for part-time students.
Students without need: 35 full-time freshmen who did not demonstrate need for aid received scholarships/grants; average award was $32,562. No-need awards available for academics.
Scholarships offered: Various memorial and endowed scholarships available.
Cumulative student debt: 33% of graduating class had student loans; average debt was $23,616.

FINANCIAL AID PROCEDURES
Forms required: FAFSA, CSS PROFILE.
Dates and Deadlines: Priority date 2/1; closing date 3/1. Applicants notified by 4/1; must reply by 5/1.
Transfers: Transfer students are awarded institutional funds only after commitments to enrolled students are met. Notification usually in late summer.

CONTACT
John DeCourcy, Director of Student Financial Aid
204 West Washington Street, Lexington, VA 24450-2116
(540) 458-8715

Wytheville Community College
Wytheville, Virginia
www.wcc.vccs.edu Federal Code: 003761

2-year public community college in small town.
Enrollment: 1,926 undergrads.
Selectivity: Open admission; but selective for some programs.

BASIC COSTS (2008-2009)
Tuition and fees: $2,615; out-of-state residents $7,779.
Per-credit charge: $82; out-of-state residents $254.
Additional info: Out-of-state students pay additional $90 capital outlay fee.

FINANCIAL AID PICTURE (2007-2008)
Students with need: Need-based aid available for full-time and part-time students.

Students without need: This college awards aid only to students with need.

FINANCIAL AID PROCEDURES

Forms required: FAFSA, institutional form.

Dates and Deadlines: Priority date 4/1; no closing date. Applicants notified on a rolling basis starting 5/1; must reply within 4 week(s) of notification.

CONTACT

Mary Gallagher, Financial Aid Coordinator
1000 East Main Street, Wytheville, VA 24382
(540) 223-4703

Washington

Antioch University Seattle

Seattle, Washington
www.antiochsea.edu Federal Code: 003010

Upper-division private university and liberal arts college in very large city.

Enrollment: 250 undergrads.

BASIC COSTS (2008-2009)

Tuition and fees: $21,435.

Per-credit charge: $468.

Additional info: For BA with Teacher Prep program, $20,025 per year, $445 per credit hour.

FINANCIAL AID PICTURE (2007-2008)

Students with need: 44% of average financial aid package awarded as scholarships/grants, 56% awarded as loans/jobs. Need-based aid available for part-time students. Work study available nights, weekends, and for part-time students.

Cumulative student debt: 72% of graduating class had student loans; average debt was $26,000.

FINANCIAL AID PROCEDURES

Forms required: FAFSA.

Dates and Deadlines: Priority date 4/15; no closing date. Applicants notified on a rolling basis starting 5/1; must reply within 2 week(s) of notification.

Transfers: Applicants notified on a rolling basis starting 5/1; must reply within 2 week(s) of notification.

CONTACT

Katy Stahl, Director of Financial Aid
2326 Sixth Avenue, Seattle, WA 98121-1814
(206) 268-4010

Art Institute of Seattle

Seattle, Washington
www.ais.edu Federal Code: 016210

4-year for-profit visual arts and technical college in very large city.

Enrollment: 2,234 undergrads, 34% part-time. 559 full-time freshmen.

Selectivity: Open admission; but selective for some programs.

BASIC COSTS (2008-2009)

Tuition and fees: $20,385.

Per-credit charge: $453.

Room and board: $10,080.

Additional info: Tuition at time of enrollment locked for 4 years.

FINANCIAL AID PICTURE (2008-2009)

Students with need: 26% of average financial aid package awarded as scholarships/grants, 74% awarded as loans/jobs. Need-based aid available for part-time students. Work study available nights, weekends, and for part-time students.

Students without need: No-need awards available for academics, art.

FINANCIAL AID PROCEDURES

Forms required: FAFSA, state aid form.

Dates and Deadlines: Priority date 4/15; no closing date. Applicants notified on a rolling basis; must reply within 4 week(s) of notification.

CONTACT

Angela Hedwall, Director of Student Financial Services
2323 Elliott Avenue, Seattle, WA 98121-1622
(206) 239-2261

Bastyr University

Kenmore, Washington
www.bastyr.edu Federal Code: 016059

Upper-division private university and health science college in small city.

Enrollment: 201 undergrads, 16% part-time.

BASIC COSTS (2008-2009)

Tuition and fees: $17,790.

Per-credit charge: $450.

Room and board: $4,100.

FINANCIAL AID PICTURE (2008-2009)

Students with need: Average financial aid package for all full-time undergraduates was $15,235. 73% awarded as scholarships/grants, 27% awarded as loans/jobs. Need-based aid available for part-time students. Work study available nights, weekends, and for part-time students.

Students without need: No-need awards available for academics.

Cumulative student debt: 80% of graduating class had student loans; average debt was $35,000.

FINANCIAL AID PROCEDURES

Forms required: FAFSA, institutional form.

Dates and Deadlines: Priority date 6/1; no closing date. Applicants notified on a rolling basis starting 5/15; must reply within 2 week(s) of notification.

Transfers: Priority date 5/1; no deadline. Applicants notified on a rolling basis; must reply within 3 week(s) of notification.

CONTACT

Carol Duke, Director of Financial Aid
14500 Juanita Drive, NE, Kenmore, WA 98028
(425) 602-3080

Bates Technical College

Tacoma, Washington
www.bates.ctc.edu Federal Code: 012259

2-year public technical college in small city.

Enrollment: 1,437 undergrads.

Selectivity: Open admission.

BASIC COSTS (2008-2009)

Additional info: Programs costs range from $4,245 to $5,606; includes tuition and fees.

FINANCIAL AID PICTURE

Students with need: Need-based aid available for full-time and part-time students. Work study available nights.

Students without need: This college awards aid only to students with need.

FINANCIAL AID PROCEDURES

Forms required: FAFSA, institutional form.

Dates and Deadlines: No deadline. Applicants notified on a rolling basis starting 9/7.

Transfers: No deadline. Applicants notified on a rolling basis.

CONTACT

Susan Neese, Financial Aid Officer
1101 South Yakima Avenue, Tacoma, WA 98405
(253) 680-7025

Bellevue Community College

Bellevue, Washington
www.bcc.ctc.edu Federal Code: 003769

2-year public community college in small city.
Enrollment: 5,017 undergrads.
Selectivity: Open admission; but selective for some programs.

BASIC COSTS (2008-2009)

Tuition and fees: $3,105; out-of-state residents $8,319.
Per-credit charge: $153; out-of-state residents $433.

FINANCIAL AID PICTURE (2007-2008)

Students with need: Need-based aid available for full-time and part-time students. Work study available nights, weekends, and for part-time students.
Students without need: No-need awards available for academics, athletics.

FINANCIAL AID PROCEDURES

Forms required: FAFSA, institutional form.
Dates and Deadlines: Priority date 4/16; no closing date. Applicants notified on a rolling basis starting 8/1.

CONTACT

Sherri Ballantyne, Director of Financial Aid
3000 Landerholm Circle SE, Bellevue, WA 98007-6484
(425) 564-2227

Bellingham Technical College

Bellingham, Washington
www.btc.ctc.edu Federal Code: 016227

2-year public technical college in small city.
Enrollment: 1,698 undergrads.
Selectivity: Open admission.

BASIC COSTS (2008-2009)

Tuition and fees: $3,420.

FINANCIAL AID PICTURE

Students with need: Need-based aid available for full-time and part-time students.
Students without need: This college awards aid only to students with need.

FINANCIAL AID PROCEDURES

Forms required: FAFSA.
Dates and Deadlines: Priority date 4/30; no closing date. Applicants notified on a rolling basis starting 7/1; must reply within 2 week(s) of notification.

CONTACT

Jack Wollens, Director of Financial Aid
3028 Lindbergh Avenue, Bellingham, WA 98225
(360) 752-8351

Big Bend Community College

Moses Lake, Washington
www.bigbend.edu Federal Code: 003770

2-year public community college in large town.
Enrollment: 1,238 undergrads, 24% part-time. 295 full-time freshmen.
Selectivity: Open admission; but selective for some programs.

BASIC COSTS (2008-2009)

Tuition and fees: $2,820; out-of-state residents $3,216.
Per-credit charge: $79; out-of-state residents $92.
Room only: $2,790.
Additional info: Tuition/fee waivers available for unemployed or children of unemployed.

FINANCIAL AID PICTURE (2007-2008)

Students with need: 73% of average financial aid package awarded as scholarships/grants, 27% awarded as loans/jobs. Need-based aid available for part-time students. Work study available nights, weekends, and for part-time students.
Students without need: This college awards aid only to students with need.

FINANCIAL AID PROCEDURES

Forms required: FAFSA, institutional form.
Dates and Deadlines: Priority date 4/15; no closing date. Applicants notified on a rolling basis starting 5/15; must reply within 2 week(s) of notification.

CONTACT

Andre Guzman, Director of Financial Aid
7662 Chanute Street, Moses Lake, WA 98837-3299
(509) 793-2034

Cascadia Community College

Bothell, Washington
www.cascadia.edu Federal Code: 034835

2-year public community college in large town.
Enrollment: 1,724 undergrads.
Selectivity: Open admission.

BASIC COSTS (2008-2009)

Tuition and fees: $2,850; out-of-state residents $8,064.

FINANCIAL AID PICTURE (2007-2008)

Students with need: Work study available nights, weekends, and for part-time students.

FINANCIAL AID PROCEDURES

Forms required: FAFSA, institutional form.
Dates and Deadlines: Priority date 4/16; no closing date.

CONTACT

Sybil Smith, Director of Student Financial Services
18345 Campus Way, NE, Bothell, WA 98011
(425) 352-8860

Central Washington University

Ellensburg, Washington
www.cwu.edu Federal Code: 003771

4-year public university in large town.
Enrollment: 9,688 undergrads, 11% part-time. 1,555 full-time freshmen.
Selectivity: Admits over 75% of applicants.

BASIC COSTS (2008-2009)
Tuition and fees: $5,540; out-of-state residents $15,411.
Room and board: $8,052.

FINANCIAL AID PICTURE (2007-2008)
Students with need: Need-based aid available for full-time and part-time students.
Students without need: No-need awards available for academics, alumni affiliation, art, athletics, job skills, leadership, minority status, music/drama, religious affiliation, ROTC, state/district residency.

FINANCIAL AID PROCEDURES
Forms required: FAFSA.
Dates and Deadlines: Priority date 3/1; no closing date. Applicants notified on a rolling basis starting 4/15; must reply within 4 week(s) of notification.
Transfers: Equal Opportunity Grant available for junior-level transfers from selected Washington counties. May receive up to $2,500/year for three years.

CONTACT
Agnes Canedo, Director of Financial Aid
400 East University Way, Ellensburg, WA 98926-7463
(509) 963-1611

Centralia College
Centralia, Washington
www.centralia.edu Federal Code: 003772

2-year public community college in large town.
Enrollment: 1,927 undergrads.
Selectivity: Open admission; but selective for some programs.

BASIC COSTS (2008-2009)
Tuition and fees: $3,002; out-of-state residents $3,397.
Per-credit charge: $76; out-of-state residents $89.
Additional info: Tuition/fee waivers available for unemployed or children of unemployed.

FINANCIAL AID PICTURE (2007-2008)
Students with need: Need-based aid available for full-time and part-time students.
Students without need: No-need awards available for academics, alumni affiliation, art, athletics, leadership, minority status, music/drama.

FINANCIAL AID PROCEDURES
Forms required: FAFSA, institutional form.
Dates and Deadlines: Priority date 5/1; closing date 9/1. Applicants notified on a rolling basis starting 7/10; must reply within 2 week(s) of notification.

CONTACT
Tracy Dahl, Director of Financial Aid
600 Centralia College Boulevard, Centralia, WA 98531
(360) 736-9391 ext. 234

City University of Seattle
Bellevue, Washington
www.cityu.edu Federal Code: 013022

Upper-division private university in very large city.
Enrollment: 1,268 undergrads, 43% part-time.
Selectivity: Open admission; but selective for some programs.

BASIC COSTS (2008-2009)
Tuition and fees: $14,580.
Per-credit charge: $324.

FINANCIAL AID PICTURE
Students with need: Need-based aid available for full-time and part-time students.
Students without need: No-need awards available for academics.
Additional info: All degree programs approved for veteran's administration education benefits.

FINANCIAL AID PROCEDURES
Forms required: FAFSA, institutional form.
Dates and Deadlines: No deadline. Applicants notified on a rolling basis.

CONTACT
Jean Roberts, Director of Financial Aid
11900 NE First Street, Bellevue, WA 98005
(800) 426-5596

Clark College
Vancouver, Washington
www.clark.edu Federal Code: 003773

2-year public community college in small city.
Enrollment: 6,098 undergrads, 55% part-time. 705 full-time freshmen.
Selectivity: Open admission; but selective for some programs.

BASIC COSTS (2008-2009)
Tuition and fees: $2,962; out-of-state residents $3,357.
Per-credit charge: $81; out-of-state residents $94.
Additional info: Tuition/fee waivers available for unemployed or children of unemployed.

FINANCIAL AID PICTURE (2007-2008)
Students with need: Need-based aid available for full-time and part-time students. Work study available nights, weekends, and for part-time students.
Students without need: No-need awards available for academics, alumni affiliation, art, athletics, job skills, leadership, minority status, music/drama, religious affiliation, ROTC, state/district residency.
Scholarships offered: Clark College Foundation Scholarships; range from $500 to full tuition; recipients selected from those completing Clark's Foundation Standard Scholarship application form.

FINANCIAL AID PROCEDURES
Forms required: FAFSA, institutional form.
Dates and Deadlines: Priority date 5/1; no closing date. Applicants notified on a rolling basis starting 5/1; must reply within 2 week(s) of notification.

CONTACT
Karen Driscoll, Director of Financial Aid
1933 Fort Vancouver Way, Vancouver, WA 98663
(360) 992-2153

Clover Park Technical College
Lakewood, Washington
www.cptc.edu Federal Code: 015984

2-year public technical college in small city.
Enrollment: 1,301 undergrads.
Selectivity: Open admission; but selective for some programs.

BASIC COSTS (2008-2009)
Tuition and fees: $3,591.
Per-credit charge: $60.
Additional info: Students in programs with high computer usage pay a $45 per quarter computer use fee.

FINANCIAL AID PICTURE (2007-2008)
Students with need: Need-based aid available for full-time and part-time students. Work study available nights, weekends, and for part-time students.

Students without need: This college awards aid only to students with need.

FINANCIAL AID PROCEDURES

Forms required: FAFSA, institutional form.

Dates and Deadlines: Priority date 6/15; closing date 8/25. Applicants notified on a rolling basis.

CONTACT

Wendy Joseph, Financial Aid Director
4500 Steilacoom Boulevard, SW, Lakewood, WA 98499-4098
(253) 589-5660

Columbia Basin College

Pasco, Washington
www.columbiabasin.edu Federal Code: 003774

2-year public community college in small city.

Enrollment: 5,904 undergrads.

Selectivity: Open admission; but selective for some programs.

BASIC COSTS (2008-2009)

Tuition and fees: $2,936; out-of-state residents $3,995.

Additional info: Tuition/fee waivers available for unemployed or children of unemployed.

FINANCIAL AID PICTURE (2008-2009)

Students with need: Need-based aid available for full-time and part-time students. Work study available nights, weekends, and for part-time students.

Students without need: No-need awards available for academics, athletics, state/district residency.

FINANCIAL AID PROCEDURES

Forms required: FAFSA, institutional form.

Dates and Deadlines: Priority date 4/10; no closing date. Applicants notified on a rolling basis starting 6/15; must reply within 2 week(s) of notification.

CONTACT

Ceci Ratliff, Director of Student Financial Services
2600 North 20th Avenue, Pasco, WA 99301
(509) 542-4715

Cornish College of the Arts

Seattle, Washington
www.cornish.edu Federal Code: 012315

4-year private visual arts and performing arts college in very large city.

Enrollment: 814 undergrads.

Selectivity: Admits 50 to 75% of applicants.

BASIC COSTS (2008-2009)

Tuition and fees: $26,100.

Per-credit charge: $1,070.

Additional info: Design majors required to have laptop computer and Adobe software, estimated cost $3,000.

FINANCIAL AID PICTURE (2008-2009)

Students with need: Need-based aid available for full-time and part-time students. Work study available nights, weekends, and for part-time students.

Students without need: No-need awards available for academics.

FINANCIAL AID PROCEDURES

Forms required: FAFSA, institutional form.

Dates and Deadlines: Priority date 2/15; no closing date. Applicants notified on a rolling basis starting 4/15; must reply by 5/1 or within 2 week(s) of notification.

Transfers: No deadline. Applicants notified on a rolling basis; must reply by 2/15.

CONTACT

Monique Theriault, Director for Financial Aid
1000 Lenora Street, Seattle, WA 98121
(206) 726-5014

DeVry University: Federal Way

Federal Way, Washington
www.devry.edu

4-year for-profit university in large city.

Enrollment: 657 undergrads, 37% part-time. 93 full-time freshmen.

BASIC COSTS (2008-2009)

Tuition and fees: $14,800.

Per-credit charge: $540.

FINANCIAL AID PICTURE (2007-2008)

Students with need: Need-based aid available for full-time and part-time students.

Students without need: This college awards aid only to students with need.

FINANCIAL AID PROCEDURES

Forms required: FAFSA.

Dates and Deadlines: No deadline. Applicants notified on a rolling basis.

CONTACT

Scott Sand, Director of Financial Aid
3600 South 344th Way, Federal Way, WA 98001-9558
(253) 943-3060

DigiPen Institute of Technology

Redmond, Washington
www.digipen.edu Federal Code: 037243

4-year for-profit visual arts and engineering college in large town.

Enrollment: 825 undergrads.

BASIC COSTS (2008-2009)

Additional info: Full-time tuition for academic year (based on 20 hours per term), $19,040; required fees, $160; per-credit-hour charge, $476. Full-time tuition for non-resident aliens for academic year (based on 20 hours per term), $24,840; per-credit-hour charge, $621.

FINANCIAL AID PICTURE

Students with need: Need-based aid available for full-time and part-time students.

Students without need: No-need awards available for job skills, leadership, minority status.

Scholarships offered: Institutional Need-Based Scholarship: $1,000; based on financial need and academic performance; 5 awarded annually. Imagine America Scholarship Program: $1,000; based on financial need, grade point average of 2.5 or greater, voluntary community service during the senior year; 3 awarded annually. First Scholarship: $2,500; based on essay and academic record; 2 awarded annually. First Scholarship: $1,000; based on essay and academic record; 5 awarded annually.

Additional info: Many aid programs are on a first-come, first-served basis.

FINANCIAL AID PROCEDURES

Forms required: FAFSA, institutional form.

Dates and Deadlines: Priority date 4/15; no closing date. Applicants notified on a rolling basis starting 1/1; must reply within 4 week(s) of notification.

Transfers: No deadline. Applicants notified on a rolling basis starting 1/1; must reply within 4 week(s) of notification. Transfer student should meet with financial aid administrator as soon as they are accepted. Need prior financial aid history to determine eligibility.

CONTACT

Kim King, Director of Financial Aid
5001-150th Avenue Northeast, Redmond, WA 98052
(425) 895-4446

Eastern Washington University

Cheney, Washington
www.ewu.edu Federal Code: 003775

4-year public university in large town.
Enrollment: 9,485 undergrads, 13% part-time. 1,305 full-time freshmen.
Selectivity: Admits over 75% of applicants.

BASIC COSTS (2008-2009)

Tuition and fees: $5,216; out-of-state residents $13,889.
Room and board: $6,756.

FINANCIAL AID PICTURE (2007-2008)

Students with need: Out of 1,015 full-time freshmen who applied for aid, 719 were judged to have need. Of these, 693 received aid, and 201 had their full need met. Average financial aid package met 90% of need; average scholarship/grant was $5,199; average loan was $2,180. For part-time students, average financial aid package was $7,744.
Students without need: 127 full-time freshmen who did not demonstrate need for aid received scholarships/grants; average award was $2,942. No-need awards available for academics, alumni affiliation, athletics, ROTC.
Scholarships offered: ***Merit:*** Killin Scholarship; $3,500; three awards; for academic excellence, must have 3.7 GPA and 1100 SAT score (exclusive of Writing). Honors Scholarship; $2,500; 38 awards; for academic excellence. Presidential Scholarship; $2,000; 75 awards; based on GPA, SAT, early admission. ***Athletic:*** 34 full-time freshmen received athletic scholarships; average amount $6,651.
Cumulative student debt: 65% of graduating class had student loans; average debt was $18,320.
Additional info: The High Demand Scholarship program helps low income students pursue "high demand" careers.

FINANCIAL AID PROCEDURES

Forms required: FAFSA.
Dates and Deadlines: Priority date 4/1; no closing date. Applicants notified on a rolling basis starting 4/1; must reply within 4 week(s) of notification.
Transfers: Educational Opportunity Grant (EOG); financially needy, place-bound students with AA or junior status, $2,500 renewable, rolling priority, first-come, first-served at end of each month beginning April 1, ending September 30.

CONTACT

Bruce Defrates, Director of Financial Aid
101 Sutton Hall, Cheney, WA 99004-2447
(509) 359-2314

Edmonds Community College

Lynnwood, Washington
www.edcc.edu Federal Code: 005001

2-year public community college in small city.
Enrollment: 7,823 undergrads.
Selectivity: Open admission; but selective for some programs.

BASIC COSTS (2008-2009)

Tuition and fees: $2,960; out-of-state residents $8,174.

FINANCIAL AID PICTURE

Students with need: Need-based aid available for full-time and part-time students. Work study available nights.
Students without need: No-need awards available for athletics.

FINANCIAL AID PROCEDURES

Forms required: FAFSA, institutional form.
Dates and Deadlines: Priority date 5/1; no closing date. Applicants notified on a rolling basis starting 6/1; must reply within 4 week(s) of notification.

CONTACT

Rae-Ellen Reas, Senior Associate Dean of Enrollment and Financial Services
20000 68th Avenue West, Lynnwood, WA 98036-5912
(425) 640-1457

Everett Community College

Everett, Washington
www.everettcc.edu Federal Code: 003776

2-year public community college in small city.
Enrollment: 4,041 undergrads, 46% part-time. 440 full-time freshmen.
Selectivity: Open admission; but selective for some programs.

BASIC COSTS (2008-2009)

Tuition and fees: $2,835; out-of-state residents $8,049.
Per-credit charge: $76; out-of-state residents $248.
Additional info: Tuition at time of enrollment locked for 2 years.

FINANCIAL AID PICTURE (2007-2008)

Students with need: Need-based aid available for full-time and part-time students. Work study available nights, weekends, and for part-time students.
Students without need: This college awards aid only to students with need.

FINANCIAL AID PROCEDURES

Forms required: FAFSA, institutional form.
Dates and Deadlines: Priority date 5/5; no closing date. Applicants notified on a rolling basis starting 4/15; must reply within 4 week(s) of notification.
Transfers: No deadline. Applicants notified on a rolling basis starting 6/15; must reply within 4 week(s) of notification.

CONTACT

Laurie Franklin, Director of Student Financial Services
2000 Tower Street, Everett, WA 98201-1352
(425) 388-9280

Evergreen State College

Olympia, Washington
www.evergreen.edu Federal Code: 008155

4-year public liberal arts college in small city.
Enrollment: 4,228 undergrads, 7% part-time. 679 full-time freshmen.
Selectivity: Admits over 75% of applicants.

BASIC COSTS (2008-2009)

Tuition and fees: $5,329; out-of-state residents $16,189.
Room and board: $8,052.
Additional info: Tuition/fee waivers available for minority students.

FINANCIAL AID PICTURE (2007-2008)

Students with need: Out of 430 full-time freshmen who applied for aid, 289 were judged to have need. Of these, 271 received aid, and 41 had their full need met. Average financial aid package met 76% of need; average scholarship/grant was $6,009; average loan was $3,480. For part-time students, average financial aid package was $3,222.

Students without need: 17 full-time freshmen who did not demonstrate need for aid received scholarships/grants; average award was $4,502. No-need awards available for academics, art, athletics, state/district residency.
Scholarships offered: 4 full-time freshmen received athletic scholarships; average amount $1,763.
Cumulative student debt: 51% of graduating class had student loans; average debt was $15,597.
Additional info: Application deadline for merit and cultural diversity scholarships February 1. Minority students may apply for tuition and fee waiver scholarships; amount of award equal to in-state tuition and fees. To meet priority deadline for required financial aid forms, official results of FAFSA must be received by March 15.

FINANCIAL AID PROCEDURES

Forms required: FAFSA, institutional form.
Dates and Deadlines: Priority date 3/15; no closing date. Applicants notified on a rolling basis starting 4/1; must reply within 8 week(s) of notification.

CONTACT

Julie Anderson, Director of Financial Aid
2700 Evergreen Parkway NW, Olympia, WA 98505
(360) 867-6205

Gonzaga University

Spokane, Washington
www.gonzaga.edu Federal Code: 003778

4-year private university and liberal arts college in large city, affiliated with Roman Catholic Church.
Enrollment: 4,442 undergrads, 2% part-time. 1,026 full-time freshmen.
Selectivity: Admits over 75% of applicants. GED not accepted.

BASIC COSTS (2008-2009)

Tuition and fees: $28,262.
Per-credit charge: $810.
Room and board: $7,860.
Additional info: Tuition/fee waivers available for adults.

FINANCIAL AID PICTURE (2007-2008)

Students with need: Out of 836 full-time freshmen who applied for aid, 567 were judged to have need. Of these, 567 received aid, and 198 had their full need met. Average financial aid package met 88% of need; average scholarship/grant was $12,464; average loan was $4,890. For part-time students, average financial aid package was $6,098.
Students without need: 264 full-time freshmen who did not demonstrate need for aid received scholarships/grants; average award was $7,316. No-need awards available for academics, alumni affiliation, athletics, leadership, minority status, music/drama, ROTC.
Scholarships offered: ***Merit:*** All freshmen are considered for Academic Merit Scholarships: awards range from $3,000 to $10,000. ***Athletic:*** 32 full-time freshmen received athletic scholarships; average amount $19,285.
Cumulative student debt: 75% of graduating class had student loans; average debt was $24,094.

FINANCIAL AID PROCEDURES

Forms required: FAFSA.
Dates and Deadlines: Priority date 2/1; closing date 6/30. Applicants notified on a rolling basis starting 3/1; must reply by 5/1 or within 3 week(s) of notification.
Transfers: No deadline. Applicants notified on a rolling basis; must reply by 4/15 or within 3 week(s) of notification.

CONTACT

Thayne McCulloh, VP for Administration and Planning; Dean of Student Financial Services
502 East Boone Avenue, Spokane, WA 99258-0001
(509) 323-6582

Grays Harbor College

Aberdeen, Washington
www.ghc.edu Federal Code: 003779

2-year public community college in large town.
Enrollment: 641 undergrads, 29% part-time. 117 full-time freshmen.
Selectivity: Open admission; but selective for some programs.

BASIC COSTS (2008-2009)

Tuition and fees: $3,167; out-of-state residents $8,381.
Additional info: Tuition/fee waivers available for adults, unemployed or children of unemployed.

FINANCIAL AID PICTURE (2007-2008)

Students with need: 94% of average financial aid package awarded as scholarships/grants, 6% awarded as loans/jobs. Need-based aid available for part-time students. Work study available nights.
Students without need: No-need awards available for academics, art, athletics, music/drama.

FINANCIAL AID PROCEDURES

Forms required: FAFSA, institutional form.
Dates and Deadlines: Priority date 5/1; no closing date. Applicants notified on a rolling basis starting 5/15.

CONTACT

Nadine Hibbs, Director of Financial Aid
1620 Edward P Smith Drive, Aberdeen, WA 98520
(360) 538-4081

Green River Community College

Auburn, Washington
www.greenriver.edu Federal Code: 003780

2-year public community college in large town.
Enrollment: 4,962 undergrads.
Selectivity: Open admission; but selective for some programs.

BASIC COSTS (2008-2009)

Tuition and fees: $3,113; out-of-state residents $3,545.

FINANCIAL AID PICTURE (2008-2009)

Students with need: Need-based aid available for full-time and part-time students.
Students without need: This college awards aid only to students with need.

FINANCIAL AID PROCEDURES

Forms required: FAFSA, institutional form.
Dates and Deadlines: Priority date 4/15; no closing date. Applicants notified on a rolling basis starting 6/30; must reply within 2 week(s) of notification.

CONTACT

Mary Edington, Director of Financial Aid
12401 SE 320th Street, Auburn, WA 98092
(253) 833-9111 ext. 2440

Heritage University

Toppenish, Washington
www.heritage.edu Federal Code: 003777

4-year private liberal arts and teachers college in small town, affiliated with interdenominational tradition.
Enrollment: 745 undergrads.
Selectivity: Open admission.

BASIC COSTS (2008-2009)
Tuition and fees: $12,205.
Per-credit charge: $405.

FINANCIAL AID PICTURE (2007-2008)
Students with need: 58% of average financial aid package awarded as scholarships/grants, 42% awarded as loans/jobs. Need-based aid available for part-time students. Work study available nights, weekends, and for part-time students.
Students without need: No-need awards available for academics, leadership, minority status.

FINANCIAL AID PROCEDURES
Forms required: FAFSA, institutional form.
Dates and Deadlines: Priority date 2/10; no closing date. Applicants notified on a rolling basis; must reply within 2 week(s) of notification.

CONTACT
Dianne Fernandez, Director of Financial Aid
3240 Fort Road, Toppenish, WA 98948-9599
(509) 865-8502

Highline Community College
Des Moines, Washington
www.highline.edu Federal Code: 003781

2-year public community college in small city.
Enrollment: 6,387 undergrads.
Selectivity: Open admission; but selective for some programs.

BASIC COSTS (2008-2009)
Tuition and fees: $2,805; out-of-state residents $3,184.
Per-credit charge: $76; out-of-state residents $89.

FINANCIAL AID PICTURE (2007-2008)
Students with need: Need-based aid available for full-time and part-time students.

FINANCIAL AID PROCEDURES
Forms required: FAFSA.
Dates and Deadlines: Priority date 5/31; no closing date. Applicants notified on a rolling basis starting 6/1.

CONTACT
Lorraine Odom, Director of Financial Aid
2400 South 240th Street, Des Moines, WA 98198-9800
(206) 878-3710

International Academy of Design and Technology: Seattle
Seattle, Washington
www.iadtseattle.com Federal Code: E01257

4-year for-profit university in very large city.
Enrollment: 511 undergrads.
Selectivity: Open admission.

BASIC COSTS (2008-2009)
Tuition and fees: $16,200.
Per-credit charge: $360.

FINANCIAL AID PICTURE (2007-2008)
Students with need: 25% of average financial aid package awarded as scholarships/grants, 75% awarded as loans/jobs.

FINANCIAL AID PROCEDURES
Dates and Deadlines: No deadline.

CONTACT
Miki Sueoka, Director of Student Finance
645 Andover Park West, Seattle, WA 98188

Lower Columbia College
Longview, Washington
www.lowercolumbia.edu Federal Code: 003782
CSS Code: 4402

2-year public community college in small city.
Enrollment: 1,313 undergrads, 33% part-time. 112 full-time freshmen.
Selectivity: Open admission; but selective for some programs.

BASIC COSTS (2008-2009)
Tuition and fees: $3,144; out-of-state residents $3,867.
Per-credit charge: $82; out-of-state residents $104.
Additional info: Full-time "border county" tuition for students in Oregon's Clatsop, Multnomah, Washington, and Columbia counties: $3,157. Tuition/fee waivers available for adults, unemployed or children of unemployed.

FINANCIAL AID PICTURE (2007-2008)
Students with need: 64% of average financial aid package awarded as scholarships/grants, 36% awarded as loans/jobs. Need-based aid available for part-time students.

FINANCIAL AID PROCEDURES
Forms required: CSS PROFILE, institutional form.
Dates and Deadlines: Priority date 5/1; no closing date. Applicants notified on a rolling basis starting 4/21; must reply within 2 week(s) of notification.
Transfers: State-need grant awards transfer with students if previously awarded at another WA institution; SEOG usually not available to transfer students. Student employment, loans, Pell Grant available.

CONTACT
Marisa Greear, Director of Financial Aid
1600 Maple Street, Longview, WA 98632-0310
(360) 442-2311

North Seattle Community College
Seattle, Washington
www.northseattle.edu Federal Code: 009704

2-year public community college in very large city.
Enrollment: 2,055 undergrads, 51% part-time. 348 full-time freshmen.
Selectivity: Open admission.

BASIC COSTS (2008-2009)
Tuition and fees: $2,969, out-of-state residents $8,183.
Per-credit charge: $76; out-of-state residents $248.
Additional info: Tuition/fee waivers available for adults, unemployed or children of unemployed.

FINANCIAL AID PICTURE (2007-2008)
Students with need: Need-based aid available for full-time and part-time students. Work study available weekends and for part-time students.

FINANCIAL AID PROCEDURES
Forms required: FAFSA, institutional form.
Dates and Deadlines: Priority date 4/30; closing date 8/31. Applicants notified on a rolling basis starting 7/1; must reply within 2 week(s) of notification.

CONTACT
Suzanne Scheldt, Director of Financial Aid
9600 College Way North, Seattle, WA 98103
(206) 528-4700

Northwest College of Art
Poulsbo, Washington
www.nca.edu Federal Code: 026021

4-year for-profit visual arts college in small town.
Enrollment: 91 full-time undergrads.

BASIC COSTS (2009-2010)
Tuition and fees: $16,200.
Per-credit charge: $665.

FINANCIAL AID PICTURE
Students with need: Need-based aid available for full-time and part-time students.
Students without need: No-need awards available for academics, art, state/district residency.

FINANCIAL AID PROCEDURES
Forms required: FAFSA.
Dates and Deadlines: Priority date 3/1; closing date 6/1. Applicants notified on a rolling basis.

CONTACT
Heidi Townsend, Financial Aid Officer
16301 Creative Drive NE, Poulsbo, WA 98370-8651
(360) 779-9993 ext. 8136

Northwest Indian College
Bellingham, Washington
www.nwic.edu Federal Code: 021800

2-year public community college in small town.
Enrollment: 467 undergrads.
Selectivity: Open admission.

BASIC COSTS (2008-2009)
Tuition and fees: $2,796; out-of-state residents $7,332.
Per-credit charge: $74; out-of-state residents $200.
Additional info: Eligibility to pay resident costs based on tribal enrollment verification. Tuition/fee waivers available for minority students.

FINANCIAL AID PICTURE
Students with need: Need-based aid available for full-time and part-time students.
Students without need: No-need awards available for academics.

FINANCIAL AID PROCEDURES
Forms required: FAFSA, institutional form.
Dates and Deadlines: No deadline. Applicants notified on a rolling basis.
Transfers: No deadline. Applicants notified on a rolling basis.

CONTACT
Mike Fentress, Director of Financial Aid
2522 Kwina Road, Bellingham, WA 98226-9217
(360) 676-2772 ext. 4206

Northwest University
Kirkland, Washington
www.northwestu.edu Federal Code: 003783

4-year private university and liberal arts college in small city, affiliated with Assemblies of God.
Enrollment: 1,094 undergrads, 14% part-time. 285 full-time freshmen.
Selectivity: Admits over 75% of applicants.

BASIC COSTS (2009-2010)
Tuition and fees: $21,994.
Per-credit charge: $905.
Room and board: $6,724.

FINANCIAL AID PICTURE (2008-2009)
Students with need: 57% of average financial aid package awarded as scholarships/grants, 43% awarded as loans/jobs. Need-based aid available for part-time students. Work study available nights, weekends, and for part-time students.
Students without need: No-need awards available for academics, art, athletics, leadership, music/drama, religious affiliation.

FINANCIAL AID PROCEDURES
Forms required: FAFSA, institutional form.
Dates and Deadlines: Priority date 3/1; closing date 8/1. Applicants notified on a rolling basis starting 3/3; must reply within 4 week(s) of notification.

CONTACT
Lana Walter, Director of Financial Aid
5520 108th Avenue, NE, Kirkland, WA 98083-0579
(425) 889-5210

Olympic College
Bremerton, Washington
www.olympic.edu Federal Code: 003784

2-year public community and liberal arts college in large town.
Enrollment: 3,111 undergrads, 46% part-time. 404 full-time freshmen.
Selectivity: Open admission; but selective for some programs.

BASIC COSTS (2008-2009)
Tuition and fees: $2,910; out-of-state residents $3,305.
Per-credit charge: $76; out-of-state residents $89.

FINANCIAL AID PICTURE (2008-2009)
Students with need: Need-based aid available for full-time and part-time students. Work study available nights.
Students without need: No-need awards available for academics, state/district residency.

FINANCIAL AID PROCEDURES
Forms required: FAFSA, institutional form.
Dates and Deadlines: Priority date 3/1; no closing date. Applicants notified on a rolling basis starting 6/1; must reply within 2 week(s) of notification.

CONTACT
Janell Whiteley, Director of Fiscal Services
1600 Chester Avenue, Bremerton, WA 98337-1699
(360) 475-7160

Pacific Lutheran University
Tacoma, Washington
www.plu.edu Federal Code: 003785

4-year private university in large city, affiliated with Evangelical Lutheran Church in America.
Enrollment: 3,265 undergrads, 4% part-time. 712 full-time freshmen.
Selectivity: Admits 50 to 75% of applicants.

BASIC COSTS (2008-2009)
Tuition and fees: $26,800.
Per-credit charge: $838.
Room and board: $8,200.

FINANCIAL AID PICTURE (2008-2009)

Students with need: Out of 641 full-time freshmen who applied for aid, 524 were judged to have need. Of these, 520 received aid, and 209 had their full need met. Average financial aid package met 91% of need; average scholarship/grant was $16,508; average loan was $6,318. For part-time students, average financial aid package was $12,989.

Students without need: 171 full-time freshmen who did not demonstrate need for aid received scholarships/grants; average award was $12,971. No-need awards available for academics, alumni affiliation, art, leadership, music/drama, religious affiliation, ROTC.

Cumulative student debt: 71% of graduating class had student loans; average debt was $22,484.

FINANCIAL AID PROCEDURES

Forms required: FAFSA.

Dates and Deadlines: Priority date 1/31; no closing date. Applicants notified on a rolling basis starting 3/15; must reply by 5/1 or within 4 week(s) of notification.

CONTACT

Kay Soltis, Director of Financial Aid
Office of Admissions, Tacoma, WA 98447-0003
(253) 535-7134

Peninsula College

Port Angeles, Washington
www.pc.ctc.edu Federal Code: 003786

2-year public community college in large town.

Enrollment: 928 undergrads, 39% part-time. 145 full-time freshmen.

Selectivity: Open admission; but selective for some programs.

BASIC COSTS (2008-2009)

Tuition and fees: $2,847; out-of-state residents $3,246.

Per-credit charge: $79; out-of-state residents $92.

Additional info: Tuition/fee waivers available for unemployed or children of unemployed.

FINANCIAL AID PICTURE (2007-2008)

Students with need: Need-based aid available for full-time and part-time students.

Students without need: No-need awards available for academics, athletics, job skills.

FINANCIAL AID PROCEDURES

Forms required: FAFSA, institutional form.

Dates and Deadlines: Priority date 4/1; no closing date. Applicants notified on a rolling basis starting 6/1; must reply within 2 week(s) of notification.

CONTACT

Krista Francis, Director of Financial Aid
1502 East Lauridsen Boulevard, Port Angeles, WA 98362
(360) 417-6390

Pierce College

Lakewood, Washington
www.pierce.ctc.edu Federal Code: 005000

2-year public community college in small city.

Enrollment: 9,939 undergrads.

Selectivity: Open admission; but selective for some programs.

BASIC COSTS (2008-2009)

Tuition and fees: $3,071; out-of-state residents $3,530.

Per-credit charge: $76; out-of-state residents $89.

Additional info: Tuition/fee waivers available for unemployed or children of unemployed.

FINANCIAL AID PICTURE

Students with need: Need-based aid available for full-time and part-time students.

Students without need: No-need awards available for academics, athletics, music/drama.

FINANCIAL AID PROCEDURES

Forms required: FAFSA, institutional form.

Dates and Deadlines: Priority date 4/15; no closing date. Applicants notified on a rolling basis starting 4/15.

CONTACT

Mary Richards, Assistant Director of Financial Aid
9401 Farwest Drive SW, Lakewood, WA 98498-1999
(253) 964-6544

Renton Technical College

Renton, Washington
www.RTC.edu Federal Code: 014001

2-year public technical college in large town.

Enrollment: 791 undergrads.

Selectivity: Open admission.

BASIC COSTS (2008-2009)

Tuition and fees: $3,105.

FINANCIAL AID PICTURE (2007-2008)

Students with need: Need-based aid available for full-time and part-time students.

Students without need: This college awards aid only to students with need.

FINANCIAL AID PROCEDURES

Forms required: FAFSA, institutional form.

Dates and Deadlines: Priority date 5/1; no closing date. Applicants notified on a rolling basis.

CONTACT

Debbie Solomon, Director of Financial Aid
3000 NE Fourth Street, Renton, WA 98056-4195
(425) 235-5841

Saint Martin's University

Lacey, Washington
www.stmartin.edu Federal Code: 003794

4-year private university in large town, affiliated with Roman Catholic Church.

Enrollment: 1,296 undergrads, 20% part-time. 209 full-time freshmen.

Selectivity: Admits over 75% of applicants.

BASIC COSTS (2009-2010)

Tuition and fees: $25,182.

Per-credit charge: $827.

Room and board: $8,360.

FINANCIAL AID PICTURE (2007-2008)

Students with need: Out of 197 full-time freshmen who applied for aid, 168 were judged to have need. Of these, 168 received aid, and 32 had their full need met. Average financial aid package met 81% of need; average scholarship/grant was $16,068; average loan was $3,147. For part-time students, average financial aid package was $14,444.

Students without need: 40 full-time freshmen who did not demonstrate need for aid received scholarships/grants; average award was $14,595. No-need awards available for academics, ROTC.
Scholarships offered: 20 full-time freshmen received athletic scholarships; average amount $5,693.
Cumulative student debt: 77% of graduating class had student loans; average debt was $27,264.

FINANCIAL AID PROCEDURES

Forms required: FAFSA.
Dates and Deadlines: Priority date 3/1; no closing date. Applicants notified on a rolling basis starting 2/15.

CONTACT

Shelle Riehl, Director, Office of Financial Aid
5300 Pacific Avenue SE, Lacey, WA 98503-7500
(360) 438-4397

Seattle Pacific University

Seattle, Washington
www.spu.edu Federal Code: 003788

4-year private university in very large city, affiliated with Free Methodist Church of North America.
Enrollment: 2,985 undergrads, 5% part-time. 712 full-time freshmen.
Selectivity: Admits over 75% of applicants.

BASIC COSTS (2009-2010)

Tuition and fees: $27,810.
Per-credit charge: $764.
Room and board: $8,544.

FINANCIAL AID PICTURE (2008-2009)

Students with need: Out of 585 full-time freshmen who applied for aid, 457 were judged to have need. Of these, 456 received aid, and 54 had their full need met. Average financial aid package met 84% of need; average scholarship/grant was $21,236; average loan was $5,479. For part-time students, average financial aid package was $16,283.
Students without need: 205 full-time freshmen who did not demonstrate need for aid received scholarships/grants; average award was $12,976. No-need awards available for academics, alumni affiliation, art, athletics, leadership, minority status, music/drama, religious affiliation, ROTC.
Scholarships offered: 17 full-time freshmen received athletic scholarships; average amount $11,309.
Cumulative student debt: 68% of graduating class had student loans; average debt was $23,066.

FINANCIAL AID PROCEDURES

Forms required: FAFSA.
Dates and Deadlines: Priority date 2/1; no closing date. Applicants notified on a rolling basis starting 3/11; must reply by 5/1 or within 30 week(s) of notification.
Transfers: No deadline. Applicants notified on a rolling basis starting 3/13; must reply by 5/1 or within 4 week(s) of notification.

CONTACT

Jordan Grant, Director of Financial Aid
3307 Third Avenue West, Suite 115, Seattle, WA 98119-1997
(206) 281-2061

Seattle University

Seattle, Washington
www.seattleu.edu Federal Code: 003790

4-year private university in very large city, affiliated with Roman Catholic Church.
Enrollment: 4,168 undergrads, 5% part-time. 883 full-time freshmen.
Selectivity: Admits 50 to 75% of applicants.

BASIC COSTS (2008-2009)

Tuition and fees: $28,260.
Per-credit charge: $628.
Room and board: $8,340.
Additional info: $200 enrollment deposit, $95 matriculation fee required. $95 per-credit-hour charge for credit by examination. $95 per-credit-hour charge for validation of field experience.

FINANCIAL AID PICTURE (2008-2009)

Students with need: Need-based aid available for full-time and part-time students. Work study available nights, weekends, and for part-time students.
Students without need: No-need awards available for academics, alumni affiliation, athletics, leadership, minority status, music/drama, ROTC, state/district residency.
Scholarships offered: Sullivan Leadership Award: full tuition, room and board for 4 years, for entering freshmen of Oregon, Washington, or Idaho residency; service, leadership, strong academics (3.5 GPA) important, 6 awarded. Presidential Scholarship: $11,000 annually for 4 years. Trustee Scholarship: $8,000 annually for 4 years. Campion Scholarship: $5,000 annually for 4 years; for first-time freshmen of U.S. citizenship or permanent resident status, strong academic and extracurricular records important.

FINANCIAL AID PROCEDURES

Forms required: FAFSA.
Dates and Deadlines: Priority date 1/15; no closing date. Applicants notified on a rolling basis starting 3/21; must reply by 5/1 or within 2 week(s) of notification.
Transfers: Closing date 3/1.

CONTACT

Janet Cantelon, Director of Financial Aid
901 12th Avenue, Seattle, WA 98122-4340
(206) 296-2000

Shoreline Community College

Shoreline, Washington
www.shoreline.edu Federal Code: 003791

2-year public community college in small city.
Enrollment: 5,823 undergrads.
Selectivity: Open admission; but selective for some programs.

BASIC COSTS (2008-2009)

Tuition and fees: $2,881; out-of-state residents $5,268.

FINANCIAL AID PICTURE (2007-2008)

Students with need: 63% of average financial aid package awarded as scholarships/grants, 37% awarded as loans/jobs. Work study available nights, weekends, and for part-time students.
Additional info: Tuition and/or fee waiver for students with need on space-available basis.

FINANCIAL AID PROCEDURES

Forms required: FAFSA, institutional form.
Dates and Deadlines: Priority date 4/1; no closing date. Applicants notified on a rolling basis starting 8/1; must reply within 3 week(s) of notification.

CONTACT

Ted Haase, Director of Financial Services
16101 Greenwood Avenue North, Seattle, WA 98133
(206) 546-4762

Skagit Valley College

Mount Vernon, Washington
www.skagit.edu Federal Code: 003792

2-year public community college in large town.
Enrollment: 2,207 full-time undergrads.
Selectivity: Open admission.

BASIC COSTS (2008-2009)

Tuition and fees: $2,905; out-of-state residents $3,300.
Per-credit charge: $76; out-of-state residents $89.
Room only: $3,420.
Additional info: Tuition/fee waivers available for unemployed or children of unemployed.

FINANCIAL AID PICTURE

Students with need: Need-based aid available for full-time and part-time students. Work study available nights, weekends, and for part-time students.
Students without need: This college awards aid only to students with need.

FINANCIAL AID PROCEDURES

Forms required: FAFSA, institutional form.
Dates and Deadlines: Priority date 3/1; no closing date. Applicants notified on a rolling basis starting 7/1; must reply within 2 week(s) of notification.

CONTACT

Steve Epperson, Financial Aid Director
2405 East College Way, Mount Vernon, WA 98273
(360) 416-7666

South Puget Sound Community College

Olympia, Washington
www.spscc.ctc.edu Federal Code: 005372

2-year public community college in small city.
Enrollment: 2,930 undergrads, 44% part-time. 323 full-time freshmen.
Selectivity: Open admission; but selective for some programs.

BASIC COSTS (2008-2009)

Tuition and fees: $2,824; out-of-state residents $3,283.
Per-credit charge: $75; out-of-state residents $89.

FINANCIAL AID PICTURE (2007-2008)

Students with need: 80% of average financial aid package awarded as scholarships/grants, 20% awarded as loans/jobs. Need-based aid available for part-time students.
Students without need: No-need awards available for academics, athletics.

FINANCIAL AID PROCEDURES

Forms required: FAFSA, institutional form.
Dates and Deadlines: Priority date 5/1; closing date 6/27. Applicants notified on a rolling basis starting 7/10; must reply within 2 week(s) of notification.

CONTACT

Carla Idohl-Corwin, Dean of Student Financial Services
2011 Mottman Road, SW, Olympia, WA 98512-6218
(360) 596-5232

South Seattle Community College

Seattle, Washington
www.southseattle.edu Federal Code: 009706

2-year public community college in very large city.
Enrollment: 3,667 undergrads.
Selectivity: Open admission; but selective for some programs.

BASIC COSTS (2008-2009)

Tuition and fees: $2,910; out-of-state residents $8,124.
Additional info: Tuition/fee waivers available for unemployed or children of unemployed.

FINANCIAL AID PICTURE (2007-2008)

Students with need: 94% of average financial aid package awarded as scholarships/grants, 6% awarded as loans/jobs. Need-based aid available for part-time students.
Students without need: No-need awards available for academics, state/district residency.

FINANCIAL AID PROCEDURES

Forms required: FAFSA, institutional form.
Dates and Deadlines: Priority date 4/16; no closing date. Applicants notified on a rolling basis starting 7/1.

CONTACT

Patricia Billings, Financial Aid Director
6000 16th Avenue, SW, Seattle, WA 98106-1499
(206) 764-5317

Spokane Falls Community College

Spokane, Washington
www.spokanefalls.edu Federal Code: 009544

2-year public community college in small city.
Enrollment: 5,783 undergrads.
Selectivity: Open admission; but selective for some programs.

BASIC COSTS (2008-2009)

Tuition and fees: $2,876; out-of-state residents $3,410.
Per-credit charge: $76; out-of-state residents $102.
Additional info: Tuition/fee waivers available for unemployed or children of unemployed.

FINANCIAL AID PICTURE

Students with need: Need-based aid available for full-time and part-time students.
Students without need: This college awards aid only to students with need.

FINANCIAL AID PROCEDURES

Forms required: FAFSA, institutional form.
Dates and Deadlines: Priority date 4/1; no closing date. Applicants notified on a rolling basis starting 5/15; must reply within 2 week(s) of notification.

CONTACT

Assistant Dean of Student Services for Financial Aid
3410 West Fort George Wright Drive, Spokane, WA 99224
(509) 533-3550

Tacoma Community College

Tacoma, Washington
www.tacomacc.edu Federal Code: 003796

2-year public community college in small city.
Enrollment: 6,090 undergrads, 41% part-time.
Selectivity: Open admission.

BASIC COSTS (2008-2009)

Tuition and fees: $2,932; out-of-state residents $3,328.
Additional info: Tuition/fee waivers available for unemployed or children of unemployed.

FINANCIAL AID PICTURE

Students with need: Need-based aid available for full-time and part-time students. Work study available nights, weekends, and for part-time students.
Students without need: This college awards aid only to students with need.

FINANCIAL AID PROCEDURES

Forms required: FAFSA, institutional form.
Dates and Deadlines: Priority date 3/26; no closing date. Applicants notified on a rolling basis starting 7/20; must reply within 4 week(s) of notification.

CONTACT

Kim Matison, Director, Financial Aid Services
6501 South 19th Street, Tacoma, WA 98466-9971
(253) 566-5080

Trinity Lutheran College

Everett, Washington
www.tlc.edu — Federal Code: 013525

4-year private Bible and liberal arts college in small city, affiliated with Lutheran Church.
Enrollment: 100 undergrads.
Selectivity: Admits less than 50% of applicants.

BASIC COSTS (2008-2009)

Tuition and fees: $19,425.
Per-credit charge: $790.
Room and board: $6,501.

FINANCIAL AID PICTURE (2008-2009)

Students with need: Need-based aid available for full-time and part-time students. Work study available nights, weekends, and for part-time students.
Students without need: No-need awards available for academics, alumni affiliation, art, leadership, music/drama.

FINANCIAL AID PROCEDURES

Forms required: FAFSA, institutional form.
Dates and Deadlines: Priority date 3/1; no closing date. Applicants notified on a rolling basis starting 3/15; must reply within 2 week(s) of notification.
Transfers: No deadline. Applicants notified on a rolling basis starting 3/15; must reply within 2 week(s) of notification.

CONTACT

Susan Dalgleish, Director of Financial Aid
2802 Wetmore Avenue, Everett, WA 98201
(425) 961-5514

University of Puget Sound

Tacoma, Washington
www.ups.edu — Federal Code: 003797

4-year private university and liberal arts college in small city.
Enrollment: 2,566 undergrads, 1% part-time. 676 full-time freshmen.
Selectivity: Admits 50 to 75% of applicants.

BASIC COSTS (2009-2010)

Tuition and fees: $35,635.
Per-credit charge: $1,118.
Room and board: $9,190.

FINANCIAL AID PICTURE (2008-2009)

Students with need: Out of 461 full-time freshmen who applied for aid, 369 were judged to have need. Of these, 369 received aid, and 128 had their full need met. Average financial aid package met 84% of need; average scholarship/grant was $21,649; average loan was $4,701. Need-based aid available for part-time students.
Students without need: 177 full-time freshmen who did not demonstrate need for aid received scholarships/grants; average award was $9,537. No-need awards available for academics, alumni affiliation, art, leadership, music/drama, religious affiliation.
Scholarships offered: Trustee Scholarships: $12,000 annually; President's Scholarships: $9,000 annually; Dean's Scholarships: $3,000 annually. Incoming students eligible based on admission application, academic performance in high school, and standardized test scores; renewable for 3 additional years.
Cumulative student debt: 64% of graduating class had student loans; average debt was $25,055.
Additional info: Cooperative education allows qualified upperclassmen to alternate semesters of full-time study and full-time work.

FINANCIAL AID PROCEDURES

Forms required: FAFSA. Students applying for Early Decision must complete the CSS PROFILE for notification of need-based financial aid eligibility.
Dates and Deadlines: Priority date 2/1; no closing date. Applicants notified on a rolling basis starting 3/15; must reply by 5/1 or within 2 week(s) of notification.
Transfers: Priority date 3/1; no deadline. Applicants notified on a rolling basis starting 3/15.

CONTACT

Maggie Mittuch, Associate Vice President of Student Financial Services
1500 North Warner Street, Tacoma, WA 98416-1062
(253) 879-3214

University of Washington

Seattle, Washington
www.washington.edu — Federal Code: 003798

4-year public university in very large city.
Enrollment: 27,365 undergrads, 9% part-time. 5,510 full-time freshmen.
Selectivity: Admits 50 to 75% of applicants.

BASIC COSTS (2008-2009)

Tuition and fees: $6,802; out-of-state residents $23,219.
Room and board: $8,640.

FINANCIAL AID PICTURE (2008-2009)

Students with need: Need-based aid available for full-time and part-time students. Work study available nights, weekends, and for part-time students.
Students without need: No-need awards available for academics, alumni affiliation, art, athletics, leadership, music/drama, ROTC.
Additional info: Tuition not due until third week of term.

FINANCIAL AID PROCEDURES

Forms required: FAFSA.
Dates and Deadlines: Priority date 2/28; no closing date. Applicants notified by 3/31; must reply within 3 week(s) of notification.

CONTACT

Kay Lewis, Director of Student Financial Aid
1410 Northeast Campus Parkway, Box 355852, Seattle, WA 98195-5852
(206) 543-6101

Walla Walla Community College

Walla Walla, Washington
www.wwcc.edu — Federal Code: 005006

2-year public community and technical college in large town.
Enrollment: 2,841 undergrads, 35% part-time. 493 full-time freshmen.
Selectivity: Open admission; but selective for some programs.

BASIC COSTS (2008-2009)
Tuition and fees: $2,970; out-of-state residents $4,069.
Per-credit charge: $92; out-of-state residents $105.
Additional info: Tuition/fee waivers available for unemployed or children of unemployed.

FINANCIAL AID PICTURE (2007-2008)
Students with need: 61% of average financial aid package awarded as scholarships/grants, 39% awarded as loans/jobs. Need-based aid available for part-time students. Work study available nights.
Students without need: No-need awards available for academics, athletics, leadership, music/drama.

FINANCIAL AID PROCEDURES
Forms required: FAFSA, institutional form.
Dates and Deadlines: Priority date 3/1; no closing date. Applicants notified on a rolling basis starting 6/1; must reply within 2 week(s) of notification.

CONTACT
Terri Johnson, Director of Financial Aid
500 Tausick Way, Walla Walla, WA 99362-9972
(509) 527-4303

Walla Walla University
College Place, Washington
www.wallawalla.edu Federal Code: 003799

4-year private university and liberal arts college in large town, affiliated with Seventh-day Adventists.
Enrollment: 1,555 undergrads, 6% part-time. 332 full-time freshmen.
Selectivity: Admits over 75% of applicants.

BASIC COSTS (2008-2009)
Tuition and fees: $21,936.
Per-credit charge: $568.
Room and board: $4,320.

FINANCIAL AID PICTURE (2007-2008)
Students with need: Out of 328 full-time freshmen who applied for aid, 239 were judged to have need. Of these, 239 received aid, and 69 had their full need met. Average financial aid package met 90% of need; average scholarship/grant was $6,219; average loan was $5,950. For part-time students, average financial aid package was $19,153.
Students without need: 86 full-time freshmen who did not demonstrate need for aid received scholarships/grants; average award was $5,002. No-need awards available for academics, leadership, music/drama.
Cumulative student debt: 79% of graduating class had student loans; average debt was $28,287.

FINANCIAL AID PROCEDURES
Forms required: FAFSA, institutional form.
Dates and Deadlines: Priority date 4/30; no closing date. Applicants notified on a rolling basis starting 3/15.

CONTACT
Cassie Ragenovich, Director of Student Financial Services
204 South College Avenue, College Place, WA 99324-3000
(509) 527-2815

Washington State University
Pullman, Washington
www.wsu.edu Federal Code: 003800

4-year public university in large town.
Enrollment: 20,690 undergrads, 13% part-time. 3,440 full-time freshmen.
Selectivity: Admits 50 to 75% of applicants.

BASIC COSTS (2008-2009)
Tuition and fees: $7,565; out-of-state residents $18,601.
Room and board: $8,482.

FINANCIAL AID PICTURE (2007-2008)
Students with need: Out of 2,404 full-time freshmen who applied for aid, 1,460 were judged to have need. Of these, 1,455 received aid, and 533 had their full need met. Average financial aid package met 84% of need; average scholarship/grant was $6,334; average loan was $3,528. For part-time students, average financial aid package was $8,049.
Students without need: 651 full-time freshmen who did not demonstrate need for aid received scholarships/grants; average award was $3,763. No-need awards available for academics, alumni affiliation, art, athletics, job skills, leadership, minority status, music/drama, religious affiliation, ROTC, state/district residency.
Scholarships offered: 81 full-time freshmen received athletic scholarships; average amount $16,379.

FINANCIAL AID PROCEDURES
Forms required: FAFSA.
Dates and Deadlines: Priority date 3/1; no closing date. Applicants notified on a rolling basis starting 4/15.
Transfers: Priority date 2/15; no deadline. Applicants notified on a rolling basis starting 3/15. President's Scholarship available for transfer students with minimum 3.9 GPA.

CONTACT
Chio Flores, Director of Student Financial Aid
370 Lighty Student Services Bldg, Pullman, WA 99164-1067
(509) 335-9711

Wenatchee Valley College
Wenatchee, Washington
www.wvc.edu Federal Code: 003801

2-year public community college in small city.
Enrollment: 2,477 undergrads.
Selectivity: Open admission; but selective for some programs.

BASIC COSTS (2008-2009)
Tuition and fees: $2,922; out-of-state residents $3,318.
Per-credit charge: $76; out-of-state residents $89.
Additional info: Tuition/fee waivers available for adults, unemployed or children of unemployed.

FINANCIAL AID PICTURE
Students with need: Need-based aid available for full-time and part-time students.
Students without need: No-need awards available for academics, athletics, leadership.

FINANCIAL AID PROCEDURES
Forms required: FAFSA.
Dates and Deadlines: Closing date 3/1. Applicants notified by 7/2; must reply within 3 week(s) of notification.

CONTACT
Kevin Berg, Financial Aid Director
1300 Fifth Street, Wenatchee, WA 98801-1799
(509) 682-6845

Western Washington University
Bellingham, Washington
www.wwu.edu Federal Code: 003802

4-year public university in small city.
Enrollment: 13,236 undergrads, 8% part-time. 2,667 full-time freshmen.
Selectivity: Admits 50 to 75% of applicants.

BASIC COSTS (2008-2009)
Tuition and fees: $5,535; out-of-state residents $17,166.
Room and board: $7,446.
Additional info: Tuition/fee waivers available for adults, minority students.

FINANCIAL AID PICTURE (2008-2009)
Students with need: Out of 1,908 full-time freshmen who applied for aid, 988 were judged to have need. Of these, 941 received aid, and 349 had their full need met. Average financial aid package met 89% of need; average scholarship/grant was $7,159; average loan was $3,197. For part-time students, average financial aid package was $9,060.
Students without need: 44 full-time freshmen who did not demonstrate need for aid received scholarships/grants; average award was $1,169. No-need awards available for academics, alumni affiliation, art, athletics, job skills, leadership, minority status, music/drama, state/district residency.
Scholarships offered: 18 full-time freshmen received athletic scholarships; average amount $5,068.
Cumulative student debt: 50% of graduating class had student loans; average debt was $15,560.
Additional info: Short-term student loans ranging from $100 to $1,000 available on a quarterly basis.

FINANCIAL AID PROCEDURES
Forms required: FAFSA.
Dates and Deadlines: Priority date 2/15; no closing date. Applicants notified on a rolling basis starting 3/20; must reply within 3 week(s) of notification.
Transfers: No deadline. Applicants notified on a rolling basis starting 3/20; must reply within 3 week(s) of notification. Some state aid not available for out-of-state transfer students.

CONTACT
Clara Capron, Director of Financial Aid
516 High Street, Bellingham, WA 98225-9009
(360) 650-3470

Whatcom Community College
Bellingham, Washington
www.whatcom.ctc.edu Federal Code: 010364

2-year public community college in small city.
Enrollment: 4,367 undergrads.
Selectivity: Open admission.

BASIC COSTS (2008-2009)
Tuition and fees: $2,799; out-of-state residents $8,013.
Per-credit charge: $78; out-of-state residents $250.

FINANCIAL AID PICTURE (2007-2008)
Students with need: 74% of average financial aid package awarded as scholarships/grants, 26% awarded as loans/jobs. Need-based aid available for part-time students. Work study available nights.
Students without need: No-need awards available for academics, athletics, state/district residency.

FINANCIAL AID PROCEDURES
Forms required: FAFSA, institutional form.
Dates and Deadlines: No deadline. Applicants notified on a rolling basis starting 7/1; must reply within 3 week(s) of notification.

CONTACT
Laura Pendleton, Director of Financial Aid
237 West Kellogg Road, Bellingham, WA 98226
(360) 383-3010

Whitman College
Walla Walla, Washington
www.whitman.edu Federal Code: 003803
CSS Code: 4951

4-year private liberal arts college in large town.
Enrollment: 1,430 undergrads, 1% part-time. 401 full-time freshmen.
Selectivity: Admits less than 50% of applicants.

BASIC COSTS (2009-2010)
Tuition and fees: $36,940.
Per-credit charge: $1,526.
Room and board: $9,260.

FINANCIAL AID PICTURE (2008-2009)
Students with need: Out of 267 full-time freshmen who applied for aid, 192 were judged to have need. Of these, 192 received aid, and 177 had their full need met. Average financial aid package met 96% of need; average scholarship/grant was $23,309; average loan was $4,088. For part-time students, average financial aid package was $34,737.
Students without need: 112 full-time freshmen who did not demonstrate need for aid received scholarships/grants; average award was $9,479. No-need awards available for academics, art, leadership, minority status, music/drama, religious affiliation, state/district residency.
Cumulative student debt: 49% of graduating class had student loans; average debt was $16,684.

FINANCIAL AID PROCEDURES
Forms required: FAFSA, CSS PROFILE.
Dates and Deadlines: Priority date 11/15; closing date 2/1. Applicants notified on a rolling basis starting 12/22; must reply within 2 week(s) of notification.

CONTACT
Tony Cabasco, Dean of Admission and Financial Aid
345 Boyer Avenue, Walla Walla, WA 99362-2046
(509) 527-5178

Whitworth University
Spokane, Washington
www.whitworth.edu Federal Code: 003804

4-year private liberal arts college in large city, affiliated with Presbyterian Church (USA).
Enrollment: 2,365 undergrads, 12% part-time. 546 full-time freshmen.
Selectivity: Admits 50 to 75% of applicants.

BASIC COSTS (2009-2010)
Tuition and fees: $28,650.
Per-credit charge: $1,180.
Room and board: $8,120.
Additional info: Tuition/fee waivers available for minority students.

FINANCIAL AID PICTURE (2008-2009)
Students with need: Out of 442 full-time freshmen who applied for aid, 353 were judged to have need. Of these, 353 received aid, and 76 had their full need met. Average financial aid package met 86% of need; average scholarship/grant was $17,899; average loan was $4,173. For part-time students, average financial aid package was $10,163.
Students without need: 175 full-time freshmen who did not demonstrate need for aid received scholarships/grants; average award was $9,880. No-need awards available for academics, art, music/drama, ROTC.

Scholarships offered: Available; $4,000 to $8,500; based on GPA, SAT/ACT scores, class rank.
Cumulative student debt: 68% of graduating class had student loans; average debt was $19,305.

FINANCIAL AID PROCEDURES
Forms required: FAFSA.
Dates and Deadlines: Priority date 3/1; no closing date. Applicants notified on a rolling basis starting 3/1; must reply by 5/1 or within 4 week(s) of notification.
Transfers: Priority date 4/1; no deadline. Applicants notified on a rolling basis starting 3/1; must reply by 5/1.

CONTACT
Wendy Olson, Director of Financial Aid
300 West Hawthorne Road, Spokane, WA 99251-0002
(509) 777-3215

Yakima Valley Community College
Yakima, Washington
www.yvcc.edu Federal Code: 003805

2-year public community college in small city.
Enrollment: 2,807 undergrads.
Selectivity: Open admission; but selective for some programs.

BASIC COSTS (2008-2009)
Tuition and fees: $2,963; out-of-state residents $3,359.
Per-credit charge: $76; out-of-state residents $89.
Additional info: Tuition/fee waivers available for unemployed or children of unemployed.

FINANCIAL AID PICTURE (2007-2008)
Students with need: Need-based aid available for full-time and part-time students. Work study available nights, weekends, and for part-time students.
Students without need: No-need awards available for academics, athletics.

FINANCIAL AID PROCEDURES
Forms required: FAFSA.
Dates and Deadlines: Priority date 5/1; no closing date. Applicants notified on a rolling basis starting 8/1; must reply within 2 week(s) of notification.
Transfers: No deadline. Applicants notified on a rolling basis starting 8/1; must reply within 2 week(s) of notification.

CONTACT
Jacinto Rodriguez, Director of Financial Aid
PO Box 22520, Yakima, WA 98907-2520
(509) 574-6855

West Virginia

Alderson-Broaddus College
Philippi, West Virginia
www.ab.edu Federal Code: 003806

4-year private liberal arts college in small town, affiliated with American Baptist Churches in the USA.
Enrollment: 591 undergrads, 5% part-time. 153 full-time freshmen.
Selectivity: Admits 50 to 75% of applicants.

BASIC COSTS (2009-2010)
Tuition and fees: $21,654.
Per-credit charge: $715.
Room and board: $7,002.

FINANCIAL AID PICTURE (2007-2008)
Students with need: Out of 151 full-time freshmen who applied for aid, 143 were judged to have need. Of these, 143 received aid, and 41 had their full need met. Average financial aid package met 82% of need; average scholarship/grant was $14,743; average loan was $4,272. For part-time students, average financial aid package was $7,781.
Students without need: 7 full-time freshmen who did not demonstrate need for aid received scholarships/grants; average award was $5,857. No-need awards available for academics, athletics, music/drama.
Scholarships offered: 4 full-time freshmen received athletic scholarships; average amount $5,375.
Cumulative student debt: 91% of graduating class had student loans; average debt was $22,002.

FINANCIAL AID PROCEDURES
Forms required: FAFSA, state aid form.
Dates and Deadlines: Priority date 3/1; no closing date. Applicants notified on a rolling basis starting 2/15; must reply within 2 week(s) of notification.

CONTACT
Brian Weingart, Director of Financial Aid
101 College Hill Drive, Philippi, WV 26416
(304) 457-6354

American Public University System
Charles Town, West Virginia
www.apus.edu Federal Code: 038193

4-year for-profit virtual university in small town.
Enrollment: 29,008 undergrads.
Selectivity: Open admission.

BASIC COSTS (2008-2009)
Tuition and fees: $7,500.
Per-credit charge: $250.
Additional info: Distance learning only.

FINANCIAL AID PICTURE
Students with need: Need-based aid available for full-time and part-time students.
Additional info: Students should complete a Federal Student Aid Intent Form and register for classes at least 37 days prior to start to allow sufficient time for financial aid process.

FINANCIAL AID PROCEDURES
Forms required: FAFSA, institutional form.
Dates and Deadlines: No deadline. Applicants notified on a rolling basis; must reply within 14 week(s) of notification.
Transfers: Must reply within 14 week(s) of notification. Students should ensure that financial aid is processed and confirmed at least 10-14 days prior to beginning a semester.

CONTACT
Missy Burke, Director of Financial Services
111 West Congress Street, Charles Town, WV 25414
(877) 468-6268

Appalachian Bible College
Bradley, West Virginia
www.abc.edu Federal Code: 007544

4-year private Bible college in rural community, affiliated with nondenominational tradition.
Enrollment: 217 undergrads.
Selectivity: Admits 50 to 75% of applicants.

BASIC COSTS (2009-2010)
Tuition and fees: $10,390.
Per-credit charge: $365.
Room and board: $5,400.

FINANCIAL AID PICTURE (2007-2008)
Students with need: 74% of average financial aid package awarded as scholarships/grants, 26% awarded as loans/jobs. Need-based aid available for part-time students.
Students without need: This college awards aid only to students with need.
Scholarships offered: Scholastic Achievement Scholarship; $1,500 per year; based on 26 ACT or 1180 SAT (exclusive of Writing).

FINANCIAL AID PROCEDURES
Forms required: FAFSA, state aid form, institutional form.
Dates and Deadlines: Closing date 6/15. Applicants notified on a rolling basis starting 6/15; must reply by 8/1 or within 4 week(s) of notification.

CONTACT
Cindi Turner, Director of Financial Aid
PO Box ABC, Bradley, WV 25818-1353
(304) 877-6428 ext. 3247

Bluefield State College
Bluefield, West Virginia
www.bluefieldstate.edu Federal Code: 003809

4-year public liberal arts and technical college in large town.
Enrollment: 1,790 undergrads, 16% part-time. 200 full-time freshmen.
Selectivity: Admits over 75% of applicants.

BASIC COSTS (2008-2009)
Tuition and fees: $4,272; out-of-state residents $8,568.
Per-credit charge: $178; out-of-state residents $357.
Additional info: Tuition for students residing in border counties is $6,288.

FINANCIAL AID PICTURE (2008-2009)
Students with need: Average financial aid package met 70% of need; average scholarship/grant was $3,400; average loan was $3,500. For part-time students, average financial aid package was $2,900.
Students without need: No-need awards available for academics, alumni affiliation, art, athletics, job skills, leadership, minority status, music/drama, state/district residency.
Cumulative student debt: 48% of graduating class had student loans; average debt was $17,600.

FINANCIAL AID PROCEDURES
Forms required: FAFSA, state aid form, institutional form.
Dates and Deadlines: Closing date 3/1. Applicants notified by 5/1.
Transfers: No deadline.

CONTACT
Tom Ilse, Director of Financial Aid
219 Rock Street, Bluefield, WV 24701
(304) 327-4020

Concord University
Athens, West Virginia
www.concord.edu Federal Code: 003810

4-year public university and liberal arts college in small town.
Enrollment: 2,384 full-time undergrads.
Selectivity: Admits over 75% of applicants.

BASIC COSTS (2008-2009)
Tuition and fees: $4,578; out-of-state residents $10,170.
Per-credit charge: $191; out-of-state residents $424.
Room and board: $6,530.
Additional info: Room and board may be paid in 2 installments each semester: 60% at registration, 40% six weeks later.

FINANCIAL AID PICTURE (2007-2008)
Students with need: Need-based aid available for full-time and part-time students.
Students without need: No-need awards available for academics, alumni affiliation, art, athletics, job skills, leadership, minority status, music/drama, state/district residency.
Additional info: March 1 priority deadline for state forms. April 15 priority deadline for FAFSA.

FINANCIAL AID PROCEDURES
Forms required: FAFSA, state aid form, institutional form.
Dates and Deadlines: Applicants notified on a rolling basis starting 3/1; must reply within 2 week(s) of notification.

CONTACT
Patricia Harmon, Director of Financial Aid
PO Box 1000, Athens, WV 24712-1000
(304) 384-6069

Davis and Elkins College
Elkins, West Virginia
www.davisandelkins.edu Federal Code: 003811

4-year private liberal arts college in small town, affiliated with Presbyterian Church (USA).
Enrollment: 531 undergrads, 4% part-time. 125 full-time freshmen.
Selectivity: Admits over 75% of applicants.

BASIC COSTS (2009-2010)
Tuition and fees: $19,800.
Room and board: $7,450.

FINANCIAL AID PICTURE (2008-2009)
Students with need: Out of 107 full-time freshmen who applied for aid, 95 were judged to have need. Of these, 95 received aid, and 46 had their full need met. Average financial aid package met 79% of need; average scholarship/grant was $4,563; average loan was $4,538. For part-time students, average financial aid package was $4,377.
Students without need: 30 full-time freshmen who did not demonstrate need for aid received scholarships/grants; average award was $4,187. No-need awards available for academics, alumni affiliation, art, athletics, leadership, minority status, music/drama, religious affiliation.
Scholarships offered: 39 full-time freshmen received athletic scholarships; average amount $5,124.
Cumulative student debt: 81% of graduating class had student loans; average debt was $25,446.

FINANCIAL AID PROCEDURES
Forms required: FAFSA.
Dates and Deadlines: Priority date 3/1; no closing date. Applicants notified on a rolling basis starting 5/1; must reply within 2 week(s) of notification.
Transfers: No deadline. Applicants notified on a rolling basis starting 5/1; must reply within 2 week(s) of notification.

CONTACT
Matthew Summers, summers@davisandelkins.edu
100 Campus Drive, Elkins, WV 26241-3996
(304) 637-1373

Eastern West Virginia Community and Technical College

Moorefield, West Virginia
www.eastern.wvnet.edu

2-year public community and technical college in rural community.
Enrollment: 420 undergrads, 76% part-time. 47 full-time freshmen.
Selectivity: Open admission.

BASIC COSTS (2008-2009)

Tuition and fees: $1,920; out-of-state residents $6,822.

FINANCIAL AID PICTURE

Students with need: Need-based aid available for full-time and part-time students.

FINANCIAL AID PROCEDURES

Forms required: FAFSA, institutional form.
Dates and Deadlines: Priority date 6/1; no closing date. Applicants notified on a rolling basis; must reply within 2 week(s) of notification.

CONTACT

Amanda Sites, Director of Financial Aid
1929 State Road 55, Moorefield, WV 26836
(304) 434-8000

Fairmont State University

Fairmont, West Virginia
www.fairmontstate.edu Federal Code: 003812

4-year public university and technical college in large town.
Enrollment: 4,046 undergrads, 13% part-time. 756 full-time freshmen.
Selectivity: Admits over 75% of applicants.

BASIC COSTS (2008-2009)

Tuition and fees: $4,804; out-of-state residents $10,370.
Per-credit charge: $200; out-of-state residents $432.
Room and board: $7,020.
Additional info: Tuition/fee waivers available for adults, minority students.

FINANCIAL AID PICTURE (2007-2008)

Students with need: Out of 579 full-time freshmen who applied for aid, 417 were judged to have need. Of these, 405 received aid, and 56 had their full need met. For part-time students, average financial aid package was $4,734.
Students without need: This college awards aid only to students with need.

FINANCIAL AID PROCEDURES

Forms required: FAFSA.
Dates and Deadlines: Closing date 3/1. Applicants notified on a rolling basis starting 4/1; must reply within 2 week(s) of notification.
Transfers: Academic transcripts required.

CONTACT

George Yanchak, Director of Financial Aid and Scholarships
1201 Locust Avenue, Fairmont, WV 26554-2470
(304) 367-4213

Glenville State College

Glenville, West Virginia
www.glenville.edu Federal Code: 003813

4-year public liberal arts and teachers college in rural community.
Enrollment: 1,180 undergrads, 5% part-time. 282 full-time freshmen.
Selectivity: Admits 50 to 75% of applicants.

BASIC COSTS (2008-2009)

Tuition and fees: $4,486; out-of-state residents $10,738.
Per-credit charge: $187; out-of-state residents $447.
Room and board: $6,250.

FINANCIAL AID PICTURE (2007-2008)

Students with need: Out of 270 full-time freshmen who applied for aid, 239 were judged to have need. Of these, 235 received aid, and 57 had their full need met. Average financial aid package met 72% of need; average scholarship/grant was $5,027; average loan was $2,983. Need-based aid available for part-time students.
Students without need: 15 full-time freshmen who did not demonstrate need for aid received scholarships/grants; average award was $1,603. No-need awards available for academics, athletics, music/drama, state/district residency.
Scholarships offered: 7 full-time freshmen received athletic scholarships; average amount $2,050.
Cumulative student debt: 69% of graduating class had student loans; average debt was $15,931.

FINANCIAL AID PROCEDURES

Forms required: FAFSA, state aid form.
Dates and Deadlines: Priority date 2/1; no closing date. Applicants notified on a rolling basis starting 4/1; must reply within 2 week(s) of notification.

CONTACT

Karen Lay, Director of Financial Aid
Office of Enrollment Services, Glenville, WV 26351-1292
(304) 462-4103

Marshall University

Huntington, West Virginia
www.marshall.edu Federal Code: 003815

4-year public university in small city.
Enrollment: 8,758 undergrads, 12% part-time. 1,661 full-time freshmen.
Selectivity: Admits over 75% of applicants.

BASIC COSTS (2008-2009)

Tuition and fees: $4,598; out-of-state residents $11,702.
Per-credit charge: $180; out-of-state residents $476.
Room and board: $7,210.

FINANCIAL AID PICTURE (2008-2009)

Students with need: Out of 1,061 full-time freshmen who applied for aid, 756 were judged to have need. Of these, 750 received aid, and 298 had their full need met. Average financial aid package met 58% of need; average scholarship/grant was $5,243; average loan was $5,635. For part-time students, average financial aid package was $5,933.
Students without need: 295 full-time freshmen who did not demonstrate need for aid received scholarships/grants; average award was $6,035. No need awards available for academics, art, athletics, minority status, music/drama, ROTC, state/district residency.
Scholarships offered: ***Merit:*** Michael Perry Scholarship; $500 based on 3.2 GPA and 20 ACT score; $750 based on 3.5 GPA and 23 ACT, or 3.2 GPA and 25 ACT; one-year only. Presidential Scholarship; $1,250; 3.5 GPA and 25 ACT; renewable with 3.5 GPA. John Marshall Scholarship; tuition waiver plus $1,250 stipend; 3.5 GPA and 30 ACT; renewable yearly with 3.5 GPA. Yeager scholarship; full tuition and fees, full room and board, book allowance, stipend, personal computer for use during program, and $4,000 toward study abroad; 28 ACT/1260 SAT (exclusive of Writing). ***Athletic:*** 56 full-time freshmen received athletic scholarships; average amount $6,918.
Cumulative student debt: 62% of graduating class had student loans; average debt was $18,718.

FINANCIAL AID PROCEDURES

Forms required: FAFSA, state aid form.

Dates and Deadlines: Priority date 3/1; no closing date. Applicants notified on a rolling basis starting 5/1; must reply within 2 week(s) of notification.
Transfers: Priority date 1/1.

CONTACT

Kathy Bialk, Director of Financial Aid
One John Marshall Drive, Huntington, WV 25755
(304) 696-3162

Mountain State University

Beckley, West Virginia
www.mountainstate.edu Federal Code: 003807

4-year private university and health science college in large town.
Enrollment: 4,266 undergrads, 25% part-time. 329 full-time freshmen.
Selectivity: Open admission; but selective for some programs.

BASIC COSTS (2009-2010)

Tuition and fees: $8,700.
Per-credit charge: $215.
Room and board: $6,116.
Additional info: Certain programs require additional costs: health science and culinary/hospitality are $320 per credit hour.

FINANCIAL AID PICTURE (2007-2008)

Students with need: Out of 258 full-time freshmen who applied for aid, 222 were judged to have need. Of these, 222 received aid. Average financial aid package met 39% of need; average scholarship/grant was $3,336; average loan was $3,378. For part-time students, average financial aid package was $5,122.
Students without need: 1 full-time freshmen who did not demonstrate need for aid received scholarships/grants; average award was $3,272. No-need awards available for academics, alumni affiliation, athletics, leadership, minority status.
Scholarships offered: 18 full-time freshmen received athletic scholarships; average amount $5,608.
Cumulative student debt: 84% of graduating class had student loans; average debt was $31,221.

FINANCIAL AID PROCEDURES

Forms required: FAFSA.
Dates and Deadlines: No deadline. Applicants notified on a rolling basis starting 4/1.

CONTACT

Michelle Sarrett, Vice President of Finance
609 South Kanawha Street, Beckley, WV 25802-9003
(304) 929-1517

Ohio Valley University

Vienna, West Virginia
www.ovu.edu Federal Code: 003819

4-year private university and liberal arts college in small city, affiliated with Church of Christ.
Enrollment: 491 undergrads, 9% part-time. 100 full-time freshmen.
Selectivity: Admits 50 to 75% of applicants.

BASIC COSTS (2009-2010)

Tuition and fees: $17,200.
Per-credit charge: $525.
Room and board: $6,676.

FINANCIAL AID PICTURE (2008-2009)

Students with need: Average financial aid package met 67% of need; average scholarship/grant was $7,972; average loan was $3,044. For part-time students, average financial aid package was $12,558.
Students without need: No-need awards available for academics, alumni affiliation, athletics, job skills, leadership, music/drama.
Cumulative student debt: 81% of graduating class had student loans; average debt was $13,480.

FINANCIAL AID PROCEDURES

Forms required: FAFSA.
Dates and Deadlines: Priority date 2/15; no closing date. Applicants notified on a rolling basis starting 3/15; must reply within 4 week(s) of notification.
Transfers: No deadline. Applicants notified on a rolling basis starting 3/15; must reply within 4 week(s) of notification.

CONTACT

Dennis Cox, Director of Student Financial Services
One Campus View Drive, Vienna, WV 26105
(304) 865-6081

Potomac State College of West Virginia University

Keyser, West Virginia
www.potomacstatecollege.edu Federal Code: 003829

2-year public branch campus and junior college in small town.
Enrollment: 1,263 undergrads.
Selectivity: Open admission.

BASIC COSTS (2008-2009)

Tuition and fees: $2,726; out-of-state residents $8,674.
Per-credit charge: $114; out-of-state residents $361.
Room and board: $6,814.
Additional info: Students residing in selected counties in bordering states receive reduced out-of-state tuition rates. Tuition/fee waivers available for adults.

FINANCIAL AID PICTURE (2007-2008)

Students with need: Need-based aid available for full-time and part-time students. Work study available nights, weekends, and for part-time students.
Students without need: No-need awards available for academics, athletics, leadership.

FINANCIAL AID PROCEDURES

Forms required: FAFSA.
Dates and Deadlines: Priority date 3/1; no closing date. Applicants notified on a rolling basis starting 4/1; must reply within 2 week(s) of notification.

CONTACT

Beth Little, Director of Enrollment Services
One Grand Central Park, Suite 2090, Keyser, WV 26726
(304) 788-6820

Salem International University

Salem, West Virginia
www.salemu.edu Federal Code: 003820

4-year for-profit university and liberal arts college in rural community.
Enrollment: 442 undergrads. 185 full-time freshmen.

BASIC COSTS (2008-2009)

Tuition and fees: $14,100.
Per-credit charge: $450.
Room and board: $6,600.

FINANCIAL AID PICTURE (2007-2008)
Students with need: Need-based aid available for full-time and part-time students. Work study available nights, weekends, and for part-time students.
Students without need: No-need awards available for academics.
Scholarships offered: Scholarships; extensive amount awarded; based on high school GPA, standardized test scores. Breed-related awards; for students in equine career and industry management program. Awards for GED diploma recipients; based on academic excellence.

FINANCIAL AID PROCEDURES
Forms required: FAFSA.
Dates and Deadlines: Priority date 4/15; no closing date. Applicants notified on a rolling basis starting 2/15; must reply within 4 week(s) of notification.
Transfers: Priority date 3/1; closing date 4/15. Applicants notified on a rolling basis starting 3/1.

CONTACT
Patricia Zinsmeister, Vice President for Financial Aid and Compliance
223 West Main Street, Salem, WV 26426
(304) 326-1303

Shepherd University
Shepherdstown, West Virginia
www.shepherd.edu Federal Code: 003822

4-year public university in small town.
Enrollment: 3,554 undergrads, 11% part-time. 699 full-time freshmen.
Selectivity: Admits 50 to 75% of applicants.

BASIC COSTS (2008-2009)
Tuition and fees: $4,898; out-of-state residents $12,812.
Per-credit charge: $200; out-of-state residents $530.
Room and board: $6,938.
Additional info: Tuition/fee waivers available for minority students.

FINANCIAL AID PICTURE (2008-2009)
Students with need: Out of 621 full-time freshmen who applied for aid, 364 were judged to have need. Of these, 352 received aid, and 98 had their full need met. Average financial aid package met 91% of need; average scholarship/grant was $4,306; average loan was $3,383. For part-time students, average financial aid package was $8,680.
Students without need: 177 full-time freshmen who did not demonstrate need for aid received scholarships/grants; average award was $8,197. No-need awards available for academics, art, athletics, job skills, leadership, minority status, music/drama, state/district residency.
Scholarships offered: ***Merit:*** Presidential scholarship; up to $5,000; requires 3.5 GPA, 26 ACT or 1200 SAT; renewable with 3.5 GPA. Academic scholarship; up to $1,500; requires 3.2 GPA, 21 ACT or 1000 SAT; renewable with 3.0 GPA. Leadership scholarship; up to $3,000; requires 3.0 GPA, 21 ACT, or 1000 SAT; nonrenewable. ***Athletic:*** 39 full-time freshmen received athletic scholarships; average amount $6,036.
Cumulative student debt: 65% of graduating class had student loans; average debt was $18,271.

FINANCIAL AID PROCEDURES
Forms required: FAFSA, state aid form.
Dates and Deadlines: Priority date 3/1; no closing date. Applicants notified on a rolling basis starting 3/15; must reply within 3 week(s) of notification.
Transfers: No deadline. Applicants notified on a rolling basis starting 11/1; must reply within 3 week(s) of notification.

CONTACT
Sandra Oerly-Bennett, Director of Financial Aid
PO Box 5000, Shepherdstown, WV 25443-5000
(304) 876-5470

Southern West Virginia Community and Technical College
Mount Gay, West Virginia
www.southernwv.edu Federal Code: 003816

2-year public community college in small town.
Enrollment: 2,264 undergrads.
Selectivity: Open admission; but selective for some programs.

BASIC COSTS (2008-2009)
Tuition and fees: $1,920; out-of-state residents $6,816.
Per-credit charge: $80; out-of-state residents $284.

FINANCIAL AID PICTURE (2007-2008)
Students with need: Need-based aid available for full-time and part-time students.

FINANCIAL AID PROCEDURES
Forms required: FAFSA.
Dates and Deadlines: No deadline. Applicants notified on a rolling basis.

CONTACT
Cindy Whitlock, Financial Aid Director
PO Box 2900, Mount Gay, WV 25637
(304) 896-7382

University of Charleston
Charleston, West Virginia
www.ucwv.edu Federal Code: 003818

4-year private university and liberal arts college in small city.
Enrollment: 1,102 undergrads, 2% part-time. 232 full-time freshmen.
Selectivity: Admits 50 to 75% of applicants.

BASIC COSTS (2008-2009)
Tuition and fees: $23,150.
Per-credit charge: $400.
Room and board: $8,325.
Additional info: Tuition for pharmacy students: $25,224.

FINANCIAL AID PICTURE (2007-2008)
Students with need: Out of 199 full-time freshmen who applied for aid, 178 were judged to have need. Of these, 178 received aid, and 75 had their full need met. Average financial aid package met 80% of need; average scholarship/grant was $4,500; average loan was $6,900. For part-time students, average financial aid package was $4,150.
Students without need: 21 full-time freshmen who did not demonstrate need for aid received scholarships/grants; average award was $19,860. No-need awards available for academics, alumni affiliation, art, athletics, leadership, music/drama, ROTC.
Scholarships offered: 8 full-time freshmen received athletic scholarships; average amount $24,250.
Cumulative student debt: 89% of graduating class had student loans; average debt was $21,530.

FINANCIAL AID PROCEDURES
Forms required: FAFSA, state aid form.
Dates and Deadlines: Priority date 3/1; no closing date. Applicants notified on a rolling basis starting 3/1; must reply by 5/1 or within 4 week(s) of notification.
Transfers: Applicants notified on a rolling basis starting 4/1; must reply by 5/1 or within 4 week(s) of notification.

CONTACT
Janet Ruge, Director of Financial Aid
2300 MacCorkle Avenue, SE, Charleston, WV 25304
(304) 357-4759

Valley College

Martinsburg, West Virginia
www.vct.edu Federal Code: G26094

2-year for-profit business and career college in small city.
Enrollment: 90 undergrads.

BASIC COSTS (2008-2009)

Tuition and fees: $7,300.
Per-credit charge: $225.
Additional info: Tuition varies according to program.

FINANCIAL AID PICTURE (2007-2008)

Students with need: Need-based aid available for full-time and part-time students.

FINANCIAL AID PROCEDURES

Forms required: FAFSA, institutional form.
Dates and Deadlines: No deadline. Applicants notified on a rolling basis.
Transfers: No deadline. Applicants notified on a rolling basis.

CONTACT

Jessica Colon, Financial Aid Administrator
287 Aikens Center, Martinsburg, WV 25404
(304) 263-0979

West Liberty State College

West Liberty, West Virginia
www.westliberty.edu Federal Code: 003823

4-year public liberal arts college in rural community.
Enrollment: 2,307 undergrads, 6% part-time. 545 full-time freshmen.
Selectivity: Admits over 75% of applicants.

BASIC COSTS (2008-2009)

Tuition and fees: $4,464; out-of-state residents $10,896.
Per-credit charge: $186; out-of-state residents $454.
Room and board: $6,282.
Additional info: Tuition for students residing in border counties is $8,896.

FINANCIAL AID PICTURE (2008-2009)

Students with need: For part-time students, average financial aid package was $6,467.
Students without need: No-need awards available for academics, alumni affiliation, art, athletics, leadership, music/drama.
Cumulative student debt: 81% of graduating class had student loans; average debt was $21,097.
Additional info: Non-need based student employment available at food service, college union, bookstore, and tutoring office. Resident assistant and campus security jobs also available.

FINANCIAL AID PROCEDURES

Forms required: FAFSA.
Dates and Deadlines: Priority date 3/1; no closing date. Applicants notified on a rolling basis starting 2/15; must reply within 2 week(s) of notification.
Transfers: Financial aid transcript required from all previous colleges attended regardless of whether aid was received.

CONTACT

Scott Cook, Financial Aid Director
Box 295, West Liberty, WV 26074-0295
(304) 336-8016

West Virginia Junior College

Morgantown, West Virginia
www.wvjc.edu Federal Code: 005007

2-year for-profit junior college in large town.
Enrollment: 157 undergrads.
Selectivity: Open admission.

FINANCIAL AID PICTURE

Students with need: Need-based aid available for full-time and part-time students.

FINANCIAL AID PROCEDURES

Forms required: FAFSA.
Dates and Deadlines: No deadline. Applicants notified on a rolling basis.

CONTACT

Patricia Callen, Executive Director
148 Willey Street, Morgantown, WV 26505

West Virginia Junior College: Charleston

Charleston, West Virginia
www.wvjc.com Federal Code: 010573

2-year for-profit junior and technical college in small city.
Enrollment: 150 full-time undergrads.
Selectivity: Open admission.

FINANCIAL AID PICTURE

Students with need: Need-based aid available for full-time and part-time students.

FINANCIAL AID PROCEDURES

Dates and Deadlines: Applicants notified on a rolling basis.

CONTACT

Bonnie Landon, Executive Director
1000 Virginia Street East, Charleston, WV 25301

West Virginia Northern Community College

Wheeling, West Virginia
www.wvncc.edu Federal Code: 010920

2-year public community and technical college in large town.
Enrollment: 2,165 undergrads, 38% part-time. 325 full-time freshmen.
Selectivity: Open admission; but selective for some programs.

BASIC COSTS (2008-2009)

Tuition and fees: $1,998; out-of-state residents $6,510.
Additional info: Tuition for students residing in border counties is $4,590. Tuition/fee waivers available for adults.

FINANCIAL AID PICTURE

Students with need: Need-based aid available for full-time and part-time students.

FINANCIAL AID PROCEDURES

Forms required: FAFSA, institutional form.
Dates and Deadlines: Priority date 3/15; no closing date. Applicants notified on a rolling basis starting 3/10.

CONTACT

Janet Fike, Director, Financial Aid
1704 Market Street, Wheeling, WV 26003
(304) 233-5900 ext. 4363

West Virginia State Community and Technical College

Institute, West Virginia
www.wvsctc.edu Federal Code: 040386

2-year public community and technical college in small town.
Enrollment: 1,737 undergrads.
Selectivity: Open admission; but selective for some programs.

BASIC COSTS (2008-2009)
Tuition and fees: $2,898; out-of-state residents $8,468.
Per-credit charge: $121; out-of-state residents $353.

FINANCIAL AID PICTURE (2007-2008)
Students with need: Work study available nights, weekends, and for part-time students.
Students without need: No-need awards available for academics, state/district residency.
Additional info: All students may apply for tuition waivers. Financial aid deadline enforced only if Federal financial aid is the only source of payment.

FINANCIAL AID PROCEDURES
Dates and Deadlines: Closing date 6/30.

CONTACT
Mary Blizzard, Director, Office of Student Financial Assistance
PO Box 1000, Institute, WV 25112-1000
(304) 766-3131

West Virginia State University

Institute, West Virginia
www.wvstateu.edu Federal Code: 003826

4-year public liberal arts and teachers college in small town.
Enrollment: 2,961 undergrads.
Selectivity: Admits 50 to 75% of applicants.

BASIC COSTS (2008-2009)
Tuition and fees: $4,466; out-of-state residents $10,466.
Per-credit charge: $186; out-of-state residents $436.
Room and board: $6,020.

FINANCIAL AID PICTURE
Students with need: Need-based aid available for full-time and part-time students. Work study available nights, weekends, and for part-time students.
Students without need: No-need awards available for academics, athletics, ROTC, state/district residency.

FINANCIAL AID PROCEDURES
Forms required: FAFSA.
Dates and Deadlines: Priority date 3/1; closing date 6/15. Applicants notified on a rolling basis starting 2/15; must reply within 2 week(s) of notification.

CONTACT
Mary Blizzard, Director of Financial Aid
Campus Box 197, Institute, WV 25112-1000
(304) 766-3131

West Virginia University

Morgantown, West Virginia
www.wvu.edu Federal Code: 003827

4-year public university in small city.
Enrollment: 21,930 undergrads, 6% part-time. 5,099 full-time freshmen.
Selectivity: Admits over 75% of applicants.

BASIC COSTS (2008-2009)
Tuition and fees: $5,100; out-of-state residents $15,770.
Per-credit charge: $213; out-of-state residents $657.
Room and board: $7,434.
Additional info: Tuition/fee waivers available for minority students.

FINANCIAL AID PICTURE (2008-2009)
Students with need: Out of 4,033 full-time freshmen who applied for aid, 3,186 were judged to have need. Of these, 2,107 received aid, and 948 had their full need met. Average financial aid package met 72% of need; average scholarship/grant was $4,082; average loan was $3,738. For part-time students, average financial aid package was $5,273.
Students without need: 1,249 full-time freshmen who did not demonstrate need for aid received scholarships/grants; average award was $1,676. No-need awards available for academics, alumni affiliation, art, athletics, job skills, leadership, minority status, music/drama, state/district residency.
Scholarships offered: 64 full-time freshmen received athletic scholarships; average amount $17,223.
Additional info: February 1 closing date for freshman scholarships.

FINANCIAL AID PROCEDURES
Forms required: FAFSA, state aid form.
Dates and Deadlines: Closing date 3/1. Applicants notified on a rolling basis starting 3/15; must reply within 4 week(s) of notification.

CONTACT
Kaye Widney, Director of Financial Aid
Admissions and Records Office, Morgantown, WV 26506-6009
(800) 344-9881

West Virginia University at Parkersburg

Parkersburg, West Virginia
www.wvup.edu Federal Code: 003828

4-year public community college in large town.
Enrollment: 3,174 undergrads, 30% part-time. 545 full-time freshmen.
Selectivity: Open admission; but selective for some programs.

BASIC COSTS (2008-2009)
Tuition and fees: $1,912; out-of-state residents $6,766.
Per-credit charge: $80; out-of-state residents $282.

FINANCIAL AID PICTURE (2008-2009)
Students with need: Out of 470 full-time freshmen who applied for aid, 440 were judged to have need. Of these, 440 received aid, and 140 had their full need met. Average financial aid package met 80% of need; average scholarship/grant was $5,450; average loan was $3,050. For part-time students, average financial aid package was $3,950.
Students without need: 68 full-time freshmen who did not demonstrate need for aid received scholarships/grants; average award was $960. No-need awards available for academics, state/district residency.

FINANCIAL AID PROCEDURES
Forms required: FAFSA.
Dates and Deadlines: Priority date 3/1; no closing date. Applicants notified on a rolling basis; must reply within 2 week(s) of notification.

CONTACT
August Kafer, Director of Financial Aid
300 Campus Drive, Parkersburg, WV 26104-8647
(304) 424-8210

West Virginia University Institute of Technology

Montgomery, West Virginia
www.wvutech.edu Federal Code: 003825

4-year public engineering and technical college in small town.
Enrollment: 1,040 full-time undergrads.
Selectivity: Admits less than 50% of applicants.

BASIC COSTS (2008-2009)

Tuition and fees: $4,964; out-of-state residents $12,748.
Per-credit charge: $207; out-of-state residents $531.
Room and board: $6,544.

FINANCIAL AID PICTURE

Students with need: Need-based aid available for full-time students. Work study available nights, weekends, and for part-time students.
Additional info: Room and board may be deferred for up to 60 days. First 50% due in 30 days.

FINANCIAL AID PROCEDURES

Forms required: FAFSA, institutional form.
Dates and Deadlines: Priority date 2/1; closing date 4/1. Applicants notified on a rolling basis; must reply within 3 week(s) of notification.

CONTACT

Sue Beaver, Director of Financial Aid
405 Fayette Pike, Montgomery, WV 25136-2436
(304) 442-3228

West Virginia Wesleyan College

Buckhannon, West Virginia
www.wvwc.edu Federal Code: 003830

4-year private liberal arts college in small town, affiliated with United Methodist Church.
Enrollment: 1,226 full-time undergrads. 382 full-time freshmen.
Selectivity: Admits 50 to 75% of applicants.

BASIC COSTS (2008-2009)

Tuition and fees: $22,880.
Room and board: $6,470.

FINANCIAL AID PICTURE (2008-2009)

Students with need: Out of 353 full-time freshmen who applied for aid, 310 were judged to have need. Of these, 310 received aid, and 82 had their full need met. Average financial aid package met 85% of need; average scholarship/grant was $18,351; average loan was $3,791. Need-based aid available for part-time students.
Students without need: 72 full-time freshmen who did not demonstrate need for aid received scholarships/grants; average award was $12,861. No-need awards available for academics, alumni affiliation, art, athletics, leadership, music/drama, religious affiliation, state/district residency.
Scholarships offered: 88 full-time freshmen received athletic scholarships; average amount $11,707.
Cumulative student debt: 73% of graduating class had student loans; average debt was $19,769.

FINANCIAL AID PROCEDURES

Forms required: FAFSA.
Dates and Deadlines: Priority date 3/1; no closing date. Applicants notified on a rolling basis starting 3/15; must reply within 4 week(s) of notification.
Transfers: No deadline. Applicants notified on a rolling basis starting 3/15; must reply within 4 week(s) of notification. Financial aid transcripts required from all institutions previously attended.

CONTACT

Susan George, Director of Financial Aid
59 College Avenue, Buckhannon, WV 26201-2998
(304) 473-8080

Wheeling Jesuit University

Wheeling, West Virginia
www.wju.edu Federal Code: 003831

4-year private university and liberal arts college in small city, affiliated with Roman Catholic Church.
Enrollment: 971 undergrads, 12% part-time. 182 full-time freshmen.
Selectivity: Admits 50 to 75% of applicants.

BASIC COSTS (2009-2010)

Tuition and fees: $24,630.
Room and board: $8,524.
Additional info: Required fees include $200 "new student fee" charged only to freshmen.

FINANCIAL AID PICTURE (2008-2009)

Students with need: Out of 171 full-time freshmen who applied for aid, 144 were judged to have need. Of these, 144 received aid, and 58 had their full need met. Average financial aid package met 96% of need; average scholarship/grant was $6,718; average loan was $4,018. For part-time students, average financial aid package was $4,810.
Students without need: 38 full-time freshmen who did not demonstrate need for aid received scholarships/grants; average award was $11,052. No-need awards available for academics, alumni affiliation, athletics, leadership, music/drama.
Scholarships offered: 15 full-time freshmen received athletic scholarships; average amount $4,519.
Cumulative student debt: 88% of graduating class had student loans; average debt was $21,383.

FINANCIAL AID PROCEDURES

Forms required: FAFSA.
Dates and Deadlines: Priority date 2/15; no closing date. Applicants notified on a rolling basis starting 3/15; must reply within 2 week(s) of notification.
Transfers: No deadline. Applicants notified on a rolling basis starting 3/15; must reply within 2 week(s) of notification. Academic scholarships available to qualified transfer students.

CONTACT

Christie Tomczyk, Director of Financial Aid
316 Washington Avenue, Wheeling, WV 26003-6295
(800) 624-6992 ext. 2304

Wisconsin

Alverno College

Milwaukee, Wisconsin
www.alverno.edu Federal Code: 003832

4-year private liberal arts college for women in very large city, affiliated with Roman Catholic Church.
Enrollment: 2,303 undergrads, 26% part-time. 252 full-time freshmen.
Selectivity: Admits over 75% of applicants.

BASIC COSTS (2009-2010)

Tuition and fees: $19,074.
Per-credit charge: $776.
Room and board: $6,504.
Additional info: Tuition and fees may vary by program.

FINANCIAL AID PICTURE (2008-2009)

Students with need: Out of 235 full-time freshmen who applied for aid, 200 were judged to have need. Of these, 200 received aid. For part-time students, average financial aid package was $8,309.

Students without need: 28 full-time freshmen who did not demonstrate need for aid received scholarships/grants; average award was $7,365. No-need awards available for academics, alumni affiliation, leadership.

Scholarships offered: Four-year academic scholarships range from $16,000 to $35,600. Alverno Scholars of Wisconsin: $10,500 scholarship, one available for each Wisconsin county.

Cumulative student debt: 91% of graduating class had student loans; average debt was $27,976.

FINANCIAL AID PROCEDURES

Forms required: FAFSA, institutional form.

Dates and Deadlines: Priority date 3/15; no closing date. Applicants notified on a rolling basis starting 3/15; must reply within 2 week(s) of notification.

Transfers: No deadline. Applicants notified on a rolling basis; must reply within 2 week(s) of notification. Transfer students are eligible for academic scholarships.

CONTACT

Dan Goyette, Director of Financial Aid
3400 South 43rd Street, Milwaukee, WI 53234-3922
(414) 382-6046

Beloit College

Beloit, Wisconsin
www.beloit.edu Federal Code: 003835

4-year private liberal arts college in large town.

Enrollment: 1,297 undergrads. 337 full-time freshmen.

Selectivity: Admits 50 to 75% of applicants.

BASIC COSTS (2009-2010)

Tuition and fees: $33,418.

Per-credit charge: $1,037.

Room and board: $6,830.

Additional info: Tuition/fee waivers available for adults.

FINANCIAL AID PICTURE (2008-2009)

Students with need: Out of 278 full-time freshmen who applied for aid, 223 were judged to have need. Of these, 223 received aid, and 213 had their full need met. Average financial aid package met 99% of need; average scholarship/grant was $21,253; average loan was $3,160. For part-time students, average financial aid package was $13,459.

Students without need: 90 full-time freshmen who did not demonstrate need for aid received scholarships/grants; average award was $12,565. No-need awards available for academics, leadership, minority status, music/drama.

Scholarships offered: Presidential Scholarships: $13,000-$15,000 per year; campus interview required. Merit-based scholarship: $4,000-$15,000 per year; 6 awarded.

Cumulative student debt: 68% of graduating class had student loans; average debt was $26,014.

FINANCIAL AID PROCEDURES

Forms required: FAFSA, state aid form, institutional form.

Dates and Deadlines: Closing date 3/1. Applicants notified on a rolling basis starting 4/1; must reply by 5/1 or within 2 week(s) of notification.

Transfers: No deadline. Applicants notified on a rolling basis starting 4/1; must reply by 5/1 or within 2 week(s) of notification.

CONTACT

Jane Hessian, Director of Financial Aid
700 College Street, Beloit, WI 53511-5595
(608) 363-2663

Blackhawk Technical College

Janesville, Wisconsin
www.blackhawk.edu Federal Code: 005390

2-year public technical college in small city.

Enrollment: 2,760 undergrads, 52% part-time. 483 full-time freshmen.

Selectivity: Open admission; but selective for some programs.

BASIC COSTS (2008-2009)

Tuition and fees: $3,118; out-of-state residents $18,034.

Per-credit charge: $97; out-of-state residents $594.

Additional info: Material fees vary by program; minimum $4 per course. $10 per credit fee for online courses.

FINANCIAL AID PICTURE (2007-2008)

Students with need: 59% of average financial aid package awarded as scholarships/grants, 41% awarded as loans/jobs. Need-based aid available for part-time students. Work study available nights.

FINANCIAL AID PROCEDURES

Forms required: FAFSA.

Dates and Deadlines: Priority date 4/30; no closing date. Applicants notified on a rolling basis starting 3/15; must reply within 2 week(s) of notification.

CONTACT

Sue Ullrick, Financial Aid Officer
Box 5009, Janesville, WI 53547-5009
(608) 757-7664

Cardinal Stritch University

Milwaukee, Wisconsin
www.stritch.edu Federal Code: 003837

4-year private university in very large city, affiliated with Roman Catholic Church.

Enrollment: 3,060 undergrads.

Selectivity: Admits over 75% of applicants.

BASIC COSTS (2008-2009)

Tuition and fees: $20,510.

Per-credit charge: $625.

Room and board: $6,020.

Additional info: Additional $55 per credit for the nursing program.

FINANCIAL AID PICTURE

Students with need: Need-based aid available for full-time and part-time students.

Students without need: No-need awards available for academics, art, athletics, music/drama.

FINANCIAL AID PROCEDURES

Forms required: FAFSA, institutional form.

Dates and Deadlines: Priority date 4/15; no closing date. Applicants notified on a rolling basis starting 3/1; must reply within 3 week(s) of notification.

CONTACT

Amy Hoss, Director of Financial Aid
6801 North Yates Road, Box 516, Milwaukee, WI 53217-7516
(414) 410-4048

Carroll University

Waukesha, Wisconsin
www.carrollu.edu Federal Code: 003838

4-year private liberal arts college in small city, affiliated with Presbyterian Church (USA).

Enrollment: 2,947 undergrads, 15% part-time. 663 full-time freshmen.

Selectivity: Admits 50 to 75% of applicants.

BASIC COSTS (2009-2010)

Tuition and fees: $22,937.

Per-credit charge: $270.

Room and board: $7,023.

FINANCIAL AID PICTURE (2008-2009)

Students with need: Out of 609 full-time freshmen who applied for aid, 513 were judged to have need. Of these, 513 received aid, and 295 had their full need met. Average financial aid package met 100% of need; average scholarship/grant was $13,249; average loan was $2,459. Need-based aid available for part-time students.

Students without need: 142 full-time freshmen who did not demonstrate need for aid received scholarships/grants; average award was $9,737. No-need awards available for academics, alumni affiliation, art, leadership, music/drama, ROTC.

Scholarships offered: Trustee Scholarship; $12,000 per year. Voorhees Scholarship; $11,000 per year. Charles Caroll Scholarship; $10,000 per year.

Cumulative student debt: 73% of graduating class had student loans; average debt was $24,097.

FINANCIAL AID PROCEDURES

Forms required: FAFSA.

Dates and Deadlines: No deadline. Applicants notified on a rolling basis starting 2/15; must reply by 5/1 or within 2 week(s) of notification.

Transfers: No deadline. Applicants notified on a rolling basis.

CONTACT

Dawn Scott, Director of Student Financial Services
100 North East Avenue, Waukesha, WI 53186-9988
(262) 524-7296

Carthage College

Kenosha, Wisconsin
www.carthage.edu Federal Code: 003839

4-year private liberal arts college in small city, affiliated with Evangelical Lutheran Church in America.

Enrollment: 2,372 undergrads.

Selectivity: Admits over 75% of applicants.

BASIC COSTS (2009-2010)

Tuition and fees: $28,250.

Per-credit charge: $400.

Room and board: $7,750.

Additional info: Tuition/fee waivers available for minority students.

FINANCIAL AID PICTURE (2008-2009)

Students with need: Need-based aid available for full-time and part-time students.

Students without need: No-need awards available for academics, alumni affiliation, art, leadership, minority status, music/drama, religious affiliation.

Scholarships offered: Lincoln Scholarship Program: range from 75% tuition to full tuition, room and board, renewable; separate scholarship application; 17 awarded. Math/Science Scholarship: three awarded; range from $17,000/year to full tuition, renewable; requires separate scholarship application, restricted to math and natural science majors. French/German Scholarship: four awarded; $17,000/year, renewable; requires separate scholarship application, restricted to French and German majors. Fine Arts Scholarships: $500-$10,000/year, renewable; requires separate audition/portfolio showing, open to majors and non majors in music and theater, and majors in studio art or graphic design. Tarble Scholarships: number awarded variable; up to $17,000 year, renewable; requires separate scholarship application, restricted to California residents.

FINANCIAL AID PROCEDURES

Forms required: FAFSA.

Dates and Deadlines: Priority date 2/15; no closing date. Applicants notified on a rolling basis starting 3/1.

Transfers: Priority date 3/1; no deadline. Applicants notified on a rolling basis starting 3/1.

CONTACT

Vatistas Vatistas, Director of Financial Aid
2001 Alford Park Drive, Kenosha, WI 53140-1994
(262) 551-6001

Chippewa Valley Technical College

Eau Claire, Wisconsin
www.cvtc.edu Federal Code: 005304

2-year public technical college in small city.

Enrollment: 5,624 undergrads.

Selectivity: Open admission; but selective for some programs.

BASIC COSTS (2008-2009)

Tuition and fees: $3,086; out-of-state residents $18,002.

Per-credit charge: $97; out-of-state residents $594.

Additional info: Material fees vary by program; minimum $4 per course. $10 per credit fee for online courses.

FINANCIAL AID PICTURE (2007-2008)

Students with need: Need-based aid available for full-time and part-time students. Work study available nights, weekends, and for part-time students.

Scholarships offered: TOP Grant: $250 per semester, up to $1,000 total; must be enrolled full-time in Wisconsin technical college within 3 years of graduating from a Wisconsin high school, maintain minimum semester 2.0 GPA, and enroll in occupational associate degree or one-two year technical diploma program.

FINANCIAL AID PROCEDURES

Forms required: FAFSA.

Dates and Deadlines: Priority date 3/15; no closing date. Applicants notified on a rolling basis starting 6/1; must reply within 2 week(s) of notification.

CONTACT

Mary Gorud, Financial Aid Officer
620 West Clairemont Avenue, Eau Claire, WI 54701-6162
(715) 833-6252

Columbia College of Nursing

Milwaukee, Wisconsin
www.ccon.edu Federal Code: 003838

4-year private nursing college in very large city.

Enrollment: 215 undergrads.

BASIC COSTS (2009-2010)

Tuition and fees: $20,500.

Per-credit charge: $620.

Room and board: $5,600.

FINANCIAL AID PICTURE (2008-2009)

Students with need: Need-based aid available for full-time and part-time students. Work study available nights, weekends, and for part-time students.

Students without need: No-need awards available for academics.

Additional info: Students must apply to and meet financial aid requirements of Mount Mary College.

FINANCIAL AID PROCEDURES

Forms required: FAFSA.

Dates and Deadlines: No deadline. Applicants notified on a rolling basis starting 2/15; must reply by 5/1 or within 2 week(s) of notification.

CONTACT

Shereen Kressin, Associate Dean, Administration and Finance
Mount Mary College Enrollment Office, Milwaukee, WI 53222-4597

Concordia University Wisconsin

Mequon, Wisconsin
www.cuw.edu Federal Code: 003842

4-year private university and liberal arts college in large town, affiliated with Lutheran Church - Missouri Synod.

Enrollment: 3,408 undergrads, 45% part-time. 422 full-time freshmen.

Selectivity: Admits 50 to 75% of applicants.

BASIC COSTS (2008-2009)

Tuition and fees: $19,990.

Per-credit charge: $830.

Room and board: $7,500.

FINANCIAL AID PICTURE (2008-2009)

Students with need: Out of 409 full-time freshmen who applied for aid, 352 were judged to have need. Of these, 352 received aid, and 130 had their full need met. Average financial aid package met 80% of need; average scholarship/grant was $12,172; average loan was $5,082. For part-time students, average financial aid package was $11,679.

Students without need: 75 full-time freshmen who did not demonstrate need for aid received scholarships/grants; average award was $9,143. No-need awards available for academics, minority status, music/drama, religious affiliation.

Cumulative student debt: 76% of graduating class had student loans; average debt was $24,351.

FINANCIAL AID PROCEDURES

Forms required: FAFSA.

Dates and Deadlines: Priority date 4/1; no closing date. Applicants notified on a rolling basis starting 2/15; must reply within 3 week(s) of notification.

CONTACT

Steve Taylor, Director of Financial Aid
12800 North Lake Shore Drive, Mequon, WI 53097
(262) 243-4392

Edgewood College

Madison, Wisconsin
www.edgewood.edu Federal Code: 003848

4-year private liberal arts college in small city, affiliated with Roman Catholic Church.

Enrollment: 1,880 undergrads, 17% part-time. 295 full-time freshmen.

Selectivity: Open admission; but selective for some programs.

BASIC COSTS (2009-2010)

Tuition and fees: $21,042.

Per-credit charge: $662.

Room and board: $7,134.

FINANCIAL AID PICTURE (2007-2008)

Students with need: Out of 263 full-time freshmen who applied for aid, 220 were judged to have need. Of these, 220 received aid, and 43 had their full need met. Average financial aid package met 82% of need; average scholarship/grant was $10,597; average loan was $4,092. For part-time students, average financial aid package was $9,406.

Students without need: 71 full-time freshmen who did not demonstrate need for aid received scholarships/grants; average award was $10,502. No-need awards available for academics, alumni affiliation, art, leadership, music/drama, religious affiliation.

Cumulative student debt: 63% of graduating class had student loans; average debt was $27,885.

Additional info: Auditions required for music scholarships, portfolios required for fine arts scholarships, essays required for a number of institutional scholarships, including AHANA Student Advancement Award, Alumni Association Scholarship, O'Connor Memorial Scholarship.

FINANCIAL AID PROCEDURES

Forms required: FAFSA, institutional form.

Dates and Deadlines: Priority date 3/1; no closing date. Applicants notified on a rolling basis starting 3/15; must reply within 2 week(s) of notification.

CONTACT

Kari Gribble, Director of Financial Aid
1000 Edgewood College Drive, Madison, WI 53711-1997
(608) 663-2206

Fox Valley Technical College

Appleton, Wisconsin
www.fvtc.edu Federal Code: 009744

2-year public technical college in small city.

Enrollment: 4,667 undergrads, 51% part-time. 623 full-time freshmen.

Selectivity: Open admission; but selective for some programs.

BASIC COSTS (2008-2009)

Tuition and fees: $3,232; out-of-state residents $18,148.

Per-credit charge: $97; out-of-state residents $594.

Additional info: Material fees vary by program; minimum $4 per course. $10 per credit fee for online courses.

FINANCIAL AID PICTURE (2007-2008)

Students with need: 40% of average financial aid package awarded as scholarships/grants, 60% awarded as loans/jobs.

FINANCIAL AID PROCEDURES

Forms required: FAFSA.

Dates and Deadlines: Priority date 4/15; no closing date. Applicants notified on a rolling basis.

CONTACT

Mary Moede, Financial Aid Director
1825 North Bluemound Drive, Appleton, WI 54912-2277
(920) 735-5645

Herzing College

Madison, Wisconsin
www.herzing.edu/madison Federal Code: 009621

3-year for-profit business and career college in small city.

Enrollment: 840 undergrads.

Selectivity: Open admission; but selective for some programs.

BASIC COSTS (2008-2009)

Tuition and fees: $11,200.

Per-credit charge: $350.

Additional info: Tuition is $350 per credit hour for most on campus courses; $390 for on-line courses. Book use included in tuition.

FINANCIAL AID PICTURE (2008-2009)

Students with need: Need-based aid available for full-time and part-time students.

FINANCIAL AID PROCEDURES

Forms required: FAFSA, institutional form.

Dates and Deadlines: No deadline. Applicants notified on a rolling basis.

CONTACT

Beverly Faga, Director of Financial Services
5218 East Terrace Drive, Madison, WI 53718
(608) 249-6611

Lac Courte Oreilles Ojibwa Community College

Hayward, Wisconsin
www.lco.edu Federal Code: 017199

2-year public community college in small town.
Enrollment: 448 undergrads, 33% part-time. 48 full-time freshmen.
Selectivity: Open admission.

BASIC COSTS (2009-2010)

Tuition and fees: $4,075.
Per-credit charge: $140.

FINANCIAL AID PICTURE

Students with need: Need-based aid available for full-time students.

FINANCIAL AID PROCEDURES

Forms required: FAFSA.
Dates and Deadlines: No deadline. Applicants notified on a rolling basis.

CONTACT

Ray Burns, Financial Aid Director
13466 West Trepania Road, Hayward, WI 54843

Lakeland College

Sheboygan, Wisconsin
www.lakeland.edu Federal Code: 003854

4-year private liberal arts college in small city, affiliated with United Church of Christ.
Enrollment: 2,839 undergrads.
Selectivity: Admits over 75% of applicants.

BASIC COSTS (2008-2009)

Tuition and fees: $18,435.
Per-credit charge: $615.
Room and board: $6,360.

FINANCIAL AID PICTURE (2008-2009)

Students with need: Need-based aid available for full-time and part-time students. Work study available nights, weekends, and for part-time students.
Students without need: No-need awards available for academics.

FINANCIAL AID PROCEDURES

Forms required: FAFSA, institutional form.
Dates and Deadlines: Priority date 3/31; closing date 7/1. Applicants notified on a rolling basis starting 2/1; must reply within 2 week(s) of notification.

CONTACT

Patty Taylor, Director of Financial Aid
Box 359, Sheboygan, WI 53082-0359
(920) 565-1297

Lakeshore Technical College

Cleveland, Wisconsin
www.gotoltc.edu Federal Code: 009194

2-year public technical college in rural community.
Enrollment: 2,238 undergrads, 62% part-time. 108 full-time freshmen.
Selectivity: Open admission.

BASIC COSTS (2008-2009)

Tuition and fees: $3,045; out-of-state residents $17,961.
Per-credit charge: $97; out-of-state residents $594.
Additional info: Materials fees vary by program; minimum $4 per course. $10 per credit fee for online courses.

FINANCIAL AID PICTURE (2008-2009)

Students with need: 55% of average financial aid package awarded as scholarships/grants, 45% awarded as loans/jobs. Need-based aid available for part-time students. Work study available nights.
Students without need: This college awards aid only to students with need.

FINANCIAL AID PROCEDURES

Forms required: FAFSA, institutional form.
Dates and Deadlines: Priority date 6/1; no closing date. Applicants notified on a rolling basis starting 6/1; must reply within 3 week(s) of notification.

CONTACT

Corey Givens-Novak, Financial Aid Manager
1290 North Avenue, Cleveland, WI 53015-9761
(920) 693-1118

Lawrence University

Appleton, Wisconsin
www.lawrence.edu Federal Code: 003856

4-year private music and liberal arts college in small city.
Enrollment: 1,452 undergrads, 3% part-time. 382 full-time freshmen.
Selectivity: Admits 50 to 75% of applicants. GED not accepted.

BASIC COSTS (2008-2009)

Tuition and fees: $33,264.
Room and board: $6,957.

FINANCIAL AID PICTURE (2008-2009)

Students with need: Out of 281 full-time freshmen who applied for aid, 258 were judged to have need. Of these, 258 received aid, and 180 had their full need met. Average financial aid package met 93% of need; average scholarship/grant was $19,410; average loan was $5,290. Need-based aid available for part-time students.
Students without need: 90 full-time freshmen who did not demonstrate need for aid received scholarships/grants; average award was $13,890. No-need awards available for academics, alumni affiliation, minority status, music/drama.
Scholarships offered: Warch Scholarships: $15,000 per year. Trustee Scholarships: $12,000 per year. Presidential Scholarships: $9,000 per year. Alumni Scholarships: $7,000 per year. Conservatory Scholarships: $2,000-$12,000 per year.
Cumulative student debt: 69% of graduating class had student loans; average debt was $26,054.
Additional info: The first $1,000 (aggregate) of independently-sponsored scholarships received by a needy student will reduce student's loan or work-study commitment. Half of scholarships in excess of $1,000 will offset loan or work-study and the other half will reduce institutional need-based grant funding.

FINANCIAL AID PROCEDURES

Forms required: FAFSA, institutional form.
Dates and Deadlines: Priority date 3/15; no closing date. Applicants notified on a rolling basis starting 3/1; must reply by 5/1 or within 2 week(s) of notification.
Transfers: Priority date 4/1. Applicants notified on a rolling basis starting 5/23.

CONTACT

Steven Syverson, Vice President for Enrollment Management
Box 599, Appleton, WI 54912-0599
(920) 832-6583

Maranatha Baptist Bible College

Watertown, Wisconsin
www.mbbc.edu Federal Code: 016394

4-year private Bible college in large town, affiliated with Baptist faith.
Enrollment: 800 undergrads, 4% part-time. 192 full-time freshmen.
Selectivity: Admits 50 to 75% of applicants.

BASIC COSTS (2009-2010)

Tuition and fees: $11,000.
Per-credit charge: $417.
Room and board: $5,990.

FINANCIAL AID PICTURE (2007-2008)

Students with need: Need-based aid available for full-time and part-time students.
Students without need: No-need awards available for academics.

FINANCIAL AID PROCEDURES

Forms required: FAFSA.
Dates and Deadlines: Priority date 3/1; no closing date. Applicants notified on a rolling basis starting 2/1; must reply within 2 week(s) of notification.
Transfers: Financial aid transcript or equivalent required.

CONTACT

Randy Hibbs, Financial Aid Director
745 West Main Street, Watertown, WI 53094
(920) 206-2318

Marian University

Fond du Lac, Wisconsin
www.marianuniversity.edu Federal Code: 003861

4-year private university and liberal arts college in large town, affiliated with Roman Catholic Church.
Enrollment: 1,903 undergrads, 27% part-time. 284 full-time freshmen.
Selectivity: Admits over 75% of applicants.

BASIC COSTS (2009-2010)

Tuition and fees: $20,900.
Per-credit charge: $315.
Room and board: $5,640.

FINANCIAL AID PICTURE (2008-2009)

Students with need: Out of 281 full-time freshmen who applied for aid, 257 were judged to have need. Of these, 257 received aid, and 120 had their full need met. Average financial aid package met 92% of need; average scholarship/grant was $11,440; average loan was $5,288. For part-time students, average financial aid package was $11,472.
Students without need: 24 full-time freshmen who did not demonstrate need for aid received scholarships/grants; average award was $5,986. No-need awards available for academics, ROTC, state/district residency.
Scholarships offered: Academic Achievement Award: $7,500; based on 3.5 GPA, 25 ACT, top 15% of class; 7 awarded. Presidential Scholarship: $5,000; based on 3.1 GPA, top 20% of class. Naber Leadership Scholarship: $3,000; based on 2.5 GPA, top 50% of class.
Cumulative student debt: 90% of graduating class had student loans; average debt was $22,200.

FINANCIAL AID PROCEDURES

Forms required: FAFSA, institutional form.
Dates and Deadlines: Priority date 3/1; no closing date. Applicants notified on a rolling basis starting 3/1; must reply within 4 week(s) of notification.

CONTACT

Debra McKinney, Director of Financial Aid
45 South National Avenue, Fond du Lac, WI 54935-4699
(920) 923-7614

Marquette University

Milwaukee, Wisconsin
www.marquette.edu Federal Code: 003863

4-year private university in very large city, affiliated with Roman Catholic Church.
Enrollment: 7,821 undergrads, 3% part-time. 1,950 full-time freshmen.
Selectivity: Admits 50 to 75% of applicants.

BASIC COSTS (2009-2010)

Tuition and fees: $29,096.
Per-credit charge: $835.
Room and board: $9,288.
Additional info: Required fees include cost of UPASS, which allows unlimited use of Milwaukee County Bus System.

FINANCIAL AID PICTURE (2008-2009)

Students with need: Out of 1,540 full-time freshmen who applied for aid, 1,185 were judged to have need. Of these, 1,180 received aid, and 378 had their full need met. Average financial aid package met 84% of need; average scholarship/grant was $16,448; average loan was $4,504. For part-time students, average financial aid package was $8,792.
Students without need: 409 full-time freshmen who did not demonstrate need for aid received scholarships/grants; average award was $9,227. No-need awards available for academics, athletics, leadership, music/drama, ROTC.
Scholarships offered: ***Merit:*** Ignatius Scholarships: $6,000-$11,000. College Scholarships: $5,000. Raynor Scholarships: full tuition; 3 awarded. National Merit Scholarships: $2,000. ***Athletic:*** 19 full-time freshmen received athletic scholarships; average amount $19,539.
Cumulative student debt: 63% of graduating class had student loans; average debt was $30,563.

FINANCIAL AID PROCEDURES

Forms required: FAFSA.
Dates and Deadlines: Priority date 2/1; no closing date. Applicants notified on a rolling basis starting 3/20; must reply by 5/1 or within 3 week(s) of notification.
Transfers: No deadline. Applicants notified on a rolling basis starting 3/15; must reply by 5/1 or within 3 week(s) of notification. Transfer scholarships available.

CONTACT

Susan Teerink, Director of Student Financial Aid
PO Box 1881, Milwaukee, WI 53201-1881
(414) 288-0200

Mid-State Technical College

Wisconsin Rapids, Wisconsin
www.mstc.edu Federal Code: 005380

2-year public technical college in large town.
Enrollment: 2,970 undergrads.
Selectivity: Open admission; but selective for some programs.

BASIC COSTS (2008-2009)

Tuition and fees: $3,206; out-of-state residents $18,122.
Per-credit charge: $97; out-of-state residents $594.
Additional info: Material fees vary by program; minimum $4 per course.

FINANCIAL AID PICTURE (2007-2008)

Students with need: Need-based aid available for full-time and part-time students. Work study available nights, weekends, and for part-time students.
Students without need: No-need awards available for academics, leadership.

FINANCIAL AID PROCEDURES

Forms required: FAFSA.
Dates and Deadlines: No deadline. Applicants notified on a rolling basis starting 5/30; must reply within 2 week(s) of notification.

CONTACT

MaryJo Green, Financial Aid Supervisor
500 32nd Street North, Wisconsin Rapids, WI 54494
(715) 422-5501

Milwaukee Area Technical College

Milwaukee, Wisconsin
www.matc.edu Federal Code: 003866

2-year public junior and technical college in very large city.
Enrollment: 15,942 undergrads, 64% part-time. 1,150 full-time freshmen.
Selectivity: Open admission; but selective for some programs.

BASIC COSTS (2008-2009)

Tuition and fees: $3,216; out-of-state residents $18,132.
Per-credit charge: $97; out-of-state residents $594.
Additional info: Material fees vary by program; minimum $4 per course. $10 per credit fee for online courses. Tuition/fee waivers available for minority students.

FINANCIAL AID PICTURE (2007-2008)

Students with need: Need-based aid available for full-time and part-time students.
Students without need: No-need awards available for academics.

FINANCIAL AID PROCEDURES

Forms required: FAFSA.
Dates and Deadlines: Priority date 3/15; no closing date. Applicants notified on a rolling basis starting 4/15.
Transfers: No deadline. Applicants notified on a rolling basis starting 4/15.

CONTACT

Lisa Lipe, Director of Financial Aid
700 West State Street, Milwaukee, WI 53233-1443
(414) 297-7042

Milwaukee Institute of Art & Design

Milwaukee, Wisconsin
www.miad.edu Federal Code: 014203

4-year private visual arts college in very large city.
Enrollment: 666 undergrads.
Selectivity: Admits over 75% of applicants.

BASIC COSTS (2008-2009)

Tuition and fees: $25,400.
Per-credit charge: $805.
Room and board: $7,400.

FINANCIAL AID PICTURE (2007-2008)

Students with need: Need-based aid available for full-time and part-time students. Work study available nights, weekends, and for part-time students.
Students without need: No-need awards available for academics, art, leadership.
Scholarships offered: One full admission scholarship; several half, 1/3 and 1/4 admission scholarships. All awards based on portfolio and grade point average.

FINANCIAL AID PROCEDURES

Forms required: FAFSA.
Dates and Deadlines: Priority date 3/1; no closing date. Applicants notified on a rolling basis starting 4/1; must reply by 5/1 or within 4 week(s) of notification.
Transfers: No deadline. Applicants notified on a rolling basis starting 4/1; must reply by 5/1 or within 2 week(s) of notification.

CONTACT

Lloyd Mueller, Executive Director of Financial Aid
273 East Erie Street, Milwaukee, WI 53202
(414) 291-3272

Milwaukee School of Engineering

Milwaukee, Wisconsin
www.msoe.edu Federal Code: 003868

4-year private university in very large city.
Enrollment: 2,418 undergrads, 10% part-time. 553 full-time freshmen.
Selectivity: Admits 50 to 75% of applicants.

BASIC COSTS (2009-2010)

Tuition and fees: $28,665.
Per-credit charge: $498.
Room and board: $7,164.
Additional info: $1,140 technology package required for all full-time first-year students. Includes laptop computer, software, Internet, insurance and repairs, upgrade every two years, wireless access, training and support, and compatibility computing throughout campus.

FINANCIAL AID PICTURE (2007-2008)

Students with need: Out of 514 full-time freshmen who applied for aid, 458 were judged to have need. Of these, 457 received aid, and 65 had their full need met. Average financial aid package met 67% of need; average scholarship/grant was $14,511; average loan was $2,304. For part-time students, average financial aid package was $10,720.
Students without need: 90 full-time freshmen who did not demonstrate need for aid received scholarships/grants; average award was $8,935. No-need awards available for academics, ROTC.
Scholarships offered: President Scholarship; full tuition; awarded to students with high academic standing; 8 awarded each year to first-time, full-time students.
Cumulative student debt: 89% of graduating class had student loans; average debt was $31,592.

FINANCIAL AID PROCEDURES

Forms required: FAFSA.
Dates and Deadlines: Priority date 3/15; no closing date. Applicants notified on a rolling basis starting 3/1; must reply within 2 week(s) of notification.

CONTACT

Steven Midthun, Director, Financial Aid
1025 North Broadway, Milwaukee, WI 53202-3109
(414) 277-7223

Moraine Park Technical College

Fond du Lac, Wisconsin
www.morainepark.edu Federal Code: 005303

2-year public technical college in large town.
Enrollment: 3,711 undergrads.
Selectivity: Open admission; but selective for some programs.

BASIC COSTS (2008-2009)

Tuition and fees: $3,043; out-of-state residents $17,959.

Per-credit charge: $97; out-of-state residents $594.

Additional info: Material fees vary by program; minimum $4 per course. $10 per credit fee for online courses.

FINANCIAL AID PICTURE (2007-2008)

Students with need: Need-based aid available for full-time and part-time students. Work study available nights.

Students without need: No-need awards available for academics, job skills, leadership, minority status, state/district residency.

FINANCIAL AID PROCEDURES

Forms required: FAFSA, institutional form.

Dates and Deadlines: Priority date 5/1; no closing date. Applicants notified on a rolling basis starting 6/15; must reply within 2 week(s) of notification.

CONTACT

Karen Zuehlke, Student Financials Partner
235 North National Avenue, Fond du Lac, WI 54935-1940
(920) 924-6320

Mount Mary College

Milwaukee, Wisconsin
www.mtmary.edu Federal Code: 003869

4-year private liberal arts college for women in very large city, affiliated with Roman Catholic Church.

Enrollment: 1,226 undergrads, 29% part-time. 174 full-time freshmen.

Selectivity: Admits 50 to 75% of applicants.

BASIC COSTS (2009-2010)

Tuition and fees: $20,736.

Per-credit charge: $596.

Room and board: $7,280.

FINANCIAL AID PICTURE (2008-2009)

Students with need: Out of 159 full-time freshmen who applied for aid, 142 were judged to have need. Of these, 138 received aid, and 12 had their full need met. Average financial aid package met 64% of need; average scholarship/grant was $10,894; average loan was $3,517. For part-time students, average financial aid package was $11,613.

Students without need: 20 full-time freshmen who did not demonstrate need for aid received scholarships/grants; average award was $11,731. No-need awards available for academics, alumni affiliation, art, leadership, music/drama.

Cumulative student debt: 86% of graduating class had student loans; average debt was $18,288.

FINANCIAL AID PROCEDURES

Forms required: FAFSA.

Dates and Deadlines: Priority date 3/1; no closing date. Applicants notified on a rolling basis starting 3/1; must reply within 2 week(s) of notification.

Transfers: No deadline. Applicants notified on a rolling basis; must reply within 2 week(s) of notification.

CONTACT

Debra Duff, Director of Financial Aid
2900 North Menomonee River Parkway, Milwaukee, WI 53222-4597
(414) 256-1258

Northcentral Technical College

Wausau, Wisconsin
www.ntc.edu Federal Code: 005387

2-year public community and technical college in small city.

Enrollment: 2,917 undergrads.

Selectivity: Open admission; but selective for some programs.

BASIC COSTS (2008-2009)

Tuition and fees: $3,062; out-of-state residents $17,978.

Per-credit charge: $97; out-of-state residents $594.

Additional info: Materials fees vary by program; minimum $4 per course.

FINANCIAL AID PICTURE (2007-2008)

Students with need: Need-based aid available for full-time and part-time students. Work study available nights.

FINANCIAL AID PROCEDURES

Forms required: FAFSA.

Dates and Deadlines: No deadline. Applicants notified on a rolling basis.

Transfers: No deadline.

CONTACT

Sue Berens, Director of Financial Aid
1000 West Campus Drive, Wausau, WI 54401
(715) 675-3331 ext. 4028

Northeast Wisconsin Technical College

Green Bay, Wisconsin
www.nwtc.edu Federal Code: 005301

2-year public community and technical college in small city.

Enrollment: 5,860 undergrads.

Selectivity: Open admission; but selective for some programs.

BASIC COSTS (2008-2009)

Tuition and fees: $3,075; out-of-state residents $17,991.

Per-credit charge: $97; out-of-state residents $594.

Additional info: Material fees vary by program; minimum $4 per course.

FINANCIAL AID PICTURE (2007-2008)

Students with need: 52% of average financial aid package awarded as scholarships/grants, 48% awarded as loans/jobs. Need-based aid available for part-time students. Work study available nights.

FINANCIAL AID PROCEDURES

Forms required: FAFSA.

Dates and Deadlines: Priority date 4/1; no closing date. Applicants notified on a rolling basis starting 5/1; must reply within 2 week(s) of notification.

CONTACT

Emily Ysebaert, Financial Aid Director
2740 West Mason Street, Green Bay, WI 54307-9042
(920) 498-5444

Northland College

Ashland, Wisconsin
www.northland.edu Federal Code: 003875

4-year private liberal arts college in small town, affiliated with United Church of Christ.

Enrollment: 624 undergrads, 4% part-time. 133 full-time freshmen.

Selectivity: Admits 50 to 75% of applicants.

BASIC COSTS (2008-2009)
Tuition and fees: $23,101.
Per-credit charge: $410.
Room and board: $6,440.

FINANCIAL AID PICTURE (2008-2009)
Students with need: Out of 123 full-time freshmen who applied for aid, 104 were judged to have need. Of these, 104 received aid, and 29 had their full need met. Average financial aid package met 91% of need; average scholarship/grant was $15,341; average loan was $3,982. Need-based aid available for part-time students.
Students without need: 27 full-time freshmen who did not demonstrate need for aid received scholarships/grants; average award was $10,433. No-need awards available for academics, alumni affiliation, art, job skills, leadership, minority status, music/drama, religious affiliation, state/district residency.
Cumulative student debt: 79% of graduating class had student loans; average debt was $23,630.

FINANCIAL AID PROCEDURES
Forms required: FAFSA.
Dates and Deadlines: Priority date 4/15; no closing date. Applicants notified on a rolling basis starting 3/1; must reply by 5/1 or within 4 week(s) of notification.

CONTACT
Paul Borans, Director of Financial Aid
1411 Ellis Avenue, Ashland, WI 54806
(715) 682-1255

Ripon College
Ripon, Wisconsin
www.ripon.edu Federal Code: 003884

4-year private liberal arts college in small town.
Enrollment: 1,037 undergrads. 282 full-time freshmen.
Selectivity: Admits over 75% of applicants.

BASIC COSTS (2008-2009)
Tuition and fees: $24,245.
Per-credit charge: $890.
Room and board: $6,770.

FINANCIAL AID PICTURE (2008-2009)
Students with need: Out of 257 full-time freshmen who applied for aid, 223 were judged to have need. Of these, 223 received aid, and 98 had their full need met. Average financial aid package met 95% of need; average scholarship/grant was $17,033; average loan was $4,551. Need-based aid available for part-time students.
Students without need: 51 full-time freshmen who did not demonstrate need for aid received scholarships/grants; average award was $9,385. No-need awards available for academics, alumni affiliation, art, leadership, minority status, music/drama, religious affiliation, ROTC, state/district residency.
Scholarships offered: Pickard Scholarships: one full tuition and ten $60,000; both by invitation only. Presidential Scholarships: $52,000; minimum 3.8 GPA, top 5% of class, ACT 30, SAT 1340; by invitation only. Knop Scholars Program: $50,000; science major, 3.8 GPA, top 5% of class, interview, by invitation only; one awarded. Faculty Scholarships: $44,000; 3.76 GPA, ACT 29, SAT 1300. Dean's Scholarships: $36,000; 3.51 GPA, ACT 27, SAT 1220. Founder's Scholarships: $32,000; 3.36 GPA, ACT 25, SAT 1140. Honor Scholarships: $24,000; 3.2 GPA, ACT 24, SAT 1110. U.S. All SAT scores exclusive of Writing. Army ROTC Scholarships: starting at $80,000. Diversity Scholarships: $20,000; application required. Forensics Scholarships: $20,000; interview. Valedictorian Scholarships: $24,000. Art Scholarships: $20,000 maximum award; portfolio. Theater Scholarships: $20,000 maximum; interview. Music Scholarships: $20,000; audition. Service Awards: $20,000; not available to academic scholarship recipients. Boy/Girl State Scholarships: $16,000 maximum award. Legacy Awards: $8,000. United Church of Christ Scholarships: $8,000; application required. National Latin Exam: $8,000.
Cumulative student debt: 96% of graduating class had student loans; average debt was $24,795.

FINANCIAL AID PROCEDURES
Forms required: FAFSA.
Dates and Deadlines: Priority date 3/1; no closing date. Applicants notified on a rolling basis starting 3/1; must reply within 2 week(s) of notification.
Transfers: Must reply within 2 week(s) of notification.

CONTACT
Steven Schuetz, Director of Financial Aid
300 Seward Street, Ripon, WI 54971-0248
(920) 748-8101

St. Norbert College
De Pere, Wisconsin
www.snc.edu Federal Code: 003892

4-year private liberal arts college in large town, affiliated with Roman Catholic Church.
Enrollment: 2,036 undergrads, 1% part-time. 543 full-time freshmen.
Selectivity: Admits over 75% of applicants.

BASIC COSTS (2008-2009)
Tuition and fees: $25,926.
Per-credit charge: $798.
Room and board: $6,781.

FINANCIAL AID PICTURE (2007-2008)
Students with need: Out of 439 full-time freshmen who applied for aid, 361 were judged to have need. Of these, 361 received aid, and 110 had their full need met. Average financial aid package met 85% of need; average scholarship/grant was $14,378; average loan was $3,904. For part-time students, average financial aid package was $7,768.
Students without need: 154 full-time freshmen who did not demonstrate need for aid received scholarships/grants; average award was $7,736. No-need awards available for academics, art, leadership, minority status, music/drama, ROTC, state/district residency.

FINANCIAL AID PROCEDURES
Forms required: FAFSA.
Dates and Deadlines: Priority date 3/15; no closing date. Applicants notified on a rolling basis starting 3/15; must reply within 2 week(s) of notification.

CONTACT
Jeff Zahn, Director of Financial Aid
100 Grant Street, De Pere, WI 54115-2099
(920) 403-3071

Silver Lake College
Manitowoc, Wisconsin
www.sl.edu Federal Code: 003850

4-year private business and liberal arts college in large town, affiliated with Roman Catholic Church.
Enrollment: 384 undergrads.
Selectivity: Admits less than 50% of applicants.

BASIC COSTS (2008-2009)
Tuition and fees: $19,194.
Per-credit charge: $595.
Room and board: $7,150.

FINANCIAL AID PICTURE (2008-2009)

Students with need: 45% of average financial aid package awarded as scholarships/grants, 55% awarded as loans/jobs. Need-based aid available for part-time students. Work study available nights, weekends, and for part-time students.

Students without need: No-need awards available for academics, art, athletics, leadership, music/drama, religious affiliation, state/district residency.

Scholarships offered: Presidential Scholarship: $8,000. Founder's Scholarship: $7,000. Dean's Scholarship: $6,000. Honors Scholarship: $5,000. All scholarships merit-based.

FINANCIAL AID PROCEDURES

Forms required: FAFSA.

Dates and Deadlines: Priority date 3/15; no closing date. Applicants notified on a rolling basis starting 3/15; must reply within 2 week(s) of notification.

Transfers: No deadline. Applicants notified on a rolling basis starting 3/15; must reply within 2 week(s) of notification. Transfer Merit Scholarships and Phi Theta Kappa Scholarships available, as well as other institutional scholarship and grant assistance.

CONTACT

Michelle Krajnik, Director of Student Financial Aid
2406 South Alverno Road, Manitowoc, WI 54220-9319
(920) 686-6122

Southwest Wisconsin Technical College

Fennimore, Wisconsin
www.swtc.edu Federal Code: 007699

2-year public technical college in rural community.

Enrollment: 971 undergrads, 40% part-time. 322 full-time freshmen.

Selectivity: Open admission; but selective for some programs.

BASIC COSTS (2008-2009)

Tuition and fees: $3,029; out-of-state residents $17,945.

Per-credit charge: $97; out-of-state residents $594.

Additional info: Materials fees vary by program; minimum $4 per course. $10 per credit fee for online courses.

FINANCIAL AID PICTURE (2007-2008)

Students with need: 51% of average financial aid package awarded as scholarships/grants, 49% awarded as loans/jobs. Work study available nights.

FINANCIAL AID PROCEDURES

Forms required: FAFSA, institutional form.

Dates and Deadlines: Priority date 4/15; no closing date. Applicants notified on a rolling basis starting 5/15; must reply within 4 week(s) of notification.

CONTACT

Joy Kite, Director of Financial Aid
1800 Bronson Boulevard, Fennimore, WI 53809
(608) 822-2319

University of Wisconsin-Baraboo/Sauk County

Baraboo, Wisconsin
www.baraboo.uwc.edu Federal Code: 003897

2-year public branch campus and liberal arts college in large town.

Enrollment: 669 undergrads.

BASIC COSTS (2008-2009)

Tuition and fees: $4,644; out-of-state residents $11,628.

Per-credit charge: $178; out-of-state residents $469.

Additional info: Minnesota reciprocity tuition: $167 per credit hour.

FINANCIAL AID PICTURE (2007-2008)

Students with need: Need-based aid available for full-time and part-time students. Work study available nights.

Students without need: This college awards aid only to students with need.

Scholarships offered: Campus scholarships; $250 to full tuition.

FINANCIAL AID PROCEDURES

Forms required: FAFSA, institutional form.

Dates and Deadlines: Priority date 4/15; no closing date. Applicants notified on a rolling basis starting 4/15; must reply within 3 week(s) of notification.

Transfers: Must reply within 3 week(s) of notification.

CONTACT

Marilyn Krump, Director of Financial Aid
1006 Connie Road, Baraboo, WI 53913-1098
(608) 263-7727

University of Wisconsin-Barron County

Rice Lake, Wisconsin
www.barron.uwc.edu Federal Code: 003897

2-year public branch campus and junior college in small town.

Enrollment: 624 undergrads.

BASIC COSTS (2008-2009)

Tuition and fees: $4,693; out-of-state residents $11,677.

Per-credit charge: $178; out-of-state residents $469.

Additional info: Minnesota reciprocity tuition: $167 per credit hour.

FINANCIAL AID PICTURE (2007-2008)

Students with need: Need-based aid available for full-time and part-time students.

FINANCIAL AID PROCEDURES

Forms required: FAFSA.

Dates and Deadlines: Priority date 4/15; no closing date. Applicants notified on a rolling basis starting 6/1.

CONTACT

Marilyn Krump, Director of Financial Aid
1800 College Drive, Rice Lake, WI 54868

University of Wisconsin-Eau Claire

Eau Claire, Wisconsin
www.uwec.edu Federal Code: 003917

4-year public university in small city.

Enrollment: 10,215 undergrads, 5% part-time. 2,026 full-time freshmen.

Selectivity: Admits 50 to 75% of applicants.

BASIC COSTS (2008-2009)

Tuition and fees: $6,203; out-of-state residents $13,777.

Per-credit charge: $218; out-of-state residents $534.

Room and board: $5,210.

Additional info: Minnesota reciprocity tuition: $270 per credit hour.

FINANCIAL AID PICTURE (2007-2008)

Students with need: Out of 1,555 full-time freshmen who applied for aid, 872 were judged to have need. Of these, 866 received aid, and 650 had their full need met. Average financial aid package met 94% of need; average scholarship/grant was $4,764; average loan was $4,264. For part-time students, average financial aid package was $5,722.

Students without need: 341 full-time freshmen who did not demonstrate need for aid received scholarships/grants; average award was $1,781. No-need awards available for academics, art, leadership, minority status, music/drama, state/district residency.

Scholarships offered: Mark of Excellence Award: $2,000; 25 awards; 25 ACT; top 25% of class. Chancellor's Award: $1,000; 35 awards; 25 ACT; top 25% of class. Wisconsin Academy Excellence Scholars: $2,250; selected H.S. valedictorians; renewable; selected by school. National Merit Scholarship finalists: full in-state tuition/fees. Diversity Scholar: 5 awards; up to $6,000 a year for 4 years; 25 ACT; top 25% of class. Blugold Fellowship; 20 awards; $1,000 scholarship and $1,200 research stipend; renewable.
Cumulative student debt: 68% of graduating class had student loans; average debt was $18,548.

FINANCIAL AID PROCEDURES

Forms required: FAFSA.
Dates and Deadlines: Priority date 4/15; no closing date. Applicants notified on a rolling basis starting 4/15.

CONTACT

Kathleen Sahlhoff, Director of Financial Aid
112 Schofield Hall, Eau Claire, WI 54701
(715) 836-3373

University of Wisconsin-Fond du Lac

Fond du Lac, Wisconsin
www.fdl.uwc.edu Federal Code: 003897

2-year public junior college in large town.
Enrollment: 732 undergrads.

BASIC COSTS (2008-2009)

Tuition and fees: $4,584; out-of-state residents $11,568.
Per-credit charge: $178; out-of-state residents $469.
Additional info: Minnesota reciprocity tuition: $167 per credit hour.

FINANCIAL AID PICTURE (2007-2008)

Students with need: Need-based aid available for full-time and part-time students.
Students without need: No-need awards available for academics, leadership, music/drama.

FINANCIAL AID PROCEDURES

Forms required: FAFSA.
Dates and Deadlines: Priority date 4/15; no closing date. Applicants notified on a rolling basis starting 6/1; must reply within 2 week(s) of notification.

CONTACT

Marilyn Krump, Director of Financial Aid
400 University Drive, Fond du Lac, WI 54935-2998
(920) 929-3600

University of Wisconsin-Fox Valley

Menasha, Wisconsin
www.uwfoxvalley.uwc.edu Federal Code: 011459

2-year public liberal arts college in small city.
Enrollment: 1,650 undergrads.

BASIC COSTS (2008-2009)

Tuition and fees: $4,502; out-of-state residents $11,486.
Per-credit charge: $178; out-of-state residents $469.
Additional info: Minnesota reciprocity tuition: $167 per credit hour.

FINANCIAL AID PICTURE (2007-2008)

Students with need: Need-based aid available for full-time and part-time students. Work study available nights, weekends, and for part-time students.

FINANCIAL AID PROCEDURES

Forms required: FAFSA.
Dates and Deadlines: Priority date 4/15; no closing date. Applicants notified on a rolling basis starting 6/1; must reply within 3 week(s) of notification.

CONTACT

Marilyn Krump, Director of Financial Aid
1478 Midway Road, Menasha, WI 54952-2850

University of Wisconsin-Green Bay

Green Bay, Wisconsin
www.uwgb.edu Federal Code: 003899

4-year public university and liberal arts college in small city.
Enrollment: 5,726 undergrads, 18% part-time. 1,000 full-time freshmen.
Selectivity: Admits 50 to 75% of applicants.

BASIC COSTS (2008-2009)

Tuition and fees: $6,308; out-of-state residents $13,881.
Per-credit charge: $212; out-of-state residents $527.
Room and board: $5,460.

FINANCIAL AID PICTURE (2008-2009)

Students with need: Out of 869 full-time freshmen who applied for aid, 586 were judged to have need. Of these, 563 received aid, and 281 had their full need met. Average financial aid package met 86% of need; average scholarship/grant was $5,278; average loan was $3,876. For part-time students, average financial aid package was $9,220.
Students without need: 23 full-time freshmen who did not demonstrate need for aid received scholarships/grants; average award was $1,294. No-need awards available for academics, art, athletics, leadership, minority status, music/drama.
Scholarships offered: 20 full-time freshmen received athletic scholarships; average amount $5,615.
Cumulative student debt: 72% of graduating class had student loans; average debt was $18,587.
Additional info: Auditions required for music and theater scholarships. Tuition is waived for children of Wisconsin soldiers and policemen who were slain in the line of duty. Tuition is also waived for all veterans.

FINANCIAL AID PROCEDURES

Forms required: FAFSA.
Dates and Deadlines: Priority date 4/1; no closing date. Applicants notified on a rolling basis starting 1/1; must reply within 3 week(s) of notification.

CONTACT

Ron Ronnenberg, Director of Financial Aid and Student Employment
2420 Nicolet Drive, Green Bay, WI 54311-7001
(920) 465-2075

University of Wisconsin-La Crosse

La Crosse, Wisconsin
www.uwlax.edu Federal Code: 003919

4-year public university in small city.
Enrollment: 8,426 undergrads, 4% part-time. 1,704 full-time freshmen.
Selectivity: Admits 50 to 75% of applicants.

BASIC COSTS (2008-2009)

Tuition and fees: $6,647; out-of-state residents $14,220.
Per-credit charge: $235; out-of-state residents $551.
Room and board: $5,420.

FINANCIAL AID PICTURE (2007-2008)

Students with need: Out of 1,228 full-time freshmen who applied for aid, 669 were judged to have need. Of these, 608 received aid, and 139 had their full need met. Average financial aid package met 79% of need; average scholarship/grant was $5,493; average loan was $3,087. For part-time students, average financial aid package was $6,503.

Students without need: 52 full-time freshmen who did not demonstrate need for aid received scholarships/grants; average award was $1,187. No-need awards available for academics, alumni affiliation, art, minority status, music/drama, ROTC, state/district residency.

Cumulative student debt: 63% of graduating class had student loans; average debt was $21,250.

FINANCIAL AID PROCEDURES

Forms required: FAFSA, institutional form.

Dates and Deadlines: Priority date 3/15; no closing date. Applicants notified on a rolling basis starting 4/1.

CONTACT

Louise Janke, Associate Director of Financial Aid
1725 State Street, 115 Graff Main Hall, La Crosse, WI 54601
(608) 785-8604

University of Wisconsin-Madison

Madison, Wisconsin
www.wisc.edu Federal Code: 003895

4-year public university in small city.

Enrollment: 29,153 undergrads, 5% part-time. 5,982 full-time freshmen.

Selectivity: Admits 50 to 75% of applicants.

BASIC COSTS (2008-2009)

Tuition and fees: $7,568; out-of-state residents $21,818.

Per-credit charge: $278; out-of-state residents $872.

Room and board: $7,700.

FINANCIAL AID PICTURE (2007-2008)

Students with need: Out of 3,498 full-time freshmen who applied for aid, 1,911 were judged to have need. Of these, 1,906 received aid, and 449 had their full need met. Average financial aid package met 78% of need; average scholarship/grant was $3,287; average loan was $4,385. For part-time students, average financial aid package was $8,190.

Students without need: 1,789 full-time freshmen who did not demonstrate need for aid received scholarships/grants; average award was $1,544. No-need awards available for academics, alumni affiliation, art, athletics, job skills, leadership, minority status, music/drama, religious affiliation, ROTC, state/district residency.

Scholarships offered: 96 full-time freshmen received athletic scholarships; average amount $16,938.

Cumulative student debt: 52% of graduating class had student loans; average debt was $21,123.

FINANCIAL AID PROCEDURES

Forms required: FAFSA, institutional form.

Dates and Deadlines: No deadline. Applicants notified on a rolling basis starting 4/1; must reply within 9 week(s) of notification.

CONTACT

Susan Fischer, Director Student Financial Aid
Armory & Gymnasium, Madison, WI 53706-1481
(608) 262-3060

University of Wisconsin-Manitowoc

Manitowoc, Wisconsin
www.manitowoc.uwc.edu Federal Code: 003897

2-year public branch campus and liberal arts college in large town.

Enrollment: 541 undergrads.

Selectivity: Open admission; but selective for some programs.

BASIC COSTS (2008-2009)

Tuition and fees: $4,946; out-of-state residents $11,929.

Per-credit charge: $178; out-of-state residents $469.

FINANCIAL AID PICTURE (2007-2008)

Students with need: Need-based aid available for full-time and part-time students. Work study available nights.

Students without need: This college awards aid only to students with need.

FINANCIAL AID PROCEDURES

Forms required: FAFSA, institutional form.

Dates and Deadlines: Priority date 3/1; no closing date. Applicants notified on a rolling basis starting 5/1; must reply within 2 week(s) of notification.

Transfers: Priority date 5/1; no deadline.

CONTACT

Christopher Lewis, Assistant Dean for Student Services
705 Viebahn Street, Manitowoc, WI 54220-6699
(920) 683-4707

University of Wisconsin-Marathon County

Wausau, Wisconsin
www.uwmc.uwc.edu Federal Code: 003903

2-year public liberal arts college in small city.

Enrollment: 1,361 undergrads.

BASIC COSTS (2008-2009)

Tuition and fees: $4,507; out-of-state residents $11,491.

Per-credit charge: $178; out-of-state residents $469.

Additional info: Minnesota reciprocity tuition: $167 per credit hour.

FINANCIAL AID PICTURE (2007-2008)

Students with need: Need-based aid available for full-time and part-time students. Work study available nights.

Students without need: This college awards aid only to students with need.

FINANCIAL AID PROCEDURES

Forms required: FAFSA, institutional form.

Dates and Deadlines: Priority date 4/15; no closing date. Applicants notified on a rolling basis starting 6/1; must reply within 3 week(s) of notification.

CONTACT

Marilyn Krump, Director of Financial Aid
518 South Seventh Avenue, Wausau, WI 54401-5396
(715) 261-6235

University of Wisconsin-Marinette

Marinette, Wisconsin
www.marinette.uwc.edu Federal Code: 003897

2-year public branch campus and liberal arts college in large town.

Enrollment: 220 undergrads.

BASIC COSTS (2008-2009)
Tuition and fees: $4,536; out-of-state residents $11,520.
Per-credit charge: $178; out-of-state residents $469.
Additional info: Minnesota reciprocity tuition: $178 per credit hour.

FINANCIAL AID PICTURE (2007-2008)
Students with need: Need-based aid available for full-time and part-time students. Work study available nights.
Students without need: This college awards aid only to students with need.

FINANCIAL AID PROCEDURES
Forms required: FAFSA.
Dates and Deadlines: Priority date 4/15; no closing date. Applicants notified on a rolling basis.

CONTACT
Cynthia Bailey, Assistant Campus Dean for Student Services
750 West Bay Shore Street, Marinette, WI 54143
(715) 735-4301

University of Wisconsin-Marshfield/Wood County
Marshfield, Wisconsin
www.marshfield.uwc.edu Federal Code: 003897

2-year public branch campus college in large town.
Enrollment: 617 undergrads.

BASIC COSTS (2008-2009)
Tuition and fees: $4,572; out-of-state residents $11,556.
Per-credit charge: $178; out-of-state residents $469.
Additional info: Minnesota reciprocity tuition: $167 per credit hour.

FINANCIAL AID PICTURE (2007-2008)
Students with need: Need-based aid available for full-time and part-time students. Work study available nights, weekends, and for part-time students.
Students without need: This college awards aid only to students with need.
Scholarships offered: Special Entering Scholarships; $1,000; based on academic excellence; 2 awarded. Ken and Ardyce Helting Scholarship; $1,000; priority given to physically challenged or learning disabled; 1 awarded. Valedictorian, Salutatorian and National Merit Finalist and Semi-Finalists; $1,000, ACT of 25 or better. Greenhouse Scholarship; priority to students in Environmental Studies; 1 awarded. Patrice Ptacek Memorial Scholarship; 2 letters of recommendation; 1 awarded. Woman of the Future Scholarship; $1,000; must be full-time female freshman entering sophomore year, well-defined career goals other than nursing; 1 awarded.

FINANCIAL AID PROCEDURES
Forms required: FAFSA.
Dates and Deadlines: Priority date 4/15; no closing date. Applicants notified on a rolling basis starting 5/15; must reply within 3 week(s) of notification.

CONTACT
Marilyn Krump, Director of Financial Aid
2000 West Fifth Street, Marshfield, WI 54449
(715) 389-6500

University of Wisconsin-Milwaukee
Milwaukee, Wisconsin
www.uwm.edu Federal Code: 003896

4-year public university in very large city.
Enrollment: 22,909 undergrads, 13% part-time. 3,937 full-time freshmen.
Selectivity: Admits over 75% of applicants.

BASIC COSTS (2008-2009)
Tuition and fees: $7,309; out-of-state residents $17,038.
Per-credit charge: $272; out-of-state residents $677.
Room and board: $7,870.
Additional info: Minnesota reciprocity tuition: $343 per credit hour.

FINANCIAL AID PICTURE (2008-2009)
Students with need: Out of 3,131 full-time freshmen who applied for aid, 2,382 were judged to have need. Of these, 2,246 received aid, and 615 had their full need met. Average financial aid package met 53% of need; average scholarship/grant was $6,190; average loan was $3,704. For part-time students, average financial aid package was $8,754.
Students without need: 38 full-time freshmen who did not demonstrate need for aid received scholarships/grants; average award was $1,953. No-need awards available for academics, art, athletics.

FINANCIAL AID PROCEDURES
Forms required: FAFSA.
Dates and Deadlines: Priority date 3/1; no closing date. Applicants notified on a rolling basis starting 3/1.
Transfers: No deadline. Applicants notified on a rolling basis starting 3/15; must reply within 2 week(s) of notification.

CONTACT
Jane Hojan-Clark, Executive Director of Financial Aid
Box 749, Milwaukee, WI 53201
(414) 229-6300

University of Wisconsin-Oshkosh
Oshkosh, Wisconsin
www.uwosh.edu Federal Code: 003920

4-year public university in small city.
Enrollment: 10,078 undergrads, 12% part-time. 1,824 full-time freshmen.
Selectivity: Admits over 75% of applicants.

BASIC COSTS (2008-2009)
Tuition and fees: $6,037; out-of-state residents $13,610.
Per-credit charge: $216; out-of-state residents $532.
Room and board: $5,510.
Additional info: Minnesota reciprocity tuition: $230 per credit hour.

FINANCIAL AID PICTURE (2007-2008)
Students with need: Need-based aid available for full-time and part-time students.
Students without need: No-need awards available for academics, alumni affiliation, art, leadership, minority status, music/drama, state/district residency.

FINANCIAL AID PROCEDURES
Forms required: FAFSA.
Dates and Deadlines: Priority date 3/15; no closing date. Applicants notified on a rolling basis starting 4/15; must reply within 2 week(s) of notification.
Transfers: Must send financial aid transcript to university.

CONTACT
Beatrice Contreras, Director of Financial Aid
800 Algoma Boulevard, Oshkosh, WI 54901-8602
(920) 424-3377

University of Wisconsin-Parkside
Kenosha, Wisconsin
www.uwp.edu Federal Code: 005015

4-year public university in small city.
Enrollment: 4,757 undergrads, 23% part-time. 831 full-time freshmen.

Selectivity: Admits over 75% of applicants.

BASIC COSTS (2008-2009)

Tuition and fees: $6,070; out-of-state residents $13,908.
Per-credit charge: $212; out-of-state residents $538.
Room and board: $5,986.
Additional info: Minnesota Reciprocity tuition and fees: $6,510 full-time; $230 per credit hour.

FINANCIAL AID PICTURE (2007-2008)

Students with need: Out of 665 full-time freshmen who applied for aid, 533 were judged to have need. Of these, 510 received aid. Need-based aid available for part-time students.
Students without need: No-need awards available for academics, art, athletics, minority status, music/drama, state/district residency.

FINANCIAL AID PROCEDURES

Forms required: FAFSA.
Dates and Deadlines: Priority date 3/15; no closing date. Applicants notified on a rolling basis starting 4/1; must reply within 2 week(s) of notification.

CONTACT

Randall McCready, Director of Financial Aid
PO Box 2000, Kenosha, WI 53141-2000
(262) 595-2574

University of Wisconsin-Platteville

Platteville, Wisconsin
www.uwplatt.edu Federal Code: 003921

4-year public university in large town.
Enrollment: 6,435 undergrads, 9% part-time. 1,459 full-time freshmen.
Selectivity: Admits over 75% of applicants.

BASIC COSTS (2008-2009)

Tuition and fees: $6,147; out-of-state residents $13,720.
Per-credit charge: $216; out-of-state residents $532.
Room and board: $5,466.
Additional info: Minnesota reciprocity tuition: $230 per credit hour.

FINANCIAL AID PICTURE

Students with need: Need-based aid available for full-time and part-time students. Work study available nights, weekends, and for part-time students.
Students without need: This college awards aid only to students with need.

FINANCIAL AID PROCEDURES

Forms required: FAFSA.
Dates and Deadlines: Priority date 3/15; no closing date. Applicants notified on a rolling basis starting 6/1; must reply within 2 week(s) of notification.

CONTACT

Liz Tucker, Director of Financial Aid
One University Plaza, Platteville, WI 53818
(608) 342-1836

University of Wisconsin-Richland

Richland Center, Wisconsin
www.richland.uwc.edu Federal Code: 003897

2-year public liberal arts college in small town.
Enrollment: 472 undergrads.

BASIC COSTS (2008-2009)

Tuition and fees: $4,836; out-of-state residents $11,820.
Per-credit charge: $178; out-of-state residents $469.
Additional info: Minnesota reciprocity tuition: $178 per credit hour.

FINANCIAL AID PICTURE (2007-2008)

Students with need: 54% of average financial aid package awarded as scholarships/grants, 46% awarded as loans/jobs. Need-based aid available for part-time students. Work study available nights, weekends, and for part-time students.
Students without need: This college awards aid only to students with need.
Scholarships offered: Richland Campus Foundation Scholarships available for new, continuing and transfer students.

FINANCIAL AID PROCEDURES

Forms required: FAFSA.
Dates and Deadlines: Priority date 4/15; no closing date. Applicants notified on a rolling basis starting 5/15; must reply within 3 week(s) of notification.

CONTACT

John Poole, Assistant Campus Dean
1200 Highway 14 West, Richland Center, WI 53581
(608) 647-6186 ext. 3

University of Wisconsin-River Falls

River Falls, Wisconsin
www.uwrf.edu Federal Code: 003923

4-year public university and liberal arts college in large town.
Enrollment: 6,050 undergrads.
Selectivity: Admits over 75% of applicants.

BASIC COSTS (2008-2009)

Tuition and fees: $6,220; out-of-state residents $13,793.
Per-credit charge: $212; out-of-state residents $527.
Room and board: $5,106.
Additional info: Minnesota reciprocity tuition and fees: $6,591 full-time, $230 per credit hour.

FINANCIAL AID PICTURE (2008-2009)

Students with need: Need-based aid available for full-time and part-time students. Work study available nights, weekends, and for part-time students.
Students without need: This college awards aid only to students with need.

FINANCIAL AID PROCEDURES

Forms required: FAFSA.
Dates and Deadlines: Priority date 3/15; no closing date. Applicants notified on a rolling basis starting 4/1; must reply within 4 week(s) of notification.
Transfers: No deadline. Applicants notified on a rolling basis starting 4/1.

CONTACT

Barbara Stinson, Director of Financial Aid
410 South 3rd Street, River Falls, WI 54022-5001
(715) 425-3141

University of Wisconsin-Rock County

Janesville, Wisconsin
www.rock.uwc.edu Federal Code: 003897

2-year public branch campus and liberal arts college in small city.
Enrollment: 1,046 undergrads.

BASIC COSTS (2008-2009)

Tuition and fees: $4,561; out-of-state residents $11,545.
Per-credit charge: $178; out-of-state residents $469.
Additional info: Minnesota reciprocity tuition: $167 per credit hour.

FINANCIAL AID PICTURE (2007-2008)

Students with need: Need-based aid available for full-time and part-time students. Work study available nights, weekends, and for part-time students.

Students without need: This college awards aid only to students with need.

FINANCIAL AID PROCEDURES

Forms required: FAFSA, institutional form.
Dates and Deadlines: Priority date 4/15; no closing date. Applicants notified on a rolling basis starting 6/1; must reply within 3 week(s) of notification.

CONTACT

Marilyn Krump, Director of Financial Aid
2909 Kellogg Avenue, Janesville, WI 53546-5699
(608) 758-6523

University of Wisconsin-Sheboygan

Sheboygan, Wisconsin
www.sheboygan.uwc.edu Federal Code: 003897

2-year public community and junior college in small city.
Enrollment: 754 undergrads.

BASIC COSTS (2008-2009)

Tuition and fees: $4,545; out-of-state residents $11,529.
Per-credit charge: $178; out-of-state residents $469.
Additional info: Minnesota reciprocity tuition: $167 per credit hour.

FINANCIAL AID PICTURE (2008-2009)

Students with need: Need-based aid available for full-time and part-time students.
Students without need: No-need awards available for academics, leadership, music/drama.
Additional info: Scholarship deadline 2/28.

FINANCIAL AID PROCEDURES

Forms required: FAFSA, institutional form.
Dates and Deadlines: Priority date 4/15; no closing date. Applicants notified on a rolling basis starting 6/1; must reply within 2 week(s) of notification.
Transfers: No deadline. Applicants notified on a rolling basis.

CONTACT

Marilyn Krump, Director of Financial Aid
One University Drive, Sheboygan, WI 53081
(920) 459-6633

University of Wisconsin-Stevens Point

Stevens Point, Wisconsin
www.uwsp.edu Federal Code: 003924

4-year public university in large town.
Enrollment: 8,558 undergrads, 4% part-time. 1,643 full-time freshmen.
Selectivity: Admits 50 to 75% of applicants.

BASIC COSTS (2008-2009)

Tuition and fees: $6,200; out-of-state residents $13,773.
Per-credit charge: $211; out-of-state residents $527.
Room and board: $5,180.
Additional info: Minnesota reciprocity tuition and fees: $6,638 full-year or $230 per credit hour.

FINANCIAL AID PICTURE (2007-2008)

Students with need: Out of 1,272 full-time freshmen who applied for aid, 809 were judged to have need. Of these, 754 received aid, and 680 had their full need met. For part-time students, average financial aid package was $6,701.
Students without need: 117 full-time freshmen who did not demonstrate need for aid received scholarships/grants; average award was $2,178. No-need awards available for academics, alumni affiliation, art, music/drama, ROTC.
Cumulative student debt: 70% of graduating class had student loans; average debt was $19,123.
Additional info: Tuition discounts offered to qualified residents from other states.

FINANCIAL AID PROCEDURES

Forms required: FAFSA.
Dates and Deadlines: Priority date 5/15; closing date 6/15. Applicants notified on a rolling basis starting 5/1; must reply within 4 week(s) of notification.
Transfers: No deadline.

CONTACT

Paul Watson, Director of Financial Aid
Student Services Center, Stevens Point, WI 54481
(715) 346-4771

University of Wisconsin-Stout

Menomonie, Wisconsin
www.uwstout.edu Federal Code: 003915

4-year public university in large town.
Enrollment: 7,666 undergrads, 11% part-time. 1,621 full-time freshmen.
Selectivity: Admits 50 to 75% of applicants.

BASIC COSTS (2008-2009)

Tuition and fees: $7,584; out-of-state residents $15,330.
Per-credit charge: $189; out-of-state residents $447.
Room and board: $5,170.
Additional info: Laptop computer included in the cost of tuition.

FINANCIAL AID PICTURE (2008-2009)

Students with need: Out of 1,310 full-time freshmen who applied for aid, 812 were judged to have need. Of these, 809 received aid, and 399 had their full need met. Average financial aid package met 87% of need; average scholarship/grant was $5,933; average loan was $3,491. For part-time students, average financial aid package was $7,187.
Students without need: 29 full-time freshmen who did not demonstrate need for aid received scholarships/grants; average award was $1,217. No-need awards available for academics.
Scholarships offered: Wisconsin Academic Excellence Scholarship: $2,250; selected by high school. National Merit Finalist Scholarship: $2,000; automatically awarded to NMSQT finalist. National Merit Semifinalist Scholarship: $1,000; automatically awarded to NMSQT semifinalist. Chancellor's Academic Honor Scholarship: $1,000; automatically awarded to top 5% of high school class with ACT of 25 who enroll by July 15.
Cumulative student debt: 75% of graduating class had student loans; average debt was $26,072.

FINANCIAL AID PROCEDURES

Forms required: FAFSA.
Dates and Deadlines: Priority date 3/15; no closing date. Applicants notified on a rolling basis starting 4/1; must reply within 4 week(s) of notification.

CONTACT

Beth Boisen, Director of Financial Aid
1 Clocktower Plaza, Menomonie, WI 54751
(715) 232-1363

University of Wisconsin-Superior

Superior, Wisconsin
www.uwsuper.edu Federal Code: 003925

4-year public university and liberal arts college in small city.
Enrollment: 2,353 undergrads, 17% part-time. 303 full-time freshmen.
Selectivity: Admits 50 to 75% of applicants.

BASIC COSTS (2008-2009)
Tuition and fees: $6,360; out-of-state residents $13,933.
Per-credit charge: $212; out-of-state residents $464.
Room and board: $5,158.

FINANCIAL AID PICTURE (2008-2009)
Students with need: Out of 216 full-time freshmen who applied for aid, 165 were judged to have need. Of these, 163 received aid, and 73 had their full need met. For part-time students, average financial aid package was $7,643.
Students without need: 13 full-time freshmen who did not demonstrate need for aid received scholarships/grants; average award was $2,256. No-need awards available for academics, alumni affiliation, art, leadership, minority status, music/drama, ROTC, state/district residency.
Additional info: Tuition Assistance Program (TAP) available to non-resident students on limited basis.

FINANCIAL AID PROCEDURES
Forms required: FAFSA.
Dates and Deadlines: Priority date 4/1; no closing date. Applicants notified on a rolling basis starting 3/15; must reply by 5/1 or within 4 week(s) of notification.
Transfers: No deadline. Applicants notified on a rolling basis starting 3/15; must reply by 5/1 or within 4 week(s) of notification.

CONTACT
Anne Podgorak, Director of Financial Aid
Belknap and Catlin, PO Box 2000, Superior, WI 54880
(715) 394-8200

University of Wisconsin-Washington County
West Bend, Wisconsin
www.washington.uwc.edu Federal Code: 003897

2-year public branch campus and liberal arts college in large town.
Enrollment: 1,018 undergrads.

BASIC COSTS (2008-2009)
Tuition and fees: $4,618; out-of-state residents $11,602.
Per-credit charge: $178; out-of-state residents $469.
Additional info: Minnesota reciprocity tuition: $167 per credit hour.

FINANCIAL AID PICTURE (2007-2008)
Students with need: Need-based aid available for full-time and part-time students. Work study available weekends and for part-time students.
Students without need: No-need awards available for academics.

FINANCIAL AID PROCEDURES
Forms required: FAFSA.
Dates and Deadlines: Priority date 4/15; no closing date. Applicants notified on a rolling basis starting 4/30; must reply within 3 week(s) of notification.
Transfers: No deadline.

CONTACT
Marilyn Krump, Director of Financial Aid
400 University Drive, West Bend, WI 53095
(262) 335-5207

University of Wisconsin-Waukesha
Waukesha, Wisconsin
www.waukesha.uwc.edu Federal Code: 003897

2-year public branch campus and junior college in small city.
Enrollment: 1,764 undergrads, 37% part-time. 791 full-time freshmen.

BASIC COSTS (2008-2009)
Tuition and fees: $4,560; out-of-state residents $11,544.
Per-credit charge: $178; out-of-state residents $469.
Additional info: Minnesota reciprocity tuition: $175 per credit hour.

FINANCIAL AID PICTURE (2008-2009)
Students with need: Need-based aid available for full-time and part-time students. Work study available nights, weekends, and for part-time students.
Students without need: No-need awards available for academics, art, leadership, minority status, music/drama.
Scholarships offered: University of Wisconsin-Waukesha Scholarship Program; numerous scholarships; amounts vary.

FINANCIAL AID PROCEDURES
Forms required: FAFSA.
Dates and Deadlines: Priority date 4/15; no closing date. Applicants notified on a rolling basis starting 5/15; must reply within 3 week(s) of notification.

CONTACT
Judy Becker, Coordinator of Financial Aid
1500 University Drive, Waukesha, WI 53188
(262) 521-5210

University of Wisconsin-Whitewater
Whitewater, Wisconsin
www.uww.edu Federal Code: 003926

4-year public university in large town.
Enrollment: 9,452 undergrads, 7% part-time. 2,105 full-time freshmen.
Selectivity: Admits 50 to 75% of applicants.

BASIC COSTS (2008-2009)
Tuition and fees: $6,162; out-of-state residents $13,736.
Room and board: $4,790.

FINANCIAL AID PICTURE (2008-2009)
Students with need: Need-based aid available for full-time and part-time students. Work study available nights, weekends, and for part-time students.
Students without need: No-need awards available for academics, alumni affiliation, art, leadership, minority status, music/drama, ROTC, state/district residency.

FINANCIAL AID PROCEDURES
Forms required: FAFSA.
Dates and Deadlines: Priority date 3/15; no closing date. Applicants notified on a rolling basis starting 4/1; must reply within 3 week(s) of notification.
Transfers: No deadline. Applicants notified on a rolling basis starting 4/1; must reply within 3 week(s) of notification.

CONTACT
Carol Miller, Director of Financial Aid
800 West Main Street, Whitewater, WI 53190-1790
(262) 472-1130

Viterbo University
La Crosse, Wisconsin
www.viterbo.edu Federal Code: 003911

4-year private university and liberal arts college in small city, affiliated with Roman Catholic Church.
Enrollment: 1,997 undergrads, 24% part-time. 358 full-time freshmen.
Selectivity: Admits over 75% of applicants.

BASIC COSTS (2009-2010)
Tuition and fees: $20,160.
Per-credit charge: $580.
Room and board: $7,510.

Additional info: Additional fees for some fine arts, dietetics, science courses, and nursing clinicals. Tuition/fee waivers available for minority students.

FINANCIAL AID PICTURE

Students with need: Need-based aid available for full-time and part-time students. Work study available nights, weekends, and for part-time students.

Students without need: No-need awards available for academics, alumni affiliation, art, athletics, leadership, minority status, music/drama, ROTC.

Scholarships offered: Fine arts scholarships: up to $10,000 per year; for incoming full-time freshmen and transfer students talented in areas of art, music or theater. Dr. Scholl Scholarship: full, 4-year tuition; must enroll full-time and maintain 3.5 GPA, 1 awarded. Viterbo University Scholarship: $1,000-$8,000 per year; based on academic history; incoming freshmen and transfers automatically considered; renewable.

FINANCIAL AID PROCEDURES

Forms required: FAFSA, institutional form.

Dates and Deadlines: Priority date 3/15; no closing date. Applicants notified on a rolling basis starting 4/1; must reply within 3 week(s) of notification.

CONTACT

Terry Norman, Director of Financial Aid
900 Viterbo Drive, La Crosse, WI 54601-8804
(608) 796-3900

Waukesha County Technical College

Pewaukee, Wisconsin
www.wctc.edu Federal Code: 005294

2-year public technical college in large town.

Enrollment: 5,076 undergrads, 61% part-time. 482 full-time freshmen.

Selectivity: Open admission; but selective for some programs.

BASIC COSTS (2008-2009)

Tuition and fees: $3,206; out-of-state residents $18,122.

Per-credit charge: $97; out-of-state residents $594.

Additional info: Materials fees vary by program; minimum $4 per course. $10 per credit fee for online courses.

FINANCIAL AID PICTURE

Students with need: Need-based aid available for full-time students. Work study available nights.

Students without need: No-need awards available for academics.

FINANCIAL AID PROCEDURES

Forms required: FAFSA, institutional form.

Dates and Deadlines: Priority date 3/31; no closing date. Applicants notified on a rolling basis.

CONTACT

Ben Dobner, Manager/Financial Aid
800 Main Street, Pewaukee, WI 53072
(262) 691-5436

Western Technical College

La Crosse, Wisconsin
www.westerntc.edu Federal Code: 003840

2-year public community and technical college in small city.

Enrollment: 3,932 undergrads, 55% part-time. 456 full-time freshmen.

Selectivity: Open admission; but selective for some programs.

BASIC COSTS (2008-2009)

Tuition and fees: $3,164; out-of-state residents $18,080.

Per-credit charge: $97; out-of-state residents $594.

Room and board: $3,896.

Additional info: Materials fees vary by program; minimum $4.50 per course. Tuition/fee waivers available for unemployed or children of unemployed.

FINANCIAL AID PICTURE (2007-2008)

Students with need: 51% of average financial aid package awarded as scholarships/grants, 49% awarded as loans/jobs. Need-based aid available for part-time students. Work study available nights, weekends, and for part-time students.

FINANCIAL AID PROCEDURES

Forms required: FAFSA, institutional form.

Dates and Deadlines: Priority date 3/1; no closing date. Applicants notified on a rolling basis starting 4/1.

CONTACT

Jerolyn Grandall, Student Financial Services Manager
PO Box 908, La Crosse, WI 54602-0908
(608) 785-9302

Wisconsin Indianhead Technical College

Shell Lake, Wisconsin
www.witc.edu Federal Code: 011824

2-year public technical college in rural community.

Enrollment: 3,007 undergrads, 53% part-time. 329 full-time freshmen.

Selectivity: Open admission; but selective for some programs.

BASIC COSTS (2008-2009)

Tuition and fees: $3,212; out-of-state residents $18,128.

Per-credit charge: $97; out-of-state residents $594.

Additional info: Materials fees vary by program; minimum $4 per course. $10 per credit fee for online courses.

FINANCIAL AID PICTURE (2007-2008)

Students with need: Need-based aid available for full-time and part-time students. Work study available nights, weekends, and for part-time students.

Students without need: This college awards aid only to students with need.

FINANCIAL AID PROCEDURES

Forms required: FAFSA.

Dates and Deadlines: Priority date 4/1; no closing date. Applicants notified on a rolling basis starting 5/9; must reply by 9/1 or within 4 week(s) of notification.

CONTACT

Terry Klein, Director of Financial Aid
505 Pine Ridge Drive, Shell Lake, WI 54871
(715) 468-2815 ext. 2243

Wisconsin Lutheran College

Milwaukee, Wisconsin
www.wlc.edu Federal Code: 014658

4-year private liberal arts college in very large city, affiliated with Wisconsin Evangelical Lutheran Synod.

Enrollment: 755 undergrads.

Selectivity: Admits over 75% of applicants.

BASIC COSTS (2008-2009)

Tuition and fees: $20,560.

Per-credit charge: $600.

Room and board: $7,300.

FINANCIAL AID PICTURE

Students with need: Need-based aid available for full-time and part-time students. Work study available nights, weekends, and for part-time students.

Students without need: No-need awards available for academics, art, leadership, minority status, music/drama, state/district residency.

Scholarships offered: Presidential Scholarship: $8,000 ($9,000 if ACT is 30 or greater); based on ACT score of 27 or higher plus top 10% of HS class or 3.7 GPA; no limit on number of awards. Academic Scholarship: $7,500; ACT score of 24 or higher and top 25% of high school class or 3.4 GPA. To qualify, students must be admitted in good standing by May 1.

FINANCIAL AID PROCEDURES

Forms required: FAFSA, institutional form.

Dates and Deadlines: Priority date 3/1; no closing date. Applicants notified on a rolling basis starting 3/15; must reply within 2 week(s) of notification.

Transfers: Transfer scholarship and transfer grant available for qualifying students.

CONTACT

Linda Loeffel, Financial Aid Director
8800 West Bluemound Road, Milwaukee, WI 53226-4699
(414) 443-8856

Wyoming

Casper College

Casper, Wyoming
www.caspercollege.edu Federal Code: 003928

2-year public community college in small city.

Enrollment: 2,701 undergrads, 31% part-time. 659 full-time freshmen.

Selectivity: Open admission; but selective for some programs and for out-of-state students.

BASIC COSTS (2008-2009)

Tuition and fees: $1,752; out-of-state residents $4,872.

Per-credit charge: $65; out-of-state residents $195.

Room and board: $3,980.

Additional info: Western Undergraduate Exchange students pay $93.50 per credit-hour and $2,244 per year for full-time students.

FINANCIAL AID PICTURE (2008-2009)

Students with need: Need-based aid available for full-time and part-time students. Work study available nights, weekends, and for part-time students.

Students without need: No-need awards available for academics, art, athletics, leadership, music/drama, state/district residency.

FINANCIAL AID PROCEDURES

Forms required: FAFSA.

Dates and Deadlines: Priority date 3/15; no closing date. Applicants notified on a rolling basis starting 4/1.

Transfers: No deadline. Applicants notified on a rolling basis starting 4/1.

CONTACT

Darry Voigt, Director of Financial Aid
125 College Drive, Casper, WY 82601
(307) 268-2510

Central Wyoming College

Riverton, Wyoming
www.cwc.edu Federal Code: 005018

2-year public community college in large town.

Enrollment: 1,150 undergrads, 40% part-time. 284 full-time freshmen.

Selectivity: Open admission; but selective for some programs.

BASIC COSTS (2008-2009)

Tuition and fees: $2,064; out-of-state residents $5,184.

Per-credit charge: $65; out-of-state residents $195.

Room and board: $4,322.

Additional info: Western Undergraduate Exchange students pay $2,592 or $98 per credit hour.

FINANCIAL AID PICTURE (2008-2009)

Students with need: Out of 169 full-time freshmen who applied for aid, 130 were judged to have need. Of these, 130 received aid. Need-based aid available for part-time students.

Students without need: No-need awards available for academics, alumni affiliation, art, athletics, leadership, minority status, music/drama, state/district residency.

Scholarships offered: Honors Scholarships: in-state tuition and general fees plus $300 book stipend; for graduating high school seniors with minimum 3.5 GPA or 25 ACT. Seniors Scholarships: in-state tuition; for graduating high school seniors with 3.0-3.49 GPA or 22 ACT. Full academic scholarships: in-state tuition, general fees, room and board, books and supplies; for Wyoming National Merit finalists.

Cumulative student debt: 30% of graduating class had student loans; average debt was $6,625.

FINANCIAL AID PROCEDURES

Forms required: FAFSA, institutional form.

Dates and Deadlines: Priority date 4/15; no closing date. Applicants notified on a rolling basis starting 5/1; must reply within 2 week(s) of notification.

CONTACT

Jacque Burns, Director of Financial Aid
2660 Peck Avenue, Riverton, WY 82501
(307) 855-2150

Eastern Wyoming College

Torrington, Wyoming
ewc.wy.edu Federal Code: 003929

2-year public community college in small town.

Enrollment: 678 undergrads, 32% part-time. 195 full-time freshmen.

Selectivity: Open admission.

BASIC COSTS (2008-2009)

Tuition and fees: $2,072; out-of-state residents $5,192.

Per-credit charge: $65; out-of-state residents $195.

Room and board: $3,666.

Additional info: Students from Western Undergraduate Exchange pay $2,232 tuition plus fees per year; $98 per credit hour.

FINANCIAL AID PICTURE

Students with need: Need-based aid available for full-time and part-time students. Work study available nights, weekends, and for part-time students.

Students without need: No-need awards available for academics, alumni affiliation, art, athletics, leadership, music/drama.

Additional info: Installment payment plan on room and board contracts offered.

FINANCIAL AID PROCEDURES

Forms required: FAFSA, institutional form.

Dates and Deadlines: Priority date 3/15; no closing date. Applicants notified on a rolling basis starting 1/1.

CONTACT

Pam Palermo, Financial Aid Director
3200 West C Street, Torrington, WY 82240
(800) 658-3195 ext. 8325

Laramie County Community College

Cheyenne, Wyoming
www.lccc.wy.edu Federal Code: 009259

2-year public community college in small city.
Enrollment: 3,165 undergrads, 44% part-time. 299 full-time freshmen.
Selectivity: Open admission; but selective for some programs.

BASIC COSTS (2008-2009)

Tuition and fees: $2,208; out-of-state residents $5,328.
Per-credit charge: $65; out-of-state residents $195.
Room and board: $5,974.
Additional info: Students from Western Undergraduate Exchange schools and Nebraska residents pay $3,000 in tuition and fees per year; $125 per credit hour.

FINANCIAL AID PICTURE (2007-2008)

Students with need: Need-based aid available for full-time and part-time students.
Students without need: No-need awards available for academics, art, athletics, music/drama.

FINANCIAL AID PROCEDURES

Forms required: FAFSA, institutional form.
Dates and Deadlines: Priority date 4/1; no closing date. Applicants notified on a rolling basis starting 6/1; must reply within 2 week(s) of notification.

CONTACT

Dennis Schroeder, Director of Financial Aid
1400 East College Drive, Cheyenne, WY 82007-3299
(307) 778-1215

Northwest College

Powell, Wyoming
www.northwestcollege.edu Federal Code: 003931

2-year public community college in small town.
Enrollment: 1,819 undergrads.
Selectivity: Open admission; but selective for some programs and for out-of-state students.

BASIC COSTS (2008-2009)

Tuition and fees: $2,107; out-of-state residents $5,227.
Per-credit charge: $65; out-of-state residents $195.
Room and board: $4,674.
Additional info: Students from Western Undergraduate Exchange schools pay $2,352 tuition; $98 per credit hour.

FINANCIAL AID PICTURE (2007-2008)

Students with need: 64% of average financial aid package awarded as scholarships/grants, 36% awarded as loans/jobs. Work study available nights.
Students without need: No-need awards available for academics, athletics.
Additional info: Interview, essay recommended for scholarships.

FINANCIAL AID PROCEDURES

Forms required: FAFSA, institutional form.
Dates and Deadlines: Priority date 5/1; no closing date. Applicants notified on a rolling basis starting 5/1; must reply within 2 week(s) of notification.

CONTACT

Beverly Bell, Director of Financial Aid
231 West 6th Street, Powell, WY 82435
(307) 754-6104

Sheridan College

Sheridan, Wyoming
www.sheridan.edu Federal Code: 003930

2-year public community college in large town.
Enrollment: 1,521 undergrads, 40% part-time. 283 full-time freshmen.
Selectivity: Open admission; but selective for some programs.

BASIC COSTS (2008-2009)

Tuition and fees: $2,131; out-of-state residents $5,251.
Per-credit charge: $65; out-of-state residents $195.
Room and board: $4,300.

FINANCIAL AID PICTURE (2007-2008)

Students with need: Need-based aid available for full-time and part-time students. Work study available nights, weekends, and for part-time students.
Students without need: No-need awards available for academics, art, athletics, leadership, music/drama, state/district residency.
Scholarships offered: Merit scholarships; in-state tuition and fees; must have 25 ACT or 1120 SAT (exclusive of Writing); renewable.

FINANCIAL AID PROCEDURES

Forms required: FAFSA, institutional form.
Dates and Deadlines: Priority date 3/1; no closing date. Applicants notified on a rolling basis; must reply within 3 week(s) of notification.

CONTACT

Randy Thompson, Director of Financial Aid
PO Box 1500, Sheridan, WY 82801-1500
(307) 674-6446 ext. 2100

University of Wyoming

Laramie, Wyoming
www.uwyo.edu Federal Code: 003932

4-year public university in large town.
Enrollment: 9,304 undergrads, 15% part-time. 1,638 full-time freshmen.
Selectivity: Admits over 75% of applicants.

BASIC COSTS (2009-2010)

Tuition and fees: $3,686; out-of-state residents $11,606.
Per-credit charge: $94; out-of-state residents $358.
Room and board: $8,006.
Additional info: International students must pay an additional $40 fee per semester.

FINANCIAL AID PICTURE (2007-2008)

Students with need: Out of 1,205 full-time freshmen who applied for aid, 711 were judged to have need. Of these, 693 received aid, and 190 had their full need met. Average financial aid package met 35% of need; average scholarship/grant was $3,085; average loan was $2,816. For part-time students, average financial aid package was $5,931.
Students without need: 167 full-time freshmen who did not demonstrate need for aid received scholarships/grants; average award was $3,475. No-need awards available for academics, alumni affiliation, art, athletics, leadership, minority status, music/drama, religious affiliation, ROTC, state/district residency.
Scholarships offered: ***Merit:*** Western Heritage Scholarship: number awarded and packages vary. President's High School Honor Scholarship: covers undergraduate fees and tuition; number awarded varies. ***Athletic:*** 63 full-time freshmen received athletic scholarships; average amount $10,403.
Cumulative student debt: 48% of graduating class had student loans; average debt was $16,307.

FINANCIAL AID PROCEDURES

Forms required: FAFSA.

Dates and Deadlines: Priority date 2/1; no closing date. Applicants notified on a rolling basis starting 3/15; must reply within 3 week(s) of notification.

CONTACT

David Gruen, Director of Student Financial Aid
1000 East University Avenue/Department 3435, Laramie, WY 82071
(307) 766-2116

Western Wyoming Community College

Rock Springs, Wyoming
www.wwcc.wy.edu Federal Code: 003933

2-year public community college in large town.
Enrollment: 2,139 undergrads, 53% part-time. 230 full-time freshmen.
Selectivity: Open admission; but selective for some programs.

BASIC COSTS (2008-2009)

Tuition and fees: $1,916; out-of-state residents $5,036.
Per-credit charge: $65; out-of-state residents $195.
Room and board: $3,900.

FINANCIAL AID PICTURE (2008-2009)

Students with need: 60% of average financial aid package awarded as scholarships/grants, 40% awarded as loans/jobs. Need-based aid available for part-time students.
Students without need: No-need awards available for academics, art, athletics, music/drama, state/district residency.

FINANCIAL AID PROCEDURES

Forms required: FAFSA.
Dates and Deadlines: Priority date 4/1; no closing date. Applicants notified on a rolling basis starting 2/15; must reply within 2 week(s) of notification.

CONTACT

Stacee Hanson, Financial Aid Director
Box 428, Rock Springs, WY 82902-0428
(307) 382-1643

Part IV

Scholarship Lists

Academic scholarships

Alabama
Alabama State University
Amridge University
Athens State University
Auburn University at Montgomery
Bevill State Community College
Birmingham-Southern College
Bishop State Community College
Calhoun Community College
Central Alabama Community College
Chattahoochee Valley Community College
Enterprise-Ozark Community College
Faulkner University
Gadsden State Community College
George C. Wallace State Community College
  George C. Wallace Community College at Dothan
  Selma
Huntingdon College
Jacksonville State University
Jefferson Davis Community College
Jefferson State Community College
Judson College
Lurleen B. Wallace Community College
Northeast Alabama Community College
Northwest-Shoals Community College
Oakwood University
Samford University
Snead State Community College
Southeastern Bible College
Spring Hill College
Talladega College
Troy University
Tuskegee University
University of Alabama
University of Alabama
  Birmingham
  Huntsville
University of Mobile
University of Montevallo
University of North Alabama
University of South Alabama
University of West Alabama
Wallace State Community College at Hanceville

Alaska
Alaska Bible College
Alaska Pacific University
University of Alaska
  Anchorage
  Fairbanks
  Southeast

Arizona
Arizona State University
Arizona Western College
Art Center Design College
Cochise College
DeVry University
  Phoenix
Dine College
Eastern Arizona College
Embry-Riddle Aeronautical University: Prescott Campus
Grand Canyon University
Mesa Community College
Northern Arizona University
Northland Pioneer College
Pima Community College
Prescott College
Scottsdale Community College
South Mountain Community College
Southwestern College
University of Arizona
Yavapai College

Arkansas
Arkansas Northeastern College
Arkansas State University
Arkansas State University
  Beebe
  Mountain Home
Arkansas Tech University
Central Baptist College
Crowley's Ridge College
Ecclesia College
Harding University
Henderson State University
Hendrix College
John Brown University
Lyon College
Mid-South Community College
National Park Community College
North Arkansas College
Northwest Arkansas Community College
Ouachita Baptist University
Philander Smith College
Phillips Community College of the University of Arkansas
Rich Mountain Community College
Southeast Arkansas College
Southern Arkansas University
Southern Arkansas University Tech
University of Arkansas
University of Arkansas
  Community College at Batesville
  Community College at Hope
  Fort Smith
  Monticello
  Pine Bluff
University of Arkansas Community College at Morrilton
University of Central Arkansas
University of the Ozarks
Williams Baptist College

California
Academy of Art University
Alliant International University
American Academy of Dramatic Arts: West
American Jewish University
Art Institute
  of California: Los Angeles
  of California: Orange County
Azusa Pacific University
Bethany University
Bethesda Christian University
Biola University
California Baptist University
California College of the Arts
California Institute of Integral Studies
California Institute of Technology
California Institute of the Arts
California Lutheran University
California Maritime Academy
California Polytechnic State University: San Luis Obispo
California State Polytechnic University: Pomona
California State University
  Chico
  Dominguez Hills
  Fresno
  Fullerton
  Long Beach
  Monterey Bay
  Northridge
  San Marcos
  Stanislaus
Chaffey College
Chapman University
Claremont McKenna College
Cogswell Polytechnical College
College of the Canyons
College of the Siskiyous
Columbia College
Concordia University
Deep Springs College
  Fremont
  Long Beach
  Pomona
  Sherman Oaks
Dominican University of California
East Los Angeles College
El Camino College
Empire College
Fashion Institute of Design and Merchandising
  Los Angeles
  San Diego
  San Francisco
Fresno Pacific University
Glendale Community College
Golden Gate University
Golden West College
Harvey Mudd College
Holy Names University
Hope International University
Humboldt State University
Humphreys College
The King's College and Seminary
La Sierra University
Life Pacific College
Loyola Marymount University
Marymount College
The Master's College
Mendocino College
Menlo College
Merced College
Mills College
Mount St. Mary's College
Mount San Jacinto College
National Hispanic University
NewSchool of Architecture & Design
Notre Dame de Namur University
Occidental College
Ohlone College
Orange Coast College
Otis College of Art and Design
Pacific States University
Patten University
Pepperdine University
Pitzer College
Riverside Community College
St. Mary's College of California
Samuel Merritt University
San Diego Christian College
San Diego State University
San Francisco Art Institute
San Francisco State University
San Joaquin Delta College
San Jose State University
Santa Clara University
Santa Rosa Junior College
School of Urban Missions: Oakland
Scripps College
Simpson University
Soka University of America
Sonoma State University
Southern California Institute of Architecture
Taft College
University of California
  Berkeley
  Irvine
  Los Angeles
  Riverside
  San Diego
  Santa Barbara
  Santa Cruz
University of California: Merced
University of La Verne
University of Redlands
University of San Diego
University of San Francisco
University of Southern California
University of the Pacific
Vanguard University of Southern California
Westmont College
Westwood College of Technology
  Westwood College: Inland Empire
Whittier College
William Jessup University
Woodbury University
Yuba Community College District

Colorado
Adams State College
Arapahoe Community College
Boulder College of Massage Therapy
Colorado Christian University
Colorado College
Colorado Mountain College
Colorado Northwestern Community College
Colorado School of Mines
Colorado State University
Colorado State University
  Pueblo
Colorado Technical University
Community College of Denver
  Westminster
Fort Lewis College
Front Range Community College
Johnson & Wales University: Denver
Mesa State College
Metropolitan State College of Denver
Northeastern Junior College
Otero Junior College
Pueblo Community College
Regis University
Remington College
  Colorado Springs
Rocky Mountain College of Art & Design
Trinidad State Junior College
University of Colorado
  Boulder
  Colorado Springs
  Denver
University of Denver
University of Northern Colorado
Western State College of Colorado
Westwood College: Denver North

Connecticut
Albertus Magnus College
Briarwood College
Central Connecticut State University
Clemens College
Eastern Connecticut State University
Fairfield University
Housatonic Community College
Lyme Academy College of Fine Arts
Mitchell College
Northwestern Connecticut Community College
Norwalk Community College
Quinnipiac University
Sacred Heart University
St. Joseph College
Three Rivers Community College
Trinity College
Tunxis Community College
University of Bridgeport
University of Connecticut
University of Hartford
University of New Haven
Wesleyan University
Western Connecticut State University

Delaware
Delaware State University
Goldey-Beacom College
University of Delaware
Wesley College

Wilmington University

District of Columbia
American University
Catholic University of America
Corcoran College of Art and Design
Gallaudet University
George Washington University
Howard University
Southeastern University
Trinity Washington University

Florida
Art Institute of Fort Lauderdale
Baptist College of Florida
Barry University
Beacon College
Bethune-Cookman University
Brevard Community College
Broward College
Carlos Albizu University
Central Florida Community College
Chipola College
Clearwater Christian College
Miramar
Orlando
Eckerd College
Embry-Riddle Aeronautical University
Embry-Riddle Aeronautical University: Worldwide Campus
Flagler College
Florida Agricultural and Mechanical University
Florida Atlantic University
Florida Christian College
Florida College
Florida Community College at Jacksonville
Florida Gulf Coast University
Florida Institute of Technology
Florida International University
Florida Keys Community College
Florida Southern College
Florida State University
Gulf Coast Community College
Hillsborough Community College
Hobe Sound Bible College
Hodges University
Indian River State College
International Academy of Design and Technology: Tampa
Jacksonville University
Johnson & Wales University: North Miami
Jones College
Lake City Community College
Lake-Sumter Community College
Lynn University
Manatee Community College
Miami Dade College
New College of Florida
North Florida Community College
Northwest Florida State College
Northwood University
Florida
Nova Southeastern University
Palm Beach Atlantic University
Palm Beach Community College
Pasco-Hernando Community College
Pensacola Junior College
Polk Community College
Ringling College of Art and Design
Rollins College
St. Leo University
St. Petersburg College
Saint Thomas University
Santa Fe College
Schiller International University
Seminole Community College
South Florida Community College
South University: West Palm Beach
Southeastern University
Stetson University
Tallahassee Community College
Trinity College of Florida
University of Central Florida
University of Florida
University of Miami
University of North Florida
University of South Florida
University of Tampa
University of West Florida
Warner University
Webber International University

Georgia
Agnes Scott College
Albany State University
Albany Technical College
Andrew College
Armstrong Atlantic State University of Atlanta
Athens Technical College
Augusta State University
Berry College
Brenau University
Brewton-Parker College
Clark Atlanta University
Clayton State University
College of Coastal Georgia
Columbus State University
Covenant College
Dalton State College
Darton College
Alpharetta
Decatur
East Georgia College
Emmanuel College
Emory University
Fort Valley State University
Gainesville State College
Georgia College and State University
Georgia Highlands College
Georgia Institute of Technology
Georgia Southern University
Georgia Southwestern State University
Georgia State University
Gordon College
Herzing College
Kennesaw State University
LaGrange College
Life University
Macon State College
Medical College of Georgia
Mercer University
Middle Georgia College
Morehouse College
North Georgia College & State University
Oglethorpe University
Oxford College of Emory University
Paine College
Piedmont College
Reinhardt College
Savannah College of Art and Design
Savannah River College
Savannah State University
Savannah Technical College
Shorter College
South Georgia College
Southern Polytechnic State University
Spelman College
Thomas University
Toccoa Falls College
Truett-McConnell College
University of Georgia
University of West Georgia
Valdosta State University
Waycross College
Wesleyan College
Young Harris College

Hawaii
Brigham Young University-Hawaii
Chaminade University of Honolulu
Hawaii Pacific University
Hawaii Tokai International College
University of Hawaii
Honolulu Community College
Manoa
West Oahu

Idaho
Boise Bible College
Boise State University
Brigham Young University-Idaho
College of Idaho
Eastern Idaho Technical College
Idaho State University
Lewis-Clark State College
North Idaho College
Northwest Nazarene University
University of Idaho

Illinois
Augustana College
Aurora University
Benedictine University
Black Hawk College
Blackburn College
Bradley University
Carl Sandburg College
Chicago State University
City Colleges of Chicago
Kennedy-King College
Malcolm X College
College of DuPage
College of Lake County
Columbia College Chicago
Concordia University Chicago
Danville Area Community College
DePaul University
Addison
Chicago
Tinley Park
DeVry University: Online
Dominican University
East-West University
Eastern Illinois University
Elgin Community College
Elmhurst College
Eureka College
Governors State University
Greenville College
Harper College
Harrington College of Design
Heartland Community College
Highland Community College
Illinois College
Illinois Eastern Community Colleges
Frontier Community College
Lincoln Trail College
Olney Central College
Wabash Valley College
Illinois Institute of Art: Schaumburg
Illinois Institute of Technology
Illinois State University
Illinois Wesleyan University
Joliet Junior College
Judson University
Kaskaskia College
Kendall College
Kishwaukee College
Knox College
Lake Forest College
Lake Land College
Lewis University
Lexington College
Lincoln Christian College and Seminary
Lincoln College
Lincoln Land Community College
Loyola University Chicago
MacCormac College
MacMurray College
McHenry County College
McKendree University
Millikin University
Monmouth College
Moody Bible Institute
Moraine Valley Community College
Morrison Institute of Technology
National-Louis University
North Central College
North Park University
Northeastern Illinois University
Northern Illinois University
Northwestern Business College
Northwestern University
Oakton Community College
Olivet Nazarene University
Parkland College
Principia College
Quincy University
Rend Lake College
Richland Community College
Robert Morris College: Chicago
Rock Valley College
Rockford College
Roosevelt University
Saint Anthony College of Nursing
St. Francis Medical Center College of Nursing
St. Xavier University
Sauk Valley Community College
School of the Art Institute of Chicago
Shimer College
South Suburban College of Cook County
Southeastern Illinois College
Southern Illinois University Carbondale
Southern Illinois University Edwardsville
Spoon River College
Springfield College in Illinois
Trinity Christian College
Trinity International University
Triton College
University of Chicago
University of Illinois
Chicago
Springfield
Urbana-Champaign
University of St. Francis
VanderCook College of Music
Waubonsee Community College
West Suburban College of Nursing
Western Illinois University
Western Illinois University: Quad Cities
Wheaton College

Indiana
Ancilla College
Anderson University
Ball State University
Bethel College
Butler University
Calumet College of St. Joseph
DePauw University
DeVry University: Indianapolis
Earlham College
Franklin College
Goshen College
Grace College
Hanover College
Holy Cross College
Huntington University
Indiana Institute of Technology
Indiana State University
Indiana University
Bloomington
East
Kokomo
Northwest
South Bend
Southeast
Indiana University-Purdue University Fort Wayne
Indiana University-Purdue University Indianapolis
Indiana Wesleyan University
Manchester College
Marian College
Oakland City University
Purdue University
Purdue University

Calumet
North Central
Rose-Hulman Institute of Technology
Saint Joseph's College
St. Mary-of-the-Woods College
Saint Mary's College
Taylor University
Trine University
University of Evansville
University of Indianapolis
University of St. Francis
University of Southern Indiana
Valparaiso University
Vincennes University
Wabash College

Iowa
AIB College of Business
Allen College
Ashford University
Briar Cliff University
Buena Vista University
Central College
Clarke College
Coe College
Cornell College
Des Moines Area Community College
Dordt College
Drake University
Ellsworth Community College
Emmaus Bible College
Faith Baptist Bible College and Theological Seminary
Graceland University
Grand View University
Grinnell College
Hawkeye Community College
Indian Hills Community College
Iowa Central Community College
Iowa State University
Iowa Wesleyan College
Kaplan University
Cedar Falls
Cedar Rapids
Davenport
Mason City
Loras College
Luther College
Mercy College of Health Sciences
Morningside College
Mount Mercy College
North Iowa Area Community College
Northeast Iowa Community College
Northwestern College
St. Ambrose University
St. Luke's College
Simpson College
Southeastern Community College
North Campus
Southwestern Community College
University of Dubuque
University of Iowa
University of Northern Iowa
Upper Iowa University
Vatterott College
Waldorf College
Wartburg College
Western Iowa Tech Community College
William Penn University

Kansas
Allen County Community College
Baker University
Barclay College
Barton County Community College
Benedictine College
Bethany College
Bethel College
Central Christian College of Kansas
Coffeyville Community College
Colby Community College
Cowley County Community College
Dodge City Community College
Donnelly College
Emporia State University
Fort Hays State University
Friends University
Garden City Community College
Hesston College
Highland Community College
Hutchinson Community College
Independence Community College
Johnson County Community College
Kansas City Kansas Community College
Kansas State University
Kansas Wesleyan University
Labette Community College
Manhattan Christian College
McPherson College
MidAmerica Nazarene University
Neosho County Community College
Newman University
North Central Kansas Technical College
Ottawa University
Pittsburg State University
Pratt Community College
Seward County Community College
Southwestern College
Sterling College
Tabor College
University of Kansas
University of Kansas Medical Center
University of St. Mary
Washburn University
Wichita State University

Kentucky
Asbury College
Ashland Community and Technical College
Beckfield College
Bellarmine University
Big Sandy Community and Technical College
Brescia University
Centre College
Clear Creek Baptist Bible College
Daymar College
Owensboro
Eastern Kentucky University
Georgetown College
Hopkinsville Community College
Jefferson Community and Technical College
Kentucky Christian University
Kentucky Mountain Bible College
Kentucky State University
Kentucky Wesleyan College
Louisville Technical Institute
Maysville Community and Technical College
Mid-Continent University
Midway College
Morehead State University
Murray State University
National College
Danville
Florence
Lexington
Louisville
Pikeville
Richmond
Northern Kentucky University
Owensboro Community and Technical College
St. Catharine College
Somerset Community College
Southeast Kentucky Community and Technical College
Spalding University
Spencerian College: Lexington
Thomas More College
Transylvania University
Union College
University of Kentucky
University of Louisville
University of the Cumberlands
Western Kentucky University

Louisiana
Baton Rouge Community College
Bossier Parish Community College
Centenary College of Louisiana
Delgado Community College
Dillard University
Grambling State University
Louisiana College
Louisiana State University
Alexandria
Louisiana State University and Agricultural and Mechanical College
Louisiana State University Health Sciences Center
Louisiana Tech University
Loyola University New Orleans
McNeese State University
Nicholls State University
Northwestern State University
Our Lady of Holy Cross College
Baton Rouge
St. Joseph Seminary College
School of Urban Missions: New Orleans
Southeastern Louisiana University
Southern University and Agricultural and Mechanical College
Tulane University
University of Louisiana at Lafayette
University of Louisiana at Monroe
University of New Orleans

Maine
Bowdoin College
College of the Atlantic
Eastern Maine Community College
Husson University
Maine College of Art
Maine Maritime Academy
New England School of Communications
St. Joseph's College
Thomas College
Unity College
University of Maine
University of Maine
Augusta
Farmington
Fort Kent
Machias
Presque Isle
University of New England
University of Southern Maine
Washington County Community College
York County Community College

Maryland
Allegany College of Maryland
Baltimore Hebrew University
Baltimore International College
Bowie State University
Capitol College
Carroll Community College
Cecil College
Chesapeake College
College of Notre Dame of Maryland
College of Southern Maryland
Columbia Union College
Community College of Baltimore County
Coppin State University
DeVry University: Bethesda
Frederick Community College
Frostburg State University
Garrett College
Goucher College
Hood College
Johns Hopkins University
Johns Hopkins University: Peabody Conservatory of Music
Loyola College in Maryland
Maryland Institute College of Art
McDaniel College
Montgomery College
Mount St. Mary's University
Prince George's Community College
St. Mary's College of Maryland
Salisbury University
Stevenson University
Towson University
University of Maryland
Baltimore County
College Park
Eastern Shore
University College
Washington Bible College
Washington College
Wor-Wic Community College

Massachusetts
American International College
Anna Maria College
Assumption College
Atlantic Union College
Babson College
Bard College at Simon's Rock
Bay Path College
Becker College
Benjamin Franklin Institute of Technology
Bentley University
Berkshire Community College
Boston Architectural College
Boston College
Boston University
Brandeis University
Bridgewater State College
Bristol Community College
Bunker Hill Community College
Cape Cod Community College
Caritas Laboure College
Clark University
College of the Holy Cross
Curry College
Dean College
Elms College
Emerson College
Emmanuel College
Endicott College
Fisher College
Fitchburg State College
Framingham State College
Franklin W. Olin College of Engineering
Gordon College
Hampshire College
Hellenic College/Holy Cross
Holyoke Community College
Lasell College
Lesley University
Marian Court College
Massachusetts College of Art and Design
Massachusetts College of Liberal Arts
Massachusetts College of Pharmacy and Health Sciences
Massachusetts Maritime Academy
Merrimack College
Montserrat College of Art
Mount Holyoke College
Mount Wachusett Community College
New England Conservatory of Music
New England Institute of Art
Newbury College
Nichols College
North Shore Community College
Northeastern University
Northern Essex Community College
Pine Manor College
Quinsigamond Community College
Regis College
Simmons College
Smith College
Stonehill College
Suffolk University
Tufts University
University of Massachusetts
Amherst
Boston
Dartmouth

Lowell
Wentworth Institute of Technology
Western New England College
Wheaton College
Wheelock College
Worcester Polytechnic Institute
Worcester State College
Zion Bible College

Michigan
Adrian College
Albion College
Alma College
Alpena Community College
Andrews University
Aquinas College
Baker College
of Auburn Hills
of Cadillac
of Clinton Township
of Flint
of Jackson
of Muskegon
of Owosso
of Port Huron
Bay de Noc Community College
Calvin College
Central Michigan University
Cleary University
College for Creative Studies
Concordia University
Cornerstone University
Davenport University
Eastern Michigan University
Ferris State University
Finlandia University
Glen Oaks Community College
Gogebic Community College
Grace Bible College
Grand Rapids Community College
Grand Valley State University
Great Lakes Christian College
Hillsdale College
Hope College
Jackson Community College
Kalamazoo College
Kalamazoo Valley Community College
Kellogg Community College
Kendall College of Art and Design of Ferris State University
Kettering University
Kirtland Community College
Kuyper College
Lake Superior State University
Lansing Community College
Lawrence Technological University
Macomb Community College
Madonna University
Marygrove College
Michigan Jewish Institute
Michigan State University
Michigan Technological University
Monroe County Community College
Montcalm Community College
Mott Community College
Northern Michigan University
Northwestern Michigan College
Northwood University: Michigan
Oakland Community College
Oakland University
Olivet College
Rochester College
Sacred Heart Major Seminary
Saginaw Valley State University
Schoolcraft College
Siena Heights University
Southwestern Michigan College
Spring Arbor University
University of Detroit Mercy
University of Michigan
University of Michigan
Dearborn
Flint
Walsh College of Accountancy and Business Administration
Washtenaw Community College
Wayne State University
Western Michigan University

Minnesota
Anoka Technical College
Augsburg College
Bemidji State University
Bethany Lutheran College
Bethel University
Brown College
Carleton College
College of St. Benedict
College of St. Catherine
College of St. Scholastica
College of Visual Arts
Concordia College: Moorhead
Concordia University: St. Paul
Crossroads College
Crown College
Dakota County Technical College
Edina
Dunwoody College of Technology
Fond du Lac Tribal and Community College
Gustavus Adolphus College
Hamline University
Inver Hills Community College
Itasca Community College
Lake Superior College
Le Cordon Bleu College of Culinary Arts
Macalester College
Martin Luther College
Metropolitan State University
Minneapolis College of Art and Design
Minnesota School of Business: Shakopee
Minnesota State College - Southeast Technical
Minnesota State Community and Technical College
Minnesota State University
Mankato
Moorhead
National American University
St. Paul
Normandale Community College
North Hennepin Community College
Northland Community & Technical College
Northwestern College
Oak Hills Christian College
Pine Technical College
Rainy River Community College
Saint Cloud State University
St. Cloud Technical College
St. John's University
St. Mary's University of Minnesota
St. Olaf College
Southwest Minnesota State University
University of Minnesota
Crookston
Duluth
Morris
Twin Cities
University of St. Thomas
Winona State University

Mississippi
Alcorn State University
Belhaven College
Blue Mountain College
Coahoma Community College
Copiah-Lincoln Community College
Delta State University
East Central Community College
East Mississippi Community College
Hinds Community College
Holmes Community College
Itawamba Community College
Jackson State University
Magnolia Bible College
Meridian Community College
Millsaps College
Mississippi College
Mississippi Delta Community College
Mississippi Gulf Coast Community College
Mississippi State University
Mississippi University for Women
Mississippi Valley State University
Pearl River Community College
Rust College
Tougaloo College
University of Mississippi
University of Mississippi Medical Center
William Carey University

Missouri
Avila University
Baptist Bible College
Calvary Bible College and Theological Seminary
Central Methodist University
Chamberlain College of Nursing
College of the Ozarks
Columbia College
Conception Seminary College
Cottey College
Crowder College
Culver-Stockton College
Kansas City
Drury University
East Central College
Evangel University
Fontbonne University
Goldfarb School of Nursing at Barnes-Jewish College
Hannibal-LaGrange College
Harris-Stowe State University
Jefferson College
Kansas City Art Institute
Lincoln University
Lindenwood University
Maryville University of Saint Louis
Metropolitan Community College: Blue River
Metropolitan Community College: Longview
Metropolitan Community College: Maple Woods
Metropolitan Community College: Penn Valley
Mineral Area College
Missouri Baptist University
Missouri Southern State University
Missouri State University
Missouri State University: West Plains
Missouri Technical School
Missouri Valley College
Missouri Western State University
Moberly Area Community College
North Central Missouri College
Northwest Missouri State University
Ozark Christian College
Park University
Research College of Nursing
Rockhurst University
St. Charles Community College
St. Louis Christian College
St. Louis Community College
Saint Louis University
Southeast Missouri State University
Southwest Baptist University
State Fair Community College
Stephens College
Three Rivers Community College
Truman State University
University of Central Missouri
University of Missouri
Columbia
Kansas City
Missouri University of Science and Technology
St. Louis
Washington University in St. Louis
Webster University
Westminster College
William Jewell College
William Woods University

Montana
Carroll College
Dawson Community College
Flathead Valley Community College
Miles Community College
Montana State University
Billings
Bozeman
Northern
Montana Tech of the University of Montana
Rocky Mountain College
Stone Child College
University of Great Falls
University of Montana
University of Montana: Western

Nebraska
Bellevue University
BryanLGH College of Health Sciences
Central Community College
Chadron State College
Clarkson College
College of Saint Mary
Concordia University
Creative Center
Creighton University
Doane College
Grace University
Metropolitan Community College
Mid-Plains Community College Area
Nebraska Christian College
Nebraska Methodist College of Nursing and Allied Health
Nebraska Wesleyan University
Northeast Community College
Peru State College
Southeast Community College
Union College
University of Nebraska
Kearney
Lincoln
Omaha
Wayne State College
Western Nebraska Community College
York College

Nevada
Art Institute of Las Vegas
DeVry University: Henderson
Sierra Nevada College
Truckee Meadows Community College
University of Nevada
Las Vegas
Reno
University of Southern Nevada
Western Nevada College

New Hampshire
Chester College of New England
Colby-Sawyer College
Daniel Webster College
Franklin Pierce University
Hesser College
Keene State College
New England College
Plymouth State University
Rivier College
St. Anselm College
Southern New Hampshire University
Thomas More College of Liberal Arts
University of New Hampshire
University of New Hampshire at Manchester

New Jersey
Berkeley College
Bloomfield College
Burlington County College
Caldwell College
Centenary College
The College of New Jersey
College of St. Elizabeth
Cumberland County College

DeVry University: North Brunswick
Drew University
Fairleigh Dickinson University
College at Florham
Metropolitan Campus
Felician College
Georgian Court University
Kean University
Mercer County Community College
Monmouth University
Montclair State University
New Jersey Institute of Technology
Ocean County College
Passaic County Community College
Ramapo College of New Jersey
Raritan Valley Community College
Richard Stockton College of New Jersey
Rider University
Rowan University
Rutgers, The State University of New Jersey
Camden Regional Campus
New Brunswick/Piscataway Campus
Newark Regional Campus
Saint Peter's College
Salem Community College
Seton Hall University
Somerset Christian College
Stevens Institute of Technology
Union County College
Warren County Community College
William Paterson University of New Jersey

New Mexico

Art Center Design College
Central New Mexico Community College
Clovis Community College
Eastern New Mexico University
Mesalands Community College
Navajo Technical College
New Mexico Highlands University
New Mexico Institute of Mining and Technology
New Mexico Junior College
New Mexico Military Institute
New Mexico State University
New Mexico State University
Alamogordo
Carlsbad
Northern New Mexico College
St. John's College
San Juan College
Santa Fe Community College
Southwestern Indian Polytechnic Institute
University of New Mexico
University of the Southwest
Western New Mexico University

New York

Adelphi University
Adirondack Community College
Albany College of Pharmacy and Health Sciences
Alfred University
ASA Institute of Business and Computer Technology
Bard College
Berkeley College
Berkeley College of New York City
Briarcliffe College
Bryant & Stratton Business Institute
Bryant & Stratton College: Albany
Bryant & Stratton College: Syracuse
Canisius College
Cayuga County Community College
Cazenovia College
City University of New York
Baruch College
Brooklyn College
City College
College of Staten Island
Hunter College
John Jay College of Criminal Justice
Lehman College
Medgar Evers College
Queens College
York College
Clarkson University
College of Mount St. Vincent
College of New Rochelle
College of Saint Rose
College of Westchester
Columbia University
School of General Studies
Columbia-Greene Community College
Concordia College
Cooper Union for the Advancement of Science and Art
Culinary Institute of America
Daemen College
DeVry
Devry College of New York
Dominican College of Blauvelt
Dowling College
D'Youville College
Eastman School of Music of the University of Rochester
Elmira College
Eugene Lang College The New School for Liberal Arts
Fashion Institute of Technology
Finger Lakes Community College
Five Towns College
Fordham University
Fulton-Montgomery Community College
Hartwick College
Hilbert College
Hobart and William Smith Colleges
Hofstra University
Houghton College
Iona College
Ithaca College
Jamestown Business College
Jamestown Community College
Jefferson Community College
Jewish Theological Seminary of America
Keuka College
King's College
Laboratory Institute of Merchandising
Le Moyne College
Long Island Business Institute
Manhattan College
Manhattan School of Music
Manhattanville College
Mannes College The New School for Music
Marist College
Marymount Manhattan College
Medaille College
Mercy College
Metropolitan College of New York
Molloy College
Monroe College
Monroe Community College
Mount St. Mary College
Nassau Community College
Nazareth College
New York Institute of Technology
New York University
Niagara County Community College
Niagara University
Nyack College
Onondaga Community College
Pace University
Parsons The New School for Design
Paul Smith's College
Polytechnic Institute of New York University
Pratt Institute
Rensselaer Polytechnic Institute
Roberts Wesleyan College
Rochester Institute of Technology
Russell Sage College
Sage College of Albany
Saint Bonaventure University
St. Francis College
St. John Fisher College
St. John's University
St. Joseph's College
St. Joseph's College: Suffolk Campus
St. Lawrence University
St. Thomas Aquinas College
Schenectady County Community College
Siena College
State University of New York
Albany
Binghamton
Buffalo
College at Brockport
College at Buffalo
College at Cortland
College at Fredonia
College at Geneseo
College at Old Westbury
College at Oneonta
College at Plattsburgh
College at Potsdam
College of Agriculture and Technology at Cobleskill
College of Agriculture and Technology at Morrisville
College of Environmental Science and Forestry
College of Technology at Alfred
College of Technology at Canton
Farmingdale
Institute of Technology at Utica/Rome
Maritime College
New Paltz
Oswego
Purchase
Stony Brook
Suffolk County Community College
Syracuse University
Tompkins Cortland Community College
Trocaire College
Union College
University of Rochester
Utica College
Vaughn College of Aeronautics and Technology
Villa Maria College of Buffalo
Wagner College
Webb Institute
Wells College
Westchester Community College
Yeshiva Mikdash Melech

North Carolina

Alamance Community College
Appalachian State University
Asheville-Buncombe Technical Community College
Barton College
Beaufort County Community College
Belmont Abbey College
Blue Ridge Community College
Brevard College
Brunswick Community College
Campbell University
Cape Fear Community College
Carolinas College of Health Sciences
Carteret Community College
Catawba College
Catawba Valley Community College
Central Carolina Community College
Central Piedmont Community College
Chowan University
Coastal Carolina Community College
College of the Albemarle
Davidson College
Davidson County Community College
DeVry University: Charlotte
Duke University
Durham Technical Community College
East Carolina University
Elizabeth City State University
Elon University
Fayetteville State University
Forsyth Technical Community College
Gardner-Webb University
Gaston College
Greensboro College
Guilford College
Haywood Community College
High Point University
Isothermal Community College
James Sprunt Community College
Johnson & Wales University: Charlotte
Johnson C. Smith University
Johnston Community College
Lees-McRae College
Lenoir Community College
Lenoir-Rhyne University
Livingstone College
Mars Hill College
Martin Community College
McDowell Technical Community College
Meredith College
Methodist University
Montgomery Community College
Montreat College
Mount Olive College
Nash Community College
North Carolina Agricultural and Technical State University
North Carolina Central University
North Carolina State University
North Carolina Wesleyan College
Peace College
Pfeiffer University
Pitt Community College
Randolph Community College
Richmond Community College
Roanoke Bible College
Roanoke-Chowan Community College
Rockingham Community College
Rowan-Cabarrus Community College
St. Andrews Presbyterian College
St. Augustine's College
Salem College
Sampson Community College
Sandhills Community College
Shaw University
Southeastern Community College
Stanly Community College
Surry Community College
University of North Carolina
Asheville
Chapel Hill
Charlotte
Greensboro
Pembroke
Wilmington
University of North Carolina School of the Arts
Vance-Granville Community College
Wake Forest University
Wake Technical Community College
Warren Wilson College
Wayne Community College
Western Carolina University
Western Piedmont Community College
Wilkes Community College
Wilson Community College
Wingate University
Winston-Salem State University

North Dakota

Bismarck State College
Dickinson State University
Jamestown College
Lake Region State College
Mayville State University
Minot State University
Minot State University: Bottineau Campus
North Dakota State College of Science
North Dakota State University
University of Mary
University of North Dakota
Valley City State University
Williston State College

Ohio

Art Academy of Cincinnati
Art Institute of Cincinnati
Ashland University
Baldwin-Wallace College
Bluffton University
Bowling Green State University
Bowling Green State University: Firelands College
Bryant & Stratton College
  Eastlake
Bryant & Stratton College: Cleveland
Capital University
Case Western Reserve University
Cedarville University
Central Ohio Technical College
Central State University
Chatfield College
Cincinnati Christian University
Cincinnati State Technical and Community College
Cleveland Institute of Art
Cleveland Institute of Music
Cleveland State University
College of Mount St. Joseph
College of Wooster
Columbus College of Art and Design
Cuyahoga Community College
  Metropolitan Campus
Defiance College
Denison University
  Columbus
Edison State Community College
Franciscan University of Steubenville
Franklin University
God's Bible School and College
Heidelberg University
Hiram College
Hocking College
James A. Rhodes State College
Jefferson Community College
John Carroll University
Kent State University
Kent State University
  Ashtabula
  East Liverpool
  Salem
  Stark
  Trumbull
  Tuscarawas
Kent State University: Geauga
Kenyon College
Kettering College of Medical Arts
Lake Erie College
Lakeland Community College
Lourdes College
Malone University
Marietta College
Marion Technical College
MedCentral College of Nursing
Mercy College of Northwest Ohio
Miami University
  Hamilton Campus
  Oxford Campus
Mount Union College
Mount Vernon Nazarene University
Muskingum College
Northwest State Community College
Notre Dame College
Oberlin College
Ohio Christian University
Ohio Dominican University
Ohio Northern University
Ohio State University
  Agricultural Technical Institute
  Columbus Campus
  Lima Campus
  Mansfield Campus
  Marion Campus
  Newark Campus
Ohio University
Ohio University
  Eastern Campus
  Southern Campus at Ironton
Ohio Wesleyan University
Otterbein College
Owens Community College
  Toledo
Pontifical College Josephinum
School of Advertising Art
Shawnee State University
Sinclair Community College
Southern State Community College
Stark State College of Technology
Terra State Community College
Tiffin University
Union Institute & University
University of Akron
University of Akron: Wayne College
University of Cincinnati
University of Cincinnati
  Clermont College
  Raymond Walters College
University of Dayton
University of Findlay
University of Northwestern Ohio
University of Rio Grande
University of Toledo
Urbana University
Ursuline College
Walsh University
Wilmington College
Wittenberg University
Wright State University
Wright State University: Lake Campus
Xavier University
Youngstown State University

Oklahoma

Cameron University
Carl Albert State College
Connors State College
DeVry University: Oklahoma City Center
East Central University
Langston University
Mid-America Christian University
Northeastern Oklahoma Agricultural and Mechanical College
Northeastern State University
Northwestern Oklahoma State University
Oklahoma Baptist University
Oklahoma Christian University
Oklahoma City Community College
Oklahoma City University
Oklahoma Panhandle State University
Oklahoma State University
Oklahoma State University
  Oklahoma City
Oklahoma Wesleyan University
Oral Roberts University
Redlands Community College
Rogers State University
Rose State College
St. Gregory's University
Seminole State College
Southeastern Oklahoma State University
Southern Nazarene University
Southwestern Christian University
Southwestern Oklahoma State University
Tulsa Community College
University of Central Oklahoma
University of Oklahoma
University of Science and Arts of Oklahoma
University of Tulsa
Western Oklahoma State College

Oregon

Central Oregon Community College
Chemeketa Community College
Clackamas Community College
Clatsop Community College
Concordia University
Corban College
DeVry University: Portland
Eastern Oregon University
Eugene Bible College
George Fox University
Lewis & Clark College
Linfield College
Linn-Benton Community College
Marylhurst University
Mt. Hood Community College
Multnomah University
Northwest Christian University
Oregon College of Art & Craft
Oregon Health & Science University
Oregon Institute of Technology
Oregon State University
Pacific Northwest College of Art
Pacific University
Portland State University
Southern Oregon University
Treasure Valley Community College
Umpqua Community College
University of Oregon
University of Portland
Warner Pacific College
Western Oregon University
Willamette University

Pennsylvania

Albright College
Allegheny College
Alvernia University
Arcadia University
Baptist Bible College of Pennsylvania
Berks Technical Institute
Bloomsburg University of Pennsylvania
Bryn Athyn College of the New Church
Bryn Mawr College
Bucknell University
Bucks County Community College
Butler County Community College
Cabrini College
California University of Pennsylvania
Cambria-Rowe Business College
Carlow University
Carnegie Mellon University
Cedar Crest College
Central Pennsylvania College
Chatham University
Chestnut Hill College
Cheyney University of Pennsylvania
Clarion University of Pennsylvania
Community College of Allegheny County
Community College of Beaver County
Delaware Valley College
DeSales University
  Fort Washington
Dickinson College
Drexel University
Duquesne University
East Stroudsburg University of Pennsylvania
Edinboro University of Pennsylvania
Elizabethtown College
Franklin & Marshall College
Gannon University
Geneva College
Gettysburg College
Grove City College
Gwynedd-Mercy College
Harcum College
Harrisburg Area Community College
Harrisburg University of Science and Technology
Holy Family University
Immaculata University
Indiana University of Pennsylvania
Johnson College
Juniata College
Keystone College
King's College
Kutztown University of Pennsylvania
La Roche College
La Salle University
Lackawanna College
Lafayette College
Lancaster Bible College
Laurel Technical Institute
Lebanon Valley College
Lehigh Carbon Community College
Lehigh University
Lincoln University
Lock Haven University of Pennsylvania
Lycoming College
Manor College
Mansfield University of Pennsylvania
Marywood University
Mercyhurst College
Messiah College
Millersville University of Pennsylvania
Misericordia University
Montgomery County Community College
Moore College of Art and Design
Moravian College
Mount Aloysius College
Muhlenberg College
Newport Business Institute: Lower Burrell
Northampton Community College
Penn State
  Abington
  Altoona
  Beaver
  Berks
  Brandywine
  DuBois
  Erie, The Behrend College
  Fayette, The Eberly Campus
  Greater Allegheny
  Harrisburg
  Hazleton
  Lehigh Valley
  Mont Alto
  New Kensington
  Schuylkill
  Shenango
  University Park
  Wilkes-Barre
  Worthington Scranton
  York
Pennsylvania College of Technology
Pennsylvania Highlands Community College
Pennsylvania Institute of Technology
Philadelphia Biblical University
Philadelphia University
Point Park University
Robert Morris University
Rosemont College
St. Francis University
Saint Joseph's University
St. Vincent College
Seton Hill University
Shippensburg University of Pennsylvania
Slippery Rock University of Pennsylvania
Susquehanna University
Swarthmore College
Temple University
Thiel College
Thomas Jefferson University: College of Health Professions
Triangle Tech
  DuBois
  Pittsburgh
University of Pittsburgh
University of Pittsburgh
  Bradford
  Greensburg
  Johnstown
  Titusville
University of Scranton
University of the Arts
University of the Sciences in Philadelphia
Ursinus College
Valley Forge Christian College
Valley Forge Military Academy & College
Vet Tech Institute
Villanova University
Washington & Jefferson College
Waynesburg University

Westminster College
Westmoreland County Community College
Widener University
Wilkes University
Wilson College
York College of Pennsylvania

Puerto Rico
Colegio Pentecostal Mizpa
Inter American University of Puerto Rico
  Aguadilla Campus
  Arecibo Campus
  Bayamon Campus
  San German Campus
National College of Business and Technology: Rio Grande
Pontifical Catholic University of Puerto Rico
Turabo University
Universidad del Este
Universidad Metropolitana
Universidad Politecnica de Puerto Rico
University of Puerto Rico
  Bayamon University College
  Cayey University College
  Humacao
  Mayaguez
  Utuado
University of the Sacred Heart

Rhode Island
Bryant University
Johnson & Wales University: Providence
New England Institute of Technology
Providence College
Rhode Island College
Roger Williams University
Salve Regina University
University of Rhode Island

South Carolina
Aiken Technical College
Allen University
Anderson University
Charleston Southern University
The Citadel
Clemson University
Coastal Carolina University
College of Charleston
Columbia College
Columbia International University
Converse College
Erskine College
Florence-Darlington Technical College
Francis Marion University
Furman University
Greenville Technical College
Horry-Georgetown Technical College
Lander University
Limestone College
Medical University of South Carolina
Morris College
Newberry College
North Greenville University
Piedmont Technical College
Presbyterian College
South Carolina State University
Southern Wesleyan University
Spartanburg Methodist College
Tri-County Technical College
University of South Carolina
University of South Carolina
  Aiken
  Beaufort
  Salkehatchie Regional Campus
  Sumter
  Union
  Upstate
Williamsburg Technical College
Winthrop University
Wofford College
York Technical College

South Dakota
Augustana College
Black Hills State University
Dakota State University
Dakota Wesleyan University
Kilian Community College
Mount Marty College
Northern State University
South Dakota School of Mines and Technology
South Dakota State University
Southeast Technical Institute
University of Sioux Falls
University of South Dakota

Tennessee
Aquinas College
Austin Peay State University
Belmont University
Bethel College
Carson-Newman College
Christian Brothers University
Columbia State Community College
Crichton College
Cumberland University
DeVry University: Memphis
Dyersburg State Community College
East Tennessee State University
Fisk University
Free Will Baptist Bible College
Freed-Hardeman University
Jackson State Community College
Johnson Bible College
King College
Lambuth University
Lane College
Lee University
LeMoyne-Owen College
Lincoln Memorial University
Lipscomb University
Martin Methodist College
Maryville College
Memphis College of Art
Middle Tennessee State University
Milligan College
Motlow State Community College
Nashville State Community College
  Nashville
National College of Business & Technology
  National College: Bristol
O'More College of Design
Pellissippi State Technical Community College
Rhodes College
Roane State Community College
Southern Adventist University
Southwest Tennessee Community College
Tennessee State University
Tennessee Technological University
Tennessee Temple University
Tennessee Wesleyan College
Trevecca Nazarene University
Tusculum College
Union University
University of Memphis
University of Tennessee
  Chattanooga
  Knoxville
  Martin
University of Tennessee Health Science Center
University of the South
Vanderbilt University
Volunteer State Community College
Walters State Community College

Texas
Abilene Christian University
Alvin Community College
Angelina College
Angelo State University
Austin College
Austin Graduate School of Theology
Baylor University
Brazosport College
Central Texas College
Clarendon College
Coastal Bend College
College of Saint Thomas More
College of the Mainland
Collin County Community College District
Commonwealth Institute of Funeral Service
Concordia University Texas
Dallas Baptist University
  Irving
DeVry University: Houston
East Texas Baptist University
El Paso Community College
Frank Phillips College
Galveston College
Hardin-Simmons University
Hill College
Houston Baptist University
Howard College
Howard Payne University
Huston-Tillotson University
Jacksonville College
Jarvis Christian College
Kilgore College
Lee College
LeTourneau University
Lon Morris College
Lone Star College System
Lubbock Christian University
McMurry University
Midland College
Midwestern State University
North Central Texas College
North Lake College
Northwest Vista College
Northwood University: Texas
Odessa College
Our Lady of the Lake University of San Antonio
Palo Alto College
Panola College
Prairie View A&M University
Rice University
St. Edward's University
St. Mary's University
Sam Houston State University
San Jacinto College
Schreiner University
South Plains College
South Texas College
Southern Methodist University
Southwestern Adventist University
Southwestern University
Stephen F. Austin State University
Sul Ross State University
Tarleton State University
Tarrant County College
Texarkana College
Texas A&M International University
Texas A&M University
Texas A&M University
  Baylor College of Dentistry
  Commerce
  Corpus Christi
  Galveston
  Kingsville
  Texarkana
Texas Christian University
Texas Lutheran University
Texas Southern University
Texas State Technical College
  Waco
  West Texas
Texas State University: San Marcos
Texas Tech University
Texas Tech University Health Sciences Center
Texas Wesleyan University
Trinity University
Tyler Junior College
University of Dallas
University of Houston
University of Houston
  Downtown
  Victoria
University of Mary Hardin-Baylor
University of North Texas
University of St. Thomas
University of Texas
  Austin
  Dallas
  El Paso
  Medical Branch at Galveston
  Pan American
  of the Permian Basin
  San Antonio
  Tyler
University of the Incarnate Word
Victoria College
Wayland Baptist University
West Texas A&M University
Western Technical College
Western Texas College
Wharton County Junior College

Utah
Brigham Young University
College of Eastern Utah
DeVry University: Sandy
Dixie State College of Utah
LDS Business College
Salt Lake Community College
Snow College
Southern Utah University
University of Utah
Utah State University
Utah Valley University
Weber State University
Western Governors University
Westminster College

Vermont
Bennington College
Burlington College
Castleton State College
Champlain College
College of St. Joseph in Vermont
Goddard College
Green Mountain College
Johnson State College
Landmark College
Lyndon State College
Marlboro College
New England Culinary Institute
Norwich University
St. Michael's College
Southern Vermont College
Sterling College
University of Vermont
Vermont Technical College

Virginia
Averett University
Blue Ridge Community College
Bluefield College
Bridgewater College
  Richmond
Central Virginia Community College
Christendom College
Christopher Newport University
College of William and Mary
  Arlington
Eastern Mennonite University
ECPI College of Technology: Virginia Beach
Emory & Henry College
Ferrum College
George Mason University
Germanna Community College
Hampden-Sydney College
Hampton University
Hollins University
J. Sargeant Reynolds Community College
James Madison University
Jefferson College of Health Sciences
John Tyler Community College
Liberty University

Longwood University
Lynchburg College
Mary Baldwin College
Marymount University
Mountain Empire Community College
- Bluefield
- Charlottesville
- Danville
- Harrisonburg
- Lynchburg
- Martinsville

Norfolk State University
Northern Virginia Community College
Old Dominion University
Patrick Henry College
Piedmont Virginia Community College
Radford University
Randolph College
Randolph-Macon College
Regent University
Richard Bland College
Roanoke College
St. Paul's College
Shenandoah University
Southern Virginia University
Southside Virginia Community College
Southwest Virginia Community College
Sweet Briar College
University of Mary Washington
University of Richmond
University of Virginia
University of Virginia's College at Wise
Virginia Commonwealth University
Virginia Military Institute
Virginia State University
Virginia Union University
Virginia Wesleyan College
Virginia Western Community College
Washington and Lee University
Wytheville Community College

Washington

Art Institute of Seattle
Bastyr University
Bellevue Community College
Big Bend Community College
Central Washington University
Centralia College
City University of Seattle
Clark College
Columbia Basin College
Cornish College of the Arts
- Federal Way

Eastern Washington University
Everett Community College
Evergreen State College
Gonzaga University
Grays Harbor College
Heritage University
Northwest College of Art
Northwest Indian College
Northwest University
Olympic College
Pacific Lutheran University
Peninsula College
Pierce College
Saint Martin's University
Seattle Pacific University
Seattle University
Skagit Valley College
South Puget Sound Community College
South Seattle Community College
Tacoma Community College
Trinity Lutheran College
University of Puget Sound
University of Washington
University of Washington Bothell
Walla Walla Community College
Walla Walla University
Washington State University
Wenatchee Valley College
Western Washington University
Whatcom Community College
Whitman College
Whitworth University
Yakima Valley Community College

West Virginia

Alderson-Broaddus College
Bethany College
Bluefield State College
Concord University
Davis and Elkins College
Fairmont State University
Glenville State College
Marshall University
Mountain State University
Ohio Valley University
Potomac State College of West Virginia University
Salem International University
Shepherd University
University of Charleston
West Liberty State College
West Virginia State Community and Technical College
West Virginia State University
West Virginia University
West Virginia University at Parkersburg
West Virginia Wesleyan College
Wheeling Jesuit University

Wisconsin

Alverno College
Beloit College
Cardinal Stritch University
Carroll University
Carthage College
Columbia College of Nursing
Concordia University Wisconsin
DeVry University: Milwaukee
Edgewood College
Lakeland College
Lakeshore Technical College
Lawrence University
Maranatha Baptist Bible College
Marian University
Marquette University
Mid-State Technical College
Milwaukee Area Technical College
Milwaukee Institute of Art & Design
Milwaukee School of Engineering
Moraine Park Technical College
Mount Mary College
Northland College
Ripon College
St. Norbert College
Silver Lake College
University of Wisconsin
- Baraboo/Sauk County
- Eau Claire
- Fond du Lac
- Green Bay
- La Crosse
- Madison
- Marshfield/Wood County
- Milwaukee
- Oshkosh
- Parkside
- Richland
- River Falls
- Rock County
- Sheboygan
- Stevens Point
- Stout
- Superior
- Washington County
- Waukesha
- Whitewater

Viterbo University
Waukesha County Technical College
Wisconsin Lutheran College

Wyoming

Casper College
Central Wyoming College
Eastern Wyoming College
Laramie County Community College
Northwest College
Sheridan College
University of Wyoming
Western Wyoming Community College

Art scholarships

Alabama
Alabama State University
Athens State University
Auburn University at Montgomery
Birmingham-Southern College
Chattahoochee Valley Community College
Enterprise-Ozark Community College
Faulkner University
Gadsden State Community College
Jacksonville State University
Jefferson State Community College
Judson College
Lurleen B. Wallace Community College
Northeast Alabama Community College
Northwest-Shoals Community College
Snead State Community College
Talladega College
Troy University
University of Alabama
University of Alabama
  Birmingham
  Huntsville
University of Montevallo
University of North Alabama
University of South Alabama

Alaska
University of Alaska
  Fairbanks

Arizona
Arizona State University
Eastern Arizona College
Northern Arizona University
Northland Pioneer College
Pima Community College
University of Arizona

Arkansas
Arkansas State University
Harding University
Henderson State University
Hendrix College
John Brown University
Lyon College
Southern Arkansas University
University of Arkansas
University of Arkansas
  Pine Bluff
University of Central Arkansas
University of the Ozarks
Williams Baptist College

California
Academy of Art University
Art Institute
  of California: Orange County
Biola University
California Baptist University
California College of the Arts
California Institute of Integral Studies
California Institute of the Arts
California Lutheran University
California Polytechnic State University: San Luis Obispo
California State University
  Chico
  Dominguez Hills
  Fresno
  Long Beach
  Stanislaus
Chapman University
College of the Canyons
College of the Siskiyous
Concordia University
El Camino College
Irvine Valley College
Loyola Marymount University
The Master's College
Mount St. Mary's College
Otis College of Art and Design
Pepperdine University
Riverside Community College
San Diego State University
San Francisco Art Institute
Santa Rosa Junior College
Sonoma State University
University of California
  Irvine
  Riverside
  San Diego
  Santa Cruz
University of La Verne
University of Redlands
University of Southern California
Westmont College
Whittier College

Colorado
Adams State College
Colorado State University
Colorado State University
  Pueblo
Fort Lewis College
Mesa State College
Metropolitan State College of Denver
Northeastern Junior College
Pueblo Community College
Rocky Mountain College of Art & Design
University of Colorado
  Boulder
  Denver
University of Denver
University of Northern Colorado
Western State College of Colorado

Connecticut
Albertus Magnus College
Fairfield University
Lyme Academy College of Fine Arts
Northwestern Connecticut Community College
Sacred Heart University
University of Connecticut
University of Hartford

Delaware
University of Delaware

District of Columbia
Corcoran College of Art and Design
George Washington University
Howard University

Florida
Barry University
Chipola College
Eckerd College
Edison State College
Flagler College
Florida Agricultural and Mechanical University
Florida Community College at Jacksonville
Florida International University
Florida Keys Community College
Florida Southern College
Hillsborough Community College
Jacksonville University
Lake-Sumter Community College
Manatee Community College
Miami Dade College
North Florida Community College
Northwest Florida State College
Ringling College of Art and Design
Rollins College
St. Petersburg College
Santa Fe College
Seminole Community College
Stetson University
Tallahassee Community College
University of Florida
University of South Florida
University of Tampa
University of West Florida
Warner University

Georgia
Albany State University
Andrew College
Armstrong Atlantic State University
  of Atlanta
Augusta State University
Berry College
Brenau University
Clark Atlanta University
Columbus State University
Covenant College
Darton College
Emmanuel College
Emory University
Gainesville State College
Georgia College and State University
Georgia Highlands College
Georgia Southern University
Georgia State University
Kennesaw State University
LaGrange College
Mercer University
Middle Georgia College
Morehouse College
North Georgia College & State University
Piedmont College
Reinhardt College
Savannah College of Art and Design
Shorter College
University of West Georgia
Valdosta State University
Wesleyan College
Young Harris College

Hawaii
Brigham Young University-Hawaii
Chaminade University of Honolulu
University of Hawaii
  Manoa

Idaho
College of Idaho
Idaho State University
Lewis-Clark State College
North Idaho College
Northwest Nazarene University
University of Idaho

Illinois
American Academy of Art
Augustana College
Aurora University
Black Hawk College
Bradley University
Carl Sandburg College
College of DuPage
College of Lake County
Columbia College Chicago
DePaul University
Eastern Illinois University
Elgin Community College
Elmhurst College
Eureka College
Greenville College
Harper College
Illinois College
Illinois Institute of Art: Schaumburg
Illinois State University
Illinois Wesleyan University
Judson University
Knox College
Lake Forest College
Lewis University
Lincoln College
MacMurray College
McKendree University
Millikin University
Monmouth College
North Central College
North Park University
Northeastern Illinois University
Oakton Community College
Olivet Nazarene University
Parkland College
Quincy University
Rend Lake College
Robert Morris College: Chicago
Sauk Valley Community College
School of the Art Institute of Chicago
South Suburban College of Cook County
Southeastern Illinois College
Southern Illinois University Carbondale
Southern Illinois University Edwardsville
Springfield College in Illinois
Trinity Christian College
University of Illinois
  Chicago
  Springfield
  Urbana-Champaign
University of St. Francis
Waubonsee Community College
Western Illinois University
Wheaton College

Indiana
Bethel College
Franklin College
Goshen College
Grace College
Huntington University
Indiana State University
Indiana University
  Bloomington
  Southeast
Indiana Wesleyan University
Marian College
Oakland City University
St. Mary-of-the-Woods College
Saint Mary's College
Taylor University
University of Evansville
University of Indianapolis
University of St. Francis
University of Southern Indiana
Valparaiso University
Vincennes University
Wabash College

Iowa
Ashford University
Briar Cliff University
Buena Vista University
Central College
Clarke College
Coe College
Cornell College
Dordt College
Drake University
Ellsworth Community College
Graceland University
Grand View University
Iowa Central Community College
Iowa State University
Iowa Wesleyan College
Kirkwood Community College
Luther College
Morningside College
Mount Mercy College

North Iowa Area Community College
Northwestern College
St. Ambrose University
Simpson College
Southeastern Community College
 North Campus
University of Iowa
University of Northern Iowa

Kansas
Allen County Community College
Baker University
Benedictine College
Bethany College
Bethel College
Coffeyville Community College
Cowley County Community College
Emporia State University
Fort Hays State University
Friends University
Garden City Community College
Hesston College
Highland Community College
Kansas City Kansas Community College
Kansas State University
Kansas Wesleyan University
McPherson College
Neosho County Community College
Newman University
Pittsburg State University
Pratt Community College
University of Kansas
University of St. Mary
Washburn University
Wichita State University

Kentucky
Asbury College
Bellarmine University
Brescia University
Eastern Kentucky University
Georgetown College
Jefferson Community and Technical College
Kentucky State University
Kentucky Wesleyan College
Louisville Technical Institute
Midway College
Morehead State University
Murray State University
Northern Kentucky University
Thomas More College
Transylvania University
University of Kentucky
University of Louisville
University of the Cumberlands
Western Kentucky University

Louisiana
Centenary College of Louisiana
Dillard University
Grambling State University
Louisiana College
Louisiana State University and Agricultural and Mechanical College
Louisiana Tech University
Loyola University New Orleans
McNeese State University
Northwestern State University
University of Louisiana at Monroe

Maine
Maine College of Art
University of Maine
University of Maine
 Machias
 Presque Isle
York County Community College

Maryland
Bowie State University
Carroll Community College
Chesapeake College
College of Notre Dame of Maryland
Goucher College
Maryland Institute College of Art
Montgomery College
Mount St. Mary's University
Salisbury University
Stevenson University
Towson University
University of Maryland
 Baltimore County
 College Park
 Eastern Shore

Massachusetts
Atlantic Union College
Boston Architectural College
Boston University
Bristol Community College
Cape Cod Community College
Endicott College
Gordon College
Holyoke Community College
Lesley University
Massachusetts College of Art and Design
Massachusetts College of Liberal Arts
Montserrat College of Art
School of the Museum of Fine Arts
University of Massachusetts
 Amherst
 Lowell

Michigan
Adrian College
Albion College
Alma College
Alpena Community College
Aquinas College
Calvin College
Central Michigan University
College for Creative Studies
Concordia University
Eastern Michigan University
Ferris State University
Glen Oaks Community College
Gogebic Community College
Grand Rapids Community College
Grand Valley State University
Hillsdale College
Hope College
Jackson Community College
Kendall College of Art and Design of Ferris State University
Lawrence Technological University
Madonna University
Marygrove College
Michigan State University
Michigan Technological University
Monroe County Community College
Mott Community College
Northern Michigan University
Northwestern Michigan College
Oakland University
Olivet College
Saginaw Valley State University
Siena Heights University
Southwestern Michigan College
Spring Arbor University
University of Michigan
University of Michigan
 Flint
Wayne State University
Western Michigan University

Minnesota
Bemidji State University
Bethany Lutheran College
Bethel University
College of St. Benedict
College of Visual Arts
Concordia University: St. Paul
Gustavus Adolphus College
Hamline University
Minneapolis College of Art and Design
Minnesota State Community and Technical College
Minnesota State University
 Mankato
 Moorhead
North Hennepin Community College
Riverland Community College
Saint Cloud State University
St. John's University
St. Mary's University of Minnesota
Southwest Minnesota State University
University of Minnesota
 Twin Cities
Winona State University

Mississippi
Belhaven College
Blue Mountain College
Copiah-Lincoln Community College
Delta State University
East Mississippi Community College
Hinds Community College
Itawamba Community College
Meridian Community College
Millsaps College
Mississippi College
Mississippi State University
University of Mississippi
William Carey University

Missouri
Avila University
College of the Ozarks
Columbia College
Cottey College
Crowder College
Culver-Stockton College
Drury University
East Central College
Evangel University
Fontbonne University
Hannibal-LaGrange College
Jefferson College
Kansas City Art Institute
Lincoln University
Lindenwood University
Maryville University of Saint Louis
Mineral Area College
Missouri Southern State University
Missouri State University
Missouri Western State University
Moberly Area Community College
Northwest Missouri State University
Park University
Rockhurst University
St. Charles Community College
St. Louis Community College
Saint Louis University
Southeast Missouri State University
Southwest Baptist University
State Fair Community College
Truman State University
University of Central Missouri
University of Missouri
 Columbia
 Kansas City
 St. Louis
Webster University
William Jewell College
William Woods University

Montana
Carroll College
Dawson Community College
Montana State University
 Billings
 Bozeman
Rocky Mountain College
University of Great Falls
University of Montana
University of Montana: Western

Nebraska
Central Community College
Chadron State College
Concordia University
Creative Center
Creighton University
Doane College
Mid-Plains Community College Area
Nebraska Wesleyan University
Peru State College
University of Nebraska
 Kearney
 Lincoln
 Omaha
Wayne State College
Western Nebraska Community College

Nevada
Sierra Nevada College
Truckee Meadows Community College
University of Nevada
 Las Vegas
 Reno

New Hampshire
Chester College of New England
Colby-Sawyer College
Keene State College
New England College
University of New Hampshire

New Jersey
Caldwell College
Centenary College
College of St. Elizabeth
Drew University
Georgian Court University
Kean University
Monmouth University
Montclair State University
New Jersey Institute of Technology
Richard Stockton College of New Jersey
Rider University
Rowan University
Rutgers, The State University of New Jersey
 Camden Regional Campus
 New Brunswick/Piscataway Campus
 Newark Regional Campus
Union County College

New Mexico
Eastern New Mexico University
New Mexico Junior College
University of New Mexico

New York
Adelphi University
Alfred University
Canisius College
City University of New York
 Brooklyn College
 College of Staten Island
College of New Rochelle
College of Saint Rose
Daemen College
Fashion Institute of Technology
Hobart and William Smith Colleges
Hofstra University
Houghton College
Jamestown Community College
Manhattanville College
Marymount Manhattan College
Molloy College
Nazareth College
Nyack College
Pratt Institute
Rensselaer Polytechnic Institute
Roberts Wesleyan College
Rochester Institute of Technology
Sage College of Albany
Saint Bonaventure University
St. John's University

School of Visual Arts
State University of New York
- Binghamton
- College at Brockport
- College at Cortland
- College at Fredonia
- College at Geneseo
- College at Plattsburgh
- College at Potsdam
- New Paltz
- Purchase
- Stony Brook

Suffolk County Community College
Syracuse University
Villa Maria College of Buffalo

North Carolina

Appalachian State University
Barton College
Brevard College
College of the Albemarle
Davidson College
Duke University
East Carolina University
Elon University
Greensboro College
High Point University
Lees-McRae College
Mars Hill College
Meredith College
Mount Olive College
Peace College
Rockingham Community College
St. Andrews Presbyterian College
St. Augustine's College
Shaw University
University of North Carolina
- Asheville
- Chapel Hill
- Greensboro
- Pembroke

University of North Carolina School of the Arts
Wake Forest University
Warren Wilson College
Western Carolina University
Wilkes Community College
Wingate University

North Dakota

Dickinson State University
Jamestown College
Minot State University
North Dakota State University
University of North Dakota

Ohio

Art Academy of Cincinnati
Art Institute of Cincinnati
Ashland University
Bluffton University
Bowling Green State University
Bowling Green State University: Firelands College
Capital University
Case Western Reserve University
Central State University
Cleveland Institute of Art
Cleveland State University
College of Mount St. Joseph
Columbus College of Art and Design
Cuyahoga Community College
- Metropolitan Campus

Denison University
Edison State Community College
Kent State University
Kent State University
- Ashtabula
- East Liverpool
- Salem
- Stark
- Trumbull
- Tuscarawas

Kent State University: Geauga
Lake Erie College
Lakeland Community College
Lourdes College
Marietta College
Miami University
- Oxford Campus

Mount Union College
Muskingum College
Ohio Northern University
Ohio State University
- Agricultural Technical Institute
- Columbus Campus
- Lima Campus
- Mansfield Campus
- Marion Campus
- Newark Campus

Ohio University
Ohio Wesleyan University
Otterbein College
Pontifical College Josephinum
School of Advertising Art
Southern State Community College
University of Akron
University of Akron: Wayne College
University of Cincinnati
University of Dayton
University of Toledo
Ursuline College
Wittenberg University
Wright State University
Wright State University: Lake Campus
Xavier University

Oklahoma

Cameron University
Carl Albert State College
Northeastern Oklahoma Agricultural and Mechanical College
Northeastern State University
Northwestern Oklahoma State University
Oklahoma Baptist University
Oklahoma Christian University
Oklahoma City Community College
Oklahoma City University
Oklahoma Panhandle State University
Oklahoma State University
Oral Roberts University
St. Gregory's University
Southeastern Oklahoma State University
Southwestern Oklahoma State University
Tulsa Community College
University of Central Oklahoma
University of Oklahoma
University of Science and Arts of Oklahoma
University of Tulsa
Western Oklahoma State College

Oregon

Art Institute of Portland
Clackamas Community College
Eastern Oregon University
George Fox University
Lane Community College
Linn-Benton Community College
Oregon College of Art & Craft
Pacific Northwest College of Art
Pacific University
Portland State University
Southern Oregon University
Southwestern Oregon Community College
Western Oregon University

Pennsylvania

Albright College
Arcadia University
Berks Technical Institute
Bloomsburg University of Pennsylvania
Bucknell University
California University of Pennsylvania
Carnegie Mellon University
Cedar Crest College
Clarion University of Pennsylvania
Drexel University
East Stroudsburg University of Pennsylvania
Edinboro University of Pennsylvania
Elizabethtown College
Franklin & Marshall College
Immaculata University
Indiana University of Pennsylvania
Juniata College
Kutztown University of Pennsylvania
Lehigh University
Lock Haven University of Pennsylvania
Lycoming College
Manor College
Mansfield University of Pennsylvania
Marywood University
Mercyhurst College
Messiah College
Moore College of Art and Design
Mount Aloysius College
Muhlenberg College
Northampton Community College
Oakbridge Academy of Arts
Point Park University
Rosemont College
Saint Joseph's University
Seton Hill University
Slippery Rock University of Pennsylvania
Temple University
University of the Arts
Ursinus College

Puerto Rico

Humacao Community College
University of Puerto Rico
- Mayaguez

Rhode Island

Rhode Island College
University of Rhode Island

South Carolina

Anderson University
Clemson University
Coastal Carolina University
College of Charleston
Columbia College
Converse College
Erskine College
Furman University
Lander University
Limestone College
University of South Carolina
University of South Carolina
- Aiken

Winthrop University

South Dakota

Augustana College
Dakota State University
Dakota Wesleyan University
Mount Marty College
Northern State University
South Dakota State University
University of Sioux Falls
University of South Dakota

Tennessee

Austin Peay State University
Belmont University
Carson-Newman College
Cumberland University
East Tennessee State University
Free Will Baptist Bible College
Freed-Hardeman University
Jackson State Community College
King College
Lambuth University
Lipscomb University
Martin Methodist College
Maryville College
Memphis College of Art
Middle Tennessee State University
Milligan College
Motlow State Community College
Pellissippi State Technical Community College
Rhodes College
Roane State Community College
Southern Adventist University
Tennessee Technological University
Union University
University of Memphis
University of Tennessee
- Chattanooga
- Knoxville
- Martin

Volunteer State Community College

Texas

Abilene Christian University
Angelina College
Austin College
Baylor University
Brazosport College
Clarendon College
College of the Mainland
Collin County Community College District
Galveston College
Hardin-Simmons University
Houston Baptist University
Howard College
Howard Payne University
Huston-Tillotson University
Kilgore College
Lee College
Lon Morris College
McMurry University
Midwestern State University
Our Lady of the Lake University of San Antonio
Panola College
Rice University
Richland College
St. Edward's University
San Jacinto College
Schreiner University
South Plains College
Southern Methodist University
Southwestern University
Tarleton State University
Texas A&M University
Texas A&M University
- Commerce
- Corpus Christi

Texas Christian University
Texas State University: San Marcos
Texas Tech University
Tyler Junior College
University of Dallas
University of Houston
University of Mary Hardin-Baylor
University of Texas
- Austin
- El Paso
- Pan American
- of the Permian Basin
- San Antonio
- Tyler

University of the Incarnate Word
Victoria College
Wayland Baptist University
West Texas A&M University
Western Technical College
Western Texas College

Utah

Brigham Young University
College of Eastern Utah
Dixie State College of Utah
Salt Lake Community College
Southern Utah University
University of Utah
Utah State University
Utah Valley University
Weber State University
Westminster College

Vermont
Castleton State College
Goddard College
Green Mountain College
Landmark College
University of Vermont

Virginia
Averett University
Bluefield College
Christopher Newport University
Eastern Mennonite University
Emory & Henry College
Hollins University
James Madison University
Longwood University
Old Dominion University
Radford University
Randolph College
Southern Virginia University
Sweet Briar College
University of Mary Washington
University of Richmond
University of Virginia's College at Wise
Virginia Commonwealth University
Virginia Intermont College
Virginia Polytechnic Institute and State University
Virginia State University

Washington
Art Institute of Seattle
Big Bend Community College
Central Washington University
Centralia College
Clark College
Everett Community College
Evergreen State College
Grays Harbor College
Northwest College of Art
Northwest University
Pacific Lutheran University
Seattle Pacific University
Trinity Lutheran College
University of Puget Sound
University of Washington
University of Washington Bothell
Washington State University
Western Washington University
Whitman College
Whitworth University

West Virginia
Bethany College
Bluefield State College
Concord University
Davis and Elkins College
Fairmont State University
Marshall University
Shepherd University
University of Charleston
West Liberty State College
West Virginia University
West Virginia Wesleyan College

Wisconsin
Cardinal Stritch University
Carroll University
Carthage College
Edgewood College
Milwaukee Institute of Art & Design
Mount Mary College
Northland College
Ripon College
St. Norbert College
Silver Lake College
University of Wisconsin
- Baraboo/Sauk County
- Eau Claire
- Green Bay
- La Crosse
- Madison
- Manitowoc
- Milwaukee
- Oshkosh
- Parkside
- Richland
- River Falls
- Stevens Point
- Superior
- Waukesha
- Whitewater

Viterbo University
Wisconsin Lutheran College

Wyoming
Casper College
Central Wyoming College
Eastern Wyoming College
Laramie County Community College
Sheridan College
University of Wyoming
Western Wyoming Community College

Athletic scholarships

Archery

Arizona
Dine College M,W

California
College of the Redwoods M

Texas
Texas A&M University W

Badminton

California
Fresno City College M,W

New Jersey
New Jersey Institute of Technology M

Wisconsin
Milwaukee Area Technical College M

Baseball

Alabama
Alabama Agricultural and Mechanical University M
Alabama State University M
Auburn University M
Auburn University at Montgomery M
Bevill State Community College M
Central Alabama Community College M
Chattahoochee Valley Community College M
Enterprise-Ozark Community College M
Faulkner State Community College M
Gadsden State Community College M
George C. Wallace State Community College
George C. Wallace Community College at Dothan M
Selma M
Jacksonville State University M
Jefferson Davis Community College M
Jefferson State Community College M
Lawson State Community College M
Lurleen B. Wallace Community College M
Marion Military Institute M
Miles College M
Northwest-Shoals Community College M
Samford University M
Selma University M
Shelton State Community College M
Snead State Community College M
Southern Union State Community College M
Spring Hill College M
Troy University M
Tuskegee University M
University of Alabama M
University of Alabama
Birmingham M
Huntsville M
University of Mobile M
University of Montevallo M
University of North Alabama M
University of South Alabama M
University of West Alabama M
Wallace State Community College at Hanceville M

Arizona
Arizona State University M
Arizona Western College M
Central Arizona College M
Chandler-Gilbert Community College
Pecos M
Cochise College M
Eastern Arizona College M
Gateway Community College M
Glendale Community College M
Grand Canyon University M
Paradise Valley Community College M
Pima Community College M
Scottsdale Community College M
South Mountain Community College M
University of Arizona M
Yavapai College M

Arkansas
Arkansas State University M
Arkansas Tech University M
Ecclesia College M
Harding University M
Henderson State University M
Lyon College M
North Arkansas College M
Ouachita Baptist University M
Southern Arkansas University M
University of Arkansas M
University of Arkansas
Fort Smith M
Little Rock M
University of Central Arkansas M
Williams Baptist College M

California
Azusa Pacific University M
Bethany University M
Biola University M
California Baptist University M
California Polytechnic State University: San Luis Obispo M
California State Polytechnic University: Pomona M
California State University
Chico M
Dominguez Hills M
Fresno M
Fullerton M
Long Beach M
Los Angeles M
Monterey Bay M
Northridge M
Sacramento M
San Bernardino M
Stanislaus M
Concordia University M
Fresno City College M
Fresno Pacific University M
Grossmont College M
Loyola Marymount University M
The Master's College M
Patten University M
Pepperdine University M
Point Loma Nazarene University M
St. Mary's College of California M
San Diego Christian College M
San Diego State University M
San Jose State University M
Santa Clara University M
Sonoma State University M
Stanford University M
University of California
Berkeley M
Davis M
Irvine M
Los Angeles M
Riverside M
Santa Barbara M
University of San Diego M
University of San Francisco M
University of Southern California M
University of the Pacific M
Vanguard University of Southern California M
Westmont College M
Yuba Community College District M

Colorado
Colorado Christian University M
Colorado Northwestern Community College M
Colorado School of Mines M
Colorado State University
Pueblo M
Lamar Community College M
Mesa State College M
Metropolitan State College of Denver M
Northeastern Junior College M
Otero Junior College M
Regis University M
Trinidad State Junior College M
University of Northern Colorado M

Connecticut
Central Connecticut State University M
Fairfield University M
Post University M
Quinnipiac University M
Sacred Heart University M
Southern Connecticut State University M
University of Bridgeport M
University of Connecticut M
University of Hartford M
University of New Haven M

Delaware
Delaware State University M
Delaware Technical and Community College
Owens M
University of Delaware M
Wilmington University M

District of Columbia
George Washington University M
Georgetown University M
Howard University M

Florida
Barry University M
Bethune-Cookman University M
Brevard Community College M
Central Florida Community College M
Chipola College M
Daytona State College M
Eckerd College M
Edward Waters College M
Embry-Riddle Aeronautical University M
Flagler College M
Florida Atlantic University M
Florida Community College at Jacksonville M
Florida Gulf Coast University M
Florida Institute of Technology M
Florida Memorial University M
Florida Southern College M
Florida State University M
Gulf Coast Community College M
Hillsborough Community College M
Indian River State College M
Jacksonville University M
Lake City Community College M
Lake-Sumter Community College M
Lynn University M
Manatee Community College M
Miami Dade College M
North Florida Community College M
Northwest Florida State College M
Northwood University
Florida M
Nova Southeastern University M
Palm Beach Community College M
Pasco-Hernando Community College M
Pensacola Junior College M
Polk Community College M
Rollins College M
Saint Johns River Community College M
St. Leo University M
St. Petersburg College M
Saint Thomas University M
Santa Fe College M
South Florida Community College M
Stetson University M
Tallahassee Community College M
University of Central Florida M
University of Florida M
University of Miami M
University of North Florida M
University of South Florida M
University of Tampa M
University of West Florida M
Warner University M
Webber International University M

Georgia
Abraham Baldwin Agricultural College M
Albany State University M
Andrew College M
Armstrong Atlantic State University M
Augusta State University M
Brewton-Parker College M
Clark Atlanta University M
Columbus State University M
Covenant College M
Darton College M
Emmanuel College M
Georgia College and State University M
Georgia Institute of Technology M
Georgia Perimeter College M
Georgia Southern University M
Georgia Southwestern State University M
Georgia State University M
Gordon College M
Kennesaw State University M
Mercer University M
Middle Georgia College M
Morehouse College M
Paine College M
Reinhardt College M
Savannah State University M
Shorter College M
Southern Polytechnic State University M
Thomas University M
Truett-McConnell College M
University of Georgia M
University of West Georgia M
Valdosta State University M
Young Harris College M

Hawaii
Hawaii Pacific University M
University of Hawaii
Manoa M

Idaho
College of Idaho M
College of Southern Idaho M
Lewis-Clark State College M
Northwest Nazarene University M

Illinois
Black Hawk College M
Bradley University M
Carl Sandburg College M
Chicago State University M
College of Lake County M
Danville Area Community College M
Eastern Illinois University M
Elgin Community College M
Highland Community College M
Illinois Central College M
Illinois Eastern Community Colleges

Lincoln Trail College M
Olney Central College M
Wabash Valley College M
Illinois Institute of Technology M
Illinois State University M
John A. Logan College M
Judson University M
Kankakee Community College M
Kaskaskia College M
Kishwaukee College M
Lake Land College M
Lewis and Clark Community College M
Lewis University M
Lincoln College M
Lincoln Land Community College M
McHenry County College M
McKendree University M
Moraine Valley Community College M
Morton College M
Northwestern University M
Olivet Nazarene University M
Parkland College M
Quincy University M
Rend Lake College M
Robert Morris College: Chicago M
St. Xavier University M
Sauk Valley Community College M
South Suburban College of Cook County M
Southeastern Illinois College M
Southern Illinois University Carbondale M
Southern Illinois University Edwardsville M
Spoon River College M
Springfield College in Illinois M
Trinity Christian College M
Trinity International University M
University of Illinois
Chicago M
Urbana-Champaign M
University of St. Francis M
Western Illinois University M

Indiana
Ancilla College M
Ball State University M
Bethel College M
Butler University M
Calumet College of St. Joseph M
Goshen College M
Grace College M
Huntington University M
Indiana Institute of Technology M
Indiana State University M
Indiana University
Bloomington M
Southeast M
Indiana University-Purdue University Fort Wayne M
Indiana Wesleyan University M
Marian College M
Oakland City University M
Purdue University M
Saint Joseph's College M
Taylor University M
University of Evansville M
University of Indianapolis M
University of Notre Dame M
University of St. Francis M
University of Southern Indiana M
Valparaiso University M
Vincennes University M

Iowa
Ashford University M
Briar Cliff University M
Clarke College M
Des Moines Area Community College M
Dordt College M
Ellsworth Community College M
Graceland University M
Grand View University M
Indian Hills Community College M
Iowa Central Community College M
Iowa Lakes Community College M
Iowa Wesleyan College M
Iowa Western Community College M
Kirkwood Community College M
Morningside College M
Mount Mercy College M
Muscatine Community College M
North Iowa Area Community College M
Northwestern College M
St. Ambrose University M
Southeastern Community College
North Campus M
Southwestern Community College M
University of Iowa M
University of Northern Iowa M
Waldorf College M
William Penn University M

Kansas
Allen County Community College M
Baker University M
Barton County Community College M
Benedictine College M
Bethany College M
Brown Mackie College
Salina M
Central Christian College of Kansas M
Cloud County Community College M
Coffeyville Community College M
Colby Community College M
Cowley County Community College M
Dodge City Community College M
Emporia State University M
Fort Scott Community College M
Friends University M
Garden City Community College M
Hesston College M
Highland Community College M
Hutchinson Community College M
Independence Community College M
Johnson County Community College M
Kansas City Kansas Community College M
Kansas State University M
Kansas Wesleyan University M
Labette Community College M
MidAmerica Nazarene University M
Neosho County Community College M
Newman University M
Ottawa University M
Pittsburg State University M
Pratt Community College M
Seward County Community College M
Sterling College M
Tabor College M
University of Kansas M
University of St. Mary M
Washburn University M
Wichita State University M

Kentucky
Alice Lloyd College M
Asbury College M
Bellarmine University M
Brescia University M
Campbellsville University M
Eastern Kentucky University M
Georgetown College M
Kentucky State University M
Kentucky Wesleyan College M
Lindsey Wilson College M
Mid-Continent University M
Morehead State University M
Murray State University M
Northern Kentucky University M
Pikeville College M
St. Catharine College M
Union College M
University of Kentucky M
University of Louisville M
University of the Cumberlands M
Western Kentucky University M

Louisiana
Bossier Parish Community College M
Centenary College of Louisiana M
Delgado Community College M
Grambling State University M
Louisiana State University
Shreveport M
Louisiana State University and Agricultural and Mechanical College M
Louisiana Tech University M
McNeese State University M
Nicholls State University M
Northwestern State University M
Southeastern Louisiana University M
Southern University and Agricultural and Mechanical College M
Tulane University M
University of Louisiana at Lafayette M
University of Louisiana at Monroe M
University of New Orleans M

Maine
University of Maine M

Maryland
Anne Arundel Community College M
Chesapeake College M
College of Southern Maryland M
Columbia Union College M
Community College of Baltimore County M
Coppin State University M
Garrett College M
Hagerstown Community College M
Harford Community College M
Mount St. Mary's University M
Prince George's Community College M
Towson University M
University of Maryland
Baltimore County M
College Park M
Eastern Shore M

Massachusetts
American International College M
Boston College M
Dean College M
Northeastern University M
Stonehill College M
University of Massachusetts
Amherst M
Lowell M

Michigan
Aquinas College M
Central Michigan University M
Concordia University M
Eastern Michigan University M
Glen Oaks Community College M
Grand Rapids Community College M
Hillsdale College M
Kalamazoo Valley Community College M
Kellogg Community College M
Lake Michigan College M
Macomb Community College M
Madonna University M
Michigan State University M
Mott Community College M
Muskegon Community College M
Northwood University: Michigan M
Oakland University M
Rochester College M
Saginaw Valley State University M
Siena Heights University M
Spring Arbor University M
University of Michigan M
Wayne State University M

Minnesota
Concordia University: St. Paul M
Minnesota State University
Mankato M
Saint Cloud State University M
Southwest Minnesota State University M
University of Minnesota
Crookston M
Duluth M
Twin Cities M
Winona State University M

Mississippi
Alcorn State University M
Belhaven College M
Copiah-Lincoln Community College M
Delta State University M
East Mississippi Community College M
Hinds Community College M
Holmes Community College M
Itawamba Community College M
Jackson State University M
Meridian Community College M
Mississippi Gulf Coast Community College M
Mississippi State University M
Mississippi Valley State University M
Northwest Mississippi Community College M
Southwest Mississippi Community College M
University of Mississippi M
University of Southern Mississippi M
William Carey University M

Missouri
Avila University M
Central Methodist University M
College of the Ozarks M
Crowder College M
Culver-Stockton College M
Drury University M
Evangel University M
Hannibal-LaGrange College M
Harris-Stowe State University M
Jefferson College M
Lincoln University M
Metropolitan Community College: Longview M
Metropolitan Community College: Maple Woods M
Mineral Area College M
Missouri Baptist University M
Missouri Southern State University M
Missouri State University M
Missouri Valley College M
Missouri Western State University M
North Central Missouri College M
Northwest Missouri State University M
Park University M
Research College of Nursing M
Rockhurst University M
St. Charles Community College M
St. Louis Community College M
Saint Louis University M
Southeast Missouri State University M
Southwest Baptist University M
Three Rivers Community College M
Truman State University M
University of Central Missouri M
University of Missouri
Columbia M
Missouri University of Science and Technology M
St. Louis M
William Jewell College M
William Woods University M

Montana
Miles Community College M
Montana State University
Billings M

Nebraska
Bellevue University M
Concordia University M
Creighton University M
Doane College M
Mid-Plains Community College Area M
Peru State College M
University of Nebraska
Kearney M

Lincoln M
Omaha M
Wayne State College M
Western Nebraska Community College M
York College M

Nevada
College of Southern Nevada M
University of Nevada
Las Vegas M
Reno M

New Hampshire
Franklin Pierce University M
Hesser College M
Southern New Hampshire University M

New Jersey
Bloomfield College M
Brookdale Community College M
Burlington County College M
Caldwell College M
Fairleigh Dickinson University
Metropolitan Campus M
Mercer County Community College M
Monmouth University M
New Jersey Institute of Technology M
Rider University M
Rutgers, The State University of New Jersey
New Brunswick/Piscataway Campus M
Saint Peter's College M
Salem Community College M
Seton Hall University M
Sussex County Community College M

New Mexico
Eastern New Mexico University M
New Mexico Highlands University M
New Mexico Junior College M
New Mexico Military Institute M
New Mexico State University M
University of New Mexico M
University of the Southwest M

New York
Adelphi University M
ASA Institute of Business and Computer Technology M
Canisius College M
City University of New York
Queens College M
College of Saint Rose M
Concordia College M
Dominican College of Blauvelt M
Dowling College M
Fordham University M
Hofstra University M
Iona College M
Le Moyne College M
Long Island University
Brooklyn Campus M
C. W. Post Campus M
Manhattan College M
Marist College M
Mercy College M
Molloy College M
Monroe College M
Monroe Community College M
New York Institute of Technology M
Niagara University M
Nyack College M
Pace University M
Saint Bonaventure University M
St. John's University M
St. Thomas Aquinas College M
Siena College M
State University of New York
Albany M
Binghamton M
Buffalo M
Stony Brook M
Wagner College M

North Carolina
Appalachian State University M
Barton College M
Belmont Abbey College M
Brevard College M
Campbell University M
Catawba College M
Davidson College M
Duke University M
East Carolina University M
Elon University M
Gardner-Webb University M
High Point University M
Lenoir Community College M
Lenoir-Rhyne University M
Louisburg College M
Mars Hill College M
Montreat College M
Mount Olive College M
North Carolina Agricultural and Technical State University M
North Carolina State University M
Pfeiffer University M
Pitt Community College M
St. Andrews Presbyterian College M
St. Augustine's College M
Shaw University M
Southeastern Community College M
University of North Carolina
Asheville M
Chapel Hill M
Charlotte M
Greensboro M
Pembroke M
Wilmington M
Wake Forest University M
Western Carolina University M
Wingate University M

North Dakota
Bismarck State College M
Dickinson State University M
Jamestown College M
Mayville State University M
Minot State University M
Minot State University: Bottineau Campus M
North Dakota State University M
University of Mary M
University of North Dakota M
Valley City State University M
Williston State College M

Ohio
Ashland University M
Bowling Green State University M
Cedarville University M
Clark State Community College M
Cleveland State University M
Kent State University M
Lakeland Community College M
Malone University M
Miami University
Oxford Campus M
Mount Vernon Nazarene University M
Notre Dame College M
Ohio Dominican University M
Ohio State University
Columbus Campus M
Ohio University M
Shawnee State University M
Sinclair Community College M
University of Akron M
University of Cincinnati M
University of Dayton M
University of Findlay M
University of Rio Grande M
University of Toledo M
Urbana University M
Walsh University M
Wright State University M
Xavier University M
Youngstown State University M

Oklahoma
Bacone College M
Cameron University M
Carl Albert State College M
Connors State College M
East Central University M
Eastern Oklahoma State College M
Northeastern Oklahoma Agricultural and Mechanical College M
Northeastern State University M
Northern Oklahoma College M
Northwestern Oklahoma State University M
Oklahoma Baptist University M
Oklahoma City University M
Oklahoma Panhandle State University M
Oklahoma State University M
Oklahoma Wesleyan University M
Oral Roberts University M
Redlands Community College M
Rose State College M
St. Gregory's University M
Seminole State College M
Southeastern Oklahoma State University M
Southern Nazarene University M
Southwestern Oklahoma State University M
University of Central Oklahoma M
University of Oklahoma M
University of Science and Arts of Oklahoma M
Western Oklahoma State College M

Oregon
Blue Mountain Community College M
Chemeketa Community College M
Clackamas Community College M
Concordia University M
Corban College M
Lane Community College M
Linn-Benton Community College M
Mt. Hood Community College M
Oregon Institute of Technology M
Oregon State University M
Portland State University M
Southwestern Oregon Community College M
Treasure Valley Community College M
University of Oregon M
University of Portland M

Pennsylvania
Bloomsburg University of Pennsylvania M
California University of Pennsylvania M
Chestnut Hill College M
Clarion University of Pennsylvania M
Duquesne University M
East Stroudsburg University of Pennsylvania M
Gannon University M
Indiana University of Pennsylvania M
Kutztown University of Pennsylvania M
La Salle University M
Lackawanna College M
Lock Haven University of Pennsylvania M
Mansfield University of Pennsylvania M
Mercyhurst College M
Millersville University of Pennsylvania M
Penn State
University Park M
Philadelphia University M
Point Park University M
Saint Joseph's University M
Seton Hill University M
Shippensburg University of Pennsylvania M
Slippery Rock University of Pennsylvania M
Temple University M
University of Pittsburgh M
University of the Sciences in Philadelphia M
Villanova University M
West Chester University of Pennsylvania M

Puerto Rico
Inter American University of Puerto Rico
Aguadilla Campus M
Bayamon Campus M
Metropolitan Campus M
Ponce Campus M,W
San German Campus M
Turabo University M
Universidad del Este M
Universidad Metropolitana M,W
Universidad Politecnica de Puerto Rico M
University of Puerto Rico
Carolina Regional College M
Cayey University College M
Humacao M
Mayaguez M
Utuado M

Rhode Island
Bryant University M
Community College of Rhode Island M
University of Rhode Island M

South Carolina
Anderson University M
Charleston Southern University M
The Citadel M
Claflin University M
Clemson University M
Coastal Carolina University M
College of Charleston M
Erskine College M
Francis Marion University M
Furman University M
Lander University M
Limestone College M
Morris College M
Newberry College M
North Greenville University M
Presbyterian College M
Southern Wesleyan University M
Spartanburg Methodist College M
University of South Carolina M
University of South Carolina
Aiken M
Sumter M
Upstate M
Winthrop University M
Wofford College M

South Dakota
Augustana College M
Dakota State University M
Dakota Wesleyan University M
Mount Marty College M
South Dakota State University M
University of Sioux Falls M

Tennessee
Austin Peay State University M
Belmont University M
Bethel College M
Carson-Newman College M
Chattanooga State Technical Community College M
Christian Brothers University M
Cleveland State Community College M
Columbia State Community College M
Crichton College M
Cumberland University M
Dyersburg State Community College M
East Tennessee State University M
Freed-Hardeman University M
Jackson State Community College M
King College M
Lambuth University M
Lee University M
LeMoyne Owen College M
Lincoln Memorial University M
Lipscomb University M
Martin Methodist College M
Middle Tennessee State University M
Milligan College M
Motlow State Community College M
Roane State Community College M
Southwest Tennessee Community College M
Tennessee Technological University M
Tennessee Temple University M

Tennessee Wesleyan College M
Trevecca Nazarene University M
Tusculum College M
Union University M
University of Memphis M
University of Tennessee
- Knoxville M
- Martin M

Vanderbilt University M
Volunteer State Community College M
Walters State Community College M

Texas
Abilene Christian University M
Alvin Community College M
Angelina College M
Angelo State University M
Baylor University M
Blinn College M
Clarendon College M
Dallas Baptist University M
El Paso Community College M
Frank Phillips College M
Galveston College M
Hill College M
Houston Baptist University M
Howard College M
Jarvis Christian College M
Lamar University M
Laredo Community College M
Lon Morris College M
Lubbock Christian University M
McLennan Community College M
North Central Texas College M
Northwood University: Texas M
Odessa College M
Paris Junior College M
Prairie View A&M University M
Ranger College M
Rice University M
St. Edward's University M
St. Mary's University M
Sam Houston State University M
San Jacinto College M
Tarleton State University M
Texas A&M University M
Texas A&M University
- Corpus Christi M
- Kingsville M

Texas Christian University M
Texas Southern University M
Texas State University: San Marcos M
Texas Tech University M
University of Houston M
University of Texas
- Arlington M
- Austin M
- Brownsville - Texas Southmost College M
- Pan American M
- of the Permian Basin M
- San Antonio M

University of the Incarnate Word M
Wayland Baptist University M
Weatherford College M
West Texas A&M University M
Western Texas College M
Wharton County Junior College M
Wiley College M

Utah
Brigham Young University M
College of Eastern Utah M
Dixie State College of Utah M
Salt Lake Community College M
Southern Utah University M
University of Utah M
Utah Valley University M

Vermont
University of Vermont M

Virginia
Bluefield College M
College of William and Mary M
George Mason University M
James Madison University M
Liberty University M
Longwood University M
Norfolk State University M
Old Dominion University M
Radford University M
St. Paul's College M
University of Richmond M
University of Virginia M
University of Virginia's College at Wise M
Virginia Commonwealth University M
Virginia Intermont College M
Virginia Military Institute M
Virginia Polytechnic Institute and State University M
Virginia State University M

Washington
Big Bend Community College M
Central Washington University M
Centralia College M
Columbia Basin College M
Edmonds Community College M
Everett Community College M
Gonzaga University M
Grays Harbor College M
Green River Community College M
Lower Columbia College M
Olympic College M
Pierce College M
Saint Martin's University M
Shoreline Community College M
Skagit Valley College M
Spokane Community College M
Tacoma Community College M
University of Washington M
Walla Walla Community College M
Washington State University M
Yakima Valley Community College M

West Virginia
Alderson-Broaddus College M
Bluefield State College M
Concord University M
Davis and Elkins College M
Marshall University M
Ohio Valley University M
Potomac State College of West Virginia University M
Salem International University M
Shepherd University M
University of Charleston M
West Liberty State College M
West Virginia State University M
West Virginia University M
West Virginia University Institute of Technology M
West Virginia Wesleyan College M
Wheeling Jesuit University M

Wisconsin
Cardinal Stritch University M
Milwaukee Area Technical College M,W
University of Wisconsin
- Milwaukee M
- Parkside M

Viterbo University M

Basketball

Alabama
Alabama Agricultural and Mechanical University M,W
Alabama State University M,W
Auburn University M,W
Auburn University at Montgomery M,W
Bevill State Community College M,W
Chattahoochee Valley Community College M,W
Enterprise-Ozark Community College M,W
Faulkner State Community College M,W
Faulkner University M
Gadsden State Community College M,W
George C. Wallace State Community College Selma M,W
Jacksonville State University M,W
Jefferson Davis Community College M
Judson College W
Lawson State Community College M,W
Lurleen B. Wallace Community College M,W
Marion Military Institute M
Miles College M,W
Northwest-Shoals Community College M,W
Samford University M,W
Selma University M,W
Shelton State Community College M,W
Snead State Community College M,W
Southern Union State Community College M,W
Spring Hill College M,W
Troy University M,W
Tuskegee University M,W
University of Alabama M,W
University of Alabama
- Birmingham M,W
- Huntsville M,W

University of Mobile M,W
University of Montevallo M,W
University of North Alabama M,W
University of South Alabama M,W
University of West Alabama M,W
Wallace State Community College at Hanceville M,W

Alaska
University of Alaska
- Anchorage M,W
- Fairbanks M,W

Arizona
Arizona State University M,W
Arizona Western College M,W
Central Arizona College M,W
Chandler-Gilbert Community College
- Pecos M,W

Cochise College M,W
Eastern Arizona College M,W
Glendale Community College M,W
Grand Canyon University M,W
Mesa Community College M,W
Northern Arizona University M,W
Pima Community College M,W
Scottsdale Community College M,W
South Mountain Community College M,W
University of Arizona M,W
Yavapai College M,W

Arkansas
Arkansas State University M,W
Arkansas Tech University M,W
Ecclesia College M,W
Harding University M,W
Henderson State University M,W
John Brown University M,W
Lyon College M,W
North Arkansas College M,W
Ouachita Baptist University M,W
Philander Smith College M,W
Southern Arkansas University M,W
University of Arkansas M,W
University of Arkansas
- Fort Smith M,W
- Little Rock M,W
- Monticello M,W
- Pine Bluff M,W

University of Central Arkansas M,W
Williams Baptist College M,W

California
Azusa Pacific University M,W
Bethany University M,W
Biola University M,W
California Baptist University M,W
California Polytechnic State University: San Luis Obispo M,W
California State Polytechnic University: Pomona M,W
California State University
- Bakersfield M
- Chico M,W
- Dominguez Hills M,W
- Fresno M,W
- Fullerton M,W
- Long Beach M,W
- Los Angeles M,W
- Monterey Bay M,W
- Northridge M,W
- Sacramento M,W
- San Bernardino M,W
- Stanislaus M,W

Concordia University M,W
Dominican University of California M,W
Fresno City College M,W
Fresno Pacific University M,W
Grossmont College M,W
Holy Names University M,W
Hope International University M,W
Humboldt State University M,W
Loyola Marymount University M,W
The Master's College M,W
Notre Dame de Namur University M,W
Pepperdine University M,W
Point Loma Nazarene University M,W
St. Mary's College of California M,W
San Diego Christian College M,W
San Diego State University M,W
San Jose State University M,W
Santa Clara University M,W
Sonoma State University M,W
Stanford University M,W
University of California
- Berkeley M,W
- Davis M,W
- Irvine M,W
- Los Angeles M,W
- Riverside M,W
- Santa Barbara M,W

University of San Diego M,W
University of San Francisco M,W
University of Southern California M,W
University of the Pacific M,W
Vanguard University of Southern California M,W
Westmont College M,W
William Jessup University M,W
Yuba Community College District M,W

Colorado
Adams State College M,W
Colorado Christian University M,W
Colorado Northwestern Community College M,W
Colorado School of Mines M,W
Colorado State University M,W
Colorado State University
- Pueblo M,W

Fort Lewis College M,W
Lamar Community College M
Mesa State College M,W
Metropolitan State College of Denver M,W
Northeastern Junior College M,W
Otero Junior College M,W
Regis University M,W
Trinidad State Junior College M
University of Colorado
- Boulder M,W
- Colorado Springs M,W

University of Denver M,W
University of Northern Colorado M,W
Western State College of Colorado M,W

Connecticut
Central Connecticut State University M,W
Fairfield University M,W
Post University M,W
Quinnipiac University M,W
Sacred Heart University M,W
Southern Connecticut State University M,W
University of Bridgeport M,W
University of Connecticut M,W
University of Hartford M,W
University of New Haven M,W

Delaware
Delaware State University M,W
Delaware Technical and Community College
Stanton/Wilmington M,W
Goldey-Beacom College M,W
University of Delaware M,W
Wilmington University M,W

District of Columbia
American University M,W
George Washington University M,W
Georgetown University M,W
Howard University M,W
University of the District of Columbia M,W

Florida
Barry University M,W
Bethune-Cookman University M,W
Brevard Community College M,W
Central Florida Community College M,W
Chipola College M,W
Daytona State College M,W
Eckerd College M,W
Edward Waters College M,W
Embry-Riddle Aeronautical University M
Flagler College M,W
Florida Agricultural and Mechanical University M
Florida Atlantic University M,W
Florida College M
Florida Community College at Jacksonville M,W
Florida Gulf Coast University M,W
Florida Institute of Technology M,W
Florida Memorial University M,W
Florida Southern College M,W
Florida State University M,W
Gulf Coast Community College M,W
Hillsborough Community College M,W
Indian River State College M,W
Jacksonville University M,W
Lynn University M,W
Manatee Community College M
Miami Dade College M,W
North Florida Community College W
Northwest Florida State College M,W
Nova Southeastern University M,W
Palm Beach Community College M,W
Pasco-Hernando Community College M
Pensacola Junior College M,W
Polk Community College M
Rollins College M,W
Saint Johns River Community College M
St. Leo University M,W
St. Petersburg College M,W
Santa Fe College M,W
Stetson University M,W
Tallahassee Community College M,W
University of Central Florida M,W
University of Florida M,W
University of Miami M,W
University of North Florida M,W
University of South Florida M,W
University of Tampa M,W
University of West Florida M,W
Warner University M,W
Webber International University M,W

Georgia
Albany State University M,W
Andrew College W
Armstrong Atlantic State University M,W
Augusta State University M,W
Brenau University W
Brewton-Parker College M,W
Clark Atlanta University M,W
Clayton State University M,W
College of Coastal Georgia M
Columbus State University M,W
Covenant College M,W
Darton College W
Emmanuel College M,W
Fort Valley State University M,W
Georgia College and State University M,W
Georgia Institute of Technology M,W
Georgia Perimeter College M,W
Georgia Southern University M,W
Georgia Southwestern State University M,W
Georgia State University M,W
Gordon College M
Kennesaw State University M,W
Mercer University M,W
Middle Georgia College M,W
Morehouse College M
North Georgia College & State University M,W
Paine College M,W
Reinhardt College M,W
Savannah State University M,W
Shorter College M,W
Southern Polytechnic State University M,W
Truett-McConnell College M,W
University of Georgia M,W
University of West Georgia M,W
Valdosta State University M,W

Hawaii
Brigham Young University-Hawaii M,W
Chaminade University of Honolulu M
Hawaii Pacific University M,W
University of Hawaii
Hilo M
Manoa M,W

Idaho
Boise State University M,W
College of Idaho M,W
College of Southern Idaho M,W
Idaho State University M,W
Lewis-Clark State College M,W
North Idaho College M,W
Northwest Nazarene University M,W
University of Idaho M,W

Illinois
Black Hawk College M,W
Black Hawk College: East Campus M,W
Bradley University M,W
Carl Sandburg College M,W
Chicago State University M,W
City Colleges of Chicago
Kennedy-King College M,W
Malcolm X College M,W
Wright College M,W
College of Lake County M,W
Danville Area Community College M,W
DePaul University M,W
Eastern Illinois University M,W
Elgin Community College M,W
Highland Community College M,W
Illinois Central College M,W
Illinois Eastern Community Colleges
Lincoln Trail College M,W
Olney Central College M,W
Wabash Valley College M,W
Illinois Institute of Technology M,W
Illinois State University M,W
John A. Logan College M,W
Judson University M,W
Kankakee Community College M,W
Kaskaskia College M,W
Kishwaukee College M,W
Lake Land College M,W
Lewis and Clark Community College M,W
Lewis University M,W
Lincoln College M,W
Lincoln Land Community College M,W
Loyola University Chicago M,W
McHenry County College M,W
McKendree University M,W
Moraine Valley Community College M,W
Morton College M,W
Northwestern University M,W
Olivet Nazarene University M,W
Parkland College M,W
Quincy University M,W
Rend Lake College M,W
Robert Morris College: Chicago M,W
St. Xavier University M
Sauk Valley Community College M,W
Shawnee Community College M,W
South Suburban College of Cook County M,W
Southeastern Illinois College M,W
Southern Illinois University Carbondale M,W
Southern Illinois University Edwardsville M,W
Spoon River College M,W
Trinity Christian College M,W
Trinity International University M,W
University of Illinois
Chicago M,W
Springfield M,W
Urbana-Champaign M,W
University of St. Francis M,W
Waubonsee Community College M,W
Western Illinois University M,W

Indiana
Ancilla College M,W
Ball State University M,W
Bethel College M,W
Butler University M,W
Calumet College of St. Joseph M,W
Goshen College M,W
Grace College M,W
Huntington University M,W
Indiana Institute of Technology M,W
Indiana State University M,W
Indiana University
Bloomington M,W
South Bend M,W
Southeast M,W
Indiana University-Purdue University Fort Wayne M,W
Indiana University-Purdue University Indianapolis M,W
Indiana Wesleyan University M,W
Marian College M,W
Oakland City University M,W
Purdue University M,W
Purdue University
Calumet M,W
Saint Joseph's College M,W
St. Mary-of-the-Woods College W
Taylor University M,W
University of Evansville M,W
University of Indianapolis M,W
University of Notre Dame M,W
University of St. Francis M,W
University of Southern Indiana M,W
Valparaiso University M,W
Vincennes University M,W

Iowa
AIB College of Business W
Ashford University M,W
Briar Cliff University M,W
Clarke College M,W
Clinton Community College M
Des Moines Area Community College M,W
Dordt College M,W
Drake University M,W
Ellsworth Community College M,W
Graceland University M,W
Grand View University M,W
Indian Hills Community College M
Iowa Central Community College M,W
Iowa Lakes Community College M,W
Iowa State University M,W
Iowa Wesleyan College M,W
Iowa Western Community College M,W
Kirkwood Community College M,W
Marshalltown Community College M,W
Morningside College M,W
Mount Mercy College M,W
North Iowa Area Community College M,W
Northwestern College M,W
St. Ambrose University M,W
Southeastern Community College
North Campus M,W
Southwestern Community College M,W
University of Iowa M,W
University of Northern Iowa M,W
Waldorf College M,W
William Penn University M,W

Kansas
Allen County Community College M,W
Baker University M,W
Barton County Community College M,W
Benedictine College M,W
Bethany College M,W
Bethel College M,W
Brown Mackie College
Salina M,W
Central Christian College of Kansas M,W
Cloud County Community College M,W
Coffeyville Community College M,W
Colby Community College M,W
Cowley County Community College M,W
Dodge City Community College M,W
Emporia State University M,W
Fort Hays State University M,W
Fort Scott Community College M,W
Friends University M,W
Garden City Community College M,W
Hesston College M,W
Highland Community College M,W
Hutchinson Community College M,W
Independence Community College M,W
Johnson County Community College M,W
Kansas City Kansas Community College M,W
Kansas State University M,W
Kansas Wesleyan University M,W
Labette Community College M,W
McPherson College M,W
MidAmerica Nazarene University M,W
Neosho County Community College M,W
Newman University M,W
Ottawa University M,W
Pittsburg State University M,W
Pratt Community College M,W
Seward County Community College M,W
Southwestern College M,W
Sterling College M,W
Tabor College M,W
University of Kansas M,W
University of St. Mary M,W
Washburn University M,W
Wichita State University M,W

Kentucky
Alice Lloyd College M,W
Asbury College M,W
Bellarmine University M,W
Brescia University M,W
Campbellsville University M,W
Eastern Kentucky University M,W
Georgetown College M,W
Kentucky State University M
Kentucky Wesleyan College M,W
Lindsey Wilson College M,W
Mid-Continent University M,W
Midway College W
Morehead State University M,W
Murray State University M,W
Northern Kentucky University M,W
Pikeville College M,W
St. Catharine College M,W

Union College M,W
University of Kentucky M,W
University of Louisville M,W
University of the Cumberlands M,W
Western Kentucky University M,W

Louisiana
Bossier Parish Community College M
Centenary College of Louisiana M,W
Delgado Community College M
Dillard University M,W
Grambling State University M,W
Louisiana State University and Agricultural and Mechanical College M,W
Louisiana Tech University M,W
Loyola University New Orleans M,W
McNeese State University M,W
Nicholls State University M,W
Northwestern State University M,W
Southeastern Louisiana University M,W
Southern University
New Orleans M,W
Southern University and Agricultural and Mechanical College M,W
Tulane University M,W
University of Louisiana at Lafayette M,W
University of Louisiana at Monroe M,W
University of New Orleans M,W
Xavier University of Louisiana M,W

Maine
University of Maine M,W
University of Maine
Augusta M,W

Maryland
Allegany College of Maryland M,W
Anne Arundel Community College M,W
Bowie State University M,W
Chesapeake College M,W
College of Southern Maryland M,W
Columbia Union College M,W
Community College of Baltimore County M,W
Coppin State University M,W
Garrett College M,W
Hagerstown Community College M,W
Harford Community College M,W
Howard Community College M,W
Loyola College in Maryland M,W
Morgan State University M,W
Mount St. Mary's University M,W
Prince George's Community College M,W
Towson University M,W
University of Maryland
Baltimore County M,W
College Park M,W
Eastern Shore M,W

Massachusetts
American International College M,W
Assumption College M,W
Bentley University M,W
Boston College M,W
Boston University M,W
College of the Holy Cross M,W
Dean College M,W
Massasoit Community College M
Merrimack College M,W
Northeastern University M,W
Roxbury Community College M
Stonehill College M,W
University of Massachusetts
Amherst M,W
Lowell M,W

Michigan
Alpena Community College M,W
Aquinas College M,W
Central Michigan University M,W
Concordia University M,W
Cornerstone University M,W
Davenport University M,W
Eastern Michigan University M,W
Ferris State University M,W
Glen Oaks Community College M,W
Gogebic Community College M,W
Grand Rapids Community College M,W
Grand Valley State University M,W
Hillsdale College M,W
Kalamazoo Valley Community College M,W
Kellogg Community College M,W
Kirtland Community College M,W
Lake Michigan College M,W
Lake Superior State University M,W
Lansing Community College M,W
Macomb Community College M,W
Madonna University M,W
Michigan State University M,W
Michigan Technological University M,W
Mott Community College M,W
Muskegon Community College M,W
Northern Michigan University M,W
Northwood University: Michigan M,W
Oakland Community College M,W
Oakland University M,W
Rochester College M,W
Saginaw Valley State University M,W
Siena Heights University M,W
Southwestern Michigan College M,W
Spring Arbor University M,W
University of Detroit Mercy M,W
University of Michigan M,W
University of Michigan
Dearborn M,W
Wayne State University M,W
Western Michigan University M,W

Minnesota
Bemidji State University M,W
Concordia University: St. Paul M,W
Minnesota State University
Mankato M,W
Moorhead M,W
Saint Cloud State University M,W
Southwest Minnesota State University M,W
University of Minnesota
Crookston M,W
Duluth M,W
Twin Cities M,W
Winona State University M,W

Mississippi
Alcorn State University M,W
Belhaven College M,W
Blue Mountain College M,W
Coahoma Community College M,W
Copiah-Lincoln Community College M,W
Delta State University M,W
East Central Community College M,W
East Mississippi Community College M,W
Hinds Community College M,W
Holmes Community College M,W
Itawamba Community College M,W
Jackson State University M,W
Meridian Community College M,W
Mississippi Gulf Coast Community College M,W
Mississippi State University M,W
Mississippi Valley State University M,W
Northwest Mississippi Community College M,W
Southwest Mississippi Community College M,W
Tougaloo College M,W
University of Mississippi M,W
University of Southern Mississippi M,W
William Carey University M,W

Missouri
Avila University M,W
Central Methodist University M,W
College of the Ozarks M,W
Columbia College M,W
Cottey College W
Crowder College W
Culver-Stockton College M,W
Drury University M,W
Evangel University M,W
Hannibal-LaGrange College M,W
Harris-Stowe State University M,W
Jefferson College W
Lincoln University M,W
Metropolitan Community College: Penn Valley M
Mineral Area College M,W
Missouri Baptist University M,W
Missouri Southern State University M,W
Missouri State University M,W
Missouri State University: West Plains M
Missouri Valley College M,W
Missouri Western State University M,W
Moberly Area Community College M,W
North Central Missouri College M,W
Northwest Missouri State University M,W
Park University M,W
Research College of Nursing M,W
Rockhurst University M,W
St. Louis Community College M,W
St. Louis Community College
Meramec M,W
Saint Louis University M,W
Southeast Missouri State University M,W
Southwest Baptist University M,W
State Fair Community College M,W
Stephens College W
Three Rivers Community College M,W
Truman State University M,W
University of Central Missouri M,W
University of Missouri
Columbia M,W
Kansas City M,W
Missouri University of Science and Technology M,W
St. Louis M,W
William Jewell College M,W
William Woods University M,W

Montana
Carroll College M,W
Dawson Community College M,W
Miles Community College M,W
Montana State University
Billings M,W
Bozeman M,W
Northern M,W
Montana Tech of the University of Montana M,W
Rocky Mountain College M,W
University of Great Falls M,W
University of Montana M,W
University of Montana: Western M,W

Nebraska
Bellevue University M
Central Community College M
Chadron State College M,W
College of Saint Mary W
Concordia University M,W
Creighton University M,W
Doane College M,W
Kaplan University
Lincoln M,W
Mid-Plains Community College Area M,W
Nebraska College of Technical Agriculture M,W
Northeast Community College M,W
Peru State College M,W
University of Nebraska
Kearney M,W
Lincoln M,W
Omaha M,W
Wayne State College M,W
Western Nebraska Community College M,W
York College M,W

Nevada
University of Nevada
Las Vegas M,W
Reno M,W

New Hampshire
Franklin Pierce University M,W
Hesser College M,W
St. Anselm College M,W
Southern New Hampshire University M,W
University of New Hampshire M,W

New Jersey
Bloomfield College M,W
Brookdale Community College M,W
Burlington County College M,W
Caldwell College M,W
Essex County College M,W
Fairleigh Dickinson University
Metropolitan Campus M,W
Felician College M,W
Georgian Court University W
Mercer County Community College M,W
Monmouth University M,W
New Jersey Institute of Technology M,W
Rider University M,W
Rutgers, The State University of New Jersey
New Brunswick/Piscataway Campus M,W
Saint Peter's College M,W
Salem Community College M,W
Seton Hall University M,W
Union County College W

New Mexico
Eastern New Mexico University M,W
New Mexico Highlands University M,W
New Mexico Junior College M,W
New Mexico Military Institute M
New Mexico State University M,W
University of New Mexico M,W
University of the Southwest M
Western New Mexico University M,W

New York
Adelphi University M,W
ASA Institute of Business and Computer Technology M,W
Canisius College M,W
City University of New York
Queens College M,W
Colgate University M,W
College of Saint Rose M,W
Concordia College M,W
Daemen College M,W
Dominican College of Blauvelt M,W
Dowling College M,W
Fordham University M,W
Genesee Community College M,W
Hofstra University M,W
Houghton College M,W
Iona College M,W
Le Moyne College M,W
Long Island University
Brooklyn Campus M,W
C. W. Post Campus M,W
Manhattan College M,W
Marist College M,W
Mercy College M,W
Molloy College M,W
Monroe College M
Monroe Community College M
New York Institute of Technology M
Niagara County Community College M,W
Niagara University M,W
Nyack College M,W
Pace University M,W
Roberts Wesleyan College M,W
Saint Bonaventure University M,W
St. Francis College M,W
St. John's University M,W
St. Thomas Aquinas College M,W
Siena College M,W
State University of New York
Albany M,W
Binghamton M,W
Buffalo M,W
Stony Brook M,W

Syracuse University M,W
Wagner College M,W

North Carolina
Appalachian State University M,W
Barton College M,W
Belmont Abbey College M,W
Brevard College M,W
Campbell University M,W
Catawba College M,W
Davidson College M,W
Duke University M,W
East Carolina University M,W
Elizabeth City State University M,W
Elon University M,W
Fayetteville State University M,W
Gardner-Webb University M,W
High Point University M,W
Johnson C. Smith University M,W
Lees-McRae College M,W
Lenoir Community College M
Lenoir-Rhyne University M,W
Livingstone College M,W
Louisburg College M,W
Mars Hill College M,W
Montreat College M,W
Mount Olive College M,W
North Carolina Agricultural and Technical State University M,W
North Carolina Central University M,W
North Carolina State University M,W
Pfeiffer University M,W
Queens University of Charlotte M,W
St. Andrews Presbyterian College M,W
St. Augustine's College M,W
Shaw University M,W
University of North Carolina
  Asheville M,W
  Chapel Hill M,W
  Charlotte M,W
  Greensboro M,W
  Pembroke M,W
  Wilmington M,W
Wake Forest University M,W
Western Carolina University M,W
Wingate University M,W
Winston-Salem State University M,W

North Dakota
Bismarck State College M,W
Dickinson State University M,W
Jamestown College M,W
Lake Region State College M,W
Mayville State University M,W
Minot State University M,W
Minot State University: Bottineau Campus M,W
North Dakota State College of Science M,W
North Dakota State University M,W
University of Mary M,W
University of North Dakota M,W
Valley City State University M,W
Williston State College M,W

Ohio
Ashland University M,W
Bowling Green State University M,W
Cedarville University M,W
Central State University M,W
Cincinnati State Technical and Community College M,W
Clark State Community College M,W
Cleveland State University M,W
Columbus State Community College M,W
Edison State Community College M,W
Kent State University M,W
Lakeland Community College M,W
Malone University M,W
Miami University
  Oxford Campus M,W
Mount Vernon Nazarene University M,W
Notre Dame College M,W
Ohio Dominican University M,W
Ohio State University
  Columbus Campus M,W
Ohio University M,W
Owens Community College
  Toledo M,W
Shawnee State University M,W
Sinclair Community College M,W
Southern State Community College M,W
University of Akron M,W
University of Cincinnati M,W
University of Dayton M,W
University of Findlay M,W
University of Rio Grande M,W
University of Toledo M,W
Urbana University M,W
Ursuline College W
Walsh University M,W
Wright State University M,W
Xavier University M,W
Youngstown State University M,W

Oklahoma
Bacone College M,W
Cameron University M,W
Carl Albert State College M,W
Connors State College M,W
East Central University M,W
Eastern Oklahoma State College M,W
Langston University M,W
Northeastern Oklahoma Agricultural and Mechanical College M,W
Northeastern State University M,W
Northern Oklahoma College M,W
Northwestern Oklahoma State University M,W
Oklahoma Baptist University M,W
Oklahoma Christian University M,W
Oklahoma City University M,W
Oklahoma Panhandle State University M,W
Oklahoma State University M,W
Oklahoma Wesleyan University M,W
Oral Roberts University M,W
Redlands Community College M,W
Rogers State University M,W
St. Gregory's University M,W
Seminole State College M,W
Southeastern Oklahoma State University M,W
Southern Nazarene University M,W
Southwestern Oklahoma State University M,W
University of Central Oklahoma M,W
University of Oklahoma M,W
University of Science and Arts of Oklahoma M,W
University of Tulsa M,W
Western Oklahoma State College M,W

Oregon
Blue Mountain Community College M,W
Chemeketa Community College M,W
Clackamas Community College M,W
Concordia University M,W
Corban College M,W
Eastern Oregon University M,W
Lane Community College M,W
Linn-Benton Community College M,W
Mt. Hood Community College M,W
Northwest Christian University M,W
Oregon Institute of Technology M,W
Oregon State University M,W
Portland Community College M,W
Portland State University M,W
Southern Oregon University M,W
Southwestern Oregon Community College M,W
Treasure Valley Community College M,W
University of Oregon M,W
University of Portland M,W
Warner Pacific College M,W

Pennsylvania
Bloomsburg University of Pennsylvania M,W
Bucknell University M,W
California University of Pennsylvania M,W
Carlow University W
Chestnut Hill College M,W
Cheyney University of Pennsylvania M,W
Clarion University of Pennsylvania M,W
Community College of Beaver County M
Drexel University M,W
Duquesne University M,W
East Stroudsburg University of Pennsylvania M,W
Edinboro University of Pennsylvania M,W
Gannon University M,W
Harcum College M,W
Holy Family University M,W
Indiana University of Pennsylvania M,W
Kutztown University of Pennsylvania M,W
La Salle University M,W
Lackawanna College M,W
Lafayette College M,W
Lehigh University M,W
Lock Haven University of Pennsylvania M,W
Mansfield University of Pennsylvania M,W
Mercyhurst College M,W
Millersville University of Pennsylvania M,W
Penn State
  University Park M,W
Philadelphia University M,W
Point Park University M,W
Robert Morris University M,W
St. Francis University M,W
Saint Joseph's University M,W
Seton Hill University M,W
Shippensburg University of Pennsylvania M,W
Slippery Rock University of Pennsylvania M,W
Temple University M,W
University of Pittsburgh M,W
University of Pittsburgh
  Johnstown M,W
  Titusville M,W
University of the Sciences in Philadelphia M,W
Valley Forge Military Academy & College M
Villanova University M,W
West Chester University of Pennsylvania M,W
Westminster College M,W

Puerto Rico
Bayamon Central University M,W
Inter American University of Puerto Rico
  Aguadilla Campus M,W
  Arecibo Campus M
  Bayamon Campus M,W
  Fajardo Campus M
  Guayama Campus M,W
  Metropolitan Campus M,W
  Ponce Campus M,W
  San German Campus M,W
Turabo University M,W
Universidad del Este M,W
Universidad Metropolitana M,W
University of Puerto Rico
  Bayamon University College M,W
  Carolina Regional College M,W
  Cayey University College M,W
  Humacao M,W
  Mayaguez M,W
  Ponce M,W
  Utuado M,W
University of the Sacred Heart M

Rhode Island
Bryant University M,W
Community College of Rhode Island M,W
Providence College M,W
University of Rhode Island M,W

South Carolina
Aiken Technical College M
Allen University M,W
Anderson University M,W
Charleston Southern University M,W
The Citadel M
Claflin University M,W
Clemson University M,W
Coastal Carolina University M,W
College of Charleston M,W
Columbia College W
Converse College W
Erskine College M,W
Francis Marion University M,W
Furman University M,W
Lander University M,W
Limestone College M,W
Morris College M,W
Newberry College M,W
North Greenville University M,W
Presbyterian College M,W
South Carolina State University M,W
Southern Wesleyan University M,W
Spartanburg Methodist College M,W
University of South Carolina M,W
University of South Carolina
  Aiken M,W
  Upstate M,W
Winthrop University M,W
Wofford College M,W

South Dakota
Augustana College M,W
Black Hills State University M,W
Dakota State University M,W
Dakota Wesleyan University M,W
Mount Marty College M,W
Northern State University M,W
South Dakota School of Mines and Technology M,W
South Dakota State University M,W
University of Sioux Falls M,W
University of South Dakota M,W

Tennessee
Austin Peay State University M,W
Belmont University M,W
Bethel College M,W
Carson-Newman College M,W
Chattanooga State Technical Community College M,W
Christian Brothers University M,W
Cleveland State Community College M,W
Columbia State Community College M,W
Crichton College M
Cumberland University M,W
Dyersburg State Community College M,W
East Tennessee State University M,W
Freed-Hardeman University M,W
Jackson State Community College M,W
King College M,W
Lambuth University M,W
Lane College M,W
Lee University M,W
LeMoyne-Owen College M,W
Lincoln Memorial University M,W
Lipscomb University M,W
Martin Methodist College M,W
Middle Tennessee State University M,W
Milligan College M,W
Motlow State Community College M,W
Roane State Community College M,W
Southwest Tennessee Community College M,W
Tennessee State University M,W
Tennessee Technological University M,W
Tennessee Temple University M,W
Tennessee Wesleyan College M,W
Trevecca Nazarene University M,W
Tusculum College M,W
Union University M,W
University of Memphis M,W
University of Tennessee
  Chattanooga M,W
  Knoxville M,W
  Martin M,W
Vanderbilt University M,W
Volunteer State Community College M,W
Walters State Community College M,W

Texas
Abilene Christian University M,W
Angelina College M,W
Angelo State University M,W
Baylor University M,W
Blinn College M,W
Clarendon College M,W
Collin County Community College District M,W
Frank Phillips College M,W
Hill College M,W
Houston Baptist University M,W
Howard College M,W
Jacksonville College M,W
Jarvis Christian College M,W
Kilgore College M,W
Lamar University M,W
Lee College M
Lon Morris College M,W
Lubbock Christian University M,W
McLennan Community College M,W
Midland College M,W
Midwestern State University M,W
Odessa College M,W
Panola College M,W
Paris Junior College M,W
Prairie View A&M University M,W
Ranger College M,W
Rice University M,W
St. Edward's University M,W
St. Mary's University M,W
Sam Houston State University M,W
San Jacinto College W
South Plains College M,W
Southern Methodist University M,W
Southwestern Assemblies of God University M,W
Stephen F. Austin State University M,W
Tarleton State University M,W
Temple College M,W
Texas A&M University M,W
Texas A&M University
- Commerce M,W
- Corpus Christi M,W
- Kingsville M,W

Texas Christian University M,W
Texas Southern University M,W
Texas State University: San Marcos M,W
Texas Tech University M,W
Texas Woman's University W
Tyler Junior College M,W
University of Houston M,W
University of North Texas M,W
University of Texas
- Arlington M,W
- Austin M,W
- Pan American M,W
- of the Permian Basin M,W
- San Antonio M,W

University of the Incarnate Word M,W
Wayland Baptist University M,W
Weatherford College M,W
West Texas A&M University M,W
Wiley College M,W

Utah
Brigham Young University M,W
College of Eastern Utah M,W
Dixie State College of Utah M,W
Salt Lake Community College M,W
Snow College M,W
Southern Utah University M,W
University of Utah M,W
Utah State University M,W
Utah Valley University M,W
Weber State University M,W
Westminster College M,W

Vermont
St. Michael's College M,W
University of Vermont M,W

Virginia
Bluefield College M,W
College of William and Mary M,W
George Mason University M,W
Hampton University M,W
James Madison University M,W
Liberty University M,W
Longwood University M,W
Norfolk State University M,W
Old Dominion University M,W
Radford University M,W
St. Paul's College M,W
University of Richmond M,W
University of Virginia M,W
University of Virginia's College at Wise M,W
Virginia Commonwealth University M,W
Virginia Intermont College M,W
Virginia Military Institute M
Virginia Polytechnic Institute and State University M,W
Virginia State University M,W
Virginia Union University M,W

Washington
Big Bend Community College M,W
Central Washington University M,W
Centralia College M,W
Clark College M,W
Columbia Basin College M,W
Eastern Washington University M,W
Edmonds Community College M,W
Everett Community College M,W
Evergreen State College M,W
Gonzaga University M,W
Grays Harbor College M,W
Green River Community College M,W
Highline Community College M,W
Lower Columbia College M,W
North Seattle Community College M,W
Northwest Indian College M,W
Northwest University M,W
Olympic College M,W
Peninsula College M,W
Pierce College M,W
Saint Martin's University M,W
Seattle Pacific University M,W
Seattle University M,W
Shoreline Community College M,W
Skagit Valley College M,W
Spokane Community College M,W
Tacoma Community College M,W
University of Washington M,W
Walla Walla Community College M,W
Washington State University M,W
Western Washington University M,W
Whatcom Community College M,W
Yakima Valley Community College M,W

West Virginia
Alderson-Broaddus College M,W
Bluefield State College M,W
Concord University M,W
Davis and Elkins College M,W
Fairmont State University M,W
Glenville State College M,W
Marshall University M,W
Mountain State University M
Ohio Valley University M,W
Potomac State College of West Virginia University M,W
Salem International University M,W
Shepherd University M,W
University of Charleston M,W
West Liberty State College M,W
West Virginia State University M,W
West Virginia University M,W
West Virginia University Institute of Technology M,W
West Virginia Wesleyan College M,W
Wheeling Jesuit University M,W

Wisconsin
Cardinal Stritch University M,W
Marquette University M,W
Silver Lake College M,W
University of Wisconsin
- Green Bay M,W
- Milwaukee M,W
- Parkside M,W

Viterbo University M,W

Wyoming
Casper College M,W
Central Wyoming College M,W
Eastern Wyoming College M,W
Laramie County Community College M
Northwest College M,W
Sheridan College M,W
University of Wyoming M,W
Western Wyoming Community College M,W

Bowling

Arkansas
Arkansas State University W
University of Arkansas
- Pine Bluff W

Delaware
Delaware State University W

Florida
Bethune-Cookman University W
Webber International University M,W

Illinois
McKendree University M,W
Robert Morris College: Chicago M,W

Indiana
Calumet College of St. Joseph M,W
Vincennes University M,W

Iowa
St. Ambrose University M,W

Kansas
Newman University M,W
Wichita State University M,W

Kentucky
Campbellsville University M,W
Pikeville College M,W

Louisiana
Southern University and Agricultural and Mechanical College W

Maryland
Bowie State University W
Coppin State University W
Morgan State University W
Prince George's Community College M,W

Michigan
Aquinas College M,W
Saginaw Valley State University M

Mississippi
Jackson State University M,W
Mississippi Valley State University M,W

Missouri
Missouri Baptist University M,W

Nebraska
University of Nebraska
- Lincoln W

New Jersey
Fairleigh Dickinson University
- Metropolitan Campus W

New York
Adelphi University W

North Carolina
Blue Ridge Community College M
Johnson C. Smith University W
Livingstone College M,W
North Carolina Central University M,W
St. Augustine's College W
Shaw University W

Pennsylvania
Cheyney University of Pennsylvania W

South Carolina
South Carolina State University W

Tennessee
Martin Methodist College M,W

Texas
Prairie View A&M University W
Texas Southern University W

Virginia
Norfolk State University W

Wisconsin
Viterbo University M,W

Cheerleading

Alabama
Bevill State Community College M,W
Chattahoochee Valley Community College M,W
Faulkner State Community College M,W
Gadsden State Community College W
Northwest-Shoals Community College M,W
Shelton State Community College M,W
Southern Union State Community College M,W
Troy University M,W
University of Alabama M,W
University of Alabama
- Huntsville M,W

University of Mobile M,W

Arizona
Glendale Community College M,W

Arkansas
Lyon College M,W
North Arkansas College W
University of Arkansas M,W
University of Arkansas
- Fort Smith M,W
- Monticello M,W

University of Central Arkansas M,W
Williams Baptist College M,W

California
California Baptist University M,W
Hope International University M,W

Delaware
University of Delaware M,W

Florida
Pensacola Junior College M,W
University of Central Florida M,W
University of Florida M,W
Warner University M,W
Webber International University M,W

Georgia
Albany State University W
Brewton-Parker College M,W
Columbus State University M,W
Georgia Institute of Technology M,W
Gordon College W
Mercer University M,W
Reinhardt College M,W
University of West Georgia M,W

Hawaii
Hawaii Pacific University M,W
University of Hawaii
Manoa M,W

Idaho
Boise State University M,W
North Idaho College M,W

Illinois
Kaskaskia College M,W
McKendree University M,W
Northwestern University M,W
Olivet Nazarene University M,W
Rend Lake College W
Robert Morris College: Chicago W
University of St. Francis W

Indiana
Ancilla College M,W
Grace College M,W
Indiana Institute of Technology M,W
Indiana Wesleyan University M,W
Marian College M,W
Oakland City University W
University of St. Francis M,W

Iowa
AIB College of Business M,W
Iowa Western Community College M,W
St. Ambrose University M,W
Waldorf College W
William Penn University W

Kansas
Allen County Community College M,W
Baker University M,W
Barton County Community College M,W
Benedictine College M,W
Bethany College M,W
Central Christian College of Kansas M,W
Coffeyville Community College M,W
Cowley County Community College M,W
Dodge City Community College M,W
Emporia State University M,W
Fort Scott Community College W
Garden City Community College M,W
Labette Community College M,W
McPherson College M,W
MidAmerica Nazarene University M,W
Neosho County Community College M,W
Ottawa University M,W
Pittsburg State University M,W
Pratt Community College M,W
Seward County Community College M,W
Southwestern College M,W
Tabor College M,W
Washburn University M,W
Wichita State University M,W

Kentucky
Bellarmine University M,W
Kentucky State University W
Murray State University M,W
Northern Kentucky University M,W
St. Catharine College M,W
Union College M,W
University of Louisville M,W
University of the Cumberlands M,W

Louisiana
Bossier Parish Community College M,W
Delgado Community College W
McNeese State University M,W
University of Louisiana at Lafayette M,W
University of Louisiana at Monroe M,W

Maryland
Morgan State University W
University of Maryland
College Park W

Michigan
Northwood University: Michigan M,W
University of Detroit Mercy M,W

Mississippi
Copiah-Lincoln Community College M,W
Itawamba Community College M,W
Mississippi Gulf Coast Community College M,W
Northwest Mississippi Community College M,W
Southwest Mississippi Community College M,W
University of Mississippi M,W
William Carey University M,W

Missouri
Avila University W
Culver-Stockton College M,W
Drury University M,W
Evangel University M,W
Hannibal-LaGrange College M,W
Harris-Stowe State University M,W
Missouri Baptist University M,W
Missouri Southern State University M,W
Missouri State University: West Plains M,W
Missouri Valley College M,W
Moberly Area Community College M,W
Northwest Missouri State University M,W
Southeast Missouri State University M,W
University of Missouri
Kansas City M,W
William Jewell College M,W

Nevada
University of Nevada
Las Vegas M,W
Reno M,W

New Mexico
New Mexico Junior College M,W

New York
ASA Institute of Business and Computer Technology W
Hofstra University M,W
Nyack College M,W

North Carolina
Brevard College M,W
Elon University M,W
Gardner-Webb University M,W
Lenoir-Rhyne University M,W
Mars Hill College M,W
Methodist University M,W
Queens University of Charlotte M,W
University of North Carolina
Wilmington M,W

Ohio
Ashland University W
Kent State University M,W
University of Rio Grande M,W
Urbana University W

Oklahoma
Bacone College M,W
Cameron University M,W
Carl Albert State College W
Eastern Oklahoma State College M,W
Langston University M,W
Northeastern Oklahoma Agricultural and Mechanical College M,W
Northwestern Oklahoma State University M,W
Oklahoma Christian University W
Oklahoma City University M,W
Oklahoma Panhandle State University M,W
Oral Roberts University M,W
Rose State College M,W
Southeastern Oklahoma State University W
Southern Nazarene University M,W
Southwestern Oklahoma State University M,W
University of Oklahoma M,W
University of Science and Arts of Oklahoma M,W
University of Tulsa M,W
Western Oklahoma State College M,W

Oregon
Southwestern Oregon Community College M,W
University of Oregon W

Pennsylvania
Kutztown University of Pennsylvania W
Lackawanna College W
Penn State
University Park M,W
St. Francis University M,W
Seton Hill University M,W
Temple University M,W
West Chester University of Pennsylvania W

Puerto Rico
University of Puerto Rico
Carolina Regional College M,W
Cayey University College M,W
Humacao M,W

South Carolina
Anderson University W
Clemson University M,W
Limestone College M,W
Morris College M,W
Newberry College W
North Greenville University M,W
Presbyterian College M,W
Spartanburg Methodist College M,W

South Dakota
Dakota Wesleyan University M,W

Tennessee
Bethel College M,W
Cumberland University M,W
Freed-Hardeman University W
King College M,W
Martin Methodist College W
Tennessee Technological University M,W
Tennessee Wesleyan College M,W
Tusculum College W
University of Memphis M,W
University of Tennessee
Martin W

Texas
Angelina College W
Clarendon College M,W
East Texas Baptist University M,W
Houston Baptist University M,W
Howard College M,W
Jacksonville College M,W
Lon Morris College M,W
Lubbock Christian University M,W
Ranger College M,W
St. Edward's University M,W
San Jacinto College M,W
South Plains College M,W
Southern Methodist University M,W
Southwestern Assemblies of God University W
Tarleton State University M,W
Texas Southern University M,W
Tyler Junior College M,W
University of Texas
of the Permian Basin M,W
Western Texas College W

Utah
Brigham Young University M,W
Snow College M,W

Virginia
Liberty University M,W
Old Dominion University M,W
Virginia Intermont College W

Washington
University of Washington M,W
Walla Walla Community College W

West Virginia
Mountain State University M,W
University of Charleston M,W

Wyoming
University of Wyoming M,W
Western Wyoming Community College W

Cricket

California
College of the Redwoods M

Cross-country

Alabama
Alabama Agricultural and Mechanical University M,W
Alabama State University M,W
Auburn University M,W
Bevill State Community College W
Jacksonville State University M,W
Lurleen B. Wallace Community College M,W
Miles College M,W
Samford University M,W
Southern Union State Community College M,W
Spring Hill College M,W
Troy University M,W
University of Alabama M,W
University of Alabama
Birmingham W
Huntsville M,W
University of Mobile M,W
University of North Alabama M,W
University of South Alabama M,W
University of West Alabama M,W
Wallace State Community College at Hanceville M,W

Alaska
University of Alaska
Anchorage M,W
Fairbanks M,W

Arizona
Arizona State University M,W
Central Arizona College M,W
Dine College M,W
Gateway Community College M,W
Glendale Community College M,W
Mesa Community College M,W
Northern Arizona University M,W
Paradise Valley Community College M,W
Pima Community College M,W
Scottsdale Community College M,W
University of Arizona M,W
Yavapai College W

Arkansas
Arkansas State University M,W
Arkansas Tech University W
Harding University M,W
Henderson State University W
Lyon College M,W
Ouachita Baptist University W
Southern Arkansas University W
University of Arkansas M,W
University of Arkansas
Little Rock M,W
Monticello W
Pine Bluff M,W
University of Central Arkansas M,W

California
Azusa Pacific University M,W
Bethany University M,W
Biola University M,W
California Baptist University M,W

California Polytechnic State University: San Luis Obispo M,W
California State Polytechnic University: Pomona M,W
California State University
- Chico M,W
- Dominguez Hills W
- Fresno M,W
- Fullerton M,W
- Long Beach M,W
- Los Angeles M,W
- Monterey Bay M,W
- Northridge M,W
- Sacramento M,W
- Stanislaus M,W

Concordia University M,W
Fresno City College M,W
Fresno Pacific University M,W
Holy Names University M,W
Humboldt State University M,W
Loyola Marymount University M,W
The Master's College M,W
Notre Dame de Namur University M,W
Pepperdine University M,W
Point Loma Nazarene University M,W
St. Mary's College of California M,W
San Diego Christian College M,W
San Diego State University W
San Jose State University M,W
Santa Clara University M,W
Santiago Canyon College M,W
Stanford University M,W
University of California
- Berkeley M,W
- Davis M,W
- Irvine M,W
- Los Angeles M,W
- Riverside M,W
- Santa Barbara M,W

University of San Diego M,W
University of San Francisco M,W
University of Southern California M,W
University of the Pacific W
Vanguard University of Southern California M,W
Westmont College M,W
William Jessup University M,W
Yuba Community College District M,W

Colorado

Adams State College M,W
Colorado Christian University M,W
Colorado School of Mines M,W
Colorado State University M,W
Colorado State University
- Pueblo W

Fort Lewis College M,W
Mesa State College W
Regis University M,W
University of Colorado
- Boulder M,W
- Colorado Springs M,W

University of Northern Colorado W
Western State College of Colorado M,W

Connecticut

Central Connecticut State University M,W
Fairfield University M,W
Post University M,W
Quinnipiac University M,W
Sacred Heart University M,W
Southern Connecticut State University M,W
University of Connecticut M,W
University of Hartford M,W
University of New Haven M,W

Delaware

Delaware State University M,W
Goldey-Beacom College M,W
Wilmington University M,W

District of Columbia

American University M,W
George Washington University M,W
Georgetown University M,W
Howard University M,W

Florida

Bethune-Cookman University M,W
Chipola College W
Embry-Riddle Aeronautical University M,W
Flagler College M,W
Florida Atlantic University M,W
Florida Institute of Technology M,W
Florida Southern College M,W
Florida State University M,W
Jacksonville University W
Nova Southeastern University M,W
St. Leo University M,W
Saint Thomas University M,W
Stetson University M,W
University of Central Florida M,W
University of Florida M,W
University of Miami M,W
University of North Florida M,W
University of South Florida M,W
University of Tampa M,W
University of West Florida M,W
Warner University M,W
Webber International University M,W

Georgia

Albany State University M,W
Andrew College M,W
Augusta State University M,W
Brenau University W
Clark Atlanta University M,W
Clayton State University M,W
Columbus State University M,W
Covenant College M,W
Georgia College and State University M,W
Georgia Institute of Technology M,W
Georgia Southern University W
Georgia Southwestern State University W
Georgia State University M,W
Gordon College M,W
Kennesaw State University M,W
Mercer University M,W
Middle Georgia College M,W
Morehouse College M
Paine College M,W
Reinhardt College M,W
Savannah State University M,W
Shorter College M,W
Truett-McConnell College M,W
University of Georgia M,W
University of West Georgia M,W
Valdosta State University M,W
Young Harris College M,W

Hawaii

Brigham Young University-Hawaii M,W
Chaminade University of Honolulu M,W
Hawaii Pacific University M,W
University of Hawaii
- Hilo M,W
- Manoa W

Idaho

Boise State University M,W
College of Idaho M,W
Idaho State University M,W
Lewis-Clark State College M,W
Northwest Nazarene University M,W
University of Idaho M,W

Illinois

Bradley University M,W
Chicago State University M,W
College of Lake County M,W
Danville Area Community College M,W
DePaul University M,W
Eastern Illinois University M,W
Illinois Central College M,W
Illinois Institute of Technology M,W
Illinois State University M,W
Judson University M,W
Lewis University M,W
Lincoln College M,W
Loyola University Chicago M,W
McKendree University M,W
Moraine Valley Community College M,W
Morton College M,W
Northwestern University W
Olivet Nazarene University M,W
Rend Lake College M,W
Robert Morris College: Chicago M,W
St. Xavier University M,W
Sauk Valley Community College M,W
Southern Illinois University Carbondale M,W
Southern Illinois University Edwardsville M,W
Trinity Christian College M,W
University of Illinois
- Chicago M,W
- Urbana-Champaign M,W

University of St. Francis M,W
Waubonsee Community College M,W
Western Illinois University M,W

Indiana

Ball State University M,W
Bethel College M,W
Butler University M,W
Calumet College of St. Joseph M,W
Goshen College M,W
Grace College M,W
Huntington University M,W
Indiana Institute of Technology M,W
Indiana State University M,W
Indiana University
- Bloomington M,W

Indiana University-Purdue University Fort Wayne M,W
Indiana University-Purdue University Indianapolis M,W
Indiana Wesleyan University M,W
Marian College M,W
Oakland City University M,W
Purdue University M,W
Saint Joseph's College M,W
Taylor University M,W
University of Evansville M,W
University of Indianapolis M,W
University of Notre Dame M,W
University of St. Francis M,W
University of Southern Indiana M,W
Valparaiso University M,W
Vincennes University M,W

Iowa

Ashford University M,W
Briar Cliff University M,W
Clarke College M,W
Dordt College M,W
Drake University M,W
Ellsworth Community College M,W
Graceland University M,W
Grand View University M,W
Iowa State University M,W
Iowa Wesleyan College M,W
Morningside College M,W
Mount Mercy College M,W
North Iowa Area Community College M,W
Northwestern College M,W
St. Ambrose University M,W
University of Iowa M,W
University of Northern Iowa M,W
William Penn University M,W

Kansas

Allen County Community College M,W
Baker University M,W
Barton County Community College M,W
Benedictine College M,W
Bethany College M,W
Bethel College M,W
Central Christian College of Kansas M,W
Cloud County Community College M,W
Coffeyville Community College M,W
Colby Community College M,W
Cowley County Community College M,W
Dodge City Community College M,W
Emporia State University M,W
Fort Hays State University M,W
Fort Scott Community College M,W
Garden City Community College M,W
Highland Community College M,W
Hutchinson Community College M,W
Johnson County Community College M,W
Kansas City Kansas Community College M,W
Kansas State University M,W
Kansas Wesleyan University M,W
McPherson College M,W
MidAmerica Nazarene University M,W
Neosho County Community College M,W
Newman University M,W
Ottawa University M,W
Pittsburg State University M,W
Pratt Community College M,W
Southwestern College M,W
Sterling College M,W
Tabor College M,W
University of Kansas M,W
Wichita State University M,W

Kentucky

Asbury College M,W
Bellarmine University M,W
Campbellsville University M,W
Eastern Kentucky University M,W
Georgetown College M,W
Kentucky State University M,W
Kentucky Wesleyan College M,W
Lindsey Wilson College M,W
Midway College W
Morehead State University M,W
Murray State University M,W
Northern Kentucky University M,W
Pikeville College M,W
Union College M,W
University of Kentucky M,W
University of Louisville M,W
University of the Cumberlands M,W
Western Kentucky University M,W

Louisiana

Centenary College of Louisiana M,W
Dillard University M,W
Grambling State University M,W
Louisiana State University and Agricultural and Mechanical College M,W
Louisiana Tech University M,W
McNeese State University M,W
Nicholls State University M,W
Northwestern State University M,W
Southeastern Louisiana University M,W
Southern University
- New Orleans M,W

Southern University and Agricultural and Mechanical College M,W
University of Louisiana at Lafayette M,W
University of Louisiana at Monroe M,W
Xavier University of Louisiana M,W

Maine

University of Maine M,W

Maryland

Bowie State University M,W
Columbia Union College M,W
Coppin State University M,W
Hagerstown Community College M,W
Loyola College in Maryland M,W
Morgan State University M,W
Mount St. Mary's University M,W
Towson University M,W
University of Maryland
- Baltimore County M,W

Eastern Shore M,W

Massachusetts
American International College M,W
Boston College M,W
Boston University M,W
Merrimack College W
Northeastern University M,W
Stonehill College M,W
University of Massachusetts
Amherst M,W
Lowell M,W

Michigan
Aquinas College M,W
Central Michigan University M,W
Concordia University M,W
Cornerstone University M,W
Davenport University M,W
Eastern Michigan University M,W
Ferris State University M,W
Grand Rapids Community College M,W
Grand Valley State University M,W
Hillsdale College M,W
Kirtland Community College M,W
Lake Superior State University M,W
Lansing Community College M,W
Macomb Community College M,W
Madonna University M,W
Michigan State University M,W
Michigan Technological University M,W
Mott Community College M,W
Northern Michigan University W
Northwood University: Michigan M,W
Oakland Community College M,W
Oakland University M,W
Saginaw Valley State University M,W
Siena Heights University M,W
Spring Arbor University M,W
University of Detroit Mercy M,W
University of Michigan M,W
Wayne State University M,W
Western Michigan University M,W

Minnesota
Concordia University: St. Paul M,W
Minnesota State University
Mankato M,W
Moorhead M,W
Saint Cloud State University M,W
University of Minnesota
Duluth M,W
Twin Cities M,W
Winona State University W

Mississippi
Alcorn State University M,W
Belhaven College M,W
Blue Mountain College M,W
Delta State University W
Jackson State University M,W
Mississippi State University M,W
Mississippi Valley State University M,W
Tougaloo College M,W
University of Mississippi M,W
University of Southern Mississippi M,W

Missouri
Central Methodist University M,W
Culver-Stockton College M,W
Drury University M,W
Evangel University M,W
Hannibal LaGrange College M,W
Lincoln University W
Missouri Baptist University M,W
Missouri Southern State University M,W
Missouri State University M,W
Missouri Valley College M,W
Northwest Missouri State University M,W
Park University M,W
Research College of Nursing M,W
Saint Louis University M,W
Southeast Missouri State University M,W
Southwest Baptist University M,W
Stephens College W
Truman State University M,W
University of Central Missouri M,W
University of Missouri
Columbia M,W
Kansas City M,W
Missouri University of Science and Technology M,W
William Jewell College M,W
William Woods University M,W

Montana
Carroll College M,W
Flathead Valley Community College M,W
Montana State University
Billings M,W
Bozeman M,W
University of Great Falls M,W
University of Montana M,W

Nebraska
College of Saint Mary W
Concordia University M,W
Creighton University M,W
Doane College M,W
University of Nebraska
Kearney M,W
Lincoln M,W
Omaha W
Wayne State College M,W

Nevada
University of Nevada
Las Vegas W
Reno W

New Hampshire
Southern New Hampshire University M,W
University of New Hampshire M,W

New Jersey
Bloomfield College M,W
Caldwell College W
Fairleigh Dickinson University
Metropolitan Campus M,W
Felician College M,W
Georgian Court University W
Monmouth University M,W
Rider University M,W
Rutgers, The State University of New Jersey
New Brunswick/Piscataway Campus M,W
Saint Peter's College M,W
Seton Hall University M,W

New Mexico
Eastern New Mexico University M,W
Navajo Technical College M,W
New Mexico Highlands University M,W
New Mexico Junior College M,W
New Mexico State University M,W
University of New Mexico M,W
University of the Southwest M,W

New York
Adelphi University M,W
Canisius College M,W
City University of New York
Queens College M,W
College of Saint Rose M,W
Daemen College M,W
Dominican College of Blauvelt W
Fordham University M,W
Hofstra University M,W
Houghton College M,W
Iona College M,W
Le Moyne College M,W
Long Island University
Brooklyn Campus M,W
C. W. Post Campus M,W
Manhattan College M,W
Marist College M,W
Mercy College M,W
Molloy College M,W
New York Institute of Technology M,W
Niagara University M,W
Nyack College M,W
Pace University M,W
Roberts Wesleyan College M,W
St. Francis College M,W
St. John's University W
St. Thomas Aquinas College M,W
Siena College M,W
State University of New York
Albany M,W
Binghamton M,W
Buffalo M,W
Stony Brook M,W
Syracuse University M,W
Wagner College M,W

North Carolina
Appalachian State University M,W
Barton College M,W
Belmont Abbey College M,W
Brevard College M,W
Campbell University M,W
Catawba College M,W
Davidson College M,W
East Carolina University M,W
Elon University M,W
Fayetteville State University M,W
Gardner-Webb University M,W
High Point University M,W
Johnson C. Smith University M,W
Lees-McRae College M,W
Lenoir-Rhyne University M,W
Livingstone College M,W
Mars Hill College M,W
Montreat College M,W
Mount Olive College M,W
North Carolina Agricultural and Technical State University M,W
North Carolina Central University M,W
North Carolina State University M,W
Pfeiffer University M,W
Queens University of Charlotte M,W
St. Andrews Presbyterian College M,W
St. Augustine's College M,W
Shaw University M,W
University of North Carolina
Asheville M,W
Chapel Hill M,W
Charlotte M,W
Greensboro M,W
Pembroke M,W
Wilmington M,W
Wake Forest University M,W
Western Carolina University M,W
Wingate University M,W
Winston-Salem State University M,W

North Dakota
Dickinson State University M,W
Jamestown College M,W
Minot State University M,W
North Dakota State University M,W
University of Mary M,W
University of North Dakota M,W

Ohio
Ashland University M,W
Bowling Green State University M,W
Cedarville University M,W
Central State University M,W
Cleveland State University W
Kent State University M,W
Malone University M,W
Miami University
Oxford Campus M,W
Mount Vernon Nazarene University M,W
Notre Dame College M,W
Ohio Dominican University M,W
Ohio University M,W
Shawnee State University M,W
University of Akron M,W
University of Dayton M,W
University of Findlay M,W
University of Rio Grande M,W
University of Toledo M,W
Urbana University M,W
Ursuline College W
Walsh University M,W
Wright State University M,W
Xavier University M,W
Youngstown State University M,W

Oklahoma
Cameron University M
East Central University M,W
Langston University M,W
Oklahoma Baptist University M,W
Oklahoma Christian University M,W
Oklahoma Panhandle State University M,W
Oklahoma State University M,W
Oklahoma Wesleyan University M,W
Oral Roberts University M,W
Southeastern Oklahoma State University W
Southern Nazarene University M,W
Southwestern Oklahoma State University W
University of Central Oklahoma M,W
University of Oklahoma M,W
University of Tulsa M,W

Oregon
Clackamas Community College M,W
Concordia University M,W
Corban College M,W
Eastern Oregon University M,W
Lane Community College M,W
Mt. Hood Community College M,W
Northwest Christian University M,W
Oregon Institute of Technology M,W
Portland State University M,W
Southern Oregon University M,W
Southwestern Oregon Community College M,W
Treasure Valley Community College M,W
University of Oregon M,W
University of Portland M,W
Warner Pacific College M,W

Pennsylvania
Bloomsburg University of Pennsylvania M,W
California University of Pennsylvania M,W
Chestnut Hill College M,W
Cheyney University of Pennsylvania M,W
Clarion University of Pennsylvania M,W
Duquesne University M,W
East Stroudsburg University of Pennsylvania M,W
Edinboro University of Pennsylvania M,W
Gannon University M,W
Holy Family University M,W
Indiana University of Pennsylvania M,W
Kutztown University of Pennsylvania M,W
La Salle University M,W
Lackawanna College M,W
Lock Haven University of Pennsylvania M,W
Mansfield University of Pennsylvania W
Mercyhurst College M,W
Millersville University of Pennsylvania M,W
Penn State
University Park M,W
Philadelphia University M,W
Point Park University M,W
Robert Morris University M,W
St. Francis University M,W
Saint Joseph's University M,W
Seton Hill University M,W
Shippensburg University of Pennsylvania M,W
Slippery Rock University of Pennsylvania M,W
Temple University M,W
University of Pittsburgh M,W
University of the Sciences in Philadelphia M,W
Villanova University M,W
West Chester University of Pennsylvania M,W
Westminster College W

Puerto Rico
Bayamon Central University M,W
Inter American University of Puerto Rico
 Aguadilla Campus M,W
 Bayamon Campus M,W
 Guayama Campus M,W
 San German Campus M,W
Turabo University M,W
Universidad del Este M,W
Universidad Metropolitana M,W
Universidad Politecnica de Puerto Rico M
University of Puerto Rico
 Carolina Regional College M,W
 Cayey University College M,W
 Humacao M,W
 Mayaguez M,W
 Ponce M,W
 Utuado M,W
University of the Sacred Heart M,W

Rhode Island
Bryant University M,W
Providence College M,W
University of Rhode Island M,W

South Carolina
Anderson University M,W
Charleston Southern University M,W
The Citadel M,W
Claflin University M,W
Clemson University M,W
Coastal Carolina University M,W
College of Charleston M,W
Converse College W
Erskine College M,W
Francis Marion University M,W
Furman University M,W
Lander University W
Limestone College M,W
Morris College M,W
Newberry College M,W
North Greenville University M,W
Presbyterian College M,W
South Carolina State University M,W
Southern Wesleyan University M,W
Spartanburg Methodist College M,W
University of South Carolina W
University of South Carolina
 Aiken W
 Upstate M,W
Winthrop University M,W
Wofford College M,W

South Dakota
Augustana College M,W
Black Hills State University M,W
Dakota State University M,W
Dakota Wesleyan University M,W
Mount Marty College M,W
South Dakota School of Mines and Technology M,W
South Dakota State University M,W
University of Sioux Falls M,W
University of South Dakota M,W

Tennessee
Austin Peay State University M,W
Belmont University M,W
Bethel College M,W
Carson-Newman College M,W
Christian Brothers University M,W
Crichton College M,W
Cumberland University M,W
East Tennessee State University M,W
King College M,W
Lee University M,W
LeMoyne-Owen College M
Lincoln Memorial University M,W
Lipscomb University M,W
Middle Tennessee State University M,W
Milligan College M,W
Tennessee Technological University M,W
Tennessee Wesleyan College M,W
Tusculum College M,W
Union University M,W
University of Memphis M,W
University of Tennessee
 Chattanooga M,W
 Knoxville M,W
 Martin M,W
Vanderbilt University M,W

Texas
Abilene Christian University M,W
Angelo State University M,W
Baylor University M,W
Clarendon College M,W
Dallas Baptist University W
Houston Baptist University M,W
Lamar University M,W
Midwestern State University W
Northwood University: Texas M,W
Odessa College M,W
Prairie View A&M University M,W
Rice University M,W
St. Edward's University M,W
Sam Houston State University M,W
South Plains College M,W
Southern Methodist University W
Stephen F. Austin State University M,W
Tarleton State University M,W
Texas A&M University M,W
Texas A&M University
 Commerce M,W
Texas Christian University M,W
Texas Southern University M,W
Texas State University: San Marcos M,W
Texas Tech University M,W
University of Houston M,W
University of North Texas M,W
University of Texas
 Arlington M,W
 Austin M,W
 Pan American M,W
 of the Permian Basin M,W
 San Antonio M,W
University of the Incarnate Word M,W
Wayland Baptist University M,W
West Texas A&M University M,W
Western Texas College M,W

Utah
Brigham Young University M,W
Dixie State College of Utah M,W
University of Utah W
Utah State University M,W
Utah Valley University M,W
Weber State University M,W

Vermont
University of Vermont M,W

Virginia
Bluefield College M,W
College of William and Mary M,W
George Mason University M,W
Hampton University M,W
James Madison University W
Liberty University M,W
Longwood University M,W
Norfolk State University M,W
Radford University M,W
St. Paul's College M,W
University of Richmond W
University of Virginia M,W
University of Virginia's College at Wise M,W
Virginia Commonwealth University M,W
Virginia Military Institute M,W
Virginia Polytechnic Institute and State University M,W
Virginia State University M,W

Washington
Central Washington University M,W
Clark College M,W
Eastern Washington University M,W
Everett Community College M,W
Evergreen State College M,W
Gonzaga University M,W
Highline Community College M,W
Northwest University M,W
Saint Martin's University M,W
Seattle Pacific University M,W
Seattle University M,W
Spokane Community College M,W
University of Washington M,W
Washington State University M,W
Western Washington University M,W

West Virginia
Alderson-Broaddus College M,W
Bluefield State College M,W
Concord University M,W
Davis and Elkins College M,W
Glenville State College M,W
Marshall University M,W
Ohio Valley University M,W
University of Charleston M,W
West Liberty State College M,W
West Virginia University W
West Virginia Wesleyan College M,W
Wheeling Jesuit University M,W

Wisconsin
Cardinal Stritch University M,W
Marquette University M,W
Milwaukee Area Technical College M,W
Silver Lake College M,W
University of Wisconsin
 Green Bay M,W
 Milwaukee M,W
 Parkside M,W
Viterbo University M,W

Wyoming
Sheridan College M,W
University of Wyoming M,W

Diving

Alabama
Auburn University M,W
University of Alabama M,W

Arizona
Arizona State University W
Northern Arizona University W
University of Arizona M,W

Arkansas
Ouachita Baptist University M,W
University of Arkansas W

California
California Baptist University M,W
California Polytechnic State University: San Luis Obispo M,W
California State University
 Northridge M,W
College of the Redwoods M
San Diego State University W
San Jose State University W
Stanford University M,W
University of California
 Berkeley M,W
 Davis M,W
 Irvine M,W
 Los Angeles M,W
University of San Diego W
University of Southern California M,W

Colorado
Colorado State University W
University of Denver M,W

Connecticut
Central Connecticut State University W
Fairfield University M,W
University of Connecticut M,W

District of Columbia
George Washington University M,W
Howard University M,W

Florida
Florida State University M,W
Indian River State College M,W
University of Florida M,W
University of Miami M,W

Georgia
Georgia Institute of Technology M,W
Georgia Southern University W
University of Georgia M,W

Hawaii
University of Hawaii
 Manoa M,W

Illinois
Eastern Illinois University M,W
Illinois Institute of Technology M,W
Illinois State University W
Lincoln College M,W
Northwestern University M,W
Robert Morris College: Chicago W
Southern Illinois University Carbondale M,W
University of Illinois
 Chicago M,W
 Urbana-Champaign W
Western Illinois University M,W

Indiana
Ball State University M,W
Indiana University
 Bloomington M,W
Indiana University-Purdue University Indianapolis M,W
Purdue University M,W
University of Evansville M,W
University of Notre Dame M,W
Valparaiso University M,W

Iowa
University of Iowa M,W

Kentucky
Asbury College M,W
University of Kentucky M,W
University of Louisville M,W
Western Kentucky University M

Louisiana
University of New Orleans M,W

Maine
University of Maine M,W

Maryland
Loyola College in Maryland M,W
Towson University M,W
University of Maryland
 Baltimore County M,W

Massachusetts
Boston College M,W
Boston University M,W
Northeastern University W
University of Massachusetts
 Amherst M,W

Michigan
Eastern Michigan University M,W
Grand Rapids Community College M,W
Grand Valley State University M,W
Hillsdale College W
Michigan State University M,W
Northern Michigan University W

Oakland University M,W
University of Michigan M,W
Wayne State University M,W

Minnesota
Minnesota State University
Mankato M,W
Moorhead M
Saint Cloud State University M,W
University of Minnesota
Twin Cities M,W

Mississippi
Delta State University M,W

Missouri
Drury University M,W
Saint Louis University M,W
University of Missouri
Columbia M,W

Nebraska
University of Nebraska
Kearney W
Lincoln W

Nevada
University of Nevada
Las Vegas M
Reno W

New Hampshire
University of New Hampshire W

New Jersey
Rider University M,W
Rutgers, The State University of New Jersey
New Brunswick/Piscataway Campus M,W
Saint Peter's College M,W

New Mexico
University of New Mexico W

New York
Fordham University M,W
Iona College M,W
Marist College M,W
Niagara University M,W
Saint Bonaventure University M,W
St. Francis College M,W
Siena College W
State University of New York
Binghamton M,W
Buffalo M,W
Stony Brook M,W
Syracuse University M,W

North Carolina
Davidson College M,W
East Carolina University M,W
University of North Carolina
Chapel Hill M,W
Wilmington M,W

North Dakota
University of North Dakota M,W

Ohio
Ashland University M,W
Bowling Green State University M,W
Cleveland State University M,W
Miami University
Oxford Campus M,W
Notre Dame College W
Ohio University M,W
University of Akron W
University of Findlay M,W
University of Toledo W
Wright State University M,W

Pennsylvania
Clarion University of Pennsylvania M,W
Drexel University M,W
Gannon University M,W
Indiana University of Pennsylvania M,W
La Salle University M,W
Penn State
University Park M,W
St. Francis University W
University of Pittsburgh M,W
Villanova University W
West Chester University of Pennsylvania M,W

Rhode Island
University of Rhode Island W

South Carolina
Clemson University M,W
College of Charleston M,W
University of South Carolina M,W

South Dakota
University of South Dakota M,W

Tennessee
University of Tennessee
Knoxville M,W

Texas
Southern Methodist University M,W
Texas A&M University M,W
Texas Christian University M,W
University of Houston W
University of North Texas W
University of Texas
Austin M,W

Utah
Brigham Young University M,W
University of Utah M,W

Vermont
University of Vermont W

Virginia
George Mason University M,W
James Madison University W
Old Dominion University M,W
Radford University W
University of Richmond W
University of Virginia M,W
Virginia Military Institute M
Virginia Polytechnic Institute and State University M,W

West Virginia
West Virginia University M,W

Wisconsin
University of Wisconsin
Green Bay M,W
Milwaukee M,W

Wyoming
University of Wyoming M,W

Equestrian

California
California State University
Fresno W

Delaware
Delaware State University W

Georgia
University of Georgia W

Idaho
College of Southern Idaho M,W

Indiana
St. Mary-of-the-Woods College W

Kansas
Kansas State University W

Kentucky
Midway College W
Murray State University M,W

Massachusetts
Stonehill College W

Nebraska
Nebraska College of Technical Agriculture M,W

New York
Dowling College W
Vassar College M,W

North Carolina
St. Andrews Presbyterian College M,W

Oklahoma
Oklahoma Panhandle State University M,W
Oklahoma State University W

Oregon
Linn-Benton Community College M,W

Pennsylvania
Seton Hill University W

South Carolina
University of South Carolina W

South Dakota
South Dakota State University W

Tennessee
University of Tennessee
Martin W

Texas
Baylor University W
Southern Methodist University W
Texas A&M University W
Texas Christian University W
West Texas A&M University W

Virginia
Virginia Intermont College M,W

Wyoming
Laramie County Community College M,W

Fencing

California
California State University
Fullerton M,W
Stanford University M,W

Illinois
Northwestern University W

Indiana
University of Notre Dame M,W

Michigan
University of Detroit Mercy M,W
Wayne State University M,W

New Jersey
Fairleigh Dickinson University
Metropolitan Campus W
New Jersey Institute of Technology M,W
Rutgers, The State University of New Jersey
New Brunswick/Piscataway Campus M,W

New York
City University of New York
Queens College W
St. John's University M,W

Ohio
Cleveland State University M,W

Pennsylvania
Penn State
University Park M,W
Temple University W

Field Hockey

California
Stanford University W
University of California
Berkeley W
University of the Pacific W

Connecticut
Fairfield University W
Quinnipiac University W
Sacred Heart University W
Southern Connecticut State University W
University of Connecticut W

Delaware
University of Delaware W

District of Columbia
Georgetown University W

Illinois
Northwestern University W

Indiana
Ball State University W

Iowa
University of Iowa W

Kentucky
Bellarmine University W
University of Louisville W

Maine
University of Maine W

Maryland
Towson University W
University of Maryland
College Park W

Massachusetts
American International College W
Boston College W
Boston University W
College of the Holy Cross W
Northeastern University W
Stonehill College W
University of Massachusetts
Amherst W

Michigan
Central Michigan University W
Michigan State University W
University of Michigan W

Missouri
Missouri State University W
Saint Louis University W

New Hampshire
Franklin Pierce University W
University of New Hampshire W

New Jersey
Monmouth University W
Rider University W
Rutgers, The State University of New Jersey
New Brunswick/Piscataway Campus W

New York
Adelphi University W
Colgate University W
Hofstra University W
Houghton College W
Long Island University

C. W. Post Campus W
Siena College W
State University of New York
Albany W
Syracuse University W

North Carolina
Appalachian State University W
Catawba College W
Davidson College W
Duke University W
University of North Carolina
Chapel Hill W
Wake Forest University W

Ohio
Kent State University W
Miami University
Oxford Campus W
Notre Dame College W
Ohio University W

Pennsylvania
Bloomsburg University of Pennsylvania W
Drexel University W
East Stroudsburg University of Pennsylvania W
Indiana University of Pennsylvania W
Kutztown University of Pennsylvania W
La Salle University W
Lafayette College W
Lock Haven University of Pennsylvania W
Mansfield University of Pennsylvania W
Mercyhurst College W
Millersville University of Pennsylvania W
Penn State
University Park W
Philadelphia University W
Robert Morris University W
St. Francis University W
Saint Joseph's University W
Seton Hill University W
Shippensburg University of Pennsylvania W
Slippery Rock University of Pennsylvania W
Temple University W
Villanova University W
West Chester University of Pennsylvania W

Rhode Island
Bryant University W
Providence College W

South Carolina
Limestone College W

Vermont
University of Vermont W

Virginia
College of William and Mary W
James Madison University W
Longwood University W
Old Dominion University W
Radford University W
University of Richmond W
University of Virginia W
Virginia Commonwealth University W

Football (non-tackle)

Alabama
Faulkner University M

Illinois
Olivet Nazarene University M

Louisiana
Southern University and Agricultural and Mechanical College M

Michigan
Southwestern Michigan College M,W

Football (tackle)

Alabama
Alabama Agricultural and Mechanical University M
Alabama State University M
Auburn University M
Jacksonville State University M
Miles College M
Samford University M
Troy University M
Tuskegee University M
University of Alabama M
University of Alabama
Birmingham M
University of North Alabama M
University of West Alabama M

Arizona
Arizona State University M
Arizona Western College M
Eastern Arizona College M
Glendale Community College M
Mesa Community College M
Northern Arizona University M
Pima Community College M
Scottsdale Community College M
University of Arizona M

Arkansas
Arkansas State University M
Arkansas Tech University M
Harding University M
Henderson State University M
Ouachita Baptist University M
Southern Arkansas University M
University of Arkansas M
University of Arkansas
Monticello M
Pine Bluff M
University of Central Arkansas M

California
Azusa Pacific University M
California Polytechnic State University: San Luis Obispo M
California State University
Fresno M
Sacramento M
Fresno City College M
Grossmont College M
Humboldt State University M
San Diego State University M
San Jose State University M
Stanford University M
University of California
Berkeley M
Davis M
Los Angeles M
University of Southern California M
Yuba Community College District M

Colorado
Adams State College M
Colorado School of Mines M
Colorado State University M
Fort Lewis College M
Mesa State College M
University of Colorado
Boulder M
University of Northern Colorado M
Western State College of Colorado M

Connecticut
Sacred Heart University M
Southern Connecticut State University M
University of Connecticut M

Delaware
Delaware State University M
University of Delaware M

District of Columbia
Georgetown University M
Howard University M

Florida
Bethune-Cookman University M
Florida Agricultural and Mechanical University M
Florida Atlantic University M
Florida State University M
University of Central Florida M
University of Florida M
University of Miami M
University of South Florida M
Webber International University M

Georgia
Albany State University M
Clark Atlanta University M
Fort Valley State University M
Georgia Institute of Technology M
Georgia Military College M
Georgia Southern University M
Morehouse College M
Savannah State University M
Shorter College M
University of Georgia M
University of West Georgia M
Valdosta State University M

Hawaii
University of Hawaii
Manoa M

Idaho
Boise State University M
Idaho State University M
University of Idaho M

Illinois
Eastern Illinois University M
Illinois State University M
McKendree University M
Northwestern University M
Olivet Nazarene University M
Quincy University M
St. Xavier University M
Southern Illinois University Carbondale M
Trinity International University M
University of Illinois
Urbana-Champaign M
University of St. Francis M
Western Illinois University M

Indiana
Ball State University M
Indiana State University M
Indiana University
Bloomington M
Marian College M
Purdue University M
Saint Joseph's College M
Taylor University M
University of Indianapolis M
University of Notre Dame M
University of St. Francis M

Iowa
Briar Cliff University M
Dordt College M
Ellsworth Community College M
Graceland University M
Grand View University M
Iowa Central Community College M
Iowa State University M
Iowa Wesleyan College M
Morningside College M
North Iowa Area Community College M
Northwestern College M
St. Ambrose University M
University of Iowa M
University of Northern Iowa M
Waldorf College M
William Penn University M

Kansas
Baker University M
Benedictine College M
Bethany College M
Bethel College M
Coffeyville Community College M
Dodge City Community College M
Emporia State University M
Fort Hays State University M
Fort Scott Community College M
Friends University M
Garden City Community College M
Highland Community College M
Hutchinson Community College M
Independence Community College M
Kansas State University M
Kansas Wesleyan University M
McPherson College M
MidAmerica Nazarene University M
Ottawa University M
Pittsburg State University M
Southwestern College M
Sterling College M
Tabor College M
University of Kansas M
University of St. Mary M
Washburn University M

Kentucky
Campbellsville University M
Eastern Kentucky University M
Georgetown College M
Kentucky Christian University M
Kentucky State University M
Kentucky Wesleyan College M
Murray State University M
Pikeville College M
Union College M
University of Kentucky M
University of Louisville M
University of the Cumberlands M
Western Kentucky University M

Louisiana
Grambling State University M
Louisiana State University and Agricultural and Mechanical College M
Louisiana Tech University M
McNeese State University M
Nicholls State University M
Northwestern State University M
Southeastern Louisiana University M
Southern University and Agricultural and Mechanical College M
Tulane University M
University of Louisiana at Lafayette M
University of Louisiana at Monroe M

Maine
University of Maine M

Maryland
Bowie State University M
Morgan State University M
Towson University M
University of Maryland
College Park M

Massachusetts
American International College M
Boston College M
Dean College M
Northeastern University M
Stonehill College M
University of Massachusetts
Amherst M

Michigan
Central Michigan University M
Eastern Michigan University M
Ferris State University M
Grand Rapids Community College M
Grand Valley State University M
Hillsdale College M
Michigan State University M
Michigan Technological University M
Northern Michigan University M
Northwood University: Michigan M
Saginaw Valley State University M
University of Michigan M
Wayne State University M,W
Western Michigan University M

Minnesota
Bemidji State University M
Concordia University: St. Paul M
Minnesota State University
  Mankato M
  Moorhead M
Saint Cloud State University M
Southwest Minnesota State University M
University of Minnesota
  Crookston M
  Duluth M
  Twin Cities M
Winona State University M

Mississippi
Alcorn State University M
Belhaven College M
Coahoma Community College M
Copiah-Lincoln Community College M
Delta State University M
East Central Community College M
East Mississippi Community College M
Hinds Community College M
Holmes Community College M
Itawamba Community College M
Jackson State University M
Mississippi Gulf Coast Community College M
Mississippi State University M
Mississippi Valley State University M
Northwest Mississippi Community College M
Southwest Mississippi Community College M
University of Mississippi M
University of Southern Mississippi M

Missouri
Avila University M
Central Methodist University M
Culver-Stockton College M
Evangel University M
Lincoln University M
Missouri Southern State University M
Missouri State University M
Missouri Valley College M
Missouri Western State University M
Northwest Missouri State University M
Southeast Missouri State University M
Southwest Baptist University M
Truman State University M
University of Central Missouri M
University of Missouri
  Columbia M
  Missouri University of Science and Technology M
William Jewell College M

Montana
Carroll College M
Montana State University
  Bozeman M
  Northern M
Montana Tech of the University of Montana M
Rocky Mountain College M
University of Montana M
University of Montana: Western M

Nebraska
Chadron State College M
Concordia University M
Doane College M
Peru State College M
University of Nebraska
  Kearney M
  Lincoln M
  Omaha M
Wayne State College M

Nevada
University of Nevada
  Las Vegas M
  Reno M

New Hampshire
University of New Hampshire M

New Jersey
Monmouth University M
Rutgers, The State University of New Jersey
  New Brunswick/Piscataway Campus M

New Mexico
Eastern New Mexico University M
New Mexico Highlands University M
New Mexico Military Institute M
New Mexico State University M
University of New Mexico M
Western New Mexico University M

New York
ASA Institute of Business and Computer Technology M
Hofstra University M
Long Island University
  C. W. Post Campus M
State University of New York
  Albany M
  Buffalo M
  Stony Brook M
Syracuse University M
Wagner College M

North Carolina
Appalachian State University M
Brevard College M
Catawba College M
Duke University M
East Carolina University M
Elizabeth City State University M
Elon University M
Fayetteville State University M
Gardner-Webb University M
Johnson C. Smith University M
Lenoir-Rhyne University M
Livingstone College M
Mars Hill College M
North Carolina Agricultural and Technical State University M
North Carolina Central University M
North Carolina State University M
St. Augustine's College M
Shaw University M
University of North Carolina
  Chapel Hill M
  Pembroke M
Wake Forest University M
Western Carolina University M
Wingate University M
Winston-Salem State University M

North Dakota
Dickinson State University M
Jamestown College M
Mayville State University M
Minot State University M
North Dakota State College of Science M
North Dakota State University M
University of Mary M
University of North Dakota M
Valley City State University M

Ohio
Ashland University M
Bowling Green State University M
Kent State University M
Malone University M
Miami University
  Oxford Campus M
Ohio Dominican University M
Ohio University M
University of Akron M
University of Cincinnati M
University of Findlay M
University of Toledo M
Urbana University M
Walsh University M
Youngstown State University M

Oklahoma
Bacone College M
East Central University M
Langston University M
Northeastern Oklahoma Agricultural and Mechanical College M
Northeastern State University M
Northwestern Oklahoma State University M
Oklahoma Panhandle State University M
Oklahoma State University M
Southeastern Oklahoma State University M
Southwestern Oklahoma State University M
University of Central Oklahoma M
University of Oklahoma M
University of Tulsa M

Oregon
Eastern Oregon University M
Oregon State University M
Portland State University M
Southern Oregon University M
University of Oregon M

Pennsylvania
Bloomsburg University of Pennsylvania M
California University of Pennsylvania M
Cheyney University of Pennsylvania M
Clarion University of Pennsylvania M
Duquesne University M
East Stroudsburg University of Pennsylvania M
Edinboro University of Pennsylvania M
Gannon University M
Indiana University of Pennsylvania M
Kutztown University of Pennsylvania M
Lackawanna College M
Lock Haven University of Pennsylvania M
Mansfield University of Pennsylvania M
Mercyhurst College M
Millersville University of Pennsylvania M
Penn State
  University Park M
Robert Morris University M
St. Francis University M
Seton Hill University M
Shippensburg University of Pennsylvania M
Slippery Rock University of Pennsylvania M
Temple University M
University of Pittsburgh M
Valley Forge Military Academy & College M
Villanova University M
West Chester University of Pennsylvania M
Westminster College M

Rhode Island
Bryant University M
University of Rhode Island M

South Carolina
Charleston Southern University M
The Citadel M
Clemson University M
Coastal Carolina University M
Furman University M
Newberry College M
North Greenville University M
Presbyterian College M
South Carolina State University M
University of South Carolina M
Wofford College M

South Dakota
Augustana College M
Black Hills State University M
Dakota State University M
Dakota Wesleyan University M
Northern State University M
South Dakota School of Mines and Technology M
South Dakota State University M
University of Sioux Falls M
University of South Dakota M

Tennessee
Austin Peay State University M
Bethel College M
Carson-Newman College M
Cumberland University M
Lambuth University M
Lane College M
Middle Tennessee State University M
Tennessee State University M
Tennessee Technological University M
Tusculum College M
University of Memphis M
University of Tennessee
  Chattanooga M
  Knoxville M
  Martin M
Vanderbilt University M

Texas
Abilene Christian University M
Angelo State University M
Baylor University M
Blinn College M
Kilgore College M
Midwestern State University M
Prairie View A&M University M
Rice University M
Sam Houston State University M
Southern Methodist University M
Southwestern Assemblies of God University M
Stephen F. Austin State University M
Tarleton State University M
Texas A&M University M
Texas A&M University
  Commerce M
  Kingsville M
Texas Christian University M
Texas Southern University M
Texas State University: San Marcos M
Texas Tech University M
Tyler Junior College M
University of Houston M
University of North Texas M
University of Texas
  Austin M
West Texas A&M University M

Utah
Brigham Young University M
Dixie State College of Utah M
Snow College M
Southern Utah University M
University of Utah M
Utah State University M
Weber State University M

Virginia
College of William and Mary M
Hampton University M
James Madison University M
Liberty University M
Norfolk State University M
Old Dominion University M
University of Richmond M
University of Virginia M
University of Virginia's College at Wise M

Virginia Military Institute M
Virginia Polytechnic Institute and State University M
Virginia State University M
Virginia Union University M

Washington
Central Washington University M
Eastern Washington University M
University of Washington M
Washington State University M
Western Washington University M

West Virginia
Concord University M
Fairmont State University M
Glenville State College M
Marshall University M
Shepherd University M
University of Charleston M
West Liberty State College M
West Virginia State University M
West Virginia University M
West Virginia University Institute of Technology M
West Virginia Wesleyan College M

Wyoming
University of Wyoming M

Golf

Alabama
Alabama State University M,W
Auburn University M,W
Central Alabama Community College M
Faulkner State Community College M,W
Faulkner University M
Gadsden State Community College M
Jacksonville State University M,W
Samford University M,W
Spring Hill College M,W
Troy University M,W
University of Alabama M,W
University of Alabama
  Birmingham M,W
University of Mobile M,W
University of Montevallo M,W
University of North Alabama M
University of South Alabama M,W
Wallace State Community College at Hanceville M

Arizona
Arizona State University M,W
Chandler-Gilbert Community College
  Pecos M,W
Eastern Arizona College M
Gateway Community College M,W
Glendale Community College M
Grand Canyon University M
Mesa Community College M
Northern Arizona University W
Paradise Valley Community College M,W
Pima Community College M,W
Scottsdale Community College M
University of Arizona M,W

Arkansas
Arkansas State University M,W
Arkansas Tech University M
Harding University M,W
Henderson State University M,W
Lyon College M,W
Ouachita Baptist University M
University of Arkansas M,W
University of Arkansas
  Fort Smith M,W
  Little Rock M,W
  Monticello M,W
  Pine Bluff M,W
University of Central Arkansas M,W

California
California Baptist University M,W
California Polytechnic State University: San Luis Obispo M,W
California State University
  Bakersfield M
  Chico M,W
  Dominguez Hills M
  Fresno M,W
  Long Beach M,W
  Monterey Bay M,W
  Northridge M
  Sacramento M,W
  San Bernardino M
  Stanislaus M
Concordia University M,W
Fresno City College M,W
Holy Names University M
Loyola Marymount University M
The Master's College M
Notre Dame de Namur University M
Pepperdine University M,W
Point Loma Nazarene University M
St. Mary's College of California M
San Diego State University M,W
San Jose State University M,W
Santa Clara University M,W
Santiago Canyon College M,W
Sonoma State University M
Stanford University M,W
University of California
  Berkeley M,W
  Davis M,W
  Irvine M,W
  Los Angeles M,W
  Santa Barbara M
University of San Diego M
University of San Francisco M,W
University of Southern California M,W
University of the Pacific M
William Jessup University M

Colorado
Adams State College M,W
Colorado Christian University M,W
Colorado School of Mines M,W
Colorado State University M,W
Colorado State University
  Pueblo M,W
Fort Lewis College M
Mesa State College W
Regis University M,W
Trinidad State Junior College M,W
University of Colorado
  Boulder M,W
  Colorado Springs M
University of Denver M,W
University of Northern Colorado M,W

Connecticut
Central Connecticut State University M
Fairfield University M,W
Post University M,W
Quinnipiac University M
Sacred Heart University M,W
University of Connecticut M
University of Hartford M,W
University of New Haven M

Delaware
Goldey-Beacom College M
Wilmington University M

District of Columbia
George Washington University M
Georgetown University M,W

Florida
Barry University M,W
Bethune-Cookman University M,W
Brevard Community College M
Daytona State College W
Eckerd College W
Embry-Riddle Aeronautical University M,W
Flagler College M,W
Florida Atlantic University M,W
Florida Gulf Coast University M,W
Florida Institute of Technology M,W
Florida Southern College M,W
Florida State University M,W
Jacksonville University M,W
Lake City Community College W
Lynn University M,W
Northwood University
  Florida M,W
Nova Southeastern University M,W
Rollins College M,W
St. Leo University M,W
St. Petersburg College W
Saint Thomas University M
Stetson University M,W
University of Central Florida M,W
University of Florida M,W
University of Miami W
University of North Florida M
University of South Florida M,W
University of Tampa M
University of West Florida M,W
Warner University M,W
Webber International University M,W

Georgia
Abraham Baldwin Agricultural College M
Andrew College M,W
Armstrong Atlantic State University M
Augusta State University M,W
Clayton State University M
Columbus State University M,W
Covenant College M,W
Darton College M
Georgia College and State University M
Georgia Institute of Technology M
Georgia Southern University M
Georgia Southwestern State University M,W
Georgia State University M,W
Kennesaw State University M
Mercer University M,W
Paine College M
Reinhardt College M
Shorter College W
Thomas University M,W
Truett-McConnell College M
University of Georgia M,W
Valdosta State University M
Young Harris College M,W

Hawaii
Chaminade University of Honolulu M,W
Hawaii Pacific University M
University of Hawaii
  Hilo M
  Manoa M,W

Idaho
Boise State University M,W
College of Idaho M,W
Idaho State University M,W
Lewis-Clark State College M,W
Northwest Nazarene University M
University of Idaho M,W

Illinois
Black Hawk College M
Bradley University M,W
Chicago State University M,W
College of Lake County M,W
Danville Area Community College M,W
DePaul University M
Eastern Illinois University M,W
Elgin Community College M
Highland Community College M
Illinois State University M,W
John A. Logan College M,W
Kaskaskia College M,W
Kishwaukee College M,W
Lewis and Clark Community College M
Lewis University M,W
Lincoln College M,W
Loyola University Chicago M,W
McKendree University M,W
Moraine Valley Community College M
Northwestern University M,W
Olivet Nazarene University M
Parkland College M
Quincy University M,W
Rend Lake College M,W
Robert Morris College: Chicago M,W
Sauk Valley Community College M
Southern Illinois University Carbondale M,W
Southern Illinois University Edwardsville M,W
Springfield College in Illinois M
University of Illinois
  Springfield M,W
  Urbana-Champaign M,W
University of St. Francis M,W
Waubonsee Community College M
Western Illinois University M,W

Indiana
Ancilla College M,W
Ball State University M,W
Bethel College M
Butler University M,W
Calumet College of St. Joseph M,W
Goshen College M
Grace College M
Huntington University M
Indiana Institute of Technology M,W
Indiana State University M
Indiana University
  Bloomington M,W
Indiana University-Purdue University Fort Wayne M,W
Indiana University-Purdue University Indianapolis M,W
Indiana Wesleyan University M
Marian College M,W
Oakland City University M,W
Purdue University M,W
Saint Joseph's College M,W
Taylor University M
University of Evansville M,W
University of Indianapolis M,W
University of Notre Dame M,W
University of St. Francis M,W
University of Southern Indiana M,W
Vincennes University M

Iowa
AIB College of Business M,W
Ashford University M
Briar Cliff University M,W
Clarke College M,W
Dordt College M
Drake University M,W
Ellsworth Community College M,W
Graceland University M,W
Grand View University M,W
Indian Hills Community College M
Iowa Central Community College M,W
Iowa Lakes Community College M,W
Iowa State University M,W
Iowa Wesleyan College M,W
Kirkwood Community College M
Marshalltown Community College M,W
Morningside College M,W
Mount Mercy College M,W
North Iowa Area Community College M,W
Northwestern College M,W
St. Ambrose University M,W
Scott Community College M,W
Southeastern Community College
  North Campus M,W
Southwestern Community College M
University of Iowa M,W
University of Northern Iowa M,W

Waldorf College M,W
William Penn University M,W

Kansas
Allen County Community College M,W
Baker University M,W
Barton County Community College M,W
Benedictine College M,W
Bethany College M
Bethel College M,W
Central Christian College of Kansas M,W
Coffeyville Community College M,W
Colby Community College M,W
Dodge City Community College M,W
Friends University M
Hutchinson Community College M
Johnson County Community College M
Kansas City Kansas Community College M
Kansas State University M,W
Kansas Wesleyan University M,W
Newman University M,W
Ottawa University M
Pittsburg State University M
Pratt Community College M,W
Southwestern College M,W
University of Kansas M,W
Washburn University M
Wichita State University M,W

Kentucky
Bellarmine University M,W
Brescia University M,W
Campbellsville University M,W
Eastern Kentucky University M,W
Georgetown College M,W
Kentucky State University M,W
Kentucky Wesleyan College M,W
Lindsey Wilson College M,W
Morehead State University M
Murray State University M,W
Northern Kentucky University M,W
Pikeville College M,W
St. Catharine College M,W
Union College M,W
University of Kentucky M,W
University of Louisville M,W
University of the Cumberlands M,W
Western Kentucky University M,W

Louisiana
Centenary College of Louisiana M,W
Grambling State University M
Louisiana State University and Agricultural and Mechanical College M,W
Louisiana Tech University M
McNeese State University M,W
Nicholls State University M,W
Southeastern Louisiana University M
Southern University and Agricultural and Mechanical College M,W
University of Louisiana at Lafayette M
University of Louisiana at Monroe M
University of New Orleans M

Maryland
College of Southern Maryland M,W
Coppin State University W
Harford Community College M
Loyola College in Maryland M
Mount St. Mary's University M,W
Towson University M
University of Maryland
    College Park M,W

Massachusetts
Boston College M,W

Michigan
Aquinas College M,W
Concordia University M
Cornerstone University M,W
Davenport University M,W
Eastern Michigan University M,W
Ferris State University M,W
Grand Rapids Community College M
Grand Valley State University M,W
Kalamazoo Valley Community College M
Kirtland Community College M,W
Lake Michigan College M
Lake Superior State University M,W
Lansing Community College M
Madonna University M,W
Michigan State University M,W
Mott Community College M
Muskegon Community College M
Northern Michigan University M
Northwood University: Michigan M,W
Oakland Community College M
Oakland University M,W
Saginaw Valley State University M
Siena Heights University M,W
Spring Arbor University M
University of Detroit Mercy M,W
University of Michigan M,W
Wayne State University M
Western Michigan University W

Minnesota
Concordia University: St. Paul M,W
Minnesota State University
    Mankato M,W
    Moorhead W
Saint Cloud State University M,W
Southwest Minnesota State University W
University of Minnesota
    Crookston M,W
    Twin Cities M,W
Winona State University M,W

Mississippi
Alcorn State University M,W
Belhaven College M,W
Copiah-Lincoln Community College M
Delta State University M
East Mississippi Community College M,W
Itawamba Community College M
Jackson State University M,W
Meridian Community College M
Mississippi Gulf Coast Community College M
Mississippi State University M,W
Mississippi Valley State University M,W
Northwest Mississippi Community College M,W
University of Mississippi M,W
University of Southern Mississippi M,W
William Carey University M,W

Missouri
Avila University W
Central Methodist University M,W
Culver-Stockton College M,W
Drury University M,W
Evangel University M,W
Hannibal-LaGrange College M,W
Lincoln University M
Metropolitan Community College: Penn Valley M
Missouri Baptist University M,W
Missouri Southern State University M
Missouri State University M,W
Missouri Valley College M,W
Missouri Western State University M
Northwest Missouri State University W
Park University W
Research College of Nursing M,W
Rockhurst University M,W
Southwest Baptist University M
Truman State University M,W
University of Central Missouri M
University of Missouri
    Columbia M,W
    Kansas City M,W
    St. Louis M,W
William Jewell College M,W
William Woods University M,W

Montana
Carroll College W
Miles Community College M,W
Montana State University
    Billings M,W
    Bozeman W
    Northern W
Montana Tech of the University of Montana M,W
Rocky Mountain College M,W
University of Great Falls M,W
University of Montana W
University of Montana: Western M,W

Nebraska
Chadron State College W
Concordia University M,W
Creighton University M,W
Doane College M,W
Mid-Plains Community College Area M
Nebraska College of Technical Agriculture M,W
Peru State College W
University of Nebraska
    Kearney M,W
    Lincoln M,W
Wayne State College M,W

Nevada
University of Nevada
    Las Vegas M
    Reno M,W

New Hampshire
Franklin Pierce University M

New Jersey
Brookdale Community College M
Caldwell College M
Fairleigh Dickinson University
    Metropolitan Campus M,W
Monmouth University M,W
Rider University M
Rutgers, The State University of New Jersey
    New Brunswick/Piscataway Campus M,W
Saint Peter's College M
Salem Community College M
Seton Hall University M

New Mexico
New Mexico Junior College M
New Mexico Military Institute M
New Mexico State University M,W
University of New Mexico M,W
University of the Southwest M,W
Western New Mexico University M,W

New York
Adelphi University M
Canisius College M
College of Saint Rose M
Daemen College M
Dominican College of Blauvelt M
Dowling College M
Hofstra University M,W
Iona College M
Le Moyne College M
Long Island University
    Brooklyn Campus M,W
Manhattan College M
Niagara University M
Nyack College M
Pace University M
Saint Bonaventure University M
St. John's University M,W
St. Thomas Aquinas College M,W
Siena College M,W
State University of New York
    Albany W
    Binghamton M
Wagner College M,W

North Carolina
Appalachian State University M,W
Barton College M
Belmont Abbey College M
Brevard College M
Campbell University M,W
Catawba College M,W
Davidson College M
Duke University M,W
East Carolina University M,W
Elon University M,W
Fayetteville State University M
Gardner-Webb University M,W
High Point University M,W
Johnson C. Smith University M,W
Johnston Community College M
Lees-McRae College M
Lenoir-Rhyne University M,W
Louisburg College M,W
Mars Hill College M
Montreat College M,W
Mount Olive College M
North Carolina Central University M,W
North Carolina State University M,W
Pfeiffer University M,W
Pitt Community College M
Queens University of Charlotte M,W
St. Andrews Presbyterian College M
St. Augustine's College M,W
University of North Carolina
    Chapel Hill M,W
    Charlotte M
    Greensboro M,W
    Pembroke M,W
    Wilmington M,W
Wake Forest University M,W
Western Carolina University M,W
Wingate University M,W

North Dakota
Dickinson State University M,W
Jamestown College M,W
Minot State University M,W
North Dakota State University W
University of Mary M,W
University of North Dakota M,W
Valley City State University M,W

Ohio
Ashland University M,W
Bowling Green State University M,W
Cedarville University M
Central State University M,W
Cleveland State University M,W
Kent State University M,W
Lakeland Community College M
Malone University M,W
Miami University
    Oxford Campus M
Mount Vernon Nazarene University M
Notre Dame College M,W
Ohio Dominican University M,W
Ohio University M
Shawnee State University M
Sinclair Community College M
University of Akron M
University of Dayton M,W
University of Findlay M,W
University of Toledo M,W
Urbana University M
Ursuline College W
Walsh University M,W
Wright State University M
Xavier University M,W
Youngstown State University M,W

Oklahoma
Bacone College M,W
Cameron University M,W
East Central University M,W
Northeastern State University M,W
Northwestern Oklahoma State University M,W

Oklahoma Baptist University M,W
Oklahoma Christian University M
Oklahoma City University M,W
Oklahoma Panhandle State University M,W
Oklahoma State University M,W
Oklahoma Wesleyan University M
Oral Roberts University M,W
Redlands Community College W
Seminole State College M,W
Southern Nazarene University M,W
Southwestern Oklahoma State University M,W
University of Central Oklahoma M,W
University of Oklahoma M,W
University of Tulsa M,W

Oregon
Concordia University M,W
Corban College M
Northwest Christian University M,W
Oregon State University M,W
Portland State University M,W
Southwestern Oregon Community College M,W
Treasure Valley Community College M,W
University of Oregon M,W
University of Portland M,W
Warner Pacific College M,W

Pennsylvania
California University of Pennsylvania M,W
Chestnut Hill College M,W
Clarion University of Pennsylvania M
Drexel University M
Duquesne University M
Gannon University M,W
Holy Family University M
Indiana University of Pennsylvania M
Kutztown University of Pennsylvania W
La Salle University M,W
Lackawanna College M,W
Mercyhurst College M,W
Millersville University of Pennsylvania M
Penn State
University Park M,W
Philadelphia University M
Robert Morris University M,W
St. Francis University M,W
Saint Joseph's University M
Seton Hill University M,W
Temple University M
University of Pittsburgh
Titusville M
University of the Sciences in Philadelphia M,W
West Chester University of Pennsylvania M,W

Rhode Island
Bryant University M
University of Rhode Island M

South Carolina
Anderson University M,W
Charleston Southern University M,W
The Citadel W
Clemson University M
Coastal Carolina University M,W
College of Charleston M,W
Erskine College M,W
Francis Marion University M
Furman University M,W
Lander University M
Limestone College M,W
Morris College M
Newberry College M,W
North Greenville University M
Presbyterian College M,W
South Carolina State University M,W
Southern Wesleyan University M
Spartanburg Methodist College M,W
University of South Carolina M,W
University of South Carolina
Aiken M
Winthrop University M,W
Wofford College M,W

South Dakota
Augustana College M,W
Dakota Wesleyan University M,W
Northern State University W
South Dakota School of Mines and Technology M,W
South Dakota State University M,W
University of Sioux Falls M,W

Tennessee
Austin Peay State University M,W
Belmont University M,W
Bethel College M,W
Carson-Newman College M
Christian Brothers University M,W
Crichton College M,W
Cumberland University M,W
East Tennessee State University M,W
King College M,W
Lambuth University M,W
Lee University M
LeMoyne-Owen College M,W
Lincoln Memorial University M,W
Lipscomb University M,W
Martin Methodist College M,W
Middle Tennessee State University M,W
Milligan College M
Tennessee Technological University M,W
Tennessee Wesleyan College M,W
Trevecca Nazarene University M,W
Tusculum College M,W
Union University M
University of Memphis M,W
University of Tennessee
Chattanooga M,W
Knoxville M,W
Martin M
Vanderbilt University M,W
Walters State Community College M,W

Texas
Abilene Christian University M
Baylor University M,W
Dallas Baptist University W
Hill College M
Houston Baptist University M,W
Lamar University M,W
Lon Morris College M,W
Lubbock Christian University M,W
McLennan Community College M
Midland College M
Northwood University: Texas M,W
Odessa College M
Paris Junior College M
Prairie View A&M University M,W
Ranger College M,W
Rice University M
St. Edward's University M,W
St. Mary's University M
Sam Houston State University M,W
Southern Methodist University M,W
Stephen F. Austin State University M
Tarleton State University W
Texas A&M University M,W
Texas A&M University
Commerce M
Corpus Christi W
Texas Christian University M,W
Texas Southern University M,W
Texas State University: San Marcos M,W
Texas Tech University M,W
Texas Wesleyan University M
Tyler Junior College M,W
University of Houston M
University of North Texas M,W
University of Texas
Arlington M
Austin M,W
Brownsville - Texas Southmost College M,W
Pan American M,W
San Antonio M,W
University of the Incarnate Word M,W
Wayland Baptist University M,W
West Texas A&M University M,W

Utah
Brigham Young University M,W
Dixie State College of Utah M
Southern Utah University M
University of Utah M
Utah State University M
Utah Valley University M,W
Weber State University M,W

Virginia
Bluefield College M
College of William and Mary M,W
Hampton University M,W
James Madison University M,W
Liberty University M
Longwood University M,W
Old Dominion University M,W
Radford University M,W
St. Paul's College M
University of Richmond M,W
University of Virginia M,W
Virginia Commonwealth University M
Virginia Intermont College M
Virginia Military Institute M
Virginia Polytechnic Institute and State University M
Virginia State University M,W
Virginia Union University M,W

Washington
Centralia College W
Columbia Basin College M,W
Eastern Washington University W
Edmonds Community College M,W
Gonzaga University M,W
Grays Harbor College M,W
Green River Community College M
Olympic College M,W
Saint Martin's University M,W
Seattle University M,W
Skagit Valley College M,W
Spokane Community College M,W
University of Washington M,W
Walla Walla Community College M,W
Washington State University M,W
Western Washington University M,W

West Virginia
Bluefield State College M
Concord University M
Davis and Elkins College M
Glenville State College M,W
Marshall University M,W
Ohio Valley University M,W
Salem International University M,W
University of Charleston M
West Liberty State College M,W
West Virginia University Institute of Technology M
West Virginia Wesleyan College M,W
Wheeling Jesuit University M,W

Wisconsin
Marquette University M
Silver Lake College M,W
University of Wisconsin
Green Bay M,W
Parkside M
Viterbo University M,W

Wyoming
Eastern Wyoming College M,W
University of Wyoming M,W

Gymnastics

Alabama
Auburn University W
University of Alabama W

Alaska
University of Alaska
Anchorage W

Arizona
Arizona State University W
University of Arizona W

Arkansas
University of Arkansas W

California
California State University
Fullerton W
Sacramento W
San Jose State University W
Stanford University M,W
University of California
Berkeley M,W
Davis W
Los Angeles W
Santa Barbara W

Colorado
University of Denver W

Connecticut
Southern Connecticut State University W
University of Bridgeport W

District of Columbia
George Washington University W
Howard University M,W

Florida
University of Florida W

Georgia
University of Georgia W

Idaho
Boise State University W

Illinois
Illinois State University W
University of Illinois
Chicago M,W
Urbana-Champaign M,W

Indiana
Ball State University W

Iowa
Iowa State University W
University of Iowa M,W

Kansas
Fort Hays State University M

Kentucky
University of Kentucky W

Louisiana
Centenary College of Louisiana W
Louisiana State University and Agricultural and Mechanical College W

Maryland
Columbia Union College M,W
Towson University W
University of Maryland
College Park W

Michigan
Central Michigan University W
Eastern Michigan University W
Michigan State University W

University of Michigan M,W
Western Michigan University W

Minnesota
University of Minnesota
Twin Cities M,W
Winona State University W

Missouri
Southeast Missouri State University W
University of Missouri
Columbia W

Nebraska
University of Nebraska
Lincoln M,W

New Hampshire
University of New Hampshire W

New Jersey
Rutgers, The State University of New Jersey
New Brunswick/Piscataway Campus W

North Carolina
North Carolina State University W
University of North Carolina
Chapel Hill W

Ohio
Bowling Green State University W
Kent State University W

Oklahoma
University of Oklahoma M,W

Oregon
Oregon State University W

Pennsylvania
Penn State
University Park M,W
Temple University M,W
University of Pittsburgh W
West Chester University of Pennsylvania W

Tennessee
Southern Adventist University M,W

Texas
Texas Woman's University W

Utah
Brigham Young University W
Southern Utah University W
University of Utah W
Utah State University W

Virginia
College of William and Mary M,W

Washington
Seattle Pacific University W
University of Washington W

West Virginia
West Virginia University W

Ice hockey

Alabama
University of Alabama
Huntsville M

Alaska
University of Alaska
Anchorage M
Fairbanks M

Colorado
Colorado College M
University of Denver M

Connecticut
Quinnipiac University M,W
Sacred Heart University M,W
University of Connecticut M,W

Illinois
McKendree University M,W

Indiana
University of Notre Dame M

Maine
University of Maine M,W

Massachusetts
American International College M
Bentley University M
Boston College M,W
Boston University W
College of the Holy Cross M,W
Merrimack College M
Northeastern University M,W
University of Massachusetts
Amherst M
Lowell M

Michigan
Ferris State University M
Lake Superior State University M
Michigan State University M
Michigan Technological University M
Northern Michigan University M
University of Michigan M
University of Michigan
Dearborn M
Wayne State University W
Western Michigan University M

Minnesota
Bemidji State University M
Minnesota State University
Mankato M,W
Saint Cloud State University M,W
University of Minnesota
Duluth M,W
Twin Cities M,W

Nebraska
University of Nebraska
Omaha M

New Hampshire
New England College M,W
University of New Hampshire M,W

New York
Canisius College M
Clarkson University M,W
Colgate University M,W
Monroe Community College M
Niagara University M,W
Rensselaer Polytechnic Institute M,W
St. Lawrence University M,W
Syracuse University W

North Dakota
Minot State University: Bottineau Campus M
University of North Dakota M,W

Ohio
Bowling Green State University M
Miami University
Oxford Campus M

Pennsylvania
Mercyhurst College M,W
Robert Morris University M,W

Rhode Island
Providence College M,W

Vermont
University of Vermont M,W

Judo

Puerto Rico
Inter American University of Puerto Rico
Aguadilla Campus M,W
Turabo University W
University of Puerto Rico
Humacao M,W

Lacrosse

California
Notre Dame de Namur University M
Stanford University W
University of California
Davis W

Colorado
Regis University W
University of Denver M,W

Connecticut
Central Connecticut State University W
Fairfield University M,W
Quinnipiac University M,W
Sacred Heart University M,W
Southern Connecticut State University W
University of Hartford M
University of New Haven W

Delaware
Delaware Technical and Community College
Terry M
University of Delaware M,W
Wilmington University W

District of Columbia
American University W
Georgetown University M,W

Florida
Florida Southern College M
St. Leo University M
University of Florida W

Illinois
Northwestern University W

Indiana
University of Notre Dame M,W

Kentucky
Bellarmine University M
University of Louisville W

Maryland
Anne Arundel Community College M,W
Community College of Baltimore County M,W
Harford Community College M,W
Johns Hopkins University M,W
Loyola College in Maryland M,W
Mount St. Mary's University M,W
Towson University M,W
University of Maryland
Baltimore County M,W
College Park M,W

Massachusetts
American International College M,W
Boston College W
Boston University W
Dean College M,W
Stonehill College W
University of Massachusetts
Amherst M,W

Michigan
Davenport University M,W
Siena Heights University M

Minnesota
University of Minnesota
Duluth M

New Hampshire
Franklin Pierce University M,W
Southern New Hampshire University M,W
University of New Hampshire W

New Jersey
Georgian Court University W
Monmouth University W
Rutgers, The State University of New Jersey
New Brunswick/Piscataway Campus M,W

New York
Adelphi University M,W
Canisius College M,W
City University of New York
Queens College W
Colgate University M,W
Dominican College of Blauvelt M,W
Dowling College M
Hofstra University M,W
Iona College W
Le Moyne College M,W
Long Island University
Brooklyn Campus W
C. W. Post Campus M,W
Manhattan College M,W
Marist College M,W
Molloy College M,W
Monroe Community College M
New York Institute of Technology M
Niagara University W
Pace University M
St. John's University M
St. Thomas Aquinas College W
Siena College M,W
State University of New York
Albany M,W
Binghamton M,W
Stony Brook M,W
Syracuse University M,W
Wagner College M,W

North Carolina
Catawba College M
Davidson College W
Duke University M
Lees-McRae College M,W
Lenoir-Rhyne University M
Mars Hill College M
Pfeiffer University M,W
Queens University of Charlotte M,W
St. Andrews Presbyterian College M
University of North Carolina
Chapel Hill M,W
Wingate University M

Ohio
Notre Dame College W

Oregon
University of Oregon W

Pennsylvania
Bloomsburg University of Pennsylvania W
Chestnut Hill College W
Drexel University M,W
Duquesne University W
East Stroudsburg University of Pennsylvania W
Gannon University W
Holy Family University W
Indiana University of Pennsylvania W
La Salle University W
Lehigh University M,W
Lock Haven University of Pennsylvania W
Mercyhurst College M,W
Millersville University of Pennsylvania W
Penn State
University Park M,W
Philadelphia University W

Robert Morris University M,W
St. Francis University W
Saint Joseph's University M,W
Seton Hill University M,W
Shippensburg University of Pennsylvania W
Slippery Rock University of Pennsylvania W
Temple University W
West Chester University of Pennsylvania W

Rhode Island
Bryant University M,W

South Carolina
Erskine College W
Limestone College M,W
Presbyterian College M,W

Tennessee
Tennessee Wesleyan College M
Vanderbilt University W

Vermont
University of Vermont M,W

Virginia
College of William and Mary W
James Madison University W
Longwood University W
Old Dominion University W
University of Richmond W
University of Virginia M,W
Virginia Military Institute M
Virginia Polytechnic Institute and State University W

West Virginia
Shepherd University W
Wheeling Jesuit University M

Rifle

Alabama
Jacksonville State University M,W

Alaska
University of Alaska
Fairbanks M,W

California
University of San Francisco M,W

Georgia
Columbus State University M,W
Mercer University M
North Georgia College & State University M,W

Kentucky
Morehead State University M,W
Murray State University M,W
University of Kentucky M,W

Mississippi
University of Mississippi W

Nebraska
University of Nebraska
Lincoln W

Nevada
University of Nevada
Reno M,W

Ohio
University of Akron W

South Carolina
The Citadel M,W

Tennessee
Austin Peay State University W
Tennessee Technological University M,W
University of Memphis M,W
University of Tennessee
Martin M,W

Texas
Texas Christian University W

Virginia
Virginia Military Institute M

West Virginia
West Virginia University M,W

Rodeo

Alabama
Troy University M,W
University of West Alabama M

Arizona
Central Arizona College M
Cochise College M
Dine College M,W

Arkansas
Southern Arkansas University M,W
University of Arkansas
Monticello M,W

Colorado
Northeastern Junior College M,W

Idaho
Boise State University M,W
College of Southern Idaho M,W

Kansas
Coffeyville Community College M,W
Colby Community College M
Dodge City Community College M,W
Fort Hays State University M
Fort Scott Community College M,W
Garden City Community College M,W
Pratt Community College M,W

Kentucky
Murray State University M,W

Louisiana
McNeese State University M,W

Missouri
Missouri Valley College M,W
Northwest Missouri State University M,W

Montana
Dawson Community College M,W
Miles Community College M,W
Montana State University
Bozeman M,W
Northern M,W
University of Montana M
University of Montana: Western M,W

Nebraska
Chadron State College M,W
Nebraska College of Technical Agriculture M,W

New Mexico
Eastern New Mexico University M,W
Navajo Technical College M,W
New Mexico Junior College M,W

North Dakota
Dickinson State University M

Oklahoma
Bacone College M,W
Eastern Oklahoma State College M,W
Northeastern Oklahoma Agricultural and Mechanical College M,W
Northwestern Oklahoma State University M,W
Oklahoma Panhandle State University M,W
Rogers State University M,W
Southeastern Oklahoma State University M,W
Southwestern Oklahoma State University M,W

Oregon
Blue Mountain Community College M,W
Eastern Oregon University M,W
Treasure Valley Community College M,W

Tennessee
University of Tennessee
Martin M,W

Texas
Clarendon College M,W
Howard College M,W
North Central Texas College M
Odessa College M,W
Panola College M,W
Ranger College M,W
Sam Houston State University M,W
South Plains College M,W
Tarleton State University M,W
Weatherford College M
Western Texas College M,W
Wharton County Junior College M,W

Utah
Southern Utah University M,W

Washington
Walla Walla Community College M,W

Wyoming
Casper College M,W
Central Wyoming College M,W
Eastern Wyoming College M,W
Laramie County Community College M,W
Sheridan College M,W
University of Wyoming M,W

Rowing (crew)

Alabama
University of Alabama W

California
California State University
Sacramento W
Humboldt State University W
Loyola Marymount University W
San Diego State University W
Stanford University M,W
University of California
Berkeley M,W
Davis W
Irvine M,W
Los Angeles M,W
University of Southern California W

Connecticut
Fairfield University W

Delaware
University of Delaware W

District of Columbia
George Washington University M,W
Georgetown University M,W

Florida
Barry University W
Florida Institute of Technology W
Jacksonville University M,W
Nova Southeastern University W
University of Central Florida W
University of Miami W
University of Tampa W

Indiana
Indiana University
Bloomington W
University of Notre Dame W

Iowa
University of Iowa W

Kansas
Kansas State University W
University of Kansas W

Kentucky
Murray State University W
University of Louisville W

Massachusetts
Boston College W
Boston University M,W
Northeastern University M,W
University of Massachusetts
Amherst W

Michigan
Eastern Michigan University W
Michigan State University W
University of Michigan W

Nebraska
Creighton University W

New Jersey
Rutgers, The State University of New Jersey
New Brunswick/Piscataway Campus M,W

New York
Dowling College M,W
Fordham University W
Marist College W
State University of New York
Buffalo W
Syracuse University M,W

North Carolina
Duke University W
University of North Carolina
Chapel Hill W

Ohio
University of Dayton W

Oklahoma
University of Oklahoma W
University of Tulsa W

Pennsylvania
Drexel University M,W
Duquesne University W
Mercyhurst College M,W
Philadelphia University M,W
Robert Morris University W
Saint Joseph's University M,W
Temple University M,W

Rhode Island
University of Rhode Island W

South Carolina
Clemson University W

Tennessee
University of Tennessee
Knoxville W

Texas
Southern Methodist University W
University of Texas
Austin W

Virginia
Old Dominion University W
University of Virginia W

Washington
Gonzaga University W
University of Washington M,W
Washington State University W

Western Washington University M,W

West Virginia
University of Charleston W
West Virginia University W

Rugby

California
University of California
Berkeley M

Illinois
Eastern Illinois University W

Pennsylvania
West Chester University of Pennsylvania W

Sailing

California
California State University
Monterey Bay M,W

Skiing

Alaska
University of Alaska
Anchorage M,W
Fairbanks M,W

Colorado
Colorado Mountain College M,W
University of Colorado
Boulder M,W
University of Denver M,W
Western State College of Colorado M,W

Idaho
College of Idaho M,W

Massachusetts
University of Massachusetts
Amherst M,W

Michigan
Michigan Technological University M,W
Northern Michigan University M,W

Minnesota
Saint Cloud State University W
University of Minnesota
Twin Cities M,W

Montana
Montana State University
Bozeman W
Rocky Mountain College M,W

Nevada
Sierra Nevada College M,W
University of Nevada
Reno M,W

New Hampshire
University of New Hampshire M,W

New Mexico
University of New Mexico M,W

Tennessee
Carson-Newman College M,W

Utah
University of Utah M,W

Vermont
University of Vermont M,W

West Virginia
Davis and Elkins College M,W

Wisconsin
University of Wisconsin
Green Bay M,W

Soccer

Alabama
Auburn University W
Auburn University at Montgomery M,W
Judson College W
Samford University W
Shelton State Community College W
Spring Hill College M,W
Troy University W
University of Alabama W
University of Alabama
Birmingham M,W
Huntsville M,W
University of Mobile M,W
University of Montevallo M,W
University of North Alabama W
University of South Alabama W
Wallace State Community College at Hanceville M

Arizona
Arizona State University W
Arizona Western College M
Chandler-Gilbert Community College
Pecos M,W
Cochise College W
Embry-Riddle Aeronautical University: Prescott
Campus M,W
Gateway Community College M
Glendale Community College M,W
Grand Canyon University M,W
Mesa Community College M
Northern Arizona University W
Paradise Valley Community College M,W
Pima Community College M,W
Scottsdale Community College M
South Mountain Community College M
University of Arizona W
Yavapai College M

Arkansas
Arkansas State University W
Harding University M,W
John Brown University M,W
Lyon College M,W
Ouachita Baptist University M,W
University of Arkansas W
University of Arkansas
Little Rock M,W
University of Central Arkansas M,W
Williams Baptist College M

California
Azusa Pacific University M,W
Bethany University M,W
Biola University M,W
California Baptist University M,W
California Polytechnic State University: San Luis Obispo M,W
California State Polytechnic University: Pomona M,W
California State University
Bakersfield M,W
Chico M,W
Dominguez Hills M,W
Fresno W
Fullerton M,W
Los Angeles M,W
Monterey Bay M,W
Northridge M
Sacramento M,W
San Bernardino M,W
Stanislaus M,W
Concordia University M,W
Dominican University of California M,W
Fresno City College M,W
Fresno Pacific University M,W
Grossmont College W
Holy Names University M,W
Hope International University M,W
Humboldt State University M,W
Loyola Marymount University M,W
The Master's College M,W
Notre Dame de Namur University M,W
Pepperdine University W
Point Loma Nazarene University M,W
St. Mary's College of California M,W
San Diego Christian College M,W
San Diego State University M,W
San Jose State University M,W
Santa Clara University M,W
Santiago Canyon College M,W
Sonoma State University M,W
Stanford University M,W
University of California
Berkeley M,W
Davis M,W
Irvine M,W
Los Angeles M,W
Santa Barbara M,W
University of San Diego M,W
University of San Francisco M,W
University of Southern California W
University of the Pacific W
Vanguard University of Southern California M,W
Westmont College M,W
William Jessup University M,W
Yuba Community College District M,W

Colorado
Adams State College W
Colorado Christian University M,W
Colorado College W
Colorado School of Mines M
Colorado State University
Pueblo M,W
Fort Lewis College M,W
Mesa State College M,W
Metropolitan State College of Denver M,W
Regis University M,W
University of Colorado
Boulder W
Colorado Springs M
University of Denver M,W
University of Northern Colorado W

Connecticut
Central Connecticut State University M,W
Fairfield University M,W
Post University M,W
Quinnipiac University M,W
Sacred Heart University M,W
Southern Connecticut State University M,W
University of Bridgeport M,W
University of Connecticut M,W
University of Hartford M,W
University of New Haven M,W

Delaware
Delaware State University W
Delaware Technical and Community College
Stanton/Wilmington M
Terry M
Goldey-Beacom College M,W
University of Delaware M,W
Wilmington University M,W

District of Columbia
American University M,W
George Washington University M,W
Georgetown University M,W
Howard University M

Florida
Barry University M,W
Eckerd College M,W
Embry-Riddle Aeronautical University M,W
Flagler College M,W
Florida Atlantic University M,W
Florida College M,W
Florida Institute of Technology M,W
Florida Southern College M,W
Florida State University W
Jacksonville University M,W
Lynn University M,W
Northwood University
Florida M,W
Nova Southeastern University M,W
Polk Community College W
Rollins College M,W
St. Leo University M,W
Saint Thomas University M,W
Stetson University M,W
University of Central Florida M,W
University of Florida W
University of Miami W
University of North Florida M,W
University of South Florida M,W
University of Tampa M,W
University of West Florida M,W
Warner University M,W
Webber International University M,W

Georgia
Abraham Baldwin Agricultural College W
Andrew College M,W
Brenau University W
Brewton-Parker College M,W
Clayton State University M,W
Columbus State University W
Covenant College M,W
Emmanuel College M,W
Georgia College and State University W
Georgia Military College M,W
Georgia Perimeter College M,W
Georgia Southern University M,W
Georgia Southwestern State University M,W
Georgia State University M,W
Gordon College M,W
Kennesaw State University W
Mercer University M,W
Middle Georgia College M,W
North Georgia College & State University M,W
Reinhardt College M,W
Shorter College M,W
Southern Polytechnic State University M
Thomas University M,W
Truett-McConnell College M,W
University of Georgia W
University of West Georgia W
Young Harris College M,W

Hawaii
Brigham Young University-Hawaii M,W
Hawaii Pacific University M,W
University of Hawaii
Manoa W

Idaho
Boise State University W
College of Idaho M,W
Idaho State University W
Northwest Nazarene University W
University of Idaho W

Illinois
Bradley University M
College of Lake County M,W
DePaul University M,W
Eastern Illinois University M,W
Elgin Community College M,W
Illinois Central College M,W
Illinois Institute of Technology M,W
Illinois State University W
Judson University M,W

Kankakee Community College M
Kishwaukee College M
Lewis and Clark Community College M,W
Lewis University M,W
Lincoln College M,W
Lincoln Land Community College M
Loyola University Chicago M,W
McHenry County College M
McKendree University M,W
Moraine Valley Community College M,W
Morton College M
Northwestern University M,W
Olivet Nazarene University M,W
Parkland College M,W
Quincy University M,W
Robert Morris College: Chicago M,W
St. Xavier University M,W
South Suburban College of Cook County M
Southern Illinois University Edwardsville M,W
Springfield College in Illinois M,W
Trinity Christian College M,W
Trinity International University M,W
University of Illinois
  Chicago M
  Springfield M,W
  Urbana-Champaign W
University of St. Francis M,W
Waubonsee Community College W
Western Illinois University M,W

Indiana
Ancilla College M
Bethel College M
Butler University M,W
Calumet College of St. Joseph M,W
Goshen College M,W
Grace College M,W
Huntington University M,W
Indiana Institute of Technology M,W
Indiana State University W
Indiana University
  Bloomington M,W
Indiana University-Purdue University Fort Wayne M,W
Indiana University-Purdue University Indianapolis M,W
Indiana Wesleyan University M,W
Marian College M,W
Oakland City University M,W
Purdue University W
Saint Joseph's College M,W
St. Mary-of-the-Woods College W
Taylor University M,W
University of Evansville M,W
University of Indianapolis M,W
University of Notre Dame M,W
University of St. Francis M,W
University of Southern Indiana M,W
Valparaiso University M,W

Iowa
Ashford University M,W
Briar Cliff University M,W
Clarke College M,W
Dordt College M,W
Drake University M,W
Graceland University M,W
Grand View University M,W
Iowa Central Community College M,W
Iowa State University W
Iowa Wesleyan College M,W
Kirkwood Community College M
Morningside College M,W
Mount Mercy College M,W
North Iowa Area Community College M
Northwestern College M,W
St. Ambrose University M,W
Scott Community College M,W
University of Iowa W
University of Northern Iowa W
Waldorf College M,W
William Penn University M,W

Kansas
Allen County Community College M,W
Baker University M,W
Barton County Community College M,W
Benedictine College M,W
Bethany College M,W
Bethel College M,W
Central Christian College of Kansas M,W
Cloud County Community College M,W
Coffeyville Community College M,W
Emporia State University W
Friends University M,W
Garden City Community College M,W
Hesston College M
Hutchinson Community College W
Johnson County Community College M
Kansas City Kansas Community College M
Kansas Wesleyan University M,W
MidAmerica Nazarene University M,W
Neosho County Community College M,W
Newman University M,W
Ottawa University M,W
Southwestern College M,W
Sterling College M,W
Tabor College M,W
University of Kansas W
University of St. Mary M,W
Washburn University W

Kentucky
Asbury College M,W
Bellarmine University M,W
Brescia University M,W
Campbellsville University M,W
Georgetown College M,W
Kentucky Wesleyan College M,W
Lindsey Wilson College M,W
Mid-Continent University M
Midway College W
Morehead State University W
Murray State University W
Northern Kentucky University M,W
Pikeville College M,W
St. Catharine College M,W
Union College M,W
University of Kentucky M,W
University of Louisville M,W
University of the Cumberlands M,W
Western Kentucky University M

Louisiana
Centenary College of Louisiana M,W
Louisiana College M
Louisiana State University and Agricultural and Mechanical College W
McNeese State University W
Nicholls State University W
Northwestern State University W
Southeastern Louisiana University W
Southern University and Agricultural and Mechanical College W
University of Louisiana at Lafayette W
University of Louisiana at Monroe W

Maine
University of Maine M,W
University of Maine
  Augusta W

Maryland
Anne Arundel Community College M,W
Chesapeake College M,W
College of Southern Maryland M,W
Columbia Union College M,W
Community College of Baltimore County M,W
Hagerstown Community College M,W
Harford Community College M,W
Loyola College in Maryland M,W
Mount St. Mary's University M,W
Prince George's Community College W
Towson University M,W
University of Maryland
  Baltimore County M,W
  College Park M,W
  Eastern Shore M

Massachusetts
American International College W
Boston College M,W
Boston University M,W
College of the Holy Cross M,W
Dean College M,W
Massasoit Community College M
Merrimack College W
Northeastern University M,W
Stonehill College M,W
University of Massachusetts
  Amherst M,W
  Lowell M,W

Michigan
Aquinas College M,W
Central Michigan University W
Concordia University M,W
Cornerstone University M,W
Davenport University M,W
Eastern Michigan University W
Grand Rapids Community College W
Grand Valley State University W
Madonna University M,W
Michigan State University M,W
Northern Michigan University W
Northwood University: Michigan M,W
Oakland University M,W
Rochester College M,W
Saginaw Valley State University M,W
Siena Heights University M,W
Southwestern Michigan College M,W
Spring Arbor University M,W
University of Detroit Mercy M,W
University of Michigan M,W
Western Michigan University M,W

Minnesota
Bemidji State University W
Concordia University: St. Paul W
Minnesota State University
  Mankato W
  Moorhead W
Saint Cloud State University W
Southwest Minnesota State University W
University of Minnesota
  Crookston W
  Duluth W
  Twin Cities W
Winona State University W

Mississippi
Alcorn State University W
Belhaven College M,W
Delta State University M,W
East Mississippi Community College M
Hinds Community College M
Holmes Community College M
Meridian Community College M
Mississippi State University W
Southwest Mississippi Community College M,W
University of Mississippi W
University of Southern Mississippi W
William Carey University M,W

Missouri
Avila University M,W
Central Methodist University M,W
Columbia College M
Culver-Stockton College M,W
Drury University M,W
East Central College M
Hannibal-LaGrange College M,W
Harris-Stowe State University M,W
Jefferson College M
Missouri Baptist University M,W
Missouri Southern State University M,W
Missouri State University M,W
Missouri Valley College M,W
Northwest Missouri State University W
Park University M,W
Research College of Nursing M,W
Rockhurst University M,W
St. Charles Community College M,W
St. Louis Community College M
Saint Louis University M,W
Southeast Missouri State University W
Southwest Baptist University W
St. Louis Community College
  Meramec M,W
Truman State University M,W
University of Central Missouri W
University of Missouri
  Columbia W
  Kansas City M
  Missouri University of Science and Technology M,W
  St. Louis M,W
William Jewell College M,W
William Woods University M,W

Montana
Carroll College W
Flathead Valley Community College M
Montana State University
  Billings M,W
Rocky Mountain College W
University of Great Falls W
University of Montana W

Nebraska
Bellevue University M,W
College of Saint Mary W
Concordia University M,W
Creighton University M,W
Doane College M,W
Wayne State College W
Western Nebraska Community College M,W
York College M,W

Nevada
University of Nevada
  Las Vegas M,W
  Reno W

New Hampshire
Franklin Pierce University M,W
Hesser College M,W
Southern New Hampshire University M,W
University of New Hampshire M,W

New Jersey
Bloomfield College M,W
Burlington County College M,W
Caldwell College M,W
Essex County College M
Fairleigh Dickinson University
  Metropolitan Campus M,W
Felician College M,W
Georgian Court University W
Mercer County Community College M,W
Monmouth University M,W
New Jersey Institute of Technology M,W
Rider University M,W
Rutgers, The State University of New Jersey
  New Brunswick/Piscataway Campus M,W
Saint Peter's College M,W
Salem Community College W
Seton Hall University M,W
Sussex County Community College W

New Mexico
New Mexico Highlands University W
University of New Mexico M,W
University of the Southwest M,W

New York
Adelphi University M,W
ASA Institute of Business and Computer Technology M
Bryant & Stratton Business Institute

Bryant & Stratton College: Syracuse M,W
Canisius College M,W
City University of New York
Queens College M,W
Colgate University M,W
College of Saint Rose M,W
Concordia College M,W
Daemen College M,W
Dominican College of Blauvelt M,W
Dowling College M
Fordham University M,W
Hartwick College M
Hofstra University M,W
Houghton College M,W
Iona College M,W
Jamestown Community College M
Le Moyne College M,W
Long Island University
Brooklyn Campus M,W
C. W. Post Campus M,W
Manhattan College M,W
Marist College M,W
Mercy College M,W
Molloy College M,W
Monroe Community College M,W
New York Institute of Technology M,W
Niagara University M,W
Nyack College M,W
Pace University W
Roberts Wesleyan College M,W
Saint Bonaventure University M,W
St. Francis College M
St. John's University M,W
St. Thomas Aquinas College M,W
Siena College M,W
State University of New York
Albany M,W
Binghamton M,W
Buffalo M,W
College at Oneonta M
Stony Brook M,W
Syracuse University M,W
Wagner College W

North Carolina
Appalachian State University M,W
Barton College M,W
Belmont Abbey College M,W
Brevard College M,W
Campbell University M,W
Catawba College M,W
Davidson College M,W
Duke University M,W
East Carolina University W
Elon University M,W
Gardner-Webb University M,W
High Point University M,W
Lees-McRae College M,W
Lenoir-Rhyne University M,W
Louisburg College M,W
Mars Hill College M,W
Montreat College M,W
Mount Olive College M,W
North Carolina State University M,W
Pfeiffer University M,W
Queens University of Charlotte M,W
St. Andrews Presbyterian College M,W
University of North Carolina
Asheville M,W
Chapel Hill M,W
Charlotte M,W
Greensboro M,W
Pembroke M,W
Wilmington M,W
Wake Forest University M,W
Western Carolina University W
Wingate University M,W

North Dakota
Jamestown College M,W
North Dakota State University W
University of Mary M,W
University of North Dakota W

Ohio
Ashland University M,W
Bowling Green State University M,W
Bryant & Stratton College
Eastlake M
Cedarville University M,W
Cincinnati State Technical and Community College M,W
Cleveland State University M,W
Kent State University W
Lakeland Community College M
Malone University M,W
Miami University
Oxford Campus W
Mount Vernon Nazarene University M,W
Notre Dame College W
Ohio Dominican University M,W
Shawnee State University M,W
Southern State Community College M
University of Akron M,W
University of Dayton M,W
University of Findlay M,W
University of Rio Grande M,W
University of Toledo W
Urbana University M,W
Ursuline College W
Walsh University M,W
Wright State University M
Xavier University M,W
Youngstown State University W

Oklahoma
Bacone College M,W
East Central University W
Northeastern Oklahoma Agricultural and Mechanical College M,W
Northeastern State University M,W
Northern Oklahoma College M,W
Northwestern Oklahoma State University W
Oklahoma Baptist University M,W
Oklahoma Christian University M,W
Oklahoma City University M,W
Oklahoma State University W
Oklahoma Wesleyan University M,W
Oral Roberts University M,W
Rogers State University M,W
St. Gregory's University M,W
Southern Nazarene University M,W
Southwestern Oklahoma State University M,W
University of Central Oklahoma W
University of Oklahoma W
University of Science and Arts of Oklahoma M,W
University of Tulsa M,W

Oregon
Concordia University M,W
Corban College M,W
Eastern Oregon University M,W
Northwest Christian University M,W
Oregon Institute of Technology W
Oregon State University M,W
Portland State University W
Southern Oregon University W
Southwestern Oregon Community College M,W
Treasure Valley Community College M,W
University of Oregon W
University of Portland M,W
Warner Pacific College M,W

Pennsylvania
Bloomsburg University of Pennsylvania M,W
California University of Pennsylvania M,W
Carlow University W
Chestnut Hill College M,W
Clarion University of Pennsylvania W
Drexel University M,W
Duquesne University M,W
East Stroudsburg University of Pennsylvania M,W
Edinboro University of Pennsylvania W
Gannon University M,W
Holy Family University M,W
Indiana University of Pennsylvania W
Kutztown University of Pennsylvania M,W
La Salle University M,W
Lackawanna College W
Lafayette College M,W
Lehigh University M,W
Lock Haven University of Pennsylvania M,W
Mercyhurst College M,W
Millersville University of Pennsylvania M,W
Penn State
University Park M,W
Philadelphia University M,W
Point Park University M,W
Robert Morris University M,W
St. Francis University M,W
Saint Joseph's University M,W
Seton Hill University M,W
Shippensburg University of Pennsylvania M,W
Slippery Rock University of Pennsylvania M,W
Temple University M,W
University of Pittsburgh M,W
Villanova University M,W
West Chester University of Pennsylvania M,W

Puerto Rico
Inter American University of Puerto Rico
Aguadilla Campus M
Bayamon Campus M
Guayama Campus M
San German Campus M
Turabo University M
University of Puerto Rico
Carolina Regional College M
Cayey University College M
Mayaguez M

Rhode Island
Bryant University M,W
Community College of Rhode Island M,W
Providence College M,W
University of Rhode Island M,W

South Carolina
Anderson University M,W
Charleston Southern University M,W
The Citadel W
Clemson University M,W
Coastal Carolina University M,W
College of Charleston M,W
Columbia College W
Converse College W
Erskine College M,W
Francis Marion University M,W
Furman University M,W
Lander University M,W
Limestone College M,W
Newberry College M,W
North Greenville University M,W
Presbyterian College M,W
South Carolina State University W
Southern Wesleyan University M,W
Spartanburg Methodist College M,W
University of South Carolina M,W
University of South Carolina
Aiken M
Upstate M,W
Winthrop University M,W
Wofford College M,W

South Dakota
Augustana College W
Dakota Wesleyan University M,W
Mount Marty College M,W
South Dakota State University W
University of Sioux Falls M,W
University of South Dakota W

Tennessee
Austin Peay State University W
Belmont University M,W
Bethel College M,W
Carson-Newman College M,W
Christian Brothers University M,W
Crichton College M,W
Cumberland University M,W
East Tennessee State University M,W
Freed-Hardeman University M,W
King College M,W
Lambuth University M,W
Lee University M,W
Lincoln Memorial University M,W
Lipscomb University M,W
Martin Methodist College M,W
Middle Tennessee State University W
Milligan College M,W
Tennessee Technological University W
Tennessee Temple University M
Tennessee Wesleyan College M,W
Trevecca Nazarene University M,W
Tusculum College M,W
Union University M,W
University of Memphis M,W
University of Tennessee
Chattanooga W
Knoxville W
Martin W
Vanderbilt University W

Texas
Abilene Christian University W
Angelo State University W
Baylor University W
Cedar Valley College M
Dallas Baptist University W
Hill College W
Houston Baptist University M,W
Lon Morris College M,W
Midwestern State University M,W
Northwood University: Texas M,W
Prairie View A&M University W
Ranger College M,W
Rice University W
St. Edward's University M,W
St. Mary's University M,W
Sam Houston State University W
Southern Methodist University M,W
Stephen F. Austin State University W
Texas A&M University W
Texas A&M University
Commerce W
Corpus Christi W
Texas Christian University W
Texas Southern University W
Texas State University: San Marcos W
Texas Tech University W
Texas Woman's University W
Tyler Junior College M
University of Houston W
University of North Texas W
University of Texas
Austin W
Brownsville - Texas Southmost College M,W
of the Permian Basin M,W
San Antonio W
University of the Incarnate Word M,W
Wayland Baptist University M,W
West Texas A&M University M,W

Utah
Brigham Young University W
Dixie State College of Utah M,W
University of Utah W
Utah State University W
Utah Valley University W
Westminster College M,W

Vermont
University of Vermont M,W

Virginia
Bluefield College M,W
College of William and Mary M,W
George Mason University M,W

James Madison University M,W
Liberty University M,W
Longwood University M,W
Old Dominion University M,W
Radford University M,W
University of Richmond M,W
University of Virginia M,W
Virginia Commonwealth University M,W
Virginia Intermont College M,W
Virginia Military Institute M
Virginia Polytechnic Institute and State University M,W

Washington
Central Washington University W
Clark College M,W
Columbia Basin College M,W
Eastern Washington University W
Edmonds Community College M,W
Everett Community College M,W
Evergreen State College M,W
Gonzaga University M,W
Green River Community College M
Highline Community College M,W
Lower Columbia College W
Northwest University M,W
Olympic College M,W
Peninsula College M
Pierce College M
Saint Martin's University M,W
Seattle Pacific University M
Seattle University M,W
Shoreline Community College M,W
Skagit Valley College M,W
Spokane Community College W
Tacoma Community College M,W
University of Washington M,W
Walla Walla Community College M,W
Washington State University W
Western Washington University M,W
Whatcom Community College M
Yakima Valley Community College W

West Virginia
Alderson-Broaddus College M,W
Concord University W
Davis and Elkins College M,W
Marshall University M,W
Mountain State University W
Ohio Valley University M,W
Salem International University M,W
Shepherd University M,W
University of Charleston M,W
West Virginia University M,W
West Virginia Wesleyan College M,W
Wheeling Jesuit University M,W

Wisconsin
Cardinal Stritch University M,W
Marquette University M,W
Milwaukee Area Technical College M,W
University of Wisconsin
Green Bay M,W
Milwaukee M,W
Parkside M,W
Viterbo University M,W

Wyoming
Central Wyoming College M,W
Laramie County Community College M,W
University of Wyoming W
Western Wyoming Community College M,W

Softball

Alabama
Alabama State University W
Auburn University W
Bevill State Community College W
Central Alabama Community College W
Chattahoochee Valley Community College W
Enterprise-Ozark Community College W
Faulkner State Community College W
Faulkner University W
Gadsden State Community College W
George C. Wallace State Community College
George C. Wallace Community College at Dothan M
Selma W
Jacksonville State University W
Jefferson Davis Community College W
Jefferson State Community College W
Judson College W
Lurleen B. Wallace Community College W
Marion Military Institute W
Miles College W
Northwest-Shoals Community College W
Samford University W
Shelton State Community College W
Snead State Community College W
Southern Union State Community College W
Spring Hill College W
Troy University W
University of Alabama W
University of Alabama
Birmingham W
Huntsville W
University of Mobile W
University of North Alabama W
University of West Alabama W
Wallace State Community College at Hanceville W

Arizona
Arizona State University W
Arizona Western College W
Central Arizona College W
Chandler-Gilbert Community College
Pecos W
Eastern Arizona College W
Gateway Community College W
Glendale Community College W
Mesa Community College W
Paradise Valley Community College W
Pima Community College W
Scottsdale Community College W
South Mountain Community College W
University of Arizona W

Arkansas
Henderson State University W
Lyon College W
North Arkansas College W
Ouachita Baptist University W
Southern Arkansas University W
University of Arkansas W
University of Arkansas
Monticello W
University of Central Arkansas W
Williams Baptist College W

California
Azusa Pacific University W
Bethany University W
Biola University W
California Baptist University W
California Polytechnic State University: San Luis Obispo W
California State University
Bakersfield W
Chico W
Dominguez Hills W
Fresno W
Fullerton W
Long Beach W
Monterey Bay W
Northridge W
Sacramento W
San Bernardino W
Stanislaus W
Concordia University W
Dominican University of California W
Fresno City College W
Grossmont College W
Holy Names University W
Hope International University W
Humboldt State University W
Loyola Marymount University W
Notre Dame de Namur University W
Patten University W
Point Loma Nazarene University W
St. Mary's College of California W
San Diego State University W
San Jose State University W
Sonoma State University W
Stanford University W
University of California
Berkeley W
Davis W
Los Angeles W
Riverside W
Santa Barbara W
University of San Diego W
University of the Pacific W
Vanguard University of Southern California W
Yuba Community College District W

Colorado
Adams State College W
Colorado Northwestern Community College W
Colorado School of Mines W
Colorado State University W
Colorado State University
Pueblo W
Fort Lewis College W
Mesa State College W
Otero Junior College W
Regis University W
Trinidad State Junior College W
University of Colorado
Colorado Springs W
University of Northern Colorado W

Connecticut
Central Connecticut State University W
Fairfield University W
Post University W
Quinnipiac University W
Sacred Heart University W
Southern Connecticut State University W
University of Bridgeport W
University of Connecticut W
University of New Haven W

Delaware
Delaware State University W
Delaware Technical and Community College
Owens W
Stanton/Wilmington M
Terry W
Goldey-Beacom College W
University of Delaware W
Wilmington University W

Florida
Barry University W
Bethune-Cookman University W
Brevard Community College W
Central Florida Community College W
Chipola College W
Daytona State College W
Eckerd College W
Edward Waters College W
Flagler College W
Florida Atlantic University W
Florida Community College at Jacksonville W
Florida Gulf Coast University W
Florida Institute of Technology W
Florida Southern College W
Florida State University W
Gulf Coast Community College W
Hillsborough Community College W
Indian River State College W
Jacksonville University W
Lake City Community College W
Lake-Sumter Community College W
Lynn University W
Manatee Community College W
Miami Dade College W
North Florida Community College W
Northwest Florida State College W
Northwood University
Florida W
Nova Southeastern University W
Palm Beach Community College W
Pasco-Hernando Community College W
Pensacola Junior College W
Polk Community College W
Rollins College W
Saint Johns River Community College W
St. Leo University W
St. Petersburg College W
Saint Thomas University W
Santa Fe College W
South Florida Community College W
Stetson University W
Tallahassee Community College W
University of Central Florida W
University of Florida W
University of North Florida W
University of South Florida W
University of Tampa W
University of West Florida W
Warner University W
Webber International University W

Georgia
Abraham Baldwin Agricultural College W
Albany State University W
Andrew College W
Armstrong Atlantic State University W
Augusta State University W
Brenau University W
Brewton-Parker College W
Clark Atlanta University W
College of Coastal Georgia W
Columbus State University W
Covenant College W
Darton College W
Emmanuel College W
Georgia College and State University W
Georgia Institute of Technology W
Georgia Perimeter College W
Georgia Southern University W
Georgia Southwestern State University W
Georgia State University W
Gordon College W
Kennesaw State University W
Mercer University W
Middle Georgia College W
North Georgia College & State University W
Paine College W
Reinhardt College W
South Georgia College W
Thomas University W
Truett-McConnell College W
University of Georgia W
University of West Georgia W
Valdosta State University W
Young Harris College W

Hawaii
Brigham Young University-Hawaii W
Chaminade University of Honolulu W
Hawaii Pacific University W
University of Hawaii
Hilo W
Manoa W

Idaho
College of Idaho W
College of Southern Idaho M,W
North Idaho College W
Northwest Nazarene University W

Illinois
Black Hawk College W
Bradley University W
Carl Sandburg College W

College of Lake County W
Danville Area Community College W
DePaul University W
Eastern Illinois University W
Elgin Community College W
Highland Community College W
Illinois Central College W
Illinois Eastern Community Colleges
  Lincoln Trail College W
  Olney Central College W
  Wabash Valley College W
Illinois State University W
John A. Logan College W
Judson University W
Kankakee Community College W
Kaskaskia College W
Kishwaukee College W
Lake Land College W
Lewis University W
Lincoln College W
Lincoln Land Community College W
McHenry County College W
McKendree University W
Moraine Valley Community College W
Morton College W
Northwestern University W
Olivet Nazarene University W
Parkland College W
Quincy University W
Rend Lake College W
Robert Morris College: Chicago W
St. Xavier University W
Sauk Valley Community College W
Shawnee Community College W
South Suburban College of Cook County W
Southeastern Illinois College W
Southern Illinois University Carbondale W
Southern Illinois University Edwardsville W
Spoon River College W
Springfield College in Illinois W
Trinity Christian College W
Trinity International University W
University of Illinois
  Chicago W
  Springfield W
  Urbana-Champaign W
University of St. Francis W
Waubonsee Community College W
Western Illinois University W

Indiana
Ancilla College W
Ball State University W
Bethel College W
Butler University W
Calumet College of St. Joseph W
Goshen College W
Grace College W
Huntington University W
Indiana Institute of Technology W
Indiana State University W
Indiana University
  Bloomington W
Indiana University-Purdue University Fort Wayne W
Indiana University-Purdue University Indianapolis W
Indiana Wesleyan University W
Marian College W
Oakland City University W
Purdue University W
Saint Joseph's College W
St. Mary-of-the-Woods College W
Taylor University W
University of Evansville W
University of Indianapolis W
University of Notre Dame W
University of St. Francis W
University of Southern Indiana W
Valparaiso University W

Iowa
Ashford University W
Briar Cliff University W
Clarke College W
Dordt College W
Drake University W
Ellsworth Community College W
Graceland University W
Grand View University W
Indian Hills Community College W
Iowa Central Community College W
Iowa Lakes Community College W
Iowa State University W
Iowa Wesleyan College W
Iowa Western Community College W
Kirkwood Community College W
Marshalltown Community College W
Morningside College W
Mount Mercy College W
Muscatine Community College W
North Iowa Area Community College W
Northwestern College W
St. Ambrose University W
Southeastern Community College
  North Campus W
Southwestern Community College W
University of Iowa W
University of Northern Iowa W
Waldorf College W
William Penn University W

Kansas
Allen County Community College W
Baker University W
Barton County Community College W
Benedictine College W
Bethany College W
Brown Mackie College
  Salina W
Central Christian College of Kansas W
Cloud County Community College W
Coffeyville Community College W
Colby Community College W
Cowley County Community College W
Dodge City Community College W
Emporia State University W
Fort Hays State University W
Fort Scott Community College W
Friends University W
Garden City Community College W
Highland Community College W
Hutchinson Community College W
Independence Community College W
Johnson County Community College W
Kansas City Kansas Community College W
Kansas Wesleyan University W
Labette Community College W
McPherson College W
MidAmerica Nazarene University W
Neosho County Community College W
Newman University W
Ottawa University W
Pittsburg State University W
Pratt Community College W
Seward County Community College W
Southwestern College W
Sterling College W
Tabor College W
University of Kansas W
University of St. Mary W
Washburn University W
Wichita State University W

Kentucky
Asbury College W
Bellarmine University W
Brescia University W
Campbellsville University W
Eastern Kentucky University W
Georgetown College W
Kentucky State University W
Kentucky Wesleyan College W
Lindsey Wilson College W
Mid-Continent University W
Midway College W
Morehead State University W
Murray State University W
Northern Kentucky University W
Pikeville College W
St. Catharine College W
Union College W
University of Kentucky W
University of Louisville M
University of the Cumberlands W
Western Kentucky University W

Louisiana
Bossier Parish Community College W
Centenary College of Louisiana W
Louisiana State University and Agricultural and Mechanical College W
Louisiana Tech University W
McNeese State University W
Nicholls State University W
Northwestern State University W
Southeastern Louisiana University W
Southern University and Agricultural and Mechanical College W
University of Louisiana at Lafayette W
University of Louisiana at Monroe W

Maine
University of Maine W

Maryland
Anne Arundel Community College W
Bowie State University W
Chesapeake College W
College of Southern Maryland W
Columbia Union College W
Community College of Baltimore County W
Coppin State University W
Hagerstown Community College W
Morgan State University W
Mount St. Mary's University W
Prince George's Community College W
Towson University W
University of Maryland
  Baltimore County W
  College Park W
  Eastern Shore W

Massachusetts
American International College W
Boston College W
Boston University W
Dean College W
Massasoit Community College W
Merrimack College W
Stonehill College W
University of Massachusetts
  Amherst W
  Lowell W

Michigan
Alpena Community College W
Aquinas College W
Central Michigan University W
Concordia University W
Cornerstone University W
Eastern Michigan University W
Ferris State University W
Glen Oaks Community College W
Grand Valley State University W
Henry Ford Community College W
Hillsdale College W
Kalamazoo Valley Community College W
Kellogg Community College W
Lake Michigan College W
Lake Superior State University W
Madonna University W
Michigan State University W
Mott Community College W
Muskegon Community College W
Northwood University: Michigan W
Oakland Community College W
Oakland University W
Rochester College W
Saginaw Valley State University W
Siena Heights University W
Spring Arbor University W
University of Detroit Mercy W
University of Michigan W
Wayne State University W
Western Michigan University W

Minnesota
Bemidji State University W
Concordia University: St. Paul W
Minnesota State University
  Mankato W
  Moorhead W
Saint Cloud State University W
Southwest Minnesota State University W
University of Minnesota
  Crookston W
  Duluth W
  Twin Cities W
Winona State University W

Mississippi
Alcorn State University W
Belhaven College W
Copiah-Lincoln Community College W
Delta State University W
East Central Community College W
East Mississippi Community College W
Hinds Community College W
Holmes Community College W
Itawamba Community College W
Jackson State University W
Meridian Community College W
Mississippi Gulf Coast Community College W
Mississippi State University W
Mississippi Valley State University W
Northwest Mississippi Community College W
Southwest Mississippi Community College W
University of Mississippi W
University of Southern Mississippi W
William Carey University W

Missouri
Avila University W
Central Methodist University W
Columbia College W
Culver-Stockton College W
Drury University W
East Central College W
Evangel University W
Hannibal-LaGrange College W
Harris-Stowe State University W
Jefferson College W
Lincoln University W
Missouri Baptist University W
Missouri Southern State University W
Missouri State University W
Missouri Valley College W
Missouri Western State University W
North Central Missouri College W
Northwest Missouri State University W
Park University W
Research College of Nursing W
Rockhurst University W
St. Charles Community College W
St. Louis Community College W
St. Louis Community College
  Meramec W
Saint Louis University W
Southeast Missouri State University W
Southwest Baptist University W
Stephens College W
Three Rivers Community College W
Truman State University W
University of Central Missouri W
University of Missouri
  Columbia W
  Kansas City W

Missouri University of Science and Technology W
St. Louis W
William Jewell College W
William Woods University W

Montana
Montana State University
Billings W
University of Great Falls W

Nebraska
Bellevue University W
College of Saint Mary W
Concordia University W
Creighton University W
Doane College W
Mid-Plains Community College Area W
Peru State College W
University of Nebraska
Kearney W
Lincoln W
Omaha W
Wayne State College W
Western Nebraska Community College W
York College W

Nevada
College of Southern Nevada W
University of Nevada
Las Vegas W
Reno W

New Hampshire
Franklin Pierce University W
Hesser College W
Southern New Hampshire University M,W

New Jersey
Bloomfield College W
Brookdale Community College W
Burlington County College W
Caldwell College W
Fairleigh Dickinson University
Metropolitan Campus W
Felician College W
Georgian Court University W
Mercer County Community College W
Monmouth University W
Rider University W
Rutgers, The State University of New Jersey
New Brunswick/Piscataway Campus W
Saint Peter's College W
Salem Community College W
Seton Hall University W

New Mexico
Eastern New Mexico University W
New Mexico Highlands University W
New Mexico State University W
University of New Mexico W
University of the Southwest W
Western New Mexico University W

New York
Adelphi University W
Canisius College W
City University of New York
Queens College W
Colgate University W
College of Saint Rose W
Concordia College W
Dominican College of Blauvelt W
Dowling College W
Fordham University W
Hofstra University W
Iona College W
Le Moyne College W
Long Island University
Brooklyn Campus W
C. W. Post Campus W
Manhattan College W
Marist College W
Mercy College W
Molloy College W
New York Institute of Technology W
Niagara University W
Nyack College W
Pace University W
Saint Bonaventure University W
St. John's University W
St. Thomas Aquinas College W
Siena College W
State University of New York
Albany W
Binghamton W
Buffalo W
Stony Brook W
Syracuse University W
Wagner College W

North Carolina
Appalachian State University W
Barton College W
Belmont Abbey College W
Brevard College W
Campbell University W
Catawba College W
East Carolina University W
Elizabeth City State University W
Elon University W
Fayetteville State University W
Gardner-Webb University W
Johnson C. Smith University W
Lees-McRae College W
Lenoir-Rhyne University W
Louisburg College W
Mars Hill College W
Montreat College W
Mount Olive College W
North Carolina Central University W
North Carolina State University W
Pfeiffer University W
Pitt Community College W
Queens University of Charlotte W
St. Andrews Presbyterian College W
St. Augustine's College W
Shaw University W
University of North Carolina
Chapel Hill W
Charlotte W
Greensboro W
Pembroke W
Wilmington W
Western Carolina University W
Wingate University W
Winston-Salem State University W

North Dakota
Dickinson State University W
Jamestown College W
Mayville State University W
Minot State University W
North Dakota State University W
University of Mary W
University of North Dakota W
Valley City State University W

Ohio
Ashland University W
Bowling Green State University W
Cedarville University W
Cleveland State University W
Kent State University W
Lakeland Community College W
Malone University W
Miami University
Oxford Campus W
Mount Vernon Nazarene University W
Notre Dame College W
Ohio Dominican University W
Ohio University W
Shawnee State University W
Southern State Community College W
University of Akron W
University of Dayton W
University of Findlay W
University of Rio Grande W
University of Toledo W
Urbana University W
Ursuline College W
Walsh University W
Wright State University W
Youngstown State University W

Oklahoma
Bacone College W
Cameron University W
Carl Albert State College W
Connors State College W
East Central University W
Eastern Oklahoma State College W
Northeastern Oklahoma Agricultural and Mechanical College W
Northeastern State University W
Northern Oklahoma College M,W
Northwestern Oklahoma State University W
Oklahoma Baptist University W
Oklahoma Christian University W
Oklahoma City University W
Oklahoma Panhandle State University M,W
Oklahoma State University W
Rogers State University M,W
Rose State College W
St. Gregory's University W
Seminole State College W
Southeastern Oklahoma State University W
Southern Nazarene University W
Southwestern Oklahoma State University W
University of Central Oklahoma W
University of Oklahoma W
University of Science and Arts of Oklahoma W
University of Tulsa W
Western Oklahoma State College W

Oregon
Blue Mountain Community College W
Clackamas Community College W
Concordia University W
Corban College W
Eastern Oregon University W
Northwest Christian University W
Oregon Institute of Technology W
Oregon State University W
Portland State University W
Southern Oregon University W
Southwestern Oregon Community College W
Treasure Valley Community College M,W
University of Oregon W

Pennsylvania
Bloomsburg University of Pennsylvania W
California University of Pennsylvania W
Carlow University W
Chestnut Hill College W
Clarion University of Pennsylvania W
Community College of Beaver County W
Drexel University W
East Stroudsburg University of Pennsylvania W
Edinboro University of Pennsylvania W
Gannon University W
Holy Family University W
Indiana University of Pennsylvania W
Kutztown University of Pennsylvania W
La Salle University W
Lackawanna College W
Lehigh University W
Lock Haven University of Pennsylvania W
Mansfield University of Pennsylvania W
Mercyhurst College W
Millersville University of Pennsylvania W
Penn State
University Park W
Philadelphia University W
Point Park University W
Robert Morris University W
St. Francis University W
Saint Joseph's University W
Seton Hill University W
Shippensburg University of Pennsylvania W
Slippery Rock University of Pennsylvania W
Temple University W
University of Pittsburgh W
University of the Sciences in Philadelphia W
Villanova University W
West Chester University of Pennsylvania W
Westminster College W

Puerto Rico
Inter American University of Puerto Rico
Aguadilla Campus M,W
Bayamon Campus M,W
Guayama Campus M,W
Ponce Campus M,W
Universidad del Este M
Universidad Metropolitana M,W
University of Puerto Rico
Carolina Regional College W
Cayey University College M,W
Humacao W
Mayaguez W
Ponce M,W
Utuado M,W

Rhode Island
Bryant University W
Community College of Rhode Island W
Providence College W
University of Rhode Island W

South Carolina
Aiken Technical College W
Anderson University W
Charleston Southern University W
Claflin University W
Coastal Carolina University W
College of Charleston W
Columbia College W
Erskine College W
Francis Marion University W
Furman University W
Lander University W
Limestone College W
Morris College W
Newberry College W
North Greenville University W
Presbyterian College W
South Carolina State University W
Southern Wesleyan University W
Spartanburg Methodist College W
University of South Carolina W
University of South Carolina
Aiken W
Upstate W
Winthrop University W

South Dakota
Augustana College W
Dakota State University W
Dakota Wesleyan University W
Mount Marty College W
Northern State University W
South Dakota State University W
University of Sioux Falls W
University of South Dakota W

Tennessee
Austin Peay State University W
Belmont University W
Bethel College W
Carson-Newman College W
Christian Brothers University W
Cleveland State Community College W
Crichton College W
Cumberland University W
Dyersburg State Community College W
East Tennessee State University W
Freed-Hardeman University W
Jackson State Community College W
King College W

Lambuth University W
Lee University W
LeMoyne-Owen College W
Lincoln Memorial University W
Lipscomb University W
Martin Methodist College W
Middle Tennessee State University W
Milligan College W
Motlow State Community College W
Roane State Community College W
Southwest Tennessee Community College W
Tennessee Technological University W
Tennessee Wesleyan College W
Trevecca Nazarene University W
Tusculum College W
Union University W
University of Tennessee
Chattanooga W
Knoxville W
Martin W
Volunteer State Community College W
Walters State Community College W

Texas
Abilene Christian University W
Alvin Community College W
Angelina College W
Angelo State University W
Baylor University W
Blinn College M
Clarendon College W
Frank Phillips College W
Galveston College W
Hill College W
Houston Baptist University W
Howard College W
Lon Morris College W
McLennan Community College W
Midland College W
Midwestern State University W
Northwood University: Texas W
Odessa College W
Paris Junior College W
Prairie View A&M University W
Ranger College W
St. Edward's University W
Sam Houston State University W
Stephen F. Austin State University W
Tarleton State University W
Temple College W
Texas A&M University W
Texas A&M University
Kingsville W
Texas Southern University W
Texas State University: San Marcos W
Texas Tech University W
Texas Woman's University W
University of Houston W
University of North Texas W
University of Texas
Arlington W
Austin W
of the Permian Basin W
San Antonio W
University of the Incarnate Word W
Western Texas College W
Wiley College W

Utah
Brigham Young University W
Dixie State College of Utah W
Salt Lake Community College W
Snow College W
Southern Utah University W
University of Utah W
Utah State University W
Utah Valley University W

Vermont
University of Vermont W

Virginia
Bluefield College W
Hampton University W
James Madison University W
Liberty University W
Longwood University W
Norfolk State University W
Radford University W
St. Paul's College W
University of Virginia W
University of Virginia's College at Wise W
Virginia Intermont College W
Virginia Polytechnic Institute and State University W
Virginia State University W
Virginia Union University W

Washington
Big Bend Community College W
Central Washington University W
Centralia College W
Columbia Basin College W
Edmonds Community College W
Everett Community College W
Grays Harbor College W
Green River Community College W
Highline Community College W
Lower Columbia College W
Olympic College W
Peninsula College W
Pierce College W
Saint Martin's University W
Seattle University W
Shoreline Community College W
Skagit Valley College W
Spokane Community College W
University of Washington W
Walla Walla Community College W
Western Washington University W
Yakima Valley Community College W

West Virginia
Alderson-Broaddus College W
Bluefield State College W
Concord University W
Davis and Elkins College W
Glenville State College W
Marshall University W
Mountain State University W
Ohio Valley University W
Potomac State College of West Virginia University W
Salem International University W
Shepherd University W
University of Charleston W
West Liberty State College W
West Virginia State University W
West Virginia University Institute of Technology W
West Virginia Wesleyan College W
Wheeling Jesuit University W

Wisconsin
Cardinal Stritch University W
University of Wisconsin
Green Bay W
Parkside W
Viterbo University W

Squash

Nebraska
University of Nebraska
Lincoln W

New York
Fordham University M

Swimming

Alabama
Auburn University M,W
University of Alabama M,W

Alaska
University of Alaska
Fairbanks W

Arizona
Arizona State University W
Northern Arizona University M,W
University of Arizona M,W

Arkansas
Henderson State University M,W
John Brown University W
Ouachita Baptist University M,W
University of Arkansas W
University of Arkansas
Little Rock M,W

California
Biola University M,W
California Baptist University M,W
California Polytechnic State University: San Luis Obispo M,W
California State University
Bakersfield M,W
Northridge M,W
San Bernardino M,W
Concordia University M,W
Fresno Pacific University M,W
Grossmont College M,W
Loyola Marymount University W
Pepperdine University W
San Diego State University W
San Jose State University W
Stanford University M,W
University of California
Berkeley M,W
Davis M,W
Irvine M,W
Los Angeles M,W
Santa Barbara M,W
University of San Diego W
University of Southern California M,W
University of the Pacific M,W

Colorado
Colorado School of Mines M,W
Colorado State University W
Mesa State College W
Metropolitan State College of Denver M,W
University of Denver M,W
University of Northern Colorado W

Connecticut
Central Connecticut State University W
Fairfield University M,W
Post University M,W
Sacred Heart University W
Southern Connecticut State University M,W
University of Bridgeport W
University of Connecticut M,W

Delaware
University of Delaware W

District of Columbia
George Washington University M,W
Georgetown University M,W
Howard University M,W

Florida
Florida Atlantic University M,W
Florida Southern College M,W
Florida State University M,W
Indian River State College M,W
St. Leo University M,W
University of Florida M,W
University of Miami W
University of North Florida W
University of Tampa M,W

Georgia
Brenau University W
Darton College M,W
Georgia Institute of Technology M,W
Georgia Southern University W
University of Georgia M,W

Hawaii
University of Hawaii
Manoa M,W

Idaho
Boise State University W
College of Idaho M,W

Illinois
Eastern Illinois University M,W
Illinois Institute of Technology M,W
Illinois State University W
Lewis University M,W
Lincoln College M,W
Northwestern University M,W
Robert Morris College: Chicago W
Southern Illinois University Carbondale M,W
University of Illinois
Chicago M,W
Urbana-Champaign W
Western Illinois University M,W

Indiana
Ball State University M,W
Indiana University
Bloomington M,W
Indiana University-Purdue University Indianapolis M,W
Purdue University M,W
University of Evansville M,W
University of Indianapolis M,W
University of Notre Dame M,W
Valparaiso University M,W

Iowa
Iowa Central Community College M,W
Iowa State University W
Morningside College M,W
University of Iowa M,W
University of Northern Iowa W

Kansas
University of Kansas W

Kentucky
Asbury College M,W
Campbellsville University W
University of Kentucky M,W
University of Louisville M,W
University of the Cumberlands M,W
Western Kentucky University M,W

Louisiana
Centenary College of Louisiana M,W
Louisiana State University and Agricultural and Mechanical College M,W
Tulane University W
University of Louisiana at Monroe M,W
University of New Orleans M,W

Maine
University of Maine W

Maryland
Loyola College in Maryland M,W
Mount St. Mary's University W
Towson University M,W
University of Maryland
Baltimore County M,W
College Park M,W

Massachusetts
Boston College M,W
Boston University M,W
Northeastern University W
University of Massachusetts
Amherst M,W
Lowell M

Michigan
Eastern Michigan University M,W
Grand Rapids Community College M,W
Grand Valley State University M,W
Hillsdale College W
Michigan State University M,W
Northern Michigan University W
Oakland University M,W
University of Michigan M,W
Wayne State University M,W

Minnesota
Minnesota State University
Mankato M,W
Saint Cloud State University M,W
University of Minnesota
Twin Cities M,W

Mississippi
Delta State University M,W

Missouri
Drury University M,W
Missouri State University M,W
Saint Louis University M,W
Stephens College W
Truman State University M,W
University of Missouri
Columbia M,W
Missouri University of Science and Technology M

Nebraska
University of Nebraska
Kearney W
Lincoln W

Nevada
University of Nevada
Las Vegas M,W
Reno W

New Hampshire
University of New Hampshire W

New Jersey
New Jersey Institute of Technology M,W
Rider University M,W
Rutgers, The State University of New Jersey
New Brunswick/Piscataway Campus M,W
Saint Peter's College M,W
Seton Hall University M,W

New Mexico
New Mexico State University W
University of New Mexico W

New York
Adelphi University M,W
Canisius College W
City University of New York
Queens College M,W
College of Saint Rose M,W
Fordham University M,W
Iona College M,W
Long Island University
C. W. Post Campus W
Manhattan College W
Marist College M,W
Monroe Community College M,W
Niagara University M,W
Saint Bonaventure University M,W
St. Francis College M,W
Siena College W
State University of New York
Binghamton M,W
Buffalo M,W
Stony Brook M,W
Syracuse University M,W
Wagner College W

North Carolina
Campbell University W
Catawba College M,W
Davidson College M,W
East Carolina University M,W
Gardner-Webb University M,W
Lenoir-Rhyne University W
Mars Hill College M,W
North Carolina Agricultural and Technical State University W
North Carolina State University M,W
Pfeiffer University M,W
University of North Carolina
Chapel Hill M,W
Wilmington M,W
Wingate University M,W

North Dakota
University of North Dakota M,W

Ohio
Ashland University M,W
Bowling Green State University M,W
Cleveland State University M,W
Miami University
Oxford Campus M,W
Notre Dame College W
Ohio University W
University of Akron W
University of Findlay M,W
University of Toledo W
Urbana University M,W
Wright State University M,W
Xavier University M,W
Youngstown State University W

Oregon
Oregon State University W

Pennsylvania
Bloomsburg University of Pennsylvania M,W
California University of Pennsylvania W
Clarion University of Pennsylvania M,W
Drexel University M,W
Duquesne University M,W
East Stroudsburg University of Pennsylvania W
Edinboro University of Pennsylvania W
Gannon University M,W
Indiana University of Pennsylvania M,W
Kutztown University of Pennsylvania M,W
La Salle University M,W
Lock Haven University of Pennsylvania W
Mansfield University of Pennsylvania W
Millersville University of Pennsylvania W
Penn State
University Park M,W
St. Francis University W
Shippensburg University of Pennsylvania M,W
University of Pittsburgh M,W
Villanova University W
West Chester University of Pennsylvania M,W
Westminster College W

Puerto Rico
Bayamon Central University M,W
Inter American University of Puerto Rico
Bayamon Campus M,W
Turabo University M,W
University of Puerto Rico
Cayey University College M,W
Humacao M,W
Mayaguez M,W
University of the Sacred Heart M,W

Rhode Island
Bryant University M,W
University of Rhode Island W

South Carolina
Clemson University M,W
College of Charleston M,W
Limestone College M,W
University of South Carolina M,W

South Dakota
South Dakota State University M,W
University of South Dakota M,W

Tennessee
University of Tennessee
Knoxville M,W
Vanderbilt University W

Texas
Rice University W
Southern Methodist University M,W
Texas A&M University M,W
Texas Christian University M,W
University of Houston W
University of North Texas W
University of Texas
Austin M,W
of the Permian Basin M,W
University of the Incarnate Word M,W

Utah
Brigham Young University M,W
University of Utah M,W

Vermont
University of Vermont W

Virginia
George Mason University M,W
James Madison University W
Radford University W
University of Richmond W
University of Virginia M,W
Virginia Military Institute M
Virginia Polytechnic Institute and State University M,W

Washington
Seattle University M,W
University of Washington M,W
Washington State University W

West Virginia
Marshall University W
West Virginia University M,W
West Virginia Wesleyan College M,W
Wheeling Jesuit University M,W

Wisconsin
University of Wisconsin
Green Bay M,W
Milwaukee M,W

Wyoming
University of Wyoming M,W

Synchronized swimming

Alabama
University of Alabama
Birmingham W

California
Stanford University W

New York
Canisius College W

Texas
University of the Incarnate Word W

Table tennis

Arizona
South Mountain Community College M,W

Puerto Rico
Inter American University of Puerto Rico
Aguadilla Campus M,W
Bayamon Campus M,W
Metropolitan Campus M,W
Ponce Campus M,W
Universidad Metropolitana M,W
University of Puerto Rico
Carolina Regional College M,W
Cayey University College M,W
Mayaguez M,W
Ponce M,W

Tennis

Alabama
Alabama Agricultural and Mechanical University M,W
Alabama State University M,W
Auburn University M,W
Auburn University at Montgomery M,W
Central Alabama Community College M,W
Faulkner State Community College M,W
Gadsden State Community College M,W
Jacksonville State University M,W
Judson College W
Marion Military Institute M,W
Samford University M,W
Snead State Community College W
Spring Hill College M,W
Troy University M,W
University of Alabama M,W
University of Alabama
Birmingham M,W
Huntsville M,W
University of Mobile M,W
University of Montevallo W
University of North Alabama M,W
University of South Alabama M,W
Wallace State Community College at Hanceville M,W

Arizona
Arizona State University W
Eastern Arizona College W
Gateway Community College M,W
Glendale Community College M,W
Grand Canyon University W
Northern Arizona University M,W
Paradise Valley Community College M,W
Pima Community College M,W
Scottsdale Community College M,W
South Mountain Community College M,W
University of Arizona M,W

Arkansas
Arkansas State University W
Arkansas Tech University W
Harding University M,W
Henderson State University W
John Brown University M,W
Ouachita Baptist University M,W
Southern Arkansas University W
University of Arkansas M,W
University of Arkansas
Fort Smith M,W
Little Rock M,W
University of Central Arkansas W

California
Azusa Pacific University M
Biola University M,W
California Baptist University M,W
California Polytechnic State University: San Luis Obispo M,W

California State Polytechnic University: Pomona M,W
California State University
- Bakersfield W
- Fresno M,W
- Fullerton W
- Long Beach W
- Los Angeles M,W
- Northridge W
- Sacramento M,W

Concordia University M,W
Dominican University of California W
Fresno City College M,W
Fresno Pacific University M,W
Grossmont College M,W
Hope International University M,W
Loyola Marymount University M,W
The Master's College W
Notre Dame de Namur University W
Pepperdine University M,W
Point Loma Nazarene University M,W
St. Mary's College of California M,W
San Diego State University M,W
San Jose State University W
Santa Clara University M,W
Sonoma State University M,W
Stanford University M,W
University of California
- Berkeley M,W
- Davis M,W
- Irvine M,W
- Los Angeles M,W
- Riverside M,W
- Santa Barbara M,W

University of San Diego M,W
University of San Francisco M,W
University of Southern California M,W
University of the Pacific M,W
Vanguard University of Southern California M,W
Westmont College M,W
Yuba Community College District M,W

Colorado

Colorado Christian University M,W
Colorado State University W
Colorado State University
- Pueblo M,W

Mesa State College M,W
Metropolitan State College of Denver M,W
University of Colorado
- Boulder W

University of Denver M,W
University of Northern Colorado M,W

Connecticut

Fairfield University M,W
Quinnipiac University M,W
Sacred Heart University M,W
University of Connecticut M,W
University of Hartford M,W
University of New Haven W

Delaware

Delaware State University M,W
Goldey-Beacom College W

District of Columbia

George Washington University M,W
Georgetown University M,W
Howard University M,W

Florida

Barry University M,W
Bethune-Cookman University M,W
Central Florida Community College W
Eckerd College M,W
Embry-Riddle Aeronautical University M,W
Flagler College M,W
Florida Atlantic University M,W
Florida Community College at Jacksonville W
Florida Gulf Coast University M,W
Florida Institute of Technology M,W
Florida Southern College M,W
Florida State University M,W
Hillsborough Community College W
Jacksonville University M,W
Lynn University M,W
Northwood University
- Florida M,W

Nova Southeastern University W
Pasco-Hernando Community College W
Rollins College M,W
St. Leo University M,W
Saint Thomas University M,W
Stetson University M,W
University of Central Florida M,W
University of Florida M,W
University of Miami M,W
University of North Florida M,W
University of South Florida M,W
University of Tampa W
University of West Florida M,W
Warner University M,W
Webber International University M,W

Georgia

Abraham Baldwin Agricultural College M,W
Albany State University W
Armstrong Atlantic State University M,W
Augusta State University M,W
Brenau University W
Clark Atlanta University W
Clayton State University W
Columbus State University M,W
Covenant College W
Darton College M,W
Emmanuel College M,W
Fort Valley State University M,W
Georgia College and State University M,W
Georgia Institute of Technology M,W
Georgia Perimeter College M,W
Georgia Southern University M,W
Georgia Southwestern State University M,W
Georgia State University M,W
Gordon College W
Kennesaw State University M,W
Mercer University M,W
Morehouse College M
North Georgia College & State University M,W
Reinhardt College M,W
Savannah State University W
Shorter College M,W
South Georgia College W
University of Georgia M,W
Valdosta State University M,W
Young Harris College W

Hawaii

Brigham Young University-Hawaii M,W
Chaminade University of Honolulu M,W
Hawaii Pacific University M,W
University of Hawaii
- Hilo M,W
- Manoa M,W

Idaho

Boise State University M,W
College of Idaho W
Idaho State University M,W
Lewis-Clark State College M,W
University of Idaho M,W

Illinois

Bradley University M,W
Chicago State University M,W
College of Lake County M,W
DePaul University M,W
Eastern Illinois University M,W
Elgin Community College M,W
Illinois State University M,W
Lake Land College M,W
Lewis and Clark Community College M,W
Lewis University M,W
McHenry County College M,W
McKendree University M,W
Moraine Valley Community College M,W
Northwestern University M,W
Olivet Nazarene University M,W
Quincy University M,W
Rend Lake College W
Robert Morris College: Chicago W
Sauk Valley Community College M,W
Southern Illinois University Carbondale M,W
Southern Illinois University Edwardsville M,W
University of Illinois
- Chicago M,W
- Springfield M,W
- Urbana-Champaign M,W

University of St. Francis M,W
Waubonsee Community College M,W
Western Illinois University M,W

Indiana

Ball State University M,W
Bethel College M,W
Butler University M,W
Calumet College of St. Joseph M,W
Goshen College M,W
Grace College M,W
Huntington University M,W
Indiana Institute of Technology M,W
Indiana State University M,W
Indiana University
- Bloomington M,W

Indiana University-Purdue University Fort Wayne M,W
Indiana University-Purdue University Indianapolis M,W
Indiana Wesleyan University M,W
Marian College M,W
Oakland City University M,W
Purdue University M,W
Taylor University M,W
University of Evansville W
University of Indianapolis M,W
University of Notre Dame M,W
University of St. Francis W
University of Southern Indiana M,W
Valparaiso University M,W
Vincennes University M

Iowa

Briar Cliff University M,W
Clarke College M,W
Dordt College M,W
Drake University M,W
Graceland University M,W
Iowa State University W
Morningside College M,W
St. Ambrose University M,W
University of Iowa M,W
University of Northern Iowa W

Kansas

Baker University M,W
Barton County Community College M,W
Benedictine College M,W
Bethany College M,W
Bethel College M,W
Central Christian College of Kansas M,W
Cowley County Community College M,W
Emporia State University M,W
Fort Hays State University W
Friends University M,W
Hutchinson Community College M,W
Independence Community College M,W
Johnson County Community College M,W
Kansas State University W
Kansas Wesleyan University M,W
Labette Community College W
Newman University M,W
Seward County Community College M,W
Southwestern College M,W
Sterling College M,W
Tabor College M,W
University of Kansas W
Washburn University M,W
Wichita State University M,W

Kentucky

Asbury College M,W
Bellarmine University M,W
Brescia University W
Campbellsville University M,W
Eastern Kentucky University M,W
Georgetown College M,W
Kentucky Wesleyan College W
Lindsey Wilson College M,W
Midway College W
Morehead State University M,W
Murray State University M,W
Northern Kentucky University M,W
Pikeville College M,W
Union College M,W
University of Kentucky M,W
University of Louisville M,W
University of the Cumberlands M,W
Western Kentucky University M,W

Louisiana

Centenary College of Louisiana M,W
Dillard University M,W
Grambling State University M,W
Louisiana State University and Agricultural and Mechanical College M,W
Louisiana Tech University W
McNeese State University W
Nicholls State University M,W
Northwestern State University W
Southeastern Louisiana University M,W
Southern University and Agricultural and Mechanical College M,W
University of Louisiana at Lafayette M,W
University of New Orleans M,W
Xavier University of Louisiana M,W

Maryland

College of Southern Maryland M,W
Coppin State University M,W
Loyola College in Maryland M,W
Morgan State University M,W
Mount St. Mary's University M,W
Towson University M,W
University of Maryland
- Baltimore County M,W
- College Park W
- Eastern Shore M,W

Massachusetts

Boston College M,W
Boston University W
Merrimack College W
Stonehill College M,W
University of Massachusetts
- Amherst W
- Lowell W

Michigan

Aquinas College M,W
Eastern Michigan University W
Ferris State University M,W
Grand Rapids Community College M,W
Grand Valley State University M,W
Lake Superior State University M,W
Michigan State University M,W
Michigan Technological University M,W
Muskegon Community College W
Northwood University: Michigan M,W
Oakland Community College W
Oakland University W
Saginaw Valley State University W
Spring Arbor University M,W
University of Detroit Mercy W
University of Michigan M,W
Wayne State University M,W
Western Michigan University M,W

Minnesota

Bemidji State University W
Minnesota State University

Mankato M,W
Moorhead W
Saint Cloud State University M,W
Southwest Minnesota State University W
University of Minnesota
Crookston W
Duluth W
Twin Cities M,W
Winona State University M,W

Mississippi
Alcorn State University M,W
Belhaven College M,W
Copiah-Lincoln Community College M,W
Delta State University M,W
Hinds Community College M,W
Holmes Community College M,W
Meridian Community College M,W
Mississippi Gulf Coast Community College M,W
Mississippi State University M,W
Mississippi Valley State University M,W
Northwest Mississippi Community College M,W
Southwest Mississippi Community College M,W
Tougaloo College M,W
University of Mississippi M,W
University of Southern Mississippi M,W

Missouri
Drury University M,W
Evangel University M,W
Lincoln University W
Missouri Baptist University W
Missouri Southern State University W
Missouri Valley College M,W
Missouri Western State University W
Northwest Missouri State University M,W
Research College of Nursing M,W
Rockhurst University M,W
Saint Louis University M,W
Southeast Missouri State University W
Southwest Baptist University M,W
Stephens College W
Truman State University M,W
University of Missouri
Columbia W
Kansas City M,W
St. Louis M,W
William Jewell College M,W

Montana
Montana State University
Billings M,W
Bozeman M,W
University of Montana M,W

Nebraska
Concordia University M,W
Creighton University M,W
University of Nebraska
Kearney M,W
Lincoln M,W

Nevada
University of Nevada
Las Vegas M,W
Reno M,W

New Hampshire
Franklin Pierce University M,W
Southern New Hampshire University M,W

New Jersey
Bloomfield College M
Caldwell College M
Fairleigh Dickinson University
Metropolitan Campus M,W
Georgian Court University W
Monmouth University M,W
New Jersey Institute of Technology M,W
Rider University M,W
Rutgers, The State University of New Jersey
New Brunswick/Piscataway Campus M,W
Saint Peter's College M,W
Seton Hall University W

New Mexico
Eastern New Mexico University W
New Mexico Military Institute M
New Mexico State University M,W
University of New Mexico M,W
Western New Mexico University M,W

New York
Adelphi University M,W
City University of New York
Queens College M,W
College of Saint Rose W
Concordia College M,W
Dowling College M,W
Fordham University M,W
Hofstra University M,W
Le Moyne College M,W
Long Island University
Brooklyn Campus W
C. W. Post Campus W
Manhattan College M,W
Marist College M,W
Mercy College M
Molloy College W
Niagara University M,W
Pace University M,W
Saint Bonaventure University M,W
St. Francis College M,W
St. John's University M,W
Siena College M,W
State University of New York
Albany W
Binghamton M,W
Buffalo M,W
Stony Brook M,W
Syracuse University W
Wagner College M,W

North Carolina
Appalachian State University M,W
Barton College M,W
Brevard College M,W
Campbell University M,W
Catawba College M,W
Davidson College M,W
Duke University M,W
East Carolina University M,W
Elon University M,W
Fayetteville State University W
Gardner-Webb University M,W
High Point University M,W
Johnson C. Smith University M,W
Lees-McRae College M,W
Lenoir-Rhyne University M,W
Mars Hill College M,W
Mount Olive College M,W
North Carolina Agricultural and Technical State University W
North Carolina Central University M,W
North Carolina State University M,W
Pfeiffer University M,W
Queens University of Charlotte M,W
St. Andrews Presbyterian College W
St. Augustine's College M,W
Shaw University M,W
University of North Carolina
Asheville M,W
Chapel Hill M,W
Charlotte M,W
Greensboro M,W
Pembroke W
Wilmington M,W
Wake Forest University M,W
Western Carolina University W
Wingate University M,W
Winston-Salem State University M,W

North Dakota
University of Mary M,W
University of North Dakota W

Ohio
Bowling Green State University M,W
Cedarville University M,W
Central State University M,W
Cleveland State University M,W
Malone University M,W
Miami University
Oxford Campus W
Notre Dame College M
Ohio Dominican University M,W
Shawnee State University W
Sinclair Community College M,W
University of Akron W
University of Dayton M,W
University of Findlay M,W
University of Toledo M,W
Ursuline College W
Walsh University M,W
Wright State University M,W
Xavier University M,W
Youngstown State University M,W

Oklahoma
Bacone College M,W
Cameron University M,W
East Central University M,W
Northeastern State University W
Oklahoma Baptist University M,W
Oklahoma Christian University M,W
Oklahoma State University M,W
Oklahoma Wesleyan University M,W
Oral Roberts University M,W
Seminole State College M,W
Southeastern Oklahoma State University M,W
Southern Nazarene University M,W
University of Central Oklahoma M,W
University of Oklahoma M,W
University of Tulsa M,W

Oregon
Portland State University W
Southern Oregon University W
Treasure Valley Community College M,W
University of Oregon M,W
University of Portland M,W

Pennsylvania
Bloomsburg University of Pennsylvania M,W
California University of Pennsylvania W
Carlow University W
Chestnut Hill College M,W
Clarion University of Pennsylvania W
Drexel University M,W
Duquesne University M,W
East Stroudsburg University of Pennsylvania M,W
Edinboro University of Pennsylvania M,W
Holy Family University W
Indiana University of Pennsylvania W
Kutztown University of Pennsylvania M,W
La Salle University M,W
Mercyhurst College M,W
Millersville University of Pennsylvania M,W
Penn State
University Park M,W
Philadelphia University M,W
Robert Morris University M,W
St. Francis University M,W
Saint Joseph's University M,W
Seton Hill University M,W
Shippensburg University of Pennsylvania W
Slippery Rock University of Pennsylvania W
Temple University M,W
University of Pittsburgh W
University of the Sciences in Philadelphia M,W
West Chester University of Pennsylvania M,W
Westminster College W

Puerto Rico
Inter American University of Puerto Rico
Aguadilla Campus M,W
Bayamon Campus M,W
San German Campus M,W
Turabo University M,W
University of Puerto Rico
Bayamon University College M,W
Carolina Regional College M,W
Cayey University College M,W
Humacao W
Mayaguez M,W
Ponce M,W
Utuado M,W
University of the Sacred Heart M

Rhode Island
Bryant University M,W
University of Rhode Island W

South Carolina
Anderson University M,W
Charleston Southern University M,W
The Citadel M
Clemson University M,W
Coastal Carolina University M,W
College of Charleston M,W
Columbia College W
Converse College W
Erskine College M,W
Francis Marion University M,W
Furman University M,W
Lander University M,W
Limestone College M,W
Morris College M,W
Newberry College M,W
North Greenville University M,W
Presbyterian College M,W
South Carolina State University M,W
Spartanburg Methodist College M,W
University of South Carolina M,W
University of South Carolina
Aiken M
Upstate M,W
Winthrop University M,W
Wofford College M,W

South Dakota
Augustana College W
Northern State University W
South Dakota State University M,W
University of Sioux Falls M,W

Tennessee
Austin Peay State University M,W
Belmont University M,W
Bethel College M,W
Carson-Newman College M,W
Christian Brothers University M,W
Cumberland University M,W
East Tennessee State University M,W
King College M,W
Lambuth University M,W
Lee University M,W
LeMoyne-Owen College M,W
Lincoln Memorial University M,W
Lipscomb University M,W
Martin Methodist College M,W
Middle Tennessee State University M,W
Milligan College M,W
Tennessee Technological University M,W
Tennessee Wesleyan College M,W
Tusculum College M,W
Union University M,W
University of Memphis M,W
University of Tennessee
Chattanooga M,W
Knoxville M,W
Martin M,W
Vanderbilt University M,W

Texas
Abilene Christian University M,W
Baylor University M,W
Collin County Community College District M,W
Dallas Baptist University W
Lamar University M,W

Laredo Community College M,W
Lee College W
Midwestern State University M,W
North Central Texas College W
Prairie View A&M University M,W
Rice University M,W
St. Edward's University M,W
St. Mary's University M,W
Sam Houston State University M,W
Southern Methodist University M,W
Stephen F. Austin State University W
Tarleton State University W
Temple College M,W
Texas A&M University M,W
Texas A&M University
Corpus Christi M,W
Kingsville M,W
Texas Christian University M,W
Texas Southern University M,W
Texas State University: San Marcos W
Texas Tech University M,W
Tyler Junior College M,W
University of Houston W
University of North Texas W
University of Texas
Arlington M,W
Austin M,W
Pan American M,W
San Antonio M,W
University of the Incarnate Word M,W
Weatherford College W

Utah
Brigham Young University M,W
Dixie State College of Utah W
Southern Utah University W
University of Utah M,W
Utah State University M,W
Weber State University M,W

Virginia
Bluefield College M,W
College of William and Mary M,W
George Mason University M,W
Hampton University M,W
James Madison University M,W
Liberty University M,W
Longwood University M,W
Norfolk State University M,W
Old Dominion University M,W
Radford University M,W
St. Paul's College M,W
University of Richmond M,W
University of Virginia M,W
University of Virginia's College at Wise M,W
Virginia Commonwealth University M,W
Virginia Military Institute M
Virginia Polytechnic Institute and State University M,W
Virginia State University M,W
Virginia Union University M,W

Washington
Eastern Washington University M,W
Gonzaga University M,W
Green River Community College M,W
Seattle University M,W
Shoreline Community College M,W
Skagit Valley College M,W
Spokane Community College M,W
University of Washington M,W
Washington State University W

West Virginia
Bluefield State College M,W
Concord University M,W
Marshall University W
Salem International University M
Shepherd University M,W
University of Charleston M,W
West Liberty State College M,W
West Virginia University W
West Virginia University Institute of Technology M,W
West Virginia Wesleyan College M,W

Wisconsin
Marquette University M,W
University of Wisconsin
Green Bay M,W
Milwaukee W

Wyoming
University of Wyoming W

Track and field

Alabama
Alabama Agricultural and Mechanical University M,W
Alabama State University M,W
Auburn University M,W
Lawson State Community College M
Miles College M,W
Samford University M,W
Troy University M,W
University of Alabama M,W
University of Alabama
Birmingham W
Huntsville M,W
University of South Alabama M,W
Wallace State Community College at Hanceville M,W

Arizona
Arizona State University M,W
Central Arizona College M,W
Gateway Community College M,W
Glendale Community College M,W
Mesa Community College M,W
Northern Arizona University M,W
Paradise Valley Community College M,W
Pima Community College M,W
Scottsdale Community College M,W
University of Arizona M,W

Arkansas
Arkansas State University M,W
Ecclesia College M,W
Harding University M,W
University of Arkansas M,W
University of Arkansas
Little Rock M,W
Pine Bluff M,W
University of Central Arkansas M,W

California
Azusa Pacific University M,W
Biola University M,W
California Polytechnic State University: San Luis Obispo M,W
California State Polytechnic University: Pomona M,W
California State University
Bakersfield M,W
Chico M,W
Dominguez Hills W
Fresno M,W
Fullerton M,W
Long Beach M,W
Los Angeles M,W
Northridge M,W
Sacramento M,W
Stanislaus M,W
Concordia University M,W
Fresno City College M,W
Fresno Pacific University M,W
Humboldt State University M,W
The Master's College M,W
Pepperdine University W
Point Loma Nazarene University M,W
San Diego State University W
Santa Clara University M,W
Santiago Canyon College M,W
Sonoma State University W
Stanford University M,W
University of California
Berkeley M,W
Davis M,W
Irvine M,W
Los Angeles M,W
Riverside M,W
Santa Barbara M,W
University of Southern California M,W
Vanguard University of Southern California M,W
Westmont College M,W
William Jessup University M,W
Yuba Community College District M,W

Colorado
Adams State College M,W
Colorado School of Mines M,W
Colorado State University M,W
Mesa State College W
University of Colorado
Boulder M,W
Colorado Springs M,W
University of Northern Colorado M,W
Western State College of Colorado M,W

Connecticut
Central Connecticut State University M,W
Quinnipiac University M,W
Sacred Heart University M,W
Southern Connecticut State University W
University of Connecticut M,W
University of New Haven M,W

Delaware
Delaware State University M,W
Goldey-Beacom College M,W
University of Delaware W

District of Columbia
American University M,W
Georgetown University M,W
Howard University M,W

Florida
Bethune-Cookman University M,W
Edward Waters College M
Embry-Riddle Aeronautical University M,W
Florida Agricultural and Mechanical University M,W
Florida Atlantic University W
Florida Memorial University M
Florida Southern College M,W
Florida State University M,W
Jacksonville University W
Nova Southeastern University M,W
University of Central Florida W
University of Florida M,W
University of Miami M,W
University of North Florida M,W
University of South Florida M,W
Warner University M,W
Webber International University M,W

Georgia
Albany State University M,W
Clark Atlanta University M,W
Columbus State University M,W
Fort Valley State University M,W
Georgia Institute of Technology M,W
Georgia Southern University W
Georgia State University M,W
Kennesaw State University M,W
Morehouse College M
Paine College M,W
Savannah State University M,W
Shorter College M,W
University of Georgia M,W

Hawaii
University of Hawaii
Manoa W

Idaho
Boise State University M,W
College of Idaho M,W
Idaho State University M,W
Lewis-Clark State College W
Northwest Nazarene University M,W
University of Idaho M,W

Illinois
Bradley University W
Chicago State University M,W
DePaul University M,W
Eastern Illinois University M,W
Illinois State University M,W
Lewis University M,W
Lincoln College M,W
Loyola University Chicago M,W
McKendree University M,W
Olivet Nazarene University M,W
Rend Lake College M,W
Robert Morris College: Chicago W
Southern Illinois University Carbondale M,W
Southern Illinois University Edwardsville M,W
Trinity Christian College M,W
University of Illinois
Chicago M,W
Urbana-Champaign M,W
University of St. Francis M,W
Western Illinois University M,W

Indiana
Ball State University M,W
Goshen College M,W
Grace College M,W
Huntington University M,W
Indiana Institute of Technology M,W
Indiana State University M,W
Indiana University
Bloomington M,W
Indiana University-Purdue University Fort Wayne W
Indiana Wesleyan University M,W
Marian College M,W
Purdue University M,W
Saint Joseph's College M,W
Taylor University M,W
University of Indianapolis M,W
University of Notre Dame M,W
University of St. Francis M,W
Valparaiso University M,W
Vincennes University M,W

Iowa
Ashford University M,W
Briar Cliff University M,W
Clarke College M,W
Dordt College M,W
Drake University M,W
Graceland University M,W
Iowa Lakes Community College M,W
Iowa State University M,W
Iowa Wesleyan College M,W
Morningside College M,W
Mount Mercy College M,W
North Iowa Area Community College M,W
Northwestern College M,W
St. Ambrose University M,W
University of Iowa M,W
University of Northern Iowa M,W
William Penn University M,W

Kansas
Allen County Community College M,W
Baker University M,W
Barton County Community College M,W
Benedictine College M,W
Bethany College M,W
Bethel College M,W

Cloud County Community College M,W
Coffeyville Community College M,W
Colby Community College M,W
Cowley County Community College M,W
Emporia State University M,W
Fort Hays State University M,W
Friends University M,W
Garden City Community College M,W
Highland Community College M,W
Hutchinson Community College M,W
Independence Community College M,W
Johnson County Community College M,W
Kansas City Kansas Community College M,W
Kansas State University M,W
Kansas Wesleyan University M,W
McPherson College M,W
MidAmerica Nazarene University M,W
Neosho County Community College M,W
Ottawa University M,W
Pittsburg State University M,W
Pratt Community College M,W
Southwestern College M,W
Sterling College M,W
Tabor College M,W
University of Kansas M,W
Wichita State University M,W

Kentucky
Bellarmine University M,W
Campbellsville University M,W
Eastern Kentucky University M,W
Kentucky State University M,W
Lindsey Wilson College M,W
Midway College W
Morehead State University M,W
Murray State University W
Pikeville College M,W
University of Kentucky M,W
University of Louisville M,W
University of the Cumberlands M,W
Western Kentucky University M,W

Louisiana
Grambling State University M,W
Louisiana State University and Agricultural and Mechanical College M,W
Louisiana Tech University M,W
McNeese State University M,W
Nicholls State University W
Northwestern State University M,W
Southeastern Louisiana University M,W
Southern University and Agricultural and Mechanical College M,W
University of Louisiana at Lafayette M,W
University of Louisiana at Monroe M,W

Maine
University of Maine M,W

Maryland
Bowie State University M,W
Columbia Union College M,W
Coppin State University M,W
Hagerstown Community College M,W
Morgan State University M,W
Mount St. Mary's University M,W
Towson University M,W
University of Maryland
- Baltimore County M,W
- College Park M,W
- Eastern Shore M,W

Massachusetts
American International College M,W
Boston College M,W
Boston University M,W
Northeastern University M,W
Stonehill College M,W
University of Massachusetts
- Amherst M,W
- Lowell M,W

Michigan
Aquinas College M,W
Central Michigan University M,W
Cornerstone University M,W
Davenport University M,W
Eastern Michigan University M,W
Ferris State University M,W
Grand Rapids Community College M,W
Grand Valley State University M,W
Hillsdale College M,W
Lake Superior State University M,W
Macomb Community College M,W
Michigan State University M,W
Michigan Technological University M,W
Northern Michigan University W
Northwood University: Michigan M,W
Saginaw Valley State University M,W
Siena Heights University M,W
University of Detroit Mercy M,W
University of Michigan M,W
Western Michigan University M,W

Minnesota
Bemidji State University M,W
Concordia University: St. Paul M,W
Minnesota State University
- Mankato M,W
- Moorhead M,W

Saint Cloud State University M,W
University of Minnesota
- Duluth M,W
- Twin Cities M,W

Winona State University W

Mississippi
Alcorn State University M,W
Hinds Community College M
Holmes Community College M
Jackson State University M,W
Mississippi State University M,W
Mississippi Valley State University M,W
Southwest Mississippi Community College M,W
University of Mississippi M,W
University of Southern Mississippi M,W

Missouri
Central Methodist University M,W
Culver-Stockton College M,W
Evangel University M,W
Hannibal-LaGrange College M,W
Lincoln University M,W
Missouri Baptist University W
Missouri Southern State University M,W
Missouri State University M,W
Missouri Valley College M,W
Northwest Missouri State University M,W
Park University M,W
Saint Louis University M,W
Southeast Missouri State University M,W
Southwest Baptist University M,W
Truman State University M,W
University of Central Missouri M,W
University of Missouri
- Columbia M,W
- Kansas City M,W
- Missouri University of Science and Technology M,W

William Jewell College M,W

Montana
Montana State University
- Billings M,W
- Bozeman M,W

University of Montana M,W

Nebraska
Chadron State College M,W
Concordia University M,W
Doane College M,W
University of Nebraska
- Kearney M,W
- Lincoln M,W

Wayne State College M,W

Nevada
University of Nevada
- Las Vegas W
- Reno W

New Hampshire
University of New Hampshire M,W

New Jersey
Essex County College M,W
Fairleigh Dickinson University
- Metropolitan Campus M,W

Felician College M,W
Georgian Court University W
Monmouth University M,W
Rider University M,W
Rutgers, The State University of New Jersey
- New Brunswick/Piscataway Campus M,W

Saint Peter's College M,W
Seton Hall University M,W

New Mexico
Eastern New Mexico University M,W
New Mexico Highlands University W
New Mexico Military Institute M
New Mexico State University W
University of New Mexico M,W
University of the Southwest M,W

New York
Adelphi University M,W
City University of New York
- Queens College M,W

Dominican College of Blauvelt W
Fordham University M,W
Houghton College M,W
Iona College M,W
Long Island University
- Brooklyn Campus M,W

Manhattan College M,W
Marist College M,W
Mercy College M,W
Pace University M,W
Roberts Wesleyan College M,W
St. Francis College M,W
St. John's University W
St. Thomas Aquinas College M,W
State University of New York
- Albany M,W
- Binghamton M,W
- Buffalo M,W
- Stony Brook M,W

Syracuse University M,W
Wagner College M,W

North Carolina
Appalachian State University M,W
Brevard College M,W
Campbell University M,W
Davidson College M,W
East Carolina University M,W
Elon University W
Fayetteville State University W
Gardner-Webb University M,W
High Point University M,W
Johnson C. Smith University M,W
Lees-McRae College M,W
Lenoir-Rhyne University M,W
Livingstone College M,W
Mars Hill College M,W
Montreat College M,W
North Carolina Agricultural and Technical State University M,W
North Carolina Central University M,W
North Carolina State University M,W
Queens University of Charlotte M,W
St. Augustine's College M,W
Shaw University M,W
University of North Carolina
- Asheville M,W
- Chapel Hill M,W
- Charlotte M,W
- Pembroke M,W
- Wilmington M,W

Wake Forest University M,W
Western Carolina University M,W
Winston-Salem State University M,W

North Dakota
Dickinson State University M,W
Jamestown College M,W
Minot State University M,W
North Dakota State University M,W
University of Mary M,W
University of North Dakota M,W

Ohio
Ashland University M,W
Bowling Green State University M,W
Cedarville University M,W
Central State University M,W
Kent State University M,W
Malone University M,W
Miami University
- Oxford Campus M,W

Notre Dame College M,W
Ohio University W
University of Akron M,W
University of Dayton W
University of Findlay M,W
University of Rio Grande M,W
University of Toledo W
Ursuline College W
Walsh University M,W
Wright State University W
Xavier University M,W
Youngstown State University M,W

Oklahoma
Bacone College M,W
Langston University M,W
Oklahoma Baptist University M,W
Oklahoma Christian University M,W
Oklahoma State University M,W
Oklahoma Wesleyan University M,W
Oral Roberts University M,W
Southern Nazarene University M,W
University of Central Oklahoma M,W
University of Oklahoma M,W
University of Tulsa M,W

Oregon
Clackamas Community College M,W
Concordia University M,W
Eastern Oregon University M,W
Lane Community College M,W
Mt. Hood Community College M,W
Northwest Christian University M,W
Oregon Institute of Technology M,W
Portland State University M,W
Southern Oregon University M,W
Southwestern Oregon Community College M,W
Treasure Valley Community College M,W
University of Oregon M,W
University of Portland M,W
Warner Pacific College M,W

Pennsylvania
Bloomsburg University of Pennsylvania M,W
California University of Pennsylvania M,W
Cheyney University of Pennsylvania M,W
Clarion University of Pennsylvania M,W
Duquesne University M,W
East Stroudsburg University of Pennsylvania M,W
Edinboro University of Pennsylvania M,W
Holy Family University M,W
Indiana University of Pennsylvania M,W
Kutztown University of Pennsylvania M,W
La Salle University M,W
Lock Haven University of Pennsylvania M,W
Millersville University of Pennsylvania M,W
Penn State

University Park M,W
Robert Morris University M,W
St. Francis University M,W
Saint Joseph's University M,W
Seton Hill University M,W
Shippensburg University of Pennsylvania M,W
Slippery Rock University of Pennsylvania M,W
Temple University M,W
University of Pittsburgh M,W
Villanova University M,W
West Chester University of Pennsylvania M,W

Puerto Rico
Bayamon Central University M,W
Inter American University of Puerto Rico
Aguadilla Campus M,W
Bayamon Campus M,W
Fajardo Campus M,W
Guayama Campus M,W
Metropolitan Campus M,W
Ponce Campus M,W
San German Campus M,W
Turabo University M,W
Universidad del Este M,W
Universidad Metropolitana M,W
University of Puerto Rico
Bayamon University College M,W
Carolina Regional College M,W
Cayey University College M,W
Humacao M,W
Mayaguez M,W
Ponce M,W
Utuado M,W
University of the Sacred Heart M,W

Rhode Island
Bryant University M,W
Providence College M,W
University of Rhode Island M,W

South Carolina
Anderson University M,W
Charleston Southern University M,W
The Citadel M,W
Claflin University M,W
Clemson University M,W
Coastal Carolina University M,W
Furman University M,W
Limestone College M,W
Morris College M,W
South Carolina State University M,W
University of South Carolina M,W
University of South Carolina
Upstate M,W
Winthrop University M,W
Wofford College M,W

South Dakota
Augustana College M,W
Black Hills State University M,W
Dakota State University M,W
Dakota Wesleyan University M,W
Mount Marty College M,W
Northern State University M,W
South Dakota School of Mines and Technology M,W
South Dakota State University M,W
University of Sioux Falls M,W
University of South Dakota M,W

Tennessee
Austin Peay State University W
Belmont University M,W
Bethel College M,W
East Tennessee State University M,W
King College M,W
Lipscomb University M,W
Middle Tennessee State University M,W
Milligan College M,W
Tennessee Technological University W
University of Memphis M,W
University of Tennessee
Chattanooga M,W
Knoxville M,W
Vanderbilt University W

Texas
Abilene Christian University M,W
Angelo State University M,W
Baylor University M,W
Dallas Baptist University W
Houston Baptist University M,W
Lamar University M,W
Northwood University: Texas M,W
Prairie View A&M University M,W
Rice University M,W
Sam Houston State University M,W
South Plains College M,W
Stephen F. Austin State University M,W
Tarleton State University M,W
Texas A&M University M,W
Texas A&M University
Commerce M,W
Corpus Christi M,W
Texas Christian University M,W
Texas Southern University M,W
Texas State University: San Marcos M,W
Texas Tech University M,W
University of Houston M,W
University of North Texas M,W
University of Texas
Austin M,W
Pan American M,W
San Antonio M,W
University of the Incarnate Word M,W
Wayland Baptist University M,W
Wiley College M,W

Utah
Brigham Young University M,W
Southern Utah University M,W
University of Utah W
Utah State University M,W
Utah Valley University M,W
Weber State University M,W

Vermont
University of Vermont M,W

Virginia
College of William and Mary M,W
George Mason University M,W
Hampton University M,W
James Madison University W
Liberty University M,W
Norfolk State University M,W
Radford University M,W
St. Paul's College M,W
University of Richmond W
University of Virginia M,W
Virginia Commonwealth University M,W
Virginia Military Institute M,W
Virginia Polytechnic Institute and State University M,W
Virginia State University M,W
Virginia Union University M,W

Washington
Central Washington University M,W
Clark College M,W
Eastern Washington University M,W
Evergreen State College M,W
Highline Community College M,W
Northwest University M,W
Saint Martin's University M,W
Seattle Pacific University M,W
Seattle University M,W
Spokane Community College M,W
University of Washington M,W
Washington State University M,W
Western Washington University M,W

West Virginia
Alderson-Broaddus College M,W
Glenville State College M,W
Marshall University M,W
University of Charleston W
West Liberty State College M,W
West Virginia State University M,W
West Virginia University W
West Virginia Wesleyan College M,W
Wheeling Jesuit University M,W

Wisconsin
Marquette University M,W
Milwaukee Area Technical College M,W
University of Wisconsin
Milwaukee M,W
Parkside M,W

Wyoming
University of Wyoming M,W

Volleyball

Alabama
Alabama Agricultural and Mechanical University W
Alabama State University W
Auburn University W
Bevill State Community College W
Central Alabama Community College W
Faulkner State Community College M,W
Faulkner University W
Gadsden State Community College W
Jacksonville State University W
Jefferson Davis Community College W
Judson College W
Lawson State Community College W
Miles College M,W
Northwest-Shoals Community College W
Samford University W
Southern Union State Community College W
Spring Hill College W
Troy University W
Tuskegee University W
University of Alabama W
University of Alabama
Birmingham W
Huntsville W
University of Mobile W
University of Montevallo W
University of North Alabama W
University of South Alabama W
University of West Alabama W
Wallace State Community College at Hanceville W

Alaska
University of Alaska
Anchorage W
Fairbanks W

Arizona
Arizona State University W
Arizona Western College W
Chandler-Gilbert Community College
Pecos W
Eastern Arizona College W
Embry-Riddle Aeronautical University: Prescott Campus W
Glendale Community College W
Grand Canyon University W
Northern Arizona University W
Pima Community College W
Scottsdale Community College W
University of Arizona W
Yavapai College W

Arkansas
Arkansas State University W
Arkansas Tech University W
Harding University W
Henderson State University W
John Brown University W
Lyon College W
Ouachita Baptist University W
Southern Arkansas University W
University of Arkansas W
University of Arkansas
Fort Smith W
Little Rock W
Pine Bluff W
University of Central Arkansas W
Williams Baptist College W

California
Azusa Pacific University W
Bethany University W
Biola University W
California Baptist University M,W
California Polytechnic State University: San Luis Obispo W
California State Polytechnic University: Pomona W
California State University
Bakersfield W
Chico W
Dominguez Hills W
Fresno W
Fullerton W
Long Beach M,W
Los Angeles W
Monterey Bay W
Northridge M,W
Sacramento W
San Bernardino W
Stanislaus W
Concordia University W
Dominican University of California W
Fresno City College W
Fresno Pacific University W
Grossmont College M,W
Holy Names University M,W
Hope International University M,W
Humboldt State University W
Loyola Marymount University W
The Master's College W
Notre Dame de Namur University W
Pepperdine University M,W
Point Loma Nazarene University W
St. Mary's College of California W
San Diego Christian College W
San Diego State University W
San Jose State University W
Santa Clara University W
Sonoma State University W
Stanford University M,W
University of California
Berkeley W
Davis W
Irvine M,W
Los Angeles W
Riverside W
Santa Barbara M,W
University of San Diego W
University of San Francisco W
University of Southern California M,W
University of the Pacific M,W
Vanguard University of Southern California W
Westmont College W
William Jessup University W
Yuba Community College District W

Colorado
Adams State College W
Colorado Christian University W
Colorado Northwestern Community College W
Colorado School of Mines W
Colorado State University W
Colorado State University
Pueblo W
Fort Lewis College W
Lamar Community College W
Mesa State College W
Metropolitan State College of Denver W
Northeastern Junior College W
Otero Junior College W
Regis University W

Trinidad State Junior College W
University of Colorado
Boulder W
Colorado Springs W
University of Denver W
University of Northern Colorado W
Western State College of Colorado W

Connecticut
Central Connecticut State University W
Fairfield University W
Post University W
Quinnipiac University W
Sacred Heart University M,W
Southern Connecticut State University W
University of Bridgeport W
University of Connecticut W
University of Hartford W
University of New Haven W

Delaware
Delaware State University W
Goldey-Beacom College W
University of Delaware W
Wilmington University W

District of Columbia
American University W
George Washington University W
Georgetown University W
Howard University W

Florida
Barry University M,W
Bethune-Cookman University W
Brevard Community College W
Eckerd College M,W
Embry-Riddle Aeronautical University W
Flagler College W
Florida Agricultural and Mechanical University W
Florida Atlantic University W
Florida College W
Florida Community College at Jacksonville W
Florida Gulf Coast University W
Florida Institute of Technology W
Florida Memorial University W
Florida Southern College W
Florida State University W
Hillsborough Community College W
Indian River State College W
Jacksonville University W
Lake-Sumter Community College W
Lynn University W
Manatee Community College W
Miami Dade College W
Northwood University
Florida W
Nova Southeastern University W
Palm Beach Community College W
Pasco-Hernando Community College W
Pensacola Junior College W
Polk Community College W
Rollins College W
St. Leo University W
St. Petersburg College W
Saint Thomas University W
South Florida Community College W
Stetson University W
University of Central Florida W
University of Florida W
University of Miami W
University of North Florida W
University of South Florida W
University of Tampa W
University of West Florida W
Warner University M,W
Webber International University W

Georgia
Abraham Baldwin Agricultural College W
Albany State University W
Armstrong Atlantic State University W
Augusta State University W
Brenau University W
Brewton-Parker College W
Clark Atlanta University W
Covenant College W
Fort Valley State University W
Georgia Institute of Technology W
Georgia Southern University W
Georgia State University M,W
Mercer University W
Paine College W
Savannah State University W
University of Georgia W
University of West Georgia W
Valdosta State University W

Hawaii
Brigham Young University-Hawaii W
Chaminade University of Honolulu W
Hawaii Pacific University W
University of Hawaii
Hilo W
Manoa M,W

Idaho
Boise State University W
College of Idaho W
College of Southern Idaho W
Idaho State University W
Lewis-Clark State College W
North Idaho College W
Northwest Nazarene University W
University of Idaho W

Illinois
Black Hawk College W
Bradley University W
Carl Sandburg College W
Chicago State University W
College of Lake County W
Danville Area Community College W
DePaul University W
Eastern Illinois University W
Elgin Community College W
Highland Community College W
Illinois Central College W
Illinois Institute of Technology W
Illinois State University W
John A. Logan College W
Judson University W
Kankakee Community College W
Kaskaskia College W
Kishwaukee College W
Lake Land College W
Lewis and Clark Community College W
Lewis University M,W
Lincoln College W
Loyola University Chicago M,W
McHenry County College W
McKendree University W
Moraine Valley Community College W
Morton College W
Northwestern University W
Olivet Nazarene University W
Parkland College W
Quincy University M,W
Rend Lake College W
Robert Morris College: Chicago W
St. Xavier University W
Sauk Valley Community College W
Shawnee Community College W
South Suburban College of Cook County W
Southern Illinois University Carbondale W
Southern Illinois University Edwardsville W
Springfield College in Illinois W
Trinity Christian College W
Trinity International University W
University of Illinois
Chicago W
Springfield W
Urbana-Champaign W
University of St. Francis W
Waubonsee Community College W
Western Illinois University W

Indiana
Ancilla College W
Ball State University M,W
Bethel College W
Butler University W
Calumet College of St. Joseph M,W
Goshen College W
Grace College W
Huntington University W
Indiana Institute of Technology W
Indiana State University W
Indiana University
Bloomington W
Southeast W
Indiana University-Purdue University Fort Wayne M,W
Indiana University-Purdue University Indianapolis W
Indiana Wesleyan University W
Marian College W
Oakland City University W
Purdue University W
Saint Joseph's College W
Taylor University W
University of Evansville W
University of Indianapolis W
University of Notre Dame W
University of St. Francis W
University of Southern Indiana W
Valparaiso University W
Vincennes University W

Iowa
Ashford University W
Briar Cliff University W
Clarke College M,W
Clinton Community College W
Des Moines Area Community College W
Dordt College W
Drake University W
Ellsworth Community College W
Graceland University M,W
Grand View University W
Indian Hills Community College W
Iowa Central Community College W
Iowa Lakes Community College W
Iowa State University W
Iowa Wesleyan College W
Iowa Western Community College W
Kirkwood Community College W
Morningside College W
Mount Mercy College W
North Iowa Area Community College W
Northwestern College W
St. Ambrose University M,W
Southeastern Community College
North Campus W
Southwestern Community College W
University of Iowa W
University of Northern Iowa W
Waldorf College W
William Penn University W

Kansas
Allen County Community College W
Baker University W
Barton County Community College W
Benedictine College W
Bethany College W
Bethel College W
Central Christian College of Kansas W
Cloud County Community College W
Coffeyville Community College W
Colby Community College W
Cowley County Community College W
Dodge City Community College W
Emporia State University W
Fort Hays State University W
Fort Scott Community College W
Friends University W
Garden City Community College W
Hesston College W
Highland Community College W
Hutchinson Community College W
Independence Community College W
Johnson County Community College W
Kansas City Kansas Community College W
Kansas State University W
Kansas Wesleyan University W
Labette Community College W
McPherson College W
MidAmerica Nazarene University W
Neosho County Community College W
Newman University W
Ottawa University W
Pittsburg State University W
Pratt Community College W
Seward County Community College W
Southwestern College W
Sterling College W
Tabor College W
University of Kansas W
University of St. Mary W
Washburn University W
Wichita State University W

Kentucky
Asbury College W
Bellarmine University W
Brescia University W
Campbellsville University W
Eastern Kentucky University W
Georgetown College W
Kentucky State University W
Kentucky Wesleyan College W
Lindsey Wilson College W
Midway College W
Morehead State University W
Murray State University W
Northern Kentucky University W
Pikeville College W
St. Catharine College W
Union College W
University of Kentucky W
University of Louisville W
University of the Cumberlands W
Western Kentucky University W

Louisiana
Centenary College of Louisiana W
Dillard University W
Louisiana State University and Agricultural and Mechanical College W
Louisiana Tech University W
McNeese State University W
Nicholls State University W
Northwestern State University W
Southeastern Louisiana University W
Southern University and Agricultural and Mechanical College W
University of Louisiana at Lafayette W
University of Louisiana at Monroe W
University of New Orleans W
Xavier University of Louisiana W

Maine
University of Maine W

Maryland
Bowie State University W
College of Southern Maryland W
Community College of Baltimore County W
Coppin State University W
Garrett College W
Hagerstown Community College W
Harford Community College W
Loyola College in Maryland W
Morgan State University W
Prince George's Community College W
Towson University W
University of Maryland
Baltimore County W

College Park W
Eastern Shore W

Massachusetts
American International College W
Boston College W
Merrimack College W
Northeastern University W
Stonehill College W
University of Massachusetts
Lowell W

Michigan
Alpena Community College W
Aquinas College W
Central Michigan University W
Concordia University W
Cornerstone University W
Davenport University M,W
Eastern Michigan University W
Ferris State University W
Grand Rapids Community College W
Grand Valley State University W
Hillsdale College W
Kalamazoo Valley Community College W
Kellogg Community College W
Lake Michigan College W
Lake Superior State University W
Lansing Community College W
Macomb Community College W
Madonna University W
Michigan State University W
Michigan Technological University W
Mott Community College W
Muskegon Community College W
Northern Michigan University W
Northwood University: Michigan W
Oakland Community College W
Oakland University W
Rochester College W
Saginaw Valley State University W
Siena Heights University M,W
Spring Arbor University W
University of Michigan W
University of Michigan
Dearborn W
Wayne State University M,W
Western Michigan University W

Minnesota
Bemidji State University W
Concordia University: St. Paul W
Minnesota State University
Mankato W
Moorhead W
Saint Cloud State University W
Southwest Minnesota State University W
University of Minnesota
Crookston W
Duluth W
Twin Cities W
Winona State University W

Mississippi
Alcorn State University W
Belhaven College W
Jackson State University W
Mississippi State University W
Mississippi Valley State University W
University of Mississippi W
University of Southern Mississippi W

Missouri
Avila University W
Central Methodist University W
College of the Ozarks W
Columbia College W
Cottey College W
Culver-Stockton College W
Drury University W
East Central College W
Evangel University W
Hannibal-LaGrange College W
Harris-Stowe State University W
Jefferson College W
Metropolitan Community College: Longview W
Mineral Area College W
Missouri Baptist University M,W
Missouri Southern State University W
Missouri State University W
Missouri State University: West Plains W
Missouri Valley College M,W
Missouri Western State University W
Northwest Missouri State University W
Park University M,W
Research College of Nursing W
Rockhurst University W
Saint Louis University W
Southeast Missouri State University W
Southwest Baptist University W
State Fair Community College W
Stephens College W
Truman State University W
University of Central Missouri W
University of Missouri
Columbia W
Kansas City W
St. Louis W
William Jewell College W
William Woods University M,W

Montana
Carroll College W
Miles Community College W
Montana State University
Billings W
Bozeman W
Northern W
Montana Tech of the University of Montana W
Rocky Mountain College W
University of Great Falls W
University of Montana W
University of Montana: Western W

Nebraska
Bellevue University W
Central Community College W
Chadron State College W
College of Saint Mary W
Concordia University W
Creighton University W
Doane College W
Mid-Plains Community College Area W
Nebraska College of Technical Agriculture M,W
Peru State College W
University of Nebraska
Kearney W
Lincoln W
Omaha W
Wayne State College W
Western Nebraska Community College W
York College W

Nevada
University of Nevada
Las Vegas W
Reno W

New Hampshire
Franklin Pierce University W
Hesser College M,W
University of New Hampshire W

New Jersey
Bloomfield College W
Fairleigh Dickinson University
Metropolitan Campus W
Georgian Court University W
New Jersey Institute of Technology M,W
Rider University W
Rutgers, The State University of New Jersey
New Brunswick/Piscataway Campus W
Newark Regional Campus M
Saint Peter's College W
Seton Hall University W

New Mexico
Eastern New Mexico University W
New Mexico Highlands University W
New Mexico State University W
University of New Mexico W
University of the Southwest W
Western New Mexico University W

New York
Adelphi University W
Canisius College W
City University of New York
Queens College W
Colgate University W
College of Saint Rose W
Concordia College M,W
Daemen College W
Dominican College of Blauvelt W
Dowling College W
Fordham University W
Genesee Community College W
Hofstra University W
Houghton College W
Iona College W
Le Moyne College W
Long Island University
Brooklyn Campus W
C. W. Post Campus W
Manhattan College W
Marist College W
Mercy College W
Molloy College W
New York Institute of Technology W
Niagara University W
Nyack College W
Pace University W
Roberts Wesleyan College W
Saint Bonaventure University W
St. Francis College W
St. John's University W
Siena College W
State University of New York
Albany W
Binghamton W
Buffalo W
Stony Brook W
Syracuse University W
Wagner College W

North Carolina
Appalachian State University W
Barton College W
Brevard College W
Campbell University W
Catawba College W
Davidson College W
Duke University W
East Carolina University M,W
Elizabeth City State University W
Elon University W
Fayetteville State University W
Gardner-Webb University W
High Point University W
Johnson C. Smith University W
Lees-McRae College M,W
Lenoir Community College W
Lenoir-Rhyne University W
Livingstone College W
Louisburg College W
Mars Hill College W
Montreat College W
Mount Olive College W
North Carolina Agricultural and Technical State University W
North Carolina Central University W
North Carolina State University W
Pfeiffer University W
Pitt Community College W
Queens University of Charlotte W
St. Andrews Presbyterian College W
St. Augustine's College W
Shaw University W
Southeastern Community College W
University of North Carolina
Asheville W
Chapel Hill W
Charlotte W
Greensboro W
Pembroke W
Wilmington W
Wake Forest University W
Western Carolina University W
Wingate University W
Winston-Salem State University W

North Dakota
Bismarck State College W
Dickinson State University W
Jamestown College W
Mayville State University W
Minot State University W
Minot State University: Bottineau Campus W
North Dakota State College of Science W
North Dakota State University W
University of Mary W
University of North Dakota W
Valley City State University W
Williston State College W

Ohio
Ashland University W
Bowling Green State University W
Cedarville University W
Central State University W
Clark State Community College W
Cleveland State University W
Edison State Community College W
Kent State University W
Lakeland Community College W
Malone University W
Miami University
Oxford Campus W
Mount Vernon Nazarene University W
Notre Dame College W
Ohio Dominican University W
Ohio University W
Shawnee State University W
Sinclair Community College W
Southern State Community College W
University of Akron W
University of Dayton W
University of Findlay W
University of Rio Grande W
University of Toledo W
Urbana University W
Ursuline College W
Walsh University W
Wright State University W
Xavier University W
Youngstown State University W

Oklahoma
Bacone College W
Cameron University W
East Central University W
Langston University W
Northeastern Oklahoma Agricultural and Mechanical College W
Oklahoma Panhandle State University W
Oklahoma Wesleyan University W
Oral Roberts University W
Redlands Community College W
St. Gregory's University W
Seminole State College M,W
Southeastern Oklahoma State University W
Southern Nazarene University W
University of Central Oklahoma W
University of Oklahoma W
University of Tulsa W

Oregon
Blue Mountain Community College W
Chemeketa Community College W
Clackamas Community College W
Concordia University W

Corban College W
Eastern Oregon University W
Lane Community College W
Linn-Benton Community College W
Mt. Hood Community College W
Northwest Christian University W
Oregon Institute of Technology W
Oregon State University W
Portland State University W
Southern Oregon University W
Southwestern Oregon Community College W
Treasure Valley Community College W
University of Oregon W
University of Portland W
Warner Pacific College W

Pennsylvania
California University of Pennsylvania W
Carlow University W
Chestnut Hill College W
Cheyney University of Pennsylvania W
Community College of Beaver County W
Duquesne University W
Edinboro University of Pennsylvania W
Gannon University W
Harcum College W
Holy Family University W
Indiana University of Pennsylvania W
Kutztown University of Pennsylvania W
La Salle University W
Lackawanna College W
Lehigh University W
Lock Haven University of Pennsylvania W
Mercyhurst College W
Millersville University of Pennsylvania W
Penn State
University Park M,W
Philadelphia University W
Point Park University W
Robert Morris University W
St. Francis University M,W
Seton Hill University W
Shippensburg University of Pennsylvania W
Slippery Rock University of Pennsylvania W
Temple University W
University of Pittsburgh W
University of Pittsburgh
Titusville W
University of the Sciences in Philadelphia W
Villanova University W
West Chester University of Pennsylvania W
Westminster College W

Puerto Rico
Bayamon Central University M,W
Inter American University of Puerto Rico
Aguadilla Campus M,W
Bayamon Campus M,W
Metropolitan Campus M,W
Ponce Campus M,W
San German Campus M,W
Turabo University M,W
Universidad del Este M,W
Universidad Metropolitana M,W
University of Puerto Rico
Bayamon University College M,W
Carolina Regional College M,W
Cayey University College M,W
Humacao M,W
Mayaguez M,W
Ponce M,W
Utuado M,W
University of the Sacred Heart M,W

Rhode Island
Bryant University W
Community College of Rhode Island W
University of Rhode Island W

South Carolina
Anderson University W
Charleston Southern University W
The Citadel W
Claflin University W
Clemson University W
Coastal Carolina University W
College of Charleston W
Columbia College W
Converse College W
Erskine College M,W
Francis Marion University W
Furman University W
Lander University W
Limestone College M,W
Morris College W
Newberry College W
North Greenville University W
Presbyterian College W
South Carolina State University W
Southern Wesleyan University W
Spartanburg Methodist College W
University of South Carolina W
University of South Carolina
Aiken W
Upstate W
Winthrop University W
Wofford College W

South Dakota
Augustana College W
Black Hills State University W
Dakota State University W
Dakota Wesleyan University W
Mount Marty College W
South Dakota School of Mines and Technology W
South Dakota State University W
University of Sioux Falls W

Tennessee
Austin Peay State University W
Belmont University W
Bethel College W
Carson-Newman College W
Christian Brothers University W
Crichton College W
Cumberland University W
East Tennessee State University W
Freed-Hardeman University W
King College W
Lane College W
Lee University W
LeMoyne-Owen College W
Lincoln Memorial University W
Lipscomb University W
Martin Methodist College W
Middle Tennessee State University W
Milligan College W
Tennessee Technological University W
Tennessee Temple University W
Tennessee Wesleyan College W
Trevecca Nazarene University W
Tusculum College W
Union University W
University of Memphis W
University of Tennessee
Chattanooga W
Knoxville W
Martin W

Texas
Abilene Christian University W
Angelo State University W
Baylor University W
Blinn College W
Clarendon College W
Dallas Baptist University W
Frank Phillips College W
Galveston College W
Hill College W
Houston Baptist University W
Jarvis Christian College W
Lamar University W
Laredo Community College W
Lee College W
Lubbock Christian University W
Midwestern State University W
North Central Texas College W
Panola College W
Paris Junior College W
Prairie View A&M University W
Ranger College W
Rice University W
St. Edward's University W
St. Mary's University W
Sam Houston State University W
Southern Methodist University W
Southwestern Assemblies of God University W
Stephen F. Austin State University W
Tarleton State University W
Temple College W
Texas A&M University W
Texas A&M University
Commerce W
Corpus Christi W
Kingsville W
Texas Christian University W
Texas Southern University W
Texas State University: San Marcos W
Texas Tech University W
Texas Woman's University W
Tyler Junior College W
University of Houston W
University of North Texas W
University of Texas
Arlington W
Austin W
Brownsville - Texas Southmost College W
Pan American W
of the Permian Basin W
San Antonio W
University of the Incarnate Word W
Wayland Baptist University W
West Texas A&M University W
Western Texas College W
Wharton County Junior College W
Wiley College W

Utah
Brigham Young University M,W
College of Eastern Utah W
Dixie State College of Utah W
Salt Lake Community College W
Snow College W
University of Utah W
Utah State University W
Utah Valley University W
Weber State University W
Westminster College W

Virginia
Bluefield College W
College of William and Mary W
George Mason University M,W
Hampton University W
James Madison University W
Liberty University W
Norfolk State University W
Radford University W
St. Paul's College W
University of Virginia W
University of Virginia's College at Wise W
Virginia Commonwealth University W
Virginia Intermont College W
Virginia Polytechnic Institute and State University W
Virginia State University W
Virginia Union University W

Washington
Big Bend Community College W
Central Washington University W
Centralia College W
Clark College W
Columbia Basin College W
Eastern Washington University W
Edmonds Community College W
Everett Community College W
Evergreen State College W
Gonzaga University W
Grays Harbor College W
Green River Community College W
Highline Community College W
Lower Columbia College W
Northwest University W
Olympic College W
Pierce College W
Saint Martin's University W
Seattle Pacific University W
Seattle University W
Shoreline Community College W
Skagit Valley College W
Spokane Community College W
Tacoma Community College W
University of Washington W
Walla Walla Community College W
Washington State University W
Western Washington University W
Whatcom Community College W
Yakima Valley Community College W

West Virginia
Alderson-Broaddus College W
Bluefield State College W
Concord University W
Davis and Elkins College W
Glenville State College W
Marshall University W
Mountain State University W
Ohio Valley University W
Salem International University W
Shepherd University W
University of Charleston W
West Liberty State College W
West Virginia University W
West Virginia University Institute of Technology W
West Virginia Wesleyan College W
Wheeling Jesuit University W

Wisconsin
Cardinal Stritch University M,W
Marquette University W
Milwaukee Area Technical College W
University of Wisconsin
Green Bay W
Milwaukee M,W
Parkside W
Viterbo University W

Wyoming
Casper College W
Central Wyoming College W
Eastern Wyoming College W
Laramie County Community College W
Northwest College W
Sheridan College W
University of Wyoming W
Western Wyoming Community College W

Water polo

Arizona
Arizona State University W

California
California Baptist University M,W
California State University
Bakersfield W
Long Beach M,W
Monterey Bay W
Concordia University M
Fresno Pacific University M,W
Grossmont College M,W
Loyola Marymount University M,W
Pepperdine University M
San Diego State University W
San Jose State University W

Santa Clara University M,W
Sonoma State University W
Stanford University M,W
University of California
  Berkeley M,W
  Davis M,W
  Irvine M,W
University of Southern California M,W
University of the Pacific M,W

District of Columbia
George Washington University M

Florida
Florida Atlantic University W

Hawaii
University of Hawaii
  Manoa W

Indiana
Indiana University
  Bloomington W

Michigan
University of Michigan W

New York
City University of New York
  Queens College M
Fordham University M
Hartwick College W
Iona College W
Marist College W
St. Francis College M,W
Siena College W
Wagner College W

Pennsylvania
Gannon University M,W
Mercyhurst College M,W

Puerto Rico
University of Puerto Rico
  Mayaguez M

Weight lifting

Puerto Rico
Inter American University of Puerto Rico
  Aguadilla Campus M,W
  Ponce Campus M,W
  San German Campus M,W
Turabo University M,W
Universidad del Este M,W
Universidad Metropolitana M
University of Puerto Rico
  Carolina Regional College M,W
  Cayey University College M,W
  Humacao M,W
  Utuado M,W

Washington
Olympic College M,W

Wrestling

Arizona
Arizona State University M
Embry Riddle Aeronautical University: Prescott Campus M
Grand Canyon University M

California
California Baptist University M
California Polytechnic State University: San Luis Obispo M
California State University
  Bakersfield M
  Fresno M
  Fullerton M
Fresno City College M
Stanford University M
University of California
  Davis M
  Los Angeles M,W

Colorado
Adams State College M
Colorado School of Mines M
Mesa State College M
University of Northern Colorado M
Western State College of Colorado M

Connecticut
Sacred Heart University M

Delaware
Delaware State University M

District of Columbia
American University M
Howard University M

Idaho
Boise State University M
North Idaho College M

Illinois
City Colleges of Chicago
  Wright College M,W
Lincoln College M
McKendree University M
Northwestern University M
Rend Lake College M
Southern Illinois University Edwardsville M
University of Illinois
  Urbana-Champaign M

Indiana
Indiana University
  Bloomington M
Purdue University M
University of Indianapolis M

Iowa
Briar Cliff University M
Ellsworth Community College M
Grand View University M
Iowa Central Community College M
Iowa State University M
North Iowa Area Community College M
Northwestern College M
University of Iowa M
University of Northern Iowa M
Waldorf College M
William Penn University M

Kansas
Colby Community College M
Fort Hays State University M
Labette Community College M
Neosho County Community College M
Newman University M
Pratt Community College M

Kentucky
Campbellsville University M
University of the Cumberlands M,W

Maryland
University of Maryland
  College Park M

Massachusetts
American International College M
Boston University M

Michigan
Central Michigan University M
Eastern Michigan University M
Grand Rapids Community College M
Michigan State University M
Muskegon Community College M
University of Michigan M

Minnesota
Minnesota State University
  Mankato M
  Moorhead M
Saint Cloud State University M
Southwest Minnesota State University M
University of Minnesota
  Twin Cities M

Missouri
Hannibal-LaGrange College M
Missouri Baptist University M
Missouri Valley College M,W
St. Louis Community College
  Meramec M
Truman State University M
University of Central Missouri M
University of Missouri
  Columbia M

Montana
Montana State University
  Northern M
University of Great Falls M

Nebraska
Chadron State College M
Concordia University M
University of Nebraska
  Kearney M
  Lincoln M
  Omaha M
York College M

New Jersey
Rider University M
Rutgers, The State University of New Jersey
  New Brunswick/Piscataway Campus M

New York
Hofstra University M
Niagara County Community College M
State University of New York
  Binghamton M
  Buffalo M
Wagner College M

North Carolina
Appalachian State University M
Campbell University M
Davidson College M
Duke University M
Gardner-Webb University M
North Carolina Agricultural and Technical State University M
North Carolina State University M
University of North Carolina
  Chapel Hill M
  Greensboro M
  Pembroke M

North Dakota
Dickinson State University M
Jamestown College M,W
North Dakota State University M
University of Mary M

Ohio
Ashland University M
Cleveland State University M
Kent State University M
Notre Dame College M
Ohio University M
University of Findlay M

Oklahoma
Bacone College M
Oklahoma State University M
University of Central Oklahoma M
University of Oklahoma M

Oregon
Clackamas Community College M
Oregon State University M
Portland State University M
Southern Oregon University M
Southwestern Oregon Community College M

Pennsylvania
Bloomsburg University of Pennsylvania M
Clarion University of Pennsylvania M
Drexel University M
Duquesne University M
East Stroudsburg University of Pennsylvania M
Edinboro University of Pennsylvania M
Gannon University M
Kutztown University of Pennsylvania M
Lehigh University M
Lock Haven University of Pennsylvania M
Mercyhurst College M
Millersville University of Pennsylvania M
Penn State
  University Park M
Seton Hill University M
Shippensburg University of Pennsylvania M
University of Pittsburgh M
University of Pittsburgh
  Johnstown M

Puerto Rico
Inter American University of Puerto Rico
  Bayamon Campus M
University of Puerto Rico
  Bayamon University College M
  Humacao M
  Mayaguez M
University of the Sacred Heart M

Rhode Island
Bryant University M

South Carolina
Anderson University M
The Citadel M
Limestone College M
Newberry College M
Spartanburg Methodist College M

South Dakota
Augustana College M
Dakota Wesleyan University M
Northern State University M
South Dakota State University M

Tennessee
Carson-Newman College M
Cumberland University M
King College M
University of Tennessee
  Chattanooga M

Utah
Utah Valley University M

Virginia
Old Dominion University M
University of Virginia M
Virginia Military Institute M
Virginia Polytechnic Institute and State University M

Washington
Highline Community College M
Yakima Valley Community College M,W

West Virginia
West Liberty State College M
West Virginia University M

Wisconsin
University of Wisconsin
  Parkside M

Wyoming
Northwest College M
University of Wyoming M
Western Wyoming Community College M

Music/drama scholarships

Alabama
Alabama State University
Auburn University at Montgomery
Bevill State Community College
Birmingham-Southern College
Chattahoochee Valley Community College
Enterprise-Ozark Community College
Faulkner University
Gadsden State Community College
Huntingdon College
Jacksonville State University
Jefferson State Community College
Judson College
Lurleen B. Wallace Community College
Northeast Alabama Community College
Northwest-Shoals Community College
Samford University
Snead State Community College
Southeastern Bible College
Talladega College
Troy University
University of Alabama
University of Alabama
  Birmingham
  Huntsville
University of Mobile
University of Montevallo
University of North Alabama
University of South Alabama
University of West Alabama
Wallace State Community College at Hanceville

Alaska
University of Alaska
  Fairbanks

Arizona
Arizona State University
Eastern Arizona College
Northern Arizona University
Northland Pioneer College
Pima Community College
South Mountain Community College
Southwestern College

Arkansas
Arkansas Northeastern College
Arkansas State University
Arkansas State University
  Beebe
Arkansas Tech University
Central Baptist College
Crowley's Ridge College
Ecclesia College
Harding University
Henderson State University
Hendrix College
John Brown University
Lyon College
National Park Community College
Northwest Arkansas Community College
Ouachita Baptist University
Phillips Community College of the University of Arkansas
Southern Arkansas University
University of Arkansas
University of Arkansas
  Fort Smith
  Monticello
  Pine Bluff
University of Central Arkansas
University of the Ozarks
Williams Baptist College

California
American Academy of Dramatic Arts: West
Azusa Pacific University
Bethany University
Bethesda Christian University
Biola University
California Baptist University
California Institute of the Arts
California Lutheran University
California Polytechnic State University: San Luis Obispo
California State University
  Chico
  Dominguez Hills
  East Bay
  Fresno
  Long Beach
  Stanislaus
Chapman University
College of the Canyons
College of the Siskiyous
Concordia University
Dominican University of California
El Camino College
Fresno Pacific University
Holy Names University
Hope International University
Irvine Valley College
La Sierra University
Loyola Marymount University
The Master's College
Mills College
Mount St. Mary's College
Mount San Jacinto College
Notre Dame de Namur University
Occidental College
Pepperdine University
Riverside Community College
San Diego Christian College
San Diego State University
San Francisco Conservatory of Music
Santa Clara University
Santa Rosa Junior College
Simpson University
Sonoma State University
University of California
  Irvine
  Riverside
  San Diego
  Santa Cruz
University of La Verne
University of Redlands
University of San Diego
University of Southern California
University of the Pacific
Vanguard University of Southern California
Westmont College
William Jessup University
Yuba Community College District

Colorado
Adams State College
Colorado Christian University
Colorado School of Mines
Colorado State University
Colorado State University
  Pueblo
Fort Lewis College
Mesa State College
Metropolitan State College of Denver
Northeastern Junior College
Pueblo Community College
University of Colorado
  Boulder
  Denver
University of Denver
University of Northern Colorado
Western State College of Colorado

Connecticut
Albertus Magnus College
Fairfield University
Sacred Heart University
University of Bridgeport
University of Connecticut
University of Hartford

Delaware
Delaware State University
University of Delaware

District of Columbia
American University
Catholic University of America
George Washington University
Howard University

Florida
Baptist College of Florida
Barry University
Bethune-Cookman University
Central Florida Community College
Chipola College
Clearwater Christian College
Daytona State College
Eckerd College
Edison State College
Flagler College
Florida Atlantic University
Florida Christian College
Florida College
Florida Community College at Jacksonville
Florida Gulf Coast University
Florida International University
Florida Southern College
Gulf Coast Community College
Hillsborough Community College
Indian River State College
Jacksonville University
Lake-Sumter Community College
Lynn University
Manatee Community College
Miami Dade College
North Florida Community College
Northwest Florida State College
Nova Southeastern University
Palm Beach Atlantic University
Rollins College
St. Leo University
St. Petersburg College
Saint Thomas University
Santa Fe College
Seminole Community College
South Florida Community College
Southeastern University
Stetson University
Tallahassee Community College
University of Florida
University of Miami
University of North Florida
University of South Florida
University of Tampa
University of West Florida
Warner University

Georgia
Agnes Scott College
Albany State University
Andrew College
Armstrong Atlantic State University
Augusta State University
Berry College
Brenau University
Brewton-Parker College
Clark Atlanta University
Columbus State University
Covenant College
Darton College
Emmanuel College
Emory University
Gainesville State College
Georgia College and State University
Georgia Southern University
Georgia State University
Gordon College
Kennesaw State University
LaGrange College
Mercer University
Middle Georgia College
Morehouse College
North Georgia College & State University
Oglethorpe University
Paine College
Piedmont College
Savannah College of Art and Design
Savannah State University
Shorter College
Spelman College
Toccoa Falls College
Truett-McConnell College
University of West Georgia
Valdosta State University
Wesleyan College
Young Harris College

Hawaii
Brigham Young University-Hawaii
Hawaii Pacific University
University of Hawaii
  Manoa

Idaho
Boise Bible College
Boise State University
College of Idaho
Idaho State University
Lewis-Clark State College
North Idaho College
Northwest Nazarene University
University of Idaho

Illinois
Augustana College
Aurora University
Benedictine University
Black Hawk College
Bradley University
Carl Sandburg College
College of DuPage
College of Lake County
Columbia College Chicago
Concordia University Chicago
DePaul University
Eastern Illinois University
Elgin Community College
Elmhurst College
Eureka College
Greenville College
Harper College
Illinois College
Illinois State University
Illinois Wesleyan University
Judson University
Kishwaukee College
Knox College
Lake Forest College
Lewis University
Lincoln College
Loyola University Chicago
MacMurray College
McHenry County College
McKendree University
Millikin University
Monmouth College
Moody Bible Institute
North Central College
North Park University
Northeastern Illinois University

Northwestern University
Oakton Community College
Olivet Nazarene University
Parkland College
Quincy University
Rend Lake College
Rockford College
Roosevelt University
St. Xavier University
South Suburban College of Cook County
Southeastern Illinois College
Southern Illinois University Carbondale
Southern Illinois University Edwardsville
Trinity Christian College
Trinity International University
University of Illinois
  Chicago
  Springfield
  Urbana-Champaign
University of St. Francis
VanderCook College of Music
Waubonsee Community College
Western Illinois University
Wheaton College

Indiana

Anderson University
Ball State University
Bethel College
Butler University
DePauw University
Goshen College
Grace College
Hanover College
Huntington University
Indiana Institute of Technology
Indiana State University
Indiana University
  Bloomington
  Southeast
Indiana Wesleyan University
Manchester College
Marian College
Oakland City University
Purdue University
Saint Joseph's College
St. Mary-of-the-Woods College
Taylor University
Trine University
University of Evansville
University of Indianapolis
University of St. Francis
University of Southern Indiana
Valparaiso University
Vincennes University
Wabash College

Iowa

Ashford University
Briar Cliff University
Buena Vista University
Central College
Clarke College
Coe College
Cornell College
Dordt College
Drake University
Ellsworth Community College
Emmaus Bible College
Faith Baptist Bible College and Theological Seminary
Graceland University
Grand View University
Iowa Central Community College
Iowa State University
Iowa Wesleyan College
Iowa Western Community College
Kirkwood Community College
Loras College
Luther College
Morningside College
Mount Mercy College
North Iowa Area Community College
Northwestern College
St. Ambrose University
Simpson College
Southwestern Community College
University of Dubuque
University of Iowa
University of Northern Iowa
Waldorf College
Wartburg College
Western Iowa Tech Community College
William Penn University

Kansas

Allen County Community College
Baker University
Barclay College
Benedictine College
Bethany College
Bethel College
Central Christian College of Kansas
Coffeyville Community College
Colby Community College
Cowley County Community College
Dodge City Community College
Emporia State University
Fort Hays State University
Friends University
Garden City Community College
Hesston College
Highland Community College
Kansas City Kansas Community College
Kansas State University
Kansas Wesleyan University
McPherson College
MidAmerica Nazarene University
Neosho County Community College
Newman University
Ottawa University
Pittsburg State University
Pratt Community College
Southwestern College
Tabor College
University of Kansas
University of St. Mary
Washburn University
Wichita State University

Kentucky

Asbury College
Ashland Community and Technical College
Bellarmine University
Brescia University
Centre College
Eastern Kentucky University
Georgetown College
Kentucky Christian University
Kentucky Mountain Bible College
Kentucky State University
Kentucky Wesleyan College
Morehead State University
Murray State University
Northern Kentucky University
Thomas More College
Transylvania University
Union College
University of Kentucky
University of Louisville
University of the Cumberlands
Western Kentucky University

Louisiana

Bossier Parish Community College
Centenary College of Louisiana
Delgado Community College
Dillard University
Grambling State University
Louisiana College
Louisiana State University and Agricultural and Mechanical College
Louisiana Tech University
McNeese State University
Northwestern State University
Southeastern Louisiana University
Tulane University
University of Louisiana at Lafayette
University of Louisiana at Monroe
Xavier University of Louisiana

Maine

University of Maine
University of Maine
  Augusta
  Machias
  Presque Isle
University of Southern Maine

Maryland

Bowie State University
College of Notre Dame of Maryland
Columbia Union College
Goucher College
Hood College
Johns Hopkins University: Peabody Conservatory of Music
Montgomery College
Salisbury University
Stevenson University
Towson University
University of Maryland
  Baltimore County
  College Park
  Eastern Shore
Washington Bible College

Massachusetts

Anna Maria College
Boston Conservatory
Boston University
Bristol Community College
Cape Cod Community College
Dean College
Emerson College
Gordon College
Holyoke Community College
Massachusetts College of Liberal Arts
Massachusetts Maritime Academy
New England Conservatory of Music
North Shore Community College
University of Massachusetts
  Amherst
  Lowell
Western New England College

Michigan

Adrian College
Albion College
Alma College
Alpena Community College
Andrews University
Aquinas College
Calvin College
Central Michigan University
Concordia University
Cornerstone University
Eastern Michigan University
Ferris State University
Glen Oaks Community College
Gogebic Community College
Grace Bible College
Grand Rapids Community College
Grand Valley State University
Great Lakes Christian College
Hillsdale College
Hope College
Jackson Community College
Macomb Community College
Madonna University
Marygrove College
Michigan State University
Michigan Technological University
Monroe County Community College
Mott Community College
Northern Michigan University
Northwestern Michigan College
Oakland University
Olivet College
Rochester College
Saginaw Valley State University
Schoolcraft College
Siena Heights University
Southwestern Michigan College
Spring Arbor University
University of Detroit Mercy
University of Michigan
University of Michigan
  Flint
Wayne State University
Western Michigan University

Minnesota

Augsburg College
Bemidji State University
Bethany Lutheran College
Bethel University
College of St. Benedict
Concordia College: Moorhead
Concordia University: St. Paul
Crossroads College
Crown College
Gustavus Adolphus College
Hamline University
Itasca Community College
Martin Luther College
Minnesota State Community and Technical College
Minnesota State University
  Mankato
  Moorhead
Normandale Community College
Northwestern College
Riverland Community College
Saint Cloud State University
St. John's University
St. Mary's University of Minnesota
St. Olaf College
Southwest Minnesota State University
University of Minnesota
  Morris
  Twin Cities
University of St. Thomas
Winona State University

Mississippi

Belhaven College
Blue Mountain College
Copiah-Lincoln Community College
Delta State University
East Mississippi Community College
Hinds Community College
Itawamba Community College
Jackson State University
Meridian Community College
Millsaps College
Mississippi College
Mississippi Gulf Coast Community College
Mississippi State University
Mississippi University for Women
Pearl River Community College
Rust College
University of Mississippi
William Carey University

Missouri

Avila University
Calvary Bible College and Theological Seminary
Central Methodist University
College of the Ozarks
Columbia College
Cottey College
Crowder College
Culver-Stockton College
Drury University
East Central College
Evangel University
Fontbonne University
Hannibal-LaGrange College

Harris-Stowe State University
Jefferson College
Lincoln University
Lindenwood University
Mineral Area College
Missouri Baptist University
Missouri Southern State University
Missouri State University
Missouri Western State University
Moberly Area Community College
North Central Missouri College
Northwest Missouri State University
Park University
Rockhurst University
St. Charles Community College
St. Louis Christian College
St. Louis Community College
Saint Louis University
Southeast Missouri State University
Southwest Baptist University
State Fair Community College
Stephens College
Truman State University
University of Central Missouri
University of Missouri
- Columbia
- Kansas City
- Missouri University of Science and Technology
- St. Louis

Webster University
Westminster College
William Jewell College
William Woods University

Montana

Carroll College
Dawson Community College
Montana State University
- Billings
- Bozeman

Rocky Mountain College
University of Montana

Nebraska

Central Community College
Chadron State College
College of Saint Mary
Concordia University
Creighton University
Doane College
Grace University
Mid-Plains Community College Area
Nebraska Wesleyan University
Northeast Community College
Peru State College
University of Nebraska
- Kearney
- Lincoln
- Omaha

Wayne State College
Western Nebraska Community College
York College

Nevada

Truckee Meadows Community College
University of Nevada
- Las Vegas
- Reno

New Hampshire

Colby-Sawyer College
Franklin Pierce University
Keene State College
New England College
Plymouth State University
University of New Hampshire

New Jersey

Caldwell College
Centenary College
Drew University
Fairleigh Dickinson University
- College at Florham
- Metropolitan Campus

Georgian Court University
Kean University
Montclair State University
New Jersey Institute of Technology
Richard Stockton College of New Jersey
Rider University
Rowan University
Rutgers, The State University of New Jersey
- Camden Regional Campus
- New Brunswick/Piscataway Campus
- Newark Regional Campus

Stevens Institute of Technology
William Paterson University of New Jersey

New Mexico

Eastern New Mexico University
Mesalands Community College
New Mexico Highlands University
New Mexico Junior College
University of New Mexico

New York

Adelphi University
Alfred University
Canisius College
City University of New York
- Brooklyn College
- College of Staten Island
- Queens College

College of Saint Rose
Concordia College
Eastman School of Music of the University of Rochester
Eugene Lang College The New School for Liberal Arts
Five Towns College
Hobart and William Smith Colleges
Hofstra University
Houghton College
Ithaca College
Jamestown Community College
Juilliard School
Manhattan School of Music
Manhattanville College
Mannes College The New School for Music
Marist College
Marymount Manhattan College
Molloy College
Monroe Community College
Nazareth College
Niagara University
Nyack College
Pace University
Parsons The New School for Design
Rensselaer Polytechnic Institute
Roberts Wesleyan College
Russell Sage College
Saint Bonaventure University
St. John's University
Skidmore College
State University of New York
- Binghamton
- Buffalo
- College at Cortland
- College at Fredonia
- College at Geneseo
- College at Oneonta
- College at Plattsburgh
- College at Potsdam
- New Paltz
- Purchase
- Stony Brook

Suffolk County Community College
Syracuse University
University of Rochester
Villa Maria College of Buffalo
Wagner College

North Carolina

Appalachian State University
Barton College
Brevard College
Campbell University
Cape Fear Community College
Catawba College
Catawba Valley Community College
Chowan University
College of the Albemarle
Davidson College
Elon University
Fayetteville State University
Gardner-Webb University
Greensboro College
High Point University
Isothermal Community College
Lees-McRae College
Lenoir-Rhyne University
Livingstone College
Meredith College
Methodist University
Montreat College
Mount Olive College
North Carolina Agricultural and Technical State University
North Carolina Central University
Peace College
Pfeiffer University
Roanoke Bible College
St. Andrews Presbyterian College
St. Augustine's College
Salem College
Shaw University
Southeastern Community College
University of North Carolina
- Asheville
- Chapel Hill
- Charlotte
- Greensboro
- Pembroke
- Wilmington

University of North Carolina School of the Arts
Wake Forest University
Western Carolina University
Wilkes Community College
Wingate University

North Dakota

Dickinson State University
Jamestown College
Lake Region State College
Mayville State University
Minot State University
Minot State University: Bottineau Campus
North Dakota State College of Science
North Dakota State University
University of Mary
University of North Dakota
Valley City State University
Williston State College

Ohio

Ashland University
Baldwin-Wallace College
Bluffton University
Bowling Green State University
Bowling Green State University: Firelands College
Capital University
Case Western Reserve University
Cedarville University
Central State University
Cincinnati Christian University
Cleveland Institute of Music
Cleveland State University
College of Mount St. Joseph
College of Wooster
Cuyahoga Community College
- Metropolitan Campus

Denison University
God's Bible School and College
Heidelberg University
Hiram College
Kent State University
Kent State University
- Ashtabula
- East Liverpool
- Salem
- Stark
- Trumbull
- Tuscarawas

Kent State University: Geauga
Lake Erie College
Lakeland Community College
Malone University
Marietta College
Miami University
- Oxford Campus

Mount Union College
Mount Vernon Nazarene University
Muskingum College
Oberlin College
Ohio Northern University
Ohio State University
- Agricultural Technical Institute
- Columbus Campus
- Lima Campus
- Mansfield Campus
- Marion Campus
- Newark Campus

Ohio University
Ohio Wesleyan University
Otterbein College
Pontifical College Josephinum
Southern State Community College
Tiffin University
University of Akron
University of Akron: Wayne College
University of Cincinnati
University of Dayton
University of Findlay
University of Rio Grande
University of Toledo
Urbana University
Walsh University
Wittenberg University
Wright State University
Wright State University: Lake Campus
Xavier University

Oklahoma

Cameron University
Carl Albert State College
Mid-America Christian University
Northeastern Oklahoma Agricultural and Mechanical College
Northeastern State University
Northwestern Oklahoma State University
Oklahoma Baptist University
Oklahoma Christian University
Oklahoma City Community College
Oklahoma City University
Oklahoma Panhandle State University
Oklahoma State University
Oklahoma Wesleyan University
Oral Roberts University
Rogers State University
St. Gregory's University
Southeastern Oklahoma State University
Southwestern Christian University
Southwestern Oklahoma State University
Tulsa Community College
University of Central Oklahoma
University of Oklahoma
University of Science and Arts of Oklahoma
University of Tulsa
Western Oklahoma State College

Oregon

Blue Mountain Community College
Clackamas Community College
Concordia University
Corban College

Eastern Oregon University
George Fox University
Lane Community College
Lewis & Clark College
Linfield College
Linn-Benton Community College
Northwest Christian University
Pacific University
Portland State University
Southern Oregon University
Southwestern Oregon Community College
Treasure Valley Community College
University of Oregon
University of Portland
Warner Pacific College
Western Oregon University
Willamette University

Pennsylvania
Albright College
Arcadia University
Baptist Bible College of Pennsylvania
Berks Technical Institute
Bloomsburg University of Pennsylvania
Bucknell University
California University of Pennsylvania
Carnegie Mellon University
Cedar Crest College
Chatham University
Clarion University of Pennsylvania
Delaware Valley College
DeSales University
Drexel University
Duquesne University
East Stroudsburg University of Pennsylvania
Edinboro University of Pennsylvania
Elizabethtown College
Franklin & Marshall College
Gannon University
Geneva College
Gettysburg College
Immaculata University
Indiana University of Pennsylvania
Kutztown University of Pennsylvania
Lancaster Bible College
Lebanon Valley College
Lehigh University
Lincoln University
Lock Haven University of Pennsylvania
Lycoming College
Mansfield University of Pennsylvania
Marywood University
Mercyhurst College
Messiah College
Moravian College
Mount Aloysius College
Muhlenberg College
Northampton Community College
Point Park University
St. Francis University
Saint Joseph's University
St. Vincent College
Seton Hill University
Slippery Rock University of Pennsylvania
Susquehanna University
Temple University
Thiel College
University of the Arts
Ursinus College
Valley Forge Christian College
Valley Forge Military Academy & College
Widener University
Wilkes University
York College of Pennsylvania

Puerto Rico
Humacao Community College
Universidad Politecnica de Puerto Rico
University of Puerto Rico
  Aguadilla
  Humacao
  Mayaguez

Rhode Island
Rhode Island College
University of Rhode Island

South Carolina
Allen University
Anderson University
Clemson University
Coastal Carolina University
College of Charleston
Columbia College
Converse College
Erskine College
Francis Marion University
Furman University
Lander University
Limestone College
Newberry College
North Greenville University
Presbyterian College
Southern Wesleyan University
Spartanburg Methodist College
University of South Carolina
University of South Carolina
  Aiken
Winthrop University
Wofford College

South Dakota
Augustana College
Dakota State University
Dakota Wesleyan University
Mount Marty College
Northern State University
South Dakota State University
University of Sioux Falls
University of South Dakota

Tennessee
Austin Peay State University
Belmont University
Bethel College
Carson-Newman College
Christian Brothers University
Crichton College
Cumberland University
Dyersburg State Community College
East Tennessee State University
Fisk University
Free Will Baptist Bible College
Freed-Hardeman University
Jackson State Community College
Johnson Bible College
King College
Lambuth University
Lee University
LeMoyne-Owen College
Lincoln Memorial University
Lipscomb University
Martin Methodist College
Maryville College
Middle Tennessee State University
Milligan College
Pellissippi State Technical Community College
Rhodes College
Roane State Community College
Southern Adventist University
Southwest Tennessee Community College
Tennessee Technological University
Tennessee Temple University
Tennessee Wesleyan College
Union University
University of Memphis
University of Tennessee
  Chattanooga
  Knoxville
  Martin
Vanderbilt University
Volunteer State Community College
Walters State Community College

Texas
Abilene Christian University
Angelina College
Angelo State University
Austin College
Baylor University
Brazosport College
Clarendon College
College of the Mainland
Collin County Community College District
Concordia University Texas
Dallas Baptist University
Dallas Christian College
East Texas Baptist University
Frank Phillips College
Galveston College
Hardin-Simmons University
Hill College
Houston Baptist University
Howard College
Howard Payne University
Huston-Tillotson University
Jacksonville College
Kilgore College
Lee College
Lon Morris College
Lubbock Christian University
McMurry University
Midland College
Midwestern State University
Odessa College
Our Lady of the Lake University of San Antonio
Panola College
Paris Junior College
Rice University
Richland College
St. Edward's University
St. Mary's University
San Jacinto College
Schreiner University
South Plains College
Southern Methodist University
Southwestern Adventist University
Southwestern University
Stephen F. Austin State University
Tarleton State University
Texas A&M University
Texas A&M University
  Commerce
  Corpus Christi
Texas Christian University
Texas Lutheran University
Texas State University: San Marcos
Texas Tech University
Texas Wesleyan University
Trinity University
Tyler Junior College
University of Dallas
University of Houston
University of Mary Hardin-Baylor
University of Texas
  Austin
  El Paso
  Pan American
  of the Permian Basin
  San Antonio
  Tyler
University of the Incarnate Word
Victoria College
Wayland Baptist University
West Texas A&M University
Western Technical College
Western Texas College
Wharton County Junior College

Utah
Brigham Young University
College of Eastern Utah
Dixie State College of Utah
Salt Lake Community College
Snow College
Southern Utah University
University of Utah
Utah State University
Utah Valley University
Weber State University
Westminster College

Vermont
Castleton State College
Goddard College
Green Mountain College
Landmark College
Norwich University

Virginia
Averett University
Bluefield College
Bridgewater College
Christopher Newport University
Emory & Henry College
George Mason University
Hampton University
Hollins University
James Madison University
Liberty University
Longwood University
Lynchburg College
Norfolk State University
Old Dominion University
Patrick Henry College
Radford University
Randolph College
Roanoke College
Shenandoah University
Southern Virginia University
Sweet Briar College
University of Mary Washington
University of Richmond
University of Virginia
University of Virginia's College at Wise
Virginia Commonwealth University
Virginia Intermont College
Virginia Military Institute
Virginia State University

Washington
Big Bend Community College
Central Washington University
Centralia College
Clark College
Everett Community College
Gonzaga University
Grays Harbor College
Northwest University
Pacific Lutheran University
Pierce College
Seattle Pacific University
Seattle University
Trinity Lutheran College
University of Puget Sound
University of Washington
University of Washington Bothell
Walla Walla Community College
Walla Walla University
Washington State University
Western Washington University
Whitman College
Whitworth University

West Virginia
Alderson-Broaddus College
Bethany College
Bluefield State College
Concord University
Davis and Elkins College
Fairmont State University
Glenville State College
Marshall University
Ohio Valley University
Shepherd University
University of Charleston
West Liberty State College
West Virginia University
West Virginia Wesleyan College

Wheeling Jesuit University

Wisconsin

Beloit College
Cardinal Stritch University
Carroll University
Carthage College
Concordia University Wisconsin
Edgewood College
Lawrence University
Marquette University
Mount Mary College
Northland College
Ripon College
St. Norbert College
Silver Lake College
University of Wisconsin
- Baraboo/Sauk County
- Eau Claire
- Fond du Lac
- Green Bay
- La Crosse
- Madison
- Manitowoc
- Oshkosh
- Parkside
- Richland
- River Falls
- Rock County
- Sheboygan
- Stevens Point
- Superior
- Waukesha
- Whitewater

Viterbo University
Wisconsin Lutheran College

Wyoming

Casper College
Central Wyoming College
Eastern Wyoming College
Laramie County Community College
Sheridan College
University of Wyoming
Western Wyoming Community College

ROTC scholarships

Air Force ROTC

Alabama
Alabama State University
Auburn University
Auburn University at Montgomery
Birmingham-Southern College
Bishop State Community College
Faulkner University
Huntingdon College
Jefferson State Community College
Marion Military Institute
Miles College
Samford University
Shelton State Community College
Spring Hill College
Troy University
Tuskegee University
University of Alabama
University of Alabama
  Birmingham
University of Mobile
University of Montevallo
University of South Alabama
University of West Alabama

Alaska
Alaska Pacific University
University of Alaska
  Anchorage

Arizona
Arizona State University
Coconino County Community College
DeVry University
  Phoenix
Embry-Riddle Aeronautical University: Prescott Campus
Estrella Mountain Community College
Gateway Community College
Mesa Community College
Northern Arizona University
Phoenix College
Pima Community College
Southwestern College
University of Arizona
Yavapai College

Arkansas
John Brown University
Northwest Arkansas Community College
University of Arkansas
University of Arkansas
  Fort Smith

California
Biola University
California Baptist University
California Institute of Technology
California Lutheran University
California State University
  Dominguez Hills
  Fresno
  Los Angeles
  Northridge
  Sacramento
  San Bernardino
  San Marcos
Chabot College
Chapman University
Claremont McKenna College
College of San Mateo
College of the Sequoias
Cuyamaca College
De Anza College
Foothill College
Fresno City College
Harvey Mudd College
Holy Names University
Irvine Valley College
The King's College and Seminary
Los Angeles City College
Los Angeles Mission College
Loyola Marymount University
Menlo College
MiraCosta College
Mission College
Mount San Antonio College
Mount San Jacinto College
National University
Occidental College
Ohlone College
Pepperdine University
Pitzer College
Point Loma Nazarene University
Pomona College
Riverside Community College
Sacramento City College
St. Mary's College of California
Samuel Merritt University
San Diego Christian College
San Diego City College
San Diego State University
San Francisco State University
San Jose State University
Santa Clara University
Scripps College
Solano Community College
Sonoma State University
Stanford University
University of California
  Berkeley
  Davis
  Irvine
  Los Angeles
  Riverside
  Santa Cruz
University of Redlands
University of San Diego
University of San Francisco
University of Southern California
University of the Pacific
Vanguard University of Southern California
West Valley College
Westmont College
Whittier College

Colorado
Aims Community College
Arapahoe Community College
Colorado Christian University
Colorado School of Mines
Colorado State University
Front Range Community College
Metropolitan State College of Denver
Regis University
University of Colorado
  Boulder
  Denver
University of Denver
University of Northern Colorado

Connecticut
Capital Community College
Central Connecticut State University
Eastern Connecticut State University
Fairfield University
Quinnipiac University
Southern Connecticut State University
Tunxis Community College
University of Connecticut
University of Hartford
Wesleyan University
Western Connecticut State University
Yale University

Delaware
Delaware State University
Delaware Technical and Community College
  Stanton/Wilmington
Goldey-Beacom College
University of Delaware
Wilmington University

District of Columbia
American University
Catholic University of America
George Washington University
Georgetown University
Howard University
University of the District of Columbia

Florida
Barry University
Bethune-Cookman University
Brevard Community College
Broward College
Clearwater Christian College
Daytona State College
Eckerd College
Embry-Riddle Aeronautical University
Florida Agricultural and Mechanical University
Florida Atlantic University
Florida College
Florida International University
Florida Southern College
Florida State University
Lynn University
Miami Dade College
St. Leo University
Santa Fe College
Tallahassee Community College
University of Central Florida
University of Miami
University of South Florida
University of Tampa
University of West Florida

Georgia
Agnes Scott College
Clayton State University
Emory University
Georgia Institute of Technology
Georgia State University
Kennesaw State University
Morehouse College
Oglethorpe University
Southern Polytechnic State University
Spelman College
University of Georgia
Valdosta State University

Hawaii
Brigham Young University-Hawaii
Chaminade University of Honolulu
Hawaii Pacific University
University of Hawaii
  Honolulu Community College
  Leeward Community College
  Manoa
  West Oahu

Idaho
Lewis-Clark State College
Northwest Nazarene University
University of Idaho

Illinois
Elmhurst College
Governors State University
Illinois Institute of Technology
John A. Logan College
Judson University
Lewis University
Lincoln Land Community College
Loyola University Chicago
McKendree University
North Central College
North Park University
Northeastern Illinois University
Northwestern University
Parkland College
St. Xavier University
Shawnee Community College
Southern Illinois University Carbondale
Southern Illinois University Edwardsville
University of Chicago
University of Illinois
  Chicago
  Urbana-Champaign
Wheaton College

Indiana
Bethel College
Butler University
DePauw University
Holy Cross College
Indiana State University
Indiana University
  Bloomington
  South Bend
  Southeast
Indiana University-Purdue University
  Indianapolis
Purdue University
Rose-Hulman Institute of Technology
St. Mary-of-the-Woods College
Saint Mary's College
Trine University
University of Notre Dame
Valparaiso University
Vincennes University

Iowa
Coe College
Grand View University
Hawkeye Community College
Iowa State University
Iowa Western Community College
University of Iowa

Kansas
Baker University
Kansas State University
Manhattan Christian College
MidAmerica Nazarene University
University of Kansas
University of St. Mary
Washburn University

Kentucky
Asbury College
Bellarmine University
Centre College
Georgetown College
Kentucky State University
Northern Kentucky University
Spalding University
Thomas More College
Transylvania University
University of Kentucky
University of Louisville
Western Kentucky University

Louisiana
Delgado Community College
Dillard University
Louisiana State University and Agricultural and Mechanical College

Loyola University New Orleans
Northwestern State University
Our Lady of Holy Cross College
Our Lady of the Lake College
Southern University
  New Orleans
Southern University and Agricultural and Mechanical College
Tulane University
University of New Orleans
Xavier University of Louisiana

Maine
University of Maine
  Augusta
University of Southern Maine

Maryland
Bowie State University
Johns Hopkins University
Loyola College in Maryland
Prince George's Community College
Salisbury University
Towson University
University of Maryland
  Baltimore County
  College Park

Massachusetts
American International College
Amherst College
Anna Maria College
Assumption College
Babson College
Bay Path College
Becker College
Bentley University
Boston College
Boston University
Brandeis University
Bridgewater State College
Clark University
College of the Holy Cross
Curry College
Elms College
Endicott College
Gordon College
Harvard College
Holyoke Community College
Massachusetts College of Pharmacy and Health Sciences
Massachusetts Institute of Technology
Massachusetts Maritime Academy
Merrimack College
Middlesex Community College
Mount Holyoke College
Northeastern University
Pine Manor College
Quinsigamond Community College
Salem State College
Smith College
Springfield College
Tufts University
University of Massachusetts
  Amherst
  Boston
  Lowell
Wellesley College
Wentworth Institute of Technology
Western New England College
Westfield State College
Williams College
Worcester Polytechnic Institute
Worcester State College

Michigan
Concordia University
Eastern Michigan University
Finlandia University
Lansing Community College
Lawrence Technological University
Michigan State University
Michigan Technological University
Oakland University
Spring Arbor University
University of Michigan
University of Michigan
  Dearborn
Wayne State University

Minnesota
Anoka-Ramsey Community College
Augsburg College
Bethel University
Century Community and Technical College
College of St. Catherine
College of St. Scholastica
Concordia College: Moorhead
Concordia University: St. Paul
Hamline University
Inver Hills Community College
Macalester College
Minnesota State University
  Moorhead
Normandale Community College
North Hennepin Community College
Northwestern College
University of Minnesota
  Crookston
  Duluth
  Twin Cities
University of St. Thomas

Mississippi
Belhaven College
Jackson State University
Mississippi State University
Mississippi University for Women
Northwest Mississippi Community College
University of Mississippi
University of Southern Mississippi
William Carey University

Missouri
Central Bible College
Central Methodist University
Columbia College
Fontbonne University
Harris-Stowe State University
Lincoln University
Saint Louis University
Southeast Missouri State University
St. Louis Community College
  Meramec
Stephens College
University of Central Missouri
University of Missouri
  Columbia
  Missouri University of Science and Technology
  St. Louis
Washington University in St. Louis
Webster University
Westminster College
William Woods University

Montana
Montana State University
  Billings
  Bozeman

Nebraska
Bellevue University
Clarkson College
College of Saint Mary
Concordia University
Creighton University
Doane College
Grace University
Nebraska Wesleyan University
University of Nebraska
  Lincoln
  Medical Center
  Omaha
York College

New Hampshire
Colby-Sawyer College
Daniel Webster College
Franklin Pierce University
Keene State College
New England College
Plymouth State University
Rivier College
St. Anselm College
Southern New Hampshire University
University of New Hampshire
University of New Hampshire at Manchester

New Jersey
Brookdale Community College
The College of New Jersey
Fairleigh Dickinson University
  College at Florham
  Metropolitan Campus
Kean University
Monmouth University
Montclair State University
New Jersey Institute of Technology
Princeton University
Ramapo College of New Jersey
Raritan Valley Community College
Rutgers, The State University of New Jersey
  Camden Regional Campus
  New Brunswick/Piscataway Campus
  Newark Regional Campus
Saint Peter's College
Stevens Institute of Technology
Union County College
William Paterson University of New Jersey

New Mexico
Central New Mexico Community College
Dona Ana Community College of New Mexico State University
National American University: Rio Rancho
New Mexico State University
New Mexico State University
  Alamogordo
University of New Mexico

New York
Adelphi University
Albany College of Pharmacy and Health Sciences
Cazenovia College
Clarkson University
College of Saint Rose
Columbia University
Columbia University
  School of General Studies
Cornell University
Dowling College
Elmira College
Fordham University
Hamilton College
Hudson Valley Community College
Iona College
Ithaca College
Jewish Theological Seminary of America
Le Moyne College
Manhattan College
Maria College
Mercy College
Molloy College
Monroe Community College
Nazareth College
New York Institute of Technology
Onondaga Community College
Pace University
Polytechnic Institute of New York University
Rensselaer Polytechnic Institute
Roberts Wesleyan College
Rochester Institute of Technology
Russell Sage College
Sage College of Albany
St. Francis College
St. John Fisher College
St. Joseph's College: Suffolk Campus
St. Lawrence University
St. Thomas Aquinas College
Schenectady County Community College
Siena College
Skidmore College
State University of New York
  Albany
  Binghamton
  College at Brockport
  College at Cortland
  College at Geneseo
  College at Old Westbury
  College at Potsdam
  College of Environmental Science and Forestry
  College of Technology at Canton
  Stony Brook
Syracuse University
Union College
University of Rochester
Utica College
Vaughn College of Aeronautics and Technology
Wells College

North Carolina
Belmont Abbey College
Bennett College for Women
Davidson College
Duke University
East Carolina University
Elon University
Fayetteville State University
Gardner-Webb University
Greensboro College
Guilford College
Guilford Technical Community College
High Point University
Johnson C. Smith University
Meredith College
Methodist University
North Carolina Agricultural and Technical State University
North Carolina Central University
North Carolina State University
Peace College
Queens University of Charlotte
St. Augustine's College
Shaw University
University of North Carolina
  Chapel Hill
  Charlotte
  Greensboro
  Pembroke
Wingate University

North Dakota
Mayville State University
North Dakota State University
University of North Dakota

Ohio
Baldwin-Wallace College
Bowling Green State University
Capital University
Case Western Reserve University
Cedarville University
Central State University
Cleveland Institute of Art
College of Mount St. Joseph
Columbus State Community College
Cuyahoga Community College
  Metropolitan Campus
Heidelberg University
Hocking College
Kent State University
Kent State University
  Ashtabula
  East Liverpool
  Salem
  Stark
  Trumbull

Tuscarawas
Lourdes College
Malone University
Miami University
Hamilton Campus
Middletown Campus
Oxford Campus
Mount Union College
Ohio Northern University
Ohio State University
Columbus Campus
Lima Campus
Mansfield Campus
Marion Campus
Newark Campus
Ohio University
Ohio University
Lancaster Campus
Ohio Wesleyan University
Otterbein College
Owens Community College
Toledo
Sinclair Community College
University of Akron
University of Akron: Wayne College
University of Cincinnati
University of Cincinnati
Raymond Walters College
University of Dayton
University of Findlay
University of Toledo
Urbana University
Wilberforce University
Wittenberg University
Wright State University
Xavier University
Youngstown State University

Oklahoma
Langston University
Northeastern Oklahoma Agricultural and Mechanical College
Oklahoma Baptist University
Oklahoma Christian University
Oklahoma City University
Oklahoma State University
Oral Roberts University
Rogers State University
St. Gregory's University
Southern Nazarene University
University of Oklahoma
University of Tulsa

Oregon
Clackamas Community College
Concordia University
Corban College
George Fox University
Linfield College
Linn-Benton Community College
Oregon State University
Pacific University
Portland State University
University of Oregon
University of Portland
Warner Pacific College
Western Oregon University
Willamette University

Pennsylvania
Bloomsburg University of Pennsylvania
Bryn Mawr College
Cabrini College
California University of Pennsylvania
Carlow University
Carnegie Mellon University
Chatham University
Drexel University
Duquesne University
East Stroudsburg University of Pennsylvania
Eastern University
Keystone College
King's College
La Roche College
La Salle University
Lackawanna College
Luzerne County Community College
Marywood University
Mercyhurst College
Misericordia University
Penn State
Abington
Altoona
Brandywine
Hazleton
University Park
Wilkes-Barre
Worthington Scranton
Philadelphia Biblical University
Point Park University
Robert Morris University
Rosemont College
Saint Joseph's University
St. Vincent College
Seton Hill University
Swarthmore College
Temple University
Thomas Jefferson University: College of Health Professions
University of Pennsylvania
University of Pittsburgh
University of Pittsburgh
Greensburg
University of Scranton
University of the Sciences in Philadelphia
Valley Forge Military Academy & College
Villanova University
Washington & Jefferson College
Widener University
Wilkes University

Puerto Rico
Bayamon Central University
Caribbean University
Inter American University of Puerto Rico
Aguadilla Campus
Bayamon Campus
Fajardo Campus
Metropolitan Campus
San German Campus
Pontifical Catholic University of Puerto Rico
Universidad Metropolitana
Universidad Politecnica de Puerto Rico
University of Puerto Rico
Mayaguez
Rio Piedras

South Carolina
Anderson University
Benedict College
Charleston Southern University
The Citadel
Clemson University
College of Charleston
Midlands Technical College
South Carolina State University
Southern Wesleyan University
Tri-County Technical College
University of South Carolina
University of South Carolina
Salkehatchie Regional Campus

South Dakota
Dakota State University
South Dakota State University

Tennessee
Austin Peay State University
Belmont University
Carson-Newman College
Christian Brothers University
Free Will Baptist Bible College
LeMoyne-Owen College
Lipscomb University
Rhodes College
Roane State Community College
Southwest Tennessee Community College
Tennessee State University
Tennessee Technological University
Tennessee Wesleyan College
University of Memphis
University of Tennessee
Knoxville
Vanderbilt University

Texas
Angelo State University
Austin Community College
Baylor University
College of Saint Thomas More
Concordia University Texas
Dallas Baptist University
Houston Baptist University
Houston Community College System
Lon Morris College
McLennan Community College
Midwestern State University
North Central Texas College
Our Lady of the Lake University of San Antonio
Rice University
St. Edward's University
St. Mary's University
San Antonio College
San Jacinto College
Southern Methodist University
Tarrant County College
Texas A&M University
Texas Christian University
Texas Lutheran University
Texas State University: San Marcos
Texas Tech University
Texas Wesleyan University
Texas Woman's University
Trinity University
University of Dallas
University of Houston
University of Houston
Downtown
University of Mary Hardin-Baylor
University of North Texas
University of St. Thomas
University of Texas
Arlington
Austin
Dallas
El Paso
San Antonio
University of the Incarnate Word
Wayland Baptist University
Weatherford College

Utah
Brigham Young University
LDS Business College
Salt Lake Community College
University of Utah
Utah State University
Utah Valley University
Weber State University
Westminster College

Vermont
Lyndon State College
Norwich University
St. Michael's College

Virginia
George Mason University
James Madison University
Liberty University
Mary Baldwin College
Piedmont Virginia Community College
University of Virginia
Virginia Military Institute
Virginia Polytechnic Institute and State University

Washington
Central Washington University
Clark College
Highline Community College
Saint Martin's University
Seattle Pacific University
Seattle University
South Puget Sound Community College
Spokane Community College
University of Washington
Washington State University

West Virginia
Fairmont State University
Shepherd University
West Virginia University

Wisconsin
Alverno College
Carroll University
Carthage College
Maranatha Baptist Bible College
Marquette University
Milwaukee School of Engineering
University of Wisconsin
Madison
Milwaukee
Stout
Superior
Whitewater
Wisconsin Lutheran College

Wyoming
Laramie County Community College
University of Wyoming

Army ROTC

Alabama
Alabama Agricultural and Mechanical University
Alabama State University
Auburn University
Auburn University at Montgomery
Birmingham-Southern College
Bishop State Community College
Chattahoochee Valley Community College
Faulkner University
Gadsden State Community College
Huntingdon College
Jacksonville State University
Jefferson State Community College
Judson College
Marion Military Institute
Miles College
Northwest-Shoals Community College
Samford University
Shelton State Community College
Spring Hill College
Talladega College
Troy University
Tuskegee University
University of Alabama
University of Alabama
Birmingham
Huntsville
University of Mobile
University of Montevallo
University of North Alabama
University of South Alabama

Alaska
University of Alaska
Fairbanks

Arizona
Arizona State University
Coconino County Community College
Embry-Riddle Aeronautical University: Prescott Campus
Gateway Community College

Grand Canyon University
Mesa Community College
Northern Arizona University
Paradise Valley Community College
Phoenix College
Pima Community College
University of Arizona
Yavapai College

Arkansas
Arkansas State University
Arkansas State University
  Mountain Home
Arkansas Tech University
Central Baptist College
Henderson State University
Hendrix College
John Brown University
Northwest Arkansas Community College
Ouachita Baptist University
Ouachita Technical College
Philander Smith College
University of Arkansas
University of Arkansas
  Fort Smith
  Little Rock
  Monticello
  Pine Bluff
University of Central Arkansas
Williams Baptist College

California
Azusa Pacific University
Biola University
California Baptist University
California Institute of Technology
California Lutheran University
California Polytechnic State University: San Luis Obispo
California State Polytechnic University: Pomona
California State University
  Dominguez Hills
  Fresno
  Fullerton
  Long Beach
  Los Angeles
  Northridge
  Sacramento
  San Bernardino
  San Marcos
Chabot College
Chapman University
City College of San Francisco
Claremont McKenna College
College of San Mateo
Cuyamaca College
De Anza College
Diablo Valley College
El Camino College
Foothill College
Fresno City College
Harvey Mudd College
Holy Names University
The King's College and Seminary
Los Angeles City College
Los Angeles Mission College
Loyola Marymount University
Menlo College
MiraCosta College
Mount San Jacinto College
National Hispanic University
National University
Occidental College
Pepperdine University
Pitzer College
Point Loma Nazarene University
Pomona College
Riverside Community College
Sacramento City College
St. Mary's College of California
Samuel Merritt University
San Diego Christian College
San Diego City College
San Diego State University
San Francisco State University
San Jose State University
Santa Clara University
Scripps College
Simpson University
Sonoma State University
Stanford University
University of California
  Berkeley
  Davis
  Irvine
  Los Angeles
  Riverside
  Santa Barbara
  Santa Cruz
University of La Verne
University of Redlands
University of San Diego
University of San Francisco
University of Southern California
Vanguard University of Southern California
West Valley College
Westmont College
Whittier College

Colorado
Arapahoe Community College
Colorado Christian University
Colorado College
Colorado School of Mines
Colorado State University
Colorado State University
  Pueblo
Colorado Technical University
Community College of Denver
Front Range Community College
Metropolitan State College of Denver
Red Rocks Community College
Regis University
University of Colorado
  Boulder
  Colorado Springs
  Denver
University of Denver
University of Northern Colorado

Connecticut
Capital Community College
Central Connecticut State University
Eastern Connecticut State University
Fairfield University
Quinnipiac University
Sacred Heart University
Southern Connecticut State University
Trinity College
Tunxis Community College
University of Bridgeport
University of Connecticut
University of Hartford
Western Connecticut State University
Yale University

Delaware
Delaware State University
University of Delaware
Wesley College
Wilmington University

District of Columbia
American University
Catholic University of America
George Washington University
Georgetown University
Howard University
Trinity Washington University
University of the District of Columbia

Florida
Barry University
Bethune-Cookman University
Brevard Community College
Broward College
Clearwater Christian College
Daytona State College
Eckerd College
Embry-Riddle Aeronautical University
Florida Agricultural and Mechanical University
Florida Atlantic University
Florida College
Florida Institute of Technology
Florida International University
Florida Memorial University
Florida Southern College
Florida State University
Hillsborough Community College
Miami Dade College
Northwest Florida State College
Pasco-Hernando Community College
Pensacola Junior College
Polk Community College
St. Leo University
Santa Fe College
South Florida Community College
Southeastern University
Stetson University
Tallahassee Community College
University of Central Florida
University of Miami
University of South Florida
University of Tampa
University of West Florida
Valencia Community College

Georgia
Agnes Scott College
Albany State University
Armstrong Atlantic State University
Augusta State University
Clark Atlanta University
Clayton State University
Columbus State University
East Georgia College
Emory University
Fort Valley State University
Georgia College and State University
Georgia Institute of Technology
Georgia Military College
Georgia Southern University
Georgia State University
Kennesaw State University
Mercer University
Morehouse College
North Georgia College & State University
Paine College
Savannah College of Art and Design
Savannah State University
Southern Polytechnic State University
Spelman College
University of Georgia
University of West Georgia

Hawaii
Brigham Young University-Hawaii
Chaminade University of Honolulu
Hawaii Pacific University
University of Hawaii
  Honolulu Community College
  Leeward Community College
  Manoa
  West Oahu
  Windward Community College

Idaho
Boise State University
Brigham Young University-Idaho
College of Idaho
Idaho State University
Lewis-Clark State College
North Idaho College
Northwest Nazarene University
University of Idaho

Illinois
Aurora University
Benedictine University
Bradley University
Carl Sandburg College
Chicago State University
DePaul University
Eastern Illinois University
Elmhurst College
Governors State University
Illinois Institute of Technology
Illinois State University
Illinois Wesleyan University
John A. Logan College
Judson University
Kankakee Community College
Kishwaukee College
Lewis and Clark Community College
Lewis University
Lincoln Land Community College
Loyola University Chicago
McKendree University
Monmouth College
North Central College
North Park University
Northeastern Illinois University
Northern Illinois University
Northwestern University
Olivet Nazarene University
Parkland College
Robert Morris College: Chicago
Shawnee Community College
Southern Illinois University Carbondale
Southern Illinois University Edwardsville
Spoon River College
University of Chicago
University of Illinois
  Chicago
  Urbana-Champaign
Waubonsee Community College
Western Illinois University
Wheaton College

Indiana
Ball State University
Bethel College
Butler University
DePauw University
Franklin College
Holy Cross College
Indiana State University
Indiana University
  Bloomington
  Kokomo
  Northwest
  South Bend
  Southeast
Indiana University-Purdue University Fort Wayne
Indiana University-Purdue University Indianapolis
Indiana Wesleyan University
Marian College
Purdue University
Purdue University
  Calumet
Rose-Hulman Institute of Technology
St. Mary-of-the-Woods College
Saint Mary's College
University of Indianapolis
University of Notre Dame
University of Southern Indiana
Valparaiso University
Vincennes University

Iowa
Allen College
Briar Cliff University
Clarke College
Coe College
Drake University
Grand View University

Hawkeye Community College
Iowa State University
Iowa Western Community College
Loras College
University of Dubuque
University of Iowa
University of Northern Iowa

Kansas
Baker University
Benedictine College
Kansas State University
Manhattan Christian College
MidAmerica Nazarene University
Pittsburg State University
University of Kansas
University of St. Mary
Washburn University

Kentucky
Asbury College
Bellarmine University
Campbellsville University
Centre College
Eastern Kentucky University
Elizabethtown Community and Technical College
Georgetown College
Jefferson Community and Technical College
Kentucky Christian University
Kentucky State University
Kentucky Wesleyan College
Midway College
Morehead State University
Murray State University
Northern Kentucky University
Spalding University
Thomas More College
Transylvania University
Union College
University of Kentucky
University of Louisville
University of the Cumberlands
Western Kentucky University

Louisiana
Delgado Community College
Dillard University
Grambling State University
Louisiana College
Louisiana State University
Alexandria
Shreveport
Louisiana State University and Agricultural and Mechanical College
Louisiana Tech University
Loyola University New Orleans
Northwestern State University
Our Lady of Holy Cross College
Southeastern Louisiana University
Southern University
New Orleans
Southern University and Agricultural and Mechanical College
Tulane University
University of Louisiana at Lafayette
University of Louisiana at Monroe
University of New Orleans
Xavier University of Louisiana

Maine
Colby College
Husson University
Maine Maritime Academy
New England School of Communications
St. Joseph's College
Unity College
University of Maine
University of Maine
Augusta
University of New England
University of Southern Maine

Maryland
Allegany College of Maryland
Bowie State University
Capitol College
College of Notre Dame of Maryland
Coppin State University
Goucher College
Hood College
Johns Hopkins University
Loyola College in Maryland
Maryland Institute College of Art
McDaniel College
Morgan State University
Mount St. Mary's University
Prince George's Community College
Salisbury University
Stevenson University
Towson University
University of Baltimore
University of Maryland
Baltimore County
College Park

Massachusetts
American International College
Assumption College
Babson College
Bay Path College
Becker College
Bentley University
Boston College
Boston University
Brandeis University
Bridgewater State College
Clark University
College of the Holy Cross
Curry College
Elms College
Emmanuel College
Endicott College
Fitchburg State College
Framingham State College
Gordon College
Hampshire College
Harvard College
Holyoke Community College
Massachusetts College of Pharmacy and Health Sciences
Massachusetts Institute of Technology
Massachusetts Maritime Academy
Mount Holyoke College
Nichols College
Northeastern University
Pine Manor College
Quinsigamond Community College
Regis College
Roxbury Community College
Salem State College
Simmons College
Smith College
Springfield College
Stonehill College
Suffolk University
Tufts University
University of Massachusetts
Amherst
Boston
Dartmouth
Wellesley College
Wentworth Institute of Technology
Western New England College
Westfield State College
Wheaton College
Worcester Polytechnic Institute
Worcester State College
Zion Bible College

Michigan
Alma College
Calvin College
Central Michigan University
Concordia University
Eastern Michigan University
Ferris State University
Finlandia University
Grace Bible College
Hope College
Kalamazoo College
Kuyper College
Lansing Community College
Lawrence Technological University
Michigan State University
Michigan Technological University
Northern Michigan University
Spring Arbor University
University of Michigan
University of Michigan
Dearborn
Washtenaw Community College
Wayne State University
Western Michigan University

Minnesota
Anoka-Ramsey Community College
Augsburg College
Bethany Lutheran College
Bethel University
College of St. Benedict
College of St. Catherine
Concordia College: Moorhead
Concordia University: St. Paul
Gustavus Adolphus College
Lake Superior College
Macalester College
Minnesota State University
Mankato
Moorhead
Normandale Community College
North Hennepin Community College
Northwestern College
Saint Cloud State University
St. John's University
St. Mary's University of Minnesota
University of Minnesota
Twin Cities
University of St. Thomas
Winona State University

Mississippi
Alcorn State University
Belhaven College
Delta State University
Hinds Community College
Jackson State University
Millsaps College
Mississippi College
Mississippi State University
Mississippi University for Women
Mississippi Valley State University
Tougaloo College
University of Mississippi
University of Southern Mississippi
William Carey University

Missouri
Avila University
Calvary Bible College and Theological Seminary
Central Bible College
Central Methodist University
College of the Ozarks
Columbia College
Drury University
Evangel University
Fontbonne University
Harris-Stowe State University
Lincoln University
Lindenwood University
Maryville University of Saint Louis
Missouri Baptist University
Missouri State University
Missouri Valley College
Missouri Western State University
Northwest Missouri State University
Park University
Research College of Nursing
Rockhurst University
St. Louis Community College
Florissant Valley
Meramec
Saint Louis University
Southwest Baptist University
State Fair Community College
Stephens College
Truman State University
University of Central Missouri
University of Missouri
Columbia
Kansas City
Missouri University of Science and Technology
St. Louis
Washington University in St. Louis
Webster University
Wentworth Military Junior College
Westminster College
William Jewell College
William Woods University

Montana
Carroll College
Montana State University
Billings
Bozeman
University of Montana

Nebraska
Bellevue University
Chadron State College
Clarkson College
College of Saint Mary
Concordia University
Creighton University
Doane College
Nebraska Methodist College of Nursing and Allied Health
Nebraska Wesleyan University
University of Nebraska
Lincoln
Medical Center
Omaha
Wayne State College
York College

Nevada
College of Southern Nevada
Sierra Nevada College
Truckee Meadows Community College
University of Nevada
Las Vegas
Reno

New Hampshire
Colby-Sawyer College
Daniel Webster College
Dartmouth College
Franklin Pierce University
Granite State College
New England College
Plymouth State University
Rivier College
St. Anselm College
Southern New Hampshire University
University of New Hampshire
University of New Hampshire at Manchester

New Jersey
Bloomfield College
Brookdale Community College
Caldwell College
The College of New Jersey
Fairleigh Dickinson University
College at Florham
Metropolitan Campus
Kean University
Middlesex County College
Montclair State University
New Jersey Institute of Technology

Princeton University
Raritan Valley Community College
Rider University
Rowan University
Rutgers, The State University of New Jersey
Camden Regional Campus
New Brunswick/Piscataway Campus
Newark Regional Campus
Saint Peter's College
Seton Hall University
Stevens Institute of Technology

New Mexico
Central New Mexico Community College
Dona Ana Community College of New Mexico State University
New Mexico Military Institute
New Mexico State University
University of New Mexico

New York
Adelphi University
Albany College of Pharmacy and Health Sciences
Alfred University
Canisius College
Cazenovia College
City University of New York
Baruch College
Lehman College
Queens College
Clarkson University
Colgate University
College of New Rochelle
College of Saint Rose
Columbia University
Columbia University
School of General Studies
Cornell University
Daemen College
Dowling College
D'Youville College
Elmira College
Erie Community College
City Campus
North Campus
South Campus
Finger Lakes Community College
Fordham University
Hamilton College
Herkimer County Community College
Hilbert College
Hofstra University
Houghton College
Hudson Valley Community College
Iona College
Ithaca College
Jewish Theological Seminary of America
Le Moyne College
Long Island University
Brooklyn Campus
C. W. Post Campus
Manhattan College
Maria College
Marist College
Medaille College
Mercy College
Mohawk Valley Community College
Molloy College
Monroe College
Monroe Community College
Nassau Community College
Nazareth College
New York Institute of Technology
New York University
Niagara County Community College
Niagara University
Onondaga Community College
Orange County Community College
Pace University
Polytechnic Institute of New York University
Rensselaer Polytechnic Institute
Roberts Wesleyan College
Rochester Institute of Technology
Russell Sage College
Sage College of Albany
Saint Bonaventure University
St. Francis College
St. John Fisher College
St. John's University
St. Joseph's College: Suffolk Campus
St. Lawrence University
Siena College
Skidmore College
State University of New York
Albany
Binghamton
Buffalo
College at Brockport
College at Buffalo
College at Cortland
College at Geneseo
College at Old Westbury
College at Plattsburgh
College at Potsdam
College of Agriculture and Technology at Morrisville
College of Environmental Science and Forestry
College of Technology at Alfred
College of Technology at Canton
Institute of Technology at Utica/Rome
Maritime College
Oswego
Stony Brook
Upstate Medical University
Syracuse University
Union College
University of Rochester
Utica College
Vaughn College of Aeronautics and Technology
Wagner College
Wells College

North Carolina
Appalachian State University
Belmont Abbey College
Bennett College for Women
Campbell University
Catawba College
College of the Albemarle
Davidson College
Duke University
East Carolina University
Elizabeth City State University
Elon University
Fayetteville State University
Gardner-Webb University
Greensboro College
Guilford College
Guilford Technical Community College
High Point University
Johnson C. Smith University
Lenoir Rhyne University
Livingstone College
Meredith College
Methodist University
North Carolina Agricultural and Technical State University
North Carolina Central University
North Carolina State University
North Carolina Wesleyan College
Peace College
Pfeiffer University
Pitt Community College
Queens University of Charlotte
St. Augustine's College
Salem College
Shaw University
University of North Carolina
Chapel Hill
Charlotte
Greensboro
Pembroke
Wake Forest University
Wingate University
Winston-Salem State University

North Dakota
Mayville State University
North Dakota State University
University of North Dakota

Ohio
Baldwin-Wallace College
Bowling Green State University
Capital University
Case Western Reserve University
Cedarville University
Central State University
Cincinnati State Technical and Community College
Cleveland Institute of Art
Cleveland State University
College of Mount St. Joseph
Columbus State Community College
Denison University
DeVry University
Columbus
Franciscan University of Steubenville
Franklin University
Heidelberg University
Hocking College
John Carroll University
Kent State University
Kent State University
Ashtabula
East Liverpool
Salem
Stark
Trumbull
Tuscarawas
Lourdes College
Malone University
Miami University
Oxford Campus
Mount Union College
Notre Dame College
Ohio Dominican University
Ohio Northern University
Ohio State University
Columbus Campus
Lima Campus
Mansfield Campus
Marion Campus
Newark Campus
Ohio University
Ohio University
Lancaster Campus
Ohio Wesleyan University
Otterbein College
Owens Community College
Toledo
Sinclair Community College
Tiffin University
University of Akron
University of Akron: Wayne College
University of Cincinnati
University of Cincinnati
Clermont College
Raymond Walters College
University of Dayton
University of Findlay
University of Rio Grande
University of Toledo
Urbana University
Ursuline College
Wilberforce University
Wittenberg University
Wright State University
Xavier University
Youngstown State University

Oklahoma
Cameron University
Langston University
Northeastern State University
Oklahoma Christian University
Oklahoma City University
Oklahoma State University
Southern Nazarene University
University of Central Oklahoma
University of Oklahoma

Oregon
Central Oregon Community College
Corban College
Eastern Oregon University
Linn-Benton Community College
Northwest Christian University
Oregon Institute of Technology
Oregon State University
Pacific University
Portland State University
University of Oregon
University of Portland
Warner Pacific College
Western Oregon University

Pennsylvania
Alvernia University
Arcadia University
Bloomsburg University of Pennsylvania
Bucknell University
Cabrini College
California University of Pennsylvania
Carlow University
Carnegie Mellon University
Cedar Crest College
Chatham University
Cheyney University of Pennsylvania
Clarion University of Pennsylvania
Community College of Philadelphia
DeSales University
Dickinson College
Drexel University
Duquesne University
East Stroudsburg University of Pennsylvania
Eastern University
Edinboro University of Pennsylvania
Gannon University
Geneva College
Gettysburg College
Harrisburg Area Community College
Indiana University of Pennsylvania
Keystone College
King's College
Kutztown University of Pennsylvania
La Roche College
La Salle University
Lackawanna College
Lafayette College
Lebanon Valley College
Lehigh Carbon Community College
Lehigh University
Lincoln University
Lock Haven University of Pennsylvania
Lycoming College
Marywood University
Millersville University of Pennsylvania
Misericordia University
Moravian College
Muhlenberg College
Neumann College
Penn State
Abington
Altoona
Berks
Brandywine
Erie, The Behrend College
Harrisburg
Hazleton
Lehigh Valley
Mont Alto
University Park
Wilkes-Barre
Worthington Scranton
Pennsylvania College of Technology

Point Park University
Robert Morris University
Rosemont College
St. Francis University
Saint Joseph's University
St. Vincent College
Seton Hill University
Shippensburg University of Pennsylvania
Slippery Rock University of Pennsylvania
Susquehanna University
Swarthmore College
Temple University
University of Pennsylvania
University of Pittsburgh
University of Pittsburgh
  Bradford
  Greensburg
University of Scranton
University of the Sciences in Philadelphia
Valley Forge Military Academy & College
Villanova University
Washington & Jefferson College
Waynesburg University
West Chester University of Pennsylvania
Westminster College
Widener University
Wilkes University
Wilson College
York College of Pennsylvania

Puerto Rico
American University of Puerto Rico
Bayamon Central University
Caribbean University
Inter American University of Puerto Rico
  Aguadilla Campus
  Arecibo Campus
  Bayamon Campus
  Guayama Campus
  Metropolitan Campus
  San German Campus
Pontifical Catholic University of Puerto Rico
Turabo University
Universidad del Este
Universidad Metropolitana
Universidad Politecnica de Puerto Rico
University of Puerto Rico
  Aguadilla
  Arecibo
  Bayamon University College
  Cayey University College
  Mayaguez
  Ponce
  Rio Piedras
  Utuado

Rhode Island
Brown University
Bryant University
Community College of Rhode Island
Johnson & Wales University: Providence
Providence College
Rhode Island College
Roger Williams University
Salve Regina University
University of Rhode Island

South Carolina
Allen University
Anderson University
Benedict College
The Citadel
Claflin University
Clemson University
Coastal Carolina University
Columbia College
Converse College
Denmark Technical College
Furman University
Lander University
Limestone College
Midlands Technical College
Morris College
Newberry College
North Greenville University
Orangeburg-Calhoun Technical College
Presbyterian College
South Carolina State University
Southern Wesleyan University
Spartanburg Methodist College
Tri-County Technical College
University of South Carolina
University of South Carolina
  Lancaster
  Salkehatchie Regional Campus
  Sumter
  Upstate
Winthrop University
Wofford College

South Dakota
Black Hills State University
Dakota State University
Mount Marty College
National American University
  Rapid City
South Dakota School of Mines and Technology
South Dakota State University
University of South Dakota

Tennessee
Austin Peay State University
Belmont University
Carson-Newman College
Christian Brothers University
Cumberland University
East Tennessee State University
Fisk University
Free Will Baptist Bible College
Jackson State Community College
King College
Lambuth University
LeMoyne-Owen College
Lipscomb University
Middle Tennessee State University
Milligan College
Pellissippi State Technical Community College
Rhodes College
Roane State Community College
Southwest Tennessee Community College
Tennessee Technological University
Tennessee Wesleyan College
Trevecca Nazarene University
University of Memphis
University of Tennessee
  Chattanooga
  Knoxville
  Martin
Vanderbilt University
Walters State Community College

Texas
Angelina College
Austin Community College
Baylor University
Central Texas College
College of Saint Thomas More
Collin County Community College District
Concordia University Texas
Dallas Baptist University
Del Mar College
El Centro College
El Paso Community College
Houston Baptist University
Houston Community College System
Huston-Tillotson University
Laredo Community College
Lon Morris College
Lubbock Christian University
Our Lady of the Lake University of San Antonio
Prairie View A&M University
Rice University
St. Edward's University
St. Mary's University
St. Philip's College
Sam Houston State University
San Antonio College
Southern Methodist University
Southwestern Assemblies of God University
Stephen F. Austin State University
Tarleton State University
Tarrant County College
Texas A&M University
Texas A&M University
  Corpus Christi
  Kingsville
Texas Christian University
Texas Lutheran University
Texas Southern University
Texas State University: San Marcos
Texas Tech University
Texas Wesleyan University
Texas Woman's University
University of Dallas
University of Houston
University of Houston
  Downtown
University of North Texas
University of St. Thomas
University of Texas
  Arlington
  Austin
  Brownsville - Texas Southmost College
  Dallas
  El Paso
  Pan American
  San Antonio
University of the Incarnate Word
Wayland Baptist University

Utah
Brigham Young University
Dixie State College of Utah
LDS Business College
Salt Lake Community College
Southern Utah University
University of Utah
Utah State University
Utah Valley University
Weber State University
Westminster College

Vermont
Castleton State College
Champlain College
Johnson State College
Middlebury College
Norwich University
St. Michael's College
University of Vermont
Vermont Technical College

Virginia
Christopher Newport University
College of William and Mary
George Mason University
Hampden-Sydney College
Hampton University
J. Sargeant Reynolds Community College
James Madison University
John Tyler Community College
Liberty University
Longwood University
Lynchburg College
Mary Baldwin College
Marymount University
Norfolk State University
Old Dominion University
Piedmont Virginia Community College
Radford University
Randolph-Macon College
Regent University
Richard Bland College
St. Paul's College
Southern Virginia University
Southside Virginia Community College
Thomas Nelson Community College
University of Mary Washington
University of Richmond
University of Virginia
Virginia Commonwealth University
Virginia Military Institute
Virginia Polytechnic Institute and State University
Virginia State University
Virginia Union University
Virginia Wesleyan College
Washington and Lee University

Washington
Central Washington University
Clark College
  Federal Way
Eastern Washington University
Gonzaga University
Highline Community College
Northwest University
Pacific Lutheran University
Pierce College
Saint Martin's University
Seattle Pacific University
Seattle University
Spokane Community College
Spokane Falls Community College
University of Puget Sound
University of Washington
Washington State University
Whitworth University

West Virginia
Fairmont State University
Marshall University
University of Charleston
West Liberty State College
West Virginia State University
West Virginia University
West Virginia University Institute of Technology

Wisconsin
Alverno College
Carroll University
Carthage College
Edgewood College
Maranatha Baptist Bible College
Marian University
Marquette University
Milwaukee School of Engineering
Mount Mary College
Ripon College
St. Norbert College
University of Wisconsin
  Eau Claire
  Green Bay
  La Crosse
  Madison
  Milwaukee
  Oshkosh
  Parkside
  River Falls
  Stevens Point
  Stout
  Whitewater
Viterbo University
Wisconsin Lutheran College

Wyoming
Laramie County Community College
University of Wyoming

Naval ROTC

Alabama
Auburn University

Arizona
Gateway Community College
Mesa Community College

Pima Community College
Southwestern College
University of Arizona

California
California Maritime Academy
California State University
    San Marcos
Contra Costa College
Diablo Valley College
Foothill College
Fullerton College
The King's College and Seminary
Los Angeles City College
Mission College
National Hispanic University
National University
Point Loma Nazarene University
Riverside Community College
Sacramento City College
Samuel Merritt University
San Diego State University
San Francisco State University
Sonoma State University
Stanford University
University of California
    Berkeley
    Davis
    Los Angeles
    Santa Cruz
University of Redlands
University of San Diego
University of Southern California

Colorado
Regis University
University of Colorado
    Boulder

Connecticut
Capital Community College
Tunxis Community College

District of Columbia
Catholic University of America
George Washington University
Georgetown University
University of the District of Columbia

Florida
Clearwater Christian College
Embry-Riddle Aeronautical University
Florida Agricultural and Mechanical University
Florida Community College at Jacksonville
Florida State University
Jacksonville University
Pasco-Hernando Community College
Tallahassee Community College
University of North Florida
University of South Florida
University of Tampa

Georgia
Armstrong Atlantic State University
Clark Atlanta University
Clayton State University
Emory University
Georgia Institute of Technology
Georgia State University
Morehouse College
Savannah State University
Southern Polytechnic State University
Spelman College

Hawaii
Brigham Young University-Hawaii
University of Hawaii
    Hawaii Community College

Idaho
Lewis-Clark State College
University of Idaho

Illinois
Illinois Institute of Technology
Judson University
Lincoln Land Community College
Loyola University Chicago
Northwestern University
Parkland College
Shawnee Community College
University of Illinois
    Chicago
    Urbana-Champaign

Indiana
Bethel College
Indiana University
    South Bend
Indiana University-Purdue University
  Indianapolis
Purdue University
Saint Mary's College
University of Notre Dame

Iowa
Hawkeye Community College
Iowa State University

Kansas
University of Kansas
Washburn University

Louisiana
Dillard University
Louisiana State University and Agricultural and
  Mechanical College
Louisiana Tech University
Loyola University New Orleans
Our Lady of Holy Cross College
Southern University
    New Orleans
Southern University and Agricultural and
  Mechanical College
Tulane University
University of New Orleans
Xavier University of Louisiana

Maine
Husson University
Maine Maritime Academy
University of Maine
University of Maine
    Augusta

Maryland
University of Maryland
    College Park

Massachusetts
Babson College
Becker College
Boston College
Boston University
Clark University
College of the Holy Cross
Harvard College
Massachusetts College of Pharmacy and Health
  Sciences
Massachusetts Institute of Technology
Massachusetts Maritime Academy
Northeastern University
Tufts University
University of Massachusetts
    Boston
Worcester Polytechnic Institute
Worcester State College

Michigan
Eastern Michigan University
Finlandia University
Lawrence Technological University
University of Michigan
University of Michigan
    Dearborn

Minnesota
Anoka-Ramsey Community College
Augsburg College
Concordia University: St. Paul
Lake Superior College
Macalester College
Normandale Community College
North Hennepin Community College
University of Minnesota
    Twin Cities
University of St. Thomas

Mississippi
East Mississippi Community College
Tougaloo College
University of Mississippi

Missouri
Columbia College
Lincoln University
Stephens College
University of Missouri
    Columbia
    Missouri University of Science and
      Technology
William Woods University

Montana
Montana State University
    Billings

Nebraska
University of Nebraska
    Lincoln
York College

New Hampshire
Rivier College

New Jersey
Montclair State University

New Mexico
Central New Mexico Community College
National American University: Rio Rancho
University of New Mexico

New York
Albany College of Pharmacy and Health
  Sciences
City University of New York
    Queens College
College of New Rochelle
College of Saint Rose
Columbia University
Cornell University
Dowling College
Eastman School of Music of the University of
  Rochester
Fordham University
Jewish Theological Seminary of America
Maria College
Molloy College
Monroe Community College
New York University
Rensselaer Polytechnic Institute
Rochester Institute of Technology
Russell Sage College
St. John Fisher College
Siena College
State University of New York
    College at Brockport
    Maritime College
Union College
University of Rochester

North Carolina
Belmont Abbey College
Duke University
Guilford College
Guilford Technical Community College
Lenoir-Rhyne University
North Carolina State University
Peace College
University of North Carolina
    Chapel Hill

Ohio
Cleveland Institute of Art
Cleveland State University
Cuyahoga Community College
    Metropolitan Campus
Miami University
    Hamilton Campus
    Middletown Campus
    Oxford Campus
Ohio State University
    Columbus Campus
    Lima Campus
    Mansfield Campus
    Marion Campus
    Newark Campus
Ohio University
    Lancaster Campus
University of Cincinnati
    Raymond Walters College

Oklahoma
University of Oklahoma

Oregon
Oregon State University
Warner Pacific College
Western Oregon University

Pennsylvania
Carlow University
Carnegie Mellon University
Chatham University
Drexel University
Duquesne University
Penn State
    University Park
Saint Joseph's University
Swarthmore College
Temple University
Thomas Jefferson University: College of Health
  Professions
University of Pennsylvania
University of Pittsburgh
Villanova University
Widener University

Puerto Rico
Caribbean University
Inter American University of Puerto Rico
    Bayamon Campus
    Ponce Campus
Universidad Metropolitana

South Carolina
The Citadel
Midlands Technical College
University of South Carolina
University of South Carolina
    Salkehatchie Regional Campus

Tennessee
Belmont University
Christian Brothers University
Fisk University
Tennessee Wesleyan College
University of Memphis
Vanderbilt University

Texas
Houston Baptist University
Lon Morris College
Prairie View A&M University
Rice University
Texas A&M University
Texas A&M University
    Galveston
University of Houston
University of Texas
    Austin

Utah
University of Utah
Weber State University
Westminster College

Vermont
Norwich University

Virginia
George Mason University
Hampton University
Mary Baldwin College
New River Community College
Norfolk State University
Old Dominion University
University of Virginia
Virginia Military Institute
Virginia Polytechnic Institute and State University

Washington
Seattle Pacific University
Seattle University
Spokane Community College
University of Washington
Washington State University

Wisconsin
Marquette University
Milwaukee School of Engineering
Mount Mary College
University of Wisconsin
Madison
Wisconsin Lutheran College

Glossary

Academic Competitiveness Grant. A federal financial aid award to students in their first two years of undergraduate study who are eligible for a Pell Grant and have successfully completed a rigorous high school academic program, as determined by their state or local education agency. The maximum award is $750 for the first year of undergraduate study and $1,300 for the second year, both of which are in addition to the Pell Grant award.

Accelerated program. A college program of study completed in less time than is usually required, most often by attending classes in summer or by taking extra courses during the regular academic terms.

Accreditation. A process that ensures that a college meets acceptable standards in its programs, facilities, and services. Only colleges that are accredited by an agency recognized by the U.S. Department of Education may distribute federal financial aid to their students. Every college described in this book is accredited by such an agency.

Advanced placement. Admission or assignment of a first-year college student to an advanced course in a certain subject on the basis of evidence that he or she has already completed the equivalent of the college's course in that subject.

Advanced Placement Program® (AP®). An academic program of the College Board that provides high school students with the opportunity to study and learn at the college level. The AP Program offers more than 30 courses and exams in a wide variety of subject areas.

AmeriCorps. A national network of community service programs for which people volunteer and from which they earn an education award that can used to pay for college or pay back student loans.

Articulation agreement. A formal agreement between two higher-education institutions, stating specific policies relating to transfer of credits and recognition of academic achievement in order to facilitate the successful transfer of students without duplication of course work.

Associate degree. A degree granted by a college or university upon completion of a two-year, full-time program of study or its part-time equivalent. In general, the associate of arts (A.A.) or associate of science (A.S.) program is similar to the first two years of a four-year college curriculum. The associate in applied science (A.A.S.) is awarded by many colleges on completion of technological or vocational programs of study.

Award letter. A means of notifying admitted students of the financial aid being offered by the college or university. The award letter provides information on the types and amounts of aid offered, as well as the students' responsibilities, and the conditions governing the awards. Usually the award letter gives students the opportunity to accept or decline the aid offered, and a deadline by which to respond.

Bachelor's degree. A degree received upon completion of a four- or five-year full-time program of study (or its part-time equivalent) at a college or university. The bachelor of arts (B.A.), bachelor of science (B.S.), and bachelor of fine arts (B.F.A.) are the most common such degrees. College catalogs describe the types of degrees awarded in each major.

Bursar. The college official responsible for handling billing and payments for tuition, fees, housing, etc.

Business college. A college that primarily prepares students to work in an office or entrepreneurial setting. The curriculum may focus on management, clerical positions, or both.

Campus-based programs. Federal financial aid programs that are administered directly by the college's financial aid office, which awards these funds to students using federal guidelines. Includes the Federal Supplemental Educational Opportunity Grant Program, Federal Perkins Loan Program, and the Federal Work-Study Program.

Candidates' reply date. The date by which admitted students must accept or decline an offer of admission and (if any) the college's offer of financial aid. Most colleges and universities follow the College Board-sponsored Candidates' Reply Date Agreement (CRDA), under which they agree to not require a decision from applicants for admission in the fall semester before May 1. The purpose of this agreement is to give applicants time to hear from all the colleges to which they have applied before having to make a commitment to any of them.

Certificate. An award for completing a particular program or course of study, sometimes given by two-year colleges or vocational or technical schools.

CLEP®. See *College-Level Examination Program®*.

College-Level Examination Program (CLEP). Thirty-four examinations in undergraduate college courses that provide students of any age the opportunity to demonstrate college-level achievement, thereby reducing costs and time to degree completion. The examinations, which are sponsored by the College Board, are administered at colleges year-round via computer, providing test-takers with instant score results.

Community/junior college. A college offering two-year programs leading to an associate degree. Community colleges are public institutions, while junior colleges are privately operated on a not-for-profit basis. Most two-year colleges offer both vocational programs (also called "career" or "terminal" programs), as well as the first two years of a four-year program ("academic" or "transfer" programs). Students in the vocational program usually go directly into a career after graduation, while students in the academic program usually intend to transfer to a four-year institution or an upper-division college.

Comprehensive fee. If the college combines tuition, fees, room, and board expenses, that single figure is called a comprehensive fee.

Consortium. A group of colleges and universities that share a common geographic location. Consortiums of colleges in the same town often allow students at one institution to take classes at neighboring consortium colleges and use facilities such as libraries at the member colleges. Larger consortiums, at the state or regional level, may offer in-state tuition to out-of-state students.

Cooperative education (co-op). A program in which students alternate class attendance and employment in business, industry, or government. Co-op students are typically paid for their work and may receive academic credit for their participation in the program. Under a cooperative plan, five years are normally required for completion of a bachelor's degree, but graduates have the advantage of about a year's practical work experience in addition to their studies.

Core curriculum. A group of courses, usually in the liberal arts, designated by a college as one of the requirements for a degree. Some colleges have both core-curriculum requirements and general-education requirements.

Cost of attendance. A number of expenses, among them tuition and fees (including loan fees), books and supplies, and the student's living expenses while attending school. The cost of attendance is estimated by the school, within guidelines established by federal regulation. The cost of attendance is compared with the student's expected family contribution to determine the student's need for financial aid.

Coverdell Education Savings Account (ESA). A federal income-tax provision (formerly referred to as the Education IRA) that enables taxpayers to establish a college savings plan. A maximum of $2,000 may be contributed annually to the account, which earns interest and/or dividends on a tax-free basis.

Credit/placement by examination. Academic credit or placement out of introductory courses granted by a college to entering students who have demonstrated proficiency in college-level studies through examinations such as those administered by the College Board's AP and CLEP programs.

Credit Hour. The standard unit of measurement for a college course. Each credit hour requires one classroom hour per week. Most college courses are offered in one to five credit-hour increments. For financial aid purposes, students taking at least 12 credit hours of classes in a semester are considered to be attending the college full-time, and students taking at least six credit hours are considered half-time.

CSS code. A four-digit College Board number that students use to designate colleges or scholarship programs to receive their CSS/Financial Aid PROFILE information. If a college requires financial aid applicants to submit the PROFILE, its CSS code will appear in its description in Part III of this book. A complete list of all CSS codes can also be downloaded from the CSS/Financial Aid PROFILE Web site.

CSS/Financial Aid PROFILE®. A Web-based application service offered by the College Board and used by some colleges, universities, and private scholarship programs to award their private financial aid funds. Students complete the online application and supplements, if required. CSS processes and reports the application data to institutions. CSS/Financial Aid PROFILE is not a federal form and may not be used to apply for federal student aid.

Deferred admission. Postponing enrollment, usually for one year, after being accepted for admission by a college.

Dependent student. For financial aid purposes, such students are either under the age of 24, attend an undergraduate program, are not married, do not have children of their own, are not orphans or wards of the court, or veterans of the active-duty armed services. The term is used to define eligibility for certain financial aid programs, regardless of whether or not the student lives with a parent, receives financial support from a parent, or is claimed on a parent's tax return. If a student is defined as dependent, parental financial information must be supplied on the Free Application for Federal Student Aid, (FAFSA), and institutional aid applications.

Direct Loan Program. See *Federal Direct Loan Program.*

District. See *In-district tuition.*

Dual enrollment. The practice in which a student enrolls in college courses while still in high school, earning both high school and college credit for his or her work.

Early Action. A nonbinding early-decision program in which a student can receive an admission decision from one or more colleges and universities earlier than the standard response date but is not required to accept the admission offer or to make a deposit before May 1. Compare to *Early Decision*, which is a binding program.

Early action single choice. An early-action program in which the student may only apply early action to one college or university.

Early Decision. A binding program where students can receive an admission decision from one college or university before applications are due for regular admission. Participating students commit to enroll at the college if admitted and offered a satisfactory financial aid package.

Elective. A course, not required for one's chosen major or the college's core curriculum, that is selected to fulfill credit hours required for graduation.

Employer tuition assistance. Money that employers offer to employees or their dependents for use in paying education costs. Tuition assistance is considered an outside resource when colleges award financial aid.

Expected family contribution (EFC). The total amount students and their families are expected to pay toward college costs from their income and assets for one academic year. The amount is derived from a need analysis of the family's overall financial circumstances. The *federal methodology* is used to determine a student's eligibility for federal and state student aid. Colleges and private aid programs may use a different methodology to determine eligibility for nonfederal financial aid. Frequently, these private institutions use the *institutional methodology.*

FAFSA. See *Free Application for Federal Student Aid.*

FAFSA on the Web. An electronic option for completing the Free Application for Federal Student Aid (www.fafsa.ed.gov).

Family Educational Rights and Privacy Act (FERPA). A federal law that protects the privacy of student education records. The law applies to all schools that receive funds under an applicable program of the U.S. Department of Education. FERPA gives parents certain rights with respect to their children's education records. These rights transfer to the student when he or she reaches the age of 18 or attends a school beyond the high school level.

Federal code number. A six-digit number that identifies a specific college to which students want their

FAFSA information submitted. Each college's federal code appears in its profile in Part III of this book. Formerly known as the Title IV code.

Federal Direct Loan Program. A program that allows participating schools to administer subsidized and unsubsidized Stafford and PLUS loans directly to student and parent borrowers. Direct loans have mostly the same terms and conditions as FFELP loans. Funds for these programs are provided by the federal government.

Federal Family Education Loan Program (FFELP). The subsidized and unsubsidized Federal Stafford Loan, PLUS Loan, and Loan Consolidation programs. Funds for these programs are provided by lenders, and the loans are guaranteed by the federal government.

Federal methodology (FM). A need-analysis formula used by colleges and universities to determine students' financial need for the purpose of awarding federal financial aid. Most colleges also use this methodology to determine need for the purpose of awarding their own institutional funds, but some colleges use the *institutional methodology* for that. The federal methodology uses information submitted by students on the FAFSA to assess their ability to pay for college and calculate their expected family contribution.

Federal Parents' Loan for Undergraduate Students (PLUS). A program that permits parents of undergraduate students to borrow up to the full cost of education, less any other financial aid the student may have received.

Federal Pell Grant Program. A federally sponsored and administered program that provides need-based grants to undergraduate students. Congress annually sets the dollar range. As of July 1, 2008, a Pell Grant cannot exceed $4,731 per year. Eligibility for Pell Grants is based on a student's expected family contribution, the total cost of attendance at the college, and whether the student is attending the college full-time or part-time.

Federal Perkins Loan Program. A federally funded campus-based program that provides low-interest student loans. The maximum amount of loan funds available to an individual for undergraduate and graduate education is $40,000. Repayment need not begin until completion of the student's education, and it may be deferred for limited periods of service in the military, Peace Corps, or approved comparable organizations. The total debt may be forgiven by the federal government if the recipient enters a career of service as a public health nurse, law enforcement officer, public school teacher, or social worker.

Federal Stafford Loan. A program that allows students to borrow money for educational expenses from banks and other lending institutions (and sometimes from the colleges themselves). Subsidized Stafford loans are offered by colleges based on need. The federal government pays the interest on subsidized loans while the borrower is in college, and repayment does not begin until completion of the student's education. Unsubsidized Stafford loans are non-need-based; anyone may apply for one regardless of their ability to pay for college. The interest on unsubsidized loans begins accumulating immediately. For both programs, the amounts that may be borrowed depend on the student's year in school.

Federal student aid. A number of programs sponsored by the federal government that award students loans, grants, or work-study jobs for the purpose of meeting their financial need. To receive any federal student aid, a student must demonstrate financial need by filing the Free Application for Federal Student Aid and meet certain other eligibility requirements.

Federal Supplemental Educational Opportunity Grant Program (SEOG). A federal campus-based program that provides need-based grants of up to $4,000 a year for undergraduate study. Each college is given a certain total amount of SEOG money each year to distribute among their financial aid applicants and determines the amount to which the student is entitled.

Federal Work-Study Program. A campus-based financial aid program that allows students to meet some of their financial need by working on- or off-campus while attending school. The wages earned are used to help pay the student's educational costs for the academic year. Job opportunities vary from campus to campus. The time commitment for a work-study job is usually between 10 and 15 hours each week.

Fee waiver. The waiver that significantly reduces the amount a student must pay for an application for admission, application for institutional financial aid, standardized tests, or other college-related expenses. Fee waivers are most commonly awarded to low-income students, but are sometimes also awarded to students who are senior citizens or in the military. See also *Tuition and fee waiver.*

Financial aid. Money awarded to students to help them pay for college. Financial aid comes in the form of gifts (scholarships and grants) and self-help aid (loans and work-study opportunities). Most aid is awarded on the basis of financial need, but some awards are non-need-based. Both need-based and non-need-based aid may or may not be offered on the additional basis of merit.

Financial aid application form. A form that collects information on the student, his or her income and assets, and (for dependent students) his or her parents' income and assets.

Financial aid award letter. See *Award letter.*

Financial aid package. The total financial aid offered to a student by a college, including all loans, grants, scholarships, and work-study opportunities.

Financial aid PROFILE. See *CSS/Financial Aid PROFILE.*

Financial need. The difference between the total cost of attending a college and a student's expected family contribution (EFC). Financial aid grants, loans, and work-study will be offered by each college to fill all or a portion of the student's need.

529 Plan. See *Section 529 Plan.*

Fixed interest rate. An interest rate on a loan that is fixed for the lifetime of the loan. Compare to *Variable interest rate.*

For-profit college/university. A higher-education institution not supported by taxes and operated as a for-profit business, either as a publicly traded corporation or as a privately held company. Sometimes referred to as a "proprietary" college.

Free Application for Federal Student Aid (FAFSA). A form completed by all applicants for federal student aid. The FAFSA is also available on the Web, at www.fafsa.ed.gov. In many states, completion of the FAFSA is also sufficient to establish eligibility for state-sponsored aid programs. There is no charge for completing the FAFSA, and you can file it anytime after January 1 of the year for which you are seeking aid (e.g., after January 1, 2010, for the academic year 2010–2011).

Full need. A student's entire financial need at a college. A college that offers a financial aid package covering the complete difference between the cost of attendance and the expected family contribution is "meeting full need." See also *Gapping.*

Full-time status. Enrollment at a college or university for 12 or more credit hours per semester. Students must be enrolled full-time to qualify for the maximum award available to them from federal grant programs.

Gapping. A practice by which a college does not meet the full financial need of an admitted student, leaving a gap that must be filled by the student's own financial resources, in addition to the student's expected family contribution.

General education requirements. Courses that give undergraduates a background in all major academic disciplines: natural sciences, social sciences, mathematics, literature, language, and fine arts. Most colleges have general education requirements that students complete in their first and second years, giving students a chance to sample a wide range of courses before selecting a major. At some colleges, general education courses are referred to as the core curriculum; at others, a few courses within the general education requirements are core courses that all students must take.

Gift aid. Financial aid in the form of scholarships or grants that do not have to be repaid.

Grant. A financial aid award given to a student that does not have to be paid back. The terms "grant" and "scholarship" are often used interchangeably to refer to gift aid, but grants tend to be awarded solely on the basis of financial need, while scholarships may require the student to demonstrate merit.

Half-time status. Enrollment at a college or university for at least 6 credit hours per semester, but fewer than the 12 credit hours required to qualify as full-time. Students must be enrolled at least half-time to qualify for federal student aid loan programs.

Health sciences college. An institution of higher education that primarily prepares students to enter work in a clinic, hospital, or private medical practice. For a complete description of health-related fields of study, see the *College Board Book of Majors*.

HOPE Education Tax Credit. A federal income tax credit of as much as $1,800 per dependent student annually. It is available to eligible taxpayers based on out-of-pocket tuition and fee expenditures for the first two years of undergraduate study, according to income eligibility guidelines. See also *Lifetime Learning Tax Credit*.

Independent student. For financial aid purposes, a student who is either 24 years old or older, married, a veteran, an orphan, or has legal dependents. Independent students do not need to provide parental information to be considered for federal financial aid programs. However, private institutions may require independent students to provide parental information on their institutional forms in order to be considered for nonfederal sources of funding.

In-district tuition. The tuition charged by a community college or state university to residents of the district from which it draws tax support. Districts are usually individual counties or cities, but sometimes are larger.

Individual Retirement Account (IRA). A retirement account that earns income tax-free. Money withdrawn for college expenses is not charged the penalty that normally would be incurred for withdrawing IRA money before age 59½, but is taxed as regular income.

In-state tuition. The tuition that a public institution charges residents of its state. Some community colleges and state universities charge this rate to students who are not residents of their district, but who are residents of their state.

Institutional form. A financial aid application form custom-made by a particular college or university. Some institutional forms are designed to collect additional information on a family's finances beyond what is collected on the FAFSA, and are required of all financial aid applicants. Others serve specific purposes and are only required from certain students, for example early-decision applicants or student athletes.

Institutional methodology (IM). A need-analysis formula used by some colleges and universities to determine students' financial need and award their own institutional funds. Compared to the *federal methodology*, the IM takes into account a broader and deeper picture of family assets to determine a student's expected family contribution. Most colleges that use the IM collect this additional information through the CSS/Financial Aid PROFILE form, but some collect it using their own customized institutional forms.

International Baccalaureate (IB). A high school curriculum offered by some schools in the United States and other countries. Some colleges award credit for completion of this curriculum. Please visit the organization's Web site for further information.

Internship. Any short-term, supervised work, usually related to a student's major, for which academic credit is earned. The work can be full- or part-time, on or off campus, paid or unpaid. Some majors require the student to complete an internship.

Junior college. See *Community/junior college*.

Lender. An organization authorized to make educational loans to students.

Liberal arts. The study of the humanities (literature, the arts, and philosophy), history, foreign languages, social sciences, mathematics, and natural sciences. Liberal arts study guides students in developing general knowledge and reasoning ability rather than specific skills.

Liberal arts college. A college that emphasizes the liberal arts in its core curriculum and academic offerings and does not offer vocation or professional programs.

Lifetime Learning Tax Credit. A federal income tax credit of as much as $2,000 per household annually; available to eligible taxpayers based on "out-of-pocket" tuition and fee expenditures, according to income eligibility guidelines. Unlike the HOPE Education Tax Credit, it can be used for any year of postsecondary study.

Major. The subject area in which students concentrate during their undergraduate study. At most colleges, students take a third to half of their courses in the major; the rest of their course work is devoted to core requirements and electives.

Maritime college/institute/academy. An institution of higher education that prepares students to operate commercial shipping or fishing vessels. Upon graduation, students of most maritime academies are commissioned as officers in the United States Merchant Marine, and simultaneously commissioned as officers in the U.S. Navy Reserve.

Master Promissory Note (MPN). A special type of promissory note used to obtain a Federal Stafford loan. The MPN is designated for use as both a single-year and a multi-year note (for four-year and graduate/professional schools). Borrowers can sign a MPN once, the time they first borrow, and then receive additional loans during the same year or in subsequent years without signing an additional note.

Merit aid. Financial aid awarded on the basis of academic qualifications, artistic or athletic talent, leadership qualities, or similar qualities. Most merit aid comes in the form of scholarships. Merit aid may be non-need-based, or the merit criteria may be in addition to a requirement that the student demonstrate financial need.

National Science and Mathematics Access to Retain Talent (SMART) Grant. A federal grant program for Pell Grant recipients who are in their third or fourth year of undergraduate study, have declared a major in the sciences, mathematics, engineering, technology, or certain foreign languages, and have maintained a GPA of at least 3.0 in that major. The maximum annual award is $4,000, in addition to the student's Pell Grant.

Need analysis. The process of analyzing the student's household and financial information to calculate an EFC and financial need. See also *Federal Methodology, Institutional Methodology.*

Need-analysis form. See *Financial aid application form.*

Need-based aid. Financial aid (scholarships, grants, loans, or work-study opportunities) given to students who have demonstrated financial need, calculated by subtracting the student's expected family contribution from a college's total cost of attendance. The largest source of need-based aid is the federal government, but colleges, states, and private foundations also award need-based aid to eligible students.

Need-blind admissions. The policy of determining whether a student should be admitted to a college without regard to his or her financial need.

Non-need-based aid. Financial aid awarded without regard to the student's demonstrated ability to pay for college. Unsubsidized loans and scholarships awarded solely on the basis of merit are both non-need-based. Some financial aid sponsors also offer non-need-based grants tied not to merit, but to other qualities, such as state of residence or participation in ROTC.

Nursing college. An institution of higher education that primarily prepares students to become registered nurses (RNs) or licensed practical nurses (LPNs).

Open admission. The college admissions policy of admitting high school graduates and other adults generally without regard to conventional academic qualifications, such as high school subjects, high school grades, and admissions test scores. Virtually all applicants with high school diplomas or their equivalent are accepted, although some programs of study may have additional requirements.

Origination fee. A fee charged to a borrower to cover the costs of processing a loan. The origination fee is usually a percentage of the total amount being borrowed. The origination fee for any loan will be disclosed in the promissory note for that loan.

Out-of-state tuition. The tuition a public college or university charges residents of other states.

Outside resources. Student financial aid granted by a source other than the college that the college must take into account when assembling an aid package. Examples of common outside resources include scholarships from private foundations, employer tuition assistance, and veterans' educational benefits.

Parents' contribution. The amount a student's parents are expected to pay toward college costs from their income and assets. It is derived from need analysis of the parents' overall financial situation. The parents' contribution and the student's contribution together constitute the total expected family contribution (EFC).

Parents' Loan for Undergraduate Students. See *Federal Parents' Loan for Undergraduate Students.*

Part-time status. Enrollment at a college or university for 11 or fewer credit hours per semester.

Pell Grant. See *Federal Pell Grant Program.*

Perkins Loan. See *Federal Perkins Loan Program.*

PLUS loan. See *Federal Parents' Loan for Undergraduate Students.*

Prepaid tuition plan. See *Section 529 Plans.*

Priority date. The date by which applications for financial aid must be received to be given the strongest possible consideration. The college will consider the financial need of applicants who make the priority date before any other applicants. Qualified applicants who do not make the priority date are considered on a first-come, first-served basis, and are only offered financial aid if (and to the extent to which) the college still has sufficient money left over after all the offers it has made. Can also refer to the priority date for admissions applications, where, again, the college will make offers to the priority applicants first, and then consider subsequent applicants on a first-come, first-served basis, making offers only if there is still room in the incoming class.

Private college/university. An educational institution of higher education not supported by public taxes and operated on a not-for-profit basis. May be independent or affiliated with a religious denomination.

PROFILE. See *CSS/Financial Aid PROFILE.*

Promissory note. A binding legal document that a borrower signs to get a loan. By signing this note, a borrower promises to repay the loan, with interest, in specified installments. The promissory note also includes any information about origination fees, grace periods, deferment or cancellation provisions, and the borrower's rights and responsibilities with respect to that loan.

Proprietary college/university. See *For-profit college/university.*

PSAT/NMSQT® (Preliminary SAT/National Merit Scholarship Qualifying Test). A preparatory tool for the SAT that is administered by high schools to sophomores and juniors each year in October. The PSAT/NMSQT® serves as the qualifying test for scholarships awarded by the National Merit Scholarship Corporation.

Public college/university. An institution of higher education supported by public taxes.

Quarter. An academic calendar period of about 12 weeks. Four quarters make up an academic year, but at colleges using the quarter system, students make normal academic progress by attending three quarters each year. In some colleges, students can accelerate their progress by attending all four quarters in one or more years.

Regular admission. At colleges with early-action or early-decision plans, "regular" admission is the round of admissions conducted in January or February, after the early-admission rounds.

Renewal FAFSA. A simplified reapplication form for federal student aid. The Renewal FAFSA allows continuing students to update the prior year's FAFSA, rather than completing the entire FAFSA for each award year.

Reserve Officers Training Corps (ROTC). Programs conducted by certain colleges in cooperation with the United States Air Force, Army, and Navy reserves. Participating students may receive a merit scholarship while they are in college, and will enter the reserves of their service branch as an officer upon graduation. Naval ROTC includes the Marine Corps. (The Coast Guard and Merchant Marine do not sponsor ROTC programs.) Local recruiting offices of the services themselves can supply detailed information about these programs, as can participating colleges.

Residency requirements. The minimum number of terms that a student must spend taking courses on campus (as opposed to independent study, transfer credits from other colleges, or credit-by-examination) to be eligible for graduation. Can also refer to the minimum amount of time a student is required to have lived in-state in order to qualify for the in-state tuition rate at a public college or university.

Rolling admission. An admission procedure by which the college considers each student's application as soon as all the required credentials, such as school record and test scores, have been received. The college usually notifies an applicant of its decision without delay. At many colleges, rolling admission allows for early notification and works much like nonbinding early-action programs.

SAR. See *Student Aid Report.*

Satisfactory academic progress. Standards set by a college or university to determine whether a student is meeting sufficient academic standards. The student must achieve these standards to continue to receive financial aid.

SAT®. The College Board's test of critical reading, writing and mathematics skills is given on specified dates throughout the year at test centers in the United States and other countries. The SAT is used by most colleges and sponsors of financial aid programs.

SAT Subject Tests™. College Board tests in specific subjects are given at test centers in the United States and other countries on specified dates throughout the year. The tests are used by colleges for help in both evaluating applicants for admission and determining course placement, and exemption of enrolled first-year students.

Scholarship. A type of financial aid that doesn't have to be repaid. Grants are often based on financial need. Scholarships may be based on need, on need combined with merit, or solely on the basis of merit or some other qualification, such as minority status.

School. In this book, used generically to refer interchangeably to colleges, universities, and other institutions of higher education. At some universities, a "school" is a subdivision of the university—for example, the administrative unit that offers nursing courses may be called the "college of nursing" at one institution, and the "school of nursing" at another.

Section 529 Plans. State-sponsored college savings programs commonly referred to as "529 Plans" after the section of the Internal Revenue Code that provides the plan's tax breaks. There are two kinds: Section 529 college savings plans and Section 529 prepaid tuition plans.

Section 529 Prepaid Tuition Plan. State-sponsored plans through which parents can pay in advance for tuition at public institutions in their state of residence.

Self-help aid. Student financial aid, such as loans and work-study jobs, that requires repayment or employment.

Semester. A period of about 16 weeks. Colleges on a semester system offer two semesters of instruction a year; there may also be an additional summer session.

SEOG. See *Federal Supplemental Educational Opportunity Grant.*

Simplified needs test. In Federal Methodology need analysis, the simplified needs test excludes assets from the Expected Family Contribution calculation for low- to moderate-income families who file simplified tax returns (1040A, 1040EZ).

SMART Grant. See *National Science and Mathematics Access to Retain Talent Grant.*

Stafford Loan. See *Federal Stafford Loan Program.*

Student Aid Report (SAR). A report produced by the U.S. Department of Education and sent to students in response to their having filed the Free Application for Federal Student Aid (FAFSA). The SAR contains information the student provided on the FAFSA as well as the federally calculated expected family contribution.

Student expense budget. A calculation of the annual cost of attending college that is used to determine your financial need. Student expense budgets usually include tuition and fees, books and supplies, room and board, personal expenses, and transportation. Sometimes additional expenses are included for students with special education needs, students who have a disability, or students who are married or have children.

Student's contribution. The amount you are expected to pay toward college costs from your income and assets. The amount is derived from a need analysis of your resources. Your contribution and your parents' contribution together compose the total expected family contribution.

Subsidized loan. A loan awarded to a student on the basis of financial need. The federal government or the state awarding the loan pays the borrower's interest while they are in college at least half-time, thereby subsidizing the loan.

Supplemental Educational Opportunity Grant. See *Federal Supplemental Educational Opportunity Grant.*

Taxable income. Income earned from wages, salaries, tips, as well as interest income, dividends, alimony, estates or trust income, business or farm profits, and rental or property income. Some scholarship awards must be reported as taxable income.

Teacher's college. A college that specializes in preparing students to teach in elementary or secondary schools. Most teacher's colleges offer a curriculum that combines a study of the liberal arts with the study of pedagogy.

Terminal program. An education program designed to prepare students for immediate employment. These programs usually can be completed in fewer than four years beyond high school and are available in most community colleges and trade schools.

Title IV code. See *Federal code number.*

Transfer program. An academic program in a community or junior college primarily for students who plan to continue their studies in a four-year college or university.

Transfer student. A student who has attended another college for any period, which may be defined by various colleges as any time from a single term up to three years. A transfer student may receive credit for all or some of the courses successfully completed before the transfer.

Trimester. An academic calendar period of about 15 weeks. Three trimesters make up one year. Students normally progress by attending two of the trimesters each year and in some colleges can accelerate their progress by attending all three trimesters in one or more years.

Tuition and fee waiver. Some colleges reduce the tuition and/or fees for some categories of students, such as adults, senior citizens, or children of alumni.

Two-year college. A college that offers only two years of undergraduate study. See *Community/junior college*; see also *Upper-division college.*

Undergraduate. A student in the freshman, sophomore, junior, or senior year of study, as opposed to a graduate student who has earned an undergraduate degree and is pursuing a master's, doctoral, or professional degree.

Unmet need. The difference between a specific student's total available resources and the total cost for the student's attendance at a specific institution.

Unsubsidized loan. An education loan that is non-need-based and therefore not subsidized by the federal government; the borrower is responsible for accrued interest throughout the life of the loan.

Upper-division college. A college that offers only the junior and senior years of study. Students must complete their freshman and sophomore years at other institutions before entering the upper-division institution to earn their bachelor's degree.

Variable interest rate. An interest rate that changes on an annual basis to better reflect market rates.

Virtual college/university. A degree-granting, accredited institution wherein all courses are delivered by distance learning, with no physical campus.

William D. Ford Federal Direct Loan Program. See *Federal Direct Loan Program.*

Work-study. An arrangement by which a student combines employment and college study. The employment may be an integral part of the academic program (as in cooperative education and internships) or simply a means of paying for college (as in the need-based *Federal Work-Study Program*).

Alphabetical Index of Colleges

More College Planning Resources from the College Board

PAYING FOR COLLEGE

Getting Financial Aid 2010

A must-have book in today's economy, this is the perfect resource for families managing the high cost of college. This easy step-by-step guide shows why, when and how to apply for financial aid.

1,050 pages, paperback

ISBN: 978-0-87447-848-8

$21.95

Scholarship Handbook 2010

The most complete and comprehensive guide to help families tap into the more than 1.7 million scholarships, internships and loans available to students each year.

624 pages, paperback

ISBN: 978-0-87447-849-5

$28.95

College Handbook 2010

The only guide listing all accredited universities, two-year and four-year colleges, and technical schools in the United States — more than 3,800 in total.

2,200 pages, paperback

ISBN: 978-0-87447-846-4

$29.95

Get It Together for College

Get organized with expert tips from collegeboard.com, the No. 1 college planning Web site. This book includes tracking charts for all college planning to-dos, easy-to-follow timelines and much more!

210 pages, paperback

ISBN: 978-0-87447-829-7

$14.95

GETTING INTO COLLEGE

The Official SAT Study Guide™: Second Edition

Introducing a new edition of the No. 1 best-selling study guide from the test maker — featuring 10 official SAT® practice tests. The updated guide contains more of the information students need to get ready for the SAT.

1,100 pages, trade paper

ISBN: 978-0-87447-852-5

$21.99

The College Application Essay

By Sarah Myers McGinty

These strategies help students craft a college essay that stands out from the crowd.

176 pages, paperback

ISBN: 978-0-87447-711-5

$15.95

Campus Visits & College Interviews

By Zola Dincin Schneider

Get the most out of college campus visits and make a good impression during interviews.

176 pages, paperback

ISBN: 978-0-87447-675-0

$12.95

Book of Majors 2010

The only book on the market providing in-depth descriptions of more than 195 majors, and listing a total of 900 majors offered at colleges nationwide.

1,350 pages, paperback

ISBN: 978-0-87447-847-1

$25.95

CollegeBoard
inspiring minds™

Available wherever books are sold.
Distributed by Macmillan

Save Time and Money

While Earning Your College Degree

The College-Level Examination Program® (CLEP®) allows you to save time and money by earning 3–12 credits per test toward your college degree for what you already know. There are 34 different examinations available to satisfy proficiency requirements, skip introductory classes and graduate on time — more affordably.

Find out more about CLEP at www.collegeboard.com/clep.

CLEP® Preparation Tools and Resources

CLEP Official Study Guide 2010

476 pages, paperback

ISBN: 978-0-87447-853-2

$24.95

The only CLEP guide written by the test-maker, the CLEP Official Study Guide 2010 features:

- Official practice questions for all 34 CLEP exams.
- Helpful guides to earning college credit, evaluating a college's CLEP policy and applying for credit.
- Valuable suggestions for preparation, including methods of self-assessment and strategies for answering exam questions.

CLEP exams are available in the following areas: Composition and Literature; Foreign Languages; History and Social Sciences; Science and Mathematics; Business

New from CLEP

On July 1, 2010, CLEP will launch two new exams: College Composition and College Composition Modular. They will replace English Composition, English Composition with Essay and Freshman College Composition.

CollegeBoard

CLEP